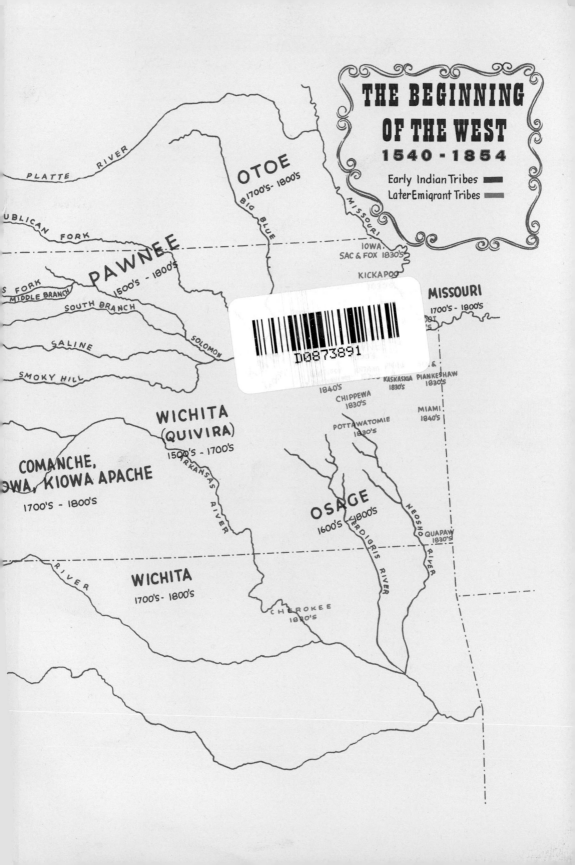

THE BEGINNING
OF THE WEST
1540-1854

Early Indian Tribes ▬▬
Later Emigrant Tribes ▬▬

PLATTE RIVER

OTOE
B 1700's - 1800's

BIG BLUE

MISSOURI

REPUBLICAN FORK

IOWA,
SAC & FOX 1830's

KICKAPOO

PAWNEE
1500's - 1800's

MISSOURI
1700's - 1800's

S FORK
MIDDLE BRANCH

SOUTH BRANCH

SOLOMON

SALINE

SMOKY HILL

KASKASKIA
1830's

PIANKESHAW
1830's

1840's

CHIPPEWA
1830's

MIAMI
1840's

WICHITA
(QUIVIRA)
1500's - 1700's

POTTAWATOMIE
1830's

COMANCHE,
OWA, KIOWA APACHE

1700's - 1800's

ARKANSAS RIVER

OSAGE
1600's - 1800's

NEOSHO RIVER

QUAPAW
1830's

VERDIGRIS RIVER

RIVER

WICHITA
1700's - 1800's

CHEROKEE
1830's

THE BEGINNING OF THE WEST

PRINTED BY
ROBERT R. (BOB) SANDERS, STATE PRINTER
TOPEKA, KANSAS
1972

The Beginning of the West

Annals of the Kansas Gateway
to the American West
1540-1854

by Louise Barry

Published by the
Kansas State Historical Society
Topeka, Kansas

In Commemoration of
the Approaching
Centennial of the
KANSAS STATE HISTORICAL SOCIETY
(founded in 1875)
and the
Bicentennial of the
UNITED STATES OF AMERICA

Foreword

Lying at the heart of the United States, a seedground and gateway for fundamental American energies, the area we now define as Kansas has been vitalized by extraordinarily varied Indian cultures, by Spanish conquistadors, French voyageurs and army officers; by Lewis and Clark, Zebulon Pike, Jedediah S. Smith, John Charles Fremont, and many other great figures in the pantheon of exploration. By a picturesque array of trappers and Indian traders, too; and by missionaries with eyes fixed on near and far horizons. The great trails to Santa Fe and to Oregon and California fanned out across the West from Kansas; and much of the military history of the Plains is rooted in Fort Leavenworth, after that post was established in 1827. Conceive as well of the canoes, pirogues, rafts, keelboats, and steamboats which over several centuries gave continental scope to Kansas waterways. How much of the history of the western half of the continent is embraced by, proceeds out of, Kansas!

Now, in Louise Barry's monumental compilation, *The Beginning of the West*, we have a book to exemplify and document the superb breadth and depth of the Kansas story, seen in larger context. There cannot be the slightest doubt that it must influence all future scholarship relating to the American West.

This ultimate significance of the book must be borne in mind, even when we double back upon our trail to observe that it is, as well, a prime contribution to the local history of Kansas, and, beyond that, the first really broad and thoroughly responsible treatment, by any Kansas historian, of the Sunflower state's rich preterritorial history, vigorous and critically acute, with minutely documented detail.

I have published my share of books relating to the American West, and not one but would have been a better piece of work had the present volume been at hand during the writing—as an aide-memoire for imperfectly remembered facts, as a guide to elusive sources, and as an index to persons, places, and events in a matrix of time. Now that *The Beginning of the West* is conveniently at hand, scholars who fail to make adequate use of it will give us eloquent testimony of their incapacity.

That is the viewpoint of a working scholar, but I think that all who are truly interested in American history and the American people may read it with profit and pleasure. Except within narrow limits, *The Beginning of the West* cannot be a work of narrative history, for it takes the form of an annals. But it is surprisingly readable, ever informative, and so organized that all the facts it contains derive fresh interest and value from their context. Read the book in a connected way or browse in it, one will find it equally absorbing.

DALE L. MORGAN,

September 2, 1970.   The Bancroft Library.

Introduction

By land, by sea and river, men came to explore, settle and develop the Great American West. Although the western half of the contiguous 48 states has a perimeter of several thousand miles, the most widely used land gateway for early access was by way of the area now called Kansas.

Of this we were not fully aware several years ago when Louise Barry, a member of the Kansas State Historical Society staff, suggested she might prepare an annals covering the known activity in the pre-Kansas region, from the appearance of the first Europeans in the mid-1500's to 1854. This cutoff date, the year Kansas territory was created and its land opened for settlement by others than Indians, has come to mark the end of an astounding era.

It was our naive judgment, when Miss Barry began her research, that the story could be contained in 300 pages! Publication of her findings began in the spring, 1961, issue of *The Kansas Historical Quarterly*, and the series of installments ran for nearly seven years. Republication of the whole in book form was not then possible. Miss Barry, however, continued to make notes and corrections, in anticipation of a time when such printing might be arranged. Happily that moment has arrived and we now present the story of the beginnings of the Great Westward movement to and through what is now Kansas in a book of well over a thousand fact-crammed pages. Citation of source materials—a feature not commonly associated with an annals—adds enormously to the value of the work. And an extensive index is the indispensable key to the entire text and the related illustrations.

Although credit for the excellence of this mammoth work must go to Louise Barry, she and all of us gratefully acknowledge the considerable help and encouragement of an eminent historian and long-time friend, the late Dale Lowell Morgan of the Bancroft Library. In exchanges of correspondence with Miss Barry he contributed much to the original annals. More recently, when this revision and book publication seemed possible, he provided new information and suggested corrections and additions. Beyond that, he agreed to express his enthusiasm for the work in a foreword, and did so only a few months before his untimely death on March 30, 1971.

Therefore, through the indefatigable research of Miss Barry and the generous help of Dale L. Morgan, this basic Western source book, *The Beginning of the West,* has reached fruition. Of course it is not claimed that every individual who moved into the early American West through the Kansas gateway will be found in these pages. Yet, in this three-century, who-was-who annals, the cast of characters seems incredibly large and inclusive.

When this book finds its place as a valued research tool for all historians of the American West, it also will become something of a memorial to Dale Morgan. And without doubt its panoramic view of America-in-motion should fascinate lovers of history everywhere.

NYLE H. MILLER, *Executive Director,*
January 5, 1972.   Kansas State Historical Society.

The Beginning of the West

1540

❡ Francisco Vasquez de Coronado (governor of a Mexican province) headed a large Spanish expedition (200 horsemen and 70 foot soldiers, well-armed; nearly 1,000 Indians and servants; perhaps 1,200 horses; pack mules; some light artillery; droves of cattle, sheep, goats, and swine) which set out from Compostela [in northwestern Mexico] late in February to search for the reportedly large and wealthy Seven Cities of Cibola. In July this great company came to the first of the Cities—a Zuñi village [on the western border of present New Mexico]. Greatly disappointed, but still hopeful of finding riches, Coronado made his headquarters among the Zuñi and sent out exploring parties. One, led by Cardenas, discovered the Grand Canyon of the Colorado. Another, under Alvarado, traveled eastward to the Rio Grande and found Indian pueblos [north of present Albuquerque] where there were food supplies. Coronado then moved to the Rio Grande valley for the winter. His next objective was the kingdom of Quivira—a land of enormous wealth, according to an Indian slave known as "Turk."

Ref: *See* next entry.

1541

❡ In search of fabled rich Quivira, Coronado and a small, selected party (30 mounted men; six foot soldiers; the Franciscan father, Juan de Padilla; some attendants; extra horses and pack animals) apparently entered present Kansas in June [possibly near present Liberal], having come from the southwest across the Texas and Oklahoma Panhandles of today. On June 29 these explorers reached and crossed the Arkansas [in present Ford county?]. A week later, east and north of the river's great bend, they came to a Quivira settlement. The friendly Indians were tall (some over six and a half feet), dark-skinned, tattooed, nearly-naked people [identified as the Wichitas], who lived in round, grass-covered houses and raised crops of corn, beans, and melons.

For 25 days Coronado and his men ranged the land of the Quiviras, particularly, it is thought, in present Rice and McPherson counties. They visited the scattered Indian villages (some had as many as 200 houses). Nowhere did they find the sought-for wealth and civilization, and they were bitterly disappointed. But the surroundings pleased them. Quivira's "rich and black" soil was "well watered by arroyos, springs and rivers." Wrote Coronado's lieutenant Juan Jaramillo: "It is not a hilly country, but has table-lands, plains, and charming rivers with fine waters. . . . I am of the belief that it will be very productive of all sorts of commodities." They found plums, grapes, mulberries, nuts; and there were the bison (the principal source of food) in numbers "as large as any one could imagine."

In mid-August, accompanied by six young Quivira guides, the expedition returned to the Arkansas crossing. By a route more direct than on the outward journey they marched to the Rio Grande where Coronado's main army awaited him.

Ref: H. E. Bolton's *Coronado on the Turquoise Trail* (Albuquerque, c1949); Geo. P. Hammond and Agapito Rey's *Narratives of the Coronado Expedition* (Albuquerque, 1940); Geo. P. Winship's *The Coronado Expedition* (in *14th Annual Report, Bureau of Ethnology*); Paul A. Jones' *Coronado and Quivira* (Lyons, 1937); W. R. Wedel's *An Introduction to Kansas Archeology* (Washington, 1959). A Kansas historical marker, "Coronado and Quivira," is west of Lyons, Rice county.

❡ Though the Spanish supposed it a part of the Mississippi (which Hernando De Soto discovered in May, 1541), Coronado had learned of the existence of the Missouri river during his 1541 visit among the Quiviras. Pedro de Castañeda's account of Coronado's expedition (written some time after the event) stated:

The great Spiritu Santo river [the Mississippi] that had been discovered by Don Fernando de Soto in the land of Florida flows from this region [Quivira]. It runs through a province called Arache [Harahey—north of Quivira], according to information which was considered reliable, though its sources were not seen, because it was said that they come from very far, from the land of the southern cordillera, where it empties into the plains and, crossing the flat lands, cuts through the northern cordillera and comes out at the place where it was sailed by Don Fernando de Soto's men. . . .

Thus the Spanish knew about the Missouri some 130 years before the first known white explorers—the French—saw its waters. (*See* 1673.)

Ref: Hammond and Rey, *Narratives of the Coronado Expedition*, p. 263.

1542(?)

❡ Father Juan de Padilla (outfitted by Coronado whose expedition he had accompanied), returned to the Quivira Indians in the spring of 1542 as a missionary. With him were Andres do Campo (a Portuguese), two Indian lay assistants (Lucas and Sebastian), some servants, and six Quiviras who had guided Coronado. Their equipment included mules, one horse, a flock of sheep, and they took church ornaments and "other trifles." After some time among the friendly Quiviras [Wichitas], at the village where Coronado had planted a cross in 1541 [said to have been near present Lyons, on Cow creek], Father Padilla determined to visit a country (the Guas) toward the east. He set out with his companions, but had not gone far when hostile Indians approached. Campo (on the horse), Lucas, and Sebastian escaped, but Father Padilla was slain by many arrows. The Indian lay assistants returned, "buried him with the consent of the murderers," and then fled with Campo. The place where Kansas' first Christian martyr met his death is not known; nor is the year certain. The event probably occurred in 1542 but may have been as late as 1544.

Ref: Castañeda, in *ibid.*; Bolton's *Coronado* . . . pp. 335-341. In Herington's city park is a monument to Father Padilla which was dedicated in 1904; ceremonies were held for a monument at Council Grove in 1931; near Lyons is a 26-foot granite cross erected to his memory in 1950; and a Kansas historical marker, "Father Juan de Padilla and Quivira," is south of Herington.

1593 or 1594

⊄ Captained by Francisco de Leyva y Bonilla and Antonio Gutierrez de Humaña, an unauthorized expedition of Spaniards left San Ildefonso [in New Mexico] in 1593 or 1594 and entered present southern Kansas after a journey which took them east and then on a northward course in search of the "gold mines of Tindan." Along a river [the Arkansas?] they found the friendly Quiviras in a "very large settlement in a great plain 10 leagues long" and some two leagues wide where there were grass houses and fine crops of corn, beans, and melons. Continuing northward across a plain, three days later the explorers came to a buffalo herd of amazing size. Then there occurred a quarrel between the leaders and Leyva was murdered by Humaña who took command. When the Spaniards had gone some ten days' travel beyond the Quivira settlements they reached a large river [possibly the Smoky Hill, or the Kansas; or the Platte?] which was about a quarter of a league wide, deep, and sluggish. At this place Jusepe and five other Indians deserted. (Jusepe, the only one to make his way back—and to give an account of the expedition—was held prisoner by Apaches for a year.)

As was later learned (by Oñate, in 1601) the Spaniards were all murdered (except one?) when Indians of the region fired the grass on all sides of them as they slept one night. (The Quiviras, in 1601, said that the massacre had occurred 18 days' travel beyond their settlements.)

[The "wide, deep and sluggish" river (which Jusepe in his account said the party had been afraid to cross) may well have been the Smoky Hill or Kansas, in flood stage.]

Ref: Hammond and Rey, *Narratives of the Coronado Expedition*, pp. 416-419, 755, 838, 940; Wedel, *op. cit.*, p. 21 (who suggests the river was the Smoky Hill or Kansas); H. E. Bolton in his *Spanish Exploration in the Southwest* . . . (New York, 1916), pp. 200, 201, decided the river was the Platte.

1601

❡ Don Juan de Oñate, governor (and colonizer, in 1598) of New Mexico, with a large force (upwards of 70 well-equipped men; two Franciscan friars, attendants; over 700 horses and mules; carts, arms, and artillery) set out late in June (from San Gabriel) for the country to the northeast where the Leyva-Humaña expedition of the 1590's had gone. Their guide was the Indian Jusepe. After more than 200 leagues of travel they came upon a large camp of Escanjaques (a roving, buffalo-hunting people). Accompanied by these Indians (who numbered 5,000 or more), Oñate's party traveled three(?) days more towards the settlement where (according to the Escanjaques) the Spaniards they sought had been slain. They crossed an east-flowing river [the Arkansas?] with "marvelous level banks . . . so wooded that the trees formed very dense and extensive forests," which had good fords but was very deep in places. A little farther on they came to a large Indian settlement of more than 1,200 grass houses, located on the banks of another fairly large river [the Little Arkansas at present Wichita?] which flowed into the larger one.

These grass-house people (unnamed by Oñate) also grew crops, and in other ways fitted the description of the Quiviras [Wichitas]. Their chief was called Catarax [the Wichitas' word for chief is Tatarrax]. The arrival of the large force of Escanjaques, their enemies, ended any possibility for friendly relations between the Quiviras and the Spaniards. Prudently deciding to turn back, Oñate and his men first had to fight and defeat the Escanjaques who had turned hostile when restrained from firing the Quiviras' abandoned houses.

Except for learning that the Leyva-Humaña expedition had been massacred by people who lived beyond the Quiviras; and that there were, in the region northward, very large settlements, Oñate's expedition accomplished nothing. He penetrated no farther than the other Spaniards before him and discovered nothing new. He and his men returned safely to New Mexico, reaching San Gabriel on November 24.

Ref: George P. Hammond and Agapito Rey's *Don Juan de Oñate, Colonizer of New Mexico* . . . (Albuquerque, 1953); Bolton's *Spanish Exploration*, pp. 250-265; Wedel, *op. cit.*, pp. 21, 22, who discusses Oñate's route in Kansas in relation to streams.

1606(?)

❦ A Quivira chief, with 600 warriors, journeyed to Santa Fe following the defeat of the Escanjaques by Oñate. He offered friendship and lands to the Spanish in return for aid against the Quiviras' enemies, the Ayjaos [who may have been the Indians Oñate had called Escanjaques].

Ref: Alfred B. Thomas' *After Coronado, Spanish Exploration Northeast of New Mexico* (Norman, Okla., 1935), p. 8; G. E. Hyde's *Indians of the High Plains* . . . (Norman, Okla., c1959), p. 13.

1670

❦ Father Jacques Marquette, writing from his mission among the Ottawas, told of the Missouri river, as reported to the French by the Indians: "Six or seven days below the Ilois [Illinois] is another great river [Missouri], on which are prodigious nations, who use wooden canoes. . . ."

Ref: J. G. Shea's *Discovery and Exploration of the Mississippi Valley* (New York, 1853), p. lvi.

1673-1674

❦ In mid-June, 1673, Louis Jolliet, Father Jacques Marquette, and five other Frenchmen, started down the Mississippi river in two canoes. At the end of June they passed by the mouth of the Pekitanoui (Missouri), and became the first known white men to see the river.

Three of the earliest existing maps based on discoveries by this expedition are noted below. They were, also, the first known which showed the Kansa Indians.

(1) A map drawn by Jolliet in 1673-1674(?)—which accompanied the *Narrative* of the expedition published in M. Thevenot's *Recueil de Voyages* (Paris, 1681). Shown as dwelling some distance up the Missouri (unnamed on the map) were the Missouris (Oumissouri); above them were the Osages (Autrechaha) and the Kansa (Kamissi) living in the same general area; and well beyond were the Paniassa. On the Arkansas river (unnamed on the map) were also the Paniassa—well upstream, with other tribes living above and below them.

(2) The so-called "Marquette" manuscript map of 1673-1674(?). The "R. Pekittanoui" was drawn as a large, but short river, ending abruptly. The same Indian tribes were noted, but under variant spellings for three: Ouchage, Oucmessourit, Kansa, and the Paniassa.

(3) The "Joliet map of 1674" (not drawn by Jolliet). The Messouris, Kansa, Ouchage, Pani, and Minengio(?) tribes (in that order ascending)

were shown on the south bank of a large, east-flowing stream (unnamed) emptying into the Mississippi. Far to the south, on the "Riviere Basire" (the Arkansas), the Paniassa were shown as the farthest west of eight tribes dwelling on its south bank.

Ref: F. B. Steck's *Marquette Legends* (New York, c1960) discusses the authorship and date of the "Marquette" map, and presents the author's theory that Marquette did not accompany Jolliet on the 1673 expedition; Tucker, *op. cit.*; Wedel, *op. cit.*

Before 1680

❦ Between 1664 and 1680 Juan de Archuleta and some soldiers were sent by the New Mexican governor to bring back several Taos Indian families which had fled Spanish rule in the middle 17th century. They found them to the northeast in the "plains of Cibola" in a fortified place to which the Spanish gave the name El Cuartelejo. The Taos Indians had copper and tin articles which they said were "from the Quivira pueblos" to which they had made a journey. The Spaniards also learned that the route to the Pawnees lay by way of Quivira; and were told (or perhaps concluded) that the French already were trading with the Pawnees.

[The Pawnees referred to were probably the Southern Pawnees—the Paniouassa (or, Black Pawnees) of the area that is now northern Oklahoma and southern Kansas. No direct trade was likely between the Pawnees and the French at this early date.]

Ref: Thomas, *After Coronado*, p. 53.

1682

❦ Rene Robert Cavalier, Sieur de La Salle, and party, descending the Mississippi in 1682, arrived at the mouth of the Missouri on February 14, camped there, and proceeded next day. Father Zenobe Membre (chaplain of the small French expedition) wrote:

The Indians assure us that this river is formed by many others, and that they ascend it for ten or twelve days to a mountain where it rises; that beyond this mountain is the sea where they see great ships; that on the river are a great number of large villages, of many different nations; that there are arable and prairie-lands, and abundance of cattle and beaver. . . .

La Salle, from information received, estimated the "grand riviere des Emisourites" to be navigable for 400 leagues or more.

Ref: G. J. Garraghan's *Chapters in Frontier History* (Milwaukee, 1933), pp. 54, 55; A. P. Nasatir's *Before Lewis and Clark* (St. Louis, 1952), v. 1, p. 4; Shea's *Mississippi Valley*, p. 167 (for quotation).

1684-1688

❦ Jean-Baptiste Louis Franquelin's *Carte de la Louisiane*, based on La Salle's map and data, was first published in 1684. La Salle's misconception of the present Platte river's eastward course as that

of the Missouri—a mistake perpetuated in Franquelin's and some later maps of the French period—thus showed "La Grande Riviere des Emissourittes" flowing almost due east, and influenced a long-held French belief that the route to the mines of New Mexico lay up the Missouri river. Franquelin's 1688 map showed the same confused network of rivers sketched in his earlier work, but gave more detailed information on the Indian tribes of the West. On the Missouri he showed the Missourits and Zages (Osages); then the Cansa well above them; and on westward, two villages of Pana, and the Panososo. On northwest branches were located the Panimaha (19 villages) and the Panetoca (four villages). Southwest of the Osages were 20 villages of Paneassa.

Ref: *The Jesuit Relations and Allied Documents,* Cleveland, v. 63, *frontispiece;* Sara J. Tucker, *Indian Villages of the Illinois Country* (Springfield, Ill., 1942); Wedel, *op. cit.; American Historical Review,* New York. v. 39, pp. 647, 650.

1693

❧ In mid-May, 1693, two French traders and some Kaskaskia Indians visited the Missouris and Osages, to make an alliance with them. Two chiefs from each village and "some elders and women" accompanied them back to Kaskaskia for a visit, and annual trade relations were established. From this contact, and others in the later 1690's, the French began to learn about other Missouri river Indians. They heard that the Pawnees traded with the Spanish "from whom they get horses of which they make use sometimes to pursue the buffalo in the hunt. . . ."

[The Pawnees acquired the Spanish horses in raids on the Padoucas (Plains Apaches), who got them from the Indians of the New Mexican frontiers. There is no record of direct trade between New Mexico and the Pawnees at this period.]

Ref: Garraghan, *op. cit.,* p. 57; *The Jesuit Relations,* v. 64, pp. 161, 169, 171; Nasatir, *op. cit.,* v. 1, p. 5.

1698

❧ Dr. Daniel Coxe outfitted two ships commanded by Captain Barr, which he sent some distance up the Mississippi river in 1698. From notes and journals of expedition members, Daniel Coxe, Jr., compiled *A Description of the English Province of Carolana, by the Spaniards Called Florida, and by the French La Louisiane,* in which the following appeared:

It will be one great conveniency of this country, if ever it comes to be settled, that there is an easy communication therewith and the South Sea, which lies between America and China . . . by the north branch of the great Yellow River, by the natives called the River of the Massorites [Missouri], which hath a course of 500 miles, navigable to its heads or springs, and which proceeds from a ridge of hills somewhat north of New Mexico, passable by horse, foot, or wagon in less than half a day. On the other side are rivers which run into a great lake, that empties itself by another great navigable river into the South Sea. . . .

Ref: B. F. French's *Historical Collections of Louisiana* (Philadelphia, 1850), pt. 2, p. 253.

1699

℄ Pierre Lemoyne, Sieur d'Iberville, with some 200 soldiers and colonists in four vessels, arrived from France in February, at a point a little east of the Mississippi's mouth, and founded Biloxi [Miss.].

Before 1700

℄ In present Scott county (12 miles north of Scott City, and about 50 miles east of the Colorado line) on a small knoll in Ladder creek valley, were found ruins of ancient stone and adobe buildings, the principal one having been a seven-room, 53 x 35-foot structure with walls 18 to 24 inches thick. Archeologists at the turn of the 20th century identified the ruins as of Pueblo origin and suggested they represented the place named El Cuartelejo (by the Spanish some 200 years earlier). More recently (1959) Dr. Waldo R. Wedel (of the Smithsonian Institution) has stated that the Scott county ruins represent ". . . a Plains Apache community of circa A. D. 1700 that included a multi-roomed stone structure, irrigation works, and other features clearly inspired by, if not the actual handiwork of, Pueblo Indians. . . ."

On at least two occasions in the latter half of the 17th century, Pueblo Indians fled from Spanish rule into the plains northeast of New Mexico. Between 1664 and 1680 when the Spaniards went after the earliest of these refugees (a group of Taos Indians) they found them among the Plains Apaches, living in structures which led the white men to call the place El Cuartelejo. (The term also was applied to the Indians in the vicinity.) In 1706 Ulibarri and a Spanish-Indian force went to El Cuartelejo to get some Picurie Indians who had left the Rio Grande in 1696 and return them to New Mexico. (*See, also,* Before 1680, and 1706 in this chronology.)

Ulibarri's diary and accounts of an expedition by Valverde in 1719 (published in 1935 in A. B. Thomas' *After Coronado*, and elsewhere noted in this chronology), seem to indicate that El Cuartelejo was in present eastern Colorado. (Thomas expressed the opinion that El Cuartelejo was either in Otero or Kiowa county, Colorado.)

Discussing El Cuartelejo's location in his *An Introduction to Kansas Archeology* (1959), Dr. Wedel commented on the fact that no archeological remains have been found in eastern Colorado to substantiate the Thomas claim, and summed up his own conclusions (p. 468) as follows:

As I see it, then, the case for El Cuartelejo in eastern Colorado rests solely on the testimony of certain historical documents. That for Cuartelejo in Scott County rests on archeological evidence, including particularly the unique association of a pueblo ruin with Plains Apache cultural remains. If Scott County pueblo and its associated archeological materials is not the very Cuartelejo rancheria from which Ulibarri rescued Don Lorenzo and his Picuris compatriots . . ., then we must conclude that it was a simultaneously occupied community (Sanasesli?) [for explanation of "Sanasesli" *see* this chronology under 1706] in which pueblo Indians from the upper Rio Grande and Plains Apaches were residing together in the late 17th and early 18th centuries.

Ref: *Kansas Historical Collections*, v. 6, pp. 124-130; Thomas' *After Coronado, see* index under El Cuartelejo; Wedel, *op. cit., see* index under El Cuartelejo, and Scott county pueblo site.

1700

❡ Father Gabriel Marest, of the Kaskaskia mission (on the Illinois) dispatched a report (dated July 10) to Iberville (at Biloxi), summing up the information he had gathered about the Missouri river and its people. For the first time, though indirectly, the Kansas river was mentioned. Marest wrote, in part:

As to the Missouri, it is a very beautiful and large-sized river extending as far as the Mississippi. It is entirely covered with different nations of Indians. . . . Its real name is the Pekitanoui and the French call it the Missouri because this people is the first you meet there. Then come the Arkansas [Kansa], who are on a little river of their own name. Then the Pana, Paniassa or rather Panis. These nations are very numerous and by way of their river, which discharges into the Pekitanoui, they carry on commerce with the Spaniards. Our warriors have brought us horses and bridles, which these nations took from the Spaniards. . . .

Ref: Marc de Villiers du Terrage, *La Decouverte du Missouri* . . . (Paris, 1925), p. 33; Garraghan, *op. cit.*, pp. 58, 59; Nasatir, *op. cit.*, v. 1, p. 6.

❡ Pierre Le Sueur (who had lived on the Upper Mississippi since the 1680's) made the voyage from France to Louisiana in 1699 with Iberville's colony. In 1700 he traveled up the Mississippi (to the mining country of present Minnesota) and passed by the mouth of the Missouri on July 13. He described the river's mouth; stated (mistakenly) that Emissourita meant "peoples of the canoe"; wrote of a tin mine 30 leagues up the river of the Osages [tributary of the Missouri]; and noted that the Aiaouez [Iowas] were enemies of the Panis [Pawnees] who lived along the Missouri. (His information on the mine came from Indians, and on the Pawnees from a Frenchman who had gone to the Iowas by way of the Des Moines river and married a woman of that nation.)

Ref: Villiers du Terrage, *op. cit.*, pp. 31, 32.

1702

❧ Seventeen Frenchmen set out in March from Tamaroa [opposite present St. Louis] to ascend the Missouri, build a trading fort in the Pawnee-Iowa country, and explore from there towards New Mexico. This earliest(?) organized trading expedition up the Missouri failed when hostile Indians, at some place not recorded, forced the French to take refuge on an island. They apparently returned safely to Tamaroa.

Ref: Garraghan, *op. cit.*, p. 62.

❧ In a *memoire* of June 20, the Louisiana colony's Iberville listed some Indian nations who lived on the Missouri and estimated their population in families. The Kansa were given as 1,500, the Panimahas as 1,200, and the Panas near Arkansas as 2,000. The Missouris were numbered at 1,500 families, but the Osages were not mentioned. Other upper river Indians in the tabulation were the Otoes, Iowas, and the Sioux.

On August 6 another Frenchman (Remonville) wrote that 14 large Indian tribes lived along the Missouri, which was a larger river than the [upper?] Mississippi.

Ref: Nasatir, *op. cit.*, v. 1, p. 8; Pierre Margry, *Decouvertes et Etablissements des Français*, v. 6 (1888), p. 179.

1703

❧ Guillaume Delisle's *Carte du Mexique et de la Floride,* published in 1703, contained data on the Missouri river country incorporated from his manuscript maps (1701 and 1702) of the Mississippi valley —data gained from Iberville and Le Sueur. Notably, the Missouri's course was sketched as from the northwest. (*See* 1684-1688.) The Osages were shown as living on the Osage river ("R. des Osages"), a tributary of the Missouri; and the Kansa ("Cansa") were placed on another branch of the Missouri some distance above, which Delisle designated as the "Metchigamiki" [the Kansas]. Farther up the Missouri, and on east-flowing tributaries, were the Pawnees ("Apana," "Panis," "Panimaha"). On the headwaters of a river north of, and paralleling the Kansas, he showed the Paniassa. Far to the south, on a tributary of the Arkansas river

("R. des Acansa") were also "2 grands Villages" of Panis; and on another branch downstream, the Paniassa.

A portion of Delisle's 1703 map is reproduced in this volume.

Ref: Tucker, *op. cit.; American Historical Review,* v. 39, pp. 652-654; Wedel, *op. cit.,* p. 28.

1706

℃ Juan de Ulibarri with a force of Spaniards and Indian allies set out from Santa Fe in mid-July to ransom some Picuries who, fleeing Spanish rule in 1696, had become slaves of the Apaches of El Cuartelejo. On July 29 they reached the river "which all the tribes call the Napestle" [the Arkansas]. (Ulibarri named it the Rio Grande de San Francisco.) Crossing, and turning eastward they arrived in the El Cuartelejo settlements on August 4. Ulibarri claimed the new country traversed for Spain. Among these friendly Apaches, he found the Picuries chief and some of his people. Next day, he dispatched men to three other Apache *rancherias.* In the one named Sanasesli (described as "forty leagues distant from the other two") were the son of a former chief, and 18 other Picuries. They were turned over to Ulibarri's scout, Jose de Naranjo, after he and his men had been entertained and given "excellent quarters" by the Sanasesli (a numerous and friendly people).

Meantime Ulibarri established relations with his Apache hosts, and gathered information. The El Cuartelejo Indians said that their enemies were the Pawnees and Jumanos. These Pawnees [*i. e.,* the Paniouassa (Black Pawnees) of present southern Kansas or northern Oklahoma] lived in two large villages on the "Sitascahe" river "seven days' journey across level land with sufficient water." The Apaches had a gun of French make and told of killing a white man and woman (but later said the gun had been taken from a Pawnee). Ulibarri got it in exchange for a Spanish gun. The Apaches said that all the tribes on the five large rivers they knew about were hostile to each other, but had trade with white people to the east. Asked about the "seas" to the north and east, they said they had heard that the one on the north was three long days' journey beyond a tribe called the Pelones [Palomas? *See* 1719 under Valverde] over a road which was all sand dunes of very fine sand without grass.

On August 11, having gathered together all the Picuries, Ulibarri's expedition left El Cuartelejo for New Mexico. The Arkansas river was reached on the 18th; and the company arrived in Santa Fe on September 2.

Ref: Thomas, *After Coronado,* pp. 16-22, 59-80, 262-265.

1706 or 1707

❡ A party of Frenchmen under Derbanne went up the Missouri "nearly 400 leagues" from its mouth in 1706 or 1707. They were (according to Derbanne's 1724 report) "the first of the French to have been so far into the interior," and they met Indians who directly, or indirectly, had been in contact with the Spaniards.

Ref: Nasatir, *op. cit.,* v. 1, p. 9; Garraghan, *op. cit.,* p. 63.

1712

❡ Antoine Crozat, a wealthy French merchant, was given a 15-year monopoly of trade in the country south of the Illinois river and between the colonies of Spain and England, in exchange for his agreement to bring two shiploads of immigrants into the Louisiana colony each year. (In 1717, the venture having been unsuccessful financially, Crozat gave up his patent.)

1712-1717

❡ Etienne Veniard de Bourgmont (a young French officer, ex-commandant at Detroit) accompanied some Missouris (who had gone north to aid the French against the Fox Indians) to their village in 1712, and lived among them for several years. He made at least two trips far up the Missouri. In 1714 he ascended to the mouth of the Pawnee [Platte] river and kept an accurate log of the "Route to Follow to Mount the Missouri." And he made a journey, also, beyond the mouth of the Niobrara, to the Arikara villages—farther, perhaps, than any white man had ascended before him.

In an account (1717?) of the Missouri and its people, Bourgmont wrote:

There are the Missouris, a nation of savages, bearing the name of the river, who are allies of the French. There are also the Auzages [Osages], another savage nation, allies and friends of the French. Their entire commerce is in furs; they are not numerous; they are a splendid race, and more alert than any other nation. All Missouri furnishes fine skins of all kinds, the climate there being very cold. Upstream is a smaller river which flows into the Missouri, called the "Rivière d'Ecanzé [Kansas] and a nation of the same name, ally and friend of the French; their trade is in furs. This is the finest country and the most beautiful land in the world; the prairies are like the seas, and filled with wild animals; especially oxen, cattle, hind and stag, in such quantities as to surpass the imagination. They hunt almost entirely with the arrow; they have splendid horses and are fine riders. Farther up is the

Rivière Large, called by the French and the Indians Nibraskier [*i. e.,* the Platte]. . . .

Ref: *Ibid.,* pp. 60, 61; *Missouri Historical Review,* Columbia, v. 35, p. 374; v. 36, pp. 282-284; Nasatir, *op. cit.,* v. 1, pp. 12, 13; *The Bulletin* of the Missouri Historical Society, v. 15 (October, 1958), pp. 3-19 (for Mrs. Max W. Myer's translation of de Bourgmont's "Exact Description of Louisiana").

1714

℄ Indians reported in Santa Fe that the Jumanos and some allied French traders had attacked El Cuartelejo.

Ref: Thomas *After Coronado,* p. 264.

1717

℄ The Company of the West (or, the Mississippi Company) secured control of Louisiana and its trade for 25 years. Though the speculative schemes of John Law, its head, quickly failed, the company continued in power for 14 years. (In 1732 it failed and surrendered its charter.) Upper Louisiana (the Illinois country) came under the supervision of lower Louisiana's government in 1717.

℄ This year, for the first time (so far as known), the Kansas river appeared by that name on a map. Vermale's *Carte Generale de la Louisiane ou du Miciscipi* (1717) showed the "R. des canzes" (and the nation "les canzes").

Notably, also, Vermale's map designated a point on the Missouri (on its left bank?, not far below the Platte's mouth?) as "F. du Missouri." (This *first* French post on the Missouri—of brief occupancy—had been established by Etienne Veniard de Bourgmont in 1715?)

Appended to the map's title (as given above) is the statement: "dressée sur plusieurs memoires et dissinee par le Sr. Vermale cy devant Cornette de Dragons."

Ref: Carl I. Wheat's *Mapping the Transmississippi West* (San Francisco, 1957), v. 1, *between* pp. 62, 63. Comment is made in Wheat's text (pp. 65, 66) that the Vermale map "apparently [was] made on the spot—at least reflective of actual experience," and that "Here French operations in the Western country make their first cartographic appearance." Mention of Bourgmont's "F. du Missouri" is made in Nasatir, *op. cit.,* v. 1, p. 14.

1718

℄ New Orleans was founded by Jean Baptiste Lemoyne, Sieur de Bienville, who recently had become governor of Louisiana. (In 1723 New Orleans became the seat of government.)

℄ Guillaume Delisle's *Carte de la Louisiane et du Cours du Mississipi* (1718) was much more detailed in its information on the Missouri, the tributaries, and the Indians, than his map of 15 years earlier. The new data had come from Bourgmont.

For the second time, so far as known, the Kansas river ("Grande Riviere des Cansez") appeared by that name on a map; and some tributaries (unnamed) were indicated. In the forks of two branches [the present Junction City area?], Delisle placed a large village of the Kansas ("Cansez"). To the west, on headwaters of the Kansas, he showed villages of Padoucas. The Padoucas (indicated in four other locations to the north and south), together with the Apaches, were shown as forming a barrier to all the region west and southwest.

On the Missouri river, some distance above the mouth of the Kansas, was shown another village of the "Cansez" Indians, below a tributary labeled "Petite Riv. des Cansez" [the village in the present Doniphan area presumably].

Delisle located villages of Paniassa (Black Pawnees) on south-flowing tributaries of the Arkansas ("Riviere des Akansas").

See reproduction of a portion of Delisle's 1718 map in this volume.

Ref: Carl I. Wheat, "Mapping the American West, 1540-1857," in *Proceedings of the American Antiquarian Society,* Worcester, Mass., v. 64, p. 50; Tucker, *op. cit., American Historical Review,* v. 39, p. 656; Wedel, *op. cit.,* pp. 28, 29, and (for discussion of the identity of the Padoucas) 77, 78; Villiers du Terrage, *op. cit.,* p. 57 (who identified the "Petite Riv. des Cansez" as the Big Nemaha of today).

1719

❧ In an attempt to reach the Padoucas by an overland route, French officer Claude Charles Du Tisné set out in the spring from Kaskaskia [on the Mississippi]. His first objective was a visit to the Big Osages [in present Vernon county, Missouri]. He was well treated in their villages, and spent some time trading among them. (Du Tisné was their first official French visitor.) Though they opposed his continuing onward to the Paniouassa (Black Pawnees), he was able to obtain a few horses from the Osages. But he left all his trading goods except three guns and a few other articles when he started southwest (accompanied by a guide-interpreter and perhaps one other person). He traveled over prairies and hills [in present southeast Kansas] where there were many buffalo. The country was fine and well wooded. He crossed four rivers, the largest, a branch of the Arkansas [the Neosho or Grand?] flowed from the northwest and had rapids. (The others were Osage tributaries.)

After four days and 40 leagues of travel Du Tisné came to a stream (12 leagues west of the large Arkansas branch) where there were two large villages of Paniouassa (a few miles apart), totaling at least 250 lodges and 500 warriors. [Whether they were in southeast

Kansas or in northeast Oklahoma has not been determined.] There, Osage meddling nearly cost him his life, but Du Tisné was saved by his own daring and boldness. He was able to secure a peace and trade alliance with the Paniouassa, but they refused to let him proceed to the country of their mortal enemies, the Padoucas, whose great village they said was 15 days' journey beyond. The Paniouassa said Spaniards had visited them, but the Padoucas were a barrier to intercourse. Du Tisné traded three guns, powder, pickaxes, and knives to the Paniouassa (who had many horses) for two horses and a mule marked with the Spanish brand.

On September 27, after placing a French flag among these Indians, Du Tisné began the homeward trip. The Osages refused him guides, and he relied on a compass to make his way back to Kaskaskia. Of his 14 horses (and a mule), six and a colt were lost during the journey.

Ref: Benard de La Harpe's *Journal Historique de L'Etablissement des Français a la Louisiane* (New Orleans, 1831), pp. 168-172, in which it is specifically stated that the largest stream Du Tisné crossed en route to the Paniouassa was a *branch* of the Arkansas (not the Arkansas itself, as given in Margry's work); Margry, *op. cit.*, v. 6, pp. 309-315; Villiers du Terrage, *op. cit.*, pp. 68, 69; *Missouri Historical Review*, v. 39, pp. 505-512; Nasatir, *op. cit.*, pp. 18, 19; *Kansas Historical Collections*, v. 9, pp. 252-254; Wedel, *op. cit.*, pp. 32, 65, 66, 533. See, particularly, Wedel, p. 533, for possible location of the Paniouassa villages sites in the Neodesha area. The identity of the Padoucas (Comanches?, Plains Apaches?) is controversial. The following excerpt from Auguste P. Chouteau's June 28, 1838, report from Fort Mason ("Okla.") bears on this matter of identity: "I was visited on the 27th May [1838] by Tabaquena (one of the principal Chiefs of the Pa-do-kah indians). . . . He brought with him a Deputation from eight of the different tribes— viz, the Ky-oh-way, Ka-ta-kah, Pa-do-kah, Yam-pa-rhe-kah or Comanche, Sho-sho-nee, Hoish, Co-che-te-kah and Wee-che-tah, among whom were 22 of their principal chiefs, and a number of warriors. . . ." (Reprinted from Grant Foreman's *Pioneer Days in the Early Southwest* [1926], pp. 236, 237.) Clearly, in this 19th century report, the Padoucas and Comanches were separate nations.

❡ Antonio de Valverde, governor of New Mexico, led an expedition against the Utes and Comanches in the fall of 1719. Unsuccessful in finding them, he was ready to return home in late October when he learned that several bands of El Cuartelejo Apaches were coming to meet him. The gathering place was on the Rio Napestle [Arkansas], in southeastern Colorado of today. From the Palomas (a band never visited by the Spanish) who came from "the most remote borderlands" of the Apaches "farther in from El Cuartelejo," Valverde heard disquieting news of white men [the French] who had made recent alliance with the Cancer [Kansa], and with the Pawnees and Jumanos, to whom they had given firearms. [Presumably these were references to Bourgmont's and Du Tisné's activities.] The Palomas told of an attack made on them earlier in the year by the Pawnees and Jumanos and said they had been forced to leave their lands. (A Paloma Indian, wounded by a bullet in the fight, in one version of his story said they had fought the Kansa Indians.) Elaborating the facts, they told of two French settlements among the Pawnees and Jumanos. [The Palomas apparently lived in present southern Nebraska and Kansas—neighbors to the Kansa and to the Black Pawnees of southern Kansas or northern Oklahoma. To the French the Paloma Apaches very likely represented a part of the people they called Padoucas.]

The Palomas spoke only of the Kansa, the Pawnees and Jumanos, and the Cadodachos Indians. When they described French settlements on a large river they perhaps referred to Bourgmont's post— see 1717 entry. Valverde's scout Naranjo, who previously had traveled as far as a large river which he named the Rio Jesús María [i. e., the Platte], where there were Pawnees, decided it was the river the Palomas meant.

The Spanish expedition returned to New Mexico in November. Valverde's report (of November 30) specifically stated: ". . . the French have their settlement on a very large river which here [Santa Fe] is known as the Jesús María. . . ."

Ref: Thomas, *After Coronado*, pp. 129-133, 143, 144.

1719-1722

❧ From lower Louisiana Benard de La Harpe made explorations by way of the Red river and the Arkansas in the 1719-1722 period—explorations which first brought him to the Arkansas river in present Oklahoma in 1719. He met representatives of nine allied Indian nations most of whom lived on a tributary (probably the Canadian of today). These people raised crops, spent their winters hunting buffalo, and bred fine horses. They were allied with the Paniouassa (the Black Pawnees) who were 40 leagues to the north. With the Osages (40 leagues to the northeast) they were at peace, but there was mutual mistrust. Other allies were some nomadic nations on the upper Red river. Their enemies were the Canecey (to the south on the Red river), the Padoucas (who had villages 15 days' journey to the west-northwest), and a few villages of Panis. The "nine-nations" people ate their captives.

They told La Harpe that a white nation [the Spaniards] traded with the Padoucas, but that they seldom went far in that direction because of their enemies. They said they knew that the Arikaras [meaning the northern Pawnees] lived in the direction of the Cances [Kansa] on the Missouri.

Knowledge gained by La Harpe's explorations was depicted on the Sieur de Beauvilliers' map of 1720 (manuscript). The "nine-nations" Indians were shown well to the west on the stream labeled "Atcanka R." [the Canadian]. The Arkansas above the junction of the Canadian was designated only as "R. decouverte en 1720." Between the two rivers and north of the nine nations were "Villages Ascanis et Ousita." (These were, actually, two of the nine nations as listed by La Harpe.)

[The Ousita may well have been the Wichita Indians of today, and if so, La Harpe provided an early reference to the Wichitas by the name which was later to be applied to them.]

Ref: La Harpe, *op. cit.*, pp. 206-209, 316-325; Wheat, *op. cit.*, p. 50, and pp. 67, 68 (for comment on manuscript maps by La Harpe, one of which is titled "Carte Nouvelle de la Partie de l'ouest de la Province de la Louisiane sur les Observations et decouvertes du Sieur Benard de la Harpe").

1720

❦ Alarmed by reports of French settlements which, as the Spanish understood, were among the Pawnees on the present Platte river, Governor Valverde of New Mexico, sent Pedro de Villasur with a small but well-equipped force to reconnoiter the French position. Villasur, with 45 Spaniards, 60 Indian allies, a priest, a French interpreter, and attendants, set out from Santa Fe in mid-June. Arriving at the El Cuartelejo settlements they stopped to rest. There some Apaches joined them, to act as guides.

On August 6 the Spaniards and their Indian cohorts crossed the Rio Jesús María [Platte]. At what point, and by what route they arrived at the river cannot be determined. (Their course had been generally northeastward.) Four days later they came to a large Pawnee village at the junction of another river with the Platte, and made a camp opposite. Though aware that the Pawnees were up to some trickery, after unsuccessful attempts to negotiate and to get news of the French, the Spaniards were ill-prepared for the surprise attack which occurred at daybreak of August 13. (The only precautions they had taken were to move their camp, and place guards, but the El Cuartelejo Apaches had realized the danger, and departed.) The Pawnees, aided by some Otoes, massacred a large part of the Spanish force. Villasur, more than two-thirds of his soldiers, and many of the Indian allies were slain. Survivors of the disastrous defeat made their way to the El Cuartelejo settlements, and then to New Mexico. Governor Valverde heard the bad news on September 6.

[There is disagreement as to where the massacre took place. It may have occurred, as some maintain, on the south side of the North Platte, near present North Platte, Neb.; others contend the Spaniards were killed near the mouth of the Loup Fork. If the Villasur massacre was in the Loup Fork vicinity, the Spanish expedition may have crossed northwestern Kansas to arrive at that locality. The French reported that the attackers were Otoes and Panimahas.]

Ref: Thomas, *After Coronado,* pp. 36-39, 13 -137, 171-175, 182-187, 226-256 *passim;* Hyde, *op. cit.,* pp. 74-80; *Nebraska History,* Lincoln, v. 6, pp. 13-19; v. 7, pp. 68-87; Garraghan, *op. cit.,* p. 64; Villiers du Terrage, *op. cit.,* p. 72. Jean-Bernard Bossu, in his *Travels* . . . (London, 1771), v. 1, pp. 151-155, related an interesting version of the Villasur expedition's massacre by the "Missouris." His account was written in a letter dated "At the Illinois, the 15th of May, 1753." *See* Bossu's *Travels in the Interior of North America, 1751-1762,* translated and edited by Seymour Feiler (Norman, Okla., c1962), pp. 85-90, for the same material.

1723

❧ Discussing possible sites for a Missouri river fort which Bourgmont had been ordered to establish, French engineer La Renaudiere wrote (on August 23):

. . . At thirty leagues in ascending [the Missouri, above Grand river] is the river of Quans [the Kansas] a beautiful river. . . . Thirty leagues higher up is a little river which runs to the north, where there is a large village of Quans, it is composed of 150 huts which border the Missouri. One finds there, on the south side, many beautiful prairies, and on the west side many mountains. . . .

[Despite the variation in distance, this was presumably the later-designated "Village of 24"—that is, the Kansa village on the Missouri said to be 24 leagues above the mouth of the Kansas—in the present Doniphan area.]

Ref: Margry, *op. cit.,* v. 6, pp. 393, 394.

❧ Etienne Veniard de Bourgmont and a party of 40 Frenchmen, journeyed up the Missouri from Kaskaskia in the fall of 1723, arriving at the Missouri Indians' village [on the south bank, in present Saline county, Missouri] on November 9. Crossing to the north side, a few miles up from the mouth of the Grand [in present Carroll county, Missouri] they erected, during the winter, a small post called Fort Orleans—the second French fortification on the Missouri. There, Bourgmont planned and prepared for his proposed expedition to the Padoucas.

Kansa chiefs apparently visited Fort Orleans either in the winter, or spring of 1724, and were given a French flag which was displayed in the Kansa village when Bourgmont arrived there the following July.

Fort Orleans was used for only five years. It probably was abandoned in 1728.

Ref: Garraghan, *op. cit.,* pp. 65, 67, 93; *Missouri Historical Review,* v. 35, pp. 373-384; v. 39, p. 525; Margry, *op. cit.,* v. 6, p. 404; Dumont de Montigny's map of Fort Orleans, in *Missouri Historical Society Collections,* v. 5 (June, 1928), *between* pp. 262, 263. The briefly-held Fort du Missouri (Bourgmont's post of 1715? origin) antedated Fort Orleans. *See* annals item p. 12.

1724

❡ Bourgmont (at Fort Orleans) in June organized his expedition to the Padoucas. It was to proceed by way of the Kansa village on the Missouri. He sent a small party under Saint-Ange upriver in canoes on June 25; and set out with seven other Frenchmen, some 100 Missouris and 64 Osages on July 3, traveling overland across present Missouri. Bourgmont's party camped, on July 7, on the Missouri opposite the Kansa village, crossing the next day. Illness among Saint-Ange's men kept the expedition in camp for over two weeks. (The Osages returned home because of the prevalent fever.) Meantime Bourgmont traded with the Kansa, obtained furs, and bought from them two Padouca slaves.

On July 24 a great throng of people set out westward across present Kansas. Accompanying the 19 Frenchmen were the two Great Chiefs, 14 war chiefs and 300 Kansa and Missouri warriors, about 300 women and 500 young people. And there were at least 300 dogs (drawing baggage). (The Kansa villagers were headed west on a buffalo hunt.)

A week later, when about three leagues from the Kansas river, Bourgmont became so ill he had to be carried back to the Kansa village on a litter (and then was taken by boat to recuperate at Fort Orleans). Before turning eastward on July 31, he delegated one of his men, Gaillard, to conduct the Padouca slaves to their people. Fifty Kansa Indians went with Gaillard. Traveling southwest and west they reached the Grand Village of the Padoucas [perhaps in Saline county?, or Ellsworth county?] on August 25. The Padoucas treated the party well, as Bourgmont was notified on September 6.

Ref: Nasatir, *op. cit.,* v. 1, pp. 20, 21; Villiers du Terrage, *op. cit.,* pp. 109-112; Margry, *op. cit.,* v. 6, pp. 398-449; Wedel, *op. cit.,* pp. 28-33; *The Colorado Magazine,* Denver, v. 14, pp. 121-128; *Missouri Historical Review,* v. 36, pp. 279-298; v. 39, pp. 521-528; A. T. Andreas and W. G. Cutler, *History of the State of Kansas* (Chicago, 1883), pp. 48, 49 (which has a translation of Le Page du Pratz's account of the Bourgmont expedition).

❡ Bourgmont left Fort Orleans again on September 20 (by way of the Missouri), arriving at the Kansa village on the 27th. On October 5 and 6 he held councils with assembled Indian chiefs and head men. Five Padoucas had returned with Gaillard to the Kansa village (and encamped not far away were great numbers of Padoucas with their families who had followed them eastward). The Missouri river Indians (Kansa, Missouris, Otoes, Iowas, and Panimahas) reluctantly agreed to make peace with the Padoucas.

On October 8, Bourgmont, with a party totaling 40, set out across present Kansas to visit the Great Chief of the Grand Village of the Padoucas. Accompanying Bourgmont were his ten-year-old son (by a Missouri woman); 14 Frenchmen; the five Padouca envoys; seven Missouris; five Kansa chiefs; four Otoe, and three Iowa chiefs. They had ten baggage-carrying horses. Proceeding west and southwest they crossed the Kansas river [near present Rossville?] on October 11; then traveled some 48 leagues farther (first southwest, and then west) during the next seven days.

On October 18 they met the Padoucas [in present Saline? or Ellsworth? county]. At the Grand Village, not far from a little river with brackish water [the Saline presumably], they were welcomed warmly. There were some 500 lodges, 800 warriors, 1,500 women, and more than 2,000 children in that village. The Padoucas had some horses, and lots of dogs. On October 19 Bourgmont presented many gifts to the Indians; then, before the assembled chiefs and head men (some 200 persons) he made a speech exhorting the Padoucas to cease warfare with the Missouri river Indians. A peace treaty was agreed to, and the Great Chief (who had been given a French flag) promised the allegiance of more than 2,000 warriors, as well as aid to Frenchmen who wished to cross to New Mexico. (The Spaniards were 12 days' travel from the village he said.) Bourgmont was presented with seven horses as a gift.

On October 22 the Frenchmen and Missouri river Indians started homeward. They took a route northeast, and east to the Kansas river (which they reached and crossed on the 27th). From that place they followed down the river valley till they came to the Missouri, near the mouth of the Kansas. On November 1 Bourgmont embarked in a canoe with some of his men (sending the rest overland with the horses) and reached Fort Orleans on November 5.

Ref: *See* preceding entry. Wedel discusses Bourgmont's route and the conclusions others have reached as to the locale of the Grand Village of the Padoucas.

1725

❧ Bourgmont, returning to France in the summer of 1725, escorted a delegation of Indians—including a Missouri, an Otoe, an Osage, and a young "Princess of the Missouri" to France. They arrived in Paris on September 20, were presented at court, and entertained by royalty. The "Princess" was baptized in Notre Dame cathedral, and married one of Bourgmont's lieutenants. After more than a year abroad these Indian "ambassadors" were returned to their own people.

Ref: Garraghan, *op. cit.*, p. 69; *Missouri Historical Review*, v. 36, p. 295; *Nebraska History*, v. 6, pp. 33-38; Nasatir, *op. cit.*, v. 1, pp. 21, 22.

1739

❈ Bound for New Mexico on a trading expedition, the brothers Paul and Peter Mallet, and six other Frenchmen, ascended the Missouri river in the late spring, at least as far as the Panimaha village [on the Niobrara? river in Nebraska] before learning they had gone far out of their way. From that place they set out over-land, with pack horses, on May 29, on a route which would take them back where they could set a course for the Spanish settlements. The river which they came to on June 2 they named the "Plate" [Platte]. Following up this stream beyond the river of the Pa-doucas [the Loup Fork?], they crossed the Platte on June 13 and set out toward the southwest. As they proceeded through present Kansas they crossed several large streams. On the 20th they lost seven merchandise-laden horses in the waters [swollen by rain?] of a river they thought was the "Cances" [possibly the south fork of the Solomon]. On June 30 they reached the banks of the Arkansas [perhaps in Ford county], where they found stones with Spanish inscriptions. Following upstream, on July 5 they came to a camp of Laitan [Comanche] Indians [perhaps in the vicinity of Lamar, Colo.]. From there, an Arikara slave guided them to the Spanish settlements. They reached Santa Fe on July 22; received good treat-ment in friendly custody; and remained for nine months. The Mallet party was the first (of record) to reach New Mexico from the Missouri country.

Ref: Margry, *op. cit.*, v. 6, pp. 455-465; *The Colorado Magazine*, v. 16, pp. 161-173; Nasatir, *op. cit.*, v. 1, p. 28.

1740

❈ Seven of the eight Frenchmen of the Mallet party left Santa Fe on May 1, intending to go to New Orleans. Arriving at the Cana-dian river on May 10, they followed downstream for three days [reaching a point probably a little east of the New Mexico-Texas boundary]. There the party split, three men deciding to "take the route of the Pani Indians" to the Illinois country. They reached their destination safely, probably more or less retracing their route of 1739 across present Kansas. No record of their journey exists.

The Mallet brothers and two companions proceeded down the Canadian [through present Oklahoma], abandoned their horses for canoes made of bark, and continued to the Arkansas river. Not long afterwards they came to a French hunting camp. From there they proceeded to the French post on the Arkansas about 45(?) miles upstream from the river's mouth, and eventually made their way to New Orleans.

An attempt by the Mallet brothers, in 1741, to guide an expedition to Santa Fe by way of the Canadian river ended in failure.

Ref: Same as preceding entry.

1744

⁋ Between 1724 and 1744 (apparently) the Kansa moved from their "Village of 24" [at present Doniphan] downstream to the site later known as the "Village of 12" [12 leagues up the Missouri from the Kansas river's mouth; in the Salt and Plum Creek valley area, Leavenworth county].

From 1744 to 1764 the French had a fortified trading post—Fort Cavagnial (or, Fort de Cavagnial) near the Kansa town. Begun in 1744 the fort was "a stockade of stout piles, 80 feet on the inside square, with bastions at each corner, the rear bastions being 'storied.'" The log buildings (most of them mud-covered) had chimneys of mud-covered logs.

French records provide some information on "Kansas'" first military post, as noted in the following chronology:

In the spring of 1744 a French engineer (the Chevalier Pierre Rene Harpin de la Gautrais) selected the site for the fort; and work was begun.

On August 8, 1744, the governor of Louisiana (Francois-Pierre Rigaud, baron de Cavagnial, marquis de Vaudreuil) officially chartered the fort, granting to Joseph Deruisseau, a Canadian, a five-year (1745-1750) monopoly of the Missouri river (and tributaries) fur trade.

It appears that the Chevalier Francois Coulon de Villiers was the first commandant at the post. Villiers, who served till 1749?, was succeeded by a lieutenant, Augustin-Antoine de la Barre, Seigneur de Jardin. La Barre, on February 24, 1751, was murdered by a soldier at the post.

Louis Robineau de Portneuf, a junior officer, succeeded La Barre, and served as commandant until the fall of 1753. (He may have returned to the post later. There is a gap in information.)

The small Santa Fe-bound expedition party of Jean Chapuis and Luis Feuilli spent the winter of 1751-1752 at Fort Cavagnial. (See separate entry.)

In the fore part of 1752, while Portneuf was absent (at Kaskaskia), Missouri Indians came to the fort on a horse-stealing raid. Two were killed. In the same, or another incident a woman was wounded, and a cow killed. And, in this same period, a windstorm destroyed all the chimneys, and damaged the buildings at Fort Cavagnial.

When, in 1752, Portneuf asked French authorities about renovating the post, repairs were approved only after it was ascertained that the Kansa Indians had *returned* to their near by village. (Portneuf earlier had complained that the post was three days' march from any Indians; that voyageurs went up the Kansas river without his permission; and for both reasons wished to rebuild the fort at a better site.

By 1757, Fort de Cavagnial was commanded by Jean Francois Tisserant de Moncharvaux. This year a report stated that the post produced 100 bundles of furs, including many beaver, but badly worked.

In 1758 Fort Cavagnial was described as "un entourage de Pieux" (fence of piles) enclosing some poor cabins and huts. The garrison consisted of the commandant, seven or eight soldiers, and some traders.

By order of January 30, 1764 (issued by D'Abbadie, the French director-general of Louisiana, at New Orleans) all the French posts in upper Louisiana were to be evacuated. Fort Cavagnial was abandoned in the late spring or early summer of 1764.

[In 1804 the Lewis and Clark expedition camped opposite Salt Creek valley on the night of July 2. They saw no traces of the old Kansa village, but "About a mile in the rear   . . .   was a small fort, built by the French on an elevation.   . . .   the situation of the fort may be recognized by some remains of chimneys, and the general outline of the fortification, as well as by the fine spring which supplied it with water.   . . ." Of the fort's one-time occupants they had no information. Extensive archeological explorations have been made in the latter part of the 20th century, but no conclusive remains have been found up to this writing.]

Fort Cavagnial is presumed to have been located about three miles north of Fort Leavenworth.

Ref: Nasatir, *op. cit.*, v. 1, pp. 28, 35, 36, 40-42, 46-48, 50, 52; T. C. Pease and Ernestine Jenison, *Illinois on the Eve of the Seven Years' War, 1747-1755* (Illinois State Historical Library *Collections*, v. 29, pp. xx, xl, 9, 338, 368, 443, 548, 549, 663, 664, 770; Charles E. Hoffhaus' "Fort de Cavagnial," in *KHQ*, v. 30, pp. 425-454; Elliott Coues' *History of the Expedition   . . .   of Lewis and Clark* (New York, 1893), v. 1, p. 37; Thomas A. Witty, Jr., and James O. Marshall, *Archeological Survey of the Lower Salt and Plum Creek Valley, Leavenworth County Kansas* (Topeka, 1968).

1748

℃ Pierre Satren, Louis Febre, and Joseph Riballo, deserters from the French post on the Arkansas, were members of a party of 12 which set out from a village of Zarca Indians [in eastern Arkansas] in the fall of 1748, for New Mexico. They went up the Rio de Napestle [the Arkansas] to the two villages of the Jumano or Panipiquet Indians [the Wichitas, possibly in present Kansas]; and were conducted by those Indians to a Comanche settlement of three villages. After remaining for a time, hunting, Satren, Febre, and Riballo accompanied some Comanches to Taos, and from there were taken by the Spanish to Santa Fe, arriving six months after leaving the Zarca Indians. They were allowed to remain as residents.

Ref: H. E. Bolton's *French Intrusions Into New Mexico, 1749-1752* (reprinted from Stephens and Bolton's *The Pacific Ocean in History* (c1917), pp. 400-404; A. B. Thomas' *The Plains Indians and New Mexico, 1751-1778* (Albuquerque, 1940).

1749-1750

⁅ Felipe de Sandoval (native of Spain) who had been at the French post on the Arkansas, and who left that place some time in 1749 with six other persons, arrived in Santa Fe, N. M., with two Frenchmen in February, 1750. Sandoval related that he and his companions had traveled up the Rio de Napestle [Arkansas] in canoes. After 50 days they reached the Jumano [Wichita] settlements where they found a French flag flying. These settled people lived along the river [possibly in the Wichita area of today] in grass houses, in two adjoining villages surrounded by stockades and ditches. They raised crops of corn, beans, and melons. The French, with whom they carried on an extensive trade, had recently paid them a visit and left gifts—and the flag. The Jumanos, who numbered about 500 warriors, were at war with the Pananas [Apaches?] and they were "fierce cannibals" according to Sandoval, who had seen them eat two captives. They had a few horses, secured from the Comanches.

Sandoval's party spent 20 days in the Jumano settlement, then set out with Indian guides, to find the Comanches. Unsuccessful, Sandoval and his companions separated, and he, after returning to the Jumanos for a few days, set out once more, this time following up the Arkansas with a Comanche guide. After 40 days of travel he reached a Comanche village, and remained among those Indians for some time. Then with two Frenchmen who had come there, and an Indian guide, he proceeded by way of Taos to Santa Fe. Sandoval thought the Jumanos were 20 to 25 days' travel to the northeast and east of Taos; and that from the Jumanos, traveling *down* the Arkansas to the French post would require about nine days.

Ref: Bolton's *French Intrusions*, pp. 396-398.

1750

⁅ Governor Velez of Santa Fe, in a report to his superiors, noted that on the northwest New Mexican frontier there were the Comanches, and the Jumanos (whom the French called Panipiquees). The alliance (in the latter 1740's) of the Comanches and Jumanos, he wrote, had resulted in their waging war against the Carlanes and other Apache bands of New Mexico; and had also made it easier for their allies, the French, to advance towards the southwest.

Velez described the Rio de Napestle [the Arkansas] which had its source in a rugged mountain range about 80 leagues from Taos. In its upper reaches the river was shallow, he wrote, but Frenchmen had told him that it was large at the Jumano [Wichita?] village, and farther down where the Colorado [Canadian] joined it, was still larger. Velez further reported that New Mexican soldiers under Lt. Gen. Bernardo de Bustamante y Tagle, pursuing some Comanches, had followed down the Rio de Napestle to the vicinity of the Jumano villages "on which expedition were acquired adequate reports of those regions, in the summer very delectable and pleasing, and inhabited by innumerable buffalo, which the Divine Providence created for the support of the barbarians and the greed of Frenchmen." (Presumably this expedition had occurred in the late 1740's.)

Ref: *Ibid.*, p. 398; H. E. Bolton's *Athanese de Mézières and the Louisiana Texas Frontier, 1768-1780* (Cleveland, 1914), v. 1, p. 48.

1751

℃ La Jonquiere (commandant at Illinois) reported (September 25) that the Great Osages had been making continual warfare on "Les Panis noirs et picqueés" [the black and tattooed Pawnees— *i. e.*, the Wichitas?] and "have completed the destruction of one of their villages, which was begun by the measles and smallpox." They [the Wichitas?] had "begged help of the Laytannes [Comanches], a tribe close to the Spaniards. This tribe . . . joined them, and they went together against the village of the Great Osages when a party of their people were at the *Cerne* [surround] killing animals. . . . the Great Osages lost twenty-two of their chiefs, and the others left twenty-seven of their people on the field of battle. . . ." The Osages then had come to get the Illinois Indians to help them avenge the defeat, but the French reminded the Illinois that "Les Panis noirs et picqueés" and the Laytannes were, like themselves, allied with the French, and induced them not to go with the Osages. La Jonquiere noted that the "Laytannes are armed with the lance like the Spaniards. They all are mounted on saddle horses, and the women go to war with them."

Ref: *Collections of the Illinois State Historical Library*, v. 29, pp. 357-359, 678; Nasatir, *op. cit.*, v. 1, pp. 44, 45.

1752

❧ After a winter at Fort Cavagnial [on the Missouri, in what is now Leavenworth county] Jean Chapuis and Luis Feuilli, joined by eight other Frenchmen, set out about the middle of March on a trading expedition to New Mexico—a trip for which Chapuis had secured a license from French authorities. They first went upriver to the Panimaha village to obtain horses. There, or later when in the Comanche country, eight men turned back. Chapuis and Feuilli, after paying a heavy toll to the Comanches were given directions to New Mexico. [Of their route across present Kansas there is no record.]

Forty days later, and four and a half months after setting out from Fort Cavagnial, the two men reached Pecos mission, on August 6. They came from the north, guided by an Ae woman (a slave fleeing New Mexico) whom they had met north of the Arkansas, and persuaded to show them the way. Chapuis and Feuilli were taken into custody and sent to Mexico (and from there to Spain). The merchandise on their nine pack horses was confiscated and sold at auction.

Ref: Bolton's *French Intrusions,* pp. 400-404; Thomas, *The Plains Indians,* pp. 21, 24, 82, 85, 93, 94, 103-106; Nasatir, *op. cit.,* v. 1, p. 42.

1753

❧ Macarty (the commandant at Illinois) reported, on May 20, these items from the Western country:

"Four men who deserted from the Missouri post [Fort Cavagnial] were killed by 'Les panis noire' [Black Pawnees]. . . .

"The Laitannes [Comanches], numerous and wandering tribes between our posts and the Spaniards, have asked . . . permission to come and see me; they said they wished to have a father. . . .

"The Spaniards have been in convoys as far as the places where they were defeated some years ago. . . ." [A reference to the Villasur massacre of 1720?]

Ref: *Collections of the Illinois State Historical Library,* v. 29, pp. 820, 821.

❧ Jean Bernard Bossu's letter, dated "At the Illinois, the 15th of May, 1753" (published in Bossu's *Travels* . . .), stated: "There are now five great villages of French inhabitants in these parts"; and a *footnote* added this information: "The five villages of the French are that of the *Kaskakias,* the Fort *Chartres,* St. *Philip,* the *Kaokias,* and the *Prairie du Rocher* (meadow on the rock); there is now a sixth, called St. *Genevieve.*"

[Two decades earlier—1732?, or 1735? (the latter, the traditional founding date) a short-lived village of Ste. Genevieve had been established.]

When, in 1763, the French territory west of the Mississippi came under Spanish control, Ste. Genevieve was the only organized community in present Missouri.

Ref: Jean Bernard Bossu's *Travels* . . . (London, 1771), v. 1, p. 127; or, Bossu's *Travels* . . ., translated and edited by Seymour Feiler (Norman, Okla., c1962), p. 76; Louis Houck's *A History of Missouri* . . . (Chicago, 1908), v. 1, p. 338; Nasatir, *op. cit.*, v. 1, p. 535; Francis J. Yealy, *Sainte Genevieve* (Ste. Genevieve, 1935). The *second* Ste. Genevieve was founded prior to 1753.

1757-1758

❡ Antoine S. Le Page du Pratz's *Histoire de la Louisiane* was published in Paris in 1758 (and later in English translation, in London). The author (resident in the Natchez-New Orleans area from 1718 to 1734), wrote extensively, and from personal observation, of the lower Mississippi country. For upper Louisiana he had to rely on others. He devoted one chapter to an abridged version of Bourgmont's 1724 journey to the Padouca village; and he related a story [fabrication?] supposedly obtained in an interview, of a Yazoo Indian named Moncacht-ape who was said to have gone far up the Missouri before 1734.) But he apparently knew nothing of La Harpe's 1719-1721 discoveries, or of the Mallet brothers' 1739 journey to Santa Fe, or even of the existence of the great Platte river. In short, both Le Page du Pratz's writings and his map of Louisiana (dated 1757, and published in the *Histoire*) were more than 20 years out-of-date in presenting French geographical knowledge of the 1750's. (Delisle's map of 1718 contained more, and better data on the country of the Arkansas and the Missouri.) Of these rivers Le Page du Pratz wrote:

[The Arkansas] . . . takes its rise in the mountains adjoining to the east of Santa Fe. It afterwards goes up a little to the north [the great bend in south-central Kansas] from whence it comes down to the south, a little lower than its source. . . .

[The Missouri] . . . takes its rise at eight hundred leagues distance, as is alleged, from the place where it discharges itself into the Mississippi . . . though the Missouri comes out of a mountain, which lies to the northwest of New Mexico, we are told that all the lands it passes through are generally rich. . . . The French [have] . . . penetrated up the Missouri only for about three hundred leagues at most. . . . According to what I have been able to learn about the course of this great river, from its source to the Canzas, it runs from west to east; and from that nation it falls down to the southward, where it receives the river of the Canzas, which comes from the west; there it forms a great elbow, which terminates in the neighborhood of the Missouris. . . . The largest known river which falls into the Missouri is that of the Canzas which runs for near two hundred leagues in a very fine country. . . .

[Of the Indian tribes of the Missouri country] The principal nations who

inhabit upon the banks, or in the neighborhood of the Missouri, are, besides
. . . [the Missouris and Osages], the Canzas, the Othoues, the White
Panis, the Black Panis, the Panimachas, the Aiouez, and the Padoucas. The
most numerous of all those nations are the Padoucas, the smallest are the
Aiouez, the Othoues, and the Osages; the others are pretty considerable.

Ref: Antoine S. Le Page du Pratz, *Histoire de la Louisiana* (Paris, 1758); Bernard
De Voto's *The Course of Empire* (Boston, 1952), pp. 566-568 (for discussion of Moncacht-ape).

1758

❦ Describing the Missouri river Indians with whom the French had
dealings, the governor of Louisiana (Louis Billouart de Kerlerec)
reported that the Kansa had only 250 to 300 warriors. They had
once been very numerous, he wrote, but wars with the Pawnees,
and smallpox had greatly weakened them. He mentioned their
great friendship for the French, and noted that Fort Cavagnial was
located at their village. He stated that the Great Osages numbered
700 warriors; the Little Osages 250; the Missouris about 150; the
Otoes 100; the Iowas 200; the Pani-Mahas on the Platte 600; the
Mahas on the Missouri 800; and the Arikaras were thought to be
more numerous than the Mahas.

Ref: Nasatir, *op. cit.*, v. 1, pp. 51-53.

1762

❦ On November 3, by the secret treaty of San Ildefonso, France
ceded Louisiana west of the Mississippi, plus the Isle d'Orleans, to
her ally Spain.

1763

❦ By the treaty of Paris, February 10, France ceded to Great Brit-
ain her territory east of the Mississippi (except the Isle d'Orleans);
and confirmed the 1762 cession of Louisiana west of the Mississippi
(and the Isle d'Orleans) to Spain.

1764

❦ St. Louis was founded in February. Auguste Chouteau (then 14)
headed the work party which began the settlement (on a site chosen
in 1763 by Pierre LaClede Liguest, on behalf of Maxent, LaClede
and Company of New Orleans, operating under a French grant of
1762).

1766

❦ Antonio de Ulloa arrived in New Orleans on March 5 as the first
Spanish governor of Louisiana.

— 28 —

1769

❧ Louis Saint-Ange de Bellerive, commandant at St. Louis, reporting (May 2) to the Spanish on the Indian tribes who came to receive presents in the District of Illinois, named the Missouris, Little Osages, Big Osages, Kansa, Otoes, and Panimahas from the district of the Missouri river.

Ref: Louis Houck's *The Spanish Regime in Missouri* (Chicago, 1909), v. 1, pp. 44, 45; Nasatir, *op. cit.*, v. 1, p. 70.

❧ Capt. Francisco Riu's report (October 29) revealed what knowledge the Spanish, from their St. Louis headquarters, had been able to gather about their recently acquired Missouri country. He wrote:

. . . From the mouth of the Misuri to that of the River of the Big Osages, there is a distance of 80 leagues. The latter river goes to the tribe called by the same name, which is some 70 leagues from the mouth.

From the mouth of the above-named river to the tribe of the Panimahas, is a distance, as is asserted by the voyageurs, of 170 leagues. That is the most distant tribe to which the traders penetrate. From the above-mentioned tribe to that of the Ayetan [Comanche], one goes overland, and it is estimated to be a voyage of 6 or 8 days. From the tribe of the Ayetan to Nuevo Mejico, the same ones calculate 6 or 8 days.

Captain Riu particularly noted the large contribution of the Kansa Indians to the fur trade. Their country, he stated, "abounds in castors [beaver]."

Ref: Houck's *Spanish Regime* . . ., v. 1, pp. 62-64; Nasatir, *op. cit.*, v. 1, p. 70. The Panimahas were the Pawnee Loups.

1770

❧ Pedro Piernas, arriving at St. Louis on May 20, took formal charge as the first Spanish (lieutenant) governor of upper Louisiana. (From 1770 to 1804 the Spanish controlled the Missouri river trade.)

Ref: Louis Houck's *A History of Missouri* (Chicago, 1908), v. 1, p. 298.

❧ The Comanches (successors on the Plains to the power and prestige formerly held by the Padoucas), were described by Athanase de Mézières (lieutenant governor at Natchitoches) in a report dated October 29:

The Comanché are scattered from the great Missuris River to the neighborhood of the frontier presidios of New Spain. They are a people so numerous and so haughty that when asked their number, they make no difficulty of comparing it to that of the stars. They are so skillful in horsemanship that they have no equal; so daring that they never ask for or grant truces; and in the possession of such a territory that, finding in it an abundance of pasturage for their horses and an incredible number of cattle [buffalo] which furnish them raiment, food, and shelter, they only just fall short of possessing all of the conveniences of the earth, and have no need to covet the trade pursued by the rest of the Indians whom they call, on this account, slaves of the Europeans, and whom they despise.

[They] . . . are obliged to follow [the buffalo herds] . . . into the more temperate country of the south [when winter arrives], whence the extreme heat of the summer again drives them along with the herds towards the cold regions. From these perpetual comings and goings it arises that the Comanches, relying upon one another, made proud by their great number, and led by their propensity to steal, let few seasons pass without committing the most bloody outrages against the inhabitants of New and Old Mexico.

Mézières recommended that "since their reduction will be one of the most costly and difficult that may be planned in this America" it would be good policy to encourage "to some extent, those who are interested in the destruction of so proud and cruel an enemy."

Ref: H. E. Bolton's *Athanase de Mézières* . . . (Cleveland, 1914), v. 1, pp. 218, 219.

1772

❡ Writing from the Great Osage village [in present Vernon county, Mo.], Rouquiere (one of several traders there), in a June 14 letter, described Osage depredations on the lower Arkansas and Red rivers (three Frenchmen killed and two young men taken captive). He also stated that a band of Osages had left the village in early April to make war on the Black Pawnees, and returned with two French scalps. The victims, slain near the Paniouassa village, had been mistaken for the enemy (so the Indians claimed). But Rouquiere added: "As for us, not a single trader up to now has any cause for complaint in the village. We have traded at our will and without any difficulty."

Ref: Lawrence Kinnaird, ed., *Annual Report* . . . *American Historical Association*, 1945, v. 2, pp. 202, 203.

1775

❡ Pedro Piernas (lieutenant governor of Upper Louisiana) reported (from St. Louis, May 19) on the ". . . nations with which we are accustomed to trade in pelts in the dependency of the Missouri River." He listed the Mahas, Panis Maha, Panis, Hotos, Cance [Kansa], Little Osages, Missouris, *Republic,* and Great Osages. (*Notable is the reference to the Pawnee Republic Indians, of whom no earlier specific mention has been found.*) Giving values of goods traded in pounds of furs, he estimated the Kansa trade at 7,500 pounds; that of the Pawnee Republic at 3,000;

the Panis at 1,200; the Panis Maha at 1,800; the Little Osages at 7,200; the Great Osages at 15,000. In 1775 trade with the latter two nations was "forbidden" (evidently to punish them for depredations committed); and after both the Kansa and Pawnee Republic entries Piernas wrote "not able to enter," but gave no explanation.

Ref: *Ibid.,* p. 228.

1776

On July 4 the 13 United States of America declared through congress assembled at Philadelphia their right to be free and independent.

Ref: The Declaration of Independence.

1777

❡ In June, or early July, five of a reconnoitering party of seven Osages were killed by a large band of Panis Piquies [Wichitas] somewhere near the Arkansas river [in present Oklahoma?]. To avenge the murders, the Osages in force returned to that area, and on the Arkansas river bank met "the man named Layones with two trappers" whom they killed and robbed. This occurred between July 15 and 18. Later in the year it was reported that the Osages were continuing "their thefts and murders along that river."

Ref: Houck's *Spanish Regime* . . ., v. 1, pp. 149, 150.

❡ Francisco Cruzat (lieutenant governor of Upper Louisiana) in a report (St. Louis, November 1) on the year's fur trade on the Missouri, indicated that the official traders among the Kansa had been Antonio Hubert and Luis Lacroix, who obtained 150 packs of tanned deerskin, one of otter, seven of beaver, and three of buckskin. The trade of the Republica [Pawnee Republic] Indians had gone to Eugenio Pouree, but "the fur of the Republica tribe has not been able to be brought down, as the river of the Canzes has no water."

Cruzat stated that Auguste Chouteau, Sylvestre Labbadie, and three others had traded among the Big Osages. (Also listed were the traders among the Little Osages, Missouris, Mahas, Panis, and Otoes; and the fur statistics for each.) He commented that "the Panis Mahas tribe, where a trader is usually sent, has again become incorporated with the tribe of the Panis Piques [Wichitas], who are settled in the territory of Nachitoches, who [the Panis Mahas] are threatened by the Sioux tribe, who are situated on the banks of Misisipy. . . ."

Ref: *Ibid.,* pp. 139, 140, 183; Nasatir, *op. cit.,* v. 1, p. 70.

❧ In a comprehensive report on the upper Missouri river Indians with whom the Spanish traded, Francisco Cruzat (from St. Louis on November 15) wrote of the "Cances" Indians:

This tribe is composed of 350 warriors. The name of the principal chief . . . is El Comy [perhaps Le Commis? in French—the earliest-located name of a Kansa chief]. They are 150 leagues from this village, and are located on the banks of the Misury river itself, at a distance of some 50 leagues from the tribe of the Misuris. Their occupation has always been, and is, that of the hunt; for although they generally plant a small quantity of maize, it does not, as a general rule, suffice for their necessary support. As a general thing, this tribe is hostile to the tribes of the said Misury river, named the Panis and La Republica [Pawnees]. For this reason they generally cause a great deal of harm to the traders who are sent to those tribes, for they do not allow those traders to ascend the river in order that those tribes may be supplied with guns and ammunition. This is the only harm experienced from this tribe. However, we have heard that they were thinking this year of making peace. This tribe has always been hostile to all those of the Misisipy. From the work of the hunt in which they are engaged, there results the profits of the trade which are made in the furs; for every year that trade produces 180 or 200 packs.

Cruzat stated that "La Republica" Pawnees numbered 350 to 400 warriors. Their principal chief was Escatape. They were located about 110 leagues up the Kansas (from its mouth), and were distant 40 or 50 leagues by land from the Kansa village. Their occupation was hunting. They were hostile to the Kansa and the Big Osages.

The Big Osages numbered 800 warriors. Their principal chief was Cleromon [Clermont]. They lived on a Missouri tributary [i. e., the Osage] 180 leagues from St. Louis by water, and about 110 overland [in present Vernon county, Mo.]. They were hostile to the tribes of "La Republica, the Hotos [Otoes], the Alkanzos [Arkansas], the Panis, the Piquies [Wichitas], and the tribes living on the Misisipy in the English district." They were hunters and accumulated from 500 to 550 packs of deerskins annually.

Cruzat's report also covered the Little Osages, the Missouris, the Otoes, the Pawnees, the Mahas, the Iowas, and the Sioux. The latter two tribes, he stated, traded with persons from "the English district." The Otoes, Pawnees, and Mahas were all enemies of the Kansa; and the Iowas were "hostile to the tribes of the Misury River."

Ref: Houck's *Spanish Regime* . . ., v. 1, pp. 141-145; Bolton in his *Athanase de Mézières* . . ., v. 2, p. 26, noted that Houck "supplied punctuation and made two tribes out of the Panis Piquies, or Wichita." In C. W. Alvord, editor, *Cahokia Records,*

1778-1790 (Illinois Historical Collections, v. 2), p. 632, in "Census of Cahokia," August, 1787, are listed "Michel Clermont, pierre Clermont, auguste Clermont"—and a note states: "from an old Canadian family."

1780

❧ In November Lieutenant Governor Cruzat (writing from St. Louis to his superior officer) referred to "the necessity which I have of using the Little Osages, with our other allied nations, to repress and punish the Kansa nation. As your Lordship knows, the last mentioned has already committed some murders on the Missouri River, assassinating and burning seven hunters who were hunting on that river. . . ."

Ref: Kinnaird, *op. cit.,* v. 2, pp. 394, 395.

1785

❧ In New Orleans Esteban Rodriguez Miró (governor-general of Louisiana) made a report (dated December 12) which included the following statements:

The Cancés is 108 leagues from the mouth of the Missouri, on its right bank. In high water one can ascend it to the village of the Republic or Panis [Pawnee Republic]. . . .

The Cancés have their villages about 140 leagues from the mouth of the Missouri on a very high cliff about two *avanzadas* from the shore of that river. They must have 200 warriors and are unquestionably the best hunters on the Missouri. They maintain peace with the Little Osages and with the Missouris, and make war on the Panis in order to obtain horses. Their hunting land is up the River de Cancés as far as the River de Nimaha. . . .

The Panis are found about 27 leagues from the Chato [Platte] River, and consist of 400 men capable of bearing arms. Their hunting grounds are on the tongue of land between their river and the Chato and extend from their village to the River of San Francisco de Arcanzás [the Arkansas].

The Indians of the Panis Republic, called Paniguaccy or Eyes of the Partridge, live on the River Cancés about 130 leagues from its mouth, and consist of 220 men capable of bearing arms. . . .

The Padós [Padoucas—Plains Apaches] were in former times the most numerous nation on the continent, but the wars which other nations have made against them have destroyed them to such an extent that at present they form only four small groups, who go wandering from place to place continually which saves them from the fury of the other nations. They number about 350 men, very skillful with the arrow and in running. . . .

The Laytanes or wandering Apaches [*i. e.,* Comanches, not Apaches] . . . inhabit the borders of New Mexico. . . . They dominate all the neighboring tribes, and although divided into several war parties . . . they all live in perfect friendship.

Of the Arkansas river Miró wrote:

. . . we find the river of San Francisco de Arkanzás on the western bank [of the Mississippi]. . . . Twelve leagues up this river is the fort of Carlos III [Arkansas Post], between which and the Mississippi at various distances is found the nation of the Arkansas divided into three villages. . . . about 100 leagues above, live the Little Osages, who are the only nation I know in this place bordering on the Kingdom of New Spain. [In mid-1785, a band of the Little Osages had left the Missouri and settled on the upper St. Francis river.]

Ref: Nasatir, *op. cit.*, v. 1, pp. 120, 121, 123, 125-127; Kinnaird, *op. cit.*, v. 3, pp. 160, 162, 164, 165, 166, 170-173. Miró's report quoted from Nasatir with a few changes supplied from Kinnaird.

1786

❧ Writing from New Orleans, August 1, Governor Miró told of steps taken to punish the Osage Indians for an outbreak of depredations. "My prohibition against carrying goods farther than the fort of Arkansas [Arkansas Post]," he stated, "may cause the Osages to molest the white hunters who are established on the upper part of the said river [in present Oklahoma, and possibly some in Kansas] to the number of some 200."

Ref: Kinnaird, *op. cit.*, v. 3, pp. 182-184.

❧ Jacobo Du Breuil (brevet lieutenant colonel of infantry), commandant at Arkansas Post [or, fort of Carlos III], in a report (December 16) on the rivers of his district, wrote of the Arkansas:

. . . its source [is] near the kingdom of New Mexico, according to the report of the hunters who have navigated it for more than 400 leagues, and it empties into the Mississippi at a point 250 leagues from the capital [New Orleans]. It abounds in fish such as the catfish, the *pargo*, seatrout, carp, *armado*, herring, eel, and turtle of two varieties. The Arkansas has several branches in which there are salt beds that give in summer a slightly salty taste to the water. The territory watered by this river has a natural growth of poplars, willows, oaks, cypress, walnut, pecans, elms, etc.

Ref: Kinnaird, *op. cit.*, v. 3, p. 193.

1787

❧ Pedro Vial, in a map showing the Mississippi watershed, part of that of the Rio Grande, and the area in between, indicated apparent first-hand knowledge of the upper Missouri. He showed that river "rising in high western mountains and flowing near settlements termed 'Riqura' [Arikara] and 'Maundane' [Mandan]."

Commenting on this map, N. M. Loomis and A. P. Nasatir, in their *Pedro Vial and the Roads to Santa Fe*, conclude: ". . . the inescapable fact is that for fifteen years (from 1787 to 1802) Pedro Vial appears to have been the only white man with an accurate knowledge of the upper Missouri River."

Ref: Carl I. Wheat, *Mapping the Transmississippi West* (San Francisco, 1957), v. 1, pp. 125-127 (including first quote above); N. M. Loomis and A. P. Nasatir, *Pedro Vial and the Roads to Santa Fe* (Norman, Okla., c1967), *facing* p. 291, and pp. 380-387.

1790

℃ Jacques d'Eglise, licensed in August to hunt on the Missouri, presumably started upriver in the late summer. At the Omaha village (in 1790?) he met Pierre Montardy and got more trading goods. By 1792, if not earlier, he had ascended the Missouri to "8 villages of a nation about which there was some knowledge under the name of Mandan, but to which no one had ever gone in this direction and by this route." (In October, 1792, d'Eglise returned to St. Louis.)

Ref: A. P. Nasatir's article on d'Eglise in *Mississippi Valley Historical Review*, v. 14 (June, 1927), pp. 47-71; Loomis and Nasatir, *op. cit.*, pp 89, 106, 107, 387.

1790-1791

℃ Auguste Chouteau was granted part of the trade of the Kansa in 1790. In pursuit of that commerce Cadet [Pierre] Chouteau spent the winter of 1790-1791 among the Kansa, and reported in St. Louis in the spring that they had not traded all their furs with him because Mississippi river Indians (representing English traders) had taken part of the pelts despite all he could do. Chouteau also stated that about the first of March some 90 Big Osages with all their chiefs and head men had come where he was camping *on the Kansas river* to ask why traders had been prohibited from visiting their villages. Angered when told it was punishment for depredations on the Arkansas (where they had been killing and plundering), some of the Osages began to blame the trader, and had to be restrained by chiefs of both nations from taking his merchandise.

[In 1785 the Kansa were reported as still living on the Missouri river; but in 1790-1791 Chouteau spent the winter with them on the Kansas; and in 1792 Pedro Vial was in the Kansa village on the Kansas. The evidence is persuasive, but not conclusive, that these Indians left their Missouri river village between 1785 and 1790. Referring to this move, but not dating it, U. S. Commr. H. L. Ellsworth, in 1833, wrote: ". . . the evidence is satisfactory that the Otoes attacked the Kansas at their old village on the Missouri near Independence creek—drove them from their village and took possession. The Kansas never afterward occupied that ground but pitched their tents 60 or 80 miles distant on the Kansas River. . . ."

[The village which Chouteau and Vial visited probably was the site about two miles east of present Manhattan in what is now Pottawatomie county; or, as it could have been described in 1794: On the Kansas river, two miles east of the mouth of the Big Blue. (During the 1906 flood, the Big Blue cut a new channel near its mouth and since then has flowed into the Kansas some four miles east of Manhattan rather than at the town site.)]

Ref: Nasatir, *op. cit.*, v. 1, pp. 135, 143, 144; Ellsworth's letter quoted from Off. of Ind. Aff. Records, Gr. 75, Treaty File in Nat. Archives, as given in Waldo R. Wedel's *An Introduction to Kansas Archeology* (Washington, 1959), pp. 37, 38.

1792

℄ Pedro (Pierre) Vial, native of France, in the employ of New Mexico's governor, set out from Santa Fe on May 21, with two young Spaniards (Vicente Villanueva and Vicente Espinosa), and some pack horses, under orders to open a line of communication between the Spanish settlements of New Mexico and those of upper Louisiana.

They went by way of Pecos; then set a course first eastward and later to the northeast. On May 29 they reached the Colorado (Canadian) river and followed down it into present Oklahoma. On June 22 they turned northeast to look for the Napestle (Arkansas). Vial's diary entry of June 27 states: "In the morning early we continued the march to the north across spacious lands to the Napestle River, where we made camp for the night, having traveled 8 [leagues]." (They were in present Kansas still to the southwest of the great bend of the Arkansas.) Vial thought they had traveled about 140 leagues up to that point.

On June 29 they followed down the river "which flowed east northeast." In the late afternoon (perhaps near Great Bend of today) they found a hunting camp of Kansa Indians on the opposite bank. Several Kansa (including a French-speaking Indian who recalled seeing Vial at the village of St. Louis) interceded to save the trio from being killed. But the Kansa gave them ill treatment—stripped them of clothing, and took possession of their horses and belongings. Vial and his companions remained in the Indians' Arkansas river camp till mid-August, when the Kansa started homeward. Vial says they "traveled ten days on a northeasterly course across broad plains all the way." He estimated the distance as 50 leagues. On August 25 they reached the Kansa village "on the banks of the Kansas river" (presumably the site two miles east of present Manhattan—*see* preceding entry).

In a goods-laden pirogue, a licensed French trader (with two? employees) arrived at the village on September 11. He supplied Vial and companions with clothes, a gun, and other items. On September 16 the explorers went down the Kansas river with the traders returning to St. Louis; and reached that place on October 3 (or 6?).

Ref: Loomis and Nasatir, *op. cit.*, pp. 369-379; Houck's *Spanish Regime*, v. 1, pp. 350-358; *Chronicles of Oklahoma*, v. 6 (June, 1928), p. 212; A. B. Hulbert's *Southwest on the Turquoise Trail* (c1933), pp. 43-54.

1793

❦ In the spring a band of Iowa Indians went to a camp of the Kansa to buy horses. While the Kansa warriors were out hunting (in order to feed their guests) the Iowas "killed, and took prisoner forty-eight women and children, and carried off all the horses." The result was renewed warfare between two nations which had long been enemies.

Ref: Nasatir, *op. cit.*, v. 1, p. 185.

❦ No traders were permitted to go up the Missouri during the year "on account of the war which was ordered declared on the Osages" to punish them for depredations in Spanish Louisiana.

Ref: *Ibid.*, v. 2, p. 530.

❦ On June 14 Pedro Vial, and his two companions of 1792, left St. Louis bound for Santa Fe. In a pirogue (with hired oarsmen), and accompanied by five traders in another boat, they journeyed up the Missouri to the Little Nemaha's mouth (near present Nemaha, Neb.), taking more than two months to make the trip. (Vial's plan to leave the Missouri earlier, and proceed directly westward overland, had been abandoned because of hostile Osages.)

At the Little Nemaha camp (rendezvous for traders with the Pawnees) Vial's party remained from August 24 till September 11. On the 12th, with Pawnee guides (who were of the Republic band), they set out overland. "We took the road through a large plain, route to the southwest," Vial wrote on the first day. Proceeding in the same direction, but turning more to the west on September 15, they came on the evening of the 17th to "a little stream [the Big Blue?] which enters the River of the Cances." Next day their route again lay "through good prairie land," and they camped on "an arm of the River of the Cances." On the 19th they noted, as they traveled, a "hill of great height which the Indians call Blue Hill." Their camp that night was on a little stream "which enters into that of the Cances." In mid-afternoon of September 20 they arrived at the Pawnee Republic village. (They had been met, around noon, by chief "Sarisere" [Sharitarish] and some of his warriors.) According to Vial's calculations, during the nine days' journey from the Little Nemaha they had traveled 49 leagues (about 125? miles). The village, on a river—the Smoky Hill, possibly in the vicinity of present Abilene, contained some 300 warriors.

The Pawnee Republic Indians maintained friendly relations with the Spanish. Their enemies were the Osages, the Taovayas [Pani-Piques—Wichitas], and the Comanches. Their allies were three other Pawnee villages (on the Platte; about 20 leagues apart; totaling some 1,000 warriors), the Mahas, the Otoes, and the Kansa (who were located about 30 leagues distant). The latter three were said to have around 1,100 men. The Osages were estimated to number 1,000 warriors; the Taovayas about 400; and the Comanches to have so many as to be countless.

Vial and his companions remained in the Pawnee Republic village till early October. They bought ten horses. On October 4, after presenting gifts to their hosts, they started for Santa Fe with seven Pawnee guides. Ten days later the party reached the Rio Napeste [Arkansas], apparently west of present Dodge City. (By Vial's calculations they traveled 68½ leagues [about 175? miles] from the Indian village before reaching the Arkansas.) Continuing on a southwesterly course to the Canadian, their homeward route took them by way of Pecos to Santa Fe on November 15.

[Early references to the Pawnee Republic Indians (see 1777 and 1785) did not specify on which fork of the Kansas they lived. A study of Vial's journal leaves little doubt that in 1793 they were, at least temporarily, on the Smoky Hill—somewhat east of the Solomon's mouth. Jean B. Truteau (see 1794) indicated the Indians' presence in that area when he wrote (in 1796) that the Republican nation was on the southwestern branch of the Kansas river, near its source. But Antoine Soulard (see 1795) located them on his map on the Kansas tributary which we call the Republican and which he plainly labeled "R. de la Republica Pani." Victor Collot (see 1796) in the text of his book stated they were on the southwest branch of the Kansas; but on his map placed them on the Republican fork (though he did not give it a name).]

Ref: Loomis and Nasatir, *op. cit.*, pp. 393-405 (for Vial's diary); *Chronicles of Oklahoma*, v. 9 (June, 1931), pp. 195-208 (also has Vial's diary); Nasatir, *op. cit.*, v. 2, pp. 383-385 (for Truteau); Bolton's *Anthanase de Mézières*, v. 1, pp. 246, 250, 294-296 (for the Taouaiazes); Wedel's . . . *Kansas Archeology*, pp. 59, 60 (for additional data on Pawnee Republic villages).

1794

❈ Early in May, at a meeting in St. Louis, arrangements were made for the year's Missouri fur trade. Four persons (Benito Vasquez, Bernal Sarpy, Laurent Durocher, and the lieutenant governor, Zenon Trudeau) were to have equal shares of the Kansa trade. Auguste Chouteau was allotted the Pawnee Republic Indians. The Grand Osages' trade was divided into 12 shares (Cerré, Robidoux, Pierre Chouteau, Papin, and Clamorgan were five of the allottees), and the Little Osages' traders (of whom there were four) included Roy and Pratte.

Ref: Nasatir, *op. cit.*, v. 1, pp. 210, 211; Kinnaird, *op. cit.*, v. 4, p. 279.

❦ At St. Louis, on May 12, an organization "La Compagnie de Commerce pour la Decouverte des Nations du haut du Missouri" (better known as the "Missouri Company") was formed for the purpose of exploring and trading on the upper Missouri. Among its members were Auguste and Pierre Chouteau, Jean Papin, Benito Vasquez, Gregoire Sarpy, Jacinto St. Cyr, Joseph Robidoux, Gabriel Cerré, Antoine Roy, and Jacques Clamorgan (who was director of the company).

Ref: Houck's *Spanish Regime* . . ., v. 2, pp. 173-178; Nasatir, *op. cit.*, v. 1, pp. 217, 218.

❦ The "Missouri Company" sent Jean Baptiste Truteau (a 45-year-old, Montreal-born, St. Louis school teacher) as head of its first upper-Missouri expedition. Truteau, in a well-loaded pirogue, manned by eight oarsmen, set out from St. Louis on June 7, and reached the mouth of the Kansas on July 12, stopping briefly there (it appears) to see a trader named Quenneville. "La riviere des cansas," he noted in his journal, was navigable for about 100 leagues in the springtime; it abounded in beavers, otters, and other fur-bearing animals. The village of the Kansa, whose men were good hunters and warriors, was 80 leagues [by water?] upstream; and ten leagues beyond began the country of the Pawnee Republic.

On July 14 Truteau and party camped on the Isles des Parques [about opposite present Leavenworth]. Next day, at 12 leagues above the mouth of the Kansas, they came to the first *old* village of the Kansas [Salt creek valley, Leavenworth co.]. On July 21 (after being delayed by a prolonged rainstorm) they reached the second *old* Kansa village [the "Village of 24" at present Doniphan] at 12 leagues above the first. By the following evening they had ascended as far as the great bend of the Missouri, near present St. Joseph, Mo. Between the Kansas and the Platte, wrote Truteau, there were three rivers (the Great Nemaha, Little Nemaha, and the Nishnabotna) which were navigable for a short distance and only in the springtime.

(Truteau's intended destination was the Mandan villages where he was to establish a fort and trading agency, but he got only as far as the Arikara country. His description [dated 1796] and information on the upper Missouri was used by French travelers Collot [1796] and Perrin du Lac [1802].)

Ref: Truteau's journal in *American Historical Review*, Lancaster, Pa., v. 19 (January, 1914), pp. 299-333; A. P. Nasatir's article on Truteau in L. R. Hafen, editor, *The Mountain*

Men and the Fur Trade of the Far West, v. 4, pp. 381-387; Nasatir, *op. cit.,* v. 1, pp. 86-93, 257-263, and pp. 262, 267, for item on "Quenneville." Annie H. Abel in her *Tabeau's Narrative of Loisel's Expedition* . . . (Norman, Okla., 1939), p. 60, offers identifications for the name. *See, also,* Stella M. Drumm's editorial note on Francois Quenneville in John C. Luttig's *Journal of a Fur-Trading Expedition* . . . (St. Louis, 1920), p. 60.

1794-1795

℄ Osage-Spanish relations improved greatly following the establishment in 1794-1795 of a small fort in the Osages' country. Short-lived Fort Carondelet [in Blue Mound? tp., Vernon co., Mo.] was built by the Chouteaus (Auguste and Pierre) in return for a six-year monopoly (1794-1800) of the Big and Little Osages' trade. Commandant Pierre Chouteau took his family there in 1795; and a few other persons, in addition to militia troops were residents for a time. Osage depredations dwindled due to the influence of the Chouteaus, who enjoyed the complete confidence of the Indians.

(But in 1802 the Chouteaus lost the Osage trading rights to Manuel Lisa and others, and all trace of Fort Carondelet quickly disappeared. Pike and Wilkinson found only a "superior growth of vegetation" at the site in 1806.)

Ref: Houck's *Spanish Regime* . . ., v. 2, pp. 100-110; Nasatir, *op. cit.,* v. 1, pp. 214, 320, 321, 326, v. 2, pp. 530, 584; *Missouri Historical Review,* Columbia, Mo., v. 35, pp. 92-95; Louis Houck's *A History of Missouri* (Chicago, 1908), v. 2, p. 252; Z. M. Pike's August 17, 1806, entry in the various editions of his *An Account of Expeditions to the Sources of the Mississippi.* . . .

℄ Antoine Soulard's maps were, so far as known, the first to show the Big Blue (tributary of the Kansas) by name; and to indicate the location of Fort Carondelet [in present Vernon co., Mo.]. There was, originally, a 1794 map, sketched expressly for Truteau's use on his "Missouri Company" expedition. But the 1795 versions (French and Spanish) are the only ones now known to exist.

On the French map, entitled "Idee Topographique des Hauts du Mississipi et du Missouri," the Big Blue was labeled "R. Eau bleue" ("R. Agua azul" on the Spanish map) meaning "Blue water." The Kansas appeared as "R. de les Cans," and the Republican fork as "R. de la Republica Pani." The Kansa village (represented by four "dots"—perhaps to indicate 400 warriors?) was shown as on the north bank of the Kansas, east of the junction of the Big Blue. The Republican Pawnees' village (represented by three "dots") was on the north bank of the branch of the Kansas named for them, at some distance upstream.

(Soulard, surveyor of Upper Louisiana and St. Louis resident, according to his own statement, had once ascended the Missouri about 500 leagues.)

Ref: **Nasatir,** *op. cit.,* v. 1, *between* pp. 46, 47 (for French map), v. 2, p. 760; Wheat, *Mapping the Transmississippi West,* v. 1, pp. 157, 158, and *facing* p. 158 (for Spanish map, which, curiously, was misdated "1785"). This map also has been reproduced in Robert W. Baughman's *Kansas in Maps* (Topeka, 1961), p. 16.

1795

❡ Benito and Quenache de Rouin, traders returning from the Kansa village, were robbed and "soundly thrashed with blows of sticks" by a party of some 160 Iowas, who carried off two of their hired men. Zenon Trudeau's report of the incident (St. Louis, March 4) stated: "They left Benito, as well as the other on the seventh of the month of January at the entrance of the Kansas river, without arms, food, or clothing. . . ." The two captives were ransomed by English traders and returned to St. Louis.

Ref: Nasatir, *op. cit.*, v. 1, pp. 316, 318.

❡ In April the "Missouri Company" sent a man named Lecuyer with a large, well-loaded pirogue, and oarsmen, on a journey to the upper Missouri. This second expedition of the St. Louis company was pillaged by the Ponca Indians. Few details of its fate are known. Lecuyer was later blamed for the disaster.

Ref: Houck's *Spanish Regime* . . ., v. 2, pp. 176, 178, 187, 190.

❡ When a distribution of medals to chiefs of the Missouri river tribes was proposed, Zenon Trudeau (lieutenant-governor of Spanish Illinois) suggested (May 30) that large medals should go to Kansa chiefs Kayguechinga (or Le Petit Chef) and Jhahoangage (or Les grands Chevaux); and small ones to Kueehagachin (or Le Batard) and Whachanguia (or Le Geur qui brule).

Ref: Nasatir, *op. cit.*, v. 1, pp. 326, 327. "Le Geur" perhaps should read "Le Coeur" (heart); and "Whachanguia" may have meant "the burning heart."

❡ Zenon Trudeau reported (from St. Louis, July 4) that Pedro [Pierre] Vial and four companions, earlier in the year had traveled from Santa Fe to the Pawnee Republic village "on the bank of the Kansas River" and spent 15 days there. He was on an official mission for the Spanish to effect peace between the Pawnee Republic Indians and the Laytanes [Comanches]. Traders from the St. Louis area who were in the village at the time said that he accomplished his purpose (and delivered a medal, a complete suit of clothes, and other gifts to the Pawnee chief). Vial had taken the traders to meet the Comanches, and wished to take them on to New Mexico, but they refused. He was reported to have made the journey from Santa Fe to the Pawnees in eight(?) days.

Ref: Nasatir, *op. cit.*, v. 1, pp. 329, 330.

❡ The "Missouri Company's" third expedition was headed by Spanish citizen (but Scottish-born) James MacKay. With 33 men and four merchandise-laden pirogues he set out from St. Louis in late August on a journey which was intended to open up commerce in the unknown parts of the upper Missouri, and to attempt explorations as far as the Pacific. The boats, making slow progress, probably passed along the Kansas bank of the Missouri in the latter part of September. By October 14 (on which date MacKay began to keep a journal) the expedition had reached only as far as the Otoe village (about a mile below the Platte's mouth). Continuing to the Maha village some distance above, MacKay built a trading fort where he spent the winter. But he sent his lieutenant, the Welshman John Evans, to explore farther upstream.

MacKay compiled a table of distances "ascending from the Missouri's mouth" (dated 1797) which included the following information:

The "beautiful" Kansas river (at 100¾ leagues) was "navigable for canoes for more than 60 leagues at all times; but not for more than 20 leagues for large boats" in times of low waters. The Kansa lived 80 leagues up their river. On the Missouri, the "First old village of the Kansas nation" (at 112⁵⁄₁₂ leagues) was "situated upon the bare hills"; and the "Second old village of the Kansas" (at 119¾ leagues) was "upon the south bank," and "about a league lower and on the same side" was an iron mine.

Wolf river (at 136⁷⁄₁₂ leagues) was a small river. The "River of the Great Nemahas" (at 141¼ leagues) was "navigable some leagues for pirogues." On that river the boats passed that carried on commerce with the Pawnee Republic nation, whose village was on a branch of the Kansas river. The "River of the Little Nemahas" (at 150⁵⁄₁₂ leagues) was a small river. The Platte (at 171¼ leagues) was "as large as the Missouri but so shallow and the course so rapid" that navigation was very difficult for any boat, except during springtime high waters.

Ref: Houck's *Spanish Regime* . . ., v. 2, pp. 181-192; and for MacKay's table: *Mississippi Valley Historical Review*, Cedar Rapids, Iowa, v. 10 (March, 1924), pp. 432-441, or Nasatir, *op. cit.*, v. 2, pp. 485-489.

1796

❦ Victor Collot (former French general) toured Louisiana in 1796 on an information-collecting expedition for his government. The data he gathered on the Missouri river (beyond the Osage tributary) however, was derived, not from personal observation, but from traders (Truteau principally) whom he met at St. Louis. Collot died in Paris in 1805. His manuscript, together with maps and sketches (including a "Map of the Missouri" probably drawn in 1796), was not published until 1826. An English edition of *Voyage in Amerique Septentrionale* appeared in the same year. Collot wrote of the Kansas:

> The river des Cans . . . is navigable an hundred leagues for barks and barges of every kind; it runs through very fertile lands, flat, well wooded, and intersected by rich meadows; but the country, such as we have already described, does not extend farther than one or two leagues from the banks. In ascending this river fifty leagues, we find a fortified point, on which is situated the great village of the Cans. The branch which runs to the West is called the River of White Water; on that of the south-west the Indian nation called Republican is established [a statement contradictory to his map location, as noted below].

Elsewhere in his work the "Cans" Indians were said to be "On the river Cans, where it divides, 60 leagues from its mouth." On his "Map of the Missouri" (1796?) Collot showed the "Can" just below the junction of the "Blue Water" with the "R. Cans." Farther upstream, on the *upper* of two forks (neither named) of the Kansas was the Republican village. The lower fork was shown to have a "S. W. Branch." But the "River of White Water" (referred to above) did not appear on the map.

Ref: Victor Collot's *A Journey in North America* (1924 reprint), v. 1, pp. 279, 310, and Plate 29 (in volume of maps and sketches); Wheat, *op. cit.*, v. 1, p. 160, and map *facing* p. 160; Abel's *Tabeau's Narrative*, pp. 14, 15.

1796-1797

❑ Fur trader Francisco Derouin [Francis Dorion?], arriving from the Platte, reported at St. Louis (on May 14, 1797) that the Kansa and Otoe Indians had spent the winter sending war parties against each other, and several had been killed. (The Otoe village was at the mouth of the Platte.)

Ref: Nasatir, *op. cit.*, v. 2, pp. 516, 517.

1798

❑ Zenon Trudeau, the lieutenant governor of Upper Louisiana, reported (from St. Louis, January 15):

> The Kancé tribe has its village located on the banks of the river of that name. They number about 400 men, and are all better hunters than the Osages, and at the least as great rogues as they. This tribe would have an easy entrance to the river of Akanzas [the Arkansas] if it were not for the Osages who prevent them, and certainly they would commit more acts of piracy and roguery than these latter. This is the only tribe whose trade is not exclusive. It is usually divided into six equal parts, each one valued at the sum of eight hundred pesos. These six parts are distributed by lot among all the

merchants of San Luis and Santa Genoveva. Those which have drawn the lot one year are excluded from it the next year, and until all have shared in this advantage. From this tribe 180 packs of furs are obtained annually.

Ref: Houck's *Spanish Regime* . . ., v. 2, p. 252.

1800

⬤ Gregoire Sarpy and [J. P.?] Cabanné, who had been traders among the Kansa for two years, suggested (in a letter, April 26) to Spanish authorities that if they were given the trade of the neighboring Panis also, they could probably mediate a peace treaty between the two nations "for a long time enemies and always at war. . . ." The conflict affected the hunting and trade of both. (Sarpy was among the Kansa again in 1801.)

Ref: Nasatir, *op. cit.,* v. 2, pp. 592, 614-616.

⬤ Régis Loisel, having (in March) been granted the right to "form an establishment in Upper Missouri," journeyed over 1,200 miles up the Missouri, and located on Cedar Island (some distance below what is now called Bad river). Loisel returned to St. Louis by July, 1801, having started(?), but not completed(?), his fort.

Hugh Heney, heading another party, also ascended the Missouri in 1800, leaving St. Louis in June(?). He, too, returned by mid-1801. (His employer, Jacques Clamorgan, said Heney's expedition had been "destroyed by the British.") At St. Louis, on July 6, 1801, Loisel and Heney reached a two-year trade agreement. (Lewis and Clark met Heney at Fort Mandan in the winter of 1804-1805.)

In 1802 Loisel again went up the Missouri, and built his fort on Cedar Island, according to Pierre-Antoine Tabeau, whose account says he accompanied the trader. Loisel (and Tabeau) returned to St. Louis this same year.

See, also, an 1803 annals entry.

Ref: *Tabeau's Narrative of Loisel's Expedition to the Upper Missouri*, edited by Annie H. Abel (Norman, Okla., 1939), pp. 22-27.

⬤ On October 1, by the secret treaty of San Ildefonso, Napoleon secured Louisiana from Spain. The territory ceded was to be the same which Spain had received from France 37 years earlier.

1801

⬤ Jacques Clamorgan, who, in 1800, had obtained exclusive trading privileges with the Otoes, Omahas and Poncas, was, on May 2, also granted the trade of the Kansa Indians.

Ref: *Tabeau's Narrative, op. cit.,* p. 23.

1802

⬤ Francois Marie Perrin du Lac (young French writer) came to the

United States in 1801 with a particular desire to visit the upper Missouri and its Indians. Chapter 24 of his *Voyages dans les Deux Lou-
isianes* (published in Paris, 1805) described that part of his travels.
(He supplemented his own observations of the region by using material from Truteau's 1796 description.) Also in the volume was his
Carte du Missouri (1802)—a map more accurate for that country
than any published earlier.

Perrin du Lac and ten others (one perhaps Truteau), set out from
St. Louis on May 18, 1802, to trade up the Missouri. When they
reached the mouth of the Kansas they turned their boat up its channel to the Kansa village [presumably the site two miles east of
present Manhattan—*see* 1790-1791]. For 12 days [in June?] they
traded and feasted among the Kansa, who, wrote Perrin du Lac,
"are tall, handsome, vigorous, and brave . . .   active and good
hunters, and trade is carried on with them by the Whites without
danger. . . ."

On returning to the mouth of the Kansas (navigable, he stated,
at all seasons for 500 miles), the traders cached their furs, and proceeded once again up the Missouri. They found the first *old* village
of the Kansa 35 miles upstream, and the second *old* village 22 miles
beyond.

Continuing to the Platte they ascended it to the Great Panis village where they spent eight days. "We were better received by the
Great Panis than we had been by the Kanses," wrote Perrin du Lac.
"They were at war with the nation called Republicans, and had only
a small number of fire-arms, without any powder. We supplied
them with some in exchange for . . .   skins. . . .   The
Great Panis are not so tall as the Kanses. They are active, and good
hunters. . . .   Their manners very closely resemble those of
the Kanses."

After visiting the Mahas and Poncas, the traders continued as far
up the Missouri as the White river (where there was a Cheyenne
village). On August 26 they started downstream. Stopping at the
mouth of the Kansas to pick up their cached furs, they saw a party
of Sioux approaching and re-embarked hastily, leaving the less valuable pelts behind. They had "hardly gained the opposite shore"
when they were "saluted with a discharge of musketry; but night
coming on, the savages abandoned their pursuit." On September
20 they reached St. Louis.

Perrin du Lac's map of the Missouri showed the "R. des Kancés"
(with the "Village des Kancés"); its tributary the Blue ("R. de l'Eau

bleue"); and its Republican fork ("Fourche des Republiques") with the "Village des Republiques" located well above the 39th parallel. Also shown were the two "Ancien" villages of the Kansa on the Missouri.

[An enlarged section of Perrin du Lac's map is reproduced in this volume.]

Ref: Nasatir, *op. cit.*, v. 2, pp. 706-712; F. M. Perrin du Lac's *Travels* . . . (1807 English ed.); Wheat, *op. cit.*, v. 1, map *facing* p. 159.

About 1802

❧ As the Lewis and Clark expedition traveled up the Missouri in the summer of 1804, a site several miles below the mouth of Wolf river [in present Doniphan county] was pointed out to the explorers as the former location of a French "settlement." William Clark's journal entry on July 9 stated:

. . . at Six Miles passed the mouth of Creek on the L. S. [larboard, or Kansas side] called Monter's [*Montain's*] Creek, about *two* miles above is some Cabins where our Bowman & Several frenchmen Camp^d. two years ago. . . .

And Sgt. Charles Floyd wrote in his journal on July 9:

. . . Passed a prarie on the South Side whare several French familyes had setled and made Corn Some Years ago Stayed two years the Indians Came Freckentley to See them and was verry frendley. . . .

Ref: Reuben G. Thwaites' *Original Journals of the Lewis and Clark Expedition* (New York, 1904), v. 1, p. 72.

1802-1803

❧ The Great and Little Osage trade, in 1802, was granted for five years to Manuel Lisa and his partners Gregoire Sarpy, Charles Sanguinet, and Francois M. Benoit. (The new four-year contract Auguste Chouteau had received from the Spanish in 1801 for the exclusive Osage trade was thus cancelled.) In 1803 Lisa acquired Sarpy's and Sanguinet's shares.

Ref: Nasatir, *op. cit.*, v. 2, pp. 591, 592.

❧ Cashesegra's band of Great Osages and some of the Little Osages (including many of the best hunters) removed from the Osage river [in present Vernon co., Mo.] in 1802 or 1803, to the lower Verdigris [in northern Oklahoma, some 60 miles above the Arkansas-Verdigris junction]. Pierre Chouteau induced them to move in order to regain part of the trade he had lost to Manuel Lisa.

[Lt. James B. Wilkinson, of Pike's 1806 expedition, reported that Cashesegra (Big Track) was the nominal leader, but Clermont was the "greatest warrior and most influential man" among them.]

Ref: *Ibid.*, pp. 539, 592, 680, 688; Lt. J. B. Wilkinson's report, April 6, 1807, Appendix to the various editions of Z. M. Pike's *Expeditions* . . .; Stella M. Drumm's editorial note in John C. Luttig's *Journal* . . ., p. 50.

❏ With two companions, James Purcell (once of Bardstown, Ky.) trapped on the Osage [Marais des Cygnes] headwaters in 1802. They were perhaps in what is now east central Kansas when some Kansa stole their horses. Purcell and his friends cached their furs and pursued the thieves into the Kansa village. The "mad Americans" (so called by the Indians) got all but one horse back, only to lose the animals again, when near the Osage river, to unknown robbers. Later their makeshift canoe overturned and the trappers' furs were lost near the mouth of the Osage. His companions then continued homeward, but Purcell joined trader Régis Loisel going up the Missouri to the Mandan country. Later, after trapping and trading with the Padoucas and Kiowas, he arrived in the upper South Platte area. (While in present Colorado he made perhaps the first gold discovery there by a white man.) In June, 1805, he reached Santa Fe and remained for 19 years. Capt. Z. M. Pike who met "Pursley" there in 1807 recorded some of his adventures.

Ref: Z. M. Pike's . . . *Expeditions* . . ., Appendix to pt. III, pp. 16, 17; H. M. Chittenden's *The American Fur Trade of the Far West* (New York, 1935), v. 2, pp. 492, 493.

1803

❏ In January President Jefferson sent a confidential message to congress urging the establishment of Indian trading houses on the United States frontier. Also, he proposed that an exploring party be sent "to trace the Missouri to its source, to cross the Highlands, and follow the best water communication which offered itself from thence to the Pacific Ocean." Congress approved and voted $2,500 "for the purpose of extending the external commerce of the United States." Jefferson chose Meriwether Lewis to head the expedition, and Lewis suggested William Clark as coleader.

Ref: W. P. Webb's *The Great Plains* (Boston and New York, 1936), p. 143; L. R. Hafen and C. C. Rister's *Western America* (New York, 1941), pp. 174, 175.

❏ Napoleon sold Louisiana (acquired just three years earlier from Spain) to the United States on April 30. Formal transfer ceremonies took place on December 20, at New Orleans.

❏ Trader Régis Loisel, en route to his fort on the upper Missouri (*see* 1800 annals entry), passed along the "Kansas" border in midyear. At St. Louis he had been commissioned to make a report on the upper country. His party included Pierre-Antoine Tabeau (clerk?) who kept a (lost) diary covering the period June 22, 1803, to May 20, 1805.

— 47 —

In the spring of 1804 Loisel journeyed down the Missouri. Explorers Lewis and Clark, just starting upriver, met him on May 25. Loisel dated his "Memorial" (report) to the lieutenant-governor of Louisiana May 28, 1804.

Tabeau, who, in 1804, moved down to an Arikara village and remained till the spring of 1805, while there, prepared a narrative (based on his diary) covering the upper river Indian tribes, trade with them, their manners, customs, beliefs, also a description of animals, birds, fish, etc. In the spring of 1805, aboard a barge Lewis and Clark sent down the Missouri, Tabeau (with a large load of peltry, and his "narrative") arrived at St. Louis. (The barge probably left Fort Mandan April 8; and perhaps early in May passed along the "Kansas" border.)

Ref: *Tabeau's Narrative, op. cit.;* Houck's *Spanish Régime, op. cit.,* pp. 355-364. Loisel died at, or near, St. Louis in October, 1804.

1804

❦ Upper Louisiana was transferred, officially, from France to the United States in ceremonies at St. Louis on March 9. Next day, Amos Stoddard (as U. S. agent) proclaimed the establishment of American authority in the district.

The newly-acquired Louisiana territory west of the Mississippi was divided (by act of congress, March 26) into the *Territory of Orleans* (which later became the state of Louisiana) and the *District of Louisiana* (which, effective October 1, was placed under the jurisdiction of the Territory of Indiana).

Ref: Clarence E. Carter, comp. and ed., *The Territorial Papers of the United States,* v. 13, pp. 8, 9; *Missouri Historical Review,* Columbia, v. 48, p. 10.

❦ The Lewis and Clark expedition (45 men in a 55-foot keelboat and two pirogues) which, on May 14, had started up the Missouri from near St. Louis, encamped on June 26 "at the upper point of the mouth of the river Kanzas," and remained for three days. In his journal, William Clark wrote:

[The Kansas river] . . . receves its name from a Nation which dwells at this time on its banks & [has?] 2 villages   one about 20 leagues & the other 40 Leagues up, [The explorers' report made clear that the Kansa were in *one* village (near the Big Blue's mouth), the location "20 leagues" up being a *former* village site.] those Indians are not verry noumerous at this time, reduced by war with their neighbours, &c, [Their population was estimated at 300 warriors and 1,300 in all, in the report.] they formerly lived on the South banks of the Missourie 24 Leagues above this river in a open & butifull plain, and were verry noumerous at the time the french first Settled the Illinois, I am told they are a fierce & warlike people [and, according to the report, a "dissolute, lawless banditti"], being badly Supplied with fire arms, [they] become easily conquered by the Aiauway [Iowa] & Saukees [Sacs] who are better furnished with those materials of War, This Nation is now out in the Plains hunting the Buffalow. . . .

Continuing up the Missouri on June 29, the explorers camped on the north bank. On the 30th, after a ten-mile journey, they stopped for the night on the south (Kansas) side where Sgt. Patrick Gass recorded in his journal "there were the most signs of game I ever saw." On July 1 camp was on one of the "Isles des Parques or field Isl'ds" near the south bank—facing a (Kansas) prairie [about opposite present Leavenworth]. The following evening, Sgt. Charles Floyd wrote in his journal:

> . . . Campt on the N Side, on the South Side was a old French fort [Fort Cavagnial, 1744-1764] who had setled hear to protect the Trade of this [Kansa] nation in the valley the Kansas Had a village between tow pints of High Praria Land a Handsome Situation for a town. [This was in Salt creek valley, northeast Leavenworth county.]

On July 3 they passed Isle au Vache (Cow Island), negotiated a stretch of sandbar, and stopped overnight on the south (Kansas) bank, half a mile beyond an old, deserted trading post [above present Oak Mills, Atchison county].

At sunrise on July 4 one shot was fired from the keelboat's swivel gun. When the travelers came to a creek flowing in from the south (Kansas) side, they named it "Fourth of July creek." Above was a high mound where three Indian paths centered, and from which there was "a very extensive prospect" [at present Atchison]. Some miles farther on they stopped on the north side, about a mile above a stream flowing in from the Kansas side—a stream which they named "Independence creek." Their camp was opposite the second old Kansa village [i. e., across the river from present Doniphan]. Wrote William Clark: ". . . we closed the [day] by a Descharge from our bow piece [and] an extra Gill of whiskey."

On July 5 the explorers spent the night on the Kansas side, and Clark recorded:

> I observe great quantity of Summer & fall Grapes, Berries & Wild roases on the banks. Deer is not so plenty as useal, great Deel of Elk Sign.

On the seventh and again on the ninth of July [on which date they passed several miles beyond Wolf river, Doniphan county] their camps were on the Kansas bank of the Missouri.

Meriwether Lewis' ". . . Summary View of Rivers and Creeks, Etc.," presumably prepared at Fort Mandan (N. D.) where the Lewis and Clark expedition wintered in 1804-1805, included these notes on the Kansas river:

> . . . it takes it's course nearly East about 300 leagues [750 miles] through fertile and leavel, plains & praries, intersperced with groves of timbered land.

. . . it has been navigated 200 leagues [500 miles] and there is good reason to believe . . . that it is navigable for perogues much further perhaps nearly to it's source.

Of more consequence was the summary's table of distances on the Kansas, which *named* (and gave distances, width, and direction of) a number of its tributaries in addition to the already-known Republican and "Bluewater" (Big Blue) rivers—among them "Wor-rah-ru za" (Wakarusa) river, "Grasshopper Creek" (now Delaware river), and "Solomon's Creek" (Solomon river). But the distances (from the mouth of the Kansas) as listed in the table were notably inaccurate.

Nicholas King prepared a manuscript map of the Missouri country which was available to several government offices early in 1806. Its data (including the Kansas tributaries' names) came from a sketch map William Clark had drawn during the winter of 1804-1805 and sent to Washington.

Ref: R. G. Thwaites, ed., *Original Journals of the Lewis and Clark Expedition* . . . (New York, 1904-1905), v. 1, pp. 60-68, v. 6, pp. 35-36 (table of distances), 84-85; *KHQ*, v. 21, pp. 402-405 (for comment on the Kansas river data); Donald Jackson, ed., *Letters of the Lewis and Clark Expedition With Related Documents* (Urbana, 1962); Wheat, *op. cit.*, v. 2, pp. 31-60; Ernest S. Osgood, ed., *The Field Notes of Captain William Clark, 1803-1805* (New Haven, 1964). In the *Letters* . . . edited by Jackson, on p. 564, William Clark's item No. 20 (in a December 7, 1810, letter) states: "The remains of the Two Kanzas Villages spoken of. Some appearance of earthen houses [several words illegible]. Part of stone chimneys where an old fort [stood?] at a short distance from the upper[?] village which was occupied by the French. . . ." *See, also*, an 1814 annals entry.

❧ Pierre Chouteau, of St. Louis, was appointed agent of Indian affairs for the District of Louisiana on July 17, by President Jefferson. He was charged to give particular attention to the Osage Indians.

Ref: *Territorial Papers of the U. S.*, v. 13, pp. 31-33.

❧ Outfitted with trading goods by William Morrison (a Kaskaskia, Ill., merchant), Jeannot Metoyer and Baptiste Lalande went up the Missouri to the Pawnee villages on the Platte in the summer[?]; and followed up the Platte to its headwaters, it is said, before making their way to Santa Fe, accompanied by some Pawnees and guided by José Gervais (who had taken some Pawnees to New Mexico in 1803, to make peace with the governor, and had returned in the spring of 1804). So far as known, these traders were the first to take goods overland from the American settlements to Santa Fe. Lalande remained in Santa Fe.

Experienced *voyageurs* Lorenzo Durocher and Jacques d'Eglise also went up the Missouri in 1804 intending to go overland to New Mexico. Both reached Santa Fe but perhaps not together. (Durocher is on record at Santa Fe in early 1805; d'Eglise is not placed there definitely till late 1806.)

It may be that none of these adventurers crossed present Kansas in traveling to Spanish territory.

Ref: *Ibid.*, pp. 182, 183; Loomis and Nasatir's *Pedro Vial*, p. 172; A. P. Nasatir, *Before Lewis and Clark*, v. 1, p. 113, v. 2, pp. 755, 756; Annie H. Abel's *Tabeau's Narrative of Loisel's Expedition* (Norman, Okla., 1939), pp. 240-245; Houck's *The Spanish Regime in Missouri* (Chicago, 1909), v. 2, pp. 356, 357, 360; Zebulon M. Pike's *Journals* . . ., edited by Donald Jackson (Norman, Okla., c1966), v. 1, pp. 378, 379 (for comment on the merchant Morrison); *New Mexico Historical Review*, Santa Fe, v. 2 (October, 1927), pp. 370, 371; A. P. Nasatir's article on d'Eglise, in *Mississippi Valley Historical Review*, v. 14 (June, 1927), pp. 47-71.

1805

❡ Gen. James Wilkinson (commander in chief of the army) was appointed governor of the Territory of Louisiana by President Jefferson on March 11. (By a March 3d act of congress, the District of Louisiana had been changed to the Territory of Louisiana which was to operate under a governor, secretary, and three judges.)

Ref: *Territorial Papers of the U. S.*, v. 13, pp. 98, 99.

❡ Trader Charles Courtin (going up the Missouri in the summer?) spent the winter of 1805-1806 among the Teton Sioux. His white companions there were Joseph Dickson and Forrest Handcock from the Illinois country.

Explorers Lewis and Clark, coming down the Missouri in 1806, on August 11 met Dickson and Handcock again ascending the river; and, on September 14, met three young men "Mr. Lacroy, Mr. Aiten & Mr. Coutau [Courtin]" also upbound.

Charles Courtin went higher up the Missouri to an Arikara village in June, 1807, where he received bad treatment. After his release, he continued upriver to the Mandan villages. From there, later in 1807 (or in 1808?) Courtin went far up the Missouri to the Three Forks where he built a stockade. Blackfeet Indians killed him, in present Montana, in February, 1810.

Ref: Alvin M. Josephy, Jr., *The Nez Perce Indians and the Opening of the Northwest* (New Haven and London, 1965), pp. 45, 660-663; Jackson, ed., *Letters of the Lewis and Clark Expedition, op. cit.*, pp. 433, 437.

❡ On September 2 the "Arkansas band" (*see* 1802-1803) of Osages (400 warriors; 1,500 persons in all) living on the Verdigris [near present Claremore, Okla.] arrived at the Great Osage village [on the Little Osage river in present Vernon county, Mo.]. Next day, Lt. George Peter (emissary of General Wilkinson) counciled with assembled chiefs and warriors about the upcoming Indian peace council, a proposed visit of Indians to Washington, and Wilkinson's plan to place a military post in Osage country. Indian Agent Pierre

Chouteau tried, unsuccessfully, to reconcile and reunite the two bands.

Lieutenant Peter estimated there were 2,000 persons, a fourth of them warriors, in the 120-house Great Osage village; and 1,400 people, 400 of them warriors, in the 85-house Little Osage village five miles to the northwest (visited by him on September 5). By his calculation the Osages had a fighting force of 1,300 men.

Ref: *Ibid.*, pp. 231, 232. When Capt. Z. M. Pike took a census of the "grand village" in 1806, he reported there were 502 men, and a total of 1,695 persons in the 214 lodges. (Pike's letter of August 30, 1806, in Appendix to editions of his *An Account of Expeditions to the Sources of the Mississippi.* . . .)

℟ At St. Louis, on October 18, through the efforts of William Henry Harrison (governor of Indiana territory) and Gen. James Wilkinson (governor of Louisiana territory), a reconciliation-and-peace treaty was effected between the Delawares, Miamis, Pottawatomies, Kickapoos, Sacs & Foxes, Kaskaskias, Sioux (of Des Moines river), and Iowas, of the one part, and the Great and Little Osages of the other part.

Ref: *Ibid.*, pp. 245-247.

℟ One Kansa was among a delegation of Indian leaders making a visit to Washington in the latter part of the year. On October 22, General Wilkinson wrote (from his St. Louis headquarters):

The Deputation destined to visit the President, will commence their journey this day under the conduct of Captn [Amos] Stoddard, and will consist of twenty six persons from eleven Nations, (to-wit) The Ottos, Missouri, Panis, Canzes, Osage, Sacque, Reynard [Fox], Ayoua [Iowa], Kickapoo, Pottowattomee, and Miamis, eight of these nations are strangers to us, and the seven last embrace the belligerents among who we have been making Peace. . . .

(When the Rev. James M. Jameson met the influential Kansa leader Wa-kan-ze-re [American Chief] in 1841, he was told that President Jefferson had appointed him a chief when he visited Washington in 1805; and that he had gone, also, to Boston on the journey.)

Ref: *Ibid.*, p. 243; *KHC*, v. 16, p. 263 (for Jameson); *Letters of the Lewis and Clark Expedition* . . . (1962), *op. cit.*, pp. 284-289, contain Indian speeches to President Jefferson (and the secretary of war)—January 4, 1806, by the above delegation.

℟ Lt. James B. Wilkinson's party, convoying a homeward-bound chief of the Arikaras up the Missouri in the late fall, encountered hostile Kansa about 20 leagues below the mouth of the Kansas river and returned the chief to St. Louis on December 8. Gov. James Wilkinson reported:

This body of Canzès after their first, very rude and unfriendly interview in which both Parties took arms, marched up the River and took Post at a difficult and narrow pass, where they decoyed two American hunters on shore who were descending the River, one of whom they killed, and the other after shooting an

Indian made his escape, but unfortunately fell in with our Camp in the night, and not answering the challenge was fired upon and mortally wounded. . . .

I am fearful this disposition of the Canzès, may be excited by agents from St Afee, but the nation has not more than three hundred warriors and a word to our friends the Osages would destroy them. . . .

Ref: *Ibid.*, pp. 297, 298.

1806

❡ In the spring the Spanish learned of the impending American expedition (Pike's) to the western frontier, and quickly assembled an imposing cavalry force (100 dragoons, 500 militia; more than 2,000 horses and mules) equipped for six months. Under command of Lt. Facundo Melgares, this company left Santa Fe about mid-June to accomplish several objectives: to intercept any American parties found in Spanish-claimed territory; to explore the northeast frontier of New Spain; to visit the Comanches, Pawnees, and Kansa.

As Pike heard the story from Melgares, the expedition descended the Red river [*i. e.*, the Canadian] for 233 leagues; met, and counciled with, the great bands of Comanches (following a ceremonial meeting at which three Spanish officers on jet black horses, attended by 500 men on white horses, rode out on a prairie to be received by 1,500 colorfully arrayed and well-mounted Comanche warriors); then moved northeastward.

Changing course to the northwest in what is now south-central Kansas (judging from Melgares' route as traced on Pike's map), the Spaniards reached the Arkansas [perhaps near present Larned] in August. Melgares left part of his force at the river crossing, and continued northward with some 350 horsemen to the Pawnee Republic village on the Republican river, arriving in late August, or early September. He held councils with assembled Grand, and Republic band, Pawnees and presented gifts (flags, commissions, grand medals, and four mules each for the head chiefs). The Indians were much impressed by the size (and the gifts) of the Spanish expedition.

The Pawnee Republic village of 1806 [located, as now interpreted, in Webster county, Nebraska] was the farthest point reached by Melgares and his men. Having no news of Americans in the area, the Spaniards turned back to the Arkansas. The reunited force then followed up the river to the mountains before turning southward. In October the expedition reached Santa Fe.

Ref: Z. M. Pike's journal (1806-1807), under entries of September 25, and November 11, 1806; *also* Pike's map; and his letter of October 1, 1806 (in Appendix to editions of his work). *The Journals of Zebulon Montgomery Pike, With Letters and Related Documents*, edited and annotated by Donald Jackson, in two volumes, was published by the University of Oklahoma Press in 1966. For an English historian's review of this definitive edition of Pike's journals, and his assessment of Pike, *see Saturday Review*, New York, September 3, 1966, issue.

❡ Capt. Zebulon M. Pike, with a company of 22 (Lt. James B. Wilkinson; Dr. John H. Robinson; three noncoms; 16 privates; and Baronet Vasquez, interpreter) set out from near St. Louis August 9, on an expedition to the West which began with a journey up the Missouri and Osage (by boat), convoying 51 Osages to their villages [in present Vernon county, Mo.]. (There were, also, two Pawnees to be escorted home.)

Pike spent two weeks (August 19-31) among the Osages; held councils with White Hair, and The Wind (chiefs of the Great, and Little villages), and other head men; took a census of the towns; collected Indian data; and with some difficulty and frustrations obtained pack horses, and arranged for a few Osages to accompany him to the Pawnee Republic village.

The overland march began on September 1. Pike and his party started out on the "Osage trace" [entering present Kansas in Bourbon? county], but left it on the 5th. They crossed the headwaters of "the [Little] Osage, White [Neosho or Grand], and Verdigrise rivers"; and halted September 11 on "a large branch of Grand river" [it was the Cottonwood's South Fork—in present Chase county]. Next day they "passed some very rough flint hills," and from one height Pike noted ". . . in one view below me, buffaloes, elks, deer, cabrie [antelope], and panthers." Camp that night was on the "main branch of Grand river" [the Cottonwood—in Chase county]. (The Osages "owing to their great fear of the Kanses" led the party "too far to the south" thereby adding many miles to the tedious journey.)

On September 17 the explorers crossed the Smoky Hill [northeast of present Lindsborg?]; and forded the Saline on the 18th [near the Saline-Ottawa county line of today?]. From a Pawnee hunter, met on the 22d, they learned of the recent presence of the Spanish expedition (*see* preceding entry). On the 23d they crossed the Solomon [west of present Glasco?]. Next day a number of Pawnees came to meet them; and on the 25th as Pike's small party neared the Republic town some 300 mounted Pawnees rode out to give them a ceremonial welcome.

[On the Republican river's south bank, in Republic county, Kansas (southwest of Republic), is the site of a Pawnee Republic town of the early 1800's. When attention was directed to it in the 1890's, conclusions were made that Captain Pike had visited the Republic band at the "Kansas site." (*See* E. B. Cowgill's 1897 address "Where Was the Pawnee Republic," in *Kansas Historical Collections* [KHC], v. 7, pp. 301-311.)

Efforts of interested parties culminated in the erection there of a Pike-Pawnee Republic monument which was dedicated in 1906 (*see ibid.*, pp. 261-317).

[Some 35 miles distant from the "Kansas site," on the Republican's south bank, in Webster county, Nebraska (southeast of Red Cloud), is the site of a Pawnee Republic town of the early 1800's. Following its identification (by A. T. Hill, in 1923) there arose a controversy over which village Pike actually visited. (*See Nebraska History*, Lincoln, v. 10, pp. 157-261; *Twenty-fifth Biennial Report . . . Kansas State Historical Society . . .*, pp. 101-129.)

[Archeologist W. R. Wedel (a native Kansan) in his *Introduction to Pawnee Archeology* (published in 1936 as the Bureau of American Ethnology's Bulletin No. 112) offered the opinion that the Nebraska or "Hill site" is the "probable site" of the Pawnee Republic village Pike visited in 1806 primarily because "it coincides in every respect with both the descriptions in the journal and the map of the expedition"—which the "Kansas site" does not.

[In addition to Pike's journals, his map, and the references noted above, essential reading for anyone probing deeply into this subject would include Elliott Coues's exhaustive study of the explorer's route in his 1895 edition of Pike's *Expeditions* (v. 2, pp. 392-441); Theo. H. Scheffer's article on Pike's trail in Saline and Ottawa counties in *KHQ*, v. 15, pp. 240-247; and *Zebulon Pike's Arkansaw Journal*, edited by S. H. Hart and A. B. Hulbert, published in 1932.] *See, also,* last annals entry for 1825.

"The immediate borders of the Republican fork near the village consist of high ridges," wrote Pike, ". . . an exception to the general face of the country." On one of the heights Pike and his men camped, but next day ". . . moved down the prairie hill, about three-quarters of a mile nearer the village . . . [and pitched] . . . camp upon a beautiful eminence," from which they could overlook the Pawnee Republic towns which, according to Lt. James B. Wilkinson, were:

. . . composed of the followers of a dissatisfied warrior [Iskatappe] who first made this establishment, and the adherents of a regular chief of the Grand Pawnees [Sharitarish] who migrated thither some few years since with his family, and usurped the power of the Republican warrior. To such a pitch does this party spirit prevail, that you easily perceive the hostility which exists between the adherents of the two chiefs.

Twelve Kansa arrived on September 26 to see Captain Pike. Two days later he called together the Osages of his party (Shingawasa and four warriors), and the Kansa (Wahonsongay and eight head men), counciled with them and "made them smoke of the pipe of peace." (*See* 1808 for the effective Osage-Kansa treaty.)

On September 29 occurred the grand council of the American party with the Pawnee Republic Indians (some 400 men), at which Captain Pike demanded that the Spanish flag displayed over the chief's door be taken down and replaced by a United States flag. The Pawnees at first ignored the request but when the demand was repeated:

. . . After a silence of some time, an old man rose, went to the door, and took down the Spanish flag, and brought it and laid it . . . [at Pike's] feet; and then received the American flag, and elevated it on the staff. . . .

The Pawnees were appeased and generally satisfied when Pike returned the Spanish flag to their keeping.

Pike's determination to continue westward to the Arkansas headwaters, in opposition to Chief Sharitarish's wishes, created a tense situation for the Americans during the remainder of their stay. But, as Lieutenant Wilkinson reported it:

On the 6th of October we made some few purchases of miserable horses at the most exorbitant prices, and on the 7th, unmoved by the threats of the Chief . . . we marched in a close and compact body until we passed their village, and took the large Spanish beaten trace for the Arkansaw river.

When some 300 Pawnees (on a buffalo hunt) overtook them on the 9th, Pike's resolute attitude again forestalled threatened trouble. He and his party continued south by west but after a time lost the Spanish trail (obliterated by a buffalo herd). Pike, Robinson, and Vasquez became separated from the others on October 15, but three days later found the company camped on the Arkansas [in the present Great Bend area]—a camp which was their headquarters for ten more days.

On October 28 Wilkinson's party (*see* second entry following) started *down* the Arkansas in two newly-made canoes (one from a cottonwood; the other of buffalo and elk skins); while Captain Pike with 16 men (and the horses) marched *up* the river toward the mountains, following the Spanish trail.

[The subsequent experiences of the expedition—the winter explorations (and terrible hardships) in the Colorado Rockies; Pike's months at Santa Fe and Chihuahua in Spanish custody; his eventual release (July 1, 1807) at Natchitoches—were also covered in Zebulon M. Pike's journal of July 15, 1806-July 1, 1807. That journal, supplemented by Pike's "Observations on . . . New Spain . . .," and his important maps and charts, was first published (at Philadelphia) in 1810 in a volume which included Pike's 1805-1806 journal of his voyage up the Mississippi to its sources.]

Appraising the country surrounding the "rivers Kanses, La Plate, Arkansaw, and their various branches," Pike commented (journal entry of February 5, 1807):

. . . it appears to me to be only possible to introduce a limited population. The inhabitants would find it most to their advantage to pay attention to the rearing of cattle, horses, sheep and goats: all of which they can raise in abundance, the earth producing spontaneously sufficient for their support. . . .

Of the great untimbered area he had traversed, it was Pike's opinion:

. . . These vast plains of the western hemisphere may become in time equally celebrated with the sandy deserts of Africa. . . . But from these immense prairies may arise one great advantage to the United States, viz., the restriction of our population to some certain limits, and thereby a continuation of the union. . . .

Ref: Same as for preceding entry; and as noted in text above.

❆ Nearing home after two years of travel and exploration in the West, the Lewis and Clark expedition, descending the Missouri, passed by the mouth of the Kansas at 11 A. M. on September 15. It was reported "very low at this time." Next day they met a boat with eight traders bound for the Pawnee village "on the river Platte about seventy or eighty miles from its mouth," and two hours later "a batteaux and two canoes going up to the Kanowas [Kansa] nation" on the Kansas river. (While coming down the Missouri, the Lewis and Clark expedition met, in all, 11 trading parties bound upstream.)

Ref: Thwaites' . . . *Journals of Lewis and Clark* . . ., v. 5, p. 385; Patrick Gass' *A Journal of the Voyages and Travels . . . Under the Command of Captain Lewis and Captain Clarke* . . . (Pittsburgh, 1807), p. 261.

❆ Lt. James B. Wilkinson, five soldiers, and two Osages left Pike's Arkansas river camp [in the present Great Bend area] on October 28 and started downstream in two makeshift canoes. In the shallow water the boats soon grounded and had to be pushed or dragged along the river bed. After a severely cold night, the Arkansas was so full of ice they could not proceed. Abandoning the canoes, they set out October 31 to "course the river by land," their only provisions "half a dozen tin cups of hard corn for each man."

They marched for a week through a desolate area, but on November 8 came to the region of game, where, according to Wilkinson:

. . . the herds of buffalo, elk, goat [antelope], and deer, surpassed credibility. I do solemnly assert, that if I saw one I saw more than nine thousand buffaloes during the day's march.

A week later, finding timber of sufficient size, they stopped to construct canoes, and to hunt for a "winter store of meat." When they set out again ten days later, shallow water again slowed their progress. They passed the "Negracka" [not the Negracka but the Ninnescah—in present Sumner county] on the 26th. A canoe-upset on November 28 caused them to lose most of their meat and ammunition. But they met a party of Great Osages on the 30th [probably south of the Kansas-Oklahoma boundary] and camped with them till December 2. (Wilkinson marched 20 miles across a prairie to visit The Wind, Little Osage chief, lying ill in a winter village.)

On December 23, after three weeks of severe hardship, Wilkinson and his half-frozen men reached the winter camp of the "Arkansas band" of Osages (whose permanent village was on the Verdigris— near present Claremore, Okla.). Four days later they passed the mouths of the Verdigris and the Grand. Making better time on the lower river, and in milder weather, they reached Arkansas Post on January 9, 1807.

Ref: Wilkinson's report, dated April 6, 1807 (written at New Orleans where he had arrived in February), published in Appendix to editions of Z. M. Pike, *op. cit.*

1807

❧ On March 3 Meriwether Lewis was commissioned (by President Jefferson) governor of the Territory of Louisiana, to succeed General Wilkinson. On March 7 William Clark was appointed (by the secretary of war) agent of Indian affairs for the nations (except the Osages) in the Territory of Louisiana. Pierre Chouteau's authority (*see* 1804), on the same date, was limited to the agency for the Great and Little Osage Indians. (Chouteau continued as Osage agent till 1818.)

Ref: *Territorial Papers of the U. S.,* v. 14, pp. 107-110, v. 15, p. 384.

❧ Manuel Lisa's first upper Missouri trading expedition (42 men in a keelboat) left St. Louis early in May and went far upriver. After successfully negotiating with the Arikara Indians, who threatened trouble, Lisa ascended to the Yellowstone river, went up it to the mouth of the Big Horn and established a fur post—Fort Manuel [in present Montana].

(Lisa's party, with a load of furs, returned to St. Louis in the summer of 1808.)

Ref: *Nebraska Historical Society Publications,* Lincoln, v. 20, p. 1; *American State Papers: Indian Affairs,* v. 2, pp. 201, 202; Richard E. Oglesby's *Manuel Lisa and the Opening of the Missouri Fur Trade* (Norman, Okla., 1963).

❧ About 95 persons were in an expedition which ascended the Missouri in the summer. They included young Auguste P. Chouteau's party of 32 (intending to trade with the Mandans); "young" Dorion's outfit of ten (headed for the Sioux country); Mandan chief Shahaka and party, also 24 Sioux Indians (all homeward bound); and a military escort for the Indians (Lt. Joseph Kimball, Ens. Nathaniel Pryor, and some 20 men).

The Sioux were returned safely to their country. But when Ensign Pryor and troops (with the Mandans), in company with Chouteau's traders, reached the Arikara village in September, those Indians (and Sioux cohorts) forced a fight, and the retreat of the whole party. Chouteau lost four? men, and several in the expedition were wounded. (Chief Shahaka was returned to St. Louis. He finally reached home in 1809. *See* pp. 61, 62.)

Ref: *Annals of Iowa,* Des Moines, 3d ser., v. 1 (1895), pp. 615-619; W. B. Douglas' editorial note in Thomas James' *Three Years Among the Indians and Mexicans* (St. Louis, 1916), p. 258; H. M. Chittenden's *The American Fur Trade of the Far West* (New York, 1935), v. 1, pp. 119-123; Jackson, ed., *Letters of the Lewis and Clark Expedition,* pp. 382, 411, 412, 414, 432-438, 446-450, 456, 457, 460, 479-484.

❡ Francis Derouen [Dorion], to trade with the "Kaas [Kansa], Ottoes and Panis," and Pierre Montardy, to trade with the Kansa, were granted licenses on August 24. One-year hunting licenses on the Kansas river were given to B. and J. Vallett (on August 31); to Lebeech and Derchette, and Louis Gonoville (On September 12).

(The trading license lists for the April-September, 1808, period contained no reference to the Kansa or their river. But Dorion apparently traded with the Kansa in the winter of 1809-1810. In 1819, "Mr. Gunville" [Louis?], a French trader, was living in the Kansa village when Say's party was there in August. *See,* under 1819.)

Ref: T. M. Marshall, ed., *The Life and Papers of Frederick Bates* (St. Louis, 1926), v. 1, pp. 202, 204, v. 2, pp. 31-33; *Missouri Historical Review,* v. 34, p. 453.

❡ From the Platte—evidently by way of Pawnee towns on that river, and the "Pike" Pawnee Republic village on the Republican (*see* 1806 annals), Jacques Clamorgan (aged 74?) together with three Frenchmen, a Negro slave, and four goods-laden pack mules, journeyed overland to Santa Fe. The route across "Kansas"—perhaps much the same as Pike's from the Pawnee Republic town, can only be conjectured. His party reached Santa Fe on December 12.

Subsequently, after being sent to Chihuahua, where he was allowed to sell his goods, Clamorgan, in 1808, returned by way of Texas and Natchitoches, to his starting point—St. Louis. As a present-day historian notes, Clamorgan was "the first American trader to earn profits on a trip to Santa Fe."

Ref: A. P. Nasatir's "Jacques Clamorgan . . .," in *New Mexico Historical Review,* v. 17 (April, 1942), pp. 101-112; Loomis and Nasatir, *op. cit.,* p. 248. At St. Louis, Clamorgan had been issued a license to trade with the Pawnee Republic Indians.

1808

❡ Gov. Meriwether Lewis, on July 1, wrote the secretary of war concerning frontier problems:

The Kanzas, Panis Republic, a considerable body of the Great Panis, the Woolf Panis, Mahas and Poncarras have all declared in favour of the Spaniards. Our friends on the west side of the Missouri are consequently reduced to the little Osages, the White Hair's party [of Big Osages], the Ottoes, Missouries and a part of the Big Panis [Grand Pawnees], not amounting to more perhaps than one thousand warriors, and those even doubtful unless measures be taken to retain them by establishing trading posts on the Missouri. . . . last winter the Mahas killed two engages, robed their traders and sent me an insolent message. the Kanzas have also robed their traders and have been extreemly insolent. . . .

The Osages generally, the Kanzas, Panis republic, and a majority of the Great Panis are by appointment at this time assembled at the Great Saline about 300 miles West of the Osage villages. The purpose of this meeting is to hold a council with the Spaniards and as it is understood by invitation of the latter. . . .

Ref: *Territorial Papers of the U. S.,* v. 14, pp. 198, 199. (The Great Salt Plains meeting was probably in Alfalfa or Woodward county of present Oklahoma.)

❡ In the early autumn, Capt. Eli B. Clemson's company of First U. S. infantry began work on a fortification (Fort Osage) on a 70-foot-high bluff of the Missouri about 340 river miles above St. Louis, and over 40 miles by water below the mouth of the Kansas. This post (first called Fort Clark) was on a site chosen by William Clark (who also supervised the start of its construction). Established for the protection of the Osage Indians, it was formally named Fort Osage on November 10. Clemson's company garrisoned the post while George C. Sibley, as factor, ran the government's trading post.

(Evacuated in June, 1813, as a War of 1812 tactic, Fort Osage was reoccupied in 1815. Until 1819 a few troops were stationed there. In 1822 the government factory system was discontinued, and in 1825 the post was abandoned officially.)

Ref: *American State Papers: Indian Affairs,* v. 1, p. 765; *Missouri Historical Review,* v. 34, pp. 439-488 (for Kate L. Gregg's "The History of Fort Osage"), v. 54, pp. 343, 344. (Today, an authentic reconstruction of Fort Osage [with block houses, factor's house, officers' quarters, barracks, interpreter's house, and stockade] stands on the original site near Sibley, Mo.) According to a table of distances on the Missouri (published in B. F. French's *Historical Collections of Louisiana* [Philadelphia, 1850], pt. 2, p. 300), based on findings of Long, Nicollet, and others, from the mouth of the Missouri to Fort Osage (at low water) was 340 miles, and from the fort to the mouth of the Kansas was 42 miles. Other tables vary considerably. David Meriwether's *My Life in the Mountains and on the Plains* (Norman, c1965), pp. 103-113, has an account of the post in 1821-1822, when Fort Osage was reoccupied by the military. He was there as sutler, and as trader with the Osages and Iowas.

❡ At the new post Fort Clark (Fort Osage) on September 27, Factor George C. Sibley counciled with chiefs and warriors of the Osage and Kansa tribes. The Indians smoked the peace pipe and effected what proved to be a permanent peace between their nations. Also, the Kansa professed to be sorry for past offenses (especially the ill treatment given their traders), and Sibley granted them permission to move near the fort. On October 10 about 1,000 Kansa arrived in the vicinity and soon began trading. Six days later their "insolent and violent conduct" caused the factor to bar them from the post.

(William Clark reported, from St. Louis on December 2, that "strong and well built" Fort Osage was nearly completed; and that Sibley's policy of refusing to trade with the Kansa was having "a very good effect," and they were "becoming verry humble" and had "given up several horses, to pay for the horses and property which they have robed the citizens of this Territory of laterly.")

Ref: *Missouri Historical Review*, v. 34, p. 445; *Territorial Papers of the U. S.*, v. 14, p. 242.

❡ On November 10 (about the time "Fort Clark" became Fort Osage) a treaty was concluded at the new post between the Osage Indians (Great and Little) of the Osage river country, and the United States (Pierre Chouteau acting for the government).

In return for the friendship and protection of the United States, a small annuity, and other promised aid, the Indians ceded millions of acres of land in present Missouri and Arkansas. In what is now Missouri they retained only a strip along the western boundary (the area south of the Missouri river and west of a line running straight south from Fort Osage).

First to sign for the Great Osages was their grand chief Papuisea (White Hair). Nicheumanee (the Walking Rain) led the Little Osage signers.

(On August 31, 1809, the "Arkansas band" of Osages [on the Verdigris, near present Claremore, Okla.] had the treaty read and explained to them by Gov. Meriwether Lewis. The first to sign was Clermont. Cashesegra, nominal leader, was the second signer. The United States ratified the treaty on April 28, 1810.)

Ref: C. J. Kappler's *Indian Affairs, Laws and Treaties* (Washington, 1904), v. 2, pp. 95-99; Kate L. Gregg, ed., *Westward With Dragoons* . . . (Fulton, Mo., 1937), pp. 69-75; *American State Papers: Indian Affairs*, v. 1, pp. 763, 764; *Missouri Historical Review*, v. 54, p. 343. A reproduction of a painting of White Hair I, by artist Charles B. J. F. de St. Mémin is in *Chronicles of Oklahoma*, Oklahoma City, v. 36 (Summer, 1958), *facing* p. 132. Reference is made to an article on St. Mémin in the American Antiquarian Society's *Quarterly Bulletin* of April, 1928.

1809

❡ The St. Louis Missouri Fur Company (an association of former fur trade rivals, organized in the winter of 1808-1809) sent its first expedition up the Missouri in the summer, to establish trading posts on the river's upper waters.

Pierre Chouteau headed the expedition (of about 150 men, in ten goods-loaded boats), but comembers Manuel Lisa (soon the company's dominant figure), Andrew Henry, Pierre Menard, and Auguste P. Chouteau were in the party; as were, also, 17-year-old Auguste A. and Paul Ligueste Chouteau (cousins), and Dr. (Peyton?) Thomas (who kept a journal of the trip). Aboard, too, was Mandan chief Shahaka's party, homeward bound.

Reaching Fort Osage on July 8, they found (as Pierre Chouteau later reported) "the Panis, Otto and Kanzas tribes . . . waiting . . . with loud Complaints because there were no merchants among them, and praying that some might be sent."

Moving on, the expedition reached the Platte on August 1; continued, with no particular trouble, to the Mandan nation and delivered Shahaka and party safely home in the latter part of September.   Henry, Menard, and most of the trappers remained in the upper Missouri country, but Lisa, the Chouteaus, and Dr. Thomas returned to St. Louis in November.

(William Clark, Benjamin Wilkinson, Reuben Lewis, Sylvestre Labbadie, and William Morrison were other members of the St. Louis Missouri Fur Company.   After three years of moderate success there was a reorganization under the name "Missouri Fur Company.")

Ref: *Territorial Papers of the U. S.,* v. 14, pp. 343-352; Thomas James, *op. cit.,* pp. 15-92; *American State Papers: Indian Affairs,* v. 2, p. 202; *Nebraska Historical Society Publications,* v. 20, p. 2 (for one part of Dr. Thomas' narrative); *The Bulletin* of the Missouri Historical Society, St. Louis, v. 20 (April, 1964), pp. 179-192 (for the rediscovered "lost" section of Thomas' narrative).   In the Kansas State Historical Society's manuscript collections are two volumes of Missouri Fur Company records.   One contains the original "Articles of Association" (January 24, 1812) and board meeting minutes (January, 1812-January, 1814), together with signatures of the members; the other is an account book.

❆ By a route (described by John Shaw at the age of 72) in the vicinity of the 37th parallel [the Kansas-Oklahoma boundary of today], Shaw recollected that he, Peter Spear, and William Miller traveled overland with pack horses from the Cape Girardeau (Mo.) area to within sight of the Rocky mountains in the spring and summer of 1809? (Shaw was perhaps several years off in dating the journey as early as 1809.)   Hostile Indians thwarted their plan to continue to the Pacific.   Returning to what is now "eastern Kansas, and western Arkansas, and Missouri" they hunted till the spring of 1811?.   Moving their furs and a quantity of bear oil by pack horses to the White river headwaters, the trio made canoes and journeyed down the White, Arkansas, and Mississippi rivers to New Orleans.

Ref: *Wisconsin Historical Collections,* v. 2, pp. 199-201 (for Shaw's reminiscences, 1855); *Missouri Historical Society Collections,* St. Louis, v. 4, p. 197; and *see* David H. Coyner's *The Lost Trappers* (Albuquerque, c1970), pp. xvi, xvii, for editor David J. Weber's comment on Shaw.

❆ Joseph McLanahan, Reuben Smith, James Patterson, Manuel Blanco (guide), and three slaves, left the Ste. Genevieve, Mo., area November 20, on a trading venture to New Mexico. (Their route is not known.)   They reached Santa Fe in late February, 1810. Subsequently they were arrested, taken to Chihuahua (Mexico), and imprisoned for two years.

Ref: Appendix to Thomas James, *op. cit.*, pp. 286-292; *Missouri Historical Society Collections*, v. 5, p. 170; Loomis and Nasatir, *op. cit.*, pp. 249-251.

❡ In the spring or early summer, a band of some 100 Kansa warriors "entered the Paunie village, or what is more generally called the Paunies Republic, and killed the principal chief and his family consisting of 15 souls; they were immediately pursued and upwards of 40 of them cut to pieces. . . ." (The mid-summer, 1809, narrative of "Dr. [Peyton?] Thomas" is quoted here.)

Thomas also stated that the Kansa lived "about 150 miles up" the "Cansas" river—a "considerable" stream "affording navigation for trading boats, up to the village." Of the nation he wrote: "The Cansas have long been the terror of the neighbouring Indians, their temerity is hardly credible . . . these people cannot be at peace with the white or red people; they rob, murder and destroy when opportunity offers; fortunately for their neighbours, they are few in number, and their daily outrages serve to lessen their number still more, their country abounds with game, particularly beaver, deer, buffaloe, elk, black bear, &c. &c. and afford the Cansas (hardly less savage) an abundance of food and raiment."

Ref: *The Bulletin* of the Missouri Historical Society, St. Louis, v. 20 (April, 1964), p. 184.

1810

❡ The advance party of the "overland" Astorians (John Jacob Astor's Pacific Fur Company men) started up the Missouri in three boats on October 21. Arriving in mid-November at a point above the mouth of the Nodaway [and across-river from present northeast Doniphan county] they encamped for the winter. There were over 40 men in the party, led by Wilson P. Hunt, with copartners Ramsay Crooks, Donald Mackenzie, and Joseph Miller. Another partner, Robert McClellan, soon joined them.

Leaving the Nodaway camp on January 1, 1811, Hunt and eight other men walked to Fort Osage, where Hunt obtained horses and reached St. Louis on January 20. His recruiting of more personnel, and other preparations for an early spring start upriver, were only slightly hampered by the delaying tactics of rival fur trader Manuel Lisa (of the St. Louis Missouri Fur Company).

Ref: Washington Irving's *Astoria* . . . (Philadelphia, 1836), v. 1; K. W. Porter's "Roll of Overland Astorians, 1810-1812," in *Oregon Historical Quarterly*, v. 34 (June, 1933), pp. 103-112.

1811

❡ On the present Oregon coast, the *Tonquin*, carrying an Astor-financed Pacific Fur Company expedition, arrived at the mouth of the Columbia river in late March (after a journey from New York around South America), and, in mid-April, a trading post—Astoria —was begun.

Ref: Irving's *Astoria, op. cit.*

❦ The "overland" Astorian expedition, led by Wilson P. Hunt, started up the Missouri, from St. Charles, in keelboats on March 14. Aboard as Hunt's guests for the river trip were two "scientific gentlemen"—English-born Thomas Nuttall, and Scottish-born John Bradbury (botanist and traveler). The latter's *Travels in the Interior of America in the Years, 1809, 1810, and 1811* (London, 1817) contained an account (largely in journal form) of the voyage upstream (and his journey back to St. Louis in mid-summer—*see* next entry). Bradbury made a brief reference to present northeast Kansas [the Doniphan area] when he wrote under date of April 15:

We passed the scite of a village which formerly belonged to the Kansas Indians. I had an opportunity of going ashore, and found the soil to have the appearance of the greatest fertility.

Two days later, across the river from what is now northeast Doniphan county, the Astorians reached the camp of the vanguard party which had wintered above the Nodaway's mouth. On April 21 the whole company (nearly 60 men), in four keelboats, proceeded upstream. Six weeks later (on June 2), the one-boat expedition of Manuel Lisa (*see* next entry) caught up with them. After a truce was arranged between the rival fur company leaders, the two parties continued onward together to the Arikara village, arriving June 12.

The Astorians spent over a month outfitting for the overland journey to the Pacific. Their party of 60 men, with 82 horses, left the Arikara village on July 18. Six months later, after a journey of hardships and difficulties, most of the expedition reached Astoria (near the mouth of the Columbia river)—in January and February, 1812.

Ref: Bradbury, *op. cit.*, pp. 1-189; and Irving, *op. cit.*, v. 1, chs. 13-30, v. 2, chs. 1-8. In Irving's work, first published in 1836, is the most complete account of all phases of Astoria's history. (He had access to company records and available source materials in preparing his narrative.)

❦ With a crew of 20 (some inexperienced) to handle his one keelboat, Manuel Lisa, and four other persons, started up the Missouri on April 2, about 20 days behind Hunt's larger and better-manned expedition. Since it was vital that his small St. Louis Missouri Fur Company party catch up with the Astorians before reaching hostile Sioux country, the journey was a race against time. Aboard as Lisa's guest was an American traveler and writer, Henry M. Brackenridge, whose journal of the voyage was later published in his *Views of Louisiana . . .* (Pittsburgh, 1814). He noted, on April 24 (as they neared Fort Osage):

Passed a canoe with four men, who had wintered up the Kansas, about five hundred miles: they had beaver, and other furs. . . .

On the afternoon of April 30 Brackenridge wrote that they:

. . . had a view of the old Kansas village . . . [the same Doniphan county scene commented on by his friend Bradbury of Hunt's party]. It is a high prairie; smooth waving hills, perfectly green, with a few clumps of trees in the hollows. But for the scarcity of timber this would be a delightful situation for a town. . . .

Over a month went by before Lisa's boat finally caught up (on June 2) with the Astorians. (See above.)

After supplying some horses (from his fur post above the Mandan village) to the Astoria-bound expedition, in trade for two of Hunt's no-longer-needed boats, Lisa arranged to send his company's collected furs downriver, placing the boats in Brackenridge's charge. John Bradbury and Amos Richardson were other passengers for the journey. Leaving the Arikara village on July 17, this small expedition reached St. Louis early in August, making the 1,440-mile trip in a little over two weeks.

Lisa (and also Thomas Nuttall of Hunt's party) remained in the Upper Missouri country for a few months, and Lisa eventually made rendezvous with his mountain partner Andrew Henry.

Ref: Brackenridge, *op. cit.*, pp. 199-264; Irving, *op. cit.*, v. 1, chs. 19-22.

℅ Factor George C. Sibley, with a servant, two interpreters, and 11 Osages (one of them war chief Sans Oreille) left Fort Osage (Mo.) May 11 on a journey to the Kansa and Pawnee villages. His mounted party headed "South 60° West, about 75 miles, along the Osage Summer hunting trace," then "North 70° West, about 65 miles" to arrive on May 19 at the Kansas river bank opposite the Kansa village [two miles east of present Manhattan]. Of the surroundings on the latter stage of the journey [Wabaunsee and southeast Riley counties of today], Sibley wrote:

This [is] a very wild but extremely beautiful and high prairie country— pretty well watered and variegated with strips of woodland, ranges of lofty rugged, naked hills, overlooking extensive tracts of meadow ground. Deer and elk are plenty, and I observed some antelope skipping among the verdant hills.

Grand Chief Shone-ge-ne-gare and more than 100 mounted Kansa warriors forded the river to assist the party in the rather difficult crossing. At the 128-lodge village, Sibley found U. S. flags flying, and the Indians both hospitable and friendly. (He had recently had occasion to deal harshly with the Kansa, and the festive reception was a pleasant surprise.)

Sibley described, at some length, the scene about him (mistakenly referring to the nearby Big Blue tributary as the Republican fork). The town, he wrote:

. . . is built without much regard to order; there are no regular streets or avenues. The lodges are erected pretty compactly together in crooked rows, allowing barely space sufficient to admit a man to pass between them. The avenues between . . . are kept in tolerably decent order and the village is on the whole rather neat and cleanly than otherwise. Their little fields or patches of corn, beans and pumpkins, which they had just finished planting, and which constitute their whole variety, are seen in various directions, at convenient distances around the villages. The prairie was covered with their horses and mules (they have no other domestic animals except dogs).

The "stout, hardy, handsome" Kansa were "fast reforming from their brutal state," but still at war with all their neighbors except the Osages (and only recently friends with them). He estimated they had "about 250 fighting men, with a full proportion of women and children."

With five Kansa added to his party, Sibley set out on May 22 for the Pawnee villages, traveling "North 40° West about 120 miles" [150?—it could have been no less in a straight line to the Platte] over a route "all prairie." Crossing the Platte "about 140 miles above its junction with the Missouri" he traveled 10[?] miles to the Loup fork, and forded it to reach the crowded 170-lodge village of three Pawnee bands (Grand and Republican) recently reunited under "venerable old Chief" Cher-a-ta-reesh (Sharitarish). [This Loup fork village may have been the "Horse Creek site," nine miles southwest of present Fullerton, Neb.] Two of the bands had lived until "about two years ago" on the "north branch of the Konsee River" [i. e., the Republican] when "successive incursions of the Konsees obliged them to abandon their old towns."

Sibley (welcomed and well treated by the Pawnees) remained in the village from May 28 to June 4. When leaders of the Loup band (living some 10? miles upriver) arrived, he called a grand council, presented flags and medals to chiefs of the four Pawnee bands; and effected a treaty of peace between the Pawnees, and the Osages and Kansa.

On a course "south about 16° East" Sibley and his party then headed for the Little Osage summer hunting camp on the Arkansas river [probably entering present Kansas in Republic county]. They crossed the Republican and "two other considerable forks of the Konsee [the Solomon and the Saline] and a number of smaller streams that flow into them," and the "same range of hills that we crossed fifty[?] miles southeast at the Konsee town." Sibley described the "enchanting prospects afforded from these heights":

. . . we overlooked a vast extent of level meadow ground to the North and Northeast, through which were to be traced a great number of rivulets and creeks, glittering in the sunshine and hastening to the main branches of the Konsee. Numerous herds of elk and antelope were frisking in the gay flowery plain, giving life and animation to the charming scene. From where we crossed the Konsee [*i. e.,* the Smoky Hill—in McPherson? county] to the Arkansas, it is about thirty-five miles and the country is much more level and less interesting. . . .

The day before reaching the Arkansas, Sibley's party came to a Kansa hunting camp "on a beautiful high spot near a small creek," and stopped overnight to help celebrate a successful kill of more than 100 "fat buffaloes." Among the Little Osages (whose camp on the river—in Reno?, or Sedgwick? county—was reached the next afternoon), Sibley spent some ten days—part of the time on the march as the Indians moved "south 50° west about thirty miles to a small prairie creek, south of the Arkansas."

From that place he rode "south 40° east" for 30 miles, to the Great Osage camp; and the next day (after a ride of "20 miles south 15° east") reached a third Osage camp—that of the "Arkansas band." With eight men (six of them Osages), Sibley then set out on a nearly-due-west course for the Grand Saline some 40 miles away. After a tour of the Saline [in present Alfalfa? county, Okla.] about June 24, he returned to the Little Osages' camp. (They had moved, meantime, near the Grand Saline and may have been on the Salt fork of the Arkansas.) Sibley, his servant, and Sans Oreille then accompanied a "war party" of 94 Little Osages on a journey of about 75 miles "south 40° West" to visit the famed Rock Saline, or "Salt Mountain."

Following this final excursion into present northern Oklahoma, Sibley began the trip (of some 300? miles) back to Fort Osage, arriving on July 11—after a two-months' and around 1,000-mile journey.

Ref: Sibley's diary, as printed in *Chronicles of Oklahoma,* Oklahoma City, v. 5, pp. 196-218, and in *Bulletin* of the Missouri Historical Society, St. Louis, v. 21 (April, 1965), pp. 167-207; W. R. Wedel's . . . *An Introduction to Kansas Archeology* (Washington, 1959), pp. 41, 42; George E. Hyde's *Pawnee Indians* (Denver, c1951), p. 105. Sibley's too-conservative mileage estimates are not compatible with actual distances traveled in any instance where comparison can be made.

❡ Scientific traveler-geographer-author Alexander von Humboldt's *Essai Politique sur le Royaume de la Nouvelle Espagne* was published in Paris during the year; and in New York an English translation of his compendious *Political Essay on the Kingdom of New Spain* also appeared. In the atlas volume was Humboldt's map of New Spain (drawn in Mexico in 1803)—the first map to present a reasonably accurate geographical view of the American southwest of today.

In writing of the province of Nuevo Mexico, Humboldt stated that within its bounds were three villas (towns), 26 pueblos (villages), three parishes, 19 missions, and no ranchos (solitary farms). He gave population figures of the towns as: Santa Fe 3,600, Albuquerque 6,000, and Taos 8,900.

Ref: Humboldt's work, American edition (as noted above), v. 2, p. 216 (for the statistics).

1812

❡ Early in May a trading expedition (two boats) of Manuel Lisa's Missouri Fur Company started up the Missouri. Clerk John C. Luttig kept a journal of the voyage (and later events) which included these June entries:

Monday. 8th fine weather, at 8 A.M. a fair Breeze sprung up. though feeble, we made 18 Miles distance, Killed 3 Deer 3 Bear, caught 17 fish, camped 2 Miles below the old Cansas Village [in Salt creek valley, Leavenworth county]. . . . [On the 9th they "made only 9 miles," but traveled 19 miles on June 10.]

Thursday the 11th, fine weather head wind but still, all hunters out, passed the upper old Cansas Village [present Doniphan area], Killed 7 Deer, distance 15 Miles. [By the 18th they had reached the mouth of Wolf river—in northeast Doniphan county—where they camped on a sand bar.]

Indian harassments (British-influenced) evidently forced an end to the Missouri Fur Company's upper river activities in the late winter of 1812-1813. (Luttig's journal ended abruptly March 3.) The St. Louis *Missouri Gazette* of June 5, 1813, reported Manuel Lisa's recent arrival from the Mandan villages; and indicated that the Arikaras, Cheyennes, Gros Ventre, Crows, and Arapahoes were arrayed on the side of the British who were inciting them to war against the Americans.

Ref: John C. Luttig's *Journal of a Fur-Trading Expedition on the Upper Missouri, 1812-1813*, edited by Stella M. Drumm. Preface and notes by A. P. Nasatir (New York, 1964), pp. 14, 15, 36.

❡ Robert McKnight, James Baird, Benjamin Shreve and Michael McDonough (partners), Samuel Chambers, and four? others, left the Missouri settlements in May on a trading expedition to New Mexico. (They were at Fort Osage on June 4.) Following Pike's directions (but by a route not recorded) they made their way safely to Santa Fe, only to be jailed as spies, and their goods seized. Most (or all?) members of the party were held in a Chihuahua prison for nine years—released only when the Mexican revolution of 1821 succeeded.

Ref: *American State Papers: Foreign Relations*, v. 4, pp. 207-213; *Missouri Historical Review*, v. 34, pp. 455, 456; Luttig, *op. cit.*, editorial note on pp. 35, 36; *Bulletin of the Missouri Historical Society*, St. Louis, v. 15, pp. 173-189; L. R. Hafen, editor, *The Mountain Men and the Fur Trade of the Far West* (1966), v. 3, pp. 27-37 (for R. W. Strickland's article on James Baird).

❦ By congressional act of June 4, the Territory of Louisiana became the Territory of Missouri, with Benjamin Howard as first governor. (The change of name was necessitated when the Territory of Orleans was admitted to the Union as the state of Louisiana on April 8.) Missouri territory's population, as of 1810, was close to 20,000. On July 1, 1813, following Howard's resignation, William Clark was appointed governor and served till Missouri became a state in 1820.

Ref: *Historic Missouri* (Columbia, Mo., c1959), p. 12; *Missouri Historical Review*, v. 54, p. 279.

❦ The United States declared war on England on June 18. (The "War of 1812" lasted for two and a half years, officially ending with the signing of the Treaty of Ghent on December 24, 1814.)

❦ Published during the year was the sixth edition of Jedidiah Morse's *The American Universal Geography* (first issued in 1789). Morse, the "father of American geography," made use of the latest information he could find on the Missouri and Arkansas rivers. But he devoted part of his comment on the Missouri to criticism of Lewis and Clark:

Had that [exploration] been made by men whose science, judgment, and accuracy could be relied on, we should have no difficulty in giving a complete description of the Missouri. But the latitude and longitude of no one place is calculated; a connected chain of distances is not given; nor are we informed on what authority a great many facts, which the travelers did not witness, are reported. . . . We ourselves believe, that the length of the Missouri . . . is, probably about 2400 miles. The waters of this river are remarkable for their muddiness and salubrious qualities. . . . The Missouri being much larger than the Missisippi branch some modern geographers are beginning to give the whole river the name of Missouri, which is probably its proper name. . . .

And from Morse's geography, students of the 1812 era learned that:

The Arkansas . . . is navigable 500 or 600 miles. It rises in Mexico. Humboldt [see 1811] supposes that it may be the same with Napestle [first mentioned in this chronology under 1706], a river which rises, according to his map, in lat. 40° N., lon. 106° W. . . . and pursues for a while a S. E. course towards the Missisippi. The Arkansas having been explored a great distance, is found to run where it should have been expected to run, if it were a continuation of the Napestle, and no other outlet for this last is known. If this be its real source, the Arkansas must be at least 1500 miles long.

Ref: Morse's . . . *Geography*, 6th ed. (1812), v. 1, pp. 122, 123, 598. In defense of Lewis and Clark, it should be noted that the complete narrative of their expedition was not published until 1814. However, some of Morse's comments have been echoed by other critics. One (W. P. Webb, in his *The Great Plains* [1936], pp. 143, 144) has referred to the explorers' journals as "meager and unsatisfactory," and noted their "lack of specific detail," the "vagueness," etc.

1812-1813

⁋ Between June 29, 1812, and April 30, 1813, young Robert Stuart (eastbound with reports for John J. Astor in New York), and a small party (seven in all) of "returning Astorians" made a hazardous, difficult journey up the Columbia, across the Rocky Mountains (of eastern Oregon, Idaho, and Wyoming of today), down the Sweetwater to the North Platte, down the Platte to the Otoe village (some 45 miles above the mouth), and by canoe down the Missouri to St. Louis. (The total distance, by Stuart's calculation, 3,768 miles.)

Stuart's party (Ramsay Crooks, Robert McClellan, Joseph Miller, and three hunters) may have been the first white men to cross the Continental Divide by way of South Pass (or in its vicinity). It was the first to discover and use the North Platte route which later became a section of the famed Oregon trail. Robert Stuart has been credited as "the first to find and follow a route from the Pacific to St. Louis that could be utilized by wagon trains."

He kept a journal (rewritten and expanded between 1813-1821 as "Traveling Memoranda") which included observations on various Indian tribes. During the last stage of the trip, as his party traveled by canoe down the Missouri in April, 1813, a stop was made at Fort Osage (Mo.) on April 24 and 25. That post, commented Stuart, was chiefly for the Osage Indians but:

. . . has been the means of reducing the turbulent Kanzes to a proper sense of the true relation in which Indians stand with their civilized neighbors.

The "returning Astorians" reached St. Louis May 2, and Stuart continued eastward to New York.

Ref: Philip A. Rollins, *The Discovery of the Oregon Trail* . . . (New York, 1935); K. A. Spaulding, ed., *On the Oregon Trail* . . . (Norman, Okla., c1953); *Oregon Historical Quarterly*, v. 17 (1916), pp. 47-51 (H. C. Dale's article, therein, includes a June 28, 1856, letter by Ramsay Crooks on the Stuart party).

1813

⁋ By canoe, trapper Ezekiel Williams set out alone from an Arapahoe camp on the Arkansas headwaters the first of March, in an attempt to reach Missouri territory. He left behind two companions (in the camp) and a cache of furs (in the mountains of present Colorado). Trapping as he proceeded down the Arkansas, Williams traveled for some 400 miles—till shallow water halted his progress. When the spring rise came (around June 1) he continued his river journey and was "within about 150 miles of the Verdigrise" [and apparently in present southern Kansas] when captured, on June 23, by a party of Kansa. As reported (in November) by Factor George C. Sibley, of Fort Osage, the Indians:

. . . robbed him of all he had with him, and very much abused him, as he says, and kept him prisoner to about the 15 Augt. when they released him and restored the greater part of his property. The balance (except a few articles they deny having taken) I have this day [November 30] caused the Kansas to refund and pay for.

(Ezekiel Williams had become a "mountain man" when he went up the Missouri with the fur company expedition of 1809?, or 1811?. After two? winters on the upper Missouri he accompanied a party of trappers Manuel Lisa sent southward towards the Arkansas headwaters. When Indian harassment began, following their first winter in the Arapahoe country, the trappers separated. Some were killed by Indians. Williams and two others finally took refuge in an Arapahoe village during the winter of 1812-1813.)

Ref: *Missouri Historical Society Collections,* v. 4, pp. 194-208; Luttig, *op. cit.,* pp. 17-19, 35; *Bulletin of the Missouri Historical Society,* v. 8, pp. 17-33; David H. Coyner's *The Lost Trappers,* edited by David J. Weber (Albuquerque, N. M., c1970). In 1963, a monument was dedicated at the grave of Ezekiel Williams "first white settler in Benton County, Missouri," by his descendants. The legend reads: "In Memory of/Ezekiel Williams/ circa 1775-1844/Western Mountain Man/Memorial Placed by/Descendants 1963." *See* Kansas City (Mo.) *Star,* July 5, 1963. The site is not stated.

❈ As late as September, 1811, there were only three bands of Osages. George C. Sibley called them the Bar-har-che (Great Osages), the Eu-jet-ta (Little Osages)—both living on the Osage river [in present Vernon county, Mo.]; and the Cha-neers (the Arkansas band) dwelling on the Arkansas [*i. e.,* on the Verdigris, near present Claremore, Okla.]. He also commented that the Osages were all "friendly and intimately connected" and the terms "Great" and "Little" referred only to the size of their towns—not to their "personal corporosity."

But Agent Pierre Chouteau's 1813 report (dated July 29) indicated a change had occurred. The Little Osages had left their "ancient village" [perhaps in 1812?]. One band (about 60 men) had reunited with the Great Osages [a move of not more than six miles]. The other band (about 150 men) was "on the great river a Branch of the arkansas River" [the Grand or Neosho—in present Neosho? county, Kansas].

When, in 1815, the westbound Chouteau-de Mun party was at the Great Osage village, de Mun wrote (in his journal, on October 2) that it was so called "to distinguish it from that belonging to the Little Osage, and that of the Grosse Côte [Big Hill]. . . ." [The Big Hill band later lived near Clermont's town.] He then confirmed the residence of the Little Osages on the Neosho [in present Kansas] in his journal (October 13):

. . . towards eleven o'clock we arrived at the *Grande Rivière,* which hunters called the *Nioncho* [Neosho or Grand] on the western bank of which is situated Ligueste's Village [Paul Ligueste Chouteau, Osage subagent, and trader] which we found deserted, the Indians having gone to hunt. This village is charmingly situated. . . .

And, in 1816, on his return journey through the same area, de Mun wrote (on March 26):

About two o'clock we reached the *Nioncho:* near the village we recognized an Osage family who told us that the old[!] village was no longer inhabited, that they had made a new one about two miles lower down. . . .

Gov. William Clark reported, in 1816, that the Great Osages on the Osage river numbered 1,600; that there were 1,800 Little Osages on the Neosho river; and that the "Arkansas band" on the Verdigris had increased to 2,600 persons.

Ref: *Chronicles of Oklahoma,* v. 5, p. 212 (Sibley); Superintendency of Indian Affairs, St. Louis, "Records" (in Kansas Historical Society, ms. div.), v. 2, pp. 21-24 (Chouteau); *Missouri Historical Society Collections,* v. 5, pp. 191, 192, 315 (de Mun); Grant Foreman's *Indians and Pioneers* . . . (New Haven, 1930), pp. 26, 27. *See,* under 1820, changes among the Osages in the 1814-1820 period.

1814

❡ Heading west to recover his cached furs (*see* 1813), Ezekiel Williams and two companions (Morris May, Braxton Cooper) left the Missouri settlements in mid-May and journeyed across present Kansas, following up the Arkansas to its headwaters.

Traveling in company were Joseph Philibert and his party of 18 hunters, bound for the Arapaho country on a trapping and trading venture. (Philibert returned to Missouri territory in 1815 to get pack horses, and supplies, for his men in the mountains.)

On the upper Arkansas, Williams retrieved his furs and hired Michael LeClerc (of Philibert's party) as an extra hand for the homeward trip. (He had learned from the Arapahoes that the two companions of 1812-1813 he had left at their village were dead— killed by Indians.)

Williams, May, Cooper, and LeClerc brought the peltries down the Arkansas for about 500 miles, but then were compelled to re-cache them [in southern Kansas?] because of low water, and continue homeward.

(Learning, during the winter, of a plot [involving Michael LeClerc] to steal the cached furs, Williams, together with Joseph and William Cooper [brothers of Braxton], went from the Missouri settlements by way of the Little Osage village [in present Neosho? co., Kan.], to the cache early in 1815. When the spring rise came, Williams was able, at last, to take his furs down the Arkansas to "the settlement" [presumably Arkansas Post, about 55 or 60 river miles from the Mississippi].)

Ref: *Missouri Historical Society Collections*, v. 4, pp. 200, 205-207; Luttig, *op. cit.*, p. 155; *Bulletin of the Missouri Historical Society*, v. 8, pp. 17-33.

℃ Gov. William Clark wrote the secretary of war on September 18:

[The British] . . . are making great exertions to gain over the Osage, Kanzis, Ottoes, & Seioux of the Missouri, which I am trying to prevent.

To deal with more distant Indian tribes, Clark earlier had appointed Manuel Lisa subagent for the nations living on the Missouri above the mouth of the Kansas. Lisa had gone upriver on his assignment August 14. (He continued as subagent till July, 1817.) An 1815 report on Indian agents stated that Manuel Lisa:

. . . has been of great service in preventing British influence the last year [1814] by sending large parties [of Indians] to war [against each other, or against tribes allied with the British, is implied].

Ref: *Territorial Papers of the U.S.*, v. 14, p. 787; *American State Papers: Indian Affairs*, v. 2, p. 76; *Missouri Historical Society Collections*, v. 3, p. 374. The treaty ending the War of 1812 was signed December 24, 1814.

℃ Published at Philadelphia during the year was a work entitled:

History of the Expedition Under the Command of Captains Lewis and Clark, to the Sources of the Missouri, Thence Across the Rocky Mountains and Down the River Columbia to the Pacific Ocean. Performed During the Years 1804-5-6. . . .

With its printing, the explorers' narrative at last became available to the public in complete form. Accompanying it was:

"A Map of Lewis and Clark's Track, Across the Western Portion of North America From the Mississippi to the Pacific Ocean . . . in 1804, 5 & 6. Copied by Samuel Lewis From the Original Drawing of Wm Clark."

More contemporaneous than its title indicated (William Clark had added data from Pike, the Astorians, etc., as current as 1812) this "cartographic achievement" was the "progenitor of many later maps, and one of the most influential ever drawn."

Ref: Carl I. Wheat, *Mapping the Transmississippi West* (San Francisco, 1957), v. 2, pp. 31, 57, 58, for map data and quote.

1815

❡ Between July 18 and September 16, at Portage des Sioux [on the west side of the Mississippi, not far above St. Louis], U. S. commissioners (Gov. William Clark, of Missouri territory; Gov. Ninian Edwards, of Illinois territory; and Auguste Chouteau, of St. Louis) negotiated treaties of peace and friendship with a number of Indian nations (most of whom had been allied actively with the British in the War of 1812). They were the Pottawatomie, Piankeshaw, Teton, Sioux of the Lakes, Sioux of St. Peter's river, Yankton Sioux, Maha, Kickapoo, Great and Little Osage, Sac, Fox, and Iowa tribes. (Several more nations signed like treaties in 1816 and 1817.)

And at Spring Wells [near Detroit, Mich.] on September 8, other U. S. special agents made a peace-and-friendship treaty with the Wyandots, Delawares, Senecas, Shawnees, Miamis, Chippewas, Ottawas, and Pottawatomies—nations living in Ohio and the territories of Indiana and Michigan.

The last of the 1815 treaties was negotiated at St. Louis—with the Kansa Indians—on October 28. (Edwards and Chouteau were agents for the government.) Nineteen chiefs and head men signed the document—the first formal peace agreement between the Kansa and the United States. The first seven Indian signers were: Cayezettanzaw (or the big chief), Needapy, Hazeware, Wahanzasby, Cayebasneenzaw (or the little chief), Manshenscaw (or the white plume), and Cayegettsazesheengaw (or the old chief).

Ref: C. J. Kappler's *Indian Affairs, Laws and Treaties* (Washington, 1904), v. 2, pp. 110-124.

❡ In the autumn Auguste P. Chouteau and Jules de Mun obtained a trading license, outfitted a small expedition in St. Louis, and started for the Arapahoe country on the Arkansas headwaters. Their party included some independent hunters and a few Shawnee Indians. With them went Joseph Philibert (returning to his company of trappers in the mountains). On the way west, Chouteau and de Mun purchased of Philibert "his furs, goods, horses, &c., and the time of his men."

Their route took them by way of the Great Osage village [in present Vernon county, Mo.], and "Liguetse's Village" of Osages [*see* 1813] on the Neosho river. (They had entered present Kansas, presumably in Bourbon county, on October 12.) On the 21st they camped "on a fork of the Arkansas and in sight of that river" [probably the Little Arkansas, near present Wichita]. They followed up the Arkansas, and as de Mun reported:

> It being late in the season, we had great difficulties to encounter; some of our horses giving out every day, we had to walk more than one-half of the way to the mountains, where we arrived on the 8th of December.

(Philibert's men were not at the rendezvous point—the mouth of Huerfano creek [some 20 miles below present Pueblo, Colo.]. In January, 1816, Jules de Mun went to New Mexico, located them, was well received in Santa Fe, and returned with the men to where Chouteau was camped in February.)

Ref: *Missouri Historical Society Collections,* v. 5, pp. 167-208; *Territorial Papers of the U. S.,* v. 15, p. 85 (for trading license item).

1815-1816

℃ Caleb(?) Greenwood and three companions who had left "Boon's Lick" (Mo.) early in September "to hunt on one of the forks" of the Arkansas, joined forces *temporarily* with the Chouteau-de Mun party on November 27, 1815, when they met on the upper Arkansas.

On March 26, 1816, Jules de Mun apparently encountered Greenwood and his friends (who recently had arrived at the Little Osage village) when he reached the Neosho river [in present Neosho? county] on his trip east [*see* next entry]. As de Mun somewhat skeptically recounted it, Greenwood's party had met a band of Pawnees:

> . . . that they had pillaged them and taken even their rifles, that they had walked for 18 days [across present Kansas] to reach this village, eating only roots on the way. . . .

Ref: *Missouri Historical Society Collections,* v. 5, pp. 171, 207, 208, 315.

1816

℃ Jules de Mun, Joseph Philibert, and some others, left the Chouteau-de Mun camp at the mouth of Huerfano creek [in present Colorado] on February 27, bound for Missouri territory. With pack horses and mules, they followed down the Arkansas (and across present Kansas) in March, finding the prairies barren of pasture for their horses, and proceeding sometimes at night to avoid Pawnee war parties.

On March 18 (the day they left the Arkansas and crossed to the Little Arkansas) they were near what is now Wichita. On the 26th they reached the Neosho, and on March 29 were at the Great Osage village. In April, after a 46-day journey, they arrived at St. Louis.

Ref: *American State Papers: Foreign Relations,* v. 4, pp. 211-213; *Missouri Historical Society Collections,* v. 5, pp. 174, 175, 311-318.

℃ Four young members of the Chouteau family were among those granted Indian trading licenses during the year:

License	Name(s)	To Trade With:
Mar. 12	Gabriel S. Chouteau (22, son of Auguste). .	Sacs and Foxes on Osage river
June 13	Jules de Mun, and Pierre Chouteau, Jr. (27)	Arapahoes, Comanches, etc.
	[Auguste P. Chouteau, 30, another son of Pierre, Sr., was de Mun's actual partner]	
Aug. 17	Gabriel S. and Francis G. Chouteau (19, son of Pierre, Sr.)	Osages, Kansa, and Pawnees
Aug. 17	Paul Ligueste Chouteau (24, son of Pierre, Sr.)	Great and Little Osages

(Two more of Pierre Chouteau, Sr's., boys were yet to enter the Indian trade—Cyprian and Frederick, aged 14 and 7 in 1816.)

Ref: *Territorial Papers of the U. S.*, v. 15, pp. 190, 191; Paul Beckwith's *Creoles of St. Louis* (St. Louis, 1893) for Chouteau family data.

❡ Probably as early as March, Auguste P. Chouteau and some 20? trappers left the upper Arkansas to bring down their furs. In present southwest Kansas, "Republican Pawnees, Ottos, and Rees," "about two hundred in number" attacked them. Taking refuge on a tree-covered island in the river [five miles southwest of present Lakin, Kearny county] they "made a sort of rampart out of their packs, forming three small redoubts, with the horses in the intermediate space," and fought off the Indians. They "had one man killed and three wounded; five Pawnees remained on the spot, and a great many wounded." The refuge was known, thenceforth, as Chouteau's Island.

Being too early for a rendezvous (on the lower Kansas) with his partner de Mun, Chouteau continued down the Arkansas to the mouth of a fork [the Little Arkansas?] and established a camp [near present Wichita?].

On July 31 Jules de Mun (camped about seven miles above the mouth of the Kansas) learned the location of his "lost" partner. *See* next entry.

Ref: *American State Papers: Foreign Relations*, v. 4, pp. 211-213; *Missouri Historical Society Collections*, v. 5, pp. 323, 324; *The Bulletin* of the Missouri Historical Society, St. Louis, v. 26 (October, 1969), p. 30; *Niles' National Register*, Baltimore, v. 11 (October 19, 1816), p. 127, wherein it is stated: "A Mr. Chouteau and party had been attacked by 150 Pawnees. He had one man killed and four wounded; but he defeated the Savages, killed seven and wounded several others and brought in 44 packs of beaver, that is about 4,400 pounds." (The *Niles' National Register* item is reprinted in Grant Foreman's *Pioneer Days in the Early Southwest* [1926], p. 78.) For text of the "Chouteau's Island" historical marker, *see* KHQ, v. 10, p. 344; and *see, also*, v. 23, p. 145 (for note on the "island" today). On the location of Chouteau's Island *see* Kate Gregg, ed., *The Road to Santa Fe* . . . (Albuquerque, c1952), pp. 256, 257.

❡ Jules de Mun's westbound party, heading for a Kansas river rendezvous with his partner Chouteau (bringing furs from the upper Arkansas), reached Fort Osage (Mo.) in early July. Some of his men had traveled up the Missouri in a barge; the rest, with the pack horses, made the journey from St. Louis overland. Several Kansa chiefs were at the fort, and one—White Plume—offered to go ahead with the pack horses to the river. De Mun and the rest of the company continued upriver in the barge, and entered the Kansas on the morning of July 11. They "went up about 3 leagues [seven or eight miles] as far as the big bank . . . [and then] were obliged to stop for lack of water."

They camped [probably on the south bank, a mile or so below, and across the river from present Muncie, Wyandotte co.] De Mun noted in his journal: "The antelope seems to be in great abundance here; our men killed three." On July 13 White Plume and the party with the horses arrived. Baronet Vasquez and some others left on July 15 to go towards the Arkansas in search of de Mun's partner Chouteau. But it was White Plume, who, two weeks later, brought word (from the Little Osage) of Chouteau's location on a fork of the Arkansas [probably near present Wichita].

Chouteau joined forces with de Mun August 10. The latter wrote: "At the Kansas river we found ourselves forty-five. We shipped the furs to St. Louis, and started again for the mountains." (No record of the journey has been found, but logically their route to the Great Bend of the Arkansas, from near the mouth of the Kansas, would have been that of the pathway soon to be known as the Santa Fe trail.)

(The Chouteau-de Mun party reached the upper Arkansas, wintered in the mountains, and accumulated furs. On May 24, 1817, by order of the Spanish governor, the whole company was arrested, taken to Santa Fe, and imprisoned for 48 days. The furs and outfit were confiscated—de Mun estimated the loss at over $30,000. Released from prison, the men were permitted to leave "each with one of the worst horses we had.")

Ref: *Missouri Historical Society Collections*, v. 5, pp. 318-326 (Jules de Mun's journal of June-August, 1816; *The Bulletin* of the Missouri Historical Society, v. 26 (October, 1969), p. 30; *American State Papers: Foreign Relations*, v. 4, pp. 209-213; *New Mexico Historical Review*, v. 36 (October, 1961), pp. 263-273.

❡ By the Comanches' own estimate, 4,000 of their people died in a smallpox epidemic during the year.

(In 1804 Pierre Chouteau had estimated the Laytanne [Comanche] population at 15,000. Despite the 1816 losses, Lt. Col. William A. Trimble's 1818 report indicated they remained the "largest and most warlike nation" in the country.)

Ref: Nasatir, *op. cit.*, v. 2, p. 760 (for Chouteau); Jedidiah Morse's *A Report* . . . *on Indian Affairs* . . . (1822), p. 259 (for Trimble).

1817

❡ Indian trading licenses granted during the year included:

Issued	Name(s)	To Trade With:
Aug. 23	Chouteau & Rivar	Great and Little Osages
Sept. 4	Francis Chouteau	Kansa and Little Osages
Sept. 23	Hugh Glenn	Cherokees and Osages
Sept. 23	Joseph Robidoux & Co.	Indians on the Missouri and its waters
Sept. 30	Cyrus Curtis	Indians on the Missouri and its waters
Oct. 6	Joseph and Francis Robidoux	Great and Little Osages

Ref: *Territorial Papers of the U. S.,* v. 15, p. 378.

❡ At "Belle Point" on the Arkansas [near the western border of what, in 1819, became the territory of Arkansas], in December, Maj. Stephen H. Long selected a site for the military post which subsequently was named Fort Smith. (By 1822 it had been only partially completed.)

1817-1818

❡ The Western Cherokees (those Cherokees who recently had moved west of the Mississippi to the Arkansas river), with allied Delawares, Shawnees, Quapaws, and some Americans, went up to the Osages' country on the Verdigris and raided Clermont's village [near present Claremore, Okla.] in the absence of the warriors. It was reported they killed more than 80 old men, women, and children and took over 100 prisoners; as well as firing the town and destroying provisions. This occurred apparently in October, or early November.

(On October 6, 1818, at St. Louis, the Cherokees and their allies (of the one part) and the Big and Little Osages (of the other part) signed a peace-and-amity treaty. But warfare was soon renewed and continued, intermittently, for several years—*see* 1821-1822.)

Ref: R. G. Thwaites' *Early Western Travels, 1748-1846,* v. 17, pp. 19, 20; *American State Papers: Indian Affairs,* v. 2, p. 172; Superintendency of Indian Affairs, St. Louis, "Records," *loc. cit.,* v. 2, p. 93; Foreman, *op. cit.,* p. 58.

1818

❡ It was reported that some 400 Pawnees ambushed a party of Osages within 50 or 60 miles of the Arkansas in the spring, and only one of 48 Osage warriors escaped. In another spring engagement, seven of a party of Spaniards on a hunting expedition "in United States territory" [possibly in present Kansas] were killed by Pawnee Loups. A ten-year-old Spanish boy taken captive (to be used in a Loup sacrificial rite) was ransomed by a trader and subsequently purchased by Manuel Lisa.

Ref: *Missouri Gazette* . . ., St. Louis, June 19, 1818 (or, *see Missouri Historical Society Collections*, v. 3, p. 388); Thwaites, *op. cit.*, v. 15, pp. 154, 155.

ℂ Chiefs and head men representing four Pawnee bands journeyed to St. Louis in the late spring and signed a peace-and-friendship treaty with the United States (William Clark and Auguste Chouteau were the U. S. commissioners.) The Grand Pawnees signed on June 18; the "Noisy Pawnees" or Pitahauerats on June 19; the Pawnee Republic band on June 20; and the Pawnee Mahas (Loups) on June 22.

Ref: Kappler, *op. cit.*, v. 2, pp. 156-159.

ℂ On September 25, at St. Louis, William Clark negotiated a treaty with the Osages which, as he put it, ceded to the United States:

. . . the country North of Arkansas [river—in present Arkansas] from their old boundary line [of 1808], to the three forks [the treaty read ". . . up the Arkansaw and Verdigris, to the falls of Verdigris river; thence eastwardly . . ."], with a width of Sixty Miles, which will include a large body of very fine land.

Ref: *Ibid.*, p. 167; *Territorial Papers of the U. S.*, v. 15, p. 454.

ℂ When the Kansa visited Fort Osage in the fall, to trade, Factor George C. Sibley (acting on William Clark's orders) made a *provisional* (and never official) treaty with the chiefs and head men, on September 30, to buy a part of the lands claimed by the Kansa. The *western* limit of the area to be ceded was described as:

[Beginning at the mouth of the Nodaway river on the Missouri [across from present northeast Doniphan county] and running from thence direct to the mouth of the River La Plane a Branch of the Kanzas River [possibly the Delaware river of today], thence due South to the Neeozho river. . . .

The document provided some information about Kansa leaders of 1818. First to sign was Sho-ge-ne-gare (head chief), followed by Ca-he-ga-wa-ton-e-ga (a son of the head chief), Waw-kun-nicha (2d chief); warriors Big Neck [Long Neck?], Big Soldier, Petit ma[i]gre [Little thin one], and several others.

(Seven years elapsed before the signing of a treaty by which the Kansa actually ceded any lands claimed by them.)

Ref: Superintendency of Indian Affairs, St. Louis, "Records," *loc. cit.*, v. 2, pp. 127-136.

ℂ Cantonment Martin (the first U. S. military post in present Kansas) was established in October, 1818, on the upper, timbered end of Isle au Vache or Cow Island [on the "Kansas" side of the Missouri's channel at that time; about equidistant from Atchison and Leavenworth of today].

Captains Wyly Martin (senior officer, for whom the post was

named), Matthew J. Magee, and Bennet Riley, with three companies of riflemen, arrived in keelboats. A little earlier (by October 18), sutler John O'Fallon and three Indians had reached Isle au Vache overland from Fort Osage (about 80 miles away), bringing cattle and horses. By mid-November the 260 troops (an advance battalion for the proposed "Yellowstone expedition" in 1819) had completed log warehouses and winter quarters. Hunting, both a sport and a necessity (to supplement meager rations), became the riflemen's chief occupation during the months Cantonment Martin was occupied. It was reported they killed "between two and three thousand deer, beside great numbers of bears, turkeys, etc."

Lt. Col. Willoughby Morgan arrived (overland from Fort Osage) on April 13, 1819, to take command at the post.

(For the first military post in present Kansas *see* 1744.)

Ref: "Napton Collection" (in the Society's manuscript division) for copies of O'Fallon letters (from the originals in the State Historical Society of Missouri); *KHC*, v. 1-2, p. 283, v. 8, pp. 436-441 (article on Isle au Vache); *KHQ*, v. 2, pp. 115, 116; Roger L. Nichols, ed., *The Missouri Expedition, 1818-1820; The Journal of Surgeon John Gale with Related Documents* (Norman, Okla., c1969), pp. 30-63. In Yale University's Coe Collection is the Henry Atkinson "Journal, 1818-1820" (mainly written by Lt. Thomas Kavanaugh) which would be a source of information for this, and subsequent items relating to the Yellowstone expedition.

1819

❡ The treaty negotiated between Spain and the United States on February 22 defined the western limits of the nation. (Also, the United States gave up claim to what is now Texas, while Spain ceded Florida, and her right to the Oregon country.) The agreed-upon boundary ran up the Sabine river to the 94th meridian; north on its line to the Red river; westwardly upstream to the 100th meridian, north on its line to the Arkansas; up that river west to the Rocky mountains and the 106th meridian; then north to the 42d parallel; and west on its line to the Pacific ocean.

[U. S. Surveyor Joseph C. Brown, while marking the Santa Fe road in the summer of 1825, made the first calculation of the 100th meridian's position, but his measurements were inexact because the longitude assigned to Fort Osage—the beginning point of his task—was incorrect. Brown was, apparently, about 10 miles west of "the Caches"—famed Santa Fe trail landmark, *see* 1822-1823—when, by his reckoning, he reached the 100th meridian. "The Caches" were about five miles west of present Dodge City; and Dodge City is on the 100th meridian. Brown, then, calculated the 100th degree of longitude to be about 15 miles west of its actual location. Army engineers later corrected all points on Brown's survey from Fort Osage to about the 102d meridian, by the "addition of 23 minutes of longitude."]

Ref: Kansas State Historical Society's *Eighteenth Biennial Report* (Topeka, 1913), p. 121 (for Brown's field notes); 33d Cong., 2d Sess., *Sen. Ex. Doc. No. 78*, v. 11 (Serial 768), p. 101 (Lt. G. K. Warren's statement); Kate L. Gregg, ed., *The Road to Santa Fe* . . . (Albuquerque, c1952), pp. 78, 79 (for G. C. Sibley's comment on Brown's work).

❏ On March 2 the act creating the Territory of Arkansas was signed by President Monroe. (Arkansas Post was the seat of government in 1819-1820, but in 1821 newly-founded Little Rock became the capital. By 1820 the population, exclusive of Indians, was over 14,000.)

Ref: D. T. Herndon's *The Highlights of Arkansas History* (c1922), pp. 27, 28, 30, 39.

❏ *A Journal of Travels into the Arkansas Territory during the Year 1819*, by Thomas Nuttall, published at Philadelphia in 1821, was one of the early-printed works of a traveler in the Arkansas-Oklahoma region.

Early in 1819 Nuttall, a botanist and ornithologist, ascended the Arkansas river to Fort Smith (Ark.). From that post he journeyed overland to the Kiamichi-Red river country (in southeastern Oklahoma of today), and back, between May 16 and June 21. In July he continued up the Arkansas to the trading houses of "Mr. [Joseph] Bougie and Mr. Prior [Nathaniel Pryor]" near the mouth of the Verdigris. There he met and talked with Osage Indians, and made excursions in present east-central Oklahoma—including a canoe trip up the Grand river to the Osage salt works; and a hazardous overland trip (impeded by a malaria-type illness) to, and back from, the Cimarron river between August 11 and September 15. After recuperating at Fort Smith till mid-October, he went down-river to New Orleans.

Ref: Nuttall's *Journal* (as noted above); also published as Volume 13 in R. G. Thwaites, ed., *Early Western Travels* (Cleveland, 1904-1906). Nuttall had ascended the Missouri river with Wilson P. Hunt eight years earlier. *See* 1811. Under 1834 his journey with N. J. Wyeth's second expedition will be noted.

❏ The *Independence*, first steamboat to ascend the Missouri, arrived at Franklin (about 200 miles above St. Louis) on May 28, after seven "*sailing* days," but 13 en route; and continued 30 miles higher, to Chariton (Mo.) before turning back. The event was celebrated by citizens of the river settlements and at Franklin cannon salutes were fired. On June 5 the Missouri's pioneer steamboat returned to St. Louis, without mishap, after a 21-day absence.

Ref: St. Louis (Mo.) *Enquirer*, May 19 and June 9, 1819; *Missouri Gazette*, St. Louis, June 9, 1819; *KHC*, v. 9, p. 277.

❏ On June 9 the *Western Engineer* (a 75-foot, light-draught, stern-wheel steamboat, designed for use on the Missouri) arrived at St. Louis after a 35-day journey from Pittsburgh, Pa. On board were Maj. Stephen H. Long and the scientific members of the "Yellowstone expedition."

The Western Engineer started up the Missouri on June 22; took aboard Indian Agent Benjamin O'Fallon and his interpreter, John Dougherty, at St. Charles on the 27th; reached Franklin on July 13 (where Thomas Say and other scientists left the boat to travel by land to Fort Osage); continued upstream past Chariton (beyond which no steamboat had been); and arrived August 1 at Fort Osage, without serious difficulties or delays.

At the fort were Col. Talbot Chambers and 260 U. S. riflemen (recently arrived in five keelboats) awaiting supplies before continuing upstream; and Say's overland party (which had been there a week).

Ref: Thwaites, *op. cit.*, v. 14, pp. 10-12; *Nebraska Historical Society Publications*, Lincoln, v. 20, pp. 18-28. Chambers and the riflemen had left St. Louis on June 14— see *North Dakota Historical Quarterly*, Bismarck, v. 5, p. 226.

❡ About July 1 (lacking provisions, and with game scarce in the Cantonment Martin area) Lt. Col. Willoughby Morgan sent Captain Martin's riflemen upriver and Captain Magee's company downstream, to hunt and subsist as best they could off the land. Captain Riley's troops and "the music" remained at Cow Island. On Independence Day Morgan wrote Gen. T. A. Smith:

I salute you on the 4th of July. Our colours are flying; and [Capt. Bennet] Riley is preparing something to eat— We shall have a pig with savory tarts to grace the table.

On the 27th Morgan reported that his command was strung out for nearly 100 miles along the Missouri, with Capt. Wyly Martin's company 60 to 70 miles upstream, where Martin "is in just such a paradise as he wants. . . . He kills sometimes twenty deer a day besides bear. Besides he floats in honey."

Ref: *KHQ*, v. 8, p. 118; "Napton Collection" (in Society's manuscript division).

❡ A "Yellowstone expedition" flotilla (three steamboats and several keelboats) carrying the Sixth U. S. infantry and supplies, left the St. Louis area early in July to go up the Missouri.

The steam craft experienced various difficulties and breakdowns. Below the Osage junction the *Thomas Jefferson* foundered (and became the first steamboat wreck on the Missouri); the *R. M. Johnson* (plagued with engine trouble) got no higher than a little below the mouth of the Kansas by mid-September; and had to remain over-winter. (*See*, 1819-1820 entry.) Only the *Expedition* managed to carry supplies as far as Cantonment Martin; and she was more than 50 days en route. The Sixth infantry made most of the journey in keelboats, which were sent on in advance of the wayward steamboats.

Ref: "Napton Collection," *loc. cit.*; *KHC*, v. 9, pp. 277, 278, 302, 309, 311; St. Louis (Mo.) *Enquirer*, July 21-October 30, 1819, issues; Nichols, *op. cit.*; *Nebraska Historical Society Publications*, v. 20, pp. 23-30; Jacob H. Holt's "Narrative" (1874), as quoted in the Kansas City (Mo.) *Times*, October 27, 1959 (or, *see* "Kansas City, Missouri, History Clippings," v. 5, pp. 82-84, in KHi); *North Dakota Historical Quarterly*, v. 5, pp. 224-226. Meriwether, *op. cit.*, and Richard G. Wood's *Stephen Harriman Long* . . . (Glendale, Cal., 1966), are additional works containing information on the Yellowstone expedition. In the Kansas City (Mo.) *Western Journal of Commerce*, February 27, 1858, is an interesting summary of the 1819 era of steamboat navigation on the Missouri river.

❡ On August 6 a company of 13 persons left Fort Osage for an overland journey. As stated in the account of Maj. Stephen H. Long's expedition:

. . . to extend our examination between Fort Osage and the Konzas river, also between that river and the Platte, a party was detached from the steamboat [*Western Engineer*], with instructions to cross the Konzas at the Konza village; thence to traverse the country by the nearest route to the Platte, and to descend that river to the Missouri. The party consisted of Mr. [Thomas] Say [a zoologist], to whom the command was intrusted; Messrs. [Augustus E.] Jessup [a geologist], [Titian R.] Peale [a naturalist] and [Samuel] Seymour [landscape artist], Cadet [William H.] Swift, J[ohn] Dougherty [interpreter and guide], and five soldiers. They were furnished with three pack-horses, and a supply of provisions for ten days. . . . they [were] accompanied by Maj. [Thomas] Biddle and his servant. . . .

Say and his companions crossed Johnson, Douglas, and Shawnee counties of today, and were, perhaps, near present Lecompton on August 13 when they came down from higher land to make their first camp on the Kansas river (south side). Two days earlier they had reached "some elevated ridges" from which they could "trace the whole course" of what they took to be Wahrengeho, or Full creek [the Mill creek of today], but which was, instead, the Warreruza [Wakarusa].

They had already coped with blowflies, rattlesnakes, high and coarse prairie grasses (which slowed their progress; wore out their clothing and moccasins), "excessive" heat, exposure, and fatigue. Dysentery and shortage of food were other problems as they traveled up the river valley. After searching on both sides of the Kansas they eventually located a trail leading up the *north* side. On the 19th they came to the Vermillion [in present Pottawatomie county], where, no other game being available, they "dined on the flesh of a black wolf."

Next day, they approached the 120-lodge Kansa village [two miles east of present Manhattan]. The chiefs and warriors "came rushing out on horseback, painted and decorated, and followed by great numbers on foot." After being escorted to a lodge, Say and his companions took part in a pipe-smoking ceremony and a talk; then feasted (on jerked buffalo meat and boiled corn) as guests of Ka-he-ga-wa-ta-ning-ga (Fool, or Little Chief), and other leaders.

(Some 150 Kansa men afterwards left for Isle au Vache to council with Agent O'Fallon.)

During the four-day visit in the town, Thomas Say collected valuable data about the Kansa—their way of life, dress, customs, beliefs, etc. Leaving on the afternoon of August 24, the Say party traveled seven miles up the "Blue Earth" [Big Blue] river and camped beside a stream [McIntyre? creek] in present Pottawatomie county. A short time later about 140 mounted Pawnee Republic Indians descended on them, drove off the pack-horses, plundered their baggage and provisions, then departed leaving the white men humiliated but unharmed.

In the morning they retraced their way to the Kansa village. That evening the hospitable Indians performed a "dog dance" to entertain them—a scene that artist Samuel Seymour portrayed in a sketch (which, as an illustration in the atlas volume [dated 1822] accompanying Edwin James' account of Long's expedition published in 1823, was, apparently, the first ever printed relating to what is now Kansas).

Abandoning the journey to the Platte, Say and his companions, on August 26, set out northeastwardly for Isle au Vache. They had the aid and guidance of "Mr. Gunville" [Gonville], a French trader living with the Kansa. (See under 1807.) Arriving at Cantonment Martin, on August 29, they learned that the *Western Engineer* had left several days earlier. All the party (except Say and Jessup who were ill), continued northward overland to the mouth of Wolf river [in present Doniphan county], where, on September 1, they caught up with the steamboat.

Ref: Thwaites, *op. cit.*, v. 14, pp. 181-211; *KHC*, v. 1-2, pp. 280-297. Samuel Seymour's sketch of the Kansa "dog dance" has been reproduced as the *frontispiece* in *KHC*, v. 1-2, and in *KHQ*, v. 15, *facing* p. 336 (cover of November, 1947, issue). The trader was probably *Louis* Gonville, though his brother Baptiste also lived among the Indians. See 37th Cong., 2d Sess., Sen. Ex. Doc. No. 58 (Serial 1122). An account (by Major Biddle?) of this journey appeared in the *Analectic Magazine*, Philadelphia, 1820, pp. 303-313. The Cahokia (Ill.) census, August 27, 1787, listed as a resident "j. B[aptis]te Gonneville." (*See* C. W. Alvord, ed., *Cahokia Records, 1778-1790* [1907], p. 627.) A footnote says: "Second name of the Desjardins. There was a Charles Desjardins at Detroit in 1761."

❦ Between August 10 and 18 the *Western Engineer* steamed up the Missouri from Fort Osage to Cantonment Martin; with a brief excursion of about a mile up the Kansas river (and an overnight stay opposite its mouth) on August 12. This first steamboat on the *upper* Missouri, and on the Kansas, was an extraordinary-looking craft— calculated to impress the Indians. As one observer described her:

The bow of this vessel exhibits the form of a huge serpent, black and scaly, rising out of the water from under the boat, his head as high as the deck, darted forward, his mouth open, vomiting smoke, and apparently carrying the boat on his back. From under the boat, at its stern, issues a stream of foaming water, dashing violently along. All the machinery is hid. . . . to the eye of ignorance, the illusion is complete, that a monster of the deep carries her on his back, smoking with fatigue, and lashing the waves with violent exertion.

. . . Objects pleasing and terrifying are at once before . . . [the savage]:—artillery [three small brass field pieces, mounted on wheel carriages on the deck]; the flag of the republic; portraits of a white man and an Indian shaking hands; the calumet of peace; a sword [these last three were on a banner prepared by artist Samuel Seymour]; then the apparent monster with a painted vessel on his back, the sides gaping with port-holes, and bristling with guns. . . .

Ref: Thwaites, *op. cit.,* v. 14 pp. 12, 172-175; *KHC,* v. 1-2, pp. 282, 283; St. Louis (Mo.) *Enquirer,* June 19, 1819, or *Niles' Weekly Register,* Philadelphia, v. 16 (July 24, 1819), p. 368 (for quote); *North Dakota Historical Quarterly,* v. 5, p. 228.

❦ Near Cantonment Martin, on August 24, at a ceremonial meeting (preceded by the firing of a few rockets and shells from aboard the *Western Engineer*), about 150 Kansa chiefs and head men (and 11 Osage warriors) counciled with Indian Agent Benjamin O'Fallon, in the presence of military officers and a few civilians.

Runners had been sent to the Kansa to summon them for a council on Isle au Vache after O'Fallon learned, while at Fort Osage, that the "impudent Kanzas" had "repeatedly plundered and insulted our traders and finally our Troops. . . ."

The "most distinguished" Indians who made the 90-mile journey from the Big Blue-Kansas junction were: Na-he-da-ba (Long Neck), one of the principal chiefs; Ka-he-ga-wa-ta-ning-ga (Little Chief), second in rank; Shon-ga-ne-ga (formerly principal chief); Wa-ha-che-ra (Big Knife), a leader of war parties; and Wom-pa-wa-ra (White Plume), a man "rising rapidly in importance."

Of the council, Agent O'Fallon commented:

A proper and I doubt not, a lasting understanding was effected—They made the fairest promises—I believe they are about to Change—This nation is at war with most of their neighbouring Tribes of red Skins, which has produced much distress upon them, within the last two or three years—They beged me to aid them in giving peace to their Nation. . . .

Many of the Kansa, still at Isle au Vache the day following the meeting, watched the departure of the *Western Engineer* upriver. They "manifested some surprise at witnessing the operations of the steamboat."

Ref: Thwaites, *op. cit.,* v. 14, pp. 176-178; *KHC,* v. 1-2, pp. 283, 284; *Territorial Papers of the U. S.,* v. 15, p. 562 (for O'Fallon quote).

⁋ The *Expedition* (second steamboat on the Missouri's *upper waters*) arrived at Cantonment Martin on August 27 or 28; followed by troop-and-supply-loaded keelboats under command of Col. Talbot Chambers; and soon after by Col. Henry Atkinson, head of the Sixth U. S. infantry.

Cantonment Martin was virtually abandoned early in September when the Sixth infantry and rifle troops started upriver on the 5th and 6th in keelboats. A trader who stopped at Isle au Vache on the 14th reported only a subaltern and 30 men remained—awaiting the arrival of a boat to take the last of the *Expedition's* cargo. (The steamboat, empty, remained at Cow Island till the ice in the Missouri broke up in the spring of 1820.)

Ref: St. Louis (Mo.) *Enquirer,* September 29, October 30, and November 27, 1819; *Nebraska Historical Society Publications,* v. 20, pp. 28, 29; "Napton Collection," *loc. cit.*; Nichols, *op. cit.*; Jacob H. Holt's "Narrative," in the Kansas City (Mo.) *Times,* October 27, 1949 (or, *see* "Kansas City, Missouri History Clippings," v. 5, pp. 82-84, in KHi); *North Dakota Historical Quarterly,* v. 5, p. 232; the Henry Atkinson "Journal," *loc. cit.* (for this, and succeeding entries).

⁋ On September 17 the *Western Engineer* was anchored for the winter a little above the Missouri Fur Company post Fort Lisa [on the Missouri's right bank a few miles above present Omaha, Neb.].

(She had left Cantonment Martin on August 25 with Major Long's party aboard, escorted by the keelboat *General Smith* carrying Lt. Gabriel Field and 15 men. Camp on the 25th was at the mouth of Independence creek [Atchison county]. On September 1, at the mouth of Wolf river [in present Doniphan county], members of Say's overland party caught up with, and reboarded the steamboat.)

From mid-September, 1819, to June, 1820, "Engineer Cantonment" (some cabins on the Missouri's right bank—in the southeast corner of present Washington county, Neb.) was headquarters for most of the *Western Engineer's* passengers. Major Long, however, returned East for the winter.

Ref: Thwaites, *op. cit.*, v. 14, pp. 221, 229, 230, 248; KHC, v. 1-2, p. 284.

⁋ About September 18 a Kansa peace delegation—Chief He-roch-che (the Real War Eagle), and five warriors—escorted by John Dougherty (acting for Agent O'Fallon), made a hurried journey from "Engineer Cantonment" (Neb.) to the Platte river villages of the Otoes, Missouris, and Iowas. (The six Kansa had arrived in the Fort Lisa area a day in advance of the *Western Engineer,* eager to achieve a peace with their enemies, but apprehensive of being killed before reaching their destination.) On the 19th(?) the

Indians counciled, smoked the peace pipe, and ended a five-year war—the latest of many conflicts between these long-hostile tribes.

Ref: Thwaites, *op. cit.,* v. 15, pp. 99-106.

¶ On October 4 at "Engineer Cantonment" agent Benjamin O'Fallon held a council with about 100 Otoes, 70 Missouris, and 50 to 60 Iowas. On the 10th, at the same place, he counciled with some 70 Pawnees of the Grand, Loup, and Republican bands. (The last-named restored much of the property taken from the Say party in August near the Kansa village.)

Ref: *Ibid.* v. 14, pp. 236-239, 244-247, v. 15, pp. 99-106.

¶ Early in October, some distance above the place called by Lewis and Clark "the Council Bluffs" [in present Washington co., Neb.] "Camp Missouri" was established by Col. Henry Atkinson and his troops (the Sixth infantry, and U. S. rifle corps—totaling over 1,100 men) who had arrived at the Bluffs in keelboats on September 29.

Atkinson (and Col. Talbot Chambers of the rifle regiment) started for St. Louis on November 3, leaving Lt. Col. Willoughby Morgan in command for the winter. After some of the barracks were completed in November, the post became officially Cantonment Missouri. [It was perhaps as much as eight miles above "Engineer Cantonment."]

Ref: *Nebraska History,* Lincoln, v. 37, pp. 121-133, 161, v. 38, pp. 229-236; "Napton Collection," *loc. cit.;* St. Louis (Mo.) *Enquirer,* October 30, and November 27, 1819; *North Dakota Historical Quarterly,* v. 5, p. 228.

¶ These comments on activities of the "2000 warriors" of the Pawnee bands were in a letter written at the Council Bluffs (Neb.) on October 9:

. . . The frontiers of New Mexico, separated by some days' ride over open plains, presents them with constant objects of plunder. A month since a war party returned from one of their excursions in that direction, bringing off about two hundred head of horses and mules, chiefly the latter. They had also killed three Spaniards. They have immense numbers of horses and mules. From four to six thousand may be seen at one view, covering the plains about their villages, all taken from the confines of Mexico.

Ref: St. Louis (Mo.) *Enquirer,* October 30, 1819.

¶ In a report on the Missouri river fur trade, Maj. Thomas Biddle wrote, on October 29 from "Camp Missouri":

Seres [Gabriel S.] and Francis [G.] Chouteau trade with the Kanzas and Osage nations. They have a trading-house not far from the mouth of the river Kanzas, and their capital is about $4,000.

These Chouteau cousins had begun trading with the Kansa, Osages, and Pawnees at least three years earlier (*see* 1816). On

November 5, 1818, George C. Sibley wrote from Fort Osage (to William Clark): "A drove of pack horses passed this way a few days ago, on their way up the Kansas River. From whence I am told they are to carry goods to trade with the little Osages, they were owned (or Controlled) by Sara [Seres] Choteau I am Informed." Apparently, then, Seres and Francis Chouteau's trading-house referred to above, was started a little later. Known as the "Four Houses" ("four log houses so arranged as to inclose a square court equal in size to the width of one of the houses"), it was the earliest trading house of record on the Kansas river; and perhaps the first 19th century fur depot in present Kansas. (But *see* "About 1802" annals entry.) It was probably in use till about 1828. After the flood of 1826 destroyed the Chouteaus' Randolph Bluffs post on the Missouri (*see* 1821-1822), it is said Francis Chouteau took his family to the "Four Houses."

As to the "Four Houses" location, it can be stated that a manuscript McCoy map of the 1830's (in KHi ms. division) shows "4 Houses" at the mouth of the small stream—now Cedar creek—which enters the Kansas some two and a half miles east of present De Soto, Johnson county. (By land this is about 20 miles from the Kaw's mouth.) the "4 Houses" is written on the south side of the river, giving the impression that the post was on the right bank. But John C. McCoy, in his "Tales of an Old Timer" (originally published in the Kansas City [Mo.] *Journal* of January 2, 1879) wrote: "In 1822[!] Col. Francis G. Chouteau established a trading post on the north[!] bank of the [Kansas] river one mile above the mouth of Cedar creek, near the P[acific] R. R. station of Lenape. It was called 'Four Houses,' being four log houses arranged in a square, answering the purpose of a fort. . . ."

Ref: *American State Papers: Indian Affairs*, v. 2, p. 202 (for Biddle); W. H. Miller's *The History of Kansas City* (1881), pp. 9, 10 ("Four Houses" description on p. 9); *KHC*, v. 8, p. 425, v. 9, p. 574; Superintendency of Indian Affairs, St. Louis, records in KHi, v. 2, p. 136 (for Sibley letter quotation); G. W. Harrington's *Historic Spots . . . of Wyandotte County* (1935), pp. 11, 12 (sums up material from various histories on the Bonner Springs "site" as the claimed location of the "Four Houses"). John C. McCoy's "Tales . . ." are also available in KHi library—in "Kansas Reminiscences," Clippings, v. 1, p. 114a.

1819-1820

℄ Aboard the *R. M. Johnson* (anchored a little below the mouth of the Kansas with a broken piston head), a small crew remained throughout the winter. Jacob H. Holt (17-year-old cabin boy) later recalled they suffered severely for bread and salt, "living entirely on venison, turkey and honey, and a little corn . . . pounded in a mortar . . ." cooked as best they could.

Before Christmas, 1819, the Missouri was frozen over; and the break up of the ice did not begin till near the end of March, 1820.

On March 1 snow stood "two feet deep in the timbered bottom below the mouth of the Kansas river." Earlier, visiting Indians (bound for Fort Osage with furs) had reported snow "very deep up the Kansas."

Early in April, the repaired *Johnson,* and the *Expedition* (from Cow Island), descended the Missouri.

Ref: Jacob H. Holt's "Narrative," as quoted in the Kansas City (Mo.) *Times,* October 27, 1949 (or, *see* "Kansas City, Missouri History Clippings," v. 5, pp. 82-84, in KHi); *North Dakota Historical Quarterly,* v. 5, p. 232.

1820

❏ Indian agent Benjamin O'Fallon, accompanied by John Dougherty, Thomas Say, Capt. Bennet Riley, three other officers, and a detachment of U. S. riflemen, left the Council Bluffs on April 20 for a trip to the Pawnee villages on the Loup Fork (and returned to "Engineer Cantonment" on May 6).

The Grand Pawnee chief, Long Hair, was at first uncivil, but "meeting a decisive tone" changed his conduct and gave O'Fallon's party a hospitable reception. The Pawnee Loups treated them "with all honor and distinction imaginable." Also very friendly were the Republican Pawnees who expressed "the greatest contrition" for robbing Say's expedition the previous autumn. It was reported that the Pawnees:

. . . lately had an engagement on the confines of Mexico with the Tetans [Ietans—Comanches] and Spaniards, and lost ninety-three warriors, killed or wounded.

Ref: Thwaites, *op. cit.,* v. 15, pp. 140-165; St. Louis (Mo.) *Enquirer,* July 5, 1820.

❏ In June, the "beautiful steamboat" *Western Engineer,* with Lt. James D. Graham in charge, descended the Missouri from "Engineer Cantonment," arriving at St. Louis (in four days running time) just over a year from the time she began her upriver journey.

Ref: Thwaites, *op. cit.,* v. 15, p. 190; *The Missourian,* St. Charles, Mo., June 24, 1820; *North Dakota Historical Quarterly,* v. 5, p. 232.

❏ Maj. Stephen H. Long's expedition (20 mounted men, with pack animals) left "Engineer Cantonment" on June 6, headed toward the Rocky mountains.

Long had returned to the Council Bluffs on May 28, accompanied overland from St. Louis by Capt. John R. Bell and Dr. Edwin James (botanist, geologist, and surgeon) who were to join his expedition—which, under amended orders, was to explore up the Platte to its source and return East by way of the Arkansas and Red rivers.

In mid-June at the Pawnee villages on the Loup Fork, two Frenchmen (an interpreter-guide Joseph Bissonette, *dit* Bijeau, and a hunter, Ledoux) were added to the party. There were 22 men, 34 horses and mules, and two dogs in the expedition as it continued up the Platte, and then up the south fork to the mountains.

Long and his men first saw the Rockies on June 30. By July 5 they were on the site of present Denver, Colo. On July 13, Dr. Edwin James, Zachariah Wilson, and Pvt. Joseph Verplank began the ascent of Pike's Peak (called "James's Peak" by Long), reaching the summit on the afternoon of the 14th—the first white men known to accomplish the feat. Moving southwest Long's expedition came to the Arkansas; ascended it as far as the Royal Gorge; then started downstream on July 19. Arriving on the 21st at a good ford of the river [present Rocky Ford?, Colo.], Long divided his force, sending Captain Bell with 11 men on down the Arkansas (*see* fifth entry following).

Long, with nine men, crossed the Arkansas and traveled almost due south to the Canadian. Mistaking it for the Red river, his party descended to the junction with the Arkansas [in present east-central Oklahoma] before discovering the error; then continued down the latter river to Fort Smith, arriving on September 13, a few days after Bell's detachment.

An Account of an Expedition from Pittsburgh to the Rocky Mountains, compiled by Edwin James from the notes of Long, Say, and others in the party was published at Philadelphia in 1823. Neither Maj. Stephen H. Long or Dr. Edwin James crossed what is now Kansas, but their disparaging words affected pre-Kansas history by fostering the theory that most of the vast region between the Missouri and the Rockies was, as Long's map labeled it, a "Great American Desert."

Major Long's summary opinion of the trans-Missouri country was:

". . . that it is almost wholly unfit for cultivation, and of course uninhabitable by a people depending upon agriculture for their subsistence. Although tracts of fertile land considerably extensive are occasionally to be met with, yet the scarcity of wood and water, almost uniformly prevalent, will prove an insuperable obstacle in the way of settling the country. . . . This region, however, . . . may prove of infinite importance to the United States, inasmuch as it is calculated to serve as a barrier to prevent too great an extension of our population westward, and secure us against the machinations or incursions of an enemy. . . ."

Edwin James made even harsher comment:

"We have little apprehension of giving too unfavourable an account of this portion of the country. Though the soil is in some places fertile, the want of timber, of navigable streams, and of water for the necessities of life, render it an unfit residence for any but a nomad population. The traveller who shall at any time have traversed its desolate sands, will, we think, join us in the wish that this region may forever remain the unmolested haunt of the native hunter, the bison, and the jackall."

Ref: Thwaites, *op. cit.*, v. 14, pp. 13-15, 20, 147, 148, v. 15, pp. 188-315, v. 16, pp. 11-63, v. 17, pp. 147-149, 257, 258; H. M. Fuller and L. R. Hafen, eds., *The Journal of Captain John R. Bell* (Glendale, Calif., 1957), pp. 31-183. The diary of Edwin James is in the Columbia University Library.

❧ Around mid-June the Missouri rose "much higher than it was ever known before." Low-lying Cantonment Missouri was inundated. Col. Henry Atkinson, who had returned to the Council Bluffs on June 14 to reassume command, wrote on the 19th:

. . . We have pitched our Camp on the Bluff, and are engaged in bringing up the materials of the Cantonment to rebuild.

On the new site [about a mile southeast of present Fort Calhoun, Neb., and 16 miles above Omaha] more permanent quarters were built; and on October 15 the post was officially designated Cantonment Council Bluffs. In January, 1821, the name was changed to Fort Atkinson.

(Fort Atkinson was abandoned in June, 1827, following the establishment of Cantonment Leavenworth.)

Ref: "Napton Collection," *loc. cit.*; *Nebraska History*, Lincoln, v. 37, pp. 132, 161, 162, v. 38, pp. 229-236, v. 40, pp. 39, 40; *Territorial Papers of the U. S.*, v. 15, p. 688.

❧ About May 19(?) Captain Craig headed the *Expedition* up the Missouri on a supply-carrying mission to the Fort Atkinson troops. The steamboat arrived at Fort Osage on June 10; presumably passed Cow Island (the high point of her 1819 trip) in the latter part of June; and reached the Council Bluffs on July 23. It was reported in August: "On account of the lowness of the water, and the loss of two anchors, it was not thought advisable for her to return [downstream] the present season."

The *Expedition* was the second steamboat to navigate the Missouri above Isle au Vache (Cow Island).

Ref: *Missouri Intelligencer*, Franklin, Mo., May 27, June 24, August 5, 1820.

❧ June.—From the Council Bluffs, David Meriwether, aged 19, and Alfred, a Negro youth, joined Big Elk's party of 17 Pawnees, at the Pawnee villages, and set out, late in June, 1820, for New Mexico. (The Indians were a raiding party; Meriwether's was a journey of exploration—agreed to by John O'Fallon and Capt. Lewis Bissell, U. S. A.—with the principal objectives of finding a wagon route to Santa Fe, and to learn "the amount of gold and silver in New Mexico.")

They traveled southwestwardly (across "Kansas") to the Arkansas; then followed upriver "for about a week" before fording the stream. Later (on the headwaters of the Canadian?), Mexicans killed all the party except Meriwether, Alfred, and three Pawnees (one of whom was badly wounded). Meriwether and Alfred were captured, and taken to Santa Fe.

Meriwether's autobiography (dictated in 1886) describes, also, his experiences as a prisoner; his (and Alfred's) release; the start homeward; the subsequent reunion with the three Pawnees (at a food cache point); and the journey back to the Council Bluffs—reached about March 1, 1821.

Ref: David Meriwether, *op. cit.*, pp. 82-103. Meriwether later (1853-1857) was governor of New Mexico territory.

❡ Dwight Mission for the Western Cherokees was founded in July by Presbyterian missionaries (sponsored by the American Board of Commissioners for Foreign Missions), near the mouth of Illinois creek [in present Pope county, Ark.]. (The missionary families arrived in May, 1821; and Dwight Mission was active thereafter at that location till the removal of the western Cherokees to the country west of the Territory of Arkansas in 1829.)

Ref: Jedidiah Morse's . . . *Report* . . . *on Indian Affairs* . . . (1822), p. 214; Herndon, *op. cit.*, pp. 36, 37; Grant Foreman's *Indians and Pioneers* . . . (New Haven, 1930), pp. 92-94; *History of American Missions* . . . (Worcester, Spooner & Howland, 1840), pp. 87, 88, 102, 110, 182, 194, 195.

❡ In Capt. John R. Bell's mounted party (detached from Maj. S. H. Long's expedition on July 21 to proceed down the Arkansas river) were Thomas Say (zoologist), Lt. William H. Swift (topographer), Samuel Seymour (landscape painter), interpreters Stephen Julien and Bijeau (Joseph Bissonette), hunter Ledoux, five soldiers, 14 horses, two mules, and two dogs.

On July 30 this eastbound company crossed the present Colorado-Kansas line; and by August 4 had reached the vicinity of what is now Dodge City. The morning of August 8 they came to "Dumun's creek" [now Big Coon creek], so called, wrote Bell:

. . . from the circumstances of a gentleman of that name from St. Louis [*i. e.*, Jules de Mun], having on a time [between 1815-1817], lost a valuable horse there, that died.

Also on the 8th they forded a stream which they named "Vulture creek" [Pawnee river of today]; and next day crossed present Walnut creek (which Bijeau mistakenly told them was the Little Arkansas). Wrote Thomas Say of their travels rounding the Great Bend of the Arkansas on that hot August 9th (noon temperature 94° in the shade):

The soil of the afternoon journey was a deep fine white sand, which rendered the travelling very laborious . . . and affected the sight, by the great glare of light which it so freely reflected. The chief produce of these tracts of unmixed sand is the sunflower, often the dense and almost exclusive occupant.

[Say's was, so far as known, the earliest *published* reference to the sunflower in what is now Kansas. He wrote the six chapters describing the trip of Bell's party down the Arkansas, as published in 1823 in James' *Account of* . . . Long's *Expedition*. . . . Captain Bell's journal entry for the same date also referred to the present Kansas state flower: "Almost the whole distance travelled during the forenoon has been over a dry loose sandy soil, covered with a luxurant growth of sun flowers, very disagreeable to travel thro' and fatigueing to the horses." But his journal (lost for many years) was not published till 1957.]

Proceeding downriver (toward Cow creek) on August 12 they met a party ("30 men and 5 squaws") of Ietans [Comanches] who had been attacked two nights earlier, while asleep, by a band of Otoes. (Three Comanches had been slain; they had six wounded; had lost 56 horses, as well as robes, moccasins, and other gear.) Bell prudently moved his men onward as soon as possible.

Describing the country between Cow creek and the Little Arkansas, Captain Bell wrote on August 14:

The timber on the river is [cottonwood] copse resembling much the lumbardy poplars, along the banks the sand is blown by the wind, or washed up by the freshes, into ridges & knobs covered with sun flowers & high plants.

Next day, arriving at the mouth of the Little Arkansas [where Wichita is today], he recorded in his journal:

. . . we discovered an old [Osage] Indian Village, or may more likely be, an Indian hunting camp for the winter season, as many of the cabins, were enclosed & covered with bark, in and about them was growing water mellons, pumpkins & corn. . . .

In succeeding days various problems arose. Their supply of food ran low. They were "lost"—to the extent that on August 16 they mistook the Ninnescah [which joins the Arkansas more than 20 miles north of the present Kansas-Oklahoma line] for the Negracka [now the "Salt Fork" which enters the Arkansas some 40 miles south of the Kansas boundary]—but came to the latter stream on August 24. On the night of August 30 three of the five soldiers deserted, taking the three best horses, saddlebags containing clothes, the irreplaceable manuscripts of Say and Swift, and other valuables. But on September 1 Bell and his companions met friendly Osages of Clermont's band; by the 5th they were at Hugh Glenn's trading post (near the Verdigris-Arkansas junction); and on September 9 reached Fort Smith (four days in advance of Major Long's party).

Ref: Thwaites, *op. cit.*, v. 14, pp. 16-18, v. 16, pp. 192-291; Fuller and Hafen, *op. cit.*, pp. 182-276; Waldo R. Wedel's *An Introduction to Kansas Archeology* (Washington, 1959), p. 44.

❡ "The Osages . . . are continually removing from one village to another, quarreling and intermarrying . . .," wrote George C. Sibley in a report from Fort Osage, October 1, which revealed the current situation, and some of the changes in that nation between 1814 and 1820.

In Missouri territory there remained but one Great Osage village (of about 1,200 population) 78 miles south of the fort, on the Little Osage [in present Vernon county, Mo.].

On the Neosho river 130 to 140 miles southwest of Fort Osage was the village of White Hair's band (of about 400) which had separated amicably from the Great Osages in Missouri some six to eight years earlier [about 1815?]. Also on the Neosho, from 120 to 140 miles southwest of Fort Osage, were three towns of Little Osages (including some 20 families of intermarried Missouris). They total about 1,000 persons. [These Neosho river towns were in Neosho and Labette counties of today.]

But the largest Osage group—Clermont's band—equaling half of all the nation, lived on the Verdigris [near present Claremore, Okla.], and did not trade at Fort Osage.

Ref: Morse, *op. cit.*, pp. 203-208.

❡ The Kansa (as reported by G. C. Sibley on October 1) were living "about three hundred miles up the Kansas river, in one village. . . ." He estimated their population at around 800. About the same time Agent Benjamin O'Fallon stated, more specifically, that the Kansa were "on the northwest side of the [Kansas] river at the mouth of the Grand Saline. . . ." [*i. e.*, some six miles east of present Salina]. He estimated their number at about 1,750 souls.

For what reason the Kansa *temporarily* moved from their town near the Big Blue-Kansas junction has not been determined. One possible explanation: A flood on the Kansas, like that on the Missouri in the spring of 1820, may have inundated the low-lying Kansa town, and forced a move. They appeared securely established at the old village when visited by Say's party in August, 1819; and were evidently back at that location by the winter of 1821-1822 when Becknell stopped with them briefly. It remained their principal abode till about 1830.

Throughout the 1700's the Kansa appeared in records as a nation of one village; and this still was true in the early 1800's. About 1820, however, after respected Chief Shon-ga-ne-ga stepped down in favor of his less-influential son Ka-he-ga-wa-ta-ning-ga (the Fool Chief), the Kansa tended to divide into partisan groups, each headed by a prominent chief. Commenting on the

Kansa in 1823, Prince Paul of Wuerttemberg (who had conversations with the American Chief in July of that year) wrote:

"Like most of the American aborigines this tribe is divided into several bands. They join each other but rarely. Such unions occur when they go on the hunt, also when they gather in their great village. By this latter term one must not think of a very stable and constant habitat. They subordinate themselves under one single head only, when the greatest danger requires it. Among the whites Wa-kan-ze-re [the American Chief] is especially highly esteemed, because he was one of the first of his tribe who induced the Kansas . . . to accept a friendly attitude and enter into trade with the Europeans. . . ."

In the 1820's there were three known bands of Kansa: Fool Chief (with 700 to 800 followers); Hard Chief (with 500 to 600 persons); American Chief (with about 100 people). Also, Chief White Plume apparently lived apart from the bands mentioned.

Ref: *Ibid.*, pp. 203, 237; *South Dakota Historical Collections,* Pierre, v. 19, p. 313 (for quote); *KHC,* v. 1-2, p. 287.

❡ Union Mission (sponsored by the United Foreign Missionary Society) for Clermont's band of Osage Indians, had its beginning in mid-November when advance members of the missionary party reached the previously-selected site, on the west bank of the Grand (Neosho) river about 25 miles above its mouth [in present Mayes county, Okla.]. After the arrival of the rest of the missionaries (from a temporary camp at Little Rock, Ark.) in mid-February, 1821, Union Mission began to function. The principal village of Clermont's band was about 28 miles to the west, on the Verdigris river [near present Claremore, Okla.]. (In January, 1833, the school at Union was discontinued; and in 1836 the mission was closed.)

Ref: Morse, *op. cit.*, pp. 217-220; G. J. Garraghan's *The Jesuits of the Middle United States,* New York (1938), v. 1, p. 187; W. W. Graves' *The First Protestant Osage Missions* . . . (Oswego, c1949), pp. 41-45, *Chronicles of Oklahoma,* Oklahoma City, v. 2, pp. 285-297; Foreman, *op. cit.*, pp. 94-104; *History of Indian Missions* . . ., pp. 170, 171, 241, 340.

1821

❡ Richard Graham (Indian agent in Illinois territory) was informed, in April, of his transfer to the Osage Nation, where he would "take charge of the Osages, and of the Delawares & Kickapoos who have removed to their neighborhood," and select an agency site in the Indian country. (The Osages had been without an agent since Pierre Chouteau's release in 1818. However, Paul Ligueste Chouteau, who lived among them, had continued to be their subagent. Neither Pierre Chouteau nor Graham maintained a residence among the Indians. They visited the Osages on occasion.)

Ref: *Territorial Papers of the U. S.,* v. 15, pp. 384, 715-717.

❡ On the Marais des Cygnes river, about 78 miles south of Fort Osage [and near present Papinsville, Mo.], a branch of the Fort Osage government factory for the Osages was constructed between July and October. This short-lived official trading post (the U. S. factory system was abolished in 1822) was some eight direct miles northeast of the Great Osage village.

Ref: Morse, *op. cit.*, pp. 222, 223; *Territorial Papers of the U. S.*, v. 15, pp. 627, 628; Graves, *op. cit.*, p. 108.

❡ Missouri's admission into the Union as a state was completed August 10 by proclamation of President Monroe. The population, as given in September, was 70,652.

Ref: *Historic Missouri* . . . (Columbia, Mo., c1959), pp. 12, 16.

❡ In August the Rev. Nathaniel B. Dodge and party of some 20 missionaries (mostly Presbyterians) under the auspices of the United Foreign Missionary Society, founded Harmony Mission for the Osage Indians on the Marais des Cygnes' left bank, about a mile and a half northwest of present Papinsville, Mo. The site (distant some eight or nine direct miles from the Great Osage village) was granted by the Indians to the missionaries at a council held on August 13. (Harmony Mission continued in operation till 1836.)

Ref: Morse, *op. cit.*, pp. 222, 223; Garraghan's *The Jesuits of the Middle United States*, v. 1, pp. 179, 180; *The Missionary Herald*, Boston, v. 18 (1822), pp. 30, 31, v. 19 (1823), p. 214; *History of American Missions* . . ., pp. 171, 229, 253, 265, 278, 340, 341; Graves, *op. cit.*, pp. 87-175.

❡ During August the Santa Fe-bound expedition (11 men) of St. Louis merchant John McKnight and trader Thomas James journeyed by keelboat up the Arkansas from Fort Smith (Ark.) as far as present north-central Oklahoma.

The McKnight-James party had left St. Louis May 10 to descend the Mississippi to the Arkansas junction and ascend the latter stream. McKnight's mission was to find his brother Robert—a Spanish prisoner since the ill-fated 1812 expedition to New Mexico. James, who carried a Spanish passport, was on a trading venture, and had goods valued at $10,000 aboard the boat.

Halted by low water some miles beyond the Cimarron's mouth, McKnight, James, and two others went cross-country to Clermont's village of Osages (two days' travel to the southeast) where James bought 23 horses. Returning to the Arkansas, they cached the heavier goods, loaded the pack animals and set out overland [from what is now Pawnee co., Okla.] for New Mexico.

Their route, by way of the Cimarron and the Canadian, took them across present western Oklahoma, and the Texas Panhandle (where they had a nearly-disastrous encounter with Comanches). On

December 1 the McKnight-James party entered Santa Fe and found the people friendly. (*See, also,* 1822.)

Thomas James' reminiscences (of his experiences from 1809 to 1824) were published at Waterloo, Ill., in 1846 in a work entitled *Three Years Among the Indians and Mexicans.* It was quickly withdrawn from circulation due to sharp criticism of the author's ill-natured characterizations of men prominent in the fur and Indian trade; and has long been an extremely rare item of Americana. The reprint edition of 1916, noted below, is scarce.

Ref: Thomas James' *Three Years Among the Indians and Mexicans,* edited by W. B. Douglas (St. Louis, 1916); and the Philadelphia [1962] reprint edition with A. P. Nasatir's introduction.

❧ Led by William Becknell, five men with goods-laden pack animals left Franklin, Mo., September 1 on a trading trip to the Comanche country. They stopped at Fort Osage; made slow progress for a time (due to illness among the party) as they headed for the Arkansas; reached it on the 24th [east of Walnut? creek]. Crossing the river, they followed up the south bank to the mountains, and on October 21 arrived at "the forks . . . and took the course of the left hand one" [Purgatoire? river]. Three weeks later, in New Mexico, they met some Spanish troops, and accompanied them, by way of San Miguel, to Santa Fe, where they were received "with apparent pleasure and joy." (Becknell's party arrived on November 16, two weeks ahead of the McKnight-James company. *See* preceding entry.)

According to Becknell, he and "Mr. M'Laughlin" left San Miguel (about 50 miles southeast of Santa Fe) on December 13 "on our return home, in company with two other men who had arrived there a few days before, by a different route." After 17 days of travel [by way of the Cimarron desert] they came to the Arkansas [in present Ford? county]; then set a course "over the highland which separates the waters of [the Arkansas] and the Caw rivers." They visited the Kansa [at their town near the Big Blue's mouth]; found them hospitable and bought corn. In 48 days from the time they left San Miguel [*i. e.,* by the end of January, 1822], Becknell and his companions were back in Franklin, Mo. Their mid-winter journey had proved less difficult than anticipated. They brought back "specie, mules, asses & Spanish . . . blankets."

Ref: William Becknell's brief 1821-1822 journal as reprinted (from the *Missouri Intelligencer,* Franklin, Mo., April 22, 1823) in *Missouri Historical Society Collections,* St. Louis, v. 2, pp 57-75; *also,* in *Missouri Historical Review,* Columbia, v. 4, pp. 71-81; G. C. Sibley letter (1825) in K. Gregg, *op. cit.,* pp. 214, 215.

❧ The Glenn-Fowler company (20 mounted men with pack horses), on a trading-trapping expedition to the Rocky mountains, left Hugh Glenn's trading house (near the Verdigris' mouth, in present east-central Oklahoma) on September 25.

Jacob Fowler (second in command), with his brother Robert and some others of the party, had reached Glenn's place earlier in the month. Kentuckian Fowler (reportedly well educated) is credited as author of the journal "Memorandum of the voige by land from Fort Smith to the Rockey mountains" which recounted the party's experiences on the outward journey, and the return trip in 1822. The journal (labeled by historian H. M. Chittenden "the best example of poor spelling and punctuation in existence"), was edited by Elliott Coues, and published in 1898 (as noted below).

Traveling northward to Clermont's Osage village, the Glenn-Fowler party crossed the Verdigris and set a northwest course; then on October 4 turned west toward the Arkansas river. On October 9 they crossed the "White River" [now Walnut river] in the vicinity of present Arkansas City; by the 13th they were at the mouth of the Little Arkansas [where Wichita is today]. On October 19 they rounded the Great Bend. Jacob Fowler's journal entry for that day stated, in part:

We set out at the ushal time and at 8 miles West We pased a point of Red Rocks about 600 yds from the [Arkansas] River and at Eleven miles Crosed the paney River [*i. e.*, it was Walnut creek they forded on the 19th—they crossed "Pawnee fork" on the 20th] . . . this is the Second Streem We Have Crosed Since pasing the little arkensaw—We found a good ford and Steered South 50 [degrees] West Six miles to the Bank of the [Arkansas] River—the land leavel as fare as the Eye Can see. Some Cottenwood on the Banks and Some Bushis. the Red Rock is evidently a volcanic production is porous like pomestone but heavier than common Sand stone. . . . [Fowler's "Red Rock" was later-famed Pawnee Rock in what is now southwestern Barton county; and he seems to have been the first to record a mention of that Santa Fe trail landmark.]

About November 4 the expedition crossed the present Kansas-Colorado line. On the 13th, at Purgatoire river, one man was fatally wounded by a bear. The company halted in the present Pueblo, Colo., area. Fowler built a blockhouse; his comrades hunted and trapped; while Hugh Glenn, with four men, went on to Santa Fe. After Glenn secured permission from Mexican authorities to trap in the Rio Grande valley, the whole party moved to that region for the rest of the winter and early spring. (*See, also,* 1822.)

Ref: Elliott Coues, ed., *The Journal of Jacob Fowler* (New York, 1898), or, the edition published, 1970, by the University of Nebraska Press, Lincoln; H. M. Chittenden's *The American Fur Trade of the Far West* (New York, 1902), v. 2, p. 503.

❡ On September 27 the independence of Mexico from Spain (proclaimed in late February) became an established fact. (Formal acknowledgment of the independence of Mexico by the United States was made in December, 1822.)

Ref: Michel Chevalier's *Mexico Ancient and Modern*, trans. by Thomas Alpass (London, 1864), v. 2, pp. 58-63; S. A. MacCorkle's "American Policy of Recognition Towards Mexico" (*The Johns Hopkins University Studies in History and Political Science*, Baltimore, v. 51, no. 3, pp. 34-36).

❐ Sixteen chiefs and head men of the Pawnee, Kansa, Omaha, Otoe, and Missouri tribes who were escorted East in the late fall by Agent Benjamin O'Fallon arrived in Washington on November 29.

They were entertained at the White House by President Monroe; and artist Charles Bird King painted several of the Indian visitors. It is believed that King's portrait of the Kansa chief White Plume (Mon-chonsia—also known as Nom-pa-wa-rah, or Wom-pa-wa-ra) was done at that time. *See* reproduction in this volume.

Ref: St. Louis *Enquirer*, October 13, 1821; Morse, *op. cit.*, pp. 241-251; J. C. Ewers' article on Charles Bird King in the *Smithsonian Report* for 1953, pp. 463-473.

1821-1822

❐ On the Missouri's right bank, less than a mile above the mouth of the Kansas river [in what is now Wyandotte county, and probably within present Kansas City, Kan.], Prince Paul of Wuerttemberg stepped ashore on June 21, 1823, to visit the "little settlement of creoles and halfbreeds" and the "two large houses" of "Curtis and Woods." (*See, also,* 1823 entry.) Despite their proximity it appears these "large houses" were *separate* fur trade posts—the former an establishment of Cyrus Curtis and Michael Eley; and the latter operated by Andrew Woods (an acting partner in the Missouri Fur Company). Because so little is known about these early 1820's "houses" above (north of) the Kansas, the available information about them is dealt with at some length below. So far as known —but *see* "About 1802" annals entry—they were the second, and third, 19th century fur posts in present Kansas, but it cannot be said with certainty what was the order of their founding.

ANDREW WOODS' *post:* The only known citation of the *location* of his place is Prince Paul's 1823 diary, noted above. But the letter-book of Thomas Hempstead (the Missouri Fur Company's acting partner at St. Louis, 1821-1823) contains references as early as June 27, 1821, which relate to Andrew Woods and to what Hempstead variously calls "Woods' establishment," "the lower house or establishment" [Fort Lisa being the *upper* house], "the Kansas Establishment," and "Fort Perkins, Kansas" [for Joseph Perkins, another partner in the Missouri Fur Company]. This post was founded on "Kansas" soil in late 1820, by Woods. It operated by virtue of licenses granted to the Missouri Fur Company (a one-year license to trade with the general tribes, of April 15, 1822, and a March, 1823, five-year license to trade with the Missouri river tribes. Woods' name is not on any lists of licenses granted).

Louis Bompart, going upriver to Fort Lisa in 1822, in the keelboat *Mary Jane*, noted in his journal on May 26 that on the lower Missouri his party met "Andrew Wood coming from the Riviere des Kans," and again, on June 8, that the boatmen stopped "at slough of the Isle de la Prairie" [Fire Prairie, below Fort Osage] "to get some corn which Mr. And. Wood had kept" [*i. e.*, stored?]. Other persons who may have spent some time at this post were Thomas Hempstead, and Charles Keemle. Whether Mrs. Andrew Woods (*see* 1823 entry relating to Prince Paul) came to "Kansas" before 1823 is unknown. The post was discontinued some time in 1824. Andrew Woods' death occurred in Jackson county, Mo., on June 10, 1832. [Ref: St. Louis (Mo.) *Beacon*, July 5, 1832.]

Andrew Woods had become a partner in the reorganized Missouri Fur Company, of which Manuel Lisa was head, in 1819. His co-partners, by the September 1, 1820, agreement, were Thomas Hempstead, Joshua Pilcher, Joseph Perkins, Moses B. Carson, John B. Zenoni, Andrew Drips(?), and Robert Jones. [Ref: F. L. Billon's *Annals of St. Louis . . . from 1804 to 1821 . . .* (St. Louis, 1888), p. 68; Dale L. Morgan, ed., *The West of William H. Ashley* (Denver, 1964), pp. xlix and l (for Drips), p. 10 (for Bompart), p. 228, and *see* index under Woods; *Missouri Historical Society Collections*, v. 3, pp. 391, 392.] Thomas Say, in January, 1820, at the Council Bluffs, noted the return of "Mr. Woods, of the Missouri Fur Company from a trading excursion" (to the Pawnee villages?). [Ref: Thwaites, *op. cit.*, v. 14, p. 277.] Some 35 miles above the mouth of the Little Sioux river, on the Missouri's right bank, was a site (of pre-1820's date?) which Prince Paul called "Cotes a Wood" in 1823 [Ref: *S. D. Hist. Coll.*, v. 19, p. 415]; and which was referred to in 1825 as "Woods' Hills" [Ref: *N. D. Hist. Quar.*, v. 4, pp. 12, 13, 50]. J. N. Nicollet, in 1839, wrote of it as "a beautiful site, formerly occupied by a Mr. Wood, an Indian trader; and it still bears his name." [Ref: 28th Cong., 2d Sess., *H. Doc.* 52 (Serial 464), pp. 33, 136. "Wood's Bluff" was noted in 1843 (May 12) by Edward Harris of Audubon's party, and editor J. F. McDermott, in a footnote, states (from Aububon's *Journals*, v. 1, p. 485) that Audubon wrote "Wood's Bluff" was so named "because a man of that name fell overboard from his boat while drunk."—*Up the Missouri with Audubon; The Journal of Edward Harris,* edited by J. F. McDermott (Norman, Okla., c1951), p. 62.]

CURTIS & ELEY's *post:* It could be that when Curtis and Eley were granted a one-year license on July 20, 1822 (to trade with the Osage, Kansa, Otoe, and Ponca Indians), *their* "large house" already stood on the Missouri's bank. Cyrus Curtis had been trading on the upper river five years or longer—*see* 1817. Michael Eley, (a native Virginian), had come to Fort Osage as assistant factor in July, 1815, and remained till June 30, 1820, it appears. Perhaps the partnership began soon afterwards. In 1823, Prince Paul (headed up the Missouri) noted in his diary on May 28: ". . . we met a large boat coming from the Kansas River. It belonged to a certain Mr. Curtis who has established himself as merchant at the mouth of that river." And on June 29 he wrote: "Near the fort [Osage] I met Mr. Curtis from the Kansas. He was in a boat. I delivered to him the letters from his trading company." The two-year license which "Curtis & Eley" obtained on September 17, 1823, is the last on record for the partnership. (However, the post was operating after the expiration date of the license.)

Following the Kansa treaty in August, 1825, the Indians were given an order for $500 worth of goods from the Curtis and Eley trading house. (But it was the Chouteau post downriver that supplied the $3,500 Kansa annuity goods later in the year.) In October, 1825 (*see* annals entry), the Atkinson-O'Fallon party on the keelboat *Antelope* stopped briefly at "Curtis & Eley's establishment." (Four days earlier they had met Curtis going upstream in a boat.) Upriver, at Fort Atkinson, on October 14, 1825, and again on December 28, James Kennerly (post sutler) mentioned Curtis in his diary. Jedediah Smith's (Ashley) party (*see* last 1825 entry) bought beef from "Ely and Curtis" in December(?), 1825. (Jim Beckwourth of that party, later had some recollections of "Messrs. Ely and Curtis.") Bvt. Maj. S. W. Kearny (who had mentioned *"Curtis & Ely's* Trading House" as being *a mile* above the mouth of the Kansas on his upriver journey in 1824), descended the Missouri in May, 1826, and on the sixth "halted for dinner at *Mr. Ely's* establishment." Kearny's is the last specific mention of the post that has been located. It does make clear that Curtis & Eley's "large house" survived the April, 1826, flood which engulfed Francis Chouteau's post some four miles downstream. Eley and Curtis had a store in Liberty, Mo., in the 1820's, and were operating a distillery there in 1826. Michael Eley went to Santa Fe in 1827 (and died there in 1832). Cyrus Curtis died at Liberty, Mo., in 1844.

Ref: *South Dakota Historical Collections,* v. 19, pp. 251, 303, 309 (for Prince Paul references); the Thomas Hempstead letterbook is in the Coe Collection, Yale University, but all the notes from it (and the opportunity to use them) are courtesy of Dale L. Morgan, of the Bancroft Library, whose generous sharing of his own research efforts have added immeasurably to this, and other annals entries dealing with the fur trade; 18th Cong., 1st Sess., *Ex. Doc. No. 7* (Serial 93)—for Missouri Fur Company licenses, 1822, 1823, *also,* the Curtis & Eley licenses, 1822, 1823; *The Bulletin* of the Missouri Historical Society, St. Louis, v. 16, pp. 16, 18 (for 1822 diary, and note on Eley); *Territorial Papers of the U. S.,* v. 15, p. 567 (for Eley at Fort Osage, 1816); Gregg, *op. cit.,* p. 34 (for Kansa treaty item); *North Dakota Historical Quarterly*, v. 5, pp. 51, 52 (for Atkinson-O'Fallon); *Missouri Historical Society Collections*, v. 6, pp. 82, 92 (for Kennerly diary); T. D. Bonner's *The Life and Adventures of James P. Beckwourth* (New York, 1856), pp. 31, 32; S. W. Kearny's ms. diary is in the Missouri Historical Society, St. Louis, but the items above, were supplied by Dale L. Morgan; *KHQ*, v. 26, p. 361; *History of Clay and Platte Counties, Missouri* (St. Louis, 1885), p. 100; other data on Curtis, Eley, and Woods from letters July, 1961, Dale L. Morgan to L. Barry.

❦ In 1821 (it is said) Francis G. Chouteau established a Missouri river fur depot about three miles below the mouth of the Kansas for the French Fur Company [*i. e.*, the Berthold, Pratte & Chouteau partnership which late in 1826 became the American Fur Company's Western Department]. Apparently the first license for that company to operate below the Council Bluffs was granted on August 21, 1822—to Chouteau, Berthold, and Pratte, to trade with the Sac, Fox, Iowa, Kansa, Ponca, and Otoe Indians, on the Missouri.

The partners had received licenses on July 19 to trade on the Missouri above the Council Bluffs, and on the Platte; and on the same date Francis G. Chouteau obtained a two-year license to trade with the Kansa and Osage Indians on the Kansas river [where he maintained his "Four Houses" post— *see* 1819].

Various 19th century writers indicated that the 1821(?) depot was on the right (or Kansas City) bank of the river. (The 1878 reminiscences of John C. McCoy, the 1881 Jackson county history, and the 1881 Miller history of Kansas City, Mo., are three examples.) From the accounts of two persons who were on the scene in the 1820's it seems clear that the short-lived post (destroyed by flood in 1826) was on the left (or Randolph Bluffs) bank of the Missouri [near the Chouteau bridge of today].

(1) In the summer of 1823 Prince Paul of Wuerttemberg (*see, also,* under 1823) spent several days at the cabin of "Grand Louis" Bertholet and family on the left (Randolph Bluffs) side of the Missouri, about three miles below the mouth of the Kansas; and hunted on the Indians' land across the river, where Kansas City, Mo., now extends. The Bertholet cabin was, apparently, the fur depot Francis G. Chouteau had founded two(?) years earlier. In 1825, and presumably in 1823, Louis Bertholet lived on Sec. 18, T. 50, R. 32, Clay co., Mo. [Ref: *History of Clay and Platte Counties* . . ., p. 113.]

(2) Frederick Chouteau (reminiscing in 1880) stated: "I came to Randolph, Clay county, Missouri, about two miles below Kansas City, on the opposite side of the Missouri river, in the fall of 1825, October or November. . . . My brothers, Francis and Cyprian, were trading there."

Bvt. Maj. S. W. Kearny (ascending the Missouri with Gen. Henry Atkinson and party) noted in his diary on October 12, 1824:

Started [from near Liberty, Mo.] at day break; morning cool, frosty & a heavy fog on the water. made 3½ to breakfast came up to Mr. Chouteaus Trading House to dinner, where we found the *Kickapoos,* & the *Kansas* were expected to-morrow made some purchases: In the afternoon passed the *Kansas River* & halted one mile above it, on the left Bank, opposite to *Curtis & Ely's* Trading House, having made 16 miles.

A year later (*see* October, 1825, entry) a journalist with Atkinson's party *descending* the Missouri made reference to "Chateau's place," but he, too, failed to state on which bank of the river it was located. If James P. ("Jim") Beckwourth's account of his own adventures in the winter of 1825-1826 (an account known to be partly fanciful) can be credited, he spent the early months of 1826 (till the ice on the Missouri broke up in the spring) "packing peltries" at G. Choteau's trading-post" ["G." meaning Gesseau—Francis Gesseau Chouteau] for $25 a month wages.

The Kansas City and Jackson county histories referred to above also say that Francis G. Chouteau brought his family to the fur depot the same year it was established. McCoy (an 1830 arrival in the Kansas City area) gave a different account. His statement: "Col. C[houteau] established a trading post on the south [right] bank of the river opposite the Randolph bluffs three miles below the city in 1821, and brought up his family and servants from St. Louis the next year[!], in barges occupying more than a month in the voyage." Apparently neither 1821 nor 1822 was correct since Prince Paul did not find the Chouteau family in the fur depot vicinity in the summer, or fall, of 1823. It would seem, then, that Mrs. Berenice Therese (Menard) Chouteau, and children, did not arrive before *late* 1823, or till 1824 (unless they were at the "Four Houses" post up the Kansas, which the Prince did not visit).

Ref: *The History of Jackson County, Missouri* . . . (Kansas City, Mo., 1881), pp. 102, 378; W. H. Miller's *The History of Kansas City* (Kansas City, 1881), pp. 9, 10; John C. McCoy's reminiscences in the Kansas City (Mo.) *Journal*, December 12, 1878 (or, *see* "Kansas Reminiscences Clippings," p. 113, in KHi); *South Dakota Historical Collections,* v. 23, pp. 300-318 (for Prince Paul), but *also see* 1823 annals entry; *KHC,* v. 8, p. 423 (for Frederick Chouteau); G. J. Garraghan's *Catholic Beginnings in Kansas City* . . . (Chicago, 1920), pp. 14, 15; C. R. Barns, ed., *The Commonwealth of Missouri* (St. Louis, 1877), pp. 748, 749 (for items on Mrs. Bertholet and Mrs. Chouteau); 18th Cong., 1st Sess., *Ex. Doc. No. 7* (Serial 93) for abstract of Indian licenses; S. W. Kearny's ms. diary is in the Missouri Historical Society, St. Louis, but the above quotation came to this writer from Dale L. Morgan, of the Bancroft Library; Bonner, *op. cit.,* p. 32. Frederick Chouteau in a May 5, 1880, letter to W. W. Cone (in KHi ms. division) stated that Mrs. Francis Chouteau had a child born in Kansas "over fifty years ago," and that "she came here 5 or 6 years before me" [before he came in 1828 as a trader].

1822

℃ In the spring White Hair and his band of Osages (who had lived on the Neosho river in present Kansas since about 1815) returned to the vicinity of the Great Osage village [in what is now Vernon county, Mo.] and set up a town within seven or eight miles of Harmony Mission. (They occupied it for a few months only. *See* autumn entry below.)

Ref: Graves, *op. cit.*, p. 132.

❧ Andrew Henry and William H. Ashley (who had formed a fur trade partnership in the summer of 1821), outfitted a large company of young men (including Jedediah Smith, David E. Jackson, James Bridger, Mike Fink, Moses ["Black"] Harris, and John H. Weber) in March; obtained licenses to enter the Indian country; and in April started their first expedition up the Missouri. Henry, with a part of the company, set out by keelboat; and Daniel S. D. Moore (with whom Smith traveled) started out with another boat in May. The second one sank below Fort Osage, but Ashley outfitted a third boat, picked up his stranded men, and joined forces with his partner in October at the mouth of the Yellowstone river where Henry built a fort as operational base for the trappers. (Ashley returned to St. Louis in the late fall. *See, also,* 1823.)

Ref: Dale L. Morgan's *Jedediah Smith* . . . (Indianapolis and New York, c1953), pp. 23, 26-29; also a letter by Dale L. Morgan, of July 15, 1961, to L. Barry, supplying data not only for the above entry, but for several other entries in this chronology—information of much value, which would otherwise have been unavailable to this writer, and acknowledged here with gratitude; Dale L. Morgan, ed., *William H. Ashley, op. cit.,* pp. 1-19; *Bulletin of the Missouri Historical Society,* St. Louis, v. 11, p. 12; J. Cecil Alter's *James Bridger* . . . (Salt Lake City, c1925), pp. 4-8; D. M. Frost's *Notes on General Ashley* . . . (Worcester, 1945), p. 59.

❧ Father Charles De La Croix, the first (Catholic) missionary to visit the Osages of western Missouri, came on horseback from Florissant, Mo., in the spring. Between May 5 and 12, at the Chouteau trading post [near present Papinsville, Mo.] he baptized 20 Osages, mostly half-French children. The first name on the list under the May 5th date was Antoine Chouteau (born in 1817), whose father was trader and subagent Paul Ligueste Chouteau. (*See, also,* under August.)

Ref: Garraghan's *The Jesuits of the Middle United States,* v. 1, pp. 178-182; also, his *Catholic Beginnings in Kansas City,* pp. 23-25.

❧ Signed on May 6 was an act abolishing the United States trading houses for Indian tribes. Among the establishments to be discontinued were the Fort Osage factory, and its branch on the Marais des Cygnes [in present Bates county, Mo.]. (The nonprofit government system had been in existence since 1796.)

Ref: *Laws of the United States of America* (Washington City, 1827), v. 7, pp. 53-55. F. S. Cohen's *Handbook of Federal Indian Law* (Washington, 1942), p. 10.

❡ Benjamin Cooper, his nephews Braxton and Stephen Cooper, and 12 other men left Franklin, Mo., early in May on a trading expedition to New Mexico. It is said their pack animals carried goods worth $4,000 to $5,000. They followed the Arkansas river to the mountains then turned southward to Taos. (On June 13, in present western Kansas, they met the eastbound Glenn-Fowler and McKnight-James party.)

Cooper, part of his original company, and some from Becknell's, recrossed present Kansas in September; and by early October had reached home again. Their expedition had been a profitable venture.

Ref: Josiah Gregg's *Commerce of the Prairies* . . . (New York, London, 1844), v. 1, p. 22; *Missouri Intelligencer*, Franklin, Mo., October 8, 1822 (reprinted in *Missouri Historical Review*, v. 4, pp. 67, 68); Coues, *op. cit.*, p. 154; James' *Three Years* . . ., pp. 167, 168. "The Book of the Muleteers" published in the *Missouri Intelligencer*, Franklin, August 5 and 19, 1825 (and reprinted in the *New Mexico Historical Review*, Santa Fe, v. 17, pp. 289-293), may have described the above expedition.

❡ Heading a mounted company of 21 men, with three loaded wagons (the first to be taken from Missouri overland to Santa Fe), William Becknell left Fort Osage about May 25 on his second trading expedition to New Mexico. Again his route varied to some extent from the soon-established road. Becknell's party crossed the Arkansas before reaching the Great Bend. It was probably in present Rice county that his company forded that river one June day, and camped on the right bank. During the night 28 horses strayed—frightened by buffalo. Eighteen were found, but two of the searchers met some "rascally Osages" who whipped them, took their horses, guns and clothing. A third man was rescued by trader Auguste P. Chouteau who was at the Indians' camp.

While Becknell's company remained in the vicinity for six days (trying to recover the stolen animals), "Mr. Heath's company" came up and joined them. The combined parties continued up the Arkansas (along the south bank) for eight days [to present Ford county], then struck southwest across the Cimarron desert. They reached San Miguel (where some of Heath's company stopped) 22 days later. Becknell went on to Santa Fe.

On his trip back to Missouri (probably in October), Becknell stated only that "we took a different course from that pursued on our way out which considerly shortened the route and arrived at Fort Osage in 48 days."

William Becknell was, probably, the first to suggest publicly (in an April, 1823, newspaper) that "An excellent road may be made from Fort Osage to Santa Fe. Few places would require much labor to make them passable."

Ref: Becknell's brief 1822 journal (first published in the *Missouri Intelligencer*, Franklin, Mo., April 22, 1823) as reprinted in *Missouri Historical Society Collections*,

v. 2, pp. 65-67, and in *Missouri Historical Review,* v. 4, pp. 79-81; *Missouri Intelligencer,* Franklin, Mo., October 8, 1822, April 22, 1823; James' *Three Years* . . ., pp. 175, 176. *Niles' Weekly Register,* v. 23 (November 23, 1822), p. 177, carried an item, from an unidentified source, on the party of traders under "col. Cooper" [*i. e.,* William Becknell!] which had "arrived [at Santa Fe] with *three wagons loaded with goods,* to the great astonishment of the people. In return for his goods, colonel Cooper [Becknell] brought back specie and mules. . . ." In Iris H. Wilson's *William Wolfskill, 1798-1866* (Glendale, Cal., 1965), p. 36, it is stated that Becknell's company of 1822 (21 men in all) included Wolfskill, Henry Ferril, and Ewing Young; and that Wolfskill and Young remained in New Mexico.

❆ From Taos, N. M., on June 1 the Glenn-Fowler and McKnight-James companies (*see* 1821) started East together. With the latter group was Robert McKnight, reunited with his brother John after nine years in Spanish custody. The united force had over 140 horses and mules—83 belonged to the McKnight-James party.

About June 11 they entered present Kansas and struck the Arkansas (after crossing what is now the southeast corner of Colorado on a direct—and original—northeast course). They followed up the south bank. On the 13th they met Cooper's westbound party (traveling up the north side of the river). On the 18th and 19th they encountered large numbers of Pawnees (fortunately not war-minded). Also on June 19th, in the Great Bend area [present Barton county], the two companies (traveling separately since the 14th) took divergent routes.

THE MC KNIGHT-JAMES PARTY continued down the Arkansas (spending one day at an Osage camp [in present Reno? county] in which were Auguste P. Chouteau and other French traders), as far as the Little Arkansas. Crossing it, they traveled eastwardly; followed an Osage trail to the Neosho; forded that stream in present Neosho county. (On the way they met more Osages, for the most part friendly.) Three days east of the Neosho they crossed into Missouri, and camped in what is now Vernon county, Mo. While they slept, Osages stole 38 of Thomas James' best animals. Finding pursuit futile, the party proceeded to the Chouteau trading post [near present Papinsville, Mo.] six miles distant. The McKnights, James, and several others then traveled by canoe and pirogue down the Osage and Missouri to St. Louis; the rest went overland with the remaining horses and mules. The journey to eastern Missouri was concluded about mid-July.

THE HUGH GLENN-JACOB FOWLER COMPANY camped June 19 on the Arkansas in what is now western Rice county; left the river next day on a course "north 60 East." By a devious and circuitous route, which took them southward as far as present Butler county, and then northeastward across Chase, Lyon, Osage, Douglas, and Johnson counties of today, they entered Missouri, near present Kansas City, on July 5, and reached Fort Osage that night. Around the middle of July they were in St. Louis.

Ref: Coues, *op. cit.,* pp. 142-174; James' *Three Years* . . ., pp. 161-186.

❆ A large delegation of Western Cherokees (from Arkansas territory), and 150 of Clermont's band of Osages (from present Oklahoma), after counciling at Fort Smith, settled their tribal differences and signed a peace treaty on August 9. (Designed to end more than a decade of warfare between the two nations, the treaty was not entirely effective for Osage-Cherokee clashes were renewed in 1823 and continued in succeeding years.)

Ref: Foreman, *op. cit.,* pp. 135-139, 147-150.

❡ In August the Rev. Charles De La Croix, on his second visit to the Osages (of Missouri), spent some three weeks among them. He performed 12 baptisms on August 11, and one on the 16th. As in May, sponsors for some of the half-Indian children who received the rite were traders Paul Liguesté Chouteau and Pierre Melicour Papin. It is probable that Father De La Croix visited the Osage towns on the Neosho [in Neosho, and Labette? counties of today] at some time during August. (On the 31st he was a witness to the treaty noted below.)

Ref: Garraghan's *Jesuits* . . ., v. 1, pp. 178-182; *KHQ,* v. 8, p. 209; *KHC,* v. 16, p. 749.

❡ At the Fort Osage sub-factory on the Marais des Cygnes [in present Bates county, Mo.] on August 31, the Osages, by treaty, and in return for merchandise worth $2,328.40 from the Fort Osage post, released the United States from its obligation (under the 1808 treaty) to maintain the trading establishment at Fort Osage. (Agent for winding up the post's affairs was Samuel Blunt; Paul Baillio, factor, handled the closing of the Marais des Cygnes branch.)

Ref: C. J. Kappler's *Indian Affairs, Laws and Treaties* (Washington, 1904), v. 2, pp. 201, 202; 18th Cong., 2d Sess., *Ex. Doc. No. 61* (Serial 116).

❡ Early in September when most of the Great Osages of Missouri left to go on their fall hunt, the missionaries at Harmony [in present Bates county, Mo.] reported: "It is understood . . . they do not intend to return to their late residence but to establish themselves sixty or seventy miles from this station."

On September 26, in the journal of Union Mission [in Mayes county, Okla., of today], it was recorded:

Mr. August P. Cheauteau with a party of Indians from White Hair's village called here. A boat of his had arrived at the mouth of Grand [or Neosho] River with goods to trade with the Indians. He intends to form an establishment on this river [about 15 miles] above this place and states that White Hair's people have left their town with the intention of moving to this [Grand or Neosho] river. [Auguste P. Chouteau took over the trading house (where Salina, Okla., is today) previously run by his associate—the half-Indian Joseph Revoir (killed by Cherokees in June, 1821).]

And in the Union Mission journal of October 17 was the comment: "Last evening arrived a company of White Hair's Indians. This is the first visit from that part of the nation. It appears that they are in an unsettled state and have not selected a place for their new home."

(On August 20, 1823, when the Osages were assembled in present Bates county, Mo., to receive their annuities, the Harmony Mission journal stated: ". . . In his talk, the Agent [Richard Graham] requested them to decide whether they would live at Neosho [in present Kansas], or at the Osage river [in Missouri], that he might know where to build houses for his interpreter and blacksmith. They finally determined to remain at Neosho." After August, 1823, there were still some Osages left in Missouri, particularly in a Little Osage village about 14 miles from Harmony Mission.)

Ref: Graves, *op. cit.*, pp. 128, 179-182; Foreman, *op. cit.*, pp. 61, 142, 143.

❧ In the autumn Missouri Fur Company peltries reportedly valued at $24,000 were brought down the Missouri from the Yellowstone country. The scope of revived interest in the fur trade was indicated by a St. Louis newspaper's comment (in September):

Since the abolition of the United States' factories a great activity has prevailed in the operation of . . . [the fur] trade. Those formerly engaged in it have increased their capital and extended their enterprize; many new firms have engaged in it, and others are preparing to do so. It is computed that a thousand men, chiefly from this place, are now employed in this trade on the waters of the Missouri, and half that number on the Upper Mississippi. The Missouri fur company . . . alone employs upwards of 300 men. . . .

Ref: *Niles' Weekly Register*, v. 23 (September 28, and November 16, 1822), pp. 53, 164; *Missouri Intelligencer*, Franklin, Mo., September 17, October 29, 1822; H. C. Dale's *The Ashley-Smith Explorations* . . . (Cleveland, 1918), p. 64.

1822-1823

❧ James Baird and Samuel Chambers (Spanish prisoners, along with Robert McKnight, from 1812 to 1820), and a company of traders left the St. Louis area in August, en route to New Mexico. Partners with Baird were William Anderson, Sr., Paul Anderson, Jr., John Foughlin, and Wilson McGunnegle. By one 1822 report there were 20 men and 60 pack animals; by another account the company numbered 50; and in 1823 it was stated 40 men made up the party. Whatever their number, the adventurers made a late-season start out of Missouri, and experienced difficulties.

On the Arkansas, in present Ford county, they were caught in a blizzard; took shelter on a large island; lost most of their animals. They were stranded for three months, enduring a severe winter. In the early spring of 1823 they dug deep pits in a slope on the north side of the river above their winter camp, stored their merchandise, and proceeded to Taos.

Writing from "Touse" June 20, 1823, McGunnegle stated "Since I came to this place I started with the two Andersons, and a few Spaniards to lift two 'Caches,' that we made on the Arkansas river; when within a short distance of them we fell in with a large War Party of the *Panis* Indians, (sixty in number,) who robbed us of 13 Mules and 1 Jack Ass, together with several other articles of less value. We were then obliged to put back to this place, which we reached after undergoing a pedestrian tour of fifteen days." On November 10, 1823, the St. Louis *Enquirer* noted that several members of the expedition had returned—"M'Gunnegle, Anderson, & company. They do not yet despair, we understand, of realising the objects of the expedition." Baird and Chambers had remained in New Mexico.

The excavations made by the Baird party were known thereafter as "the Caches," and remained for years a noted landmark on the Santa Fe trail [about five miles west of present Dodge City]. In 1846 a woman traveler (Mrs. Susan Shelby Magoffin) wrote in her diary: ". . . 'the Caches' . . . are large holes dug in the ground somewhat the shape of a jug. . . . They are situated about a quarter of a mile from the River, on rather an elevated piece of ground, and within a hundred yards of the road, which runs at present between them and the river. They are quite as noted as any point on the road and few travellers pass without visiting them."

Ref: St. Louis (Mo.) *Enquirer,* September 2, 1822, November 10, 1823; *Missouri Intelligencer,* Franklin, September 3, 1822 (reprinted in *Niles' Weekly Register,* v. 23, p. 177); *Missouri Republican,* St. Louis, August 27, September 3, November 8, 1823; *Bulletin of the Missouri Historical Society,* St. Louis, v. 15, pp. 190, 191; Stella M. Drumm, ed., *Down the Santa Fe Trail . . . the Diary of Susan Shelby Magoffin . . .* (New Haven, 1926), pp. 53, 54; R. W. Strickland's article on Baird, in L. R. Hafen, editor, *The Mountain Men and the Fur Trade of the Far West* (1966), v. 3, pp. 27-37. Alphonso Wetmore in his *Gazetteer of the State of Missouri* (1837), p. 269, called the pits "Anderson's Caches on the Arkansas."

1823

❡ The keelboats *Yellow Stone Packet* and *The Rocky Mountains* carried the second large Ashley-Henry fur expedition up the Missouri along the present northeast Kansas boundary in April. (They had left St. Louis on March 10 with 70 or more persons aboard.) Led by William H. Ashley, the company on this trip included such young men as Thomas Fitzpatrick, William Sublette, Hugh Glass, and James Clyman.

On June 2, at the Arikara villages, in what is now South Dakota, the Indians defeated and routed Ashley's men in a treacherous surprise attack. In the battle 13 trappers or boatmen were killed, 11 were seriously wounded (two died later); and all of the party's horses were lost. From Fort Atkinson [Neb.] Col. Henry Leavenworth led a punitive expedition against the Arikaras in July and August. It ended, indecisively, in negotiations, and a peace treaty on August 11.

Ref: Morgan, *Jedediah Smith, op. cit.*, pp. 50-77; Morgan, ed., *William H. Ashley, op. cit.*, pp. 19-39, 52-57; *Bulletin of the Missouri Historical Society*, St. Louis, v. 11, p. 12; J. E. Sunder's *Bill Sublette, Mountain Man* (Norman, Okla., c1959), pp. 34-45; L. R. Hafen and W. J. Ghent, *Broken Hand; the Life Story of Thomas Fitzpatrick* (Denver, 1931), pp. 18-30; C. L. Camp, ed., *James Clyman, American Frontiersman* . . (San Francisco, 1928), pp. 12-22; Frost, *op. cit.*, pp. 71-126.

❡ Thirty-one men were in the Santa Fe-bound expedition captained by Stephen Cooper which left Missouri in May. Joel P. Walker was another leader of this company. Each trader had one or two pack horses and an average of about $200 in goods. On June 1 on the bank of the Little Arkansas [present Rice? county] Indians stampeded and ran off all but six of their horses. Cooper and five others went back to Missouri to buy more animals. When they returned to their party they found some 1,500(?) Kansa (on a buffalo hunt) camped near by. Cooper took his company over the Cimarron desert route where they nearly succumbed to thirst; but finding water in time, they reached Santa Fe safely.

Walker later recollected that this company of "1822" (*i. e.*, 1823) lost 50 horses and mules in the raid; that "Cooper, Walker, Bird and McKenny" returned to Missouri for more animals; that later, out on the Arkansas, they encountered Joseph R. Walker (brother of Joel P.) and his company of trappers (who, having recovered cached furs, were also Santa Fe-bound). The combined party (55 men and 200 animals), subsequently (on the Jornada, evidently) suffered so from thirst the men killed buffalo and drank the blood.

On their return to Missouri in November(?), it was reported they had brought back "400 Jacks and Jennets and mules, a quantity of beaver and a considerable sum in species. . . ."

Ref: *Missouri Historical Review*, v. 4, pp. 69, 70; *Niles' Weekly Register*, v. 25 (December 13, 1823), p. 230; *History of Howard and Chariton Counties, Missouri* (St. Louis, 1883), pp. 153, 154; Gregg, *op. cit.*, pp. 251, 252; Joel P. Walker, *A Pioneer of Pioneers* (Los Angeles, Glen Dawson, 1953).

❡ John McKnight (of the 1822 McKnight-James expedition to New Mexico) was killed by Comanches in May, in the country south of the North Fork of the Canadian.

(The McKnight brothers, John and Robert, with Thomas James and some 20 others had taken a pack train up the North Fork in the early part of the year. While most of the company began to construct a trading "fort" in what is now Blaine county, Okla., McKnight and three others went to locate the Comanches. After leaving the Indians' camp alone he was slain.)

Ref: James' *Three Years* . . . pp. 190-227; *Arkansas Gazette*, Little Rock, July 22, 1823; *Missouri Republican*, St. Louis, July 30, 1823.

❡ Prince (later Duke) Paul Wilhelm of Wuerttemberg and his

hired hand Louis Caillou spent the night of June 16 at the new town of Liberty, Mo. Next day, on horseback, they traveled "five miles on the slope of a chain of hills" to the cabin of "Grand Louis" Bertholet (and his family) on the Missouri's left bank, some three miles below the mouth of the Kansas—a site later known as Randolph Bluffs, Mo.

Prince Paul, 25, traveler and naturalist, had arrived at New Orleans in December, 1822. At St. Louis in May, 1823, he obtained passage up the Missouri for himself and two employees on a keelboat of the "French Northwest Trading Company" [i. e., the Berthold, Pratte & Chouteau firm]. At Franklin on June 12 the Prince and Caillou left the slow-moving boat (after arranging a mouth-of-the-Kansas rendezvous), and set out overland for that vicinity. They proceeded mostly afoot, crossing the Missouri twice, and reaching Liberty, Mo., on the 16th.

"Grand Louis" Bertholet's cabin was Prince Paul's headquarters for several days. [This was, apparently, the fur depot which Francis G. Chouteau established about 1821. See 1821-1822.] On June 18 the Prince crossed the Missouri to hunt [in present Kansas City, Mo.]. Intense heat, nettles, and dense forest made the going difficult, and he brought back only one deer. Three days later, in company with Caillou, "Grand Louis," and a man named Roudeau, he went in a pirogue to the Kansas river. Before ascending it, he paid a visit to the "two large houses" of fur traders "Curtis and Woods" [see 1821-1822 entry] which were "scarcely more than a half mile further up on the right bank of the Missouri" [in present Kansas City, Kan.]. Of this place Prince Paul wrote:

Neither of them [Cyrus Curtis; Andrew Woods] was at home but the wife of the latter was there. She was a creole, a daughter of old Mr. Chauvin . . . [of] St. Charles. The whole population of this little settlement consists of only a few persons, creoles and halfbreeds, whose occupation is the trade with the Kansas Indians, some hunting and agriculture. Here I also found a youth of sixteen years of age, whose mother . . . [Sacajawea], had accompanied the Messrs. Lewis and Clark, as an interpreter, to the Pacific Ocean, in 1804-1806. This Indian woman married the French interpreter, Toussaint Charbonneau. Charbonneau later served me in the capacity of interpreter, and Baptiste, his son, whom I mentioned above, joined me on my return, followed me to Europe and has since then been with me. I remained for dinner with Mrs. Woods and after the meal went to the Kansas again.

If Marie Louise Chauvin Woods, wife of Andrew Woods (and daughter of Francis and Helene Tayon Chauvin) was not the first white woman to reside in present Kansas, she has the distinction of being the first white female "Kansas" resident whose name is known. (See, also, "About 1802" annals entry.)

The Prince and his party proceeded "eight English miles up stream" and "spent the night without food on a sandbar" of the Kansas river. Their next day's (June 22) hunt was hampered by insects. Wrote Prince Paul:

. . . we were swarmed about and covered by mosquitoes to such an extent that we could scarcely see and recognize each other at a distance of twenty paces.

But "Grand Louis" killed a large black bear, and "turtle eggs and bear meat afforded . . . a delicious noonday meal." Because of the mosquitoes the Prince gave up his plan to go further up the Kansas.

On June 24 Prince Paul and Caillou set out *down* the Missouri— their craft two small canoes tied together and a seat put across— to hunt for the slow-to-arrive fur company boat. They got as far as recently-abandoned "picturesque" Fort Osage that evening; and next morning met and boarded the upbound keelboat.

Reaching "Grand Louis" Bertholet's cabin again on July 4, the Prince learned that Kansa chief Wa-kan-ze-re (the American Chief) and his band were camped across the river [opposite Randolph Bluffs] waiting to meet him. He went over in a canoe and was the honored guest among the Indians. (In his diary Prince Paul made some notes on the Kansa, particularly of their appearance, clothing, and weapons.) Next day, the American Chief and several other Kansa repaid the visit, and there was an exchange of gifts.

The keelboat continued upstream on July 6. The Prince caught up with it and went aboard on the 7th. As they proceeded he noted such landmarks as the *old* Kansa "Village of the Twelve," "Ile a la vache" (Cow Island), and the "Village de vingt quatre" (Village of 24—the second *old* Kansa town). On July 18 they passed the mouth of Wolf river [in present Doniphan county]; and on that same date the Prince noted in his account:

"The whole day long canoes with men of Mr. [William H.] Ashley's party had come down the stream. Most of them were wounded men, who had taken part in the fight with the Arikaras. . . ."

Prince Paul's river journey ended above the Platte's mouth on July 29. During August he visited the Otoes, and then traveled overland to the Missouri Fur Company's post near the White river's mouth [in present South Dakota], where his host was Joshua Pilcher. He returned to the Council Bluffs (by boat) on September 9. On the 17th he left Fort Atkinson (accompanied by Capt. Bennet Riley, a few soldiers, and an interpreter) and journeyed overland to the Pawnee villages. During his three-day stay among the Grand Pawnees and the Pawnee Loups (on the Loup Fork of the Platte) he was given honored and preferential treatment. Returning to the fort on September 29 the Prince then continued (by boat) down the Missouri again on October 2. At the mouth of the Kansas, on the 9th, a stop of a few hours was made. (As noted above, Baptiste Charbonneau there joined Prince Paul and accompanied him to Europe.) They arrived at St. Louis on October 24.

Ref: *South Dakota Historical Collections*, v. 19 (1938), pp. [7]-471, contains Wm. G. Bek's translation from the German of *First Journey to North America in the Years 1822 to 1824*, by Duke Paul Wilhelm of Wuerttemberg, originally published at Stuttgart in 1835. In (Francis A.) *Chardon's Journal at Fort Clark*, edited by Annie H. Abel (Pierre, S. D., 1932), pp. 231, 232, is published Prince Paul's letter, dated "St louis May 5th 1823," to William Clark, regarding his passport (and noting his German companion named J. G. Shlape, and his Creole hunter); also, Clark's May 18, 1823, letter to the secretary of war relating to Prince Paul and the passport given him. For notes on "Grand Louis" Bertholet, *see* Louis Houck's *Spanish Regime in Missouri* (Chicago, 1909), v. 2, pp. 381, 391 (note 31); C. R. Barns, ed., *The Commonwealth of Missouri* (St. Louis, 1877), pp. 15, 748, 749; and Garraghan's *Catholic Beginnings in Kansas City*, pp. 18, 121. For trader Cyrus Curtis *see* 1821-1822 entry. Data on Mrs. Andrew Woods from the Missouri Historical Society, St. Louis; and from *The Bulletin*, v. 16, p. 16, of that Society. *See* 1821-1822 entry for Frederick Chouteau's statement on his brother's Randolph Bluffs fur post; also Garraghan, *Catholic Beginnings in Kansas City*, p. 14.

❦ Between September 3 and October 16 the western boundary of Missouri, from the mouth of the Kansas river southward, was surveyed by Joseph C. Brown, of St. Louis, for the federal government.

Ref: *Missouri Republican*, St. Louis, August 13, 1823 (for item on survey party); the Missouri Historical Society, St. Louis (which has Brown's field notes) supplied the inclusive dates.

❦ Returning from a raid against the Caddo Indians, some 200 Osages (led by Mad Buffalo, a son of Clermont) attacked a camp of Arkansas hunters on Blue Water river in present southern (Bryan county) Oklahoma, on November 17. During the battle five of the Arkansans (Curtis Welborn; men named Sloan, Lester, and Deterline, and a Negro, Ben) were killed; the camp was plundered; and 30 horses were taken.

In June, 1824, five Osages gave themselves up to Little Rock authorities. At trials held in November, Mad Buffalo and Little Eagle were convicted, and sentenced to be hanged in December. (The other Osages were acquitted.) The executions were postponed; and on March 21, 1825, President Adams pardoned the two Indians. They were set free in May.

This incident particularly, plus other Indian depredations, focused attention on the need for military posts on the frontier. (*See* 1824.)

Ref: *Arkansas Gazette*, Little Rock, July 22, December 9, 16, 23, 1823, June 22, 1824; *Missouri Intelligencer*, Franklin, January 15, 29, November 13, 27, 1824, June 4, 1825; *Niles' Weekly Register* (December 4, 1824), v. 27, p. 219; Foreman, *op. cit.*, pp. 189-201.

❦ Missionaries Epaphras Chapman and William C. Requa of Union Mission [in present Mayes county, Okla.], in December began a new Osage mission station, Hopefield, about four miles higher up Grand (Neosho) river, and on the opposite side.

In the spring of 1824 they moved their families from Union to Hopefield. Among the difficulties which the missionaries survived were devastating flood losses in 1826 and Indian troubles in the same year.

Ref: Graves, *op. cit.*, p. 60; Foreman, *op. cit.*, pp. 245, 246; *History of American Missions* . . ., p. 171.

❦ Late in the year Auguste P. Chouteau (who had taken over the Osage trading post on Grand river [at present Salina, Okla.] in September, 1822) bought a post near the mouth of the Verdigris. A Union Mission report, dated December 10, stated:

Mr. Chouteau now owns the establishment formerly occupied by Messrs. Barber and Brand near the falls of the Verdigris, about four miles above its entrance into the Arkansas and 22 miles from this place.

Ref: Graves, *op. cit.*, p. 60. See, also, A. P. Chouteau's statement (1831) in 22d Cong., 1st Sess., Sen. Doc. 90 (Serial 213), p. 60.

❦ A man who called himself John Dunn Hunter had a book published at Philadelphia in 1823 under the title:

Manners and Customs of Several Indian Tribes Located West of the Mississippi; to Which Is Prefixed the History of the Author's Life During a Residence of Several Years Among Them.

As the more colorful title—*Memoirs of a Captivity Among the Indians of North America, From Childhood to the Age of Nineteen; with Anecdotes Descriptive of Their Manners and Customs*—of the London edition (also 1823) indicated, the writer claimed to have spent most of his first 20 years as an Indian captive—first among the Kickapoos; briefly with a Pawnee band; and for a span of years among the Kansa and Osages.

Hunter's popular work was accepted as factual in England; but in the United States the author was denounced as an imposter and his verisimilar autobiography was labeled fiction by such prominent men as William Clark ("It is not possible that he could have lived with the tribes he mentions, and gone through with the scenes he describes, without some knowledge of him, and of his history, having reached me."); Pierre Chouteau (". . . my acquaintance with the Osages has been since 1775 to this day [September 3, 1825], in the capacity of trader, agent, or otherwise, and . . . during that period, there never was any white boy living or brought up by them. . . ."); Baronet Vasquez (". . . I have been engaged in trade with the Kansas tribe of Indians nineteen years, between the years 1796 and 1824, and . . . during the whole of that time, there was no white man a prisoner, of any age or description among them; nor do I believe that such a circumstance has occurred for the last thirty years."); and by John Dunn, a Missouri legislator, who wrote he had "never known such a person as John Dunn Hunter" (contrary to Hunter's claim).

Ref: *North American Review*, Boston, v. 22 (January, 1826), pp. 105, 106 (for quotes

—all from letters written in September, 1825). John Dunn Hunter was killed by Indians in 1827—*see* H. Yoakum's *History of Texas* . . . (New York, 1856), v. 2, pp. 246-250.

1824

❧ On February 19, at the Council Bluffs, Antoine Robidoux was given authorization to cross through the Indian country to New Mexico.

While on this trapping expedition, after reaching Taos, he ventured as far northwest as the Green river. He and his party returned to Taos in February, 1825. By late June Robidoux was back in St. Louis.

Ref: Morgan, ed., *William H. Ashley, op. cit.*, p. 154.

❧ Jedediah S. Smith "rediscovered" (or made the "effective discovery" of) the South Pass [in present Wyoming] in March, while he and a trapping party (including James Clyman and William Sublette) were seeking a way to the rich fur country beyond the Wind River mountains. (*See* 1812-1813 for an earlier discovery of the passageway.)

A hint of the future—that the South Pass would become the great emigrant route to Oregon and California—was to be found in a St. Louis newspaper item (reprinted widely) in the autumn of 1824:

We learn that his party [referring to Andrew Henry, partner of Smith's employer, William H. Ashley] have discovered a passage by which loaded wagons can at this time reach the navigable waters of the Columbia River. This route lies South of the one explored by Lewis and Clarke, and is inhabited by Indians friendly to us.

Ref: Morgan, *Jedediah Smith, op. cit.*, pp. 89-92, 154, 155; *Arkansas Gazette*, Little Rock, November 16, 1824; or, *see Niles' Weekly Register*, v. 27 (December 4, 1824), p. 224.

❧ In April Cantonment Gibson was established by Col. Matthew Arbuckle and five companies of the Seventh U. S. infantry in present east-central Oklahoma—on the east side of the Grand (or Neosho) river about two miles from the "three forks" (the Grand, and Verdigris junctions with the Arkansas).

(Fort Gibson, for many years an important post in the Indian territory, was discontinued in 1857 as a military establishment, and turned over to the Cherokee Nation; but during the Civil War it was reoccupied, and not permanently abandoned till 1890.)

In May, some 120 miles to the south, Cantonment Towson was established by Maj. Alexander Cummings and two companies of the Seventh infantry near the present Oklahoma-Texas boundary, not far from the mouth of the Kiamichi river.

(Fort Towson was abandoned as a military post in 1854.)

Ref: Foreman, *op. cit.*, pp. 193, 195, 196, 204, 205; W. B. Morrison's *Military Posts and Camps in Oklahoma* (Oklahoma City, c1936), pp. 28-58.

❡ The largest Santa Fe-bound caravan of the year (83 persons), which left the Franklin, Mo., area in mid-May, had 156 horses and mules, but was notable for its extensive use of wheeled vehicles (20 dearborns, two road wagons, two carts, and one "small piece of cannon"). The trading goods carried was estimated to total $30,000. In this company were Alexander Le Grand (the elected captain), Meredith M. Marmaduke (later governor of Missouri), Augustus Storrs (soon to be U. S. consul at Santa Fe), and "other gentlemen of intelligence." Paul Anderson (elected first lieutenant) and Thomas L. (Pegleg) Smith went to Santa Fe with this caravan; and so, it appears, did Jacob Gregg (older brother of Josiah).

Except for the loss of some stock (frightened by buffalo), the traders' journey was without particular incident. They left the Arkansas on June 28 to take the Cimarron route; and reached Santa Fe a month later—their total trip an estimated 931 miles.

Most of the company returned to Missouri in September. It was *reported* they brought back $180,000 in gold and silver, and furs valued at $10,000. M. M. Marmaduke (whose "Journal of a Tour to New Mexico" is a principal source of information on the expedition) made the homeward journey in 1825.

Ref: *Missouri Historical Review,* v. 6, pp. 1-10 (for Marmaduke's diary as reprinted from the *Missouri Intelligencer,* Franklin, September 2, 1825); *New Mexico Historical Review,* v. 29, p. 84; *Glimpses of the Past,* St. Louis, v. 5, pp. 70, 88-90; *Niles' Weekly Register,* v. 27 (January 15, 1825), pp. 312-316 (for Storrs' statement); *Diary and Letters of Josiah Gregg* . . ., edited by M. G. Fulton (Norman, Okla., 1941), v. 1, pp. 9, 126; *The Overland Diary of James A. Pritchard* . . . *1849,* edited by Dale L. Morgan (1959), p. 157 (for "Pegleg" Smith). Morgan, ed., *William H. Ashley, op. cit.,* p. 259.

❡ An act providing for the appointment of an agent for the Osage Indians west of the state of Missouri and Arkansas territory was signed on May 18 by President Monroe. Alexander McNair (ex-governor of Missouri) was appointed to the post on June 1. (Following McNair's death in the spring of 1826, John F. Hamtramck became Osage agent.)

Ref: *Statutes at Large,* v. 4, p. 25; Foreman, *op. cit.,* p 200; *KHQ,* v. 16, p. 2.

❡ May 25.—An act passed "to enable the President to hold Treaties with certain Indian Tribes . . ." included a provision:

That it shall be the duty of Indian Agents to designate, from time to time, certain convenient and suitable places for carrying on trade with the different Indian Tribes, and to require all traders to trade at the places thus designated, and at no other place or places.

Ref: *U. S. Statutes at Large,* v. 4, pp. 35, 36.

❡ In June the steamboat *Mandan* (which had left St. Louis May 26) passed up the Missouri, bound for the Council Bluffs (and Fort

Atkinson). She reached her destination some time after July 9. One passenger was Agent Benjamin O'Fallon, who, because of the *Mandan's* slow progress, journeyed the last 50-some miles by land. She was the first commercial steamboat to ascend to the Council Bluffs.

Ref: St. Louis *Enquirer*, May 24, 31, 1824; Morgan, ed., *William H. Ashley, op. cit.*, p. 253 (for the *Mandan*), and p. 82 (for O'Fallon letter of July 8, 1824).

❡ Mission Neosho—the first Indian mission and school in what is now Kansas—was started in mid-September by the Rev. Benton Pixley and his wife Lucia F. (Howell) Pixley, who came from Harmony. They had the use of a trader's log house located near a small Osage village on the Neosho's west bank [not far from present Shaw, Neosho county]. The site was some 60 miles west-southwest of Harmony Mission (*see* 1821), of which it was a branch; and about 110 miles north of Union Mission (*see* 1820). Before the end of the year the Pixleys opened a Protestant school for Osage children. Samuel B. Bright and his wife Charlotte (Stocker) Bright were in charge of Mission Neosho's farm and household affairs during the early part of its existence.

Most of the near by villagers soon moved to White Hair's town, about six miles distant, where other small Osage bands had also congregated, forming (as reported in 1828) a village of nearly 2,000 Indians (living in lodges or mud houses spread over four or five acres of land).

Because of the opposition of the Osages' traders and subagents, Mission Neosho was only modestly successful; and, following a controversy between Pixley and Agent John F. Hamtramck, the school and mission closed abruptly in the spring of 1829 after less than five years of operation.

(The Pixleys, who were married in August, 1812, eventually had a family of six children. A statement that some of them were born at Mission Neosho, while quite possibly correct, has not been verified. But *see* under 1827.)

Ref: Graves, *op. cit.*, pp. 182-196; *Report of the American Board of Commissioners for Foreign Missions . . . at the Nineteenth Annual Meeting . . .* (1828), pp. 94, 95; *History of American Missions . . .*, pp. 171, 194, 340, 341.

❡ A delegation of 26 Spaniards (sent by Bartolome Baca, the New Mexican governor) traveled from Santa Fe to the Council Bluffs [Neb.] in the summer, and, with the assistance of Agent Benjamin O'Fallon and Fort Atkinson authorities, concluded a peace treaty with their long-time enemies—the Pawnee Indians. O'Fallon, arriving at Franklin, Mo., the latter part of September, reported the Spaniards were "highly delighted" with the reception given them and had left the Council Bluffs September(?) 11 on the homeward journey. Their route across present Kansas is not known.

Ref: *Niles' Weekly Register*, v. 27 (November 6, 1824), p. 151, *see, also, ibid.*, v. 26 (June 19, 1824), pp. 252, 253; *The Bulletin* of the Missouri Historical Society, St. Louis, v. 16, pp. 20-29. The St. Louis *Enquirer* of May 24, 1824, printed a Bartolome Baca letter of February 21, 1824, to O'Fallon, stating that the two Spanish commissioners would leave Santa Fe in May. In the Superintendency of Indian affairs, "Records" (in KHi ms. division), v. 21, p. 6, is a record that O'Fallon, on September 27, 1824, paid "Charleville & Moreau" $39.00 for "services rendered the Indian deputation during the visit of the Spaniards."

❡ In September Manuel Alvarez and Francois Robidoux headed a Robidoux fur trade party of 12 which set out from the Council Bluffs for New Mexico.

On August 30, 1825, "Robideaus party from Tous" returned to the Council Bluffs. These fur returns may have been brought in by Francois or Louis Robidoux.

Ref: Morgan, ed., *William H. Ashley, op. cit.*, p. 155; *Missouri Historical Society Collections*, v. 6, p. 75; W. S. Wallace's *Antoine Robidoux, 1794-1860* . . . (Los Angeles, 1953), pp. 10, 52.

❡ At the beginning of November, William H. Ashley's fur trade expedition to the Rocky mountains left Fort Atkinson [Neb.], traveling up the north side of the Platte. Ashley and his 25 "mountaineers," began the journey with 50 pack horses, and a wagon (soon abandoned?) and team.

Ref: Morgan, ed., *William H. Ashley, op. cit.*, p. 100.

❡ In November Augustus Storrs, of Franklin, Mo. (replying to queries addressed to him by Missouri's U. S. Sen. Thomas H. Benton) supplied a variety of information on the "Trade Between Missouri & Mexico" which was presented by Benton to the second session of the 18th Congress on January 3, 1825.

According to Storrs, three companies, in addition to the large May caravan of which he was a member, had gone from Missouri to Santa Fe in 1824— in February, August, and November; and the last one (departing November 10) had taken $18,000 in goods. [William Becknell, on his third trip to New Mexico was in the August(?) party.]

Ref: 18th Cong., 2d Sess., *Sen. Doc. No. 7; also*, published in *Niles' Weekly Register*, v. 27 (January 15, 1825), pp. 312-316; for Becknell, *see Missouri Historical Review*, v. 4, p. 81.

1825

❡ On March 3 a bill authorizing the President "to cause to be marked out" a road from Missouri's frontier to the New Mexican boundary, was signed by President Monroe (shortly before he left office). The act provided the sum of $10,000 to survey and mark the road; and $20,000 to treat with the Indians for a right of way.

President Adams, on March 16, appointed three Santa Fe road commissioners: Benjamin H. Reeves (of Howard county, Mo.); Pierre Menard (who resigned and was replaced by Thomas Mather of Kaskaskia, Ill.); and George C. Sibley (of Fort Osage, Mo.). *See, also,* under July.

Ref: *Statutes at Large,* v. 4, pp. 100, 101; K. Gregg, *op. cit.,* pp. 5-7.

❧ The caravan of 105 New Mexico-bound traders, with 34 wagons and 240 horses and mules, which stopped at Fort Osage on May 16 carried "a much larger & better assortment of merchandise" than any previously taken over the Santa Fe trail. Augustus Storrs was elected captain; Robert McKnight, Elisha Stanley, Ira Emmons, and men named Thompson and Shackleford drew up the company's code of laws. A party of 33 persons (which included a Doctor Willard of St. Charles, Mo.) probably part of the caravan, was, by Willard's account, beyond the Missouri settlements on May 16; at the Arkansas on June 8; and had reached Taos (by way of the Cimarron desert route) early in July.

Ref: *Niles' Weekly Register,* v. 28 (July 16, 1825), p. 309; K. Gregg, *op. cit.,* pp. 29, 216, 254, 264; James O. Pattie's . . . *Personal Narrative* . . . (1831), pp. 255-300, for Doctor Willard; or, *see* Thwaites, *op. cit.,* v. 18, pp. 325-347. Josiah Gregg's older brother, John, went overland to Santa Fe this year. *See Diary & Letters of Josiah Gregg, op. cit.,* v. 1, p. 126; and it *appears* that Jacob Gregg—who had made the trip in 1824—also went to New Mexico in 1825. William M. Paxton's *Annals of Platte County, Missouri* (Kansas City, Mo., 1897), p. 977, states that Jacob Gregg went to Santa Fe in 1825 "with a caravan of twenty-four wagons piloted by Hi Emmons."

❧ A company of some 40 Tennesseeans crossed present Oklahoma (traveling west from Fort Smith, Ark.) in May, en route to Santa Fe. Each trader was mounted, and led one or more goods-carrying pack horses.

Ref: Foreman, *op. cit.,* p. 244.

❧ At St. Louis, the Osages (on June 2), and the Kansa (on June 3), signed treaties with the United States (William Clark acting for the government) which (as described by Thomas L. McKenney of the Indian affairs office in a November 30 report) extinguished Indian titles to three or four million acres of land in the state of Missouri and Arkansas territory, and to nearly 100,000,000 acres west of Missouri and Arkansas. Reservations within the latter acreage were secured to the Osages and Kansa, he noted: ". . . to the first, a tract of fifty miles front, parallel to, and about twenty-five miles West of, the Western boundary of Missouri, and to the Kanzas a tract of thirty miles front, parallel also to the Western boundary of Missouri, and about fifty miles West of it; both running back to the Spanish line [*see* 1819]. A judicious arrangement as to space between those two reservations, and between the frontier of Missouri, has been effected. Thus, all the titles of Indians to lands within the limits of Missouri, except a few reservations, have been extinguished; and a country, represented to be fertile, and in all respects desirable, provided, and in sufficient extent, beyond the boundaries of Missouri and Arkansas, for the accommodation of all the tribes within the States, which, should they incline to occupy it, it is the policy of the Government to guarantee to them lasting and undisturbed possession. . . ."

The GREAT AND LITTLE OSAGES' *reserve* was described in the treaty of June 2 as follows: "Beginning at a point due east of White Hair's village [on the Neosho, in present Neosho county], and twenty-five miles west of the western boundary line of the State of Missouri, fronting on a north and south line, so as to leave ten miles north, and forty miles south, of the point of said beginning, and extending west, with the width of fifty miles, to the western boundary of the lands hereby ceded and relinquished. . . ." Their treaty also provided (1) for a government survey of the reserve; (2) payment of a $7,000 tribal annuity for 20 years; (3) that the Osages would be furnished 600 head of cattle, 600 hogs, 1,000 domestic fowls, 10 yoke of oxen, six carts, some farming utensils; (4) that the government would support a blacksmith among them; (5) that a house for each of the four principal chiefs would be built at their respective villages. In addition to the tribal reserve, 640-acre tracts were specified for each of 42 Osage half-breeds (including Noel Mongrain's 10 children and four grandchildren; William Sherley ["Old Bill"] Williams' daughters Mary and Sarah; and James G. and Alexander Chouteau); 54 other tracts (of a mile square each) were reserved (these to be sold to provide funds for educating Osage children); two sections of land at Harmony Mission, and one at the Union establishment were also reserved.

The KANSA *land cession* was described in the treaty of June 3 as follows: "Beginning at the entrance of the Kanzas river into the Missouri river; from thence north to the northwest corner of the State of Missouri; from thence westwardly to the Nodewa [Nodaway] river, thirty miles from its entrance into the Missouri; from thence to the entrance of the Big Nemahaw river into the Missouri, and from that river to its source; from thence to the source of the Kanzas river, leaving the old village of the Pania [Pawnee] Republic to the west; from thence, on the ridge dividing the waters of the Kanzas river from those of the Arkansas, to the western boundary of the State line of Missouri, and with that line, thirty miles, to the place of beginning."

The KANSA *reserve* was briefly described: "From the cession aforesaid . . . a tract of land, to begin twenty leagues up the Kanzas river, and to include their village [east of present Manhattan] on that river; extending west thirty miles in width, through the lands ceded in the first article. . . ." The treaty also provided (1) for a government survey of the reserve; (2) payment of a $3,500 tribal annuity for 20 years; (3) that the Kansa would be furnished 300 head of cattle, 300 hogs, 500 domestic fowls, 3 yoke of oxen, two carts, farming implements; (4) that the government would support a blacksmith among them. In addition to the tribal reserve, 23 one-mile-square tracts were reserved for the Kansa half-breeds. These were to be located on the north side of the Kansas river "commencing at the [east] line of the Kanzas reservation [not far west of present Topeka—North Topeka is on Tract No. 4], and extending down the Kanzas river for quantity" [*i. e.*, for 23 miles—to the vicinity of present Williamstown, Jefferson county]. The Kansa half-breeds included four children of trader Louis Gonville, and two of Baptiste Gonville. On the Big Blue river (of Missouri) 36 sections of land were reserved (these to be sold to provide funds for educating Kansa children). The United States was granted "the right to navigate freely all water-courses or navigable streams" in the Kansa reserve. [In 1968, Congress paid the approximately 400 heirs to the 23 half-breed tracts the 1862 appraised valuation of $5 per acre, in part settlement of the Kaw Indian tribal council's longstanding claims for reparations. Still at issue (November, 1970) is the several-million dollar claim for accumulated interest dating back to 1862. *See* news stories in the Kansas City (Mo.) *Star*, July 9, 1961, March 27, 1967, and November 4, 1970.]

Ref: 19th Cong., 1st Sess., *House Ex. Doc. No. 1*, pp. 89-92 (Serial 131) for McKenney; Kappler, *op. cit.*, v. 2, pp. 217-225.

❡ Headed for Missouri, and probably captained by Bailey Hardeman, a good-sized expedition of American and Mexican traders with "a great number of Mules, Asses, &c." (nearly 500, by report), set out from Santa Fe about June 1. They traveled towards the Canadian's headwaters; descended that river's left bank for some 300 miles; then set a course to the northeast; and reached the Arkansas river not far from present Wichita on July 12. As reported (to G. C. Sibley) by expedition members M. M. Marmaduke and James Moore, they met a large band of Osages "not far from the Mouth of the Little Arkansas, the 14th of July, by whom they were robbed of about 120 head of Animals, & some other property, and were otherwise illy Treated." (Osage Agent Alexander McNair later recovered some of the stolen stock.)

Ref: *Missouri Republican*, St. Louis, August 15, 1825; *Niles' Weekly Register*, v. 29 (September 24, 1825), p. 54, and v. 29 (October 22, 1825), p. 100; *Missouri Historical Review*, v. 4, p. 84 (for item on Hardeman as captain); K. Gregg, *op. cit.* (for quote from Sibley's journal, July 27, 1825, entry).

❡ Between July and October (in present North and South Dakota, or at the Council Bluffs, [Neb.]) the following Indian tribes (in peace treaties with the United States) agreed not to molest American citizens who traversed the Santa Fe road: the Sioux and Ogallalahs (July 5); the Cheyennes (July 6); the Crows (August 4); the Otoes and Missouris (September 26); the Pawnees (September 30); the Mahas (October 6).

Ref: Kappler, *op. cit.*, v. 2, pp. 230-261 *passim*.

❦ The Santa Fe road surveying-and-marking expedition (40 men; 57 horses and mules; seven baggage wagons) left Fort Osage on July 17. Heading the company were U. S. Commrs. Sibley, Reeves, and Mather (*see* March entry); their secretary Archibald Gamble; and surveyor Joseph C. Brown. Stephen Cooper was pilot and captain. The work party included such men as Benjamin Jones (one-time Astorian), Joseph R. Walker (later-famous mountain man), and Benjamin Majors (father of freighter-to-be Alexander Majors).

Reaching the Neosho on the morning of August 5 the expedition camped in a "Large & beautiful Grove of fine Timber" 160 miles from Fort Osage. Wrote George C. Sibley in his journal:

As we propose to Meet the Osage Chiefs in council Here, to negotiate a Treaty with them for the Road &c. I suggested the propriety of naming the place "Council Grove" which was agreed to, & Capt. Cooper directed to Select a Suitable Tree, & to record this name in Strong and durable characters— which was done. . . . From our camp, near the great Oak that is Marked, just at the eastern edge of the Grove, to the Crossing of the Nee Ozho the distance is 25 chains [550 yards].

Three days later about 50 Osages arrived with their interpreter William S. ("Old Bill") Williams. Next day a council was held; and on August 10 Chief White Hair (of the Great Osages), the Foolish Chief (of the Little Osages), and other leading men, signed a treaty giving the United States the right to mark the Santa Fe road through their land, and the free use of the road forever, in return for $800 compensation.

Having hired interpreter Williams for the rest of the journey, the commissioners sent him to the Kansa village (about 45 miles north— near present Manhattan) to summon the Kansa for a similar treaty council at a point farther west on the Santa Fe trail (where game was more plentiful). To "the Sora Kanza Creek" (a small branch of present Turkey creek, about five miles southeast of McPherson) some 50 Kansa came and counciled with the commissioners on the 15th, and signed a right-of-way treaty on August 16, receiving $800 in payment. For the Kansa, their great chief Shone-gee-ne-gare signed first; followed by his eldest son Ke-hea-bash-ee [another name for the Fool Chief, apparently]; then Hu-ra-soo-gee, the red eagle? [probably the same as He-roch-che (the Real War Eagle) of the September, 1819, entry]; and other leaders. White Plume was not present, but a warrior signed as his deputy.

On September 11 the expedition reached a point on the Arkansas

calculated to be the 100th meridian [the U. S.-Mexican boundary—
see 1819]; and camped till the 20th in a futile wait for permission
to extend the survey into Mexico. It was then agreed that Sibley,
Brown, Williams, and nine others would continue on to Taos and
Santa Fe (to obtain authority for continuing the survey); and that
Reeves, Mather, Gamble, and the rest of the party would return
to Missouri—which they did, reaching Fort Osage on October 25.

Sibley's party crossed the Arkansas on September 25; left the
river on the 27th at Chouteau's Island; and struck out across the
sand hills for Taos, arriving there on October 30. (A month later
Sibley moved on to Santa Fe.)

It was June 16, 1826, before official permission came for examination (but
no marking) of the Santa Fe road in Mexican territory. As stated in the report later prepared: "He [Sibley; and Joseph C. Brown] accordingly commenced a Survey at San Fernando [in the valley of Taos] on the 24th. of
August, Ran it through the Mexican Territory, and on the 16th of September,
connected it with the former [1825] Survey at the line, on the Arkansas
River." Subsequently (between May and July, 1827—*see* 1827 entry),
Sibley made some corrections in the *eastern* section of the 1825 survey.

Commrs. Mather, Reeves, and Sibley submitted their Santa Fe
road report (written by Sibley) under date of October 27, 1827
(and Surveyor Brown's field notes also carried that date). The
report (first printed in 1952, after 125 years had elapsed) presented
a picture of the "Space between the Missouri River and the Rio
Grande del Norte" which contrasted with Maj. Stephen Long's and
Dr. Edwin James' "Great American Desert" descriptions (*see* 1820):

[It] . . . is occupied by an almost unbroken plain or Prairie. Taken
as one great whole, this vast expanse . . . presents but little more variety
of Surface, than the face of the Atlantic Ocean. Its features are generally
proportioned to its great magnitude, except as to its Streams. Numerous
Rivulets, Creeks & Small Rivers flow through it, the most of which are marked
in their courses by narrow fringes of forest Trees, & thickets of underbrush.
Prominent Ridges frequently occur, which . . . Relieve in Some degree,
the dull *monotony* of the Scene. . . .

The Herbage of this Plain is in general Rich & luxuriant, consisting chiefly
of Strong and Succulent Grasses, of many varieties; Some of which would
doubtless prove valuable additions to the cultivated grasses of the United
States. In the Season of flowers, a very large portion of this great plain presents one continual *carpet* of Soft verdure, enriched by flowers of every tint—
these beauties afford pleasure for a time; but the traveller is apt Soon to lose
the Relish for them, as he pursues his tedious way, under a cloudless Sky,
and exposed to the unbroken Rays of a burning Sun, which, but for the brisk
flow of air that usually prevails, would be Scarcely Supportable.

(The 1855 legislature made the Santa Fe trail, as far west as Council Grove, a territorial road. In 1868 the Kansas legislature passed an act declaring the Santa Fe road from the eastern to the western boundaries of Kansas, a state road.)

Ref: K. Gregg, *op. cit.*; Kansas State Historical Society's *18th Biennial Report*, pp. 107-116 (for Santa Fe road data and map), and pp. 117-125 (for J. C. Brown's field notes); Kappler, *op. cit.*, v. 2, pp. 246-250 (for Osage and Kansa treaties); *Special Laws of the State of Kansas . . . 1868* (Lawrence, 1868), p. 83.

❡ With the errors and discrepancies that accompany an account written from memory, *The Personal Narrative of James O. Pattie, of Kentucky . . .* (edited by Timothy Flint) was published at Cincinnati in 1831. In it, young Pattie described his 1825-1830 adventures in the West. His "Kansas" experiences were limited to the late summer of 1825 [not 1824, as in the *Narrative—see* explanation below]. *But his account is particularly notable because it is one of the very few existing records of a journey to New Mexico in the 1820's from the Council Bluffs area; and to describe a route north of the Kansas river.*

In July, 1825, at the Bernard Pratte & Co. trading post [six miles or so below Fort Atkinson], a large New Mexico-bound expedition (112 men; 300 mules and some horses) was outfitted, and placed in charge of Sylvester Pratte (Bernard's 26-year-old son) who arrived from St. Louis on July 26. At a rendezvous camp on the Platte river in early August, this company was augmented by Sylvester Pattie (a War of 1812 hero), his son James Ohio Pattie, and two other tyro traders (whose upper-Missouri trip had foundered for lack of an Indian trading license).

The expedition moved upstream on August 6, to the Pawnee Loup village. After five days there (during which Pratte bought 600 buffalo skins and some horses; and Sylvester Pattie ransomed a captive Indian child), the journey to the southwest, across the Plains, began on August 11.

The route cannot be determined with any accuracy from young Pattie's account. It would appear this expedition reached the Republican fork on the 19th; repelled an attack by Arikaras on the 22d (the Indians lost five warriors); encountered large herds of buffalo and wild horses on the 26th; reached, that evening, what Pattie referred to as "a fork of the Platte called Hyde Park" [a *Republican* tributary], in an area where there were "multitudes of prairie dogs"; attacked a "Crow" camp (after finding the arrow-riddled bodies of two white men) on August 31 (killing 30 Indians and losing one man); arrived at the Republican-Smoky Hill dividing ridge on September 9; had an encounter with a grizzly bear on the 11th (one man died of wounds received); came to a fork of "Smoke Hill river" on the 14th [they were probably in far-western Kansas of today at this time]; and after some fairly steady traveling, reached the Arkansas river [in present eastern Colorado] on September 22. A little over a month later (October 26)—11 weeks after leaving the Loups' village—the large trading expedition arrived at Taos.

Ref: Thwaites, *op. cit.*, v. 18 (in which Pattie's *Narrative* is reprinted). To Dale L. Morgan, of the Bancroft Library, I am indebted for information (generously offered) that he has ascertained Pattie to be a year off in his dates—that Bernard Pratte & Co.'s expedition went to New Mexico in 1825, not 1824. This is fully established by documents in the "Chouteau Collection," Missouri Historical Society, St. Louis. In that perspective, a corroborative note is added by the James Kennerly diary entry of July 27, 1825, at Fort Atkinson: ". . . young Pratte & party arived last night from St Louis at Mr Cabannies" [J. P. Cabanné operated the trading post]. Kennerly's published diary (1823-1826) is in the *Missouri Historical Society Collections,* v. 6, pp. 50-97 (for above quote *see* p. 78). George C. Sibley, at Taos, N. M., mentioned "Messrs. Pratt, Robidoux and others" as recent arrivals there under date of November 12, 1825—*see* K. Gregg, *op. cit.,* p. 114, *also, see* p. 150. Pattie perhaps meant Kansa Indians when he wrote of the "Crow" camp.

❡ Indian traders who obtained licenses during 1825 which specifically entitled them to trade (for one year) *at the mouth of the Kansas river* were:

License issued to		*Date of license*
Joshua Pilcher, Lucien Fontenelle,	)	
William Vanderburgh, Charles Bent,	)	July 4
& Andrew Drips [successors to the old	)	
Missouri Fur Company]		
Bernard Pratte & Co. [Pratte,		
Chouteau & Berthold]		July 5
Russel Farnham [associated with the		August 17
American Fur Company]		
Michel Robidoux		October 8

On December 5 Bernard Pratte & Co. also was licensed to trade at the "Kanzas Village, on Kanzas River."

Ref: 19th Cong., 1st Sess., *House Doc. 118* (Serial 136); 19th Cong., 2d Sess., *Sen. Doc. 58* (Serial 146). *See KHQ,* v. 18, pp. 159, 160, for an 1841 "Kansas" item on Michel Robidoux. An account of Russel Farnham is in *The Quarterly of the Oregon Historical Society,* Portland, v. 24, pp. 338-344. He had been a witness to the Kansa treaty of June 3, 1825, at St. Louis.

❡ On September 14 Antoine Robidoux (and possibly his brother Isidore), with a Robidoux fur trade party, left the Council Bluffs for New Mexico.

This expedition made a fairly rapid trip. The company was in Taos in November.

Ref: Morgan, ed., *William H. Ashley, op. cit.,* pp. 156, 306; *Missouri Historical Society Collections,* v. 6, pp. 78, 80; Wallace, *op. cit.,* pp. 10, 52; Gregg, *op. cit.,* p. 114.

❡ September.—Returning from the Rocky mountains, William H. Ashley and his "mountaineers" (*see* p. 118), on the Missouri, in a keelboat, passed along the "Kansas" border in the latter part of the month. They arrived at St. Louis November 4, with what was reported to be "one of the richest cargoes of fur that ever arrived at St. Louis"—variously estimated worth $40,000 to $50,000.

(From the Yellowstone's mouth, where he met the Atkinson-O'Fallon expedition, Ashley, his men, and the fur returns had been convoyed downriver to Fort Atkinson [Neb.] in the boats of that expeditionary force, reaching the post September 19.)

Ref: Morgan, ed., *William H. Ashley,* op. cit., pp. 131-137, 298.

❆ While camped near the mouth of Walnut creek, at the Great Bend of the Arkansas on September 29, the eastbound party of U. S. (Santa Fe road) Commrs. Reeves and Mather met other travelers. Archibald Gamble (the commissioners' secretary) reported:

. . . a company of 20 adventurers, with a great many mules and horses laden with merchandize, arrived from Missouri [they had left Fort Osage around September 14], bound for Santa Fee; and an hour afterwards a company of 81 persons, returning from Santa Fee, also arrived at . . . camp.

The westbound company later took the "Mule Trace" through the mountains (from the upper Arkansas) and arrived at Taos on October 28 (by G. C. Sibley's report). Gamble, who joined the eastbound party (to get back to Missouri more quickly), learned from one trader that they had left New Mexico with $18,568 in silver, $182 in gold, 2,044 beaver furs (valued at $10,220), 630 animals (416 mules; 25 jacks & jennets; 189 horses) valued at $15,700. (The total figure: $44,670.) However, before reaching Walnut creek, 100 head of the stock had stampeded and not been recovered.

Ref: Gamble's October 24, 1826, letter, in K. Gregg, *op. cit.,* pp. 85, 112, 230, 256; *Missouri Republican,* St. Louis, October 24, 1825 (for accurate statistics), or, *see, Nebraska Historical Society Publications,* Lincoln, v. 20, p. 47.

❆ Gen. Henry Atkinson, Agent Benjamin O'Fallon, Capt. Bennet Riley, Lt. Samuel McRee, Lt. Jason Rogers, and 18 other persons were aboard the keelboat *Antelope* which left the Council Bluffs on October 7.

Atkinson and O'Fallon were en route to St. Louis after serving since May as U. S. commissioners on a treaty-making mission to the upper Missouri Indians. Their expedition (nine keelboats, with a 476-man First, and Sixth infantry escort) had been active on the upper river from May 16 to September 19; and the commissioners had concluded 12 treaties between May and October—the last three being made at Fort Atkinson. (The keelboats, by Atkinson's order, were equipped with paddle wheels—operated by crewmen—which were utilized on the upper Missouri.)

A journalist (name not established—quite possibly Lt. Samuel McRee) who recorded the expedition story, and the downriver trip of the *Antelope* in October, as well, included these comments relating to present Kansas.

[Under date of October 12, as the keelboat passed along the northeast Kansas boundary, in the Doniphan-Atchison county area of today] . . . proceeded at 9 o. c. at 11 saw a deer come into the water from the right bank, pursued it with the Antelope, came up with & succeeding in taking it after it was twice shot by Maj. O'Fallon, the deer had been driven into the water by a panther as appeared on examination the deer being wounded by the claw of the animal on the thighs & around the tail. Passed Cow Island at 5 & halted 2 miles below on the right [Kansas] bank for the night. Saw several Indians on the lower point of the Island & some 20 Horses.

Thursday [October] *13th* Proceeded at ½ past 5 & ran till 8 & came to on the right bank for breakfast—proceeded at ½ past 8, saw a party . . . [of] Kansas on the right bank arrived at Curtis & Eley's establishment [*see* 1821-1822] at 12 o. c. Here we saw the [chief] white plume & several other Kansas Indians—proceeded at ½ past 12 passed the Kansas river [mouth] & arrived at Chateau's place [Francis Chouteau's Randolph Bluffs post—*see* 1821-1822] at one o. c. & halted for dinner. F. Chateau had gone with his Father [Pierre Chouteau, Sr.] across to the Osage river.

The *Antelope* and its passengers, after various other stops on the way downstream, reached St. Louis on October 20.

Ref: "Journal of the Atkinson-O'Fallon Expedition," in *North Dakota Historical Quarterly*, v. 4, pp. [5]-56 (p. 52 for quote above).

❡ With goods valued at $3,500, purchased from the Chouteaus' Randolph Bluffs, Mo., post, Subagent Baronet Vasquez made the first annuity payment to the Kansa Indians late in the year. According to Frederick Chouteau (reminiscing in 1880):

. . . [Vasquez] took the goods in my brothers' [Francis G. and Cyprian's] boat across the Missouri river and up to the yellow banks, just above where Wyandotte [Kansas City, Kan.] is. [They] . . . were landed on a sand-bar there.

Ref: *KHC*, v. 8, p. 423; Janet Lecompte's article on Vasquez, in Hafen, ed., *Mountain Men, op. cit.*, v. 7, pp. 321-333. (Baronet Vasquez had accompanied Capt. Z. M. Pike on the 1806 expedition as interpreter [*see* 1806]; had traded with the Kansa since 1796 [*see* last 1823 entry]; and served from late 1822 to 1825 as interpreter and acting subagent for the Iowas.)

❡ At St. Louis on November 7 the Shawnee Indians *of Missouri*, in a treaty with the United States (William Clark acting for the government), agreed to cede their land claims in Missouri (in the Cape Girardeau area) for (1) a tract equal to 50 miles square, west of that state within the bounds of the recent Osage cession— a tract which would also be for the use of the *Ohio* Shawnees (subject to their agreement to move west); and (2) $14,000 as payment for improvements on the lands given up.

The Missouri Shawnees were granted $11,000 to settle indemnity claims against white men; and the United States agreed to maintain a blacksmith among them for five years. Another treaty article provided that if, on examination of the Osage-lands tract, the Shawnees were dissatisfied, then the government would ". . . assign to them an equal quantity of land, to be selected on the Kansas river, and laid off either south or north of that river, and west of the boundary of Missouri, not reserved or ceded to any other tribe."

The Indians chose a reserve which was bounded on the north by the Kansas river, bordered Missouri on the east for 28 miles, and extended west 120 miles. This tract (not fully described till the Shawnee-United States treaty of 1854) was estimated to contain 1,600,000 acres.

At the beginning of 1825 the Shawnees *of Missouri* were reported to number 1,383 persons. (At the same time, the *Ohio* Shawnees were *estimated* at 800.) The movement of these first immigrant Indians into present Kansas began late in 1825; continued in 1826 (with accessions from Ohio, also); and extended as late as 1833 for the last of the Shawnee bands.

Ref: Kappler, *op. cit.,* v. 2, pp. 262-264; *KHC,* v. 8, p. 78, v. 9, pp. 162, 163; 18th Cong., 2d Sess., *Ex. Papers* No. 64-3 (Serial 116), or *American State Papers: Indian Affairs,* v. 2, p. 544, or *Niles' Weekly Register,* v. 27 (February 15, 1825), p. 264 (for population figures, 1825); *History of American Missions . . .,* p. 540; 23d Cong., 1st Sess., *Sen. Doc. 512,* v. 3 (Serial 246), pp. 408, 409, 634, 635, 649, 650.

℃ As reported by Gen. Henry Atkinson and Agent Benjamin O'Fallon (on November 23) the Grand Pawnees (estimated at 5,500 souls; 1,100 warriors) and the Pawnee Loups (3,500 in all; 700 warriors) were living on the Platte. The Republican Pawnees (1,250 persons; 250 warriors) were situated *on the Republican fork of the Kansas river.*

The return (for something like a decade, as indicated below) of the Republican Pawnees to the Kansas tributary named for them deserves attention (which it has not previously had) for its connection with one, or the other, of the two known Pawnee Republic village sites on the Republican river [*i. e.,* the Republic county, Kan., and the Webster county, Neb., sites—*see* comment under 1806]. These Indians dared to move southward in the 1820's because their chief (Iskatappe) had made peace with the Kansa.

When Pike visited the Republican Pawnees in 1806 their town was on the Republican river (where they had lived for some time—*see* 1793 for notes on their 18th century homes). When Sibley visited the Pawnees in 1811, the Republican band had moved northward and was sharing a new and uncompleted village on the Platte's Loup Fork with the Grand Pawnees. (The latter, by Robert Stuart's 1813 comment, had removed from the main Platte about 1809; and by Sibley's statement the former had left the Republican about the same time.) Between 1811 and 1820, when O'Fallon (in May) and Long (in June) visited the Pawnee villages on the Platte's Loup Fork, the Republican band had left the Grand Pawnees' town, but their village was only a few miles distant. However, three years later (September, 1823) when Prince Paul of Wuerttemberg visited the Grand and Loup Pawnees (on the Loup Fork), he made only passing reference to the existence of the Republican Pawnees—and the inference is that they had already left that area (between 1820 and 1823) and were on the Republican where O'Fallon reported them to be in 1825 (as noted above). On September 24, 1823, Louis Vasquez was licensed to trade with the Pawnees on "Republic Fork."

[At the Republic county, Kan., site, once a village of 30 to 40 lodges, inhabited (it is thought) in the 1820's and early 1830's, 22 lodge sites now are visible on a six-acre tract. One of the large ones, enclosed by a building completed in 1967 (*see KHQ*, v. 35, p. 77) is a Pawnee Indian Village Museum, administered by the Kansas State Historical Society.]

When, in a letter of August 27, 1824, Agent O'Fallon advised Indian traders on locations, he stipulated: "For the convenience of the Panis Loups and Panis Republics all trade and intercourse will (for one year from the date of this) be confined to their two Dirt Villages one on the Loup fork of the River Platte and the other on the Republican fork of the Kansas River."

Jedediah Smith's (Ashley) party, en route to the mountains in the winter of 1825-1826, spent some time with the Republican Pawnees in early 1826 at their village *on the Republican river* 50 miles south of the Platte. (*See* last 1825 annals entry for comment on Smith's journey and the "Fremont-Gibbs-Smith" map which traces his route and *shows the location of the Republican Pawnees' village at that time.* Also, *see* a segment of the map, reproduced in this volume.)

In a February, 1829, report on Indian affairs (by the secretary of war), it was stated of the Pawnees:

There are four great bands of this tribe: the Pawnee Republicans, living on the Republican fork of the Kanzas, the Pawnee Loups, living on the Loup fork of the Platte, the Grand Pawnees, living on the main branch of the Platte, and the Pawnee Piques [the Wichitas and related tribes], living in Texas. . . .

Two years later a superintendency of Indian affairs, St. Louis report (November 28, 1831) referred to "the Grand Panis, Loup and Republican Panis.—At their present Dirt villages, two on the Loup fork of the Platte, and one on the Republican fork of the Kanzas."

Before the Pawnee-United States treaty of October 9, 1833, the Republican Pawnees again moved northward. In late 1834 the Rev. John Dunbar, missionary, wrote that the Grand Pawnees were on the south side of the Platte; the "Tapage and a part of the Republican band" were in a village on the north side of the Loup Fork, 30 miles above its mouth; and the other part of the Republican band was in a "little village four miles above the Tapage on the

same stream." Above them three miles was the Pawnee Loups'
town.

Ref: 19th Cong., 1st Sess., *House Doc. 117* (Serial 136), pp. 7, 8 (for 1825 report);
The Bulletin of the Missouri Historical Society, St. Louis, v. 16, p. 25 (for item on the
Republican Pawnee-Kansa peace treaty); for Sibley, *see* under 1811; K. A. Spaulding, ed.,
On the Oregon Trail . . . (c1953), pp. 155-157 (for Robert Stuart); for O'Fallon
and Long in 1820, *see* 1820 entries; for Prince Paul, *see* under 1823; 18th Cong., 2d Sess.,
House Ex. Doc. 54 (Serial 115) for Vasquez; O'Fallon's 1824 directive quoted by courtesy
of Dale L. Morgan, who helpfully supplied this item from the Bancroft Library's filmed
copy of O'Fallon's letterbook, 1822-1829; 20th Cong., 2d Sess., *Sen. Doc. 72* (Serial 181),
p. 103 (for 1829 report); 22d Cong., 1st Sess., *Sen. Doc. 90* (Serial 213), p. 63 (for
1831 report); 23d Cong., 2d Sess., *House Ex. Doc. 97* (Serial 273) (for 1834 license to
"Soublette and Campbell"); *KHC*, v. 11, p. 328 (for Dunbar); W. R. Wedel's *An Introduction to Kansas Archeology* . . . (Washington, 1959), pp. 58-60 (for some comment
on Pawnee Republic village sites). The "tour" Henry L. Ellsworth took of the Pawnee
villages in October, 1833, makes clear that the Republican band was on the Platte in that
year.—*See* J. T. Irving, Jr., *Indian Sketches* . . ., edited by John F. McDermott (Norman, Okla., c1955), p. 150.

❦ Jedediah Smith (William H. Ashley's new partner) led the company of about 60 Ashley-Smith men (with 160 horses and pack-
mules; an outfit worth $20,000) which left St. Louis on November 1
for the Rocky mountains. Making this trip were such experienced
hands as Jim Beckwourth (who later told a partially fanciful version
of this journey), Louis Vasquez, Moses ("Black") Harris, Hiram
Scott, and Albert G. Boone; as well as novice Robert Campbell.

They crossed the Kansas near its mouth; bought beef at the Curtis
& Eley post; proceeded up the north bank of the Kansas (camping
for a time at, or near, the Kansa village, according to Beckwourth);
and reached the Smoky Hill-Republican junction on January 1,
1826 (as Robert Campbell recalled it, in 1870). The slow (two
months') journey from St. Louis to the present Fort Riley site was
probably due to shortage of food, and severe weather. According
to Campbell they ". . . wintered all along the Republican Fork,
and suffered very much for want of provisions." A third of their
mules died, and Smith sent back to St. Louis for others. (From
Beckwourth's account, he and "Black" Harris had this mission.)
Up on the Republican they came to the dirt village of the Republican Pawnees (in present Republic county, Kansas—*see* preceding entry); found the absent Indians' cached corn; paid the
Pawnees (on their return from a hunt) for what they took; and
remained in the Indian town, apparently, till some time in March.
Jedediah Smith and Robert Campbell were guests in Chief Iskatappe's lodge.

Leaving the Republican river, above the Indian village (which
Campbell later said was 50 miles from the Platte), Smith's company

crossed to the Platte in two days of travel. Early in April William H. Ashley, coming up that river with supplies, overtook them at Grand Island. The expedition continued up the north side of the Platte to the forks, then on to South Pass via the North Platte and the Sweetwater.

(A "lost" map by Jedediah Smith, which over a century ago was available to mapmaker George Gibbs, included a showing of his 1825-1826 journey up the Kansas-Republican-Platte rivers. Gibbs, using a "Fremont" printed map of 1845, copied thereon some data from Smith's map, including the route of 1825-1826 taken by the Smith-Ashley party to the Rockies, and the location of the Pawnee Republic village. A segment of the "Fremont-Gibbs-Smith" map showing the "Kansas" section is reproduced on p. 197.)

Ref: Robert Campbell's 1870 dictation in the Bancroft Library, made available for use and quoting by courtesy of Dale L. Morgan (of the Bancroft Library) to whom a special debt of gratitude is due for the opportunity to include this "new" chapter of Kansas-Republican river history in the annals (and since published in Morgan, ed., *William H. Ashley, op. cit.,* pp. 143-145); Dale L. Morgan and Carl I. Wheat, *Jedediah Smith and his Maps of the American West* (San Francisco, 1954), pp. 56, 57, and the "Fremont-Gibbs-Smith" map (folded, in back pocket); Dale L. Morgan's *Jedediah Smith . . .,* pp. 175, 331, 408; Bonner, *op. cit.,* pp. 23-32. Campbell made no reference in his recollections to passing the Kansa village, but the Kansa played a part in Beckwourth's account. The original manuscript of Campbell's dictation is in the Missouri Historical Society, St. Louis.

1826

❡ Mountain man Ewing Young, partners-in-trade Thomas H. Boggs and James Dempsey, Paul Baillio, six men of the Santa Fe road survey crew (sent East by Comm'r G. C. Sibley for economy's sake), and several other persons—around 20 in all—were in the company with laden pack horses and mules which left Taos, N. M., for Missouri in mid-February. They crossed present Kansas in March, and probably reached Fort Osage around April 1. Somewhere on the Santa Fe road a band of perhaps 200 Pawnees robbed members of this party.

Ref: Kate L. Gregg, ed., *The Road to Santa Fe . . .* (Albuquerque, c1952), pp. 41, 42, 84, 140-150, 227, 231, 260, 263, 275. Ceran St. Vrain may have been with this party.—*See* comment in David Lavender's *Bent's Fort* (Garden City, N. Y., 1954), pp. 65, 375.

❡ Francis G. Chouteau's "Randolph Bluffs" (Mo.) depot (*see* 1821-1822) was "washed away entirely" in early May (or late April) by a flood on the Missouri. Chouteau, it is said, removed his family to the "Four Houses" post (*see* 1819) some 20 miles up the Kansas river (in present Johnson? county). Then he relocated on higher ground, and higher up the Missouri—a mile or so above the "Randolph Bluffs."

The new site was on the river's *south* bank (within what is now

"Guinotte's Addition" to Kansas City, Mo.), and about two miles below the mouth of the Kansas. Frederick Chouteau was quoted (in 1880) as saying: "My brother Francis . . . built his house at [what is now] Kansas City in 1828—a frame house—where he lived with his family."

(Within the next 12 years—before his death in 1838—Francis Chouteau's establishment came to include "one of the largest and best farms in the county, with a steamboat landing [built in 1832, perhaps near what is now Olive street, Kansas City, Mo.], warehouses, and costly dwellings, and out-houses. . . ." All of this was swept away by the great flood of 1844.)

Ref: *Kansas Historical Quarterly* (*KHQ*), v. 16, p. 7; W. H. Miller's *History of Kansas City* . . . (Kansas City, 1881), p. 10; *Kansas Historical Collections* (*KHC*), v. 8, p. 425; *The Kansas Monthly*, Lawrence, v. 2 (June, 1879), p. 83 (John C. McCoy's statement on Chouteau's farm, etc., and the flood of 1844); Kansas City (Mo.) *Times*, February 10, 1951 (or "Kansas City, Mo., History Clippings," v. 5, p. 146, in Kansas State Historical Society library). For W. F. Vaill's report of the 1826 floods on the Grand (Neosho—in "Kansas") river as it affected the Union and Hopefield Missions in present Oklahoma, see *KHC*, v. 8, pp. 479, 480.

❏ Late in May a caravan (80 to 100 persons) left Missouri for New Mexico. (In mid-April the Franklin, Mo., paper had reported the company would include "all those lately returned"—and it is known that Ewing Young, Paul Baillio, and Thomas H. Boggs made this journey.) There were "waggons and carriages of almost every description," and the "amount of merchandise taken . . . [was] very considerable." The Franklin editor commented:

It has the air of romance to see splendid pleasure carriages, with elegant horses journeying to the Republic of Mexico, yet it is sober reality. In fact the obstacles exist rather in the imagination than in reality. Nature has made a fine road the whole distance.

Spanish trader Escudero, who left Missouri in the fore part of June with "six or seven new and substantial [goods-laden] wagons," may have caught up with the large caravan, but probably traveled the route separately.

Ref: *Missouri Intelligencer*, Franklin, Mo., April 14, June 9, 1826; *Independent Patriot*, Jackson, Mo., July 8, 1826; Lavender, *op. cit.*, pp. 65, 375 (for notes on Ceran St. Vrain's presence? with this company); R. E. Twitchell's *Old Santa Fe* . . . (Santa Fe, c1925), p. 217.

❏ Baronet Vasquez—first subagent for the Kansa—was assigned that post in April, 1825, and served till his death in August, 1828. The only persons employed for the Kansa up to September, 1826 (according to the St. Louis Indian superintendency report), were Subagent Vasquez and Gabriel Philibert, blacksmith. (The latter probably was hired in mid-1826—a record of tools purchased for Philibert bears the date July 11, 1826.)

During his tenure Antoine Francois (Baronet) Vasquez maintained a home, and the agency headquarters, within present Kansas City, Mo. He brought his wife, Emilie Forastin (Parent) Vasquez, and children upriver from St. Louis, perhaps as early as 1825. (Frederick Chouteau was quoted, in 1880, as stating: "His [Vasquez's] family was [in 1828] at my brothers' agency at Randolph, where he had lived since 1825." This could be interpreted to mean that the Vasquez family had quarters supplied by Francis Chouteau—first at "Randolph Bluffs"; and after the 1826 flood, at Chouteau's new location within present Kansas City, Mo.) According to the Rev. G. J. Garraghan (whose source of information was Vasquez family letters): "The Vasquez house [of 1828], a good-sized comfortable sort of building, was apparently rented at Government expense for the use of the Kansa Indian agent. It stood on the south bank of the Missouri just below the mouth of the Kaw, probably [i. e., possibly] at what is now the foot of Gillis Street in Kansas City [Mo.]."

Ref: 19th Cong., 2d Sess., *H. Ex. Doc. 112* (Serial 156), Sig. 40; G. J. Garraghan's *Catholic Beginnings in Kansas City* . . . (Chicago, 1920), pp. 28-30; *KHC*, v. 8, pp. 423, 425 (for Frederick Chouteau); Superintendency of Indian Affairs, St. Louis, "Records" (hereafter cited as SIA), v. 29, p. 29—in KHi ms. division. For a biographical note *see* Morgan, ed., *William H. Ashley, op. cit.*, p. 243.

❧ On August 16 fur trader Joseph Robidoux (aged 43), up to then associated with the Chouteau (and company) interests in the Council Bluffs vicinity, obtained a trading license in his own name. In 1826, and a year later (when he and a partner, Baptiste Roy, were issued a license on August 14, 1827), the listed places of operation were: Bellevue; mouth of the Papillion; the Omaha villages; the Pawnee villages; "a little above Roy's grave"; and mouth of L'eau qui court [Niobara river].

It is *said* that Robidoux landed at "Roy's Branch" above the Blacksnake Hills (Mo.) in the fall of 1826; and that he soon afterwards removed to the mouth of Blacksnake creek—where St. Joseph, Mo., was later founded.

Robidoux and Roy obtained a license in 1828 (August 6) to operate in the same locations as before. Eight days later they were issued a license permitting them to trade *at the Blacksnake Hills,* near the Iowa subagency. However, in October, the Chouteau interests (American Fur Co., Western Dept.) bought out rival Robidoux, agreeing to pay him "$1,000 a year for two years to stay out of the Indian country." When he returned to the Blacksnake Hills post (late 1830? or 1831?) he was an employee of the American Fur Company. But in 1834 he purchased the post from the company, and became sole proprietor. A license issued to Robidoux on July 30, 1834, indicated that he traded with the Iowas, Sacs, and Foxes, and employed eight men. Nine years later (1843) Robidoux founded the town of St. Joseph, Mo., at that location.

Ref: 19th Cong., 2d Sess., *Sen. Doc. 58* (Serial 146); 20th Cong., 1st Sess., *Sen. Doc. 96* (Serial 165); *The History of Buchanan County, Missouri* (St. Joseph, Mo., 1881), pp. 391-396; *History of Buchanan County and St. Joseph, Mo.* (St. Joseph, [1899], pp. 335-337; 20th Cong., 2d Sess., *Sen. Doc. 47* (Serial 181); Morgan, ed., *William H. Ashley, op. cit.*, p. 157; Dale L. Morgan's *Jedediah Smith* . . . (Indianapolis and New York, c1953), p. 319; R. G. Thwaites, ed., *Early Western Travels* . . . (Cleveland, 1904-1906), v. 24, p. 121; 23d Cong., 2d Sess., *H. Ex. Doc.* 97 (Serial 273).

❧ Francis G. and Cyprian Chouteau obtained a license on August 17 to trade (for a year) at "Mouth of Kanzas River, and [at] the Dirt Village of the Kanzas" (over 100 direct land miles upstream, near the Big Blue junction). Apparently the "Four Houses" post (of 1819? origin)—20 miles up the Kansas—continued to serve as their base of operations on that river till late in 1828 when they built at a new location about 12 miles from the Kaw's mouth. (*See*, under 1828.)

Ref: 19th Cong., 2d Sess., *Sen. Doc.* 58 (Serial 146); 20th Cong., 2d Sess., *Sen. Doc.* 57 (Serial 181) for September 3, 1827, license issued to Pierre Chouteau, Jr. (American Fur Company agent), to trade near the mouth of the Kansas, with the Kansa nation—a license covering the trading operations of his brothers, Francis and Cyprian, for the 1827-1828 year.

❧ Between August 21 and October 10, surveyor Angus L. Langham's party meandered the Kansas river from its mouth to the Kansa village (near the Big Blue-Kansas junction). Langham's assistants were Thomas Swearingen, William S. ("Old Bill") Williams (also serving as interpreter), and eight hired hands. The outfit included horses. (Subsistence of men and horses from August 1 to December 31 was a $382 item in the surveyor's accounts.) It is said the party had a small military escort—*see* below.

This company reached the "mouth of Warhusa" (Wakarusa) on September 2; passed the "Necushcutebe, Soutrielle or Grasshopper" (Delaware river of today) on September 13; and reached Langham's first objective—a point "20 leagues up," or "60 miles on a straight line from the mouth of Kansas river" on October 2. (By the Kansa treaty—*see* June, 1825—this survey point was to mark the *east* line of the Kansa reserve. It was about three and a half miles west of the center of present Topeka, in what is now Sec. 27, T. 11, R. 15 E., in Silver Lake township, Shawnee county.)

Continuing upriver, Langham noted they were near the "old [Burning] Heart village" of the Kansa on October 5; that they passed the "bl[ack] Vermillion" [now called the Red Vermillion] on the 8th; and arrived at "the Kansa Village, 125 dirt lodges" on October 10.

Of the surveyors' subsequent movements no contemporaneous account has been located. It appears that Langham and his men retraced their path to the east line of the Kansa reserve; surveyed the approximately 22-mile section of the *east* line from the river northward; and then spent the rest of the year marking off, down along the Kansas, the 23 one-mile-square Kansa half-breed reserves (which extended eastward from the east Kansa boundary to about four miles below the mouth of the "Grasshopper"). Writing in 1885, John C. McCoy (surveyor in the 1830's, who likely heard the story direct from Langham) stated that Langham "passed the winter of 1826-7 on Soldier Creek [known as Heart river at that time] about 4 miles north of [present] Topeka, and about 3 miles east of the Kaw village of the 'Fool Chief' [a location dating from 1829?—*see* map p. 167—not in existence when Langham was in the vicinity]. He had with him a small guard of infantry detailed from Fort Osage. . . . [But Fort Osage no longer existed in 1826, so the troops came from elsewhere.] The name 'Soldier Creek' was adopted afterwards in honor of the flag that proudly waved over the Major's [*i. e.*, Langham's] shanty and the warlike aspect of the camp where the trophies secured during the winter were chiefly possums strung up by their tails curled over ropes and tugs stretched from tree to tree." (Isaac McCoy, in 1830, called the stream Soldier creek.)

At some time in 1827 Langham surveyed the approximately eight-mile portion of the Kansa *east* boundary south of the Kansas river, and then proceeded west for 200 miles marking a length of the *south* line of the reserve.

Ref: Photostats of A. L. Langham's 1826 field notes; his 1826 accounts; and two William Clark letters (July 9 and October 9, 1826), all in KHi ms. division; John C. McCoy letter, February 9, 1885, in KHi ms. division; Isaac McCoy statement, 1832, in 23 Cong., 1st Sess., *Sen. Doc. 512*, v. 3 (Serial 246), p. 486; John C. McCoy statement, 1885, in *KHQ*, v. 5, p. 352; John C. McCoy statement, 1889, in *KHC*, v. 4, p. 302. The time of occupancy of the Kansa "Heart village" has never been satisfactorily determined. For McCoy's 1830 references to Soldier creek *see KHQ*, v. 5, pp. 352-354, 364.

❡ The company of traders (size unknown) which left Fort Osage in August and reached Santa Fe in November, included James Collins (at a later date Indian affairs superintendent in New Mexico), Elisha Stanley, Solomon Houck, Edwin M. Ryland, James Fielding, Thomas Talbott, and William Wolfskill. All these men remained in Mexico for nearly a year. (*See, also,* October, 1827.) Apparently with this party was Andrew Broadus, who, at the Walnut creek camp (near present Great Bend), underwent, and survived, emergency amputation of an arm (injured earlier in a gun accident). And if Broadus was in this company, so was the runaway 17-year-old Christopher ("Kit") Carson (who, by his own account, witnessed the surgery while on his first journey to the Southwest in 1826).

Ref: *KHQ*, v. 21, pp. 561-563; Josiah Gregg's *Commerce of the Prairies* (1844), v. 1, pp. 59, 60; Blanche C. Grant, ed., *Kit Carson's Own Story of His Life* (Taos, N. M., 1926), p. 10; *Missouri Historical Review*, Columbia, v. 38, p. 497; Lavender, *op. cit.*, p. 380; Harvey L. Carter, *'Dear Old Kit'* (Norman, Okla., c1968), p. 38.

❡ After a 70-day march William H. Ashley and party (over 50 men; more than 100 pack animals) reached St. Louis the last week in September (returning from a spring and summer overland expedition beyond the Rocky mountains—*see* last 1825 entry). It was reported that each horse and mule carried nearly 200 pounds of beaver fur, and that the 123(?) packs of beaver were valued at $60,000. According to St. Louis editor Charles Keemle:

. . . The whole route lay through a level and open country, better for carriages than any turnpike road in the United States. [East of the Rockies, Ashley's route, generally, was along the Sweetwater, Platte, and apparently on the north side of the Missouri—a pathway he had first used in the fall and winter of 1824-1825; and had traversed again, westbound, in the spring of 1826.] Wagons and carriages could go with ease as far as General Ashley went, crossing the Rocky Mountains at the sources of the north fork of the Platte; and descending the valley of the Buenaventura [Bear River] towards the Pacific Ocean. . . .

Ref: Dale L. Morgan, *Jedediah Smith, op. cit.,* pp. 156-161, 187, 190-192; Morgan, ed., *William H. Ashley, op. cit.,* p. 153; *Missouri Republican,* St. Louis, September 21, 1826; D. M. Frost's *Notes on General Ashley* . . . (Worcester, 1945), pp. 146, 147; J. E. Sunder's *Bill Sublette* . . . (Norman, Okla., c1959), p. 62.

❡ Describing the Indian peace council held at St. Louis in late September and early October, William Clark (superintendent of Indian affairs, St. Louis) wrote:

. . . a deputation from the Great and Little Osage Nation met one from the Delaware, Shawanoes, Piankeshaws, Peorias, Weas, Senecas, and Kickapoos, at this place, on the 25th day of September, and, after [my] recommending that they should make an attempt to effect a permanent peace, without the interference of the Government, they met in Council, and, after six days warm debate and recriminations, I was forced to take my seat among them, and with much difficulty obtained their entire approbation to the Treaty . . . [on October 7 and 8].

The tribes with whom the Osages made the reluctantly-arrived-at peace treaty were nations (or, rather, portions of nations) then residing in Missouri and Arkansas territory which the government hoped could be induced to emigrate to reserves west of Missouri and Arkansas, where some Shawnees already had moved (*see* November, 1825).

Ref: 19th Cong., 2d Sess., *House Doc. 9* (Serial 149), pp. 9-12; *American State Papers: Indian Affairs,* v. 2, pp. 673, 674; also a William Clark letter of October 9, 1826 (photostat in Langham survey papers, ms. division, KHi).

❡ A harvest of 260 bushels of corn from the farm at the little station Mission Neosho (in present Erie township, Neosho county) on the Neosho river—*see* 1824—was reported for the year 1826. As a result, "the expense of supporting the mission families [the Pixleys and the Brights] was very moderate."

Ref: *Report,* of the American Board of Commissioners for Foreign Missions for 1827, p. 136.

1827

❡ Eastbound on a perilous, heart-of-winter, 1,500-mile journey overland to St. Louis (from a January 1 starting point in the Great Salt Lake valley), snowshoe-equipped William L. Sublette and Moses ("Black") Harris, with their Indian-trained pack dog—all three exhausted and starving—left the Platte near Grand Island and headed southeast towards the Kansas. In their extremity, the men finally killed and ate the dog. Later they shot a rabbit; and after that, in a timbered area, brought down some wild turkeys. Meantime, they had found an old Kansa trail which eased their way through the deep, uncrusted snow. After traveling down the Big Vermillion (in present Marshall county) they made their way to the Kansa village (near the Big Blue's mouth) in the latter part of February. There they got food and other aid. Sublette traded his pistol for a horse (to give Harris—who had sprained an ankle—transportation), and the two men hastened on down the Kansas valley to Missouri. They arrived in St. Louis on March 4—three days late for the all-important business date with William H. Ashley which had occasioned the epic winter journey. (Ashley fulfilled the contract anyway.)

Earlier (in mid-July, 1826), in the Rocky mountains, Jedediah S. Smith, David E. Jackson, and William L. Sublette had formed a partnership and bought out fur trader William H. Ashley. Ashley then had returned to St. Louis—*see* 1826 entry—where he was, by contract, to supply Smith, Jackson & Sublette supplies and goods at certain prices, *provided* the partners gave him their order by March 1. *See* March, 1827, entry for a westbound journey over this new route—"Sublette's Trace."

Ref: *Weekly Picayune*, New Orleans, January 1 and March 18, 1844. After journalist Matthew C. Field heard, from Sublette, in 1843, the story of the 1827 winter trip, he wrote two articles ("Death of a Dog," and "A Perilous Winter Journey") which were published in the *Picayune* (as noted above), and in the daily issues of December 27, 1843, and March 14, 1944. *Also, see* Matthew C. Field's *Prairie and Mountain Sketches* . . . (Norman, Okla., c1957), pp. 165, 166 (for Field's diary notes, August 21, 1843). For Smith, Jackson & Sublette partnership *see* Dale L. Morgan, *op. cit.*, pp. 189-193, 225.

❦ At, or near, the Osage towns on the Neosho (in present Neosho county), several log buildings were erected during the year. On January 12 a contract was let for construction of a house for each of the three principal Osage chiefs living on that river. (This was in accordance with Article 4 of the Osage treaty of June 2, 1825. The total cost—$5,700—suggests they were substantial homes.)

On February 1 David Bailey (native of New Hampshire; hired as "agriculturist" to the Great Osages in late 1826) was given $450 to build quarters for his use. Bailey, and his wife—who was "instructress to Osage Women"—continued to work among the Osages, and to reside in present Kansas, till sometime in 1831. (Nothing has been learned of the Baileys' family, if any.)

Between March 16 and August 20, Richard Brannin (native of Virginia; hired as "agriculturist" to the Little Osages in November, 1826) was given $445.40 to build quarters for his use. Brannin, and his wife—an "instructress to Osage Women"—continued among the Little Osages till the spring(?) of 1831. (Nothing is known of their family, if any).

Other log houses and buildings already in the vicinity of the Osage towns were those at the Osage Agency; at the "Trading House"; and at Mission Neosho. The headquarters of Agent John F. Hamtramck (of Indiana; a May, 1826, appointee; and the first *resident* agent) was on the right bank of the river, "on a Rock Ridge one half a mile from the Neosho," "surrounded by Indian villages, some within half a mile," on the former site of White Hair's town (White Hair and a band of his people had moved six miles downstream). Other persons at the Osage Agency included Robert Dunlap (a Virginian, blacksmith to the Osages since late 1824), and Baptiste Mongrain (hired as interpreter in April, 1827). At the "Trading House" were Paul Ligueste Chouteau (Osage subagent), Pierre Melicour Papin (trader), and others. (*See*, August, 1827, entry.)

Ref: SIA, v. 6, pp. 100, 101, v. 25, pp. 26, 44, v. 29, pp. 2, 3, 5, 23, 25, 37; 19th Cong., 1st Sess., *House Doc. No. 112* (Serial 137), Sig. 69; 19th Cong., 2d Sess., *House Ex. Doc. 112* (Serial 156), Sig. 40; 22d Cong., 1st Sess., *Sen Doc. 90* (Serial 213), p. 64; *KHQ*, v. 13, pp. 448, 449.

❡ A site for the Kansa Agency was selected by the Kansa chiefs and Subagent Baronet Vasquez early in 1827 (or possibly late in 1826). The place chosen was just east of the last half-breed reserve (No. 23), over four miles below the Grasshopper's (Delaware's) mouth, on the north bank of the Kansas river—65 miles below the Kansa village (as then located—near the Big Blue's mouth).

It was something like 50 miles from Subagent Vasquez's residence (within present Kansas City, Mo.—*see* first 1826 annals entry). Described in relation to other present-day place names, the Kansa Agency was in the southern part of Jefferson county, seven miles upriver from Lawrence.

Perhaps the agency's first white resident was Daniel Morgan Boone (a son of the famous Daniel) who had been hired as "agriculturist" for the Kansa Indians at least as early as March, 1827. An account dated March 19-21 shows transfer to him of $450 for construction of buildings; also that he had spent $114 for a cart and yoke of oxen, and had purchased two other yokes (at $35 and $40), as well as tools and sundries. Besides Boone and his family, other "first residents" were Gabriel Philibert (the blacksmith), Clement Lessert (interpreter), Louis Gonville with his Kansa family, and half-Kansa Joseph James (holder of reserve No. 23). Two miles to the northwest, a good-sized stone house was built (in 1827?) for Chief White Plume (in accordance with a promise made to him by William Clark), and a number of Kansa families lived near him.

Isaac McCoy (an 1830 visitor) noted the "comfortable hewed log buildings" of the subagent, blacksmith, interpreter, and agriculturist, and White Plume's "large stone building" two miles distant. John T. Irving, Jr., after a brief stay at the Kansa Agency in 1832, wrote this description (for a work of fiction):

It was a half savage white settlement. . . . Three cabins built of unbarked logs, and thrown together in the rudest style of architecture, composed the dwelling of the workmen belonging to the agency. A little apart from the rest stood a house of larger dimensions, but scarcely more finished in its construction. This was the dwelling of the agent. Attached to it was a large field of Indian corn, almost the only grain raised by a backwoodsman; and in front was a small yard, surrounded by a slender white railing. Not only the cornfield, but a large space around the hamlet was filled with burnt and scathed trunks, giving intimation that a luxuriant growth of giant forest trees had once covered the spot, but had yielded to the unsparing inroads of man.

Ref: SIA, v. 4, pp. 196, 197, v. 29, pp. 4, 31; KHC, v. 9, pp. 194, 195; J. F. McDermott, ed., J. T. Irving, Jr.'s *Indian Sketches* (c1955), p. 238; Kansas City (Mo.) *Journal*, September 14, 1879 (or *see* KHi "Scrapbook," v. 2, pp. 223, 224); 23d Cong., 1st Sess., *Sen. Doc. 512*, v. 2 (Serial 245), p. 437 (Isaac McCoy's 1831 comments on the Kansa Agency settlement).

❡ Outfitted by William H. Ashley, and the American Fur Company, a party of about 60 men, headed by James B. Bruffee and Hiram Scott, left St. Louis late in March for the trappers' summer rendezvous at Bear Lake (where they arrived about the end of June). They took with them "a piece of artillery (a four-pounder) on a carriage which was drawn by two mules"—the first wheeled vehicle to be taken across South Pass. (It was also the first wheeled vehicle known to have crossed what is now northern Kansas.)

William L. Sublette accompanied this expedition, which (it seems established) traveled "Sublette's Trace" (pioneered in February by the eastbound Sublette and his companion "Black" Harris—*see* first 1827 entry)—the pathway which led up the Kansas valley, turned northward beyond the Red Vermillion's crossing (in present Pottawatomie county) toward the Little Blue, and near the head of that river, crossed to the Platte—the route of the future Oregon trail. (However, this year, and in 1829?, the turning-north point may have been farther up the Kansas valley—near the Big Blue's mouth. By 1830 the shorter "cut-off" route was in use.)

The returning expedition, piloted by James Clyman (over the same line of march as on the the outward journey, apparently), brought down over 7,000 pounds of beaver from the mountains, leaving Bear Lake July 13 and reaching

Lexington, Mo., about October 1. (Clyman, westbound on the section of the Oregon trail between the Little Vermillion and the Big Blue, on June 24, 1844, noted in his diary: "to day struck our old trail made on our return from the mountains in the summer of 1827. . . .") Reoutfitted by Ashley, William L. Sublette and David E. Jackson promptly started back to the mountains and reached the Rockies by the end of November, but had to winter east of the Divide because of severe weather. (There was no caravan to the mountains in 1828, this second outfit of 1827 having taken its place.)

Ref: H. C. Dale's *The Ashley-Smith Explorations* . . . (Cleveland, 1918), p. 172; Morgan, ed., *William H. Ashley, op. cit.*, pp. 164-176, 180; Dale L. Morgan's letters of October 25, and November 11, 1961, to L. Barry; Sunder, *op. cit.*, pp. 74, 75; C. L. Camp, ed., *James Clyman* . . . (San Francisco, 1928), p. 70; or *ibid.*, *definitive edition* (Portland, 1960), p. 77.

❦ Between April 27 and May 24, surveyor Angus L. Langham and his assistant, R. P. Beauchamp, ran a line to determine "the beginning of the Osage reservation"; and then surveyed the 50-mile stretch of eastern boundary.

(The Osage treaty of June 2, 1825, had specified that the reserve would have a beginning point "due east of White Hair's village" [in present Neosho county], and 25 miles west of the Missouri boundary; and that the east line would run 10 miles north of the village from the beginning point, and 40 miles south of it.)

The surveyors began work on the Neosho's east bank where they "had a view" of White Hair's town but could not reach it because of high water. They proceeded due east to the Missouri boundary, intersecting it 102 miles south of the Kansas river's mouth. Turning back, they then established the northeast corner of the Osage reserve—on May 11; and set out southward to mark off the 50-mile east line. On May 14 they crossed the road leading from "the [Chouteau] Trading House" to Harmony Mission. Ten days later they completed the east line survey at a point on the Neosho river. Langham discharged his work crew on May 30 at Harmony Mission (Mo.), reporting that they had, with one exception, refused to "go westward on the south or north boundary" through fear of Indians.

By John C. McCoy's account (in 1889) Langham's camp had been invaded one day by a large party of "naked, painted, yelling Osages" chasing one of the workmen. They had dashed through "in a solid phalanx," "trampling down tents and camp fixtures," and bowling over Surveyor Langham, who was seated, writing. The Indians "wound up the demonstration with an impromptu war dance, and an emphatic demand for the surveyor and his party to vamose, with which command they complied with alacrity." (McCoy, who ran the Osage *north* line in 1836, probably heard the story from Langham.)

In the early winter of 1827-1828, apparently, Langham surveyed the *south* boundary of the Osage lands. His letter of January 4, 1828, from "Neosho

Saline" advised of expenditures for Osage surveys; and on February 2 he wrote (from Franklin, Mo.) that he had arrived from the Osage country on January 31, and had completed all the Osage and Kansa surveys except the north boundaries of their reserves.

Ref: Langham's field notes and letters (photostats from National Archives) in KHi ms. division; Office of Indian Affairs (OIA), "Registers of Letters Received," v. 2, p. 294 (microfilm from National Archives); KHC, v. 4, pp. 308, 309.

❦ Cantonment Leavenworth was founded in the spring by Col. Henry Leavenworth, commander of the Third U. S. infantry. He wrote, on May 8, that he had chosen a location for a permanent military post atop a 150-foot bluff on the Missouri's *right* bank (the March 7 orders had specified the *left* bank, but he found no suitable place there), 20-odd miles above the Little Platte's mouth; and reported that Bvt. Maj. Daniel Ketchum and a battalion of Sixth infantry (having evacuated Fort Atkinson [Neb.] as required by the March 7 orders) had stopped on their way down the Missouri to deposit army property and stores from the upriver post.

Ketchum's command, in four keelboats, had reached the Little Platte's mouth on May 3. Leavenworth, coming from Liberty, Mo., arrived on the 4th, as recorded (in his diary) by James Kennerly (who, with his family, was aboard the *Otter*). On May 5, Kennerly wrote: "Col L. started up in Barge to select a side [*sic*] for a garison. Mr. [John] Dougherty with him"; and, on the 7th, noted: ". . . Col L. come down, about 12 oc. . . ."

Four companies of the Third infantry, under Capt. William G. Belknap, which had started up the Missouri in keelboats from Jefferson Barracks (Mo.) on April 17, arrived shortly afterwards and were put to work on temporary quarters. (These were huts of logs and slabs of bark, it is said.) "Cantonment Leavenworth" was named *after* the war department officially approved (September 19) the site selected. Upon Colonel Leavenworth's departure for Jefferson Barracks, Maj. Daniel Baker (a late arrival) took over command.

The post's garrison (B, D, E, and H companies, Third infantry) had, for the quarter ending October 31, a strength of 14(?) officers and 164 enlisted men. The officers then present were: Major Baker, commanding, Asst. Surg. Clement A. Finley, Capt. John Bliss, Capt. William G. Belknap, Capt. Andrew Lewis, Lt. Benjamin Walker, Lt. Samuel W. Hunt, Lt. Otis Wheeler, Lt. Lewis N. Morris, Lt. Henry H. Loring, 2d Lt. Joseph Bennett, 2d Lt. William R. Montgomery, 2d Lt. N. Sayre Harris, Bvt. 2d Lt. E. B. Babbitt. There were some women and children at Cantonment Leavenworth in 1827. Two ladies present whose names are known: Ann (Clark) Belknap, wife of the senior captain, who had come with her husband in the spring; and Mary (Hertzog) Dougherty, wife of the new "Upper Missouri" Indian agent (*see* a following entry), who was a late September arrival. During an outbreak of malarial fever in the autumn, one of the victims was the six-year-old son of Lt. Samuel W. Hunt.

Ref: Elvid Hunt and W. E. Lorence's *History of Fort Leavenworth 1827-1937* (Fort Leavenworth, 1937), pp. 13-20; Kennerly Papers, Missouri Historical Society, St. Louis (courtesy of Dale L. Morgan); F. B. Heitman's *Historical Register and Dictionary of the United States Army* . . . (Washington, 1903), v. 1 (for army officers' names); *Annals of Iowa, 3d series*, v. 7 (October, 1906), pp. 533-537 (for data on the Belknap family); Fort Leavenworth post returns.

❡ The large Santa Fe caravan (about 105 men; 53 wagons; and pleasure carriages) which left Missouri in May had Ezekiel Williams (*see* 1813, 1814) as its elected captain. Among other officers of this highly organized company were David Workman (one of nine "commanders of the guard"), Richard Gentry (marshal), and the Rev. John Pearson (chaplain). Another traveler was Augustus Storrs (newly appointed U. S. consul at Santa Fe) whose letter dated "Santa Fe Trace, 120 miles west of Franklin, May 18, 1827" is the principal source of information on the expedition.

Of this caravan ("the largest which has traversed this route") it was reported that the "line of march" was "at least one mile in length"—a sight "extremely beautiful to the eye of the spectator."

Ref: *Missouri Intelligencer*, Fayette, Mo., May 24, 1827; *Niles' Weekly Register*, Baltimore, v. 32 (June 30, 1827), p. 292.

❡ George C. Sibley and a work party of 14 (including Andrew Carson, Jacob Gregg, and Benjamin Majors) spent from May 25 to July 1 in present Kansas, making corrections in the 1825 Santa Fe road survey and putting up sod-mound markers on a section of the route west of Missouri. They reached Council Grove (westbound) on June 7. (Sibley *estimated* he had cut the distance from Fort Osage—162 miles by the 1825 survey—to 149 miles. In J. C. Brown's final field notes it was entered as 142 miles.) Continuing 16 miles southwest of Council Grove on June 10, this party camped at "the Springs." Wrote Sibley in his journal:

. . . This Spring [called "Jones' Spring" by Sibley in 1825] is very large, Runs off boldly among Rocks, is perfectly accessible and furnishes the greatest abundance of most excellent, clear, cold Sweet water. It may be appropriately called "The Diamond of the Plains" and So I had it Marked [by "Big John" Walker] on an Elm which grows near & overhangs it.

In this fashion Diamond Spring(s) received its name; and the near by creek, which to Sibley was "Otter Creek" subsequently became "Diamond creek." Turning homeward from this place the party reached Council Grove again on June 12. Next day, by Sibley's account, they

. . . Coursed and chained the Cut off from C[ouncil] Grove to Gravel

Creek. . . . Here halted for the day. . . . Found an excellent Spring near Camp—which I had Marked [on a Big Oak near by] *"Big John's Spring"* as it was first discov[ere]d by John Walker. . . .

Thus another landmark on the Santa Fe road received its name; and the stream—Sibley's "Gravel Creek"—became "Big John creek."

On July 1 the tour of correction was completed to the Missouri boundary. Sibley reached home (near old Fort Osage, Mo.) a week later.

Ref: K. Gregg, *op. cit.,* pp. 45-47, 175-195 (Sibley's journal), also pp. 60, 272; *The Western Journal,* St. Louis, v. 5 (December, 1850), pp. 178-181.

❤ Successor to Benjamin O'Fallon (resigned) as head of the "Upper Missouri" Indian agency (headquarters at the Council Bluffs— "Bellevue" [Neb.]), was John Dougherty, who had been interpreter and subagent there since 1819. Before Dougherty wrote (on May 30) to accept the position, Cantonment Leavenworth had been founded, and Colonel Leavenworth had requested that the Upper Missouri agent locate there. The move—as a temporary expedient till the end of 1828—was approved by William Clark at St. Louis.

On September 25 Dougherty and his family arrived at Cantonment Leavenworth. At that post, despite controversy, he maintained his "headquarters" till sometime in 1832.

Ref: *Missouri Republican,* St. Louis, February 15, 1827; "Records of the Office of Indian Affairs, Registers of Letters Received" (microfilm, from National Archives), v. 2, pp. 140, 157, 160, 292; "Dougherty Collection" (typed copy of Dougherty's March 9, 1832, report) in KHi ms. division; *KHQ,* v. 22, p. 102; Hunt and Lorence, *op. cit.,* pp. 18, 19.

❤ Six Osage Indians (four men, two young women) and Paul Loise (half-Osage interpreter) were conducted to Europe in the summer by David Delaunay and Francis Tesson of St. Louis (who calculated to make money exhibiting them abroad). Three years later, two of the men, both women, and an infant, returned to their Neosho river [Kansas] homes and kinsmen.

(For a time, after arriving in France on July 27, the Indians attracted great crowds, and were entertained by royalty. But the financial schemes of Delaunay failed; he was imprisoned for debt; and the Osages wandered through Europe in 1828 and 1829, suffering many hardships. Two Osage children were born— one was adopted by a Belgian woman. In the latter part of 1829 funds were raised to return the Indians to America. On board ship two of the men died. It was the spring of 1830 before the others reached the Indian country.— William Clark wrote on May 15 that he had sent the Osages who returned from France to their nation, except Paul Loise.)

During 1827, when the visitors from America were still a novelty, two slim (and now rare) volumes relating to the Osage Indians were published at Paris. One, credited to Paul Vissier, was titled: *Histoire de la Tribu des Osages* (Paris, C. Bechet, 1827) in which about a dozen of the 92 pages dealt with the six Osages, and their travels up to August 21 when they were presented to the French king. The shorter work—*Six Indiens Rouges de la Tribu des Grands Osages*—was devoted wholly to the subject of its title. The imprint of the Society's third edition copy of this latter book reads: "Paris. Delaunay, Libraire de son altesse royale Madame la duchesse d'Orleans, Palais-Royal, No. 243. 1827."

Ref: *KHQ*, v. 16, p. 24; *Niles' Weekly Register*, v. 37 (September 5, 1829), p. 19; *Missouri Historical Society Collections*, St. Louis, v. 5, pp. 109-128 (for Grant Foreman's article on the Osages, which has reproductions of contemporaneous portraits of the Indians); SIA, v. 4, pp. 119, 120 (for William Clark).

❦ Public sale of lots in the new town of Independence—seat of recently organized Jackson county, Mo.—was held on July 9. (The Missouri general assembly, by an act approved December 15, 1826, had established Jackson county.)

(By 1832 Independence was to become the dominant outfitting point for, and eastern terminus of, the Santa Fe and southwestern trade.)

Ref: *The Bulletin* of the Missouri Historical Society, St. Louis, v. 16, pp. 33-46; *Laws of . . . the State of Missouri, Passed Between . . . 1824 & 1836 . . .* (Jefferson City, 1842), v. 2, pp. 83, 84.

❦ In July(?) 25 mounted Missourians (from Lafayette and Jackson counties), captained by James Cockrell, crossed "Kansas" en route to "Colorado" in search of a silver mine discovered by Cockrell some four(?) years earlier while on a hunting-trapping expedition in the West. Benjamin Majors, Mark Foster, and Clark Davis were members of this party.

From Missouri they traveled "across the prairie a little south of west" to the Great Bend of the Arkansas, then followed up the river to the foothills. After some search, the "silver" was found, and the party started home with specimens. In the vicinity of present Dodge City, during October, Indians stampeded the horses. Making the rest of the journey on foot, and after hardships and privations, all 25 men eventually reached home.

Ref: Alexander Majors, *Seventy Years on the Frontier* (1893), p. 32. Note that Benjamin Majors was in G. C. Sibley's employ till July 1, 1827.—*See* p. 142.

❦ In June, apparently, Louis Robidoux, Thomas Boggs, Paul Baillio, Samuel C. Lamme, Gervais Nolan, Manuel Alvarez, and 11 others who left Taos, N. M., April 7, crossed "Kansas" by way of the Santa Fe trail.

The arrival at Franklin, Mo., in mid-July, of this party of some 20 traders with "about $30,000 in specie, and several hundred mules"—concluding a "very profitable" trip—was noted in the Fayette newspaper.

Ref: H. H. Dunham's article on Manuel Alvarez, in L. R. Hafen, ed., *Mountain Men and the Fur Trade of the West*, v. 1, p. 183; *Missouri Intelligencer*, Fayette, July 19, 1827.

❦ The Rev. Charles Felix Van Quickenborne, S. J., arrived August 24 at the house of Osage Subagent Paul Ligueste Chouteau, on the Neosho river (present Neosho county), after a 16-day overland journey from near St. Charles, Mo., with a lay companion. He spent two weeks among the Osages of that vicinity. The day following his arrival he said "the first verifiable mass in Kansas."

Of the 17 half-Osage children baptized by Father Van Quickenborne (on August 27 and September 2), the first was two-year-old Henry Mongrain (son of Noel Mongrain and Tonpapai). Surnames of the others baptized were: Vasseur, Chouteau, Quenville, and Williams. ("Clemence Williams" was doubtless a child of William S. ["Old Bill"] Williams, whose half-Osage daughters, Sarah and Mary, had been given land under the June, 1825, Osage treaty.) Sponsors of the baptisms were Subagent Chouteau, Pierre Melicour Papin (trader), Agent John F. Hamtramck, Louis Peltier, Alexander Peter, P. L. Mongrain, and Christophe Sanguinet.

Ref: G. J. Garraghan's *The Jesuits of the Middle United States* (New York, 1938), v. 1, pp. 179, 191; *KHQ*, v. 8, p. 209.

❦ BORN: at Mission Neosho, either in 1827, or the latter part of 1826, Lucia Francis Pixley, daughter of the Rev. Benton and Lucia F. (Howell) Pixley. Insofar as records are available, it would appear she may have been the *first white child* born in what is now Kansas. (For Mission Neosho, *see* under 1824.)

Ref: U. S. census, 1850, Jackson county, Mo., No. 1187 (household of Mrs. Lucia Pixley, aged 61, of Blue township), as recorded on September 19, 1850. Listed in the household, also, were: Harriet N. Pixley (aged 33, born in Virginia); *Lucia F. Pixley (aged 23, born in "Ind. Ter.")*; Flora A. Pixley (aged 21, born in Missouri); also Mrs. Lucia Pixley's daughter-in-law(?) and her infant; and Madison Meador (aged 22, farmer). Though no substantiation from any other source has been located, there is every reason to suppose that Lucia Francis Pixley was, in fact, born in present Neosho county, Kansas, where her parents lived as missionaries to the Osages from September, 1824, to March, 1829. According to W. W. Graves, in his *First Protestant Osage Missions* . . . (Oswego, c1949), p. 244, the Pixleys had six children, some(?) of whom were born at Mission Neosho: Harriet N., Levi P., Mary Jane (who married Madison Meador), Lucia F., Flora A., and A. B. Graves also stated (p. 243) that the Rev. Benton Pixley is said to have died at Independence, Mo., April 11, 1835.

❦ In September, after a four months' absence, about 60 members of the large spring caravan of Santa Fe traders returned to Missouri, bringing "a considerable amount of money," and around "800 head of jacks, jennets, mules, etc.," valued (it was reported) at nearly $28,000.

Ref: *Missouri Intelligencer*, Fayette, Mo., September 20, 1827.

❦ While the Kansa were gathered near the mouth of the Kansas river in September to collect their annual annuities, the greater part of the nation fell ill, and some 70 Indians died of the epidemic malady. Agent John Dougherty, learning of the disaster upon his arrival at Cantonment Leavenworth in late September, hired a Liberty, Mo., doctor to go to the aid of the Kansa. On the advice of the post medical officer, Asst. Surg. Clement A. Finley, Dougherty also "procured several barrels of flour and some salt provisions and took them to the Indians."

Ref: SIA, v. 4, pp. 72, 73; "Dougherty Collection," KHi ms. division.

❦ Early autumn(?)—A party of 32, including Louis Robidoux, Michel S. Cerré, Thomas Boggs, Paul Baillio, Manuel Alvarez, Francois Guerin, and other traders and trappers, under permit (by William Clark, St. Louis) dated July 23, "to pass through the Indian country to the Province of Mexico," probably traveled the Santa Fe trail across "Kansas" in September or October.

Alvarez later estimated it as a 770-mile journey. The passport was not presented in Santa Fe till November 12.

Ref: H. H. Dunham's article on Alvarez, *loc. cit.*, p. 184; Dale L. Morgan and Eleanor T. Harris, editors, *The Rocky Mountain Journals of William Marshall Anderson* . . . (San Marino, Cal., 1967), p. 281; R. G. Cleland, *This Reckless Breed of Men* (New York, 1950), *facing* p. 202 (reproduction of passport).

❦ En route to Missouri from New Mexico, with "horses, mules, asses, and specie," the small party of 12 to 15 traders which included Messrs. Collins, Stanley, Houck, Ryland, Fielding, Talbott, and Wolfskill (*see* August, 1826), camped on October 12 about 25 miles west of Pawnee Fork crossing [probably at Little Coon creek, present Edwards county]. A band of perhaps 30 Pawnees made a midnight raid on their stock and ran off 166 animals—all but three the party had. Next day, by good fortune, the traders found about 66(?) head (either abandoned by, or escaped from, the Indians). The arrival of this party in the Missouri settlements was noted in early November (by the Fayette newspaper).

Ref: KHQ, v. 21, pp. 561-563; *Missouri Intelligencer*, November 9, 1827, as reprinted in the *Arkansas Gazette*, Little Rock, December 4, 1827. According to Alphonso Wetmore's 1831 statement, the 1827 robberies totaled 130 head of stock.—*See* 22d Cong., 1st Sess., *Sen. Doc. 90* (Serial 213), p. 176. In 32d Cong., 1st Sess., *H. Ex. Doc. No. 103* (Serial 647), p. 391, it is recorded that the following payments (from Indian dept. disbursements) were made (under terms of an act of congress, approved March 3, 1849, for the relief of Thomas Talbott and others): October 13, Thomas Talbott, $2,515; October 15, Elisha Stanley $935, William Wolfskill, $105, James Collins, $160, Solomon Houck, $120, Ed. M. Ryland, $150, James Fielding, $120.

1828

❧ On April 14 the steamboat *Liberator* set out from St. Louis for Cantonment Leavenworth—presumably carrying freight. On April 23 the steamboat *Illinois* (advertised in March as a "new and substantial" craft) left Jefferson Barracks, Mo., for the same place, with Companies A, F, I, and K, Third U. S. Infantry aboard. Col. Henry Leavenworth, head of the regiment, accompanied them. The troops' arrival (early in May) placed eight out of 10 companies of the Third infantry at Cantonment Leavenworth.

These steamboats may have been the first on the "upper" Missouri (*i. e.*, above the mouth of the Kansas) since 1824. The *Liberator* returned to St. Charles, Mo., on April 27; the *Illinois* was back at St. Louis "from the Platt" on May 6.

Ref: *KHQ*, v. 16, pp. 140n, 144-146, 148. *The Jeffersonian Republican*, Jefferson City, Mo., January 26, 1839, referred to the year *1826* as follows: "In 1826 there was but one steamboat (the Muskingum) up [the Missouri] during the whole year. The 'Liberator,' a new boat having failed the same year to get higher than Belle Fontaine." Presumably the *Muskingum* did not go above Jefferson City?

❧ The Western Cherokees (those living west of the Mississippi) in a treaty with the United States signed on May 6, were *guaranteed* a reserve of "seven millions of acres" of land and a "perpetual outlet" to the west, in what is now Oklahoma. This tract (40 by 300 miles) was to be for *all* of the Cherokees:

. . . a *permanent* home . . . which shall, under the most solemn guarantee of the United States, be and remain theirs forever—a home that shall never, in all future time, be embarrassed by having extended around it the line, or placed over it the jurisdiction of a territory or state, nor be pressed upon by the extension, in any way, of any of the limits of any existing territory or State. . . .

Ref: C. J. Kappler's *Indian Affairs, Laws and Treaties* (Washington, 1904), v. 2, pp. 288-292; 23d Cong., 1st Sess., *H. R. No. 474* (Serial 263), p. 15.

❧ The large Santa Fe caravan (about 150? men) which left Missouri in the fore part of May is said to have taken merchandise valued at $150,000 to New Mexico; and, by report, the smaller caravan (about 50 persons) which left the last of May, carried goods worth $41,000. Alphonso Wetmore captained the latter expedition which rendezvoused at the Blue Springs (Mo.) on May 28th. [His brief diary (May 28-August 2), with its graphic, colorful comments, enlivened an otherwise staid senate document published in 1831.]

Wetmore's company reached Council Grove on June 11; met a *return* caravan on the 12th; crossed Cow creek (in present Rice county) on the 24th; and on July 4 arrived at the Caches (Wetmore called them "Anderson's caches") of 1823 origin. There the caravan crossed the Arkansas and proceeded by way of the Cimarron desert route to New Mexico.

A biographical sketch of Dr. Henry Connelly states that in 1828 "he joined a party under a man named Stephenson, bound for Chihuahua, Mexico," and that Stephenson's party (having traveled to Santa Fe with the caravan leaving in *early* May?) arrived at Chihuahua "after many adventures with the Indians and much suffering from hunger and thirst."

Ref: H. M. Chittenden's *The American Fur Trade of the Far West* (New York, 1902), v. 2, p. 509; 22d Cong., 1st Sess., *Sen. Doc. 90* (Serial 213), pp. 34-40 (for Wetmore's diary), or, see *Missouri Historical Review*, v. 8, pp. 184-195. Wetmore's company, it appears, included John Hardeman. See *Arizona and the West*, Tucson, v. 6 (Winter, 1964), p. 314. Hardeman left Franklin, Mo., late in May; arrived at Santa Fe in August. For Connelly and Stephenson, *see* W. E. Connelley's *Doniphan's Expedition* . . . (Topeka, 1907), p. 279.

❦ At Cantonment Leavenworth, on May 29, a post office was established—the first in what is now Kansas. Philip G. Randolph, first appointee, was succeeded as postmaster by Dr. Thomas S. Bryant on October 16.

Ref: Robert W. Baughman's *Kansas Post Offices* (Topeka, c1961), pp. 21, 156, 197; *KHC*, v. 1-2, p. 255, or, v. 7, p. 441.

❦ Died: in May, Clermont, I, long-time chief of the large band of Osages residing on the Verdigris river (in present Oklahoma)— first mentioned in this chronology under 1777. It is stated that he had four wives and 37 children. (His son, Clermont, II, also a distinguished man, died in 1838.) The town of Claremore, Okla., near the one-time Osage village site, was named for the chiefs "Clermont." Of Clermont, I, the missionary W. F. Vaill wrote:

. . . a man of noble countenance and stately figure, of robust constitution, and vigorous intellectual powers. . . . He was a jealous, subtle man—a wily, intriguing politican, and a most eloquent speaker. . . .

Ref: *Report* of American Board of Comm'rs for Foreign Missions for 1828, pp. 90, 91; Grant Foreman's *Indians and Pioneers* . . . (New Haven, 1930), pp. 22, 157, 158.

❦ In the spring Father Charles Felix Van Quickenborne made a second journey (*see* August, 1827) to the Osages of the Neosho river, stopping en route at Harmony Mission, on the Marais des Cygnes, in Missouri. It is known that he performed 17 baptisms, but there is no record of the names. A little Osage "prince" accompanied him on the return trip—to be educated at the Jesuits' Indian school at Florissant, Mo.

Ref: Garraghan's *Jesuits* . . ., v. 1, p. 193.

❦ On June 4 Indian Agent John Dougherty paid Calice "Montargu" (Montardy) $7.25 for "his services and use of his ferryboat in crossing the Kansas Nation across the Missouri." This transaction—

listed in a Superintendency of Indian affairs, St. Louis, record book—is the earliest item located concerning a ferry operation at, or near, the mouth of the Kansas.

(Other ferry operators had been licensed in Clay county, Mo., as early as 1825—Joseph Boggs, John Thornton, and Richard Linville—all of whom had ferries within a few miles of the Kaw's mouth. Linville's location on the Missouri, in 1825, was in Sec. 18, T. 50, R. 32 W., Clay co., Mo., "where Louis Barthelette . . . lives." Presumably this was at the Randolph Bluffs location where Louis ("Grand Louis") Bertholet lived in 1823, and earlier—*see* annals entries for 1821-1822, and June, 1823. It is said that Linville sold his ferry to "an old[?] Frenchman named Calisse Montarges" in 1826. After the spring, 1826, flood, if not before, "Calisse" doubtless moved the ferry nearer the mouth of the Kansas, and across the river(?). A land entry of October 31, 1832, shows Calice Montardy on the W.½ of Lot 2, in Sec. 5, T. 49, R. 33 W., in present Kansas City, Mo. He is said to have operated his ferry till 1830. Catholic records of Kansas City, Mo., state that "Calice Montredie" died June 18, 1847, aged 49 years.)

Ref: SIA, v. 21, p. 26 (for the June 4, 1828, item); *History of Clay and Platte Counties, Missouri* . . . (St. Louis, 1885), p. 113; *KHQ*, v. 2, p. 5; D. A. R., Kansas City (Mo.) chapter, *Vital Historical Records of Jackson County, Missouri, 1826-1876* (Kansas City, Mo., c1934), p. 266. Mrs. Alfred Garrison, Bartlesville, Okla., has records of the family "Montardy." The name has elsewhere appeared as Montardeau.

❡ Delegations from the Pawnee Republic band, the Omaha, Otoe, Iowa, Sac, Kansa, and the immigrant Shawnee Indians, called together by Agent John Dougherty, met in council at Cantonment Leavenworth on June 23, and made a peace treaty. Also present were Subagent Jonathan L. Bean (from the Iowa subagency), Lt. Samuel W. Hunt (of the Third infantry), and Levi Benjamin.

Ref: SIA, v. 21, p. 30; "Dougherty Collection," in KHi ms. division.

❡ During the summer, it is said, a "military" road was opened from a point opposite Cantonment Leavenworth to the town of Barry, near Liberty, Mo. Troops from the post worked on the section from the Missouri river eastward, while Clay county, Mo., residents built westward from the settlements.

Ferries were required at the crossings of the Missouri and the Little Platte river. By Joseph Thorp's recollections (in the 1880's) Robert Todd was authorized to keep the first ferry at the cantonment (and held the job for several years); while John Thorp (brother of Joseph) operated the first Little Platte ferry, but sold out in less than a year to a partner, Zadoc Martin.

Ref: Joseph Thorp's *Early Days in the West* . . . (Liberty, Mo., 1924), p. 62; Hunt and Lorence, *op. cit.*, p. 22; W. M. Paxton's *Annals of Platte County, Missouri* (Kansas City, Mo., 1897), pp. 9-12.

❡ DIED: on August 5, Kansa Subagent Baronet Vasquez, of cholera, while returning from St. Louis to his post. Two companions on the journey—Dunning D. McNair (20-year-old Indian superintendency clerk), and the Rev. Joseph Anthony Lutz—reached the Vasquez residence (within present Kansas City, Mo.) on August 12.

Ref: G. J. Garraghan's *Catholic Beginnings in Kansas City* . . ., p. 28. The *St. Louis Catholic Historical Review*, v. 2 (April-July, 1920), pp. 76-84.

❏ Intent on establishing a Catholic mission among the Kansa Indians, the Rev. Joseph Anthony Lutz (aged 26) arrived at the mouth of the Kansas river on August 12 (*see* preceding entry). After a week's stay there, at the Vasquez residence, he accompanied acting subagent Dunning D. McNair 65 miles up the Kansas valley, where, for the next six weeks, he made his headquarters at the Kansa Agency (with McNair), as the first missionary visitor to that nation. On August 20, the day after his arrival, he met Chief White Plume who was cordial; on the 24th, and subsequently, he visited the 16 Indian families (including White Plume) who lived two miles northwest of the agency. But he did not meet the main body of the Kansa till September 17, and they were then preparing to go on their fall hunt—not to return till mid-December.

On September 18 Father Lutz started for Cantonment Leavenworth (37 miles to the northeast) where his visit was the first by a Catholic priest at that post. Returning to the Kansa Agency, he remained till September 29. With McNair, he then went downriver to the mouth of the Kansas, and stayed with Mrs. Vasquez and her children—ministering to the "little community of nine families at the mouth of the Kaw" [present Kansas City, Mo.] till December 2. On that date he left for St. Louis.

Though it appears that Father Lutz returned to the Kansa Agency, briefly, in 1829 (to pick up some personal possessions left there), the plan to establish a Catholic mission among the Kansa was abandoned. There is no record that he baptized any Indians in 1828 or 1829.

Ref: Garraghan's *Catholic Beginnings* . . ., pp. 27-33; *St. Louis Catholic Historical Review*, v. 2 (April-July, 1920), pp. 76-84.

❏ In mid-August a company of perhaps 70 traders with about 1,200 head of stock left Santa Fe to return to Missouri. While heading for the Cimarron, two men, traveling ahead of the main party, were shot by unknown Indians. Young McNees died at the scene— near a little stream (a tributary of Beaver creek, in Union co., N. M.), then named "McNees' creek" for him. Daniel Munroe, fatally wounded, was carried 40 miles to the Upper Cimarron Springs, where both men were buried. Soon afterward, some of the traders fired on (and killed most of) a small party of (Pawnee?) Indians that rode up to them—thereby precipitating an Indian war which was to be costly to Santa Fe traders. (It was the *Pawnees* who were reported, in November, to have gone "en masse in a war excursion against the whites.")

It is said that Meredith M. Marmaduke and Milton G. Sublette were in the party firing on the Indians. These men, a William Taylor, and four others, had a narrow escape from death a few days later when they met a large band of hostile Indians while hunting—according to the recollections of William Waldo.

In September, probably in the Great Bend area, Pawnee Indians raided this company of around 700 horses and mules.

Ref: *Missouri Intelligencer* . . ., Fayette, September 12, 1828; *Missouri Republican*, St. Louis, September 23, 1828; William Waldo's "Recollections . . ." in *Glimpses of the Past*, St. Louis, v. 5, pp. 68-71; 20th Cong., 2d Sess., *Sen. Doc.* 67 (Serial 181), pp. 17, 18; 22nd Cong., 1st Sess., *Sen. Doc.* 90 (Serial 213), pp. 31, 40; *KHQ*, v. 13, p. 411—for Isaac McCoy's statement concerning his own 1828 expedition: "We afterwards ascertained that we had been within 75 miles of the place where the last attack of the Pawnees was made on the first party defeated on the Santa Fe road, which happened in September while we were in that country." McCoy's party got as far west as present Marion county, to the Cottonwood, apparently. Also, in *ibid.*, p. 433, is his comment, "While I was in that country two caravans, at different times were robbed by those western Indians [*i. e.*, Pawnees?]. The first company had two men killed, and lost about 700 mules and horses." *Ibid.*, v. 16, p. 170 (for Pawnee war excursion).

❆ BORN: on August 22, at the Kansa Agency (present Jefferson county) Napoleon Boone, 12th (and last) child of Daniel Morgan and Sarah Griffin (Lewis) Boone. This grandson of famed frontiersman Daniel Boone was the second white child, and the first white *boy* born in present Kansas of whom there is record. (Napoleon Boone died, aged 21 and single, in California, May 20, 1850.)

Ref: *KHC*, v. 1-2, p. 289, v. 8, pp. 260n, 433, 434; *Missouri Historical Review*, v. 41, pp. 365, 369.

❆ A party of 21(?) homeward-bound traders, with 150 mules and horses, four wagons, and a quantity of silver money, left Santa Fe on September 1. Near the Upper Cimarron Springs they came on a large Comanche camp. The caravan's captain, John Means, was killed and scalped when the Indians attacked the rear guard. Thomas Ellison and Milton E. Bryan, riding with him, escaped. The traders moved on, followed and harassed by the Indians, who, some days later, succeeded in stampeding all the horses and mules. William Y. Hitt, ambushed by the raiders, received several wounds and narrowly escaped death.

Forced to abandon their wagons and baggage, the merchants set out on foot, at night, on a northward course, each carrying as much silver as he could manage. On reaching the Arkansas (at

Chouteau's Island?) they buried most of the money, and headed for Missouri, some 350 miles distant. It was a journey of hardship and suffering. They reached Cow creek in a group, but some, from exhaustion, hunger, and exposure, could go no farther. Five of the stronger men continued to the settlements. A rescue party went out from Independence and picked up the stragglers, who were scattered along the Santa Fe road for 150 miles. In the latter part of October these traders reached home.

According to Milton E. Bryan, and others, the buried money was recovered in 1829 when the Santa Fe caravan and military escort reached the vicinity of Chouteau's Island in July.

Ref: Milton E. Bryan's "The Flight of Time . . .," in *The Kansas Chief*, Troy, June 9, 1887 (clipping in KHi library); *Missouri Republican*, St. Louis, October 24, 1828; Otis E. Young's *The First Military Escort on the Santa Fe Trail . . .* (Glendale, Cal., 1952), pp. 17-29, 86, 87; William Waldo's "Recollections," *loc. cit.*, p. 70; Isaac McCoy (*see KHQ*, v. 13, p. 433) stated, in 1828, that the traders carried with them "about $6,000 in specie on their backs," when they abandoned the wagons.

❡ Between September 4 and 24, U. S. Comm'r Isaac McCoy (a Baptist missionary at Carey [Mich.]) conducted a small Indian delegation (three Ottawas, two Pottawatomies, and a half-Pottawatomie interpreter) on an exploratory tour into present Kansas.

Though McCoy's party had reached St. Louis (on horseback, from Carey) in mid-July, it was after the middle of August before McCoy, the Indians, and two hired hands—nine persons in all—left that town for Harmony Mission (Mo.). There, Noel Mongrain (an elderly half-Osage) joined them as "guide." On September 4 they crossed into "Kansas" and camped on the Marais des Cygnes [in present Linn county]. As McCoy outlined the journey in his report (of October 7):

". . . I proceeded westwardly up the Osage [Marais des Cygnes] river, generally on the north side. Passing the sources of Osage we bore South west across the upper branches of Neosho until we intersected the main river at a point eighty miles south, and 127 west of the mouth of Kanzas river, and [a]bout 25 miles southeast of the Santa Fe road. We then bore north west until we reached the Santa Fe road [in present Marion county] . . . 140 [miles] due west of . . . [Missouri]. . . . We turned eastward along and near to the Santa Fe road, to a point due South of the upper Kanzas village, then travelled north to said village on the Kanzas river, 125 miles west of . . . [Missouri]."

It was on September 18 that they came to the "upper" Kansa town of about 15 huts—in the vicinity of Junction City of today. Heading eastward they passed between two other small Kansa camps; and early on the afternoon of the 19th sighted "the principal Kanzau village . . . say 7 miles off"—two miles east of present Manhattan. Bearing southeast from that area they crossed Mill creek [in what is now Wabaunsee county]; reached the Wakarusa headwaters; continued eastward on the divide between the Kansas and Marais des Cygnes rivers, and on September 24 reached the Shawnee settlements near the mouth of the Kansas.

Isaac McCoy, summing up his impressions of the country traversed, noted its high rolling character; the abundant limestone; the "exceedingly fertile" soil; the sufficiency (though not abundance) of water; the scarcity of wood (though it "is not so great as has sometimes been reported"); and the abundance of game ("Elk, Deer & Bear plenty," also they had seen "a few Antelopes"). The Pottawatomies and Ottawas, he wrote, "while they lament the scarcity of wood, and especially the almost total absence of the sugar tree, pronounce it a fine country."

Ref: *KHQ*, v. 5, pp. 227-268 (for McCoy's journal; and brief report, on pp. 264, 265), v. 13, pp. 408-415 (for a longer report by McCoy), v. 26, pp. 152-157 (for a discussion of McCoy's route, the Kansa village locations, and a map showing the general route of the exploring party).

❡ The situation of the Shawnee Indians in present Kansas was described by the Rev. Isaac McCoy in late September:

The Shawanoes arrived in this country last Spring late. [The *first* immigrant Shawnees had come late in 1825—*see* annals entry.] They [now] consist chiefly of about one half of those who resided at Waupaugkonetta in Ohio, some from Merimack [river, Mo.] . . ., some from Lewistown, O[hio] & elsewhere. With some aid from government, chiefly in food & clothing, & farming utensils, they are in three or four settlements of villages putting up with their own hands very neat log cabbins [in present Shawnee township, Wyandotte county—south of the Kansas river, and in Johnson county—also south of the Kansas].

McCoy also noted the presence of the "old prophet"—Ten-squata-wa (brother of Tecumseh). Among other Shawnee chiefs of prominence already in "Kansas" by the fall of this year were William Perry and Cornstalk.

Ref: *KHQ*, v. 5, pp. 260, 261, v. 13, p. 442.

❡ On the Kansas river's south bank, about six miles (by land) west of the Missouri boundary, within the Shawnee reserve, in the autumn, the Chouteau brothers built a new American Fur Company trading house—a post of some permanence—known as Cyprian Chouteau's establishment by the 1840's. At the scene in 1828 was Father Joseph A. Lutz, who wrote, on November 12: "Messrs. Francis, Cyprian and Frederick Chouteau have begun to erect at the Kanzas River a large building which will soon be looked upon as a sort of emporium for the sale and exchange of goods among the Shawnee and Kanzas Indians." (The site seems to have been a mile or so north of present Turner, Wyandotte county, in Sec. 13, T. 11, R. 24 E.)

An 1830 trading license issued for its operation referred to the post's location as "On the Kanzas river about 12 miles from the mouth . . ."; in 1831 (and later) it was described as "opposite the old half breed establishment[?] on the Kanzas, about 12 miles from the mouth." Frederick Chouteau (in 1880) was quoted as saying: "In 1828 and 1829 we built some trading-houses [the 1829 post was Frederick's—farther upstream] four or five miles [by land] above [what was later] Wyandotte, on the north [*i. e., south*—he must have been misquoted!] side of the Kansas river. . . . The houses built in 1828, in the fall, were for trading with the Shawnees and Delawares." An early confirmation that the post was on the *south* bank can be found in the January, 1830, annals entry of Prince Paul's visit there. Also, Isaac McCoy's surveying party stopped there in August, 1830, and, as Prince Paul had done, crossed the Kansas at that point, to proceed to Cantonment Leavenworth.

As for the occupants of the trading house, the following statement from the Rev. Benedict Roux's letter of November 24, 1833, strongly implies that both Francis G. Chouteau (together with his family), and Cyprian were then living there. Father Roux wrote:

"I am at present at the trading house of the Messrs. Chouteau. . . . I cannot . . . speak too highly in praise of Mr. [Francis] Guesseau and of his wife and brother. . . . But I do not expect to remain long with them, as they are right in the Indian country and too far away from the Catholics [referring to the French settlement which had developed on the site of present Kansas City, Mo.] for me to carry on my ministry with convenience.

Ref: G. J. Garraghan's *Catholic Beginnings* . . ., pp. 32, 47, 48; 21st Cong., 2d Sess., *House Ex. Doc. 41* (Serial 207); 22d Cong., 2d Sess., *House Doc. No. 104* (Serial 234); *KHC*, v. 8, p. 425, v. 9, pp. 573-575; *ibid.*, v. 4, p. 302, and *KHQ*, v. 5, p. 346 (for McCoy—the latter reference gives the *date* but does not specifically mention the trading post). In William J. Dalton's *The Life of Father Bernard Donnelly* (Kansas City, Mo., 1921), the name "Roux" appears as "Le Roux."

❡ Between November 8 and early December a party of Chickasaws, Choctaws, and Creeks was conducted on an exploring tour of present "Kansas and Oklahoma," from the Kansas river southward to the Canadian, along a line of march at no place more than 48 miles west of the Missouri and Arkansas boundaries. By Isaac McCoy's report, the company which set out on November 8 from a camp (in present northeast Johnson county) about five miles south of the Kansas river's mouth, consisted of:

. . . Cap. G. H. Kennerly, leader, Lieut. [Washington] Hood Topographist, Mr. John Bell assistant topographist, and G. P. Todson surgeon. To me [McCoy] had been instrusted the monied matters. The Chickasaws Delegation consisted of 12 Indians, and an interpreter, accompanied by three white men chosen by themselves, in all 16, with Mr. John B. Duncan Sub. Agent, as their leader. The Choctaw delegation was composed of six Indians, and lead by Mr. D. W. Haley. The Creek delegation consisted of three, and was lead by Mr. Luther Blake. We had one interpreter to Osages and Kanzas [Noel Mongrain], seven hired men, and a black servant belonging [to] a Chickasaw Chief. In all 42. We had with us upwards of sixty horses.

The expedition moved "a little west of south" to the Marais des Cygnes (crossed it about 20 miles west of Missouri), continued southwest to the Neosho, and followed downriver to the Osage Agency (present Neosho county) on November 17. After four days of Indian councils and peace talks Kennerly's party proceeded about six miles down the Neosho to camp on the night of the 20th near White Hair's village. They were entertained in the houses of White Hair and Belle Oiseau. (The latter accompanied McCoy's party southward on the 22d.)

From the Osage towns they "took the road to the Creek agency on the Verdigris river, within four miles of its junction with the Arkansaw." There, and near Fort Gibson (Okla.), they remained five days before continuing to the mouth of the Canadian river's south fork—260 miles south of the Kansas river's mouth. By December 10 all the Indian delegations had set out for their homes. Kennerly, Hood, Bell, Todson, McCoy, together with the hired hands and pack horses retraced their way to the Osage Agency (arriving on December 15), crossed the Neosho there, and "took the direct route to Harmony Mission" 70 miles to the northeast. From that place they returned to St. Louis on December 24th.

Ref: *KHQ*, v. 13, pp. 400-462 (for Isaac McCoy's journal and report; and the reports of Kennerly, Hood, and Bell); Isaac McCoy's *History of Baptist Indian Missions* . . . (Washington, 1840), pp. 350-369.

❡ BORN: on December 7, at Cantonment Leavenworth, Lewis Bissell Dougherty, son of Indian Agent John and Mary (Hertzog) Dougherty. He was, so far as known, the third white child and second white *boy* born in present Kansas. (Lewis B. Dougherty died at Liberty, Mo., in 1925.)

Ref: *KHC*, v. 8, p. 260n; "Dougherty Collection," in KHi ms. division; *Missouri Historical Review*, v. 24, pp. 359-363.

❡ Four years before the treaties of October 27 and October 29, 1832, legalized and defined their tribal reserves in what is now Kansas, the bands of Piankeshaw and Wea Indians, and the Peorias, residing in southwestern Missouri, took William Clark's advice and moved to lands already set aside for them, south of the Shawnee reserve. (In 1828 Angus Langham partially surveyed the two tracts—one for the Weas and Piankeshaws, the other for the Peorias and Kaskaskias—in present Miami and Franklin counties.)

It was during 1828 that these Indians first established villages in present Kansas. The exact time is unknown—a January 3, 1829, report on Indian tribes noted that 350 Shawnees "with all the Weas and Piankeshaws" had removed from Missouri to lands assigned them. (*See, also,* July, 1830, and March, 1831, entries.)

Ref: 20th Cong., 2d Sess., *Sen. Doc.* 27 (Serial 181), p. 2 (for 1829 report); 23d Cong., 1st Sess., *Sen. Doc. 512,* v. 2 (Serial 245), p. 115 (for Clark's "advice" reference); Langham map showing 1828 survey of Wea and Piankeshaw, etc., lines (photostat), in KHi ms. division.

❧ Subagent John Campbell came from Missouri in (the latter part? of) 1828 to occupy (perhaps build?) the Shawnee Agency (present Johnson county, near the Missouri line), where his particular charges (as subagent) were the Piankeshaws, Weas, and Peorias (whose tracts of land were south of the Shawnee reserve). In a February 9, 1829, report by the secretary of war, Subagent Campbell was listed as residing at "mouth of Kanzas river." He was subordinate to Agent Richard Graham in 1828-1829 (then to Graham's successor George Vashon, in 1829-1830, and to his successor, R. W. Cummins, in 1830-1833).

The beginnings of Shawnee Agency are obscure, and whether a building was erected prior to 1828 has not been ascertained. Agent Graham (in charge of the Delawares, Shawnees, Kickapoos, Piankeshaws, Weas, and Peorias residing in Missouri, Arkansas, and west of Missouri) had his headquarters near St. Louis, and visited the various Indians under his supervision when business demanded.

Shawnee Agency was well established by 1829. (The location, by present-day description, was on the E.½ of the S.E.¼, Sec. 10, and W.½ of the S.W.¼, Sec. 11, T. 12, R. 25 E.—*See KHQ,* v. 5, p. 342.) As 2d Lt. Philip St. George Cooke saw it in June, 1829: ". . . [on the edge of a] light and airy grove . . . was delightfully situated . . . the house . . . of the subagent of the Delawares—the hospitable old Major C[ampbell] . . . with ready joke and julep, did his best to make our long farewell to the settlements, a lively one." Surveyor Isaac McCoy, westbound from Independence (Mo.), wrote, on August 21, 1830: "In the evening reached the Shawanoe & Delaware agency, at the house of Maj. J. Campbell the Sub. Agt. by whom we were kindly received. Our tents were pitched for the company, while I accepted an invitation to take quarters with Maj. Campbell." (For an earlier Shawnee Agency event of that year, *see* January 12, 1830, annals entry.)

Ref: 20th Cong., 2d Sess., *Sen. Doc.* 72 (Serial 181), pp. 6, 7; Philip St. George Cooke's *Scenes and Adventures* . . . (Philadelphia, 1857), pp. 4, 42; *KHQ,* v. 5, p. 342 (for McCoy). Campbell had been Graham's subagent, in Missouri, since April, 1825. *See* William Clark letter (photostat) of April 13, 1825, in KHi ms. division in the "Christopher Collection."

❧ Author-editor-missionary Timothy Flint's two-volume popular and "romantic" work, *A Condensed Geography and History of the*

Western States, published at Cincinnati during the year, contained a chapter on "Missouri Territory" (defined as the area bounded by the British possessions on the north; the Northwest Territory, Illinois, and Missouri on the east; the Mexican republic on the south and southwest; and the Rocky mountains on the west). By his description (but not from his own observation), beyond the partially wooded belt of country extending from 200 to 400 miles west of the Mississippi:

There commences that ocean of prairies, that constitutes so striking and impressive a feature in the vast country beyond the Mississippi and Missouri. This vast country is for the most part, a plain, more or less covered with grass, in great extents fertile; in other extents almost a moving sand. It is pastured, and trodden by countless numbers of buffaloes, elk and other wild animals, that graze upon it. . . .

Ref: Flint's work, as noted above, v. 2, p. 435.

1829

❡ William L. Sublette's party ("52 men and two Indians") left St. Louis around mid-March to take the Smith, Jackson & Sublette pack-mule train to the fur traders' rendezvous in the Rockies, ending up at Pierre's Hole. (Sublette had brought the partners' furs down to Missouri in September, 1828, and had remained over the winter at St. Louis.)

In this company were George W. Ebbert, Joseph L. Meek, Samuel Parkman, and Robert Newell—new recruits among the more experienced mountain men like Milton Sublette. After a brief stop at Independence, Mo., this expedition followed out the Santa Fe trail for some miles, then, apparently, turned northwest, forded the Kansas, moved up its valley, then headed north to the Little Blue and on to the Platte—traversing "Sublette's Trace" (*see* March, 1827 entry)—the future Oregon trail route.

Ref: Dale L. Morgan, *op. cit.,* pp. 302, 303, 429; Sunder, *op. cit.,* pp. 76-80; D. O. Johansen, ed., *Robert Newell's Memoranda* . . . (Portland, 1959), p. 31; Frances F. Victor's *The River of the West* (Hartford and Toledo, 1870), pp. 45-58. Newell's *Memoranda,* as printed, gives the departure date from St. Louis as "March 7, 1828"—a misprint(?). The year was 1829 (no caravan went to the mountains in 1828—*see* p. 140). Newell says "55 men in all" started on this "hunting expedition for beever." The rendezvous ("when all together about 175 men") at Pierre's Hole was held August 20.

❡ Visiting Cantonment Leavenworth in March, on an inspection trip, Col. George Croghan made a report (dated March 31) which included these remarks:

. . . A great deal has been done [since 1827], much more in truth than could have been expected of a garrison so reduced by sickness; still the work is not half accomplished. . . . A good hospital has been erected, and four houses originally intended to quarter one company each (though now occupied by officers) have been put up and very nearly completed, but there yet remains to be provided for: Officers quarters, store houses, guard house, magazine, etc., etc. . . . I am . . . at a loss . . . as to the operating causes of [the cantonment's] . . . sickness. There is certainly nothing apparently in its location to render it unhealthy, on the contrary, the site might be considered an admirable one.

Cantonment Leavenworth was then garrisoned by Companies A, B, D, E, F, H, I, and K of the Third U. S. infantry, with Bvt. Maj. John Bliss as commanding officer. Maj. Surg. John Gale was the overworked medical officer.

Ref: *KHQ*, v. 15, pp. 353-355; Heitman, *op. cit.* (for officers' names).

❧ In the spring, probably in March, Mission Neosho (which had been operated since 1824 by the Rev. Benton Pixley and his wife for the Osages of Neosho river) ceased operation. The hostility of Agent John F. Hamtramck towards Pixley brought about the abrupt closing of the mission, and the removal of the mission family from present Neosho county to Missouri.

(*See* under 1830 for a "revival" of the mission, in another location, with different personnel, and under a new name—Boudinot.)

Ref: Graves, *op. cit.*, p. 194.

❧ On April 13 the small, side-wheel steamboat *Wm. D. Duncan* (Captain Crooks), from Pittsburgh, Pa., left St. Louis for Franklin, Mo. (and returned on the 23d)—the first of several trips she made during the 1829 season, between the two towns. Her series of voyages may be said to have ushered in the era of regular steamboat travel on the Missouri. (*See* March 15, 1830, entry.)

Ref: *KHQ*, v. 16, pp. 284, 285; St. Louis (Mo.) *Beacon*, April 13 and July 4, 1829. (Though H. M. Chittenden in his *Early Steamboat Navigation on the Missouri River* (1903)—*see KHC*, v. 9, p. 278—stated that the *Duncan* ran to "Fort" Leavenworth in 1829, as a regular packet, this does not seem to have been the case.)

❧ The April 18 issue of the Fayette *Missouri Intelligencer* carried Bvt. Brig. Gen. Henry Atkinson's notice (of the same date) that about June 1 a detachment of 200 Sixth infantrymen, under Bvt. Maj. Bennet Riley, would leave Cantonment Leavenworth for the Santa Fe road and proceed to the Arkansas river for the protection of trading caravans bound for New Mexico. The notice concluded: "The detachment will halt at some position on the Arkansas, for the return of the caravans, till some time in October, when it will fall back upon the frontier." (The Sixth infantry was stationed at Jefferson Barracks, Mo.)

Ref: Young, *op. cit.*, pp. 39, 40, 49, 50.

❧ At Cantonment Leavenworth, on May 15, a 15-gun salute greeted the steamboat *Diana*, arriving with Bvt. Maj. Bennet Riley and four companies of Sixth infantry; and also bringing some of the soldiers' families ("the boat swarmed with their wives and children; the deck was barricaded with beds and bedding . . .").

The *Diana* had made the voyage in record time—10 days—from Jefferson Barracks, Mo.

Ref: *Ibid.*, pp. 50-54; KHQ, v. 16, p. 287; [Philip St. G. Cooke's] "Journal" in *New Mexico Historical Review*, Santa Fe, v. 3, pp. 268-270; also Cooke's *Scenes and Adventures* . . ., pp. 40, 41.

❧ Five companies of the Third infantry left Cantonment Leavenworth in keel and mackinaw boats on May 16 for Jefferson Barracks. Next day, the rest of the Third (three companies) left that post on the *Diana*, for the lower river. (The *Diana* reached the Barracks on May 20; the "3 keels and 4 small boats" arrived on May 23.)

Ref: *Ibid.*, p. 270; KHQ, v. 16, pp. 288, 289; Young, *op. cit.*, p. 54.

❧ The latter part of May, Marston G. Clark ("General Clark" in various records of the time), new subagent for the Kansa Indians, arrived at the Kansa Agency (which was to be his headquarters for the next five years). A native of Virginia, but resident of Indiana, Clark had been appointed in February, to fill the vacancy created by the death of Baronet Vasquez in August, 1828, and filled interim by Dunning D. McNair. John T. Irving, Jr., who met him in the fall of 1833, described Clark as a "tall, thin, soldier-like man, arrayed in an Indian hunting-shirt and an old fox-skin cap."

Ref: KHQ, v. 16, p. 288. The letter of appointment was dated February 19, 1829; Clark accepted in March.—This information from Dale L. Morgan, who cites "Records Group 75, National Archives."

❧ Agent George Vashon (newly appointed to succeed Richard Graham, discharged) left St. Louis on June 4 for the mouth of the Kansas, to make an annuity payment to the Shawnee Indians. Probably he did not remain long at the Shawnee Agency (where Subagent Campbell resided), but in October he was back at "Indn Ag[enc]y, mouth of Kanzas River," issuing (on the 21st) a trading license to Francis G. Chouteau; reporting (October 27) on the condition of the agency Indians, and forwarding (to William Clark) a treaty he had made with the Delawares on September 24, "at Council camp, on James's fork of White river, in the State of Missouri."

(Vashon served only briefly as agent to the Shawnees, Delawares, &c. of Missouri, Arkansas, and present Kansas. He left in mid-July, 1830, to become agent for the Western Cherokees.)

Ref: OIA, "Registers of Letters Received," v. 2, pp. 496, 497, 499; 21st Cong., 2d Sess., *House Ex. Doc. 41* (Serial 207); SIA, v. 29, p. 34.

❧ On June 11 the first military escort for Santa Fe traders—Bvt. Maj. Bennet Riley and 200 Sixth infantry troops—reached the traders' rendezvous at Round Grove (on the headwaters of Cedar creek, in present Johnson county). These soldiers were Companies A, B, F, and H, captained by William N. Wickliffe and Joseph Pentland. Among the junior officers was 2d Lt. Philip St. George Cooke, who, as a captain, in 1843, would lead a military escort on the same road.

Riley's expedition (with 20 heavily-laden wagons and four carts, drawn by *oxen*—an innovation on the Santa Fe trail; and a six-pounder, mule-drawn on a carriage) had left a camp across the Missouri from Cantonment Leavenworth on June 4; traveled down the river's *left* bank; and recrossed (on the 8th and 9th) near the Kaw's mouth, to head out on the prairie past the Shawnee Agency.

From June 12 to July 9, Riley's command marched—ahead of the traders—over the Santa Fe road, to the vicinity of Chouteau's Island (present Kearny county—*see* 1816).

Ref: [Cooke's] "Journal," *loc. cit.,* v. 3, pp. 271-273; Cooke's *Scenes and Adventures* . . ., pp. 41, 42; Young, *op. cit.,* pp. 65-85; *New Mexico Historical Review,* v. 2, p. 288.

❧ Charles Bent (on his first journey to the southwest) was elected captain of the moderate-size Santa Fe caravan (about 70? men, and 37? wagons) which left Round Grove (*see* preceding entry) on June 12, following in the rear of the military escort. Among the traders were William Bent, David and William Waldo, James L. Collins, and Milton E. Bryan. (The names of a good many others on this trip are known, also.) The caravan reached Council Grove on June 18; left there on the 20th; and proceeded without special incident to the Upper Crossing of the Arkansas (near Chouteau's Island), on July 9.

Ref: Young, *op. cit.,* pp. 74-85; Cooke's *Scenes and Adventures* . . ., pp. 42-46; William Waldo's "Recollections," *loc. cit.,* pp. 72, 73; *The Western Monitor,* Fayette, Mo., March 24, 1830 (for a list of more than 30 traders); and *see* Young's book, p. 184.

❧ MARRIED: Clement Lessert (interpreter at the Kansa Agency), and Julia Roy, on June 13, in Jackson county, Mo., by Andrew P. Patterson, J. P.

Ref: Marriage records, Jackson County, Mo. Lessert (Kansa interpreter from 1827 to 1834) died July 20, 1854, aged 58—*see* D. A. R., Kansas City, Mo., *Vital Historical Records of Jackson County, Missouri, 1826-1876* (Kansas City, Mo., c1934), p. 267.

❧ On July 10 the Santa Fe traders forded the Arkansas river (below Chouteau's Island, in present Kearny county) and camped on Mexican soil. Next day they took leave of the military escort and started across the sand hills for Santa Fe. They had traveled only six to nine miles when a party of about 50? Indians ambushed three men riding in advance—killing merchant Samuel Craig Lamme. (This incident presumably occurred in what is now Kearny county.) The traders, under Charles Bent's direction, corraled the wagons, dug rifle-pits, and got their small cannon into use. Nine volunteers rode back to the Arkansas for aid. Major Riley led his entire command into Mexican territory, rescued the traders from their predicament, and escorted them on through the sand hills. On July 15 Riley and the Sixth infantry battalion turned back to the Arkansas.

(The traders had a difficult journey to Santa Fe. Indians harassed them constantly, and the caravan, though augmented by a party of 120 Mexicans met on the road, might not have reached its destination except for aid from the west. Ewing Young and some 95 trappers from Santa Fe and Taos fought through the Indian lines and came to their rescue.)

Ref: Young, *op. cit.*, pp. 85-102, 140, 141; Waldo's "Recollections," *loc. cit.*, pp. 64, 72-77; [Cooke's] "Journal," *loc. cit.*, pp. 280-282. In the Sand Hills battle the traders thought the Indians numbered several hundred (Waldo "recollected" their number at from 500 to 2,000!). Cooke's journal suggests there were probably not more than 50 in the party which killed Lamme.

❡ Carrying dispatches and mail, Corporal Arter and Pvt. William Nation of the Sixth infantry, on July 12, left Cantonment Leavenworth on horseback for Major Riley's camp on the Arkansas. On July 23, when only "some 25 miles below" their destination, a small party of Indians (armed with bows and lances) wounded both men, took their horses and the mail. Though Nation was in poor condition, the two managed to travel perhaps 15 miles upriver. On August 10 Arter, alone, stumbled into Riley's camp. Forty soldiers with a cart went out and rescued Nation. He died on August 28, in present Kearny county; but the skirmish with the Indians *apparently* occured in what is now Finney county.

Ref: [Cooke's] "Journal," *loc. cit.*, pp. 287, 288; Bennet Riley's report in *American State Papers: Military Affairs*, v. 4, p. 279; Young, *op. cit.*, p. 124.

❡ A clash between Big Neck's band of Iowas, and some settlers in the Grand Chariton region of northern Missouri, in mid-July, created an Indian war scare. At Cantonment Leavenworth where Capt. Zalmon C. Palmer, and about 20 men of the Sixth infantry (all but six of them ill) composed the entire force to defend the inhabitants which included "eight or nine ladies and about twenty camp women." The ladies (and children?) "assembled every night in a large hospital which was surrounded by about 16 cannon." A request was sent to Liberty, Mo., for aid, and 40 men came to bolster the garrison.

Missouri's Gov. John Miller asked for troops from Jefferson

Barracks (Mo.) to quell the "war." Bvt. Brig. Gen. Henry Leavenworth hastily organized an expedition of Sixth and Third infantrymen which proceeded to Cantonment Leavenworth on the steamboat *Crusader*. At that place, some Iowa, Sac, and Fox leaders met Leavenworth in council, in the fore part of August. They expressed regret for the actions of Big Neck's band and offered 19 chiefs and warriors as hostages (to insure surrender of the Iowas involved in the July affray). By August 19 Leavenworth, his command, and the 19 Iowas, aboard the *Crusader*, had reached St. Louis.

(Big Neck and nine others of his band were captured in September and taken to Jefferson Barracks in October. The hostages were sent home early in December.)

Ref: O. W. Pollock's *A Sketch of the Life of Mrs. Jane Foster Wheeler (Wallace)* . . . (San Francisco, 1910), pp. 24, 25; Young, *op. cit.*, p. 62; *Western Monitor*, Fayette, Mo., August 29, 1829; St. Louis *Beacon*, December 20, 1830; *KHQ*, v. 16, pp. 294, 300, 302, 303; Dorothy J. Caldwell's "The Big Neck Affair," in *Missouri Historical Review*, v. 64 (July, 1970), pp. 391-412. An account of John Thornton's life, in *The U. S. Biographical Dictionary, Missouri Volume* (1878), says, on p. 603, that Thornton (of Liberty, Mo.) had received a letter from Lt. Francis Lee, in command at Cantonment Leavenworth, dated July 24, 1829, in regard to the trouble with the Iowa Indians in Randolph county, and the need for militia.

❦ Returning from Mexican territory after aiding the Santa Fe-bound traders (*see* July 10 entry), Major Riley, on July 26, selected a summer camp site for his command on the left bank of the Arkansas (in U. S. territory), opposite Chouteau's Island.

The days were uneventful till July 31, when four discharged soldiers, Simmons, Fry, Colvin, and Gordon, set out on foot for Missouri. About 10(?) miles downriver they met some 30 mounted, "friendly" Indians. George Gordon was killed while shaking hands with one of them. His more prudent companions had moved on, but they retaliated by shooting an Indian. Fortunately for the three besieged men, a hunting party from Riley's camp came along late in the day and rescued them. (Gordon's body was found, and buried, several days later. His death perhaps occurred in what is now eastern Kearny county. Cooke's journal says the men were "perhaps 18 miles" from Chouteau's Island; Riley's report says "not more than eight or ten miles.")

On the afternoon of August 3, several large parties of Indians made a raid on the stock. One of the guards, Pvt. Samuel Arrison, was severely wounded and died an hour or so later. The troops engaged the 300 to 400 Indians in a skirmish that lasted about 45 minutes. The raiders lost eight warriors, but succeeded in driving off 50 oxen and some 20 horses and mules, and they wounded other animals. (It was later reported by Mexican traders that these were Kiowas and Comanches.)

The morning of August 11 Capt. Joseph Pentland and 18 men, with six oxen and a wagon, left camp to bring in meat from three buffaloes which had been shot earlier in the day. A party of perhaps 150 mounted Indians swooped down on them. Bugler Matthew King, and the team and wagon, were abandoned by Pentland, who fled, followed by his men, to a sandbar refuge. King was killed and scalped. Riley sent additional troops and the Indians withdrew, leaving the wagon and team unharmed. (Pentland was later court-martialed, and dismissed from the service, for his action in this affair.)

There were no further Indian depredations; in fact, the Indians disappeared. On August 16 Riley moved camp four miles downriver. All of September was a quiet month, with good buffalo hunting for the soldiers. The week of September 21st the move back upstream to Chouteau's Island was begun—in anticipation of the arrival of the returning trading caravan, scheduled for not later than October 10.

Ref: [Cooke's] "Journal," *loc. cit.*, pp. 283-291; Riley's report, *loc. cit.*, p. 278; Young, *op. cit.*, pp. 104-136.

℃ August.—Robert Campbell (after a four-year stay in the mountains) headed a party of mountain men returning to the States. He brought in Smith, Jackson & Sublette fur returns. On the Platte(?) he met Andrew Drips (en route to the Council Bluffs). It would appear that Campbell (and party) subsequently came down from the Platte to the Little Blue and crossed "Kansas" on his way to Missouri. He reached Lexington in mid-August.

Ref: Morgan, *op. cit.*, p. 430; Robert Campbell's 1870 dictation, and letters, August 9, 1829, by Andrew Drips and Lucien Fontenelle—originals in Floyd E. Risvold's collection—courtesy of Dale L. Morgan. Five days after he and Campbell parted, Drips reached his destination, on or before August 9.

℃ In the Missouri-bound caravan which left Santa Fe about September 1, there were 96 traders, some well-to-do Spanish refugees (10 men and six *women*), fewer than 30 wagons, and about 2,000 head of horses, mules, and jacks. Col. Jose Antonio Viscarra and a force of 200 men (some 75 Mexicans, 91 "hired whites," and 34 "hired Indians") provided escort all the way to the Arkansas. Also in the party was Santiago Abreu, a New Mexican official.

On October 6, at the Cimarron (in the Oklahoma Panhandle of today), three(?) of the escort party were killed when the Mexicans had a skirmish with a large band of Indians following a "friendly" parley. In saving Viscarra's life, one of the Pueblo Indians lost his own. With the traders' assistance, the Indians were driven off, and several were killed.

On October 11, still more than 20 miles from the Arkansas river, and already a day late for the Chouteau's Island rendezvous, the traders sent messengers to find Major Riley and inform him of their approach.

Ref: Young, *op. cit.*, pp. 136-144; Cooke's *Scenes and Adventures* . . ., pp. 83-85; Josiah Gregg's *Commerce of the Prairies* . . . (1844), v. 1, pp. 47, 48, has comment on early female travelers on the Santa Fe trail, but does not state what year the first woman went over that route.

⟪ On September 23 the Rev. Isaac McCoy, his son Dr. Josephus McCoy, Gosa (an Ottawa Indian), and a hired hand arrived at the Kansa Agency. (This small party had left Fayette, Mo., on horseback, September 17 to make a "tour of exploration" at McCoy's own expense, in order "to acquire a more definite knowledge of a portion of the Indian territory . . ." in present Kansas.)

"We left the agency on the 29th," wrote McCoy, "having added to our company [the agent] General [Marston G.] Clark, White Plume [principal Kansa chief] . . . and Plume's son-in-law [Louis] Gunville [Gonville], a Frenchman, who, though he could speak very little English, was our only interpreter."

Two weeks later—on October 13th—they returned to the Kansa Agency. Where did these seven people travel during the two weeks of early October? Isaac McCoy was careful *not* to say! Beyond mention of the prairies he gave no geographical clue; and he did not state the direction of their journey.

Ref: Isaac McCoy's *History of Baptist Indian Missions* . . . (Washington, 1840), pp. 393, 394.

⟪ At sunrise on October 11, after firing one shot from the cannon, Bvt. Maj. Bennet Riley and his Sixth infantry battalion left the camp near Chouteau's Island and headed homeward. But three miles downstream they halted upon learning that the caravan from Santa Fe was within a day's journey of them. (*See* September 1 entry.)

On the afternoon of the 12th the traders' caravan, and its large escorting party under Colonel Viscarra, reached, and forded the Arkansas near Riley's camp. By evening over 500 persons (Mexicans, Spaniards, Indians of several tribes, Creoles, Frenchmen, and Americans), and an immense number of animals (Riley's oxen, and more than "2,000 horses, mules, [and] jacks, which kept up an incessant braying") were gathered together on the river's left bank—a few miles below Chouteau's Island (and within present Kearny county). Lieutenant Cooke wrote that it was "the strangest collection of men and animals that had perhaps ever met on a frontier of the United States."

The two days this congregation spent together were highlighted by exchanges of military and social courtesies, buffalo hunting, feats of horsemanship, Indian songs and rituals. Riley's Sixth infantry troops were displayed in review and drill for Colonel Viscarra; he in turn, showed his troops in formation. Whereas the American officers could offer as festive menu only buffalo meat, salt pork, bread, raw onions, and "a tin cup of whiskey," served on a green blanket "table-cloth," Colonel Viscarra (on the evening of the 13th) provided an elaborate dinner including fried ham, "various kinds of cakes, and delightful chocolate; and . . . several kinds of Mexican wines"—all served on a low table set with silver.

Taking leave of each other on the morning of October 14, the Missouri-bound company (more than 300 persons; some 1,800? animals) started downriver; while Colonel Viscarra and his 200 men prepared to return to Santa Fe. Riley's battalion, the traders, and the Spanish refugees reached the Caches on October 17; took the dry "cut-off" towards the Great Bend; by October 23 were past that point and encamped on Cow creek. On the 25th the traders' caravan split up in several parties, each proceeding at its own pace. Riley and his battalion continued to follow the Santa Fe trail till November 5; then (somewhere in present Douglas county) they crossed the Wakarusa, and pursued a northward course 12 miles to the Kansas river; forded it (on the 5th and 6th) opposite the Kansa Agency (seven miles above present Lawrence). Lieutenant Cooke wrote: ". . . the log-houses there, were the first habitations of men we had seen for five months."

An hour was spent at the Agency, where they got a guide, and sent out an advance party to make a trail for the oxen (only 24 yoke were left) and wagons, across Jefferson and Leavenworth counties of today, to Cantonment Leavenworth. On the evening of November 8 the battalion "marched into garrison in Column of Companies, by field music"; and was received with a 15-gun salute. The Sixth infantrymen's post quarters were "the miserable huts and sheds left by the Third infantry the preceding May."

Ref: [Cooke's] "Journal," *loc. cit.*, pp. 293-300; Cooke's *Scenes and Adventures* . . ., pp. 84-92; Young, *op. cit.*, pp. 139-163.

❧ In the autumn Frederick Chouteau (20, youngest of Pierre Chouteau, Sr's., eight sons) opened a trading house for the Kansa Indians at Horseshoe Lake, on the south side of the Kansas (in what is now Douglas county), across the river and about a mile from the Kansa Agency (seven miles above present Lawrence). He remained at that location for over two years, moving in 1832 [not 1830 as printed in *KHC*, v. 8, p. 425] to a location higher up the Kansas, near the mouth of American Chief [Mission] creek. (*See, also,* under 1832.)

In 1829, it appears, the Kansa Indians abandoned their large town near the Big Blue-Kansas junction to form three separate villages some distance downstream. (*See* next entry.) It was Frederick Chouteau's intention, in 1831, to move from Horseshoe Lake upriver to the vicinity of the new Kansa towns. The annual license issued on October 10, 1831 (to the American Fur Company), specified that his trade would be at "A point between the two upper villages of the Kanzas, on the Kanzas river." However, in December young Chouteau was still at the site opposite the Agency. On December 20 his brother Francis G. Chouteau (in person) applied to Kansa Subagent M. G. Clark for permission for Frederick to continue at that place. Clark wrote Chouteau a letter that same day, referred to the license of October 10, and stated: " . . . you have been vending goods at your old stand for some days [disregarding the license] both to Indians and to whites thereby bringing down on this agency, large bodies of Indians to the great annoyance of the few whites at this place by killing their stock, crowding their houses and begging for provisions. . . . You had, I conceive, full time to have reached the point designated in the license and to have made your cabins, but the Kansas trade is unprofitable this year and you may think proper to abandon it this year. . . .

Ref: *KHC*, v. 8, p. 425; 22d Cong., 2d Sess., *House Doc. No. 104* (Serial 234); *SIA*, v. 6, p. 413 (M. G. Clark's letter of December 20, 1831). A biographical sketch of Frederick Chouteau on p. 45 of E. F. Heisler and D. M. Smith's *Atlas Map of Johnson County, Kansas* (Wyandott, 1874) states that his first wife was Nancy Logan, a [Shawnee] Indian whom he married in 1830, and that they had four children before her death in 1846.

❮ It was apparently in 1829 that the Kansa abandoned their long-occupied 125-lodge village near the Big Blue-Kansas junction (*see* 1790-1791 annals entry) to move some 40 miles downstream and form three towns—all west of present Topeka, within what is now Shawnee county. Discussing the Kansa, Agent John Dougherty commented, on January 30, 1830: "not until the last year, were they located in such manner as to enjoy any advantage from opening fields and cultivating the earth." His statement seems to imply a move in 1829. Unquestionably, the Kansa were well established in their new abodes by the end of 1830.

Fool Chief's village (700 to 800 people) was *north* of the Kansas river, and six miles west of the mouth of Heart river [Soldier creek]. On September 6, 1830, Isaac McCoy's surveying party was at work about four miles west of present Topeka, and McCoy noted in his journal: "About a mile and a half north of us between the [Soldier] creek and [the Kansas] river is the village of Chachhaa hogeree, *Prarie-village*. It contains about 50 houses, with say three families

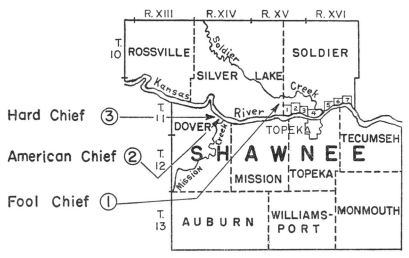

Hard Chief ③

American Chief ②

Fool Chief ①

From a Shawnee county map of 1874 which shows seven of the Kansa half-breed reserves.

to the house." (Fool Chief's town was on the S. E. ¼ of Sec. 16, T. 11, R. 15 E., in present Menoken township.)

About seven miles to the west, and on the *south* side of the Kansas was *Hard Chief's village* (500 to 600 people), on high ground, but near the river. (His town was on the N. E. ¼ of the N. W. ¼ of Sec. 28, T. 11, R. 14 E., in Dover township.)

American Chief's village (about 100 people), described as 20 dirt lodges of good size, was in the bottoms on the west side of American Chief [Mission] creek, about a mile and a half from the Kansas river, and about a mile below Hard Chief's town. (American Chief's town was, apparently, in Sec. 27 of T. 11, R. 14 E., in Dover township.)

Ref: 21st Cong., 1st Sess., *Sen. Doc. 110* (Serial 193), p. 10 (for Dougherty's statement); *KHQ*, v. 5, p. 353 (for McCoy); *KHC*, v. 9, p. 573 (for locations of the Kansa villages), v. 8, p. 425, and v. 9, p. 196 (for other data on the Kansa towns, according to Frederick Chouteau's recollections [1880]).

1830

❡ Bound for the Rocky mountains on a scientific expedition, Prince Paul of Wuerttemberg, together with two servants, a clerk (H. Crossler), and two American Fur Company hands, left St. Louis December 23, 1829. (*See* 1823 for the prince's earlier Western expedition.) Journeying across Missouri on horseback, this small party reached Francis G. Chouteau's establishment on the Missouri (within present Kansas City, Mo.) on January 5, 1830; and from that place continued westwardly a few miles, along the Kansas river's south bank, to the Chouteaus' American Fur Company post on the Shawnees' land (in Wyandotte county of today). Commenting on the Missouri-"Kansas" border scene, Prince Paul wrote:

. . . the country presented to me a few wooded hills and small prairies . . . clusters of lofty trees intermingled with a few sumach and dwarf oak bushes. The land includes that section of the country lately ceded to the Delawares, Peorias, and Shawnee Indians. . . . Traces of cultivated ground, and the possession of cattle, and even of a few black slaves, already indicate the change which may be wrought in the course of time, and under a free, mild, and pacific government. . . .

Heading for Cantonment Leavenworth, Prince Paul forded the Kansas near the Chouteaus' trading house. ("The ice presented some difficulties to swimming my horse . . .," he noted.) At the military post he found his "old friend" Maj. Bennet Riley, in command.

By February, Prince Paul was at the Council Bluffs. When spring arrived he continued up the Missouri to the American Fur Company post Fort Tecumseh (Fort Pierre). On August 20 he left that post in a pirogue, accompanied by a trapper named James Andrews (a Canadian), to return to St. Louis. By September 24 they had passed Cantonment Leavenworth. On reaching St. Louis Prince Paul embarked for New Orleans.

Ref: *KHQ*, v. 16, p. 304; St. Louis (Mo.) *Beacon*, October 7, 1830; *Arkansas Gazette*, Little Rock, February 23, 1831; *South Dakota Historical Collections*, Pierre, v. 19, pp. 463-473; (Francis A.) *Chardon's Journal at Fort Clark*, edited by Annie H. Abel, pp. 221, 222, 229-231. The 1830 federal census shows that Francis G. Chouteau had three slaves (an adult male, an adult female, and a child under 10); and that several other Jackson county, Mo., residents also owned slaves.

❡ Starting from the Rocky mountains late in December, 1829, William L. Sublette and "Black" Harris, with a pack dog train, made a winter journey to St. Louis, reaching that town, apparently, on February 11, 1830. Little is known of their trip—presumably they traveled "Sublette's Trace" which would have brought them from the Platte to the Little Blue and down across Marshall and Pottawatomie counties of today to the Kansas river valley. (Compare with January-March, 1827, Sublette-Harris journey.)

Ref: Dale L. Morgan's *Jedediah Smith* . . . (Indianapolis and New York, c1953), p. 315; J. E. Sunder's *Bill Sublette* . . . (Norman, Okla., c1959), p. 84.

❡ BORN: on January 12 Susannah (Susan) A. Yoacham, daughter of Daniel and Rosannah (May) Yoacham, at the Shawnee Agency, in present Johnson county. She was, perhaps, the fourth white child, and second white *girl* born in what is now Kansas.

The Yoachams then lived with Subagent John Campbell (cousin of Mrs.

Yoacham). Later they ran a tavern in Westport, Mo. Susan married William J. Dillon; had seven(?) children; and died in December, 1912, at Kansas City, Mo., aged 82.

Ref: May H. (Dillon) Tinker's April 25, 1916, letter, in a "Remsburg scrapbook," Kansas State Historical Society (KHi) library; letter by John C. McCoy, August, 1879, in KHi ms. division (McCoy says Yoacham was employed as a farmer for the Shawnees); Kansas City (Mo.) *Star*, July 16, 1950 (for an account of Yoacham's tavern). Rosannah (May) Yoacham was the daughter of Samuel and Mary Ann (Sevier) May, of Overton county, Tenn. (*See* data in "Christopher Collection," KHi ms. div.) *Also, see* Cora B. Sevier and Nancy S. Madden, *Sevier Family History* (Washington, D. C., 1961), pp. 301, 302 (for Campbell), and pp. 244, 301, 302 (for Yoacham).

¶ Reporting, January 30, on the civilization of the Missouri river Indians, Agent John Dougherty stated:

. . . they have made no advance . . . of agriculture [they know] nothing more than they have perhaps always known . . . to raise in a very rude manner, a little corn, a few beans and pumpkins; and even this confined to a very few, out of the numerous tribes on the Missouri; and as to "education," there is not a single Indian man, woman, or child, to my knowledge, from the head of the Missouri to the mouth of the Kanzas river, that knows one letter from another. . . .

[As to] . . . the "condition" of the Indians in Missouri [agency] generally, I can only say, that the Kanzas, Iowas, Omahas, Ottoes, and the Yankton band of Sioux, from the diminution and scarcity of game in this country, starve at least half the year, and are very badly clad. The other tribes, who reside higher up the river, and near the mountains, in the buffalo country, live plentifully, and are well clothed.

Ref: 21st Cong., 1st Sess., *Sen. Doc. 110* (Serial 193), pp. 9, 10.

¶ Expanding from its Missouri river posts to compete for the Rocky mountain fur trade, the American Fur Company (Western Department) organized an overland expedition at St. Louis in February. (From Fort Union, in 1829, a party headed by William Vanderburgh, had gone into the mountains.)

From a rendezvous at Liberty, Mo., a mounted party of 45, with a good-sized pack train (more than 100 animals), traveled through present northwest Missouri, and southwestern Iowa between March 20 and the end of the month; crossing the Missouri (in a keel boat) to the Fontenelle & Drips trading post at Bellevue (Neb.), eight or nine miles above the Platte's mouth, on March 31st. At the end of April, the expedition, headed by Lucien Fontenelle (with Andrew Drips and Michel Robidoux, traveling in company) began the journey to the mountains, up the Platte and to South Pass.

Warren Angus Ferris (aged 19), who was in this party, kept a diary of his experiences (1830-1835) which was the basis of a work he prepared entitled *Life in the Rocky Mountains* (first published in issues of the *Western Literary Messenger*, Buffalo, N. Y., between January, 1843, and May, 1844). His narrative, aside from its merit as an account of fur trade life and of the

Indians of the Far West, is notable in that it presents the American Fur Company side of the fur trade "war" of the early 1830's.

Ref: W. A. Ferris' *Life in the Rocky Mountains* . . ., edited by Paul C. Phillips (Denver, 1940).

❧ The steamboat *Wm. D. Duncan* (*see* April, 1829) was scheduled to begin regular trips between St. Louis and Franklin, Mo., on March 15; and her operators stated she would go as far as Cantonment Leavenworth whenever quantity of cargo justified the journey.

(At one Fayette, Mo., social event in March a toast was offered "to the captain of the steamboat W. D. Duncan. May his exertions in proving the practicability of navigating the Missouri river be long remembered.")

Another steamboat—the *Globe* (John Clark, master)—advertised a departure for Franklin and Cantonment Leavenworth on March 28, and again, in May, another trip to the same places.

Ref: St. Louis (Mo.) *Beacon*, March 25, May 20, and October 28, 1830; *Western Monitor*, Fayette, Mo., March 31, 1830.

❧ In March, Boudinot Mission—successor to Mission Neosho (*see* 1824, 1829) and about 10 miles downriver from its site—was established for the Osage Indians by the Rev. Nathaniel B. Dodge and his wife, on the Neosho's *east* (left) bank near the mouth of Four Mile creek. White Hair's main town was across the Neosho and about two miles westward. (The location of Boudinot is now described as on the S.W.¼ of Sec. 10, T. 29, R. 20 E., some two and a half miles west and north of present St. Paul, Neosho county.)

Nathaniel B. and Sally (Gale) Dodge (formerly of Harmony Mission and more recently of Independence, Mo.) were the principal missionary workers at Boudinot. When Isaac McCoy stopped there in June, 1831, he commented that Dodge "had erected . . . pretty comfortable buildings." During the winter of 1831-1832 the Dodges were on leave in the East. Mary B. Choate, of Vermont, came in the autumn(?) of 1832 to teach the Dodge children. A few Osage pupils also attended her school. But she left in March, 1834, to marry outside the missionary family. In 1835 Boudinot was abandoned by the Dodges who found it unsafe to stay longer, due to Indian troubles not explained. However, William C. Requa (from New Hopefield—*see* next entry) moved there, probably early in 1836, and occupied the place as "farmer and catechist" till May, when he went East on leave. He may have returned in the fall, but he abandoned Boudinot either in 1836 or very early in 1837. (*See*, under 1837, for Hopefield [No. 3], the successor to Boudinot.)

Ref: *Reports* of the American Board of Comm'rs for Foreign Missions: 1830 (pp. 90, 91), 1831 (p. 87), 1834 (p. 118), 1836 (pp. 94, 96), 1837 (p. 111); *History of American Missions* (Worcester, Spooner and Howland, 1840), pp. 278, 340, 341; W. W. Graves' *First Protestant Osage Missions* . . . (Oswego, c1949), pp. 211-217; Isaac McCoy's *History of Baptist Indian Missions* (Washington, 1840), p. 416; *Missionary Herald*, Boston, v. 27, pp. 46, 287, 288, v. 30, p. 258, v. 31, p. 26. The Dodges (married in 1803) had eight children: (Dr.) Leonard, Philena, Sally, Nathaniel B., Jr., Jonathan E., Samuel N., Thomas S., and Harriet. Some were adults by 1830. How many of them were in "Kansas" during the 1830-1835 period is not known.—*See* J. F. McDermott, ed., *The Western Journals of Washington Irving* (Norman, 1934), pp. 89, 90.

❡ Early in the spring the missionaries and about 15 Osage families comprising Hopefield Mission (*see* 1823) moved some 20 miles up Grand (Neosho) river, to a site just below Big Cabin creek's mouth (in present Mayes co., Okla.). By summer, 20 Indian families had settled there.

New Hopefield prospered till 1834 when about a fourth of the Osages there died of cholera, and other illnesses, in the summer and fall. Two adults and four children among the missionary families also were victims. On October 30, 1835, the wife of the remaining missionary, William C. Requa, died. New Hopefield closed late in 1835, or very early in 1836. (*See* preceding entry for Requa's stay at Boudinot Mission; and *see* under 1837, for the third Hopefield—which was in present Kansas.)

Ref: Spooner and Howland's *History of American Missions*, pp. 206, 253, 278; 23d Cong., 1st Sess., *H. R. No. 474* (Serial 263), pp. 113-115; Graves, *op. cit.*, p. 202; *Reports of the American Board of Comm'rs for Foreign Missions*: 1831 (pp. 88, 90), 1832 (p. 114), 1835 (pp. 96, 97); Grant Foreman's *Advancing the Frontier* (Norman, 1933), pp. 120, 143.

❡ On April 10 William L. Sublette's company of 81 mule-mounted men and a "caravan of ten wagons, drawn by five mules each, and two dearborns, drawn by one mule each" (also a dozen cattle for food, and a milk cow) set out from St. Louis for the fur trappers' summer rendezvous in the Wind river valley (of present Wyoming). The route was "nearly due west to the western limits of the State; and thence along the Santa Fe trail about forty miles; from which the course was some degrees north of west, across the waters of the Kanzas, and up the Great Platte river. . . ." (*See* illustration, p. 398.)

Sublette's notable expedition—*the first to take wagons as far as the Rocky mountains*—proceeded at the rate of 15 to 25 miles per day, and with no particular difficulty reached the rendezvous on July 16. Partners David E. Jackson and Jedediah S. Smith were there awaiting him, with a sizable collection of furs. (*See* August entry for the homeward journey.)

A year earlier (*see* March, 1829) Sublette had, perhaps, first made use of a section of the Santa Fe trail (that is, traveled *south* of the Kansas for a distance) en route to the Rocky mountains, and at the same time had pioneered the path branching away from the Santa Fe trail northwestward to the Kansas river. Where Sublette forded the Kansas in 1829 (with a pack train) and in 1830 (with wagons) is not on record. But it seems probable his party crossed near the Kansa Agency, for it is known that two years later (*see* May, 1832, annals entries) Sublette's pack train crossed the Kansas in that vicinity, and about a week prior, Captain Bonneville's expedition (with its 20 wagons) had also forded the river near the Agency. (*See* Spring, 1827, annals entry for location of the Kansa Agency.)

From the Kansas crossing, up to the Platte, the expedition traversed "Sublette's Trace" (*see* March, 1827, and March, 1829, entries), the future Oregon trail pathway.

Ref: Morgan, *op cit.*, pp. 315-317; Dale L. Morgan and C. I. Wheat's *Jedediah Smith and His Maps of the American West* (San Francisco, 1954), p. 80, and folded Fremont-Gibbs-Smith map; 22d Cong., 2d Sess., *Sen. Doc. 39* (Serial 203), pp. 21-23 (for Smith-Jackson-Sublette letter containing above-quoted statements); Sunder, *op. cit.*, pp. 84-86. The 1827 company, headed by Scott and Bruffee, which included Sublette, *could* have initiated use of the Santa Fe trail section. See annals, p. 139.

❡ A party of 48 men, nominally led by Robert Bean, left the vicinity of Fort Smith, Arkansas territory, May 7, on a trapping expedition to the Rocky mountains.

This trip had been organized and financed by John Rogers, of Fort Smith, and three associates. Each of the adventurers had his own rifle, and two or three pack animals in charge. Among these "trappers" were George and Mark Nidever, Alexander and Pruett Sinclair, Frederick Christ, Jacob P. Leese, Job Dye, and Dr. James S. Craig. (The names of most of the others are known, also.)

Beyond the Cross Timbers (as these men were proceeding across present Oklahoma by way of the Canadian river country—the North Fork, apparently), they had a fight with Comanches. Ten of the party then turned back, while the others changed direction and moved northward. On reaching the Arkansas river (possibly near the Little Arkansas junction, as Craig stated; or higher up, as implied in George Nidever's account), they followed its course. Some days later, in a skirmish with a band of Pawnees, they lost seven horses, and had several others wounded. From this point Alexander Sinclair became the party's leader, by tacit agreement.

Subsequently, in the mountains, three of this party were killed by Indians (Mark Nidever and Frederick Christ in 1830; Alexander Sinclair in 1832, at the battle of Pierre's Hole). A fourth man died in the mountains. Some of the party returned to Arkansas territory. Others eventually settled in California.

Ref: L. R. Hafen's "The Bean-Sinclair Party . . .," in *The Colorado Magazine*, Denver, v. 31, pp. 161-171; W. H. Ellison, ed., *The Life and Adventures of George Nidever* . . . (Berkeley, 1937); *Pony Express Courier*, Placerville, Calif., v. 4, no. 2 (July, 1937), p. 6; Henry R. Wagner and Charles L. Camp, *The Plains and the Rockies* . . ., 3d ed. (Columbus, Ohio, 1953), pp. 70, 71.

❡ From a rendezvous at Blue Springs (Mo.) a large trading caravan departed for Santa Fe around the middle of May. This expedition (unaccompanied by a military escort, as in 1829) undoubtedly was well-armed and efficiently organized. Some of the wagons probably were pulled by ox teams. (Josiah Gregg later stated that oxen were first used by *traders* in 1830.) If so, this journey marked another "first" in Santa Fe *trade* annals (though the military escort in 1829 had pioneered in the experiment with ox teams on the trail). Ceran St. Vrain was one of the merchants, and perhaps the captain(?) of this caravan. It appears that Charles Bent also made this trip. By one report there were 120 men, with 60 wagons. (Josiah Gregg's later-day tabulation for 1830 was 140 men and 70 wagons.) The expedition reached Santa Fe on August 4.

Before the end of October a company of traders had returned from New Mexico to Missouri—reportedly "with less profit than usual."

Ref: *Western Monitor*, Fayette, Mo., March 31, April 7, 1830; *Missouri Intelligencer*, Columbia, May 22, October 30, 1830; Josiah Gregg's *Commerce of the Prairies* (New York, 1844), v. 2, p. 160; *Colorado Magazine*, v. 31, p. 110 (for L. R. Hafen's statement on St. Vrain as captain); David Lavender's *Bent's Fort* (New York, 1954), pp. 123, 124, 383, 385. Conceivably Gregg's 1830 totals covered another expedition in addition to the large caravan. But in view of the 1828-1829 Indian troubles, a small party on the trail in 1830 seems unlikely.

❈ The "Indian Removal Bill," which had evoked bitter congressional debate before its passage, was signed by President Jackson on May 28. This act provided "for the exchange of lands with the Indians residing in any of the states or territories, and for their removal west of the Mississippi river." It was, in the words of Isaac McCoy, "the first efficient step taken by the Government towards settling the policy of colonizing the Indians."

Ref: Isaac McCoy's *History of Baptist Indian Missions*, p. 400; *Statutes at Large*, v. 4, p. 411; Grant Foreman's *The Last Trek of the Indians* (Chicago, c1946), p. 59.

❈ In May, Paul Liguiste Chouteau, long-time subagent to the Osages of Neosho river, was promoted to head the Osage Agency (in present Neosho county), succeeding John F. Hamtramck.

In the same month, or in June, Richard W. Cummins was appointed to head the Shawnee Agency in present Johnson county. He succeeded George Vashon who went to the Western Cherokee Agency. (Vashon turned over his accounts to Cummins on July 17.)

(Ref: Superintendency of Indian Affairs, "Records" (SIA), v. 4, pp. 118, 119, 142, v. 29, p. 34; Office of Indian Affairs (OIA), "Registers of Letters Received," v. 2, p. 385.

❈ The Rev. Charles Felix Van Quickenborne visited the Osage Indians (for a third time—*see*, 1827, 1828) in the early summer. Presumably he went to the Neosho river towns, but the tangible evidence of his 1830 journey relates to locations on the Marais des Cygnes and the Marmaton—sites which *probably* were in present Kansas. A Catholic *Osage Register* contains the record of his three baptisms "Done [on June 8] at the house of Francis D'Aybeau near the banks of the Marmiton river, opposite the place where formerly was the village of the *grand Soldat* [Big Soldier]"; and of three marriages he performed, also on June 8, at D'Aybeau's house; also of six baptisms "Done [on June 9] at the house of Joseph Entaya near the Marais des Cygnes."

Most of the persons involved in the three marriages listed below were, according to Van Quickenborne, from good half, or metif (three-quarter) Osage families which had left the Indian towns to commence civilized life. The two witnesses to the marriages—Christophe Sanguinet and Louis Peltier—had been sponsors of baptisms which the Catholic father had performed on his 1827 visit to the Neosho river villages. The ceremonies of June 8, at the Marmaton, were for:

Francis D'Aybeau, *alias* Brugiere (a Frenchman), and Mary (an Osage woman).

Joseph Brown, *alias* Equesne (a Frenchman, son of Stephen Brown and Acile Giguiere), and Josette D'Aybeau (a metif Osage girl, daughter of Francis D'Aybeau).

Basile Vasseur (son of Basil Vasseur, half-Osage), and Mary (an Osage woman, daughter of Kanza Shinga).

Assuming that Francis D'Aybeau's house was in present Bourbon county, then his is *the first recorded marriage in what is now Kansas.*

Ref: G. J. Garraghan's *The Jesuits of the Middle United States* (New York, 1938), v. 1, pp. 193, 194; Osage Mission records, v. 1 (microfilm in KHi). In the Cahokia census of August 27, 1787 (in C. W. Alvord's *Cahokia Records, 1778-1790,* p. 632), is an entry for "Michel Peltier." A footnote states: "Pelletier called Antaya. The family was among the early arrivals in Canada. About 1665 one of the family married an Indian woman, from whom came the name Antaya. The family was in Cahokia as early as 1751."

℄ Leaders of the small bands of Piankeshaw, Wea, and Peoria Indians living in present Miami and Franklin counties wrote William Clark on July 28 about their troubles:

. . . [we] moved on the lands you gave us [in 1828], and are satisfied with them, and have remained quiet and peaceable with all our neighbors; but now . . . we are in trouble . . .; our neighbors, the Kansas, infest us constantly; they beg every thing from us, and what we do not give them, they steal from us; they are now commencing on our corn fields; we can not lay a hoe or an axe down, but what they steal it, and strip our horses of all our bells.

. . . our friend Campbell [Subagent John Campbell] came this spring, and broke ground enough for us to make plenty to live upon, and our crops are good. . . . the Osages—they do not trouble us much now; they would not let our women gather pecans last fall, they drove them away, and told them that the land was theirs. . . .

Ref: 23d Cong., 1st Sess., *Sen. Doc. 512,* v. 2 (Serial 245), p. 115.

℄ Partners Jedediah Smith, David Jackson, and William Sublette, with a company of 50 to 70 men, left the Wind river valley (Wyo.)

on August 4 for St. Louis. Their outfit included the 10 pioneer wagons (now loaded with furs), the same mule teams which Sublette had taken to the Rockies in the spring and summer, also a large number of horses and mules, four of the cattle, and the milk cow which had made the journey from Missouri. (*See* April annals entry.)

The homeward route was "over the same ground nearly as in going out." A large number of the mountain men, with the wagons, reached St. Louis on October 11. But the arrival of "Messrs. Smith and Jackson" on October 7 had been reported and it appears the party may have separated into detachments on the latter stage of the march, with "Smith and Jackson" perhaps moving down the *north* side of the Kansas (possibly beginning a divergent route at the Kansa Agency).

On the way to Missouri, Jedediah Smith wrote a letter (to a brother in Ohio) dated September 10, at "Blue River, fork of Kanzas, 30 miles from the Ponnee [Republic] Villages," and later added a postscript after he overtook the letter on September 22 "at the Kanzas Fairry, 30 miles from Cantonment Leavenworth." (The operator, and location, of this Kansas river ferry have not been identified. *See* January, 1831, entry.)

Smith, Jackson and Sublette (in a letter of October 29 to the secretary of war) commented that the round trip with wagons, made with "ease and safety," proved "the facility of communicating overland with the Pacific ocean"; and stated that from the South Pass (where their wagons had stopped) to the Columbia river was an "easier and better" pathway than east of the mountains. (*See,* under 1832, Bonneville's expedition—the first to take loaded wagons over the Continental divide.)

Ref: Morgan, *op. cit.,* pp. 315-317, 320, 322, 343, 431; Jedediah Smith's letter of September 10, 1830, in KHi ms. division; 22d Cong., 2d Sess., *Sen. Doc.* 39 (Serial 203), pp. 21-32; Sunder, *op. cit.,* pp. 88, 89; and *see,* KHQ, v. 5, p. 366, for Isaac McCoy's journal entry of October 22, 1830, mentioning his party's crossing the wagon train's trail.

❧ In the fore part of August (after August 7 and before the 16th), at Cantonment Leavenworth, head men of the Otoes, Omahas, Iowas, Sacs, Delawares, Shawnees, and Kickapoos (of western Missouri) assembled for a peace council at Agent John Dougherty's request. Co-operatively, the Indians pledged amity and friendship.

Ref: "Dougherty Collection," in KHi ms. division (in a typed copy of Dougherty's March, 1832, report).

❧ Maj. William Davenport, Sixth U. S. infantry, became commanding officer at Cantonment Leavenworth in the latter part of August. (He replaced Maj. Bennet Riley.)

An August, 1830, visitor at the post, recalled many years later—in August, 1879—that half a dozen or more white *families* were then at Cantonment Leavenworth including those of Major Davenport, Indian Agent John Dougherty, Subagent R. P. Beauchamp, Dr. Benjamin F. Fellowes, U. S. A., and Alexander G. Morgan (post sutler).

Ref: *KHQ*, v. 5, p. 347; SIA, v. 6, p. 91; John C. McCoy letter, August, 1879, in KHi ms. division. That Fellowes was at the post in 1830 is doubtful. He was an army officer from March 2, 1833, to May 30, 1839; and Maximilian says Fellowes was on the upbound *Yellowstone* in 1833 (Thwaites, v. 34, p. 114).

❡ In mid-September Maj. Stephen W. Kearny, of the Third U. S. infantry (who had married Mary Preston Radford, stepdaughter of William Clark, on September 5, near St. Louis), and his bride arrived at Cantonment Leavenworth. (They were at the post over the winter—leaving in March, 1831, when Kearny's orders called him elsewhere.)

Ref: *KHQ*, v. 16, p. 401; D. L. Clarke's *Stephen Watts Kearny* . . . (Norman, c1961), p. 47.

❡ Throughout September a surveying party headed by Isaac Mc-Coy—a party which included his sons Rice and John C., two chainmen (Congreve Jackson and Albert Dickens), three hired hands, an interpreter, and a nine-man military escort—was at work in present eastern Kansas north of the Kansas river. By October 2 these surveyors had run the lines of the Delaware Indians' general reserve, and marked out the bounds of Cantonment Leavenworth.

In the course of accomplishing these tasks, McCoy entered "Kansas" on August 21, at the Shawnee Agency; moved northward to the cantonment on the 28th (accompanied by Delaware chief John Quick); departed on September 1 for the Kansa Agency (some 37 miles southwest); visited Chief White Plume (two miles to the northwest) on the 3d; and on September 6 (not far west of present Topeka) "arrived at the Kansas land, and commenced . . . surveying where their eastern line crossed Kansas river." (*See*, under 1826, Langham's Kansa survey.) From that point the line was run northward to ten miles beyond the northeast corner of the Kansa reserve (or, to the northwest corner of the Delaware reserve); and from there McCoy proceeded to Cantonment Leavenworth's vicinity to survey the post's boundaries. They were completed on October 1. (*See*, under October, for McCoy's Delaware "outlet" survey.)

Ref: *KHQ*, v. 5, pp. 339-361 (for Isaac McCoy's 1830 journal covering the above period of survey); 23d Cong., 1st Sess., *Sen. Doc. 512*, v. 2 (Serial 245), pp. 430-440 (for Isaac McCoy's 1831 report on his 1830 Delaware lands survey); *KHC*, v. 4, pp. 302-305 (for John C. McCoy's account of the survey).

❡ About 100 Pawnee Republic Indians arrived at Cantonment Leavenworth on September 22, "from their village on the Republican Fork of the Kansas river."

Agent John Dougherty had sent for a few of their head men to visit him to talk about the Kansa, whose recent horse-stealing raid had violated the peace between the two tribes; and to win the Pawnees' consent for a survey of the Delaware "outlet" (the north line of which would pass near their country).

By way of entertainment, the Indians performed the "Discovery Dance" on the evening of the 23d. The council was held next day. Among those attending were surveyor (and Baptist missionary) Isaac McCoy, and "venerable old" John Quick (second chief of the Delawares). Principal speaker for the Pawnee Republic band was the head chief Capote Bleu (Blue Coat)—described by an unidentified onlooker [probably 2d Lt. Philip St. George Cooke] as the "best looking Indian" he had ever seen, "his manners are actually fine, a man of natural grace and dignity. . . ." The Pawnees gave consent for the survey; and Dougherty advised them concerning their relationship with the Kansa.

Ref: St. Louis (Mo.) *Beacon*, October 7, 1830; *KHQ*, v. 5, pp. 357, 358.

❏ Early in October, at Cantonment Leavenworth, Isaac McCoy (and his sons Rice and John C.) prepared to survey the north line of the Delaware "outlet" (a 10-mile-wide strip of land north of the Kansa reserve, which, by terms of the 1829 treaty, was to provide the Delawares access to western hunting grounds). "At the garrison we refitted," wrote McCoy, "the number of soldiers being increased to 15, who, together with a Kansas interpreter, who joined us 26 miles west, and an interpreter for Pawnees, Ottoes, and others who joined us 92 miles west, made our whole company 23."

The "outlet" survey began at a point about 46 miles northwest of Cantonment Leavenworth (in what is now northern Jackson county). McCoy's party, on horseback, reached that spot on October 13, and then set a course *due west*. It was a "remarkably dry" season—"an uncommon drought had prevailed throughout that whole region" McCoy later reported. After October 14, when a prairie fire "swept away the grass on both prairies and woodlands . . ." the journey was made with some difficulty. Grass for the horses could rarely be found and the animals failed rapidly. Winds carrying dust and sand, as well as smoke and ashes from the burned prairies, added to the travelers' discomfort.

On October 22 the expedition crossed the Mon-e-ca-to, or Blue Earth (Big Blue) river; reached the Pa-ne-ne-tah, or Pawnee (Republican) river on the 29th; crossed it next day (near present Clifton). On November 5, the north line of the "outlet" having been run 150 miles west, the survey was terminated at a point in southeast Smith county of today—"on the top of a ridge west of Oak creek, not many miles from the present town of Cawker City." "We stopped," McCoy reported, "about forty miles within the region abounding with buffaloes, elks, antelopes, &c." "The country *is* habitable thus far," he wrote in his journal.

Heading homeward (on November 6) down the Solomon (called "Nee-pa-holla"—water on the top of a hill—by the Kansa), McCoy and some of his party took time to visit the great natural curiosity later known as Waconda (or Great Spirit) Spring (about two and a half miles southwest of present Cawker City). To the Kansa it was "Nee-woh-kon-da-ga"—Spirit Water. Moving southeastwardly, the expedition left the waters of the Solomon and crossed to "Nishcoba" (now Chapman) creek, followed it for a time, then turned east to the Republican, and on November 13 camped on the point of land where that river and the Smoky Hill join (near present Junction City, on the Fort Riley reserve). After crossing the Republican, McCoy's weary party, with nearly worn out horses, moved on down the north side of the Kansas river, and on November 19 arrived at the Kansa Agency (in south Jefferson county of today). Isaac McCoy reached the Shawnee Agency (present Johnson county) on November 21.

Ref: *KHQ*, v. 5, pp. 339-377 (especially pp. 361-377) for Isaac McCoy's journal of the 1830 Delaware surveys; 23d Cong., 1st Sess., *Sen. Doc. 512*, v. 2 (Serial 245), pp. 430-440 for Isaac McCoy's comprehensive report covering the 1830 Delaware surveys, the character of the country traversed, the state of the Kansa Indians, with recommendations for improving their lot, and lengthy descriptions of such landmarks as the Indian mounds (near Cantonment Leavenworth) and the Great Spirit Spring (present Mitchell county); *KHC*, v. 4, pp. 304-306 for John C. McCoy's account; Isaac McCoy's *History of Baptist Indian Missions*, pp. 404-412. Now Lake Waconda (formed by water impounded by Glen Elder Dam) covers the Great Spirit Spring.

❧ MARRIED: 2d Lt. Philip St. George Cooke (aged 21) of the Sixth U. S. infantry, and Rachel Wilt Hertzog, of Philadelphia, on October 28, at the Cantonment Leavenworth quarters of Agent John Dougherty and his wife Mary (Hertzog) Dougherty (sister of the bride), by the Rev. John Edwards.

This was *the first wedding of record in present Kansas in which both bride and groom were white persons.* (See Van Quickenborne's June 8, 1830, ceremonies for earliest recorded "Kansas" marriages.)

Ref: St. Louis (Mo.) *Beacon*, November 11, 1830; *KHQ*, v. 22, pp. 97-103. The Cooke-Hertzog marriage was recorded at the Clay county, Mo., courthouse, Liberty, Mo.

❧ In October about 100 of the Delaware Indians living on James' Fork of White river in southwestern Missouri, led by their aged principal chief William Anderson, began the journey to a reserve set aside for them west of the Missouri, north of the Kansas river (and north of the Shawnees). (In late August and early September Chief John Quick had inspected and approved the reserve lands, after making a brief tour with surveyor Isaac McCoy.) By mid-November Anderson's party had established a settlement in present Wyandotte county several miles west of the Kaw's mouth. Many more Delawares had arrived by December 3d. Agent R. W. Cummins wrote on that date:

"Since the arrival of Chief Anderson, the balance of the Nation except those that are on a hunting Expedition, and a few that are still left on James's Fork of White River fifteen or twenty they say, *past my Agency a few days agoe* to the Lands alloted to them on Kansas River. I have not as yet been able to ascertain the precise number, they say about four hundred in all. . . . The principal part of them that are here, are old Men, Women and Children."

Treaties of August 3, 1829 (with the Delawares of Sandusky river, Ohio), and of September 24, 1829 (with the Missouri Delawares), had implemented the land cessions and removal of these Indians. The latter treaty had described the Delawares' reserve and had specified, additionally, an "outlet" to western hunting grounds. Also by its terms the government agreed to provide assistance in moving; farming utensils and tools to build houses; a year's provisions after removal; a grist and saw mill (within two years); an annuity increase from $4,000 to $5,000; and 36 sections of the relinquished Missouri lands were to be set aside to provide funds to educate Delaware children.

On September 22, 1831, Chief Anderson wrote the secretary of war: "I inform you that nearly all our nation are on the land that Government has laid off for us; and I hope . . . that before many years the balance of my nation, who are now scattered, some on Red River and some in the Spanish country, will all come here on this land. We are well pleased with our present situation. The land is good, and also the wood and water, but the game is very scarce."

Ref: SIA, v. 6, pp. 65, 66, 81; *KHQ*, v. 5, pp. 343, 344, 350, 356, 376; C. J. Kappler's *Indian Affairs, Laws and Treaties* (Washington, 1904), v. 2, pp. 303-305; 23d Cong., 1st Sess., *Sen. Doc. 512*, v. 2 (Serial 245), p. 438 (for an Isaac McCoy statement), p. 599 (for Chief Anderson's letter).

❅ In November the Rev. Thomas Johnson and the Rev. Alexander McAlister (Methodists from Missouri) visited the Shawnee Indians and obtained the permission of Fish's (William Jackson's) band to begin a mission among them. It is said that by December 1 the Rev. Thomas Johnson (aged 28) and his bride Sarah T. (Davis) Johnson (aged 20) were established at the chosen site—on a wooded bluff, not far from the Chouteau brothers' Kansas river American Fur Company post. (By present-day description, this first Shawnee Methodist Mission's location was three-fourths of a mile southeast of Turner, Wyandotte county, on the N. E. ¼ of the S. W. ¼, Sec. 24, T. 11, R. 24 E.)

On January 13, 1831, Richard W. Cummins (Shawnee agent) wrote that "Mr. Johnson is at this time making arrangements, and I think shortly after the winter breaks will have the school in operation." He also noted that "the managers of the institution intend instructing the Indian children the arts of Mechanism as well as that of literature." The extent of the Johnsons' missionary efforts during the winter of 1830-1831 is not known. It is thought that the large building (a two-story double log-house, with rooms about 20 feet square) which was to be the Shawnee Methodist Mission headquarters for eight years, was completed by the spring of 1831. (*See* illustration, p. 399.)

Except for a suspension in the latter half of 1831 (when a smallpox epidemic temporarily scattered the Indians), the Methodists' school and mission flourished and prospered. In 1839 the site in present Wyandotte county was abandoned for another near the Missouri line, in what is now Johnson county, where an enlarged Indian manual labor school was built—a school which was in operation till 1862.

Ref: *KHC*, v. 9, pp. 161-174, v. 12, p. xiii (for the mission's location), v. 16, pp. 187-197 (for Turner monument dedication, 1917); SIA, v. 6, p. 96 (Cummins' letter, 1831); Martha B. Caldwell, comp., *Annals of Shawnee Methodist Mission* . . . (Topeka, 1939), especially pp. 8-32, 111. *See, also,* Thomas Johnson's August 16, 1833, letter (copy in "Christopher Collection," in KHi ms. division); Thomas Johnson's letter of July 21, 1834, to Isaac McCoy (in "McCoy Collection," in KHi ms. division); and, for a description of the mission buildings, etc., *see* Office of Indian Affairs (OIA), "Letters Received from the St. Louis Superintendency," National Archives Microcopy 234, Roll 751, under William Clark's letter of November 15, 1836, enclosing Johnson's report, and R. W. Cummins' report.

❡ A short-lived Kansa Methodist Mission was established on December 19 when the Rev. William Johnson (aged 25, brother of Thomas) opened a school at the Kansa Agency. (He had reached that place earlier in the month, to make his home with Daniel M. Boone's family.)

As early as April, 1830, the Rev. Alexander McAlister (presiding elder of the Cape Girardeau, Mo., district) had corresponded with Agent M. G. Clark, and Boone, on the subject of a Methodist school among the Kansa. And in November (from the 19th to the 21st?) McAlister and Johnson had visited the agency to select a site. Baptist missionary Isaac McCoy, in his capacity as U. S. surveyor, had met them there—and noted the fact in his journal on November 20.

Missionary William Johnson, on June 26, 1831, reported:

I opened a school in a room which the agent invited me to occupy; but for three months the weather was so extremely cold that I did but little, there being but few children in a situation to attend school. [The nearest Kansa village was more than 20 miles upriver.] At the close of the winter, we prepared a school house which I now occupy with a small school ["of about ten Indian and six or seven white children"]. We have preaching every Sabbath but there are few who understand the English language well enough to be profited by hearing. . . . [I have] no suitable interpreter . . . [I] apply all my convenient time to study of their language. I have formed a vocabulary of about 600 words. . . .

This is a large and needy field of labour. There are about 1,500 souls in the Kanzas tribe. . . . I view them on the threshold of destruction. . . .

In July, or August, 1831, William Johnson left the Kansa Methodist Mission to attend meetings in Missouri. (Before his departure he had converted some of the Boone family, but no Indians.) He returned to the mission, apparently, for part of the winter of 1831-1832, but then abandoned the field till the fall of 1835.

Ref: William Johnson's letters of June 26 and August 30, 1831, reprinted in *KHC*, v. 16, pp. 227-229; also, *ibid.*, v. 1-2, p. 276, v. 9, pp. 160, 161, 193, 194 (for McAlister), and v. 16, pp. 237, 239, 240; *KHQ*, v. 5, p. 375 (for McCoy); SIA, v. 6, pp. 78, 79 (for M. G. Clark letter of November 21, 1830); Spooner & Howland's *History of American Missions*, p. 543.

❡ Near the Kaw's mouth—where Kansas City, Mo., subsequently developed—these were the residents as listed in the 1830 federal census (so far as can be determined from the Jackson county, Mo., entries): Francis G. Chouteau, Calice Montardy, Francis Tremblé, Pierre Revalette, Louis Roy, and James H. McGee.

Chouteau had settled there in 1826, and with him had come French trappers and voyageurs employed in the Chouteaus' fur trade activities. When Father Joseph A. Lutz (*see* August, 1828, annals) was briefly a resident at the Kaw's mouth in the latter part of 1828, he noted the "little community of nine families" there. Other Frenchmen—besides Chouteau, Montardy, Tremblé, Revalette, and Roy, above—known to have been in the vicinity prior to 1830 (and already mentioned in these annals) were: Gabriel Philibert, Clement Lessert, and "Grand Louis" Bertholet. The McGee family arrived in 1828, apparently.

James H. McGee (in November, 1828) was the first to enter a land claim in the bounds of present Kansas City, Mo. (when a land office opened at Franklin, Mo. that year). Others who made land entries in "Kansas City" in 1831 and 1832 were: Joseph and Gabriel Philibert, Louis ("Grand Louis") Bertholet, Gabriel Prudhomme, Francis G. Chouteau, Clement Lessert, Oliver Caldwell & H. Chiles, W. B. Evans, Calisse Montardy, Pierre La Libertie, Louis Roy, and William Gilliss.

Ref: U. S. census, 1830, Jackson co., Mo. (as abstracted by Mrs. H. E. Poppino, 1956); W. H. Miller's *History of Kansas City* (1881), pp. 12, 13 (for land entry list); G. J. Garraghan's *Catholic Beginnings in Kansas City* . . . (Chicago, 1920), p. 32 (for Lutz).

1831

❡ In January, it is said, Moses R. Grinter (a Kentuckian, aged 21) began operating a Kansas river ferry, from a site on the *north* bank within the Delaware reserve. This was three to four miles above, and across the river from, the Chouteaus' trading post and the newly-founded Shawnee Methodist Mission, in what is now Wyandotte township, Wyandotte county, on the N. W. ¼ of Sec 28, T. 11, R. 24 E. (*See* p. 175 for a ferry operating in 1830.)

For lack of tangible evidence, the date and circumstances of the founding of Grinter's ferry cannot be stated with certainty. According to one account young Grinter arrived in present Kansas in 1828, as a soldier at Cantonment Leavenworth; another says he came from Bardstown, Ky., in 1831. Both versions indicate he was "appointed" by the government in January, 1831, to run a ferry. This suggests an arrangement between Cantonment Leavenworth officials and the Delawares for travel through the Indians' lands, and transportation across the Kansas river. The first records located for this ferry consist of two items in James Kennerly's May, 1833, list of expenditures in conducting Kickapoo immigrants to their reserve above Fort Leavenworth: "Moses R. Grinter, for ferriage of Indians, four wagons and baggage, across the Kansas river [the amount of] $38.75," and "Moses Grinter, for ferriage of 5 wagons and teams across the Kansas river [the amount of] $9.25." In a July 22, 1833, letter, the Rev. Isaac McCoy wrote of a cholera threat which "so alarmed the Delawares, that they removed their ferry boat to prevent travellers from crossing to them." In a July 29, 1833, letter, the Rev. W. D. Smith mentioned that there was, on the Kansas, about 12 miles from the Missouri and two miles from a Shawnee village, "a tolerably good ferry, at which the mail crosses once every week going and returning between the Shawanoe Agency and Cantonment Leavenworth."

Subsequent development of the military road from Fort Leavenworth to Fort Scott in the early 1840's brought increased use of Grinter's ferry (sometimes referred to as Delaware crossing; later as the military crossing; still later, as Secondine crossing). Also, a good many emigrants to Oregon and California crossed the Kansas by way of this ferry in the 1840's and early 1850's. Accounts say that James C. Grinter (a younger brother of Moses) assisted as ferryman from late 1849 to about 1855.

See, also, January, 1836, entry for item on Moses Grinter's marriage.

Ref: *KHC,* v. 9, p. 203n; 23d Cong., 1st Sess., *Sen. Doc. 512,* v. 5 (Serial 248), pp. 74, 79 (for Kennerly items); *KHQ,* v. 2, pp. 264-266 (McCoy item on p. 264), v. 23, p. 178; J. T. Irving, Jr.'s *Indian Sketches,* ed. by J. F. McDermott (Norman, c1955), p. 17 (for Smith item); *Portrait and Biographical Album of Jackson, Jefferson and Pottawatomie Counties, Kansas* (Chicago, 1890), pp. 662, 663 (for James C. Grinter); the 1855 census of Kansas, which listed, in the 16th district, p. 2, Moses and James Grinter (but not their families); the federal census of 1870 for Wyandotte tp., Wyandotte co., listed Moses R. Grinter as aged 61, a native of Kentucky.

❦ January.—Three Mormon missionaries (Oliver Cowdery, Parley P. Pratt, and one other), from a party of five recently arrived at Independence, Mo., entered "Kansas" to visit the Shawnees and newly-arrived Delawares. When Chief Anderson and the Delawares showed interested in Mormon teachings, the missionaries remained with them several days, lodging with James Pool, government blacksmith.

Pratt (at a later time) wrote: ". . . we were soon ordered out of the Indian country as disturbers of the peace," as a result of having "stirred up the jealousy and envy of the Indian agents and sectarian missionaries." At Independence, where the Mormons continued proselytizing efforts among the people of Jackson county, Oliver Cowdery, on February 14, 1831, addressed a letter to William Clark, St. Louis, in which he stated that he had been appointed by a "society of Christians" in the state of New York, to superintend establishment of missions among the Indians; and applied for permission for himself, and others, to "have free intercourse with the several tribes." No further efforts were made by the Mormons to reach the "Kansas" immigrant Indians.

Ref: SIA, v. 6 (typed copy), p. 198; Joseph Smith, *History of the Church of Jesus Christ of Latter-day Saints* (Salt Lake City, 1902), v. 1, pp. 118, 120; Parley P. Pratt,

Autobiography (New York, 1874), pp. 54-61; Warren A. Jennings, "The First Mormon Mission to the Indians," *KHQ*, v. 37 (1971).

❡ About 50 young Kansa warriors, in late March, made a "bloody and unprovoked" raid on the village of the Republican Pawnees (on the Republican river) and returned home with scalps of nine women and children. Kansa leader Hard Chief and his brother Gray Eyes, who went to Cantonment Leavenworth to inform Agent Dougherty, also admitted that within the "last twelve months" Kansa warriors had taken 14 scalps, and stolen between 20 and 30 horses from the Pawnees.

In a report (April 23), Kansa Agent Marston G. Clark, gave a broader picture of his wards' situation:

> The Kanzas Indians are at this time as Retched as human beings can well be the severity of the winter prevented them from hunting and distroyed nearly all their Horses which rendered them incapable to resume their hunting or packing provisions from the white settlements if they had any thing to purchase with; but that is not the case. They ar[e] roving about on foot beging and stealing both food and horses. . . . There natural disposition drivin on allso by distress they have renued the war with the Pawoneys [and] has lately taken scalps and horses. . . .

Ref: SIA, v. 6, p. 164 (for Dougherty's letter of April 7), and pp. 179, 180 (for M. G. Clark's letter).

❡ Late in March some Wea Indians who had removed from Indiana in the autumn of 1830 and spent the winter "in the Mississippi [river] swamps" joined their relatives (*see* 1828 and July, 1830, entries) on the Wea and Piankeshaw reserve in present Miami county. About the same time 19 Kaskaskia Indians—the entire remnant (it was stated) of a once-populous nation—reached the village of their relatives, the Peorias, on the Marais des Cygnes in what is now Franklin county. (The Peoria and Kaskaskia reserve adjoined the Wea and Piankeshaw reserve on the west, and both were immediately south of the Shawnee lands.)

Agent R. W. Cummins reported that the Wea newcomers were in a starving condition and that he had furnished them with two wagon loads of corn, and some pork. They were, he wrote, too poor to purchase farming tools, but appeared very humble and willing to work.

Ref: SIA, v. 6, pp. 166-168 (for Cummins' letters of April 2 and 3, 1831); 23d Cong., 1st Sess., *Sen. Doc. 512*, v. 2 (Serial 245), p. 117; and *ibid.*, v. 5 (Serial 248), pp. 4, 7, 502. In July, 1826, when the Kaskaskias had arrived at St. Louis (en route to a Missouri "home," where they remained till 1831) it was reported that the "whole remnant of that great Nation consists at this time of 31 Soles[!]—15 men mixed, 10 women, 6 children."—*see* KHQ, v. 16, p. 14.

❡ Between the 1st and 22d of April, Missionaries Nathaniel B.

Dodge (of Boudinot), William F. Vaill (of Union), and Cephas Washburn (of Dwight), made a tour, on horseback, of Western Creek, and Osage settlements.

They went first to the Western Creek (or Muscogee) Indians—departing from Union Mission (in present Mayes co., Okla.) on April 1, and traveling about 25 miles southward. (Some 2,500 to 3,000 Creeks had emigrated from Georgia and Alabama between 1827 and 1831 and settled near the junction of the Arkansas and Verdigris rivers.) The Protestant ministers spent two days among them, and returned to Union on April 4.

On April 6 the three missionaries set out for Clermont's village of Osages— about 25 miles west and a little north of Union. (Young Clermont gave them indifferent treatment.) They returned to Union on April 8, but started next day for New Hopefield (*see* Spring, 1830, entry) about 20(?) miles northward. (There, they had a better reception.) On April 11 they rode to "La Bett" creek crossing (in present Labette county) 40 miles distant; and next day reached Boudinot (*see* March, 1830, entry) 30 miles above "La Bett" and on the north side of the Neosho (in present Neosho county).

At White Hair's town (two miles from Boudinot, and across the river) on April 13, the missionaries preached before a good-sized audience assembled at White Hair's house (the chief was absent, however). Two days later they held services at Wasooche's town 16 miles upriver (where they met Agent P. L. Chouteau), and visited other small towns of White Hair's people. On April 16 they rode to the Little Osages' (or Walk-in-Rain's) town—the farthest north Osage village (also in present Neosho county). It was, Vaill reported, ". . . probably larger than either of White Hair's, but not so large as Clermont's."

The missionaries returned to Agent Chouteau's residence (15 miles south, between the two White Hair villages) on April 18, where, after dinner, they spoke before an assemblage of persons—Americans, Frenchmen, Negroes, and Osages—to the number of 50 or 60. They proceeded to Boudinot; and from there, on April 19, Vaill and Washburn set out for Union Mission, reaching it on the 22d.

Ref: *Missionary Herald*, v. 27, pp. 286-289 (for Vaill's journal); J. O. Choules and T. Smith's *The Origin & History of Missions*, 4th ed. (Boston, 1837), v. 2, p. 385.

❡ The American Fur Company's new and handsome *Yellowstone* (the first steamboat to be employed in the mountain trade) left St. Louis April 16 on her initial upper Missouri voyage. She arrived at Cantonment Leavenworth on May 1. Aboard, as a passenger, was Pierre Chouteau, Jr., the company's Western Department head, on whose orders the boat had been constructed during the winter of 1830-1831. (*See* reproduction of a Charles Bodmer 1833 painting of the steamboat, p. 400.)

By June 19 the *Yellowstone* had reached the company's post Fort Tecumseh (in present South Dakota)—the high point of her trip.

[*Continued on p. 201*]

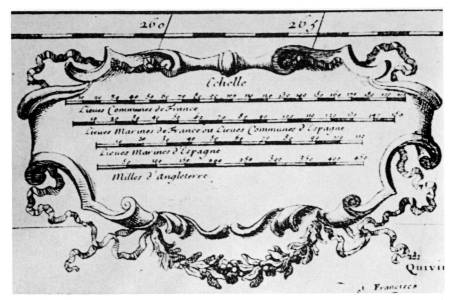

Above (enlarged from Delisle's map of 1703) is a scale of distances showing comparative lengths of (1) the French land league, (2) the French marine league and Spanish land league [same], (3) the Spanish marine league, and (4) the English mile.

The *league* as a measure of distance has varied for different times and countries from 2.4 to 4.6 miles. Historians, tracing routes of the pre-19th century Spanish and French explorers, have estimated the league, generally, as between 2.5 and 3 miles; and seldom as more than 2.6 miles for the *land* league.

Above is a section of Guillaume Delisle's *Carte du Mexique et de la Floride* . . 1703. The Cansa Indians are shown living on the Metchigamiki river, a name not found in later records.

Kansa Indians sketched by George Catlin, probably in 1832. From left to right: Sho-me-kos-see (The Wolf), a chief; Wa-hon-ga-she (No Fool); Chesh-oo-honga-ha (The Man of Good Sense); Mesch-o-shin-ga (The Little White Bear). In front are one Kansa's wife and child. Sketch courtesy of the New York Public Library.

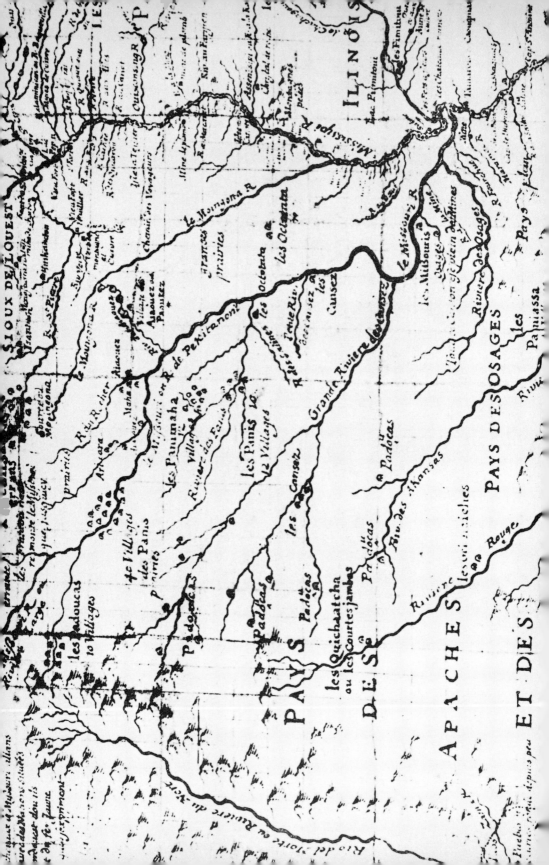

A portion of Guillaume Delisle's *Carte de la Louisiane et du Cours du Mississipi* . . . 1718. Here, the Kansas river ("Grande Riviere des Cansez") appeared by that name for the second time on a map, so far as is known. As located by Delisle, the Kansa Indians were living in the early 18th century in two, far-apart villages, one, between the forks of a Kansas tributary, the other, on the Missouri, at the mouth of a stream labeled "Petite Riv. des Cansez."

". . . Upstream is a smaller river which flows into the Missouri, called the 'Rivière d'Ecanzé' [Kansas]. . . This is the finest country and the most beautiful land in the world; the prairies are like the seas, and filled with wild animals; especially oxen, cattle, hind and stag, in such quantities as to surpass the imagination. . ."

—Quoted from the 1717 account of Bourgmont, whose explorations up the Missouri supplied much new information for Delisle's 1718 map.

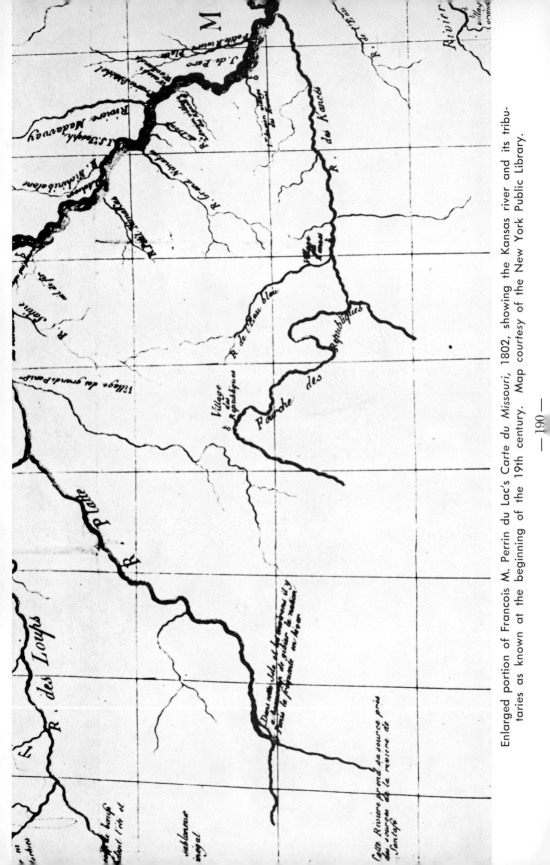

Enlarged portion of Francois M. Perrin du Lac's *Carte du Missouri*, 1802, showing the Kansas river and its tributaries as known at the beginning of the 19th century. Map courtesy of the New York Public Library.

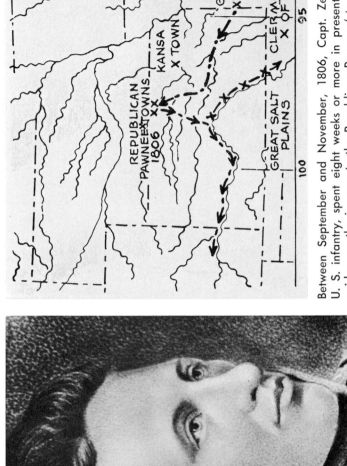

Between September and November, 1806, Capt. Zebulon M. Pike, First U. S. infantry, spent eight weeks or more in present Kansas. His Osage guides, on the journey to the Republican Pawnees' town on the Republican river, carefully avoided the country of the Kansa—their enemies. (But Pike arranged a tentative Osage-Kansa peace treaty while at the Pawnee village when a small party of Kansa visited him there.)

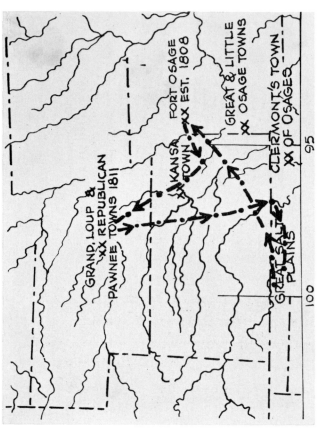

Between May and July, 1811, George C. Sibley, Fort Osage factor, spent about six weeks in present Kansas. With Osage companions he visited the Kansa and the Pawnees. (In the five-year interval—1806-1811—notable changes had occurred: the Republican Pawnees had moved to the Loup Fork of the Platte; Fort Osage had been established; and a permanent Kansa-Osage peace had been effected—through Sibley's efforts.)

Pawnee pictograph of a Pawnee-Kansa battle which occurred (at some time prior to 1819) when 18 Kansa warriors, approaching a Pawnee town on foot to steal horses and take scalps, were discovered, attacked, and killed to the last man in a stubborn fight, by a larger, mounted band of Pawnees. (See, also, the following page.)

Auguste P. Chouteau (headed west with Jules de Mun and some trappers) first crossed present Kansas in the fall of 1815. His fight with Pawnees during an early-1816 trip *down* the Arkansas led to the naming of "Chouteau's Island" in what is now Kearny county. Returning to the mountains, Chouteau, de Mun, and party fell into Spanish hands during the winter of 1816-1817; were jailed for 48 days; had their furs, equipment, and best horses confiscated. Chouteau then concentrated on trade with the Osage Indians. In 1821 (and probably in earlier years) he accompanied the Osages on their summer hunt in what is now Kansas.

←—— Photograph of a hand-colored engraving which reproduced Artist Titian R. Peale's 1819 *sketch* of the Pawnee artist's pictograph portrayed in bright red, yellow, green, and black on a buffalo robe presented to Agent Benjamin O'Fallon at a Pawnee council in 1819. The engraving was published in 1822 in the volume of maps and illustrations which accompanied the first (1823) edition of Edwin James' *An Account of an Expedition* [by Maj. S. H. Long] *From Pittsburgh to the Rocky Mountains.*

Sixteen of the Pawnees are armed with shields. The heads of many of them are decorated with buffalo horns and feathers, or feathers only. They are armed with spears, battle axes, and one or two with firearms. One carries a flag of feathers; another a whip. In the original pictograph the Pawnee figures were marked so they could be identified. Many of the horses are shown with human scalps hanging from their mouths (a common ornament for warriors' horses); two have brands. The Kansa are armed with bows and arrows, and firearms. Nine are shown headless; wounds are indicated by the flowing of blood from the wounded part.

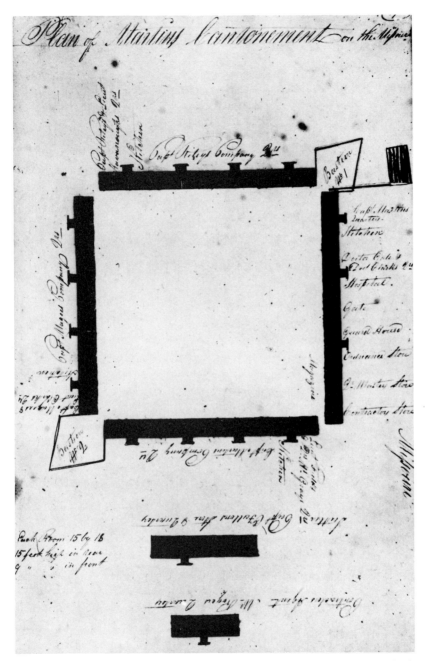

"Plan of Martin's Cantonment on the Missouri, October 31, 1818," which accompanied the ms. Henry Atkinson "Journal," 1818-1820. It is in Yale's Coe collection, and is reproduced here through the *courtesy of* the Yale University Library, New Haven, Conn. (*See* pp. 79, 80.)

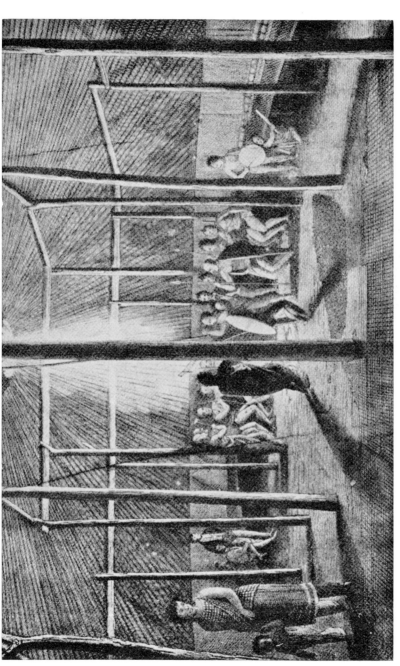

A dog dance by the Kansa Indians, August 24, 1819, at their village two miles east of present Manhattan, as sketched by Samuel Seymour of Maj. Stephen H. Long's expedition, and published in 1822.

A section of the Fremont-Gibbs-Smith map, reproduced from Robert W. Baughman's *Kansas in Maps*. The dotted line following up the Kansas and Republican rivers, then looping northeast to the Platte, shows the route Jedediah Smith and fur trappers took in the winter of 1825-1826. (See pp. 130, 131.)

White Plume (Mon-chonsia; or Nom-pa-wa-rah), who was for some years considered head chief of the Kansa Indians. Portrait (1821?) by artist Charles Bird King, as reproduced from the McKenney and Hall *History of the Indian Tribes of North America.*

Duke Paul Wilhelm of Wuerttemberg in 1844. As a prince in 1823, on his first journey to North America, he traveled up the Missouri in the summer of 1823 and returned in the fall. A planned excursion up the Kansas, in June, was abandoned when the hordes of mosquitoes his party encountered a few miles upriver spoiled the outing. ("Photograph" reproduced, by permission, from the *New Mexico Historical Review*, Albuquerque, July, 1942.)

"Arrival of the Caravan at Santa Fe" (from Josiah Gregg's Commerce of the Prairies, first published in 1844). The earliest extensive use of wheeled vehicles on the trail was in 1824, when 20 dearborns, two road wagons, two carts, and one "small piece of cannon" were in the Santa Fe-bound trading caravan.

[Continued From p. 184]
(No previous steamboat had gone beyond the Council Bluffs.) On July 15, with a cargo of furs, she was back at St. Louis, having inaugurated a new era in steamboat travel on the Missouri. American Fur Company boats thereafter made annual voyages to the river's upper waters, carrying men, supplies, and a few passengers.

Ref: St. Louis (Mo.) *Beacon*, April 14, 1831; H. M. Chittenden's *History of Early Steamboat Navigation on the Missouri River* . . . (New York, 1903), v. 1, pp. 112, 134-137; *KHC*, v. 9, p. 280; John Dougherty's March, 1832, report (typed copy), p. 22, in Dougherty Collection (KHi ms. division) for May 1 date.

❡ Other steamboats scheduling trips on the Missouri in April were the *Globe* (to Cantonment Leavenworth), the *Liberty* (to Franklin, Mo.), and the *Missouri* (to Liberty, Mo.). (Beginning in July, the *Chieftain* also entered the Missouri river trade, advertising runs to Liberty and intermediate ports.)

Ref: *Missouri Republican*, St. Louis, March 29, April 12, July 5, 26, and November 1, 1831 (as examples)—as noted in *Nebraska Historical Society Publications*, Lincoln, v. 20, p. 52.

❡ John Gantt and Jefferson Blackwell headed an overland trapping-and-trading expedition of 70 mounted men which left St. Louis on April 24 for the Rocky mountains. At Fort Osage (Mo.) they obtained food supplies. At the mouth of the Kansas they spent two or three days trading with Indians, then proceeded up the river, along its north bank, as far as the "Republican" fork. These adventurers then followed the "Republican's" course for many miles, turning northward only when provisions ran low and little game could be found. They reached the Platte several days' travel below its forks. (The Gantt-Blackwell party subsequently wintered on Laramie river, undergoing severe hardships.)

In 1839 a small volume entitled *Narrative of the Adventures of Zenas Leonard* . . . was published at Clearfield, Pa. Author Leonard opened the *Narrative* with an account of his journey west with the Gantt-Blackwell expedition in 1831 (when he was 22), and described subsequent adventures during five years of trapping and trading in the Rockies. Zenas Leonard, retiring from mountain life at the age of 26, settled at Sibley, Mo. (adjoining old Fort Osage), in 1836; died there in 1857 at the age of 48.

Ref: John C. Ewers, editor, *Adventures of Zenas Leonard* . . . (Norman, Okla., c1959), especially pp. xvii-xxiv, 3-7; 22d Cong., 1st Sess., *House Doc. 121* (Serial 219) for item on a three-year trading license issued to Gantt & Blackwell on April 5, 1831. It may be that this party went up the Big and Little Blue rather than the Republican.

❡ From a camp 10 miles southwest of Independence, Mo., a good-sized caravan set out about May 4 for New Mexico. This was the initial venture in the Santa Fe trade of Jedediah Smith and his former partners David Jackson and William Sublette. The outfit totaled 74 men and 22 mule-drawn wagons (one carrying a six-pounder). Smith owned 11 wagons; Jackson and Sublette had 10; and the gun carrier was joint property. Among this company were Peter and Austin Smith (Jedediah's brothers), Samuel Parkman, Jonathan T. Warner; and mountain man Thomas Fitzpatrick joined the party late. A few more men and two wagons (one belonging to Samuel Flournoy of Independence, Mo.) had joined near the frontier. There were, apparently, 85 persons in all, in the expedition.

On the "pawnee fork" on May 19 a young man, E. S. Minter (clerk to Jackson and Sublette), was killed by Indians ("we supose by the pawnees," wrote Sublette), while some distance from his comrades in pursuit of antelope. A few days later the caravan forded the Arkansas and began the 60-mile journey across the Cimarron desert (during a particularly dry season). On May 27 when lack of water had created a situation critical for the teams, parties set out in search of the Cimarron. Jedediah Smith and Fitzpatrick headed south. The two separated and Smith was never seen again by his comrades. Later, some time after the expedition (which did locate water) reached Santa Fe (on July 4), Smith's fate was learned. Austin Smith purchased his brother's gun and pistols from Mexicans who had obtained them, and an account of Jedediah's death, while bartering with the Comanches who had slain him. He wrote home to his father, in September:

> Your Son Jedediah was killed on the Semerone the 27th of May on his way to Santa Fé by the Curmanch Indians, his party was in distress for water, and he had gone alone in search of the above river which he found, when he was attacked by fifteen or twenty of them—they succeeded in alarming his animal not daring to fire on him so long as they kept face to face, so soon as his horse turned they fired, and wounded him in the shoulder he then fired his gun, and killed their head chief it is supposed they then *rushed* upon him, and despatched him. . . .

It has been said that Jedediah Smith was killed at or near Wagon Bed Spring in present Grant county. Ezra D. Smith (in a letter in 1915) stated that his great-uncle was killed

> at a water hole known in my time as Fargo Spring, to the later Santa Fe traders as Wagon Body Spring. Do not confuse this with Wagon Bed Spring just above the confluence of the dry Cimarron with the Cimarron. This water hole was . . . on the north side of the Cimarron at the mouth of a canyon which comes down from the north, and is near the west line of Seward county, Kansas.

Whether in Grant or Seward county, there seems little doubt that Jedediah Smith met his death in present southwest Kansas.

Ref: Morgan, *op. cit.*, pp. 325-330, 433-436; Austin Smith's letter of September 24, 1831, in KHi ms. division; an article on Jedediah Smith by Ezra D. Smith is in *KHC*, v. 12, pp. 252-260, but his letter quoted above is printed in Morgan, *op. cit.*, p. 436; William L. Sublette's letter of September 24, 1831, is quoted in *ibid.*, pp. 435, 436. In *Robert Newell's Memoranda*, edited by Dorothy O. Johansen, p. 32, Newell says (from the upper Missouri): "The Spring of 1831 Mr. Fitzpatrick went to St. Louis for Supplies. . . ." *The 1962 Brand Book of the Denver Posse of The Westerners* (Denver, 1963), pp. 273-290, contains Harry E. Chrisman's article, "Here They Killed Jed Smith" (on the Wagon Body, or Fargo Spring site). The David E. Jackson estate papers, in the Ste. Genevieve county, Mo., courthouse, show that the young man "Minter" was E. S. Minter. (This item courtesy of Dale L. Morgan.)

❧ Repenting their past winter's depredations against the Western Creeks (Muscogees), and the Cherokees of Arkansas river, Clermont's band of Osages (residing on the Verdigris, near present Claremore, Okla.) asked Agent Paul Ligueste Chouteau to arrange peace talks. At Cantonment Gibson [Okla.] on May 5 a delegation representing all the Osage bands met with the Western Creeks and a peace-and-friendship treaty was signed on May 10. A similar treaty was made with the Western Cherokees on May 18. In both instances the Osages agreed to return stock stolen, and to pay for property destroyed. Most of the 1831 annuity funds of Clermont's band were required to make restitution.

Ref: SIA, v. 6, pp. 209-212, 215, 216; 23d Cong., 1st Sess., *Sen. Doc. 512*, v. 2 Serial 245), pp. 457-459, 497-506 (the treaties are on pp. 500-506), v. 3 (Serial 246), pp. 238, 449.

❧ Daniel M. Boone, agriculturist for the Kansa Indians (with headquarters at the Kansa Agency) since early 1827, was dismissed in May, but approved of the "alteration in the farming business" which cost him his job. (He asked, however, to be reimbursed for hogs and cattle stolen by the Kansa; and to remain at the agency till fall to harvest his crops.)

Agent Marston G. Clark was enthusiastic about the new plan of maintaining farms *at the Kansa towns*. He wrote William Clark on July 5:

. . . I have men fencing a 16 acre field, build[ing] a large cabbin at the Upper Village [Hard Chief's?], I can now do something for the Kansas with the Money formerly thrown away on the Agriculturists.

By October an agriculturist was again on the Kansa Agency pay roll (*see* September, 1832, entry). In succeeding years a number of other men served for brief periods as farmers for the Kansa.

Ref: SIA, v. 6, pp. 187-189 (for Boone's letter), and pp. 225, 226 (for Clark's letter).

❧ On May 27 the annual spring caravan for Santa Fe, captained by Elisha Stanley, left the rendezvous at Council Grove. There were more than 200 persons (including a few Spanish women returning home—*see* autumn, 1829, eastbound trip), nearly 100 wagons (*about half were drawn by oxen*, the rest pulled by mules), 12 dearborns, and other light vehicles, also two small cannon. (For first? use of oxen by Santa Fe *traders see* May, 1830, entry.) The merchandise carried was estimated at $200,000.

In this company, on his first journey to the southwest, was 24-year-old Josiah Gregg, whose later-written *Commerce of the Prairies* (published in 1844) was to become the classic account of the first 20-odd years of the Santa Fe trade.

The caravan crossed the Arkansas on June 11; pitched camp that evening "opposite the celebrated 'Caches' . . ."; proceeded on the 14th by way of the desert route. In the Cimarron valley on the 19th, a horde of Indian warriors (Blackfeet and Gros Ventres, by Gregg's account) and their families (perhaps 3,000 persons in all) descended to the same vicinity and camped. Either in late July or early August the expedition reached Santa Fe. (By October 11 some of these traders, traveling with the regular fall eastbound company, were back in Missouri, their trip a successful one.)

Ref: Gregg, *op. cit.*, v. 1, pp. 50-111, 305; *Missouri Intelligencer*, Columbia, October 15, 1831; 22d Cong., 1st Sess., *Sen. Doc.* 90 (Serial 213), pp. 31, 76; also Josiah Gregg's *Commerce of the Prairies*, ed. by Max L. Moorhead (Norman, Okla., c1954), pp. xviii, xix, 26-77.

❧ DIED: Dunning D. McNair, recent appointee as Osage subagent (at Neosho River Agency), on June 2, McNair was killed by a bolt of lightning while crossing a prairie. He was buried at Union Mission (Okla.).

DIED: Nathaniel Pryor, subagent to the Osages of the Verdigris (Clermont's band), on June 9. He had made his headquarters at Cantonment Gibson (Okla.). (*See* 1807 annals for earliest reference to Pryor.)

Ref: SIA, v. 6, pp. 208, 209, 215; St. Louis (Mo.) *Beacon*, July 31, 1831. For the subagents who replaced McNair and Pryor, *see* September, 1832, annals entry.

❧ Baptist missionary and physician Johnston Lykins, his wife Delilah (McCoy) Lykins, and family, arrived at the Shawnee Agency on July 7 to found a mission for William Perry's and Cornstalk's bands of Shawnee Indians. (Isaac McCoy had obtained the chiefs' permission for the mission in November, 1830.)

In the late summer (when the Baptist board failed to provide building funds in 1831), Lykins bought "a small tract of U. S. land, immediately on the line of the State of Missouri" [just east of the Shawnee reserve—in Jackson county, Mo.] and built "at his own cost" a home for his family. Little missionary work was accomplished in 1831—due largely to the smallpox outbreak among the Indians.

In June, 1832, money was available for erection of the Shawnee Baptist Mission buildings. The site chosen was something over two miles northwest of the Shawnee Agency, and about three miles south (and a little east) of the Shawnee Methodist Mission (as *then* situated—*see* November, 1830, entry). By present-day description, the Baptist mission was in the N. E. ¼ of Sec. 5, T. 12, R. 25 E., in Mission township, Johnson county. (*See* sketch in this volume.)

The Rev. Alexander Evans, who (with his wife and family) had arrived before mid-June, was conducting a small school for Indian children at least as early as September. After visiting Shawnee Baptist Mission on October 3, Isaac McCoy wrote:

"Their houses are not completed, but are so that they can be occupied, except in school house. . . . They will be substantial and comfortable buildings and are pretty well situated. A few Indian children attend though not regularly and study lessons in school. They [the Evans] have opened their house for public religious worship few Indians as yet attend Bro. Evans [is] a little discouraged."

By November, 1832, another missionary, Daniel French, had come from Ohio as assistant to Dr. Johnston Lykins.

Shawnee Baptist Mission continued in operation till the mid-1850's.

Ref: Johnston Lykins' "Journal," and Isaac McCoy's "Journal," in KHi ms. division; Isaac McCoy's *History of Baptist Indian Missions*, pp. 347, 404, 422; Spooner & Howland's *History of American Missions* . . ., p. 540; *KHQ*, v. 5, pp. 343, 376, 377 (for McCoy's activities, 1830). *The Herald of Freedom*, Lawrence, March 3, 1855, issue, contains an article on the mission.

¶ At Cantonment Leavenworth, on July 8, Alexander G. Morgan, post sutler, was appointed postmaster—an office he continued to hold for more than six years. Alexander G. Morgan and his wife America (Higgins) Morgan had been "Kansas" residents for at least a year, and probably somewhat longer.

Ref: *KHC*, v. 1-2, p. 255, or v. 7, p. 441; Fayette county, Ky., Marriage Book 1, p. 63, has record of marriage of Alexander G. Morgan to America Higgins on September 25, 1823 (this information courtesy Kentucky Historical Society). Lacking any information to the contrary, this compiler has assumed it was America Morgan who came to live in "Kansas."

¶ Surveyors Isaac McCoy, John Donelson, and Dr. Rice McCoy (with some hired hands), left Union Mission (Okla.) July 9, on horseback, to travel northeastwardly to the southwest corner of Missouri. At that place, on July 18, their paths diverged, each to undertake a separate project.

Donelson moved southward. He ran a traverse line to Fort Smith—the 77-mile boundary between the Cherokee lands and the Territory of Arkansas. Dr. Rice McCoy moved northward. After marking the line between the Cherokees' reserve and the state of Missouri, he then determined where the northeast corner of the Cherokees' lands should be. (Later, in mid-August,

Isaac McCoy and two Cherokee delegates visited that area for final agreement on the northeast corner location.)

Isaac McCoy (with a servant, and an interpreter, Stephen Van Rensselaer—half-Osage), headed northwest towards the Osage Agency. He reached Boudinot Mission July 23, and arrived on July 25 at the agency where a military escort—Capt. Edgar S. Hawkins, Asst. Surg. John W. Baylor, and 25 Seventh U. S. infantrymen from Cantonment Gibson (Okla.)—awaited him. McCoy and party set out July 28 on a tour of exploration ("to explore the Osage lands . . . with a view of ascertaining whether the Chickasaws might not be located there, and the Osages [moved northward] to be placed along side of the Kansas"). McCoy later reported: "We proceeded along the northern boundary of the Osage lands west about 120 miles from the State of Missouri [into present Butler county]; thence, south across the Osage reserve [through Butler and Cowley counties], which brought us to the Arkansas river [probably a little south of the Kansas-Oklahoma line of today]. We then turned east along the southern boundary of the Osage lands." On August 6 the party turned southeast; reached Clermont's town on August 12; and arrived at Union Mission (McCoy's headquarters) late that night. The soldiers continued on to Fort Gibson.

In his report (dated August 18) covering all these activities, Isaac McCoy recommended that the Chickasaws be located "on the south bank of Canadian and Arkansas river" if "an arrangement to that effect can be made with the Choctaws"; and suggested "that the removal of the several bands of . . . [non-reservation] Osages—one . . . in Arkansas Territory, one on the Creek lands, and one on the lands of Cherokees to a tract adjoining their kindred, the Kansas, is exceedingly desirable."

Ref: 23d Cong., 1st Sess., *Sen Doc. 512*, v. 2 (Serial 245), pp. 561-564 (for McCoy's report); McCoy's *History of Baptist Indian Missions*, pp. 418-421.

BORN: at Shawnee Methodist Mission (present Wyandotte county), on July 18, Alexander McAlister Johnson, first child of the Rev. Thomas and Sarah T. (Davis) Johnson. (He died less than a month later—on August 15.)

Ref: *KHC*, v. 12, p. xii.

❧ In the summer Lucien Fontenelle, Andrew Drips, and some 30 trappers came down from the mountains, reaching the Missouri (probably at Bellevue, "Neb."), in September(?). They were accompanied by three Nez Perces and one Flathead, bound for Missouri to seek information on Christianity. The Indian delegation, traveling down the Missouri with Fontenelle (Drips going back to the mountains), reached St. Louis by October 1.

Black Eagle (Nez Perce war chief) died there on October 31; and the Flathead died soon afterwards. (The two remaining Nez Perces were on the *Yellowstone* going up the Missouri in 1832. One died on the upper river; the other was killed by Blackfeet before he reached home.)

Ref: Ferris, *op. cit.*, p. 96; Bernard De Voto, *Across the Wide Missouri*, pp. 7-10, 13-15.

❆ Smallpox broke out among the Shawnees in mid-summer; and about October 1 it spread to the Delawares (north of the Kansas river).

When Dr. Johnston Lykins, in company with Subagent Campbell, visited the Shawnee settlements on July 18 to vaccinate "a considerable number" of persons, more than 20 Indians had been stricken, with one death reported. (At Cantonment Leavenworth, during the summer, Dr. Thomas S. Bryant also vaccinated some Indians.) When the disease struck the Delawares, Agent R. W. Cummins advised them to scatter to avoid an epidemic. The Rev. Thomas Johnson, returning to Shawnee Methodist Mission on October 21 (after a journey to Missouri) found everything "in a state of confusion; the small pox was raging among different tribes, and the Indians flying in different directions."

It was reported in November that about a dozen Shawnees had died but that "among them the disease appears to be discontinued"; among the Delawares "it still exists . . . and many of them have died." By late December the outbreak had subsided and the Indians were returning home. Isaac McCoy (in March, 1832) stated that the toll was nine Shawnees and 15 Delawares. (*See, also,* October entry.)

Ref: Johnston Lykins' "Journal," *loc. cit.,* Isaac McCoy's "Journal," *loc. cit.;* SIA, v. 6, p. 375 (Cummins' November 9, 1831, letter); KHC, v. 16, pp. 236, 237 (Johnson's December 29, 1831, letter); 22d Cong., 2d Sess., *H. Doc. No. 137* (Serial 235), p. 3 (for Cantonment Leavenworth item); 23d Cong., 1st Sess., *Sen. Doc. 512,* v. 3 (Serial 246), p. 239. A John Campbell letter of 1831, in the Isaac McCoy collection (KHi ms. division) is another reference source.

❆ Bound for Taos, N. M., Charles Bent, with 30 to 40 mounted men and 10 wagons drawn by oxen, left Independence, Mo., on September 10. In this party was a young Easterner, Albert Pike (afterwards prominent in Arkansas as journalist, lawyer, and Confederate officer), who had joined at St. Louis. According to his later-written account, this small expedition reached Taos by November 10, after being delayed in the mountains for a week by a blizzard.

William Rogers Schenck, of Warren County, Ohio (according to a descendant's letter), left Cincinnati February 3, 1831; went to St. Louis, then to Independence, and from there to Santa Fe in the party which included Albert Pike. This account says there were 75(?) men; that the 10-wagon train (all but one drawn by oxen) was fitted out by "Carter" Bent, Frederick Billon, and a man named Holliday. The party left St. Louis August 10; set out from Independence between September 5 and 10; got into Taos (some on one day, some on another) between November 9 and 15, 1831. (Schenck came back with the party of early 1833.)

The advantages of oxen were noted by Thomas Forsyth (writing from St. Louis, to the secretary of war, October 24, 1831): ". . . if he [Charles

Bent] succeeds with his ox wagons, the oxen will answer the tripple purpose of, 1st, drawing the wagons; 2d, the Indians will not steal them as they would horses and mules; 3d, in cases of necessity, part of the oxen will answer for provisions." (Forsyth seemingly was unaware that traders of the Santa Fe-bound spring caravan of 1831, and probably of the 1830 expedition, too, had made use of ox teams.)

Ref: 22d Cong., 1st Sess., Sen. Doc. 90 (Serial 213), pp. 31, 77 (for Forsyth letter); Maurice Fulton and Paul Horgan, editors, *New Mexico's Own Chronicle* . . . (Dallas, c1937), pp. 103, 104; William Waldo's "Recollections . . ." in *Glimpses of the Past*, St. Louis, v. 5, p. 91; Lavender, *op. cit.*, pp. 128, 129, 385; *Old Santa Fe*, Santa Fe, v. 2 (October, 1914), pp. 207-211 (for the Schenck material). Annie H. Abel, in *Chardon's Journal* . . ., p. 235, cites, as an Albert Pike reference source, a "MS. Autobiography" in the Scottish Rite Temple, Washington, D. C.

❡ Dɪᴇᴅ: William Anderson, aged head chief of the Delaware nation, in the latter part of September, at his home on the Delaware reserve, present Wyandotte county. He had been a "Kansas" resident less than one year. Though Anderson had some white blood, according to missionary Johnston Lykins, he had "shewed but little disposition to embrace . . . [white man's] manners and customs. . . ."

The chief's death (*possibly* from the then-prevalent smallpox) occurred after September 22, on which date Anderson wrote a letter in which he made mention of his four sons: Captains Shounack (Shawanock), Pushkies, Secondyan (Secondine), and Sacacoxy (Sarcoxie).

Ref: 23d Cong., 1st Sess., Sen. Doc. 512, v. 2 (Serial 245), pp. 599, 718; Johnston Lykins' "Journal," *loc. cit.*, in an 1831 entry (for item on Anderson's death). At a latet time "Secondine" was the name of a Wyandotte county post office (from 1856-1859), and "Sarcoxie" was the name of a Jefferson county post office (from 1889-1901).

❡ Smallpox was epidemic among the Pawnee Indians in October. Agent John Dougherty reported (from Cantonment Leavenworth) on October 29:

I have returned from a visit to the four Pawnee villages, all of whom I found in a most deplorable condition. Indeed their misery defies all description. Judging from what I saw during the four days I spent with them, and the information I received from the chiefs and two Frenchmen who reside with them . . . I am fully persuaded that one half the whole number of souls of each village have and will be carried off by this cruel and frightful distemper. They told me that not one under 33 years of age escaped the monstrous disease, it having been that length of time [*i. e.*, 1798?] since it visited them before.

They were dying so fast, and taken down at once in such large numbers, that they had ceased to bury their dead. . . . Their misery was so great and so general, that they seemed to be unconscious of it, and to look upon the dead and dying as they would on so many dead horses. . . .

Dr. Johnston Lykins reported (in February, 1832) that John Dougherty *believed* that more than 4,000(?) Pawnees, Otoes, Omahas, and Poncas had died of the smallpox. About 160(?) Indians of the three latter tribes had succumbed before vaccination checked the disease among them.

Ref: 22d Cong., 1st Sess., *H. Ex. Doc. 190* (Serial 220), pp. 1-3; 23d Cong., 1st Sess., *Sen. Doc. 512,* v. 2 (Serial 245), p. 718, v. 3 (Serial 246), p. 239; Isaac McCoy's *History of Baptist Indian Missions,* pp. 442, 443.

❡ MARRIED: Capt. William N. Wickliffe, of the Sixth U. S. infantry, and Ann Hertzog, on November 14, at the Cantonment Leavenworth residence of Agent John Dougherty and Mary (Hertzog) Dougherty, by the Rev. John Edwards. (The bride was a sister of the agent's wife and of P. St. George Cooke's wife.)

Ref: St. Louis (Mo.) *Beacon,* December 15, 1831. The marriage was recorded at the Clay county, Mo., courthouse, Liberty, Mo.

❡ In late November, five men of a Wyandot exploring delegation from Ohio—a delegation headed by William Walker (a white man married to a Wyandot)—spent six days in the lower Little Platte country (across the Missouri from present Leavenworth county); and then returned home after making an adverse report on the lands they had "examined." James B. Gardiner (agent), who had arranged the $1,000 trip, subsequently wrote the secretary of war about the Wyandots' junket:

. . . The delegation *never saw the country* which I had proffered to them in behalf of the Government. They spent but *one night* in the woods. They were but six days in all on the western line of the State of Missouri, and . . . they occupied most of that time in the sports of bear-hunting on horseback, and with dogs. [The Wyandots were supposed to cross west of the Missouri on their tour if they were displeased with the Little Platte country.] Their 'report,' . . . is, I am thoroughly convinced, an ingenious tissue of preconcerted misrepresentation. . . .

(The Wyandots—the last Indians to leave Ohio—retained their homes in that state for 12 more years—moving in 1843 to present Wyandotte county—on lands purchased from the Delawares.)

Ref: 23d Cong., 1st Sess., *Sen. Doc. 512* (Serial 246), pp. 7, 8, 10, 11, 153-168; *KHQ,* v. 15, pp. 248-262.

❡ On December 19 a party of 17 left Union Mission (Okla.) to travel northward. Isaac McCoy, his wife, son John C., and younger McCoys totaled seven persons. The others were McCoy's assistant surveyors (one of them John Donelson, of Tennessee), and hired hands, returning to homes in Missouri. (Winter weather had forced the discontinuance of surveying.)

They made camp on "La Bete" creek (in present Labette county) on December 21st; passed White Hair's Osage towns (in present Neosho county) next day; reached Harmony Mission (Mo.) on Christmas Day and remained over night; arrived at Independence, Mo., on December 28. From that place the McCoys proceeded (the same day) to Dr. Johnston Lykins' residence.

Ref: Isaac McCoy's "Journal," *loc. cit.*

❆ BORN: on December 28, at Fort Leavenworth, Montgomery Bryant, son of Asst. Surg. Thomas S. Bryant, the post's medical officer.

Ref: Wichita *Evening Eagle*, August 10, 1943 (in Victor Murdock's article).

1832

❆ MARRIED: Lindsay Boone, and Sarah Groom, on January 14, by the Rev. Thomas Johnson.

MARRIED: Daniel Boone, and Marie Constance Philibert, on January 19, by the Rev. Thomas Johnson.

Lindsay and Daniel were sons of Daniel Morgan Boone (agriculturist to the Kansa, 1827-1831), and grandsons of the famous Daniel Boone. Sarah Groom was, perhaps, the daughter of Joseph Groom—"striker" to the Kansa blacksmith in 1831 and later. Marie Philibert was a sister of Gabriel Philibert —Kansa blacksmith, 1827-1831. These marriages, subsequently recorded in Jackson county, Mo., may have taken place in "Kansas."

Ref: Jackson county, Mo., marriage records, Independence, Mo.; Garraghan's *Catholic Beginnings* . . ., p. 121 (though Garraghan confused the Boone family generations, and erred in suggesting that Gabriel Philibert—born about 1805—was Mary's father); Hazel A. Spraker in her *The Boone Family* (Rutland, Vt., 1922), p. 124, noted the "Lindsey" Boone marriage. *A Memorial and Biographical Record of Kansas City and Jackson County, Mo.* (Chicago, 1896), p. 354, states that Daniel Boone married Marie Constance Philibert; that her brother Gabriel was a gunsmith with the Kansa Indian Agency; that her father's name also was Gabriel; that both her parents died early in life; that while visiting her brother at the agency, she became the wife of Daniel Boone, the marriage being performed by the Rev. Thomas Johnson. Implied here is that the marriage ceremony was at the Kansa Agency, in south Jefferson county of today.

❆ By a War Department order of February 8, all *cantonments* were directed to be called forts. The redesignated Western frontier posts were Fort Leavenworth (founded 1827); and Forts Gibson and Towson (founded 1824) in present Oklahoma.

❆ Early in the year, apparently, a Delaware Methodist Mission was established. On February 19, Johnston Lykins (Baptist missionary) wrote that "Mr. Wm. Johnson (Meth Misry) has located a school near Andersons town on Kanzas River for the Del[aware]s which they expect to put into operation, soon. . . ." In September, at the Missouri conference, missionaries William Johnson and Thomas B. Markham were assigned to the Delaware mission and school.

In 1833 the *church* membership was given as five whites and 27 Indians. That fall the Rev. Edward T. Peery was assigned to the mission, but may not have arrived till late in the year. (An October 27 visitor—Mrs. Moses Merrill— wrote of the Merrills' party spending the day "at the Methodist Episcopal mission of the Delaware's, with Rev. Mr. Dunlap." And a July, 1834, visitor— John Dunbar—wrote that "the Methodist missionary [Peery] at this station

. . . commenced his labors with the Delawares five or six months previous to our visit.") In 1834 it was reported the mission had 40 church members, the school 24 Indian children, and the Sabbath school 14 male and 10 female scholars, conducted by three teachers and a superintendent. In 1835 Thomas Johnson wrote: "The Delaware mission is still gaining ground, and the members of the society appear to enjoy much of the influence of religion, though they are greatly persecuted by the pagan part of the nation." In the fall of 1837 the Rev. L. B. Stateler was assigned to the mission, and he relocated it. (*See* autumn, 1837, annals.)

The "Rev. Mr. Dunlap" (above) was, in fact, Robert Dunlap, *government blacksmith* for the Delawares, who may have been care-taking the mission for a time in 1833. The site of the 1832-1837 mission is not known, but indications are it was not far from Grinter's (the Delaware) crossing of Kansas river. John Dunbar (in 1834) described the mission as "23 miles below [Fort Leavenworth] on the Konzas," and stated that the Shawnee Methodist Mission (the 1830-1839 "Turner" site) was across the river and five miles distant. Isaac McCoy (in May, 1837) wrote that the Delaware Methodist school was "near Cap[tain] Ketchum's." L. B. Stateler stated that it was "at a place where there was a fountain of water and the soil was good. . . . But it was not central[ly located among the Delawares]"—which was his reason for relocating it.

Missionaries Edward T. and Mary S. (Peery) Peery—they were cousins— had two children born at the *above* mission site: Martha Jane (b. March 15, 1834; d. November 17, 1835), and Mary [Margaret?] Jane (b. February 25, 1836).

Ref: Isaac McCoy Collection, *loc. cit.* (for Lykins); D. R. McAnally's *History of Methodism in Missouri* . . . (St. Louis, 1881), pp. 630, 635; *KHC*, v. 9, pp. 203-207, v. 14, pp. 576, 587 (for Dunbar), v. 16, p. 238 (for 1835 Johnson statement); Nebraska State Historical Society *Transactions* . . ., Lincoln, v. 5 (1893), p. 222 (for Mrs. Merrill's statement); E. J. Stanley's *Life of Rev. L. B. Stateler* . . . (Nashville, 1907), pp. 80, 86; 23d Cong., 1st Sess., *H. R.* 474 (Serial 263), p. 70 (for an 1834 statement not quoted above); Isaac McCoy's "Journal," May 20, 1837, entry; Si and Shirley Corn's *Our Family Tree* (1959), Section 4 (for Peery family data). The statement in *KHC*, v. 9, p. 574, that mission buildings are shown on Sec. 3, T. 11, R. 23 E., of the original land survey plats (in the state auditor's office) and that they "are supposed to have been" those of the Delaware Methodist Mission established in 1832, is an error which has been perpetuated in other publications. The plat in question does not show any buildings on Section 3; and the mission buildings shown on Section 10 (immediately south of Section 3) represent those of the second Delaware Baptist (or "Pratt") Mission. The *Vital Historical Records of Jackson County, Missouri*, compiled by the Kansas City chapter, D. A. R. (c1934), p. 313, shows the tombstone record for Martha Jane Peery's death as November 17, 1835 (not March 17, as elsewhere given). Thomas Johnson's letter of August 16, 1833 (typed copy in KHi ms. division under Shawnee Indian history) is another reference on the Delaware mission.

❡ In March(?) a party of Delawares (and some Shawnees) which included the young chiefs (and brothers) Shawanock and Pushkies was attacked by Pawnee Indians while hunting on lands claimed by the Pawnees. Pushkies and two other Delawares (one a woman) were killed; another was wounded. (*See* July, 1833, entry for the Delawares' retaliatory action.)

(It appears the Delawares had left their reserves in October, 1831, on an extended hunt; and that they did not return till late March or early April, 1832. Writing about the incident on April 24, 1832, William Clark stated that Agent R. W. Cummins had warned the Delawares "against hunting in the Panis country, notwithstanding which, they went in October last.")

Ref: 23d Cong., 1st Sess., *Sen. Doc. 512*, v. 1 (Serial 244), p. 523 (in which William Gordon, in a report dated August 12, 1833, refers to the attack as occurring "some 15 or 18 months ago"); *ibid.*, v. 3 (Serial 246), pp. 238, 306; SIA, v. 4, pp. 358, 359.

❆ The American Fur Company's S. *Yellowstone* (Andrew S. Bennett, master) left St. Louis March 26 on her second upper Missouri journey. (*See* April, 1831, annals entry.) Among her passengers were Pierre Chouteau, Jr., the artist George Catlin (who, before the boat's departure, painted the "Steamboat 'Yellow Stone' Leaving St. Louis"), John F. A. Sanford (Mandan agent), and some Indians returning from a trip East. After a successful 2,000-mile voyage, the *Yellowstone* reached the company's post, Fort Union, at the mouth of the Yellowstone river, in mid-June. (She was back at St. Louis in the fore part of July.)

Ref: Chittenden, *op. cit.*, v. 1, p. 137; Harold McCracken's *George Catlin and the Old Frontier* (New York, 1959), pp. 39, 40, has a reproduction of Catlin's 1832 "Yellow Stone" painting; *Missouri Historical Review*, Columbia, v. 29, p. 338. William Banks' reminiscences, in *The History of Holt and Atchison Counties, Missouri* (St. Joseph, 1882), pp. 311-313, relate that he was a deckhand on the *Yellowstone* in 1832.

❆ Steamboats (other than the *Yellowstone*) scheduled to depart from St. Louis in March and April for Missouri river ports included: the *Globe* (John Clark, master), for Fort Leavenworth, on March 11; the new *Otto* (James B. Hill, master), for "mouth of Kanzas river" on April 19; and the *Freedom* (A. Harkins, master), for Fort Leavenworth, on April 26.

Ref: St. Louis (Mo.) *Beacon*, March 8, April 19, 26, 1832.

❆ Within this year, probably in the early spring, Frederick Chouteau moved his trading post from Horseshoe Lake (*see* autumn, 1829, annals entry) to a location near the mouth of American Chief (now Mission) creek. The site was not far from Valencia of today, in Sec. 27, T. 11, R. 14 E., Dover township, Shawnee county. An Indian trading license issued on October 18 described the site as "On the Kanzas river, between the two present [upper] villages of the Kanzas [*i. e.*, Hard Chief's and American Chief's towns], on their lands. . . ."

Ref: SIA, v. 6, p. 303; 23d Cong., 1st Sess., *H. Doc. No. 45* (Serial 254); Frederick Chouteau's letters of May 6 and 10, 1880 (in KHi ms. division). The May 6 letter contains the phrase: "When I built my trading post above Topeka in 1832 . . ."; and the May 10 letter refers to "when I went and built near the American chief creek in 32. . . ." These items (supplementary to other facts noted in the autumn, 1829, annals entry) make it clear that Chouteau's statement "In 1830 I made my house on the American Chief creek . . ." in *KHC*, v. 8, p. 425, was a misquote, or a misprint.

⊄ Capt. Benjamin L. E. Bonneville's well-equipped expedition (110 men, 20 wagons, horses, mules, oxen, a cow, and a calf), heading for the Rocky mountains and Far West, left Fort Osage, Mo., on May 1. Joseph R. Walker and Michel S. Cerré were the "lieutenants" of this company which included experienced trappers, adventurers, and a few Delaware Indians hired as hunters.

(Captain Bonneville, having been granted a two-year furlough from the U. S. army had outfitted his combined exploration-fur trade venture with the financial backing of New York capitalists.)

His party followed out the Santa Fe trail for some distance (across Johnson and Douglas counties of today) then turned to the northwest, camping on the bank of the Kansas on May 12. Next day the river was forded (after a raft had been constructed to ferry the wagons). The crossing was near the Kansa Agency (or, seven miles above present Lawrence). By evening the entire party had reached the agency. Bonneville visited White Plume at his stone house some two miles northwest) and made a friend of the chief (who traveled for a day with him).

The expedition moved up the left bank of the Kansas, then turned northward, following, in general, the pathway of "Sublette's Trace," and the future Oregon trail (across present Pottawatomie and Marshall counties). On May 21 (*see* next entry) the Sublette-Wyeth pack train overtook, and passed this wagon caravan. Bonneville reached the Platte on June 2, near Grand Island apparently.

On July 24, at South Pass, this company crossed the Continental divide, and headed for Green river. *Bonneville's wagons were the first to make that crossing.* (*See* April and August, 1830, entries for the first wagons to go as far as South Pass.) It *appears*, too, that some of Bonneville's wagons were pulled by oxen, and if so he was the first to use ox teams on this mountain route and across the divide. Washington Irving (*see* below) described Bonneville's ". . . train of twenty wagons, drawn by oxen, or by four mules or horses each . . .," and the Crow Indians' astonishment "at the long train of wagons and oxen. . . ."

Captain Bonneville returned to Missouri in the summer of 1835, after three years in the mountains and Far West. Subsequently, in the East, he met Washington Irving who (after purchasing and rewriting Bonneville's manuscript account of his experiences—an account based on a now-lost journal), published, in 1837, a two-volume work entitled *The Rocky Mountains. . . .* This book, renamed *The Adventures of Captain Bonneville . . .,* in later editions, has been appraised by historian H. M. Chittenden as "a true and living picture of those early [fur trade] scenes. . . ."

Ref: Washington Irving's *The Adventures of Captain Bonneville . . .,* edited by E. W. Todd (Norman, Okla., c1961), especially pp. xvii-liv, and 13-32, 379-400; Bernard De Voto's *Across the Wide Missouri* (Boston, 1947), pp. 50-59; *Evening and Morning Star,*

Independence, Mo., June, 1832, which noted that "Captain Bonaville's company [150] passed this town" early in May.

❏ William L. Sublette headed a pack train (transporting supplies to the Rocky Mountain Fur Company) which left Independence, Mo., on May 12. His party of about 60 included Andrew Sublette, Robert Campbell, and Thomas Fitzpatrick. Their destination was the trappers' summer rendezvous at Pierre's Hole (Idaho). Traveling in company was Nathaniel J. Wyeth's party of about 25 men—mostly New Englanders—bound for the Oregon country. Wyeth's group included his brother Dr. Jacob Wyeth (who turned back at the Platte), an 18-year-old cousin John B. Wyeth, and John Ball, of Baltimore, Md.

The combined force of 80 to 85 men (with some 300 horses and mules, 15 sheep and two yoke of oxen) headed out the Santa Fe trail for three days' travel, but turned northwest on May 15 towards the Kansas river—crossing it above present Lawrence, near the Kansa Agency (about May 16?). The Sublette-Wyeth companies proceeded up the left bank of the Kansas, passing Fool Chief's village (west of present Topeka) perhaps about May 18. By May 21 they had left the Kansas valley and were well to the northward on "Sublette's Trace"—camping that night on the Big Blue. They crossed it next day and soon overtook Captain Bonneville's slower-moving wagon caravan (*see* preceding entry). John Ball, in his journal, noted: "We stopped a few moments to salute and passed on." Continuing up the waters of the Little Blue to its source, they crossed, on May 28, in a day's march of 25 miles, to the Platte —apparently reaching it at Grand Island. (The Sublette-Wyeth expedition subsequently reached Pierre's Hole about July 6.)

Ref: St. Louis (Mo.) *Beacon*, October 11, 1832 (for William Sublette's letter of September 21, 1832); N. J. Wyeth's journals (the "Kansas" section for the 1832 trip is lacking—having been torn out), and related correspondence (1831-1836), in *Sources of the History of Oregon*, Eugene, v. 1 (1899), parts 3-6; John B. Wyeth's *Oregon . . .* (Cambridge, Mass., 1833), as reprinted in R. G. Thwaites' *Early Western Travels* (Cleveland, 1904-1906), v. 21 (young Wyeth's comments on the Kansa Indians are of some interest, though unscientific); John Ball's journal, in the *Oregon Historical Society Quarterly*, Salem, v. 3 (1902), pp. 82-106 (offers the best information on the "Kansas" section of the trip—*see* pp. 84-88); John Ball's "Itinerary," from copy of typed transcript in Oregon Historical Society (for date of departure); Sunder, *op. cit.*, pp. 101-108; De Voto, *op. cit.*, p. 65 (for comment on John B. Wyeth and his book *Oregon*); *The Rocky Mountain Letters of Robert Campbell* (printed for F. W. Beinecke, 1955), p. 8; *Evening and Morning Star*, Independence, Mo., June, 1832—has item: "About the middle of May, Capt. Soublett's Company (70) passed, for the Rocky Mountains . . . At which time, also, Capt. Wyeth of Mass with a Company of 30, passed for the mouth of Oregon river. . . ." *Robert Newell's Memoranda*, edited by Dorothy O. Johansen, p. 32, has information on the Sublette party at the rendezvous.

❏ An act of congress, signed May 5, provided "the means of extending the benefits of vaccination, as a preventive of the small-pox, to the Indian tribes. . . ." (*See* Summer, and October, 1831, entries for smallpox among the Indians.) Before the end of May, doctors had been appointed for this emergency service at the Upper Missouri Agency of John Dougherty (Dr. __ __ Davis); the Osage Agency of P. L. Chouteau (Dr. J. R. Conway); and the Shawnee-Delaware (etc.) Agency of R. W. Cummins (Drs. __ __ Crow, Ware S. May, and Benjamin S. Long).

It was reported on February 1, 1833, by the commissioner of Indian affairs, that 3,000 Sioux and other Indians (in Dougherty's agency), 2,177 Osages (in P. L. Chouteau's agency), and 1,695 Shawnees, Kickapoos, and others (in Cummins' agency) had been vaccinated. Among the Kansa there had been some opposition (said to have been caused by trader Frederick Chouteau). Whether the Kansa were vaccinated is not made clear in the report. There had been no trouble with any other Indians, but some tribes and some individuals remained untreated.

Ref: SIA, v. 4, p. 329; 22d Cong., 2d Sess., H. Doc. No. 82 (Serial 234); 23d Cong., 1st Sess., H. Ex. Doc. 490 (Serial 259), pp. 3, 136; F. S. Cohen's *Handbook of Federal Indian Law* . . . (Washington, 1942), pp. 491, 492. W. E. Connelley's *Doniphan's Expedition* (Topeka, 1907), p. 279, has mention of Dr. Ware S. May. *The Weekly Tribune*, Liberty, Mo., December 3, 1847, noting May's death on November 30, 1847, stated he was a resident of Platte county, Mo., and that he had but recently returned from Santa Fe (where he had served as surgeon of Col. Price's regiment).

❰ In May, or early June, apparently, Chief White Hair, head of the Osages, died. Missionary W. B. Montgomery reported, on June 16, from Clermont's town (on the Verdigris) where he was visiting:

"An invitation has just come from Whitehair's for a united expedition against the Pawnees, in honor of their chief, who has deceased since our [missionary] tour in April."

When Washington Irving passed through White Hair's town (in Neosho county), early in October, he noted the "monument of chief who died lately—mound on a hill surrounded by railing—three poles with flags—trophies—a scalp, scalping knife &c. He had killed 4 Pawnees."

It appears the deceased chief had no children and that the White Hair who succeeded him was a sister's son. The new leader was called "Majakita." He was deposed in 1843.

Ref: *Missionary Herald*, v. 29, p. 134 (for Montgomery); J. F. McDermott, ed., *The Western Journals of Washington Irving* . . ., p. 100; J. F. McDermott, ed., *Tixier's Travels on the Osage Prairies* (Norman, 1940), pp. 127, 128, 143, 144 (for discussion of the various chiefs named White Hair, and their relationship to each other).

❰ In May the annual trading expedition departed for New Mexico. By Josiah Gregg's tabulation, the year's traffic from Missouri to the southwest totaled 150 men (40 of them proprietors), 70 wagons, and goods estimated at $140,000. But the size of the spring caravan is not known, and the figures above may have represented more than one Santa Fe-bound party.

Ref: Gregg, *op. cit.*, v. 2, p. 160; Lavender, *op. cit.*, p. 131, asserts Charles Bent headed the spring caravan; but L. R. Hafen (in *The Colorado Magazine*, v. 31, pp. 112, 113) presents a different view; *Morning and Evening Star*, Independence, Mo., June, 1832, which states: "During the month of May there also passed one company bound to Santa Fe."

❡ An act of June 15 authorized the President to raise a battalion of Mounted Rangers for one year's service.

Maj. Henry Dodge headed the Mounted Rangers—a force of 660 (plus officers)—six companies of 110 men each. Four of the companies served (for varying lengths of time) on the Western frontier. Those headed by Capts. Jesse Bean, Nathan Boone, and Lemuel Ford were assigned to the Fort Gibson (Okla.) area. The last company formed—that of Capt. Matthew Duncan—was ordered to Fort Leavenworth in 1833—*see* February, 1833, entry.

This battalion of mounted troops was the predecessor of the First U. S. cavalry—*see* March 2, 1833, entry.

Ref: 22d Cong., 2d Sess., *H. R. No. 17* (Serial 236); O. E. Young's article on the Mounted Rangers in *The Mississippi Valley Historical Review*, Cedar Rapids, Iowa, v. 41, pp. 453-470; Louis Pelzer's *Henry Dodge* (Iowa City, 1911), pp. 67-69; Foreman's *Advancing the Frontier*, p. 40.

❡ "About the 8th or 9th" of June, Jefferson Blackwell's company— "60 or 70" men—passed through Independence, Mo., en route to the mouth of Laramie river.

Blackwell—of the Gantt-Blackwell expedition of 1831—had returned to the States in the fall of 1831, in company with Thomas Fitzpatrick and five others (traveling across "Kansas"?). He now carried provisions, merchandise, and ammunition to Gantt and the other trappers who had wintered in the mountains.

Ref: *Evening and Morning Star*, Independence, Mo., June, 1832; Zenas Leonard, *Adventures, op. cit.*, pp. 9, 52; Dale L. Morgan and Eleanor T. Harris, *The Rocky Mountain Journals of William Marshall Anderson*, San Marino, Cal., 1967, p. 302.

❡ In the early summer, Baptist missionary (and surveyor) Isaac McCoy bought a tract of land just east of the "Kansas"-Missouri line (in present Kansas City, Mo.). During June and July he had six or eight workmen building log dwellings there "in the woods" for his family. By the end of July one "hewed log" cabin was finished, and the main house (35 x 22 feet) was covered in, doors cut out, etc., but lacked chimneys and "shutters to doors and windows."

Ref: Isaac McCoy's "Journal," *op. cit.* J. F. McDermott, in his *The Western Journals of Washington Irving*, p. 91n, locates McCoy's land as "55th Street to 64th Street, Belleview Avenue to the State line," in Kansas City, Mo., of today.

❡ On July 4 a party of Seneca Indians from Sandusky river, Ohio, reached their new reserve (of about 67,000 acres) west of the southwestern corner of Missouri—adjoining the Cherokees' lands.

Conducted by Henry C. Brish, these Indians had left their Ohio homes the previous autumn, after ceding their Eastern lands in a treaty made February 28,

1831. Their six months on the road had been a chaotic journey of hardship and suffering. By one report they totaled 352 persons on arrival. In December, by official count, they numbered 275 souls.

Ref: Foreman's *The Last Trek of the Indians*, pp. 66-71, 83; Kappler, *op. cit.*, v. 2, pp. 325-327; SIA, v. 27, pp. 1-24.

❦ An act of July 9 authorized the President to appoint a commissioner of Indian affairs, who was to serve under the secretary of war's direction. The first commissioner (1832-1836) was Elbert Herring.

Another provision of the act was a general prohibition against taking liquor into the Indian country.

Since the beginning of United States government it had been illegal to give, sell, or trade liquor to the Indians, but the traffic in "ardent spirits" had become such a scandal that—as one writer has put it—"in 1832 the government forbade the importation into the Indian Country of the liquor whose use there was already forbidden.")

Ref: Cohen, *op. cit.*, pp. 10, 11, 73; DeVoto, *op. cit.*, pp. 120, 121 (for quote).

❦ BORN: at the Shawnee Methodist Mission (present Wyandotte county), on July 11, Alexander Soule Johnson, son of the Rev. Thomas and Sarah T. (Davis) Johnson.

(Twenty-three years later, in the first Kansas territorial legislature, Thomas Johnson was council president and Alexander Soule Johnson was the youngest member of the house.)

Ref: *KHC*, v. 8, p. 260n, v. 9, pp. 162n, 168, 190n, v. 12, p. xii; KHi's *Fifteenth Biennial Report*, p. 35.

❦ An act of July 14 provided for the appointment (by the President) of three commissioners to treat with the Indians in the Western country and handle various matters relating to the immigrant and native tribes there. The final appointees were Montfort Stokes, of North Carolina, Henry L. Ellsworth, of Hartford, Conn., and the Rev. John F. Schermerhorn, of Utica, N. Y.

Ref: Cohen, *op. cit.*, p. 492; Foreman's *The Last Trek of the Indians*, p. 60.

❦ On July 26 John Calvin McCoy and two assistants set out (from present Kansas City, Mo.) to survey a 34,000-acre reserve, in what is now Franklin county, for the Ottawa Indians (then living east of the Mississippi, some of them in Ohio). Surveyor Isaac McCoy joined his son at the end of July. By August 6 the task was completed, and the party had reached home again.

(The site for the reserve—south of the Shawnees, and west of the Peorias and Kaskaskias—had been chosen earlier by Isaac McCoy. *See* November 30 entry for arrival of the first of the Ottawas in "Kansas.")

Ref: 23d Cong., 1st Sess., *Sen. Doc. 512*, v. 3 (Serial 246), p. 420; Isaac McCoy's "Journal," *loc. cit.*

❡ In the fore part of September, William L. Sublette, Robert Campbell, 60 (or more) mounted trappers, and a mule train carrying 169 beaver packs, came down from the Platte to the Kansas river valley over "Sublette's Trace." They reached Independence, Mo., about September 18.

(A few days later, east of Lexington, traveler Charles J. Latrobe met "the long train of Trappers . . . their mules laden with . . . skins. . . . They were about seventy in number . . .; men worn with toil and travel. . . .")

Ref: St. Louis (Mo.) *Beacon*, October 11, 1832 (for Sublette's letter of September 21, 1832); C. J. Latrobe's *The Rambler in North America* . . . (London, 1835), v. 1, p. 126; *Missouri Intelligencer* . . . Fayette, September 29, October 20, 1832; Robert Campbell dictation (in Bancroft Library, Berkeley, Cal.); Sunder, *op. cit.*, pp. 112, 113.

❡ A Baptist missionary—the Rev. Charles E. Wilson—who had arrived at "Shawanoe" mission on August 10, located among the Delawares in September(?). But after spending a few weeks at their settlements he left (in mid-December) to go to the Choctaws.

Ref: Isaac McCoy's *History of Baptist Indian Missions*, pp. 450, 451, 453, 455.

❡ It was probably in September that artist George Catlin, and his two traveling companions "Ba'tiste [and] Bogard," beached their canoe at Fort Leavenworth's landing.

"My voyage from the mouth of Teton River to this place has been the most rugged, yet the most delightful, of my whole Tour," wrote Catlin. (He had gone *up* the Missouri aboard the S. *Yellowstone* in the early spring.) "I . . . descended . . . in my little canoe, with my two men at the oars, and myself at the helm. . . . In addition to the opportunity which this descending Tour has afforded me, of visiting all the tribes of Indians on the river, and leisurely filling my portfolio with the beautiful scenery which its shores present—the sportsman's fever was roused and satisfied; the swan, ducks, geese, and pelicans—the deer, antelope, elk, and buffaloes, were 'stretched' by our rifles. . . ."

At Bellevue, "about nine miles" above the Platte's mouth, they had been guests of Upper Missouri agent John Dougherty. On their arrival at Fort Leavenworth, Lt. Col. William Davenport gave them comfortable quarters in the barracks, and Catlin entered into the post's social activities.

"I have joined several times in the deer-hunts, and more frequently in grouse [prairie chicken] shooting," he wrote. "They [the grouse] make their appearance in these parts in the months of August and September . . . and the whole garrison, in fact, are almost subsisted on them at this time. . . ."

Catlin witnessed, wrote about, and may have painted a prairie fire, while at the military post. He also proceeded to paint Indians, and make notes about the tribes he met. In his next letter from

Fort Leavenworth he indicated "some considerable time" had elapsed. "I have been moving about and using my brush amongst different tribes in this vicinity," he wrote.

It was in this letter that he described the young Iowa chief White Cloud (son of a recently-deceased White Cloud), and two other Iowas he had painted; wrote of the "Konzas" Indians, and Chief White Plume—whom he did not paint; noted four "Konzas" Indians he had portrayed; dwelt at some length on the custom of "shaving the head, and ornamenting it with the crest of deer's hair" which was common to the Kansa, Osages, Pawnees, Sacs, Foxes, and Iowas, and to no other tribe that he knew of; discussed the Pawnees, Omahas, Otoes, and Missouris; and described the men of these nations whom he had painted.

Some time in October, Catlin, with his hired hands Baptiste and Bogard, left Fort Leavenworth, and paddled on downriver in their canoe to St. Louis. On October 26, at Castor Hill, outside St. Louis, he was a witness to a treaty William Clark negotiated with certain Shawnees and Delawares.

Bernard De Voto (in his *Across the Wide Missouri*, c1947) discussed artist George Catlin at some length, describing him as the "first painter of the West who had any effect," and as "an extraordinary man, a man with a certain greatness in him. . . ." Repeatedly he stated that Catlin's first trip to the West was in 1832. So far as this writer knows, no *evidence* has come to light which refutes that statement.

However, Lloyd Haberly, in his highly romantic and *completely undocumented* biography of Catlin (*Pursuit of the Horizon*, 1948), has described a trip the artist made in 1830! to Cantonment Leavenworth, and from there, in William Clark's company, to the Kansa towns; also, another journey, in 1831!, in company with Agent John Dougherty, to the Platte river and the tribes residing there. These statements have been echoed by John C. Ewers ("George Catlin, Painter of Indians and the West," in the Smithsonian *Report* for 1955, pp. 483-528), and by Harold McCracken (*George Catlin and the Old Frontier*, 1959).

As for the alleged journey by Catlin and William Clark to the Kansa towns in 1830, it needs to be pointed out that Haberly's description of "General Clark" ("the gaunt, erect old General in his stained buckskins and mangy coonskin cap"—p. 43) seems to have been borrowed from John T. Irving, Jr.'s *Indian Sketches*, wherein Irving described Marston G. Clark, the Kansa agent ("met the Kanza agent, General Clark, a tall, soldier-like man, arrayed in an Indian hunting-shirt and an old fox-skin cap"). Had Indian Sup't William Clark gone up the Missouri that fall his departure, or return, or both, would certainly have been recorded in the Clark "diary" (*see KHQ*, v. 16, pp. 396-405, for latter part of 1830).

As for the alleged 1831 spring journey up the Missouri in Dougherty's company, a Dougherty report (of March, 1832—typed copy in KHi ms. division) outlines that agent's movements in 1831, and indicates his only trip to the Platte river Indians that year was in September.

See a Catlin *sketch* of some Kansa Indians in this volume. The same group of Kansa, in a Catlin *painting*, has been reproduced in color in Harold McCracken's *George Catlin and the Old Frontier.*

Ref: George Catlin's *North American Indians* (Philadelphia, 1913), v. 2, pp. 1-33; Marjorie (Catlin) Roehm, ed., *The Letters of George Catlin and His Family* (Berkeley, 1966), pp. 55-57 (for Dale L. Morgan's comments on Catlin and his 1831-1833 activities).

❡ U. S. Comm'r Henry L. Ellsworth and the English traveler Charles Joseph Latrobe left Independence, Mo., on September 27, in company with Kansa agent Marston G. Clark, to visit Isaac Mc-Coy "at his house" (a mile east of the Missouri line). They also crossed into "Kansas" where they remained overnight with Agent R. W. Cummins at the Shawnee Agency (present Johnson county).

On September 28 Ellsworth and Latrobe "struck across wide prairies" in a southeasterly direction to overtake a small party (including Auguste P. Chouteau, Washington Irving, and a young Swiss count) which had left Independence on the 27th bound for Fort Gibson (Okla.). Before nightfall they found Chouteau's camp somewhere east of the Missouri line. (*See, also,* next entry.)

Ref: Latrobe, *op. cit.,* v. 1, pp. 126-143; 23d Cong., 1st Sess., *Sen. Doc. 512,* v. 3 (Serial 246), p. 481 (Ellsworth's October 9, 1832, letter); J. F. McDermott, ed., *The Western Journals of Washington Irving,* pp. 4-21, 90-92; Isaac McCoy's "Journal," *loc. cit.*

❡ Led by Auguste P. Chouteau, Comm'r Henry Ellsworth and party (en route to Fort Gibson—*see, also,* preceding entry) arrived at Harmony Mission (Mo.) on September 30, after a journey southward from Independence begun on September 27.

In this little cavalcade were Chouteau (and his two servants), Ellsworth, Charles Joseph Latrobe, Washington Irving, a 19-year-old Swiss count—Albert-Alexandre de Pourtalès, Dr. Thomas O'Dwyer, and two half-Indian factotums. The outfit included wagons (dearborns) and some riding horses. And there were eight dogs belonging to Chouteau.

These travelers left Harmony on October 1; journeyed southwest; and entered present Bourbon county some time the following day. On the 3d (in present Neosho county) they reached "Rev. N. Dodge's house — near Osage Village" (Boudinot Mission — *see* March, 1830, entry), and remained overnight. On October 4 they left Boudinot early and crossed the Neosho. Wrote Washington Irving in his journal:

"We have a journey of 30 miles to make over open Prarie before we can find a camping place, there being water in the interim but no wood—pass thro the village of the White Hair (Osages). . . . Passed over vast prarie —here not a tree or shrub was to be seen—a view like that of the ocean. . . . About 3 oclock arrived at a grove on the banks of stream & encamp— place called La Bête—wood entangled with rich underwood—grape vines— pea vines, &c. Fine trees—flights of Perroquets—called la Bête, or the Beast, because the Indians saw a great & terrible animal there, the like of which they never saw before or since. [The camp was, apparently, in southeastern Labette county of today.]

The journey to Fort Gibson (which most of the party reached on October 9) was made by way of New Hopefield mission, Auguste P. Chouteau's Grand Saline trading post (where Salina, Okla., is today), and Union Mission.

Subsequently, between October 13 and November 10, Ellsworth, Irving, Latrobe, and Pourtalès accompanied Capt. Jesse Bean's company of the Mounted Rangers on a 400-mile expedition in present Oklahoma which Irving described as "a wide exploring tour, from the Arkansas to the Red [Cimarron] river, including a part of the Pawnee [Pawnee Pict, or Wichita] hunting grounds, where no party of white men had as yet penetrated."

Ref: J. F. McDermott, ed., *The Western Journals of Washington Irving*, especially pp. 97-101 (for "Kansas" journey); Henry L. Ellsworth's *Washington Irving on the Prairie . . .*, ed. by S. T. Williams and B. D. Simison (New York, 1937), pp. 2-146; Latrobe, *op. cit.*, v. 1, pp. 144-242; Washington Irving's *A Tour on the Prairies . . .* (Chicago and New York), pp. 27-274; 23d Cong., 1st Sess., *Sen. Doc. 512*, v. 3 (Serial 246), p. 481; Albert de Pourtalès, *On the Western Tour With Washington Irving . . .*, ed. by George F. Spaulding (Norman, Okla., c1968).

❡ As reported for the year October 1, 1831-September 30, 1832, the following persons had been employed at the Indian agencies in "Kansas":

At the *Kansa Agency*—Marston G. Clark (agent); Clement Lessert (interpreter); John McGill (gun and blacksmith); Joseph Groom (striker to blacksmith); Matthew Jefferies (agriculturist, October--December, 1831); William Elledge (agriculturist, January-June, 1832); George Lumpkin (agriculturist, July-September, 1832).

At the *Osage Agency*—Paul Ligueste Chouteau (agent); Thomas Anthony (subagent); Alexander W. McNair (subagent); Baptiste Mongrain (interpreter); Gabriel Philibert (gunsmith); Joseph Trumblee (blacksmith); Louis Peletrie [Peltier] (striker); A. Woodruff (blacksmith); Solomon Hoyle (laborer).

At the *Delaware-Shawnee Agency*—Richard W. Cummins (agent); John Campbell (subagent); Anthony Shane, James Connor, and Baptiste Peoria (interpreters); Harmon Davis and James Pool (gun and blacksmiths from July, 1831-March, 1832); Robert Dunlap and Lewis Jones (gun and blacksmiths from April, 1832). Also, Davis Hardin [*i. e.*, Harmon Davis?] and James Pool had been paid for labor in completing agents' and blacksmiths' buildings.

[Cummins' agency included the Shawnees, Delawares, Weas, Peorias, Piankeshaws, and Kickapoos (of western Missouri).]

Ref: 22d Cong., 2d Sess., *H. Doc. No. 137* (Serial 235), pp. 67-69, 73, 114, 115.

❡ An Indian trading license issued October 18 to the American Fur Company (*i. e.*, to the Chouteaus) renewed the permit for the Chouteaus' Shawnee reserve post on the Kansas river's south bank (in present Wyandotte county); and sanctioned the establishment of another post to be located on a branch of the Marais des Cygnes "at a point about one mile east of the present village of the Weas." This trading place, for the "Piankeshaws, Kickapoos [of western Missouri], Weas, and Peorias," was within a few miles of present Paola, Miami county.

Ref: 23d Cong., 1st Sess., *H. Doc. No. 45* (Serial 254); SIA, v. 1, p. 56 (McCoy map); also, *see* 23d Cong., 2d Sess., *H. Ex. Doc. 97* (Serial 273), for 1834 for a renewal of the license for the Wea (etc.) trade.

❡ Charles Bent's eastbound caravan traveled the Santa Fe trail across present Kansas in October; and reached western Missouri, apparently, early in November. As reported later that month, from *eastern* Missouri:

Captain Bent and Company have just returned from Santa Fe. The amount of property in coin, gold and silver bullion, mules, furs, etc., is very considerable, although few have returned rich. What this company has may be considered as the avails of nearly two years. . . . Supposed amount $190,000.

Ref: *Missouri Intelligencer,* Columbia, November 10, 1832; *Colorado Magazine,* v. 31, p. 113 (for quotation—from the *Upper Missouri Advertiser,* as reprinted in the Little Rock [Ark.] *Advocate* of December 5, 1832).

❡ In a treaty made October 26 (at Castor Hill, near St. Louis), the last claims of the Delawares and the Shawnees to lands in Missouri (in the Cape Girardeau area) were extinguished.

That portion of the Delawares having such claim had already left Missouri and were either on the reserve in "Kansas," or had gone to present Oklahoma and Texas. For benefits given the Delawares who had removed to the reserve, *see* March 30, 1833, entry.

The only Shawnees involved were some small bands living on the White river in Arkansas territory. (They had refused to join their kinsmen on the reserve in "Kansas.") The treaty (which granted them $1,200—$800 in cash and $400 in clothing and horses) anticipated their removal to the reserve, but these Indians did not come to "Kansas." One of the "White river" Shawnees who signed this treaty was La-lah-ow-che-ka. Artist George Catlin, a treaty witness, painted his portrait.

Ref: Kappler, *op. cit.,* v. 2, pp. 370-372; 23d Cong., 1st Sess., *Sen Doc. 512,* v. 3 (Serial 246), pp. 408, 409, 635; McCracken, *op. cit.,* p. 31 (for portrait of the Shawnee "chief"), and p. 32 (wherein McCracken asserts that "Lay-law-she-kaw's" portrait was painted at Fort Leavenworth).

❡ Treaties of October 27 (with the Kaskaskia and Peoria Indians) and October 29 (with the Piankeshaw and Wea Indians), made at Castor Hill, Mo. (William Clark for the U. S.), extinguished these Indians' land claims in Illinois and Missouri, and ceded to them reserves totaling 400 sections of land in present Kansas, south of the Shawnee lands.

Except for a band of Weas in Indiana, and some bands of Illinois Indians united with the Kaskaskias, the people of these four small nations had already moved west of the Mississippi. Most of them had lived for several years on the reserves (in Miami and Franklin counties of today) referred to in the treaty. (*See* March, 1831, annals entry.)

The Kaskaskias' and Peorias' treaty included provisions that the government would build them four log houses; and that they would be paid an annuity of $3,000 for 10 years. In the Piankeshaws' and Weas' treaty it was stated that the government would support a blacksmith's shop for five years at a location on their reserve which would be convenient for *all four tribes*. Both treaties specified certain agricultural aid.

Ref: Kappler, *op. cit.*, v. 2, pp. 376, 377, 382, 383; 23d Cong., 1st Sess., *Sen. Doc. 512*, v. 3 (Serial 246), pp. 637-640.

❦ At Fort Leavenworth, on November 26, a deputation of four Kickapoo Indians (having concluded an examination of the reserve offered their nation on the Missouri river, north of the Delawares' lands, signed a treaty article which defined the reserve's bounds. Comm'rs Frank J. Allen and Nathan Kouns, who had accompanied the delegation, represented the government. James Kennerly was also present, as the commissioners' secretary.

A month earlier (October 24, at Castor Hill, Mo.) Kickapoo chiefs and head men had signed the treaty to which the above article was supplemental. (Pa-sha-cha-hah, or Jumping Fish, and Kennekuk, the Kickapoo Prophet, headed the list of signers.) For removing from Illinois, and the Osage river in Missouri, the Kickapoos were to receive: a one-year annuity of $18,000 ($12,000 to pay debts); an annual annuity of $5,000 for 19 years; $1,000 per year for five years to support a blacksmith and strikers; $3,700 for the erection of a mill, and a church; $500 per year for 10 years to support a school, buy books, etc.; $3,000 for farm implements; $4,000 for labor and improvements on the land; $4,000 in cattle, hogs, and other stock.

See May, 1833, annals for removal of the Kickapoos to their "Kansas" reserve.

Ref: Kappler, *op. cit.*, v. 2, pp. 365-367; 23d Cong., 1st Sess., *Sen. Doc. 512*, v. 5 (Serial 248), pp. 48, 49, 54-56; Foreman's *The Last Trek of the Indians*, pp. 61-63.

❦ In charge of Lt. Col. James J. Abert, and conducted by G. W. Pool, 334 Shawnees and 73 Ottawas arrived at the Shawnee Agency on November 30, after an overland journey from Ohio begun in September. Most of the adults had traveled on horseback, and the children in the baggage wagons. These Indians were:

(1) Wapaghkonetta and Hog creek Shawnees from Allen county, Ohio, who, by treaty of August 8, 1831, had ceded their Eastern lands for 100,000 acres stipulated to be within, or contiguous to, the existing Shawnee reserve in present Kansas. Among these immigrants to "Kansas" were Chief John Perry, Henry and James Bluejacket, Peter Cornstock, John Woolf, and the families of each.

(2) Blanchard's Fork and Oquanoxa's village Ottawas from northwestern Ohio, who, by treaty of August 30, 1831, had ceded their lands for a 34,000-acre tract which was to adjoin the Shawnee reserve on the south or west. Intermarriages connected these Ottawas with the Shawnees; on their reserve the Ottawas remained till the summer of 1834.

Ref: 23d Cong., 1st Sess., *Sen. Doc. 512*, v. 1 (Serial 244), pp. 396-400, v. 3 (Serial 246), pp. 566, 567, v. 4 (Serial 247), pp. 4-10 (for Abert's January 3, 1833, report); SIA, v. 5, pp. 23-27 (for Shawnee and Ottawa muster rolls); Kappler, *op. cit.*, v. 2, pp. 331-334 (Shawnee treaty), pp. 335-339 (Ottawa treaty); Foreman's *The Last Trek of the Indians*, pp. 72, 76-88. In Superintendency of Indian Affairs, St. Louis, "Records," v. 8 (typed copy), p. 6, an R. W. Cummins letter of May 14, 1839, states that 24 Shawnees *of the River Huron* moved west with the Shawnees arriving in "Kansas" in 1832; and that 14 more arrived in "Kansas" on September 15, 1833, making, in all, 38. Chief George Bluejacket died in 1833 before the party came. In 1839, according to Cummins, the Huron river Shawnees in "Kansas" totaled 39.

❏ In charge of Lt. John F. Lane, and conducted by Daniel M. Workman, a mixed band of Seneca and Shawnee Indians (258 persons in all) from the vicinity of Lewistown, Ohio, arrived December 13 on the Cowskin (now Elk) river in present northeastern Oklahoma, where they camped, temporarily, on the reserve of the Senecas from Sandusky, Ohio. (*See* July 4 annals entry.)

These Seneca and Shawnee Indians had ceded their Ohio lands in a treaty made July 20, 1831. Their overland journey to a new reserve in present northeastern Oklahoma had begun in late September. Shortly after their arrival, they joined with the Sandusky Senecas to form a confederacy, calling themselves the "United Nation of Senecas and Shawnees." This became a formal agreement on December 29 when the "United Nation" made a treaty with the United States—a treaty which also granted the mixed band of Senecas and Shawnees a 60,000-acre reserve adjoining the Sandusky Senecas on the north (in lieu of the tract west of Grand river originally intended for them).

Ref: 23d Cong., 1st Sess., *Sen. Doc. 512*, v. 4 (Serial 247), pp. 10-12, 77-84; Foreman's *The Last Trek of the Indians*, pp. 71-83; Kappler, *op. cit.*, v. 2, pp. 383-385.

1833

❏ About the first of January, Kiowa (and Comanche?) warriors attacked 12 Missouri-bound traders on the Canadian river route, in the present Texas Panhandle. (With "Judge" [J. H.?] Carr as captain, these men, with a mule pack-train carrying $10,000, or more, in gold and silver, had left Santa Fe in December.)

"Pratt and Mitchell" were killed, several other men were wounded, and all the party's animals were lost during a 36-hour siege. Under cover of night, leaving their baggage and most of the money behind, the 10 survivors headed eastward on foot. Five of them soon left the river, took a direct route (crossing "Kansas"), and reached Missouri safely. Three of those who continued down the Canadian, near starvation, arrived at the Western Creek settlements after 42 days; while the last two (one of them William R. Schenck) were never heard from again.

Ref: James Mooney's "Calendar History of the Kiowa Indians," in *Seventeenth Annual Report of the Bureau of American Ethnology* . . ., 1895-96, Pt. I, pp. 254-257; Josiah Gregg's *Commerce of the Prairies* . . . (New York, London, 1844), v. 2, pp. 49-53; Albert Pike's *Prose Sketches and Poems* . . . (Boston, 1834), pp. 80, 132; *Missionary Herald*, Boston, v. 29 (1833), p. 369; *Missouri Republican*, St. Louis, March 5, 1833; *Niles' Weekly Register*, Baltimore, v. 44 (March 23, 1833), p. 51; *Arkansas Gazette*, Little Rock, March 20, 1833; William Waldo's "Recollections," in *Glimpses of the Past*, St. Louis, v. 5, pp. 66-68 (Waldo identified four of the party as: Thomas Eustace, Judge Carr, Washington Chapman, and John Harris). The Kiowas recorded the event in their "calendar," but some accounts say the Indians were Comanches. See *Old Santa Fe*, Santa Fe, v. 2 (October, 1914), pp. 207-211, for W. R. Schenck material.

❧ On February 5 Agent R. W. Cummins wrote Sup't William Clark about property lost by Delaware chief Captain Pipe, William Monture, Isaac Hill, and Solomon Jonnicake (later "Journeycake"), while their party (about 30 persons) was en route from the Little Sandusky river, Ohio, to present Kansas. These men—all influential in their nation—were among the last of the Delawares to emigrate to the West.

Captain Pipe and his group left Ohio in the autumn of 1831, and spent the winter of 1831-1832 in Indiana. Presumably, despite the date of Cummins' letter, they had arrived in "Kansas" in the spring or summer of 1832. (Sup't William Clark's St. Louis records of emigrating Indians show a payment of $25 on April 29, 1832, for a "horse furnished Captain Pipe, a Delaware chief"; another of $10 on May 15 to "Moonshine" to "defray expenses" of some Delawares "on their way to Kansas river"; one of $15 to George Ketchum [a Delaware], on June 4, for the same purpose; and other payments as late as September 30, 1832, to various persons supplying provisions to small parties of "emigrating Shawnees, Delawares, Kickapoos, and Kaskaskias.")

Ref: Superintendency of Indian Affairs, St. Louis, "Records" (SIA), v. 5, pp. 321, 330; 23d Cong., 1st Sess., *Sen. Doc. 512*, v. 2 (Serial 245), pp. 691, 705, 722, 725, v. 4 (Serial 247), pp. 125, 126, v. 5 (Serial 248), pp. 12, 13, 57-61, 100-103; Grant Foreman's *The Last Trek of the Indians* (Chicago, c1946), p. 69. For note on the "Journeycake" family see KHC, v. 12, p. 186.

❧ Following a three-day visit (February 23-25) by Baptists Johnston Lykins and Daniel French among the Delawares, the missionaries of "Shawanoe" Baptist Mission began regular preaching trips to Chief Nah-ko-min's village—the most remote of the Delaware settlements—over 10 miles from "Shawanoe" (and across the Kansas river—near present Edwardsville, Wyandotte co.). In this way Delaware Baptist Mission got its start.

On April 3 Isaac McCoy wrote: "We have made an arrangement with Mr. Blanchard . . . to remain with them [the Delawares]. . . . He will put up a little cabin for himself, and make a small garden—all by consent of the Indians." (Ira D. Blanchard, of Ohio —a young, self-appointed missionary—had been living among the Delawares for more than a year, learning their language. On April 21 he was baptized at "Shawanoe" Baptist Mission.)

Early in 1834 Nah-ko-min finally gave permission for Blanchard to build a house near the settlement. It was erected in the spring and early summer (on a site now within the S. W. ¼ of the N. E. ¼ of Sec. 26, T. 11 S., R. 23 E., Delaware tp., Wyandotte co.); and on July 28, 1834, Jotham Meeker wrote: "Br. Blanchard commences housekeeping alone." McCoy's report, at the end of 1834, referred to the "small comfortable [18' x 20', story-and-a-half log] dwelling"; and stated that Blanchard was giving lessons at his house and at three other places among the Delawares; that arrangements had recently been made for erection of a schoolhouse; and that the Delawares who were Baptists met for church at "Shawanoe" Baptist Mission.

In February, 1835, Blanchard went East. He returned in June with his bride—Mary (Walton) Blanchard, and Sylvia Case (teacher). Meantime, work had been started on the 20-foot-square school, a kitchen, and other buildings.

The Blanchards and Miss Case were missionaries at Delaware Baptist Mission for some 12 years thereafter, and conducted a boarding (manual labor) school—almost as long as the mission was at the "Edwardsville" site. In the 1840's they had a native assistant—Charles Johnnycake (Journeycake). Another dwelling (18' x 20'; one-and-a-half stories) was added in 1843. Though the 1844 flood caused the nearby Delawares to move several miles away, the mission was unharmed, and work was disrupted for a few months only. In December, 1846, a frame meeting house (36' x 26') was completed—on a new site; and the mission was prospering in 1847. Late in 1847(?) Delaware Baptist Mission was turned over to the Rev. John G. Pratt, who moved it to a new location (about four miles northwest) before the year was over. The dismissal of the previous missionaries was stated to be: "on account of immoralities of two of . . . [the mission's] members. . . ."

Ref: Isaac McCoy's "Journal," in Kansas State Historical Society (KHi) ms. division (especially entries in the February, 1833-December, 1835, period); Meeker's "Diary," in KHi ms. division, July 28, 1834, February 9, June 15, 27, 1835, entries (and various others, scattered); Isaac McCoy's *Annual Register,* January, 1835, pp. 25-27; a ms. report of the Shawnee and Delaware missions (dated September 10, 1835), in Isaac McCoy manuscripts, (in KHi ms. division) for description of buildings; *The Baptist Missionary Magazine,* Boston, vols. 16-28 (1836-1848)—particularly the annual reports of North American missions; Comm'r of Indian Affairs (CIA) "Reports" (for 1842 and 1843); W. A. Seward Sharp's *History of Kansas Baptists* (Kansas City, 1940), pp. 33, 34; KHC, v. 12, p. 183n; KHQ, v. 2, pp. 227-250; Isaac McCoy's *History of Baptist Indian Missions* (in lieu of his "Journal"), pp. 455, 456, 463; Johnston Lykins' letter of March 26, 1836, in Isaac McCoy manuscripts; A. J. Paddock papers (in KHi ms. division) for some biographical data on the Blanchards. Five daughters (Lydia, Olive Ann, Myra, Abigail, and Rebecca) were born to the Blanchards at Delaware Baptist Mission. In the "Barker Collection," in KHi ms. division, are letters on the subject of the Blanchard dismissal.

❧ At Fort Leavenworth, in February, Maj. Bennet Riley's command (four Sixth U. S. infantry companies—about 120 men) was enlarged when Capt. Matthew Duncan's Company F (over 100 men) of the Mounted Rangers reported for duty.

(This sixth, and last-formed ranger company had been enlisted from the Vandalia, Ill., area, and mustered into service there, on November 5, 1832. Other officers of Company F were: 1st Lt. Benjamin D. Moore, 2d Lt. William

Bradford, 3d Lt. Henry B. Roberts. Captain Duncan, subsequently, commanded Company C, First U. S. dragoons.)

For the Mounted Rangers' service in "Kansas," *see, also,* entries of May 15, and October.

Ref: *The Mississippi Valley Historical Review,* Cedar Rapids, Iowa, v. 41, pp. 462-464; R. G. Thwaites, *Early Western Travels* (Cleveland, 1904-1906), v. 22, pp. 253, 254 (for Maximilian's comment on the post garrison in April, 1833); J. T. Irving, Jr., *Indian Sketches . . .,* edited by John F. McDermott (Norman, c1955), pp. 24, 28, 44. This work is hereinafter cited as: J. T. Irving (McDermott edition). John F. McDermott's extensive research, and editorial notes, for this volume, and other works he has edited, have been of much help to the compiler of these annals. Special acknowledgment is due him, and herewith given.

❡ An act of March 2 provided for the raising of a United States dragoon regiment, to be headed by a colonel, with a command of 10 companies (60 privates to a company), and a complement of officers and noncoms; also, the President was authorized to discharge the Mounted Rangers.

[The U. S. dragoon regiment of 1833 became the *First U. S. dragoons* when, by act of May 28, 1836, another dragoon regiment was authorized. In 1861, by act of August 23, the First U. S. dragoons became the First U. S. cavalry.]

Henry Dodge (ranger commander) was made colonel of the (First) U. S. dragoons. Stephen W. Kearny (Third infantry) was selected as lieutenant colonel; and Richard B. Mason (First infantry) became the regiment's major. Appointed as captains were ex-infantry officers Clifton Wharton, Edwin V. Sumner, Reuben Holmes, Eustace Trenor, David Hunter; and ex-ranger officers Lemuel Ford, Nathan Boone, Jesse B. Browne, Jesse Bean, Matthew Duncan. (Holmes died November 4, 1833; and, as of that date, David Perkins was promoted captain.) The senior first lieutenant was Philip St. George Cooke.

Companies A-E were organized at Jefferson Barracks, Mo., during the summer and autumn. Under Col. Henry Dodge they set out November 20 for Fort Gibson (Okla.), and arrived at that post December 17 (after a journey, of some hardship, across Missouri and Arkansas territory).

Ref: *U. S. Statutes at Large,* v. 4, p. 652; [James Hildreth's] *Dragoon Campaigns to the Rocky Mountains . . .* (New York, 1836), pp. 35-37, 59; *Niles' Weekly Register,* v. 44 (March 16, 1833), p. 36, v. 45 (November 16, 1833), p. 192; *American State Papers: Military Affairs,* v. 5, p. 280; Louis Pelzer's *Henry Dodge* (Iowa City, 1911), pp. 80-87; Grant Foreman's *Pioneer Days in the Early Southwest* (Cleveland, 1926), pp. 108, 109, 115.

❡ About 800 Osages from the Neosho towns (on the reservation in "Kansas"), and from the Verdigris towns (in "Oklahoma"), were present at Fort Gibson (Okla.) between March 13 and 28 when U. S. Comm'rs Stokes, Ellsworth, and Schermerhorn held treaty councils with them in an *unsuccessful* attempt to promote an exchange of the existing Osage reserve (granted under the 1825 treaty), for another farther north (between the Neosho and Kansas rivers). The commissioners also met continued resistance from

Clermont's band to removing from the Verdigris to the Osage reservation in present Kansas. (The Verdigris Osages—more than a third of the whole nation—were some 50 miles south of the reserve.) Auguste P. Chouteau (trader) and his brother Paul Ligueste Chouteau (Osage agent) had influential roles at these councils.

In a letter of April 2, the commissioners stated:

The Osages are a poor, almost naked and half starved people. The unexampled freshets in the fall [of 1832] swept away most of the corn and vegetables they had stored up for winter's use. The number of Osages is estimated by the agent at 6,000, and all but Requoius's [Missionary William C. Requa's, or the Hopefield] band were suffering from the want of food when the council was called. . . .

The Osage tribe have been divided by many jealousies and private feuds . . . Great rivalry as to rank has existed in the nation, and . . . at the council, it was a matter of contest who should be head chief. . . . [Clermont was considered the "principal or first chief" of the Osage nation. Of the reservation Osages, White Hair was the leader; Walking Rain (the Little Osages' chief) was subservient to him.]

Ref: 23d Cong., 1st Sess., Sen. Doc. 512, v. 4 (Serial 247), pp. 207-230.

❡ By letter of March 30, Sup't William Clark, St. Louis, was notified (by the comm'r of Indian affairs) that his office would receive the following funds for the Delawares formerly of Missouri (per October 26, 1832, treaty terms):

To purchase stock and open farms—$3,000; to pay "a person to attend their mill [then under construction?—see July entry], and for repairs for same for 1833"—$500 (and Clark was instructed to take measures to establish the school and select a teacher); for merchandise—$5,000; for payment of some Delaware debts (money owed to traders William Gilliss and William Marshall)— $12,000; annuities of $100 each for Delaware chiefs Patterson, Tah-whee-la-len (or, Ketchum), and "Nea-coming" (Nah-ko-min; Nat-coming, etc.)—$300.

Ref: 23d Cong., 1st Sess., Sen. Doc. 512, v. 3 (Serial 246), pp. 634, 635; C. J. Kappler's Indian Affairs, Laws and Treaties (Washington, 1904), v. 2, pp. 370-372.

❡ The Assiniboine (Bernard Pratte, Jr., master), new steamboat of the American Fur Company (and larger, but lighter-draught than the Yellowstone), was sent up the Missouri early in the spring—in advance of the older craft.

Ultimately the Assiniboine went as far as Fort Union (at the mouth of the Yellowstone); left that place on June 26 with a full cargo of peltries, and reached St. Louis again on July 11.

Ref: Thwaites, op. cit., v. 22, p. 240, v. 23, p. 12; H. M. Chittenden's The American Fur Trade . . . (New York, 1902), v. 1, pp. 357, 358; Missouri Republican, St. Louis, July 16, 1833.

❡ April 21.—The Yellowstone, on her third voyage to the upper Missouri, passed the mouth of the Kansas. Maximilian, prince of

Wied-Neuwied (on a scientific journey), his servant, and a young Swiss artist, Charles Bodmer, were passengers; as were, on some stages of the journey, Indian agents John Dougherty and John F. A. Sanford; also Asst. Surg. Benjamin F. Fellowes; and the American Fur Company's Kenneth McKenzie and Lucien Fontenelle. (Fontenelle, bound for the mountains with the outfit for Fontenelle & Drips, subsequently set out overland from Fort Pierre, and remained in the mountains till late summer, 1834.) In all, about 100 persons, mostly company employees, were aboard.

Maximilian noted the Kansas river's "clear green water," as contrasted with the muddy Missouri. "The steam-boat," he wrote, "has navigated the Konzas about seven miles upward, to a trading-post of the American Fur Company [the Chouteaus' post, of late 1828 origin]. Which steamboat?; and when (between 1828 and 1832) was the trip made? From the time of the *Western Engineer's* 1819 excursion of about a mile up the Kansas, to the voyage (or voyages?) referred to by Maximilian, no other steamboat had ventured up the river, so far as known. *See* further comment below.

Early on April 22 the *Yellowstone* reached the Fort Leavenworth landing—where she was thoroughly searched for contraband liquor. About seven barrels of "shrub," one of rum, one of wine, and two of whisky, were confiscated. Late in the afternoon, the trip upriver was continued.

On the 23d the steamboat passed Cow Island (Isle au Vache—*see* p. 49) "six miles in length, and covered with poplars [cottonwoods] and shave grass." Above the mouth of Independence creek, Maximilian noted the "naked grassy eminences, where a village of the Konzas formerly stood . . . [and the] Spaniards [*i. e.,* the French] had a post of a few soldiers. . . ." [*See* comment following.]

The *Yellowstone* reached Fort Pierre (S. D.) the last of May; and shortly set out on the return trip. She arrived at St. Louis on June 21 with "a rich cargo of skins." Maximilian and Bodmer continued upriver to other American Fur Company posts, then spent the winter of 1833-1834 at Fort Clark (N. D.). For their return to St. Louis *see* May, 1834, annals.

Ref: Thwaites, *op. cit.,* v. 22, pp. 237-328 (for Maximilian); *Missouri Republican,* June 25, 1833 (for the *Yellowstone's* return); Chittenden's *The American Fur Trade,* v. 1, p. 357. In the 1839 Coblenz edition of Maximilian's *Reise in das Innere Nord-America* . . ., v. 1, p. 271, the item on a steamboat voyaging up the Kansas reads: "Mit dem Dampfschiffe hat man den Konzas etwa 7 Meilen weit aufwärts beschifft, bis zu einem Handelsposten (Trading-Post) der American-Fur-Company, welchem gegenwärtig ein Bruder des Herrn Pierre Chouteau vorstand." The April 19, 1832, issue of the St. Louis (Mo.) *Beacon* noted that the steamboat *Otto* "will leave today" for the "mouth of Kanzas river." Was it, perhaps, the *Otto* which went up the Kansas to the Chouteaus' post? Or, could it have been the *Yellowstone,* which, in 1832, took an unusually long time (from April 16 to May 1) to travel from St. Louis to Fort Leavenworth? Maximilian's comment on the (French) fort location was misinformation. Fort Cavagnial (*see* 1744 annals) was near the Kansa village in the Salt creek valley area, not at Independence creek.

℃ In late April or early May White Hair and some 200 Osages (on foot) clashed with a mounted Kiowa war party (also around 200? in number), somewhere in northern Oklahoma of today. A heavy rainstorm terminated the battle. Probably this was the engagement reported by missionary W. F. Vaill—*see* May 7 entry—in which 22 "Pawnees" [Kiowas], and two Osages were reported killed.

Meantime, in late April, Clermont and some 300 Osage braves, having found and *back-tracked* the trail of the Kiowa war party, attacked the defenseless village (in present southwestern Oklahoma); massacred the women, children, and old men therein; cut off their victims' heads; burned the lodges; and departed for home with (it is said) over 100 new and old (Kiowa-taken) scalps, and two Kiowa prisoners (a brother and sister, about 10 and 12).

At Clermont's town, in early May, the Osages spent several days celebrating the great "victory" over the Kiowas; while to the northward, at White Hair's and other Neosho river towns, at nearly the same time, Osages were celebrating a victory over the "Pawnee" (Kiowa) war party.

Ref: Grant Foreman's *Advancing the Frontier* . . . (Norman, 1933), pp. 118-119; *Missionary Herald*, v. 29 (1833), pp. 368-370 (W. F. Vaill's journal); Foreman's *Pioneer Days* . . ., pp. 117-119; *Seventeenth Annual Report of the Bureau of American Ethnology* . . ., *1895-96*, Pt. II, pp. 257-260. Although Vaill called Clermont's Kiowa victims "Pawnees," it appears that White Hair's braves battled Kiowas rather than "Pawnees." As noted in Foreman's *Pioneer Days* . . ., p. 116: "Pawnee was the elastic term by which they roughly classified prairie Indians in the southwest and denoted particularly Pawnee Picts or Pique, Tawehash or Wichita Indians."

❦ MARRIED: William Thomas Ward, of Fayette, Mo., and Christiana McCoy, on May 2, at the home of the bride near "Westport," Mo., by her father, the Rev. Isaac McCoy. (This was one of the first marriages in the vicinity of soon-founded "Westport.") *See, also,* September 10 entry.

(In June, 1832—*see* p. 216—Isaac McCoy had started building a house east of state line. As later recollected by pioneer William Mulkey: "Isaac McCoy came with his family and settled out just south of where Westport is now. He built the first house in that section, a big double log cabin . . . which stood on a big hill. . . .")

Ref: McCoy's "Journal," May 2, 1833; Kansas City (Mo.) *Star*, March 21, 1933 (for Mulkey quote—in article by W. H. Harris on Westport, Mo.), also in "Wyandotte County Clippings," v. 6, p. 8, in KHi library. McCoy, in his "Journal," gave the groom's name as "Mr. T. I. Ward," but in the Jackson county, Mo., "Marriage Records," it is correctly entered as "William Thomas Ward." *See*, McCoy's "Journal," September 5, 1838, entry for item on Ward's death, September 2, 1838.)

❦ On May 7 four missionaries—William B. Montgomery and William F. Vaill (of Union), John Fleming (of the Creek mission), and Hugh Wilson (of the Chickasaw mission) left Union Mission (Okla.) on a 17-day preaching tour to the Osage villages.

They rode 25 miles to Clermont's town; found the Indians celebrating the great "victory" over the Kiowas (*see* a preceding entry); remained three days despite the commotion, excitement, and "unusual signs of depravity"; left for Hopefield on May 11; preached there next day; then moved northward to the towns on the Neosho (in present Neosho county), but found those Indians also in a state of excitement, having just come in from a buffalo hunt cut short by a fight with some Pawnees (Kiowas); 22 enemy warriors killed and two Osages lost, as Vaill was told. The missionaries (joined by the Rev. Amasa Jones of Harmony [Mo.]) were at White Hair's village on May 15; at another town farther north on the 16th (returning to Boudinot Mission to spend the night); at Wasoshi's village on May 17, where they found the occupants preparing for a female dance. Wrote Vaill: ". . . great preparations were going on. Some were opening the roof of a lodge that spectators may look in; females dressing in their best attire, with scarlet calico, ribbons, and feathers; and the men were shaving and painting, caparisoning the horses for the mounted grooms who dash about the streets to keep order. . . ."

After spending the night at the Osage Agency, the missionaries returned to Wasoshi's town on May 18 and "obtained an audience for an hour or two." But the Indians were impatient to go to a dance at White Hair's village. (On this tour, the Little Osages, whose town was still higher up the Neosho, were not visited. According to Vaill, they were then "dispersed as follows—300 had gone to war, a party on a buffalo hunt, and the women planting their corn.") The missionaries returned to Boudinot for the night; recrossed the Neosho again next day (fordable despite a heavy rain during the night); gathered a small audience at White Hair's (the day was Sunday); then returned to Boudinot once more, where services were held. On May 20th the four men started home, reaching Union Mission on May 22d.

Ref: *Missionary Herald*, v. 29 (1833), pp. 366-371 (for Vaill's journal of the tour—he mistakenly referred to the Indians killed by Clermont's warriors as Pawnees, rather than Kiowas).

⟨ From the Lexington-Liberty, Mo., area, in May, newly associated partners William Sublette and Robert Campbell launched their fur trade activities for the year. (Sublette was to direct operations on the Missouri, and open trading posts in competition with the American Fur Company. Campbell was to make the journey overland— to the trappers' rendezvous—with supplies it was hoped the Rocky Mountain Fur Company would buy; then with acquired furs, he was to join Sublette at the mouth of the Yellowstone—which place the latter would reach by keelboat. There they would build a fort in opposition to Fort Union.)

Robert Campbell's expedition—a mule pack-train, and company of 50— 45 employees, three guests, and an Arapaho boy (whom Fitzpatrick had found on the Plains in 1831—the day Jedediah Smith was killed), left Lexington about May 7, and shortly thereafter headed west, bound for the upper Green river valley, beyond the continental divide. Campbell's chief assistants were "old mountain man" Louis Vasquez, and "Mr. Johnesse" [Antoine Jaunisse or Janis?], a clerk. Making the journey as a pleasure trip were Capt. William Drummond Stewart (a later-wealthy Scotchman, and half-pay British army captain), Dr. Benjamin Harrison ("wild and adventurous" son of the former President), and Edmund Christy of St. Louis (who subsequently entered into a copartnership with the Rocky Mountain Fur Company). In the outfit were some 120(?) mules, a number of horses, two bulls, and three cows. Provisions included "twenty sheeps two loads of Bacon 500 weight of corn meal. . . ."

From the statements of Charles Larpenteur, then aged 25 (whose later-written journal and narrative provide details of this trip—his first to the mountains), it appears that the expedition left Independence about May 12; traveled the Santa Fe trail for two or three days; then turned northwestward to the Kansas—following the established pathway. Larpenteur wrote: "the first river of any consiquence that we crossed was the Caw river where there is an agensey for the Caw Indians which is kept by General [Marston G.] Clark relation of old General [William] Clark. . . ." The party forded the river on May 15, and after camping for one or two days near the agency, resumed the journey to the mountains by way of "Sublette's Trace"—across Jefferson, Shawnee, Pottawatomie, and Marshall counties of today. On May 23 Campbell's expedition reached the Platte; and on July 5 arrived at the rendezvous on Horse creek, well ahead of the "opposition" party led by Lucien Fontenelle which set out from Fort Pierre on June 8.

Ref: Charles Larpenteur's *Forty Years a Fur Trader* . . ., ed. by Elliott Coues (New York, 1898), v. 1; Dale L. Morgan's letter of May 10, 1962, to L. Barry, containing pertinent data, including a quotation from a Robert Campbell letter of September 12, 1833 (Campbell estate papers, Missouri Historical Society, St. Louis) that his party numbered "fifty men in all including two or three who went on a trip of pleasure"; Bernard De Voto's *Across the Wide Missouri* (Boston, 1947), pp. 27-34; John Sunder's *Bill Sublette* . . . (Norman, Okla., c1959), pp. 116, 123-130; 23d Cong., 1st Sess., H. Doc. No. 45 (Serial 254) for "Soublette and Campbell" trading license of April 15. Robert Campbell's diary, September-December, 1833, in *The Bulletin* of the Missouri Historical Society, St. Louis, v. 20 (October, 1963; January, 1964), pp. 3-24, 107-118, contains information on the 1833 expedition.

❮ About May 12, from the Lexington-Liberty, Mo., area camp (*see* preceding entry) William Sublette's river expedition got under way. His keelboat *Gallant* (and another which was left "at the Sioux"), towed up the Missouri to the last settlements by the steamboat *Otto,* passed along the "Kansas" border in mid-month; reached Bellevue (Neb.) May 28; and arrived at the Yellowstone on August 29. (On the way up Sublette established trading posts.) Andrew W. Sublette apparently was along on this trip.

By way of the Rockies, his partner Robert Campbell (accompanied by Nathaniel Wyeth and Milton Sublette) reached the Yellowstone camp on August 30. At that site, two miles below the Yellowstone's mouth (and several miles below the American Fur Company's Fort Union) construction immediately got under way on Sublette and Campbell's principal trading post, Fort William. Robert Campbell supervised its construction, remaining on the upper Missouri till the middle of 1834. (*See* p. 250 for Sublette's return trip.)

Ref: John Sunder's *Bill Sublette, op. cit.,* pp. 124-129; Robert Campbell's diary (1833) in *The Bulletin* of the Missouri Historical Society, St. Louis, v. 20, pp. 3-24, 107-118.

❮ In a treaty signed May 13, the Quapaws (remnant of the Arkansa Indians, numbering fewer than 500? persons) were granted 150 sections of land "between the lands of the Senecas and Shawnees" (*i. e.*, west of Missouri's southwest corner); and gave up the tract of land on Red river, Louisiana (in the Caddo country), occupied by most of the nation following the November 15, 1824, treaty, when they had been persuaded to cede their Arkansas territory lands. ("They were the first Western Indians to feel the ill effects of the removal scheme."—*KHC*, v. 8, p. 81.)

The 1833 treaty stipulated the Quapaws would be moved at government expense; be furnished stock and agricultural implements; a government farmer, and a blacksmith would live among them; educational aid of $1,000 a year would be provided; cabins would be built for them; also, there was an annuity provision.

Distrusting Wharton Rector (appointed to remove them), only about 160(?) of the 460(?) Quapaws journeyed to their new home in 1834. More arrived before 1838—the year in which the reserve was surveyed and discovery was made that these Indians had been settled on the Seneca-Shawnee lands. It is said this knowledge—that they would be required to move again—so disheartened the Quapaws that many wandered off, and about 250 established a village on the Canadian river. Eventually most of the nation gathered on their own reserve.

The Quapaws' reserve was laid out *above*, rather than *between*, the lands of the confederated Senecas & Shawnees. It was principally in the northeast corner of present Oklahoma; but 12 of the 150 sections of land were north of the 37th parallel, in what is now southern Cherokee county, Kansas.

Ref: Kappler, *op. cit.*, v. 2, pp. 395-397; 23d Cong., 1st Sess., *Sen. Doc. 512*, v. 4 (Serial 247), pp. 724-726; CIA "Report," 1839, p. 474; *KHC*, v. 8, p. 81; Foreman's *The Last Trek of the Indians*, pp. 308-311. See *KHQ*, v. 1, p. 105, for this statement in its proper context: ". . . the thirty-seventh parallel did not become the effective southern boundary of Kansas until the treaty of February 23, 1867, when the Quapaws, last of the tribes to conform, ceded all their right, title and claim to land in Kansas."

❏ "Round Prairie, near Missouri line," on May 15, was the set rendezvous for the spring caravan to Santa Fe. When Capt. William N. Wickliffe (Sixth U. S. infantry) and the government-provided military escort (144? men) reached that place (from Fort Leavenworth) on May 23d, most of the traders were still at Independence, Mo. Heavy rains and muddy roads had caused delays.)

The rendezvous was shifted to Council Grove—about 115 miles westward. Wickliffe's command (Capt. Matthew Duncan's company of more than 100 Mounted Rangers; and 25 Sixth infantry troops, under a lieutenant; also a fieldpiece and six wagons), hampered (as were the traders) by bad weather, arrived at Council Grove three weeks later—on June 13. The trading caravan which assembled there, and set out for Santa Fe on June 19(?), totaled 184(?) men, 103(?) wagons and carriages, goods variously listed as worth $100,000 and $180,000. (It was reported that Charles Bent took merchandise estimated at $40,000.)

At Diamond Spring(s)—15 miles beyond Council Grove—on June 20, the traders elected Charles Bent as their captain; and Messrs. Legrave, Barnes,

Smith, and Branch, as lieutenants. On July 2, at the Great Bend of the Arkansas, the shorter, direct "dry route" to the Arkansas crossing was selected. Wickliffe's command lost the trail, and before reaching the river again on July 6, the troops' horses suffered for lack of water and forage.

The caravan forded the Arkansas, at the lower crossing, on July 10. Next day the traders and the military escort parted company. The former, including Capt. Richard B. Lee (on leave from the army) who had been with the escort, began the march through Mexican territory—reaching Santa Fe safely August 4; the latter headed back to Fort Leavenworth—arriving there August 3d. (*See* September entry for return of the caravan.)

Ref: *Missouri Republican*, April 23, July 12, 1833; *Missouri Intelligencer*, Columbia, July 20, 1833; *Niles' Weekly Register*, v. 44 (issue of August 3, 1833), p. 374; *Arkansas Gazette*, August 7, 1833; *The Mississippi Valley Historical Review*, v. 41, pp. 462-464 (for military escort data); J. T. Irving (McDermott edition), pp. 16, 18, 19, 28 (for other information on the rangers); Josiah Gregg (*op. cit.*, v. 2, p. 160) gave the 1833 statistics as: 105 wagons, 185 men (60 proprietors), goods worth $180,000; *Colorado Magazine*, Denver, v. 31 (1954), p. 114 (for quote of a statement by James Aull, May 15, 1833, on Charles Bent's goods); Fort Leavenworth post returns (microfilm, KHi).

❧ About May 21, 375 Kickapoos, and 119 Pottawatomies (attached to the Prophet's band), reached the new Kickapoo reserve (north of the Delawares' land) after an overland trip from southwest Missouri. Their conductor was James Kennerly. At the settlement site, about five miles above Fort Leavenworth, Special Agent William Alley first issued rations to the 494 immigrants on May 21.

Sup't William Clark had estimated the Kickapoos (and Pottawatomies attached) in Illinois and Missouri, at about 650 persons—the Prophet's band of 352 (including 110 Pottawatomies), on the Vermilion river, Illinois; and Kishko's band of about 300 on the Kickapoo reserve in southwest Missouri. Kennekuk (the Prophet) and his followers departed from Illinois in the fall of 1832; attended the Castor Hill (Mo.) treaty councils (of late October) *en masse;* and after the treaty were conducted (by John McCausland) to the Kickapoo reserve in Missouri, to spend the winter of 1832-1833.

Though Pa-sha-cha-hah (Jumping Fish) was head chief (the first signer of the 1832 treaty), Kennekuk (the Prophet) was the dominant figure who "exercised unlimited sway over the larger portion of the Kickapoos, but the rest despised him" (according to Missionary J. C. Berryman). Kishko (a "war chief"—13th on the list of 1832 treaty signers), and some of his band (about 70?), after migrating to "Kansas" in May, 1833, refused to live on the reserve (*see* September 2 entry). It was Kishko's influence which, for several months, kept the Kickapoos in turmoil. The Rev. W. D. Smith (Presbyterian), then visting "Kansas," stated in a July 29 letter:

"They [the Kickapoos] are not yet settled. . . . They live at present in the only unhealthy place I have seen in the [Indian] country. Their village is . . . on the northern edge of a low wet Prairie which runs up along a creek from the low bottoms of the Missouri. Their huts are built so closely as to prevent a free circulation of air, and to accelerate the accumulations of filth."

Between May 21 and June 30 store houses and an "issuing house" were built in the settlement. (Workmen on the project were John Bridges, Louis Chamezous, Solomon Groom, James Kennerly's "negro boy Ananias," and Smith Story's Negro man.) It was, presumably, the latter building which J. T. Irving, Jr., saw in August: "In the centre of the town is a small log house, the residence of the agent appointed to reside with the tribe. . . . (He referred to disbursing agent William Alley—hired by Sup't William Clark at $50 a month—to distribute rations to the Kickapoos and Pottawatomies.)

Ref: SIA, v. 5, pp. 55, 56; 23d Cong., 1st Sess., Sen. Doc. 512, v. 1 (Serial 244), pp. 644, 647, v. 3 (Serial 246), pp. 511, 512, 518, 640, 706, 707, v. 5 (Serial 248), pp. 68-81; Presbyterian Historical Society, American Indian Missions correspondence, microfilm, KHi ms. division, for W. D. Smith quotation); J. T. Irving (McDermott edition), p. 42 (for Irving's statement); Hiram W. Beckwith's *The Illinois and Indiana Indians* (Chicago, 1884), p. 137.

℃ In May there was a flood of unprecedented proportions on the Arkansas river—at least on the lower Arkansas—in the Fort Gibson (Okla.) and Fort Smith, Ark. ter., areas. The waters of two of its tributaries—the Verdigris and the Grand (Neosho) rivers—were also reported "higher than ever known before."

On the lower Verdigris, the flood swept away the trading houses of Auguste P. Chouteau (his loss was said to be over $10,000), and Hugh Love; and the government lost two of its Creek Agency buildings, together with contents.

How high upstream these rivers flooded does not seem to be recorded. As noted (*see* May 15 for the rain-delayed Santa Fe traders; and next entry for comment on the "great and continued fall of heavy rains"), the spring of 1833 was an extraordinarily wet one.

Ref: Foreman's *Pioneer Days in the Early Southwest,* pp. 107, 108, 201.

℃ William Gordon (special agent for Sup't William Clark, St. Louis), arrived in "Kansas" in May or June, to distribute annuity merchandise and agricultural equipment to several Indian nations (in accordance with the October, 1832, treaty terms—*see, also,* March 30, 1833, entry).

Gordon delivered the items for the Kaskaskias & Peorias and the Weas & Piankeshaws to Agent R. W. Cummins "near his agency" (present Johnson county). He later reported: "The great and continued fall of heavy rains . . . kept the roads in an impassable state for a considerable length of time after my arrival in the vicinity of the Indians." The Delawares received their goods on June 25. After more delay, Gordon reached Fort Leavenworth with supplies for the Kickapoos. The tribe accepted the agricultural tools, but refused the goods; and Gordon was forced to arrange to pay their annuities in cash—which he did on July 20th. By report, the merchandise was worth less than half the represented value; and was also rejected by post sutler Alexander G. Morgan, who had considered buying it. Subsequently, the *John Nelson* freighted the goods back to St. Louis! (Compare with October 13, 1834, entry.)

Ref: 23d Cong., 1st Sess., *Sen. Doc. 512*, v. 4 (Serial 247), pp. 522-525 (Gordon's letter of August 12, 1833), v. 5 (Serial 248), pp. 62, 66, 71; SIA, v. 10 (an unpaged "Clark" daybook); Presbyterian Historical Society, American Indian Missions correspondence (the Rev. W. D. Smith letter of July 22, 1833, for item on Morgan, and other comment on quality of the goods).

❏ In June a school was opened at the Peoria Methodist Mission by the Rev. James H. Slavens and his wife. The mission (founded in 1832?—*see* below) was on the Marais des Cygnes' north bank, near the Peoria & Kaskaskia village (and near present Peoria, Franklin co.). It was a one-story, hewed-log structure (dwelling and school house combined), 42 by 18 feet, with a 10-foot passageway in the middle, and a chimney at either end. There was a separate "cooking house" 16 feet square.

(Probably the Peoria Methodist Mission had its origin in late 1832. Slavens was appointed missionary to the Peorias at the Methodists' Missouri conference in the fall of 1832. Isaac McCoy [in his January, 1835, *Annual Register*] stated that the Peoria Methodist Mission was "commenced in 1832.")

On August 5, 1833, the Rev. W. D. Smith (a visitor) commented: "Among the Peorias . . . the Methodists have a station with a school . . . which is doing well." The Rev. Thomas Johnson reported (on August 16, 1833) that the Peoria school had 24 young students (23 males and one female). In the autumn of 1833 the Rev. Nathaniel Talbott was appointed to the Peoria mission (and Slavens was assigned to Chariton, Mo.). The *church* membership, in 1835, was given as two whites and 26 Indians.

Talbott and his wife continued as the principal missionaries to the Peorias till late 1841, when they were succeeded by the Rev. Nathan T. Shaler and wife. Mrs. Shaler died in March, 1843. Though a July, 1843, report described the mission as "doing well," and having a church membership of over 40, it appears the Peoria Methodist Mission closed before the end of that year.

Ref: Thomas Johnson's letters of August 16, 1833 (typed copy in KHi ms. division), and July 21, 1834 (Isaac McCoy manuscripts); D. R. McAnally's *History of Methodism in Missouri* (St. Louis, 1881), pp. 629-631; *KHC*, v. 9, pp. 168, 199, 200, 211, 226, 227 (though some of Lutz's statements are inaccurate), v. 16, pp. 238, 249-251, 253, 254; Isaac McCoy's *Annual Registers* for 1835, 1836; Presbyterian Historical Society, American Indian Missions correspondence, for W. D. Smith item; 23d Cong., 1st Sess., *H. R.* 474 (Serial 263), p. 70 (for May, 1834, report); CIA *"Reports"* for 1834, 1837, 1838. The Talbotts had three children according to a July, 1834, report Thomas Johnson wrote Isaac McCoy—McCoy manuscripts. For a description of the Peoria mission buildings, *see* Office of Indian Affairs, "Letters Received from the St. Louis Superintendency" (National Archives Microcopy 234, Roll 751), William Clark's letter of November 15, 1836, enclosing R. W. Cummins' report on Methodist mission schools.

❏ From June 18 to late August, Presbyterian missionary William D. Smith was a visitor in eastern "Kansas"—on a tour to determine mission locations.

Smith made his headquarters at the home of Joseph Barnett (a well-educated, part-Shawnee) and family, on the Shawnee reserve. Accompanied by Barnett, he began a journey about June 20, which took him first to the Delaware settlements; then to Fort Leavenworth (where he met Chief Ietan of the Otoes, and Chief Big Elk of the Omahas and visited the nearby Kickapoos); then southwest to the Kansa Agency (about July 12) and to the Kansa villages; then back to the Shawnee reserve. Subsequently, he paid visits to the Ottawas (in late July); to the Weas & Piankeshaws, and Peorias & Kaskaskias (in early August); went again to Fort Leavenworth; and from there to the Iowas (in mid-August); then returned to Barnett's house. In late August he visited the Weas & Pianke-shaws again; and made preliminary arrangements for a Presbyterian mission among them. (Among the Iowas, also, he had found a promising field for a mission.)

Ref: Presbyterian Historical Society, American Indian Missions correspondence, for William D. Smith's six letters—all written at Shawnee Village, Kansas river—dated June 19, July 22, 29, August 5, 20, 27, 1833; Joseph Barnett's letter of June 23, 1833, in *ibid.*

❧ "On the 24th June," wrote Isaac McCoy, "Shawanuk [a young chief] . . . & 22 others started from Delaware Town on a War excursion against the Pawnees, to avenge the death of some Dela-wares killed by the Pawnee last summer or fall [*see* March, 1832, entry]. The party passed thru the Kanza villages, the latter were to join them in the expedition."

Shawanock (Sou-wah-nock) and his warriors reached the Platte early in July(?); found the Grand Pawnees' village deserted (the 2,500 inhabitants were absent on a hunt); burned the town, and also destroyed the near-by fields of corn and vegetables.

(When Comm'r Henry Ellsworth and his party visited the Grand Pawnees in October they found that the Indians had completed the rebuilding of their village.)

Ref: McCoy "Journal," entry of July 7, 1833; 23d Cong., 1st Sess., *Sen. Doc. 512,* v. 4 (Serial 247), pp. 523, 654; J. T. Irving (McDermott edition), pp. 6, 130, 242, 247.

❧ In the summer (June?, or July?), the Friends (of Indiana yearly meeting) sent a committee of three (Henry Harvey, Simon Hadley, and Solomon Haddon) to visit the Shawnees—particularly the Shawnees who had removed from Wapaghkonetta, Ohio, to "Kan-sas" late the year before (*see* November 30, 1832, entry), among whom the Friends had maintained a mission, in Ohio, for about 11 years. The report they submitted included this statement:

"The Indians are settled on an excellent tract of land, nearly one-half of which is rich, dry prairie; the remainder well timbered, with good mill streams, and apparently healthy, and they appear to be satisfied." (The Shawnee re-serve included Johnson, Douglas, and parts of Shawnee, Osage, Wabaunsee, Morris, and Geary counties of today. How much of it the committee personally inspected is not known.)

Three more years elapsed before a Shawnee Friends Mission was constructed (in 1836) in "Kansas"; and the mission school was not opened till 1837.

Ref: *KHC,* v. 8, pp. 261 262, 267, 268; *KHQ,* v. 13, p. 36; Henry Harvey's *History of the Shawnee Indians* . . ., *1681 to 1854* . . . (Cincinnati, 1855), p. 234.

❧ About July 8—the date can only be approximated—cholera broke out aboard the steamboat *Yellowstone.* She was then ascending the

Missouri (on her second voyage upstream in 1833) and approaching present Kansas City, Mo. In a short space of time eight(?) men died—leaving only the captain (Andrew S. Bennett) and Joseph La Barge (aged 17, a company clerk).

La Barge is quoted as stating (at a later time): "There is a spot just below Kansas City . . . where I buried eight cholera victims in one grave." Captain Bennett started for St. Louis to hire another crew. Frightened Jackson county, Mo., residents threatened to burn the *Yellowstone* (which was lying below the Kaw's mouth). La Barge fired up the boilers and piloted the boat out of Missouri jurisdiction—anchoring her on the Missouri's right bank, but *above* the Kaw's mouth (present Wyandotte county). Then he set out, afoot, for the Chouteaus' Shawnee reserve post—about eight miles distant—for instructions on handling the Chouteaus' supplies aboard. A guard posted (because of the cholera threat) about a mile from the trading house, relayed his message. When a reply came, it was late in the day, and La Barge prepared to camp out overnight. Later, young Edward Ligueste Chouteau (a former school chum, visitor at the Chouteaus' post) brought him food, and a buffalo robe to sleep on. Next day he returned to the *Yellowstone*.

Isaac McCoy's journal entry of July 13 adds this note to the episode: ". . . A boat had, a few days ago, been compelled by Cholera to stop on her way up. Some eight or ten had died. She stopped, and is still lying about 5 miles from our [Westport, Mo.] house. Our neighbourhood is considerably uneasy."

Some time elapsed before Captain Bennett and a new crew arrived—aboard the *Otto*—to resume the voyage. The *Yellowstone* reached "Cabanne's" (Pilcher's) post at the Council Bluffs in August.

Ref: *KHC,* v. 9, pp. 281, 282; H. M. Chittenden's *History of Early Steamboat Navigation on the Missouri River; Life and Adventures of Joseph La Barge* (New York, 1903), v. 1, pp. xi, xii, 13, 19, 31-37; McCoy's "Journal"; *Missouri Republican,* St. Louis, July 16, 1833. The *Assiniboine,* which reached St. Louis on July 11, had met the *Yellowstone*—then at the Kaw's mouth, three hands and her pilot dead—but did not stop because of the cholera.

❡ July 13.—Baptist missionaries Moses and Eliza (Wilcox) Merrill (from Michigan territory) arrived at Isaac McCoy's home near "Westport," Mo. (They had reached Independence Landing about July 11, after a journey up the Missouri on a steamboat which had "three cases and one death of cholera" aboard.)

Before July 21 the Merrills moved into quarters at Shawnee Baptist Mission, in "Kansas." According to Eliza Merrill's journal, they had arrived to find the empty house "filled with fleas, and . . . very dirty. . . . Mr. Merrill killed a rattlesnake in the house. . . ." By the end of the month, however, they were settled. On Sunday, August 4, Moses Merrill journeyed to the Delawares to hold service, while Eliza Merrill walked a mile and a half to collect some Shawnee children for her first Sunday school. On August 10 she noted: "The past week we opened our day school with seven scholars. The second day we had eight. They are very wild. Some of them had nothing on but a shirt." On a later Sunday she wrote: "This morning Mr. Merrill and myself walked to the Indian village. . . . We succeeded in gathering 14 children to teach. . . . The men, most of them, were out racing horses, or gambling or hunting, and the women were at their work." One Friday she recorded: ". . . [today] we had 18 scholars. I gave those who had been a week some clothing. They appeared very happy as they exchanged their ragged, filthy garments for new ones. . . ."

After residing for 15 weeks in "Kansas," the Merrills left to found a Baptist mission at Bellevue (Neb.), for the Otoes. *See* October 27 entry for their departure; but, *see, also,* September 5 entry.

Ref: Nebraska Historical Society *Transactions*, Lincoln, v. 5 (1893), pp. 205-240 (wherein are excerpts from Eliza Merrill's journal); Isaac McCoy's "Journal," July 13 and 21, 1833, entries.

❡ By July, if not earlier, the Delawares' saw and grist mill (provided by the government under terms of the October 26, 1832, treaty) was in operation. *It was the first such mill in "Kansas."* Construction probably had been started early in the spring. The first known reference to its being in use is in a July 29 letter by a "Kansas" visitor, the Rev. W. D. Smith, who wrote: "They [the Delawares] have also a good grist mill and saw mill in operation."

Up to September 30 Agent R. W. Cummins had paid out: $2,975.50 to Michael Rice "for building Delaware mills and bolt, and repairing the same"; $10 to James and Robert Aull "for saw for Delaware mill"; $32 to Edward Brafford and $6 to William Barnes "for attending Delaware mill." On October 1 William Barnes was appointed miller at a salary of $500 per year. (He was still in charge in 1836.)

Comm'r Henry Ellsworth (in a November 8 letter) noted that the Kickapoos "are anxious to have a mill erected soon, and Mr. Cummings [Cummins], their agent, has some experience in this business, having just finished a mill for the Delawares, and also one for himself." (Cummins' mill was east of the state line, probably just north of "Westport" in Jackson county, Mo.) The following items from the diary of Jotham Meeker—then residing at Shawnee Baptist Mission (present Johnson county)—indicate at least three grist mills were operating within a half-day's journey of the mission in 1834-1835: February 8, 1834, "Go with wagon to [James H.] M'Gee's mill [within present Kansas City, Mo.]. Bring home chopped corn & meal"; November 6, 1834, "Take load of corn to Delaware Mill"; November 24, 1834, "Return home [from the Delaware reserve] and bring meal from the Delaware Mill"; September 9, 1835, "Purchase and bring from Cummins' Mill, Flour & Bran"; December 15, 1835, "Rode to Cummins' mill,—bro't home a bag of flour"; December 16, 1835, "Went again to mill, and engaged 500 lbs. flour."

Ref: Presbyterian Historical Society, American Indian Missions correspondence, for Smith's letter; 23d Cong., 1st Sess., *H. Ex. Doc. 490* (Serial 259), p. 160; 23d Cong., 1st Sess., *Sen. Doc. 512*, v. 4 (Serial 247), p. 659 (for Ellsworth; 23d Cong., 2d Sess., *H. Doc. No. 150* (Serial 274), p. 26 (for Barnes' salary, 1833-1834); 24th Cong., 1st Sess., *Sen. Doc. 109* (Serial 280), p. 7 (for an 1836 reference to Barnes); Jotham Meeker's "Diary," in KHi ms. division. On the original land plat (of the mid-1850's), of Sec. 21, T. 11, R. 24 E., on Mill creek, about a mile and a half west and south of Muncie, Wyandotte co., is shown a Delaware mill site (not necessarily, but perhaps, the same location as the mill of the 1830's).

❡ Between July 29 and August 14, Isaac McCoy, his son John C. McCoy, and nine assistants, were occupied in surveying the lines of the small Peoria & Kaskaskia reservation (bounded on the east by the Wea & Piankeshaw lands; and on the west by the Ottawa reserve).

The McCoys' assistants were: Stephen Cantrell and Peter Duncan, chainmen; hired hands C. Bowers, B. C. Cooper, Thomas Linville, Ira Hunter, W. H. H. Cantrell, Charles Morris, and George Brace. Also along was John C. McCoy's servant to serve as cook and hostler. They had a dearborn drawn by two horses; and three pack horses.

Ref: SIA, v. 1, pp. 60-65 (for survey field notes dated "Shawanoe Jackson Co. Mo. Aug. 31, 1833"), and p. 56 (for plat); 23d Cong., 1st Sess., *Sen. Doc. 512*, v. 5 (Serial 248), pp. 248-250 (for itemized expenses of the survey); Isaac McCoy's "Journal," July 29-August 16, 1833, entries.

❡ About August 1 eight(?) of the 10 residents at the Upper Missouri Indian Agency—Bellevue (Neb.)—were stricken with cholera. Seven died; Agent John Dougherty barely survived an attack. (Bellevue was 170 miles above Fort Leavenworth.)

Joshua Pilcher (American Fur Company agent) wrote, on August 21: "The cholera was very fatal at *Belle Vue:* the Sub Agent [R. P. Beauchamp], both Blacksmiths [George Casner (or Cassner?), and Vincent Guitar(?)], Mrs. Cossner [Cassner?], the Interpreter [Francis Sanssouci] & wife all went off in a few hours, and Major Daugherty escaped narrowly and is still in verry bad health. . . ." (Some persons died of cholera at Pilcher's near-by post, also.)

Ref: J. T. Irving (McDermott edition), pp. xxix, 45n; SIA, v. 21, p. 80 (for names of Bellevue Agency employees, as of June 30, 1833); Thwaites, *op. cit.,* v. 24, p. 14 (for Maximilian's comment on the deaths at Bellevue, and at Pilcher's post). On a visit to Fort Leavenworth (in August), the Rev. W. D. Smith *heard* that the cholera had been taken up to Bellevue by the *Yellowstone* (which had not been allowed to land at the military post because of *reported* cholera aboard).—Smith's letter of August 27, 1833, in Presbyterian Historical Society, American Indian Missions correspondence.

❡ August 3.—U. S. Comm'r Henry L. Ellsworth, Edward A. Ellsworth (his son), John Treat Irving, Jr. (nephew of Washington Irving), and John Dunlop ("a Scotch gentleman"), arrived at Fort Leavenworth, on horseback. With them was Lt. John Nicholls, Sixth U. S. infantry, who had joined the group at Independence, Mo.

From St. Louis, the party's journey (begun at Washington early in July) had been overland, with hired hands driving two supply-laden dearborns. Ellsworth and his companions, it appears, spent the night of August 2 at blacksmith Lewis Jones' log cabin (exact location unknown), on the Shawnee reserve. They crossed the Kansas, on the morning of August 3, by way of Grinter's ferry, and stopped, briefly, at the house of the Delawares' blacksmith, Robert Dunlap, before proceeding to Fort Leavenworth, 23 miles northward.

John Treat Irving, Jr. (aged 20), who spent about three and a half months (August to mid-November) in "Kansas" and "Nebraska" in company with the Ellsworths and Dunlop, subsequently wrote of his 1833 adventures in a work entitled *Indian Sketches* . . . (first published at Philadelphia in 1835).

This book is a principal source of information on Comm'r Henry Ellsworth's activities during the summer and autumn of 1833—activities which are noted in some following annals entries.

Ref: Used for the above (and later) entries—J. F. McDermott's edition of John T. Irving, Jr.'s *Indian Sketches* . . ., which includes valuable introductory material, extensive and useful footnotes, and incorporates pertinent information from the 1888 revised edition of the *Indian Sketches*.

❦ At Fort Leavenworth, in August, there were (by later report) "a great number" of cholera cases, but very few fatalities. It would appear, from available information, that the presence of this often-swiftly-fatal malady created no great alarm at the post. The army doctor—Asst. Surg. Benjamin F. Fellowes—was commended by Comm'r Henry Ellsworth (whose son, Edward, got the cholera, but survived) as "a skillful man and well qualified for the situation."

In May, 1834, Fellowes told Maximilian "He had been very successful with his cholera patients [in 1833], for, out of a great number, one only had died, because he always attacked the disorder at its very commencement." Three Mounted Rangers died at the post in August (Samuel Carey on the 20th; John K. Green and Benjamin F. Phelps on the 28th), but *perhaps* only one was a cholera victim.

Ref: *Ibid.*, pp. xxix, 44n; Thwaites, *op. cit.*, v. 24, p. 114 (for Maximilian).

❦ August 26.—In charge of Lt. William R. Montgomery, a party of 68 Prairie Pottawatomies, headed by Chief Qui-qui-to (Que-ah-que-ah-ta), and Michi-che-cho-ca-ba (who was "next in authority among the religious Indians to the celebrated Kickapoo prophet"), arrived at Fort Leavenworth aboard the steamboat *Otto.* Their destination was the Kickapoo reserve—a few miles northward—where they had been invited to live.

In December, 1832, "two Pottawatomie chiefs from the prairies in Illinois, with their bands, amounting to 200," had gone to the Logansport, Ind., vicinity "in a very distressed situation," and asked permission (of Indian Agent William Marshall) to remain till spring, when they would remove west. In the summer of 1833, after much manoeuvering, 68 of these Prairie Pottawatomies, were induced to begin their migration westward. They left Logansport, Ind., on July 27th; traveled overland to Alton, Ill.; reached that place August 14; and departed August 16, aboard the *Otto,* for the mouth of the Missouri, and the journey upstream.

Ref: 23d Cong., 1st Sess., Sen. *Doc. 512*, v. 1 (Serial 244), pp. 276, 277, 775-780, 800, 897, v. 3 (Serial 246), p. 734, v. 4 (Serial 247), pp. 135-137, 187, 416-418.

❦ September 2.—Comm'r Henry Ellsworth journeyed from Fort Leavenworth to the Kickapoo settlement (five miles northward) and held a council with some of the chiefs. Kishko—leader of the dissident faction which was holding out for a reserve on the Marais des Cygnes river—presented his objections to the assigned lands.

Ellsworth reported there were 30 camps of Indians on the reserve; and that the Kickapoos who had refused to move there (Kishko's 70? followers) were "on the other side of the Kanzas river, on the Shawnee lands, occupied I think in drinking and rioting." Nothing in particular was accomplished at this meeting. But, *see* November 13 entry.

Ref: 23d Cong., 1st Sess., *Sen. Doc. 512,* v. 4 (Serial 247), pp. 639-642.

❐ The first week of September Comm'r Henry Ellsworth, his son Edward, John T. Irving, Jr., John Dunlop, Dr. Ware S. May, and Agent John Dougherty, left Fort Leavenworth to travel to the Otoe and Missouri village. Seven Sixth infantrymen served as escort; also there were drivers for two dearborns, and two ox-drawn, heavy wagons; and a Negro cook. Traveling northward—keeping from 20 to 30 miles west of the Missouri river—this mounted company arrived at the Indians' town (near the Platte) on September 17, after a journey of about 180 miles.

Ellsworth negotiated a treaty with the Otoes and Missouris on September 20 and 21. The Indians ceded claim to lands south of the Little Nemahaw river. Also, they declared their willingness to "abandon the chase" for an agricultural life. In return, the government was to continue their annuities (to 1850); provide agricultural aid of various kinds, money for educational purposes, etc. Witnesses to the treaty included Edward Ellsworth, Dougherty, May, Dunlop, Irving, and Ira D. Blanchard (Baptist missionary to the Delawares).

For two weeks following the treaty-signing, Ellsworth and his party remained among the Otoes and Missouris; then, on October 4, accompanied by Chief Ietan and some of his warriors, and three of the infantrymen, they set out for the Grand Pawnees' town—some 80 miles higher up the Platte. (*See, also,* October 7 entry.)

Ref: J. T. Irving (McDermott edition), pp. xxxiii, 44-113; Kappler, *op. cit.,* v. 2, pp. 400, 401.

❐ September 5.—A mounted party of three—the Rev. Moses Merrill, of Shawnee Baptist Mission, Ira D. Blanchard (Baptist affiliate, residing among the Delawares), and a guide—set out from the Kansas river, northward, for the Otoe-Missouri village on the Platte river, 200 miles distant. They were making a preliminary investigation of the route, and of conditions at Bellevue (Neb.) where the Baptists proposed to establish a mission.

On September 16 they reached the Otoe-Missouri village (a mile? from the Platte, and some 20? miles above its mouth); next day they crossed the Platte and rode 35(?) miles to the Bellevue Agency, on the Missouri river. (Apparently they left the Indians' village the same day Comm'r Henry Ellsworth's party arrived.) Merrill and Blanchard were, again, at the Otoe-Missouri town on September 20 when Ellsworth held a treaty council there. On September 21, the day the treaty was signed (Blanchard was a witness), they started the

200-mile homeward journey. The missionaries were back at the Kansas river by October 2d. (*See* October 26 entry for their second journey to Bellevue.)

Ref: Nebraska Historical Society *Transactions*, v. 4 (1892), p. 160, v. 5 (1893), p. 221; J. T. Irving (McDermott edition), pp. 47, 73, 89, 103. In June, 1831, Lt. Philip St. George Cooke, on a leave of absence from Cantonment Leavenworth, had journeyed from that post to the villages of the Otoe and Omaha Indians, and to "Bellevue," in company with "Mr. B.," an "officer of the Indian Department" (presumably Subagent R. P. Beauchamp). *See* his *Scenes and Adventures* . . . (Philadelphia, 1857), pp. 95-107. Their route must have been much the same as that of Merrill and Blanchard.

❡ MARRIED: Thomas Jefferson Givens, of Potosi, Mo., and Sarah McCoy, on September 10, at the home of the bride near "Westport," Mo., by her father, the Rev. Isaac McCoy. (*See, also,* May 2, entry.)

Ref: Jackson county, Mo., "Marriage Records"; letters in Isaac McCoy manuscripts, for general information.

❡ September 15.—Conducted by their interpreter, Joseph Parks (an educated, and much-respected quarter-Shawnee), 67 Shawnee Indians from Wapaghkonetta, Ohio, arrived at the Shawnee reserve in "Kansas." (*See* November 30, 1832, entry for earlier migrants from Wapaghkonetta.)

These Indians had left Ohio early in June, and traveled overland, by way of St. Louis. Originally the emigrating party numbered more than 80, but Parks reported that two had died on the way, one family ("Barnett's bro.") turned back, three "went over to the Delawares," and one family did not leave Ohio. Leading men in this band of Shawnees were: Little Fox, George Williams, Quilina, and Peculse-coe(?). They were among the last of their nation to remove to "Kansas."

Ref: Joseph Parks' mss. (in KHi ms. division); 23d Cong., 1st Sess., *Sen. Doc. 512*, v. 2 (Serial 245), pp. 594, 595, v. 3 (Serial 246), pp. 649, 650, 698, v. 4 (Serial 247), pp. 174, 200, 201; *KHC*, v. 8, pp. 252-255, and v. 10, pp. 399-401 (for notes on Joseph Parks). Parks later became head chief of the Shawnees. He died in the early part of April, 1859, and was buried "at the Shawnee burial ground" with Masonic honors.—Leavenworth *Daily Times*, April 13, 1859, p. 2, col. 4. The Shawnee treaty of August 8, 1831, describes Joseph Parks as one-quarter Shawnee.

❡ Between September 18 and October 12, Isaac McCoy, his son John C. McCoy, and nine assistants (all well armed), were occupied in surveying the Shawnees' *southern* boundary (which extended 120 miles west from the Missouri line), and the 19-mile-long *western* boundary. The Shawnees' west line ran through present Morris and Geary counties. The stream labeled "Boundary Cr[eek]" on the map is, evidently, Lyons creek of today.)

The McCoys' assistants were: Stephen Cantrell and Peter Duncan, chainmen; hired hands Thomas Linville, Jacob and Daniel Crandell, William Lovelady, Hiram Abbot, W. H. H. Cantrell, and Charles Morris; and a servant who was cook and hostler.

On September 18, at a point 20 miles west of Missouri, on the Shawnees' south line, the McCoys and party started westward; on the 26th they camped at the 60th mile point. From that place they digressed 19 miles straight northward (crossing the Santa Fe trail) to the southeast corner of the Kansa reserve, in order to "ascertain the situation of the Shawanoe lands at this place." Their camp on the 27th was on a creek four miles from the Kansas river. (This would seem to place them on present Shunganunga creek, southwest of Topeka, in Mission township.) On September 30 and October 1 they returned southward to the 60th mile point on the Shawnees' southern line; and then started westward again. On October 10 they reached the 120-mile point (the southwest corner of the Shawnee reserve) and turned north; on the 12th they established the northwest corner of the Shawnee lands (a few miles south of present Junction City, near the Smoky Hill river). This was the end of the survey.

Ref: SIA, v. 1, pp. 106-119 (for field notes of the survey), and p. 120 (for plat); 23d Cong., 1st Sess., Sen. Doc. 512, v. 5 (Serial 248), pp. 249, 250 (for Isaac McCoy's itemized expenditures in making the survey); Isaac McCoy's *History of Baptist Indian Missions,* p. 464.

℃ September 27.—Nathaniel J. Wyeth, traveling down the Missouri in a "bull boat," with a few voyageurs, arrived at Fort Leavenworth. (For Wyeth's overland expedition of 1832 to the Far West, *see* May, 1832, annals.) In his journal, Wyeth wrote:

I . . . was received with . . . politeness . . . [and] was offered all the stores which I might require by Leiut. [Asa] Richardson the officer of the day. . . . I took . . . ["my boy Baptiste and the Indian"] to Doct [Benjamin F.] Fellow[e]s quarters to be vaccinated the Docts wife and another lady ["really beautiful women"] happened to be present. . . . Baptiste . . . told the other boys . . . that he had seen a white squaw white as snow and so pretty."

Wyeth (whose journey down the Bighorn, the Yellowstone, and the Missouri had begun in mid-August) continued downriver on September 28, to Liberty, Mo. At Liberty Landing, on the 30th, he boarded the steamboat *John Nelson* which was going *up* as far as Fort Leavenworth. About October 3d he was again at the military post, where, he wrote, "I . . . was treated with great politeness by the officers . . . especially a Capt. Nichols [*i. e.,* Lt. John Nicholls] who invited me to dinner." The *John Nelson,* with Wyeth as a passenger, reached St. Louis on October 9th.

Ref: *Sources of the History of Oregon,* Eugene, v. 1 (1899), pp. 71, 209, 218, 219; SIA, v. 10 (an entry in this daybook of the St. Louis Indian superintendency shows payment, on October 12, to the *John Nelson* for freight of Kickapoo goods); Jotham Meeker in his "Diary," on October 2, noted the Meekers' arrival at Independence Landing on the upbound *John Nelson;* J. T. Irving (McDermott edition), footnotes on pp. xxiii and 15 for items on Lt. John Nicholls. Wyeth took the two Indian boys East with him. *See* Daniel Lee and J. H. Frost's *Ten Years in Oregon* (New York, 1844), p. 112.

℃ As reported for the year ending September 30 (*i. e.,* October 1, 1832-September 30, 1833), the following persons had been employed at the Indian agencies in "Kansas":

At the *Kansa Agency:* Marston G. Clark (subagent); Clement Lessert (interpreter); John McGill (gun and blacksmith); Joseph Groom (striker to blacksmith); Joseph Jim [Joseph James] (sundry work); Andrew Gordah [Gordon?] (blower and striker, April 1-September 30, 1833). Among other agency payments were these: to Daniel M. Boone $120 for transporting 12,000 pounds of flour, bacon, corn meal, salt, tobacco, lard, powder, lead, and $3,600 in specie to the agency; to James P. Hickman $220 for his labor in putting up a double log house (this was, apparently, for Fool Chief), and for instructing the Kansa in agriculture; to William Ward $21 for making fence, gathering corn, and aid in agriculture; also for aid in agriculture, $142 to Moses Grantham, $131 to Joshua Hitchcock, and $14 to George Sawyer.

At the *Osage Agency:* Paul Ligueste Chouteau (agent); Alexander W. McNair (subagent); Thomas Anthony (subagent for nine months); Baptiste Mongrain (interpreter); Gabriel Philibert (gunsmith); Joseph Trumblee [Tremblé] (blacksmith); Joseph Bertrand (blacksmith from June 30-September 30, 1833); Louis Peltier (striker, for six months).

At the *Shawnee-Delaware Agency:* Richard W. Cummins (agent); John Campbell (subagent); Anthony Shane, James Connor, and Baptiste Peoria (interpreters); Robert Dunlap (gun and blacksmith for Delawares); Lewis Jones (gun and blacksmith for Shawnees). Among the Jackson and Clay county, Mo. merchants who had supplied provisions for the agency Indians were: James E. E. Sloan, James and Robert Aull, S. G. Flournoy, Samuel C. Owens, Richard Fristoe, Francis G. Chouteau, and Cyrus Curtis. Another payment ($101.55) went to the Steamboat *Heroine,* for transporting annuities.

Ref: 23d Cong., 1st Sess., *H. Ex. Doc. 490* (Serial 259), pp. 74, 75, 136, 158-160. Noted in a preceding entry are the Shawnee-Delaware Agency disbursements for the Delawares' mill.

❲ October 1.—Dr. F. W. Miller officially succeeded John Campbell as subagent at the Shawnee Agency (headed by R. W. Cummins). Campbell (subagent since April, 1825) had been notified in August of his "removal from office," but was paid through September; and Miller did not arrive to assume his duties till October 29.

(In a letter of April 9, Agent Cummins had referred to his subagent as being old and inefficient. The Rev. Thomas Johnson, of Shawnee Methodist Mission, subsequently made charges against Campbell—charges which Campbell answered, without avail, in a May 20th letter to Sup't William Clark, St. Louis.)

Miller was subagent for only nine months. His job ended in July, 1834.

Ref: Office of Indian Affairs (OIA), "Registers of Letters Received," v. 4, pp. 53, 58, 267; 23d Cong., 2d Sess., *H. Doc. No. 150* (Serial 274), pp. 26, 52; Christopher Collection, in KHi ms. division, for photostat of Campbell's May 20, 1833, answer to charges, and for other data on Campbell collected by Mrs. Orville H. Christopher, of Kansas City, Mo. Miller was addressed as "Doctr. F. W. Miller" in an OIA circular sent to all subagents on July 2, 1834—*see* OIA, "Letters Sent," v. 13, p. 94. In SIA, v. 5, p. 76, is one letter ("Shawnee Agency Apl 1st 1834") by Miller to Sup't William Clark. *See* p. 156 for Campbell's arrival in "Kansas." John Campbell eventually was cleared of the charges made against him.

❲ October 4.—Baptist missionaries Jotham and Eleanor D. (Richardson) Meeker (from a mission among the Ottawas in Michigan territory), and Cynthia Brown (also a missionary), arrived at Isaac McCoy's home near "Westport," Mo. (They had reached Independence Landing on October 2, after a trip up the Missouri on the *John Nelson.*)

Jotham Meeker brought with him a printing press (purchased in Cincinnati, Ohio) which subsequently was set up at Shawnee Baptist Mission. It was the *first printing press in "Kansas."* (*See* March 8, 1834, annals entry for the first items printed on the "Meeker" press.)

Meeker, on October 13 and 14, paid a visit to the small Ottawa settlement; set out on the 19th for the Kickapoo reserve; arrived on the 20th, interviewed Kennekuk (the Prophet), and returned on the 22d; then visited the Delawares on the 24th and 25th (in company with Agent R. W. Cummins, Dr. Johnston Lykins, and Ira D. Blanchard). On October 29 Jotham and Eleanor Meeker moved to Shawnee Baptist Mission (from McCoy's home) and became "Kansas" residents. (They occupied the quarters vacated two days earlier by the Merrills —*see* October 27 entry.)

The Meekers remained at Shawnee Baptist Mission till 1837; then opened a mission among the Ottawas in Franklin county of today.

Ref: Jotham Meeker's "Diary"; *KHC*, v. 8, p. 80; Isaac McCoy's *History of Baptist Indian Missions*, p. 464.

¶ About October 7 Comm'r Henry Ellsworth and party—about 30 in all—(*see* p. 242) arrived at the Grand Pawnees' village, on the Platte's south bank—distant about 80 miles from the Otoe and Missouri town (which they had left about October 4).

On October 9 the commissioner began councils with delegations from all the Pawnee bands assembled there; and on October 10 the Pawnees signed a treaty. By its terms, they *ceded all claim to lands south of the Platte river,* in return for annuities, and agricultural and educational aid.

Heading the treaty signers were: Shah-re-tah-riche (for the Grand Pawnees), Blue Coat (for the Pawnee Republicans), Little Chief (for the Tappage Pawnees), and Big Axe (for the Pawnee Loups). Members of Ellsworth's party were witnesses (Edward Ellsworth, Dougherty, May, Dunlop, Irving); as were, also, trader Alexander La Force Papin and interpreter Louis La Chapelle.

Ellsworth and party (including the Otoes), a few days later, crossed the Platte and journeyed up the Loup Fork to the villages of the three other bands (Tappage-Republican, Little Republican, and Pawnee Loup); afterwards they returned to the Grand Pawnees' town; and set out from there (the company now enlarged by some 80? Pawnees—including four Indian-peace-council delegates from each band) about October 18(?) for Fort Leavenworth. At least part of this company reached the fort before the end of October.

Ref: J. T. Irving (McDermott edition), pp. xxxiii, 113-219, 240; 23d Cong., 1st Sess., *Sen. Doc. 512,* v. 4 (Serial 247), pp. 601-604 (for the Pawnee council proceedings); Kappler, *op. cit.,* v. 2, pp. 416-418.

¶ October 9.—To John O. Agnew, and to J. H. Flournoy & Co., licenses were issued (by Agent R. W. Cummins) which permitted them to trade with the Kickapoos, the Delawares, and the Kansa— at a specified location within each of the three Indian reserves.

These were apparently the first permits issued for trading places on the Kickapoo and the Delaware lands. As described in the Agnew and Flournoy licenses, and in those given to other traders subsequently, the specified locations were:

On the *Kickapoo* reserve: "At the first point of bluffs above the mouth of Salt creek, about 3½ miles above Fort Leavenworth" (present northeast Leavenworth county).

On the *Delaware* reserve: "a bluff on the north side of the Kanzas river, near the mouth of the second creek [present Mill? creek] which empties into that river, where the Delaware blacksmith now lives" (present Wyandotte county—and the place is further identified by J. T. Irving's account [August, 1833] of crossing the Kansas at Grinter's ferry: "We disembarked and galloped up the bank. On the top was a large log house, inhabited by the blacksmith of the Delaware Indians. . . .").

Agent Cummins, on October 10, licensed Francis G. Chouteau (agent for the American Fur Company) to trade with the Kickapoos at the location on their reserve described above. But, *see, also,* October 25 entry.

(The *Kansa* reserve trading point had been specified earlier—when Frederick Chouteau was granted a license in 1832.)

Ref: 23d Cong., 2d Sess., *H. Ex. Doc.* 97 (Serial 273); J. T. Irving (McDermott edition), p. 18. Agnew and Flournoy, were Independence, Mo., merchants.

❆ October.—During this month the fall caravan of returning Santa Fe traders crossed "Kansas." Apparently this company was accompanied by a military(?) escort (*see* below). At Columbia, Mo., a November 9 newspaper issue noted the traders' return with "from 80 to 100 thousand dollars in specie, furs, mules, etc."; and it was reported the party included about 100 of those who had gone out in the spring. Josiah Gregg (who had traveled to Santa Fe in the spring of 1831) was in this company.

Earlier (on September 21) the Columbia paper had stated that the returning caravan had a Mounted Ranger escort. Possibly it was the same force which had accompanied the traders in the spring (*see* May 15 entry), and then had returned to Fort Leavenworth on August 3d. But no *official record* has been found which shows that the Fort Leavenworth-based rangers made an autumn trip westward to rendezvous with the fall caravan. The Columbia newspaper report might be written off as hearsay, except for this additional item supplied by Maximilian, prince of Wied-Neuwied (a surprising source, since he was then—about December 19—on the upper Missouri, at Fort Clark). He wrote:

"Some of Mr. Soublette's people arrived [at Fort Clark] from St. Louis, which they had left on the 14th of October. . . . They told us . . . that the party escorting the caravan from Santa Fe had been so closely hemmed in by the Indians (probably Arikkaras), that they had been compelled, by want of provisions, to slaughter fourteen of their horses."

Ref: *Missouri Intelligencer,* September 21, November 9, 1832; Thwaites, *op. cit.,* v. 24, p. 46 (for Maximilian); Gregg, *op. cit.,* v. 1, p. 305; R. E. Twitchell's *Old Santa Fe* . . .

(Santa Fe, c1925), p. 218. Gregg, in his table of Santa Fe trade statistics—1822-1843—published in v. 2, p. 160, of his *Commerce of the Prairies*, recorded under *1834:* "2nd U. S. escort." He certainly knew of the 1829 escort; and had returned in 1833 (above) with a caravan perhaps under military escort. (In any case the *westbound* 1833 caravan had been escorted by the Mounted Rangers.) So, for *1834*, he should have recorded: 3d U. S. escort.

℃ October 25.—Issued to the American Fur Company (by Sup't William Clark, at St. Louis) were trading licenses which renewed permits for three fur posts in "Kansas," and granted permission, additionally, for trade with the Kickapoos, and with the Delawares.

The old sites were: (1) Francis & Cyprian Chouteau's Kansas river (south bank) post, on the Shawnee reserve (present Wyandotte county); (2) Frederick Chouteau's mouth-of-American Chief (Mission) creek post on the Kansa reserve (present Shawnee county); (3) the Chouteau brothers' branch-of-the-Marais des Cygnes post on the Wea & Piankeshaw reserve, about one mile east of the Wea villages (present Miami county).

The new sites were: (1) a Chouteau-operated post on the Delaware reserve; and (2) a trading house operated by Laurence Pensineau on the Kickapoo reserve. (For locations, *see* October 9 entry.)

Though these October licenses listed only five American Fur Company trading houses in "Kansas," there was still one more—the post on the Osage reserve (present Neosho county) for which a renewal permit had been granted on January 1, 1833.

Ref: 23d Cong., 2d Sess., *H. Ex. Doc.* 97 (Serial 273); 23d Cong., 1st Sess., *H. Doc. No.* 45 (Serial 254)—for Osage reserve license. For references to Laurence Pensineau as trader among the Kickapoos, *see* G. J. Garraghan's *Catholic Beginnings in Kansas City . . .* (Chicago, 1920), pp. 53, 54, and his *The Jesuits of the Middle United States* (New York, 1938), v. 1, p. 387.

℃ Late in October, in the Big Nemaha country, John Treat Irving, Jr., of Comm'r Henry Ellsworth's party, became separated from his companions on the journey from the Platte to Fort Leavenworth (*see* p. 246). Though he reached the military post not long after the others—around the first of November(?)—the experiences during several days of solitary travel provided material for three chapters in his subsequently-written *Indian Sketches* (1835).

Irving's wanderings brought him southward, so that he arrived on the bank of the Kansas—probably in the general area of present Topeka. There he met a mounted Kansa, who, reluctantly (as Irving tells the story in light-hearted vein) gave him assistance, and eventually guided him (by a circuitous route) towards the Kansa Agency some miles downriver. In the middle of the night, after a rest-stop, they forded the Sauterelle—now Delaware—river; then passed White Plume's abandoned stone house (*see* p. 139); and, near daylight, reached the Kansa Agency. Irving was fed and housed by the government blacksmith (John McGill, apparently). A few hours later, he met Agent Marston G. Clark; and in his company (Irving riding a mule), set out that evening for Fort Leavenworth, about 40 miles distant. They arrived at the post early next morning.

Ref: J. T. Irving (McDermott edition), pp. xxxiii, 218-240.

❏ October 27.—Missionaries Moses and Eliza Merrill, and Cynthia Brown (who had come with the Meekers—*see* October 4 entry) left Shawnee Baptist Mission to travel some 230 miles northward—beyond the Platte—to Bellevue (Neb.), where they were to open a Baptist mission for the Otoe and Missouri Indians. Ira D. Blanchard accompanied them to the vicinity of the Platte, then returned to his place among the Delawares (on November 29). Also in the party were a guide, and a teamster to handle the oxen and wagon. (*See* July 31 entry for the earlier Merrill-Blanchard round-trip over much this same route.)

Mrs. Eliza Merrill's journal (excerpts only are available) discloses their three-weeks' journey was one of privations and hardships. They were nearly surrounded by prairie fires (in present Leavenworth? county) on the 29th; then became lost; ran short of food; became both exhausted and disheartened before finally reaching the Platte on November 13. There they made a raft, but could not cross till the 17th, because of high winds. Late on November 17 the three missionaries reached Bellevue, and occupied a log house there. Seven days later they opened a Baptist mission school.

(On April 1, 1835, Moses Merrill was appointed government teacher for the Otoes and Missouris. On September 18, 1835, the Merrills and Miss Brown moved from Bellevue to a new mission site—near the place selected for the relocation of the Otoes—on the north side of the Platte, about six miles above its mouth.)

Ref: Nebraska Historical Society *Transactions*, v. 5 (1893), pp. 222-226; Jotham Meeker's "Diary," October 26 and 27, 1833, entries; *The Baptist Missionary Magazine*, v. 16 (June, 1836), pp. 129, 130; 24th Cong., 1st Sess., *Sen. Doc. 109* (Serial 280), p. 8 (for Merrill's 1835 appointment).

❏ October 28.—Alexander G. Morgan (sutler, and postmaster, at Fort Leavenworth) was issued three Indian trading licenses (by Sup't William Clark, St. Louis). They permitted him (and one associate) to trade with (1) the Kickapoos, (2) the Kansa, and (3) the Delawares. (*See* October 9 entry, for trading location on each reserve.)

On November 1 Morgan was also licensed to trade on the Des Moines river, at the Sac & Fox village—again with one other person. It appears that Alexander G. Morgan's associate was "free hunter" Johnson Gardner (by report, also "one of the best pilots on the whole course of the Missouri"). Maximilian's party (coming down the Missouri in 1834) included Gardner, and the prince made this comment: "Near this post [Fort Leavenworth] is the village of the Kickapoos. . . . Major Morgan [*i. e.*, Alexander G. Morgan] who kept a large store of provisions and other necessaries, had a share in Gardner's fur trade; the latter accordingly quitted me at this place."

Ref: 23d Cong., 2d Sess., *H. Ex. Doc. 97* (Serial 273); Thwaites, *op. cit.*, v. 24, p. 114 (for Maximilian). In Chittenden's *The American Fur Trade*, v. 2, pp. 941-945, are items relating to "Johnson Gardner," including a copy of a free hunter's contract of July 5, 1832,

with Gardner's X-mark "signature." More information on Gardner is to be found in Dale
L. Morgan, editor, *The West of William H. Ashley,* pp. 286, 287. In 23d Cong., 1st Sess.,
H. Doc. No. 45 (Serial 254), is an item on the trading license issued to "Johnston Gardiner"
(by William Clark) on July 3, 1833, for 13 persons to trade "On the Cowskin [now Elk]
river," etc., with the Senecas of Sandusky (in present northeastern Oklahoma).

❦ About November 1 the difficulties which had been accumulating
between the Mormons and anti-Mormons of Jackson county, Mo.,
began to involve the settlers in serious clashes.

Jotham Meeker (at Shawnee Baptist Mission) noted on November 2: "A
very great excitement about the Mormons. Fear disastrous consequences."
Isaac McCoy (a Jackson county resident) wrote on November 4: "A war
among our neighbours is about commencing"; he also described the clash which
occurred late that day. Meeker (on the 5th) noted the "battle . . . fought
yesterday evening in real warlike style between the Mormons and Anti-Mormons, in which several[?] were killed and wounded on both sides." McCoy
envisioned having his property destroyed, and considered taking his family
elsewhere.

By November 10 the "warfare" had subsided (for the time being). Meeker,
on November 11, wrote: ". . . Learn that the Mormons have all fled."
(Some 1,200 Mormons were "forcibly expelled" from Jackson county. Most
went to Clay county on the other side of the Missouri.) In January and February, 1834, there were further "Mormon troubles."

Ref: McCoy's "Journal," and Meeker's "Diary"; *see, also,* W. A. Jennings' "Isaac McCoy
and the Mormons," in *Missouri Historical Review,* v. 61 (October, 1966), pp. 62-82, and
his "The Army of Israel Marches Into Missouri," in *ibid.,* v. 62 (January, 1968), pp.
107-135.

❦ By November 2 (and perhaps at the end of October) William
Sublette, his brother Milton (also Andrew?), and about 30 others,
arrived at Fort Leavenworth in the keelboat *Gallant.* (They had
left the Yellowstone on September 20.)

Continuing downriver, the *Gallant* passed Independence, Mo., November
5; and reached St. Louis in mid-month.

Ref: Sunder's *Bill Sublette, op. cit.,* pp. 129, 130; *The Bulletin,* of the Missouri Historical Society, St. Louis, v. 20, pp. 5, 117.

❦ November 4.—Hiram W. Morgan began work as blacksmith to
the Kickapoos (under terms of the October 24, 1832, treaty).

He was thus employed till March 21, 1835. Agent R. W. Cummins spent
$250 in erecting buildings for a blacksmith on the Kickapoo reserve, apparently
in the spring of 1834.

Ref: 23d Cong., 2d Sess., *H. Doc. No. 150* (Serial 274), pp. 29, 56; SIA, v. 8, p. 129.
Possibly Morgan was related to the Fort Leavenworth sutler—Alexander G. Morgan.

❦ The Indian peace council (called by Comm'r Henry Ellsworth)
opened at Fort Leavenworth about November 8. Some 100 Pawnees, Otoes, and Omahas met delegates from the immigrant nations
—the Delawares, Shawnees, Kickapoos, Pottawatomies, Ottawas,

Weas, Peorias & Kaskaskias. (The Kansa arrived late—on the 14th; the Iowas and Sacs on the 15.)

Ellsworth wrote, on the 8th: "Peace will be concluded at this council between the hostile Indians upon terms highly satisfactory; the wampum has been exchanged, but the speeches not finished." (Baptist missionaries Johnston Lykins and Jotham Meeker attended the November 8 and 9 meetings; Methodists Thomas Johnson and Jerome Berryman were present for some council sessions.)

The treaty, signed on November 12 by the nations then present, contained agreements: to cease all hostile acts; to take no private or personal revenge; and to allow other tribes to become parties to it. Signers included:

Delawares: Patterson, Nah-ko-min, Ketchum, Nonon-do-quo-mon, Sha-wah-nock, and Long House; *Shawnees:* John Perry, William Perry, Wy-lah-lah-piah, Cornstalk (and four others); *Kickapoos:* Pa-sha-cha-hah and Kennekuk; *Pottawatomies:* Qui-qui-to and Noh-sha-com; *Ottawas:* Oquanoxa and Chi-cah (She-Kauk); *Peorias & Kaskaskias:* White Shield, Big Harry, Jim Peorias, and Le Coigne; *Weas:* Quih-wah (Negro legs), Wah-pon-quah (Swan) (and three others). Ietan headed the Otoe signers; Wah-con-ray signed first for the *Omahas;* Shah-re-tah-rich for the *Grand Pawnees;* Ska-lah-lay-shah-ro for the *Tappage Pawnees;* Ah-shah-lay-roh-she for the *Republican Pawnees;* and Pah-kah-le-koo for the *Pawnee Loups.* On November 16 the *Kansa* delegates—11 of them, headed by Nom-pa-wa-rah (White Plume), Ky-he-ga-wa-ta-ninga (Fool Chief), and Ky-he-ga-war-che-ha (Hard Chief)—signed; as did, also, the Iowa and Sac Indians. But most of the delegates had left for home by this date.

Witnesses, on the 12th, included all of Comm'r Henry Ellsworth's party, several army officers (Maj. Bennet Riley, Capt. William N. Wickliffe, Lieutenants Asa Richardson, John Nicholls, Robert Sevier, and John Conrad), Indian agents John Dougherty and Richard W. Cummins; Subagents A. S. Hughes, J. L. Bean, and F. W. Miller; post sutler A. G. Morgan; interpreters Anthony Shane, James Connor, Baptiste Peoria, Peter Cadue, and Louis La Chapelle. Agent Marston G. Clark, and interpreter Clement Lessert were among the witnesses to the Kansa signers. (*See, also,* November 20 annals entry.)

Ref: 23d Cong., 1st Sess., *Sen. Doc. 512,* v. 4 (Serial 247), pp. 654, 659, 702, 703, 726-732; 23d Cong., 1st Sess., *H. R. No. 474* (Serial 263), pp. 80, 105-112 (for treaty, *with Osage signers*); J. T. Irving (McDermott edition), pp. 241-254.

❦ November 12-13.—A great meteor "shower" which (as reported) began around midnight of the 12th and lasted for several hours, was a phenomenon memorable to all who saw it. (The "falling of the stars" was visible "all over eastern North America.")

Missionary Jotham Meeker (at Shawnee Baptist Mission), arising at five A. M. on November 13, witnessed "a constant flying of innumerable meteors." He also noted (in his diary): "The Ind[ian]s are much alarmed about it."

On his way to "Kansas" (and camping out in western Missouri), another Baptist missionary, Robert Simerwell, "awoke [on the night of the 12th] and beheld an innumerable quant[it]y of vapors or shooting stars passing toward the earth which was magnificent beyond description."

At Fort Leavenworth, on the 13th (as Methodist missionary Jerome C. Berryman later recalled), Comm'r Henry Ellsworth told the Indians assembled in council that the Great Spirit had caused the shower of stars to show Divine approval of their councils, and of the peace treaty which had been negotiated on the 12th. This amused the more enlightened of the Indians present, but doubtless impressed many of the delegates.

The Kiowas (then camped on a tributary of Elm fork of Red river, in present Greer county, Oklahoma) looked upon the meteor shower as "something ominous or dangerous"; watched it "with dread and apprehension until daylight"; and recorded it on their calendar as the "Winter that the stars fell." —James Mooney.

Ref: Meeker "Diary," and Simerwell "Diary," in KHi ms. division; McAnally, *op. cit.*, p. 438 (for Berryman's story); *Seventeenth Annual Report of the Bureau of American Ethnology* (1895-1896), Pt. I, pp. 260, 261 (for Mooney). The *Encyclopaedia Britannica* [1968], v. 15, p. 267, says: "Serious study of the subject [of meteors and meteorites] was really initiated by the great meteor shower of Nov. 12, 1833 . . . [and that] Hundreds of thousands of shooting stars were observed in one night, some leaving persistent trains, but none reaching the earth. It was noted that all the meteors seemed to radiate from a point in the constellation Leo."

❡ November 13.—At Fort Leavenworth, Comm'r Henry Ellsworth held a second council (*see September 2*) with the Kickapoos. This talk was with all the chiefs. Of its results Ellsworth wrote:

"There is an entire satisfaction [of the assigned reserve], if Kishkoo and a few followers are excepted. . . . When Kishkoo's followers find he is not able to give them land on the Osage [Marais des Cygnes] river, most of them, I think, will leave him, and join their friends [here] on the Missouri river."

In a June 25, 1834, letter, the Rev. Joseph Kerr of Wea Presbyterian Mission in present Miami county, mentioned the presence of a "roving band" of Kickapoos near the Piankeshaw settlements. These Indians, he wrote, had planted corn and would probably remain for the summer. Presumably this was Kishkoo's band.)

Ref: 23d Cong., 1st Sess., *Sen. Doc. 512*, v. 4 (Serial 247), pp. 639-644; Presbyterian Historical Society, American Indian Missions correspondence.

❡ November 14.—Baptist missionaries Robert and Fanny (Goodridge) Simerwell, and their three children, recently of Michigan territory, arrived at Isaac McCoy's home near "Westport," Mo.

From Decatur, Ill., on October 10, they had set out overland (in two covered wagons—one horse-drawn, and driven by an Indian youth; the other pulled by oxen), on the last stage of the journey westward. The Simerwells spent the winter of 1833-1834 in a rented house about two miles east of the state line. On May 16, 1834, they moved five miles westward to Shawnee Baptist Mission, and became "Kansas" residents. They took over the quarters vacated by the Rev. Alexander Evans (recently dismissed by the Baptists); and shared the mission premises with the Jotham Meekers.

Ref: Robert Simerwell's "Diary"; Bessie E. Moore's "Life and Work of Robert Simerwell" (thesis, 1939); Jotham Meeker's "Diary," entries of November 14, 1833, and May 16,

1834, and his letter of November 29, 1833. The Simerwells' children (as of November, 1833) were: William (7), Sarah (4), and Ann (1).

❦ November 14.—The Rev. Benedict Roux (Jesuit missionary, from the St. Louis diocese) arrived at "mouth of the Kansas," overland, from Independence, Mo. On the 18th he journeyed to the Kickapoo settlement (above Fort Leavenworth), and spent a few days at Laurence Pensineau's American Fur Company trading house.

Kennekuk (the Prophet) was absent—60 miles away. But a messenger brought back an address he dictated; and on November 22, in the presence of several Indians, the trader, and his brother Paschal Pensineau, the Prophet's speech was given in Pottawatomie, translated into Kickapoo by "Mechouet," and into French by Laurence Pensineau.

Father Roux, after a "short week" among the Kickapoos and Pottawatomies, returned to the Kansas river and spent the winter of 1833-1834, also the following spring, as guest at Francis and Cyprian Chouteau's Shawnee reserve trading house. (He was "about ten miles from the majority of the French families . . ."—the "Kaw's mouth" residents of "Kansas City," Mo.)

Ref: Garraghan's *Catholic Beginnings* . . ., pp. 35, 42-54; and his *The Jesuits of the Middle United States*, v. 1, p. 387. John Reynolds' *The Pioneer History of Illinois*, second edition (1887), pp. 362-364 has data on the Pensineau family.

❦ Kickapoo Methodist Mission had its beginning in November, when the Rev. Jerome C. Berryman (with the Rev. Thomas Johnson's aid), selected a site, and got work started on temporary buildings—a dwelling and a schoolhouse (both of round logs)—on a high bluff overlooking the Missouri, three (or more?) miles above Fort Leavenworth.

(Berryman, his wife, Sarah C. [Cessna] Berryman, and her assistant, Dyza Tucker, had arrived at Shawnee Mission early in November, after a journey overland from eastern Missouri. The two women remained there till the Kickapoo Mission—some 30 miles distant—was habitable.)

Perhaps around the beginning of January, 1834, the mission opened. On March 4, 1834, Berryman started a day school. In January, 1835, he reported the school had averaged 45 students. Also, beginning in January, 1835, Berryman became a government teacher (by appointment), and thereafter conducted classes in the U. S. schoolhouse (*see* December 1, 1833, entry), about a quarter of a mile from the mission. Subsequently (in 1835?), permanent Kickapoo Methodist Mission buildings were erected on the government school grounds (in present northeast Leavenworth county).

There was a flourishing church society. The 1834 report showed two white members, and 230 Kickapoo and Pottawatomie members. (In 1838 the figures given were: three whites and 161 Indians.) Berryman also preached at Fort Leavenworth, by invitation, and the missionaries enjoyed their relations with the army people. The school continued to do well till the summer of 1839.

(From 1835 on, it was operated chiefly as a boarding school, with as many as 16 Indian children living at one time at the mission.) In 1834-1835 the Rev. John Monroe taught there; in 1837-1838 the Rev. David Kinnear was the government teacher; and in 1839 Elizabeth Lee conducted the school. After a son of Kennekuk (the Kickapoo Prophet) killed the government blacksmith in mid-July, 1839, the Kickapoos showed increasing reluctance to have their children at the mission. Apparently no school was conducted after 1839. (A few Kickapoo children went to Shawnee Mission.)

But the Kickapoo Methodist Mission continued to function till the late 1850's. When the Berrymans removed to Shawnee Mission in late 1841, their replacements (for two years) were the Rev. Nathaniel Talbott and his wife (from the Peoria Mission). After that the changes of missionaries were frequent.

Ref: KHC, v. 9, pp. 207-211, 226-230, v. 16, pp. 209, 211-219, 241, 242; CIA "Reports," for 1834, 1837-1839, 1845, 1848, 1853, 1859-1861; Isaac McCoy's *Annual Registers* for 1835 (p. 30), 1836 (p. 31), 1837 (p. 33), 1838 (p. 67); 24th Cong., 1st Sess., *Sen. Doc. 109* (Serial 280), p. 8. For description of the government's and the Methodists' buildings at Kickapoo settlements, *see* "Letters Received by OIA," St. Louis Superintendency, R. W. Cummins' report enclosed with William Clark's November 15, 1836, letter (National Archives Microcopy 234, Roll 751).

❧ On November 20(?) Comm'r Henry Ellsworth left Fort Leavenworth and began a journey to the Osages' country, and to Fort Gibson. He was accompanied to "Oklahoma" by about 50 Pawnee and Otoe Indians (on foot); also Agent John Dougherty, Edward A. Ellsworth, and the interpreter Baptiste Peoria were in the party.

At Shawnee Agency (present Johnson county), Ellsworth added *Piankeshaw* signers to the Indian peace treaty he carried with him (*see* p. 251). On the 22d in the morning, he conferred with the Rev. Isaac McCoy; on the 23d, from Independence, Mo., he forwarded a *copy* of the treaty to Washington. Evidently he then took the road south from Independence to Harmony Mission; crossed back into "Kansas" to approach the Osage towns by way of Boudinot Mission (as later noted by the Rev. N. B. Dodge). On December 3 he wrote from "Osage Agency," of his party's safe arrival there. Many of the Osages were absent, hunting, he reported.

If Ellsworth followed his stated intention, his party then went on to Fort Gibson, and afterwards visited Clermont's band of Osages. His actual movements are, apparently, not on record. It was perhaps around mid-December when Clermont, Tallia, White Hair, and other Osages added their names to the Indian peace treaty. Comm'r Montfort Stokes was present on that occasion. Witnesses were the two Ellsworths, Stokes, Dougherty, Auguste P. Chouteau, Agent Paul Liguesté Chouteau, Subagent Thomas Anthony, Edward L. Chouteau, Lt. Jefferson Van Horne, Samuel B. "Wright" ["Bright?"—of Harmony Mission], interpreters Baptiste Peoria and James Lee.

Ref: 23d Cong., 1st Sess., *H. R. No. 474* (Serial 263), pp. 109-112; 23d Cong., 1st Sess., *Sen. Doc. 512*, v. 4 (Serial 247), pp. 744, 745 (Ellsworth's December 3, letter); Isaac McCoy's "Journal," November 22, 1833; W. W. Graves' *The First Protestant Osage Missions* . . . (Oswego, c1949), pp. 215, 216 (for Dodge); J. T. Irving (McDermott edition), p. 254.

❡ December 1.—John D. Swallows went on the pay roll as *government teacher* to the Kickapoos. (This was in accordance with Article 7 of the Kickapoo treaty of October 24, 1832.)

In the spring of 1834, apparently, a schoolhouse (costing $300) was erected on the Indians' reserve. No report by Swallows of his Kickapoo school has been located. On January 1, 1835, the Rev. J. C. Berryman (whose school at the Kickapoo Methodist Mission was started early in 1834) also became a government-paid teacher to the Kickapoos. Both Swallows and Berryman (at annual salaries of $480) were listed as teachers to the Kickapoos in a January 30, 1836, report by Comm'r of Indian Affairs Elbert Herring.

Ref: 23d Cong., 1st Sess., *Sen. Doc. 512*, v. 5 (Serial 248), p. 71; 23d Cong. 2d Sess., *H. Doc. No. 150* (Serial 274), pp. 29, 56; 24th Cong., 1st Sess., *Sen. Doc. 109* (Serial 280), p. 8; Robert Simerwell's "Diary" contains mention of Swallows.

❡ On December 4, from a point above Fort Leavenworth, Isaac McCoy, his son John C. McCoy, and eight hands, began a survey of the Kickapoo reserve. The outfit included horses—probably riding animals, as well as pack horses.

Work was started in present Leavenworth county—where the north boundary of the Delaware lands crossed Salt creek. The party then meandered Salt creek to its mouth; and on December 7 turned northward up the Missouri. (Isaac McCoy went back to his home near "Westport," Mo., on business, on December 7; and returned to Fort Leavenworth on December 19, where two of the party, in for supplies, met him). The surveyors, on December 10 were about where Oak Mills, Atchison co. is today—a point opposite the foot of Cow Island (as recorded in the field notes). By the 23d they had reached Independence creek. "Christmas day proceeded along the bluff," state the field notes. Isaac McCoy's journal entry for the 25th was: "Encamped on bank of Missouri in a bottom of Rushes, which is pretty good food for our horses." On December 30 they camped "opposite [Joseph] Robardeaux's trading house."

The New Year began with a snowstorm and a siege of bitter weather. (On January 1, 1834, the surveyors were 55 miles from the mouth of Salt creek by the course of the Missouri [30 miles direct route].) They huddled around a huge campfire for two or three days (*see* January, 1834, entry), then headed home. On January 7 they camped near the mouth of Salt creek; and on the evening of the 9th, the McCoys reached home—crossing the Kansas river on the ice. (*See* June, 1834, entry for completion of the Kickapoo reserve survey.)

Ref: SIA, v. 1, pp. 156-160 (for manuscript copy of field notes), and pp. 154, 155 (for copy of the plat of Kickapoo lands); Isaac McCoy's "Journal," December 2, 1833-January 9, 1834, entries. Curiously, these field notes (signed by Isaac McCoy and John C. McCoy) are dated: "Westport, Jackson County, Missouri Feb. 10th 1834"—and thus *appears* to be the earliest document showing the name "Westport," Mo. However, *at that date, and until May, 1834*, the McCoys were still using the address "Shawanoe," Jackson co., Mo., in their correspondence.

❡ A late-in-the-year journey down from the mountains was made by Moses ("Black") Harris, Dr. Benjamin Harrison, and one or two others. They left Ham's Fork November 13, or soon after. Supposedly, George Holmes (bitten by a rabid wolf at the rendezvous) was along, and died of rabies en route.

Doubtless the party crossed "Kansas" but no information on the route, or exact time of arrival in the States is available.

Ref: Morgan, *The Rocky Mountain Journals of William Marshall Anderson, op. cit.,* p. 327.

1834

❡ January 1.—"Until now we have had a remarkably pleasant winter. This day has been very cold.—the snow has fallen about six inches deep."—Jotham Meeker, writing at Shawnee Baptist Mission, present Johnson county.

January 2-9.—Meeker, on the 2d, wrote: "Mercury fell this eve. to 18 deg. below zero." Isaac McCoy (from a surveyors' camp on the Missouri, in present Doniphan county) wrote, under dates of the 2d and 3d:

The weather is excessively cold, and sometimes the wind is high. . . . We have a fire of logs twelve or fourteen feet long, piled up. . . . Our tents upon each side front this large fire, which we keep up day and night, and still we suffer with cold, and not a little from smoke.

After returning to his home near "Westport," Mo., on January 9, McCoy wrote:

We ascertained that at the garrison [Fort Leavenworth] the Mercury had sunk to 30 below zero. At our house and by our Farenhiet, the mercury had ranged for several days below zero, and sometimes as low as 26 below. This has been the coldest weather ever known in these regions. It is still cold.

Ref: Meeker's "Diary," and McCoy's "Journal."

❡ Available sources suggest that "Bent's Fort"—the large, fortified, adobe trading post of Bent & St. Vrain (Charles Bent and Ceran St. Vrain)—may have been under construction in the summer of 1833; but that the work was not completed till 1834.

This soon-famous post (originally "Fort William" for William Bent—younger brother of Charles—who supervised its erection) was located on the Arkansas river's north bank, seven miles east of present La Junta, Otero co., Colo.—and about 530 miles west of Independence, Mo.

In a letter written at Fort Pierre (S. D.) on January 10, 1834, fur trader William Laidlaw stated: "I understand from the Sioux that Charles Bent has built a Fort upon the Arkansas for the purpose of trade with the different bands of Indians. . . ." A St. Louis newspaper of October 14, 1834 (*see* a September, 1834, annals entry), reported the arrival of a "Messrs. St. Vrain, Bent and Company" wagon train from "the trading posts on the Arkansas river." (With the inclusion of William Bent, the partnership became Bent,

St. Vrain & Company.) At St. Louis on December 13, 1834, Charles Bent was issued a two-year license to trade (employing 29 men) with the Arapahoes, Cheyennes, Kiowas, Snakes, Sioux, and Arikaras, at several upper Arkansas river locations—including "Fort William, on the north side of the Arkansas about 40 miles east of the Rocky Mts. . . ." A map by Capt. Lemuel Ford (see *March of the First Dragoons to the Rocky Mountains in 1835; the Diaries and Maps of Lemuel Ford* . . ., by Nolie Mumey [Denver, 1957], *between* pp. 56, 57) shows Fort Cass and a "Fort William" (in close proximity) about where Pueblo, Colo., is today; and also shows "Bents Fort" farther down the Arkansas—at the location east of present La Junta, Colo.

Ref: L. R. Hafen's "When Was Bent's Fort Built," in *The Colorado Magazine*, v. 31 (April, 1954), pp. 105-119; H. W. Dicks' "The Excavation of Bent's Fort, Otero County, Colorado," in *ibid.*, v. 33 (July, 1956), pp. 181-196; Janet Lecompte's "Gantt's Fort and Bent's Picket Post," in *ibid.*, v. 41 (Spring, 1964), pp. 111-125; 23d Cong., 2d Sess., *H. Ex. Doc* 97 (Serial 273)—for the trading license issued to Charles Bent in late 1834; David Lavender's *Bent's Fort* (New York, 1954), pp. 131-140, 386 (the trading license year is incorrect as given in his book); also *see* G. B. Grinnell's "Bent's Old Fort and Its Builders," in *KHC*, v. 15, pp. 28-91 (for an early account of the trading post, the Bents, and Ceran St. Vrain).

❡ MARRIED: Joseph La Suisse (half-Osage), and Julia Mongrain (daughter of half-Osage Noel Mongrain), on February 6, at the Osage Agency, Neosho river (present Neosho county), by the Rev. Nathaniel B. Dodge, of Boudinot Mission.

A large crowd of Osages attended the wedding, and the "remarks and ceremony were interpreted into the Osage language . . ." Agent Paul Ligueste Chouteau provided a dinner for 40 or 50 persons (eight, or more, were chiefs and head-men); and another feast, on February 7, for perhaps 100 Osages.

According to Dodge, it was "The first marriage among the Indians on the Neosho." No doubt it was the first Protestant marriage among the Osages of Neosho river (in "Kansas"), but for earlier marriages (Catholic) of Osages from the Neosho towns, *see* a Spring, 1830, annals entry.

Ref: *Missionary Herald*, v. 30 (July, 1834), p. 259 (for Dodge's letter of March 1, 1834), or Graves, *op. cit.*, p. 216.

❡ Early in February the Catholic congregation (12 French, two American, and two Indian families) at "mouth of the Kansas" (the future Kansas City, Mo.), rented a "chapel" (house), where Father Benedict Roux officiated till April, 1835. Until summer (1834) he "commuted" from the Chouteaus' post on the Kansas river (*see* November 14, 1833, entry); then removed to a rented dwelling two miles from the "chapel."

Father Roux's first baptisms (13 children) were on February 23, 1834. Kansa interpreter Clement Lessert's daughters Mary and Martha (by his wife Julia Roy) were in this group. Others baptized by the Rev. Benedict Roux, during his 1834-1835 tenure, included: Francis G. and Berenice (Menard) Chouteau's son Benedict Pharamond (born February 22, 1833); Kickapoo trader Laurence Pensineau's eight-year-old son Louis (by Nina—a Kickapoo?), baptized March 3, 1834; Daniel and Marie Constance (Philibert) Boone's daughters Elizabeth (born February 3, 1833) and Eulalia (born February 13, 1835)—granddaughters of Daniel Morgan Boone (formerly agriculturist for the Kansa); and Louis Gonville's 18-year-old daughter Mary Josephine—also called "Josette" (whose mother was a daughter—or niece?—of Kansa chief White Plume), baptized on April 19, 1835 (the sponsors were Francis G. and Berenice Chouteau, in whose home she had been raised). Of these, probably the only one "Kansas-born" was Mary Josephine Gonville—whose father had traded with, and lived among, the Kansa Indians since about 1807.

Ref: Garraghan's *The Jesuits* . . ., v. 1, pp. 257, 258, 386, 387; D. A. R., Kansas City chapter, *Vital Historical Records of Jackson County, Missouri, 1826-1876* (c1934), pp. 90-92; Frederick Chouteau's May 5, 1880, letter (in KHi ms. division) in which he states: "My brother [Francis] raised Louis' [Louis Gonville's] daughter Josephine Gonville and she married Joseph Papin at his house"; 37th Cong., 2d Sess., *Sen. Ex. Doc. No. 58* (Serial 1122), p. 2. Clement Lessert had two children (Clement and Adel) by his Kansa wife Me-ho-yah, who were born in "Kansas"; but his family by wife Julia (Roy) Lessert had, so far as known, no "Kansas" connection.

℄ Work was started on the Wea Presbyterian Mission late in February—at a site (chosen by the Rev. Wells Bushnell) about a mile from the larger Wea village (on Wea creek, a branch of the Marais des Cygnes, in present Miami county). On April 17 the hewed-log mission house (built by part-Shawnee Joseph Barnett and four hands), though not completed, was occupied by the Bushnells, the Rev. Joseph Kerr and his wife, and Nancy Henderson (teacher).

These persons, in the service of the Western Foreign Missionary Society of the Presbyterian Church, had arrived at Independence, Mo., on December 31, 1833 (from Pittsburgh, Pa.), and spent the winter there.

In a June 25 letter Wells Bushnell reported that a school (opened late in May, in a room of the dwelling) had been temporarily suspended due to Mrs. Kerr's illness; that a 24-foot-square, hewed-log, school-and-meeting house had been built, also a stable, a smoke house, corn crib, spring house, and "some other little conveniences." Henry Bradley (hired to run the farm) arrived not long after the missionaries. He wrote, on August 5, that the Wea Mission occupants had been ill with fever and ague. On August 5 Bushnell and his family left.

For a brief time in 1835 Elihu M. Shepard (teacher) was at Wea Mission. That summer Francis H. Lindsay (teacher) and his wife joined the mission staff. The personnel in December, 1835, as stated by Joseph Kerr: the Kerrs, the Lindsays, Henry Bradley, Nancy Henderson, and Mrs. Rosetta Hardy. However, Miss Henderson was absent during the winter of 1835-1836—teaching school for three months at *Westport,* Mo. (the winter before, she had taught at Independence). (The Weas and Piankeshaws were away, hunting, in the winter months.)

The Kerrs left when Mrs. Mary Ann Kerr's health failed in 1836. Henry Bradley, his wife (an 1836? arrival), Nancy Henderson, and James Duncan were at the mission in late 1836. In July, 1837, the Rev. John Fleming and his wife arrived. Fleming, in a December, 1837, letter stated that he thought the Wea band too small and the Indians too closely settled to the Peoria Methodist Mission to justify keeping the Presbyterian mission open. Wea Mission closed in 1838. The buildings were sold to the government for the Indians' use.

Ref: Presbyterian Historical Society, American Indian Missions correspondence; Spooner & Howland's *History of American Missions* (1840), pp. 723, 724; Isaac McCoy's *Annual Registers*, 1835 (p. 21), 1836, (p. 22), 1837 (p. 25), 1838 (p. 60). Comm'r of Indian affairs, "Report," 1837, p. 609 (for location of the mission). In the McCoy manuscripts (in KHi ms. division) is an April 18, 1836, letter by Elihu M. *Shepard*. (The spelling "Sheppard" for his name, as in some records, is thus incorrect.)

❡ March 8.—At Shawnee Baptist Mission, where he had set up his press in February, Missionary Jotham Meeker wrote in his diary: "Took an impression of Blanchard's first form [*see* March 21 entry, below]. Also printed [50 copies of] a Shawanoe hymn for Br. [Alexander] Evans." On March 10 he wrote: " . . . Print [50 copies of] the Shawanoe Alphabet & Hymns for Br. Evans."

These were the first items printed on the "Meeker press"; and they were the first items printed in "Kansas." (See March 21 entry for the first "Meeker press" book.)

Ref: Meeker's "Diary," and Meeker's February 10, 1835, report, in KHi ms. division; *see* KHQ, v. 4 (1935), pp. 61-73 (for Kirke Mechem's article on "The Mystery of the Meeker Press").

❡ BORN: on March 15, at Delaware Methodist Mission (present Wyandotte county), Martha Jane Peery, daughter of the Rev. Edward T. and Mary S. (Peery) Peery. (She died November 17, 1835.)

Ref: Si and Shirley Corn's *Our Family Tree* (1959), Section four. *See, also,* 1832 annals item on p. 211.

❡ March 21.—At Shawnee Baptist Mission (present Johnson county), Jotham Meeker recorded in his diary: "Complete the first Ind. book in the Territory containing 24 pages besides the cover. . . ." He referred to Ira D. Blanchard's *Linapie Lrkvekun, Apwivuli Kavuni Vawinj Wato* . . . (Shawnee Mission, J. Meeker, Printer, 1834).

This "Delaware Primer and First Book" (the edition was 300 copies) was the *first book printed in "Kansas."*

The second "Meeker press" *book* was Missionary Alexander Evans' 18-page Shawnee First Book—300 copies were printed on March 29; and the third *book* was Missionary Robert Simerwell's 32-page Pottawatomie First Book— 300 copies were printed on June 2. The translations were all based on a Meeker-devised system of using the English alphabet characters to represent Indian language sounds—a system which proved to be a simple and popular method of teaching the Indians to read.

At least two copies of the *first* book printed in "Kansas" (Blanchard's Delaware elementary book) exist—one is in the New York Public Library and the other in the Boston Athenaeum. The Kansas State Historical Society has none of the three books noted above. It does however, have a later Delaware book by Blanchard. On February 6, 1837, Jotham Meeker (still resident at Shawnee

Baptist Mission) wrote in his diary: "Commence setting types on the Harmony of the Gospels in Delaware by Br. [Ira D.] Blanchard." It is this 221-page "Harmony of the Gospels"—the last book published by Meeker before he moved from Shawnee Mission to work among the Ottawa Indians—of which the Society has a copy (800 were printed). Illustrations of the book's two title pages (English, and Delaware) are reproduced in this volume.

Ref: Meeker's "Diary," and Meeker's February 10, 1835, report; *KHC*, v. 8, pp. 80, 81. *Also, see* D. C. McMurtrie's *Jotham Meeker* . . . (Chicago, 1930), and J. C. Pilling's *Bibliography of the Algonquian Languages* (Bureau of Ethnology *Bulletin No. 13*), especially p. 314 (and for comparative purposes, p. 51).

❡ BORN: on March 26(?), about one half mile east of Shawnee Methodist Mission (present Wyandotte county), Julia Ann Beauchemie, daughter of Mackinaw and Betsy [or Mary] (Rogers) Beauchemie.

(Betsy [or Mary] Rogers' father was Henry Rogers, a white man kidnapped from his Virginia home as a child, by the Shawnees, and raised in Chief Blackfish's family. Her mother was a daughter of Blackfish.)

Ref: Notes from interviews with Julia Ann (Beauchemie) Stinson, July 16, 1895 (in which she says her mother's name was "Betsy"), April 21, 1906 (in which her birth date is given as March 26, and her mother's name as "Mary," or "Polly," also sometimes called "Betsy"), in KHi ms. division; Shawnee County Historical Society *Bulletin*, No. 22 (December, 1954), p. 52 (gives the birth date as March 28); *KHC*, v. 9, p. 171*n* (for family data); *Kansas City Sun*, June 22, 1917 (for statement she was born "less than one-half mile of the First Mission"), or *see* "Wyandotte County Clippings," v. 4, p. 304—in KHi library.

❡ April 1.—The Rev. Henry Rennick, Jr., a Cumberland Presbyterian minister, went on the pay roll as government teacher to the Delawares. A school house, and "buildings attached thereto," worth $278.50 (as reported by Isaac McCoy, in late 1834), probably were built about this same time; but McCoy also stated no school had yet been started (as of December, 1834).

At the end of 1835 McCoy reported that Rennick was teaching at the Delaware Methodist Mission house; that he had 19 scholars, three of whom were supported by the mission; at the end of 1836, he stated merely that the schoolhouse erected by the United States was unoccupied. Henry Rennick was government teacher for several years, but no other record of his work, or accomplishments, has been located.

Ref: 23d Cong., 2d Sess., *H. Doc. No. 150* (Serial 274), p. 27; 24th Cong., 1st Sess., *Sen. Doc. 109* (Serial 280), p. 8; *Report* of the American Board of Comm'rs for Foreign Missions, 1834, p. 171; McCoy's *Annual Registers* for 1835 (p. 26), 1836 (p. 28), 1837 (p. 31). In the U. S. census records, 1830, 1840, and 1850, for Jackson county, Mo., the name appears both as "Rennick" and "Renick."

❡ BORN: on April 4, at the Kickapoo Methodist Mission (present Leavenworth county), Sarah Emily Berryman, daughter (and first child) of the Rev. Jerome C. and Sarah C. (Cessna) Berryman. (She died three years later.)

Ref: Leavenworth *Times*, September 21, 1925 (or, Remsburg "Stork" clippings, in KHi library); *KHC*, v. 16, p. 214.

❡ In April the post office of "Shawnee," Jackson co., Mo. (established in June, 1832; Dr. Johnston Lykins, postmaster) was changed to "West Port," Mo., and John C. McCoy was appointed postmaster. (His certification bears the date May 27, 1834.)

The post office was in McCoy's small log house (built in 1833, at a location on the public road from Independence, Mo., to state line) in which he had opened a general store (stocked with goods owned by J. P. Hickman & Co.— i. e., partners Hickman, J. H. Flournoy, and J. C. McCoy). The site was the northeast corner where Westport and Pennsylvania avenues, Kansas City, Mo., now intersect—in the S.E.¼ of Sec. 19, T. 49 N., R. 33 W., a tract of land purchased by McCoy from Johnston Lykins in 1833. (The Santa Fe trail route westward from Independence ran some eight(?) miles south of McCoy's store.) In the spring of 1834 (as McCoy recollected in 1879) the steamboat *John Hancock*[?] put ashore a stock of goods for him at the nearest point on the Missouri river—about four miles north of the store—where the future Kansas City, Mo., had its beginning.

John C. McCoy wrote (in 1879) that he had no idea who "first conceived the idea of laying off a town at this point [i. e., Westport] . . . but . . . previous to about 1834 no such project was spoken of or suggested in this region." His own town lots then, were probably first laid out in 1834. But, just to the southeast, on adjacent land, John Campbell (recently subagent at Shawnee Agency) also laid out a town "West Port" in 1834 (on a tract in the S.W.¼ of Sec. 20, T. 49 N., R. 33 W., purchased from Robert Johnson by deed of August 9, filed August 13, 1834). John C. McCoy bought three lots in Campbell's town of "West Port" on August 31, 1834.

McCoy was the first to file his town plat for record (the date was February 13, 1835). It showed an area labeled "Campbell's Addition. . . ." John Campbell's "West Port" plat was filed on March 26, 1835. But death curtailed any plans he had for the development of a town. (He died in the East, in 1836, where he had gone to fight charges which had caused his dismissal as Indian subagent [see p. 245].) So, it was John C. McCoy's "West Port" which subsequently expanded as the town of Westport, Mo.

Ref: Kansas City (Mo.) *Journal*, January 16, 1879 (or, "Kansas Reminiscences" clippings, v. 1, pp. 127, 128, in KHi library); Isaac McCoy manuscripts (for J. C. McCoy's certificate as postmaster and for J. P. Hickman & Co. document); photostats of Jackson co., Mo., deed records (particularly from Book C, pp. 427-429 and Book D, pp. 1, 238-240) and other documents relating to John Campbell, collected by Mrs. Orville H. Christopher, of Kansas City, Mo., and graciously lent to this compiler for annals use; Kansas City (Mo.) *Star*, July 12, 1925, March 12, 1933 (or, "Wyandotte County Clippings," v. 6, pp. 2-8). The steamboat *John Nelson* was operating on the Missouri in 1834; and the *John Hancock* may have been, but the earliest record of this boat on the Missouri seems to be 1835.

❡ April 28.—From a camp about four miles west of Independence, Mo., Nathaniel J. Wyeth's *second* expedition to the Far West got under way. His was the first party on the trail to the Rocky mountains in 1834, but following after were three other companies.

In 1832 Wyeth had gone west with William L. Sublette. (*See* May, 1832, annals; and September, 1833, for his return.) This year (1834) Milton G.

Sublette (brother) was accompanying Wyeth—associated in taking supplies to the Rocky Mountain Fur Company. And William L. Sublette was readying a rival expedition—*see* next entries. Also preparing to cross "Kansas" to the mountains shortly, were (1) an American Fur Company party (with supplies for Fontenelle, Drips & Co.), headed by Etienne Provost, and (2) a company taking supples to Bonneville, headed by Michel S. Cerré. (No narratives of these two expeditions exist, so far as known.)

From a journalistic viewpoint, Wyeth's 1834 expedition was the "best-covered" overland journey of the fur trade era. Quotations from the diarists and narrators who "reported" it, have been linked, below, to present an account of the "Kansas" portion of the trip— the *early* Oregon trail route ("Sublette's Trace") across "Kansas," when expeditions crossed the Kansas river about seven miles above present Lawrence.

At the journey's beginning, according to *Osborne Russell* (a Wyeth employee): "Our party consisted of forty men engaged in the service [of Wyeth] accompanied by Mess[rs Thomas] Nuttall and [John K.] Townsend Botanists and Ornithologists with two attendants; likewise Rev's Jason and Daniel Lee Methodist Missionaries with four attendants [With the Lees were Cyrus Shepard (teacher), Philip L. Edwards (lay helper) of Richmond, Mo., and Courtney M. Walker (assistant) of Missouri; also a wagoner—as far as Kansas river.] . . . which brot. our numbers (including six independent Trappers) to fifty Eight[?] men. . . ." [Subsequently, there were some desertions and a few additions to the party.]

[April 28] *Daniel Lee:* "On the 28th we raised camp, and began our march. . . . The whole party . . . all mounted on horses or mules, and armed with rifles. . . . The mules and horses altogether were over 150. . . ." *Russell:* ". . . about forty men leading two loaded horses each were marched out in double file . . .: led by Mr. Wyeth . . . whilst the remainder of the party with twenty head of extra horses and as many cattle to supply emergencies brot. up the rear under the direction of Capt. Joseph Thing . . . who had been employed by . . . [Wyeth's] Company in Boston to accompany the party and measure the route across the Rocky Mountains by Astronomical observation." *John K. Townsend:* "The band of missionaries, with their horned cattle, rode along the flanks." *Russell:* "We travelled slowly . . . untill about 2 clk P. M. and encamped at a small grove of timber near a spring."

[April 29] *Jason Lee:* "[I] Started early, accompanied by Bro. [P. L.] Edwards, to find Bro. T[homas] Johnson at the Shawnee [Methodist] Mission, about 7 miles from camp . . . was much pleased to find Sister Johnson surrounded with Shawnee sisters engaged in quilting. Stayed over night. . . ." [On the 30th, Lee bought a beef cow from Johnson, and with Edwards, journeyed to Wyeth's camp—the company had, meantime, progressed not more than 20 miles, it appears.]

[May 1] *Townsend:* "We encamped this evening on a small branch of the Kanzas river. . . . we were joined by a band of Kanzas Indians. . . .

They were encamped in a neighboring copse where they have six lodges."
[May 2] *Jason Lee:* "Did not decamp. Some of our com[pany] visited the
Indian camp. . . ."

[May 3] *Jason Lee:* "Struck tent—came ahead of the Com[pany] and found
a number of wigwams on the bank of the Kansas. They are Caws—came here
to visit the agent General Clark. . . ." [They were awaiting Agent Marston
G. Clark's arrival, according to *Cyrus Shepard*, who also wrote]: ". . . we
crossed [the Kansas] in a flat-bottomed boat with our goods. . . . Swam
our horses & cows over, except our beef cow which got into the woods and
eluded all further search." *Townsend:* "[we] . . . landed on the opposite side near our horse pen [the animals, after swimming the river, had been
driven into a fenced lot] where we encamped [*i. e.,* at the Kansa Agency]. The
[Indian] lodges are numerous here, and there are also some good frame[!]
houses inhabited by a few white men and women, who subsist chiefly by raising
cattle, which they drive to the settlements below. They, as well as the Indians,
raise an abundance of good corn; potatoes and other vegetables are also plentiful. . . . In the evening the principal[?] Kanzas chief paid us a visit in our
tent. He is a young man about twenty-five years of age, straight as a poplar
and with a noble countenance and bearing. . . . a very lively, laughing,
and rather playful personage." [Fool Chief?—or, more likely, old White Plume's
son, White Plume II.]

[May 4—Sunday] *Shepard:* "Passed day at the yesterday's encampment
. . . on the bank of the Kanzas river . . . surrounded by a wicked,
profane & licentious company of white men and some scores of indians. . . ."
Jason Lee: "No regard paid by any of Capt. W's company to the Sabbath."

[May 5] *Jason Lee:* "Started early before breakfast from the agency and
travelled till 12 o'clock and then took breakfast." [Lee had left letters with
"General Clark's son"—probably "George B." Clark, *see* August 15, 1834, entry
—for mailing. This is the only known reference to the presence in "Kansas" of
any member of Agent Marston G. Clark's family.] *Nathaniel J. Wyeth:* "Made
this day along the Kanzas about 16 miles [camped] on a small stream [Soldier
creek?] having crossed one called the Saut[e]relle ["Grasshopper"; now Delaware river]. . . ."

[May 6] *Wyeth:* "Moved along the Kansas and made about 12 miles to
noon . . . made this day about 18 miles." *Jason Lee:* "Stopped to dine
and bait our animals a little distance from the Caw Village." [Fool Chief's
town—in present Shawnee county—*see* p. 167]. *Townsend:* "[a] village
. . . consisting of about thirty lodges, and situated in the midst of a
beautiful level prairie." [May 7] *Wyeth:* "Made about 15 miles and camped
on Little Vermillion" [now Red Vermillion, in present Pottawatomie county].

[May 8] *Wyeth:* "In the morning Mr [Milton G.] Sublette finding that his
leg would not bear travelling turned back made this d[a]y about 15 miles
This day left Kanzas River." *Jason Lee:* "Are now [camped] on a stream
about as large as the little Vermillion [Rock creek]. . . ." [May 9] *Wyeth:*
"Made about 20 miles and camped on a small river this day our hunter killed
our first deer." *Jason Lee:* "Encamped on a brook in a beautiful place.
. . ." [May 10] *Wyeth:* "Made 15 miles to Big Vermillion [Black Vermillion, present Marshall county] and then 5 miles more and camped in the prairie

with but little wood and a little stagnant water." [May 11] *Jason Lee:* "Decamped early this morning but lost the trail came to a stop about 11 o'clock." *Wyeth:* "Sent a man to hunt the trail." *Shepard:* ". . . Halted to feed our animals on the bank of a creek a branch of *Blue* river in Lat. 40° 18′ North[?] . . . On starting from this place we lost the trail . . . encamped near a verdant grove. . . ."

[May 12] *Townsend:* "Our scouts came in this morning with the . . . [news] that they had found a large trail of white men, bearing N. W. We have no doubt that this is Wm. Sublette's party, and that it passed us last evening. . . ." *Wyeth:* "Spent the morning mending hobbles . . . in afternoon started and in about 8 mil[e]s found a camp of Sublettes for nooning and marched until dark and camped. . . ."

[May 13] *Wyeth:* "Started and travelled 7 hours and camped on a fork of the Blue." *Jason Lee:* "Encamped on . . . a large Brook clear . . . water. Capt. Thing took a lunar observation and found we were 97° 7′ West from Greenwich. . . ." [May 14] *Wyeth:* "Made W. S. W. 21 miles and struck the main Blue [Little Blue of today]." *Jason Lee:* "We decamp about ½ past 7 o'clock stop about 2 hours at noon and camp about ½ past 6: Make near 50 [*i. e.,* 20] m. per day which is as much as the horses can endure for they are heavily loaded. . . ." [May 15] *Wyeth:* "Made about W. 9 miles [Lat. 40° 17′] then made 12 mils W. by N. over a very level prairie and again struck the main Blue [Little Blue] and camped." *Jason Lee:* "Mr. [Courtney M.] Walker caught two cat fish. . . . Saw a number of antelope the hunters killed two."

[May 16] *Wyeth:* "Made 10 miles about W. by N. to Dinner (Lat. 40° 23′) and 12 more to the Pawnee trail to the head of the Arkanzas[?] and found that a very large party [of Pawnees] had passed it about 10 days before and a smaller one this morning." *Jason Lee:* "Crossed the Pawnee trail just before we camped it is worn by travel so that it appears like a wagon road. [The Pawnees] . . . had just passed and I perc[e]ive our camp is arranged with more care than usual."

[May 17] *Jason Lee:* "Started this morning at 7 o'clock. Made a severe march of 9 hours from the Blue to the Platte. . . . We came to day 15 m. N. W. and 10 m. W. Total 25 m."

By Daniel Lee's table of distances they reached the Platte in 17 days, and 340 miles from Independence, Mo.; 29 days (and 580 miles) later, Wyeth's company reached the Green river rendezvous. (On June 1, after crossing the Laramie river, they had found some of William L. Sublette's men building a trading post—"the first Fort Laramie.") On reaching the rendezvous, Wyeth got the bad news that the Rocky Mountain Fur Company was unable to fulfill the contract to purchase his goods. (From Thomas Fitzpatrick he received the $500 forfeit.) Wyeth subsequently went on to build Fort Hall at a Snake river site selected in mid-July. The missionaries, in company with Thomas McKay's Hudson's Bay Company trading party, went on to "Fort Wallah-wallah"—arriving there September 1st.

Ref: N. J. Wyeth's "2nd Journal" (1834), in *Sources of the History of Oregon*, Eugene, v. 1 (1899), Pts. 3-6, pp. 221-225, and *ibid.*, pp. 129-132, for Wyeth's April, and May, 1834, letters; Osborne Russell's *Journal of a Trapper*, edited by Aubrey L. Haines (Portland, 1955), pp. i, vi, 1, 2; John K. Townsend's *Narrative of a Journey Across the Rocky*

Mountains . . . (Philadelphia, 1839), pp. [9], 21, 27-42 (or, *see* in Thwaites, *op. cit.*, v. 21, pp. 107-369); "Diary of Rev. Jason Lee," in Oregon Historical Society *Quarterly*, v. 17 (1916), pp. 116-123; *also,* Jason Lee's "Diary," as published in A. B. Hulbert's *The Oregon Crusade* (1935), pp. 147-160, 167-184; Daniel Lee and J. H. Frost's *Ten Years in Oregon* (New York, 1844), pp. 109-123; Cyrus Shepard's "Diary" (1834), pp. 42-64 (Coe Ms. No. 421, Yale University—used by permission); P. L. Edwards' letter, in *Niles' Weekly Register*, v. 47 (October 11, 1834), p. 92; De Voto, *op. cit.*, p. 389; Dale L. Morgan and Eleanor T. Harris, editors, *The Rocky Mountain Journals of William Marshall Anderson* (San Marino, Cal., 1967), pp. 14-29, 130-137, 389, 390.

❡ Spring.—The *Assiniboine* (American Fur Company boat; new in 1833) made her second trip up the Missouri. (One passenger was Andrew W. Sublette, going upriver as an agent for his brother William.) She reached Fort Clark (N. D.) on June 18, and Fort Union (at the Yellowstone) on the 26th.

Coming downriver in July, *1835* (after "wintering" at Fort Union) the *Assiniboine* "was burnt a little below Heart river, and all her cargo—1100 Packs and some Beaver [valued at $60,000 to $80,000], distroyed." Also aboard, and burned, with a large part of Maxmilian's natural history collection.

Ref: Francis A. *Chardon's Journal at Fort Clark, 1834-1839,* edited by Annie H. Abel (Pierre, S. D., 1932), pp. 3, 37, 272, 301, 379, 381; Morgan and Harris, *op. cit.*, p. 361.

❡ The fifth of May William L. Sublette's pack train (37 men; 95 horses and mules) "encamped at the Sapling grove," west of Missouri's boundary, en route to the Rocky mountains by way of "Sublette's Trace."

(In New York, late in January, Sublette and the American Fur Company had reached agreement on a division of the West. To Sublette & Campbell would go most of the mountain country fur trade, while the American Fur Company would retain the Missouri river trade, buying Sublette & Campbell's river posts.)

William Marshall Anderson—a supernumerary with this expedition—is its only known diarist, but his journals and narrative provide much information on the "Kansas" travels.

Under way before dawn on May 6, the party stopped to breakfast "at the Round grove," which had only seven or eight trees. Camp for the night of May 7 was opposite the Kansa Agency. They met some Kansa ("Kaws, or, as they call themselves, Kawsies."—Anderson). (Also, they met a wrinkled, white-haired old man (interpreter for the Indians) who "called himself Vieil, spoke a little French"—and who was, very likely, Louis Gonville. On the 8th, the "whole cavalcade, horses, cows and mules," crossed the Kansas to the Agency (where they visited with Marston Clark). After breakfast May 9 "on the bank of a creek called Soldier," the party passed "through a village, named the new Kansas village. . . . It is very, small." [?] (This same day they met Milton Sublette eastward bound.) Camp on the 10th was "about 5 miles from Vermillion [the Red Vermillion of today]"; Next day they "Crossed a creek on Sublettes trace, which he made for ten wagons, 4 years past, called by some of his hands cannon ball creek [now Rock creek]." At night they camped on a Big Blue tributary they called "bee river, from finding a bee-tree near our tents" (the Black Vermillion of today).

On May 12 Sublette (and company) passed Wyeth's party (*see* preceding entry). But he was not far in advance, for on May 15 John K. Townsend (with Wyeth) noted in his journal: "This morning a man was sent ahead to see W. Sublette's camp, and bear a message to him, who returned in the evening with the information that the company is only one day's journey beyond. . . ."

At the end of May, after crossing the Laramie river, Sublette detached some 13 men to build a log trading post at that point—the first "Fort Laramie" (founded May 31, and formally christened "Fort William"); then continued on—to the Green river rendezvous.

On July 10 William Sublette's homeward-bound party (with 60 to 70 packs of beaver) left the trappers' rendezvous on Ham's Fork, to return to Missouri. Edmund Christy and Michel Cerré accompanied him. Sublette reached Lexington, Mo., before August 27.

Ref: Morgan and Harris, editors, *The Rocky Mountain Journals of William Marshall Anderson;* De Voto, *op. cit.,* pp. 186, 190, 194, 437; *Frontier and Midland,* Missoula, Mont., v. 19 (Autumn, 1938), pp. 54-63; John K. Townsend's *Narrative of a Journey Across the Rocky Mountains* (Philadelphia, Boston, 1839), p. 41; *Missouri Republican,* St. Louis, August 26, 1834; *Annals of Wyoming,* Cheyenne, v. 12 (January, 1940), pp. 56-62.

❛ In May the spring caravan was on its way to Santa Fe, captained by Josiah Gregg. There were about 160 men, 80 wagons, and goods estimated at $150,000. Among the 50 proprietors were Gregg, James Sutton, Thomas J.[H?] Boggs, Dr. Philippe A. Masure, Edward Charless, J. L. Collins, James B. Turley, A. J. Rains, J. T. Wood and Ira G. Smith (brother of the noted Jedediah). (Charles Bent may have been still another. *See* below.)

Meantime, on May 13, from a camp near Fort Gibson (Okla.) Capt. Clifton Wharton and 50 men of the recently-organized (First) U. S. dragoons, with pack animals, one wagon, and some beeves, had started northward to meet the traders. Junior officers in Wharton's Company A command were Lt. Lancaster P. Lupton, and 2d Lt. John L. Watson. (Earlier, Col. Henry Leavenworth had sent Lt. John Henry K. Burgwin to Franklin, Mo., for news of the traders.) On May 19 (in present Labette? county) Wharton met Burgwin (returning). Two days later the dragoons reached the Osage Agency (southwest of present Erie, Neosho co., on the Neosho's *right* bank); and halted—to repair the wagon, shoe horses, and search for strayed beeves. They marched again on the 24th and camped about three miles above the Little Osages' town (present Neosho county). There, Wharton set a course for the nearest Santa Fe trail point. On June 3 the dragoons reached the Cottonwood crossing (near present Durham, Marion co.) The traders arrived on June 8; and next day accepted Wharton's offer of military escort westward.

The caravan, and the dragoons, left Cottonwood crossing on June 10. They halted at Walnut creek on the 17th and 18th. Some Kansa and their chief showed up in the vicinity, but the traders did not allow them in the camp. About the 26th(?), a party of Comanches approached, and for a time a clash seemed imminent. Subsequently, the Comanches (perhaps 100 in all) remained in the vicinity of the caravan, and camped about a mile away when the traders and dragoon escort halted, soon afterwards, at the Arkansas crossing.

Wharton made peaceful overtures to the Comanches (to the traders' dismay), and arranged for a council; but it was forestalled when Josiah Gregg and four other traders (without Wharton's knowledge) met the Comanche delegation (of five) on the right bank of the river, and warned the Indians to keep away.

On June 27 the caravan, accompanied by the dragoons, crossed the Arkansas. Gregg (who had requested Wharton to provide escort as far as the Canadian— which Wharton could not do) resigned as captain of the traders, and Ira G. Smith was elected in his place. (Wharton had *offered* to provide escort to the crossing of the Cimarron.) That night the Comanches broke camp and moved off eastward.

Next day (the 28th), after seeing the caravan on its way, the dragoons recrossed the river and started home. (Wharton's men and the animals were "Reduced in flesh," and short of rations; also the broken-down wagon had to be abandoned.) However, their journey eastward was without special incident except for a meeting with a party of "Pawnee Mahaus" (Pawnee Loups). On July 13 the dragoons were again at Osage Agency; and on the 20th Capt. Clifton Wharton and Company A, (First) U. S. dragoons, were back at Fort Gibson (Okla.).

Ref: *New Mexico Historical Review*, Santa Fe, v. 2 (July, 1927), pp. 269-304) for Capt. Clifton Wharton's report, dated at Fort Gibson, July 21, 1834); *Niles' Weekly Register*, v. 47 (September 20, 1834), p. 38 (for [Wharton's] letter of August 4, 1834—in which he stated the dragoons had been away 68 days on military escort duty); [James Hildreth's] *Dragoon Campaigns . . .*, p. 116. For item that Charles Bent declared goods in New Mexico on August 21, 1834—giving as reference the Ritch papers, 150, Huntington Library —*see* Lavender, *op. cit.*, p. 391. Josiah Gregg, in his *Commerce of the Prairies* (1844)—10 years after this journey—stated (in v. 1, p. 311) that the track across the Jornada (the desert route from the Arkansas crossing to the Cimarron—about 60 miles) had been made a *permanent* track in the year *1834*, owing to continuous rains during the passage of the caravan of that year. Since 1833 was a year of continuous rains; and because there is no indication (from available records) that the 1834 caravans (either east, or west, bound) encountered rains on the Jornada, it seems possible Gregg was a year off in his date. Apparently a printing press was taken to New Mexico in this caravan. *See* discussion of this in George R. Gibson, *A Soldier Under Kearny and Doniphan*, edited by R. P. Bieber (Glendale, Calif., 1935), p. 103. The identification of "I. G. Smith" (younger brother of Jedediah) is made by Dale L. Morgan, Bancroft Library, Berkeley, Calif.

❧ On the morning of May 16, Maximilian, prince of Wied-Neuwied, Charles Bodmer (artist), David Dreidoppel (the prince's servant), and a small party (mostly crewmen), journeying down the Missouri in a large, flat-bottom boat, passed the mouth of Wolf river (present Doniphan county); and in the afternoon arrived at the Blacksnake Hills post operated by Joseph Robidoux (where St. Joseph, Mo., now is).

Maxmilian and his two companions were enroute to St. Louis after nearly a year in the upper-Missouri country. (*See* April, 1833, entry.) They had left Fort Pierre (S. D.) on April 29. Johnson Gardner was Maximilian's boat pilot on the downriver trip.

On the night of May 17 camp was made on the river bank about two miles below the Kickapoo settlement (present Leavenworth county), and some of the company walked the three miles to Fort

Leavenworth. Next morning (according to Maximilian) when his party arrived at the post:

> The sentinel informed us that we must immediately appear before the commanding officer, and compelled us, in an imperious manner, to keep close and march before him. We arrived like prisoners at the house of the commander, where Major Ryley [Bennet Riley] received us with tolerable politeness, and supplied me with the provisions, meat, bread, &c., which I required, taking care, however, to be well paid for them.

Maximilian, and companions, reached St. Louis on May 27.

Ref: Thwaites, *op. cit.*, v. 24, pp. 92, 101, 110-125.

❡ Appended to a May 20 report (*H. R. No. 474*) of the (23d Cong., 1st Sess.) house committee on Indian affairs, were several documents, which included two tables giving the numbers (estimated in some cases) of Indians west of the Mississippi. The figures for the nations then in "eastern Kansas" are listed below. (The first column presumably represents Office of Indian Affairs statistics; the second column's figures are from the February 10, 1834, report of U. S. Comm'rs Stokes, Ellsworth, and Schermerhorn; and the third column [for comparison] gives the statistics from the January, 1835, issue of Isaac McCoy's *Annual Register.*)

Indians	OIA	U. S. Comm'rs	McCoy
* Osages	5,510	5,200	about 5,510
* Ottawas	200	200	about 75
Peorias & Kaskaskias	130	128	140
* Weas & Piankeshaws	394	405	400
Shawnees	1,250	1,250	of Kansas river 750
Kansa	1,440	1,496	about 1,500
Delawares	830	835	800
* Kickapoos	513	555	575
* Pottawatomies	....	....	250

* Some comment is necessary in relation to these figures: From one-third to one-half of the *Osages* were in present Oklahoma; fewer than 100 *Ottawas* were in "Kansas" at this time, according to reliable sources; the U. S. comm'rs' statistics gave the *Weas* as 220 souls, the *Piankeshaws* as numbering 185; the figures for the *Kickapoos* would have to include the Pottawatomies (approximately 110) attached to the Prophet's band—*see* May 21, 1833, entry. McCoy's Pottawatomie total includes the immigrants of 1834.

Ref: 23d Cong., 1st Sess., *H. R. No. 474* (Serial 263), pp. 39, 87; Isaac McCoy's *Annual Register* . . ., 1835, pp. 5, 16.

❡ On June 8 Maj. Alexander R. Thompson, Sixth U. S. infantry, replaced Maj. Bennet Riley as commandant at Fort Leavenworth. By unofficial report only about 60 soldiers (infantrymen) were stationed at the post during the summer. (Thompson's tenure was brief—*see* a late September entry for arrival of Col. Henry Dodge and the [First] U. S. dragoons.)

Ref: *KHC*, v. 14, pp. 578, 584, 693. Isaac McCoy in his *Annual Register*, January, 1835, p. 41, stated that Major Riley was at the post when Colonel Dodge and the dragoons arrived, but this was incorrect. Thompson's letter of October 7, 1834, refers to *his* having turned over command to Captain Hunter, earlier, because Dodge had not returned.—Office of Indian affairs, "Letters Received from St. Louis Superintendency." A personal letter Thompson wrote from Fort Leavenworth on July 23, 1834, giving some details of life there, is in *The Trail Guide* (published by the Kansas City Posse, The Westerners), v. 1, No. 3 (July, 1956), p. 16. *See, also,* Fort Leavenworth post returns.

¶ June 9.—Resuming the Kickapoo reserve survey (halted by cold weather five months earlier—*see*, under December 4, 1833, entry), Isaac McCoy and a work party began at a point on the Missouri's bank 30 direct miles—and 55 by the Missouri's meanders—above the mouth of Salt creek (in present Doniphan county). They proceeded due west (40? miles) to the northwest corner of the Kickapoos' land (in present Brown county); then turned due south till they came to the Delawares' north boundary (at a point in Jackson county of today). Probably this location—the end of their task—was reached before the end of June.

The field notes (signed by Isaac McCoy, surveyor, and William McCoy, assistant surveyor) summarized the work of the entire 1833-1834 survey; and were dated "Westport Jackson County Missouri August 1st 1834." The manuscript copy of the *plat* of the Kickapoos' reserve shows the following-named streams: Salt creek, Independence creek, "Kickapoo" creek [for the second stream, on the plat, about Independence creek], Wolf river, "Sauterelle" [Grasshopper—now Delaware] river, and Stranger river.

Ref: *SIA*, v. 1, pp. 161-167 (for field notes), and pp. 154, 155 (for plat, dated August 10, 1834). There is no Isaac McCoy "Journal" available for the June-December, 1834, period.

¶ From June 15 to August 15 the (First) U. S. dragoons (then stationed in the Fort Gibson [Okla.] area) were engaged in an expedition to the Comanche, Wichita, and Kiowa country of present southwest Oklahoma. At the beginning Col. Henry Leavenworth commanded the 500 troops. In the cavalcade were two former Osage captives—a Kiowa girl and a Wichita girl; also, artist George Catlin, and a German botanist, Heinrich Karl Beyrick.

Beyond the Washita (crossed near its mouth, not far from Red river), Colonel Leavenworth, and many of the dragoons—ill from a prevailing fever—were left in a temporary camp. Col. Henry Dodge took command on July 4, and on the 7th, with a reorganized force of 250, continued westward. More troops (Catlin too) fell ill on the march. On July 14 Dodge held a parley with some Comanches; subsequently, he reached a large Comanche camp (over 200 skin lodges; more than 3,000 horses). The sick, with a guard, remained there, while a depleted force (about 190) men continued on, beyond the Wichita mountains, to the Wichita's village of nearly 200 grass houses, on the North Fork of Red river (in present Greer county, Okla.)—arriving there July 21. (On the same day, at "Camp Smith," about 25 miles west of the Washita, Col. Henry Leavenworth died.)

Dodge held a general council with the Comanches, Wichitas, and Kiowas on July 24. The atmosphere was particularly friendly as a result of the restoration of the captive girls to their people, and the handing over (by the Kiowas) of a white boy prisoner. On July 25, accompanied by representatives of the three nations, the dragoons started home. Dodge's command, and the Indians reached Fort Gibson August 15. (The troops left on the Washita, in Lt. Col. S. W. Kearny's command, arrived August 24.) Though the (First) U. S. dragoons' expedition took a heavy toll in lives, it was considered a success for the contacts made with the western tribes. (*See* September 2 entry for the Indian council at Fort Gibson.)

[*The body of Brig. Gen. Henry Leavenworth (he had been promoted July 25—four days after his death, then unknown in Washington) was originally interred at Delhi, N. Y. But, 68 years later, his remains were removed to the National Cemetery at Fort Leavenworth—the fort which he had founded in 1827—and there reinterred, with ceremony, on May 30, 1902.*]

Ref: *American State Papers: Military Affairs,* v. 5, pp. 373-382 (for Lt. Thompson B. Wheelock's official journal), or, 23d Cong., 2d Sess., *H. Ex. Doc. No. 2* (Serial 271), pp. 70-91; *Chronicles of Oklahoma,* Oklahoma City, v. 3 (1925), pp. 175-215 (Sgt. Hugh Evans' journal); *Iowa Journal of History and Politics,* Iowa City, v. 7 (1909), pp. 341-360; [James Hildreth's] *Dragoon Campaigns . . .,* pp. 102-189; *Niles' Weekly Register,* v. 47 (September 6, 20, October 4, 1834, February 7, 1835), pp. 4, 38, 74-76, 403, 404; Foreman's *Pioneer Days . . .,* pp. 122-152; *KHC,* v. 7, p. 577 (for General Leavenworth's burial at Fort Leavenworth); also Henry Shindler, compiler, "Correspondence relating to removal of remains . . ." (typescript), in KHi library.

℄ From June 26 till September the Rev. John Dunbar, and Samuel Allis, Jr. (in the service of the American Board of Comm'rs for Foreign Missions; and bound for the Pawnee country), were visitors in eastern "Kansas."

They had come up the Missouri, on the *Ioway,* reaching Liberty, Mo., on June 14; and after 10 days there, had set out afoot, on the 24th, for Fort Leavenworth. At the fort they were guests, for a time, in the home of Alexander G. Morgan (post sutler). In July they were invited to make the Kickapoo Methodist Mission their headquarters. Both men made a July 3-7 journey to the Shawnee and Delaware missions; and Dunbar accompanied the Rev. J. C. Berryman to the Kansas river missions again in late July—*see* July 25 entry.

On September 1 Allis boarded the *Diana* to go upriver to Bellevue (Neb.)— the Upper Missouri Agency. (He arrived there on the 7th.) Dunbar (who had bouts with a bilious fever in August, and early September) left "Kansas" on September 22, on horseback—crossing to the Missouri's left bank (via the military post ferry). There, on the 23d, he joined the Rev. Moses Merrill (of the Otoe Baptist Mission) and two other persons, to travel northward. They reached Bellevue October 2d, after crossing the Missouri from a point opposite Joshua Pilcher's American Fur Company post.

The Pawnees arrived at Bellevue in mid-October. Agent John Dougherty gave them their annuities on the 18th. Next day Missionaries Dunbar and Allis set out with the Indians—to spend the winter among them. Dunbar went with the Grand Pawnees; Allis accompanied the Pawnee Loups; and they did not meet again till early April, 1835.

John Dunbar and Samuel Allis, Jr., had a long association with the Pawnee Indians, and with the mission subsequently opened (in 1836) at Bellevue—as will be noted in later entries. Dunbar's 1834-1835 journal, and letters (1831-1849), and Samuel Allis, Jr.'s, letters (1834-1839), as published in the *Kansas Historical Collections*, v. 14, contain a wealth of data on the Pawnees, their customs, habits, beliefs, etc., as well as on the events related to the Pawnee mission.

Ref: *KHC*, v. 10, pp. 99-104 (for a summary account of John Dunbar's work among the Pawnees), v. 11, pp. 323-332 (for an article by John Dunbar on the Pawnee mission, 1834-1836), v. 14, pp. 570-595, and 692-695; *Missionary Herald*, v. 31 (1835), pp. 343-349, 376-381, and 417-421 (for the Dunbar "Journal," 1834-1835—which is also in *KHC*, v. 14, pp. 578-619).

❡ On June 30—"perhaps the most significant date in the history of Indian legislation"—there were enacted two "comprehensive statutes which, in large part, form the fabric of our law on Indian affairs to this day."—Cohen's *Handbook of Federal Indian Law.*

(1) *The act regulating trade and intercourse with the Indian tribes.* It was "the final act in a series of acts [dating back to 1790] 'to regulate trade and intercourse with the Indian tribes.'" It defined the Indian country ("all that part of the United States west of the Mississippi, and not within the States of Missouri and Louisiana, or the Territory of Arkansas . . ."); provided the controls over Indian traders, and regulated licenses; prohibited (again) the introduction of liquor into the Indian country; provided penalties, etc.

(2) *The act organizing the Department of Indian affairs* (within the War Department). This statute "was intended to deal comprehensively with the organization and function of the Indian Department." Its provisions (and the resulting War Department regulations of July 7)—as they particularly affected the "Kansas" area—are summarized below:

The Indian country was divided into three superintendencies: (1) Michigan, (2) St. Louis, and (3) the "acting superintendency." The *Superintendency of St. Louis* (headed by William Clark, till his death in 1838) was defined (in the regulations) to "include all the Indians and Indian country *west of the Mississippi river* and *north of the Osage reservation,* and *as far west as De Mun's [Big Coon] creek* and thence . . . will be *bounded on the south by the Santa Fe road, to where it crosses the Arkansa,* and thence *by the Arkansa, to its source in the Rocky Mountains.* And the said Superintendency shall include all the Indians and Indian country west of the Rocky Mountains." The *"acting superintendency"* was (by War Department regulation) given the name *Superintendency of the Western Territory,* and was defined as including the Indians and Indian country *west of the Mississippi river,* and *south of the southern line of the superintendency at St. Louis, as far west as the Rocky mountains.* (The Osages were the only "Kansas" *resident* Indians in this new superintendency.)

Section 4 provided for 12 Indian agencies (some of them temporary). Only *three* were west of the Mississippi: two were "Western Territory" agencies, which (by War Department regulation) were designated as (1) *Northern Agency of the Western Territory* and (2) *Southern Agency of the Western Territory;* the third was the (3) *Upper Missouri Agency.* [Agencies (1) and (3) were in the Superintendency of St. Louis; and (2) was in the Superintendency of the Western Territory.]

John Dougherty continued to head the *Upper Missouri Agency* which was to include all the Indians and the Indian country west of the State of Missouri, north of the Northern Agency of the Western Territory, and to extend west and north so as to include the Otoes, Pawnees, Omahas, and Poncas.

Richard W. Cummins was appointed to head the *Northern Agency of the Western Territory* which was to include all of the Superintendency of St. Louis south of the Upper Missouri Agency, *except* the Shawnees, Ottawas, Peorias & Kaskaskias, and Weas and Piankeshaws (these nations to be in a separate *subagency*). When Comm'r Elbert Herring sent Cummins his commission as agent (on July 14), he stated: "Your agency will include the Delawares and Kanzas. . . ."

(Prior to the June 30, 1834, act there had been three Indian agencies in "Kansas": Cummins' Shawnee [Delaware, etc.] Agency; Marston G. Clark's Kansa Agency; and Paul Liguste Chouteau's Osage Agency. As will be seen from the above, all three were eliminated. In brief, Cummins' Shawnee Agency was split and reorganized, Clark's Kansa Agency was closed, and Chouteau's Osage Agency was reduced to a subagency, as will be noted hereafter.)

See July 2 entry for further reorganization of the Indian department—on the subagency level.

Ref: *U. S. Statutes*, v. 4, pp. 729, 735; Felix S. Cohen's *Handbook of Federal Indian Law* . . . (1945), pp. 72-75; OIA "Letters Sent," v. 13, pp. 111-113, and p. 180 (for the July 14, 1834, letter to Cummins); OIA, "Registers of Letters Received," v. 5, for item on Cummins' August 20, 1834, letter accepting appointment as agent.

❧ July 2.—From the Office of Indian Affairs a circular was sent to 10 Indian subagents, notifying them that their jobs had been terminated by the act of June 30 organizing the Indian department; but also stating that the same act provided for the appointment by the President of a number of subagents within the new departmental organization. The new subagencies, as specified by the act, included two for "Kansas": (1) a subagency for the Shawnees, Ottawas, Weas & Piankeshaws, Peorias & Kaskaskias; (2) a subagency for the Osages.

Two men in "Kansas" received the circular dismissal notice: Osage subagent Alexander McNair (whose address was "near Neosho river, via Independence, Mo."); and Dr. F. W. Miller, subagent to the Shawnees, etc. (whose address was given as "near Kanzas river via Shawnee P. O., Mo.")

Also on July 2 Comm'r Elbert Herring sent Paul Liguste Chouteau a letter informing him that his office as Indian Agent for the Osages had been discontinued; and offering him the office of subagent for the Osages. (Chouteau accepted.)

On July 3 Commissioner Herring wrote Marston G. Clark, informing him that "the office of Agent for the Kanzas has ceased." (*See* August 15 entry.) Five days later Herring again wrote Clark—this time offering him the appointment as subagent for the Shawnees, Ottawas, etc. (Clark accepted in August; but was subagent less than a year—leaving early in 1835.)

Ref: OIA "Letters Sent," v. 13, pp. 93, 94 (for the circular), p. 91 (for letter to Chouteau), pp. 105 and 131 (for letters to Clark); OIA, "Registers of Letters Received,"

v. 5 (for items on William Clark's letter of August 27, 1834, with M. G. Clark's letter of August 16, 1834, accepting subagency); Isaac McCoy letter (copy) of January 19, 1835, in McCoy manuscripts.

❡ Early in July a delegation of four Wyandots from Ohio was in eastern "Kansas." On Sunday, the 6th, at Shawnee Methodist Mission, one of them preached in his language. According to Samuel Allis, Jr., the sermon was "enterpeted by a Frenchman."

(Comm'r of Indian Affairs Elbert Herring had written Agent R. W. Cummins on June 13, 1834, that his office had learned the delegation was en route to the Indian country ostensibly to select a suitable location for a permanent location of the Wyandots; but that it was believed "that this delegation are unfriendly to emigration and intend making such unfavorable report as will deter the tribe from removing. . . ." He urged Cummins to attempt to produce a favorable impression on the Wyandots' minds, etc.)

Agent Cummins wrote, from Shawnee Agency, on July 13, that the Wyandots had examined the country and were pleased with it. (Compare with a Wyandot delegation's 1831 trip west.) The Wyandots did not move to "Kansas" till 1843.

Ref: *KHC*, v. 14, p. 694; OIA, "Letters Sent," v. 13, pp. 37, 38; *ibid.*, "Registers of Letters Received," v. 5.

❡ In July, Robert Campbell, from Fort William (the 1833-established Sublette and Campbell trading post at the Yellowstone), came down the Missouri. He and his party passed Fort Clark (N. D.) on July 11; and reached St. Louis early in August.

Ref: Morgan and Harris, *op. cit.*, p. 274; *Chardon's Journal, op. cit.*, p. 3.

❡ July 25 and 26.—A "conference of the Missionaries . . . in this [eastern 'Kansas'] section of the Indian country" was held at Shawnee Baptist Mission. It was the first in a series of *annual* meetings.

Present were Methodists J. C. Berryman, E. T. Peery, and Thomas Johnson; Baptists Isaac McCoy, Johnston Lykins, Jotham Meeker, Robert Simerwell, and Ira D. Blanchard; Presbyterians Joseph Kerr, Benton Pixley (formerly of Mission Neosho), and John Dunbar (bound for the Pawnee country).

Kerr was moderator, and Lykins the clerk. Amity ended on the 26th when a resolution was offered "relating to the manner members should be received from one mission church to another of a different denomination." The Baptists and Methodists disagreed on this subject. According to Dunbar "feelings were manifested that should have found no place at such a meeting." Before adjourning, however, a conference was scheduled for 1835—to be held at Shawnee Methodist Mission. (And it was held there on May 15, 1835. In 1836, on May 12, a third annual meeting was held—at Shawnee Baptist Mission.)

Ref: *KHC*, v. 14, pp. 589, 590; Jotham Meeker's "Diary," entries of July 25, 26, 1834, May 15, 1835, and May 12, 1836; Joseph Kerr's letter of September 25, 1834 (enclosing a copy of the "Minutes" of the July 26 meeting) in Presbyterian Historical Society, American Indian Missions correspondence.

¶ In the summer an elementary book in the Osage language—prepared by Missionaries William B. Montgomery and William C. Requa of New Hopefield Mission (in present Mayes county, Okla.) —was published at Boston, Mass., under the patronage of the American Board of Comm'rs for Foreign Missions.

According to a bibliography of Indian language books published under the auspices of the above board, 500 copies were printed of the 126-page *Washashe Wageressa Pahugreh Tse* (Osage First Book).

Ref: *Missionary Herald*, v. 31 (January, 1835), p. 26, v. 32 (July, 1836), p. 269. The Kansas State Historical Society has a copy of this book.

¶ Apparently in July, or August, Ottawa chief Oquanoxa, and his small band of about 75 persons, left the Shawnee reserve—where they had lived since coming to "Kansas" in November, 1832, from Ohio—and moved to their own reservation (south of the Shawnees and west of the Peorias & Kaskaskias), in present Franklin county.

Oquanoxa, and seven of his young men, had been escorted to their reserve (to examine it) in February, 1833, by Agent R. W. Cummins, and Isaac McCoy. And in May Cummins had, it appears, advanced the Ottawas $2,000 of their funds for the erection of houses and opening of farms. But, fearing the Osages and the Pawnees, the Ottawas (few in number) had chosen to settle at a site (which has not been identified) about 20 miles from the Shawnee settlements, and on the Shawnees' land.

In July, 1834, when Missionary Jotham Meeker (then of the Shawnee Baptist Mission) was in their camp (on the 18th), the Ottawas told him they were preparing to remove to their own reserve (20 miles further—40 miles in all—from the Shawnee settlements). On a subsequent visit, at the beginning of October, Meeker lodged in the Ottawas' camp on the "Osage" [Marais des Cygnes] river, in present Franklin county.

A delegation of Ottawas from the Maumee river in northwest Ohio arrived at Shawnee Baptist Mission on October 14, 1834; traveled the 40 miles southwest to the Ottawa reserve; examined it; approved it; and returned to "Shawanoe" on the 17th—en route back to Ohio. (But they did not emigrate to "Kansas" till 1837.)

Ref: 23d Cong., 1st Sess., *Sen. Doc. 512*, v. 4 (Serial 247), pp. 7-9; 23d Cong., 1st Sess., *H. Ex. Doc. 490* (Serial 259), p. 54; Isaac McCoy's "Journal," February 19-21, 1833, entries; Jotham Meeker "Diary," *loc. cit.* (various entries from October, 1833, through October, 1834); also, Meeker's October 30, 1834, letter. *Also, see,* Grant Foreman's *Last Trek of the Indians* (c1946), pp. 90, 91.

¶ During most of August the Rev. Cyrus Kingsbury and the Rev. Cyrus Byington (in the service of the American Board of Comm'rs for Foreign Missions) were in present eastern Kansas, on a tour of the Indian settlements and Indian missions.

In June and July they had voyaged up the Mississippi, as far as the Sac & Fox Agency at Rock Island, Ill., and returned to St. Louis; then had ascended the Missouri. Their complete itinerary in "Kansas" is not known. They were at Shawnee Baptist Mission on August 14; at Kickapoo Methodist Mission from August 23 to about the 26th (where they conferred with the Rev. John Dunbar —also an "American Board" missionary, and a guest there); at Westport, Mo., by the 28th; again at Shawnee Baptist Mission on September 1. Byington visited the Wea mission on September 2.

Kingsbury and Byington, in a report dated at Westport, Mo., September 4, made note of the two Shawnee missions (Methodist and Baptist); the two Delaware missions (Methodist and Baptist), and the government teacher among the Delawares; the Kickapoo mission (Methodist), and the government teacher among the Kickapoos; the absence of any Kansa mission; the Otoe mission (Baptist); the *prospective* Omaha mission (Baptist); the *prospective* Iowa mission (Presbyterian); and the *prospective* Pawnee mission ("American Board"). [Not mentioned: the Methodists' Peoria & Kaskaskia mission; or the Presbyterians' Wea & Piankeshaw mission; or the "American Board's" Osage missions— Harmony (Mo.) and Boudinot (present Neosho county).] On leaving Westport, Mo., Kingsbury and Byington, en route southward to the missions west of Arkansas territory, traveled by way of Harmony and Boudinot.

Ref: *Missionary Herald*, v. 30 (December, 1834), pp. 453-455; *Report of the American Board of Comm'rs for Foreign Missions* . . ., 1834, pp. 112, 113, 171-174; Jotham Meeker's "Diary," entries of August 14, September 1, 1834; *KHC*, v. 14, pp. 591, 592, 695; Presbyterian Historical Society, American Indian Missions correspondence—for item on Byington at Wea mission (in Joseph Kerr's letter of October 1, 1834).

❧ Pratte, Chouteau & Company received licenses on August 7 to trade with the (1) Kickapoos, (2) Delawares, and (3) Kansa; and on August 9 additional permits were given them for trade with the (4) Weas, etc., and (5) Shawnees. The licenses indicated seven traders, in all, were employed.

(Two months earlier—on June 1—the "American Fur Company" had undergone a change, with the retirement of John J. Astor. What had been the Northern Department, went to Ramsay Crooks and associates; while the Western Department, which Pierre Chouteau, Jr., headed, became Pratte, Chouteau & Company in the reorganization.)

Ref: 23d Cong., 2d Sess., *H. Ex. Doc.* 97 (Serial 273); Chittenden's *The American Fur Trade*, v. 1, p. 364 (for Pratte, Chouteau & Company).

❧ Born: on August 11, at Shawnee Methodist Mission (present Wyandotte county), Sarah Elizabeth Johnson, daughter of the Rev. Thomas and Sarah T. (Davis) Johnson. (She died June 8, 1840.)

Ref: *KHC*, v. 12, p. xii; KHi's 15th *Biennial Report*, p. 35.

❧ Some 300 to 400 Osages, particularly of the Neosho river settlements, were estimated to have been cholera victims in the summer. About a fourth of the Indians at the small New Hopefield Mission (Okla.) died. Trader Auguste P. Chouteau advised the Osages of Clermont's village to scatter, and the spread of cholera among them was thus prevented.

Ref: Foreman's *Advancing the Frontier*, p. 143. *Also, see* a spring, 1830, annals item, p. 171.

❡ August 15.—Upon Marston G. Clark's receipt, this date, of Comm'r of Indian Affairs Elbert Herring's July 3d letter, the Kansa Agency officially—and abruptly—closed.

Herring (in the letter) thanked Clark for past services (since May, 1829) and instructed him to deliver all public property in his possession to Agent R. W. Cummins. In a final accounting (covering the January-August 15 disbursements) dated "Kanzas Agency, August 17, 1834," Marston G. Clark listed these payments: to himself (as agent) $625; to Clement Lessert (interpreter) $250; to John McGill (gun and blacksmith) $250; to Lindsey Boone (assistant to McGill) $150; to George B. Clark $45, and to C. C. Mounts $110, for "labor and assisting the Kansa in agriculture"; to James King $110 for his "labor on chief's house, per contract"; to George B. Clark $10 for "taking express from Kanzas to Independence, 89 miles . . . [etc.]"; to S. Arthur $300 for "provisions furnished for feeding the Kanzas at the reception of their annuities"; to "Johnson & Fristoe" $125 for transporting provisions; and to John O. Agnew $150 for "presents to Indians."

See July 2 entry for Marston G. Clark's subsequent employment.

Ref: OIA, "Letters Sent" (June 1-September 30, 1834), v. 13, p. 105 (for Herring's July 3, 1834, letter); 23d Cong., H. Doc. No. 150 (Serial 274), pp. 18, 19 (for M. G. Clark's August 17, 1834, accounts). George B. Clark was, probably, Agent Clark's son, mentioned earlier by Jason Lee—see under April 28, 1834, entry.

❡ September 2-4.—At Fort Gibson, Okla., Col. Henry Dodge and Francis W. Armstrong (acting sup't of Indian affairs for the Western Territory) conducted councils with Indian representatives of the eastern tribes (Seneca, Choctaw, Cherokee, Creek, and Osage), and the western tribes (Kiowa, Comanche, Wichita, and Waco). (The western delegates had arrived at the post in mid-August, with Dodge and the dragoons.)

On September 5 the western Indians, having been given U. S. medals and flags (also some guns and goods), and the assurance that their request for a peace treaty the following year would be given consideration, started home— escorted out of the settlement by a small force of dragoons, and some Cherokees —the latter accompanying them as far as the Cross Timbers.

Ref: Foreman's Pioneer Days . . ., pp. 152-155.

❡ BORN: on September 4, at Shawnee Baptist Mission (present Johnson county), Maria Meeker, daughter of missionaries Jotham and Eleanor (Richardson) Meeker.

(Maria Meeker married Nathan L. Simpson, of Westport, Mo., on December 10, 1851.)

Ref: Jotham Meeker's "Diary," and KHi's 15th Biennial Report, p. 35, for her birth; KHi's Biographical Scrapbook, "S," v. 3, p. 273. Maria (Meeker) Simpson died January 15, 1885, as stated in "Miscellaneous Genealogical Records from Kansas Society, D. A. R.," v. 3, p. 9 (in KHi library).

❡ In September a small (11-wagon) eastbound train of Bent, St.

Vrain & Company crossed "Kansas." As reported in a St. Louis paper of October 14, the party had left Santa Fe

". . . early in August, taking Taos in the route, and thus extending the journey across the Rocky Mountains to the trading posts [most particularly new Fort William—better known as "Bent's Fort"] on the Arkansas river. They met with very few Indians and suffered no interruption whatever in their progress home. . . . The present company brought with them eleven wagons which, with the contents, belong to Messrs. St. Vrain, Bent and Company."

The above brief account is notable as an early reference to the upper Arkansas trading posts in connection with the partnership of Ceran St. Vrain, Charles (and William) Bent; and also, because it presaged the opening of another regular pathway to Santa Fe—the upper Arkansas, or mountain route— a longer, but better-watered, and therefore safer route, by way of "Bent's Fort," Raton Pass, and Taos.

Ref: *Missouri Republican*, October 14, 1834; or, *Colorado Magazine*, v. 31 (April, 1954), p. 114. Capt. Richard B. Lee (army officer on leave) was with this company on part of the journey. In an official letter of November 4, 1834, after his return to Washington, he stated that on August 5 he had joined an eastbound party of 29 men.—For this item I am indebted to Dale L. Morgan, of the Bancroft Library. David Lavender in his *Bent's Fort*, p. 389, says Lee "captained" the wagon train, but this seems unlikely—especially since he left the train (with four other men) 300 miles west of the settlements to hasten on to Independence, arriving there October 3d.—The source for this is the same letter noted above.

❦ September 22.—William Marshall Anderson, homeward-bound from the mountains (*see* p. 265), and traveling down the Missouri in company with 16 mountain men (superintended by Etienne Provost) in a fur-laden "big canoe" (two canoes lashed together), stopped briefly at Fort Leavenworth. He was "very unexpectedly & cordially received by Mssrs. Morgan, Wickliffe, Hughes & Doherty." (Alexander G. Morgan, sutler; Capt. William N. Wickliffe, Sixth U. S. infantry; Andrew S. Hughes, Iowa subagent; John Dougherty, Upper Missouri Indian agent.)

Anderson had traveled from the Rockies to the Missouri (reaching the Council Bluffs September 11) in the 57-man company of Lucien Fontenelle. From Bellevue (Neb.) on the 18th, the Provost-headed party had started downriver. Part of Sunday, the 21st, had been spent at Robidoux's Blacksnake Hills post (St. Joseph, Mo., site), and camp that night had been "within gun sound" of Fort Leavenworth. The night of September 22 was spent "below the mouth of the Kansas river."

Ref: *The Rocky Mountain Journals of William Marshall Anderson, op. cit.*, pp. 218-220.

❦ September-October.—The autumn eastbound company of traders began to move out of Santa Fe around September 1. From a "Red River" (Canadian) rendezvous, on the 10th, the caravan of about 140 men and 40 wagons, captained by "Mr. Kerr," set out for Missouri. It was later reported they "met with no Indians." By October 18 they had reached Columbia, Mo. A St. Louis paper, a few days later, stated:

The Company brought in, as near as can be ascertained, $40,000 in gold, $140,000 in specie, $15,000 worth of Beaver, 50 packs Buffalo Robes, 12,000 pounds of Wool, and 300 head of mules, valued at $10,000. (This wool shipment in 1834 is noteworthy. Wool did not become an important item in the Santa Fe trade till the 1850's.)

Ref: *Missouri Intelligencer*, October 18, 1834; *Niles' Weekly Register*, v. 47 (November 8, 1834), p. 147; *Missouri Republican*, October 24, 1834; Missouri Historical Society, St. Louis, *Collections*, v. 5 (June, 1928), p. 286.

℄ About September 7(?) Capt. David Hunter and three (First) U. S. dragoon companies (C, D, and G) left Fort Gibson (Okla.) under orders to proceed to Fort Leavenworth.

According to Sgt. Hugh Evans, they rendezvoused September 8 on the Verdigris, in the Creek nation; remained two days; then began the journey northward. En route they passed some of the Osage towns, but whether these dragoons crossed present southern Kansas on their march is uncertain. Near the end of the journey they entered "Kansas" (probably in present Johnson county) to cross (ford?) the Kansas river—*about two miles from its mouth* (in present Wyandotte county), by Evans' statement. "This river," he wrote, "is very wide and shallow by no means suitable for navigation at least any distance up it." On the 22d(?) Hunter and his command reached Fort Leavenworth. (If, as Evans stated, they were about 18? days en route, the arrival date was later than the 22d.)

Col. Henry Dodge, and Company A, apparently left Fort Gibson on September 14, and reached Fort Leavenworth on the 27th.

Ref: *Chronicles of Oklahoma*, v. 3 (1925), p. 215 (Sgt. Hugh Evans' journal); [Henry Shindler's] "The History of Fort Leavenworth" (typescript), in KHi library, pp. 69, 70; H. P. Beers' *The Western Military Frontier, 1815-1846* (Philadelphia, 1935), p. 113.

℄ In the autumn Fort Leavenworth (designated headquarters of the [First] U. S. dragoons by war department G. O. No. 41, of May 19, 1834) became regimental headquarters in fact—upon the arrival, late in September, of Capt. David Hunter with three dragoon companies, followed soon after by regimental commander Col. Henry Dodge and a fourth company—all from Fort Gibson (*see* preceding entry). The two companies of Sixth infantry troops which had been the post's summer garrison, departed for Jefferson Barracks, Mo.

Colonel Dodge's officers at Fort Leavenworth were: *Captains* David Hunter (Co. D), Lemuel Ford (Co. G), Matthew Duncan (Co. C); *First Lieutenants* Lancaster P. Lupton, Thomas Swords (A. A. Q. M.), Thompson B. Wheelock, James W. Hamilton (Adjt.), Benjamin D. Moore; *Second Lieutenants* John S. Van Derveer, Enoch Steen, John L. Watson, Burdett A. Terrett; *Brevet Lieutenants* Gaines P. Kingsbury and Asbury Ury. Asst. Surg. Benjamin F. Fellowes was the medical officer.

From a letter Dodge wrote on October 20, 1834, it appears that no stables or shelter for the horses had been built prior to his arrival; and that, despite an allotment of $10,000 made by the war department, required additional quarters (subsequently constructed of brick) had not been started.

The secretary of war's 1834 report (dated November 27) showed Col. Henry Dodge's Fort Leavenworth command to have an aggregate strength of 230, with 213 present at the time of report. (Companies B, H, and I, of the dragoons—under Lt. Col. Stephen W. Kearny—were then stationed at newly established Fort Des Moines; and Companies E, F, and K, under Maj. R. B. Mason, were at Fort Gibson.)

Ref: *Ibid.; Chronicles of Oklahoma,* v. 3, p. 215; Elvid Hunt and W. E. Lorence's *History of Fort Leavenworth, 1827-1937* (Fort Leavenworth, 1937), pp. 51, 52; *KHC,* v. 14, p. 693; McCoy's *Annual Register,* January, 1835, pp. 41, 42 (for names of Dodge's officers); *American State Papers: Military Affairs,* v. 5, pp. 369, 370 (for secretary of war's report); *Niles' Weekly Register,* v. 46 (August 2, 1834), p. 388. In *March of the First Dragoons to the Rocky Mountains in 1835; the Diaries and Maps of Lemuel Ford . . .,* by Nolie Mumey, on p. 101, is a Ford diary entry indicating his "Compy G horses were stabled 15th December 1834. . . ."

❧ Between October 13 and 23, at Fort Leavenworth, the immigrant Indians of "Kansas," were paid their annuity funds by 2d Lt. Jonathan Freeman (A. A. Q. M.), Sixth U. S. infantry.

The use of the military post as a central distribution point, and the disbursements in cash by the military, were innovations of this year—resulting from the June 30 act regulating the Indian department. The annuity payments were:

INDIANS	DATE	AMOUNT	
Kickapoos [of Missouri]	October 13	$5,000	
Kickapoos of Illinois	" "	2,000	
Delawares	" 16	6,500	also $100 each to chiefs Patterson, Nahkomin, and Ketchum
Ottawas	" 18	900	
Shawnees	" 20	3,000	
Piankeshaws	" 23	800	
Weas	" "	3,000	
Peorias & Kaskaskias	" "	3,000	

Ref: 23d Cong., 2d Sess., H. Doc. No. 150 (Serial 274), p. 71; OIA, "Letters Sent," v. 13, p. 95 (War Department, July 3, 1834, "Regulations concerning the payment of Annuities"—"All annuities payable by treaty stipulations will be hereafter paid by a military officer . . ." and "the annuities will be paid in specie . . .").

❧ In October Marston G. Clark (recently Kansa agent), subagent (since August) for the Shawnees, Ottawas, Weas & Piankeshaws, and Peorias & Kaskaskias, issued four licenses for trade with the Shawnees, and the Weas. Flournoy & Co. (three men) was issued a permit on October 4; and on October 17 licenses were given to John O. Agnew (two men); to Henry McKee; and to George B. Clark.

Ref: 23d Cong., 2d Sess., *H. Ex. Doc.* 97 (Serial 273). *See* July 2, and August 15, 1834, entries for Marston G. Clark's change of positions.

❡ DIED: Fish, a Shawnee chief ("alias William Jackson, a white man, raised with the Shawnees"), late in October, in present Wyandotte county.

Missionary Thomas Johnson, in a letter of November 4, wrote: ". . . one week ago we were called to mourn the death of our old friend Fish, the head man of the band of Shawnees, among whom our [Methodist] mission is established. . . ." (*See* November, 1830, annals item.)

Fish's sons included one named "Paskal" or (Paschal) who was described (in 1830) as a moral, good, English-speaking man with a family; another named Charles; and a third who was referred to (by Johnson in 1834) as a "prodigal son."

Ref: *Christian Advocate,* New York, v. 9, no. 17 (December 19, 1834); Mary Greene's *Life of Rev. Jesse Greene* (Lexington, Mo., 1852), pp. 45, 46; *KHC,* v. 9, pp. 166, 167, 186, 198.

❡ Capt. Lemuel Ford, Lt. Thomas Swords (A. A. Q. M.), and Agent R. W. Cummins left Fort Leavenworth on December 24 to superintend payment of the Kansa Indians' annuities, at their villages. (Ford stated that the Kansa population totaled 1,552 persons.) They returned to the post on December 31.

The Kansa chiefs' names, as recorded on December 29, at the Kansa villages, were: "Nompe warrow" (White Plume), "Kehiga wat i inga" (elsewhere given as "Ka-he-ga-wa-ta-ning-ga"), "Kihega watcha" (Hard Chief—elsewhere given as "Ki-ha-ga-wah-chuffe"), "Micho chinga" (The Little White Bear—elsewhere given as "Mesch-o-shin-ga"), and "Wah con chia."

Ref: *March of the First Dragoons* . . ., by Nolie Mumey, p. 102 ("Hausiel Indians" in the reference is a misprint for *Kansa* Indians). Office of Indian Affairs, "Letters Received from St. Louis Superintendency" (National Archives Microcopy 234, Roll 750), Richard W. Cummins' letter of January 25, 1835, therein.

❡ Anthony L. Davis, "emigrating agent" for the Pottawatomies of Indiana, in a letter of December 31, reported his arrival at "Kickapoo Camp" (present Leavenworth county), with his family, "all in good health."

Appointed "emigrating agent" in July (by Secretary of War Cass), Davis had made an earlier trip to "Kansas"—probably arriving in September, for he had written on October 1 from Fort Leavenworth, asking that the Pottawatomie annuities be forwarded.

At the end of 1834, according to Isaac McCoy, there were 250 Pottawatomies in "Kansas"—all residing on the Kickapoo reserve. (About 110 had come in May, 1833, with the Kickapoos; Qui-qui-to's band of 68 had come in August, 1833. The additional 70 or so immigrants apparently arrived in 1834.)

Ref: OIA, "Letters Sent," v. 13, pp. 135, 136 (for Davis' appointment); *ibid.,* "Registers of Letters Received," v. 5 (for Davis' October 1, 1834, letter); *Indiana Historical Collections,* Indianapolis, v. 26, pp. 97, 98 (for Davis' December 31, 1834, letter); Isaac McCoy's *Annual Register,* January, 1835, p. 19. McCoy also stated that the Pottawatomie "removing agent," Abel C. Pepper, of Indiana, had brought a Pottawatomie exploring delegation to "Kansas" in 1834. No information on this has been located, but *see Indiana Historical Collections*, v. 26, p. 50.

1835

❡ January 17.—The printing of 1,000 copies of Isaac McCoy's 52-page *The Annual Register of Indian Affairs Within the Indian (or Western) Territory . . . January 1, 1835*, was completed at Shawnee Baptist Mission, by Jotham Meeker. (McCoy had turned over his manuscripts to Meeker on December 15, 1834, and the printer started typesetting the next day.)

In this pamphlet McCoy described the state of civilization of each of the native and emigrant tribes of "Kansas"; listed the names of leading chiefs, of government employees (interpreters, blacksmiths, etc.), and of missionaries; also he gave some information about each mission. In format, and content, this first (of four) *Annual Registers* set the pattern for succeeding issues. (*See* December 9, 1835, annals, for item on the second issue.)

A change among the Kansa—a move westward by part of the nation (apparently some of Hard Chief's band) to be nearer the buffalo country—was recorded by McCoy. He located this group (about a third of the Kansa) on the *north* bank of the river "about 40 miles from their eastern boundary" [in present Pottawatomie county—roughly between St. George and Wamego]. He placed the rest of the Kansa in two locations: (1) about a third on the Kansas river's north bank within three miles of the Kansa eastern boundary [Fool Chief's village]; and (2) the other third a few miles higher up, on the *south* bank [American Chief's and Hard Chief's towns]. (These were the approximate sites of the villages of 1829.)

Ref: Jotham Meeker's "Diary" (for printing information). In a March 5, 1834, letter, Missionary Wells Bushnell had written: "The Konzas, since last summer, have burnt their old villages[?] & moved 8[?] miles further up the river, & are building new ones." Though inaccurate, Bushnell's statement may indicate the time (autumn of 1833?) when the removal began. (His letter is in Presbyterian Historical Society, American Indian Missions correspondence—microfilm, Kansas State Historical Society.)

❡ BORN: at Shawnee Baptist Mission (present Johnson county), on January 21, Elizabeth Simerwell, daughter (and fourth child) of Missionaries Robert and Fanny (Goodridge) Simerwell.

(On March 1, 1866, she married John S. Carter. They resided near Auburn, Shawnee county, and had six children living at the time of her death, January 3, 1883.)

Ref: Meeker's "Diary"; KHC, v. 8, p. 260 (where the birth date is given, erroneously, as January 24); and Topeka *Commonwealth*, February 24, 1883 (In KHi "Scrapbook," v. 6, p. 46), which also gives the date as January 24.

❡ February 2.—In Washington, Rep. William H. Ashley, of Missouri, presented to the house a petition, signed by 33 eastern "Kansas" and western Missouri residents (and forwarded by Isaac McCoy), asking "that a mail route be established from Fort Leavenworth to Fort Towson [on the Red river], on which the mail shall be transported weekly on horseback." The route outlined in the petition (dated November, 1834) is summarized here:

Miles

From Fort Leavenworth,° through the "Delaware Settlements":

	Miles
To West Port ° (on the west line of Missouri; near the Shawnee Agency)	about 35
" "Wea Smithery and Mission House" (10 miles *west* of the Missouri line)	" 40
" Harmony Mission (15 miles *east* of the Missouri line)	50
" The Osage Village (five miles *east* of the Osage Agency; and 30 miles *west* of Missouri)	70
" "Requa's Osage Settlement" (within the Cherokee country, southwest of the Senecas & Shawnees of Neosho; and 30 miles *west* of Arkansas territory)	80
" The west bank of Neosho (Grand) river at (Auguste P.) Chouteau's crossing	15
" "Union Mission House"	16
" The late "Agency of the Creek Indians on Verdigris River"	22
" Fort Gibson ° (50 miles *west* of Arkansas territory	4
Thence, passing the Cherokee Agency (on the *north* side of Arkansas river)	
" Choctaw Agency (on the *south* side of the Arkansas, within the Choctaw Nation)	65
" Fort Smith ° (on the western line of Arkansas territory)	7
" Fort Towson ° (20 miles *west* of Arkansas territory)	120

About 524

(° At these five locations there were post offices.)

The 33 signatures on the petition (original in the National Archives; photostat in KHi) present an interesting collection of autographs. The names:

H[enry] Dodge   Col.   U S Dragoons
Matthew Duncan   Capt.
   U. S. Dragoons
D[avid] Hunter, Capt. U. S. Drag.
J[ames] W. Hamilton   1st. Lt.
   & Adjt.   Dragoons
B[enjamin] D. Moore   1st. Lieut
   Dragoons
A. B. Duncan of Clay County
A[sbury] Ury   Lt.   Dragoons
Benj. F. Fellowes   Asst Surgeon
Isaac McCoy of Jackson Co. Mo.
James P. Hickman of Jackson Co. Mo.
John C. McCoy   P[ost] M[aster]
   Westport Mo.

M[arston] G. Clark   S[u]b.
   Agent for Shawonees & others
George B Clark   [son of M. G. Clark]
Richd W Cummins   U. S. Ind
   Agent for Delawares, Kickapoo,
   & Kanzas Indians
William Johnson   Missionary
   to Shawnees
Asa Jones   Farmer at Shawnee
   Mission
Jotham Meeker, Printer, Ind. Ter.
Robert Simerwell   Missionary to
   Potawatomie
I[ra] D Blanchard   [missionary to]
   Delawares

Anthony L. Davis   Emgt. Agt
Potawatomies
Johnston Lykins   Supt. Ind schools
&c., Indian Territory
Joseph Kerr   Missionary to Weas
& Piankeshaws
Henry Bradley   Missionary to Weas
& Piankeshaws
Elisha Shepard   missionary to Weas
& Piankeshaws
Robert Johnson   Westport

Joseph Russell   Westport
Thomas W. Polke   West Port
Missouri
Lemuel Ford   Capt   U S Dragoons
L[ancaster] P Lupton   1st. Lieut
Dragoons
G[aines] P Kingsbury   Lt   Dragoons
Jno L Watson   Lt   Dragoons
C[laiborne] B Lykins
Thos J. Givens of Washington Co
Mo   [son-in-law of Isaac McCoy]

(On December 16 Representative Ashley again presented the petition to the house, where it was referred to the post office and post roads committee. *See, also,* January 5, 1836, entry.)

Ref: Isaac McCoy's letter of December 29, 1834 (in McCoy manuscripts, KHi ms. division); W. H. Ashley letter of January 30, 1835 (in *ibid.*); the petition (among the records of the United States House of Representatives in the National Archives). Dr. Johnston Lykins and Dr. C. B. Lykins were brothers. *See* J. Lykins' letter of January 28, 1839, and Isaac McCoy's March 1, 1839, letters—both in McCoy manuscripts.

❡ February 24.—Jotham Meeker (at Shawnee Baptist Mission, present Johnson county) printed the first number of the *Shawnee Sun*. (He had, on the 18th, started "setting types" for this small "newspaper.") The *Siwinowe Kesibwi* (*Shawnee Sun*) was "the first periodical publication to be printed in what is now Kansas" (McMurtrie); and "the first newspaper ever published exclusively in an Indian language" (McCoy). Dr. Johnston Lykins was the *Sun's* editor.

From 1835 up to as late as May, 1842, this publication was issued at irregular intervals, and presumably in small editions. Accompanying Douglas C. McMurtrie's article "The Shawnee Sun," in *KHQ*, v. 2, pp. 339-342, is an illustration of the first page of a November, 1841, issue of the *Siwinowe Kesibwi*. It was photographed from the only known extant copy of this publication—a copy then (1933) in private hands, and now in the Snyder collection of the library of the University of Missouri at Kansas City.

Ref: Meeker "Diary"; Isaac McCoy's *History of Baptist Indian Missions* (1840), p. 486; letter by Kenneth J. LaBudde (director of libraries, University of Kansas City, Kansas City, Mo.), June 8, 1962, to L. Barry; D. C. McMurtrie's and A. H. Allen's *Jotham Meeker* . . . (Chicago, 1930), p. 159.

❡ In a February 26 report (based on incomplete returns), Comm'r Elbert Herring listed Indian agents, subagents, and other field employees hired subsequent to the Indian department reorganization act of June 30, 1834. In "Kansas" these employees were:

Richard W. Cummins, *agent,* Northern Agency, Western Territory; Marston G. Clark, *subagent* for the Ottawas, Shawnees, etc. (but *see* Clark's resignation, p. 284); Paul Ligueste Chouteau, *subagent* for the Osages; *interpreters* Joseph James (for the Kansa), James Connor (for the Delawares), Peter Cudjoe

["Cadue" in later lists] (for the Kickapoos), Baptiste Mongrain (for the Osages), Henry Clay (for the Ottawas and Shawnees); *blacksmiths* Robert Dunlap (for the Delawares), James McGill (for the Kansa); *teachers* Henry Rennick (for the Delawares), J. C. Berryman (for the Kickapoos).

The Kickapoos' blacksmiths were paid by the tribe (not by the Indian department). From April 1, 1835, to November 15, 1837, I. O. Smith was that nation's smith, and W. V. Smith was "striker" (or assistant smith).

Ref: 23d Cong., 2d Sess., *H. Doc. No. 181* (Serial 275). Some errors in the printed list have been corrected; also some data have been added above, to link names correctly with tribes, etc. For I. O. and W. V. Smith, *see* Superintendency of Indian Affairs, St. Louis, "Records," v. 8, typed copy, p. 129.

ℭ Early in the year Marston G. Clark resigned as subagent "for the Shawanees, Ottawas and other emigrant tribes, including the Kickapoos, the Weas and Piankeshaws, the Kaskaskias and Peorias"—a post he had held since the closing of the Kansa Agency, August 15, 1834. His resignation was accepted effective March 31.

Comm'r Elbert Herring, in a March 20 letter, wrote Isaac McCoy that "The Secretary of War has determined not to fill that Sub Agency, but to attach it to some other agency." (Until 1837 Agent R. W. Cummins had the added responsibilities.)

Clark (a "Kansas" resident since May, 1829) returned to his Salem, Ind., home and was elected to the state legislature in August. (He had been an Indiana state senator, and a representative from Washington county, prior to his appointment to the Indian service.)

Ref: Office of Indian Affairs records (OIA) in the National Archives, Records Group No. 75; McCoy manuscripts (for Herring letter); *Indiana Historical Collections,* Indianapolis, v. 24, p. 134, v. 40, pp. 187, 189, 198, 226; William H. English's *Conquest of the Country Northwest of the River Ohio 1778-1783* . . . (Indianapolis and Kansas City, Mo., 1896), v. 1, p. 34, v. 2, pp. 866, 978. When Clark first came to "Kansas" he was *subagent* to the Kansa; by a July 12, 1832, appointment he became Kansa *agent.*

ℭ MARRIED: John Dement (who held the rank of colonel in the Black Hawk war) and Mary Louise Dodge, daughter of post commandant Col. Henry and Christiana (McDonald) Dodge, on April 1, at Fort Leavenworth.

Ref: T. R. Woodward's *Dodge Genealogy* (Chicago, 1904), pp. 66, 67; Reynolds, *op. cit.,* p. 139; *History of Lee County* . . . [Illinois] (Chicago, 1881), p. 218 (for data on John Dement).

ℭ By April 18 German botanist Charles A. Geyer was on the "western borders of the state of Missouri," preparing for a botanical tour beyond the frontier. He later described this trip (made with only one companion) as a "journey to the Pawnee-loups Indians on the Big Nemahaw[?] and lower North Fork of the Platte river." (If his point of departure was Independence, Mo., as seems likely, or Liberty, he presumably crossed present northeast Kansas to reach the Big Nemaha country.)

The tour "turned out abortive on account of fever and maltreatment by a party of Indians." Geyer was barely able to make it back to the Missouri border, where he spent a long time recuperating. About September 9 he embarked "from the mouth of the Kansas river," on an American Fur Company steamboat bound for St. Louis. He met, on board, French scientist and explorer Joseph N. Nicollet, and Scottish traveler Charles A. Murray.

Ref: Susan D. McKelvey's *Botanical Explorations* . . . (1955), p. 660; Charles A. Murray's *Travels in North America* . . . (London, 1839), v. 2, pp. 107, 108. In McKelvey, and some other sources, the botanist's name is given as "Karl Andreas Geyer."— See *Oregon Historical Quarterly*, v. 41 (June, 1940), p. 184.

❡ Robert Campbell (partner of William Sublette) and a small party probably crossed "Kansas" by way of "Sublette's Trace" in the latter part of April. Campbell had left St. Louis on April 9, bound for "Fort Laramie" to transfer his and Sublette's property at that post to the fur company formed the preceding summer—the merger of Fontenelle & Drips with Fitzpatrick, Milton Sublette, and Bridger— to which they had sold out. He remained some 15 days at Laramie river.

On the return journey, in June and July, Campbell made successful use of boats on the North Platte and Platte to transport his buffalo robes down to Missouri; but also had a land party (which included Andrew Sublette) with fur-laden pack mules, which followed down the Platte's north bank.

At the forks of the Platte Campbell was able to avoid trouble with the hostile Arikaras then located there. On June 27 his party met the westbound American Fur Company expedition headed by Lucien Fontenelle (*see* May 14 entry). Of this encounter Dr. Marcus Whitman wrote: "met Messrs Campbell & Sublit returning from the mountains with twelve men"; and the Rev. Samuel Parker noted: "met Messrs. Campbell and Sublette with a small caravan, returning from the Black Hills."

Campbell and the land party crossed the Missouri at, or near Bellevue, and came down the left bank to Joseph Robidoux's Blacksnake Hills post (St. Joseph, Mo. now); and continued on to St. Louis where they arrived July 15.

Ref: Robert Campbell dictation in the Bancroft Library (courtesy of Dale L. Morgan); *Niles' Weekly Register*, v. 48 (August 8, 1835), p. 406; *Missouri Republican*, St. Louis, July 18, 1835; Samuel Parker's *Journal of an Exploring Tour Beyond the Rocky Mountains* . . ., 3d edition (Ithaca, N. Y., 1842), p. 47; Marcus Whitman's "Journal and Report," in Archer B. and Dorothy P. Hulbert, *Marcus Whitman, Crusader, Part One, 1802 to 1839* (c1936), p. 151; and in *Oregon Historical Society Quarterly*, v. 28, p. 245; D. B. Nunis, Jr., *Andrew Sublette* . . . (Los Angeles, 1960), pp. 55, 56; John E. Sunder, *Bill Sublette*, . . . (Norman, Okla., c1959), pp. 145, 146.

❡ In the spring(?) Joseph V. Hamilton became sutler at Fort Leavenworth. He replaced Alexander G. Morgan; and continued to hold the position till 1839.

(In an 1839 letter Col. S. W. Kearny—commandant at Fort Leavenworth— stated that Hamilton had by then been sutler [and "a very bad one" in his opinion] for *four years;* that in May, 1839, the "Council at this Post" had renominated him; that he [Kearny] had objected; and subsequently he had found it necessary to discipline Maj. Clifton Wharton and the two other council officers when they persisted in choosing Hamilton. On his own behalf, Joseph V. Hamilton then went to Washington, saw the secretary of war; failed to get the sutler's post; received, instead, appointment as an Indian agent.)

Ref: *The Trail Guide* (publication of the Kansas City Posse, The Westerners), Kansas City, Mo., v. 1, No. 3 (July, 1956), pp. 18, 19 (for Kearny's letter). Though the relationship, if any, has not been determined, it is noteworthy that the post adjutant at Fort Leavenworth in early 1835 was Lt. James W. Hamilton.

❦ May 9-10.—The Rev. Samuel Parker, of New York, left his temporary abode at Liberty, Mo., and rode to Fort Leavenworth where he was a guest at "Lieut. S's" [probably Lt. Enoch Steen's] home. On Sunday, the 10th, he preached three times "and most of the people of the garrison assembled."

(Parker, and Dr. Marcus Whitman, employed by the American Board of Comm'rs for Foreign Missions to determine the missionary needs in the "Oregon country," had been at Liberty since mid-April, awaiting the arrival of the American Fur Company's westbound caravan.)

Ref: Parker, *op cit.*, pp. 31, 22. (The first edition of Parker's *Journal* was published in 1838.)

❦ May 14.—Leaving Liberty, Mo., the American Fur Company caravan (headed by Lucien Fontenelle) moved northward—up the Missouri's left bank—en route to Bellevue (Neb.), from which place they would follow up the Platte towards the Rocky mountains, and the rendezvous on the Green river (Wyo.). With this party were the Rev. Samuel Parker, Dr. Marcus Whitman (*see* preceding entry), and, as far as Bellevue, the Rev. Moses Merrill, missionary to the Otoes.

On the 18th this party arrived at Joseph Robidoux's Blacksnake Hills trading post [St. Joseph, Mo.]; and on May 30, crossed the Missouri to Bellevue, where the missionaries remained till June 22. Cholera broke out among the mountain men on June 10—many, including Fontenelle, were stricken. Doctor Whitman's efforts helped save most of them, but at least three died.

The caravan which set out on June 21 (between 50 and 60 men, six wagons, three yoke of oxen, and nearly 200 horses and mules—each man a horse to ride, and a horse and a mule to pack) arrived at Fort Laramie (Wyo.) on July 26. There, Thomas Fitzpatrick took charge and got the party to the rendezvous on August 12 (some five weeks late). At Green river it was arranged that Samuel Parker should continue west to examine the Oregon country (he reached Fort Walla Walla on October 6); while Marcus Whitman was to return East to gather a missionary party for a station among the Indians of the Far West. (*See* October 26 annals entry.)

Ref. Marcus Whitman's "Journal and Report," *loc. cit.*, pp. 239-250; Parker, *op. cit.*, pp. 33-86; A. B. Hulbert's *Marcus Whitman, Crusader* . . . (1936), pt. 1, pp. 89-135 (Samuel Parker's journal), pp. 146-165 (Marcus Whitman's journal—varying slightly from the one noted above); Bernard De Voto's *Across the Wide Missouri* (Boston, 1947), pp. 218-238. A statement by William Clark (in "Letters Received," St. Louis Superintendency, letter of April 28, 1835—microfilm from the National Archives), notes the issuance of a trading license to Fontenelle, Fitzpatrick & Co. on April 21, 1835.

❈ The annual spring caravan to Santa Fe rendezvoused "west of Independence"—presumably in May. According to Josiah Gregg's compilation (in 1844) a total of about 140 men (40 of them proprietors) and some 75 wagons took merchandise estimated at $140,000 to the southwest during 1835.

Ref: *Niles' Weekly Register*, Baltimore, v. 48 (July 18, 1835), p. 337; Josiah Gregg, *Commerce of the Prairies* . . . (New York, London, 1844), v. 2, p. 160.

❈ May 27.—Capt. David Hunter and Company D, (First) U. S. dragoons left Fort Leavenworth on a summer patrol. Sgt. Hugh Evans stated that Hunter's command was "Dispatched to Fort Gibson to range along the Osage boundary to keep them [the Osages] from commiting depridations they are so frequently engaged in." (On July 18, Hunter and his men returned to Fort Leavenworth.)

Ref. *Mississippi Valley Historical Review*, Cedar Rapids, Iowa, v. 14 (September, 1927), p. 193 (for Sgt. Hugh Evans' statement); *Iowa Historical Record*, Iowa City, v. 8 (April, 1892), p. 254 (Col. Henry Dodge's May 12, 1835, letter); 24th Cong., 1st Sess., H. Doc. No. 181 (Serial 289); C. A. Murray's *Travels in North America* . . . (London, 1839), v. 2, p. 105; Fort Leavenworth post returns.

❈ From Fort Leavenworth, on May 29, Col. Henry Dodge and three (First) U. S. dragoon companies (a total force of 125), headed northward to the Platte, on the first leg of a circuit tour up that river and its South Fork as far as the Rocky mountains, and then homeward by way of the Arkansas river and Santa Fe trail. John Gantt (ex-army officer; and fur trader since 1831) was guide for the expedition.

Capt. Lemuel Ford, Capt. Matthew Duncan, and Lt. Lancaster P. Lupton commanded the dragoon companies (G, C, and A). Lt. Gaines P. Kingsbury was acting adjutant and journalist, Lt. Burdett A. Terrett (A. A. Q. M.) the commissary officer, Lt. Enoch Steen in charge of ordnance, and Asst. Surg. Benjamin F. Fellowes the medical officer. Agent John Dougherty was along as far as the Grand Pawnee village; and Samuel P. Winter's trading party (which included William O. Fallon) traveled in company beyond the forks of the Platte (losing one man—drowned in the "Grand Nemaha"—en route). Four Delawares were in the party, principally as hunters. The cavalcade included pack mules, 25 beef cattle, two small wheel-mounted swivels, and (part of the way) two flour-laden ox wagons. Captain Duncan's small wagon made the entire journey.

Crossing Wolf river (present Doniphan county) on June 1, and the "Grand Nemahaw" on the 3d, the dragoons arrived June 10 at the Otoe-Missouri village, on the Platte. Dodge held council with these Indians on the 11th; and with the Omahas (at the same camp) on the 17th. Next day the march up the Platte was resumed; and on the 21st the expedition camped near the Grand

Pawnees' village. There, on the 23d, Dodge met assembled delegates of the Pawnee bands for a talk; then marched again upriver, on the 24th.

The dragoons passed the forks of the Platte on July 4, and camped some 20 miles up the South Fork. On the 5th chiefs and head men of the "savage and treacherous" Arikaras came to Dodge's camp for a council. (John Gantt had persuaded these Indians that the troops were not on a punitive expedition). They were sternly advised to change their ways. The march upriver continued on the 6th. Near the base of the Rockies, on July 24, the dragoons left the South Fork and turned southward towards the waters of the upper Arkansas, stopping for the night of the 26th "opposite" Pikes Peak, and making their first camp on the Arkansas river, July 30th.

They passed John Gantt's abandoned trading post (Fort Cass) on August 1. Five days later, and some 60 miles down the Arkansas, they came to "Messrs. Bent and St. Vrain's trading establishment"—the recently-built "Bent's Fort" (Fort William)—and made camp a mile below it.

On August 11 Colonel Dodge met assembled Cheyennes, Arapahoes, and Gros Ventres of the Prairie (also a few Blackfeet and Pawnees) in council.

(See August 12 entry for the dragoons' homeward journey.)

Ref: *Iowa Historical Record,* v. 8 (April, 1892), pp. 254, 256-265; *American State Papers: Military Affairs,* v. 6, pp. 130-146, or 24th Cong., 1st Sess., *H. Doc. No. 181* (Serial 289) for Lt. G. P. Kingsbury's official journal of Dodge's 1835 expedition; Capt. Lemuel Ford's journal, edited by Louis Pelzer, is in the *Mississippi Valley Historical Review,* v. 12 (March, 1926), pp. 550-579, and has also been published (with two manuscript maps of the Santa Fe trail-Arkansas river route, and additional data) in *March of the First Dragoons to the Rocky Mountains in 1835 . . .* (Denver, 1957) by Nolie Mumey; Sgt. Hugh Evans' journal (which ends August 19) is in the *Mississippi Valley Historical Review,* v. 14 (September, 1927), pp. 192-214; "A Summer Upon the Prairie" (a narrative of the expedition, ending August 16), by "F," originally published in the *Army and Navy Chronicle* (vols. 2 and 3, 1836), is more accessible in A. B. Hulbert's *The Call of the Columbia* (Denver, 1934), pp. 228-305 (Hulbert arbitrarily assigned authorship to Capt. Lemuel Ford); [James Hildreth's] *Dragoon Campaigns to the Rocky Mountains* (New York, 1936) is another source; Lt. Enoch Steen's 1836 map—one of two maps that accompanied the expedition report—has been reproduced, and discussed, in Carl I. Wheat's *Mapping the Transmississippi West* (San Francisco, 1958), v. 2, pp. 149, 150, and *facing* p. 157.

❦ The American Fur Company's steamboat *Diana,* which left St. Louis on May 20 to ascend the Missouri, passed along the "Kansas" shore around the end of May; and, again, on the downward journey, in the fore part of July.

The *Diana* was scheduled to go to Fort Union at the mouth of the Yellowstone river; but despite a fine stage of water, she apparently went no higher than Fort Pierre (Pierre, S. D.) according to Kenneth McKenzie (of Fort Union), who later wrote: ". . . there was no person on board to direct the self-willed Captain & no one at Fort Pierre to enforce his proceeding to this place." The St. Louis *Missouri Republican* of July 16, reporting the *Diana's* return, stated she arrived "from the mouth of the Little Missouri" (as the Teton, or Bad river, often was called in this era). Two, out of 30 persons stricken by cholera while aboard, had died.

Ref. *Nebraska Historical Society Publications,* Lincoln, v. 20, p. 63 (for items from the *Missouri Republican*); Francis A. *Chardon's Journal at Fort Clark,* edited by Annie H. Abel (1932), p. 380 (for McKenzie letter of December 10, 1835).

❡ In a letter of June 16 the Rev. Thomas Johnson wrote of a recent visit to the Kansa Indians:

I found but few of them at home. The most of the tribe had started to hunt buffalo two days before we reached the villages. These Indians live on the Kansas river . . . and have their villages on both sides . . ., but a part of the nation have removed 40 miles higher up the river, for the purpose of getting near the buffalo. I never before saw any part of the human family in so wretched a condition. They live chiefly in dirt houses. They cultivate only a small portion of ground, and this done chiefly by the women, with hoes. They do not plough. They have no fences. Their only dependence for meat is on the chase, and the deer have entirely disappeared from their prairies. They have to go 250 miles, or farther, to find the buffalo, and then are frequently driven back by their enemies; and should they succeed in finding the buffalo, if they bring any of the meat home, it frequently has to be packed by their women, for many of them have no horses to ride; and their means of support are becoming more difficult every year, for the buffalo, like the deer, are fast retiring.

Ref: *Christian Advocate and Journal*, New York, v. 9 (July 31, 1835), p. 194; or *KHC*, v. 16, p. 237.

❡ July 2.—Conducted by William Gordon, a delegation of 38 Pottawatomies from Lake Michigan—en route to examine the lands (in southwestern "Iowa") assigned to them under the treaty of Chicago, 1833—passed through Westport, Mo., and took the route through "eastern Kansas" to Fort Leavenworth and its vicinity (where several hundred Pottawatomies—immigrants of 1833 and 1834—were living). Chief Alexander Robinson was a member of the party.

Congress, on March 3, had appropriated $9,453 to defray the expenses of this tour. It may have been the end of July before the delegation reached, and began exploring, the reserve in "Iowa." (Gordon's journal of the expedition covers only the dates July 30 to September 12.) Upon returning to Chicago, in the early autumn, the delegation reported the country unsuitable, being scarce in timber, and more remote than anticipated (with hostile Sioux near by).

Ref: Isaac McCoy's "Journal," July 2, 1835; *U. S. Statutes at Large*, v. 4, p. 791; 24 Cong., 1st Sess., *Sen. Doc. No. 348* (Serial 283), pp. 3-7, or *Indiana Historical Collections*, v. 26, pp. 265, 266; Isaac McCoy's *Annual Register* . . . *January, 1836*, p. 20; Grant Foreman's *The Last Trek of the Indians* (Chicago, c1946), pp. 105, 122; William Gordon's "Journal" (not seen by this compiler) in the National Archives; G. J. Garraghan's *The Jesuits of the Middle United States* (New York, 1938), v. 1, pp. 426, 427 (for references to Chief Robinson).

❡ July 2-4.—Late on the 2nd, the Hon. Charles Augustus Murray, of Scotland, arrived at Fort Leavenworth, accompanied by his Scotch servant, and a "young gentleman from Germany" named Vernunft. Murray's objectives: to make "a tour . . . [to acquaint himself with] the manners and habits of the extreme West, and of the tribes beyond the American settlements"—as stated in his subsequently-published *Travels in North America*—first edition, London, 1839.

This trio had left St. Louis late in June; traveled upriver on the *John Hancock;* outfitted at Liberty, Mo.; and started west, on horseback, with pack animals early on July 2—crossing the Missouri in the evening. At the fort, "Lieutenant C____" [Lt. George H. Crosman, of the Sixth infantry, probably], who was in charge of the small summer garrison, gave them a hospitable reception. (*See* May 27 and 29 entries for dispersal of the post's dragoons.)

The Fourth of July was celebrated with a 24-gun salute; followed by a festive dinner (with Madeira and champagne). While the officers and their guests were still at table, Agent John Dougherty arrived from the Platte with 150 Pawnee chiefs and warriors. A dozen or so leading men joined the party, by invitation. Outside, around numerous campfires, the rest of the Indians roasted "on rough sticks huge fragments of a newly-killed ox." (*See, also,* July 7 entry.)

Ref: Murray, *op. cit.*, v. 1, pp. 237-253. Lt. P. St. G. Cooke—the only dragoon officer who could be identified with "Lieutenant C____" was in the East; also, Murray, later, in his book (v. 2, p. 91) seems to indicate that the lieutenant was *regularly* stationed at Jefferson Barracks, where the garrison was composed of Sixth infantry troops. *See* Otis E. Young's *The West of Philip St. George Cooke* (Glendale, Calif., 1955) for Cooke.

❰ July 4-18.—The Rev. Charles Felix Van Quickenborne arrived at the Kickapoo settlements (above Fort Leavenworth) on the 4th; said Mass on Sunday (the 5th) at the house of Laurence Pensineau, American Fur Company trader; remained among the Kickapoos, apparently, till July 13 or 14; received assurances that Catholic missionaries would be welcomed by the chiefs and head men; and was, from July 15-18(?), a visitor at the Kaw's mouth, before returning to St. Louis.

(Father Van Quickenborne had left St. Louis on June 20 on a steamboat; reached Independence 10 days later; and subsequently had spent a few days as guest of "a gentleman of the American Fur Company" [presumably Francis G. Chouteau] at his residence near the junction of the Kansas with the Missouri; then traveled by way of Grinter's ferry and the Fort Leavenworth road to the Kickapoo reserve.)

Ref: G. J. Garraghan's *Catholic Beginnings in Kansas City* . . . (Chicago, 1920), pp. 89, 90; and his *The Jesuits of the Middle United States*, v. 1, pp. 258, 387-389.

❰ July 7.—The Hon. Charles A. Murray and party of three (his servant; the young German, Vernunft; and a teen-age hired hand, John Hardy), departed from Fort Leavenworth with 150 Pawnees, bound for the upper Republican river, to join the main body of Indians (then moving down from the Platte) and accompany them on the summer buffalo hunt. Murray's particular "host" was the aging "Sa-ni-tsa-rish" (Sharitarish), former head chief of the Grand Pawnees. (A French-Pawnee "interpreter—Louis La Chapelle— with these Indians, spoke no English.)

Traveling west-northwest, they crossed the "Great Nimahaw" on July 13; reached the Little Blue and traveled up its bank for some time; forded it, and moved west-southwest to strike the Republican; followed up that river some six days. Two weeks after leaving the fort, they joined the huge Pawnee camp (600 buffalo-skin lodges; some 5,000 persons, and several thousand horses). Missionary John Dunbar was with the Indians. (Murray described him as taciturn, indolent, and phlegmatic.)

Continuing their journey, the Pawnees (after crossing the Republican— probably near its forks, north of present Phillips county) traversed (apparently on a southwest course) a "barren and desolate prairie" where the prairie dog and the owl abounded (in the region of the stream now called Prairie Dog creek), and entered the buffalo country. On July 22 the Indians killed some 80 animals. They continued to hunt and to move camp from time to time. On July 30 Murray noted: "We must hereafter make a southeastern march in order to avail ourselves of the sources of the Saline River and other streams falling into the Kanzas. . . ." By August 3 they were in an area which, by description ("gigantic columns of some mighty though ruined portico" 60 to 70 feet high; huge broken pillars; a region of fast-eroding cliffs, and of ravines 30 to 50 feet deep and as wide) seems to place them in what is now Logan county or Gove county. The Indians made a "grand *chasse*" (a great surround of buffalo) on August 5. Next day they moved camp a few miles south, where, wrote Murray (who had a telescope), it was possible to see "the distant fringe of timber marking the Upper Arkansas."

Weary of life with the Pawnees, Murray and his three companions made a start for "home," on August 8. On the 9th Vernunft was thrown from his horse and trampled; and the quartet had to return to the Indian camp. But, on August 11, accompanied by two Pawnee guides, they made a second start. (Vernunft traveled with his injured arm in a sling; and on a different horse.)

They set a northeast course. Traveling on barren ridges, on the 14th, they saw below them a stream the Pawnee guides called "Snake River" (apparently the Saline). After descending the declivity to the water (which was extremely salty), Murray wrote: "I never should have believed it possible that so many rattlesnakes could have assembled together as I saw in that ravine. I think there must have been nearly enough to fatten a drove of Missouri hogs." This same day the two Pawnees left them. Murray (resolute and competent in every crisis) took over as guide. He had a compass, and it was his aim to move northeast—and return to the Republican. He located a buffalo trace which led them out of the cul-de-sac of "Snake" river gorge, and northward.

By August 18 they had come to a large stream bearing east-northeast which they followed about 14 miles. They then struck an Indian trail; followed it northward; found a merging trail; entered an area of more vegetation; traversed a swampy and marshy region (in present southeast Jewell? county); and on August 21 or 22 arrived at the "Kanzas" (Republican fork).

In descending to the river they came to a spot commanding a beautiful view of the Republican's course, where, wrote Murray, there had evidently *once been a permanent Indian village* (the Republican Pawnee town in Republic county of today). He also noted that on the journey west (in July), the Pawnees had shown him a site "about fifty miles west of the spot where we now were" where they had once lived (*i. e.*, the Webster co., Neb., site). [For more on these locations, *see* pp. 54, 55.]

After crossing the Republican, Murray led his companions north, in order to strike the trail made on the outward journey. On August 25 they found the sought-for trace and proceeded joyfully eastward on it. After 10 days of following the July-made path, they arrived at Fort Leavenworth on September 3.

Capt. David Hunter (commanding officer) was Murray's host for several days. About September 9, having disposed of his outfit and horses, the Scotsman boarded a steamboat (of the American Fur Company—*see* April 18 entry), and reached St. Louis September 12.

Ref: Murray, *op. cit.*, v. 1, pp. 258-473, v. 2, pp. 1-90. The St. Louis *Daily Union* of December 22, 1846, stated: "C. A. Murray, son of an English Peer owns 30,000 acres in Wisconsin which he purchased at a Government sale." Was this the same Murray?

❧ "Chouteau's [Catholic] Church at the mouth of the Kansas river" (approximately at the south line of Eleventh street, at the intersection with Pennsylvania avenue, present Kansas City, Mo.) apparently was built in the late spring, and first used in July.

This log structure (20' x 30' with presbytery) was erected on land which the Rev. Benedict Roux (*see* p. 257) had obtained before his departure in late April, and with money chiefly supplied by the Chouteaus. (The contract had been let before Roux left.)

In "Chouteau's Church," on July 15, the Rev. Charles F. Van Quickenborne (*see* July 4 entry) baptized Louis Lessert (son of Clement and Julia [Roy] Lessert); and on the 18th, he baptized Cyprian Terrien (son of Ignatius and Louise [Vallé] Terrien).

(About November, 1839, "Chouteau's Church" was first called the church of "St. Francis Regis"—and under that name it appeared in Catholic records thereafter.)

Ref: G. J. Garraghan's *Catholic Beginnings. . . .*, facing p. 80, 90; also, his *The Jesuits of the Middle United States*, v. 1, pp. 258-261. Mrs. Alfred Garrison, Bartlesville, Okla., a descendant of Cyprian Terrien, provided this compiler with much help on the French families of the Kaw's mouth area.

❧ Two French tourists—Louis Richard Cortambert, and a younger man "Laurent"—arrived at Independence, Mo., by steamboat, around midyear. (They had already traveled for several weeks through Eastern United States.) With a notion to camp on a Missouri river bluff in the Indian country, they hired a wagon and driver, and took the road to Fort Leavenworth. After crossing the Kansas at "Ferry-town, petit village d'Indiens" (the Delaware, or Grinter, ferry), they met a government agent (Cummins?) whose warnings of dangers and difficulties caused them to reconsider, and to return to Missouri.

Several days later, on foot, the two again set out from Independence— heading southward. At Harmony Mission they were delighted to find a small inn run by a Frenchman. Determined to spend some time far from all habitation, Cortambert and "Laurent" obtained a horse and journeyed as far as the bank of the Marmaton river, where, in an area rich in coal and other minerals, they built a shelter and resided for about three weeks. (Their camp was *probably* west of Missouri, in present Bourbon county.) Near the end of

August, both men fell ill of the prevalent "fever and ague"; were eventually rescued by Missourians; and spent a long period of recuperation at Harmony, at the Frenchman's inn.

In December Cortambert, his health recovered, began a journey to Fort Gibson. En route he visited the Chouteaus' trading post in the Osage village of "Manrinhabatso" (on the Neosho's west bank, over four miles west and north of present St. Paul, Neosho co.), where he gathered information about the Osages, and met two of the Indians (a man and a woman) who had gone to France in 1827 (*see* p. 143). Continuing down the Neosho, Cortambert stopped at Auguste P. Chouteau's Saline trading post (in the Cherokee country) around Christmas-time; and probably reached Fort Gibson (in the Creek country) before year's end. (Later, he left for France from the port of New Orleans.)

Louis R. Cortambert's *Voyage au Pays des Osages* . . . (the book which described his travels in America) was published at Paris in 1837. Of particular interest is his listing of the six principal Osage settlements—four in "Kansas" (all in present Neosho county), and two in "Oklahoma." The Neosho river towns: (1) "Manrinhabatso" (or "celui qui touche au ciel"); (2) two leagues *below*, and also on the right bank, the town usually known as White Hair's ("les Cheveux blancs"); (3) *above* Manrinhabatso, a town known as the Peaceful Heart ("Coeur tranquille"); (4) and still higher, the village of the Little Osages. On the Verdigris ("Vert-de-gris") river, to the southwest were two Osage bands: the Big Hill ("Grosse Côte") to the north, and Clermont's large settlement ("la Chénière") to the south.

Ref: Louis R. Cortambert's *Voyage au Pays des Osages* . . . (Paris, 1837); Mrs. Max W. Myer's translation of Cortambert's "Journey to the Land of the Osages, 1835-1836," is in *The Bulletin* of the Missouri Historical Society, St. Louis, v. 19 (April, 1963), pp. 199-229. The *Missouri Republican*, St. Louis, January 29, 1852, has information on "L. R. Cortambert" (the same man?).

❡ In mid-July it was reported at St. Louis, that 10 persons had died of cholera at Fontenelle's post, about a mile from Bellevue [Neb.].

When Dr. Marcus Whitman subsequently spent a few October days at Bellevue he was told the Omahas had lost 180 of their people, and the Otoes 60, to cholera.

Ref: Nebraska Historical Society *Publications*, v. 20, p. 63 (for St. Louis *Missouri Republican* item); *Oregon Historical Quarterly*, v. 28, p. 252 (for Whitman).

❡ Died: on August 11, at Wea Presbyterian Mission (present Miami county), Kerwin Swift Kerr (aged three months and eight days), son of the Rev. Joseph and Mary Ann Kerr.

(It is probable this child was born at Independence, Mo., for his mother, ill, had spent some time there in the spring of 1835.) He was the Kerrs' second infant son to be buried in "Kansas."

Ref: Joseph Kerr's August, 1835, letter, in Presbyterian Historical Society, American Indian Missions correspondence (microfilm, KHi).

❡ On August 12 Col. Henry Dodge and his (First) U. S. dragoon command left camp, below Bent's Fort (*see* May 29 entry), and began the homeward march, down the Arkansas, to Fort Leavenworth. Lt. G. P. Kingsbury's journal states:

"The command . . . was in a most perfect state of health. . . . The horses in fine order. . . . The colonel had seen all the Indians he expected to see, and had established friendly relations with them all; had marched one thousand miles over a beautiful and interesting country, and we started for home with that joyous and self-satisfied feeling . . . of having accomplished the full object of the expedition."

They came to a Cheyenne camp on the 14th (50 miles below Bent's Fort); then a party of Pawnee Loups and Arikaras arrived; and on the 16th Colonel Dodge held a last council with the Indians of the region. The dragoons marched again on August 17; crossed the "Colorado-Kansas" line on the 18th(?); and reached Chouteau's Island on the 19th. They came to the Santa Fe trail crossing of the Arkansas (55 miles below Chouteau's Island) on the 23d; took the dry route; arrived at rain-swollen Pawnee fork on the 29th; crossed the baggage in a buffalo boat and swam the horses, on the 30th; passed, on the same day "a noted Rock Sandy called Pawney rock where was found a great many of the Rocky Mountain adventurer names engraved" (Capt. Lemuel Ford added his); and camped that night at Walnut creek. They reached the Little Arkansas on September 2; were delayed by rain at Cottonwood crossing till the 7th; and arrived at Council Grove the next evening (". . . a most butifull rich grove of timber near one mile in width the richest groth of timber thickly covered with Peavine where our horses fared sumptously. we found Several Bea trees with fine honey. encamped on the East Side of the timber in the edge of the preurie [prairie]").

Pvt. Samuel Hunt, of Company A, aged 23, died on September 11. He was buried on a high prairie—five miles west of present Burlingame, Osage county, and not far from the stream now called Dragoon creek. A stone with the incription "S. Hunt, U. S. D." still marks the grave of the only casualty of the 1835 expedition.

The dragoons passed "Round and Elm groves" on the 15th, then proceeded northwardly to Grinter's (or Delaware) crossing of the Kansas. Using both a flat ferry and a pirogue, the command crossed by early evening, making camp in a lot at Robert Dunlap's (the Delawares' blacksmith), only 22 miles from "home." On September 16 Colonel Dodge and his dragoons returned to Fort Leavenworth, after an absence of three and a half months, and a journey of about 1,645 miles.

Ref: Same as for May 29 entry. Capt. Lemuel Ford's sketch maps (reproduced in Nolie Mumey's edition of Ford's diaries) are notable for their showing of "Fort Cass," "Fort William," and "Bent's Fort" on the Upper Arkansas; and in the "Kansas" section of the Santa Fe trail for the designation of present Big Coon creek as "Racoon cr."; also for the showing of "Old Kansas lodges" west of Big Coon creek, and of alternate routes from above Big Coon creek to the Cottonwood crossing.

❡ In August Capt. Benjamin L. E. Bonneville (after three years in the West—see p. 213), and a company of trappers, having come down from the Rocky mountains by way of the Platte, crossed "Kansas" (presumably on "Sublette's Trace"—the established route), and arrived at Independence on the 22d, looking like a "procession of tatterdemalion savages."

Zenas Leonard (who had gone to the Rocky mountains in 1831—*see* p. 201) was in this party; and, in his later-written narrative, stated that they reached "the Pawnee Village" about July 25(?), traded with the Indians for some corn, and continued to Independence, arriving August 29 [*i. e.*, the 22d].
See, also, May 1836, annals.

Ref: Washington Irving's *The Adventures of Captain Bonneville* . . ., edited by E. W. Todd (c1961), pp. 370, 394; John C. Ewers, editor, *Adventures of Zenas Leonard* . . . (c1959), p. 161.

℄ August 24.—The Comanches and the Wichitas signed a peace treaty with the United States, and with representatives of the Cherokees, Muscogees (Western Creeks), Choctaws, Osages, Senecas, and Quapaws at temporary "Camp Holmes" (about 150 miles southwest of Fort Gibson, and some five miles northeast of present Purcell, Okla.), within the country assigned by the United States to the Western Creeks.

This first treaty with the western prairie Indians also contained a provision that the "eastern" Indians could hunt and trap as far west as the limits of the United States; and granted to U. S. citizens passage to Santa Fe across the western Indians' country.

(Camp Holmes had been established on June 2 by Maj. R. B. Mason and U. S. dragoons from the Fort Gibson area. Seventh infantry troops joined them in July, as the western Indians gathered, and Comanche hostility was rumored. The Kiowas came, grew tired of waiting, and departed before the council. The U. S. commissioners [Gen. Mathew Arbuckle and Montfort Stokes], accompanied by two Seventh infantry companies and some of the eastern Indian delegates, did not arrive at Camp Holmes till August 19.)

Soon after the treaty, Auguste P. Chouteau established a small fortified post on the Camp Holmes site, and traded with the Comanches, Kiowas, Wichitas, and other western tribes, till his death in 1838.

Ref: Grant Foreman's *Pioneer Days in the Early Southwest* (Cleveland, 1926), pp. 159-164; also, his *Advancing the Frontier* . . . (Norman, 1933), p. 232; H. P. Beers' *The Western Military Frontier* . . . (Philadelphia, 1935), pp. 113, 114; C. J. Kappler's *Indian Affairs, Laws and Treaties* (Washington, 1904), v. 2, pp. 435-439; *Chronicles of Oklahoma*, Oklahoma City, v. 18, pp. 281-292 (Dr. Leonard McPhail's journal, June-August, 1835).

℄ During the late summer the incidence of "fever and ague"—"the scourge of the Mississippi and Missouri valleys"—apparently was abnormally high in Missouri and "Kansas."

Scottish traveler Murray, arriving at Fort Leavenworth (from the west) on September 3, wrote: "it was painful to see the number of sunken eyes and ashy cheeks" (Capt. David Hunter's wife was one of the convalescents); and later remarked "the wan and unhealthy appearance of all the settlers on the banks of the Missouri between the Fort and St. Louis," stating that on his downriver steamboat journey he had landed perhaps 20 times, and that the "fever and ague" seemed to have struck every family, leaving "haggard and emaciated" men, women, and children.

French traveler L. R. Cortambert, who spent some three months (September through November) recuperating from "fever and ague" at Harmony, Mo., stated that very few persons escaped the malarial illness which was then epidemic from the Missouri to the Arkansas.

Ref: Murray, *op. cit.*, v. 2, pp. 74, 75; L. R. Cortambert's *Voyage au Pays des Osages* . . . (Paris, 1837), pp. 26-28.

❧ September 19.—Missionaries John Dunbar and Samuel Allis, Jr., in company with 16 Pawnee Loups and an interpreter, arrived at Fort Leavenworth; and remained five days. (The Indians made the trip to receive some of their annuities.)

(The party had left the Pawnee Loup village [some 60 miles above the mouth of the Platte's Loup Fork] on September 12. Only a few days before that, Dunbar and Allis had returned to the village after accompanying Pawnee bands on the summer buffalo hunt in western "Kansas" and southwestern "Nebraska.")

From Fort Leavenworth the Indians and the missionaries set out for Bellevue (Neb.)—arriving there October 3. They spent two days at the American Fur Company post (a mile distant) where Dr. Marcus Whitman (en route East) was a guest. Then, on October 9, started up the Platte—Dunbar stopping at the Grand Pawnee village and Allis continuing with the Pawnee Loups. (With these bands they spent the winter.)

Ref: *KHC*, v. 14, pp. 619, 705, 706; *Oregon Historical Quarterly*, v. 28, pp. 250, 251.

❧ BORN: at Kickapoo Methodist Mission (present Leavenworth county), on September 22, Gerard Q. Berryman, son of the Rev. J. C. and Sarah C. (Cessna) Berryman.

Ref: Leavenworth *Times*, September 21, 1925; or, Remsburg "Stork" clippings, in KHi library.

❧ DIED: on September 23, at a Wea village near the Marais des Cygnes (in present Miami county), Maquakononga, or Negro Legs, aged about 90(?), principal chief of the Weas.

(He had signed the 1809, 1816, and 1820 treaties made by his nation with the United States, in Indiana. Probably he came to "Kansas" in 1831—*see* p. 183.)

Ref: Mary Ann (Mrs. Joseph) Kerr's letter of September 28, 1835, in Presbyterian Historical Society, American Indian Missions correspondence (microfilm, KHi).

❧ In October the annual fall caravan returning from Santa Fe crossed "Kansas." At Columbia, Mo., it was reported on the 24th that most of the traders had arrived there after a successful trip and that the returns included $200,000 in specie, 300 mules, some horses, furs, and other items.

Ref: *Missouri Intelligencer*, Columbia, October 24, 1835; *Niles' Weekly Register*, v. 49 (November 21, 1835), p. 188.

❡ October 26-31.—Dr. Marcus Whitman, traveling down the Missouri (from Bellevue [Neb.]) by boat, in company with J. P. Cabanné, stopped, briefly, at Fort Leavenworth on the 26th. With him were two Nez Perces boys he was taking East.

(From the Green river rendezvous—departing August 27—Thomas Fitzpatrick had headed a company of returning trappers [including some families?] as far as Fort William [Laramie]—reached September 8. Cotravelers were Whitman [*see* May 14 entry] and Captain Stewart [who had journeyed west in 1833]. Warren A. Ferris [a trapper since 1830—*see* p. 169] was another in the party of about 80 persons that Lucien Fontenelle brought down from Fort William. They traveled down the Platte to near its mouth, and arrived at the Council Bluffs and Bellevue area around October 10. There the company dispersed, to proceed to Missouri by various routes, and at different times. Whitman, a guest at Bellevue from October 12 to the 20th, then started downriver [as noted above]. There is no definite information on Stewart's travels from Bellevue to St. Louis. Ferris, and a few others, set out on the 17th, on horseback; reached Fort Leavenworth September 28; and remained till the 31st.)

❡ On October 31, at Fort Leavenworth, visitors, including Ferris (and Captain Stewart?) witnessed a review of Colonel Dodge's (First) U. S. dragoon command.

Ref: Marcus Whitman's "Journal and Report," in *Oregon Historical Quarterly*, v. 28, pp. 250-253, and in Hulbert, *Marcus Whitman, Crusader, op. cit.*, pp. 158-160; W. A. Ferris' *Life in the Rocky Mountains* . . ., edited by Paul C. Phillips (Denver, 1940), p. 288; Morgan and Harris, *op. cit.*, pp. 270, 304, 310.

❡ December 2.—A party of 252 Pottawatomies (and Ottawas and Chippewas united with them) from Lake Michigan, under the charge of Capt. John B. F. Russell (Fifth U. S. infantry), arrived in the Little Platte country (across the Missouri from Fort Leavenworth, and from the Kickapoo reserve—where 454 Pottawatomies already were residing).

(About 460 other Pottawatomies from this company of emigrants spent the winter of 1835-1836 on Skunk river, in southeastern "Iowa." The intended destination of all these Indians was a reserve in southwestern "Iowa," which had been assigned under the Chicago treaty of September 26, 1833.)

Reluctant to proceed northward to the reserve (influenced by the adverse report of the Pottawatomie exploring delegation—*see* July 2 entry), the party of 252 Indians remained in the Little Platte country till 1837. Their location was described as "on Todd's Creek about fourteen miles below [and across the Missouri from] the Garrison [Fort Leavenworth] on the road to Liberty." Subagent Anthony L. Davis (residing at "Kickapoo Town" several miles above the fort) was given temporary charge of the new arrivals.

Ref: *Indiana Historical Collections*, v. 26, pp. 184-186, 207, 208, 231, 265, 266; A. L. Davis' letter of January 1, 1836, in McCoy manuscripts (KHi ms. division); Isaac McCoy's "Journal," December 14, 1835; Foreman's *The Last Trek of the Indians*, p. 106; 24th Cong., 1st Sess., *Sen. Doc. No. 348* (Serial 283), pp. 2, 3.

❡ December 9.—The second issue of Isaac McCoy's *Annual Register of Indian Affairs,* bearing a title-page date of January 1, 1836, was published at the Shawnee Baptist Mission. Jotham Meeker printed 1,500 copies of this 91-page, revised edition of the *Register.*

Among the changes, and events, of the year, as reported by McCoy:

(1) New missionaries at Shawnee Methodist Mission were: the Rev. William Ketron and wife, the Rev. David G. Gregory and wife, and Mrs. ___ ___ Miller.

(2) Captain Patterson, the Delawares' head chief had died; and his successor as principal chief was Nah-ko-min. [Patterson's death occurred prior to July 22, 1835.]

(3) At the Kansa lower village (Fool Chief's) the government had fenced 20 acres of land; plowed 10 acres; and erected a good, hewed-log house for the principal chief (White Plume, apparently, since McCoy listed "Nam-pa-war-rah or White Feather" as the Kansa "principal chief"). Also, the "smithery" had been removed from the old Kansa Agency (closed in 1834—*see* p. 276), and relocated "near their lower village."

(4) On the Kickapoo reserve a church (to cost $700), and a saw and grist mill (worth $3,000) were being erected by the government.

Ref: McCoy's *Annual Register* . . . *1836,* pp. 24, 28-31; Meeker's "Diary"; D. C. McMurtrie and A. H. Allen, *op. cit.,* pp. 146, 147; OIA, "Registers of Letters Received," v. 6, lists a letter by William Clark of March 28, 1835, enclosing an R. W. Cummins letter asking for money to enable him to remove the Kansa blacksmith shop, and in the margin is a note: "Apr 9 authorized to remove it"; 24th Cong., 2d Sess., *H. Doc. No. 137* (Serial 303), p. 12 (contains a statement that during the year ending September 30, 1836, Michael Rice was paid $3,000 for his services in erecting a saw and grist mill for the Kickapoos), and p. 29 (during the same period, J. Milburn was paid $700 "for [erecting] church for Kickapoos"). In "Letters Received" by the Office of Indian Affairs (microfilm from the National Archives), is a July 22, 1835, letter listing Nah-ko-min as head chief of the Delawares.

❧ December 24.—A memorial was placed before the U. S. senate from the citizens of Clay county, Mo., asking for (1) protection from Indians, and (2) the establishment of a line of frontier posts from the upper Mississippi to Red River in the south, linked by a military road to be patrolled by U. S. dragoons.

The memorial (signed by John Thornton, chairman, and Edward M. Samuel, secretary) was an endorsement of Indian Agent John Dougherty's plan for protection of the frontier—a plan proposed by him in a letter of December 16, 1834.

See, also, July 2, 1836, entry.

Ref: *American State Papers: Military Affairs,* v. 5, pp. 729-731, v. 6, pp. 12-15; H. P. Beers' *The Western Military Frontier* . . . (Philadelphia, 1935), p. 118.

❧ December 29.—The Cherokee Indians, in a treaty with the United States made at New Echota, Ga., relinquished claim to all lands east of the Mississippi and agreed to remove, within two years, to the 7,000,000-acre reservation west of Arkansas territory and Missouri guaranteed to them by the treaty of May 6, 1828 (*see* p. 147).

However, the 1835 treaty provided an additional reserve of about 800,000 acres at the Cherokees' request (and at a cost to them of $500,000). This tract was the rectangle of land between the Osage reserve and the State of Missouri, in present southeastern Kansas. Its bounds ran from the southeast corner of the Osage reserve northward, 50 miles, to the northeast corner of that reserve, then east 25 miles to the Missouri line, then south for approximately 50 miles, then west 25 miles to the place of beginning. It was unassigned land, except for a few Osage half-breed tracts (granted by the treaty of 1825), to which the government extinguished title before selling the 800,000-acre area to the Cherokees in 1836. The new owners made little use of this tract which came to be known as the *Cherokee Neutral Lands*.

As one writer has pointed out: "Had the Cherokees contented themselves with . . . [the original] seven million acres they could not have properly been called Kansas emigrants; because their [original] reserve extended only a very short distance [a little over two miles] beyond [north of] the thirty-seventh parallel" [the southern Kansas boundary of today].

Ref: Kappler, *op. cit.*, v. 2, pp. 439-448; *KHC*, v. 8, pp. 77, 82 (for quote).

1836

❆ January 5. — From Westport, Mo., Isaac McCoy mailed Rep. William H. Ashley a *memorial*, addressed to the house of representatives, asking that the mail route (in "Oklahoma") from Fort Towson to Fort Gibson be extended from the latter post to Fort Leavenworth (*see* item on *petition* of 1834 under February 2, 1835, entry).

As set forth in the memorial (dated "Western Territory 1835") the distance would be 318 miles: Fort Gibson to the Creek subagency, seven miles—Union Mission, 22 miles—A. P. Chouteau's, on east bank of Neosho river, 16 miles—W. C. Requa's [Hopefield Mission], 15 miles—Osage Agency, 65 miles—Harmony Mission, a few miles within Missouri, 75 miles—Wea Mission, 50 miles—Westport, Mo., 35 miles—"Delaware Smithery" (near the Delaware's Kansas river ferry), 10 miles—Fort Leavenworth, 23 miles. (The distances vary from those given in the 1834 petition noted earlier.)

The memorial's 38 signers were: Col. Henry Dodge, Capt. David Hunter, Capt. Matthew Duncan, Lt. G. P. Kingsbury, Lt. Asbury Ury, *Lt. Enoch Steen,* Lt. L. P. Lupton, Lt. B. D. Moore, *Lt. J. S. Van Derveer, Lt. B. A. Terrett, Asst. Surg. S. Preston Moore,* Lt. J. W. Hamilton, *L. V. D. Stryker,* J. H. Freligh, Anthony L. Davis (emigrating agent for Pottawatomies), John P. Smith (Kickapoo blacksmith), Wea missionaries the Rev. Joseph Kerr, Henry Bradley and *Francis Lindsay,* Agent Richard W. Cummins, the Rev. Isaac McCoy, Capt. Lemuel Ford, *Dr. J. A. Chute, W. W. Kavenaugh, C. M. H. Loudon, W. T. Loudon, Charles Findlay,* Nat. H. Scruggs, *H. C. Davis, J. B. Chiles, Michael Farmer*(?), *Peter Duncan, James M. Hunter* [these last 11 were Westport, Mo., residents], the *Rev. J. C. Berryman,* Jotham Meeker, Robert Simerwell, Dr. Johnston Lykins, John C. McCoy. [The persons whose names are in italics were *not* among the signers of the 1834 *petition* for a post route. One name notably absent from both lists in that of the Rev. Thomas Johnson.]

(*See, also,* March 19 entry.)

Ref: Isaac McCoy's copy of the memorial (in McCoy manuscripts, KHi ms. division), with note on verso of attached page that he has enclosed the original to Ashley with a letter of January 5, 1836.

❡ MARRIED: Moses R. Grinter (aged 26?), operator of the Delawares' Kansas river ferry, and Anna Marshall (aged 16), half-Delaware, daughter of Indian trader William Marshall, in January, on the Delaware reserve (present Wyandotte county).

To this couple 10 children were born. The Grinters' land (north of the ferry site), was on Sec. 20 and 21, T. 11, R. 24 E., in Wyandotte township of today. A two-story brick house, erected by Moses Grinter in the late 1850's, on his farm, still remains (1971), and is scheduled for preservation as an historic site under supervision of the Kansas State Historical Society. Grinter died June 12, 1878. Anna (Marshall) Grinter died June 28, 1905.

Ref: Goodspeed's *Wyandotte County and Kansas City, Kansas* . . . (Chicago, 1890), pp. 622, 623; Wyandotte *Gazette*, June 14, 1878 (or, see Biographical Clippings, "G," v. 3, p. 287, in KHi library); Kansas City (Mo.) *Star*, June 28, 1905 (or *see* Biographical Clippings, "G," v. 7, p. 321); U. S. census, 1870, Wyandotte tp., Wyandotte co., p. 4 (which lists Moses R. Grinter, 61, native of Kentucky; his wife Ann, 50, native of Indiana; and son William, 28, born in "Kansas").

❡ On January 29 John C. McCoy, founder (in 1834) of Westport, Mo. (also its first storekeeper, and first postmaster), wrote (in a letter to his father): "We have sold out our stock of goods to Col. [William M.] Chick of Chariton [Mo.] for cost and 12 per cent and I have rented my house to him for one year." Chick succeeded McCoy as Westport postmaster, also.

("We" referred to McCoy and his partners J. H. Flournoy and J. P. Hickman—operating under the name J. P. Hickman & Co. The partnership was dissolved on February 6, 1836.)

Ref: Isaac McCoy manuscripts, *loc. cit.*

❡ As shown by Comm'r Elbert Herring's January 30, report, employees of the Department of Indian affairs in "Kansas," were:

Northern Agency of Western Territory—Agent Richard W. Cummings; *Interpreters* Joseph James, James Connor, Peter Cudjoe [Cadue], Henry Clay, Joseph Parks; *Blacksmiths and gunsmiths* John P. Smith, Claybourne Colbert, William Donalson, Lewis Jones, Robert Dunlap, William Carlisle, and *assistants* William V. Smith, Preston Moore, R. D. McKinney, John Barnes, Samuel Boydston, and —— Jackson; also William Barnes, *miller* for the Delawares and Shawnees; *Teachers* Jerome C. Berryman and John D. Swallows for the Kickapoos, and Henry Rennick for the Delawares.

Osage Subagency—Subagent Paul Ligueste Chouteau; *Interpreter* Baptiste Mongrain; *Blacksmith* Gabriel Philibert, and *assistant* E[tienne] Brant.

Ref: 24th Cong., 1st Sess., *H. Doc. No. 95* (Serial 288). Spellings of some names have been corrected from the printed listing.

❦ BORN: at Delaware Methodist Mission (present Wyandotte county), on February 25, Mary (or Margaret?) Jane Peery, daughter of the Rev. Edward T. and Mary S. Peery.

Ref: Si and Shirley Corn's *Our Family Tree* (1959), Section 4. Mary Jane Peery married Henry B. Bouton on September 2, 1852 (Jackson county, Mo., marriage records). In 1860 they were Westport, Mo., residents and had two children—Julia (4) and Edward H. (1), according to the U. S. census, 1860, Jackson county, Mo.

❦ BORN: at Kickapoo Methodist Mission (present Leavenworth county), on March 4, Gustavus P. Smith, son of the government blacksmith for the Kickapoos, John P. Smith, and his wife Elizabeth.

Ref: KHi 16th *Biennial Report,* p. 66; G. J. Remsburg, in Atchison *Daily Globe,* April 13, 1914. In 1837[?] the John P. Smith family moved to Platte county, Mo. A Remsburg letter of May 5, 1908 (in KHi ms. division), states that the Smiths came to Kickapoo mission in the spring of 1834, from Clinton county, Missouri, with two children—Mary A. and Lucretia. They remained three years.

❦ Early in March, about a mile above the mouth of American Chief (now Mission) creek (in present Shawnee county), a party of workmen, supervised by the Rev. William Johnson, began erecting two log cabins for a Kansa Methodist Mission. (By survey description, the site was the N. W. ¼ (apparently) of Sec. 33, T. 11, R. 14 E., Dover township.) American Chief's village (*see* p. 167) was not far away; and down near the creek's mouth, was Frederick Chouteau's American Fur Company trading post (*see* p. 212).

Appointed missionary to the Kansa at the Methodists' Missouri conference in the fall of 1835, Johnson twice had visited the Indians before winter set in, to make preliminary arrangements. *See* p. 180, for his earlier, short-lived Kansa Mission.)

On June 7, 1836, William Johnson wrote: "We have now 20 acres of good soil, fenced and planted; two cabins built, and a garden nearly finished. We removed into our cabins about two weeks since. [He had married Mary Jane Chick, of Chariton, Mo., in May, 1834.] The Indians have . . . gone out to hunt for buffalo. . . . We are preparing to instruct these people . . . but shall not be able to do much before winter, as we have our dwelling house to build—also to depend upon our new farm for provision, as we are 100 miles from the nearest white settlement. . . .[The Kansa] have some corn, and but little of anything else . . . no cattle or hogs, and few horses . . . The . . . agent [R. W. Cummins] . . . is at this time having about 300 acres of land [near the mission] fenced and planted for them."

As reported in February, 1837, the mission buildings were: a not-yet-completed, hewed-log dwelling (36' x 18') a story and a half high; a kitchen, and a smoke house (each 18' x 18') under the same roof, with a 10-foot passageway between. The occupants were the Johnsons, and a farmer. A 20-acre fenced farm was ready for cultivation.

Apparently no formal school ever was undertaken. A few Kansa children lived at the mission for brief periods, and were taught as time permitted. The

Johnsons also labored faithfully among the adult Indians till William Johnson's death in 1842. The Kansa Methodist Mission on American Chief creek was maintained (though twice suspended in the 1840's) till the end of 1846.

Ref: *Christian Advocate and Journal,* New York, v. 10, pp. 138, 186, v. 11, p. 130; *KHC,* v. 1-2, pp. 277, 278 (contains errors, especially in dates), v. 8, pp. 426, 428, v. 9, pp. 196-201 (also has errors), v. 16, pp. 229-236, 239-241, 251, 253-266; J. S. Chick letter, April 19, 1906 (in KHi ms. division); J. T. Peery letter, December 30, 1880 (in *ibid.*); Comm'r of Indian Affairs (CIA) *Reports,* 1838-1846; *Baptist Missionary Magazine,* Boston, v. 20 (1840), pp. 42, 43.

❧ According to a March 8 report (published as *Senate Report 288,* 24th Congress, 1st session) on the number and situation of Indians on the frontiers, about 31,000 Indians had been removed west of the Mississippi, and some 72,000 were yet to be removed. Below are some statistics relating to "Kansas" from the report's "Census of Indian Tribes." Also listed, for comparative purposes, are figures published in Isaac McCoy's *Annual Register* for 1837—statistics apparently obtained in late 1836, which, for the emigrant tribes, are more realistic than those of the "census." (*See* p. 268 for 1834 statistics.)

Indigenous Tribes	*"Census"*	*McCoy*
Kansa	1,471	about 1,606
Osages *	5,120	about 5,510
Emigrant Tribes		
Pottawatomies from Indiana	441	444
Kickapoos	588	625
Delawares	826	921
Shawnees	1,250	of Kansas river 823
Ottawas	200	79
Weas	222	206
Piankeshaws	132	157
Peorias and Kaskaskias	132	142

* From one-third to one-half of the Osages were in "Oklahoma."

Ref: 24th Cong., 1st Sess., *Sen. Report 228* (Serial 281); Isaac McCoy's *Annual Register* for 1837, p. 7 (McCoy states most of his materials were collected prior to January, 1837). *Niles' Weekly Register,* Baltimore, v. 50 (August 27, 1836), pp. 435, 436, has a table (with varying figures) prepared "at the topographical bureau."

❧ March 19.—A resolution of congress authorized the postmaster general to establish the following post roads: (1) from Fort Towson (in present southern Oklahoma) to Fort Gibson (in present east-central Oklahoma); and (2) from Fort Gibson by way of Fayette [ville] in Arkansas territory, Barry [county, Mo.] courthouse [*i. e.,* Cassville, Mo.], Van Buren [county, Mo.] courthouse [now *Cass* county, Mo., county seat Harrisonville], Jackson [county, Mo.] courthouse [*i. e.,* Independence], Fort Leavenworth, Liberty (Clay county, Mo.), Plattsburgh (Clinton county, Mo.), and Fort Des Moines, to the town of Dubuque [Iowa].

Ref: *U. S. Statutes at Large*, v. 5, p. 131. The name of Van Buren county, Mo., was changed to Cass county on February 19, 1849.—See J. N. Kane's *The American Counties* (New York, 1960), p. 326.

❧ April 7.—Reaching Liberty, Mo., from the East (after a trip up the Missouri on the *Chariton*) was a missionary party in the service of the American Board of Comm'rs for Foreign Missions. Bound for the Oregon country were Dr. Marcus Whitman and his bride Narcissa (Prentiss) Whitman, the Rev. Henry H. Spalding and his wife Eliza (Hart) Spalding; and with them two(?) Nez Perces boys (brought East the previous autumn by Whitman—*see* October 26, 1835, entry). Also, there were Dr. Benedict Satterlee (sent out as missionary to the Pawnees), with his seriously-ill wife, and Emeline Palmer (bride-to-be of Samuel Allis—*see* April 17 entry), whose destination was Bellevue (Neb.).

The Whitman-Spalding party, by previous arrangement, was to join the American Fur Company's caravan at Bellevue for the overland journey to Oregon. Remaining at Liberty for three weeks, this group outfitted while awaiting arrival of the American Fur Company's *Diana* for passage of some of the group to the Council Bluffs. During this interval William H. Gray (a skilled mechanic), arrived to join the Oregon party.

See, also, next entry, and April 27 and May 1 entries.

Ref: Eliza S. Warren's *Memoirs of the West* . . . (Portland, Ore., 1916[?]), pp. 57, 58 (Mrs. Spalding's diary); Oregon Pioneer Association *Transactions,* Portland, 1891, pp. 81-94 (Mrs. Whitman's letters); C. M. Drury's *Marcus Whitman* . . . (Caldwell, Ida., 1937), pp. 133-140; also his *Henry Harmon Spalding* (Caldwell, Ida., 1936), pp. 120-131; C. M. Drury, editor, *First White Women Over the Rockies* (Glendale, Cal., 1963-1966), v. 1.

❧ April 17-23.—The steamboat *Diana,* which had left Bellevue (Neb.) April 15th, stopped at Fort Leavenworth on the 17th, en route to St. Louis. A passenger who disembarked, and remained three days, was Missionary Samuel Allis (who had reached Bellevue on April 1, after spending the winter with the Pawnee Loups).

(The *Diana,* on her first upriver voyage of the season, had left St. Louis in March, but—as reported—hit a snag below Lexington; sank in shallow water; was delayed for repairs and drying of cargo; and did not get to Bellevue till April.)

Samuel Allis arrived at Liberty, Mo. (overland from Fort Leavenworth), on April 21; and on the 23d was married to Emeline Palmer of Ithaca, N. Y. (who had reached Liberty on the 7th, in company with the Whitman-Spalding party). The Rev. Henry H. Spalding officiated.

Ref: *KHC*, v. 9, p. 301, v. 14, p. 710; C. M. Drury's *Henry Harmon Spalding*, pp. 111, 126, 131; Oregon Pioneer Association *Transactions* (19th annual reunion), 1891, p. 81 (for Mrs. Narcissa Whitman's comment on the *Diana's* mishap); *op. cit.*, p. 58; C. M. Drury's *First White Women, op. cit.*, v. 1, p. 42.

❆ BORN: at Shawnee Methodist Mission (present Wyandotte county), on April 20, Eliza Shallcross Johnson, daughter of the Rev. Thomas and Sarah T. (Davis) Johnson.

Ref: *KHC*, v. 12, p. xii; KHi 15th *Biennial Report*, p. 35. (Eliza S. Johnson married John Wornall. She died July 5, 1865, aged 29.)

❆ April 21.—On the San Jacinto river (about 22 miles east of present Houston, Tex.) Samuel Houston's Texas army defeated a Mexican force under Santa Anna in a brief battle which won independence for Texas, and avenged the massacres at the Alamo (March 6) and Goliad (March 27).

One inscription on the San Jacinto Monument (at the battle site) reads (in part):

"Measured by its results, San Jacinto was one of the decisive battles of the world. The freedom of Texas from Mexico won here led to annexation and to the Mexican War, resulting in the acquisition by the United States of the states of Texas, New Mexico, Arizona, Nevada, California, Utah, and parts of Colorado, Wyoming, Kansas, and Oklahoma. . . ."

Ref: Walter P. Webb, editor-in-chief, *The Handbook of Texas* (Austin, 1952), v. 2, p. 554.

❆ In the spring, on a 320-acre tract leased from the Shawnees (a tract some four miles west of Westport, Mo.), native workmen employed by the committees of Ohio, Indiana, and Baltimore yearly meetings, Society of Friends, began erection of three Shawnee Mission buildings ("two houses of hewn logs, twenty feet square, one and one-half stories high, with a brick chimney in each end, and another for school and meeting-house, of same dimensions, to be warmed by a stove").

The original land survey plat of the 1850's shows the Friends' mission land principally within the S. E. ¼ of Sec. 7, and extending southward into the N. E. ¼ Sec. 18, T. 12, R. 25 E. It is now partly within the city limits of Merriam, Johnson county.

Apparently the log houses of 1836 were completed by midsummer. Jotham Meeker, of the Baptist mission two miles to the northeast, wrote in his diary on August 29: "Attend at the Quakers' buildings to witness the Shawanoe Councils, &c preparatory to their drawing their annuities on to-morrow."

Beginning in mid-1837 (*see*, June, 1837, entry) and continuing, except for brief interruptions, till 1869, a boarding school for Indian children was maintained by the Friends. In 1845 a 24 by 70-foot, three-story, stone-and-frame permanent mission house was erected. During the 1860's most of the pupils were orphans.

Ref: *KHC*, v. 8, pp. 250-269, especially pp. 262, 267, 268; Meeker "Diary," in KHi ms. division; CIA reports, from 1838; *KHQ*, v. 10, p. 348 (gives the text of the historical marker for Shawnee Friends Mission). In the Shawnee census of 1857 (in KHi archives), the Friends Labor School, consisting of 320 acres, is described as located on the S½ of Sec. 7, T. 12 S., R. 25 E.

❡ April 27.—The Rev. Henry H. Spalding, William H. Gray, three Nez Perces boys, and a hired man, left Liberty, Mo. (*see* April 7 entry), with the Whitman-Spalding party's outfit (two loaded wagons, horses, mules, and 17 head of cattle) to cross the Missouri at Fort Leavenworth (which they did, after delays, on May 2) and head northward across "Kansas" to the Otoe Mission (six miles above the Platte's mouth). Some 40 miles beyond the fort, a young man traveling alone joined them. He was Miles Goodyear (aged 19) who later became "the first white settler in what is now the State of Utah." *See, also,* May 1-19 entry.

Ref: William H. Gray's *History of Oregon* (Portland, 1870), pp. 113-142; *KHC*, v. 14, pp. 710, 711; *Utah Historical Quarterly*, Salt Lake City, v. 21 (July, 1953), pp. 195-218 (for Dale L. Morgan's article on Miles Goodyear); C. M. Drury's *Henry Harmon Spalding*, pp. 131-133; and his *Marcus Whitman*, p. 140.

❡ In April, after a tour of the Southwest during the winter of 1835-1836 (on a mission for U. S. commissioners Montfort Stokes and Gen. Mathew Arbuckle), Paul Ligueste Chouteau reported on the Indians of that region, as follows:

Comanches—Claim and occupy all the country bounded North by the Arkansas river, South by the Mexican Settlements, West by the Grand Cordillera, and East by the Cross Timbers. The numerical Military force of the Comanches . . . is estimated . . . by the Mexican Government at 8,000; but, from my own personal observation I have been induced to calculate the number of Comanche warriors at 4,500.

Kaywahs [Kiowas]—Occupy at pleasure during the different seasons of the year, such parts of the Comanche Country as suit their immediate convenience. This is done by full consent of the Comanches, who consider the Kaywas their closest allies, Number of Warriors (at least) 1,500.

Cah-tah-kahs or a band of Apaches; Reside generally with and under the protection of the Kaywahs. Military force estimated at about 300.

Wee-che-tah [Wichita], Tow-wac-car-ro, Wacco and Keetz-sah Bands of Pawnee Picts; Are corn planters—occupy several permanent villages and reside within the limits of the Comanche Country; which last nation together with the Kaywahs are supplied by them with corn and other production of the earth. Their force has been variously estimated but I think it would not be exagerated at 1,000 men.

Calculating the respective numbers . . . as one to six, to the whole population, would make the latter amount to 43,800. [Comanches: 27,000; Kiowas: 9,000; "Cah-tah-kahs": 1,800; Wichitas (and other Pawnee Pict bands): 6,000.]

Ref: Grant Foreman's *Advancing the Frontier 1830-1860* (Norman, 1933), p. 148, quotes P. L. Chouteau's April 25, 1836, report.

❡ May 1-19.—The *Diana* (upbound on her second trip of the season, and with a new captain) passed Liberty Landing, Mo., on May 1, refusing to stop, or "take a pound for any person." This occurred as the Oregon-bound missionary party (*see* April 7 and 17 entries), awaiting the steamboat at Liberty, was preparing to bury Mrs. Benedict Satterlee (who had died the day before).

On May 3, having made hasty arrangements to journey *overland* to the Council Bluffs, the Whitmans, Mrs. Eliza Spalding, Doctor Satterlee, and the Allises, started for Fort Leavenworth. (Allis purchased a wagon and three yokes of oxen; Doctor Whitman hired a team, wagon, and driver; the three women rode on horseback.) They reached the fort on May 5. Samuel Allis set out to overtake Spalding, Gray, and the wagons (*see* April 27 entry). The others remained at the post—guests of Capt. Matthew Duncan, and of Alexander G. Morgan (postmaster-trader)—till the evening of May 7; then continued five miles northward to the Kickapoo Methodist Mission, where they spent Sunday, the 8th, with the Berrymans, and journeyed northward again on May 9. Allis, meantime, had traveled to within 30 miles of Bellevue before overtaking Spalding, Gray, and the wagons on May 8. Gray and Allis returned to the Big Nemaha, and from there Allis continued to backtrack till he met his party about 45 miles north of Fort Leavenworth. On May 11 they all reached the Big Nemaha.

The Whitman-Spalding-Gray group, in haste to join the American Fur Company caravan setting out from Bellevue, hurried on ahead, crossing the Platte on May 19 and 20. (The Allises and Doctor Satterlee proceeded more slowly; stopped for three days at the Otoe Mission; and reached Bellevue on the 27th.)

Headed by Thomas Fitzpatrick, the American Fur Company caravan (which included Capt. William Drummond Stewart's party) had started up the Platte from Bellevue on May 15. The Whitmans, Spaldings, and Gray set out in pursuit on May 21; and by making forced marches caught up with the caravan four and a half days later.

Subsequently, the fur traders, Stewart's party, and the Oregon-bound missionaries reached "Fort Laramie" on June 13; crossed the continental divide by way of South Pass on July 4; and reached the rendezvous (on a branch of Green river, near present Daniel, Wyo.) on July 6.

Under escort of John McLeod (and Thomas McKay) of the Hudson's Bay Company, the missionaries continued westward reaching Fort Hall on August 3, Fort Boise on August 19, and Fort Walla Walla at the beginning of September.

Narcissa (Prentiss) Whitman and Eliza (Hart) Spalding were the first white women to cross the Rocky mountains. The Spaldings' light wagon, though not the first to cross the mountains, was the first wheeled vehicle (at Snake river it was converted to a two-wheeled cart) to go as far as Fort Boise, in present Idaho.

Ref: C. M. Drury's *Marcus Whitman*, pp. 141-154; C. M. Drury's *Henry Harmon Spalding*, pp. 132-152; C. M. Drury's *First White Women, op. cit.*, v. 1, pp. 48-88 (Mrs. Narcissa Whitman's diary), and pp. 188-197 (Mrs. Eliza Spalding's diary); *KHC*, v. 14, pp. 710, 711 (for Samuel Allis' journal); *Oregon Historical Quarterly*, Salem, v. 38, pp. 355-369 (for William H. Gray's journal); Oregon Pioneer Association *Transactions* (19th annual reunion), 1890, pp. 40-68 (for Mrs. Narcissa Whitman's journal); Warren, *op. cit.*, pp. 59-68 (for Mrs. Eliza Spalding's diary); Bernard De Voto's *Across the Wide Missouri* (Boston, 1947), pp. 244-250, 440 (for the American Fur Company party). The Lees and Shepard had driven cattle to Oregon in 1834. Of the Whitman-Spalding party's 17 cattle, eight completed the journey to Fort Walla Walla.

❡ About May 7 Capt. Benjamin L. E. Bonneville left the Missouri frontier on his second journey to the Rocky mountains (where he would "make a final close" of his fur trade interests). Presumably he crossed "Kansas," but nothing is known of his route, his companions, or even the point of departure (which may have been Fort Leavenworth). (*See* August, 1835, entry, *also*, for item on Bonneville.)

He reached Fort William (Fort Laramie) after June 6; probably did not go beyond Powder river (Wyo.); left the mountains in July; and by August 6 had reached Fort Leavenworth.

Awaiting at the army post was a War Department order (of April 22) reinstating Bonneville as a captain in the Seventh U. S. infantry. He set out, at once from Fort Leavenworth, on horseback, for his designated station—Fort Gibson (Okla.).

Ref: Washington Irving's *The Adventures of Captain Bonneville* . . ., edited by E. W. Todd (c1961), pp. xxx, xxxvii, xxxviii, xliii; Lt. G. K. Warren's "Memoir," in *Reports of Explorations and Surveys . . . for a Railroad . . . to the Pacific Ocean* (1861), v. 11, p. 33 (for quote of Bonneville's letter of August 24, 1857: "I left the mountains in July, 1836, and reached Fort Leavenworth, Missouri, the 6th of August following"); *Niles' Weekly Register*, v. 51 (September 3, 1836), p. 16; Dale L. Morgan's letter of June 9, 1962, to L. Barry, for the "after June 6" statement; 23d Cong., 2d Sess., *H. Ex. Doc.* 97 (Serial 273) for trading license issued to "Astor, Bonnville & Co." on April 16, 1834; William Clark's statement of licenses granted from March 7 to May 3, 1836, in "Letters Received by the Office of Indian Affairs" (microfilm from National Archives), for April 19, 1836, license issued to B. L. E. Bonneville to trade with the Arapahoes at a point of timber (on the south side of the Platte) called "Laramai's point."

❡ May.—A steamboat named *Kansas* was advertised for the Missouri river trade. On May 21 a St. Louis newspaper carried notice that the *Kansas* and the *John Hancock* would leave soon for Missouri river; and a June 25 issue noted the scheduled departure of these same two steamboats for the Missouri on June 27.

Other boats advertised for the Missouri between April and July included: the American Fur Company's *Diana* (the only one to go beyond the Council

Bluffs), the *Iowa*, the *Howard*, the *Boonville*, the *St. Charles*, the *Tiskilwa*, the *Chariton*, and the *Dart*. On November 30 the *Missouri Republican*, St. Louis, stated that five steamboats had been lost on the Missouri during the season past. One was the *Diana* which sank "in Diana bend," above Rocheport, Mo., on October 10, 1836, with a valuable cargo of furs. A few days later the *Chariton* went down (but was apparently salvaged—*see* April, 1837, annals). On November 26 the *John Hancock* (heavily laden), hit a snag "at Bellefontaine" and sank in 10 feet of water.

Ref: Nebraska Historical Society *Publications*, Lincoln, v. 20, pp. 65, 66; *KHC*, v. 9, pp. 301, 305 (the *Kansas* is said to have been piloted by Joseph La Barge); *Jeffersonian Republican*, Jefferson City, Mo., October 22, 1836.

❑ May 23.—By an act of this date, the President was authorized to raise an additional regiment of dragoons.

As a result the existing U. S. dragoon regiment (organized in 1833) commanded by Col. Henry Dodge, and headquartered at Fort Leavenworth, became the *First* U. S. dragoons. *See, also,* July 4 entry.

Ref: *U. S. Statutes at Large,* v. 5, pp. 32, 33.

❑ Beginning May 25, and ending in the fore(?) part of June, John C. McCoy and a party of "seven or eight poorly-armed men," surveyed the north line of the Osage reservation (treaty of 1825)— from the northeast corner (a point now in southwest Bourbon county), due westward as far as the Arkansas river (in present Sedgwick county).

Nine years earlier—*see* p. 140—Angus Langham had canceled a survey of this line, due to Osage hostility. McCoy, too, met opposition. In an address, in 1889, he told of the experience. As he and his crew approached the Neosho they worked only about three miles above the Little Osages' village (the uppermost Osage town—north of present Chanute, Neosho co.). Braves on horseback, watching and following them, became increasingly restive—claiming their land extended much farther north. McCoy found it expedient to pay a visit to the head chief Nicheumanee (Walking Rain). He and Charles Findlay, with an Indian escort, rode to the village (over 100 lodges), "situated on a high prairie hill a mile or so west of the Neosho." There, in the chief's large, centrally-located lodge (of bark, over a framework of poles), the surveyor faced Nicheumanee and several hundred head men and braves of the Little Osages. He remained firm in the face of threats. The council (much of it conducted in sign language, for lack of an interpreter) ended in a stalemate. McCoy says: "Findlay and I took our departure. . . . We found our horses at the [lodge] door, with the tail of my horse completely denuded of hair. I was glad to get the horse, even with his corn-cob tail." Back at the surveyors' camp, meantime, an Osage attempt at robbery had been thwarted.

The survey westward was continued "without serious molestation." The line of march—across Township 26 South of today—ran a few miles south of present Eureka and El Dorado. (McCoy states that the Arkansas tributary now called Walnut river was then known as the "Little Neosho"; and the stream now named Whitewater river was then called the "Little Verdigris"!). They reached the Arkansas at 124 miles from the point of beginning, about five miles above the mouth of the Little Arkansas.

Ref: *KHC*, v. 5, pp. 308-311 (for McCoy's 1889 address), v. 8, p. 199 (where the *northwest* corner of the Cherokee Neutral Lands [identical with the *northeast* corner of the Osage line—as noted by McCoy, v. 5, p. 309] is described as 20 rods south of the north line and three-fourths of a mile east of the west line of Sec. 26, T. 26 S., R. 21 E., Bourbon county); SIA, v. 1, pp. 267-269 (for McCoy's plats) and pp. 276-283 (for his field notes, dated "West Port, Mo., Septr 16th 1836"). The field notes contain little of interest beyond the comment that, on the highlands, as they approached the Neosho they crossed "an Indian Trace [running north and south] leading from the Little Osage village to the Wea settlements. . . ."

❡ May.—The annual spring caravan to Santa Fe was overtaken several days out on the trail by Charles Bent's seven-wagon train which traveled in company (for protection from Indians) as far as Cimarron crossing of the Arkansas. The experienced mountain man Robert ("Doc") Newell was one of Bent's party.

Another hand, not experienced, was young Richens Lacy ("Dick") Wootton (hired as a mule driver) whose account of the journey (his first to the west) was included in reminiscences published in 1890. By Wootton's recollection, the caravan numbered some 150 men and 57 wagons. (Josiah Gregg, in 1844, listed the Santa Fe-bound trade statistics for 1836 as 135 men [35 of them proprietors], 75 wagons, and $130,000 in merchandise.)

On night guard at the Little Cow creek camp (present Rice county), Wootton shot "Old Jack" (a mule) mistaking it for an Indian. At Pawnee Fork 250 or more Comanches "charged through the camp three or four times, trying to make the mules break loose." They failed, and lost three warriors in the attempt. After leaving the caravan at Cimarron crossing, to continue up the Arkansas, Bent's small train was met by Ceran St. Vrain and a mounted party from Fort William ("Bent's Fort") and escorted to that post.

Ref: H. L. Conard's *"Uncle Dick" Wootton* (Chicago, 1890), pp. 28-42; Josiah Gregg, *Commerce of the Prairies* . . . (New York, London, 1844), v. 2, p. 160; *Robert Newell's Memoranda, op. cit.*, p. 33; David Lavender's *Bent's Fort* (Garden City, N. Y., 1954), pp. 166, 167, 393, 394. Henry Inman, in a tale entitled "How 'Pawnee Rock' Was Named" (published in his *Stories of the Old Santa Fe Trail* [Kansas City, Mo., 1881], pp. 1-10), first attributed a mule-shooting incident to "Kit" Carson on an *alleged* first trip west in 1833. But Carson's first journey on the Santa Fe trail was in 1826. James Hobbs may have been another tyro hand with this Bent, St. Vrain & Co. party. In his reminiscences (*Wild Life in the Far West*—first published in 1872) Hobbs told of being taken captive by Comanches (near the Arkansas, west of "The Caches") during his first trip west in 1835 (but perhaps, correctly, 1836) as a Bent, St. Vrain & Co. employee; and of being ransomed four[?] years later by William Bent.

❡ Kickapoo Catholic Mission had its beginning on June 1, when the Rev. Charles F. Van Quickenborne, S. J., and three lay brothers (Andrew Mazzella, Edmund Barry, George Miles) debarked from a Missouri river steamboat at Kickapoo Landing (about five miles, by water, above Fort Leavenworth), and took up temporary residence in a log cabin of American Fur Company trader Laurence Pensineau, whose post was at the landing. (They had left St. Louis on May 25.)

At a site over a mile west of Pensineau's post, and near both Kickapoo settlements—Chief Pa-sha-cha-hah's village (half a mile southwest) and Kennekuk's town (a quarter-mile south)—the first mission building (a one-story, hewed-log schoolhouse, 16' x 15') was erected, after some delays. Ready for use in October, it served as mission headquarters during the winter, and until completion, in the spring of 1837, of a log house and chapel house (48'x20'x16'). Father Christian Hoecken (who had arrived some weeks after Van Quickenborne's party) then opened a school which, in the autumn, was reported to have 20 pupils.

At the end of 1836 the mission church had only two Kickapoo members (both children). The chief obstacles to converting these Indians were: (1) their addiction to whisky, and (2) the increasing opposition of the Kickapoo Prophet (Kennekuk) who had his own religion, many followers, and a government-built church in which to preach. Nor did the school prosper, for the Kickapoos felt they did not need it—having already the government school run by Methodist missionary J. C. Berryman.

Father Felix L. Verreydt replaced Van Quickenborne in July, 1837. Later, Father Anthony Eysvogels became head of the mission. Chief Pa-sha-cha-hah and his followers moved some 20 miles distant in 1839(?), leaving the Catholics few supporters. The school dwindled to eight students and the government withdrew its $500 per annum support (given since 1837) in 1840.

On September 19, 1840, the decision was made to close the Kickapoo Catholic Mission. Apparently its last use for church services was in late December.

Ref: G. J. Garraghan's *The Jesuits of the Middle United States* . . . (New York, 1938), v. 1, pp. 395-421 (p. 421 contains a footnote on the subsequent use of the mission house); R. J. Bollig's *History of Catholic Education in Kansas* . . . (Washington, D. C., 1933), pp. 10-12. See *KHC*, v. 16, p. 256, for comment, 1843, on the mission.

❡ June 7.—An act of this date provided for the extension of Missouri's western boundary to the Missouri river. (The existing line ran due north and south from the mouth of the Kansas—*see* map of 1834 in this volume.)

Prerequisites for adding this area (the "Platte Purchase") to Missouri: (1) extinguishment of Indian title to the land lying between Missouri's boundary and the Missouri (*i. e.,* the Little Platte country), and ceding of jurisdiction to the State of Missouri, (2) assent of the State of Missouri to the act's provisions, (3) a Presidential proclamation—*see* March 28, 1837, annals entry.

Ref: *U. S. Statutes at Large*, v. 5, p. 34.

❡ June 11.—At Fort Leavenworth, Capt. Matthew Duncan (the

commanding officer), together with Agent John Dougherty, held a council with 49 chiefs and head men of the Missouri band of Sac (and Fox) Indians who had arrived the day before to seek redress of grievances (relating to a claim for annuities; and in regard to their removal to the southwest side of the Missouri).

Ref: Capt. Matthew Duncan's June 18, 1836, report, in "Letters Received by the Office of Indian Affairs"—microfilm from National Archives. Col. Henry Dodge—*see* July 4 entry —had already left Fort Leavenworth.

❦ June 13.—Capt. Matthew Duncan and Agent R. W. Cummins, at Fort Leavenworth, counciled with the Kickapoo Indians in regard to a war dance recently held at their upper village (Pa-sha-cha-hah's settlement)—a dance reportedly in celebration of an Indian victory over U. S. troops in Florida.

Ref: Capt. Matthew Duncan's report, *loc. cit.*

❦ June 15.—Arkansas, a territory since 1819, was admitted to the Union as a state.

Ref: *U. S. Statutes at Large*, v. 5, p. 50.

❦ July 2.—President Jackson approved the enabling act for the better protection of the Western frontier. It provided: (1) for the surveying and opening of a military road from a point on the upper Mississippi to Red river in the south; (2) that the road should pass *west of Missouri and Arkansas* (after getting the assent of the Indians through whose territory it would run); (3) for the construction of military posts along the road (locations unspecified; (4) for the use of U. S. troops to perform the required labor; (5) the sum of $100,000 to accomplish the objects of the act.

Ref: *Ibid.*, p. 67; *KHQ* v. 11, p. 117.

❦ At the northeast corner of the Kansa lands (in present Jackson county), on July 2, John C. McCoy and a work party began a survey of the north boundary of the Kansa reservation (treaty of 1825). Before July ended they had proceeded west for 206 miles (to Rooks county of today), where they terminated the survey "on [a] high level prairie covered with short curley Buffalo grass. . . . Solomons fork about 1½ miles to S[outh]."

Ten years earlier (1826-1827) Angus Langham had surveyed the east and south Kansa lines (*see* p. 134); and six years earlier (1830), John C. McCoy had accompanied his father on a survey of the Delaware Outlet's north line (*see* p. 177)—a boundary which paralleled the Kansa north line and ran only 10 miles above it. (See map of 1834 in this volume.)

It appears that the northeast corner of the Kansa lands was (by current description), about the southwest corner of Sec. 22, T. 7 S., R. 15 E., Franklin township, Jackson co. The line then ran due west through Township 7. McCoy, in his field notes, mentions "Soldier creek" (crossed beween 10 and 11 miles from the beginning point); "Egoma Saba (or Black paint) Creek" [since McCoy was in present Pottawatomie county, the stream referred to is the Red Vermillion creek of today]; the "blue earth river" [Big Blue] crossed between 52 and 53 miles west; the "Republican fork of Kanzas" between 79 and 80 miles west; and the bank of "Solomon's fork" between 121 and 122 miles west. This last-named stream is mentioned again at 151 miles, at 192-193, and 195-198 miles, as well as at the end of the survey.

Ref: Superintendency of Indian Affairs, St. Louis "Records" (SIA), v. 1, pp. 271-275 (for McCoy's survey plats) and pp. 284-294 (for his field notes, dated "West Port, Mo., September 16, 1836").

❡ July 4.—Col. Henry Dodge (whose resignation as head of the First U. S. dragoons was effective this date) took the oath of office as governor of the newly created Territory of Wisconsin, at Mineral Point (Wis.).

To rank from July 4, Lt. Col. Stephen Watts Kearny was promoted colonel of the First U. S. dragoons, Maj. Richard B. Mason became the regiment's lieutenant colonel, and Capt. Clifton Wharton its major.

Colonel Kearny, who had been at Fort Des Moines since the autumn of 1834, received orders in July to move to Fort Leavenworth and assume command. See p. 176, for his earlier, brief, tour of duty there.)

Ref: *Iowa Historical Record*, Iowa City, v. 8 (July, 1892), pp. 300, 302; D. L. Clarke's *Stephen Watts Kearny* . . . (Norman, c1961), pp. 69, 70; F. B. Heitman's *Historical Register and Dictionary of the United States Army* . . . (Washington, 1903).

❡ July 18.—In the settlement of Frenchmen and Indians, at the mouth of the Kansas (present Kansas City, Mo.), Father C. F. Van Quickenborne (of Kickapoo Catholic Mission) baptized 14 mixed-blood Indian children (Flatheads, Kutenai, Iroquois, etc.), all, apparently, from 12 families which had "lately come down from the Rocky Mountains." (Probably they had come in with the Fontenelle and Whitman party in the late summer of 1835—*see* p. 297.) Also on the 18th he performed two marriage rites (the earliest recorded in that vicinity). Both parties in the first ceremony were Iroquois Indians: Benjamin Lagautherie (son of Victor) and Charlotte Gray (daughter of John and Marianne). The other rite—for Clement "Liserte" (Lessert) and Julia Roy—renewed a civil marriage of 1829 (*see* p. 160).

In a letter of October 4, 1836, Van Quickenborne referred to the recent settlement on the "low level ground that skirts the right bank of the Kaw at its junction with the Missouri" of 12 families which had "lately come down from the Rocky Mountains"; and stated that on the second of two visits to the Indians he "found them all sick, and, in despair of being able to live here, they were talking of going back to their mountains." With his sketch map of "the Indian country" (also October 4, 1836) he wrote this descriptive note relating to the Kaw's mouth settlement: "Place where the American Fur Company has built a small church ["Chouteau's Church"—*see* July, 1835, entry]—here live 25 families—20 of which are Indians or half breeds. . . ."

Ref: Garraghan, *op. cit.*, v. 1, pp. 259, and *between* 402 and 403 (for map). Benjamin "Logatree" was deeded land near "mouth of the Kansas," on April 10, 1836, by Francis G. Chouteau—Jackson County (Mo.) courthouse, in Book E, p. 564.

❡ BORN: within the Kickapoo reserve (present Leavenworth county), on July 23, Brigitte Aimable Pensineau, daughter of trader Paschal Pensineau and Catharinette, "an Indian woman (Kickapoo) *vulgo Greenwood.*" (She was baptized January 4, 1837, at "Kickapootown," by the Rev. C. F. Van Quickenborne, S. J.)

Ref: "Kickapoo Register" (microfilm in KHi). Charles Pensineau and Laurence Pensineau were present at the baptismal ceremony.

❡ Gholson Kurcheval (appointed July 2) superintended the removal west, during the summer, of several hundred more Pottawatomies of Illinois. Capt. John B. F. Russell was the disbursing agent. Apparently they were the Indians who had spent the preceding winter in southeastern "Iowa"—*see* December 2, 1835, entry.)

These Pottawatomies joined the emigrants of 1835 in the Little Platte (Mo.) country. They were placed under the temporary supervision of Emigrating Agent Anthony L. Davis (whose residence was at "Kickapoo town" above Fort Leavenworth).

Expenditures by the government for the emigrants included payments of $2,352.20 and $7,977.30 to [J. T. V.] Thompson and [Hiram] Rich for provisions; $56 to N. W. Hutchins for transporting Indians on the steamboat *Siam;* $8 to Francis L. Vallier for service as interpreter.

Though a December 1, 1836, report stated that the number of Pottawatomies (and united Chippewas and Ottawas) removed west of the Mississippi was 1,712, a later report (1840) estimated their number did not exceed 1,455. (In November, 1835, the figure had been given as 1,200[?].)

Ref: Grant Foreman's *The Last Trek of the Indians* (Chicago, c1946), p. 107; 24th Cong., 2d Sess., *H. Doc. No. 137* and *H. Doc. No. 141* (both in Serial 303); 24th Cong., 2d Sess., *Sen. Doc. 1* (Serial 297) for CIA report of December 1, 1836; 24th Cong., 1st Sess., *Sen. Report 228* (Serial 281), p. 5, for November 24, 1835, report; *Report* of the Comm'r of Indian Affairs for 1840 (Document 3, with the report).

❡ August 26.—After an official inspection of Fort Leavenworth, Col. George Croghan wrote:

. . . it is not only not a fort but is even devoid of the regularity of a common barrack. Of defences it has none. Colonel [S. W.] Kearny [the new commandant] having very wisely recommended the erection of block houses, has . . . contracted for the building of two . . . both of them will be finished, it is believed, by December. . . .

Ref: F. P. Prucha, ed., *Army Life on the Western Frontier* . . . (c1958), p. 24.

❡ William Clark's journey to Fort Leavenworth in September

(*see, also,* next entry) may have been his first and only visit to that post. He traveled there aboard the steamboat *Boonville,* leaving St. Louis on August 30. George Rogers Hancock Clark (his 20-year-old son, serving as secretary), an interpreter, and a servant, accompanied him. After the treaty was concluded in mid-September, Clark returned to St. Louis on the American Fur Company's *Diana.*

In 1804, bound up the Missouri with the Lewis & Clark expedition, and again in 1806, returning, he had passed the site of the future fort. But there does not appear to be any record that William Clark returned to that vicinity in the 30 years between 1806 and 1836, though he was situated no farther away than St. Louis, as superintendent of Indian affairs, during most of the intervening time.

Ref: "Letters Received by the Office of Indian Affairs," St. Louis Superintendency (National Archives microcopy 234, Roll 751)—George Maguire's September 2, 1836, letter, and William Clark's abstract of disbursements from October 1, 1836, to September 30, 1837. *See, also,* next entry references.

❦ September 17.—At Fort Leavenworth William Clark (sup't of Indian affairs, St. Louis) negotiated a treaty with the Iowas, and the band of Sacs and Foxes of the Missouri. By its terms, the Indians

(1) Gave up all claim to lands lying between the State of Missouri and the Missouri river and received a present of $7,500. (This was the "Platte Purchase" country, where they were residing.)

(2) Were assigned a reserve across the Missouri—a small strip of land between the Kickapoos' north line and the Grand Nemaha, extending "back and westwardly" from the Missouri to encompass 400 sections, to be divided equally between the Iowas and the Sacs & Foxes. (See map of 1834 in this volume for general location.) The rectangular tract of land as surveyed in 1837-1838, was divided by a diagonal line into "twin reserves." (*See* May, 1837, entry.)

(3) Agreed to move as soon as arrangements could be made. In return, the government was to do these things for the *Iowas:* build five comfortable houses; fence and break up 200 acres of land; furnish a farmer, blacksmith, teacher, interpreter; provide agricultural implements (for five years), rations for one year, a ferry boat, a mill, 100 cows and calves, five bulls, 100 stock hogs; and assist in removing them to the extent of $500. For the *Sacs & Foxes* the terms were the same, except only three houses were to be built, and but $400 provided for removal.

"Mo-hos-ca" (White Cloud), "Nau-che-ning" (No Heart), and 10 others signed for the Iowas. "Cau-ca-car-mack" (Rock Bass), "Sea-sa-ho" (Sturgeon), and 13 others signed for the Sacs & Foxes.

Treaty witnesses were: Col. S. W. Kearny (commandant at Fort Leavenworth), Agent John Dougherty, George R. H. Clark (son of William Clark), Subagent Andrew S. Hughes, William Duncan (farmer for the Iowas), Sutler Joseph V. Hamilton, Joseph Robidoux, Jr., Sgt. Maj. William Bowman (of the First dragoons); interpreters Jeffrey Dorion, Peter Cadue, Jacques Mette, and Louis M. Dorrion.

Ref: C. J. Kappler's *Indian Affairs, Laws and Treaties* (Washington, 1904), v. 2, pp. 468-470; *KHQ*, v. 16, p. 2 (for item on George R. H. Clark); *KHC*, v. 8, p. 82.

❧ About September 19 John C. McCoy and a work party left Westport, Mo., and set out southward, to survey the Cherokees' reserve. They reached a beginning point on the Arkansas (location not identified) on October 14. (A dragoon escort from Fort Leavenworth, detailed to accompany McCoy, did not leave that post till October 19.) After completing between 60 and 70 miles of the survey, illness and bad weather forced suspension of work till 1837.

Ref: Isaac McCoy manuscripts (Isaac McCoy letter of December 15, 1836).

❧ September 26.—At Fort Leavenworth Col. Stephen W. Kearny was dinner host to British army captain William Drummond Stewart, who was en route East after a summer's hunting expedition in the Rocky mountains.

Captain Stewart's party (a companion "Mr. Sillem, a German gentleman"; three servants; two light wagons; some fine horses; and two dogs) had traveled *to* the mountains with the American Fur Company caravan (headed by Thomas Fitzpatrick) which left Bellevue (Neb.) on May 15 and followed up the Platte. It is supposed that Stewart and party returned to Bellevue with Fitzpatrick, by the same route, in August and September. (*See, also,* October 26-31, 1835, entry.)

Ref: Clarke, *op. cit.,* p. 73; De Voto, *op. cit.,* pp. 244, 270.

❧ BORN: at Delaware Baptist Mission (present Wyandotte county), on October 7, Lydia Blanchard, daughter of the Rev. Ira D. and Mary (Walton) Blanchard.

Ref: Jotham Meeker's "Diary," October 7, 1836, entry; A. J. Paddock correspondence, in KHi ms. division.

❧ October 15.—At Bellevue (Neb.) the Otoes, Missouris, Omahas, and Yancton & Santee bands of Sioux, after a council with Agent John Dougherty and Subagent Joshua Pilcher, signed a "convention" giving up all claim to lands lying between the State of Missouri and the Missouri river. (*See* the June 7, 1836, "Platte Purchase" annals item.)

The acting secretary of the proceedings, who also signed the document as witness, was "J[oseph] Varnum Hamilton, sutler, [First] U. S. dragoons," of Fort Leavenworth.

Ref: Kappler, *op. cit.,* v. 2, pp. 479-481.

❧ October 21.—The chiefs and leading men of the Delawares, Shawnees, Piankeshaws & Weas, Peorias & Kaskaskias met in council with Agent Richard W. Cummins (head of Northern Agency, Western Territory), and signed an agreement giving "our full consent that the United States, open and establish a road through each of our countries, and establish therein such military posts, as the Government of the United States may think proper. . . ." (*See* July 2, entry.)

In return, the Indians were paid $900 in goods (the Delawares and Shawnees, $300 each; $150 each to the two smaller Indian groups). Delaware signers were Nah-comin, Captain Ketchum, Nonon-da-gomin, Captain Swanock, "Sackindeattun" (Secondine), and four others; for the Shawnees, John Perry, George Williams, Young Blackhoof, Letho, Little Fox, Peter Cornstalk, and two others signed; Charley, Swan, Go-to-cop-wah, and six others signed for the smaller nations. Witnesses to the agreement were: Dr. J. Andrew Chute, W. W. Kavanaugh, Angus G. Boggs; also, interpreters Joseph Parks and Baptiste Peoria.

Ref: SIA, v. 1, pp. 262, 263, v. 26, p. 78.

❆ November 5.—Jesse Overton received payment (from Lt. Thomas Swords, assistant quartermaster) of $1,795 for having made three farms for the Kansa Indians.

(According to Isaac McCoy, these fields, "fenced and ploughed," were at the "lower village" and of 130, 140, and six acres in size. Earlier, 10 acres had been ploughed and fenced.)

Ref: 25th Cong., 2d Sess., *H. Doc. No. 362* (Serial 330), p. 86; Isaac McCoy's *Annual Register* for 1837, p. 32.

❆ In November Capt. Edwin V. Sumner, and Company B, First U. S. dragoons, arrived at Fort Leavenworth, from Fort Des Moines. They had left the latter post on October 30.

Ref: Louis Pelzer's *Marches of the Dragoons in the Mississippi Valley* . . . (Iowa City, 1917), p. 62.

❆ DIED: Ten-squa-ta-wa (the Shawnee Prophet), in November, at his small settlement (four huts) on the Shawnee reserve (within the bounds of present Kansas City, Wyandotte co.). He was probably about 68. (The year of his birth is given as 1768.)

A brother of famed chief Tecumseh, Ten-squa-ta-wa ("the open door"— a self-given name) was, in the early 1800's, a powerful and influential man. (Throughout his life he claimed to have direct communication with the Great Spirit.) He abetted Tecumseh in the plot to unite the Indian nations against the United States. When the Battle of Tippecanoe (1811, in Indiana) ended in defeat for the Indians, Ten-squa-ta-wa's prestige declined, and he became an obscure figure.

It is said that he came to "Kansas" in 1828, from the Shawnee settlement in the Cape Girardeau, Mo., area, where he had lived two years; that he settled on the N. E. ¼ of Sec. 32, T. 11, R. 25 E., but moved to the N. E. ¼ of

Sec. 30 about a year before his death. *See* his portrait (by Catlin) in this volume, p. 401.

Ref: *KHC*, v. 9, pp. 164n, 165n; Kansas City *Sun*, March 5, 1909; the Kansas City (Mo.) *Star*, March 27, 1950, shows a picture of "White Feather" spring (described as "in a ravine which bisects Ruby avenue," in the block west of 38th street, Kansas City, Kan.) and notes that the Shawnee Prophet is buried near by; Bureau of American Ethnology, *Fourteenth Annual Report*, pt. 2, pp. 673, 674.

❡ According to the December 3 report of the secretary of war, the army's Western Department force (under Maj. Gen. Edmund P. Gaines) totaled only 2,458 troops.

At Fort Leavenworth the aggregate strength was 321 men— seven companies of the First U. S. dragoons. In present Oklahoma there were 132 men at Fort Gibson, 44 at new Fort Coffee, and 158 at Fort Towson.

Ref: 24th Cong., 2d Sess., *Sen. Doc. 1* (Serial 297), pp. 107, 146.

❡ MARRIED: The Rev. Robert Clark Ellifrit and Ann Eliza Jefferson (teacher), both of the Kickapoo Methodist Mission, on December 20, at Shawnee Methodist Mission, by the Rev. Thomas Johnson.

(In the fore part of 1837 the Ellifrits were at Delaware Methodist Mission, but moved, in the latter part of the year, across the Missouri, where they were early settlers in the "Platte Purchase.")

Ref: Jackson County, Mo., marriage records, Independence, Mo., v. 1, p. 102; W. M. Paxton's *Annals of Platte County, Mo.* (Kansas City, Mo., 1897), *see* index; *KHC*, v. 9, p. 206; "Remsburg Scrapbook," v. 1, p. 252 (in KHi library); Isaac McCoy's *Annual Register* for 1837, p. 30. It is said that Mrs. Ann Eliza Ellifrit was a relative (grand niece?) of Thomas Jefferson.

❡ A gold mine (or buried treasure) was the quest of a party of men who were guided, in 1836, by Jesse Chisholm, from Arkansas to the mouth of the Little Arkansas river (present Sedgwick county).

James Mead told of this journey in an address made in 1907, and thereby contributed an item to "Kansas" buried treasure lore. He stated that the search was undertaken partly because Antoine S. Le Page du Pratz's map of 1757 (*see* reference on p. 27) showed "A Gold Mine" in that vicinity; and also because of a tradition "that long ago a party from New Mexico, descending the river in boats, were surrounded by Indians in the night at this point, and after a siege of several days were all killed but one, who escaped, after he had buried their gold and silver."

Ref: *KHC*, v. 10, p. 9. Mead no doubt heard this tale direct from Chisholm.

❡ Employed in "Kansas" by the Indian Department during all, or part of the year 1836, were the following persons:

In the *Northern Agency, Western Territory*—*Agent* Richard W. Cummins [whose headquarters was the old Shawnee Agency (present Johnson county, near state line)]; *Interpreters* Joseph James [Kansa], Joseph Parks [Delawares, etc.]; *Gun and blacksmiths* John P. Smith [Kickapoos], Lewis Jones [Shawnees], savage countrymen.") In July he removed his belongings and abandoned Hopefield (No. 3).

In a journal entry of September 5, 1837, the Rev. David B. Rollin (en route from Shawnee Baptist Mission to visit the Creek Indians) wrote: "Arrived at Harmony, [Mo.—where the first mission to the Osages had been founded in 1821 (*see* p. 96)]. Here, about fifteen years ago, missionary efforts were commenced on a large scale, for the benefit of the Osages. Labors have of late been suspended. At this place, I was introduced to Mr. Requa, the last of many missionaries who have left these degraded sons of the forest. The Osages have recently been very abusive, and Mr. Requa has concluded to quit their country, after a service of about sixteen years. There is now no missionary among this people, and their prospects, for time and eternity, are indeed gloomy."

Ref: *Report* of the American Board of Comm'rs for Foreign Missions for 1837, pp. 111, 112; *Missionary Herald,* Boston, v. 33, p. 476; *Baptist Missionary Magazine,* v. 18, p. 42.

❡ March 28.—President Van Buren proclaimed the Indian title extinguished to the lands lying between the State of Missouri and the Missouri river—the "Platte Purchase" (act of June 7, 1836—*see* p. 310), thereby making the area a part of Missouri, and opening it to settlement.

Six northwestern Missouri counties—Platte, Buchanan, Andrew, Holt, Nodaway, and Atchison) subsequently (1838-1845) were organized from the "Platte Purchase."

Ref: James D. Richardson's *Messages and Papers of the Presidents 1789-1902* (1905), v. 3, p. 32; State Historical Society of Missouri, comp., *Historic Missouri* . . . (Columbia, c1959), p. 27.

❡ At the beginning of April seven steamboats were reported "engaged in the commerce of the Missouri." They were the *Chariton, Phillos, Kansas, Howard, Dart, Bridgewater,* and *Fayette.* The first four had arrived on the same date (April 4?) at St. Charles, Mo., *from the upper river,* after a long absence. The *Dart* was still to come down.

Ref: *Missouri Argus,* St. Louis, April 7, 1837 (copied from the St. Charles [Mo.] *Clarion*).

❡ April 13.—Revised regulations adopted by the Indian Department included these changes in the superintendencies, agencies, and subagencies, as organized under the July 7, 1834, regulations.

THE SUPERINTENDENCY OF ST. LOUIS (William Clark, sup't) was enlarged to include the united Pottawatomies, Chippewas & Ottawas north of the Missouri river, in addition to all the other Indians south of the Missouri and north of the northern line of the Osage reservation. Its subdivisions:

*Fort Leavenworth Agency** (Richard W. Cummins, agent)—for the Delawares, Kansa, Shawnees, and Kickapoos. [Location: the old Shawnee Agency buildings, in present Johnson county, near the state line.]

Council Bluffs Agency (John Dougherty, agent)—for the Otoes, Missouris, Omahas, and Pawnees.

Upper Missouri Agency (Joshua Pilcher, agent)—for the Sioux of the Missouri, Cheyennes, and Poncas.

Upper Missouri Subagency (W. N. Fulkerson, subagent)—for the Mandans, Blackfeet, etc.

Council Bluffs Subagency (Dr. Edwin James, subagent—appointed April 28)—for the United Pottawatomies, Ottawas, & Chippewas north of Missouri river.

Great Nemahaw Subagency* (Andrew S. Hughes, subagent)—for the Iowas, Sacs & Foxes of Missouri. [Location: on the Missouri, just above the mouth of Wolf river, present Doniphan county.]

Osage [Marais des Cygnes] River Subagency* (Anthony L. Davis, subagent—appointed April 28)—for the Ottawas, Peorias & Kaskaskias, Weas & Pianke-shaws, and the Pottawatomies south of Missouri river. [Location: on Wea creek, present Miami county, at Wea Presbyterian Mission.]

THE ACTING SUPERINTENDENCY OF THE WESTERN TERRITORY (William Arm-strong, acting sup't), was to have three agencies (Choctaw, Creek, and Chero-kee), and two subagencies: *Osage Subagency** (Paul Ligueste Chouteau, sub-agent) for all of the Osages [Location: on the Neosho river, present Neosho county]; and *Neosho [Grand] River Subagency* for the Senecas, united Senecas & Shawnees and the Quapaws.

* Agency, and subagencies with headquarters in "Kansas."

Ref: *Report* of the Comm'r of Indian Affairs, 1837, pp. 660-664 (for new regulations); 25th Cong., 2d Sess., *H. Doc. No. 135* (Serial 326) for names of officials. For data on sites, see A. T. Hughes' letter of August 14, 1837, A. L. Davis' letter of May 15, 1838, and R. W. Cummins' letter of May 18, 1838—all in OIA, Letters Received from SIA, St. Louis (National Archives, Microcopy 234, Roll 751).

❡ April 20.—Anthony L. Davis ("emigrating agent" for the Pot-tawatomies from Indiana, residing on the Kickapoo reserve) set out from Westport, Mo., with Isaac McCoy, Robert Simerwell, Dr. J. A. Chute, Robert Polke and son, of Indiana, "Mr. Holliday" (a Pottawatomie), and Lewis McNeff (a Chippewa) to view the country in which he would soon relocate as subagent (appoint-ment date: April 28) of the new Osage River Subagency.

This party reached Wea Presbyterian Mission (present Miami county) on April 21; proceeded next day south and west to the "Osage" [Marais des Cygnes] river; followed up its course to the Peoria & Kaskaskia line; crossed the river and camped. On April 24th these explorers arrived at an "Osage" tributary which (wrote McCoy) "we named Putawatomie creek, supposing that the first settlement of the [soon-to-arrive] Putawatomies would be on it."

Crossing and moving southward, they camped on the Neosho on the 25th. On the night of April 27, after traveling up the Neosho's north bank, they were (according to McCoy) some 70 to 75 miles west of the state of Mis-souri (in present Lyon? county). On the 28th the line of march was north-east for about 12 miles, then east for perhaps 13 more, to a branch of "Puta-watomie Creek." Continuing east on the 29th, McCoy noted: "We . . .

Wakarusa—40 miles

Kansas river—25 miles

A small creek near the [Kansa] Agency—4 miles

Sauterelle, or Grasshopper river [now the Delaware]—into the Kansas—
6 miles

Soldier creek—15 miles (6 miles from the Kansa village it empties into
the Kansas)

to Prairie creek—15 miles

Black [now Red] Vermillion—18 miles

Big black creek [Black Vermillion] a fork of the Blue—30 miles

North fork of the Blue [the Big Blue, of Nebraska and Kansas]—15 miles

Big Sandy creek—40 miles

The west fork of the Blue [Little Blue river]—"136[?] to the Paune [Paw-
nee] trails"—25 miles

Across to the Big Platte—20 miles

Ref: David L. Brown's "Three Years in the Rocky Mountains," in Cincinnati *Daily Morning Atlas*, September 8, 10-13, 1845 (microcard, KHi); De Voto, *op. cit.*, pp. xvii, 309-319, 391, 409, 414, 415, 444; Marvin C. Ross' *The West of Alfred Jacob Miller* (Norman, Okla., c1951), pp. xvii, 17, 48; William H. Gray's "Diary" for July 13, 1837 (typed copy of the Oregon Historical Society's original, supplied to this compiler by Dale L. Morgan, of the Bancroft Library, who also gave additional valuable help on this entry in his letter of December 10, 1962, to L. Barry). Though De Voto's account places Thomas Fitzpatrick at the head of the 1837 caravan, there is no evidence that he was with the expedition while it traveled from Missouri to Fort Laramie.

❦ May.—On her way to the American Fur Company's upper Missouri trading posts, the *St. Peters* probably passed along the "Kansas" shore in the latter part of the month. Among the passengers were Indian agents John Dougherty and Joshua Pilcher; and the boat's cargo included annuity goods for their Council Bluffs and Upper Missouri agencies. (The *St. Peters* reached Fort Clark on June 19.)

At, or near, Fort Leavenworth, a Company employee—a mulatto—became ill. Before the *St. Peters* arrived at Bellevue [Neb.]—the Council Bluffs Agency—his disease—smallpox—was fully developed and "had been communicated to several other persons subject to it."

From this introduction (according to Joshua Pilcher) there followed the devastating smallpox epidemic of 1837-1838 which destroyed some, and nearly wiped out others of the upper Missouri Indian nations; and thereby altered the river fur trade. (The nations most affected were the Mandans, Arikaras, Minnetarees, Assiniboines, Blackfeet, and Sioux.)

According to Isaac McCoy, upper Missouri fur traders "conjectured" 15,000 Indians had perished of smallpox by year's end.

Ref: Joshua Pilcher's February 5, 1838, letter to William Clark (copy in John C. McCoy Collection, KHi ms. division); Isaac McCoy's *Annual Register* for 1838, pp. 22-24. There are other versions of the origin of the epidemic. Bernard De Voto has discussed them in his *Across the Wide Missouri*, pp. 279-301, 442. Apparently he did not know of the Pilcher letter referred to above.

❦ A *Gazetteer of the State of Missouri*, compiled by Alphonso

Wetmore, was published at St. Louis in the spring. The western border county of *Jackson* (created in December, 1826; county seat, Independence, established in 1827—*see* p. 144) was listed as having a population of 4,522 in 1836 (as against 2,823 in 1830).

In the *Gazetteer* is a table of distances "From Jackson county to Santa Fe" (calculated as an 897-mile journey). The indications are that it was compiled by Wetmore when he captained an 1828 expedition to Santa Fe.

Another table gives the mileage by water, from St. Louis to Fort Leavenworth. By this reckoning the distance up the Missouri from St. Louis to Franklin and Boonville was 204 miles; 115 more to Lexington; 32 miles to Sibley [Fort Osage]; 20 to Liberty; eight to Independence; 12 to [Francis G.] "Chouteau's"; and 40 to Cant. [*i. e.*, Fort] Leavenworth—a total of 431 miles. [An up-to-date table would have listed Westport Landing.]

Ref: Wetmore's *Gazetteer* . . . (as noted above); *Missouri Argus*, St. Louis, May 12, 1837 (contains editorial comment on, and long quotes from, the *Gazetteer*); J. F. McDermott, ed., *The Early Histories of St. Louis* (St. Louis, 1952), p. 21.

❦ May 12.—John G. Pratt (missionary and printer), with his bride Olivia (Evans) Pratt, reached Shawnee Baptist Mission (where they would replace the Jotham Meekers who were preparing to settle among the Ottawa Indians).

Ref: Isaac McCoy's "Journal," May 14, 1837, entry; Jotham Meeker's "Diary," May 11, 1837, entry; J. W. Manning's "John Gill Pratt" (dissertation, 1951, on microfilm in KHi). He states the Pratts arrived at Westport Landing on May 11; and reached the mission on May 12.

❦ May.—According to Josiah Gregg's statistics (as compiled for his *Commerce of the Prairies*, 1844), the goods taken to the Southwest over the Santa Fe trail in 1837 were estimated to be worth $150,000. The merchandise, belonging to some 35 proprietors, was carried in about 80 wagons; and around 160 men made the journey. Gregg, southwest bound for the third time, was one of the merchants. (He returned in May, 1838.) Not all the traders, necessarily, went in the *spring* caravan.

Ref: Gregg, *op. cit.*, v. 1, p. 305.

❦ During the spring and early summer, the Iowa Indians, and the Sac & Fox Indians of Missouri, assisted by their subagent Andrew S. Hughes, moved across the Missouri from their old homes in the "Platte Purchase" (northwestern Missouri) to the lands provided by treaty of September 17, 1836 (*see* p. 314), settling in present Doniphan county, north of the Kickapoos' reserve.

Subagent Hughes wrote in mid-May that he recently had taken the Iowas to the new reserve. On July 31 Brig. Gen. Henry Atkinson (from "Independence landing") sent Isaac McCoy (at Westport) a letter stating: "The Iowas & Sauks have generally crossed the river to their own lands, a few being permitted to remain a short time to gather their crops of corn." He urged McCoy to go up at once and mark out the division line between the two bands' reserves as the Indians were fighting over their rights of location. (McCoy went, a few days later, and before August 12 had straightened out the difficulties.)

With his August 14 letter to the Indian department, Subagent Hughes sent a rough sketch showing the new Indian settlements at "Eagle Point," "on the Prairie" along the Missouri's right bank. The Sacs & Foxes were just north of the mouth of Wolf river (now Wolf *creek*), and the Iowa Indians a little higher up the Missouri (elsewhere, the distance between settlements was given as one mile). Hughes wrote that it was about four miles between Wolf river and the next Missouri tributary to the north—which he called "Mill creek" (now Clear creek)—and that the Indians were located right on the river between these two streams.

On August 26 Subagent Hughes reported that the Indians had erected 41 bark houses, and that the early-arriving families had small fields or patches of corn, pumpkins, beans, and other vegetables. "According to the best count I can make," he wrote, "the Ioways consist of 992 souls; the Sacs consist of 510 souls."

Ref: Isaac McCoy's "Journal," May 19, 1837; Isaac McCoy manuscripts (for McCoy letters of August 2 and September 23, 1837, and for an A. S. Hughes letter of July 8, 1837); Presbyterian Historical Society, American Indian Missions correspondence (microfilm, KHi), for S. M. Irvin and Aurey Ballard letter of August 12, 1837; OIA, Letters Received from SIA, St. Louis (National Archives Microcopy 234, Roll 751) for Hughes' August 14, 1837, letter, and August 26, 1837, report (the latter is, also, in *Report* of the Comm'r of Indian Affairs for 1837, but undated there).

❡ May 26.—At Fort Gibson (Okla.) delegations of chiefs and leading men from the Kiowa, Kiowa Apache, and Tawakoni tribes, entered into a treaty of peace and friendship with the United States—the first such treaty negotiated with these western prairie Indians.

Also present were representatives of two "eastern" tribes—the Muscogees (Western Creeks) and the Osages of the Verdigris. Auguste P. Chouteau and Montfort Stokes signed for the United States. Ta-ka-ta-couche (Black Bird) headed the Kiowa signers; Roly McIntosh signed first for the Muscogees; and Clermont for the Osages.

Ref: Kappler, *op. cit.,* v. 2, pp. 489-491; Grant Foreman's *Pioneer Days in the Early Southwest* (Cleveland, 1926), p. 231.

❡ June 6.—The steamboat *Kansas* reached Fort Leavenworth (from St. Louis) with 62 dragoon recruits, in the charge of two lieutenants—one of them 2d Lt. Philip Kearny (nephew of post commander Col. Stephen W. Kearny).

Ref: Clarke, *op. cit.,* p. 75. Philip Kearny was commissioned a second lieutenant in the First dragoons as of March 8, 1837.—Heitman, *op. cit.,* v. 1, p. 586.

❡ Between June 7 and 18 Methodist ministers Andrew Monroe, William W. Redman, and Nelson Henry, all of Missouri, visited the Peoria, Shawnee, Delaware, and Kickapoo missions of their church, holding business and religious meetings. They left for home on June 20.

Ref: *Christian Advocate and Journal*, v. 12 (September 8, 1837), p. 10; or, *KHC*, v. 9, pp. 199, 200.

❧ In June Lt. Col. Richard B. Mason and the remaining troops (18 men) of Companies H and I, First U. S. dragoons, arrived at Fort Leavenworth from Fort Des Moines (which had been abandoned on June 1, by War Department order).

(The ranks were depleted because many dragoons had completed an enlistment period and left the army.)

Ref: Pelzer, *op. cit.*, pp. 62, 63.

❧ Ottawa Baptist Mission had its beginning on June 18 when Missionary Jotham Meeker and family unloaded their wagons at a site (selected in March) on the north bank of the Marais des Cygnes, near present Ottawa, and moved into temporary living quarters ("a small rough cabin intended for a stable"). Before mid-October the mission house had been completed.

Two days earlier the Meekers had left Shawnee Baptist Mission (some 40 miles distant) which had been their home since October, 1833. On the Ottawa reserve there were only 79 Indian residents in June, 1837, but 170 more arrived in October (*see* p. 334).

Jotham Meeker's first teaching efforts were in the Ottawa language. By report, a school of 26 men, women, and children was opened in January, 1838—conducted by visits of the missionary to the homes of Indians who were interested (many were not). In February, 1838, Meeker went to the Shawnee Baptist Mission and printed 400 copies of an Ottawa First Book. This stimulated interest in reading, and in the summer he built a schoolhouse, where, on July 9, he commenced teaching *in English* (at the chief's request). His day school was conducted with some success. In February, 1839, Meeker reported that 17 Indians attended, but he averaged nine or ten students. Many Indians refused to send their children because the missionaries did not board and clothe them.

Ottawa Baptist Mission was moved, after the flood of 1844, to a site "back on to the hills" some five miles northeast of present Ottawa. Following Jotham Meeker's death in January, 1855—the mission was discontinued.

Ref: Jotham Meeker's "Diary"; *Baptist Missionary Magazine*, v. 18 (June, 1838), p. 140, v. 19 (May, 1839), p. 117, also, later issues; Spooner & Howland's *History of American Missions* . . . (1840), pp. 545, 546; *Report* of the Comm'r of Indian Affairs for 1837, p. 609; *KHC*, v. 8, pp. 472-475.

❧ At Shawnee Friends Mission a school was opened in June. (For construction of the mission buildings—in 1836—and other data, *see* p. 304.) The first superintendents were Moses Pearson and his wife Sarah (Pearson) Pearson, who came out in covered wagons, from Miami county, Ohio, with their five children (Rhoda, aged 12,

Mahala, Timothy, Ann, and three-year-old Joshua), in the late(?) spring. Mary H. Stenton (assistant matron) and Elias Newby (teacher) also came in 1837.

As reported in 1838, the Friends' school had 17 scholars, who were instructed in English, and fed and clothed by the mission. The Pearsons remained in "Kansas" for three years—their appointed time—and were succeeded in mid-1840 by Henry and Ann Harvey.

Ref: Isaac McCoy's *Annual Register* for 1838, p. 64; *KHC*, v. 8, pp. 267, 268; *The History of Miami County, Ohio* (Chicago, 1880), p. 849; W. W. Hinshaw's *Encyclopedia of American Quaker Genealogy*, Ann Arbor, Mich., v. 5 (1946), pp. 790, 819; Comm'r of Indian Affairs *Report*, 1840, pp. 150, 151. As noted hereafter, two sons were born to the Pearsons during their "Kansas" stay—one in 1837, the other in 1840.

❧ June-July.—As reported at St. Louis in late July, "Captain White's company" of Santa Fe traders recently had returned to Fayette, Mo., bringing between $80,000 and $100,000 in gold dust and silver bars. During the journey east this party had lost most of its mules. Presumably these traders crossed "Kansas" in June.

Ref: *Missouri Republican*, St. Louis, July 28, 1837 (as reprinted in Nebraska State Historical Society *Publications*, v. 20, p. 67).

❧ On the Shawnee reserve, by mid-year, a saw and grist mill had been completed, at a reported total cost of about $8,000. Michael Rice received a payment of $6,994.40 (from Capt. E. A. Hitchcock, handling disbursements for the St. Louis superintendency) for erecting this mill. (Rice, in 1833, had built a mill—costing less than half as much, apparently—for the Delaware Indians. *See* p. 239.)

Ref: OIA, Letters Received from St. Louis Superintendency (Hitchcock's disbursements for the half year ending September 30, 1837), National Archives Microcopy 234, Roll 751; Isaac McCoy's *Annual Register* for 1837, p. 27.

❧ About July 1 the third issue of Isaac McCoy's *Annual Register of Indian Affairs* (with a title-page date of May, 1837) was published at Shawnee Baptist Mission, by John G. Pratt, in a 1,500-copy edition. So far as known this was the first work printed by Pratt on the Shawanoe Mission Press (or, "Meeker press"). He had arrived on May 12.

Ref: McCoy's *Annual Register* . . . (as noted above); his *History of Baptist Indian Missions* (1840), p. 524; D. C. McMurtrie's and A. H. Allen's *Jotham Meeker* . . . (Chicago, 1930), p. 154.

❧ July 9.—Maj. Gen. Edmund P. Gaines arrived at Fort Leavenworth on an inspection trip. He subsequently reported: "the first Dragoons as drilled by Colonel [S. W.] Kearny are the best troops I have ever seen."

Ref: Clarke, *op. cit.*, p. 76.

❡ BORN: on July 15, at Shawnee Friends Mission, present Johnson county, Abram Pearson, son of the mission superintendent Moses Pearson and his wife Sarah. (*See* June annals entry.)

Ref: *The History of Miami County, Ohio* (1880), p. 849; W. W. Hinshaw's *Encyclopedia of American Quaker Genealogy,* v. 5, p. 819.

❡ In July and August the emigrant bands of united Pottawatomies, Chippewas, and Ottawas residing (since 1835 and 1836) across the Missouri from Fort Leavenworth in the "Platte Purchase," were removed (under the management of Maj. Gen. Edmund P. Gaines) to the Council Bluffs reserve (southwestern Iowa) set aside for them by the treaty of September 26, 1833.

Aboard the steamboat *Kansas,* Brig. Gen. Henry Atkinson, Col. S. W. Kearny, Dr. Edwin James (the Indians' newly appointed subagent), and some 100 Pottawatomie women, children, and invalids, arrived at the new location on July 28. A second group of Indians (about 75) reached the Council Bluffs on August 8, aboard the *Howard.* Meantime the main body traveled overland—up the left bank of the Missouri—and probably arrived before the end of August.

By November 842 more Pottawatomies had "removed themselves" from east of the Mississippi to this reserve; and on November 26 Lewis H. Sands "delivered" an additional 287 Indians. At the end of 1837 some 2,500 Pottawatomies were under the care of the Council Bluffs Subagency. By official report, up to 1840 a total of 2,734 had been removed there.

The united Pottawatomies, Chippewas, & Ottawas also were called the "Prairie Band of Pottawatomies." In 1847 they moved to "Kansas"—to the new Kansas river reserve for *all* of the Pottawatomies provided by the treaty of June 5, 1846.

Ref: Nebraska State Historical Society *Transactions,* Lincoln, v. 4, p. 184; *Missouri Argus,* St. Louis, August 8, 1837; *Iowa Journal of History and Politics,* Iowa City, v. 11, pp. 341-363; *Indiana Historical Collections,* Indianapolis, v. 26, pp. 405, 412, 423, 424, 457-462; *Nebraska History Magazine,* Lincoln, v. 18, pp. 5-9; *Report* of the Comm'r of Indian Affairs for 1840 (document No. 3, accompanying report); Grant Foreman's *The Last Trek of the Indians* (c1946), pp. 107-109.

❡ July 20-22.—Anthony L. Davis, head of the new Osage River Subagency, moved from the Fort Leavenworth vicinity (where he had been, since December, 1834, agent for the Pottawatomies squatting along the Missouri in that region) to the "Osage" (Marais des Cygnes) river country.

The "temporary" subagency (to which he had already moved his family) was at Wea Presbyterian Mission, on Wea creek (present Miami county). In May, 1838, Davis was of the opinion his residence had been purchased by the government from the missionaries, and wrote that he considered it eligible for use with $100 to $150 repair; and in his 1840 report the subagent stated his headquarters was still on the Wea lands—for lack of orders to erect buildings on the site selected in April, 1837, within the Pottawatomie reserve.

Ref: *Indiana Historical Collections,* v. 26, p. 419; A. L. Davis' letter of May 15, 1838 (cited under April 13, 1837, entry); A. L. Davis, report for 1839, in *Report* of the Comm'r of Indian Affairs for 1839.

❧ Late July and early August.—Aboard the American Fur Company's *St. Peters* (Bernard Pratte, Jr., captain), Count Francesco Arese (aged 32, from a noble family of Milan, Italy) journeyed up the Missouri from St. Louis to the Council Bluffs. (He was the only passenger not connected with the fur trade.)

"Fort Leavenworth," wrote tourist Arese, "is the last American post. It has a regiment of dragoons and artillery to keep the savages respectful. Some wretched barracks and a second-rate blockhouse is all there is to what is called the military establishment." Present at the fort "because it so happened that several chiefs of different tribes were . . . on their way to Washington to see the President," was "a big gathering of savages . . . all in their finest costumes."

A few hours later, above Fort Leavenworth, the *St. Peters* stopped "at a post of the American Fur Company and landed the boss [Laurence? Pensineau] of the [Kickapoos'] trading station . . . The boat was instantly flooded with savages, to whom tobacco and brandy[!] were given. They greeted the boss . . . affectionately, wringing his hand and calling him 'Papá, Papá.' They played cards with great enthusiasm and even passion, and remained on board very late that night; and three young Indian women remained on board all night . . . with the consent of the Kickapoo chief. . . .'"

The *St. Peters* reached the Council Bluffs "after 11 days on the Missouri." Arese, with two companions, subsequently traveled on horseback across present Minnesota; then, by canoe, and dug-out, made his way to Prairie du Chien; traversed Wisconsin (mostly in canoes); spent some time in the Great Lakes region; eventually reached Boston; and then returned to Italy.

Ref: Francesco Arese's *A Trip to the Prairies and in the Interior of North America* . . ., translated . . . by Andrew Evans (New York, 1934); *Mississippi Valley Historical Review,* Cedar Rapids, Iowa, v. 20 (December, 1933), pp. 381-399.

❧ Late in the summer the Pottawatomies residing on the Kickapoo reserve above Fort Leavenworth left that location and journeyed 70 miles southward to the "Osage" (Marais des Cygnes) river reserve which had been provided for the Pottawatomies of Indiana by the treaty of February 11, 1837. (*See* pp. 318, 319.)

Jotham Meeker reported that the first migrants arrived at the "Osage" on August 16, but indications are that most of them (681) made the journey in September. An abstract of Indian department expenditures for September 13 shows the following items relating to removing the Pottawatomies from Fort Leavenworth to "Osage" river: to Johnston Lykins $617.50 for his services as assistant agent, and $372 for aiding in the Indians' removal; to Joseph Barrette[?] $60 for "ferriage over Kansas river" of 552 Indians and their horses, etc.; to "Sacarocpy" [Sarcoxie—a Delaware] $16.12 for "ferriage over Kansas river" of 129 Indians and their horses, etc.; also, to Charles Johnson, William Mattingly, John P. Smith, William M. Chick, and Joseph "Barrette" (*i. e.*, Barnett), payments for "hire of a wagon" (two wagons in the case of Chick) in removing the Indians.

These Pottawatomies made their camps along the *south* side of Pottawatomie creek. According to Isaac McCoy and Subagent A. L. Davis, many of the Pottawatomies who migrated to the "Osage" river reserve *in 1837* were either "Kankakee" (Ill.) Indians, or "St. Joseph river" (Mich.) Indians, formerly enrolled in the Chicago Agency—and therefore not *Indiana* Pottawatomies.

On September 27, coming direct from east of the Mississippi, 53 Pottawatomies under the care of George Proffit, reached the Marais des Cygnes. This group left "Crooked creek" on August 23. According to George Winter (Indiana artist), Kee-wau-nay, O-ga-maus, and Nas-waw-kay were among these emigrants. Joseph Barron accompanied them. They moved slowly, Proffit being ill; and reached the destination in "Kansas" on *October 23* (by Winter's statement)! Nearly all this party returned to Indiana within a year, it is said. (And *see* pp. 337, 338 for November arrivals.)

Ref: Meeker "Diary," August 16, 1837, entry; 25th Cong., 3d Sess., *H. Doc. No. 174* (Serial 347), p. 59; *Indiana Historical Collections*, v. 26, pp. 405, 419-424, 459-461, 465, 466; *Report* of the Comm'r of Indian Affairs for 1837 (A. L. Davis' report, incorporated); *ibid.*, for 1840 (Document No. 3 accompanying report); Johnston Lykins' "Journal," April, 1839 (in KHi ms. division); also, the references cited for Pottawatomie Baptist Mission—*see* p. 336; *The Journals and Indian Paintings of George Winter, 1837-1839* (Indianapolis, 1948), p. 147.

❧ MARRIED: William Smith Donohoe and Eleanor McCoy, on August 22, at the home of the bride, near Westport, Mo., by her father the Rev. Isaac McCoy.

Ref. Jackson county, Mo., marriage records, v. 1, p. 119.

❧ August 30.—A Chippewa "exploring deputation" from Michigan (three chiefs of the Saginaw band, three from the Swan creek and Black river bands, their conductor, Albert J. Smith and attendants— 10 persons in all), accompanied by the Rev. Isaac McCoy, left Westport, Mo., to examine the country west and south, of the Ottawas' reserve—in present Franklin county—which McCoy (as agent for the government) had selected for the Chippewas' 8,320-acre reservation (promised under terms of the May 9, 1836, treaty).

[Conductor Smith's abstract of disbursements shows payment, on August 17, 1837, to the Steamboat Kansas of $20 "for self," and of $72 "for Indian chiefs," from St. Louis to Westport. Residents who supplied goods or services were: Daniel Yoacham (who boarded the party), merchants William M. Chick, and Parks & Findlay (who outfitted the deputation), and Thomas J. Colbert (who was paid for "Transportation of Indians from Westport to Independence" when the Chippewas started home). Notably, this abstract contains one of the early specific references to Westport as an outfitting point.]

On August 31 the deputation reached newly founded Ottawa Baptist Mission (on the Marais des Cygnes, near present Ottawa); and on September 3, after several days of exploring, was back at the mission, en route to Westport.

The Chippewas, and their aides, returned to St. Louis on the *Boonville*, boarding her at Independence, Mo., about September 9. By the end of the month they had reached their Michigan homes.

(In November, 1839, 62 of the Swan creek Chippewas came to "Kansas" to make their home in present Franklin county.)

Ref: 25th Cong., 3d Sess., *H. Doc. No. 174* (Serial 347), pp. 19-21 (for Smith's abstract of disbursements); *KHC,* v. 11, p. 314; Jotham Meeker's "Diary," August 31, September 3 and 4, 1837, entries; Isaac McCoy "letters" of September 6, 1837, in McCoy manuscripts.

❧ Between September 1 and November 8 the route subsequently known as the Fort Leavenworth-Fort Gibson military road was located and surveyed by a party made up of Col. Stephen W. Kearny, Capt. Nathan Boone, Lts. Philip Kearny and Philip R. Thompson, Charles Dimmock (civil engineer), Mr. Minor (his assistant), and Company H, First U. S. dragoons as escort.

On the exploratory journey southward, through what is now the eastern tier of Kansas counties (after leaving Fort Leavenworth on September 1), the line of march was never more than a few miles within the Indian country, and, on occasion, approached within yards of the Missouri boundary. In the latter part of September, the Kearny-Boone party arrived at short-lived Fort Coffee (on the Arkansas, about eight miles west of the state of Arkansas)—the chosen terminus for this middle section of the Western military road (*see* p. 311 for note on the July 2, 1836, frontier protection act).

The actual survey was made (by Dimmock) on the return trip, beginning at the Arkansas river, opposite Fort Coffee ("Okla.") on September 27. (Colonel Kearny left the party, and returned to Fort Leavenworth October 9—reassuming command of that post.) In his report of the survey (which was completed to Fort Leavenworth November 8) Dimmock commented on the extensive rolling prairies in the "Kansas" portion of the route—the 158 miles between Spring river (in present Cherokee county) and Fort Leavenworth. The streams to be forded he listed as "Spring river," "Pomme de Terre" [Cow? creek, Cherokee county], "Wildcat" [Drywood?], "Mermiton" [Marmaton], "Little Osage," "Cotton Wood [Mine?] creek," "Marias des Lygne" [Marais des Cygnes], "Blue" [Big Blue, Missouri tributary], and the "Kanzas."

(*See, also,* October 15, 1838, annals entry.)

Ref: *KHQ,* v. 11, pp. 115-121, also map *facing* p. 129. Fort Coffee (Okla.) was abandoned in the autumn of 1838.—*Ibid.,* p. 123; Fort Leavenworth post returns (microfilm in KHi); *Chronicles of Oklahoma,* v. 19 (December, 1941), p. 335; Otis E. Young's *The West of Philip St. George Cooke* . . . (Glendale, Cal., 1955), p. 92.

❧ September 7.—En route east from Oregon, missionary William H. Gray and two other men arrived at Fort Leavenworth, in a canoe (from Bellevue, ["Neb."]; left August 31). Gray "called on Mrs. Morgan, Major [former sutler Alexander G. Morgan] being absent . . . [and] also called on Capt. [Edwin V.] Sumner, . . . the Commanding Officer." (On the 8th, Gray continued downriver; boarded the *Boonville* when met on the Missouri; and reached St. Louis September 13.)

Gray's party, on setting out from the trappers' rendezvous (at Horse Creek) July 25, had numbered four whites, and five (or six) Indians (several of them Flatheads) who were in his charge. The result of Gray's foolhardiness in venturing overland with so small a group had been the massacre (on August 8, at Ash Hollow, by Sioux) of all the Indians entrusted to his care.

Ref: *Whitman College Quarterly*, June, 1913, issue reprint(?), for W. H. Gray's journal (quoted above); Bernard DeVoto's *Across the Wide Missouri* (c1947), pp. 329-332.

℃ September 18.—Lt. Thomas Swords (acting quartermaster) made a contract with J. B. Wells to prepare and sow in timothy seed, 100 acres of land near Fort Leavenworth; also a contract with Jesse Overton to prepare, sow in timothy seed, and fence in, by the 31st of October (1837), and the 31st of May (1838), 500 acres of prairie near Fort Leavenworth.

Ref: 25th Cong., 2d Sess., *Sen. Doc. 200* (Serial 316), pp. 352, 353, 360.

℃ September 27.—An exploring delegation of 18 to 20 New York Indians, conducted by the Rev. John F. Schermerhorn, of Utica, N. Y., left Westport, Mo., to examine a tract north of the Cherokee Neutral Lands and the Osage reserve.

This party first entered "Kansas" some 70 miles south of Westport—probably a little above the Linn-Bourbon county line of today; proceeded to tour the Little Osage river country, and some tributaries of the Neosho; visited the Osage Subagency; descended the Marmaton; crossed the Missouri line to Harmony; and by October 13 was back at Westport, en route East.

Subsequently, by treaty of January 15, 1838 (which was signed by all the groups of New York Indians—those who had emigrated to Wisconsin in the 1820's, as well as those residing in New York), a large rectangular reserve (1,824,000 acres) in the "Kansas" area described above, was assigned to these tribes. (The negotiations involved an exchange of 435,000 acres of the land in Wisconsin which had been given them by the treaty of 1831.) On June 11, 1838, the U. S. senate amended the treaty, but only part of the New York Indians signed the final document.

Though something like 200 New York Indians finally came out to the reserve —in 1846—only 32 received patents (for 320 acres each) provided by terms of the treaty, and none settled permanently in "Kansas."

After President Buchanan, in 1860, declared the vacant reserve public domain, open for settlement, the New York Indians filed suit for indemnity. In 1898 their claim was allowed.

Ref: John F. Schermerhorn letter of October 13, 1837 (in McCoy manuscripts; also Isaac McCoy letter of November 23, 1837, in *ibid.*; Felix S. Cohen's *Handbook of Federal Indian Law* . . . (Washington, 1942), p. 420; *KHC*, v. 8, pp. 83-85; Kappler, *op. cit.*, v. 2, pp. 502-512; 52d Cong., 1st Sess., *Senate Report No. 910* (Serial 2915), p. 5, 6. In *KHC*, v. 4, p. 301, John C. McCoy (in 1889) stated that he surveyed, *in 1837*, "a tract south of the Pottawatomies and north of Fort Scott [established in 1842] for the New York Indians. . . ."

℃ Late in September(?) some 100(?) Shawnee and Delaware men, who had been enlisted for six months' service in the war against the Seminoles, left "Kansas" for Florida. The leading Delaware chief —Nah-ko-min—was in this company, but the captain was Joseph Parks (one-quarter Indian; later Shawnee head chief). By one report about 80 of each nation went; however, Capt. Thomas Swords (AQM, Fort Leavenworth), on September 27, made a contract with Joseph White to transport 100 Indians, and the officers in command, from mouth of Kansas river to Jefferson Barracks, Mo.

Thirty Delawares (led by Captain Parks) took part in the battle near Lake Okeechobee, Fla., on December 25. (It was in this engagement that Missouri volunteer troops suffered heavy casualties, and lost their leader, Col. Richard Gentry.) Prior to the battle, the "greater part" of the Shawnees had been detached, and the rest had refused to accompany Col. Zachary Taylor "under the pretext that a number of them were sick, and that the remainder were without moccasins." It is said that all these Indians returned to "Kansas" safely in 1838.

Ref: Jotham Meeker's "Diary," October 6, 1837, entry; 25th Cong., 3d Sess., *H. Doc.* 94 (Serial 346), p. 54; Isaac McCoy letter of December 15, 1837 (published in *Indiana Historical Collections*, v. 26, p. 474); 25th Cong., 1st Sess., H. Doc. 27 (Serial 311); 25th Cong., 2d Sess., *Sen. Doc.* 227 (Serial 316); *KHC*, v. 10, p. 400; E. C. McReynolds' *The Seminoles* (Norman, c1957), pp. 193, 201; Isaac McCoy letter of July 1, 1839 (for item on Nah-ko-min). In the "John G. Pratt Collection" (in KHi div. division) among the Kansas Agency papers, 1851-1854, there are copies of muster rolls of Delaware volunteers who served in the Florida War; and in the same collection, among the Indian subagency Wyandot papers, in an 1851 packet, are lists of Shawnees and Delawares who served in the Florida War.

❡ October 6-20.—Conducted from Maumee, Ohio, by John McElvain, a party of 170 Ottawas arrived at Chouteau's Landing on the 6th, aboard the *St. Peters*. Ten wagons and teams, supplied (at $4 a day per team) by Westport merchant William M. Chick, then transported the Indians (between October 7 and 11) to the reserve, in present Franklin county, occupied by approximately 80 Ottawas who had come to "Kansas" in 1832 (*see* pp. 223, 224.)

The reserve assigned these new arrivals (the Roche de Boeuf and Wolf Rapids Ottawas) was both south, and west, of the tract already occupied; but Jotham Meeker, of the newly founded Ottawa Baptist Mission (near present Ottawa), wrote in his diary on October 20: "Our new Indians have just decided to settle near us." (In August, 1839, 108 more Ottawas came to "Kansas.")

Ref: Jotham Meeker's "Diary," October 6-20, entries; 25th Cong., 2d Sess., *Sen. Doc.* 200 (Serial 316), pp. 2-4; Isaac McCoy manuscripts, for McCoy's letter of September 30, 1837, and a September 22, 1837, letter by Disbursing Agent Criger; *KHC*, v. 13, pp. 373-375 (for Joseph B. King's article, which contains errors in dates, etc., but is, in general, correct); Grant Foreman's *Last Trek of the Indians*, p. 91.

❡ October 9.—The Rev. Learner B. Stateler and his bride Melinda (Purdom) Stateler arrived at Delaware Methodist Mission (present Wyandotte county)—*see* p. 210 for its 1832-1837 history— where the Rev. E. T. Peery and his family recently had resided.

Stateler first preached to the Indians on October 15. Subsequently he was occupied for some weeks in repairing the mission buildings. On January 4, 1838, he opened a school for Delaware children. (The Statelers were transferred to Shawnee Methodist Mission in 1840.)

Ref: E. J. Stanley's *Life of Rev. L. B. Stateler* (1907), p. 81, 87, 88, 104; *Christian Advocate and Journal*, v. 12 (February 16, 1838), p. 102 (for Thomas Johnson's report of December 27, 1837—wherein he notes that the Munsees who arrived in December, 1837, settled about three miles from the Delaware Methodist Mission); portraits of L. B. and Melinda Stateler are in *KHC*, v. 9, pp. 222, 223.

❡ October 11.—The Rev. Lorenzo Waugh (a single man) arrived at Shawnee Methodist Mission, to serve as assistant missionary. He lived with the Rev. Thomas Johnson family.

As he later recollected: "At the old Shawnee Mission [in Wyandotte county] then we had only a small farm, and all the mission buildings were poor and inconvenient." (Waugh left the Indian country in 1840. Besides teaching the Shawnees, he had also spent some months at the Kansa Methodist Mission assisting Missionary William Johnson.)

Ref: Lorenzo Waugh's *Autobiography* . . ., 2d edition (San Francisco, 1884), pp. 112, 117, 126, 134; *KHC*, v. 9, pp. 168, 226.

❡ MARRIED: the Rev. Nathan T. Shaler, and Annie Beauchemie (aged 17?, of Chippewa, Shawnee, French, and English ancestry), daughter of Mackinaw and Betsy (Rogers) Beauchemie, in the autumn, at, or near, Shawnee Methodist Mission (present Wyandotte county).

Ref: *KHC*, v. 16, p. 253 (for the Rev. E. T. Peery's statement concerning this marriage); *ibid.*, v. 9, p. 171n, and annals, p. 260 (for items on Mrs. Betsy Beauchemie, and another daughter). Nathan T. Shaler had arrived at Shawnee Mission in late 1836.—*KHC*, v. 9, p. 170. Annie Beauchemie had been educated at the mission.—*Ibid.*, pp. 171n and 211. She died in March, 1843.—*Ibid.*, v. 16, p. 253.

❡ MARRIED: Joseph Papin and "Kansas"-born Mary Josephine ("Josette") Gonville (daughter of the Frenchman Louis Gonville and a Kansa woman [who was either a daughter, or niece, of Chief White Plume]), on October 25, at "Chouteau's Church," in present Kansas City, Mo., by the Rev. Felix L. Verreydt, S. J. (*See, also,* p. 258.)

Ref: Frederick Chouteau's May 5, 1880, letter (in KHi ms. division); 37th Cong., 2d Sess., Sen. Ex. Doc. No. 58 (Serial 1122), p. 2; G. J. Garraghan's *The Jesuits of the Middle United States*, v. 1, pp. 95, 260 (where the bride's name is given as Mary "Cave"— doubtless because of difficulty in deciphering Verreydt's handwriting in the original *Kickapoo Register*. As early as 1833 a "J. Papin" was an employee of the American Fur Company; and a company trader whom Missionary William Gray described as "a Frenchman by the name of Joseph Papair" [Joseph Papin?], was credited by Gray as saving him from death at the hands of the Sioux in the summer of 1837.—De Voto, *op. cit.*, pp. 331, 332. James Beckwourth, in his reminiscences (*op. cit.*, pp. 394, 395) referred to a "Joseph Pappen," on the Missouri river in 1837.

❡ October 28.—Capt. Edwin V. Sumner, with Companies A and

B, First U. S. dragoons, left Fort Leavenworth on an expedition to the "Osage Country." (They returned November 20, or 21?)

Ref: Fort Leavenworth post returns (microfilm in KHi).

❧ Late in October Pottawatomie Baptist Mission was established when Robert Simerwell moved his family (wife and four children) from Shawnee Baptist Mission (their home since May, 1834—*see* p. 252) to a log cabin 50 miles southwest, near the newly arrived Indians.

The mission station, as constructed in 1839-1840, was on the south side of Pottawatomie creek, in southeastern Franklin county of today. On good evidence it appears the site was on the S. W. ¼ of Sec. 9, T. 19, R. 21 E., about two and a half miles above present Lane, and the ford known as "Dutch Henry's crossing." As described in October, 1840, the recently completed hewn-log mission buildings were: a story-and-a-half dwelling 32'x18', divided into two apartments above and below, with a stone chimney, shingle roof, and plank floor; a 16'x16' cookhouse, with a stone chimney; and a 20'x18' schoolroom, with three 12-light windows and one door. (It is said the Simerwells' original cabin was a little farther downstream.)

When Simerwell began visiting the Pottawatomie camps in January, 1838, almost everybody seemed anxious to be taught to read. But in the spring the Indians "commenced drinking," and later the "sickly season" arrived. Many Pottawatomies died; and all the Simerwells were ill. Following the arrival of more Indians in 1838, there was a movement of many Pottawatomies (beginning in March, 1839) to a settlement on Sugar creek (in present Linn county). In October, 1839, the missionary reported that a day school, begun in January for the Pottawatomie creek Indian youths and his own children, had been attended by nine to 14 Pottawatomies. This school was soon suspended. Simerwell subsequently took employment as a government blacksmith, in order that the Baptist Board in Boston might apply his salary for a minister at the mission. But no minister was sent. Jotham Meeker, of Ottawa Baptist Mission (about 14? miles northwest), had pastoral charge, for a time, beginning in May, 1840. A letter Jotham Meeker wrote February 24, 1842, stated: "At the Potawatomie Station Br. Simerwell still works in the smith shop—he occupies one end of the mission buildings, and Dr. Lykins the other. . . . Brn. Jones and Fuller and an old woman continue to be the only Potawatomie Ch[urch] members there."

In April, 1844, the Board in Boston "judged it expedient to suspend the station," and "dissolve their connexion with Mr. Simerwell." Four months later Robert and Fanny (Goodridge) Simerwell were appointed missionaries by the American Indian Mission Association (a new Baptist organization, headed by the Rev. Isaac McCoy, with headquarters in Louisville, Ky.). Under the A. I. M. A., Pottawatomie Baptist Mission was continued at the Pottawatomie creek location till 1848; and then was re-established in present Shawnee county after the Indians moved, in 1847 and 1848, to a reservation on the Kansas river.

Ref: Jotham Meeker's "Diary," particularly October 27, 1837, and May 4, 1840, entries; *Reports* of the Comm'r of Indian Affairs for 1837, 1839, 1840; Jotham Meeker letter, January,

1838 (in McCoy manuscripts); *Baptist Missionary Magazine*, v. 18 (June, 1838), p. 139, v. 19 (April, 1839), pp. 90, 91, v. 20 (June, 1840), p. 128, v. 23 (June, 1843), p. 140, v. 24 (July, 1844), p. 182; Johnston Lykins' "Journal," for April, 1839; Malin, *op. cit.*, pp. 714-717 (wherein Doctor Malin's thorough research for the history of "Dutch Henry's crossing," and vicinity, provides evidence of the Pottawatomie Baptist Mission location); Bessie E. Moore's "Life and Work of Robert Simerwell" (thesis, May, 1939), pp. 40-56; Spooner & Howland's *History of American Missions*, pp. 543, 544; Meeker collection, in KHi ms. division, for Meeker letter of 1842.

❡ About November 1 the Rev. Samuel M. and Eliza H. Irvin occupied a recently built log cabin on the Iowa reserve, above the mouth of Wolf creek (in present Doniphan county) and established in "Kansas" the Presbyterian mission for the Iowa Indians which had been founded, in 1835, across the river at the old Iowa Agency in the "Platte Purchase" of Missouri.

(On October 12 Irvin had written: "We have one building put up at the new station and as much hay as will support our cattle through the winter." The location for the cabin had been determined in mid-August—after Isaac McCoy surveyed the dividing line between the Iowas and the adjoining Sacs & Foxes of Missouri—*see* pp. 325, 326.)

Whereas the mission east of the Missouri had been for the Iowas only, the school at the new station (at the invitation of Subagent A. S. Hughes) was to include the Sacs & Foxes. Near the end of December (*see* p. 339), the Rev. William Hamilton and his wife joined the Irvins at the Iowa, Sac & Fox Presbyterian Mission. (To the missionaries it was the "Ioway and Sac Mission.")

In 1844 a decision was made to form a "manual-labor boarding-school." A three-story stone and brick building (containing 32 rooms) started in 1845 was completed in 1846. The site of this mission (the surviving portion of the original building is a state museum) is some two miles east of present Highland, within Sec. 24, T. 2, R. 19 E.

Ref: Presbyterian Historical Society, American Indian Missions correspondence (microfilm, KHi), for S. M. Irvin and Aurey Ballard's letter of August 12, 1837, S. M. Irvin's letters of May 16, and October 12, 1837, Eliza H. Irvin's letter of June 2, 1837, and Aurey Ballard's letter of November 20, 1837; *Reports* of the Comm'r of Indian Affairs, 1842-1861 (especially 1844-1847); *KHC*, v. 10, pp. 312-321; *KHQ*, v. 10, p. 348, v. 23, pp. 124, 125; and Spooner & Howland's *History of American Missions*, pp. 724, 725.

❡ In the middle of November, To-pen-e-bee (or, To-pin-a-bee)— the *principal chief of the Pottawatomie nation,* and 164 of his people, arrived in "Kansas" to settle on the "Osage" (Marais des Cygnes) river reserve. They were from St. Joseph river in Michigan.

Under the superintendence of Lewis H. Sands, and conducted by Capt. Robert H. McCabe, nearly 500 Pottawatomies from Michigan and Illinois had started overland in September—crossing the Mississippi at Quincy, Ill., beginning September 24. The larger number (287) of these emigrants went to the Council Bluffs (Iowa) reserve; but through the efforts of Luther Rice (part Pottawatomie, whose family was in the party), Moses H. Scott (assistant emigrant agent), and Isaac McCoy, Chief To-pen-e-bee and his followers diverged from the route to Council Bluffs at a point about 40 miles above Westport, Mo., and came down to the Marais des Cygnes, and the settlement on Pottawatomie creek (*see* pp. 330, 331).

With this accession, the total Pottawatomie population in the Osage River Subagency at the end of the year was between 850 and 900.

Ref: Grant Foreman's *The Last Trek of the Indians*, pp. 107, 108; *Indiana Historical Collections*, v. 26, pp. 433, 438, 439, 457-462; 25th Cong., 2d Sess., *Sen. Doc. 395* (Serial 318), p. 2; McCoy manuscripts (A. L. Davis' letter of January 22, 1839).

❦ During mid-November Bishop Jackson Kemper, the Protestant Episcopal Church's "missionary bishop of the Northwest," made an overland tour of Missouri river towns, as far as Westport, and also journeyed to Fort Leavenworth to discuss with Col. S. W. Kearny the need for a chaplain there. (He was accompanied from Fayette, Mo., by the Rev. Mr. Peake.)

As a result of this brief visit—the first by Episcopalian clergymen to the post—a minister of Bishop Kemper's church was appointed, in 1838, as Fort Leavenworth's first chaplain. (*See* December 17, 1838, annals.)

Ref: *KHC*, v. 16, p. 355; *Historical Magazine of the Protestant Episcopal Church*, Richmond, Va., v. 4 (September, 1935), pp. 198, 199; John Wilson's letter of November 13, 1837, in McCoy manuscripts.

❦ November 19.—The steamboat *Boonville*, en route to Fort Leavenworth (and laden principally with stores for that post) hit a snag a few miles above Independence, Mo., and went down—a total loss.

Ref: *Missouri Republican*, St. Louis, November 28, 1837, as reprinted in Nebraska State Historical Society *Publications*, v. 20, p. 69; the Rev. William Hamilton's November 20, 1837, letter (in Presbyterian Historical Society, American Indian Missions correspondence—microfilm KHi).

❦ December.—Accompanied by the Rev. Jesse Vogler, Moravian (United Brethren) missionary, John Kilbuck's party of Munsee (or, Christian) Indians—72 persons in all—arrived at the "mouth of Kansas river" early(?) in the month, aboard the *St. Peters*. By the end of December, these Indians, and their missionary, were established on the reserve of the Delawares (kindred of the Munsees) at a site some eight miles above the Kaw's mouth, and north of the river. Their settlement—or the Munsee Moravian Mission in its midst—was called "Westfield." (The location: at, and near present Muncie, Wyandotte co., in Sections 14, 15, and 16(?) of T. 11, R. 24 E.)

More Munsees arrived, in 1839, with some Stockbridge Indians. The Rev. J. Christopher Micksch (and wife) succeeded Vogler at the Moravian mission; and after Micksch's death, in 1845, other missionaries came. Although "Westfield" was within that part of the Delawares' reservation which they granted to the Wyandot Indians late in 1843, the Munsees continued to live there till about the end of 1853. (The Wyandots finally requested them to move.) By the Delaware treaty of May 6, 1854, the Munsees were granted four sections of land located about three miles below present Leavenworth— land now occupied by the Wadsworth veterans' facility and Mount Muncie cemetery. They lived at "Shekomeko" (as the new settlement, or the Moravian mission, was called) for only four years (1854-1858); then sold the reserve; confederated with the Swan creek Chippewas who came to "Kansas" in October, 1839; and moved, as did their missionaries, to present Franklin county. The Munsee Moravian Mission, which began in (or, was transferred from Canada to) "Kansas" in 1837, continued in operation till 1905.

Ref: OIA, Letters Received from SIA, St. Louis (Microcopy 234, Roll 751—National Archives), William Clark's abstract of requisitions for 1837 (item for December 4—$432 for transportation of John Kilbuck's party of "72 Delawares from Canada" on the *St. Peters*); *Baptist Missionary Magazine*, v. 18 (June, 1838), p. 139; E. J. Stanley's *Life of Rev. L. B. Stateler* (1907), p. 87; KHC, v. 11, pp. 314, 317-323; Henry R. Schoolcraft's *Personal Memoirs* . . . (Philadelphia, 1851), pp. 564, 565; *Reports*, of the Comm'r of Indian Affairs, especially 1840, 1844, 1845; KHC, v. 8, pp. 85, 86; KHQ, v. 21, pp. 454, 459, 485 (for "Shekomeko"). A Munsee[?] burial place is shown on the land plats of the 1850's in Sec. 16, T. 11 S., R. 24 E. *The History of Jackson County Missouri* . . . (Kansas City, Mo., 1881), p. 684, states: "At this time [1855] Isaiah Walker [Wyandot Indian] . . . lived in the old Moravian Mission House . . . at Muncie town."

❬ MARRIED: John Calvin McCoy and Virginia Chick (daughter of William M. and Ann Eliza Chick), on December—(?), at Westport, Mo., by the Rev. Isaac McCoy (father of the groom).

(The William M. Chick family had moved to Westport from Howard county, Mo., in 1836 [*see* p. 300]. Earlier, in 1834, Mary Jane Chick [older sister of Virginia] had married the Rev. William Johnson, missionary to the Shawnees and the Kansa.)

Ref: *The Annals of Kansas City*, Kansas City, Mo., v. 1 (October, 1924), p. 467; KHC, v. 9, p. 178n. No exact date of this marriage has been located. Apparently it was not recorded at the Jackson county, Mo., courthouse though other McCoy marriages are to be found at Independence, Mo.

❬ On December 28 the Rev. William Hamilton, afoot, and his wife Julia Ann N. (McGiffin) Hamilton, on a mule, crossed the Missouri on the ice from Joseph Robidoux's trading post (now St. Joseph, Mo.) and proceeded cross-country (through present Doniphan county) towards the new home of the Iowa, Sac & Fox Presbyterian Mission 25 miles to the northwest, above Wolf creek.

With them, on a pony, were two small girls (one? an Indian) from "Mr. [Aurey] Ballard's family." (The Ballards still occupied the former Iowa mission station [founded 1835] at the old Iowa Agency east of the Missouri, some nine miles below the Robidoux post.)

Late in the afternoon of December 29, after a night out on the prairie, and some hardships, these travelers reached their destination—the mission cabin occupied (since November—*see* p. 337) by the Rev. Samuel M. and Eliza T. Irvin.

The Hamiltons remained in "Kansas" as missionaries to the Iowa and Sac & Fox Indians till 1853. Of five daughters born to them during the 16-year interval, four were living when the family removed to "Nebraska."

Ref: Presbyterian Historical Society, American Indian Missions correspondence (microfilm, KHi), for Hamilton's November 20, 1837, and September 29, 1852, letters; Nebraska State Historical Society *Transactions*, v. 1, pp. 60-73.

❦ John Treat Irving, Jr.'s *The Hunters of the Prairie, or the Hawk Chief. A Tale of the Indian Country,* was published at London in 1837. The locale of the novel was "Wolf Hill" [Fort Leavenworth], and the frontier to the west and north (the country of the Kansa, Pawnees, Otoes, Sioux, and Omahas)—a region which the author had visited in 1833.

In the introduction to this work of fiction, young Irving wrote: "The tract of country . . . is a wild and luxuriant region of prairies, glowing with gorgeous flowers and rich herbage, and here and there intersected by small rivers of crystal waters, bordered by groves of lofty trees. It is, in truth, a fairy-land, and fitted for wild adventure." The plot, concerning hunters, Indians, and mounted rangers, was an implausible adventure tale.

Ref: J. T. Irving, Jr.'s *The Hunters of the Prairie* . . . (London, R. Bentley, 1837).

❦ Employed in "Kansas" by the Indian Department during all, or part of the year 1837 were the following persons:

Fort Leavenworth Agency—*Agent* Richard W. Cummins; *Interpreters* Henry Tiblow (appointed May 14, 1837), and Clement Lessert (appointed July 15, 1837); *Gun and blacksmiths* David Shahan (for Shawnees), William Donalson (for Shawnees), John P. Smith (for Kickapoos), Nelson A. Warren (for Kansa), and William F. Newton (for Delawares); *Assistant gun and blacksmiths* Paschal Fish (for Delawares), John Bluejacket (for Shawnees), William V. Smith (for Kickapoos), Silas Dougherty (for Kickapoos?), John M. Owen (for Kansa), William Pechalker (for Kansa), and Charles Fish (for Kansa); *Farmer* Cephas Case (for Kansa?); *Teachers* the Rev. J. C. Berryman, John D. Swallows, and David Kinnear (all for the Kickapoos), Henry Rennick (for Delawares); *Millers* James and John Allen (for Delawares and Shawnees).

Great Nemahaw Subagency—Subagent Andrew S. Hughes; *Interpreters* Jeffrey Dorney (for Iowas), and Nimrod Henderson (for Sacs & Foxes); *Gun and blacksmiths* James Duncan (for Iowas), James Gilmore (for Sacs & Foxes); *Assistant gun and blacksmiths* Joseph H. Ficklin (for Iowas), Madison Gilmore (for Sacs & Foxes); *Farmers* William Duncan (for Iowas), and Leonard Searcy (for Sacs & Foxes).

Osage [Marais des Cygnes] River Subagency—*Subagent* Anthony L. Davis (appointed April 28); *Interpreters* Francis Le Vallier, and John T. Jones (paid for December only); *Gun and blacksmiths* William Carlisle, and Perry G. Crafton (assistant).

Osage Subagency—*Subagent* Paul Ligueste Chouteau; *Interpreter* Baptiste Mongrain; *Blacksmiths* Etienne Brant and Louison Brequier (assistant).

Ref: 25th Cong., 2d Sess., *H. Doc. No. 135* (Serial 326); 25th Cong., 2d Sess., *H. Doc. No. 362* (Serial 330), pp. 84, 86, 87; 25th Cong., 3d Sess., *H. Doc. No. 174* (Serial 347), pp. 58-60.

1838

❡ Robert Polke (recently of Indiana) opened a trading house for the Pottawatomies (on Pottawatomie creek, about where present Lane, Franklin county is today) in the latter part of 1837, but no reference earlier than the January 3, 1838, diary entry of the Ottawas' missionary Jotham Meeker has been located. He wrote: "Visit Quaquatau [Qui-qui-to, Pottawatomie chief], do some business at Mr. Polks ["Robert Polke & Co."] and ride [12 miles] home. . . ."

(Subagent A. L. Davis had met Polke—a brother-in-law of Isaac McCoy—in the spring of 1837 and promised him a trading license when the Pottawatomies removed to the Marais des Cygnes country.)

In a July, 1838, journal entry, McCoy recorded that on July 21 he took his wife "to Mr. Polke's among the Putawatomies," after a journey from Westport, Mo., and overnight stop at Davis' "Agency among the Weas. . . ." (Reminiscing, in 1879, John C. McCoy stated that "Robert Polk and Moses H. Scott, traders among the Pottawatomies . . . [in the 1830's] broke and put in cultivation a large field in the valley of Pottawatomie creek, near Osawatomie, which they cultivated for several years . . . [with indifferent success].") It appears that W. W. Cleghorn was also trading at Pottawatomie creek, as early as 1839.

Robert Polke was still living on Pottawatomie creek at the time of his death in 1843. Apparently he, his wife Elizabeth (Widener) Polke (and some? of their children) had been "Kansas" residents during the intervening years. His oldest son Thomas W. Polke (about 23 in 1838) probably was associated with the trading house from the beginning; and his second son, John W. Polke (about 18 in 1838) later(?) became a trader.

Ref: Jotham Meeker's "Diary," in Kansas State Historical Society (KHi) ms. div., January 3, 1838, and occasional subsequent entries, also May 26, 1843 (for Polke's death); Isaac McCoy's "Journal," in KHi ms. div., as noted above; *Indiana Historical Collections*, Indianapolis, v. 26, pp. 362, 398; 26th Cong., 1st Sess., *H. Doc. No. 173* (Serial 366), p. 93 (for an August 25, 1839, item on "Robert Polke & Co.," and mention of "W. Cleghorne"); 27th Cong., 2d Sess., *H. Doc. No. 164* (Serial 403), p. 97; *Vital Historical Records of Jackson County, Missouri,* compiled by the Kansas City chapter, D. A. R. (c1934), p. 415 (Polke burials in McCoy cemetery); *Indiana Magazine of History,* Bloomington, v. 10 (March, 1914), pp. 86 and 107 (for biographical data on Robert Polke and family). Kansas City (Mo.) *Journal,* February 6, 1879 (or, "Kansas Reminiscences," clipping volume in KHi library) for John C. McCoy's statement. The Polkes are not in the 1840 U. S. census of Jackson county, Mo., but Elizabeth Polke (Robert's widow), and five sons, are listed in the 1850 census under Jackson county, Mo. (These sons were: Thomas W., John W., Oliver H. Perry, Charles, and Robert T.; Robert Polke's only daughter, Mary A., married Pierre Menard Chouteau, son of Francis G. Chouteau, in 1849). A "Moses G. Scott" is listed in the 1850 U. S. census of Jackson county, Mo. "Mr. Cleghorn," of Pottawatomie creek, is mentioned in Meeker's "Diary," under date of December 26, 1840.

❡ Born: on January 15, at Shawnee Methodist Mission (present Wyandotte county), Mary Cummins Johnson, daughter of the Rev. Thomas and Sarah T. (Davis) Johnson.

Ref: *KHC,* v. 12, p. xii; or, 15th *Biennial Report* of the Kansas State Historical Society, p. 35. (This infant died two months later—on March 19.)

❆ January.—The Rev. Christian Hoecken (of Kickapoo Catholic Mission), after a difficult eight-day, 80-mile winter journey, arrived at Pottawatomie creek (near the present Miami-Franklin county line) on his first visit to the Pottawatomie Indians. He remained for "about a fortnight" as guest of the chief "Nesfwawke" (Naswaw-kee) and his band of Catholic Indians (formerly of Indiana).

On January 30 Father Hoecken performed marriage ceremonies for two Pottawatomie couples. Both "brides" were daughters of "Nesfwawke." These marriages (of Wawiakächi to Josette, and Chachäpäki to Wawasemokwe) are the earliest of record among the Pottawatomies of the Marais des Cygnes country. They were, it appears, ceremonies revalidating irregular marriages.

Ref: Christian Hoecken's "Diary," as published in T. H. Kinsella's . . . *The History of Our Cradle Land* . . . (Kansas City, 1921), pp. 225, 226; G. J. Garraghan's *The Jesuits of the Middle United States* . . . (New York, 1938), v. 1, pp. 190, 191, and 195. In Isaac McCoy's *Annual Register* for 1838, p. 59, the chief's name is given as "Naswaugee." The April 22, 1836, Pottawatomie treaty "signature" is "Nas-waw-kee."

❆ January-February.—Smallpox was prevalent among the Pawnees. (*See* p. 324.) It had been transmitted first to the Pawnee Loups by captives (some 20 women and children, most of whom succumbed to the disease) and plunder taken in a winter battle with the Sioux. "Multitudes" of Pawnee children died as smallpox spread to the other villages. According to Missionary John Dunbar, the mortality among the adults was not so great. The victims were chiefly those persons born since the 1831 epidemic.

The Pawnee Loups, in order to "retrieve their good fortune," resorted to a custom for which this Pawnee band was notorious, killing one of the remaining Sioux prisoners (a 14-year-old girl) in a human sacrifice rite. "The chiefs of the other bands refused to witness the bloody spectacle though specially invited to be present." This incident occurred on February 22.

Ref: *KHC*, v. 14, pp. 630-632, 640; Isaac McCoy's *Annual Register* for 1838, pp. 22-24; Henry R. Schoolcraft's *Personal Memoirs* . . . (Philadelphia, 1851), p. 614; John B. Dunbar's *The Pawnee Indians, A Sketch* (reprint from *Magazine of American History*).

❆ BORN: on February 10, at Kickapoo Methodist Mission (present Leavenworth county), Emily Greene Berryman, daughter of the Rev. Jerome C. and Sarah C. (Cessna) Berryman.

Ref: 15th *Biennial Report* of the Kansas State Historical Society, p. 35.

❆ February 15.—The "fast running St. Peters" (the steamboat which in 1836 and 1837 had carried American Fur Company employees and supplies to the upper river trading posts, and brought back fur returns) was advertised to leave for Fort Leavenworth "as soon as the navigation will permit," and to "run as a regular packet in the Missouri trade" during the ensuing season.

On October 11 the *Missouri Republican*, St. Louis, reported the return (on

October 9 or 10) of the *St. Peters*—perhaps completing her last run of 1838 on the Missouri. This boat was also in service during 1839.

Ref: Nebraska State Historical Society *Publications*, Lincoln, v. 20, pp. 70, 86.

❰ March 23.—In an altercation between some Missourians and a party of Osages (over Indian depredations on livestock), Nathaniel B. Dodge, Jr., aged 30, was killed, another white man was wounded; and the Osages had two men killed and one wounded. This border incident perhaps occurred in Bourbon county of today.

Ref: Isaac McCoy manuscripts, in a McCoy "document" of 1839, labeled "Remarks to aid Genl Tipton in speaking on Ind Affs. . . ."; *History of Vernon County, Missouri* . . . (St. Louis, 1887), p. 157. A photograph of Dodge's tombstone appeared in the Kansas City (Mo.) *Star*, June 27, 1970. It is stated that he was the first person "to be buried at Little Osage, later known as Balltown" (in Vernon county, Mo., "just west of Horton").

❰ Late in March Parks & Findlay (Joseph Parks, prominent member of the Shawnee nation; and James Findlay, of Jackson county, Mo.) erected a trading house near the Ottawa Indian settlements (present Franklin county) and within a few miles of Ottawa Baptist Mission. Missionary Jotham Meeker assisted in the "raising" of this "store house" on March 29.

(On September 8 Meeker noted in his diary: "Visit Mr. Findlay who arrived with his goods on yesterday at his Post." On December 25 he "Attended the Ottawa [annuity] payment at Findlay's store. . . . The Agent [Anthony L. Davis] and Paymaster [Dr. John C. Reynolds] . . . [left] at sunset.")

Ref: Jotham Meeker's "Diary," entries of February 23, March 29, September 8, 21, December 25, 1838, January 19, 1839 (and subsequent entries). In the 1850 U. S. census of Jackson county, Mo., James Findlay is listed as aged 34. He was about 22, apparently, in 1838. *See, also,* June 16, 1838, annals entry.

❰ In late March(?)—taking advantage of an early break-up of ice in the Missouri—the American Fur Company's new steamboat *Antelope* passed along the "Kansas" shore, en route to the upper river trading posts. Trader Charles Larpenteur and Robert Christy (coming down from Fort Union in a canoe, with two oarsmen) met the steamboat at the Platte's mouth some time in April, apparently.

The *Antelope* returned in mid-July. On arrival (July 16) at St. Louis, it was reported that most of the 1,000 packs she brought were buffalo robes; and that the more valuable furs were coming down in Mackinaw boats.

Ref: Charles Larpenteur's *Forty Years a Fur Trader* . . . (New York, 1898), v. 1, p. 136; Nebraska State Historical Society *Publications*, v. 20, p. 78.

❰ April 3.—Joseph V. Hamilton, sutler (since 1835) at Fort Leavenworth, was also appointed postmaster, succeeding Alexander G. Morgan (who had been Hamilton's predecessor as sutler).

See, also, June 27, 1839, entry.
Ref: *KHC,* v. 1-2, p. 255.

❡ DIED: Francis Gesseau Chouteau, on April 18, at his farm on the Missouri's right bank, two to three miles below the Kaw's mouth, in present Kansas City, Mo. (*See* pp. 131, 132, for his settlement there.) He was 41 years old, and died suddenly. Notably, his death occurred at a time when the American Fur Company's caravan was organizing in the Westport and Chouteau's landing area. *See* next entry.

Francis G. Chouteau (son of Pierre Chouteau, Sr.) had entered the fur trade about 1816 (*see* p. 76). At the time of his death, "Chouteau's Landing" (on the river front of his property) was at the height of its prominence as a shipping point on the Missouri. This *lower* landing (where his warehouses served as a base for American Fur Company—or, Pierre Chouteau, Jr., and Company—operations) was the steamboat port generally used for traffic and commerce bound to Westport, Mo., or the Indian Country beyond. The *upper,* or "Westport Landing,"—some two miles above, near the Kaw's mouth—was, as yet, the lesser-used shipping point.

The following quotations (from a sequence of letters Sup't Joshua Pilcher wrote Subagent A. L. Davis in the latter part of 1839) show that Cyprian Chouteau (younger brother of Francis G., whose own trading place was on the Kansas river, a few miles above its mouth, in present Wyandotte county) took over the operations at Chouteau's Landing. Pilcher, on September 9, wrote: [about goods for the Pottawatomies] "which I wished you to be prepared to receive by the 13th at Chouteaus landing . . ."; and on September 25: "I will ship the property . . . and have it consigned to Mr. Ciprien Chouteau's landing . . ."; and on November 4: "the property . . . was shipped on board the *Pizarro,* and Mr. Chouteau, being absent, it was taken to the upper [Westport] landing, and placed in charge of Mr. [Thomas A.] *Smart.* . . ."

Ref: The following information was supplied to this compiler by James Anderson, historian of The Native Sons of Kansas City, Mo., and his help is acknowledged with gratitude. There is extant a Bible inscribed "To Delia from her Grandma" [*i. e.,* to Odille Chouteau from Mme. Berenice Chouteau (widow of Francis G. Chouteau)] which is at the Boatman's Bank, St. Louis. On a page in this Bible are Chouteau family vital records, apparently recorded there by Mme. Berenice Chouteau; and therein the death date for Francis G. Chouteau is entered as April 18, 1838. Also, the *Missouri Saturday News,* St. Louis, of April 28, 1838 (in Mercantile Library, St. Louis, Mo.), reported the sudden death (on an April day unspecified) of "Mr. Francis Chouteau" at the "mouth of the Kansas river," and stated that his remains had been brought to St. Louis "on Tuesday last [*i. e.,* April 24] and interred in the Catholic burying grounds." This tends to corroborate the April 18 death date. Sup't Joshua Pilcher's letters, noted above, are to be found in Superintendency of Indian Affairs (SIA), St. Louis, "Records," v. 7, typed copy, pp. 44, 46, and 55.

❡ April 22-28.—Andrew Drips headed the American Fur Company's caravan which left Westport, Mo., on Sunday, the 22d, for the Rocky mountains. Moses ("Black") Harris was his lieutenant; additionally there were perhaps 45 company employees; and an outfit of 17 carts and some 200 horses and mules.

With the caravan were Capt. William Drummond Stewart (making his fourth trip West) and party of five(?) which included William Clark's son William Preston Clark and step-son John Radford (Stewart and Clark each had a wagon); also, Swiss-born John Augustus Sutter (who would become prominent in California's development after his settlement there in 1839), and a friend named "Welter," or "Wetler?"

By April 27 (having followed a section of the Santa Fe trail and the general pathway up the south side of the Kansas river—across present Johnson, Douglas, and Shawnee counties—soon to be known as the "Oregon trail") the American Fur Company caravan reached a point of timber on the Kansas river, *above(?) present Topeka*, and encamped. At that place (*apparently for the first time*) the crossing would be made, after the arrival of a company flatboat then on its way upriver with supplies. (For crossing apparently used on the 1837 journey, *see* p. 323.)

On April 28 a party of missionaries, Oregon-bound, reached the camp of Drips and party, to travel in company as far as the Rocky mountain rendezvous. (*See, also,* following entries.)

Ref: Oregon Pioneer Association *Transactions*, Portland, 1889, pp. 54-88 (for Mrs. Myra F. Eell's "Journal"); C. M. Drury, editor, *First White Women Over the Rockies, op. cit.,* v. 2 (contains diaries of Mrs. Mary Walker and Mrs. Myra F. Eells) and v. 3 (contains Mrs. Sarah Smith's diary, and other documents); *Pacific Northwest Quarterly*, Seattle, v. 29 (1938), pp. 277-282 (for W. H. Gray's "Journal"); C. M. Drury, editor, *The Diaries and Letters of Henry H. Spalding and Asa Bowen Smith Relating to the Nez Perce Mission 1838-1842* (Glendale, Calif., 1958), pp. 43-79; Ruth Karr McKee's *Mary Richardson Walker, Her Book* (Caldwell, Ida., 1945), pp. 140-157; C. M. Drury's *Elkanah and Mary Walker* . . . (Caldwell, Ida., 1940), pp. 67-95; Cornelius Rogers' letter of July 2, 1838 (microfilm, KHi); J. Cecil Alter's *Jim Bridger* (Norman Okla., c1962), p. 182 (for names of William Clark's son and stepson; J. P. Zollinger's *Sutter, The Man and His Empire* (New York, 1939), pp. 26-38, 41, 345; S. G. Gudde's *Sutter's Own Story* . . . (New York, 1936), pp. 11, 12; Myron Eell's *Father Eells* . . . (Boston, c1894); "Personal Reminiscences of General John Augustus Sutter" (in Bancroft Library), typed copy, courtesy of Dale L. Morgan; Kansas City, (Mo.) *Journal*, January 23 and 30, 1879, or, "Kansas Reminiscences," clipping volume, in KHi library, for John C. McCoy's statements on Sutter.

❡ April 23-28.—Nine missionaries (four couples, and a single man) left Westport, Mo., on Monday, the 23d, to begin an overland journey to the Oregon country (where they would serve as re-enforcements for the Indian mission sponsored by the American Board of Comm'rs for Foreign Missions). They were: William H. Gray (who had gone to "Oregon" in 1836, and returned in 1837), his bride Mary A. (Dix) Gray, the Rev. Cushing Eells, his bride Myra (Fairbanks) Eells, the Rev. Asa B. Smith, his bride Sarah G. (White) Smith, the Rev. Elkanah B. Walker, his bride Mary (Richardson) Walker, and Cornelius Rogers (bachelor). Their companion, and guide, on the first stage of the journey was Dr. J. Andrew Chute, of Westport. *The four women in this party were the first white females to cross "Kansas" by the Oregon trail pathway.* (Compare with the route which Narcissa Whitman and Eliza Spalding traveled in May, 1836—*see* p. 306.)

(The Eells, Smiths, Walkers, and Rogers had debarked at Independence Landing Mo., on April 15, from the steamboat *Howard;* the Grays had reached Independence a few days earlier. At this town they outfitted; then moved 12 miles to Westport, where the American Fur Company caravan was organizing. There they hired mountain man John Stevens, as their packer. At Westport, Mary Walker and Mary Gray were guests at Isaac McCoy's home; the others stayed in quarters Doctor Chute found for them.)

At the start the missionaries had 25 horses and mules, 12 horned cattle (including two fresh milch cows), and a light one-horse wagon. The available journals (of Gray, Smith, Myra Eells, and the Walkers) provide detailed information of their journey across present Johnson, Douglas, and Shawnee counties; and make it clear that they traveled nearly 100 miles to reach the Kansas river crossing (just above present Topeka) where the American Fur Company caravan was encamped. (By a direct route this would have been little more than 70 miles.)

From Westport, on the 23d, their course was south of West—towards the Santa Fe road (which they would follow for a time). According to the journal of William H. Gray (whose log is used here because he was the experienced traveler in the party) their first day's journey was *eight miles*—to "Sapling Grove," where a little stream ran northwest into the Big Blue of Missouri.

On April 24, after 25 *miles* of prairie travel, their night's camp was on "a little stream called Brush Creek" [headwaters of Bull creek]. (Myra Eells wrote that it was "one of the head branches of the Osage river.")

After eight miles of travel on the 25th, they "proceeded onto a beautiful stream called the WaKorusah from a root found in abundance on its banks made use of for food by the Natives," according to Gray. [There are several versions of the meaning of "Wakarusa."] Late in the day they crossed this stream. (Smith recorded: "Had one small river to cross just before we encamped wh. we forded without any difficulty.") They had traveled 20 *miles*.

On the 26th they "proceeded over high rolling prairie . . . on the top of the divide between the waters of the Wakerusah and the Kansas . . ." (Gray's journal), and camped on the open prairie, after a *20-mile* journey.

They traveled 17 *miles* on the 27th, and (according to Gray) camped on the west bank of a "stream running into the Kansas" [the Shunganunga, or a branch] at a spot "about 9 miles East of the Kansas Village." [Hard Chief's? prominently located village in Dover township, Shawnee co.—*see* p. 167.] During the night three of their best horses disappeared—presumably stolen by Kansa Indians.

On April 28 they "proceeded about 7 miles do [due] North" to the Kansas river where they "found the Fur Co. encamped on its South bank in a point of timber . . ." (Gray's journal).

Gray's "distances" total 97 miles. (By the estimates of two others in his party, the journal to the Kansas crossing, from Westport, was slightly over 100 miles.) If Gray's statements can be taken literally (as to traveling *due* north to the river after camping "about 9 miles" east of the Kansa village), the caravan crossed the Kansas just above present Topeka. But, *see* annals entry for the American Fur Company party of (May) 1839.

Ref: Same as for preceding entry. *See, also,* preceding entry, and entries of April 28 and April 29.

❡ April 28(?)—The American Fur Company's supply-carrying
flatboat, cordelled up the Kansas river to the overland caravan's
camp (above present Topeka), made rendezvous late on the 28th
(or early on the 29th?). (*See* preceding entry.)

In 1906—nearly 70 years after the event—Joseph S. Chick (aged nine in
April, 1838) wrote: "In 1838 I was visiting my sister, Mrs. William Johnson
. . . [at the Kansa Methodist Mission a few miles above the caravan's
camp] when the Chouteaus [about April 30] brought a 'Periogue' to the
mouth of Mission Creek [where Frederick Chouteau had his trading post—*see*
p. 212]. Everybody living near there, whites and Indians, went to see it."
In an interview (1908) Chick stated: "Chouteau's pirogue was cordelled up
the Kaw river. It had a plank deck. The goods were all down in the hold.
There was no awning over the boat." Chick (in 1906) also wrote: "I have
no recollection of any keel boats on the Kansas river. The Chouteaus did use
pirogues on both the Missouri and Kansas."

However, Frederick Chouteau stated (*see KHC,* v. 8, p. 428) that *keelboats*
were used for the Chouteaus' trading activities on the Kansas. He described
them as "ribmade boats, shaped like the hull of a steamboat, and decked over.
They were about eight or ten feet across the deck and five or six feet deep
below deck. . . ." Chick and Chouteau seem to describe the same type
of craft, but Chick called them *pirogues,* and Chouteau called them *keelboats.*

Ref: *See* April 22-28, and April 23-28 entries; and Joseph S. Chick's letter of May 3,
1906, and interview of October 19, 1908 (in KHi ms. division).

❡ On Sunday, April 29, the rendezvous-bound American Fur Company caravan and the Oregon-bound missionary party crossed the
Kansas river not far above present Topeka. The baggage was
ferried on the Company's flatboat, and the animals swam. After
camping for the night on the north bank, the cavalcade (stretching
for nearly half a mile) set out, on the 30th, up the Kansas valley.
According to Myra Eells, there were about 60 men, and besides
the four females of the missionary party, "ten or fifteen Indian
women and [half-breed] children."

The further "Kansas" travels of this company (while spelled out in considerable detail in the missionaries' journals) are not here outlined since the
route from this point was the now "old" and familiar "Sublette's Trace" (or,
"Oregon trail") previously noted in these annals (and dealt with at some
length on pp. 262-264).

On May 13 the cavalcade crossed from the Little Blue to the Platte. (The
camp that night was "about 27 miles below the head of the Grand or Big
Island in the Platt River on its South East Bank."—Gray.) On the 30th these
travelers crossed Laramie's Fork and came to "Ft. Laramy or Ft. William at
the foot of the black hills." (Gray stated: "As near as we can make or calculate
the distance it is 790 miles [although] it is called . . . [by those who
travel with pack animals] but 750." (Myra Eells' estimate to this point was
776 miles; Asa B. Smith calculated it as 740 miles.)

After reaching the Wind river rendezvous on June 21, the missionaries remained in camp till July 12; then continued westward (to Fort Hall) with Francis Ermatinger (of the Hudson's Bay Company) and a small company (about 20 men) which included John Augustus Sutter and party of five. Eventually—on August 29—(after four months and one week en route from Westport) the nine missionaries reached the mission at Wallula, where they were greeted by the Whitmans and Spaldings (pioneers of 1836).

Ref: Same as for April 22-28 entry; *also, see The Missionary Herald*, Boston, v. 35 (July, 1839), p. 269, and v. 36 (January, 1840), pp. 15 and 33.

❦ DIED: Clermont, II, chief, since 1828, of the Osages on the Verdigris river, in "Oklahoma," in the spring(?).

On June 5 Montfort Stokes wrote (from Fort Gibson): "The recent death of their [Osages'] Principal Chief Clermont, will cause their turbulent warriors to go to war before winter with the Pawnees, Kiawas, and other tribes of the great Prairies, with whom they have been at peace ever since our late Treaties."

Ref: Grant Foreman's *Pioneer Days in the Early Southwest* (1926), p. 239, footnote. A successor, Clermont (III), signed the Osage treaty of January 11, 1839.

❦ Beginning May 9, and continuing into June, John C. McCoy surveyed the Pottawatomie reserve—completing a project on which preliminary work had been done in August, 1837. (*See* p. 319.)

Ref: Isaac McCoy manuscripts (for survey field notes); "Plat of the Potawatomie Lands Surveyed in 1838 by J. C. McCoy" (photostat from National Archives, in KHi ms. division); 25th Cong., 3d Sess., *H. Doc. No. 174* (Serial 347), p. 105. In these references August, 1837, is indicated as the time the preliminary survey was made.

❦ May 10.—This was the *scheduled* date for the annual traders' caravan to depart from Independence, Mo., for Santa Fe (as announced in the St. Louis *Missouri Argus* of April 5).

Little information has been located which relates to the 1838 season. Overland trade to Mexico was in a "languishing condition," partly due to recently imposed higher duties at Santa Fe for American traders, and also because of an uprising—a revolutionary movement (lasting till the spring of 1838)— which had begun in the province of New Mexico in the summer of 1837. A memorial that the General Assembly of Missouri addressed to congress in December, 1838, stated "only seven [Missourians'?] wagons" had gone to Mexico "during the last season." According to Josiah Gregg's later-published estimate, some 50 wagons (carrying goods worth $90,000), and around 100 men (20 of them proprietors) made the trip to Santa Fe in 1838. It may be that the wagons of *Mexican* traders carried the bulk of the 1838 New Mexico-bound trade.

Ref: *Missouri Argus*, St. Louis, April 5, 1838; 26th Cong., 1st Sess., *Sen. Doc. 472* (Serial 360), p. 6 (for memorial of December 27, 1838); R. E. Twitchell's *Leading Facts of New Mexico History* (1912), v. 2, pp. 53-60; Josiah Gregg's *Commerce of the Prairies* (New York, 1844), v. 2, p. 160. The 1838(?) expedition recollected by Oliver P. Wiggins (*see* E. L. Sabin's *Kit Carson Days* [1935], v. 1, pp. 307, 308; *The Trail*, Denver, v. 3, No. 7 [December, 1910], p. 6; and M. M. Estergreen's *Kit Carson* [c1962], pp. 77-79), has been omitted here for lack of substantiation, and because of discrepancies in Wiggin's accounts. For lack of time, the files of certain St. Louis newspapers (not available in KHi) have not been examined. The *Missouri Republican*, particularly, may contain items which throw additional light on the Santa Fe trade of 1838.

❡ May 11.—In the party of 22 Americans (with 12 Mexican servants, and outfit of seven wagons, one dearborn, and two small fieldpieces) arriving at Independence, Mo., after a 38-day journey from Santa Fe, were traders Josiah Gregg, and "Messrs. Ryder and Payne." Gregg and the other principal proprietors brought with them about $150,000 in specie and bullion. (Ryder and Payne were later reported as reaching St. Louis with $65,000 in gold and silver.)

(This company left Santa Fe on April 4; John J. Langham died after they had proceeded some 130 miles; at a camp in the Cimarron valley, below the Willow Bar, Pawnees attempted, but failed, to stampede the stock; the rest of the trip was without incident.)

Ref: Gregg, v. 1, pp. 308-313; *Missouri Argus*, St. Louis, May 31, 1838.

❡ BORN: on May 12, at Shawnee Baptist Mission (present Johnson county), Ann Eliza Pratt, daughter (and first child) of Missionaries John G. and Olivia (Evans) Pratt.

Ref: Pratt Collection (KHi ms. division); J. W. Manning's "John Gill Pratt . . ." (dissertation, May, 1951; microfilm copy in KHi).

❡ May 21.—About this date there arrived at Kickapoo Catholic Mission (five miles above Fort Leavenworth) a small party of Jesuits: the Rev. Peter Joseph Verhaegen (superior of the Missouri Jesuits), as a visitor, the Rev. Anthony Eysvogels and Brother William Claessens (who were to remain at the mission), and the Rev. Pierre-Jean De Smet (whose ultimate destination was the Pottawatomie settlements at Council Bluffs [Iowa]).

All had traveled from St. Louis on the *Howard* as far as Independence, Mo. There Father Verhaegen had disembarked and made his way overland, on horseback, to Fort Leavenworth—reaching that post four days later. The others remained on the *Howard* till the boat put in at the fort's landing. Father De Smet (who stayed to supervise baggage unloading) was a day later than the others in reaching the mission.

Ref: De Smet's letter of July 20, 1838, in Chittenden and Richardson, *op. cit.*, v. 1, p. 161; Garraghan, *op. cit.*, v. 1, p. 433. Verhaegen previously had visited Kickapoo mission in 1837—*see ibid.*, pp. 403-406.

❡ May 25.—The Rev. Pierre-Jean De Smet and two missionaries from the Kickapoo Catholic Mission (the Rev. Felix L. Verreydt and Brother Andrew Mazzella) boarded the upbound steamboat *Wilmington* at a landing near the mission (five miles above Fort Leavenworth), to journey to the Pottawatomie settlements at Council Bluffs (Iowa), where they were to establish a mission.

The night of May 25 the *Wilmington's* stopping place was "two miles from the village of Pashishi" (Pa-sha-cha-hah—Kickapoo head chief). De Smet paid the chief a visit that evening at his town "situated on the river." Subsequently, the steamboat stopped at the Blacksnake Hills (the future St.

Joseph, Mo.) for two hours, and De Smet had a "long talk with J[oseph] R[obidoux, Jr.] who keeps a store and runs his father's fine farm." "The place is one of the finest on the Missouri for the erection of a city," wrote Father De Smet. Later, as the *Wilmington* passed "up by the Sauk country, the bank for more than a quarter of a mile presented nothing but groups of savages, warriors, women and children, accompanied by an army of dogs." At the Iowa village, where the boat stopped for several hours, De Smet talked with young head chief Mahaska (Francis, or Frank, White Cloud). Farther up the Missouri he visited the Otoes. On May 31, in the afternoon, the Catholic missionaries reached their destination—the Pottawatomie settlements at Council Bluffs (Iowa).

Ref: Chittenden and Richardson, *op. cit.*, v. 1, pp. 150-157, 161, 162; Garraghan, *op. cit.*, v. 1, p. 418 (which refers to a move by Pa-sha-cha-hah and his band in 1839[?] to a locality about 20 miles from the Kickapoo mission). De Smet, in 1838, found this band living on the bank of the Missouri—a location which apparently is not the same as the 1837 village site shown in Father Verhaegen's sketch (of 1837 date) published in Garraghan, *op. cit.*, v. 1, *facing* p. 403.

❦ May-June.—In company with the Rev. Peter Joseph Verhaegen ("the Superior of the Missouri Jesuits"), the Rev. Christian Hoecken (of Kickapoo Catholic Mission) paid a second visit to the Catholic Indians on Pottawatomie creek. (*See* January, 1838, entry.) Their particular host was Joseph Napeoleon Bourassa—an educated Pottawatomie, and one of the nation's prominent young men. Though Verhaegen's stay was brief, Hoecken remained about three weeks among the Pottawatomies. (*See, also,* October 2 entry.)

Ref: Christian Hoecken's "Diary," in Kinsella, *op. cit.*, p. 226; Garraghan, v. 2, pp. 191-193. On December 10, 1838, Father Hoecken performed a marriage ceremony for (Joseph) Napoleon Bourassa and Memetekosikwe.—*Ibid.*, pp. 193 and 195.

❦ June 16.—Licenses to trade with the Indians in the Fort Leavenworth Agency (the Kickapoos, Delawares, Shawnees, and Kansa) were issued by Agent R. W. Cummins to: (1) C[yprian] Chouteau, (2) William M. Chick, (3) J[oseph] Parks and Charles Findlay, (4) A[lbert] G. Boone.

For earlier mention of Cyprian Chouteau, *see*, particularly, pp. 76 and 153. (Kansa trader Frederick Chouteau, though not named, was "covered" by Cyprian's license.) William M. Chick had arrived in Westport, Mo., to make his home, in 1836 (*see* p. 300). Joseph Parks had resided on the Shawnee reserve since 1833 (*see* p. 243).

Traders James Findlay (*see* March, 1838, annals) and Charles Findlay were, apparently, brothers. They are listed in the 1840 U. S. census of Jackson county, Mo. (both in the 20-30 age bracket). Two letters of 1840 written from "West Port," by Mrs. H. C. D. Findlay to her daughter Margaret C. Findlay (then aged 17), and addressed to "Lone Jack Jackson Co., Mo.," refer to trading activities. The August 14 letter mentions "William" (probably William S. Chick—son of William M. above—whom Margaret later married), and James Findlay's store (at Lone Jack), also "Charles" (Findlay) at Westport. The August 27 letter includes these statements: "Mrs. [Joseph?] Parks is sick the new [trading] goods has been here some eight or ten days . . .," and "Your brother [Charles] has gone to Park's since supper to try and get a horse to send for you."

Albert G. Boone (son of Jesse Bryan Boone; and grandson of frontiersman Daniel Boone) brought his family to live in Westport, Mo., about 1838, it is said. He had been a resident of Callaway county, Mo.

Ref: Office of Indian Affairs (OIA), Letters Received from St. Louis Superintendency (R. W. Cummins' letters of June 28, 1838), Microcopy 234, Roll 751, National Archives; Mrs. Carrie W. Whitney's *Kansas City Missouri, Its History and Its People* . . . (Chicago, 1908), v. 1, pp. 649-651 (for Findlay letters); *KHC*, v. 9, p. 565 (for W. R. Bernard's statement regarding A. G. Boone); Hazel A. Spraker's *The Boone Family* (1922), pp. 125, 126, 189. Charles and James Findlay, it appears, were nephews of Governor Findlay of Pennsylvania. See OIA, Letters Received from Fort Leavenworth Agency (National Archives Microcopy 234, Roll 302), June 19, 1845, memorial.

ℭ June(?).—At Fort Leavenworth on an inspection trip, Col. George Croghan commented favorably on the "experiment" there to grow forage for the garrison's horses and cattle. (*See* September 18, 1837, annals entry.)

"About 1,000 acres of prairie are now under fence and in corn," he wrote, "from which 20,000 bushels may be expected, that is to say, 20 bushels an acre or half a crop and no more, such being the average of prairie lands that have been broken up during the fall previous to planting." (He anticipated a second-year crop of 40 bushels to the acre given a reasonably favorable season in 1839.)

Ref: F. P. Prucha, editor, *Army Life on the Western Frontier* (c1958), p. 83.

ℭ July 3.—Iowa became a territory. (The organic act of June 12 had provided for the division of the territory of Wisconsin, and the establishment of the territorial government of Iowa.)

Ref: *U. S. Statutes at Large,* v. 5, p. 235.

ℭ July.—Dr. J. Andrew Chute, of Westport, Mo. (employed by the Indian department), gave smallpox vaccinations to the Ottawas at the beginning of the month; and proceeded to the Pottawatomie settlements on July 4. He also visited some of the other Indian reserves in "Kansas" on this mission during the summer. Probably he had vaccinated the Kansa in April. See p. 345.

Doctor Chute, aged 27, died at Westport, Mo., on October 1, 1838.

Ref: Jotham Meeker's "Diary," June 30, July 2, 4, and October 8, 1838; C. M. Drury, editor, *First White Women, op. cit.,* v. 2, p. 59. See, also, September 6, 1839, annals entry.

ℭ July 5.—The act of this date to increase the "present military establishment" of the United States, included a provision for the organization of the *Corps of Topographical Engineers* (to replace the previous Bureau); and a provision which permitted "the officers composing the council of administration at any post . . ." to employ a *chaplain*.

Capt. Washington Hood (appointed a captain in the topographical corps effective July 7) arrived at Westport, Mo., not long afterward (in the summer?) to make surveys in the Indian territory. (For this purpose congress, in 1838, appropriated $10,000). He began, at the mouth of the Kansas river, an initial project to determine the eastern boundary of the Indian territory. John C. McCoy was hired to assist in the survey. Work on this line (which was also the western boundary of Missouri) was continued some 40 miles southward, then abandoned when Captain Hood became incapacitated and had to return East. McCoy, in reminiscences, indicated Captain Hood found Joseph C. Brown's 1823 survey of the western boundary of Missouri (*see* p. 113) accurate, and made no changes.

The provision of the July 5 act which related to *chaplains* was amended on July 7, by limiting to 20 the number of posts permitted to have such an officer. *See* December 17, 1838, entry for Fort Leavenworth's first chaplain.

Ref: *U. S. Statutes at Large*, v. 5, pp. 257, 258; Kansas City (Mo.) *Journal*, February 13, 1879, or "Kansas Reminiscences," clipping volume, in KHi library (for McCoy); also *KHC*, v. 4, p. 301.

❧ July 12.—Fur trader Lancaster P. Lupton's small caravan, bound for Fort Lupton (or, Fort Lancaster) on the South Platte, started out from Independence, Mo., on the Santa Fe trail. Seth E. Ward (aged 18), beginning his career in the West, was one of the hired hands. His recollections provide the only information located on this journey, which took about six weeks. (*See, also*, July 26, 1839, entry.)

Soon after reaching the South Platte, young Ward joined fur traders Thompson & Craig; crossed the continental divide to their post (Fort Davy Crockett) at Brown's Hole [in the northwest corner of present Colorado]; and spent some seven years in the mountains, and among the Indians, before becoming an independent trader, and a freighter. Later, from 1857 to 1871, Seth Ward was sutler at Fort Laramie. Subsequently, he lived in the Kansas City, Mo., area. Alexander Majors, in 1893, described the Wards' home as a spacious, two-story brick house, two-and-a-half miles south of Westport, on the old Santa Fe trail.

Ref: *The United States Biographical Dictionary* . . . *Missouri Volume* (New York, etc., 1878), pp. 466-469; H. L. Conard, editor, *Encyclopedia of the History of Missouri* . . . (1901), v. 6, p. 372; Alexander Majors' *Seventy Years on the Frontier* (Chicago, etc., 1893), pp. 119-124; *A Memorial and Biographical Record of Kansas City and Jackson County, Mo.* (Chicago, 1896), pp. 567-570; *Annals of Wyoming*, Cheyenne, v. 5 (July, 1927), pp. 5-18; L. R. and Ann W. Hafen, editors, *To the Rockies and Oregon, 1838-1842* (Glendale, Calif., 1955), p. 57 (Obadiah Oakley's journal). Theodore Talbot, in his journal, 1843 (arriving at "St. Vrain's Fort"—Fort George—on July 14), recorded that Marcellin St. Vrain was in charge, James Barry was clerk, and "Mr. [Seth E.] Ward, Chief trader."— *The Journals of Theodore Talbot 1843 and 1849-52,* . . . edited by C. H. Carey (Portland, Ore., 1931), p. 23.

❧ July.—Outfitting at Independence, Mo., partners Louis Vasquez and Andrew W. Sublette moved out on the Santa Fe trail (about mid-month?) with ox-drawn supply wagons, and a company which included James Beckwourth, bound for their trading post "Fort

Vasquez" (of autumn, 1835, origin)—the first of the forts on the South Platte river.

(These partners had received their first trading license for the South Platte country on July 29, 1835, at St. Louis. "Fort Vasquez"—about one and a half miles south of present Platteville, Colo.—was maintained by Vasquez and Sublette till the spring of 1840.)

As Beckwourth later recollected it, the particular incidents of this journey on the Santa Fe trail and upper Arkansas route (past Bent's Fort) were (1) his own illness from sunstroke (suffered while crossing the Arkansas-Platte dividing ridge), and (2) Louis Vasquez's encounter (on the upper Arkansas) with a war-party of Pawnees (on foot). By his account, it was after this 1838 company reached the post that "suitable buildings" were erected at "Fort Vasquez."

Ref: T. D. Bonner's *The Life and Adventures of James P. Beckwourth* (New York, 1856), pp. 422-424; OIA, "Registers of Letters Received" (National Archives microfilm), for William Clark's August 3, 1835, letter; E. W. Smith's "Journal," in *To the Rockies and Oregon . . .*, edited by L. R. and Ann W. Hafen, p. 161; Dale L. Morgan's letter, June 9, 1962, to L. Barry; *The Colorado Magazine*, Denver, v. 29 (October, 1952), p. 241; *Mississippi Valley Historical Review*, Cedar Rapids, Iowa, v. 12 (December, 1925), pp. 335-341. Since Beckwourth says he spent July 4, 1838, on a Missouri river steamboat en route to Independence, Mo., it seems the overland journey may have commenced by mid-July.

❡ July 14-26.—Conducted by James L. Schoolcraft (with four assistants), a delegation of 26 Ottawas and Chippewas from Michigan arrived at Westport, Mo., on the 14th, en route to examine lands for a future home.

Under Isaac McCoy's direction, this party set out on the 19th for the Ottawa settlements (present Franklin county), traveling by way of the Osage River Subagency (on the Weas' land, present Miami county), and across the Peoria & Kaskaskia reserve. On July 22 McCoy joined the group, which proceeded, on the 23d, to examine the Marais des Cygnes country adjoining the existing Ottawa reserve. After a noon council on the 24th, at a crossing of the river, the company started home. Schoolcraft's party was back at Westport, Mo., by July 26.

Ref: Isaac McCoy's "Journal," July 18-26, 1838, entries; Isaac McCoy's *History of Baptist Indian Missions* (1840), p. 543; Jotham Meeker's "Diary," July 23 and 25, 1838.

❡ Between July 18(?) and August 10 William S. Donohoe surveyed the "twin" reserves of the Iowa, and Sac & Fox Indians, on the Missouri river in northeastern "Kansas," under instructions from John C. McCoy. (Preliminary surveying had been done in August, 1837—*see* pp. 325, 326.)

The Iowas' lands extended, on the north, to the Great Nemaha river (in southeastern "Nebraska"). The Sac & Fox lands (below the Iowa reserve) extended southward to the Kickapoos' north line. The two reserves were divided by a diagonal line having a beginning point near the mouth of Wolf river and running to the northwest.

Ref: Isaac McCoy manuscripts (for the field notes); Isaac McCoy's "Journal,"

July 28 and August 8, 1838, entries; survey plat (in KHi ms. division); 25th Cong., 3d Sess., *H. Doc. No. 174* (Serial 347), p. 98. The field notes were dated "Westport, Mo., Sept. 15, 1838." P. L. Gray's *Doniphan County History* (Bendena, Kan., 1905), p. 29, has a statement regarding the boundaries of the Sac & Fox, and Iowa reserves.

❧ BORN: on August 3, at "Ioway and Sac Mission" (present Doniphan county), Anna Maria Hamilton, daughter of the Rev. William and Julia N. (McGiffin) Hamilton.

Ref: "Highland Presbyterian Church Records, 1843-1890" (microfilm in KHi), where, under January 16, 1843, is noted the baptism of Annie Maria Hamilton; Presbyterian Historical Society, American Indian Missions correspondence, Box 100 (microfilm, KHi), William Hamilton's letter of September 29, 1851. Though some sources have suggested that the Rev. S. M. Irvin's son—Elliott Loury Irvin—was born at the above mission in 1838 or 1839, it appears that he was born in Pennsylvania. (The Irvins returned East in the fall of 1838, because of Mrs. Irvin's health, and she remained there till the spring of 1840.) *Also, see, Illustriana, Kansas* . . . (1933), p. 580 (biographical sketch of Elliott Samuel Irvin); and Mrs. Mary Irvin Leigh's letter of February 25, 1907, in KHi ms. division.

❧ August.—On the Arkansas river a war party of about 80 Kansa and Osage Indians surprised a party of Pawnees and took 11 scalps. Their own losses were four killed and two wounded. In a separate skirmish, warriors from the same party killed five Pawnees.

Isaac McCoy, who reported these incidents, also wrote: "On the first of September a party of about 20 Kanzas, headed by the 3d Chief of the nation named 'The Hard Chief,' was absent on a war and stealing expedition, the result of which I have not yet heard. In August last a large drove of horses was stolen from the Osage villages. Besides many horses stolen from other Indian tribes, the Osages have among them some valuable horses stolen from the whites."

Ref: Grant Foreman's *Advancing the Frontier 1830-1860* (Norman, Okla., 1933), p. 197 (quoting McCoy's letter of November 27, 1838, from OIA, Western Superintendency records in National Archives); Isaac McCoy manuscripts (1839), also contain McCoy's statements, in a copy of lengthy "Remarks" he originally prepared for Sen. John Tipton.

❧ In late August and early September the American Fur Company caravan (including some 30 fur-laden wagons and carts) homeward bound from the summer rendezvous (held near present Riverton, Wyo.), crossed "Kansas"—doubtless retracing the "Oregon trail" pathway utilized on the westward march in April and May. Indications are that Moses ("Black") Harris, and probably Lucien Fontenelle, too, made this journey.

Capt. William Drummond Stewart returned with the caravan; presumably William Preston Clark and John Radford were with him. Some travelers from the Oregon country also were in the party. They included the Rev. Jason Lee (going East for re-enforcements to the Methodist mission on the Willamette river), Philip L. Edwards (missionary assistant; now homeward bound to Missouri), F. Y. Ewing (who had gone West with the 1837 party), and five Indian youths (in Lee's charge) who were to be educated in the East. (Lee and Edwards had crossed "Kansas" westbound, in 1834, with N. J. Wyeth's second expedition.)

(Capt. William Drummond Stewart learned, after he arrived at St. Louis on, or before, September 28, that his brother, Sir John A. Stewart, had died in Scotland on May 20. As successor to the title, he thus became "Sir William.")

On September 5 Jason Lee arrived at Shawnee Methodist Mission (the "old" mission, present Wyandotte county) and remained for several days. At one o'clock on the morning of September 9 two messengers from the West reached the mission to notify Lee that his wife and infant son had died in "Oregon" in late June. (One of the men who had left Fort Hall [Ida.], after July 27, on this mission was Paul Richardson.)

Ref: Drury's *Elkanah and Mary Walker*, pp. 87, 88, 91; *Christian Advocate and Journal*, New York, v. 13 (November 9, 16, 23, 30, 1838, January 4, 1839), pp. 46, 54, 60, 77, 78; William Drummond Stewart's letter of August 27, 1838, from "Head of the Blue Fork," en route to Missouri (item—not seen by this compiler—available by courtesy of Dale L. Morgan, of the Bancroft Library, from the original in the Missouri Historical Society, St. Louis); Oregon Pioneer Association *Transactions*, 1889, pp. 79, 83; Dale L. Morgan's letter of March 5, 1963, to L. Barry (for Harris and Fontenelle); Jason Lee's "Diary," in *Oregon Historical Quarterly*, Portland, v. 17 (December, 1916), pp. 403-430; *Pacific Northwest Quarterly*, v. 29 (July, 1938), p. 282; Alter, *op. cit.*, pp. 181, 183; Bernard DeVoto's *Across the Wide Missouri* (Boston, 1947), p. 358 (for "Sir William" data); C. J. Brosnan's *Jason Lee* . . . (New York, 1932), pp. 92-103.

❡ DIED: William Clark (sup't of Indian affairs at St. Louis since 1822), on September 1, at the home of his son Meriwether Lewis Clark, in that city. He was 68 years old. The *Missouri Republican* was of the opinion Clark was "probably the oldest American settler residing in St. Louis."

Ref: Nebraska State Historical Society *Publications*, v. 20, pp. 80-82 (for item from *Missouri Republican*, St. Louis); *KHQ*, v. 16, pp. 1-3 (for brief sketch of Clark's life).

❡ In the autumn (or late summer), Henry Bradley, his wife, and Mrs. Rosetta Hardy—the last of the Wea Presbyterian Mission personnel—removed to the "Ioway and Sac Mission" in present Doniphan county. The Wea mission buildings (on Wea creek, near present Paola, Miami co.) were sold to the government for $750, and the Osage River Subagency headquarters, established there in 1837, by Subagent A. L. Davis, remained at that location till after 1843(?).

Ref: Presbyterian Historical Society, American Indian Missions correspondence (microfilm, KHi), Box 100; Spooner & Howland's *History of American Missions* (1840), p. 724; *Journal of the Presbyterian Historical Society*, Philadelphia, v. 28 (December, 1950), pp. 244, 245; Isaac McCoy's *Annual Register* for 1838, p. 60.

❡ Pottawatomie Methodist Mission was opened in the autumn at a site near one of the Indian settlements on Pottawatomie creek—not far from the Miami-Franklin county line of today. (No information has been found on its exact location.) The main building was a story-and-a-half "double log house, standing east and west, with a hallway between." Mackinaw Beauchemie (half-Chippewa, but raised among the Pottawatomies) and his family may have moved into quarters there before the Rev. Edward T. Peery (with his family) arrived in the latter part of 1838.

A missionary had been assigned (by the Missouri conference) in the fall of 1837, to work among the Pottawatomies, but failed to arrive. Meantime, the Rev. Thomas Johnson (of Shawnee mission) visiting the Pottawatomies, and finding them unsettled, determined not to build a mission in 1837; but "employed a native exhorter [Beauchemie] from the Shawnee mission . . . who speaks the language to labor among them this winter [1837-1838] and to act as interpreter for the missionary when he arrives."

According to an October 15, 1839, report, Pottawatomie Methodist Mission had opened, within the preceding year, despite strong opposition from various sources; the missionary [Peery] had "suffered much from affliction himself, and in his family," yet had been able "to collect a little band of 23 Indians. . . ." The 1840 report indicated that "on the whole," prospects were encouraging. In the fall of 1840 the Rev. Nathaniel M. Talbott (of nearby Peoria Methodist Mission) was assigned to minister also to the Pottawatomies. (The Peerys were reassigned to Delaware mission.)

Pottawatomie Methodist Mission was maintained till the Indians removed (in the latter 1840's) to a reservation on the Kansas river. Mackinaw Beauchemie died May 12, 1848. His family perhaps continued to occupy the mission house till the death of Mrs. Beauchemie in 1849.

Ref: *KHC*, v. 9, pp. 211, 212, 226, 227; *Christian Advocate and Journal*, v. 12 (February 16, 1838), p. 102 (for Johnson letter of December 27, 1837), v. 13 (November 9, 1838), p. 28 (for 1838 report), v. 14 (November 22, 1839), p. 54 (for 1839 report), v. 14 (March 20, 1840), p. 122 (for 1840 report); *Report* of the Comm'r of Indian affairs for 1839, p. 518; Isaac McCoy's *Annual Register* for 1838, p. 59; *Christian Advocate and Journal*, v. 13 (September 21, 1838), p. 18, for a Thomas Johnson letter of August 17, 1838. See *KHC*, v. 10, p. 401, for Beauchemie's death; and *see, also*, James O. Andrew, *Miscellanies* . . . (Nashville, 1855), p. 167.

❆ Pottawatomie Catholic Mission (present Miami county) had its beginning on October 2 when the Rev. Christian Hoecken reached the Pottawatomie creek settlements to serve the Indians of Catholic persuasion already there, and await the arrival of the "Wabash and St. Joseph" Pottawatomies (then en route from northern Indiana). The location, by Father Hoecken's description (in an 1837 diary) was southwest of present Osawatomie—five miles from the mouth of Pottawatomie creek.

Chief Nas-waw-kee's new cabin served as Father Hoecken's headquarters for over a month. The large immigrant party reached Pottawatomie creek on November 4—*see* p. 358. (They were accompanied by Father Benjamin-Marie Petit, who remained two months—in poor health.) The newcomers "immediately constructed a church 40 feet long and 22 feet wide; and by means of wood and bark and canvas they raised shanties for a temporary shelter, until they could select a fixed abode." In January, 1839, Father Hoecken reported there were 600 Catholics among the Pottawatomie creek Indians, and that his mission was thriving.

See March 10, 1839, annals for continuation of Pottawatomie Catholic Mission at a new site—on Big Sugar creek (in present Linn county).

Ref: Christian Hoecken's "Diary" of 1837 (microfilm copy in KHi), and of 1838 in Kinsella, *op. cit.*, pp. 226, 227; Garraghan, *op. cit.*, v. 2, pp. 193, 194, 200; Indiana Historical Society *Publications*, v. 14 (1941), especially p. 131.

❡ MARRIED: James Hays, "agriculturist for the Kansas Indians," and Rebecca Lemons, of Jackson county, Mo., on October 13, by the Rev. William Johnson, of Kansa Methodist Mission.

Ref: Jackson county, Mo., marriage records. The place of the ceremony is not indicated.

❡ October 15.—Contracts were let (at Independence, Mo.) to (1) Aaron Overton and (2) D[aniel] M[organ] Boone and others, by Capt. George H. Crosman (AQM), for the "construction and completion" of the 72-mile section of the Western military road between Fort Leavenworth and the Marais des Cygnes (in present Linn county). Work was started at once, but not completed till the fore part of 1839. (*See, also,* October 29, 1839, annals entry.)

Ref: 25th Cong., 3d Sess., *H. Doc. No. 194* (Serial 346), p. 57; 25th Cong., 3d Sess., *H. Ex. Doc. No. 2* (Serial 344), p. 122; *KHQ*, v. 11, pp. 123, 125.

❡ DIED: White Plume (principal chief of the Kansa for at least 13 years), also four Kansa braves, during the Indians' autumn hunt. (Some died of fever, others of whiskey, as reported by Missionary William Johnson).

(A year earlier, the aging chief had made his last visit to St. Louis. There is a record of payment on November 11, 1837, by the Indian department, of $36 to "E. Flenister" for "transportation of White Plume, principal chief of the Kanzas, and six Indians, from St. Louis to Liberty, Mo.")

Commenting on the Kansa Indians, after an April, 1839, visit to their villages, the Rev. Henry Gregory wrote: "An old chief [White Plume], who was opposed to the abandonment of their Indian habits, recently died, and now the two principal chiefs, both active and intelligent men, are in favor of civilization."

Whereas Isaac McCoy, in his *Annual Register of Indian Affairs* for 1835, 1836, and 1837, had listed "Nam-pa-war-rah or White Feather" [White Plume] as principal chief for the Kansa (followed by "Ka-he-ga-wa-ta-ne-ga" [Fool Chief], and others), in the 1838 edition (not published till early 1839?), there was a significant change—with "Nam-pa-war-rah, (Fury)" [or, White Plume, II] as first chief, followed by "Ka-he-ga-wa-ta-in-ga (Reckless [or, Fool] Chief)," "Kia-he-ga Wah-cha-ha (Hard Chief)," and "Me-chu-shing-a (Little White Bear)," as second, third, and fourth chiefs.

Ref: *KHC*, v. 16, p. 230 (for William Johnson's statement); 25th Cong., 3d Sess., *House Doc. No. 174* (Serial 347), p. 52 (for Capt. E. A. Hitchcock's disbursement of November 11, 1837); *Baptist Missionary Magazine*, Boston, v. 20 (February, 1840), p. 42 (for Henry Gregory's statement); Isaac McCoy's *Annual Register* for 1838, p. 66. White Plume, first mentioned in these annals in 1815, was head chief, apparently, by 1825, since he was the first to sign the June 3, 1825, Kansa treaty.

❡ October 19.—At the Great Nemahaw Subagency (present Doniphan county), John Dougherty (as commissioner for the United States) concluded a treaty with the Iowa Indians which confirmed cession of all claims by them to lands between the Missouri and Mississippi which had been held in common with the Sacs & Foxes.

In return, the government was to invest (at not less than five per cent interest) $157,500 for the tribe's use; and to pay the income annually, in October, to the Iowas (less a $50 lifetime annuity to their interpreter Jeffrey Dorion); also, 10 houses were to be built for the Iowas (in addition to the five promised under the treaty of September 17, 1836).

Heading the 13 Iowa signers were "Frank White Cloud" (*i. e.*, young Mahaskah, or White Cloud) and "Non-gee-ninga, or No Heart" (second chief, whose name also appears as "Nacheninga," etc.).

Ref: C. J. Kappler's *Indian Affairs, Laws and Treaties* (Washington, 1904), v. 2, pp. 518, 519; *Report* of the Comm'r of Indian affairs for 1839, p. 328; T. L. McKenney and James Hall, *The Indian Tribes of North America* . . . (Edinburgh, 1934), v. 1, pp. 283, 301, v. 2, pp. 110, 111, 114 (for biographical data on the chiefs White Cloud and No Heart).

❡ October 30.—Maria Pensineau, daughter of trader Paschal Pensineau and a Kickapoo(?) woman "Dutchi," was baptized by the Rev. Anthony Eysvogels. Joseph Robidoux (of Blacksnake Hills, Mo.) was sponsor.

Maria, or Mary Pensineau (born June 25?, 1838) apparently did not have the same mother as Brigitte Pensineau (*see* July 23, 1836, annals entry). In the 1850's Mary Pensineau married Tom Whipple. In 1883 she was living in Mexico, separated from her husband (who was residing with the Cherokees); and their son, aged 26 (born in 1857?) was on the Kickapoo reserve in Kansas.

Ref: "Kickapoo Register" (microfilm copy in KHi); Paschal Pensineau's dictation, in KHi ms. division. Paschal Pensineau was the son of Louison and Lizette Pensineau, of Cahokia, Ill.—John Reynolds' *The Pioneer History of Illinois*, second edition, *op. cit.*, pp. 362-364. In the "dictation," Pensineau says that his father was a Frenchman, and his mother had some Pottawatomie blood.

❡ MARRIED: William Turner and Mary Bowers, on November 1, at Ottawa Baptist Mission, by Missionary Jotham Meeker, in the presence of about 30 Ottawa Indians.

(After the wedding dinner, the couple removed into their own house. Both had lived with the Meekers for over four years. Turner, on January 15, 1838, had received permission to settle on the Ottawa reserve, and that same day had selected a site for a cabin and a field near the mission.)

Ref: Jotham Meeker's "Diary," January 15 and November 1, 1838, entries.

❡ November 4.—Some 750 emigrating Pottawatomies (of Wabash river, Ind., and St. Joseph river, Mich.), under the conductorship of William Polke, arrived at the settlements of their kinsmen on Pottawatomie creek (near the present Miami-Franklin county line), after a two-months' overland journey.

Their trip had begun on September 4, from a camp near Plymouth, Ind., where *some* of the reluctant-to-move Pottawatomies had been collected forcibly by a volunteer militia force headed by John Tipton (U. S. senator from Indiana). The emigrating party (by report over 850 persons) had been escorted to the Illinois line by Tipton and a few militiamen, and turned over to Polke's charge on September 20 near Danville, Ill.

Among the chiefs who made the journey were Ash-kum, I-o-weh, and Pe-pish-kay. Father Benjamin-Marie Petit accompanied the Indians, and his presence helped to reconcile the Catholic bands to the move westward. (Menominee, Black Wolf, and Pepinowah—all "improperly called chiefs"— leaders of these bands, had been among those in militia custody early in September.)

The Pottawatomies crossed the Mississippi at, or near, Quincy, Ill., on October 8, and the Missouri at Lexington, Mo., on October 27. (At the end of October, Ass't Conductor Jacob Hull, with 23 Pottawatomies, caught up with Polke's party.) The company which crossed the Missouri line on November 2 (some 18 miles southwest of Independence) totaled about 750 Pottawatomies. (On the long march some had dropped out because of illness; others had "deserted"; and around 43 persons had died.)

On November 3 the immigrants camped near the Wea settlement on Bull creek (present Miami county); on November 4, at 2 P.M., they began crossing the Marais des Cygnes; and around 3:30 P.M. they reached the end of their journey. Subagent A. L. Davis being absent, Conductor Polke (and his son Benjamin C. Polke, an assistant conductor) remained in the Indian Country till Davis' return at the beginning of December.

Ref: *Indiana Magazine of History*, v. 21 (December, 1925), pp. 315-336, v. 44 (December, 1948), pp. 393-408, v. 45 (September, 1949), pp. 285-288; Indiana Historical Society *Publications*, v. 14, no. 1 (1941), especially pp. 87-110; *Reports* of the Comm'r of Indian affairs for 1838, 1839, and 1840; *Indiana Historical Collections*, v. 26, pp. 659-769; *Niles' National Register*, Washington City, v. 55 (October 6, 1838), p. 88.

❡ November.—As reported by the army's commander-in-chief, Fort Leavenworth's garrison consisted of six First U. S. dragoon companies—with Col. Stephen W. Kearny's command having an aggregate of 329 (24 commissioned officers and 305 troops); additionally 99 recruits were "on march." (The other four First dragoon companies were at Fort Gibson [Okla.].)

On August 31 Lt. Col. J. B. Brant had arranged (by contract with J. P. Moore) for transportation of four officers and 190 recruits from Jefferson Barracks, Mo., to Fort Leavenworth; and on October 8, had made a contract with T. Dennis for carrying up to Fort Leavenworth two officers, one surgeon, and 180 recruits. (The November report obviously did not include all the late arrivals.)

Ref: 25th Cong., 3d Sess., *H. Ex. Doc. No. 2* (Serial 344), table *between* pp. 120, 121; 25th Cong., 3d Sess., *H. Doc. No. 94* (Serial 346), pp. 50, 58.

❡ November 14.—The Gabriel Prudhomme estate—a 257-acre Missouri river front property which included "Westport Landing," was sold for $4,220 to a hastily-organized town company of 14 persons, who were: William L. Sublette, of St. Louis, Moses G. Wilson, John C. McCoy, William Gilliss, Fry P. McGee, Abraham

Fonda, William M. Chick, Oliver Caldwell, George W. Tate, Jacob Ragan, William Collins, James Smart, Samuel C. Owens, and Russell Hicks, all of Jackson county, Mo.

The proprietors reached an agreement that their projected town (the future Kansas City, Mo.) should be called "Kansas." John C. McCoy made out a plat for about 15 acres of the "Westport Landing" area, which William S. Donohoe (his brother-in-law) then surveyed. Because the legality of the Prudhomme estate title sale was undetermined till 1846, little was done in the intervening eight years to develop the town of "Kansas."

Nine town lots were sold in May, 1839, but these sales were never effective. Some time in 1839, Thomas A. Smart located at Westport Landing (operating the first trading house in that vicinity). The steamboat *Pizarro*, in October, 1839, delivered some Indian goods at the "upper landing" and placed it "in charge of Mr. Smart." It may be that he occupied the small (20′ x 40′) hewed-log warehouse which the town company built (in 1838?, or 1839?) at "Kansas."

In 1843, according to the later recollection of Washington H. Chick (son of W. M.), aside from the warehouse, the only building within the original 15-acre town limits was a two-story double log house built by William B. Evans and "occupied by him as a dwelling and hotel." Joseph S. Chick (son of W. M.) wrote, in 1906: "At that time [1843] there was, as I remember, the Evans tavern at the foot of Main Street and Levee, a warehouse and two other houses [not in the 15-acre area?]. My father built the next houses, a warehouse [in the winter of 1843-1844] on the Levee and the first residence on the hills in Kansas City [Mo.]."

By 1846 instead of 14 town of "Kansas" shareholders there were only *seven:* Robert Campbell, of St. Louis (four shares), William Gilliss (three shares), Fry P. McGee (two shares), John C. McCoy (two shares), Jacob Ragan, William B. Evans, and Henry Jobe, each one share.

Ref: *The History of Jackson County, Missouri* . . . (Kansas City, Mo., 1881), pp. 396-398; C. C. Spalding's *Annals of the City of Kansas* (reprint of 1858 edition), pp. 15-20; Superintendency of Indian Affairs (SIA), St. Louis, "Records," v. 7, typed copy, p. 55 (for item on Smart); letter of February 22, 1963, James Anderson (historian of The Native Sons of Kansas City, Missouri) to L. Barry, and enclosures with the letter; John C. McCoy's statements in Kansas City (Mo.) *Journal*, February 17, 1884; W. H. Chick's recollections, and J. S. Chick's letter of May 3, 1906, are in the KHi ms. division. In the Isaac McCoy manuscripts (in *ibid.*), is a fragment of what may be J. C. McCoy's original(?) outline plat of "Kansas" which, on the back, records 15 lot numbers with corresponding names of would-be(?) purchasers, and the price to be paid. The names on this list are: D[aniel] Yoacham, J. C. McCoy, M[ilton] McGee, C. Young, W. L. Sublette, H. Weymeyer, [W. S.] Donohoe, E. Downing, J[acob] Ragan, A. Justice, O[liver] Caldwell, J. C. McCoy, Jr.[?], and [Fry P.] McGee.

❧ For use at the Kansa Methodist Mission, 300 copies of a 24-page book in the Kansa language were published, probably in the latter part of the year, by the Shawnee Baptist Mission press (John G. Pratt, printer).

No copy is known to exist. Isaac McCoy, in his *Annual Register* for 1838 (published in late 1838, or early 1839) stated: "A small book in the Kauzau language, upon the New System, has been published and brought into use."

Ref: *Baptist Missionary Magazine*, v. 19 (June, 1839), p. 125; McCoy, *Annual Register,* 1838, p. 67; D. C. McMurtrie and A. H. Allen, *Jotham Meeker* . . . (1930), p. 125; *KHC,* v. 10, pp. 366, 367.

❦ December 17.—Newly arrived Rev. Henry Gregory, of the Protestant Episcopal Church, was appointed chaplain at Fort Leavenworth, by the council of administration. He was the first chaplain there (*see* July 5 entry), and the first resident Episcopalian clergyman in "Kansas." (He resigned September 30, 1839.)

During his brief tenure, Chaplain Gregory officiated at four marriages, and three funerals; baptized one child; distributed Bibles, prayer books, and tracts— in addition to preaching. Also, he made two tours into the Indian country (visiting the Kansa in April, 1839, with Agent Cummins; and accompanying Colonel Kearny's party to the Otoe and Missouri village, and to the Pottawatomie settlements around Council Bluffs, [Iowa] in September, 1839).

Ref: *KHC,* v. 16, p. 355; David C. Skaggs, Jr.'s, thesis "Military Contributions to the Development of Territorial Kansas" (microfilm, KHi); *Historical Magazine of the Protestant Episcopal Church,* Richmond, Va., v. 4 (September, 1935), pp. 201, 202; *Baptist Missionary Magazine,* v. 20 (February, 1840), pp. 42-44 (for Gregory's account of tours in the Indian country).

❦ DIED: Auguste P. Chouteau (long-time trader with the Osages, and other nations on the frontier), on December 25, at Fort Gibson (Okla.). He was 52 years old.

(For first mention of him in this chronology, *see* an 1807 annals entry; and *see* his portrait [together with a summary of his connection with "Kansas" history] in an illustrations section of this volume.)

Ref: Grant Foreman's *Pioneer Days in the Early Southwest,* p. 239.

❦ December 31.—An act by the general assembly of Missouri to organize the counties of Platte and Buchanan (both bordering on the Missouri river; and formed from the "Platte Purchase") was approved on this date.

Ref: *The History of Buchanan County, Missouri* . . . (St. Joseph, Mo., 1881), pp. 152-154.

❦ Between December, 1838, and March, 1839, over 11,000(?) Cherokees, removed *by force* from their southeastern United States homes, arrived in "Oklahoma" to join the Western Cherokees (residents for more than 20 years in the Indian country—*see* p. 78), and some 3,000 other Eastern Cherokees (arrivals in late 1837 and during the summer of 1838), on the large Cherokee reserve (*see* pp. 147 and 298).

The Indians in the 13 detachments which made the late 1838-early 1839 journey overland endured hardships which caused them much misery and distress. (Chief John Ross placed the number of deaths en route at 424.) The Cherokees' phrase for this trek, "the Trail of Tears," has endured as a fitting description for an event of great tragedy in their history.

Ref: Grant Foreman's *Indian Removal* (Norman, Okla., 1932), pp. 229-312; Grace S. Woodward's *The Cherokees* (Norman, Okla., c1963), pp. 192-218; *Missouri Historical Review*, Columbia, v. 56 (January, 1962), pp. 156-167 (article by B. B. Lightfoot, "The Cherokee Emigrants in Missouri, 1837-1839"); *Report* of the Comm'r of Indian affairs, 1839 ("Of the Indians removed last year [1838-1839] there are now . . . upon subsistence . . . 10,000 Cherokees, whose 12 months will expire at different periods from December [1839] to March, next.").

❦ Employed in "Kansas" by the Indian Department during all, or part of the year 1838, were the following:

FORT LEAVENWORTH AGENCY—*Agent* Richard W. Cummins; *Interpreters* Henry Tiblow and Clement Lessert; *Gun and blacksmiths* William Donalson (for Shawnees), Robert Dunlap (for Shawnees), James M. Simpson (for Shawnees), Andrew Potter (for Kickapoos), William F. Newton (for Delawares), and Nelson A. Warren (for Kansa); *Assistant gun and blacksmiths* Mathew King (for Shawnees), Wilson Rogers (for Shawnees), Charles Fish (for Kickapoos), Paschal Fish (for Delawares), J. Bezain (for Delawares; appointed in October), William Pechalker (for Kansa); *Farmer* James Hays (for Delawares; appointed January 30, 1838, subsequently, farmer for the Kansa); *Teacher* David Kinnear (for Kickapoos); *Millers* James Allen (for Delawares), Edward Brafford (for Delawares), and Azariah Holcomb for Shawnees).

GREAT NEMAHAW SUBAGENCY—*Subagent* Andrew S. Hughes (with notation: "Discontinued"—John Dougherty "acting temporarily"); *Interpreter* Jeffrey Dorion; *Gun and blacksmiths* Hiram W. Morgan (for Iowas) and James Gilmore (for Sacs & Foxes); *Assistant gun and blacksmiths* Francis Brishnell (appointed in April), Benjamin F. Catlett, and Samuel M. Gilmore; *Farmers* William Duncan (for Iowas) and Leonard Searcy (for Sacs & Foxes); *Teacher* Aurey Ballard (for Iowas; appointed May 31).

OSAGE [MARAIS DES CYGNES] RIVER SUBAGENCY—*Subagent* Anthony L. Davis; *Interpreter* John T. Jones; *Blacksmith* William Carlisle; *Assistant blacksmith* Perry G. Crafton; *Clerk* (in payment of goods) Joseph N. Bourassa.

OSAGE SUBAGENCY—*Subagent* Paul Ligueste Chouteau (with notation: "Resigned—Mr. [Robert A.] Calloway [of the Neosho River Subagency] acting temporarily."); *Interpreter* Baptiste Mongrain. [No other employees listed.]

Ref: 25th Cong., 3d Sess., *H. Ex. Doc. No. 103* (Serial 346); OIA, Letters Received from SIA, St. Louis (Maj. E. A. Hitchcock's disbursements for July, 1838)—National Archives Microcopy No. 234, Roll 751; John Dougherty's requisitions, for quarters ending June 30, and September 30, 1838, in *ibid.*, Roll 752; Isaac McCoy's *Annual Register* for 1838. *Also, see,* October 13, 1838, annals entry.

1839

❦ January 11.—At Fort Gibson [Okla.], Brig. Gen. Mathew Arbuckle (as U. S. commissioner) negotiated a treaty with the Osage Indians. The government, taking cognizance of the long-neglected Osages' destitute condition (*see* p. 228), found it imperative to (1) induce the Osage bands still living on the Verdigris (in the Cherokees' reserve), to join the rest of the nation, and (2) to extinguish title to the "half-breed" tracts (of 640 acres each) granted under the 1825 treaty. By the above negotiation these purposes were accomplished.

The Osages ceded all claims under the treaties of 1808 and 1825 (except Article 6 of the latter); and the bands on the Verdigris promised to remove to the reservation in "Kansas." The government agreed to pay the Osages annually, for 20 years, $12,000 in money and $8,000 in goods; and to furnish blacksmiths; mills and millers; stock; agricultural tools, etc.; also to furnish each of 22 chiefs with a house worth $200. (The first eight chiefs on this list were: Pa-hu-sca [White Hair], Clermont, Chiga-wa-sa [Shingawassa], Ka-he-gais-tanga, Tawan-ga-hais, Wa-cho-chais, Ni-ka-wa-chin-tanga, and Tally.) Also, the United States arranged to buy the "half-breed" tracts (some in "Oklahoma" on Grand, or Neosho river; others on the Marais des Cygnes, or Osage, in "Kansas") at $2 an acre (and specified that the fund of $69,120 should be invested to produce annual income of $3,456 for the Osages).

Sup't William Armstrong (of the Western Superintendency), in his report for 1839, stated that the Osages were "concentrating in their country, where, with the attention of an agent lately appointed for them [Congreve Jackson], they will probably turn their attention to labor. . . . Their character has been greatly misunderstood. They are represented as fierce, and disposed to war; they are on the contrary civil and easily governed. They are a fine looking race of Indians, but little removed in point of civilization from the prairie Indian. They have been reduced very much in numbers within a few years. . . ."

Ref: Kappler, *op. cit.*, v. 2, pp. 525-527; Comm'r of Indian affairs *Report* for 1839.

❦ January.—The steamboat *Kansas,* upbound on the Missouri, stopped at Jefferson City, Mo., on the 20th, and the local paper commented on "the novel spectacle of a steam boat landing at our shore in January."

During the last week of January, the *Pirate* (a new craft) ascended the river (above Jefferson City), and the *Kansas* came down. Floating ice was thick in the Missouri, and the water level low.

Ref: *Jeffersonian Republican,* Jefferson City, Mo., January 26 and February 2, 1839.

❦ January.—A petition (relating to withheld annuity funds) from the Pottawatomies of Pottawatomie creek, Osage River Subagency, which Subagent A. L. Davis forwarded to Washington on January 22(?), was signed by about 110 Indians.

The principal chief of the Pottawatomie Nation—To-pen-e-bee headed the list. Other leading chiefs who signed were O-ke-mas, Che-bas, Pash-pa-ho, We-we-say, Ash-kum, Sin-ba-nim, Au-be-nah-ba, and I-o-way. Louis "Bernott" [Burnett?] and Abraham Burnett were 14th and 15th on the list of chiefs. Among the prominent Indians in the section headed "young men" of the

Pottawatomie Nation were J[oseph] N[apoleon] Bourassa, Luther Rice, and Stephen Bourassa.

Ref: Isaac McCoy manuscripts.

❏ February.—The last day of the month, the *Kansas* (again up-bound—*see* January) was at Jefferson City; and departed March 1 for Independence, Mo. The Missouri was reported "higher than in many months," and excellent for navigation.

(In the latter part of February, the *Howard,* going downriver, sank and was "entirely lost.")

Ref: *Jeffersonian Republican,* March 2, 1839.

❏ March 4.—Joshua Pilcher was appointed to head the superintendency of Indian affairs, St. Louis (as successor to William Clark, deceased).

Ref: 26th Cong., 1st Sess., *Sen. Doc. 126* (Serial 357), p. 5; OIA, Letters Received from SIA, St. Louis (National Archives Microcopy No. 234, Roll 752) contains Pilcher's March 13, 1839, letter of acceptance.

❏ March 10.—With their missionary, the Rev. Christian Hoecken, the Catholic band of Pottawatomies (600? Indians—*see* p. 356) moved, in a body, from Pottawatomie creek to a new home 15 miles southward, on (Big) Sugar creek, present Linn county. A small log church (replaced in 1840 by a larger one) was built immediately after they were settled, the Indians erecting it in three days' time. Thus the Pottawatomie Catholic Mission of October, 1838, origin was re-established on (Big) Sugar creek, where it would remain till 1848 when the Indians again moved—to a Kansas river reserve.

The location of these Pottawatomies was approximately four miles (in a direct line) northeast of present Centerville, Linn co. (The government survey plat of the 1850's, shows an "old Indian field" in Sections 12 and 13, T. 21 S., R. 22 E., which coincides, generally, with the above description.) In 1843 Father Felix Verreydt wrote that the mission was "about 15 miles directly west from the point where the military road leading from Fort Leavenworth to Fort Scott crosses the Osage River" (*i. e.,* 15 miles west of present Trading Post, Linn co.—*see* July, 1839, annals entry p. 376).

On April 26, 1839, Father Herman G. Aelen and Brother Francis Van der Borght arrived at Sugar creek. For two months Aelen worked among other tribes (Peorias, Ottawas, etc.). But when Father Hoecken left the Indian country in July, because of illness, Father Aelen took charge of Pottawatomie mission. It is recorded in Hoecken's diary that after he left the Indians "were sorely tried by sickness and disease" and "being without medicines, they died in great numbers in . . . [1839] and . . . 1840." (Hoecken returned to Sugar Creek mission in 1841.) A school for Indian boys was opened July 7, 1840.

Ref: Christian Hoecken's "Diary," in Kinsella, *op. cit.*, p. 227; Garraghan, *op. cit.*, v. 2, pp. 194-196; Felix Verreydt's report in *Report* of the Comm'r of Indian affairs for 1842. In Kinsella, *op. cit.*, the location of the Pottawatomie settlement of Sugar creek is stated as "Five and a half miles northeast, on the Michael Zimmerman farm, but about four miles in a direct line from Centerville." The *St. Louis Catholic Historical Review*, v. 2 (April-July, 1920), p. 95, has Aelen's 1839 report from "Sugar Creek."

❦ March 11.—At the first term of the Platte county (Mo.) court, Isaac M. C. Ellis was licensed to keep a ferry on the Missouri between the Platte county side and the Kickapoo village in "Kansas." His location was some three and a half miles above Weston, Mo. (*See* Hutawa's map, 1842, p. 408 in this volume.)

Ref: The name is "Isaac McEllis" in W. M. Paxton's *Annals of Platte County, Missouri* (Kansas City, Mo., 1897), p. 26, and in the *History of Clay and Platte Counties, Missouri* . . . (St. Louis, 1885), p. 572; but in Edwards Brothers' *An Illustrated Historical Atlas of Platte County, Missouri* (Philadelphia, 1877), p. 10, a tax roll of 1839 lists "Isaac M. C. Ellis," and several other taxpayers with the surname "Ellis." *See, also, KHQ*, v. 2, p. 25.

❦ In the spring (March?, or April?), Capt. John D. Keiser's new steamboat *Shawnee*, built for the Missouri river trade at Pittsburgh, Pa., and chartered there early in the year by the Rev. Jerome C. Berryman, arrived at Westport Landing, Mo., with a load of materials for the new Shawnee Methodist Mission and Indian manual labor school, in present Johnson county. (*See* May 23, 1839, annals item.)

Berryman, sent East (by the Rev. Thomas Johnson) to make the purchases, had spent a month at Pittsburgh on this mission.

Ref: *KHC*, v. 16, p. 219.

❦ April 6.—A commission as subagent for the Osage Indians was forwarded from St. Louis to Congreve Jackson, of Howard county, Mo. (The Osages, since the resignation of their long-time agent-subagent Paul Ligueste Chouteau, had been in the temporary charge of Robert A. Calloway, head of the Neosho River Subagency [in northeastern "Oklahoma"].)

Ref: SIA, St. Louis, "Records," v. 7, typed copy, pp. 2, 3; 25th Cong., 2d Sess., *H. Doc. No. 135* (Serial 326).

❦ April.—The American Fur Company's *Antelope* (Edward F. Chouteau, master) left St. Louis April 4 on the annual journey to the upper Missouri trading posts. She carried about 12 clerks and 120 hands. Around mid-month this steamboat passed along the "Kansas" shore.

French scientist Joseph N. Nicollet (in U. S. government service) was aboard, and in his party were Lt. John C. Fremont (of the U. S. Topographical Engineers), Charles A. Geyer (botanist), Etienne Provost (mountain man), Louis Zindel (former Prussian soldier), and one other person. They were to be convoyed to Fort Pierre [S. D.]; there to begin an overland journey which would take them as far as Devil's Lake [N. D.], for the purpose of collecting data for Nicollet's subsequently-prepared map of the "Hydrographical Basin of the Upper Mississippi River.")

Company employees making this journey (or part of it) included John F. A. Sanford, William Laidlaw, and James Kipp. From Council Bluffs (Iowa) as far as the Vermilion river (some 360 miles upstream), Father Pierre-Jean De Smet was also a passenger on the *Antelope.*

In a report (dated September 13, 1843), Nicollet observed that they were 69 days (April 4-June 12) in ascending a distance of 1,271 miles (from St. Louis to Fort Pierre), "which, on the Mississippi, and with a steamboat of the same power, could have been accomplished in twelve days." Neither Nicollet's report, or his journal (begun April 21, 1839, in the Council Bluffs vicinity) contain mention of the "Kansas" area of the Missouri.

Ref: 28th Cong., 2d Sess., *House Doc. 52* (Serial 464), for Nicollet's report; *Missouri Republican,* St. Louis, April 5, 1839, item, as quoted in Nebraska Historical Society *Publications,* v. 20, p. 97; *South Dakota Historical Collections,* Pierre, v. 10, pp. 98-129; *North Dakota History,* Bismarck, v. 21, pp. 75-82; Annie H. Abel, editor, *Chardon's Journal at Fort Clark* (Pierre, S. D., 1932), p. 270 (Note 257); John C. Fremont's *Memoirs* . . . (1887), pp. 30-54; Chittenden and Richardson, *op. cit.,* v. 1, pp. 179-182; Susan D. McKelvey's *Botanical Exploration of the Trans-Mississippi West* . . . (1955), pp. 659-667. The notice in the St. Joseph (Mo.) *Gazette* of October 22, 1851: "DIED: Wm. Laidlaw, aged about 60, in Clay Co. on the 10th," probably refers to the above Laidlaw.

❆ April 20(?)—The *Pirate,* which had started up the Missouri from St. Louis on April 2, hit a snag and sank about seven miles below Council Bluffs (Iowa).

The total damage was estimated at $40,000. She carried government provisions for the Council Bluffs Pottawatomies, and for scientist Joseph N. Nicollet's party (traveling on the *Antelope*). Supplies for Father De Smet's Catholic mission at Council Bluffs also were lost.

Ref: Chittenden and Richardson, *op. cit.,* v. 1, p. 183; Garraghan, *op. cit.,* v. 1, p. 441; Abel, *op. cit.,* p. 270 (Note 257): In OIA, Letters Received from SIA, St. Louis (National Archives Microcopy 234, Roll 752), Agent John Dougherty's requisitions for the quarter ending June 30, 1839, include one of April 8 date for transportation (upriver) of himself, John Gantt, and Jeffery Dorion on the *Pirate.* In *ibid.,* is Dougherty's letter of April 4, 1839, from Liberty, Mo., referring to his impending journey to the Council Bluffs with the disbursing agent. He *planned* to go up on the *Antelope.*

❆ April.—After a journey to the Kansa villages, in company with Agent R. W. Cummins (and five other persons), Fort Leavenworth's chaplain, the Rev. Henry Gregory, wrote:

"The number of the Kauzas, as ascertained from the pay roll, during my visit, is 1588. They are settled principally in the eastern part of their country, on the Kauzas river, and continuously[?] to each other, as respects the three several villages. . . . Their missionary [the Rev. William Johnson], his assistant[?], and the farmer [James Hays] are Methodists, and speak more or less of the Kauzas language.

"The U. S., within the last two or three years, have made . . . [the Kansa] several fields for corn, and have furnished them with a farmer and blacksmith. (The assistant blacksmith [Charles Fish] is a Shawanoe Indian, and a good workman too.) . . . nearly every head of a family is beginning to engage in agriculture. . . . They are abandoning their filthy wigwams of earth, and beginning to erect dwellings of logs. Several of them have recently fenced and cultivated little fields of their own."

(Agent R. W. Cummins, in his annual report for 1838, had stated: "This tribe number about 1,700; they are divided into three bands, each band having a village or town, all located on the Kanzas river; two of which, one on the north [Fool Chief's] and the other [Hard Chief's, apparently] on the south bank [are] nearly opposite each other. . . . [The third] is on the north bank, about 30 miles higher up. . . ." In February, 1839, Missionary William Johnson had written: "The Kanzas . . . number two thousand souls. . . .")

Ref: *Baptist Missionary Magazine*, v. 20 (February, 1840), p. 42 (for Gregory's letter reprinted from *Spirit of Missions*). As quoted above, the order of the letter's contents has been altered. See Comm'r of Indian affairs *Report* for 1838 (for Cummins); and *KHC*, v. 16, p. 230 (for Johnson). The chief, *in 1839*, of the "third" village (which soon changed location again) is not known. By 1841 Chief E-ya-no-sa had a village eight miles *above* the Kansa mission, on the *south* side of the Kansas river, near the mouth of present Mill creek, Wabaunsee co.—*See KHC*, v. 16, p. 264.

❡ May 1.—Bound for Chihuahua, by way of Santa Fe, Josiah Gregg's trading caravan (fitted out by Gregg and George C. Pickett), left Van Buren, Ark., to follow a route across "Oklahoma," on the north side of the Canadian river. There were 34 men, 14 road wagons (carrying about $25,000 in goods), half drawn by mules, half by oxen, a carriage, a Jersey wagon, and two swivels on one pair of wheels.

Lt. J. M. Bowman and some 40 First U. S. dragoons were detailed to meet the traders at Camp Holmes (*see* p. 295) and escort them westward (to the boundary?). If the dragoons actually performed this service, Josiah Gregg signally failed to mention it in his *Commerce of the Prairies* (1844).

Gregg's caravan reached Santa Fe on June 25; subsequently departed for Chihuahua in August; arrived on October 1; left there October 31; and was back at Santa Fe on December 6. Leaving Santa Fe on February 25, 1840, 47 men, Gregg's 27 wagons, one belonging to Samuel Wethered and James R. Ware, and some 200 mules, made up the returning caravan. The route was "in the vicinity" of the 1839 journey west, except that the party traveled much of the way on the south side of the Canadian. On April 22 the caravan reached Van Buren, Ark.

Ref: *Arkansas State Gazette*, Little Rock, May 15, 1839; Gregg., *op. cit.*, v. 2, pp. 9-155; M. G. Fulton, editor, *Diary & Letters of Josiah Gregg* . . . (Norman, Okla., 1941), pp. 43-69; Grant Foreman's *Pioneer Days of the Early Southwest*, pp. 241, 242. See Carl I. Wheat's *Mapping the Transmississippi West* (San Francisco, 1957), v. 2 (1958), pp. 174-170 for the Garland-Gregg map of 1841 and comment on it. Gregg's route to Santa Fe in 1839, and his return route of 1840 are shown on this manuscript map. The dragoon escort is noted in the *Arkansas Gazette* issue (noted above); also, Maj. Gen. Alexander Macomb in his 1839 report (26th Cong., 1st Sess., Sen. *Doc. No. 1* [Serial 354], p. 56) mentioned the two squadrons of the First dragoons "currently engaged" in building Fort Wayne. "These squadrons," he wrote, "also furnished last spring an escort to a caravan of traders to Santa Fe in Mexico."

❡ May 4.—At Sapling Grove (about eight miles from Westport,

Mo., in the Shawnee reserve) the various persons—27 in all—who were to comprise the American Fur Company caravan of 1839, gathered for their first overnight camp. (Most of them had set out from Westport—the organizing point—that morning.)

Moses ("Black") Harris headed the expedition. There were eight other Company hands; and an outfit of four two-wheeled mule-drawn carts, plus pack animals. (The mules and horses of the entire party totaled between 50 and 60.)

Two independent Oregon-bound missionary couples made this trip: the Rev. John S. Griffin and his bride Desire C. (Smith) Griffin; Asahel Munger (a carpenter) and his wife Eliza. (The Mungers' diary is one source of information on the journey.) With the missionaries was Paul Richardson, hired as hunter. Among the travelers, it appears, was Peter Lassen (*see below*).

Another cotraveler was Dr. Frederick A. Wislizenus, of St. Louis (who had been at Westport since debarking from the *St. Peters* at Chouteau's Landing sometime in mid-April). The narrative of Wislizenus (as translated from the German) states: "All the rest [including himself] joined the expedition as individuals," and most were headed for the Columbia, or California "actuated by some commercial motive." (*See, also,* September 17 entry.)

Sapling Grove, says Wislizenus, was "in a little hickory wood, with fresh spring water." From the Grove, on May 5, the company "marched over the broad Santa Fe road, beaten out by the caravans." Then, turning to the right, they "took a narrow wagon road, established by former journeys to the Rocky Mts., but often so indistinctly traced, that our leader at times lost it, and simply followed the general direction . . . through prairie with many undulating hills of good soil . . . [and through a region] watered with a few brooks and rivulets. . . ." [Wislizenus thus pictures for us "Sublette's Trace" as it was in 1839, just prior to becoming known as the "Oregon trail."]

On the fifth day of travel (May 8) the caravan "reached the Kanzas, or, as it is commonly called, Ka River . . ." [Wislizenus]. Camp was made "on an elevation near the river," to await the arrival of the Company's "canoe" (bringing supplies up the Kansas). Wislizenus says this camp was "some miles" below the Kansa village, and implies that they had traveled about 100 miles to reach the crossing point. [This fits the general description of the American Fur Company's 1838 crossing place—*see* p. 346.] But Asahel Munger wrote that the camp (the missionaries' camp, at least) was "within 2½ miles" of the Kansa village. This would *seem* to place the crossing higher above present Topeka than is indicated by the other accounts.

For about two and a half days the caravan remained on the Kansas river's south bank. On May 9 the Mungers visited Missionaries William and Mary Jane (Chick) Johnson at the not-far-distant Kansa Methodist Mission (*see* p. 301, and p. 347), where they exchanged three horses for two horses and two mules. Next day, the Griffins called on the Johnsons.

Doctor Wislizenus, too, made a "side trip"—to the deserted Kansa village. ("The greater part of the inhabitants were hunting buffalo. The rest had gone to our camp.") This settlement—presumably Hard Chief's town—was "on an elevation from which one can enjoy a pleasant and wide view." "The whole village consists of 50 to 60 huts, built, all in one style, in four somewhat irregular rows. The structure is very simple. On a round, arched frame of poles and bark, earth is placed with grass or reeds; at the top, in the middle, an opening is left for light and smoke; in front, at the ground, a similar opening as an entrance; and the shanty is finished. At the open door there is usually a reed-covered passage, extending a few steps into the street. There are about twelve cut braces inside the house; the fireplace is under the opening in the roof; at the side are some bunks of plaited strips of wood. The whole is rather spacious."

The "canoe" having arrived, the American Fur Company caravan crossed the Kansas river on May 11. The boat was utilized to carry the baggage over; the carts (empty) were driven across, and the animals swam the river. The travelers repacked and "drove on 3 hours and camped." From this point they were again on "Sublette's Trace."

Apparently, on May 23d the expedition crossed from the Little Blue to the Platte; on June 14 Fort Laramie was reached; and on July 5 this company arrived at the Green river rendezvous. The missionaries eventually reached their "Oregon" destination. Of the noncompany travelers, Dr. Frederick A. Wislizenus, Paul Richardson, and two others reappear on the "Kansas" scene— *see* September 17, entry.

Ref: *Oregon Historical Quarterly*, v. 8 (December, 1907), pp. 387-405 (for the Mungers' diary); F. A. Wislizenus, *A Journey to the Rocky Mountains in the Year 1839* (St. Louis, 1912), pp. 27-105; *Missouri Republican*, St. Louis, April 12, 1839, item on the Griffins (reprinted in Nebraska Historical Society *Publications*, v. 20, p. 102); De Voto, *op. cit.*, pp. 379, 380; H. H. Bancroft's *History of Oregon* (1886), v. 1 (1834-1848), pp. 239, 240, lists a number of the "individuals" in the party. T. J. Schoonover's *The Life and Times of Gen. John A. Sutter*, rev. and enl. edition (Sacramento, 1907), p. 287, states that Peter Lassen (b. August 7, 1800, in Denmark; to Boston in 1824) "left Missouri in 1839 in company with twenty-seven men and two women"—who crossed the plains, reaching Oregon in the autumn; and that Lassen remained there till spring. From Oregon he went down to California. In Georgia W. Read and Ruth P. Gaines, eds., *Gold Rush—The Journals, Drawings, and Other Papers of J. Goldsborough Bruff* . . . (New York, 1949), p. 666, it is stated that Peter Lassen left Missouri in the spring of 1839 in company with 12 others; and that they arrived at The Dalles in Oregon, in October.

❡ May 7.—Julius C. Robidoux was licensed by the Buchanan county (Mo.) court to keep a ferry on the Missouri river at Robidoux's Landing (at, or near present St. Joseph, Mo.).

Ref. *The History of Buchanan County, Missouri* . . . (St. Joseph, Mo., 1881), p. 167.

❡ May 11.—In Platte county, Mo., William Hague was granted a license to operate a ferry on the Missouri at the Fort Leavenworth crossing.

Ref. Paxton, *op. cit.*, p. 27.

❡ May-June.—The annual spring caravan which crossed "Kansas" to Santa Fe contained, by one report, "93 men with 53 wagons." (Another traveler wrote that the train contained about 40 "immense waggons" and nearly 400 mules.) Dr. David Waldo and

Manuel Alvarez headed the caravan, and presumably were the principal proprietors.

On June 19, after this wagon train had corraled for the night on the east bank of Pawnee Fork (near present Larned), the "Peoria party" (*see* p. 371) came up and joined the traders, to travel in company as far as the Arkansas crossing—a point which was reached on June 28. (The Kansa Indians, on their summer hunt, were on the west bank at Pawnee Fork crossing.)

Solomon P. Sublette (youngest of the five Sublette brothers) may have been with this wagon train. It is known that he left Independence, Mo., by the late spring of 1839, to return to Santa Fe.

The ledgers of Manuel Alvarez seem to indicate that he had (during his trip East in the winter of 1838-1839) purchased goods in New York, Philadelphia, etc., valued at $9,411.93, which were carried to Santa Fe in the above caravan; and that his wagons, teams, and other equipment were given a valuation of about $2,500 (at Independence, prior to starting on the overland journey).

Ref: R. G. Thwaites, ed., *Early Western Travels* (Cleveland, 1904-1906), v. 28, pp. 80-93 (for Thomas J. Farnham's account); L. R. and Ann W. Hafen, *op. cit.,* pp. 38-45, 100-102, 297; *New Mexico Historical Review,* Santa Fe, v. 21 (April, 1946), p. 136 (for Alvarez ledgers), and v. 36 (January, 1961), p. 52 (for item on Solomon P. Sublette).

❆ In early May, by report, Captain Kelly's train (14 wagons; about 30 men) started from Independence, Mo., for Santa Fe. But this company did not leave Council Grove till early June. (Untrained mules, and a "long . . . spell of rainy weather" contributed to the delay.)

On June 12, at Cottonwood Crossing, the mounted "Peoria party" (*see* p. 371) overtook and passed Kelly's wagon train.

Ref: Thwaites, *op. cit.,* v. 28, pp. 57, 68 (for Farnham's mention of Kelly and company); L. R. and Ann W. Hafen, *op. cit.,* pp. 30, 34, 35 (for Oakley's account), p. 71 (for Sidney Smith's mention); J. E. Sunder, editor, *Matt Field on the Santa Fe Trail* (Norman, Okla., c1900), p. 81.

❆ May.—New missionaries at Shawnee Baptist Mission (present Johnson county) were: the Rev. Francis Barker (who began work on the 20th), and Elizabeth Churchill (who arrived on the 25th). (*See, also,* October 23 entry.)

Ref: *Baptist Missionary Magazine,* v. 19 (September, 1839), p. 228.

❆ May 23.—At the site of the new Shawnee Methodist Mission and Indian manual labor school (present Johnson county), about 40 men were at work on the project (which had been started late in January).

The location (as described by Agent R. W. Cummins in October, 1838, when he and the Rev. Thomas Johnson chose it): about six miles nearly due south of the mouth of the Kansas river, and about half a mile west of the Missouri line. (By current survey description: the S. W. ¼ of Sec. 3, T. 12, R. 25 E.) "The site," he wrote, "is on a beautiful elevated ritch prairie near

& adjoining a beautiful grove of timber on the south on a small creek known by the name of brush creek . . . there are also three springs which are in a line in the edge of the timber. . . ."

Accomplishments on the project, as of May 23, by Cummins' report: 400 acres of land rail-fenced (12 acres in orchard, and in vegetables; 176 in corn, 85 in oats; "five ploughs . . . breaking the balance . . . which is intended for timothy and blue grass"). "The buildings are under way," he wrote, "mechanics preparing brick, 30,000 feet of lumber at the place, 15,000 of it dressed ready for laying floors, 2,500 lights of sash made, stone quarried for the first building, nails, glass, hinges, locks &c ready on the premises."

See, also, October 22-29, 1839, annals entry.

Ref: R. W. Cummins' letter of October 18, 1838 (photostat from National Archives, in KHi ms. division); SIA, St. Louis, "Records," v. 8, pp. 4, 5 (for Cummins' May 23, 1839, report); *Christian Advocate and Journal,* v. 13 (March 8, 1839), p. 113 (for Johnson's January 22, 1839, letter).

❦ May 29.—With Thomas J. Farnham as captain, 18 mounted men (mostly from Peoria, Ill., and all novices in the West), set out from a camp west of Independence, Mo. (Seven pack mules carried provisions.) Oregon was their destination (they called themselves the "Oregon Dragoons"), but their pathway (on the advice of traders Andrew W. Sublette and Philip F. Thompson) was the Santa Fe trail and upper Arkansas route.

[A book Farnham subsequently wrote, together with the journals of Obadiah Oakley and Sidney Smith, and Robert Shortess' later-written narrative, give detailed information on the experiences of this company.]

The Peoria party crossed the Big Blue (of Missouri) on May 31 and encamped that evening at Elm (or Round) Grove [about 33? miles west of Independence] in the Shawnee reserve. By the evening of June 7 (after several days of delays) they were at 110-mile creek. Next day three men turned back (accompanying a returning wagon party which had been out to Council Grove). At Cottonwood Crossing the Peorians overtook, and passed, Captain Kelly's train (*see* p. 370); on June 13, about eight miles east of the Little Arkansas, they met Charles Bent's Missouri-bound wagons (*see* p. 372); on the 16th a hunting detachment of the Peorians caught up with the large Santa Fe-bound traders' caravan (headed by Dr. David Waldo and Manuel Alvarez); and on the 19th, at Pawnee Fork, the rest of the party joined this wagon train to travel in company as far as the Arkansas crossing (*see* p. 370).

On June 21, in a gun accident, Sidney Smith severely wounded himself. (Doctor Waldo removed the bullet, and gave other assistance.) At the Arkansas crossing (on June 28) three more of the "Oregon Dragoons" deserted— to head for Santa Fe with the caravan. A man named Blair (from the wagon train) joined the dissension-split Peoria party, which with this accession, totaled 13. Continuing up the Arkansas (Smith despite his wound managed to ride a mule) the group traveled together as far as Bent's Fort—reached on July 6.

Robert Shortess headed the party of eight which then proceeded to Fort St. Vrain on the South Platte. (Eventually six of these men arrived in Oregon —five, at least, in 1840.) Farnham, Smith, Oakley, Joseph Wood, and Blair, hiring a trapper named Kelly to guide them across the Rockies, made their way to Fort Davy Crockett on Green river. There, Oakley and Wood turned back, but the other three went on to Oregon.

Ref: L. R. and Ann W. Hafen, *op. cit.*, pp. 20-120 (Obadiah Oakley's journal, pp. 25-64; Sidney Smith's diary, pp. 67-93; Robert Shortess' narrative pp. 94-120). Thomas J. Farnham's *Travels in the Great Western Prairies* from the London, 1843, edition (as reprinted in Thwaites, *op. cit.*, v. 28). The Shortess narrative was also published in 1896, in the *Transactions* (24th annual reunion) of the Oregon Pioneer Association.

❧ June-October.—G. S. Tuttle's contract with the war department called for delivery at Fort Leavenworth of 1,000,000 "well-burnt bricks"—200,000 each month beginning June 1—for which he was to receive $7.39 per thousand.

(In November, 1838, the quartermaster general had noted the satisfactory progress "during the past season in the work of enlarging and repairing the quarters at Fort Leavenworth, and in the erection of stables, rendered indispensably necessary by the increase of the dragoon force stationed at that post. . . .")

In November, 1839, the quartermaster general reported: "The barracks at Fort Leavenworth are in rapid progress; and if an adequate appropriation be made, they may be completed during the next year."

(At the end of 1840, out of an 1840 appropriation of $30,000 for barracks, quarters, etc. at Fort Leavenworth, $10,000 had been spent.)

Ref: 25th Cong., 3d Sess., *House Ex. Doc. No. 2* (Serial 344), p. 123 (for 1838 report); 26th Cong., 1st Sess., *H. Doc. No. 89* (Serial 365), p. 19 (for Tuttle contract, made by Capt. Thomas Swords, AQM, on December 31, 1838); 26th Cong., 1st Sess., *Sen. Doc. No. 1* (Serial 354), p. 113 (for 1839 report); 26th Cong., 2d Sess., *H. Doc. No. 74* (Serial 383), p. 4 (for 1840 item). For a sketch of Fort Leavenworth in 1838, *see KHQ*, v. 22, *facing p. 113.*

❧ BORN: on June 9, at Delaware Baptist Mission (present Wyandotte county), Olive Ann Blanchard, daughter of Missionaries Ira D. and Mary (Walton) Blanchard.

Ref: A. J. Paddock correspondence, in KHi ms. division.

❧ June.—En route from Bent's Fort to St. Louis, Charles Bent, and "Larout" [Antoine Leroux?], with 30 to 35 men, 10 ox-and-mule-drawn wagons (carrying peltries), and 200 "Santa Fé sheep," crossed "Kansas" on the Santa Fe trail. On June 13, in present McPherson county, the westbound "Peoria party" met this eastbound train. (Bent, earlier, had lost 30 mules and seven horses. These strays were found by the Peorians and taken to Bent's Fort.)

Ref: Thomas J. Farnham's *Travels in the Great Western Prairies* (as reprinted in Thwaites, *op. cit.*, v. 28, p. 71); L. R. and Ann W. Hafen, *op. cit.*, pp. 36, 37, 40, 50 (in Obadiah Oakley's journal); Oregon Pioneer Association, *Transactions* (24th Annual Reunion), 1896, p. 95 (Robert Shortess' narrative).

❏ MARRIED: the Rev. Jesse Greene (a presiding elder in the Methodists' Missouri conference) and Mary Todd (teacher at Shawnee Methodist Mission), on June 21, by the Rev. Thomas Johnson, at the "old" mission (present Wyandotte county). Mary Todd had come to Shawnee mission late in December, 1838.

Ref: Belle Greene's letter of November 13, 1906, in KHi ms. division; Jesse Greene's [Note Book], in *ibid.*; Jackson county, Missouri marriage records (where the date is given as June 25—perhaps the date of recording?); *KHC*, v. 9, p. 165 (footnote), v. 16, p. 196; Kansas City (Mo.) *Star*, January 23, 1925 (reminiscences of T. J. Greene).

❏ BORN: on June 22 at the "old Shawnee Methodist Mission (present Wyandotte county), William Thomas Johnson, son of the Rev. Thomas and Sarah T. (Davis) Johnson.

Ref: 15th *Biennial Report* of the Kansas State Historical Society, p. 35; *KHC*, v. 12, p. xii. This infant died less than a year later—on April 2, 1840.

❏ June 24.—Agent R. W. Cummins reported the completion of a house for the Shawnee blacksmiths (who were, in 1839, Robert Dunlap and James M. Simpson). J. J. Edwards had built this residence at a cost of $650.

(Cummins, in 1838, had stated: "The Blacksmiths' shops are located about six miles southwest of the northeast corner of [the Shawnees'] lands." This seems to be the same location referred to by Dr. Wilson Hobbs [who was at Shawnee Friends Mission in 1850]. He recollected that: "Adjoining us [the mission] on the east was the government blacksmith and shop.")

Ref: SIA, St. Louis, "Records," v. 8, typed copy, p. 12 (and *see* v. 7, typed copy, p. 28); *Report* of the Comm'r of Indian affairs for 1838 (for Cummins' 1838 statement); *KHC*, v. 8, p. 255 (for Hobbs). For names of blacksmiths *see* last 1839 annals entry.

❏ June 27.—Joseph V. Hamilton (sutler, and postmaster, at Fort Leavenworth) was appointed agent of the Council Bluffs Agency (for the Otoes, Missouris, Omahas, and Pawnees) to succeed John Dougherty.

On August 1 Sup't Joshua Pilcher wrote Hamilton: "so much has the public service suffered on the Upper Missouri for months past, that it is found necessary to order you *forthwith* to your post. . . . You will please proceed immediately to Bellevue . . . & receive from Major Dougherty . . . [if he is there] all books, papers [etc.]. . . ." Agent Hamilton reached Fort Leavenworth about August 12, and left for Bellevue on the 24th(?).

Ref: SIA, St. Louis, "Records," v. 7, typed copy, pp. 32, 33, v. 8, pp. 8, 11; 26th Cong., 1st Sess., *Sen Doc. No. 126* (Serial 357), p. 6; *KHC*, v. 14, p. 638.

❏ About July 1 a small caravan (18 men, with a few wagons) left Independence, Mo., for Santa Fe. In the company were several

Mexican citizens—among them Don Antonio José Luna and Captain Branch (José de Jesús Branch, of Taos). There were also a number of Americans, one of whom was actor Matthew ("Matt") C. Field.

(A journal Field kept, mostly in verse, provides an account of the party's progress from Cottonwood Crossing to Bent's Fort; and his later-written series of 85 "Sketches of the Mountains and the Prairies," based, in part, on his experiences in 1839, contain much Santa Fe trail information and description, as well as some fiction.)

Matt Field and his companions came to the great bend of the Arkansas on July 21; at rain-swollen Walnut creek (reached on the 22d) they were delayed three days; on the 28th they passed near Pawnee Rock. (Later, Field wrote of this landmark: "Pawnee Rock springs like a huge wart from the carpeted green of the prairie. It is about thirty feet high, and perhaps an hundred around the base. One tall, rugged portion of it is rifted from the main mass of rock, and stands totally inaccessible and alone. Some twenty names are cut in the stone, and dates are marked as far as ten years back." In another of his "sketches," he recounted a "Legend of Pawnee Rock.")

At Big Coon creek, on July 31, these travelers were delayed by heavy rains; next day they came to the Arkansas again, and continued up its north bank, arriving at Fort William (Bent's Fort) about mid-August. Several days later they crossed the Arkansas and continued the journey. Matt Field reached Santa Fe after a stopover at Taos. The caravan, taking a direct route, arrived there in the fore part of September.

(See October annals entry for Matt Field's return journey.)

Ref: Sunder, *op. cit.*, pp. xvii-xxix, 3-50, 60-142 *passim* (especially p. 100, for Pawnee Rock description). The sketch on Pawnee Rock was published in the New Orleans *Weekly Picayune* of November 9, 1840. All 85 "sketches" appeared in both the daily and weekly issues of the *Picayune* between December, 1839, and October, 1841. Editor J. F. McDermott (in Matthew C. Field, *Prairie and Mountain Sketches*, c1957, p. 80) remarks that James Barry (to whom Field wrote a letter in 1843, while Barry was at Bent's Fort—and Field at Fort Laramie) was probably one of the *four* young men who had accompanied Field to Santa Fe in 1839.

❦ DIED: Daniel Morgan Boone "one of the two surviving sons of [famed frontiersman] Daniel Boon," on July 13, "near West Port, Mo.," reportedly of cholera(?). He was 69 years old. (From 1827-1831 he had been a "Kansas" resident, as government farmer for the Kansa Indians.)

Ref: *Jeffersonian Republican*, Jefferson City, Mo., August 31, 1839 (which gave his age as 72); Hazel A. Spraker's *The Boone Family* . . . (Rutland, Vt., 1922), pp. 65 (where his birth date is listed as December 23, 1769), and 123, 124 (where it is stated he was aged 71 years, 1 month, and 19 days on July 13, 1839); Lilian H. Oliver, *Some Boone Descendants and Kindred* . . . (1964), pp. 19-23 (gives birth date as December 23, 1769); Samuel Lewis' letter of March 16, 1839, from Westport—*see Bulletin of the Missouri Historical Society*, St. Louis, v. 4, p. 114—referred to Boone's "feeble health." A list of Daniel Morgan Boone's children (with birth dates) is in *KHC*, v. 8, p. 434. In *Vital Historical Records of Jackson County, Missouri*, compiled by the Kansas City chapter, D. A. R. (c1934), p. 411, Boone's birth date is given as December 23, 1769, and death date as July 13, 1839; and his wife, Sarah Griffin (Lewis) Boone is stated to have died June 19, 1850.

❧ Born: on July 13, at Fort Leavenworth, Mary Kearny, daughter of Col. Stephen W. and Mary (Radford) Kearny.

Ref: D. L. Clarke's *Stephen Watts Kearny* . . . (Norman, Okla., c1961), p. 77.

❧ Married: Martin Greene and Sarah Ann Pugh, both of Shawnee Methodist Mission, on July 14, by the Rev. Thomas Johnson, at the "old" mission (present Wyandotte county).

Ref: Jackson county, Mo., marriage records.

❧ July.—Weston, Mo. (as later recollected by W. M. Paxton, who had been there from July 14 to 20), was a "busy, bustling town of three hundred people."

(Early-day histories state that Joseph Moore, ex-soldier, from Fort Leavenworth, selected the town site in the fall of 1837; that in 1838 Bela M. Hughes [then just 21] purchased a half interest in it; that after he took control, in the winter of 1838-1839, the town began to prosper; and that the plat of Weston was recorded in 1839.)

In May, 1840, Weston was reported to have 400 inhabitants.

Ref: Paxton, *op. cit.*, pp. 23, 24; *History of Clay and Platte Counties, Missouri* . . ., p. 561; Nebraska State Historical Society *Publications*, v. 20, p. 119.

❧ July 16.—Andrew Potter, recently blacksmith for the Kickapoos, was stabbed and killed by a drunken Indian named Wapuatuck (a son of Kennekuk, the Prophet) at the subagency building on the Kickapoo reserve, in the presence of Potter's family and others (white men and Indians).

Dragoons arrested Wapuatuck and he was put in the Fort Leavenworth guardhouse. (In April, 1841, he was sentenced to 18 months' imprisonment, and fined $500. Apparently he was given clemency by the President in May(?), 1841.) One result of the incident, as reported by Agent R. W. Cummins, was the subsequent "backwardness in some of the parents of the children in sending or letting them remain at the school [for the Kickapoos, supported by the government, and taught by a Methodist missionary]."

Ref: SIA, St. Louis, "Records," v. 7, typed copy, p. 65, v. 8, pp. 9, 10, and in typed copy, p. 129; *Report* of the Comm'r of Indian affairs, 1839; "Remsburg Scrapbook," v. 1, p. 200 (in KHi library), or Atchison *Daily Globe*, June 19, 1908; OIA, "Letters Received from SIA, St. Louis" (Microcopy 234, Roll 752, National Archives), *see* secretary of war's letter of May 17, 1841; New Orleans *Weekly Picayune*, June 28, 1841.

❧ July.—The trading licenses issued by Joshua Pilcher (sup't of Indian affairs, St. Louis) in 1839 *which had a "Kansas" connection* were all issued during this month:

Joseph Robidoux	July 17	At Robidoux's trading house "five miles west of Blacksnake Hills," Mo.; and, on the south [Kansas] side of the Missouri, with the Iowas, Kickapoos, and Sacs & Foxes
Joseph Lafleche	July 23	With the Iowas and Sacs of Missouri at their villages [in Kansas]; also with the united Pottawatomies at their [Council Bluffs, Ia.] villages; at Bellevue, Cabanne's post, and at the Pawnee villages [all in present Nebraska]

P[ierre] Chouteau,   July 25   With the Chippewas, Ottawas and Pottawato-
Jr. & Co.   mies at their villages [Council Bluffs, Ia.]
                                    and on the Marais des Cygnes [in Kansas];
                                    and with the Osages near their villages on
                                    Grand [Neosho] river [in Kansas]

The license for Pierre Chouteau, Jr., & Co. is notable for mention of the location *on the Marais des Cygnes*—the American Fur Company's *new post* (of 1839 origin?) for the *newly arrived* Pottawatomies' trade, on the river's south bank at the ford on the *new* Fort Leavenworth-Fort Gibson military road, about three miles west of the Missouri line, where now is the village of Trading Post, Linn co. Michel Giraud headed this establishment, and for some years it was known as Giraud's trading post.

(Trading Post was the locale of the May, 1858, "Marais des Cygnes massacre" in which five Free-State men were murdered and five wounded by a Proslavery gang from Missouri—*see KHQ*, v. 10, p. 356 for historical marker text. William P. Tomlinson who visited "Chotteau's Trading Post" [his spelling] in 1858, wrote: "It is an old place, having been established as a frontier post to trade with the Indians long before Kansas was organized as a Territory. The buildings are chiefly log—long, low, and ruinous. . . .")

See February 21 and August 10, 1840, annals for other information on Giraud, his associates, and an early marriage at "Trading Post."

Ref: OIA, Letters Received from SIA, St. Louis (National Archives Microcopy No. 234, Roll 752), Pilcher's abstract of licenses granted in SIA, St. Louis for the year 1839; William P. Tomlinson's *Kansas in Eighteen Fifty-Eight* . . . (New York, 1859), p. 62; M. Giraud is mentioned in Abel, *op. cit.*, pp. 210 and 407; W. A. Mitchell's *Linn County, Kansas* . . . (c1928), pp. 197, 198, contains an account of the Giraud-Chouteau trading post. In 22d Cong., 2d Sess., H. Doc. No. *137* (Serial 235), p. 73, Osage agent P. L. Chouteau's expenditures for the October, 1831-September, 1832, period, include one to "M[ichel] Giraud" for transportation of annuities.

❧ In July, *apparently*, a party of 159 Shawnees from "Neosho, Arkansas," arrived to join their kinsmen on the reservation in "Kansas." Agent R. W. Cummins wrote, on July 23, that he had made a contract with John C. McCoy to "furnish and issue provisions" to these Indians, and was forwarding a muster roll of the immigrants to Sup't Joshua Pilcher.

As Cummins explained it, the Shawnees west of the Mississippi [*i. e.*, those living in Missouri] who made the November 7, 1825, treaty (*see* p. 127) had separated afterwards; some (Fish's band) had moved to the reservation in "Kansas"; Lewis Rogers' party had stopped on the Osage river till 1832(?); a third party (the above band) had gone to Arkansas.

In his annual report for 1838, Cummins had stated: "This tribe [Shawnee] numbers about 975, besides those who still remain on the Neosho, Arkansas"; yet in his 1839 report (*after* the above 159 Shawnees arrived in "Kansas"), he gave the number of Shawnees in his agency as 963! (Perhaps he meant to write "including" rather than "besides," in 1838.)

Ref: SIA, St. Louis, "Records," v. 8, typed copy, pp. 15, 16; 26th Cong., 2d Sess., *Sen. Doc. 161* (Serial 378), p. 57; *Reports* of the Comm'r of Indian affairs for 1838 and 1839.

❡ July 25.—A delegation of five or six Wyandots from Ohio arrived at Westport, Mo., to explore possible locations in "Kansas" to which their people might emigrate.

This party, which paid its own expenses, returned to Ohio without making a decision, but according to Isaac McCoy, who assisted them, they inclined to a location which included parts of the Shawnee and Delaware reserves. (*See*, *also*, November 7 entry.)

Ref: *Report* of the Comm'r of Indian affairs, 1839; Isaac McCoy's *History of Baptist Indian Missions*, p. 559.

❡ About July 26th trader Lancaster P. Lupton left Independence, Mo., with six goods-laden, ox-drawn wagons and a small party of men, taking the Santa Fe road to head for his trading post "Fort Lupton," on the South Platte (some 50 miles north of present Denver).

On the upper Arkansas, on August 30, Vasquez & Sublette's faster-moving company overtook and passed Lupton's outfit. Presumably Lupton reached his destination in mid-September.

Ref: L. R. and Ann W. Hafen, *op. cit.*, pp. 161-167 (E. Willard Smith's journal).

❡ July-August.—Two-year licenses to trade with the Indians of the Fort Leavenworth Agency, as issued by Agent R. W. Cummins, were as follows:

C[yprian] Chouteau	July 25	with the Delawares, Shawnees, and Kansa
Charles Finley [Findlay]	August 21	with all agency tribes [*i. e.*, the above, plus the Kickapoos]
James M. Hunter	" " " " " "	
Robert Johnston	" " " " " "	
William McCoy	" " " " " "	
T[homas] J. Guthrie	" " " " " "	

Ref: OIA, Letters Received from SIA, St. Louis (National Archives Microcopy No. 234, Roll 752), Abstract of licenses granted in SIA, St. Louis for 1839. William McCoy (and his brother John) arrived in Independence, Mo., in 1838—*see The Bulletin* of the Missouri Historical Society, St. Louis, v. 4 (April, 1948), p. 188—but McCoy is not listed in the 1840 U. S. census of Jackson county, Mo. Nor are James M. Hunter or Robert Johns(t)on in that census; but Findlay and Guthrie are.

❡ Among the steamboats plying the Missouri during the middle and late summer, as reported at St. Louis, were the following:

In July, the *Shawnee*, *Wilmington*, and *Smelter* (which departed on the 25th for Independence, Mo.), and the *General Leavenworth* (which arrived from Independence on the 30th, with 50 cabin and 36 deck passengers).

In August, the new *Naomi* (George Taylor, master), the *St. Peters*, *Kansas*, *Wilmington*, *Pizarro*, *Smelter* (which arrived from Independence on the 15th), *Rhine*, *Malta*, and *Shawnee*.

In September, the *Rhine* (which reached St. Louis on the 7th, had met the *Pizarro* at Glasgow, Mo., on the 4th, the *St. Peters* on the 5th, aground at Pinkney bar, and the *Malta*, near the Missouri's mouth on the 6th). The *Rhine* reported the river very low and falling. However, the *Pizarro* (Cleveland, master) advertised to leave for Weston, Mo., on the 14th.

Ref: *Missouri Daily Argus*, St. Louis, issues of July 23 through September 13, 1839 (microfilm, KHi).

☾ August.—On the 6th partners Louis Vasquez and Andrew W. Sublette, with four goods-laden wagons, and a party totaling 32 men, took the Santa Fe road out of Independence to head for "Fort Vasquez" on the South Platte (some 10 days' journey north of Bent's Fort). The teams (and most of the mounts) were mules. Sublette, at least, had a fleet horse.

Trader Philip F. Thompson (of Fort Davy Crockett, on Green river, beyond the continental divide) was in this company. (Apparently he had his trading goods on pack animals.) Baptiste Charbonneau (son of Sacajawea) was one of the two half-breeds employed as hunters. Another traveler was E. Willard Smith (a young civil engineer), whose journal is the chief source of information on the journey.

The Vasquez-Sublette party arrived at Council Grove on August 15. Four more persons joined the group on the 16th. Beyond the "Kansas"-"Colorado" line, on August 30, this cavalcade overtook trader Lancaster P. Lupton (whose ox-teams moved slowly). On September 3 the company passed Bent's Fort; and on the 13th reached Fort Vasquez.

(On August 2, west of the continental divide, Obadiah Oakley of the "Peoria party" met some of a company of 10 men under "Captain Craig" [one of Philip F. Thompson's partners at Fort Davy Crockett]. The party of 10 was en route to the South Platte to meet Thompson, who, as noted above, was on that date about to leave Independence, Mo.)

Ref: L. R. and Ann W. Hafen, *op. cit.*, p. 56, and pp. 151-195 (for E. Willard Smith's journal); *The Colorado Magazine*, v. 27 (July, 1950), pp. 161-188, contains the same material; and the *Oregon Historical Quarterly*, v. 14 (September, 1913), pp. 250-279, also contains Smith's journal (but with some slight variations). *The Colorado Magazine*, v. 29 (January, 1952), p. 20, has information on Philip F. Thompson. "A. Sublette and Phil Thompson" had arrived at Independence, Mo., from the mountains late in May, 1839— as noted by Robert Shortess in *To the Rockies and Oregon* (cited above), on p. 98. *See, also,* D. B. Nunis, Jr., *Andrew Sublette . . .* (Los Angeles, 1960), pp. 59, 60.

☾ BORN: on August 19, at Fort Leavenworth, Clifton Ormsby Wharton, son (and first child) of Maj. Clifton and Oliveretta (Ormsby) Wharton.

Ref: *Pennsylvania Magazine of History and Biography*, Philadelphia, v. 2 (1878), p. 217; Wharton biographical data (in KHi ms. division and in KHi library). [Henry Shindler's] "History of Fort Leavenworth" (ms., in KHi library) states that all *six* Wharton children were born at Fort Leavenworth. The first reference above names four other Wharton children (without giving birth date) as Oliver Franklin, John Burgwin (died young), Josephine, and Mary Etta (died young).

☾ August.—A party of 108 Ottawa Indians from the Maumee Valley of Ohio, in charge of R. A. Forsyth, arrived at St. Louis by steamboat on the 14th. It appears they were then transported by steamboat up the Missouri to Chouteau's Landing; and that the last stage of the journey was made in wagons. These Maumee Ottawas reached the reserve (in present Franklin county) before August 29. (*See* earlier—1837—migration of the Maumee Ottawas to "Kansas," on p. 334.)

As reported, two chiefs were with this band—Autokee (the head chief), and Petonoquette "a much younger man," half French. Both were said to be "very good men, well informed, and not much inclined to barbarity." Autokee was a son of the "celebrated chief" Tushquaquier, whom the Ottawas looked upon as "the father of the tribe."

Ref: SIA, St. Louis, "Records," v. 7, typed copy, p. 37, v. 8, typed copy, pp. 70, 71, 100, 101; *Report* of the Comm'r of Indian affairs, 1839; 26th Cong., 1st Sess., *Sen. Doc. No. 126* (Serial 357), p. 8 (for emigrating officers); Henry R. Schoolcraft's *Personal Memoirs* . . . (Philadelphia, 1851), p. 666; 26th Cong., 1st Sess., *H. Doc. No. 89* (Serial 365), p. 3. By inference, the war department contracts from this last reference, as listed below, relate to the Ottawas of Maumee: (1) J. Throckmorton, August 15, 1839, Transportation of "Indians &c" to "Chouteau's Landing" as "soon as practicable"; (2) W. M. Chick, August 22, 1839, Transportation of "Indians" from "Chouteau's Landing" "to their homes, west," $4.50 for each wagon per day. Grant Foreman's *The Last Trek of the Indians* (c1946), pp. 91, 92, contains some additional information about the early stages of the Ottawas' journey, but is incorrect as to their trip west from St. Louis and the Indians' experiences after reaching "Kansas." *Niles' National Register*, v. 57 (October 12, 1839), p. 112, says R. A. and D. C. Forsyth were the conductors.

❅ During August and early September "*Señores* Thompson and Cordero" crossed "Kansas" with a large trading caravan (reportedly over 100 wagons) en route to Santa Fe.

"Cordero" was José Cardero of Chihuahua, Mexico—and presumably he was bound for that place. Thompson's identity seems to be in question. It is possible he was P. W. Thompson, agent for the St. Louis trading house of Powell, Lamont, & Co.

Matt Field, eastbound on the Santa Fe trail, noted the meeting of his party with the Thompson-Cardero wagon train on September 29, at a point within a week's travel of Santa Fe. In his diary he referred to the caravan as "*Senór* Cordero's Companero," and mentioned that he dined with the "American Drivers."

Ref: Sunder, *op. cit.*, pp. 54, 277. The Philip Thompson who was at Independence in June, 1839, left there August 6 (*see* annals entry) with the Vasquez-Sublette party; and therefore was not the same Thompson who went to Santa Fe. *The Bulletin* of the Missouri Historical Society, St. Louis, v. 9 (July, 1953), p. 425, under "acquisitions," lists some Santa Fe "Papers." One is an inventory of goods turned over by Robert W. Morris to P. W. Thompson, agent for Powell, Lamont, & Co., merchants, St. Louis, May 12, 1837; and there are two letters concerning collection of bill for above goods, one signed by Levi Keithly, L. Roubidoux, and Antonio Martinez, June 6, 1839, at Santa Fe; the other signed Charles Bent, Arkansas River, Road to Santa Fe, October 18, 1839.

❅ August-September.—The Santa Fe-bound 36-wagon caravan of Hicks & Marney which, on October 1, was approaching Rabbit Ear creek, and then within 10 days' travel of its destination, apparently crossed "Kansas" in late August and the fore part of September.

Eastbound traveler Matt Field noted the meeting of his party with the caravan. He recorded the traders' names as "Hick & Barney."

Ref: Sunder, *op. cit.*, p. 54; James J. Webb, in *Adventures in the Santa Fé Trade, 1844-1847* (Glendale, Calif., 1931), p. 133, refers to traders "Hicks and Marney." "Amos Marney, a freighter for Dr. Henry Connelly," is mentioned in W. E. Connelley's *Doniphan's Expedition*, pp. 142, 143.

❦ September 5.—From Fort Leavenworth, Col. Stephen W. Kearny, Maj. Clifton Wharton, and two First U. S. dragoon squadrons commanded by Capts. Nathan Boone and James Allen marched northward on the "Council Bluffs road" (across Leavenworth, Atchison, and Doniphan counties of today) toward the Platte.

(Other officers on this expedition were: Surg. Edward Macomb, and Lts. Philip R. Thompson [Adjt.], Enoch Steen, Levi P. Davidson, Robert H. Chilton, and William Bowman. Chap. Henry Gregory was along, too.)

At the Council Bluffs Agency, Bellevue (Neb.), on September 16, Colonel Kearny counciled with the Otoes and Missouris (against whom complaints had been made). The Indians' new agent, Joseph V. Hamilton, assuming responsibility for their future good conduct, dissuaded the colonel from punishing them.

On the 17th the dragoons crossed the Missouri and camped at a Pottawatomie village (at the Council Bluffs, Iowa, settlements) for the night. Next day Kearny counciled with some of the chiefs. The expedition then began the homeward march (the route is not recorded). On September 25 Kearny and his command returned to Fort Leavenworth.

Ref: Louis Pelzer's *Marches of the Dragoons* . . . (Iowa City, 1917), pp. 82-85; *Arkansas Gazette*, Little Rock, December 25, 1839; SIA, St. Louis, "Records," v. 8, pp. 8, 11, 56; 26th Cong., 1st Sess., Sen. Doc. No. 1 (Serial 354), p. 56; Chittenden and Richardson, *op. cit.*, v. 1, pp. 176, 177; *Baptist Missionary Magazine*, v. 20 (February, 1840), pp. 42-44 (for Gregory).

❦ September 6.—In a report on his summer's work for the Indian department, Dr. Joseph R. De Prefontaine, of Westport, Mo., stated he had given smallpox vaccinations to 517 Delawares, 809 Shawnees, and 237 Kickapoos in the Fort Leavenworth Agency; also, to 312 Pottawatomies, 90 Ottawas, 44 Peorias & Kaskaskias, and 33 Weas & Piankeshaws in the Osage River Subagency.

The Pottawatomies, suffering from the prevalent fever and ague, had been too ill to assemble for vaccination. De Prefontaine had visited as many Indian dwellings (in July) as time permitted. The Kansa (out hunting) could not be reached as a body, so had been omitted (but their agent stated they had been vaccinated in 1838).

Ref: SIA, St. Louis, "Records," v. 7, typed copy, pp. 20, 21 (in KHi ms. division); Jotham Meeker's "Diary," July 17 and 18, 1839, entries; OIA, Letters Received from SIA, St. Louis (National Archives Microcopy No. 234, Roll 752), for De Prefontaine's report, with Joshua Pilcher's letter of September 27, 1839.

❡ Born: on September 18, at Ottawa Baptist Mission (present Franklin county) Emeline ("Emma") Meeker, daughter of Missionaries Jotham and Eleanor (Richardson) Meeker.

Ref: Jotham Meeker's "Diary"; 15th *Biennial Report* of the Kansas State Historical Society, p. 35. On December 22, 1859, Emeline Meeker married Peter Byram, of Atchison. She died April 22, 1880. *See* L. A. Alderson's *A Brief Sketch of the Life and Character of Mrs. Emma Meeker Byram* . . . (1880), pp. 2-5.

❡ The regular autumn eastbound Santa Fe caravan, numbering 20 wagons, crossed "Kansas" during September and reached Missouri early in October. By report, the traders brought back close to $200,000 in specie.

Ref: John E. Sunder's statement in *Matt Field on the Santa Fe Trail*, p. xxiv (in which he used as reference the *Daily Missouri Republican*, St. Louis, October 4, 5, and November 12, 1839); *Niles' National Register*, v. 57 (October 19, 26, 1839), pp. 128, 133.

❡ On September 17 a small mounted party—Dr. Frederick A. Wislizenus, Paul Richardson (the leader), Charles Kline, "Mr. Koontz," and a French trapper ("Swiss")—with pack animals, set out from Bent's Fort (Colo.) to follow down the Arkansas river and the Santa Fe trail to Missouri.

(For the journey of Wislizenus, Richardson, Kline, and Koontz *to* the mountains, *see* May 4 annals entry. After reaching Fort Hall [Idaho] in late July, they, and two others, had determined to return to Missouri, but by a different route. Joined by "Swiss" (Suisse) they had traveled across the Rockies and down to Bent's Fort by way of Fort Davy Crockett [on Green river] and the trading posts on the South Platte. They arrived at "Penn's Fort"— as the doctor termed it—on September 15.)

These five men crossed the present Colorado-Kansas line about September 20; by the 26th they had reached Pawnee Fork; on the 27th they passed Pawnee Rock ("which is accounted as half way between the boundary of Missouri and Penn's [Bent's] Fort," wrote Wislizenus). On the 28th, after they had crossed Walnut creek, the doctor became lost (in foggy weather) from his companions, veered several miles north of the Santa Fe road and found himself in "a great swamp" [the Cheyenne Bottoms in Barton county of today]. With his riding horse, pack horse, and dog, he crossed this "swamp." Wislizenus described Cheyenne Bottoms and his experience as follows:

"Toward north and south I could see no end to . . . [the swamp], but it seemed to extend only a few miles toward the east. The water was not very deep and the ground pretty firm. . . . I rode my horse forward at the slowest pace, but it often slid down on grass and reeds. My pack animal I led after me with a rope. All sorts of water birds swarmed around from all sides. Never have I seen together such quantities of swans, cranes, pelicans, geese and ducks, as were here. The swamp was fairly covered with them, and they seemed to feel themselves so safe that I could have killed hundreds of them with the shot barrel of my double-barreled weapon. . . . I finally reached . . . [some] tall reeds, and the second half of the swamp still lay before me. My horse now would not budge for either whip or spur; so I dismounted and dragged it after me by the bridle. The water sometimes reached to my chest. With slow and measured step I moved onward; my dog swam usually in the rear of our stately procession. The sun was sinking when I finally reached the other side of the swamp."

After camping overnight, Wislizenus continued eastward; finally, on the fifth day of his solitary travel, he came out on the Santa Fe road. The next day he "went 25 miles on a stretch of Cottonwood Creek" where he caught up with his companions. (This was on October 4.) Reaching Council Grove on October 6, these travelers stayed three days (because of continuous rains), and set out again on the 9th. On October 14 they rode into Westport, Mo.

Ref: Frederick A. Wislizenus, *A Journey to the Rocky Mountains in the Year 1839* [as translated from the original German edition of 1840] (St. Louis, 1912), pp. 85-147 (the Cheyenne Bottoms account can be found on pp. 143, 144); L. R. and Ann W. Hafen, *op. cit.*, p. 62 (for Obadiah Oakley's list of persons with Wislizenus); Walter H. Schoewe (in *Transactions* of the Kansas Academy of Science, v. 56, June, 1953, p. 164) states: "The Cheyenne Bottoms are in Barton County, primarily in T. 18 S., Rs. 12 and 13 W., about six miles northeast of Great Bend. Hoisington is in the northwest corner of the Bottoms, Ellinwood lies to the southeast. . . ."

❦ In the late summer and during the autumn the Kansa "suffered dreadfully with sickness," and perhaps 100, or more, of the nation died. Commenting on this in February, 1840, the Rev. Thomas Johnson also wrote: "They left their villages in the time of their sickness and have not all returned yet."

Agent R. W. Cummins, in his October, 1839, report, stated, of the Kansa: "This tribe has been exceedingly sickly this season; many of them died; their number at present is 1,602. (*See* April, 1839, entry for other comment on the Kansa population.)

Ref: *Christian Advocate and Journal*, v. 14 (March 20, 1840), p. 122 (for Thomas Johnson's statement—his source it may be assumed was either his brother William [missionary to the Kansa], or Agent Cummins); Lorenzo Waugh in his *Autobiography* (2d, enlarged edition, 1884), p. 126, stated that when he arrived at the Kansa mission [either in 1839, or 1840] to serve as assistant missionary for a few months, "sickness was prevailing among these Indians at a terrible rate, and many were dying off." The latter part of 1840 was also a time of much illness among the Kansa—see KHC, v. 16, p. 231.

❦ BORN: on September 30, at Kickapoo Methodist Mission (present Leavenworth county), John Wesley Berryman, son of the Rev. Jerome C. and Sarah C. (Cessna) Berryman.

Ref: 15th *Biennial Report* of the Kansas State Historical Society, p. 35.

❦ October 5.—About this date, apparently, Ewing, Clymer, & Co., opened a store and trading establishment in Westport, Mo. An extant account book (October, 1839-October, 1840) of the firm states, on a front page: "These Books commenced October 5th 1839."

"Clymer" was Joseph Clymer ("of the firm of Ewing Walker & Co.," of Logansport, Ind.), who had arrived in western Missouri in the spring(?) with letters of introduction from Sen. John Tipton and George W. Ewing, both of Logansport.

The largest (and longest) accounts in this record are labeled "Sugar Creek outfit" (*i. e.*, the Pottawatomie Indians of Sugar creek, present Linn county), to whom were sold blankets, scarlet cloth, calico, shoes, gloves, coats, bridles, spurs, beads, knives, axes, pans, kettles, salt, flour, bacon, etc.

Listed below are the names of individuals (largely Westport residents) who purchased goods (gloves, coats, fur caps, blankets, and a wide variety of merchandise items) from Ewing, Clymer, & Co., *in 1839:*

Daniel Yoacham, Johnston Lykins, Milton McGee, James Johnston, Jos. R. De Prefontaine, A. L. Davis [Indian subagent], Allen McGee, James McGee, Joseph Parks [of the Shawnee Nation], Robert Weathered, Jonathan J. Piert, Boone Hays, A. B. Van Bibber, William M. Chick, John C. McCoy, Samuel C. Roby, William Parks [of the Shawnee Nation?], John W. Polke, Baptiste Peoria [Indian interpreter], Francis Philibert, Lewis Vogel, Jacob Ragan, Andrew H. Stinson [brother-in-law of A. L. Davis], Seth Hays [later trader at Council Grove], Greenup Dodson, David H. Burnett, Hamilton McDowell, Luther Rice [part-Pottawatomie], Wesley Mulkey, William Bowers, David Lock, Stephen Bourassa [part-Pottawatomie], James B. Devenport, Robert Wilson, John ["Tauy"] Jones, Samuel J. Hensley, John B. Young, William Pelott, Isaac McCoy, George W. Yoacham, John Self, Charles Cummins, Samuel Wade, Walter Bales.

Ref: Ewing, Clymer, & Co., account book (microfilm, KHi). The original is now located at the Kansas City (Mo.) Public Library. An account item of April, 1840, date "Recd De Smith" (for six yards of "Canadian Jeanes," etc.) may represent a sale to the Rev. Pierre-Jean De Smet. The Isaac McCoy manuscripts contain the Tipton and Ewing letters of February 28 and March 16, 1839, respectively. "J. Climer" and "G. N. Ewing" (as transcribed) are listed in the 1840 U. S. census of Jackson county, Mo. *The History of Cass and Bates Counties, Missouri* . . . (St. Joseph, Mo., 1883), p. 807, lists Joseph Clymer as an early resident of West Boone township, Bates co.—near the "Kansas" line—and states that he moved to Texas after the Civil War.

❡ In a small (five-wagon) eastbound caravan of Mexican merchants (one of them Don José Chavez) which crossed "Kansas" in October, Matthew C. Field was the only "American." From Council Grove, on October 24, he and three Spanish companions (also three servants) rode on ahead to Independence, Mo., arriving there October 30.

This party, which left San Miguel, N. M., September 23 to take the Cimarron route, had been accompanied to the Arkansas crossing by a military escort (25 mule-mounted soldiers) headed by Lt. José Hernandez. A brass cannon served the traders as protection from that point to Cottonwood Grove, where it was cached.

Matt Field, in his journal, recorded Spanish names (and translations) for "Kansas" streams and places: *Nepeste* [Arkansas] river, *Rio de Pananas* [Pawnee Fork], *Rio de Nuezes* [Walnut creek], *Punta la Circuila* [Plum Buttes], *Rio de Nepestita* [Little Arkansas river], *Rio de Alamos* [Cottonwood river], and *Concilio Arboleda* [Council Grove].

Ref: Sunder, *op. cit.,* pp. xxiv, 50-59 (for the journal), 288-293, 304-311. On p. 300, Field states: "The party was composed entirely of Mexicans, the writer forming one solitary exception." Evidently Dr. David Waldo (*see* p. xxiv) traveled in company only as far as San Miguel. *Niles' National Register,* v. 57 (November 30, 1839), p. 217, stated that the *Pizarro* which reached St. Louis on November 11, had on board $60,000 in specie brought from Santa Fe; and that her passengers included Matt Field and five Mexican gentlemen from Santa Fe.

❧ October 22-29.—In this interval, the following events occurred at the *new* Shawnee Methodist Mission and Indian manual labor school (present Johnson county):

On the 22d the Rev. Thomas Johnson moved his family down from the old mission (some six miles northwest, near present Turner, Wyandotte co.— *see* p. 179) to the new location. (A report of October 15 had stated that a frame building sufficient for two families was nearly completed; and a brick building, intended for a boarding house, cook room, and family residence, was in progress. —*See, also*, May 23, 1839, annals item.)

On the 23d the Indian students were moved to the new institution. On the 25th the centenary of Methodism was celebrated there. On the 29th the Indian manual labor school opened. The missionaries were ministers Thomas Johnson (and his wife), Jesse Greene (and his wife), Wesley Browning (who arrived on October 14), David Kinnear (formerly at Kickapoo mission), and Elizabeth Lee (recently of Kickapoo mission).

Ref: Martha B. Caldwell, compiler, *Annals of Shawnee Methodist Mission* . . . (Topeka, 1939), pp. 31, 32; also, Miss Caldwell's typescript compilation (with sources of data), which was the basis for the published *Annals* (on file in KHi ms. division).

❧ MARRIED: the Rev. Francis Barker, and Elizabeth Churchill, both of Shawnee Baptist Mission, on the evening of October 23, at the mission (present Johnson county), by the Rev. Jotham Meeker (of Ottawa Mission).

Ref: *Baptist Missionary Magazine*, v. 20 (March, and June, 1840), pp. 58, 126; Jotham Meeker's "Diary," October 23, 1839.

❧ MARRIED: Patrick Brown (son of Jacob and Maria Henry Brown), of Fort Leavenworth, and Catharine Sweany (daughter of Hubert and Johanna Boys Sweany), on October 27, at the home of the groom, by the Rev. Anthony Eysvogels, S. J., of Kickapoo Catholic Mission.

Ref: "Kickapoo Register" (microfilm in KHi).

❧ October 29.—At Fort Leavenworth contracts were let for construction of sections of the Fort Leavenworth-Fort Gibson military road principally in the area between the Marais des Cygnes and Spring river crossings. (*See, also*, October 15, 1838, annals.)

In the middle of 1840, when Capt. Thomas Swords returned to Fort Leavenworth after inspecting the road as far as the Arkansas river crossing (in present Oklahoma), he reported it "very nearly finished."

Ref: 26th Cong., 1st Sess., *H. Doc. No. 89* (Serial 365), p. 41; F. P. Prucha, *op. cit.*, p. 86; *KHQ*, v. 11, pp. 124, 125.

❧ Late in October(?) 62 Chippewa Indians of the Swan Creek band, conducted from their Michigan homes by Albert J. Smith, arrived at their small (two by six mile) reserve on the Marais des

Cygnes (west of the Ottawas' lands), in present Franklin county. In the party were Chief Esh-ton-o-quot (Clear Sky), or Francis McCoonse, his family, some relatives, and a few followers.

Of their journey to "Kansas," no account has been found. Sup't Joshua Pilcher, at St. Louis, learned of their emigration *after* the Chippewas reached their destination. Abraham S. Schoolcraft and William P. Patrick assisted Smith in conducting the party to the Indian Country.

By report, these Chippewas "immediately began to clear lands and make preparation for building and fencing. The mildness of the climate permitted them to labor uninterruptedly through the winter. . . . By the 20th of April, 1840, each head of a family had cleared and fenced and planted a number of acres, and most of them had built comfortable log cabins. . . . The chief had from twelve to fifteen acres enclosed, and had completed a good log dwelling. . . ."

(For the confederation of the Munsee Indians with these Chippewas, in 1859, *see* December, 1837, annals entry, and *see, also,* August 30, 1837.)

Ref: SIA, St. Louis, "Records," v. 7, typed copy, p. 60; *Report* of the Comm'r of Indian affairs for 1839; Henry R. Schoolcraft's *Personal Memoirs* . . . (1851), p. 670; *KHC*, v. 11, pp. 314-316; 26th Cong., 1st Sess., *Sen. Doc. No. 126* (Serial 357), p. 8 (lists Smith, Schoolcraft, and Patrick as emigrating officers; and gives October 29, 1839, as the date their service ended).

❡ November.—Col. S. W. Kearny and five companies of Fort Leavenworth's First U. S. dragoons journeyed as far as Fort Wayne [Okla.] and home again over the new military road. (The troops marched south on October 28, and returned November 20.) Factional difficulties in the Cherokee Nation prompted this hasty trip. As Colonel Kearny put it, concisely, in a letter he wrote in December:

"Genl. [Mathew] Arbuckle, assisted by the Arkansas people, tried hard to get up an alarm against the Cherokees. I marched down with 250 Dragoons, found all quiet but the Genl. and then marched home again. Great men have done the same before me. . . ."

Ref: 26th Cong., 1st Sess., *Sen. Doc. No. 1* (Serial 354), p. 56; *Report* of the Comm'r of Indian affairs for 1839 (*see* Secretary of War J. R. Poinsett's letter of November 9, 1839, to Brig. Gen. Mathew Arbuckle); Fort Leavenworth post returns; *The Trail Guide* (published by the Kansas City posse, The Westerners), v. 1, no. 3 (July, 1956), p. 19 (for quote from Kearny's letter of December 17, 1839, to Maj. E. A. Hitchcock); *Niles' National Register,* v. 57 (December 14, 1839), p. 241. An article on Nathan Boone, in the *Chronicles of Oklahoma,* v. 19 (December, 1941), p. 337, states that the dragoons remained but three days at Fort Wayne; and that "The return trip was made in nine days," the troops returning to Fort Leavenworth November 20, after marching almost 300 miles.

❡ About November 2(?) Nicholas Boilvin (agent to explore lands for a Winnebago reserve) debarked at Westport Landing, Mo., from the *Malta.* (The Winnebagoes who were to have accompanied him had decided it was too late in the year for such a tour.)

The prospective reserve (suggested by Isaac McCoy) was north of the Delawares, south of the Otoes, and west of the Kickapoos, Iowas, and Sacs &

Foxes. McCoy later wrote: "early in November, I gave direction to a tour of exploration by N. Boilvin, Esq. . . ." and "I spent seven days in the wilderness at the commencement of this tour."

Other facts about the trip can be deduced from Boilvin's expense account. At Westport, on November 9, he settled with Daniel Yoacham (for board and room?). This was likely the starting date of his late-in-the-year overland journey. On November 25 (having concluded his exploration of the prospective reserve?) he paid the Rev. William Hamilton (of the Iowa, Sac & Fox Mission) for expenses "at Great Nemahaw." On November 30 (back at Kansas river?) he paid out nine dollars to "C[yprian] and F[rederick] Choteau" for blankets. On December 2 he settled with William M. Chick (at Westport) a merchandise bill of $235.23, paid "Tom Captain" for the use of a horse for 22 days, and paid Benjamin Lagoterie (an Iroquois) $22 for his services (at a dollar a day?) as guide. On December 21 Richard Brooks received $33 for his services as a "hand" for one month.

Ref: Isaac McCoy manuscripts (for Boilvin's letters of October 20 and November 4, 1839; also McCoy's letter of November 5, 1839, to J. C. McCoy); Isaac McCoy's *History of Baptist Indian Missions* (1840), p. 558 (for quotes, above); 26th Cong., 2d Sess., *Sen. Doc. 161* (Serial 378), p. 47 (for Boilvin's disbursements).

❧ November 7.—Seven Wyandots from Ohio (described as "Hicks & Co.") arrived at Westport, Mo., to consider a location for a reserve in "Kansas" which an earlier delegation (*see* July 25 entry) had reported as desirable. Probably Francis A. Hicks, aged 39, headed this group, rather than his father Chief John Hicks. U. S. Comm'r William H. Hunter (congressman from Ohio) joined them later in the month, with instructions to purchase land from the Delawares and Shawnees, contingent on the Wyandots' acceptance of it as their future home.

When negotiations ended, in December, both the Delawares and Shawnees had agreed to sell certain acreage from their reserves. But the Wyandots failed to carry the matter further. Four more years elapsed before they made a treaty for removal.

Ref: *Report* of the Comm'r of Indian Affairs, 1839; Isaac McCoy's *History of Baptist Indian Missions* (1840), p. 559; *KHC*, v. 9, pp. 82-85, 225. In the Ewing, Clymer, & Co. (Westport, Mo.) 1839-1840 account book (microfilm, KHi) an entry under December 10, 1839, is for halters, saddles, bridles, etc. sold to "Hicks & Co. ('Wiandott') . . . Bording at D[aniel] Yoachams."

❧ November.—In his annual report the army's commander-in-chief in Washington listed Fort Leavenworth's garrison as six First U. S. dragoon companies—with Col. Stephen W. Kearny's command having an aggregate of 436 (23 commissioned officers and 413 troops). This compared with a six-company aggregate of 329 in 1838 (*see* p. 359).

Ref: 26th Cong., 1st Sess., *Sen. Doc. No. 1* (Serial 354), table pp. 72, 73.

❧ November 30.—Indian department disbursements of this date

show payment to the following persons for services to the Iowas, and to the Sacs & Foxes in "Kansas," as fulfillment of some September 17, 1836, treaty terms—*see* p. 314.

For the *Iowas:* to J. T. V. Thompson "for breaking up and enclosing grounds," $2,800; to W. J. Norris "for live stock," $1,163.62; to R. B. Mitchell "for erection of houses," $5,500; and to Garnet M. Hensley "for a ferry boat," $100.

For the *Sacs & Foxes:* to William J. Norris "for livestock" $1,163.62; to R. B. Mitchell "for erection of houses," $2,100; to J. T. V. Thompson "for breaking up and enclosing grounds," $2,800; also, on November 16, to Garnet M. Hensley "for erection of mills, etc.," $2,786. (This last item may have been for both the Sac & Fox and Iowa mills.)

Ref: 26th Cong., 2d Sess., *Sen. Doc. 161* (Serial 378), p. 55.

❡ BORN: on December 3, at Pottawatomie Methodist Mission, present Miami(?) county, James Andrew Peery, son of the Rev. Edward T. and Mary S. (Peery) Peery.

Ref: Si and Shirley Corn's *Our Family Tree* (1959), Section IV; U. S. Census, 1850, Jackson County, Mo., Kaw township, no. 86 (for Edward T. Peery family). James Andrew Peery died February 28, 1853.

❡ December 5.—Albert G. Wilson was appointed postmaster at Fort Leavenworth. It is probable that Wilson had received appointment as sutler at the military post some weeks earlier.

The preceding postmaster had been Joseph V. Hamilton (*see* an item on his sutlership, p. 285; also the April 3, 1838, item on his appointment as postmaster; and the June 27, 1839, item on his appointment as Indian agent at Council Bluffs). According to Col. S. W. Kearny, the Fort Leavenworth council of administration nominated "a Mr. Miller [Daniel Miller?], a young Country Merchant" to succeed Hamilton as sutler, and Miller subsequently was appointed [temporarily?] against Kearny's wishes. But Kearny states: "I insisted upon my right to have a voice in the appointment. . . ." Apparently, then, Albert G. Wilson was Kearny's choice. Wilson was succeeded in mid-1841 by Hiram Rich.

Ref: *KHC*, v. 1-2, p. 255 (or, v. 7, p. 441); *The Trail Guide* (Kansas City posse, The Westerners), v. 1, no. 3 (July, 1956), p. 18 (for Kearny's letter of December 17, 1839). For a comment on "Daniel Miller," *see KHC*, v. 14, p. 649.

❡ December 5(?)—With John W. Newcom (a Stockbridge, of Buffalo, N. Y.) as their conductor, a party of Stockbridge and Munsee Indians from Wisconsin territory arrived at Westport, Mo.; and on December 6(?) reached the Delaware reserve, north of Kansas river.

The *Munsees* joined their people—the 72 Munsees who had come to "Kansas" in December, 1837 (*see* p. 338)—at the "Westfield" settlement (where Muncie, Wyandotte co. is today). Newcom stated 84 Munsees were in his party. Agent R. W. Cummins, in February, 1840, put their number at 105[!]

(In September, 1840, he reported the total Munsee population in the Fort Leavenworth Agency as about 183 persons.)

The *Stockbridges* (84 by Newcom's count; 74 by Cummins' reports), after councils with the Delawares, were given permission to settle on the latter's reserve (if the Stockbridges would see that the government added a tract of land to the Delawares' original holdings). On February 4, 1840, Cummins wrote that the Stockbridges would "in a few days remove from where they are now encamped and settle near Fort Leavenworth"—nearly 20 miles from the Munsees. In September he described the location as "about four or five miles below . . . Fort Leavenworth." Among the heads of families in the Stockbridge emigrating party (as listed on a roll accompanying the Stockbridge and Munsee treaty of September 3, 1839) were: Thomas T. and Eli Hendrick, Robert Konkapot (also, other Konkapots), John W. Newcom (who brought his family from New York, later), Jonas Littleman, Henry Skickett (or "Skiggett," who had been in "Kansas" prior to 1839), Eli Williams, and James Rain (a Munsee, but enrolled with the Stockbridges).

Ref: SIA, St. Louis, "Records," v. 7, typed copy, p. 181, v. 8, typed copy, pp. 32-34, 43, 60, 76; Isaac McCoy manuscripts, for draft of December 26, 1839, letter, a December 31, 1839, memorandum, and a January 2, 1840, item; *Report* of the Comm'r of Indian Affairs for 1840 (for Cummins' September, 1840, report); *Baptist Missionary Magazine*, v. 20 (March, 1840), p. 58; Kappler, *op. cit.*, v. 2, pp. 529-531; *Report* of the American Board of Comm'rs for Foreign Missions for 1840, pp. 184, 185; 26th Cong., 1st Sess., *Sen. Doc. 42* (Serial 355); 26th Cong., 2d Sess., *Sen. Doc. 161* (Serial 378), pp. 54, 55. In OIA "Letters Received from Fort Leavenworth Agency" (National Archives Microcopy 234, Roll 301), is Cummins' (February 27, 1840) muster roll of 69 Stockbridges emigrated from Wisconsin territory; and (same date) roll of a party of 105 "Delaware and Munsee" Indians. In *ibid.*, the 1842 census gives the Munsee total as 208; and the Stockbridge total as 70.

❡ December 21.—The Rev. David E. Griffith (Episcopalian) became Fort Leavenworth's second chaplain.

See December 17, 1838, annals entry.

Ref: F. B. Heitman's *Historical Register and Dictionary of the United States Army* (1903), v. 1, p. 479.

❡ Employed in "Kansas" by the Indian Department during all, or part of the year 1839 were the following persons:

FORT LEAVENWORTH AGENCY—*Agent* Richard W. Cummins; *Interpreters* Henry Tiblow and Clement Lessert; *Blacksmiths* Robert Dunlap (for Shawnees), James M. Simpson (for Shawnees), William F. Newton (for Delawares), John Van Horn (for Kansa); *Assistant blacksmiths* Wilson Rogers (for Shawnees), Benjamin Rogers (for Shawnees), John Pemesco (for Delawares), Charles Fish (for Kansa); *Farmer* James Hays (for Kansa); *Teacher* David Kinnear (for Kickapoos).

Within the "discontinued" GREAT NEMAHAW SUBAGENCY—John Dougherty, acting, succeeded by Joseph V. Hamilton, acting; *Blacksmiths* Hiram W. Morgan (for Iowas), Stewart M. (or L?) Reynolds (for Sacs & Foxes); *Assistant blacksmiths* John B. Rubetie (for Iowas) and Andrew Gilmore (for Sacs & Foxes); *Farmers* James Duncan (for Iowas) and Benjamin F. Catlett (for Sacs & Foxes); *Millers* William P. Trippets (for Iowas) and D. Smith (for Sacs & Foxes).

OSAGE [MARAIS DES CYGNES] RIVER SUBAGENCY—*Subagent* Anthony L. Davis; *Interpreter* Luther Rice; *Issuing agent* (at $3 per diem) Andrew H. Stinson; *Blacksmiths* Jesse King and Robert Wilson; *Assistant blacksmith* Andrew Fuller. (The three smiths, all for the Pottawatomies, were appointed April 16, 1839).

OSAGE SUBAGENCY—*Subagent* Congreve Jackson. [No other employees listed.]

Ref: 26th Cong., 1st Sess., Sen. Doc. 126 (Serial 357), pp. 5, 6; 26th Cong., 2d Sess., Sen. Doc. 161 (Serial 378), pp. 42, 43, 50, 55; SIA, v. 7, typed copy, pp. 5, 13, 14, 40; Letters Received by OIA (National Archives Microcopy No. 234, Roll 752), R. W. Cummins' return for September 30, 1839.

1840

❦ DIED: Wau-sa-on-o-quet (or "Wossaonukwut"), principal chief of the Ottawas, on January 10, at the Ottawa settlement in present Franklin county.

Ref: Jotham Meeker's "Diary," in KHi ms. division, January 10, 1840. As a treaty signer, in 1833, the chief's name was listed as "Wau-sa-on-o-quet."—*See* C. J. Kappler's *Indian Affairs, Laws and Treaties* (Washington, 1904), v. 2, p. 393.

❦ DIED: the Rev. Moses Merrill, missionary to the Otoes and Missouris, on February 6, at the Otoe Baptist Mission (in "Nebraska") which he had founded in October, 1833.—*See* p. 249.

Ref: *The Baptist Missionary Magazine*, Boston, v. 20 (June, 1840), p. 129; Nebraska State Historical Society *Transactions*, Lincoln, v. 4, pp. 157-159.

❦ MARRIED: John Baptiste Chaurette and Elise Braconier, on February 21, at the American Fur Company trading house of Michel Giraud on the Marais des Cygnes (at present Trading Post, Linn co.), by the Rev. Herman G. Aelen, S. J.

This ceremony renewed an earlier marriage. A son, Jean Baptiste Chaurette, born to this couple on July 5, 1839, was baptized on February 21, 1840, by Father Aelen. Michel Giraud was sponsor at the ceremony.

Ref: "Pottawatomie Marriage Register," and "Pottawatomie Baptismal Register" (microfilm in KHi).

❦ DIED: Au-to-kee (or, "Ottowukkee"), principal Ottawa chief (since January—*see* above), on March 18, at the Ottawa settlement in present Franklin county. He had come to "Kansas" in August, 1839.

"Ottowukkee' (according to Jotham Meeker) was much opposed to Christian teachings among his people. Just prior to his death he had been working actively toward the expulsion of the Baptist missionaries (the Meekers) and some of the leading Christian Ottawas.

Ref: Jotham Meeker's "Diary," January 19, 1840; *The Baptist Missionary Magazine*, v 20 (June, 1840), p. 128, and v. 21 (June, 1841), p. 173. As a treaty signer, in 1833, the chief's name was "Au-to-kee" (then second chief of the Ottawas).—*See* Kappler, *op. cit.*, v. 2, p. 393.

❡ March 25.—Capt. Nathan Boone, with Companies B and I, First U. S. dragoons, left Fort Leavenworth (crossing the Missouri at the post) and began a march up the river's left bank to settle difficulties between northwest Missouri settlers, and the Otoe and Iowa Indians.

The Otoes had raided stock in Buchanan county; while the Iowas (a band living on the "Council Bluffs" Pottawatomies' reserve in southwest Iowa) had destroyed cattle of Nishnabotna valley settlers. By report, several detachments of volunteers joined Captain Boone's troops. The troubles were quickly settled, and on April 10 the dragoons were back at Fort Leavenworth.

Ref: *Missouri Argus* (daily), St. Louis, April 4, 11, 1840; Louis Pelzer's *Marches of the Dragoons* . . . (Iowa City, 1917), p. 86; O. E. Young's *The West of Philip St. George Cooke* . . . (Glendale, Calif., 1955), p. 98; *Chronicles of Oklahoma*, v. 19 (December, 1941), pp. 337, 338.

❡ Spring—Among the steamboats in the Missouri river trade were the: *Naomi, Malta, Shawnee, Bedford, Rienzi, Euphrasie* (new; W. B. Miller, master), *Thames* ("splendid, fast-running"; Thomas Dennis, master), *Rhine, Albany, Platte,* and *General Leavenworth.*

On April 25 the *Naomi* sank in about six feet of water at the mouth of Grand river. The *Osceola* (an Osage river boat) took her passengers down to St. Louis.

Ref: *Missouri Argus* (daily), March and April, 1840, issues; *Missouri Daily Republican*, St. Louis, April 30, 1840 (in Nebraska State Historical Society *Publications*, Lincoln, v. 20, p. 108). Though "Euphraise" in some advertisements, this boat generally was listed as the "Euphrasie." During 1840, 28 steamboats made 147 trips on the Missouri (many in the lower river only), according to a tabulation published in *Niles' National Register*, Baltimore, v. 72 (July 31, 1847), p. 351. In 1838, 17 steamboats had made 96 trips; and in 1839, 35 steamboats had made 141 trips.—*Ibid.*

❡ April 1.—About this date the steamboat *Antelope* (American Fur Company) left St. Louis for the annual trip to the upper Missouri trading posts. Presumably she passed along the "Kansas" shore in the latter half of the month.

Ref: *Missouri Argus* (daily), April 1, 1840. Charles Larpenteur, in his *Forty Years a Fur Trader* . . . (New York, 1898), v. 1, p. 161, implied that the *Trapper* went up to Fort Union in 1840, but he may have meant 1841 for the *Trapper's* first trip.

❡ Born: on April 3(?), at "Ioway and Sac Mission" (present Doniphan county), Margaret Elcy Hamilton, daughter of the Rev. William and Julia Ann N. (McGiffin) Hamilton.

Ref: Presbyterian Historical Society, American Indian Missions correspondence, Box 100 (microfilm, KHi), William Hamilton's letter of September 29, 1851. The Highland Presbyterian church records, 1843-1890 (microfilm in KHi), in recording the baptism of three daughters of William Hamilton, on January 16, 1843, entered the birth date of Margaret E. Hamilton as April 3, 1840. In the above reference the date is April 7.

❡ April 17.—The first issue, dated April 3, of the Independence (Mo.) *Chronicle* (a weekly Democratic paper, published by William C. Reed), received this comment from the editor of the St. Louis *Missouri Argus:*

"The establishment of such a journal within twelve miles of the western limits of the Union, and almost within sight of the wigwam of the aboriginal savage, is a rich illustration of the rapid uniformity with which intellectual culture spreads among the American people. . . ."

Ref: *Missouri Argus* (daily), April 17, 1840. The Library of Congress, Washington, D. C., has a copy of the April 3, 1840, issue of the *Chronicle*, according to the *Union List of Newspapers*.

❦ April 19.—Agent Joseph V. Hamilton (of the Council Bluffs Agency) and Missionary (to the Pawnees) John Dunbar, set out from Bellevue [Neb.] to visit the *six* Pawnee villages (along the Platte and the Loup Fork). They completed the tour, and returned on May 2.

While on this trip Hamilton obtained custody of seven Mexican youths (aged 12 to 16) held by the Pawnees, who had captured them on the southwest frontier. (In late September, 1840, they were still in his care, but were to be sent home at the first opportunity.)

Also, he had a census taken—the first "accurate" count of the Pawnees. (John Dunbar was of the opinion that the figures were "nearly correct.") The *Pawnee Loups* (836 males and 1,070 females) totaled 1,906; the *Republican band* (775 males and 1,048 females) totaled 1,823; the *Grand Pawnees* (746 males and 1,035 females) totaled 1,781; and the *Tappage band* (380 males and 452 females) totaled 832. The grand total was 6,342.

Hamilton reported that a count of the Otoes & Missouris had been made "recently," and their number was found to total 943 souls.

Ref: Superintendency of Indian Affairs (SIA), St. Louis, "Records," v. 8, typed copy, p. 58, or, Comm'r of Indian affairs *Report*, 1840 (for Hamilton's September 30, 1840, letter); *KHC*, v. 14, pp. 641, 642; *Niles' National Register*, v. 58 (June 20, 1840), p. 241, stated of the Mexican youths, "Two of them were . . . drowned." The Grand Pawnee census totals 1,781, not 1,683 as appears in Hamilton's report. Thus, the grand total, revised, would be 6,342, not 6,244 as he gave it.

❦ April 22.—Ewing, Clymer & Co. received an Indian department contract to erect a "church and parsonage house" at Sugar Creek (Catholic) Mission for the Pottawatomies (in present Linn county). The buildings were to be completed in four months at a cost of $1,640.

Arrival of more Pottawatomies (over 500?) early in October, required an enlargement of the new facility; and on October 23 Joseph Clymer, Jr., got the contract for "making certain additions to a church lately built," to cost $360.

On December 25 the new log church was blessed by the Rev. Herman G. Aelen, S. J., then in charge of Sugar Creek Mission.

Ref: 26th Cong., 2d Sess., *H. Doc. No. 72* (Serial 383), p. 2; 27th Cong., 2d Sess., *H. Doc. No. 34* (Serial 402), p. 39, T. H. Kinsella's *The History of Our Cradle Land* . . . (1921), p. 227; G. J. Garraghan's *The Jesuits of the Middle United States* (New York, 1938), v. 2, pp. 199, 200; SIA, St. Louis, "Records," v. 7, typed copy, p. 124, v. 8, typed copy, pp. 29, 30. The 1840 federal census of Jackson county, Mo., lists heads of households "G. N[?]. Ewing" and "J. Climer" [Clymer].

❦ Crossing "Kansas" in April, the year's first eastbound company on the Santa Fe trail arrived at Independence, Mo., early in May.

William S. Messervy was one of the principal merchants in this train of about 40 wagons (some of them from Chihuahua). The traders brought "a quantity of gold and silver."

See, also, June 30 annals entry.

Ref: *Daily Missouri Republican,* May 11, 1840 (as reprinted in Nebraska State Historical Society *Publications,* v. 20, p. 108); *The Weekly Picayune,* New Orleans, May 25, 1840 (or, *see* J. E. Sunder, editor, *Matt Field on the Santa Fe Trail* [Norman, c1960], p. xxiv); *Niles' National Register,* v. 58 (May 23, 1840), p. 192.

❅ April 30.—Andrew Drips headed the American Fur Company's caravan which set out for the Rocky mountains. Cotraveler Father Pierre-Jean De Smet wrote: "I started from Westport on the 30th of April in company with the Annual Expedition. . . ." Joel P. Walker later recollected there were 40 men, 30 carts (two-wheeled; each drawn by two mules *tandem*), and some 60 pack mules, in the traders' outfit. Seven of the carts, and 16 mules (also eight horses), belonged to Henry Fraeb and Jim Bridger (new partners). Some of the 40 men were in their employ.

Father De Smet (en route to explore the prospects for establishing an Indian mission in the northwest) had reached Westport on April 11, and by the 20th had purchased four horses and three mules for the journey. (Walker recollected that De Smet joined them "at Kaw river with six or eight men and pack mules.")

With Joel P. Walker (brother of mountain man Joseph R. Walker) were his wife, Mary (Young) Walker, their four children (John, Joseph, Newton, Isabella), also, Mrs. Walker's sister, Martha Young. They had two wagons. (The Walkers, residents for some years of the Independence, Mo., area, planned to settle in California. One historian has referred to them as the "first family of avowed emigrants that came to Oregon or the Pacific coast.")

Also accompanying the fur traders were six Oregon-bound missionaries: the Rev. Harvey Clark (a Congregationalist) with his wife; and laymen Philo B. Littlejohn and Alvin T. Smith, with their wives. The missionaries' outfit included two wagons.

Of the journey across "Kansas" (over the route of 1839—the "Oregon trail") Father De Smet wrote: "Until the 17th of May we traveled westward over immense plains, destitute of trees or shrubs, except along the streams, and broken by deep ravines, where our voyageurs lowered and raised the carts by means of ropes. . . . often the thermometer would be as low as 27 in the morning, through it might rise to 90 by noon. The strong winds that prevail unceasingly in these vast plains make the heat supportable. . . ."

On May 18 the caravan crossed the 30-mile plain from the Little Blue to the Platte river; and on June 30 reached the mouth of Horse creek, in the Green river valley, where the 16th (and last) annual trappers' rendezvous was to be held.

Subsequently the three missionary couples, and the Walkers, made their way to Oregon (but in 1841 the Walkers went overland to California). Father

[*Continued on p. 409*]

Artist Henry Worrall's reconstruction of the Kansa Agency (1827-1834?) and Chief White Plume's stone house (inset)—as sketched in 1879 after he visited the site (with its then fragmentary remains), and gathered other information from pioneers' recollections. The location was on the Kansas river in present south Jefferson county.

SOME HISTORIC SITES OF PRE-1826 ORIGIN

(See corresponding numbers on map)

	Site	Date	Location	See Annals
1.	Pueblo ruins ("El Cuartelejo")	Early 1700's	Ladder creek valley, Scott county.	"About 1700"
2.	Osage villages	17th?-early 18th centuries	Vernon county, Mo.	
3.	Kansa "Village of 24"	Early 18th century	Doniphan, Doniphan county.	1723
4.	Kansa "Village of 12"	Mid-18th century	Salt (or Plum) Creek valley, Leavenworth county.	1744
5.	Fort Cavagnial	1744-1764	Salt Creek valley, Leavenworth county.	1744
6.	Kansa village	1790's?-1829	In Pottawatomie county, two miles east of Manhattan, Riley county.	1790-1791
7.	Pawnee Republic village	One was occupied 1790's?-1809; the	Southwest of Republic, in Republic county, Kan.	1806; 1825
8.	Pawnee Republic village	other from 1822?-1831?	Southeast of Red Cloud, in Webster county, Neb.	1806; 1825
9.	Clermont's Osage village	1802 or 1803	Near Claremore, Rogers county, Okla.	1802-1803
10.	Fort Osage	1808-1822	Near Sibley, Jackson county, Mo.	1808
11.	Little Osage village	1812?	In Neosho county, on west bank of Neosho river.	1813
12.	Chouteau's Island	1816	Southwest of Lakin, Kearny county.	1816
13.	Isle au Vache (Cow Island) Cantonment Martin site	1818-1819	Island in Missouri river, between Atchison and Leavenworth.	1818
14.	"Four Houses" trading post (of Chouteau brothers)	1819?-1828?	At mouth of Cedar creek? in Leavenworth county?	1819
15.	Union Mission	1820-1836	In Mayes county, Okla., on the Grand river.	1820
16.	Osage villages; including White Hair's town	18__?	In Neosho county.	1820; 1822
17.	Andrew Woods' (Missouri Fur Co.) trading post	1820?-1824?	On the Missouri, above the mouth of the Kansas river.	1821-1822
18.	Francis G. Chouteau's (French Fur Co.) depot	1821?-1826	On the Missouri, about three miles below the mouth of the Kansas, at Randolph Bluffs, Mo.	1821-1822
19.	Harmony Mission	1821-1836	Near Papinsville, Bates county, Mo.	1821
20.	Fort Osage sub-factory	1821-1822	Near Papinsville, Bates county, Mo.	1821
21.	Cyrus Curtis-Michael Eley trading post	1822?-1826?	On the Missouri, above the mouth of the Kansas river.	1821-1822
22.	"The Caches"	1823	About five miles west of Dodge City, Ford county.	1822-1823
23.	Hopefield Mission (No. 1)	1823	In Mayes county, Okla., on the Grand river.	1823
24.	Mission Neosho	1824-1829	Near Shaw, Neosho county.	1824
25.	Council Grove	1825	On the Neosho river, in Morris county.	1825
26.	Shawnee settlement (first immigrant Indians)	1825	In Shawnee township, Wyandotte county.	1825

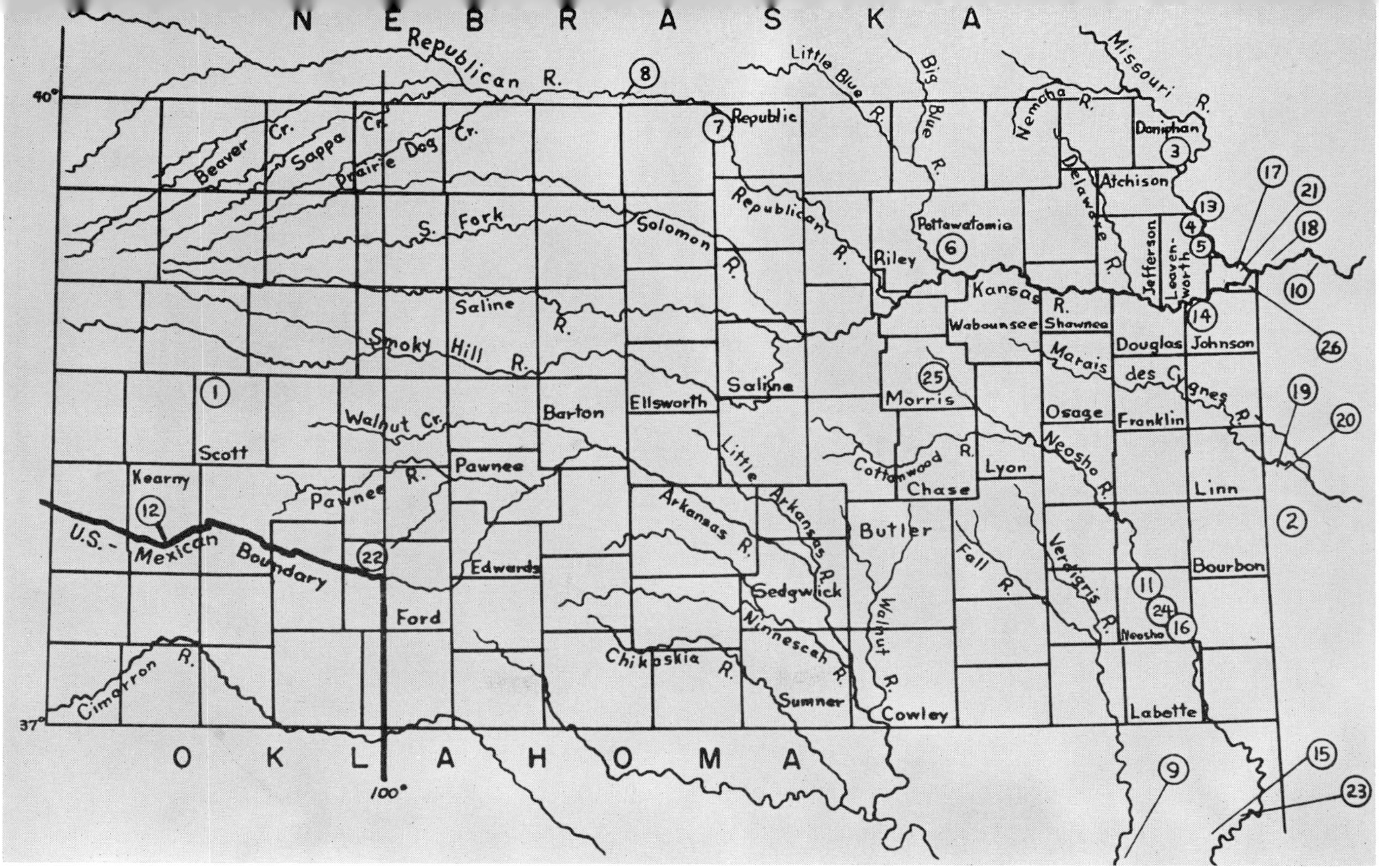

NEBRASKA

OKLAHOMA

Missouri R.

Nemaha R.

Doniphan

Atchison

Delaware R.

Jefferson

Leaven-worth

Douglas Johnson

des Cygnes

Franklin

Linn

Bourbon

Labette

Neosho

Verdigris R.

Shawnee

Marais

Osage

Neosho R.

Wabaunsee

Kansas R.

Pottawatomia

Lyon

Chase

Cottonwood R.

Fall R.

Butler

Cowley

Walnut R.

Morris

Riley

Republican R.

Big Blue R.

Little Blue R.

Saline

Little Arkansas

Sedgwick

Ninnescah R.

Sumner

Republic

Solomon R.

Ellsworth

Arkansas R.

Chikaskia R.

Beaver Cr.

Sappa Cr.

Prairie Dog Cr.

S. Fork

Saline R.

Smoky Hill R.

Barton

Edwards

Ford

Walnut Cr.

Pawnee R.

Scott

Kearny

Pawnee

U.S.-Mexican Boundary

Cimarron R.

Republican R.

40°

37°

100°

— 395 —

CYPRIAN CHOUTEAU
(1802-1879)
His trading post (from late 1828) was on the Shawnee reserve, south bank of the Kansas (present Wyandotte county).

FREDERICK CHOUTEAU
(1809?-1891)
His Kansa trading post (founded 1829) was, after 1831, near the mouth of Mission creek (present Shawnee county).

Fool Chief's Kansa Village (dating from 1829?) between Soldier creek and the Kansas river (northwest of present Topeka), as drawn by George Lehman (from Nicholas Point's sketch). Fathers Pierre-Jean de Smet and Point paid a brief visit to the town in May, 1841, while en route west with an emigrant caravan. De Smet stated there were about 20 of the "wigwams" (like stacks of wheat), each one about 120 feet in circumference—large enough to shelter 30 to 40 persons. He estimated the village population at 700 to 800 souls.

The Smith-Jackson-Sublette expedition (81 mounted men, and "caravan of ten wagons, drawn by five mules each, and two dearborns, drawn by one mule each"—the first wagons to go as far as the Rocky mountains), which William L. Sublette piloted across "Kansas" in the spring of 1830 (see p. 171), as portrayed 100 years later by Artist William H. Jackson. The scene is the departure from St. Louis. (From water color in Oregon Trail Museum, Scotts Bluff National Monument, Neb., courtesy National Park Service.)

Mrs. Thomas (Sarah Davis) Johnson (1810-1873)

The Rev. Thomas Johnson (1802-1865)

SHAWNEE
METHODIST
MISSION
and
Its
Founders
(See November, 1830, annals.)

The 1830-1839 log mission, in present Wyandotte county. Sketched (from a description) by C. P. Bolmar.

The mission premises, 1830's, in present Johnson county. Woodcut, from a contemporary sketch.

SHAWNEE
BAPTIST
MISSION
and
Its
Founders
(See July, 1831, annals.)

Dr. Johnston Lykins (1800-1876)

The Rev. Isaac McCoy (1784-1846)

A Charles Bodmer painting (1833) of the Steamboat *Yellowstone* on her third voyage to the American Fur Company's upper Missouri trading posts. The *Yellowstone*'s first journey—in the spring of 1831—had opened a new era in boat travel on the upper Missouri. A painting of the *Yellowstone* (departing from St. Louis in 1832) was made by Artist George Catlin.

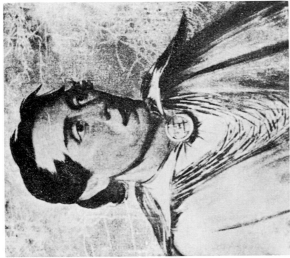

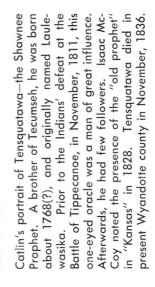

Kennekuk—the Kickapoo Prophet, portrait by Catlin. Born about 1797(?), this "tall bony Indian, with a keen black eye, and a face beaming with intelligence," had risen to power before he arrived in "Kansas" (present Leavenworth county) in May, 1833. Kennekuk's self-evolved religion (despite its absurdities) had a beneficial influence on his people. He died on the reserve above Fort Leavenworth in 1852. Photos courtesy Smithsonian Institution.

Catlin's portrait of Tensquatawa—the Shawnee Prophet. A brother of Tecumseh, he was born about 1768(?), and originally named Laulewasika. Prior to the Indians' defeat at the Battle of Tippecanoe, in November, 1811, this one-eyed oracle was a man of great influence. Afterwards, he had few followers. Isaac McCoy noted the presence of the "old prophet" in "Kansas" in 1828. Tensquatawa died in present Wyandotte county in November, 1836.

Three "distinguished and ambitious young men . . . of the best families in the Osage nation"—according to Artist George Catlin, who painted them in 1834. "These portraits," he added, "set forth fairly the modes of dress and ornaments of the young men of the tribe, from the tops of their heads to the soles of their feet. The only dress they wear in warm weather is the breech-cloth, leggings, and moccasins of dressed skins, and garters worn immediately below the knee, ornamented profusely with beads and wampum." Elsewhere, Catlin wrote: "The Osages may justly be said to be the tallest race of men in North America . . . few . . . of the men . . . are less than six feet in stature, and very many of them six and a half, and others seven feet."

RLATHEMWAKUNEK

WTCLAWSWAKUN

NRVLALKWF KRTHWVALKWF

NHESUS KLYST?

CNTU

JIJWANUKIF WUNTUNASW

CNTU

LINEXSIF TCLEXTWNRW

MPLCNHES.

NAIIME TCLI WEHWMAT.

JAWANOUR,

TALI REJETWN.

1837.

JOTHAM MEEKER

(1804-1855)

Baptist Missionary and Pioneer "Kansas" Printer.

Between March, 1834, and March, 1837, at Shawnee Baptist Mission (present Johnson county), Meeker printed numerous Indian language publications. The two title pages of the last book he printed there (before going to the Ottawas as missionary) are shown here—reproduced from the Society's copy. (See annals entry of March 21, 1834, for further details.)

THE HISTORY

OF

OUR LORD AND SAVIOUR JESUS CHRIST?

COMPREHENDING ALL THAT THE

FOUR EVANGELISTS

HAVE RECORDED CONCERNING HIM;

ALL THEIR RELATIONS BEING BROUGHT TOGETHER IN ONE NARRATIVE, SO THAT NO CIRCUMSTANCE IS OMITTED, BUT THAT INESTIMABLE HISTORY IS CONTINUED IN ONE SERIES, IN THE VERY WORDS OF SCRIPTURE, BY THE REV. SAMUEL LEIBERKUHN, M. A.

TRANSLATED INTO THE

DELAWARE LANGUAGE, IN 1806,

BY REV. DAVID ZEISBERGER,

Missionary of the United Brethren.

RE-TRANSLATED, SO AS TO CONFORM TO THE PRESENT IDIOM OF THE LANGUAGE,

BY I. D. BLANCHARD.

J. MEEKER, PRINTER, SHAWANOE BAPTIST MISSION.

1837.

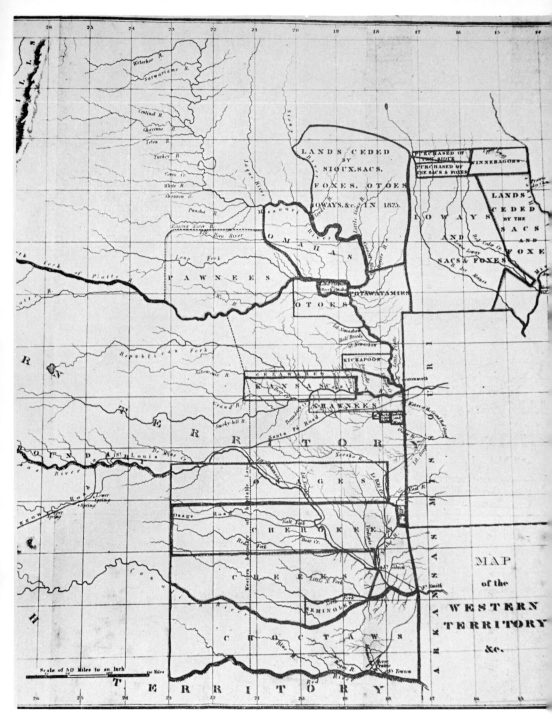

Section of a map published with House Report No. 474 (dated May 20, 1834), 23d Cong., 1st Sess. The three small reserves below the Shawnees are (left to right) those of the Ottawas, the Peorias and Kaskaskias, and the Weas and Piankeshaws.

Henry Dodge (1782-1867) was colonel of the (First) U. S. dragoon regiment from its organization in 1833 to mid-1836, when he resigned to become governor of the new terrritory of Wisconsin. From Autumn, 1834, to Spring, 1836, he was commandant at Fort Leavenworth, headquarters of the (First) dragoons. Reproduced is Catlin's portrait of Dodge, in hunting garb, painted during the 1834 expedition to the Comanche and Wichita country. (From *Iowa Historical Record*, Iowa City, October, 1889, *courtesy* State Historical Society of Iowa.)

Col. Henry Leavenworth (left) for whom Fort Leavenworth was named. The portrait was painted by George Catlin in 1834, only a few weeks before the death of the officer (see pp. 269, 270). The original watercolor, 2⅞" x 3½", is on display at the Fort Leavenworth museum, through whose courtesy it is here reproduced. (Right) Stephen Watts Kearny (1794-1848) became colonel of the (First) U. S. dragoons on July 4, 1836. He succeeded Col. Henry Dodge as commandant at Fort Leavenworth, arriving in mid-1836 and remaining till August, 1842. For brief periods he was at the post again: in 1845 (heading a dragoon expedition to South Pass), in 1846 (as commander of the Army of the West), and in 1847. On June 30, 1846, Kearny became a brigadier general; in August, 1847, he was brevetted major general. (From oil portrait, courtesy Missouri Historical Society, St. Louis.)

"Crossing the Kansas"—Artist Alfred Jacob Miller's water color showing the American Fur Company's caravan of 1837 fording the river (some seven or eight miles above present Lawrence) en route to the Rocky mountains. (See p. 323.) Reproduction courtesy of the Walters Art Gallery, Baltimore, Md., and the University of Oklahoma Press.

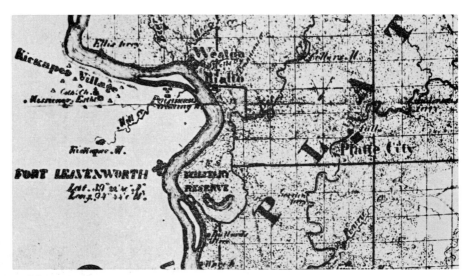

Reproduced here is an enlarged segment of Hutawa's map (1842) of the "Platte Country." East of the Missouri (in the dark background) is shown a part of Platte county, Mo. (organized following the 1837 Platte Purchase addition to the state of Missouri). West of the river, in present Leavenworth county, is Fort Leavenworth, and to the north, a part of the Kickapoo Indians' reserve.

ON THE "KANSAS" SIDE: *Fort Leavenworth* was founded in May, 1827 (see p. 141); the *Kickapoo Village[s]* were of May, 1833, origin (see p. 234); *Pensineau's trading post* was opened about October, 1833 (see p. 248); *Kickapoo [Method:st] M[ission]* was founded in November, 1833 (see p. 253); *Kickapoo Catholic Mission* ("Cathc. Ch. [and] Missionary Estbt.") was begun in June, 1836, and closed in December, 1840 (see p. 309). *Mill cr[eek]* presumably was so labeled by Hutawa because the Kickapoos' mill (built in 1835-1836—see p. 298) was located on it, but the stream's name, at least as early as 1833 (see p. 247) was *Salt creek*. (The 18th century French post, Fort de Cavagnial, of 1744 origin, was located near the mouth of Salt creek—see p. 22.) The large island in the bend of the Missouri (opposite Weston, Mo.) is Kickapoo Island. On maps of later decades it appears in varying shape and size.

ON THE MISSOURI SIDE: The *U. S. Military Reserve* (a tract of some 6,840 acres) was created June 21, 1838, to prevent whisky sellers and other undesirables from settling opposite the fort. It was reduced in size, in 1844, to 936 acres. *Rialto* (or, "the Rialto"), at the mouth of *Pensineau's creek*, was known, also, as Pensineau's Landing. *Weston*, selected for a town site in 1837 by ex-soldier Joseph Moore (for whom *Moore's creek* evidently was named), had a population of some 300 persons in 1839 (see p. 375). *Ellis ferry* was licensed on March 11, 1839 (see p. 365).

[Continued From p. 392]

De Smet went on to Pierre's Hole; then, in the company of Flatheads and Pend d'Oreilles, journeyed to the Three Forks of the Missouri (in Montana) before starting home. He returned via "Bozeman pass" to the Yellowstone, and thence down to Fort Union (having traveled from Fort Alexander—the American Fur Company post for the Crows—with only one companion). From Fort Union De Smet came down the Missouri (by horseback and canoe) to Council Bluffs [Iowa]; left there December 14; reached Westport on the 22d; and arrived at St. Louis on the last day of 1840.

Ref: H. M. Chittenden and A. T. Richardson's *Life, Letters and Travels of Father Pierre-Jean De Smet, S. J.* (New York, 1905), v. 1, pp. 198-258, 270; Joel P. Walker's narrative, *A Pioneer of Pioneers* . . . (Los Angeles, Glen Dawson, 1953); H. H. Bancroft's *History of Oregon,* v. 1, 1838-1848 (San Francisco, 1886), pp. 239-241; *The Pacific Northwest Quarterly,* Seattle, v. 35 (January, 1944), pp. 29-43 (especially p. 34, for De Smet's letter dated Westport, April 20, 1840); *Robert Newell's Memoranda* . . ., edited by Dorothy O. Johansen (Portland, Ore., 1959), p. 39; "Chouteau Account Books" (in Missouri Historical Society, St. Louis), items of March 13-16, 1840 (courtesy of Dale L. Morgan, of the Bancroft Library); *Glimpses of the Past,* St. Louis, v. 8 (January-June, 1941), p. 42; *History of Sonoma County* . . . (San Francisco, 1880), pp. 482-484.

❡ Within this year (in the spring?), it is said, Joseph Papin and his half-Kansa wife, "Josette" (Gonville) Papin (*see* p. 335 for their marriage) took up residence on Kansa "half-breed" reserve No. 3 (across the Kansas river from present south Topeka), which had been allotted under the 1825 treaty to "Josette" Gonville.

(For location—on the north side of the Kansas, in present Soldier township, Shawnee co.—*see* outline map p. 167.)

In December, 1841, Isaac McCoy (employed by the government in an abortive effort to extinguish all 23 Kansa "half-breed" reserves) indicated that 22 of the 640-acre tracts should be purchased at $800 ($1.25 an acre) each; but that Josette Papin had made improvements on her section worth $250, and ought to receive $1,050.

Ref: W. W. Cone's *Historical Sketch of Shawnee County* . . . (Topeka, 1877), p. 7; Isaac McCoy manuscripts (for McCoy's December 22, 1841, report to the secretary of war); A. T. Andreas and W. G. Cutler, *History of the State of Kansas* (Chicago, 1883), pp. 531, 532. The fact that Father Point's 1840 list of Kaw's mouth residents (*see* November 1 entry) does not include the Papin name, tends to corroborate the Papins' presence in "Kansas" prior to November, 1840.

❡ April.—The Rev. Isaac McCoy's *History of Baptist Indian Missions*—a 611-page volume, written from the viewpoint of his more than 20 years of missionary operations, and based upon a journal he had kept during that span of time—was in process of publication at Washington and in New York.

McCoy's preface was dated "Shawanoe Baptist Mission, Indian Territory, December, 1839," and his history was inclusive to that date. A receipt of April 18, 1840 (in the McCoy manuscripts), shows payment by Isaac McCoy of $500 to printer Peter Force, of Washington, for his work on the *History.*

Ref: Isaac McCoy's *History of Baptist Indian Missions* . . . (Washington and New York, 1840); Isaac McCoy manuscripts.

❧ May(?)—The spring caravan to Santa Fe—a small one—was made up principally of Mexican proprietors. Don José Chavez y Castillo and his party had merchandise valued at $75,000 (goods purchased in the East during the preceding winter) which was freighted in 11 wagons. One of the U. S. citizens had three wagons.

The caravan reached Santa Fe in July. Don José Chavez y Castillo paid $1,200 in duties to Mexican customs officials, but the U. S. citizen with only three wagons was compelled to pay $1,286. Dr. John H. Lyman perhaps traveled to New Mexico with this company. Darby H. Cantrell was in charge of wagons and some 30 mules belonging to Manuel Alvarez on this trip.

Ref: *The Weekly Picayune*, June 12, 1840 (or, see Sunder, *op. cit.*, p. xxiv); H. H. Dunham's "Sidelights on Santa Fe Traders 1839-1846," in *1950 Brand Book* (Denver, c1951), p. 286; H. R. Wagner and C. L. Camp, *The Plains and the Rockies* . . ., 3d edition (Columbus, Ohio, 1953), p. 128; Office of Indian Affairs (OIA), National Archives Microcopy 234, Roll 301.

❧ May 22.—Edward Papin, son of Pierre Melicour Papin (the American Fur Company's trader with the Osages) and his part-Osage wife Sophie Mongrain, was baptized near the Marais des Cygnes (in present Linn? county) by the Rev. Herman G. Aelen, S. J.

Edward Papin was born, it appears, July 12, 1838. Sponsor of the baptism was Michel Giraud, of the American Fur Company's Marais des Cygnes post.

Ref: "Pottawatomie Baptismal Register," p. 34 (microfilm in KHi).

❧ On May 25 tourist Victor Tixier (young French medical student), three companions (James De Berty Trudeau, Alexandre Guérin, "Foureau"), and two half-blood Osage guides entered present Bourbon county. Moving southwest, this mounted party camped for the night near the "Pânie-Tanga" (Big Pawnee), now Pawnee creek (a tributary of the Marmaton's South Fork); and on May 27, following several hours of travel (and after fording the "Nion-Chou" [Neosho]), reached the Osage town of *Manrinhabotso* ("The Village Which Scrapes the Sky"—*see* p. 293), and the home of trader Pierre M. Papin, their host (in present Neosho county).

[Tixier and his friends, while passengers on a New Orleans-to-St. Louis steamboat, early in May, had met Paul Ligueste Chouteau who influenced them to make the journey to the Osages' country. Before May 19 they had reached Independence, Mo. (and made a trip to Westport, and the Shawnee reserve, in search of horses); then moved southward on May 20; and reached George Douglass' Vernon county, Mo., farm (northeast of present Deerfield, Mo.) on the 22d. There they remained two days before starting west into "Kansas."

Tixier's account of his journey to, and subsequent experiences among, the Osages, together with much valuable commentary on the Indians (their situation, civilization, culture, etc.) was originally published in France in 1844, under the title *Voyage aux Prairies Osages, Louisiane et Missouri, 1839-40*.]

Besides *Manrinhabotso* (where Baptiste Mongrain was "chief"), there were, by Tixier's description, three other Great Osage towns within a few miles: *Naniompa* ("The Village of the Pipe") where old White Hair (about 80; uncle of the Osages' great chief) and young [George] White Hair (cousin of the Osages' great chief) lived; *Maisons Cailles,* the town of Chief White Hair, the reigning chief of *all* the Osage Indians, who was called Majakita (or, The Lips); *Coeurs Tranquilles* (village of the "Quiet Hearts")—a town of young warriors known as the "Bande-des-Chiens" (Band of Dogs)—whose chief was Man-chap-ché-mani. Also, there was an "independent republic" village not far away, where Ouachinka-lâgri (Bel Oiseau; or, Handsome Bird) was chief.

On June 4 the Osages set out for the summer hunt, heading west (northwest at first) to the Verdigris. At the camp that first night out, there were some 200 lodges, 1,500 men, the same number of dogs, and 3,000 horses (by Tixier's estimate). Pierre M. Papin, his Indian family, and entourage, plus his four guests, constituted one lodge of some 15 persons.

Several days' travel beyond their fording of the Arkansas, the Osages reached the buffalo country. Near the camp they set up were some 200 lodges of Kansa. Tixier remarked how different "the Kansa lodges were from ours." "Each frame," he wrote, "was covered with skins decorated with red, yellow, blue, and black designs which, through their primitive simplicity, recall the ancient Egyptian paintings." And he noted that the Kansa girls were "much prettier" than the Osage.

The Kansa head chief "White Feather" [White Plume II], invited "Majakita, Baptiste, and some of the principal [Osage] chiefs, and us, the white warriors" to a banquet, wrote Tixier. He described "White Feather" as "a short, wiry man with an aquiline nose and piercing eyes." [White Plume II, leading chief since Autumn(?) 1838, apparently died prior to February, 1841. Tixier's comment, plus Artist Alfred Jacob Miller's portrait—*see* note p. 323 and Isaac McCoy's mention of him p. 357, give the only information known about White Plume II, who was so briefly leader of the Kansa.]

After hunting and traveling together for six days, the two nations separated. The Osages moved on west till near the end of June when they reached the "warpaths." Then they changed course to the southwest so as to approach the Great Saline. Around July 20 they made a one-day, 25 mile-each-way round trip to the Saline for a supply of salt. [*See* account of G. C. Sibley's trip in 1811, with the Osages, to the "Grand Saline."]

Then the Indians headed for the Arkansas river; and continued eastward to their Neosho river villages. Tixier noted that the Osages had "secured rather large provisions," and that the place where they had found the "largest number of bison" was on the "River Bahabêh" [or, "Pa-ha-bee"?—probably the present Bluff creek (tributary of the Chikaskia), which crosses present Harper and Sumner counties in Kansas, and Kay county, Okla.]. The night before they reached home the Osages camped on the "river 'A-la-bete' " [Labette creek].

On August 8 Victor Tixier and his three companions left Pierre M. Papin's house to retrace their pathway of May to George Douglass' farm in Missouri. Tixier reached St. Louis late in August (he had gone down the Osage to its mouth in a canoe, then boarded the steamboat *Thames*); proceeded to New York; and sailed for France on September 25, reaching home a month later.

Ref: *Tixier's Travels on the Osage Prairies,* edited by John F. McDermott (Norman, Okla., 1940); R. A. Calloway's report of September 1, 1843, in SIA, St. Louis, "Records," v. 8, typed copy, pp. 228-239, helps to clarify the identity of the head chief White Hair (or, Pahuscah).

❧ May-June.—"Messrs. Bent & St. Vrain" arrived in St. Louis at the beginning of July on the steamboat *Euphrasie* with 15,000 buffalo robes and a considerable amount of furs. These traders had left Fort William ("Bent's Fort") in May to bring their laden wagons across "Kansas" on the Santa Fe trail. They reached Independence, Mo., in June.

Ref: *Daily Missouri Republican,* June 12, July 3, 1840 (as reprinted in Nebraska State Historical Society *Publications,* v. 20, pp. 108, 109).

❧ BORN: on June 7, at Shawnee Friends Mission (present Johnson county), Nathan Pearson, son of mission superintendent Moses Pearson and his wife Sarah. (*See* June, 1837, annals entry.)

Ref: *The History of Miami County, Ohio* (1880), p. 849; W. W. Hinshaw's *Encyclopedia of American Quaker Genealogy,* Ann Arbor, Mich., v. 5, p. 819.

❧ June 10.—At Joseph Robidoux's "Blacksnake Hills" trading post (present St. Joseph, Mo.) a post office was established. Julius C. Robidoux (a son of Joseph) was the first postmaster. (His successor was appointed August 7, 1841.)

Ref: *The History of Buchanan County, Missouri* (1881), p. 413; and *see* KHC, v. 10, p. 319.

❧ June 13.—New superintendents Henry and Ann (Maden) Harvey, with six of their children (aged 3 to 18), from Clinton county, Ohio, arrived at Shawnee Friends Mission (present Johnson county). David Jones, a teacher they had hired, had preceded them—and was at the mission when they arrived.

[The Harveys replaced Moses and Sarah Pearson (*see* June, 1837, annals); they stayed two years; and were succeeded in 1842 by Thomas and Esther (Cattell) French.]

By July 1, the mission school (with 27 pupils) had been resumed. (It had been discontinued in March with the departure of teacher Elias Newby.) At the beginning of September there were 36 children (22 males, 14 females) attending. All except two were Shawnees.

Ref: W. W. Hinshaw's *Encyclopedia of American Quaker Genealogy,* v. 5, pp. 544d, 572; KHC, v. 8, p. 252, v. 13, p. 348; *Some Account of the Conduct of the Religious Society of Friends Towards the Indian Tribes* . . . (London, 1844), p. 241; Henry Harvey's *History of the Shawnee Indians, From* . . . *1681 to 1854* . . . (Cincinnati, 1855), p. 250. The Harveys' children (and their ages) as of spring, 1840, were: George M. (21), who, it appears did not come to "Kansas," Caleb E. (18), Mary (16), Deborah (14), Samuel (9), Henry C. (6), and Ann B. (3). "Maden" seems to be correct as Mrs. Harvey's maiden name, but the common spelling is "Madden."

❧ June.—Dr. Joseph R. De Prefontaine, of Westport, Mo., was employed to give smallpox vaccinations to "such Indians as may stand in need of the Operation" in R. W. Cummins' Fort Leavenworth Agency and A. L. Davis' Osage [Marais des Cygnes] River Subagency. (*See* September, 1839, annals for his work in 1839.)

The Indian department had authorized only $200 for this purpose. On July 20 the physician visited the Ottawas, who gathered at the Baptist mission for their vaccinations.

Ref: SIA, St. Louis, "Records," v. 7, typed copy, p. 90 (Joshua Pilcher's May 28, 1840, letter); Jotham Meeker's "Diary"; 27th Cong., 2d Sess., *H. Doc. No. 164* (Serial 403), p. 20.

❡ June.—E. Willard Smith and six companions who had come down the South Fork and main Platte in a Mackinaw boat, arrived at the Platte's mouth on June 22; and subsequently continued down the Missouri, arriving at St. Louis on July 3. (Baptiste Charbonneau was the party's hunter.)

Aboard their boat (36′ x 8′), built at Fort Vasquez (the point of departure), were 700 buffalo robes and 400 buffalo tongues. They had set out on April 26. Navigation of the South Fork of the Platte—a venture rarely attempted—had proved to be a difficult operation. Smith wrote: "We were obliged to wade and push the boat along most of the way for about three hundred miles, which took us forty-nine days." From the forks of the Platte eastward they made better progress, traveling sometimes 50 miles a day.

Ref: E. Willard Smith's "Journal," in L. R. and Ann W. Hafen, eds., *To the Rockies and Oregon, 1839-1842, op. cit.*

❡ June 30(?)—"Hicks and Marney," of Boone county, Mo., arrived at Independence, Mo., from Santa Fe. Between 20 and 30 wagons (as reported) were in the train which they headed.

At St. Louis (in mid-July) it was stated: "This company and the one which arrived in May have brought about $200,000 in specie and bullion." (One wagon, from Chihuahua, of the above train, was said to have brought into St. Louis $50,000 in bullion and $30,000 in specie.)

Ref: *Missouri Daily Argus*, July 9, 23, 1840.

❡ As July opened it was harvest time at Shawnee Methodist Mission and Indian manual labor school (present Johnson county). The farmer in charge, "Mr. Kline," had 90 acres of wheat to cut; and also had the care of 100 acres of timothy and 125 of oats. "Our wheat and oats are first rate," wrote Missionary Thomas Johnson, "and if we can save them will very much lessen the current expenses of the institution."

In mid-September a report of the institution gave these crop statistics: "about 2,000 bushels of wheat, 4,000 bushels of oats, 3,500 bushels of corn, 500 bushels of potatoes. . . ."

Ref: *Christian Advocate and Journal*, New York, v. 15 (November 25, 1840), p. 58; Comm'r of Indian affairs *Report* for 1840 (Agent R. W. Cummins' report). The identity of "Mr. Kline" has not been determined. Perhaps he was Charles Kline who had journeyed to the Rocky mountains with the 1839 American Fur Company expedition, and returned in the autumn, by way of Bent's Fort, and the Santa Fe trail, with Dr. F. A. Wislizenus and Paul Richardson.

❡ July 3.—At Delaware Methodist Mission (present Wyandotte county) a newly erected hewed-log meeting house (22' x 27'), which the Indians themselves had constructed, was dedicated.

The Rev. Thomas Johnson (of Shawnee Mission) made the principal address; and the Delawares' second chief (Ketchum, apparently), who was a Christian, also made a speech.

Ref: *Christian Advocate and Journal,* v. 15 (November 25, 1840), p. 58.

❡ July 7.—The Jesuits opened a school for Indian boys at Pottawatomie Catholic Mission, on Sugar creek (present Linn county). (*See, also,* March 10, 1839, entry.)

The school was maintained at Sugar creek till 1848; then was transferred to the Pottawatomies' new Kansa river reserve.

Ref: G. J. Garraghan's *The Jesuits of the Middle United States,* v. 2, pp. 202, 208, 209, 213.

❡ July.—Inspecting at Fort Leavenworth, Col. George Croghan wrote: "The Captain [Thomas Swords, acting quartermaster] has in cultivation a field of about 800 acres in corn, oats, and timothy, which promises fairly. [*See* June, 1838, annals entry.] When the harvest is gathered in, an estimate of costs may be made out from which a correct decision can be drawn as to the propriety of continuing this system of cultivation."

[In 1842 Colonel Croghan, again at Fort Leavenworth, wrote: "The Farm is still kept up, but as yet without profit, nor need profit ever be expected so long as it is cultivated by soldiers and under the direction of a military officer, ignorant (as most officers are) of even the first principles of farming. There are a few hired citizens at work on the farm. . . ."]

See, also, October 11, 1842, entry.

Ref: F. P. Prucha, ed., *Army Life on the Western Frontier* (c1958), pp. 86, 88. The colonel's 1842 report was dated August 16.

❡ MARRIED.—John Tecumseh ("Tauy") Jones (well-educated; half Chippewa and half English, but counted as a Pottawatomie), and Rachel Littleman (a Stockbridge Indian), on July 20, at Ottawa Baptist Mission (present Franklin county), by Jotham Meeker, in the presence of 30 Indians. (*See* Jones' portrait in this volume.)

(In his diary entry of July 21, Meeker recorded: "Br. & Sis. Jones leave for Putawatomie"—meaning the settlement at Pottawatomie creek, 12 miles distant.)

Ref: Jotham Meeker's "Diary," July 20, 21, 1840; Lewis Henry Morgan's *The Indian Journals 1859-62* (Ann Arbor, v1959), pp. 38, 39 contains some autobiographical information on Jones, and a portrait).

❡ MARRIED: Jean Baptiste St. Michel (half? Osage), and Elizabeth

Quenneville (half Osage), daughter of Francois Quenneville (Canville), on August 10, "a la riviere des Osages, American Fur Compy's trading post" (*i. e.*, on the Marais des Cygnes, at present Trading Post, Linn co.), by the Rev. Herman G. Aelen, S. J.

Witnesses to the ceremony were: Michel Giraud, Marguerite Renaud, Charles Cardinal, Wossosta, Louis Peltier, Thomas Mongeon, Martin Belhumeur, Francois St. Michel, Joseph Marie, Auguste Kans, Antoine Payne, Solomon Bienville, Francois Queneville, A. Janis. These persons were dwellers near, or employees of, the American Fur Company's Marais des Cygnes post.

Among the Osage "half-breeds" mentioned in the treaty of June 2, 1825, who were to be assigned 640-acre reserves on the north side of the Marais des Cygnes, above Harmony Mission (Mo.) were Baptiste St. Mitchelle, Jr. (also Julia and Francis St. Mitchelle), and Marguerite Reneau (Renaud).

Ref: "Pottawatomie Marriage Register" (microfilm, KHi); also, in Osage Catholic Mission "Records," v. 1 (microfilm, KHi); W. A. Mitchell's *Linn County, Kansas* . . . (c1928), pp. 197, 198, mentions "Jean Baptiste" (whose marriage is noted above), and "Michael Giareau" of the Trading Post; Stella M. Drumm, ed., John C. Luttig's *Journal* . . . (1920), p. 60, has data on Francois Quenneville and his descendants.

❡ August.—Bound for Santa Fe, a small caravan carrying goods owned by U. S. citizens apparently crossed "Kansas" during this month. It reached Santa Fe in October. The proprietors had to pay duties higher than those charged their compatriots in July. (*See* May annals entry.)

According to Josiah Gregg's statistics, 1840 was a poor year in the Santa Fe trade. Not since 1824 had such a small valuation of goods been taken from Missouri to New Mexico. He estimated the merchandise transported to Santa Fe in 1840 at $50,000 (perhaps excluding the Mexican nationals' goods?), with five proprietors, employing some 60 men, and about 30 wagons, in the trade.

Ref: *1950 Brand Book* (Denver, c1951), p. 268; Josiah Gregg's *Commerce of the Prairies* (New York, 1844), v. 2, p. 160.

❡ August(?)—The trading expedition of "Metcalf and Richard" (Archibald C. Metcalf and John Richard) may have crossed "Kansas" during this month. A St. Louis newspaper of July 9 had stated these traders would "depart for the Rocky Mountains in ten or fifteen days."

Ref: *Missouri Argus* (daily), July 9, 1840. In a journal entry of July 16, 1843, Theodore Talbot (of Fremont's second expedition) referred to "Metcalf, a trader," as bringing "news from the North Fork of the Platte" to "St. Vrain's Fort" (on the South Platte). In a diary entry on July 5, 1843, Matthew C. Field (with Sir William Drummond Stewart's pleasure party) wrote of encamping "opposite Richard's fort" ["Fort Platte"—purchased by Sibille & Adams in 1842 from Lancaster P. Lupton]. It appears that John Richard was, for a time, a copartner with Sibille & Adams. Sources for the preceding: *The Journals of Theodore Talbot* . . ., edited by C. H. Carey (Portland, 1931), p. 23; Matthew C. Field's *Prairie and Mountain Sketches* . . ., edited by Kate L. Gregg and John F. McDermott (Norman, c1957), p. 74; Dale L. Morgan's letters of June 15 and 28, 1963, to L. Barry. *And, see* Janet Lecompte's article on Metcalf in L. R. Hafen, editor, *The Mountain Men and the Fur Trade of the Far West* (Glendale, Cal., 1966), v. 4, pp. 217-224.

❧ August-September.—Among the Kansa Indians, and at the Kansa Methodist Mission (present Shawnee county), sickness ("fever, and other diseases") was prevalent.

Residing at, and near, the mission were 14 white persons—the Rev. William Johnson, his wife, and two children; assistant [Martin?] Greene, his wife; a "young lady" (not identified); also, Kansa farmer David Benzley, his wife, and five children. At one time, Johnson and the "young lady" were administering to 10 sick people. The Kansa farmer's wife—[Margaret (Ligget)?] Benzley —died; several weeks later, the Johnsons lost their young daughter Mary Frances.

Wrote Missionary Johnson: "While we were sick at the mission, the Indians were suffering equally as much. In some families as many as five died. [Young Kansa head chief White Plume II may have been one of the victims.] But few families escaped disease; and the number of deaths was great in proportion to the number sick. . . . The Indians were gloomy, and not inclined to do anything but prepare for their fall hunt; believing that they would be better off if scattered in the woods, where fresh meat could be obtained. . . . The last two summers have been sickly here [*see* Autumn, 1839, annals, p. 382], though we have always considered the country very healthy."

Ref: *KHC*, v. 16, p. 231 (for William Johnson's December 30, 1840, letter). In the Jackson county, Mo., marriage records, the marriage of David Benzley and Margaret Ligget is entered as occurring on September 10, 1830. It has been assumed she was the Mrs. Benzley who died in "Kansas" in 1840. For the Greenes, *see* July 14, 1839, annals entry. In June, 1840, Victor Tixier met the *then* Kansa head chief White Plume II; but eight months later, in February, 1841, it was "Kihigawatinga" (Fool Chief) who received $1,000, by tribal order, at the payment of the Kansa annuities—evidently as head chief of the nation.

❧ BORN: on September 5, at the new Shawnee Methodist Mission (present Johnson county), Thomas Johnson Greene and Mary Elizabeth Greene, son and daughter of the Rev. Jesse and Mary (Todd) Greene. They were, so far as known, the first white twins born in "Kansas."

Ref: KHi's 15th *Biennial Report*, p. 36; Kansas City (Mo.) *Star*, January 23, 1925 (for T. J. Greene's recollections of early days at Shawnee Mission).

❧ DIED: Jacques Ash-kum (chief of the Wabash Pottawatomies), on September 10(?), at the Sugar creek settlement (present Linn county). He was upwards of 70 years old. Burial was on September 11. (*See* his portrait on p. 602 in this volume.)

Ref: "Pottawatomie Burial Register" (microfilm in KHi).

❧ DIED: Cynthia (Burr) Mercer, wife of Reuben Mercer (of Jackson county, Mo.), on September 11, at Pottawatomie creek (present Franklin county), where the couple was living while Mr. Mercer worked on "Mr. Simerwell's houses"—the new buildings at Pottawatomie Baptist Mission (*see* p. 336).

The Mercers had been married at Otoe Baptist Mission, near the Council

Bluffs (Neb.) on August 18, 1836, by the Rev. Moses Merrill. Theirs was one of the early marriages of white persons in "Nebraska."

Ref: Jotham Meeker's "Diary," September 12, 1840; Jackson county, Mo., marriage records (for affidavit by Merrill, made at Independence, Mo., February 23, 1837, of the Mercer-Burr marriage); Delilah (McCoy) Lykins' letter of March 31, 1840 (in Isaac McCoy manuscripts), for item on Mercer's work in "Kansas." Mrs. Lawrence G. Kellerman, and others, in December, 1970, reported that Cynthia Mercer's tombstone is located on a hill southeast of "Ritchel Crossing" on the Pottawatomie, between Lane and Greeley, in Franklin county. The still-legible marker gives her age as 33.

❦ September-October.—A small party of British army officers (from Canada), headed by Lt. Col. William Greenwood, Grenadier Guards, and accompanied by "Gen." Robert Patterson (of Pennsylvania), camped near Shawnee Methodist Mission on September 13, en route west, via the Santa Fe trail, on a hunting expedition.

They sighted the first buffalo September 27; on the 29th, west of "Cottonwood Creek," they rode in pursuit of a buffalo herd; on October 4 reached the Walnut creek area; hunted on the Pawnee fork in mid-October; began the journey home on the 16th (prairie fires made the return trip a hazardous one); reached Westport at the end of October.

Ref: John E. Sunder's article, "British Army Officers on the Santa Fe Trail," in *The Bulletin* of the Missouri Historical Society, St. Louis, v. 23 (January, 1967), pp. 147-157; SIA, St. Louis, "Records," v. 7, typed copy, pp. 110, 111.

❦ September 21.—Col. Stephen W. Kearny and 165 First U. S. dragoons left Fort Leavenworth, crossed the Missouri, and marched up the left bank towards the Pottawatomie settlements near present Council Bluffs, Iowa. Capt. Philip St. George Cooke made this trip, and by report, Captains Nathan Boone and James Allen, with their companies, were on the expedition.

By the 29th they were encamped on Mosquito creek (about a mile and a half "from that part of the Missouri river opposite to Belleview" [Bellevue, "Neb."], where they remained till October 7. During that time the Pottawatomies received their annuities under dragoon supervision; and Colonel Kearny held councils with the Indians. A problem relating to a band of some 150 Iowas residing on the Pottawatomies' reserve was resolved when the latter requested that the Iowas not be forced to remove. Pottawatomie chiefs Joseph LaFromboise, Wam-goe-see, Sau-ke-nosh [Sagaunash?—Billy Caldwell?], and Half Day were among those who took part in the proceedings.

On October 14 Colonel Kearny and his command were back at Fort Leavenworth.

Ref: Office of Indian Affairs (OIA), Letters Received from SIA, St. Louis (National Archives Microcopy No. 234, Roll 752), Col. S. W. Kearny's report, October 16, 1840; *Missouri Argus* (daily), September 28, 1840; Comm'r of Indian Affairs *Report* for 1840; Fort Leavenworth post returns.

❦ October 6.—Emigrant Pottawatomies (from northern Indiana and southern Michigan), reported to number 524 persons on arrival, reached the reservation in "Kansas"—south of the Marais des Cygnes river. Their conductor was Samuel P. Brady.

[The subsistence and transportation west of this party was by war department contract of June 13 (made by Bvt. Brig. Gen. Hugh Brady) with Alexis Coquillard, of South Bend, Ind., who agreed to remove the Indians for the sum of $55 each.]

It appears that the Rev. Stanislaus A. Bernier (Catholic) accompanied (but did not remain with) this party; and that most (or all?) of the immigrants settled with the Sugar creek Pottawatomies (in present Linn county).

See, also, November 25 entry.

Ref: 26th Cong., 2d Sess., *Sen. Doc. No. 161* (Serial 378), p. 37; 27th Cong., 2d Sess., *H. Doc. No. 143* (Serial 403), pp. 26-29, 151; SIA, St. Louis, "Records," v. 7, typed copy, pp. 126-128; G. J. Garraghan's *The Jesuits of the Middle United States,* v. 2, p. 190; *Niles' National Register,* v. 59 (September 12, 26, 1840), pp. 17, 50.

❡ BORN: on October 8, at Shawnee Baptist Mission (present Johnson county), Mary Frances Barker, daughter (and first child) of the Rev. Francis and Elizabeth F. (Churchill) Barker. (*See* October 23, 1839, annals entry.)

Ref: Elizabeth F. Barker's *Barker Genealogy* (New York, 1927), p. 199; "Barker Collection," in KHi ms. division. In KHi's 15th *Biennial Report,* p. 36, the name is incorrectly given as "Frances Elizabeth Mary Barker." Mary Frances Barker married William L. Miles in 1873; died in 1917.

❡ MARRIED: Thomas Mongeon (half Osage) and Helene De'haitre (the widow Bastien), on October 26, at the American Fur Company's Marais des Cygnes post (present Linn county), by the Rev. Herman G. Aelen, S. J. (*See, also,* August 10 entry.)

Witnesses were: John Basile, Michel Giraud, Andrew Drips, Louis Peltier, J. Arquoite, John Michel [St. Mitchelle?], N(?) Woester(?), J. Petre, J. Michel [St. Mitchelle?], Solomon Bienville, J. Queneville, B. L'Habitant, A. Payne.

Ref: "Pottawatomie Marriage Register" (microfilm in KHi); also in Osage Catholic Mission "Records," v. 1 (microfilm, KHi); and *see* G. J. Garraghan's *The Jesuits of the Middle United States,* v. 2, p. 230. The "Pottawatomie Baptismal Register," p. 66, has record of the baptism, on August 7, 1841, of this couple's son Joseph. The mother's name is given as "d'Etre." "Mongeon" is, presumably, a form of the name "Mongrain."

❡ October 31 and November 2.—At Sugar creek (present Linn county), Comm'r Alexis Coquillard held councils with the Pottawatomies (all except Chief To-pin-a-bee and part of his band attended) on the subject of reuniting the nation by removing the Council Bluffs (Iowa) Pottawatomies to the reserve in "Kansas."

[Bvt. Brig. Gen. Hugh Brady had appointed Coquillard, of South Bend, Ind., and the Rev. Isaac McCoy, of Westport, Mo., commissioners to treat with the Indians on this matter. Coquillard arrived at Westport on October 26; consulted with McCoy (who drew up a treaty form); then proceeded southward to the Marais des Cygnes. George Crawford (secretary) accompanied him.]

"Sag-au-naw"[?] was principal spokesman for the "Kansas" Pottawatomies at both councils. Other chiefs who indicated approval of the plan included

Che-bas, We-we-saw, Che-chaw-cose, Be-se-ah, Pa-ma-di-si, Louison, and Ioway. Witnesses to the unilateral agreement were Crawford, and Pottawatomies Abram Burnett (interpreter), Andrew Jackson, Richard Furman, Joseph N. Bourassa, and Lewis Compant.

See, also, November 9 entry.

Ref: 27th Cong., 2d Sess., *H. Doc. No. 143* (Serial 403), pp. 23, 24, 139-144; Isaac McCoy's letter of January 1, 1841, in McCoy manuscripts.

❦ November 1.—The Rev. Nicholas Point, S. J., arrived at Westport Landing to take charge of the St. Francis Regis (originally "Chouteau's Church"—*see* p. 292) parish, in present Kansas City, Mo. He remained till May 10, 1841.

"The district [at the Kaw's mouth] in which I took up my abode," wrote Father Point, "was peopled by an assemblage of 23 Indian families each family group comprising a Frenchman with his Indian wife and half-breed children." He sketched a map of his parish, listing the residents' names (including several non-French persons). Some of these people (listed below) had been connected with "Kansas"' history in the early 1800's; and others (or their relatives) became "Kansas" residents in the 1840's, or later:
(1) Mission-church, (2) [Moyse] Bellemare and Clement [Lessert], (3) Gerber, (4) [Pierre?] Carboneau, (5) [Antoine] De Laurier, (6) Tremblé, (7) [Joseph] Vertefeuille, (8) [Pierre] Laliberté, (9) [Joseph] Rivard, (10) Petit Louis [Louis Prieu, step-son of Grand Louis Bertholet], (11) [Andrew B.] Campville [Canville], (12) Cadoret, (13) Widow Rivard, (14) Widow Chouteau [Berenice (Menard) Chouteau, widow of Francis G.], (15) Grand Louis [Bertholet], (16) [Gabriel?] Philibert, (17) Peria, (18) Benjamin [Lagautherie], (19) [John?] Gray, (20) Prud'homme, (21) Edouard, (22) Bowird [William Bowers], (23) Ben., (24) [Andrew] Drips, (25) [Thomas A.] Smart, (26) Meguille.

Ref: G. J. Garraghan's *Catholic Beginnings in Kansas City, Missouri* (Chicago, 1920), pp. 101, 102; also his *The Jesuits of the Middle United States,* v. 1, p. 261; Kansas City (Mo.) *Times,* November 4, 1948 (also, in KHi library, in Kansas City, Mo., history "Clippings," v. 5, pp. 74, 75). Probably "Gerber" was Joseph Jarboe. "Widow Rivard" was, it appears, Frances (Roy) Rivard, widow of Joseph Rivard. "Peria" was, perhaps, "Perrier." The Prud'homme household doubtlessly included Mrs. Gabriel Prudhomme. "Edouard," according to Mrs. Blanche O. Garrison, of Bartlesville, Okla., was Edouard La Chasse. "Meguille" is generally supposed to be a spelling of Magill, or McGill. Mrs. Garrison (in letter of April 11, 1964, to L. Barry) noted that Pierre Charbonneau (Carboneau) went by the name Pierre Revalette. He, and his sister Elizabeth, received grants of land as Kansas "half-breeds" under the 1825 Kansa treaty provisions.

❦ November 9.—The Rev. William Hamilton (of "Ioway and Sac Mission," present Doniphan county) wrote that the resident missionaries were Samuel M. Irvin, Henry Bradley, William Hamilton, and their wives.

The summer school had averaged about 30 students, who were taught in English. The Iowas were decreasing rapidly; the five houses for the chiefs (per September, 1836, treaty) had been erected; their mill (for lack of a substantial dam) was doing little business; many Iowas had sold their farming tools to whisky traders; and had also killed their stock. They had dismissed their government farmers and smiths about a year earlier. Some of the Iowas were on the Pottawatomies' reserve (in Iowa). The Sacs had torn down most of their mill (no water had ever run in the mill race); and had also destroyed part of their houses. They were averse to missionary operations.

In 1841(?) Isaac McCoy was told by the Rev. S. M. Irvin that the Iowas numbered about 600 (450 on the reserve; 150 among the Pottawatomies); that the principal chiefs were White Cloud and No Heart; and that this tribe had employed Francis Irvin (father of Samuel M.) as their farmer. The "Sauks" (Sacs & Foxes of Missouri) were supposed to number about 600. Their principal chiefs were Nesoquot and Shakopee.

Ref: Isaac McCoy manuscripts (for Hamilton's letter dated "Liberty Nov. 9th 1840"; and McCoy's notes from Irvin, a few pages following the letter).

❈ November 9.—Comm'rs Alexis Coquillard and Isaac McCoy, their secretary George Crawford, Dr. Johnston Lykins, with part Pottawatomies Luther Rice and Joseph Bertrand, Jr. (interpreters), also J. B. Bertrand (in charge of the pack horse), set out from Westport, Mo., for Council Bluffs (Iowa).

They reached the Pottawatomie reserve on the 16th; found the Indians had left in October for the hunting grounds; sent out runners to bring them in for a council. Finally, on January 2, 1841, the commissioners met with *some* of the Pottawatomie chiefs (one being "Wau-pen-say"—Wau-bon-seh) and discussed the subject of removal from the Council Bluffs reserve to the Pottawatomie reserve in "Kansas" (south of the Marais des Cygnes). "Shaw-be-my" was spokesman for the Council Bluffs Indians at this meeting (which accomplished nothing).

Ref: 27th Cong., 2d Sess., *H. Doc. No. 143* (Serial 403), pp. 144-146; McCoy manuscripts (for Isaac McCoy's letter of November 22, 1840).

❈ November 16.—Missionary (and printer) John G. Pratt and his wife, Olivia (Evans) Pratt, returned to Shawnee Baptist Mission, after a year in the East where Mrs. Pratt had been restored to good health. A teacher, Abigail Ann Webster, accompanied them to "Kansas," and on December 1, under the superintendence of the Rev. Francis Barker, assumed charge of the mission school of 10 pupils.

Ref: *The Baptist Missionary Magazine*, v. 20 (June, 1840), p. 127, v. 21 (March, 1841), p. 80. The Pratts had come to "Kansas," originally, in May, 1837.

❈ November 25.—About 439 Pottawatomies (from southern Michigan and northern Indiana), conducted by Robert A. Forsyth, reached the reservation in "Kansas"—south of the Marais des Cygnes river. Apparently most (or all) these Indians settled with their kinsmen on Pottawatomie creek (in present Miami and Franklin counties). *See, also,* October 6 entry.

Bvt. Brig. Gen. Hugh Brady, with 200 soldiers, and 100 mounted volunteers had rounded up these very reluctant emigrants in the late summer and early autumn; then herded them cross-country to Peru, Ill., where they were placed aboard a steamboat. (For the capture of a chief[?] named Muc-mote [Muck-e-moote], one citizen received payment of $100.) The "bold and determined conduct" of Robert A. Forsyth in handling the Pottawatomies made it unnecessary to send a military escort on the steamboat. Before November 11 the emigrants had reached St. Louis and were encamped about 20 miles from the city, awaiting transportation to "Kansas." The Rev. Isaac S. Ketchum (an assistant Indian agent) accompanied this party; and "Mr. [Gholson?] Kercheval" was assistant conductor.

The subsistence and transportation West of these Pottawatomies was by war department contract (made by General Brady on August 4) with James J. and Peter Godfroy (who were to receive $60 per Indian). The emigrants' destitute condition, the late traveling season, and early severe weather required the government to furnish them with over $6,000 worth of clothing. After their arrival in "Kansas," Subagent Anthony L. Davis made further contracts for their subsistence.

Chiefs, or head men, Os-met, Was-saw-we, Ken-kosh, Kapes-co-wet, To-pen-ebi, 2d, and others (some 30 in all), of the above party, wrote a letter dated "Pottawatomie Creek, Feb. 3, 1841," to the secretary of war, stating that "Muck-e-moote" and three others of the tribe who had started to Washington in January(?), with the Rev. Isaac S. Ketchum, "are not considered by us as chiefs. . . ."

Ref: 26th Cong., 2d Sess., *H. Doc. No. 72* (Serial 383), p. 3 (for Godfroy contract); 27th Cong., 2d Sess., *H. Doc. No. 143* (Serial 403), pp. 28-32, 34, 50, 51, 138; 27th Cong., 2d Sess., *H. Doc. No. 164* (Serial 403), p. 70; *Niles' National Register,* v. 59 (November 7, 1840), p. 148; SIA, v. 7, typed copy, pp. 141, 142, v. 8, typed copy, p. 63; *Michigan Pioneer and Historical Collections,* Lansing, v. 21 (1892), pp. 305-311; S. W. Durant's *History of Ingham and Eaton Counties, Michigan* . . . (Philadelphia, 1880), p. 350.

¶ December.—As Agent R. W. Cummins reported it: "The Kanzas Indians while in the buffaloe grounds this winter, sent out a war party of Sixty five men, they came across a party of (Seventeen lodges) Pawnees, the men were absent in search of buffaloe, the Kanzas rushed into the lodges, killed they say, Sixty or upwards women and children and took eleven prisoners, five women and six children. . . ."

According to another account (via Fort Leavenworth), the Kansa "laid in ambush near the ill-fated encampment until they saw the Pawnee warriors, numbering but 17, depart for their hunting ground. The Kanzas warriers, 65 in all, then commenced a murderous fire upon the defenceless women and children [and three men, one blind], which they continued until they supposed all within the encampment had been killed.—On entering the scene of carnage they tomahawked and scalped more than 70 of their victims—they found 12 (six women and as many children) unhurt, whom they decided to retain as prisoners. . . ." (One of these women fought her captors and was killed.) These Indians were stated to be "Pawnee Republics."

Kansa missionary William Johnson wrote that there were 19 Pawnee lodges (a camp of around 150? Indians); that the Kansa "killed and scalped about 93, and took 11 prisoners, 10 horses, and all the articles they could pack, out of their houses [lodges], burned the balance, and then fled. . . . they shot some dead, and others they thrust through with the spear. . . ."

Ref: SIA, St. Louis, "Records," v. 8, typed copy, pp. 69, 70 (for Cummins' March 1, 1841, letter); *Arkansas State Gazette*, Little Rock, April 7, 1841 (reprinting of a St. Louis *Gazette* article), or, see *KHQ*, v. 11, p. 399; *KHC*, v. 16, pp. 232, 233; *Niles' National Register*, v. 60 (April 3, 1841), p. 68. Father DeSmet, in 1841, referred to the "ninety" Pawnee scalps taken by the Kansa.—See Chittenden and Richardson, *op. cit.*, v. 1, p. 285.

⁅ Employed in "Kansas" by the Indian Department during all, or part of the year 1840 were the following persons:

FORT LEAVENWORTH AGENCY—*Agent* Richard W. Cummins; *Interpreters* Henry Tiblow and Clement Lessert; *Blacksmiths* William F. Newton (for Delawares), Robert Dunlap (for Shawnees), Greenup Dodson (for Shawnees), W. J. Baugh (for Kansa); *Assistant blacksmiths* W. H. Newton (for Delawares), Benjamin Rodgers, Wilson Rodgers, James M. Simpson, and Jackson Pitman (all for the Shawnees); Charles Fish (for Kansa); *Farmers* James Hays (for Kansa), and David Benzley (for Kansa).

GREAT NEMAHA SUBAGENCY (re-established)—*Subagent* Congreve Jackson (beginning November 15); *Interpreter* Jeffrey Dorion; *Assistant blacksmith:* John B. Rubeti (for Iowas).

OSAGE [MARAIS DES CYGNES] RIVER SUBAGENCY—*Subagent* Anthony L. Davis; *Interpreter* Luther Rice; *Blacksmiths* Robert Simerwell (appointed June 1) and Robert Wilson (both for Pottawatomies); *Assistant blacksmiths* John Leib (appointed June 1) and D. Moreland (both for Pottawatomies).

OSAGE SUBAGENCY—*Subagent* Congreve Jackson (transferred to Great Nemaha Subagency late in 1840), succeeded by Robert A. Calloway (beginning near end of 1840?); *Interpreter* Charles Mongrain; *Blacksmiths* John Lemons, and John C. Brashears (appointed March 4); *Assistant blacksmiths* Peter Kannab, and E. W. Black (appointed March 4).

Ref: 27th Cong., 2d Sess., H. Doc. No. 41 (Serial 402); 27th Cong., 2d Sess., *H. Doc. No. 164* (Serial 403), pp. 63, 73, 75, 89, 90, 96, 97; SIA, St. Louis, "Records," v. 7, typed copy, pp. 55, 57, 72, 142, 143, 145, 146, 387, and v. 8, typed copy, p. 257.

1841

⁅ MARRIED: Moyse Bellemare (a French-Canadian, from Yamachiche, Quebec) and Adele Lessert (half-Kansa daughter of Clement Lessert, a French-Canadian), on January 7, at present Kansas City, Mo., by the Rev. Nicholas Point, S. J.

In the Kansa treaty of June 3, 1825, "Adel" (then a child) and her brother "Clement" (who died young) were the first-named of the 23 half-breeds who were each to receive a 640-acre reserve on the Kansas river. Some time in the 1840's Moyse and Adele (Lessert) Bellemare moved from the Kaw's mouth [Kansas City, Mo.] to present Shawnee co., to make their home on reserve No. 2 (*see* Shawnee county map, p. 167). "Moses Bellemore," but not his family, was recorded in the Kansas territorial census of 1855. The state census of 1865 listed the "Bellmore" family as follows: Moses (52), Adell (42), Joseph (17; born in Missouri[?]), Julia (12), and Leonard (4), both born in Kansas.

Ref: "Westport Register" (microfilm in KHi); G. J. Garraghan's *The Jesuits of the Middle United States*, v. 1, p. 263; Isaac McCoy manuscripts (McCoy's December 22,

1841, report); *KHC*, v. 8, pp. 482, 483; 37th Cong., 2d Sess., *Sen. Ex. Doc. No. 58* (Serial 1122), pp. 2, 11; Kansas territorial census, 1855, 12th district, p. 5; Kansas state census, 1865, Soldier township, Shawnee co.; Kansas City chapter, D. A. R., *Vital Historical Records of Jackson County, Missouri* . . . (c1934), pp. 92, 95, 266 (for items on children born to the Bellemares). Mrs. Theodore Bellmard, in a letter of April 17, 1962, to L. Barry, wrote that Joseph Napoleon Bellmard's application for a Civil War pension states he was born at "Topeka," August 1, 1847. (He was the "Joseph" aged 17 in 1865, noted above.) The Bellemares were not listed in the 1860 or 1870 federal censuses.

❧ January.—The Kansa Indians returned from the buffalo country to their villages, bringing the prisoners taken in the December massacre at the Pawnee Republic encampment.

Wrote Missionary William Johnson, at the end of January: "Since the Indians came in, the war song and scalp dance constitute their daily employment. All other matters . . . are laid aside. The effect of this massacre upon the tribe at large, in paralyzing all our operations, is now felt to an alarming extent. There are but few men . . . of the Kanzas now disposed to think of anything but a defense against the attacks of the Pawnees, now exasperated at the slaughter of their women and children.

"The upper village of Kanzas have fled from their town, and expect to wander to and fro for the balance of the year. They talk of planting a little corn at their town, but even that is uncertain. The village near the mission are so elated with their past act of bravery, that they have done little else than dance since they came in. The few families who were building houses near the mission are now the subjects of laughter and sport by the new-made braves. The number who are now disposed to build houses and provide for their families is small, not more than 15 families in all. . . . The prospect of reforming these people is truly gloomy at present. . . . ."

Ref: *KHC*, v. 16, pp. 233, 234 (Johnson's letter of January 30, 1841, reprinted from the *Christian Advocate and Journal*, v. 15, p. 122).

❧ February.—Agent R. W. Cummins, accompanied by a First U. S. dragoon escort (Capt. Eustace Trenor, Asst. Surg. Alfred W. Kennedy, and Company F), arrived at the principal Kansa village on the 22nd. (The troops had left Fort Leavenworth on February 17.) Cummins' two-fold purpose: (1) to make the annual annuity payment ($2,500 to the tribe; also, $1,000 to chief "Kihigawatinga" [Fool Chief] by order of the Kansa), and (2) to recover the 11 women and children of the Pawnee Republic band held captive by the Kansa since December, 1840.

The agent later reported: ". . . they gave up the prisoners the same evening [February 22] without hesitation, they were much alarmed at the approach of the troops . . . As the prisoners were naked I was compelled to purchase them some clothing and blankets."

The dragoons, with the 11 Pawnees, returned to Fort Leavenworth on March 1. On the 5th Lt. Charles F. Ruff, with a few troops, set out from the post "to convey the Pawnee prisoners to Bellevue [Neb.]," where they would "meet their missionaries and some members of their own tribe."

Ref: *Arkansas State Gazette*, Little Rock, April 7, 1841 (or, *see KHQ*, v. 11, p. 399); SIA, St. Louis "Records," v. 8, typed copy, pp. 69, 70, and v. 7, typed copy, pp. 175-177; 27th Cong., 2d Sess., H. Doc. No. 164 (Serial 403), p. 90 (for item on "Kihigawatinga," also for items that Frederick Chouteau was paid $45 for "blankets furnished Pawnee prisoners," and William Johnson received $29.20 "for transportation of Kanzas annuity &c and shirts for Pawnee prisoners."

❡ BORN: on March 9, at Fort Leavenworth, Louisa Kearny, daughter of Col. Stephen W. and Mary (Radford) Kearny.

(The colonel also noted in his diary: "Snowed all day to a depth of ten inches.")

Ref: D. L. Clarke's *Stephen Watts Kearny* . . . (Norman, c1961), p. 81.

❡ March.—While the Osages received their annual annuity, Subagent Robert A. Calloway had a census taken. There were, he reported, 1,484 men, 1,436 women, and 1,375 children—a total of 4,295 souls.

(In 1840 it had been estimated the Osages had 1,024 "warriors." The report of the Comm'r of Indian affairs, in late 1841, gave the Osage population as 5,120. Also, *see* March, 1836, annals.)

Ref: Calloway's report, and the commissioner's, are in *Report* of the Comm'r of Indian affairs, 1841; 26th Cong., 1st Sess., Sen. Doc. No. 379 (Serial 359), for the 1840 "warriors" figure.

❡ April.—At Shawnee Baptist Mission (present Johnson county), a new printing office was under construction. (The former office was to be used "as a place of religious worship and school-house.")

Missionary-printer John G. Pratt (despite ill health; the move to the new office; and other interruptions) proceeded to print the following works on the "Meeker press" between April, 1841, and April, 1842: 750 copies of *Matthew* (a 68-page book) in Shawnee; 500 copies of *Matthew* (a 125-page book) in Ottawa; 750 copies of *Matthew* (48 pages; reprinted) in Shawnee; 500 copies of a 24-page, reprinted *First Book* in Delaware; occasional issues (totaling 12 pages and 800 copies) of the *Shawanoe Sun* (newspaper); and a "small hymn book, in Shawanoe," was reported as "in press, and nearly completed."

Ref: *The Baptist Missionary Magazine*, v. 21 (June, 1841), p. 173, v. 22 (June, 1842), p. 161.

❡ April.—The *Trapper* was the American Fur Company's steamboat sent to the upper Missouri trading posts in 1841. Upbound, she presumably passed along the "Kansas" shore in April, reaching Fort Union (at the mouth of the Yellowstone) after an 80-day journey from St. Louis.

At St. Louis, on July 14, a "fleet" of 10 "barges" from the headwaters of the Missouri and Yellowstone, reached port "all richly laden, upwards of 20,000 Buffalo robes, and an indefinite amount of beaver skins, buffalo tongues and other luxuries. . . ." The *Trapper's* arrival was expected hourly, with other peltries.

Ref: *Daily Missouri Republican*, July 15, 1841 (as reprinted in Nebraska State Historical Society *Publications,* v. 20, p. 114); *Weekly Picayune,* August 2, 1841; H. M. Chittenden's *The American Fur Trade of the Far West* (New York, 1935), v. 2, p. 956. Charles Larpenteur (*see* his *Forty Years a Fur Trader* . . ., v. 1, p. 161) may have been aboard the up-bound *Trapper* in 1841 (not 1840 as his narrative suggests). He stated: "On the 31st of March I was on the steamer Trapper, and after a long, tedious trip we reached Union on the 27th of June."

❡ April.—Among the steamboats in the Missouri river trade were the: *General Leavenworth, Shawnee* (B. P. Clifford, master), *Colonel Woods* (L. C. Dickerson, master), *Thames* (Thomas Dennis, master), and the new *Oceana* (W. B. Miller, master).

Others which were on the Missouri during the spring and summer season included: *Bowling Green, Malta, Iatan,* the new *Emilie* (J. W. Keiser, master), and the new *Mary Tompkins* (B. J. Byer, master).

Ref: *Daily Missouri Republican,* April-July, 1841, issues; SIA, St. Louis, "Records," v. 7, typed copy, pp. 177, 183, 195, v. 8, typed copy, pp. 93, 94. According to statistics published in *Niles' National Register,* v. 72 (July 31, 1847), p. 351, there were 32 steamboats on the Missouri in 1841.

❡ MARRIED: Anthony A. Ward (wheelwright at the Methodists' Indian manual labor school, present Johnson county) and Mary Jane Foster (of Jackson county, Mo.) on April 7, at Independence(?), Mo., by the Rev. James Porter.

From 1841 till after 1851, the Wards lived at Shawnee Mission. During that time they had six children born (two of whom died young). John Allen Ward, their first child, apparently was born early in 1842.

In 1854 (after a brief stay at Union Town), the Wards bought Kansas riverfront property just west of what became the original Topeka town site. Five acres of that farm, and the "Ward-Meade house" on the tract, now belong to the city of Topeka. A "Garden Center" is maintained there.

Ref: Jackson county, Missouri, marriage records; Cone, *op. cit.,* p. 5; *Bulletin of the Shawnee County Historical Society,* Topeka, v. 3 (March, 1949), pp. 9-13; Allen T. Ward letters (in KHi ms. division); Kansas territorial census, 1860, v. 9, p. 36 (Shawnee county); Kansas state census, 1865, Topeka township, Shawnee co. (which lists the Ward family: Anthony A. (53), Mary J. (48), and their "Kansas-born" children, J. A. (23), Mary E. (20), Emily J. (17), Alice (13), Anthony (11), and William (9).

❡ MARRIED: John W. Polke (son of trader Robert Polke, resident on Pottawatomie creek, "Kansas") and Sarah Ann Chick (daughter of William M. Chick, Westport, Mo., merchant), on April 11, presumably at Westport, by the Rev. Thomas Johnson (of Shawnee Mission, "Kansas").

Ref: Jackson county, Missouri, marriage records.

❡ May.—Under construction at Shawnee Methodist Mission and Indian manual labor school (present Johnson county) was a large two-story brick building, 110 feet by 34 feet, to contain 14 rooms "for the accommodation of Teachers & children & for school and lodging rooms."

(In this building, in 1855, the first Kansas territorial legislature met, and passed the "bogus" laws.)

Ref: SIA, St. Louis, "Records," v. 8, typed copy, pp. 73, 74; Martha B. Caldwell, compiler, *Annals of Shawnee Methodist Mission* . . . (Topeka, 1939), pp. 40, 41.

❡ May.—A Shawnee Methodist meeting house (within present Shawnee, Johnson co.) was being built. It had been promoted by the Rev. Learner B. Stateler of Shawnee Mission. The Indians were doing much of the work (including the log-hewing), and also had raised nearly $100 to help pay for the building (a 25′ x 50′ structure, with one large door and nine windows). The church was ready for use by early summer.

The location (by a description of 1857): within the N. ½ of the S. E. ¼ of Sec. 11, T. 12 S., R. 24 E. It was in a grove about four miles west of the Indian manual labor school.

Ref: *Christian Advocate and Journal*, New York, v. 15 (May 5, 1841), p. 150; E. J. Stanley's *Life of the Rev. L. B. Stateler* (1907), pp. 104, 105 (Stateler had been transferred from Delaware Mission to Shawnee in the fall of 1840); "Shawnee Census, 1857" (ms. in KHi archives division), which describes the site (the five acres "including the meeting house and grave yard") of Shawnee Methodist Church.

❡ May 7.—The Rev. Ambler Edson and his wife arrived at Bellevue [Neb.] as Baptist missionaries to the Otoe and Missouri Indians.

Since the death of Missionary Moses Merrill in February, 1840, the condition of the Otoes (as reported) had "greatly deteriorated," and their number had been "diminished by intemperance and civil feuds." The Missouris had crossed to the south side of the Platte and refused to return; and others of the Indians were "roaming at large, having no fixed abode."

During the summer Missionary Edson "collected a school . . . of 20 pupils." Later, illness forced him to close it. The Edsons journeyed to St. Louis in March, 1842, but returned in April, in improved health. The Otoe Baptist Mission school (with 13 pupils) was reopened. However, the Indians became "increasingly intemperate and quarrelsome," and in August, 1842, it became expedient to abandon the mission.

Ref: *The Baptist Missionary Magazine*, v. 21 (June, 1841), p. 172, v. 22 (June, 1842), p. 160, v. 23 (June, 1843), p. 138. *See* annals p. 249, for the founding of Otoe Baptist Mission in 1833.

❡ May 8.—"Messrs. [Solomon] Houck, [William S.?] McKnight, Mazerva [William S. Messervy] and [a man named] Martin" were the principal merchants in the spring caravan which departed from Independence, Mo., for Santa Fe. On the 9th "the few last wagons . . . left." "Many other individuals" besides traders were co-travelers. Some were "going . . . for pleasure, some for health, and others for the curiosities and botanical plants." The naturalist William Gambel (who went on from Santa Fe to California with the Rowland-Workman party) was one of the latter group.

When this company organized, at Cow creek (some 235 miles out), late in May, the personnel totaled 87 males and one female (a "nice little Dutch woman," accompanying her husband); the vehicles "large and small, of various and quaint construction," numbered 33 (one, an "artillery wagon" with a cannon); and there were about 200 mules, also some oxen.

Twelve days after leaving Independence the caravan reached Council Grove; and stopped three days to overhaul and reload wagons, while waiting for laggards to arrive. About May 28, at Cow creek, Solomon Houck was elected captain, the company was enrolled, and guard duty assigned.

Just before the train reached this crossing, eight late-starting travelers (who left Independence about May 19), with their "three little wagons . . . and three riding mules," caught up with the caravan. Among the eight were Isaac L. Given, John McClure, Wade Hampton, and Albert G. Toomes. These four, after reaching Santa Fe, went on to California with the Rowland-Workman party.

On June 1 the caravan was at Ash creek; on June 5, at a point apparently below any of the usual crossings, the rising Arkansas river was forded; then the 60-mile "Jornada" was traversed; and by the 12th the line of march was up the Cimarron. The wagon train reached Santa Fe early in July—completing the trip in less than two months.

Ref: *Daily Missouri Republican,* May 19, November 23, 1841. The latter issue contains the unsigned letter from Santa Fe, of July 29, 1841, originally published in the Evansville (Ind.) *Journal,* which was widely reprinted, appearing in *Niles' National Register,* v. 61 (December 4, 1841), p. 209, the New York (weekly) *Tribune,* November 13, 1841 (*see KHQ,* v. 8, pp. 104-106), and various other publications in 1841 and 1842. *Santa Fe and the Far West* . . . (Los Angeles, 1949), is a reprint of this same letter, with a note by Dale L. Morgan, outlining his reasons for concluding that John McClure probably wrote it. Other references: "Isaac Given Biography" (ms. in Bancroft Library); Richard L. Wilson's *Short Ravelings From a Long Yarn* . . . (Santa Ana, Calif., 1936); Susan D. McKelvey's *Botanical Exploration of the Trans-Mississippi West 1790-1850* (1950), pp. 731-735, 744-746 (for Gambel); *1950 Brand Book* . . . (Denver, 1951), p. 269.

℃ On May 10 and 11 four Methodist ministers (Thomas Johnson, E. R. Ames, W. W. Redman, James M. Jameson) journeyed 80 miles on horseback from Shawnee Mission (present Johnson county) to Kansa Methodist Mission (present Shawnee county).

They traveled about half way on the 10th; camped some three miles west of the Wakarusa crossing for the night; reached Mission creek on the evening of the 11th. The delegation found Missionary William Johnson and his family "in good health." Also on hand to greet them were the "venerable" American Chief, his son ("a vile wretch"), and a few other Kansa.

On May 12, at a vacant house half a mile distant, these Kansa Indians and some 25 others (men and women) gathered for a council with the Methodists. On this day, too, Chief E-ya-no-sa (meaning "Big both ways"—an apt description), who was living eight miles up the Kansas, came to invite the white men to his village.

Early on the 13th the ministers set out for E-ya-no-sa's town which was in a "most delightful" location, "in the fork, between the Kansas and the Wa-nun-ja-hu, a large creek which empties itself into the Kansas" [present Mill creek, Wabaunsee county]. Crossing the Wa-nun-ja-hu, to reach the village, they found that it consisted of about 25 lodges "constructed of the bark of trees, so as to form a pleasant summer house, but require to be differently fixed for the winter." After a council with the chief, the Methodists returned to the Kansa mission. They were back at Shawnee before May 20.

Ref: *KHC*, v. 16, pp. 263-265, contains the Rev. James M. Jameson's letter of May 20, written at Shawnee Mission, describing the May 10-13 experiences of his party.

❡ May 12.—From the Sapling Grove rendezvous (15? miles west of Independence, and eight from Westport, Mo.) on the Shawnee reserve (present Johnson county), the men, and families, of the *first emigrant wagon train to set out for the Pacific* (the "Bidwell-Bartleson" party) began the journey across "Kansas" on the "Oregon trail."

The emigrants (and a few men traveling for pleasure, health, or other reasons) numbered, at the outset, around 60 persons, including five women and perhaps 10(?) children. They had eight mule-and-horse-drawn wagons; five larger wagons drawn by 17 yoke of oxen; and riding animals; but took no milk cows.

In advance was the Jesuit missionary party (11 men) of Father Pierre-Jean De Smet (bound for the Flathead Indians' country), whose guide, Thomas Fitzpatrick, was to pilot the combined company to the West. The missionaries had four carts and a small wagon—all two-wheeled, (drawn by two mules each, hitched in tandem); and riding horses. With De Smet (who had set out from Westport on May 10, after arriving there 10 days earlier on the *Oceana*) were Father Nicholas Point (a Westport resident during the winter of 1840-1841), Father Gregory Mengarini, three lay brothers, an English tourist "Romaine," James Baker (a trapper), and John Gray (an Iroquois; and Kaw's mouth resident), hired as hunter. Two others of this party (who had taken a baggage-loaded pirogue upriver) were waiting at the Kansas crossing (at, or near, present Topeka), when De Smet and his companions arrived about May 16(?). On hand to help the horses swim the river were two Kansa Indians. "Baggage, wagons and men" crossed in the pirogue (a "hollowed tree trunk," which, at a distance, reminded Father De Smet of a Venetian gondola). Camp was made "on the banks of the Soldier's river . . . six miles from the [Kansa] village." "We had scarcely pitched our tents when the great chief [Fool Chief] presented himself with six of his bravest warriors, to bid us welcome," wrote De Smet. The chief supplied the missionaries with two armed guards for "the three days and three nights" spent at Soldier creek camp.

The emigrants arrived at, and crossed the Kansas, on May 17, and proceeded to the Soldier creek camp (two miles west of the river) where they spent two nights. Nancy (Mrs. Benjamin) Kelsey later recollected: ". . . the Indians towed us across the . . . river in rawhide boats made of buffalo skins. Our oxen crossed the river with the empty wagons."

On the 18th the company organized. "Talbot H. Green"—whose real name was Paul Geddes—presided; and young John Bidwell—recently a schoolteacher in Platte county, Mo.—served as secretary. John Bartleson (aged 54, of Jackson county, Mo.) was elected captain.

When the caravan set out on the 19th, there were (according to Father De Smet) 70 souls, "fifty of whom were capable of managing the rifle." He, Father Point, and young Romaine, left the procession to spend an hour at Fool Chief's 20-lodge village (to the left of their line of march). [Point sketched the town—*see* p. 397 in this volume—and De Smet, in a letter, described the Kansa village, and its occupants, at some length.]

Overtaking the caravan on May 23 were three men, Joseph B. Chiles, of Jackson county, Mo. (with a wagon), Charles M. Weber, and James John who had left Westport on May 16. Also joining north of Kansas river were Robert Rickman, of Jackson county, Mo., James Shotwell, and Henry Peyton. [Others in the company who had left Jackson county, Mo., homes were Charles Hopper, William P. Overton, Grove Cook (a brother-in-law of the fur-trading Sublettes), and some (if not all) of the Kelsey family.] On May 27 the Rev. Joseph Williams caught up with the wagon train (*see* May 21 entry). He was the last accession to the "very mixed crowd"—now 79(?) in all.

As far as the Platte (reached June 1) the journey was fairly routine. Between Grand Island and Green river (reached on July 23) a number of events occurred—including two weddings, one death (James Shotwell's) by accident, some "desertions," a few accessions, and Nicholas Dawson's encounter with Indians. On August 10-11, at Soda Springs [Ida.], the travelers came to a parting of ways. The missionaries, with guide Thomas Fitzpatrick, and 24(?) Oregon-bound emigrants (including all but one family), turned north towards Fort Hall (the Rev. Joseph Williams accompanied this group); while 32 men, one woman and her infant daughter, took a route towards California.

Among those who reached California (after a difficult journey; and after abandoning their wagons en route) were: John Bartleson, John Bidwell, Charles Hopper, Robert Rickman, Grove Cook, Joseph B. Chiles, Charles M. Weber, Josiah Belden, James P. Springer, "Talbot Green," Andrew Kelsey, Benjamin Kelsey, his wife and child; and George Henshaw. (The names of the rest are on record, but not listed here.) Some returned to Missouri in the fall of 1842, as will be noted in these annals.

Ref: John Bidwell, *A Journey to California* . . . (San Francisco, 1937); Doyce B. Nunis, Jr., editor, *Josiah Belden 1841 California Overland Pioneer: His Memoir and Early Letters* (Georgetown, Calif., 1962); Chittenden and Richardson, *op. cit.*, v. 1, pp. 275-286; C. L. Camp, editor, *Narrative of Nicholas "Cheyenne" Dawson* . . . (San Francisco, 1933); Joseph Williams, *Narrative of a Tour* . . . (New York, 1921); John Bidwell's *Echoes of the Past* (Chicago, 1928); H. H. Bancroft's *History of California* (San Francisco, 1886), v. 4, pp. 265-280; Nicholas Point's "Recollections . . .," in *Woodstock Letters*, Woodstock, Md., v. 12 (1883), pp. 3-22, 133-143; Gregory Mengarini's "The Rocky Mountains . . .," in *ibid.*, v. 17 (1888), pp. 298-309; Nicholas Point, *Wilderness Kingdom* . . . *The Journals & Paintings of Nicolas Point, S. J.*, trans. by Joseph P. Donnelly, S. J. (New York, Chicago, etc., c1967]; *Daily Missouri Republican*, May 19, 1841; *Transactions* of the 19th Annual Reunion of the Oregon Pioneer Association for 1891, p. 139; *Oregon Historical Quarterly*, Salem, v. 31 (September, 1930), pp. 253, 254; from the Bancroft Library, Berkeley, Calif. (courtesy of Dale L. Morgan), typed copies of manuscripts by James John, Nicholas Dawson, J. B. Chiles, Charles Hopper, Mrs. Benjamin Kelsey, and A. S. Taylor; also, courtesy of Dale L. Morgan, a typed copy of a James John journal in the Rosenbach Foundation library, Philadelphia; W. J. Ghent, *The Early Far West* . . . (New York, 1931), pp. 314-319; George R. Stewart's *The California Trail* . . . (New York, c1962), pp. 7-29; Helen S. Giffen, *Trail-Blazing Pioneer Colonel*

Joseph Ballinger Chiles (San Francisco, 1969); H. E. Tobie's "From the Missouri to the Columbia, 1841," in *Oregon Historical Quarterly*, v. 38 (June, 1937), pp. 135-159; John C. McCoy's "Tales of an Old Timer" (from Kansas City [Mo.] *Journal*, January 30, 1879), in "Kansas Reminiscences" clippings, KHi library; Dale L. Morgan's letter of June 8, 1966, to L. Barry.

❦ May 14.—"Mr. Hinkley" began work on the Ottawas' mill (in present Franklin county, not far from Ottawa Baptist Mission). On the 19th Jotham Meeker sent the "Ottawa Mill up to its place after its having set in . . . [the mission] door yard near 3 years." It was declared operational on May 25.

(The building for the mill had been put up in 1840; and additional work had been done on it by the Ottawas in April, 1841.)

Meeker wrote on June 14 "it [the mill] still does not do well"; but on the 16th he recorded: "It grinds pretty well."

Ref: Jotham Meeker's "Diary," January 10, 11, 13, March 2, 3, 1840, May 14, 19, 25, June 14, 16, 1841.

❦ May.—A caravan from Santa Fe, in which the principal proprietors were "Messrs. [James M.] Giddings, from Fayette, McGuffin [James W. Magoffin], Garvis [Chavez] and some other Spanish gentlemen," reached Independence, Mo. This company had 22 wagons, a large number of mules (around 100 extra ones), and brought, by report, $180,000 to $200,000 in specie.

(About May 14 and 15, in present Douglas and Osage counties, travelers in the Santa Fe-bound spring caravan had met some of the above train. Richard L. Wilson recorded (on the 14th?): "we met about 20 Spanish Mexicans of the Chihuahua return Company . . . headed by Chavez . . ." and next day, west of 110-mile creek, "four Mexican wagons hove in sight." With this rear detachment was "Black Wolf," a Delaware chief.)

Ref: *Daily Missouri Republican*, May 19, 1841; Wilson, *op. cit.*, pp. 19-22. Chavez was probably either Don Antonio José Chavez, or Don José Chavez y Castillo.

❦ About May 20 a small mounted party—Missionary William Johnson, Fool Chief (head of the Kansa nation), another chief, and nine Kansa boys (aged from nine to 13)—arrived at the Indian manual labor school (present Johnson county), where the youths were to be enrolled.

Meeting, on this occasion, the man who had recently (late 1840?) become leader of the Kansa, the Rev. James M. Jameson wrote: "Ki-ha-ga-wa-ti-in-ga . . . signifies the chief who accomplishes what he undertakes at all hazards. He is known by the phrase 'Fool-chief;' but our word reckless would better express the meaning of the original. He is a man of middle stature, of strong native mind, and of fine address, and speaks with ease and force."

Ref: *KHC*, v. 16, p. 265 (from *Western Christian Advocate*, Cincinnati, v. 8, January 28, 1842, p. 161). "Ki-he-ga" (or "Ki-ha-ga") signifies "chief." Fool Chief's name appears in varying forms, for example "Ca-he-ga-wa-tan-nin-ga,' "Ky-he-ga-wa-ti-nin-ka." The above Fool Chief was at least the second Kansa leader to bear the name. The

"Ky-he-ga-wa-ti-nin-ka" who signed the June 3, 1825, Kansa treaty probably was the father of this young Fool Chief.

⊄ May 21.—En route to Oregon, 64-year-old Methodist preacher Joseph Williams arrived at Shawnee Methodist Mission, after a journey on horseback from his Indiana home.

With Missionary William Johnson, and two Kansa chiefs (*see* preceding entry), he rode westward on May 22 as far as Wakarusa river. The next day's 45-mile journey brought them to Kansa Methodist Mission (present Shawnee county). On the 24th, supplied with provisions by the Johnsons, and accompanied by "Mr. Brensill" (the Kansa Indians' farmer David Benzley?), Williams crossed the Kansas (the water was over their horses' backs); and, after a few miles, was left to hasten on, alone, in pursuit of the Oregon-and-California-bound companies. He carried no gun or weapon. By good fortune he avoided hostile Pawnees in the area, and, after two nights and most of three days on the prairies, caught up with the caravan on May 26. (*See* May 12 entry.)

Ref: Williams, *op. cit.*, pp. 25-33; John Bidwell, *A Journey to California*, p. 3.

⊄ May 25.—At Ottawa Baptist Mission (present Franklin county), John Clayter and his work crew (under a contract let by Jotham Meeker) began to erect new mission buildings which cost $832.

On September 22 the family moved into the not-yet-completed structures. "The houses are well built with substantial stone chimneys," wrote Meeker. "There are four rooms—one for a dwelling room, a meeting room, a kitchen, and an Indian house."

Ref: Jotham Meeker's "Diary"; and his letter of February 7, 1842.

⊄ May.—Eastbound from Fort William ("Bent's Fort"), a Bent, St. Vrain & Co. train (18 fur-laden wagons), transporting the previous winter's "fine trade" crossed the Santa Fe trail en route to Missouri. Charles Bent headed this expedition which had left the upper Arkansas on April 30.

Around May 27, in present McPherson county, the spring caravan bound for Santa Fe met Bent's party. As Richard L. Wilson described the encounter: ". . . a troop of Mountain Trappers hove in sight, and came up like a herd of buffalo, with their pack-mules laden with furs and robes, and 17 wagons in train. Fine specimens of bronzed humanity were they all. . . ."

A St. Louis newspaper reported Charles Bent's arrival in that city on June 10. He brought a "large lot of Buffalo robes and furs."

Ref: *Daily Missouri Republican*, June 12, 1841; *New Mexico Historical Review*, Santa Fe, v. 30 (April, 1955), p. 159 (has Bent's April 30, 1841, letter, with the statement "Our Wagons 18 in number left this morning. . . . I think I shall be in St. Louis . . . by the 10th June . . ."); Wilson, *op. cit.*, pp. 27, 28; "Isaac Given Biography" (ms. in Bancroft Library).

⊄ June 1.—A trading license issued to Pierre Chouteau [Jr.] and Company (by Sup't Joshua Pilcher, at St. Louis) specified trade with the Pottawatomies, Peorias, Weas, and "Maumis" at these places:

(1) on the Marais des Cygnes near the mouth of Sugar creek [*i. e.*, present Trading Post, Linn co.]—Michel Giraud's headquarters.

(2) at Sugar creek [the Pottawatomie settlements, also in present Linn county, but 15 miles west of Giraud's place].

(3) at Pottawatomie creek near the Issue House [the Pottawatomie settlements in present Franklin and Miami counties, about 15 miles north of the Sugar creek settlements].

(4) also, the 15 employees in the Marais des Cygnes outfit of the American Fur Company could trade "at the respective villages of the above tribes."

Ref: OIA, Letters Received from SIA, St. Louis (National Archives Microcopy 234, Roll 753), December 31, 1841, list of licenses issued in 1841. The license of June 27, 1842, was nearly identical; but only 11 men were employed.

❡ Around the first of June, at the lower Cimarron Spring (in present Grant county), some 500 "Arapahoes" met a party of Pawnees, and in the ensuing battle the Pawnees lost over 70 men (72 or 76, by varying reports), and their horses. The "Arapahoes" had six warriors killed.

The Santa Fe-bound spring caravan met the still-elated "Arapahoes" at the lower spring in June, 10 days after the battle, and (as reported by John McClure?) "gratified them with encamping on the battle ground, where the unburied bodies were yet almost unbroken."

Ref: *Daily Missouri Republican*, November 23, 1841 (for McClure's? letter—*see* May 8, 1841, annals entry); Rufus B. Sage's *Scenes in the Rocky Mountains* as reprinted in *Rufus B. Sage . . .*, edited by L. R. and Ann W. Hafen (Glendale, Calif., 1956), v. 1, p. 137; Wilson, *op. cit.*, pp. 71-74. It may be that the "Arapahoes" were Comanches. In September, 1846, Robert Bliss, of the Mormon Battalion, recorded in his journal: "On the 22 we passed the Battle Ground of Indians our Pilot was passing at the time he says he had encamped [in 1841] & in the morning 4 or 5000 Camanches & Pawnees came down in the valley & had a Great Battle." (*Utah Historical Quarterly*, v. 4 [July, 1931], pp. 67-96.) Mormon Henry Standage, in his 1846 journal, identified the informant as "Our Pilot Mr. Thompson." (F. S. Golder's *The March of the Mormon Battalion . . .* [N. Y., c1928], pp. 166, 167.)

❡ June.—The "six waggons with 18 men, with Furs and Robes on their way from Ft. Larimie, to St. Louis," which the westbound emigrant-and-missionary caravan met on May 31 while on the head of the Little Blue, crossed "Kansas" during this month. John Bidwell further described the party: "The waggons were drawn by oxen and mules . . . the rusty mountaineers looked as though they never had seen razor, water, soap, or brush. . . ."

Ref: John Bidwell's *A Journey to California . . .*, p. 4.

❡ BORN: on June 8, near Sugar creek (present Linn county), Genevieve Caroline Wilson, daughter of government-blacksmith-for-the-Pottawatomies Robert Wilson and Genevieve C. Wilson. She was baptized on June 9 by the Rev. Herman G. Aelen, S. J.

Ref: "Pottawatomie Baptismal Register" (microfilm in KHi).

❦ July 15 (or 17?).—Four nuns from the Society of the Sacred Heart (Mothers Philippine Duchesne, Lucille Mathevon, A. O'Connor, and lay sister Louise Amyot) opened a school for Indian girls at Sugar Creek (Pottawatomie) Mission, in present Linn county. (*See* March 10, 1839, entry.)

(From Mother Mathevon's journal it is known that they left St. Louis June 29, by steamboat, escorted by the Rev. P. J. Verhaegen [superior of the Missouri Jesuits]; arrived at Westport Landing about July 6[?]; proceeded, by wagon, southward on the Fort Leavenworth-Fort Gibson military road; spent the night of July 7 at the house of American Fur Company trader Michel Giraud [at present Trading Post]; and, on July 8, traveled the last miles of the journey with an escort of some 150 mounted Pottawatomies, arrayed in colorful finery [including feathered head-dresses], led by Fathers Aelen and Eysvogels of Sugar Creek Mission.)

The building of a school (in July), and a two-story, six-room log house (in August) was supervised by the nuns' Negro servant. The location was "close to the mission-church on a bluff or eminence that commanded a view of the surrounding country." Here the well-attended girls' school was maintained till 1848, when it was transferred to the Pottawatomies' new Kansas river reserve. The aged Mother Duchesne left in July, 1842. In her place came Mothers Thiefry and Xavier, who remained till 1845.

Ref: G. J. Garraghan's *The Jesuits of the Middle United States*, v. 2, pp. 204-213; Kinsella, *op. cit.*, pp. 18-22, 227.

❦ Born: on July 17, at Shawnee Baptist Mission (present Johnson county), Lucius Bolles Pratt, son (and second child) of Missionaries John G. and Olivia (Evans) Pratt.

(On March 2, 1860, at Delaware Baptist Mission, 19-year-old Lucius B. Pratt married Nannie May Journeycake [daughter of Charles Journeycake, Delaware Indian]. Young Pratt died five years later—on September 7, 1865.)

Ref: Pratt Collection (in KHi ms. division); Jack W. Manning's "John Gill Pratt . . ." (dissertation, May, 1951).

❦ July.—Santa Fe trader [James M.] Giddings and party left Independence, Mo., for New Mexico on the 23d. James W. Magoffin's company (bound for Chihuahua) was to join him. On July 27 a number of wagons belonging to "Mr. Ward," of Rocheport, Mo., passed through Independence "on their way to Santa Fe and Chihuahua."

Ref: *Daily Missouri Republican*, August 6, 1841; *Weekly Picayune*, September 6, 1841.

❦ August.—Hiram Rich (a Liberty, Mo., trader, aged 42) was appointed sutler at Fort Leavenworth. (On October 19 he was also appointed postmaster.) He succeeded Albert G. Wilson (*see* December 5, 1839, annals) in both positions. For the next 20 years (till his sudden death in April, 1862), Rich remained as the post's sutler and postmaster.

As early as 1829 Hiram Rich was established as a merchant at Liberty. By 1837 his trading ventures extended to the South Platte. The license granted on November 2, 1837, to Hiram Rich (for 11 employees) specified trade "At a point on the South Fork of the Platte about 30 miles below the mountains" with the Arapahoes, Cheyennes, and Sioux. (That he ever journeyed to that region himself has not been ascertained.)

On July 16, 1838, he received a one-year contract to supply rations for immigrant Pottawatomies (and other Indians) in the Osage [Marais des Cygnes] River Subagency. A year later (August 14, 1839) Sup't Joshua Pilcher, of St. Louis, wrote: "This [1838] contract with Mr. Rich was the offspring of necessity; but fortunately for the government, that necessity will soon cease to exist. Those Liberty birds have *feathered their nest*, but I shall take measures to check their career." On November 10, 1840, Rich was given a one-year license to trade (23 men in all) with the bands of Sioux on the upper Missouri.

Ref: *KHC*, v. 7, p. 441; SIA, St. Louis, "Records," v. 7, typed copy, p. 37 (for Pilcher), v. 10 (bottom of page headed "St Louis Dec 2nd 1834" has an early reference to Hiram Rich); OIA, Letters Received from SIA, St. Louis (National Archives Microcopy No. 234, Roll 751 and Roll 753); 25th Cong., 3d Sess., *H. Doc. No. 94* (Serial 346), p. 4 (for 1838 contract); Leavenworth *Daily Times*, April 30, 1862 (for obituary). Hiram Rich is buried in the Fort Leavenworth national cemetery. The inscription states he was born at Charlotte, Vt., September 21, 1799, and died April 28, 1862, aged 62 years, seven months, and seven days. In *KHC*, v. 13, p. 335, the Hiram Stone diary entry of April 24, 1862, recording Rich's funeral as occurring on that date is evidently a misprint for April 29.

ℭ August.—The Osages, returning to their towns (in "Kansas") from the summer hunt "on the southwestern part of the Grand Prairie," brought two white persons they had purchased from the Comanches. One was a young Spanish woman; the other a nine- or ten-year-old Texas girl.

The Osages reported the Comanches had many white prisoners; and were only "waiting for the leaves to fall . . ." before making a general attack on the whole Texas frontier.

Ref: Osage Subagent Robert A. Calloway's August 23, 1841, letter to the editors of the Houston (Tex.) *Telegraph,* as reprinted in *Niles' National Register,* v. 61 (October 2, 1841), p. 66; also reprinted in *Weekly Picayune,* September 20, 1841.

ℭ August.—Around the middle of the month the Delawares' black-smith shop (just north of the Delaware, or Grinter, crossing of the Kansas river, on the Fort Leavenworth-Fort Gibson military road) burned, and nearly all the tools were destroyed.

(In 1842, by Indian department authorization, the shop was rebuilt at a cost of $140, and the sum of $75 was provided for replacement tools.)

Ref: SIA, St. Louis, "Records," v. 7, typed copy, p. 223, v. 8, typed copy, pp. 77, 78, 92, 93; annals p. 247 (for location of the shop).

ℭ Born: on August 16, at Shawnee Methodist Mission (present Johnson county), Andrew Monroe Johnson, son of the Rev. Thomas and Sarah T. (Davis) Johnson.

Ref: *KHC*, v. 12, p. xii.

ℭ August 29.—Jesuit fathers Felix L. Verreydt and Christian

Hoecken, with lay brothers Andrew Mazzella and George Miles arrived at Pottawatomie mission on Sugar creek (present Linn county). (*See* portrait of Father Verreydt in this volume.)

(They came from Council Bluffs [Iowa], where a Pottawatomie Catholic mission had been abandoned. Verreydt succeeded the Rev. Herman G. Aelen as superior, and remained at the head of Sugar Creek mission till it was transferred to the Kansas river in 1848.)

Another recent arrival was Father Anthony Eysvogels, who had come in May or June.

Ref: G. J. Garraghan's *The Jesuits of the Middle United States*, v. 1, p. 446, v. 2, pp. 195, 196.

❧ Early in September a wagon train from Santa Fe reached Independence, Mo. As reported, there were only one or two "old traders," the majority being the freighters who had gone out in the spring. Some Mexican citizens with this company "brought along with them 70, or 80,000 dollars, and a quantity of valuable furs." An unidentified Independence writer called it the "most expeditious . . . [trip] ever performed."

Ref: *Daily Missouri Republican*, September 28, 1841, or, *Niles' National Register*, v. 61 (October 16, 1841), pp. 100, 101; Sage, *op. cit.*, v. 1, pp. 132-135.

❧ September 4.—Lancaster P. Lupton's caravan, bound for new Fort Platte [Wyo.], set out from a camp on the Shawnee reserve, in present Johnson county, to follow the "Oregon trail" across "Kansas," up to the Little Blue and Platte rivers.

Around 18(?) men (mountaineers, apprentices, and greenhorns) were in the company at the outset. (A small advance party was picked up at the Wakarusa, and two voyageurs joined beyond the Kansas crossing, making the total personnel about 24.) Of the six (or more) wagons, at least four were large Conestogas; and there was a dearborn, also, in the outfit. The freight included illegal cargo—24 barrels (perhaps more) of alcohol for the Indian trade.

[One of Lupton's employees was Rufus B. Sage (aged 24), westbound, for the first time, to gather material for a book. His *Scenes in the Rocky Mountains*, subsequently published (in 1846), described what Sage learned and experienced during his travels in 1841, 1842, and 1843.]

Lupton's caravan reached, crossed, and camped by the Wakarusa on September 6. On the 7th, after some 12 miles of travel, the over-night stop was "at a place known as the Springs" (Big Springs, Douglas co., of today). Camp on the 8th was "at a small creek within six miles of the crossing of the Kansas river" (the Shunganunga, or a branch). Most of September 9 was spent fording the Kansas (at, or near, present Topeka). "This proved rather difficult," according to Sage, "as the water was deep and the bottom sandy," and the river was "not far from six hundred yards wide, with steep banks of clay and sand." The caravan then proceeded some six miles before making camp.

Sage noted that the Kansa Indians' "main village" (Fool Chief's) was "on the left bank . . . a few miles above the crossing." He mentioned the

"Protestant mission" (the Methodists' establishment—on the opposite side of the river). Without specifying a location, he wrote that there were "two or three families of half-breeds in the neighborhood, who "occupy neat houses, and have splendid farms and improvements." (The "splendid farms" doubtless were those which had been plowed and prepared by the government farmers.)

When Lupton and his company reached the "North Fork of Blue" (Big Blue) in mid-month they were detained till September 24 by high water. Their sojourn, in present Marshall county, was not unpleasant. Sage wrote: "During our stay no less than four bee-trees were levelled, and every . . . [container] in the whole camp was filled to overflowing, and every stomach to repletion, with honey of almost crystalline transparency. The great abundance of deer, turkey, and other game in the vicinity, also contributed their share of amusement, and enlivened the interval of detention."

On September 27 the caravan reached the Little Blue; crossed to the Platte about October 10; and arrived at Fort Platte [Wyo.] on November 2. This new trading post was on the left bank of the North Platte, not far from the mouth of Laramie river, and a mile or so from the American Fur Company's opposition post Fort John (Fort Laramie).

(Sage, and some other trappers, made an unsuccessful attempt to descend the Platte with a boatload of furs in the spring of 1842; finally arrived at Council Bluffs [Neb.] afoot; then descended the Missouri in canoes, reaching St. Louis about July 20, 1842. *See, also*, August 10, 1842, entry.)

Ref: Sage, *op. cit.*, v. 1, pp. 84-87, 125-221.

❦ September 5.—A "party of Americans [from Santa Fe] with six or eight waggons and a large number of horses and mules" was met by L. P. Lupton's mountain-bound caravan west of Elm Grove, in present Johnson county.

These travelers from Santa Fe (possibly stragglers from the fall caravan—*see* p. 435), had with them a nearly full-grown elk, two blacktailed deer, an antelope, and a white-tailed fawn.

Ref: Sage, *op. cit.*, v. 1, pp. 132-135.

❦ September.—At least six men (including John Gray, the Iroquois; Henry Peyton; [J. M.?] Jones; the Englishman Romaine; and Amos E. Frye) who had accompanied the Oregon-and-California-bound wagon train of emigrants and missionaries to the Rocky mountains in the spring and summer, retraced the Oregon trail across "Kansas," and reached Missouri in mid-September.

On September 21, an Independence, Mo., writer reported: "Nine or ten of the California company returned a few days since having left the remainder on some of the tributaries of Green River . . . [on July 23]. . . . The returning party were attacked six or eight times[!], but not seriously injured. They seem satisfied completely with their Quixotic adventure."

Ref: John Bidwell, *Echoes of the Past* . . ., p. 11; also, his *A Journey to California* . . ., p. 11; James John's "Diary" (in Bancroft Library); *Daily Missouri Republican*, September 28, 1841; or, *Niles' National Register*, v. 61 (October 16, 1841), p. 101.

❅ September(?)—Partners John Sibille and David Adams, taking their first trading outfit (with perhaps 10 men in all) out to Laramie's Fork, crossed "Kansas" (via the "Oregon trail" route) during this month. By mid-November this company had reached its destination.

(On July 31 Sibille & Adams had been issued their first license, at St. Louis, to trade on Laramie's fork, the Cheyenne, and Wind rivers. James Adams, brother of David, was one of the "sureties" for the partners; Bernard Pratte [the younger?] was another.)

Ref: OIA, Letters Received from SIA, St. Louis (National Archives Microcopy No. 234, Roll 753), for D. D. Mitchell's December 31, 1841, list of licenses issued during the year; Dale L. Morgan's letters of March 26, and June 15, 1963, to L. Barry, noting David Adams' fragmentary 1841 diary, at Missouri Historical Society, St. Louis; and see Bulletin of the Missouri Historical Society, St. Louis, v. 13 (October, 1956), p. 101; Glimpses of the Past, v. 8, p. 42.

❅ September 17; October 5.—In New Mexico the advance, and main, parties of the Texan Santa Fe expedition (which had left Austin in June), surrendered to Gov. Manuel Armijo's army, after being defeated by the arid plains, where they had been lost for days and suffered privations. (The captives were cruelly treated; marched, on foot, to Mexico City and imprisoned; most were released in April, 1842.)

President Mirabeau B. Lamar had anticipated that this combined diplomatic-military-commercial venture (of 303? men, with 24? ox-drawn merchandise-and-supply-carrying wagons) would establish Texas jurisdiction over part of New Mexico, or at least gain for his republic some of the Santa Fe trade which Missouri enjoyed.

The expedition, though a failure, focused United States and Mexican attention anew on Texas. In New Mexico there were some demonstrations against, and an increased suspicion of, U. S. citizens.

Ref: G. W. Kendall's Narrative of the Texan Santa Fe Expedition (New York, 1844); W. C. Binkley's The Expansionist Movement in Texas, 1836-1850 (Berkeley, 1925), pp. 68-95; Southwestern Historical Quarterly, Austin, v. 27 (1923), pp. 85-107; Thomas Falconer's Letters and Notes on the Texan Santa Fe Expedition . . . (New York, 1930).

❅ September 20.—David D. Mitchell was appointed to head the superintendency of Indian affairs, St. Louis. (He replaced Joshua Pilcher—appointed March 4, 1839—whose removal in 1841 was a matter of politics.)

Ref: 27th Cong., 2d Sess., H. Doc. No. 41 (Serial 402). SIA, St. Louis, "Records," v. 7, typed copy, p. 192 (for Pilcher's departure on June 11, 1841), p. 199 (for D. D. Mitchell's October 6, 1841, letter—one of his first in office); Daily Missouri Republican, April 12, June 7, 1841 (for comment on Pilcher and his politics).

❅ September-October.—A small party of mountain men (unidentified, except that they had connections with Fort Davy Crockett [in northwestern "Colorado"] and the activities of trader Philip F.

Thompson) brought "a large drove of horses, and several domesticated buffalo" down from the mountains, crossing "Kansas" apparently by way of the "Oregon trail."

L. P. Lupton's party met this outfit in the latter part of September, west of the Big Blue (near the north "Kansas" line). Rufus B. Sage (westbound with Lupton) stated: "Their horses had been mostly obtained from Upper California, the year previous, by a band of [22] mountaineers, under the lead of one Thompson. This band . . . had made a descent upon the Mexican *ranchoes* and captured between two and three thousand head of horses and mules," but then lost at least half of them before reaching their rendezvous.

Ref: Sage, *op. cit.*, v. 1, p. 137; L. R. and Ann W. Hafen's *Old Spanish Trail* (Glendale, 1954), pp. 236-241; *Colorado Magazine*, Denver, v. 29 (January, 1952), p. 17, for location of Fort Davy Crockett.

❦ Early in October (before the 9th) a large caravan, in which were some 30 wagons (carrying 72 tons of merchandise), and around 350 mules, set out from Independence, Mo., for Santa Fe. "Seignoirs Armeho [Armijo], Charvois [Chavez] and Monsieur D. Gordis [De Gordin?]" headed this expedition.

(*See* May annals entry, p. 430.)

Ref: *Daily Missouri Republican*, October 20, 24, 1841.

❦ October 11.—A "few gentlemen" arrived at Independence, Mo., from Santa Fe, by way of Bent's Fort. They had come down from the upper Arkansas in company with "an express" sent to meet the westbound wagon train of Charles Bent. From the meeting point (some 150 miles west of Independence) the eastbound travelers had proceeded without escort.

(The "express" probably carried news relating to the Texan Santa Fe expedition. The *Weekly Picayune*, New Orleans, of August 30, 1841, had reported: "The brothers Bent have just left Missouri [*i. e.*, St. Louis?] for their fort upon the Arkansas intending to go into Santa Fe with a hundred men, in anticipation of the Texan expedition and afford any and every facility in their power in forwarding whatever object shall be set forth in [Texas president Mirabeau] Lamar's proclamation." The *Picayune's* source of information was not indicated.)

Ref: *Daily Missouri Republican*, October 15, 1841; *Weekly Picayune*, as noted above.

❦ October.—The Rev. Jerome C. Berryman succeeded the Rev. Thomas Johnson as head of the Methodists' Indian manual labor school (present Johnson county). (*See* his portrait, p. 603.)

Johnson (who retired because of ill health) had been for 11 years in the Indian country. (*See* p. 179 for his founding, in 1830, of Shawnee Mission, the first Methodist mission in "Kansas.") Berryman (eight years among the Indians) had established Kickapoo Mission in 1833.—*See* p. 253. (In 1847 Thomas Johnson returned to head the school.)

Ref: Stanley, *op. cit.*, p. 106. Caldwell, *op. cit.*, p. 61.

❦ DIED: Robert S. Bent (youngest of the four Bent brothers associated with the history of Bent's Fort [Colo.]), on October 19, at St. Louis, Mo., aged 25 years.

(The notice published in the *Missouri Republican*, St. Louis, October 21, 1841—"Died on the 19th instant; in this city, Robert S. Bent, son of the late Judge [Silas] Bent."—disproves the several-times-published "tale" that Robert was killed by Comanches on the Santa Fe trail.)

Ref: *Daily Missouri Republican*, October 21, 1841. George B. Grinnell, quoting an October 15, 1913, letter by Robert's nephew, George Bent (the half-Cheyenne son of William Bent and Owl Woman), in *KHC*, v. 15, p. 51, was probably the first to publish the "tale." Other writers, since, have accepted as factual George Bent's statement: "Robert Bent, my father's brother, was killed by Comanches near Pawnee Fork. . . ." According to Allen H. Bent's *The Bent Family in America* (Boston, 1900), Robert S. Bent was born February 23, 1816.

❦ October.—A hunting party (16 Delawares and one Pottawatomie) was surrounded and massacred by a large force of Sioux, on a fork of "Mink Creek" [in Iowa?]. The Pottawatomie, badly wounded, escaped; 14 Delawares were slain and scalped (and two taken prisoners?); while 28 dead Sioux were found on the battleground (as reported to Subagent W. P. Richardson of the Great Nemaha Subagency on January 17, 1842, by a five-man Delaware search party).

Ref: SIA, St. Louis, "Records," v. 7, typed copy, pp. 249, 250, 266, v. 8, typed copy, pp. 84, 85, 338, 481, 482.

❦ November.—Antoine Robidoux, it is said, lost one or two men and over 100 mules and horses—all frozen to death in a blizzard (the same endured by the Alvarez party?)—while at, or in the vicinity of, Cottonwood Crossing, on the Santa Fe trail.

Joseph Robidoux, Jr., headed the relief party which arrived from Blacksnake Hills (St. Joseph), Mo., to assist his brother's company.

Ref: William S. Wallace's *Antoine Robidoux 1794-1860* . . . (Los Angeles, 1953), pp. 30, 31, 56 (which uses as a source James L. Collins' letter of December, 1852, recounting the above episode, published in *El Palacio*, Santa Fe, v. 19 [1925], pp. 206-211; also, the St. Joseph [Mo.] *Gazette* of August 29, 1860). Collins referred to the Alvarez party as being ahead of Robidoux on the trail. P. St. George Cooke, in his *Scenes and Adventures in the Army* . . . (Philadelphia, 1859), p. 243, writing while at Cottonwood Fork on September 6, 1843, stated: "I find Mr. [Antoine] Robidoux here, with a dozen light horsecarts; he has a trading house three hundred miles beyond Santa Fe. The snow-storm of the 8th of November last [but it was 1841, not 1842!] fell upon him in this vicinity; more than a hundred horses and mules perished, and indeed one man; he had lost his only axe, or he could have cut down cotton-woods for food to save his animals."

❦ MARRIED: (1) Francis St. Michel and Mary Jane Prior (Pryor), (2) Charles Cardinal and Angelique Wot-sing-a, (3) Louis Peltier and Angelique Osinga, all on November 17, near Marmiton (now Marmaton) river, by the Rev. Herman G. Aelen, S. J.

Witnesses to the first of these Osage (or half-blood) marriages were Pierre Melicour Papin and Louis Peltier; to the second marriage, Papin, and Francis

St. Michel; and to the third, Charles Cardinal and Joseph Swiss (or, La Suisse—"Lasweese"—*see* p. 257, for *his* marriage).

Ref: "Pottawatomie Marriage Register" (microfilm in KHi). Joseph Swiss (or, Suisse) was probably the "Swiss" who came down from the Rocky Mountains in the autumn of 1839 with Dr. Frederick A. Wislizenus, Paul Richardson, and two others—*see* p. 381. (For other data on Joseph Suisse *see* Victor Tixier's *Travels on the Osage Prairies*, p. 153, in editor John F. McDermott's footnote.) A daughter, Pelagie, of "Francois Michel" (St. Michel) and "Marie Jeanne Prior," born October 13, 1844(?), was baptized June 20, 1845, by Father F. L. Verreydt, S. J.—"Westport Register" (microfilm in KHi). *See, also,* August 10, 1840, annals entry.

❆ December 13.—Manuel Alvarez (acting U. S. consul at Santa Fe), who, with 16 Americans, and 67 horses and mules, had set out from New Mexico late in October, arrived at Independence, Mo., with seven men and 27 animals. Cold weather and a blizzard (with deep and drifting snow) had caused these travelers much suffering during their 50-day journey.

On the Arkansas five of the party had turned southward to head for Texas. On the plains one man froze to death. At Cottonwood Crossing (present Marion county) three men ("one badly frozen, one sick . . ." and a third to assist them) had been left—to whom Alvarez dispatched aid on the 14th(?) One of the three died; and the other two reached Independence on the 24th.

The unseasonable trip had been undertaken because of the precarious situation for Americans in New Mexico (a result of the capture of the Texan Santa Fe expedition—*see* p. 437). Alvarez, for one, had difficulty getting a passport to leave. (Earlier, his home at Santa Fe had been attacked, and he had suffered a severe facial wound.)

Ref: *Daily Missouri Republican,* December 24, 1841; *Niles' National Register,* v. 61 (January 8, 1842), p. 304; *1950 Brand Book* (v. 6), Denver, pp. 273, 274.

❆ December 14.—The license issued to Joseph Robidoux, Sr. (by Sup't D. D. Mitchell, at St. Louis) specified trade with the Iowas and the Sacs & Foxes of the Missouri, at Robidoux's "establishment on the Great Nemaha Sub Agency" (in present Doniphan county), and at such other points as the subagent might designate. Ten men were employed in this activity.

(In the 1842 license—July 15, 1842—Robidoux's trading locations in "Kansas" were "at a point opposite Blacksnake Hills, south of the Missouri river," and at the Ioway and Sac villages; and his trade was with the Kickapoos also. Nine men were employed.)

Ref: OIA, Letters Received from SIA, St. Louis (National Archives Microcopy 234, Roll 753), D. D. Mitchell's lists of licenses issued: (1) during 1841, dated December 31, 1841; and (2) for January 1-September 30, 1842. See *KHQ,* v. 18, pp. 159-163, for an article on Robidoux creek in present Marshall county, and an 1841 item on Joseph Robidoux's brother Michel in "Kansas."

❆ December 22.—"Waubaunse," an "old and very influential" Pottawatomie chief, accompanied by his son, and four others (three of whom were Pottawatomie chiefs residing on the Kickapoo reserve above Fort Leavenworth) arrived at Westport, Mo., to discuss with Isaac McCoy the desire many of their people had to exchange the reserve in southwestern Iowa for lands in "Kansas."

Chief Wabaunsee (who, in 1845, was described as having "the snows of eighty winters on his head") had come from his home in present Mills county, Iowa, where he had lived since 1836. Once he had been the principal war chief of the Prairie Pottawatomies (when their home was on the Kankakee river in Illinois).

Though Wabaunsee died before the Pottawatomies left Iowa to settle on a Kansas river reserve in the late 1840's, a town, a township, and a county in present Kansas bear his name. (His death occurred in Ohio, apparently in December, 1845, when a stage upset in which he and other Pottawatomie chiefs were riding while homeward-bound from Washington.)

Ref: Isaac McCoy manuscripts, for McCoy's December 22, 1841, letter; *History of Mills County, Iowa* . . . (Des Moines, 1881), p. 379; *Annals of Iowa*, Des Moines, 3d series, v. 35 (Fall, 1959), pp. 81-100; *The Palimpsest*, Iowa City, v. 29 (December, 1948), pp. 353-361; T. L. McKenney and James Hall's *The Indian Tribes of North America* . . . (Edinburgh, 1934), v. 2, p. 194; R. S. Elliott's *Notes Taken in Sixty Years* (St. Louis, 1883), p. 212 (for item on Wabaunsee's death).

❡ Employed in "Kansas" by the Indian Department during all, or part of the year 1841 were the following persons:

FORT LEAVENWORTH AGENCY—*Agent* Richard W. Cummins; *Interpreters* Clement Lessert and Henry Tiblow; *Blacksmiths* James M. Simpson (for Shawnees), Greenup Dodson (for Shawnees; till November), William Donalson (for Shawnees; beginning November 1), William F. Newton (for Delawares), W. J. Baugh (for Kansa; till August 4), Charles Fish (for Kansa; promoted from assistant smith); *Assistant blacksmiths* Wilson Rodgers (for Shawnees), Jackson Pitman (for Shawnees), W. H. Newton (for Delawares), Charles Fish (for Kansa; promoted to smith), Mab Frankier (for Kansa); *Farmer* David Benzley (for Kansa).

GREAT NEMAHAW SUBAGENCY—*Subagent* Congreve Jackson (till August 3), succeeded by William P. Richardson on August 4 (but appointed on June 25); *Interpreters* Peter Cadue (for Sacs & Foxes), John Rubeti (for Sacs & Foxes; appointed August 5), Jeffrey Dorney (for Iowas), Elisha P. Swift (for Iowas, from November 4); *Blacksmith* James Gilmore (for Sacs & Foxes; appointed August 7); *Assistant blacksmith* William Davies [or, Daviess?] (for Sacs & Foxes; appointed August 7); *Farmer* Preston Richardson (for Sacs & Foxes; appointed October 1); *Assistant farmer* Pleasant Johnson (for Sacs & Foxes); *Teacher* William Hamilton (for Sacs & Foxes, appointed September 23).

OSAGE [MARAIS DES CYGNES] RIVER SUBAGENCY—*Subagent* Anthony L. Davis; *Interpreter* Luther Rice; *Blacksmiths* Robert Simerwell and Robert Wilson (both for Pottawatomies); *Assistant blacksmiths* D. Moreland, Thomas Evans, William A. Simerwell (all for Pottawatomies); *"Issuing agent"* for the Pottawatomies Andrew H. Stinson (from April 1 to November 24).

OSAGE SUBAGENCY—*Subagent* Robert A. Calloway; *Interpreter* Charles Mongrain; *Blacksmiths* John Mathews (appointed January 1), John C. Brashears (till March 4), Silas Moser (appointed March 5; died on, or before, September

4), Edwin B. Lowther (from September 5); *Assistant blacksmiths* E. W. Black (till March 4), William (half Osage; appointed January 1), and Jacob (an Osage; appointed March 5).

Ref: 27th Cong., 2d Sess., *H. Doc. No. 41* (Serial 402); 27th Cong., 2d Sess., *H. Doc. No. 164* (Serial 403); 27th Cong., 3d Sess., *H. Doc. No. 76* (Serial 403); 27th Cong., 3d Sess., *H. Doc. No. 162* (Serial 422); SIA, St. Louis "Records," v. 8, typed copy, pp. 240, 257-259.

1842

❧ MARRIED: Andrew Bernard Canville (born about 1801?; native of France) and Mary Louise Terrien (daughter of Ignatius and Louise [Vallé] Terrien), on January 2, at the Kaw's mouth French settlement (in present Kansas City, Mo.) by the Rev. Christian Hoecken, S. J.

Ignatius Terrien (a French-Canadian; and American Fur Company employee) had brought his family to the Kaw's mouth (from Carondelet—now part of St. Louis) before March, 1834. A. B. Canville arrived there prior to November, 1840.

It has long been *said* that Canville established a trading post among the Osages, in present Neosho county, in 1844. He may have had trade connections with them in the 1840's, but evidence now compiled shows that he did not move to the Osage reserve till 1852. Items of proof: (1) Canville, his wife (French, and one-quarter Osage), and two children (Missouri-born) are recorded in the 1850 federal census of Jackson county, Mo.; and other Canville children born in the 1840's who died before 1850, are listed in Catholic baptismal and burial records of "Kansas City." (2) In the 1860 Kansas territorial census, the 1865 Kansas state census, and the 1870 U. S. census of Kansas, the children born *after* 1852 are all listed as Kansas natives. (Although a son, Henry Alfred, born in 1852, is recorded in the 1860 census as Kansas-born, in the censuses of 1865 and 1870 he is listed as a native of Missouri; and his baptism is to be found in the Catholic records at Kansas City—but this is not true for his younger brothers and sisters.) (3) Records of Jackson county, Mo., show transfers of property by A. B. Canville in 1851 and 1852. (4) Noting Canville's current annual visit to the city to buy a large bill of groceries, a Kansas City, Mo., newspaper of August, 1858, referred to his having been a resident and storekeeper there as early as 1840; remarked that he had built several of the oldest houses in town—one being the brick building occupied (1858) by the City Hotel, and another W. J. Jarboe's "store house"; stated that Canville had left Kansas City "several years ago" to settle among the Osages, and that the property he disposed of when he left, for a few hundred dollars, had become worth $60,000 to $80,000. (5) In June, 1876, when A. B. Canville (then a resident of "Oklahoma") visited Osage Mission (present St. Paul), he "entertained" the local newspaper editor "with reminiscences of the early settlement of . . . [Neosho] county to which he came in 1852." (6) A newspaper item of 1878— the year of his death—referred to him as "A. B. Canville, who settled in 1852 above Erie. . . ." (*See* 1852 annals for additional data on the Canvilles, and on Canville Trading Post.)

Ref: Mrs. Blanche O. Garrison, of Barlesville, Okla. (who is descended from Ignatius

Terrien [her great-grandfather] and his son Cyprian), has graciously shared with this compiler some data from her research on the Terrien (now spelled "Tayrien") family, and also
on the Canville (Quenneville) family. (Her mother was La Reine "René" [Tayrien] Mickels.)
Other sources: "Liber Matrimoniorum," microfilm in KHi (for the marriage record); *Vital
Historical Records of Jackson County, Missouri,* compiled by Kansas City chapter, D. A. R.
(c1934), pp. 91-93, 266; U. S. census records (as noted above); and Kansas state census,
1865; *KHC,* v. 17, pp. 692, 693 (which has many inaccurate statements concerning the
Canville family); *Western Journal of Commerce,* Kansas City, Mo., August 14, 1858; *Neosho
Valley Journal,* Osage Mission, June 14, 1876; W. W. Graves' *Annals of Osage Mission* (St.
Paul, c1935), p. 229; *also,* his *History of Neosho County* (St. Paul, 1949), v. 1, pp. 125,
127; *The History of Jackson County, Missouri* (Kansas City, Mo., 1881), p. 398.

❦ BORN: on January 10, at Delaware Methodist Mission (present Wyandotte county), Susan Talbott Peery, daughter of the Rev. Edward T. and Mary S. (Peery) Peery.

Ref: Si and Shirley Corn's *Our Family Tree* (June, 1959), Section IV; *KHC,* v. 9, p. 227 (for location of the Peery family in 1842).

❦ February 7.—Isaac Coffman and Frantz Blattman, of Jackson county, Mo., agreed to take over and operate Isaac McCoy's ferry on the Missouri river "at or near the Town of Kansas" [present Kansas City, Mo.], until February 1, 1843.

This was the ferry originally established by Peter Roy (about 1837?), located near the foot of present Grand avenue, Kansas City, Mo. The second owner (for less than a year) was James H. McGee, who sold it to Isaac McCoy. John Bidwell (an 1841 emigrant to California), who taught school in Platte county, Mo., in the winter of 1840-1841, recalled that he crossed by "the ferry at Westport Landing" on two or three trips to Jackson county; that crossing there was "always dangerous in winter, when ice was running"; and that the Independence Landing ferry, 10 miles downstream was "safer." In 1843 John C. McCoy (son of Isaac) became the ferry's owner.

Ref: Isaac McCoy manuscripts; *KHQ,* v. 2, p. 6; John Bidwell's *Echoes of the Past* (Chicago, 1928), pp. 20, 21.

❦ BORN: on February 26(?), at Fort Leavenworth, Medora Easton Rich, daughter of post sutler Hiram Rich and his wife Julia.

Ref: Fort Leavenworth national cemetery, tombstone inscription (which records that Medora died July 31, 1847, aged 5 years, 5 months, and 5 days). The 1860 federal census of Fort Leavenworth's civilian population lists the Rich family, and shows a son Hiram, aged 16 (therefore born about 1844), as a native of "Kansas."

❦ BORN: on March 10, at Fort Leavenworth, Julia Turner Cooke, daughter of Capt. Philip St. George and Rachel (Hertzog) Cooke.

She was the last-born of the Cookes' four children, and the only one a native of "Kansas." Her parents had been married at Fort Leavenworth in 1830— *see* p. 178.

Ref: *KHQ,* v. 22, p. 109, v. 28, p. 177.

❦ March 25.—John Hambleton signed a contract to build a school house for the Sacs & Foxes (in present Doniphan county). It was to cost $285.50, and be completed in a month.

In September Subagent Richardson wrote: "There is no public building on the Sac & Fox land except the school house and the Sub Agency Blacksmith's shop and dwelling which were built by James Gilmore the Blacksmith."

Ref: 27th Cong., 3d Sess., *House Doc. No. 68* (Serial 420), p. 8; *Report* of the Comm'r of Indian Affairs, 1842; Superintendency of Indian Affairs (SIA), St. Louis, "Records," v. 8, typed copy, pp. 150-161; 27th Cong., 3d Sess., *House Doc. No. 162* (Serial 422), p. 43.

❡ Spring.—Buildings for the Great Nemaha Subagency headquarters were under construction on the Iowa reserve (in present Doniphan county).

The site was "within five miles of what is called Iowa Point, about five miles from the mouth of Wolf River, and four miles from the Missouri River . . ." (Subagent W. P. Richardson's description). The Iowas' principal village (where half the nation lived) was less than a mile away.

In September Richardson wrote: "The buildings are of hewn logs, of one story high, two rooms & a hall, clap board roof, puncheon floor, two doors, two windows, a kitchen fifteen feet by seventeen, wooden chimneys with stone jambs to dwelling house and kitchen; a spring house, stable and other fixtures *all* of which have been built at the expense of your Sub Agent." (He estimated the outlay at $400 which included putting into cultivation 10 acres of ground.)

Ref: Comm'r of Indian Affairs *Report*, 1842; SIA, St. Louis, "Records," v. 7, typed copy, pp. 209, 210, v. 8, typed copy, pp. 75, 76, 150-161; *KHC*, v. 10, p. 318 (Pryor Plank notes that the above subagency site was a mile southwest of the Iowa, Sac & Fox Presbyterian Mission; and that up to the time of the treaties of 1854, when the Indians' reserves were diminished and they moved northward, little change or improvement had been made in the buildings erected in 1842.)

❡ Around April 1 Thomas and Esther (Cattell) French became superintendents at Shawnee Friends Mission (succeeding the Henry Harveys—*see* June 13, 1840, annals—who returned to Ohio).

Thomas H. and Mary (Wilson) Stanley had arrived about March 21 to serve, respectively, as principal farmer, and housekeeper; and with them came John Steward as assistant farmer. The autumn, 1842, report listed the mission personnel as totaling eight persons. Mary Crew was assistant housekeeper; Thomas and Hannah (Dukemineer) Wells were teachers.

(In the spring[?] of 1843 the Stanleys became superintendents when the Frenches returned East; and remained in charge till August, 1845, then went home to Ohio.)

Ref: Henry Harvey's *History of the Shawnee Indians* . . . (Cincinnati, 1855), p. 250; *Reports* of the Comm'r of Indian Affairs for 1842, 1843; H. Pearl Dixon's *Sixty Years Among the Indians* . . . (1922), pp. 20-32; W. W. Hinshaw's *Encyclopedia of American Quaker Genealogy*, v. 4, pp. 86, 707, v. 5, pp. 49, 139.

❡ BORN: on April 3, at Shawnee Methodist Mission (present Johnson county), William C. Berryman, son of the Rev. Jerome C. and Sarah C. (Cessna) Berryman.

Ref: Leavenworth *Times*, September 21, 1925; or, Remsburg "Stork" clippings, in KHi library.

❡ April 9.—John C. McIntosh was issued a license (at St. Louis) to trade at the Iowas' village, at the mouth of the Big Nemaha, and at such other points on the Iowa and Sac & Fox reserves as the resident subagent might designate.

(Why this trader was licensed in 1842 is not clear, for his illegal trafficking in liquor was known at St. Louis. Subagent W. P. Richardson, in a November 12, 1841, letter had reported that it was Jeffrey Doraway [Dorney] who had got "McIntosh to settle so near to them [the Iowas] with poison by the bottle or bowl as they might want it," and that "McIntosh brought 100 Bbls of Liquid fire here only 4 months since and I believe he has but little left.")

Ref: Office of Indian Affairs (OIA), Letters Received from SIA, St. Louis (National Archives Microcopy 234, Roll 753), for Mitchell's list of licenses, January 1 to September 30, 1842; OIA, Letters Received from Fort Leavenworth Agency (National Archives Microcopy 234, Roll 307), for Richardson's letter.

¶ April 9.—Capt. Benjamin D. Moore, Asst. Surg. Jacob R. Motte, and a detachment of First dragoons, accompanied by Missouri residents George Douglass and Abraham Redfield, arrived at the Marmaton crossing of the Fort Leavenworth-Fort Gibson military road. Near the ford (in present Bourbon county), Moore and Motte (commissioners for this task) selected a site for a new military fort—a post first known as "Camp Scott" (named for Gen. Winfield Scott).

The military party had left Fort Wayne (a new and brief-lived post on the Cherokees' land in "Oklahoma") April 1. Having made the Marmaton crossing selection (because a preferred Pomme de Terre [Spring] river site on the Cherokee neutral lands was unavailable), Captain Moore and Asst. Surgeon Motte returned to Fort Wayne, leaving Sgt. John Hamilton and a work party of dragoons to begin temporary log structures at "Camp Scott."

(Writing 30 years later, Hamilton recollected that buildings [temporary?] for the commanding officer, a hospital, and a quartermaster and commissary storehouse were up, and a garden planted, before garrison troops arrived.)

See, also, May 30 entry.

Ref: KHQ, v. 11, pp. 126, 127; 28th Cong., 1st Sess., Sen. *Doc. No. 136* (Serial 433).

¶ DIED: the Rev. William Johnson (founder of Kansa Methodist Mission in 1836), on April 10, of pneumonia, at Shawnee Mission (where he was buried). He was 37 years old.

Missionary Johnson (four years among the Delawares and Shawnees; and seven among the Kansa) could speak in Shawnee, and may have been the only white man to learn the Kansa language with grammatical accuracy.

In July, 1842, the Rev. E. T. Peery wrote: "Our operations at the Kanzas Mission are wholly suspended, owing to the death of the Missionary, Rev. Wm. Johnson." *See, also,* October, 1842, entry.

Ref: KHC, v. 16, pp. 234, 235, 251; Comm'r of Indian Affairs *Report*, 1842 (see Agent R. W. Cummins' report therein).

¶ Near dusk, on April 13, Methodist Bishop Robert R. Roberts and the Rev. E. R. Ames (northward-bound on the Fort Leavenworth-Fort Gibson military road), in a horse-drawn covered carriage, arrived at the "falls of the Marie des Cygnes"—present Trading Post, Linn county.

As Ames described it: "Here was an Indian trading-house, occupied by a Frenchman and two or three squaws. Several Osage Indians, some Pottawatomies, and two or three negroes were about." The Frenchman (Michel Giraud, presumably) became hospitable upon learning a *bishop* was at his door; and, says Ames, "both ourselves and horses fared exceedingly well."

(Bishop Roberts, touring Methodist Indian missions, had left the Cherokee-Seneca border, in northeast "Oklahoma," with Ames, on April 5. They had traveled part of the time on the "Old Harmony mission trace" in Missouri; but left it on the morning of the 13th to strike off over the prairie "in a due west course" for some 10 miles, to the military road—entering "Kansas" somewhere in present Bourbon county.)

Leaving "Trading Post" on April 14, they crossed the Marais des Cygnes and continued northward. While "nooning" at a grove of timber where there was a large spring (a popular camp spot, called, by other travelers, "Cold Water Grove"—in present Miami county), the horses bolted, left the carriage with top crushed, tongue and a whipple-tree broken, at the bottom of a ravine, and later were found, grazing, a couple of miles away. Ames (foresightedly equipped with tools) spent the night repairing the carriage and harness; and the 63-year-old bishop made do as best he could during the chilly hours. Early on April 15 they were under way again—traveled hard all day, not stopping to eat—and reached the Indian manual labor school (present Johnson county) about dark.

Bishop Roberts' subsequent "Kansas" travels (between mid-April and early May) included the Friends (Shawnee) and Moravian (Munsee) missions as well as Methodist stations. On May 4 he disposed of his carriage and ponies to take passage on the *Oceana* (at Kansas Landing—present Kansas City, Mo.) for St. Louis.

Ref: Charles Elliott's *The Life of the Rev. Robert R. Roberts* . . . (Cincinnati, 1844), pp. 342-348; *Western Christian Advocate*, Cincinnati, v. 9 (May 13, 1842), p. 14 (for E. R. Ames' letter—copy in ms. division, KHi).

❡ **April 18.**—Col. Stephen W. Kearny and his five First U. S. dragoon companies (described by their commander as 350 "efficient and well mounted men ready for service") departed for Fort Gibson (Okla.) to report to Brig. Gen. Zachary Taylor (under army orders of March 26). The dragoons' summer replacement at Fort Leavenworth was a company of First U. S. infantry. Capt. John H. K. Burgwin, First dragoons, was in command at the post from April 18 to May 21, and Capt. Eustace Trenor, First dragoons, from May 21 to July 11, when Kearny returned.

The Independence (Mo.) *Western Missourian,* noting the dragoons' southward march, complained: "This takes from our frontier the whole force assigned by the Government for its protection." The troop movement was said to be "owing to the unsettled state of our relations with Mexico. . . ."

By the end of April, Kearny and his command were at Fort Gibson; and on June 6 they were in camp near that post.

See, also, August 4 entry.

Ref: *Niles' National Register,* Baltimore, v. 62 (April 9, 1842), p. 84 (for army general orders of March 26); *Daily Missouri Republican,* St. Louis, May 4, 1842 (reprinted in Nebraska State Historical Society *Publications,* Lincoln, v. 20, p. 117); Otis E. Young's *The West of Philip St. George Cooke* . . . (Glendale, 1955), p. 103; Fort Leavenworth post returns.

℄ April.—David Adams (accompanied by Daniel Simons), from Sibille & Adams' post on Laramie river (left March 26), crossed "Kansas" in the last third of the month, traveling with P. D. Papin's small party (in which were Henry Chatillon, Charles Lajeunesse and "Decoto").

Papin had two light wagons. They crossed from the Platte to the Little Blue April 17; probably reached the Big Blue about the 21st (being at "sandy fork" on the 20th).

Ref: David Adams Papers, Missouri Historical Society, St. Louis (courtesy of Dale L. Morgan, Bancroft Library).

℄ Assembled Oregon-bound emigrants left the Independence, Mo., area on May 4; crossed into the Shawnee reserve and encamped at Elm Grove (present Johnson county) to await late-comers. Dr. Elijah White, chief promoter of the 1842 overland emigration, and recently appointed as Oregon's first subagent of Indian affairs, arrived from Independence on the 14th.

Officers were elected on May 15—White as captain (to serve for one month); Columbia Lancaster, Lansford W. Hastings, and Asa L. Lovejoy as a scientific corps; James Coates as pilot; Nathaniel Crocker as secretary; Hugh Burns as master blacksmith; and John Hoffstutter as master wagonmaker. Dr. Elijah White (a Methodist missionary in Oregon, 1837-1840) had never crossed the Rocky mountains. Traveling in his care were two homeward-bound half-Chinook youths—John and Alexander McKay, sons of Hudson's Bay Company's Thomas McKay—who had journeyed over the Oregon trail (en route to Eastern schools) in 1838, with Missionary Jason Lee.

On May 16 the caravan got under way. Medorem Crawford (in his journal) wrote: "In our company were 16 waggons & 105 persons including children & 51 men over 18 years of age." White indicated there were 18 wagons and 112 persons when the company organized; and that later additions brought the personnel to 125. (Lt. John C. Fremont had information there were 64 men, and 16 or 17 families. "They had a considerable number of cattle," he noted, "and were transporting their household furniture in heavy wagons.") Lansford Hastings' later-published figures "our company consisted of 160 persons, giving us a force of 80 armed men," evidently were exaggerated.

Stephen H. L. Meek (brother of Joe Meek), and two other men, with one wagon, joined on the 17th. On May 18 Captain White issued an unpopular decree that the emigrants' dogs must be killed (22 were put to death) to prevent a rabies outbreak. Bad weather, and a sick child, slowed the company's progress for several days. On May 21 the Columbia Lancasters' 16-months-old daughter died and was buried (in present Douglas county). Next day—Sunday —the caravan traveled 25 miles, camping in Shawnee county of today. On the 24th, as Crawford recorded it: "Started at 9 o'clock M. drove to the Kansas river [present Topeka area] and crossed with saf[e]ty, Distance 10 miles."

The night of May 26 camp was on Vermillion creek. From the 27th to the 30th Mrs. Lancaster's illness delayed the company. The Lancasters turned back; and were escorted to the Kansas crossing by Captain White and others. The caravan camped on Blue river the night of May 31. White rejoined the emigrants on June 1. On the 3d Crawford wrote: "The company started at 5 oclock M. & left myself with 3 others to wait for Mr. [Hugh] Burns and others who were detained by Mr. Lancaster." On the 4th Crawford "Met Mr. Burns & his company together with O'Fallen [William O. Fallon] 2 miles back, turned & came on with them." On the 5th they all joined the caravan.

The emigrants crossed the 25-mile stretch from Little Blue river to the Platte on June 9. Lansford W. Hastings ("an aspiring sort of man"—Lovejoy) was elected captain in place of White on June 15. As a result, the company split, and Dr. Elijah White's smaller party went on ahead next day. But at Fort Laramie, in late June, there was a temporary reuniting of forces. F. X. Matthieu and two other trappers joined the emigrants; and Thomas Fitzpatrick, just arrived from the Flatheads' country, was hired by White (at $500, government expense) to guide them to Fort Hall.

Subsequently, in the Independence Rock area, a man named Bailey died in an accidental shooting; and on July 13 Hastings and Lovejoy, caught by Sioux Indians, were rescued from their precarious situation by Thomas Fitzpatrick. The emigrants, long since traveling in two separate parties, reached Fort Hall (where Fitzpatrick left them) in mid-August. By this time the Hastings group had only seven wagons; and the rest of the emigrants were using pack animals.

All of the 1842 overland company went to Oregon (but in 1843, a party headed by Hastings went on to California). Early in October, 1842, the long journey was completed. Crawford logged the distance from Independence to Willamette Falls as 1,746 miles.

Ref: Medorem Crawford's "Journal," in *Sources of the History of Oregon*, Eugene, v. 1, no. 1, pp. 1-26; A. J. Allen's *Ten Years in Oregon* . . . (Ithaca, 1850), pp. 139-155; L. W. Hastings' *The Emigrants' Guide to Oregon and California*, edited by C. H. Carey (Princeton, 1932); John C. Fremont's *Report of the Exploring Expedition* . . . (Washington, 1845), pp. 12, 40; H. H. Bancroft's *History of Oregon* (San Francisco, 1886), v. 1, pp. 254-262; W. J. Ghent's *The Early Far West* . . . (New York, 1931), pp. 319-323; *Oregon Historical Quarterly*, Salem, v. 31 (September, 1930), pp. 240-243 (for Asa L. Lovejoy's narrative); Oregon Pioneer Association, *Transactions of the Fifty-first Annual Reunion* . . . 1923, p. 27 (for item on David Weston and companions of the 1842 journey), and *Transactions of the Fifty-fifth Annual Reunion* . . . 1927, pp. 16-20 (for William McKay's article—he did not return with the 1842 emigrants; but his two brothers John and Alexander did); New York *Weekly Tribune*, April 13, 1844 (has long letter from "New Madrid, Mo., March 19, 1844," signed "A Pioneer" [evidently L. W. Hastings] who says he was with a "party of 160 persons" arriving overland in Oregon October 5, 1842; and has recently returned to the United States "via California, Mexico City and Vera Cruz").

❡ Born: on May 5, at Iowa, Sac & Fox Presbyterian Mission, Mary Elizabeth, daughter of the Rev. William and Julia A. N. Hamilton.

Ref: Highland Presbyterian Church Records, 1843-1890 (microfilm in KHi), under January 16, 1843, baptismal record.

℄ May.—The spring caravan to Santa Fe was made up of a "large company of Americans and Spaniards"—around 15 proprietors and 120 men in all. The 62 wagons, mule-drawn (about 800 animals in all), carried merchandise (from English and Eastern markets) valued at between $150,000 and $160,000. Manuel Alvarez was one of the proprietors.

Ref: *Daily Missouri Republican*, St. Louis, May 4, 1842 (in Nebraska State Historical Society *Publications*, v. 20, p. 118); *The Bulletin* of the Missouri Historical Society, St. Louis, v. 16 (October, 1959), p. 39; *New Mexico Historical Review*, Santa Fe, v. 21 (April, 1946), p. 136; Josiah Gregg, *Commerce of the Prairies* (1844), v. 2, p. 160.

℄ May.—The caravan from Santa Fe which reached Independence, Mo., early in May numbered about 80 men. It was said the proprietors in the party had brought about $200,000 in specie, and intended to invest $150,000 in goods.

Probably in this company were the six Mexican traders who, later in May, were "in Pittsburg for the purpose of making contracts for waggons, harness, & purchasing other articles intended to cross the desert for the Mexican market." It was *reported* they had brought with them "17 boxes of specie, containing $350,000[?]" to make purchases in the United States.

Ref: *Daily Missouri Republican*, May 9, 11, 1842 (reprinted in Nebraska State Historical Society *Publications*, v. 20, p. 118); *Weekly Picayune*, New Orleans, May 30, 1842 (from the daily of May 28).

℄ May.—Bent, St. Vrain & Company's wagon train reached Missouri after an April-early May journey across "Kansas" on the Santa Fe trail, from Bent's Fort on the upper Arkansas. Kit Carson (who brought with him his young half-Arapaho daughter to be cared for and educated in Missouri) was with Charles Bent on this trip.

A St. Louis newspaper of May 19 stated: "A part of Bent & St. Vrains Santa Fe traders arrived yesterday bringing 283 packs of buffalo robes, 30 packs of beaver, 12 sacks of tongues, and 1 pack of deer skins."

Ref: *Daily Missouri Republican*, May 19, 1842; Blanche C. Grant, editor, *Kit Carson's Own Story of His Life* (Taos, N. M., 1926), p. 50; Harvey L. Carter's *'Dear Old Kit' the Historical Christopher Carson* (Norman, Okla., [c1968]), p. 81; *Montana the Magazine of Western History*, v. 18, no. 4, p. 80, v. 19, no. 2, p. 91 and no. 3, p. 79; David Lavender's *Bent's Fort* (New York, 1954), pp. 206-211; John C. Fremont's *Memoirs of My Life* . . . (Chicago, 1887), p. 74.

℄ On May 15 Subagent A. L. Davis reported that the Pottawatomies in his Osage [Marais des Cygnes] River Subagency totaled 1,949 souls. In the "Wabash band" were 625 persons; and the "St. Joseph & Prairie bands" including "those [260 or 270 souls] who have joined from the Council Bluffs" [the Pottawatomie reserve in southwestern Iowa], numbered 1,324 persons.

In September, Davis wrote: "The Settlement on Sugar Creek are notorious for sobriety and industry, they nearly all live in good comfortable log cabins, have fields fenced with rails and well cultivated, and have ploughed and fenced a large quantity of Prairie ground the present Season, while the other settlements [on Pottawatomie creek] have indulged in drunkenness, and idleness followed as a necessary consequence. . . ."

According to records kept at Sugar Creek Mission, the Catholic Pottawatomies in the Marais des Cygnes country numbered 812 in 1841, and in 1842 totaled 940. (*See* pp. 358, 364.)

Ref: SIA, St. Louis, "Records," v. 8, typed copy, pp. 106-110, 137; G. J. Garraghan's *The Jesuits of the Middle United States,* v. 2, p. 229.

❏ May.—Martias Dias (a Mexican), *by his own account,* crossed "Kansas" alone, coming down from Bent's Fort to Independence, Mo., over the Santa Fe trail.

Martias' story (published in the *Picayune* after he reached New Orleans in June) was that he had dug out of the Santa Fe, N. M., jail, in April, with tools supplied by friends. (He had been held there for serving as a spy with the Texan Santa Fe expedition.) Reaching Taos, he stole a horse and mule; made his way to Bent's Fort (where he obtained provisions); then continued eastward, reaching Missouri after a 26-day journey. The *Picayune's* reporter concluded: "If his story is correct he is probably the first traveller who has ever 'gone it alone' across the immense prairies of the West. . . ." (There was a "Martias," or "Matias," with the Texans. He is mentioned in published accounts of that ill-fated expedition.)

Ref: *Weekly Picayune,* June 13, 1842; Thomas Falconer's *Letters and Notes on the Texan Santa Fe Expedition* . . . (New York, 1930), p. 40.

❏ May.—At Kansa Methodist Mission the occupants were the government farmer William H. Mitchell and his family. (*See* April 10 entry.) On May 18 a delegation of Methodists (among whom were ministers Andrew Monroe, E. T. Peery, and David Kinnear), with a Delaware guide, arrived for a brief visit among the Kansa.

(This party had left Shawnee Mission on the 16th; camped near the Wakarusa that night; and spent the night of the 17th at a "creek [the Shunganunga?] and camping ground, ten miles from the mission." After leaving the Kansa, the ministers returned to the Indian manual labor school arriving there by May 23.)

Ref: *KHC,* v. 16, pp. 260, 261.

❏ About May 23 Capt. John H. K. Burgwin and a company of First U. S. dragoons left Fort Leavenworth for present Council Bluffs, Iowa, and reached their destination at the beginning of June. They were to prevent further hostilities between the Pottawatomies and the Sioux.

Agent R. W. Cummins (of the Fort Leavenworth Agency), on special assignment, had arrived at Council Bluffs on May 30. On June 4 he held a council with the Pottawatomies, which Burgwin attended. The Indians informed the agent they wanted two points guarded—one, the line between them and the Sioux; the other, between them and whisky sellers.

The troops set up "Camp Fenwick"—subsequently renamed "Fort Croghan" (within present Council Bluffs). (In October, 1843, this post was abandoned, and Captain Burgwin and his troops returned to Fort Leavenworth.)

Ref: SIA, St. Louis, "Records," v. 8, typed copy, pp. 111-114; *Annals of Iowa*, Des Moines, 3d series, v. 3 (April-July, 1898), p. 471 (the date here given for Burgwin's arrival is April, 1842; but Cummins' letter of June 14, 1842, in the SIA "Records" is explicit); H. P. Beers' *The Western Military Frontier, 1815-1846* (Philadelphia, 1935), p. 140. Edward Harris, in his journal—*Up the River With Audubon* . . ., edited by John F. McDermott (Norman, c1951)—under dates of May 9 and October 5 and 6, 1843, mentioned Fort Croghan.

❮ Born: on May 28, at Iowa, Sac & Fox Presbyterian Mission, Mary Jane, daughter of the Rev. Samuel M. and Eliza H. Irvin.

Ref: Highland Presbyterian church records, 1843-1890 (microfilm in KHi).

❮ May 30.—Capt. Benjamin D. Moore, Lt. William Eustis, Asst. Surg. Josiah Simpson, and Companies A and C (about 120 men) of the First U. S. dragoons arrived at new "Camp Scott" (*see* April 9 entry) after a journey northward from Fort Wayne (Okla.), which was officially abandoned when they departed from it on May 26. (Government records designate May 30 as the founding date of Fort Scott.)

On October 23 Bvt. Maj. William M. Graham arrived, with Company D, Fourth U. S. infantry, to command the post. Permanent buildings were started before the end of 1842—*see* August 15 entry.

Ref: *KHQ*, v. 11, pp. 127, 128; 28th Cong., 1st Sess., Sen. Doc. No. 136 (Serial 433); Fort Scott post returns (microfilm from National Archives, in KHi).

❮ June 6.—Lt. John C. Fremont (of the U. S. Topographical Engineers), and the 27(?) other persons who were members of his first exploring expedition to the Rocky mountains, moved overland about 12 miles—from Chouteau's Landing on the Missouri (where they had debarked June 4 after a steamboat trip from St. Louis)— to Cyprian Chouteau's trading house on the Kansas (in present Wyandotte county—*see* p. 153). There they stayed six days, making final arrangements.

In Fremont's employ were Kit Carson (met on the steamboat, and hired as guide), Charles Preuss (as assistant topographer), Lucien Maxwell (as hunter), and 22 Canadian and Creole-French voyageurs. Also along were two youths, Randolph Benton (12) and Henry Brant (19), son and grand-nephew of Missouri's U. S. senator Thomas H. Benton (Fremont's father-in-law).

On June 10 this company left Chouteau's post to take the Oregon trail across "Kansas." "We were," wrote Fremont, "all well armed and mounted, with the exception of 8 men, who conducted as many carts, in which were packed our stores, with the baggage and instruments, and which were drawn by two mules. A few loose horses, and four oxen, which had been added . . . completed the train."

Arriving, late on June 14, at the crossing of the rain-swollen Kansas ("by our route, the ford was 100 miles from the mouth"—Fremont), the animals were made to swim over; six of the eight carts were taken across, one at a time (each dismantled, and with its accompanying load) in an India-rubber boat (20' x 5'), handled by a crew of three, with paddles. The crowding of two carts as one load for a last trip, resulted in the boat capsizing. Two men nearly drowned; and some supplies were lost.

June 15 was spent on the river's north bank (not far west of present North Topeka). Kansa Indians came to visit; brought vegetables and other articles for barter. Fremont was able to obtain 20-some pounds of coffee from "Louis Pepin" (brother of Joseph Papin, apparently); and exchanged a yoke of oxen for a "fine cow and calf." On the 16th the company moved about seven miles upriver and camped for two days on a "handsome, open prairie."

On the 18th the journey was "along the foot of the hills which border the Kansas valley." Fremont rode off "some miles to the left" to examine a cluster of huts—a deserted Kansa village—scattered in an open wood near the Vermillion's mouth (not far from present Belvue, Pottawatomie co.). "The Pawnees had attacked it in the early spring," he wrote. "Some of the houses were burnt, and others blackened with smoke." The expedition's camp that night was on the west bank of the (Red) "Vermillion," at the ford.

"Quitting the river bottom" for the uplands, the company traveled 19 miles on June 19. Lieutenant Fremont noted "many large boulders . . . of various shades of red, some of them 4 or 5 tons in weight . . . scattered along the hills; and many beautiful plants in flower . . ." (in present Pottawatomie county). On the 20th the "Big Vermillion" (Black Vermillion) was crossed; and after a day's march of 24 miles the party "reached the Big Blue, and encamped on the uplands of the western side, near a small creek, where was a fine large spring of very cold water." (By Fremont's observations [inexact?] they were in longitude 96° 32' 35"; latitude 29° 45' 08".) Kit Carson "brought a fine deer" to camp. On June 22 they were near the Little Blue; four days later they crossed to the Platte. (The Oregon-bound emigrants had reached the Platte 17 days earlier.)

Subsequently, on July 5, near the forks of the Platte, Fremont sent the main party on to "Fort Laramie" by the emigrant route; while he, Lucien Maxwell, and three others, traveled up the South Platte as far as Fort St. Vrain before heading for Laramie's fork.

From the American Fur Company post "Fort John, or Laramie" (where the main party arrived on July 13, and Fremont on July 15), the exploring expedition (leaving behind young Benton and Brant) proceeded west on the "Oregon trail." Crossing South Pass on August 8 the party entered the Wind River mountains on the 10th.

The return trip (begun about August 18) was made by the same route as on the outward journey, except that the party followed down the Platte all the way to its mouth, arriving at the Missouri on October 1. Lieutenant Fremont and his men embarked October 4 from Bellevue (Neb.) in a boat built at the trading post there, and reached St. Louis on October 17. (See, also, October 10 entry.)

According to a speech Sen. Lewis F. Linn, of Missouri, made on August 8,

"The object of . . . [Fremont's] expedition was to examine and report upon the rivers and country between the frontiers of Missouri and the base of the Rocky Mountains; and especially to examine the character, and ascertain the latitude and longitude of the South Pass, the great crossing place in those mountains on the way to the Oregon." He noted that all this had been accomplished, and that Fremont had returned ". . . with a vast mass of useful observations and many hundred specimens in botany and geology."

John C. Fremont's biographer, Allan Nevins, has referred to him as "the first distinctively scientific explorer produced by the United States." (Fremont, during the next 10 years (1843-1853) made *four* more expeditions to the West.)

Ref: John C. Fremont's *Report of the Exploring Expedition to the Rocky Mountains in the Year 1842* . . .; John C. Fremont's *Memoirs of My Life* . . ., pp. 73-163; Charles Preuss, *Exploring With Frémont* . . ., translated and edited by E. G. and Elisabeth K. Gudde (Norman, c1958), pp. 3-77; Allan Nevins, editor, [John C. Fremont's] *Narratives of Exploration and Adventure* (New York, 1956), pp. 23, 183, particularly; Donald E. Jackson and Mary Lee Spence, eds., *The Expeditions of John Charles Frémont* (Urbana, etc., c1970), v. 1, pp. 143-158.

❦ June 19.—Visiting the Sugar Creek (Pottawatomie) Mission (present Linn county), the Rt. Rev. Peter R. Kenrick, of St. Louis, officiated at a ceremony confirming 300 Indians. He was "the first Catholic bishop to administer the Sacrament of Confirmation within present Kansas."

Ref: T. H. Kinsella's *The History of Our Cradle Land* . . . (Kansas City, 1921), pp. 87, 228.

❦ June 21.—Beeby Robinson was awarded a contract to construct a horse mill for the St. Joseph and Prairie bands of Pottawatomies living on Pottawatomie creek (present Miami and Franklin counties). This grist mill was to cost $1,150, and to be completed within five months.

(In May, 1844, the Indians' subagent wrote that it was an "absolute necessity" that he be authorized to appoint a miller for the two-year-old mill, which had no one in charge of it.)

Ref: 27th Cong., 3d Sess., *House Doc. No. 68* (Serial 420), p. 14; SIA, St. Louis, "Records," v. 8, typed copy, pp. 106-110, 114, 115, 322, 323.

❦ June 23.—Four children of Frederick Chouteau (trader among the Kansa since 1829—*see* pp. 165, 212) and his part-Shawnee wife, Nancy (Logan) Chouteau, were baptized at present Kansas City, Mo., by the Rt. Rev. Peter R. Kenrick, Catholic bishop. They were: William (9), Benjamin (7), Amanda (5), and Francis X. (3). (All were natives of "Kansas.")

Ref: "Westport Register" (microfilm in KHi), on a slip of paper labeled "To be recorded in Westport's Baptismal records."

❦ Summer (and autumn).—Among the Missouri river steamboats making trips as high as Weston, Mo., (or still farther upriver—to Blacksnake Hills, or Council Bluffs) were the *Edna, Emilie, Omega,*

Huntsville, Bowling Green, Rowena, and *Oceana.* The *Thames* and *General Brooke* made stops at "Westport" [Landing] and probably went higher.

Records indicate there were 26 steamboats in the Missouri river trade in 1842; but some ran in the lower river only. At least 44 persons died after more than 60 "emigrant passengers" were scalded when the *Edna's* boiler burst, at the mouth of the Missouri, on July 3.

Ref: Nebraska State Historical Society *Publications*, v. 20, pp. 117, 119-121 (items from the *Daily Missouri Republican*, 1842); SIA, St. Louis, "Records," v. 7, typed copy, p. 275; 27th Cong., 3d Sess., *H. Doc. No. 162* (Serial 422), pp. 42, 47, 48; 28th Cong., 1st Sess., *H. Doc. No. 240* (Serial 441), pp. 38, 39; *Niles' National Register*, v. 72 (July 31, 1847), p. 351.

❡ On August 1, according to the recollections (in 1915) of Washington H. Chick, a company of traders left Westport, Mo., for Santa Fe. William McCoy had wagons in this train; "Pruitt" (Benjamin W.[?] Pruett) had one wagon; and young Chick (then 16) also had one—which his father (W. M. Chick) had outfitted.

At Big John spring the oxen turned Pruett's wagon too short and smashed a wheel. The train was delayed and hindered by rains, high water, and muddy roads as far as the Cimarron. There, William McCoy (who had a law suit pending at Independence), Chick, and another man, left the train and returned (on muleback) to Missouri (reaching Westport in mid-November). The wagons (in charge of a "good man" hired by McCoy) went on to Santa Fe; and some were taken to Chihuahua, to return in the spring of 1843.

Ref: Washington H. Chick's reminiscences (in KHi ms. division), from an article published in the *Weekly Democrat-News*, Marshall, Mo., April 8, 1915.

❡ August 1.—Subagent R. A. Calloway reported that most of the Osages were still living in large towns, and not much disposed to lead an agricultural life. However, some 10 or 12 families of George White Hair's and Clermont's bands had fenced and ploughed fields in the spring. (Ploughs and horse-gear—200 of each—received at the subagency in April, had been reserved for those Indians who "showed intent.")

The principal Osage chief, Pa-hus-ca (or, White Hair)—The man whom Tixier in 1840 (*see* p. 215) had called "Majakita"—was much opposed to farming. He had received the only wagon and team issued under the 1839 treaty, then sold them to Joseph Swiss ("Suisse"—a half-Osage living across the line in Missouri). Calloway's estimate of head chief White Hair: "he is a bad man."

In April, at annuity payment time, the Osages had numbered 3,788 souls (1,302 men, 1,222 women, and 1,264 children). The decrease from 1841 (when the total had been 4,301—*see* March, 1841, entry) was because Sho-tal-sah-bas (Black Dog) and his band (about 50 lodges) had moved "lower down on the Verdigris," in Cherokee country, and had not come in for their annuities. (In April, 1843, the census of Osages was 1,388 men, 1,322 women, and 1,392 children—4,102 souls.)

Ref: Comm'r of Indian affairs *Report*, 1842; SIA, St. Louis, "Records," v. 8, typed copy, pp. 228-239 (has Calloway's 1843 report).

❦ BORN: on August 2, at Shawnee Methodist Mission (present Johnson county), William Hunneywell Eisele, son of Andrew M. and Rosina (Lose) Eisele.

It is said the Eiseles went to the Indian manual labor school in 1840, where Andrew M. was cook and baker. Some years later they settled at Westport, Mo., where Eisele established a bakery at "the northeast corner of Mill street and Westport avenue."

Ref: W. H. Eisele's letter of November 20, 1908, and R. C. Eisele's letter of January 23, 1916, in KHi ms. division; *KHC*, v. 9, p. 564. The 1860 census of Westport, Jackson co., Mo. (taken on June 25), lists A. M. "Eisle" (46), Rosina (40), William (17), and five younger children born in Missouri. In the 1850 census, the entry for the Eisele family is: Andrew M. (33), Rosina (29), Louisa S. (10; born in Germany), "John W." (8; born in Indian [ter.]—who is, evidently, the William H., above), Rosena (5) and Margaret (2), both born in Missouri. Sup't J. C. Berryman's August 15, 1842, report on the school personnel (National Archives Microcopy 234, Roll 301) lists "Mr. M. Eisle, baker and cook."

❦ August 4.—Col. Stephen W. Kearny (promoted, with rank unchanged, to command the Third Military Department of the army) left Fort Leavenworth with his adjutant and staff for Jefferson Barracks, Mo.—his new headquarters.

Capt. Eustace Trenor, First dragoons, was Fort Leavenworth's commandant during the latter part of 1842; and still the ranking officer in March, 1843.

Ref: D. L. Clarke's *Stephen Watts Kearny* . . . (Norman, c1961), pp. 83, 410; Otis E. Young's *The West of Philip St. George Cooke* . . ., p. 107; OIA, Letters Received from Fort Leavenworth Agency (National Archives Microcopy No. 234, Roll 302) for Capt. E. Trenor's March 4, 1843, letter.

❦ Early in August the upbound steamboat *Lebanon*, carrying the merchandise of several Santa Fe traders, sank in five feet of water some 50 miles below Independence, Mo., resulting in "entire loss of $80,000 worth" of goods (a third of the fall's outfit, by report).

Manuel Armijo, governor of New Mexico, had an investment of goods valued at between $18,000 and $20,000 on the *Lebanon*. When he learned of his losses he "became excited to a high degree against all the citizens of the United States," according to acting U. S. consul Manuel Alvarez.

Ref: *Glimpses of the Past*, v. 8 (January-June, 1941), p. 43; *1950 Brand Book* (Denver, c1951), p. 278; *Daily Missouri Republican*, August 6, 1842.

❦ August 10.—Rufus B. Sage, and two experienced mountain men, all mounted on mules, and well equipped, left Independence, Mo., for the Rocky mountains, taking the Oregon trail across "Kansas." (For Sage's first trip West *see* September 4, 1841, annals.)

Successive rains made the early days of the journey unpleasant. They had to "raft" the Wakarusa; and the Kansas was so high it was forded with "great difficulty." Near the head of the Little Blue they met Pawnees who were, fortunately, friendly. At the forks of the Platte, this trio took the route up the South Platte, and arrived at Fort Lupton (Colo.) on September 2d.

(Sage spent two winters in the mountains, on the move much of the time. His travels extended as far south as Taos, N. M., and as far west as Fort Hall [Idaho]. He returned East in the spring of 1844.)

Ref: Rufus B. Sage's *Scenes in the Rocky Mountains*, as reprinted in *Rufus B. Sage . . .*, edited by L. R. and Ann W. Hafen (Glendale, Calif., 1956), v. 1, p. 92, v. 2, pp. 46-80.

℄ August.—The seven small American Fur Company boats "having on board 20,000 buffalo robes and a few packs of other furs," which reached St. Louis on the 16th (after taking two months to descend from the Yellowstone river), probably passed along the "Kansas" bank of the Missouri early in August.

Ref: St. Louis *Bulletin* of August 17, 1842, as reprinted in the *Weekly Picayune*, New Orleans, August 29, 1842, and in *Niles' National Register*, v. 63 (September 3, 1842), p. 16.

℄ August 15.—Capt. Thomas Swords (AQM) let three contracts "for furnishing and delivering" at "Camp Scott, Mo." (Fort Scott, "Kansas") materials for the construction of permanent buildings: (1) to Samuel Wilson, for 500,000 laths, at $1.45 per 1,000 (Edward L. Chouteau and Caleb Darby, sureties); (2) to Samuel B. Bright, for 100,000 bricks, at $4.98 per 1,000 (John Shirley and John Shelton, sureties); (3) to Nehemiah Beardslee, for 300,000 shingles, at $2.97 per 1,000 (W. B. Hagan and Jacob Lutzenlizes, sureties). (*See, also,* May 30 entry.)

Other army contracts for Fort Scott in 1842: Lt. Richard S. Ewell (AAQM), on July 15, with Jesse B. Winscott (for 250 tons of hay, at $4.98 per ton), and with William Moore (for 1,000 bushels of lime, at 18¾ cents per bushel); on August 1 with Calvin Waldo, and with Staples & Butts, for commissary items (Waldo's contract, totaling $1,522.50 was to begin October 1, and end June 1, 1843; Staples & Butts', for $1,132.20, ran from December 31 to June 1, 1843). On August 20 Capt. Thomas Swords (AQM) made a contract with Bennet Ford to supply 1,200 bushels of "good sound merchantable oats," at 25 cents per bushel.

Ref: 27th Cong., 3d Sess., H. *Doc. No. 68* (Serial 420), pp. 33, 36, 49. Edward L. Chouteau (son of Paul Ligueste Chouteau, former agent to the Osages) had a farm on the north side of the Marmaton, in Missouri, near the state line.—*See Tixier's Travels on the Osage Prairies*, edited by John F. McDermott (Norman, 1940), pp. 87, 98.

℄ August 15(?)—2d Lt. John W. T. Gardiner, of the First dragoons, and 20 men, dispatched from Fort Leavenworth on the 14th, overtook Fort Platte-bound trader John Sibille and his outfit (two wagons; seven men) at a point "five miles North of the Kansas villages." They seized and destroyed 11 barrels of contraband alcohol (the equivalent of 55 barrels of whisky). Sibille and his men) with the confiscated wagons and other property) were escorted to the military post, and from there were taken to Platte

City, Mo., for confinement; but the local magistrate refused to act, and set them free.

Sibille, having recruited his outfit (men, wagons, oxen, and goods—he still had several barrels of alcohol) following the August 15(?) disaster, was at the Kansas river ford (present Topeka area) on the 27th, preparing to move westward. He traveled to Laramie's Fork in company with [P. D.?] Papin's Fort Laramie-bound party, arriving at Fort Platte on October 12.

Making a later start, partner David Adams, with another small outfit, was camped on the north bank of the Kansas crossing (present Topeka area) in mid-September. (While there, some of his party, one day, helped Joseph Papin—*see* p. 409—raise a corn crib.) Adams' party (which included James McClosky—later a Marshall county, Kansas, resident, and "Mr. Baker") was on the move again on the 18th; reached Fort Platte late in October.

Ref: OIA, Letters Received from Fort Leavenworth Agency (National Archives Microcopy 234, Roll 301) for Gardiner's report of August 24, 1842; some letters of John Sibille and David Adams, and excerpts from Adams' diaries (originals in Missouri Historical Society, St. Louis), courtesy of Dale L. Morgan, Bancroft Library, who has most generously shared the results of his research on these traders; OIA, Letters Received from SIA, St. Louis (National Archives Microcopy 234, Roll 753), for D. D. Mitchell's list of licenses issued, January 1-September 30, 1842; *Glimpses of the Past*, St. Louis, v. 8 (January-June, 1941), p. 42, for Sublette letter; *Bulletin* of the Missouri Historical Society, St. Louis, v. 13 (October, 1956), p. 101; Francis A. *Chardon's Journal at Fort Clark*, edited by Annie H. Abel (1932), p. 406, and *see* pp. 221, 228, 248.

❧ August 15.—Superintendent Berryman's report listed the following personnel at Shawnee Methodist Mission and Indian manual labor school: Rev. J. C. Berryman, principal; Rev. David Kinnear and wife, teachers; William Honeywell, assistant; Rev. L. M. Carter, carpenter; Rev. William Tuggle, blacksmith; Anthony A. Ward, wagonmaker; E. Curell, shoemaker; and A. M. Eis[e]le, baker and cook. Also, about "an average of eight farm hands" were employed by the month, some of them Indians.

(In a report of May 23, 1843, the Rev. E. R. Ames wrote that there were employed at the institution 10 single men and one single woman; 11 married men having in their families 20 children. These, plus 100 Indian students, made a total "population" of some 150 persons.)

Ref: OIA, Letters Received from Fort Leavenworth Agency (National Archives Microcopy 234, Roll 301); Martha B. Caldwell, compiler, *Annals of Shawnee Mission* . . . (1939), p. 48.

❧ August(?)—Crossing "Kansas"—presumably by the Oregon trail —to the Rocky mountains, during the early autumn, were new partners Louis Vasquez and Jim Bridger. In a September letter, William Sublette, at St. Louis, wrote: "Vasquez and Bridger has left here lately with about 30 or 40 men fitted out by the American

Fur Co. to trap on the watters of Missouri, Say near the 3 forks."
(This partnership lasted for 13 years—till 1855.)

(Bridger's recent partner, Henry Fraeb—*see* p. 392—had been killed by
Indians in August, 1841; and Bridger had come down from the mountains in
the summer of 1842 "with about 20 men and 30 packs of Beaver." Louis
Vasquez and his former partner, Andrew W. Sublette, had sold Fort Vasquez,
on the South Platte, and their business, to Locke, Randolph & Co. in 1841.)

Ref: *Glimpses of the Past,* v. 8 (January-June, 1941), pp. 42-44; *The Colorado Magazine,* Denver, v. 7 (May, 1930), p. 3, and v. 10 (January, 1933), p. 19.

❡ August-September.—Nine men (members of the "Bidwell-Bartleson" company which had left the Missouri frontier for California in
May, 1841), en route home from the Pacific coast, crossed "Kansas"
on the Santa Fe trail, reaching Missouri September 9.

Originally 13(?) men had set out from Sutter's Fort in April, 1842, to make
the return journey. *Joseph B. Chiles, Robert Rickman, John Bartleson, Charles
Hopper* (all from Jackson county, Mo.), *James P. Springer,* Ambrose Walton,
Major Walton, John McDowell, and A. Gwinn Patton, were, it appears, in this
party. En route, four men dropped out. The rest, via the Spanish trail(?),
reached New Mexico, where they began the last stage of the trip home in the
late summer. (Joseph Williams, arriving overland from the West at Independence, Mo., on October 25, met there Robert Rickman who had just returned.)
Almost certainly among the *nine*(?) were those whose names appear above in
italics.

Ref: J. B. Chiles' dictation, 1878 (in Bancroft Library), and published (1970) as a
keepsake of the Friends of the Bancroft Library with the title "A Visit to California in
1841," and an introduction by George R. Stewart; Charles Hopper's "Narrative," 1871
(Bancroft Library); A. S. Taylor, "The Discoveries, Founders and Pioneers of California"
(Bancroft Library); George R. Stewart's *The California Trail* . . . (New York, c1962),
pp. 31-35; H. H. Bancroft's *History of California* (1886), v. 4, p. 343. On May 20, 1843,
westbound Peter Burnett met Bartleson and Rickman in Jackson county, Mo.—*See* his *Recollections and Opinions* . . . (1880), p. 101. Chiles returned to California, overland,
in 1843. Dale L. Morgan's letter of January 30, 1864, to L. Barry, notes that George Henshaw (or Hinshaw?) made the return trip by sea; and gives other information used above.
For Williams, *see* his *Narrative of a Tour From the State of Indiana to the Oregon Territory*
(New York, 1921), p. 91.

❡ September.—Ten Iowa chiefs, for whom government-built houses
had been promised in the October 19, 1838, treaty, were moving
into the just-completed homes (erected by John W. Forman, under
contract, for $3,000). Subagent W. P. Richardson reported the
Indians liked the well-built structures.

The Iowas, with the help of government farmer Francis Irvin, and the
"labor of the squaws," had raised a crop of nearly 15,000 bushels of corn,
and ample quantities of pumpkins, squashes, Irish potatoes, and other vegetables.

A census, taken on September 5, showed a total of 470 Iowas on the
reservation (about 30 were absent). The agent noted that the "upper Ioways
or pouting party as they are called" (the Iowas living on the Pottawatomies'

reserve in southwest Iowa), composed nearly half the nation; but some were moving down to "Kansas."

Ref: *Report* of the Comm'r of Indian affairs, 1842; SIA, St. Louis, "Records," v. 8, typed copy, pp. 150-161. In *ibid.*, pp. 161-164, in a December 1, 1842, letter, Subagent Richardson stated that the Iowas on the Pottawatomie reserve numbered "nearly 200."

❡ September.—Commenting on the Kickapoos' agricultural status, Agent R. W. Cummins wrote: ". . . their trader Mr. [William H.] Hildreth takes all the corn, beef, pork, hides and potatoes that they have to spare at a fair price for goods. . . ." According to the 1842 census, the Kickapoos in "Kansas" numbered 505 persons.

Ref: OIA, Letters Received from Fort Leavenworth Agency (National Archives Micro-copy No. 234, Roll 301); a letter by Geo. H. Swords, of New York, February 13, 1843, to the Comm'r of Indian affairs (CIA), in *ibid.*, mentions W. H. Hildreth of Fort Leaven-worth—an Indian trader to the Kickapoos and other tribes. *Apparently* the Pensineau trad-ing post was no longer in operation.

❡ September 15.—At Richmond, Mo., Philip Leget Edwards (who had journeyed across "Kansas" to the Far West with Wyeth's expedi-tion of 1834—*see* p. 262; spent four years in "Oregon"; and then returned East with the Rev. Jason Lee, coming down from the Rocky mountains with the American Fur Company's caravan of 1838—*see* p. 354) wrote a long letter describing the Oregon coun-try, outlining the recommended route for overland travelers, also giving information and advice to prospective emigrants. It was his opinion that wagons could not be taken to the Columbia river valley.

Before the end of 1842 the Liberty (Mo.) *Herald* office pub-lished Edwards' letter as a 20-page pamphlet, entitled *Sketch of the Oregon Territory or, Emigrants' Guide.* Only one copy (in the Coe Collection at Yale University's library) is known to exist of this *first guidebook to the Far West.*

Ref: A reprint of Edwards' *Sketch* . . . [1953?], with added paper covers; H. R. Wagner and C. L. Camp, *The Plains and the Rockies* . . . 3d edition (Columbus, Ohio, 1953) p. 133; *The Washington Historical Quarterly*, Seattle, v. 24 (July, 1933), p. 178 (has a brief biographical sketch of Edwards); *California Historical Society Quarterly*, San Francisco, v. 3 (April, 1924), pp. 73-83 (has C. L. Camp's article "Colonel Philip Leget Edwards and His Influence Upon Early Immigration to the Far West"). C. M. Drury, in his *Marcus Whitman, M. D., Pioneer and Martyr* (Caldwell, Idaho, 1937), p. 330, stated that the St. Louis *New Era* of May 25, 1843, in "two columns of fine print," published P. L. Edwards' letter of September 15, 1842.

❡ September 16.—Alexander Barclay (recently a Bent & St. Vrain employee), en route to the mountains, arrived at the Kansas crossing (present Topeka area), with one companion, and one wagon (de-scribed by David Adams as "a 3 hors wagon" (but actually pulled by mules), carrying "about 1500 hundred lbs."

Barclay had left Westport, Mo., on, or about, September 2, and intended to overtake a company ahead of him on the trail. He reached Fort George, on the South Platte, November 24.

Ref: Alexander Barclay Papers, Bancroft Library; David Adams' diary, *loc. cit.*

℄ September 23.—The Rev. Leander Ker (author of a pamphlet entitled *Slavery Consistent With Christianity,* first published at Baltimore, Md., in 1840) became Fort Leavenworth's third chaplain. He remained for over 16 years (till March 31, 1859).

[His predecessors had been Episcopalians—the Rev. Henry Gregory (December 17, 1838-September 30, 1839), and the Rev. David E. Griffith (December 21, 1839-December 31, 1840). Ker was a Presbyterian.]

During the border warfare years (1854-1858) Chaplain Ker was a controversial figure in Kansas territory because of his avowed Proslavery stand. (A third, revised and enlarged, edition of his *Slavery* pamphlet was printed at Weston, Mo., in 1853. A second edition had been published in 1842, at Jefferson City, Mo.)

Ref: F. B. Heitman's *Historical Register and Dictionary of the United States Army* (1903), v. 1, pp. 477, 479, 593 (for dates of Gregory, Griffith, and Ker); Library of Congress catalog cards (for the editions of Ker's pamphlet); 34th Cong., 1st Sess., H. R. No. 200 (Serial 869), pp. 859, 860; John McNamara's *Three Years on the Kansas Border* (New York, 1856), p. 140, in particular. *Niles' National Register,* v. 63 (October 29, 1842), p. 129, noting Ker's appointment, stated: "Mr. Ker is the author of several letters to the late Dr. [William Ellery] Channing [Unitarian minister], on the slave question and the Creole case." Fort Leavenworth post returns (microfilm from National Archives in KHi).

℄ October 6.—American Fur Company employee Andrew Drips (with connections in the Kaw's mouth area) was appointed Indian agent for the Upper Missouri Agency. At the beginning his assignment was as special agent to enforce the intercourse law, or, as John F. A. Sanford put it: "to exercise a surveillance over the Traders & put a stop to the introduction of spirits & liquor into the Indian Country."

(On July 11 Sup't D. D. Mitchell, St. Louis, had written Agent R. W. Cummins, of the Fort Leavenworth Agency: "The Government is *now* determined to use every possible exertion to Suppress this illegal, pernicious traffic, and no agent will be held guiltless who fails to exert himself in the cause. . . .")

Drips received his instructions at St. Louis on October 8; and left at once for Fort Pierre (S. D.), arriving there November 24. His first report, January 2, 1843, indicated lack of success. But Mitchell still hoped the experiment would work and that by "vigilance and assiduity" on Drips' part, the "pernicious traffic" could be "either suppressed or greatly abated."

For his services as "special agent" from October, 1842, to March 31, 1843, Andrew Drips was paid $729.84. He headed the Upper Missouri Agency till "removed" in 1846. As fur trade historian H. M. Chittenden has pointed out, securing the reactivation of the Upper Missouri Agency and getting one of its own men appointed agent, was a shrewd move by the American Fur Company to strengthen its own position in fighting opposition fur traders.

Ref: 28th Cong., 1st Sess., *H. Doc. No. 240* (Serial 441), p. 22; 29th Cong., 2d Sess., *H. Doc. No. 36* (Serial 499), p. 4; 30th Cong., 1st Sess., *H. Ex. Doc. No. 5* (Serial 514), pp. 92, 93; OIA, Letters Received from SIA, St. Louis (National Archives Microcopy 234, Roll 753), Mitchell's October 8, 1842, letter, and Drips' letter of January 2, 1843; SIA, St. Louis, "Records," v. 7, typed copy, pp. 300-303, 349, for Mitchell's letters of October 6, 1842, and April 20, 1843; Francis A. *Chardon's Journal at Fort Clark*, edited by Annie H. Abel, p. 405 (for Sanford quote); H. M. Chittenden's *The American Fur Trade of the Far West* (c1954), v. 1, p. 367.

❡ October 10.—Lt. John C. Fremont and the members of his first Rocky mountain exploring expedition, homeward-bound on the Missouri in a boat propelled by 10 oarsmen, "halted [early in the morning] to make some astronomical observations at the mouth of the Kansas." It was "exactly four months," Fremont noted, "since we had left the trading post of Mr. Cyprian Chouteau, on the same river, ten miles above." (*See* June 6 entry.)

(They reached St. Louis on October 17.)

Ref: John C. Fremont's *Report of the Exploring Expedition to the Rocky Mountains in the Year 1842* . . ., p. 79.

❡ October 11.—James M. Estill leased, for three years, the "United States farm" at Fort Leavenworth, under terms of a contract made with Lt. Ferdinand Coxe (AAQM), First U. S. infantry.

Estill agreed to supply 12,000 bushels of corn and 8,000 bushels of oats (per year?) for the sum of 22½ cents per bushel; and was to receive $3.50 "for every ton of hay he may make." (The "sureties" were Archibald Woods and Hiram Rich.) (*See* July, 1840, annals entry.)

A supplementary contract of January 16, 1843, granted Estill "the privilege of passing his wagons, teams &c over the Missouri river by the ferry at Fort Leavenworth" while in possession of the public farm, "at half the rate charged to other individuals."

Ref: 27th Cong., 3d Sess., *H. Doc. No. 68* (Serial 420), p. 39; 28th Cong., 1st Sess., *H. Doc. No. 42* (Serial 441), p. 27.

❡ October.—A mounted party of five—Solomon P. Sublette, Alfred Shutes, James Ross, "Mr. M'Carty," and the Rev. Joseph Williams—coming down from Bent's Fort (which they had left on September 26), crossed "Kansas" by way of the Santa Fe trail en route to Missouri.

[Shutes, Ross, and Williams had traveled together from Oregon by a route which included Fort Hall, the *first* Fort Bridger (of August, 1841, origin; on Green river), Antoine Robidoux's fort (on the Uinta), Taos, N. M., and then Bent's Fort. Both Ross and Williams had been in the Oregon-bound emigrant train of 1841.]

Of their Santa Fe trail journey, Williams wrote: "We traveled for fourteen days without being out of sight of buffaloes. . . . After we crossed the Pawnee fork . . . we saw no more . . . [of them]." At Council Grove the five men "remained . . . parts of two days, and two nights" to trade with the Kansa Indians.

Williams left his companions six miles east of Council Grove, and traveled on alone. He reached Elm Grove the third day of his solo journey, after having come, on the last morning, to a camp of four hunters, two of whom were "Colonel Boon's grandsons." About October 23 he arrived at Shawnee Methodist Mission (from which place he had departed on May 22, 1841, for the Far West—*see* p. 431); and on the 25th he started for Independence, Mo., on the last stage of his journey to Indiana, where he eventually arrived safely.

Ref: Joseph Williams' *Narrative of a Tour From the State of Indiana to the Oregon Territory* . . . (New York, 1921), pp. 70-93; *New Mexico Historical Review*, v. 36 (January, 1961), p. 53; Dale L. Morgan's letter of July 5, 1963, to L. Barry.

❆ October 27-29.—The American Indian Mission Association (a Baptist organization) was founded at Cincinnati, Ohio. The Rev. Isaac McCoy (its chief promoter) was elected corresponding secretary (and thereupon removed from Westport, Mo., to Louisville, Ky., the association's headquarters).

Subsequently, the AIMA operated missions in "Kansas" (principally for the Weas, Pottawatomies, and Miamis), and in "Oklahoma." It became affiliated (in 1845) with the Southern Baptist Convention.

Ref: American Indian Mission Association (AIMA) *Proceedings* (microfilm, KHi); *Baptist Missionary Magazine*, Boston, v. 25 (November, 1845), p. 293.

❆ October.—Father Pierre-Jean De Smet, S. J., returning from the Rocky mountains (where he had gone in 1841—*see* p. 428), came down the Missouri from Fort Union in a steamboat (the *New Haven?*) which had just brought up a load of merchandise for a trading post at the mouth of the Yellowstone.

According to De Smet, this was "the first boat that had ever attempted to ascend [so far up] the river in that season of the year." The owners—"four gentlemen from New York" [of the firm Fox, Livingston and Company (or, Union Fur Company) which was opening trading posts in opposition to the American Fur Company]—were aboard.

The descent (begun about mid-September) was particularly hazardous and difficult because of low water. At journey's end (46 days later—October 30?) the steamboat "appeared to be little more than a mere wreck."

Ref: H. M. Chittenden and A. T. Richardson's *Life, Letters and Travels of Father Pierre-Jean De Smet, S. J.* . . . (New York, 1905), v. 1, p. 392; H. M. Chittenden's *The American Fur Trade of the Far West* (New York, 1935), v. 1, p. 369 (for Fox, Livingston and Company—also known as the Union Fur Company). Charles Larpenteur in his narrative, *Forty Years a Fur Trader* . . . (New York, 1898), v. 1, p. 174, gives the impression that De Smet went downriver with an American Fur Company boat. His statement: "Mr. Chouteau returned from St. Louis to Fort Union, having gone down with Father De Smet, who was on his way from the Columbia to the States. His most important news was that a strong Opposition had arrived; the firm was Fox, Livingston and Co. of New York. They had come up in a steamer with a large outfit, and were building a Mackinaw boat for the Crows' trade of the Yellowstone; so that we should have opposition here." Audubon (*see ibid.*, p. 179), in 1843, referred to the opposition firm as "C. Bolton, Fox, Livingstone & Co., of New York."

❧ October.—The Rev. George W. Love, appointed in September by the Missouri conference to take charge of the Kansa Methodist Mission on American Chief (Mission) creek (present Shawnee county), was at Delaware Mission in mid-October recovering from a bilious fever attack. Probably he reached his own station before the end of the month.

Love left the Kansa in May, 1843, apparently, to serve at Delaware Mission during the summer, and, so far as known, did not return.

Ref: *KHC*, v. 9, pp. 118, 227, v. 16, pp. 253, 258, and 262. *See* April 10, 1842, annals item for death of the previous Kansa missionary—William Johnson.

❧ In late(?) October, on a tour of various Indian nations, John D. Lang and Samuel Taylor, Jr., arrived at Westport, Mo. (after a steamboat journey up the Missouri), and proceeded overland about nine miles to Shawnee Friends Mission.

(They had left the East in August on this mission for the Yearly Meeting of Friends of New England and New York, but did not reach St. Louis till early in October—having first visited the Winnebago Indians.)

In "Kansas" they inspected Shawnee Friends Mission; stopped at Shawnee Methodist Mission (three miles distant); talked to Indian families; hired horses and a guide and rode northward to the Kickapoo reserve. On November 3 they were at the Stockbridge settlement; and then continued southward to the Delaware Baptist and Munsee Moravian missions. Next they journeyed to the Kansa reserve, but most of the Indians were absent on the fall hunt.

Lang and Taylor returned to Shawnee Friends Mission, then traveled some 40 miles southwest, to A. L. Davis' "Osage River" subagency, on November 10. Because of a heavy snowfall, few Indians (Weas, Piankeshaws, Peorias, Kaskaskias, and Ottawas) attended the called council next day. Proceeding to the Simerwells' home (18 miles southwest), the two men visited the Pottawatomie creek Pottawatomies (the St. Joseph river band; also some of the Prairie band); then moved on 12 miles to the Sugar creek Pottawatomies (the Wabash band; also some Prairie band) and the Jesuit mission.

Learning that the Osages were away hunting, Lang and Taylor omitted a journey to their country and moved on to "Oklahoma"—visiting the united Shawnees & Senecas, the Cherokees, the Creeks, the Seminoles, and the Choctaws—concluding their tour about the end of the year.

The Lang-Taylor report (dated "Fourth Month 19, 1843"), containing a variety of information about the situation and condition of the "Kansas" and "Oklahoma" Indian nations, was published at New York in 1843 under the title *Report of a Visit to Some of the Tribes of Indians Located West of the Mississippi River.* . . .

Ref: John D. Lang and Samuel Taylor, Jr., *Report* . . . (as noted above).

❧ October 28.—On the Arkansas, in present Pawnee(?) county, mountain man Thomas Fitzpatrick and a companion, "Vandusen," traveling east on the Santa Fe trail, met a war party of some 20 Pawnees "coming from the Sioux." In a scuffle with the Indians,

Vandusen fled (back to Bent's Fort), and Fitzpatrick was robbed of all his "travelling equipage" except his horses, which were "politely returned."

The two men had left Fort Hall (Idaho) on August 20; made their way safely to Bent's Fort (Colo.); and were only 300 miles or so from Independence when the robbery occurred. Wrote Fitzpatrick: "The loss . . . is very trifling, but the insult is very great to have occurred as it were on the very borders of the Settlement." He was later reimbursed from Pawnee annuities for a "double barrel & twist gun" valued at $50.00, a "spy glass" worth $25.00, a "Super broad cloth dress coat" listed at $34.00, and other items of less value, totaling $207.50.

Ref: *KHQ*, v. 19, pp. 50, 51, reprinted from SIA, St. Louis, "Records," v. 8, pp. 109-111. (On p. 50 of the above reference, "Fort Scott" should read "Fort Hall.") Pawnee Fork crossing, on the Santa Fe trail, was 303 miles from Independence, according to Josiah Gregg's tables of distances.

❧ BORN: on November 10, at Shawnee Baptist Mission (present Johnson county), Francis Churchill Barker and William Bowen Barker, twin sons of the Rev. Francis and Elizabeth F. (Churchill) Barker.

Ref: Elizabeth F. Barker's *Barker Genealogy* (New York, 1927), p. 199. One twin—Francis C.—died on December 25, 1842.

❧ DIED: Non-on-da-gum-un (Nonon-do-quo-mon), a Delaware chief of some prominence, on November 11, after a lingering illness, at his home on the Delaware reserve north of Kansas river.

Prior to his conversion (by the Methodists) some eight years earlier, he had been "a degraded drunkard, a noted juggler, a furious blood-thirsty heathen. . . ." According to Missionary E. T. Peery, Non-on-da-gum-un had been "summoned to trial before a heathen council" of Delawares about 1840(?), and accused of killing people by witchcraft. The chief asserted his innocence, and the council decided to let him live a little longer, on probation. "Three of the chief men were then pointed out to him, and he was told that whenever any one of them died, sooner or later his life . . . should be taken without pity."

George Catlin's portrait of "Non-on-dá-gon," reproduced in this volume, probably was painted in 1832 when the artist was at Fort Leavenworth.

Ref: *KHC*, v. 16, pp. 251, 252.

❧ December 1.—The "connexion of Mr. and Mrs. [Johnston] Lykins with the [Shawnee Baptist] mission" ended this day, following months of dissension and conflict between Lykins and his fellow missionaries at "Shawanoe." (In 1831 Lykins had founded Shawnee Baptist Mission—the first [and principal] station of the American Baptist Board of Foreign Missions in "Kansas"—*see* p. 205.)

Ref: *Baptist Missionary Magazine*, v. 23 (June, 1843), p. 139; Jotham Meeker's "Diary," April 5, August 13, 1841, May 12, 1842, February 4, 1843, etc.

¶ December 22-25—A Frenchman named Ducote, residing about half a mile from the Iowas' subagency (present Doniphan county), with his Iowa wife, was fatally wounded on the 22d while drunk and during an argument with his wife, her father, and her sister. He died on the 25th.

Subagent W. P. Richardson was of the opinion that the "squaws" had done the killing, and that they should be "severely dealt with."

Ref: SIA, St. Louis, "Records," v. 8, p. 88. No information has been found on subsequent developments in this affair.

¶ Employed in "Kansas" by the Indian Department during all, or part of the year 1842 were the following persons:

FORT LEAVENWORTH AGENCY—*Agent* Richard W. Cummins; *Interpreters* Clement Lessert and Henry Tiblow; *Blacksmiths* William Donalson and James M. Simpson (for Shawnees), William F. Newton (for Delawares; till March 24), Isaac Munday (for Delawares; appointed January 29), Charles Fish (for Kansa); *Assistant blacksmiths* Wilson Rogers and Jackson Pitman (for Shawnees), W. H. Newton (for Delawares; till March 24), Powhatan Phifer (for Delawares; appointed January 29), Mab Frankier (for Kansa; till July?); *Farmer* William H. Mitchell (for Kansa; appointed January 29).

GREAT NEMAHA SUBAGENCY—*Subagent* William P. Richardson; *Interpreters* Samuel M. Irvin appointed January 1; for Iowas) and John Rubeti (for Sacs & Foxes); *Blacksmith* James Gilmore for Sacs & Foxes); *Assistant blacksmith* William Daviess (for Sacs & Foxes); *Farmers* Preston Richardson (for Sacs & Foxes), Francis Irvin (appointed April 1; for Iowas); *Assistant farmer* Pleasant Johnson (for Sacs & Foxes; appointed October 1); *Teacher* William Hamilton (for Sacs & Foxes).

OSAGE RIVER [MARAIS DES CYGNES] SUBAGENCY—*Subagent* Anthony L. Davis; *Interpreter* Luther Rice; *Blacksmiths* Robert Simerwell and Robert Wilson (for Pottawatomies); *Assistant blacksmiths* William A. Simerwell and Michael Nadeau (for Pottawatomies).

OSAGE SUBAGENCY—*Subagent* Robert A. Calloway; *Interpreter* Charles Mongrain; *Blacksmiths* John Mathews, Edwin B. Lowther (left in May), Elias N. Beardon (hired November 10); *Assistant blacksmiths* William (half-Osage) and Jacob (an Osage).

Ref: 27th Cong., 3d Sess., H. Doc. No. 76 (Serial 420); 27th Cong., 3d Sess., H. Doc. No. 162 (Serial 422); 28th Cong., 1st Sess., H. Doc. No. 240 (Serial 441); SIA, St. Louis, "Records," v. 7, typed copy, p. 387, v. 8, typed copy, pp. 240, 258, 259. Isaac Munday (Mundy) was long employed as blacksmith for the Delawares. His death, at the age of 43, in a hunting accident, occurred February 27, 1858. Isaac Mundy is buried at the White church, 85th and Lafayette, present Wyandotte county. Some information on the Mundy family is in W. M. Paxton's *Annals of Platte County, Missouri* (Kansas City, Mo., 1897), pp. 251, 252; and a story on Mundy (with a picture of his grave-marker) appeared in the Kansas City (Mo.) *Times*, February 5, 1971.

1843

¶ MARRIED: the Rev. David Lykins (a Westport, Mo., resident) and Abigail Ann Webster (teacher at Shawnee Baptist Mission), on January 7, at Westport, by the Rev. Johnston Lykins (older brother of the groom).

(*See* October 27-29, 1842, annals entry.)

Ref: *The Kansas City Genealogist,* Kansas City, Mo., v. 2, no. 6 (August 1, 1961), p. 5; *Vital Historical Records of Jackson County, Mo.,* compiled by Kansas City chapter, D. A. R., p. 38; *Baptist Missionary Magazine,* v. 23 (June, 1843), pp. 133, 139, v. 26 (July, 1846), p. 239; D. C. Gideon's *Indian Territory* . . . (Chicago, 1901), p. 444; American Indian Mission Association *Proceedings* . . . *1843,* p. 18. In the Isaac McCoy manuscripts, in an account covering the 1837-1839 period, is an item of "4 Feb. 1839" for "Mr. David Lykens, Dr." making a purchase from Wm. M. Chick of Westport, Mo.

❬ January.—In a period of fine weather and break up of ice in the Missouri (during a winter described as "a long, hard one"), the steamboat *Ione* came up to Westport Landing (Kansas City, Mo.).

"On the day of her arrival," says John C. McCoy, "it turned suddenly cold, the river froze up again and so remained until near the 1st of May, during which time the boat remained near the foot of Grand Avenue." Peter Burnett wrote: "the ice in the Missouri River at Weston only broke up on the 11th of April."

Ref: *The History of Jackson County, Missouri* . . ., p. 403; Peter H. Burnett's *Recollections and Opinions of an Old Pioneer,* p. 102.

❬ January-February.—On his famous winter ride from Oregon to the East, Dr. Marcus Whitman, coming down from Bent's Fort (Colo.) in company with a party of mountain men, crossed "Kansas" on the Santa Fe trail, and reached Westport, Mo., February 15. (He had arrived at, and departed from, the Bent, St. Vrain & Co. post early in January. A Whitman draft, dated at Fort William, January 6, was for $501.35.)

(Whitman—motivated chiefly by matters concerning the Oregon Mission to make this epic journey—had as traveling companion, from Oregon to Bent's Fort, Asa L. Lovejoy of the 1842 emigrant company. Their journey—on horseback—had begun on October 3, 1842. After following up the Snake river to Fort Hall, they had then been piloted to Taos, by the way of Soda Springs, Brown's Hole, Colorado of the West, the Wina [Uinta], and the waters of the del Norte.)

After a week in western Missouri, Marcus Whitman proceeded to St. Louis (he was there by March 7, and left on March 9); then to Washington (where, during his talk with the secretary of war, it is presumed he recommended that military posts be established along the Oregon trail); and by March 28 was in New York (en route to Boston). Following Whitman's visit to the New York *Tribune* office, on March 29, editor Horace Greeley described the appearance of this "hardy and self-denying" missionary: "He was dressed in an old fur cap that appeared to have seen some ten years' service, faded and nearly destitute of fur; a vest whose natural color had long since fled, and a shirt—we could not see that he had any—an overcoat every thread of which could be easily seen, buckskin pants, &c.   . . ."

Ref: C. M. Drury's *Marcus Whitman, M. D.* . . ., pp. 277-307; W. H. Gray's *A History of Oregon* (Portland, 1870), pp. 324-326 (for Lovejoy's letter of 1869); New York *Weekly Tribune*, April 1, 1843; W. J. Ghent's *The Early Far West* . . . (New York, 1931), pp. 323-325; B. Clapp's March 7 and 9, 1843, letters (in Chouteau collection, Missouri Historical Society, St. Louis), courtesy of Dale L. Morgan.

❦ February 2.—In Louisville, Ky., at its meeting to begin operations, the board of the (Baptist) American Indian Mission Association appointed Dr. Johnston Lykins and Delilah (McCoy) Lykins, his wife, as missionaries. (*See* January 7, 1843, annals entries.)

Ref: AIMA *Proceedings* . . ., *1843*, p. 17.

❦ MARRIED: Abraham Burnett (a full blood Pottawatomie) and Marie Knoffloch (a native of Germany, daughter of John and Elizabeth Knoffloch), on February 16, at Sugar creek (present Linn county), on the Pottawatomie reserve, by the Rev. Felix L. Verreydt, S. J. (Witnesses were part-Pottawatomie Joseph Bertrand, Jr., and his wife Elizabeth Ann [Jackson] Bertrand.)

"Abraham Burnett" was born in November, 1812, in Indiana. His parents (who died when he was young) were Shau-uque-be and Cone-zo-qua. The name they gave him is not known. Cone-zo-qua was a daughter of Chief Chebas. Chebas was a brother of Topenibee (considered head chief of all the Pottawatomies); and they had a sister Cakimi. She married a white man, William Burnett, and had seven children (*Abraham,* James, John, Isaac, Jacob, Rebecca, and Nancy). Cakimi's son, *Abraham* Burnett (half-Pottawatomie), had no children of his own, but adopted the son of Shau-uque-be and Cone-zo-qua, gave him (or let him take) the name "Abraham Burnett," provided for his care, and sent him to the Choctaw Academy to be educated.

When the Pottawatomies began the emigration to "Kansas" in the latter 1830's, "Abraham Burnett" was in his mid-20's. He made several trips between Indiana and "Kansas," serving as an interpreter, before settling at Sugar creek, where he lived 11 or 12 years. In 1848, after the Pottawatomies removed to a reserve on Kansas river, Abraham Burnett and his family lived in present Mission township, Shawnee county. "Burnett's Mound," Topeka, is named for him. (His home was on the north side of Shunganunga creek, in the S. E. ¼ of Sec. 9, T. 12, R. 15 E.) Abraham (or Abram B.) Burnett died June 14, 1870.

Ref: Abraham Burnett's deposition, of March 23, 24, 1870 (copy in KHi, courtesy of Indiana Historical Society); "Pottawatomie Marriage Register" (microfilm in KHi); *Indiana Historical Collections*, Indianapolis, v. 24, pp. 715, 815; *Indiana Magazine of History*, Bloomington, v. 22 (March, 1926), pp. 28-36; *KHC*, v. 13, pp. 371-373, (has a biographical sketch, which contains errors, particularly as to Burnett's parentage); Garraghan, *op. cit.*, v. 2, p. 230. The deposition was signed "Abraham Burnett." On the tombstone his name was inscribed "Abram B. Burnett."—*Bulletin* of the Shawnee County Historical Society, Topeka, no. 18 (March, 1953), p. 14.

❦ March 3.—Sutler John A. Bugg, Fort Scott, was appointed as the first postmaster for the military post. He served for six years. It is said he arrived with the Fourth infantry troops, as sutler, in 1842. (*See, also,* September 13 entry.)

Ref: Robert W. Baughman's *Kansas Post Offices* (c1961), pp. 156, 161; T. J. Robley's *History of Bourbon County, Kansas* . . . (Fort Scott, 1894), p. 12.

❡ DIED: on March 13, at Peoria Methodist Mission (present Franklin county), Annie (Beauchemie) Shaler, part-Indian wife of the Peorias' missionary, the Rev. Nathan T. Shaler. (*See* p. 335 for their marriage.)

Ref: *KHC*, v. 16, p. 253; *Bulletin* of the Missouri Historical Society, v. 10 (January, 1954), pp. 177, 180.

❡ March 27.—The Rev. Samuel G. Patterson opened a Methodist manual labor school on the east bank of the Pomme de Terre (or, Spring) river, in the Quapaw Indians' small reserve (which was adjacent to present Cherokee county, southeast Kansas—*see* p. 232).

Named "Crawford Seminary" by 1845, the school was moved about five miles northward in April, 1848, to a site east of present Baxter Springs, Cherokee co., near the Quapaws' north boundary.

Ref: Comm'r of Indian affairs, *Reports* for 1843-1848; *KHC*, v. 16, pp. 247, 729; *KHQ*, v. 1, p. 107, v. 28, p. 325.

❡ April 1.—Fifteen men, captained by John McDaniel (said to be "lately from Texas"), left the Westport, Mo., area and headed out the Santa Fe trail with the avowed purpose (as was common knowledge in Jackson county, Mo.) of robbing "the [Mexican] Caravan from Santa Fe . . . as well as the one going out."

(McDaniel had been recruited by "Texan Colonel" Charles A. Warfield the preceding year to raise a company and join his volunteers in plundering Mexican wagon trains in 1843. Citizens of Independence, Mo., in a letter of March 13, had alerted Sup't D. D. Mitchell, St. Louis, that McDaniel's "banditti" planned to enter the Indian country.)

Upon Agent R. W. Cummins' requisition of April 1, 60 First dragoons were dispatched from Fort Leavenworth on April 3(?), with seven days' rations, in pursuit of the gang, to arrest them (since they had no passports). The troops crossed the Kansas river on April 4, but failed to overtake McDaniel and his followers.

Ref: SIA, St. Louis, "Records," v. 7, typed copy, pp. 345-347, v. 8, typed copy, pp. 181, 186, 187; OIA, Letters Received from SIA, St. Louis (Microcopy 234, Roll No. 753, National Archives), D. D. Mitchell's April 21, 1843, letter, and accompanying items; *Southwestern Historical Quarterly*, Austin, v. 54 (January, 1951), pp. 274-277. Mitchell, in his letter (noted above) stated that Warfield, having recruited in the summer of 1842, had left in the fall for the Rocky mountains to get trappers to join his company; and that the appointed rendezvous was "point of rocks," within "Mexican Territory," about May 15, 1843.

❡ About April 7(?) Mexican merchant Antonio José Chaves, east-bound on the Santa Fe trail with five servants, one wagon, and five mules, was intercepted by John McDaniel and his 14 "banditti" (*see* preceding entry), perhaps near the Rice-McPherson county line of today. Chaves had left New Mexico in February with 15(?) men (ten of whom deserted), two wagons, and 55(?) mules (most died as a result of severe weather).

McDaniel's gang took Chaves prisoner, robbed him, and forced him to march westward with them for two(?) days. Then they divided the spoils $10,000 or $11,000 in specie and gold bullion; also a small lot of furs). Seven who were averse to killing the trader took their booty and departed, but had to bury the silver on the prairie when the horses stampeded and left them afoot. The other eight (John McDaniel, his brother David, Joseph Brown, William Mason, Gallatin and Christopher Searcy, Schuyler Oldham, and Thomas Towson), after taking Chaves and his wagon four or five miles south of the trail, murdered the trader, and threw his body into a ravine (on a small Cow creek tributary which still bears Chaves' name—in corrupt spelling—the present Jarvis creek, Rice county). Apparently all 15 of the "banditti" returned to Missouri.

Trader Reuben Gentry (and three others, coming from Santa Fe) arrived at Independence, Mo., on April 19, and spread the alarm (knowing only that Chaves had vanished from the trail). Ten of the gang were quickly apprehended; and much of the "money" recovered. (Josiah Gregg wrote a long account, published in a Van Buren, Ark., newspaper, giving many details of this sordid affair, which involved several individuals from Clay and Jackson county, Mo.) Mason turned state's evidence, and named all the participants. Those who took part in the robbery, only, were Dr. Joseph R. De Prefontaine, Samuel O. Berry, William and B. F. Harris, Nathaniel Morton, John McCormick, and B. F. Talbert. Doctor De Prefontaine (previously mentioned in these annals) was arrested at Council Grove (where he had gone to get the buried loot). He had in his possession "about $2600 silver coin"; was subsequently sentenced to pay a $1,000 fine, and serve a year in jail. John McDaniel and Brown, tried and convicted of murder, were hanged (publicly, before a large crowd) at St. Louis, August 16, 1844. (No concise information on the fate of the others has been located; some served prison terms; clemency was recommended in several cases; five men, including three of the "murder party," never[?] were caught.)

Chaves' name appeared in some accounts of the time as "Garvis," or "Charvis," and the spelling "Jarvis" replaced the correct form of the name, not only in the geographical name for the creek where the trader was murdered; but also in the name of a short-lived Rice county "town" called Jarvis View (four miles east of Lyons) which had a post office from 1878 to 1880. (A Rice county map of 1878, published in the state board of agriculture's *First Biennial Report*, p. 294, shows the location of Jarvis View.)

Ref: Josiah Gregg's account, of May, 1843, reprinted in *New Mexico's Own Chronicle* . . ., edited by M. G. Fulton and Paul Horgan (Dallas, c1937), pp. 130-135; New York *Weekly Tribune*, May 13, 20, 27, September 30, October 14, 1843; *Niles' National Register*, v. 64 (May 13, June 10, July 1, 1843), pp. 163, 234, 280, v. 65 (October 7, 1843), p. 96; St. Louis *Democrat*, April 29, May 2, 11, 12, June 1, September 1, 1843, April 30, June 10, August 17, 1844; J. C. McCoy's "Tales of an Old Timer" in Kansas City (Mo.) *Journal of Commerce*, January 23, 1879 (or, see "Kansas Reminiscences" clippings, pp. 126, 127—in KHi library); *KHC*, v. 9, pp. 552, 553; Baughman, *op. cit.*, p. 64.

¶ Spring (or later).—Steamboats operating on the Missouri this year included the *Weston* (new), *Oceana, John Aull, Tobacco Plant, Rowena, Iatan, Edna, Colonel Woods, Mary Tompkins, Vermillion, General Brooke, Ione,* and *Omega.*

On June 1 the *Weston* was "entirely consumed" by fire a few miles above St. Charles, Mo. Passengers, crew, baggage, and most of the 500 bales of hemp aboard were saved. The *Omega,* after returning from her (first and only) trip to the American Fur Company's Upper Missouri trading post in June (*see* p. 488) went into the regular river trade. By report, 26 steamboats made 205 trips on the Missouri in 1843.

Ref: *Missouri Republican,* issues of 1843; New York *Weekly Tribune,* June 17, 1843 (for the *Weston* fire); *Niles' National Register,* v. 72 (July 31, 1847), p. 351 (for 1843 steamboat report).

⁅ April.—A printing press—the second to be set up in "Kansas"— arrived at "Ioway and Sac Mission" (present Doniphan county). Including type and fixtures it had cost the Presbyterian Board of Foreign Missions about $250.

Missionaries Samuel M. Irvin and William Hamilton, after mastering the use of the press and working out a system of representing Iowa language sounds by letters of the alphabet, printed at least two books during 1843.

One of these was a 225-copy edition of a 101-page *An Elementary Book of the Ioway Language, With an English Translation,* by Hamilton and Irvin, with J[ohn] B[aptiste] Roy, interpreter. The imprint: "Ioway and Sac Mission Press, Indian Territory. 1843." (This book was about 3¾ x 5½ inches in size.) The other was the missionaries' coauthored 62-page work entitled *Original Hymns in the Ioway Language,* which had a like imprint.

Neither of the above is represented in the Kansas State Historical Society's collection. The society has a copy of the 152-page book: *An Ioway Grammar, illustrating the principles of the language used by the Ioway, Otoe, and Missouri Indians. Prepared and printed by Rev. Wm. Hamilton and Rev. S. M. Irvin. Under the direction of the Presbyterian B. F. M.* Ioway and Sac Mission Press, 1848.

Ref: D. C. McMurtrie and A. H. Allen, *A Forgotten Pioneer Press of Kansas* (Chicago, 1930); *KHQ,* v. 1, pp. 6, 7.

⁅ April 22.—By Indian department contracts of this date, J. M. Hunter was to deliver eight yoke of oxen and yokes (for $324.48), and J. C. Berryman was to supply 30 bushels of potatoes and 30 bushels of seed corn (for $68.75), at the "Kanzas Village," before May 1.

Agent R. W. Cummins subsequently reported, in September, that the Kansa had been "almost in a state of starvation" in the spring and had "subsisted a part of the year on roots"; that "at their pressing request" he had "employed about 18 hands and cultivated about 200 acres of corn & planted 30 bushels of irish potatoes for them" after they agreed to "turn in and plant & tend as much corn as they could"; and to his surprise "they raised themselves more than they have done for many years" and would probably "have corn plenty to do them" over the winter. Cummins also mentioned that their horse mill was in contract, and would soon be completed.

Ref: 28th Cong., 1st Sess., *H. Doc. No. 42* (Serial 441), p. 16; SIA, St. Louis, "Records," v. 8, typed copy, p. 287. In *ibid.*, v. 7, p. 293, Sup't D. D. Michell had written Cummins (on August 12, 1842) that if the Kansa should "consent and deserve" the horse mill which the late Rev. William Johnson had requested for their use, Cummins was authorized to spend $400 for that purpose.

❧ April.—White Hair (Pah-ha-skah), III, was deposed, or close to being deposed, as head chief of the Osage Nation—a position he had held since an election in 1832 following the death of his uncle(?), White Hair, II. This young, and bad, chief—one of the ugliest men in the nation—was known by the name "Majakita" because of his big lips. (*See, also,* August 1, 1842, entry.)

Subagent R. A. Calloway reported (in September, 1843): "Pah-ha-skah has for years been very unpopular amongst his people. . . . Last summer [1842] a party of 25 or 26 chiefs & principal men visited Capt. [William] Armstrong the Supt. . . . [and] had him broke & another chief (Shingah, wah,sah) made in his stead." But there was disagreement over the choice of Shinga-wassa, and "Pah-ha-skah was therefore still recognized as the chief" till in April, 1843, when Pah-ha-skah "grew still more saucy and at length . . . drove the Blacksmiths ["Beardon & Rhinehart, one with, & the other without a family"] out of their buildings [the former Boudinot Mission—"two old log cabins, (double cabins) nearly rotted down"] & took possession of them himself." Calloway then "called a few braves, and after talking to the people of his town (which was nigh) on the subject, . . . went to the place, & had his little effects moved back to his lodge." The subagent wrote that it was his intention to present the matter to the whole nation when the Osages gathered for annuity payments, adding that "I seldom ever saw or heard more indignation felt & expressed against any man, than was done against Pah-ha-skah." In the letter he referred to White Hair, III, as the Osages' "late principal man."

Ref: SIA, St. Louis, "Records," v. 8, typed copy, pp. 228-239 (for Calloway's September 1, 1843, report); Victor Tixier's . . . *Travels on the Osage Prairies,* edited by John F. McDermott, pp. 143, 144; and *see* annals, p. 215.

❧ Ministers William Patton and Wesley Browning, of Missouri, beginning a tour of Methodist Indian missions in "Kansas," arrived at the Indian manual labor school (present Johnson county) on April 27.

They "examined" the school on May 1, found 62 boys and 39 girls, representing some 12 tribes, in attendance. Accompanied by the Rev. Thomas Johnson, they started for Kickapoo Mission on May 4, crossing the Kansas at the Delaware (or, Grinter) ferry, and stopping overnight at Delaware Mission (present Wyandotte county) where the Rev. Edward T. Peery was in charge. Next day, joined by Peery, they rode some 25 miles northward to Kickapoo Mission (present Leavenworth county) where the Rev. Nathaniel M. Talbott was missionary. William Patton, in his journal, noted that "in sight of the mission house" there was a "Roman Catholic establishment . . . which has not been in operation for some two or three years"; and that there was also a house belonging to Kennekuk, "a heathen prophet," whose one-time 250 followers were, in 1843, perhaps only a quarter that number. Kennekuk, he noted, "has some two or three wives, and is considered as a great sinner."

On May 8 the travelers returned to Delaware Mission, and met the "Rev. Mr. Meech [J. Christopher Micksch] and his wife," of near by Munsee Moravian Mission. A meeting with the Delawares was held on the 9th.

Rains, from May 10 to 14, caused cancellation of plans to visit Pottawatomie Mission (present Miami? county) where part-Indian assistant Mackinaw Beauchemie was in charge, and Peoria Mission (present Franklin county) where the Rev. Nathan T. Shaler was missionary.

On May 15 Browning, Peery, and Patton, set out for Kansa Mission (present Shawnee county) 80 miles distant, camping that night near the "lower ford," of the Wakarusa; and because of delays, stopping overnight on the 16th at the "upper ford." Crossing the full stream early on May 17, they traveled some 55 miles to the Kansa station. The missionary there—Rev. George W. Love—was in good health, but somewhat discouraged with his progress among the Kansa. A meeting held with chiefs and braves on May 18, accomplished little. But on the 19th, when the travelers started home, they were accompanied by "brother Love, and some nine or ten of the Caw children, destined for the school." The party arrived safely at the Indian manual labor school on the 20th. At the Shawnees' log meeting house, a camp meeting was in progress; and on Sunday, the 21st, the assembled Methodist church members, Shawnees and whites, heard the Rev. Thomas Johnson's funeral address for Annie (Beauchemie) Shaler—*see* March 13 annals entry.

Ref: *Bulletin* of the Missouri Historical Society, v. 10 (January, 1954), pp. 167-180; *KHC*, v. 16, p. 258.

❧ At the end of April the Missouri river was at flood stage. On board the upbound *Omega*, on May 2, Naturalist John J. Audubon (*see* next entry) wrote in his journal: "We . . . stopped at Madame Chouteau's plantation [Chouteau's Landing, Mo.]. . . . The water had been two feet deep in her house, but the river has now suddenly fallen about six feet."

On May 3, reaching Fort Leavenworth, Audubon and his companions reluctantly gave up their intended "walk across the Bend" above the post upon learning "that the ground was overflowed, and that the bridges across two creeks had been carried away. . . ."

Ref: Maria R. Audubon's *Audubon and His Journals* (New York, 1897), v. 1, p. 467.

❧ May 3.—Naturalist John J. Audubon and party (John G. Bell, taxidermist, Isaac Sprague, artist, Lewis M. Squires, secretary, Edward Harris, gentleman-farmer and bird specialist) were aboard the American Fur Company's *Omega* (Joseph A. Sire, master and Joseph La Barge, pilot) which reached Fort Leavenworth Landing at 6 A. M., en route to Fort Union (at the mouth of Yellowstone river). Edward Harris, in his journal, wrote: "Stopped at Fort Leavenworth to take in some cargo. Saw abundance of Parrokeets [the Carolina parrakeet—a species now long extinct]. . . ." (He had first mentioned these birds on April 29.)

The *Omega* had left St. Louis on April 25, her other passengers being "a hundred and one trappers . . . [mostly] French Canadians, or Creoles . . . ." (according to Audubon's journal), and some Iowa Indians. Captain Sire, in his log, noted that "a stop was made on May 2 at 'Madame Chouteau's' [Berenice Therese (Menard) Chouteau, widow of Francis G.—of Chouteau's Landing two miles below Westport Landing (or 'Kansas')], where I find everything abandoned." After sunset that evening the steamboat "Passed the bad place at the mouth of the Kansas river," and, wrote Sire, "The weather was so fine that I decided to run all night. At 6 a. m. we reached Leavenworth."

Audubon evidently went ashore for he wrote: "This situation of the fort is elevated and fine, and one has a view of the river up and down for some distance." He did not meet Lt. Col. Richard B. Mason (the commandant was ill); but "saw two officers who came on board, also a Mr. Ritchie" [sutler Hiram Rich?].

Two hours were spent at the post landing. Though carrying contraband liquor, the *Omega* safely passed inspection by the military, and continued her journey, experiencing delays by running aground on May 3, and, on succeeding days, by encountering winds which (as Harris wrote) "blew so strong up stream that the boat would not steer. . . ." On May 5 the *Omega* made a stop at Joseph Robidoux's Blacksnake Hills post (where, a few months later, St. Joseph, Mo. was founded); and on the 6th the Indians aboard were deposited at the Iowa village (present Doniphan county).

The *Omega* reached Fort Pierre (S. D.) at the end of May, and arrived at Fort Union (on the west border of present North Dakota) on June 12, having made the 1,760-mile trip in a record time of only 49 days.

Audubon and his friends spent two months at Fort Union, and the naturalist traveled overland some distance up the Yellowstone river, having as guide the noted mountain man Etienne Provost. As writer Bernard De Voto has pointed out: "To this journey we owe his buffalo, the grizzlies, and other plates in *The Quadrupeds of America*." (For Audubon's return trip, *see* October annals item.)

Ref: Edward Harris' journal, *Up the Missouri With Audubon* . . ., edited by John F. McDermott; SIA, St. Louis, "Records," v. 7, typed copy, pp. 347, 348 (D. D. Mitchell's April 19, 1843, letters to Agents Andrew Drips, Daniel Miller, and R. W. Cummins); *North Dakota Historical Quarterly*, Bismarck, v. 10 (April, 1943), pp. 63-82 (A. O. Stevens' "Audubon's Journey Up the Missouri River 1843"); John J. Audubon, *Audubon in the West*, compiled and edited by John F. McDermott (Norman, Okla., 1965); H. M. Chittenden's *History of Early Steamboat Navigation on the Missouri River* (New York, 1903), v. 1, pp. 141-153; and his *The American Fur Trade of the Far West*, v. 2, pp. 985-1003; *Niles' National Register*, v. 64 (May-July), pp. 176, 233, 234, 288, 297, 298, 312, 347; Susan D. McKelvey's *Botanical Exploration of the Trans-Mississippi West*, 1790-1850 (c1955), pp. 830-841. Another principal source is John J. Audubon's *Journal* . . . *1840-1843*, edited by Howard Corning (Cambridge, Mass., 1929), of which general extracts are to be found in Maria R. Audubon's *Audubon and His Journals* (New York, 1897).

❡ Early in May Sir William Drummond Stewart, of Scotland, with upwards of 20 gentlemen, and retinue of 30—participants in his long-planned, well-publicized pleasure jaunt to the Rocky mountains—debarked at Chouteau's Landing, Mo., after a voyage upriver from St. Louis.

By May 10 "Camp William" (10 tents—Sir William's a very elegant, large one) had been set up a mile west of the Missouri line, near Shawnee chief Joseph Parks' home (present Johnson county); and here the party remained nearly two weeks. William L. Sublette (traveling overland), with three men, and two slave lads, arrived on May 11, bringing about 50 mules.

Other guests joined the luxury excursion at "Camp William," and the company which set out, under Sir William's command, on May 22, numbered 60 or more. Sublette wrote that there were "Some of the armey [Lts. Richard H. Graham and Sidney Smith, Fourth infantry, on furlough from Jefferson Barracks, Mo.], Some professional Gentlemen, Come on the trip for pleasure, Some for Health, etc etc. So we had doctors, Lawyers, botanists [there were four; and two—German Botanists Charles A. Geyer and Friedrich Lüders— went on to Oregon], Bugg Ketchers, Hunters and men of nearly all professions. . . . One half or rather more was hired men Belonging to Sir William [among them: Antoine Clement and Baptiste Charbonneau (son of Sacajawea)]. . . ." The guests were from diverse places—including Paris, London, Baltimore, New Orleans, Pittsburgh, Alton, Ill., Scotland, and Luxemburg. Among the St. Louis group were 'teen-agers Jefferson K. Clark and W. Clark Kennerly; and Matthew C. Field (with St. Louis connections) was the excursion's journalist. Cyprian Menard, of Kaskaskia, Ill., and Edmund F. ("Guesso") Chouteau (eldest son of Francis G.), of Chouteau's Landing, were also among those from the "mid-west."

"Sir William had 10 Carts & one small 2 mule yankee waggon. There were Some 30 other Carts and small 2 horse wagons in Company Belonging to Individual gentlemen." According to Clark Kennerly, each guest supplied his own horse and manservant. William L. Sublette (and several men, with two carts) remained in the Westport vicinity till May 27; then set out to catch up with Stewart and what a later-day writer has termed "the West's first dude expedition."

The excursionists took a route somewhat north of the emigrant-crowded Oregon trail; crossed the Kansas, on May 27, above present Lawrence, at the *old* ford ("upon a pirogue. . . . Our vehicles and their contents were floated over . . . [and with much difficulty] the animals were made to swim across"—Matt Field); made camp near the ruins of the Kansa Agency. (*See* reproduction on p. 407 of Alfred J. Miller's painting of this crossing; and p. 323 for Stewart's fording of the river here in 1837. On the *north* side of the Kansas Sir William and company found the 20 miles to Soldier creek (where they arrived at the end of May) "a bad Road for muddy Creeks."

Meantime, Sublette had traveled up the *south* side of the Kansas, via the Oregon trail, and among the emigrants. (His diary entry of May 28 states: "passt Some 40 or 50 Santa-fee waggons . . . Left the Santafee Trace and took Sublette's Old Trace to the Mountains made about 25 miles.") He rafted the river on May 30 (at present Topeka) in Joseph Papin's boat; camped on Soldier creek; sent his two carts ahead on May 31 "to a creek 8 miles distance to Encamp [on a stream] Called Muddy [now Cross creek] . . ."; returned to assist Sir William and the caravan over the Soldier. *Perhaps* traveling with Sublette from the Westport area were the Jesuits (Fathers Peter De Vos and Adrian Hoecken, lay brother John B. McGean) and their party, led by William's brother Solomon P. Sublette, who also crossed the Kansas on May 30.

At the Muddy creek camp, on June 1(?), Sir William's excursion caravan was joined by "Solomon P. Sublette with 2 Carts and 2 priests or Missionaries with 3 Carts, 1 waggon, and one Small Cariole . . . with some 15 men or 20 more and animals in proportion." The combined company which moved on, over the Oregon trail, in advance of the main emigrating parties, numbered some 80 men "with 18 carts, one 6 mule waggon, & 2 2 mule waggons & a smal[l] Barouche, Some Cows, and Oxen . . ."—also, by report, 50 or 60 fine horses.

Sir William and his company (minus some 15? who had turned back on the Platte, or before), arrived at Forts Platte and Laramie on July 5, and Solomon P. Sublette remained there. On August 3, beyond the Continental divide, on the Little Sandy, the Jesuit party (bound for the Flatheads' country), accompanied by botanists Geyer and Lüders, separated from them, to continue westward on the Oregon trail. From August 7 to 12 the pleasure party camped beside Fremont Lake, on Green river; and spent from the 12th to 17th at a site between the Upper Forks. On August 17 the excursionists started home. (*See, also,* October annals entry.)

Ref: Matthew C. Field, *Prairie and Mountain Sketches* . . ., edited by Kate L. Gregg and John Francis McDermott (Norman, c1957); William L. Sublette's "Journal," in *Mississippi Valley Historical Review*, Cedar Rapids, Iowa, v. 6 (June, 1919), pp. 102-110; William Clark Kennerly's story *Persimmon Hill*, as told to Elizabeth Russell (Norman, 1948), pp. 143-167, 257; John E. Sunder's *Bill Sublette* . . . (1959), pp. 197-216; H. M. Chittenden and A. T. Richardson's *Life, Letters and Travels of Father Pierre-Jean De Smet, S. J.* . . ., v. 1, p. 44; *Quarterly of The Society of California Pioneers*, San Francisco, v. 7 (September, 1930), p. 153; *Bulletin* of the Missouri Historical Society, v. 11 (October, 1954), pp. 41-53 (for reports of Lt. R. H. Graham and Lt. Sidney Smith); *Niles' National Register*, v. 64 (May 20 and July 8, 1843), pp. 192, 297; *New Mexico Historical Review*, v. 36 (January, 1961), pp. 53, 54; McKelvey, *op. cit.*, pp. 773-778, 818, 819, 837; Bernard De Voto's *Across the Wide Missouri* (1947), p. 363; Overton Johnson and W. H. Winter's *Route Across the Rocky Mountains* (Princeton, 1932), p. 16; *Washington Historical Quarterly*, v. 3 (October, 1912), p. 314.

❬ By mid-May all of the spring caravan from Santa Fe (about 180 men, 42 wagons, and 1,200 mules) had reached Independence. This company (largely Mexican traders) had started for Missouri about April 1, traveling by the "lower trace" to the Arkansas river, thereby avoiding "Texan Colonel" Charles A. Warfield and his marauders, who were on the "upper trace."

The "principal men" reached St. Louis on May 17, "having with them sixteen bales and twelve boxes of silver [the bullion by two reports totaled around $250,000; by another, $300,000], and a quantity of furs" [50 packs], belonging to José Gutierrez, "John Pravis" [José Chavez?], James Floris, P. Arando, "J. Olaro" [Otero?], M. Sandrue[?], J. C. Armijo, R. Armijo, W.[?]

Glasgow, and N. W. Greene." Eleven traders went on to New York to make purchases.

(An account states that young Francisco Perea, Joaquin Perea, and J. Francisco Chavez, in charge of Juan and José Leandro Perea, and José Chavez, were brought to St. Louis in this caravan, to be entered as students "in a Jesuit college.")

Ref: *Niles' National Register,* v. 64 (May 27, June 3, 17, August 26, 1843, issues), pp. 195, 224, 241, 406; New Orleans *Weekly Picayune,* May 22, 1843; New York *Weekly Tribune,* June 3, 1843; *Old Santa Fe,* Santa Fe, v. 1 (October, 1913), p. 212. "W." Glasgow was W. H. Glasgow, probably. In 30th Cong., 1st Sess., *H. R. No. 458* (Serial 525), both W. H. and Edward I.[J.?] Glasgow are listed as Santa Fe traders.

❡ On May 17 some 300 Oregon-bound men, women, and children, with about 50 wagons, were at the "Indian Creek" rendezvous (just west of the Missouri line, in present Johnson county). By June 1 (at Soldier creek, near what is now Topeka) the "Great Emigration" of 1843—great only as compared with previous years—probably numbered upwards of 800 persons, with 110 wagons; and the final count of this year's emigrants, it would appear, totaled around 850 persons (though some claimed up to 1,000), with 120, or more, wagons. The peak livestock census (work oxen, loose cattle, horses, and mules) may have totaled 3,000 animals (though estimates ranged up to 5,000).

The "Great Emigration" (slowed by a late spring) got under way from eastern "Kansas" on May 21 and 22. Committees (appointed on the 18th and 20th) had sought advice from Dr. Marcus Whitman (who would be traveling with them), and hired John Gantt (ex-army officer and one-time fur trader) as pilot to Fort Hall.

Stopping on May 22 at a famous camp site, Peter H. Burnett (from Weston, Mo.) noted: "Elm Grove stands in a wide, gently undulating prairie. . . . There are only two trees . . . both elms. . . . The small elm was most beautiful . . . and the large one had been so, but its branches had been cut off for fuel. . . ." (The same night, James W. Nesmith recorded in his journal: "Encamped at the grove, consisting of one old elm stump.")

By May 24 the Oregonians were crossing the Wakarusa—letting their wagons down the steep bank with ropes, unaware that "a very practicable ford . . . [was] about one hundred yards above." Their pilot, John Gantt, joined the camp on the Wakarusa's west bank that night. On the 25th the vanguard reached the Kansas crossing (at "Topeka"); the rest arrived next day. Since the river was high and unfordable, a committee (appointed May 27) "attempted to hire Pappa's [Joseph Papin's] platform, but no reasonable arrangement could be made with him." The emigrants then built their own ferryboat, completing it on the 28th. Meantime, some persons paid Papin and crossed the Kansas as early as May 26 on his "platform made of two canoes." (It sank on May 28 and "several men, women, and children came near being drowned, but all escaped with the loss of some property.")

On May 31 the last of the emigrants, and their wagons, reached the Kaw's north bank, and joined those already at "Camp Delay" (as one man styled it) on the bank of Soldier creek ("Black Soldier," or "Black Warrior" to those who mentioned it in journals), where the stock "were constantly sticking fast in the mud upon its banks," and where dissension was mounting over guarding the great number of loose cattle. (It is said Jesse Applegate had "over 200 head," and other individuals "over 100 head.")

Organizing on June 1, the company elected Peter H. Burnett "commander in chief" and James W. Nesmith "orderly sergeant." (Nesmith, as adjutant, made a roll. The men "numbered 254," he wrote, and "The number of wagons was 111." Burnett stated that there were 263 men "able to bear arms," and about 110 wagons.) The caravan set out from "Camp Delay" that afternoon, up the north side of the Kansas. Next day Burnett divided his command into "four marching divisions."

An Iowan who dated his letter "Oregon Emigration Company, Kansas River, June 3d, 1843," wrote there were upwards of 120 wagons, "over 3,000, and perhaps 5,000 head of cattle, mules and horses"; that the stock-guarding issue might split the emigrants; and that "Dr. Whitman . . . advises . . . [they] divide into 3 or 4 parties for speed and convenience."

On June 6, 80 Osages and Kansa, returning from a fight with Pawnees, were met; that night a heavy wind-and-rain storm blew down tents and flooded the camp; and more torrents of rain fell on two succeeding days. Jesse Applegate and others, with 25 (or more?) wagons, "withdrew" on June 8 and formed a separate company (the "cow column"); also, Peter H. Burnett resigned and William J. Martin was elected "colonel" of the larger company (the "light column"), said to number about 175 men and 75 wagons. (Before the division, a report, from near Big Blue, stated there were 990 persons, 121 wagons, 1,967 head of cattle.)

The two columns (never far apart) continued westward; crossed from the Little Blue to the Platte in mid-June; reached Fort Laramie in mid-July; later on, traveled in smaller parties. En route, perhaps only eight turned back. At Fort Hall (in mid-September) a few joined the California-bound parties (see p. 484), but almost all of the emigrants of 1843 went to Oregon, continuing west under the guidance of Dr. Marcus Whitman; and taking their wagons (for the most part) with them!

Jesse Looney, writing from "Waiilatpu, October 27, 1843," stated: "the company of emigrants came through safely this season to the number of a thousand[?] persons with something over a hundred wagons to this place . . . and, with the exception of myself, and a few others, have all gone on down . . . [to the Willamette Valley]. . . . There were five or six deaths on the road . . . and there were some eight or ten births. Upon the whole we fared better than we expected." But Missionary Jason Lee wrote (on October 28?) that three detachments of emigrants had arrived at the Columbia river, and some had suffered severely by sickness and want of provisions.

Ref: *Washington Historical Quarterly*, v. 2 (1908), pp. 372, 373, v. 3 (1912), pp. 168-176, 250-256, 314-330, v. 4 (1913), pp. 60-80, 218, 219; Peter H. Burnett's letters, in *Oregon Historical Quarterly*, v. 3 (1902), pp. 398-420; J. W. Nesmith's diary, in *ibid.*, v. 7 (1906), pp. 329-359; W. T. Newby's diary, in *ibid.*, v. 40 (1939), pp. 219-242; P. B. Reading's journal, in *Quarterly of The Society of California Pioneers*, v. 7 (1930), pp. 148-198; Jesse Looney's October 27, 1843, letter, in *Told By the Pioneers* . . . ,[Olympia?], v. 1, pp. 75, 76; J. A. Stoughten's recollections, in *ibid.*, pp. 73, 74; Peter H. Burnett's *Recollections and Opinions* . . . (1880); New York *Weekly Tribune*, June 24, July 1, August 5, 1843, March 30 and September 21, 1844; Jesse Applegate's "A Day With the Cow Column in 1843," reprinted in *Oregon Historical Quarterly*, v. 1 (1900), pp. 371-383; *ibid.*, v. 3, pp. 395-398 (for Tallmadge B. Wood letter); *Bulletin* of the Missouri Historical Society, St. Louis, v. 11 (1954), p. 43; H. H. Bancroft's *History of Oregon* (1886), v. 1, pp. 391-400; E. H. Lenox, *Overland to Oregon* . . . (Oakland, Calif., 1904); *Niles' National Register*, v. 64 (July 22, 1843), p. 323; Nebraska State Historical Society *Publications*, v. 20, pp. 121-124; L. R. Hafen and C. C. Rister's *Western America* . . ., 2d edition (c1950), p. 239 (for statement on size of emigration—reprinted from *Niles' National Register*); Ghent, *op. cit.*, pp. 327-331; Samuel Penter's "Recollections," in *Oregon Historical Quarterly*, Salem, v. 7, pp. 56-61; Maude A. Rucker, *The Oregon Trail and Some of Its Blazers* (New York, 1930), which has information on the Applegates and other emigrants of 1843. Samuel M. Gilmore's November 11, 1843, letter, from Fort Vancouver, was published in the Weston (Mo.) *Journal* of March 15, 1845, and reprinted in the *Oregon Historical Quarterly*, v. 16, pp. 280-284. "We left Westport on the 27th[?] of May [1843], and crossed the Kansas river near the old village [he wrote]; thence up the north side of the Kansas, where we had a great deal of rain and stormy weather to encounter, which made it very disagreeable traveling. We then crossed over the Platte, about eighty miles above the Pawnee village. . . . [He said they reached Fort Hall *August* 25] we were 6 mos. today [to a day] from the time we left home in getting to this place." Gilmore returned to Platte City, Mo., in 1844. The St. Joseph (Mo.) *Gazette* of January 23, 1846, published his advice to prospective emigrants; and his recommendation of St. Joseph as a starting point. He returned to Oregon, overland, in 1846.

❡ May.—Five American Fur Company Mackinaw boats which had left Fort Pierre (S. D.) about May 13(?), reached St. Louis on the 27th—only 14 days in descending—said to be "the quickest [trip] ever made by several days." They brought down 1,400 packs of buffalo robes (10 to a pack), and a small amount of furs.

Ref: New York *Weekly Tribune*, June 17, 1843 (from Missouri *Republican*, St. Louis, May 29, 1843).

❡ May 25.—Col. Jacob Snively, and 176 mounted Texan partisans, crossed the northern "Oklahoma" line and entered present Comanche county, heading northward to the Arkansas. They reached the river on May 27, in what is now southwest Edwards county.

(On February 16 Snively had been authorized by the Texan government to organize an expedition of not over 300 men "for the purpose of intercepting and capturing the property of Mexican Traders" [in retaliation and to "make reclamation for injuries sustained by Texan citizens"]. He was specifically instructed "not to infringe" on U. S. territory. The colonel, with his self-equipped "Battalion of Invincibles," had left Fannin county, Texas, on April 25.)

Between May 27 and June 30 (when confronted by Captain Cooke and his First U. S. dragoons—*see* p. 487), the Texans ranged the south side of the Arkansas in the area of the Cimarron crossings, and sent spies (some north of the river) to watch the Santa Fe trail. When a Bent, St. Vrain & Company caravan passed, about May 31, Texas spies accompanied it eastward. About June 4(?) "Texan Colonel" Charles A. Warfield and several companions arrived (coming down from the upper Arkansas with Ceran St. Vrain), in near-destitute condition after making an unprofitable May raid in New Mexico with some 24 freebooters. On June 20(?) about 15 miles below the Cimarron crossing, a part of the Texans (led by Warfield) engaged 100(?) poorly armed Mexicans (an advance guard of the force Gov. Manuel Armijo was bringing up the trail to escort the Mexican caravan home) in a brief battle, killing 18(?), wounding 18(?), and capturing 62(?) others. No Texans were killed. [Governor Armijo, on hearing of the fight, returned to Santa Fe with 500(?) men.] On June 28 the Texans reformed into two separate companies; also, they released the Mexican prisoners. On the 29th both companies left the camp on Crooked creek, one supposedly to return to Texas, the other to return to the Arkansas. The smaller band, about 76 men, was led by Eli Chandler; the other, 107 Texans, was headed by Jacob Snively. The latter Texan force was encamped about 10(?) miles east of present Dodge City by June 30.

[Subsequently, those Texans who remained with Snively after the surrender to Captain Cooke on June 30, joined Eli Chandler's "home party"—on July 2. Snively resigned command on the 9th (while the Texans were still considering an attack on the caravan—which the U. S. troops had left on July 4); and the "home party" set out for Texas; then Warfield was elected to head those remaining. On July 14 Warfield resigned and Snively was re-elected; also, most of the party started home. Some got to Bird's Fort, Tex., on August 6.]

Ref: W. C. Binkley's *The Expansionist Movement in Texas, 1836-1850* (Berkeley, 1925), pp. 107-116; *Southwestern Historical Quarterly*, v. 44 (July, 1940), pp. 16-32, v. 54 (January, 1951), pp. 261-286; New Orleans *Weekly Picayune*, July 17, 31, August 14, September 11, 1843; *Niles' National Register*, v. 64 (August 26, 1843), p. 406; H. Yoakum's *History of Texas* . . . (New York, 1856), v. 2, pp. 399-405; H. H. Bancroft's *History of the Northern Mexican States and Texas* (1889), v. 2, p. 372; 28th Cong., 2d Sess., *Sen. Ex. Doc. No. 1* (Serial 449), pp. 91-112; *Rufus B. Sage* . . ., edited by L. R. and Ann W. Hafen, v. 2, pp. 248-252; *Mississippi Valley Historical Review*, v. 12 (June, 1925), pp. 227-238; an interview with Capt. R. P. Crump, in Porter's *Spirit of the Times,* New York, October 16, 1860, v. 9, no. 8, reprinted, as an 18-page pamphlet, by Edward Eberstadt and Sons, New York, December, 1949. In 1846 Dr. Frederick A. Wislizenus (with Albert Speyer's trading caravan), crossed the Arkansas on June 10, and noted: "pitched our night camp on 'Battle Ground' (15 miles from Arkansas)." He further commented that this was where Snively's Texans engaged the vanguard of Armijo's army and "made a dreadful havoc among them."—Wislizenus' *Memoir of a Tour to Northern Mexico* . . . *in 1846 and 1847* (Washington, 1848), p. 11.

❢ DIED: Robert Polke (trader among the Indians on Pottawatomie creek), on May 26, at his home in present Franklin county. He had been a "Kansas" resident since 1837 (*see* p. 341).

Ref: Jotham Meeker's "Diary," entry of May 26, 1843; Kansas City chapter, D. A. R., *Vital Historical Records of Jackson County, Missouri*, p. 415 (gives Robert Polke's tombstone inscription [in McCoy cemetery] as born June 7, 1797; died May 26, 1843).

❢ May.—Two young men from Indiana, Overton Johnson and William H. Winter, left Independence, Mo., in "the latter part of May . . ." and, having "traveled up the Kanza River 90 miles" (via the Oregon trail), came "to where the Emigrants were crossing" on the 30th. They crossed the rain-swollen river (perhaps on Papin's "ferry"?) the same day; and "after delaying one day and a half" on the north side, "succeeded in making . . . [their] company eight persons, and again began to travel."

Proceeding, most of the time, apart from the other emigrants, Johnson, Winter, and companions, made the journey safely to Oregon. Winter went to

California in 1844. In 1845 (as will be noted in the annals) Johnson and Winter returned East by way of the Oregon trail. A coauthored account of their travels, entitled *Route Across the Rocky Mountains, With a Description of Oregon and California,* published in 1846 at Lafayette, Ind., has long been one of the rarest of Western travel narratives. A "Bill of the Route" (a table of distances; with comment on camping spots) included in this work, also puts it in the category of "guide-book." Summarizing the "Kansas" section of the guide, these were the distances as compiled by Johnson and Winter (undoubtedly on the 1843 journey, rather than in 1845):

From Independence to "Crossing of the Kanzas," 90 miles; to "Muddy Creek" [Cross creek], 17; to "Honey Creek" [Little Vermillion—now Red Vermillion], 20; to "Can[n]on-Ball Creek" [Rock creek], 18; to [Black] "Vermillion," 21; to "Big Blue," 20; to "Battle Creek"[?], 11; to "Little Blue," 68; "to the point where the road leaves Little Blue," 51; to "The Great Platte," 25. Total: 341 miles.

Of the "Crossing of the Kanzas," the authors commented: ". . . The Kanzas River is generally full in the Spring, but emigrants will probably hereafter be accommodated, by a Frenchman [Joseph Papin] who resides at the crossing place, with a ferry-boat."

Ref: Johnson and Winter, *op. cit.;* Overton Johnson letter, dated "Fort Hall . . . September 15, 1843," in New York *Weekly Tribune,* March 2, 1844. For another Oregon trail table of distances compiled in 1843 see Peter H. Burnett's letter of January 18, 1844, in *Oregon Historical Quarterly,* v. 3 (1902), pp. 406, 407.

❡ May 27(?)—May 31.—Dr. Marcus Whitman (accompanied by his 13-year-old nephew, Perrin B. Whitman) was a guest at Shawnee Methodist Mission. On May 31 he (and Perrin) set out, overland, for Oregon. (*See* p. 466 for his winter trip East.)

Whitman was at Fremont's camp the night of June 1; by the 3d he had joined the Oregonians. Jesse Applegate later wrote that Whitman's "great experience and indomitable energy were of priceless value to the migrating column." At Fort Hall, where the emigrants were advised to abandon their wagons and cattle, he was able to persuade some of them that the wagons could be taken through to Oregon.

Ref: Drury, *op. cit.,* pp. 331-338; Hulbert, *Marcus Whitman, Crusader, Part Two, op. cit.,* pp. 312-321; *also* Oregon Pioneer Association *Transactions,* 19th annual reunion, 1891, pp. 177-179 (for letters by Whitman, dated at Shawnee Mission, May 27 and 28, 1843); C. H. Carey, editor, *The Journals of Theodore Talbot* (1931), p. 8; New York *Weekly Tribune,* July 1, August 5, 1843; *Oregon Historical Quarterly,* v. 40 (September, 1939), p. 223; Peter H. Burnett's *Recollections and Opinions* . . ., p. 101. See September 15, 1842, annals entry for P. L. Edwards' contrary view on feasibility of getting wagons through to the Columbia river.

❡ May 27.—Capt. P. St. George Cooke and 162(?) First U. S. dragoons (Companies C, F, and K), with two mountain howitzers, and 11 baggage wagons (mostly mule-drawn), left Fort Leavenworth for Council Grove to serve as escort for the Santa Fe-bound spring trading caravan. Cooke's command included Capt Benjamin D. Moore, Lt. William Bowman, 2d Lieutenants George T. Mason,

John Love, Daniel H. Rucker, and Asst. Surg. Richard F. Simpson. Also making this journey was the commander's 10-year-old son, John Rogers Cooke.

They marched (in mud) down the military road on the 27th; reached the Delaware (or Grinter) crossing of the Kansas on the 28th, got one company and the baggage train across on the ferry flatboats; and on the 29th, at an early hour, left the river and soon veered right toward the Santa Fe trail, striking it, on May 30, a little east of Elm Grove (where, wrote Cooke, there was "no wood," and "little water").

Their travel on the trail to Council Grove was routine; they reached the traders' rendezvous on June 3, about noon, and camped on the southwest bank of the Neosho in the prairie bottom. Captain Terrett and troops joined Cooke's command on June 4—*see* next entry. *See, also,* June 6 entry.

Ref: *Mississippi Valley Historical Review,* v. 12 (June, 1925), pp. 72-78, 80; *KHQ,* v. 22, pp. 107, 110.

❡ Leaving Fort Scott on May 26, Capt. Burdett A. Terrett, with 23 Company A First dragoons, and two wagons (25 troops in all), arrived at Council Grove on June 4, after a 200-mile march, chiefly on the divide between the Marais des Cygnes and Neosho rivers. Terrett joined Captain Cooke's command. *See* June 6 entry.

Ref: *Mississippi Valley Historical Review,* v. 12 (June, 1925), pp. 73, 78, 79; and *see ibid.,* p. 248, for Terrett's homeward journey, in July; Fort Scott post returns (microfilm in KHi).

❡ May 28.—Lt. John C. Fremont (U. S. Topographical Engineers), bound for Oregon (and northern California), left "the little town of Kansas" (Kansas City, Mo.) with his second exploring expedition (some 39 men; 12 two-mule carts; a light spring wagon for the instruments; a 12-pounder brass howitzer; a band of loose horses and mules); crossed the state line, and encamped two nights four miles from Westport, near "the [Shawnee] Methodist Mission House." (*See* June 6, 1842, entry for his first expedition.)

In Fremont's party were Thomas Fitzpatrick (guide), Charles Preuss (a topographer), Theodore Talbot (whose journal gives many particulars of the march as far as "Idaho"), Frederick Dwight (a Pacific-bound tourist), Lucien Maxwell (hunter; en route to Taos), Louis Zindel ("cannonier"), Philibert Courteau (cook), Jacob Dodson (a free Negro; Fremont's servant), and 29 voyageurs (principally "creole and Canadian French, and Americans"). The explorer and most of his company had reached the "town of Kansas" (notably, Fremont did not refer to it as Westport Landing, though Talbot did), by steamboat (from St. Louis) on May 18. They spent 10 days at "Kansas" making final preparations. Fitzpatrick, with seven men and 40 horses and mules, arrived, overland, on the 23d; and he brought in more animals on the 27th.

On May 30 the company was at Elm or Round Grove ("only two elm trees remain of what was once a beautiful grove"—Talbot), where there were some emigrant wagons; and where Oregon-bound William Gilpin (later governor of Colorado) joined them. On May 31 the march was 27 miles to the "Wahka-loosa" (Wakarusa) where they camped, and placed a "signal as agreed" on "Blue Mound" (present Douglas county) in sight of the home of Shawnee(?) Indians James (Jim) Rogers and his son Thomas Jefferson Rogers, who arrived around noon next day to accompany the expedition out to the South Platte, as hunters. (Fremont called them Delawares.)

The June 2 stopping point was about 100 miles (as traveled) from "Kansas landing," apparently near Shunganunga creek, in present south Topeka. At this camp, on the morning of the 3d, instead of turning northward to the Kansas crossing, Fremont's expedition *left the Oregon trail* and *continued up the south side of the river*. Progress was much delayed by numerous small streams which had to be bridged. The company "nooned" near a Kansa village whose chief was "The Little Turtle"(?), according to Talbot. He also recorded (perhaps inaccurately) the three Kansa divisions: "that under 'The American Chief' counts 50 wigwams, the 'Little Blue' 30 and the 'Yellow Banks' 20 wigwams"; adding that " 'The Black Soldier' is now one of the most distinguished [chiefs]."

The expedition halted June 3 on a "handsome stream"—present Mill creek, Wabaunsee co. (which Fremont called "Otter creek"; and Talbot recorded as "Beaver Creek"). Next day they met a returning Delaware hunting party; traveled 18 miles; camped on "Buck Cr." (apparently Deep creek, Riley co.). On June 5, about due south of what is now Manhattan, a mounted war party of Osages chased Lucien Maxwell; overran Fremont's outfit in pursuit; went off with some of the best horses (which were recovered with difficulty after a hard ride). The night of June 7 probably was spent on present McDowell creek, Riley co. Next day the expedition reached the junction of the Smoky Hill and Republican rivers (at the future Fort Riley), and camped two nights "upon the banks of the Kansas" just below the junction.

On June 10, using a raft (constructed the day before) and an India rubber boat, the company crossed the Smoky Hill, went about a mile and camped in the point formed by the two branch streams (present Junction City area; Isaac McCoy and party had stopped there in 1830—*see* p. 178).

Between June 11 and June 14 the expedition traveled some 82 miles up the Republican's right bank. At "Big timber creek" camp (present Buffalo? creek, Cloud co.; in lat. 39° 32' 54" and long. 98° 11' 41") the explorer divided his company—moving on ahead on the 16th with "a light party of 15 men," and taking the howitzer and Jersey wagon; leaving Thomas Fitzpatrick with 25 men "in charge of the provisions and heavier baggage" to follow. Fremont headed westward to "Solomon's fork of the Smoky-hill river," traveling on its North Fork, apparently, for several days. On June 21 he moved up "to the affluents of the Republican"; and on the 25th(?) crossed "Republican fork of the Kansas" (in the vicinity of present Benkelman, Neb.).

At the end of June he came to the South Platte; arrived at Fort St. Vrain (not far from Greeley, Colo., of today) on July 4. Fitzpatrick's party, probably via much the same route, reached the "Padouca" (South Platte) on July 8; and arrived at "St. Vrain's Fort" on July 14.

Again ready to move Fremont separated his company, which now included Kit Carson, taking him and a small party on what was intended (Talbot wrote) as "a bee line . . . across the mountains to Fort Hall." (But en route, Fremont had to alter his plans and cross South Pass. Subsequently he and a few men made a detour to the Great Salt Lake, leaving the Oregon trail at, or just west of, Soda Springs on August 26. He rejoined his company at Fort Hall September 18.) Fitzpatrick and the rest of the party reached Fort Hall by way of Fort Laramie and South Pass. From Fort Hall (where 11 men were discharged), the emigrant route to Oregon was followed, but Fremont and a few companions pushed on ahead, reaching The Dalles ahead of Fitzpatrick's group. On November 21 they were united. Four days later the explorer (with 25 men) set out on a winter expedition into northern California which concluded with a foolhardy, but successful, scaling of the Sierras that brought them to Sutter's fort in the fore part of March, 1844.

Ref: John C. Fremont's *Report of the Exploring Expedition to . . . Oregon and North California in the Years 1843-'44;* Carey, *op. cit.;* Charles Preuss, *Exploring With Fremont . . .,* translated and edited by E. G. and Elisabeth K. Gudde (Norman, c1958), p. 81; H. H. Bancroft's *History of California,* v. 4, pp. 435-439; also his *History of Oregon,* v. 1, pp. 419, 420; Ghent, *op. cit.,* pp. 329-332; New York *Weekly Tribune,* September 23, 1843 (for William Gilpin's? July 26, 1843, letter). Despite Fremont's calling them Delawares, the hunters were, apparently, Shawnees—Talbot says so, Gilpin(?) says so; and, more convincingly, the Rogers family evidently lived on the Shawnee reserve. Fremont's dates do not always tally with those of Talbot. The latter's journal dates have seemed more reliable where there are discrepancies. W. E. Connelley's *Doniphan's Expedition . . .,* p. 147, has some comment on William Gilpin and the trip with Fremont.

❦ May 29.—Capt. Nathan Boone and 90 First dragoons (including Lt. Abraham R. Johnston, Lt. Richard H. Anderson, Lt. Abraham Buford, and Asst. Surg. Josiah Simpson) marching northward from "Oklahoma" to "make a reconnoisance of the Western prairies," entered "Kansas" in present Harper county. (They had left Fort Gibson in mid-month.)

To-wan-ga-ha's band of Osages, met on the 29th, with whom they were in company till June 3, stole 10 horses and two mules; Boone seized some Indian ponies to replace them. Continuing northward, the dragoons crossed the Arkansas (June 5) near present Hutchinson, and came to the Santa Fe trail (June 7) on the headwaters of the Little Arkansas (near the Rice-McPherson county line of today). They found the site where the McDaniel gang had camped; searched in vain for the body of the murdered Chaves (*see* p. 469); took in tow "a small party of traders, five persons and one wagon" bound for California by way of Santa Fe (these persons later joined the caravan Cooke escorted); then, in need of buffalo meat, left the trail; marched southwest. (On June 9 they had been at the Little Arkansas crossing.) On June 10 the dragoons crossed the Arkansas again (not far from present Alden, Rice co.); moved up the right bank (fording Rattlesnake creek after seven miles of travel); camped after a 10-mile march. Captain Boone, Lieutenants Buford, Anderson, and 12 others, hunted, and found buffalo on June 11. Moving upriver again on June 13, the Fort Gibson dragoons soon saw the Fort Leavenworth dragoons on the opposite side of the Arkansas. (About this same time, Lt. Abraham R. Johnston accidently shot himself, suffering a severe foot injury, which required that he be carried, for the rest of the trip, in one of the (three) supply wagons. Captain Boone made camp across river from the mouth of Walnut creek (and across from Captain Cooke's force), in present Barton county; and remained in that vicinity through June 21.

On the homeward-march, begun June 22, the Fort Gibson dragoons traveled across Stafford, Pratt, and Barber counties of today. They met a large band of Osages headed by "To-ca-sa-ba" [Tshonga Sabba—Black Dog] on the 27th; left "Kansas" on the 29th in southwest Barber county; visited the "Rock Salt" (salt plains of "Oklahoma") on June 30; met Osage chief "Tallee" on July 1; subsequently had some fine buffalo hunting before descending the Canadian to proceed to Fort Gibson—reached July 31.

Ref: Nathan Boone's journal in *Chronicles of Oklahoma*, Oklahoma City, v. 7 (March, 1929), pp. 58-105; *Mississippi Valley Historical Review*, v. 12 (June, 1925), pp. 81-92.

❮ On May 30th a small party of California-bound men, women, and children spent the night at Elm Grove. Lt. John C. Fremont, also camping there, noted this "company with several [five?] emigrant wagons . . . under the direction of Mr. J. B. Childs [Joseph B. Chiles], of [Jackson co.] Missouri. . . ."

Chiles (who had gone to California, overland, in 1841, and returned in 1842—*see* pp. 429 and 458) now was moving out to the Sacramento Valley. The party *at this time* included his friend William Baldridge, and, probably, Milton McGee, both of Jackson county, Julius Martin, his wife and three young daughters, Bartlett Vines, his wife, and her unmarried sister; also John Boardman, who left at Fort Hall and went to Oregon. (No complete list is available.) Fremont noted that the party's wagons were "variously freighted with goods, furniture, and farming utensils"; and that Chiles was taking "an entire set of machinery for a mill. . . ."

The Californians arrived at "Caw River" on June 3; crossed "on a raft, half canoe and half raft"; "fell in with four wagons and 90 head loose cattle, bound for Oregon" [the Daniel Waldo party?] on June 5; were delayed by rains on subsequent days; came to the "fresh track of the Oregon Company" on the 20th; camped on "Big Blue" [Little Blue!] that night; left the "head of Blue for the Platte" on the 23d; caught up with the Great Emigration at the Platte's South Fork. West of Fort Laramie they met mountain man Joseph R. Walker, and Chiles was able to hire him as guide. They arrived at Fort Bridger on August 13; and on September 12 reached Fort Hall, where Chiles (because of a scarcity of food) divided his company. Joseph R. Walker, with the wagons, the families, and some others, by one route (and having to abandon the wagons on the way) finally reached the California destination in December. Joseph B. Chiles, Milton McGee and 11 other men (among them John Gantt, Pierson B. Reading, and William J. Martin of the "Oregonians"), on horseback, by another route, reached Sutter's Fort on November 10.

Ref: John C. Fremont's *Report* . . ., pp. 106, 107, 247; John Boardman's journal in *Utah Historical Quarterly*, Salt Lake City, v. 2 (October, 1929), pp. 99-121; J. W. Nesmith's journal in *Oregon Historical Quarterly*, v. 7 (December, 1906), pp. 331, 337, 339, 342, 345; P. B. Reading's journal in *Quarterly of The Society of California Pioneers*, v. 7 (September, 1930), pp. 161-198; H. H. Bancroft's *History of California*, v. 2, p. 759, v. 4, pp. 392-395, 732, v. 5, p. 764; George R. Stewart's *The California Trail* (1963), pp. 36-48. The following is quoted from Georgia W. Read and Ruth Gaines, *op. cit.*, p. 650: "With [E. Milton] McGee in this Chiles-Walker party of '43 were his Missouri friends 'Maj. S. J. H.' and 'J. M.' ('Autobiography,' MS, Native Sons of Kansas City, Mo.; courtesy James Anderson), whom we suppose to be Maj. Samuel J. Hensley and J. Myers, both listed by Reading. . . ." [The Native Sons of Kansas City, Mo., records, are now at the Kansas City (Mo.) Public Library.] Samuel J. Hensley made a second(?) trip to California in 1848, and John J. Myers (same person as J. Myers?) made the overland journey, for a second, or third time, in 1849, as later noted. As regards the Daniel Waldo party referred to above, in Mary C. Withington, compiler, *A Catalogue of Manuscripts in the Collection of Western Americana Founded by William Robertson Coe, Yale University Library* (New Haven, 1952), on p. 291, reference is made to a three-page typed item— Daniel Waldo's "Critiques, Narrative and remarks" (the original being in the Bancroft Library, Berkeley, Calif.). Comment is made: "Waldo emigrated from Virginia to Missouri in 1819 and was a neighbor of the Applegates. . . . He joined the 1843 emigration to Oregon. The ms. summarizes the events of the journey and expresses critical opinions of W. H. Gray, Whitman, and the [Oregon] missions. . . ." Fred Lockley's *History of the Columbia River Valley* . . . (Chicago, 1928), pp. 1060-1094, contains William Henry Rector's autobiography. (Rector moved to Independence, Mo., in the late 1830's; and formed a partnership with "Lorance Flournoy" to build a steam sawmill.) On p. 1068 Rector is quoted as stating "in 1842 [*i. e.*, 1843] I was at the Shawney mission [Shawnee Methodist Mission] puting up a steam engin for their mills when the emigrants war randavouseing near by I see there was a number of families of respectible people. the applegates Waldo and many others of like good caractor. . . ."

❦ June.—A grand council of Indian nations, held from June 5 to July 3, at Tahlequah (Okla.)—the Cherokees' council ground—had a peak attendance of nearly 4,000 persons.

It was said that 22 tribes (out of 36 invited), sent representatives; but the 18 which had official delegates (totaling 211) were: Cherokees (17), Creeks (50), Seminoles (12), Chickasaws (12), Osages (9), Delawares (24), Shawnees (18), Kickapoos (4), Iowas (5), Pottawatomies (21), Chippewas (4), Stockbridges (6), Wichitas (1), Piankeshaws (2), Weas (6), Senecas (10), Peorias (6), and Ottawas (4). Notably absent were the Pawnees, Kansa, Comanches, and Kiowas; and the Choctaws did not take part in the proceedings, which were presided over by the Cherokees' head chief John Ross. Among those who came from some distance were aged chief Wabaunsee and orator Op-te-gee-zheek (or, Half Day) of the Council Bluffs (Iowa) Pottawatomies. Captain Ketchum headed the delegation of Delawares from "Kansas." The principal Osage chiefs present, it appears, were Shingawassa (or, Handsome Bird) and Black Dog.

Gen. Zachary Taylor attended the council; and Artist John Mix Stanley was on hand to do portraits of distinguished delegates, as well as a painting of the council in session. Other invited guests included some missionaries and Indian agents. According to the Rev. William H. Goode (a visitor June 22-25), it was costing the Cherokees $250 a day to feed the Indian congregation. He commented that the "only two tribes present that seemed . . . fully to retain their primitive customs in dress and manners, were the Iowas and Osages. . . ." The latter nation's delegates were tall men (all over six feet) weighing not less than 200 pounds each, by his estimate.

A peace-and-friendship treaty was signed on July 3 by the Cherokees, Creeks, and Osages.

Ref: *Niles' National Register*, v. 64 (July 22, 1843), p. 341; William H. Goode's *Outpost of Zion* . . . (Cincinnati, 1864), pp. 55-85, 90; Grant Foreman's *Advancing the Frontier 1830-1860* (Norman, 1933), pp. 205-214.

❏ June.—John Richard, associated with Indian traders John Sibille and David Adams, of Fort Platte (on the North Platte about a mile from Fort Laramie), came down the Oregon trail, across "Kansas," with "some cows & 6 Buffalo Calves & one young Elk also 5 or 6 One (horse) Waggons Loaded with Robes," as recorded by William L. Sublette (of Sir William Drummond Stewart's westbound expedition) who met him June 6 on the Big Blue.

Richard recrossed "Kansas," in July, en route to Fort Platte (a Pratte, Cabanne & Co. post), with an outfit of eight or nine men, and some 15 pack animals, carrying, principally, kegs of contraband alcohol (said to total nearly 300 gallons). He arrived at the trading post in "Wyoming" about August 15.

See, also, August entry, p. 493.

Ref: SIA, St. Louis, "Records," v. 7, typed copy, p. 363; OIA, Letters Received from SIA, St. Louis (National Archives Microcopy 234, Roll, 753), Agent Andrew Drips' letter of October 15, 1843, with enclosures: *Quarterly of The Society of California Pioneers,* v. 7 (September, 1930), p. 156; *Washington Historical Quarterly,* v. 3 (October, 1912), p. 318; for Pratte & Cabanne's license, issued at St. Louis, July 27, 1843, for trade (with 26 men) on the Upper Missouri, Laramie's Fork, South Platte, etc., *see* OIA, Letters Received from SIA, St. Louis (National Archives Microcopy No. 234, Roll 753), D. D. Mitchell's list of licenses issued from October 1, 1842, to September 30, 1843.

❏ Early on June 6 the spring caravan for Santa Fe—over 50 wagons and around 140 persons, headed by "Dr. [George?] East, & L[i]eut, Armijo & Ortiz"—left the Council Grove rendezvous; followed by a large military escort—Capt. P. St. George Cooke and upwards of 190 First U. S. dragoons (*see* May 27 entry).

In this train, as Cooke later reported, there were: "American owners 10; Mexican owners 5; Armed Americans 68; Armed Mexicans, about the same; Wagons large & *small,* American owners, 24; Wagons Large, Mexican owners, 32." (Earlier, Cooke had told Captain Boone there were 47 wagons, including three dearborns.)

Camp on June 6 was at Diamond Spring; next day Cooke took the lead, marching to Cottonwood Crossing, while the traders moved more slowly. On June 11, from a camp on a branch of Cow creek, Cooke sent Capt. Benjamin D. Moore's Company C to backtrack the trail and remain near the laggard caravan. On the 13th he wrote (in his journal): "This has been our great day: our first meeting with buffalo. . . . Encamped between 3 & 4 o'clock on Walnut Creek. Capt [Nathan] B[oone]'s tents on the other side of Arkansas are visible." [Boone remained there till June 23—*see* p. 483 for his expedition.]

Captain Cooke and his command stayed at Walnut Creek Crossing for 12 days—awaiting the caravan. Charles Bent and his 14-wagon train came from the west on June 14 (*see* p. 487)—camped to wait for his partner whose wagons arrived on June 24; remained till June 25. Accompanied by Captain Moore and Company C, the traders reached Walnut creek on June 23—after being bogged down for days by mud and flooded streams in present Rice county.

At last, on June 25, the whole expedition was on the move again, the military escort marching in advance. Five days later came the meeting with the Texas battalion.

Early on June 30 Captain Cooke and the dragoons reached a point on the Santa Fe trail (near the junction of two branches) about 10 miles east of present Dodge City, and saw across the river the camp of Col. Jacob Snively and his 107 Texans (*see* p. 479). The Texans believed the site was west of the 100th meridian (the United States-Mexican boundary in the Arkansas river vicinity); while Cooke's information was that the 100th meridian struck the Arkansas "about, or above the 'Caches' " (which landmark was west of present Dodge City).

The dragoons, having two howitzers, as well as a stronger force than the Texans, were in a commanding position. Cooke marched his dragoons across the river, demanded, and got, the surrender of the Texans. Snively's men (having secreted many of their firearms) gave up the weapons they carried, but a few were returned to them (for hunting purposes). Most of the Texans remained with Snively (and supposedly were to head homeward), but Cooke gave escort (Capt. B. A. Terrett and 60 men) to those who requested it, and started that party east, toward Missouri, on July 1.

The caravan, and the military escort, moving on up the Arkansas, spent the night of July 1 west of the Caches. Next day the dragoons reached the Cimarron crossing and camped; and the caravan came up next day. On July 4 Cooke wrote in his journal: "The traders are crossing their wagons in a gale . . . Some hundred mules and oxen, and half as many Mexicans floundering incessantly in the water, sound like a great water fall. . . . [later] The last wagon is over—ten hours were consumed in crossing." Without escort for the balance of the journey, this caravan reached Santa Fe safely.

On July 5 Captain Cooke and his command started eastward; caught up with Captain Terrett's party east of Pawnee fork, on July 8. Cooke was plagued by Texans on the homeward route; gave passports to some who traveled with him; found others following him on the trail. On the 13th, east of Cottonwood fork, he sent out troops to disarm every one of the "bold outlaws" they found armed. Camp on July 15 was at Council Grove. A little east of Elm Grove, on the 20th, Capt. B. A. Terrett and his troops diverged to march toward Fort Scott. Cooke's own dragoons (Companies C, F, and K) crossed the Kansas on July 20 and 21, marched into Fort Leavenworth the afternoon of the 21st.

Ref: *Mississippi Valley Historical Review*, v. 12 (June, 1925), pp. 72-98, 227-249 (for Cooke's journal, May 27-July 21, 1843); *KHC*, v. 9, pp. 553-556; and *see* references under May 25 annals entry. In the National Archives is Cooke's 1843 "Map of the Santa Fe Trace from Independence to the Crossing of the Arkansas, with part of the military road, from Fort Leavenworth, W. Mo." "Dr. East" probably was the "George East"—trader of the 1840's on the Santa Fe route—mentioned in 30th Cong., 1st Sess., *H. R. No.* 458 (Serial 525), a document which relates to the claim of Manuel X. Harmony (Santa Fe trader).

❧ June.—Charles Bent, coming down from Fort William, on the upper Arkansas, with 14 well-laden wagons drawn by ox and mule teams, and some "Colorado"-raised cattle for his Jackson county, Mo., farm, reached the Santa Fe trail's Walnut Creek crossing on the 14th, and camped on the left bank (near Captain Cooke and his dragoons) to await the rest of his company.

Manuel Alvarez (recently U. S. consul at Santa Fe) was in his party; and so was Kit Carson (who left express to Santa Fe via Bent's Fort on June 24, accompanied by Dick Owens). Also traveling with Bent had been spies from the Texan camps upriver.

Ceran St. Vrain (delayed by a "not altogether unsuccessful experiment of boating [furs] from the 'Fort' down the Arkansas") arrived on June 22 with five peltry-laden wagons. (En route he had met the Texans encamped at the Arkansas crossing.) He was able to cross flooded Walnut creek on the 24th. Next day the Bent, St. Vrain & Company caravan started east. St. Vrain arrived at St. Louis on July 5.

Ref: *Mississippi Valley Historical Review*, v. 12 (June, 1925), pp. 85-93; *Kit Carson's Own Story of His Life* . . ., edited by Blanche C. Grant (Taos, 1926), pp. 52-54; New Orleans *Weekly Picayune*, July 17, 1843; *Niles' National Register*, v. 64 (July 22, 1843), p. 323.

❧ Before June 14, three Missourians (two of them white), on a buffalo-calf hunting expedition, were slain by Indians on Pawnee Fork (in present Pawnee county), according to information Charles Bent gave Captain Cooke.

Cooke noted that two other parties hunting buffalo were in the area—one of them (he wrote, on June 15, at Walnut creek) "is here with 35 calves."

Ref: *Mississippi Valley Historical Review*, v. 12, p. 85.

❧ June 18(?).—The American Fur Company's steamboat *Trapper*, which had wintered on the upper Missouri, left Fort Pierre (S. D.) on June 12, and arrived at St. Louis on June 21. She probably passed Fort Leavenworth around the 18th. In her cargo were some 1,200 packs of buffalo robes.

The captain brought reports of hostilities by Sioux, and Otoe Indians against fur traders and trappers. At the Council Bluffs (Neb.), Agent Daniel Miller, because of threats against his life, had sent his family to Blacksnake Hills (St. Joseph) Mo., aboard the *Trapper*, for safety. The Sioux were gathering to "come down and attack the Indians" [*i. e.*, the Pawnees].

Ref: New York *Weekly Tribune*, July 8, 1843 (from a St. Louis paper); Nebraska State Historical Society *Publications*, v. 20, p. 122.

❧ June 26.—Returning from Fort Union (N. D.), and making record time, the American Fur Company's steamboat *Omega*, according to Capt. Joseph A. Sire's log book, on this day "Stopped at Robidoux (St. Joseph, Mo., site). . . . Finally we camped at [Fort] Leavenworth Met the steamboat Admiral at Weston."

On the 27th the boat "Stopped at Madame Chouteau's"; and on June 29 those aboard "Reached St. Louis in time for breakfast," wrote Captain Sire. The *Omega* (having left Fort Union on June 14) had made the trip in 15 days.

Ref: H. M. Chittenden's *The American Fur Trade* . . ., v. 2, p. 973.

❦ June 27.—In "Nebraska," some 300 Sioux Indians led by chiefs Bull Tail and Iron Shell (as reported) raided a new Pawnee village on the Loup fork's north bank (about 30 miles above the river's mouth; and a mile from Pawnee Mission), killing 69(?) men, women, and children, and wounding "upwards of 20" others. Missionary John Dunbar wrote: "The Pawnees lost in all, killed outright, died of their wounds, and taken prisoners 70," and stated that reports from the Sioux country indicated around 40 of the 500 attackers had been killed at the scene, and others had since died of wounds.

Twenty (or 21?) of the largest Pawnee lodges in the 41-lodge compound were burned, and the enemy also stole some 200 horses. Missionary Samuel Allis reported: "Of the number killed, were 35 Tappags, 28 Republicks & 6 Grand Pawnees. The men that were killed, were mostly Rplks. [Republic band] . . . [including] the first chief (Cappo Blue) [Blue Coat] who was one of the first if not the first man in the nation. Several chiefs & braves were killed, also the interpreter (La Shapell) [Louis La Chapelle] who was a half breed Pawnee. The first Tappags chief, who has been sick for a long time . . . died thrue excitement. . . ." Allis also wrote: "Since the first of March there has been from 200 to 250 Pawnees killed, and probably 400 horses stolen by their enemies."

Ref: *KHC*, v. 14, pp. 656, 657, 659, 730, 731, and for village location, *see ibid.*, pp. 647-649; SIA, St. Louis, "Records," v. 8, typed copy, pp. 215, 251-256 (here, Agent Daniel Miller reports 136 Pawnees as having "died in wars during the past spring"—1843 —a figure at variance with Allis' statement); *Niles' National Register*, v. 64 (July 22, 1843), p. 323, for the Sioux chiefs' names, and p. 341, for an account of the massacre.

❦ June 28-July 2.—En route to Shawnee Methodist Mission from Tahlequah, Cherokee Nation, Missionaries Learner B. Stateler and William H. Goode, in the latter's horse-drawn buggy, entered "Kansas," at its southeast corner, on June 28. (They were now in the Cherokee Neutral Lands.) In his later-written *Outposts of Zion* (evidently based, in part, on a journal), Goode told of the trip northward—much of it on the Fort Leavenworth-Fort Gibson military road.

After noon on the 28th they came to the Pomme de Terre (Spring) river at a point (in present Cherokee county) where "Joseph [John?] Rogers," a mixed-blood Cherokee, had his home. When Rogers attempted to ferry the buggy and baggage across the rain-swollen stream on a large "canoe," the boat capsized. Stateler and Goode spent the night at the Cherokee's home while their goods (recovered) dried out.

Next morning, they took the military road; found it expedient to camp most of the day (in a grove of trees, with a smudge fire going) to avoid the plague of horseflies; traveled all night; stopped for breakfast on the Drywood (they found a bed of "stone-coal, lying upon the surface" of this stream); proceeded (on July 30) to Fort Scott. "The only accommodation for travelers was at a cabin hotel, some hundreds of yards from the fort, but very difficult of access. This was crowded to overflowing with a class of men who cared little for the comfort of a weary stranger. . . ." So, they left (after a further unpleasant experience with the "little acting Quarter-Master" over a matter of buggy repairs). Again, they camped by day; traveled part of the night. (In September, the Osages' subagent, R. A. Calloway, wrote: "[The horse] flies . . . are fifty per cent worse than for many years in this country—so as to make it entirely impossible to use horse or ox unless at night, and a dark one at that.")

On July 1 (in the daytime) they forded the Little Osage (with some difficulty); arrived at "Jeru's [Michel Giraud's] Trading House"; crossed the Marais des Cygnes there; reached "Cold Water Grove" in the early afternoon; spent the night on the open prairie; and on Sunday, July 2, arrived at Shawnee Mission.

Ref: Goode, *op. cit.*, pp. 85-95; SIA, St. Louis, "Records," v. 8, typed copy, pp. 228-239, has Calloway's September 1, 1843, report.

❏ Between June and September, Sup't D. D. Mitchell, St. Louis, issued these Indian trading licenses for locations in "Kansas":

June 14	P. Chouteau, Jr. & Co. (11 men emloyed)	At the Marais des Cygnes near mouth of Sugar creek [now Trading Post, Linn co.]; at Pottawatomie creek near the issue house [at, or near present Lane, Franklin co.]; at the villages of the Weas, Peorias, Miamis [in present Miami and Franklin counties]; and at Sugar creek near the [Catholic] church [northeast of present Centerville, Linn co.] — with the Pottawatomies, Peorias, Weas, and Miamis [Piankeshaws]
July 17	Jos. Robidoux, Senr. (8 men employed)	At the villages of the Sacs of Missouri, Iowas, and Kickapoos; and at a point in the Kickapoo country on the Missouri river opposite Blacksnake Hills (Mo.)—with the above-named tribes, and the Pottawatomies (of Council Bluffs, Iowa) [The above locations were in Doniphan and Leavenworth counties of today.]
August 2	Boone & Hamilton [Albert G. Boone and James G. Hamilton] (6 men employed)	At a point on the Miamis' [Piankeshaws' & Weas'] lands near the line dividing them from the Pottawatomie lands [present Miami county]; and at a point on Sugar creek near the [Catholic] church of the Wabash Pottawatomies [northeast of

		present Centerville, Linn co.]—with the Pottawatomies, Weas, Ottawas, and Piankeshaws
August 24	Ewing & Clymer [George W. Ewing and Joseph Clymer]	At or near the old issue house on Pottawatomie creek [at, or near present Lane, Franklin co.]—with the Pottawatomies and others
August 24	Ewing & Clymer	At a point on the eastern shore of the Neosho river [in present Neosho? county]; and at other points in the Osage Subagency as designated by the subagent—with the Osages
September 29	Cornelius Davy (3 men employed)	At Sugar creek near the Catholic Church; at Pottawatomie creek [locations as above]—with the Pottawatomies and others

Ref: OIA, Letters Received from SIA, St. Louis (National Archives Microcopy No. 234, Roll 753). Cornelius Davy is listed in the federal census of 1850, in Jackson county, Mo., as aged 58, born in Ireland; with a son Thomas, 16 (born in Kentucky), and a son Cornelius, 5 (born in Missouri).

❡ July 3.—Indian department contracts, for the "Wabash Pottawatomies of Sugar Creek" (residents of present Linn county, northeast of Centerville) were awarded as follows:

John Cummins to supply 93 yoke of oxen, and yokes (for $2,500) within 42 days

John Cummins to supply 134 cows and calves, and one bull (for $1,000) within 42 days

D. W. Smelser to supply 69 breeding sows and five boars (for $150) within 42 days

Ref: 28th Cong., 1st Sess., H. Doc. No. 42 (Serial 441), p. 20.

❡ July 5(?)—William H. Goode—then at "town of Kansas," Missouri—wrote: "Since coming here [on July 5] I have seen a company of 'Mackinaw boats' . . . from the Upper Missouri, freighted with skins and furs, the property of the American Fur Company, as they glided rapidly down the stream."

These were, evidently, the "eight or ten Mackinaw boats" which a St. Louis newspaper on June 22 had reported were "expected" to arrive at that port.

Ref: Goode, op. cit., p. 100; Nebraska State Historical Society Publications, v. 20, p. 122.

❡ About July 6 a party of independent fur traders, en route to the upper Arkansas, left Independence, Mo., to travel the Santa Fe trail westward. One of the small company was Alexander Barclay.

(In May Barclay had crossed "Kansas" eastbound, having left the South Platte on April 28. Coming in by way of Fort William [Bent's Fort], which he passed May 5, he reached Westport, Mo., on June 7.)

Ref: Barclay Papers, Bancroft Library.

❡ July 6.—Sup't D. D. Mitchell, St. Louis, was notified that the Osage Subagency (previously in the Western superintendency) had been transferred to the St. Louis superintendency (and henceforth was under his charge).

Ref: SIA, St. Louis, "Records," v. 7, typed copy p. 360. For earlier history of the subagency *see* annals pp. 272 and 321.

❡ Early in July, south of the Arkansas, in present Ford county, Comanches killed six or seven men of the Texan expeditionary force, in three separate incidents.

Cooke's information (from some of the Texans) was that Snively's party was attacked, and two men killed, while on the way to join Chandler's party; "that they found a junction and were again attacked—two or three more were slain & 60 horses & mules driven off . . ."; that, subsequently the Texans sent out spies to see what had become of Cooke's "convoy" (*i. e.*, the traders' trains), and two "well mounted" men who "should have returned in two, but had not in six days . . . were supposed to have been killed . . . [by Indians]."

Ref: *Mississippi Valley Historical Review,* v. 12, p. 245. Cooke recorded the above under date of July 13.

❡ July.—East of Cottonwood fork, on the 13th, eastbound Capt. P. St. George Cooke met "13 wagons with ox & mule teams, freighted by an Englishman [Edward J. Glasgow?] for Chihuahua, via Santa Fe." On the 15th, at Council Grove, Cooke found "about 20 wagons for Santa Fe; the 13 we met are to wait for them at Pawnee Fork." On the 17th Cooke "Met this morning . . . 9 more wagons (& two carriages) & Dr. Connolly [Dr. Henry Connelly, of Chihuahua] . . ." the rear detachment of the 42-wagon caravan en route to the southwest without escort.

One of the party (perhaps Connelly) sent a letter (dated "Pawnee Rock July 20") to Missouri, by Lupton's company, stating (in part): "Our teams, as well as ourselves, are very much annoyed by the musquitoes they are worse than I ever saw them."

Ref: *Mississippi Valley Historical Review,* v. 12 (June, 1925), pp. 245-247; *Niles' National Register,* v. 64 (August 26, 1843), p. 406.

❡ July.—Trader Lancaster P. Lupton, and party, came down from the South Platte by way of the Santa Fe trail. New Mexico-bound merchants met him on July 20 at Pawnee Rock. Some of Lupton's company reached Independence, Mo., on August 4.

Ref: *Niles' National Register,* v. 64 (August 26, 1843), p. 406.

❡ July 15.—George W. Tate was given an Indian department contract to supply the Kickapoos with 87 cows and calves, and 25 sows, for the sum of $1,000. He had 45 days in which to complete delivery.

Ref: 28th Cong., 1st Sess., *H. Doc. No. 42* (Serial 441), p. 20.

❡ July 28 and 31.—About 630 Wyandot Indians, removing from northern Ohio to "Kansas," were put ashore at Westport Landing, Mo., from the small steamboat *Republic* and the larger *Nodaway*.

They set up camp just west of the Missouri line, on the right bank of the Kansas, near its mouth; remained there till October. A few families rented homes in, or near, Westport. (Matthew R. Walker and the young men of the Nation, bringing a herd of horses overland, arrived several weeks after those who came by water.) Methodist minister James Wheeler accompanied the Wyandots; stayed till autumn; returned in 1844 (from Ohio).

The civilized Wyandots (more white than Indian through intermarriage with captives adopted into their tribe), brought a code of laws, a Methodist church, a Masonic lodge; set up their school and their own trading store. It is said that when the Nation (then numbering about 700) came to "Kansas," no Wyandot was more than one-quarter Indian. Some were well-educated and well-to-do. Their first subagent in "Kansas"—Jonathan Phillips—wrote (in 1844): "The half breeds controul the tribe; a majority of them are stubborn, and vindictive, subtile, lazy and deceptious. The form of Govt. of the Wyandot tribe is an oligarchy, all power being vested in Seven Chiefs. . . . They have no written constitution, nor do the chiefs want any. Their feeling towards the U. S. is that of hostility. . . ." (Phillips was replaced in the spring of 1845.)

See, also, October annals entry.

Ref: New York *Weekly Tribune*, August 12, 1843 (for item from St. Louis paper of July 25, 1843, reporting arrival there on July 24, of 630 Wyandots on the *Republic* and *Nodaway*); A. T. Andreas and W. G. Cutler's *History of the State of Kansas* (Chicago, 1883), p. 1227; Goodspeed's *Wyandotte County and Kansas City, Kansas* . . . (Chicago, 1890), pp. 150, 151; SIA, St. Louis, v. 8, typed copy, pp. 343-348 (for Phillips' report); *KHC,* v. 15, pp. 181-185; James Wheeler's June 28, 1845, letter in KHi ms. division. *Also, see* Wheeler's September 30, 1843, letter, in *KHC,* v. 16, pp. 267, 268.

❡ Summer.—At Shawnee Friends Mission (present Johnson county) where 45 Indian children were in school (27 boys and 18 girls, aged five to 18), an additional two-story "apartment" had been added to the dwelling-house. On the farm 320 "dozens"[?] of wheat, 960 of oats, and about two tons of hay had been harvested. There were 44 acres in corn, four and a half acres in buckwheat, and one in potatoes—all in promising condition. The livestock numbered four horses, 35 head of cattle (17 of them milk cows), and upwards of 40 hogs.

Ref: *Some Account of the Conduct of the Religious Society of Friends Towards the Indian Tribes* . . . (London, 1844), pp. 245, 246.

❡ August 17.—David Adams, trader, on the way to Fort Platte (Wyo.) via the Oregon trail, with supply-laden wagons, was, on this day, at "Cances Rivr crosing of mr [Joseph] papan" (present Topeka).

On September 23, near Ash Hollow, when Matt Field of Sir William Drummond Stewart's eastbound company met Adams' outfit, he identified two of the men as Dan Finch and Julius Cabanne.

See, also, June entry, p. 486.

Ref: Field, *op. cit.,* p. 202; W. C. Kennerly's story, *Persimmon Hill,* p. 163; Dale L. Morgan's letter of June 29, 1963, to L. Barry.

❡ On August 21, 2d Lt. Richard S. Ewell, and a platoon from Company A, First U. S. dragoons, left Fort Scott for Council Grove (presumably traveling by way of the divide between the Marais des Cygnes and Neosho rivers); and arrived before the 31st—*see* next entry.

Ref: *Mississippi Valley Historical Review,* v. 12 (June, 1925), p. 250, and p. 253 (for Ewell's homeward route, in October; Fort Scott post returns (microfilm in KHi).

❡ August 24.—Capt. P. St. George Cooke and 150(?) First U. S. dragoons (Companies C, F, and K; also detachments of Companies E and H) left Fort Leavenworth for Council Grove to begin a mission as protective escort for the autumn caravan of Santa Fe-bound traders. (The threat of Texan marauders was not yet ended.) Cooke anticipated a march beyond the U. S. boundary, possibly even to Santa Fe! He and his command reached the rendezvous on August 31; found dragoons from Fort Scott (*see* preceding entry) awaiting at the Grove.

Ref: *Ibid.,* pp. 249, 250, 253. Cooke says "I prepared to march with 150 men provided for an excursion . . . beyond the U. S. boundary. . . ." He may have included in the 150 the platoon from Fort Scott—*see* above entry.

❡ August-September.—Capt. Enoch Steen, of the First U. S. dragoons, with 54 men, marched from Fort Gibson (Okla.) up to the Santa Fe trail, under orders to assist in escorting the autumn caravan of Mexican traders to the U. S. boundary.

His route northward across "Kansas" was probably much the same as Captain Boone's (*see* p. 483). On September 10 Captain Cooke (westbound on the trail) met Captain Steen on the Little Arkansas "marching Eastward," short of provisions and with two-thirds of his horses unfit for service. Cooke attached two young officers, and 25 of the best-mounted men to his command; sent Steen (ill), Asst. Surg. Charles McCormick, and the rest of the detachment, to Missouri where they "could obtain succor, and thence by the military road . . ." to Fort Gibson.

Ref: *Mississippi Valley Historical Review,* v. 12 (June, 1925), p. 250; Grant Foreman's *Pioneer Days in the Early Southwest* (1926), p. 302; New York *Weekly Tribune,* September 9, 1843.

❡ September 2.—The autumn caravan to Santa Fe—an all-Mexican train of about 150(?) wagons, which had left Independence, Mo., on August 24—set out from Council Grove, accompanied by Capt. P. St. George Cooke and at least 177 First dragoons (perhaps more —*see* preceding entries).

Captain Cooke stated: "I marched with the caravan of about 140 wagons: the merchants were all Mexicans. I was more fortunate than some of them, in remaining no longer at the Grove where the air was filled with miasma. A succession of rains followed and the result was that the overloaded and ill-managed wagon train advanced but 87 miles in the next 12 days. . . . [then] We were again exposed to a long spell of cold rains: very many of the Mexican drivers were sick and six or eight died. [It was later reported that "13 Spaniards died on the way—12 of them from fever and ague."] The caravan advanced in the next three weeks but 126 miles: Sept. 25th there was a severe frost."

On October 1 the expedition was still 25 miles from the Arkansas crossing, and Cooke was faced with logistics problems. The arrival, from Missouri, of Bent, St. Vrain & Company supply wagons was opportune. On October 3, the dragoons marched to "within 9 miles of the crossing; and learned . . . that a Mexican [escort] force had arrived at the river the night before." "This was a great surprise to *all*," Cooke later reported. Moving next day to the crossing, the caravan forded the Arkansas, and joined the Mexican escort.

Captain Cooke and his troops started homeward on the 5th. The journey was a slow one—the average daily march being "less than 16 miles." (There was insufficient grass for the horses.) On October 18 the dragoons arrived at Council Grove. Cooke "pushed on" leaving five wagons and a small party to follow. On the 24th, near the military road, the troops for Fort Scott, under 2d Lt. Richard S. Ewell, were detached. The Fort Leavenworth dragoons reached their post on October 25. Cooke wrote: "The march from Council Grove began amid flames and billows of smoke tossed by violent winds . . . it ended with two days of snow storm and severe winter weather. . . ."

Ref: *Mississippi Valley Historical Review*, v. 12 (June, 1925), pp. 249-254; Nebraska State Historical Society *Publications*, v. 20, p. 122 (from *Missouri Republican* of August 28, 1843, which states: "The largest caravan—175 wagons—that ever started from Independence, left on the 24th."); New York *Weekly Tribune*, January 27, 1844 (which says Norris Colburn reported there were 150 wagons in the train reaching Santa Fe; that the trip had been 106 days in length).

❧ Of the new Osage Subagency headquarters Subagent Robert A. Calloway wrote, in September: "This Agency is located on the river Neosho, about equidistant from the northern & southern boundaries—and near the Eastern boundary of this reservation." (By description this site was south of the present Neosho-Labette county boundary.)

[From 1838 (when Paul L. Chouteau resigned) to 1842, no subagent had maintained residence on the Osage reserve. But Calloway had "found it impossible to attend to his business while living in the Seneca country," and Sup't William Armstrong had "thought it best" to erect buildings "in the Osage nation"—as Calloway reported in a September 1, 1842, letter. William Sherer (or Sharer?), the contractor, finally received $2,000, in 1844, for the

Osage Subagency quarters he built, though Indian department officials thought his claim "extravagently high."]

Also new on the Osage reserve were two houses for Osage millers (built between April 20 and June 20, 1843, for $217.50 each, by contractor Edward L. Chouteau), at a location not specified, on the Neosho river, where a site for a mill had been selected, but no mill, as yet, built, or even started.

Calloway stated that the blacksmiths' shop was on the Neosho, 12 to 15 miles above the subagency; and still five or six miles higher up was the American Fur Company's trading house, whose agent Pierre Melicourt Papin (an "excellent man, well qualified . . .") had been in the Indian trade for 30 years. He noted, too, the recent trading application by a Mr. Clymer [Joseph Clymer] of the firm Ewing & Clymer," who came "well recommended."

About two-thirds of the Osages—the bands of White Hair and the Little Osages—were on the Neosho, the subagent reported. The other two bands—Clermont's and Paw-ne-no-pashees [the Big Hill band?]—lived on the Verdigris near the Osages' southern boundary.

Ref: SIA, St. Louis, "Records," v. 7, typed copy, pp. 406, 407; and *ibid.*, v. 8, typed copy, pp. 228-239 (for Calloway's report of September 1, 1843); 28th Cong., 1st Sess., *H. Doc. No. 42* (Serial 441), p. 15; 29th Cong., 1st Sess., *H. Doc. No. 91* (Serial 483), p. 2; OIA, Register of Letters Received (National Archives Microcopy 18, Roll 23) for Calloway's letter of September 1, 1842.

❡ In September Father Felix L. Verreydt (superior at Sugar Creek Mission) reported: "I have secured the services of Messrs. Thomas Watkins, and John Tipton (a Pottawatomie?) as school-masters; the former teaches the English language . . . and the latter the English and the Potawatomie languages conjointly . . . both belonging to the nation and very popular."

It is presumed that the former was the Thomas Watkins who taught school in Chicago during the early 1830's; later served as chief clerk in the Chicago post office (under the first postmaster there); and married a daughter of Joseph LaFromboise (Pottawatomie chief). The Watkins-LaFromboise wedding was an important social event in Chicago, according to Mayor John Wentworth, who was present. However, the couple subsequently were divorced; and Mrs. Watkins afterwards married Menard Beaubien, "son of Jean Baptiste Beaubien of Chicago and later a resident of Silver Creek [Silver Lake?], Kansas."

Ref: Garraghan, *op. cit.*, v. 2, p. 209.

❡ September 13.—Hiero T. Wilson (recently employed as clerk for his brother Thomas E. Wilson, sutler at Fort Gibson) arrived at Fort Scott. A partnership (or half-interest) arrangement he made with John A. Bugg (*see* March 3 entry) for the post sutlership lasted six years.

(In 1849 Bugg went to California and Wilson became sole proprietor.)

Ref: *The United States Biographical Dictionary. Kansas Volume* . . . (Chicago and Kansas City, 1879), pp. 39, 40; Robley, *op. cit.*, pp. 12, 13.

❡ After a September journey across present Kansas, "Mr. Weatherhead's [Samuel? Wethered's] company of Santa Fe traders, 140 in number" arrived at Independence, Mo., about the end of the month. Twelve of the party (including Wethered), at St. Louis early in October, were reported to have in their possession "500 pounds weight of gold and silver in bars," and to be en route East to purchase goods.

Out on the Arkansas, on September 15, Capt. P. St. George Cooke (westbound) had met this "small[?] American portion of the Spring caravan returning with a few empty wagons."

Ref: *Missouri Democrat*, St. Louis, October 4, 1843; *Mississippi Valley Historical Review*, v. 12 (June, 1925), p. 251.

❡ September.—The first general sale of lots took place at the new town of St. Joseph, Mo.—formerly "Blacksnake Hills, the old Indian trading station of Monsieur Joseph Robidoux." (The town had been laid out in June; and a plat had been certified by Robidoux, at St. Louis, on July 26.)

Subagent Richard S. Elliott who had debarked from the *John Aull* at Blacksnake Hills on May 20, 1843, later wrote: "Mons. Robidoux's warehouse . . . was a building of stockade fashion, split logs, set upright and roofed with clapboards. . . . His ample [old] log house for dwelling and trade . . . stood a short distance away on the gentle slope of a hill, with his little corn-cracking mill on a 'branch' in the foreground." That very day "the active old gentleman . . . was mounting his horse for a ride to the land office, to be opened next day at Plattsburg. He wanted to be on hand early to enter his quarter section, which it was said the people of Buchanan county intended to take from him for a county seat. They wanted to lay out a town and sell lots; but so did Mons. Robidoux. . . . With proper self-regard, he named the town after himself, ST. JOSEPH. . . ."

On November 20, 1843, the name of the post office was changed from Blacksnake Hills to St. Joseph.

Ref: Richard S. Elliott's *Notes Taken in Sixty Years* (St. Louis, 1883), pp. 166-169; *The History of Buchanan County, Missouri* (St. Joseph, 1881), pp. 405, 409, 413. *See, also,* annals, pp. 133, 412 and 538.

❡ September.—As related by Missionary Ira D. Blanchard, 23 pupils (12 boys and 11 girls) were attending Delaware Baptist Mission's manual labor school; during the year a new house, 18 by 20 feet, a story and a half high, had been added to the mission buildings; and the farm crops (some not yet harvested) would provide an abundant supply for the station.

Ref: Blanchard's September 25, 1843, report in Comm'r of Indian Affairs *Report* for 1843.

❡ September-October.—Leaving the Missouri frontier, on the Santa Fe trail, in the fore part of September, the wagon train headed by

Charles Bent and Ceran St. Vrain overtook Capt. P. St. George Cooke (and the Mexican traders' caravan) about October 1.

Cooke, on October 1, wrote in his journal: "I was 25 miles below the [Arkansas] crossing: and the caravan was strung out on desperate roads 10 or 15 miles behind . . . when the arrival of Bent & . . . [St. Vrain] announcing the approach of provisions for wintering in the wilderness, relieved me in some degree."

(At St. Louis, in late August, the traders had contracted to transport about 35,000 pounds of government "stores and provisions" from Westport, Mo., to "the trading house on the Arkansas river, called Fort Williams" [Bent's Fort] and store them up to October 1, 1844, at eight cents per pound. Subsequently [in 1844] there was some difficulty over this contract.)

Ref: *Mississippi Valley Historical Review*, v. 12 (June, 1925), p. 251; 28th Cong., 1st Sess., *H. Doc. No. 42* (Serial 441), p. 36; and *see* documents quoted in Nolie Mumey's *Old Forts* . . . (1956), pp. 64-70.

❡ Late September(?)—Two Otoe Indians, held prisoners at Fort Leavenworth for outrages of the previous summer, made a break for freedom. One was shot and killed by a sentinel; the other escaped.

Ref: *Niles' National Register*, v. 65 (October 21, 1843), p. 115 (from St. Louis (Mo.) *Gazette* of October 8); SIA, St. Louis, "Records," v. 7, typed copy, p. 411.

❡ DIED: Wy-lah-lah-piah, or Wa-wa-la-peah (a leading chief of the Shawnee nation), on October 3, at his home in present Johnson county.

J. C. Berryman described him as "a man of imposing personal presence, superior intellect, and eloquent speech, mighty in exhortation and prayer, his influence was a power for good among his people." James G. Hamilton, of Westport, Mo., wrote that "Wawalapi" was one of the most talented Shawnees he ever knew, and the "greatest orator in the tribe."

Ref: F. H. Cross and K. J. Moore's *Notebooks of James Gillespie Hamilton* . . . (c1953), p. 5; *KHC*, v. 16, p. 218, *See, also,* annals, p. 251.

❡ On October 1, from a camp near the Platte's South Fork, 22 men of Sir William Drummond Stewart's homeward-bound "pleasure excursion" set out in advance of the main company. (The journey back from the "hunting frolic" to the Wind River mountains had begun August 17—*see* p. 475.)

This group, made up of persons either at odds with Sir William's autocratic ways, or impatient with his slow homeward pace, included Lt. Richard H. Graham and Lt. Sidney Smith (whose furloughs were rapidly expiring), Cyprian Menard, Edmund F. Chouteau, Jefferson K. Clark, and W. Clark Kennerly (who kept a diary of the trip eastward). Isaac Greathouse was appointed captain.

In "Kansas," at the Oregon trail Kansas river crossing (present Topeka), Graham, Smith, Clark, and two men from the main party who caught up with them, left the trail to follow "precisely the road we had taken going up" (as stated in the Graham-Smith report)—that is, along the north side of the river to the old ford at the one-time Kansa Agency (nearly 20 miles below present Topeka). The others, it appears, all kept to the Oregon trail, crossing the Kansas at Papin's (*i. e.*, at "Topeka"). Some 20 of the splinter party arrived at St. Louis on October 23, aboard the *Omega*.

Sir William, William L. Sublette, and the rest of the company came down the Oregon trail not far behind the Greathouse party. Matt Field, and two mess-mates, reached Joseph Papin's cabin early on October 15, a day ahead of the others. Field wrote, in his diary, on October 16: "Camp [Stewart, Sublette, *et al*] came to the [Kansas] crossing at noon, and we got everything over in a 40 foot pirogue of Charles Choteau's by sundown . . . swam the animals over beautifully." On October 30, aboard the steamboats *Iatan* and *John Aull*, most, if not all, of these expedition members, reached St. Louis.

Ref: Field, *op. cit.*; W. C. Kennerly's diary in *Persimmon Hill*, pp. 158-167, 257; *Bulletin* of the Missouri Historical Society, v. 11 (October, 1954), pp. 50-53 (for Graham-Smith report of the homeward journey). Charles B. Chouteau (1808-1884), a son of Pierre Chouteau, Sr., and his second wife, was a full brother of Francis G., Cyprian, and Frederick Chouteau. The above is the earliest mention found linking him with the Kansas river trade (and Frederick Chouteau's post—a few miles above present Topeka).

❧ October 5-10.—Descending the Missouri in a Mackinaw boat, naturalist John J. Audubon, accompanied by Edward Harris, J. G. Bell, L. M. Squires, Isaac Sprague—*see* May 3 entry, mountain man Etienne Provost, and some oarsmen, arrived at Fort Croghan (at present Council Bluffs, Iowa) on October 5. Next day, accompanied by another boat carrying Lt. James H. Carleton and 18 men of the First dragoons, the journey downriver was resumed. On October 10, at 4 P. M. they put in at Fort Leavenworth's landing. At half-past six, Audubon's boat departed, proceeding to the Independence lower landing by sunset. Audubon and his friends reached St. Louis on October 19. (They had left Fort Union [N. D.] on August 16; and Fort Pierre [S. D.] on September 8.)

Ref: Edward Harris' journal—*see* May 3 annals entry; *North Dakota Historical Quarterly*, v. 10 (April, 1943), pp. 63-82; John J. Audubon's manuscript journal, August 16-November 6, 1843, is in the E. D. Graff collection of the Newberry Library, Chicago.

❧ October 6.—Fort Croghan, Iowa (*see* above entry) was abandoned on this day. Capt. John H. K. Burgwin and part of his First dragoons started overland for Fort Leavenworth; while Lt. James H. Carleton and 18 men left for the post by water.

(*See* p. 451 for short-lived Fort Croghan's founding, in June, 1842.)

Ref: Edward Harris' journal, *op. cit.*, p. 183.

❧ October.—The Wyandot Indians (now scarcely more than 600? in number), who had been encamped (since the end of July) on the Kaw's right bank, near its mouth, moved across the river to the east end of the Delawares' reserve (on lands subsequently

Large numbers of Indians met en route—150 lodges of Cheyennes and a larger camp of Arapahoes (25 miles below Fort William), also, a war party of about 150 Cheyennes (looking for Pawnees) about 100 miles farther east— had been friendly. Those in the rear of Colburn, by report, sent to Independence for provisions and clothing; apparently did not reach Missouri till January, 1844.

Ref: New York *Weekly Tribune*, January 13, 27, 1844.

℃ Employed in "Kansas" by the Indian Department during all, or part of the year 1843 were the following persons:

FORT LEAVENWORTH AGENCY—*Agent* Richard W. Cummins; *Interpreters* Clement Lessert and Henry Tiblow; *Blacksmiths* William Donalson and James M. Simpson (for Shawnees), Isaac Mundy (for Delawares), Charles Fish (for Kansa); *Assistant blacksmiths* Jackson Pitman and Joseph Parks' "coloured boy" (for Shawnees), Powhatan Phifer (for Delawares), Mab Frankier (for Kansa); *Farmer* William H. Mitchell (for Kansa).

GREAT NEMAHAW SUBAGENCY—*Subagent* William P. Richardson; *Interpreters* John Rubeti (for Sacs & Foxes), Samuel M. Irvin (for Iowas); *Blacksmiths* James Gilmore (for Sacs & Foxes), Benjamin Stewart (for Iowas); *Assistant blacksmiths* William Daviess (for Sacs & Foxes), Elisha P. Dorion (for Iowas); *Farmers* Preston Richardson (for Sacs & Foxes), Aurey Ballard (for Iowas); *Assistant farmer* Pleasant Johnson (for Sacs & Foxes); *Teacher* William Hamilton (for Sacs & Foxes).

OSAGE RIVER [MARAIS DES CYGNES] SUBAGENCY—*Subagent* Anthony L. Davis (removed from office in July), Joshua Carpenter (appointed November 23); *Interpreter* Luther Rice (for Pottawatomies, till May 15; he died on May 21); *Blacksmiths* Robert Simerwell and Robert Wilson (for Pottawatomies); *Assistant blacksmiths* Thomas N. Stinson and D. Moreland (for Pottawatomies); *Miller* Peter Perillard (at Pottawatomie creek, for Pottawatomies; from January 1).

OSAGE SUBAGENCY—*Subagent* Robert A. Calloway (removed during 1843), Hector Bell (appointed December 16; but did not take office); *Interpreter* Charles Mongrain; *Blacksmiths* Elias N. Beardon, John Mathews (dismissed in April), Jesse Rhinehart (appointed May 12); *Assistant blacksmiths* William (half-Osage) and Jacob (an Osage).

WYANDOT SUBAGENCY—*Subagent* Jonathan Phillips (appointed October 24). (In Ohio, prior to the Wyandots' removal to "Kansas," Purdy McElvain had been subagent from October 1, 1842, to October 30, 1843.); *Interpreter* James Rankin; *Blacksmith* Charles Graham; *Assistant blacksmith* Abraham Trager.

Ref: SIA, St. Louis, "Records," v. 7, typed copy, pp. 352, 369, 371, 375, 377, 378, 383, 385, 393, 395, v. 8, typed copy, pp. 240, 257-259, 292, 300, 305, 438; 28th Cong., 1st Sess., *H. Doc. No. 67* (Serial 441); 28th Cong., 1st Sess., *H. Doc. No. 240* (Serial 441); 29th Cong., 1st Sess., *H. Doc. No. 91* (Serial 483), p. 2 (gives "Peter Peryard"—*i. e.*, Peter Perillard); Jotham Meeker's "Diary," May 24, 1843, entry (for Luther Rice's death).

1844

℃ January 4.—Thomas H. Harvey, succeeding David D. Mitchell, wrote his Indian agents and subagents: "You are hereby notified that I have entered upon the discharge of my duties as Supert. of Indn Affairs at . . . [St. Louis]."

Ref: Superintendency of Indian Affairs (SIA), St. Louis, "Records," v. 7, typed copy, p. 384; 28th Cong., 2d Sess., *H. Doc. No. 139* (Serial 465), pp. 2, 5; 30th Cong., 1st Sess., *H. Ex. Doc. No. 26* (Serial 516), p. 4. Harvey's original date of commission was October 3, 1843.

❦ BORN: on January 18, at Delaware Methodist Mission, present Wyandotte county, Sarah Ann Peery, daughter of the Rev. Edward T. and Mary S. (Peery) Peery.

Ref: Si and Shirley Corn's *Our Family Tree* (June, 1959), Section IV; *KHC*, v. 9, p. 227 (for location of Peery family in January, 1844).

❦ March 2.—The Oregon-bound Cornelius Gilliam family (including married sons and daughters), and, probably, some other families who were also ex-residents of western Missouri counties, crossed the Missouri at a point about nine miles above St. Joseph (near, or at, present Amazonia, it is said), and encamped in the river bottoms (of present Burr Oak township, Doniphan county).

At that location, on the Sac & Fox reserve (evidently by agreement with the Indians and the subagent), these prospective Oregonians remained for over two months. By early April 30 families were in the "Kansas" camp; and many more persons were preparing to join them. *See* May 9 entry.

(In the late summer of 1843 Cornelius Gilliam, of Platte county, Mo., had published a notice that he intended to emigrate to Oregon in the spring of 1844; and that the rendezvous would be on the Missouri's right bank "opposite Owen's Landing, five miles west of Savannah [Mo.]," on the first Monday in May [*i. e.*, May 6].)

Ref: New York *Weekly Tribune*, September 16, 1843, and June 15, 1844; Oregon Pioneer Association *Transactions*, Portland, 16th annual reunion (1888), pp. 82-122 (E. E. Parrish diary), 18th annual reunion (1890), pp. 61-66 (John Minto's sketch of Mrs. Nancy Morrison), 31st annual reunion (1903), pp. 202-208 (W. S. Gilliam reminiscences); *Washington Historical Quarterly*, Seattle, v. 18 (April, 1927), pp. 93-102 (W. H. Rees article); *Oregon Historical Quarterly*, Salem, v. 2 (1901), pp. 119-167, 209-254, v. 17 (1916), p. 360; H. H. Bancroft's *History of Oregon* (San Francisco, 1886), v. 1, pp. 448-466 (pp. 465 and 466 contain a long list of names of the 1844 emigrants—the above party, and those who started from other points); Nebraska State Historical Society *Publications*, Lincoln, v. 20, p. 126, or *Daily Missouri Republican*, St. Louis, May 28, 1844; SIA, St. Louis, "Records," v. 8, typed copy, p. 304 (Subagent W. P. Richardson's November 22, 1843, letter); C. L. Camp, editor, *James Clyman Frontiersman* (c1960), pp. 57, 317.

❦ Writing March 3, from "Fort Scott, Indian Territory," Capt. George A. McCall, Fourth U. S. infantry, described the hunting to be had in the "Marmiton" [now Marmaton] river country:

Of each in its season, we have the deer, turkey, grouse, partridge, woodcock, snipe, plover, of half a dozen or more species; and on the lakes near the river, swans, geese, of two or three species; and ducks without number; pelicans, sand-hill cranes, &c. [Earlier he had mentioned quail and "pinnated grouse" —prairie chickens.] Altogether, including its fine climate, it is a glorious country for the sportsman. Deer I always hunt on horseback, and shoot them as they bounce from the tall grass or hazel-bushes that line the streams. . . .

Ref: George A. McCall's *Letters From the Frontiers* . . . (Philadelphia, 1868), pp. 416-418. McCall, at Jefferson Barracks, Mo., 1842-1843, was at Fort Scott by October, 1843, for, in *ibid.,* p. 418, he describes, under date of October 9 [1843], a jaunt on the branches of the "Marmiton," and mentions "Carlos' Branch," five miles below the post, and the "two Drywoods."

❧ March 15.—A "menagerie" of nine Osages, an interpreter, two Mexicans, and 12 buffaloes—all in charge of "Messrs. Dade and Wilkins" (Boonville, Mo., entrepreneurs), and en route East "to be exhibited at Baltimore during the conventions in May"—arrived at St. Louis aboard the steamboat *Wapello.*

A Baltimore publication stated that the "bison" had reached that city March 29. Early in May, a St. Louis paper reported that 15 Osages, two Mexicans, and 12 buffaloes (presumably the same travelling exhibition) had just come down the Missouri aboard the S. *White Cloud,* in care of "Mr. Bassett, of Boonville," who planned to show them in Kentucky, Virginia, and Tennessee.

Six of the exploited Osages, including a middle-aged chief, returned to St. Louis in July, "emaciated and nearly naked," after being abandoned and left destitute at Louisville, Ky.

Ref: *Missouri Democrat,* St. Louis, March 16, May 6, 1844; *Niles' National Register,* Baltimore, v. 66 (March 30, August 10, 1844), pp. 160, 394.

❧ March 31.—Mexico's president, Santa Anna, rescinded, in part, decrees of August, 1843, which had "entirely closed to all commerce" the frontier ports of entry (Taos, N. M., Paso del Norte, and Presidio del Norte, Chihuahua). But news that the custom-houses had been opened to restricted American trade did not reach Missouri till late(?) May; and there was *no spring caravan to Santa Fe in 1844.*

Ref: Josiah Gregg's *Commerce of the Prairies* (New York, 1844), v. 2, p. 177; M. G. Fulton, editor, *Diary & Letters of Josiah Gregg* (Norman, 1941), p. 132; J. J. Webb's *Adventures in the Santa Fé Trade, 1844-1847,* edited by R. P. Bieber (Glendale, 1931), p. 25.

❧ April 16.—On a tour of the "Indian Territory" for the domestic missions board of the Protestant Episcopal Church, the Rev. N. Sayre Harris, on horseback, entered southeastern "Kansas" (in present Cherokee county) and arrived at the "house of Mr. R [half-Cherokee John Rodgers, presumably], who, with thirty Cherokee families," lived, detached from the main body of the nation, on the 800,000-acre Cherokee Neutral Lands tract.

Subagent B. B. R. Barker, of the Neosho Subagency (in northeast "Oklahoma"), had guided Harris (and one? dragoon companion) to Rodgers' "substantial and commodious edifice," located in "a beautiful spot on the Spring river. . . ."

On the 17th Harris continued his journey northward—traveling 15 miles, and camping out; early the next afternoon, after a 42-mile ride he reached Fort Scott. Almost immediately Harris set out for "the Osage village"—on a fresh horse (supplied by Capt. Thomas Swords), and with 2d Lt. Allen H. Norton (Fourth U. S. infantry), and two dragoons as guides. Reaching the Neosho, Osages swam their horses over; and the white men crossed in a canoe. The near by village had about 50 lodges ("some nearly 100 feet long, others not more than 30"). Harris was entertained by Baptiste Mongrain (part-Osage), and by trader "Monsieur [Pierre M.] Papan, of the American Fur Company," in whose lodge he spent the night.

Next day Harris met "the chief of the band Pah-sha-sha" [Pa-hus-cah]—George White Hair, evidently, since he called him "a fine-looking man . . . favourably disposed to the improvement of his people." In the afternoon, many Osages, and Harris, crossed the Neosho and traveled several miles to greet the new subagent, John Hill Edwards (a Virginian), whose arrival with two well-filled wagons of specie and goods delighted the Indians. (Edwards, appointed February 14, served but briefly; he resigned in August.)

Returning to Fort Scott, Harris, in company with "Major W.," and some discharged soldiers, ferried the rain-swollen Marmaton river on the 22d; and, after a 28-mile journey up the Fort Leavenworth-Fort Gibson military road, reached the Marais des Cygnes. (Here, after dark, "Torches were lighted, spears seized, and fishing parties organized.") On the 23d the travelers nooned at "Cold Water Grove"; and spent the night at "Bartleston's" (John? Bartleson's) 40 miles north of the Marais des Cygnes, in Jackson county, Mo. Next day, Harris rode to the Fort Leavenworth Agency (present Johnson county—near state line); saw Agent R. W. Cummins; moved on to the Shawnee Methodist Mission; then visited the Baptist and Friends missions among the Shawnees; and spent the night with the Rev. E. T. Peery family at Delaware Methodist Mission, north of the Kansas river.

On April 25th Harris moved on to Fort Leavenworth where he was a guest of the commandant—Maj. Clifton Wharton. (*In 1827, as a Third infantry second lieutenant, and regimental adjutant, N. Sayre Harris had been present when "Cantonment Leavenworth" was founded!*) After visiting the Kickapoos, and the Iowa, Sac & Fox Presbyterian Mission on the 26th, he boarded a steamboat, at Fort Leavenworth, on the 27th, and went down the Missouri to St. Louis, en route to New York.

Ref: N. Sayre Harris' *Journal of a Tour in the "Indian Territory"* . . . (New York, 1844).

❧ April.—On the Kickapoo reserve, above Fort Leavenworth, a trader (presumably William H. Hildreth) was operating from a "portable store," which had been purchased in Ohio, and shipped by steamboat. Manufactured by "P[hilip] Hinkle" of Cincinnati, the "pannel work" building, 33 by 16 feet in size, had been "erected [on the spot] in one morning . . . with the aid of three men." So far as known, this was the first prefabricated house in "Kansas."

Ref: Harris, *op. cit.* Harris was so impressed by this building which was "proof against the weather," that he stopped in Cincinnati on his return East to inspect "Mr. P. Hinkle's [pattern] portable house," which had "two partitions, making three rooms." (*See KHQ,* v. 21, pp. 112, 113, for information on the Hinkle, Guild & Company "Cincinnati houses" of the 1850's erected in Kansas territorial towns.) *The Cincinnati Business Directory for the Year 1844* (Cincinnati, 1844), p. 25, under "Carpenters and Builders" listed: "Hinkle, Philip, Vine bet 2nd and Pearl." For Hildreth, *see* Agent R. W. Cummins' report on the Kickapoos in Comm'r of Indian Affairs *Report* for 1845.

❡ Late in April the Wyandots held first services in a not-yet-completed Methodist Episcopal church—a project promoted by Esquire Greyeyes in January. Approximately 200 (or one-third) of the Wyandots were Methodists when they arrived in "Kansas."

The hewn-log church (about 30' by 40') was located "near the center of the nation" (and near present 23d street and Washington boulevard, Kansas City, Kan., it is said). It was dedicated at the beginning of June (*see* p. 512). In 1847 a brick meeting house was erected (near what became 10th and Walker).

Ref: Comm'r of Indian Affairs *Report*, 1844 (Subagent Jonathan Phillips' report); A. T. Andreas and W. G. Cutler, *History of the State of Kansas* (Chicago, 1883), p. 1227; *KHC*, v. 9, p. 214; G. W. Harrington's *Historic Spots . . . of Wyandotte County, Kansas* (Merriam, 1935), pp. 121-124.

❡ In "Kansas" the season of "spring opened very early; but after about three weeks' pleasant weather in March, rains commenced, and continued up to the 1st of June so constant, as to render it quite impossible to plough or plant. . . ." (Ira D. Blanchard, June 30, 1844).

"After a mild winter and a delightsome opening of spring at the latter part of April the rains commenced falling in such torrents as to remind us of Noah's day. . . ." (Francis Barker, July 23, 1844).

Ref: *Baptist Missionary Magazine*, Boston, v. 24 (September, 1844), p. 284; "Barker Collection," in KHi ms. division.

❡ April.—At Munsee Moravian Mission (where Muncie, Wyandotte co., is today), the "venerable Brother [J. Christopher] Micksch" was building a new church.

This missionary died in "Kansas" in 1845, but no record of the month, or day, has been found. Sup't Thomas H. Harvey, St. Louis, in his September 10, 1845, report, mentioned the Munsees' "severe loss during this year by the death of the Rev. Mr. Mi[ck]sch," adding that the missionary was "remarkable for his piety and simplicity of manner," and that he had taught not only religion and letters, but had devoted his time "to the general improvement of the Indians."

Ref: Harris, *op. cit.*; Comm'r of Indian Affairs, *Report*, 1845 (Thomas Harvey's report, therein). *See* annals, p. 338, for an account of Munsee Moravian Mission.

❡ April-May.—Three men who had left Santa Fe about April 5, arrived at Independence, Mo., on May 13.

Numerous Indians (Comanches, Cheyennes, and Arapahoes) met en route, though friendly, had exacted tolls of tobacco and extra clothing.

Ref: New York *Weekly Tribune*, June 15, 1844.

❦ From about May 1 to June 22 Sup't Thomas H. Harvey, St. Louis, was absent from his headquarters on a tour of the Indian tribes in "Kansas."

His itinerary, in part: May 15, among the Weas and Piankeshaws (present Miami county); May 17, at the near by Peoria & Kaskaskia settlements; May 18-20, a guest at Pottawatomie Catholic Mission on Sugar creek (present Linn county); at "Clymer's Trading House" (present Neosho? county) May 22-25, to meet the Osages; at Fort Scott May 26, 27; May 29, at Pottawatomie creek, to visit the Pottawatomie Indians residing in that vicinity (present Franklin and Miami counties); June 1, at the Ottawa settlements (present Franklin county); June 4, at Shawnee Baptist Mission (present Johnson county); June 6-7, at Fort Leavenworth; June 8, among the Kickapoos (north of the military post); June 11, at the Stockbridge settlements (present Leavenworth county); June 12, among the Delawares (present Wyandotte county).

Flooded streams prevented Harvey from visiting the Iowa and Sac & Fox Indians (but he paid a "flying visit" to the Great Nemaha Subagency in August, while en route, by steamboat, to the Council Bluffs); and such was "the overwhelming state of the waters" that he could not get to the Wyandot settlements. Nor did he visit the Kansa.

Ref: Office of Indian Affairs (OIA), Letters Received from SIA, St. Louis (National Archives Microcopy 234, Roll 753), for Harvey's June 24, 1844, letter; *Niles' National Register*, v. 66 (August 10, 1844), pp. 393-395; T. H. Kinsella's *The History of Our Cradle Land* . . . (Kansas City, 1921), p. 229; Comm'r of Indian Affairs, *Report*, 1844 (Harvey's October 8, 1844, report, therein); OIA, Letters Received from Osage Subagency (National Archives Microcopy 234, Roll 632), for Harvey's May 27, 1844, letter.

❦ Early in May the American Fur Company's new steamboat *Nimrod* (Joseph Sire, captain) passed along the "Kansas" shore, on her way to Fort Union on the Upper Missouri. (She had left St. Louis April 30.)

The passengers included wealthy, gregarious, pleasure-seeking le Comte d'Otranto (son of Bonaparte's minister of police), with a retinue of servants; also le Comte de Peindry; and, apparently, Scotsman Alexander H. Murray was aboard.

Delayed by low water at the Omaha village, the *Nimrod* did not arrive at the mouth of the Yellowstone till June 22. She started back on the 24th; and reached St. Louis July 9 (or 11?). In her cargo were 1,250 packs of buffalo robes, about 20 packs of furs, and several packs of buffalo tongues and meat. She brought down, also, six buffaloes, an elk, and two beavers.

Ref: *Niles' National Register*, v. 66 (July 27, 1844), p. 352; H. M. Chittenden's *History of Early Steamboat Navigation* . . . (New York, 1903), v. 1, pp. 154-166; SIA, St. Louis, "Records," v. 7, typed copy, pp. 446, 447; St. Louis *Democrat*, July 12, 1844; Alexander H. Murray's April, 1844, letter stating: "I am off for the Rocky Mountains on the 25th instant, having made arrangements with the American Fur Co. to proceed on my way thither . . ."—as quoted in Eberstadt & Sons *Catalogue 161*, p. 54. The *Publications of the Canadian Archives*, Ottawa, No. 4 (1910), which contains Murray's "Journal of the Yukon 1847-48," states that he entered the service of the Hudson's Bay Company as a senior clerk in 1846. Joseph Fouché, duke of Otranto, who was minister of police under Napoleon, had died in 1820. John E. Sunder's *The Fur Trade on the Upper Missouri, 1840-1865* (Norman, Okla., 1965), pp. 72-75, contains data on the American, and Union, Fur Company activities on the Missouri in 1844.

❈ May.—Union Fur Company traders John A. N. Ebbetts, Fulton
Cutting, and some companions coming down from the Yellowstone
(and reaching St. Louis May 8), reported a mild winter, with but
little snow in the upper Missouri country. (At Weston, Mo., they
had boarded a steamboat.)

Three of the Company's Mackinaw boats, "richly laden with Buffalo robes
and furs" arrived at St. Louis May 22. By the sinking of a fourth boat, a few
days earlier, about 150 bales of buffalo robes had been lost.

Ref: *Niles' National Register*, v. 66 (June 1, 1844), p. 224; St. Louis *Democrat*, May
23, 1844; OIA, Letters Received from SIA, St. Louis (National Archives Microcopy No. 234,
Roll 753), has D. D. Mitchell's abstract of trading licenses issued January 1-September 30,
1842, which includes the Ebbetts & Cutting license of July 16, 1842; Sunder, *op. cit.*, p. 72.

❈ May 9.—The Oregon-bound emigrants whose starting-point was
in present Doniphan county, on the Missouri river, some nine miles
above St. Joseph, Mo.—*see* March 2 annals entry—began their
journey West, heading first for the Great Nemaha Subagency, about
20 miles distant.

The vanguard crossed Wolf river (creek) and set up a camp
near the Subagency (not far from present Highland) on May 11.
Heavy rains fell that night sending streams out of their banks and
washing away Wolf river bridge on the 12th. (On this day, too,
an invalid named Bishop died. Rev. William Hamilton of the
near by Presbyterian mission conducted his funeral services.)

Two "canoes" were built to get the stranded emigrants' wagons
across the "river." (Rains continued, and it was May 17 before
all stragglers had caught up, and the company was under way
again.) At the camp near the Subagency, about May 15, the emigrants organized. Cornelius Gilliam was chosen to command the
brigade, which, at first, was divided into three companies, captained by Robert W. Morrison, William Shaw, and Richard Woodcock. Willard H. Rees was named adjutant. In a letter written
on the 15th, "General" Gilliam, stated that the emigrants then
numbered 323 (48 families, 108 men—60 of them younger men, 167
children), with 72 wagons, 713 head of horned cattle (410 oxen,
160 cows, 143 young cattle), 54 horses, and 41 mules; and more
persons were yet to arrive. According to Rees, the three companies
averaged 27 wagons each; and some half dozen wagons joined
afterwards. He also stated there were, finally, 115 men, rank and
file. John Minto recollected there were 84 wagons when the emigrants left this camp.

The theft of some cattle by Iowa Indians (a matter amicably settled by
Subagent W. P. Richardson) caused some delay. But rains and sickness were

the chief causes for the wagon train's slow progress. (Another factor was inept leadership.) John Minto later wrote: "During the first two months we were on the way, we only had eight days in which it did not rain. . . . This dampness told against the health of the camp." Apparently two persons— one a child—died while the emigrants were in the Big Nemaha area.

Happier events were the wedding of Martin Gilliam and Elizabeth Asabill on the night of May 20 (at a camp in present Brown county); and the first birth in camp, which was on May 31. Rev. Edward E. Parrish (whose diary is a principal source of information on this detachment of Oregonians) performed the marriage ceremony.

On June 7, after nearly a month on the road, "General" Gilliam's company arrived at the "Creek Vermillion" (Black Vermillion of today, in Marshall county). They had traveled westward less than 100 miles! Wrote E. E. Parrish: "We found the creek up and rising, and are waterstayed until we build a boat." From the 8th through the 14th, heavy rains fell. On the 17th and 18th, using newly built "canoes," the emigrants finally crossed "Creek Vermillion," and proceeded to the Big Blue some 13(?) miles distant.

The first section of the train (Woodcock's company) got across the Big Blue on June 19(?) using two canoes and platform left by some earlier-passing emigrants (who had started from Independence). But it was June 24 before the last of the cattle were on the west bank (presumably a few miles below present Marysville). Under way again on June 26, the emigrants now traveled the established Oregon trail to the Platte—reaching it on July 7.

Subsequently, on the South Platte, General Gilliam resigned, and the companies reorganized. No great calamities befell these emigrants. Most of them went to Oregon, some reaching their destination in October; but the families did not arrive till the fore part of November.

Ref: Same as for March 2 annals entry. James Clyman (*op. cit.*, p. 77) wrote that on June 24 at "Burr oak creek" (Black Vermillion) they "Found the date of Mr. Gillhams [Gilliam's] company having crossed 4 days previous." See KHC, v. 16, pp. 276, 277, and J. H. Carleton's *The Prairie Logbooks* . . . (Chicago, 1943), August 16-18, 1844, entries, for (not entirely accurate) statements on the emigrants.

❦ May 13.—A grist and saw mill (costing $2,400) for the Pottawatomies of Sugar creek (present Linn county) was completed by millwright James B. Yager about May 10, and "accepted" on the 13th. But there was "no one suitable" among the Indians to run it. (On October 9 Joel Grover was appointed miller.)

Ref: 28th Cong., 1st Sess., *H. Doc. No. 42* (Serial 441), p. 20; SIA, St. Louis, "Records," v. 8, typed copy, pp. 322, 323. Yager's Indian department contract, dated July 6, 1843, called for completion of the mill by June 1, 1844.

❦ May 14.—Some 350 Oregon-bound emigrants (who had assembled at Independence, Mo., and come by way of Westport, Mo., into "Kansas") set out from "Lone Elm" rendezvous (present Johnson county). They had hired as pilot the experienced mountain man Moses ("Black") Harris; and their captain (formally elected at Wakarusa camp on the 25th) was Nathaniel Ford, of Howard county, Mo.

First-published statistics (in the *Western Expositor,* Independence, Mo.) indicated "Colonel" Ford's company contained 358 persons—55 married men with their wives (110), 80 single men, 168 children; and that there were 54 wagons, 500 head of cattle, 60 horses, and 28 mules. Yet to join (according to the *Expositor*) were several small parties "embracing in all 27 families, numbering about 125 souls," who had 10 wagons, 130 cattle, and some horses.

A notable member of the company was ex-fur trapper James Clyman (who had left the Rocky mountains in 1827—*see* p. 139). Clyman's diary, and some letters he wrote, supply almost all of the information known about these travelers. His mid-May diary entries indicate the conditions under which the company set out. He wrote, on the 14th: "Roads extremely bad owing to the Leate greate rains." (It rained "all day" on the 14th, too.) On the 15th he commented: "This morning the whole prairie covered in water Shoe mouth deep. . . ."

From May 22 through May 25 (in continuing rainy weather), many of the emigrants were stalled at flooded Wakarusa river (present Douglas county). Their camp was "about 8 or 10 miles" above its mouth. After the crossing was effected on May 26 it was "assertained that there ware 92 men present"; but more travelers were coming behind them.

Clyman, in a letter penned at Shunganunga creek (south of the Kansas river, in present Shawnee county) on May 30, wrote: "We arrived here yesterday; 39 wagons, about 100 men, and about the same no. of women and children. . . . [there are] 20 or 30 teams yet behind. 41 teams are [already] north of the Kansas river, and 10 teams three or four days ahead of us. You will perceive by this time that we muster about 100 wagons, and from 5 to 700 souls, when we are fairly collected."

He also stated: "We have had almost one continued shower of rain since we left the settlements. We are commencing to cross the Kansas river today, which will occupy all our exertions for the next two or three days. We shall not all get collected in one company in less than eight or ten days. . . ."

In his diary, on May 30, Clyman wrote: "our ferrying goes on Slowly it being difficult to get to the boat on account of the low grounds being overflown." (The emigrants were also occupied in trying to locate some horses stolen by Kansa Indians.) On June 4 "all hands still engage getting our stock across the river which is beginning to fall." On the 5th Clyman and others "crossed over the river [and] went 10 miles up . . . to the village of the head chief [Fool Chief] . . ." who promised to help get the stolen horses back.

Before they returned, camp had been moved to "Knife river" (present Cross creek, Shawnee county). Rains began anew, and on June 10 "Knife river" rose 15 feet during the day. On June 13, in mid morning, "after 80 hours steady rain," the sun came out. (*See, also,* June 10-19 entry.)

By June 18 all the wagons and stock were across "Knife river." The emigrants took to the uplands and made progress, though rainy weather continued. On the 20th they found a ford over the "Black vermillion" [*i. e.,* now Red Vermillion creek, Pottawatomie county]; and on June 23 "Struck the oregon trace on Cannon Ball Creek [present Rock creek] greate Joy at finding the trail and a good ford. . . ." On the 24th they reached "Burr oak creek" (Black

Vermillion, in Marshall county), where they "Found the date of Mr Gillhams [Gilliam's] company [the emigrants who had set out from the vicinity of St. Joseph, Mo.] having crossed 4 days previous." (*See* May 9 entry.)

The company with which Clyman traveled came to the Big Blue (some miles below present Marysville) on June 25; but the vanguard (10 wagons) of the Nathaniel Ford company of Oregonians had reached there about June 5. (Clyman, and companions, crossed on the 26th and 27th.)

Their subsequent adventures are not recounted here. James Clyman, in a letter from "Willamet Falls, Oregon, October 27, 1844," wrote that he had arrived October 13, "having been on the way 151 days from Independence . . . which was at least one month longer than were the last year's company of emigrants. This was owing to the unusual rains that fell during the first two months after our departure from Missouri."

Ref: Camp, *op. cit.*, pp. 57-118, 317; Bancroft's *History of Oregon*, v. 1, pp. 448-466.

℃ May.—Starting from Council Bluffs, Iowa ter., the last week of May, a combined Oregon-California emigrant company (about 40 men; 27 wagons), crossed the Missouri and pursued a westward course, *north of the Platte,* to Fort Laramie. Captained by Elisha Stephens, and guided, at times, by mountain man Caleb Greenwood and his sons, these emigrants traveled the route subsequently known as the Mormon trail, less delayed by bad weather than those who traveled "Kansas" routes this spring. West of South Pass they opened the route known till 1849 as the Greenwood cutoff, thereafter as the Sublette cutoff, to Bear river.

The California contingent (about 26 men, 8 women, 17 children; with from 11 to 20 wagons)—now referred to as the Stephens-Townsend-Murphy party—managed to get most of their wagons across the Sierra Nevada, opening "the trail up the Truckee River and over Donner Pass which became, until 1849, the primary avenue for overland travel into and out of California."

The Oregon contingent, captained by John Thorp (or Tharp), reached the Willamette well ahead of the companies from Independence and St. Joseph.

Ref: George R. Stewart, editor, *The Opening of the California Trail* (Berkeley, 1953); George R. Stewart's *The California Trail* (New York, c1962), pp. 53-82; Dale L. Morgan, editor, *Overland In 1846* . . . ((1963), v. 1, pp. 17-19 (p. 18 for quote above); New York *Weekly Tribune,* June 29, 1844; *Oregon Historical Quarterly,* v. 1 (September, 1900), pp. 272-276 (for "Reminiscences of William M. Case"), and *see, also,* v. 2, p. 233, v. 6, p. 358, v. 17, p. 360; Camp, *op. cit.,* pp. 317, 318. The compiler is much indebted to Dale L. Morgan, of Bancroft Library, for assistance on the above entry.

℃ May.—The Rev. James Wheeler, accompanied by his family (wife Caroline; children John, Thomas, and Mary), arrived at the Kaw's mouth by steamboat (from Sandusky, Ohio), to resume his work as pastor of the Wyandots' Methodist Episcopal church. (*See* p. 493.)

On June 2, in the recently completed log meeting house (*see* p. 506) Missionary Wheeler baptized infants born since the preceding fall. A two-story parsonage (costing about $1,500; located half a mile from the Kansas-Missouri junction)—said to have been the first *frame* structure erected in present Wyandotte county—was completed in July. It was the Wheelers' home for two years. (They left May 5, 1846.)

Ref: James Wheeler's letter of June 28, 1845, copy in KHi ms. division; W. E. Connelley, *The Provisional Government of Nebraska Territory and the Journals of William Walker* . . . (Lincoln, Neb., 1899), p. 178 (for Walker's diary entry of May 5, 1846); Andreas and Cutler, *op. cit.*, p. 1227; *KHC*, v. 9, pp. 214, 215.

❡ May 20-22.—At St. Louis, on the 20th, the Mississippi was "within two feet of the great flood in 1826." The Missouri was "rising fast"; and the Osage was out of its banks.

The steamboat *Lexington*, which had left Weston, Mo., on the 16th, and reached St. Louis on the 21st, reported a "rise of five or six feet behind." On May 22 the Mississippi crested at St. Louis—having come within a foot of its height in the 1826 freshet. The river began falling on the 24th. (The rise which preceded St. Louis' *second* flood of 1844 began about June 1.)

Ref: St. Louis *Democrat*, May 20-25, June 1, 1844.

❡ May 21.—At Pawnee Fork (present Pawnee county), eastbound Santa Fe trail travelers (nearly 100 men, with upwards of 50 wagons), long delayed by the flooded river, were able to effect a crossing. Some had been waiting since April 23.

The assembled traders' caravan included Bent, St. Vrain & Company's train (with proprietors Charles Bent, William Bent, and Ceran St. Vrain); a Mexican traders' train (in which were "three or four Mexican ladies and several children"); also some Indians of note: Cheyenne chief Slim Face (going east on a mission for his people), aging Shawnee war chief Spy Buck (returning home); and the young Arapahoe "Friday" (whom Thomas Fitzpatrick had rescued in 1831).

Traveler Rufus Sage (one of those who had spent four weeks on Pawnee Fork's west bank) wrote that the "dense bands of buffalo that thronged the vicinity abated somewhat the annoyance of delay." He also remarked that Pawnee Fork—called by the Indians "Otter creek" because of the "great number of those animals found upon it"—had "an inexhaustible supply of cat-fish, which were caught in great numbers by our party."

Having crossed Pawnee Fork on the 21st, the "caravan" progressed 20-some miles in the next three days—to Walnut creek, where, wrote Sage: "The bottoms were so completely flooded that we were forced to occupy an adjoining eminence for a camp." From May 24 till after mid-June, Walnut creek was impassable.

Ref: *Rufus B. Sage* . . ., L. R. and Ann W. Hafen, editors (Glendale, 1956), v. 2, pp. 292-298; David Lavender's *Bent's Fort* (1954), pp. 230, 231. The Missouri-bound "Mexican traders' train" undoubtedly was headed by James Wiley Magoffin (a Kentuckian who first had engaged in trade at Chihuahua in the 1820's; served as the first U. S. consul there; and married, about 1830, Mary Gertrude Valdez, of Chihuahua). Stella M. Drumm, ed., *Down the Santa Fe Trail* . . . (1926), quoted James W. Magoffin's son Joseph as follows: "In 1844 my father and family and my Uncle Samuel [Magoffin], who was not then married, left Chihuahua for the States, and my father settled near Independence, Missouri. He bought a farm there, and my mother died there in January, 1845. Of course, our journey from Chihuahua to Independence [in 1844] was overall."

❡ May 22-25.—Sup't Thomas H. Harvey, of St. Louis, writing from "Clymer's Trading House, Osage Sub Agency" (in present Neosho? county) on the 25th:

I arrived at this place on the 22d instant. . . . It has rained ever since I arrived [in the Indian country?], except one day. The Neosho . . . is very high, having overflowed its banks and covered the bottoms to a considerable depth, which makes the river in most places more than a mile wide. The canoes used by the whites have been mostly carried off by the flood. . . . Notwithstanding the rains and high water, a considerable number of Osages, with their principal chiefs, called to see me, many of them swimming the river. . . .

Ref: *Niles' National Register*, v. 66 (August 10, 1844), p. 395. Harvey had reached present Kansas before mid-May—*see* annals, p. 507.

❡ May.—A Jesuit priest and 20(?) other young men, referred to by their guide, Andrew W. Sublette, as the "company of Catholicks," left Westport, Mo., some time after May 21, to travel the Oregon trail. Half of the group were invalids, seeking health by making a journey West.

About June 8, beyond the Kansas crossing, the party caught up with the Oregon emigrants at flooded "Knife river" (present Cross creek, Shawnee co.). Ten days elapsed before any of the westbound travelers were under way again. (The Catholic company traveled alone most of the time.) Two of the invalids were then so ill Sublette thought they would "not stand many days longer." The first to go was James H. Marshall, of St. Louis, who was buried on June 27, apparently near the Black Vermillion crossing (present Marshall county). Mr. Ketchum, also of St. Louis, died July 3 (and he was buried on "Ketchum's creek" some 10 miles beyond the Big Blue crossing). Mr. Browning died on July 6; and before July 13 a fourth death occurred—according to emigrant E. E. Parrish.

Upon reaching Fort Laramie, in early August, the party dispersed. Andrew Sublette went no farther West; but at least one of the group did. On October 1 the "Roman priest, with several French Indians" made camp near Fort Boise [Ida.].

Ref: C. L. Camp, *op. cit.*, pp. 58, 78, 81-83, 267; Oregon Pioneer Association *Transactions*, 16th annual reunion (1888), pp. 94, 98, 101, 111, and 31st annual reunion (1903), p. 204; John E. Sunder's *Bill Sublette* (1959), p. 225; *The Colorado Magazine*, Denver, v. 10 (September, 1933), pp. 179-184; *Pacific Historical Review*, Berkeley and Los Angeles, v. 28 (November, 1959), pp. 337-339; New Orleans *Weekly Picayune*, April 23, 1844; *Niles' National Register*, v. 68 (July 12, 1845), p. 292 (for J. H. Marshall). William Findley, en route to Oregon in 1845 (with a company starting from St. Joseph, Mo.) in his "Overland Journal," noted, under date of June 2, "Passed the grave of Mr. I. P. W. Chutheson[?] of St. Louis. Died June 29, 1844." The site was just beyond the Big Blue crossing.

❡ May 30.—"Never saw such a time of rain," wrote the Ottawas' missionary Jotham Meeker, from his home on the Marais des

Cygnes (in present Franklin county). "It has fallen almost every day in the last three weeks. The river has overflown its banks, and the bottoms in many places have been inundated more or less for three weeks. . . ." (*See, also,* June 10-17 entry.)

Ref: Meeker's "Diary," in KHi ms. division.

❡ June 1.—Dr. Johnston Lykins (Baptist missionary) was appointed "Physician for the Potawatomies" of the Osage [Marais des Cygnes] River Subagency—*i. e.,* the approximately 2,000 Pottawatomies in "Kansas."

Ref: SIA, St. Louis, "Records," v. 7, typed copy, p. 438.

❡ Summer.—Missouri river steamboats making two or more trips up to, or beyond, the "Kansas" area during the season included the *John Aull, Lewis F. Linn, Missouri Mail, Iatan, Mary Tompkins, Tobacco Plant, Omega, Nodaway, Lexington, Balloon, Admiral, Annawan, Ione,* and *Western Belle.*

The *Nimrod* (American Fur Company), in addition to the spring trip to Fort Union, made a journey up to the Council Bluffs in August; and the *Frolic* (Union Fur Company boat) went to the upper Missouri in August. In the autumn the *Yucatan* made an October trip to Weston, Mo.; and the *General Brooke* went up to St. Joseph in November.

It is said that the *Annawan, Lexington,* and *Colonel Woods* ascended the Little Platte river to Platte City, Mo., during the flood (*i. e.,* in June?); and that a small steamboat sank below the Falls of the Platte.

Ref: *Niles' National Register,* v. 44 (July 20, 1844), p. 331; St. Louis *Democrat,* issues between May-September, 1844; SIA, St. Louis, "Records," v. 7, typed copy, pp. 455, 456, 459, 476; T. A. Morris, *Miscellany* (1853), p. 346; R. S. Elliott, *Notes Taken in Sixty Years* (1883), p. 191; Remsburg "Clippings," v. 2, p. 6 (in KHi library), or Atchison *Daily Globe,* April 17, 1924; W. M. Paxton's *Annals of Platte County, Missouri* . . . (1897), p. 62. The St. Louis *Democrat* of April 20, 1844, had noted the arrival of the *Frolic* "from Pittsburgh." For other information on the *Frolic* see Sunder's *The Fur Trade, op. cit.,* p. 73.

❡ June.—Early in the month Santa Fe traders Edward J. Glasgow and [George S.] Simpson, accompanied by "enterprising" William Bent, reached St. Louis—in advance of their flood-stalled wagons.

"Mr. [Ebenezer W.] Pomeroy, from Santa Fe," arriving about June 12, stated "no less than 60 wagons" had been delayed by high water at Pawnee Fork (*see* May 21 entry). Later in the month there was news that the Santa Fe traders had "thrown a bridge across Pawnee Fork."

Ref: New Orleans *Weekly Picayune,* June 11, 24, July 1, 1844; *Niles' National Register,* v. 66 (June 29, 1844), p. 281. See an article on Simpson, by H. L. Carter and Janet Lecompte, in L. R. Hafen, ed., *The Mountain Men, op. cit.,* v. 3, pp. 285-299. Ebenezer W. Pomeroy was Robert Aull's brother-in-law.—*See* Missouri Historical Society, St. Louis, *Collections,* v. 5 (June, 1928), p. 295.

❡ June 10-17.—Missionary Jotham Meeker (living near present

Ottawa) described the "great freshet" of 1844 on the Marais des Cygnes:

June 10.—The river is very high. . . . Put things away and prepare for the flood.

June 12.—At sunrise the water began to overflow the bank at our house, and continued to rise rapidly all day. At three P. M. it came into the dwelling-house, when we fled to the hills near us, the rain descending in torrents. . . . The river still continued to rise for thirty-six hours after we left, until the whole bottom country was from six to twelve feet deep. . . .

June 17.—Find that none of my crops or fences are left. . . . All my out-houses and all that was within them are swept away. Nothing left but the [much-damaged] dwelling house and office. . . .

The Ottawas have lost all of their fences and new crops, with a very small exception; some of their dwellings have been carried down the stream—many of them are lodged against trees. All their old corn has either been washed away or . . . become unfit to eat. Much of their stock, viz., fowls, hogs, cattle, and horses, have been drowned. I think there is not breadstuff in the nation to subsist them one week from this time [June 26]. . . .

Ref: Jotham Meeker's "Diary" (*loc. cit.*); and Meeker letter of June 26, 1844, in *Baptist Missionary Magazine*, v. 24 (September, 1844), pp. 282, 283; or, see *KHC*, v. 8, pp. 472-474.

❡ June.—At Pottawatomie Catholic Mission on (Big) Sugar creek —a Marais des Cygnes tributary—Father Christian Hoecken recorded that it had been raining for "forty days in succession," and that "great floods covered the country . . . [but] damage . . . was not great [in the mission area]."

Ref: Father Hoecken's "Diary," as published in Kinsella, *op. cit.*, p. 229.

❡ June.—The Fort Leavenworth-Fort Gibson military road was "greatly injured" by the excessive rains. Bridges over many of the small streams were destroyed in the flood waters; and the 275-foot "substantial" structure over Sugar creek was also carried away.

(Passing over this route in mid-October, Bishop Morris, and companions, found travel difficult because of the boggy sloughs to be crossed where the bridges were out.)

Ref: 28th Cong., 2d Sess., *Sen. Doc. No. 1* (Serial 449), p. 147; Morris, *op. cit.*, p. 348.

❡ June 10-19.—In present Shawnee county, on the 10th "it commenced raining . . . [and] rained all day without a moments cesation. . . . Knife river [present Cross creek] . . . rose 15 feet during the day." (Thus wrote James Clyman, in his diary, as the Oregon-bound emigrants remained in camp near flooded "Knife river.") On the 11th rain fell again; on the 12th it rained all night. On the 13th, there was more rain, but at "10 A. M. we [the emigrants] saw the sun & a general shout was raised through all the camp after 80 hours steady rain we saw the Kanzas river from the Bluffs & it shews 8 or 10 miles wide . . ." (Clyman).

There was more rain on the 17th; and on the 19th "torrents of rain" fell, but the sun broke out about noon, and the emigrants (by then a few miles beyond "Knife river" crossing) "had several views of the Kanzas river which was overflown from Bluff to Bluff 8 or 10 miles wide . . .," as they moved westward.

Ref: Camp, *op. cit.*, pp. 74-76; *KHQ*, v. 20, pp. 73-81 (p. 73 "Available records indicate that the flood of 1844 was five to six and one half feet higher than the disastrous flood of 1951 from Manhattan to below Lawrence on the Kansas river, and at Ottawa on the Marais des Cygnes [Osage] river."—S. D. Flora).

❦ June.—On the 14th Agent R. W. Cummins, eastbound after "running some lines between The Kaws & Pawnees," reached the west bank of flooded Cross creek (present Shawnee county), opposite the camp of the Oregon emigrants.

Of Cummins' journey (outward, or returning) there is, apparently, only one other contemporary reference. The agent's statement of expenditures for June included this item: "J Pappe [Joseph Papin] For ferriage of agent's horses, &c $2.50." An account published 33 years later stated that "During the [1844] flood, Major Cumings [*i. e.*, Indian agent R. W. Cummins], wishing to cross from the south to the north side of the Kaw river, stepped into a canoe at about the corner of Topeka Avenue and Second street, and was rowed by an Indian from there to the bluffs . . . the water being twenty feet deep over the ground where North Topeka now stands. One of the Papans lived in a house on [what was in 1877] the island just above the bridge. This house stood the flood until the water came above the eaves and then was washed away. This island, at that time, was part of the main land."

Writing of the Kansa Indians (then, for the most part, residents of what is now "Shawnee county"), in his September report, Cummins commented: "they farm mostly in the bottom lands of the Kanzas river, which was [as he had witnessed] overflown from Bluff to Bluff, sweeping off all . . . [their] fencing, houses &cc."

Ref: Camp, *op. cit.*, p. 75; 28th Cong., 2d Sess., *H. Doc. No. 139* (Serial 465), p. 53; W. W. Cone's *Historical Sketch of Shawnee County, Kansas* . . . (Topeka, 1877), p. 7; Comm'r of Indian Affairs *Report* for 1844 (Cummins' September 21, 1844, report, therein); *KHQ*, v. 20, p. 76.

❦ June.—From about the 13th to the 16th the flood on the *lower* Kansas river was at its peak.

Missionary Ira D. Blanchard, of Delaware Baptist Mission (present Wyandotte county), wrote on June 30:

The first days of June were . . . fine . . .; but, to the surprise of all, the rain again commenced, and for two weeks fell in perfect torrents. The Kanzas river rose at least 20 feet above what had been supposed to be high 'water mark,' carrying with it houses, farms, cattle, horses, &c., and sweeping the whole bottom country. Thousands of families along the water courses are without any thing to shelter them from the storms, and many of them have lost their last morsel of food. The state of things beggars all description. This [mission] station is three-fourths of a mile from the Kanzas, and on grounds a little raised from the bottom, so that the water was just to us, and did no damage. But the [Delaware] village near us, is all destroyed. There is not even a stalk of corn left in all their fields; and their old stock [of grain] all carried away by the flood. . . . [Of the destroyed Delaware village, it was later reported that the inhabitants—most of them—moved up "on the *high* prairie, distant nearly six miles" from the Baptist mission.]

Missionary Francis Barker, of Shawnee Baptist Mission (present Johnson county), wrote (on July 23) of the June flood:

The waters came up over the banks of the creeks and rivers so as to be in many places fifteen feet high where they were never known to come before. Fences were swept away invariably, the newly planted crops destroyed, young orchards, &c., among the rest, the most of the buildings within several miles of the rivers or as far as the river bottoms extended, were swept away, corn cribs and all. Hogs were drownded, many horses and cattle also. Many persons barely escaped with their lives leaving all behind. Many[?] have been drowned in the white settlements. I have not heard of any of the Ind[ian]s drownding. . . .

Our Mission is several miles from the [Kansas] river bottom . . . but our crops have been very much injured by the continued rains as is universally the case throughout the region. We still have the clouds lowering around us with only here and there a day of sunshine. The roads are almost impassable on acc[oun]t of the mud. . . .

Agent R. W. Cummins, from his headquarters (present Johnson county), wrote on January 6, 1845:

There are about 80 Munsees, 171 Shawnees, & 240 Delawares, that were deprived of bread stuffs by the freshets last spring—the most of these families lost their houses as well as their crops & fences, and many of them their old corn in their cribs or houses, and a great many hogs, some cattle & horses."

Ref: *Baptist Missionary Magazine*, v. 24 (September, 1844), p. 284 (for Blanchard), v. 25 (July, 1845), p. 163; "Barker Collection" (in KHi ms. division); SIA, St. Louis, "Records," v. 8, typed copy, p. 419.

❮ June.—Missionary John G. Pratt (of Shawnee Baptist Mission in 1844), at a later time, recalled that during the flood a large steamboat came up the Kansas as far as the Delaware (or Grinter, or military road) Crossing; and that it brought "a lot of lumber for the use of traders."

Ref: "Pratt Collection" (in KHi ms. division).

❮ June 13-16.—At the Kaw's mouth, on the 13th, the Missouri river was "only a few feet over the bottom lands" (according to an account published 37 years later), "but the great volume of water that came down the Kansas River madly rushing against the mighty Missouri, caused the seething waters to pile up at the mouth. . . ." In a 12-hour period, on the 14th, there was an enormous rise of eight to ten feet.

Swept away were all the buildings in the low areas—the homes of the French-Indian settlers, the Kansas Town Company warehouse, and all other buildings in the Westport Landing, Mo., area. At Chouteau's Landing, some two miles below the Kaw's mouth, the flood "left not a vestige of the entire homestead [dwellings, warehouses, etc.], and [when the water receded] the surface of the entire farm [of Mme. Berenice Chouteau, widow of Francis G.] was a wide expanse of sand in many places five feet deep." (John C. McCoy)

Ref: W. H. Miller's *The History of Kansas City* . . . (Kansas City, Mo., 1881), pp. 36, 37, or *The History of Jackson County, Missouri* . . . (Kansas City, Mo., 1881), pp. 403-406; *The Kansas Monthly*, Lawrence, v. 2 (June, 1879), p. 83 (for quote from McCoy). At the Kaw's mouth, the Missouri, in 1844, was said to have crested six feet or more above its rise in late May and early June, 1843.

❡ June 17.—Mule-mounted, Rufus Sage (stranded, since May 24, with the eastbound wagon trains at flooded Walnut Creek Crossing —*see* May 21 entry) forded the Arkansas above the mouth of Walnut creek and proceeded down the river's right bank some four miles to make camp. His only companion was a young Arapahoe Indian—"Friday."

On the 18th these two recrossed the Arkansas, striking the Santa Fe trail near Plum Buttes. Continuing eastward "by easy stages," they reached Council Grove five days later (June 22?).

Sage (later) wrote: "We were detained [at Council Grove] . . . for five or six days [June 23-27?] by a continuous rain which raised the creek [*i. e.,* Neosho river] to an extraordinary height,—overflowing its banks and completely flooding its extensive bottoms. So sudden was the rise that we were compelled to move camp three times in the course of an hour, and were finally driven to an adjoining hill."

When it was possible to travel again, Sage (bound for Van Buren, Ark.) said good by to Friday and struck off down the Neosho. About the end of June he reached "the Osage village," where he was "kindly entertained by a chief," and stayed two days. He reached his destination late on July 4, after crossing the lands of the Quapaws, Shawnees, and Cherokees (in present eastern Oklahoma).

Ref: L. R. and Ann W. Hafen, eds., *Rufus Sage* . . ., *op. cit.,* v. 2, pp. 298-310.

❡ June 21.—The Liberty (Mo.) *Pioneer* estimated the Missouri to be five feet higher than in the 1826 flood; and related that the steamboat *Mary Tompkins,* to the terror of all aboard, had been swept out of the river's channel into "the Wacondah prairies," where she broke down many of the tallest cottonwoods in her path. From Weston to the Missouri's mouth, the lowlands were flooded, with crops destroyed; cattle, sheep, hogs, etc., drowned; homes inundated or swept away. The inhabitants had taken refuge "on high ground, or aboard steamboats or flatboats."

Ref: *Niles' National Register*, v. 66 (July 20, 1844), pp. 330, 331.

❡ June 24.—By noon, in St. Louis, the Mississippi had risen to "38 feet 7 inches of a plumb rise above low water mark." (This was well over four feet higher than during "the great flood of 1785.") But the crest was on June 26, or the day after. On the 28th the water began to recede.

Ref: *Niles' National Register*, v. 66 (July 20, 1844), pp. 330, 331; St. Louis *Democrat*, June 24-27, 1844.

❡ June 25.—At Weston, Mo., the Missouri river had gone down about four feet (as reported by the *Western Belle*, which left there the morning of the 25th; and reached St. Louis on, or before, the 29th).

Ref: *Niles' National Register*, v. 66 (July 20, 1844), p. 306.

❡ Summer.—Fourteen Iowa Indians, and their interpreter (mulatto Jeffrey Dorney), went abroad on an exhibition tour, under the conductorship of George H. C. Melody. Frank White Cloud (Mahaska), first chief of the nation, Walking Rain (Neumonya), third-ranking chief, five warriors, one youth, four women, one girl, and one infant, were in the party. (*See* illustration, p. 607.)

The Iowas had left their reserve in (or by) December, 1843. (They were in St. Louis on December 25.) Part of the winter of 1843-1844 was spent in New Orleans. They set out across the Atlantic in the summer of 1844 (from New York?) and reached London in mid-July. Artist George Catlin and Melody joined forces to exhibit Indian paintings and the Iowas. While in England the Iowas met some of the royal family; and once were entertained at breakfast by Disraeli. They appeared in Scotland in February, 1845; and in Ireland in March. On April 21, in France, they were received by King Louis Philippe. Three of the group died abroad—Roman Nose, and the infant "Corsair" in England; O-kee-we-me (wife of Little Wolf), in France.

Eleven Iowas arrived in Boston aboard the *Versailles* on August 27, 1845; They remained in the East for over two months; finally reached their "Kansas" homes (present Doniphan county) in mid-November.

Subagent W. P. Richardson, in his October 6, 1844, report on the Iowa Nation, suggested the year's notable decrease (of over 50 per cent) in liquor consumption by the Iowas was probably due to the absence of "two of their Chiefs, and their old interpreter Jeffery Derroway."

Ref: George Catlin's *Notes of Eight Years' Travels and Residence in Europe* (New York, 1848), v. 1, p. 294, v. 2, pp. 1-275, 327, 328; *Colorado Magazine*, v. 26 (April, 1949), pp. 143-151; Carolyn T. Foreman's *Indians Abroad* . . . (Norman, 1943), pp. 185-198; Comm'r of Indian Affairs, *Reports*, 1844, 1846; T. L. McKenney and James Hall's *The Indian Tribes of North America* . . . (Edinburgh, 1934), v. 2, p. 114; *Niles' National Register*, v. 65 (December 9, 1843), p. 226, v. 68 (June 14, August 2, 1845), pp. 229, 339, v. 69 (September 6, 1845), p. 6; Robert R. Wright's September 8, 1939, letter (copy) to OIA (in L. Barry's files); New York *Weekly Tribune*, August 2, 1845;

KHQ, v. 28, p. 280. Wright Howes, in his *U. S. iana* . . . (New York, 1962), p. 386, lists a 24-page book (with eight plates) by George H. C. Melody, entitled *Notice sur les Indiens Ioways* . . . *venu des plaines du Haut-Missouri* . . ., published in 1845. (Not seen by this compiler.)

ℂ MARRIED: Abelard Guthrie, recently of Ohio, and Quindaro Nancy Brown, daughter of Adam Brown (a Wyandot Indian) and his Shawnee wife, "in the early summer," [*i. e.*, June?] within present Kansas City, Kan., presumably by the Rev. James Wheeler.

The one-time town "Quindaro" (now part of Kansas City), founded in late 1856, was named for Mrs. Guthrie.

Ref: Connelley, *op. cit.*, pp. 103-107. (Connelley says Guthrie arrived in "Kansas" in January, 1844; that he had met Miss Brown while working for the Indian agent at Upper Sandusky, Ohio, and that subsequent to the marriage Guthrie was adopted into the Wyandot Nation.) *KHC*, v. 6, p. 98; *KHQ*, v. 22, p. 305, 306 (for Quindaro).

ℂ June.—On the Smoky Hill river (perhaps near the present Colorado-Kansas line?), "a band of Sioux consisting of about 60 lodges, and 25 lodges of Chyans, came on a small [hunting] party of 15 Delawares . . . and killed them all." The victims included several men "highly esteemed" in the nation. "Captain Swanac [Shawanock] the great Delaware War Chief was one of the number."

The Cheyennes told George Bent that the Delawares killed three and wounded three of their men; and killed four Sioux and wounded five. Lt. John C. Fremont, and party, starting east from Bent's Fort on July 5, met the Sioux-Cheyenne "village" that day on the upper Arkansas. Wrote Fremont: "They were desirous that we should bear a pacific message to the Delawares on the frontier, from whom they expected retaliation." The massacre had occurred a "few days previous."

Ref: SIA, St. Louis, "Records," v. 8, typed copy, pp. 339 and 482; John C. Fremont's *Report* . . ., *1843-'44* (Washington, 1845), p. 288; *Niles' National Register*, v. 66 (August 17, 1844), pp. 397, 398; E. J. Stanley's *Life of Rev. L. B. Stateler* (1907), pp. 122, 123. On August 9, 1845, at Bent's Fort (Colo.), the Delawares and Cheyennes held a council on the subject of the 1844 massacre. Lts. J. W. Abert and G. W. Peck were among the few white men present.—*See* 29th Cong., 1st Sess., *Sen. Doc. No. 438* (Serial 477), pp. 4, 5.

ℂ Off the press in June were first copies of Josiah Gregg's two-volume *Commerce of the Prairies* (with illustrations, and a valuable map)—a work which was to become the classic account of the Santa Fe trail and Santa Fe trade. The New Orleans *Picayune's* reviewer wrote:

. . . so rich and varied are its contents that you cannot, if you would, skim through its pages at one or two sittings. . . . It should be in the possession of every one who feels any interest in the destinies of this country, as connected with the ultimate occupation and settlement of the prairies and the north-western portion of Mexico by the Anglo-Saxon race. (*See* portion of Gregg's map on p. 606 in this volume.)

Ref: Fulton, *op. cit.*, pp. 140-144; *Weekly Picayune*, New Orleans, September 23, 1844.

❡ July 1.—John M. Armstrong (a lawyer; "an accomplished scholar"; one-eighth Wyandot) opened a school in present Kansas City, Kansas (a site described in 1879 as "on the east side of Fourth street, between Kansas and Nebraska avenues in Wyandott City"), in a newly completed frame school building.

Mrs. Lucy Armstrong stated (in 1879): "Though the school was for Wyandotts, and supported by their money [from a fund provided by the 1842 treaty], yet white children were admitted free of charge. Mr. Armstrong taught until 1845. . . ."

Because the Wyandot Council met in the building (at night, or during vacations), it was sometimes called the "Council House." On April 16, 1852, it was last used as a school house. Mrs. Armstrong was then the teacher.

Ref: Kansas City (Mo.) *Journal*, September 21 (or 20?), 1879, and June 8, 1901 (or, Kansas Biography Clippings, "A," v. 2, pp. 190, 191, and 197, in KHi library); Andreas and Cutler, *op. cit.*, p. 1228; Comm'r of Indian Affairs, *Report*, 1845 (Subagent Richard Hewitt's report); Harrington, *op. cit.*, pp. 133-137.

❡ Early July.—The "remainder of the Santa Fe Company" (from the caravan long stranded in "Kansas" by flooded streams) reached St. Louis on the 6th, aboard the *Missouri Mail*, bringing (by one report) "$90,000 in specie." Another account put the returns at "over $100,000 in specie, and a quantity of furs and Spanish hides." A small party, from Bent's Fort, was yet to arrive.

Ref: St. Louis *Democrat*, July 8, 1844; *Niles' National Register*, v. 66 (July 27, 1844), p. 352; New Orleans *Weekly Picayune*, October 14, 1844. Santa Fe traders Eugene and Thomas Leitensdorfer, it appears, were among those who had reached St. Louis, from Santa Fe, on June 21, 1844. See Webb, *op. cit.*, p. 41, footnote (reference to *Daily Missouri Republican*, St. Louis, June 22, 1844).

❡ July 9.—Homeward-bound, but still exploring, Lt. John C. Fremont, and his small company (perhaps around 20?), including Thomas Fitzpatrick, Charles Preuss, and Theodore Talbot, probably entered present Wallace county this day, after arriving July 8 at the headwaters of the Smoky Hill river (in eastern "Colorado").

(Now returning from California, where his second exploring expedition to the West—which had left eastern "Kansas" in May, 1843—see p. 481—had culminated in March, 1844, Fremont's circuitous marches eastward had brought him, and his men, to Bent's Fort [Colo.] on July 1. Four days later, on the march again, they had camped 20 miles down the Arkansas; and on July 6 had turned northeastward toward the upper reaches of the Smoky Hill.)

Moving downstream (along the north bank), on the 10th they marched 28 miles and entered the buffalo range; spent the 11th hunting and re-provisioning; "made a detour to the north [of the river] to get out of the way of the Comanches" on the 12th. Their camp of the 13th (apparently in southeast Gove county of today), was on a "high river prairie," by "an insignificant little stream." But a cloudburst in the night caused the bottomlands to flood, and the river (Fremont reported) "broke into the camp so suddenly, that the baggage was instantly covered, and all our perishable collections almost entirely ruined, and the hard labor of many months destroyed in a moment." Preuss wrote, on the 14th: "To dry the herbarium and everything else we are having a day of rest today, a Sunday."

After traveling 10 miles on the 15th, they came to a "deep branch" of the river. Neither this stream, nor the Smoky Hill, were yet fordable for the pack animals, so camp was made "at this fork" [which was, it appears, near the mouth of Hackberry creek in what is now southwestern Trego county]. A march of 23 miles was made on July 16. Next day, having proceeded some 17 miles (and now on the river's right bank), they "discovered a large village of Indians [nearly the entire Pawnee Nation] encamped at the mouth of a handsomely wooded stream" [Big Timber creek, entering the Smoky Hill near the present Ellis-Rush county line]. The Indians were returning from the Arkansas crossing where they had met the Kiowa and Comanche Indians. (Note the route of "Pawnee Trail" shown on the Fremont map in this volume.) The Pawnees treated Fremont's small force with "unfriendly rudeness" and "insolence." After "some delay, and considerable difficulty," the white men got out of the Indian village; and traveled 15 miles downriver before encamping. (Fremont later learned the Pawnee Loups had intervened to prevent the Grand Pawnees from massacring his party that night!)

About July 20(?), after having traveled "directly along . . . [the Smoky Hill's] banks [since July 8] for 290 miles," the explorer and his men left the river "where it bore suddenly off in a northwesterly direction [*i. e.*, northeasterly! direction], towards its junction with the Republican fork of the Kansas. . . ." [They left the river in present McPherson county.] Continuing an "easterly course" they came to the Santa Fe trail after about 20 miles' travel; and followed it to Missouri, arriving "on the last day of July . . . at the little town of Kansas . . ." [Kansas City, Mo.]. Lieutenant Fremont and most of his party reached St. Louis on August 6.

Ref: John C. Fremont's *Report* . . . (Washington, 1845), pp. 287-290, 293, 322; Charles Preuss, *Exploring With Fremont* . . . (c1958), pp. 138, 139; L. R. Hafen's *Broken Hand, The Life Story of Thomas Fitzpatrick* . . . (Denver, 1931), p. 161; H. H. Bancroft's *History of California* (San Francisco, 1884-1890), v. 4, pp. 436-439; New York *Weekly Tribune*, August 24, 1844 (from St. Louis *Missourian* of August 2), notes the arrival of Theodore Talbot at St. Louis on August 1; Agent Daniel Miller's September 6, 1844, report, in Comm'r of Indian Affairs *Report*, 1844, or, *see* SIA, St. Louis, "Records," v. 8, typed copy, pp. 352-363; Pawnee items from the journal of Clifton Wharton's 1844 expedition, in *KHC*, v. 16, pp. 296-299.

❡ July 11.—Bent, St. Vrain & Company's 20-wagon train (bringing 700 packs of buffalo robes, and four of beaver furs), arrived at Independence, Mo.—68 days after leaving Bent's Fort (on May 5), and a month later than usual (as a result of delays in "Kansas" due to flooded streams).

Charles Bent, and 25 of the company, reached St. Louis, aboard the *Lexington*, on July 18.

Ref: New York *Weekly Tribune*, August 3, 1844.

❡ July.—Three Union Fur Company Mackinaw boats, from the

Yellowstone, brought 550 packs of buffalo robes and furs down the Missouri; reached St. Louis on the 14th or 15th.

Ref: St. Louis *Democrat*, July 17, 1844; *Niles' National Register*, v. 66 (July 27, 1844), p. 352; Sunder's *The Fur Trade, op. cit.*, p. 72.

℃ July.—The steamboat *John Aull*, coming down from St. Joseph, Mo., carried some 200 passengers—many of them flood victims "returning to their old homes in other states." She reached St. Louis about July 17.

Ref: Nebraska State Historical Society *Publications*, v. 20, p. 128.

℃ BORN: on July 21, at Shawnee Methodist Mission, present Johnson county, Elizabeth C. Berryman, daughter of the Rev. Jerome C. and Sarah C. (Cessna) Berryman.

Ref: Remsburg "Stork Clippings," in KHi library; or, Leavenworth *Times*, September 21, 1925. (Elsewhere, Remsburg refers to correspondence he had with the Rev. Jerome C. Berryman, as the source of his information on the Berryman children.)

℃ July 26.—A letter from "Kansas, Mo." (Kansas City, Mo.—or, Westport Landing) stated: "A part of the California company has just arrived [by way of the Santa Fe trail]. They left Lower California on the 24th of May last. . . ."

Probably at Bent's Fort (Colo.) this returning party (size and personnel unknown) had met Lieutenant Fremont and his men; and traveled briefly (one day?) in company.

Ref: *Niles' National Register*, v. 66 (August 17, 1844), pp. 397, 398.

℃ Late July.—The steamboat *John Aull*, reaching the port of St. Louis on 29th, from Weston, Mo., reported a four-foot rise in the Missouri, "principally from the Kanzas and Little Platte rivers"; and that the Osage river was "very full."

Ref: St. Louis *Democrat*, July 30, 1844.

℃ Summer.—A blacksmith shop (of frame construction; and costing $197.50) for the Wyandot Indians was erected about half a mile from the mouth of the Kansas river, in present Kansas City, Kan.

Blacksmith Charles Graham (who arrived in the winter of 1843-1844) had selected the site—later described as near the northwest corner of Nebraska and Thirds streets. Samuel Ellis built the shop.

Ref: Comm'r of Indian Affairs, *Report*, 1844 (Subagent Jonathan Phillips' report, therein); SIA, St. Louis, "Records," v. 8, typed copy, pp. 299, 300, 343-348, 511; Andreas and Cutler, *op. cit.*, p. 1227; 28th Cong., 2d Sess., H. *Doc. No. 139* (Serial 465), p. 43.

℃ August.—At the Stockbridge Indian settlement (below Fort Leavenworth, in present Leavenworth county—*see* p. 387), teacher Jane Kelley opened a day school—the initial step in founding a separate Stockbridge Baptist Mission. (Since 1843 Stockbridge had been an out-station of Shawnee Baptist Mission, 30 miles distant.)

Though the school soon was suspended (due to prevalent sickness), and not reopened till January, 1845, buildings for the Stockbridge mission were commenced in the fall of 1844; and, before year's end, it appears, the Rev. John G. Pratt (missionary and printer) and his wife, Olivia (Evans) Pratt, removed there, from the Shawnee mission. They remained till the institution was discontinued in 1848.

Jane Kelley left in June, 1845. The day school, for a time, was taught by Sarah Wallace. In 1846 there were from 12 to 16 students; in 1847, 17 were in regular attendance.

Stockbridge Baptist Mission Church, organized April 13, 1845, had 16 members in the spring of 1846; and 16 in 1848, prior to merging with the Delaware Mission Church.

The "Meeker press" (at Shawnee Baptist Mission since 1834) was removed to Stockbridge Baptist Mission in the summer(?) of 1846; and was kept there till 1849. Items printed by Pratt at Stockbridge during 1846-1847 included "the gospel of John in Shawnee," a "new edition of part of the Shawanoe hymn book," and a "book of hymns in Delaware and Ojibwa for the Methodist Mission. . . ."

Ref: *Baptist Missionary Magazine*, v. 23 (1843), p. 139, v. 24 (1844), pp. 181, 182, v. 25 (1845), pp. 141, 162, 163, 273, v. 26 (1846), pp. 205, 206, v. 27 (1847), pp. 258-260, v. 28 (1848), p. 280; *KHQ*, v. 2, pp. 243-250; Comm'r of Indian Affairs, *Report, 1845* (R. W. Cummins' report, therein).

❡ August 12.—Maj. Clifton Wharton and five First U. S. dragoon companies (headed by Capts. P. St. George Cooke, John H. K. Burgwin, Benjamin D. Moore, Burdett A. Terrett, and Lt. Philip Kearny) left Fort Leavenworth and began a march to the Pawnee villages on the Platte. The expedition was undertaken to impress the Indians with the power of the U. S. government; and to reconcile, if possible, Pawnee-Sioux difficulties. The cavalcade included two 12-pound howitzers; a train of 15 mule-drawn wagons (two were sent back at the Big Blue); and perhaps 350 animals in all.

Other officers were Capt. William M. D. McKissack (AQM), Surg. Samuel G. I. De Camp; Lts. Andrew J. Smith, J. Henry Carleton (a "logbook" he kept provides some colorful details), John Love, Thomas C. Hammond, George T. Mason, and Chaplain Leander Ker. Also along was artist Charles Deas. A 72(?)-year-old Indian guide—Jim Rogers—proved to be of more hindrance than help.

On the 14th Wharton and his command veered left from the old Council Bluffs road and set a northwestward course to search out a new, more direct pathway to the Pawnee towns. (Also, on this date, Private Clough died.) The major's journal tells of many difficulties encountered as the dragoons pursued this "experimental" route. On the 16th they intersected, and followed the track made in the spring by the Oregon emigrants (Gilliam's company);

but abandoned it on the 17th when led into a cul-de-sac. On August 22 they reached, and crossed the Big Blue, apparently not far from what is now the Kansas-Nebraska line.

From the waters of the Little Blue they crossed to the Platte, striking it (on the 27th) "nearly opposite the mouth of the *Loup-fork.*" (Another trooper —Private Thompson—died on the 26th.) Moving up the Platte's valley some 30 miles, the dragoons camped near a Pawnee town on the 29th; and on August 30, Major Wharton counciled with the chiefs of the Grand and Republican Pawnee bands. In the afternoon he and his men crossed the Platte and moved 18 miles northward to the Loup Fork. On the 31st they crossed; and Wharton counciled with the Loup and Tappage Pawnee bands.

On September 1 the expedition started down the river valley; reached the bank of the Missouri on the 6th, and camped about a mile from Bellevue (agency). Wharton counciled with the Otoes on the 7th; on the 10th and 11th the dragoons crossed the Missouri to the Pottawatomies' reserve; and the major had an informal talk with Chief Wabaunsee, and others. Then the dragoons marched, on the 12th, down the Missouri's left bank; reached the northern line of Missouri on the 13th; crossed the Big Tarquio (by ferry) on the 15th. On the 17th Wharton sent most of the wagons, and a small dragoon detachment, to Fort Leavenworth by way of Carrollton and Weston.

He and his command reached "Jeffrey's, or Iowa Point" (on the Missouri's left bank) the evening of the 17th; crossed next day on a ferry boat (the horses were made to swim over); and by evening the dragoons were encamped near the Great Nemaha Subagency—some seven miles from Iowa Point. Wharton noted: "There is quite a little village here, consisting of the houses of the Sub-Agent, of two Missionaries, Blacksmith, Farmer, and others. We are not a little astonished to find so many White persons living at this place."

On the 19th he met the Iowa, and Sac & Fox Indians in council. "Na-cha-min-ga" (No Heart), second chief of the Iowas, spoke for his nation. (Head chief White Cloud was in Europe at this time). "Ne-so-quot," Sac chief, spoke for his people. Company K remained at the subagency to assist in the forthcoming payment of annuities to the Indians. Wharton and the rest of his command continued the homeward march on the 19th; reached Fort Leavenworth on September 21.

Ref: *KHC*, v. 16, pp. 272-305 (for Wharton's journal); Carleton, *op. cit.*, pp. 3-152; also, *see* P. St. G. Cooke's *Scenes and Adventures in the Army* . . . (Philadelphia, 1857). *See* annals index for citation on Iowa Point. Also, *see* the reminiscences of William Banks, in *The History of Holt and Atchison Counties, Missouri* . . . (St. Joseph, 1882), for data on "Jeffrey's, or Iowa Point." Capt. Burdett A. Terrett (Company A, First dragoons) had come from Fort Scott (left July 5) to join Wharton's command. He brought to Fort Leavenworth with him, three sergeants, three corporals, a bugler, a farrier, a blacksmith, and 45 privates. The Fort Scott post returns (microfilm in KHi) show that Terrett and company returned from the summer trip on September 28, 1844.

❡ August.—The first Santa Fe-bound caravan of the year (*see* March 31 entry) left Council Grove rendezvous some time after mid-month. Samuel C. Owens was elected captain of the company, which (at the beginning) numbered 40 men, with 23 wagons, 140 mules, and 80 yoke of oxen.

Owens had eight wagons; partners Samuel Wethered & Thomas J. Caldwell, four; Eugene and Thomas Leitensdorfer, three; Christopher C. Branham, three; Nicholas Gentry (the wagonmaster), two; Lewis D. Sheets, ___ ___ "Saucer" [Saucier?], and James J. Webb (making his first trip West) each had one. In the party were John Tulles, Benjamin Pruett, also men named Sénécal, Leblanc, and Langelier. One of Gentry's two wagons was driven by 17-year-old William Boggs.

At Pawnee Fork this company took the "dry route" and reached Big Coon creek "without accident or adventure." Another contingent joined them somewhere en route; and the caravan "mustered sixty men and thirty-four wagons, with two dearborns," when Samuel C. Owens was re-elected captain at a meeting held at "the Farther Coon creek" about September 7(?).

The Arkansas was "in fair fordable condition," and the wagons were got across in one day by doubling teams. Here, on September 13, the traders determined to send a delegation ahead to Taos, to make arrangements at the port of entry. The Leitensdorfer brothers, and Caldwell, accompanied by Webb and Sénécal, formed this party, which continued up the Arkansas; reached Bent's Fort on the 17th; and got to Taos in mid-October.

Meantime the caravan crossed the *jornada* safely; later encountered a severe storm; eventually reached Santa Fe about October 20.

Ref: Webb, *op. cit.,* pp. 26, 27, 45-91; *Niles' National Register,* v. 67 (January, 1845), p. 385; *New Mexico Historical Review,* Santa Fe, v. 30 (April, 1955), p. 167; *The Colorado Magazine,* v. 7 (March, 1930), p. 58, v. 11 (November, 1934), p. 226; David Lavender's *Bent's Fort* (1954), pp. 233-235.

❦ September 3.—Trader David Adams, with a small outfit, in company with John Anson (Hansen?) and two Robidouxs (Joseph [Jr.?] and Sellico), set out from Hickory Grove—on the Shawnee reserve, for Laramie river. During the day Lancaster P. Lupton, also mountain-bound, joined them. Camp that night was at Elm Grove.

Leaving the Santa Fe trail September 4 they stopped at "black Jack" [Captain's?] creek that night; camped at the Wakarusa on the 5th; and at "the spring" [Big Springs] on the 6th. Adams, delayed at this place three days (searching for lost horses), arrived at Joseph Papin's on the Kansas (at present Topeka) on September 13. The Robidouxs had preceded him and others of the party to the river crossing. Here they found Kansa Indians just back from a buffalo hunt (and a fight with Pawnees).

From the 13th to the 21st, Adams and his cotravelers remained at the Kaw river camp. (Papin, at this time, and as a result of the 1844 flood, was located on the *right,* or *south,* bank of the river; and had no ferryboat.) On the 16th Joseph Robidoux sent Joseph Papin and J. Lucas to Westport, Mo., on business; on the 17th other mountain-bound travelers arrived—two Frenchmen and one Spaniard. On the 19th Michel Dubray (seriously ill for days) died. With "Rouville" acting as minister, Dubray was given a burial service. (It would seem likely that this was the first white funeral in Topeka.) On the 20th

Papin and Lucas returned. They brought Adams two horses, to replace the lost animals.

On September 21 the combined Adams-"Anson"-Robidoux-Lupton pack-horse party (11 men, or more) started West, proceeding up the Kaw's south bank to Frederick Chouteau's trading post. Chouteau lent his pirogues so the travelers could get their "plund[e]r" to the north bank; then the horses were taken across. They were near a great many Kansa Indians at the camp made there. The party halted at Cross creek on the 22d; camped at the Little Vermillion on the 24th; and at the Big Vermillion on the 26th. They crossed the Big Blue on the 27th; camped at Wyeth's creek on the 29th; reached the Platte on October 5.

Adams, in company with "mr anson and lupton" arrived at Fort Platte on October 24. His partner John Sibille, and Dan Finch were there ahead of him (having gone up the Missouri on the steamboat *Frolic* in August—*see* p. 514— and hauled trading goods in).

Ref: Adams' diary, 1844-1845 (in the David Adams Papers, Missouri Historical Society, St. Louis), courtesy of Dale L. Morgan, Bancroft Library, Berkeley, Cal.

❦ September.—During this month three caravans left Independence, Mo., to take the Santa Fe trail. (1) A Bent, St. Vrain & Co. train (about 20? wagons), headed by Charles Bent and Ceran St. Vrain, returning to Bent's Fort, departed about September 6. (2) Albert Speyer, with 25 wagons left in mid-month. (3) Partners Dr. Henry Connelly and Edward J. Glasgow (also [Francisco?] Elguea), with 20(?) wagons set out about September 19.

They crossed "Kansas" with no particular difficulty, but "not far from Willow Bar," on the Cimarron, Speyer and Connelly & Glasgow were caught in a severe sleet-and-rain storm. Both trains lost many mules (Speyer over 75 in a single night); and were stranded till replacement stock reached them. (Speyer and Connelly went into the New Mexican settlements to purchase mules.) Their wagons had not reached Santa Fe up to November 24.

Ref: Fulton, *op. cit.*, pp. 146-148; Webb, *op. cit.*, p. 107; *Niles' National Register*, v. 67 (January, 1845), p. 385; David Lavender's *Bent's Fort* (1854), pp. 235, 404; James Hobbs' *Wild Life in the Far West* . . . (Hartford, Conn., 1875), pp. 59-61; *Old Santa Fe*, Santa Fe, v. 1 (October, 1913), p. 212 (for Francisco Elguea's name). Wislizenus, in his *Memoir* . . ., pp. 13, 14, noted, in passing the "Willow creek" area on June 15, 1846, the skulls and bones of about 100 mules "which Mr. Speyer had lost here several years ago." In James J. Webb, *Adventures in the Santa Fé Trade* . . . (Glendale, Cal., 1931), pp. 107, 108, mention is made of Speyer's and Glasgow's losses in the 1844 storm.

❦ DIED: Delilah (McCoy) Lykins, aged 35, wife of the Rev. Johnston Lykins, on September 23, apparently at Pottawatomie Baptist Mission, on Pottawatomie creek, present Franklin county. Also surviving her were three children.

Ref: Calvin McCormick's *The Memoir of Miss Eliza McCoy* (Dallas, 1892), p. 45;

American Indian Mission Association report for 1844, p .15. Delilah McCoy was a daughter of the Rev. Isaac McCoy.

℄ September.—At Iowa, Sac & Fox Presbyterian Mission (present Doniphan county) preparations were being made to build the new "manual labor boarding school" which the Presbyterian Board had authorized.

Missionaries Samuel M. Irvin and William Hamilton, in their September 30 report, wrote that "upwards of 70 acres of land has been fenced, and part broken. A contract for making 200,000 brick has been let, and 100,000 are now ready to lay up. . . . Hands are employed to commence the foundation, forward stone, &c. . . ."

Ref: Comm'r of Indian Affairs, *Report*, 1844 (Irvin and Hamilton report, therein).

℄ September.—John W. Forman, operator of the Sac & Fox "pattern farm" (located on the reserve uplands, in present Doniphan county), reported harvests of 1,600 bushels of corn; more than 2,000 bushels of potatoes; 500 bushels of turnips. The wheat crop, due to rust—an aftermath of the excessive rainfall—was but a third of normal. When milled, the 400(?) bushels had produced 80 barrels of flour. The Sac & Fox Indians' own farms—all in the Wolf creek bottoms—had been "almost entirely destroyed" by flood waters.

Ref: Comm'r of Indian Affairs, *Report*, 1844 (Foreman's report, therein).

℄ September.—The new Independence (Mo.) *Journal*, in an article on the Santa Fe trade of 1844, estimated the imports (brought by the caravans after the June flood waters subsided) at "$400,000 in specie, and buffalo robes, furs, &c., to the amount of $50,000 more." The lower-than-normal exports (the merchandise taken by the four companies departing in August and September, in which were, altogether, 160 men, 92 wagons, 780 mules and 60 oxen) totaled "at Eastern cost," perhaps $200,000.

Ref: New Orleans *Weekly Picayune*, October 14, 1844; or New York *Weekly Tribune*, October 19, 1844.

℄ MARRIED: John Thompson Peery, Methodist minister, and Mrs. Mary Jane (Chick) Johnson, widow of the Rev. William Johnson (Methodist missionary to the Kansa), on October 3, at Westport(?), Mo.

Ref: "Marriage Record No. 2," Jackson county, Mo., p. 89; *KHC*, v. 9, pp. 194, 198.

℄ October.—In a letter, of the 16th, Methodist Bishop Thomas A. Morris wrote of debarking from the steamboat *Yucatan*, on the 10th, at "the landing, one mile below the mouth of the Kansas" [Westport Landing, or Town of Kansas, Mo.], and provided a brief contemporary descriptive note on the "town" area.

Here I came ashore alone ["between sundown and dark"], in a strange land
. . . far from my family and friends, on the border of the Indian country
. . . without porter or guide . . . and my lodging yet to hunt. . . .
Shouldering my baggage, which consisted of a heavy carpet-bag, cloak, umbrella, and a small bundle, I ascended the steep hill, between the base of
which and the river there was scarcely room for a warehouse and a few other
small buildings [of post-flood construction evidently]; and after resting several
times by the way, much heated, and nearly out of breath, I reached a new cabin
on the summit, occupied by Colonel [William M.] Chick, who, having been
'washed out' by the late freshet, removed above high-water mark. . . .

Ref: Morris, *op. cit.*

❧ October 10.—Josiah Gregg and companions returned to Independence, Mo., after a brief hunting trip out the Santa Fe trail to
the headwaters of the Marais des Cygnes.

"We went [wrote Gregg] some 50 or 80 miles beyond the border [to present
Osage county?], and occupied our time in hunting game and bees. Of the
former we found but little. . . . Of 'wild honey' we found at least a
sufficiency for our use. . . ."

Ref: Fulton, *op. cit.*, pp. 150, 151.

❧ October 14.—Bishop Thomas A. Morris (who had arrived at
Shawnee Mission on the 11th, after a journey up the Missouri),
together with Missionaries Edward T. Peery, Thomas Hurlburt,
and Learner B. Stateler, set out, in two buggies (and with camping
equipment), to attend the Methodists' first Indian Mission conference—to be held near Tahlequah, the Cherokees' capital.

They traveled the military road; made about 25 miles to "Hickory Camp"
on the 14th; stopped, on the 15th, some 38 miles beyond, on the Marais des
Cygnes' south bank; on the 16th (at the Little Osage) overtook the buggy of
conference-bound Rev. Thomas H. Ruble (missionary to the Pottawatomies)
and his young Indian companion, Washington Beauchemie; camped that night
on the Marmaton, near Fort Scott; made 15 miles to Drywood creek on the
17th; journeyed 30 miles in stormy weather on the 18th, to the residence of
Widow Adams on the Seneca reserve (in northeast "Oklahoma"); arrived at
their destination on October 22.

Ref: *KHC*, v. 9, pp. 177-179, 206, v. 16, pp. 258, 259; Morris, *op. cit.*, pp. 350-358;
Stanley, *op. cit.*, p. 113.

❧ October.—At Shawnee Methodist Mission (present Johnson
county) a third large brick—now known as the north—building was
under construction, to enlarge the Indian manual labor school. Also,
machinery to saw lumber was being added to the mission's year-old
steam mill. Since put in operation (*see* p. 500), the flouring mill
(capable of grinding 300 bushels of wheat a day) had netted $1,800
(which would be applied toward paying off the $4,000 cost).

Ref: Morris, *op. cit.*, p. 350; Comm'r of Indian Affairs, *Report,* 1844 (Thomas H.
Harvey's October 8, 1844, report, therein).

❧ October 15.—The seven-man Wyandot Council addressed a complaint to Sup't Thomas H. Harvey, St. Louis, asking for the "early removal of Jonathan Phillips as sub agent."

One of the charges: "he is at heart really hostile to our people and he hesitates not openly to avow it." The council members were: Henry Jacques [or, Jaquis], Squeen-dehty, Sarahass, John Gibson, John Arms, Francis A. Hicks, and James Sharlow [or, Cherloe]. (See June 6, 1845, entry for Phillips' successor.)

Ref: SIA, St. Louis, "Records," v. 8, typed copy, pp. 405-407 (the name of John Arms appears to be "Aeris" in v. 8—an error).

❧ October(?).—Alfred J. Vaughan (appointed July 5), new head of the Osage River Subagency, arrived in "Kansas" in the autumn.

On October 20 Father Christian Hoecken, at Pottawatomie Catholic Mission, noted in his diary: "new Indian agent [Vaughan] visited the mission [present Linn county] in company with Mr. Joshua Carpenter [former sub-agent], who was lately put out of office by the American government."

Carpenter had moved the subagency (which had been in present Miami county) to Pottawatomie creek early in 1844. It appears that the "new" subagency headquarters was the one-time "Issue house" for the Pottawatomies, in the vicinity of what is now Lane, Franklin county. (See December 18 entry.)

Ref: Kinsella, op. cit., p. 229. For Vaughan, see, also, list of Indian department employees, annals p. 533. Joshua Carpenter (appointed November 23, 1843) reached "Kansas" in January, 1844—see OIA, Letters Received from Osage River Subagency (National Archives Microcopy 234, Rolls 642 and 643).

❧ October 22.—William Gilpin and several other persons who had left Bent's Fort on September 22, arrived at Independence, Mo. They had met a number of westbound parties on the Santa Fe trail: (1) Charles Bent, Manuel Alvarez, and Mr. (Alexander C?) Ferguson, at Chouteau's Island; (2) Ceran St. Vrain, this side of Coon creek, "with waggons, going on well"; (3) Dr. Henry Connelly "with Lucas," between Ash creek and Pawnee Fork, and 25 miles ahead of (4) Albert Speyer's company, "which was near Walnut Creek." (The latter's mules were "poor and much worn out," and he had lost a number of animals soon after leaving Independence.)

(William Gilpin had gone out to Oregon in 1843 with Fremont's second expedition—see p. 482.)

Ref: *Oregon Historical Quarterly*, v. 4 (September, 1903), pp. 271, 272 (from Independence [Mo.] *Journal*, October 24, 1844). There is mention of trader J. S. Lucas in *The Daily Reveille*, St. Louis, March 26, 1850.

❧ Born: on October 22, at Shawnee Methodist Mission, present Johnson county, Mary Elizabeth Ward, daughter of Anthony A. and Mary Jane (Foster) Ward.

Ref: KHi's 15th *Biennial Report*, p. 36; Topeka *Journal*, April 15, 1916.

❑ October 24.—In the evening a "dreadful hurricane passed over
. . . [Shawnee Methodist Mission and school], demolishing
many of the buildings and injuring some few individuals, but no
lives were lost." East of the mission, near the state line, the Fort
Leavenworth [Indian] Agency was "torn to pieces . . . all the
roof was carried off several hundred yards, and torn all into pieces
& scattered, hardly two pieces at the same place."

At Westport, Mo., the schoolhouse and one dwelling were blown over. Of
the settlement's 31 occupants, one, a little girl, was killed; and several were
injured. John C. McCoy's two-story frame house was "thrown from its founda-
tions," and the "gable ends . . . were carried upwards of 50 yards.
. . . Some of the large beams were taken 50 feet. Pieces of furniture were
found a great distance in the woods." Near Independence, the tornado killed
10 persons.

On October 26 Missionary Jotham Meeker (then residing at Shawnee Baptist
Mission, present Johnson county), recorded in his diary: "Ride to Westport
and other places, where I witnessed terrible destruction from a tornado which
passed about a mile from us on day before yesterday evening. Nearly all the
fences, trees, houses, etc., in its course are prostrated. Many people are
wounded. Hear of eight lives being lost."

Ref: Stanley, *op. cit.*, p. 116; SIA, St. Louis, "Records," v. 8, typed copy, p. 427;
McCormick, *op. cit.*, pp. 48-50; Elizabeth Hayward's *John M'Coy His Life and His Diaries*
(New York, c1948), p. 247; Jotham Meeker's "Diary," (in KHi ms. division), or, *see* KHC,
v. 8, p. 477.

❑ November 7.—Eliza McCoy (newly arrived from Indiana)
opened a "small day school taught in English" at Pottawatomie
Baptist Mission (on Pottawatomie creek, in present Franklin county
—*see* p. 336) as the beginning effort of the American Indian Mission
Association, of Louisville, Ky., in maintaining a Baptist mission
among the Pottawatomies.

Also living at the mission in the 1844-1847 period were the Robert Simerwell
family, and widower Dr. Johnston Lykins (most of the time). But the Simerwells were not paid by the A. I. M. A. (Lykins had a post as physician to the
Pottawatomies; and Simerwell was employed as blacksmith for the same nation.)

Eliza McCoy maintained her day school, and Johnston Lykins usually
preached to the Pottawatomies on Sundays, till early December, 1847, when
the Indians began removing to their new Kansas river reserve. In 1848 Pottawatomie Baptist Mission personnel moved to present Shawnee county. The
mission, as reopened, was a manual labor school, receiving government support.

Ref: The reports of the American Indian Mission Association, 1843-1852 (on microfilm
in KHi); Jotham Meeker's letters of May 6, 1845, and December 9, 1847 (in KHi ms.
division); Comm'r of Indian affairs, *Report*, 1845 (Eliza McCoy's September 18 report
therein); McCormick, *op. cit.*, pp. 41*ff*.; Hayward, *op. cit.*, pp. 269, 270.

❑ November.—The steamboat *General Brooke* ("Capt. Throckmorton on deck and Joseph E. Gorman in the office") made a
late-in-the-year trip up the Missouri to Council Bluffs (Iowa).

Passengers included "dignitaries of the Missouri Legislature, and . . . some of those who had helped to make them," also, Richard S. Elliott, subagent of the Council Bluffs [Iowa] Subagency.

Ref: Elliott, *op. cit.,* p. 191.

❡ December.—At 18-months-old Fort Scott, construction of buildings was still "in progress." There had been delays because of the troops being used for other duty. Two blocks of officers' quarters, and three sets of soldiers' barracks were "nearly completed." Materials were on hand for another set of officers' quarters. The commandant was Bvt. Maj. William M. Graham; his troops were two companies (C and D), Fourth U. S. infantry, and one company (A), First U. S. dragoons.

(Passing by the post in mid-October, Bishop T. A. Morris and his companions had thought the Fort Scott troops appeared to "have but little to do," as they had seen some of the men "miles beyond, sporting with greyhounds.")

Ref: 28th Cong., 2d Sess., *Sen. Doc. No. 1* (Serial 449), pp. 144, 145; 29th Cong., 1st Sess., *H. Doc. No. 51* (Serial 482), p. 46; *KHQ,* v. 11, p. 127, and v. 29, pp. 437, 442; Morris, *op. cit.,* pp. 346-361.

❡ December 18.—On Wea creek (in present Miami county) the Rev. David Lykins, his wife Abigail Ann (Webster) Lykins, and teacher Sarah Ann Osgood, opened Wea Baptist Mission by "taking into the mission family a few boarding scholars," and commencing a school. This institution of the American Indian Mission Association, Louisville, Ky., remained active till 1857. (As late as October, 1856, 30 Indian children were attending the school.)

At the beginning, the mission property (obtained from the government—it had been headquarters for Osage River Subagency—*see* pp. 329 and 530) consisted of one dwelling (38' x 18') a story and a half high (divided into four rooms), with two stone chimneys; and a one-story cookhouse (17' x 18') connected to it by passageway.

In August, 1845, the Rev. Barzillai M. and Caroline M. (Hickman) Adams, of Jackson county, Mo., replaced David Lykins and wife (who returned to the Westport area to work among the Shawnees). In August, 1847, the Adamses left missionary service; whereupon David Lykins and wife returned to Wea mission.

As described in 1845, Wea Baptist Mission was "about seven miles north of the Osage [Marais des Cygnes] river, and 14 miles west of the Missouri line." Gov. John W. Geary's executive minutes of October 20, 1856, contain this statement: "The Baptist mission school, under the charge of Dr. [*i. e.,* the Rev. David?] Lykins, assisted by three white teachers, is about one mile and a half [east] from Paola." (Most descriptions say: "a mile east of Paola.") In 1876 the principal mission building was still standing, on the farm then owned and occupied by "Mrs. McGraw."

Ref: The reports of the American Indian Mission Association, 1843-1852 (on microfilm in KHi); Comm'r of Indian Affairs, *Reports* for 1845, 1846; Jackson county, Mo., marriage records (the Adamses were married on July 1, 1841); McCormick, *op. cit.*, pp. 43-51; Hayward, *op. cit.*, pp. 232, 242, 243; *KHC*, v. 4, p. 619 (for Geary, 1856), v. 9, p. 570; Miami *Republican*, July 21, 1876; annals, p. 465 (for item on Lykins' marriage).

℃ DIED: Squeen-dehty, aged 61, a prominent man of the Wyandot Nation, in December. He was buried at present Kansas City, in Huron Place Cemetery.

Ref: Wyandotte county "Clippings," v. 3, p. 103 (in KHi library); and *see* October 15, 1844, annals entry.

℃ Employed in "Kansas" by the Indian Department during all or part of the year 1844 were the following persons:

FORT LEAVENWORTH AGENCY—*Agent* Richard W. Cummins; *Interpreters* Clement Lessert and Henry Tiblow; *Blacksmiths* William Donalson, James M. Simpson (resigned in July?), and Calvin Perkins (appointed September 19) for Shawnees, Isaac Mundy for Delawares, Charles Fish for Kansa; *Assistant blacksmiths* Powhatan Phifer, Richard Simpson, Joseph Parks' colored boy, and Jackson Pitman for Shawnees, Duke W. Simpson's colored man Hiram for Delawares, Mab Frankier for Kansa; *Farmer* William H. Mitchell for Kansa.

GREAT NEMAHAW SUBAGENCY—*Subagent* William P. Richardson; *Interpreters* Samuel M. Irvin (to September 17) and John Baptiste Roy (appointed September 17) for Iowas, John Rubite for Sacs & Foxes; *Blacksmiths* Benjamin Stewart for Iowas and James Gilmore for Sacs & Foxes; *Assistant blacksmiths* Elisha P. Dorion (dismissed in April?) and Thomas Stewart (began work May 1) for Iowas, William Daviess (died in May?) and Andrew Meyer (appointed May 20) for Sacs & Foxes; *Farmers* Preston Richardson, for Iowas, and John W. Forman (appointed April 1) for Sacs & Foxes; *Assistant farmer* Harvey W. Forman for Sacs & Foxes.

OSAGE RIVER [MARAIS DES CYGNES] SUBAGENCY—*Subagent* Joshua Carpenter (removed), Alfred J. Vaughan (appointed July 5); *Interpreters* Joseph N. Bourassa and John Tecumseh Jones; *Blacksmiths* Robert Simerwell and Robert Wilson; *Assistant blacksmiths* Samuel L. Bertrand and Andrew Fuller (both appointed January 1); *Physician* Johnston Lykins (from June 1); *Millers* Peter Perillard (at Pottawatomie creek; to March 31), Joel Grover (at Sugar Creek; appointed October 9). *Note: All of the above, except the subagent, were employed for the Pottawatomie Indians only.*

OSAGE SUBAGENCY—*Subagent* John Hill Edwards (appointed February 14; resigned in August), Joel Cruttenden (appointed September 18); *Interpreters* Charles Mongrain (to April 20), Joseph Swiss (or, "Suisse"); *Blacksmith* John Gibson (from August 1); *Assistant blacksmiths* Louis Gotte (from January to April), Francis Mitchell, and Joseph Captain.

WYANDOT SUBAGENCY—*Subagent* Jonathan Phillips; *Interpreter* John M. Armstrong; *Blacksmith* Charles Graham; *Assistant blacksmith* James B. Post.

Ref: 28th Cong., 2d Sess., *H. Doc. No. 38* (Serial 464), pp. 5-7; 28th Cong., 2d Sess., *H. Doc. No. 139* (Serial 465), pp. 7, 9, 35, 43, 50, 53; 29th Cong., 1st Sess., *H. Doc. No. 91* (Serial 483), pp. 2, 39-41, 45, 46, 66, 85, 86; SIA, St. Louis, "Records," v. 7, typed copy, pp. 383-468, *passim*, v. 8, typed copy, pp. 292-467, *passim*.

1845

℃ January.—To provide "bread stuff" for the Indians of "Kansas" whose crops had been ruined or destroyed by the previous year's rains and floodwaters, Sup't Thomas H. Harvey, St. Louis, arranged for the purchase, and distribution, of 13,840 bushels of corn:

For the Osages, 5,000 bushels; Kansa, 3,000; for the Pottawatomies, Peorias, Weas, and Kaskaskias, 4,000; Delawares, 342; Shawnees, 480; Munsees, 178; Ottawas, 760; and Chippewas, 80.

Ref: Superintendency of Indian Affairs (SIA), St. Louis, "Records," v. 7, typed copy, pp. 491, 492; 29th Cong., 1st Sess., *H. Doc. No. 91* (Serial 483), pp. 4, 7.

℀ KILLED: Fool Chief (head chief of the Kansa Nation), on January 28, at a camp near the Shawnee Nation's meeting house, by Wa-ho-ba-ke (a Kansa brave), in a fight. He was buried on the prairie at, or near, present Shawnee, Johnson county.

Fool Chief and his band were (by Frederick Chouteau's recollection) en route to Missouri on a "begging and stealing expedition." Wa-ho-ba-ke fled to the Osages; but returned in 1846(?).

In June, 1844, James Clyman had described the Kansa "head chief" as "a tall lean wrinkld faced Filthy looking man with a forehead indicating deceed Dissimilution and intriegue and more like a Beggarly scape gallows than a Chief." According to Chouteau Fool Chief was a "fine-looking fellow," but addicted to drinking; James G. Hamilton (of Westport, Mo.) referred to the Kansa leader as "a great scoundrel."

Ref: F. H. Cross and K. J. Moore, editors, *Notebooks of James Gillespie Hamilton* . . . (c1953); *KHC*, v. 8, pp. 426, 427, v. 10, p. 349; C. L. Camp, editor, *James Clyman, Frontiersman* . . . (c1960), p. 73. *Presumably* it was Fool Chief Clyman met, but he did not refer to him by name.

℀ MARRIED: 2d Lt. Thomas Clark Hammond, First U. S. dragoons, and Mary A. Hughes, daughter of Judge Matthew M. Hughes, Platte county, Mo., on January 28, at Pilot Knob ("a picturesque landmark . . . [about] five miles from Fort Leavenworth").

The clandestine wedding ceremony was performed on horseback. (The name of the clergyman apparently is not on record.) Lieutenant Hammond was killed in the battle of San Pasqual, Cal., on December 6, 1846; as was, also, Hammond's brother-in-law Capt. Benjamin D. Moore of the First dragoons (who had married Martha M. Hughes, sister of Mary A.). A monument to their memory was erected in the Platte City, Mo., cemetery.

Ref: *History of Clay and Platte Counties, Missouri* . . . (St. Louis, 1885), p. 944; W. M. Paxton's *Annals of Platte County Missouri* . . . (Kansas City, Mo., 1897), pp. 80, 81, 271, 272; Susan S. Magoffin's *Down the Santa Fe Trail and Into Mexico* . . ., edited by Stella M. Drumm (New Haven, 1926), pp. 63, 113, 145, 146; J. H. Carleton, in *The Prairie Logbooks* . . . (1943), p. 163, P. St. G. Cooke, in *Scenes and Adventures* . . . (Philadelphia, 1859), p. 431, and J. W. Abert in 30th Cong., 1st Sess., *H. Ex. Doc. No. 41* (Serial 517), all make mention of "Pilot Knob"; and *see KHC*, v. 16, p. 274.

℀ February 1.—A contract to build (by July 1) 21 houses for Osage chiefs and head men (under terms of the January 11, 1839, treaty) was awarded to Thomas B. Arnett and William C. Brown, of Van Buren (now Cass) county, Mo. Ten of these, for the leading chiefs, were to cost $200 each; the others, $100 per cabin.

The two-room, hewed-log, clapboard-roofed, plank-floored dwellings (each 18 feet square), were to be located on sites selected by Subagent Cruttenden. Most, but probably not all of the houses, were erected in present Neosho county. (The bands of Clermont and Black Dog lived at "Big Hill on the Verdigris" at this period.)

Other Osages built homes in what is now Neosho county in 1845. The subagent reported, in the late summer, that "the half-breeds are mostly in the nation," having come "within the last year . . . bringing with them considerable stocks of horses, hogs, &c., and permanently locating themselves, built themselves houses, fenced fields, and are making preparation to plant corn, &c."

Ref: Office of Indian Affairs (OIA), Letters Received from Osage Subagency (National Archives Microcopy 234, Roll 632), 1845 records, therein; Comm'r of Indian Affairs, *Report*, 1845 (Joel Cruttenden's September 1, 1845, report); C. J. Kappler's *Indian Affairs, Laws and Treaties* (Washington, 1904), v. 2, pp. 525-527; annals, pp. 362, 363.

❦ February 17.—The *John Golong* (William W. Baker, master) reached Weston, Mo.—the first of 118 steamboat arrivals at that port in 1845.

In May the *John Golong* was advertised (under date of May 23) to run as a regular packet between St. Louis and St. Joseph, Mo.; and was, thus, one of the (as reported) 31 steamboats which went to places higher up the Missouri than Weston during the year.

Ref: *The Western Journal*, St. Louis, v. 5 (March, 1851), p. 326; *The Gazette*, St. Joseph, Mo., May 23, 1845.

❦ February 19.—Subagent Alfred J. Vaughan was authorized (by Sup't Thomas H. Harvey) to let contracts (not to exceed $300) "for the improvement & erection of buildings" at the Osage [Marais des Cygnes] River Subagency (at, or near, present Lane, Franklin county), on the Pottawatomie reserve. (*See, also*, p. 530.)

Vaughan's disbursements for the third quarter of the year showed payment of $230 to John W. Polke "For erecting and repairing agency buildings," and of $66 to C. D. Fulton "For making and hauling rails to enclose agency buildings." The subagent, on September 20, reported the structures "good and substantial" ones.

August Bondi, Franklin county pioneer of 1855, stated in his *Autobiography:* "Dutch Henry [Sherman] . . . with his two brothers William and Jacob, or James, lived on what had been a large farm, and Agents' Headquarters of the Pottawattomies . . . Dutch Henry had come from Northern Germany . . . [in the 1830's] and had worked for the Indians. When they left [by 1848], he squatted in the buildings. . . ." *See, also*, pp. 322 and 336, for mention of Dutch Henry's Crossing.

Ref: SIA, St. Louis, "Records," v. 7, typed copy, p. 512; Comm'r of Indian Affairs, *Report*, 1845 (Vaughan's report, therein); 29th Cong., 1st Sess., *H. Doc. No. 91* (Serial 483), p. 47; August Bondi's *Autobiography* . . . (Galesburg, Ill., 1910), p. 38. Jotham

Meeker (missionary to the Ottawas) first mentioned "Henry Shearman" [Sherman] in his diary under date of April 18, 1847.

❧ February.—In an exchange of property effected by Subagent Joel Cruttenden, the dwelling and farm of part-Osage Charles Mongrain became the Osage Subagency. The new location "on [Flat] Rock Creek" (in present Neosho county) was "on high ground & in the Centre of the Osage Nation," on the main road leading from "the white settlement to the Villages."

Involved was a deal, suggested by Mongrain, that he take over the costly, but badly situated subagency building (remote from the Indian villages; and subject to the Neosho's overflow) which had been erected during Subagent Robert A. Calloway's tenure (see p. 495), and turn over his home to the government, if paid $500. Cruttenden's contract with Mongrain later received official sanction; and Mongrain gave a quitclaim deed to his property in January, 1846.

The new Osage Subagency consisted of a log dwelling, 50' x 16' (two rooms, connected by a coverway), with two chimneys, plank floors, and glass windows; two smoke houses, a barn, and three corn cribs (all in good repair except the last-named). The house lacked only a kitchen, which could be added for $100, according to Cruttenden.

Ref: OIA, Letters Received from Osage Subagency (National Archives Microcopy 234, Roll 632), various 1845-1846 letters and documents therein; Comm'r of Indian Affairs, *Report*, 1845 (Cruttenden's September 1, 1845, report); SIA, St. Louis, "Records," v. 8, typed copy, p. 539; 30th Cong., 1st Sess., *H. Ex. Doc. No. 5* (Serial 514); p. 5. Subagent Cruttenden had reached the Osage reserve in November, 1844; and, until the above property was obtained, had lived, by Edward L. Chouteau's invitation, at the American Fur Company's Neosho river trading post (long operated by Pierre Melicourt Papin—*see* annals, p. 496).

❧ March.—Seven Santa Fe traders who had "made the tedious winter journey across the ["Kansas"] prairies," arrived at Independence, Mo., in the fore part of March. They had left Santa Fe early in January, and traveled by way of Bent's Fort (Colo.).

Ref: New Orleans *Weekly Picayune*, March 17, 1845.

❧ Died: Capt. Burdett A. Terrett, First U. S. dragoons, on March 17, at Fort Scott, from a bullet wound. A pistol, held in his hand, accidentally discharged as the captain dismounted from his horse.

Ref: *Niles' National Register*, Baltimore, v. 68 (April 5, 1845), p. 66; F. B. Heitman's *Historical Register . . . of the United States Army* (Washington, 1903), v. 1, p. 951.

❧ Born: on March 21, at Shawnee Baptist Mission (present Johnson county), Maria Barker, daughter of the Rev. Francis and Elizabeth F. (Churchill) Barker.

Ref: Elizabeth F. Barker's *Barker Genealogy* (New York, 1927), p. 199; Barker Collection (in KHi ms. division). In the *Genealogy* she is listed as *Maria Deleno* Barker; but in papers of the "Collection" she is *Maria C.* Barker. She died July 30, 1847—*see* Jotham Meeker's diary (in KHi ms. division), July 31, 1847, entry.

❧ April 3.—Two companies (I and K) of the Third U. S. infantry, stationed at Fort Leavenworth, left that post under orders to Fort Jesup (on the Texas frontier).

On April 3, at Fort Leavenworth, Capt. William M. D. McKissack (AQM) made a contract with steamboat captain W. B. Miller for transportation of these troops (five commissioned officers, 15 noncoms, and 57 men) to St. Louis.

Ref: *Niles' National Register*, v. 68 (April 26, 1845), p. 117; 29th Cong., 1st Sess., *H. Doc. No. 51* (Serial 482), p. 34; Fort Leavenworth post returns.

❦ April(?)—Kansa Methodist Mission (on Mission creek, present Shawnee co.), inactive since 1843(?), was occupied by the Rev. John T. Peery and his wife Mary Jane (Chick) Johnson Peery, who went there "with a view of establishing a Manual Labor School." On April 9 Peery also received appointment as government farmer for the Kansa Indians. Mrs. Peery—as the wife of Rev. William Johnson (who had died in 1842)—had been a missionary among the Kansa for seven years—*see* p. 301.

The Peerys "kept a few [Kansa] children & taught them through 1st year." As the missionary recollected (in 1880), the spring (*i. e.,* summer) of 1845 was "very wet & unfavorable, & we failed to raise a good crop." His employees included three young men—James Foster, [John D.?] Clark, and Samuel M. Cornatzer.

[According to Peery, "Pi-hu-sca-goth-ra" (or, "Loy-a-tunga") was then chief of the Kansa town on a hill about a mile north of the mission; and American Chief's village was some 10 miles west, on what is now called Mill creek (in present Wabaunsee county). Charles B. Chouteau and Seth M. Hays were in charge of Frederick Chouteau's trading post (located on what is now Mission creek, within two miles of the Kansa Methodist Mission.)]

Because of the nation's approaching move to a new reservation, following the signing of the Kansa treaty in January, 1846, the mission was discontinued some time in 1846. California-bound travelers who visited it on May 18, that year, apparently found the missionaries still in occupancy.

Ref: John T. Peery's letter, December 30, 1880 (in KHi ms. division); *KHC,* v. 9, pp. 198-201; SIA, St. Louis, "Records," v. 7, typed copy, p. 520; Comm'r of Indian Affairs, *Reports,* 1845, 1846 (Thomas H. Harvey's reports, therein); Edwin Bryant's *What I Saw in California* . . ., 4th ed. (1849), pp. 45, 46. John D. Clark was a witness to the Kansa 1846 treaty, as were Peery, Chouteau, and Hays. "Pi-is-cah-cah," third signer of the treaty, evidently was the chief "Pi-hu-sca-goth-ra," named by Peery. There were two Kansa villages *north* of the Kansas river, also; the town of recently-deceased Fool Chief (near Big Soldier creek), and Hard Chief's town (near the mouth of the Little—now Red—Vermillion). These were in present Shawnee, and Pottawatomie counties, respectively.

❦ Spring.—The Missouri river, in early April, was "very low," with "snags so numerous that boats could scarcely pass between them," and one St. Louis newspaper listed 11 steamboats reported aground at various places.

In mid-May the Missouri was said to be "in a worse condition now for navigation than it has been known for many years before. The channel has almost formed anew [a result of the 1844 floods], and is terribly beset with snags, stumps, and sandbars." About May 22 there was a rise of over four feet in the St. Joseph area.

Some of the steamboats which managed to reach the Kansas area (or beyond), in April and May, were the *General Brooke, Nimrod, Independence, John Golong, Huntsville, Ohio, Henry Bry, Annawan, Balloon, Lexington,* and *Boreas No. 2.*

Ref: *Niles' National Register,* v. 68 (April 26, May 31, June 7, 28, 1845), pp. 128, 208, 224, 258; SIA, St. Louis, "Records," v. 8, typed copy, p. 431; *The Gazette,* St. Joseph, Mo., May 23, 1845.

℃ April.—Around the 16th, a small party of Santa Fe traders—Dr. Eugene Leitensdorfer, Thomas Leitensdorfer, Christopher C. Branham, James J. Webb and perhaps a dozen others—arrived at Independence, Mo.

They had left Santa Fe at the beginning of March, with wagon-and-mule outfits, to take the Raton route and come by way of Bent's Fort. Most of the trip had been made on short rations, but without special incident.

Ref: *Niles' National Register,* v. 68 (May 10, 1845), p. 148; J. J. Webb's *Adventures in the Santa Fé Trade* . . . (1931), pp. 118-123.

℃ Spring.—The "vagrant band of Iowas" (numbering perhaps 150), which had been living since 1837 on the "Council Bluffs" Pottawatomies' reserve in southwestern Iowa, joined their kinsmen on the Iowa reserve in "Kansas" (present Doniphan county). *See* pp. 417, 420, 458, 459.

Ref: Comm'r of Indian Affairs, *Report,* 1845 (Subagent W. P. Richardson's report, therein).

℃ May 1.—The Methodist Episcopal Church was "rent asunder" (over the slavery issue) by the organization of the Methodist Episcopal Church, South, at a convention held in Louisville, Ky.

Subsequently, the Missouri conference, and the Indian Mission conference (which included the "Kansas" missions) were drawn into the church South. *See* October 12 annals entry.

Ref: *KHC,* v. 9, p. 179; Charles Elliott's *South-Western Methodism* . . ., edited and revised by L. M. Vernon (Cincinnati, 1868), p. 22.

℃ May.—Fast-growing St. Joseph, Mo., scarcely 18 months old (*see* p. 497), now contained 682 inhabitants; 12 large mercantile establishments; three hotels; a "host of mechanics of all trades"; and one small church. (These were statistics published in an early issue of the town's first newspaper—*The Gazette.*)

Oregon-bound William Findley wrote (in his journel) on May 21: "St. Joseph is a flourishing town. Contains 650 inhabitants." In March, 1846, a town booster asserted that "in the last two years" two Oregon emigrant companies had outfitted at St. Joseph—the first (*i. e.,* 1844), of about 100(?)

wagons, and the latter (1845), of around 300(?); the wagons averaging six(?) persons in each.

Ref: *The Gazette*, St. Joseph, Mo., May 9, 1845, and March 6, 1846; William Findley's 1845 "Overland Journal" (microfilm of ms. in Coe Collection of Yale University library).

❡ May.—Four Oregon-bound emigrant companies started West from the St. Joseph, Mo., area in 1845. Between May 1 and May 24, they passed the Great Nemaha Subagency (in present Doniphan county); and Subagent W. P. Richardson (who commented: "The character of the emigration is very much improved from last year.") compiled these totals (as published in the St. Joseph paper): 223 wagons and 954 persons, with 545 firearms, 9,425 cattle, and 108 horses and mules. The four companies (listed under their elected commanders) were:

(1) Captain William G. T'Vault's company. (Historian H. H. Bancroft says: "61 wagons and 300 persons"; but more likely the total was under 275, since available figures indicate the trains of 1845 averaged about 4.3 persons per wagon.) The gathering point of these emigrants was "4 miles below St. Joseph, on the opposite side of the Missouri river" (in present Doniphan county). They left this camp in two groups, one on April 29, the other on April 30. About April 26, at a general meeting, they had elected William G. T'Vault (of Kosciusko county, Ind.) their captain; and John Waymire, lieutenant; also, they hired "Mr. [John] Clark" to pilot them to the Junction with the Independence-to-Oregon trail. On May 7, in present Brown county, there was "a wedding in camp between Mr. Geo. Shafer and Miss Margaret Packwood" (as recorded in emigrant Jesse Harritt's diary). In mid-May the St. Joseph *Gazette* reported: "We heard from Capt. Tvault's company 70 miles from Wolf river, they were doing well and were one days travel in advance of Capt. Tutherlow company." On May 24 these emigrants left the head of Little Blue to cross to the Platte—reached that river on May 25, and while spending a day in camp "were passed by a company . . . from Independence, consisting of about 30 wagons."

(2) Captain Solomon Tetherow's company (66 wagons; 293 persons). At now-extinct Elizabethtown, Andrew co., Mo. (adjoining present Amazonia), on April 5, the "Savannah Oregon Emigrating Society" was organized (the Rev. William Helm, chairman; the Rev. Lewis Thompson, secretary). (Elizabethtown boasted an "excellent, large, new ferryboat," and low crossing rates.) By March 8 prospective emigrants from Andrew county had arranged with the Sac & Fox Indians "for the privilege of range, wood, and water, opposite Elizabethtown" (*i. e.*, across the river in present Doniphan county). On April 28, at "Oregon Encampment, Missouri bottom," the "Savannah Society" chose James Officer temporary commander, and Zachariah Moreland, lieutenant— who were to obtain John Clark's services to pilot them to the "Independence Trace." At the final organization, May 5, at "Oregon Encampment—Wolf River," Solomon Tetherow was elected captain, and Hardin D. Martin, lieutenant. Company records show that there were: 100 armed men; 293 persons (63 females over 14, 56 under 14, 68 males under 16); 66 wagons; 170 guns

and pistols; 1,022 cattle (398 oxen, 624 loose cattle); 74 mules and horses. Among these emigrants were Samuel Hancock (whose *Narrative*, published in 1927, is discussed below), William A. Goulder (whose *Reminiscences* was printed in 1909), and Sarah J. (Mrs. Benjamin) Walden (whose *Autobiography* [as Mrs. Sarah J. Cummins] was published in 1914).

(3) Captain Samuel Parker's company (about 46? wagons; less than 200? persons). The starting point was St. Joseph, which place Parker left on May 5. On the 7th, at "Musketo Creek," 23 wagons were gathered. From this camp, the company went on to the Great Nemaha Subagency and awaited the arrival of other wagons. Parker was elected captain on May 11. The figures, above, have been reckoned from Richardson's statistics, and those available for the other three trains.

(4) Captain Abraham Hackleman's (Hackelman?) company (50? or 52? wagons; 214 persons). This was the last emigrant company to leave the St. Joseph, Mo., area in 1845. In a letter, from St. Joseph, on May 14, the Rev. Ezra Fisher stated: "We have now 14 wagons in company and suppose there are at least 50 behind." In his letter of May 23, from "Indian Territory, Nemaha Agency, 25 miles west of St. Joseph, Mo." (where his party had been for a week), Fisher enclosed proceedings of the "New London Emigrating Company for Oregon." He mentioned a committee of seven which included himself and "A. Hackelman"; and wrote: "Our company consists of 50 wagons, 214 souls, and about 666 head of cattle." (According to H. H. Bancroft: "A . . . company, with 52 wagons, left St. Joseph under the command of Hackleman, to which belonged W. W. Buck of Oregon City.") Fisher went on to say: "275[?] wagons have already passed this point before us, and about 1000 souls." "Every facility," he noted, had been "rendered" to them by Subagent Richardson and family.

Another Oregon-bound Baptist missionary—the Rev. Hezekiah Johnson— in a May 18, 1845, letter from St. Joseph, Mo., mentioned that he had two wagons, four oxen, and 13 cows; and that Fisher had gone on ahead to the "Indian Agency." (The Fishers and Johnsons had left Iowa early in April "with a large company of emigrants.") Writing from "Nimeha Agency" on May 23, 1845, Johnson stated: "Ours is the fourth caravan that has come this way [*i. e.*, via St. Joseph]. The three that have gone before us contained 175 wagons, 1000 persons, and 2000 cattle. We have 50 wagons, 214 persons, 666 cattle, and a few horses. A caravan of 500 wagons has left Independence. Another is about to leave Independence containing about 60 or 100 wagons. In all 825 wagons, probably 4214 persons and 8666 cattle."

William Findley, of Oquawka, Ill., must have been in the "Hackleman company" *at the outset*, but he nowhere mentions (in his journal) the number of wagons, or name of the captain. Findley crossed the Missouri at St. Joseph on May 19; "joined the Company at the Indian Agency" on May 22; set out from there on the 24th; crossed the Big Blue and "Struck the Independence Trail" on May 31. His "Roster of the Company as of June 11th" lists 77 men —Joseph Moist and John B. Courtney being officers of the guard. Probably there had been a division of the "Hackleman company" by that time for the only name among the 77 which is also (in variant spelling) on Fisher's com- mittee of seven (Fisher, A. Hackelman, Eckenburg, Knox, Gallaheir, Hezekiah

Johnson, and Wm. Bruck [Buck?]) is N. C. Gallaher. Findley's group of emigrants reached Fort Laramie on July 11, Fort Hall on August 31, and the Grand Ronde, in Oregon, on October 5.

Ref: *The Gazette*, St. Joseph, Mo., May 16 ("Three companies have already been organized and have left the Missouri river"), May 23 ("The last company of emigrants left on yesterday"), and June 6, 1845 (for Richardson's totals). The *Gazette's* March 6, 1846, issue referred to "Mr. Clarke," a mountain trader, as the pilot of 1845.

For T'Vault's Company: *The Gazette*, St. Joseph, May 2, 16, 1845; *Oregon Historical Quarterly*, Salem, v. 24, p. 66, v. 25, pp. 353-356, 359; H. H. Bancroft's *History of Oregon* (San Francisco, 1886), v. 1, p. 509 ("A . . . company of 61 wagons and 300 persons, starting from St. Joseph . . . was commanded by W. G. T'Vault . . ."); *Oregon Pioneer Association Transactions* of the 38th and 39th annual reunions, Portland, 1910 and 1911, pp. 506-526 (for the diary of Jesse Harritt).

For Tetherow's Company: *Oregon Historical Quarterly*, v. 16, pp. 278, 284 (for Weston, Mo., newspaper items), v. 25, pp. 365-473, and Fred Lockley's *History of the Columbia River Valley* . . . (Chicago, 1928), pp. 1021-1029, both contain some records of this company; W. A. Goulder's *Reminiscences* . . . (Boise, Idaho, 1909), pp. 111-117; Sarah J. Cummins' *Autobiography* . . . (c1914), pp. 22-39; *History of Andrew and DeKalb Counties, Missouri* (1888), p. 179 (item on Elizabethtown); Samuel Hancock's . . . *Narrative* . . . (New York, 1927), pp. 1, 2. (His statements about his "departure from Independence, Mo., in company with two hundred others . . .," and "Our party after leaving Independence proceeded up the Missouri river for four days . . . [halted and remained a week, and at this camp the company] all collected together numbering about forty wagons," are difficult of interpretation, and have been misinterpreted in the past. One fact is certain—Hancock's name is on the roll of the "Savannah Society." Just possibly he meant St. Joseph instead of Independence, Mo. If, in 1845, a company of 200 persons, having arrived at Independence, Mo., then proceeded overland to St. Joseph's vicinity to start for Oregon, the journey was not recorded in contemporary sources.)

For Parker's Company: *The Gazette*, St. Joseph, June 6, 1845; and items from a copy of Samuel Parker's diary, courtesy Oregon Historical Society.

For Hackleman's Company: *Oregon Historical Quarterly*, v. 16, pp. 379-411 (Ezra Fisher's letters); H. H. Bancroft's *History of Oregon*, v. 1, p. 509; William Findley's *1845 Overland Journal; Pacific Northwest Quarterly*, Seattle, v. 37 (January, 1946), pp. 19 and 20 (for Johnson's letters); *Baptist Home Missions in North America . . ., 1832-1882* (New York, 1883), p. 338.

❡ May.—At Independence, Mo., "We're in a perfect Oregon fever," wrote the *Western Expositor's* editor in the May 3d issue, ". . . we suppose that not less than two or three thousand people are congregating at this point." In another issue (May 10?) he remarked the departure of 200 wagons from Independence; noted, additionally, the passage of 28 wagons (from Fort Madison, Iowa ter., and vicinity); and the approach of another 50 (as reported to him).

From "Camp Oregon," on the Big Blue (in Jackson county, Mo.) the "main company" of emigrants (about 100 wagons) set out on May 2; crossed into "Kansas" to spend four final-preparation days at "Spanish Camp" near the border; and resumed travel on May 6. Other trains (but none so large) were either in advance, or close behind.

Emigrant John E. Howell (in a diary) recorded the movements of the "main company." Camp on May 7 was at Lone Elm ("one elm with all the limbs trimmed off"); the "Wappaloosa" (Wakarusa) was crossed on the 9th; camp on the 11th was at Shunganunga creek; on the 12th some of the emigrants crossed the Kansas river (at present Topeka). Joel Palmer (who had caught up with the "main company" on the 11th) wrote: "We were obliged to be ferried over . . . [the Kansas] in a flat boat; and so large was our company, and so slowly did the ferrymen carry on the necessary operations, that darkness overtook us before half the wagons had crossed the stream." During the night, the emigrants' cattle scattered during a thunderstorm. But by noon of the 13th they had been rounded up; and all the wagons had reached the north bank. Camp was made about three miles from the Kansas—near the bank of Big Soldier creek—where, by prearrangement, the "main company" was to organize, and elect officers. (About a mile distant was the Kansa village which had been Fool Chief's—*see* p. 534.) Emigrant William B. Ide wrote, on May 13, that this "main company" numbered 107 wagons; that 35 wagons were "a few miles ahead"; and "a few days behind" were some 70 others.

On May 14 the emigrants "held a confused meeting and adjourned abruptly" to meet at 8 A. M. the next day. (There were two candidates for pilot—T. M. Adams [a promoter of the 1845 emigration] and Stephen H. L. Meek [*see* p. 447, for his 1842 journey west]). On the 15th the emigrants chose Meek for pilot, and Dr. Presley Welch (of Cooper county, Mo.) as captain. The *Western Expositor* editor (who rode out 100 miles from Independence) apparently arrived about election time. He reported that the Welch-Meek company had 104 wagons "arranged in an oval ring" . . . linked together with ox-chains" to form an immense stock corral; and that 100 more wagons were "encamped in groups at small distances." He published these census figures (collected during his visit): males, 421; females, 138; children, 448 (240 boys, 208 girls)—totaling 1,007 persons; wagons, 233 *; cattle, 3,261; horses, 182. [*As printed in *Niles' Register*. The St. Joseph *Gazette* printed it "223." No file of the *Expositor* is known to exist.]

On the 16th, west of present Cross creek, 16 wagons left the Welch-Meek company, but 15 others joined (according to Palmer). Making slow progress, some of the emigrants camped, on the 17th, by the Little (now Red) Vermillion, "in sight of a Caw village," where (wrote Palmer) "the principal chief, [*i. e.*, Hard Chief—successor to Fool Chief] resides." On the 18th, at a camp some 12 miles north of the Kansa town, Pilot Stephen H. L. Meek and a young woman emigrant—Elizabeth Schoonover—(said to be an orphan), were married by a "quondam justice of the peace."

A reorganization took place on May 19. John E. Howell put it succinctly: "Divided company in three Divisions." (Each was to take its turn at traveling in advance, for a week at a time. Captain Welch was to accompany whichever train was in the lead; but each division was to choose its own officers. Meek was retained as pilot.) William B. Ide (in a May 21 letter, from a camp west of the Big [now Black] Vermillion), stated that the Welch-Meek company then consisted of 131 wagons; and that they were divided into the "anti-stock go-ahead division . . . the small stock division, and the large stock division." "We," he wrote, "have 350 head of loose stock, twenty-seven wagons, and fifty-one women and children." (Joel Palmer says he was chosen to captain a company [*i. e.*, division?] of 30 wagons. If Palmer headed a "division" it must have been the one in which the Ide family traveled.) Emigrant Jacob R. Snyder (then behind the Welch-Meek company) wrote, on May 21, that its "Rear Division" was said to number about 80 men and 50 wagons. (Fifty wagons, plus 27, subtracted from 131, would seem to indicate the third division may have had some 54 wagons.) Palmer refers to Captain [Thomas F.] Stephens as head of a company [*i. e.*, "division"?], but does not mention its size.

Palmer's company reached the Platte on June 1; but had been preceded there by Captain Stephens' company. In advance of both were many other emigrants—some who had started from Independence; but principally those in the first three(?) companies which had set out from St. Joseph or Elizabethtown.

Ref: Joel Palmer's *Journal*, as reprinted in R. G. Thwaites, editor, *Early Western Travels*, v. 30; John E. Howell's diary, in *Washington Historical Quarterly*, Seattle, v. 1 (April, 1907), pp. 138-158; Jacob R. Snyder's diary, in *Quarterly of the Society of California Pioneers*, San Francisco, v. 8 (December, 1931), pp. 224-260; H. H. Bancroft's *History of Oregon*, v. 1, pp. 508-531; and his *History of California* (San Francisco, 1884-1890), v. 2, pp. 732, 733 (for data on John Henry Brown), and v. 4, pp. 571-585; Fred B. Rogers' *William Brown Ide Bear Flagger* (San Francisco, 1962); New York *Weekly Tribune*, June 21, July 12, August 2, 16, September 6, 20, December 6, 20, 1845; *Niles' National Register*, v. 68 (May 3, 31, June 14, 21, July 5, 12, August 30, 1845), pp. 129, 203, 241, 246, 277, 292, 416; Carleton, *op. cit.*, pp. 180-251; Nebraska State Historical Society *Publications*, Lincoln, v. 20, pp. 129-132, 161 (items from the *Missouri Republican*, St. Louis); *Oregon Historical Quarterly*, v. 24 (March, 1923), pp. 36-55 (for B. F. Bonney's recollections), v. 25 (December, 1924), pp. 353-377 (for article on the McNemees and Tetherows), v. 26 (September, 1925), pp. 209-219 (for article on Samuel K. Barlow); *The Gazette*, St. Joseph, Mo., June 6, July 11, August 15, October 3, November 21, 1845; W. H. Gray's *A History of Oregon . . .* (Portland, 1870), p. 453; George R. Stewart's *The California Trail* (New York, c1962), pp. 83-126; Stephen H. L. Meek's *The Autobiography of a Mountain Man . . .* (Pasadena, Cal., 1949), p. 9 (for name of Meek's bride). Beyond Fort Boise (Idaho), Stephen H. L. Meek had the misfortune to become lost while attempting to pilot a large train (214? wagons) of "St. Joseph company" emigrants over a "nearer" route from Snake river to The Dalles. Returnees of 1846 reported that "some seventy-five" of the "St. Joseph company" had died as a result of hardships suffered.—*See* Dale Morgan, editor, *Overland in 1846* (Georgetown, Cal., 1963), v. 2, pp. 590, 594, 595, 601, 602; Keith Clark and Lowell Tiller, *Terrible Trail: the Meek Cutoff, 1845* (Caldwell, Idaho, 1966); *The Gazette*, St. Joseph, Mo., July 17, 1846 (for Hiram Smith's letter of July 7, 1846). According to his daughter, Samuel K. Barlow captained one of the *divisions* all the way to The Dalles. For Barlow, and Barlow's road, *see Oregon Historical Quarterly*, v. 3 (March, 1902), pp. 71-81, v. 26 (September, 1925), pp. 209-224.

❡ May.—One of the trains which started from Independence, Mo., but traveled apart from the "main company" of Oregon-bound emigrants, consisted of "38 wagons, with about 1,000 head of loose cattle, all under the direction of a Mr. [John Henry?] Brown."

On May 8, in eastern "Kansas," this good-sized party was just behind the "main company." But a month later (on June 11), at the Platte lower crossing, Joel Palmer noted that encamped on the west bank was "Brown's company, which passed us whilst we were organizing at Caw River." (A week earlier, Brown's train had been augmented by "Mr. Loulard and his party"—who had left, on June 3, the company in which Jacob R. Snyder then traveled.) According to emigrant William Knight, Captain Brown lost command at Fort Laramie, to William B. Ide.

Historian H. H. Bancroft, writing of California pioneer John Henry Brown (who, *by his own account,* had gone to live among the Cherokees around 1840; then journeyed overland to California with a party of Cherokee fur traders in 1843; returned east in the spring of 1844; and traveled back to California in 1845 with the Grigsby-Ide party), stated: "there is little doubt that he [Brown] came overland in '45, in a party that was with the Grigsby-Ide part of the way, and about which there is much confusion. . . ."

Ref: Joel Palmer's "Journal," in Thwaites, *op. cit.,* v. 30, pp. 34, 52; Jacob R. Snyder's diary, in *Quarterly of The Society of California Pioneers,* v. 8 (December, 1931), p. 230; Rogers, *op. cit.,* p. 22 (for William Knight); Bancroft's *History of California,* v. 2, pp. 732, 733. The April 12, 1850, St. Joseph (Mo.) *Gazette* reprinted a St. Louis *Union* item which noted the return East (by sea?) of "Capt. Griggsby," once of southwest Missouri; and indicated he would take the overland route on his return to California.

❡ May 7.—Two companies (A and B) of the First U. S. infantry arrived at Fort Leavenworth, by steamboat, from Jefferson Barracks, Mo.

Ref: 29th Cong., 1st Sess., *H. Doc. No. 51* (Serial 482), p. 29 (for War Department contract of May 1, 1845—Maj. Aeneas Mackay, QM, with George W. Atchison, for transportation of these companies). The dragoons' absence for the summer, with Kearny's expedition, prompted the above move, but by November, 1845, the Fort Leavenworth garrison had reverted to four companies of First dragoons, and one company of First infantry.—29th Cong., 1st Sess., *H. Doc. No. 2, between* pp. 220, 221; Fort Leavenworth post returns.

❡ In May, at an American Indian Mission Association (Baptist) meeting held in Georgia, Corresponding Secretary Isaac McCoy's report included this table:

NAMES AND NUMBERS OF TRIBES WITHIN THE INDIAN TERRITORY

[In "Kansas"]		[In "Oklahoma"]	
Kansa	1,700	Cherokees	25,911
Osages	4,102	Choctaws and	
Shawnees	887	Chickasaws	16,521
Delawares	1,059	Creeks and Seminoles	27,730
Peorias and Kaskaskias	150	Senecas and Shawnees	462
Weas and Piankeshaws	272	Quapaws	400
Kickapoos	588		
Ottawas	240		71,024
Sacs and Foxes	414	[In "Nebraska"]	
Iowas	270	Pawnees	8,000
Pottawatomies	2,000	Otoes and Missourias	931
Stockbridges,		Omahas	1,301
Munsees, etc.	278	Poncas	777
Chippewas	62		
Wyandots	585		11,009
	12,567	Grand Total	94,600

Agent R. W. Cummins, in his September 14, 1845, report gave these statistics: Kansa, 1,607; Shawnees, 929; Delawares, 1,059; Kickapoos, 516; Munsees, 208; Stockbridges, "about 60." *See* December, 1845, annals entry for additional Indian emigrants to "Kansas."

Ref: *Baptist Missionary Magazine*, Boston, v. 25 (September, 1845), pp. 246, 247; SIA, St. Louis, "Records," v. 8, typed copy, pp. 479-488; or Comm'r of Indian Affairs, *Report*, 1845.

¶ May 12.—On, or by, this date Col. Stephen W. Kearny, head of the Third Military department, arrived at Fort Leavenworth from St. Louis.

Capt. William Eustis and Company A, First U. S. dragoons, from Fort Scott, had preceded Kearny to Fort Leavenworth, to join the colonel's command for the upcoming expedition to the Rocky mountains—*see* May 18 entry. They reached the post May 7.

Ref: Carleton, *op. cit.*, pp. 157 and 160; Fort Leavenworth post returns.

¶ May.—A trading caravan which left Santa Fe on April 16, reached the Missouri frontier by mid-May, having had "very favorable weather" en route. On May 16 the St. Louis *Reveille* reported the arrival of "Mr. Sausser [Saucier?] and several gentlemen of Mr. [Edwin?] Norris's company" aboard the steamboat *Lexington*, and of "another party" of these traders on the *Henry Bry*.

Josiah Gregg (writing on August 27) stated: ". . . a number of small caravans . . . crossed the prairies last spring [all eastbound?], amounting in all to considerable more than a hundred wagons."

In a May issue of the Independence (Mo.) *Western Expositor*, the editor discussed trade with Mexico as affected by the strained relations between that country and the United States. He thought the overland trade would be considerable anyway, adding the comment: "Already we have goods arriving here to be transported thither. Messrs Houck, Magoffin, and McKnight, we believe, are determined to go out—the first we know positively." (*See* July-August annals entry.)

Ref: New Orleans *Weekly Picayune*, June 2, 1845; Josiah Gregg's *Diary & Letters* . . . (1941), v. 1, p. 168; *The Gazette*, St. Joseph, Mo., May 30, 1845. Both Edwin and Henry Norris were Chihuahua traders.—*See* 30th Cong., 1st Sess., *H. R. No. 458* (Serial 525), pp. 30, 42, 43.

¶ May 18.—Col. Stephen W. Kearny, his command of some 280 "well-mounted and equipped" First U. S. dragoons (Companies A, C, F, G, K), and guide Thomas Fitzpatrick, marched from Fort Leavenworth towards the Platte, and a junction with the Oregon trail, on the first leg of a summer's expedition to the Rocky mountains—an expedition undertaken for purposes of military reconnaissance, also to protect the emigrants, and impress the Indians. (The colonel and his troops would return 99 days later, by way of the Santa Fe trail, after a 2,200-mile march—the longest undertaken by the dragoons.—*See* map of Kearny's march in this volume; (*also, see* pp. 548, 549 and 558.)

On Kearny's staff were Capt. William M. D. McKissack (AQM), Surg. Samuel G. I. De Camp, Lt. Henry S. Turner, Lt. J. Henry Carleton, and Lt. William B. Franklin (of the U. S. topographical engineers; who joined on May 28). His line officers were Capts. P. St. George Cooke, Benjamin D. Moore, John H. K. Burgwin, and William Eustis; Lts. Philip Kearny, Andrew J. Smith, Richard S. Ewell, John Love, Henry W. Stanton, and Thomas C. Hammond. There were, also, three guests: Alexander S. Macomb (ex-Second dragoons captain), "Henry Loring, Esq., of Boston" (from May 19), and "Mr. Simpson, of St. Louis" (from May 28). Eustis, and 54 Company A, First dragoons, had left Fort Scott on May 3, 1845, en route to Fort Leavenworth.

Besides extra horses and mules, the cavalcade (at the outset) included 19 mule-drawn wagons (mountain howitzers mounted on two), over 50 beef cattle and 25 or more sheep. (Two wagons were sent back from the Big Blue.)

Kearny's march from the Missouri to the Big Blue was made with intent to find a "direct road" from the military post to the "Great Oregon Trace" (the Independence-to-Oregon road); and the path he blazed was the antecedent of the later-established Fort Leavenworth-Fort Kearny military road. For the first two days (May 18 and 19) the dragoons followed "the trails of previous marches." On the 20th they traveled W. N. W. over the ridge dividing the waters of Wolf and Stranger rivers; on the 21st the course was N. W. all day; two "considerable branches" of Stranger [*i. e.*, Delaware?] river were forded; and late in the afternoon they crossed a divide and camped on a Nemaha tributary. *On this divide (in present Nemaha county) "the Oregon trace from St. Joseph runs* [wrote Carleton], *and where we intersected it, it bore due south: evidently making an immense detour to avoid the branches of the Nemaha that here cut up the country in every direction like the sticks of a fan. Our course is nearly the chord of the arc it describes, but that trace [the emigrants'] keeps clear of the streams, while ours passed them with but little trouble."*

On the 22d, marching "through the broken land drained by the Nemaha" (now South Fork Nemaha river), they crossed this stream on a "smooth lime-stone ford." On the 23d (some 90 miles from the fort) they turned toward the south; traversed a "vast elevated and nearly level plain . . ." and camped not far from the Big Blue (in present Marshall county). Next day, after bridging a tributary stream, they reached the Big Blue; spent some time locating a ford; found one (well above the Oregon trail crossing, and probably near present Marysville); graded the river's banks and began crossing. "In one hour the whole command was over. Nothing had to swim but the sheep. . . ." After about five miles' travel beyond, they saw, on a distant ridge, "a long train of wagons"; and at one o'clock in the afternoon (on May 24), after a six-and-a-half day, 120-mile march, Kearny and his dragoons reached the Independence-to-Oregon trail.

Moving ahead at a rapid pace (and "continually overtaking and passing the emigrants" for the next 20 days) the military party reached the Platte on May 29; and arrived at Fort Laramie on June 14. At this trading post, where some 1,200 Sioux were gathered, Colonel Kearny, on June 16, counciled with Bull's Tail and other chiefs. While Company A remained in camp near Fort Laramie,

Kearny and four dragoon companies continued west on the Oregon trail to South Pass (which they reached at the end of June). They started back on July 1; and were in the Fort Laramie area again on the 13th. Subsequently, the dragoons marched southward (*see* map of Kearny's march), passed along the base of the Rocky mountains, and arrived on the bank of the Arkansas river (at a point about 60 miles above Bent's Fort), on July 26. *See* August annals entry, p. 558, for Kearny's journey back to Fort Leavenworth.

Ref: 29th Cong., 1st Sess., *H. Doc. No. 2* (Serial 480), pp. 210-213 (Kearny's report, 1845), and pp. 214-217 (Lts. W. B. Franklin's and H. S. Turner's journal abstracts); Carleton, *op. cit.*, pp. 155-280; Cooke, *op. cit.*, pp. 282-432; *Niles' National Register*, v. 68 (May 10, June 7, and July 12, 1845), pp. 160, 224, 292, v. 69 (October 25, 1845, and January 10, 1846), pp. 123, 124 (for a letter [of October date?] by Cooke), 303 (Kearny's report); New York *Weekly Tribune*, July 26 (for letters of May 30 and June 3 from Platte river), and November 1, 1845 (for a letter reprinted from Boston *Atlas*); *The Colorado Magazine*, Denver, v. 30 (October, 1953), pp. 246-269; D. L. Clarke's *Stephen Watts Kearny* (Norman, Okla., c1961), pp. 92-98; Joel Palmer's *Journal*, as reprinted in Thwaites, *op. cit.*, v. 30, p. 444, 445; Fort Scott post returns (microfilm in KHi).

℄ May.—The *Independence*, which left St. Louis on the 15th with some 125 tons of government cargo (principally corn and flour for the Iowas and Pawnees) reached Bellevue (Neb.) on May 29 "after a difficult and dangerous passage. . . ." By one account she had spent six days aground on a sandbar. The *Independence* was the first steamboat of the year to reach the Council Bluffs.

Leaving the Bellevue (Neb.) area on June 2, this boat was back at St. Louis on the 8th, bringing 430 packs of robes, peltries, and furs—mostly belonging to the American Fur Company.

Ref: New York *Weekly Tribune*, June 28, 1845 (from the St. Louis *New Era* of June 9), and January 31, 1846 (R. S. Elliott letter on Missouri river navigation); *Niles' National Register*, v. 68 (June 28, 1845), p. 258. The *Independence* was at St. Joseph, Mo. (again) early in July—see *The Gazette*, St. Joseph, Mo., July 4, 1845.

℄ May.—From Fort Pierre (S. D.) on the 18th, Indian agent Andrew Drips wrote: "The Union Fur Company has sold their entire stock in the [upper Missouri] country to P. Chouteau, Jr., & Company" (the American Fur Company).

Via the *Independence*, news reached St. Louis early in June that: "The fur companies in . . . [the Council Bluffs area] are fast consolidating into the powerful and extensive associations known as the American Fur Company, who have this last winter, purchased, besides the claims of the Union Fur Company, those of John Baptiste Roy and the Coopers, and arrangements are about to be made between them and the companies of Pierson and Ewing, by which it is said they will obtain the whole business in that section."

Ref: H. M. Chittenden's *The American Fur Trade of the Far West* . . . (New York, 1935), v. 1, p. 374; *Niles' National Register*, v. 68 (June 28, 1845), p. 258 (from St. Louis *New Era* of June 9, 1845).

℄ May 21-25.—On their way to northwestern Missouri to begin a "summer's campaign" of surveying, seven men afoot (with provisions and camp equipage in a small one-horse wagon), entered eastern "Kansas" on the "cold and rainy" morning of May 21. (They left Independence, Mo., on the 20th; and came through Westport early on the 21st.) Surveyor Alexander W. McCoy, in a June 3 letter, described the four-day journey in northeastern "Kansas."

From Shawnee Methodist Mission, reached in mid-day of May 21, they moved on; crossed the Kansas 12 miles from Westport (at the Delaware, Grinter, or military road ferry); spent the rainy night "in a Delaware store house" on the north bank. On the 22d, heading northward (on the military road) they "struck the Grand Prairie," and followed a pathway which was "a single track in the grass."

McCoy, impressed with the scene, wrote: "as far as the eye could reach on every side of us nothing was to be seen but swell after swell of the immense field of green—without a single object to break the view. . . . Here the plants and flowers of the Rocky Mountains region were to be seen about us. The snow berries of every variety, verbenas from a pink to a variegated scarlet, the buffalo berry, the sweet scented heartflower . . ., currants of every kind and strawberries in profusion, [and] the 'Polar plant' [rosinweed, or, compass plant] whose leaves point directly north and south an unerring guide to the lost wanderer on the plains."

The surveyors camped 10 miles below Fort Leavenworth. Several(?) days later (McCoy says on "Sunday"—which was the 25th), they crossed the Missouri and reached the "banks of [Little] Platte river"; and subsequently proceeded to the Nodaway and Tarkio river country to begin work.

Ref: *Pioneering on the Plains* (c1924 by John McCoy, Kaukauna, Wis.); for the polar plant, *see* F. C. Gates' *Wild Flowers in Kansas* (Topeka, 1933), pp. 135, 251.

❧ May.—Fur traders "from the head waters of the Arkansas," with six wagons ("bringing 187 packs of furs and Buffalo robes"), coming down by way of Bent's Fort, and the Santa Fe trail, reached Westport, Mo., around May 22. (Some of the party, including William Tharp, arrived at St. Louis, aboard the *Nimrod*, on May 25.) Very likely Alexander Barclay was one of these traders.

Ref: *Niles' National Register*, v. 68 (June 7, 1845), p. 224 (from St. Louis *New Era* of May 26); Barclay Papers, in Bancroft Library.

❧ May 23.—Lt. William B. Franklin (of the topographical engineers), with a small troop escort, left Fort Leavenworth to make a rapid march across northeast "Kansas" and overtake Col. Stephen W. Kearny's expedition.

On the 28th, a day in advance of his escort, Franklin and "Mr. Simpson, of St. Louis") caught up with the First dragoons on the Little Blue's headwaters, having traveled 217 miles over "the unknown prairie" in a little more than five days.

The "Map of the route pursued by the late expedition under the command of Col. S. W. Kearny . . . [in 1845] by W. B. Franklin . . ."—reproduced in this volume—is thus explicably deficient (as well as misleading) in marking out the dragoons' path, and in attempting to show the water-courses, for the area between Fort Leavenworth and the Little Blue.

For the Santa Fe trail section, comparison of place names with those on Josiah Gregg's 1844 map shows only one variation. The stream, now "Switzler creek," which Gregg (and others of the period) called "Bridge Cr." is labeled "Switzers" on the Franklin map. (When Pvt. M. B. Edwards, of Saline county, Mo., crossed this stream on June 29, 1846 [at what is now Burlingame, Osage co.], he wrote: "Switzler creek—so named by John Switzler, formerly a citizen of Saline, who built a bridge across it when the road was first opened.")

Ref: Carleton, *op. cit.*, p. 195; New York *Weekly Tribune*, July 26, 1845 (for a May 30, 1845, letter); R. P. Bieber, editor, *Marching With the Army of the West, 1846-1848* (Glendale, Cal., 1936), p. 122. Joseph C. Brown, surveyor with the 1825 Santa Fe road survey expedition (*see* KHi's *18th Biennial Report*, p. 117), in his 1827 report had stated: "Bridge Creek [105 miles from Fort Osage] . . . affords good water, timber and grass. The bed of this creek is muddy and must of necessity be bridged." A diary entry (February 10, 1826) by Santa Fe road Comm'r George C. Sibley, mentions a draft "for $200 fav[o]r John Switzler at 10 days"—which *may* relate to the original bridge construction. Switzler was *not* a member of the Santa Fe road survey expedition.—*See* Kate L. Gregg, editor, *The Road to Santa Fe* . . . (c1952), p. 142.

❦ May 24.—The Union Fur Company's steamboat *Frolic* (which had been near the mouth of the Yellowstone over-winter) arrived at St. Joseph, Mo., on her way to St. Louis.

Because of the Missouri's low stage, she carried little cargo; and half her cabin had been "thrown away" to lighten her. Earlier in May, traders from the mountains had reported the *Frolic* was "lying high and dry" on the upper river.

Ref: *The Gazette*, St. Joseph, Mo., May 23 and 30, 1845; Sunder's *The Fur Trade* . . ., *op. cit.*, p. 81.

❦ May.—The American Fur Company's *General Brooke* (Joseph A. Sire, master), which left St. Louis on the 22d for the upper Missouri, probably passed along the "Kansas" shore before the end of May. She went as far as the mouth of the Yellowstone.

One passenger, it appears, was the Count of Otranto (son of Joseph Fouché, minister of police under Napoleon), who also had gone upriver in the spring of 1844. Aboard, too, were Subagent Richard S. Elliott (of the Council Bluffs [Iowa] Subagency), and his family.

On her return journey in July (arriving at St. Joseph, Mo., on the 15th; and St. Louis on the 18th), the *General Brooke* brought about 500 packs of buffalo robes.

Ref: H. M. Chittenden's *Early Steamboat Navigation* . . ., (New York, 1903), v. 1, p. 177; R. S. Elliott's *Notes Taken in Sixty Years* (1883), pp. 191-194; *Niles' National Register*, v. 68 (August 2, 1845), pp. 339, 340; *The Gazette*, St. Joseph, Mo., July 18, 1845.

❦ May.—Workmen began relocating Ottawa Baptist Mission (present Franklin county) at a new site about two and a half miles northward—a location out of reach of flood waters. Jotham Meeker and family took up quarters there on May 27, occupying a building "designed for the stable." On October 11 they moved into the not-yet-completed mission house.

Ref: Jotham Meeker's "Diary," (in KHi ms. division), entries of July 2, August 2, September 4, 17-19, 1844, and May, August 9, and October 11, 1845.

❦ MARRIED: John Tecumseh ("Tauy") Jones (half-English; half-Chippewa), and Jane Kelley (Baptist teacher at Stockbridge Mission), on June 2.

For Jones' earlier marriage (his first wife died in February, 1844), *see* p. 414; and *see* his portrait on p. 602. His 30-acre farm *of the 1840's* was on Pottawatomie creek, present Franklin county. Missionary Jotham Meeker, on September 1, 1845, noted that "Br[other] J. T. Jones" had accepted an appointment from the American Baptist Board of Foreign Missions to work among the Pottawatomies as a native assistant.

Ref: *Baptist Missionary Magazine*, v. 26 (June and July, 1846), pp. 205, 239; Jotham Meeker's diary (from 1838 on, for references to John T. Jones); Goodspeed's *Wyandotte County and Kansas City, Kansas* . . . (Chicago, 1890), pp. 131-133; Lewis H. Morgan's *The Indian Journals 1859-62* (Ann Arbor, c1959), p. 38 (for autobiographical data on Jones); B. Smith Haworth's *Ottawa University Its History and Its Spirit* [1957], p. 161 (has a brief chronology of facts about J. T. Jones); John G. Pratt's statement on Jane (Kelley) Jones (in KHi ms. division).

❦ Around June 1, six American Fur Company Mackinaw boats, "heavily laden" with buffalo robes, were in the St. Joseph, Mo., area, en route from Fort Pierre (S. D.) to St. Louis.

On June 13 the St. Joseph *Gazette* stated: "Within the last three days, eight mackinaw boats have passed down, heavily laden with robes and furs. They bring from the mountains near two thousand bales. Other boats are looked for in a few days, belonging to the American Fur Company."

Ref: *Niles' National Register*, v. 68 (June 28, 1845), p. 258 (from St. Louis *New Era* of June 9; *The Gazette*, St. Joseph, Mo., June 13, 1845.

❦ June 6.—Dr. Richard Hewitt, accompanied by his family (wife Hannah; and six? children) came from Jackson county, Mo., to succeed Jonathan Phillips as head of the Wyandot Subagency.

There was no subagency building (Phillips had lived in Missouri). On September 1 the Hewitts moved into a rented house [the Henry Jacquis residence?] in present Kansas City, Kans. Doctor Hewitt served as subagent four years, returning to Missouri July 15, 1849.

Ref: SIA, St. Louis, "Records," v. 8, typed copy, pp. 497, 511; Comm'r of Indian Affairs, *Report*, 1845 (Hewitt's report); William Walker's journal (printed in W. E. Connelley's *Provisional Government of Nebraska Territory* . . . [Lincoln, Neb., 1899]), entries of June 7, 1845, and July 15, 1849; KHC, v. 10, p. 272 (states that Hewitt was a strong Proslaveryman; returned to Kansas [after 1860, apparently] to live; was a legislator in 1867; and died in Wyandotte county in 1879). From the listing of Doctor Hewitt's family in the 1850 Jackson county, Mo., census (p. 502), it would appear that his children, in 1845, were Eldridge (17?), Jane (15?), Experience (12?), Louisa (7?), Richard M. (3?), and Roxana (1?). The Goodspeed history of *Wyandotte County*, p. 352, says "Henry Jaques" erected his "second residence" where "Dunning's Hall" was later built, and that: "From May, 1845, to the spring of 1849, this was occupied as a United States agency."

❦ On June 9 Capt. John C. Fremont and some of the men who

were to participate in his third exploring expedition, debarked, with baggage and equipment, from the *Henry Bry*, at the "little port of Kansas" (Kansas City, Mo.). This party included Lt. James W. Abert and (2d Lt.) William G. Peck (of the topographical engineers), Edward M. Kern (artist), and Dr. James McDowell (surgeon and naturalist; who returned East from Bent's Fort), and a number of "recruits." In company also, were two young artists —Alfred S. Waugh and John B. Tisdale (would-be members of the expedition, but rejected by Fremont on July 1). (Theodore Talbot [of the second expedition], handling final details at St. Louis, arrived at Kansas, Mo., some six days later, aboard the *White Cloud*.)

Men and gear were transported in wagons to a camp six miles west of Westport, Mo. Hired hand Isaac Cooper called this place "Boone's Fork." (Edward Kern's letter of June 19 was from "Camp, at the head of Boon Creek, Mo. Ter.") Waugh described the site as "a gentle eminence" nearly surrounded by forest, with "a clear spring a short distance below" flowing sufficiently to form a rivulet. At "Boone's Fork," in present Johnson county, Fremont's company remained two weeks (a period of heavy rainfall). Abert, Peck, and Kern had quarters at Westport.

On June 23 a six-mile march was made. At this second camp (on a little plateau near a creek) three nights were spent. After Fremont made a speech to all hands laying down his "martial law" regulations, about 10 men quit (on the 26th). When the march resumed, around noon on June 26, the company numbered about 70, including two Delaware Indians. (Talbot wrote: "many of our men are of very respectable families more than two thirds of them are Americans the remainder French.") Heading the cavalcade was a "little [instrument-carrying] Yankee wagon on springs" with square black top and buttoned-down cutains; followed by four heavier mule-drawn vehicles. There were around 200 horses and mules; also a number of beeves. Three ox-drawn supply-carrying wagons were in the procession, too. (They were sent back about July 4.) Camp, on the 26th, apparently was at Lone Elm— a site known (up to about 1844) as Elm Grove, or Round Grove.

Journeying down the Santa Fe trail, and making slow progress due to bad roads, the expedition, at the close of travel on July 3, crossed a small creek and "camped on the hill beyond." Here the company remained over July 4. Fremont called the stream "Independence creek." (Probably this was the branch of Dragoon creek now called Soldier creek—placing the camp near the Osage-Wabaunsee county line of today. *See* Abert's statement, in 1846, below.) Some of the hands celebrated the Fourth with a "discharge of firearms at daybreak." Fremont issued a "small quantity of fire-water" to his men; and at a rifle-shoot held later in the day, brandy, and clothing were the prizes. (For this expedition the captain had "procured about a dozen rifles, the best that could be found.")

After crossing Pawnee Fork, about July 17, Fremont and company *left the Santa Fe trail* and "struck off in a direction north of west," up the Pawnee Fork's right bank, and into the buffalo range. From the head of this stream they "struck over to the Smoky hill Fork of Kansas River." The going was rough, and the wagons delayed them. Retracing, generally, the route of 1844 (but in the opposite direction—*see* p. 521), they reached the Arkansas at a point 25 miles below Bent's Fort, on August 1, and on the 2d arrived at the trading post. (Kearny and the First dragoons, there on July 29, had continued down the Arkansas, on the 30th.)

Bent's Fort was "the real point of departure" for the expedition. Here, Lts. James W. Abert and William G. Peck were detached to "make a survey of the prairie region to the southward, embracing the Canadian and other rivers." (Abert's party, with guides Thomas Fitzpatrick [recruited from Kearny], and John L. Hatcher [for part of the trip], 30 hired hands [including Isaac and Stephen Cooper], also four wagons and 63 animals, starting August 15, concluded "explorations" in October; arriving at Fort Gibson [Okla.] on the 21st.)

Fremont, with over 50 men (and no wagons), set out, up the Arkansas, on August 16. Kit Carson and Dick Owens were newly added members of his force, as were six Delaware Indians (all distinguished for bravery) as hunters. These included Jim Shawanock (son of the chief killed in 1844—*see* p. 520), Jim Secondine, and Jim Connor. Joining still later were Lucien Maxwell (as hunter) and Joseph R. Walker (as guide).

The explorations westward from Bent's Fort to California—too complex for brief summation—are not outlined here. Fremont, and a small party, arrived at Sutter's Fort on December 9. The larger force, under Talbot (and including Kern), with Walker as guide, also reached California safely, but this company was not reunited with Captain Fremont till mid-February, 1846.

Ref: *Niles' National Register*, v. 68 (May 3, 1845), p. 129; *New York Weekly Tribune*, August 2, 1845; *The Western Journal and Civilian*, St. Louis; v. 9 (October, 1852-March, 1853), pp. 71-73, 146-148, 221-222, 290-293, 366-368, 433-436, and v. 10 (April-September, 1853), pp. 69-73, 149-152, 222-226, 295-301, 370-375, 441-445) contain the "memoranda" of "Francois des Montaignes"—identified as Isaac Cooper); John C. Fremont's *Memoirs* . . . (1887), pp. 424-602; Theodore Talbot letters, June 9-August 16, 1845 (from originals in the Library of Congress); *Bulletin* of the Missouri Historical Society, St. Louis, v. 6 (April, July, 1950), pp. 288-322, 503-509 (for Waugh and Tisdale), or, *see* the same data in A. S. Waugh's *Travels In Search of the Elephant*, ed. by J. F. McDermott (1951); 30th Cong., 1st Sess., *H. Ex. Doc. No. 41* (Serial 517), p. 393 (for statement of Lt. J. W. Abert, who, marching with Kearny in 1846, camped July 2, 1846, at 110-mile creek, and on July 3, wrote: "Having marched 15 miles, we reached Independence creek, so called by Colonel Fremont, in consequence of our encamping here [Soldier? creek, in southeast corner of Wabaunsee county?] on the 4th of July, one year previous); 29th Cong., 1st Sess., *Sen. Doc. No. 438* (Serial 477), pp. 1-75 (for Abert's report of the 1845 explorations); DeWitt C. Peters' *The Life and Adventures of Kit Carson* (any edition) for the journey beyond Bent's Fort; D. Morgan, *op. cit.*, outlines Fremont's explorations of 1845 in his introduction, *see* v. 1, pp. 44-49; James W. Abert, *Through the Country of the Comanche Indians in* . . . *1845*, edited by John Galvin (San Francisco, 1970). To Dale Morgan the compiler is indebted for access to (1) items from Edward M. Kern papers—in the Huntington Library, and (2) notes on financial records covering Fremont's third expedition (from the National Archives, Washington, D. C.), which have been most useful in verifying data relating to personnel of the expedition. David Lavender, in his *Bent's Fort* (1954), p. 246, notes Hatcher's role as guide for Abert. In 1857 Fremont stated that the Delawares with his 1845-1846 expedition were James Swanuck, James Saghundai, James Conner, Delaware Charley, Wetowka, Crane, Solomon Everett and Bob Skirkett.—58th Cong., 1st Sess., *Sen. Doc. No. 16* (Serial 4563), p. 159.

❡ **Mid-June.**—On the 14th(?), or 16th(?), the foremost companies of emigrants reached Fort Laramie. They were just behind Colonel

Kearny and his First dragoons, who, almost daily from May 24 to June 14, had overtaken wagon trains on the Oregon trail.

For the most part, the emigrants in advance were those who had set out from St. Joseph, or that vicinity. (Goulder, of Tetherow's company, recollected he reached Fort Laramie on June 14; Harritt, of T'Vault's company, got there June 17. Palmer, and Snyder—in companies which started from Independence—were at Fort Laramie on June 23, and Howell on June 27.) The intended destination of nearly all these 1845 emigrants was Oregon. At Fort Hall some were persuaded to alter their course, but it appears that fewer than 200 went to California.

The size of the year's emigration was estimated, calculated, or "counted" by a number of people. Because 1845 was a "large-migration" year, and one in which all(?) the overland emigrant traffic to Oregon or California crossed "Kansas," contemporary statements on "size" are of particular interest.

Col. S. W. Kearny (in his September, 1845, report): "We found the emigrants on the Oregon trail to be about 850 men, 475 women, 1,000 children [i. e., 2,325 persons], driving with them about 7,000 head of cattle, 400 horses and mules, with 460 wagons." [Compare with Subagent Richardson's figures for the "St. Joseph" companies, and the *Western Expositor's* census of the "Independence" companies—pp. 539 and 542.]

Capt. P. St. G. Cooke (in a letter): "The emigrants amounted to about 2,500 souls."

Trader Daniel Finch (eastbound on the Oregon trail in May) was reported to have met "at least 500 wagons and the usual proportion of emigrants and cattle."

Joseph V. Hamilton (who left Fort Laramie about June 14, for Missouri) was said to have met "573 emigrant wagons."

John M. Shively (returning from Oregon in the summer) was quoted as stating: "The emigrants numbered about 2,375 souls, large and small." (A figure obtained from the dragoons?)

From a count made by traders in the Fort Laramie area in June: "550 wagons of Oregon immigrants," and an estimated 2,750 persons (calculated at five persons per wagon).

Emigrant James H. McMillen (at Fort Laramie, June 27): "In all we number over 3,000 persons."

Emigrant John E. Lyle (at Fort Laramie, June 25): "There have several companies passed this [place] in advance of us—there are also some in our rear." "Some wise men says there are 600 wagons and that they will average four souls to each wagon; I think 500 high enough with 4 persons each."

The Rev. George Gary (Oregon City resident), on October 11, wrote: "from the statements of all so far the emigration will perhaps number more than 2,000, and more than 500 wagons." On October 27 he wrote: "The probability is the entire number of this year's emigration is about 3,000 souls, 600 wagons and 15,000 head of cattle; So writes Mr. Brewer who has a pretty good opportunity to ascertain the number. A large proportion of this large emigration are as high up the Columbia as the Dall[e]s and some still further back. . . ."

Ref: 29th Cong., 1st Sess., *H. Doc. No. 2* (Serial 480), p. 212 (for Kearny); *Niles' National Register,* v. 69 (October 25, 1845), pp. 123, 124 (for Cooke); *ibid.* (September 6,

1845), p. 5 (for Fort Laramie traders); *ibid.*, v. 68 (June 14, 1845), p. 241 (for Finch); *Daily Missouri Republican*, St. Louis, July 15, 1845 (for Hamilton); New York *Weekly Tribune*, September 6, 1845 (for Shively), and September 20, 1845 (for McMillen); *The Gazette*, St. Joseph, Mo., October 3, 1845 (for Lyle); *Oregon Historical Quarterly*, v. 24 (September, 1923), pp. 291, 293.

❏ Mid-June.—The St. Joseph, Mo., newspaper noted the recent arrival at that place of three "independent" steamboats; the *White Cloud, John Aull,* and *Lexington.*

Theodore Talbot (of Fremont's expedition), who was aboard the *White Cloud* from St. Louis to Kansas (City), Mo., indicated the "June rise" of the Missouri had occurred soon after June 9.

Ref: *The Gazette*, St. Joseph, Mo., June 20, 1845; Theodore Talbot's letter of June 15, 1845 (original in Library of Congress).

❏ June.—By the 23d, in the Marais des Cygnes valley (present Franklin county), the "bottoms . . . [were] all covered with water from three to eight feet deep."

On the 26th Missionary Jotham Meeker wrote: "The constant heavy rains keeps the river up. . . ." The same day "Br[other] David Green [one of the most faithful of Meeker's converts, and often his assistant in translating into the Ottawa language], while trying to swim across the creek [near Ottawa Baptist Mission] to attend a prayer meeting, was drowned."

In September Sup't Thomas H. Harvey, St. Louis, reported: "the Indians on the Osage [Marais des Cygnes], embracing parts of the Pottawatomies, Chippewas, Ottawas, and Weas, have again [as in 1844] had their crops destroyed by the high water of that river and its tributaries."

Ref: Jotham Meeker's "Diary"; *Baptist Missionary Magazine*, v. 25 (September, 1845), p. 273; Comm'r of Indian Affairs, *Report*, 1845 (Harvey's report, therein).

❏ June 23.—The Kansas, in flood stage from recent rains, had "overflown its bottoms for miles to the high bluffs on either side" —at least on the lower river.

At the Delaware (or Grinter) crossing on the military road, ferry operations were halted. So Theodore Talbot, bound from Westport, Mo., to Fort Leavenworth (on a mission for Capt. John C. Fremont—*see* p. 551) "went round to the Missouri" and boarded an upbound steamboat. That river's current was so powerful the boat could "scarcely battle against it."

Returning, on horseback, via the military road, on the 24th, Talbot "slept at 'Delaware Town'" (and attended a "grand dance" there, which lasted till daylight). He was able to cross the Kansas on June 25.

Ref: Theodore Talbot's letter of June 25, 1845 (from original in Library of Congress).

❏ Summer.—Under construction at Shawnee Friends Mission (present Johnson county) was a new three-story building, 24 by 70 feet. The first floor, or basement, of stone, contained the kitchen, dining-room, and cellar; the upper stories, of frame, had "school rooms in each end, dormitories above, with four rooms in the middle . . . for the family."

Sup't Thomas H. Stanley, and his brother James, had chopped the logs, hauled them to the mill [presumably the new saw mill at Shawnee Methodist Mission], hewed the framing timber, and built most of the mission themselves.

In August Thomas H. and Mary (Wilson) Stanley returned to Ohio, after three and a third years of service in "Kansas." Thomas and Hannah (Duke-mineer) Wells (teachers at the mission since 1843) succeeded the Stanleys as superintendents. Zeri and Miriam H. Hough were listed as teachers in the 1845 report. The school then had around 50 students (male and female).

Ref: H. Pearl Dixon's *Sixty Years Among the Indians* [1921?]; *KHC*, v. 8, pp. 252, 268; annals, p. 444; Comm'r of Indian Affairs, *Report*, 1845 (Agent R. W. Cummins' report, therein).

❡ Summer(?)—The Delaware Indians, "out of their own means," (but apparently by an arrangement with the Methodists) built a "good saw & grist mill with two run of stones—one for corn and the other for wheat." Both mills were "of a superior order, [with] good bolting apparatus, screen, fan & elevators all complete." The location was on the Stranger river (in present Leavenworth county), about 10 miles west of the Missouri, and about equidistant from the Delawares' north and south boundaries.

In 1851 Agent Thomas Moseley, Jr., wrote: "The Delaware mill, which was built by the Methodist missionary board as a boon for their education for a term of years, is now a complete wreck. I have visited it, and recommended the chiefs to retain $3000 out of the money they received from the Wyandots, which they did for the purpose of rebuilding the mill. . . . The tribe is anxious it should be rebuilt, as there is not a mill in the Indian country near, but the chiefs seem to feel indifferent." No information on the fate of the government-built Delaware mill of the 1830's (*see* p. 239) has been located. Perhaps it was ruined by the 1844 flood, if still in operation then.

Ref: Comm'r of Indian Affairs, *Reports* for 1845 (*see* R. W. Cummins' report, therein) and 1851 (*see* Thomas Moseley, Jr.'s report, therein); *KHC*, v. 9, pp. 205, 206.

❡ MARRIED: Silas Peirce and Mary Shook, employees at the Iowa, Sac & Fox Presbyterian Mission (present Doniphan county), on July 3, by the Rev. William Hamilton.

Witnesses (as stated in a later-day account) included: the Rev. Samuel M. and Eliza H. Irvin, Ann Eliza Richardson (daughter of Subagent W. P. Richard-son), Mrs. Rachel McCreary (sister of Mrs. Irvin), her son (T. J.) and daughter (Flora), Elizabeth Masters (daughter of John Masters), Mary White Cloud (wife of the Iowas' head chief, Frank White Cloud), also carpenters "Garvin," Henry Adamson, and J. C. Waterson (Waterman?), working on the new mission.

Ref: *Weekly Kansas Chief*, Troy, November 23, 1893 (special edition). The Peirces left the mission in 1846; settled on a farm across the Missouri, near Oregon, Mo.

❡ July-August.—En route to New Mexico and Chihuahua were four different companies of traders "numbering over 160 wagons and over double that number of men"—as reported by Glasgow's party (reaching Independence August 9). (Compare with statistics in December 31 annals entry.)

Kearny's homeward-bound expedition (leaving Bent's Fort July 30; striking the Santa Fe road, at the Arkansas Crossing on August 7; and branching from the trail on August 22) "met with several parties of traders going to Taos and Santa Fe, they were getting along without . . . difficulty."

Fremont's out-bound expedition had overtaken "several companies on the trace to Santa Fe," before digressing from the trail July 17 at Pawnee Fork.

Ref: New York *Weekly Tribune,* August 30, 1845 (from St. Louis *New Era* of August 14); 29th Cong., 1st Sess., *H. Doc. No. 2* (Serial 480); Theodore Talbot's letter of August 10, 1845 (original in Library of Congress).

❡ July 3.—"Today [wrote Theodore Talbot, of Fremont's expedition] we met Bent's convoy of wagons 14 in number coming into the States laden with robes & furs. *None* of the gentlemen were [with] them, having come in advance from Pawnee Cr." This encounter was in the vicinity of Dragoon creek crossing on the Santa Fe trail.

Ref: Theodore Talbot's July 3, 1845, letter (original in Library of Congress); *The Western Journal and Civilian,* St. Louis, v. 10 (June, 1853), p. 224 (wherein Isaac Cooper mentions this "train of fourteen wagons . . . from Bent's Fort . . . destined for the States)."

❡ In July's first week, by report, the "trading party of Mr. [Charles?] Bent of Bent's Fort," was preparing to leave the Missouri frontier. (Charles Bent had come East in April—reaching St. Louis May 9.)

C. C. Spalding's *Annals of the City of Kansas* (first published in 1858) states: "In 1845 Messrs. Bent & St. Vrain landed the first cargo of goods at Kansas City, [Mo.] that was ever shipped from this point to New Mexico in wagons that went out in a train. This train consisted of 18 wagons, with 5 yoke of cattle to the wagon, and about 5,000 lbs. of freight to each team." If correct, it must apply either to the Bent, St. Vrain & Co. caravan above, or the one which set out in October (*see* p. 564).

Seth E. Ward, making his first independent trading venture, *may* have been in this train (with one small ox-drawn wagon-load of goods).

Ref: *Daily Missouri Republican,* St. Louis, May 12, 1845 (for Charles Bent's arrival at St. Louis); *Bulletin* of the Missouri Historical Society, St. Louis, v. 6 (July, 1950), p. 509; C. C. Spalding's *Annals,* reprint edition, p. 32; biographical accounts of Seth E. Ward state that he returned to Missouri in the spring of 1845 (in company with Ceran St. Vrain[?]), after seven years in the mountains; that he used his $1,000 pay to purchase trading goods; then went out in the summer, with one wagon, in company with his old employers (Bent, St. Vrain & Co.)—*See The United States Biographical Dictionary . . . Missouri Volume* (New York, 1878), p. 466; *A Memorial and Biographical Record of Kansas City and Jackson County, Mo.* (Chicago, 1896), p. 568. If Ceran St. Vrain came to Missouri in 1845 he was back at Bent's Fort by July 29—welcoming Kearny and his dragoons; and, a few days later, host to Fremont. According to Theodore Talbot (who reached Bent's Fort with Fremont on August 2) the only one of the Bent brothers then at the fort was George. *Apparently* P. St. George Cooke, with Kearny, erred in writing that Charles Bent was there on July 29! *See, also,* Lavender, *op. cit.,* pp. 243, 405. J. S. Chick said that Bent, St. Vrain & Co. began using W. M. Chick's Kansas, Mo., warehouse in 1845.—*See* A. Theodore Brown's *Frontier Community Kansas City to 1870* (c1963), p. 56.

❡ Mid-July.—"Mr. Hicks" (with eight wagons) was captain of a train (27? wagons) which set out from the Council Grove rendez-vous for Santa Fe. The company included partners George P. Doan and James J. Webb (who had three ox-drawn wagons—two large ones carrying 5,500 pounds each; the other with a 1,500-pound load), "Mr. [Norris] Colburn," Bethel Hicks (cousin of the captain), "Mr. [Smallwood V.?] Noland," and "Tom Otobus [Auto-bees]."

They went by way of Bent's Fort; and some of the traders went on to Santa Fe, in advance. It was, presumably, this company of whom Theodore Talbot wrote, on August 10 (while at Bent's Fort with Fremont): "There has . . . been a Caravan of 27 Wagons belonging to Santa Fe traders camped at the Fort. . . ." The wagons reached Santa Fe early in September.

Ref: Webb, *op. cit.*, pp. 128-138; Theodore Talbot's August 10, 1845, letter (original in Library of Congress). The "trading wagons of Mr. [George P.] Doan of St. Louis" were nearing Council Grove around July 4—*see* Isaac Cooper's statement in *The Western Journal and Civilian,* St. Louis, v. 10 (July, 1853), p. 295.

(MARRIED: William John Dillon and Susannah (Susan) Adams Yoacham, daughter of Daniel and Rosannah (May) Yoacham, on July 17, at Westport, Mo., by the Rev. James Porter.

The bride, born at Shawnee Agency (later Fort Leavenworth Agency) in present Johnson county on January 12, 1830—*see* p. 168—was the second white girl known to have been born in "Kansas."

Ref: "Marriage Record No. 2," Jackson county, Mo., p. 107.

(In July Fort Scott had a change of command. Capt. William M. Graham and Companies C and D, Fourth infantry departed for Jefferson Barracks, Mo., on July 21. Capt. Sidney Burbank, who, with Company B, First infantry had arrived at the post July 14, assumed command on the 21st. Company A, First dragoons, already stationed there (but with Kearny's expedition during the spring and summer), returned on August 24.

Ref: H. P. Beers' *The Western Military Frontier 1815-1846* (Philadelphia, 1935), p. 142; 29th Cong., 1st Sess., *H. Doc. No. 51* (Serial 482), p. 46 (for War Department contract of July 26, 1845, Lt. C. Hoskins, AAQM, with John McCloy, for transportation, by steamboat *Lexington*, from Independence Landing to Jefferson Barracks, of Companies C and D, Fourth infantry, consisting of five officers, 99 men, five women, and five servants, with baggage, etc.); 29th Cong., 1st Sess., *H. Doc. No. 2* (Serial 480), *between* pp. 220, 221; Fort Scott post returns (microfilm in KHi).

(July 23.—The steamboat *Big Hatchee*, en route from St. Louis to Weston, Mo., "burst her starboard boiler" while leaving the landing at Hermann, Mo.

The casualties, as of July 31: 12 known dead, and nine injured (some critically) under medical treatment. The boat "suffered severely."

Ref: New York *Weekly Tribune,* August 9, 16, 1845 (from St. Louis newspapers—one the *New Era* of July 31); *The Gazette,* St. Joseph, Mo., August 15, 1845.

The emigrant company of which Jacob R. Snyder was a member, met (on June 29, west of Fort Laramie) ". . . Antoine Roubidoux from the Spanish Country." Snyder added: "He was obliged to come through this way [from 'Utah'] on account of the Indians, 8 of his men having been killed."

Ref: *The Gazette*, St. Joseph, Mo., August 15, 1845; *Quarterly of the Society of California Pioneers*, v. 8 (December, 1931), p. 237.

❦ August 11.—Seven men (including John M. Shively and "Mr. Sappington"), eastward bound from Oregon, and California, reached Independence, Mo., after a journey over the Oregon trail (and across "Kansas").

Shively was one of 12 "Oregonians" who had set out on April 19; "Mr. Sappington" was one of 15 who had left Sutter's Fort in California on May 12. The parties having met near Fort Hall, *some* had traveled the rest of the way together to Missouri. (For later arrivals, via the Oregon trail, from the same company *see* August 29 entry.)

In 1846 John M. Shively's *Route and Distances to Oregon and California, With a Description of Watering-Places, Crossings, Dangerous Indians, &c., &c.*, (one of the rarest, and earliest, of the guides to Oregon and California), was published at Washington, D. C. The author noted therein: "From Independence to the Crossings of Kanzas, [is] 102 miles"; "When you arrive at the crossings of the Kanzas, if it be past fording, there is a ferry there . . ."; "202 miles from the crossings of Kanzas . . . you will come to the river Platte."

Ref: *Niles' National Register*, v. 68 (August 30, 1845), p. 416; New York *Weekly Tribune*, September 6, 1845; D. Morgan, *op. cit.*, v. 1, pp. 18-21, and v. 2, pp. 734-742 (for a reprinting of the Shively guidebook). *See* reproduction of cover and table of distances (from original copy owned by the Kansas State Historical Society) in this volume.

❦ August.—A "few days" before the 27th, Wethered & Caldwell's train of some 20 wagons left Independence, Mo., for Santa Fe. Traders Samuel Wethered and Thomas J. Caldwell apparently reached that place in November.

Ref: J. Gregg, *op. cit.*, v. 1, p. 168; Webb, *op. cit.*, pp. 139, 145, 148.

❦ August 17(?)—Lansford W. Hastings and a small party of men on horseback, with pack animals, left a camp west of Independence Mo. (near "Fitzhugh's on the Santa Fe road"), and set out for California by way of the Oregon trail. By August 24 they were three days' travel beyond the Kansas crossing (present Topeka). From Fort Laramie to the Fort Bridger area, this party used a detour; then continued the regular trail route to Fort Hall [Ida.].

(Hastings had journeyed overland to Oregon in 1842, and from there to California in 1843—*see* p. 447; then returned East by way of the "roundabout Mexican route." His *The Emigrants' Guide, to Oregon and California* . . . had been published at Cincinnati early in 1845.)

Originally Hastings' California-bound party of 1845 numbered 23 persons. (The Independence *Western Expositor* of August 16 listed the prospective travelers' names.) But over half the party backed out. The 10 who made this late-in-the-year start were fortunate, reaching Sutter's Fort safely, and without particular difficulty, on December 25.

Ref: *Niles' National Register*, v. 69 (September 6, 1845), p. 7 (for the *Expositor* item, incorrectly dated therein as from the July 6 issue; D. Morgan, *op. cit.*, v. 1, pp. 21-35 (for all the pertinent data relating to Hastings); Overton Johnson and W. H. Winter's *Route Across the Rocky Mountains* (Princeton, 1932), p. 165 (for August 24 item); L. W. Hastings' *The Emigrants' Guide* . . ., edited by C. H. Carey (1932), p. xv; Stewart, *op. cit.*, pp. 104, 105.

❡ Died: Doctor Greyeyes, aged 50, a prominent man of the Wyandot Nation, in August. He was buried at present Kansas City, Kan., in Huron Place cemetery.

Ref: Connelley, *op. cit.*, p. 254. "Greyeyes" is variously spelled—"Gray Eyes," etc.

❡ August.—The *General Brooke*, bound for Council Bluffs, with only 90 tons of freight, left St. Louis on August 25. Such was the low stage of water in the Missouri that this "light boat" spent three days on a sandbar at Lexington, Mo.; above St. Joseph was "obliged to divide the load and leave one half"; finally reached the "Bluffs" about 15 days after starting.

Returning, in mid-September, with no cargo, the *General Brooke* was frequently aground; and spent 10 days running the 750 miles to St. Louis. The former Indian subagent Richard S. Elliott (who gave the above information) also reported: "The price of freight from St. Louis to Council Bluffs is often as high as $60 per ton. From St. Louis to Weston, Mo., freights are 50 to 60 cents and higher, per 100 lbs. more months than a lower rate."

Ref: New York *Weekly Tribune*, January 31, 1846.

❡ August 29.—Seven men (Overton Johnson, William H. Winter, Father Soderena, of Kalispell mission [Mont.], and four others) who had left Fort Laramie near the end of July, reached the Westport, Mo., vicinity, after a journey over the Oregon trail (and across "Kansas").

Johnson and Winter had traveled to Oregon in 1843—*see* p. 479—and Winter had gone on to California in 1844. They were reunited in June, 1845, when their eastbound parties (*see August* 11 entry) met near Fort Hall and joined forces. Of the 17 from this company who reached Fort Laramie on July 27, the above seven continued down the Oregon trail together.

On the Platte, in the Pawnee country, on August 13, these travelers were surrounded and harassed by a large band of Pawnees, but took a resolute stand which influenced the Indians to let them go unmolested. To avoid further encounters, the white men left the trail; then had some difficulty determining the route from the Platte to the Little Blue's headwaters. However, they reached the Little Blue safely, and on August 16 "came again to the emigrant's trail." On the 22d they forded the Big Blue (in present Marshall county); on the 24th "met a small company bound for California" (Lansford W. Hastings' party); on the 25th met some wagons bound for Fort Platte. In fording the Kansas river (at what is now Topeka) on the 27th, the men found the water too deep to take the baggage on their horses, and carried it over on their shoulders. On August 29th, late at night, they crossed the state line and encamped near Westport.

Ref: Johnson and Winter, *op. cit.*, pp. 120-132. As noted in these annals, p. 480, their book (principally a narrative, but, in part, guidebook) was originally published at Lafayette, Ind., in 1846. It contained a section with "Instructions to Emigrants" on supplies and equipment needed, the manner of traveling, etc., and a table of distances. *See, also,* D. Morgan, *op. cit.*, v. 1, pp. 18-21. Josiah Gregg, in a letter from Independence, Mo., August 27, 1845, wrote: "We have lately had an arrival from Oregon and California—a small party of a dozen or so men from each region, who came in together."—J. Gregg, *op. cit.*, v. 1, p. 168.

❊ August 30.—Col. Stephen W. Kearny arrived at St. Louis from Fort Leavenworth (to which post he had returned, from the Rocky mountain expedition, on August 24—*see* p. 558).

Ref: New York *Weekly Tribune,* September 20, 1845 (from a St. Louis newspaper).

❊ Early in September, apparently, Albert Speyer and other traders —a party of some 20(?) men, and six(?) wagons, from Chihuahua, and Santa Fe—reached Independence, Mo. (Josiah Gregg stated that the "avant-couriers" of this company had arrived on August 26.)

Ref: J. Gregg, *op. cit.*, v. 1, p. 168.

❊ September.—Daniel Finch "with eight or nine ox teams, heavily loaded with trading goods for Indians," crossed "Kansas" by way of the Oregon trail during this month (presumably). On October 17 he was within a day's travel of his(?) trading fort (located on the Platte, seven to eight miles below Fort Laramie [Wyo.]). Probably traveling in company most of the way was "Mr. Spane" and party who "had several teams loaded with goods for trading with the Sioux."

(Finch, eastbound in the spring, with five peltry-laden wagons, had traveled through "Kansas" in May.)

Ref: New York *Weekly Tribune,* December 6, 1845; A. J. Allen's *Ten Years in Oregon* (Ithaca, N. Y., 1850), p. 296; *Niles' National Register,* v. 68 (June 14, 1845), p. 224. *Quarterly of The Society of California Pioneers,* v. 8 (December, 1931), p. 226 (for Jacob R. Snyder's meeting with Finch on May 21 near the Kansas river). "Mr. Spane," whose partner died about October 17, was, on the 18th, a day behind Finch on the trail.

❊ September.—Mountain man Miles M. Goodyear, with a few companions, and a pack train, left Independence, Mo., in mid-month, to travel the Oregon trail out to the Fort Bridger vicinity. It was his announced intention to build a trading fort—"a sort of *half way house*"—somewhere on the emigrants' route.

(Goodyear's summer visit to Missouri had been his first in nine years. *See* p. 305, for his original trip to the mountains.)

Where Ogden, Utah, is today, Miles Goodyear, in the late summer of 1846, founded his trading post—Fort Buenaventura.

Ref: *Utah Historical Quarterly,* Salt Lake City, v. 21 (July, October, 1953), pp. 195-218, 307-329 (for Dale L. Morgan's articles on Miles Goodyear); D. Morgan, *op. cit.,* v. 1, pp. 280, 379, 385, 442, 443.

❆ Mid-September.—The new (north) building, "intended for the female school," at Shawnee Methodist Mission (present Johnson county) was "up to the Square," and was expected to be finished by December 25.

This two-story, 100-by-20 foot brick structure (begun in 1844—*see* p. 529) had a "piazza the whole length, with the exception of a small room at each end taken off. . . ."

During the year "137 male and female scholars from sundry tribes" had attended the Indian manual labor school.

Ref: Comm'r of Indian Affairs, *Report,* 1845 (R. W. Cummins' report of September 15, 1845, therein).

❆ September 16.—Bound from Weston, Mo., to St. Louis, the *Lexington* (valued at $7,000 to $8,000) hit a snag at "Rock Castle Bar" and sank—nearly a total loss. (The upper part of the boat could be salvaged; but not the freight and hull.)

Other steamboats on the Missouri in the "Kansas" area during the autumn included the *Republic, Amaranth, Radnor, Archer, Mendota,* and *Tributary.*

Ref: 29th Cong., 1st Sess., *H. Doc. No. 91* (Serial 483), pp. 43, 107, 199; 30th Cong., 1st Sess., *H. Ex. Doc. No. 5* (Serial 514), pp. 50, 133; *The Western Journal,* St. Louis, v. 5 (March, 1851), p. 326; Nebraska State Historical Society *Publications,* v. 20, pp. 133, 134; *The Gazette,* St. Joseph, Mo., October 3, 1845.

❆ September.—At Iowa, Sac & Fox Presbyterian Mission (present Doniphan county), the "main building for the [new manual labor boarding] school was under roof on the 21st instant."

Missionary Samuel M. Irvin described the building as 106 feet long by 37 feet wide; with a first, or basement, story of limestone; the two upper stories of brick, and the roof of good pine. Subagent W. P. Richardson wrote: "The boards for the flooring, the window sash, blinds, doors, &c., &c., are in a forward state of preparation, which will enable the workmen to complete the building by the first of June next, at farthest." A grain mill (to be operated by horse-power), and out-houses, were also in progress.

Principal workmen on the project during 1845-1846 were J. W. Glazebrook, J. C. Waterman, Henry Adamson, and Andrew McCormick. G. & C. Todd built the grain mill (for $224.32).

Among the persons paid for their services at the mission in the 1845-1846 period (prior to April, 1846), were Samuel M. Irvin (missionary), Paul Bloohm and M. E. Higby (teachers), Francis Irvin (father of Samuel M.), John Meyer, and R. Waugh (farmers), and Findley C. McCreary.

Ref: Comm'r of Indian Affairs *Report,* 1845 (*see* S. M. Irvin's report, and W. P. Richardson's report, both dated September 30, 1845, therein); 30th Cong., 1st Sess., *H. Ex. Doc. No. 5* (Serial 514), p. 81. Missionary William Hamilton, and family were in the East at this time.

❦ September.—Visiting the Kansa, late in the month, to pay the *last annuity under the 1825 treaty,* Agent R. W. Cummins found them in a deplorable situation. Just prior to his arrival about 200 persons had died—68(?) men and women, the rest, children.

In addition, the Kansa had raised but little corn, their fields "having been overflown [again] last spring [as in 1844]"; and their horses were all dying from a disease (characterized by a swelling under the chest) which also was killing deer and raccoons.

Perhaps it was in this time of sickness that the elderly American Chief (Wa-kan-ze-re) died. His death apparently occurred before the Kansa treaty of January 14, 1846, was signed.

Ref: *Niles' National Register,* v. 69 (November 1, 1845), p. 134.

❦ September.—Residents—Indian and white—of present Doniphan county were suffering from attacks of fever, which had caused the death of some 40 Iowas and about 20 Sacs (mostly adults).

Ref: Comm'r of Indian Affairs, *Report,* 1845 (Subagent W. P. Richardson's September 30, 1845, report, therein).

❦ October 12.—Convening at Shawnee Methodist Mission's Indian manual labor school, the second session of the Indian Mission conference (Bishop Joshua Soule presiding) elected ministers Jerome C. Berryman and Wesley Browning as delegates to the Methodist Episcopal Church, *South,* convention (to be held May 1, 1846, at Petersburg, Va.). *See* May 1 annals entry.

Of this movement which brought the Methodist missions (and the manual labor school) in "Kansas" into the Southern convention of the divided Methodist Episcopal Church, the Rev. William H. Goode wrote: "The influence of the large mission establishment at the manual-labor school was strong. There were few to counteract or explain; and at the separation the main body of our Shawnee membership was carried, *nolens volens,* into the Church South. . . . They have a large meeting-house and camp-ground, and exert a powerful influence over the tribe. Our [M. E.] membership is reduced to about twenty—a faithful band." Except among the Wyandot Indians, where the Methodist Episcopal Church was strong, the transition to the Church South was effected without strife.

From 1845 till its close in 1862, the Indian manual labor school (present Johnson county) was under the Methodist Episcopal Church, South.

Ref: *KHC,* v. 9, pp. 179, 180; Martha B. Caldwell, compiler, *Annals of Shawnee Methodist Mission* . . . (Topeka, 1939), p. 56. The first session of the Indian Mission conference had been held near Tahlequah, [Okla.]—*see* annals, p. 529.

❦ Around October 15 the wagons of "Messrs. Bent, Alvarez," and others, were at Council Grove, westbound on the Santa Fe trail (as noted by "Messrs. Kaufman" [Hoffman] and party, who met them there).

The Bent, St. Vrain & Co. wagons (with William Bent in charge?), presumably included the 14 which had reached Missouri in July (*see* July 3 annals entry). Manuel Alvarez (U. S. consul at Santa Fe; and a trader) had arrived at Independence a few days prior to June 18 (by his own statement).

Ref: New York *Weekly Tribune*, November 15, 1845 (from *Western Expositor*, Independence, Mo., of October 25); *1950 Brand Book* (Denver, c1951), p. 280 (for Alvarez).

❡ October.—On the 22d(?) Santa Fe traders "Messrs. Kaufman [Hoffman] and Goldstein, Bean, [George H.?] Peacock [all of Jackson county, Mo.], and four of the Armijos (Mexicans)" arrived at Independence, Mo., with 12 wagons, 300 mules, and $30,000 in specie. Their 30-day journey had been uneventful.

Ref: New York *Weekly Tribune*, November 15, 1845 (from *Western Expositor*, Independence, Mo., of October 25, 1845); Stella M. Drumm, editor, in Magoffin, *op. cit.*, p. 4, says the Armijos "passed through St. Louis on their way to New York in December, 1845, to purchase their winter outfit. They carried with them over $50,000 in specie."

❡ November.—Dr. Elijah White, accompanied by William Chapman, Orus Brown, and Charles Saxton, direct from Oregon, by way of the Oregon trail, arrived at Westport, Mo., on November 15, after a 90-day journey.

(White, who had gone out in 1842 as Oregon's first subagent of Indian affairs—*see* p. 447—now carried a petition from the Oregon legislature to congress, asking "for an extension of the laws of the Union" to protect that territory. Chapman and Brown had made the overland journey west in 1843; Saxton in 1844.)

Starting east, these men left Oregon City on August 16; crossed the continental divide on October 4; reached Fort Laramie on October 15. Two weeks later, on the Platte, they fell into the hands of abusive, pillaging Pawnees who stripped them of clothing and most other possessions, and held them prisoners overnight.

On November 1 the four white men were put on "poor lame ponies," given a "few scant garments," three old rifles (with little ammunition), and a supply of "raw corn," then turned adrift. (White retained 541 letters he had brought to be mailed to persons in the East.) They were further endangered by a prairie fire, set behind them, but kept ahead of the flames. Crossing safely from the Platte to the headwaters of the Little Blue, they struck the Oregon trail on November 2, and some six(?) days later reached the bank of the Big Blue (in present Marshall county).

One account says that (about November 12) the men obtained a turkey and a little flour from an Indian family met on the trail; then "pressed down the river, and arrived at a Frenchman's" [Joseph Papin, probably] where they managed to get a little more flour. Two days later they "entered the house of Mr. Charles Fish [part Shawnee], who was . . . blacksmith among the Shawnee [*i. e., Kansa*] Indians," and who lived "30 miles from the U. S. line." Mrs. Fish "prepared them a noble repast of pork, dried venison, potatoes, and bread." White and his companions remained overnight; resumed their journey on the 15th; and by evening reached Westport, Mo., where they received a "kind and handsome" reception from Mr. [Albert G.] Boon[e] . . . and "spent the night at Mr. [Samuel] Geer's hotel."

On November 17, the Independence, Mo., *Western Expositor* published an *extra*, headlined: "Overland Mail From Oregon—Arrival of Dr. White, direct from Oregon—Unprecedented despatch—Through in Ninety Days!!"

As computed by these travelers the distance from Oregon City to Fort Hall was 800 miles; from Fort Hall to Green river, 195 miles; from Green river to Fort Laramie, 400 miles; and from Fort Laramie to Independence, Mo., 630 miles—a total of 2,025 miles.

Dr. Elijah White continued east to Washington, and on December 10 the Oregon Memorial was presented to the house of representatives.

Ref: Allen, *op. cit.*, pp. 275-314; New York *Weekly Tribune*, December 6, 1845 (for the "Independence Express [*i. e.*, *Western Expositor*], Nov 17th Extra" and other items); *Niles' National Register*, v. 69 (December 6, 1845), p. 224; Henry R. Wagner and Charles L. Camp, *The Plains and the Rockies* . . ., Third edition (Columbus, Ohio, 1953), pp. 200, 201; Thwaites, *op. cit.*, v. 30, p. 100; D. Morgan, *op. cit.*, v. 1, p. 160.

❧ DIED: John Perry, principal chief of the Shawnees, and "quite an old man," on November 16, at his home on the Shawnee reserve. He had been a "Kansas" resident since 1832—*see* p. 223.

Ref: Cross and Moore, *op. cit.* In the order of their signing a March 30, 1844, letter, the Shawnee chiefs were: John Perry (first chief), Pe-a-ta-cumme (second chief), Joseph Parks (third), Sah-qua-we (fourth), Blackhoof (fifth), and Letho (sixth).—OIA, Letters Received from Fort Leavenworth Agency (National Archives Microcopy 234, Roll 732).

❧ November.—Chiefs Wah-bon-seh (Wabaunsee), Op-te-ke-shiek (Op-te-gee-zheek), or Half Day, and Me-ah-mis (Mi-au-mise), headed a delegation of "Council Bluffs" Pottawatomies arriving in Washington, D. C., to meet the President, and to negotiate a land cession treaty.

This party (which included "half-breeds" Peerish [or Pierre] Le Clerc, Holliday, and M. B. Beaubien, interpreter) traveled east by steamboat (the *Amaranth*, on the Missouri) as far as Pittsburgh. Richard S. Elliott (recently their subagent; now employed by the Indians to look out for their interests), accompanied them to Washington. About November 24(?) the councils concluded (a protocol was signed, but not a final treaty), and the Pottawatomies left. Elliott (not with them) later wrote: "On their way home [to southwestern Iowa], a stage was upset in Ohio, and Wah-bon-seh was killed [and buried in Ohio]. Some of the others were hurt, but not fatally." (*See* pp. 440, 441, 485.)

A portrait of the Pottawatomies' venerated chief Wabaunsee (for whom a county, township, and town in Kansas are named) is reproduced on p. 614. In Shawnee county is a Big Soldier tributary creek now spelled "Halfday," named for Chief Half Day (the Pottawatomies' noted orator, above), who removed to "Kansas" in 1847?)

Ref: R. S. Elliott, *op. cit.*, pp. 198-213.

❧ November 19.—The *Tributary* arrived at Weston, Mo.—the last steamboat of the year to reach that port.

Ref: *The Western Journal*, St. Louis, v. 5 (March, 1851), p. 326.

❧ MARRIED: Hiram M. Northrup (a Westport, Mo., resident since

1844), and Margaret Clark (part Wyandot; daughter of Thomas Clark—who died in 1843), on November 27, at the Wyandots' Methodist parsonage, in present Kansas City, Kan., by the Rev. James Wheeler.

Northrup first established a mercantile business in the new town of Kansas, Mo., and built a log house near the corner of Main and Fourth streets, in 1847. But in 1855 he removed to "Wyandotte"—present Kansas City, Kan.; and had a log house "on the south side of what is now Minnesota Ave. at the crossing of Eighth street."

Ref: Jackson county, Mo., marriage records (wherein the bride is listed as "Margaret Clark of Wyandott City, Ind. Ter."); *United States Biographical Dictionary, Kansas Volume* (1879), pp. 80-82; Connelley, *op. cit.*, p. 303; Goodspeed's *Wyandotte County and Kansas City* . . . pp. 163, 174; *The History of Jackson County, Missouri* . . . (1881), p. 406. Margaret (Clark) Northrup (b. August 28, 1828; d. June 29, 1887) is buried in Huron cemetery, Kansas City, Kan.—*See The Kansas City Genealogist*, v. 4 (July 1, 1963), p. 3.

❦ December 22.—James J. Webb, Benjamin Pruett, four other Americans, and two Mexicans, with one small wagon, and about 20 mules and horses, arrived at Westport, Mo., from New Mexico. Pruett and Webb (who had set out from Santa Fe on November 2) brought about $8,000 in gold and specie. Their party had encountered storms en route; and excessively cold weather in "Kansas." Great numbers of buffaloes had been seen on the Arkansas.

Ref: Webb, *op. cit.*, pp. 145-170. Webb's partner—George P. Doan—had left Santa Fe for Missouri with a "return train" apparently in late September; and his company must have reached Independence in November.—*Ibid.*, p. 139.

❦ December.—Newly arrived from the Des Moines and Raccoon rivers country, Iowa (ter.), perhaps 900(?) of the "Mississippi" Sac & Fox Indians were encamped, by year's end, on the Shawnee reserve, south of Kansas river (in present Douglas county). Sac chief Keokuk and his band, plus some 250 "attached" Foxes (so far as can be determined from available information) were the Indians who arrived in 1845. They remained on the "borrowed" land till autumn, 1846, before removing southward to the new Sac & Fox reserve (*see* May, 1846, annals), on the Marais des Cygnes' headwaters (principally in Franklin and Osage counties of today).

At removal (from Iowa) time—October, 1845, by terms of the 1842 treaty— Agent John Beach stated the Sacs numbered 1,207 and the Foxes 1,271. Sac chief Keokuk and a large party started for "Kansas" in September, 1845. "These Indians looked decidedly well," reported the St. Joseph (Mo.) *Gazette*, in mid-October, "they have good horses, good clothing, and . . . are a much superior indian to the Sacs and Iowas that live opposite us [the 'Missouri' Sacs & Foxes—residents of 'Kansas' since 1837—*see* p. 325]. Old Keokuk wore quite a military appearance, having on a 'soldier's coat,' with epauletts, and being mounted on a fine horse."

Another large Sac (& Fox) contingent (some of Keokuk's people, and Hard Fish's band), setting out from Iowa in October, traveled southward—to Brunswick, Mo.—where some (apparently a good-sized band), together with their government employees, "wintered"—and did not reach "Kansas" till late April, 1846. But perhaps 300(?) continued overland from Brunswick, and around 200(?) boarded the steamboat *Amaranth*. At Lexington, Mo., on November 23, the "river party" went ashore, and was reunited on the 24th with the "land party." It appears that Long Horn (a Sac councilman) headed this migrating company, which included 21-year-old Keokuk, Jr., or Waw-naw-ke-saw (later known as Moses Keokuk), also Nash-she-wah-skuk and his younger brother, Aw-tha-me-saw—both sons of famed Sac chief Black Hawk. The Independence (Mo.) *Western Expositor* of December 6, 1845, said that some 500 Sac & Fox Indians had passed through town "a few days since," traveling cheerfully, despite five-below-zero weather; and were reported to have with them the "bodies of two or three children . . . who had been frozen to death, which they were taking to their new locations." Agent John Beach (ill, and on leave in the East) did not come to "Kansas" till 1846. "S." Vaughan [Leonidas Vaughan?] and Thomas Clements accompanied the emigrants.

At the end of 1845 approximately four-fifths (or, about 1,000) "Mississippi" Foxes were still in Iowa, but Chief Powashiek, and a majority of his nation, had moved, in October, 1845, as far as the Council Bluffs Pottawatomies' reserve in southwestern Iowa, where they remained on "borrowed" land, till the fall of 1846. *See, also*, annals entries of March, April, May, and October, 1846, for items on the "Mississippi" Sacs & Foxes.

Ref: *The Gazette*, St. Joseph, Mo., October 24, November 7, 1845, May 8, 1846; New York *Weekly Tribune*, December 20, 1845; *Daily Missouri Republican*, St. Louis, December 15, 1845; Comm'r of Indian Affairs, *Reports*, 1845, 1846; *Bulletin* of the Missouri Historical Society, St. Louis, v. 7 (January, 1951), pp. 228-233 (for A. S. Waugh's account of the Sac & Fox Indians at Lexington or, *see* McDermott, *op. cit.*, pp. 79-83; *KHC*, v. 8, *footnote* on pp. 130, 131, v. 11, pp. 333-395; 30th Cong., 1st Sess., *Sen. Ex. Doc. No. 48* (Serial 508), p. 12 (for an item on Vaughan and Clements); OIA, Letters Received from Sac & Fox Agency (National Archives Microcopy 234, Roll 732), records of 1845 and 1846, therein; Mason Wade, editor, *The Journals of Francis Parkman* (New York, 1947), v. 2, p. 417 (on May 5, 1846, Parkman "Rode from Westport to find the Sac encampment. They had gone" [from near the border to the Wakarusa vicinity]); Waugh referred to "Young Keokuk" as "Wa-som-e-saw," and to the elder son of Black Hawk as "Nash-a-ash-kuk." The spellings, in text above, are from *KHC*, v. 11. "Keokuk, Jr." was the second Sac signer of the 1842 treaty. His father was first, as head of the "Mississippi" Sacs.

❡ December 29.—President Polk signed the measure that admitted the former Republic of Texas as a state of the Union.

Ref: *Dictionary of American History* (New York, 1940), v. 5, pp. 251, 253.

❡ December 31.—A letter summarizing trade imports of the year, written at Santa Fe, stated: "There left at Independence and arrived at Santa Fe in 1845, 141 wagons, 21 carriages, 1,078 oxen, 716 mules, 39 horses, and 203 men employed as drivers etc." Not included were "two companies [still] detained by snow at Bent's Fort."

Ref: The Santa Fe correspondent of the *Daily Missouri Republican* wrote the December 31 letter from Santa Fe. It was published in the *Republican* of March 19, 1846, and reprinted in *The Gazette*, St. Joseph, Mo., April 3, 1846. Compare with Glasgow's(?) statistics—*see* July-August annals entry.

¶ Employed in "Kansas" by the Indian department during all, or part of the year 1845, were the following persons:

FORT LEAVENWORTH AGENCY—*Agent* Richard W. Cummins; *Interpreters* Clement Lessert and Henry Tiblow; *Blacksmiths* Calvin Perkins and William Donalson for Shawnees, Isaac Mundy for Delawares, Charles Fish for Kansa; *Assistant blacksmiths* Joseph Parks' colored boy and Powhatan Phifer for Shawnees, Duke W. Simpson's colored man for Delawares; *Farmer* John T. Peery (appointed April 9) for Kansa; and as temporary assistant farmers for the Kansa: O. Noland, J. Walsh, L. Noland, Henry Smith, Hugh Murdock, W. Marsh, and F. W. Chambers.

GREAT NEMAHAW SUBAGENCY—*Subagents* William P. Richardson (removed in summer), Armstrong McClintock (appointed July 26); *Interpreters* John Rubite for Sacs & Foxes and John Baptiste Roy for Iowas; *Blacksmiths* William M. Carter and James Gilmore for Sacs & Foxes; *Assistant blacksmith* Andrew Meyer for Sacs & Foxes; *Farmers* John W. Forman and Hugh J. McClintock for Sacs & Foxes, Preston Richardson for Iowas; *Assistant farmers* Harvey W. Forman (resigned in March), Martin Meyer (appointed April 1), Andrew Meyer, and Harmon Gill for Sacs & Foxes.

OSAGE RIVER [MARAIS DES CYGNES] SUBAGENCY — *Subagent* Alfred J. Vaughan; *Interpreters* Joseph N. Bourassa (to April?), Joel W. Barrow (appointed February 6); *Blacksmiths* Robert Simerwell and Robert Wilson; *Assistant blacksmiths* Andrew Fuller and Samuel L. Bertrand; *Physician* Johnston Lykins; *Millers* Jude W. Bourassa (at Pottawatomie creek; appointed May 1), Joel Grover (at Sugar creek), Pierre Perillard (at Sugar creek; appointed August 6. *Note: All of the above, except the subagent, were employed for the Pottawatomie Indians only.*

OSAGE SUBAGENCY—*Subagent* Joel Cruttenden; *Interpreter* Joseph Swiss; *Blacksmiths* Akin Brant (appointed June 24), Jesse Rhinehart, Roger Shopleigh, Alexander Woodruff (appointed July 1), J. Simons; *Assistant blacksmiths* Joseph Captain and Francis Mitchell.

WYANDOT SUBAGENCY—*Subagent* Jonathan Phillips (to April?), Richard Hewitt (appointed April 24); *Blacksmith* Charles Graham; *Assistant blacksmith* Patrick McShafer (dismissed), Ira Hunter (from November 10).

Ref: 29th Cong., 1st Sess., *H. Doc. No. 91* (Serial 483), pp. 42, 43, 46-48, 67, 85, 107; 29th Cong., 2d Sess., *H. Doc. No. 36* (Serial 499), *passim;* 30th Cong., 1st Sess., *H. Ex. Doc. No. 5* (Serial 514), pp. 27, 28, 30, 31, 50, 72, 73, 133; OIA, Letters Received from SIA, St. Louis (Microcopy 234, Roll 753, National Archives), for report of persons employed in SIA on September 30, 1845; SIA, St. Louis, "Records," v. 8, typed copy, pp. 423, 434, 436, 497, 499, 501, 505, 512, 522-524, 526, 528.

1846

¶ January 14.—The Kansa Indians, in a treaty negotiated by Thomas H. Harvey (sup't of Indian affairs, St. Louis) and Richard W. Cummins (head of the Fort Leavenworth Agency), at Kansa Methodist Mission (near the mouth of Mission creek, in Shawnee county of today), ceded a Kansas river reserve of 2,000,000 acres to the United States and agreed to move to a new location (not specified) in 1847.

Of the $202,000 the Kansa were to receive for their land, $200,000 was to be funded at five per cent interest (this to be paid annually for the first 30 years—$1,000 each year for educational purposes; $1,000 for agricultural purposes; and $8,000 to the Kansa Nation). The $2,000 not funded was to pay: treaty expenses; $400 to the Missionary Society of the Methodist Episcopal Church for their Kansa Mission establishment; $600 for a mill at the Kansa Indians' new location; and the balance would go to provide some food for the destitute and starving nation.

The first four (of the 19) Kansa treaty signers were: Ki-hi-ga-wah-chuffe, or Hard Chief; Me-cho-shin-gah, or Broken Thigh; Pi-is-cah-cah ("Pi-hu-sca-goth-ra," according to Missionary Peery); and Ish-tal-a-sa, or Speckled Eyes. Eleventh on the list was No-pa-war-ra (a son? of the deceased White Plume II); and the 13th to sign was Ke-hi-ga-wat-ti-in-ga (a son? of the Fool Chief killed in 1845).

Treaty witnesses were: James M. Simpson (secretary), Clement Lessert (interpreter), John T. Peery (Kansa missionary), John D. Clark (mission employee), Charles Chouteau and Seth M. Hays (of the Chouteaus' Kansa trading post), Nelson Henry (a young, educated, Kansa Indian), and R. M. Parrett.

Ref: C. J. Kappler's *Indian Affairs; Laws and Treaties* (1904), v. 2, pp. 552-554.

❦ January.—Several traders who had left Santa Fe on December 21, crossed "Kansas" in January and arrived at St. Louis in the latter part of the month.

They had "experienced exceedingly severe weather on the plains"; had "crossed the Arkansas on the ice, and observed a greater quantity of buffalo on the bottoms than had ever been seen before by the oldest traders of their party."

Ref: New York *Weekly Tribune*, February 7, 1846 (from a St. Louis newspaper).

❦ February 3.—"Messrs. Houck and Beck, of Boonville, and Hicks of Boone county" (in all, seven men with three mule teams) arrived at Independence, Mo., after a 34-day journey from Santa Fe. They brought about $35,000 in specie "forwarded by residents of New Mexico to meet their indebtedness in eastern cities."

On December 1, 1845, these traders had left Chihuahua; and on January 1, 1846, had set out from Santa Fe, encountering only one snowstorm, and meeting few Indians on the road to Missouri.

Ref: *Missouri Republican*, St. Louis, February 16, 1846 (from the *Western Expositor*, Independence, Mo., of February 7), or, *see* Nebraska State Historical Society *Publications*, Lincoln, v. 20, p. 137. *The Gazette*, St. Joseph, Mo., March 13, 1846, also using the *Western Expositor's* article, gave the names as quoted above. *See* June 20 annals entry for the arrival of "Mr. Houck" from Santa Fe. If both references are to the same man, then Solomon Houck made an unheralded (and unprecedented?) *return* trip to New Mexico, in the spring of 1846, to reach Santa Fe by the end of May, and come back in June to Missouri. One or the other may have referred to the lesser-known *Philip* Houck, but this seems unlikely. The New Orleans *Picayune* of December 30, 1846 (as quoted in the New York *Weekly*

Tribune, January 16, 1847) stated: "We yesterday saw and conversed with Mr. Philip Houck, brother of the well-known Santa Fe trader, who left the city of Orizava [Mexico] late in November. . . ."

⁋ February 6.—Most of the Kansa Nation (*see* January 14 entry) arrived at the Fort Leavenworth Agency (present Johnson county) to receive some provisions. Agent Cummins reported (on the 14th) to Sup't Thomas H. Harvey:

I have furnished them with 1818 bushels of corn, 2513 pounds of bacon, 466 pounds of Fresh pork, there are a few others yet to serve, I expect them down soon. [The Kansa] . . . seem to be in better health & spirits— As they came down they called and paid a visit to the [recently-arrived "Mississippi"] Sacs & Foxes, this tribe seeing the distressed condition of the Kanzas from poverty and disease, gave them a considerable quantity of clothing, blankets, shirts, domestics, calicos &cc.—between 40 and 50 guns and 70 Horses.

On arriving here, they had nothing to eat, and were the most greedy people for provisions I ever saw, the little meat I gave them only served to make them howl and beg for more; it was painful to my feelings that I could not give them enough to do them some good. I gave to each family as much corn as they could pack off; they came well prepared with Bags, and all the horses and mules they could raise; some families that had but few horses went off with packs on their backs, both men and women; I assure [you] they all went off heavily laden.

Ref: Superintendency of Indian Affairs (SIA), St. Louis, "Records," v. 8, typed copy, pp. 528, 529; Office of Indian Affairs (OIA), "Letters Received from Fort Leavenworth Agency" (National Archives Microcopy 234, Roll 302).

⁋ March 7.—The *John Golong* reached Weston, Mo.—the first of 132 steamboat arrivals at that port in 1846. Under date of March 27 the "light draught" *John Golong* (William W. Baker, master) was advertised (as she had been in 1845) to run as a regular packet between St. Joseph, Mo., and St. Louis.

Ref: *The Western Journal,* St. Louis, v. 5 (March, 1851), p. 326; William Walker's journal, March 7, 1846, in W. E. Connelley's *Provisional Government of Nebraska Territory* . . . (Lincoln, 1899), p. 170; *Daily Missouri Republican,* St. Louis, March 12, 1846; *The Gazette,* St. Joseph, Mo., March 27, 1846.

⁋ March 7.—At Cow creek, on the Santa Fe trail, Pawnees raided the stock of some Missouri-bound traders. Norris Colburn lost 17 mules. Two horses and 27 mules were taken from Messrs. Armijo & Co. (A. Armijo, James Flores, Mr. Elliott, and Mr. Lussard).

The Armijo party, left nearly destitute of animals, had to walk the remaining 200 miles, and reached Independence about March 17. Colburn, who had taken in charge their baggage and money (350 pounds of gold dust), was delayed, and arrived some days later. All these traders were aboard the *Tobacco Plant* which docked at St. Louis March 25. They had left Santa Fe on February 16.

Ref: New York *Weekly Tribune,* April 14, 1846 (from *Daily Missouri Republican,* St. Louis, of March 26).

❡ March.—Leaving Fort Des Moines, Iowa (ter.) on the 8th, 2d Lt. Patrick Noble, and 25 Company I, First U. S. dragoons, began a march to Fort Leavenworth (where they would be stationed), escorting 125 "Mississippi" Fox Indians (principally the band of Wetemah—brother of Powashiek) who had remained over-winter on the "Forks of the Des Moines" in violation of treaty terms (*see* December, 1845, annals).

After reaching Fort Leavenworth (in mid-March?) the Indians squatted on the Kickapoo reserve instead of joining the "Mississippi" Sacs & Foxes south of the Kansas river. It appears they did not move on to the Marais des Cygnes country (where the new Sac & Fox reserve was located—in present Franklin and Osage counties) till 1847.

Ref: *Annals of Iowa,* Des Moines, 3d ser., v. 4 (October, 1899), pp. 175, 176; OIA, "Letters Received from Sac & Fox Agency" (National Archives Microcopy 234, Roll 732), *see* Lt. William N. Grier's February 13, 1846, letter, Brig. Gen. George M. Brooke's February 23, 1846, letter, and Thomas H. Harvey's letters of May 7, 1846, and February 3, 1847, therein; 30th Cong., 1st Sess., *Sen. Ex. Doc. No. 70* (Serial 510), p. 91.

❡ March.—Lt. William N. Grier, and the remainder of Company I, First U. S. dragoons (*see* preceding entry), abandoned Fort Des Moines, Iowa (ter.) on March 10, and set out for Fort Leavenworth where they would join the post garrison.

Grier anticipated overtaking Noble's party about March 13, and probably did so. (Company I, First dragoons, was Capt. James Allen's command.)

Ref: *Annals of Iowa,* 3d ser., v. 4 (October, 1899), pp. 175, 176. Fort Des Moines (No. 2) was abandoned under order of February 23, 1846.

❡ MARRIED: William Garrett and Mary Ann Long (both of the Wyandot Nation), on March 15, at the Wyandots' Methodist parsonage (in present Kansas City, Kan.), by the Rev. James Wheeler.

Ref: William Walker's journal, March 15, 1846, entry (in W. E. Connelley's *The Provisional Government* . . ., p. 171).

❡ BORN: on March 20, at Shawnee Methodist Mission, present Johnson county, Jeremiah Dummer Peery, son of the Rev. Edward T. and Mary S. (Peery) Peery.

Ref: Si and Shirley Corn's *Our Family Tree* (June, 1959), Section four. Though Peery was assigned to the Wyandots in the fall of 1845, William Walker's journal entry of May 9, 1846 (*see* May 5 annals entry), makes clear the Peerys did not move to the Wyandot Mission till that day.

❡ March 27.—For the Oregon-California emigrants' notice, Evan Parrott advertised his Missouri river ferry, four miles above St. Joseph, Mo., as the shortest road to Wolf river and the "Iowa [Great Nemaha] Sub-Agency" (in present Doniphan county).

Ref: *The Gazette,* St. Joseph, Mo., March 27, 1846.

❡ March.—From Santa Fe, by way of Bent's Fort, Dr. Eugene Leitensdorfer and his family, with three wagons and 100 mules, crossed

"Kansas"—arriving at Independence, Mo., around the end of the month, perhaps in company with Norris Colburn (*see* March 7 entry). The trader's wife—Soledad (Abreu) Leitensdorfer—who made this journey, was the daughter of Santiago Abreu (New Mexico's governor, briefly, in 1832-1833).

A newspaper report stated the "Messrs. E. and F. J. Leitensdorfer" had left Santa Fe on February 10, and, en route, had "met some obstruction from Indians . . . losing a part of their provisions."

(On February 3, 1847, while camped on the Arkansas, in present Ford county, Lt. James W. Abert recorded, as printed in his report: "On a fallen tree, against which we built our fires, we read that which follows: 'J. Abrea, Y. Litsendorfer, C. Estis, March 11, 1846.' 'A storm.'")

Ref: New York *Weekly Tribune,* April 14, 1846 (from *Missouri Republican,* St. Louis, March 26); Josiah Gregg's *Diary & Letters . . .* (1941), v. 1, p. 191; 30th Cong., 1st Sess., *H. Ex. Doc. No. 41* (Serial 517), p. 532, 533.

❡ DIED: Shawnee chief Henry Clay, on April 4, in present Johnson county, on the Shawnee reserve; and on the 8th, "Blackboddy or Cottawaheothi," one of the Shawnees' principal "medicine men."

Clay, according to J. G. Hamilton, of Westport., was an educated man, and talented, but lacked "moral honesty," and thus never had become a leader of his nation.

Ref: F. H. Cross and K. J. Moore's *Notebooks of James Gillespie Hamilton . . .* (c1953), p. 5. "Blackbody"—on March 28, 1846—had been one of 18 Shawnees "signing" a letter relating to an old claim against the Indians.—OIA, "Letters Received from Fort Leavenworth Agency" (National Archives Microcopy 234, Roll 302).

❡ April.—Sixteen Pawnees (15 men and a woman) ventured into the Neosho river country to make peace with the Osages. Two were killed when they approached the Little Osages' town, and the villagers then chased down and massacred nine others. Five Pawnee men escaped. Subagent Joel Cruttenden, reporting on April 11, said this occurred "on the Neosho" at and near the Little Osages' town (present Neosho county).

Ref: OIA, "Letters Received from Osage Subagency" (National Archives Microcopy 234; Roll 632), Cruttenden's letter, therein.

❡ In mid-April the "fine steamer" *Tobacco Plant,* bound for Fort Leavenworth with government supplies, struck a "snag or rock" near Richfield, Mo., and sank in shallow water. Boat and cargo, both in a damaged state, were salvaged.

Ref: *The Weekly Tribune,* Liberty, Mo., April 18, 1846.

❡ April.—D. G. W. Leavitt and party of 60(?) men, bound for California by way of southern trails, left Napoleon, Ark.; were joined at Fort Smith by Hiram Hudson and some Cherokees; proceeded westward in mid-month.

They had Gregg's map and route description; traveled up the Canadian;

arrived at Santa Fe before June 20. From that place, Leavitt and 11 others set out June 21 on the Spanish trail. It appears all these men were murdered, but mystery surrounds their exact fate. Hudson and his followers (who had obtained Mexican passports, and gone to Albuquerque) were arrested and held as American spies, till Doniphan's force captured the town.

Ref: *Arkansas Historical Quarterly*, Fayetteville, v. 6 (Spring, 1947), p. 9; Dale Morgan, editor, *Overland in 1846* (Georgetown, Cal., 1963), v. 2, pp. 459, 472-474, 477-479, 488, 491-493, 500, 509, 642-645, 769, 773; New York *Weekly Tribune*, August 15, 1846 (from *Missouri Republican*, of August 3), contains statement relating to New Mexico in June, that "A small body of Texans [Arkansans?], emigrating to California, thirteen in number, who had lost their way, were taken prisoners [at Santa Fe?] under the supposition that they were spies, or the advance of the Americans, but they were finally released."

❡ April 24.—A party of "Mississippi" Sacs & Foxes, en route from Iowa (ter.), by way of Missouri (where they had wintered, at, or near, Brunswick, apparently), passed through Independence, and probably entered "Kansas" this same day. The Indians were accompanied by "their mechanics and farmers"—*i. e.*, the tribes' gunsmiths and blacksmiths.

It appears they camped for a time near the Missouri-"Kansas" line, but when, on May 5, young Francis Parkman "Rode from Westport to find the Sac encampment," the migrants had gone—having moved on westward to present Douglas county where Chief Keokuk and about 900(?) Sacs & Foxes were squatting—*see* May 8 entry.

Ref: *The Gazette*, St. Joseph, Mo., May 8, 1846; Mason Wade, ed., *The Journals of Francis Parkman* (New York, 1947), v. 2, p. 417.

❡ April 27-29.—Arriving at Independence, Mo., in this three-day period were several traders (the whole party numbering about 45 men, with 17 wagons) who had left Chihuahua on March 3, and Santa Fe on the 30th. The "principals" were "Mr. Lewis Jones & Co.," of Independence, (Samuel) Wethered and (Thomas J.) Caldwell, of Baltimore, Md. Theirs had been "a very expeditious trip."

Ref: *The Weekly Tribune*, Liberty, Mo., May 9, 1846 (from *Western Expositor*, Independence); Gregg, *op. cit.*, v. 1, p. 191; J. J. Webb's *Adventures in the Santa Fé Trade* . . . (1931), p. 45 (for home of Wethered and Caldwell); D. Morgan, *op. cit.*, v. 2, p. 510 (from *Weekly Reveille*, St. Louis, April 27, 1846). The 1850 federal census for Washington township, Jackson county, Mo., lists "Lewis P. Jones," aged 56, and family.

❡ April.—For rebuilding the storm-damaged Fort Leavenworth Agency (in present Johnson county, near the state line), Robert Mundy was paid $282.99—as shown in Agent R. W. Cummins' April accounts. *See* p. 531 for the 1844 tornado.)

Originally Shawnee Agency (1828-1834); then Northern Agency of the Western Territory (1834-1836); and Fort Leavenworth Agency from 1837 on, this establishment, by 1846, consisted of a "queer irregular string of log houses," according to Jessie (Benton) Fremont's description (in 1848).

Ref: OIA, "Letters Received from Fort Leavenworth Agency" (National Archives

Microcopy 234, Roll 302); 30th Cong., 1st Sess., *H. Ex. Doc. No. 5* (Serial 514), p. 28; Allan Nevins' *Frémont Pathmarker of the West* (New York, 1939), p. 350.

❦ April 30.—At the revitalized Missouri river town of Kansas (Kansas City), Mo., a sale of lots was held. The expanded city limits (as resurveyed by town company member John C. McCoy) embraced 256 acres. Around 300 persons (as later estimated) were *area* residents at this time. (For a summary history of Kansas, Mo., from 1838 to 1845, *see* p. 359; and for its situation in October, 1844, *see* pp. 528, 529.)

A year later—May 1, 1847—when the Rt. Rev. Aug. M. A. Blanchet debarked at Kansas, Mo., he wrote: "This town, just coming into existence, numbers eight houses, some of which are not yet finished. At Kansas and in the neighborhood there are 180 Catholics, almost all Canadians. They have a frame chapel a mile from town. Rev. Mr. [Bernard] Don[n]elly is their resident pastor. . . . Mrs. [Berenice (Menard)] Chouteau . . . widow [of Francis G.] . . . seems to be the soul of this colony."

Among the lot buyers on April 30 were the following men who, prior, or subsequent to 1846, had some part in Kansas (state) history: John C. McCoy (as a surveyor of Indian lands); Gabriel Philibert (blacksmith for the Kansa, and gunsmith for the Osages, 1826-1833); John Park[s] (if, as presumed, he was the part-Shawnee John Parks); William Gilliss (as an Indian trader with the Delawares); Isaac Zane (of the Wyandot Nation); Moyse Bellemare (who married a half-Kansa woman; and moved to present Shawnee county about 1847); Hiram M. Northrup (who married a Wyandot; and moved to Wyandotte in 1855); Benjamin Pruett (who, as a Santa Fe trader, crossed "Kansas" several times prior to 1847); Fry P. McGee (who settled at 110-mile creek, at the Santa Fe trail crossing, in 1854).

Ref: C. C. Spalding's *Annals of the City of Kansas* (1858), p. 17; *Illinois Catholic Historical Review*, Chicago, v. 9 (January, 1927), p. 212; W. H. Miller's *The History of Kansas City* . . . (1881), pp. 40-42; A. Theodore Brown's *Frontier Community Kansas City to 1870* (Columbia, Mo., c1963), p. 44. For McCoy, Philibert, Bellemare, and Northrup *see* annals index; for McGee *see* KHC, v. 8, p. 237, *footnote*. Benjamin Pruett was one of the men massacred at Moro, N. M., on January 19, 1847, during the Mexican-Pueblo revolt.—Saint Louis (Mo.) *Weekly Reveille*, March 31, 1847.

❦ May.—From St. Joseph, Mo., or points upriver, the launching of 1846's Oregon-California emigration began on April 26 when William J. Martin's party ferried the Missouri (at St. Joseph); and ended about May 22 as the last wagons to join Smith's company crossed at Parrott's ferry (four miles above). A Weston, Mo., writer commented on May 17: "They [the emigrants] have been crossing . . . at as many different points as there are ferries between here and the [Council] Bluffs, but the largest body crossed at Iowa Point, Elizabethtown and St. Joseph. . . . they continue upon their long journey without stopping. . . . the road from the Iowa village [or, Great Nemaha Subagency—25 miles west of St. Joseph] to the Pawnee [Platte] is strung with them like some great thoroughfare in the States. . . ." He also stated that all the wagons passing the subagency were ox-drawn; that there were "generally four yoke" to each team; and that the quantity of loose stock was "very great" (including work oxen, "at least 5,000 head").

About two-thirds of the emigrants were said to be California-bound; and by estimate there were "five or six souls" per wagons. The final (June 7) statistic—that 224 wagons had passed the Great Nemaha Subagency—did not include 50(?) which had ferried the Missouri above Iowa Point to travel a route not before used by wagons, so far as known (*see below*). From St. Joseph, or upriver locations, then, some 274(?) wagons, and probably not fewer than 1,350 persons, set out for California or Oregon in 1846. (Council Bluffs, except as used by the Mormons—*see* p. 596—was not an emigration point in 1846.)

A company in the van of the year's emigration all the way West was that of William J. Martin, Platte City, Mo. (an emigrant to Oregon in 1843, who returned in 1844, with Fremont). His party (12 wagons when crossing the Missouri on April 26) journeyed some 40 miles out and formed a camp to await other arrivals. Diarist William E. Taylor (in the small "Craig-Stanley" party) who crossed the Missouri on April 29, at Parrott's ferry, and, on May 4, passed the Great Nemaha Subagency, wrote, two days later: "We overtook 18 waggons at the Nemihaw River crossed over . . . 6 wagons encamped making 27 waggons and 50 men [Martin's growing company]. By Taylor's record, they forded the Big Blue on May 10 and "Came to Independence trail." For a time the Martin train traveled as part of a large company (altogether 130? wagons and over 1,000 head of stock) which elected Elam Brown as captain; but eventually seceded from all the rest and "struck out ahead." On June 10 the eastbound Palmer party met Martin's train (ahead of all others) at Fort Laramie. At the Sweetwater on July 11, an emigrant wrote: "The . . . advance company . . . [is] some 10 days' travel beyond any previous emigration. . . . By this time the leading company numbering eleven wagons, is at Fort Bridger."

Later, at Soda Spring(?), eight men (John Craig, Larkin Stanley, Taylor, and five others) left Martin's train to head for California—and became the "first company to bring wagons across the Sierra in 1846."

Fifty wagons (or 57?) which crossed the Missouri near Oregon, Mo.—at "Thompson; Hameys Ferry" (as diarist Nicholas Carriger recorded it at the time; and later referred to by him as "Thompson and Hayman's ferry")—near the present Kansas-Nebraska line, traveled to the Platte by a route not previously used by wagons so far as known. This road, pioneered(?) by the Riley Gregg train (which Carriger's party joined at the Missouri), became, essentially, the trail subsequently known as the "Old Fort Kearny" road. It was on May 14 that Gregg's train of 50 wagons left "Honey Creek" camp, on the Missouri's right bank (very near the 40th parallel) to begin the trip over the new(?) route. On May 25, when well on the journey to the Platte, Stephen Cooper's California-bound, seven-wagon party joined the company. Before long there were the usual divisions, and splits, and regroupings of wagons; especially on the Platte, after passing the Pawnee country. (The junction of the "Old Fort Kearny" road with the Independence-to-Oregon trail was near the head of Grand Island—a few miles east of the place where the second ["new"] Fort Kearny was established in 1848.) Carriger went to California; Gregg to Oregon, presumably.

The last train to leave the St. Joseph area in 1846 was "Smith's company"— or at least [Fabritus?] Smith was captain on the Platte. This Oregon-bound train—43 wagons—left the Missouri on May 23 (after being joined by late arrivals west of Parrott's ferry on the 22d). The eastbound Joel Palmer party came upon "Smith's company" below the crossing of the Platte's South Fork, on June 18, "lying by," having lost 150 head of cattle. Emigrant Edward Trimble was killed by Pawnees that same day, while searching for the lost stock. "About twenty of this party, with four wagons, returned to the frontier, guarded by a company of Messrs. Palmer and Smith."

Ref: D. Morgan, *op. cit.*, v. 1, particularly pp. 90-100, 105, 116, 118-158, 369-388, v. 2, pp. 476-592, *passim*, 610, 731, 743-747, 798; *Oregon Historical Quarterly*, Salem, v. 4 (September, 1903), pp. 251-253 (Anson S. Cone's "Reminiscences"). In *The History of Holt and Atchison Counties, Missouri* . . . (St. Joseph, 1882), pp. 311-313, the reminiscences of William Banks include the information that in 1841 he landed at what had been known as "Jeffrey's point"; purchased from Jeffrey Dorway (Dorney) the projection of land (long since washed away) then included in S. W. ¼ of Sec. 15, T. 59, R. 38, Holt county, Mo.; renamed it Iowa Point; and in the summer of 1844 established a flatboat ferry there (Major Wharton and the First dragoons of the 1844 expedition—*see* annals, p. 525—were the first to use it!), which he ran till 1856. (Also, it is stated, on p. 313, that "By permission of William Banks, the point in Kansas opposite the original Iowa Point, Missouri, was so named by John Pemberton and Harvey Foreman [in 1855?].") Since Banks was the ferry operator in 1846 at Iowa Point, Mo., the ferry called "Thompson and Hayman's"—*see above*—must have been upriver from Iowa Point.

❦ May 5.—The Rev. James Wheeler (missionary to the Wyandots since 1839?), and his family, "embarked on board the *Radnor*" to return to Ohio.

On the 9th the Rev. Edward T. Peery (superintendent of the Methodists' Indian manual labor school in 1845), and his family, moved over from Shawnee Mission to the Wyandots' parsonage (in present Kansas City, Kan.).

Ref: William Walker's journal, in Connelley's *Provisional Government* . . ., pp. 178, 181; Martha B. Caldwell, comp., *Annals of Shawnee Methodist Mission* (Topeka, 1939), p. 56; *KHC*, v. 9, p. 214.

❦ May 5.—The steamboat *Archer* (H. Moore, captain) was advertised to run as a regular packet between St. Joseph, Mo., and St. Louis. She was scheduled to leave St. Joseph on May 18; and again on June 6.

Ref: *The Gazette*, St. Joseph, Mo., May 8, June 5, 1846.

❦ May 8.—A table of "Distances on the Missouri River"—from the *mouth of the Missouri* (a location 20 miles above St. Louis) to

Council Bluffs—as supplied by "one of the oldest and most experienced Pilots on the Missouri river," appeared in the St. Joseph (Mo.) *Gazette*. It is reprinted below (in part), together with some mileages from another table—published in 1883, and based on St. Louis as a beginning point—for comparative purposes.

1846 From "Mouth [of the] Missouri" to:	Miles	Miles	*1883* From St. Louis to:	From Mouth of Missouri to:
			Miles	Miles
Lower Independence Landing		404		
Liberty Landing	6	410	Liberty [Landing], 436	[416]
Wayne City [upper Independence landing]	5	415		
Mouth Big Blue	3	418		
Randolph [Bluffs]	5	423		
Westport Landing [Town of Kansas, Mo.]	6	429	Kansas City	457	[437]
*Mouth [of the] Kansas	2	431	Kansas river	459	[439]
Parkeville [Parkville]	10	441		
			Leavenworth [town]	472	[452]
Mouth [of the] Little Platte	1	442	Little Platte	473	[453]
*Fort Leavenworth	25	467		
Weston	8	475	Weston	506	[486]
Iatan	15	490		
*First Indian Village[?]	7	497		
			Atchison	521	[501]
*Independence Creek	13	510		
*Twenty-four League Village [old Kansa town, present Doniphan]	1	511	Doniphan	528	[508]
Owen's Landing	3	514		
Sullivan's Landing	25	539		
St. Joseph	5	544	St. Joseph	591	[571]
Bond's Landing	15	559		
Cable's [Caples'] Landing,	7	566		
Savannah or Samuel's Landing	1	567		
West Union, Head Nodaway Isl[and]	8	575		
*Iowa point [on Missouri side; *see* p. 577]	38	613	Iowa point [Kan.]	646	[626]
Council Bluffs ["Nebraska"?]	250	863	Council Bluffs [Iowa]	757	[737]

    * Sites in, or related to, "Kansas."

Ref: *The Gazette*, St. Joseph, Mo., May 8, 1846; J. T. Scharf's *History of Saint Louis City and County* . . . (Philadelphia, 1883), v. 2, p. 1042. *See* annals, pp. 22, 112, for information on the "Twenty-four League Village" (Village of 24). Not identified is the "First Indian Village." (The old "Village of 12" was above Fort Leavenworth.) Caples' Landing (for Charles and William Caples, who, in the 1840's laid out a town, Nodaway City, on land adjoining present Amazonia, Mo.).—*History of Andrew and DeKalb Counties, Missouri* (1888), pp. 171, 172. This same history, p. 22, states that in February,

1842, the Andrew county court authorized a tobacco inspection warehouse (one-story, 20' by 70') to be erected at Nicholas C. Owens' landing on the Missouri.

❡ May 8.—Counciling with Chiefs Keokuk, Hard Fish, and others (at Keokuk's encampment, south of present Lawrence—*see* December, 1845, annals), Agent John Beach learned that the more than 1,400 "Mississippi" Sacs & Foxes then in "Kansas" had decided to accept a reserve on the upper Marais des Cygnes; and that Hard Fish's band (about 500 souls) was already en route there— some 30 miles southward.

Present, and representing Fox chief Powashiek, but taking no part in the council, were chiefs Wetemah (*see* p. 572) and Keoququart. (*See, also,* October 16, 1846, entry for more on the "Mississippi" Foxes.)

Chief Keokuk, and his more than 700 Sacs and 250 Foxes, remained on the Shawnees' land till fall, apparently in several camps. James Clyman (eastbound on the Oregon trail), on July 20 passed "immediately through a small settlement of Saukie Indians." "Their small farms had a Thrifty appearance," he wrote. (He, and his companions, spent that night on the "Waukarusha.")

Ref: OIA, "Letters Received from Sac & Fox Agency" (National Archives Microcopy 234, Roll 732), Agent John Beach's May 11, 1846, letter, therein; C. L. Camp, editor, *James Clyman Frontiersman* . . . (c1960), p. 229; 30th Cong., 1st Sess., *Sen. Ex. Doc. No. 70* (Serial 510), pp. 107, 108; *Iowa Journal of History and Politics,* Iowa City, v. 14 (July, 1916), p. 385 (for a statement that Hard Fish's band was largely composed of followers of the deceased Chief Black Hawk).

❡ May.—Four trading outfits (all previously licensed for the "Mississippi" Sac & Fox trade prior to the Indians' removal from Iowa territory) were permitted to establish themselves on the new Sac & Fox reserve in "Kansas." They located, not far apart, in what is now Greenwood township, Franklin county, south of Pomona.

(1) Pierre Chouteau, Jr., & Co., whose Sac & Fox outfit was "Phelps & Co." (William and Sumner S. Phelps—the latter in charge in "Kansas"). Employees included Isaac G. Baker and John Goodell.

(2) "Messrs. Scott" (Willson A. and John B. Scott—the latter resident, 1847, in "Kansas").

(3) W. G. & G. W. Ewing (with Alexander Street as "Kansas" agent).

(4) John H. Whistler (with whom was associated his brother-in-law, Robert A. Kinzie—"in a clandestine manner" during Agent Beach's tenure; but by license afterwards [late 1847?]).

Sac chief Hard Fish, in a December, 1847, speech, said: "We came **here** [to the Marais des Cygnes reserve] last spring was a year [May, 1846], **with** the intention to remain in this country; in a short time the traders commenced pouring in, and destroying all of our timber and making large fields; **we** supposed that they would only build trading and other houses for themselves to live in. . . . Their accounts and papers follow us all around, and we never get done paying them; it's pay all the time and never scratch out. There are most as many whites as Indians at the trading houses."

Ref: SIA, St. Louis, "Records," v. 8, typed copy, p. 558; 30th Cong., 1st Sess., *Sen. Ex. Doc. No. 70* (Serial 510), items *passim.* John H. Whistler (son of Col. William Whistler

—commandant at Fort Dearborn in 1832) subsequently removed (with his family) to Coffey county about 1857; died there in 1873(?). Robert A. Kinzie (son of John Kinzie—"the father of Chicago") lived in "Kansas" part of the time between 1846 and 1861. (His son John, aged 10 in 1860, was "Kansas"-born.) From about 1857 to 1861, the Robert A. Kinzie family resided in Coffey county. See A. T. Andreas' *History of Chicago* (1884), v. 1, pp. 72, 99; A. T. Andreas' and W. G. Cutler's *History of Kansas* (1883), p. 656; *KHC*, v. 11, pp. 387, 388; U. S. census, 1860, Burlington township, Coffey co., Kansas, pp. 37, 44, 45; *Annals of Iowa*, v. 4 (October, 1899), p. 170, 3d ser., v. 13 (April, 1922), pp. 243-262; F. B. Heitman's *Historical Register . . . of the United States Army . . .* (1903), v. 1, pp. 603 (Kinzie), and 1026 (Wm. Whistler).

ℂ Between May 8 and May 14 several trading companies from Chihuahua arrived at Independence, Mo. In the van were "Messrs. Aguira [Francisco Elguea] and [Henry] Skillman," who had made the entire trip in 46 days. They were followed by traders "Peo Semirane, José Gonzales, and Louis Yaulwager"; and by James W. Magoffin (who had 30 wagons).

These various companies were reported to have brought "an immense quantity of specie, amounting to about $350,000," and mule herds totaling perhaps 1,000 animals.

Ref: *Missouri Republican*, St. Louis, May 15 and 21, 1846, or, *see* Nebraska State Historical Society *Publications*, v. 20, pp. 144, 145; *Niles' National Register*, Baltimore, v. 70 (June 6 and July 4, 1846), pp. 213, 281; D. Morgan, *op. cit.*, v. 2, p. 547 (from *Missouri Reporter*, St. Louis, May 20, 1846); Edwin Bryant's *What I Saw In California* (New York, 1849), p. 33; Missouri Historical Society *Collections*, St. Louis, v. 5 (June, 1928), pp. 291, 292 (for item on John Otero's forwarding $12,000 to Samuel C. Owens, by James Magoffin); G. R. Gibson's *Journal of a Soldier Under Kearny and Doniphan*, in v. 3, R. P. Bieber, ed., *Southwest Historical Series* (Glendale, Cal., 1935), p. 332 (for a mention of Henry Skillman, trader).

ℂ May 8-16.—From Independence, Mo., on the 8th, Josiah Gregg wrote: "The earliest caravans [for Santa Fe] are now just starting. . . ." On the 16th a correspondent reported: "About forty wagons have left [Independence] for Santa Fe and Chihuahua this week, and others are preparing to leave shortly."

George Doan and James J. Webb set out on May 9. They, and most of the other traders, had ox teams. According to Webb: "Besides our five wagons, there were three of W. S. McKnight, [Norris] Colburn, Juan Armijo [who "had a train of wagons ahead of us"] . . . J. B. Turley, and some others." Francis X. Aubry, who left Independence May 9 on his first Santa Fe-trade venture, must have been in this company. About May 29 "Webb, Doan and others" crossed Ash creek. The Armijo wagons (property of New Mexico's governor, Manuel Armijo) were then in the rear. At the Arkansas crossing these traders reorganized; delegated George Doan, and others of the company, to travel ahead (by the upper Arkansas route) to Santa Fe; then started the wagons across the Jornada. "About half way up the Cimarron," in mid-June, they were overtaken by Albert Speyer's caravan—*see* May 22 entry; but entered Santa Fe, at the end of June, only "half a day behind him."

Among the traders who left Independence around May 15 (and subsequently traveled together) were: Benjamin Pruett, George H. Peacock, "Weick," "Mayer," Charles Blumner, Samuel Ralston, and (Adam?) Hill. A cotraveler was artist Alfred S. Waugh. When Speyer's caravan caught up with these traders at the Arkansas crossing on June 9 they were camped on the river's right bank. They, too, reached Santa Fe in the latter part of June. Henry and Edwin Norris' train, which left Missouri "about mid-May," perhaps joined this caravan. (Their wagons, also, reached Santa Fe in late June.)

Ref: Gregg, *op. cit.,* v. 1, p. 192; *Missouri Republican,* St. Louis, May 21, June 25, July 17, 1846; Saint Louis *Daily Union,* August 24, 1846; *The Pacific Historian,* Stockton, Cal., v. 5 (August, 1961), pp. 111-123 (for Aubry); A. S. Waugh's *Travels In Search of the Elephant* (1951), pp. 97-133; Missouri Historical Society, St. Louis, *Bulletin,* v. 6 (April, 1950), p. 292; New York *Weekly Tribune,* June 13, 1846; Webb, *op. cit.,* pp. 179-182; F. A. Wislizenus' *Memoir of a Tour To Northern Mexico* (Washington, 1848), p. 11; 30th Cong., 1st Sess., *H. R., No. 458* (Serial 525), pp. 42, 43 (for H. and E. Norris); Gibson, *op. cit.,* pp. 41, 42. A letter by Norris Colburn, dated at Santa Fe, July 17, 1846, which refers to the loss of 34 mules and a horse, and "Mr. Cooper's" loss of six mules—stolen by Apaches—"while we were on the way from the Pueblo fort on the Arkansas," seems to show that Colburn took his stock (but not his wagons?) beyond Bent's Fort before turning southward for Santa Fe.—See D. Morgan, *op. cit.,* v. 2, p. 645.

❊ May 9.—Two young Bostonians—Francis Parkman and his cousin Quincy A. Shaw—together with their guide-hunter Henry Chatillon, and cart-driver Antoine De Laurier (of the Kaw's mouth French settlement), set out from Westport, Mo., on a summer's excursion to the Rocky mountains. (Four and a half months later—on September 26—they returned to Westport, by way of the Santa Fe trail.) Parkman's "classic" account of this journey—his narrative *The Oregon Trail*—was published serially in the *Knickerbocker Magazine,* February, 1847-February, 1849; then first appeared in book form—in February, 1849—under the title *The California and Oregon Trail.* His more valuable *journals* of the 1846 expedition were not published till 1947.

Parkman, Shaw, and Chatillon had reached Kansas Landing (Kansas City), Mo., (aboard the *Radnor,* from St. Louis) on May 3; and they "put up" for several days at the "solid log house of Col. [William M.] Chick" while buying horses and mules, and organizing for the journey. Parkman spent some time at Westport, and Independence; crossed into the Indian country twice—visiting the Wyandots on May 6.

Beginning the overland march on May 9, Parkman and his three companions crossed the Shawnee reserve and camped at the Delaware (or military, or Grinter) crossing of the Kansas (Kaw) river; ferried over on the 10th; traveled northward on the military road; and, on the 11th, near Fort Leavenworth, joined the British hunting party (Capt. Bill Chandler, Jack Chandler, Romaine—"an English gentleman," and three hired hands) with whom, as earlier agreed, they were to travel the Oregon trail. (The Chandler-Romaine party—the latter "virtually the leader"—had left Westport on May 8. For Romaine's travels across "Kansas" in 1841 see pp. 428, 429.)

On May 12, still camped near Fort Leavenworth, Parkman and Shaw rode four miles to the Kickapoo settlements; visited the trader (W. H. Hildreth) on the way back; then stopped at the fort and (as Parkman wrote) "sat down to the Colonel's [Kearny's] table with Romain[e] and the Capt. [Chandler]—the last Madeira, the last fruits that we shall enjoy for a long time."

Resuming travel on the 13th, Parkman's and the British party missed the turn-off they intended to take (the route cross-country to the Oregon trail blazed in 1845 by Kearny's dragoons—*see* p. 546); traveled the northward path leading toward the Great Nemaha Subagency; finally, on the 16th, struck the St. Joseph branch of the Oregon trail, and followed it westward. On May 23 they reached the Big Blue; built a raft and crossed; next day "struck upon the old Oregon Trail," and had first contact with the emigrants. Parkman's party (separating from Chandler's on June 10, near Ash Hollow) reached Fort Laramie on June 15—five days behind the advance companies of emigrants.

After several weeks in the Fort Laramie area (most of the time with Sioux Indians), Parkman and his companions started southward (on August 4), and after a journey along the base of the Rockies, arrived, August 20, at the Pueblo, on the upper Arkansas. (*See* September 26 entry for return journey.)

Ref: Wade, *op. cit.*, v. 2, pp. 385-483; Francis Parkman's *The Oregon Trail* (any edition); D. Morgan, *op. cit.*, v. 1, pp. 101-110; annals, p. 419 (for prior mention of Antoine De Laurier).

❦ May.—Indian traders Joseph Bissonette, John Sibille, and three hands, with some goods-laden wagons, westbound from Missouri to the upper North Platte, crossed "Kansas" by way of the Oregon trail.

On June 4, probably near the head of Grand Island (Neb.), Pawnees robbed this party of a "considerable amount of goods." Bissonette reached his destination—Fort Bernard (eight miles below Fort Laramie)—on June 28.

Ref: D. Morgan, *op. cit.*, v. 1, p. 59, v. 2, pp. 573-575, 753, 759; Camp, *op. cit.*, p. 225. The Cahokia, Ill., census of 1787, lists a "Joseph Bissonet." *See* Alvord, *op. cit.*, p. 627.

❦ May.—At Independence, Mo., on the 11th (by which time most of the year's Pacific-bound emigration had passed beyond Missouri's border) a writer commented: "Our town for the last few weeks, has presented a scene of business equal to a crowded city. Emigrants . . . have been pouring in from all quarters. . . . There are, this spring [*in contrast to previous years*], two distinct companies, one to Oregon, and the other to California. . . ."

The total emigration which channeled out of Independence is difficult to determine. A man who reached Independence on May 25, after a journey out to the "California camp" near the Kansas crossing, reported that 230 wagons had crossed before he left, and perhaps some 60(?) were yet south of the river. (Presumably the latter "statistic" did not include the 25-wagon train, largely Mormons —*see* p. 588—which, at the end of the procession, left Independence on May 27.) But Joel Palmer (eastbound in June, *see* p. 623) presumably met all the various companies, and counted only 541 wagons. If (as indicated by the figures on p. 576) the emigration from St. Joseph and upriver points was a minimum 274 out of the 541, the wagons which had started from Independence numbered 267. On this assumption (allowing a "count" of five to a wagon), perhaps 1,300 persons traveled the "old" Oregon trail.

❡ May 11.—"The Oregon emigrants have all moved on to the Kanzas river, where, I presume, they will organize," wrote a man in the California-bound company, on the 11th. However, some of the Oregonians organized late that same day at a camp west of Wakarusa crossing. Virgil Pringle (from St. Charles, Mo.), whose party included Orus Brown (emigrant to Oregon in 1843; returned East, 1845), recorded in his diary on May 11 that their wagons "came into Carel" (at the above camp) in the evening "with the whole emigration in sight"; that the emigrants gathered there proceeded to divide into two parties (about 20? wagons in each). Pringle's party chose William Keithly as captain; John Robinson headed the other. Orus Brown was to pilot both.

On May 13 these Oregonians camped by the Kansas river (at present Topeka); next day Robinson's and some of Keithly's wagons crossed; the rest were ferried over on the 15th. (Pringle states that the "two flat boats [were] owned by a Shawnee Indian named Fish." *See* Pvt. Jacob Robinson's statement under "Ref:" below; and *see, also,* p. 584.) Five days later (May 20) the two companies reached the Big Blue crossing [the "Independence" crossing as it came to be known—some four miles northwest of present Blue Rapids, and above five miles southwest of Marysville, in Sec. 31, T. 3 S., R. 7 E.]. The river was rising rapidly and only 20 wagons were able to ford that day. The rest had to wait three days. On the 23d, after all were on the west bank, the company "burst asunder" (as Pringle recorded it), "leaving 27 with us." Captain Keithly was one of those who separated and went on ahead. At the camp beside the Big Blue, that night, Mrs. Aaron Richardson's child was born.

The journey cross-country of these emigrants is not followed further here, except to note that Robinson's advance company (with which Orus Brown traveled) reached the Willamette Valley of Oregon in September (via the Barlow Road); and that Pringle's party, taking the "Applegate Cutoff," did not enter that valley till November 22.

There were emigrants-for-Oregon besides the above who started from Independence, but information about other parties of them while in "Kansas" is fragmentary. One person conspicuous in the throng at Missouri's border early in May was a young Navy man on leave—Passed Midshipman Selim E. Woodworth (who later had a role in the rescue of the Donner party). Woodworth (whom Francis Parkman called "a great busybody . . . ambitious of taking a command among the emigrants") wrote from Westport on May 6 that he would leave for the "Ford of Kanzas" next day; and that his (mounted?) party would remain there till the 10th to recruit their horses. He was at Ash Hollow on June 8; and he reached Oregon City on August 25, in the forefront of the arriving emigrants, having crossed the Rocky mountains, as reported, "in company with three other gentlemen destined to Oregon." Subsequently he went to California.

❡ May 11.—California-bound emigrants (55 wagons), gathered at an Indian creek camp (present Johnson county), elected this day William Henry Russell

("Colonel" Russell), of Callaway county, Mo., as their captain. At another camp, half a mile away, also on the 11th, other emigrants-for-California—the George Harlan train (then 20 wagons)—chose Josiah Morin ("Judge" Morin) as leader, after Harlan declined the honor.

The Russell company or, "main body of the California emigrants" (which included wagons bearing Oregon legends), set out from Indian creek on May 12 (now 63[?] wagons in all; with 119 men; 59 women; 110 children); encamped after a six-mile march; and organized into four sections (with a leader for each). Most wagons reached the Wakarusa to camp on May 14. Next day the company was overtaken by a party (nine[?] wagons) which included Lilburn W. Boggs (governor of Missouri, 1836-1840), his family, and J. Quinn Thornton, of Illinois, with his wife. Camping on the west side of the Wakarusa the night of May 15 the company totaled (by Thornton's count) 72 wagons (with 130 men, 65 women, and 125 children). Edwin Bryant thought the daily-use oxen numbered about 700; and that there were some "300 mules, horses, and other loose animals." According to Thornton, John Baker and David Butterfield (who had with them some 140 head of cattle, plus five ox teams) were expelled on the 16th because of their excess stock. (He later came up with Baker, and Butterfield—a Jackson county, Mo., man, on the Platte.)

At the Shunganunga creek camp on May 17 dissension arose. James G. T. Dunleavy (a Methodist minister, recently of Independence, Mo.) was spokesman for the "disaffected party." Next day, with a storm imminent, and an urgency for getting across the Kansas (some five miles distant), the Dunleavy "disaffected party" stayed in camp; while 35(?) wagons moved forward with leader William H. Russell to the river. Edwin Bryant wrote that "two half-breed Indians" owned the two flatboats (each capable of taking two wagons a trip) and that 35 (Curry says 40) wagons (at a dollar each) had been ferried (i. e., "pushed across . . . with long poles handled by Indians") by six P. M. [Pringle—see p. 583—said a Shawnee named Fish owned the boats. Thornton, in his book, wrote: "Near the ferry was a small cabin . . . occupied by a Frenchman who kept the ferry. His wife was a Kansas squaw. . . ." The Frenchman residing near the ferry evidently was Joseph Papin; but Thornton appears to have been wrong in referring to him as the ferry operator in 1846.] The stock was made to swim the Kansas. Russell's company went three or four miles further, to make camp on Soldier creek; remained at that location on May 19. Early on the 19th, twin boys were born to Martha (Mrs. Reason) Hall (and were named Reuben and William for Dr. Reuben P. Rubey and William H. Russell). This day, also, "nine wagons from Illinois, belonging to Mr. [James F.] Reed and the Messrs. [George and Jacob] Donner" joined. A census now showed 98 men, 40 (or 50?) women, 57 children; and 46 wagons, 320 (or 250?) oxen, 50 horses. (Russell's and Bryant's figures, as printed, vary.)

The march was resumed on May 20; six more wagons (unidentified) joined this day; and on May 21 Alphonso Boone's expected party (11 wagons) caught up (making 67 wagons in all.) But on the 22d, 13 wagons (the Joseph Gordon-Gallant D. Dickenson party) separated, going on ahead. When the large Russell company reached the Big Blue on May 26 it was unfordable. The

California emigrants were forced to camp five nights on the left bank— eventually crossing the flooded stream on May 30 (when nine wagons were ferried over) and May 31 when the rest were taken across on the "canoes"— the "Blue River Rover"—a "nondescript craft" the emigrants constructed. During the enforced stop on the Big Blue's left bank, Edwin Bryant discovered (half a mile east of the ford) "Alcove Spring" (still a noted landmark—*see* p. 583 for location of the Independence crossing where Russell's company was in camp). George McKinstry says eight wagons joined on the 28th. Early on the 29th Mrs. Sarah Keyes ("a lady aged 70," mother-in-law of James F. Reed) died; and was buried that day under a tree near the camp.

On June 1 the Russell Company continued the journey West. Russell, near Fort Laramie, resigned command, traded his wagons for pack mules, and with a few others, including Bryant and McKinstry, went on ahead, reaching Sutter's Fort on August 31, in the van of the "Californians." The further travels of the other emigrants is not followed here, except to remark that to the Donner and Reed families (and their cotravelers) great tragedy occurred in the sierras —and that 1846 has come to be remembered chiefly as the year of the Donner party.

The before-mentioned Harlan-Morin California company (which left Indian creek on May 12); the Dunleavy company (which separated from Russell's at the Shunganunga on May 18); and the Gordon-Dickenson party (which left Russell's on May 22)—all crossed the Big Blue *before* the flood on May 26. With the Harlan-Morin company, for a time were "Five German Boys" from St. Louis whose story has been told by one of them—Heinrich Lienhard—who records that the party grew to 32 or 33 wagons at one time; but fell apart before reaching the Big Blue. With the Dunleavy company (at least as far as Fort Laramie) was T. H. Jefferson (he reached California in October)— maker of the map which historian Dale L. Morgan has termed "one of the great American maps . . . a trail document of high importance." (*See* a "Kansas" section of Jefferson's map in this volume.)

Ref: Dale Morgan, editor, *Overland In 1846; Diaries and Letters of the California-Oregon Trail* (Georgetown, Cal., 1963), two volumes. (This comprehensive study of the 1846 emigration includes not only heretofore unpublished letters, and journals [those of W. E. Taylor, Nicholas Carriger, Virgil Pringle, and George McKinstry having special "Kansas" interest]; but also reprints two rare items—the John M. Shively guide, and the T. H. Jefferson map; as well as the collected newspaper source material.) Bryant, *op. cit.*; J. Quinn Thornton's *Oregon and California In 1848* . . . (New York, 1849), v. 1 (of two); Francis Parkman's *Journals* . . ., ed. by Mason Wade (1947), v. 2, pp. 385-483; Heinrich Leinhard, *From St. Louis to Sutter's Fort, 1846*, tr. and ed. by E. G. and Elisabeth K. Gudde (Norman, c1961); H. H. Bancroft's *History of Oregon* (San Francisco, 1886), v. 1, pp. 552-568; *KHQ*, v. 5, pp. 208-212, and v. 23, p. 154 (for some Alcove Springs, and Sarah Keyes items); Jacob S. Robinson's *A Journal of the Santa Fe Expedition* . . ., reprint ed. (Princeton, 1932), p. 3 (Pvt. Jacob Robinson, of Doniphan's regiment, crossing the Kansas on Charles Fish's ferry, *at the Wakarusa's mouth*, on June 25, reported: "The keeper of the boat said he had made four hundred dollars this season, by the crossing [at the upriver "Topeka" Oregon trail crossing] of emigrants bound to Oregon."). Selim E. Woodworth's letter of May 6, 1846, is in National Archives—"Officers' Letters in the Records of the Navy Department" (and used here courtesy of Dale L. Morgan).

❡ May 13.—The existence of a state of war between the United States and Mexico was proclaimed by President Polk.

Also on the 13th the War department took steps to organize an overland expeditionary force (the "Army of the West") which would march from Fort Leavenworth to protect the property of Santa Fe traders and occupy the New Mexican capital. To Col. Stephen W. Kearny (who, on the 14th was given command *) went the organization plans (which called for combining First U. S. dragoon companies with volunteer troop units); and to Gov. John C. Edwards, of Missouri, went an initial request for volunteers to make up an eight-company mounted regiment, and two companies of light artillery. (* Kearny received his formal orders on May 26.)

Ref: Allan Nevins, ed., *Polk The Diary of a President 1845-1849* . . . (1929), p. 90; Ralph P. Bieber's introduction to *Marching With the Army of the West 1846-1848*, v. 4 of the *Southwest Historical Series* (Glendale, Cal., 1936), pp. 19, 23, 24, 29-31; also, his introduction to G. R. Gibson's "Journal," v. 3 of the *Southwest Historical Series*, pp. 23-29.

❰ In mid-May, traders [John S.] Shaw and Robert Pope, from Fort George (the Fox, Livingston & Co. post) on the "Little Missouri" (Bad river), who had left Fort Laramie on March 31, arrived at St. Louis. (*See, also,* p. 644, for Shaw.)

Ref: D. Morgan, *op. cit.*, v. 2, p. 547 (from *Missouri Reporter*, St. Louis, May 19 and 20, 1846); *Historical Record*, Salt Lake City, v. 9 (January, 1890), entry for October 17, 1847, mentions "John Shaw" then en route to Fort Laramie. The *Missouri Republican*, St. Louis, December 21, 1849, issue, in noting the death of Samuel M. Fox (aged 50), head of the house of Fox & Livingston, on the "9th instant," stated that some 20 years earlier, the house of C. Bolton, Fox & Livingston had succeeded that of Francis Depau; that a little later Mr. Bolton retired; and that Messrs. Fox and Livingston (who had married the two daughters of Depau and inherited a share of a large fortune) had continued the business.

❰ May 15.—Bound for Table creek (Neb.) to establish a new army post—the first, short-lived, Fort Kearny (located where Nebraska City is today)—Col. Stephen W. Kearny, also Maj. Clifton Wharton and Lt. William E. Prince), in company with Brig. Gen. George M. Brooke, and a command of First dragoon (Company C) and First infantry (Company A) troops, left Fort Leavenworth on the steamboat *Amaranth* (which carried materiél including "flooring, stoves, &c." for the new post). They reached Table creek (15 miles below the Council Bluffs) about May 21.

A detachment of Company C, First dragoons, under 2d Lt. Andrew J. Smith (dispatched overland from Fort Leavenworth on May 12), arrived at Table creek on the 22d. General Brooke and Colonel Kearny determined the location for "Camp Kearny" on May 23(?) and departed downriver on the *Amaranth* the same day. (Kearny was back at Fort Leavenworth by May 26 [*see* May 13 entry]; the general reached St. Louis on the 29th.)

On May 30, 55 of the First dragoons started back to Fort Leavenworth, reducing Major Wharton's "Camp Kearny" command to 39 enlisted men (some ill) and seven "citizen mechanics." When, early in June, Wharton departed, Lt. William E. Prince was left to supervise construction of the fort. At a later time (1858) he wrote: "I succeeded in erecting a [log] blockhouse, when

I was ordered to abandon the place. . . ." On July 13 Wharton (now commandant at Fort Leavenworth) reported: "Company A, First infantry (53 aggregate), under command of First Lieut. Prince, First infantry, arrived here this morning from Table Creek."

The blockhouse, and other public property at the original Fort Kearny was put in charge of William R. English. Subsequently, "Oregon battalion" troops built log huts and wintered there in 1847-1848. Some of them served as escort to Lt. Daniel P. Woodbury (of the army engineers), who supervised construction of the second Fort Kearny, at Grand Island on the Platte.

Ref: Nebraska State Historical Society *Publications*, v. 20, pp. 150, 151, and *see* v. 21, pp. 250-259. Parkman (*see* Wade, *op. cit.*, v. 2, p. 422) mentioned the overland dragoon party under date of May 13; 30th Cong., 1st Sess., *H. Ex. Doc. No. 29* (Serial 516), p. 20 (for contract, of July 9 date, with English).

❡ May 19.—An act to provide for raising a regiment of Mounted riflemen, and for establishing military posts on the Oregon trail, was signed by President Polk.

Ref: *U. S. Statutes at Large*, v. 9, pp. 13, 14. The first U. S. Mounted rifleman to cross "Kansas" was 2d Lt. Julian May—*See* p. 590. Capt. John C. Fremont, in California, was commissioned lieutenant colonel of the new regiment.

❡ May 20.—Osage chiefs who signed a letter complaining about their new agent (Samuel H. Bunch—appointed in February, but not in "Kansas" till mid-April?) were: (1) George White Hair, (2) Big Chief (of the Little Osages), (3) Clermont (the 3d), (4) Pa-ne-non-pa-sha (principal chief of the Big Hill band).

Ref: OIA, "Letters Received from SIA, St. Louis" (National Archives Microcopy 234, Roll 754).

❡ May 22.—Albert Speyer's Santa Fe-bound caravan—"22 large wagons, (each drawn by 10 mules,) several smaller vehicles, and 35 men"—set out from "Big Blue camp" (about 20 miles west of Independence, Mo.). In two wagons were munitions (purchased in England) for the governor of Chihuahua.

"Big Blue camp," wrote cotraveler Dr. Frederick A. Wislizenus, of St. Louis, is a "charming spot . . . just on the western boundary . . . of Missouri, the military road from Fort Towson [La.] to Fort Leavenworth passing by it." Wislizenus, with a "small wagon on springs" to carry his baggage and instruments, and a servant, was making a privately financed expedition, principally to collect scientific data. His 1848-published *Memoir of a Tour to Northern Mexico . . . in 1846 and 1847* (issued as a government document, by senate resolution) included a travel journal, a "botanical appendix," three maps, and meteorological tables. [For his 1839 travels across "Kansas" *see* pp. 368 and 381.]

On May 24 Wislizenus wrote: "This morning we passed the road to Oregon, that leaves, about eight miles from Round Grove, the Santa Fe road, and turns to the right towards the Kansas [river]. A way post had been put there, marked: 'Road to Oregon.' . . ." Camp on the 29th was at Council Grove. ("For agriculture, as well as raising stock, the place would be excellent," was Wislizenus' opinion.)

West of Walnut creek, on June 5, the "whole plain" was "covered with bands of buffaloes; their number must have been at least 30,000." Later that day, about six miles east of Ash creek, the "yellow [and red] sandstone" Pawnee Rock was seen, to the right of their path. On the 8th Speyer and company camped at "The Caches"; next day moved "about 20 miles up the Arkansas" and "arrived at the usual fording place of the Arkansas." Across the river, was "a corrál of wagons, belonging to some smaller companies that had started before . . . [them]." (On the 19-day journey to the Cimarron crossing, Speyer's caravan had averaged nearly 18½ miles' travel per day.)

His train forded the river on the morning of June 10; struck out in the evening on the Cimarron route; reached Santa Fe 20 days later. Despite the new war status (*see* June 17 entry), Governor Armijo was still treating the traders as usual. A duty of $625 was imposed on each wagon; passports to the Mexican interior were available for those persons (Speyer and Wislizenus included) who wanted them.

Ref: 30th Cong., 1st Sess., *Sen. Misc. Doc. 26* (for Wislizenus' *Memoir*); F. A. Wislizenus, *A Journey to the Rocky Mountains . . . 1839* (1912), p. 9; Webb, *op. cit.*, p. 181; G. R. Gibson, *op. cit.*, pp. 41, 42. The Saint Louis *Daily Union*, April 4, 1848, noted the arrival at New Orleans of "Speyers," who was said to be thoroughly anti-American —a German using a British protection in Mexico. The April 8, 1848, issue had some comments by J. S. Dougherty on "Mr. Speyers."

❡ May 25.—"A small company of three wagons . . . from the mountains" (coming by way of Bent's Fort and the Santa Fe trail?) arrived at Independence, Mo.

Ref: *Missouri Republican*, June 1, 1846, as reprinted in Nebraska State Historical Society *Publications*, v. 20, p. 154.

❡ May 27.—Manuel X. Harmony ("a native of Spain"), whose train of 12 heavy merchandise-filled wagons (each drawn by 12 oxen), and two other chartered wagons left Independence, Mo., for Santa Fe on the 27th, was overtaken in the Pawnee Fork vicinity about June 17 by Capt. Benjamin D. Moore's command; and detained there some 20 days. (He had goods valued at $38,739, and a $10,000 outfit.)

Subsequently Harmony followed Moore to Bent's Fort (arriving there about July 26); reached Santa Fe a month later, behind Kearny's Army of the West.

Ref: 30th Cong., 1st Sess., *H. R. No. 458* (Serial 525), pp. 1, 2; Missouri Historical Society *Collections*, v. 5 (June, 1928), pp. 291-293 (for reference to Peter Harmony & Co. of New York); Susan S. Magoffin, *Down the Santa Fe Trail and Into Mexico*, edited by Stella M. Drumm (New Haven, 1926), p. 50, footnote, states that "P. Harmony, Nephews & Co." engaged in trade in northern Mexico; W. E. Connelley's *Doniphan's Expedition . . .* (Topeka, 1907), p. 477.

❡ May 27.—A train of 25 wagons, captained by William Crosby, left Independence, Mo., to travel the Oregon trail. Crosby, and the personnel of 19 wagons (24 men; 43 persons in all)—a company (mostly from Southern states) now referred to as the "Mississippi

Saints" were Mormons who expected to meet their Nauvoo (Ill.) brethren out on the plains. The occupants of the other six wagons were Oregon-bound emigrant families (a party mustering 13 or 14 men).

One of the "Saints"—John Brown—in a later-written narrative, related that when, in the Indian country (*i. e.*, "Kansas"), their "Oregon friends" learned they were traveling with Mormons, they became "a little uneasy and somewhat frightened," but remained in company, most of the time, till reaching the Platte; then went on ahead. Joel M. Ware, who left Independence June 2 (the last emigrant to set out from the frontier), joined the above train; then proceeded with the six Oregon-bound wagons.

The "Mississippi Saints," finding no trace of the Mormons from Nauvoo, continued out the Oregon trail to the vicinity of Fort Laramie (the only Mormon company to reach that area in 1846); met trader John Richard a few miles below that post; decided to follow him to Pueblo, on the upper Arkansas, to winter. Starting south with Richard on July 10, they arrived at Pueblo (Colo.) August 7. There the Mormon *families* remained till the spring of 1847 (when they retraced the route to Fort Laramie). (*See* p. 647 for a return East of some men from this party.)

Ref: D. Morgan, *op. cit.*, v. 1, pp. 60, 62, 111-115, v. 2, pp. 512, 633, 647, 659, 746, 753, 764, and *see, also*, index, under "Mississippi Saints"; John D. Lee's "Diary" published in *New Mexico Historical Review*, v. 42 (July and October, 1967), pp. 165-209 and 281-332 —*see* September 14, 1846, entry, therein.

❧ May 28(?)—The 22-wagon Bent, St. Vrain & Co., train (*possibly* headed by Marcellin St. Vrain?) which left Bent's Fort in mid-May (and reached Missouri in the middle of June), lost one man about the 28th—killed and scalped by Comanches(?) west of Pawnee Fork. Two of the victim's companions "had to run for it— just escaping."

Near Pawnee Fork, on September 9, Robert S. Bliss, of the Mormon battalion, found "a paper enclosed in two rappers reading thus 'look out for Indians for one of our men was killed   supposed by a Camanche'   signed by an officer & dated May 18th [*i. e.*, 28th?] 1846." Earlier—on June 6—Dr. F. A. Wislizenus (bound for Santa Fe with Speyer's train) recorded having seen, on June 6, west of Pawnee Fork, the grave of the above victim, who "but a week ago had been killed by Indians, as his companions, from Bent's Fort, had already told us [when met on June 3 near the Little Arkansas]."

Ref: *Missouri Republican*, St. Louis, June 1, 1846 (for May 25 letter from Independence, Mo., mentioning that "St. Vrain, of Bent's Fort [and not Ceran St. Vrain for he was elsewhere] is expected in a few days"); F. A. Wislizenus, *Memoir of a Tour to Northern Mexico*, pp. 8, 10; Lewis H. Garrard, *Wah-To-Yah, and the Taos Trail* (Cincinnati, 1850), p. 25; *Utah Historical Quarterly*, Salt Lake City, v. 4 (July, 1931), p. 72 (for Bliss quote). William H. Richardson in his *Journal*, 2d edition (Baltimore, 1848), p. 14, shortly after passing Pawnee Fork, westbound, on September 7, 1846, wrote: "we saw near the road side a little mound of stones, on one of which was engraved the name of R. T. Ross. It was supposed to be the grave of a man who was murdered by the Indians in 1840[?]" It may be that Ross was the above Indian victim.

❧ May.—Seven mountain men, from the upper Arkansas "beyond

Bent's Fort," reached St. Louis on May 28, with around 300 packs of buffalo robes and a few packs of furs. About 150 miles from Missouri (west of Council Grove?) they had met the first "outward bound Santa Fe traders and from there passed a great many wagons and parties of traders."

Ref: New York *Weekly Tribune,* June 13, 1846.

❡ May 29.—The *General Brooke,* en route to the upper Missouri with goods for trading posts of the American Fur Company (Pierre Chouteau, Jr. & Co.), passed St. Joseph, Mo.

Ref: *The Gazette,* St. Joseph, Mo., June 5, 1846.

❡ BORN: on May 30, at Fort Leavenworth, Henry Stephen Kearny, son of Col. Stephen W. and Mary (Radford) Kearny.

Ref: D. L. Clarke's *Stephen Watts Kearny* . . . (Norman, c1961), p. 106.

❡ As June began, several Santa Fe-bound wagon trains were leaving the Missouri frontier. About June 9 an eastbound traveler met "Messrs. [Christopher C.?] Branham and [James P.?] Hickman and Col. Davis [*i. e.,* Cornelius Davy, of Independence, Mo.] near Rock Creek"; and the next(?) day met "Messrs. [Alexander C.] Ferguson, [Edward J.] Glasgow & Clark" at 110-mile creek.

Capt. Benjamin D. Moore's dragoon command (*see* June 5 entry) would (on Colonel Kearny's orders) halt their wagons (and those of all other trains en route to New Mexico) at Pawnee Fork.

Ref: *Missouri Republican,* St. Louis, June 25, 1846; or, *see,* Waugh, *op. cit.,* p. 107, footnote; W. E. Connelley's *Doniphan's Expedition,* pp. 646, 647. It seems likely that "Clark" was George R. Clark, St. Louis (son of William Clark, explorer, and Indian superintendent).

❡ June 1.—George T. Howard (on a War department mission) en route from Washington to New Mexico, and accompanied by 2d Lt. Julian May (of the U. S. Mounted riflemen), left Agent R. W. Cummins' house with an escort of "7 Draggoons [from Fort Leavenworth] and about as many Shawanee & Delaware Inds. say 16 or 17 in all."

Two days later (and 50 miles out on the Santa Fe trail), Howard dispatched word to Fort Leavenworth that Speyer and Armijo (ahead of him) were freighting some arms and ammunition to New Mexico. Colonel Kearny sent back instructions to catch up with, and detain the traders till a dragoon force arrived.

Howard made a futile attempt to overtake the wagon trains, but his pack mules gave out. When eastbound "Messrs. Bent, St. Vrain, and Folger" met him, on June 16, at the crossing of the Arkansas, he was preparing to travel on, slowly, to Taos, having entrusted to two emissaries (who had left on fresh mules) the task of entering Santa Fe.

Subsequently, Howard's agents barely escaped capture as spies in the New

Mexican capital (which they reached about June 24—*after* the arrival of war news; and left prior to June 30). They rejoined Howard, at Taos; and his party traveled to Bent's Fort early in July. (*See* p. 630 for return journey.)

Ref: New York *Weekly Tribune,* August 15, 1846 (from *Missouri Republican,* St. Louis, of August 3); OIA, "Letters Received from Fort Leavenworth Agency" (National Archives Microcopy 234, Roll 302), Cummins' May 30, 1846, letter; *Niles' National Register,* v. 70 (July 11, 1846), p. 304; 31st Cong., 1st Sess., H. Ex. Doc. No. 17 (Serial 573), p. 235; G. R. Gibson's *Journal* . . ., pp. 28, 29; R. P. Bieber, ed., *Marching With the Army of the West* . . ., p. 86; W. E. Connelley's *Doniphan's Expedition,* p. 139; John T. Hughes' *Doniphan's Expedition* . . . (Cincinnati, 1848), p. 50. Texan George T. Howard (a leader in the ill-fated Texan Santa Fe expedition of 1841—*see* annals, p. 437), after reaching Washington, got a captain's commission, in the volunteers, on August 27, 1846; became a major on June 21, 1847; and was honorably discharged October 15, 1848. Heitman, *op. cit.,* v. 1, p. 546.

⟪ **June 5.**—Capt. Benjamin D. Moore, of the First U. S. dragoons, got orders (from Col. S. W. Kearny) to "march this day" from Fort Leavenworth with his own and "Capt. [John H. K.] Burgwin's Comps. (C & G)," to overtake, and detain, the Santa Fe-bound wagons of traders Armijo and Speyer (*see* May 8-16, May 22, and June 1 entries), reported to be carrying "a large quantity of arms and ammunition."

The captain was also directed to "stop the progress of the whole [traders'] Caravan, our own Citizens, as well as the Mexican," till he (Kearny) caught up with them; and to "take 2 12 pdr. Mountain Howitzers" along. Moore, accompanied by mountain man Thomas Fitzpatrick, set out with "only 8 hrs. notice"; and camped "at Kansas river" on June 6. (An eastbound traveler, meeting the dragoons at Big John's spring about June 7, reported they numbered 180.) By forced marches (over "roads exceedingly dry and dusty"), Moore and troops reached the Arkansas crossing in 11½ days from Fort Leavenworth. (When Charles Bent's eastbound party met them on June 17, between Pawnee Fork and "The Caches," they were "six or eight days" behind Speyer's wagons; and had lost the race to overhaul the arms-carrying traders. Speyer had forded the Arkansas on June 10.)

In a July 10 letter, from Pawnee Fork "Head Qr's Advance Guard, U. S. A.," Moore wrote: "On our arrival at the crossing, finding no Mexicans, nor sign of any, and the grass scarce and insufficient, I fell back, with my command [enlarged around June 30 by Company I dragoons—*see* June 12 entry], to this point, about 80 miles [east] . . ., in tolerable grass, where I have remained since; but to-morrow I shall take up the line of march for Bent's Fort. . . ." (*See* July 11 entry.) Also in the Pawnee Fork vicinity were the wagon trains of all Santa Fe traders who had left Independence, Mo., on, or after, May 27. (*See* pp. 590, 600.)

Ref: R. P. Bieber, ed., *Marching With the Army of the West, 1846-1848,* pp. 73, 114 (footnote) 121, 131; G. R. Gibson, *op. cit.,* p. 43; New York *Weekly Tribune,* August 22, 1846 (for Moore's letter—originally published in St. Louis *Reveille* of August 11); *Missouri Republican,* St. Louis, June 25, 1846; *Niles' National Register,* v. 70 (July 11, 1846), p. 304 (for Charles Bent's party); 30th Cong., 1st Sess., H. R. No. 868 (Serial 525), p. 2; Magoffin, *op. cit.,* pp. 42-47. Capt. Benjamin D. Moore was killed at the battle of San Pasqual, December 6, 1846; Capt. John H. K. Burgwin was killed at Pueblo de Taos, in February, 1847.

❡ June 5 and 17.—The Pottawatomie Nation, in a treaty signed on the 5th by the "Council Bluffs" Indians (the united Pottawatomies, Chippewas, and Ottawas—sometimes called the Prairie band—about 2,000 in number), and on the 17th by the "Kansas" Pottawatomies (principally the St. Joseph and Wabash bands—nearly 2,000 souls), ceded the reserves (1) in southwestern Iowa territory, and (2) on the Marais des Cygnes' waters in eastern "Kansas," for a 30-mile-square tract (576,000 acres) on the Kansas river (the eastern part of the reserve given up by the Kansa Nation in January), and agreed to remove there within two years. U. S. Comm'rs Timothy P. Andrews, Thomas H. Harvey, and Gideon C. Matlock negotiated the treaty. The Pottawatomies, altogether, gave up about 6,000,000 acres.

Of the $850,000 the Pottawatomies were to receive, the balance ($643,000), after applying various sums for specified purposes ($87,000 for the Kansa lands; $50,000 for tribal debts, compensation for property, improvements, etc.; $30,000 for removal expenses; $40,000 for 12 months' subsistence) was to be held in a trust fund, with five per cent interest to be paid the Indians annually, at their new homes, for 30 years; after which time other arrangements were provided.

Chiefs Mi-au-mise (the Young Miami) and Op-te-gee-shuck (or Half Day) headed the signers at Council Bluffs Subagency on June 5. Among other leading men of the nation on the list were Francois Bourbonnai[s], Charles H. Beaubien, Joseph Le Frambeau [La Fromboise], interpreter, Pierre or Perish Le Clerk [Le Clerc], and M. B. Beaubien, interpreter. Subagent R. B. Mitchell, Richard Pearson, Albert G. Wilson, S. W. Smith, and John H. White-head were some of the witnesses.

At the Osage River Subagency, on Pottawatomie creek (in present Franklin county), the first four signers on June 17 were chiefs To-pen-e-be, We-we-say, Gah-gah-amo, and I-o-way. Further down the list were (among others) Abraham Burnett, Joseph Napoleon Bourassa, Jude W. Bourassa, and "Bossman" (Mackinaw Beauchemie). Witnesses were: Joseph Bertrand, Jr. (part Pottawatomie), Agent R. W. Cummins, Leonidas W. Vaughan (son of Subagent A. J. Vaughan), Robert Simerwell (government blacksmith), Thomas Hurlburt (Methodist missionary), John W. Polke (trader), Johnston Lykins (government physician), Moses H. Scott (trader), Washington Bossman (son of Mackinaw Beauchemie), John Tecumseh Jones (part-Indian; and Baptist missionary), James A. Poage, Joseph Clymer, Jr. (trader), and W. W. Cleghorn (trader).

Ref: Kappler, *op. cit.*, v. 2, pp. 557-560. The "Kansas" Pottawatomies, according to Subagent Vaughan's September 4, 1846, statement (in Comm'r of Indian Affairs, *Report,* 1846), totaled 1,941 persons (735 of the Wabash, 710 of the St. Joseph, and 496 of the Prairie bands).

❡ June 6-27.—Arriving at Fort Leavenworth were 13 Mexican War volunteer companies (totaling over 1,300 men) from Missouri counties bordering on the Missouri river, or from St. Louis and vicinity.

Alexander W. Doniphan
(1808-1887)

Eleven were mounted companies; eight (some 830 men) were organized as the First regiment Missouri volunteers (or, "Doniphan's"
regiment); another—the "Laclede Rangers" (107 in number)—was
attached to the First U. S. dragoons; and two light artillery companies were formed as a battalion (about 232 men). The infantry
battalion (two companies) numbered 145 men. These 13 companies, and about 430 First U. S. dragoons (some on the road in
advance of the Missourians—*see* June 5 and June 12 entries; others
behind—*see* July 6 entry) made up Col. Stephen W. Kearny's Army
of the West. Various data on the Missouri companies are summarized below. They were enlisted for 12 months' service.

Ar-rived June	Captain of company	Company from	Assign-ment	Left the fort June	Remarks
6	David Waldo	Jackson county (mounted)	"Doni-phan's" regt., Co. A	22	Organized at Independence. Dr. David Waldo had been promi-nent as a Santa Fe trader since 1829.
''	William P. Walton	Lafayette county (mounted)	'' Co. B	26	
''	Oliver P. Moss	Clay county (mounted)	'' Co. C	26	Organized at Liberty. Moss was brother-in-law to Doniphan. Both Doniphan (col.) and Ruff (lt. col.) were privates in the company till June 18.
9	John W. Reid	Saline county (mounted)	'' Co. D	22	Reid was a coleader of the Pro-slaverymen (the 2,700 Missouri-ans) who invaded Kansas in September, 1856.

Pvt. John T. Hughes (of "C"), in a "Ft. Leavenworth, June 9" letter, stated: "There are 4 companies of volunteers here and more are expected every day. . . . The companies generally, are nearly full (114) . . . Our quarters here are *only tolerable*, not altogether *comfortable*. We do not live in *palaces* or feast upon dainties; but we use up Uncle Sam's beef and pork with railroad speed."—*The Weekly Tribune*, Liberty, Mo., June 13, 1846.

10	Thomas B. Hudson	St. Louis (mounted)	"Laclede Rangers"— attached (June 27) to First dragoons	29	The "Laclede Rangers" arrived aboard the *Pride of the West*— chartered for their trip. Richard S. Elliott, formerly Indian sub-agent at Council Bluffs, was 1st lieutenant.
15	M. Monroe Parsons	Cole county (mounted)	"Doniphan's" regt., Co. F	26	
"	William Z. Angney	Cole county (infantry)	Battalion of infantry Co. A	29	Angney (on June 29) was placed in command of the two-company battalion of infantry. 2nd Lt. Lucian J. Eastin later published the Proslavery *Kansas Weekly Herald*, at Leavenworth.
"	Congreve Jackson	Howard county (mounted)	"Doniphan's" regt., Co. G	27?	Jackson (earlier) had been an Indian subagent in "Kansas." When Ruff resigned, Jackson became the regiment's lieutenant colonel. Horatio H. Hughes then headed Company G.

In a June 16 letter Pvt. John T. Hughes wrote: "Fort Leavenworth at this time presents quite the appearance of a military camp. . . . The whole Fort is full of life and cheerful good humor. . . . Twice a day we parade . . . about 700 strong."—*The Weekly Tribune*, Liberty, Mo., June 20, 1846.

| 18 | Richard H. Weightman | St. Louis (light artillery) | Battalion of light artillery Battery A | 30 | Maj. M. Lewis Clark (son of ex-plorer-Ind. sup't William Clark) was the battalion's field officer. Antoine Clement (*see* pp. 323, 474) served in Battery A. |

On June 18 the First regiment Missouri volunteers was organized by the election of field officers. Chosen as colonel was Alexander W. Doniphan, a Liberty, Mo., lawyer. Charles F. Ruff (a West Point graduate; and a First dragoons second lieutenant, 1838-1843) was elected lieutenant colonel. William Gilpin (later Colorado's first governor; for his overland travels of 1843-1844, *see* p. 530) became the regiment's major.

| 20 | Woldemar Fischer | St. Louis (light artillery) | Battalion of light artillery Battery B | 30 | Fischer (whose company was composed of Germans) was placed in *temporary* command of the battalion on June 27. Maj. M. Lewis Clark took charge on July 9 when he joined the battalion. |

"The *Missouri Mail*, on the 23d brought up Clay county ladies, to Fort Leavenworth, with a flag for Capt. Moss's company."—*The Weekly Tribune*, Liberty, Mo., June 27, 1846.

23	Charles B. Rodgers	Callaway county (mounted)	"Doni-phan's" regt., Co. H	29	
26	John D. Stevenson	Franklin county (mounted)	" Co. E	29	
27	William S. Murphy	Platte county (infantry)	Battalion of infantry Co. B	29	Jonas S. Woods succeeded Murphy as captain of this company on May 1, 1847.

Ref: W. E. Connelley's *Doniphan's Expedition* . . .; John T. Hughes' *Doniphan's Expedition* . . . (Cincinnati, 1850); and his letters in *The Weekly Tribune*, Liberty, Mo., particularly the issues of June 6, 13, 20, 27, July 4, August 1, September 5, 26, 1846; Marcellus B. Edwards' "Journal" in R. P. Bieber, ed., *Marching With the Army of the West* . . .; Abraham R. Johnston's "Journal," in *ibid.*; Frank S. Edwards' *A Campaign in New Mexico With Colonel Doniphan* (Philadelphia, 1847); Robinson, *op. cit.*; Charles F. Ruff's notes (copy in KHi ms. division); Richard S. Elliott's *Notes Taken in Sixty Years* (St. Louis, 1883), pp. 217-225; George R. Gibson, *op. cit.*; William C. Kennerly's *Persimmon Hill* . . . (Norman, Okla., 1948), pp. 184-186.

❡ June 9.—"210 Senecas landed to-day [at the mouth of the Kansas river] from Cattaraugus, Tonawanda and Buffalo [New York]. . . ." William Walker (Wyandot), resident at the Kaw's mouth, thus recorded the arrival of a party of New York (or, "Six Nation") Indians—composed principally of Tuscaroras, but including some Senecas and Cayugas. (The exact size of this party is uncertain, but it probably numbered above 200.)

Emigrating agent Dr. Abraham Hogeboom, who had brought these immigrants to "Kansas" unauthorized, continued southward with them to the sizeable, and up-to-now unoccupied New York Indian reserve—north of Fort Scott (the reserve erroneously labeled "Wyandots" on Gregg's map —*see* in this volume; and *see* p. 333); where he left them, on June 16(?). ("There they were abandoned without shelter, without care, without the means of planting . . .," as the New York *Tribune* later reported it.) The Rev. James N. Cusick (a native preacher) and his party of 14 Indians came in July, and were taken, in three wagons, to join the earlier arrivals. (Agent Cummins wrote, on August 4; "It was very difficult to get waggons to undertake the trip, the flies were so exceedingly bad, [and] the weather . . . [so] very hot, that they had to make nearly the whole trip in the night. Joseph Parks [Shawnee chief; and Westport, Mo., trader] furnished the waggons . . . and [they] were ten days in service. . . .")

Cusick, in a September 14 letter, wrote that his people were "alarmed because so many are dying [more than 30 since their arrival!] . . . it is most extremely hot, that we had melted down like as snow before the sun." In October a St. Louis newspaper reported the arrival, on the 25th, of "Eight or 10 Seneca Indians," en route East. "They represent that nearly all their people they have left behind, are sick." In a letter dated "Fort Scott Mo Nov 28th 1846," James N. Cusick, Peter Elm, and Matthew Jack stated that only about 32[?] of their people remained on the New York reserve (and that the "larger portion" of them were "widows and orfant children"). Some of the Indians, it appears, went (temporarily, at least) to live with the

Sandusky Senecas in northeastern "Oklahoma" (*see* pp. 216, 224). Not clear is where the rest spent the winter of 1846-1847.

In July, 1847, 65 Senecas were at St. Louis, "bound for their former homes" in New York. (As reported, the emigrants to "Kansas" had "suffered greatly from sickness," and a "large number of them" had died.) Subagent W. P. Angel (of New York state) reported in September, 1847, the return in August of about 94 Indians from Hogeboom's party; and stated that some 10 or 12 more were expected to arrive. He *thought* about 186 had been in the original emigrating company; and stated that 82 had died "at the west" (*i. e.*, in "Kansas").

Ref: William Walker's journal, in W. E. Connelley's *Provisional Government* . . ., p. 198; 29th Cong., 2d Sess., *H. Doc. No. 36* (Serial 499), p. 9 (for Hogeboom); 30th Cong., 1st Sess., *H. Ex. Doc. No. 5* (Serial 514), p. 9 (item on Cusick); SIA, St. Louis, "Records," v. 8, typed copy, pp. 569, 570; OIA, "Letters Received from SIA, St. Louis" (National Archives Microcopy 234, Roll 754), for Cusick's letters; Comm'r of Indian Affairs, *Report*, 1846, 1847 (and later years, also); New York *Weekly Tribune*, May 8, August 7, 1847; Saint Louis *Daily Union*, October 26, 1846; *The Weekly Tribune*, Liberty, Mo., July 17, 1847 (from *Missouri Republican*, St. Louis of July ——?); *Baptist Missionary Magazine*, Boston, v. 27 (January, July, 1847), pp. 31, 60, 61, 258 (this page has statement: "The Tuscarora branch . . . are now located in the immediate neighborhood of Shawanoe, under the care of Rev. James Cusick."); Felix S. Cohen's *Handbook of Federal Indian Law* . . . (Washington, 1945), p. 420; 52d Cong., 1st Sess., *Senate Report No. 910* (Serial 2915), pp. 5, 6; Charles & William B. King, *Brief on Behalf of Settlers in Kansas Upon Public Lands in Which it Is Claimed That Certain New York Indians, Have an Interest Under the Treaty* . . . [of] *1838* (Washington, D. C., 187—?)—copy in KHi.

❡ June 12.—2d Lt. Patrick Noble, and 50 men of Company I, First dragoons, were sent from Fort Leavenworth to reinforce Captain Moore's command (*see* June 5 entry).

Susan (Mrs. Samuel) Magoffin, June 15, noted that this company, "some seventy[?] in number, . . . passed on before us and camped" not far from 110-mile creek. Company I must have joined Moore at Pawnee Fork around the end of June.

Ref: R. P. Bieber, ed., *Marching With the Army of the West*, p. 73; Magoffin, *op. cit.*, p. 9; G. R. Gibson, *op. cit.*, p. 43.

❡ On June 13 the advance companies of the Mormons emigrating westward from Nauvoo, Ill., reached the Missouri river at Council Bluffs. Their slow journey across Iowa during a very wet spring had been one of hardship and suffering. On the way, camps had been established at Garden Grove, on Grand river, and at Mount Pisgah, Iowa. By July 1 perhaps 800 wagons of Mormon families had reached the Council Bluffs camp. (A ferry built opposite Bellevue [Neb.] by the advance Mormons was not completed till June 29.)

Mormon leader Brigham Young, on July 7, stated that in addition to the estimated 800 wagons already on the Missouri's east bank, 1,005 teams had been counted on the road between the Mount Pisgah camp and Council Bluffs. (*See* annals entry, p. 632, for the Mormon battalion organized in mid-July from the men among these emigrants.)

In mid-summer the "main body of the Church" crossed the Missouri river, via the ferry, at Sarpy's point; traveled up the west side some 15 to 20 miles; and established a large camp—"Winter Quarters"—on the Omahas' land, just north of present Omaha, Neb. This was the westernmost point of the collective Mormon migration in 1846.

Not all of the emigrants spent the winter of 1846-1847 at "Winter Quarters" camp. They were, also (by Thomas L. Kane's statement) "Upon the Potta-watamie lands, scattered through the border regions of Missouri and Iowa, in the Sac and Fox country, a few among the Iowas [in "Kansas"?], [and] among the Poncas in a great company. . . ."

Ref: Orson Pratt, *Exodus of Modern Israel* . . . *Diary* . . . (Salt Lake City, 1947; William Clayton's *Journal* (Salt Lake City, 1921); D. Morgan, *op. cit.*, v. 1, p. 89, v. 2, pp. 745, 747; *Missouri Republican*, St. Louis, July 7, 1846; Daniel Tyler's *A Concise History of the Mormon Battalion* . . . (1881), pp. 64-102 (for Thomas L. Kane's discourse, 1850), pp. 138, 139; *Niles' National Register*, v. 70 (July 25, 1846), p. 327.

❡ June 14 and 17.—The Pawnees' large town on the Platte's Loup Fork (some 30 miles above its mouth) was twice raided by bands of Sioux in June, while the villagers were absent. In addition to burning the lodges, the raiders destroyed cornfields and turned lose their enemies' horses. Pawnee Mission, a few miles distant, was abandoned as a result of the renewed Sioux hostilities, the missionaries going to Bellevue, on the Missouri.

An emigrant writing from Fort Bernard (on the North Platte) June 25, reported some 1,500 Sioux had been there a couple of weeks earlier with 35 recently obtained Pawnee scalps.

Ref: D. Morgan, *op. cit.*, v. 2, pp. 574, 588; *KHC*, v. 14, pp. 683-689, 739, 740.

❡ June 15.—The United States formally ratified the British-drafted treaty establishing the 49th parallel as the boundary in the Oregon country.

Ref: Ray A. Billington's *The Far Western Frontier 1830-1860* (New York, c1956), p. 159; *Dictionary of American History* (New York, 1940), v. 4, pp. 186, 187.

❡ June 16.—"Already near 100 provision waggons have been dis-patched [from Fort Leavenworth] on the *Route* to Santa Fe," wrote Pvt. John T. Hughes. "A great number of beef cattle will be driven along with the army [Kearny's Army of the West]."

"Mr. McKenney" [McKenzie?], who arrived at Westport, Mo., on June 15 (from Bent's Fort), had met 25 provision wagons east of Black Jack; and Charles Bent, reaching Westport on June 27, reported he had "met two long trains of provision wagons—the first within 20 miles of Council Grove and the other at Dragoon creek." (It is unlikely that *these* supply trains traveled the new branch road [see next entry]. Presumably they ferried the Kansas at the Delaware [or Grinter] crossing on the Fort Leavenworth-Fort Scott military road.)

Pvt. Frank S. Edwards (who reached Fort Leavenworth June 18 and left on the 30th) wrote: "For some time previous and during our stay, every second or third day would witness the departure of long trains of government wagons, which, loaded with provisions, were dispatched with orders to push on as fast as possible to Bent's Fort . . . about 500 miles [*i. e.*, 565? miles] . . . to await our arrival."

Ref: *The Weekly Tribune*, Liberty, Mo., June 20, 1846 (for Hughes); *Missouri Republican*, St. Louis, June 25, 1846; *Niles' National Register*, v. 70 (July 11, 1846), p. 304; F. S. Edwards, *op. cit.*, p. 22. The "Mr. McKenney" (above) possibly was the man mentioned as being (again?) eastbound on the Santa Fe trail in August. Daniel Tyler (in his *A Concise History of the Mormon Battalion* . . ., p. 141) stated that "On the 25th [of August, 1846; and somewhere east of Council Grove] . . . we met Bro. McKenzie, who had been to Bent's Fort as Indian interpreter to General . . . Kearney." And John D. Lee (in his "Diary"—original in Utah Historical Society), on September 3, at Fort Leavenworth ". . . unexpectedly met Bro McKenzie who had just arrived with the express from Santa Fe—for which he received $250.00."

❡ About mid-June a fatigue party was sent out from Fort Leavenworth to work on a new military road leading to Fish's Kansas river ferry (at the Wakarusa's mouth), and thence on southwestwardly to a junction with the Santa Fe road in the vicinity of "The Narrows" (east of Willow Springs, present Douglas county; and 65 miles west of Independence, Mo.). This was the 50 to 55-mile trail—traveled only once previously—which Col. S. W. Kearny and his First dragoons had blazed in 1845 (*see* p. 558). No official name applied to this pathway. It could be termed the Fort Leavenworth branch of the Santa Fe trail.

The first Army of the West troops to march for Santa Fe by way of the new route left the fort on June 22 (*see* p. 617). Part of them, and others who followed, got lost because the fatigue party "did but little good," and the path was "scarcely visible in many places." There were some detachments that got on the wrong trail while traveling between the post and the ferry. More went astray south of the Kansas, in the Wakarusa valley, by taking the Oregon-California trail (intersected by the military path eight miles southwest of Fish's ferry, at a point about one mile from the Wakarusa crossing), and overlooking the "faint and indistinct" trail which "struck out to the left for the Santa Fe road." (On June 30, Lt. A. R. Johnston wrote: "Some mistakes having occurred by cross roads, orders were sent back to the commanding officer at Fort Leavenworth to send out a plough and have the crossings all marked with a furrow in the direction of Santa Fe.")

Pvt. M. B. Edwards (who crossed the Kansas on June 25) wrote: "The ferry consists of two flatboats, or bateaux, which are poled across by some Indians who have the management of them. It has been chartered by the government to ferry the troops across." Lt. J. W. Abert (on June 29) wrote: "In the river we found two large flat boats or scows manned by Shawnee Indians, dressed in bright-colored shirts, with shawls around their heads. . . . [The river's rapid current] required the greatest exertions on the part of our ferrymen to prevent the boats from being swept far down the stream. We landed just at the mouth of the Wakaroosa creek." Several soldiers mentioned the Shawnee (and Delaware) Indians' fine farms in the area. Pvt. Frank S. Edwards referred to the "house of one Charles Fish, a French [*i e.*, part-

Shawnee] settler on the Kaw." Another mentioned a Rogers family of Shawnees at the crossing. Lt. A. R. Johnston recorded on July 1: "Marched to Kaw (or Kansas) river and crossed it in ferry flats, it being too deep to ford; it is sometimes fordable for horses, but not for wagons on account of the quicksands. The crossing is known as Fish's ferry."

Pvt. John T. Hughes wrote this description of his journey from the Kansas crossing to the Santa Fe trail on July 1: "Left the Kansas river and struck off in a southwesterly direction. . . . After a tiresome march of about 12 miles through the tall prairie grass and peavine, over hill and dale, mound and mountain, sometimes marching west, sometimes south, we struck upon the Old Santa Fe Trace and encamped for the night near the Black-Jack-Grove. [Later, in his book, Hughes wrote: "encamped for the night near the black-jack grove or the Narrows."] To-day we encountered a formidable hill, which we were compelled to surmount, as it was impossible to avoid it by turning either right or left. The ascent was steep, rugged, and at least 200 feet high, being the projecting spur of the high Table Land which divides the waters of the Kansas from those of the Osage [Marais des Cygnes]. The mountain is a solid ledge of limestone." 2d Lt. George R. Gibson wrote: "The big hill is between the Oregon and Santa Fe roads, and is a high, steep, and rocky ridge requiring hard pulling to get up. It is about three miles from the Santa Fe road, and the prospect from its summit is magnificent and extensive."

Ref: M. B. Edwards, "Journal . . . 1846-1847," in *Marching With the Army of the West, 1846-1848,* v. 4 of *The Southwest Historical Series,* pp. 118-122; Hughes, *op. cit.,* pp. 31-33, or Connelley, *Doniphan's Expedition,* pp. 141, 143, 144; Hughes' letter of July 5, 1846, in *The Weekly Tribune,* Liberty, Mo., August 1, 1846; Robinson, *op. cit.,* pp. 2, 3; Ruff's notes (*loc. cit.*); J. W. Abert, in 30th Cong., 1st Sess., *H. Ex. Doc. No. 41* (Serial 517), pp. 160*ff* and 386-391; J. W. Abert, *Western America in 1846-1847, the Original Travel Diary of Lieutenant J. W. Abert . . .,* edited by John Galvin (San Francisco, Cal., 1966); F. S. Edwards, *op. cit.,* pp. 23-25; A. R. Johnston, *op. cit.,* pp. 74-77; Gibson, *op. cit.,* pp. 126-132. For other data on Fish's ferry see *KHQ,* v. 2, pp. 276, 277.

❡ June 17-30.—News reached Santa Fe on the 17th that a state of war existed between the United States and Mexico. "This was confirmed on the 26th by the arrival of the first . . . traders from Independence, Mo."—according to U. S. consul Manuel Alvarez.

The early-arriving traders were referred to as "Messrs. [George] Doan & Co.," who had entered Santa Fe "in advance of their goods." Apparently Albert Speyer's wagons (on June 30) were the first to reach the town. Doan & Webb's (and others) were "but half a day behind him."

Ref: *1950 Brand Book* . . . (Denver, c1951), p. 281; New York *Weekly Tribune,* August 15, 1846 (from *Missouri Republican,* St. Louis, August 3); D. Morgan, *op. cit.,* v. 2, pp. 643, 644; Webb, *op. cit.,* pp. 180, 181. See May 22, 1846, annals entry for Speyer.

❡ Around June 20(?) "Mr. [Solomon?] Houck" arrived at Independence, Mo., direct from Santa Fe in the remarkable time of 20 days (as reported). (*See* February 3 annals entry.)

Solomon(?) Houck was on the trail bound *for* Santa Fe again(?), no later than the end of June. Susan Magoffin, whose husband's wagons were also in the traders' caravan following Kearny to Santa Fe, wrote, on August 17 (while in Raton Pass): "Before we left camp some two hours, one of the traders Mr. Howk of Boonvill[e], Mo. came up with his wagons and passed us. . . ."

Ref: *The Gazette*, St. Joseph, Mo., June 25, 1846 (from a Lexington [Mo.] *Express* extra); or, New York *Weekly Tribune*, July 4, 1846; also, Magoffin, *op. cit.*, pp. 82, 83. Later while the traders' battalion was en route with Doniphan's regiment to Chihuahua, Pvt. John T. Hughes (in his diary) noted that "Mr. Houke, Trader, lost 85 to 90 oxen by the Apaches."—Connelley, *Doniphan's Expedition*, p. 98.

❦ DIED: the Rev. Isaac McCoy (associated with "Kansas" history —as a government surveyor-explorer of Indian lands, and as a Baptist missionary to the Indians—from 1828 up to 1843), on June 21, at Louisville, Ky.

In tribute, the *Baptist Missionary Magazine* noted his "many years devoted to the civilization and spiritual welfare of the Indian tribes"; his "energy, perseverance, and self-denial"; and concluded "the red man has lost a sincere friend, and the cause of Indian reform a most indefatigable laborer."

Ref: *The Baptist Missionary Magazine*, v. 26 (August, 1846), p. 269. *See* annals, p. 152, for McCoy's first entry into "Kansas," and p. 462, for his departure—to Louisville —in 1842.

❦ June 21.—Several Santa Fe-bound traders who arrived at Council Grove—"the great rendezvous"—on the 19th and 20th, set out together—a caravan of 45 wagons—on the 21st. They included Samuel Magoffin, Samuel C. Owens & James Aull, Dr. Eugene Leitensdorfer (whose wife accompanied him), Frank McManus, Gabriel Valdez, and one of the Armijo family. One cotraveler was Dr. Philippe Masure; and another, artist John Mix Stanley, who accompanied the Owens-Aull train. Owens was said to be taking $50,000 in merchandise.

With Samuel Magoffin was his bride, Susan Shelby Magoffin, whose diary—the earliest contribution to Santa Fe trail literature by a woman—was published in 1926 under the title: *Down the Santa Fé Trail and Into Mexico*. The Magoffin train (which had left Independence June 10) consisted of 14 large ox-drawn wagons, a baggage wagon, a dearborn and a carriage (both mule-drawn), some 200 oxen, nine mules, two riding horses, and "Ring," a greyhound; and it numbered 20 men ("Mr. Hall," wagonmaster), and two women (Mrs. Magoffin and her maid).

The caravan reached Pawnee Fork early in July (the Magoffins—the last? to arrive—got there on the 4th). Susan Magoffin wrote: "we found all the companies which have come on before us [*i. e.*, Harmony's train—*see* p. 588— and those who had been behind him on the trail], having been stoped by an order of government." She commented (on July 5): "We are quite a respectable crowd now with some seventy-five or eighty wagons of merchandise, besides those of the soldiers. When all that are behind us come up we shall number some hundred and fifty."

[*Continued on p. 617*]

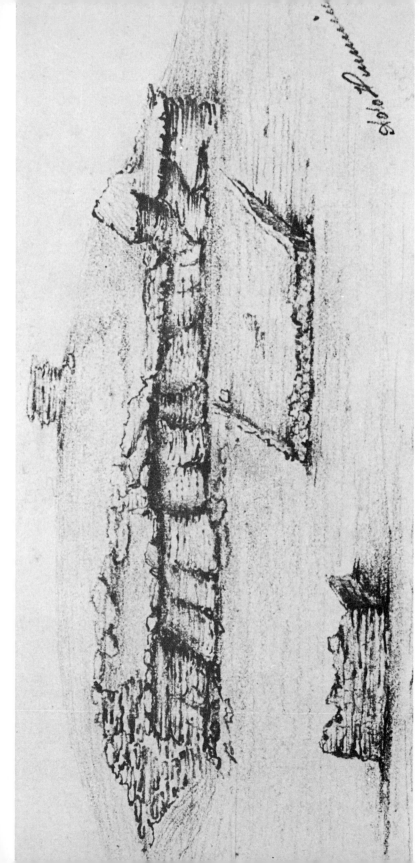

PAWNEE ROCK, FAMED LANDMARK ON THE SANTA FE TRAIL

To Jacob Fowler (in 1821) it was "the Red Rock," in a region otherwise "leavel as fare as the Eye Can see." To Matt Field (in 1839) it was "like a huge wart" in the prairie, some 30 feet high, and about 100 feet in circumference; with "one tall, rugged portion . . . [standing] totally inaccessible and alone." The Ado Hunnius sketch reproduced above shows Pawnee Rock as it appeared in 1867 before the settlement of southwestern Barton county and the subsequent stripping of some of the rock for building materials.

22—4138

John Tecumseh "Tauy" Jones (1808?-1872), half English, half Chippewa, was born in Canada, and educated at Baptist schools. He came to "Kansas" in 1837(?) with the Pottawatomies. In the 1840's he was an assistant Baptist missionary among the Pottawatomie creek Indians. In 1848(?) Jones and his second wife (Jane Kelley) were adopted by the Ottawas. Their home was northeast of present Ottawa. Jones was ordained a minister in 1864.

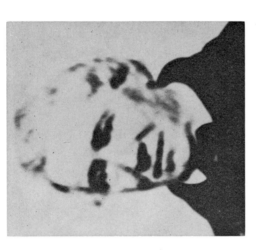

The Rev. Felix L. Verreydt, S. J. (1798-1883), spent 12 years as an Indian missionary. He was at Kickapoo Catholic Mission in 1837 and 1838 (p. 310); the superior at Pottawatomie Sugar Creek Mission from 1841 to 1848 (see p. 434); and head, from September, 1848, till autumn, 1849, of the Pottawatomie St. Mary's Mission (built on the site Verreydt selected, at present St. Marys Pottawatomie co.). Photograph courtesy of old St. Mary's College, St. Marys.

Jacques Ash-kum, head of the Pottawatomies' Wabash band, as painted by Indiana artist George Winter, who described him (then about 70) as "an orator of some distinction and possessed [of] some diplomatic qualities." Ash-kum came to "Kansas" in November, 1838 (p. 359), and died at the Sugar creek settlement in September, 1840 (see p. 416). Portrait reproduced courtesy of the Tippecanoe County Historical Association, Lafayette, Ind.

After visiting Shawnee Methodist Mission and Indian Manual Labor School in May, 1843, and meeting Supt. Jerome C. Berryman (portrait above), California-bound P. B. Reading wrote: "The improvements are two large brick buildings with a large barn, stables, wheelwright, blacksmith and shoemaker shops. . . This establishment cost about $45,000." The illustration (from the Heisler and Smith Johnson county *Atlas*) shows the two large brick buildings erected between 1839 and 1841 (see pp. 370 and 425) as they appeared in 1874.

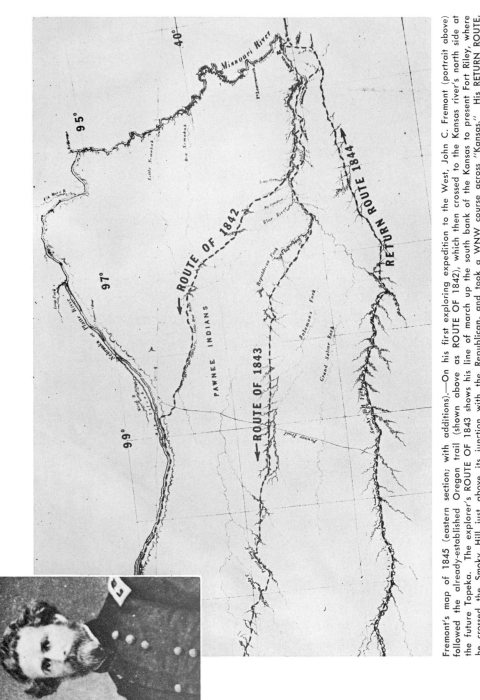

Fremont's map of 1845 (eastern section; with additions).—On his first exploring expedition to the West, John C. Fremont (portrait above) followed the already-established Oregon trail (shown above as ROUTE OF 1842), which then crossed to the Kansas river's north side at the future Topeka. The explorer's ROUTE OF 1843 shows his line of march up the south bank of the Kansas to present Fort Riley, where he crossed the Smoky Hill just above its junction with the Republican, and took a WNW course across "Kansas." His RETURN ROUTE, 1844, was by way of the Smoky Hill river, and the Santa Fe trail.

Fort Leavenworth—presumably as it appeared to an artist in the 1840's. Reproduced here from a picture of the painting. (No information is available, at this time, concerning the location of the original work, or the identity of the artist.)

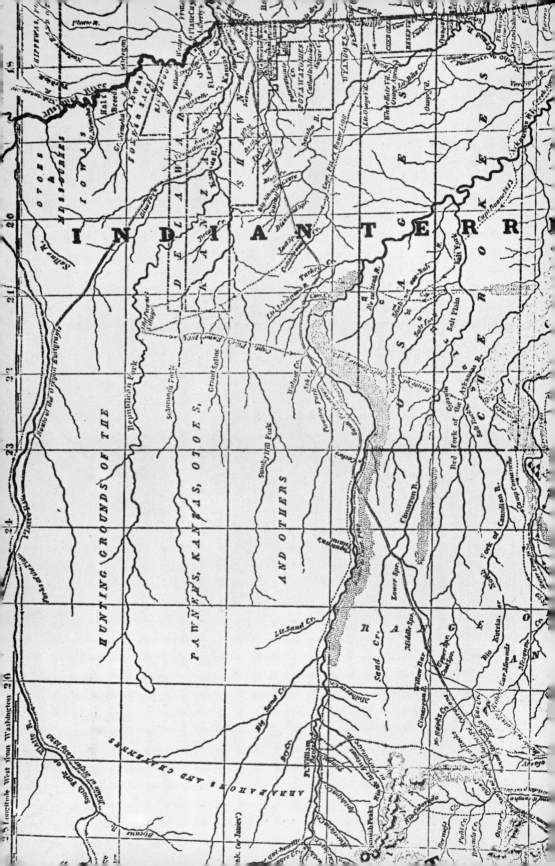

A section of Josiah Gregg's map (1844), as published in his *Commerce of the Prairies* (see p. 520). Note that Fort Scott (of 1842 origin) and the Pottawatomies' briefly-held (1837–1846) Marais des Cygnes reserve are shown. However, the Indian reserve south of it was *not* for the "Wyandots," but for the New York Indians.

Fourteen Iowas went abroad in 1844 (see p. 519), headed by the nation's first chief, Mahaska, or Frank White Cloud. At right, their conductor, George H. C. Melody, and Jeffrey Dorney, interpreter. Two Indians died in 1844 in England before the London engraving, reproduced above, was made. Later, in Paris, one of the women in this group died. The remaining 11 Iowas returned to their "Kansas" homes late in 1845.

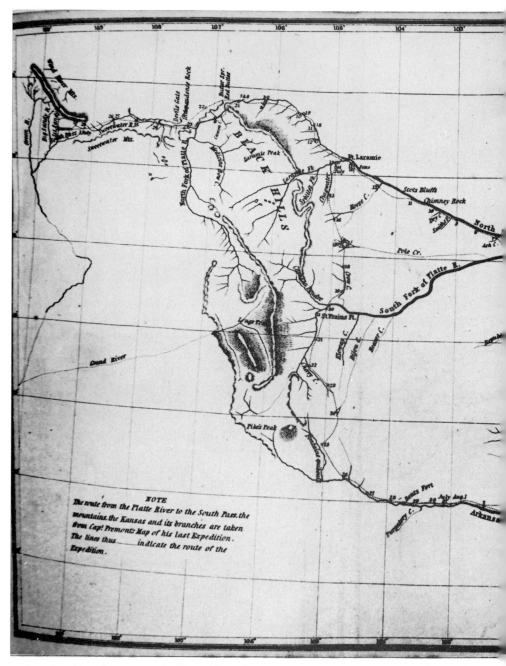

Leaving Fort Leavenworth May 18 and returning August 24, 1845, Col. Stephen W. Kearny and some 280 First U. S. dragoons, made a 2,200-mile, 99-day march, traver

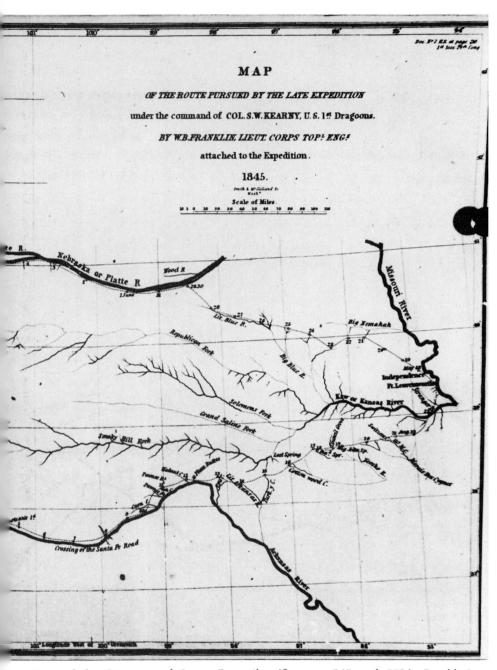

MAP

OF THE ROUTE PURSUED BY THE LATE EXPEDITION

under the command of COL. S.W. KEARNY, U.S. 1st Dragoons.

BY W.B. FRANKLIN, LIEUT. CORPS TOP! ENG!

attached to the Expedition.

1845.

Smith & McClelland Sc
Wash?

Scale of Miles.

sections of the Oregon and Santa Fe trails. (See pp. 545 and 558.) Franklin's
o shows the expedition's day-to-day (May 18–August 23) camp sites. (Serial 470.)

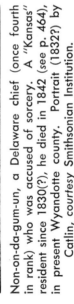

Non-on-da-gum-un, a Delaware chief (once fourth in rank) who was accused of sorcery. A "Kansas" resident since 1830(?), he died in 1842 (see p. 464), in present Wyandotte county. Portrait (1832?) by Catlin, courtesy Smithsonian Institution.

Matthew R. Walker (1810-1860), one-quarter Wyandot, was prominent in the civilized Wyandot Nation which removed from Ohio to "Kansas" in 1843 (see p. 493). He lived in present Kansas City; is buried in now famous (litigation-involved) Huron cemetery.

DISTANCE FROM INDEPENDENCE TO ASTORIA.

From Independence to the Crossings of Kanzas, 102 miles.
Crossings of Blue, - - - 83
PlatteRiver, - - - 119
Crossings of South Platte, - - 163
To North Fork, - - - 20
To Fort Larima, - - - 153   640

From Larima to cross'g of North fork of the Platte, 140
To Independence Rock on Sweet Water, - 50   830

Fort Bridger, - - - 229
Bear River, - - - 68
Soda Springs, - - - 94
To Fort Hall, - - - 57   1278

Salmon Falls, - - - 160
Crossings of Snake river, - - 22
To crossings of Bosie river, - - 69
Fort Bosie, - - - 45
Dr. Whitman's Mission, - - 190
Fort Walawala, - - - 25
Dallis Mission, - - - 120
Cascade Falls, on the Columbia, - 50
Fort Vancouver, - - - 41
Astoria, - - - 90   2117

☞In preparation by the author a concise description of the Oregon and California Countries; climate, soil, natural productions, together with a map of the same.

ROUTE
AND
DISTANCES
TO
OREGON AND CALIFORNIA,
WITH A DESCRIPTION OF
WATERING-PLACES, CROSSINGS, DANGEROUS INDIANS, &c. &c.
BY J. M. SHIVELY.
WASHINGTON, D.C.
WM. GREER, PRINTER.
1846.

John M. Shively, returning from Oregon, crossed "Kansas" in August, 1845 (see p. 560). His 1846-published guidebook was crammed with specific directions and practical, pertinent advice for the families, and single men, migrating to Oregon or California. He cautioned: "When you start over these wide plains, let no one leave dependent on his best friend for any thing; for if you do, you will certainly have a blow-out before you get far."

JOURNAL OF TRAVELS

OVER THE

ROCKY MOUNTAINS,

TO THE

MOUTH OF THE COLUMBIA RIVER;

MADE DURING THE YEARS 1845 AND 1846:

CONTAINING MINUTE DESCRIPTIONS OF THE

VALLEYS OF THE WILLAMETTE, UMPQUA, AND CLAMET;

A GENERAL DESCRIPTION OF

OREGON TERRITORY;

ITS INHABITANTS, CLIMATE, SOIL, PRODUCTIONS, ETC, ETC.;

A LIST OF

NECESSARY OUTFITS FOR EMIGRANTS;

AND A

Table of Distances from Camp to Camp on the Route.

ALSO;

A Letter from the Rev. H. H. Spalding, resident Missionary, for the last ten years, among the Nez Percé Tribe of Indians, on the Koos-koos-kee River; The Organic Laws of Oregon Territory; Tables of about 300 words of the Chinook Jargon, and about 200 Words of the Nez Percé Language; a Description of Mount Hood; Incidents of Travel, &c. &c.

BY JOEL PALMER.

CINCINNATI:
J. A. & U. P. JAMES, WALNUT STREET,
BETWEEN FOURTH AND FIFTH.
1847.

TABLE OF DISTANCES FROM INDEPENDENCE, MISSOURI; AND ST. JOSEPH, TO OREGON CITY, IN OREGON TERRITORY.

	MILES.
From Independence to Rendezvous	20
" Rendezvous to Elm Grove	13
" Elm Grove to Walkarusha	20
" Walkarusha to crossing of Kansas river	28
" Kansas to crossing of Turkey creek	14
" Turkey creek to Little Vermilion	24
" Little Vermilion to branch of same	12
" To Big Vermilion, with intermediate camps	29
" Vermilion to Lee's branch	8
" Lee's branch to Big Blue	6
" Big Blue to the junction with St. Joseph's trail	10

The distance from St. Joseph, Missouri, to the Independence trail, striking it ten miles west of Blue river, is about one hundred miles. Good camps can be had from eight to fifteen miles apart.

From forks of road as above, to Big Sandy, striking it near its junction with the Republican Fork of Blue river, with intermediate camps	42
" Sandy to Republican fork of Blue river	18
" up Republican fork, with good camps	53
" Republican fork to Big Plate	20
" up Big Plate to the crossing of South fork	120

Camps can be had at suitable distances, with wood for fuel upon the islands.

From lower to upper crossings of South fork	45

There is a road on each side of the river, and but little choice in them.

From South to North fork, at Ash Hollow	20
" Ash Hollow to opposite Solitary Tower, on Little creek	42
" Little creek to opposite Chimney rock	16
" Chimney Rock to where the road leaves the River	15
" thence to Scott's Bluffs (Good Spring)	10
" Scott's Bluffs to Horse creek	12
" Horse creek to Fort Laramie	24
" Laramie to Dry Branch and Big Spring	12
" to Bitter Cottonwood	10

Joel Palmer crossed "Kansas" for the first time in May, 1845 (see p. 542), en route to Oregon, and retraced the trail (eastbound) in midsummer, 1846. In the spring of 1847 (just as his *Journal of Travels* was being published) he started west from Indiana with his family, and was elected to captain an Oregon-bound emigrant company. There were later editions (in 1851 and 1852) of his popular guidebook.

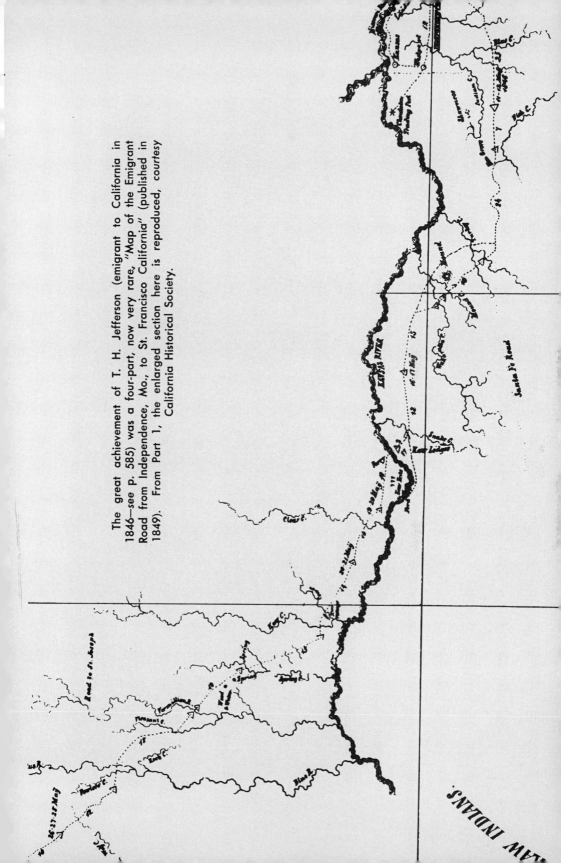

The great achievement of T. H. Jefferson (emigrant to California in 1846—see p. 585) was a four-part, now very rare, "Map of the Emigrant Road from Independence, Mo., to St. Francisco California" (published in 1849). From Part 1, the enlarged section here is reproduced, courtesy California Historical Society.

Wah-bon-seh (Wabaunsee), a chief of the Pottawatomie Indians, who was killed in a stagecoach accident before his portion of the Pottawatomies (residing at Council Bluffs, Iowa) removed to Kansas (*see* p. 566). A county, township, and town in Kansas are named for this venerated chief. Copy of the 1835 painting, by Charles Bird King, *courtesy* the Redwood Library and Athenaeum, Newport, R. I., and the Mills County Historical Society, Glenwood, Iowa.

Na-che-ning-a (No-Heart-of-Fear) was second chief of the Iowas and about 35 years old when Charles Bird King painted his portrait in 1837. In 1848, the year he became principal chief, missionaries to the Iowas wrote of him: "under good influence [he] will always be a fine man"; he "shows some concern for the welfare of his people"; is "a friend to the whites"; is "very friendly to education. . . ." Portrait *courtesy* Smithsonian Institution.

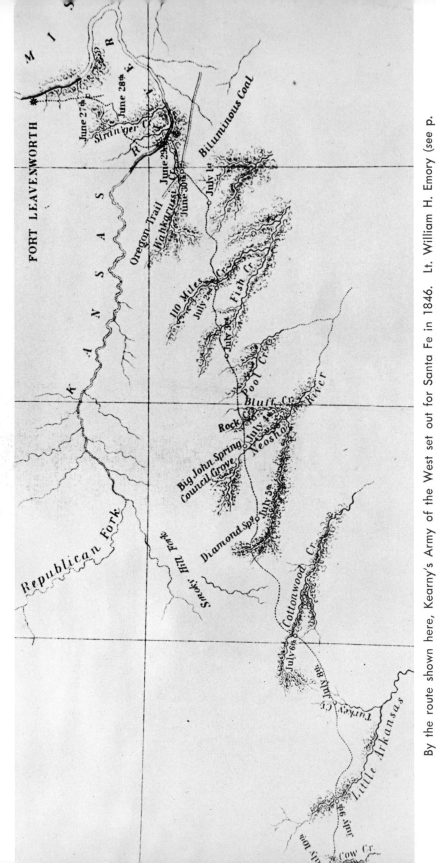

FORT LEAVENWORTH

M I S S O U R I

June 27th
June 28th
Stranger R.
June 29th
Wakarusa Cr.
June 30th
Oregon Trail
July 1st

Bituminous Coal

K A N S A S

KANSAS

110 Miles Cr.
July 2nd
Fish Cr.

Republican Fork

Rock Cr.
Big John Spring
Council Grove
July 4th
Neosho River
Bluff Cr.
Pool Cr.

Smoky Hill Fork

Diamond Spg. July 5th

Cottonwood Cr.
July 6th

Turkey Cr.
July 8th

Little Arkansas

July 9th

Cow Cr.

By the route shown here, Kearny's Army of the West set out for Santa Fe in 1846. Lt. William H. Emory (see p. 619) made the map (of 1847 date) from which this section is reproduced. The dotted line of march from the military post to the (Emory) camp labeled "July 1st" shows the new Fort Leavenworth-Santa Fe trail pathway Kearny had pioneered in 1845 (see pp. 558, 559), which crossed the Kansas river just below the Wakarusa's mouth at Fish's ferry (not labeled by Emory). Though the new fort-to-Santa Fe trail road was used extensively in 1846, it seems to have fallen into disuse in 1847.

[Continued From p. 600]

On July 8 Mrs. Magoffin wrote: "This is our fourth day here. . . . The soldiers [of Kearny's Army of the West] are coming in, and if we have to travel behind them, it will be poor living both for man and beast." Next day permission was given the traders to move on to the Arkansas crossings, or to Bent's Fort. The Magoffins renewed their journey on July 11—taking the dry route, while most of the companies followed (according to Susan) "a new road along the river." They reached Bent's Fort on July 26; later journeyed (as did the other traders) to Santa Fe in the rear of Kearny's Army of the West.

Ref: Magoffin, *op. cit.; KHQ*, v. 20, pp. 5, 6, for note on John M. Stanley, and his now-lost (destroyed by fire) portrait of Sac chief Keokuk, painted in "Kansas" in 1846; *Missouri Republican*, St. Louis, June 25, 1846; or, *see* Waugh, *op. cit.*, p. 107, footnote; Gregg, *op. cit.*, v. 1, pp. 195-198; *Missouri Reporter*, St. Louis, May 20, 1846 (reprinted in D. Morgan, *op. cit.*, v. 2, p. 547).

❧ June 22-30.—Leaving Fort Leavenworth for the march to Santa Fe (via the Santa Fe trail and its Bent's Fort, or upper Arkansas branch) were the following units (principally Missouri volunteer companies—*see* June 6-27 entry) of Col. Stephen W. Kearny's Army of the West:

DEPARTING JUNE 22—

Companies A and D, First regiment Missouri volunteers ("Doniphan's" mounted regiment), numbering over 200 men, captained by David Waldo and John W. Reid. (They were, apparently, the earliest Army of the West troops to travel the new military branch road to the Santa Fe trail—*see* p. 598.)

In "D" were two men—Pvt. Jacob S. Robinson and Pvt. Marcellus B. Edwards—who kept journals of the march. Reid's company crossed the Kansas (on Fish's ferry flatboats) June 25, in mid-afternoon "and with considerable difficulty got . . . [the] wagons up the steep hill on the south side." Waldo's "A" company ferried over on the 26th. On the 27th, "D" company, intersecting the Oregon-California trail, followed it westward; learned of the error after crossing the Wakarusa; but decided to proceed up that stream. Recrossing some miles above on the 28th, the men "cut a road across a branch" on the 29th to arrive at the Santa Fe trail east of 110-mile creek. Company A, and "D's" wagons, reached the Santa Fe road on the 28th and continued to 110-mile creek; were joined there by "D" company on the 29th.

On July 4 (before leaving Cottonwood Fork camp) the troops had a drink of whisky in honor of the day; then marched 25 miles. On the 8th they "travelled 4 miles to Walnut Creek, and 25 miles to Pawnee Fork," passing Pawnee Rock en route. Robinson wrote: ". . . from the top of . . . [it] I witnessed one of the grandest sights ever beheld. Far over the plain to the west and north was one vast herd of buffaloes; some in column, marching in their trails, others carelessly grazing. Every acre was covered, until in the dim distance the prairie became one black mass . . . extending to the horizon. . . . Most of them were travelling south . . . so as to come across our path. Their front ranks very obligingly made way for us for about two miles; but as the main body moved on they could be kept off no longer. They rushed through our ranks, throwing us into complete confusion; stopped the further progress of our wagons; and though an hundred shots were fired at them, we could not drive them away until the crowd passed. We killed 40 of them—cooking our meat by fires made of buffalo-dung, which burns as well as charcoal."

After three days at Pawnee Fork (where they had joined Captain Moore's command on the 8th—*see* p. 591) these two companies (except Reid and some sick troops) proceeded to the Bent's Fort area—arriving there on July 21 and 22.—(Ref: Robinson's, and M. B. Edwards', journals—*op. cit.*)

Departing June 26 (and 27)—

Companies B, C, F (W. P. Walton, O. P. Moss, M. M. Parsons, captains), of "Doniphan's" regiment, on the 26th; and Company G (Congreve Jackson, captain), on the 27th. These more than 400 Missouri volunteers were under command of the regiment's Lt. Col. Charles F. Ruff.

On June 29, at Stranger river camp, Ruff organized the four companies as a battalion. On the 30th "every man & horse & mule & wagon & oxe crossed [the Kansas river] before dark together with 70 head Beef cattle"; and Ruff settled with the ferryman for "425 men & horses & 14 wagons." Next day the battalion went astray—by taking the Oregon-California trail—and had to retrace four miles, but reached the Santa Fe road and camped at "Black Jack point." Ruff and his troops arrived at Council Grove on July 5. (Their "glorious 4th" had been "a temperance celebration"; and they had marched from 22 to 27 miles.) The evening of July 11 Major Gilpin's command (Companies E and H) and Colonel Doniphan—short of provisions—overtook Ruff's command at Cow creek.

The next night they all encamped at Walnut creek. (In a letter of July 12, Pvt. John T. Hughes wrote: "The Army is generally in tolerable condition. . . . There are from 75 to 90 on the sick-list in this command, though but few are seriously ill. . . . Many of our animals have either died or been left on the prairie. . . .) On their July 13 march "innumerable herds of Buffalo" were to be seen—"the whole plain . . . black with them" as far as the eye could reach. Many were killed, and the troops "feasted sumptuously." (Pvt. Nehemiah Carson, of Howard county, who died this day, was buried on the 14th in an excavation hollowed out of Pawnee Rock.) When Ruff's command reached Pawnee Fork on the 14th, to encamp, the river was in flood stage. (Pvt. Arthur E. Hughes, a "Laclede Ranger"—*see* following— on "express" duty, drowned, and was buried on the 15th near the stream.) On the 16th Colonel Kearny (who had arrived the day before) expedited the crossing of swollen Pawnee Fork, and after a night on the right bank, the march was resumed. Ruff's command reached the Bent's Fort vicinity by July 29. (Ref: Ruff's notes, *loc. cit.*; Hughes' letters, *loc. cit.*; Hughes' *Doniphan's Expedition;* Conelley's *Doniphan's Expedition.*)

Departing June 27—

Lt. William H. Emory (corps of topographical engineers) and party—2d Lt. James W. Abert, 2d Lt. William G. Peck, and 10(?) hired hands. (Their mission: to make a military reconnaissance— collecting meterological, geographical, and "natural history" data.)

This small party (equipped with mules, horses, provisions, and an instrument-carrying carriage) crossed the Kansas (at Fish's ferry) late on June 29; camped on the right bank, spent the night of the 30th in the Wakarusa valley (after a nine-mile march, and having had to reverse their course when led out of the way by a young Shawnee guide). Shortly after intersecting the Oregon trail, they had come to a steep-banked stream (a Wakarusa tributary—once called "Coal," but now "Cole" creek) where "a seam of bituminous coal" outcropped. "This is worked by the [Shawnee] Indians," wrote Emory, "one of whom we met driving an ox-cart loaded with coal, to Westport." Next day (July 1) they got on the right trail and reached the Santa Fe road. On July 2, at 110-mile creek "young Mr. Nourse" from Washington joined them. The Fourth of July Emory's party camped at Big John Spring (water temperature 53°); passed Council Grove, to camp at Diamond Spring (54°) on the 5th; reached the Little Arkansas on July 9; camped, on the 11th, at the Great Bend of the Arkansas; arrived at flooded Pawnee Fork on the 13th; constructed a raft on the 15th; and crossed on the 16th. From this point, to Bent's Fort, Emory's party traveled more "in company" with the Army of the West than previously; arrived there July 29. A "Table of geographical positions" which accompanied the Emory report included these mileages:

	Distance From Camp To Camp	Total Distance From Fort Leavenworth
Fort Leavenworth, on the Missouri, to:		
Oregon trail, about one mile from where it strikes the Wakarusa,	43	43
Big John Spring	81	124
Diamond Spring	20	144
Cottonwood creek	29	173
Cow creek	58	231
[Great] bend of the Arkansas river, where the road strikes it	22	253
Pawnee Fork	35	288
Jackson Grove (where Cooke confronted Snively's Texan force in 1843—*see* p. 487)........	64	352
Bent's Fort	[212]	564

Abert (who fell ill in southwestern "Kansas"; recuperated at Bent's Fort) and Peck, went only as far as Santa Fe with the Army of the West, but Emory continued westward to the Pacific with Kearny. *See,* on pp. 616, 682, two small (enlarged) "Kansas" segments of Lieutenant Emory's map "Military Reconnaissance of the Arkansas, Rio del Norte and Rio Gila," which accompanied his report, published in 1847. (Ref: 30th Cong., 1st Sess., *H. Ex. Doc. No. 41* [Serial 517]; Gibson, *op. cit.,* pp. 45, 46. And *see* Abert's travel diary, *op. cit.*)

DEPARTING JUNE 29—

Companies E and H (J. D. Stevenson and C. B. Rodgers, captains) of "Doniphan's" regiment, in charge of Maj. William Gilpin, accompanied by Col. Alexander W. Doniphan; the "Laclede Rangers" (headed by Capt. T. B. Hudson); and the two-company Missouri infantry battalion (under Capt. W. Z. Angney).

Doniphan, Gilpin, and Companies E and H (some 220 men) crossed the Kansas at Fish's ferry (after having gone astray earlier) on July 1, apparently. Little is known of their travel up to July 12, when (having run short of provisions) they overtook Ruff's command at Cow creek (*see* above). The (107) "Laclede Rangers" went 60 miles out of their way by taking the "lower ferry road" (the Fort Leavenworth-Fort Scott military road). They crossed the Kansas at the Delaware (or Grinter) ferry and got on the Santa Fe trail in the Westport, Mo., area. On July 4 the "Rangers" reached 110-mile creek; remained a day; and were overtaken there July 5 by Colonel Kearny (*see below*). Angney's Company A (68 in all) of the infantry ferried the Kansas (at Fish's) on July 1; marched on next day. Murphy's Company B (77 in all) of the infantry spent July 2 in camp near the Kansas after crossing (at Fish's) early in the day; then marched on the 3d and reached the Santa Fe trail, having learned meantime that Angney's company had traveled (by error) 10 miles out the Oregon trail and "were a long day's march out of their way." On July 4, after a very hard, nearly-30-mile journey (which caused great fatigue and suffering) Murphy's company arrived at 110-mile creek (and the "Laclede Rangers" came up that night—*see above*). On July 8 Company A (Murphy's) camped at Diamond Spring. "The general [Kearny], [the] artillery, Captain Hudson's [Laclede Rangers"] company, and [Angney's] company A [of infantry] all came up . . .," wrote 2d Lt. George R. Gibson, "company A considerably worsted and in low spirits." He added: "We presented a more military and warlike appearance than we have before. . . . Besides the soldiers, there is a heavy train of commissary and quartermaster teams and baggage wagons . . . and with the loose mules adds to the magnitude and display of the rear." In succeeding days the foot soldiers kept up remarkably well with the mounted forces. Of the Army of the West contingent which left Fort Leavenworth between June 26 and 30, the infantry companies were first to reach the Bent's Fort area—arriving there July 28. (Ref: Gibson's and Johnston's journals.)

DEPARTING JUNE 30—

Col. Stephen W. Kearny (commander, Army of the West), his staff, and escort of First dragoons; the Missouri volunteers' two-company light artillery battalion (Capt. R. H. Weightman's Battery A; Capt. Woldemar Fischer's Battery B), in Fischer's (temporary) charge.

Kearny's regular army officers on this march included Capt. Henry S. Turner, Lt. Abraham R. Johnston (adjutant, and journalist), Lt. William N. Grier, Lt. John Love, Lt. William H. Warner (ordnance officer). Antoine Robidoux (interpreter) and Hiram Rich (Fort Leavenworth sutler and postmaster) were also in his party. On July 1 Kearny's headquarters command ferried the Kansas (at the Wakarusa's mouth); encamped on the right bank; and remained three nights. (On July 2 the colonel wrote a letter from Fish's ferry to the governor of Missouri, in which he expressed a desire for more infantry troops.) Weightman's Battery A (without the captain—ill at the fort, he joined on July 8) also reached the Kansas river on July 1, encamping on the north bank. In his company were (Lt.) Edmund F. Chouteau, (Sgt.) W. Clark Kennerly, and (Pvt.) Antoine Clement (famed hunter)—for their earlier journeys across "Kansas" see annals index; also Pvt. Frank S. Edwards—whose book, A Campaign In New Mexico With Colonel Doniphan, was published in 1847. By the evening of July 3 Fischer's (all-German) Battery B, the artillery and ammunition trains, and a provision train, had arrived at Fish's ferry. (Pvt. Frank Edwards wrote that there were "eight long brass six pounders and two twelve pound howitzers; and to each of these, as well as to the caissons, were harnessed four fine dragoon horses.") On July 4 the march was resumed. Kearny and his command reached the Santa Fe trail that day. ("It being the Fourth . . . of July, the men were permitted to buy liquor from the sutler to celebrate as best they might," Johnston wrote.) At 110-mile creek, on the 5th, Kearny overtook Angney's infantry company, and the "Laclede Rangers" (see above under June 29 departures). On the 8th, at Diamond Spring, he came up with Murphy's infantrymen. Maj. M. Lewis Clark joined on July 9 and took charge of the artillery battalion. On July 14 camp was made on the Arkansas, about six miles from Walnut creek. Next day Kearny's command (now including the battalions of artillery and infantry, and the "Laclede Rangers") marched 34 miles to flooded Pawnee Fork ("the infantry . . . poor fellows, came into camp long after dark") where they found "Doniphan's six companies [also Col. A. W. Doniphan, Lt. Col. C. F. Ruff, Maj. William Gilpin] and the topographical engineers and some traders." Upwards of 1,200 men were now in the Pawnee Fork crossing area.

On July 16, to get his large command beyond flooded Pawnee Fork, Kearny "caused trees to be felled across the deep, rapid current. On the trunks of these trees the men passed over. . . . In this manner the principal loading of the wagons was also transported." The animals were forced to swim; and the wagons were floated across. Soon after noon the infantrymen (in advance of the rest) crossed; and camped a few miles beyond. One of them (2d Lt. G. R. Gibson) described the scene on the 17th: "The different mounted companies have been coming up all day, with stragglers, wagons, oxen, beef cattle, etc., and as far as can be seen, both in front and rear, we had a column like the picture in the journey of the Israelites. . . ." He also recorded (on the 18th) a less attractive picture: "the whole country from the Little Arkansas is like a slaughter pen, covered with bones, skulls, and carcasses of animals in every state of decay. . . ."

The Army followed along the Arkansas instead of the shorter "dry" route. On the 20th (a day on which Kearny became ill, but quickly recovered) the troops passed "The Caches" and camped at the Arkansas crossing (the Cimarron route crossing); on the 22d passed "Pawnee Fort, an old decayed stockade" (Sgt. Augustus Leslie who died this day was buried on the 23d four miles above it); continued a daily march up the Arkansas; and arrived at the Bent's

his family (who would go out in an 1847 wagon train), and Smith, were among those who took passage, at St. Joseph, on the *Balloon;* and debarked at St. Louis on July 16. (*See, also,* June 30 entry.)

Palmer, whose party met the first (Martin's company) of the Oregon-California migration on June 10, at Fort Laramie, and "continued for two hundred miles" to meet other trains (of six to 40 wagons each), reported that a count of 541 wagons had been made; and that an estimate of five persons to each wagon was not an exaggeration. (This would place the total emigration for 1846 at around 2,700 persons.)

Ref: Joel Palmer's *Journal* . . . as reprinted in R. G. Thwaites, editor, *Early Western Travels,* v. 30, pp. 222-256; D. Morgan, *op. cit.,* v. 1, pp. 62-68, v. 2, pp. 593-601, 759; Wade, *op. cit.,* v. 2, p. 437; Thornton, *op. cit.,* v. 1, p. 80; Bryant, *op. cit.,* pp. 94, 97. George L. Curry (Oregon immigrant, 1846) wrote, on April 23, 1847, that the emigration to California in 1846 "comprised about the same number of wagons as the Oregon emigration"—about 250.—Saint Louis *Reveille* (daily), August 6, 1847.

❡ July 8.—The 12-mile Independence-to-Westport, Mo., U. S. mail route (with twice-a-week service; under contract to W. H. Younger), was extended "five miles" to the town of Kansas, Mo.

(Beginning May 1, 1847, to the twice-a-week, 17-mile Independence-Westport-Kansas, Mo., service, was added one additional weekly trip from Independence to Westport only.)

Ref: 30th Cong., 1st Sess., *H. Ex. Doc. No. 64* (Serial 521), pp. 45, 46.

❡ Leaving Fort Leavenworth early(?) in July, Maj. Thomas Swords (chief quartermaster to the Army of the West) crossed "Kansas" by the Santa Fe trail and its Bent's Fort branch (apparently); caught up with Kearny on August 15 (at Las Vegas, N. M.). The mail he carried included Kearny's brigadier general's commission (dated June 30, 1846).

With Swords, on August 15, were Lt. Jeremy F. Gilmer (of the U. S. engineers) and Capt. Richard H. Weightman (of the Missouri volunteers' artillery battalion). Gilmer may have traveled from Fort Leavenworth with the major; but Weightman probably joined at Bent's Fort.

Ref: Gibson, *op. cit.,* pp. 199, 200; Johnston's journal, *loc. cit.,* p. 99 (for biographical note on Swords); Connelley, *Doniphan's Expedition,* p. 190.

❡ July.—The following description of Fort Leavenworth was published in the St. Louis *New Era* of the 10th:

"The nearest buildings and block-houses . . . are situated about 400 yards from the steamboat landing, on the summit of the first swell of land which gradually rises from the river. . . . The area of ground occupied by the buildings, lawns and streets, is but little short of 20 acres, in the form of a square. At each corner is planted a block-house, to be used by artillery-men or rifle-men.

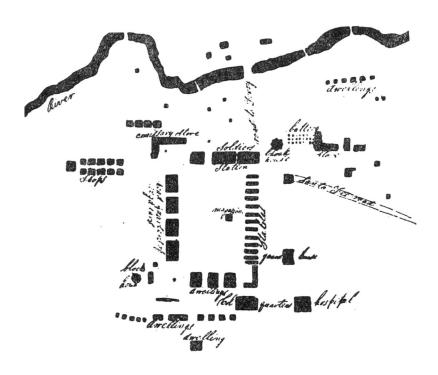

Fort Leavenworth in the Mexican War era, as drawn by Pvt. Uriah Thomas ("First" regiment Illinois volunteers) in a letter dated July 9, 1847. (Reproduced courtesy of Lee H. Cornell, Wichita, and Floyd E. Risvold, Minneapolis, Minn.) See *KHQ,* v. 15, facing p. 352, for a plan of the fort in 1828; v. 22, facing p. 113, for an 1838 drawing; v. 20, facing p. 416, for an 1849 sketch; *ibid.,* cover of May, 1952, issue, for an 1872 photograph showing post headquarters; and see, on p. 605 of these annals, a painting of the 1840's(?), by an unidentified artist.

"On the east side the buildings are of brick, two stories high, with double porticoes running their whole length, used by the troops as quarters. On the north side, the buildings are principally of brick, two stories, and occupied by the principal officers of the Fort as offices and family residences. These buildings are also fronted by porticoes and piazzas. The west side is not so closely built up. The arsenal and two or three buildings near the southwest corner of the Fort, are of brick, and the balance are large frame houses, occupied as quarters for officers and privates. The south side is altogether occupied by a long line of stables, and yard for artillery. South of the arsenal about 100 yards, on a beautiful piece of ground,

— 625 —

stands the hospital, a building of considerable size and very comfortably constructed. . . . [It] is completely surrounded by porticoes, which afford pleasant retreats for the convalescent.

"Besides the public buildings of the Fort, several small log and frame houses are to be seen on the northern and western suburbs occupied by the families of regular soldiers, and of persons laboring for the Government. The powder magazine is located near the centre of a beautiful lawn finely shaded by forest trees, and in the heart of the Fort. It is completely fire and bomb proof. West of the Fort, is the parade ground. It is a beautiful space, and admirably calculated for the purpose. South-west, at a distance of half a mile, is the Government farm, about 1100 acres of which is now under cultivation. Provender for the horses in the Fort, is the principal production."

Ref: St. Louis *Daily New Era*, July 10, 1846, as reprinted in Gibson, *op. cit.*, pp. 122, 123.

❡ July 11.—Capt. Benjamin D. Moore and his First dragoons (Companies C, G, and I) broke camp at Pawnee Fork (where they had been for some 20 days—*see* June 5 and 12 entries) and marched westward for Bent's Fort. With the dragoons were most of the troops from Companies A and D (Waldo's and Reid's) of "Doniphan's" regiment (who had reached Pawnee Fork on July 8). Moore's command arrived at Bent's Fort on July 21 and 22.

Also departing Pawnee Fork for the same destination, were the Santa Fe traders' trains which Captain Moore had detained there, and 25 government supply wagons. By July 27(?) they were encamped near Bent's Fort.

Ref: New York *Weekly Tribune*, August 22, 1846 (for Moore's July 10 letter, from the St. Louis *Reveille* of August 11; M. B. Edwards' journal, *loc. cit.*, Magoffin, *op. cit.*, pp. 43, 59; Charles F. Ruff's notes (copy in KHi ms. division); D. Morgan, *op. cit.*, v. 2, pp. 652, 771; Robinson, *op. cit.*, pp. 13-15.

❡ July 11-14.—A "large [Santa Fe-bound] train of wagons, belonging to Messrs. Hoffman, of Baltimore," camped on July 11 at the Great Bend of the Arkansas (about eight miles west of Plum Buttes). On the 12th, before daybreak, this train set out for Walnut creek, and stopped there for the night. Lt. Col. Charles F. Ruff and his command (*see* p. 618) also arrived at Walnut Creek crossing on the 12th. Ruff recorded in his notes: "meet Messrs Hoffman's traders for Santa fe Jew trader Goldstein with whiskey sells to men— exhorbitant prices $1 per pint for 18¢ whiskey—increased price to 50¢ per drink, Sergeant & file of men ordered to close the concern— trader liable to confiscation of goods &c. . . ."

Lt. James W. Abert, who had caught up with the Hoffman train at the

Great Bend on the 11th, and passed it at Walnut creek on the 12th, again encountered these traders at Pawnee Fork. Abert wrote, on July 14: "We were obliged to remain here all day . . . [because of the flooded river]. . . . In the evening some of us went over to visit Mr. Hoffman's camp."

Ref: 30th Cong., 1st Sess., *H. Ex. Doc. No. 41* (Serial 517), p. 398; Charles F. Ruff's notes (copy in KHi ms. division); *Niles' National Register*, v. 71 (September 26, 1846), p. 62 (has comment: "Among the list of traders we observe the name of the following Baltimoreans—Messrs. Hoffman and Barney [or Barnum?], and Edmund Hoffman, having with them 9[?] wagons."). In April, at Independence, Edwin Bryant had met "A party of gentlemen from Baltimore, bound for Santa Fe on a pleasure excursion, among whom were Messrs. Hoffman, Morris, and Meredith. . . ." See his *What I Saw in California* . . . (pp. 17, 18). These three may have gone out with advance companies; but were doubtless connected (Hoffman at least) with the above Baltimore traders.

❡ July 12.—Bound for the upper Missouri, under charter to the newly formed St. Louis Fur Company (otherwise known as "Harvey, Primeau & Co."), the *Clermont No. 2* (D. G.? Taylor, captain) passed St. Joseph, Mo.

On leaving St. Louis July 7 this steamer was reported to have aboard the partners, some 45 employees (these to be reinforced by perhaps 50 others "on the way up"), and about $50,000 worth of merchandise (principally for the Sioux and Blackfeet trade). Another passenger was Charles P. Cassilly, of Cincinnati, on a pleasure trip. The *Clermont No. 2* made the voyage to Fort Union (N. D.) in 37 days. (See p. 643 for her return trip.)

Ref: *The Gazette*, St. Joseph, Mo., July 17, 1846; *Saint Louis Daily Union*, September 21, 1846 (gives the captain's initials as "D. S."); Nebraska State Historical Society *Publications*, v. 20, pp. 160, 166 (from the *Missouri Republican*, St. Louis, July 7 and September 20?, 1846); *Niles' National Register*, v. 70 (July 18, 1846), p. 311 (from the St. Louis *New Era*); Scharf, *op. cit.*, v. 2, p. 1104. For some information on Harvey, Primeau & Co. origins, see Historical Society of Montana *Contributions*, Helena, v. 10 (1940), pp. 265, 302-305; and for the 1846 expedition see, also, Sunder, *op. cit.*, pp. 87, 93, 94. Alexander M. Harvey and Charles Primeau had as co-partners Joseph Picotte and Anthony R. Bouis.

❡ July 13-29.—James Clyman (emigrant to Oregon in 1844—*see* pp. 510, 511) returning from California (where he had journeyed in 1845) crossed "Kansas" eastbound on the Oregon trail. His companions were A. H. Crosby, "Mr. McKissick," five other men, two women, and a boy—a detachment of the only party to leave California in 1846 by the northern route.

Clyman's journal indicates he entered "Kansas" about July 13; crossed the Big Blue to camp on its east bank July 15 ("here," he wrote, "I observed the grave of Mrs. Sarah Keys agead 70 yares who had departed this life in may [the 29th] last [*see* p. 585] at her feet stands the stone that gives us this information."). On the 17th Clyman's party left the Big Blue, soon passed "Burr oak creek" (Black Vermillion); nooned, that day, at "cannon Ball Creek" (Rock Creek); crossed the "Black vermillion" (now Red Vermillion) on the forenoon of the 18th ("today the Trail runs nearly East") "came to knife [now Cross] creek for Breakfast" on the 19th; later that day crossed the Kansas river ("got our Baggage taken over in a canoe and Swam our animals across"); camped on the Wakarusa on the 20th; passed through Westport ("a small ordinary village") on the 22d, and reached Independence, Mo., before nightfall. Clyman, Crosby, and four other men were aboard the steamboat *Nimrod* which docked at St. Louis on July 29.

Ref: Camp, *op. cit.*, pp. 199-299; D. Morgan, *op. cit.*, v. 1, pp. 51-62, v. 2, pp. 623-630, 763; *also, see, ibid.*, pp. 575 and 753 (note 68) for others of the California party; Thornton, *op. cit.*, v. 1, pp. 110, 111.

❡ About July 15 James W. Magoffin (formerly U. S. consul to Chihuahua, Mexico, and long a trader there), accompanied by José Gonzales (a Chihuahua merchant) set out from Independence, Mo., in a buggy; and after a rapid trip over the Santa Fe trail and up the Arkansas, arrived at Bent's Fort on July 31.

Magoffin, on a secret mission for the United States government, subsequently accompanied Capt. P. St. George Cooke's advance party to Santa Fe; and, accounts say, was instrumental in making it possible for Kearny to occupy New Mexico without bloodshed.

Ref: Gibson, *op. cit.*, pp. 55, 57; W. E. Connelley's *Doniphan's Expedition*, pp. 183, 196-199.

❡ July.—A blacksmith-wheelwright and an assistant were dispatched (about mid-month?) from Fort Leavenworth to establish a government smithy at Council Grove (140 miles from the post). Capt. Robert E. Clary (AQM) reported in a July 18 letter that he had sent the two men (unidentified) to open the shop and perform such repairs as the wagoners, or troops, might require.

No blacksmith shop existed at the Neosho crossing when Doniphan's regiment, and Colonel Kearny, were there in early July. Pvt. John T. Hughes (in a letter of July 5), wrote: "We are now at the Council Groves. . . . Here the traders procure timbers for the repairing of waggons which may fail on the road across the Great Plain. . . . The Council Grove is nothing more than a forest or grove of timber about a mile in width, irrigated by a beautiful stream of clear water, one of the head branches of the Neochio [*i. e.*, the main Neosho]. Out of the bluff, in the open prairie, on the west bank of the stream, and near the road, flows a bold spring of cold water, sufficient for the use of a large army." 2d Lt. George R. Gibson (at Council Grove on July 8), wrote in his journal: "A settlement at this point, where supplies could be obtained or fresh animals for any given out, would very much diminish the drawbacks of a march across the plains. . . . A blacksmith and wagon shop with a few soldiers, established here by the government, would be of great benefit. . . ."

The earliest located references to the blacksmith shop *by travelers* are the following:

Pvt. William H. Richardson (with "Price's" regiment) in a journal entry of August 29:

"This morning we caught some black trout and cat fish in the Big John [creek] . . . at 12 o'clock we struck our tents, passed Council Grove, and encamped at 2 o'clock a few miles further on, where there is a blacksmith shop, established by the government. Here I left letters for my friends in Maryland, to be carried back by the return mail to Fort Leavenworth."

John D. Lee (westbound to overtake Mormon Battalion) in a diary entry of September 10:

"At this grove is a blacksmith shop employed by government. We here tryed to get them to repair our carriage as Government Property but they refused unless we would show U S on our mules or an order from Head Quarters. They said that they would assist us for pay—we all went to work built a new axle tree and shod one of the mules . . . at 5 we took a cup of Tea. The Smiths (blacksmiths) partook with us. About 6 we resumed our travel. . . ."

Francis Parkman (coming down from the upper Arkansas) in a journal entry of September 20:

"Came at noon to Council Grove—beautiful meadows and woods. Here was a blacksmith's shop, and a train of waggons repairing. . . ."

Lewis H. Garrard (with a Bent, St. Vrain & Co. wagon train, westbound):

"On the 30th September, we arrived at Council 'Grove'—considered the best camping spot on the road. On the west skirt of the belt of timber, under the widespreading protection of a huge oak, was a diminutive blacksmith's shop, sustained by government, for the purpose of repairing wagons *en route* to the army at Santa Fe."

But no habitation was mentioned by Lt. James W. Abert when he reached Council Grove on a "stormy and cold" winter's day in 1847. His journal of February 24 states: "Here we found grateful shelter in that noble grove whose huge walnut trees raise their limbs aloft, as if to battle with the clouds in our defence while their lower boughs were stretched over us to shield us from the pitiless pelting of the storm. . . ."

Ref: L. H. Garrard's *Wah-to-yah and the Taos Trail*, ed. by R. P. Bieber (Glendale, Cal., 1938), pp. 35 and 61 (for Clary, and Garrard); W. H. Richardson's *Journal*, p. 11; Wade, *op. cit.*, v. 2, p. 481; *The Weekly Tribune*, Liberty, Mo., August 1, 1846 (for Hughes' letter); W. E. Connelley's *Doniphan's Expedition*, p. 156 (for Hughes' *Doniphan's Expedition* [reprint]); 30th Cong., 1st Sess., *H. Ex. Doc. No. 41* (Serial 517), p. 544 (for Abert); John D. Lee's "Diary," in *New Mexico Historical Review*, v. 42 (July, 1967), p. 184.

❰ July 18-19.—Completion of the three-story, 32-room, brick-and-stone "manual labor boarding school," at the Iowa, Sac & Fox Presbyterian Mission, on the Iowa's reserve (in present Doniphan county), was celebrated on the 18th with a dinner for the construction crew; and on Sunday, the 19th, the Rev. Samuel M. Irvin preached a dedication sermon. (*See, also,* pp. 528 and 563.)

(A remaining portion of the above building stands today, at a point two miles east and a little north of Highland. It is state-owned, and houses a museum which is under the direction of the State Historical Society.)

Ref: *The Gazette*, St. Joseph, Mo., July 24, 1846; Comm'r of Indian Affairs, *Report*, 1846 (contains Thomas H. Harvey's September 5, 1846, statement: "The school among the Iowas [Presbyterian] . . . is now about to go into operation upon an extensive scale."). In a letter of May 28, 1847, Jane M. Bloohm (then a resident), described the interior arrangement of "Ioway and Sac Mission."—See George Catlin's *Notes of Eight Years Travels and Residence in Europe With His North American Indian Collection* . . .

(New York, 1848), v. 2, p. 329. The Indians contributed $6,000 towards the cost (nearly $8,000) of the boarding school. In 29th Cong., 1st Sess., *H. Doc. No. 91* (Serial 483), p. 85, is shown Subagent W. P. Richardson's payment (under date of March 31, 1845), to Walter Lowrie (secretary of the Board of Foreign Missions of the Presbyterian church) of $1,719.05 "for building and supporting manual labor school on land of the Iowas." *See KHQ*, v. 23, pp. 124, 125, for present-day status of the mission.

❡ July.—About the 23d(?) the *Tributary* (John McCloy, master), returning from a trip to St. Joseph, Mo., took aboard at Boonville, Mo., "Capt. [James] Kipp," 55 other American Fur Company employees, and the large lot of "peltries" which they had brought down from Fort Union (N. D.) in seven Mackinaw boats.

The fur company's cargo consisted of 18,000 buffalo robes and 2,500 buffalo tongues, as well as packs of skins, furs, and peltries.

Ref: *The Weekly Tribune*, Liberty, Mo., August 1, 1846; Nebraska State Historical Society *Publications*, v. 20, pp. 161, 162 (from *Daily Missouri Republican*, St. Louis, July 25, 1846; Saint Louis *Daily Union*, August 22, 1846 (and following issues), for advertisement of the *Tributary* as a regular packet to Weston and St. Joseph.

❡ Died: Mrs. Sarah C. (Cessna) Berryman, wife of Methodist missionary Jerome C. Berryman, on July 28, at the Shawnee Mission Indian manual labor school, present Johnson county.

On August 7, at the mission, a funeral sermon was preached by the Rev. William Patton.

Ref: *KHC*, v. 9, p. 209; William Walker's journal, August 7, 1846, in Connelley's *Provisional Government* . . ., p. 191.

❡ July.—George T. Howard and 2d Lt. Julian May (*see* June 1 entry), together with 20 others, left Bent's Fort (Colo.) around the 10th(?); reached Missouri safely at the end of the month. (Howard and May were aboard the *Amaranth* which docked at St. Louis August 2.)

On the Santa Fe trail this party had met Captain Moore's dragoons, the large caravan of traders, and the various units of Colonel Kearny's Army of the West. Lt. Abraham R. Johnston (Kearny's adjutant), on July 17, recorded the arrival of Howard and May at their Arkansas river camp, in the Big Coon creek area (present southwestern Pawnee county). "They appeared to know very little of the prospects ahead of us," he wrote. "They remained an hour or two with us and went on towards 'the States.' "

Ref: Same as for June 1 entry.

❡ In the early days of August, 14 mounted companies of Missouri volunteers were assembling at Fort Leavenworth. (Six were there, by report, prior to August 1.) These were organized into a 10-company Second Missouri regiment ("Price's" regiment), and a four-company "Extra" (or, separate) battalion—all commanded by Col. Sterling Price (recently a congressman from Missouri); and numbering around 1,200 men. (*See, also,* p. 635, for the departure from Fort Leavenworth.)

Sterling Price
(1809-1867)

The Second regiment, Missouri mounted volunteers (Lt. Col. David D. Mitchell; Maj. Benjamin B. Edmondson; Robert Walker, adjutant; Dr. Ware S. May, surgeon) was comprised of the following companies:

Captain	Missouri County	Date the Company Reached Santa Fe
Napoleon B. Giddings	Monroe	October 7 (via Bent's Fort)
Samuel H. McMillan	Boone	" 2 (with Edmonson)
William Y. Slack	Livingston	" 10 (with Mitchell)
Hancock Jackson	Randolph	" " " "
John Holloway	Benton	" 2 (with Edmonson)
Thomas M. Horine	Ste. Genevieve	" " " "
William C. Halley	Chariton	" 10 (with Mitchell)
Thomas Barbee	Linn	" " " "
John C. Dent	St. Louis	" 2 (with Edmonson)
Richard E. Williams	Carroll	" 10 (with Mitchell)

The "Extra" battalion, Missouri mounted volunteers (Lt. Col. David Willock; Samuel Shepard, adjutant; Dr. E. S. Gale, assistant surgeon) was made up of these companies:

Captain	Missouri County	Date the Company Reached Santa Fe
Jesse B. Morin	Platte	October 12 (via Bent's Fort)
Israel R. Hendley*	Ray	" 8 (with Willock)
Benjamin F. Robinson	Polk	" " " "
Anson Smith*	Marion	" " " "

* Hendley died January 25, 1847, and was succeeded by William M. Jacobs. Anson Smith became the Marion county company's captain when Willock

was elected lieutenant colonel; subsequently Smith resigned as captain, and was succeeded by Samuel Shepard.

Ref: W. H. Robarts' *Mexican War Veterans; A Complete Roster* . . . (Washington, D. C., 1887), pp. 61, 62; Connelley (Hughes reprint), pp. 256, 257; *History of Carroll County, Missouri* (St. Louis, 1881), pp. 268, 269; *History of Howard and Chariton Counties, Missouri* (St. Louis, 1883), p. 522; *The History of Marion County, Missouri* (St. Louis, 1884), pp. 284-287; *The History of Ray County, Mo.* . . . (St. Louis, 1881), p. 278. See F. A. Golder's *The March of the Mormon Battalion* (New York, c1928), p. 141, for Henry Standage's August 1 journal entry: ". . . There are 6 companies of Missouri Volunteers here."

❡ August.—There arrived at Fort Leavenworth on August 1 (after an overland march from Council Bluffs, Ia., via St. Joseph and Weston, Mo.) a five-company Mormon infantry battalion (around 500 men), enlisted for a year's Mexican War service, and bound for California by way of Santa Fe, to serve with Brig. Gen. Stephen W. Kearny. With the Mormon foot-soldiers, and traveling in wagons, were a number of families (a few elderly persons, about 31? women —wives of the volunteers, and upwards of 30 children). The Mormons (who found at the fort some 70 U. S. "regulars," and perhaps 400 Missouri volunteers of Price's command) were issued tents, and set up their camp on the west side of the "public square."

[The battalion had been recruited in Iowa from the Mormons emigrating from Illinois (*see* p. 596), on Kearny's order, by Capt. James Allen, First U. S. dragoons. Having organized it, he became the commanding officer, with rank of lieutenant colonel.]

At the fort, Allen fell seriously ill. (Some of the Mormons—men, women and children—were suffering from the prevailing ague and fever.) Thus it happened that Companies A, B, and C set out for Santa Fe on August 13 (and Companies D and E on the 15th?) in charge of the battalion's senior captain—Jefferson Hunt (Co. A). The other captains were: Jesse D. Hunter (Co. B), James Brown (Co. C), Nelson Higgins (Co. D), and Daniel C. Davis (Co. E). All five had their families with them.

The advance companies crossed the Kansas (at Fish's ferry) on August 16. ("We were ferried over in flat boats by some half-civilized Delaware and Shawnee Indians who were living there and cultivating the soil."—Daniel Tyler.) They camped that evening at Spring creek, in present Douglas county ("where we found more than a dozen springs within twenty yards of each other"—Tyler). After a two-day stay they moved (because their cattle were invading the Shawnees' fields) four miles beyond, to "Stone Coal Creek" (present Cole creek, Douglas county), where they found some of Price's Missouri troops encamped; and where they were joined by the rest of the battalion. (A tornadic wind-and-rain storm on the 19th at "Stone Coal Creek" camp caused the Mormons to name the place "Hurricane Point.")

On August 22 the journey was resumed. A courier brought news, on the

26th, of Lt. Col. James Allen's death (*see* p. 640). At Council Grove, reached on the 27th (where they found some companies of Price's command), the Mormon battalion encamped four days. Here died two elderly members of Capt. Jefferson Hunt's family—Jane Bosco (on the 28th), and her husband, John Bosco (on the 29th). (Pvt. Robert S. Bliss wrote: "we carryed Rock from the Bluff built a wall 7 by 10 ft. around their Graves and covered the graves over with stone level with the wall.") Here, too, the Mormons were joined by Lt. Andrew J. Smith (of the First dragoons), who had come to take over command of the battalion; and by Surg. George B. Sanderson (of Platte county, Mo.; and an anti-Mormon), who had been assigned August 1 as the medical officer.

Under Smith's command, the battalion set out again on August 31. Quite a few men were ill when mustered that night at Diamond Spring. Neither Smith or Sanderson showed much sympathy for the sick (then, or in succeeding days). The Mormons rebelled against the doctor's remedies (said to be principally calomel, arsenic, and bitters). Marching about 15 miles each day, the Mormon infantry (and the families) camped on September 4 at Cow creek (where they overtook their 30 provision wagons). On the 7th they reached Walnut creek; camped at Pawnee Fork on the 9th (after a difficult crossing of that river). An express brought news, on the 10th, of Kearny's entry into Santa Fe, and Kearny's advice for the troops to take the Cimarron route.

The Mormon battalion reached the Arkansas crossing on September 15. Pvt. Henry Standage's journal for that date reads (in part): ". . . not so much water running here as would turn the smallest water power. [Some of] Col Price's Regiment of Missouri Volunteers encamp'd here. We are now on the South side of the Arkansas. . . . Some of our train staid on the other side of the river including those families that were removing to California. Our officers giving their consent to cross the Arkansas at this place and proceed to Santa Fe instead of going to Bents Fort. 10 men detailed to go with [some of] the families up the river to Bents Fort and Cap[tain] Higgins of D. Co. and Quarter Master Seargeant [S. C.] Shelton, also, their families being along." This party of Mormons set out, up the Arkansas, on the 16th; traveled on past Bent's Fort to Pueblo, where they, and other families of Mormons wintered (*see* p. 589). Pvt. Alva Phelps, who died this day, was buried on the 17th near the crossing.

Marching again on the 17th, the Mormon battalion "travelled 25 miles . . . across one of the most dreary deserts that ever man saw, suffering much from the intense heat of the sun and for want of water."

On October 3, while on "Red" river, "Lieu Smith and Dr. Sanders[on] caused most of our leading officers to consent to a division of the battalion," wrote Standage, "leaving the sick and lame behind and taking the stoutest of the company on a forced march to Santa Fe. . . ." Three Mormon companies arriving at Santa Fe on October 9 received a 100-gun salute, on Col. A. W. Doniphan's orders. The rest of the battalion and some families (25 women and "many children"—according to Cooke) reached Santa Fe on October 12.

Subsequently, Capt. James Brown (of Co. C) was appointed to take a "sick detachment" northward to Pueblo to join the Mormons wintering there. This party (87 men and 20 women, by one account—and the children) set out from Santa Fe on October 18; reached Pueblo on November 17. The Mormon battalion, traveling under the command of Capt. (Acting Lt. Col.) P. St. George Cooke (of the First dragoons) went on to California. Most of these infantrymen were mustered out of service at Los Angeles on July 16, 1847. Some re-enlisted.

Ref: Tyler, *op. cit.;* Golder, *op. cit.;* Iowa Adjutant General's *Roster and Record of Iowa Soldiers* . . . (Des Moines, 1911), v. 6, pp. 825-881; *Utah Historical Quarterly,* v. 4 (January and July, 1931), pp. 6-23 (N. V. Jones' journal), 67-96 (R. S. Bliss' journal); v. 5 (April, 1932), pp. 35-64 (H. W. Bigler's journal), v. 6 (January, 1933), pp. 3-28 (John Steele's journal); Connelley, *Doniphan's Expedition,* pp. 75, 76, 81 (Hughes diary), and 257-259, 353-355 (Hughes reprint); *Niles' National Register,* v. 70 (August 1, 1846), p. 352 (from *Missouri Republican,* St. Louis, June 24); Gibson, *op. cit.,* pp. 250-252; 30th Cong., 1st Sess., *H. Ex. Doc. No. 41* (Serial 517), p. 551 (for Cooke); Robert W. Whitworth's (Mormon battalion) diary, in *Arizona and the West,* Tucson, v. 7 (Summer, 1965), pp. 127-160; Bernard DeVoto's *The Year of Decision, 1846* (Boston, 1943).

❡ August 1.—An overland party of 10(?), or 11(?) persons, "direct from Oregon," arrived at St. Joseph, Mo. (On the 15th, aboard the *Amaranth,* they reached St. Louis.)

This company (perhaps 16, originally, when setting out from Oregon in April) included B. Genois, probably included A. F. Davidson, S. Eikenburg, J. B. Holliday, J. A. Hunt, and Henry Williamson; and another member may have been a "Mr. Hockerman" (Abraham Hackelman?).

Ref: D. Morgan, *op. cit.,* v. 1, p. 371, v. 2, pp. 640-642, 768, 769. A. F. Davidson had made the overland journey West in 1845. On the return trip he drew a series of 22 maps showing the return route—maps covering the last five weeks, from June 26(?) to August. "They show location of the road, changes in route, location of water and fuel, and the camps, with some 1845 camps as well. . . ."—*See* Mary C. Withington, *op. cit.,* pp. 56-60; and Carl I. Wheat, *op. cit.,* v. 3, p. 29.

❡ August 2-17.—Charles Bent's mounted party (he was accompanied by trader Thomas J. Caldwell, Lt. Charles F. Wooster, of the Fourth U. S. artillery, and others?) left Independence, Mo., on the 2d (or 3d?); made a swift journey across "Kansas" over the Santa Fe trail; and reached Bent's Fort on the 17th. (Returning trader Norris Colburn met them at the Arkansas crossing on August 12 [or 13?], "only ten days from Independence.")

Charles Bent went on to Santa Fe; and on September 22 was appointed governor of New Mexico territory by Brig. Gen. Stephen W. Kearny.

Ref: *Missouri Republican,* St. Louis, September 2, 1846, as reprinted in *The Gazette,* St. Joseph, Mo., September 11, 1846; Magoffin, *op. cit.,* p. 21 (footnote), and *see* p. 148; Lavender, *op. cit.,* pp. 263, 407; 29th Cong., 2d Sess., *H. Doc. No. 19* (Serial 499), p. 26 (for Kearny's appointments).

❡ August 3.—News reached Fort Leavenworth that the steamboat *Radnor* (John T. Douglass, captain), upbound with about 60 tons of ammunition and provisions for the Army of the West, had sunk (boat and cargo reported "lost") after hitting a stump above Boonville, Mo.

Ref: Golder, *op. cit.,* p. 142 (Henry Standage's journal item); *The Gazette,* St. Joseph, Mo., August 21, 1846; Saint Louis *Daily Union,* February 9, 1847.

❧ The first week in August the American Fur Company's *General Brooke,* returning from the mouth of the Yellowstone (*see* May 29 entry), passed along the "Kansas" shore, and reached St. Louis on the 6th.

In her cargo were 450 packs of buffalo robes, 20 packs of assorted furs, and 1,400 buffalo tongues; also aboard were a young grizzly bear, an elk, and the stuffed skin of an enormous (1,200-pound) grizzly bear.

Ref: Nebraska State Historical Society *Publications,* v. 20, p. 162 (from *Daily Missouri Republican,* August 6, 1846); Sunder, *op. cit.,* p. 86.

❧ August.—Between the 10th(?) and 23d(?) Col. Sterling Price's command—the approximately 1,200 mounted Missouri volunteers of the Second regiment, and the "Extra" battalion—marched out of Fort Leavenworth, in separate detachments, on the road to Santa Fe. Price "had [additionally] a considerable number of heavy pieces of artillery, and artillerymen to manage them (commanded by regular army officers), and a great number of baggage and provision wagons." Also with Colonel Price were U. S. army paymasters Maj. Dunham Spalding and Maj. Benjamin Walker; and Albert G. Wilson, sutler. All of this "army" except two Missouri companies (which went via Bent's Fort and Raton Pass) reached Santa Fe *by way of the Cimarron route.* (*See* p. 631 for organization of Price's command.)

The advance Missouri troops (leaving August 10?) were Captain Giddings' Second regiment company and Captain Morin's "Extra" battalion company. On the 22d they were in the Cottonwood crossing area; were met September 2, above the Arkansas crossings, by Francis Parkman (who referred to them as "two companies of Munroe and Platte City mounted volunteers"); encamped at Bent's Fort on September 9. Giddings, and company, entered Santa Fe on October 7. Morin reached there October 1; but his company, escorting a commissary train, did not arrive till the 12th.

Six(?) more companies started out between August 11th and 18th. The Second regiment companies of Captains McMillan and Horine; also a "command of 12 men and 4 howitzers"—all of which were met on August 23d at Council Grove by an eastbound trader; and "Maj. [Dunham] Spalding, Asst Paymaster, with 12 wagons and 2 pieces of artillery '24 pounders,'" were in the advance. Maj. Benjamin B. Edmonson, who left the fort August 18, was to take command of four(?) Second regiment companies ahead of him (McMillan's, Horine's, Holloway's, and Dent's, apparently). On the 19th(?) Lt. Col. David Willock with the Ray, Polk, and Marion county companies of the "Extra" battalion started; and so did Lt. Col. David D. Mitchell. In the Carroll county Second regiment company which left on the 20th was "journalist" Pvt. William H. Richardson. The last two companies of the

Second regiment set out on the 22d(?). Col. Sterling Price, and his staff, departed on August 23(?).

Several companies of the Missouri volunteers were camped on Stone Coal creek (now Cole creek, in Douglas county) on the night of August 19 when a tornadic wind-and-rain storm struck. Their animals stampeded, and (an account says) "several days were spent in searching before they could be recovered. As a result, a portion of Price's cavalry did not overtake the [Mormon] battalion until after . . . [it] arrived at Santa Fe." (It was possibly this same "estampeda" which John T. Hughes [not present] later described [erroneously? placing it "somewhere on the Arkansas"]: "Wildly and madly they plunged over the plain, near a thousand head. . . . After great labor the majority of them were recovered. . . .")

It was also Hughes who later reported: "Col. Price's forces feeling entirely secure against . . . [hostile Indian parties] placed out no picket guards as the other [Kearny's] command had done, and sometimes had no sentinels about the camps at night."

On September 10, from a point "12 miles West of the crossing of the Arkansas" (and now at the forefront of his "army"), Colonel Price wrote Brig. Gen. S. W. Kearny (at Santa Fe) that he had with him four Second regiment companies (and that two had proceeded up the Arkansas towards Bent's Fort). Pvt. William H. Richardson, whose company reached the Arkansas crossing on September 14, wrote: "We were then 362 miles from Fort Leavenworth. Our course has been along the margin of the river for 75 miles. At this place are steep bluffs[?] difficult to descend. There are multitudes of fish in the river, many of them were killed by the horses' feet in crossing. We caught several varieties by spearing. A number of antelopes were killed here." On the 17th Richardson's company prepared "to cross a sandy desert 60 miles wide."

At the Cimarron Springs Colonel Price sent another express to General Kearny—this time an urgent request for supplies (which were dispatched). Price ("in a very feeble state of health") and Major Spalding reached Santa Fe on September 28. By October 12 all of the 14 Missouri mounted volunteer companies (around 85 men each?), and the Mormon infantry battalion (some 500 men)—more than 1,650 troops in all—had entered Santa Fe.

Ref: Connelley, *Doniphan's Expedition*, pp. 74-76 (Hughes' diary) and 256-261 (Hughes reprint); or, Hughes, *Doniphan's Expedition*, pp. 132-138; Richardson, *op. cit.*; New York *Weekly Tribune*, August 29, September 12, 1846; Tyler, *op. cit.*, p. 140; Wade, *op. cit.*, v. 2, pp. 476-480; *The Gazette*, St. Joseph, Mo., September 11, 1846; Charles F. Ruff's notes (copy in KHi); Gibson, *op. cit.*, pp. 241-252; annals, p. 387 (for an item on Albert G. Wilson); Golder, *op. cit.* (for Standage's journal, pp. 141, 147, 148 [for date of storm], and p. 161 [for his September 10 entry which records the arrival of the express from Santa Fe announcing Kearny's entrance into Santa Fe, and bringing Kearny's advice to Price and to the Mormon battalion's commander] *to take the Cimarron route*, instead of going by Bent's Fort).

❏ August 13.—Samuel Ralston, of Jackson county, Mo., and some others (a mounted party, apparently) who had left Santa Fe in July, arrived at Independence, after a trip, by way of the Cimarron route, of 37(?) days.

The Independence *Expositor* reported that Ralston had "made the trip in 35 days and the entire trip from here to Santa Fe and back in 104 days, allowing 14 days' stay in Santa Fe." (*See* p. 580.)

Ref: Saint Louis *Daily Union*, August 21 and 24, 1846; Waugh, *op. cit.*, p. 98.

❧ August 13.—At the Arkansas crossings a Bent's Fort-bound government supply train (43 wagons; 54 men) was in distress, and "lying by for repairs" (with 15 yoke of oxen "lost," many teamsters ill, ammunition low, and hostile Indians frequenting the area). Eastbound "Major Clark" and Norris Colburn gave the men "all the powder which they could spare."

At Bent's Fort, on August 26, Francis Parkman noted: "Yesterday, 40 waggons of supplies for the Santa Fe expedition came up in very poor plight. Lt. James W. Abert (also at Bent's Fort), wrote: "On the 26th August, a commissary train of 42 wagons arrived. The teamsters refused to go beyond this place. . . ."

Ref: *The Gazette*, St. Joseph, Mo., September 11, 1846 (from *Missouri Republican*, St. Louis, September 2); Wade, *op. cit.*, v. 2, p. 474; 30th Cong., 1st Sess., *H. Ex. Doc. No. 41* (Serial 517), p. 420 (for Abert).

❧ August 13.—"Mr. Turly's [Simeon? Turley's] company of three wagons, for Taos" was at the Arkansas crossings. (Returning trader Norris Colburn met him there.)

Ref: *The Gazette*, St. Joseph, Mo., September 11, 1846 (from *Missouri Republican*, St. Louis, September 2). This may have been Simeon Turley, proprietor of a mill and distillery at the Arroyo Hondo about eight miles above Taos, N. M. At that place, he and six other Americans were murdered on January 19, 1847.—*See* W. E. Connelley's *Doniphan's Expedition*, p. 514; Saint Louis *Daily Union*, March 20, 1846; L. H. Garrard's *Wah-to-yah* . . ., ed. by R. P. Bieber (1938), p. 32.

❧ August 14.—An express which had left Bent's Fort on August 1, arrived at Fort Leavenworth. (The courier presumably brought news of Colonel Kearny's arrival at Bent's Fort with his Army of the West.) To make the 565-mile journey in 14 days, the express had to average 40 miles' travel per day.

Ref: St. Louis *Weekly Reveille*, August 21, 1846 (as reprinted in *Arkansas State Gazette*, Little Rock, September 14, 1846); 30th Cong., 1st Sess., *H. Ex. Doc. No. 41* (Serial 517), p. 176 (for Fort Leavenworth-Bent's Fort distance as 564 miles); M. B. Edwards, *op. cit.*, p. 137, gave the distance as 566 miles; Gibson, *op. cit.*, p. 170, estimated the journey as 607 miles.

❧ August 14.—During a night attack on their camp, in the vicinity (east?) of Pawnee Fork, the company of "Mr. Campbell and Mr. Coons, of St. Louis" (22 government wagons, en route to Bent's Fort) killed one Indian and wounded another (as they reported).

Ref: *The Gazette*, St. Joseph, Mo., September 11, 1846 (from *Missouri Republican*, St. Louis, September 2). Francis Parkman (who left Bent's Fort on August 27, eastbound), noted, on August 30 (*see* his *Journals*, ed. by Mason Wade, v. 2, p. 475): "Afternoon, met a train of govt. wagons. They say that the road is dangerous. 'Coates' [possibly Coons?] the master driver." G. R. Gibson, *op. cit.*, p. 258 (at Santa Fe, under date of October 20), noted the arrival of "Mr. Campbell" from "the States").

❧ August 16.—Sixty wagons "loaded with merchandise" belonging to "Armijo, Magoffin, and others"—en route to Santa Fe—were at Pawnee Fork on this day.

(Eastbound John McKnight and F. X. Aubry [see next entry] met "The company of Armijos . . . at different points, progressing slowly. Mr. William Magoffin at or near Arkansas; Samuel[?] Magoffin, a little nearer, this way. . . .")

Francis Parkman (who had left Bent's Fort on August 27) nooned on the Arkansas on the 29th, later in the day "met a train of Santa Fe waggons, belonging to McLaughlin [Magoffin]" and learned of hostile Pawnees ahead. (Magoffin had reburied Swan's remains— see p. 640. The Indians who killed him had dug up Swan's body to scalp him.) Lt. James W. Abert, at Bent's Fort, noted, on September 2: "In the afternoon Mr. McGoffin arrived; he had been 35 days on the road since leaving Independence, Mo., and has a train of 25 wagons."

Ref: *The Gazette*, St. Joseph, Mo., September 11, 1846 (from *Missouri Republican* of September 2); Saint Louis *Daily Union*, August 21, 1846; Wade, *op. cit.*, v. 2, p. 475; 30th Cong., 1st Sess., *H. Ex. Doc. No. 41* (Serial 517), p. 426.

❧ August 17.—With two wagons and "a very small party of men," traders John McKnight (from Chihuahua) and Francis X. Aubry (who had gone to New Mexico in May), arrived at Independence, Mo. (They had left Santa Fe on July 16, and traveled the Cimarron route.) When they reached St. Louis, on August 22, aboard the *Balloon*, it was reported that "Messrs. McKnight and Aubrey . . . brought in . . . between 50 and 60,000 dollars in specie."

Others in the party were Adam Hill, of Jackson county, Mo. (presumably the Hill who had gone to Santa Fe in May—see p. 580), "Mr. Stephenson, direct from Chihuahua" (a former Boone county, Mo., resident who had been out of the States for 22 years), and (apparently) two young sons of trader Dr. Henry Connelly, of Chihuahua.

Ref: *The Gazette,* St. Joseph, Mo., September 11, 1846 (from *Missouri Republican,* v. 5 (August, 1961), pp. 111-123 (for article on Aubry); Missouri Historical Society, *Collections,* v. 5 (June, 1928), p. 293, quotes Gov. Manuel Armijo's July 15, 1846, letter from Santa Fe, to S. C. Owens: "With Mr John Mc night I sent to Mr. P. Harmony & Co. six thousand eagle dollars, & nineteen ounces of gold from the placer, amount that I owe him." See W. E. Connelley's *Doniphan's Expedition,* p. 280 (for an item on Stephenson and an 1828 journey) and p. 281 (for Adam Hill, and Connelly's sons).

❧ August 17.—"Messrs. Barnes and Allen" with 31 government wagons and 43 men, bound for Santa Fe, were at Cow creek on this day. (Returning trader Norris Colburn met them.)

Lt. James W. Abert (at Bent's Fort) apparently referred to the Barnes and Allen train when he wrote on September 7: "This evening a party of teamsters arrived; they seemed to be very insubordinate, and refused to go on to Santa Fe. . . ."

Ref: *The Gazette,* St. Joseph, Mo. September 11, 1846 (from *Missouri Republican,* September 2); 30th Cong., 1st Sess., *H. Ex. Doc. No. 41* (Serial 517), p. 431.

❧ August 18.—Brig. Gen. Stephen W. Kearny and his Army of the West, "after a tiresome march of near nine hundred miles in less than fifty days," took possession of Santa Fe "without firing a gun or spilling a drop of blood."

(*See, also,* July 15, and September 22 entries.)

Ref: Connelley, *Doniphan's Expedition,* p. 198; Hughes, *Doniphan's Expedition,* p. 78; Gibson, *op. cit.,* pp. 77 and 199 (for item on Kearny's receiving his appointment as brigadier general on August 15, as he neared Santa Fe), pp. 204-206 (for entry into the town); 29th Cong., 2d Sess., *H. Doc. No. 19* (Serial 499), p. 21.

❧ August 18.—"Mr. Horner's company" of 18 Santa Fe-bound government wagons, camped at Owl creek (in present Rice county), was attacked about three A. M. by a large body of Indians.

Apparently there were no losses; but they were left "almost without powder." "Major Clark" and Norris Colburn, who met them, gave the teamsters all they could spare.

Ref: *The Gazette,* St. Joseph, Mo., September 11, 1846 (from *Missouri Republican,* September 2).

❧ August 18(?)—On, or about this day, the 46-wagon train of "Algueir and Paris [Francisco Elguea and J. Calistro Porras], the latter in charge of Messrs. Stillman, Waldo, and Noland" (Henry Skillman, L. L. Waldo, and S. V.? Noland), crossed the Little Arkansas river, en route to Santa Fe. (Returning trader Norris Colburn met them there.)

Earlier, two of the train's wagons had been struck by lightning, and one man slightly injured.

Ref: *The Gazette,* St. Joseph, Mo., September 11, 1846 (from *Missouri Republican,* September 2). For Elguea and Porras see 30th Cong., 1st Sess., *H. R. No. 458* (Serial 525), pp. 46-48. It appears Porras himself was not with this train. For Henry Skillman *see* R. P. Bieber, editor, *Exploring Southwestern Trails, 1846-1854* (Glendale, Cal., 1938), pp. 311, 312.

❧ August 20.—East of the Little Arkansas (in present McPherson county), Missouri-bound Norris Colburn met "Doyle and Garvey's [*i. e.,* Joseph B. Doyle and William Guerrier's] 6 wagons, with goods for the [upper Arkansas] Indian trade."

At Bent's Fort, on September 8, Lt. James W. Abert noted the arrival of "Bill Garey" who had served as "interpreter last year [1845] at the council held in August at this place, by a deputation of Delawares and the Cheyenne nation. He is now engaged in trading with the Indians in the vicinity of Peublo[*sic!*], or Hardscrabble."

Ref: *The Gazette,* St. Joseph, Mo., September 11, 1846; 30th Cong., 1st Sess., *H. Ex. Doc. No. 41* (Serial 517), p. 432 (for Abert); *also, see* Lavender, *op. cit.,* pp. 212, 238, 246, 349 (for mention of Doyle, and Guerrier).

❧ August.—All except one of an eastbound company numbering

about 30 (some mounted men; the drivers of 10 empty provision wagons; and 11 sick volunteer soldiers) which had set out from Bent's Fort on July 29(?), reached Council Grove on August 22, and Independence, Mo., about the 27th(?).

Among the mounted travelers, at the start, were George R. Clark and artist Alfred S. Waugh of St. Louis, William L. (or Z.?) Swan, of Northampton, Mass., and "Fay . . . an Italian"—all(?) returning from Santa Fe; also Robert M. Ewing and E. Hewitt who had left the Oregon trail in the Fort Laramie area in July and journeyed southward to the upper Arkansas.

Soon after leaving Bent's Fort, Ewing, Hewitt, and Fay had an encounter with "friendly" Cheyennes. Near Chouteau's Island (present Kearny county), on August 11 or 12, Swan was shot and killed by a Cheyenne(?) within 75 yards of camp. At Cow creek a large band of Indians attempted to stampede the party's animals, and got three fine mules. Ewing killed one raider, and two others, perhaps, were slain.

Ref: D. Morgan, *op. cit.*, v. 2, pp. 583, 650-654, 770, 771; New York *Weekly Tribune*, September 12, 1846; Waugh, *op. cit.*, pp. xiii, xiv, 95; *Daily Missouri Republican*, St. Louis, September 2, 1846; *The Gazette*, St. Joseph, Mo., September 11, 18, 1846; Wade, *op. cit.*, v. 2, p. 475; and *see, also,* Parkman, *op. cit.*, ch. 23, "Indian Alarms."

❡ August 22.—"McCaulley and Sandford's wagons with merchandize"—en route to Santa Fe—were met this day by returning trader Norris Colburn, probably in present McPherson county.

Ref: *The Gazette*, St. Joseph, Mo., September 11, 1846 (from *Missouri Republican*, September 2). "Sandford" was perhaps "Sanford."

❡ August 23.—At Council Grove, en route to Santa Fe, were "43 wagons loaded with merchandize belonging to R[euben] Gentry" (according to returning trader Norris Colburn).

A month later (September 22) while on the Cimarron, Pvt. W. H. Richardson, of Price's regiment, wrote: "On arriving where we had to encamp we found 42 wagons, laden with goods. They were the property of a Mr. Gentry, a trader who has amassed great wealth, in merchandising between Independence, Santa Fe and Chihuahua. He speaks the Spanish language, and had nearly a dozen Spaniards in the caravan. . . ." Nearer Santa Fe, on October 3, Capt. Charles F. Ruff (eastbound) met "42 wagons of Miles[?] Gentry, at Whetstone creek." Pvt. John T. Hughes (in New Mexico), passing "Gentry's Train of wagons" on November 23, commented "he has the largest train [owned by one individual?] ever brought from the U. S."

Ref: *The Gazette*, St. Joseph, Mo., September 11, 1846 (from *Missouri Republican*, September 2); Charles F. Ruff notes (copy in KHi ms. division); W. H. Richardson, *op. cit.*, p. 17; W. E. Connelley's *Doniphan's Expedition*, p. 81 (for Hughes). In 30th Cong., 1st Sess., *H. R. No. 458* (Serial 525), p. 43, reference is made to traders "Messrs Kerford and Gentry" who escaped from Doniphan's command (or broke the blockade) at El Paso del Norte, and got to Chihuahua without molestation.

❡ DIED: Lt. Col. James Allen, commander of the Mormon battalion, on August 23, at Fort Leavenworth. (*See, also,* pp. 632, 633.)

Ref: Tyler, *op. cit.*, pp. 150, 151. John T. Hughes, in Connelley, *Doniphan's Expedition*, p. 259, and some other sources, including *The Weekly Tribune*, Liberty, Mo., August

29, 1846, stated that Allen died on the 22d, but Tyler offers evidence that the correct date is August 23.

❡ August 24-September 14.—Around 1,000 men—nine companies of Missouri volunteers—arrived at Fort Leavenworth during this period; and were mustered in for 12 months' service as an infantry regiment (which had been authorized on July 18). John Dougherty (former Indian agent), of Liberty, Mo., was elected colonel. But on September 12 Secretary of War Marcy wrote General Kearny that "orders to muster . . . [this third Missouri regiment] into service have been countermanded." The official news reached the fort about a week later, creating "great excitement and dissatisfaction among the troops." Between September 29 and October 2 the regiment was disbanded and the men departed for home.

Over half these volunteers were from St. Louis, or southeastern Missouri. Capt. Thomas H. Holt's company (the first?) had left St. Louis August 16, on the *Tributary*, and probably reached the fort about the 22d; Capt. Washington L. McNair's company (the last?) went up on the *Galena*, and must have disembarked by September 14. The others were captained by: Alfred M. Julian, Augustus Rainey, Francis M. Boing, Benjamin W. Smithson, Firman A. Rozier (whose men were from Madison, Cape Girardeau, and Perry counties), John W. (or T.?) Franciscus (his "Governor's Guards" company was from St. Louis), and Napoleon Koscialowski (whose company left St. Louis, on the *Archer*, September 1).

Commented the St. Louis *New Era* (when the Presidential order became known): "The Regt. of Vols. now at Leavenworth and ordered to be disbanded will, at the time of its discharge, have cost the Government upward of *fifty thousand dollars*. But the expenses, trouble and loss of time of the officers and privates will amount to a much larger sum. . . ."

Ref: 29th Cong., 2d Sess., *H. Doc. No. 19* (Serial 499), p. 5 (Marcy's letter); Saint Louis *Daily Union*, August 17, 24, 25, 27, 29, September 2, 17, 21, 22, October 1, 5, 16, 19, 1846, January 16, 1847; New York *Weekly Tribune*, October 3, 1846 (from St. Louis *New Era*); Robarts, *op. cit.*, p. 62; John T. Hughes' *Doniphan's Expedition* (1850), pp. 138, 139; Connelley's *Doniphan's Expedition*, p. 261. Rozier's company had 115 men and Koscialowski's had 113, so the nine companies of the intended 10-company regiment presumably totaled over 1,000 men. Sec. W. L. Marcy (in the *Union*, January 16, 1847) stated the companies were mustered in on August 24 and 31 and on September 1, 3, 5, 7, 8, and 14; and were mustered out on September 29 and 30 and October 1 and 2, 1846.

❡ August 24.—A new steamboat—the *Amelia*—"just built here by Capt. Thomas Miller," and designed for the Missouri river trade, was described in the Saint Louis *Daily Union*. She was a "sidewheeler," valued at $12,000.

Ref: Saint Louis *Daily Union*, August 24, 1846. The *Amelia* was named for the daughter of E. B. Cordell of Jefferson City, Mo.

❡ August 25.—Seven wagons "belonging to Tharp and Lee [William Tharp and Elliott Lee], with merchandise for the mountains and Taos" were met at Switzler's creek, on the Santa Fe trail (present Osage county) by eastbound Norris Colburn.

(However, Elliott Lee journeyed to Bent's Fort with St. Vrain's train which left Kansas, Mo., on September 1. *See* p. 645.)

Ref: *The Gazette*, St. Joseph, Mo., September 11, 1846; Lavender, *op. cit.*, pp. 287, 289 (for mention of Tharp), 295, 306 (for Lee); *KHC*, v. 15, p. 84 (for Grinnell's mention of Tharp).

❡ August 26-27.—"Armijo, with 13 wagons loaded with merchandize" for Santa Fe was met at Hickory Point (present Douglas county) on the 26th by returning trader Norris Colburn. On the 27th, not far from Independence, he met "4 wagons belonging to Miller and Reed, and Mr. A. Armijo who had been detained by sickness. . . ."

On October 5 Capt. Charles F. Ruff (who had left Santa Fe September 27) "met Miller's (of Fayette) waggon [waggons?] near Rabbit Ear creek"; and on the 7th "met Armijo's wagons about 6 miles north of upper [Cimarron] spring."

Ref: *The Gazette*, St. Joseph, Mo., September 11, 1846 (from *Missouri Republican*, September 2); Charles F. Ruff's notes (copy in KHi ms. division).

❡ August 27.—This day the new steamboat *St. Joseph*, owned and commanded by Capt. William W. Baker, was scheduled to depart from St. Louis for Weston, Mo.

Ref: Saint Louis *Daily Union*, August 25, 1846.

❡ August 27.—Trader Norris Colburn, accompanied by "Major Clark" (George R. Clark, of St. Louis, apparently), reached Independence, Mo., after an eventful 24½-day journey from Santa Fe (left on August 3) by the Cimarron route. His train had reached the Arkansas crossings in 10 days (the 12th, or 13th?), "the quickest trip ever made to that point in wagons." Numerous parties, en route to Santa Fe or the Rocky mountains (some in difficulties; and others harassed by Indians) had been met from the Arkansas to Missouri.

On August 15, at Colburn's camp on Coon creek, Indians made an unsuccessful raid on the train's stock. Two days later, at Cow creek, in another stampede attempt, Indians stole three of "Major Clark's" mules.

Ref: *Missouri Republican*, St. Louis, September 2, 1846, as reprinted in *The Gazette*, St. Joseph, Mo., September 11, or, in the New York *Weekly Tribune*, September 12; St. Louis *Daily Union*, September 3, 1846. *See, also*, August 13 annals item.

❡ September.—An Independence, Mo., compiler of statistics on the year's exports from Missouri in the Santa Fe trade wrote that some 39 firms had engaged in the trade (including parties yet to start?), employing 351 goods-carrying wagons, 12 smaller "kitchen wagons," and about 50 carriages—total: 413 vehicles.

He estimated 750 to 800 men had gone with these Santa Fe-bound trains. The merchandise—mostly "baled up"—he calculated at 9,588 bales in all; which, if worth $95 to $100 each, could be considered to have a total value of around $950,000, and "perhaps the whole, in round numbers might safely be extended to a million of dollars."

At Independence, on June 30, Josiah Gregg had stated that 216 wagons were then " '*en masse*' upon the Santa Fe trail" in detached parties, and yet to start were some 150 wagons and 50 smaller vehicles (carriages, buggies, etc.)—mostly belonging to Mexicans. The whole—416 vehicles—carried "an amount of merchandise . . . [estimated at] a fraction *over one million of dollars*"—"more than treble that of any previous season." Traders, wagoners, loungers, connoisseur travelers, loafers, and others in the Santa Fe-bound trains might total about 1,000 men.

Ref: New York *Weekly Tribune*, September 19, 1846 (from *Missouri Republican*, St. Louis, September 3); *Niles' National Register*, v. 70 (August 1, 1846), p. 343; Gregg, *op. cit.*, pp. 200, 201.

❧ September.—Steamboats plying the Missouri and making trips to Fort Leavenworth, Weston, or St. Joseph, during this month, included the *Archer, Balloon, St. Joseph, St. Croix, Galena, Tributary, Tobacco Plant, Bertrand, Little Missouri,* and *Amelia.*

Ref: Saint Louis *Daily Union*, September, 1846, issues.

❧ September.—Early(?) in the month the *Clermont No. 2* passed along the "Kansas" shore, on her return from the upper Missouri (Fort Union, N. D.)—*see* p. 627—finally reaching St. Louis on the 20th. She had been detained for two weeks at Antelope Island because of the river's low stage.

By this steamboat, news reached St. Louis that Fort Defiance was under construction at the mouth of Medicine creek; and that the rest of the St. Louis Fur Company personnel had been left near Fort Union, to go up Marias river in Mackinaw boats.

Passengers on the homeward-bound *Clermont No. 2* were: "S. Parkman and T. Coburn" from Fort Pierre, "H. S. Sanford" from Vermillion (trading post), "C. Cassil[l]y" (who had made the voyage up in July), "S. H. Wilson and Capt. White" from Fort Leavenworth.

Ref: Same as for July 12 annals entry.

❧ September 6.—Leaving Fort Leavenworth to overtake the Mormon Battalion on the Santa Fe trail were John D. Lee and Howard Egan (dispatched, by Brigham Young, from the Mormon camp above present Omaha on August 31), and Lt. James Pace (battalion member, who joined at the fort). Lee's mission was to collect the battalion pay (to be received at Santa Fe) and return with the money to Mormon headquarters.

By Lee's reckoning (as recorded in his diary) it was 26 miles to the Stranger river crossing; and 11 miles further to the Kansas river ferry at the Wakarusa's mouth. He wrote: "The ferry over this stream is managed & owned by the 2 nations [Delawares and Shawnees]. . . . 3 Flats were running constant. They have a contract of Ferr[y]ing for the Government at $1.00 per waggon." Lee's party crossed on September 7; traveled till very late; finally camped 10 miles beyond 110-mile creek, having passed some 90 provision wagons during the day's journey.

On the 8th the Mormon trio met "3 large waggons & [some] oxen & about 24 men bound for the Ft. Leavenworth"; passed, on the 9th, Capt. Henry Hensler's provision wagons; overtook, on the 11th "Capt Martin & Moore"—leaving them "forming their Co's for the night," and learning from them of recent Pawnee depredations (stock-stealing) upon another company. On September 12 they "met a waggon, 6 or 8 persons and about 40 or 50 Santafe horses & mules," and a few oxen. (These were traders moving to Missouri from New Mexico.) Also on the 12th they met the Santa Fe-Fort Leavenworth express (six men); and overtook "Capt Brown's Co." at the Little Arkansas. On the 13th they passed the wagons of Wilson & Goddard (sutlers to the Mormon battalion); next day overtook "Capt Armeho's & Co (A Spaniard trader)," also met the returning small party of "Mississippi Saints" (see p. 647), and overtook "Capt Jas Thompson with a co of 30 waggons loaded with Provisions for the army."

At the Arkansas crossing, on September 17, Lee, Egan, and Pace caught up with the Mormon battalion, and traveled with the troops to Santa Fe. (See, also, November 14 entry.)

Ref: John D. Lee's "Diary" in *New Mexico Historical Review*, v. 42 (July, 1967), pp. 165-199.

❡ September.—Solomon P. Sublette, in company with Charles Taplin (who had journeyed West with Fremont in 1845), Walter Reddick, and one other man—all homeward-bound from California —left Bent's Fort on August 18; crossed "Kansas" by way of the Santa Fe trail, and reached Missouri before September 11. (On the 11th Sublette and party arrived at St. Louis aboard the *Little Missouri.*)

The journey of these four, from "Pueblo de los Angeles" to Fort Bridger (Wyo.), had been made by way of a southern route, in company, at least part of the way, with Joseph R. Walker (driving a herd of horses and mules east). Leaving Fort Bridger early in July, they had proceeded down the Oregon trail to Fort Laramie (Wyo.); and from there, southward, to Bent's Fort (reached August 17).

Ref: D. Morgan, *op. cit.*, v. 1, pp. 114, 127, 371-373, 378, v. 2, pp. 609, 611, 646-649, 654, 655, 760, 769-771. At Bent's Fort, 2d Lt. James W. Abert noted, under date of August 26: "Captain Walker . . . has a party encamped on the banks of the [Arkansas] river, about 8 miles north of the fort, and is there awaiting the arrival of Colonel Price's regiment, for which he has a supply ["some 60 head"] of mules."—30th Cong., 1st Sess., *H. Ex. Doc. No. 41* (Serial 517), p. 420.

❡ About September 12 the "company of Messrs. [Zenas] Leonard, of . . . [Jackson] county and [John S.] Shaw, of St. Louis" (eight men, with wagons carrying from 125 to 130 packs of buffalo robes) was reported to be within a few days' travel of Independence, Mo., after a "long and tedious trip." On the Platte, Pawnees had robbed these traders of 140 packs of robes.

(Unable, in the spring, to get their furs down the Platte in Mackinaw boats, due to the river's "extreme lowness," John S. Shaw had made his way to Missouri and obtained wagons and teamsters. (*See* p. 586.)

Ref: Saint Louis *Daily Union*, September 21, 1846 (reprinted from the *Western Expositor*, Independence, Mo.). Presumably Shaw's partner (or fellow trader) was Zenas Leonard of Fort Osage (Sibley), Mo.—first known as a mountain man in the 1830's.

❡ On September 15(?) Ceran St. Vrain's train of 23 mule-drawn wagons left the Westport, Mo., area for Bent's Fort. Frank De Lisle was wagonmaster; "Bransford," the company clerk; "Beauvais," trader; and there were some 23 teamsters (mostly French-Canadians), also three Mexican herders. Traveling with St. Vrain were Jared W. Folger, Elliott Lee, Charles Beaubien (all with connections in New Mexico), Lancaster P. Lupton, Edmund Chadwick, T. B. Drinker, and 17-year-old Lewis H. Garrard (the latter two from Cincinnati; and on a pleasure trip). Garrard's account, in his *Wah-to-yah, and the Taos Trail* (published in 1850) is the chief source of information on the journey.

Camp on September 16 was at Lone Elm. On the 22d, east of 110-mile creek, Francis Parkman returning to Missouri (*see* p. 646), recorded meeting "Messrs. Folger, Lee, and Upton [Lupton], connected with Bent & St. Vrain, whose waggons were encamped a few miles behind"; and on September 23 noted: "Met Bent's train this morning. St. Vrain was there, as also a brother of [artist George] Catlin's friend, Joe Chadwick. . . ." (Thus it was that near the Osage-Douglas county line of today Parkman and Garrard —future authors of "classic" narratives of the West—passed and doubtless greeted each other on the Santa Fe trail.)

St. Vrain's train got to Council Grove on September 30 (camped for two days); reached the Arkansas crossings on October 23; reached Chouteau's Island (and spent a day) on the 26th; and, without having met *hostile* Indians, arrived at Bent's Fort as October ended.

Ref: Lewis H. Garrard's *Wah-to-yah and the Taos Trail*, ed. by R. P. Bieber (Glendale, Cal., 1938); Wade, *op. cit.*, v. 2, p. 482; *The Colorado Magazine*, v. 6 (November, 1929), pp. 220-226.

❡ September 15.—The *Ohio*, bound for Fort Leavenworth with a "large quantity of government stores," struck a snag below Arrow Rock, Mo., and sank in six feet of water. The uninsured boat was a total loss (except for engine and boilers); her cargo, though in a damaged state, could be salvaged.

Ref: Saint Louis *Daily Union,* September 18, 1846.

❡ About September 22(?) an express from Santa Fe reached Fort Leavenworth, bringing the news that General Kearny and his Army of the West had entered Santa Fe without the firing of a gun. (The St. Louis newspapers of September 25 reported this, having got the information from persons aboard the *Little Missouri* which arrived on the 24th.) The express brought at least 997 letters and packages.

This was the small party which Pvt. John T. Hughes (of Doniphan's regiment) mentioned in his journal under date of August 25: "Express left [Santa Fe] for Fort Leavenworth—5 men, 3 Dragoons & 2 Volunteers. R[obert] W. Fleming & W[illiam] C. Gunter. . . ." (Fleming and Gunter, as well as Hughes, were from Company C [Clay county, Mo.].) John D. Lee (of the three-man Morman party, westbound—*see* p. 643) noted, on September 12, when near the Little Arkansas: "About 6 eve we met an express from Sante Fe carried by 6 men bound to Ft. Leavenworth."

Ref: New York *Weekly Tribune,* October 10, 1846 (from *Missouri Republican,* St. Louis, of September 25); Connelley, *Doniphan's Expedition,* p. 64 (for Hughes' diary), and p. 544; Gibson, *op. cit.,* p. 221; Golder, *op. cit.,* p. 161 (for Standage's September 10 diary entry); John D. Lee's "Diary," *loc. cit.*

❡ September 26.—After a journey eastward from "the Pueblo" (Colo.), down the Arkansas, and across "Kansas" on the Santa Fe trail, Francis Parkman and Quincy Shaw, with their guide Henry Chatillon, and muleteer Antoine De Laurier, returned to Westport, Mo.—which place they had left on May 9 (*see* p. 581) to make their Oregon trail excursion. (Ten days earlier, in present McPherson county, Parkman had celebrated his 23d birthday.)

These four had reached Pueblo on August 20; spent three days riding down the Arkansas to Bent's Fort; there had added four others to their party (Hodgeman, a Missouri volunteer; two men from California—"Jim Gurney," and Munroe; Ellis—a homesick Missouri emigrant); then continued downriver on August 26.

On the Santa Fe trail they met buffalo herds, companies of traders, units of Price's regiment, the Mormon battalion, and government trains; but encountered no hostile Indians. Parkman and party reached Pawnee Fork on September 12 (having left the Arkansas on the 9th to travel the "Ridge Road," the shorter dry route); crossed Walnut creek on the 13th; camped at the Little Arkansas on the 15th; "Munroe, Jim, and Ellis" left to go on ahead, on the 18th; nooned on the 19th at Diamond Spring; passed Council Grove on the 20th; met Ceran St. Vrain's train on the 23d; nooned at Elm Grove on the 25th; next day entered Westport—where Parkman and Shaw "sold off" their outfit; and about three(?) days later—after spending the intervening days at

William M. Chick's Kansas (City), Mo., home—boarded a steamboat for St. Louis.

Ref: Wade, *op. cit.,* v. 2, pp. 473-483; Parkman, *op. cit.* Parkman was born September 16, 1823.

℃ September 29.—Capt. Philip R. Thompson, First U. S. dragoons (under appointment to head the Mormon battalion) left Fort Leavenworth with an escort of 15(?) men to make a rapid journey down the Santa Fe trail.

Eastbound travelers "met Col. Thompson with a party of 13 men and 3 wagons" at Rock creek—making forced marches. About two days later, west of Cottonwood crossing, Thompson "with three light wagons, and an escort of ten[?] dragoons" came up to the camp of Ceran St. Vrain's train. On October 13 the captain reached the Arkansas crossings; and he got to Santa Fe (by the Cimarron route) on the last day of October.

Ref: *The Weekly Tribune,* Liberty, Mo., October 17, 1846; New York *Weekly Tribune,* October 31 (from *Missouri Republican,* St. Louis, October 13) and November 7, 1846 (from St. Louis *New Era,* October 26); Lewis H. Garrard's *Wah-to-yah* . . ., ed. by R. P. Bieber, p. 62; G. R. Gibson, *op. cit.,* pp. 264, 307, and 250-252 (for arrival at Santa Fe of the Mormons). Instead of Thompson, it was Capt. P. St. George Cooke who, at Santa Fe, took command of the Mormon battalion, on Kearny's order.

℃ September 30.—Seven(?) of the "Mississippi Saints"—William Crosby, John Brown, and five(?) others (*see* pp. 588, 589); also an Ohio-bound wayfarer named Wales B. Bonney (emigrant to Oregon in 1845), arrived at Independence, Mo., from the upper Arkansas by way of the Santa Fe trail. They had left Pueblo (Colo.) —two days' travel above Bent's Fort—on September 1.

The Mormons were returning to the States for their families. On September 14, between Walnut creek and Pawnee Fork, westbound John D. Lee, and his Mormon companions, "discovered several men on horse back with 3 or 4 waggons in co—coming toward us—what when they came up proved to be Br. Wm Crowsby, John Brown, John D. Hollody [Holliday], Geo W. Bankhead & Daniel Thomas from Miss[issippi] Co. Bro Crowsby said that he led a co 43 persons & 19 waggons when at Independence Mo. . . ."

Bonney's trip from Oregon (begun May 13) had been a curious and bold enterprise. He had journeyed part of the way alone. West of Fort Laramie, Solmon P. Sublette and party (*see* p. 644) had overtaken, and aided, Bonney— then afoot—after he had been robbed by Sioux Indians of horses, provisions, and clothing. From Fort Laramie he managed to get to Pueblo safely.

Ref: D. Morgan, *op. cit.,* v. 1, pp. 63, 65, 94, 95, 114, 115, v. 2, pp. 604, 608, 614, 647, 655, 768-773; John D. Lee's "Diary" in *New Mexico Historical Review,* v. 42 (July, 1967), pp. 165-199.

℃ October 1.—Santa Fe trader Norris Colburn, *making his second trip of the year to New Mexico,* left the Missouri border with a train of 19 wagons "loaded with goods, implements of husbandry, ploughs, etc." The Independence (Mo.) *Western Expositor* commented of this second venture: "a thing unprecedented in the annals of prairie travel." (For the earlier journeys of 1846 *see* pp. 581 and 642.)

Eastbound Capt. C. F. Ruff met Colburn's train near Pawnee Rock on October 20. On the 31st eastbound John D. Lee "Came to the last point on the Simeroan [Cimarron] & struck up camp . . . about 1 P M met Capt Hall Colburn & co (Sante Fe traders) with 26 waggons arrived in camp . . . left Ft Leavenworth [Independence] on Oct 1st met with no accidents on the way. . . ." Norris Colburn treated Lee's party (Mormons) most hospitably.

Ref: New York *Weekly Tribune*, October 24, November 21, 1846; Saint Louis *Daily Union*, October 8, 1846; John D. Lee's "Diary," *loc. cit.* For "Hall" *see* next annals entry.

❦ October 2.—"Messrs. [A. P.] Kean & [Jacob] Hall," of Independence, Mo., started for Santa Fe with nine(?) wagon-loads of provisions and goods—aiming at a market among the Army of the West troops in New Mexico.

In the fore part of November, some eastbound travelers (who had left Santa Fe on October 26), met Hall & Kean "getting along fine," and within 250 miles of the New Mexican capital.

Ref: New York *Weekly Tribune*, October 24, 1846; St. Louis *Daily Union*, October 8 and December 8, 1846. In KHi library is a brief in circuit court of U. S. for District of Kansas, *Hall vs. Huffaker*, in which Jacob Hall says (in evidence taken June 24, 1862): "I reside at Independence, Missouri, where I have been residing for over 20 years. I commenced trading to Santa Fe, N. M., in the fall of 1846. I took out, in company with Mr. A. P. Kean, in that year, some 14 or 15 wagon loads of goods. I returned in the Spring of 1847." Hall, subsequently (1850) was mail contractor on the Independence-Santa Fe route. Alonzo P. Kean was killed September 2(?), 1850, at Independence, Mo., in a warehouse explosion. —Independence *Commonwealth*, September 2, 1850. Both Hall and Kean are listed in the 1850 federal census of Jackson county, Mo.

❦ October 2.—The one-year Indian trading license (renewal) issued by Agent R. W. Cummins to Cyprian Chouteau (representing Pierre Chouteau, Jr. & Co.) showed that the "persons engaged" were Frederick Chouteau, Charles Chouteau, Thomas Elliott, and John Owens (the first three as "clerks and salesmen," the latter as "teamster, cook," etc.).

Though licensed to trade with the Kickapoos, Delawares, Shawnees, and Kansa, the Chouteaus' trading houses *in the Fort Leavenworth Agency*—once four in number—were now reduced to two: (1) the post occupied since 1828 by Cyprian Chouteau (see p. 153), 12 miles up the Kansas (on the *south* bank, and on the Shawnee reserve, in present Wyandotte county); (2) the post located on a bluff, on the *north* side of the Kansas, near the mouth of the second creek emptying into it, above the Delawares' blacksmith shop (on the Delaware reserve, apparently at the Kansas crossing variously known as Grinter, military road, or Delaware crossing, in present Wyandotte county —*see* p. 434).

Ref: OIA, "Letters Received from Fort Leavenworth Agency" (National Archives Microcopy 234, Roll 302), Cummins' list forwarded from St. Louis to OIA on September 27, 1847. No longer maintained were: (1) the post among the Kickapoos, on Salt creek, present Leavenworth county, and (2) the post among the Kansa *on the Kansas river*. The latter site was abandoned in 1847(?) as a result of the Kansa tribe's forthcoming move to the upper Neosho country. *See KHC,* v. 8, pp. 256, 257, for mention of John Owens (who had married a Shawnee woman). Cyprian Chouteau's post is shown on T. H. Jefferson's map—*see* segment in this volume.

❦ October 3.—On or about this date Richard Grant, Jr. (son of the Hudson's Bay Company's Fort Hall factor) arrived at Kansas (City), Mo., from "Idaho." Letters written at Fort Hall as late as August 14, and sent in his care, were postmarked at Kansas, Mo., on October 3.

Of his route and journey no other information is presently known. One of his companions may have been A. L. Davidson of Oregon who reached the states in the fore part of October. Young Grant (about 20), on a mission for his father, was to return home in 1847 with the Oregon-bound emigrants. Davidson, as reported, had come East to get his parents, and return to Oregon.

Ref: D. Morgan, *op. cit.,* v. 2, pp. 635, 636, 640, 765, 766; New York *Weekly Tribune,* November 7, 1846, reprinted an account of Davidson's lecture on Oregon—a column and a half of it—as published in the Sangamo (Ill.) *Journal* of October 22.

❦ October.—Dr. (James S.) Craig, a Kentuckian (who for 15 years had been a resident of New Mexico and California) arrived at Independence, Mo., prior to October 11 (on which date he reached St. Louis). He had left Santa Fe on September 6.

He brought in a mail, and Kearny's dispatches. His party, traveling the Cimarron route, had met Price's regiment, the Mormon battalion, and Capt. Philip R. Thompson with his escort.

Craig reported that the Arkansas was "perfectly dry for the whole distance" he traveled along it—"an evidence of drouth which has not been known for many years." (While on the river, a small party of Indians had made an attack on his camp.) As reported: "Along the whole route the grass was abundant, but water very scarce."

Ref: New York *Weekly Tribune,* October 31, 1846 (from *Missouri Republican,* St. Louis, October 13). Almost certainly the above was Dr. James S. Craig of the "Bean-Sinclair" party which went West in 1830—*see* annals, p. 172. Apparently he was not with the Ware-Ferguson company (*see* next annals item) at least on the early stages of the trip—since Craig encountered hostile Indians, and they did not. The departure dates varied by three days.

❦ October 3 and 4.—Some 10 to 15 persons who left Santa Fe on September 9 arrived at Independence, Mo., and brought with them a "large number of letters." The company included John Ware, of Baltimore, Charles Ferguson, of Philadelphia, several men from Jackson county, Mo., and (apparently) "Mr. Hill" of Lafayette county, Mo.

As reported, the company had "no difficulty en route except scarcity of wood and water on the Cimarron." These men had met various New Mexico-bound trains; and some of the party (originally 20 to 25 in number) had taken employment with them, and returned to Santa Fe.

Ref: Saint Louis *Daily* Union, October 9, 12, 1846; New York *Weekly Tribune,* October 24, 1846 (from *Missouri Republican,* St. Louis, October 9).

❧ October 6-14.—Brant Chapman and five other persons, setting out from Fort Leavenworth on the 6th, traveled down the Missouri in a skiff, and reached St. Louis in midmonth. The river was reported "falling, with but thirty inches on the principal bars."

They met a number of upbound steamboats: the *Algoma* at Lexington, Mo., on the 8th; the *St. Joseph* on the 9th; the *Clermont No. 2* and *Archer* "hard aground" at Portland Bar; the *General Brooke* which had "hauled over" at the mouth of the Osage; the *Tributary* and *Little Missouri* "both hard aground" there on the 11th.

Ref: St. Louis *New Era*, October 15, 1846, as reprinted in New York *Weekly Tribune*, October 31, 1846. Probably Brant Chapman was a steamboat captain. The Saint Louis *Daily Union* of September 22, 1846, mentioned "Capt. Chapman, of the *Galena*, who came passenger on the *Bertrand* from Fort Leavenworth. . . ."

❧ Around October 11, Capt. A. W. Enos (AQM), 2d Lt. Alexander B. Dyer (U. S. ordnance), and (presumably) an escort party, left Fort Leavenworth for Bent's Fort (where Enos was to serve as assistant quartermaster). They reached their destination on November 3.

Ref: New York *Weekly Tribune*, November 7, 1846 (from St. Louis *New Era* of October 26); L. H. Garrard's *Wah-to-yah and the Taos Trail*, ed. by R. P. Bieber (1938), p. 129. In Heitman's *Historical Register* Enos is entered as "Elanson W. Enos"; but Bieber, using primary sources, lists him as "A. W. Enos."

❧ October 12, or 13.—The 28-wagon train of Messrs. (James H.) Bullard, Hooke & Co., Lexington, Mo., with partner Isaac McCarty as "superintendent," left the Missouri border for Santa Fe. The Independence *Expositor* commented: "This is the latest company that has ever started before for the plains from here. . . . The company have brought corn here and haul it out with them to Council Grove."

Late in November, south of the sand hills on the Cimarron, disaster—in the form of a blizzard—struck Bullard, Hooke & Co.'s camp. During the storm 20 head of oxen escaped in a stampede; and some mules died. The traders cached goods "near the Semirone," and returned to the Arkansas with the rest; then proceeded upriver to Bent's Fort; intending to winter there and continue to Santa Fe in the spring. On January 31, 1847, 2d Lt. James W. Abert, coming down from Bent's Fort, "met a train of six wagons belonging to Messrs. Bullard & Hook, of Missouri. It had been to the crossing of the Arkansas to raise some 'caches,' which some of the proprietors of this train had been obligated to make early in the fall."

Ref: New York *Weekly Tribune*, November 7 (for the *Expositor* quote), 21, 1846, January 9, 1847; Saint Louis *Daily Union*, December 8, 28, 1846; *Missouri Republican*, St. Louis, December 23, 28, 1846; 30th Cong., 1st Sess., *H. Ex. Doc. No. 41* (Serial 517), p. 530; *KHQ*, v. 26, p. 364. John D. Lee (*see* his Diary, *loc. cit.*) met, on November 5, at Pawnee Fork, "Capt. Bulliard Russell's co. . . . with 30 wagons & 50 men were encamped there."

❧ October.—At Independence, Mo., a man was "building a waggon to run across the prairies to Bent's Fort, to be propelled by the wind."

With masts and sails, the inventor expected his wind-wagon to run at 15 miles an hour; and planned to *"blaze the way"* before year's end. (But in April, 1847, the Independence *Western Expositor* reported that "Mr. Thomas" was *soon* to make an experimental trip on the plains with his newly invented "wind ship.")

Ref: *The Weekly Tribune,* Liberty, Mo., October 24, 1846; Saint Louis *Daily Union,* April 12, 1847.

¶ October 13(?)—A government mule train (headed by "Harlowe"?), en route to Bent's Fort, was attacked by Pawnees at Pawnee Fork. The Indians slipped up on the teamsters as they were at supper, killing one man and slightly wounding (by an arrow) the wagonmaster.

Ceran St. Vrain's train (westbound) camped at Pawnee Fork on October 14; on the 17th (as noted by Lewis Garrard) his party overtook and "nooned" near the train "from which the man was killed at Pawnee Fork." Capt. C. F. Ruff (eastbound) "met Harlowe train of Waggons on 17 [Oct.] at coon creek." (He did not meet the St. Vrain train, which must have passed beyond the point where Ruff crossed the Arkansas before his arrival.)

Ref: *The Gazette,* St. Joseph, Mo., November 20, 1846 (from St. Louis *New Era* of November 9), or *see* New York *Weekly Tribune,* November 28, 1846; Lewis H. Garrard's *Wah-to-yah,* ed. by R. P. Bieber, p. 79; Charles F. Ruff's notes (copy in KHi ms. division).

¶ October 16-24.—Chief Powashiek and most of the "Mississippi" Foxes (after squatting on Pottawatomie and Kickapoo lands for a year—*see* December, 1845, annals entry), reached the Sac & Fox Agency on the upper Marais des Cygnes (in present Franklin county) on the 16th. Reluctant immigrants, the Foxes were drawn to their new reserve by the forthcoming annuity payment.

Sup't Thomas H. Harvey, of St. Louis (with the annuity funds—$30,000 for the Sacs and $30,000 for the Foxes) also arrived at the agency on October 16 (and remained till after the 24th). Under his watchful supervision, the payments were made as determined by the Indians (and not according to the traders' wishes). Half of the Sacs' $30,000 was divided among the individuals of the nation. (This amounted to $14 for each person, indicating a total of 1,071 Sacs.) Chiefs Keokuk and Hard Fish received the other $15,000— $7,500 went to each. (Harvey commented, in an October 24 letter, that Keokuk turned his money over to Pierre Chouteau, Jr. & Co., traders; and that Hard Fish "probably" turned his over to R. A. Kinzie.) The Foxes also divided half (or $15,000) among the members of the nation. (Each person received $17.50, indicating a total of 857 Foxes.) Chief Powashiek, to whom went $15,000, paid out (according to Harvey) $10,000 to trader "Scott," and $3,000 to "Ewing." (*See* p. 579 for other data on these traders.)

Ref: OIA, "Letters Received from Sac & Fox Agency" (National Archives Microcopy 234, Roll 732), Harvey's October 24, 1846, letter; 30th Cong., 1st Sess., *Sen. Ex. Doc.*

No. 70 (Serial 510), p. 93 (for comment by Harvey, in 1848, that the Sac & Fox "are the only Indians within my knowledge that object to have schools or missionaries among them").

℄ October 17.—An express which had left Santa Fe on September 17, arrived at Fort Leavenworth—having met the Mormon battalion on the Cimarron; Capt. Philip R. Thompson's party at Cottonwood crossing; and Capt. A. W. Enos (en route to Bent's Fort) at Council Grove.

Ref: New York *Weekly Tribune,* November 7, 1846 (from St. Louis *New Era,* October 26); Saint Louis *Daily Union,* October 24, 1846; Gibson, *op. cit.,* p. 239 (Gibson, at Santa Fe, wrote on September 17: "This morning an express with the mail left for 'the States' and is expected to reach Independence in twenty-four days").

℄ In mid-October, at a point some 20 miles below the Arkansas crossings, Pawnees attacked and captured 19 wagoners. The ill-equipped teamsters (said to have only five guns among them!) were robbed of all possessions, then allowed to continue afoot.

The Pawnees "carried off all the arms and clothing . . . and about 50 head of mules." They destroyed the wagons, and any contents unwanted—which included about 300 sacks of flour that they cut open and scattered to the four winds. "The prairie for miles around the spot was . . . as white as if covered with snow" (according to an account supplied by two of the teamsters). The Pawnees frolicked in the flour—powdered themselves, snow-balled each other; then made use of the flour sacks—one wound his as a turban; some devised other garb. It was reported they seemed to prize the lettering on the sacks, "as in all the breech clothes made of them the U. S. was contrived to be preserved in front."

John D. Lee's diary entry of October 27 evidently described the above attack. On the 27th, a week out of Santa Fe, returning by the Cimarron route, Lee "Met Capt Gipson [Gibson?] with a train [of] 31 waggons, from Ft. Gibson . . . [and learned from him that "Gipson" earlier had] sent 19 of [his] co back which were rob[b]ed of all their blankets, guns, provisions & even took the clothes of[f] their backs—all but 2 sick men that were lying down—if I mistake not 2 of the no. escaped with their horses—after rob[b]ing them the chief & braves shook hands & left them there was about 150 [Indians] in no.—the last robbery [*i e.,* this one] was committed about 25 ms beyond the crossing of the Arkansas—the 2 men that made their escape followed up the trains of waggons to report their defeat."

Ref: *The Gazette,* St. Joseph, Mo., November 20, 1846 (from St. Louis *New Era,* November 9); New York *Weekly Tribune,* December 12, 1846; Saint Louis *Daily Union,* November 23, 1846; G. F. Ruxton's *Adventures in Mexico and the Rocky Mountains,* new ed. (London, 1861), p. 290 (has mention of the incident); John D. Lee's "Diary," in *New Mexico Historical Review,* v. 42 (October, 1967), p. 313.

℄ October 28.—The 24-wagon, Santa Fe-bound government supply train (Daniel P. Mann, captain; "Buchanan," wagonmaster) which camped 25 to 30 miles below the Arkansas crossings on October 27, was attacked next morning by a large band of Pawnees (400 to 500, reports said). The 40 teamsters (who had 29 guns and 80 cartridges) corralled their wagons, except one (loaded with bacon; and Mann's belongings) which was captured and burned. In the fighting John H. Dougherty was killed, John C. Northrup was shot through both legs, and three other men ("F. Valet," "John Anthony," "Peter Hurman") were wounded slightly. After the Indians succeeded in getting possession of all the mules and horses (except about a dozen), they departed.

When darkness came Mann and some others set out, upriver, taking the wounded; and after traveling some 30(?) miles came up with McElvaine's train. The latter's mules were subsequently taken to the battle site to bring up all abandoned wagons and salvagable contents. Mann's party then fortified about four miles from the Arkansas crossing; sent the wounded to Bent's Fort; and awaited the arrival of teams. Buchanan and two others reached Bent's Fort on November 5. Aid probably was dispatched to the stranded men soon thereafter.

On November 1, John D. Lee's small party, eastbound, "reached & crossed the Arkansas & encamped. Here we found [wrote Lee] capt Hornback & McLevain [McElvaine] with a Mule Train (130 Waggons government Provisions) Capts Man[n] Yates & Buckhannon were also here but their Trains of 40 men was 30 miles back where they on the 28 of Oct were attacked by 300 Pawnees—about 10 in the morning. The fire [engagement] lasted 4 hours when Yates, Mann & Buckhannon & their co retreated with the loss of one man wounded[?] The Indians lost one of their chieves—took about 160 mules—some blankets & clothing—burned 1 waggon loaded with Bacon & Flour—after making this raise they soon toddled. . . . Capt McLevain sent back teams to bring up the rear of Capt Mann's waggons."

Ref: *The Weekly Tribune*, Liberty, Mo., December 5, 1846; Saint Louis *Daily Union*, December 28, 1846; New York *Weekly Tribune*, January 6, 1847; L. H. Garrard's *Wah-to-yah . . .*, ed. by R. P. Bieber (1938), p. 94; W. E. Connelley's *Doniphan's Expedition*, pp. 522, 523, or John T. Hughes' *Doniphan's Expedition* (1850), pp. 404, 405; John D. Lee's "Diary," in *New Mexico Historical Review*, v. 42 (October, 1967), pp. 316, 317. The Pawnees' agent, in 1847, reported the *Grand* Pawnees (living south of the Platte) were very hostile to the whites; and that they were the Indians who "robbed the United States wagon train last fall, killing one man and driving off 160 head of mules."—Saint Louis *Reveille* (daily), June 20, 1847.

❡ October 30.—Capt. Charles F. Ruff, of the Mounted riflemen (recently lieutenant-colonel of "Doniphan's" regiment) reached Fort Leavenworth, after a 34-day journey from Santa Fe (left on September 27) by the Cimarron route. He had in charge some First dragoon horses which General Kearny had sent back to headquarters post. His own destination was Jefferson Barracks, Mo., and then southward to join Gen. Zachary Taylor's forces.

Ruff's notes of the trip include this statement: "10 horses gave out on 16th [October] in a winter's storm between the old road from 'cachee's' & coon creek on river road 3 more left on morning of 17th unable to get up—effects of the cold after a march of 20 miles" Young "Mr. Nourse" who returned with Ruff's one-wagon(?) party as far as Council Grove (and reached St.

Louis November 6) reported that nearly half the horses perished during this "severe storm on the plains."

Ref: *The Weekly Tribune,* Liberty, Mo., November 7, 1846; Saint Louis *Daily Union,* November 7, 1846; New York *Weekly Tribune,* November 21, 1846; Charles F. Ruff's notes (copy in KHi ms. division); W. E. Connelley's *Doniphan's Expedition* . . ., pp. 74, 247-249. Ruff had resigned from the Missouri volunteers on September 17, 1846. His commission as a captain in the U. S. Mounted riflemen dated from July 7, 1846.

❧ November 3.—Indian trader William H. Hildreth, whose post was near the mouth of Salt creek (three and a half miles above Fort Leavenworth) on the Kickapoo reserve, was granted a trading license (renewal) good for *two* years, by Agent R. W. Cummins. (*See* p. 505.)

(On May 12, young Francis Parkman, from a camp near Fort Leavenworth, had ridden over to the Kickapoo reserve. "Returning, we stopped at the trader's," he wrote in his journal. "We were hot and tired; and the trader showed us into a neat, dark, and cool parlor, where he gave us iced claret and an excellent lunch. . . . His mistress, a yellow woman, brimful of merriment, entertained us with her conversation.")

Ref: OIA, "Letters Received from Fort Leavenworth Agency" (National Archives Microcopy 234, Roll 302), *see* Cummins' list, forwarded from St. Louis on September 27, 1847; Wade, *op. cit.,* v. 2, p. 422. In 1850, W. H. Hildreth was at Davenport, Iowa.—*See* OIA, "Letters Received from Fort Leavenworth Agency" (National Archives Microcopy 234, Roll 303).

❧ November 3.—From Santa Fe, by the Cimarron route, four men —Capt. William S. Murphy (of the Missouri volunteers), in company with "H. P. Paulsel, F. Roubedou and a Mr. [C.] Perry, the bearers of an express"—arrived at Westport, Mo. Murphy's mission: "to get specie funds for the troops" and return to New Mexico. (He reached St. Louis on November 8. *See* p. 658 for his journey back.)

The express trio, with one wagon, had left Santa Fe on October 7. Murphy, setting out on the 9th, with a pack mule, overtook them. They traveled the Cimarron route; encountered one snow storm; and "lay by four days." At the Arkansas crossings on October 23 they met St. Vrain's company going upriver to Bent's Fort.

Ref: New York *Weekly Tribune,* November 28, 1846 (from St. Louis *New Era,* November 9); *The Gazette,* St. Joseph, Mo., November 20, 1846; Lewis H. Garrard's *Wah-to-yah,* ed. by R. P. Bieber, p. 81 (which lists other sources); G. R. Gibson, *op. cit.,* p. 250, and pp. 226, 234, for mention of Perry. Murphy was captain of Company B (Platte county), infantry battalion, Missouri volunteers.

❧ By November 5 head chief Francis La Fontaine and a party of 323 Miami Indians (142 males; 181 females), newly arrived from Indiana, were encamped on Sugar creek (a mile or so west of the military road, and some 13 miles north of the American Fur Company's Marais des Cygnes post—now Trading Post, Linn co.), in what is now the southeastern corner of Miami county. They had been conducted to "Kansas" by Joseph Sinclair (recently their subagent); but the person who had looked out for their welfare on the journey (the Indians said) was Alexis Coquillard, one of the contractors for their removal.

Early in October (and *six* years after the 1840 treaty in which they had agreed to emigrate within *five* years) about 328 Miamis had been rounded up and forcibly removed from their Wabash river homes. (Some 300? yet remained in Indiana.) On the steamboat *Colorado* (from Cincinnati) this party reached St. Louis October 20; then boarded the *Clermont No. 2* on the 22d, and after a slow journey (because of low water), arrived at Kansas (City), Mo., on November 1. The same day, the overland party (12 men, with the Miamis' horses and several wagonloads of their possessions) which had left Peru, Ind., on October 8, also reached the Kaw's mouth. The united company set out for Little Sugar creek on November 2.

Subagent Alfred J. Vaughan, visiting the new arrivals on November 9 and 10, reported they seemed pleased with their new location. He appointed his son, Leonidas Vaughan, as their "issuing Commissary of Subsistence." Among the Miamis were many half-bloods (and there were Miami women with white husbands; as well as some Indian men with white wives—according to the Cincinnati *Enquirer*). By year's end, 25 "good and substantial log houses" (built under contract by Joseph Clymer, Jr.,) had been completed; but Subagent Vaughan also noted that "not less than 30" deaths (some the result of intemperance) had occurred among these immigrants.

The Miamis' "old and much respected" (also well-to-do) Chief La Fontaine, who left "Kansas" about the end of March, 1847, (with 40? of his people) to return to Indiana, died at Lafayette, on April 13, before reaching home. His wife (a daughter of former head chief John B. Richardville) and seven children survived him. Also in 1847, about 70 more Miamis came to "Kansas."

Ref: SIA, St. Louis, "Records," v. 8, typed copy, pp. 575-579 (Vaughan's November 12, 1846, letter); OIA, "Letters Received from Osage River Subagency" (National Archives Microcopy 234, Roll 643); *The Weekly Tribune*, Liberty, Mo., October 31, 1846; Saint Louis *Daily Union*, October 17, 20, 23, 1846, March 30, 1847; 29th Cong., 2d Sess., *H. Doc. No. 36* (Serial 499), p. 9; 30th Cong., 1st Sess., *Sen. Ex. Doc. No. 48* (Serial 508), p. 191; 30th Cong., 1st Sess., *H. Ex. Doc. No. 5* (Serial 514), pp. 109, 110; 31st Cong., 1st Sess., *H. Ex. Doc. No. 11* (Serial 572), p. 6; Comm'r of Indian Affairs, *Report*, 1847; Grant Foreman's *The Last Trek of the Indians* (c1946), pp. 125-131; New York *Weekly Tribune*, May 1, 1847 (for death of La Fontaine).

⁋ In (the first week of?) November a Mackinaw boat from the upper Missouri, carrying "190 packages of [buffalo] Robes, and 40 of Beaver," consigned to Pierre Chouteau, Jr., & Co., passed along the "Kansas" shore of the river. The voyage (a difficult one, because of low water) ended at St. Louis on November 12.

Ref: Saint Louis *Daily Union*, November 13, 1846.

⁋ November 10.—Gov. Charles Bent included in his report (as *ex officio* sup't of Indian affairs in New Mexico), these statements:

"The Cheyennes and Arapahoes range through the country of the Arkansas and its tributaries. . . . They live almost entirely on the buffalo, and carry on a considerable trade with the Americans and Mexicans in buffalo robes. . . . They are a roving people, and have for many years been on friendly terms with the New Mexicans. The Arapahoes number about 400 lodges, or 2,000 souls; the [southern] Cheyennes 300 lodges, or 1,500 souls.

"The Comanches range east of the mountains of New Mexico—a numerous and warlike people, subsisting entirely by the chase. The different bands number in all about 2,500 lodges, or 12,000 souls. They have been at peace for many years with the New Mexicans, but have carried on an incessant and destructive war with the States of Chihuahua, Durango, and Coahuila. . . .

"The Cayugas [Kiowas] range through a part of the same country, and are similar in habits and customs, and are considered a more brave people than the Comanches. They number about 400 lodges, or 2,000 souls."

Ref: 31st Cong., 1st Sess., *H. Ex. Doc. No. 17* (Serial 573), pp. 191-194. Indian Agent Thomas Fitzpatrick, in his December 18, 1847, report stated: "I believe that the Camanche Indians do not exceed 1000 lodges, and as it is rare that more than one warrior occupies a lodge amongst them, we may put them down at the very utmost 1200 warriors." —Report published in *The Westerners New York Posse Brand Book,* v. 10 (1963), see p. 88. For Indian statistics Charles Bent gave at St. Louis, in August, see *Niles' National Register,* v. 70 (August 29, 1846), p. 404.

❦ About November 13(?) Thomas Fitzpatrick (en route to Washington, D. C., with Com. Robert F. Stockton's California dispatches, and letters from Lt. Col. John C. Fremont) reached the Missouri border. (He had left Santa Fe on October 14; and he arrived at St. Louis on November 15.)

On this journey east he learned of his appointment (dated August 3) as Indian agent for the new Upper Platte (and Arkansas) Agency. Before the end of November he delivered the dispatches in Washington. (These dispatches, and Fremont's letters, had left California in Kit Carson's care; and had been transferred to Fitzpatrick's charge, on General Kearny's orders, at the meeting point of Kearny's command with Carson's eastbound party, some 175 miles west of Santa Fe.)

Ref: Saint Louis *Daily Union,* November 16, 1846; New York *Weekly Tribune,* November 28, 1846 (from *Missouri Republican,* St. Louis, November 16); *The Gazette,* St. Joseph, Mo., November 27, 1846; Edwin L. Sabin's *Kit Carson Days* . . . (1935), v. 2, pp. 509-516; 29th Cong., 2d Sess., *H. Doc. No. 36* (Serial 499), p. 5 (for Fitzpatrick's date of appointment); L. R. Hafen and W. J. Ghent's *Broken Hand The Life Story of Thomas Fitzpatrick* . . . (Denver, 1931), pp. 186, 187, 191, 192; G. R. Gibson, *op. cit.,* p. 251.

❦ November 14.—A party of four Mormons arrived at Fort Leavenworth, having avoided both the hostile Indians and the bad weather which plagued most other late-autumn Santa Fe trail travelers. They were John D. Lee and Howard Egan (for their trip *to* Santa Fe *see* p. 643), Samuel L. Gully, and Roswell Stevens; and they had left San Miguel, N. M., on October 22.

Lee's and Egan's mission was to bring back the Mormon battalion soldiers' pay—received at Santa Fe—to Mormon headquarters (above present Omaha). They (and the others) paused but briefly at the fort; reached "Winter Quarters" on the evening of November 21.

John D. Lee, in his diary, recorded mention of numerous government and traders' wagon trains met en route: *October 26* (near Round Mound) "Capt Woods & Campbell [John P. Campbell, of Springfield, Mo.] with about 800 head of beef for Santafe" and (later) "Capt M. M. Bynum with a train of 21 [government] waggons," also "Capt Mills & J. D. Bradsley's co of 26 waggons-Provision trains." *October 27* (at Cedar Springs, or vicinity of) "Capt Gipson [Gibson?] with a Train of 31 waggons from Ft Gibson," and (later) "Capt Belle's train." *October 28* (at head of the Cimarron) "Capt Overfelt with his Train of 25 waggons loaded with provisions for the Mor. Bat[talion]." *October 29* (on the Cimarron) "Adams & Harry trading co of 11 waggons." *October 30* (on the Cimarron) "Capt Hall [and] Coulbourn [Colburn] & co (Santefe Traders) with 26 waggons arrived & encamped." *November 1 and 2* (on the Arkansas) "Capt Hornback & McLevain [McElvaine] with a Mule Train (30 Waggons government Provisions)"; also Capt. Daniel P. Mann (with Yates and Buchanan)—*see* p. 652. *November 4* (at Pawnee Fork) "Capt Bulliard Russel [Santa Fe traders] with 30 waggons & 50 men."

Ref: John D. Lee's "Diary," in *New Mexico Historical Review*, v. 42 (October, 1967), pp. 281-332; W. E. Connelley's *Doniphan's Expedition*, pp. 77, 96, 107, 260, 405, 451, 452 (for items on John P. Campbell, the founder of Springfield, Mo.); Tyler, *op. cit.*

❡ November.—Dr. George Penn (recently surgeon with Doniphan's regiment) who set out with 15(?) others from Santa Fe on October 8 or 9, reached Missouri in mid-November (he was at 110-mile creek the night of November 11), and St. Louis on the 16th. John Thurman and a "Mr. Billingsby" were in this party; and so was Michael McEnnis, who later recollected they numbered 16 men; and that they encountered hostile Navajos[?] on the Cimarron, and severely cold weather (also snow) on the plains.

The appointment as assistant treasurer of the United States for St. Louis, for which Penn left the regiment, finally materialized (when Robert Campbell of St. Louis declined the post), in January, 1847; and on March 18 he was reported to be setting up his office.

Ref: Saint Louis *Daily Union*, November 9, 17, December 14, 16, 1846, January 26, March 18, 1847; New York *Weekly Tribune*, November 28, 1846 (from St. Louis *New Era* of November 9); W. E. Connelley's *Doniphan's Expedition*, pp. 529, 627; G. R. Gibson, *op. cit.*, pp. 248, 249; John D. Lee's "Diary," *loc. cit.*, October 28 and November 9, 11, 1846, entries. Lee heard (from "Capt Gipson") that "the Indians had made 2 attempts to rob Dr. Penn & co but failed—on the upper Cimeroan at the willow bar. . . ."

❡ November 19.—The *Amelia* arrived at Weston, Mo. She was the last steamboat of the year to reach that port. Her return to St. Louis, on November 25, was noted in newspapers of the 26th.

Just preceding the *Amelia*, the *Cora* had made a trip to Weston. She returned to St. Louis on November 21. The Liberty, Mo., paper of November 14 stated that pilots on the Missouri said the river was the lowest it had been in 15 years. Only small steamboats could operate, and they had much difficulty. Passenger and freight rates were "at least double the usual price."

Ref: *The Western Journal*, St. Louis, v. 5 (March, 1851), p. 326; New York *Weekly Tribune*, December 12, 1846 (from St. Louis *New Era*, November 26); *The Weekly Tribune*, Liberty, Mo., November 14, 1846.

❡ Around November 22 Capt. William S. Murphy (*see* p. 654) and an escort left Fort Leavenworth to convoy wagons carrying $120,000 in gold (the Missouri volunteers' pay) to Santa Fe. "Provisions and forage . . . for the whole train" were taken along because of the late season. They reached Santa Fe safely, and apparently without particular difficulty, by way of the Cimarron route.

But "a company of men who had been sent from Bent's Fort, with a wagon load of corn, to meet Captain Murphy at the crossing of the Arkansas" fared less well. Lt. James W. Abert, eastbound from Bent's Fort, saw these men on January 23, 1847, in the Big Timbers area. Because of heavy snows, "they had only succeeded in getting thus far on their return to the fort," he wrote.

Ref: *The Weekly Tribune,* Liberty, Mo., November 21, 1846; St. Louis *New Era,* November 26, 1846, as reprinted in New York *Weekly Tribune,* December 12, 1846; 30th Cong., 1st Sess., *H. Ex. Doc. No. 41* (Serial 517), p. 527 (for Abert); L. H. Garrard in his *Wah-to-yah,* ed. by R. P. Bieber, p. 147.

❡ November.—Arriving at Fort Leavenworth about the 23d, from Santa Fe (left on October 18) were Maj. Edwin V. Sumner (reassigned to the *Second* dragoons), Lt. William Armstrong (Second artillery), 2d Lt. Henry W. Stanton (adjutant, First dragoons), also Lt. John Love (First dragoons) and about a dozen other mounted men.

They had traveled the Cimarron route; met numerous wagon trains; had no trouble with Indians. At 110-mile creek (present Osage county) Sumner had sent Eli Danna (or Dana), of St. Louis (an ex-Laclede Ranger), ahead with dispatches.

Danna was aboard the *Amelia* which docked at St. Louis November 24. Major Sumner and Lieutenant Armstrong arrived in that city on the 28th.

Ref: Saint Louis *Daily Union,* November 25, 1846; *The Weekly Tribune,* Liberty, Mo., November 28, 1846; New York *Weekly Tribune,* December 12, 1846 (from *Missouri Republican,* St. Louis, November 28); Heitman, *op. cit.,* (for identification of Armstrong and Stanton); G. R. Gibson, *op. cit.,* p. 258 (under date of October 20, Gibson referred to the departure from Santa Fe of "Major Sumner, Lieutenant Love [on recruiting service], and Lieutenant Stanton").

❡ November 23-28.—Father Pierre-Jean De Smet, S. J., and some companions, who had launched their skiff on the upper Missouri (in present Montana) on September 28, landed at St. Joseph, Mo., the 23d of November.

Five days later, Father De Smet reached Westport, Mo. (by steamboat?, from Fort Leavenworth?). Probably he spent about a week in Jackson county, Mo. An entry in Father Christian Hoecken's diary for 1846 reads: "In December, Father [Felix L.] Verreydt proceeded [from Sugar Creek Mission, present Linn county] to Independence, Mo., to meet Father Peter J. de Smet, who was expected to land there on his return from the Rocky Mountains." De Smet reached St. Louis (by stage?) on December 10.

Ref: H. M. Chittenden and A. T. Richardson's *Life, Letters and Travels of Father Pierre-Jean De Smet, S. J.* (New York, 1905), v. 1, p. 56, v. 2, pp. 600-612; T. H. Kinsella's *The History of Our Cradle Land* . . . (Kansas City, 1921), p. 234 (for Hoecken diary quotation); Saint Louis *Daily Union*, December 19, 1846 (indicates arrival date as December 11).

❡ Early in December Dr. Isaac P. Vaughan, of Howard county, Mo. (recently assistant surgeon in "Doniphan's" regiment) arrived at Independence, Mo. He had left Santa Fe on October 26.

Nothing on the size of his party, or their route and experiences, has been located. Vaughan brought mail to Missouri.

Ref: Saint Louis *Daily Union*, December 14, 1846; W. E. Connelley's *Doniphan's Expedition*, pp. 181, 244, 530 (for items on Vaughan).

❡ December 11-16.—Between the Little Arkansas and Diamond Spring three men from Buchanan county, Mo., froze to death. They were Messrs. Bartlett (who died on the 11th), Thompson (or, Thomason? Tomlinson?; on the 11th or 12th), and Long (about the 16th).

In a company of 27 (a First dragoons sergeant and 26 teamsters), with one wagon and seven mules, they had set out from Santa Fe on November 2. All three had been ill (of dysentery) for several days before a blizzard—on December 9 and 10—subjected the party to a very heavy snow, and bitter cold. Subsequently the wagon had to be abandoned; and several of the mules were left behind (or died). Some of the men suffered frostbitten feet. The sergeant, and three teamsters, who went on ahead from Council Grove, on the 18th, to get help, arrived at Fort Leavenworth on December 22. (They had met, on the 21st, a party sent to aid the stranded men.) Four of the company reached Westport, and Independence, Mo., on January 8, 1847.

Ref: New York *Weekly Tribune*, February 6 and 27, 1847; Saint Louis *Daily Union*, January 18, 1847.

❡ December.—A census taken at St. Joseph, Mo., on the 18th and 19th showed the town's population to be: 510 white males; 385 white females; 70 slaves (27 males; 43 females); and two free Negroes (1 male; 1 female)—a total of 967 persons.

Ref: *The Gazette*, St. Joseph, Mo., December 25, 1846.

❡ DIED: Matthew Sarrahess, of the Wyandot Nation, aged 60, on December 18, in present Wyandotte county. He was buried in Huron Place cemetery (in Kansas City, Kan., of today).

Of Sarrahess, William Walker wrote: "He was a fine orator."

Ref: William Walker's journal, December 21, 1846 (in W. E. Connelley's *The Provisional Government* . . ., p. 193.

❡ MARRIED: George Armstrong and Hannah (Charloe) Barnett, widow of John Barnett, on December 24, at the home of William Walker, by the Rev. Edward T. Peery, Methodist minister. All, except Peery, were members of the Wyandot Nation.

Ref: William Walker's journal, in W. E. Connelley's *Provisional Government* . . ., p. 193, and *see, also,* pp. 192 and 194. John Barnett may have been part-Shawnee.

❡ December.—On the 24th Thomas Fitzpatrick (Indian agent) and Solomon P. Sublette left St. Louis for Fort Leavenworth. The latter was bound for Santa Fe as a "Government Express" (but he did not set out from the fort till January 8, 1847). Both had been in Washington, D. C.

On December 18 the Saint Louis *Daily Union* had quoted a letter from Sen. Thomas Hart Benton (in Washington) giving notice that "A Government Express for Santa Fe, and perhaps, California" would "pass through St. Louis in a few days. . . ."

Ref: Saint Louis *Daily Union,* December 18, 24, 1846, January 18, 1847.

❡ December.—2d Lt. John O. Simpson (of Maj. M. Lewis Clark's battalion, Missouri volunteers) arrived at St. Louis on the 26th from Bent's Fort (where he had been stationed as acting quartermaster). The party of Pawnees met while crossing "Kansas" had "not seriously molested" him.

Ref: *Missouri Republican,* St. Louis, December 28, 1846; St. Louis *Daily Union,* December 28, 1846; New York *Weekly Tribune,* January 6, 1847; W. E. Connelley's *Doniphan's Expedition,* p. 574 (for Simpson's rank, etc.); Nolie Mumey's *Old Forts* . . . (Denver, 1956), p. 83 (for Capt. A. W. Enos' letter of December 12, 1846, mentioning Simpson's duty at Bent's Fort).

❡ In December a new chapel was completed at a location some four miles north of Delaware Baptist Mission (*i. e.,* the mission near present Edwardsville, Wyandotte co., occupied from 1833-1847 —*see* p. 225). The new meeting house was in the vicinity of the Delaware village which had moved a distance of "nearly six miles" from the mission following the 1844 flood (*see* pp. 516, 517).

The church was described (in 1847) as "a framed house, 36 feet by 26; . . . arched, ceiled, floored and painted; . . . capable of seating 300 persons." It had cost about $450, "including $161.50 contributed in labor &c., by the Delawares, and $74.55 by the missionary [Ira D. Blanchard]."

Ref: *The Baptist Missionary Magazine,* v. 27 (January and July, 1847), pp. 31 and 259; and *see* item in KHC, v. 12, p. 183 (for a reference to the frame chapel), and p. 188 (for mention of the distance to the "old" mission, above, from the "Pratt mission," which was opened in 1848).

❡ Employed in "Kansas" by the Indian department during all, or part of the year 1846 were the following persons:

FORT LEAVENWORTH AGENCY [*Kickapoos, Delawares, Shawnees, Kansa, Stockbridges, and Munsees*] — *Agent* Richard W. Cummins; *Interpreters* Clement Lessert and Henry Tiblow; *Blacksmiths* Calvin Perkins and William Donalson for Shawnees, James B. Franklin (appointed February 13) for Delawares, William H. Mitchell (appointed January 26) for Kansa; *Assistant blacksmiths* Joseph Parks' colored boy and Powhatan Phifer for Shawnees,

Cornelius Yager (appointed February 13) for Delawares, Nelson Henry (a Kansa Indian; appointed February 24) for Kansa; *Farmer* John T. Peery for Kansa.

GREAT NEMAHA SUBAGENCY [*Iowas and Sacs & Foxes of the Missouri*]— *Subagent* Armstrong McClintock (removed in spring?), William E. Rucker (appointed June 17); *Interpreters* John Rubite for Sacs & Foxes, John B. Roy for Iowas; *Farmers* John W. Forman for Sacs & Foxes, Findley C. McCreary (appointed April 15) for Iowas; *Assistant farmers* Andrew Meyer and Martin Meyer for Sacs & Foxes.

OSAGE RIVER SUBAGENCY [*Ottawas, Chippewas, Weas, Piankeshaws, and Pottawatomies*]—*Subagent* Alfred J. Vaughan; *Interpreter* Joel W. Barrow; *Blacksmiths* Robert Wilson and Robert Simerwell; *Assistant blacksmiths* Samuel L. Bertrand, Andrew Fuller (died August 5), Jonas P. Lykins (appointed August 6); *Millers* Jude W. Bourassa and Joel Grover; *Physician* Johnston Lykins. *Note: All of the above, except the subagent, were employed for the Pottawatomie Indians only.*

OSAGE SUBAGENCY [*Osages*]—*Subagent* Joel Cruttenden (removed—served to April 12), Samuel H. Bunch (appointed February 13); *Interpreter* Charles Mongrain (appointed in April); *Assistant blacksmiths* Henry Hill, Joseph Captain, T. R. Hunt, Francis Mitchell; *Gunsmith* John R. McKinney.

WYANDOT SUBAGENCY [*Wyandots*]—*Subagent* Richard Hewitt; *Interpreter* John M. Armstrong; *Blacksmith* Charles Graham; *Assistant blacksmith* Ira Hunter (appointed November 1).

SAC & FOX AGENCY [*Sacs & Foxes of the Mississippi—newly arrived, from Iowa*]—*Agent* John Beach; *Interpreter* Josiah Smart; *Gunsmiths* James Drake (resigned May 20) and Harvey Sturdevant; *Blacksmiths* Charles H. Withington and Arthur Ingraham Baker; *Assistant blacksmiths* Jonathan Parsons and James Garlick; *Physician* Volney Spalding (appointed April 8). *Note: Except for Spalding, all these persons had been employed for the Sacs & Foxes while in Iowa. The dates of original appointment to the positions held are listed below: Agent John Beach (May 29, 1844), Josiah Smart (July 1, 1839), James Drake (1842 or 1843), Harvey Sturdevant (September 15, 1835), Charles H. Withington (October 1, 1838), Arthur Ingraham Baker (November 1, 1844), Jonathan Parsons (August 1, 1840), and James Garlick (November 1, 1844).*

Ref: 29th Cong., 2d Sess., H. Doc. No. 36 (Serial 499), pp. 4-6; 30th Cong., 1st Sess., Sen. Ex. Doc. No. 48 (Serial 508), pp. 13, 58, 59, 67, 79, 80 (on p. 80 is item of payment of $83.33, under date of December 31, 1846, to Prudence Fuller, adm. for Andrew Fuller); 30th Cong., 1st Sess., H. Ex. Doc. No. 5 (Serial 514), pp. 28, 31, 32, 52, 56, 57, 133, 134; 30th Cong., 1st Sess., H. Ex. Doc. No. 26 (Serial 516), p. 6 (for J. P. Lykins, and Ira Hunter); 31st Cong., 1st Sess., H. Ex. Doc. No. 79 (Serial 579), p. 15 (for Charles Mongrain); SIA, St. Louis, "Records," v. 8, typed copy, pp. 524, 527, 528, 530, 556-558; OIA, "Letters Received from Sac & Fox Agency" (National Archives Microcopy 234, Roll 732), for Drake's May 20, 1846, letter; OIA, "Letters Received from Osage River Subagency" (National Archives Microcopy 234, Roll 643), for A. Fuller's death and Jonas Lykins' appointment.—See T. H. Harvey's January 26, 1847, letter.

1847

❡ January 8.—Snow on the "Kansas" plains was 10 inches deep. Bound for Santa Fe with dispatches (brought from Washington— see p. 660), Solomon P. Sublette (accompanied by Bill Garmon,

Fred Smith, and "an amateur") set out from Fort Leavenworth on muleback.

Sublette says: "I crossed the Kanzas river on the 11th near the Caw mission [on Mission creek, present Shawnee county] where I procured enough of corn for my mules untill we reached Council Grove. . . . I took the new[?] trail from Council Grove, and have found it better travelling for pack animals than the old road—more timber and better camping grounds."

At Pawnee Fork, on January 23, in "very cold and stormy" weather, the Sublette party met "twelve men [teamsters employed by "Harvey, of Boonville"] on foot returning from Santa Fé . . . [and] then 46 days out." Two had frozen feet. Their mules had been lost (part stolen; the rest dead from cold). The teamsters were given some provisions; and directed to Missouri by the nearest route. Evidently they carried Sublette's letter dated "Pawnee Fork, Jan. 24, 1847"—written in the midst of the *third* storm he had encountered since leaving Fort Leavenworth. In it he says: ". . . what I mean by *storm* one of those old-fashioned, searching visiters, peculiar to this region."

Early in February Sublette and companions reached Bent's Fort; and had to remain at "Ft. William" till February 17 because of the uprising in New Mexico. Sublette reached Taos on the 21st; and delivered the dispatches to Col. Sterling Price on February 23. (On March 26 he started back to Missouri —*see* April 21 entry.)

Ref: The quotes (combined above) are from Sublette's January 24, 1847, letter in the Saint Louis *Reveille*, March 4, 1847, and his May 1, 1847, account in Sublette mss., Missouri Historical Society, St. Louis—as published in L. H. Garrard's *Wah-to-yah and the Taos Trail*, ed. by R. P. Bieber (Glendale, Calif., 1938), pp. 200, 201; Saint Louis *Daily Union*, January 18, April 28, 1847; 30th Cong., 1st Sess., *H. Ex. Doc. No. 41* (Serial 517), p. 530; New York *Weekly Tribune*, April 24, 1847 (St. Louis *Weekly Reveille*, April 10).

❡ January.—The Osages' first grist and saw mills were completed and ready for use. They had been built by "Messrs. Foster and Redfield." Subagent Samuel H. Bunch appointed William S. Sims and R. B. Coleman as millers; L. Brenizier and Samuel Bevenue as assistant millers.

On January 18 Chiefs George White Hair, Clermont, Kahegahlangah (of the Little Osages), and Pa-ni-non-pa-sha (of the Big Hill band) wrote Sup't Thomas H. Harvey recommending Abraham Redfield, of Bates county, Mo., and Henry Clemens (Clements) to replace Sims and Coleman (who were Bunch's brother-in-law and son-in-law).

Ref: Office of Indian Affairs (OIA), "Letters Received from Osage Subagency," National Archives Microcopy 234, Roll 633 (the chiefs' letter of January 18, 1847, and Bunch's letter of February 22, 1847).

❡ Died: Francis Driver (Wyandot Indian), aged 45, on January 24, in present Wyandotte county. He was buried in Huron Place cemetery, in Kansas City, Kan., of today. (*See, also,* May 24 annals entry.)

Ref: William Walker's "Journals," in William E. Connelley, *The Provisional Government of Nebraska Territory and the Journals of William Walker* (Lincoln, Neb., 1899), p. 203.

❡ February 9, or 10.—Thomas O. Boggs, mail express from Santa Fe (which he had left about December 15, 1846), arrived at Fort Leavenworth. He, two assistants, and a five-man party headed by "Mr. Seymour of St. Louis," had traveled the trail during a period of severe cold weather; and walked all the way from Coon creek. (Seymour and his companions reached Independence, Mo., on February 10, looking "more like icicles of the north pole than human beings.")

As appears from three newspaper accounts, the Boggs-Seymour company came by way of Bent's Fort; found, at Chouteau's Island, some 80(?) teamsters (afoot; many too frostbitten to travel; and short of supplies); traveled through snow a foot and a half deep, in places, on the Arkansas; had nine mules stolen by Pawnees at Coon creek; and, by necessity, walked the rest of the way to the Missouri border.

Nearly 40 years later, Boggs recollected of this trip that they were caught in a blizzard the night of January 8, on the Arkansas. When the storm was over several mules were dead, and the rest had disappeared. Proceeding afoot, in deep snow, and after two weeks of wandering, "half frozen and nearly starved," they came upon a camp of Osages, who, says Boggs, "supplied us with a few ponies when we were rested sufficiently to go on. We followed the river down to the Caw [Kansa] village and here secured guides, two Indian boys, who escorted us across country to Ft. Leavenworth."

Ref: Saint Louis *Reveille* (daily), February 18, 1847; *Niles' National Register*, Baltimore, v. 72 (March 6, 1847), p. 7; New York *Weekly Tribune*, March 6, 1847; *The Gazette*, St. Joseph, February 26, 1847; Thomas O. Boggs' account, as published in Garrard, *op. cit.*, pp. 161-163; 30th Cong., 1st Sess., *H. Ex. Doc. No. 29* (Serial 516), p. 71 (for Boggs' contract to transport mail to Fort Leavenworth, and back to Santa Fe for the sum of $650— the government to furnish the necessary pack mules and subsistence; Boggs to supply, at his own expense, the men to make the round trip with him); *Missouri Republican*, St. Louis, February 19, 1847; *The Colorado Magazine*, Denver, v. 7, pp. 156, 157. Both February 9 and 10 are given as the date of Boggs' arrival at the fort.

❡ February 9 and 10.—Newsletters from Fort Leavenworth reported winter tragedies in "Kansas." Capt. Robert E. Clary (AQM) had sent "a few days since" to the Kansa village to bring in two men found on the prairie "half starved and frozen." Near Council Grove, at the foot of a tree (the bark eaten all around the trunk), had been found (by the Boggs-Seymour party) the bodies of two men (said to be "volunteers, one of them with 'D. B.' marked on his canteen"). At Diamond Spring, some weeks earlier, westbound Captain Murphy had come upon (and buried) two dead men.

Ref: New York *Weekly Tribune*, March 6, 13, 1847; *Niles' National Register*, v. 72 (March 6, 1847), p. 7.

❡ February 15.—Marvin L. Kritzer, of Independence, Mo., returned home from Santa Fe—which place he, and three companions, had left December 29, 1846. His party had suffered from the severe weather, but not from hunger. En route they had met no one!

On the 16th "another [small] company arrived from the plains," bringing Santa Fe mail with dates up to January 7.

Ref: Saint Louis *Daily Union,* February 25, March 2, 1847; *The Weekly Tribune,* Liberty, Mo., February 20, 1847; New York *Weekly Tribune,* March 13, 1847 (from a *Missouri Republican* extra of February 26 which mentioned "Mr. M. L. Kritser" a trader from Independence, and a "party of 9 men with 2 wagons direct from Santa Fe" (the second company?)—all from "B's" letter dated Independence, Mo., February 15. Martin L. Kritzer, grocer, aged 43, is in the 1850 U. S. census for Jackson county, Mo.

❡ About February 22(?) "Mr. [B. F.] Coons," a "young gentleman" of St. Louis, and three others, who had started from Santa Fe on January 14, reached the Missouri border. Their trip, by way of the Cimarron route, and for over 200 miles through deep snow, had been one of hardship and suffering. They had walked the last 200 miles, after their mules gave out.

As reported, they met on the way, government wagons which had left Fort Leavenworth on December 8, 1846; and found the teamsters in "very destitute condition"—20(?) having subsisted for 10 days on the meat of one mule.

Ref: Saint Louis *Reveille* (daily), February 26, 1847, or, New York *Weekly Tribune,* March 13, 1847. Coons had gone to Santa Fe the preceding summer—*see* annals, p. 637. Elihu H. Shepard in his *Autobiography* (1869), p. 147, refers to Coons as "Frank Coons."

❡ February 25.—John A. Mathews, of Missouri, was granted a two-year license to trade with the Great and Little Osage Indians, by Subagent Samuel H. Bunch. (The subagent noted that Mathews "has a trading house in the Creek and Quapaw nations.")

Ref: OIA, "Letters Received from Osage Subagency," National Archives Microcopy 234, Roll 633. (Bunch spelled the name "Mathes" in his letter of February 25, 1847.) John A. Mathews is the same "John Mathews" who was blacksmith for the Osages in 1841-1843.

❡ February 28.—The *Amelia* (which passed the mouth of the Kansas on the 27th) reached Weston, Mo. She was the first of 182 steamboats recorded as arriving there in 1847. (By the same record, 47 upbound steamboats went to points beyond Weston during this year.)

Ref: *The Western Journal,* St. Louis, v. 5 (March, 1851), p. 326; William Walker's "Journals," *loc. cit.,* p. 195; *KHC,* v. 9, p. 298; annals, p. 641; Saint Louis *Daily Union,* March 2, 1847 (says the Boonville [Mo.] *Bulletin* of February 25 announced the *Amelia's* arrival at Boonville on the 23d as "the first boat to go so far up the Missouri this season").

❡ March 1.—Lt. James W. Abert (of the topographical engineers; recently at Santa Fe; now en route to Washington, D. C.) arrived at Fort Leavenworth after an adversity-filled winter journey across "Kansas." He, and 14 well-armed companions, with two mule-drawn wagons, had set out from Bent's Fort on January 20.

Abert's party included men named Pilka, Laing, Brown, Preston, Wiseman, Pilcher, and J. Dobson. Four of their mules froze to death during a "norther," on February 1; the rest were stolen by Pawnees on the 6th. From this raided camp (near "Jackson's grove" on the Arkansas) they subsequently hauled one wagon (containing essential provisions, Abert's New Mexico-gathered mineralogical specimens, and a sick man—Pilcher) for 65 miles (by the river route) to Pawnee Fork, using two "broken down" oxen (found on the trail), and with the men also "in the traces" pulling. An oddity of this march was that, on February 9, after a parley with 17 "friendly" Pawnees, Abert shared his tent overnight with the chief and five attendants!

At Pawnee Fork (on February 12) Brown, Preston, and the sick man, Pilcher, remained to await the expected mail express. The others forged on. At Cow creek, on the 17th, they were overtaken by the Hoffman-Miller party (*see* next entry), and by the mail express headed by James Brown (*see* p. 666). Abert's and Brown's combined company was at the head of Turkey creek on February 19 when caught in a blizzard. During the 36-hour storm, Pilcher died (he was carried to Cottonwood Fork for burial); and James Brown lost eight mules. Abert wrote: "I had to dig some of my men out of the snow, that lay above them to the depth of 5 feet."

On reaching Cottonwood Fork, after a difficult 27-mile march on the 22d, they found "Mr. Smith" (a government wagonmaster) who had plenty of provisions for them. From that point (leaving the rest to accompany Brown's party), Abert and Smith went on in advance. ("Mr. Smith made me mount his horse, while he journeyed on foot," wrote the lieutenant.) They overtook the Hoffman-Miller party; camped at Council Grove on the 24th, and at "110 creek" on the 26th; left the Santa Fe trail at "Willow spring" (after traveling 25 miles on the 27th), to take the branch road to Fort Leavenworth.

On February 28 they reached the Kansas river (at the Wakarusa's mouth); found it full of ice; got to the opposite bank by the "perseverance and good management" of Smith, who maneuvered a flatboat across (after the Indian ferrymen on the other side failed to operate their craft). Abert arrived at the fort the next afternoon (after a night's camp by the river).

Ref: 30th Cong., 1st Sess., *H. Ex. Doc. No. 41* (Serial 517), pp. 507-546 (for Abert's journal); James W. Abert, *Western America in 1846-1847,* . . . *Travel Diary* . . ., edited by John Galvin (San Francisco, 1966); Saint Louis *Daily Union,* March 9, 11, 1847 (for Abert's letter from "Turkey Creek" [Kansas], February 20, 1847, to Robert Campbell); Saint Louis *Reveille* (daily), March 11, 1847; New York *Weekly Tribune,* April 3, 1847 (from *Missouri Republican,* St. Louis, March 11).

❡ March 1.—There arrived at Independence, Mo., Mr. H. Hoffman, of Baltimore, Md., Mr. [Henry C.] Miller, of Saline county, Mo., Mr. Harris, and one or more others, who had left Santa Fe on January 13. This party (evidently traveling by way of Bent's Fort), brought to Missouri first news of the uprising at Taos (the killing of Gov. Charles Bent, and others) on January 19.

The Hoffman-Miller party suffered from the bitter cold weather encountered on the "Kansas" plains; ran short of food; and after enduring a 36-hour blizzard (on February 19 and 20), east of Turkey creek, "had been obliged to leave their wagon, and pack all their camp furniture on their mules."

Ref: *Jefferson Inquirer,* Jefferson City, Mo., March 6, 1847; *The Weekly Tribune,* Liberty, Mo., March 6, 1847; Saint Louis *Reveille* (daily), March 9, 1847; New York *Weekly Tribune,* March 27, April 3, 1847; 30th Cong., 1st Sess., *H. Ex. Doc. No. 41* (Serial 517), pp. 540-546.

❧ Early in March mail-carrier James Brown reached Fort Leavenworth, by way of Bent's Fort, from Santa Fe (which he had left on January 9). He (and his party) traveled with at least one wagon.

At Pawnee Fork (in mid-February) Brown had picked up three of Lieutenant Abert's party (*see* March 1 entry); and on February 17 he had overtaken, and assisted, Abert and the rest of his company. During the 36-hour blizzard of February 19-20 (while camped with Abert on Turkey creek), Brown lost eight mules (frozen to death). He reached Fort Leavenworth (soon?) after Abert.

Ref: Saint Louis *Daily Union*, March 9, 1847 (Abert's February 20, 1847, letter); 30th Cong., 1st Sess., *H. Ex. Doc. No. 41* (Serial 517), pp. 541, 542 (Abert's report); *Niles' National Register*, v. 72 (April 3, 1847), p. 73 (for reprint of a letter dated "Bent's Fort, February 1, 1847," which begins: "By an express from Santa Fe, en route for Fort Leavenworth, I avail myself of writing you . . ."; Saint Louis *Reveille* (daily), March 9, 1847 (notes anticipated arrival of the "express" at St. Louis on March 10).

❧ March 3.—A statute passed this day "impressed a lasting mark upon federal Indian law," and "amended in various respects the comprehensive legislation of June 30, 1834." (*See* pp. 271, 272, for some provisions of the 1834 act.)

One amendment was a "broadening of the language of the Indian liquor legislation"; another "relaxed the requirement that had been established by the 1834 legislation to the effect that moneys due tribes should be paid to tribal officers [*i. e.*, the chiefs], and authorized payments of such moneys 'to the heads of families and other individuals entitled to participate therein.' This, in effect, substituted the judgment of federal officials for that of tribal government on the question of tribal membership, so far as the disposition of funds was concerned. This provision was the first in a long series of statutes designed to individualize tribal property."

[By illegal means and disgraceful connivance the "Mississippi" Sac & Fox Indians' traders managed to thwart application of the latter amendment in the payment of annuities in 1847 (so that they might collect large debts owed by the tribal chiefs)—*see* September 20 entry.]

Ref: The quotations above are from Felix Cohen's *Handbook of Federal Indian Law* . . . (Washington, 1942), p. 76.

❧ March 3.—"Steamboat *John J. Hardin* came up."—William Walker's journal entry. This was the second arrival of the year at the Kansas river's mouth. The *Hardin* went on up to Weston, Mo.; left there March 4; and was back at St. Louis on March 10.

Ref: Walker's "Journals," *loc. cit.*; Saint Louis *Daily Union*, March 11, 1847; New York *Weekly Tribune*, April 3, 1847 (from *Missouri Republican*, St. Louis, March 11—which noted the arrival of Lt. James W. Abert—*see* annals, p. 664—and H. Hoffman—*see* p. 665 —on the *J. J. Hardin*); Saint Louis *Reveille* (daily), February 10, 1847 (which reported John T. Douglas[s] had purchased this boat, in February, for $14,000).

❧ MARRIED: Willson A. Scott, Sac & Fox trader, and Mrs. Louisa

Laclair (Le Clerc), on March 4, at Ottawa Baptist Mission (present Franklin county), by the Rev. Jotham Meeker.

Ref: Jotham Meeker's "Diary" (in KHi ms. division); *Annals of Iowa*, Des Moines, 3d ser., v. 13 (April, 1922), pp. 243-262 (for an article on "Willson Alexander Scott"). W. A. Scott and his cousin John B. Scott were Iowans who traded with the "Mississippi" Sacs & Foxes in Iowa, and then, for a time, in "Kansas" after the Indians removed westward in 1845-1846.—*See* annals, p. 579. The marriage is recorded in "Jackson County [Mo.] Marriage Records," v. 2, p. 140.

❡ On March 11(?) 2d Lt. John O. Simpson (a Missouri volunteer —*see* p. 660), with "two wagons and 10 men, conducting a heavy mail," left Fort Leavenworth for Santa Fe. In mid-month he was at 110-mile creek (where eastbound Thomas J. Caldwell met him).

Apparently this was the express which had been scheduled to leave March 1 (but delayed starting due to bad weather?). Thomas O. Boggs—*see* p. 663—whose mail contract was for a round-trip, and who evidently returned with Simpson, later said he left the fort for Taos on March 11.

Ref: Saint Louis *Reveille* (daily), February 2, March 31, June 2, 1847; Saint Louis *Daily Union*, February 22, 1847; *Missouri Republican*, St. Louis, August 11, 1847 (for return of Simpson to Fort Leavenworth on August 6); David Lavender's *Bent's Fort* (1954), p. 410, note 3 (item on Boggs); *Niles' National Register*, v. 72 (July 17, 1847), p. 320 (for item that "Mr. [Thomas O.] Boggs" was, on June 3, in the Taos, N. M., area, serving as guide to Lt. Col. David Willock).

❡ March 19.—Andrews Drips (former Indian agent; now in charge of the American Fur Company's Fort Pierre) arrived at the mouth of the Kansas from the upper Missouri post, "having made the entire trip by land, during an unusually inclement season." (He had set out from Fort Pierre on February 27.)

En route, Drips had "passed through numerous Mormon settlements or camps from Poncha Creek down as far as Cabanne's old farm, below Council Bluffs." Whether, from that area, he traveled down the right bank of the Missouri (and across "Kansas"), or, as is more likely, along the left bank (through northwestern Missouri), is not stated.

Ref: Saint Louis *Daily Union*, March 30, 1847; John Palliser's *Solitary Rambles . . .* (London, 1853), p. 104 (for 1847 reference to Andrew Drips being in command at Fort Pierre).

❡ Mid-March.—Keokuk (head chief of the "Mississippi" Sacs) and 10 of his nation left their "Kansas" reserve to visit St. Louis— arriving there March 23 aboard the *Amelia*.

The Saint Louis *Daily Union* of March 25, stated: "To-night we are informed that the celebrated Indian Chief Keokuk with 10 warriors will appear at the Circus."

(Reproduced in this volume, p. 809, is a daguerreotype of Keokuk, made at St. Louis, in 1847, presumably in March, by Thomas M. Easterly.)

Ref: Saint Louis *Daily Union*, March 24, 25, 1847; *The Bulletin*, Missouri Historical Society, St. Louis, v. 24 (July, 1968), p. 332. The departure homeward of "celebrated" chiefs Keokuk and "Appanoose-o-Keemar" on the *Amelia*, March 27, was noted in the Saint Louis *Reveille* (daily) of March 28, 1847.

❦ March 25.—Leonidas Vaughan, appointed March 8 (by Indian agents and commissioners John Beach and Alfred J. Vaughan), began a survey of the small (13-section; 8,320-acre) reserve belonging to the Chippewas of Swan creek and Black river (immigrants to "Kansas" in 1839—*see* pp. 331, 384).

This reserve (in present Franklin county) adjoined, on the west, the recently arrived "Mississippi" Sacs' & Foxes' land; on the east the Chippewas' neighbors were the Ottawas, residents since the 1830's.

Ref: OIA, "Letters Received from Superintendency of Indian Affairs (SIA), St. Louis (National Archives Microcopy 234, Roll 754).

❦ March 25.—Trader Thomas J. Caldwell, who had started from Santa Fe on February 3, and traveled the Cimarron route, arrived at Independence, Mo. He was some 10 to 12 days (as supposed) in advance of his company (12 men with several wagons, carrying a large mail) which he had left (evidently snow-stalled) 25 miles east of the Arkansas crossing. He reported that snow had fallen "almost uninterruptedly" on the plains from February 16 to March 10. (Caldwell reached St. Louis, aboard the *Bertrand,* March 30.)

Ref: Saint Louis *Daily Union,* March 30, 31, April 1, 1847; *The Weekly Tribune,* Liberty, Mo., March 27, 1847; Saint Louis *Reveille* (daily), March 30, 31, April 10, 1847. A passenger on the *Amelia,* arriving at St. Louis on April 9, reported that the mail Caldwell had left on the plains had reached Independence.

❦ Late in March, near "Hickory Point" (in present Douglas county), Missouri-bound Santa Fe trader Norris Colburn was murdered. But several weeks elapsed before his body was found (by a search party, early in May) in a ravine, wrapped in a blanket, and weighted down with stones. By report, people on the frontier thought he had not been killed by Indians.

Colburn was traveling alone at the time. His brother-in-law, Eugene Leitensdorfer, carrying the large sum of money they had brought from New Mexico, had forged ahead from "Elm Grove" (65 miles out) after Colburn's mule gave out. (*See, also,* March 31 entry.) For a time, suspicion fell on Leitensdorfer. Apparently the case was solved in 1849. Sac & Fox agent Charles N. Handy (in his annual report for that year) stated: "During my spring payment I arrested one of the murderers of Mr. Colburn. . . . His accomplice was found in the Pottawatomie Nation. There is no doubt of their guilt and they . . . will be tried in April [1850] at St. Louis." The accused were Sac Indians (according to Sup't D. D. Mitchell, St. Louis).

Ref: Saint Louis *Daily Union,* April 17, 19, May 3, 6, 7, 11, 1847; *The Weekly Tribune,* Liberty, Mo., May 15, 1847; Saint Louis *Reveille* (daily), April 10, 18, 1847; St. Louis *Daily New Era,* September 15, 1849; New York *Weekly Tribune,* July 14, 1849; St. Joseph (Mo.) *Gazette,* July 20, 1849 (which says the Indians were Foxes); Comm'r of Indian Affairs, *Report,* 1849 (Handy's report, therein); SIA, St. Louis, "Records," v. 9, typed copy, p. 424 (for Mitchell); *Kansas Historical Collections (KHC),* v. 11, p. 344. *The Weekly Tribune,* Liberty, Mo., August 31, 1849, has article from Independence *Expositor* re the dragoons having brought in two "Fox" Indians "suspected" of Colburn's murder. In SIA,

St. Louis, "Records," v. 9, typed copy, p. 424, D. D. Mitchell (April 11, 1850) refers to a Sac woman as chief witness against the two accused Sacs.

❡ March 31.—Among the men arriving at Independence, Mo., from Santa Fe, were George H. Peacock and Alonzo P. Kean (traders; and Jackson county, Mo., residents), "Major Ewing of Lafayette," and "Orderly Sgt. White of Major [M. Lewis] Clark's [Missouri volunteers] batt[alio]n," also men named Hambright and Hudspeth.

Apparently this was the company (long delayed by snow and cold en route) departing Santa Fe on February 3, with which trader Caldwell traveled to the Arkansas (see March 25 entry), and traders Colburn and Leitensdorfer accompanied as far as Walnut creek (see p. 668). However, since "news up to the 28th ult. [i. e., February] from Col. [Sterling] Price" was brought by this party, some of the personnel must have left Santa Fe at the end of February, and overtaken the wagon company.

Ref: Saint Louis Reveille (daily), April 10, 1847; Saint Louis Daily Union, April 19, 1847. Ebenezer W. Pomeroy, in a letter written at Santa Fe on May 29, 1847, referred to his having (earlier) sent $16,000 of James Aull's money east "by Ewing."—Missouri Historical Society Collections, St. Louis, v. 5 (June, 1928), p. 295. "Hambright" was Amos Hambright of Buchanan county, Mo., who died in Chihuahua in October, 1849.— See St. Joseph (Mo.) Gazette, January 11, 1850.

❡ April.—On the 1st, Thomas C. Gordon contracted to deliver fresh beef at Fort Leavenworth (beginning that day); on April 15 "W. W. Wadell" (William B. Waddell?) contracted to supply flour at the fort on May 15. Lt. William E. Prince, AQM, was the negotiating officer.

Ref: 30th Cong., 2d Sess., Sen. Ex. Doc. No. 17 (Serial 529), pp. 9, 10.

❡ DIED: William Miles Chick, pioneer merchant of Westport, Mo., and of Kansas [City], Mo., on April 7. He had removed from Howard county, Mo., to Westport in 1836; and had built a warehouse early in 1844 at Kansas, Mo. (see p. 360).

Ref: William Walker's "Journals," loc. cit., KHC, v. 9, pp. 178, 281, 282 (for Joseph S. Chick's recollections).

❡ April.—On the Santa Fe trail, near the Arkansas, and within sight of "The Caches" (west of present Dodge City), a small stockaded government depot—Mann's Fort (or, "Fort Mann")—was in process of erection. Its builders were civilians—a party of 40 teamsters, headed by wagonmaster Daniel P. Mann (see p. 652)— sent there by Capt. W. M. D. McKissack (army quartermaster at Santa Fe), who (later) wrote of his project: "Owing to the great number of Wagons abandoned on the plains I made arrangements to erect Wheelwright, Smith, & Store houses near [i. e., some 20? miles below] the crossing of the Arkansas: the work was performed by Teamsters, and occupied by them."

Mann's Fort (about 60 feet square, with walls 20 feet high) consisted of "four log houses, connected by angles of timber framework, in which were cut loop-holes for the cannon and small arms." The flat roofs were "made of small poles, laid parallel, with six inches of mud piled on." Not until May 16 were the "large gates— two ponderous wooden puncheon concerns, a foot in thickness" placed in position and secured on their hinges; and the making of adobes (mud bricks) for chimneys and breastworks continued, intermittently, up to mid-June. On June 23 Mann's Fort was abandoned. Though used as a refuge, subsequently, during the summer, it was not reoccupied *as a post*, till November. During its first brief occupancy there were no military tenants. (Pvt. E. N. O. Clough who examined "Fort Mann" on July 24, wrote: "It is a log fort, eight buildings and log walls, connecting angles, &c., &c." Indian agent Thomas Fitzpatrick, in a December 18 report, commented: "Fort Mann . . . is nothing more than rough, uneven, and very crooked cotton wood logs, raised eight or ten feet high, without form or design. . . .") The following chronology lists events connected with the first phase of the "fort's" history.

Late April—The Peck-McKnight party (*see* p. 682), harassed by Indians, fell back to Mann's Fort (apparently) till the Carson-Beale-Talbot party arrived. *May 9.*—Comanches killed and scalped a teamster fishing in the Arkansas, in sight of his comrades within the stockade. *May 11.*—Indians stampeded, and carried off, 15 yokes of oxen and 40 mules. *May 15.*—Captain Enos' train (*see* p. 687) arrived from Bent's Fort, bringing a "sixpounder," and a new "commander" (John S. Smith—*see* p. 688) for Mann's Fort; also, Lewis H. Garrard, of Enos' party, volunteered for employment there. *May 16.*— Enos' train departed; and with it went Daniel P. Mann and 25(?) of Mann's Fort's builders. The "garrison" left there consisted of 10 well men and three sick ones; the other occupants were Smith's Cheyenne wife and two children, Raymond's "half-breed Rosalie," a few mules, horses, and steers, and a dog. *May 20.*—Callahan's eastbound train passed by; one man joined the garrison. *May 24.*—Bent, St. Vrain & Co's. train, and Tharp (*see* p. 686) stopped briefly; when they left, so did John S. Smith (and family). Thomas Sloan assumed command of the stockade. *May 26.*—Some Arapahoes attempted to run off the animals. In a parley with the would-be raiders the fort's occupants were told the Comanches planned to wipe them out. *May 28.*—About 300 Arapahoes (80 lodges) arrived; set up a village within cannon-range; soon struck camp and moved half a mile away. Fowler's government train, from Santa Fe, arrived and corralled near the gate. One man—John Nagle—joined the garrison. In mid-afternoon a company of Santa Fe-bound traders (the parties which left Missouri late in April—*see* p. 674) arrived and camped close by. Their train had been harassed for three days by Comanches and the above-noted Arapahoes. *May 29.*—The two trains (totaling some 120 men, and 60 wagons) departed—one heading east (the three sick men at the fort leaving with it), the other going west. *May 30.*—Ceran St. Vrain and party (*see* p. 690) arrived and camped overnight near by.

June 11(?)—"Mr. Coolidge [or, Goodrich?], with four wagons and five men from the Arkansas Pueblo and the Platte, arrived"; and decided to remain till reinforced. *June 15.*—Lewis H. Garrard celebrated his 18th birthday; also the Russell-Bell company (*see* p. 693) came from the west, and camped near "The Caches." *June 16.*—The Russell-Bell train departed; with it went "Coolidge's" party, and Lewis H. Garrard (who had spent a month at Mann's Fort). *June 19-21.*—About 400 Indians made several attacks on the post. Thomas Sloan and nine others inside, with effective use of the cannon, killed 15 of the Comanches (and Arapahoes?); wounded some 30 to 40 more. Three defenders (Johnson, of Independence; Roy, of Lexington; and John Nagle, of Linn county, Mo.) who went outside the stockade were killed (and scalped) before going 300 yards. *June 23*(?)—On or by this date the seven remaining Mann's Fort occupants destroyed much of the stockade's contents (throwing some stores into the well); rigged up two teams; placed the cannon at the forefront; joined a passing Santa Fe-bound train; and "left the fort to the mercies of the Indians." On June 26, on the Jornada, Houck's eastbound company met two government trains, accompanied by the seven men from Mann's Fort, with their cannon.

Ref: Garrard, *op. cit.*, pp. 35, 36, 325-359; New York *Weekly Tribune*, June 5 (from *Missouri Republican*, St. Louis, May 18), July 31, 1847; Saint Louis *Daily Union*, July 19, 1847; *The Weekly Tribune*, Liberty, Mo., July 17, 1847 (from *Missouri Republican*, July 19?); Saint Louis *Reveille* (daily), July 18, 1847; *Democratic Standard*, Leavenworth, August 10, 1883 (for Clough); *The Westerners New York Posse Brand Book*, v. 10, no. 4 (1963), p. 76 (for Fitzpatrick).

❦ April.—At Council Grove, on the Santa Fe trail, traders (Albert G.) Boone & (James G.) Hamilton, of Westport, Mo., opened a store (by virtue of their Kansa trading license), placing bachelor Seth M. Hays in charge. (Boone & Hamilton's announcement in the Saint Louis *Reveille* is reproduced in this volume.)

Several Santa Fe trail travelers of 1847 recorded the changing scene at Council Grove. (Compare the following with descriptions of 1846, on pp. 628 and 629.)

George F. Ruxton (British traveler and sportsman; eastbound in May), in a later-written narrative (after noting that "Council Grove is one of the most beautiful spots in the western country," and further describing the locale), commented: "A trader [*i. e.*, Seth Hays] amongst the Caw Indians had erected himself a log house at the grove, which appeared to us a magnificent palace. Himself, his cows and horses, looked so fat and sleek, that we really thought them unnaturally so. [Ruxton had spent a rugged winter in the Rocky mountains.] . . . There was one lodge of Caw Indians at the grove, the big village being out on the prairie, hunting buffalo. . . ."

E. N. O. Clough (Missouri volunteer in "Easton's" battalion; westbound) reached Council Grove on July 2: "There are here [he wrote] three new log houses and several bark wigwams. . . . There is a trader here who is making money hand over hand. . . . Here are some of his prices, molasses, $2 per gallon, cheese 35 cents per pound, tobacco 75 cents a plug and rotten at that, shoes, a very course brogan, $3.50 per pair. There is also a black-smith shop here and his prices are just about as reasonable as the trader's."

Richard S. Elliott (a "Laclede Rangers" lieutenant—*see* p. 594—now re-turning to St. Louis) in a July 13 letter at Independence, Mo. (using the pseudonym "John Brown"), stated: "I wrote you [on July 8] from the trading station of Messrs. Boone & Hamilton at Council Grove, where Mr. Hays is in charge. Mr. H. treated us with all attention. We found corn bread, milk, butter, &c., which go very well, I assure you, after a journey like ours. The houses have shingle roofs. . . ."

A *correspondent* of the *Missouri Republican,* St. Louis, wrote, in July: "Council Grove is a cluster of timber skirting a small stream. . . . It is 126 miles from Fort Leavenworth. The Govt. has a smith shop here, for the purpose of repairing wagons, shoeing horses, &c. There is also a store and dwelling, owned by whites, and 20 or 30 Indian wigwams. . . ."

Philip G. Ferguson (Missouri volunteer in "Ralls'" regiment; westbound) camped on July 15 and 16 "at the famous Council Grove." He noted: "Near the Grove are numerous mounds, some of them nearly 100 feet high, the graves of red men. . . . There is a village of Kaw here—a dirty, lazy set, whose doleful songs at night disturbed my slumbers. . . . there is a store owned by a white man, and a government blacksmith shop."

Ref: Saint Louis *Reveille* (daily), April 23 and 24, 1847 (for comment on Boone & Hamilton's advertisement; and first appearance of the "ad"—on page 2, column 4, bottom of page); George F. Ruxton's *Adventures in Mexico and the Rocky Mountains,* new ed. (London, 1861), pp. 308, 309; *Democratic Standard,* Leavenworth, August 10, 17, 1883 (for Clough's diary-and-letters extracts); Saint Louis *Reveille* (daily), July 20, 1847 (for Elliott's letter); *Missouri Republican,* St. Louis, July 31, 1847 (for next-to-last item above), as reprinted in Nebraska State Historical Society *Publications,* Lincoln, v. 20, p. 173; P. G. Ferguson's "Diary," in R. P. Bieber, editor, *Marching With the Army of the West, 1846-1848,* v. 4 of *The Southwest Historical Series* (Glendale, Cal., 1936), pp. 299, 300. Seth M. Hays, a Council Grove resident from 1847 till his death in 1873, was a son of William Hays, Jr. (whose parents were William and Susannah [Boone] Hays). Susannah Boone was a daughter of frontiersman Daniel Boone and Rebecca (Bryan) Boone.—Lilian Hays Oliver's *Some Boone Descendants and Kindred of the St. Charles District* (1964), pp. 16, 265-267.

❡ April 16.—Capt. Joseph La Barge's "fine new boat"—the *Martha* (a side-wheeler)—arrived at St. Joseph, Mo. (en route to Council Bluffs?), on her initial voyage up the Missouri. (*See, also,* May 22 entry.)

The *Martha's* dimensions: keel, 150 feet; on deck, 170 feet; beam 26 feet; hold five feet. Her hull had been built in Cincinnati; the cabin and machinery at St. Louis. She had two engines. Her draught was a "scant two feet."

Ref: St. Louis *Daily Union,* March 24, 1847; *The Gazette,* St. Joseph, Mo., April 16, 1847. The *Gazette's* issues of April 23 and 30 carried an advertisement that the *Martha* ("Robert Labard, master"[?]) would run as a regular packet between St. Louis and St. Joseph. But *see* May 22 annals entry. H. M. Chittenden, in his *Early Steamboat Navigation on the Missouri River* (1903), v. 1, p. 179, says the *Martha* was a side-wheeler.

❡ April 16.—Headed by Brigham Young, a Mormon "pioneer band" of 148 persons (143 men and boys, three women, and two children), with 72 wagons, and livestock, set out from a camp in eastern "Nebraska" (about 47 miles from the Mormon "Winter Quarters" on the Missouri) to find a new home for the Saints in the West. Their route (north of the Platte and its North Fork) from Council Bluffs to Fort Laramie came to be known as the Mormon trail.

The "pioneer band" reached Fort Laramie on June 1; crossed South Pass on June 26 and 27; and the first of these Mormons entered the Great Salt Lake valley on July 21.

Starting some two months later ("about the 1st of July the emigration was fairly under way") "upwards to 2,000" Mormons, with 566 wagons, left the same "Nebraska" camp area; followed the route of the "pioneer band"; began arriving at Salt Lake in mid-September; and by mid-October the last of these westbound Mormon emigrants of 1847 had completed the 1,032-mile journey to "Utah."

Ref: *Historical Record*, Salt Lake City, v. 9 (January, 1890); *Annals of Wyoming*, v. 21 (July-October, 1949), p. 130 (for addition, at Fort Laramie, of three Mormon families—some of the "Mississippi Saints" who had wintered at Pueblo [Colo.]), and p. 152 (for item that the final pioneer band total was 77 wagons and one cart).

❡ April 21.—Solomon P. Sublette, direct from Santa Fe with government dispatches and mail, arrived at Fort Leavenworth. (For his trip *to* Santa Fe *see* January 8 annals entry.)

Sublette had left Santa Fe March 26, with two men and six mules; and was joined on the 27th by mountain man Joseph R. Walker and two companions. The arrival at Independence, Mo., on April 18 of a "small party that accompanied an express in" [*i. e.,* Walker's party] was noted by a local correspondent (writing on April 22). Sublette, aboard the *Amaranth* (from Fort Leavenworth?) reached St. Louis on April 28. The *Reveille* said he had "lost but two mules, a mess pan, and a lariat rope," on the "trip out and in"; and that "considering the season, the distance, and the dangers together," Sublette's "feat of safely bearing these despatches will compare with any thing on record."

Ref: Solomon Sublette's May 4, 1847, letter (in "Sublette Collection," Missouri Historical Society, St. Louis); Saint Louis *Reveille* (daily), April 24, 28, 1847; Saint Louis *Daily Union*, April 28, 1847; New York *Weekly Tribune*, May 15, 1847 (from *Missouri Republican*, St. Louis, April 28).

❡ April 27.—"Mr. Cuniffe" (Henry J. Cuniffe), of St. Louis, a trader who had been out of the States for "some two years," arrived at Independence, Mo., after a 22-day journey across the plains with one companion—his Mexican servant boy. They had left Santa Fe on April 5; and had "met with but little adventure." Cuniffe reached St. Louis May 10.

Ref: Saint Louis *Daily Union*, May 3, 8, 11, 1847; Saint Louis *Reveille* (daily), May 11, 1847. The dates above are from the *Union's* May 8 issue which quoted the Independence *Expositor's* May 1, issue.

❡ April(?)—Apparently in advance of other Santa Fe-bound traders, "Mr. Brown" left Independence "with a few wagons" en route to New Mexico. By mid-May there was concern for him, on the

Missouri border, when incoming parties reported they had not seen his party on the trail.

At Westport, Mo., on May 22, A. G. Boone wrote: ". . . rumor says that he [Brown] was robbed and lost two men[?] with all his wagons, stores, &c., having reached Bent's Fort with the rest of his party with safety." At Independence, Mo., about the same time, J. McKnight "learned" that Brown had been robbed, on the Arkansas, by Comanches[?], who had taken his oxen and such portion of his goods (which belonged to "Rich & Pomeroy") as they wanted. The St. Louis *Union,* on June 1, reported: "Mr. Mead from the plains says he met Mr. Brown near Pawnee Fork and the latter says he had been captured by the Pawnees, robbed and whipped and would have been killed but for the intervention of the principal Indians. Mr. B. succeeded in escaping and his clothes were finally restored to him."

In no account is "Mr. Brown" further identified. Probably he was **the** James Brown who had brought in the mail from Santa Fe in March—*see* p. 666, or the "Judge or Col. [James] Brown" of Eastin's party—July 23 entry.

Ref: *Missouri Republican,* St. Louis, May 18, 1847 (reprinted in New York *Weekly Tribune,* June 5, 1847); Saint Louis *Reveille* (daily), May 28, 1847; Saint Louis *Daily Union,* May 22, June 1, 1847.

❡ April—Charles Primeau, of Harvey, Primeau & Company, who had left the company's trading post at the mouth of Medicine creek (some 1,500 miles up the Missouri) on April 6, and descended the river (with a few others?) in a skiff, as far as Fort Leavenworth, was a passenger on the *Archer* arriving at St. Louis (from the army post) about the end of April.

Ref: Saint Louis *Daily Union,* April 30, 1847. For "Charles" Primeau, *see* Charles Larpenteur's *Forty Years a Fur Trader* (1898), v. 1, p. 227; Historical Society of Montana, *Contributions,* v. 10 (1940), p. 305.

❡ April.—Santa Fe traders leaving western Missouri around the end of the month included James C. Bean, Thomas G. Clarkson, and "Reynolds" (all from Jackson county, Mo.), McCauly & Shaw, Dr. [G. W.?] Hereford (of St. Louis), Bullard, Hooke & Co. (of Lexington, Mo.).

News reached Missouri that Bullard, Hooke & Co.'s wagons, and two other trains, were at Pawnee Fork in mid-May "waiting on account of high water." Bean's partner (on June 25, at St. Louis) heard that 1,000[!] Indians had attacked the traders on the Arkansas, compelling them to corral for three days. But "Christopher" wrote (after reaching Santa Fe) that, at Coon creek: "We awoke one morning and found ourselves surrounded by near 700 well mounted warriors [Arapahoes and Comanches] with more than 400 formidable weapons called lances; and we were only thirty fighting men strong. . . . we owe our lives to Capt. Thomas G. Clarkson . . . whose knowledge of the Indian character caused him to turn the three first scoundrels that came to us into the correl formed by our wagons, and disarmed them. . . . [One attempted to escape and was shot down.] On the next day we wounded several others, and fought them every day for about 70 miles. . . . there was little sleeping done in our camp from Pawnee Fork to the crossing of Big Arkansas River; here the Indians left us . . . [But] In the *Jornada* . . . we met with . . . [270] renegade Mexicans [and had to be on the defensive against them]. . . . We arrived at Santa Fe on the 25th of June, after a trip of 58 days from Independence, losing 51 head of oxen, stolen . . . on Coon Creek, and some 20 were lost for want of grass . . . [in New Mexico]." About June 19(?), at "Ocate, near the wagon mound," an eastbound party had met "McDowell, Herriford [Hereford] and others," who had "preserved stock enough to get through."

It would appear that most (or all?) of the above-mentioned traders were in the company which arrived at Mann's Fort on May 28 (and camped overnight) whose train had been harassed for three days by Indians (*see* p. 670).

Ref: Saint Louis *Daily Union*, May 8, 11, 29, June 2, 26, September 7, 1847; New York *Weekly Tribune*, September 18, 1847 (from *Missouri Republican*, St. Louis, September 7); *The Weekly Tribune*, Liberty, Mo., July 17, 1847; *History of Saline County, Missouri* . . . (St. Louis, 1881), p. 694. Dr. G. W. Hereford, a St. Louis Medical College graduate, had moved to Saline county, Missouri, in 1844.

❡ From April 28 to June 15, Bvt. Maj. (John M.) Scott was commandant at Fort Leavenworth. Lt. Col. Clifton Wharton, in this interval, was at St. Louis (or, Jefferson Barracks) for the purpose of mustering in Missouri volunteer companies for Mexican War service.

Ref: Saint Louis *Daily Union*, May 6 (notes Wharton's presence at St. Louis), 26 (a Fort Leavenworth letter writer notes return of Wharton on June 15), 1847. Reference is made in the letter that during his absence "Bvt. Major Scott" had been commandant. John M. Scott, since September 23, 1846, had been brevet major in the First U. S. infantry; and one company of the First infantry was at Fort Leavenworth in 1847. Fort Leavenworth post returns (microfilm in KHi).

❡ April 30.—Francis X. Aubry, carrying mail to Santa Fe, set out from "town of Kansas" (Kansas City, Mo.). His trading goods had been sent on ahead three days earlier.

Aubry was met (about June 25?, or 26th), south of the Arkansas, by Houck's eastbound train. He warned the eastbound travelers of hostile Indians ahead. One of his men (name not reported) had been killed and scalped a few rods from the train (place not indicated). With Aubry were two men he had rescued from Mann's Fort, where they had defended themselves for nearly two days, after being chased by Indians while trying to overtake a party in advance of them. This would indicate Aubry's train passed Mann's Fort no earlier than June 24—*if* it was not abandoned by Sloan (and the six others "garrisoning" the post) until June 23.

Ref: *The Pacific Historian*, Stockton, Cal., v. 5 (August, 1961), pp. 111-123 (for article on Aubry); James J. Webb's *Adventures in the Santa Fé Trade* (1931), p. 287.

❡ May.—The Oregon-California migration which crossed "Kansas" in the spring of 1847 was (1) considerably (perhaps by 2,000 persons) larger than in 1846; (2) nearly all of it was bound for Oregon; (3) about two-thirds of the traffic crossed the Missouri at St. Joseph—or in that area (whereas in 1846 nearly half the emigrants had started from Independence, Mo.).

As for its size, a June issue of the St. Joseph *Gazette* stated, flatly, that 867 wagons (704 of them prior to May 28) had crossed "at this point" (but evidently including area ferries), and 433 had crossed at Independence—making a total of 1,300 wagons. The editor (after reducing from five, to four, his estimated average of persons per wagon) arrived at a figure of 5,200 emigrants. (He also calculated that the companies had, altogether, about 13,000 head of cattle, 1,200 horses, 700 sheep and 90 mules.)

From the viewpoint of some eastbound travelers, the Oregon-California emigration appeared as follows. On July 28, at the Sweetwater, Capt. Henry S. Turner (returning with General Kearny from California) wrote in his journal: "Met the rear-most party of emigrants [a company which had left St. Joseph about June 6]. . . . With very few exceptions the entire emigration this year is to Oregon: a few families were destined to California; a good deal of pains having been taken to obtain correct information, the following statistical list is the result & may be relied on:

   1336 Men—789 women—1384 both sexes under 16 years of age
   [Total: 3,509]
   929 Horses & Mules—7946 Cattle—469 Sheep—941 Wagons."

The Kearny company traveled the Greenwood (or Sublette) cutoff, and therefore Turner's 941-wagon count could not have included some of the emigrants who took the "detour" trail by way of Fort Bridger. Similarly, R. H. Holder (returning from Oregon—*see* July 28 entry), taking one, or the other trail, would have missed wagons then on the alternate route. Holder reported having "met 975 wagons of emigrants" on their way "to Oregon." N. N. Osburn (who left Oregon with Holder, but apparently was one of a group traveling a different route part of the journey) reportedly "met on his return 1,050 wagons belonging to emigrants on their way to Oregon and 750 Mormon teams. . . ." (Notably, Turner's statistics show an average of 4.0 persons per wagon. In Capt. Joel Palmer's 99-wagon train [*see* following] the figure was slightly above 3.7.)

Late in the year, the *California Star,* San Francisco, reported (using information garnered from the *Oregon Spectator,* Oregon City): "Of the emigration, we learn of the safe arrival of 600 wagons in the valleys of the Oregon, while we are credibly informed of the manifest anxiety for the welfare of the remainder . . . one half only of the emigration is enumerated above."

THE "ST. JOSEPH" EMIGRATION. Upwards of 300 wagons had crossed at St. Joseph, Mo., by May 7; the town was crowded with Oregon emigrants; an Illinois company of 100 wagons was expected on the 8th; wagons, in large numbers, were crossing at Iowa Point (*see* p. 577). By May 28, 704 wagons had ferried the Missouri in the St. Joseph area; and more emigrants were arriving daily. If, as the local *Gazette* later reported, the final count was 867 wagons, 163 of them crossed on May 28 or later. The last company to leave St. Joseph departed about June 6.

In its May 28 issue, the *Gazette's* editor published information on the emigrants obtained from James Cochran (who had traveled out some 250 miles, apparently with the leading wagons). Cochran had left "the foremost company" near the head of Little Blue river on May 16. This combined party (captain not given) had 37 wagons (17 from Independence, Mo.; 20 from St. Joseph). [An item (in 1848) on the death of Miss Sarah Boggs of Putnam county, Mo., of the 1847 emigration, stated she had "belonged to Cochran and Johnson's company"—not elsewhere mentioned in the 1847 accounts.]

The returning James Cochran met these companies (all of which had started from St. Joseph): On May 16—"Capt. Bowman's" (53 wagons); "Capt. James Curl's" (41 wagons); "Capt. Davidson's" (48 wagons). On May 17—"Capt. Hawes'" (28 wagons); "Capt. Vahn's" (48 wagons); "Capt. Claypool's" (23 wagons); "Capt. Sawyer's" (27 wagons). On May 18—"Capt. Palmer's" (99 wagons); "Capt. Carter's" (19 wagons). On May 19—"Capt. Patton's" (35 wagons). On May 20—"Capt. Whitcomb's" (109 wagons). On May 21— "Capt. White's" (37 wagons); and 21 unorganized wagons. The *Gazette's* editor added: "Since that time 75 wagons have crossed; and we were informed yesterday by an emigrant that several companies are still behind—one numbering 70 wagons."

"Capt. Bowman's" company, according to diarist Isaac Pettijohn (who gave the captain's name as Nathaniel "Bowen"), had crossed the Missouri on May 1 at "Caples Landing" (*see* p. 578), 12 miles above St. Joseph. It then contained 12 wagons from Illinois; but joined a Missouri company of about 30 wagons on May 2. (In the latter group were "Judge Samuel Burch of Chariton county" [*see* Saint Louis *Daily Union*, April 20, 1847] and his party of six or eight wagons.) This company crossed the Big Blue on May 8, and "came into the independence road" next day; and (evidently enlarged) arrived on the evening of May 16 at the head of the Little Blue river. Before reaching Fort Laramie the company split into three divisions.

"Capt. Vahn" was William Vaughan, Platte county, Mo., resident since 1839 (who had gone to Oregon in 1845 with a pack party, and returned in 1846). His family (wife, and nine children) now accompanied him West. Vaughan's outfit included three ox-drawn wagons, some cattle, and 258 sheep. (An account says the 100 which survived the journey were the first "blooded" sheep to reach Oregon overland.)

"Capt. [Joel] Palmer's" company had numbered some 85 wagons when organizing at Wolf creek on May 6; but Thomas Cox's "Chicago company" joined when overtaken in the "Nemaha country." Experienced Joel Palmer, of Indiana (*see* index of these annals) had a census taken of his 99-wagon company (which later subdivided). There were 129 males and 72 females over 16; 85 males and 83 females 16 and under. The cattle numbered 1,012 head; and there were 66 horses, two mules, 45 sheep. On June 27, at the North Platte, "a Company of 11 wagons drove up Mr Cox foreman," and crossed by the Mormon ferry. Palmer's division, arriving there July 1, contained 35 wagons.

"Capt. [Lot] Whitcomb's" company—109 wagons early in the journey, was said to number 22 wagons, on July 6 at the North Platte. But "Capt. White's" 37-wagon company apparently had increased to about 50 before arriving there July 9. Diarist Loren B. Hastings (of this company) stated that White was a Methodist preacher; that the wagons crossed the Missouri on May 18; that White was elected leader on the 20th; and that on the 22d a division into four sections was made. Also under May 22 he wrote: "A wedding in camp this night and a very tall spree; we put the married couple to bed in a wagon and then hauled the wagon over the prairie through the brush. When the wagon was under good headway down the hills we would drop logs before the wheels; we called this 'rocking them to sleep.'" Hugh Cosgrove later recollected that among a party of 13 families which left Joliet, Ill., in April, 1847, and crossed overland to the Missouri, were Lot Whitcomb's, Cosgrove's (and James McKay's?). In a subsequent division of the 114(?)-wagon train, Cosgrove (who had three) and others, with a total of 13 wagons, made up one of the splinter parties.

Wiley Chapman captained one of the companies which left the St. Joseph area in the rear of the emigration. His "command" numbered about 50 wagons (according to the recollections of James E. R. Harrell) before the division (after which William Jolly headed one group). On July 10 "Capt Chapman Co of 16 waggons" crossed the Mormons' North Platte ferry and "said that they ware the Last Co this Season that is they Knowed of no others on the road they had lost all their horses since they Left the States. . . . Capt Chapman Co said that 40 head of their stock ran off with the buffalow. . . ."

THE "INDEPENDENCE" EMIGRATION. On May 15, a St. Louis newspaper reported: "The [Independence, Mo.] Expositor [of May 8?] says 200 families have left that place this year for Oregon and California." Summing up the year's emigration, in June, the St. Joseph, Mo., *Gazette* stated (without indicating source of information) that 433 wagons had started from Independence. Allen T. Ward (Shawnee Methodist Mission employee) wrote, in an August letter: "The emigration to Oregon & California appears to be increasing. I think something over 500 wagons left here [the Independence-Westport, Mo., area] for those parts last spring. . . ."

Just ahead of all other Oregon-California wagons arriving at Fort Laramie in (early June) 1847, was a company of "11 waggons" (nine wagons, a cart, and a two-horse carriage) which had started from Independence on April 22. The diarists among the Mormon "pioneer party" which had contact with this Oregon-bound company west of Fort Laramie, mentioned the name of only one member: Gabriel Prudhomme (half-Indian son of the Kaw's mouth Gabriel Prudhomme—*see* annals index; now returning to the Catholic mission on St. Mary's river [after accompanying Father De Smet east in 1846?]). Mormon William Clayton recorded: "They left Independence on the 22nd of April. They are expecting the mail soon on mules[?], but they anticipate keeping ahead of all the companies."

In February and March various newspapers published notices similar to the New York *Tribune's* item: "Mail for Oregon.—J. M. Shively [appointed postmaster for Astoria on March 9, 1847], of Oregon is preparing to start for that territory from Washington [D. C.], on the 30th of March. He will leave Independence, Mo. in April and will take charge of all letters directed to him at that place, post-paid, for settlers in Oregon. . . ." (For Shively's journey East in 1845 *see* p. 560.) On August 19 the *Oregon Spectator,* Oregon City, reported (from information by a man "from the States" who arrived August 16): "The immigrants are bringing a very large mail through with them, which is carried in a wagon expressly set apart for it and which is kept in the advance company." The *Spectator's* September 2 issue noted that "Mr. Shively . . . with a large quantity of papers and letters for the settlers in Oregon" was (on August 28) near The Dalles with "the advance company of wagons, consisting of 16, under the guidance of Capt. Nat Bowman [*see* under 'St. Joseph' emigration]"; but one wagon, and about 10 persons had reached The Dalles on August 22. A *Spectator* "Extra" of September 8 reported the arrival at Oregon City. on the 7th, of "John M. Shively, Esq., Deputy Postmaster at Astoria . . ."; and, in its September 30 issue, discussing the daily arrival of emigrants, stated: "The first wagons, those belonging to Mr. Lampson [*i. e.,* Jeremiah Lamson] arrived at this point [Oregon City] on the 7th [September] being about one week in advance of the time of arrival of last year's immigration." (In 1848, the Rev. G. E. Atkinson wrote, in his diary, on June 14: "We met Mr. Lamson and Mr. Hereford from Clatsop. They came from Des Moines Co. Iowa last year . . . [with wives and families]. They left [the Missouri frontier] on May 5 [1847] and arrived at Oregon City Sept. 7.")

On May 19, west of Kansas river, a caravan of 76 or 78 wagons effected a short-lived organization, captained by William Wiggins (who was returning to California). A good many of the relatively few emigrants California-bound in 1847 were in this train. One of them Chester Ingersoll (with his family)—recorded (in a letter) that he crossed the Kansas river on the 18th; and that the wagons "had to be ferried over, at a cost of one dollar each." (No mention was made of the ferry's operators.) In a matter of days, after organizing under Wiggins, the emigrants divided "into a company for Oregon, and the other for California"—the latter with 30 wagons, 45 able-bodied men, and "a guide that has travelled the route eight times [Charles Hopper?]." Samuel Scott (also California-bound) was reported as stating that the company which had numbered "76 wagons" on May 18, was, on June 16, reduced to 16 wagons; and that on June 17 Captain Wiggins resigned and left the 16-wagon company of still-quarreling emigrants. On

July 3 the Mormons "ferryed Capt Ingersols Co of 11 waggons" across the North Platte. (They had ferried "Capt Higgins [*i. e.*, Wiggins?] Co of 23 waggons" on June 30.) From Fort Hall, in a 20-wagon company, Ingersoll set out for California on August 9; and arrived at Johnson's Ranch on October 2. A company (18 wagons and around 75 persons) headed by Wiggins attempted to reach California by a cut-off route, but had to turn north into Oregon; finally reached California by sea. William A. Trubody, James Findla, and some others bound for California, who, at Fort Hall, formed a 20-wagon company headed by Charles Hopper (*see* pp. 429, 458), had set out from Independence. Trubody recollected that a company of some 30 or more wagons and about 100 persons started from Independence. Findla remembered that there were 200 persons and 47 wagons in the company with which he set out; and his "Statement" says: "The first trouble we had with the Indians was at Caw Village, when they stole some of our cattle. We kept two of the Indians prisoners, and as they started to run away, they were killed by the guard."

Traveling from about May 10 to May 21 in the company (captained, for a time, by Wiggins) which included the Californians, was a party which Ingersoll described as "7 priests and one bishop for Oregon." Headed by Aug. M. A. Blanchet (who became the first bishop of Walla Walla on arriving in Oregon), this Catholic party included, besides the bishop and seven priests, several employees (one being Joseph Huneau [Hunant, Uno, etc.] connected with the Kaw's mouth French settlement), and cotraveler Richard Grant, Jr. (*see* p. 649), returning to Fort Hall. Blanchet and most of his group (whose outfit consisted of three ox-drawn wagons, several riding horses, and two? cows) had arrived at Kansas, Mo., aboard the *Tamerlane* on May 1. About May 13 they joined other emigrants setting out for the West; crossed the Kansas on May 18; and camped on "Soldier River," where the bishop met "Kakinga, chief of the Kansas Indians." On May 26 (the day they reached the Big Blue) the Blanchet party, having left the Californians some days earlier, joined "Capt. McGowan's caravan" which was near by.

"Capt. McGowan" (who appears in James Jory's reminiscences as "Joseph Magone'; and in Sarah [Hunt] Steves' recollections as "Major Magoon") then had in charge a large wagon train. By one account, the company of about 90 wagons which organized with McGowan as captain, had started west on May 17. A census taken June 10 (on the Platte) showed a total of 172 persons, and indicates a division must have taken place by then. One of the "separations" was "Capt John McKinneys Co of 27 waggons" which was ferried over the North Platte by the Mormons on July 4; and another(?) the Capt. Elijah Patterson 16-wagon company which had crossed on June 30. On July 7 "Capt Magones Co" of 36 wagons [including "a catholick bishop & 7 priests"] crossed by the same ferry, and "8 waggons of the same Co went above to ford making 44 waggons in Said Co."

W. A. Hockett (aged nine in 1847), in a later-day account, wrote of four Salem, Ia., Quaker families (the families of Nathan H. Hockett, Henderson Luelling, John W. Fisher, and Enos Mendenhall), 17 people, with seven wagons, and 75 head of stock cattle, who went first to St. Joseph, then to Savannah, Mo., but ended up by crossing the Missouri at Independence, on May 14. (This seems a most unlikely procedure!) On May 17 they started west, evidently in the company which became "Capt McGowan's" caravan. But after several days' travel, the Salem company and 13 other Oregon-bound wagons separated; elected Thomas Hockett (Nathan's single brother) as captain; and continued the journey on May 20. Though the Hockett company numbered 20 wagons when arriving at the North Platte crossing on July 6 (as noted by a Mormon ferryman), the Luelling family was not then of the party, and John W. Fisher had died a month earlier. (Both Nathan Hockett and his wife also died, in August, on the journey west.) Hockett's account does not mention the remarkable "traveling nursery" which Henderson Luelling successfully transported to Oregon. Mormon ferryman W. A. Empey wrote (in his journal) on July 11: ". . . we ferryed a nursery of 700 trees they ware apple peach plumb pare Curnd Grapes rasberry and cherryes all growing in a clover patch and were owned by M. H. Lieulling a Quaker from Salim Iowa." Emigrant Ralph Geer later wrote: "That load of living trees and shrubs brought more wealth to Oregon than any ship that ever entered the Columbia river."

Ref: (GENERAL) *The Gazette*, St. Joseph, Mo., June 11, 25, 1847; *Saint Louis Daily Union*, February 10, March 15, 26, June 12, August 5, 1847; *The Weekly Tribune*, Liberty, Mo., September 3, 1847; New York *Weekly Tribune*, March 6, June 12, August 21, 1847, and May 13, 27, 1848; New York *Daily Tribune*, September 6, 1847; *Annals of Wyoming*, v. 21 (July-October, 1949), pp. 130-145, 149-166; *Utah Genealogical and Historical Magazine*, Salt Lake City, v. 16 (July, 1925), pp. 119-122 (Orson Pratt diary); William Clayton's *Journal* . . . (Salt Lake City, 1921), pp. 217, 218; Appleton M. Harmon's *Journals* . . . (Berkeley, Cal., 1946), pp. 28-39; H. H. Bancroft's *History of Oregon* (San Francisco, 1886), v. 1, pp. 623-626; H. S. Lyman's *History of Oregon* . . . (New York, 1903), v. 3, pp. 408-411; Dale Morgan, editor, *Overland In 1846* (Georgetown, Cal., 1963), v. 2, pp. 796, 797; Fred Lockley's *History of the Columbia River* . . . (Chicago, 1928), pp. 226, 489; *Oregon Spectator*, Oregon City (items from issues August 19 to September 16, 1847, inclusive, courtesy of Miss Priscilla Knuth, of the Oregon Historical Society, and Dale L. Morgan, Bancroft Library, Berkeley, Cal.).

(THE "ST. JOSEPH" EMIGRATION) New York *Weekly Tribune*, May 29, 1847 (from *Missouri Republican*, St. Louis, May 15); *The Gazette*, St. Joseph, Mo., March 12, 26, April 23, May 14, 21, 28, June 11, 25, 1847, March 10, 1848; *Saint Louis Daily Union*, August 17, 1847; *Oregon Historical Quarterly*, Salem, v. 1 (September, 1900), pp. 255-269 (Hugh Cosgrove's reminiscences), v. 24 (June, 1923), pp. 186-192 (James E. A. Harrell's reminiscences); Isaac Pettijohn's "Diary" (original in Bancroft Library), courtesy Dale L. Morgan; Oregon Pioneer Association *Transactions*, 51st annual reunion, Portland, 1923 (for Loren B. Hastings' diary); *ibid.*, seventh annual reunion, Salem, 1879 (for Ralph C. Geer's address); *ibid.*, 35th annual reunion, Portland, 1907 (for Mrs. Elizabeth D. Smith's diary); *Portrait and Biographical Record of the Willamette Valley, Oregon* . . . (Chicago, 1903), p. 1356 (for William Vaughan).

(THE "INDEPENDENCE" EMIGRATION) *Saint Louis Daily Union*, May 15, 1847; *California Historical Society Quarterly*, San Francisco, v. 16 (June, 1937), pp. 122-143 (for W. A. Trubody narrative, and James Findla items); *Illinois Catholic Historical Review*, Chicago, v. 9 (January, 1927), pp. 208-222 (for Bishop Blanchet's journal); W. A. Hockett's account (typed copy in KHi ms. division); Fred Lockley's *To Oregon By Ox-Team in '47* (Portland, n. d.), pp. 1-7; Chester Ingersoll's *Overland to California in 1847* (Chicago, 1937); *Oregon Historical Quarterly*, v. 3 (1902), pp. 271-286 (for James Jory's reminiscences), v. 40 (June, 1939), pp. 174, 175 (for Lamson and Hereford families); Allen T. Ward's August 29, 1847, letter, in *KHQ*, v. 33, p. 351; George R. Stewart's *The California Trail* . . . (New York, c1962), pp. 185-192.

❡ May 10.—Under supervision of the Rev. John Schoenmakers, S. J., with the Rev. John Bax, S. J., assisting, Osage Catholic Mission began formal operation by opening a boys' manual labor school in the log buildings erected in 1845-1846 (*see* p. 559) near the Flat Rock creek-Neosho river junction, at present St. Paul, Neosho county. The first pupils were three half-Osage boys; before the end of May, 14 Indian youths were enrolled. *See, also,* October 10 entry.

Fathers Schoenmakers and Bax, with three(?) others had reached the mission site on April 28, coming from St. Louis to the Kaw's mouth by steamboat, and then journeying southward by ox-drawn wagon.

Ref: G. J. Garraghan's *The Jesuits of the Middle United States* (New York, 1938), v. 2, pp. 495-504; Sister Mary Paul Fitzgerald's *Beacon on the Plains* (Leavenworth, 1939), pp. 65-77; Comm'r of Indian Affairs, *Report,* 1846, and following years.

❡ May 13.—At the Delawares' meeting house (present Wyandotte county), a deputation of Pawnees counciled with the Wyandots, Delawares, Shawnees, and Kickapoos; and all "Entered into a treaty of peace and amity."

According to A. G. Boone, of Westport, Mo., the commanding officer at Fort Leavenworth paid a visit to the Pawnee delegation to ask them "about those animals they robbed the Fort of last year" (*see* p. 652); and the Indians promised to "go up the next day, have a friendly talk, and give up the animals, but that night *they stole 10 horses of the Delawares,* and left for their villages."

Ref: William Walker's "Journals," *loc. cit.,* May 12 and 13, 1847, entries; Saint Louis *Reveille* (daily), May 28, 1847.

❡ Mid-May.—Three small parties which had left Santa Fe separately, in April, reached Missouri together. They were: (1) Lt. William G. Peck, with "Messrs. Sanford and Woods" (a wagon train); (2) J[ohn?] McKnight (trader, from Chihuahua); (3) a company from California headed by Carson, Beale, and Talbot—all of whom, as well as Peck, were aboard the *John J. Hardin* which docked at St. Louis May 16.

The first two parties, taking the Cimarron route, joined forces before reaching the Arkansas. Lieutenant Peck (of the topographical engineers) made a "reconnaissance" survey of this route during the journey. In late April when these travelers arrived at a point about nine miles east of "The Caches," some 90 Comanches attacked, made off with 10 animals, and forced them to fall back to Mann's Fort, apparently, and wait for reinforcements. On the second day the Indians struck again. In this fight a man named Williams was severely lanced; and the Comanches got away with the rest of the stock—39 mules and horses (owned principally by Sanford and Woods). By the arrival that night of the California party, they were supplied with more animals, so as to continue the journey.

Christopher ("Kit") Carson, Acting Lt. Edward F. Beale, U. S. N., Theodore Talbot (recently lieutenant and adjutant in Fremont's California battalion, and a member of the explorer's third expedition)—all carrying dispatches and letters (and bound for Washington, D. C.)—had left southern California, with an escort, about the beginning of March. They had reached Santa Fe in April; and then started (on April 19?) for Missouri by way of

Bent's Fort. With them now (*see, also*, p. 687) were Robert Eugene Russell, Lt. Charles Taplin (of the U. S. army), and (apparently) Anthony Cosgrove—all of whom had crossed "Kansas" westbound with Fremont's third expedition (*see* June 9, 1845). Russell and Cosgrove evidently came direct from California; but Taplin must have joined the party in New Mexico, having returned overland in 1846 (*see* p. 644).

At the Great Bend of the Arkansas, the above combined force was attacked by Pawnees, who failed to stampede the stock, but stole two horses.

Ref: New York *Weekly Tribune*, May 29, June 5, 1847 (from *Missouri Republican*, St. Louis, May 17 and 18); Saint Louis *Reveille* (daily) May 18, 28, 1847; Saint Louis *Daily Union*, May 18, 20, 22, 1847; items on financial records covering Fremont's third expedition (*loc. cit.*); Lt. W. H. Emory's map "Military Reconnaissance . . ." of 1847 shows the "Cimarron route as Surveyed by Lt. W. G. Peck in 1847"; Lt. G. K. Warren, in his "Memoir" (33d Cong., 2d Sess., Sen. Ex. Doc. No. 78, v. 11 [Serial 768], p. 54), quotes a Peck letter of 1854 regarding his survey of the Cimarron route "in the month of April, 1847"; Edwin L. Sabin's *Kit Carson Days* . . . (New York, 1935), v. 2, pp. 550-569; Stephen Bonsal's *Edward Fitzgerald Beale* . . . (1912), pp. 25-31; F. B. Heitman's *Historical Register* . . . *of the United States Army* . . . (1903), v. 1, p. 943 (for Talbot), and p. 944 (for Taplin—who had been commissioned March 5, 1847, as a first lieutenant; and assigned April 9 to the 12th U. S. infantry); Ruxton, *op. cit.*, p. 299 (for Peck and party in Mann's Fort vicinity).

❡ May 13.—William N. Thompson and Samuel C. Hall (both of St. Joseph, Mo.?) came in from the "waters of the Nemahaw" (where they had gone with Capt. Joel Palmer's company of Oregon emigrants), having, on the homeward trip, "returned on the South side of Wolf river," and selected a shorter, better road by which future emigrants could avoid "the difficult stream of Wolf river, and the Great Nemaha."

Ref: The Gazette, St. Joseph, Mo., May 14, 21, 1847.

❡ May 17 and 18.—Three government trains of 30 wagons each left Fort Leavenworth for Santa Fe. Two more were scheduled to start about May 22. (Albert G. Boone, Westport, Mo., merchant, reported their departure.)

A correspondent "F. C. A.," who was "On the Arkansas, Caches, June 21, 1847," apparently was in one of the early-departing trains. "For four days past [he wrote], we have been greatly molested by the Indians of the Camanche and Arapaho tribes. We have fought them twice. In the first engagement, we wounded one, and in the last, which took place this morning, we killed four, and wounded six or eight.

"They succeeded this morning in running off six Govt. mules, of a train under charge of Mr. Smith, of St. Louis. Day before yesterday [the 19th], about 400 Indians made several attempts to take possession of the fort [Mann's Fort—near 'The Caches']. . . . [F. C. A. told, also, of the killing of three Mann's Fort defenders; and of Sloan's conclusion to abandon it, and to go to Santa Fe 'with his men and cannon'—*see* p. 671.] A Govt. train, under charge of Mr. Sweeney of Weston, has been sent out, with only 15 rounds of ammunition—some of the men have only two rounds left."

Sloan, his men, and the cannon, joined the above two government trains

(Smith's, and Sweeney's, apparently). A few days later, on the Jornada, Houck's eastbound train met "two quartermaster's trains, accompanied by Mr. Smith [*i. e.,* Thomas Sloan] who had been in command of the little fort on the Arkansas [and his six companions]. . . ." "These trains were marching in two columns each driver with a loaded rifle on his shoulder, and in front of all, a piece of artillery [the Mann's Fort cannon]. . . ."

Ref: Saint Louis *Reveille* (daily), May 28, 1847; New York *Weekly Tribune,* July 31, 1847 (from *Missouri Republican,* St. Louis); Saint Louis *Daily Union,* July 19, 1847; *The Weekly Tribune,* Liberty, Mo., July 17, 1847.

❡ May.—The steamboat *Archer,* upbound from St. Louis, reached St. Joseph, Mo., on the 20th; where she took aboard "a large quantity of flour, wheat, corn and bacon" for "the [Council] Bluffs."

St. Joseph's ability to supply all commercial demands was emphasized by the *Gazette's* appended statement: ". . . and this too after the immense caravan of Oregon wagons have taken their departure with good outfits."

The *Archer,* returning from Council Bluffs, reached St. Louis May 31 with a "full cargo of produce and peltries."

Ref: *The Gazette,* St. Joseph, May 21, 28, 1847; Saint Louis *Reveille* (daily), June 1, 1847.

❡ May.—Arriving on Missouri's border (apparently at Westport) after mid-month, from Fort Laramie, by way of the Oregon trail, were Pierre D. Papin, Charles Beaumont, and seven other fur traders, with three wagons carrying about 1,100 packs of "buffalo robes, &c."

They had left Fort Laramie on April 20; had traveled at night to avoid Indians; had seen "immense herds of buffaloes"; had met the "advance of Mormon emigrants" on the Platte (May 4); the first Oregon-California emigrants "at Ketchum's Fork"(?); and then had encountered them "scattered all along to the Wakarusa," in companies of 40 to 50 wagons; in all, between 400 and 500 wagons. Six of these traders reached St. Louis on May 24. Papin may have boarded the *Martha* (*see* May 22 and July 7 entries).

Ref: *Missouri Republican,* St. Louis, May 28, 1847 (as reprinted in New York *Weekly Tribune,* June 12, 1847); Orson Pratt, and others, *Exodus of Modern Israel* (Salt Lake City, n. d.), p. 31, or, reprint edition, 1947; *Historical Record,* Salt Lake City, v. 9 (January, 1890); *William Clayton's Journal* . . . (Salt Lake City, 1921), p. 128 (Clayton understood the traders were bound for Council Bluffs).

❡ Between May 21 and June 15, five companies of troops—the newly organized Missouri battalion of infantry volunteers, and their unanimously elected commander, Lt. Col. Alton R. Easton, arrived at Fort Leavenworth (aboard the steamboats *Mandan, Amaranth,* and *Little Missouri*), from St. Louis.

[Raised under a war department requisition of April 19, this force had been recruited (for the Mexican War's duration) at St. Louis (and vicinity); and mustered in there by Lt. Col. Clifton Wharton, of the First U. S. dragoons.]

The company commanders were Capts. Elihu H. Shepard (Company A), Nicholas Woechner (Company B), Noble L. Cunningham (Company C), Edward W. Paul (Company D), and William A. Barnes (Company E). Lt. Samuel H. Holmes was Easton's adjutant; and the battalion's surgeon was Dr. Joseph Malin.

Between June 17 and June 21 these foot soldiers left Fort Leavenworth for Santa Fe (as hereafter noted), where they would replace Missouri volunteers whose 12-months' enlistments were expiring.

Ref: Saint Louis *Daily Union*, April 26, May 10, 11, 13, 15, 17, 29, 31, June 1, 3, 8, 9, 15, 1847; Saint Louis *Reveille* (daily), May 4, 15, 16, 18, June 1, 1847; J. T. Scharf's *History of Saint Louis City and County* . . . (1883), v. 1, pp. 378, 379; 30th Cong., 1st Sess., *H. Ex. Doc. No.* 29 (Serial 516), pp. 81, 82; *Democratic Standard*, Leavenworth, August 10, 1883; New York *Weekly Tribune*, July 31, 1847 (from *Missouri Republican*, St. Louis, July 19); R. P. Bieber, editor, *Marching With the Army of the West*, p. 57 (for summary of secretary of war's requisitions, March 31 and April 19, 1847, on state of Missouri); Shepard, *op cit.*, pp. 143-146.

❐ May 22.—The *Martha* (Joseph La Barge, captain), under charter to Pierre Chouteau, Jr., & Co., and en route to Fort Union, at the Yellowstone's mouth, passed St. Joseph, Mo. She had left St. Louis on May 15. (*See, also,* July 7 entry.)

Ref: Saint Louis *Daily Union*, July 9, 1847; *The Gazette*, St. Joseph, Mo., May 27, 1847; H. M. Chittenden, *op. cit.*, v. 1, pp. 177-183. (Chittenden *says* Mrs. La Barge made this trip; and that she was said to be the first white woman to make the river journey to Fort Union. But *see* June, 1851, annals.

❐ May 23.—Upwards of 65 persons (14 "Americans," and about 54 Mexicans by one account) arrived at Independence, Mo., from Santa Fe. Among the Americans (all of them Missouri volunteers, discharged for ill-health) were H. L. Caldwell and J. T. Hook, of Ste. Genevieve county, Missouri. They had accompanied Mexican traders whose wagons totaled 18, and who had with them $65,000 in specie. (The ex-soldiers, who brought in a mail, had left Santa Fe in detached parties, the last departing on April 21.)

On May 12, at Pawnee Fork, a Comanche-Arapahoe band of about 100 had attacked the train. In the fight, an Indian leader had been killed, and several of the raiders wounded, but the train lost 105 head of horses and mules. About 100 belonged to Emanuel Armijo (or the Armijo family).

When these traders reached St. Louis (on May 28), it was reported that another Mexican party was "on their way in," also bringing a large amount of money. On May 31 there arrived at St. Louis (aboard the *Tamerlane*), from Independence, "Senors St. Jago Archivali, Michael Ortaro [Otero], Emanuel Armijo, and James Armijo" (aged about 14, educated in the United States).

At a later time, Francisco Perea recollected that he, his brother Joaquin Perea, J. Francisco Chavez, Miguel A. Otero, and Jose Gutierrez (all youths) came East over the Santa Fe trail in the spring of 1847; that the Otero and Gutierrez boys were placed in school at St. Louis; and the other three went on to a school in New York, "in company with José Leandro Perea and Juan Montoya" (who presumably were among the traders in the trains noted above).

Ref: New York *Weekly Tribune,* June 12, 1847 (from *Missouri Republican,* St. Louis, May 29); *Niles' National Register,* v. 72 (June 12, 1847), p. 235 (from St. Louis *New Era,* May 28); Saint Louis *Daily Union,* May 29, September 7, 1847; Saint Louis *Reveille* (daily), May 29, June 1, 1847; *Old Santa Fe,* Santa Fe, v. 1 (October, 1913), p. 213; P. G. Ferguson's "Diary," in R. P. Bieber, editor, *Marching With the Army of the West,* p. 306.

❑ MARRIED: Francis A. Hicks (head of the Wyandot Nation), and Mrs. Matilda (Stephenson) Driver (widow of Francis—*see* January 24 entry), on May 24, in present Wyandotte county.

Ref: William Walker's "Journals," *loc. cit.;* KHC, v. 9, p. 225 (for a biographical note on Hicks). Matilda Stephenson, a Wyandot by adoption, was originally from Lancaster county, Pa.

❑ May.—"Mr. Richards" (John Richard) who had left Fort Laramie on the 26th of March(?), with two other traders, apparently crossed "Kansas" in May. He arrived at St. Louis with "more than 30 packs" of buffalo robes, on June 11.

As reported, he had met, at "Elm Grove," 400 Delawares, Shawnees, etc., on their way to fight the Pawnees. If (as the account stated) he met an emigrant party out of St. Joseph "on the great Nemaha," it would appear that Richard came in by way of the Oregon trail's St. Joseph route.

Ref: Saint Louis *Daily Union,* June 12, 1847; Saint Louis *Reveille* (daily), June 13, 1847.

❑ May 28.—Bent, St. Vrain & Co.'s eastbound train, accompanied by trader William Tharp and his wagons, was attacked by mounted Indians, supposed to be Arapahoes, at Walnut Creek. Tharp was killed and "brutally mangled."

This occurred in the morning (with the wagons still corralled at the overnight camp), while Tharp, and Frank De Lisle (in charge of the Bent train) were out shooting buffalo. "A simultaneous attack was made on them, on the wagons, and cattle and mules which had been turned out to graze."

Tharp (a young man, formerly of St. Louis) "had been trading very successfully during the winter, and was supposed to have made some $5,000, but by the robbery of about 60 mules, at this time, he lost more than one half of his earnings. Bent, St. Vrain & Co. lost about 40 mules and cattle." Tharp was buried at Walnut creek crossing.

Ref: New York *Weekly Tribune,* June 26, 1847 (from *Missouri Republican,* St. Louis, June 14, 1847); Ruxton, *op. cit.,* p. 290 (says the Indians were Pawnees); Garrard, *op. cit.,* pp. 338, 339, 345, says the Indians were Comanches); *Weekly Reveille,* St. Louis, June 14, 21, 1847, April 3, 1848. The *Missouri Republican's* account is quoted above. The information therein would have been obtained from Ceran St. Vrain's party which overtook the Bent, St. Vrain & Co. train *after* the attack, and reached St. Louis on June 12, ahead of the wagons. John S. Smith and his Cheyenne family who joined the above train at Mann's Fort on May 24, were still "in company" when the above attack took place. Smith lost seven animals.

❑ MARRIED: Paul Bloohm and Jane M. Greasham, both recently from England, on May 29, in the new boarding-school building at

Iowa, Sac & Fox Presbyterian Mission, by the Rev. William Hamilton.

Present, also, at the ceremony: the Rev. Samuel M. Irvin, his wife, his parents (the Francis Irvins), Walter Lowrie (of the Presbyterian foreign missions board), and George H. C. Melody (another visitor). The Bloohms were to assist at the mission—he with the boys, and she to have "full charge of the girls."

Ref: George Catlin, . . . *Eight Year's Travels and Residence in Europe* . . . (New York, 1848), v. 2, pp. 327-331. The arrival of "Miss Greasham" at the mission, on May 28, was noted by Irvin in a May 30, 1847, letter. The Bloohms left before the end of 1847.—*See* Presbyterian Historical Society, American Indian Missions correspondence, Box 102 (microfilm, KHi), Iowa & Sac mission, 1845-1849; Highland Presbyterian church records, 1843-1890 (microfilm in KHi) wherein the bride's name is spelled "Gresham."

❧ Near the end of May five men and a young California Indian—late-arriving members of the Carson-Beale-Talbot party from California (*see* p. 682)—reached the Missouri frontier; and were aboard the *Monona* docking at St. Louis June 1. Marion Wise, J. C. Davis, Thomas E. Brackenridge, Joseph Steppe, and Aaron Hamilton—all members of Fremont's third expedition—had crossed "Kansas" westbound in June-July, 1845 (*see* June 9, 1845, annals entry).

On the trip East (still in Fremont's employ) they had been left behind, "below Santa Fe," in charge of the party's mules (which needed recruiting). Subsequently, from the Bent's Fort area to Pawnee Fork, they had traveled under Capt. A. W. Enos' protection (*see* below); then had "pushed on ahead" and brought the mules in safely, and without interference from hostile Indians.

Ref: Saint Louis *Daily Union*, June 2, 1847; Saint Louis *Reveille* (daily), June 2, 1847; items from financial records of Fremont's third expedition (from National Archives, Washington, D. C.), courtesy of Dale L. Morgan; Sabin, *op. cit.*, v. 2, pp. 563, 564; Ruxton, *op. cit.*, p. 291; Garrard (ed. by Bieber), *op. cit.*, p. 325.

❧ Before the end of May, Lt. John Love and new recruits of Company B, First U. S. dragoons, after a journey overland from St. Louis, reached Fort Leavenworth. They were under orders to Santa Fe (*see* June 7 entry).

On May 15 "Lt. Love's troop" had paraded at St. Louis Park. Some two weeks later, George F. Ruxton (British traveler), coming in from Bent's Fort, and nearing the Missouri border, met this "troop of dragoons from St. Louis," on their way to the fort. "They were superbly mounted . . . [but] The dragoons themselves were all recruits, and neither soldierlike in dress nor appearance."

Ref: Saint Louis *Reveille* (daily), May 16, 1847; Ruxton, *op. cit.*, p. 311.

❧ Early in June, Capt. A. W. (or Elanson? W.) Enos, of the army quartermaster's department, arrived at Fort Leavenworth, from Bent's Fort, his party bringing in some 33 empty government wagons, and a lot of loose stock.

On leaving Bent's Fort early in May (with about 20? wagons), Enos'

cotravelers were (as one of them—Lewis H. Garrard—put it) "a motley party
. . . [of] wagonmasters, teamsters and amateurs." (Many of the teamsters were ill from scurvy; and seven[?] died on the journey.) The "amateurs"
included young Garrard, and T. B. Drinker (both Ohioans, and pleasure
seekers)—*see* p. 645, for previous mention. British traveler George F. Ruxton, and two companions, joined the train on the upper Arkansas; and so did
five "Californians"—the Marion Wise party (*see* above). At the Cheyenne
village, at "Pretty Encampment" (a location near the "Colorado-Kansas" line,
in present Hamilton county), mountain man John S. Smith, and his Indian
family (of three) were added to the cavalcade.

At new Mann's Fort (reached on May 15) the train was further enlarged,
by the addition of Daniel P. Mann and 25(?) "resident" teamsters; also some
more wagons. Leaving Enos' company here were John S. Smith (hired to
replace Mann as "commander" of Mann's Fort), his Cheyenne family, and
adventurous Lewis H. Garrard (who volunteered for employment).

So far as known, Captain Enos' train made the trip East without encountering hostile Indians. The Marion Wise party reached the Missouri border in
advance of the wagons; and George F. Ruxton arrived at Fort Leavenworth
(late in May) also ahead of the main company.

Ref: Ruxton, *op. cit.*, pp. 290-314; Garrard (ed. by Bieber), *op. cit.*, pp. 323-333;
Saint Louis *Daily Union*, June 1, 2, 1847 (also, the issue of June 29, for mention of arrival
at St. Louis of T. B. Drinker). *The Gazette*, St. Joseph, Mo., June 11, 1847, notes statement
(made by "our old friend Samuel Wildbahn" on June 7, at St. Joseph) that "seven men
of his train died on their way home." An account of Drinker's death (with biographical
data) is in the Saint Louis *Daily Union* of April 6, 1848. *The Daily Reveille*, St. Louis,
September 1, 1848, noted Ruxton's death.

℃ June 3(?)—Near Walnut creek, on the Santa Fe trail, Indians
attacked two men of an eastbound train. "One who was a Spaniard,
escaped without his scalp; the other, an American [McGuire], was
killed on the spot."

This train was in command of "Captain Fowler," according to Lewis H.
Garrard. (It had camped overnight, on May 28, near Mann's Fort.) But a
St. Louis newspaper referred to it as "Barclay's government train." A Mis-
souri volunteer (E. N. O. Clough) who saw the scalped victim at Fort Leaven-
worth, on June 21, thought he was about 16 years old. (Garrard said the
Mexican youth lived for a month.)

Ref: Garrard, *op. cit.*, pp. 349, 372; Saint Louis *Daily Union*, June 21, 1847; E. N. O.
Clough's "Recollections" in *Democratic Standard*, Leavenworth, August 10, 1883. Garrard,
at Walnut creek, eastbound, in June, 1847, saw "the graves of Tharpe [slain May 28] and
McGuire, both killed by the Camanches[?]."

℃ The first week of June the *Tributary* brought from St. Joseph,
Mo., and landed at Fort Leavenworth, 50 tons of army stores.

Ref: Saint Louis *Daily Union*, June 7, 1847.

℃ Around June 5(?) a party of 27 persons, with four wagons,
reached the Missouri border after a journey by the Cimarron route
from Santa Fe (left on May 3). The mail they brought was deposited at Fort Leavenworth. Among these travelers were "Dr.

[R. T.] Edmondson and Lieut. [Benjamin M.] Hawkins" (the latter from Willock's "Extra" battalion—*see* p. 631; and the doctor from "Price's" regiment—*see* p. 631). Indians (though none were seen) had stolen three mules from the party en route.

Ref: *Niles' National Register*, v. 72 (June 26, 1847), p. 266; Saint Louis *Daily Union*, June 11, 1847. "Edmondson" (Edmonson?) and Hawkins arrived at St. Louis, on the *John J. Hardin*, June 10.

❲ June 7.—Lt. John Love and Company B (some 80 men), First U. S. dragoons (*see* p. 687), left Fort Leavenworth as guard to Santa Fe for paymaster Maj. Charles Bodine, who had in charge nearly $350,000 in specie for the troops in New Mexico. On June 10, some 75 miles out on the Santa Fe trail, Indian agent Thomas Fitzpatrick joined the command. (*See, also,* June 9, 24-26, entries.)

Ref: New York *Weekly Tribune*, August 7, 1847 (for Love's report of June 27, 1847); Comm'r of Indian Affairs, *Report*, 1847, appendix (for Fitzpatrick's report, September 18, 1847); *Bulletin* of the Missouri Historical Society, St. Louis, v. 4 (July, 1948), p. 274.

❲ June 8.—Under instructions (of May 15) from Sup't T. H. Harvey, St. Louis, Agent Richard W. Cummins set out from the Missouri border to select a location suitable as a future home for the Kansa Indians (*see* pp. 569, 570 for their January, 1846, land cession treaty). He was accompanied by interpreters Clement Lessert and Henry Tiblow, also by James M. Simpson; and joined by six Kansa (three chiefs; three warriors).

Spending some 16 days on this mission, Cummins (and party) went, first, *west* of the Kansa reserve ceded in 1846; but this area he rejected—partly because of the proximity to hostile Indians, but more specifically because "there is no timber on the waters of the Kansas River west of the grand point [Smoky Hill-Republican river junction] suitable for Agricultural purposes, except cottonwood. . . ." The area next inspected—west of the Shawnee reserve—likewise lacked sufficient timber. Thirdly, he examined "the country known as the Council Grove and headwaters of the Neosho," and was satisfied that though a very small country for 1,500 Indians, this was the place to which the Kansa should remove.

Cummins' July 17 report "bounded" the chosen Kansa reserve in these words: *"To commence at a point ten miles due north of the Trading house of Boon & Hammilton and the Government blacksmith shop, both of which are on the bank of council grove creek [i. e., the Neosho river!] at the crossing of the santifee road, from thence due west five miles to corner, thence due south twenty miles to corner, thence east twenty miles to corner, thence due north twenty miles to corner, thence due west fifteen miles to the place of beginning."*

Ref: OIA, Letters Received from Fort Leavenworth Agency (National Archives Micro-copy 234, Roll 302).

❧ At Westport, Mo., on June 9, Albert G. Boone (in a letter) wrote: "Our old friend Major Thos. Fitzpatrick [Indian agent], left this place yesterday in company with Major John Dougherty [ex-Indian agent], who is taking some 500 head of beef cattle, for the Govt. to Santa Fe."

He added: "They will be accompanied by Lieut. [John] Love, command-ing a co. of dragoons [see June 7 entry] and will join the co. tomorrow on the Santa Fe road. . . ." (On May 15 John Dougherty, of Liberty, Mo., had made a contract with Lt. W. E. Prince, AAQM, Fort Leavenworth, "To deliver at Santa Fe N. M. 550 head of beef cattle at $2.50 per 100 pounds. . . .")

At Council Grove, in mid-June, Dougherty's herd stampeded, and about 150 cattle escaped. On July 16 St. Louis newspapers reported that he had recovered "nearly all" his cattle; had "sent them on with the [Missouri volunteer] troops that went out under [Lt.] Col. [Alton R. Easton] and re-turned to Fort Leavenworth."

See reproduced, on p. 812, John Dougherty's bill for purchases at Boone & Hamilton's (new) Council Grove store in 1847. The original (in the Dougherty Collection, KHi) perhaps was kept as a memento of his Council Grove experience.

Ref: Saint Louis *Reveille* (daily), June 15, July 16, 1847; Saint Louis *Daily Union*, June 23, July 16, 1847; 30th Cong., 2d Sess., Sen. Ex. Doc. No. 17 (Serial 529), p. 55.

❧ June 9.—Ceran St. Vrain, George Bent, Jared W. Folger, Francis P. Blair, Jr., Edmund Chadwick, Asa Estes, of Taos, J. T. Hoffman, of Baltimore, and "other gentlemen" arrived at Westport, Mo., from Santa Fe, by way of Bent's Fort.

Leaving Santa Fe on May 13, they had reached Taos on the 16th, Bent's Fort on the 26th, and about May 30 passed Mann's Fort. (At that place Lewis H. Garrard noted the party had one wagon, and 25 horses and mules "in prime order.") The journey from Bent's Fort to Westport was made in 14 days (about 40 miles per day), and without trouble from Indians. These travelers were aboard the *Monona* which docked at St. Louis June 12.

Ref: Saint Louis *Reveille* (daily), June 15, 1847; New York *Weekly Tribune*, June 26, 1847; Lavender, *op. cit.*, p. 299; Garrard, *op. cit.*, pp. 351, 352.

❧ June 17-21.—Bound for Santa Fe, "Easton's" infantry battalion, Missouri volunteers (see May 21 entry) left Fort Leavenworth in three detachments:

On the 17th, Capt. Elihu H. Shepard's Company A (an effective force of 85 men and officers), as escort for a government train of 40 ox-drawn wagons (which had started on the 15th). Shepard's "separate" command reached Council Grove on the morning of July 2; departed next day; spent the Fourth on the march; camped at Diamond Spring on July 5; but traveled, sub-sequently, in the *rear* of Easton's force; reached Santa Fe on August 25.

"Frank Coons' train of merchant wagons" traveled with Shepard from Council Grove.

On the 19th, Capt. Nicholas Woechner's Company B. At Council Grove (reached July 1) Woechner's "separate" command became escort for traders assembled there (most?, or all? of those listed on p. 696). His command left the Grove on July 5; and apparently traveled not far from Easton's throughout the journey to Santa Fe.

On the 21st, Lt. Col. Alton R. Easton, his staff, and Companies C, D, and E (headed by Captains Cunningham, Paul, and Barnes); also a government wagon train. Pvt. E. N. O. Clough (of Paul's Company D), in his diary, provides details that make clear the battalion traveled from the fort to the Santa Fe trail on the old Fort Leavenworth-Fort Scott road (and not by the branch road which Kearny's army used in 1846). Under June 23 he wrote: "Crossed the Kaw river to-day and camped four miles this side of the crossing. . . . We camped about 3 p. m. and found a beautiful gum spring right at the side of the Shawnee church. We are only about six miles from Westport and just at the starting point of the Santa Fe trail. The place is known as Gum Spring among the people." (As shown on a map of 1857, Gum Spring was about on the line of Sec. 11 and Sec. 12, T. 12 S., R. 24 E.; within the limits of present Shawnee, Johnson county.)

Easton's command reached Council Grove the afternoon of July 2; remained three days. On July 3 his force was enlarged by the arrival of Lt. James M. Allen with McNair's Company A, Third regiment, Missouri mounted volunteers. When Easton set out again on the 5th he had with him three infantry companies, one of cavalry, 33 wagons (and their teamsters), 200 mules, 100 horses, 600 loose cattle (most of them Dougherty's animals—*see* p. 690), and 30 herdsmen mounted and armed.

News of "Love's defeat" (*see* p. 694) had reached Council Grove on July 3; and some of "Dougherty's" cattle were needed to replace Hayden's lost oxen. Easton moved his command westward with all speed. He was at the Little Arkansas on July 11; camped at Walnut creek on the 14th; crossed Pawnee Fork on the 16th; and, on the 19th, having taken the "Ridge road" and found no water available on it, "struck off for the lower [river] road." Up to this time his command had not been troubled by Indians.

See July 20 entry for further account of Easton's battalion.

Ref: Saint Louis *Reveille* (daily), June 27, July 10, 13, 18, August 5, 12, 15, 1847; Saint Louis *Daily Union*, June 25, 26, July 10, 14, 19, August 2, 12, 16, 19, September 7, 1847; New York *Weekly Tribune*, July 10, 24, 27, 31, August 28, October 9, 1847; *Niles' National Register*, v. 72 (July 17, 1847), p. 320; *Democratic Standard*, Leavenworth, August 10, 17, 1883 (for Clough's diary and letters [excerpts]); Shepard, *op. cit.*, pp. 146, 147.

❡ June 19.—Four (out of 10) companies of the new Third regiment, Missouri mounted volunteers arrived at Fort Leavenworth from the rendezvous—Independence, Mo. (where the companies had been assembling since before May 24; and where, on June 17, seven companies had voted for regimental officers).

Later in June, and in July, the six other companies left Independence (one— the last?—on July 15). Elected to head Missouri's Third regiment (raised under a March 31 requisition by the secretary of war for duration-of-the-war service) were Col. John Ralls, of Ralls county, Lt. Col. Richard H. Lane, of Madison county, and Maj. William W. Reynolds, of Osage county.

See July annals entry, p. 696, for the departure of these troops for Santa Fe.

Ref: New York *Weekly Tribune*, July 17, 1847 (from *Missouri Republican*, St. Louis, June 29?); *The Gazette*, St. Joseph, Mo., July 23, 1847; Saint Louis *Reveille* (daily), May 29, 1847; Saint Louis *Daily Union*, July 8, 1847; W. H. Robarts' *Mexican War Veterans* . . . (1887), pp. 62, 63.

❮ On (and around) June 21, the "First" regiment, Illinois infantry volunteers (headed by Col. Edward W. B. Newby, Lt. Col. Henderson P. Boyakin, and Maj. Israel B. Donalson) arrived at Fort Leavenworth, by steamboat, from Alton, Ill. (where, on June 7, the regiment had been organized).

Destined for Santa Fe, these foot-soldiers remained at the "Kansas" post till early July (see July 7 entry). About a dozen Illinois volunteers died—some from measles—at Fort Leavenworth.

[This Illinois regiment's major—Israel B. Donalson—later had a role in Kansas territorial history, as U. S. marshal (appointed by President Pierce), serving from November 10, 1854, till November 4, 1856.]

Ref: Illinois Adjutant General's *Record of the Services of Illinois Soldiers* . . . (Springfield, Ill., 1902), v. 9, pp. xxx, 208-228; Saint Louis *Daily Union*, July 10, 13, 14, 1847; A. T. Andreas' *History of Chicago* (Chicago, 1884), v. 1, pp. 280-283; *History of Marion and Clinton Counties, Illinois* . . . (1881), pp. 121, 122. For Donalson, *see* *KHC*, v. 3, p. 228, v. 7, p. 332, v. 9, p. 543, v. 16, p. 660. The above Illinois regiment was the *fifth* to be organized in that state, but the first to be mustered in for duration-of-the-war service.

❮ June.—The *Tributary*, reaching St. Louis on the 21st, from St. Joseph, Mo., had aboard American Fur Company clerks Henry Goulet (or Gonlette?), Cifears Ayotte, and some 14 other employees, together with the cargoes (1,265 packs of robes, furs, &c.) of three Mackinaw boats in which they had left Fort Pierre on May 9.

The transfer to the steamboat had been made near St. Joseph, from which place the *Tributary* had transported 25 tons of army stores to Fort Leavenworth, Below the mouth of the Kansas, cargoes of two Harvey, Primeau & Company (or, St. Louis Fur Company) Mackinaw boats had also been taken aboard. These fur returns, in charge of "Capt. Jacob Picott[e]," had been brought down the Missouri from the mouth of Medicine creek, and were consigned to Robert Campbell, of St. Louis.

Ref: Saint Louis *Daily Union*, June 22, 1847; Saint Louis *Reveille* (daily), June 22, 1847; Sunder, *op. cit.*, p. 97 (which contains some variations from annals account).

❮ June 22-23.—Camped on the left bank of Pawnee Fork, on the 22d, waiting for floodwaters to recede, was a Santa Fe-bound company which Lewis H. Garrard (who swam over to visit) described as "a government train [*i. e.*, two trains—one in charge of 'Hayden'; the other headed by 'Fagan,' of Platte City, Mo.], some traders' wagons [James S. Wethered's, Henry C. Miller's, and others], any quantity of gaping men, and a *whitewoman*—a real whitewoman!"

Comanches (about 50 in number) attacked one train on the morning of June 23; failed to raid the stock; and lost a warrior. "Mr. Smith, of Platte county" ("Van Buren [now Cass] county"—according to Garrard) was lanced in seven places (including his throat), but recovered(?); and two, or more others were wounded, also; but no property was lost. ("Smith" was from Wethered's party.)

Lt. John Love took these trains under escort on June 24—*see* p. 694.

Ref: Saint Louis *Daily Union*, May 29, 1847 (quoted an Independence, Mo., letter of May 22: "The Messrs. Wethered and others are just about starting. . . ."), and *see* issue of August 1, 1847, for "Fagan." The New York *Weekly Tribune*, July 31, 1847 (reprints a letter by James S. Wethered to Baltimore, Md., friends); Garrard, *op. cit.*, pp. 369-372; *Niles' National Register*, v. 72 (July 17, 1847), p. 320; J. M. Cutts' *The Conquest of California and New Mexico* . . . (Philadelphia, 1847), pp. 240-242. A Thomas Fitzpatrick letter of July 6, 1850 (written at St. Louis) in regard to a claim made against "Osages" by "Messrs. Thompson, Miller [Henry C. Miller], and Turl[e]y" for depredations committed on the Santa Fe trail near Pawnee Fork in June, 1847, describes the incidents relating to the claim; and says positively the Indians were Comanches and Kiowas (not Osages), etc.—OIA, "Letters Received from Osage Agency" (National Archives Microcopy 234, Roll 633). Fitzpatrick was with Lt. John Love's command.

⁋ June 22-23.—An eastbound company (some 85 men) corralled, on the 22d, near flooded Pawnee Fork's right bank at the Santa Fe trail crossing. In it were William H. Russell's mounted party of 16 or 17, from California, "Bell's" train of 25(?) ox-drawn government wagons, and fur trader "Coolidge's" (or, Goodrich's?) outfit, with four large robe-and-peltry-laden wagons. "Coolidge," and young Lewis H. Garrard, had joined at Mann's Fort on June 16 (*see* p. 671). Prior to reaching Pawnee Fork, some of the company (particularly Russell's men, "Coolidge," and Garrard) had been in two skirmishes with Indians.

At Pawnee Fork, on June 23, Comanches first attacked the train across the river (*see* preceding entry), then made a raid on Bell's and "Coolidge's" stock —running off 160 head of cattle (which they drove some two miles off, then wantonly killed, with lances, cutting off the tails as trophies).

There were no casualties in the half-hour's engagement. The "green" teamsters (some of them unarmed!) put up little resistance; and the Indians were only after the oxen. Russell's and "Coolidge's" men (hunting buffalo when the raid began) managed to save 30 cattle. The fur trader (who lost 27 animals) had only two left. (He had to cache some of his robes and furs; Russell carried a few packs on his wagon; the rest were sent back to Mann's Fort.) Bell, with enough oxen for three wagons, had to abandon 22(?) others, and "any amount of extras." Before (or after?) the much-altered train crossed Pawnee Fork on June 24, 26 wagons, and some contents, were burned. Garrard estimated the loss at upwards of $9,000. Lt. John Love and his First dragoons (*see* p. 687) came up soon after the company started eastward. He promised revenge.

At Council Grove, on July 3, troops westbound met "Bell's party of traders [*i. e.*, government teamsters] coming in from Santa Fe." *See* July 2 entry for more on Russell's party.

Ref: Garrard, *op. cit.*, pp. 359-372, said the fur trader was "Coolidge"; whereas M. W. Murphy, also with Russell's party, said it was "Goodrich"; New York *Weekly Tribune,* July 24, 1847 (from *Missouri Republican,* St. Louis); *The Weekly Tribune,* Liberty, Mo., July 10, 1847; Saint Louis *Daily Union,* July 7, 1847; Saint Louis *Reveille* (daily), July 13, 1847; Cutts, *op. cit.*, pp. 240-242.

❦ June 24-26.—Lt. John Love, his 80 (Company B) First U. S. dragoons, Maj. Charles Bodine (with his paymaster's outfit), and Indian Agent Thomas Fitzpatrick, en route to Santa Fe (*see* June 7 entry), arrived at Pawnee Fork on June 24. Love took under his protection the two government trains (Hayden's and Fagan's), and accompanying traders (Wethered, Miller, and others) corraled there. (*See* p. 693.)

Crossing Pawnee Fork, and marching on the lower road, the combined force camped near the Arkansas, in the Coon creek vicinity, the night of June 25. Love's troops were "on the bank of the river, between the two trains." About sunrise on the 26th, the men in Hayden's train (some 500 yards west of the dragoons' guard-tent) started to drive their oxen out of corral to graze. "All were scarcely out, when a large band (250 to 300) of Cumanches and Mexicans emerged from a ravine called Coon creek . . . and charged furiously on the teamsters and herdsmen, wounding three and driving off 130 yoke of government oxen and 30 yoke belonging to a trader [Henry C. Miller, of Arrow Rock, Mo.]. . . ."

Lieutenant Love sent Sgt. Ben Bishop and about 25 mounted men to retake the cattle; meantime he prepared to defend his own camp as another large band of Indians appeared on the river bank, opposite. Bishop's mounted troops (whose horses became unmanageable) were surrounded by the attackers; and, though the inexperienced dragoons put up a gallant fight, five were killed (Privates —— Arlidge, John Dickhart, —— Short, George Gaskill, J. H. Blake); and six were wounded (Sgt. Ben Bishop, Privates Vancaster, Lovelace, and Ward, severely; Bush [or Burk?] and Wilson had minor injuries. The Comanches and their cohorts (Mexicans; and a few white men, it was said) suffered losses too—12 or 15 fell, by one report.

The raid left Hayden's 30 government wagons stranded. (*see* p. 700 for Miller's solution to *his* problem.) Love got off an express to Fort Leavenworth; "encamped both trains together," and remained near the battle site (a location afterwards called "Love's defeat"; apparently in the vicinity of present Garfield, Pawnee county), from June 26 to July 2. When the wounded could travel, he moved on up the Arkansas to Mann's Fort. Left at "Love's defeat" were "17 wagons and seven[?] graves" (according to Pvt. E. N. O. Clough, who camped near by on July 17), and a cache of Hayden's ox-yokes.

Having got the remains of Hayden's train to Mann's Fort, Lt. John Love's party (with Fagan's train, also Wethered and other traders in company) continued the journey; crossed the Arkansas about July 11; reached Santa Fe on August 6. (For Hayden, see also p. 705.)

Ref: Lt. John Love's report, June 27, 1847 (reprinted from the Washington [D. C.] *Union*), in New York *Weekly Tribune*, August 7, 1847, and in *Niles' National Register*, v. 72 (July 31, 1847), p. 343; [Sgt. Ben Bishop's] letter, July 1, 1847, in Cutts, *op. cit.*, pp. 240-242; Thomas Fitzpatrick's report, September 18, 1847, in Comm'r of Indian affairs, *Report*, 1847 (appendix); *The Weekly Tribune*, Liberty, Mo., July 10, 1847 (has letter from "Camp near Battle Ground, Arkansas River, June 27, 1847," by unidentified writer); New York *Weekly Tribune*, July 31, 1847 (has James S. Wethered's letter describing the battle); Webb, *op. cit.*, pp. 290-293; *Bulletin* of the Missouri Historical Society, St. Louis, v. 4 (July, 1948), p. 274; 34th Cong., 1st Sess., *Sen. Ex. Doc. No. 96* (Serial 827), p. 616 (notes the "Affair of Lt. Love, 1st dragoons at Grand Prairie, Arkansas river June 26, 1847," in which five men were killed, and six wounded); Saint Louis *Daily Union*, July 10, 29, September 7, 1847 (says, by one report, the Indians were led by a Negro "whom the late Col. Sublette set free in the mountains several years ago); *ibid.*, August 2 and September 7, 1847 (for Love's movements after June 26); Percival G. Lowe, in his *Five Years a Dragoon* (Kansas City, Mo., 1906), gives Bishop's name as "Ben"—*see* pp. 104, 114, 137; R. P. Bieber, editor, *Marching With the Army of the West*, p. 295, lists other newspaper references; *Niles' National Register*, v. 72 (August 14, 1847), p. 375; OIA, "Letters Received from Osage Subagency" (National Archives Microcopy 234, Roll 633), R. S. Elliott's September 27, 1847, letter, therein identifies Miller as "Henry C. Miller." The Osages later had some of Miller's oxen. Chief George White Hair said the cattle had been purchased from the Comanches.—Brig. Gen. Mathew Arbuckle's October 13, 1847, letter in *ibid.* Pvt. Thomas B. Lester, on the Santa Fe trail in the summer of 1847, camped near Coon creek on August 6. He wrote: "Where this crk empties into the Ark. is the spot where Lieut Love . . . was attacked."—Thomas B. Lester's diary (from photostats in Western Historical Manuscripts Collection, The University of Missouri, Columbia, Mo.).

❦ MARRIED: Paschal Pensineau (a Frenchman, formerly resident among the Kickapoos) and Katakaukwe (a Pottawatomie?), on June 28, at Sugar Creek Pottawatomie settlement (present Linn county), by the Rev. Christian Hoecken, S. J. (Witnesses were: the Rev. Felix L. Verreydt, S. J., and James Sidney.)

Evidently this "regularized" an earlier marriage, for on June 28, also, their daughter Rosalie Pensineau (aged three years) was baptized by Father Hoecken. Three years later—on November 16, 1850—"at Kansas river" (present Pottawatomie county) their son Joseph Pensineau, aged nine months, was baptized by Father Maurice Gailland, S. J., of St. Mary's Mission.

Ref: "Pottawatomie Marriage Register," and "Pottawatomie Baptismal Register," pp. 179, 275 (microfilm in KHi).

❦ June 28.—In search of Neosho valley floral specimens, Lucille St. Pierre (about 20), of New Orleans, set out from trader Michel Giraud's home (west of present Erie, Neosho county), accompanied by a young French-speaking Osage girl, "Angelica Mit-ce-ke." They crossed the river in a skiff; subsequently lost the boat; could not find their way back; and (not located by search parties) were believed to have drowned. By a fortunate circumstance Michel Giraud and part-Osage Isaac Swiss (Suisse) found them, alive, on June 30. By July 3 they had recovered sufficiently to return to the trader's house.

A long account of this incident (written many years later) by the Rev. Paul M. Ponziglione, S. J., of Osage Catholic Mission, supplies the basic facts set forth above. Miss St. Pierre (daughter of Anthony St. Pierre) had come up the Mississippi to St. Louis in the spring; and continued by steamboat (the *Martha*), in the Chouteaus' care, to Kansas (City), Mo., where she was a guest of Mrs. Berenice Therese (Menard) Chouteau till escorted overland to the Neosho valley by Edward L. Chouteau (son of P. Ligueste), whose home was at the mouth of Flat Rock creek (some seven miles below Giraud's residence). St. Pierre (according to Ponziglione) was an agent for a French botanist (Benoit DeBonald) "whose charge was to supply the Paris Botanical Gardens with a special collection of complete North American flora."

Ref: *St. Louis Catholic Historical Review*, St. Louis, v. 4 (January-April, 1922), pp. 51-64; and reprinted in St. Paul (Kan.) *Journal*, May 7, 1942. American Fur Company trader Michel Giraud, from 1839 to about 1845(?) had operated the company's post on the Marais des Cygnes at present Trading Post, Linn county (*see* annals, p. 376).

℘ July.—Among the Santa Fe-bound traders camped near Council Grove "waiting until reinforcements should come up," as the month began, were "Coon & Gallaghers train of nine wagons each with seven yoke of cattle," also "Cunifee" (H. J.? Cuniffe—*see* April 27 entry), and others. ("Messrs. [B. F.] Coons & Gallagher's train" had left Independence, Mo., some three weeks earlier.)

The arrival of "Easton's" troops (Company B, in particular) at Council Grove on July 1 and 2 (*see* p. 691) supplied the awaited escort. When, on August 8, eastbound F. X. Aubry met Easton's large command at "McKneis' [McNees'] creek"—within two weeks' travel of Santa Fe—the traders then in company were "Messrs. Stevenson, Coons, McIntosh, Cuniffe, McGill, Drace, Williams, Estis, Carr, Rohman and [Charles E.] Kearn[e]y, with 40 wagons filled with dry goods and provisions."

Ref: Saint Louis *Reveille* (daily), July 13, 1847; E. N. O. Clough's diary, in *Democratic Standard*, Leavenworth, August 10, 1883; New York *Weekly Tribune*, July 24, 1847 (from *Missouri Republican*, St. Louis, July 7); *Niles' Weekly Register*, v. 72 (July 17, 1847), p. 320; Saint Louis *Daily Union*, September 7, 1847 (for Aubry); Garrard, *op. cit.*, p. 374. "Williams" may have been William S. ("Old Bill") Williams, who was on the Santa Fe trail this summer of 1847. At Mann's Fort, on July 23, Pvt. E. N. O. Clough, of Easton's battalion, wrote: "Old Bill Williams, the trapper, came into our camp this evening. . . . He stayed in my tent while here." "Estis" possibly was Asa Estes, of Taos, who had come East with Ceran S. Vrain—*see* June 9 annals entry. Charles E. Kearney entered the Santa Fe trade in 1847—*see The United States Biographical Dictionary* . . . *Missouri Volume* (1878), p. 155.

℘ July.—Eight companies of the Third regiment, Missouri mounted volunteers (headed by Col. John Ralls—*see* June 19 entry) were on the Santa Fe trail, in detachments (most of them escorting government or traders' wagon trains). On August 1 the last two companies, with the regimental officers, bringing up the rear, set out from Fort Leavenworth. Summarized below are some data on "Ralls'" regiment of cavalry.

Capt. Washington L. McNair's Company (A), from St. Louis: arrived at Independence, Mo., on June 13; and at Fort Leavenworth on June 19; under Lt. James M. Allen, joined "Easton's" infantry battalion at Council Grove on July 3. *See* June 17-21 annals entry. McNair was still at Independence on July 13; traveled to Santa Fe with Ralls.

Capt. Gabriel de Korponay's Company (B), from St. Louis: arrived at Independence on June 13; and at Fort Leavenworth on June 19; was east of Council Grove from about July 3 to July 10 (or later); was at Cottonwood crossing on July 18 and 19 (as were Clarkson's and Boake's companies); was at Middle Cimarron spring on August 13 (with the same, and Smithson's companies; also two trains of government wagons, and some traders); reached Santa Fe without losing any men, and had but few ill on the way. (Two men of Korponay's company, earlier reported as missing on the march—and supposed killed by Indians—evidently turned up later.)

Capt. Louis Geis' Company (C), from St. Louis: was mustered in at St. Louis on May 28; was referred to as a "German company"; apparently did not leave Fort Leavenworth till August 1.

Capt. Augustus Jones' Company (D), from Washington county: arrived at Independence July 1; left for Fort Leavenworth on the 3d; part of the company left a camp below the fort on July 9 (under orders to assist Lt. John Love). *See* July 9 annals entry. Under 2d Lt. Stephen D. Mullowny, the rest of Jones' company served as escort for "Kit" Carson. *See* July 17 annals entry.

Capt. William S. Lofland's Company (E), from Ralls county: arrived at Fort Leavenworth on June 19; was at Council Grove on July 21; reached the Arkansas crossing on August 13; eastbound travelers, on the Jornada, August 16, met "Lofflin's [Loffland's] Co." and a train of government wagons; reached San Miguel, N. M., on September 9.

Capt. James I. Clarkson's Company (F), from Dade county: reached Independence before May 24; was east of Council Grove on July 10; traveled with Korponay's and Boake's companies for a time; was, on July 22, at Cow creek with Boake; reached Santa Fe in August.

Capt. Samuel A. Boake's Company (G), from Greene county: arrived at Fort Leavenworth on June 19; was at Cow creek, on July 22 (*see* above); four men died on the journey (one of them was Second Lieutenant Oliver, on August 15), and there was much sickness in the outfit; when 250 miles from Santa Fe (on August 17) a company member wrote that they had seen no Indians, that most of their horses were in bad condition (and they had lost six).

Capt. Moses H. Simonds' Company, from Gentry county: was camped near Council Grove on July 15 and Simonds was then very ill (he died on July 25, or 26?, at or near Council Grove); was at Middle Cimarron spring on August 14; reached Santa Fe on, or about September 7.

Capt. [Benjamin W.?] Smithson's Company, from Polk(?) county: was camped with Simonds' company a few miles west of Council Grove on July 21; was attacked near Pawnee Rock on August 1 by about 400 Indians (*see* under the July 17 entry for "Kit" Carson); lost 11 men on the march to Santa Fe from sickness and fatigue.

Capt. John Haley's Company, from Madison(?) county: left Independence for Fort Leavenworth on July 13; apparently did not leave Fort Leavenworth till August 1.

On August 1 a government train left Fort Leavenworth escorted by Lt. Col. Richard H. Lane. Colonel Ralls and his staff (and the tenth company?) probably followed soon thereafter. A letter (apparently by Ralls) dated "Council Grove, Aug. 17, 1847" stated that a few days were being spent there, waiting for the government trains which were to be escorted. ("Our march [here] was agreeable and without inconvenience or accident.") The writer also mentioned the death of "Capt. Simonds, of my command" (*see* above) on "the 25th ulto. His death we do lament. A little rude mound upon the hill side . . . [marks his grave]."

At the Little Arkansas, on August 28, eastbound F. X. Aubry met Col. John Ralls with two companies (Haley's and Geis') of the Missouri cavalry, also Captains McNair (of Company A—*see* above), Haley and Geis, together with five government trains, and some traders (including Stone, and Goldstein). Two days later, at Cow creek, a volunteer wrote that the train (which included 180 wagons with army stores) was getting along well, and stated: "We have over 3500 animals to guard and as yet have not lost one from any cause. Indian signs abundant."

On September 6 Colonel Ralls was on the lower Coon creek road (and eastbound "Colonel" Price, traveling the upper road, rode down to see him). When, about September 15, Ralls learned (from eastbound travelers) that the Illinois regiment's Colonel Newby, already in Santa Fe, had ordered several companies of troops to El Paso, he turned over command of his large force to Maj. William W. Reynolds (not to Lt. Col. Richard H. Lane, who was, it appears, unpopular), and set out in haste for Santa Fe with an escort of 20 men. (On the 20th he was well beyond McNees' creek; and before September 27 he reached New Mexico's capital.)

Major Reynolds' command camped at Middle Cimarron spring on September 29. A volunteer wrote: "we have made a rapid march considering that our train consists of 300 wagons [180 government; 120? traders'] with 1,500 yoke of cattle and 500 head of beef cattle. . . . We expect to reach Santa Fe by October 5."

Ref: Saint Louis *Reveille* (daily), July 18, September 17, 22, November 2, 1847; Saint Louis *Daily Union,* June 3, 23, August 2, 9, September 1, 7, 20, 23, October 4, December 22; New York *Weekly Tribune,* July 31, August 14, October 2, 9 (from *Missouri Republican,* St. Louis, July 19, August 2, September 20, 22); *The Weekly Tribune,* Liberty, Mo., October 1, 1847; *Jefferson Inquirer,* Jefferson City, Mo., September 17, 1847; *Democratic Standard,* Leavenworth, August 17, 1847; *see, also,* references under June 19 annals entry.

❈ July 2.—At Independence, Mo., a correspondent wrote: "This morning Col. [William Henry] Russell, Sec. of the Ter. of Calif. [under Fremont's brief administration], arrived at this place, with a party of 18 men." Russell (a Callaway county, Missouri, resident; emigrant West in 1846—*see* p. 583), carrying dispatches from Commodore Stockton and Lieutenant Colonel Fremont, had left California on March 25 "with a party of 15 men," and traveled, by southern routes, to Santa Fe; from there, on May 29, he set out, with Bell's government train, for Missouri. (*See* p. 693 for the train's loss of stock to the Comanches; and the Indian skirmishes of Russell's party.

From the Pawnee Rock vicinity, Russell, his escort (of 15?), also Michael W. Murphy (an ex-Laclede Ranger), Charles McCarty, and Lewis H. Garrard, and a few others—25 mounted men in all, with one light wagon, had come in ahead of the slow wagon train. Russell, McCarty, Murphy, "the colonel's [California] Indian," and Garrard, with two pack mules, reached Westport, Mo. (from Council Grove), one day in advance of their companions. Garrard went up to Fort Leavenworth (to collect pay for his services at Mann's Fort—*see* pp. 670, 671), before continuing homeward to Ohio.

Ref: New York *Weekly Tribune,* July 24, 31, 1847; *Niles' National Register,* v. 72 (July 17, 1847), p. 320 (from *Missouri Republican,* St. Louis, July 7); Saint Louis *Daily Union,* July 7, 8, 1847; Saint Louis *Reveille* (daily), July 8, 1847; Garrard, *op. cit.,* pp. 357-377. Garrard was not always accurate on names in his book *Wah-to-yah.* Murphy, for example, he called "Henry" instead of Michael. William H. Russell's escort was headed by a young man named Brown (an emigrant to California in 1845, from western Missouri). William H(enry) Russell and family are listed in the federal census of 1850 in Jackson county, Mo.

❈ July 4.—Army regulars and volunteer troops paraded at Fort Leavenworth in observance of Independence day. Participating were: Col. Clifton Wharton's First U. S. dragoons staff, a company of First U. S. infantry, the entire First ("Newby's") regiment, Illinois infantry volunteers, and one company of the Third ("Ralls'") regiment, Missouri mounted volunteers.

Ref: Thomas B. Lester's diary, 1847-1848, from photostats in Western Historical Manuscripts Collection, University of Missouri, Columbia, Mo.

❈ July 7.—Captained by Solomon Houck, a company from Santa Fe—traders, discharged Missouri volunteers, and others—about 70 men in all (with eight wagons, and a small mule herd), arrived at Council Grove. They had met no hostile Indians en route.

The merchants were Houck, of Boonville, James J. Webb, of St. Louis, Cornelius Davy, of Independence, Christopher C. Branham, of Platte City, his brother —— —— Branham, of Columbia, also, Henry C. Miller, of Arrow Rock. Some 23 ex-Laclede Rangers (*see* p. 594), including Richard S. Elliott (whose letters, written under the alias "John Brown," describe the journey) were among the Missouri volunteers (now civilians) in the party. Another cotraveler was Lt. George T. Andrews, newly commissioned in the U. S. artillery. Peter Joseph, who had been in the company, turned back from the Arkansas (to Santa Fe) after effecting there a deal for the goods of Henry C. Miller (*see* above, and p. 694), a westbound trader whose oxen had been taken by Indians on June 26; and Miller reversed direction, also.

Houck and company met many Santa Fe-bound trains while journeying eastward. Among the travelers who warned them of Indian dangers ahead were Francis X. Aubry (met south of the Arkansas) and Agent Thomas Fitzpatrick (with Lt. John Love and the First dragoons—*see* p. 694), who rode up on June 30 as they traveled the "bluff road" (dry, or cut-off route) between the Arkansas and Pawnee Fork.

Houck, Webb, and the Laclede Rangers, in advance of some of the company, reached Independence on July 13; and St. Louis on July 17, aboard the *Monona*.

Ref: Webb, *op. cit.,* pp. 287-300; Saint Louis *Reveille* (daily), July 18, 20, 1847; *The Weekly Tribune,* Liberty, Mo., July 17, 1847; Richard S. Elliott's *Notes Taken in Sixty Years* (1883), pp. 254, 255; New York *Weekly Tribune,* July 31, 1847 (from *Missouri Republican,* St. Louis, July 19).

❦ July 7.—The *Martha* (returning from the American Fur Company's Fort Union—*see* May 22 entry) passed the mouth of the Kansas on the 7th; and reached St. Louis the evening of July 8. She had made the homeward journey, without accident (though there were reports contrariwise), in less than 13 days (and the round trip in 57 days).

Her cargo included 1,300 packs of buffalo robes, 280 packs of furs, 96 sacks of buffalo tongues, and 237 beef hides. Among her passengers were John B. Sarpy, Honoré D. Picotte, Pierre D. Papin—all connected with the fur trade; and the Rev. Nicholas Point, S. J. (missionary to the Blackfeet Indians), who disembarked at the Kaw's mouth and stopped at Westport, Mo., for about three(?) weeks.

Ref: Saint Louis *Daily Union,* July 9, 1847; Saint Louis *Reveille* (daily), July 9, 1847; Garraghan, *op. cit.,* v. 2, pp. 446, 447, 451; Sunder, *op. cit.,* pp. 97, 98. For a December 17, 1847, letter by Sup't T. H. Harvey concerning "spirits" having been sold aboard the *Martha* while on the upper Missouri, see SIA, St. Louis, "Records," v. 9 (typed copy), pp. 29, 30.

❦ July 7.—Beginning this day, and in three detachments, the First ("Newby's") regiment, Illinois infantry volunteers, departed from Fort Leavenworth on the 800-mile march to Santa Fe.

Lt. Col. Henderson P. Boyakin (of Clinton county, Ill.) with Companies B, C, and E (Capts. John M. Cunningham, Vantrump Turner, and George W. Hook) started on July 7, escorting a train of 30 government wagons, in charge of "Captain Finley [Findlay], of Westport, Mo." His command ferried the Kansas on the 10th (at the military road, or Delaware, or Grinter, crossing); stopped at the Shawnee camp ground; attended church at the Indians' large log meeting house on the 11th; traveled to "Lone Elm" on the 13th (Pvt. John W. Collins was buried here); at Pool creek, on the 20th, Pvt. Aaron J. Campbell was buried; reached Council Grove on July 22d; left on the 25th with 30 more wagons (a train in charge of "Captain Elliott") in company; reached Pawnee Fork on August 5 (Pvt. Robert Easley was buried this day); passed Mann's Fort on the 12th ("there was no person there," wrote Pvt. Thomas B. Lester); reached the Arkansas crossing on the 13th; laid by on the 14th; crossed the river on the 15th; on August 19, at the Lower Cimarron spring, an express from Newby arrived with orders to wait for his command (which arrived on the 20th). [Pvt. Benjamin L. Wiley, of Company B, and Pvt. (later acting assistant surgeon) Thomas B. Lester, of Company C, kept diaries of the march of Boyakin's detachment over the Santa Fe trail; their records supply many details of the journey. In contrast, little information is available about the other two commands—particularly Donalson's.]

Maj. Israel B. Donalson (of Pike county, Ill.) and four companies (A, H, I, and K), headed by Capts. Thomas Bond, James Hampton, Franklin Niles, and William Kinman, evidently left Fort Leavenworth soon after Boyakin's detachment; apparently escorted across the plains a large number of cattle. The Illinois adjutant general's records show that Capt. Franklin Niles "died at 110 Creek . . . July 24, 1847." On August 19, Donalson, his four companies, and "Huntington's train of government wagons, were met by eastbound F. X. Aubry at the Arkansas crossing; on the 29th (in the [Middle?] Cimarron springs area) other Missouri-bound men met Donalson's command—described as four companies of Illinois volunteers, a government train of wagons, and 400 government cattle.

Col. Edward W. B. Newby (of Brown county, Ill.), and the remaining three companies (D, F, and G), headed by Capts. John C. Moses, Thomas B. Kinney, and Henry J. Reed, presumably left Fort Leavenworth not long after the others. On August 18, about a day's travel in *advance* of Donalson's command, Newby, his three companies, together with traders Barclay, of Lexington, Mo., and Tharp, of St. Louis (with seven wagons), were met by eastbound F. X. Aubry, at "Battle Ground," south of the Arkansas crossing. On August 20 the colonel and his detachment (with a train of 24 government wagons—perhaps Huntington's train) arrived at the Lower Cimarron spring, joining Boyakin's command.

Colonel Newby divided his six-company, 84-wagon force, detaching Captain Hook and Company E, with Elliott's train on the 22d; placing Findlay's train with Kinney's and Reed's companies on the 25th; and himself proceeding with Boyakin, Companies B, C, D, and 18 wagons. About September 10 the Illinois troops began to arrive at Santa Fe. Newby reached there on September 11.

Ref: Saint Louis *Daily Union*, June 10, July 14, August 2, 26, September 7, 21, 30, 1847; Saint Louis *Reveille* (daily), November 2, 1847; New York *Weekly Tribune*, October 9, 1847 (from *Missouri Republican*, St. Louis, September 22); Benjamin L. Wiley's Mexican War journal, "Benjamin Wiley Papers," Southern Illinois University, Carbondale, Ill. (Wiley, in a table of distances, recorded a total of 803 miles from Fort Leavenworth to Santa Fe);

Thomas B. Lester's diary, 1847-1848, from photostats in Western Historical Manuscripts Collection, University of Missouri, Columbia, Mo. *Also, see* references under June 21 entry. Lester later lived in Kansas City, Mo.

❡ DIED: Mary (Mrs. Charles) Graham, wife of the Wyandots' government blacksmith, on July 9, in present Kansas City, Kan.

Ref: William Walker's "Journals," *loc. cit.*

❡ July 9.—Capt. Augustus Jones and part of Company D, ("Ralls'") Third regiment, Missouri mounted volunteers, with two six-pounders (for Easton's command), and seven mule-drawn wagons, left Fort Leavenworth under orders to proceed by forced marches to Lt. John Love's relief (*see* p. 694). The express with news of "Love's defeat" on the Santa Fe trail had arrived at the fort on July 5.

Pvt. Philip G. Ferguson, in a diary, recorded details of the march, and varied items of "Kansas" interest. He noted there were two ferries (flat-bottomed boats, "pushed along by poles") at the military road (or Grinter) crossing—one operated by Delaware Indians, the other by Shawnees; and he mentioned the presence at Fort Leavenworth, in early July, of Maj. Nathan Boone (the only living son of frontiersman Daniel Boone), of the First dragoons.

Jones and his command reached Council Grove on July 15; left on the 17th, accompanied by a Mexican trader's train of nine wagons "owned by R. Armijo & Co." (according to Ferguson), but with Emanuel Armijo in charge (as stated by F. X. Aubry). On July 25 the Missouri volunteers and the merchant train crossed Pawnee Fork; on the 29th they passed Mann's Fort (and learned that Lt. John Love had left some days earlier). They entered Santa Fe on August 23, one day behind Easton's command.

Ref: Saint Louis *Daily Union*, May 29, June 8, 21, July 8, September 7, 1847; New York *Weekly Tribune*, July 31, 1847; Scharf, *op. cit.*, v. 1, p. 379; Saint Louis *Reveille* (daily), July 18, 1847; R. P. Bieber, editor, *Marching With the Army of the West*, pp. 283-361 (for Ferguson's diary).

❡ July 11.—The *Lake of the Woods*, with $40,000 to $50,000 in supplies, and 50 to 60 men, left St. Louis for Harvey, Primeau and Co's. upriver posts. (She returned to St. Louis on September 5.)

Ref: Sunder, *op. cit.*, pp. 100-103.

❡ July 13(?) and 14(?)—At, or near Pawnee Fork, Indians killed two(?) or three(?) men belonging to returning government trains. (Travelers' "reports" provide inconclusive information.)

Pvt. E. N. O. Clough (in his diary, July 15) wrote: "Met Kraven's [Cravens'?] train, of Buchanan co., Mo. which left Santa Fe May 28th last. They had one man killed and another[?] scalped night before last." On the 16th, near Ash creek, Clough's company "Met a train of wagons just in from

Santa Fe which left there May 28th. They lost one man near the Fork."
[Did Clough refer, in both entries, to one incident?, or two separate killings?]

Lt. L. J. Eastin (eastbound; and at Pawnee Fork around June 14) wrote
of an occurrence the previous day to a government train: "Indians captured
twenty-one oxen and killed [and scalped] a negro man belonging to Moses
Payne, of Boone County, Mo., within 150 yards of camp. A white man narrowly escaped with his life." (Homeward-bound with this train were Capt.
William Z. Angney and his company of Cole county, Missouri, volunteers
[*see* p. 594]. Angney's company reached Fort Leavenworth on July 30; and
was discharged on the 31st.)

A westbound Missouri volunteer wrote, on July 16: "This letter will be
taken to Independence by Capt. Grooms [wagonmaster], whom we have just
met. Ind's attacked Capt. G. & his party night before last at Pawnee Fork,
scalped one, took many head of cattle and a wagon." (Probably this was the
same incident noted by Eastin.)

Ref: *Democratic Standard,* Leavenworth, August 10, 1883; New York *Weekly Tribune,*
August 11, 1847 (from *Missouri Republican,* St. Louis, August 2); Saint Louis *Daily
Union,* August 5, 1847; Saint Louis *Reveille* (daily), July 18, August 5, 1847; W. E.
Connelley's *Doniphan's Expedition* (1907), p. 566. Pvt. Thomas B. Lester, at Pawnee
Fork on August 5, wrote: "Here we found the graves of two persons killed by Indians—
one a negro boy [Payne's Negro man?] who went down to spring; the other person is not
known to me."—Thomas B. Lester's diary, 1847-1848, from photostats in Western Historical
Manuscripts Collection, University of Missouri, Columbia, Mo.

❦ July 14.—Lt. Daniel P. Woodbury (Army engineers) arrived at
Fort Leavenworth, from St. Louis; and remained till September.

His further journey, and his mission—to select a site for a military post on the Oregon-California trail—were delayed by the slow
outfitting of the "Oregon battalion"—*see* August 9 and 28 entries.

Ref: Nebraska State Historical Society *Publications,* v. 21, p. 250.

❦ July 14.—An American Fur Company Mackinaw boat, bound
for St. Louis with some 2,500 buffalo robes, struck a snag in the
Missouri about a mile below St. Joseph, Mo., and sank. The men
aboard escaped.

Ref: *The Gazette,* St. Joseph, Mo., July 16, 1847.

❦ July.—Santa Fe traders leaving Council Grove in mid-month
were "Messrs. Murphy and Post, Wm. McKnight, Owens and
Woods, with 20 wagons," also "Messrs. Emerson, Turner, Allen and
Teabout, of St. Louis . . . with 10 wagons." (They made
the journey to New Mexico under escort of detachments of ["Ralls' "]
Third regiment, Missouri mounted volunteers—which also had in
charge government trains.)

On August 12, above Middle Cimarron spring, eastbound F. X. Aubry met
the first group; and on the 13th, at Middle spring met the other party traveling
with four companies of "Ralls' " troops, and two government trains (Thompson
and Hayden, wagonmasters).

Ref: Saint Louis *Daily Union*, September 7, 1847.

❧ About July 17 (?), Lt. Christopher ("Kit") Carson (commissioned June 9 in the U. S. Mounted riflemen by President Polk) left Fort Leavenworth carrying dispatches (brought from Washington, D. C.) to be delivered in New Mexico and in California. He had as escort, to Santa Fe, 2d Lt. Stephen D. Mullowny and 50 men of Capt. Augustus Jones' Company D, Third regiment, Missouri mounted volunteers. (This company was from Washington county.)

On July 25 Carson's party camped at Diamond Spring (as did the portion of First Illinois regiment troops under Lt. Col. H. P. Boyakin's command). The journey, as far as the Pawnee Rock vicinity, was uneventful. But at Ash creek, on August 1 (as Carson later related), he and his escort camped "about 300 yards from a company of [Missouri] Volunteers [Captain Smithson's company of the Third regiment] enroute for New Mexico having with them a very large train of wagons.

"At daylight the men of said company were leading out their horses to picket them in new grass. They were attacked by a party of Commanches and had 26 horses and all their cattle driven off. The cattle taking a turn near our camp, I was enabled to retake them from the Indians . . . [six or eight Comanches were killed, and as many more wounded, by report].

"The company lost 26 and would have lost all of their cattle, if I and my party had not been there to assist them. Also had three men wounded. I lost two horses. . . . We then continued our march and arrived at Santa Fe [on August 27] without any difficulty."

Carson went on to California, reaching his destination there in October. On January 28, 1848, the senate negatived his commission.

Ref: 31st Cong., 1st Sess., *H. Ex. Doc. No. 17* (Serial 573), p. 247; *Kit Carson's Own Story of His Life* . . ., ed. by Blanche C. Grant (Taos, N. M., 1926), pp. 85, 86; H. L. Carter's *Dear Old Kit* . . ., *op. cit.*, pp. 117, 118; Sabin, v. 2, pp. 571-576; Saint Louis *Reveille* (daily) June 23, 26, July 18, 1847; Saint Louis *Daily Union*, July 29 (for letter dated Fort Leavenworth, July 16, 1847, noting Carson's presence there), September 20, 1847; Benjamin L. Wiley's Mexican War journal ("Benjamin Wiley Papers," Southern Illinois University, Carbondale, Ill.); Thomas B. Lester's diary (from photostats in Western Historical Manuscripts Collection, University of Missouri, Columbia, Mo.); Philip G. Ferguson's diary, in *Marching With the Army of the West* . . ., ed. by R. P. Bieber, p. 319; Heitman, *op. cit.*, p. 286.

❧ July(?)—Sac & Fox Agency buildings (costing $1,432), under construction (off and on) since January, were completed about this time by contractor Allen B. H. McGee, Westport, Mo.

The agency headquarters consisted of a one-and-a-half-story, hewed-log, double house of four rooms (15' x 16' each), with passageway between, and kitchen (15' x 15') at one end; also a smokehouse (16' x 16') and a stable (18' x 18'), both of round logs. By present-day description, the location was near the center of the NW¼ of Sec. 16, T. 17, R. 18 E. (south of Pomona, and a mile or more south of the Marais des Cygnes, in Greenwood township, Franklin co.).

There were, also, two two-room blacksmith shops (16' x 24'), built by John

Barham and George Sharp(e), for $380. For digging wells, H. Netherton received $212.75, and James Taylor $48.

Ref: OIA, "Letters Received from Sac & Fox Agency" (National Archives Microcopy 234, Roll 732), for John Beach's "ad," dated November 19, 1846, and his letters of February 15 and May 25, 1847; 30th Cong., 1st Sess., Sen. Ex. Doc. No. 48 (Serial 508), p. 14; KHC, v. 11, p. 341; U. S. survey plat (state auditor's office).

❡ July 20.—At Fort Scott (present Bourbon county), John L.(?) Kline agreed, in a war department contract made with Lt. George W. Wallace (AAQM), First U. S. infantry, to furnish 50 tons of "good sound, well cured prairie hay" (for the sum of $2.60 per ton) at the U. S. sawmill near the fort.

George Douglass (on September 28) signed a contract to furnish 150 tons of hay (at $5.90 per ton) at Fort Scott; and John S.(?) Kline (on September 29) agreed to supply 50 tons of hay (at $5.47 per ton).

Ref: 30th Cong., 1st Sess., H. Ex. Doc. No. 29 (Serial 516), pp. 49, 84.

❡ July 20.—Lt. Col. Alton R. Easton, en route to Santa Fe (*see* p. 690) with a command of four companies of Missouri volunteers (three infantry; one cavalry), escorting a government train and 600 loose cattle, camped for the night about 25 miles below Mann's Fort, after a 15-mile march along the Arkansas. (The location was in present eastern Ford county.)

Some 25 to 50 infantrymen "in parties of two and three, and entirely unarmed," were gathering firewood on the opposite (right) bank of the river when mounted Indians (thought to be Comanches), waiting in ambush, attacked. Before help could arrive, eight of the Missourians had been killed ("horribly lanced and scalped"), and four others wounded. Capt. William A. Barnes' Company E lost six men: William Duncan, Francis Turcott, Ludwick Tanner, Jacob Johnson, Valentine Regg, and Henry Barlow; Benjamin Frost, though severely wounded, and scalped, survived. Of Capt. Edward W. Paul's Company D, Philander Porter and Charles Fuss were killed; Michael McBride and William Warner were wounded, severely; and Acuzi Stanley, slightly. (The Comanches? lost only one warrior.) The dead were buried in one grave.

Easton's command continued upriver on July 21; and on the 22d camped "in sight of [and two miles from] Manns Fort"; spent the next three days there. Pvt. E. N. O. Clough, in a letter dated "Mann's Fort July 25, 1847," wrote: "We have several hundred head of loose cattle with us, and we will yoke up 180 yoke of them, to haul Hayden's train [*see* p. 694], when the yokes [cached, after "Love's defeat" of June 26, near present Garfield?, Pawnee county] are brought in." (Also at Mann's Fort in this period were Companies A and B of Easton's battalion with the trains under their escort—*see* p. 690. Shepard's ["A"] command departed on July 24; Woechner's ["B"] command left on July 25.)

"Press Gang" (a Missouri volunteer), in a July 23 letter, added a puzzling item to the history of Mann's Fort. He wrote: "The report that this fort had been consumed by the Indians proves to be erroneous. . . . Mann, who built it, and has charge of it[?], says he will abandon it, unless he can get some 30 men from our battalion to remain with him—of which I think there is no probability." (This *seems* to place wagonmaster Daniel P. Mann, who left the fort on May 16—*see* p. 670—back there, briefly, in mid-July.)

Easton's command left Mann's Fort on July 26; forded the Arkansas (some 25? miles upriver) on July 27. Private Clough wrote (later) that from the Arkansas crossing "till we crossed the Cimarron we travelled from daylight in the morning till . . . [late at night]." Eastbound trader F. X. Aubry met Easton with "five" companies of Missouri volunteers, a train of government wagons, and 40 traders' wagons, on August 8 at McNees' creek. According to Clough, the date of arrival at Santa Fe was August 22.

Ref: Same as for June 17-21 entry. The Saint Louis *Daily Union, December* 21, 1847 (quoting the Santa Fe [N. M.] *Republican* of October 23, 24, 1847), stated: "Mr. Frost . . . who was scalped by the Indians on the Arkansas is now here [Santa Fe], hearty and well, and swears vengeance against all of the copper colored race. . . ."

❰ Sumner.—At Ottawa Baptist Mission (present Franklin county) a new meeting house was nearing completion. The hewed-log structure (for which the "first round" had been laid on October 5, 1846), was 40 feet by 25 in size, with shingle roof. Inside were "26 seats or slips and a pulpit." The total cost would be about $500.

On October 21 Missionary Jotham Meeker wrote (in his diary) that the Indian subagent had examined the meeting house, and promised to "certify to the U. S. Govt that it is worth 700 or 800 dolls." On November 5 Meeker "Cut holes through the M[eeting] H[ouse] ceiling and roof, and put up a stove."

Ref: *The Baptist Missionary Magazine*, Boston, v. 27 (July, 1847), p. 259; Jotham Meeker's "Diary."

❰ July 21.—On the *Haydee,* from Weston, Mo., arriving at St. Louis were "Messrs. [James] Murray, [James] Kipp, and [John] Sebille [Sibille]," and a number of American Fur Company employees. The 1,307 packages of buffalo robes they had brought down from the upper Missouri (as far as Weston) in Mackinaw boats, were also aboard the *Haydee.* Murray had left Fort Alexander, on the upper Yellowstone, June 6; Kipp had left Fort Union on June 12; Sibille had joined at Fort Pierre.

On, or about, the same day the *Amaranth* docked at St. Louis, having aboard some 40 American Fur Company employees, and the cargoes (consisting of peltries) from two Mackinaw boats.

Ref: Saint Louis *Reveille* (daily), July 22, 1847; Saint Louis *Daily Union*, July 22, 1847; *Contributions to the Historical Society of Montana*, Helena, v. 10, p. 284 (for "James" Murray—in charge of Fort Alexander); Sunder, *op. cit.*, p. 97.

℄ July 23.—"Judge, or Col. [James] Brown [of Pettis county, Mo.]," in company with Lt. Lucian J. Eastin (of Angney's Cole county, Mo., infantrymen—*see* p. 703), and "young Mr. Hughes," of Howard county, Mo., arrived at Westport, Mo., in advance of co-travelers (military and civilian) with whom they had journeyed from Santa Fe (left June 20 and 21) as far as the Little Arkansas. (Fourteen of Angney's men reached Fort Leavenworth on July 29.)

On July 4, while on the Cimarron, a combined force of Comanches and renegade Mexicans had attacked their party "in the middle of the day, when . . . least expected . . . and succeeded in taking one mule and killing another. Judge Brown, at the same time, lost 17 oxen."

Ref: Saint Louis *Daily Union*, August 2, 3, 5, 1847; Saint Louis *Reveille* (daily), July 30, 1847; New York *Weekly Tribune*, August 14, 1847 (from *Missouri Republican*, St. Louis, August 2). Capt. W. Z. Angney did not return from Santa Fe with his company.

℄ July 28.—The year's first party *from* Oregon arrived at St. Joseph, Mo. R. H. Holder (of the 1846 emigration West) and 14(?) other men were in this company. Holder and a man named Shaw were aboard the *Tributary* which reached St. Louis on August 4.

These travelers had made the trip in 83 days. They had left Oregon City on (and about) May 5; traveled the Applegate cutoff (or "southern") route (having as guide to Fort Hall, Levi Scott); separated into two parties for part of the journey in. Several outbound travelers mentioned meeting the two divisions. The advance party of eight was at South Pass on June 26, and was said to have "over 20 horses and mules with them, mostly laden with packs of robes, skins, etc." Among these eight, as far as the Mormon ferry on the North Platte, was Moses ("Black") Harris. Ferryman Appleton M. Harmon recorded, on July 3: "the oregon mail arived [and crossed] a bout Sun down thare ware 8 men of them & several pack horses & mules they had been ever since the 5th of May on the rout. . . ." Of the *second* division he noted, on July 7: "8 men from oregon arived with pack horses & mules we ferryed them & their packs."

On July 16 this company (reunited?) met about 1,000 Sioux (who were on their way to attack the Pawnees); and on the 20th met some 2,000 Pawnees (going up the Platte on a hunt) who detained Holder and his party, but decided not to rob them.

Ref: New York *Weekly Tribune*, August 21, 1847 (from *Missouri Republican*, St. Louis, August 5); *The Gazette*, St. Joseph, Mo., July 30, 1847; Saint Louis *Daily Union*, August 5,

1847; Saint Louis *Reveille* (daily, August 5, 1847 (which stated that R. H. Holder, of Illinois, who went West "last May a year ago" was in the company of A. J. Grayson, G. L. Curry, and others); *Illinois Catholic Historical Review*, v. 9 (January, 1927), p. 217; Pratt, *op. cit.*, p. 63; or, *The Utah Genealogical and Historical Magazine*, v. 16 (July, 1925), p. 166; *Annals of Wyoming*, Cheyenne, v. 21 (July-October, 1949), pp. 111-167 (for "The Mormon Ferry on the North Platte; The Journal of William A. Empey . . .," edited by Dale L. Morgan—*see*, particularly, pp. 137, 138, 159, 160); *Niles' National Register*, v. 72 (August 14, 1847), p. 370 (which mentions "Messrs. Shaw and Bolden [Holder]," but subsequently refers to "Messrs. Shaw and Thompson[?]," without further mention of Holder).

❧ **August 6.**—A government train from Santa Fe, in charge of Isaac McCarty (of Bullard, Hooke & Co., Lexington, Mo.) arrived at Fort Leavenworth. Some returning Missouri volunteers had traveled with McCarty—among them Capt. John C. Dent's company ("Price's" regiment—*see* p. 631), Sgt. G. N. Coulter (ex-"Laclede Ranger"), and 2d Lt. John O. Simpson (who had stopped at Council Grove).

Ref: Saint Louis *Daily Union*, August 12, 1847; *New York Weekly Tribune*, August 28, 1847 (from *Missouri Republican*, St. Louis, August 11); Saint Louis *Reveille* (daily), *August* 12, 1847; *The Weekly Tribune*, Liberty, Mo., August 14, 1847.

❧ **August 9.**—At Fort Leavenworth, Dr. Ludwell E. Powell, of St. Charles, Mo., was elected lieutenant colonel of the "Oregon battalion"—a force of Missouri mounted volunteers requisitioned with a view to the establishment of military posts on the Oregon trail—*see* p. 587. (Powell won, by 72 votes, over Andrew W. Sublette.)

Early in July the first of the five companies composing the battalion had arrived at the fort. Heading the slow-to-be-outfitted companies were: Capt. Andrew W. Sublette (Company A), Capt. David McCausland (Company B; from St. Charles county); Capt. James Craig (Company C, from Holt and Atchison counties); Capt. William H. Rodgers (Company D; Andrew county); Capt. Robert M. Stewart (Company E; from Buchanan county).

The "Oregon battalion," with an aggregate strength of 477 (25 officers, 452 men), finally prepared, left Fort Leavenworth near the end of August—*see* p. 712. Capt. Stewart Van Vliet, U. S. A., was quartermaster for the Missouri volunteers.

Ref: *The Gazette*, St. Joseph, Mo., June 11, 25, July 2, 16, 1847; Saint Louis *Daily Union*, May 27, June 21, July 9, August 9, 1847; *The Weekly Tribune*, Liberty, Mo., August 21, 1847; Robarts, *op. cit.*, p. 63; *The History of Buchanan County, Missouri* (St. Joseph, 1881), p. 200; 30th Cong., 1st Sess., Sen. Doc. No. 1 (Serial 503), p. 79; W. S. Bryan and Robert Rose, *A History of the Pioneer Families of Missouri* . . . (St. Louis, 1876), p. 188. Rodgers also is mentioned as "Rogers"; and Stewart as "Stuart." The correct spellings have not been ascertained.

❧ **August.**—About the 17th or 18th, a company of 14 men, overland from Oregon, and California, reached St. Joseph, Mo. The 10(?) from Oregon included Capt. T. G. Drake of the British navy (whose ship—the *Modeste*—had been at Fort Vancouver), John G. Campbell, of Philadelphia (said to be a nephew of Robert Campbell, St. Louis), also William and Samuel L. Campbell.

The "Californians" were John Craig (emigrant West in 1846; returning to Ray county, Mo.), Samuel(?) Truitt (of Shelby county, Ill.), and two unidentified men, one of whom may have been James Stice. Captain Drake and J. G. Campbell were noted as arriving at St. Louis on August 22.

Drake, and the three Campbells (it appears) started from Oregon on May 6, traveling as far as Fort Hall with a Hudson's Bay Company brigade. Subsequently their party of four overtook "another party of seven" from Oregon; and were overtaken by the four men from California. Craig and companions (seven at the start) had set out, near the first of June, from the Sutter's Fort area. They traveled the Hastings cutoff. Miles Goodyear and two Indian herders (taking a band of horses to Goodyear's new trading post—see p. 562) were the three in this party who traveled only as far as Bear river.

When, on July 16, the 14 reached the Mormon ferry on the North Platte, ferryman W. A. Empey wrote: "about sunset there came fourteen men in company from oragon with 40 horses and mules a going to ohio . . . they started from oragon the 6 of may . . ."; and ferryman Appleton M. Harmon wrote: "a Company of 14 men arived from oregon with 50 pack horses & mules a going to the States a part of which [the four "Californians"?] came by way of fort Bridger. . . ."

Ref: *Missouri Republican*, St. Louis, August 24, 1847; Saint Louis *Daily Union*, August 5 (for advance notice of Drake and Campbell's journey. which stated they would be accompanied by a few others, principally servants), 23 (for arrival of Drake), 1847; *The Gazette*, St. Joseph, Mo., August 20 (for general mention of parties arriving), 27 (for "S. L. Campbell"), 1847; Oregon Pioneer Association *Transactions* of the seventh annual reunion, 1879, p. 35; *Annals of Wyoming*, v. 21 (July-October, 1949), pp. 140, 164-166; Dale Morgan, editor, *Overland in 1846* (1963), v. 1, pp. 119, 141 (for John Craig, Miles Goodyear, and others of the California party); Pratt, *op. cit.*, p. 70; Rhoads-Esrey Papers, in Bancroft Library, Berkeley, Calif. (for Stice). The *Missouri Republican* reported that Drake would head east to take the earliest steamer to Liverpool; and that J. G. Campbell planned to return "this Fall" to Oregon by some southern route.

❡ August 18.—Capt. Jonas S. Woods' Platte county, Mo., infantry company (formerly headed by Capt. William S. Murphy—see p. 595) was mustered out at Fort Leavenworth, after returning overland from Santa Fe.

Ref: W. E. Connelley's *Doniphan's Expedition*, p. 568; Saint Louis *Reveille* (daily), July 18, 1847; New York *Weekly Tribune*, August 28, 1847 (from *Missouri Republican*, St. Louis, August 16).

❡ August 19.—Capt. Woldemar Fischer's St. Louis (German) light artillery company (see p. 594) was mustered out at Fort Leavenworth, having arrived, overland from Santa Fe, by way of Bent's Fort, on the 18th.

On July 28, 12 miles east of Mann's Fort, westbound troops had camped "near Captain Fischer's company of German Jagers, returning home after a year's service in N. M. . . ." Three of Fischer's men who had left Bent's Fort in advance of the others, arrived at the Missouri border some eight days ahead of their comrades. They had come through without difficulty "by the route marked out for them by a Frenchman at Bent's Fort."

Ref: W. E. Connelley's *Doniphan's Expedition*, p. 577; Saint Louis *Reveille* (daily), July 18, August 24, 1847; Saint Louis *Daily Union*, August 17, 23, 1847; New York *Weekly Tribune*, August 14, 1847 (from *Missouri Republican*, August 2); R. P. Bieber, editor, *Marching With the Army of the West*, p. 307.

❡ August 20.—James M. Estill, of Weston, Mo., contracted (with Lt. William E. Prince, AQM) to deliver fresh beef at Fort Leavenworth on September 1.

Ref: 30th Cong., 2d Sess., *Sen. Ex. Doc. No. 17* (Serial 529), p. 10.

❡ August.—The St. Joseph, Mo., *Gazette* of the 20th noted: "For the last three or four days several companies of [returning] Oregon emigrants have arrived in our town." Among them were some (if not all) of the travelers in the parties described below (in addition to the Drake-Campbell-Craig party—*see* August 17 entry).

William Findley (emigrant to Oregon in 1845—*see* p. 538) left The Dalles on May 31 to return East. He (and others) reached Fort Bridger about July 7. Brigham Young (the Mormon leader) in a letter of July 8, from that post, wrote: "Col. Findley left here this morning for the states, direct from Oregon. . . ." Prior to this, on July 4 (on Bear river?), westbound emigrant Isaac Pettijohn—who had been at Fort Bridger three days earlier—recorded: "we met three men from Oregon to day." One of these may have been William Findley; and possibly another was eastbound John E. Howell (emigrant West in 1845—*see* p. 541) who, by his own statement, was at Smith's Fork of Bear river on July 4, 1847. Probably during most of the journey, both Findley and Howell traveled with the foremost company Hastings and Empey mentioned (*see* following).

On July 17 (on the Sweetwater?), westbound Loren B. Hastings wrote: "This day met a returning company from Oregon. In the company was a man and his wife and family . . . going back to Adams county, Illinois." The woman rode astride, and to Hastings: "This is the greatest curiosity I have seen yet, it knocks everything else into the shade." (Another emigrant— Ralph C. Geer—later recollected meeting, "At the last crossing of Sweetwater," a man named Grant, "with his whole family on his way back to Missouri[?].") On July 21 William A. Empey (at the Mormons' North Platte ferry) wrote: "a Company of 18 men from oragon with 60 horses & mules a going to the States passed us 2 of them that Came by way of Fort Bridger said they saw the campt of [Mormon] peioniers at the fort there ware in their Company 1 famley a going back on horse back 3 of them Famely were woomin. . . ."

On July 18 Oregon-bound emigrant Hastings (*see* above) recorded in his diary: "Met another returning company from Oregon. In the Company was a missionary . . . and his family with him. His ladies rode [astride] like the ladies we met yesterday. . . . A little child not old enough to talk was lashed on to a pony and they drove the pony before them." Another westbound emigrant—Isaac Pettijohn—ahead of Hastings' company, had written in his diary on July 7—west of Bear river: "met a company of men from Oregon . . . amongst them was Mr [Philo B.] Littlejohn his wife [Adeline (Saddler) Littlejohn] and two children he has been in Oregon eight years [*i. e.*, since 1840—*see* p. 392] as a Missionary." Mormon ferryman Empey (*see* above), recorded on July 22: "there came a company of 10 men from oragon with a bout 40 ponies and mules there were also a famley with them going to the states & Davenport [Mormon James Davenport] bought a poney and started with them back to winter quarters on Friday [the 23d]." On August 19 the "Littlejohn party" and Davenport had reached Wolf creek (according to a traveler who overtook them), and were nearing St. Joseph, Mo.

Ref: *The Gazette*, St. Joseph, Mo., August 20, 1847; *Annals of Wyoming*, v. 21 (July-October, 1949), pp. 141, 164, 165 (for Empey; and for Dale L. Morgan's editorial notes); Oregon Pioneer Association, *Transactions* of the 51st annual reunion, Portland, 1923, p. 17 (for Hastings); *ibid.*, seventh, 1879, pp. 35, 36 (for Geer); *Utah Historical Quarterly*, Salt Lake City, v. 4 (January, 1931), p. 23; Isaac Pettijohn diary transcript (courtesy of Dale L. Morgan), from original diary in Bancroft Library, Berkeley, Cal.; *Illinois Catholic Historical Review*, v. 9 (January, 1927), p. 218; *The Washington Historical Quarterly*, Seattle, v. 1 (April, 1907), p. 157 (for Howell); *Oregon Spectator*, Oregon City, August 19, 1847.

❡ August 22.—Overland from the Sacramento valley, by way of the California-Oregon trail, in 66 days (every one spent in travel), Brig. Gen. Stephen W. Kearny returned to Fort Leavenworth (after an absence of nearly 14 months—*see* p. 620). "The old General . . . was welcomed back by his friends, and a salute of 13 guns fired in honor of his return," wrote "Prairie." "He is a great soldier, one who knows no fear, and minds not fatigue."

Over 60 persons (there had been 66 on leaving California) arrived in "Kansas" with General Kearny. There were, in his own party, Maj. P. St. George Cooke, Maj. Thomas Swords, Capt. Henry S. Turner, Lt. William Radford (U. S. N.), Asst. Surg. George Sanderson, Hon. Willard P. Hall, of Missouri (*see* p. 723), Edwin Bryant, of Kentucky (*see* p. 584), William H. Peterson, —— Duff, guides William O. Fallon and "Mr. Murphy," an escort of Mormon battalion troops (15 at the start), a few discharged dragoons, and some servants. Also arriving with Kearny (and under his command) was the Fremont party of 28 persons—Lt. Col. John C. Fremont (virtually under arrest) and 19 men of his 1845-1846 exploring party (*see* pp. 550-552) the principals in this group.

[Both Major Swords and guide William Fallon recorded mileages traveled on the march eastward. Whereas Swords listed the Fort Laramie to Fort Leavenworth distance as 613 miles, Fallon's memoranda gave it as 601 miles; and the latter entered the distance from Grand Island to Fort Leavenworth as 284 miles, while Swords gave it as 295 miles (from the "head").]

On the afternoon of August 22, when Lt. Col. John C. Fremont came into Fort Leavenworth headquarters (from his camp about two miles distant), General Kearny placed Fremont under arrest and ordered him to proceed to Washington. Fremont and his party moved on toward the town of Kansas (Kansas City), Mo., the same day—probably arrived on the 23d. (The colonel's wife, coming from the East to meet him, had already reached that place.)

Brig. Gen. Stephen W. Kearny left Fort Leavenworth (for the last time) aboard the *Amelia*, on August 23; arrived at St. Louis on the 25th; and set out for Washington on the 30th.

Aboard the *Martha*, Lt. Col. John C. Fremont and lady, and 23 persons of his "suite," reached St. Louis on August 28; on September 1 the colonel started for Washington, D. C.

Noting the departure of Kearny (on Monday), and of Fremont (on Wednesday), for the nation's capital, the Saint Louis *Reveille* commented: "Now comes the tug of war!" But the court-martial proceedings against Lt. Col. John C. Fremont (growing out of his conflict with Kearny in California) did not begin till November.

Ref: *The Weekly Tribune*, Liberty, Mo., August 28, September 3, 1847; Saint Louis *Reveille* (daily), August 26, 27, 29, September 2, 4, 1847; Saint Louis *Daily Union*, August 26, 30, 31, 1847; New York *Weekly Tribune*, September 11, 1847 (from *Missouri Republican*, St. Louis, August 26); *The Original Journals of Henry Smith Turner and Stephen Watts Kearny to New Mexico and California, 1846-1847* (Norman, Okla., c1966); 30th Cong., 2d Sess., *H. Ex. Doc. No. 1* (Serial 537), pp. 229-236 (for Swords' October 8, 1847, report); 30th Cong., 1st Sess., *Sen. Ex. Doc. No. 33* (the Fremont court-martial proceedings); N. V. Jones' diary (excerpts) in *Utah Historical Quarterly*, v. 4 (January, 1931), pp. 18-23, and additional entries (not in above), courtesy Dale L. Morgan; items from Isaac Pettijohn's diary (original in Bancroft Library), also courtesy of Dale L. Morgan; W. A. Empey's journal, in *Annals of Wyoming*, v. 21 (July-October, 1949), pp. 144, 145, 166, 167; *Historical Record*, Salt Lake City, v. 9 (January, 1890), August 4, 1847, item therein; Daniel Tyler's *A Concise History of the Mormon Battalion* . . . (1881), pp. 299-304; Edwin Bryant's *What I Saw in California* (London, 1849), p. 399; D. L. Clarke's *Stephen Watts Kearny* . . . (c1961), pp. 319-337. The Saint Louis *Reveille* (daily), of September 4, 1847, noted above, contains William O. Fallon's (*not* O'Fallon!) "memoranda" (table of distances) of the "Route between California and Fort Leavenworth." Kearny traveled by way of the Greenwood (or Sublette) cutoff.

❡ August 28-30.—Three companies of the "Oregon battalion," Missouri mounted volunteers, headed by Lt. Col. Ludwell E. Powell, with orders (soon countermanded) to march to Grand Island on the Platte, left Fort Leavenworth on the 28th; the other two companies followed on the 30(?); and on September 2, Lt. Daniel P. Woodbury (*see* July 14 entry) set out to overtake them.

On September 3 the battalion received new orders—to proceed to Table creek (*i. e.*, "old" Fort Kearny—*see* p. 586), build quarters, and winter there. En route there, on September 15, Capt. James Craig's company was detached for service at Council Bluffs (Ia.) Subagency—to protect the Pottawatomie payments. The rest of the battalion (in two detachments) reached "old" Fort Kearny on September 15 and 18.

Lt. Daniel P. Woodbury, escorted by Captain Sublette and about 70 men, set out for Grand Island on the Platte, on September 23; on arriving there Woodbury selected a site for a military post ("new" Fort Kearny). He and his escort returned to Table creek October 22. On October 9 Capt. David McCausland and 272 men of the battalion started out northward, on a futile expedition against the Sioux and Ponca Indians (who had massacred some Otoes). They returned a month later, with horses worn out and dying, having seen no Indians.

The "Oregon battalion" wintered at Table creek. A November 9 letter from Fort Kearny stated: "We have erected, and nearly completed some 60 or 70 log cabins. with slab, dirt and straw roofs. . . ." These were the Missouri troops' quarters.

Ref: *The Weekly Tribune,* Liberty, Mo., August 28, October 8, 1847; New York *Weekly Tribune,* October 16, December 25, 1847 (from *Missouri Republican,* St. Louis); Nebraska State Historical Society *Publications,* v. 20, pp. 174-176, 250-254 (from *Missouri Republican,* September 30, October 2, November 30, December 6, 1847); *ibid.,* v. 21 (inside back cover) for Woodbury's map; Saint Louis *Reveille* (daily), September 4, 1847; 30th Cong., 1st Sess., *Sen. Doc. No. 1* (Serial 503), pp. 77, 79; *The History of Buchanan County, Missouri* (1881), p. 200; *Historical Record,* Salt Lake City, v. 9 (January, 1890), entry for October 9, 1847.

❡ August 29-30.—On the stretch of Santa Fe trail between Cottonwood crossing and Hickory Point, these were the westbound travelers, met by F. X. Aubry on his rapid journey to Missouri:

". . . at Cottonwood [on the 29th] Symington & Renning's train of Govt. wagons. At Council Grove, [Ceran] St. Vrain's ([Frank] Delisle and Bauvais, of St. Louis) 20 wagons. Aug. 30 At creek 142 Mr. [Ceran] St. Vrain and [Alexander] Barclay with 6 wagons of provisions. At Soldiers creek . . . Messrs. Noland, Har[r]ison, Herrald and Oldham of Independence, with 12 wagons of provisions. At Bridge [or, Switzler's] Creek, Mr. Colter [G. N. Coulter?] and lady, of St. Louis, and Smith, of the firm of Colburn and Smith. At Willow Spring, Mr. [Seth M.] Hays, Indian trader [going to Council Grove]. At Hickory Point, Messrs. White & Simpson, sutlers to Ralls' [Third] regt. [Missouri mounted volunteers], and trader [traders?] to Santa Fe."

(Barclay, and Kellog Estes, with St. Vrain, left the Missouri border August 24. Ten days out on the trail, at Lost Spring, they overtook William Bent's wagons. [Bent had started west on the 22d.] St. Vrain and Barclay, in advance of the train, reached Bent's Fort September 20; and continued their journey on the 24th.)

Ref: Saint Louis *Daily Union,* September 7, 1847 (as reprinted from *Missouri Republican,* St. Louis); Saint Louis *Reveille* (daily), November 2, 1847 (for other reference to Noland, Oldham, and White); Alexander Barclay Papers, Bancroft Library, courtesy of Dale L. Morgan.

❡ On August 31(?) Francis X. Aubry reached Independence, Mo., in advance of the large company with which he had journeyed part of the way (as far as Pawnee Fork?) from New Mexico. In his last four days of travel (as reported) he had covered 300 miles. He brought a large mail.

On July 28 Aubry had left Santa Fe with "Mr. Barnum, of Baltimore (direct from Chihuahua), Capt. [Thomas C.] McKinney's company [of "Price's" regiment] from Monroe Co. [Mo.], and a train of 65 U. S. wagons, under the charge of Mr. King." ("McKinney" and his company arrived at Fort Leavenworth on September 11, along with other returning Missouri volunteer companies.)

Ref: Saint Louis *Daily Union*, September 7, 1847; Saint Louis *Reveille* (daily), September 7, 21, 1847; New York *Weekly Tribune*, September 18, 1847 (from *Missouri Republican*, St. Louis); *The Pacific Historian*, Stockton, Cal., v. 5 (August, 1961), pp. 111-123 (article on Aubry). Robarts, *op. cit.*, p. 61, lists "Thomas C. McKamey" (second lieutenant to March, 1847) as a captain in "Price's" regiment, replacing N. B. Giddings. "McKamey" *probably* is an error, since he is "McKinney" or "McKinny" in the newspaper accounts, but the name has not been verified.

℄ September 1.—Andrew Goodyear (brother of mountain man Miles Goodyear), from Connecticut, making his first journey West, left Independence, Mo., "in company with four others, mounted upon mules, having a wagon and four yoke of oxen to draw . . . [the] baggage." They had a few sheep along for provisions. (At Independence, Goodyear had encountered old Bill Williams, who had arrived in the fore part of August. Williams, he reported "has been upon the mountains some twenty-three years.")

He wrote (from Fort Laramie, on October 18) that (because of rains) they had found it necessary to unload the wagon at the Kansas crossing (present Topeka) "and convey the loading across in a canoe by the help of some Canadian French [members of the Papin family presumably] and Indians living there."

At a camp on a branch of the Little (Red) Vermillion, on September 15, they were overtaken by Joseph R. Walker and two others (*see* p. 715). On the 18th, at "Ketchum's" creek, the Goodyear-Walker party found, and was joined by, Pierre D. Papin and six men (all bound for Fort Laramie). The combined company of 15 men (two of them quite ill and confined to the wagons) continued out the Oregon trail; came to the Platte on September 26; found buffalo on the 27th; arrived at Fort Laramie on October 16, without trouble from Indians.

Andrew Goodyear later wrote that "Captain Walker and his men, with the exception of myself and another wintered on Henry's Fork. I left him on Green River, on the 8th of November, and arrived at Miles' [his brother's] fort [where Ogden, Utah is today] on the 13th of the same month."

Ref: Charles Kelly and M. L. Howe's *Miles Goodyear First Citizen of Utah* (Salt Lake City, 1937), pp. 77-82.

℄ September 1.—E. M. Campbell contracted (with Lt. G. W. Wallace, AAQM) to deliver flour at Fort Scott, beginning in October, and ending in March, 1848.

Ref: 30th Cong., 2d Sess., Sen. Ex. Doc. No. 17 (Serial 529), p. 10.

℄ September 1-18.—Arriving at Fort Leavenworth were five companies (two cavalry, two infantry, and one unmounted artillery) of Missouri volunteers, totaling about 500 men (raised under a July 20 requisition by the secretary of war). Best known as

"Gilpin's battalion" (for its commander Lt. Col. William Gilpin, who had been major of "Doniphan's regiment"), this force also was known as the "Indian battalion," "Arkansas battalion," and "Santa Fe trace battalion," because of its service on the Santa Fe trail. Some data on "Gilpin's battalion" are summarized below; but *see, also,* pp. 720 and 727.

Capt. John C. Griffin's cavalry *Company A* (110 officers and men), from Grundy county, Mo.; arrived at Fort Leavenworth September 1; was mustered in September 3; left around September 23(?); spent the winter of 1847-1848 near Bent's Fort on the upper Arkansas (in eastern "Colorado").

Capt. Thomas Jones' cavalry *Company B* (113 officers and men), from Dallas county, Mo.; arrived at Fort Leavenworth September 8; was mustered in September 11; left around September 23(?); spent the winter of 1847-1848 near Bent's Fort.

Capt. William Pelzer's foot artillery *Company C* (104 officers and men), an all-German outfit, from St. Louis and vicinity; arrived at Fort Leavenworth (on the *Bertrand*) September 8; was mustered in September 10; left between October 4-6; spent the winter of 1847-1848 at "Fort Mann," on the Arkansas (in present Ford county, Kan.).

Capt. Paul Holzscheiter's infantry *Company D* (80 officers and men), an all-German outfit, from St. Louis and vicinity; arrived at Fort Leavenworth (on the *St. Joseph*) about September 17(?); was mustered in September 18; left between October 4-6; spent the winter of 1847-1848 at "Fort Mann," in "Kansas."

Capt. Napoleon Koscialowski's infantry *Company E* (86 officers and men), from the St. Louis area; arrived at Fort Leavenworth (on the *Amelia*) about September 17(?) was mustered in September 18; left October 4; spent the winter of 1847-1848 at "Fort Mann," in "Kansas."

Ref: W. E. Connelley's *Doniphan's Expedition* (1907), pp. 147-149; Saint Louis *Daily Union,* August 6, September 13, 14, October 2, 10, December 14, 1847; Saint Louis *Reveille* (daily), September 3, 9, 11, 12, 22, October 31, November 2, December 12, 15, 16, 19, 31, 1847; *The Weekly Tribune,* Liberty, Mo., September 24, October 16, November 19, December 31, 1847; *Jefferson Inquirer,* Jefferson City, Mo., September 1, 1847; 30th Cong., 2d Sess., *H. Ex. Doc. No. 1* (Serial 537), pp. 136, 223; *KHQ,* v. 30, pp. 1-14. For this and subsequent entries on Gilpin *see, also,* Thomas L. Karnes' *William Gilpin . . .* (Austin and London, c1970).

❡ September 2.—"Mr. Jo[seph R.] Walker, the mountain guide, in company with Frank McClelland, and five others [as reported]," left Westport, Mo., for California, by way of the Oregon trail. Of the "others," one was James T. Walker (later described as a cousin of McClellan[d]); and his father, Samuel Walker (brother of Joseph R.), also was in the party. Joseph R. Walker, on a rare visit to the States, had been in Missouri since April—*see* p. 673.

Ref: Saint Louis *Reveille* (daily), September 16, 1847; Saint Louis *Daily Union,* August 24, 1847; Kelly and Howe, *op. cit.,* pp. 72-82; item on James T. Walker supplied courtesy of Dale L. Morgan, Bancroft Library, Berkeley, Cal.; *see, also,* C. L. Camp, ed., *James Clyman, Frontiersman* (c1960), p. 237.

❧ September.—In a narrative (*Solitary Rambles* . . ., published at London in 1853), British sportsman John Palliser described a horseback journey he made from Independence, Mo. (starting September 2), up the Missouri's *left bank* to Fort Union (at the Yellowstone's mouth) with an American Fur Company party (17 or 18 men) headed by James Kipp ("hardy old veteran . . . over 60"), and including "Mr. [James] Murray, a Scotchman" (in charge of the Company's Crow trading post—Fort Alexander—high up the Yellowstone). The party reached Fort Union on October 27.

Fur trader Kipp (by this account) had made the trip 20 times or more (returning downriver each spring in a Company boat). (*See* July 21 entry.) Palliser's is a rare account of the annual trek to the upper Missouri by this (non-"Kansas") overland route.

Ref: Palliser, *op. cit.*, pp. 77-110.

❧ BORN: on September 5, at Shawnee Baptist Mission (present Johnson county), Ellen Sophronia Barker, daughter of the Rev. Francis and Elizabeth F. (Churchill) Barker.

Ref: "Barker Collection" (in KHi ms. division); Elizabeth F. Barker's *Barker Genealogy* (New York, 1927), p. 199 (which gives the year, erroneously?, as 1846). The statement in the "Barker Collection" is of 1908 date, and has been *assumed* correct.

❧ September 11-30.—Most troops of the Second ("Price's") regiment, Missouri mounted volunteers, and "extra" battalion (*see* pp. 631, 635) en route home after expiration of their 12-months' Mexican War service, arrived at Fort Leavenworth in this period. The returning companies (by reason of casualties, re-enlistments, etc.) were said to average fewer than 40 men each. One Marion county, Mo., volunteer was "lost" (presumed killed by Indians) on the march eastward, while hunting buffalo (on September 3) near the Arkansas crossing.

A party which reached the fort on September 11 included "Major [Benjamin B.] Edmonson, Capts. [Benjamin F.] Robinson, [William M.] Jacobs, [John] Holloway, [Thomas M.] Horine, [Jesse B.] Morin and several others." The reporter stated: "These officers [are] to be followed in about fifteen days by their respective companies." "Colonel" Price, who had accompanied his men from a rendezvous camp on the Moro, in New Mexico (left August 19) to the vicinity of the Great Bend of the Arkansas, arrived at Fort Leavenworth six days behind the above officers (*see* September 17 entry).

According to John T. Hughes (of Liberty, Mo.), the remains of Capts. John H. K. Burgwin, First U. S. dragoons, Israel R. Hendley, of Ray county, Mo. (*see* p. 631), several lieutenants, and sutler Albert Wilson, were exhumed at Santa Fe, brought back by the returning troops, and reinterred at Fort Leavenworth on September 22 (except Hendley, who was buried at Richmond, Mo., on the 23d).

Ref: New York *Weekly Tribune,* October 2, 9, 1847 (from *Missouri Republican,* St. Louis, September 20, 22); Saint Louis *Reveille* (daily), September 19, 23, October 7, 1847; Saint Louis *Daily Union,* September 20, 25, October 4, 1847; W. E. Connelley's *Doniphan's Expedition,* pp. 517, 523, 524.

❡ MARRIED: A. D. Jones and Saphronia Reeves, on September 15, at Scott's Sac & Fox trading house (in present Franklin county), by the Rev. Jotham Meeker.

Ref: Jotham Meeker's "Diary." The marriage is recorded in "Jackson County (Mo.) Marriage Records," v. 2, p. 158 (the bride's name is entered there as "Saphrona Rives").

❡ September 17.—"Boon & Hamilton" (Albert G. Boone and James G. Hamilton, of Westport, Mo.) were issued a one-year Indian trading license (by Agent R. W. Cummins). The post location was on the Pottawatomies' new reserve (recently the Kansa Indians' land) "at a point on the Kansas river about a half mile below the mouth of the creek that the [former] Kansas Mission is located on" (*i. e.,* where, from 1832 to 1846, Frederick Chouteau had maintained a trading post for the Kansa; on Mission creek, present Shawnee county). (In 1848 all Pottawatomie traders were centralized at a new site—"Union Town.")

Ref: OIA, "Letters Received from Fort Leavenworth Agency" (National Archives Microcopy 234, Roll 302), *see* Cummins' list forwarded from St. Louis on September 27, 1847. *See* annals, p. 212, for establishment of Chouteau's trading post in 1832.

❡ September 17.—"Simpson & Hunter" (James M. Simpson and James M. Hunter) were issued a one-year Indian trading license (by Agent R. W. Cummins), to operate on the Delaware reserve, at a location north of Kansas river, above the Delawares' blacksmith shop (*i. e.,* near the military road crossing—the Delaware, or Grinter ferry site).

Ref: OIA, "Letters Received from Fort Leavenworth Agency" (National Archives Microcopy 234, Roll 302, Cummins' list forwarded from St. Louis on September 27, 1847. For earlier items on Simpson, and Hunter, *see* index to annals.

❡ September 17.—Sterling Price, newly commissioned a brigadier general, arrived at Fort Leavenworth (overland from Santa Fe), accompanied by Surg. Samuel G. I. De Camp, U. S. A., Hiram Rich (sutler—*see* p. 621), and a small escort.

On September 11, while marching eastward with discharged troops of his Second regiment, Missouri mounted volunteers, and in present Barton(?) county, "Colonel" Price had received his commission (of July 20 date)—delivered to him from a westbound wagon train. The general, De Camp, Rich, and escort, then set out post-haste "with provisions and blankets only," and traveled for seven days more than 40 miles a day to Fort Leavenworth.

See, also, November 3 annals entry for Price's return to New Mexico.

Ref: New York *Weekly Tribune,* October 9, 1847 (from *Missouri Republican,* St. Louis, September 22).

℃ September.—In a Santa Fe-bound caravan which left Independence, Mo., in mid-month were 11 wagons containing merchandise of "Mr. Root" (sutler for "Newby's" Illinois regiment), freighted by "Mr. Brown"; also, "Messrs. Bullard, Russel[1], & Cos. wagons, 19 in all, under the charge of Mr. Isaac McCarthy [McCarty]"; and some 200 beef cattle.

Ref: Saint Louis *Daily Union,* September 27, 1847; Saint Louis *Reveille* (daily), November 2, 1847 (for "Mr. McShane's" report of travelers met on the Santa Fe trail— including "Messrs. Bullard and McCarthy," also "Messrs. Brown and Root of Quincy, Ill."). Isaac McCarty, of Lexington, Mo., died at Santa Fe on October 10, 1850.—St. Joseph (Mo.) *Gazette,* December 18, 1850.

℃ In mid-September (about the 20th), a party of 16 men reached the Missouri border from Santa Fe. Among them were Lt. Col. David Willock, of Marion county, Mo. (*see* p. 631), Dr. [G. W.?] Hereford, of St. Louis, Elliott Lee, of Taos, N. M., and James C. Bean, of Independence, Mo.

From New Mexico they had traveled to the vicinity of the Arkansas crossing in company with "Brig. Gen. [Sterling] Price and a portion of his regiment." They had met no Indians; but at Pawnee Rock nearly had lost their horses and mules in a buffalo stampede.

Ref: *The Weekly Tribune,* Liberty, Mo., October 1, 1847; Saint Louis *Reveille* (daily), September 28, 1847 (notes arrival of Elliott Lee at St. Louis on the 27th, via the *Bertrand,* from Fort Leavenworth). Bean left Santa Fe August 9; Lee left there August 15.

℃ September 20.—At Fort Leavenworth was held a public sale of a large number of government mules, horses, and oxen, and other property, beginning at 10 A. M. The sale had been advertised (by Capt. Langdon C. Easton, AQM) in the St. Joseph, Mo., *Gazette* (and probably in other area newspapers).

Ref: *The Gazette,* St. Joseph, Mo., September 17, 1847.

℃ September 20.—Irregularities connected with the annuity payment, this day, to the "Mississippi" Sacs & Foxes, at the agency in present Franklin county, resulted in: Agent John Beach's resignation (on October 4); an investigation by the Indian department; the revocation (on November 22) of W. G. & G. W. Ewing's license to trade with these tribes; and the closing of their Sac & Fox trading house (not far from the agency) on December 2.

The secretary of war's report covering the investigation reveals that Beach went to St. Louis in August for the annuity money; got it, and left for his agency on September 3, "expressly directed . . . not to make the payment until he received instructions in relation to the manner in which it was required to be done under the new law" (*see* March 3 annals entry); that the letter of instructions, which arrived at Westport, Mo., on the 15th, and left there on the 16th, fell, on the 17th, into the hands of William D. Harris (employee of the Ewings), who suppressed it; and that there was, at least, connivance by the other Sac & Fox traders whose financial interests were at stake. On the 20th Beach was induced (or intimidated by threats from the chiefs—manipulated by the traders) to proceed with the annuity payment—following the procedure of previous years.

The testimony indicates the Sacs paid out (through their chiefs) to Pierre Chouteau, Jr. & Co. $10,000, to Robert A. Kinzie $6,000, and that the heads of families of the nation received $11 each. The Foxes (through their chiefs) paid the Ewings $21,600, and the Scotts (W. A. & J. B.) $9,000; the heads of families of the nation got $3 each. According to Sup't Thomas H. Harvey, Pierre Chouteau, Jr., & Co. received "over $45,000 of the money in bulk; having furnished the other traders with goods, they received all the money [paid Kinzie, the Ewings, and the Scotts]." *See* p. 579, for other information on the Sac & Fox traders.

Ref: *30th Cong., 1st Sess., Sen. Ex. Doc. No. 70* (Serial 510).

❪ September.—Trader John S. Shaw's party of 12 men with four wagons, en route from Independence, Mo., to Fort Laramie was, on October 17, traveling up the Platte, not far above the head of Grand Island. Probably this outfit had left the Missouri frontier after the middle of September.

(An article on John S. Shaw—who was connected both with the Indian trade, and with Missouri river steamboating—notes that Shaw had sold the *Tobacco Plant* in August, 1847, to re-enter trading activity; and "in connection with" Robert Wilson [sutler to the "Oregon battalion"], started with a "large outfit" for the Sioux country. His 1847-1848 venture was later reported a profitable one.)

Ref: *Historical Record*, Salt Lake City, v. 9 (January, 1890); *The United States Biographical Dictionary . . ., Missouri Volume* (1878), pp. 762-764.

❪ About September 25 "Messrs. [Francis X.] Aubry, Boggs, [A. P.] Kean & Co.," traders, left Independence, Mo., with 15 wagons, bound for Santa Fe. Probably "Messrs. Peacock and Flournoy," also of Independence, traveled in company (since one returning traveler mentioned meeting them with "Boggs").

Near the border of New Mexico this party had an encounter with Indians; but reached Santa Fe safely on October 29, before the onset of cold weather.

Ref: Saint Louis *Daily Union*, October 1, 1847; *The Pacific Historian*, v. 5 (August, 1961), pp. 111-123 (article on Aubry); Saint Louis *Reveille* (daily), November 2, 1847. The identities of this Boggs, and of Flournoy, have not been ascertained. George H. Peacock was, very likely, the above trader.

❪ The last week of September, Lt. (Cyrus?) Hall arrived at Fort Leavenworth with 66 recruits for Company A, First U. S. infantry, bringing the company total to 112.

The adjutant general's November 30, 1847, report indicated Lt. Col. Clifton Wharton's command at the fort consisted of one company, First U. S. infantry, and a detachment (of First dragoons?).

Ref: Saint Louis *Daily Union,* October 2, 1847; 30th Cong., 1st Sess., *Sen. Doc. No. 1* (Serial 503), p. 79, and chart F, between pp. 96, 97. The St. Louis *Tri-Weekly Union,* November 2, 1847, noted the arrival there of "Lieut. [John W. T.] Gard[i]ner," with 37 men of Company D, First dragoons, from Fort Leavenworth, on the *Archer;* and that others of the company were on the *Amelia* and had gone to Jefferson Barracks—all under orders to Vera Cruz, Mexico.

℃ October 1.—"[I] Ride to the Pottawatomie payment ground," wrote diarist Jotham Meeker (the Ottawas' Baptist missionary). The payment was distributed at the subagency—on Pottawatomie creek, near present Lane, Franklin county. Meeker made the trip to watch the Indians "receive their annuity, their improvement money, and their removal & subsistence money, in all about $60,000"—incident to the Pottawatomies' removal (under the June, 1846, treaty—*see* p. 592) to their new Kansas river reserve.

Meeker further recorded (in his diary): "The Sub-Agent commences paying the annuity money this afternoon [October 1]. Some 16 or 17 stores open —a great many wagons with flour, bread, apples, &c. . . . hundreds of whites, blacks, Weas, Peorias, Piankeshaws, Kaskaskias, Miamis, Shawanoes, Foxes, Sauks, Chippewas, and Ottawas, selling horses, beef, pork, vegetables, bread, goods, &c. Twelve tables kept on the ground by Inds. . . ."

Ref: Jotham Meeker's "Diary," September 24 and October 1, 1847, entries.

℃ October 4-6.—Lt. Col. William Gilpin with the three unmounted companies of his battalion (*see* September 1-18, entry) set out from Fort Leavenworth for "Fort Mann," on the Arkansas. (Griffin's and Jones' cavalry companies had started out the Santa Fe trail some two weeks earlier.)

"I concentrated my whole battalion on the 1st November, at Walnut creek," Gilpin later reported. From that point, in detachments, the march was continued westward. An eastbound traveler who met the troops early in November at Pawnee Fork, reported their animals were "in deplorable condition" for want of grass (unavailable because of the burned prairies). About November 6 part of the battalion reached the "little stockade of fort Mann." (Adjt. Henry L. Rouett stated they were 30 days en route.) Gilpin (arriving November 9?) remained only long enough to place his three foot companies "in garrison," with orders to "repair and enlarge" the post; then continued (on the 10th?), with his two cavalry companies, up the Arkansas to Bent's Fort; and set up camp near that post "in the midst of the winter residences of the Cheyennes and Arapahoes" till March, 1848.

At "Fort Mann" (by one description "a miserable dog hole, surrounded by desolation, destitute of shelter [and] of fuel"; and which Lieutenant Rouett thought must be "certainly the most desolate and uninteresting place upon the face of the earth"), the two all-German infantry companies and the foot artillery company —a force of about 270 officers and men—spent the winter. Company C's Capt. William Pelzer (as senior officer present) was "Fort Mann's" commandant. (*See, also,* November 16 entry.)

Ref: Saint Louis *Daily Union*, October 10, December 14, 1847; Saint Louis *Reveille* (daily), October 31, November 2, December 15, 1847; *The Weekly Tribune*, Liberty, Mo., November 19, December 31, 1847; 30th Cong., 1st Sess., *H. Ex. Doc. No. 1* (Serial 537), pp. 136, 137.

❧ October 10.—At Osage Catholic Mission a manual labor school for Osage girls was opened by four newly arrived Sisters of Loretto —Mother Concordia Henning, superior, Sisters Bridget Hayden, Mary Petronilla van Prater, and Vincentia Van Cool. Their first pupils were four in number—one full-blood Osage girl, and three who were half-Osage. (*See, also,* May 10 entry.)

These ladies, recruited by Osage mission's superior, Father John Schoenmakers, had traveled from Kentucky to "Kansas" in his care. They left St. Louis September 20 on the steamboat *John J. Hardin;* were guests of Mme. Berenice Therese Chouteau (widow of Francis) while in the Kaw's mouth area; then journeyed in ox-drawn lumber wagons for eight days (camping out at night). On the day they reached the mission, October 10, their school opened.

Ref: Sister M. Lilliana Owens' "The Early Work of the Lorettines in Southeastern Kansas," in *KHQ,* v. 15, pp. 263-276; and *see* references under May 10, 1847, annals entry.

❧ October 13.—Trader Samuel Wethered, of Baltimore, arrived at Independence, Mo., from Santa Fe. He (and his party?) had left there August 25. Wethered reported that grass on the plains was very dry, and water scarce.

Ref: *The Weekly Tribune*, Liberty, Mo., October 22, 1847.

❧ BORN: on October 15, at the Sac & Fox Agency, present Franklin county, Albert P. Withington, son of government blacksmith Charles H. and Dorinda (White) Withington.

Ref: KHi's 15th *Biennial Report*, p. 36. The 1855 and 1860 censuses of Kansas territory indicate the Withington family, as of October 1, 1847, consisted of Charles H., his wife, two young daughters (Kate J. and Mary Ellen), and a son (George E., aged one year)— the three children all born in Iowa. Another daughter—Catherine G.—was born in "Kansas" in 1851 or 1852.

❧ In mid-October the new *St. Peters* (returning from St. Joseph, Mo.?) took aboard, below Fort Leavenworth, the voyageurs, and cargo (5,245 buffalo robes, &c.) from three American Fur Co. Mackinaw boats which had started downriver from Fort Pierre (S. D.) about September 17. Another passenger was John B. Sarpy (a Pierre Chouteau, Jr. & Company partner) who had been in "Kansas" (and "Nebraska"?) on company business. The *St. Peters* reached St. Louis on October 21.

Ref: New York *Weekly Tribune*, November 6, 1847 (from *Missouri Republican*, St. Louis, October 22); Saint Louis *Daily Union*, October 6, 13, 1847; 30th Cong., 1st Sess.,

Sen. Ex. Doc. No. 70 (Serial 510), pp. 48, 49, 55, 56, 61-64 (for items on Sarpy in "Kansas" in September, 1847). The *Union* of October 6 stated that the "fine, light draught" *St. Peters* ("entirely new, having made only one or two trips") had been engaged by Captain Kennett to run in the Missouri river trade during low water; and that Captain Jewett of the *Rowena* "also goes on the *St. Peters.*"

☾ October 19.—Indian Agent Thomas Fitzpatrick, in a report (from Bent's Fort) wrote: "In all the skirmishing, and 'scrapes' on the Santa Fe road last summer and spring, I cannot make out more than twenty-seven white men killed; but an Aripahoe has told me that the Camanche and Kiaway, together, counts sixty, and can produce that number of scalps; but I am disposed to think it much exaggerated." (This figure—27 whites killed on the trail in 1847—accounts for almost the exact number of victims noted in the 1847 annals as here compiled.)

In a report written at "Fort Mann," August 1, 1848, Lt. Col. William Gilpin stated: "By careful inquiry, I estimated the losses sustained from Indian attacks, during the summer of 1847 to have been: Americans killed 47 [*i. e.,* 27?]; 330 wagons destroyed, 6,500 stock plundered."

Ref: *New Spain and the Anglo American West* (Los Angeles, 1932), v. 2, p. 133; 30th Cong., 2d Sess., *H. Ex. Doc. No. 1* (Serial 537), p. 136.

☾ October 27.—Overland from the Sacramento Valley (left on July 19), by way of the California-Oregon trail, Com. Robert F. Stockton, U. S. N., together with his staff (Lt. William H. Thompson, of the Navy, Lt. Archibald H. Gillespie, of the Marines), also a private secretary and escort, arrived at St. Joseph, Mo. The probability is that mountain man Caleb Greenwood, and his sons John and Britton, guided the party east. This mounted company (with pack mules, and one wagon) totaled upwards of 45 persons. The commodore was welcomed by a large crowd at the ferry landing; and later made an address at the Mansion House.

Stockton (whose ultimate destination was Washington, D. C., to testify at Fremont's trial), and most of his party, departed for Weston, Mo., on the 29th; boarded the *Meteor* there; and reached St. Louis on November 4. One cotraveler from California was Samuel J. Hensley (an 1843 immigrant; once of Jackson county, Mo.—*see* p. 383); and another (apparently) was Joseph B. Chiles (also formerly of Jackson county—*see* p. 429). Both testified at Fremont's trial; and returned to California overland (Chiles for the third time) in 1848. Still another was Peter Lassen (overland emigrant to Oregon in 1839), who got lost from Stockton's company on the South Platte; existed for 13 days on four buffalo tongues; arrived on the Missouri frontier in advance of the commodore. (Lassen, too, went back to California in 1848.) Guide Moses ("Black") Harris, who had joined the commodore west of South Pass, traveled only to St. Joseph with Stockton.

Ref: *The Gazette,* St. Joseph, Mo., October 22, 29, and (December 3), 1847; St Louis *Tri-Weekly Union,* October 29, 1847; *Missouri Republican,* St. Louis, November 5, 1847;

Saint Louis *Reveille* (daily), November 5, 1847; *Historical Record*, Salt Lake City, v. 9 (January, 1890), items under dates of September 25, 26, October 2, 17, 1847; New York *Weekly Tribune*, November 13, 1847 (item, by telegraph—Cincinnati, November 9—says Stockton and 46 men arrived at St. Louis on the 5th); Charles Kelly and Dale L. Morgan, *Old Greenwood* . . . revised edition (Georgetown, Cal., 1965), pp. 257-277. *California Pioneer Register 1542-1848* . . . (as reprinted, Baltimore, 1964), p. 99 (for Chiles), p. 184 (for Hensley), and p. 216 (for Lassen).

❡ MARRIED: Hon. Willard P. Hall (congressman-elect from Missouri) and Ann Eliza Richardson (whose father, William P. Richardson, had headed the Great Nemaha Subagency, 1841-1845), on October 28, at St. Joseph, Mo., by the Rev. William Hamilton, of the Iowa, Sac & Fox Presbyterian Mission. They left for Washington, D. C., a few days later.

Hall, just back from California with Kearny's party (*see* p. 711), had been out of the States since June, 1846. He had left Missouri as a private in "Doniphan's" regiment; and later in 1846 (after special service at Santa Fe) journeyed to California with Cooke and the Mormon battalion. *See* p. 555 for other mention of Ann Eliza Richardson.

Ref: *The Gazette*, St. Joseph, Mo., October 29, 1847; Saint Louis *Daily Union*, June 1, September 4, 1847; *Biographical Directory of the American Congress* . . . (1961), p. 993. William P. Richardson, Great Nemaha subagent 1841-1845, also held the same post from late 1849 to (up to?) 1853. Hall had been elected in August, 1846, while in Mexican War service—*see History of Clay and Platte Counties, Missouri* . . . (St. Louis, 1885), p. 137.

❡ October 30.—From Shawnee Friends Mission (present Johnson county), Richard Mendenhall wrote a letter on the subject of "the existence of slavery in this Territory [*i. e.*, 'Kansas'], contrary to the restrictions of the Missouri Compromise." *The National Era*, Washington, printed his communication on December 23.

"We are," wrote Mendenhall, "situated near the south side of the Kansas River, and a little to the south of the 39th degree of north latitude; consequently, the existence of slavery here is not legal, and yet it does exist. It is true, it does not exist to any great extent, for there are perhaps not more than twenty slaves in this region; but if there was only one, it would be a grievance calling for redress." He noted that "one of the chiefs among the Shawnees [*i. e.*, Joseph Parks] owns a number of slaves . . . the only Indian in this part of the Territory, so far as I am informed, that either owns slaves, or has them in his employ. But it is white men in the service of the Government of the United States, and missionaries, that have introduced slavery here. . . . a very extensive missionary establishment . . . under the care of the Methodist church South . . . have some half dozen or more slaves."

Mendenhall further commented: ". . . many of the Indians are decidedly opposed to slavery; but there are others who, no doubt, would own slaves if they were able to buy them. Some of them will take up runaway slaves whenever they find them [and return them to their masters], whilst others will quietly let them pass."

Ref: *The National Era*, Washington, December 23, 1847; or, *see* Martha Caldwell's typescript used as basis for her *Annals of Shawnee Methodist Mission*, in KHi ms. division.

℄ November 3.—Brig. Gen. Sterling Price, accompanied by Maj. Benjamin L. Beall (First dragoons), Lt. William E. Prince (First infantry), and a small escort (about 15? soldiers and 12? teamsters), set out from Fort Leavenworth for New Mexico—making his second march westward over the Santa Fe trail. (*See* August, 1846, annals entry.)

By November 15 Price was at Walnut creek; on the 19th, arriving at Fort Mann, he was "received with military honors," but remained only a few hours; continued up the Arkansas, passing Bent's Fort November 30. On reaching Santa Fe in December, the general assumed command of Ninth Military department troops (among them "Easton's battalion, Missouri infantry; "Ralls'" regiment, Missouri cavalry; and "Newby's" regiment, Illinois infantry).

Ref: Saint Louis *Daily Union*, November 13, December 14, 1847; Saint Louis *Reveille* (daily), November 19, December 12, 15, 1847, January 12, 1848; *Jefferson Inquirer*, Jefferson City, Mo., November 13, 1847; *The Westerners New York Posse Brand Book*, v. 10, No. 4 (1963), p. 76.

℄ November 4.—B. F. Coons, of St. Louis, who had left Santa Fe on October 18, arrived at Independence, Mo. His journey "in the short space of 17 days," was said to be "the quickest trip on record." Trader [James?] Wethered, with whom Coons traveled part of the way, got to Independence some days later. (For Coons' July trip *to* Santa Fe, *see* p. 696.)

Wethered's party (19 in number), with wagons, and "Express mail," left Santa Fe on October 8. Coons (who carried dispatches), starting 10 days later, alone, apparently overtook Wethered at the Arkansas crossing. On the Arkansas Pawnees attacked the train two successive nights (the first time—October 25, near "Fort Mann"—attempting to raid the stock, they lost a warrior; the second time their motive was revenge). Once past the area of hostile Indians, Coons went on, in advance, to Missouri.

As he reported it: "The whole country, to within 18 miles of Independence, is nothing but a vast black crisp, the grass and all kinds of vegetation having been entirely burnt up by the Indians."

Ref: *The Weekly Tribune*, Liberty, Mo., November 19, 1847; New York *Weekly Tribune*, November 20, 1847; Saint Louis *Daily Union*, November 11, 1847. Apparently Coons' wagons had been sent on ahead. A "Mr. McShane" who left Santa Fe on September 7, reached St. Louis November 1, having accompanied the "return wagons of Messrs. Coons, Murphy & McKnight, the well known traders." McShane had been forced to leave his wagons behind because the grass from the Great Bend to Council Grove had been destroyed by fire.—Saint Louis *Reveille* (daily), November 2, 1847.

℄ November.—"Kansas [City, Mo.] . . . we understand is improving with a rapidity unprecedented in the history of western towns," wrote the editor of *The Weekly Tribune*, Liberty, Mo., in the November 6 issue. "The general impression, we believe is, that it will eventually become the starting point for traders and emigrants, owing to its being on the river. The site of the town is said to be a beautiful one."

In the November 12 issue, the *Tribune's* editor wrote of St. Joseph, Mo.: "We recently paid a visit to this place, and was astonished to see it improving with such rapidity. It . . . now numbers, we suppose, between 1500 and 2000 inhabitants. . . . [In] our opinion . . . it is destined ere many years to become a city of considerable note."

Ref: *The Weekly Tribune*, Liberty, Mo., November 6, 12, 1847.

❧ November.—A reuniting of the Pottawatomie Nation on a Kansas river reserve (recently the home of the Kansa Nation) occurred this month, as the "Council Bluffs" Pottawatomies began arriving in "Kansas" from southwestern Iowa; and the "Marais des Cygnes" Pottawatomies moved up to the new reserve, leaving the settlements on Sugar creek (present Linn county), and on Pottawatomie creek (present Miami and Franklin counties). By the spring of 1848, the Pottawatomies residing in "Kansas" totaled some 3,235 souls.

The "Council Bluffs" Pottawatomies. A correspondent at the Council Bluffs (Ia.) Subagency, on October 13, wrote: "This place . . . is now almost as still as a church-yard—the Indians having nearly all left for their new homes. Many . . . leave in comfortable order. One family . . . with four wagons, and a buggy. . . . When the Supt. [Thomas H. Harvey, St. Louis] arrived here [to oversee annuity, and other payments totaling some $90,000], he informed the Indians that he did not intend to leave until they were on the road for their new homes; . . . he is still here but will leave this evening." (Harvey remarked, on November 22, that Joseph LaFromboise, Pierre Le Clerc, and Half Day were the three chiefs who "manifested the greatest zeal in inducing their people to emigrate from the Bluffs.") About November 10 (according to Agent R. W. Cummins), Chief LaFromboise "and many others of the Bluffs party," reached Kansas river. But a large portion of them were still on the road, "scattered hunting" as they moved westward (finding a good many deer between "their country and the Kickapoos"); they were expected in two or three weeks. Early in December, Cummins wrote that the Kansa Indians' blacksmith, W. H. Mitchell, occupying the old Kansa Methodist Mission (*south* of the Kansas river, on Mission creek, present Shawnee county) had given up two rooms for LaFromboise (and family) "to winter in." But it appears that many of the "Council Bluffs" Pottawatomies settled *north* of the Kansas, upon their arrival.

The "Marais des Cygnes" Pottawatomies. Subagent A. J. Vaughan, in a November 17 letter (from his Pottawatomie creek headquarters), wrote that the Sugar creek and Pottawatomie creek Indians, in council, had agreed to move; that "some have gone, others will be off in a day or two"; the rest were pledged to leave "in a body" on the 29th, if sufficient teams could be procured; and he planned to get some 15 wagons from Missouri for this purpose. The subagent also noted that Topenebee (the principal chief), who had been at the point of death for a fortnight, was making a rapid recovery. On December 9 Jotham Meeker (of Ottawa Baptist Mission) wrote that the Pottawatomies had commenced moving "last week"; and Dr. Johnston Lykins (government physician; and Baptist missionary) had accompanied them. He meant the Indians of Pottawatomie creek (who were under Baptist, or Methodist, influence). On November 1, Father Felix L. Verreydt, S. J., and a party of the Sugar creek (Catholic) Indians had set out to explore the new Kansas river reserve, and select a Catholic church site. (Though some authorities believe the chosen location was on Mission creek, best available information indicates it was on the Wakarusa, in present Auburn township, Shawnee co.)

The move of the Sugar creek Indians was stated by Father Christian Hoecken, S. J., as follows: "During the month of November [1847], we changed our home and departed for the Kansas valley—Nov. 22." About 20 log cabins were erected on the Wakarusa by the Pottawatomies, a later-day history says. But the location was outside (south of) the boundary of their own reserve, on the Shawnees' land, and subsequently they had to leave. (Father Paul M. Ponziglione, in 1891, recollected: "I myself saw the poor little shanties they put all along that creek [the Wakarusa]. In the spring of 1847 [*i. e.*, 1848] they moved again. . . ."

Sup't Thomas H. Harvey, St. Louis, wrote, on January 4, 1848: ". . . it appears that the emigration of the Pottawatomies was completed in the month of Novr last with the exception of a few straggling hunters. . . . that emigration was effective in October by those from the Council Bluffs; and in November by those on the Osage [Marais des Cygnes]. . . ."

Ref: St. Louis *Tri-Weekly Union,* October 29, 1847; OIA, "Letters Received from Fort Leavenworth Agency," National Archives Microcopy 234, Roll 302 (Harvey's November 22, 1847, letter; Cummins' letters of November 12 and December 6, 1847); OIA, "Letters Received From Osage River Sugagency," National Archives Microcopy 234, Roll 653 (Vaughan's November 17, 1847, letter); T. H. Kinsella's *The History of Our Cradle Land . . .* (Kansas City, 1921), p. 235; Jotham Meeker's "Diary", *loc. cit.*, (December 9, 1847, entry); *The Dial,* St. Mary's College, v. 2 (February, 1891), pp. 85-88; SIA, St. Louis, "Records," v. 9, typed copy, pp. 10, 40; Augustin C. Wand's *The Jesuits in Territorial Kansas 1827-1861* (1962), pp. 10, 11; Comm'r of Indian affairs, *Reports,* 1847, 1848; *KHC,* v. 14, pp. 492, 493; W. W. Cone's *Historical Sketch of Shawnee County* (Topeka, 1877), Auburn township section.

❡ BORN: on November 12, at Wea Baptist Mission, present Miami county, Wayland C. Lykins, son of Dr. David and Abigail Ann (Webster) Lykins, missionaries of the American Indian Mission Association.

Ref: D. C. Gideon's *Indian Territory, Descriptive, Biographical and Genealogical . . .* (New York and Chicago, 1901), pp. 444-446 (in which the place is erroneously given as Miami county, Texas"); in U. S. census, 1860, Kansas, v. 8, p. 41, under Paola, Lykins (now Miami) county, are listed David Lykins, age 34; Wayland C. Lykins, age 12 —born in Kansas; and Edward W. W., age 10—born in Kansas (in 1849?). A biographical sketch of Wayland C. Lykins in the A. T. Andreas-W. G. Cutler, *History of the State of Kansas* (Chicago, 1883), p. 1158, says he was born in Missouri; as does, also, the Kansas state census, 1875, Cherokee county, Salamanca township; but the 1860 census seems the more reliable source.

❡ Mid-November.—Bearer of dispatches from Santa Fe, Capt.

Vantrump Turner (of the First ["Newby's"] regiment, Illinois infantry volunteers), accompanied by Lieutenant "Hooper" (and an escort?) arrived at the Missouri border around November 15. They had left Santa Fe October 11; and carried a large "letter mail." Turner and "Hooper" reached St. Louis, aboard the *Bertrand,* on November 18.

Ref: Saint Louis *Daily Union,* November 19, 1847; Saint Louis *Reveille* (daily), November 19, 1847.

❡ November 16.—At "Fort Mann" (occupied for some 10 days by Missouri volunteers of Gilpin's battalion—*see* p. 715, and October 4-6 entry), in mid-afternoon, a party of Indians was seen "coming down the hights opposite the fort," on the south side of the Arkansas. The German post commander—Capt. William Pelzer—called his garrison "to arms"; went out (with Lt. Caleb S. Tuttle) to parley with the Pawnee chief and three braves who approached the gate; then invited the four inside the fort; smoked a peace pipe with the chief; showed his visitors around; meantime allowed the party of some 60 Indians to enter the stockade (where they seated themselves in a circle).

Several versions are extant of the *"melee"* which resulted when Pelzer gave an order to detain the whole party, and the Indians rushed to the gate to escape. "Three [Pawnees] were shot down the first volley we fired—one killed, the other two wounded," wrote "Mc. K." (The fleeing Indians were pursued about two miles from the fort.) Remaining inside the stockade were three Pawnees who took refuge in Captain Pelzer's quarters. One dashed out, and was killed outside the fort; the other two refused to surrender. "The guard then commenced firing in on them from the door and window of the room . . . and the Indians, to prevent being too plainly seen, commenced throwing on the fire such materials as . . . officers' cloaks, coats, uniforms, &c." But they "were perfectly riddled with balls, as also were the clothing and effects of the officers who occupied the quarters." "There were in all four [Pawnees] killed, two taken prisoners, and some fifteen or twenty wounded," according to "Mc. K."

The St. Louis *New Era* publishing an account of the "atrocious massacre," editorialized: "We are satisfied that whatever blame attaches to anybody rests on Capt. Peltzer. We have reason to believe that he was strongly advised to refuse the Indians admission into the fort, but he utterly disregarded such counsel."

Ref: Saint Louis *Reveille* (daily), December 15, 16, 19, 31, 1847; *The Weekly Tribune,* Liberty Mo., December 31, 1847; *The Westerners New York Posse Brand Book,* v. 10, No. 4 (1963), p. 76; Saint Louis *Daily Union,* January 1, February 8, 9, 1848.

❡ November 20.—The *Cora* arrived at Weston, Mo.—the last steamboat to reach that town in 1847.

Ref: *The Western Journal,* St. Louis, v. 5 (March, 1851), p. 326.

❧ November.—"Mr. [Jabez?] Smith, a "Santa Fe trader," direct from that place, arrived at St. Louis November 26, on the *Cora*. (Probably he was the Smith of "Colburn and Smith"—*see* August 29-30 annals entry.)

Ref: 30th Cong., 2d Sess., *Sen. Ex. Doc. No. 17* (Serial 529), p. 10.

❧ November 25.—J. McHenry contracted (with Lt. George W. Wallace, AAQM) to deliver fresh beef at Fort Scott, beginning January 1 and ending December 31, 1848.

Ref: 30th Cong., 2d Sess., *Sen. Ex. Doc. No. 17* (Serial 529), p. 10.

❧ November 25.—A military party (seven officers and 15 privates) from Santa Fe, in charge of Capt. Gabriel de Korponay, reached Independence, Mo. (with one wagon, the mail, and part of their baggage), after a journey in severe winter weather during which 29 of their 37 pack mules died.

The officers (detached for recruiting service) were Korponay, Lieutenants Dillon and Hawkins—all of "Ralls'" Missouri cavalry; Capt. George W. Hook and Lieutenant Madison [Relly Madeson?] of "Newby's" Illinois infantry; Lt. Abram Allen, of "Easton's" Missouri infantry; and Lt. William B. Royall, adjutant of the "Santa Fe battalion," organized in Santa Fe, and composed largely of Missourians.

Leaving Santa Fe on October 21, this party endured a severe snow storm two days later; lost some 20 animals (by starvation and freezing) in the Arkansas crossing vicinity; spent November 10 and 11 at Fort Mann (having arrived just after Lt. Col. William Gilpin and his command reached there; met General Price at Walnut creek on the 15th; ran out of food at the Little Arkansas; whereupon Korponay, Allen, and three others, on foot, traveled (in an incessant snow-and-rain storm) to Council Grove for assistance; reached the States after being on the road 36 days.

Ref: Saint Louis *Reveille* (daily), December 6, 12, 1847; Saint Louis *Daily Union*, December 14, 1847. In the Illinois Adjutant General's *Record of the Services of Illinois Soldiers* . . . (1902), v. 9, Madison's(?) name is entered as "Relly Madeson."

❧ Around December 1 provision trains of "Gilpin's battalion" arrived "in very good order," at "Fort Mann." (An eastbound party had met "Col. Gilpin's sutler" east of Walnut creek—at "Arkansas Bend"—in mid-November.)

The night (prior to December 7) that the empty train started back to Missouri Pvt. "Bill" Newcome "came up missing" at the fort; but was located next morning with the returning wagons (corraled a few miles away). "He" was brought back to the outpost, and "frankly acknowledged that he was a woman [Caroline, instead of Bill, Newcome]."

Ref: Saint Louis *Daily Union*, December 14, 1847; Saint Louis *Reveille* (daily), December 31, 1847; *KHQ*, v. 30, p. 5.

❧ MARRIED: on December 12, at the Miami Indian village, present

Miami county, by the Rev. Charles Truyens, S. J., the following couples:

Joseph Bourdon (son of Francois and Lisette [Peret] Bourdon), and Sophie Gibeau (daughter of Louis and Marie Louise [Robidoux] Gibeau).

Charles Gibeau (son of Louis and Marie Louise [Robidoux] Gibeau), and Adeline Prayon (daughter of Etienne and Aloise [Prebert?, or Robert?] Prayon).

Also, *apparently* at the same time (though no date appears in the record), Joseph Gibeau (son of Louis and Marie Louise [Robidoux] Gibeau), and Mathilde Prayon (daughter of Etienne and Aloise [Robert?] Prayon).

Ref: Kinsella, *op. cit.,* pp. 240-242, and *see, also,* p. 24. Twin sons (Moisis and Michael) born September 19, 1848, to Charles and Adeline Gibeau, and a daughter (Archange Rosaly Philomena) born September 28, 1848, to Joseph and Sophia Bourdon, were baptized by the Rev. Henry Van Mierlo, S. J.

℄ December 26.—At a Wyandot Methodist church meeting, members made liberal subscriptions for finishing their new brick meeting house (under construction during the year; and first used about November 1).

This brick church (promoted chiefly by the Wyandots' pastor, Rev. Edward T. Peery) was a 50′ x 35′ building, with basement. The location (it is thought) was near what became the junction of Tenth street and Freeman avenue, Kansas City, Kan. About 240 Wyandots were members of the Methodist Episcopal church in 1847.

Ref: William Walker's journal, *loc. cit.; KHC,* v. 9, pp. 215-218; Andreas and Cutler, *op. cit.,* p. 1228.

℄ BORN: on December 31, at Wyandot Methodist Mission (present Wyandotte county), Francis Theodore Peery, son of the Rev. Edward T. and Mary S. (Peery) Peery.

Ref: Si and Shirley Corn's *Our Family Tree* (June, 1959), section IV; *KHC,* v. 9, p. 228, for location of the Peery family in 1847; William Walker's "Journals," *loc. cit.,* entry of December 31, 1847 ("The Deacon [Peery] has had the good fortune to have a son born to him on the last day of the year, 1847.")

℄ Employed in "Kansas" by the Indian Department during all, or part of the year 1847 were the following persons:

FORT LEAVENWORTH AGENCY [*Kickapoos, Delawares, Shawnees, Kansa, Stockbridges, and Munsees*]—*Agent* Richard W. Cummins; *Interpreters* Clement Lessert and Henry Tiblow; *Blacksmiths* William Donalson and Calvin Perkins for Shawnees, James B. Franklin for Delawares, William H. Mitchell for Kansa; *Assistant blacksmiths* Joseph Parks' colored boy and Powhatan Phifer for Shawnees, Cornelius Yager for Delawares, Nelson Henry (died February 13) for Kansa.

GREAT NEMAHA SUBAGENCY [*Iowas and Sacs & Foxes of the Missouri*]— *Subagent* William E. Rucker; *Interpreters* John B. Rubite, John B. Roy, and Francis Bricknelle (appointed July 1); *Blacksmiths* William M. Carter, Andrew Meyer, and William T. Harris (appointed April 1); *Farmers* John W. Forman, Frederick Lyda (appointed March 1), Alfred Rucker; *Assistant farmer* Martin Meyer.

OSAGE RIVER SUBAGENCY [*Ottawas, Chippewas, Weas, Piankeshaws, Pottawatomies, and Miamis.*]—*Subagent* Alfred J. Vaughan; *Interpreter* Joel W. Barrow; *Blacksmiths* Robert Wilson and Robert Simerwell; *Assistant blacksmiths* Samuel L. Bertrand and Jonas P. Lykins; *Millers* Jude W. Bourassa and Joel Grover; *Physician* Johnston Lykins. *Note: "This sub-agency, by direction of the Secretary of War, has been discontinued, and the tribes within it, excepting the Pottawatomies, transferred to the charge of the agent of the Sacs & Foxes. The Pottawatomies of this and the Council Bluffs [Iowa] subagency are to be united on the lands purchased for them of the Kanzas, with Mr. [Alfred J.] Vaughan for their sub-agent."*—30th Cong., 1st Sess., *H. Ex. Doc. No. 26* (Serial 516), pp. 6, 7.

OSAGE SUBAGENCY [*Osages*]—*Subagent* Samuel H. Bunch ("Removed"), John M. Richardson (appointed November 15); *Interpreter* Charles Mongrain; *Blacksmith* John R. McKinney; *Assistant blacksmiths* Francis Mitchell and Joseph Captain; *Millers* William S. Sims and R. B. Coleman; *Assistant millers* L. Brenizier and Samuel Bevenue. Returns incomplete for 1847.

WYANDOT SUBAGENCY [*Wyandots*]—*Subagent* Richard Hewitt; *Interpreter* John M. Armstrong; *Blacksmith* Charles Graham; *Assistant blacksmith* Ira Hunter.

SAC & FOX AGENCY [*Sacs & Foxes of the Mississippi*]—*Agent* John Beach ("Resigned"—on October 4), Solomon P. Sublette (appointed October 21); *Interpreter* Josiah Smart; *Gunsmiths* Harvey Sturdevant and Newman York; *Blacksmiths* Charles H. Withington and Arthur Ingraham Baker; *Assistant blacksmiths* Jonathan Parsons and James Garlick; *Physician* Volney Spalding ("Removed"). In 1848 roster *see* Osage River Agency.

Ref: 30th Cong., 1st Sess., *H. Ex. Doc. No. 26* (Serial 516), pp. 4-7; 31st Cong., 1st Sess., *H. Ex. Doc. No. 11* (Serial 572), p. 107; 31st Cong., 1st Sess., *H. Ex. Doc. 79* (Serial 579), pp. 15, 16; 30th Cong., 1st Sess., *Sen. Ex. Doc. No. 70* (Serial 510), p. 113 (for John Beach's abrupt resignation); SIA, St. Louis, "Records," v. 9 (typed copy), p. 36 (for death of Nelson Henry—an educated Kansa Indian, who left a mother and two small brothers).

1848

❧ January 2.—Mountain man James P. Beckwourth (recently express *from* Santa Fe) left Fort Leavenworth to make the return journey. Across "Kansas," and as far as Bent's Fort, he had (it appears) but one companion.

The Santa Fe (N. M.) *Republican* of February 12, reporting his safe arrival, gave Beckwourth's account of an encounter with 11 Pawnees (when two days' travel west of Fort Mann). He claimed to have killed two Indians and wounded three others.

See, also, July 13 entry.

Ref: *The Gazette*, St. Joseph, Mo., March 31, 1848; Saint Louis *Daily Union*, April 1, 1848.

❧ January 5.—Francis X. Aubry (alone) arrived at Independence, Mo., after a rapid (14-day) journey overland from Santa Fe (and several days in advance of an express which had started East three days before him).

Aubry had left behind "at the Cottonwood," his servant—last to wear out of five men who departed Santa Fe December 22, 1847, with him.

See, also, May 28 and September 17 entries for swifter Aubry "rides."

Ref: Saint Louis *Daily Union,* January 12, 1848; *The Weekly Tribune,* Liberty, Mo., January 28, 1848 (from *Missouri Republican,* St. Louis); *The Daily Reveille,* St. Louis, January 12, 1848; New York *Weekly Tribune,* January 29, 1848; *The Pacific Historian,* Stockton, Calif.; v. 5 (August, 1961), pp. 111-123 (for Aubry article). By one account Aubry had 10 mules stolen by Mexican robbers; was detained by Indians one-half day; and lost another half day in a snowstorm. The *Reveille's* Independence correspondent wrote that Aubry saw no Indians en route; killed three mules by hard riding; had four days of "severe cold weather"; and traveled 306 miles on the last three days of his journey.

❧ January 5.—Lt. Col. Stephen H. Long's table *"Probable extent of steam navigation on the western waters"* (published in Col. J. J. Abert's report [of above date] on "Commerce of the Lakes and Western Rivers") gave these estimates for the Missouri and tributaries:

River	Miles Navigable
Missouri proper	1,800 miles
Yellowstone	300 miles
Platte	40 miles
Kansas	150 miles
Osage	275 miles
Grand	90 miles

Ref: 30th Cong., 1st Sess., *H. Ex. Doc. No. 19* (Serial 516), pp. 18-20.

❧ DIED: Henry Jacquis (prominent in the Wyandot Nation), at "12 o'clock at night [of January 5]," in present Kansas City, Kan.

Subagent Hewitt wrote that Jacquis had been "one of their most active, useful, and influential chiefs." The Rev. Edward T. Peery officiated at his funeral on January 7; William Walker was the orator.

Ref: William Walker's "Journals" (in William E. Connelley's *The Provisional Government of Nebraska Territory* . . . [Lincoln, Neb., 1899]), January 6, 1848, entry; Comm'r of Indian affairs, *Report,* 1848 (Richard Hewitt's report, therein). The Wyandots pronounced the name Jacquis "Jocko."

❧ Mid-January.—At Fort Mann, on the Arkansas (present Ford county), the troops—three companies of Gilpin's battalion, Missouri volunteers—were said to be in good health generally, though some were suffering from scurvy; but the garrison's horses—once numbering around 75—were reduced to "about a dozen . . . barely able to stand upon their feet"; only six or eight were left of 144 mules brought there in November, 1847; fewer than 100(?), out of 800 oxen, still survived, and the wolves were daily devouring them.

Ref: New York *Weekly Tribune,* February 26, 1848 (from *Missouri Republican,* St. Louis, February 7, 1848); Saint Louis *Daily Union,* February 8, 1848.

❧ In January, at the Catholic Pottawatomie mission station south of Kansas river (on the Wakarusa in present Auburn township, Shawnee co.), where Father Christian Hoecken had removed (from Sugar Creek) in November, 1847—*see* p. 726—a log house (residence and church under one roof) was started with the aid of Indians. It was occupied on February 26.

Short-lived "Mission creek" station prospered during the spring, then served as base of operations for the establishment of the mission where St. Mary's College, St. Marys, Kan., later was founded. The Rev. Felix L. Verreydt (superior at Sugar Creek), after spring visits to Father Hoecken's station, and to the reserve area across the Kansas, determined, in June, to locate the "permanent" Pottawatomie Catholic Mission at a site north of the Kansas. *See* September 9 annals entry for the founding of St. Mary's mission. In mid-October Father Hoecken, and some Indian families, removed to month-old St. Mary's.

Ref: *The Dial*, St. Mary's College, St. Marys, Kan., v. 2 (February, 1891), pp. 85-88; Augustin C. Wand, S. J., *The Jesuits in Territorial Kansas* . . . (1962), pp. 10-15. In G. J. Garraghan's *The Jesuits of the Middle United States* (New York, 1938), v. 2, pp. 601, 603, 604, Father Gailland is quoted that the "Mission creek" station was on the "Waggerousse" [Wakarusa]; and W. W. Cone in his *Historical Sketch of Shawnee County* . . . (1877), p. 8, also gives that location.

❦ January 17.—"Mr. [Thomas] Glendy" (a "practical woodsman" from St. Charles county, Mo.), and one companion, who had set out from Oregon City on September 23, 1847, and traveled the Oregon trail eastward (across present Idaho, Wyoming, and Nebraska), arrived safely (though with badly frostbitten feet) at "old" Fort Kearny (on Table creek; where Nebraska City, Neb., is today).

On their adventurous (and notable) winter's journey, most of the time afoot, Glendy and his cotraveler had taken circuitous routes, on occasion, to avoid hostile Indians (and had seen none on the entire trip).

Ref: *The Weekly Tribune*, Liberty, Mo., February 4, 1848; New York *Daily Tribune*, February 9, 1848. Glendy the "Glendry" who, in 1849, was guide to the U. S. Mounted riflemen on their march from Fort Leavenworth to Oregon—*see* R. W. Settle, editor, *The March of the Mounted Riflemen* . . . (Glendale, Calif., 1940), p. 284. In 33d Cong., 1st Sess., Sen. Ex. Doc. No. 17 (Serial 694), p. 4, "Thomas Glendy" is listed as having received payment at Sutter, Calif., in September, 1849 (from Lt. D. R. Jones, U. S. A.), for services as guide.

❦ January 21.—From Fort Mann (present Ford county) Capt. Napoleon Koscialowski's Company E (infantry) and a light artillery detachment set out (under orders received by express on January 15) to join Lt. Col. William Gilpin's command (two cavalry companies) above Bent's Fort.

After a tedious 35 days of travel up the Arkansas (delayed by their starving oxen—140 head reduced to around 70 by journey's end), the Missouri volunteers reached Gilpin's camp on February 24.

On March 10 (or 11?) Gilpin and enlarged command—now close to

300 men—headed southward for Moro, N. M.; arrived there March 26; received supplies; and in the first week of April, set out, eastward, on a campaign against the Comanches, other hostile Indians, and renegade Mexicans reported to be collecting on the Canadian (preparing, as in 1847, to maraud on the Santa Fe trail in the spring).

Gilpin's mule-mounted expedition force consisted of his battalion's Companies A and B (cavalry), Company E (infantry—now mounted?), Lt. Phillip Stremmel's artillery section (with a six-pounder); also, three Delawares, three Cheyennes, one Blackfoot, and three mountain men (as guides, spies, etc.); and there were 26 mule-drawn supply wagons.

A letter written from Las Vegas, N. M., on May 4, reported the arrival there of a Mexican (a prisoner among the Comanches for several years) who said he had escaped when Gilpin and troops surrounded a Comanche village and "made considerable slaughter" among the Indians. The Santa Fe *Republican* learned the Indians' loss in men and stock had been great; and that one or two of Gilpin's men had been killed.

See, also, May 30 annals entry.

Ref: *The Weekly Tribune,* Liberty, Mo., March 17, May 26, June 2, 1848; New York *Weekly Tribune,* February 26, June 17, 1848 (from *Missouri Republican,* St. Louis, February 7 and June 3, 1848); Saint Louis *Daily Union,* February 8, April 11, May 23, June 9, 1848; *The Daily Reveille,* St. Louis, February 8, April 12, 1848.

❧ January 24.—Gold was discovered at Sutter's Mill in California.

News of the gold finds began to reach the East Coast in August; but it was the arrival of firsthand accounts, in mid-September, and later, that generated public gold excitement. (*See, also,* October, and December annals entries.)

Ref: Carl I. Wheat's *Mapping the Transmississippi West* (San Francisco, 1957), v. 3, pp. 49-63, outlines the year 1848, see p. 63, for the development of gold excitement in the East. L. R. and Ann W. Hafen, in *Old Spanish Trail* (1954), pp. 338, 339, comment on overland news carriers.

❧ January 27.—Lt. Caleb S. Tuttle (Company E, Gilpin's battalion) arrived at Fort Leavenworth, from Fort Mann. He, Lt. Christian Boecking, and 14(?) other Missouri volunteers had made the trip to the Missouri border, on foot, in 14 days, with a one-day stopover at Council Grove.

Tuttle's party (11 to 16 men—reports vary) had left the post on the Arkansas on January 13. Some of the company apparently went directly to Independence, Mo. The Boonville (Mo.) *Bulletin,* noting "Lieut. Bicking's" arrival there, January 30, stated he had reached Independence on the 25th(?).

Early in February, Lieutenant Tuttle, with only one companion(?)—Corporal Gaines—left Fort Leavenworth to cross "Kansas" again, and rejoin his company (then en route to Bent's Fort—*see* January 21 entry).

Ref: *The Daily Reveille,* St. Louis, February 6, 26, March 30, 1848; Saint Louis *Daily Union,* February 8, 1848.

❧ About the end of January an express (several? men, with pack animals) from Santa Fe reached Fort Leavenworth.

This small party arrived at Bent's Fort on January 8; left next day; reached Fort Mann on the 15th (bringing Gilpin's order for troops to join him—*see* January 21 entry); continued east on the 16th; did not overtake Tuttle's party on the road—*see* January 27 entry.

Ref: *The Westerners New York Posse Brand Book*, v. 10 (1963), p. 80 (in a Thomas Fitzpatrick letter from Bent's Fort); *The Daily Reveille*, St. Louis, February 8, 1848; New York *Weekly Tribune*, February 26, 1848 (from *Missouri Republican*, February 7).

❡ January-June—Licenses (new and renewal) to trade with Indians in "Kansas," as granted by agents and subagents of the St. Louis Indian superintendency, were:

Traders	Indians	Issued by	Rec'vd at St. Louis
(A. G.) Boone & (J. G.) Hamilton	Sacs & Foxes	S. P. Sublette	January
Joseph Clymer	Miamis	S. P. Sublette	January
A. G. Boone & Co.	Pottawatomies	A. J. Vaughan	March
(J. M.) Simpson & (J. M.) Hunter	Pottawatomies	A. J. Vaughan	March
W. W. Cleghorn	Pottawatomies	A. J. Vaughan	March
Moses H. Scott	Miamis	S. P. Sublette	March
J. B. Scott	Sacs & Foxes	S. P. Sublette	March
John Cummins	Sacs, and Miamis	S. P. Sublette	March
(R. A.) Kinzie & (J. H.) Whistler	Sacs & Foxes	S. P. Sublette	March
Porter[?] & Chouteau	Weas & Miamis	S. P. Sublette	March
Cyprian Chouteau	Shawnees and Delawares	R. W. Cummins	April
Richard Pearson	Pottawatomies	R. W. Cummins	April
P. Chouteau, Jr. & Co.	Pottawatomies	R. W. Cummins	April
W. H. Hildreth	Kickapoos, Delawares, and Pottawatomies	R. W. Cummins	May
A. B. H. and A. G. McGee	Sacs & Foxes	[S. P. Sublette?]	May
(M. H.) Scott & (Ezekiel) French	Pottawatomies	R. W. Cummins	June

See pp. 769, 770, for July-September traders' licenses.

Ref: Superintendency of Indian Affairs (SIA), St. Louis, "Records," v. 9, typed copy, pp. 48, 49, 120, 137-139, 141, 209, 211, 212. Albert G. Boone, James G. Hamilton, Joseph Clymer, James H. Simpson, and James M. Hunter were all from Westport, Mo.; also from Jackson county, Mo., were Moses H. Scott, Allen B. H. (and Albert G.?) McGee. For W. W. Cleghorn, *see* annals, p. 341; for John B. Scott (an Iowan), Robert A. Kinzie, John H. Whistler, and W. H. Hildreth, *see* annals. Ezekiel French, of Oswego, Ind. (partner of Moses H. Scott), is mentioned in a May 17, 1848, document—*See* Office of Indian Affairs (OIA), Letters Received from Fort Leavenworth Agency (National Archives Microcopy 234, Roll 302). For some data on Allen B. H. McGee (and Albert G. McGee) *see The United States Biographical Dictionary . . . Missouri Volume* (1878), pp. 317, 318. Apparently John C. Pearson was clerk for Richard Pearson (*see* SIA, v. 9, p. 212—noted above); and Thomas N. Stinson was clerk, in 1848, for Simpson & Hunter (*see* T. N. Stinson Collection, ms. div., KHi; *also, see* W. W. Cone's *Historical Sketch of Shawnee County*, p. 10.

❡ Between January and July there were important changes at

Delaware Baptist Mission (present Wyandotte county). (1) Early in January, the Rev. Ira D. Blanchard (long-time missionary to the Delawares—*see* p. 225) was dismissed. He and his family left, apparently, before month's end. (2) On January 8 a new mission house—some four miles northwest of the old station (where the Blanchards had lived—at present Edwardsville)—was described as "advancing towards completion." (3) The Rev. John G. and Olivia (Evans) Pratt, assigned to the Delawares, removed from nearby Stockbridge station (in the early spring?) to the new mission (not yet finished on April 1). (4) On July 3 the Delaware "boarding school" reopened—with Pratt as superintendent, and Elizabeth S. Morse (recently at Ottawa mission) as teacher. (There were 28 children at the beginning.)

New Delaware Baptist Mission (as described by John G. Pratt in 1851) consisted of "a principal dwelling-house 36 feet square, a frame building, with kitchen, and usual small out-buildings, a school, and meeting house." (The church had been constructed in 1846—*see* p. 660.) By survey description the site was on the NW¼ of Sec. 10, T. 11 S., R. 23 E., some four miles north of the Kansas river.

Ref: Barker Collection (in KHi ms. division); Comm'r of Indian affairs, *Reports*, 1848, 1851; *The Baptist Missionary Magazine*, Boston, v. 28, pp. 280, 408, 469; *KHQ*, v. 23, p. 179. Although Elizabeth S. Morse stated (in *The Baptist Missionary Magazine*) that Delaware Baptist Mission was 56' by 56', Pratt's description—that it was "36 feet square"—undoubtedly was correct.

❡ February 1.—A brief history of the Iowa and Sac tribes, of this date, by Missionaries S. M. Irvin and William Hamilton of the "Iowa and Sac [Presbyterian] mission," included comment on the Iowa Nation's three leading chiefs. Some excerpts follow:

WHITE CLOUD (head chief): "not remarkable for any trait except an insatiable thirst for spirits"; "very regardless of the interests of his nation"; "has sustained his influence . . . heretofore, by . . . [treating] a few braves (so called) . . . [as] favorites . . ."; "offers no encouragement to the [mission] school"; "has three wives, and sometimes four"; "[is] a man of middle size, one eye out from the constant use of liquor"; "about 35 or 36 years of age"; "a poor speaker, and says but little in council, usually." (White Cloud distinguished himself in May, 1848—*see* p. 752. *Also, see* his portrait in this volume.)

NA-CHE-NING-A, or NO-HEART-OF-FEAR (second chief: "the principal business-man of the nation [and] . . . is at this time chief speaker"; "under good influence will always be a fine man"; "shows some concern for the welfare of his people"; "[is] a friend to the whites"; "very friendly to education"; "the school and mission owe much to him"; "a man of good appearance"; "has but one wife"; "is almost 45 years of age." (*See* his portrait in this volume.)

NEU-MON-GA, or WALKING-RAIN (third chief): "a man of most dignified and fine appearance"; "of a shrewd and cunning mind"; "modest and well-behaved among the whites"; "ambitious and selfish among his people, and generally of doubtful reputation"; "[is] a ready speaker"; "nearly 50 years of age"; "has one wife."

Ref: Henry S. Schoolcraft's *Archives of Aboriginal Knowledge* . . . (Philadelphia, 1860), v. 3, pp. 259-265. This chief White Cloud (Mahaska) was also known as Frank White Cloud—*see* index to annals; *also, see*, p. 607 for a group illustration of Iowas, and p. 519 for their trip abroad.

❆ Early in February, Sup't T. H. Harvey, St. Louis, visited the Miamis; rode over their reserve; and selected a site for a Catholic mission school, also a place near by for a new Miami village (by designating where the blacksmith and traders should locate). This "Miamitown" or "Miami Village" was near the Marais des Cygnes, some seven miles southeast of present Paola, according to available information, in Sec. 18, T. 18 (or 19?) S., R. 24 E., Miami township, Miami co.

By early May (when Harvey returned, to pay annuities) a number of Miami families had moved up to the new site (the "old" town—*see* p. 654—was on Sugar creek, in the area of present Rockville, Miami co.); Joseph Clymer, Jr., trader (by contract, for $1,439), had fenced and broken 225 acres of land for the Indians; and the Miami Catholic mission school was in process of construction. (*See, also,* a November entry, p. 789.) By September over half the Miamis had moved to new "Miamitown," where all the traders had been relocated, and where the Indians' blacksmith shop was in operation.

Ref: SIA, St. Louis, "Records," v. 9, typed copy, pp. 56, 142; 31st Cong., 1st Sess., *H. Ex. Doc. No. 11* (Serial 572), p. 6; Comm'r of Indian affairs, *Report,* 1848 (Harvey's and Agent Fains' reports therein). Harvey, after visiting "Kansas" a third time in 1848, wrote in a November 21, 1848, letter that "A large portion of the Miamies have moved up to the vicinity of the school and it is expected that nearly all will during the winter & spring."—SIA, St. Louis, "Records," v. 9, typed copy, p. 238. For location of Miamitown—or Miami Village, see Ely Moore's notation on a printed map in Moore papers, KHi ms. division, which shows the site as on the W½ of the E½ of Sec. 18, T. 18 S., R. 24 E. (The 1878 Miami county atlas map of T. 18 S., R. 24 E. does not indicate where the town had been; but on the NW¼ of the SW¼ of Sec. 19, an "Indian cemetery" is marked.) Since Ely Moore lived at the Osage River Subagency in 1854 (his father was agent), the location he specified for "Miami village & agency" has been presumed correct. (Note: *KHC,* v. 9, p. 570, gives the location—wrongly—as Sec. 24, T. 18 S., R. 23 E.; and *ibid.,* v. 11, p. 463, gives it—wrongly—as Sec. 24, T. 18 S., R. 24.)

❆ In (mid?) February.—"Fisher's express" left Fort Leavenworth for Santa Fe. The men in this party "suffered much" on the journey, and several had their ears frozen—as reported by Tharp and his eastbound company who met them March 5, on the trail.

Ref: *The Weekly Tribune,* Liberty, Mo., April 14, 1848; New York *Weekly Tribune,* April 8, 1848.

❆ February 17.— Hugh Hamilton obtained the contract to furnish 30,000 pounds of flour (at $3.00 per 100 pounds) for the Sac & Fox Indians of the Mississippi—as approved by Agent Solomon P. Sublette.

Other bidders were: Jeremiah Farmer, John Jackson, Z[enas] Leonard,

Solomon Young, Isaac G. Baker, Oliver Caldwell, William G. Childs, E. M. Campbell, George W. Rhodes, Joseph Clymer, Hiram M. Northrup, A[mazon] Hays, M[ichael?] Rice, John W. Campbell, and Rice & Aull.

Ref: OIA, Letters Received from Osage River Agency (National Archives Microcopy 234, Roll 643). Amazon Hays was a son of Boone Hays, who had emigrated to western Missouri in 1837—*see* Lilian Hays Oliver's *Some Boone Descendants and Kindred of the St. Charles District* (1964), pp. 38, 306.

❦ February 23.—The *Tamerlane* reached Weston, Mo.—the first of 193 steamboat arrivals at that port in 1848. (*See, also,* April 5 entry.)

(Sixty-eight steamboats went to points higher up the Missouri before year's end. The last boat of 1848 to arrive at Weston was the *Cora*, on November 22.)

Ref: *The Western Journal*, St. Louis, v. 5 (March, 1851), p. 326. The *Tamerlane* returned to St. Louis, from the above trip, on March 2—*see The Daily Reveille*, St. Louis, March 2, 1848.

❦ February.—Agent Thomas Fitzpatrick (of the Upper Platte Agency), counciled with chiefs of the Kiowa Nation (in the Bent's Fort vicinity?). Subsequently, the Kiowas severed their alliance with the Comanches (hostile to the white man), came up to the Arkansas, and joined the peaceful Cheyennes and Arapahoes. (*See* May 30 entry for Gilpin's meeting with these three tribes on the Arkansas.)

Explorer John C. Fremont, writing from Bent's Fort on November 17, noted his recent visit with Fitzpatrick at "Big Timber," and commented: "He is a most admirable agent, and has succeeded in drawing out from among the Cumanches the whole Kiowa nation, with the exception of six lodges and brought over among them a considerable number of lodges of the Apaches and Cumanches. . . ."

Ref: Comm'r of Indian affairs, *Report*, 1848 (Fitzpatrick's report, therein); New York *Weekly Tribune*, March 10, 1849 (for Fremont's letter, reprinted from the Washington *National Intelligencer*, February 26).

❦ DIED: Nah-ko-min ("Captain Nah koo min"), principal chief of the Delawares (since 1835—*see* p. 298), "about the 1st March 1848," on the reserve north of Kansas river (in present Wyandotte county).

His successor was "Captain Ketchum." Following Chief Ketchum in rank were Sakendiathen (Secondine) and Sah-coc-sa (Sarcoxie).

Ref: OIA, Letters Received from Fort Leavenworth Agency (National Archives Microcopy 234, Roll 303), R. W. Cummins' March 28, 1849, letter.

❦ Early in March, Agents R. W. Cummins and A. J. Vaughan chose a location for "the smith & traders for the Potawatomies." Vaughan, in a March 7 letter, reported: "I have accordingly stuck my stake and christened it union town . . ."; and Cummins (on March 12) wrote: "The point selected by us is on the south side of the Kansas ["on high ground, near the river"] . . . & very nearly in the center of their [the Pottawatomies'] country, east & west & as nearly so north and south as good timber . . . could be had. . . ."

Union Town, by survey description, was in the NE¼ of Sec. 23, T. 11 S., R. 13 E., near the western edge of Shawnee county. The Pottawatomies north of the river (where most of the "Council Bluffs" Indians had settled) were opposed to a single trading site for the Nation (Chiefs Me-ah-mies, Half Day, and many others, in a petition, pointed out the dangers of having to cross the Kansas, and asked for "our Blacksmith," and "our traders"). But Union Town was the only official trading point from 1848 until about 1853.

When Capt. L. C. Easton visited "Uniontown" on September 15, 1849, he remarked: "[It is] situated a mile from the Kanzas on the South side, there are a few dwellings and four or five Stores, which contain Indian Goods and a variety of such Articles as Emigrants would probably require at this point." (Beginning in 1849 some of the California-Oregon trail traffic followed up the Kansas valley on the *south* side of the river past Union Town—instead of ferrying, or fording, at present Topeka—and crossed the Kansas a little west of what is now Willard, Shawnee county.)

See the January and July annals entries (1848-1854) listing licensed traders for the Pottawatomies (and other tribes).

Ref: OIA, Letters Received from Fort Leavenworth Agency (National Archives Microcopy 234, Roll 302), for Vaughan's and Cummins' letters, and the petition; *KHQ*, v. 20, p. 412 (for Easton); W. W. Cone's *Historical Sketch of Shawnee County*, p. 11 (Cone gave the location as in the NW¼ of Sec. 23, but rather, it was in the NW¼ of the NE¼ of Sec. 23—according to George Root's notations on Dover township map in 1873 Shawnee county atlas (in KHi map division), and other information. The main street of Union Town ran (north and south) just east of the present (1971) homesite of Ernest Ray Green—*see* affidavits relating to Union Town's location in KHi ms. division. The Oregon trail (crossing Union Town on the main street) forded Post creek "almost directly north of the present homesite," according to these affidavits. For other data on Union Town *see* Thomas N. Stinson Collection (in KHi ms. division). One item therein seems to show that Simpson & Hunter (with Stinson as clerk) began trading at Union Town in April, 1848. Also, *see* J. S. Chick's April 19, 1906, letter, and an interview (1908) with Chick which are in KHi ms. division; and "Memoranda" of an 1880 trip by F. G. Adams and W. W. Cone to the Union Town site, in *ibid*. *See* the Topeka *Daily Capital* of July 20, 1958, and August 17, 1961, for articles on Union Town, and the E. R. Green farm.

❧ In early March a number of persons (mostly traders) reached Missouri from New Mexico. The Santa Fe *Republican* of January 29 had reported that "a party of Traders" including "Mr. M'Knight, Redmon, Murphy, Estes, Gardiner, Beck and Manies" would leave for the States on February 1.

At St. Louis the *Reveille* announced the arrival from New Mexico of "Messrs. McKnight and Meyer [or, Mayer]," on March 8, with wagons, in 22 days (32?—to the Missouri-"Kansas" border?), and stated they had "met" (*i. e.*, passed) on the way traders Bullard and Murphy whose mules were nearly worn out. The *Union's* story stated "Messrs. McKnight and Owens, and four or five Mexican traders" reached St. Louis aboard the *John J. Hardin;* and in a later issue, noting the arrival on March 17(?) of Murphy, stated he had left Santa Fe on January 28; had seen no Indians en route; and had carried a mail to Fort Leavenworth. ("A. B.," writing from Taos on January 26, had reported that "Mr. Easter" [Estes] of that place would leave in a few days "with an express" for Missouri.)

Ref: *The Daily Reveille*, St. Louis, March 9, 1848; Saint Louis *Daily Union*, March 10, 18, 1848. Perhaps "Manies" was trader Frank McManus.

❦ March.—From Fort Mann, on the 7th, a correspondent wrote of a mutiny a day or two before, with such strong demonstrations made against the commanding officer—Capt. William Pelzer—that he had been forced to "order out the Battalion" to quell the trouble.

Another news item in the letter: a first lieutenant, wrestling with an Indian (the Pawnee prisoner?), had got his leg fractured.

Ref: *The Weekly Tribune*, Liberty, Mo., April 7, 1848. For Pelzer's difficulty, in 1847, at Fort Mann *see* annals, p. 727.

❦ March.—Andrew Drips (American Fur Company agent), from Fort Pierre (which he had left around February 8), reached St. Louis March 8 aboard the *John J. Hardin*.

Other steamboats on the Missouri in March included the *Haydee* (back at St. Louis on the 21st, after a trip up to Weston, Mo.), the *Martha* (which left St. Louis, upbound, on the 22d, reached St. Joseph and departed downriver prior to March 31).

Ref: Saint Louis *Daily Union*, March 10, 1848; *The Daily Reveille*, St. Louis, March 21 and 28, 1848; St. Joseph (Mo.) *Gazette*, March 31, 1848. The *Union* did not state how far up the *Hardin* went; nor where Drips boarded her.

❦ March 14.—Comment on fast-growing Kansas (City), Mo., appeared in St. Louis newspapers of this date:

"H" (in the St. Louis *Union*) wrote: "Kansas [is] one of the most thriving towns on the Missouri River. . . . The accommodations for strangers are fully equal to those of any town on the Missouri river. . . . Many of the largest traders for Santa Fe, all the Indian traders, and nearly all the mountain traders[?], already make Kansas their starting point, and the time is not far distant when Kansas will be the main point for the great Western Prairie trade."

The *Reveille*, noting the growing importance of the Santa Fe trade to St. Louis, stated: "The Messrs. Leitsendorffer [Leitensdorfer] have shipped their goods to Kansas landing by which they save 40 miles of travel. Messrs. Webb & Doane, traders, intend traveling in company with . . . [them]."

On April 7, the Liberty (Mo.) *Tribune* wrote of Kansas, Mo.: "This is going to be quite a flourishing town. Within a few months, it has been gaining fast, both in trade and population. Some of the heaviest Santa Fe traders start now from this point. The landing is one of the best, if not the very best, on the Missouri river; there is a good road to the prairie, a good ferry, and a clever ferry-man—namely Mr. [John] Calvin McCoy."

Bishop James O. Andrew, viewing Kansas, Mo., on October 21, had this comment: "the site is a very unsightly one, being a perfect pile of steep hills, yet I think it is destined to be a thriving, prosperous place for business."

On October 29 Allen T. Ward (employed at Shawnee Methodist Mission), wrote in a letter: "The town of Kansas . . . now contains I think upwards of 300 houses & is rapidly improving. It is one of the best landings on the [Missouri] river, and the town is founded on a ledge of rocks that are as permanent as gibralter; it is also destined to be the starting point to Santa fee California Oregon &c. A considerable portion of the goods for the Santa fee market are now landed at Kansas, besides all this it is as good a point for the Indian trade as can be found in this country. . . ."

Ref: Saint Louis *Daily Union*, March 14, 1848; *The Daily Reveille*, St. Louis, March 14, 1848; *The Weekly Tribune*, Liberty, Mo., April 7, 1848; James O. Andrew's *Miscellanies* . . . (Nashville, 1855), p. 156; Allen T. Ward's October 29, 1848, letter, in *KHQ*, v. 33, p. 358. See annals, p. 575, for Kansas City's status in 1846.

❆ In mid-March, weeks in advance of other traders, Francis X. Aubry (*see* January 5 entry) left Independence, Mo., for Santa Fe with some 15 merchandise-laden wagons. (To supply feed for his animals as far as Fort Mann, Aubry had corn hauled out to Diamond Spring—present Morris county.)

On April 21 he reached his destination, safely; and sold his goods at wholesale before the wagons got to Santa Fe. *See, also,* May 28 and October 8 entries.

Ref: *The Daily Reveille*, St. Louis, March 19, April 11, 1848; *The Gazette*, St. Joseph, Mo., June 2, 1848; *The Weekly Tribune*, Liberty, Mo., June 9, 1848; *The Pacific Historian*, v. 5 (August, 1961), p. 113.

❆ March 20.—Trader Lewis Tharp's pack party (eight men; 13 mules) which had left "Fort Spaulding" (an upper-Arkansas trading post, 80 miles above Bent's Fort) on February 25, arrived at town of Kansas (Kansas City), Mo.

(During a winter clash with Indians, Tharp had been robbed of merchandise, and three of his men had been killed. Also, a few days prior to starting East, his brother, Edward Tharp, had been murdered by a white man—James Waters.)

While on the Santa Fe trail, in March, Lewis Tharp and companions had been obliged to backtrack to Fort Mann (after passing it two days earlier) hunting their mules which had wandered off during a severe storm. On this "retrograde march" they met three men, express from Santa Fe, with worn-out animals; and, after recovering their own mules, assisted the mail carrier's party to reach Council Grove (where trader Seth Hays provided further aid).

Lewis Tharp, aboard the *St. Joseph,* arrived at St. Louis, from "Kanzas," on March 26.

Ref: St. Louis *Daily Union*, March 27, 1848; *The Weekly Tribune*, Liberty, Mo., April 14, 1848; New York *Weekly Tribune*, April 8, 1848; Janet Lecompte's article on William Tharp, in Hafen, ed., *Mountain Men, op. cit.*, v. 3, p. 307. William Tharp, brother of Lewis and Edward Tharp, had been killed by Indians at Walnut creek in 1847—*see* annals index.

❧ March 20.—An express from Santa Fe reached Fort Leavenworth. Newspapers dated as recently as February 24 were brought by the mail carrier—who was, apparently, "Mr. Palmer." (Palmer's arrival at St. Louis, aboard the *Amelia,* on March 26, was noted by the *Union.*)

The express was reported (by "Cacero"—writing from Fort Leavenworth on March 20) to have left Las Vegas, N. M., March 1; and to have made the trip in 26 days from Santa Fe. *See, also,* preceding entry.

Ref: *The Weekly Tribune,* Liberty, Mo., March 24, 1848; Saint Louis *Daily Union,* March 27, 31, 1848.

❧ March 20.—At a new location (selected by Dr. Johnston Lykins and Agent R. W. Cummins), near the center of present Shawnee county, Pottawatomie Baptist Mission (operated by the American Indian Mission Association) reopened, in temporary quarters (an old Indian log house).

The mission (1837-1847) had been in present Franklin county—*see* pp. 336 and 531. In the party which arrived at the new site (described in 1849 as a half mile south of the Kansas, nine miles below Union Town, and one and a half miles "west of the great California road . . ."; and by later survey description as on the NW¼ of Sec. 32, T. 11 S., R. 15 E.), on the 24th of February, from Westport, Mo., were Dr. Johnston Lykins (physician to the Pottawatomies), Eliza McCoy (mission teacher), Robert Simerwell (blacksmith to the Pottawatomies), and his daughter Sarah Simerwell.

From March 20 to August 20 Eliza McCoy maintained a school for 17 children (16 boarders). There were 11 Pottawatomie girls (aged five to 14), five boys (six to 12), also one white girl (stepdaughter of a Pottawatomie man).

On September 1, 1848, Johnston Lykins was appointed superintendent; and in late October, the AIMA reported government contracts had been signed for establishment of a large (90-pupil) manual labor school; with $5,000 for buildings, agricultural improvements, &c., and an annual appropriation of $4,500, to be provided for operation. *See, also,* September 30, 1849, annals entry.

Ref: Comm'r of Indian Affairs, *Reports,* 1848, 1849; American Indian Mission Association (AIMA) *Proceedings,* 1848, pp. 9, 10, 19 (microfilm, KHi); Shawnee County Historical Society *Bulletin* No. 23 (July, 1955), pp. 11-13 (includes Eliza McCoy's letter from "Kansas River, March 8, 1848"); W. W. Cone's *Historical Sketch of Shawnee County,* p. 9 (the account here is, for the most part, factual); *Atlas of Shawnee County* (New York, 1873), Mission township.

❧ DIED: Osage chief Black Dog (Tchong-tas-sab-bee, Shonkah-sabe), March 24, at his home on Dog creek, near present Claremore, Okla. He was "about" seven feet tall and weighed some 275 pounds.

In 1834 artist George Catlin had met this chief; painted a full-length portrait of him; described his huge size ("in height and in girth, above all of his tribe"); noted that he was "blind in the left eye"; and remarked the admiration and respect accorded him by most army officers, traders, and other white men. Artist J. M. Stanley (in 1843) also painted this chief's portrait; and stated his height to be six feet six inches.

Black Dog (according to the *Cherokee Advocate*) was "courteous in his Indian ways," "warm-hearted, and generally beloved."

Ref: *The Daily Reveille*, St. Louis, April 25, 1848 (from the *Cherokee Advocate*); George Catlin's *Letters and Notes on . . . North American Indians* (New York, 1841), v. 2, p. 42, and Plate 42; J. F. McDermott, ed., Tixier's *Travels on the Osage Prairies* (Norman, Okla., 1940), p. 268, has summarized data on Black Dog; Grant Foreman's *Marcy & the Gold Seekers . . .* (Norman, Okla., 1939), p. 69.

℃ About March(?) a "double geared inclined wheel Grist Mill" for the Sac & Fox Indians (of the Missouri), was completed—at, or near, the Great Nemaha Subagency (present Doniphan county).

Subagent W. E. Rucker, in advertising for bids on construction (in the St. Joseph *Gazette*) under date of July 2, 1847, had specified the main wheel was to be 28 feet in diameter with 36 feet tread in diameter; and the mill was to be enclosed in a "substantial and durable frame" 38 by 50 feet in size. In March, 1848, W. H. High was paid $850 for "services as carpenter in erecting mill, &c." John W. Forman, the first miller, was succeeded before year's end by James F. Forman.

Ref: *The Gazette*, St. Joseph, Mo., July 2, 1847; 31st Cong., 1st Sess., *H. Ex. Doc. No. 11* (Serial 572), p. 175. See last 1848 annals entry for the Formans as millers.

℃ April 1.—George Douglass, of Missouri, received a contract (from Lt. George W. Wallace, of the First U. S. infantry) to supply fresh beef at Fort Scott for one year, commencing April 1.

Ref: 30th Cong., 2d Sess., *Sen. Ex. Doc. No. 17* (Serial 529), p. 11.

℃ April 1.—Crawford Seminary—a Methodist Church, South, manual labor school for the Quapaw Indians—reopened at a new location "about five miles distant" (*i. e.,* upriver) from the old one (*see* p. 468). The new site perhaps was in "Kansas"—in present Cherokee county.

The Rev. Samuel G. Patterson (sup't) wrote (on September 8) that the buildings were "plain and substantial," and large enough to house "two families, several work hands, and 40 Indian children" (but the school's average attendance in 1848 was 24 pupils, only six of them girls). He described the location as "near the east bank of the Pomme de Terre, or Spring river, immediately on the military road leading from Fort Leavenworth to Fort Smith, five miles west of Newton county, Mo."

Subagent B. A. James reported: "The Quapaws numbered, on the 18th August [1848], 53 men, 59 women, and 109 ch[ildren] total 221."

See, also, August 22 entry.

Ref: Comm'r of Indian Affairs, *Report*, 1848 (S. G. Patterson's September 8 report, and B. A. James' September 9 report, therein).

❦ April.—The *Tamerlane* (William B. Miller, captain), leaving St. Louis on April 5, finally reached St. Joseph, Mo., on the 18th—according to passenger Rudolph Friederich Kurz (Swiss artist). (The Missouri was at low stage, delaying steamboat travel.)

Kurz made St. Joseph (and vicinity) his headquarters from April, 1848, to May, 1850. In this interval he became well acquainted with Iowa chief "Kirutsche" (who, in the summer of 1848, taught Kurz the Iowa dialect). "Kirutsche" (one of the Indians who had gone abroad in 1844—*see* annals, p. 519) was described by Kurz in his journal (in 1848) as "a man of middle age, agreeable in manner, not tall but extremely agile," who had "seen a great deal of the world; had been received by Louis Philippe himself in Paris." He was chief of an Iowa band numbering about 30 lodges.

Ref: R. F. Kurz's *Journal* (Bureau of American Ethnology *Bulletin No. 115*, Washington, 1937), pp. 27-29. "Kirutsche" was not the name by which this man was known on the European trip.

❦ April.—Steamboats running in the "upper" Missouri river trade (to points above the Kansas river's mouth), this month, included the following:

St. Joseph (returned to St. Louis April 11; and again on the 26th), *Wyandotte* (left Weston April 12; at St. Louis on the 18th), *Tamerlane* (upbound for St. Joseph—*see* preceding entry), *Cora* (went to Fort Kearny—and Council Bluffs?; back at St. Louis on April 22), *Boreas No. 3* (returned, from Weston?, to St. Louis April 20; and was again(?) at Weston on the 29th), *St. Croix* (returned to St. Louis, from St. Joseph, April 24), *Julia* (went up—to Weston?), *Martha* (was at Fort Kearny April 28; reached St. Louis May 2), *Kansas* (advertised to depart St. Louis April 11; at Weston on the 21st; back at St. Louis on the 25th), *Mandan* (advertised this spring as a regular packet to Weston and St. Joseph), *Haydee* (to Weston?), *Alton* (was at Fort Leavenworth on April 21). Some of these boats also went up past town of Kansas, Mo., in April: *Bertrand, Mustang, Whirlwind, War Eagle, Lightfoot, Amelia, Mary,* and *Eliza Stewart.*

Ref: *The Daily Reveille*, St. Louis, April 9, 11, 18, 25, 26, May 3, 1848; Saint Louis *Daily Union*, April 13, 22, 24, 1848; *Oregon Historical Quarterly*, Salem, v. 31 (March, 1930), p. 56. The above steamboat *Kansas*—the second of this name on the Missouri (*see* entry in annals index, for the earlier one) had been built in 1847. The *Reveille* of September 8, 1847, reported that the "*Kanzas*"—"a stanch little craft, built for the Missouri trade," had "dropped down to the levee," and would "make her first trip to New Orleans"; and that her captain was Isaac McPherson. The *Kansas* was 185 feet "deck length"; beam, 28 feet; had two engines and two boilers; her cabin was built by Bitts & Corey. In 1848, on the Missouri, the *Kansas* was commanded by J. J. Mitchell—*see The Daily Reveille*, April 11, 1848, and 30th Cong., 2d Sess., Sen. Ex. Doc. No. 17 (Serial 529), p. 80.

❦ In mid-April a company of some 30 men (mostly traders) reached the Missouri border after a 27-day journey from Santa Fe. "Capt. [P.] Emerson" (once of the steamboat *White Cloud*), and 15 to 20 others (including discharged soldiers) of the party, arrived at St. Louis, aboard the *St. Joseph,* on April 26. (They brought newspapers dated as recently as March 18.)

Ref: Saint Louis *Daily Union*, April 26, 27, 1848; New York *Weekly Tribune*, May 13, 1848 (from St. Louis *New Era* of April 26); *The Gazette*, St. Joseph, Mo., May 5, 1848.

❧ April 29.—The Independence (Mo.) *Expositor*, reported that many Santa Fe traders had been detained for some days due to lack of grass on the plains for their animals; noted that the season had been remarkably dry, also quite cold at times, retarding vegetation growth; and stated that rain had commenced falling the night of the 27th.

Ref: Saint Louis *Daily Union*, May 9, 1848.

❧ Spring.—James M. Simpson, Westport, Mo., supplied 40 yoke of work oxen for the Kickapoo Indians, and was paid $2,270 (an average $28 per ox).

Ref: 31st Cong., 1st Sess., H. Ex. Doc. No. 11 (Serial 572), p. 110 (Agent R. W. Cummins' accounts for quarter ending June 30, 1848).

❧ April.—At Fort Leavenworth, as the month ended, there were, apparently, around 670 Mexican War volunteers—recruited over-winter in Missouri and Illinois—who would, in May or June, march for Santa Fe to fill depleted ranks of military volunteer units from the two states.

In the last third of April, the nearly 370(?) Missouri volunteers had arrived. The *Kansas* and *Alton* each had brought 100 men and 100 horses; the *Wyandotte*, 100 men and 50 horses. Two principal recruiters for these cavalry troops: Capt. Gabriel de Korponay and Lt. John K. Hawkins, both of "Ralls'" (third) Missouri regiment. Upwards of 50 other mounted Missourians, mustered in at Weston, Mo., by Lt. William B. Royall, apparently crossed the river to Fort Leavenworth in this same period. (Ultimately, Royall's command numbered over 70 men.)

As appears from a later mention, some 300 Illinois volunteers—infantrymen—under the command of Capt. Vantrump Turner of "Newby's" "First" Illinois regiment, their chief recruiter, were also at Fort Leavenworth in late April. But information about them is meager.

Ref: Saint Louis *Daily Union*, February 8, April 14, 1848; *The Daily Reveille*, St. Louis, April 13, 14, 1848; *The Weekly Tribune*, Liberty, Mo., April 21, 1848; St. Joseph (Mo.) *Gazette*, May 5, 1848; 30th Cong., 2d Sess., Sen. Ex. Doc. No. 17 (Serial 529), p. 80. Lt. William B. Royall was adjutant of the Santa Fe battalion in New Mexico. Organized at Santa Fe in 1847, it was composed, in large part, of reenlisted Missouri volunteers from Doniphan's regiment and other units of 1846-1847 service. The commanding officer was Maj. Robert Walker.

❧ April-May.—Compared with 1847, the Oregon-California emigration of 1848 was small. Indications are it did not exceed 1,700 persons. Indian Agent Thomas Fitzpatrick, who (eastbound in the spring) met nearly the entire emigration, provided the most illuminating statistics of the year. He counted 364 wagons; and estimated (on a five-per-wagon basis) that about 1,700 persons were en route to Oregon, and around 150 to California. (The "rule of thumb" Fitzpatrick, and others, used has been shown unreliable—four per wagon being a more nearly accurate calculation.)

By June 9 the St. Joseph (Mo.) *Gazette* had concluded (from "best information") that the year's Oregon-California emigration would not exceed 350 wagons—about 1,600 souls. Out on the trail, eastbound from Oregon, was Isaac Pettijohn (emigrant West in 1847). Between June 23 (near South Pass) and July 2 (below the North Platte crossing), diarist Pettijohn recorded meeting 343 wagons of emigrants for Oregon or California; and at Ash Hollow, on July 10, "met the [Mormon] Brethren . . . 350 waggons strong."

For a later perspective there is the statement of Mr. E. Whipple (a Mormon from Salt Lake City), published in the New York *Weekly Tribune* of February 10, 1849, that in 1847 the Oregon-California emigrant wagons had numbered about 1,000, but in 1848, there had been only around 350.

THE "ST. JOSEPH" EMIGRATION. The *Gazette* of May 5 reported that St. Joseph had been "literally crowded" for the "last two weeks" with Oregon and California emigrants "laying in their supplies"; also, that 210 wagons had crossed the Missouri there, and some 40 or 50 others at the ferry (ferries?) above. This was not the final count for the St. Joseph area. However, except for one 11 or 13-wagon train which (inferentially) ferried the Missouri the second week in May, no supplemental figure is available. The *Gazette* on May 5 noted, also, the arrival of Moses ("Black") Harris "from the front camp of the Oregon emigrants," with a report the various trains for Oregon and California were all getting on well except the last-met company (unidentified) which was camped (some 35 miles from St. Joseph) distant from water, leaderless, and "in utter confusion," having lost nearly all their oxen (strayed, or stolen by Indians).

One company (the first?) on the road from this area had "Tom Fallon" (William O. Fallon—*see* p. 711) as guide, and included Pierre B. Cornwall, who recollected leaving St. Joseph "early in April." (It was probably at least late April before any company left the frontier.) Most (if not all) of this party (including Cornwall, Orvin Kellogg, emigrant West in 1845, and his son Joseph) were headed for Oregon. Fallon, and a man named "Guthrie" were killed by Indians west of Fort Hall.

At Mosquito creek (present Doniphan county), on April 27, 42 men of a train then said to have 15 to 20 wagons, chose M. N. Wambough as "Camp Master." Oregon-bound Riley Root (in a diary) recorded that this company reached the Great Nemaha Subagency on the 28th; remained in the area three days; on May 14, in the Little Blue country, killed the first buffalo; on May 15 was joined by a "few wagons" coming up behind, "making in all about thirty wagons." This addition probably was the party of James Clyman (one-time mountain man; now California-bound to stay), including the McCombs family, and others, which (it is known) did travel with the Wambough company (later further enlarged?) out to the turning-off point for California. Clyman's statement is that his group left "west of Missouri" on May 1. Subsequently, he captained the train that went to California. The (later-written) narrative of Rufus G. Burrows (aged 14 in 1848), who left Kansas (City), Mo., with his stepfather Rufus Hitchcock, and uncle, Street Rice, to go to California in the spring of 1848, states: "After our arrival at Fort Laramie, our train was soon organized and . . . Wm. Wambo [elected] as the Captain. . . ." Burrows' account says there were 51 wagons, about 200 people, 250 head of oxen, also 200 or 300 head of stock cattle and about 50 saddle horses; and that the company [now?] included mountain man Caleb Greenwood, together with his family. (Whether Burrows and his family traveled via St. Joseph, or started with a company out of Independence, is not clear.) His narrative mentions, also, P. B. Cornwall (*see* above), "a half breed Cherokee Indian and a man by the name of Stone" (*see* "David Stone" below) as being of the party (from Fort Laramie?).

Joseph Watt (Oregon immigrant, 1844; now westbound with his family, including brother Ahio Watt) was ahead of Porter's train (*see* below) on the trail (having started from the St. Joseph area?). Porter mentions a campsite (on the Little Blue?) where "Mr. Watts company had buried a child the day before." An account (1903) says that Joseph Watt was "looked to as a leader" for the party with which he traveled in 1848; that the Watt family had two large wagons, also a band of sheep; and indicates that William Greenwood, and his family, from Iowa, were among those in the company.

Oregon-bound William Porter's brief diary mentions leaving "Peters Creek six miles from St. Joseph" (in present Doniphan county) on May 5. His own party (then four wagons?) included John Purvine. Porter reached the Great Nemaha Subagency May 6. Perhaps the company was organized there with Bolivar Walker as captain. Porter, with Walker's train, reached Pacific Springs July 8. If Oregon-bound W. L.(?) Adams (who wrote a letter July 8 from Pacific Springs) was also in the company, there were some 50 wagons at that time. Walker's train reached Oregon City October 1. John Purvine (mentioned above), by one account, captained a train reaching Oregon. Five "packers" arriving at Oregon City August 30, were the first to bring news that Joe Meek (whom they had met on May 7, some 60-70 miles west of St. Joseph) had reached the States safely. One of these men was George Luther Boone, son of Alphonso Boone (an 1846 Oregon immigrant). Another was William Bristow (later) said to have been of Captain Purvine's train.

In a narrative, James D. Miller says the "last company [David Stone, captain?] that crossed the plains to Oregon in 1848" (*i. e.*, the last out of St. Joseph?) was composed of 11 or 13(?) wagons, with 31 men able to bear arms; that in the party were the Joseph Miller family (James D.'s father), David Stone and family, George A. Barnes and wife, and others (quite a few are named) including two Catholic priests—the Rev. J. Lionet and Father Lampfrit. He further states: "The ferryboat that brought our last wagon over [the Missouri] took back on the return trip . . . Joseph L. Meek . . . [and party]." (If this was so, the date was May 11, since Meek reached St. Joseph that day.) Some of the party had arrived at Weston, Mo. (via the *Boreas No. 3* from St. Louis), on April 29; but others were en route overland from Indiana. Bancroft's *History of Oregon* states that David Stone captained the company with which George A. Barnes (of Fort Wayne, Ind.) traveled. Two added notes from Miller's narrative: He says that at Steamboat Springs they "found a part of Whitaker's train"[?]; and that his own company arrived at Oregon City the first week in November.

Daniel Hunsacker and family (wife, at least) from Atchison county, Mo., were overland emigrants in 1848. Hunsacker's April 10, 1849, letter, from Benicia City, Calif., was published in the St. Joseph papers in June, 1849.

THE "INDEPENDENCE" EMIGRATION. James P. C. Allsopp (from New Orleans) recollected that his all-male party joined a train of "about 25 wagons" at Independence, Mo., around April 10. According to Allsopp his party reached Fort Laramie early—May 31. Probably the start from the frontier was not before late April. Allsopp's group went by way of Salt Lake City, where some of the men stayed. He and six others went on to California, reaching San Francisco in December.

California-bound Edward L. B. Smith (who kept a journal) left the frontier April 29, traveled 12 miles, and encamped at "Elm Grove." His party then numbered, it appears, not over two wagons. Beyond the Wakarusa (and after May 3) there was a union, of sorts, with an Oregon-bound train of 23 wagons. (Possibly this was the same company—"about 25 wagons"—with which Allsopp's party traveled.) Some four miles beyond the "Chunga-Lung" (Shunganunga) these emigrants arrived at the bank of Kansas river (present Topeka area). The Oregonians forded it with great difficulty; the Smith party ferried over. Several(?) days later Edward Smith's group was joined by other Smiths (a man, his wife, children, and his two brothers) who left the Oregon company. Now forming a party of three families (nine men, plus women and children) and four wagons, the Smiths followed the regularly-traveled Oregon trail. But the Oregon company digressed for a time. *Edward L. B. Smith's brief diary is of special interest in its mention of a point five miles east of the Little (now Red) Vermillion crossing, where a branch road turned off from the regularly-traveled route. (He referred to the branching-off point as the "junction of the Oregon trail which runs over the ridge some miles north of the Kansas River.")* The ridge road was traveled by the Oregon company, Smith says; and the two parties came together again at the "Big [now Black] Vermillion," in present Marshall county. At that point, the Smith party formally united with the Oregon company. Arriving at the Big Blue, Edward Smith visited Alcove Spring—described it, and the grave of Mrs. Sarah Keyes (*see* pp. 585, 627). Beyond the junction with the St. Joseph trail (where Smith estimated 200 wagons had passed a few days earlier), his journal (or fragment thereof) ends abruptly.

Joseph B. Chiles' California-bound train left the Missouri frontier (from Independence, Mo.) May 12. (Chiles was returning home—*see* annals index for references to his earlier cross-country travels.) Having learned, by an express, that Richard May's party (which left Independence May 12) would join him, Chiles traveled slowly; but it was May 21 (beyond the Big Blue crossing?) before the latter group came up. On May 22 the Chiles-May company (now 29? wagons) passed the junction with the St. Joseph trail. [May's party, earlier, had found the Kansas river "Verry Low (Fordable)" but the sand bar on which they crossed had tried the strength of their teams.] When the Chiles-May company left the Little Blue, on June 1, May recorded

"We number Men Women & Children 112 . . .[37 being men]." More were yet to come—a train of 18 wagons and 12 men with pack mules. At the head of Grand Island, on June 3 the 29-wagon train "passed 4 Companies of the oregon Battaleon They were Layin off a fort [*i. e.*, new Fort Kearny— *see* p. 755]. . . ." Two days later, Samuel J. Hensley (one of the 12 "packers") arrived in camp; and on June 7 the awaited 18-wagon train corralled just below the Chiles-May company. Among the newcomers were David and John Plemmons, and evidently Peter Lassen. Richard M. May stated (on June 9) "The number now is 47 (Wagons) near 80 men quite a formidable force." (No attempt will be made here to carry these travelers on to California. Chiles, Hensley, and Lassen, all pioneered new routes before reaching their destinations.)

One final note: The Independence *Expositor* of May 27 reported that a gentleman who had accompanied the *Oregon* (but meaning California?) emigrants out beyond the crossing of Kansas river 200 miles, had returned "this morning" with a report that they were in fine health and spirits. "There are 50[?] wagons in all, with a considerable number of loose stock."

Ref: (GENERAL) L. R. Hafen and W. J. Ghent's *Broken Hand* . . . (Denver, 1931), p. 209 (for Fitzpatrick—his June 24, 1848, report is cited as source); St. Joseph (Mo.) *Gazette*, June 9, 1848; Isaac Pettijohn's diary (some items from the original in Bancroft Library, Berkeley, Calif., courtesy Dale L. Morgan; others, from C. L. Camp, ed., *James Clyman, Frontiersman* [c1960], p. 292); New York *Weekly Tribune*, February 10, 1849.

(The "ST. JOSEPH" EMIGRATION) St. Joseph (Mo.) *Gazette*—issues of April and May, 1848; Camp's *Clyman* (*op. cit.*), pp. 236, 288 (for Cornwall), 235-237, 282, 283, 286, 287, 338 (for Wambough; Clyman, etc.), 237 and 288 (for Porter-Walker, etc.), 338 (Note 210, for "Mr. Watts" company); Riley Root's "Journal" in *California Historical Society Quarterly*, San Francisco, v. 10 (December, 1931), pp. 396-400; Rufus G. Burrows' narrative (typescript) is in the California State Library; Robert H. Down's *A History of the Silverton Country* (Portland, 1926), pp. 60-69 (for Wm. Porter's diary); H. E. Tobie's article "Joseph L. Meek," in *Oregon Historical Quarterly*, v. 40 (September, 1939), p. 264 (for Purvine, Boone, Bristow, etc.); Tobie's *No Man Like Joe* (Portland, Ore., 1949), p. 160, states it was *August* 30 when Boone and four other packers arrived at Oregon City; *Oregon Historical Quarterly*, v. 42 (September, 1941), pp. 220-229 (for Boone relationships); H. H. Bancroft's *History of Oregon* (San Francisco, 1886), v. 1, pp. 751-754 (for items on the 1848 immigrants); *Oregon Historical Quarterly*, v. 4 (June, 1903), pp. 150-161 (for the Watts, Greenwoods, etc.); *ibid.*, 40 (September, 1939), p. 263 (for Watt); *ibid.*, v. 31 (March, 1930), pp. 55-60 (for James D. Miller); Bancroft, *op. cit.*, p. 752 (for Barnes and Stone); St. Joseph (Mo.) *Gazette*, June 29, 1849 (for Daniel Hunsaker). The name "Whittacer" is mentioned in a biographical sketch of Edward L. B. Smith (a typed copy of the sketch accompanied the typed copy of Smith's diary, made available by courtesy of George C. Deckard, and Dale L. Morgan, Bancroft Library, Berkeley, Calif.—*see* reference following).

(The "INDEPENDENCE" EMIGRATION) Camp's *Clyman* (*op. cit.*), pp. 236, 288 (for Allsopp); Topeka *Daily Capital*, July 19, 1959 (for an article on the Edward L. B. Smith diary—original privately owned); typed copy of the Edward L. B. Smith diary (courtesy of George C. Deckard, and Dale L. Morgan, Bancroft Library, Berkeley, Calif.); Camp's *Clyman*, pp. 237, 238, 289 (for the Chiles-May company); items from Richard M. May's diary (other than those in Camp), courtesy of Dale L. Morgan, Bancroft Library, Berkeley, Calif.; Saint Louis *Daily Union*, June 6, 1848 (for Independence [Mo.] *Expositor* item). For Chiles, Hensley, and Lassen, and the routes they pioneered, *see*, in addition to Camp's *Clyman*, Georgia W. Reed and Ruth Gaines, editors, *Gold Rush—The Journals, Drawings, and Other Papers of J. Goldsborough Bruff* . . . (New York, Columbia University Press, 1949), pp. xxxvi, xxxvii, 630, 631; Helen S. Giffen, *Trail-Blazing Pioneer Colonel Joseph Ballinger Chiles* (San Francisco, 1969), pp. 68-73; and for Hensley and Chiles *see* *Utah Historical Quarterly*, Salt Lake City, v. 19 (1951), pp. 249-251. Lassen's journey to Missouri in 1847 (which some writers have questioned) is given specific mention in the annals on p. 722. The journeys of Hensley and Chiles to the States in 1847 are noted there, too.

(DIED: Dr. Jesse Harvey, superintendent since 1847 at Shawnee Friends Mission (present Johnson county), in the fore part of May (about the 11th)? He was a man "highly esteemed."

His widow—Elizabeth (Burgess) Harvey (as superintendent), and the three Harvey "children" (all adults by 1848) continued to operate the mission until 1850 (or late 1849). Dr. William F. Harvey and Sarah T. Harvey were teachers; Thomas B. Harvey operated the mission farm.

Ref: Allen T. Ward's May 21, 1848, letter (in *KHQ*, v. 33, p. 356), which states: "Doctor Jesse Harvey . . . departed this life some ten days ago."; *KHC*, v. 8, p. 268; Comm'r of Indian affairs, *Reports*, 1848 and 1849; W. W. Hinshaw's *Encyclopedia of American Quaker Genealogy*, Ann Arbor, Mich., v. 5 (1946), pp. 189 and 573.

(May 11.—Overland from Oregon, Joseph L. Meek (bearer of a memorial to congress) and his escort of six (or eight?) men, arrived at St. Joseph, Mo.—in about 69 days, on horseback, and afoot, from the Whitman mission.

Meek, George W. Ebbert, Nathaniel Bowman, and others—10 in all at the outset—had started from Oregon City early in January; and two months later— March 4 (or 5?) had left the mission (where the massacre of the Whitmans, and others, on November 29, 1847, had touched off an Indian war which necessitated the memorial [request for federal aid] to congress).

Ebbert later recollected of the Oregon trail journey eastward that they had met westbound emigrant companies including those with which Sol Emerick and Joseph Watt traveled (on the Little and Big Blue); that at the "Kaw Agency" [the Great Nemaha Subagency?] they "tried to get provisions, but failed," and "in a few miles met a man who gave us some bread and a bottle of whiskey." Four(?) days later on "the 4th day [*i. e.*, the 11th] of May, 1848" they reached St. Joseph.

Meek took the steamboat *Mandan* to St. Louis (arriving there on May 17), and reached Washington the last week of May.

See, also, August 14, and September 10 entries.

Ref: *The Gazette*, St. Joseph, Mo., May 12, 1848 (which says Meek and escort of "six men" arrived there the 11th); Saint Louis *Daily Union*, May 18, 20, 1848; H. E. Tobie's *No Man Like Joe* . . ., pp. 151-162; *Oregon Historical Quarterly*, v. 19 (September, 1918), pp. 262-267 (for Ebbert's account); *ibid.*, v. 40 (September, 1949), pp. 263, 264; H. H. Bancroft, *op. cit.*, v. 1, pp. 755-757. The *Mandan* had been up to Council Bluffs, and left there on May 13, arriving at St. Louis May 17—see *The Daily Reveille*, St. Louis, May 18, 1848.

(DIED: on May 12, at the old Pottawatomie Methodist Mission (present Miami? county; on Pottawatomie creek), the Rev. Mackinaw Beauchemie, of pneumonia.

In the early 1830's Beauchemie (half-Chippewa) had been converted by the Rev. Thomas Johnson; and in 1837, employed by him as a native preacher among the Pottawatomies. He was ordained deacon (minister), in the M. E. Church, South, in 1847. Bishop James O. Andrew characterized Beauchemie as "probably the greatest and best of the Pottawatomies . . . a man of rare gifts and ardent and consistent piety."

Ref: *KHC*, v. 9, pp. 212, 227, v. 10, pp. 401, 402; Andrew, *op cit.*, p. 167. *See, also,* annals, pp. 355 and 472.

❧ May.—From Council Grove, "R" wrote, on the 12th: "The road from this place [east] to Independence is almost one continued encampment of Santa Fe and Chihuahua traders. McKnight, Mayer, Hall, Slaughter and Bean, Reynolds and Clarkson, Coons, and many others, in all perhaps 200 wagons, heavily freighted with merchandise of every description, are scattered all along the road from here to the State line, besides at least 100 wagons that have already passed on. The amount of goods taken out this year will far exceed the exports of any preceding year."

Ref: Saint Louis *Daily Union*, May 26, 1848; SIA, St. Louis, "Records," v. 9, typed copy, p. 151, for May 12 letter written by Sup't Thomas H. Harvey, St. Louis, stating: "Since I have been here [he arrived at Council Grove on the 10th] some hundred heavy waggons have passed on to Santa Fe (commercial traders)."

❧ Around May 15, five miles south of the Arkansas crossing (in present Gray county), Maj. William Singer (paymaster) abandoned "his entire baggage, including his pay rolls, horses, four mules and his wagon" to a large band of well-mounted Indians presumed hostile; and with six companions, fled to Fort Mann. (Singer, with driver and a servant, had left Santa Fe about May 3, escorted by a four-man express bound for the States.)

Fort Mann's notorious Capt. William Pelzer (with 65 men) made a show of going after the Indians, but found it expedient to turn back when he discovered the "enemy" numbered around 150. Lt. Caleb S. Tuttle, continuing to scout the Indians, arrived at the camp of Leitensdorfer and Webb (bound for Santa Fe with merchandise). The traders went to the Indian village— Kiowas, newly friendly to whites—and recovered all Major Singer's lost property.

From Fort Mann Singer accompanied a government train to Cow creek; then with his driver and servant journeyed the rest of the way without escort; and arrived at Fort Leavenworth on May 26 "having been but 23 days out from Santa Fe."

Ref: *The Daily Reveille*, St. Louis, June 1, 10, 1848; *The Weekly Tribune*, Liberty, Mo., June 9, 1848; New York *Weekly Tribune*, June 17, 1848 (from *Missouri Republican*, St. Louis, June 3, 1848).

❧ Between May 15 and 20 (as deduced from fragmentary information) some 300 Illinois infantry recruits and 71 Missouri cavalry recruits marched from Fort Leavenworth for New Mexico. (Remaining at the post, to depart in June, were about 300 other Missouri volunteers—*see* April entry, p. 744.) As far as Council Grove, Capt.

Vantrump Turner (of "Newby's" Illinois regiment) had charge of all these troops.

At Council Grove, Lt. William B. Royall and his 71 Missouri volunteers, were assigned to escort Major Bryant (paymaster) to Fort Mann, and government trains to Santa Fe—*see* June 5-20 entry. (Royall reached Fort Mann on June 20.)

Perhaps 10 days later Turner and his Illinois troops left Council Grove, escorting other government trains. California-bound Orville C. Pratt, in his diary, recorded (on June 30) that near Fort Mann his party passed a train of 100 wagons and 400 head of beef cattle, and some 300 infantry troops under Captain Turner of Illinois, going to Santa Fe.

Ref: 30th Cong., 1st Sess., *H. Ex. Doc. No. 1* (Serial 537), p. 141 (Royall says that on June 5, at Council Grove, he was placed "by Captain V. Turner, of the Illinois volunteers [who had the direction of all the troops who left Fort Leavenworth for Santa Fe on the 15th and 20th of May], in charge of two government trains . . . [etc.]"); Orville C. Pratt's "Diary" (microfilm of original in Coe Collection, Yale University Library).

❧ May 17.—James Brown (in a contract negotiated with Capt. Langdon C. Easton, AQM) agreed to transport 200,000 pounds of government stores from Fort Leavenworth to Santa Fe, N. M., for $11.75 per 100 pounds. Sureties signing his $50,000 bond were: G[eorge] R[appeen] Smith, John S. Jones, and David Waldo.

On the 18th, by another contract, James Brown agreed to transport from the fort to Santa Fe "such government stores as may be delivered to him by the said Easton," at the same rate; and to take, "at the price they cost the government," a number of wagons (not exceeding 120), also such ox yokes, chains, etc., "as can be spared," and to pay for them in specie on receipt. For his $600,000 bond, the sureties were Jabez Smith, David Waldo, John McCoy, William McCoy, S. H. Woodson, and Cornelius Davy.

Ref: 31st Cong., 1st Sess., *Sen. Ex. Doc. No. 26* (Serial 554), p. 12. For a biographical sketch of George Rappeen Smith *see The United States Biographical Dictionary . . . Missouri Volume* (1878), p. 130. Brown was a Pettis county, Mo., resident—*see* annals, p. 707. Jabez Smith (one of the above bondsmen) on August 28, 1848, at Las Vegas, N. M., contracted (as "Jabez Smith & Co.") to transport, in wagons, to Independence, Mo., "such stores as may be required for use of the [homeward-bound] Third Missouri Volunteers" (at the rate of six cents per pound from Point of Rocks, and eight cents per pound from Las Vegas).—31st Cong., 1st Sess., *Sen. Ex. Doc. No. 26* (Serial 554), p. 22.

❧ In mid-May two, out of three, Mackinaw boats which had come down the Missouri in Joseph Picotte's charge, reached Weston, Mo. Their cargoes ("upwards of" 800 bales of buffalo robes, consigned to Messrs. Harvey, Primeau & Co.) were put aboard the *Amelia* at Weston, and arrived at St. Louis on May 20. Earlier, above Council Bluffs, the third boat (carrying 100 packs of furs) had "snagged" and sunk.

Ref: *The Daily Reveille*, St. Louis, May 21, 1848; Saint Louis *Daily Union*, May 23, 1848.

❧ May.—Ceran St. Vrain, William Bent, E. T. Hempstead, "Mr. [Hugh N.] Smith, the Attorney General for . . . [New Mexico]

Territory," and others, crossed "Kansas" eastbound on the Santa Fe trail, arriving in St. Louis, on the *Whirlwind,* May 21. They had left "Fort William" (Bent's Fort) April 22; endured cold weather on the journey; had seen no Indians.

St. Vrain (Bent, and Smith, also?) had left Taos, N. M., on April 12 for Bent's Fort. He, and Bent, had gone *to* New Mexico, from "Fort William," early in March to procure supplies for Gilpin's campaign (*see* under January 21 entry).

Ref: *The Daily Reveille,* St. Louis, May 23, 1848; Saint Louis *Daily Union,* May 23, 1848; New York *Weekly Tribune,* June 10, 1848 (for a letter by "'T. S.," dated at Taos, April 11, 1848, published in the Cincinnati *Republican*). H. N. Smith, "Dist. Atty.," returned to Santa Fe, from Washington, D. C., on October 29, 1848—*see* St. Joseph (Mo.) *Gazette,* February 23, 1849.

❧ May.—White Cloud (head chief of the Iowas) and a band of his "braves" left their village (present Doniphan county) on the 14th; traveled up to "Nebraska"; ambushed the rear detachment of a large body of Pawnees (westbound after journeying to Council Bluffs for corn); killed six women, three men, and two children; returned home, rejoicing, about May 25, with the scalps of their victims. (*See* a portrait of White Cloud on p. 813.)

Sup't T. H. Harvey, St. Louis, called it "one of the most outrageous and inexcusable acts of butchery, even among the wild Indians" that had come to his knowledge. "White Cloud," he wrote, "is a desperate bad man . . . he [has] . . . seen much of the world [having gone to Europe in 1844] and is sensible of the criminality of his conduct." Harvey also stated that White Cloud's son (a young man of education, who had "lived a considerable time in the Settlements with the Whites") was in the war party, and had "committed the horrible act of cutting off the head of a wounded boy. . . ." Horse stealing by Pawnees was the Iowas' excuse for the massacre. Neither the Iowas' second or third chiefs had participated in the affair; nor had the Sacs & Foxes (of the Missouri).

Ref: OIA, Letters Received from Great Nemaha Subagency (National Archives Microcopy 234, Roll 308), A. J. Vaughan's June 1, 1848, account, therein; SIA, St. Louis, "Records," v. 9, typed copy, pp. 206, 207 (Harvey's September 4, 1848, letter); Comm'r of Indian affairs, *Report,* 1848 (Harvey's report); *The Gazette,* St. Joseph, Mo., June 2, 1848.

❧ DIED: Keokuk, celebrated Sac chief, aged 60(?), "Kansas" resident since late 1845, in May (or April?), at his settlement on the Marais des Cygnes, near the Osage-Franklin county line of today. (*See* his portrait on p. 809.)

It was June 6 when Sup't T. H. Harvey, St. Louis, first learned of Keokuk's death. The first report was that Keokuk had been poisoned by one of his people; that the "murderer" had confessed his guilt and had been executed (shot) by other Sacs. But in a June 14 letter to the Indian department, Harvey wrote that Keokuk's death was caused "by a dysentery brought on by a drunken frolic." Apparently Keokuk died near the end of May (but *see* below). Harvey had been in "Kansas" in May (*e. g.,* at Council Grove on May 12) and (presumably) would have been informed of the chief's death then, had it occurred prior to his visit.

Keokuk's grave, in a Franklin county burial area a little west of the Sac & Fox Agency, subsequently was marked with a marble slab bearing the inscription: SACRED TO THE MEMORY OF KEOKUK DISTINGUISHED SAC CHIEF BORN AT ROCK ISLAND IN 1788 DIED IN APRIL 1848. (This slab, in 1883, was removed to Keokuk, Iowa, and embedded in the east side of a monument to Keokuk erected in the town's Rand Park. "This monument [says the inscription on the west side] is erected by popular subscription in memory of the Sac Chief Keokuk for whom this city is named." It goes on to state that in 1883 his remains together with the marble slab were brought from Franklin county, Kansas, where he died, and was buried; and that his grave was located about 3½ miles southeast of the "village of Pomona Franklin County Kansas," on the SE¼ of NW¼ of Sec. 16, T. 17 S., R. 18 E., and had been covered by the slab above mentioned; also that his remains, and other matter of historical value are "deposited in the base of this structure." A statue of Chief Keokuk, sculptured by Nellie V. Walker, and placed atop the 1883-erected monument, was dedicated October 22, 1913.)

Ref: Saint Louis *Daily Union*, May 29, June 8, 1848; St. Joseph (Mo.) *Gazette*, June 16, 1848; *The Daily Reveille*, St. Louis, June 7, 1848; SIA, St. Louis, "Records," v. 9, typed copy, pp. 162, 168 (for Harvey's letters); *KHC*, v. 11, pp. 337, 343; OIA, Letters Received from Osage River Agency (National Archives Microcopy 234, Roll 643), also has Harvey's June 6 and 14, 1848, letters; Ottawa *Daily Republican*, October 22, 1883, p. 4, col. 3 (has account of Keokuk's "removal" to Iowa in 1883); Charles R. Green's *In Keokuks Time on the Kansas Reservation* (Olathe, c1913), pp. 8-12; Edward McCoonse's letter of August 24, 1875 (in KHi ms. division) tells of Indian graves—Keokuk's and Hard Fish's included—in Franklin county, being robbed (medals, etc., stolen) and bones strewn about. Grant Foreman, in his *The Last Trek of the Indians* (Chicago, c1946), p. 226, mentions McCoonse's August 24, 1875, letter; and further states that "McCoonse later secured the medals [taken] which he restored to the graves, together with the bones of the dead Indians, and replaced the inscribed slabs. . . ." Foreman's reference is a Sac and Fox "Letter Book" in the Oklahoma Historical Society archives. The inscriptions (all four sides) on Keokuk's monument in Rand Park, Keokuk, Iowa, were copied for this compiler by a friend, who also sent a clipping from *The Daily Gate City*, Keokuk, Iowa, March 11, 1965, p. 16, which contains a story on Nellie V. Walker, sculptor of the Chief Keokuk statute. James B. Finley's *Life Among the Indians* . . . (Cincinnati, 1857), pp. 531-543, contains vivid word descriptions of Chief Keokuk. George Catlin, Charles Bird King, and John Mix Stanley were some of the artists who painted Chief Keokuk. Stanley's portrait of him was destroyed by fire. F. W. Hodge, in his *Handbook of American Indians* . . . (Washington, 1907), v. 1, pp. 673, 674, mentioned a bronze bust of Keokuk—in the Capitol at Washington, D. C.

❧ May.—The arrival at St. Louis, on May 30, of "Mr. Fink," who had left Santa Fe April 18, was noted by the *Reveille*, which stated: "The party he was with was attacked, when about 30 miles this side of Fort Mann, by [about 25 well-mounted] Comanches. One of the traders, a Mexican, was wounded by a lance."

Ref: *The Daily Reveille*, St. Louis, May 31, 1848.

❧ May 28.—Francis X. Aubry (who had left Santa Fe, N. M., the night of May 19) rode into Independence, Mo., about an hour before sunrise—having traveled the 780-mile length of Santa Fe trail in "the incredible short space of *eight days and ten hours!!!*" (This broke his own previous record—*see* January 5 entry—by about five and one-half days. But *see* September 17 entry for Aubry's fleetest Santa Fe trail trip.)

The Independence *Expositor* published an extra on May 29 to herald Aubry's feat. On June 3 the St. Louis *Republican,* reporting his arrival in that city on the previous evening, wrote of Aubry's "unexampled" travelling that "he lost, from detention by the Indians [near Pawnee Fork], more than a day [also lost his "baggage, provisions, packages of letters, &c."], and really made the distance . . . in seven days"; that six men who left Santa Fe with him gave out in the first 300 miles; that he "killed three horses and two mules [by hard riding]"; walked 40 [about 30!] miles [to Fort Mann, where he got a horse]; was three days without provisions; slept "only four or five hours on the route."

See, also, July entry, p. 764.

Ref: *The Gazette,* St. Joseph, Mo., June 2, 1848 (reprinting the *Expositor* article of May 29); New York *Weekly Tribune,* June 17, 1848 (from *Missouri Republican,* St. Louis, June 3); Saint Louis *Daily Union,* June 5, 1848; *The Daily Reveille,* St. Louis, June 3, 1848; *The Pacific Historian,* v. 5 (August, 1961), p. 113; G. D. Brewerton's *Overland With Kit Carson* . . . (New York, 1930), p. 252.

❡ May 29.—Mail carriers A. Smith and G. R. Gibson (who had left Santa Fe on April 28), reached the Missouri border—one day *after* Aubry (who had brought Santa Fe newspapers of May 19 date).

Ref: New York *Weekly Tribune,* June 17, 1848 (from *Missouri Republican,* St. Louis, June 3); Saint Louis *Daily Union,* August 23, 1848 (from Santa Fe *Republican*). See, also, June 29 annals entry.

❡ About the end of May a large traders' caravan left Council Grove for Santa Fe and Mexico. It included the wagons of John McCoy, Independence, Mo., John Simpson, Westport, Mo., and others—a train of some 75 wagons and 100 men.

McCoy (who went to Chihuahua; and came home in 1849) wrote his recollections of the outbound journey after his return. His account mentions the passing by of Aubry (on his swift May ride); the finding of large buffalo herds on the "third of July" [*i. e.,* June!], east(?) of the Little Arkansas; the arrival at "Mann's Fort" where disgruntled Missouri volunteers (of "Gilpin's battalion") destroyed the caravan's "hospital stores" of "costly wines and brandies." (A day earlier, Lt. Col. William Gilpin had confiscated two wagon-loads of beer brought to the post by a German trader, and caused the beer to be poured out.)

"Fourteen miles from the Caches near Mann's Fort and eight miles from the crossing of the Big Arkansas," they experienced a "fearful" storm; but were able to ford the river next day. By the Fourth of July the caravan had reached "point of rocks"; and probably the wagons arrived in Santa Fe in midmonth.

Ref: *Pioneering on the Plains* . . . (Kaukauna, Wis., c1924), "Along the Santa Fe Trail in 1848," by John McCoy (dated May, 1849), therein.

❦ May 30.—The Mexican War came to a formal end with the ratification, this day, by the Mexican government, of the February 2 treaty of Guadalupe Hidalgo (which the U. S. senate had accepted on March 10). New Mexico and California now became part of the American Union.

On July 4 President Polk issued a proclamation declaring the termination of the war between the United States and Mexico.

Ref: 30th Cong., 2d Sess., *H. Ex. Doc. No. 1* (Serial 537), pp. 45, 173, 174; F. J. Turner's *The United States: 1830-1850* (New York, c1935), pp. 569, 570.

❦ May 30.—Lt. Col. William Gilpin and his 300(?) Missouri volunteers, ending the Indian expedition begun in March (*see* January 21 entry), arrived in the vicinity of Fort Mann (where the rest of "Gilpin's battalion" formed the garrison), and set up a cavalry camp on the south side of the Arkansas.

They had left the Canadian river on May 18, in western "Oklahoma," at a point near the "Antelope buttes" (and near the 100th meridian), to strike northward for the Arkansas. En route they had crossed the Wolf, Beaver, and Cimarron rivers—the last-named after entering "Kansas" in present Clark county.

In the Fort Mann area Gilpin found "the chiefs of the Kiowa, Cheyenne, and Arapahoe tribes" awaiting his return, and "desiring to enter into treaties of peace." He ordered them to move their villages away from the Santa Fe road, and to "wait further instructions upon the waters of the Platte." These tribes complied.

News reached St. Louis (a month later) that Gilpin, immediately on his return from the "Comanche tour," had placed Fort Mann's Capt. William Pelzer under arrest; and had taken other disciplinary action at that post.

Ref: 30th Cong., 1st Sess., *H. Ex. Doc. No. 1* (Serial 537), p. 138; *The Daily Reveille*, St. Louis, July 2, 1848.

❦ Late May, or early June.—At Walnut creek, one man in "Brown's train" was killed by Comanches. He was, so far as known, the only white man killed by Indians in "Kansas" in 1848.

A Fort Mann correspondent (writing June 21 from the "Cavalry Camp" there) referred to the large band of Indians (mostly Comanches) which had infested the "Coon Creek Bottom" for "some weeks past," and succeeded in "robbing several trains, as well as wounding several persons," besides murdering (James?) Brown's employee.

Ref: New York *Weekly Tribune*, July 29, 1848 (from *Missouri Republican*, St. Louis). See May 17, 1848, annals entry for James Brown.

❦ At the beginning of June, in "Nebraska," a new military post (first known as "Fort Childs"; officially named Fort Kearny December 30, 1848) was established near the head of Grand Island on the Platte river, and near the Oregon-California trail. (The site had been chosen in October, 1847—*see* p. 712.)

These were some of the developments at new Fort "Kearny" in 1848: *June 1.*—Lt. Col. Ludwell E. Powell and three companies (Sublette's, McCausland's, and Craig's) of his "Oregon battalion" Missouri volunteers arrived at the new post site—after an overland journey (of about 190 miles) across "Nebraska" from Fort Kearny (on the Missouri). *June 3.*—Lt. Daniel P. Woodbury (U. S. engineers), in charge of construction, proposed the name "Fort Childs" for the post. About this same time the Pawnee Indians agreed to cede certain land as the fort reserve (*see* August 6 entry for formal treaty). *June 6 or 7.*—The rest of the "Oregon battalion" (Rodgers' and Stewart's companies) arrived. *June 26.*—Capt. A. W. Sublette was reported in charge; and a brickyard (for adobes) and sawmill was said to be in "full operation." *August 22.*—A Missouri volunteer wrote (in a letter dated "Fort Childs, Nebraska Terr'y") that two buildings were "*nearly* half completed," one of them a sod stable; that the "Oregon battalion" men (construction workers by necessity) were "tired of the war" and anxious to return home; and that old Pawnee chief "Si-re-cherish" [Shah-re-ta-riche] was a prisoner at "Fort Childs"—held for past misdeeds. (He was released prior to October 6.) *Early in September,* Lt. Col. L. E. Powell allowed three "Oregon battalion" companies to go home; leaving at "Fort Childs" a portion of Sublette's and McCausland's companies. *October 6.*—The "entire garrison" at the post consisted of "the [Oregon battalion] headquarters [soon to depart] . . . and some 18 or 20 men." Those left would be able to defend themselves "as each man is armed with a fine brass 12-pounder, and some 500 rounds of fixed ammunition." *About October 28,* Capt. Charles F. Ruff and two companies of U. S. Mounted riflemen (127) arrived—relieving Lt. Antoine Lefevre and the few remaining Missouri volunteers. (See October 15 and November 16 annals entries.) *October 31.*—Lt. D. P. Woodbury reported the first buildings completed at "Fort Childs." (Others were finished by December 7.)

Ref: *The Gazette*, St. Joseph, Mo., May 17, 1848; *The Daily Reveille*, St. Louis, June 20, July 18, 1848; Saint Louis *Daily Union*, June 21, 30, 1848; *The Weekly Tribune*, Liberty, Mo., September 1, 1848; Lyle E. Mantor's "Fort Kearny and the Westward Movement" in *Nebraska History*, Lincoln, v. 29 (September, 1948), pp. 175-207; Nebraska State Historical Society *Publications*, v. 16, pp. 227-267, v. 21, pp. 211-314.

❡ June.—In one of the westbound merchant trains on the Santa Fe trail this month were Preston Beck, Samuel Wethered, G. Estes, Elliott Lee, Charles Towne, his brother, Smith D. Towne, Thomas O. Boggs, and H. O'Neil. By report, their company had left the Missouri border (*i. e.*, Council Grove?) around May 28.

At the Arkansas Crossing the train took the Cimarron route, but Lee, Charles Towne (and others?) went on upriver to Bent's Fort. Subsequently, near the Raton mountains, en route to Taos, on June 19, a company of 14 men (including these three) was attacked by Apaches. Killed were Towne, a Mexican, and a Frenchman; while Lee (reported killed; later found alive by a search party) and Lucien Maxwell were wounded. (Maxwell had joined the party at the Arkansas crossing.)

Ref: Saint Louis *Daily Union,* July 26, August 23, October 16, 1848; *The Daily Reveille,* St. Louis, August 8, 1848; New York *Weekly Tribune,* August 12, 1848 (from *Missouri Republican,* St. Louis, July 26; W. A. Keleher's *Turmoil in New Mexico, 1846-1868* (Santa Fe, c1952), p. 128, note 54 (for some data on Preston Beck). *The Daily Reveille,* St. Louis, April 11, 1848, had noted the arrival at St. Louis on April 9 of Charles Towne, who had left Taos February 25. The *Union* of August 23 (*see* above) reprinted this item from an issue of the Santa Fe *Republican:* "Amongst some of the late arrivals: P. Beck, G. Estos, S. Weatherhead, L. Maxwell, T. Boggs, and Mr. H. O'Neil, who left the States on the 28th of May." The *Union* of October 16 printed Elliott Lee's letter of July 19, 1848 (from Lodo Moro, N. M.), giving an account of the Indian attack. Smith D. Towne is mentioned as at Santa Fe in 1849-1850, in James S. Calhoun's *Official Correspondence,* Annie H. Abel, editor (Washington, 1915). Janet Lecompte's article, "The Manco Burro Pass Massacre," in *New Mexico Historical Review,* v. 41 (1966), pp. 305-318, gives a complete account of the Apache attack.

❛ **June 5.**—"Mr. [John S.] Shaw," fur trader with the Sioux, arrived at St. Joseph, Mo., from "Fort John on Platte river." He had met around 300 wagons of Oregon-or-California-bound emigrants, and some 200 wagons of westbound Mormons.

Emigrant R. M. May, of Chiles' company noted meeting, near the end of May, on the Little(?) Blue, 22 fur traders' wagons "Laden with Buffalo Robes & Tongues principally"; and stated that one train of seven belonged to "Mr. Shaw who [in 1847] commanded the Steamer Tobacco Plant [on the Missouri]."

Ref: St. Joseph (Mo.) *Gazette,* June 9, 1848; *The United States Biographical Dictionary . . . Missouri Volume* (1878), pp. 762-764; R. M. May's diary quoted courtesy of Dale L. Morgan, Bancroft Library.

❛ **June 5-20.**—Lt. William B. Royall, U. S. V., with a command of 71 "raw recruits" (mostly young backwoods Missourians—signed up for the Santa Fe battalion), set out from Council Grove about June 5 to escort government trains (Messrs. Burnham and Fulton's 60-some wagons; Fagan's 425 beef cattle), and Maj. Thomas S. Bryant, U. S. paymaster (accompanied by his nephew, John Y. B. Dietz), to Fort Mann.

Royall's recruits—*see* p. 744—having spent part of April and May at Fort Leavenworth, departed for Council Grove on (or about) May 18.

West of Walnut creek, on June 14, Royall's command was augmented by the arrival (from the west) of Lt. Phillip Stremmel and 64 "Gilpin's battalion" artillerymen, with two six-pounders (*see* June 7 entry). The combined military-civilian party totaled upwards of 200 men.

On June 17 this company "encamped on the Arkansas, about five miles from Lieutenant Love's fight in 1847"—Royall's statement. (For "Love's defeat"—which, on best available evidence, appears to have occurred near present Garfield, Pawnee county—*see* p. 694.) Birch's later-day account states: "Crossing Coon creek we spread our tents on the banks of the [Arkansas] river, close by the present town of Kinsley." But it would appear that the camp was several miles to the northward—perhaps near the Pawnee-Edwards county line of today. (One writer in 1848 referred to Royall's "Coon Creek Bottom" camp; and another gave the locale as "near the mouth of Coon Creek.")

At sunrise on June 18 an alarm was given. The whole plain seemed covered with (Comanche and Apache) Indians—some 200 off to the north, about the same number to the south, and from 200 to 300 warriors coming at full gallop towards the camp. There was a "short, severe fight" with the attackers. Royall's recruits, the artillerymen, and the civilians "gave them a hot reception." An attempt to charge through the tents on Major Bryant's side was foiled; next a penetration on Royall's side was turned back; and after that a strike at the corralled wagons was repulsed. When the Indians began to withdraw, effective use was made of the two six-pounders. Nine of the enemy were believed killed in the fighting. The camp's losses were 15 "military" horses, five horses and four mules from the trains.

Lieutenant Royall and 38 mounted men then pursued a body of Indians across the river; were soon surrounded by 500 to 700 savages; managed to charge through to an elevated point; fought off several attacks, killing probably 14 of the enemy, and wounding a good many others. (During this action they saw a female dressed in scarlet, with silver ornaments, who rode about the field of combat directing care of the wounded.) When the Indians drew off some distance, Royall got his command (with four wounded men) back across the river to "Coon Creek Bottoms."

Royall (whom one writer described as "cool and heroic") had praise for Lt. Phillip Stremmel and 2d Lt. William "Khulan," also for their artillerymen, his own recruits ("my men acted gallantly"), Mr. Dietz, Lance Sergeant Selkirk, and others. He noted that Major Bryant had killed two Indians (with a six-pounder), Johnston (a teamster), one, and Mr. Burnham, one. The four wounded men (apparently all recruits) were James Moody, J. L. Henry, John C. Slocum, and James Roop.

By 10 A. M. Royall had his company "on the road" and the night's encampment was made about 10 miles upriver. Two days later— the evening of June 20—Major Bryant, the troops, and the trains arrived at Fort Mann. (Bryant was at the fort till about July 1; then returned to Missouri.)

Royall and his recruits subsequently continued the journey to New Mexico. A Santa Fe newspaper of July 18 noted the arrival, on the 17th, of "Lt. Royal [three or four days in advance of his men] and Mr. Owens."

Ref: 30th Cong., 1st Sess., *H. Ex. Doc. No. 1* (Serial 537), pp. 141-144 (Royall's report), 146; *The Weekly Tribune*, Liberty, Mo., July 28 (from Weston *Herald*) and August 11 (from *Missouri Republican*, St. Louis), 1848; New York *Weekly Tribune*, July 29 and August 19, 1848 (from *Missouri Republican*); Saint Louis *Daily Union*, July 20, August 23, 1848; *KHC*, v. 10, pp. 409-413. One account says Royall was a nephew of Sterling Price.

"Khulan" is "Khulon" in some accounts, and also is found as "Khulow," "Kuhlow" and even "Cooley." The correct spelling has not been ascertained.

❦ June 7.—Eastbound (detached from Fort Mann's force on June 3, to meet and escort Major Bryant [paymaster]), Lt. Phillip Stremmel and his command (64 artillerymen, Company C, "Gilpin's battalion"; with two six-pounders), while encamped at Pawnee Fork, underwent attack by a large band of Indians, believed to be mostly Comanches. (Some 200 of the enemy were seen— armed for the most part with lances, or bows and arrows.)

"We were . . . surrounded on all sides," Stremmel reported. "We succeeded in keeping them from our animals with our small arms, doing some execution among them." The Indians began to retreat; but when one of the six-pounders was fired, the troops' animals stampeded. 2d Lt. William "Khulan," with 30 men, went out and recovered five mules; the Indians (using a white horse as decoy) got away with 22 mules and horses. No artillerymen were wounded in the 10-minute engagement. It was thought the Indians lost five killed and twice that number wounded. *See* preceding entry.

Stremmel sent an express back to Fort Mann, and Gilpin (on June 10) dispatched Lt. Ashley Gulley with 50 mounted men. This force, after relieving Stremmel, set out to scout the surrounding country. The artillerymen (now accompanied by a Santa Fe-to-Fort Leavenworth express) continued eastward on the Santa Fe road; and on the 14th, a little west of Walnut creek, met Major Bryant and accompanying troops under Lt. William B. Royall (who assumed charge of the united command).

Ref: 30th Cong., 1st Sess., *H. Ex. Doc. No. 1* (Serial 537), pp. 138, 141, 144-146; New York *Weekly Tribune*, July 29, 1848 (from *Missouri Republican*, St. Louis).

❦ June 7.—In "Nebraska," Sioux Indians crossed the Platte, destroyed a deserted Pawnee village, and the near by cornfields—as witnessed by Capt. Stewart Van Vliet (AQM at "Fort Childs").

Two days earlier (the day he left the fort, with three companions, on a mission to St. Louis), Van Vliet had met 300 Cheyennes "lying in wait" for the Pawnees; and on June 6th he had met the "whole Pawnee nation—several thousands" heading for the buffalo grounds.

Ref: *The Daily Reveille*, St. Louis, June 20, 1848; Nebraska State Historical Society *Publications*, v. 20, pp. 177, 178; Saint Louis *Daily Union*, June 21, 1848. An Oregon-bound traveler, writing May 26 from the forks of the Platte area, stated that the Pawnees had lost 20 braves and 60 horses some two weeks earlier in a fight with the Sioux.—Saint Louis *Daily Union*, June 19, 1848. In his 1848 report, Agent John Miller stated: "The Pawnees number about 2,500 . . . owing to their potent enemies, the Sioux, they still reside on the south side of the Platte. . . ."—Comm'r of Indian Affairs, *Report*, 1848.

❦ June-July.—From Fort Leavenworth on June 9 a Santa Fe-bound supply-and-specie-carrying government train (53 wagons) set out with an escort of 143 Missouri mounted volunteers (recruits—*see* p. 744), all in charge of Capt. George W. Hook (of "Newby's" Illinois regiment). Maj. Noah Johnston (paymaster), Capt. George H. Kennerly (QM's dep't), and Orville C. Pratt (a lawyer en route to California, who kept a diary of the trip) were of this party. At Council Grove (reached June 16) Hook halted his command to await another company coming up behind. (Kennerly, while here, got orders to return to St. Louis; and left on June 21.)

On June 10 a "detachment 150 strong [of Missouri mounted volunteers—recruits—under Capt. Gabriel de Korponay], besides wagons and traders," left Fort Leavenworth; headed southward on the military road; and on the 11th camped seven miles south of the Kansas river crossing ("Delaware," or "Grinter" ferry), not far from Westport, Mo., to wait for Bvt. Lt. Col. John Garland (Fourth U. S. infantry) and Lt. Col. Clifton Wharton (Fort Leavenworth's commandant). These two officers—under orders to Fort Mann to investigate charges preferred against Capt. William Pelzer and other officers there—arrived late on June 13(?). The company (under way again on June 14?) reached Council Grove on the 17th (but Wharton, ill, had turned back for Fort Leavenworth).

At the end of June, Hook's and Korponay's commands reached the Fort Mann vicinity and went into camp. (It is not clear what escort was provided the government trains from this point to Santa Fe.) Colonel Garland began his investigation of several Fort Mann officers; and on July 7 (after seeking lawyer Orville C. Pratt's advice) Capt. William Pelzer and Lt. Amandus Schnabel resigned. (Garland left for the States about July 8?.)

Late on July 7 Pratt joined Captain Hook's command (at camp 12 miles above Fort Mann). Hook's force proceeded up the Arkansas to Bent's Fort; thence to Santa Fe (reached July 31). Pratt went to California—setting out from Santa Fe on August 27.

Korponay (by one report) was still in the Fort Mann area on July 10. But 100 of his Missouri recruits (instead of continuing to Santa Fe) were homeward-bound (the end of the Mexican War having brought about change of orders); some, or all, served as escort to Bvt. Lt. Col. John Garland; and reached Fort Leavenworth at the end of July. Maj. Thomas S. Bryant (*see* June 5-20 entry), and Garland, both arrived there near the end of the month, within a few days of each other, but with separate escorts.

The St. Louis *Reveille* of August 3 reported the arrival (on the 2d) of the steamboat *Wyandotte* having on board as passengers, Garland and Bryant, Lt. Dillon and 50 mounted men of Captain de Korponay's company, also 30 discharged soldiers, Company A, First U. S. infantry (from Santa Fe and Chihuahua). The St. Louis *Union* of August 5 reported the arrival (on August 3?) of the "remainder of Capt. Korponay's company"—56 men with 24 horses—aboard the *Mandan*.

Ref: Orville C. Pratt's "Diary" (microfilm of original in Coe Collection, Yale University Library); *The Daily Reveille*, St. Louis, June 10, 30, August 3, 11, 1848; *The Weekly Tribune*, Liberty, Mo., August 11, 1848; Saint Louis *Daily Union*, August 3, 5, 1848; 31st Cong., 1st Sess., *Sen. Ex. Doc. No. 26* (Serial 554), p. 10; L. R. and Ann W. Hafen, *op. cit.*, pp. 341-359 (for data on Orville C. Pratt).

❡ June.—The *St. Croix* (G. W. Atchison, Jr., master), a regular packet to Weston and St. Joseph since April, made a record trip this month. She returned to St. Louis on June 13(?), having gone up to Weston and back in the unparalleled time of five days and 18 hours.

Ref: Saint Louis *Daily Union*, June 14, 1848; *The Daily Reveille*, St. Louis, April 9, June 13, 1848.

❡ June.—The *Mandan,* coming down from St. Joseph, Mo. (and arriving at St. Louis on the 14th), carried a cargo of 1,833 packs of buffalo robes consigned to R. & W. Campbell, P. Chouteau, Jr. & Co., and Houseman and Lawry.

Ref: *The Daily Reveille*, St. Louis, June 15, 1848.

❡ June.—The St. Louis *Reveille* of the 15th stated: "Maj. [Thomas] Fitzpatrick [of the Upper Platte Agency—headquarters at Bent's Fort] arrived a few days since [via the Platte; and the Oregon trail, to Westport, apparently] from the plains. He has taken an extended tour through the Indian tribes whose hunting grounds skirt the base of the Rocky Mts." On the way in Agent Fitzpatrick had met almost all the emigrants bound for Oregon and California.

Ref: L. R. Hafen and W. J. Ghent, *op. cit.,* pp. 208, 209; *The Daily Reveille*, St. Louis, June 15, 1848. Fitzpatrick's valuable June 24, 1848, report (which Hafen and Ghent cite) was not seen by this compiler.

❡ June 15.—Some 170 government wagons, in charge of (David) Waldo & Company, passed Fort Mann. (This was one of the trains operating under James Brown's government contract—*see* May 17 annals entry.)

Ref: New York *Weekly Tribune*, July 29, 1848 (from *Missouri Republican*, St. Louis).

❡ June 18.—A few miles below St. Joseph, Mo., an American Fur Company Mackinaw boat struck a snag and sank. Baptiste Picotte drowned; and the boat's heavy load of furs was lost.

Ref: *The Gazette*, St. Joseph, Mo., June 23, 1848.

❡ June.—Council Grove's white inhabitants (as listed by traveler Orville C. Pratt) were: William H. Mitchell (blacksmith for the Kansa Indians), his wife ("a sprightly good natured old lady"), his son (assistant smith), "Mr. Brown" (wagonmaker and repairer), Charles Chouteau and Seth Hays—both Indian traders.

Mrs. William H. Mitchell—*Council Grove's first white woman resident*—earlier had lived among the Pottawatomies "several years" according to Pratt. He also noted that she spoke the Kansa language "quite well," and seemed to be popular among the Indians.

Ref: Orville C. Pratt's "Diary," entry of June 19, 1848 (microfilm of original in Coe Collection, Yale University Library). In 1844 William H. Mitchell was *farmer* for the Kansa (*see* annals, p. 533); his name is not on the list of 1845 employees; on January 26, 1846, he was appointed *blacksmith* for the Kansa (*ibid.*, p. 660), and was so employed in 1847 and 1848; but not in 1849. It appears he went to New Mexico and was a clerk for St. Vrain and McCarty. In late 1849, James S. Calhoun (newly arrived Indian agent at Santa Fe) referred to "William H. Mitchell" as being of little assistance to him because of poor health. —James S. Calhoun, *op. cit.*, pp. 49, 335. In *KHC*, v. 16, p. 556, it is stated that the "Choteau brothers'" store ("a small log building") was on the site where the "Pioneer Store" later was erected.

¶ June.—Traders Ebenezer W. Pomeroy, Joseph P. Hamelin, Edward J. Glasgow, all from Chihuahua, and others, crossed "Kansas," eastbound; reached the Missouri border about July 2. They had left Santa Fe early in June. (On the 4th some of these men were at Lexington, Mo.)

Westbound traveler Orville C. Pratt had met Pomeroy's train on June 26 at the great bend of the Arkansas. He remarked "Their train looked bad."

Ref: Missouri Historical Society *Collections*, v. 5 (June, 1928), pp. 306, 307 (Aull correspondence—Robert Aull wrote, in a July 14 letter, that Pomeroy, Hamelin, and Glasgow had brought the "balance of effects of Owens & Aull"—the sum of $51,295.62—from Chihuahua. Perhaps referring to the same party, the St. Louis *Reveille* of July 16, 1848, reported the arrival there, on the 15th, of "Mr. J. S. Glasgow [with $41,000 in bullion] and several other men recently from Santa Fe," aboard the *Whirlwind*.

¶ June 29.—James S. Rains, appointed Indian agent to succeed Solomon P. Sublette (resigned), reached his post—the Osage River Agency.

The Osage River *Agency*—new in 1848—included the Sacs & Foxes of the "Mississippi" (their former "Sac & Fox Agency" being abolished), the Kansa (formerly in the Fort Leavenworth Agency), the Ottawas, Chippewas, Weas, Miamis, etc.—all recently in the Osage River *Subagency* (abolished). For the changes in 1848 (from 1847), *see* annals, pp. 730, 792.

Rains' tenure as agent was brief—he was removed early in 1849.

Ref: OIA, Letters Received from Osage River Agency (National Archives Microcopy 234, Roll 643), Rains' letter of June 29, 1848. The headquarters of the Osage River Subagency had been on Pottawatomie creek in the southeast corner of present Franklin county (*see* annals, pp. 530, 535); and the Sac & Fox Agency headquarters had been established in west-central Franklin county of today, about four miles west of the present Osage county line (*see* annals, p. 704). In his September 7, 1848, report Rains stated "the Kansas [Indians] . . . [are] about ninety miles fom the agency." This would seem to indicate he was making use of the quarters at the Pottawatomie creek location.

¶ June 29(?)—Expressman A. Smith left the Missouri border for Santa Fe. He arrived there the evening of July 17, in "precisely" 19 days from Fort Leavenworth. The Santa Fe *Republican* believed this "the quickest trip ever made by any person who has had charge of the mail."

See, also, May 29 entry.

Ref: Saint Louis *Daily Union*, August 23, 1848 (from Santa Fe *Republican*).

¶ July 1.—William R. McClure announced he had "just opened" the "Missouri Hotel [on] Water st[reet], [in the town of] Kansas, Jackson County, Mo." His "house for the accommodation of travelers and boarders" was in "a large new brick building, with commodious and pleasant rooms. . . ."

Ref: Saint Louis *Daily Union*, July, 1848, and later, issues.

❦ Early(?) in July, "high up" the Kansas river—in the buffalo range—a hunting party of Pottawatomies, accompanied by a few Sacs and Kickapoos, was invited to join a large body of Kansa, who also were after buffalo. The united company, in a day or two, met some Pawnees (long hostile to the Kansa) hunting with a band of "Comanches." There was a show of "friendly greetings by smoking, &c" by the chiefs of each group, and an agreement was reached to meet next day for a council and feast. However, an incident occurred which resulted in an Indian battle—a conflict which thenceforth made the Pawnees enemies of the Pottawatomies and Sacs.

Conflicting versions of what happened make it difficult to determine the true events. Just after the Pottawatomies returned, a detailed account was written, dated "Kansas River, Pottawatomie Nation, July 26." In this it was stated that two young Pawnees with a peace pipe approached the Kansa camp; a Kansa brave shot and killed one; a Pottawatomie (defying his chief) pursued and dispatched the other Pawnee with a spear. Then the Pawnees and "Comanches" attacked. In the fight (it was said) they (the attackers) lost a good many warriors. The Pottawatomies brought home five scalps. Father Gailland (on September 17) wrote that the Pottawatomies "killed many Pawnee warriors and ponies." (The version which reached official quarters apparently made no mention of the murder by the young Pottawatomie, for the report to Washington suggested the Indians in company with the Kansa were blameless.)

From Independence, Mo., on August 21, "Roving Bill" wrote that the trouble had started when a Pawnee struck a Kansa; and that the Kansa Indians had brought scalps back to Council Grove. (An 1849 account said the Kansa lost seven warriors; and had Pawnee prisoners, but were forced to release them.) Agent J. S. Rains, in his September 7, 1848, report, stated that "while Keokuk, a Sac [*i. e.*, Moses Keokuk, son of the recently deceased Chief Keokuk] was handing to a Pawnee the pipe of peace, a Kansa Indian that was in company fired and killed the Pawnee"; and that in the fight which ensued "they killed and scalped five of the Pawnees. No other Indians were killed but several wounded."

(The Pottawatomies—since many of them lived north of Kansas river—were vulnerable to attacks from the Pawnees. Within two months after the fight, the Pawnees had retaliated by stealing some 40 horses from their settlements; and other depredations occurred later.)

Ref: New York *Weekly Tribune*, September 2, 1848 (reprinting an account from "Kansas River, Pottawatomie Nation, July 26"), July 21, 1849 (a June 7, 1849, letter from Council Grove); *The Weekly Tribune*, Liberty, Mo., August 25, 1848 (for "Roving Bill's" August 21 letter from Independence, Mo.); Comm'r of Indian Affairs, *Report*, 1848; *KHC*, v. 11, p. 342; *KHQ*, v. 20, p. 507 (for Gailland). The Council Grove letter of June 7, 1849, is reprinted in *KHQ*, v. 18, p. 324.

❈ July 7-12.—Capt. John C. Griffin and 100 Missouri volunteers (of "Gilpin's battalion"), with a six-pounder, set out from the Fort Mann area on a Comanche-hunting expedition, at noon of July 7.

July 7.—They marched southward 25 miles; camped on Crooked creek. July 8.—They continued downstream (across present Meade county) to Crooked creek's mouth; then followed down the Cimarron's left bank till near sunset; crossed to the south bank and camped (the day's march had been more than 40 miles). July 9.—This day, after traveling 12 miles, the Missourians reached a grove (sighted the day before from an eminence) where they found "the deserted camp of the enemy"—a village of "thousands" (Griffin's estimate). Lt. Joseph C. Eldridge and 20 men went scouting; came upon a Mexican boy; learned the Comanche village was "not more than three leagues off, down the Cimar[r]on." Griffin at once marched his force in pursuit. "In three hours," he reported, "we came in sight of their warriors, about 600 strong, posted on a well chosen piece of ground on the north side of the Cimar[r]on." At noon, on July 9, the engagement commenced; lasted three hours; ended with a retreat by the Indians. Griffin also reported: "The enemy could not have lost less than 30 of their best men. . . . We lost on our side, in killed, none. Wounded: Lieutenant Eldridge . . . slightly . . . and Sergeant Gibson . . . slightly." (By contrast, letters from Fort Mann to Missouri indicated that only a few Indians [not 25 or 30] had been killed, and several wounded; and one stated that Captain Griffin's conduct in the action had been censured.) The locale of this fight must have been in what is now Woods county, Okla.

Griffin's force encamped on the battle ground; found no sign of the enemy next morning (the 10th); and marched northward towards Mulberry creek (in Ford county of today); reached the stream on July 11 "almost famished for water." On the 12th the expedition returned to Fort Mann.

Ref: 30th Cong., 1st Sess., *H. Ex. Doc. No. 1* (Serial 537), pp. 146-149; *The Daily Reveille*, St. Louis, August 24, 1848; New York *Weekly Tribune*, August 19, September 9, 1848. The latter issue reprinted a Fort Mann letter of July 28, from the St. Louis *New Era*, which stated: "On the 7th a party went out under Capt. Griffin, who broke up a village of about 1,000 lodges of Camanches, though without serious fighting."

❈ July.—One Santa Fe-bound merchant caravan on the trail this month consisted of "some sixty-odd heavy mule wagons" which were "for the most part [*i. e.*, 30? of them] owned by Aubrey [Francis X. Aubry]," according to 2d Lt. George D. Brewerton (whose eastbound company met the westbound traders at the Arkansas crossing in late July).

Aubry, taking his second train of the year to Santa Fe (*see* mid-March entry), arrived there August 5, in advance of his wagons. *See, also,* September 17 entry.

Ref: G. D. Brewerton, *op. cit.*, p. 252; *The Pacific Historian*, v. 5 (August, 1961), p. 113.

❈ July 13.—Express from Santa Fe, mountain man James Beckwourth (accompanied by half-Cherokee Charles McIntosh, and Henry Hamilton) arrived at Fort Leavenworth. It was *stated* the trio had left Santa Fe on June 26(?) and had made the journey in 17 days. (An express from Chihuahua to Fort Leavenworth passed Fort Mann on July 2—as recorded in O. C. Pratt's diary.) Hamilton, aboard the *Wyandotte*, reached St. Louis on July 18.

On July 15 Beckwourth and McIntosh started back to New Mexico. (At a later time, Beckwourth said of this return trip that "we overtook Bullard and Company's train of wagons, which were on their way to Santa Fé with supplies for the army"; and that Bullard and his partner [leaving the wagons in charge of employees] traveled "with us as far as the Moro . . . where we were compelled to leave them, as they were tired out. . . .")

Ref: Saint Louis *Daily Union*, July 20, August 3, 1848; *The Daily Reveille*, St. Louis, July 19, 1848; T. D. Bonner, ed., *The Life and Adventures of James P. Beckwourth* (1931), pp. 342, 343; Orville C. Pratt's "Diary" (microfilm of original in Coe Collection, Yale University Library). In Georgia W. Read and Ruth Gaines, eds., *op. cit.*, p. 599, is a compilation of some data on Charles McIntosh. By the southern route, he guided the Ithaca company of packers from Salt Lake to California in 1849. For the return east of Bullard, in 1848, *see* annals entry of September 28.

❧ DIED: Lt. Col. Clifton Wharton, First U. S. dragoons, aged 46, on July 13, at Fort Leavenworth, where he had been post commandant since 1844(?).

"He was a man of fine accomplishments and stood high in the esteem of all who knew him," according to "Roderick" (writing from the fort on July 14), who also stated that Wharton "leaves a wife and five ["Kansas"-born] children."

Ref: *The Daily Reveille*, St. Louis, July 20, 1848; Saint Louis *Daily Union*, July 20, 22, 1848; *The Gazette*, St. Joseph, Mo., July 21, 1848; *The Weekly Tribune*, Liberty, Mo., July 28, 1848; *Pennsylvania Magazine of History and Biography*, Philadelphia, v. 2 (1878), pp. 56, 217; annals, p. 378; Louis Pelzer's *Marches of the Dragoons in the Mississippi Valley* . . . (Iowa City, 1917), p. 169; a typed page of Wharton biographical data, in KHi library. Wharton's remains were taken to Alleghany cemetery, near Pittsburgh, Pa.

❧ On July 13 Sup't Thomas H. Harvey, St. Louis, forwarded to Washington (for approval) the licenses Agent Thomas Fitzpatrick had granted: (1) William W. Bent (of Bent's Fort), and (2) Messrs. Ward & Guerrier, to trade in the Upper Platte and Arkansas Agency.

An article (1878) on Seth Edmund Ward's life states that in 1848 he formed a partnership with "William Le Guerrier," in the Indian trade, "each of them having about $1,500 in cash"; that five large goods-laden wagons (the merchandise purchased at Westport, Mo., from Boone & Hamilton, on 10 months' credit) were taken to the upper Arkansas; and that the partners made a very successful expedition, "securing 6,000 buffalo robes, with which they returned to Westport, May, 1849." (The robes were shipped to New York; and Ward went East to attend to their sale.)

Ref: SIA, St. Louis, "Records," v. 9, typed copy, p. 179; *The United States Biographical Dictionary* . . . *Missouri Volume* (1878), p. 468. For other data on Ward, *see* annals, pp. 352 and 556. The SIA "Records," v. 9, typed copy, pp. 348, 461, 569, 693, and 918, show that "Ward & Guerrier" also were granted licenses to trade within the same agency from 1849 through 1854 (and later?).

❡ July.—The *Martha* (Joseph La Barge, master), under charter to the American Fur Company, returned from the upper Missouri (having left the mouth of the Yellowstone June 29), and reached St. Louis July 14.

Her passengers included F. C. [Ferdinand] Culbertson, from Fort Benton, and British sportsman John Palliser (*see* p. 716). In her cargo were 1,722 packages of buffalo robes, 262 bales of furs, and 5,000 buffalo tongues.

On May 9 the *Martha* had set out from St. Louis for the trip upriver. One voyager on *that* journey was Etienne Provost making his last trip to the mountains.

Ref: *The Daily Reveille,* St. Louis, July 15, 1848; Saint Louis *Daily Union,* July 17, 1848; John Palliser's *Solitary Rambles* . . . (London, 1853), pp. 286, 287 (Palliser later recounted that the *Martha* reached the upper Missouri "Late in July"—but it was June, rather); H. M. Chittenden's *Early Steamboat Navigation* . . . (1903), v. 1, p. 184, gives confused details of the *Martha's* trips for the fur company. The Saint Louis *Daily Union* of July 20, 1848, stated that "Major [Joseph V.] Hamilton, Mr. [Alexander] Culbertson, Mr. [Pierre Didier] Papin," and 70 men connected with the American Fur Company had arrived "yesterday" (but probably meaning July 18) aboard the *Wyandotte*. *Missouri Republican,* St. Louis, May 11, 1848 (for the departure from St. Louis); Morgan and Harris, *The Rocky Mountain Journals of William Marshall Anderson, op. cit.,* pp. 350, 351.

❡ July 14.—At Weston, Mo., 10 or 12 Mackinaw boats, containing large quantities of buffalo robes had arrived from the upper Missouri (having started downriver on May 17). The *Wyandotte* would carry the boats' cargoes from Weston to St. Louis.

Ref: Saint Louis *Daily Union,* July 20, 1848.

❡ July 15-23.—Capt. Thomas Jones with a command of 101 mounted Missouri volunteers (of "Gilpin's battalion"), seven guides and hands, and a "brass six-pounder," set out from the Fort Mann area July 15, to hunt Comanches.

On the 15th and 16th Jones and his troops marched down the Arkansas; camped the night of July 16 at a point below the mouth of Mulberry creek (present Ford county); learned from Bullard & Hook's Santa Fe-bound train that no Indians had been seen on the trail. Leaving the Arkansas on July 17, Jones' command traveled southward; camped on the Cimarron July 19; and on the 20th marched "up" [*i. e.,* east, and *down*river] to locate the Comanches Captain Griffin had dispersed on July 9. About 10 A. M. Micheau (guide) came up with news of Indians seen in timber ahead.

Jones deployed his troops so as to hide the six-pounder, and dispatched Lt. Oliver Bain with 30 mounted men to examine the woods. Bain's force "on entering, was quickly attacked and hotly engaged" by Indians "lying in ambush." Jones then sent Lt. Joseph C. Eldridge with 30 men to the head of the grove; and they "met and drove back" the ambushers who were retreating from Bain's troops. The fighting was (by Jones' report) "hand to hand, and muzzle to muzzle." "The two parties having the Indians between them . . .

soon completed their destruction." Of 41 Indians seen, 21 were killed, six escaped unhurt, and the rest (not found) either fell in the creek, or crawled into the brush. Of the Missouri troops, Lieutenant Eldridge and Privates Phillip Kinchle, G. W. Vance, James B. Hoover, and Robert Williams were wounded severely by arrows. Jones wrote: "These Indians I believe to have been a party of Pawnees, but they refused to make themselves known, and began the fight."

The locale of this engagement was not far from the abandoned Comanche village (in present Woods county, Okla.) that Griffin had dispersed. After the battle Jones reconnoitered the area and found the large village, where lodge poles, saddles, bags of salt and provisions remained strewn about.

Having injured men to care for, and finding no signs of Comanches in the area, Jones marched his troops back to Fort Mann; arrived there July 23.

Ref: 30th Cong., 1st Sess., *H. Ex. Doc. No. 1* (Serial 537), pp. 149, 150; New York *Weekly Tribune*, September 9, 1848 (from *Missouri Republican*, St. Louis).

❦ July 17.—Bvt. Capt. Abraham Buford and Company H, First U. S. dragoons, set out from Fort Gibson ("Okla.") for Santa Fe, N. M.; and arrived there on September 9, having explored a "hitherto untraveled route" across "Oklahoma"—a route which he considered "the best and shortest" between the States and Santa Fe.

Buford's path followed up the north side of the Cimarron; and "by the way of the Salt Rock, through the Cross Timbers"; thence south, and westward, to the Santa Fe trail, striking it at the Middle Cimarron Spring. One of his party was lost on the march—supposedly killed by Comanches.

Ref: New York *Weekly Tribune*, October 7, 1848 (from *Missouri Republican*, St. Louis, September 23?—which got its news from the Santa Fe *Republican* extra dated September 12); Saint Louis *Daily Union*, October 10, 1848; *Chronicles of Oklahoma*, Oklahoma City, v. 27 (Summer, 1949), p. 199; R. P. Bieber, ed., *Southern Trails to California* (Glendale, Calif., 1937), pp. 325, 326; Grant Foreman, *Marcy & the Gold Seekers* (Norman, Okla., 1939), pp. 7-9; 35th Cong., 1st Sess., *H. Ex. Doc. No. 104* (Serial 958), for map "Boundary of the Creek Country," which shows part of Buford's path. Evidently Buford's party returned to Fort Gibson via a Canadian river route—*see* New York *Weekly Tribune*, February 17, 1849 (from Fort Smith [Ark.] *Herald*).

❦ Midsummer.—The Santa Fe (N. M.) *Republican* of July 18(?) stated: "Not a day passes now without the arrival of large trains from the United States, laden with all kinds of merchandise."

Lt. Col. William Gilpin (at Fort Mann, on the Arkansas) wrote, August 1, that more than 3,000 government and traders' wagons had already passed that post "during the present season"; along with perhaps 12,000 persons, and some 50,000 head of stock (which he considered "probably a low estimate").

A traveler reaching St. Louis on August 27, from Chihuahua and New Mexico, reported a train of 250 wagons had come into Chihuahua before his departure; on his journey east he had met "over 1,000 wagons in different trains, bound for Santa Fe, El Paso and Chihuahua" (of which nearly 400 belonged to the government); and another large train on the Santa Fe trail was not met because it had gone by the Bent's Fort route.

Ref: Saint Louis *Daily Union*, August 23, 1848 (quoting the Santa Fe *Republican* of July 18?); 30th Cong., 1st Sess., *H. Ex. Doc. No. 1* (Serial 537), p. 139 (for Gilpin); New York *Weekly Tribune*, September 16, 1848 (from *Missouri Republican*, St. Louis, August 30).

❏ July 21.—Overland from California, and en route to Washington with official dispatches, Christopher ("Kit") Carson, with his pack train, arrived at Fort Leavenworth. (On July 25, on the *St. Joseph*, boarded at Weston, Mo., he reached St. Louis; and set out next day for his destination—reporting at Washington in the fore part of August.)

Accounts state that Carson made the entire journey (to the Missouri border) "with the same set of animals." From Los Angeles (left May 5) to Santa Fe his company had numbered 28 persons; but he set out from Taos, N. M., (in late June), with only three(?) men (who later turned back, after Carson joined eastbound fur traders on the Platte). His route from Taos was northward (avoiding hostile Indians) to the Pueblo (Colo.), and to Bijou creek (South Platte tributary), thence cross-country, eastwardly, to the Platte, down that river past new Fort Childs (Kearny), and presumably to Fort Leavenworth by the established Oregon-California trail(?). Though as Carson later put it, from "Fort Kearney" he had "then struck for the Republican Fork [*i. e.*, Little Blue?] and from thence to Fort Leavenworth, having no trouble on the march."

See, also, October 2 entry.

Ref: Saint Louis *Daily Union*, July 26, 1848; New York *Weekly Tribune*, August 5, 12, 1848 (from *Missouri Republican*, and via telegraph news); Blanche C. Grant, ed., *Kit Carson's Own Story of His Life* (Taos, N. M., 1926), pp. 87-89; Edwin L. Sabin's *Kit Carson Days* (New York, 1935), v. 2, pp. 581-604.

❏ July 21.—Ten men, direct from Oregon by way of the Oregon-California trail, arrived at St. Joseph, Mo., after an 87-day journey, and no serious difficulties en route. One of the travelers was "Dr. Derby" (emigrant West in 1847).

R. M. May (of Chiles' California-bound train), on June 28, near Fort Laramie, noted meeting the 10 men from Oregon. "7 out of the ten disliked the Country and was returning home," he wrote.

Ref: St. Joseph (Mo.) *Gazette*, July 21, 1848; *The Weekly Tribune*, Liberty, Mo., August 11, 1848 (from St. Joseph *Adventure*); New York *Weekly Tribune*, August 26, 1848; *The Daily Reveille*, St. Louis, August 3, 1848; Charles L. Camp, ed., *op. cit.*, p. 289; Richard M. May's diary quoted courtesy of Dale L. Morgan, Bancroft Library, Berkeley, Calif.

❏ July.—The St. Louis Fur Company's *Bertrand* (Morrison, captain), came down from the upper Missouri, arriving at St. Louis July 24. She brought "a large lot of robes, skins and peltries consigned to Messrs. R[obert] & W[illiam] Campbell." Aboard as clerk: Alexander K. McLean.

The *Bertrand* (purchased in May, for $8,000, by Harvey, Primeau & Co.—the St. Louis Fur Company) had left St. Louis, upbound, on June 1; had gone 50 miles above the Yellowstone's mouth—higher than any other steamboat had voyaged (so accounts stated); and had made the round trip in 53 days—"the shortest yet accomplished."

Ref: *The Daily Reveille,* St. Louis, May 17, July 25, 1848; Saint Louis *Daily Union,* July 26, 1848. For the early-1848 journey (mostly afoot) of "Messrs. [Alexander M.] Harvey, [Alexander K.] McLean, and three others" of the company, from the upper Missouri to St. Louis, *see* the *Reveille,* March 30, 1848; and the *Union,* March 31, 1848.

❡ July 28.—James T. V. Thompson, of Platte county, Mo., contracted (with Capt. L. C. Easton, AQM) to transport 400 head of beef cattle from Fort Leavenworth to Santa Fe.

Ref: 30th Cong., 2d Sess., *Sen. Ex. Doc. No. 17* (Serial 529), p. 56. For items on James T. V. Thompson *see* W. M. Paxton's *Annals of Platte County, Missouri* . . . (1897).

❡ During July, Auguste A. L. Trécul (sent from Paris by the Museum National d'Histoire Naturelle to gather plants and animals in America) arrived in "Kansas," and was at work on the prairies west of Missouri.

Trécul collected botanical specimens on the Marais des Cygnes in July, and from the vicinities of "Sugar creek au Neosho," the "village Osage de Neosho," the "Mission de Sugar creek, chez les Potowatomies [the about-to-be-closed Catholic mission in present Linn county]," also around Fort Scott, in August. He was on the Neosho in late August and early September; then moved westward to work on the Arkansas and Little Arkansas, till some time in October, when he turned southward to the Grand Saline (of "Oklahoma").

Where Trécul spent the winter of 1848-1849 is not indicated in his records. But during March, 1849, he was in "Kansas"—on the Pawnee and Little Pawnee creeks of present Bourbon county, and also at, and around, Fort Scott. His last "Kansas" notation was in March, from "Prairies du Neosho à la frontiere de l'état du Missouri. . . ."

Ref: Susan D. McKelvey's *Botanical Exploration of the Trans-Mississippi West 1790-1850* (1955), pp. 1048-1052.

❡ Summer.—Alexander Majors, of Jackson county, Mo., supplied the Kickapoo Indians with 19 cows and 19 calves. He received as payment $237.64.

Ref: 31st Cong., 1st Sess., *H. Ex. Doc. No. 11* (Serial 572), pp. 111, 116 (Agent R. W. Cummins' accounts, 1848).

❡ July-September.—Licenses (new and renewal) to trade with Indians in "Kansas," as granted by agents of the St. Louis Indian superintendency, were:

Traders	Indians	Issued by	Month received at St. Louis
William F. Dyer	Delawares, Kickapoos, and Pottawatomies	R. W. Cummins	August
Josiah Smart	Sacs & Foxes (in the Marais des Cygnes country)	J. S. Rains	August

John Walsh	Pottawatomies (in the Kansas river country)	R. W. Cummins	September
Whitehead & Peltier	Pottawatomies (in the Kansas river country)	R. W. Cummins	September
Isaac G. Baker	Sacs & Foxes (in the Marais des Cygnes country)	J. S. Rains	September
(J. M.) Simpson & (J. M.) Hunter	Sacs & Foxes (in the Marais des Cygnes country)	J. S. Rains	September
C[harles] and F[rederick] Chouteau	Kansa	J. S. Rains	September
Farmer & Gardner	Miamis	J. S. Rains	September
Hay [Hays?] & Stateler	Miamis	J. S. Rains	September
B. D. Mosier	Miamis	J. S. Rains	September
Robert A. Kinzie	Pottawatomies (in the Kansas river country)	R. W. Cummins	?
Peter A. Sarpy	Pottawatomies (in the Kansas river country)	R. W. Cummins	September

Ref: SIA, St. Louis, "Records," v. 9, typed copy, pp. 169, 195, 201, 208, 211-213, 233, 301. Kinzie's clerk in the Pottawatomie trade was Paul Campbell (p. 211, *ibid.*). In OIA, Letters Received from Osage River Agency (National Archives Microcopy 234, Roll 643) is a July 18, 1848, document re Isaac G. Baker's purchase, from P. Chouteau, Jr. & Co., all right, title, etc., to one third of the Osage River Agency trading establishment.

❦ Around August 1 a company of 36 men, overland from Oregon, reached St. Joseph, Mo. (They had set out early in May.) Other arrivals from the West were Mr. Gray (a Virginian) and his small party from California (left early in May).

Some of the Oregonians had been (evidently) in the party with which Isaac Pettijohn started East. (Pettijohn, on May 1, had written "on tomorrow we start on our Journey [from Oregon], being about 35 in number besides three small children." But there was a division en route; and on June 10 Pettijohn wrote: "Oure company now consists of twelve men and the children." Subsequently his party reached new Fort Kearny on July 17; and took "the new rout down platt"; and on the 25th crossed the Missouri at "old" Fort Kearny.) California-bound R. M. May, on July 4 (below the North Platte crossing), recorded in his diary: "took a Stroll up the Creek to an encampment of about 20 Oregon Gentlemen Rough & Rude were their appearance. . . ." He noted that one of them was "Mr. Umphet" who was returning to Ohio. How to account for a party of 36—rather than 20—is a problem yet to be solved.

Gray's party (as reported) carried "a copy" of the San Francisco *California Star* special (*see* p. 772). Incidentally, this issue stated that San Francisco had a white population of 575 males, 177 females, 60 children of school age; 812 white persons in all.

Ref: *The Weekly Tribune*, Liberty, Mo., August 11, 1848 (from St. Joseph [Mo.] *Adventure* of August 4); *The Daily Reveille*, St. Louis, August 12, 1848 (from the *Adventure*); New York *Weekly Tribune*, August 26, 1848; Isaac Pettijohn's and Richard M. May's diaries quoted courtesy of Dale L. Morgan, Bancroft Library, Berkeley, Calif.

❡ August 6.—The Pawnees signed a treaty (negotiated in early June by Lt. Col. Ludwell E. Powell of the "Oregon battalion") giving up claim to Grand Island (in the Platte), and a strip of land adjacent on either side of the river.

Finalities of the treaty, made at new "Fort Childs" ("Neb."), had awaited the arrival of $2,000 worth of Indian goods (brought by Capt. Stewart Van Vliet, AQM, U. S. army). "Ma-laigne"—as principal chief of the four confederated bands—headed the list of Pawnee signers.

Ref: C. J. Kappler's *Indian Affairs; Laws and Treaties* (1904), v. 2, pp. 571, 572; *The Gazette*, St. Joseph, Mo., June 16, 1848; New York *Weekly Tribune*, June 24, 1848 (from *Missouri Republican*, St. Louis, June 20); Nebraska State Historical Society *Collections*, v. 20, pp. 182, 183 (from *Missouri Republican*, St. Louis, September 8, 1848).

❡ August 10.—In a train of 25 goods-laden wagons leaving Independence, Mo., for New Mexico was Alexander Majors, of Jackson county, Mo., with a "little outfit of six wagons and teams"—his first venture in freighting to Santa Fe.

En route this company met homeward-bound Mexican War volunteers, and, in mid-September, Francis X. Aubry on his fleet ride to Independence.

In his memoirs Majors stated: "I made that trip [to Santa Fe and back in 92 days] with remarkable success . . . the quickest on record with ox teams." (The good condition of many of his oxen, when he returned, gave him "quite a reputation among the freighters and merchants. . . .")

Ref: Alexander Majors' *Seventy Years on the Frontier* . . . (Chicago, c1893), pp. 74, 75, 156; Kansas City (Mo.) *Globe*, February 10, 1890 (or, *see The Pacific Historian*, v. 5 [August, 1961], p. 115) for Majors' statement: "I was on my way to Santa Fe with a train of 25 wagons [in 1848] . . . and knew nothing of Aubry's design . . . [etc.]."

❡ August 14.—Oregon territory was created by act of congress.

For governor, President Polk appointed Joseph Lane, of Indiana, recently a brigadier general (for two years) in Mexican War service; and appointed as U. S. marshal Joseph L. Meek (*see* May 11 entry). Within a month Lane and Meek were in "Kansas," heading for Oregon, overland—*see* September 10 entry. (Other officials went by water.)

Ref: *U. S. Statutes*, v. 9, p. 323; 30th Cong., 2d Sess., *H. Ex. Doc. No. 1* (Serial 537), p. 18; Bancroft, *op. cit.*, v. 1, pp. 770, 776-778.

❡ Mid-August.—"Mr. Estes and another individual," express from Santa Fe, in 25 days (having left there July 21), apparently reached Fort Leavenworth August 14; and were at Weston, Mo., on the 16th. From Fort Mann eastward, Lt. Col. William Gilpin had accompanied them.

Gilpin (ill) went downriver to Independence, Mo.—arriving there August 18—and took rooms at the Noland House. His battalion troops (to follow later) would be mustered out at Independence.

Ref: New York *Weekly Tribune*, September 16, 1848 (from Weston [Mo.] *Journal* of August 19); Saint Louis *Daily Union*, August 29, 1848 (from Independence *Expositor* of August 19); *The Weekly Tribune*, Liberty, Mo., August 25, 1848.

❡ August 15.—Jacob Thierer, of Weston, Mo., signed a contract (Capt. Langdon C. Easton, negotiator) to supply fresh beef at Fort Leavenworth for one year, commencing September 1.

Thierer, emigrant from Germany to St. Louis in the early 1840's, moved from Weston, by early 1855, to Riley county, Kansas territory. A farm on which he settled in the 1850's still (1971) is owned by his descendants.

Ref: 30th Cong., 2d Sess., *Sen. Ex. Doc. No. 17* (Serial 529), p. 11; Matt Thomson's *Early History of Wabaunsee County* (Alma, 1901), p. 261 (has sketch of Gus Thierer—son of Jacob, which says he was born [1851] in Weston, Mo.). Jacob Thierer (but not his family) is listed in the 1855 Kansas territorial census.

❡ August.—Arriving at Independence, Mo., during this month was a large caravan (three trains—totaling more than 100 wagons and about 500 loose cattle) which had left New Mexico in July. In the company (made up of some 100 teamsters—mostly young Missourians, plus "sundry traders, travelers, and Mexican herdsmen") was 2d Lt. George D. Brewerton, First U. S. infantry (who later wrote an account of the journey).

Brewerton referred to Mann's Fort as "a little government post, or half-way dépôt, then garrisoned by a handful of volunteers, who drank corn whisky, consumed Uncle Sam's bacon and hard tack . . . [etc.]."

Ref: Brewerton, *op. cit.*, pp. 219-282 ("In the Buffalo Country"). Brewerton had traveled from California to New Mexico with expressman Kit Carson. For the liquor situation at Fort Mann in June, *see* the entry on John McCoy, May, 1848, annals entry.

❡ August 21.—Traders Joseph H. Reynolds, John Hurd, and others from Independence, Mo., who had taken wagons out to Santa Fe in the spring, returned home with their trains "in fine condition." Very likely they came with the caravan mentioned in the preceding entry.

Ref: Saint Louis *Daily Union*, September 6, 1848; *The Weekly Tribune*, Liberty, Mo., August 25, 1848. The *Tribune* reported they had left Santa Fe on August 4 (*i. e.*, July? 4, probably).

❡ August 22.—A post office was established at Crawford Seminary (a Methodist Church, South, school—*see* April 1 entry) on the Quapaw Indian reserve, and on the Fort Leavenworth—Fort Scott —Fort Gibson—Fort Smith military road. The school's superintendent, Rev. Samuel G. Patterson, served as postmaster.

It is believed Crawford Seminary was in "Kansas"—near, and east of, present Baxter Springs. The other "Kansas" post offices in 1848 were at Fort Leavenworth and Fort Scott.

Ref: Robert W. Baughman's *Kansas Post Offices* . . . (Topeka, c1961), pp. 31, 156.

❡ August.—A private overland mail from San Francisco (a special *California Star* express) reached the Council Bluffs ("Neb.") Mormon headquarters "about the middle of August." Some of the mail carriers traveled down the Platte, from Fort Laramie (either via the Mormon trail, or the "old" Fort Kearny route) to the Missouri.

On March 25 Samuel Brannan had advertised in his newspaper: "The 'California Star' Express (60 days) to Independence, Mo., will leave this place on the first of April, and New Helvetia on the 15th. Postage on letters 50, on papers 12½ cents." William Hawk, his son Nathan, four other Mormons, and four gentiles started East, as scheduled, with this mail. Leaving Salt Lake City, there were nine in the party. Four men (the Hawks, and two other Mormons, presumably) were (later) mentioned as arriving at the Council Bluffs Mormon headquarters in August. (The journey had required more than twice 60 days!) It appears that the four non-Mormons (Mr. Gray's party?—*see* p. 770) may have carried a mail to Independence, Mo., by way of St. Joseph, Mo.

Ref: Daniel Tyler's *Concise History of the Mormon Battalion* (1881), pp. 341, 342; *Journal History* (ms. in L. D. S. Church Historian's Office, Salt Lake City), entry of October 2, 1848 (courtesy of Dale L. Morgan, Bancroft Library); Sabin, *op. cit.*, v. 2, pp. 580, 581 (for the *California Star* information); L. R. and Ann W. Hafen, *op. cit.*, p. 339. Juanita Brooks, ed., *On the Mormon Frontier* [Hosea Stout's diaries] (Salt Lake City, 1965), v. 1, p. 321 (for mention of the westbound Mormons meeting Hawk's party on July 26); R. P. Bieber, ed., *op. cit.*, pp. 19, 20.

❡ August.—A contract to transport, in covered wagons, from Fort Gibson ("Oklahoma") to Fort Leavenworth, 14,260 pounds of clothing, equipage, etc., for the sum of $4 per 100 pounds, was signed by James Wilkins at Fort Smith, Ark., on the 14th.

(Presumably the wagons reached Fort Leavenworth in late August, or early September.)

Ref: 31st Cong., 1st Sess., *Sen. Ex. Doc. No. 26* (Serial 554), p. 11.

❡ Late in August, Jesse B. Thompson, of Buchanan county, Mo., reached Weston, Mo., from Chihuahua (left July 15), by way of Santa Fe (left August 1).

Thompson reported meeting several government trains and trading companies on the plains—getting along well; and that all was quiet at Fort Mann.

Ref: *The Weekly Tribune*, Liberty, Mo., September 1, 1848 (from the *Frontier Journal*, Weston, Mo.). The size and character of his party is not stated.

❡ August 28.—The Osages' subagent, John M. Richardson, forwarding (for Indian department approval) a trading license he had issued to Elias Brevoort, stated that Brevoort "heretofore had been a clerk for the Messrs. [W. G. and G. W.] Ewing."

Ref: OIA, Letters Received from Osage Subagency (National Archives Microcopy 234, Roll 633). The Osage Subagency was *not* in the St. Louis superintendency.

❡ September 9.—The Pottawatomie Catholic mission named St. Mary's, north of Kansas river, was founded with the arrival at the site (where St. Mary's College, St. Marys, Kan., later was built) of Fathers Felix L. Verreydt (superior) and Maurice Gailland, four Ladies of the Sacred Heart (headed by Mother Lucille Mathevon), a lay brother, Charlot (an Indian boy), and Joseph Bertrand (as guide). On the grounds were two half-finished log houses—alike in dimensions. The west building, assigned to the nuns, had two stories and five rooms.

The site had been selected in June (*see* January entry, p. 732) by Father Verreydt. On August 16 his party had left old Sugar Creek mission (in present Linn county—*see* p. 364) en route to St. Mary's; had spent from August 19 to September 7 at Father Hoecken's mission station (*see* January entry, p. 731); and then set out again on the 7th. Father Gailland's diary records that they were "delayed a whole day" at "the trading post" (Union Town), because of a rise in the Kansas river; but, on the 9th, forded the stream "some in wagons, others on horseback"; and arrived, in the afternoon, at St. Mary's Mission.

Some events during the rest of the year: Brother Mazzella arrived (from Sugar Creek) on September 26; at St. Louis, on October 4, an Indian department contract was signed, providing financial assistance for operation of the boarding school; Father Christian Hoecken (from the station south of Kansas river) removed to St. Mary's on October 12; a small temporary chapel was erected, and first used on November 12; between November 25 and December 11 five male boarding students were taken in, also about the same number of girls, in the same period.

Ref: *The Dial*, St. Mary's College, v. 2 (February, 1891), pp. 85-88; *KHQ*, v. 20, pp. 501-510; Garraghan, *op. cit.*, v. 2, pp. 594-612; Augustin C. Wand, *op. cit.*, pp. 12-15.

❡ September 10.—Two of Oregon's newly appointed territorial officials—Joseph Lane, governor, and Joseph L. Meek, U. S. marshal—set out, overland, from Fort Leavenworth, to travel by way of Santa Fe, other southern trails, and California, to their destination. (*See, also,* May 11 and August 14 entries.)

Escorted by Lt. George W. Hawkins and 24(?) men of Company C, U. S. Mounted riflemen, their party also included Doctor Hayden (of the military detachment), Lane's eldest son, Nathaniel, a guide (or guides), teamsters (for the 10? wagons), and servants—a company of perhaps 50(?) in all.

On the 14th Lane, Meek, and party were at Willow Springs (present Douglas county); about the 16th, at Council Grove, the eastbound Francis X. Aubry met them; on the 22d they were at the "Big Bend of Arkansas"—where troops returning from Mexican War service encountered them. It was probably on the 23d, between Great Bend and Pawnee Fork, that two Mexican War generals (U. S. volunteers) met on the Santa Fe trail—the Oregon-bound ex-Bvt. Maj. Gen. Joseph Lane, and Missouri-bound Brig. Gen. Sterling Price.

The Lane-Meek party entered Santa Fe on October 18; remained about four days; set out (with pack horses) to take the Gila route to California. Subsequently, on March 2, 1849, just two days before President Polk's term of office expired, Lane and Meek reached Oregon City; and on March 3 (having been sworn in as governor) Lane proclaimed the establishment of Oregon's territorial government.

Ref: Saint Louis *Daily Union*, September 2, 10, 16, 19, 1848; New York *Weekly Tribune*, September 30, October 7, 1848 (from *Missouri Republican*, St. Louis of September 18 and 23); SIA, St. Louis, "Records," v. 9, typed copy, pp. 204, 205, 215, 216; *The Gazette*, St. Joseph, Mo., December 1, 1848 (from *Missouri Republican* of November 23); H. E. Tobie's *No Man Like Joe*, pp. 180-185; Bancroft, *op. cit.*, v. 1, pp. 777, 778; F. B. Heitman, *Historical Register . . . of the U. S. Army* (1903), for Lane's and Price's military ranks. The *Biography of Joseph Lane*, by "Western" (Washington, 1852), p. 24, says Lane arrived at Fort Leavenworth September 4, and left on the 10th with "22 men including guides &c."

❆ In September(?) "Reed's train from Lexington" crossed "Kansas" bound for Santa Fe. (J. M. White, who left Santa Fe October 18, met Reed's wagons at "Cedar Springs" on the 25th.)

Ref: St. Joseph (Mo.) *Gazette*, December 1, 1848.

❆ Mid-September.—On the Santa Fe trail between Fort Mann and Pawnee Fork these were some of the eastbound travelers swift-riding F. X. Aubry (*see* next entry) passed, about the 14th and 15th, on his journey to Missouri:

Lt. Col. Alton R. Easton's infantry battalion, at the fort; Maj. William W. Reynolds (*see* p. 778) with three companies of Ralls' Third Missouri (mounted) regiment, the Santa Fe battalion (Maj. Robert Walker, commander), Lt. John Love and 25 First U. S. dragoons, "Messrs. Findl[a]y, Allen, and Cary & McCarty [traders]" —all water-bound at "Sand Creek"; Col. John Ralls, and others, water-bound at the "Battle Ground"; Brig. Gen. Sterling Price and his staff, Maj. Israel B. Donalson's division of Illinois volunteers, and "Lt. Cooley" (Khulan) of Gilpin's battalion—all water-bound at Pawnee Fork.

(At Independence, Mo., on September 29, a party just in from Santa Fe reported Pawnee Fork, Walnut, and Coon creeks were "very high" and difficult to cross; and that grass and water, on the Santa Fe trail, were more abundant than "within the recollection of the oldest traders.")

Ref: *The Weekly Tribune*, Liberty, Mo., September 29, 1848; New York *Weekly Tribune*, October 7, 1848.

❆ September 17.—"Skimmer of the Plains" Francis X. Aubry (who had left Santa Fe, N. M., alone, the morning of September 12) rode into Independence, Mo., late at night—having traversed the 780-mile stretch of Santa Fe trail in *five days and 16 hours* (breaking his earlier trip record of eight days and 10 hours—*see* May 28 entry).

Taking the *Bertrand* down the Missouri to St. Charles, thence by buggy, he arrived at St. Louis the night of September 22—in a fraction over 10 days from the New Mexican capital.

Of the 23-year-old Aubry's extraordinary (and never-surpassed) Santa Fe trail ride, the *Missouri Republican* had this to say: "On his way he had to swim every stream, was delayed by the transaction of business at Fort Mann, with his own teams which passed that way, and with the various parties of troops; and beside breaking down six horses and walking 20 miles on foot, he made the trip, traveling time only counted, in about four days and a half! During this time, he slept two and a half hours and ate only six meals. It rained upon him 24 consecutive hours, and nearly 600 miles of the distance was performed in the mud, and yet, what is strange, the rain did not reach Council Grove. . . . We learn from Mr. A. that he made some portion of the trip between Santa Fe and Independence at the rate of 190 miles to the 24 hours. He had no one to accompany him."

Ref: New York *Weekly Tribune,* October 7, 1848 (from *Missouri Republican,* St. Louis); *The Daily Reveille,* St. Louis, September 24, 1848; *The Pacific Historian,* v. 5 (August, 1961), p. 114; *Missouri Republican,* September 11, 1854 (typed copy of article from, in KHi library); *The Weekly Tribune,* Liberty, Mo., September 29, 1848, published the Independence *Expositor's* account of Aubry's ride—an account which states Aubry arrived at Independence "on the 18th before daylight." Joseph Tassé's *Les Canadiens de l'Ouest* (Montreal, 1878), v. 2, p. 180, gives Aubry's birth date as December 4, 1824.

❡ September 21.—Arrivals at Fort Leavenworth this day: Capt. Charles F. Ruff (whose company of U. S. Mounted riflemen—traveling overland—reached the post on the 26th or 27th), and a company (two officers; 50 men) of the Sixth U. S. infantry, aboard the *Highland Mary,* from Jefferson Barracks, Mo. (For Ruff, *see, also,* October 15 annals entry.)

Ref: Saint Louis *Daily Union,* September 30, 1848 (from the *Frontier Journal,* Weston, Mo., September 23); *The Weekly Tribune,* Liberty, Mo., September 29, 1848; 31st Cong., 1st Sess., *Sen. Ex. Doc. No. 26* (Serial 554), p. 11 (September 15 contract).

❡ September.—Missionaries S. M. Irvin and William Hamilton reported they had printed more than 30,000 pages, during the year, on the "Iowa and Sac Mission" press—the principal work being a "small grammar of the Iowa language."

Ref: Comm'r of Indian Affairs, *Report,* 1848; annals, p. 470 (for other information on the press, and on the grammar of 1848).

❡ September 25.—Western Academy—the first high school in "Kansas"—opened at Shawnee Methodist Mission (present Johnson county).

Sup't Thomas Johnson's advertisement (of August 17) had announced the plan to open this school "of high order" (for "both males and females") at "Ft. Leavenworth Indian Manual Training School." The Rev. Nathan Scarritt, A. M. (27 years of age; recently head of the male department, Howard High School, Fayette, Mo.), hired as principal, served till the summer of 1851.

Writing from "Ind M L School & Western Academy," on February 11, 1849, Allen T. Ward stated: "Our High School . . . has gone on prosperously, & we have as many students as we can accommodate; this high school . . . is for both white & red. . . ." (For a modest tuition, young people from western Missouri, could [and a number did] take the course of instruction ["all the branches of a complete English education together with the Latin and Greek languages"—as advertised].)

Ref: *The Annals of Kansas City*, Kansas City, Mo., v. 1 (October, 1924), pp. 434-445 (article on Nathan Scarritt); Allen T. Ward's letter in *KHQ*, v. 33, p. 359; Martha B. Caldwell, comp., *Annals of Shawnee Methodist Mission* . . . (1939), pp. 61, 62, 67, 72.

❡ September 28.—A party arriving at Independence, Mo., from Santa Fe, included "Mr. [James H.] Bullard, of Bullard, Russell, & Co.," and a member of Lt. Col. Alton R. Easton's battalion.

Lt. John Love, Company B, First U. S. dragoons (and 25 men?), who "passed up to Fort Leavenworth" the same day, perhaps reached the border with the above party.

Ref: Saint Louis *Daily Union*, October 10, 1848.

❡ September.—At Shawnee Baptist Mission (present Johnson county), a "neat and commodious" frame church (28 by 40 feet, with a belfry), erected during the summer by the Indians, was dedicated. Missionary Francis Barker reported the building was well constructed, of good materials.

Ref: *The Baptist Missionary Magazine*, v. 29 (July, 1849), p. 269; Comm'r of Indian Affairs, *Report*, 1848 (Barker's report, therein).

❡ September-October.—Mexican War volunteer troops from Missouri, and Illinois, homeward-bound by way of the Santa Fe trail (*down* which they had marched in 1846, 1847, or 1848), crossed "Kansas"; began to arrive at the Missouri border (Fort Leavenworth for the Illinois men; Independence for the Missourians) about September 18; and continued coming in, at intervals, up through October 6.

AT FORT LEAVENWORTH:

Between September 20 and October 1 there arrived the "First" regiment, Illinois infantry volunteers—Col. Edward W. B. Newby (and escort of 23? men) on the 20th; Maj. Israel B. Donalson (with the third and last detachment) at the end of the month. Newby had left Santa Fe about August 15. He and his troops traveled the Santa Fe trail without special incident; except that Major Donalson's command was detained at rain-swollen Pawnee Fork, in mid-September.

Via Missouri river steamboats, and between September 22 and October 10, the Illinois veterans reached Alton, Ill., where they were paid and mustered out of service. The St. Louis *Union* of September 25 noted the arrival of Lt. Col. Henderson P. Boyakin, Dr. R. N. Handley (regimental surgeon), Maj. N[oah] Johns[t]on (U. S. paymaster), and his clerk, T. J. Bradley, on the *Plough Boy*; the St. Louis *Reveille* of the 29th reported the arrival of Colonel Newby (and others) on the *Highland Mary*. The *Tamerlane, Cora, St. Joseph, Plough Boy* (a second trip), and *Eliza Stewart*, also took aboard Illinois troops at Fort Leavenworth and carried them downriver. (The *Plough Boy's* military passengers, Companies I and K, reached Alton aboard the *Amelia*, which picked them up after the *Plough Boy* "snagged" and sank above Portland, Mo., on

October 6.) Major Donalson (with six officers and 132 men), on the *Eliza Stewart,* reached Alton, Ill., about October 9.

AT INDEPENDENCE, MO.:

Between September 18(?) and October 7 there arrived the Missouri volunteers—troops of three battalions (Gilpin's, Easton's, and the Santa Fe battalion), one regiment (Ralls' Third Missouri), and some unassigned recruits. Apparently it was well into November before all had been mustered out (by Col. Ethan A. Hitchcock) and paid off (by Maj. Thomas S. Bryant).

First to be mustered out were Griffin's, Jones', and Holzscheiter's companies of "Gilpin's battalion" from Fort Mann. (The rest of Gilpin's men were discharged on September 30 and October 2, followed on the 3d by the lieutenant colonel, his "field and staff.")

On September 29 Brig. Gen. Sterling Price (who had left Santa Fe about August 26) reached town, accompanied by Capt. William M. D. McKissack, U. S. A., Capt. Amos F. Garrison, U. S. V., Maj. Charles Bodine (paymaster), Lt. William E. Prince, U. S. A. (Price's aid-de-camp), Lt. Alexander B. Dyer (army ordnance); and escorted by Lt. William B. Royall, U. S. V. (and his recruits—*see* below, and *see* June 5-20 entry).

Lt. Col. Alton R. Easton "with his entire[?] command [infantry battalion]" arrived on October 3 and camped near town. (Also encamped "in the suburbs" were "Lts. Royall and Allen and their detachments of recruits" who had been to New Mexico and back without having been assigned to companies.) On October 4 Captains Shepard, Barnes, and Cunningham of Easton's battalion reached town; also Captain McNair of Ralls' regiment, three lieutenants named Allen (James, Abraham, Charles), and other officers. On October 6 the townspeople witnessed "the return of the brave Missouri boys under Colonel Ralls [the Third regiment, Missouri mounted volunteers]"; and on the 7th, the Santa Fe battalion, commanded by Maj. [Robert] Walker arrived; but encamped at Wayne City, three miles away, on the Missouri river.

At St. Louis, the *Reveille* of November 1 noted the arrival (on October 31) of 78 officers and men of the Third (Ralls') regiment, from Wayne City, on the *Mary Blane.* About 100 Third regiment men were aboard the *Alexander Hamilton* which reached St. Louis November 7. (Probably these were among the last of the troops to return home.)

Ref: ILLINOIS TROOPS—Saint Louis *Daily Union,* September 25, 26, 30, October 4, 6, 10, 1848; *The Daily Reveille,* St. Louis, September 29, October 10; New York *Weekly Tribune,* September 30, October 7, 1848 (from *Missouri Republican,* St. Louis); 31st Cong., 1st Sess., *Sen. Ex. Doc. No. 26* (Serial 554), p. 21. MISSOURI TROOPS—Saint Louis *Daily Union,* September 18, 22, 25, October 9, 10, 17, 24, 1848; *The Daily Reveille,* St. Louis, October 6, 10, 11, 17, November 1, 8, 1848; *The Weekly Tribune,* Liberty, Mo., September 29, 1848; W. E. Connelley's *Doniphan's Expedition* (1907), pp. 149, 150 (for data on Gilpin's battalion); New York *Weekly Tribune,* October 7, 1848.

℄ DIED: Maj. William W. Reynolds, of the Third ("Ralls'") regiment, Missouri volunteers, in October (or September?), at Fort Mann, of a fever, while returning home from Santa Fe with his command. He was an Osage county, Mo., resident.

Ref: *The Daily Reveille,* St. Louis, October 11, 1848 (quoted an Independence, Mo., letter of October 5, which stated Reynolds had been left "quite sick" at Fort Mann (according to just-arrived troops); *ibid.,* November 9, 1848 (quoted the Independence *Expositor* of October 28th to the effect that this "gallant young officer," a "nephew of the late Gov. [Thomas] Reynolds [of Missouri]," had died "recently" of fever at Fort Mann; C. R. Barns' *The Commonwealth of Missouri* (St. Louis, 1877), p. 263 (says Reynolds died "in October, 1848, at Fort Mann . . ."). *See, also,* annals, pp. 692, 698.

❡ October.—At Wea Baptist Mission (present Miami county), according to the American Indian Mission Association's annual report, "a new and commodious school and meeting house" had been erected during the year; the boarding-school session had ended with 32 pupils; and the mission farm (enlarged by 16 acres) had produced a good corn crop.

In November, Sup't T. H. Harvey, St. Louis, wrote: "This little school & mission, I am persuaded, is doing much good."

Ref: AIMA *Proceedings,* 1848, pp. 20, 21; SIA, St. Louis, "Records," v. 9, typed copy, p. 245. For brief history of Wea mission *see* annals, p. 532. The Rev. David Lykins, his wife Abigail (Webster) Lykins, and Sarah Ann Osgood (teacher) were the missionaries in 1848.

❡ October 2.—Kit Carson (at Independence, Mo., on September 29) was reported to be leaving "on Monday" (the 2d) from the town of Kansas, Mo., for "the Far West."

By his own (later) statement he reached New Mexico (his destination Taos) in October. Eastbound J. M. White met him at "Whetstone" on October 24. About November 1 he was at Santa Fe.

Ref: *The Daily Reveille,* St. Louis, October 10, 1848; *The Gazette,* St. Joseph, Mo., December 1, 1948 (from *Missouri Republican,* St. Louis, November 23); New York *Weekly Tribune,* February 24 and March 3, 1849 (from telegraph news, and *Missouri Republican,* February 13).

❡ October.—"Mr. Newman" (mail carrier), who probably left the Missouri border early in the month, reached Santa Fe on the 29th. Hugh N. Smith (New Mexico's district attorney), evidently was in the express party since he, too, was an October 29 arrivee.

(In November—on the 20th—he set out again, eastbound, with a mail for the States, but "was compelled to return, after reaching the Cimerone [Cimarron], on account of the depth of snow, and the coldness of the weather.")

Ref: New York *Weekly Tribune,* March 3, 1849 (from *Missouri Republican,* St. Louis, February 13); Saint Louis *Daily Union,* February 15, 1849.

❡ October.—Items and stories of gold discoveries in California began to appear in western Missouri newspapers.

The Liberty *Tribune,* October 6, reprinted a New Orleans *Picayune* story on the arrival of Navy Lt. Edward F. Beale at Mexico City, August 17 (en route from the West Coast to Washington, D. C., with dispatches), bringing news of gold finds in "Upper California." The same paper, on October 13, carried an account of B. F. Chouteau's arrival at Santa Fe from California (left July 4), with a report that a man had found two pieces of virgin gold near San Francisco, worth $2,000.

The St. Joseph *Gazette,* about October 20(?), reprinted a "gold" article from the New York *Sun;* and on October 27, quoted the Washington *Union* in stating: "An immense bed of gold, 100 miles in extent, has been discovered in California. . . ."

Ref: *The Weekly Tribune*, Liberty, Mo., October 6, 13, 1848; *The History of Buchanan County, Missouri* (St. Joseph, 1881), p. 201; St. Joseph (Mo.) *Gazette*, October 27, November 24, 1848; New York *Weekly Tribune*, September 30, 1848 (has Washington *Union* story, September 19, 1848, re Beale's reaching Mexico City on August 17 and arriving at Washington, D. C., on September 16). B. F. Chouteau's government mail contract, March 5, 1848 (Santa Fe to California, and back) is listed in 31st Cong., 1st Sess., *Sen. Ex. Doc. No. 26* (Serial 554), p. 12.

❰ October 8.—At Fort Leavenworth, Capt. L. C. Easton, AQM, arranged for the *Sacramento* (William Atkinson, master) to transport two companies of First U. S. infantry (one from the fort, the other from "Kanzas"—Kansas City, Mo.) to Jefferson Barracks, Mo.

Ref: 31st Cong., 1st Sess., *Sen. Ex. Doc. No. 26* (Serial 554), p. 10.

❰ October 8.—Heading for Santa Fe with a large stock of merchandise—his third trip of the year to New Mexico—Francis X. Aubry set out from Independence, Mo., this day.

He was at Cow creek (present Rice county) on October 21 (and got word there, of an Apache attack [near Las Vegas, N. M.] on October 13, in which the raiders had run off 240 government animals, and some of Aubry's mules; also killed stockherder Williams). Eastbound J. M. White, about October 27 met "F. X. Aubry and [ex] Captain [William Z.] Angney . . . at the Lower Cimarron Springs going on well." (Aubry was hastening on, in advance of his wagons, to Santa Fe, to obtain forage and extra animals. When he set out, *from* Santa Fe, in December, with 15 men, to meet his train, he got as far as the "Red" river vicinity, then was forced to turn back when seven men deserted. Aubry's goods eventually reached Santa Fe, but he lost around 150 mules altogether—some by severe weather, the rest stolen by Indians.

Ref: *The Weekly Tribune*, Liberty, Mo., November 24, 1848; New York *Weekly Tribune*, October 28, December 2, 1848, April 14, 1849 (all from St. Louis newspapers); *The Daily Reveille*, St. Louis, October 17, 1848; St. Joseph (Mo.) *Gazette*, December 1, 1848 (from *Missouri Republican*, St. Louis, November 23). Summarizing Aubry's Santa Fe trail activities in 1848: He arrived at Independence (from Santa Fe) on January 5; left Independence (with wagons) in mid-March; returned to Independence (after fast ride) May 28; left Independence (with wagons) late June or early July; returned to Independence (after swiftest ride) September 17; left Independence (with wagons) October 8.
The Daily Reveille of August 8, 1848, reported "Capt. Angney of Cole County" had just arrived in St. Louis *from* Santa Fe.

❰ October.—Spruce M. Baird (appointed in May, by Texas governor George T. Wood, as judge of newly created Santa Fe county— an area east of the Rio Grande, now in New Mexico, to which Texas laid claim) crossed "Kansas" this month, arriving at Santa Fe on November 10. His mission was to establish Texan jurisdiction over the county.

Ref: *New Spain and the Anglo-American West* (Los Angeles, 1932), v. 2, pp. 157-183; W. C. Binkley's *The Expansionist Movement in Texas 1836-1850* (1925), pp. 160-164; St. Joseph (Mo.) *Gazette*, February 23, 1849; W. P. Webb, editor-in-chief, *The Handbook of Texas* (1952), v. 1, p. 97; 31st Cong., 1st Sess., *Sen. Ex. Doc. No. 24* (Serial 554). Baird left Texas in late May, 1848, and went to New Mexico by way of St. Louis, Mo. Possibly he traveled the Santa Fe trail with Aubry—*see* October 8 annals entry. A letter dated "Santa Fe, N. M., Dec. 2, 1848," states: "A few weeks since, the Judge sent from Texas to preside over her *Eleventh Judicial District*, arrived in town with his sheriff and other dignitaries, for the purpose of claiming jurisdiction over the whole of New Mexico, established by an act of Texas legislation, into 'the county of Santa Fé, Texas.' "—New York *Daily Tribune*, March 12, 1849.

¶ October 10-17.—A "Great Council" of Indian tribes residing in "Kansas" was held near Fort Leavenworth, on the Delawares' reserve. Present were representatives of immigrant nations long linked in confederacy—the Wyandots, Delawares, Shawnees, Pottawatomies, Ottawas, Chippewas, Miamis, Weas, and Peorias; also the Sacs & Foxes (who left in the midst of proceedings, following a speech reciting incidents in their ancient war with the Wyandots), the Kickapoos, and the Kansa. (Not present, and probably not invited: the Osages.)

Wyandot delegates, arriving the evening of the 10th, found the "Delawares, Shawnees, Miamis, Peoris, Kanzas, Sacs and Foxes already on the ground, and the Kanzas camp in a bustle, making preparations for a grand dance." Subagent Richard Hewitt (a visitor in midweek) was impressed by the panorama— the "grandeur of Indian costume . . . the social and friendly feeling exhibited amongst the people there congregated, the enjoyment of the dance, and the great numbers engaged in them, contrasted with the sober and staid countenances of the older chiefs, the harmless countenance and the musical voice of the females present. . . ."

The journal of this Indian congress (which met daily from the 11th through the 17th) later was lost. But it is recorded that "all the former arrangements of the league were solemnly renewed"; that the Kickapoos and Kansa joined (by invitation) and "agreed to incur the responsibilities and abide by the regulations and joint acts of the league." (The renewal of "former arrangements" confirmed the position of the Wyandots as "keepers of the Council-fire of the Northwestern Confederacy.")

Ref: W. E. Connelley, *The Provisional Government of Nebraska Territory* . . . pp. 4, 62, 63, 265, 266; Comm'r of Indian Affairs, *Report* for 1848 (Richard Hewitt's report, therein); *KHC*, v. 6, p. 104; Andrew, *op. cit.*, p. 146 (Bishop Andrew, on October 18, a few miles below Fort Leavenworth, "met a party of Indians, mostly Kickapoos, returning from a council, composed of leading men from a number of surrounding tribes, who had met in the Delaware nation, for the purpose of consulting upon the best measures for promoting peace and good neighborhood among themselves. . . .")

¶ October.—Ceran St. Vrain (with a train of wagons?), accompanied by Thomas Fitzpatrick, traveled the Santa Fe trail, westbound, across "Kansas" this month. On November 1, at the Arkansas Crossing, eastbound trader J. M. White met St. Vrain and the Indian agent.

Fitzpatrick, a few days later, stopped at the Big Timbers to council with "about 600 lodges of . . . Apaches, Cumanches, Kiowas and Arapahoes." Fremont's party, reaching that area about November 11(?), found Fitzpatrick "holding a talk with . . . [the Indians] making a feast, and giving small

presents." Fremont further says: "We were three or four days among them.—
The number of their lodges would indicate about 6,000." (*See, also,* October
20 entry.)

Ref: St. Joseph (Mo.) *Gazette,* December 1, 1848 (from *Missouri Republican* of November 23), for J. M. White; Comm'r of Indian Affairs, *Report,* 1848 [Fitzpatrick's October 6, 1848, report therein says: "I will leave here (St. Louis) in two days for Bent's Fort, on the Arkansas river . . ."]; Blanche C. Grant's *When Old Trails Were New* (New York, 1934), pp. 123, 127; New York *Weekly Tribune,* March 10, 1849 (for Fremont's November 17, 1848, letter).

❆ October 15.—Capt. Charles F. Ruff, with Companies C and I,
U. S. Mounted riflemen, left Fort Leavenworth for "Fort Childs"
(new Fort Kearny—*see* June annals entry, p. 755). His command
(127 men) reached the head of Grand Island in just 12 days; and
there relieved the small "Oregon battalion" detachment (18 or 20
men) left in charge.

Ref: Nebraska State Historical Society *Publications,* v. 20, pp. 185, 189; *Missouri Historical Review,* Columbia, v. 24 (April, 1930), pp. 359-364 (for L. B. Dougherty's recollections of the winter of 1848-1849 at Fort Kearny); *The Weekly Tribune,* Liberty, Mo., January 19, 1849. The Liberty paper, in its issue of November 3, 1848, published a biographical article on Charles F. Ruff.

❆ October 17.—At Fort Leavenworth, Francis C. Hughes signed
a contract (Capt. Langdon C. Easton, AQM, negotiator) to "take
charge of and winter" 3,862 oxen, 2,062 mules, and 195 horses,
for the rate of 86½ cents each per month. Sureties for his $100,000
bond were George B. Sanderson, Benjamin Holladay, "J." F. (*i. e.,*
Theodore F.) Warner, and David Hughes.

Ref: 31st Cong., 1st Sess., *Sen. Ex. Doc. No. 26* (Serial 554), p. 13.

❆ October 18-23.—Bishop James O. Andrew, M. E. Church, South,
spent upwards of five days in "Kansas," after attending a conference
at Weston, Mo., in mid-October.

On the 18th (in a carriage, with "Brother [B. H.] Russel," and a driver)
the bishop crossed the Missouri below Weston; rode some three miles to (and
on past) Fort Leavenworth (where there were "hundreds of wagons" and a
large number of the "poorest" mules he had ever seen); late in the day arrived
at the Delaware Methodist Mission (the Rev. Nathan T. Shaler, in charge);
preached (with James Ketchum as interpreter) at the Delawares' church (half
a mile distant) that night. On the 19th Bishop Andrew continued his tour—
riding four miles to the Kansas river ferry ("jointly owned" by the Delawares
and Shawnees). South of the river, en route to Shawnee Mission, he passed
the "Quaker establishment" with its "very neat and prosperous looking farm";
also the "church and camp ground" of the Shawnees. At the "Manual Labor
School" (reached around noon) he was greeted by the Rev. Thomas Johnson
(who had returned as superintendent in the fall of 1847).

Bishop Andrew spent two days at Shawnee Mission—an institution so
diverse in its operations as to give "the air of a clever, thriving village"; and
its over-500-acre farm "one of the most extensive, and well-managed" the

bishop had ever seen. On the evening of the 21st Andrew journeyed some eight miles to the Wyandot Mission—going by way of Westport, and Kansas, Mo., then by the Wyandots' Kansas river ferry, to reach his destination. On the 22d (Sunday) he preached at the Indians' church; afterwards returned to Shawnee; and departed "Kansas" on October 23.

Ref: Andrew, *op. cit.*, pp. 137-170; William Walker's "Journals" (*loc. cit.*), entries of October 21 and 22, 1848.

❮ October 20.—From "Boone Creek" camp (about three miles from Westport, Mo.), John C. Fremont (now a civilian) and the men of his fourth West-exploring expedition (privately financed) traveled some five miles to "Mission Creek." On the 21st his mounted party (with pack mules) moved westward 14 miles to "Mill Creek." (It was this day that Bishop James O. Andrew—inspecting Shawnee Methodist Mission—saw "a company of men [Fremont's] singularly equipped, passing just below the mill.") On October 22, after a 22-mile march, camp was made "near the Wakerloos [Wakarusa]." Here, Jim Secundi (Secondine) and several other Delawares (as guides out to the Smoky Hill) joined the party.

Fremont was now bound for the Pacific by a path (across the mountains) south of all his former routes—in search of a way practicable for a railroad; and he planned to "seek a (believed) pass between 37 and 38 [degrees] in the Sierra Nevada"—Fremont's statement. The explorer and "35 young and athletic men," had arrived at Kansas, Mo., on October 8—after setting out from St. Louis on the 3d aboard the *Martha*. (Jessie Benton Fremont, and an infant son who died on the way upriver, were also on the steamboat. Mrs. Fremont was a guest at R. W. Cummins' Fort Leavenworth Agency house when her husband set out for the West.) The expedition members included Alexis Godey, Edward M. Kern (artist), Charles Preuss (topographer), Charles Taplin, Henry King, Raphael Proue, Henry J. (or Marion) Wise, Thomas E. Brackenridge, and several more who had served with Fremont before. Two other Kern brothers—Richard H. (artist) and Dr. Benjamin J. (physician), were in the party; also Frederick Creutzfeldt (botanist), and Capt. Andrew Cathcart (adventurer; formerly of the British army).

On October 23 Fremont and his men passed "a small trading town of the Pottawattomie nation, built in a small hallow"; and during the 25-mile day's journey traveled with prairie fires "blazing in all directions" around them. After a march of some 28 miles on the 24th they "camped at the old Pota [*i. e.,* Kansa] Mission composed of 3 or four log houses now occupied by a Mr. Monday [Isaac Mundy], blacksmith to the [Pottawatomie] nation   about 1½ [*i. e.,* 4½] miles from here is their [Union Town] trading post."—Edward M. Kern's diary.

On the 28th Richard H. Kern (in his diary) noted "one of the

Smoky Hills . . . looming-up blue and far off [to the right]"; and he sketched "Buttes [off to the left] in the direction of Council Grove." The company crossed the Smoky Hill (near present Salina) on October 29; saw buffalo for the first time; traversed an immense, level, grass-covered plain (with "Smoky Hill Buttes . . . far off and solitary"), then came to a "more hilly and rugged" country. (On the 30th Richard Kern recorded descriptions of rock masses "singular in shape.")

On October 31 they arrived, again, at the Smoky Hill (presumably in present Russell county); proceeded up the right bank on November 1; crossed, on the 2d (in Ellis county?) "near a very bald high & perpendicular bluff" (and near what had been the Pawnees' summer camp while buffalo hunting); headed (southwesterly?) toward the Arkansas; on the 7th reached it (having endured some wintry weather in the intervening days). Richard Kern wrote on November 8: "Our object today was to reach Choteaux Island supposed to be about 25 miles off." But they traveled 52 miles before camping (and crossed the icy Arkansas to the shelter of some cottonwoods). About November 12 the exploring party arrived (and remained three? days) at the Big Timbers, where Agent Thomas Fitzpatrick was holding councils with some 6,000 Indians (Apaches, Comanches, Kiowas, and Arapahoes—according to Fremont).

After reaching Bent's Fort, November 16, Fremont wrote (on the 17th) of his route across "Kansas":

"I followed the line of the southern Kanzas, (the true Kanzas River) [i. e., the Smoky Hill]. . . . We find that the valley of the Kanzas affords by far the most eligible approach to the mountains. The whole valley soil is of a very superior quality, and the route very direct, (between thirty-eight and thirty-nine degrees). This line would afford continuous and good settlements certainly for four hundred miles, and is therefore worthy of consideration in any plan of approach [for a railroad!] to the mountains."

From Bent's Fort Fremont and his party (33 men; about 100 horses and mules) continued upriver to Pueblo (where "Old Bill" Williams was hired as guide); and then on to the uppermost settlement—Pueblo San Carlos, where final preparations were made. Lancaster P. Lupton (writing from Pueblo on November 28) stated: "On the 26th Col. Fremont commenced the ascent of the Snowy Mountains."

The fourth expedition came to disaster before reaching the continental divide. (That story is not related here.) Ten of Fremont's men died, during January, 1849, in the mountains, from starvation or freezing. Fremont lost his entire outfit; but went on to California (by already established routes) leaving many of his men behind.

Ref: New York *Weekly Tribune*, October 21, 1848, March 3, 10, 31, April 7, 14, 21, 1849 (for a quantity of information—news reports, letters, etc.); L. R. and Ann W. Hafen, *Fremont's Fourth Expedition* . . . (Glendale, Calif., 1960) for the documentary material (diaries of the three Kern brothers; narratives, etc.); Blanche C. Grant, *When Old Trails Were New* . . ., pp. 119-127 (has Richard H. Kern's diary, also); Andrew, *op. cit.*, pp. 154, 155; Allan Nevins' *Frémont, Pathmarker of the West* (New York, 1939), especially pp. 348, 349, and 627-629 (for Edward M. Kern's February 11, 1849, letter to Antoine Robidoux—reprinted from the St. Joseph [Mo.] *Gazette* of April 13, 1849); Charles Preuss, *Exploring With Frémont* . . . (Norman, Okla., c1958), pp. xii, 143; Alpheus H. Favour's *Old Bill Williams* . . ., reprint ed. (Norman, Okla., c1962), pp. 173-204. For Frémont's earlier expeditions, *see* annals index, and map, for the routes of 1842, and 1843-1844.

❡ October 22.—David Waldo, trader, arrived at Independence, Mo., "in about 11 days" from Santa Fe.

Ref: *The Weekly Tribune*, Liberty, Mo., November 10, 1848 (which also stated that Doctor Waldo had "left Col. Washington's command about a day's march from Santa Fe." W. A. Keleher in his *Turmoil in New Mexico* . . ., pp. 36, 37, notes that Bvt. Lt. Col. John M. Washington (newly appointed military commander and provisional governor for New Mexico) had left Monterey, Mexico, July 28 and [by way of Chihuahua? where Waldo joined him?] arrived at Santa Fe on October 10, 1848.

❡ October 22.—The ferry boat at Rialto, Mo. (a mile below Weston, and not far above Fort Leavenworth—*see* Hutawa's map), in crossing the Missouri with nine men and six horses, struck a snag in midstream, and sank. All aboard were saved. The passengers included Lt. Col. Ludwell E. Powell, Capt. Andrew W. Sublette, and two lieutenants of the "Oregon" battalion, also Francis C. Hughes.

Ref: *The Daily Reveille*, St. Louis, November 4, 1848.

❡ DIED: Gen. Stephen Watts Kearny, on October 31, at the residence of M. Lewis Clark, in St. Louis.

Ref: *The Daily Reveille*, St. Louis, November 1, 1848; Dwight L. Clarke's *Stephen Watts Kearny* (Norman, Okla. c1961), pp. 387, 388. See a portrait of Kearny on p. 406 of this volume, and *see* index for his connections with "Kansas" history.

❡ November 3.—The St. Joseph (Mo.) *Gazette* noted that "Mr. [Miles] Goodyear [*see* pp. 305, 562], with a party of 10 persons [one of them his brother Andrew], recently [had] arrived in . . . town from California and the Rocky Mountains via South Pass, bringing with them 120 horses, and several packs of peltries."

Goodyear had left southern California (where he purchased the animals driven East) in April. (Earlier, he had sold his post "Fort Buenaventura"— where Ogden, Utah, is now.) Finding no market for his horses at Fort Leavenworth, or at St. Joseph, Miles Goodyear (and Andrew) spent the winter of 1848-1849 in the States; and in 1849 took his band of horses (and some mules) back West—to Salt Lake City, and on to California, where there were willing buyers among the gold seekers.

Ref: St. Joseph (Mo.) *Gazette*, November 3, 1848, February 16, April 13 (adv.), 27, 1849; Charles Kelly and M. L. Howe's *Miles Goodyear* . . . (Salt Lake City, 1937), pp. 101-109.

❡ November 16.—Lt. Antoine Lefevre (Lefaivre?), and a small "Oregon battalion" detachment (18 to 20 men?), arrived at Fort

Leavenworth, from "Fort Childs" (new Fort Kearny) on the Platte. They were mustered out and paid—the last of Lt. Col. Ludwell E. Powell's Missouri volunteers battalion to be discharged. (The rest of the troops had been released the preceding week.)

See, also, June annals entry on founding of new Fort Kearny, and October 15 entry.

Ref: Nebraska State Historical Society *Publications*, v. 20, pp. 185, 189. In W. H. Robarts' *Mexican War Veterans* . . . (1887), p. 63, the lieutenant's name is spelled "Antoine Lefevre." A newspaper account gave his name as "Ant. Lefaivre."

(Mid-November.—Passengers boarding the *Highland Mary* at Fort Leavenworth included Father Pierre-Jean De Smet, Jesuit missionary, Col. Ethan A. Hitchcock, U. S. A., and (Lt. Col.) Ludwell E. Powell (also some officers and men of his mustered-out-of-service "Oregon battalion"). The steamboat reached St. Louis prior to November 18.

Father De Smet had gone up the Missouri in August—by steamboat to the Council Bluffs; thence overland to Fort Pierre. His tour of Indian tribes (particularly the Sioux) had ended in October. Coming downriver he traveled part way by skiff, then by horse and wagon to St. Joseph, Mo. The *Highland Mary* had left there prior to his arrival, but De Smet (on horseback?) overtook her at the fort.

Ref: H. M. Chittenden and A. T. Richardson, eds., *Life, Letters and Travels of Father Pierre-Jean De Smet, S. J.* . . . (New York, 1905), v. 2, pp. 613, 614, 617, 635-637; Saint Louis *Daily Union*, November 18, 1848.

(November.—James M. White (who had left Santa Fe on October 18), reached the Missouri border in mid-November, and St. Louis on the 23d. He brought to the States $58,000 in gold and silver coins and bullion.

His party (size not indicated) had experienced some severe storms en route, and cold weather most of the way.

Ref: *The Gazette*, St. Joseph, Mo., December 1, 1848 (from *Missouri Republican*, St. Louis, November 23).

(November.—Bvt. Maj. Philip R. Thompson and his company of First U. S. dragoons (61 men), on November 6, began a march across Missouri, from St. Louis (or Jefferson Barracks?), to Fort Scott where they would form part (about half?) the garrison. *See, also,* December 2 annals entry.

Ref: *The Daily Reveille*, St. Louis, Mo., November 7, 1848.

(Mid-November.—Lt. Edward F. Beale, U. S. N. (courier, overland, from Washington, D. C., to military officials in New Mexico and California), departed Fort Leavenworth for Santa Fe with (as later described) "seventeen mounted men, all raw recruits and a few adventurers." One of the "adventurers" was Andrew W. Sublette—recently a captain in the "Oregon battalion."

(For Beale's summer journey from the West Coast to Washington, D. C., *see* October annals entry, p. 779. He started the above trip, from Washington, in mid-October; reached Fort Leavenworth, from St. Louis, aboard the *Cora*.)

Beale and his escort were at Council Grove on November 19. (One letter from that trading post, dated the 19th, stated that Beale and Sublette intended to investigate a reported murder on reaching the vicinity of Cottonwood Fork—45 miles west.) By December 3 the party had reached the Big Timbers. Here Beale wrote a letter in which he remarked: "I have had a most unpleasant journey so far, and the men I have with me are so utterly worthless that I anticipate many difficulties. . . . I have had two [potentially serious] affairs with the Indians. . . . The weather here is most cruelly, bitterly cold, it is snowing and freezing. . . ." He also related: "I find here three Americans trading with the Indians. They have built a couple of miserable huts, but appear . . . to be making a very excellent business. There are thousands of Indians here but most of them friendly tribes. . . ."

Continuing up the Arkansas to Bent's Fort, Beale and party arrived 16 days after Fremont [*i. e.*, about December 2] with some men severely frostbitten, and animals in poor condition. Subsequently, Beale and his men reached Santa Fe on December 25, after encountering "all the severities of Winter" in the Raton mountains.

At Santa Fe seven of the party dropped out (but not Sublette, apparently); Beale recruited replacements and left for California in the fore part of January (Fremont says January 9); eventually (after enduring bitter winter weather; and later, intense heat in the desert) reached San Francisco about April 10, 1849.

Ref: New York *Weekly Tribune*, September 30, 1848, March 10, April 14, and June 9, 1849; Saint Louis *Daily Union*, December 12, 1848 (reports on a letter received at Independence, Mo., dated Council Grove, November 19); *The Weekly Tribune*, January 19, 1849; *Jefferson Inquirer*, Jefferson City, Mo., November 4, 1848; Stephen Bonsal's *Edward Fitzgerald Beale* . . . (New York, 1912), pp. 32, 33, 49, 50, 52; Doyce B. Nunis' *Andrew Sublette* (Los Angeles, 1960), pp. 88-90 (quotes from a letter Sublette wrote at Council Grove on November 19, 1848); 31st Cong., 1st Sess., *Sen. Ex. Doc. No. 24* (Serial 554), pp. 4, 7. The dates in the Mobile (Ala.) *Register's* May 23, 1849, story on Beale (reprinted in the *Tribune*, and in Bonsal) are unreliable. For Beale's 1847 journey on the Santa Fe trail (eastbound), *see* annals, p. 682. Beale, in the above references (except in the *Sen. E.x Doc. No. 24*, where he is called "Midshipman," by Lt. Col. John M. Washington) is given the title "Lieutenant." But Thos. H. S. Hamersly's *Complete General Navy Register* . . . (New York, 1888), p. 59, lists Beale as "Passed Midshipman, 1 Jl 1842. Master, 1 Aug 1849. Lieut, 28 Feb 1850."

ℂ November.—The St. Joseph *Gazette* (of Friday, the 24th) reported the arrival ("on Wednesday last") of a small party, overland, from California "bringing with them large quantities of the Feather river gold dust, a portion of which was assayed by a chemist of our town, and pronounced pure gold."

Apparently this was the party of (or including) Jacob Wittmer, who (some accounts state) was dispatched by John Augustus Sutter to escort—in 1849—members of his family (arriving from Switzerland) overland to California. Artist Rudolph F. Kurz (residing at St. Joseph, Mo., in 1848 and 1849) later wrote that he "and many other people as well," had regarded "this much-discussed discovery of gold" as a "make-believe" on the part of the U. S. government to get newly acquired California "quickly populated." "However, when a certain Widmer [Wittmer] arrived here in the autumn [of 1848] having been sent on by Solothurn von Sutter in California to conduct his wife and daughter over the prairie, no one could longer doubt the truth of the reports."

Ref: St. Joseph (Mo.) *Gazette*, Friday, November 24, 1848; Kurz, *op. cit.*, p. 46, E. G. Gudde's *Sutter's Own Story* (New York, 1936), pp. 197, 220, 224 (on p. 224, Sutter, in March, 1849, refers to the anticipated arrival of some of his family from Switzerland); T. J. Schoonover's *The Life and Times of Gen. John A. Sutter*, rev. and enl. ed. (Sacramento, 1907), p. 284, states that "General Sutter paid a man ten dollars a day and expenses to go to Switzerland[?] and bring his family to California." H. H. Bancroft's *California Pioneer Register* . . . reprinted (Baltimore, 1964), p. 387, lists Jacob Wittmer—a Swiss in Sutter's employ. Kurz, noted, in 1849, "Widmer's" return to St. Joseph, "he was now conducting a large company of gold seekers" ("as Sutter's family had taken the route through Panama").

❡ November 22.—At Fort Leavenworth, T. M. Ewing signed a contract (Capt. Langdon C. Easton, AQM, negotiator) to "take charge of and winter" 700 mules for the sum of 74¾ cents each per month. Sureties for his $20,000 bond were W. P. Ewing and E[benezer] W. Pomeroy.

Ref: 31st Cong., 1st Sess., Sen. Ex. Doc. No. 26 (Serial 554), p. 13.

❡ November 30.—At Independence, Mo., a correspondent wrote: "Some few traders and teamsters are arriving occasionally from the Plains. . . . The weather is said to be very severe, beyond Council Grove. Winter set in on the Plains nearly two months ago. . . ."

Ref: Saint Louis *Daily Union*, December 9, 1848.

❡ November-December.—Among the Wyandots, church difficulties (the Methodist Episcopal Church *vs.* the Methodist Episcopal Church, South—or, the abolitionists *vs.* the proslaveryites) headed towards a crisis with (1) the arrival of the Rev. John Thompson Peery (missionary appointee of the Church, South) who moved into the Wyandots' parsonage on November 28; (2) the arrival of the Rev. James Gurley (appointed missionary by Bishop Morris of the Northern church) on December 1.

William Walker (Wyandot) whose sympathies lay with "the Church, South," wrote, on December 1: "So I suppose we are to have religious dissensions in full fruition." On February 6, 1849, Subagent Richard Hewitt reported that since Mr. Gurley's arrival "our church windows are all broken, fights and riots have been frequent at almost every religious meeting"; and stated that he had requested Gurley to leave. (The Wyandots' subagent, soon after, was removed as a result of the action taken.)

Ref: OIA, Letters Received from Wyandot Subagency (National Archives Microcopy 234, Roll 950), letters of November 10, 1848, and February 6, 1849 (by Dr. M. Simpson and Richard Hewitt); SIA, St. Louis, "Records," v. 9, typed copy, pp. 239, 274, 275, 287; William Walker's diary (*loc. cit.*), p. 271, *also* pp. 260 and 267 (for W. E. Connelley's comments); *KHC*, v. 9, pp. 216, 217; A. T. Andreas and W. G. Cutler's *History of the State of Kansas* (Chicago, 1883), p. 1228; annals, p. 729 (for item on the Wyandots' new brick church of 1847-1848). Note that it was Edward T. Peery—not John Thompson Peery —who was missionary when the brick church was built.

❡ Late in the year—November, or December—at new Miami Catholic Mission (present Miami county—*see* February entry, p. 736), a boys' school was opened. Father Charles Truyens, S. J. (superior), assisted by Father Henry Van Mierlo, and two lay brothers, ran this short-lived institution. Located on an "elevated piece of table-land," the mission had two main buildings (of hewed logs) each two stories high 51' x 11' (divided into four rooms, about 20' square); and a 40-acre field (fenced and broken).

The mission school had been authorized by the Miamis in March, 1847; and in November, 1847, the Jesuits had signed a contract to open a manual labor school. Some $3,500 were available ($1,500 from the Miamis' annuities; $2,062 from other Indian department funds). Among the itemized disbursements for "Miami Manual Labor School" (as made by the Rev. J. Van de Velde, S. J.) were these: J. Robideau, building $30; C. Truyens, carpenter $255; M. Giraud, two horses $70; George Miles, wagon $70; James Allen, wagon $50; Anson Eccleson, breaking and fencing school farm $250—all under date of September 30, 1848; and under date of December 31, 1848, were these: Thomas Morgan, erecting two buildings for manual labor school $600; George Miles, shingles $63; Anson "Enliston" [Eccleson?], digging well $70, transportation of plank $18, building stable $35; Charles Truyens, services as superintendent of school $74; A. Tolle, carpenter $71.75.

Miami Catholic Mission did not prosper. Part of the blame attached to the Indians who were leaderless and dissipated. The most pupils at one time in the school were eight; in July, 1849, only one child was attending. Whereas a majority of the Miami children were girls, the school was for boys only; and it was not a manual labor school, as intended.

In May, 1849, the Jesuits asked to be released from their contract; after investigating, Sup't D. D. Mitchell, St. Louis, wrote to Washington, August 1, recommending "a change of Teachers & that the contract with the Catholics be annulled." Before the end of 1849 the institution closed.

Ref: Garraghan, *op. cit.*, v. 2, pp. 231, 232; Comm'r of Indian Affairs, *Report*, 1848 (Harvey's report, therein), 1849 (Handy's report); 31st Cong., 1st Sess., *H. Ex. Doc. No. 11* (Serial 572), pp. 6, 7, 250; 31st Cong., 1st Sess., *H. Ex. Doc. No. 61* (Serial 577), p. 107; SIA, St. Louis, "Records," v. 9, typed copy, pp. 354, 355.

❡ December 2.—The adjutant general's office reported there were at Fort Leavenworth   3 companies, Sixth U. S. infantry; and 1 com-

(on the Missouri)   pany, First U. S. dragoons; with Capt. William S. Ketchum (Sixth infantry) commanding.

FORT SCOTT   1 company, Sixth U. S. infantry; and 1 com-
(on the Marmaton)   pany, First U. S. dragoons; with Bvt. Maj. Albemarle Cady (Sixth infantry) commanding.

GRAND ISLAND   2 companies, U. S. Mounted riflemen;
(Fort Kearny—on the Platte)   with Capt. Charles F. Ruff commanding.

Ref: 30th Cong., 2d Sess., H. Ex. Doc. No. 1 (Serial 537), p. 162 and *between* pp. 184, 185 (or, p. 184 d.). Albert G. Brackett's *History of the United States Cavalry* . . . (New York, 1865), p. 124, notes that the rest of the First dragoons were located as follows: one company at Fort Washita (southern "Oklahoma"), three companies in New Mexico, three in California, and one on the Mississippi, above Fort Snelling.

❦ December 2.—George Douglass signed a contract (with Bvt. Capt. Alexander Morrow, AQM) to deliver 100 tons of well-cured prairie hay at Fort Scott by January 31, 1849. His bond signers were Edward L. Chouteau and Abraham Redfield.

Ref: 31st Cong., 1st Sess., *Sen. Ex. Doc. No. 26* (Serial 554), p. 7. Captain Morrow was in the Sixth U. S. Infantry.

❦ December 5.—President Polk's message to congress contained this reference to the California gold discoveries:

"The accounts of the abundance of gold in that territory are of such an extraordinary character, as would scarcely command belief, were they not corroberated [*sic*!] by the authentic reports of officers in the public service, who have visited the mineral district and derived the facts which they detail, from personal observations."

Ref: 30th Cong., 2d Sess., H. Ex. Doc. No. 1 (Serial 537). Col. Richard B. Mason and Lt. William T. Sherman, together, had visited "the newly discovered Gold Placer in the valley of the Sacramento."

❦ December 11.—"Smith, Brown & Co., who undertook a large Government contract for freight to Santa Fe last Summer [*see* May 17 annals entry], are losing great numbers of cattle, by the severe weather on the Plains, and no doubt many of their hands are suffering severely, for they are not near all in," wrote an Independence, Mo., correspondent.

The same writer noted that the Missouri was frozen over at Independence, and the weather "very severe—6 below zero." At Wyandotte (present Kansas City, Kan.) on December 11, William Walker recorded in his journal: "At daylight thermometer 18 below zero." (On the 4th he had written of a great snow and sleet storm; on the 5th "sleet, sleet . . ."; on the 6th "cold, cloudy . . . sleet all day; on the 7th "at daylight, snow, sleet and rain! When is this horrible tempest to come to an end. . . . In the evening the weather cleared up . . . the moon shone with unusual brilliancy.") Walker reported it was 10 degrees below zero on December 12. (*see, also,* December 21 entry.)

A traveler westbound on the Santa Fe trail in May, 1849, in the area between 110-mile creek and Bridge (Switzler's) creek, "passed immense numbers of Skeletons of Dead Oxen government having about one thousand Froze to death here last winter Some places thirty would lye in one pile."

Ref: Saint Louis *Daily Union*, December 19, 1848; William Walker's "Journals" (*loc. cit.*), p. 272; John R. Forsyth's "Journal" (microfilm of typed copy in KHi). Lt. E. F. Beale, westbound to Santa Fe, via Bent's Fort, wrote from Big Timbers on December 3, 1848, "a trader who passed some sixty miles to the southward of me lost in one snowstorm *ninety* mules frozen to death in a single night. I counted in one day myself, seventy-two animals dead and dying, belonging to a large company returning to the United States."— Bonsal, *op. cit.*, pp. 49, 50.

❧ December.—"St. Joseph [Mo.] has 1542 inhabitants, and 373 votes," reported the Liberty (Mo.) *Tribune,* in midmonth.

Ref: *The Weekly Tribune*, Liberty, Mo., December 15, 1848. *See, also,* February, 1849, annals entry.

❧ December 21.—At Wyandotte: "Horrible! Sleet and snow in all its fury 2 below," wrote William Walker.

On the 22d: "At daylight 20 below zero"; on the 23: "29 below zero!"; on the 24th: "Cold and freezing weather"; and on the 25th: "A merry Christmas!"

Ref: William Walker's "Journals" (*loc. cit.*), pp. 273, 274.

❧ December 27.—A Fort Leavenworth correspondent reported the arrival of "a Santa Fe party with the oxen for the government contractors—they lost one man who perished in the snow; and 1,600 oxen died on the way." (*See* December 11 entry.)

Ref: *The Weekly Tribune*, Liberty, Mo., January 19, 1849 (from St. Louis *New Era*).

❧ December 27.—Robert Wilson signed a contract (Capt. Langdon C. Easton, AQM, negotiator) to furnish and deliver at Fort Leavenworth 30,000 bushels of corn, and 5,000 bushels of oats for 34⅜ cents per bushel, each. His $10,000 bond was signed by Hiram Rich (post sutler) and Charles A. Perry.

Ref: 31st Cong., 1st Sess., *Sen. Ex. Doc. No. 26* (Serial 554), p. 13.

❧ At Osage Mission (present St. Paul), during the year 1848, there was erected a 30′ by 30′ log structure—the first Catholic church in what is now southern Kansas. The month of its completion apparently is not on record.

(In 1858 an addition, also of logs, enlarged the church to 60 by 33 feet; and in 1861 there was an addition of frame. In 1882 "an imposing stone structure begun ten years before was dedicated. . . .")

Ref: Garraghan, *op. cit.*, v. 2, p. 508. *See* annals, pp. 559, 681, for the beginnings of Osage Catholic Mission.

❧ Employed in "Kansas" by the Indian Department during all, or part of the year 1848 were the following persons:

FORT LEAVENWORTH AGENCY [*Kickapoos, Delawares, Shawnees, Pottawatomies, Stockbridges, and Munsees*]—*Agent* Richard W. Cummins; *Interpreters* Henry Tiblow, and Joseph LaFromboise (appointed June 19; for the Pottawatomies); *Blacksmiths* William Donalson and Calvin Perkins for Shawnees, James B. Franklin for Delawares, Isaac B. Mundy, Michael P. Newman (appointed June 19), and Robert Simerwell for Pottawatomies; *Assistant blacksmiths* Lindsey T. Cook (appointed February 3), Thomas A. Cook (appointed March 31; died during 1848), and Powhatan Phifer (part time) for Shawnees, Cornelius Yager for Delawares, Henry Scruggs, John LaFromboise (suspended September 12), and John L. Ogee (all three appointed June 19) for Pottawatomies; *Physician* Johnston Lykins for Pottawatomies.

OSAGE RIVER AGENCY [*Sacs & Foxes of the Mississippi, Kansa, Ottawas, Chippewas, Weas, Piankeshaws, Peorias & Kaskaskias, Miamis, and New York Indians west of the Mississippi*]—*Agent* Solomon P. Sublette (resigned), James S. Rains (appointed May 11; arrived June 29); *Interpreters* Baptiste Peoria, Josiah Smart (resigned), Thomas J. Connolly, Clement Lessert, and John Bouice; *Blacksmiths* Charles H. Withington and Arthur I. Baker for Sacs & Foxes, Robert Wilson, for Miamis, William H. Mitchell for Kansa; *Assistant blacksmiths* Jonathan Parsons, James Garlick, Morris Baker (from April 1) and Emanuel Mosier for Sacs & Foxes, James Wilson for Miamis; *Gunsmiths* Harvey Sturdevant (died September 25) and Newman York for Sacs & Foxes; *Physician* S. G. Harlan for Sacs & Foxes.

GREAT NEMAHA SUBAGENCY [*Iowas, and Sacs & Foxes of the Missouri*]—*Subagent* William E. Rucker (resigned), Alfred J. Vaughan (appointed March 1); *Interpreters* John B. Rubite and Francis Bricknelle; *Farmers* F. Lyda, John W. Forman (resigned), Findley C. McCreary, and James F. Forman; *Blacksmiths* William T. Harris and George Tinker; *Millers* John W. Forman (resigned) and James F. Forman.

OSAGE SUBAGENCY [*Osages*]—*Subagent* John M. Richardson; *Interpreter* Charles Mongrain; *Blacksmiths* Akin Brunt and John R. McKinney; *Assistant blacksmiths* Joseph Captain and Francis Mitchell; *Millers* George T. Arthur and Fenwick Fisher; *Assistant millers* Augustus Captain and Dodridge Barnabey.

WYANDOT SUBAGENCY [*Wyandots*]—*Subagent* Richard Hewitt; *Blacksmith* Charles Graham; *Assistant blacksmith* Ira Hunter.

Ref: 30th Cong., 2d Sess., Sen. Ex. Doc. No. 7 (Serial 529), pp. 2-8; 31st Cong., 1st Sess., H. Ex. Doc. No. 11 (Serial 572), pp. 3-6, 107, 109-111, 117, 118, 170, 175, 176, 179, 205, 206, 272; 31st Cong., 1st Sess., H. Ex. Doc. No. 61 (Serial 577), pp. 36, 39, 58, 68; OIA, Letters Received from Osage River Subagency (National Archives Microcopy 234, Roll 643); SIA, St. Louis, "Records," v. 9, typed copy, pp. 106, 111, 119, 120, 130-132, 209, 234, 249; OIA, Letters Received from Osage Subagency (National Archives Microcopy 234, Roll 633); Jotham Meeker's "Journal" (in KHi ms. division), September 25, 1848, entry, for Harvey Sturdevant's death. Alfred J. Vaughan, appointed March 1 to the Great Nemaha Subagency, had been head of the discontinued Osage River Subagency (see annals, p. 730).

1849

℄ January 4.—Matthew M. Hughes (of Platte county, Mo.) agreed (by contract) to take charge of Fort Leavenworth's farm for the year. He was to furnish the government 12,000 bushels of corn and 8,000 bushels of oats, at 24 cents per bushel; and all the timothy hay produced, for $3.77½ per ton.

Ref: 31st Cong., 1st Sess., Sen. Ex. Doc. No. 26 (Serial 554), p. 15. Hiram Rich (post sutler) and J. B. Martin were "sureties" for Hughes.

❡ "At the end of January 1849 the first gold seeker showed himself in St. Joseph [Mo.] . . ."—so wrote Swiss artist Rudolph F. Kurz, then a resident.

These first arrivals were "two rich merchants [wealthy speculators—not duffers] from New York," who had "traveled in a sleigh direct from their home to this place . . . in order to be the first to reach California."

Ref: Bureau of American Ethnology Bulletin No. 115 (Kurz's "Journal"), p. 46. Kurz did not identify the men; and of their subsequent travels no item has been located.

❡ January-June.—Licenses to trade with Indians in "Kansas," as granted by agents and subagents of the St. Louis Indian superintendency, were:

Traders	Indians	Issued by	Rec'vd at St. Louis
Forman & Vaughan	Iowas, Sacs & Foxes (of the Missouri)	A. J. Vaughan	January
John B. Scott	Kansa	R. W. Cummins	February
(R. A.) Kinzie & (J. H.) Whistler	Sacs & Foxes	R. W. Cummins	February
(A. G.) Boone & (J. G.) Hamilton	Sacs & Foxes	R. W. Cummins	February
Moses H. Scott	Miamis	R. W. Cummins	February
Josiah Smart	Sacs & Foxes	R. W. Cummins	February
P. M. Chouteau	Miamis, Weas & Piankeshaws	R. W. Cummins	April
Albert G. McGee	Sacs & Foxes	R. W. Cummins	April
Cyprian Chouteau	Kickapoos, Delawares, and Shawnees	R. W. Cummins	April
Robert A. Kinzie	Pottawatomies	R. W. Cummins	April
(J. D.) Lasley & (Elias) Brevoort	Pottawatomies	R. W. Cummins	May
(M. H.) Scott & (Ezekiel) French	Pottawatomies	R. W. Cummins	May
John B. Scott	Sacs & Foxes	C. N. Handy	May

Ref: Superintendency of Indian Affairs (SIA), St. Louis, "Records," v. 9, typed copy, pp. 272, 273, 285, 300, 312, 315, 321, 324, 337; and ibid., pp. 309, 312, 313, 330 for (1) Hiram Byington as clerk for Boone & Hamilton, (2) William B. Watts as clerk for Josiah Smart, (3) N. Spear as clerk for Scott & French. "P. M." Chouteau, presumably, was Pierre Menard Chouteau (son of Francis Gesseau Chouteau). Except in the case of the first license above, the Sac & Fox Indians were those "of the Mississippi."

❡ February 7.—Turner & Allen, St. Louis, began to advertise a projected "Pioneer Passenger Train for California! Overland by the South Pass" which, at a future date, would set out from Independence, Mo. A $200 fare would cover transportation of a passenger, also 100 pounds of baggage; and rations (for 100 days

—as later specified). Covered, elliptic-spring wagons, seating six persons, would be provided.

On March 9 the "Pioneer Passenger Line for California" advertised to start a first train on April 25, and a second one on May 20 (but the departure dates would be, instead, May 13, and June 18). A *Missouri Republican* notice of March 21 mentioned the Turner & Allen line's superior type of (mule) teams, its well-adapted wagons, etc.

Ref: Saint Louis *Daily Union*, February 7, 1849; *Missouri Republican*, St. Louis, March 9, 21, April 29, 1849.

❧ February.—St. Joseph, Mo. (according to the local *Gazette*), contained nearly 1,800 inhabitants[?]; and, by one resident's claim, was the fourth largest town in Missouri.

In addition to 19 stores, there were two steam flour mills, two steam saw-mills, nine blacksmith shops, four wagon factories, two tin and sheet iron ware manufactories, two large saddleries and harness-making establishments, etc.

On May 3 James Tate, of Callaway county, Mo., en route to California, wrote: "St. Jo is beautifully situated and improving very fast, it is now a population of 14 hundred, three churches, Presbyterian, Methodist, and Catholic."

Ref: St. Joseph (Mo.) *Gazette*, February 9, 16, 23, 1849; James Tate's "Diary" (typescript), in the Western Historical Manuscripts Collection, University of Missouri, Columbia.

❧ February 10.—David Hunt (by contract) agreed to furnish and deliver at Fort Leavenworth, by November 1, 1,000 cords of wood, for $3.38 per cord.

Ref: 31st Cong., 1st Sess., *Sen. Ex. Doc. No. 26* (Serial 554), p. 13. John H. Winston was surety for Hunt's $3,000 bond.

❧ February 10.—"There were some twelve or fifteen desertions from Fort Leavenworth on Saturday night last [the 10th]," reported the Weston (Mo.) *Frontier Journal*. "They were principally from the command destined for Oregon."

Capt. Michael E. Van Buren's Company A, U. S. Mounted riflemen (the regiment "destined for Oregon"), had left Jefferson Barracks, Mo., to march overland to the "Kansas" post in the fore part of January; and some "C" company men may have been at the fort in early February, also—*see* next entry.

Ref: R. W. Settle, ed., *The March of the Mounted Riflemen* . . . (Glendale, Cal., 1940), p. 16; Saint Louis *Daily Union*, February 26, 1849 (for Weston newspaper item).

❧ February 12.—Bvt. Lt. Col. Benjamin S. Roberts and a small detachment of Mounted riflemen paid a visit to St. Joseph, Mo.— sent there by Fort Leavenworth's commandant, Bvt. Col. Edwin V. Sumner, to check the trespassing by citizens of that town and vicinity, on the Kickapoo Indians' timbered lands.

Ref: St. Joseph (Mo.) *Gazette*, February 16, 1849. Roberts was head of Company C, U. S. Mounted riflemen, but some of his men had gone overland, via the Santa Fe trail, in 1848, as escort for Oregon's Gov. Joseph Lane.

❧ February.—"Emigrants for California or Oregon, by the way of

Independence, Kansas landing, or Westport will find an excellent ford across the Kansas river, at Uniontown . . . [trading post for the Pottawatomies—*see* March, 1848, annals, p. 737], in the event of high water," advised a correspondent of the St. Louis *Missouri Republican*. "At Uniontown [near west boundary of present Shawnee county], the traders with the Indians have a good supply of all articles of provisions, &c. . . . at reasonable rates."

Comments on Union Town, and the Kansas ford (and ferry)—the "upper crossing"—as recorded by some westbound travelers in the April-June, 1849, period are quoted below:

William Kelly (April 22?—perhaps later)—"The trading post is a small hamlet, composed of some half-dozen shops, and a little straggling suburb of wigwams. The shops are kept by white men, licensed to supply the Indians around with the flimsy, fantastic, and trumpery articles they require; liquor being specially interdicted, and very properly so. . . . There are not many Indians living immediately at the trading-post. . . ."

"One of the white traders . . . having built what they call a skow, a large flat-bottomed boat, capable of carrying a waggon loaded, together with the team—a very unwieldy craft, propelled with long poles and clumsy oars, we chartered her for the occasion [of crossing] rather than run the risk of fording. . . . The loose animals were got over by swimming. . . ."

James A. Pritchard (May 7)—[He referred to Union Town as "a mission[?] and trading post called Potiwatimi."] "There are several white familys liveing there & some 4 or 5 stores blacksmith shop &c. A number of the Indians are liveing in the village. . . . There was 2 ferry boats, one Kept by a half breed Indian (Michegan) & the other by a white man. . . ."

Samuel R. Dundass (May 8)—"The village is constituted of a few Indian huts and log cabins, with two or three small stores, reasonable in their prices considering the difficulty and distance of transportation." [He had crossed the Kansas at the "lower" ferry—present Topeka area—and started up the north side of the river; then, with two companions, had left the train to pay a visit to Union Town—some five miles distant and south of the Kansas. After crossing (by ferry) they found that the "village was . . . about two miles, and a bad road."]

[Unidentified emigrant] (May 12?-15)—[This man, and three companions, reached the Union Town *area* around May 12?, spent some three days "refreshing themselves with the last glimpses of civilized life in the mission and agent's families," and visits among the Indians.] "The Kansas River was crossed at two trips [on May 15?], in a ferry-boat kept by a venerable but stalwart Indian, a knowing and most entertaining old fellow, who charged five dollars for the transit."

[A Jackson county, Mo., resident who left Union Town May 13, to return to "the settlements," wrote (on the 26th): "There are two ferries at the crossing of Kansas each about 15 miles apart [*i. e.*, the one near Union Town; and the Papin ferry at "Topeka"], and two boats at each ferry; each ferry was said to cross from 65 to 70 wagons per day, cost of ferriage $1 per wagon. . . ."]

George Mifflin Harker (May 18)—"To-day we journeyed through a beautiful country—arrived at this place, sometimes called Uniontown, a trading post for the American Fur Company, and several individual fur companies, among the Pottawatomie Indians; about three o'clock, passed on to the ferry, a half mile distant, and proceeded to cross our teams, which we accomplished without accident, just before night. . . . The ferryman here informed me that he had crossed about seven hundred teams already this season. He has, or rather the company, two small boats propelled by poles, and is very successful in passing over teams safely."

David Dewolf (May 28)—"passed Pattawatama town which is situated near the Bank of the Kansas river & contains about 25 log houses. We had to swim our cattle over . . . towards evening we cross our wagons on two flat Boats & encampt on the bank among the sand . . . The kansas is quite a large stream with muddy water."

Kimball Webster (June 4)—"We cross two or three small streams and pass some Indian settlements, and arrive at the Kaw River Ferry in season to cross our horses and mules and a part of our baggage before night. The ferry-boat is made from hewn planks framed together, bearing a very strong resemblance to a raft. . . .

"On the right bank of the river [*i. e.*, south side] is situated a small Indian village, known as Uniontown, which, together with the Indian population, contains a few white men who have taken Indian women for their wives."

John Hale (about June 11)—"We came to a trading post near the Kansas ferry. Here was an Indian village, the Indians partly civilized; who lived in log-houses; and a few stores were kept by white men. . . . We left this settlement, and crossed the ferry one mile from it. . . ."

Ref: *Missouri Republican*, St. Louis, February 16, 1849 (or, *see* New York *Weekly Tribune*, March 10, 1849); William Kelly, *An Excursion to California* . . . (London, 1851), v. 1, pp. 59, 60; Dale L. Morgan, ed., *The Overland Diary of James A. Pritchard* . . . (San Francisco, 1959), p. 57, and *see* pp. 145, 146, for mention of "emigrants" D. Jagger and Amos Batchelder, who, in their journals (not seen by this compiler), also recorded mention of Union Town and environs; Samuel R. Dundass' *Journal* . . . (Steubenville, O., 1857); unidentified emigrant's narrative in Chambers' *Journal of Popular Literature No. 100* (December 1, 1855); *Missouri Republican*, June 4, 1849; G. M. Harker's letter (from "Fort Kansas, May 18th, 1849"), in *The Daily Reveille*, St. Louis, June 9, 1849; David Dewolf's "Diary," in Illinois State Historical Society, *Transactions* . . . 1925, p. 188; Kimball Webster, *The Gold Seekers of '49; a Personal Narrative* . . . (Manchester, N. H., 1917), p. 41; John Hale's *California As It Is* [a narrative], reprint edition (1954), p. 10. W. W. Cone's *Historical Sketch of Shawnee County, Kansas* (Topeka, 1877), p. 13, states: "A [Kansas river] ferry was started in 1849 by Chas. B[e]aubien and Louis Ogee, and run for three or four years, from near the mouth of Cross Creek, to a point directly opposite, and now in [eastern] Wabaunsee county [west of Union Town—which was within Shawnee county, but near its west line]. It was a pole ferry, and probably the first ferry on the river above the Papans [*i. e.*, the old 'lower crossing' ferry, Topeka vicinity]." Perhaps part-Pottawatomie Charles Beaubien was the "half breed Indian (Michigan)" to whom Pritchard (above) referred. Cone, on p. 13, states that Thomas N. Stinson was the first trader to build at Union Town (*see* March, 1848, annals entry); followed, within two months, by "P. E. Sarpie" [Peter Sarpy], "R. A. Kinsey" [Robert A. Kinzie], "O[liver] H. P. Polk[e]," "T. D. S. McDonald" (this name, it appears, was Macdonell, or McDonnell), and "W. W. Cleghorn"; and traders who arrived in 1849 were: "J. R. Whitehead," "J. D. Leslie" (Lasley), and "William Dyer." Compare with the list of traders licensed to deal with the Pottawatomies in 1848 (*see* annals, p. 769), and in 1849 (*see* annals, pp. 793, 879). Note that Harker stated the ferry was "a half mile" from Union Town; Hale recorded it as "one mile"; Dundass thought it "about two miles."

❡ Mid-February.—"An arrival at Independence from Santa Fe brings news two days later than any previously received," the St. Louis *Union* stated on the 17th (thus indicating winter travel on the Santa Fe trail by two eastbound parties).

Information on a battle between the Kansa and Pawnees (occurring "some time since" on "one of the forks of Kansas river") in which seven Kansa and 20 Pawnees were reported killed, probably came from the above source.

Ref: Saint Louis *Daily Union*, February 17, 1849.

❡ February 23.—Mountain man Miles M. Goodyear (in a letter written at St. Joseph, Mo.) recommended the upriver point Old Fort Kearny (present Nebraska City, Neb.) as a starting point for emigrants heading west. (*See, also,* April 13 entries.)

Ref: *Missouri Republican*, St. Louis, March 6, 1849. For Goodyear's journey east, in 1848, *see* annals, p. 785.

❡ February.—The town of Kansas, Mo., now contained "some eight or ten stores, several blacksmith's shops, a gunsmith's shop, wagon maker's shops, three hotels; &c. &c."

Ref: Saint Louis *Daily Union*, February 26, 1849.

❡ February 26.—At Fort Scott, Hiero T. Wilson became postmaster —succeeding John A. Bugg (California-bound) who had held the office since 1843 (*see* p. 467).

After Bugg's departure, Wilson was sutler until the fort was abandoned in 1853. Present-day Wilson (in Ellsworth county), and Wilson county were named for Hiero T. Wilson.

Ref: *KHC*, v. 1-2, p. 256, v. 7, pp. 442, 474, 486; *KHQ*, v. 6, p. 15 (footnote).

❡ Around March 1 "Messrs. Newman, Hall, Rees and others, express from Independence [*i. e.,* Fort Leavenworth?]" to Santa Fe, left the Missouri border; reached their destination April 1.

Bvt. Lt. Col. John M. Washington (in command at Santa Fe) wrote: "one of the express men who had been sent to Fort Leavenworth in December [1848], returned with a mail [on April 1] and relieved apprehensions then entertained in regard to the route." He added: "Another mail from [the States] . . . of much more recent date, is daily expected." But apparently it was May 11 (*see* annals entry) before the next express reached Santa Fe.

Ref: New York *Weekly Tribune*, April 21, 1849 (from the Glasgow [Mo.] *Times*, March 29, which reported O. P. Hovey's meeting with the above express at Walnut creek); 31st Cong., 1st Sess., *Sen. Ex. Doc. No. 24* (Serial 554), p. 13 (for Washington's April 8, 1849, letter). On December 20, 1848, at Santa Fe, Jared W. Folger had contracted to carry U. S. mail from that place to Fort Leavenworth, and return, for $600 (31st Cong., 1st Sess., *Sen. Ex. Doc. No. 26* [Serial 554] p. 23), but it appears that Newman, not Folger, carried the December mail.

❡ March 3.—An act which created the Department of the Interior also provided (in Section 5) for transfer of "supervisory and appellate powers" over the Commissioner of Indian affairs from the secretary of war to the secretary of the interior. This marked the end of direct War Department control over Indian matters.

Ref: Felix S. Cohen's *Handbook of Federal Indian Law* . . . (Washington, 1942), p. 76.

℃ March.—On the 8th the Missouri river steamboat *St. Joseph* got up to the vicinity of Kansas (City), Mo., "but owing to the ice not being broken up" above that area, returned to St. Louis. On the 9th the *Amelia* reached the mouth of the Kansas (and on the 11th was at Weston, Mo.—the first of 216 steamboat arrivals there in 1849). On March 10 the *Mandan* passed the mouth of Kansas river, upbound.

Ref: William Walker's "Journals," published in W. E. Connelley's *The Provisional Government of Nebraska Territory* . . . (1899); *The Western Journal*, St. Louis, v. 5 (March, 1851), p. 327.

℃ At "Union Town   Pott   March 8th 1849" Thomas N. Stinson (a trader with the Pottawatomies; and Union Town resident for nearly a year) opened an account book in which he made a few entries during 1849-1850.

Recorded therein were these names: John Hardin, L. R. Darling, R. A. Kinzie, James B. Franklin, G. T. Dearing [Deering?], Half Day (Pottawatomie chief), Lewis Ogee, Enoch Stevens, Noah Danell [Daniel]. One page—headed "Building House"—itemizing costs of logs, plank, sash, doors, clapboards, etc. totaling $125.32, undoubtedly related to Stinson's own log house at Union Town.

Ref: Thomas N. Stinson Collection (KHi ms. division). See annals, p. 737, for Union Town's beginning.

℃ March.—Capt. Noah Newton and his Company B, U. S. Mounted riflemen, traveling overland from Jefferson Barracks, Mo. (left in mid-February?), arrived at Fort Leavenworth early in the month, after a hardship-filled journey.

Trooper William H. Packwood (at a later time) stated: "We crossed the Kaw river in open flat boats [the military road ferry—better known as Delaware or Grinter], with the ice breaking up and running in large chunks. . . ."

Ref: *Oregon Historical Quarterly*, Salem, v. 16 (March, 1915), pp. 42, 43; Settle, *op. cit.*, p. 16.

℃ March.—From Fort Smith, Ark., on the 12th, a pack-mule train of Forty-niners (24 men, captained by W. W. Heath, of Illinois) set out for Santa Fe, and California; traveled a route north of the Canadian (part of the way); reached New Mexico's capital May 4.

Another train (the third to take a Canadian river route?) which started in March from Fort Smith was the Knickerbocker Mining Company of New York (John A. N. Ebbetts, captain—*see* p. 508; 12 wagons with ox and mule teams), which set out on the 20th; and reached Santa Fe on May 27. One member of this 65-man company was Samuel Y. Lum, who, in September, 1854, became a pioneer resident (and Congregational minister) of Lawrence, Kansas territory.

Historian R. P. Bieber has estimated that during the spring and summer of 1849 about 3,000 gold seekers chose Fort Smith (and vicinity) as the area of departure for California. "Most of the emigrants [starting] from Arkansas passed the vicinity of Santa Fe between May and August, and reached the gold mines of California in about seven or eight months."

See, also, April 4 annals entry (Marcy's expedition).

Ref: *Missouri Republican,* St. Louis, July 1, 1849; New York *Weekly Tribune,* July 2, 21, 1849; New York *Daily Tribune,* July 20, 24, 1849; *KHQ,* v. 25, p. 39; Grant Foreman, *Marcy & the Gold Seekers* . . . (Norman, Okla., 1939); R. P. Bieber, ed., *Southern Trails to California in 1849* (1937), pp. 42-48).

❡ March 16.—The St. Joseph (Mo.) *Gazette* reported the Missouri river "clear of ice," and noted the arrivals of the *Mandan* and *Kansas* during the week, with "cargoes . . . for our business houses," and "a large number of emigrants who have come here to make their outfit."

Ref: St. Joseph (Mo.) *Gazette,* Friday, March 16, 1849.

❡ March 17.—At Fort Leavenworth, St. Patrick's day "was the occasion of a grand military ball."

Ref: *Oregon Historical Quarterly,* v. 16 (March, 1915), p. 43 ("Reminiscences of William H. Packwood," then a Mounted rifleman).

❡ March 17.—Green Jones, of Independence, Mo., arriving home from Santa Fe, brought a February 2 issue of the Santa Fe *Republican,* containing letters from Taos, N. M., giving accounts of the disaster which had befallen Fremont's expedition (*see* October, 1848, annals entry).

Ref: *The Weekly Tribune,* Liberty, Mo., March 23, 30, 1849. The *Tribune's* March 23 story was from the Independence *Expositor* of March 17, 1849.

❡ March.—On the 19th the *Mary,* having aboard Capt. Thomas Duncan, Bvt. Capt. Thomas Claiborne, Jr., Asst. Surg. John F. Hammond, and Companies E and F, U. S. Mounted riflemen (about 156 troops), together with their horses, equipment, etc., left Jefferson Barracks, Mo., for Fort Leavenworth.

At St. Louis, on the 19th, contracts were made to transport other Mounted riflemen (and their horses, etc.) to Fort Leavenworth: the *Alexander Hamilton* to carry two officers and 76 men; the *Alice,* and the *Eliza Stewart* also, to take two officers and 76 men each. These boats started up the Missouri March 21. On the 27th arrangements were made for the *Dacotah* to transport two officers and 61 men to Fort Leavenworth.

Ref: *Missouri Republican,* St. Louis, March 19, 1849; 31st Cong., 1st Sess., *Sen. Ex. Doc. No. 26* (Serial 554), pp. 18, 19, 28; *The Daily Reveille,* St. Louis, March 22, 1849.

❡ March 21.—A notice listing the advantages of the emigrant routes via Independence, Mo., to California and New Mexico—an advertisement signed by William Gilpin and other Independence-area residents—first appeared in the Saint Louis *Daily Union.*

Gilpin (who had accompanied Fremont to Oregon in 1843; and traveled the Santa Fe trail as recently as 1848—in Mexican War service), earlier had written a description of the route to California—issued first in a small circular under date of January 8, 1849, and some, or all, reprinted in the *Saturday Morning Visitor,* Warsaw, Mo., February 3, 1849.

Ref: Saint Louis *Daily Union,* March 21, 1849 (and subsequent issues); *Missouri Historical Review,* Columbia, v. 39 (January, 1945), p. 143.

❦ March.—Advertised as "California Guide Books" by St. Louis book dealer John Halsell were: "[Joseph E.] Ware's [just-published] Emigrants Guide to California . . ." (60¢ or 75¢ in cloth); "[Edwin] Bryant's [issued late in 1848] What I Saw in California [in 1846-1847] . . . " ($1.25); "[Lt. William H.] Emory's [1847-published] Overland Journey [in 1846] from Fort Leavenworth to San Diego . . ." (25¢); "California Guide Book, comprising Fremonts, Emorys . . . [and other data]" (50¢).

In addition to the works by Bryant, Fremont, Emory, and Ware, W. D. Skillman of St. Louis, listed for sale these maps, books, and guides for California emigrants: Mitchell's new map of California; Foster's work on the "Gold Mines" (Charles Foster, ed., *The Gold Placers of California* . . . [1849]); "[Jessy Quinn] Thornton's [1849-published] Oregon and California"; "T. H. Jefferson's Guide . . ." (map and "Accompaniment"), published in 1849; and "Lieutenant Reveer's [Revere's] Tour to California." Another 1849-issued publication was E. Sandford Seymour's *Emigrant's Guide to the Gold Mines of Upper California* (the *Missouri Republican* of April 14 commented that the map in this guide was defective in several respects); and there was, also, Francis Parkman's book, published, *in 1849,* under the title *The California and Oregon Trail.*

Joseph E. Ware's well-publicized *The Emigrants' Guide to California* was little more than a compilation of material from Fremont's reports, Hastings' (1845) guide, Bryant's book, and William Clayton's *Latter-Day Saints Emigrant Guide* (1848). Ware (of St. Louis), from the evidence, had never been to Missouri's western border. His 1849-issued (but out-of-date) guide stated: "About ten miles above [the Kansas crossing—present Topeka area], there is a mission station of the M. E. church." [This Kansa mission had been closed in 1846; and the Kansa had removed to the Council Grove reserve—on the Santa Fe trail—in 1847. However, in the spring of 1849, a blacksmith for the Pottawatomie Indians (who *now* resided on the Kansas river) was living at the old Kansa mission. A few miles *down*river from it, travelers in 1849 would find a Pottawatomie Baptist Mission (established in 1848); and a few miles *up*river from it they would pass the Pottawatomies' trading post Union Town (established in 1848), and near by, find a new crossing (called the "upper crossing") of the Kansas. On the north side of the river, some miles above, they would pass by new St. Mary's (Catholic) mission.] Neither Old Fort Kearny (on the Missouri) or new Fort Kearny (on the Platte) were mentioned in Ware's *Guide*.

Ref: *The Daily Reveille*, January 29, 1849; *The Weekly Tribune*, Liberty, Mo., February 16, March 23, 1849; *Missouri Republican*, St. Louis, March 29, 1849; Joseph E. Ware's *The Emigrants' Guide to California* . . . reprint edition (Princeton, 1932). For some comment on Ware's book, see Morgan, *op. cit.*, p. 147, note 20, and H. R. Wagner and C. L. Camp's *The Plains and the Rockies* . . . 3d edition (1953), pp. 239, 240. According to Alonzo Delano (in his *Life on the Plains and Among the Diggings* [Auburn and Buffalo, 1854], pp. 152, 153), Joseph E. Ware died on the Oregon-California trail, east of Fort Laramie, in the early summer of 1849. But the *Daily Reveille*, St. Louis, August 5, 1849, made mention of "Mr. Joseph E. Ware," and stated "We take pleasure in noticing the connection of this talented gentleman and artist with the *Valley Farmer*." Also, Ware is listed in St. Louis directories through 1851.

❧ March 23-30.—The St. Joseph (Mo.) *Gazette* of the 23d reported the Missouri "in fine boating order," and listed the steamers *Martha, Sacramento, Algoma, Alton,* and *St. Joseph* (bringing "large freights for our merchants," and "a large number of emigrants bound for California") as having arrived during the week (March 18-23).

The *Gazette* of the 30th stated: "There are now in St. Joseph and surrounding country upwards of 500 emigrants. . . ."

Ref: St. Joseph (Mo.) *Gazette*, Friday, March 23 and 30, 1849, issues.

❧ March.—Agent R. W. Cummins, on the 24th, forwarding a contract made with Thomas C. Banning as a "sawyer & attendant" on one of the portable circular saw mills purchased for the Pottawatomie Indians, wrote: "I have made arrangements for the transportation of the saw mills & ploughs to the Potta. Country I shall proceed up there myself early next week to make locations for the mechanics shops and other buildings and to deliver the ploughs. (At St. Mary's Mission, on April 5, Father Gailland recorded in his diary: "The agents arrived with the ploughs, and the mills.")

In May several Forty-niners made mention of a mill, as they passed up the Kansas river valley after fording Cross creek (at present Rossville).

James A. Pritchard, on May 8, having got over Cross creek early in the morning, wrote: "We crossed a number of creeks & mud holes, with steep banks. We passed an Indian village about 9 A.M. where their was a saw mill, and a temporary bridge thrown across a bad muddy creek by an old Indian who charged us 25 cts apiece for our wagons. In about 10 m[ile]s from where we started this morning we came to a Catholic mission, surrounded with a number of [Pottawatomie] Indian Wigwams."

Jasper M. Hixson (in a letter), on May 10, wrote: "We traveled up the Kansas some distance over a beautiful bottom. The Pottowatomies live on this bottom. . . . We encamped on Mill creek, [after] travelling 20 miles. Here there is a Circular Saw Mill, owned by a half Indian—this was quite a novel scene, after traveling 5 days in an Indian country, to come to a large farm and an excellent saw mill." In his diary, Hixson noted: "Peter Bullbony, a half-breed, Indian and French resided here. He owned, or at least claimed and exercised authority over thirty miles square[?] of as fine land as a crow ever flew over. He had a number of comfortable hewn-log cabins, a circular sawmill, etc." "Bullbony" charged Hixson's party fifty cents each to use his bridge. (Another diarist—Joseph C. Buffum—and his party crossed what he called "Crooked Creek," on May 13, for "1 dime per waggon.") [Peter Bull-bony apparently was Peter Bourbonnais; the same man Kansas pioneer William Darnell (years later) called "old" Bourbonnais, who died around 1861—*see* *KHC*, v. 17, p. 499. Darnell also stated that "He was a big man in the councils of the Pottawatomies, but was not a chief"; and mentioned that "An Indian graveyard was located on the farm of Frank Bourbonnais on Bourbonnais creek, about two miles east of St. Marys. Old Bourbonnais was buried there. . . ."]

Henry J. Shombre (traveling up the Kansas valley) wrote on May 16: "we past a hors power S[aw] mill and a toll bridge a bridg it was."

William G. Johnston, on May 5 (having camped the previous night on what he called "Deer . . . [or] Deep Creek"—Cross creek) wrote: "The march resumed, our way led over a low, flat, marshy ground. . . . We also encountered some small streams the crossing of which gave us trouble. . . . A Catholic mission established among the Pottawatomies was passed, the houses belonging to it presenting appearances of comfort and neatness. Around one, a long, low structure used as a school house, a number of Indian lads were playing. . . . A sawmill was passed which had probably been erected for sawing the lumber used in the mission houses. Near the mill were a number of huts constructed of the boughs of trees and covered with bark. Most of them appeared to be deserted, but in some were seen males and females of the Potta. tribe. . . ."

Ref: Office of Indian Affairs (OIA), Letters Received from Fort Leavenworth Agency, National Archives Microcopy 234, Roll 303 (for Cummins); *KHQ*, v. 20, p. 518; *The Weekly Tribune*, Liberty, Mo., June 8, 1849 (for Hixon's letter, the original of which is in the Miller Papers, at Missouri Historical Society, St. Louis); Morgan, *op. cit.*, pp. 57, 58, 146 (for quote from Hixson diary, and Buffum diary); Henry J. Shombre's "Diary," in KHi ms. division; William G. Johnston's *Overland to California* (Oakland, Calif., 1948), p. 42. The small stream two miles east of St. Mary's Mission, where the "temporary bridge" and circular sawmill were located in May, 1849, is shown on present-day maps of Shawnee county as "Bourbony creek." State board of agriculture maps of 1878 and 1882 labeled it "Boubien Cr." An 1898 atlas of Shawnee county shows the stream as "Bourbon creek"; and so does a 1913 atlas.

❡ March 25.—Overland from Santa Fe (left February 10), Oliver P. Hovey (editor of the Santa Fe *Republican*), a man named "Woods," and a Mexican youth, reached Independence, Mo., in advance of four companions (left at the Little Arkansas).

At the Lower Cimarron Springs, some time in February, the original party (seven men with one wagon) had lost their stock—except two animals—in a pre-dawn Indian raid. Caching their belongings and abandoning the wagon, the seven men packed 15 days' food, clothing, bedding, etc., on the two mules remaining; and traveled afoot some 60 miles ("amid continued rain and sleet," and very cold weather), in three days and four nights, to Fort Mann (vacated in 1848) on the Arkansas. After a search these travelers found a salt pork cache left by Gilpin's troops. Several days later (men and mules somewhat recruited) "the little party again took up the line of march, but were stopped [briefly] at Walnut creek by high water"; at this point, however, they met the Santa Fe-bound express and obtained "a fresh animal and some provision, from Mr. Newman"; two days later reached the Little Arkansas. Hovey, Woods, and the young Mexican, with the animals (but taking no food) pushed on to Council Grove—reaching that haven two days later. (Presumably help was dispatched to the men at Little Arkansas Crossing.) Hovey and companions, with renewed supplies, arrived at Independence on March 25, "having been on the road 43 days, and walked over 350 miles on the route."

Ref: New York *Weekly Tribune*, April 21, 1849 (articles from Cincinnati *Commercial*, and Glasgow [Mo.] *Times*, March 29, 1849); *The Weekly Tribune*, Liberty, Mo., April 6, 1849.

❡ Around March 27 "Messrs. Austin and [James J.] Webb," who had left Santa Fe on March 1, arrived at the Missouri border.

Ref: New York *Weekly Times*, April 21, 1849 (from Glasgow [Mo.] *Times*, March 29, 1849, which, also, stated: "We conversed a few minutes with Mr. Austin as he passed down the river."). Joseph P. Hamelin *perhaps* returned to Missouri with this party. He was back at Lexington, from Chihuahua(?) before March 29—see Robert Aull letter of that date in Missouri Historical Society, *Collections*, St. Louis, v. 5 (June, 1928), p. 307. Or, Hamelin may have traveled the Santa Fe trail with St. Vrain's party—*see* next entry.

❡ Late March.—Ceran St. Vrain (carrying mail from Santa Fe under contract), accompanied by Jared W. Folger, and others, arrived at Independence, Mo., about the 27th(?). Folger reached St. Louis March 29, and St. Vrain (aboard another steamboat) a day later.

Newspaper accounts stated these travelers had left Santa Fe on February 24. Their route was via Bent's Fort, and they brought news that William Bent had "made a good winter's trade," and expected to be in Missouri in May.

Ref: *The Daily Reveille*, St. Louis, March 30, 1849; New York *Weekly Tribune*, April 14, 1849 (from *Missouri Republican*, St. Louis, March 30); 31st Cong., 1st Sess., Sen. Ex. Doc. No. 26 (Serial 554), p. 26 (for item on January 31, 1849, contract, Capt. T. L. Brent, AQM, Santa Fe, with St. Vrain & McCarty, to carry the U. S. mail from Santa Fe to Fort Leavenworth and return to Santa Fe with the mail from Fort Leavenworth, for the sum of $800).

❡ DIED: Pierre (Peter) Le Clerc, one of the leaders among the "Chicago" Pottawatomies, on March 28, near St. Mary's Catholic Mission (present St. Marys, Kan.).

Le Clerc (also Pierish, or Perish La Clair, or Le Clair) had been present at the Fort Dearborn massacre in 1815; and served as interpreter when surrender terms were arranged. With the "Council Bluffs" Pottawatomies he removed to "Kansas" (from Iowa) late in 1847.

Ref: *KHQ*, v. 20, pp. 517, 518; and *see, also*, annals index.

❡ Between March 31 and April 6, these steamboats (carrying large numbers of California-bound emigrants) arrived at St. Joseph, Mo.: *Kansas, Consignee* (on March 31), *San Francisco, Timour, Algoma, St. Ange, Sacramento, Tamerlane, Falcon,* and *Alton.*

The *Consignee*, from Pittsburgh, Pa., chartered by Capt. William J. Ankrim's "Pittsburgh Enterprise Company" of gold seekers, carried some 240 (of the 280) company members, nearly 100 tons of gear (clothing, gold-digging and gold-washing implements, etc.), 70 wagons, also betwen 80 and 90 head of mules. Of the *Consignee's* passengers, the *Gazette* commented: "This is the largest, best organized and most complete company that has reached St. Joseph." (The Pittsburghians did not remain a cohesive group for long.)

Another boat—the *Alice*—would have made port there on April 6, but that morning, about 15 miles above Weston (having tied up for the night of April 5 on land "belonging to the Kickapoo nation"), developed boiler trouble. Her passengers and freight were transferred to the *Mary* (an April 6 or 7 arrival at St. Joseph).

Three of the above steamboats were new—launched in March for the Missouri river trade:

Name	Captain	Built at:	Keel	Deck	Boilers: No.	Diam.	Length
Timour	William Miller	St. Louis	164'	180'	3	40"	26'
St. Ange	Joseph La Barge	St. Louis	170'	180'	2	42"	28'
San Francisco	Mortimer Kennett	Pittsburgh	165'	182'	2	42"	32'

The *Kansas* (which returned to St. Louis on April 5) reported having met 22 upbound steamboats.

Ref: *The Daily Reveille*, St. Louis, March 4, 18, 22, 24, 1849; St. Joseph (Mo.) *Gazette*, March 23, 30, April 6, 1849; Saint Louis *Daily Union*, March 24, April 6, 1849; *Missouri Republican*, St. Louis, March 19, 1849; *Indiana Magazine of History*, Bloomington, v. 56 (December, 1960), pp. 281, 282. Emigrant Lucius Fairchild, in an April 24, 1849, letter from St. Joseph, stated: "There is a very large company from Pittsburg and some hard cases among them. They fight and quarell continually some have seperated in anger."— *Wisconsin Historical Collections*, Madison, v. 31, p. 14. See, also, annals entry, p. 808.

❡ April 4.—A military expedition, headed by Capt. Randolph B. Marcy (Fifth U. S. infantry), with whom was Lt. James H. Simpson (U. S. topographical engineers), left Fort Smith, Ark., for Santa Fe. In Marcy's command were some 75 troops, guide Black Beaver (Delaware), and others.

The expedition's dual purpose, as Simpson expressed it: "the escorting of a [large] number of California emigrants, and at the same time the exploration, survey, and construction of a wagon road from that post [Fort Smith] to Santa Fe, by way of the south side of the Canadian river."

Marcy reached Santa Fe on June 28. By the route traveled (across "Oklahoma," Texas, and New Mexico) the distance was 819.5 miles.

Ref: 31st Cong., 1st Sess., *Sen. Ex. Doc. No. 64* (Serial 562); 31st Cong., 1st Sess., *H. Ex. Doc. No. 45* (Serial 577); *Chronicles of Oklahoma*, Oklahoma City, v. 38 (Summer, 1960), pp. 154-179; R. P. Bieber, *op. cit.*, pp. 42-46; Grant Foreman, *op. cit.*

❡ Between April 6 and 13, these steamboats arrived at St. Joseph, Mo.: the *Mary* (left St. Joseph the 8th for return trip), *North Carolina* ("in port" on the 8th; still there on the 10th), *Mustang* ("in port" on the 8th; destination Council Bluffs), *Bay State* (left St. Joseph on the 10th), *Alexander Hamilton* ("in port" on the 10th; started down same day), *St. Joseph* (left for Council Bluffs on the 10th), and the *Martha*. (The *Meteor No. 3*, within 12 miles of St. Joseph on April 10, apparently went on above that port.) The *Gazette* reported these boats "crowded, as usual, with emigrants and . . . large numbers of oxen, mules, wagons &c."

The *Ne Plus Ultra* which had been to Kansas, Mo. (but no higher?), returned to St. Louis on April 12.

Ref: St. Joseph (Mo.) *Gazette*, April 13, 1849; St. Louis *Daily New Era*, April 12, 14, 17, 1849.

❡ April 13.—Via steamboat—the *St. Joseph*, apparently—some California-bound travelers debarked at Old Fort Kearny (present Nebraska City, Neb.). One of the men ("L."), addressing his letter to the St. Louis *Reveille*, wrote: "We arrived at this place this morning about nine o'clock. We [the St. Louis "Telegraph Company"?] are the first on the ground, although we expect several companies in the course of a week or so. In starting from this point we avoid crossing several creeks and rivers, having only one to cross between this and Fort Childs, or *new Fort Kearny*. . . ."

(Both the *Mustang* and *St. Joseph,* en route to Council Bluffs, were in the Old Fort Kearny vicinity on April 13, but it was probably from the latter boat that "L." and his companions [also their wagons, mules, supplies, etc.] were landed this day. On April 19, at St. Louis, the *Missouri Republican* reported: "The St. Joseph, Capt. Baker, returned last evening from [Old] Fort Kearny after a successful trip up with the Telegraph Company from this city, and bound for California.")

The Old Fort Kearny trail (south of the Platte) was referred to by one Forty-niner as "a central route between [the starting points of] St. Joseph and Council Bluffs." The road was traveled by many companies in 1849, but there is uncertainty as to which California-bound party was the first to "jump off" from this Missouri river point. Emigrant "M. M.," while "On Board Steamer Eliza Stewart, Near Fort Kearny, May 2d, 1849," wrote: "Capt. Miller, with a small company, will leave in 2 or 3 days from [Old] Fort Kearny." (Earlier he had stated: "We have heard of but one company that has started yet, that of Col. Jarrott [who crossed the Missouri at St. Joseph], and he had encamped a short distance out.") Emigrant John Boggs, of Howard county, Mo. (who had wintered at Council Bluffs), began a diary on May 3—the day he crossed the river near Old Fort Kearny. The "Telegraph Company," may have been in the van. N. Grant, of Miles Goodyear's party, at new Fort Kearny, on May 17, wrote: "the Telegraph Company of St. Louis left here a day or two ago"—indicating an early May departure from the Missouri; also, a member of the St. Louis company, in a letter the St. Louis *Reveille* printed on May 22, wrote of being overtaken, on *May 3*, while traveling, by Pawnees fleeing from a Sioux war party. (This date does not quite reconcile with "M. M.'s" statement above.)

Departing Old Fort Kearny on May 8 was Miles Goodyear (*see* next entry). On May 9 one company which set out was the "E[benezer] & T[haddeus] Pomeroy" 33-wagon (160 yoke of oxen) mercantile train, from Lexington, Mo. (with cotraveling groups—*e. g.*, Joseph P. Hamelin's five wagons, the Higgins brothers, Peebles' party)—around 70 persons in all.

Among the last to leave in 1849, from this point (after a trip, overland, from St. Joseph, Mo.) was the "Washington City and California Mining Association"—on June 4. This company reached Fort Kearny on the Platte, June 15. J. Goldsborough Bruff ("President and Commander") kept one of the more-detailed of Forty-niner journals; but more importantly (as a skilled map maker) produced some valuable emigrant-trails-of-1849 maps.

Ref: St. Louis *Daily New Era*, April 14, 17, 1849; *The Daily Reveille*, St. Louis, April 20, 1849; *Missouri Republican*, St. Louis, May 11, 1849; Morgan, *op. cit.*, pp. 20, 181. For the "Telegraph Company" *see Mo. Rep.*, April 19; *Daily Reveille*, April 29, May 22; St. Joseph (Mo.) *Gazette*, June 22, 1849. For Pomeroy train *see Mo. Rep.*, May 13, June 21; New York *Weekly Tribune*, November 3, 1849; Morgan, *op. cit.*, p. 188 (for Hamelin). For Bruff *see* Georgia W. Read and Ruth Gaines, eds., *Gold Rush—The Journals, Drawings, and Other Papers of J. Goldsborough Bruff* . . . (New York, 1949); Morgan, *op. cit.*, pp. 173-176 (for discussion of the Bruff maps, and *see* reproduced Bruff maps therein); and *ibid.*, for chart recording data on 12 diarists of the 1849 emigration West who traveled the Old Fort Kearny trail.

❧ April 13.—In the St. Joseph (Mo.) *Gazette* Miles M. Goodyear advertised he would "leave [Old] Fort Kearny for California as soon as practicable"; and was prepared to provide transportation "on liberal terms" for "12 or 15" persons.

Goodyear's party (14 men—Miles Goodyear, his brother Andrew, two California Indians, and nine gold seekers) set out April 27—traveling northward (up the Missouri's left bank) to cross near present Nebraska City, Neb.; subsequently left Old Fort Kearny May 8; arrived at new Fort Kearny by (or before) the 17th; went on to reach Sacramento, Calif., in mid-July, in, or near, the forefront of the 1849 overland emigration via South Pass.

Ref: St. Joseph (Mo.) *Gazette*, April 13, 27, June 15, 22, October 5, November 2, 1849; Morgan, *op. cit.*, pp. 25, 26; Charles Kelly and M. L. Howe's *Miles Goodyear* . . . (1937), pp. 103-109. "Sawtell and Company" left St. Joseph with Goodyear, and may have traveled west with his party—*see* Lucius Fairchild's April 24, 1849, letter in *Wisconsin Historical Collections*, v. 31, p. 13.

❧ Between April 13 and 20, these steamboats arrived at St. Joseph, Mo.: the *Mandan* ("in port" on the 13th; left the 14th), *San Francisco* ("in port" on the 18th), *Algoma* (left on 17th), *Haydee*, *St. Joseph* (returning from Council Bluffs), *Highland Mary* ("in port" on the 17th), *John Hancock, St. Ange* (left on the 18th), *Mustang* (returning from Council Bluffs), *Alice, Embassy* (which had left St. Louis with over 450 "Californians for Independence and St. Joseph"), and *Alton.*

All these boats (except the downbound *St. Joseph* and *Mustang*) carried large number of emigrants, and quantities of their freight. The *Tamerlane*, at Weston, Mo., on April 19, probably reached St. Joseph on the 20th. She was "in port" there April 21.

On the *Highland Mary's* upward journey some deaths occurred aboard—14 before she reached Lexington (according to the *Martha's* officers); but the *Mandan's* captain (at St. Louis on April 18) stated that the number of *cholera* deaths aboard her was eight (and not "eighteen as before reported"); and an emigrant confirmed the "eight deaths positively on board of one boat [presumably the *Highland Mary*] on her way up." Up to Independence, the *St. Ange* had one fatal case of cholera, the *San Francisco* two, and the *Algoma* four.

In a letter from Independence, Mo., April 15, emigrant John A. Johnson wrote: "every boat that now arrives from St. Louis has cholera on board and more or less die on every one of them. . . . Independence is some three miles from the river and mostly out of reach of the river influence and not a place liable to Cholera." (But *see* April 25 annals entry.)

"F. W. M.," who reached St. Joseph on April 19 (aboard either the *Alice, Embassy,* or *Alton?*), wrote (in a letter on the 21st): "We had five or six cases of the cholera on board of our boat on the way up, but were all cured. We had a St. Louis physician on board."

Ref: St. Joseph (Mo.) *Gazette*, April 20, 1849; St. Louis *Daily New Era*, April 17, 18, 20, 23, 24, 1849; *The Daily Reveille*, St. Louis, April 17, May 9, 1849; *Pioneering on the Plains* (Kaukauna, Wis., c1924), for Johnson's letters of April 15 and 29, 1849; Chicago *Daily Journal*, May 7, 1849 (for "F. W. M.'s" letter).

℄ In mid-April a mail express left Fort Leavenworth for Santa Fe; and arrived there May 11. (Eastbound travelers who reached Independence, Mo., on April 22 had met "the mail, on its way to Santa Fe, at Council Grove.")

Ref: *The Daily Reveille*, St. Louis, April 29, 1849 (The account here says "This mail will be the first that will have reached Santa Fe for months. . . ." But *see* March 1 annals entry.); 31st Cong., 1st Sess., *Sen. Ex. Doc. No. 24* (Serial 554), p. 14 (for Bvt. Lt. Col. John M. Washington's May 15, 1849, letter, at Santa Fe, acknowledging receipt of a February 24 communication from the secretary of war, on May 11 "by the express from Fort Leavenworth").

℄ April 14.—The first Forty-niner train starting out the Oregon-California trail from Independence, Mo., or vicinity, was (so far as known) one captained by G. W. Paul, of St. Louis. With his company of 10 Missourians and Easterners was a party from Upper Sandusky, Ohio.

"At nine o'clock [April 14, from near Independence] the neighboring camps of Paul and Johnston struck their tents, to begin the march westward; being the foremost . . . [etc.]," wrote Ohioan W. G. Johnston (whose own company did not set out till April 28). By, or before April 28, Captain Paul's train reached the Big Blue, after delays due to the early season. John Fuller, aged 20, a driver for Paul, died of an accidental gunshot wound on the east bank, on the 28th. (News reached the Independence area on April 29 that "the Sandusky City Company [and Paul's?] had "gone 50 miles beyond the Kansas river and stopped for want of grass and had to send back to Kansas river for corn for their animals. . . .") On April 30, beyond the Big Blue (Independence-route) ford, Captain Paul's party nailed a board to a tree with information on it that Paul, in the lead of the emigration (on both the Independence and St. Joseph branches), had left there that day.

Around May 7 Paul's train passed Fort Kearny; and about May 10(?) reached the forks of the Platte. An incoming trader who met this *leading* company, reported that "immediately following" Paul was Captain Winter's company (organized at Independence; composed of men from various southern states); next, several Pittsburgh companies (out of St. Joseph?); and afterwards, Captain Jarrot's (*see* p. 825) and Captain "Harvy's" companies (both from Illinois). Paul led the 1849 emigration at least most of the way to California.

Ref: *Missouri Republican,* St. Louis, April 7, 12, 23, June 9, 1849; *The Weekly Tribune,* Liberty, Mo., March 23, June 8, 1849; *The Daily Reveille,* St. Louis, June 10, July 6, 1849; Johnston, *op. cit.,* pp. 17, 47, 99, 108, 143; John A. Johnson's April 29, 1849, statement in *Pioneering on the Plains;* Morgan, *op. cit.,* pp. 19-24; Edward Eberstadt & Sons, N. Y., *Catalogue 159,* in listing John A. Johnson's manuscript diary, states: "We further learn . . . [from this diary] that a company from Upper Sandusky, Ohio, made up part of the company of G. W. Paul . . ."; St. Joseph (Mo.) *Gazette,* October 19, December 7, 1849; *Utah Historical Quarterly,* Salt Lake City, v. 19 (1951), pp. 265, 266.

❰ April 15.—Emigrant Henry J. Shombre, visiting Westport, Mo. (which was, as he recorded in his diary, "¾ of a mile from the boundry of U. S."), wrote that it had a population of 500; four(?) stores, two doctors, one church, one school, two smiths, and "Some other mechanicks."

Ref: Henry J. Shombre's "Diary," in KHi ms. division.

❰ April 17.—Alexander Majors signed a contract to plough and plant 300 acres of prairie land (near Council Grove) for the Kansa Indians. (He fulfilled the contract—made with Agent R. W. Cummins—promptly; but two years elapsed before he received $1,500 compensation.)

Ref: SIA, St. Louis, "Records," v. 9, typed copy, pp. 315, 463, 480 (and *see* p. 151 for account of an unsuccessful attempt to break ground for the Kansa in 1848—when a contractor, with six heavy teams, found the prairie soil so hard the work could not be done); 32d Cong., 1st Sess., *H. Ex. Doc. No. 103* (Serial 647), p. 632; OIA, Letters Received from Fort Leavenworth Agency (National Archives Microcopy 234, Roll 303), for Cummins' April 17, 1849, letter.

❰ April.—At Independence, Mo., on the 17th, a correspondent wrote: "At this time there are between 2,000 and 2,500 persons [emigrants] at this place," perhaps 100 at Westport, and about the same number at Kansas, Mo.

On the 21st, at Independence, the (same?) writer reported: "To be sure of 'being first,' several [California-bound companies] have already moved as

[*Continued on p. 825*]

Keokuk, chief of the Sacs.—In March, 1847, Keokuk (a "Kansas" resident since December, 1845—see p. 567) left the "Mississippi" Sacs & Foxes' reserve, briefly, for a trip to St. Louis (see p. 667). The daguerreotype (of 1847) from which the above portrait evolves, was made at that time. Keokuk died just a year later—in May(?), 1848. (The year of his birth is variously given as "about 1780," "about 1781," and "1788.")

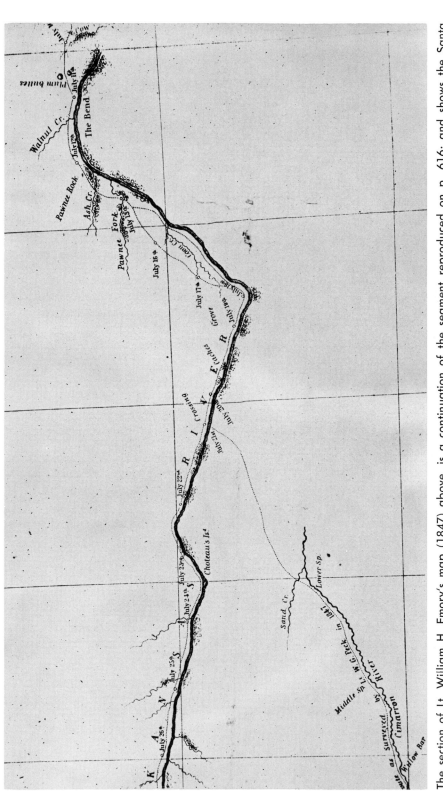

The section of Lt. William H. Emory's map (1847) above, is a continuation of the segment reproduced on p. 616; and shows the Santa Fe trail from the Great Bend of the Arkansas to the western and southwestern limits of present Kansas. Emory outlined two routes available to travelers beyond Pawnee Fork, in the Coon creeks area. He noted, also, Lt. W. G. Peck's (cursory) survey, in 1847 (see p. 682) of the Cimarron route.

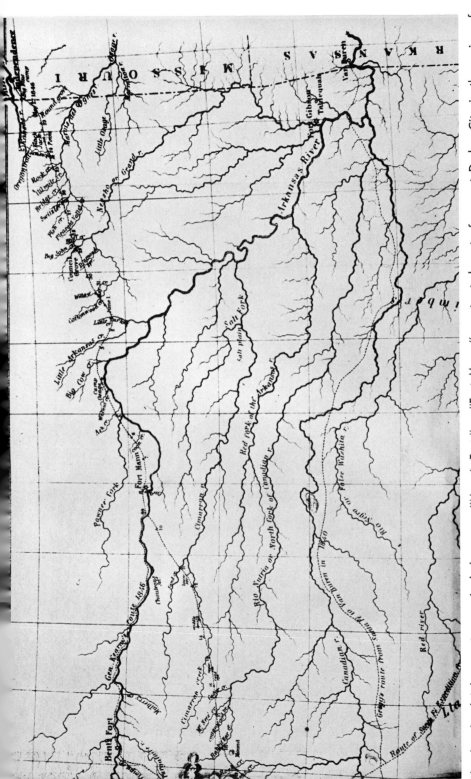

The short-lived Arkansas river stockade known as "Mann's Fort," or "Fort Mann," constructed west of present Dodge City in the spring of 1847 (see pp. 669-671), and first occupied by troops late that year (see p. 720), was shown on Dr. F. A. Wislizenus' "Map of a tour from Independence to Santa Fe, Chihuahua, Monterey and Matamoras" (reproduced, in part, above), published with his Memoir, in 1848, as Sen. Doc. No. 26, 30th Cong., 1st Sess.

At Council Grove in the spring of 1847, Westport, Mo., merchants Albert G. Boone and James G. Hamilton (licensed traders for the Kansa Indians) opened a store (see p. 671), operated by Seth M. Hays. (Both Boone and Hays were descendants of frontiersman Daniel Boone.) The above advertisement first appeared in an April, 1847, issue of the Saint Louis Reveille. Copy courtesy The Newberry Library, Chicago.

In the summer of 1847, John Dougherty, of Liberty, Mo., incurred this debt for groceries "Bo[ugh]t of S M Hays," at Boone & Hamilton's Council Grove store. (Note that the arithmetic is faulty.) See p. 690 for Dougherty's connection with Santa Fe trail history.

An 1837 painting of "Young Mahaska" (White Cloud) —Iowa head chief—attributed to artist Charles Bird King. White Cloud was deposed in 1848 for murdering defenseless Pawnees (see p. 752).

Sac chief Moses Keokuk (Keokuk, Jr.), born in 1824(?) near Rock Island, Ill.; came to "Kansas" late in 1845; became head chief in 1848 (see p. 752); removed to "Oklahoma" in 1869; died there in 1903.

JOHN A. BINGHAM—1848					JOSIAH GREGG—1844
To:	Miles	Aggregate miles	miles	Miles	To:
State Line	17				
Lone Elm	15	32		35	Round Grove
Bull creek	8	40			
Black Jack	15	55			
Willow Spring	10	65	65	30	Narrows
110 creek	25	90	100	35	110-mile creek
Bridge [or, Switzler's] creek	10	100	108	8	Bridge creek
Bluff creek	25	125			
Big John Spring	8	133	148	40	Big John Spring
Council Grove	2	135	150	2	Council Grove
Diamond Spring	15	150	165	15	Diamond Spring
			180	15	Lost Spring
Cottonwood Fork	36	186	192	12	Cottonwood creek
Turkey creek	24	210	217	25	Turkey creek
Little Arkansas	20	230	234	17	Little Arkansas
Big Owl creek	12	242			
Little Owl creek	4	246			
Cow creek	8	254	254	20	Cow creek
Plum Buttes	9	263			
Big Bend of Arkansas	7	270	270	16	Arkansas river
Walnut creek	8	278	278	8	Walnut creek
Pawnee Rock	15	293			
Ash creek	5	298	297	19	Ash creek
Pawnee Fork	5	303	303	6	Pawnee Fork
Coon creek [divides into Big Coon and Little Coon]	10	313			
			336	33	Coon creek
Mann's Fort	52	365			
			372	36	Caches [within sight of Mann's Fort]
Crossing of Arkansas	30	395	392	20	Ford of Arkansas
Sand creek	50	445	442	50	Sand creek (leave Arkansas river)
Lower Springs	12	457	450	8	Cimarron (Lower spring)
Middle creek	30	487	486	36	Middle spring (up Cimarron river)
. . .					. . .
Santa Fe		781	775		Santa Fe

Young John A. Bingham, of St. Louis, traveled the Santa Fe trail in 1848, and in 1849 sent a table of distances on the route (in a letter) to a friend. *Arizona and the West*, Tucson, v. 6 (Winter, 1964), pp. 317-319, published Bingham's letter. The original is in the State Historical Society of Missouri, Columbia. Josiah Gregg's table first appeared in his *Commerce of the Prairies* (1844), p. 313.

TABLES OF DISTANCES ON THE SANTA FE TRAIL ("KANSAS" SECTION)
From Fort Leavenworth

	DYER–CARLETON—1846-48			KENDRICK—1849	
To:	Miles	Aggregate miles	miles	Miles	To:
Upper ferry [mouth of Waka-rusa]	35			30	"Camp Kanzas" [south of lower ferry—"Delaware," or "Grinter"]
			44	14.00	Lone Elm
			54.91	10.91	Bull creek
			64.19	9.28	Black Jack Point
Willow Spring	17	52	76.52	12.33	Miller's Spring
			91.22	14.70	Pelican creek
110 creek	24	76	102.42	11.20	110-mile creek
Beaver creek	12	88	114.54	12.12	Waldo creek, Big creek, &c., Dragoon; Independence
Dragoon creek	8	96	129.81	15.27	140-mile creek
Bluff creek	13	109	142.96	13.15	Rock creek
Council Grove	12	121	152.04	9.08	One mile beyond Council Grove
Diamond Spring	15	136	168.54	16.50	Diamond Spring
Lost Spring	14	150	184.29	15.75	Lost Spring
Cottonwood	15	165	201.24	16.95	Cottonwood Spring
Main Turkey creek	18	183	220.22	18.98	Little Turkey creek
Little Arkansas	26	209	246.22	26.00	Little Arkansas
			257.42	11.20	Owl creek
Big Cow creek	21	230	267.92	10.50	Big Cow creek
			285.92	18.00	Arkansas river ("Two miles above Osage camping ground")
Walnut creek	25	255			
			314.07	28.15	Ash creek
Pawnee Fork	25	280	321.17	7.10	Pawnee Fork
Coon creek	12	292	337.74	16.57	On the Arkansas ("Guide called this 'Love's defeat' ")
			354.65	16.91	On the Arkansas
Fort Mann	55	347	373.30	18.65	" "
			395.60	22.30	"Near Fort Mann"
Crossing of Arkansas	26	373	418.59	22.99	Crossing of Arkansas
			420.09	1.50	"Crossed Arkansas to Camp"
			435.77	15.68	At a water hole
Sand creek	50	423	465.79	30.02	Found two water holes
Lower spring on Cimarron	8	431	479.93	14.14	Lower Cimarron Springs
			499.93	20.00	Some pools of water
Middle Spring	34	465	518.95	19.02	Middle Springs of Cimarron
Santa Fe		757	821.68		Santa Fe

Bvt. Maj. James H. Carleton (using data from Bvt. Capt. Alexander B. Dyer's notes) compiled the table *(above, left)*, which was published (reprinted) in Stryker's *American Register and Magazine*, v. 4 (July, 1850), pp. 247-249. Carleton's covering letter was dated February 1, 1850; but Dyer had crossed the Santa Fe trail during the Mexican War period. Bvt. Maj. Henry L. Kendrick's table of distances (measured by viameter) was compiled between May 16 and July 22, 1849, as he traveled to Santa Fe. It was published in 31st Cong., 1st Sess., *H. Ex. Doc. No. 17* (Serial 573), p. 92.

South view of new Delaware Baptist Mission (see p. 735), published in the May, 1851, *Baptist Missionary Magazine*, along with a letter by teacher (and artist?) Elizabeth S. Morse, describing "Briggsvale School." The *framed main building* (36' x 36') had eight rooms; the log (18' x 20') addition served as "kitchen and dining room"; next was a storeroom. On the far right was the "too-small" *school house* (20' x 20'). In later years this institution was known as "Pratt Mission"—for long-time missionaries John G. Pratt and wife.

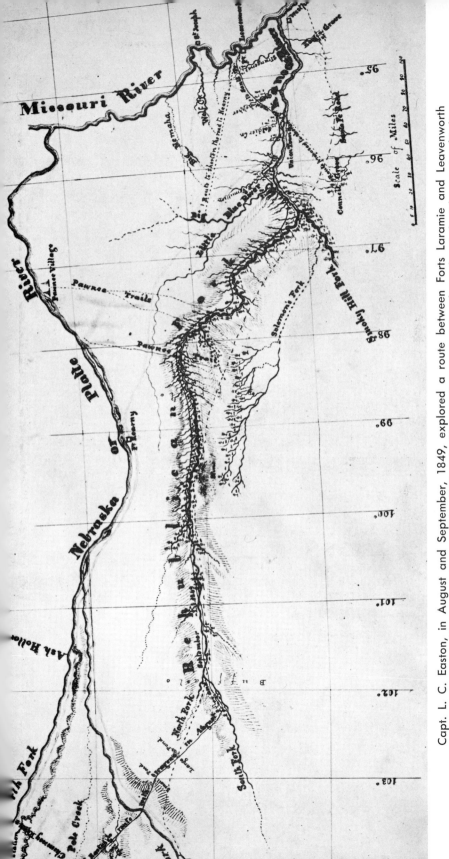

Capt. L. C. Easton, in August and September, 1849, explored a route between Forts Laramie and Leavenworth by way of the Republican river (see pp. 886, 887). On his map (eastern portion shown here), besides tracing his line of march, he showed such new frontier locations as Union Town (on the Kansas), and Fort Kearny (on the Platte). Both were established in 1848 (see pp. 737, 738 and 755, 756). Old Fort Kearny (on the Missouri, nearly directly east of the new post) is not on his map. Easton's report of his 1849 journey (and a full map reproduction) can be found in *KHQ*, v. 20, pp. 392-416.

Relics of 1849

Burial markers of Forty-niners who didn't make it (see p. 845). Found on the Oregon-California trail in Pottawatomie county, the markers are now preserved in the museum of the Kansas State Historical Society.

At the right are views of the Pottawatomie Baptist Mission's large stone building (a little west of Topeka—see pp. 889, 890) which show the structure's post-mission use as a barn. The building was under construction in 1849, but cholera, and the exodus to California, caused delays. The upper photograph was taken in 1897; the lower in 1954.

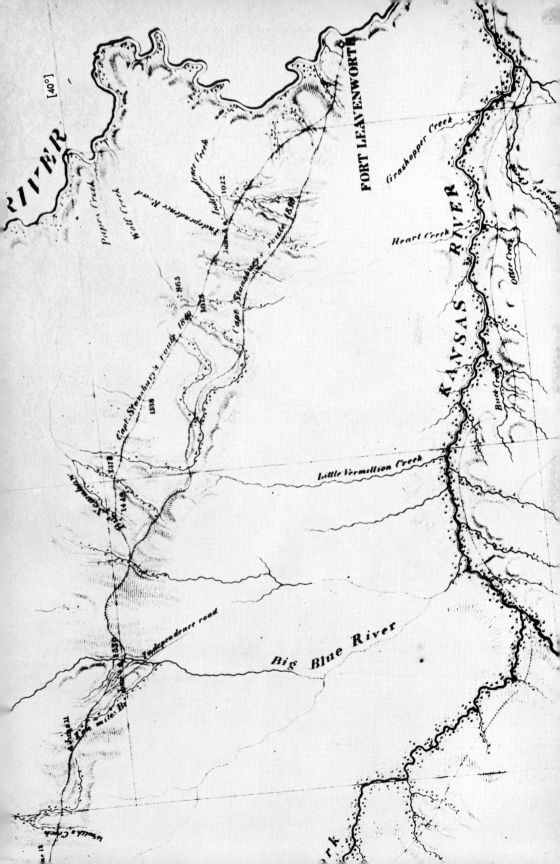

Reproduced on preceding page is the eastern "Kansas" section of a map (drawn by Lt. J. W. Gunnison and Charles Preuss) published with Capt. Howard Stansbury's report of his Great Salt Lake Valley expedition. (See pp. 972-974.) From Fort Leavenworth out to a junction (east of the Big Blue) with the Oregon-California trail's St. Joseph branch, Stansbury, in 1849, marched over a circuitous "old" road. Returning, in November, 1850, he traveled the new (more direct) military road which Bvt. Maj. E. A. Ogden had laid out in April (see p. 908). Both routes are shown, but the map's defect is an inaccurately-sketched relationship of the Oregon-California trail to the 40th parallel. The St. Joseph branch crossed the Big Blue (at present Marysville) some 11 miles below the "Kansas-Nebraska" line; and the junction of the St. Joseph branch with the Oregon-California trail from Independence (west of the Big Blue) was nine miles south of the 40th parallel.

The Kaw Methodist Mission at Council Grove, built in 1850-1851 (see p. 962), is shown here about 1910, when it was a private residence, and as it appears today. Purchased by the state in 1951, it is now a historical museum administered by the Kansas State Historical Society.

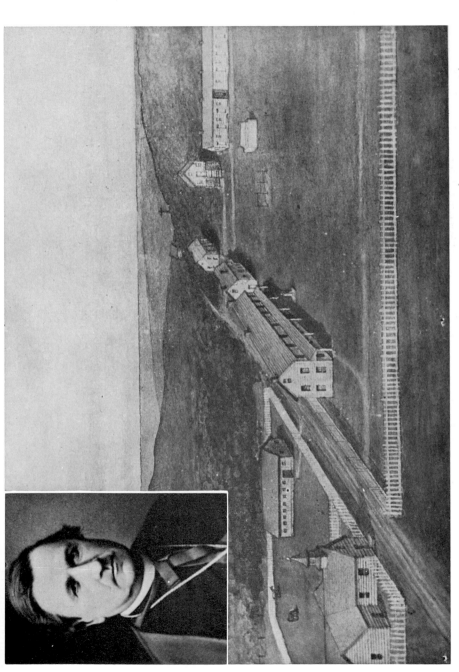

The Rt. Rev. John B. Miege, S. J., first Catholic bishop of "Kansas" (see p. 1007); and a representation (drawn in 1924) of the early-day St. Mary's Mission, present St. Marys. At lower left is the building which served as a cathedral from 1851 to 1855. (See photograph of the church in *KHQ*, v. 20, *facing p. 512.*) Sketch used courtesy of Father Augustin C. Wand, S. J., of old St. Mary's College, which ceased operation in 1967.

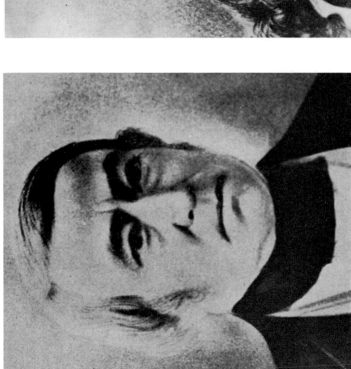

Four famed men of the West who were on the Santa Fe trail in 1851: *(upper left)* Indian agent Thomas Fitzpatrick (1799-1854); *(upper right)* Santa Fe trader Christopher ("Kit") Carson (1809-1868); *(lower left)* Indian trader William Bent (1809-1869); *(lower right)* Santa Fe trader and trail explorer Francis X. Aubry (1824-1854).

For first mention in the annals, see p. 109, Fitzpatrick to the Rockies in 1823; p. 135, Carson on the Santa Fe trail in 1826; p. 160, William Bent to Santa Fe in 1829; p. 580, Aubry's initial Santa Fe trading venture, 1846. Fitzpatrick's portrait is from Hafen & Ghent's *Broken Hand.*

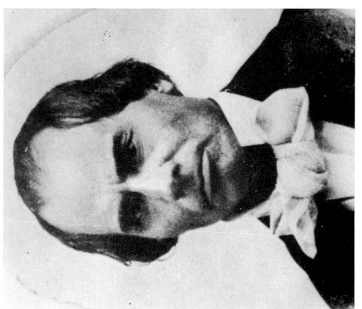

Charles Bluejacket (1816?-1897), a mixed-blood Shawnee (son of Captain Bluejacket), came to "Kansas" in 1832, aged 16; remained nearly 40 years; removed to "Oklahoma" in 1871. Mission-educated, he was an influential, much-respected man; and in 1859 was licensed to preach by the Methodist Church, South. The substantial log house he built (in 1851?)—see p. 1030 for reference to what may have been the building—is shown here (after being weather-boarded) as sketched in Heisler's Johnson county *Atlas*, 1874. (The location was in Shawnee township, Sec. 2, T. 12, R. 24 E.)

[Continued From p. 808]

far as Kaw River [*i. e.*, to present Shawnee county], are there in camp, and ready to proceed when others appear. [*See* April 14 entry.] . . . The companies in camp [in the Independence vicinity] ready to move comprise 2,500 persons, who will carry at least 3,000 head of stock, in oxen and mules. This body of men, with this amount of stock, intend moving the coming week."

On April 27 "A." wrote from Independence: "The weather here at this time is warm, and the grass growing fine. . . . Most of the emigrants have moved out, and are camped at various points from this to the Kanzas river."

At Independence on May 4 a man wrote: "Thousands [of California gold seekers] have left our town this week, and may be considered as started."

W. C. Skinner, coming in from Santa Fe, began to meet emigrants on that trail around May 8, when about 70 or 80 miles from Missouri, and reported that from there in he met the Forty-niners in "one unceasing, everlasting flood." (He reached Independence May 10; and would have passed, on the 9th, the point where the Oregon-California trail branched off the Santa Fe route.)

Ref: *Missouri Republican*, St. Louis, April 23, 1849; New York *Daily Tribune*, May 11, 1849; *The Daily Reveille*, St. Louis, May 5, 10, 1849.

❡ April 18.—Moses ("Black") Harris, overland from "Fort John" (Laramie), arrived at St. Joseph, Mo.

He reported there had been a "very successful" trapping season—the traders having "procured a large number of robes, skins, &c."; and that there was deeper snow at Fort John than for many years past.

Ref: St. Joseph (Mo.) *Gazette*, April 20, 1849. *See* May 13, 1849, annals entry for Harris' death.

❡ April 19.—David D. Mitchell, replacing Thomas H. Harvey, entered upon his duties as Sup't of Indian affairs, St. Louis.

Mitchell had been superintendent before (from September, 1841, to January, 1844—*see* p. 437, and p. 502); Harvey had held the office over five years.

Ref: SIA, St. Louis, "Records," v. 9 (which show Harvey's last letter as April 18, 1849, and Mitchell's first letter as dated April 19, 1849). During the Mexican War Mitchell had been lieutenant colonel of "Price's" regiment, Missouri volunteers—*see* annals, pp. 631, 635.

❡ April 19.—The first company of Forty-niners to set out on the St. Joseph branch of the Oregon-California trail got under way— starting from a camp "at the foot of the [Missouri river] Bluffs," in present Doniphan county, Kansas, about four miles from St. Joseph, Mo.

Ahead of all others (but not for long) was Col. Vital Jarrot's "St. Clair [County, Ill.] Mining Company," (with mule teams and 13? wagons) which traveled on the 19th, about 15 miles; on the 20th reached the banks of Wolf Creek ("in crossing which our foremost team stalld . . .," wrote Joseph W. Berrien). "Found here several families of the Sac Indians Encamp'd by the creek. . . ." (There were 13 wagons in the "St. Clair" train on May 10. One had joined, and one? had left prior to that date.)

The Illinois men traveled slowly; met incoming fur traders April 26 on the

"Nemahaw"; were overtaken that night by Kentuckians (with three wagons) who moved on the next day; remained in camp on the 27th; were overtaken that evening by a seven-wagon company from Pittsburgh ("driving energetic fellows," whose captain was said to have accompanied Edwin Bryant to California in 1846); on the 29th they lost team-driver Nicholas Boismenue (in a gun accident); carried his body on to the Big Blue; camped on the Blue's left bank that night. (The Kentuckians had crossed the river around 2 P. M. that day—the 29th; and about 10 P. M. the seven-wagon Pittsburgh company reached the ford; crossed by moonlight; and camped on the other side.)

Jarrot and his party (after burying Boismenue) forded the Big Blue on April 30; went into camp on the right bank, and "lay by" on May 1, for repairs. While they were crossing (on the 30th), an Iowa company with 19 ox-drawn wagons "arrived at the ford and commenced crossing"; encamped near by. Berrien, in his diary entry of the 30th, wrote: "The Pittsburgh waggons left this afternoon and there is one or two companies ahead of us on the Independence Road [the junction of the St. Joseph with the Independence road was some nine miles west of the crossing]." On or before May 1, one wagon (Captain Lafferty's) left the Illinois train because of the slow rate of travel.

While Jarrot's company was in camp at the Big Blue, on May 1, "Some 3 or 4 ox teams and 5 or 6 six and four horse teams arrived," forded the river, and most of them went on; several more wagons came up "just at night," and crossed—except for one which broke in mid-stream and was left there till the next day. (The "Delaware [Ohio] Mining Company" reached the Big Blue ford on May 1, according to diarist Joshua D. Breyfogle, and some, or all, of the above wagons were probably the Ohioans.)

When the "St. Clair Mining Company" arrived at Fort Kearny on May 9, Berrien wrote in his diary: "We learned . . . that there are some 50 teams ahead of us on the road . . ."—*see* May annals entry for Fort Kearny, p. 848. On the 10th he recorded: "At sunrise this morning we discovered the Ox teams we passed on the Blue camped on the bank of the [Platte] river 2 miles below us. There are 2 companies of them 10 in one and 23 in the other which together with our 13 and 54 before us make the number of waggons we know of in the valley at present 100. . . ."

Ref: *Missouri Republican,* St. Louis, April 20, 29, May 11, 1849; New York *Weekly Tribune,* May 26, 1849; *Indiana Magazine of History,* v. 56 (December, 1960), pp. 273-353 (for J. W. Berrien's diary); Morgan, *op. cit.,* pp. 18-21, 181 (for item on Joshua D. Breyfogle's diary), 186 (for item on Daniel W. Gelwick's diary), p. 200 (for note on Berrien diary), and *see* folded chart for other data on diarists of 1849. Col. Vital Jarrot's father, Nicholas Jarrot (who came to Illinois in 1794 from France; died in 1823), was one of Cahokia's most prominent settlers.—*History of St. Clair County, Illinois* . . . (Edwardsville, Ill., 1881), p. 327, and *see* p. 329, for mention of Col. Vital Jarrot. On July 23, 1849, J. C. Parks, writing from Sacramento, reported "Capt. Laferday [Lafferty] was within six days' travel of that place—near the forefront of the Forty-niners traveling via South Pass."—St. Joseph (Mo.) *Gazette,* October 12, 1849.

❡ In mid-April Solomon P. Sublette was on the Santa Fe trail, with wagons, bound for New Mexico. His small(?) train, met in present Rice county about April 25(?) by Fitzpatrick and Bent (*see* May 1 entry), perhaps was the advance trading outfit of the year.

Ref: *The Daily Reveille,* May 6, 1849; Doyce B. Nunis, Jr.'s *Andrew Sublette* (Los Angeles, 1960), p. 95, notes a letter Thomas A. Hereford wrote to Solomon P. Sublette on March 9, 1850. Sublette was then in Chihuahua, Mexico. In OIA, "Letters Received from Osage River Agency," National Archives Microcopy 234, Roll 644, a letter by M. Sarver, dated at St. Louis, May 23, 1850 (and addressed to Orlando Brown, Comm'r of Indian affairs), comments on the activities of Solomon P. Sublette as Indian agent; notes Sublette's subsequent journey to Santa Fe "upon a commercial enterprise," and from there to Chihuahua—"from which place he returned in February, 1850."

❮ On April 21 the *Embassy*, and the *Alton* departed St. Joseph, Mo., for St. Louis (reaching there on the 24th and 25th). This same day the *Sacramento* arrived, unloaded, and departed downriver. (On this boat, one passenger had died of cholera.)

The *Embassy's* log showed the *Alton* and *Tamerlane* in port at St. Joseph when she left. During the return trip she met the *Sacramento* "above Independence creek," the *Timour* "at Houston's wood-yard," the *Dacotah* "at Iatan," the *Bay State* "below Iatan Bend," the *Cambria* "at Kansas [Mo.]," the *Mary* "at Randolph [Bluffs]," the *Amelia* "at Liberty [Mo.]," and other boats below.

The *Alton*, on her downriver trip met the *Timour* (bound for Savannah, Mo.) within six miles of St. Joseph, the *Bay State* above "Independence [creek] Prairie," and the *Dacotah* (bound for Council Bluffs) below that point; on the 22d (after leaving Weston, Mo., at 8. A. M.) she met the *Mary* at Fort Leavenworth; *passed* the *Sacramento* at Parkville, Mo., met the *Tamerlane*, at Liberty Landing; the *Kansas, Alexander Hamilton,* and others, below.

Bay State passenger, Lucius Fairchild, wrote of his "very pleasant trip from St. Louis being six days coming up." Emigrant Henry Page knew of two cholera deaths aboard this steamboat (which reached St. Joseph on April 21). Jasper S. Hill (who debarked from the *Timour* at St. Joseph on the 21st) wrote: "The *Bay Stat[e]*, a boat that had all kinds of stock & filth, such as mules & cattle, had the greatest number of deaths, caused by the cholera." He also stated: "There have been a considerable number of cases of the cholera on several other boats; some of which . . . kept along with our boat, sometimes ahead & other times behind." *Timour* passenger Palmer C. Tiffany wrote: "We were told that there was a number of cases of cholera on board [the *Bay State*] and that there had been some deaths on her."

Ref: St. Louis *Daily New Era,* April 25, 26, May 4, 1849; Chicago *Daily Journal,* May 7, 1849 (for the *Sacramento's* April 21 arrival); Elizabeth Page, *Wagons West* . . . (New York, c1930), pp. 98-100 (for Henry Page); *Wisconsin Historical Collections,* v. 31, p. 7 (for Lucius Fairchild's April 23, 1849, letter); Doyce B. Nunis, Jr., ed., *The Letters of a Young Miner* . . . (San Francisco, 1964), for Jasper S. Hill's April 23, 1849, letter.

❮ April 22.—A large company of Mexican traders (Juan Perea, Dr. Henry Connelly, and others) arrived at Independence, Mo. "Some of their wagons were drawn by as many as ten mules," noted California-bound W. G. Johnston (who was camped near town).

Apparently this was the party (40 Mexicans "with a train of 15 or 20 wagons") with which Samuel "Trussdail" (Trousdale?) traveled the Santa Fe trail. "Trussdail," who reached St. Louis (aboard the *Tamerlane*) on April 27, brought with him the coffined remains of "Major Samuel Hackelton, of the Illinois regiment, formerly Speaker of the House of Representatives in Illinois." The journey (as reported) had been made in 30 days.

Amos Andrews (who had quit Fremont's company at Bent's Fort in November, 1848; spent the winter there; and started east in March with William Bent) probably arrived with the above company. On the plains he had joined a Mexican party which was traveling "with more expedition" than the Bent-Hatcher train.

Ref: Johnston, *op. cit.*, p. 24; New York *Weekly Tribune*, May 12, 19, 1849; *The Daily Reveille*, St. Louis, April 29, 1849. For Perea and Connelly, see *Old Santa Fe*, Santa Fe, N. M., v. 1 (October, 1913), p. 214. The St. Joseph (Mo.) *Gazette* of May 11, 1849 (and other newspapers), noted that "A party [the above?] of 12 wealthy Mexican gentlemen, accompanied by their families, have arrived in Cincinnati [from Santa Fe, presumably]. They design spending the entire summer in the United States."

❬ April 23.—David Waldo received the contract (made with Bvt. Maj. E. A. Ogden, AQM) to transport government stores from Fort Leavenworth to Fort Laramie (in covered wagons; at the rate of $8.91 per 100 pounds). Waldo's bond was set at $150,000; his sureties were William McCoy and Jabez Smith.

Ref: 31st Cong., 1st Sess., *Sen. Ex. Doc. No. 26* (Serial 554), p. 19. Emigrant John A. Johnson, in a letter of April 30, 1849, from a camp eight miles from Independence, Mo., wrote: "A friend of ours, William McCoy . . . [of] Independence . . . says he has a contract to deliver Government supplies for the Army at . . . [Fort Laramie] . . . and that his train on their return will bring back all letters to the States. . . ." (*Pioneering on the Plains* [Kaukauna, Wis., c1924].) *See, also,* October, 1849, annals entry.

❬ April 23.—The *St. Paul* (George Cable, captain) started up the Missouri, bound for Fort Leavenworth, having aboard 11 officers, 340 troops (detachments of artillery, Third U. S. infantry, and Mounted riflemen), and their horses, baggage, etc.

Lt. Col. Samuel McRee, St. Louis, had made the contract with Captain Cable on April 19. Earlier, he had arranged, on the 11th, for the *Dacotah* (Capt. D. Finch) to carry 25 U. S. troops (with baggage, etc.) up to the fort; and on the 13th, for the *Bay State* (Capt. D. Collier) to transport two officers, 60 men, laundresses, etc. On April 27, Capt. W. H. Fulton agreed to carry two officers, 100 men, laundresses, etc., on his boat, the *Alton.*

The *St. Paul* returned to St. Louis on May 3. Her officers reported there had been considerable sickness among the troops on the passage up, ten having died of cholera. A cabin passenger—E. Alexander, from Georgia—also had succumbed to cholera. An emigrant ("Hunt") wrote from Independence (on May 2) that the *St. Paul* "Upon her arrival at this landing . . . buried three, which made eleven in all."

Ref: *Missouri Republican*, St. Louis, April 21, 1849; 31st Cong., 1st Sess., *Sen. Ex. Doc. No. 26* (Serial 554), pp. 24, 29; St. Louis *Daily New Era*, May 4, 1849; *The Daily Reveille*, St. Louis, May 9, 1849.

❡ April 25.—At St. Joseph, Mo. a correspondent wrote: ". . . there appears to be a greater number of emigrants rendezvousing at this point than at Independence. . . . The roads, in every direction, are lined with wagons of emigrant parties from the lower counties, of Missouri, and from Iowa, Wisconsin, Michigan and Illinois." He estimated 3,000 or more California-bound emigrants had arrived, up to then, at St. Joseph. Several companies, already under way, were perhaps 100 miles out on the trail. (*See* April 19 entry.)

The *Gazette* of Friday, April 27, stated that some 1,200 emigrants had arrived at St. Joseph during the week; many who had been camped in the area had departed; up to Thursday nearly 300 wagons had crossed at "Duncan's ferry" four miles above town, and 600 or more had ferried the river at St. Joseph; several hundred wagons were reported to have crossed at points upstream; and hundreds were still in the St. Joseph vicinity.

Ref: *Missouri Republican*, St. Louis, May 2, 1849; St. Joseph (Mo.) *Gazette*, April 27, 1849.

❡ April 25.—The new "fine steamer" *Dacotah* (owned by "Messrs. Chouteau & Co., St. Louis"; valued at $20,000; insured for $15,000), carrying a large number of Mormon emigrants, around 20 tons of freight (baggage, wagons, provisions), and 60 head of mules, struck a snag 25 miles below Old Fort Kearny, and sank in 20 feet of water. No lives were lost; the wagons and mules were saved.

Ref: St. Joseph (Mo.) *Gazette*, May 4, 1849; *The Daily Reveille*, St. Louis, May 5, 1849; New York *Daily Tribune*, May 16, 1849; St. Louis *Daily New Era*, May 4, June 16, 1849. The name of this boat was spelled "Dahcota" in some accounts.

❡ About April 25 cholera deaths began to occur in the town of Kansas (City), Mo. Items below, give some clues to the extent of the April-May epidemic in the Kansas-Westport-Independence, Mo., area; and on the movement of cholera into the Kansas river valley.

April 26.—"Asiatic cholera broke out in K[ansas]," recorded William Walker (Wyandot) in his diary, "Isaac McCoy [son of the Rev. Isaac McCoy (1784-1846)] departed this life to-day." (Leonidas Chick, aged nine, had died on the 25th.)

April 27.—"A few cases of cholera, in mild form, have occurred here; two deaths last week," wrote "A" in a letter from Independence.

April 29.—"There have now . . . been over seven deaths by Cholera in Independence in all and eight at Kansas at the mouth of the Kansas river, but it does not spread in town nor extend into the country," wrote emigrant John A. Johnson (from a camp some miles out of town).

April 30.—"the Cholera is at Kansas, and . . . 15 persons there have died within 3 or 4 days now past, and . . . among the dead is Mrs. John C. McCoy," Jotham Meeker recorded in his diary, at Ottawa mission, from news just received by the arrival from the Kaw's mouth of Agent C. N. Handy. (Virginia [Chick] McCoy had died on the 28th.) A Jackson county, Mo., resident later (May 26) referred to the April epidemic at Kansas "where in 2 or 3 days it took off fifteen persons, some of whom were inhabitants."

May 1.—William Bent (and Thomas Fitzpatrick), coming in the Santa Fe trail, and passing the junction with the California-Oregon trail (in present Johnson county) on the 29th of April, arrived at Westport. On reaching St. Louis, Bent was reported as estimating that six to 10 deaths from cholera had occurred "from each [emigrant] encampment."

May 2.—"In the streets of Independence the moving crowd is considerable . . .," wrote "Hunt" (an emigrant who had arrived there May 1), ". . . [cholera] prevails in and about Independence to a slight extent, and probably some twenty of the emigrants have died in the last two weeks."

May 3.—"Cholera abating in Kansas," wrote William Walker in his diary. (But was it?) "It is estimated that the deaths at Kansas for the two weeks previous to the 8th inst. [the April 25-May 7 period] averaged full ten daily," reported the St. Louis *New Era* of May 12. (This exaggeration of the facts probably stemmed from a statement, elsewhere, that as high as 10 persons had died there in a day.) The *New Era* also said that cholera was still "raging to some extent" at Kansas and Independence; and that both places were "nearly depopulated."

May 6-8.—Emigrant Caleb N. Ormsby (whose party was encamped some miles out of Independence) wrote (on May 14): ". . . but few deaths were reported till about the 6th inst., when the indications were that it [cholera] was to take a wider and more effectual range. On the 6th [Sunday], 7th and 8th a pretty general alarm was manifest; deaths were common both among the emigrants and citizens; gloom pervaded all classes, even to such a degree that the gambling shops in town were closed on the Sabbath."

May 7.—Emigrant Isaac J. Wistar (whose party was just getting under way from the Independence area) wrote: "There is quite a populous graveyard at the crossing of the Big Blue [of Missouri], and numerous single graves along the trail." (On May 6 he had noted: "There is a large camp below us on the Blue, badly afflicted with cholera, of which five have died, two of them last night.")

May 9.—This day six or seven deaths occurred at Kansas—according to the *Highland Mary's* officers (arriving at St. Louis May 11).

May 10.—"The Cholera is increasing at Kansas and Independence, among the California emigrants, and along the river," wrote Jotham Meeker (at Ottawa mission). Emigrant George M. Harker, in a letter (of the 10th) from Independence, stated: "The deaths from cholera for the past few days in this place and immediate vicinity have ranged in number from five to eleven. Two or three citizens have died, and the rest have been strangers." (*See* May 13 "Turner & Allen" annals entry for names of some victims.)

By May 13 or 14 there were "only a few cases of cholera at either Independence or Kansas"; and but three deaths at the latter place on the 13th—as reported by persons on the *Boreas No. 3* (which reached St. Louis May 16). The deaths of Dr. Joseph H. Palmer, and Mr. Knapp of Ann Arbor, Mich., at Independence, on May 14, were noted in the Chicago *Daily Journal*. An emigrant had stated on May 11: "The cholera has raged at this place

[Independence] severely for several days, but is now apparently subsiding, as emigration ceases. . . . The alarm among the people was excessive . . . [cholera] is now reported . . . prevailing with great violence among the emigrants encamped on the Kansas and the Blue."

A man who left Union Town (in western Shawnee county of today) on May 13, to return to the "settlements," and who probably reached the Missouri line around the 16th, wrote (later) that he had seen eight graves (presumed cholera victims) on his way in. "A number of deaths have occurred in the camps, about Independence, thence to the line, and in the neighborhood of Westport," he added; and noted, too, "At Westport some deaths have occurred" (but only two or three were residents). A May 25 cholera victim was 26-year-old Charles K. Cummins (son of Indian agent R. W. Cummins), who lived near Westport.

On June 15 an Independence correspondent stated that cholera had "disappeared entirely" for the last eight or 10 days; and the *Highland Mary's* officers (having left Weston June 20; and arriving at St. Louis on the 23d) reported there was no cholera at the river towns.

See p. 878 for the second epidemic in the Kansas-Independence area.

Ref (aside from those noted above): *The Annals of Kansas City,* Kansas City, Mo., v. 1 (October, 1924), p. 469; W. H. Chick's reminiscences (typed copy in KHi ms. division); *Missouri Republican,* St. Louis, May 12, 17, June 4, 21, 1849; *The Daily Reveille,* St. Louis, May 5, 6, 9, 13, 23, 1849; St. Louis *Daily New Era,* June 4, 1849; *Glimpses of the Past,* St. Louis, v. 6, p. 45; *The Weekly Tribune,* Liberty, Mo., May 18 and June 1, 1849; John A. Johnson's April 29, 1849, letter, in *Pioneering on the Plains* (Kaukauna, Wis., c1924); Bieber, *op. cit.,* p. 354; Russell E. Bidlack, *Letters Home* . . . (Ann Arbor, Mich., 1960), p. 18 (for Ormsby); Isaac J. Wistar's *Autobiography* . . . (Philadelphia, 1937), pp. 52, 53. Lists of persons who died of cholera at Independence in 1849, were published in the *Missouri Republican* of August 12, 1849.

❦ April 27.—The *Boreas No. 3,* leaving St. Joseph for St. Louis, met this day the *Meteor No. 3* "in Sullivan's Bend," the *St. Joseph* (bound for Council Bluffs) at the "foot of Sullivan's Bend," the *Mandan* "above Independence creek," the *Martha* "above Cow Island"; on the 28th, met the *Eliza Stewart* at Wayne City (landing point for Independence, Mo.), and others below; arrived at St. Louis the morning of May 3.

Ref: St. Louis *Daily New Era,* May 3, 7, 1849.

❦ April.—On the 28th, at Fort Scott ("Kansas"), a correspondent wrote: "During the last week about 40 wagons [for California] have passed here from the southwest part of this State [*i. e.,* southwest Missouri], and some eighteen wagons are expected to-morrow from the Cherokee nation [but not an all-Cherokee party?], for the Plains. A majority of these wagons will not touch at any of the river towns, but will go through the Old Pottawatomie nation [the old reserve is shown on Gregg's map, reprinted, in part, on p. 606], and strike the Santa Fe road at the Council Grove. There are many emigrants from the southwest who will take this route. Large companies from

Polk, Cedar, and Dade counties [in southwestern Missouri] are expected in a few days, to take the above named route."

[So far as known, 1849 was the first year in which California-bound traffic traveled the Fort Scott-Council Grove pathway. Travelers on this wagon trail crossed Pottawatomie creek near present Lane, Franklin county (*see* pp. 322, 336, 535). This was the fording point later(?) known (and notorious during John Brown's time in Kansas) as "Dutch Henry's Crossing." Henry Sherman, for whom it was named—and possibly the name was applied as early as 1849—had been in the vicinity since about 1847.]

Of the "about 40 wagons" (above) some 24 were in Captain Bogue's Springfield, or, Greene county, Mo., company, which pioneered(?) the Fort Scott-Council Grove trail. (*See, also,* May-June entry, p. 855.) Perhaps most of the others went into the company formed when the "some eighteen wagons" from the Cherokee Nation arrived on April 29(?). The recollections of W. W. Buffington (a Cherokee) seem to indicate that "Judge Tully of Missouri" was elected captain of the combined train. Going by way of Westport, and Independence(?), the company, in early June, was traveling up the Platte. It appears that the Cherokees in the party numbered 15—headed by Dr. Jeter L. Thompson. Between June 8 and about June 11(?), near the Forks of the Platte, nine of them died of cholera. Others of the train were cholera victims, also. For further mention of Dade county, Mo., emigrants, *see* May-June entry, p. 855, item on Capt. L. C. Bostick's company.

James W. Evans, a '49er, wrote (in an October 27, 1850, letter) of his overland journey: "I left Home on the 24th day of March [1849]; left Fort Smith on the 30th: Remained 3 weeks in Benton Co. Ark., Apr 23rd got into the State of Mo.; Got to Fort Scott, May 1st; Left Mo. at West Point—and struck out West, May 8th. . . . Passed Fort Kearney May 28th Fort Laramie, June 16th. . . ."

Ref: *Missouri Republican,* St. Louis, May 14, 1849; for the Cherokees *see:* Foreman, *op. cit.,* pp. 82-87; Bieber, *op. cit.,* pp. 345, 346; Settle, *op. cit.,* pp. 73, 74; *Colorado Magazine,* Denver, v. 15 (May, 1938), p. 104; *Missouri Historical Review,* Columbia, v. 43 (October, 1948), pp. 38-47 (for Evans' letter).

❡ April 28-29—F. Robidoux, who had left the American Fur Company's trading post at Fort Laramie on March 24, and new Fort Kearny (U. S. military post) on, or about, April 18, arrived at St. Joseph, Mo., on the 28th. He brought a large mail from "Fort Childs" (*i. e.,* new Fort Kearny); and apparently was one day in advance of cotravelers. "Messrs. Bissonette, McLean, Richard and Bordeau," who, also, had left Fort Laramie March 24, reached St. Louis on May 9; and newspaper accounts stated *they* had arrived at St. Joseph on April 29.

These incoming traders had met the first California-bound party from the St. Joseph area (a company headed by "Capt. [Vital] Jarrot of Cahokia") on the Nemaha April 26—as elsewhere noted.

Ref: St. Joseph (Mo.) *Gazette,* May 4, 1849; *The Daily Reveille,* St. Louis, May 11, 1849; New York *Weekly Tribune,* May 26, 1849 (from Saint Louis *Daily Union*).

❈ April 30.—James Brown and William H. Russell ("Brown & Russell") received the contract (made with Bvt. Maj. E. A. Ogden, AQM) to transport government stores from Fort Leavenworth to Santa Fe (in wagons; for $9.88 per 100 pounds; with the addition of five percent to the weight of bacon).

The bond was $150,000; sureties were John S. Jones, Charles O. Jones, Amos Fristoe, George Scrogin, John S. Brown, W. Watson, David Thompson, George R. Smith, William B. Waddell, H. W. Waddell, J. W. Waddell, James H. Graham, and Robert B. Bradford.

Ref: 31st Cong., 1st Sess., Sen. Ex. Doc. No. 26 (Serial 554), p. 24.

❈ April-May.—A few of the Forty-niner trains or companies which set out from the Independence, Mo., area to travel the Oregon-California trail across "Kansas" (in addition to some mentioned in other annals items) are listed below.

William Henry Russell, of Callaway county, Mo. (to California, 1846; back east, 1847), captained a large (all? mule-drawn wagons) train which left the Missouri border around April 24. David Willock was first lieutenant; and in the party was (Robert) Eugene Russell. The company (numbering 88, or more, on April 17; but further enlarged before starting) included a group of Newark, N. J., men (the "mule" division from "Gen." John S. Darcy's company), and, also, a party of Monroe, Mich., gold seekers. At least part of the way there were some families. By May 5 Russell's train had passed the Big Blue; and the South Platte was forded on May 21(?). The company broke up en route west. Russell reached Sutter's Fort on August 8.

Ref: Morgan, op. cit., pp. 100, 157; Missouri Republican, St. Louis, April 17, 23, 1849; Johnston, op. cit., pp. 13, 20, 21, 47, 62, 63; St. Joseph (Mo.) Gazette, January 4, 1850; New York Daily Tribune, May 5, 11, 1849. See annals index for earlier mention of W. H. Russell, Willock, and R. E. Russell.

Amos P. Josselyn, of Zanesville, Ohio, and six companions (with two wagons) who left Independence April 24, joined (there?) seven men (with two wagons) from Newark, Ohio; then, at Kansas river, became part of a company of 53 men (which soon divided into two parties—Josselyn's group, 26 men); later (beyond South Pass) separated from the Steubenville, Ohio, men who made up part of the 26. Josselyn's group reached Salt Lake City on July 14.

Ref: Western Humanities Review, Salt Lake City, v. 3 (April, 1949), pp. 102-104; Morgan, op. cit., p. 190.

A large company from Cincinnati, "well equipped," who "wore uniforms similar to those of Uncle Sam's soldiers," made a start from the Missouri border in the latter part of April. When W. G. Johnston's party reached the "Topeka" Kansas river ferry on May 2, "The Cincinnati company so handsomely equipped . . . was in the act of crossing." "Its members present a fine appearance in their blue uniforms, but only a few seem inclined to work," wrote Johnston. Their 12 wagons, "built of iron," proved unsuitable for ferrying by themselves. On May 24, near the South fork of the Platte, emigrant James A. Pritchard noted: ". . . we passed the Cincinnati Train a joint Stock association of

50 members. They had 8 mules to the wagon." This probably was the company of Cincinnatians above, which, at Independence, on April 6, was said to number 51 men, 10 wagons and 11 mules per wagon. [Dr.] J. H. Levering was listed as "president."

Ref: *Missouri Republican*, April 11, 1849; Johnston, *op. cit.*, pp. 24, 34-36, 42, 43; Morgan, *op. cit.*, pp. 69, 70 (for Pritchard); *KHQ*, v. 18, pp. 324, 325 (for an item on "Dr. Levering's party").

James Stewart (experienced on the Santa Fe trail) headed an early-starting company built around a small Palmyra, Mo., group which included "E. R. Pye & Son." William G. Johnston, of Pittsburgh, Pa. (whose 1849 journal is among the best), and companions, joined this train (mule-drawn wagons) which left the Missouri border on April 28. At Kansas river, May 2, with additions, the party numbered 24 men; but had a further accession of 10 (with two wagons and 25 mules). They organized, formally, west of Cross creek; elected Stewart as captain, "Lt. Blakey" as guard captain, "Captains" Pye, Karkuff, and Washington as a rules committee. As did most companies, this one later split up.

Ref: W. G. Johnston, *op. cit.*; C. W. Haskins, *The Argonauts of California* (1890), p. 405.

"Capt." Sublette headed a party of some 38 men (Mississippians, Texans, and Missourians) who traveled by ox-train. (Reuben Reynolds was one of the Missourians.) On May 6 Sublette's company was in the Little (Red) Vermillion area. Emigrant James A. Pritchard, on May 16, on the Little Blue, passed "the large train of 50[!] wagons commanded by Capt Sublett." But the company had just split—27 wagons staying with him.

Ref: Doyce B. Nunis, Jr., *Andrew Sublette* (1960), pp. 91-93; Morgan, *op. cit.*, pp. 61, 62, 147; Johnston, *op. cit.*, pp. 43-45. It now seems established that "Capt." Sublette was *not* Andrew W. Sublette (who, in the summer of 1849 was in Sonora, Calif.). See biographical account of Andrew in Dale L. Morgan and Eleanor T. Harris, *The Rocky Mountain Journals of William Marshall Anderson, op. cit.*, p. 363.

Benoni M. Hudspeth (mountain man) guided a large ox-wagon train which started at the beginning of May. "S."—writing from Independence May 4— stated it was "composed chiefly of persons of this [Jackson] and adjacent [Missouri] counties." Among these Forty-niners were John J. Myers (who had gone to California in 1843 in the Chiles party), J. C. McCarty (Santa Fe trader), of Lexington, Mo., and four brothers of Benoni Hudspeth. On May 6, west of the Wakarusa, emigrant Bennett C. Clark stated this train contained about 40 wagons, with some 600 head of stock. There were Ohioans in the train, but not all remained with it. John A. Johnson, and nine others (with mule teams), from Lower Sandusky, Ohio, left the border on May 2. On May 8 Johnson wrote: "Fox and Titus and Headspeth's train up with us on road together"—this at a point 15 to 20 miles before reaching the Kansas river. Some of Hudspeth's train (including the Johnson party) crossed the Kansas near Union Town on May 10; but others ferried at present Topeka. In a letter from Fort Kearny, May 23, Johnson wrote: "We have separated from that part of our travelling Company from Missouri leaving only ourselves and the Seneca and Tiffin [Ohio] boys, 18 in all." The Hudspeth ox-train did not reach Fort Kearny till June 10. Before then, another Ohio party of seven wagons, 26 yoke of oxen, headed by Alexander W. McCoy (and including his brother Samuel F.) had joined up (caught up). [These McCoys were brothers of John and William McCoy, Independence, Mo., residents, and Santa Fe traders.] However, on June 11, the McCoys left the Hudspeth train (which then seemed about to split). Beyond Fort Laramie, June 22, emigrant Isaac J. Wistar noted in his diary: "Overtook the Missouri train of 47 wagons and 200 men, guided by Hudspeth."

Ref: *The Daily Reveille*, St. Louis, May 10, 1849; *Pioneering on the Plains* (Kaukauna, Wis., c1924); *Missouri Republican*, St. Louis, May 13, 1849; Morgan, *op. cit.*, pp. 27, 165; Read and Gaines, 1949 ed., *op. cit.*, pp. 139, 621, 635, 692; *Missouri Historical Review*, v. 23 (October, 1928), p. 7. *A Memorial and Biographical Record of Kansas City and Jackson County, Mo.* (Chicago, 1896), p. 249, states that Thomas Hudspeth, of Fort Osage township (since 1828), crossed the plains in 1849, but died in California November 16, 1849. The Fort Osage township, Jackson county, Missouri, 1850 census (taken September 26, 1850) lists the household of William Hudspeth (73) in which were sons Silas (35), Benoni (33), Joel (31), George (29), and Robert (26); also the households of Joseph Hudspeth (41) and family, Nathan Hudspeth (47) and family, and Cyntha Hudspeth (female; 36) and family. Was Cyntha the widow of Thomas?

Milton McGee (later prominent in Kansas City, Mo.'s development), who had gone to California in 1843 (with Chiles), piloted a Forty-niner company (chiefly from Ray county, Mo., apparently)—and pioneereed a trail into California. He left his family in Jackson county (with his brother Mobillon, an account says); but his brother Fry P. McGee, who traveled overland West in 1849 (with Milton?) took his family. The Fry McGee family returned to Missouri in 1850, and, in July, 1854, settled at 110-mile creek crossing on the Santa Fe trail. Milton McGee, it is said, came back "with all the gold he could carry."

Ref: G. R. Stewart's *The California Trail*, pp. 223, 269; *KHC*, v. 8, p. 237; Kansas City (Mo.) *Star*, November 20, 1904.

"[William] Waldo's large [ox] train from Jackson County, Missouri," and "the large ox train led by Captain _____ Boone of Kentucky" (*i. e.*, Daniel Boone, of Jackson county, Mo.?) were encamped near, or by, the Shunganunga on May 12. On the 15th, having crossed the Kansas river, and camped near Soldier creek, emigrant Henry Shombre (of an Indiana company) "went to a large ox camp close by   saw Mrs & Mr Boon gds of old D Boon   she was very inteligent and good looking   he tol[erably] so." Waldo's train was in the Little (Red) Vermillion area on May 17. Boone's train, on the 29th was camped not far from Fort Kearny.

Ref: Wistar, *op. cit.*, pp. 56, 57, 60, 75; Shombre "diary," *loc. cit.*; *Glimpses of the Past*, v. 5 (April-June, 1938), p. 60 (for William Waldo). Daniel Boone (son of Daniel Morgan Boone) aged 40, and his wife Marie Constance (Philibert) Boone, of Jackson county, Mo., went to California overland in 1849. It seems likely it was this Daniel Boone (who *was* a grandson of the famous Daniel) who captained the above train. Boone Hayes (another Daniel Boone descendant), also of Jackson county, Mo., and his three sons (Amazon, Linville, and Upton) crossed the plains in 1849, with ox teams. Perhaps they were with the Boone company. *See A Memorial and Biographical Record of Kansas City and Jackson County, Mo.* (1896), pp. 78, 79 (for Boone Hayes), and p. 354 (for Daniel Boone); also, *KHC*, v. 8, p. 434. "Hayes," or "Hays"? Elsewhere, and by others of this family (*e. g.*, Seth M. Hays), it was spelled "Hays." By inference, Napoleon Boone (so far as known, the first white boy born in "Kansas") probably went West with his brother (the above Daniel) in 1849. Napoleon Boone (born August 2, 1828—*see* annals, p. 151) died in California on May 20, 1850.

Edwin Bryant (to California in 1846; east with Kearny, 1847; author of

What I Saw in California) headed a pack-mule train of Kentuckians and In-dianans (principally) which set out May 8. His company of around 60 men, with from 155 to 180 mules (accounts vary), reached Fort Kearny by, or before, May 21.

Ref: *Missouri Republican,* St. Louis, April 17, May 21, 1849; *The Daily Reveille,* St. Louis, April 28, June 9, 1849; New York *Weekly Tribune,* February 24, April 7, June 2, 1849; *Glimpses of the Past,* St. Louis, v. 6, pp. 46, 49; Shombre "diary," *loc. cit.;* Read and Gaines, *op. cit.,* p. 39; Wistar, *op. cit.,* May 11 entry; Johnston, *op. cit.,* pp. 16, 18, 25; Haskins, *op. cit.,* p. 408.

The "Wolverine Rangers," an "ox company," from Michigan, was a stock company (each member paying into the treasury $85). The captain "Judge [James D.] Potts" (who replaced J. J. Baker, after 10 days), was (according to Oliver Goldsmith) "made of the right kind of stuff and proved worthy." It was May 28 before the "Wolverine Rangers" reached (or crossed?) the Kansas river ferry. Later, if not at the beginning, there were women in this party.

Ref: Read and Gaines, *op. cit.,* pp. 130, 134, 135, 613, 636, 637; Morgan, *op. cit.,* p. 195 (items on James Pratt letters), and p. 198 (William Swain, diarist).

Lewis Jones, of Jackson county, Mo., headed a company which probably left the Missouri border about May 18. A Jackson county history states that "Lewis Jones, John Bartleson, L. W. Boggs, Major Hickman, and others, fitted out an expedition [in 1849] to California [and later returned to Independence]." "S." (from Independence, on May 14) noted: "There is also quite a large company from this county, yet to start. [It] . . . will go out under guidance of Lewis Jones, Esq., an old hand upon the plains." On May 21 Jones' train was beyond the Wakarusa crossing; on June 5, at Wyeth's creek on the Little Blue, the McCoy party (above mentioned) "passed Jones' company."

Ref: *The History of Jackson County, Missouri* (Kansas City, Mo., 1881), p. 644; *The Daily Reveille,* St. Louis, May 22, 1849; *Pioneering on the Plains, op. cit.* Another Boggs— John O.—"crossed the plains with ox teams [in 1849], leaving Jackson county on the 7th of May [possibly with the Hudspeth-led train?], and arriving at the gold diggings on the 7th of September." He returned in 1850. *See A Memorial and Biographical Record of Kansas City and Jackson County, Mo.* (1896), p. 132.

Joseph Thing (who had gone West with N. J. Wyeth in 1834) captained a pack-mule train composed of two companies organized at Boston, Mass.— the "Granite State and California Mining and Trading Company" (some 29 men); and the "Mount Washington Company" (about 40 members). Several from both parties died of cholera while encamped near Independence, in May. It was May 26 or 27 when Thing's train crossed the Missouri line. On June 12, west of the Big Blue, on Wyeth's creek, Capt. Howard Stansbury (U. S. A.) observed: "We have been in company with multitudes of emigrants the whole day. . . . We passed a company from Boston, consisting of seventy persons, one hundred and forty pack and riding mules, a number of riding horses, and a drove of cattle for beef. The expedition, as might be expected, and as is too generally the case, was badly conducted: the mules were overloaded [poorly packed, etc.]. . . ."

Ref: Stansbury, *op. cit.,* pp. 24, 30; O. T. Howe's *Argonauts of '49* (1923), pp. 44, 195, 196, 201; Webster, *op. cit.;* annals, p. 262 (for Thing in 1834); Haskins, *op. cit.,* pp. 411, 412.

Another of the at least six companies organized at Boston was the Sagamore and Sacramento Mining and Trading Company from Lynn, Mass., commanded by seven-footer Francis Dixon, and numbering (at the start) 52 men. Stillman Churchill and Joseph Sedgley were two members who kept diaries. By May 20 this group was on the plains 300 miles beyond Independence, and reported to be in fine spirits and condition. The party, earlier, had been described as having gray uniforms, with silver braid; driving made-to-order wagons (one for every four men), drawn by "four horses resplendent in silver-plated harnesses and from the rear of each wagon projected a swivel gun."

Ref: New York *Weekly Tribune*, March 17, 1849; Howe, *op. cit.*, p. 43. *See* Morgan, *op. cit.*, pp. 183 and 196, for items on Churchill and Sedgley.

The "Congress and California Mutual Protection Association" was another New England company organized at Boston. "Major" John Webber, of Boston, was president and captain. (The officers wore navy blue; the noncoms and privates had gray uniforms.) *Dr. Charles Robinson, Fitchburg, Mass. (the company's surgeon), from 1854 to 1861 had a leading role in Kansas territorial history; and in 1861 became the first Kansas state governor.* When the CCMPA reached Kansas (City), Mo. (via steamboat on April 10), there was a split into two parties, and a subsequent division of the jointly held equipment and supplies, while the New Englanders spent a month in the Kansas (City) area. Printed excerpts from Charles Robinson's '49er diary (the original not in existence?) describe his party's experiences in the Kaw's mouth area; and give details of the "Kansas" section of the overland journey (begun on May 10).

Ref: Octavius T. Howe's *Argonauts of '49* (Cambridge, Mass., 1923), pp. 41-43; Frank W. Blackmar, *The Life of Charles Robinson* . . . (Topeka, 1902), pp. 43-51; *Nebraska and Kansas, Report of the Committee of the Massachusetts Emigrant Aid Co.* . . . (Boston, 1854), p. 11*ff* (for Robinson diary excerpts). *See, also,* "Charles Robinson— Yankee '49er: His Journey to California" (compiled by L. Barry), in *KHQ*, v. 34, pp. 179-188.

The "Colony Guards," from New York City, commanded by Dr. J. McNulty, also wore special garb. Indianan J. W. Berrien described "a party of New Yorkers . . . dressed in uniforms of Blue Cassimere, armed with Government Rifles Bowie Knives and Colts Revolvers," who were "the most lackadaisycal Milk and Waterish fellows" he ever saw. "They are as green as a pumpkin vine," he added. The New Yorkers debarked (from the *Alice*) at Kansas landing, Mo., on April 5. Far out on the trail—beyond Fort Kearny, J. G. Bruff, on June 24, "dined & supped with Capt. McNulty commandg a New York Compy called the Colony Guards." He referred to them as "a very clever set of adventurers—a company . . . with mule wagons also, but the members were mounted on mules."

Ref: Read and Gaines, *op. cit.*, pp. 587, 588; *Indiana Magazine of History*, v. 56, p. 279.

❧ May.—Among the trains or companies of Forty-niners starting from St. Joseph, Mo., or its vicinity, the following were a *few* (not noted in other annals items) which traveled across "Kansas" by way of the Oregon-California trail (St. Joseph branch).

James Craig was elected captain of a company (about 75 persons; at least two families) which left Oregon, Holt county, Mo., around May 1; and crossed the Missouri at Iowa Point. The train of 25 wagons organized in the Great

Nemaha Subagency area. [John Utt (later a White Cloud, Kan., resident) recollected that he took two barrels of brandy along.] On the North Platte, "Doctor Westerfield" replaced Craig as captain. These Missourians reached Sacramento in October; most of them came back "home."

Ref: *The History of Holt and Atchison Counties, Mo.* (St. Joseph, 1882), pp. 567-571.

William B. Almond ("an old mountaineer") captained a Platte county, Mo., company of "seven waggons & 37 men" which organized on February 3, 1849, and set out May 3. This party reached Sutter's Fort on July 30, all the wagons going through safely. Almond later lived (and died) in Kansas.

Ref: *Pony Express Courier,* v. 9, no. 4 (September, 1942), p. 5. W. M. Paxton's *Annals of Platte County, Missouri* (1897), p. 110. In a biographical sketch of Almond, published in Sheffield Ingalls' *History of Atchison County, Kansas* (Lawrence, 1916), p. 98, it is stated that Almond's company of '49ers included Benjamin Holladay.

Another famous mountain man—Antoine Robidoux—"guided a party from St. Joseph to California in 1849; he was encountered along the trail by [Ansel J.] McCall and others, and mentioned by [Augustus R.] Burbank as far west as Green River" (quote from Dale L. Morgan).

Ref: Morgan, *op. cit.,* p. 151.

J. C. Davis (an experienced man, who had been with Fremont—*see* annals, p. 687) headed a train built around the "Mound City Association," from St. Louis. A company member wrote from Fort Bridger, July 4, that the "party consists of several Western associations who have combined together on the way and get on well under Col. [J. C.] D[avis]'s skillful management." They had reached Fort Bridger on July 3.

Ref: *Missouri Republican,* St. Louis, April 23, 1849; New York *Daily Tribune,* October 2, 1849. St. Joseph was the starting point for the "Mound City Assn."

The "Mt. Pleasant [Henry county, Ia.] Mining Company" left St. Joseph May 1. (Some had reached that town by steamboat; others, with the wagons, traveled overland.) On May 11, beyond the Big Blue, the company organized; electing Presley Saunders as captain. At Fort Kearny, on May 18, Jasper S. Hill wrote that the train (of ox-drawn wagons) numbered 15; and the company contained 42 men, one woman and a child.

Ref: Doyce B. Nunis, Jr., ed., *The Letters of a Young Miner* (San Francisco, 1964).

Joseph H. Cutting, of Lockport, Ill. (to California in 1847; back in 1848), was guide, and J. A. Gooding, captain, of the train (mule-drawn wagons) known as the "Banner Company"—composed of men from Wisconsin and Illinois—which set out early in May. "F. T. S.," writing from Fort Kearny on May 22, stated: "We are now 240 miles from St. Joseph, with about 1400 emigrant teams ahead of us, and about 7000 behind. . . I think we have got the best train that has started upon the plains, and I believe Mr. Gooding is well pleased with all the boys and his company." Later, it was reported this company had passed all but about 20 teams before reaching the "diggings."

Ref: Chicago *Daily Journal,* June 19, 1849; St. Joseph (Mo.) *Gazette,* November 16, 1849; Gustavus C. Pearson, *Overland in 1849* . . . (Los Angeles, 1961), p. 7.

The "Illinois Sucker Company" (H. Buffum, president; mountain man David Adams, of St. Louis, guide) encamped, before April 13, in "Kansas" across the river from St. Joseph; probably numbered some 120 persons (including eight ladies and four children) when starting. There were 40 wagons—both ox and mule teams.

Ref: *Missouri Republican*, April 20, 1849; New York *Weekly Tribune*, February 24, 1849; St. Joseph (Mo.) *Gazette*, April 27, 1849; Haskins, *op. cit.*, p. 403. For David Adams, *see* annals index.

James Tate, of Callaway county, Mo. (one of three known diarists who described the journey overland across Missouri), and part of his train, crossed the Missouri, by the St. Joseph ferry, on May 5; camped 10 miles out (in "Kansas"); were joined by expected arrivals on the 8th; organized on the 9th, "having 15 wagons, 58 men and 2 ladies"; reached Fort Kearny on May 21. Tate (aged 53) died October 22, 1849, near Sacramento, Calif.

Ref: James Tate's diary (typescript), in Western Historical Manuscripts Collection, University of Missouri, Columbia, Mo.; Morgan, *op. cit.*, p. 198.

A Boone county, Mo., company, originally about 42(?) persons, which perhaps left the Missouri about May 7, organized at the Big Nemaha on May 11 after increasing the group to 57 by adding some 15 "strangers." William Y. Hitt was elected captain. Before June 3 (and before reaching Fort Laramie) a split occurred. A group which included the correspondent "Old Boone" (name not ascertained), and William B. Royall (*see* p. 728), and consisted of six wagons and 27 men, broke off from the others, and chose M. C. Stone as captain. They reached Sutter's Mill on August 20.

Ref: W. D. Wyman, ed., *California Emigrant Letters* (New York, c1952), pp. 46, 47, 55-58, 78, 117, 118; St. Joseph (Mo.) *Gazette*, February 1, 1850. For William Y. Hitt on the Santa Fe trail *see* annals, p. 151.

The "Illinois Union Band"—a train of 26 wagons, left St. Joseph May 11; at a rendezvous on Wolf creek (18 miles out), where nine other wagons were to join (as reported), officers were elected (Dr. H. [or J. C.?] Gray was chosen as captain). This train crossed the Big Blue on May 19.

Ref: St. Joseph (Mo.) *Gazette*, May 11, 1849; *The Daily Reveille*, St. Louis, June 2, 1849 (from St. Joseph *Adventure*).

The "St. Joseph Mining Company" (a small pack-mule party of 19? men) left the Missouri river May 12; lost one man (Samuel Wilson) from cholera, about 75 miles out; later (not in "Kansas"), another died in a gun accident. Some, or all, of the party reached Sacramento, Calif., on August 5. Joel Ryan of this company later lived in Doniphan county, Kan.

Ref: St. Joseph (Mo.) *Adventure*, November 2, 1849; St. Joseph (Mo.) *Gazette*, May 4, 25, June 22, November 2, 1849, January 4, February 1, 22, 1850; P. L. Gray's *Doniphan County History* (1905), Pt. 2; *The History of Buchanan County, Missouri* (St. Joseph, 1881), p. 206.

The Rev. Isaac Owen, of Bloomington, Ind., headed a large company of Indianans (principally) which, on April 27, encamped "across the river six miles south of St. Joseph," was said to number 107 persons. On the Little Blue, May 24, P. A. Athearn's company "Overtook and passed several large trains, numbering in all this day 200 waggons. Owens train from Bloomington amongst the number." A Mr. "Brubanks" (Augustus R. Burbank) of Naples, Ill., writing from Fort Laramie June 19, stated: "The Bloomington, Indiana company has broken up into many small divisions, many deserted, and would not keep the Sabbath. The final breaking up was on June 6. Myself and others formed a company of 13 wagons of which I have command. The Rev. Isaac Owen and family, Rev. James Corwine, and the most of the families are with us. . . ."

Ref: St. Joseph (Mo.) *Gazette,* April 27, August 3, December 14, 1849; *The Pacific Historian,* Stockton, Calif., v. 2, p. 7 (for Athearn); New York *Weekly Tribune,* January 27, 1849. *See* Morgan, *op. cit.,* p. 182, for note on Burbank, and his diary.

The Charlestown, Va., Mining Company (80 men; each paying $300 for membership) reached St. Joseph, Mo., on April 19 (or most of the party did) aboard the *Embassy* (one member had died of cholera on the boat). Frank Smith (an experienced man) was obtained as guide. The Virginians, and their 16-wagon, mule-drawn train, left a camp on the Missouri river bluffs (in "Kansas") on May 12; crossed the Big Blue on May 20. On the 26th, as Vincent Geiger recorded in his diary: "we had a general meeting of the company, and by a unanimous vote, we took our Guide in as a full member of our company. Our Captain & Lieutenants then resigned and placed the entire command & supreme control of our company in the hands of Mr. Smith, and declared him our leader & Captain." The Charlestown Company reached Fort Kearny on May 28; arrived at the "diggings" at the end of August.

Ref: David M. Potter, ed., *Trail to California* . . . (1945); Edward W. McIlhany, *Recollections of a '49er* . . . (Kansas City, Mo., 1908); St. Joseph (Mo.) *Gazette,* April 27, 1849.

Dr. Thomas James White, of St. Louis, his wife, two daughters, a son, a niece, a nephew, three servants, accompanied (only as far as the Big Blue) by Almarin B. Paul, composed a company that traveled near, or with Loring's Mounted riflemen command. On the Little Blue, May 24, "Capt. Jas. White's" train had passed emigrant George M. Harker's company. "In this co. are Dr. White and family, and two other families," he wrote. (Loring passed the same day.) White's party reached Fort Kearny on June 3; and Fort Laramie on the 23d. ("Joaquin" wrote from there on July 21: "Dr. White's company . . . was getting along better than any other train on the road.") The St. Louis *Reveille* published an August 1 letter from Fort Laramie which stated: "Miss Fanny White, reported dead was married at Scott's Bluffs to Mr. McKewen. Her father Dr. White is said to be acting as Army Surgeon."

Ref: *Missouri Republican,* June 24, 1849; *The Daily Reveille,* St. Louis, May 23, August 9, September 6, 1849; St. Louis *Daily New Era,* May 12, 1849; *Quarterly of the Society of California Pioneers,* San Francisco, v. 4 (1927) pp. 25, 26; New York *Daily Tribune,* June 25, 1849; New York *Weekly Tribune,* September 15, 1849; St. Joseph (Mo.) *Gazette,* October 19, 1849.

❡ May 1.—Charles N. Handy, appointed March 30 to head the Osage River Agency (replacing James S. Rains), arrived at his headquarters—the recent "Sac & Fox Agency" house.

Ottawa missionary Jotham Meeker, under date of April 30, wrote: "The new agent Handy arrives— stops with us for the night. . . ."

Ref: Comm'r of Indian Affairs, *Report,* 1849 (Handy's report, therein); Jotham Meeker's "Diary." Whereas Rains apparently had lived at the former Osage River Subagency house on Pottawatomie creek (*see* June 29, 1848, annals entry), Handy "repaired to the Agency house which is located in the Sac and Fox nation, on the south side of the Marais des Cygnes . . . about 65 miles southwest of Westport . . . Missouri." The Washington *Whig* (quoted in the New York *Weekly Tribune*, April 14, 1849) stated that Handy, a native of Worcester county, Md., and "quite a young man," had removed to Warsaw, Mo., about 1845.

❡ May 1.—John Dougherty received the contract (made with Bvt. Maj. E. A. Ogden) to transport government stores from Fort Leavenworth to Fort Kearny (in wagons; for six cents per pound; with addition of five percent to the weight of bacon). Surety for his $20,000 bond was Robert Campbell, St. Louis.

Ref: 31st Cong., 1st Sess., *Sen. Ex. Doc. No. 26* (Serial 554), p. 24. Dougherty was sutler at Fort Kearny.

❡ May 1.—From the "Iowa and Sauk Indian Agency" (the Great Nemaha Subagency, about two miles west of Wolf river, in present Doniphan county) an emigrant (who signed his letter "E. Pluribus One of 'Em") wrote to the New York *Tribune's* Horace Greeley: "The anxiously-expected and long-awaited-for grass has come, and we are now enroute, to the number of about 300 wagons, from this one point of outset—St. Joseph. [The subagency was about 25 miles "out," as the road ran.] In all probability the same number has set off from Independence, and as many more are on the Fort Kearney [Old Fort Kearny] . . . trail. Thus in about 18 days 900 wagons will be on the California road proper, beyond Grand Island, where all the before-mentioned roads converge into one [below Fort Kearny]. Three men to each wagon is a fair average, which would make nearly three thousand, allowing for the considerable number who go with pack mules. [Compare with the May 18 statistics at Fort Kearny, p. 848.] So far as St. Joseph is concerned, not nearly half are yet set off. . . ."

This same man stated: "A most remarkable degree of health prevails among us, and with the exception of some cases of cholera morbus on the river boats, there has been no sickness among the Californians. [*See* mid-May entry, p. 845, for a changed situation.] A few deaths occurred at St. Joseph's from that cause."

Ref: New York *Daily Tribune*, June 7, 1849, or *Weekly Tribune*, June 16, 1849.

❡ May 1.—Agent Thomas Fitzpatrick (of the Upper Platte Agency) and Indian trader William Bent arrived at Westport, Mo., after a 46-day journey from Bent's Fort. They were in advance of the "Bent & [John] Hatcher's party" wagons (heavily laden with buffalo robes, which they had left at a point 16 miles "beyond" Cow creek.

With Fitzpatrick were three Arapahoes—a chief, his wife, and their son; and accompanying William Bent was his eight-year-old son, Robert Bent (half-Cheyenne).

Ref: *The Daily Reveille*, St. Louis, May 6, 1849; New York *Weekly Tribune*, May 19, June 2, 1849; David Lavender's *Bent's Fort* (c1954), p. 314 (for Robert Bent). Amos

Andrews had set out from Bent's Fort with William Bent on March 17; but (late in March?) joined a Mexican train—*see* April 22, entry. Fitzpatrick reached St. Louis on May 8—*see* L. R. Hafen and W. J. Ghent, *Broken Hand* . . . (Denver, 1931), p. 303.

❦ May 3-7.—The *St. Joseph,* down from the Council Bluffs (left May 3), arrived at St. Louis May 7. She brought the season's "first important shipment of robes and furs." "R[obert] & W[illiam] Campbell" were the consignees.

Ref: St. Louis *Daily New Era,* May 7, 1849.

❦ May.—Among the great throng of emigrants on the Oregon-California trail from Independence who crossed the Kansas river at the Papin, or "lower ferry" (where Topeka now is) were diarists who recorded the following descriptions:

May 3. (William G. Johnston) "About eight o'clock the operation of ferrying the Kansas began. By means of a rope, one end of which was coiled about a tree, the wagons were let down the steep banks of the river, and placed in the boat. Two wagons and twelve mules were taken over at a time, the boat being propelled by poles. A Frenchman and his two sons, who are half-breed Kaws, own and work the ferry. Their charge is two dollars for each wagon, twenty-five cents for a mule, and ten cents for each man. Double teams were required to haul the wagons up the northern bank, and through the deep sand extending a quarter of a mile back from the river."

May 8. (Jasper M. Hixson) "We reached the Kansas late on the evening of the 8th, and crossed just at dark, by ferrying our wagons and swimming our mules. The Ferry is owned by a Frenchman, who had been living with the Indians 14 years."

May 8. (Bennett C. Clark) "Just after passing down the bluff [his party had reached the lower Kansas Ferry early, but other wagons ahead caused a delay of some 4 hours] we had to cross a sand beach of some width before getting to the boat, through which the wagons draged very heavy. . . . We rolled [the wagons] into the boat by hand. Finally we got all our wagons over and then forded our animals. . . . The lower Kansas crossing is from all I could learn much the best and the road to and from it far superior to the upper [Union Town] one."

May 13. (Isaac J. Wistar) "Sunday, May 13th. Rolled out early [from a Shunganunga creek camp] to reach the [Kansas] crossing, if possible, in advance of the [two heavy ox-] trains near us. As we passed these, some were burying a man just dead of cholera. . . . The five or six miles of road leading to the crossing was bad, and we stalled and had to double teams several times, but reached the place by 8 A. M. to find still other trains ahead, all squabbling for precedence. Some enterprising emigrants . . . had built a small scow capable of transporting a single wagon without the team, and naturally every one wanted to be the first. We rushed our wagons in [Wistar detailed the procedure]. . . . We worked hard most of the day, in crossing our [five] wagons and stores . . . and in making our initial mule crossing. The mule ford was narrow and crooked, with swimming depth in the middle, and a rapid current. . . ." Wistar did not mention the regular ferry.

May 26. (David J. Staples) "at the lower crossing here [Kansas river] we had to be ferried over in flat boats owned by half breeds the wind blew and we could not persuade them to take us over till tomorrow . . . Sunday 27th 49 This morning we got ferryed across at a cost of 10 cents a head for our animals and $1.00 for our waggons we got all over at noon"

Ref: Johnston, *op. cit.*, pp. 39, 40; *The Weekly Tribune*, Liberty, Mo., June 8, 1849 (for Hixson); *Missouri Historical Review*, v. 23 (October, 1928), p. 9 (for Clark); Wistar, *op. cit.*, pp. 56, 57; *California Historical Society Quarterly*, v. 22 (June, 1943), p. 124 (for Staples).

❑ May 4.—The *Alton* left Weston, Mo., for St. Louis. She met the *Amelia* at Fort Leavenworth; the *Sacramento, Haydee,* and *Tamerlane* at Kansas (City, Mo.); and other steamboats farther downriver; arrived at St. Louis the morning of May 7.

Ref: St. Louis *Daily New Era*, May 7, 1849.

❑ May 4.—The St. Joseph (Mo.) *Gazette* reported that every steamboat arriving at the wharf was crowded with emigrants; within the "last few days" several hundred wagons had come through by land from Iowa, Illinois, Indiana, Michigan, and Wisconsin; and up to 12 o'clock on May 3, 8,318[?] persons had made St. Joseph their point of departure for the Plains.

(The editor estimated some 5,000 more would ferry the Missouri there; while at the Council Bluffs perhaps 4,000 emigrants, in all, would cross. He guessed 18,000 persons, altogether, would leave the frontier from St. Joseph and points on up the river, plus 6,000 to 8,000 from Independence—for a total around 25,000.)

E. W. Roberts ("Hunt"), an emigrant whose departure point would be Independence, paid a visit to St. Joseph, and asserted in a May 8 letter: "The number of emigrants at St. Joseph far exceeds that at Independence. I am well satisfied that at least 6,000 persons had crossed the ferries at that town up to this date, and at the upper ferry [four or five miles above] probably 1,000 more!" He guessed perhaps 5,000 had left from the Independence area, though "they[?] pretended to estimate the number who had already left Independence at 8,000." He added: "There is a great disposition to overrate all these things, yet the number is most extraordinary." It was his opinion that "greater numbers" were "backing out" at St. Joseph than at Independence.

The St. Joseph *Gazette* of May 11 placed the emigration which had passed through that town at upwards of 13,000 persons. (In the June 22 issue it was stated: "Between 17,000 and 18,000 emigrants left this point [St. Joseph *and* upriver points?] for California this spring." A week earlier [June 15] the editor had commented: "From the best information we can get, about 10,000 persons have left Independence, which will increase the [total] number of persons [emigrants] to 27,000.")

Ref: St. Joseph (Mo.) *Gazette*, May 4, 11, June 15, 22, 1849; *The Daily Reveille*, St. Louis, May 13, 1849, October 2, 1850 ("Hunt" is here identified as "Mr. E. W. Roberts, late of Ill.").

❑ May.—These were the comments of some Forty-niner diarists

traveling the St. Joseph branch of the Oregon-California trail, while in the Big Blue vicinity, and on reaching the junction with the Independence road (about nine miles beyond the river ford).

May 4. (Charles Tinker) "we arrived at the Big Blue at 1 A. M.   crossed by raising our wagon boxes."

May 6. (Peter Decker) "Approaching Big Blue is hilly, scenery pretty, some pretty high ridges of peculiar stones or rocks piled in places perpindicular. . . . Big Blue deep, half way up side of a horse."

May 16. (Israel F. Hale) Arriving at 10 A. M. "at the fork of the St. Joseph and Independence Road" (having camped the night before on the Big Blue's west side), "the road is nearly filled with wagons and teams; as many as eight or ten trains in sight at one time, and some of them large."

May 16. (Henry Tappan) "This morning crossed the [Big] Blue (forded) 10 miles brought us to the Santa Fee Trail [*i. e.*, Independence road]."

May 16. (Joseph Hackney) "Traveled 15 miles . . . crossed the big blue at nine o'clock   this is a beautiful stream about 50 yards wide and from 2 to three feet in depth . . . [had a hard time getting] our team [over] . . . theare was two graves on the bank of the stream   both made this year."

May 17. (Sterling B. F. Clark) "Crossed the Big Blue River in morning. Water 3½ feet deep."

May 18. (James Tate) "Crossed the [Big Blue] river   it was near the beds on most of the waggons."

May 19. (John Edwin Banks) "Early this day we crossed the Big Blue. Two big trains immediately behind us. The water is nearly three feet deep, the stream wide. . . . Today we passed the intersection of the Independence road. Saw two graves. The crosses: 'I. H. Snow, here lies a Catholic,' and 'John Graham, died March 21, 1847'[?]   The only old[?] graves I have seen."

May 20. (Vincent Geiger) "we came to the Big Blue. This is a stream of beautiful, clear water, and is very palatable to a thirsty man. The stream is about 40 yards wide, deep enough to touch the wagon beds, but is neither swift or rough. On either side the banks are rather steep. . . . Near this river we found the lava or rocks formed by some volcanic eruption. The ground was covered with the rocks. From St. Joseph to this place the road is good & easily found—plenty of wood, grass & water."

May 21. (Vincent Geiger) After crossing the Big Blue, and camping a mile or two beyond, on the 20th, the Charlestown, Virginia, Mining Company, set out on the 21st. "In nine miles from camp we struck the Independence Trail."

See, also, Capt. Howard Stansbury's statements under May 31 annals entry.

Ref: *Ohio State Archaeological and Historical Quarterly*, Columbus, v. 61 (January, 1952), p. 73 (for Tinker); The Society of California Pioneers, San Francisco, *Publication for the Year 1953*, p. 17 (for Decker), or, *see Diaries of Peter Decker; Overland to California in 1849 and Life in the Mines, 1850-1851*, edited by Helen S. Giffen, (Georgetown, Cal., 1966), p. 66; *Quarterly of the Society of California Pioneers*, San Francisco, v. 2, (1925), p. 64 (for Hale); *Annals of Wyoming*, Cheyenne, v. 25 (July, 1953), p. 119 (for Tappan); Elizabeth Page's *Wagons West* . . . (New York, c1930), pp. 126-130 (for Hackney); Sterling B. F. Clark, *How Many Miles from St. Jo?* (San Francisco, 1929), p. 10; James Tate's "Diary," in Western Historical Manuscripts Collection, University of

Missouri, Columbia, Mo.; Howard L. Scamehorn's *The Buckeye Rovers in the Gold Rush* (Athens, Ohio, 1965), for J. E. Banks' diary; D. M. Potter, ed., *Trail to California* . . . (New Haven, 1945), pp. 81, 82 (for Geiger).

❡ May.—On the Oregon-California trail west of St. Mary's Mission, in what is now Pottawatomie county, a number of Forty-niners died of cholera. The observations of two emigrants show that the death toll was heaviest in the latter part of May; but there is no way of determining the complete count of victims in this area in 1849.

Jasper M. Hixson, of Liberty, Mo., and party, crossed the stream then called Little Vermillion (now Red Vermillion) on May 10, and camped on a high ridge. Hixson wrote: "On the 11th we passed the grave of an emigrant with this inscription, 'Henry Roush, of Ill., died May 8, 1849.' In the morning another, T. Adams—I do not know where he was from." [Hixson, later, noted passing the grave of James H. Marshall (d. 1844—*see* p. 513); and at the Big Blue, saw the markers for Sarah Keyes (d. 1846), and John Fuller (d. April 28, 1849), elsewhere mentioned in these annals; and recorded by other Forty-niner diarists.]

David Dewolf, in a May 31 diary entry, wrote: "we next crossed the little [Red] Vermillion which has very steep banks & rapid current. . . . On the bank of this stream there was 6 graves, all died with the Colery & out of a company of seven from Tenn. . . ." On June 1 Dewolf's company "Got an early start rolling on a high rolling prairie passed several small streams & in one we saw some fine fish. . . . we passed this day 11 graves of Californians. . . ."

As for the graves mentioned above, in the 1870's (and later) the stone marking the burial place of Henry Roush (or Roushi?) was still in one piece, and the inscription legible. (Its location: on the NW¼ of Sec. 32, T. 8, R. 9 E.—or, the NW¼ of Sec. 32, Union township, Pottawatomie co.) Also, the marker for "T. S. Prather, May 27, 1849," (with others not identifiable) was then to be found on the east bank of the Red Vermillion, on the NW¼ of Sec. 24, T. 9, R. 10 E.—or, the NW¼ of Sec. 24, Louisville township, near the Vieux cemetery, and Vieux Crossing of the Red Vermillion. Prather could have been one of the Tennesseeans mentioned by Dewolf.

The 11 graves Dewolf noted evidently were in the present Westmoreland area, where, it is known, a number of Forty-niners were buried. On a hill a mile and a half north and west of Westmoreland (up to 1928), stood a boulder bearing the inscription: "S. M. Marshall Wadesboro Ky Died May 27 1849." (This stone and the remnant of the Roush marker are in the Kansas State Historical Society's museum. As of 1971 the Prather marker remains at, or near, its original location.)

Farther out the Oregon-California trail, emigrant George M. Harker wrote, from "Ford [Fork] of Little Blue River May 26, 1849": "As near as I have been able to ascertain from the emigrants, from 50 to 70 deaths have occurred on the St. Joseph and Independence roads . . . [mostly cholera victims]."

Kimball Webster (traveling near the tail-end of the year's procession) wrote, on June 10, from a point west of the Big Blue: "The great bulk of the immigration, which is very large, is in advance of us. That very much dreaded scourge, the Asiatic cholera, is making such sad havoc among the Californians that almost every camp-ground is converted into a burial-ground, and at many[?] places twelve or fifteen graves may be seen in a row."

Ref: *The Weekly Tribune,* Liberty, Mo., June 8, 1849, for Hixson; Illinois State Historical Society, *Publication No. 32,* for Dewolf diary (on pp. 183-222); *KHC,* v. 17, pp. 442-449 (and accompanying maps); *The Daily Reveille,* St. Louis, June 15, 1849, for Harker; Kimball Webster, *The Gold Seekers of '49* (1917), pp. 43, 44.

❡ May and June.—These were the comments of some Forty-niner diarists traveling the Oregon-California trail route from Independence, Mo., while in the Big Blue (of Kansas) vicinity, and on reaching the junction (about 10 miles beyond the river ford) with the St. Joseph branch of the trail.

May 9-10 (William G. Johnston) "A short way from camp this morning, we came to a wooden tombstone marking the grave of 'Mrs. Sarah Keyes, aged 70, who died May 29th, 1846. [*See* pp. 585, 627.] Mr. [Edwin] Bryant mentions the death and burial of this lady in his work; and the little headstone served to determine our locality; for by it we knew we were nigh the Big Blue River. . . . [After an overnight stop.] A short march from camp brought us to the Big Blue River. . . . Its banks at the crossing being low, we got over without difficulty, and soon again reached the open plains. . . . Rising from the valley of the Big Blue, our line of march was over high table lands, across which there was an extensive range for the eye. . . . [Some time later] we . . . reached a point where the road, leading from St. Joseph, Mo. joins the Oregon trail which we have been pursuing. From an elevation at the point of intersection we had an extensive view, and in looking behind over the road just traveled, or back over the St. Joseph road, or forward over that to be taken; for an indefinite number of miles, there seemed to be an unending stream of emigrant trains, whilst in the still farther distance along these lines could be seen great clouds of dust, indicating that yet others of these immense caravans were on the move. It was a sight which once seen can never be forgotten; it seemed as if the whole family of man had set its face westward."

May 10-11 (James A. Pritchard) "[At] 4 P. M. . . . we came to the big Blue. This is a fine large Stream with a bold rapid current & gravelly bottom. We had here to lower our wagons down with ropes, which consumed the ballance of the evening in crossing all the train. The Soil is very fine on this river, and the bottoms are well timbered. This will doubtless become a fine farming country—and that before many years." [On May 11] "By noone today we came to where the St. Joseph road & Indipendance road came togeather. It was allarming to see the long strings of wagons that were on the road. I counted just passing before us as we came into the St. Jo. road 90 Ox teams in one string. And as far as the Eye could reach forward and back the road was just lined with them. It would appear from the sight befor us that the Nation was disgorgeing its self and sending off its whole inhabitance."

May 13-14 (Jasper M. Hixson) "We crossed the Big Blue the 13th, which is a most beautiful stream. On the eastern bank are two graves, one Sarah Keys, of Springfield, Ill. . . . and John Fuller, aged 20 years, accidentally shot himself April 28th, 1849." . . . We came to the St. Joseph road on the 14th. This road we found much more travelled than the one from Independence. About this time trains are very frequent, principally cattle. At this point there were some 100 wagons in sight. One train from Cooper [co.], Mo., one from Holt [co.], Mo., one from Ohio, one from old Franklin, Mo., and one from Peoria, Ill. . . ."

May 17 (Samuel R. Dundass) "to big Blue by 4 p. m. [after crossing the "Big Vermillion" and traveling 15 miles]. This river is generally fordable, except after heavy rains. There is no ferry, and all emigrants think themselves fortunate when it is fordable . . . we . . . found it in a fordable condition. . . . He, too, noted Sarah Keyes' and John Fuller's graves "under a large spreading oak, which had been barked, and their inscription cut on the tree."

May 20 (Isaac J. Wistar) "We reached and crossed it [the Big Blue—but he called it the Little Blue] about 1 P. M., descending the eastern side with ropes and surmounting the far bank without much difficulty. At our crossing, it was about four feet deep and eighty yards wide, with a large island in the middle, and a rapid current." [Wistar, ill, did not comment on the traffic at the trails junction when his party passed it two or three days later.]

June 4 (David Dewolf) ". . . we crossed the big blue which is a fine stream, the water being quite blue we crossed without any difficulty passed through a fine strip of timber & then crossed a small creek where we halted for dinner. Here we found a fine spring of water which comes out of a perpendicular rock about eight feet high. One mile up the blue on the left side is a spring called cover [Alcove] spring which is a most beautiful place."

Ref: Johnston, *op. cit.*, pp. 46-48; Morgan, *op. cit.*, pp. 58, 59; *The Weekly Tribune*, Liberty, Mo., June 8, 1849; Dundass, *op. cit.*, Wistar, *op. cit.*, p. 63; Illinois State Historical Society, *Publication No. 32*, p. 189 (for Dewolf).

❢ May 5-9.—The *Eliza Stewart*, leaving Council Bluffs on the 5th and arriving at St. Louis May 9, met the *Amelia* at the Nodaway's mouth, the *Tamerlane* at Savannah, Mo., the *Highland Mary* and *Sacramento* at St. Joseph, the *Kansas* at Parkville, Mo., the *Timour* in "Kansas bend"; and others below.

Ref: St. Louis *Daily New Era*, May 10, 1849.

❢ May.—At St. Joseph, between the 6th and 11th, six cholera cases (all persons off steamboats) "terminated fatally." The *Gazette* of the 11th also reported that cholera was "raging to an alarming extent" at Fort Leavenworth; that 25 deaths had occurred there on one day; and that business at the military post was "entirely suspended."

Between May 18 and 25 four emigrants and one townsman died of cholera at St. Joseph. The week following, there was no case reported in the town; and but few were occurring on the steamboats ("indeed a number are now making trips to this place without a single case on board").

Two persons died of cholera at St. Joseph between June 22 and 29. One was a passenger from the *Mary Blane*.

Ref: St. Joseph (Mo.) *Gazette*, May 11, 18, 26, June 1, 8, 29, 1849; New York

Weekly Tribune, May 26, 1849 (quoting the Philadelphia *Inquirer's* statement: "We have seen a letter dated St. Joseph's, Mo. May 1, which says that only one or two cases of cholera had occurred at that place.").

❡ May.—At Fort Kearny ("Nebraska") on the 6th, the first California-bound gold seeker made his appearance. Not far behind were others of the "advance guard." As recorded at this post (and reported by correspondents and journalists) the following were some statistics on the *"emigrant" wagons* which channeled past new Fort Kearny, in May, from Missouri river jumping-off points *south of the Platte* (principally Independence, St. Joseph, and Old Fort Kearny; but also, Weston, Fort Leavenworth, Savannah, etc.):

May	Passed up to this date	Passed on this date	Total	Source
9	("We learned from the garrison at the fort that there are some 50 teams ahead of us on the road. . . ."—Joseph W. Berrien.)			
17	("About three hundred wagons have passed; the foremost train about ten days ago. They are said to be go-ahead boys from St. Louis [Captain Paul's train]. . . . There is every variety of conveyance—ox, mule, and horse trains, foot travelers, &c."—Miles M. Goodyear, in a "Fort Kearney, May 17, 1849," letter.)			
18	476 wagons	180 wagons	656 wagons	*Mo. Rep.,* June 4
21		214 wagons	1,203 wagons	*Mo. Rep.,* June 9
22		232 wagons	1,435 wagons	*Mo. Rep.,* June 9
23			1,980 wagons	Page, May 24 lr.
26			2,527 wagons	Wyman, p. 49
27	2,600 wagons (mule co's.—"packers"—not included)			N. Y. W. T., June 23
28		460 wagons	[3,160] wagons	*Mo. Rep.,* June 21
29		381 wagons	[3,541] wagons	*Mo. Rep.,* June 21
30		[276] wagons	3,739 wagons	*Mo. Rep.,* June 21
31		194 wagons	[3,933] wagons	*Mo. Rep.,* June 21

("Already have four thousand wagons passed Fort Kearny . . . and most of the ox trains are still behind. . . ."—George M. Harker's May 31, 1849, letter.)

("In consequence of the immense Emigration [some 4,000 Wagons having already passed this point and a large number following] I have determined to divide my supply train."—Bvt. Col. W. W. Loring's May 31, 1849, letter from "Camp at Fort Kearny.")

See, also, June annals entry, p. 871.

Ref: *Indiana Magazine of History,* v. 56 (December, 1960), p. 298 (for Berrien); *Missouri Republican,* St. Louis, July 6, 1849 (for Goodyear); Nebraska State Historical Society *Publications,* v. 20, pp. 200-202 (includes Loring item); Page, *op. cit.,* pp. 130-132, for Henry Page's May 24, 1849, letter); W. D. Wyman, ed., *California Emigrant Letters* (New York, c1952), p. 49, or, *Missouri Republican,* June 16, 1849; New York *Weekly Tribune,* June 23, 1849 (for May 6 and 27 items); *Glimpses of the Past,* St. Louis, v. 6, p. 53 (for Harker), or *The Daily Reveille,* St. Louis, June 24, 1849.

❡ This was the scene on May 7 in present Doniphan county, Kansas, across the Missouri river from St. Joseph, Mo., as a visitor saw it:

"I rode out some sixteen or eighteen miles. . . . In starting up the bluffs, after leaving the river bottoms, the California and Oregon trail winds around very much so that several miles of it are closely in view at once. The whole length of this, as far as the eye could range, was covered with moving wagons, with ox and mule trains of every variety—whilst almost every ravine and grove by the road-side, within a mile, contained a camp of one to a dozen wagons, with tents pitched and, in many instances, the United States flag waving over them, in the bright sun and pleasant breeze of a lovely spring morning."

Ref: "Hunt's" May 8, 1849, letter, from St. Joseph, Mo., published in *The Daily Reveille*, St. Louis, May 13, 1849.

❡ **May 8.**—St. Joseph's two ferryboats ("very indifferent scows," in J. G. Bruff's opinion) "though running all day and most of the night," were inadequate to the demands of Forty-niners endeavoring to cross. Some persons were paying $5, and up to $10, for transportation of a single wagon and team over the Missouri. The steamboats *Sacramento* and *Highland Mary* made several trips as "ferries" while in port.

A visitor wrote, on May 8: "They have two ferries at the town, each of which transports at least thirty-five trains in twenty-four hours, and these trains will average more than four persons. . . . They have been crossing at that rate for more than three weeks past, at night hiring their boats to emigrants who ferry themselves over in parties of fifteen, twenty, and thirty wagons in a night." He commented, also: "at St. Joseph [contrasted with Independence, some three miles distant from the Missouri] all the excitement is immediately in the town itself, three-fourths of the ferriage being down at the steamboat landing. . . . The streets are crowded with wagons and their trains, and the pavements are alive with people. It is a perfect Babel. . . ."

Emigrant J. B. Witt (aboard the *Mary*, passing St. Joseph May 10?) wrote (on the 16th, after reaching Council Bluffs): "At St. Joseph, the country on both sides of the river was lined as far as the eye could reach. . . . They [the emigrants] were and had been for the last two weeks, crossing day and night. There were two ferry boats [at the town] . . . and two more a few miles above. Two steamboats had been engaged one or two days, and still the accommodation was insufficient. Many had gone to other places to cross [*i. e.,* Savannah Landing, Mo., Iatan, Mo., Old Fort Kearny, "Neb."—above; Weston, or Fort Leavenworth—below]. . . . A considerable number had concluded to go by Santa Fe and some few were on the retreat."

Ref: *Missouri Republican*, St. Louis, May 12, 1849; St. Joseph (Mo.) *Gazette*, May 11, 1849; St. Louis *Daily New Era*, May 12, 1849; *The Daily Reveille*, St. Louis, May 13, 1849; Chicago *Daily Journal*, May 28, 1849; Read and Gaines, *op. cit.*, p. 7 (for Bruff). Early arriving emigrants had found only one ferry boat at St. Joseph (but there was another, four miles upriver). On April 11 J. W. Berrien wrote: "The Ferry Boat is an old flat Boat which the passengers have to row across themselves and is an unwieldy and unmanageable affair."—*Indiana Magazine of History,* v. 56 (December, 1960), pp. 285, 286.

❡ In the fore part of May, several Missouri river steamboats had high incidence of cholera aboard; and heavy loss of lives. Many of the victims were Mormons—emigrants from England, just arrived by way of New Orleans—bound for Council Bluffs.

On the *Mary* (carrying over 250 Mormons), 35 persons had died by May 8 when the *Highland Mary* met her "above Kansas [City, Mo.]"; the toll had risen to 39 when she passed Weston; and to 47 by the time she reached St. Joseph (where the citizens "rose *en masse*"—according to passenger J. B. Witt —to prevent the landing there of freight or passengers. Witt, on arrival at Council Bluffs, May 16, wrote: "There have been ten deaths since we left St. Jo and one now dying, making in all 58 since we left St. Louis out of 300 persons [including crew])."

The *Kansas,* upbound, and at Independence on May 9 or 10, had lost "some eight of ten" passengers, by cholera, up to that point.

The *Monroe* (carrying many Mormons) reached Jefferson City about May 11, where her officers, crew, and most of the passengers deserted the boat. Up to the morning of May 12, cholera had killed 53 persons aboard.

On the *Mary Blane,* eight cholera deaths had occurred by May 12 when she reached the vicinity of Weston. "Maj. Armour," a passenger, later reported that a number of persons had died of cholera between St. Louis and Fort Leavenworth; that one of the victims was a "Mr. Treadwell, a merchant of Southport [now Kenosha], Wisconsin, who was on his way to superintend the starting of several companies of emigrants which he had fitted out for California"; and that his remains were taken to Fort Leavenworth and (by permission) "interred in the officers' burial ground."

The pilot of the *Lightfoot* (bound for Council Bluffs with a load of Mormon passengers) died of cholera near Iowa Point, Mo. (opposite present Iowa Point, Kan.) about May 17(?). (Earlier, before reaching St. Charles, Mo., three aboard had died of cholera, and other were ill.) The *St. Croix* took the freight and passengers of the *Lightfoot* from St. Joseph up to Council Bluffs.

Ref: St. Louis *Daily New Era,* May 12, 15, 1849; *The Daily Reveille,* St. Louis, May 8, 13, 15-17, June 9, 1849; Saint Louis *Daily Union,* May 25, 1849; *Missouri Republican,* St. Louis, May 8, 12, 17, 23, 1849; St. Joseph (Mo.) *Gazette,* May 11, 1849; Chicago *Daily Journal,* May 28, 1849 (for J. B. Witt letter).

❧ May 10.—William Curtis Skinner (who had left Chihuahua March 20; and Santa Fe in mid-April) arrived at Independence, Mo., in advance of some other traders with whom he had journeyed the Santa Fe trail as far as Big Cow creek. (He reached St. Louis on the 16th aboard the *Boreas No. 3.*)

Skinner's companions had been John McCoy, David Hickman, Solomon Houck, Christopher Branham, Marcellin St. Vrain, Duncan, Rees, Stettinius, Hambright, Nash (some of these from Chihuahua; others from Santa Fe), and Olivares, from Guaymas. In their 10-wagon train these merchants brought about $125,000 in specie and bullion. They all arrived at Independence by May 12.

Ref: *Missouri Republican,* St. Louis, May 17, 1849 (two items); St. Louis *Daily New Era,* May 17, 1849; *The Daily Reveille,* St. Louis, May 17, 1849; St. Joseph (Mo.) *Gazette,* May 25, 1849. The *New Era* of July 31, 1849, mentioned the arrival of Solomon Houck, Boonville, Mo., at St. Louis (aboard the *Rowena*), with $13,000 in specie (mostly bullion) he had brought from Mexico. David Lavender in his *Bent's Fort,* p. 310, states that Marcellin

St. Vrain (long a mountain man) married Elizabeth Jane Murphey, on June 26, 1849, in Missouri. John McCoy's brother, Samuel F. McCoy (from Chillicothe, Ohio), in a diary entry of May 19, 1849, wrote: "Taking brother John's outfit, with which he had just returned from Mexico over the Santa Fe route, I left Independence . . . in company with brother Alexander . . . [to travel the Oregon-California trail]."—*Pioneering on the Plains.*

❡ May 10.—Emigrant Israel F. Hale (who had crossed the Missouri at Savannah Landing—above St. Joseph, near present Amazonia, Mo.—on the 6th; and camped at Wolf river on the 9th) rode up to the Great Nemaha Subagency (*see* May 1 entry) to look around. He recorded in his diary: "They have a large farm, I think one hundred and fifty or two hundred acres, four or five dwellings, a [Sac & Fox] mill, a store and a blacksmith shop. The mill [new in 1848—*see* p. 742] is by far the best building. It is frame, the balance log and not good."

One of Hale's fellow travelers—Nathaniel Clark—stricken with cholera at Wolf river camp, died, and was buried, on the 10th.

Ref: *Quarterly of the Society of California Pioneers,* San Francisco, v. 2 (1925), pp. 61, 62.

❡ May 10.—Lt. Col. Benjamin L. E. Bonneville (assigned to command Fort Kearny), set out from Fort Leavenworth on his journey to that post.

Apparently he went by steamboat up the Missouri to Old Fort Kearny; there joined Lt. Levi C. Bootes and Company D, Sixth U. S. infantry; traveled overland from that point on the trail south of the Platte; reached new Fort Kearny May 29; assumed command (from Bvt. Maj. Charles F. Ruff) on the 30th. (See, *also*, May 23 entry.)

Bonneville (under new orders) departed Fort Kearny in mid-July. The post's commandant from July 16 was Bvt. Maj. Robert H. Chilton, First U. S. dragoons.

Ref: St. Louis *Daily New Era,* May 17, 1849 (for Bonneville's May 9 letter); Settle, *op. cit.,* p. 56, and p. 302 (for George Gibbs' May 30 journal entry); Nebraska State Historical Society *Publications,* v. 20, p. 202, and v. 21, pp. 258, 259 (for statements by Lt. D. P. Woodbury); *Nebraska History,* Lincoln, v. 29 (September, 1948), p. 189.

❡ May 10.—From "Camp Sumner" (established in late March?; on Salt Creek's west bank, about five miles from Fort Leavenworth) Bvt. Col. William W. Loring (head of the U. S. Mounted riflemen), with Companies A, D, F, H, and K of his regiment, 700 horses, a train of 171 wagons, 1,200 mules, and some oxen, set out for Oregon. (This same day?, or prior to the 10th?, the separate command of Fort Laramie-bound Maj. Winslow F. Sanderson and Company E began the journey westward.) Bvt. Maj. Gen. David E. Twiggs (who had come up the Missouri by steamboat, accompanied by deputy quartermaster Bvt. Col. Aeneas Mackay, to superintend) gave the order which put Loring's Oregon expedition in motion.

[Eight companies of Mounted riflemen had arrived at Fort Leavenworth, in detachments, between January and May—*see* pp. 794, 798, 799, 828. Companies G and I had been at Fort Kearny (on the Platte) over winter. After the above departures on May 10 (and an earlier departure, by way of Old Fort Kearny, of Bvt. Maj. John S. Simonson and some men of "B" company), there remained at "Camp Sumner" part of Company B (*see* June 5 entry) and Company C (*see* mid-June entry, p. 872).]

Colonel Loring had Bvt. Maj. James Belger as his chief quartermaster from "Camp Sumner" out to Fort Kearny (where Maj. Osborne Cross—*see* May 20 entry—replaced him). His guide was "Tom Glendry [Glendy?]." The families of some (a few?) officers were along. The civilians who made this journey included artist George Gibbs—who kept a journal describing the day-to-day travel in some detail; and later prepared a map (the Fremont-Gibbs-Smith map—*see* p. 131, for item on this; and *see, also,* on p. 197 a portion of the map, on which is shown "Col. Loring's Route 1849," from Fort Leavenworth as far as the Platte). Loring's report, and Asst. Supt. Israel Moses' table of distances, supply other information on the march to Fort Kearny (and beyond).

It was May 15 before Loring and his Mounted riflemen reached Wolf creek. Gibbs wrote: ". . . about three miles from Wolf creek the [road from Fort] Leavenworth strikes into the great trail from St. Joseph, now the most traveled of all the routes. . . . We have begun to encounter the emigrant trains in numbers. . . . Our route was intersected or joined by a number of smaller trails, some of them . . . [Indian paths?]. Others . . . made by emigrants from distant points on the Missouri." The military camp that night was beyond the junction of the trails, and "some twelve[?] miles from the Missouri" (according to Gibbs). The total distance traveled from Fort Leavenworth (according to Moses) was 59 miles.

On the 16th (a nontravel day) Gibbs noted: "The trail . . . very broad and beaten like a turnpike, was covered with emigrant parties, who continued passing at intervals during the day." And he observed that they varied much as to "appearance of the individuals and the apparent completeness of their outfit"; that "but few women or children accompanied them"; that they were "chiefly made up from single towns or districts, less often of combined parties, and as yet . . . [were] not banded in large companies; that "most of their wagons . . . [were] drawn by oxen, from three to seven yoke to a team."

Loring's expedition reached the "Great Nemaha" (where "the pioneers had . . . constructed a tolerable road and we passed [across] safely") on May 19. At 10 o'clock on the 21st (having "kept more westerly," since crossing the Great Nemaha, and "following the ridge between that stream and the Little Nemaha") the Mounted riflemen "struck the valley of the Big Blue itself." The crossing was made safely ("The river was at this time about twenty-five yards wide, and up to our saddle girths at the ford, with steep banks some twenty feet high."); and "Camp on the Big Blue," for the night, was about a mile beyond "to the left." The day's travel had been on a general course "to the south and west." On the 22d the troops marched 8¼ miles; and on the 23d, soon after leaving camp, came to the juncture with the "great trail from Independence."

The Mounted riflemen reached Fort Kearny May 31 (where Bvt. Maj. Charles F. Ruff and Company I joined Loring for the march to Oregon). Major Sanderson's command had reached Fort Kearny on May 25 or 26 (and subsequently arrived at Fort Laramie on June 16). Loring's expedition reached Fort Laramie on June 22; and his troops arrived at Oregon City on October 8 and 9.

Ref: Settle, *op. cit.*, contains Loring's report; Moses' table; and George Gibbs' journal, referred to, and quoted, above; also Cross' journal; *Oregon Historical Quarterly*, v. 16 (March, 1915), p. 43; Nebraska State Historical Society *Publications*, Lincoln, v. 20, pp. 192, 199-201. An item on the wounding of "famous guide Tom Glendry" (shot by an Indian in an altercation, 20 miles from Fort Leavenworth, early in May), appeared in *The Daily Reveille*, St. Louis, May 23, 1849. *See* annals entry of January 17, 1848, for items on Thomas Glendy.

❧ May 12-16.—The *Boreas No. 3* left St. Joseph on the 12th. (The *Tamerlane* was then "in port.") On the downward trip she met the *Alice* and *Mary Blane* at Weston, Mo., the *St. Ange* below Parkville, Mo.; and others; arrived at St. Louis on the 16th.

Ref: St. Louis *Daily New Era*, May 16, 1849.

❧ May 12-13.—Coming up from northeastern "Oklahoma" *by a route newly blazed for wagons,* Capt. Lewis Evans' California-bound train (40 wagons; 130 persons) struck the Santa Fe trail at Turkey creek, in present McPherson county. They had crossed into "Kansas" around May 1, in what is now Chautauqua county. Those who arrived first at the junction "obtained a large stone and planted it in the fork of the road," inscribing thereon: "to Fayetteville, Ark. 300 miles—Capt Evans Com'y. May 12, 1849."

Men from northwestern Arkansas made up the train's majority (some other southern states were represented); but 15 Cherokee Indians were also an important segment of the company. (Additionally, there were three women; and five Negroes.) Organizing near present Salina, Okla., on April 24, Lewis Evans, of Evansville, Ark., was elected captain. James S. Vann, a Cherokee, was voted secretary. The 40-wagon train set out April 24 and 25. After crossing the Verdigris (above present Claremore, Okla.) the route was northwest, the course "being almost entirely on a dividing ridge"—first between the Verdigris and Caney rivers; then between the waters of the Neosho and Arkansas.

At Turkey creek, on May 14, the company (divided in views) voted to proceed via the Santa Fe trail, and the upper Arkansas, to Bent's Fort. (The alternative: to open a trail northward from Turkey creek to the Platte.) As they started west, losses of oxen (45 at the Little Arkansas; 14 earlier; only 21 strays recovered) caused delays. Four persons (one wagon) from northwestern

Missouri, overtaken at the Little Arkansas, joined up—making the count 41 wagons and 134 "emigrants." (About May 4, west of Council Grove, eastbound W. C. Skinner had met the "company of four persons bound for California who gave him information on the number behind." Who these Missourians were has not been ascertained.)

On May 29 Captain Evans' company reached (abandoned-in-1848) Fort Mann (and saw there some 50 discarded government wagons). By June 4 (having passed by the Arkansas Crossing on June 2?) the train was 40 miles above the fort (where the eastbound Ward & Guerrier trading wagons were met). From available evidence, the Arkansans and Cherokees were in the forefront of Forty-niner parties out on the Santa Fe trail west of Council Grove (except for the above-noted Missouri wagon). Other groups (starting from Independence, or thereabouts) were, by now, close on their heels. With a few exceptions, the companies which followed kept to the main Santa Fe trail—the Cimarron route—crossing the Arkansas about 26 miles above Fort Mann.

At Pueblo, Colo., the Evans company split. Thirty men (including some of the Cherokees) left the others, to pack the rest of the way; hired mountain man "Dick" Owens as guide; and took a northward route (which become known as the Cherokee trail) to Fort Bridger. Four wagons turned back East. The 90-some persons led by Evans (among whom were some Cherokees), hired a part-Osage guide to take them (and their 30 wagons) northward, by way of St. Vrain's fort on the South Platte. (Their further travels are not outlined here.)

Of the wagon trail which Captain Evans and his Arkansans and Cherokees had opened across Kansas to Turkey creek, James R. Mead (early day Kansas resident) had this to say at a later date:

"What is known as the 'old California trail' passed through Fayetteville, Ark., thence across the corner of the Indian territory, entering Kansas about the southwest corner of Chautauqua county; thence northwest between the Caney rivers across the corner of Elk [county], entering Butler [county] near its southeast corner, reaching the Walnut [river] at the Osage crossing near El Dorado; thence northwest to the Whitewater crossing below Plum Grove [in Butler county], and pursuing the same course to the Santa Fe trail at Turkey creek, in McPherson county. This trail bore evidence of heavy wagon travel in former times. The writer passed over it in 1863. It was then abandoned, and in places grown over with grass." *[To distinguish this road from other California trails crossing "Kansas," it will be referred to in these annals as the "Chero-kee trail."]*

Ref: *Missouri Republican*, St. Louis, June 30, July 4, 1849; New York *Weekly Tribune*, August 11, 1849; Bieber, *op. cit.*, pp. 48, 49, 325-350; Foreman, *op. cit.*, pp. 66-81; Morgan, *op. cit.*, p. 16; *KHC*, v. 5, pp. 90, 91 (for Mead quote); St. Joseph (Mo.) *Gazette*, May 25, 1849 (for Skinner).

❲ May (and June).—California-bound (and other) companies setting out on the Santa Fe trail from Independence (or, from other points), in late April or May, were encountered, in June, by the incoming train of Seth Ward (Ward & Guerrier, fur traders), which included "W. A. T."—who reported on the traffic met. From "W. A. T." and from emigrant P. B. Marple (quoted below), a continuity to the procession of gold seekers westbound on the Santa Fe trail can be determined.

[To set the scene: Seth Ward and companions, coming down from the upper Arkansas (*see* June 28 entry), were some 15 miles *above* the Arkansas Crossing, on June 4, when they met the advance California-bound company—Capt. Lewis Evans' Arkansans and Cherokees (*see* May 12-13 entry)—en route to Bent's Fort, and Pueblo. On June 5 the fur traders reached the crossing in time to meet the first (so far as known) of the Forty-niner companies (Captain Bogue's train) taking the Cimarron route to Santa Fe. In succeeding June days, Ward, "W. A. T.," and companions met much traffic on the Santa Fe road, including the gold seekers and emigrants noted below.]

On May 25, at Turkey creek, on the Santa Fe trail (where, May 12, Capt. Lewis Evans and his company, pioneering the "Cherokee trail," had set up a monument to mark their feat), P. B. Marple (whose train had just reached that point, from the east) wrote a letter in which he stated: "Our information is, that since the passing of Mr. Evans' company, and which was the first, only one company of emigrants has passed this point; this was commanded by Capt. Bogue, numbering about 20 wagons—all from Greene county, Mo."

(1) Capt. Lewis Evans' company of Arkansans, Cherokees, and others.—See May 12-13 annals entry.

(2) Captain Bogue's company (*see* April entry, p. 832), from Springfield, and Greene county, Mo. "W. A. T." met this train, June 5, at the Arkansas Crossing; reported 24 wagons. (At the Upper Cimarron Spring, on June 13, eastbound Capt. Abraham Buford, U. S. A., "met a party of California emigrants . . . the most advanced of those embarking from Independence[?] —all well." Presumably this was Bogue's company.)

(3) Capt. L. C. Bostick's company. "W. A. T.," meeting this train on June 7, above Fort Mann, recorded 22 wagons. P. B. Marple (of Jasper county, Mo.), in this company, stated it was composed of (Missouri?) emigrants "from different parts." The 21(?) wagons had been organized at Council Grove on May 21. Marple indicated they had intended to take the

South Pass route, but found it too crowded; and that some persons had turned back near Willow Springs from fear of cholera, etc.

(4) Captain Berry's company, from Callaway county, Mo., camped near Turkey creek on May 25. "W. A. T. saw this train at Fort Mann on June 7; and stated there were 15 wagons and 53 men. (On the Gila route, in November, A. M. Heslep mentioned Berry's ox train from Missouri—reduced to three wagons, with some of the company afoot.)

(5) Captain Barber's (or, Barke's?) company, from Linn, Chariton, Livingston, Sullivan, and Saline counties, Missouri. "W. A. T." met "Capt. Barber's" train on June 8 "above Jackson's Grove"—27 wagons and 90 men. They were "bound for the Taos gold mines," he stated. George W. Withers (from Salt Lake City, in August) wrote that his "Sullivan County and California Mining Assn." had left Independence, Mo., about May 14, with wagons and ox teams; and at Council Grove had joined the Linn, Chariton, and Saline county men under "Captain Barke" (as printed). Barber's company followed the Arkansas river up to Pueblo (reaching there June 23) and on to Greenhorn, where the party split, to follow different trails.

(6) Captain Galley's company was, according to "W. A. T." (who met the train on June 8, in the Jackson's Grove area), from Marion county, Mo., and composed of 44 wagons and 120 men, going via Santa Fe to California. In a narrative written about 1905, John Hudgins recollected that his wagon and six more from Livingston county, Mo., joined with others at Diamond Spring(s) to form a train of "38 wagons [apparently all ox-drawn] and about 150 men and boys, one woman and three children," which "Captain Gully" was elected to head. The train included "some 10 or 15" Missourians who had served in the Mexican War ("and some of us had crossed the plains twice before," wrote Hudgins). Whether Captain Jackson's train from Marion county, Mo. (never mentioned by "W. A. T.," but referred to by A. Williamson) was connected with Galley's (Gully's) Marion county company is not clear. Williamson, on June 1, noted, among the several companies camped that night near Turkey creek, Captain Jackson's train from Hannibal (Marion county), Mo., and Captain Rodgers'[?] company from Howard county, Mo. (a coincidence of names and not Doctor Rogers' Menard county, Ill., group?—See No. 8). Earlier, on May 15, A. M. Heslep, nine miles out of Independence, Mo., mentioned finding Col. Congreve Jackson and a company of some 20 persons encamped; and on May 19, west of Bull creek, H. M. T. Powell learned that "Colonel Jackson is only a day or two ahead." As a surmise, "Galley's" 44-wagon company was a combination of Missouri companies from Marion, Howard, Livingston (and other?) counties. If so, there evidently was a separation at the Cimarron crossing. Hudgins described their fording the Arkansas at that point; and stated that on July 2, they were near Las Vegas, N. M. (Hudgins and companions went on to California by way of Tucson and the Gila route.) "Jacksons train of Waggons" was on the upper Arkansas on June 15 (as noted by J. R. Forsyth in his diary). The Liberty (Mo.) *Tribune* of September 7 reported that "Col. Congreve Jackson, of Howard county, and his party," had arrived at the Taos mines; and that the colonel was trying to arrest the murderers of his brother Johnson Jackson. (*See* annals index for reference to Congreve Jackson's earlier connections with "Kansas" history.)

California-bound A. Williamson, "In Camp, near Turkey Creek June 1st,

1849," wrote a letter of particular interest. He had set out from Fayetteville, Ark., on April 1; journeyed to Independence, Mo.; left there on May 17; and, deciding the Oregon-California trail was too crowded, had stayed on the road to Santa Fe. He remarked: "I have out-traveled all, except a mule train from Ithaca, N. Y. [see below]." At Cottonwood Crossing, on May 31, Williamson had counted 187 vehicles; and he thought the "teams in advance" might total 700. He stated: "Several trains have left the Oregon route after crossing the Kansas, and intersected this road this side of Council Grove." [Here he apparently referred either to (1) the Fort Leavenworth branch of the Santa Fe trail (see pp. 559, 598), which C. E. Pancoast, for one, traveled—(see, following); or, (2) the new trail (mentioned by Easton—see p. 886) which ran from St. Joseph, Mo., to Union Town (on the Kansas river), and southward from there, to the Santa Fe trail near (east of) Council Grove.]

(7) The Ithaca and California Mining Company pack-mule train, captained by Charles V. Stuart, was, on June 8, west of Pawnee Fork. "W. A. T." (who did not meet the company) inexplicably referred to it as "Capt. Tuttle[?], with 50 men, and pack animals [which, on June 8] took the Cut Off, leaving the Arkansas river." The Ithaca and California Mining Company was a "joint Stock association . . . with a capital invested of $25,000.00. . . ." Its president was Dr. Elijah White—chief promoter of the 1842 emigration to Oregon. Originally equipped as a wagon train, the Ithaca company (which included some Auburn men) had set out from New York state on March 21. Subsequently it was reported the company would "cross the plains with pack-mules, three mules to the man," going "by way of Independence and the Middle Pass." At Independence, Mo., Charles V. Stuart was appointed captain; and the party started west from a Missouri border camp on May 15. Dr. A. M. Heslep (of the large train under pilot James Kirker—see, below), in a July 8 letter from Greenhorn, wrote: "We left that [Ithaca] company at 110 mile creek [in mid-May] to recruit. . . . we were not overtaken by them until after our arrival at Council Grove. Up to that time and [as] late as June 27 [at Pueblo], the Ithaca company has been alternately in advance or rear of our company." From Pueblo, the Ithaca men took an unusual route—"via the Cache la Poudre, Laramie Plains, Browns Hole, and Fort Uintah to Utah Valley" (quoting historian Dale L. Morgan). It was this route that George Withers and others of Captain Barber's company (above) also traveled.

An item in the New York *Tribune* of March 3, 1849, noted that Capt. C. S. Tuttle, who had been "with the Plains Battalion" (Gilpin's battalion, 1847-1848), was on his way to Independence and hoped to organize an early-starting pack-mule company for the Santa Fe route. (For Caleb S. Tuttle, see, also, pp. 727, 733, and 750.) If he traveled with the Ithaca company, he must have been one of the four men (including Jerome B. Howard) who joined west of Independence on May 15(?). Howard (in a February 12, 1850, letter) commented: "Too large a company, fifty-four in all, and a deplorable want of system, occasioned by a difficiency in the early pack-mule education of our Captain [i. e., Stuart], together with considerable sickness, caused a slowness of movement that foretold a late arrival at the 'diggins.'"

(8) James Kirker, pilot, with three "conjointed" Illinois companies numbering over 150 (144 "fighting men, exclusive of the clergy and boys"—as one

member put it), was met by "W. A. T." on June 9, between Jackson's Grove and Coon creek. "Their object is to examine the Taos mines and then if not satisfied to leave Santa Fe in September for California," he reported. The mule-drawn wagons (Joseph Heslep, captain) perhaps numbered 15; and there were about 29 in the ox train division (Doctor Rogers, captain). Under Kirker's pilotage were the following:

The Morgan county (Ill.) and California Rangers (Joseph Heslep, captain), composed of 40 men with 12 wagons (and including "guide and interpreter James Kirker" as a company member), had reached Independence May 1; camped in the vicinity; added, before May 11, about 20 men (five from Racine, Wis. ter.; and an ox-team group under "Dr. Rogers of Petersburg, Menard county Ills."); headed out the Santa Fe trail on May 17 "some sixty strong, with mule teams [mostly], splendid outfit, military organization. . . ." They had delayed their start, awaiting the coming of a "company of about eighty men from Peoria, Illinois . . . also, two or three smaller companies."

Most of the Peoria (Ill.) ox-team contingent (some 90 men in all; a few non-Peorians) joined the Morgan county train at Council Grove around May 25 (having come down from Fort Leavenworth via the old military road), crossing the Kansas at the Delaware, or Grinter's ferry—as J. R. Forsyth's diary shows, and the Santa Fe trail (from the Westport area). Both "Obadiah Oakley," and "Joseph Wood," whose names appear on a list of the Peoria Forty-niners, presumably were the same men, who, as members of the Peoria "Oregon Dragoons," in 1839, had accompanied Thomas J. Farnham across "Kansas" to the Rocky mountains (see pp. 371, 372). John R. Forsyth (whose diary is the principal source of information on the Peorians' travels in 1849) is listed in the same roster. Others therein include "Capt Phillips," "M[yron] Angel," and "J [Eugene] Angel" who are mentioned in the narrative (written in 1890, mostly from memory) of Charles E. Pancoast (published, in 1930, under the title A *Quaker Forty-Niner*). These men (and nine? others) were the last of the "Peorians" to join the Kirker-piloted "conjointed" companies, catching up near Cottonwood Crossing. Pancoast's narrative (off as to dates; and with obvious exaggerations, and some inaccuracies) is of particular interest in showing the use, in 1849, of the Fort Leavenworth branch of the Santa Fe trail (the road pioneered in 1845 by Kearny, and used in 1846 by his Army of the West—see pp. 559, 598, and Emory's map, segment in this volume). Pancoast recollected traveling some 43(?) miles from Fort Leavenworth; reaching the Kansas at "a place called Rope Ferry, where I suppose Topeka now stands" (but, rather, at the Wakarusa's mouth); and where "a lone Settler [Charles? Fish] with his Wife and Family" lived in a "double Log Cabin with Port Holes and a door four inches thick. . . ." The ferry operator charged Pancoast and companions "less [he said] than he charged the Santa Fe Traders" to cross on his rope-pulled "substantial Flat Boat." "This man," wrote Pancoast, "had no doubt made a great deal of money there, as the government had sent many teams that way during the Mexican War, beside the constant[?] traffic to Santa Fe, and this year many Emigrants."

The Kirker-piloted Illinois men traveled up the Arkansas to Pueblo; on to Greenhorn; and from there a detachment of 50 men explored for gold on

"Sangre de Cristo creek." Eventually, some of the company, without Kirker, took the Gila route to California.

(9) The South Carolina ("Palmetto"), (Greenville, Bond co.) Illinois, and Mormon companies from Johnson and Henry counties, Mo., were met by "W. A. T." at noon on June 11, near Coon creek. The diary of H. M. T. Powell records that his Greenville, Ill., party met (on May 21, in the Black Jack area) five wagons of South Carolinians who wanted to join them; and that on May 27, east of Council Grove, a "fine Company [including some families] with 14 waggons" from Johnson county, Mo., passed them. (The Greenville party lost a man—Dr. Edmund C. Park—to cholera, this same day; earlier two other men had died.) West of Diamond Spring, on May 31, these three companies (22 wagons) united under Captain Lightner, of the Missouri train. The Henry county, Mo., group apparently joined farther out on the trail.

(10) "Germans & Hungarians" made up part of the all-Wisconsin train, bound for California by way of southern routes, which "W. A. T." met on June 12 near Pawnee Fork. In this group was the family of Hungarian noble-man Count Agostin Haraszthy (including his father "General" Haraszthy), "Mr. Rheiner" (partner of the count), also Thomas W. Sutherland (former district attorney for Wisconsin territory) and wife. With them traveled the Walworth County Mutual Mining Company, originally 12 men, with three wagons. David Brainard, of this group, kept a diary. After reaching St. Joseph, Mo., May 15, the combined party had crossed the Missouri (above Fort Leavenworth) on the 18th, and the Kansas river on the 26th (the crossing point is not identified). A newspaper-published, unsigned letter, dated "Council Grove, Indian Territory, June 4, 1849," evidently written by Sutherland, in-cluded these statements: "We start this morning for Santa Fe, having re-mained here two days repacking, and washing, and resting our cattle. . . . The crowd is not very great on this road. We have organized our company. H. [Count Haraszthy] is captain and I am judge. . . . A Dr. McE_____ of Mississippi, travels with us. He is a wealthy gentleman; has his servant, &c. He travels with a mule carriage. . . . Our cattle are strong, and are the better for having been driven from the northwest [Wisconsin territory] and fed on corn. . . ." The Wisconsinites crossed the Arkansas on June 18; arrived at Albuquerque July 29. Subsequently, by way of the Gila route, they reached California.

(11) "Captain Carr's" company, met by "W. A. T." on June 14 near Plum Buttes (present Rice county) was the military-civilian party of Capt. Croghan *Ker,* Second dragoons, and James Collier (*see* p. 869).

(12) "June 19th, passed ex Gov Edwards' and maj. Hart's cos. for Calif.," "W. A. T." reported. Missouri's former governor John C. Edwards was in a late-starting company which, at one time, was stated to number five wagons and 30 men. Hart evidently was the same person referred to as "Adjutant Hart" (*see* July Council Grove annals entry, p. 879) who was bound for Chi-huahua, not California. Joseph R. Simmons (nephew of ex-Gov. John C. Edwards) kept a diary of the journey. Though Edwards' party reached West-port, Mo., on April 28, the move into "Kansas" was not made till May 29. (On June 1 and 2, the camp was near Lone Elm.) Edwards was at Council Grove as early as June 9; his company arrived there June 12; and was joined

on the 15th by "Maj. Hart"; and Hart's trains caught up, west of the Grove, on the 16th. That same day "another company . . . Dr. Richardson's" joined them. (Of Edwards' group, "Saling" died on June 6 and "Taffinder" on the 10th; "Mr. Williams of Richardson's Co." died June 30 on the Arkansas.) Simmons' July 3 entry states that they camped two miles beyond Mann's Fort; and that "The Fort is all in ruins, having been torn down by Indians, and by the Emigrants for fuel." On July 4 they met four wagons of "Capt. Evans'" company of Californians, returning from Taos(!) and going back home to Arkansas. After passing the Moro, on July 25, Simmons wrote in his diary: "A Fort is being built here by Mr [Alexander] Barclay: to be called Fort Alexander. . . ." (But to Santa Fe trail travelers it was "Barclay's Fort.") On October 9, on the "road to Santa Cruz," L. D. Aldrich (a '49er traveling a southern route) "came up with Governor Edwards from Missouri & encamped."

Ref: (General) Missouri Republican, St. Louis, June 30 (for "W. A. T.'s" letter, dated Westport, Mo., June 25, 1849), and July 4, 1849 (for the Turkey creek letters of P. B. Marple—May 25, and A. Williamson—June 1); for (2) New York Weekly Tribune, August 11, 1849; for (5) The Weekly Tribune, Liberty, Mo., December 7, 1849 (for G. W. Withers' August 13 letter); Morgan, op. cit., p. 143, under note 1; for (6) The Weekly Tribune, Liberty, Mo., September 7, 1849 (for a Congreve Jackson item); John Hudgins' recollections, "California in 1849," in The Westport Historical Quarterly, v. 6 (June, 1970), pp. 3-16; and John R. Forsyth's "Journal," as listed under No. 8; for (7) Morgan, op. cit., pp. 16, 49, 143; Bieber, op. cit., pp. 364, 366, 367; New York Daily Tribune, March 3, April 7, May 16, September 21, 1849; letters by Dr. Elijah White (May 14) and J. G. Morse (June 24), in the Ithaca (N. Y.) Journal of June 13 and August 29, 1849, courtesy of Dale L. Morgan, Bancroft Library; letters of Jerome B. Howard in Thomas D. Clark, editor, Gold Rush Diary Being the Journal of Elisha Douglass Perkins . . . 1849 (Lexington, Ky., 1967), pp. 175-185; for (8) The Daily Reveille, St. Louis, May 9, 13, 23, 1849, February 16, 1850 (for letters by "Hunt," of the Morgan county, Ill. company); Bieber, op. cit., pp. 353-381; John R. Forsyth's "Journal" (microfilm of typed excerpt in KHi); C. W. Haskins' The Argonauts of California . . . (New York, 1890), pp. 412, 413 (for names of the Peorians); Charles E. Pancoast's A Quaker Forty-Niner . . . (Philadelphia, 1930); for (9) Douglas S. Watson, editor, The Santa Fe Trail to California, 1849-1852, the Journal and Drawings of H. M. T. Powell (San Francisco, c1931); for (10) Wisconsin Historical Publications, v. 31, pp. 2, 3, 6, 7, 14, 15, 24, 25 (for references in Lucius Fairchild's letters, to Sutherland, the Hungarians, etc.); David Brainard's diary (typescript copy in State Historical Society of Wisconsin); Bieber, op. cit., p. 381; KHQ, v. 7, p. 205 (for Sutherland letter); for (12) KHQ, v. 7, pp. 204, 205; Joseph R. Simmons' diary, in the Western Historical Manuscripts Collection of the University of Missouri; Lorenzo D. Aldrich's A Journal of the Overland Route to California & the Gold Mines (Los Angeles, 1950), p. 49.

❡ May.—The number of known diaries, or journals, kept by Forty-niners who traveled the Oregon-California trail across "Kansas" in May, 1849, exceeds 100. Of 101, 63 were written by persons who started from St. Joseph, Mo. (or vicinity thereof); and 38 by individuals who set out from Independence, Mo. (or that area). Traffic on the St. Joseph branch was heavier than on the Independence trail, perhaps about in proportion to the diarists for each route.

One of these journal-keepers, Henry J. Shombre, of Richmond, Ind. (whose diary ended at Fort Laramie), is given particular mention because: (1) the original manuscript is in the Kansas State Historical Society; (2) Shombre had a later, very brief,

Kansas connection—at the head of a Free-State company, he entered Kansas territory early in August, 1856, to take part in the struggle against Proslaveryites, and was mortally wounded less than two weeks later (August 16) during the attack on "Fort Titus."

Shombre, and other Indianans, arrived at Independence early in April, 1849; camped near the town; on the 11th, numbering 44 men, they elected William F. Davis as captain. When they crossed the Missouri line on May 4, the train numbered 10 wagons, 57 men, 81 horses, mules, oxen, and three dogs. One man died on May 18; the company passed the Wakarusa on the 9th; pitched tents on May 11 "on a little creek 3 ms E of the lower ferry on the caw [Kansas]" (Shombre noted the new grave of an emigrant there); remained two more days because of a sick man (Shombre climbed what is now called "Burnett's Mound"—"I went to a high mound from which I could see . . . all the surrounding country   there are 3 Ind monuments rudely made of common lime stone   . . .   teams passing all day mostly ox teams."); on May 14 they "conclud to cross the river   . . .   reached the river at 9 A.M. 40 waggons then to cross but we got over by 1 oc P M   the river is 150 yds wide full of Islands   . . .   going into the stream you decend a tol steep hill ¼ mile from the water   the valley is very rich   the wagons has to be puled up a steep 30 feet bank out of the boat   . . .   soldiers creek runs to the west and the Caw to the north   . . ."; on the 15th lost another man from cholera. On the 21st, in the Big (Black) Vermillion area, another company was taken in (the "Ge[orgia] Co"—with 21 men, five wagons, and 37 mules); David B. Wood was here elected captain; and Davis became wagonmaster. Shombre's company reached Fort Kearny on May 31; and arrived at Fort Laramie June 16.

Ref: Henry J. Shombre's "Diary" (in KHi ms. division); Morgan, *op. cit.*, for information on the diarists of 1849—*see* pp. 177-200, and folded chart; Haskins, *op. cit.*, pp. 397, 404; Bernhard Knollenberg, *Pioneer Sketches of the Upper Whitewater Valley* . . . (1945), pp. 130-134; *KHC*, v. 1-2, pp. 227, 228, 230, 231, v. 8, pp. 309, 340; *Herald of Freedom*, Lawrence, November 1, 1856.

❧ May 13.—Turner & Allen's (or, Turner, Allen & Co's.) "Pioneer [commercial] Line" first train (behind schedule—*see* February 7 entry) left a camp (established in April) about 10 miles west of Independence, Mo., to begin the journey to "Upper California," by way of the Oregon-California trail. There were 20 passenger carriages, six persons to each, "drawn by but two mules, and small ones at that"; and 20 (overloaded) baggage and supply wagons— all mule drawn. Passengers and personnel must have numbered upwards of 160 souls. Mr. Turner was with the company as late as May 17.

Several cholera deaths already had occurred among the company: "Capt. Gillespie" (described as "one of the principal managers of the line") on May 5; mountain man Moses ("Black") Harris (employed as guide), and the Rev. Mr. Goheen on the 6th; O. Trowbridge and William Miller on the 7th;

teamster Robert Rudles on the 9th. Two "Pioneer Line" passengers died of cholera near Lone Elm on May 17(?). (The train had gone on.)

Making slow progress due to rainy weather, and much sickness in camp, the Turner Allen & Co. first train apparently crossed the Kansas river about May 22. C. M. Sinclair, from Ann Arbor, Mich., died May 29 or 30, of "bilious fever," and was buried on the (Black?) Vermillion's west bank (in present Pottawatomie county). After the train reached Fort Kearny on June 8, a passenger said 11 persons had died of cholera up to that time. The date of arrival at Fort Laramie was June 27. By one report, the Pioneer Line first train reached the California mines on October 12.

See, also, June 18 entry.

Ref: *Missouri Republican,* St. Louis, April 29, May 17, June 19, July 6, November 19, 1849; *The Daily Reveille,* St. Louis, May 10, 17, June 9, December 25, 1849; *New York Weekly Tribune,* June 2, July 28, September 15, 1849; Bidlack, *op. cit.,* pp. 13-23; Read and Gaines, *op. cit.,* p. 631; R. P. Bieber, *op. cit.,* pp. 361, 362; *Journal of American History,* New Haven, Conn., v. 2, (1908), pp. 129-154 (John E. Brown's journal); St. Joseph (Mo.) *Gazette,* July 20, 1849.

❧ May 14.—The *Timour* arrived at St. Louis, from St. Joseph, Mo. In her cargo: 742 bales of hemp, and 680 bales of buffalo robes.

Ref: St. Louis *Daily New Era,* May 15, 1849.

❧ Mid-May.—On the 15th, from "Third Camp—Wolf Creek Bottom, Iowa Nation of Indians" (on the St. Joseph branch of the Oregon-California trail), Dr. B. B. Brown, St. Louis, wrote: "The Cholera is sweeping over the trains on this road with fearful mortality. . . . Death seems to have visited every camp but mine, and not a train passes without Cholera cases." On the "13th" (*i. e.,* 18th?), in another letter, he wrote (from "Near the Iowa Mission"): "The Cholera is making fearful head on the road. . . . Up to this time I have lost no case."

Prince A. Athearn (in the Great Nemaha Subagency area?), on May 16, "Passed a grave where three men were buried—all died in one camp within 20 hours of cholera." (These may have been Marion county, Mo., men. A history states: "About the 15th of May, Mr. Theodore Jones . . . Mr. John Newbower and John Tatlow, of Palmyra; Mr. Samuel Muldrow, of Ralls co., and others, had died of cholera, near an Indian Agency 25 miles west of St. Joseph"; and that several of them had been buried in the same grave.)

Vincent Geiger, on May 19, west of the Nemaha (apparently) wrote: "Passed over a rolling country. Today we saw a grave in which three emigrants are burried who died with cholera in 10 hours after they were taken. Every day we have passed fresh made graves. . . ."

"Maj. Armour," who returned from St. Joseph to St. Louis (after a futile attempt to overtake the train he intended to travel with, out on the trail) reported that 12 out of 13 members of a New York emigrant company had died of cholera; and that 12 of another New York state party "had shared a like fate."

Ref: St. Louis *Daily New Era,* May 28, June 2, 1849; Saint Louis *Daily Union,* May 25, 1849; *The Pacific Historian,* Stockton, Calif., v. 2 (February, 1958), pp. 6, 7 (for Athearn);

Potter, *op. cit.*, p. 80 (for Geiger); *The History of Marion County, Missouri* . . . (St. Louis, 1884), p. 296.

❧ May-June.—"Veni" (who had left Fort Leavenworth May 16 and camped near the Missouri border, south of the Kansas river, till May 31), wrote on June 9, from Council Grove: "The cholera carried off a great number of soldiers and emigrants at the fort [including five out of "Veni's" train] and other points on the river, and is not entirely out of some of the trains on the route yet, as every camp ground between here.[Council Grove] and Fort Leavenworth and Independence is marked with two or three fresh graves, as well as all along on the roadside."

He stated, also: "the Indians have all left the road at every settlement contiguous to the roadside, on account of the cholera. I noticed at Bull creek, Kaw river and Willow Springs, among the Delawares and Shawnees, that they had all run off, and left their houses and gardens, with vegetables growing, to the mercy of travelers . . ."

A. Williamson, who had left Independence May 17 to travel the Santa Fe trail, stated on June 1, at Turkey creek, that he had seen "29 [cholera] cases which terminated fatally" since leaving the Missouri state line; but that cholera was "now abating."

Ref: New York *Daily Tribune Supplement*, July 6, 1849 (or, *see KHQ*, v. 7, pp. 204, 205); *Missouri Republican*, St. Louis, July 4, 1849.

❧ May 18.—"Up to the present time there have crossed the river at St. Joseph about 1200 wagons; at Duncan's ferry four miles up the river 600 wagons, at Bontown 6 miles above 500 wagons, and at the Savannah landing 550 wagons—making 2850 wagons," the St. Joseph *Gazette* reported. Also, "a large number have crossed here who go with pack mules which will increase the number at least 200 more." It was said not over half a dozen emigrant wagons remained in St. Joseph on May 18; but there were still camps across the Missouri in "Kansas."

Forty-niners entering "Kansas" from the St. Joseph area, to mid-May, perhaps totaled around 11,600. "Near all the wagons have oxen and average about four yoke to the wagon," the *Gazette's* editor stated. (Roughly, then, some 22,800 oxen and mules pulled these 2,850 wagons; and there were additionally, the pack animals, riding horses, some milk cows, etc.)

At the ferries between Savannah and the Council Bluffs (principally at the Old Fort Kearny starting point), an estimated 1,500 wagons had crossed the Missouri up to mid-May; and (on a four-per wagon assumption) perhaps 6,000 persons.

Compare June 15, 1849, St. Joseph statistics with these.

Ref: St. Joseph (Mo.) *Gazette*, May 18, 1849; *Niles' National Register*, v. 75 (June

13, 1849), p. 383 (from St. Joseph [Mo.] *Adventure* of May 18); *Missouri Republican,*
St. Louis, May 23, 1849.

❡ May-August.—Nearly all the Indian tribes in "Kansas" were affected by the cholera outbreak in 1849, some more than others, as
the items below indicate.

On May 18, at Ottawa Baptist Mission (present Franklin county), Jotham
Meeker recorded in his diary: ". . . the Cholera is approaching . . .
it is on the Miami, Shawanoe, Delaware, Wyandotte, Kickapoo and Pottawatomie lands; and is within 10 miles of 'us'—is at Westport, Blue, Gr. River,
Westpoint, Leavenworth and Uniontown, and all along the road to California
among the emigrants."

Meeker learned, on May 22, that cholera had "broken out severely among
the Miamis and Shawanoes, and . . . is just commencing among the
Sauks [Sacs & Foxes]. So we are surrounded by it." [Frances Barker, at
Shawnee Baptist Mission wrote, in a September letter, that during May, June,
July, and part of August, meetings had been much interrupted by the cholera.
He thought two-thirds of the Shawnees had been "more or less affected" with
the disease; though not many had died; and severe cases had been comparatively few. John G. Pratt, at Delaware Baptist Mission wrote, in August, that
eight Delawares had died of cholera; many others had been sick; and nearly
all the Indians "forsook their dwellings and fled into the interior . . . to
avoid contact with the whites" during the epidemic. The Wyandots' agent
Thomas Moseley, Jr., reported, in the fall, that only six of that nation had
died of cholera.]

At St. Joseph, Mo., on May 25, the *Gazette* stated there had been a large
number of cholera deaths among the tribes across the Missouri (Iowas, Sacs
& Foxes, Kickapoos, and some Pottawatomies); and on June 15, reported:
"Some 15 Iowa Indians have died of Cholera at the [Presbyterian] Mission."

In May the Pottawatomies, in fear of cholera, "started on their hunt without
waiting for their spring annuity." Of those who remained on the reserve, a
number were stricken. The diary of Father Maurice Gailland, St. Mary's
Mission, recorded a few items on the outbreak. (June 2) "Father [Christian]
Hoecken is called to Uniontown in order to care for four persons sick of
cholera . . . [all died the day they became ill; and so did two others
'far away']." On June 3 Father Gailland went to Uniontown, where "There
were four new victims of the cholera." Next day he and Father Hoecken
"visited the Indians at Wakarusa, but frightened by two successive funerals,
they have all fled except one family." This day (June 4) Mrs. John Gallimore, wife of the Pottawatomies' government physician, died at Union Town;
and so did an Indian woman. On June 5 Dr. John Gallimore became ill (and
died a few days later). The next day the wife of Nicholas Jarveau (*not*
Janveau) became ill; and Gailland also noted "Almost all have fled." On
June 7 he returned to St. Mary's Mission (across the river) "as the country
was almost deserted." On the 8th he wrote: "There is no school at this
time because of the danger of contagion." Two more persons died on or
about the 10th. Under June 12-13, he recorded: "The doctor [Gallimore]
died."

On June 15 Jotham Meeker learned that "the Cholera rages with great violence among the Pottawatomies and the Kansas." A Sac & Fox chief told Meeker, on August 8, that cholera had attacked his people while out buffalo hunting (some 2,000 were on the Plains); that 20 to 30 deaths occurred; and fearing that all would become ill, the Indians left the dead unburied, and the dying, and fled. On August 9 Meeker recorded in his diary: "30 of the Sauk & Fox men have just died with Cholera besides women & children . . . [and] about 100 Kaws [Kansa], and many of the Osages, Otoes & Pawnees have also just died."

Many Osage Indians died of cholera. Acting Agent John M. Richardson reported, in October, that the "malignancy of the disease" had been "more terrible and fatal than among them in 1832, as it appears none, or at least very few, recovered from it when attacked during the past summer." The epidemic had occurred while the Osages were out on the high and open prairie, in June. After the first onslaught, they separated into small parties, and roamed till some time in August.

Ref: St. Joseph (Mo.) *Gazette*, May 25, June 15, 1849; Jotham Meeker's "Diary" (in KHi ms. division); Comm'r of Indian Affairs, *Report*, 1849 (for Moseley and Richardson); SIA, St. Louis, "Records," v. 9, typed copy, pp. 357, 358, 361, 413; *KHQ*, v. 20, pp. 520, 521 (for Gailland's diary items); *Baptist Missionary Magazine*, v. 29 (November, December, 1849), pp. 403-405, 430; Pierre-Jean De Smet's *Western Missions and Missionaries* . . . (New York, 1859), p. 369. Dr. John Gallimore, when appointed physician for the Pottawatomies, lived at Harrisonville, Mo.

℃ May 20.—Maj. Osborne Cross (quartermaster's department), who had arrived at Fort Leavenworth May 19 after a nine-day journey up the Missouri on the *San Francisco*), set out for Fort Kearny "to catch up" with Bvt. Col. W. W. Loring and his Oregon-bound Mounted riflemen—*see* May 10 entry. His wagons were pulled by unbroken, weak mules; the drivers were unskilled; and the start of the journey was inauspicious.

On May 22 Cross reached Wolf creek; and on the 23d (having, the preceding days, traveled "on a trail made partly by the Oregon expedition") he and his party "came into a road as large as any public highway in the United States, leading from St. Joseph and Weston." In his journal, Cross also noted that "Large trains were coming in from all points on the Missouri river on trails intersecting this great highway. . . . All these trails followed ridges, which placed the wagons frequently in such position that they seemed to be crossing the prairies in every direction . . . they looked at a distance not unlike vessels on the wide ocean steering for different parts of the globe." This same day Cross overtook Bvt. Capt. Gordon Granger, of the Mounted riflemen. (Gibbs, of Loring's command, in his journal entry of June 5, stated that Granger "reached camp [west of Fort Kearny] from Forts Leavenworth and Kearny. He had measured the distance between those two points by an odometer and fixed it at 325 miles.")

Cross "arrived on the Nemaha, about eleven o'clock" of May 24 (and found cholera prevalent among the emigrants camped in this area). On the 25th he reached "within five miles of . . . the Big Vermilion." During the 30-mile trek on the 26th, Cross noted the many graves along the road—

evidence "that the cholera was prevailing to an alarming extent." (Loring had lost two men—cholera victims—before reaching the Platte.)

On the 27th the major and his party overtook "at least 100 wagons" ("many of these people were from Illinois"). On the 30th Cross left the Little Blue to cross to the Platte; and on the 31st, joined Loring's command (then going into camp about two miles above Fort Kearny).

Ref: Settle, *op. cit.*, pp. 33-272 (for Maj. Osborne Cross' journal), and *ibid.*, p. 303 (for Gibbs' mention of Cross) and p. 308 (for Gibbs' mention of Granger); the Cross journal was first published in 31st Cong., 2d Sess., *H. Ex. Doc. No. 1*, Pt. 2 (Serial 587), pp. 126-244. Moses' table (in Settle, p. 345), lists the Fort Leavenworth-Fort Kearny distance as 310 miles.

❡ May 23.—Bvt. Maj. Robert H. Chilton and his Company B, First U. S. dragoons (also Asst. Surg. John F. Hammond), from Fort Leavenworth (left early in May?), arrived at Fort Kearny—where they would form part of the garrison, and replace U. S. Mounted riflemen (now leaving for Oregon) who had been at the post since October, 1848. No information on Chilton's journey (departure, route, etc.) has been located. His family was in the party.

Also under orders to Fort Kearny were Bvt. Lt. Col. B. L. E. Bonneville, and two companies of Sixth U. S. infantry. They arrived (by way of the trail from Old Fort Kearny) on May 28 and 29, under the command of Lts. Thomas O. Davis and Levi C. Bootes, respectively. *See* a May 10 entry.

Ref: *Missouri Republican*, St. Louis, June 16, 21, 1849; Settle, *op. cit.*, pp. 56, 302; Nebraska State Historical Society *Publications*, v. 21, pp. 258, 259; *Nebraska History*, v. 29 (September, 1948), pp. 175-207 (for Fort Kearny article).

❡ May 25.—A mail from Salt Lake City, carried by Allen Compton's (Mormon) party (11 men on horseback), arrived at Kanesville (Council Bluffs), Iowa. (On June 7 a St. Louis dispatch noted the arrival there, from the Great Salt Lake, of an express "with advices to the 15th of April.")

Compton's party had left Salt Lake City April 14; reached Fort Laramie on May 8; met the first California-bound "emigrants" near the Forks on the Platte about May 14 or 15; was at Fort Kearny May 17 and 18; continued eastward to the Missouri, via the Old Fort Kearny trail across "Nebraska." The Mormons had "a good many other loose horses with them, also one wagon," according to emigrant Jasper S. Hill.

Ref: Morgan, *op. cit.*, p. 200; New York *Weekly Tribune*, June 16, 23, 1849. N. Grant (of Miles M. Goodyear's westbound party) wrote from Fort Kearny on May 17, 1849, that a company of 11 men had just come in from Salt Lake—having left there in April.—St. Joseph (Mo.) *Gazette*, June 22, 1849. Joseph W. Berrien (in Col. Vital Jarrot's company), on May 14, on the South Platte "met a party of Mormons from Salt Lake proceeding to St. Joseph[?] . . . They had been 30 days on the road and were carrying the mail."— *Indiana Magazine of History*, v. 56 (December, 1960), p. 301. Doyce B. Nunis, ed., *The Letters of a Young Miner*, *op. cit.*, (for Jasper Hill's May 18 letter, at Fort Kearny).

❡ Before the end of May, James J. Webb and other traders set out from Council Grove for Santa Fe. At the Little Arkansas, on June 5, an emigrant (in his journal) noted: "Just after breakfast Webb's and Meier's [Henry Mayer's] Train came up . . ."

An eastbound party met "Mr. Webb and others" on June 11 near Coon creek; later that day met "a party for California, and traders for Santa Fe; some Germans in company"; on the 15th met "Mr. Ross' " company in the Great Bend area. Another Missouri-bound company, about the 15th, met "Webb with train of self and others—40 wagons" at "the [Arkansas] Crossings"; also met "Ross and others [traders]" at Fort Mann (the same, or following day). "Messrs. Webb & Ross" arrived in Santa Fe before July 7.

The *Missouri Republican* received a June 5 letter from "A Blamner [Blumner?]," whose party, en route to Santa Fe, included Mr. Mellen and family, Mr. Colly, Mr. Roberts, Mr. M'Lean, and Mr. Richter's wagon train— 21 persons in all. On June 5 "Blamner's" company was two days' travel behind "Mr. Webs" (Webb?), "Le Blanis," and two brothers Dennis.

Ref: Watson, *op. cit.*, p. 34; *Missouri Republican*, St. Louis, June 30, July 4, 8, 1849; Saint Louis *Daily Union*, August 16, 1849.

❦ May 28.—Two westbound travelers who were in the Council Grove vicinity this day wrote comments on the small settlement.

Dr. Augustus M. Heslep (*"Rambler"*): "Our supplies of timber for repairs being obtained at Council Grove, we left that beautiful spot on the 27th of May [*i. e.*, May 28] . . . The Grove is an oasis in the wilderness . . . A splendid grove of choice timber, with a beautiful, clear, pebbly stream [Neosho river] running through it—a fertile soil, with the bluffs along the stream, combined, adds beauty and enchantment to the scene. Six houses and three or four shops are here located; and though in the Indian country, the inhabitants live in safety and comfort. The Grove is the headquarters of the Kansas, or Caw Indians [and he called them a "filthy, lazy, thieving, worthless set of beings"]. . . ."

H. M. T. Powell: "We descended the bluff, passed the bottom timber and a fine running stream and entered a little village consisting of 2 blacksmith shops, 2 stores and 3 or 4 houses."

Ref: Heslep's letter was reprinted in the New York *Daily Tribune*, September 21, 1849 (from the *Missouri Republican*, St. Louis); or *see* Bieber, *op. cit.*, pp. 368, 369. For Powell, *see* Watson, *op. cit.*, p. 27.

❦ May 31.—The "Wyandott Mining Company"—a party of Wyan- dot Indians and some whites (later described, by Agent Thomas Moseley, Jr., as "fifteen in number, chiefly young men [who had] organized themselves into a joint stock company") set out for the gold mines by way of the Oregon-California trail.

A list gives the names of *Irving P. Long, Theodore F. Garrett* (captain), William Bowers, William Lynville, Ira Hunter, *Matthew Brown, C. B. Garrett, Philip Brown, Adam Hunt, R. Palmer, Russell Garrett*, Dr. E. B. Hand. (Names of Wyandots are italicized.) Washington H. Chick (in reminiscences) stated that he, Evan G. Hewitt and F. B. Tibbs (the latter two being "merchants down on the [Kansas, Mo.] levee") "bought a pony apiece and a wagon and four oxen"; and "joined a company of Wyandotte Indians and with

25 wagons altogether[?] started out across the Plains in May, 1849"; and that they "got along nicely until about 100 miles out, when cholera broke out among some of the emigrants and a great many died."

The Wyandots were mentioned as having arrived in California, in October, by emigrant J. Goldsborough Bruff. An account says these Indians went to the North Fork of Feather river "and were successful" in their gold mining.

Ref: William Walker's "Journals," in Connelley, *op. cit.*, p. 290 (also *see* pp. 275, 276, 340); Comm'r of Indian Affairs, *Report*, 1849 (Moseley's report, therein); Washington S. Chick's reminiscences (typed copy in KHi ms. division); Read and Gaines, *op. cit.*, pp. 210, 667.

❧ May 31.—Capt. Howard Stansbury (U. S. topographical engineers)—under orders to "survey . . . the Great Salt Lake, and [make] an exploration of its valley"—having outfitted at Fort Leavenworth, set out from that post on his expedition West.

In Stansbury's own party were 18 men (Lt. John W. Gunnison; assistant "Mr. Langdall"; artist F. R. Grist, and geologist Dr. James Blake, of St. Louis; guide Auguste Archambault; teamsters, hunters, and other "hands"—"principally . . . experienced voyageurs"), outfitted with five wagons, 46 horses and mules. A California-bound party in which were Charles C. Sackett, his wife, and four others (men), with one wagon, a carriage, and 15 animals, traveled in company. (A seventh person of this group—Elbridge Lawrence—died of cholera at Fort Leavenworth on June 1. Sackett, who had remained there with his friend, left on June 2 to catch up with the expedition.)

Stansbury's report stated: "We followed the 'emigrant road,' (already broad and well beaten as any turnpike in our country) . . ." The first day's march was only six miles. On June 5 after traveling (by the captain's table of distances) about 46½ miles from the army post, they "entered the main emigration road from Kansas," (he also called it "Independence Road—Crossing of the St. Joseph's and Independence Road," perhaps referring to the intersection with the new trail running from St. Joseph southwestward to Union Town on the Kansas river, which Capt. L. C. Easton described later in the year —*see* September 3 entry, p. 886). It was, in any case, by way of the regular emigrant road from St. Joseph that Stansbury and company traveled on out to the Big Blue (reached, and *crossed* on June 9). At the Big Blue ford (where the river was "about 70 yards wide and three feet deep, flowing with a bold current"), they found "the trees and stumps on its banks carved all over with the names of hundreds of emigrants" who had preceded them, along with "the dates of their passing, the state of their health and spirits . . ." (They had passed seven graves this day; and were continuing to meet emigrants returning—mostly because of illnesses or deaths in their companies.)

Over Sunday, June 10, the Stansbury expedition remained in camp "on the right bank of the Big Blue, near a spring of fine water, on the margin of a level prairie, bordered with huge trees." Some of the party caught some "good-sized catfish" in the river; and gathered "hatfuls" of "fine quality" strawberries in the rich bottomland behind the camp. On June 11, "eight miles from the Blue," they "struck the emigration road from Independence," and met a sizeable company of California-bound emigrants with some 20 wagons.

Stansbury subsequently reached Fort Kearny June 19 (by his reckoning the distance from Fort Leavenworth was 311 miles); from July 12-18 he was at Fort Laramie (647 miles); on August 28 he arrived at Salt Lake City. (His wagons had reached there the 23rd.)

Ref: Howard Stansbury, *An Expedition to the Valley of the Great Salt Lake of Utah* . . . (Philadelphia, 1852); *The Daily Reveille*, St. Louis, June 3, 12, July 14, 1849 (for C. C. Sackett's letters of May 27, June 2, and July 14).

❧ On May 31, from "Camp Kanzas" (near Shawnee chief Blackhoof's home—present Johnson county), a large military-civilian company set out for Santa Fe. "Camp Kanzas" had been the stopping-point (or "delaying-point") for two weeks of:

(1) New Mexico-bound Bvt. Lt. Col. Edmund B. Alexander's force (four companies—D, F, G, H—Third U. S. infantry; Bvt. Maj. Henry L. Kendrick's two companies [B and D] Second U. S. artillery —having six 12-pounder mountain howitzers; with which was the party (upwards of 14 persons, including four females) of James S. Calhoun (appointed Indian agent at Santa Fe); also a baggage-and-supply train of ox-drawn wagons (which, at Council Grove, was put in charge of Capt. A. W. Reynolds). Date of departure from Fort Leavenworth: May 16.

(2) California-bound Capt. Croghan Ker's Company K, Second U. S. dragoons; with which was the party ("some 15 persons"— clerks, assistants, &c.—looking more like gold diggers!) of James Collier (appointed collector at the port of San Francisco); also a baggage-and-supply train of mule-drawn wagons. The date of departure from Fort Leavenworth was May 17.

After two or three days' march on the Santa Fe trail, the Ker-Collier company (in a hurry, and able to travel faster) went on ahead; reached Council Grove by June 7; probably left on the 8th. The Alexander-Calhoun company camped a mile beyond the Grove on June 9; left on the 11th.

On June 19, at Jackson's Grove on the Arkansas, Bvt. Capt. Abraham Buford (and party), eastbound, met the Ker-Collier company, "all well, and moving ahead rapidly." He noted that the party included Bvt. Maj. Enoch Steen and Bvt. Maj. William N. Grier (both of the First U. S. dragoons), also Jared W. Folger "sutler of New Mexico." David Brainard, a '49er in another party, stated (in his diary) that Ker (he spelled it "Carr") had as guide "Mr. [George S.] Simpson"; and noted that Mrs. "Carr" (Ker), and Elder and Mrs. Reed (Read) were in the company. The Ker-Collier company arrived at Santa Fe July 11; subsequently, under the guidance of John L. Hatcher, by way of the Gila route, and San Diego, *Collier's* party (and other '49ers) reached California.

At Pawnee Fork, on June 21, Buford met the Alexander-Calhoun company (which, he noted, included Maj. Marshall S. Howe, of the Second dragoons). The party was "all well, and no Cholera," but "a short time previous" there had been a "few fatal cases." The Alexander-Calhoun company arrived at Santa Fe on July 22. "All the companies, from the effects of cholera and other causes before starting, are much reduced in numbers, and present very little more than skeleton forms," wrote Bvt. Lt. Col. John M. Washington (military commander at Santa Fe), on July 30.

Ref: *Missouri Republican*, St. Louis, May 24, June 2, 1849; *KHQ*, v. 7, pp. 204, 205 (for a June 9, 1849, letter from Council Grove—reprinted from New York *Daily Tribune* supplement, July 6, 1849), v. 18, pp. 324, 325 (for a June 7, 1849, letter from Council Grove—reprinted from New York *Weekly Tribune*, July 21, 1849); New York *Daily Tribune*, June 12, 1849; David Brainard's diary (typescript copy in State Historical Society of Wisconsin); New York *Weekly Tribune*, August 11, 1849 (for Buford's "diary" entries); 31st Cong., 1st Sess., *H. Ex. Doc. No. 5* (Serial 569), p. 184; 31st Cong., 1st Sess., *Sen. Ex. Doc. No. 24* (Serial 554), p. 18; 31st Cong., 1st Sess., *H. Ex. Doc. No. 17* (Serial 573), p. 92 (for Bvt. Maj. H. L. Kendrick's table of marches of Alexander's command); James S. Calhoun's *Official Correspondence* . . ., ed. by Annie H. Abel (Washington, 1915), pp. 2-17. Calhoun was from Georgia; Collier came from Steubenville, Ohio. (Samuel R. Dundass in the foreword to his *Journal* [Steubenville, Ohio, 1857] mentions Collier. The New York *Weekly Tribune*, December 22, 1849, has an article on the journey of Collier's party from Santa Fe to San Diego, Calif.); *also, see, Deseret News*, Great Salt Lake City, v. 1, no. 11, August 24, 1850, pp. 85, 86.

❲ May-June.—"Of [William H.] Russell's [government] train from Fort Leavenworth [bound for Santa Fe], nine have died from Cholera, and seven were ill at last accounts," wrote a correspondent at Independence, Mo., on June 18. "The remainder of his teamsters, numbering some 35 or 40, left their teams on the plains, and cut for 'tall timber.' This you may rely upon, as there are now a number of them in this place on their way home."

Ref: *Missouri Republican*, St. Louis, June 30, 1849. See, also, April 30 annals entry for item on the "Brown & Russell" contract with the government.

❲ May-June.—Crossing the Missouri at the Council Bluffs on May 25, and traveling the Mormon trail (north of the Platte) out to Fort Laramie, Almon W. Babbitt (with a five-man guard, a light carriage and 12 horses), carried a United States mail westward to Salt Lake City, reaching there on July 1. (He set out for the East again July 27.)

Babbitt (after returning to the States) said that while en route to Fort Laramie he had "counted" (as he passed up the Platte's north side) upwards of 6,000 wagons westbound on the Oregon-California trail south of the river. (His count probably included the government wagon trains—*not* included in the Fort Kearny statistics—*see* below). It was his guess that some 500 of these wagons subsequently were abandoned (burned, or left standing by the road) in the Fort Laramie vicinity (as the "emigrants" discarded goods and provisions to lighten loads).

Ref: St. Joseph (Mo.) *Gazette*, October 19, 1849; Latter Day Saints *Journal History*.

❲ June.—Fort Kearny statistics on the emigrant *wagons* passing the post during this month included the following:

June	Passed up to this date	Passed on this date	Total	Source
1 & 2		470 wagons	4,403	Mo. Rep., June 21

(Lt. Daniel P. Woodbury, in a June 2 letter, stated: "4,400 wagons have already passed by this post—nearly all destined for California. There are 4 men and 10 draft animals to each wagon—very nearly. Many not included above have traveled on the other side of the Platte [on the Mormon road] and many—probably more than 1,000—are still to come on this side.")

June	Passed up to this date	Passed on this date	Total	Source
5	4,804 wagons	(not counting 250 gov't wagons)		Mo. Rep., June 24
7	4,862 wagons			Mo. Rep., June 24
9		(At sundown)	5,092	Mo. Rep., July 6
15	[5,436] wagons			N. Y. D. T., July 24
19	5,493 wagons			Sackett

(Charles C. Sackett, in a June 19 letter, wrote that by Capt. Stewart Van Vliet's records, 5,493 wagons had passed on the south side of the Platte "up to last evening," and from 500 to 600 had traveled the [Mormon] road north of the Platte—making in all about 6,000 Forty-niner wagons; and not including government trains, or pack-mule parties. Sackett, calculating three persons per wagon (Col. B. L. E. Bonneville's guess was two and a half; Captain Van Vliet's estimate was four per wagon), thus arrived at a figure of 18,000 emigrants "and if we add for those who are with pack mules, and parties not yet here, 2000—we get a total of 20,000. . . .")

June	Passed up to this date	Passed on this date	Total	Source
23			5,516	Mo. Rep., Aug. 6

("Pawnee" [Capt. Stewart Van Vliet] wrote from Fort Kearny on June 23: "The great California caravan has at length swept past this point, and the prairies are beginning to resume their wonted state of quiet and loneliness. . . . 5,516 wagons up to the present, have passed here, on this bank of the [Platte] river, while, on the other, from the best information that can be obtained, about 600 have gone along. . . . At a moderate calculation, there are 20,000 persons, and 60,000 animals now upon the road between this point and Fort Hall [Idaho]. This is below the actual number, as the numerous trains of pack mules are thrown in.") See, also, the Fort Laramie entry of June 26.

Ref: *Missouri Republican*, St. Louis, August 6, 1849 (for "Pawnee's" letter); *The Daily Reveille*, St. Louis, July 14, 1849 (for Sackett); Nebraska State Historical Society *Publications*, v. 21, p. 259 (for Woodbury); New York *Daily Tribune*, July 24, 1849 (as *printed*, the number of wagons up to June 15 was "7,436"—evidently a misprint, and intended to read "5,436"). Morgan, *op. cit.*, p. 22, says one emigrant who passed Fort Kearny after June 23 was diarist James M. Hutchings—on June 24.

❡ June 3.—The *St. Ange* (Joseph La Barge, captain) arrived at St. Louis (from St. Joseph; left May 30), having aboard 1,098 packs of buffalo robes, bear skins, and sundry smaller lots of furs and peltries for Pierre Chouteau, Jr. & Co. (the American Fur Company). Four Company Mackinaw boats had brought these returns from the upper Missouri to St. Joseph.

On May 30 the *St. Ange* had met the *Tamerlane* nearing St. Joseph, the *Algoma* at Fort Leavenworth, and the *Monroe* above Kansas, Mo.

Ref: *Missouri Republican*, St. Louis, June 4, 1849; *The Daily Reveille*, St. Louis, June 5, 1849; St. Louis *Daily New Era*, June 4, 1849; John E. Sunder's *The Fur Trade on the Upper Missouri* (1965), p. 119.

❡ June 5.—From Fort Leavenworth the party of Agent John Wilson (of Howard county, Mo.; appointed to head the new "Salt Lake in California" Indian Agency) set out for Fort Kearny, en route to the West. In company, as escort, were Bvt. Capt. Robert M. Morris and 25 Company B, Mounted riflemen.

Wilson's outfit included seven wagons (teamsters to drive them), and mules for his carriage. With the agent were his wife, two sons, and two daughters, Dr. Lewis A. Birdsall, and daughter Sophia, Milton S. Latham (who turned back near Fort Kearny), and botanist Augustus Fendler. Maj. Robert B. Reynolds (regimental paymaster), and his two wagons, traveled in company out to Fort Laramie.

This late-starting party reached Fort Kearny on, or about, June 23; crossed South Pass on July 22. Trooper William H. Packwood (of the escort) later wrote: "We were five months to a day [from Fort Leavenworth] reaching Sacramento." They had passed over the summit of the Sierras on October 25.

Botanist Fendler (having lost much of his equipment by a freshet on the Little Blue), spe t upwards of a week at Fort Kearny; then joined an eastbound party, and journeyed back to Missouri. He was at Fort Kearny as late as July 1; by July 10 was 10 miles west of the Big Blue; crossed it about the 13th; reached Wolf creek on the 20th; and was back at Fort Leavenworth by July 23.

Ref: *The Daily Reveille*, St. Louis, June 12, 1849; New York *Weekly Tribune*, August 18, October 6, 1849; Read and Gaines, *op. cit.*, p. 586; *Oregon Historical Quarterly*, v. 16, (March, 1915), pp. 33-43 (for Packwood); Susan D. McKelvey, *Botanical Explorations of the Trans-Mississippi West* (1955), pp. 1027-1030 (for Fendler); *Missouri Historical Review*, Columbia, v. 51 (July, 1947), pp. 350-356; St. Joseph (Mo.) *Gazette*, March 22, 1850; *California Historical Society Quarterly*, v. 26 (December, 1947), pp. 321-348, v. 30 (March, 1951), pp. 56-65.

❡ June 7.—"Mr. Brulet [Rouville Brunet?], a French trader, from Fort Laramie, with a large train of wagons, laden with packs of buffalo-robes, bound for St. Louis," was met by westbound Captain Stansbury, in present Nemaha county, on the St. Joseph branch of the Oregon-California trail.

"Brulet," 40 days en route from Fort Laramie, said he "had met not less than four thousand wagons, averaging four persons to a wagon."

Ref: Stansbury, *op. cit.*, p. 18. Emigrant Henry Tappan, on May 23, the day he reached the Platte from the Little Blue, "met a party Traders coming into the States with furs & Buffalo Robes." Five days later he noted meeting another such train—these "Traders from Fort Laramie" were "26 days out" from that post; and their wagons were loaded with "Buffalo Robes, Elk Skins & Furs."—*Annals of Wyoming*, v. 25 (July, 1953), pp. 120, 121.

❆ June 7-8—"Capt. Hughes" of Platte county, Mo., who had taken 600 head of government cattle out to Fort Kearny, started home June 7 via the Old Fort Kearny road; was robbed of "teams, provisions, saddlery, &c." on June 8 or 9, when "about thirty miles this side of the Fort" by some 400 Cheyenne and Sioux warriors (on a foray against the Pawnees).

Ref: New York *Weekly Tribune*, August 11, 1849 (from *Missouri Republican*, St. Louis). Perhaps this was Francis C. Hughes.

❆ June 10.—"The advance of a train from St. Joseph, Mo., belonging to Messrs. Bissonet [Joseph Bissonette] and Badeau [James Bordeaux], bound on a trading expedition among the Sioux," passed Captain Stansbury's expedition (in camp) on the Big Blue's west bank.

Ref: Stansbury, *op. cit.*, p. 23. For mention of James Bordeaux *see Annals of Wyoming*, Cheyenne, v. 5 (July, 1927), pp. 13, 14.

❆ June (and later).—On the Arkansas, between Coon creek and the Cimarron Crossing, Indians in large numbers, and friendly, were encountered by emigrants and traders traveling the Santa Fe trail.

On June 10, while encamped about four miles below Fort Mann, the Kirker-piloted train of Forty-niners (*see* pp. 857, 858) became aware of mounted Indians, in force, across the Arkansas; prepared for trouble; but found these "Arapaho and Kiowa, with a few Cheyenne" peaceable. One chief—Buffalo Heart—carried a letter Agent Thomas Fitzpatrick had given him.

East of Jackson's Grove, on June 20, Capt. Abraham Buford's party "Passed the camps of some 3,000 or 4,000 Indians of the various tribes that inhabit the Praires. They were all very friendly, and were awaiting the arrival of Fitzpatrick . . . with whom they were to have a big talk." (Fitzpatrick had set July 15 for his return; but *see* below.)

"At and near the Arkansas Crossing [on June 24 and 25]," wrote New Mexico-bound Agent James S. Calhoun, "we found several thousand Indians of various tribes assembled, awaiting the return of Mr. Fitzpatrick. . . . The Arapahoes, Cheyennes, Keoways, Comanches & Utahs were the principal tribes in lodges at the . . . Crossing."

Traders reaching Independence about July 10 reported that both sides of the "Big Arkansas," from "the crossing to Mann's fort," were "literally lined" with "Indian camps, themselves and their animals." One man stated that the very friendly Indians had gone so far as "to assist in getting a wagon out of the Arkansas River that stalled."

T. J. Slaughter (who left Santa Fe July 7, and reached Independence August 6) had found "The Kiowas, Cheyennes, Arrapahoes . . . near the road, beyond and this side of the Arkansas. The Camanches had abandoned the route, and gone South. The Cholera was committing great ravages among those who remained, particularly the Kiowas." Another account stated: "Mr. S. found 4,000 Indians on the Arkansas, all friendly, but greatly scourged with Cholera."

For Agent Fitzpatrick's return, *see* mid-November entry, p. 336.

Ref: Bieber, *op. cit.*, pp. 371-373 (Dr. A. M. Heslep's July 8, 1849, letter); New York *Weekly Tribune*, August 11, 1849 (from Van Buren [Ark.] *Intelligencer*, July 14); Calhoun, *op. cit.*, p. 17; 31st Cong., 1st Sess., *H. Ex. Doc. No. 17* (Serial 573), pp. 92, 198-200; New York *Weekly Tribune*, August 4, September 1, 1849 (from *Missouri Republican*, St. Louis); Saint Louis *Daily Union*, August 16, 1849.

❧ June 12.—At Ottawa Baptist Mission (present Franklin county) the Jotham Meekers' third daughter—Eliza—was born.

Her sisters Maria (14) and Emeline (9), also "Kansas-born," were in the States receiving an education at this time.

Ref: Jotham Meeker's "Diary" (in KHi ms. division). In March, 1892, Eliza Meeker (Mrs. W. T.) Keith, of Oakland, Calif., gave the Kansas State Historical Society her father's diary (covering the entire period of his life in "Kansas," 1833 to 1854), and other family papers. *See* annals, p. 276, and p. 381, for the births of Maria and Emeline Meeker.

❧ On June 13(?) Bvt. Col. Aeneas Mackay, QM (up from St. Louis), left Fort Leavenworth to journey out to Fort Laramie (on an inspection tour). The colonel's party included Capt. Langdon C. Easton, AQM, "Dr. Russell, U. S. A.," Dr. George B. Parks (a Bostonian), the Rev. John Robertson (a Scotch gentleman), Mackay's 13-year-old son; and he had, as escort, Bvt. 2d Lt. Nathan G. Evans and 10 First U. S. dragoons.

The Mackay party evidently traveled west with Bvt. Lt. Col. Benjamin S. Roberts, Lt. Washington L. Elliott, and 60 Company C Mounted riflemen, who left Fort Leavenworth (the last of their regiment to depart) on June 13(?), also. The date of arrival at Fort Laramie for all the above was July 26. (At Fort Kearny, Capt. Stewart Van Vliet, AQM, had joined them.) Roberts and his company remained at the new post on the Laramie (*see* June 26 entry). *See* entries of September 3, and 14, for the return trips of Easton, and Mackay.

Ref: *Missouri Republican*, St. Louis, September 1, 15, 26, 1849; New York *Daily Tribune*, September 11, 1849; KHQ, v. 20 (May, 1953), p. 393.

❧ In mid-June a number of traders set out from Council Grove for Santa Fe and points beyond. Eastbound travelers met "Mr. Harley's train for Santa Fe" west of the Little Arkansas on June 15; and the same day "Captain [Ceran] St. Vrain and Mr. Jones" (traveling with Bvt. Lt. Col. E. B. Alexander's infantry-artillery force—*see* May 31 entry). On the 16th they met four companies of traders en route to Santa Fe and Chihuahua; on June 21, near Diamond Spring, passed "F[rank] McManus and others for Chihuahua"; later in the day saw "Judge [James] Brown's [government] train" in camp near Council Grove, and met "Buteris" (with three wagons), bound for Rio Abajo, N. M.

Around July 28 "a large train of Santa Fe traders, from St. Louis, about thirty-five [wagons] in number, loaded with various descriptions of merchandise, with teams bearing six or seven thousand pounds weight, drawn by three or more yoke of oxen," reached a camp near San Miguel, N. M. "They had left

St. Louis on the 22d of May," reported the emigrant (Lorenzo D. Aldrich) who recorded the above in his journal.

"W. M.," wrote from Santa Fe, on August 15, that "Hardy [Harley?], Hickman, Adams and McManus, with 60 wagons," had arrived and "gone on to Chihuahua"; and that other traders "for the lower country" would be in "in a fortnight."

Ref: *Missouri Republican*, St. Louis, June 12, 30, September 12, 1849; Aldrich, *op. cit.*, p. 33; New York *Weekly Tribune*, September 29, 1849.

❡ June 14-24.—Late starting California-bound parties setting out from St. Joseph (as noted in the *Gazette*) were these: on the 14th nine men, with two ox-drawn wagons (they had arrived at St. Joseph on June 4; and anticipated wintering at Salt Lake City); on the 24th, seven men—all Missourians (they had bought their entire outfit at St. Joseph).

The first group included the Rev. Henry Kroh, of Cincinnati, described as "missionary chaplain to Monterey, Cal."; the Missourians were from Howard, Randolph, and Chariton counties.

Ref: St. Joseph (Mo.) *Gazette*, June 15, 29, 1849. Names of all the men were listed in the newspaper issues.

❡ June 15.—"The wagons that [have] crossed the [Missouri] river at . . . [St. Joseph], by ferry and steamboats, number 1508, at Duncan's ferry, four miles above . . ., 685, at Bontown, Savan[n]ah, and the ferries as far up as the [Council] Bluffs, say 2000. This makes the number of wagons 4,193."—St. Joseph (Mo.) *Gazette*.

At four men, and eight mules or oxen, to each wagon, the *Gazette's* editor estimated there were 16,772 persons and some 33,544 mules and oxen traveling with these wagons. The pack-mule emigrants would raise the total to at least 17,000 souls, and the livestock to 34,000 or more.

Ref: St. Joseph (Mo.) *Gazette*, June 15, 1849.

❡ June 16.—The *Tamerlane* (owned by R. & W. Campbell) left St. Louis for the Harvey, Primeau and Company trading posts on the upper Missouri. She carried supplies, and some 100 persons (traders, passengers, crew); reached the Yellowstone's mouth July 21; went a little higher; started back about July 23; and returned to St. Louis on August 8.

Ref: Sunder, *op. cit.*, p. 119; *The Daily Reveille*, St. Louis, August 10, 1849.

❡ June 18.—At Independence, Mo., on the 15th, it was reported that Turner, Allen & Co's. second "Pioneer line" train (*see* May 13 entry for the first) had advanced to Missouri's western border, and would "take final leave" on the 18th. Early notices had said there would be 75 passengers.

This second train (with less heavily loaded wagons) arrived at Fort Kearny on July 11 (in 14? days from Independence, by one account); on August 1 was at Fort Laramie; on August 17, took the Sublette cutoff; apparently (after hardships and losses on the Carson river route) reached the California settlements late in October. George M. Harker (not of either train), in an October 25, 1849, letter from the "Dry Diggings," wrote: "The June train of the Pioneer Line came near overtaking the May train. It was only three or four days behind when it arrived at Pleasant Valley [Calif.]."

Ref: *Missouri Republican*, St. Louis, May 17, June 21, August 1, October 25, 1849; New York *Weekly Tribune*, August 11, 1849; *The Daily Reveille*, September 6, 1849, January 22, 1850; Read and Gaines, *op. cit.*, p. 631.

❧ June 19.—The *Amelia* (D. Finch, captain), under charter to Pierre Chouteau, Jr., & Co., passed St. Joseph en route to the upper Missouri. She had set out from St. Louis on June 9.

In the fore part of July the *Amelia* came downriver to the Council Bluffs (where her cargo of robes and furs was transferred to St. Louis-bound packets); then she started back up in mid-July (losing on this trip, nine men by cholera, and 30 others, "mountaineers who had deserted"). *See, also,* July 16 and September 14 entries.

Ref: St. Joseph (Mo.) *Gazette*, June 22, 1849; New York *Daily Tribune*, September 4, 1849; *The Daily Reveille*, St. Louis, August 10, 1849; Sunder, *op. cit.*, pp. 117, 118.

❧ June 23.—At Turkey creek, on the Santa Fe trail (in present McPherson county), Capt. Abraham Buford and eight First dragoons (from an escort party of 10), took leave of the companies with whom they had journeyed from New Mexico, and set a course (southeastward) for Fort Gibson ("Okla.").

Captain Buford's notes of the trip state that he reached Turkey creek on June 23; and "considering the mail near enough the settlements to be entirely out of danger, took eight men of the escort" and left the rest of the party; then "followed the trail made by Capt. [Lewis] Evan's [Evans'] company . . . [*see* May 12-13 annals entry], down between the Verdigris and Arkansas Rivers"; crossed the Verdigris at Big Island; followed the divide between the Verdigris and Grand rivers; arrived at Fort Gibson on June 29, having made the trip (with wagons) in 25(?) days.

The civilians who continued on the Santa Fe trail to Missouri included mail contractor "Mr. Haywood" [George Hayward?], "Messrs. Mulliken, Heister, Hagan, and Lucas, Chihuahua merchants," and "Mr. Martin, a California [bound] emigrant" who had turned back. At Independence, Mo., on June 29, a correspondent wrote: "Today we had an arrival from the Plains. Messrs. Mullin, of St. Louis, Heisterhagen[?] and Jas. Lucas, together with some others. I learn that an express has gone on to Fort Leavenworth. By these men we have dates to May 16 from Chihuahua and to June 8 from Santa Fe."

Ref: New York *Weekly Tribune*, August 11, 1849 (from Van Buren [Ark.] *Intelligencer*, July 14); *Missouri Republican*, St. Louis, July 8, 1849. Buford had left Santa Fe on June 6; so had the traders, and Martin; the escort of dragoons had joined at (Alexander) Barclay's Fort on the Moro, June 8. 31st Cong., 2d Sess., *H. Ex. Doc. No. 23* (Serial 599), p. 14 (for May 28, 1849, contract, Capt. T. L. Brent, Santa Fe, with "George Hayward," to carry U. S. mail from Santa Fe to Fort Leavenworth; and return to Santa Fe from the

fort with a mail, for $450). At Independence, Mo., on June 18, a reporter stated that a
train from Chihuahua and Santa Fe was daily expected and that it would bring some
$350,000.—New York *Weekly Tribune,* July 14, 1849 (from *Missouri Republican*). Pre-
sumably the above-mentioned traders were those referred to. "Mr. Haywood" arrived at
St. Louis June 30—*Missouri Republican,* St. Louis, July 1, 1849.

❡ June 26.—The American Fur Company's Fort Laramie (Wyo.),
on the Oregon-California trail, was sold for $4,000 to the govern-
ment, for use as a military post.

The transaction was between the Company's agent, Bruce Husband, and Lt. Daniel P. Woodbury (acting on request of Maj. W. F.
Sanderson, U. S. Mounted riflemen, who had reached that post June
16—*see* May 10 entry).

California-bound emigrants and gold seekers had reached Fort Laramie in
May—the first train (Capt. G. W. Paul's company from St. Louis) arriving on
the 22d. By July 1 most of the traffic heading for California (or Oregon) had
gone by; and on July 21, post records showed that 5,500 wagons (with an
average 3½ souls each, as estimated—and only 100 families) had passed. One
correspondent thought that the number of deaths occurring on the various
routes "from the Missouri River" to Fort Laramie had equaled about 1½ per
mile (but this was probably far above the mark). In the Fort Laramie area,
where a great many "emigrants" abandoned "goods and provisions to an astonishing extent," they (in some cases) "carefully interred in the style of a grave,
with head and foot stone" the most valuable of the cast-aside property. To the
uninformed, these were graves. Doctor Price (a returning "emigrant") who left
Fort Laramie June 22, and reached St. Joseph on July 19, estimated some 300
persons had died on the trail between the two points. There had been only
two deaths from cholera at Fort Laramie.

On August 1 a correspondent wrote: ". . . The old Fort is now used for
store houses, stables, &c. . . . The American Fur Company . . . intend to erect a trading post at Scott's Bluffs, some 40 miles below."

An August 27 letter from Fort Laramie stated that the latest of the California emigrants ("a train of 70 or 80 pack mules"—from St. Louis?) had
passed that post on the 26th (in 25 days from Independence); and the trains
of Mormons (for Salt Lake) were still coming through. Troops were busy
building quarters, stables, putting up hay for the winter, etc.; and the fur
company's agents were about to move to the Scott's Bluff post, on the Platte,
50 miles eastward.

Ref: *KHQ,* v. 20, p. 393; *Missouri Republican,* St. Louis, August 29, 1849; Nebraska
State Historical Society *Publications,* v. 20, pp. 200, 201, 207-209; New York *Weekly
Tribune,* April 14, September 15, October 16, 27, 1849; New York *Daily Tribune,* Septem-
ber 11, 1849; St. Joseph (Mo.) *Gazette,* July 20, October 19, 1849; David L. Hieb's *Fort
Laramie* (Washington, D.C., 1954); Le Roy Hafen and F. M. Young's *Fort Laramie*
(Glendale, Calif., 1938). See annals index for Fort Laramie references, also. The *Missouri
Republican,* St. Louis, September 15, 1849, reported (by arrivals from Fort Laramie) that
the last emigrant trains had passed that post between August 14 and 17.

❡ June 27.—Five Mackinaw boats, heavily laden with American
Fur Company furs and peltries arrived at St. Joseph, Mo., from the
upper Missouri.

Ref: St. Joseph (Mo.) *Gazette,* June 29, 1849.

❧ About June 28 Seth E. Ward (Indian trader) created a little excitement at Independence, Mo., when he arrived from the upper Arkansas (and Platte) with some gold dust. Ward & Guerrier's train had left Pueblo ("Colo.") May 9, and Bent's Fort ("Colo.") on the 26th.

Ward may have reached the Missouri border a little in advance of his wagons. In the Coon creek area, on June 11, an emigrant en route to California "met a return train of waggons from the Mountains near the head waters of the South fork of Platte River; they came by Bent's Fort, and were laden to the very top of their bows with Buffalo robes." East of Ash creek, on June 12, '49er David Brainard recorded in his diary: "This afternoon we met a train of nine wagons from the mountains near Fort Laramie. They were a trading company, and been out a year. . . . Their loading consisted of robes entirely, numbering seven thousand." (*See, also,* p. 765.)

It was reported (when he reached St. Louis aboard the *Highland Mary*) that Ward had with him about $2,000 in gold, purchased, on his way in "at the crossing of the Platte," from an Arapahoe who said he had dug it "at the head of Ash Hollow. . . ."

Ref: *Missouri Republican,* St. Louis, June 30, July 8, 1849; St. Joseph (Mo.) *Gazette,* July 20, 1849; Douglas S. Watson, *op. cit.,* p. 41; David Brainard's diary, *loc. cit.* Ward returned to the upper Arkansas late in the year with Thomas Fitzpatrick—*see* mid-November annals entry; and for mention of Ward in 1848, *see* July 13, 1848, annals entry.

❧ June-July.—Cholera, in a form as virulent as before, returned to the town of Kansas, Mo., late in June. By July 12 the second epidemic (*see* April-May entry for first outbreak) had resulted in 20 deaths there; and across the Kansas river, on the Wyandot reserve, four Indians had died.

At Shawnee Methodist Mission (south of the Kansas), an employee wrote on July 8: ". . . we have not yet had one real case of Cholera in this numerous family of 150 or more persons, while all around us . . . [cholera] has been, and still is, prevailing to an alarming extent. . . . many, very many since it first made its appearance ["some two months ago"] in Kansas & Westport have fallen victims. . . ."

In June, Independence, Mo., also had a second outbreak of cholera, and more deaths. Later (August 6) a correspondent wrote from there: ". . . the dread scourge has again visited our place . . . [and] deprived us of many valuable citizens."

Ref: OIA, Letters Received from Wyandot Subagency (National Archives Microcopy 234, Roll 950), for Thomas Moseley, Jr.'s letter of July 12, 1849; Allen T. Ward's letter of July 8, 1849 (in KHi ms. division); St. Joseph (Mo.) *Gazette,* July 13, 1849. The *Missouri Republican,* St. Louis, August 12, 1849, published a list of cholera victims at Independence, Mo., in the July 21-August 6 period; also a list of earlier victims there.

❧ July-December.—Licenses to trade with Indians in "Kansas," as granted by agents and subagents of the St. Louis Indian superintendency, were:

Traders	Indians	Issued by	Rec'vd at St. Louis
C(yprian) & F(rederick) Chouteau	Kansa	C. N. Handy	July
(J. M.) Simpson & (J. M.) Hunter	Delawares and Pottawatomies	R. W. Cummins	July
W(illiam) F. Dyer	Kickapoos, Delawares, and Pottawatomies	R. W. Cummins	July
Whitehead & Peltier	Pottawatomies	R. W. Cummins	Aug.
Michael D. Richardville	Miamis	C. N. Handy	Aug.
P. Chouteau, Jr. & Co.	Pottawatomies	R. W. Cummins	Aug.
W. B. Watts	Sacs & Foxes	C. N. Handy	Oct.
Joseph Clymer	Miamis	C. N. Handy	Nov.
Oliver H. P. Polke	Pottawatomies	Luke Lea	Nov.
P. M. Chouteau	Miamis, Weas & Piankeshaws	C. N. Handy	Dec.

Ref: SIA, St. Louis, "Records," v. 9, typed copy, pp. 343, 346, 358, 359, 365, 368, 370, 379, 402, 405, 412.

❡ July.—From Council Grove a large number of Santa Fe and Chihuahua traders set out for the southwest this month.

Mexican trader Olivares (with some 20 wagons) had left Independence, Mo., on June 15; on, or about the 17th, James Magoffin's train (40 wagons "each drawn by six yoke of steers, and probably conveying goods to the amount of $150,000") had passed through that town. (A mid-June issue of the *Expositor* had noted that trains yet to start for Santa Fe included those of "Adjutant Hart [whose party, taking out machinery, planned to settle in Chihuahua], McGoffin [Magoffin] and Lightner, Armijo and Olivares.") On June 18 an Independence correspondent wrote: "Goldstein's, Parae's [Perea's] and Armijo's [trains], intend starting in a few days. J. M. White also sends a number of wagons loaded with dry-goods, groceries, &c. to Sante Fe. . . ."

An eastbound traveler noted meeting "Lightner & McGoffin's trains" in camp at 110-mile creek on June 23; and later in the day he passed "Domingo's wagons for Mexico" at Willow Springs. On June 24 (the day he reached Westport, Mo.) he met "Armijo's wagons for Rio Abajo."

Dr. Henry Connelly's train started from Westport, Mo., early in July (bound for Paralto, Mex.). At Independence, on July 10, a correspondent wrote: "Several trains left here last week for Santa Fe. Messrs. Goldstein, Flournoy, Oldham, Thompson, J. M. White & Bro. and Wheeler"; and noted that James Magoffin was to depart on July 11, and expected to "overhaul his train" at the Little Arkansas.

In August eastbound travelers reaching Missouri told of having seen Armijo's train at Round Mound, N. M., about August 8; Magoffin's train at Middle

Cimarron Springs about the 11th; and Connelly's wagons, also one of James Brown's government trains (from Fort Leavenworth) "at or near the Arkansas" before August 15(?). Connelly reached Santa Fe prior to September 11, but his train, and others, were at Las Vegas around the 15th "getting on pretty well."

Ref: *Missouri Republican*, St. Louis, June 21, 30, July 8, 17, August 25, October 12, 1849; New York *Weekly Tribune*, July 14, 1849; *Old Santa Fe*, v. 1 (October, 1913), pp. 214, 215; *The Daily Reveille*, St. Louis, June 20, 1849.

❡ July.—Early in the month, the *Monroe* (Elisha Fine, captain) transported a contingent of U. S. troops (four officers, 164 enlisted men) from St. Louis to Fort Leavenworth. (*See, also,* July 25 entry.)

Ref: 31st Cong., 2d Sess., *H. Ex. Doc. No. 23* (Serial 599), p. 11. Fine's contract was dated July 4, 1849.

❡ July 5.—Thomas Moseley, Jr., newly appointed subagent for the Wyandots, arrived in "Kansas." On July 15 Dr. Richard Hewitt (subagent since June, 1845—*see* p. 550) moved "from the Wyandott Territory to give place to his successor."

Moseley, in a July 12 letter, declared that the two-room rented house which had been the subagency headquarters was unsuitable for his family (not yet arrived) or himself; and that he would live (temporarily) at Westport, Mo.

On November 23 Sup't D. D. Mitchell, St. Louis, forwarded a deed of conveyance made by Joel Walker (half-Wyandot), of his "house & appurtenances in the Wyandot country," to the United States, "for the purpose of a residence for the Indian subagent." Mitchell stated that Moseley was already in possession of the property. In December he forwarded deeds executed by Wyandots Robert Robitaille and Isaac Zane, Jr., for properties (two houses) for the residences of the Wyandots' blacksmith and assistant.

Ref: Moseley's July 12, 1849, letter, in "Pratt Collection," KHi ms. division; William Walker's "Journals" (*loc. cit.*), July 7, 1849, entry; OIA, St. Louis, "Records," v. 9, typed copy, pp. 392, 399, 400, 422, 469. On a later occasion—October 12, 1851—Walker, paying a visit to Major Moseley (who was ill), "found him recovering; but Oh! what an ill tempered, wicked old sinner. . . . [he can] swear like a pirate"; and further noted: "His son John arrived on Saturday [the 11th]."

❡ July 7.—George Douglass (in a contract made with Capt. Alexander Morrow, AAQM) agreed to deliver at Fort Scott 225 tons of hay (for $4.87½ per ton). His sureties were Abram Redfield and J. Dodge.

Ref: 31st Cong., 1st Sess., *Sen. Ex. Doc. No. 26* (Serial 554), p. 26.

❡ July 14.—The last Mormon emigrant train of the year (upwards of 300 wagons) left "Winter Quarters" (in eastern Nebraska) and started for Salt Lake City via the Mormon trail north of the Platte. The leaders were George A. Smith and Ezra T. Benson.

Four other Mormon (organized) companies had taken that route earlier in the season. Prior to all these, a Mormon party captained by **Howard Egan**, had set out in May, by way of the Old Fort Kearny route south of the Platte.

The Mormon emigration of 1849, to Utah, is reckoned at about 1,400 persons.

Ref: St. Joseph (Mo.) *Gazette*, August 3, 1849 (from *Frontier Guardian*, Kanesville, Ia., July 25); Morgan, *op. cit.*, pp. 17, 20.

❧ July 16.—The Missouri river boats *St. Croix* and *Mustang,* from Council Bluffs, arrived at St. Louis. Together they brought down nearly 1,200 packages of American Fur Company buffalo robes and furs (transferred from the *Amelia*—*see* June 19 entry), and a number of the company's employees.

Ref: *The Daily Reveille*, St. Louis, July 17, 1849.

❧ July 18.—From South Pass (left June 18) and Fort Laramie, expressman A. L. Johnson (with one Indian companion) arrived at Fort Leavenworth with about 350 pounds of "letter mail." On the 30-day trip he had "laid by" 10 days (some of the delay due to high water).

Mountain man Johnson (who had not been in the States since 1841) was scheduled to start west again on July 26; and hoped to make the 640-mile journey to Fort Laramie in 15 days.

Ref: *The Frontier Guardian*, Kanesville, Ia., August 22, 1849 (from the Glasgow [Mo.] *Times*).

❧ July 20.—The *Mary Blane,* down from St. Joseph, Mo., brought to St. Louis upwards of 600 packs of buffalo robes—consigned to "the house of R[obert] & W[illiam] Campbell. . . ."

Ref: *The Daily Reveille,* St. Louis, July 21, 1849; St. Louis *Daily New Era,* July 20, 1849.

❧ Died: Pierre Melicourt Papin (long-time American Fur Company agent among the Osage Indians; and many years a resident of present Neosho county), on July 20, at St. Louis, of "the prevailing epidemic"—cholera. He was 56 years old.

His funeral took place the same day, "at 6 o'clock, from the residence of Michael [Michel] Giraud, Esq. . . ." (also for some years an agent of the American Fur Company in "Kansas").

Ref: St. Louis *Daily New Era*, July 20, 1849 (the *Era* was an evening newspaper); *Missouri Republican*, St. Louis, July 21, 1849. Pierre Melicourt Papin was first mentioned in the annals in 1822—*see* p. 107; and last mentioned in 1845—*see* p. 505. Michel Giraud was first mentioned in the annals in 1839—*see* p. 376; and last mentioned in 1848—*see* p. 789. John F. McDermott, editor, *Tixier's Travels on the Osage Prairies* (1940), p. 117, gives some additional information on Papin. The *Missouri Republican* commented that Papin, a "resident of the Indian country," usually came to St. Louis to "spend the summer months among relatives and friends."

❧ Around July 25(?) the *Princeton* brought 150 U. S. troops to the Fort Leavenworth landing. This boat (Samuel S. Dickinson, captain), previously in the Mississippi river trade, was on her first trip up the Missouri (and bound for St. Joseph). She had left St. Louis July 22. The troops were from Jefferson Barracks, Mo.

Ref: *The Daily Reveille,* St. Louis, July 21, 1849; *Missouri Republican,* St. Louis, July 21, 1849; St. Louis *Daily New Era,* July 23, 1849. Presumably some(?) of these, and part(?) of the troops noted under the early July entry, p. 880, went to Santa Fe with Bvt. Lt. Col. John Munroe—*see* p. 885.

❧ July.—Quarters for the Baptists' printing press—the "Meeker press" (see pp. 245, 246, 259, and 524)—were being prepared at Ottawa Baptist Mission. Jotham Meeker, on July 27, recorded in his diary: "I with two Indian men, build a house for a printing office."

In an October 6 letter Missionary Meeker wrote: "Br[other] Hendrick"—a Stockbridge—"brought the press and types from Delaware [mission] last week." Also on the 6th he noted in his diary: "Put up the printing press and a stove in the office."

Ref: Meeker's "Diary" (in KHi ms. division); *The Baptist Missionary Magazine,* v. 29 (December, 1849), p. 432.

❧ July-August.—"The road from Independence to Santa Fe, is thronged with California emigrants, who are pressing forward with ease and rapidity, the grass being more abundant and of better quality than for years past, and water in profusion." (This was the report of William Mitchell, a member of Aubry's train which left Santa Fe July 21 and reached Independence, Mo., on August 23.)

Ref: New York *Daily Tribune,* September 10, 1849 (from Saint Louis *Daily Union,* August 31).

❧ August 6.—At Independence, Mo., a correspondent wrote: "A day or two since, Mr. Angus Boggs, and today Messrs. Thos. Slaughter, Wm. Wheatley, Jas. Bean, and Benj. Bartleson, Munday, and others, arrived from Chihuahua [left June 4] and Santa Fe."

James C. Bean (under contract as a mail carrier), carried more than 400 letters which had arrived at Santa Fe from California, and a large mail for Fort Leavenworth (delivered there August 9). Thomas J. Slaughter ("merchant, of Independence, Mo.") had left Santa Fe on July 7 or 8. At St. Louis, after "Messrs. Slaughter & Harmens" arrived August 15, aboard the *Princeton,* a newspaper commented: "The specie imports of Mr. S. and company was but little short of $100,000." (On July 10 an Independence man had written that several local traders, with large amounts of specie and trains of mules, were expected any day, from Chihuahua—among them Thomas Slaughter of Slaughter & Bro., Boggs & Clarke, Charles W. White of J. M. White & Co., and Cornelius Davy.) Davy presumably returned with the above, or about the same time. On June 29, near Rabbit Ear creek (N. M.), westbound travelers had met "a train coming from Santa Fe," and sent letters by "Mr. Davy, an Irishman, owner of the waggons, a Santa Fe and Chihuahua trader."

Ref: *Missouri Republican,* St. Louis, July 17, August 12, 1849; *The Daily Reveille,* St. Louis, August 16, 1849; 31st Cong., 1st Sess., *Sen. Ex. Doc. No. 26* (Serial 554), p. 31 (for item on Bean's mail contract of July 7, 1849, date); Watson, *op. cit.,* p. 61.

❧ MARRIED: Emanuel Mosier and Sarah C. Baker, on August 9, at the house of Arthur I. Baker (a trader with the "Mississippi" Sacs & Foxes), by the Rev. Jotham Meeker, of Ottawa Baptist Mission.

Ref: Meeker's "Diary"; also Meeker's certification (in Meeker Collection, KHi ms. division). The Mosier's daughter Kate was born at Council Grove on February 29, 1852(?) As listed in KHi's 15th *Biennial Report*, p. 36, her birth year was 1851; but 1852 was a leap year!

❧ August 15.—"Messrs. Ross and Johnson" of Independence, Mo., returned from New Mexico after a 22-day routine journey on the Santa Fe trail.

Ref: Saint Louis *Daily New Era*, August 28, 1849.

❧ August 20 or 21.—Famed "Bent's Fort" (built in 1833?-1834, originally named "Fort William"), on the upper Arkansas (in present Otero county, Colo.) was destroyed by its owner, William Bent.

Ref: James S. Calhoun's letter of October 5, 1849 (in his *Official Correspondence . . .*, ed. by Annie H. Abel, Washington, 1915), pp. 41-43, stated: "One of the owners [William Bent] of Bent's Fort, has removed all property from it, and caused the Fort to be burnt . . ."; Lavender, *op. cit.*, pp. 315-317, 413, 414; *Missouri Republican*, St. Louis, October 2, 1849 (which printed a letter from Independence, Mo., September 27, 1849, giving an account of just-arrived travelers who had heard the loud report [explosion] signaling the post's destruction, and who, a day or two later, came to the still-smoking ruins of Bent's Fort). This letter is reprinted in Nolie Mumey's *Old Forts . . .* (Denver, 1956), pp. 103-105. See, also, annals, p. 256 (for founding of Bent's Fort).

❧ On, or before, August 21, Andrew Drips (American Fur Company agent) reached Kansas, Mo. He had come down from Fort Pierre, as far as the Council Bluffs, aboard the *Amelia*, in July.

Ref: New York *Daily Tribune*, September 4, 1849 (from *Missouri Republican*).

❧ August 21.—"Messrs. Jones, Harley, and two other men" who had left the Moro settlement in New Mexico on August 4, arrived at Independence, Mo.

Ref: *Missouri Republican*, St. Louis, August 25, 1849.

❧ August 23.—Some (or all?) of the persons in Francis X. Aubry's train (13 "Americans," seven Mexicans; a number of wagons, and 120 mules) from Santa Fe (left July 21) arrived at Independence, Mo.

At Ash creek, Pawnees had made a night attack on the camp, "firing at intervals for about two hours, wounding two mules, and riddling several wagons and wagon covers." After the moon came up the Indians had been dislodged from their position.

William Mitchell (one of the 13 "Americans") was, at the end of August, in St. Louis, purchasing goods for the Santa Fe trade.

Robert Carson (brother of "Kit") who reached Missouri after mid-August, may have traveled with the above train. An account stated he had left Santa Fe on July 17(?) with a small company; and that at Pawnee Fork(?) Indians had attempted to rob them.

Ref: New York *Daily Tribune*, September 10, 1849 (from the Saint Louis *Daily Union*,

August 31); *Missouri Republican,* St. Louis, August 25, 1849. *The Weekly Tribune,* Liberty, Mo., September 7, 1849 (for Carson).

❡ August 29.—On the Little Blue (in present southern Nebraska), Thomas Fulton's Fort Kearny-bound wagon train was attacked by a band of Pawnees. Fulton was robbed; the wagons' contents were destroyed; and he was then turned loose.

Ref: *The Weekly Tribune,* Liberty, Mo., December 7, 1849. Fulton returned to Liberty the first week in December.

❡ August 30.—About 25 miles above Weston, Mo., the *Haydee* (bound for Council Bluffs) burst a steam connecting pipe. Capt. G. Fishback was killed, pilot George Martin was seriously injured, engineer Robert Lindsay, and three lady passengers, also were scalded.

Ref: St. Joseph (Mo.) *Gazette,* September 7, 1849; *The Weekly Tribune,* Liberty, Mo., September 14, 1849.

❡ August 31.—The Rev. B. H. Russell, of the Methodist Episcopal Church, South, replaced the Rev. John Thompson Peery as missionary to the Wyandots.

Ref: William Walker's "Journals" (*loc. cit.*).

❡ August-September.—Of wagon trains westbound—either to Santa Fe, or points beyond, an Independence, Mo., man wrote, on August 21: "The companies [gold seekers] from Liberty [Clay co.], Davis [Daviess] county and Caldwell [county, Mo.] have already gone out as far as safety will permit, their numbers not being sufficiently great to venture very far." He noted, too, that "Messrs. Lucas and others" would leave the week following, for Santa Fe, and "Messrs. Houck, Miller and others for California by way of Santa Fe, at the same time."

Eastbound James Brown (who left Santa Fe September 7; reached Missouri the 25th) met (about September 10?), at "Red River," a pack-mule train of California-bound emigrants from northern Missouri (*i. e.,* the Daviess and Caldwell county companies); next met, at "Cimerone Springs," a company of 60 men from Clay county, Mo.; subsequently met "Mr. [Solomon] Houck, of Boonville" September 19(?) "this side" of Cow creek (another traveler met "Messrs. Houck and Stone" on the Arkansas); "Mr. [James] Lucas," on the 20th(?) at Cottonwood Fork; "[James M.] White & Auburn's [Francis X. Aubry's]" train, on the 22d(?), at 110-mile creek; and that of St. Vrain and McCarty around the 23d(?) at "Blackjack Point." (It was elsewhere stated that the goods of "Messrs. St. Vrain & McCarty's Company, consisting of eight or ten wagons," had left Kansas [City], Mo., about September 15—"freighted out by Mr. Aubrey's mule train.") Later arrivals at Independence mentioned meeting "Messrs. White, [William] Mitchell and [Charles L.] Spencer" at Cottonwood Crossing, near the end of September; and still later arrivals had met "Lucas and others" at Mann's Fort, "Messrs. McCarty, Mitchell and Spencer and trains" at or near the Big Arkansas. ("Spencer & Sabine's" five-wagon train had left Missouri in mid-September.)

Merchant James M. White, who was, this fall, removing from Independence to Santa Fe, had with him his wife, small daughter, employees, cotravelers, and 13 goods-laden wagons. In New Mexico, on October 23, the Whites and six or seven other persons, left the White and Aubry wagons, to go on in advance. Late the 24th, or early the 25th, near Point of Rocks an Apache band murdered James M. White, William Callaway (an Aubry employee), "Ben Bushman" (a mulatto), two or three Germans, and a Mexican. Mrs. Ann (Dunn) White, her small daughter, and a Negro woman servant, were taken prisoners. (In November, when a military search party overtook the Apaches, the Indians killed Mrs. White, young Virginia White (then, or later), and the servant; then fled.

On October 27 Charles L. Spencer (who had come upon the White massacre scene), together with "Mr. [Alexander] Barclay, Geo. Simpson and Mr. [Isaac] Adamson," reached Las Vegas, N. M. Spencer had left his wagons at Cold Spring (and planned to send out corn "to meet them"). Francis X. Aubry lost 20 mules—frozen to death in a severe early storm, and had to cache two wagon loads of his goods (according to a correspondent writing from Santa Fe on October 28.)

Ref: *Missouri Republican*, St. Louis, August 25, September 29, October 1, 12, November 1, December 12, 15, 1849; New York *Daily Tribune*, September 4, 1849; New York *Weekly Tribune*, October 13, 1849; St. Joseph (Mo.) *Gazette*, October 12, 1849; Calhoun, *op. cit.*, p. 63; Alexander Barclay Papers, Bancroft Library. For the White family, *see, also*, St. Joseph (Mo.) *Gazette*, December 14, 21, 1849; *The Daily Reveille*, St. Louis, December 9, 1849, May 2, 1850; New York *Daily Tribune*, December 20, 1849, February 23, 1850; New York *Weekly Tribune*, December 22, 29, 1849, January 5, February 2, 1850. Isaac McCarty, of Lexington, Mo., died at Santa Fe on October 10, 1850.—*Missouri Republican*, St. Louis, December 7, 1850.

❧ September.—From Fort Leavenworth (perhaps starting in late August?), Bvt. Col. John Munroe (Second U. S. artillery), and 250 men (100 dragoons, 150 infantry), set out, overland, for Santa Fe (where Munroe would replace Bvt. Lt. Col. John M. Washington as military commander and governor). About September 18 eastbound James Brown met Munroe's expedition, and the cotraveling "company of Tennessee emigrants under the direction of Gen. Anderson," at Walnut creek (in present Barton county).

Alexander O. Anderson (ex-U. S. senator) and his large, "well-organized" "East Tenn. Mining Company," traveling by land, had passed through St. Louis on June 7 (then having 17 wagons and 100 horses and mules); subsequently had arrived at St. Joseph, Mo., on July 1. Tennesseean "Quincy" wrote, on July 24, from St. Joseph: "After much delay . . . in procuring mules and other requisites . . . we will leave this place, for Santa Fe, via Weston and Fort Leavenworth, tomorrow." But more than a month went by before Anderson's company took the Santa Fe trail!

Bvt. Col. John Munroe and his troops (also the cotraveling Tennesseeans?)

reached Santa Fe on October 22. Munroe assumed command of the military district.

The incomplete diary of Tennesseean Jacob Stuart shows that some, if not all, of the Anderson company members were still in New Mexico as late as July 25, 1850.

Ref: *Missouri Republican*, St. Louis, September 29, 1849; F. B. Heitman, *Historical Register . . . of the U.S.* (1903), for Munroe's rank, etc.; *The Daily Reveille*, St. Louis, June 9, August 5, 1849; *Tennessee Magazine of History*, Nashville, 2d series, v. 1 (1931), pp. 279-285 (for Jacob Stuart's diary); *Biographical Directory of the American Congress* (for Alexander O. Anderson as U. S. senator); New York *Weekly Tribune*, January 5, 1850 (for Munroe's arrival at Santa Fe); St. Joseph (Mo.) *Gazette*, October 12, November 23, 1849.

❧ On September 3 (or 4) Capt. Langdon C. Easton, AQM (engaged in an exploration of the Republican river) crossed from "Nebraska" into present Jewell county, Kan. Under instructions received from Col. Aeneas Mackay, at Fort Laramie on August 1 (*see* June 13 entry), the captain was proceeding to Fort Leavenworth by way of the Republican Fork, and the Kansas, in search of a better, or more direct route (which he did not find) between that post and Fort Laramie. Aside from the Republican river portion of his report, Easton's journal contained "Kansas" information of some importance in its descriptive data on a new branch road from St. Joseph, Mo., to Union Town on the Kansas river, and leading on southward to Council Grove—*see* following.

Easton's small, well-armed party (composed of Dr. George B. Parks, Boston; Col. Aeneas Mackay's 13-year-old son, Thomas; an escort—Lt. N. George Evans and 10 dragoons; guide Joseph "Hunoit"; 10 teamsters and "hands"; also two servants), with traveling outfit of ample size (four wagons with six-mule teams, a light wagon drawn by four mules, riding animals, etc.), left Fort Laramie on August 2; traveled first south, then southeastward (across present Wyoming and Colorado); forded the South Fork of the Platte August 10; reached the Arickaree on the 14th (after an 86-mile journey without water); followed it to the junction with the Republican (reached on the 16th; after passing across what is now the northwestern tip of Kansas); then proceeded down the Republican's left bank (and across southern "Nebraska").

Camp of September 4 apparently was in the vicinity of present Republic, Kan. On the 11th, Easton's party struck the Kansas river at a point about three miles below the Republican-Smoky Hill junction (on the future Fort Riley reservation); on September 12 came to the Big Blue—near its mouth (until the 1906 flood it entered the Kansas at present Manhattan); crossed at an upstream ford (with a "hard sandy bottom") on the 13th; on the 14th (in south-central Pottawatomie county of today) came to the Oregon-California trail out of Independence, Mo.; and proceeded eastward on it.

On September 15, at a point "within 3 Miles of the Ferry at Uniontown," Easton "directed the Waggons to turn off [the trail], and take an East direction, until they came into the [new in 1849?] Waggon road leading from Uniontown to St. Joseph Mo"; and to make camp on that road. (Easton crossed the Kansas and obtained some supplies at the Pottawatomies' trading post; returning, he "took the St. Joseph road to Camp . . . about 5 miles from the Ferry.") On the 16th the captain and his party continued to follow the "St. Joseph road" which "runs East 8 Miles and then crosses Soldier Creek. . . . After crossing the Creek the road runs N. E." Camp that night was on the Grasshopper (now Delaware), after a day's journey of some 26 miles. On the 17th they "Followed the Saint Joseph road 7 miles travelling N. E. where we left it and travelled an indistinct Waggon trail, which turns off to Fort Leavenworth." Marching (E. N. E.) 15 miles farther, they stopped for the night on Stranger river. Easton, mule-mounted, rode on two miles (E. N. E.); came to the "road leading to Fort Kearny"; and followed it nine miles into Fort Leavenworth.

Easton, in his report, stated that the "distance from Fort Leavenworth to Union Town," by the "fine" road he traveled, was 64 miles; and that from Union Town to Council Grove—45 miles—there was (he was told) "an equally good road." He remarked that the road currently used by military trains traveling between Fort Leavenworth and Council Grove was 160 miles in length— "making a difference in the distance of the two routes of 51 Miles in favor of the Uniontown route." By cutting "timber out sufficiently wide for Waggons, on the Stranger, Grasshopper and Soldier," and digging the banks down on the "Stranger and Grasshopper," an excellent road could be made from the fort to Union Town.

Ref: *KHQ*, v. 20 (May, 1953), pp. 392-415 (for Easton's report, edited by Merrill J. Mattes). On Easton's map, reproduced (in part) in these annals, is the earliest showing of "Union Town," and of the new (in 1849?) road from northeast "Kansas" to Union Town, and on to Council Grove (and the Santa Fe trail). See p. 680 for previous mention of the guide, Joseph "Hunoit" (Hunant). Easton's trip was noted in the *Missouri Republican*, St. Louis, September 26, 1849.

❡ September 4.—John Phillips and James M. Clay, express mail carriers from Santa Fe (left August 15), arrived at Fort Leavenworth.

A Santa Fe *Republican* extra, dated August 8, brought by the mailmen, contained an order from Bvt. Lt. Col. John M. Washington, establishing a monthly mail between Fort Leavenworth and Santa Fe, scheduled to leave on the 15th of each month. Phillips and Clay evidently returned, at once, to Santa Fe, *See* December annals entry, p. 894.

Ref: *Missouri Republican*, St. Louis, September 12, 1849. Indian depredations subsequently disrupted the "monthly mail"; also, Bvt. Col. John Munroe succeeded Washington as military commander at Santa Fe in late October, 1849.

❡ DIED: Mrs. Mary Steen, wife of Bvt. Maj. Enoch Steen (First U. S. dragoons), at Fort Leavenworth, on September 8.

Ref: St. Joseph (Mo.) *Gazette*, November 23, 1849. The same issue contains a story: "Late from New Mexico"—an account which mentions Major Steen's fight with Apaches on August 15.

❡ September 14.—In present Doniphan county, a young Pawnee girl (about 16), traveling with "Mr. [Christopher?] Ritson's" small party (en route from Fort Kearny to St. Joseph, Mo.) was seized by some "Missouri" Sacs & Foxes, who then murdered her (cutting off her head and limbs).

Subagent Vaughan sent an express to Fort Leavenworth for troops. On September 15 Bvt. Col. Edwin V. Sumner dispatched Bvt. Maj. James H. Carleton and 15 First dragoons to the Great Nemaha Subagency. They arrived on the 16th; proceeded to the Sac & Fox village; and arrested the Indians involved (the son of Chief Nesoquot was the principal murderer). At Vaughan's request, Carleton also made a prisoner of White Cloud (ex-head chief of the Iowas; deposed in 1848—*see* p. 752), because of his general bad conduct, and threats made against the subagent, and the Presbyterian missionaries.

Ref: OIA, Letters Received from Great Nemaha Subagency (National Archives, Microcopy 234, Roll 308), for Vaughan's September 19, 1849, report, and Carleton's September, 1849, report; St. Joseph (Mo.) *Gazette*, September 28, 1849. After a period of confinement at Fort Leavenworth, the Indians were released without further punishment, according to an 1855 account reprinted in the White Cloud (Kan.) *Chief* of November 12, 1857, and in P. L. Gray's *Doniphan County History.*

℄ September 14.—The *Amelia,* from the upper Missouri (*see* June 19 entry), bringing returns for the American Fur Company, reached St. Louis. Passengers on the trip down included Col. Aeneas Mackay (who debarked at Fort Leavenworth), Doctor Russell, and the Rev. John Robertson—all of whom had journeyed from Fort Leavenworth overland to Fort Laramie in June and July, and then to Fort Pierre in August (*see* p. 874).

Ref: *Missouri Republican,* St. Louis, September 1, 15, 26, 1849; Sunder, *op. cit.,* p. 118.

℄ September 22.—A man at Oregon City, Ore., wrote: "A few of the immigrants have arrived. They repeat that there will not be above one hundred wagons of the overland immigration come into Oregon this fall. The California wagons are estimated by them at from 8,000 to 15,000."

On October 18 the *Oregon Spectator* commented: "Emigrant parties are coming in slowly from the mountains. Inclusive of a company of 27 wagons, the arrival of which is daily expected, there have some 55 wagons arrived in this Valley. Others are reported as coming."

A letter written at Fort Hall ("Idaho"), early in October, stated: "Some [emigrants] left this place on the 1st of October for Oregon."

The emigration to Oregon in 1849 has been estimated at 400 to 500 persons.

Ref: New York *Weekly Tribune,* January 19, February 16, 1850; St. Joseph (Mo.) *Gazette,* December 7, 1849; H. H. Bancroft's *History of Oregon* (San Francisco, 1886), v. 1, p. 64. See Morgan, ed., *The Overland Diary of James A. Pritchard, op. cit.,* pp. 180, 194 and 199, for information on three Oregon immigrants of 1849 (Lewis Baldwin, David E. Pease, and William J. Watson) who kept overland journals.

℄ September 24.—Overnight guests at Ottawa Baptist Mission (present Franklin county) were Father Provincial John Anthony Elet, S. J., and Father Pierre-Jean De Smet, S. J. Missionary Jotham Meeker recorded in his diary: "Two noted Catholic priests, De Smett and Elet of the St. Louis University stop with us. . . ."

An account says that Elet and De Smet had ascended the Missouri to "Westport" [*i. e.,* Kansas], Mo., in August; traveled overland via Fort Scott to Osage Catholic Mission; then visited the Miamis, and other tribes, while en route to St. Mary's (Pottawatomie) Mission. They arrived at St. Mary's on September 27 (having met Father Christian Hoecken south of Kansas river; where was held a council and barbeque with a large gathering of Pottawatomies). When they departed St. Mary's on the 29th, in company was Father Felix L. Verreydt (now leaving missionary service in "Kansas").

Ref: Jotham Meeker's "Diary"; H. M. Chittenden and A. T. Richardson, eds., *Life, Letters and Travels of Father Pierre-Jean De Smet* (New York, 1905), v. 2, p. 614; *KHQ,* v. 20, pp. 524, 526, 527; G. J. Garraghan's *The Jesuits of the Middle United States* . . . (New York, 1938), v. 2, p. 614. De Smet, *op. cit.,* pp. 486-491, contains a biographical account of Father Elet, vice-provincial of the vice-province of Missouri.

❡ September 25.—"Judge [James] Brown" (of Brown & Russell, government freight contractors), Moses Goldstein (trader), of Independence, Mo., and one other man, reached Independence overland from Santa Fe (left about September 7).

East of Rabbit Ear creek (N. M.) they had been captured by a party of some 40 Arapahoes and Apaches who robbed them, debated killing them, finally gave them some mules, and allowed the trio to proceed. (Brown carried $84,000 in "government receipts" which he saved; Goldstein lost around $600.) At the Lower Cimarron Springs, three days later, the three met California-bound travelers who supplied them with provisions, blankets, etc.

Around the 25th one of "Judge Brown's [government] trains reached the Missouri border, from Santa Fe, having had a "pleasant and agreeable" trip home.

Ref: *The Weekly Tribune,* Liberty, Mo., October 5, 1849 (from Independence and Boonville, Mo., newspapers); New York *Weekly Tribune,* October 6, 13, 1849.

❡ September 25.—"Mr. W. F. Dewebber and others" arrived at Independence, Mo., overland from Santa Fe. They had been "a long while on the route, detained by circumstances beyond their control"—one of which was a clash with marauding Indians (on the Cimarron—in New Mexico) who stampeded a few of their mules.

Ref: *The Weekly Tribune,* Liberty, Mo., October 5, 1849; New York *Weekly Tribune,* October 13, 1849 (from *Missouri Republican,* St. Louis).

❡ September 30.—At Pottawatomie Baptist Mission (present Shawnee county—*see* March 20, 1848, annals entry), as reported by Sup't Johnston Lykins, a large stone building for the manual labor school was in "process of completion." He described it as "85 feet long and 35 feet wide, with two cross-walls of stone, three stories high, divided into twelve rooms, having sixty doors and windows; walls of first story two feet thick, balance one and a half foot thick." Estimated cost (when finished in 1850) about $4,800. (For views of its post-mission use, *see* p. 818.)

Other mission structures were: a one-story, hewed-log dwelling (36' x 18'); a one-story, hewed-log mechanic's house (18' x 16'); a hewed-log kitchen and meat house (each 16' square); a "root house"; a hewed-log "lodging room for hired men" (16' x 18'); and another 16-foot-square kitchen. Of 60 acres "ploughed prairie" 25 were in corn, one in potatoes, two in beans and other garden vegetables. Fencing of 13,000 rails and stakes had been "made and put up." The whole farm would (on completion) have 65 acres plowed, and 40 acres in pasture.

California-bound Samuel F. McCoy, had recorded in his diary, on May 23: "We passed the Baptist Mission to the Pottawottamies, which presented a motley frontier scene with its few log houses built on the banks of a small stream."

The missionaries (as of September 30): Dr. Johnston Lykins, the Rev. B. W. Sanders and his wife, Miss Eliza McCoy, Robert Simerwell and his wife. The Sanders had arrived July 24, replacing the Rev. N. Dille and wife (who reached the mission in February; and departed May 4, 1849).

Ref: Comm'r of Indian Affairs, *Report*, 1849 (Dr. J. Lykins' report, therein); American Indian Mission Association, *Proceedings*, 1849, pp. 10, 22-24; *Pioneering on the Plains* (Kaukauna, Wis., c1924), for McCoy "Diary"; Lykins' letter of June 7, 1849, regarding contracts for the buildings, in OIA, "Letters Received from Fort Leavenworth Agency" (National Archives Microcopy 234, Roll 303).

❡ October 1.—Agent John E. Barrow reported that over 1,200 Pawnees had died of cholera during the spring and summer. This epidemic, and some losses suffered in fights with hostile tribes, had reduced the tribe by nearly one-fourth within a six-months' period.

Barrow also stated: "With the exception of the 'Ottoe,' 'Omaha,' and 'Comanche' Indians, this tribe is at variance with the red men of the whole western territory."

Ref: Comm'r of Indian Affairs, *Report*, 1849 (Barrow's report, therein).

❡ Around October 1 "Judge [James] Brown," of Pettis county, Mo. (*see* September 25 entry), with a 20-wagon merchandise train, set out from Independence, Mo., for Santa Fe. "Forty miles beyond the main Arkansas," on November 17, his party was caught in a severe three-day snow storm; during which all the oxen died, leaving the train stranded 30 miles from timber.

Upwards of 10 men were left in charge of the wagons. In January, 1850, it was reported that young Mr. Brown—nephew of the judge—had returned to the settlements to purchase new teams.

Ref: St. Louis *Reveille*, January 26, 1850.

❡ The first week in October, Smallwood ("Uncle Wood") Noland, John Calvin McCoy, and others, left the Independence-Westport, Mo., area on an expedition into "Kansas." It was said they had gone out about 160 miles to look for a gold mine "that was known of years back."

An account of October 26 stated the party had returned "lately," with "high hopes of accomplishing something worth while at some future day." The writer asserted: "Gold, Tin, Iron Ore and Coal can be found in abundance on the waters of the Kansas."

In February, 1850, there was a flurry of excitement over the "gold mine" lately discovered by Mr. Noland; then came a report that Noland's find had been tested and "is not gold."

Ref: *Missouri Republican*, St. Louis, October 12, November 1, 1849; St. Joseph (Mo.) *Gazette*, February 15, 22, 1850.

❧ Early in October the steamboat *Cumberland Valley* (upbound with equipment—pumps, diving bells, etc.—to raise the *Dacotah*— (*see* April 25 entry) struck a snag at the mouth of the Kansas river and sank.

Ref: St. Joseph (Mo.) *Gazette*, October 12, 1849.

❧ October 8.—"Messrs. Hall, Woods, Harrold, Harrison, and Owens" (son of Samuel Owens) arrived at Independence, Mo., from Santa Fe. These traders (Independence residents) had left the New Mexican capital on September 11.

Ref: *Missouri Republican*, St. Louis, October 12, 1849.

❧ October.—"Mr. S. Thomas," express from Fort Hall ("Idaho") to Fort Leavenworth, arrived at his destination around mid-month. He had passed "Green River" (Fort Bridger?) on August 19; and was at Fort Laramie on September 18.

Ref: *Missouri Republican*, St. Louis, October 25, 1849.

❧ October.—Luke Lea, Esq., of Cleveland, Tenn., appointed (August 9) to head the Fort Leavenworth Agency, arrived in "Kansas." (He had left St. Louis on the 19th.) Lea replaced Richard W. Cummins, who, for *19 years*, had served as Indian agent at the same headquarters—a location near the eastern border of the Shawnee Indians' reserve (south of the Kansas river, and just west of the Missouri state line), in present Johnson county.

Ref: OIA, Letters Received from Fort Leavenworth Agency (National Archives Microcopy 234, Roll 303) for Lea's October 1, 1849, letter, Cummins' November 12, 1849, letter, and others; SIA, St. Louis, "Records," v. 9, typed copy, pp. 361, 370, 382. In KHi's manuscript division is a July 24, 1905, letter by W. R. Bernard, on the subject of Richard W. Cummins. Among other things, he stated that no portrait of Cummins had been located But Bernard remembered him as a "commanding figure," six feet, two inches tall, broad-shouldered, with large head and ears; and weighing about 200 pounds. In 1860 Cummins and some of his family were residents of Spruce township, Bates co., Mo. His son-in-law James M. Simpson, and family, formerly of Jackson county, Mo., also resided there in 1860. The 1860 U. S. census listed Cummins as aged 73, native of Pennsylvania.

❧ October.—On the 21st, three mail carriers en route from Fort Kearny to Fort Leavenworth, were obliged to turn back when they met some 60 hostile Pawnees on the Little Blue.

Bvt. 2d Lt. Charles H. Ogle, and 20 First dragoons, were then dispatched as escort for the mailmen. Near the Little Blue they met and engaged the Pawnees in a fight. Three Indians were killed and several wounded. Seven dragoons were wounded, two severely. (Ogle was struck in the mouth by an arrow.) These, and an express, returned to Fort Kearny. Bvt. Maj. Robert H. Chilton, with more troops, joined Ogle, but the Pawnees were not located. David Waldo, and his train of about 50 government wagons, brought the mail in to Fort Leavenworth. (Pierpont Perry, who accompanied Waldo, supplied most of the above information.) Prior to October 26 the "second and third of [William] McCoy & [David] Waldo's trains from Fort Laramie" reached Independence, Mo.

Ref: New York *Weekly Tribune,* December 8, 1849; New York *Daily Tribune Supplement,* December 10, 1849; *Missouri Republican,* St. Louis, November 1, 24, 1849. For Waldo's government contract *see* April 23, 1849, annals entry.

❧ October 26.—Peter H. Norris and William Barclay arrived at Independence, Mo. They had left Santa Fe September 25; and traveled in company with one of "Judge" James Brown's (government) trains as far as the Little Arkansas.

In the vicinity of Cottonwood Crossing they had encountered a "violent" snow storm of brief duration.

Ref: *Missouri Republican,* St. Louis, November 1, 1849.

❧ November 2.—E. Kelly, of St. Louis, and others, just in from Santa Fe (left September 27) and El Paso (left on the 12th), arrived at Independence, Mo.

Near Fort Mann (on the Arkansas) they had encountered a "violent" snow storm. Grass on the prairies between the Little Arkansas and Council Grove had been burned off by the Indians.

Ref: *Missouri Republican,* St. Louis, November 8, 1849.

❧ November.—At St. Mary's (Pottawatomie Catholic) Mission, on the 2d, the new "house for the [boys'] school" (under construction since mid-June), was occupied. On the 3d the Rev. John B. Duerinck, S. J. (replacing Father Verreydt as superior), arrived from St. Louis. With him were two lay brothers and a teacher.

Ref: *KHQ,* v. 20, pp. 521-526, *passim.*

❧ November 5.—"On the subject of the Pacific Railway," "Col." William Gilpin addressed a mass meeting of the citizens of Jackson county, Mo.

Ref: The speech (over six columns in print) was published in the *Missouri Republican,* St. Louis, June 7 and 8, 1850.

❧ November 6.—An Independence, Mo., correspondent stated that 16 or 17 Missourians, returning overland from California, recently had passed through town. They had made the journey, with pack mules, in 68(?) days.

Ref: New York *Weekly Tribune,* December 1, 1849 (from *Missouri Republican,* St. Louis).

℃ November 10.—President Taylor received the Osage Nation's principal chief, George White Hair, and his delegation (six in all) in the East Room of the White House. Earlier in the morning, the Indians had visited Orlando Brown, Comm'r of Indian affairs, and Thomas Ewing, secretary of the interior. Both then accompanied them to the interview with the President.

Chief White Hair, War Eagle, Cas-she-ge-ne-ga, Man-he-ca-cha, War-shaw-wa-ta-sa, and Antyne Penn (interpreter), en route east from the Osage reserve (on the waters of the Neosho and Verdigris in "Kansas"), had passed through St. Louis on October 29; and reached Washington on November 9. Until their departure, on November 25(?), they were guests at "Maher's Globe hotel."

A reporter present at the interview noted the tact displayed by the President in his "reply to the address of the head Chief." (The Osages' grievance was the delay in payment of annuities—a delay caused by the illness of an agent appointed for the nation.) Chief White Hair "presented the President with several small paintings executed by the young people of his tribe . . . and also a beautiful bead purse [made by an Osage girl]. . . ."

During the November 10-24 period of their stay in Washington, the Osages were escorted by "Mr. Loughry and Mr. [William] Devereux" on visits to the public buildings of the city—the "Capitol . . . the Patent Office, the Navy Yard, the Arsenal, etc." At least one daguerreotype was taken of the Osage delegation (a disbursement item mentions daguerreotypist "M. B. Breedy" [Brady?]). Chief White Hair asked for, and got, a general's uniform; and the other Osages were given military coats.

Ref: New York *Weekly Tribune,* November 17, December 1, 1849; *Missouri Republican,* St. Louis, November 20, 1849; *The Daily Reveille,* St. Louis, November 1, 1849 (which referred to Chief George White Hair as "Wah-ka-pi-hah"); SIA, St. Louis "Records," v. 9, typed copy, p. 384; 32d Cong., 1st Sess., *H. Ex. Doc. No. 103* (Serial 647), p. 221; Garraghan, *op. cit.,* v. 2, p. 505. National Archives failed to locate this 1849 Osage daguerreotype taken by "Breedy" or Brady.

℃ Mid-November.—Thomas Forsyth "just in from the Salt Lake," arrived at Westport, or Kansas (City), Mo.; and, aboard the *St. Joseph,* on the 20th, was voyaging down the Missouri to St. Louis (his home).

Forsyth had left Salt Lake near the end of September, and Fort Bridger around October 1. Subsequently he had "crossed over the Plains to the head waters of the Arkansas"; thence to Bent's Fort (ruins), and east via the Santa Fe trail. Above the Big Timbers he had passed the Cheyenne-Arapaho-Kiowa encampment; below, he had met Agent Thomas Fitzpatrick and party (including trader Seth Ward); farther down the Arkansas he had met Ceran St. Vrain's New Mexico-bound wagons (*see* August-September entry p. 884); and at Cow creek another Santa Fe-bound traders' train which had lost "a large portion of their stock."

Ref: New York *Weekly Tribune*, December 8, 15, 22, 1849; *Missouri Republican*, St. Louis, November 28, December 4, 1849.

❧ November 28.—The *Highland Mary* reached Weston, Mo.—the last steamboat of the year to visit that port. *See, also,* December 9 entry.

Ref: *The Western Journal*, St. Louis, v. 5 (March, 1851), p. 327.

❧ November 28(?)—Robert Wilson (sutler at "Bear River Post") arrived at Platte City, Mo., from the West. He had left Fort Hall (with a returning government train?) on October 15; and made the journey (via Forts Laramie and Kearny) in 37 traveling days.

Ref: *The Weekly Tribune*, Liberty, Mo., December 7, 1849 (from Platte *Argus*).

❧ December 3.—A party of 18(?) men reached the Missouri border. (They had left Las Vegas, N. M., on November 3.) "Messrs. [John] Phillips & [James M.] Clay," mail-carriers, with escort of six(?) First dragoons went to Fort Leavenworth. The travelers reaching Independence included Hugh N. Smith (delegate to congress from New Mexico; en route to Washington), Benjamin F. Thompson, John Ware, "Mr. Miller," Squire Asbury (from Chihuahua), "Mr. Mundy, a Santa Fe trader," John W. H. Patton (who, on December 5, supplied the *Commonwealth* with an account of the J. M. White party massacre—*see* p. 885), and "Mr. McKnight."

From Las Vegas to the Lower Cimarron Springs(?), an escort of 20 First dragoons had accompanied the party—supplied because of the hostile Apaches.

Ref: St. Joseph (Mo.) *Gazette*, December 21, 1849 (from Independence [Mo.] *Commonwealth* of December 5); *Missouri Republican*, St. Louis, November 1, 8, December 12, 1849; *The Daily Reveille*, St. Louis, December 9, 1849; New York *Daily Tribune*, December 24, 31, 1849; New York *Weekly Tribune*, December 29, 1849. See August 6 annals entry for an eastbound trader named "Munday" (the same as Mr. Mundy above?). Percival G. Lowe in his *Five Years a Dragoon* (Kansas City, Mo., 1906), p. 22, arriving at Fort Leavenworth December 25, was assigned to quarters where was also "a detachment of six men of I Troop, First Dragoons, just in [recently] from Riado, New Mexico, with the mail."

❧ December 9.—The *Anna*, which had been up to St. Joseph, Mo., returned to St. Louis. Her officers reported the Missouri low, and falling; no ice in the river yet, but the weather very cold; and the end of navigation for the season at hand.

On the 6th the *Anna* had met the *Sacramento* and *Amelia* (the only two boats "up") at "Smith's landing." The *Amelia*, on the 11th, struck a snag above Glasgow, and sank.

Ref: *Missouri Republican*, St. Louis, December 10, 17, 19, 1849.

❧ About December 10 the *Haydee*, having aboard Bvt. 2d Lt. Charles W. Field (of the Second dragoons), and the 75 First dragoon recruits in his charge, attempted to navigate the Missouri; but ice in the river forced a return to St. Louis on the 14th. Her military passengers had been put ashore at Portland, Mo. (about 140 miles up).

Lieutenant Field and his men made the rest of the journey to Fort Leavenworth (some 300 miles) overland. Trooper Percival G. Lowe later recounted details of the winter march in his *Five Years a Dragoon ('49 to '54.)*.

It was Christmas eve ("cold, with plenty of snow on the ground") when the dragoons arrived at "Grinter's Ferry" (the Kansas river crossing for the Fort Leavenworth-Fort Scott military road). By Lowe's account "the old ferryman [Grinter—'an old soldier'] and his wife [then] lived on the south[!] side." After ferrying the "Kaw" the 75 men were furnished with a good supper (and breakfast on the 25th) by Isaac Mundy (the Delawares' blacksmith— *see* below) and his wife. For the night, some dragoons "occupied an old store-room," or huddled around a big fire outdoors, while the Mundys took in all they could accommodate.

On Christmas Day, Lieutenant Field and troops, marched the 22 miles northward to Fort Leavenworth. Their dinner, on arrival, consisted of boiled pork, bread, and coffee.

Ref: *The Daily Reveille*, St. Louis, December 15, 1849; 31st Cong., 2d Sess., *H. Ex. Doc. No. 23* (Serial 599), p. 20; Lowe, *op. cit.*, pp. 7-28. Lowe, on pp. 15, 16, gives some information of the Mund(a)ys. On p. 12 he notes that the 74 dragoon recruits were: 16 for K company (then at Fort Leavenworth); 34 for F company (then at Fort Scott)— and these men (*see* p. 24) about December 27(?), left for that post, having been provided transportation; 24 for B company (Lowe's), assigned to Fort Kearny (but to remain at Fort Leavenworth over the winter).

☙ December.—At the end of the year, Bvt. Col. Edwin V. Sumner's Fort Leavenworth command consisted of Bvt. Maj. James H. Carleton's Company K, First U. S. dragoons, some 30 "B," and "I" company men, and two Sixth infantry companies. Bvt. Maj. Philip R. Thompson's Fort Scott troops were Company F, First dragoons, and one Sixth infantry company.

Ref: 31st Cong., 1st Sess., *H. Ex. Doc. No. 5* (Serial 569), p. 188d; Lowe, *op. cit.*, pp. 22-28.

☙ Employed in "Kansas" by the Indian Department during all, or part of the year, 1849 were the following persons:

FORT LEAVENWORTH AGENCY *[Kickapoos, Delawares, Shawnees, Pottawatomies, Stockbridges, Munsees, and New York Indians]*—*Agents* Richard W. Cummins ("removed"—he was paid to November 1), Luke Lea (appointed August 9); *Interpreters* Henry Tiblow and Joseph La Fromboise; *Physicians* Johnston Lykins and John Gallimore (appointed March 2) for Pottawatomies, and James B. Stone (appointed April 10) for Delawares; *Wagonmaker* Henry R. Samuel (appointed January 30) for Pottawatomies; *Gunsmith* James B. Franklin and *Assistant gunsmith* William H. Franklin (both appointed January 31) for Pottawatomies; *Blacksmiths* William Donalson (resigned March 31) and Calvin Perkins (for Shawnees), Cornelius Yager (for Delawares), Isaac Mundy * and Granderson T. Deering (for Pottawatomies); *Assistant black-*

smiths Lindsey T. Cook and Valentine C. Warden (for Shawnees), Thomas C. Peers (for Delawares), John L. Ogee (quit, in spring?), William H. Scruggs,* and William F. Deering (for Pottawatomies); *Miller* Joel Grover (for Pottawatomies); *Sawyers* Thomas C. Banning, John W. Tucker (appointed July 6) and *Assistant sawyer* Thomas G. Campbell (appointed August 29) for Pottawatomies; *Laborers* William H. Huffman (Hoffman?), Thomas Merander, and Peter Moose (for Pottawatomies).

OSAGE RIVER AGENCY *[Sacs & Foxes of the Mississippi, Kansa, Ottawas Chippewas, Weas, Piankeshaws, and Miamies]—Agents* James S. Rains ("removed"); Charles N. Handy (appointed March 30); *Interpreters* Thomas J. Connolly, John Goodell (for Sacs & Foxes), and Baptiste Peoria (for Miamis, Weas, etc.); *Blacksmiths* Arthur I. Baker (resigned), Alfred Laws, and Matthew R. Johnson (for Sacs & Foxes), Robert Wilson (for Miamis); *Assistant blacksmiths* Thomas C. Warren, Morris Baker (removed to the Kansa, where reemployed as assistant blacksmith), and Rolin McDaniel (all for Sacs & Foxes), James P. Wilson (for Miamis), Emanuel Mosier (for Kansa); *Gunsmiths* Charles H. Withington and John Gray (for Sacs & Foxes); *Laborer* Peter Thorpe (for Sacs & Foxes?); *Physicians* S. G. Harlan (services ceased in April) and F. McKnight (for Sacs & Foxes); *Miller* Henry L. Hicks (from August 1, 1849, to January 8, 1850).

GREAT NEMAHA SUBAGENCY *[Iowas and Sacs & Foxes of the Missouri]—Subagents* Alfred J. Vaughan ("removed"), William P. Richardson (appointed December 18); *Interpreters* John B. Roy and John B. Rubite; *Farmer* James F. Forman.

OSAGE SUBAGENCY *[Osages]—Subagents* John M. Richardson ("resigned"), William H. Bell (did not serve), Henry Harvey (appointed December 18); *Interpreter* Charles Mongrain; *Blacksmiths* Akin Brant, John R. McKinney and Elijah Pennington; *Assistant blacksmiths* Francis Mitchell and Joseph Captain; *Millers* George T. Arthur ("resigned") and Augustus Captain; *Assistant millers* Dodridge Barnaby and Peter Chouteau.

WYANDOT SUBAGENCY *[Wyandots]—Subagents* Richard Hewitt ("removed"), Thomas Moseley, Jr. (appointed May 29); *Interpreter* William Walker (appointed March 31); *Blacksmith* Charles Graham, *Assistant blacksmith* Guilford D. Hurt, appointed July 30.

---

* In August, Isaac Mundy (smith), and William M. Scruggs (assistant smith) left the Pottawatomies and were given contracts for the Delawares.

Ref: 31st Cong., 1st Sess., *H. Ex. Doc. No. 61* (Serial 577), pp. 37, 40, 61; 31st Cong., 1st Sess., *H. Ex. Doc. No. 79* (Serial 579), pp. 11-16; 32d Cong., 1st Sess., *H. Ex. Doc. No. 103* (Serial 647), pp. 102, 326, 356, 357, 780, 783; 33d Cong., 1st Sess., *H. Ex. Doc. No. 37* (Serial 718), p. 361 (for Henry L. Hicks); SIA, St. Louis, "Records," v. 9, typed copy. pp. 273, 274, 280, 281, 301, 337, 346, 349, 358, 369, 371, 380, 393, 400. William H. Bell, of Columbia, Miss., accepted commission as Osage subagent on August 1, 1849; but (without serving) resigned the post November 25, 1849. See OIA, Letters Received from Osage Subagency (National Archives Microcopy 234, Roll 633); and OIA, Letters Received from Fort Leavenworth Agency (National Archives Microcopy 234, Roll 303).

1850

❐ January-June.—Licenses to trade with Indians in "Kansas," as granted by agents and subagents of the St. Louis superintendency, were:

Traders	Indians	Issued by	Rec'vd at St. Louis
Arthur I. Baker	Sacs & Foxes	C. N. Handy	January
Robidoux & Vaughan	Iowas, and Sacs & Foxes (of the Missouri)	A. J. Vaughan	January
(A. G.) Boone & (J. G.) Hamilton	Sacs & Foxes	C. N. Handy	January
(R. A.) Kinzie & (J. H.) Whistler	Sacs & Foxes	C. N. Handy	January
Josiah Smart	Sacs & Foxes	C. N. Handy	January
J. B. Scott	Kansa	C. N. Handy	February
(A. G.) Boone & (W. R.) Bernard	Kansa, and Sacs & Foxes	C. N. Handy	April
Robert A. Kinzie	Pottawatomies	Luke Lea	May
John D. Lasley	Pottawatomies	Luke Lea	May
(J. M.) Simpson & (J. M.) Hunter	Pottawatomies	Luke Lea	May
Cyprian Chouteau	Delawares, Shawnees, and Kickapoos	Luke Lea	May
C(yprian) & F(rederick) Chouteau	Kansa	C. N. Handy	June
J. B. Scott	Sacs & Foxes	C. N. Handy	June

Ref: Superintendency of Indian Affairs (SIA), St. Louis, "Records," v. 9, typed copy. pp. 405, 409, 417, 422, 429, 439, 440. Except as noted, the Sacs & Foxes were the "Mississippi" Sacs & Foxes (whose head chief was Moses Keokuk—"Keokuk, Jr.").

❐ January 1.—The St. Louis *Intelligencer*, v. 1, no. 1, and in subsequent issues, ran a table of distances on the Missouri from "St. Louis to St. Joseph"—as shown (in part) in column "A" below. The (partial) Missouri river table in column "B" combines nearly identical data from an 1850 J. Calvin Smith *Illustrated Hand-Book*, and an 1852 J. H. Colton *Guide-Book*. . . . In column "C" the mileages have been compiled from a table in the 1851-published *James's Traveler's Companion*. (Compare with the distance tables on p. 578.)

A			B			C	
From St. Louis to:	*Miles*		*From St. Louis to:*	*Miles*		*From St. Louis to:*	*Miles*
Mouth of Missouri	20		Mouth of the Missouri	18		Mouth of the Missouri	[18]°
St. Charles	35					° (This mileage assumed correct; and supplied here.)	

· · · · · ·   · · ·

			Sibley [old Fort Osage]	345			
Liberty Landing	381		Liberty Landing	366		Liberty Landing	[358]
Independence [Landing]	387		Independence [Landing]	369		Wayne City [one landing for Independence]	[363]
						Randolph	[370]
Kansas River	404		Kansas River Landing	381		Kansas [City]	[375]
						Parkville	[385]
[Little] Platte River	413		Little Platte River	391		Mouth of Little Platte	[386]
Fort Leavenworth	438		Fort Le[a]venworth	411		Fort Leavenworth	[406]
Weston	443		Weston	418		Weston	[413]
St. Joseph	488		St. Joseph	478		St. Joseph	[468]
			Mouth of Nodaway River	492		Nodeway City	[493]
			Wolf River	508		Iowa Point	[523]
			Grand Nemahaw River,	526			
			Nishnebotna River	551			
			Little Nemahaw River,	563			

· · ·

			Platte River	633		Mouth of Platte River	[658]
			Bellevue Trading House	645		Bellevue Trading House	[673]
						Traders' Point	[694]
			Council Bluffs	685		Council Bluffs	[698]

Ref: St. Louis *Intelligencer*, January 1, 1850; J. Calvin Smith's *The Illustrated Hand-Book, a New Guide for Travelers Through the United States of America* . . . (New York, 1850); (J. H.) *Colton's Traveler and Tourist's Guide-Book Through the United States of America and the Canadas* . . . (New York, 1852); S. L. Massey, *James's Traveler's Companion* . . . (Cincinnati, 1851), in which the distances are listed from mouth of the Yellowstone down to the Missouri's mouth, and for the above table have been compiled in reverse assuming the distance from St. Louis to the mouth of the Missouri as 18 miles.

❦ January.—William P. Richardson, St. Joseph, Mo., who had headed the Great Nemaha Subagency, 1841-1845, received appointment to the post—replacing Alfred J. Vaughan.

Ref: *Missouri Republican*, St. Louis, January 23, 1850; *Missouri Statesman*, Columbia, Mo., January 18, 1850; New York *Weekly Tribune*, February 23, 1850.

❦ January 15.—Daniel P. Mann, and two companions, with the express mail from Santa Fe, arrived at Fort Leavenworth, having been "about 40 days" en route.

Ref: St. Joseph (Mo.) *Gazette*, January 25, 1850 (from Weston [Mo.] *Reporter* of January 19). "Mann's Fort," or, "Fort Mann," on the Arkansas, was named for Daniel P. Mann—*see* annals index. The *Missouri Republican*, St. Louis, January 28, 1850, noted receipt of a November 28, 1849, issue of the Santa Fe *New Mexican*—presumably from the above mail.

❦ January 18.—At St. Joseph, Mo., "Ralph Ringwood" (corre-spondent for the New York *Tribune*) wrote: "From present appear-ances, it is likely that the overland emigration for California will commence here at least a month earlier than last season. The Missouri opposite this town has never once been closed over since Winter set in, and we have every indication of an early Spring. . . ." (It proved to be a *late* spring, "owing," as "Ringwood" stated on April 23, "to a constant succession of cold rains. . . .")

He reported, also: "Large and extensive outfitting stores have been newly established, commodious hotels fitted up, and a considerable amount of stock suitable for the trip collected. . . . Many of our citizens who intend taking up the line of march are awaiting impatiently the time [when first grass appears]. . . .

"Numerous passenger and freight lines are advertised to start at the earliest possible day. S. Roundy & Co. give notice that they will take passengers from Council Bluffs to Sutter's Fort for $300—freight at $12.50 per 100 lbs. A passenger and freight train will also leave this point, and an other will start from Independence. . . ."

Ref: New York *Weekly Tribune*, February 23, 1850.

❦ February 1.—From Fort Leavenworth, with accompanying letter, Bvt. Maj. James H. Carleton, First dragoons, sent to the St. Louis *Intelligencer* the table of distances, below, on the "Route from Fort Leavenworth to Fort Kearny."

(Since May, 1845, when Col. S. W. Kearny had supervised some route improvements—*see* p. 546, and the map on pp. 608, 609—this had been the military path utilized. But part of the Fort Leaven-worth-Big Blue section remained "circuitous and objectionable." Two months after Carleton's letter was written, Bvt. Maj. Edmund A. Ogden laid out a new route through this area—*see* p. 908. On the Stansbury map—*see* segment on p. 819—both the old and new roads are shown.)

From Fort Leavenworth to [Miles]	[Total Miles]	
Independence creek 16		Good wood, water and grass
Clough creek 16	[32]	Good wood, water and grass
Wolf creek 10	[42]	Good wood, water, and grass fine stream, good fishing, &c.
Stranger creek 24	[66]	Good grass, but wood and wa-ter indifferent several good places of encampment in the last distance
Big Nemaha 30	[96]	Excellent road for this distance, but wood and water no where found together on the route

Little Nemaha	10	[106]	This stream, is a remarkably fine one, and affords everything desirable for an encampment
Branch of Nemaha	20	[126]	A very fine camping ground, with plenty of wood, water, and grass
Little Blue [*i.e.*, Big Blue]	12	[138]	Fine river, about 50 yards wide, good fishing, plenty of wood, water, and grass; very good ford
Good encampment	12	[150]	Wood, water and grass plenty
Sandy creek	20	[170]	Wood, water and grass plenty
A running stream	12	[182]	Good encamping ground
Little Sandy creek	18	[200]	Good encamping ground
Little Blue	15	[215]	This is where the road first strikes the Little Blue
Encampments on Little Blue	5	[220]	
Encampments on Little Blue	23	[243]	
Encampments on Little Blue	21	[264]	The roads that leads along this river, is obstructed by many ravines, running perpendicular to the stream; road heavy. Here the road leaves the river to strike the *NeoBraska*, or *Platte.* Between the Blue and the Platte the road is *very heavy,* it is filled with difficult ravines and broken ground, no good places for camping. The distance along the river bottom to the fort level and *marshy,* and in wet weather would be exceedingly difficult for wagons.
Through the bluffs to river bottom	22	[286]	
Fort Kearny	15	[301]	

301

Ref: Stryker's *American Register and Magazine,* Philadelphia, v. 4 (July, 1850), pp. 249, 250 (for Carleton's table, reprinted from the *Intelligencer*). The Philip L. Platt and Nelson Slater *Traveler's Guide Across the Plains Upon the Overland Route to California* originally published in 1852 (reprinted, 1963, John Howell, publisher, with an introduction by Dale Morgan), in a section "Appendices No. 1," describes the old and new military routes out of Fort Leavenworth, and gives the "old road" distances (identical to those above) fom the fort to the Big Blue crossing. See 32d Cong., 1st Sess., Sen. Ex. Doc. No. 1 (Serial 611), Bvt. Maj. E. A. Ogden's report, 1851, therein, for the phrase "circuitous and objectionable" as quoted above.

❡ Early(?) February.—An express mail left Fort Leavenworth for Santa Fe. W. C. Skinner, departing the New Mexican capital on March 19, met the carriers 20 miles out.

Presumably the westbound mail party met, en route, "Mr. [Robert] Brent and party" who left Santa Fe on January 25 (and carried letters for Indian

Agent James S. Calhoun); also the Fort Leavenworth-bound mail which left Santa Fe at the beginning of February.

Ref: New York *Weekly Tribune*, May 11, 1850; *The Daily Reveille*, St. Louis, March 31, 1850; James S. Calhoun's *Official Correspondence* . . ., ed. by Annie H. Abel (1915), pp. 104, 105. "D." wrote from Santa Fe on January 31 that it had been more than 100 days "since our latest news from the United States"; and a mail was daily expected. If a January express left Fort Leavenworth for Santa Fe—and reached there in February—no information on it has been found.

❈ MARRIED: Stephen Cole, of Gentry county, Mo., and Mrs. Lydia Youcht, formerly of Jersey Shore, Lycoming county, Pa., on February 13, at "Ioway and Sac Mission" (present Doniphan county) by the Rev. William Hamilton.

Ref: St. Joseph *Gazette*, February 22, 1850.

❈ In the fore part of February an express mail from Santa Fe arrived at Fort Leavenworth. Issues of the Santa Fe *New Mexican* up to January 3 reached Missouri by this party.

Ref: *Missouri Republican*, St. Louis, February 18, 1850. The mail got to St. Louis (from Fort Leavenworth) on February 17, via "the regular mail" across Missouri.

❈ February 18.—Preston Beck (trader), and seven other men who had left Santa Fe January 27, reached Independence, Mo. Their 23-day journey, in a wagon, had been made across plains covered with "snow to the depth of ten inches."

Ref: New York *Weekly Tribune*, March 9 (by telegraph from St. Louis), and March 30, 1850 (from St. Louis *Daily Union* of March 9). Beck arrived at St. Louis on March 8.

❈ February 24.—The *St. Ange* reached Weston, Mo.—the first of 226 steamboats to arrive there in 1850. *See, also,* March 6 entry.

Steamboats which went to places higher up the Missouri during the year numbered 160. The last boat of the 1850 season at Weston was the *Mary Blane*, on November 30.

Ref: *The Western Journal*, St. Louis, v. 5 (March, 1851), p. 327.

❈ February 25.—David Waldo obtained a contract (made with Bvt. Maj. E. A. Ogden, AQM) to transport government stores overland from Fort Leavenworth to Fort Laramie. (Rate: $7.74 per 100 pounds; bond: $40,000; sureties: William McCoy and Jabez Smith.)

Ref: 31st Cong., 2d Sess., *H. Ex. Doc. No. 23* (Serial 599), p. 15.

❈ February 26.—Joseph Clymer, Westport, Mo. (connected with the Ewings—W. G. and G. W.), received a contract (made with Bvt. Maj. E. A. Ogden) to freight government supplies from Fort Leavenworth to Santa Fe. (Rate: $8.87½ per 100 pounds; bond: $50,000; sureties: William G. Ewing, Joseph A. Sire, and Edward Walsh.)

Ref: 31st Cong., 2d Sess., *H. Ex. Doc. No.* 23 (Serial 599), p. 17; 32d Cong., 1st Sess., *Sen. Com. Report No.* 304 (Serial 631); A. Theodore Brown's *Frontier Community Kansas City to 1870* (c1963), p. 56.

❦ February 27.—*A Journey to California*—a guidebook by "Major" John Stemmons, Rocheport, Mo., published by Fisher & Bennett, St. Louis—was first advertised in the St. Louis *Reveille*. So far as known, no copy is extant.

The *Reveille* "ad" stated it embraced "a description of the country, incidents of the overland route, with directions to future emigrants in making up outfits." The St. Joseph (Mo.) *Gazette*, in April, mentioned this "guide to California emigrants"—priced at 25 cents—containing notes of Stemmons' overland journey "last year." (*See* an item on Stemmons, p. 1075.)

Ref: *The Daily Reveille*, St. Louis, February 27 (and later issues), 1850; St. Joseph *Gazette*, April 5, 1850; *Missouri Statesman*, Columbia, Mo., March 1, 1850. The St. Louis *Intelligencer* also advertised Stemmons' guide.

❦ March 2.—James C. Ogden (by contract made with Bvt. Maj. E. A. Ogden) agreed to furnish and deliver at Fort Leavenworth, by December 31, 800 cords of "good quality" wood, for the sum of $2,774.

Ref: 31st Cong., 2d Sess., *H. Ex. Doc. No.* 23 (Serial 599), p. 15.

❦ March 5.—James Brown and John S. Jones obtained the contract (made with Bvt. Maj. E. A. Ogden, AQM) to freight government stores from Fort Leavenworth to the new military post in the vicinity of Fort Hall ("Idaho"). (Rate: $14.15 per 100 pounds; bond: $75,000; sureties: A. Fristoe, George Scrogin, and A. M. Forbes.)

The St. Joseph *Gazette* of March 15 reported: "Mr. John S. Jones, of Georgetown, Mo., advertises in Boonville Democrat to take 80 persons through to California if they will drive a team from Fort Leavenworth to Fort Hall . . . and after arriving at that post [Jones] will proceed to California with Empty Wagons. Each man will be furnished with one month's provisions after arrival at the mines." (*See, also*, May 21 entry.)

Ref: 31st Cong., 2d Sess., *H. Ex. Doc. No.* 23 (Serial 599), p. 15; St. Joseph *Gazette*, March 15, 1850; *The Daily Reveille*, St. Louis, May 3, 1850. The "Fort Hall" post was abandoned in the early summer of 1850. Jones freighted the army supplies to Fort Laramie. The *Reveille* ran James Brown & Co.'s advertisement (dated April 27) for a "mule train of Passenger Cars from Kansas [Kansas City, Mo.] to California [to start] between the 15th and 20th of May. The train . . . [to be] fitted out by men of experience; James Brown, of Pettis county, Missouri, the great Government contractor . . . being at its head. The price of passage will be $175. . . ." Brown, from the evidence, backed out on the passenger train enterprise. His freight wagons were on the trail, however, apparently in charge of John S. Brown (who, in 1849—*see* p. 833—had been a Brown & Russell "surety"). Henry A. Stine (of the Glenn & Co. passenger train), west of South Pass on July 30, wrote: "A number of the passengers have purchased oxen from John Brown's Government Freight Train at $100 per yoke and intend to leave the [Glenn & Co.] train. . . ."—Stine's diary quoted from typed copy courtesy California State Library, Sacramento.

❦ March 6.—David Waldo received a contract (made with Bvt.

Maj. E. A. Ogden, AQM) to transport government supplies from Fort Leavenworth to El Paso del Norte. (Rate: $13.47 per 100 pounds for the first 125,000 pounds; $13.87½ per 100 pounds for the remainder; bond $75,000; sureties: Jabez Smith and William McCoy.)

Ref: 31st Cong., 2d Sess., *H. Ex. Doc. No.* 23 (Serial 599), pp. 15, 18. A supplemental contract of June 28, altered the above to read: "The delivery of stores . . . shall be made by said Waldo at Santa Fe or at such of the interior posts of New Mexico not more remote than El Paso. . . ."

❦ March 6.—The *Kansas* left Weston, Mo., to return to St. Louis. Among the upbound boats she met were the *Anna, Haydee, Cora, St. Ange, Minnesota, Rowena, Gen. Lane, Alleghany Mail* (the last three? all lower-river boats), *Sacramento, Saluda, Highland Mary,* and *Duroc.*

On March 10 the *Haydee* and *Cora* arrived at St. Joseph, Mo.—the first steamboats to reach there in 1850. Both departed downriver, on the 11th. The Missouri was reported to be in "good boating condition."

Ref: *The Daily Reveille,* St. Louis, March 12, 1850; St. Joseph *Gazette,* March 15, 1850.

❦ March 7.—Promoting Independence, Mo., over St. Joseph, Mo., as the starting point for westbound emigrants, "California" (in a communication published by the *Missouri Republican,* St. Louis) wrote: ". . . the crossing [crossings?] of the Kansas river (where six new boats are provided,) is a 'mere circumstance,' when viewed with the difficulties of crossing the Missouri."

Emigrants starting west from Independence, or Westport, or Kansas, Mo., in 1850, could ferry the Kansas at Delaware (or, Grinter) crossing, about eight miles west of the Missouri line, and take the military road up past Fort Leavenworth to join the St. Joseph branch of the Oregon-California road. Or, having crossed the Kansas at the point above-mentioned, they could proceed northward on the military road till they intersected a new (in 1849?) north-of-the-Kansas road which had its eastern origin point at Parkville, Mo. [*See* annals p. 1076, and the notice advertising Parkville, Mo., as "the best point to cross the Missouri," for mention of this road.] Or, emigrants could remain on the south side of the Kansas river, traveling either the "old" Oregon-California road westward [to one of three crossing points—all in present Shawnee county: the (so-called) "lower ferry" at present Topeka; the ferry upstream at Pottawatomie Baptist Mission; or the "upper ferry" a little above the Pottawatomies' trading post "Union Town"]. Or, they could take the Santa Fe trail.

Later in March, in a circular addressed to California emigrants, signed by 46 Independence merchants and residents (also published in the *Republican*), it was stated: "At the crossing[?] of the Kansas on this route there will be twelve new ferry boats, by the arrival of the first emigrants."

Ref: *Missouri Republican,* St. Louis, March 7, 21, 26, 1850.

❡ March 15.—A mail express from Fort Leavenworth to Santa Fe, which left the post on the 15th, was met by eastbound W. C. Skinner on the Cimarron about March 29; and reached Santa Fe about April 15.

From Santa Fe, in March, Frank Hendrickson and James Clay set out for Fort Leavenworth with the mail (in a wagon); reached their destination, safely, in April. *See, also,* April 18 entry.

Ref: New York *Weekly Tribune*, May 11, 1850; Calhoun, *op. cit.*, p. 198; George A. McCall, *Letters From the Frontiers* . . . (Philadelphia, 1868), p. 492.

❡ March.—Several parties of Santa Fe traders, overland from New Mexico, reached Missouri this month.

On the 15th, "H. M[a]yer, from Chihuahua and J. S. Lucas and H. Lightner from El Paso," arrived at Independence. It was stated the party had left Santa Fe on February 10, "making the journey in 22 [*i. e.,* 33?] days." Young James Belt (16 or 17), son of Dr. W. S. Belt, Independence, was a cotraveler.

"McCarty's train" (eight "Americans" and four Mexicans), which had set out from Santa Fe on February 6, was overtaken by the above traders between the Little Arkansas and Cottonwood Crossing, traveling afoot, their animals (some 25 mules and horses) having been stolen at Big Bend of the Arkansas by Indians (Pawnees, or Kansa). "Some relief for this party was sent back from Council Grove," Belt reported. By March 20 all (or part) of the hapless McCarty train reached Missouri. "T. L." [John L.] Hatcher (one of the "Americans") boarded the *Highland Mary* at Kansas, Mo.; arrived at St. Louis on the 21st.

Upwards of 20 men—James Webb, (Charles L.?) Spencer, James E. Sabine, George Estes, Thomas Flournoy, William Mitchell, among them—were in a third traders' company eastbound on the Santa Fe trail in March. By one account they left Santa Fe on February 10, but were not expected to reach Missouri till the last of March.

Ref: New York *Daily Tribune*, April 2, 1850; New York *Weekly Tribune*, March 9, 16, 30, April 6, 1850; *Missouri Republican*, St. Louis, March 22, 25, 1850; *The Daily Reveille*, St. Louis, March 26, 1850; *Jefferson Inquirer*, Jefferson City, Mo., April 6, 1850.

❡ In mid-March, by report, not less than 80 out of Parkville, Mo.'s, 150 inhabitants started "in search of gold, high up on Caw [Kansas] River, in the Indian territory." The Liberty *Tribune* "understood" the expedition numbered about 40 men, with nine wagons. (*See, also,* April 8 entry.)

Ref: St. Louis *Intelligencer*, March 29, 1850; *The Weekly Tribune*, Liberty, Mo., March 29, 1850.

❡ March 19.—At Fort Scott, the Rev. David Clarkson (Episcopalian; from the New Jersey diocese) became chaplain. (He remained till Fort Scott was abandoned in 1853.)

Some time in 1850 Father John J. Bax, S. J., of Osage Mission (about 40 miles distant) established a Catholic missionary station at Fort Scott, continuing it until, and after, the military post closed.

Ref: F. B. Heitman's *Historical Register & Dictionary of the United States Army* . . . (1903), v. 1, p. 308, which gives the name as "Daniel" rather than "David." *KHC*, v. 16, pp. 355-389. If Fort Scott had a chaplain prior to March, 1850, the record has not been located. Clarkson's tour of duty there ended April 26, 1853. For Father Bax, *see* G. J. Garraghan's *The Jesuits of the Middle United States* (New York, 1938), v. 2, p. 569.

❡ **March 19.**—From St. Joseph, Mo., "Ralph Ringwood" wrote Horace Greeley: "With the opening of steamboat navigation they [California-bound emigrants] have been pouring in upon us, and a few of them are now ready for their long tramp. . . . As yet the arrivals are confined chiefly to those who have come from our neighboring Western States. A few Virginians are now on the ground. . . . Some will leave as early as the 1st of April, taking along corn enough to last their cattle and mules [until there is grass to sustain them]. . . ."

(The first emigrant train reached Fort Kearny on April 13—*see* p. 934. But Lorenzo Sawyer, traveling up the Little Blue on May 15, wrote: "The bend [a 10-mile stretch between river points] is full of emigrants waiting for grass to become better; some of whom left St. Joseph as early as the 2nd of April.")

The New York *Tribune's* correspondent also reported: "Mules and cattle are selling at round prices—supply not over plentiful. Good American mules range from $150 to $200 per pair. Santa Fe mules from $200 to $300 per pair. Well broken cattle of the proper age are selling at from $60 to $100 per yoke, and few in the market that are fit for the trip. Everything else necessary for the emigrants' outfit in great profusion and selling low.

"Whilst I write the steamboats *Daniel Boon* and *Saranak* are at the wharf, landing emigrants. The former has on board a company of 80 from the Hoosier State [Indiana]. . . . To judge from present appearances, the emigration from the Western States will be considerably larger than it was last season. . . ."

Ref: New York *Weekly Tribune*, April 6, 1850; Lorenzo Sawyer, *Way Sketches* . . . 1850 (New York, 1926), p. 28. The *Missouri Republican*, St. Louis, of March 12, 1850, reported: "The Steamer Daniel Boon reached this city night before last, from the Wabash River, with a company of California emigrants on board. They number between 70 and 80 and have their camp equipage, wagons, mules, &c. on board. This is the first organized company that has reached here this season, and they depart to-day on the same boat for Independence [*i. e.*, St. Joseph]."

❡ **March 19-27.**—The *Mary Blane* left St. Louis on the 19th (with some 250 cabin passengers, and perhaps 200 more on deck); reached Weston, Mo., on the 26th, and St. Joseph, on the 27th.

Landing at St. Joseph (to travel overland to Fort Pierre—up the Missouri's left bank) were Alexander Culbertson (the American Fur Company's principal upper Missouri agent) and his brother Thaddeus A. Culbertson (who, under auspices of the Smithsonian Institution, would spend part of the summer on an expedition to the Bad Lands).

Ref: Thaddeus A. Culbertson's "Journal of an Expedition to the Mauvaises Terres and the Upper Missouri in 1850," ed. by J. F. McDermott (Bureau of American Ethnology, *Bulletin No. 147*, Washington, 1952).

❡ March 20.—Agent Luke Lea (head of the Fort Leavenworth Agency—near State Line, present Johnson county) sent a letter to "The Rev. Mr. [Thomas B.] Markham Wyandott Nation" forbidding him to preach among the Shawnee Indians.

Markham (missionary of the northern Methodist church), assigned to the Wyandots and Shawnees in August, 1849, by the Missouri conference, had reached the Wyandot reserve sometime after October 4; made his residence there; and was preaching to the northern-church Wyandots from a small log chapel. (The Wyandots' brick Methodist meeting house—erected 1847-1848— was in the hands of the Church, South. *See* pp. 729 and 788, for the controversy between the Anti-slavery and Proslavery church factions.)

On April 20 a letter protesting Lea's action was addressed to the Comm'r of Indian affairs by Shawnee Indians Charles Fish, James Captain, John Fish, William Rogers, Crane, and Paschal Fish. (All were "northern church" members; as was their amanuensis, Wyandot John M. Armstrong.) They blamed the persons in charge of Shawnee Methodist Mission and manual labor school (the Rev. Thomas Johnson, and others of the southern church) for influencing Lea to make the ruling against Markham; and accused them of other "improper acts."

Ref: Office of Indian Affairs (OIA), Letters Received from Fort Leavenworth Agency (National Archives Microcopy 234, Roll 303); Comm'r of Indian Affairs, *Report*, 1849, Thomas Moseley's report, therein; A. T. Andreas and W. G. Cutler, *History of the State of Kansas* (Chicago, 1883), p. 1228; *KHC*, v. 9, p. 230.

❡ March 21.—Passengers boarding the St. Louis-bound *Sacramento* at Kansas (City), Mo., included Baptist-missionary-to-the-Ottawas Jotham Meeker, "19 Sauks [including head chief (Moses) Keokuk], the Sauk Agent [Charles N. Handy] & family, [Josiah] Smart, [John] Goodel[l] & Gardner [Sac traders] from the Agency, King & Nonedowah [Ottawa? Indians]. . . ." Already aboard was Baptist-missionary-to-the-Delawares John G. Pratt. (The *Sacramento* reached St. Louis on March 25.)

Meeker's diary entry of March 21 also stated: "We have a great Sauk dance on the Boat in the evening." The Indians were making the journey to attend the trial of two tribesmen accused of murdering Santa Fe trader Norris Colburn in 1847—*see* p. 668.

Ref: Meeker "Diary" (in KHi ms. div.); St. Louis *Intelligencer*, March 26, 1850; SIA, St. Louis, "Records," v. 9, typed copy, p. 424; *The Weekly Tribune*, Liberty, Mo.; St. Louis *Daily New Era*, September 15, 1849; *The Daily Reveille*, St. Louis, March 29, 1850, which stated that "I-thi-thi-mar and Es-co-tah, two Osages[?]," charged with Colburn's murder, would be tried during the U. S. district court session beginning "next week."

❡ March 24.—The St. Joseph (Mo.) *Gazette* reported: ". . . there are now at this landing 3 large flat boats, and a new and excellent horse boat, and a steam ferry boat will be here in April next. In addition to the above, there are two new flat boats at the ferry a few miles above St. Joseph."

(Aaron Lewis, John Duncan, and William Lewis had advertised on February 15 that they would "have in operation by April 1," a "good and substantial horse ferry boat" at St. Joseph.)

The St. Joseph *Adventure* of May 17 stated that "three ferries—one steam ferry boat and four flats" had been "constantly employed for the last four weeks." Emigrant N. A. Cagwin, at St. Joseph on May 5, ". . . prepared for crossing over the River. Done so about 1-O'clock P. M. on a Steam ferry Boat. . . ." On May 20 emigrant James Bennett "Reached St. Joseph's at 9 o'clock this morning. . . . Crossed the Missouri at 4 p. m. in a steam ferry-boat. . . ."

Ref: *The Daily Reveille*, St. Louis, March 24, 1850; St. Joseph *Gazette*, February 15, March 24, 1850; *Adventure*, St. Joseph, Mo., May 17, 1850; N. A. Cagwin's "Diary," 1850 (from typed copy, courtesy California State Library, Sacramento); James Bennett, *Overland Journey to California* . . . (New York [1933]), p. 11.

❦ **March 26-29.**—Leaving Savannah Landing (Mo.) on the 26th (weather very cold and snow falling) to return to St. Louis, the *Pocahontas* met the *Minnesota* at "Lost Lake," the *Mary Blane* at "Grand Prairie"; on the 27th met the *El Paso* at Weston, *Haydee* at Blue Mills, *Cora* and *Princeton* at Camden; on the 28th met the *Consignee* at Waverly, *Melodeon* and *Julia* at "Hill's Lodge,' *Saluda* at Glasgow, *Lightfoot* "just below," *Highland Mary* at Lamoine, *Embassy* at Boonville; and on the 29th met the *Duroc, Alton, Sacramento, Lake of the Woods,* and *Kansas.*

At Glasgow, Mo., the *El Paso* (passing up on the 25th) was reported to have over 200 California immigrants aboard; and to be making her first trip up the Missouri. The new *Melodeon*, passing Glasgow on the 27th, was said to have some 300 passengers aboard, mostly bound for California; and to be one of the roomiest boats on the river.

Ref: *Missouri Republican*, St. Louis, April 1, 1850; Glasgow (Mo.) *Weekly Times*, March 28, 1850.

❦ **March 29.**—The St. Joseph *Gazette* reported: "Every boat that arrives at our wharf is crowded with Californians. Within the last week several hundred have arrived at this place. We suppose there are now in this place, and vicinity, upwards of 1,500. . . ."

Ref: St. Joseph *Gazette*, March 29, 1850.

❦ **March 31.**—Joseph D. Ellis and party (17 Americans—returning from California?) arrived at Independence, Mo., from Santa Fe (left March 5), via the Bent's Fort route. They reached St. Louis April 8. (Ellis was in the Santa Fe trade.)

The account sent east from St. Louis by telegraph stated there were 17 Mexicans as well as 17 "emigrants" in the company. The "Americans" reported they had found Agent Thomas Fitzpatrick "at the Big Timbers, engaged in conference with several tribes of Indians."

Ref: *Missouri Republican,* St. Louis, April 10, 1850 (from Independence [Mo.] *Commonwealth* of April 2); New York *Weekly Tribune,* April 6, 27, 1850. The news sent by telegraph frequently became garbled in transmission.

℃ March.—Santa Fe trader Moses Goldstein, of Independence, Mo. and seven other men who had spent the winter "in an open prairie' on the Jornada, "about 30 miles on the south side of the Arkansas," with James Brown's 20 stranded wagons (freighting goods for "Goldstein, Thompson and Flournoy") were reported (by parties reaching Independence March 31 and April 14) to be "in good health and good spirits," "patiently awaiting the arrival of oxen from the States." (A relief train "with provisions and cattle" left Independence in March—*see* April entry, p. 916.) During a period of freezing weather Goldstein, and companions, had found it necessary to burn two wagons for self-preservation. (*See* p. 890, for the November 17, 1849, disaster to Brown's train.)

Ref: *Missouri Statesman,* Columbia, January 25, 1850; *Missouri Republican,* St. Louis, April 24, June 21, 1850; New York *Weekly Tribune,* April 6, 22, 1850.

℃ April 2.—Bvt. Maj. Edmund A. Ogden (post quartermaster) left Fort Leavenworth, accompanied by "a lot of Kickapoo Indians as guides," and a "negro named Morgan, who lived with them, as interpreter," to lay out an improved (shorter) military road from the fort to a junction with the St. Joseph branch of the Oregon-California trail. (For the "old" road *see* February 1 annals entry.) In company with Ogden were "a number of officers and their families" bound for Forts Kearny and Laramie; also a detachment of Company B, First dragoons, and some infantry recruits, as their escort. (Trooper P. G. Lowe later recollected three officers who made the journey were Lt. Col. Gustavus Loomis, Capt. Henry W. Wharton [accompanied by his family], and Bvt. Capt. Alexander B. Dyer.) Ogden stopped at the Big Blue (where his project ended); presumably he and his guides returned to Fort Leavenworth well before month's end.

If Ogden made a report on his April, 1850, road survey it has not been located. Trooper Lowe, in his *Five Years a Dragoon* (1906), stated: "The first night out we camped at the springs near where Lowemont, Kansas, is now located. We followed the military road to Santa Fe about eight miles, and from there to the intersection of the St. Joe road about 120 miles we followed the divide on account of excessive wet weather, heading, or crossing near the head of the streams running northeast into the Missouri and those running southeast into the Kaw [Kansas], crossing the Delaware where is now Kinnekuk [Kennekuk], the Nemaha where is now Seneca, intersecting the road from St. Joe between Seneca and Marysville [Big Blue crossing]."

Dr. J. S. Shepherd (a Wisconsinite on his way to California) traveled Ogden's road before it was a month old. His party reached Fort Leavenworth April 24; encamped within half a mile; set out for the West on May 1. Shepherd's recorded mileages (May 1 to May 7) to the point where he "struck the high road from St. Joe West . . ." total 122. He wrote: "From Fort Leavenworth, the road we have travelled, is a new one made by Uncle Sam's men this spring, and is better than any road leading from Racine, not excepting even the plank. . . ." Shepherd noted that the distance from St. Joseph, Mo., to the junction was said to be 120 miles.

Philip L. Platt and Nelson Slater, in their *Travelers' Guide* (published in 1852) discussed the "route from Fort Leavenworth to its intersection with the St. Joseph Road, a little east of the Big Blue river" as follows: "This road, after passing out from the fort 14 miles, divides; the right hand road being the old one [*see* February 1 entry; and *also* the Stansbury map on p. 819] and the left hand road the new one, which was surveyed and first traveled in the spring of 1850. . . . The left-hand or new road is the shortest and the best. It intersects the St. Joseph road 103 miles out from the fort. [Shepherd had reckoned it 122 miles.] It is somewhat crooked, like all other routes to miss the hills and hollows, and to strike the streams at the best points for fording. This road has been remarkably well laid out by the government surveyors, being located more nearly on a level, and running with more directness than any one would suppose it could, judging from the rolling aspect of the country through which it passes." (*See, also,* the November 6 entry on Stansbury.)

Commenting on the road "surveyed by myself" in 1850, Bvt. Maj. Edmund A. Ogden, in his October, 1851, report, wrote: ". . . the principal obstacle is . . . the Big Blue, which is often swollen by floods and impassable, so that the troops, contractors' and emigrant trains frequently encounter there very serious delay. At this place [the future Marysville] there should be a bridge and a party of twenty soldiers stationed for its protection. . . ." [In 1852 the military permitted private enterprise to handle the situation, by allowing Francis J. Marshall to establish a ferry and trading post at this "Marysville" crossing of the Big Blue.] Ogden also recommended bridging the "Sauterelle" [Grasshopper; now Delaware] 40 miles west of the fort, to eliminate detours and "indifferent fords" on the forks of that stream.

Ref: P. G. Lowe, *Five Years a Dragoon* (1906), pp. 34, 35; *KHC*, v. 3, p. 360; J. S. Shepherd, *Journal of Travel Across the Plains to California* (reprinted 1945), pp. 2-4; Platt and Slater, *op. cit.*, 32d Cong., 1st Sess., Sen. Ex. Doc. No. 1 (Serial 611), Ogden's 1851 report, in War Department report, therein.

¶ April 5-12.—The St. Joseph *Gazette* of the 5th stated: "Several hundred emigrants have arrived at this place during the past week. . . ." The issue of April 12 reported: "Californians continue to arrive daily in large numbers. Several hundreds have already crossed the river, some of whom *have left for the plains,* taking with them forage for their horses and mules."

April 5—The season's first ox train (10 wagons, D. Burroughs, of Kendall county, Ill., captain) was scheduled to leave St. Joseph (according to the St.

Louis *Republican*). Capt. D. Burroughs and 19 men had arrived at St. Joseph on March 17.

April 9.—A large Wayne County (Ohio) Company (around 260 names were on the roster, including some Pennsylvanians), which had arrived at St. Joseph, on the *Consignee* from Pittsburgh, March 31 (and subsequently had crossed the Missouri to camp on the "Kansas" bluffs six miles out, on April 7 and 8) began the journey overland. (This mule and horse train reached Fort Kearny April 20; arrived at Fort Laramie on May 4; and on July 4 encamped near Lawson's Ranche in California.)

April 10—L. D. Dick, and nine companions, from Rock Island, Ill., with horse-drawn wagons, left St. Joseph for the West.

April 11—A company of footmen (Tacitus P. Zander, of Milwaukee, and 26? others from Illinois, Ohio, New York, Indiana, etc., were listed in this party) started from St. Joseph with 40 days' provisions. ("There was a company of twenty-two left here on foot, with their knapsacks on their backs, on the 10th?; they expect to walk through in 40 days!" a St. Joseph correspondent stated on April 13.)

"Cheyenne," at Fort Laramie, wrote that the first company of emigrants— 24 men, with six light wagons, from Kendall county, Ill., captained by S. B. Craw—arrived at that post on April 29. (Presumably this company—from St. Joseph—had been the first to arrive at Fort Kearny—on April 13.) East of Fort Bridger, on May 15, an eastbound Mormon party met "Captain Craw's company of five wagons from Kendall County, Illinois, with twenty-five men. They had performed their journey from the Missouri River in thirty-nine days. Their horses looked well."—A. M. Harmon's *Journal*.

"Cheyenne," on May 4, listed the day's arrivals at Fort Laramie as: Captain Denison's company (250 men; 50 wagons) from Wayne county, Ohio; Captain Burrough's company (50 men; 14 wagons) from Kendall county, Ill.; and five men with one wagon, from Rock Island, Ill.

"Cheyenne," in a May 14 letter, reported that, up to then, 950 men and 215 wagons had passed Fort Laramie (whereas, in 1849, no emigrant had yet arrived on that date!). He commented "The strangest set of all, however, that has yet made its advent is a party of footmen, numbering some 15 or 20. These men carry everything on their backs—provisions, blankets and all. They look a little the worse for wear, but appear to get along well."

Ref: St. Joseph *Gazette*, March 29, April 5, 12; *Missouri Republican*, St. Louis, April 16, June 9, 16; *Missouri Statesman*, Columbia, April 26, 1850; George Keller, *A Trip Across the Plains, and Life in California* . . . (Massillon, Ohio, 1851); Maybelle H. Anderson, ed., *Appleton Milo Harmon Goes West* (Berkeley, 1946). *Also, see,* Edward Eberstadt & Sons, N. Y., *Catalogue 159* [n. d.], p. 92, for item on Henry M. Wertz's letters. (Wertz was a member of the Wayne County [Ohio] Company.)

❡ On April 7 Franklin Street (with ox teams; and with Ohio? companions) set out across "Kansas" from St. Joseph, Mo., on the St. Joseph branch of the Oregon-California trail. He arrived in Salt Lake City on June 23; and reached California in August. At Cincinnati, in 1851, his guidebook *California In 1850, Compared With What It Was In 1849* was published. Reprinted here (with added notes) is the St. Joseph-to-Fort Kearny section from Street's "Table of Distances, From Point to Point."

	Miles	Total Miles
From *St. Joseph* the road runs through the bottom, which is covered with a dense growth of cotton-wood and other timber. It is very crooked, and in some places extremely muddy.		
Clear Creek, at the foot of the Bluffs is a fine place for camping. From here, the road is somewhat hilly, to	6	
Mosquito Creek; low bottom on the east side of this Creek, some timber on both sides. From here the road is quite hilly.	15	21
Wolf Creek—Low wide bottom on the east side. There are some old dilapidated Indian huts, and farms, in the bottom near the Bluffs. Banks of the Creek very steep and miry. The Indians have a temporary bridge across the stream. They charge twenty-five cents for each wagon that crosses.	5	26
Indian Agency—At this place there is quite a number of Americans living, in the employment of Government. It is the agency of the Miami and Kickapoo Indians. [The Great Nemaha Subagency, in 1850—and earlier—embraced the Iowa, and the Sac & Fox Indians "of the Missouri."] There is a [Presbyterian] Missionary Station here, several fine farms, and a good school for the education of Indians.	4	30
Mill Creek, is a small stream in the prairie, some green elm trees standing on its banks, a few rods above the road. [Now Clear creek, Doniphan county.]	5	35
Small Creek—left of the road; some timber on its banks; good place to camp. [Now Walnut creek, Brown county.]	22	57
Grove, half mile north of the road; good place to camp.	6	63
Grove, on a small creek, to the right of the road; nice place, and a good camping ground.	10	73
Small Creek, one mile north of road. Plenty of timber and water.	12	85
Nemehaw Creek—This is a beautiful stream of clear water; plenty of timber, and a delightful place to camp; banks a little rocky on the east side. [Now South Fork Nemaha river, Nemaha county.]	7	92
Little Nemehaw—Plenty of timber and good water. [Now Turkey creek, Nemaha county. A. H. Thomasson, an 1850 emigrant, wrote: "After we crost the creek and got on top of the hill look back the road is so crooked some of the teemes looks as tho they was going back. . . ."]	12	104

Small Creek in the prairie; plenty of water and some timber.	12	[116]
Rock Creek—Some green elms on the banks of the creek; plenty of good water. [The upper waters of West Branch Vermillion river, Marshall county. The Platt and Slater *Travelers' Guide*, 1852, called this "Stony Creek," and noted: "In the bottom of this stream are large stones. The Indians call it Vermillion Creek. From its banks they get red clay with which to paint their faces."]	4	120
Blue River—Should this stream be up, you will have to build a raft to cross on. It is about fifty yards wide, and a very rapid current; the stream abounds with excellent fish. [The crossing at what became Marysville, Marshall county.]	18	138
[The "Independence" Oregon-California trail, and the St. Joseph branch, joined (according to Stansbury) 8 miles beyond the Blue. By other accounts the distance was 9 or 10 miles. Street, oddly, made no mention of the junction.]		
Small Creek in the prairie; some timber half a mile from the road, on each side.	10	148
Small Creek—Plenty of standing water. ["Ketcham's Creek—sometimes called Ten-mile Branch."—Stansbury]	10	158
Small Creek—Plenty of water, and some green timber, half mile north of the road. ["Turkey Creek."—Stansbury]	7	165
Wythe Creek—Plenty of timber, and good water. After this, several small streams to cross, and steep hills to ascend and descend. ["Wyeth's Creek—Trib. of Big (*i. e.*, Little) Blue."—Stansbury]	7	172
Big Sandy—Good water, and some timber. ["Sandy Creek."—Stansbury]	13	185
Dry Sandy—This stream is very wide, the bed of which is composed of loose sand, in which the water sinks, in dry weather. ["Big Sandy Creek."—Stansbury]	13	198
Little Blue River, or American Fork—This is a deep narrow stream, of beautiful, clear, running water. Its banks are skirted with a thin growth of cottonwood. You travel up it forty-four miles;—camping places all along the river.	12	210
Road leaves the River	44	254
Platte River	[24]	278
Fort Kearney [Kearny] (near the head of Grand Island)	10	288

Ref: Franklin Street's *California in 1850* . . . (Cincinnati, 1851)—from microfilm, Library of Congress copy; Platt and Slater, *op. cit.*; Howard Stansbury's *An Expedition to the Valley of the Great Salt Lake of Utah* . . . (Philadelphia, 1852), pp. 270-277; A. H. Thomasson's "Diary" of journey to California in 1850 (from typed copy, courtesy California State Library, Sacramento, which has the original diary).

❧ April 8.—By report from Independence, Mo., "a party of enter-prising persons," guided by Smallwood Noland, was to set out this day on an expedition "to test the reported existence of gold" on the Kansas river some 160 miles due west.

On May 6 a St. Joseph, Mo., man wrote: "The grand bubble of the gold mines on the 'Caw' River, or Kansas, is exploded at last. Those who went out there some weeks ago to dig for the 'dust' have returned with their 'pockets full of rocks,' but they happen to be not of the right sort."

Ref: *The Daily Reveille*, St. Louis, April 10, 1850; New York *Daily Tribune*, May 21, 1850.

❧ April 9.—An auction was held at Fort Leavenworth to dispose of some 350 wagons, 200 ox yokes, bows, etc., no longer "required for the public service." (The sale advertisement, dated March 16, stated that about 200 Spanish mules, 350 oxen, and 200 horses would "probably be sold at the same time.")

Ref: St. Joseph *Gazette*, March 22, 1850.

❧ April 11.—The Boonville (Mo.) *Observer* published a table of distances "Camping Grounds on the [Independence] route to Cali-fornia," by C. Q. Lewis (a returned '49er?). Of his 2,140-mile itinerary (via South Pass, Fort Bridger, Fort Hall, Humboldt river, the Truckee route, Johnson's ranch, and Sacramento) to San Fran-cisco, the section of the "old" Oregon-California trail out as far as Fort Kearny is reprinted here.

From the [Fort Leavenworth-Fort Scott] military road 25 miles South of Independence. The road leads over a dividing ridge between Grand [Neosho] river and Bull creek. By turning to the right a camp can be had at a distance of five or six miles.

	Miles	[Total Miles]
To the head of Grand River	20	
To Santa Fe road	10	[30]
To Rogdger's [Rogers, or Rodger's] settlement (an Indian farm)	10	[40]
To the Oregon [California] road	3	[43]
To a tributary of Walkerrusha [Wakarusa]	7	[50]
To main Walkerrusha, intermediate camp	10	[60]
To Willow Spring, intermediate camp	18	[78]
To Forks of Upper and Lower [Kansas river] ferry roads, good camp	10	[88]
To Lower Ferry [Topeka vicinity]	4	[92]
To Upper Ferry [Union Town area], it is supposed the lower ferry road is the best	14	[106]
To an Indian [Pottawatomie] settlement, good camp	2	[108]
To a bend in Kaw [Kansas] river, good camp	10	[118]

To next water and camp ground 5   [123]
To Indian settlement, good camp 4   [127]
To crossing of Vermil[l]ion int'diate. camps 18   [145]
To Big Vermil[l]ion, intermediate camps 30   [175]
To Big Blue [Alcove Spring vicinity], camps scarce 24   [199]
To St. Joseph road [junction] 10   [209]
To Otter Creek, camps scarce 34   [243]
To Republican Fork of Blue [i. e., Little Blue], camps scarce, 24   [267]
To Where the road leaves the river, camps good 40   [307]
To the next water, good camp 6   [313]
To Pawnee trail, good camp a little ahead 4   [317]
To Platte river, a couple of lakes to the right in the distance, 18   [335]
To Fort Kearney [Kearny], good camps 20   [355]

Ref: Boonville (Mo.) *Observer*, April 11, 1850. *See* in this volume the "Pawnee trail" as shown on the Fremont map of 1845.

℄ April.—The St. Joseph *Gazette* of April 12 stated: "There are more steamboats now in the Missouri trade than was ever in it before . . . from 15 to 20 being [at this time] on the river between St. Louis and St. Joseph. . . ."

The *Melodeon* had left St. Joseph on April 1 (and reached St. Louis April 8). Just behind was the *Highland Mary* (departing on the 2d; and taking aboard at Kansas, Mo., "Some twelve or fifteen Kaw [Kansa] Indians" going to St. Louis "to buy farming utensils"). She left the *Embassy*, *Consignee*, and *Lightfoot* "in port" at St. Joseph; met the *Saluda* (hard aground) at Iatan; [passed the *Cora* at Weston, apparently]; met the *Alton* and *Duroc* at Fry's Point; the *Sacramento* at Liberty; other boats below; and reached St. Louis on April 8. (The *Consignee*, from Pittsburgh, Pa., with a charter load of Ohio and Pennsylvania emigrants-for-California—246 of them the *Missouri Republican* reported when the boat stopped overnight at St. Louis on March 21—had reached St. Joseph on the 31st. The *Lightfoot* had been chartered at St. Louis to take 400 English Mormons to "a point high up the Missouri.")

Also on the Missouri, and bound for Kansas river, or higher, in the first-half-of-April period were the *Kansas*, *St. Paul*, and *Anna* (all of which returned to St. Louis April 13), the *Robert Campbell*, *Saranak*, *J. L. McLean*, *St. Ange*, *Pocahontas*, *Tuscumbia*, *El Paso* (the last three of these returned to St. Louis on April 18), *Pride of the West* (which reached Weston April 14; then returned to St. Louis), *Bay State* (which had left St. Louis, April 9 with "about 300 passengers" mostly California-bound, but including Missionary Jotham Meeker, and two daughters, who debarked at Kansas, Mo., on the 13th), and the *Princeton*. (The *Robert Campbell* and *St. Ange* went up to Council Bluffs; the latter reached there April 15, but the *Robert Campbell*, on the 17th, was reported to be "a few miles below . . . in the ice . . . with heavy freight and [a load of English Mormons] passengers." The *Bay State* left St. Joseph for St. Louis on April 15; the *Princeton* started upriver for Council Bluffs the same day.)

Ref: St. Louis *Intelligencer*, March 23, April 8, 13, 18, 20, 1850; *The Frontier Guardian*, Kanesville, Ia., April 17, 1850; *The Daily Reveille*, St. Louis, March 24, 26, April 14, 1850;

Jotham Meeker's "Diary," *loc. cit.; Missouri Republican*, St. Louis, March 22, 1850 (or, New York *Daily Tribune*, April 2); Keller, *op. cit.*; C. W. Smith's *Journal* . . . N. Y. [1920]), for *Pride of the West*.

❑ April 12.—At Independence, Mo., a correspondent wrote: "For some unknown cause, this town is extraordinarily dull this season; as yet, compared to last season there are but few California emigrants here. . . . The prospect is quite discouraging for an early start; the nights are cold and frosty, clear and dry. . . ." (*See* May 14 entry.)

The St. Joseph *Gazette* of April 12 stated: "We learn, by a gentleman just from Independence, that there are only about five hundred emigrants at that place."

Ref: New York *Daily Tribune*, May 3, 1850; St. Joseph *Gazette*, April 12, 1850.

❑ April 13-19.—At St. Joseph, Mo., on the 13th, a man wrote: "This place is all bustle at this time with emigrants for California. From the best estimate that can be had, there have been 8,200 arrivals at this place, and a great many of them have crossed over the river [into "Kansas"] and started on their journey. . . . There are in this place and across the river encamped, about five thousand. None of the Missouri boys have gotten here yet, except some five or six from Ralls county. . . ."

Ohio emigrant Walter G. Pigman reached St. Joseph on the 15th (by stage from Weston, Mo.). His journal states: "April 15 . . . found my company ashore but all in a bustle Hundreds of waggons and thousands of persons for the diggings. April 16 Rain and snow fast stop the crossing. Both sides of the river are literally crowded. . . . April 19 Start for the Ferry five miles above the town. . . ." [Pigman and company had to wait their turn—finally got across on the 21st.]

Reaching St. Joseph on April 17 (via steamboat) Ohio emigrant John Wood wrote in his journal: "The excitement here is almost alarming. There are now about 10,000 emigrants in this place and all are hurrying to make a start." He remarked on the "quarreling and wrangling in the town"; stated that "considerable sickness also prevails now among the emigrants, in this town." [Wood's company "concluded to move up the river about forty miles" to recruit stock for "a few weeks" before starting.]

The St. Joseph *Gazette* of April 19 stated: "During the past week upwards of three thousand California emigrants have arrived at this place by land and water. From the best estimate we can make, we suppose upwards of eight thousand have arrived at this place, during the present spring." (*See* the *Gazette's* April 26 estimate.)

Emigrant Silas Newcomb wrote in his journal on April 19: "This place [St. Joseph] contains some two thousand five hundred inhabitants and at present is a very busy place. . . . Hills and dales are white with . . . [emigrants'] camps. Many have crossed the river and encamped on the west side in the Indian Territory. . . . [St. Joseph] contains four good sized Hotels, about twenty Stores and the residue is made up of groceries, bakeries, &c."

Ref: *Missouri Statesman*, Columbia, April 26, 1850; Ulla S. Fawkes, ed., *The Journal of Walter Griffith Pigman* (Mexico, Mo., 1942); St. Joseph *Gazette*, April 19, 1850; Sawyer, *op. cit.*, p. 17 (for quote from Silas Newcomb's "Journal"—the original being in the Coe Collection, Yale University Library); John Wood, *Journal* . . . 1850 (Chillicothe, Ohio, 1852).

❧ April 14.—Travelers (some 25 in all) arriving at Independence, Mo., from Santa Fe (left around March 19) included William C. Skinner, Dr. Henry Connelly, Messrs. James L. Collins, Charles E. Kearney, of Taos, N. M., George H. Peacock, of Independence, F. Y. Ewing, W. T. Pigott, and Dr. J. F. Hassel, of Lexington, Mo., Mr. Frazer, of Santa Fe, and Henry Martin, of Jefferson City, Mo.

They were in advance of Manuel Armijo's cotraveling party. S. L. Hubbell (who had started from Pajarilo, N. M., with Armijo) reached St. Louis April 30 (on the *J. L. McLean*), leaving Don Manuel at Council Grove. His train had lost 20 mules (frozen) at Walnut creek, and had been detained, otherwise, by severe weather.

Ref: New York *Daily Tribune*, May 11, 1850 (from *Missouri Republican*, St. Louis, April 24); New York *Daily Tribune*, May 13, 1850; St. Joseph *Gazette*, May 3, 1850; *The Daily Reveille*, St. Louis, May 1, 1850.

❧ April.—On the 18th James Clay, Frank Hendrickson, and a man named Branton left Fort Leavenworth with the express mail for New Mexico. On the Santa Fe trail they overtook a relief train, headed by Thomas W. Flournoy, which was going out to James Brown's stranded wagons—*see* p. 890. (Flournoy's party was at Little Cow creek on April 11.) Around the end of April "Mr. Thos. Flournoy and mail carriers" were "near to Brown's wagons," on the Jornada.

Subsequently, in the fore part of May, 10 men were in the mail carriers' party when, at a camp near Wagon Mound, N. M., Apaches attacked, and massacred all of them. Killed were Clay, Hendrickson, Branton, Flournoy, Moses Goldstein (who had spent the winter with the stranded Brown wagons), also Benjamin Shaw, John Duty, John Freeman, John Williams, and a German teamster—some (or all) of whom had joined from an eastbound company en route. The bodies were found on May 19, but the men had died perhaps as early as May 7. Most of the mail was recovered.

Ref: *Missouri Republican*, St. Louis, June 21, 1850; *The Weekly Tribune*, Liberty, Mo., June 21, 1850; Calhoun, *op. cit.*, pp. 198-200, 206-209; New York *Daily Tribune*, May 29, July 1, 1850; *The Daily Reveille*, St. Louis, May 1, June 28, August 27, 1850; McCall, *op. cit.*, pp. 493, 494; St. Louis *Intelligencer*, November 1, 1850; Bvt. Maj. E. A. Ogden's Fort Leavenworth, June 18, 1850, letter (typed copy in KHi ms. div.), which gives the massacre date as May 12. Lt. A. E. Burnside (*see* Calhoun, p. 198), and others, put the date earlier in May—around the 7th.

❡ April.—Henry Harvey, from Clinton county, Ohio, new head of the Osage Subagency (a post to which he had been appointed in December, 1849) arrived in "Kansas" with his family. (Earlier— 1840-1842—the Harveys had been "Kansas" residents while in charge of Shawnee Friends Mission—see pp. 412, 444.)

On April 21 Matilda Smith (a Shawnee Friends Mission teacher) wrote in her diary: "Henry Harvey and wife, 3 sons and daughter and Lindsay Cook and wife were here to meeting. . . . After dinner George Harvey [Henry's eldest son], Joseph Parks [Shawnee chief] and another man came . . . the Harveys went to J. Parks and stayed all night. They were on their way to the Osage Indians."

Henry Harvey was Osage subagent till mid-1851, when, in the Indian department reorganization, Neosho Agency was created, and Osage Subagency discontinued. In December, 1850, his accounts included an item: "Building a house for subagent . . . $800." (See p. 536, for previous subagency residence.)

Ref: 32d Cong., 1st Sess., *H. Ex. Doc. No. 103* (Serial 647), pp. 357, 429, 704, 706; *Shawnee Indians in Kansas* (Kansas City, Kan., n. d.)—a 32-page booklet (copy in KHi) in which are some extracts from Matilda Smith's diary 1849-1850; *KHC*, v. 13, p. 348; OIA, Letters Received from Osage Subagency (National Archives, Microcopy 234, Roll 633) has Henry Harvey letters of August 25, 1850, and May 5, 1851, from Osage Subagency. By 1855 the Henry Harveys were again in Kansas—early territorial settlers on Dragoon creek in Wabaunsee county. In 1855, also, Mr. Harvey's *History of the Shawnee Indians, 1681-1854* was published (in Ohio). Mrs. Ann Harvey died July 8, 1859, near Wilmington, Kan.—See Topeka *Tribune*, July 21, 1859. Caleb E. Harvey (second son of Henry and Ann) married a Shawnee widow—Mrs. Sally Bobb—about 1850—see "Census of . . . Shawnees" [1857], in KHi archives div. Henry Harvey returned to Ohio after his wife's death.

❡ April 23.—At Weston, Mo., emigrant C. W. Smith wrote: "The ferry boats here are very poor and make slow passages. Common flat boats are used, propelled with oars; they have to tow them up the shore a quarter of a mile before crossing, to prevent landing below their mark on the other side. They carry about two wagons each time, beside several head of cattle or horses. We are now to cross."

On May 14 the company with which John A. Stauder traveled, arrived at Weston, and "camped ¾ of a mile above town." "Weston [wrote Stauder] is a beautiful place fine buildings 1400 inhabitants a good wharf on the Missouri river." But his party "crossed the Missouri River 4 miles above Weston . . . [on May 15 and 16]."

Ref: Smith, *op. cit.*, p. 17; John A. Stauder's "Memorandum of Travels . . ." ("typescript," in Western Historical Manuscripts Collection, University of Missouri, Columbia).

❡ April 23-26.—At St. Joseph, Mo., on the 23d, "Ralph Ringwood" wrote to the New York *Tribune:* "The Californians still continue to pour into this place in one constant stream. . . . A few days since I crossed the Missouri to visit them at their encampments [in "Kansas"]. I found it impossible to make out a list of the companies. . . . From the river bank out to the bluff, a distance of some five miles, their camps are strung all along." (About 6,000 emigrants, by estimate, were in the St. Joseph vicinity around April 25—as reported at St. Louis on the 28th by officers of the *Kansas.*)

"Ringwood's" letter included these comments: "As near as it can be computed there are now 1,000 wagons between this point and Grand Island [Fort Kearny]. Most of them carry with them corn sufficient to feed their cattle on for three weeks. Over 5,000 persons have already rendezvoused at this point alone. One of our papers sets it down at 8,000.—There are now at Council Bluffs over 1,000[?], and at Independence between 2,000 and 3,000, to say nothing of the various other points of departure on the frontier of lesser note. . . . Among those now here are a few from the western part of New York. The Eastern emigration overland is small in comparison with that from the Western States. . . ." [The St. Louis *Reveille* of March 15, in a paragraph headed "California Fever," had observed: "All the papers of Missouri, Iowa, Wisconsin, Illinois, Indiana and Ohio come to us filled with accounts of preparations by companies, in all the towns and counties, for California. Double the emigration of last season is a moderate estimate of that likely to go this spring and summer."]

The St. Joseph *Gazette* of April 26 stated: "From the best estimate we have been able to make, 15,000 emigrants have made this place a point of departure for California . . ."; and "about 3,000 teams are reported to be at Council Bluffs." "It is estimated that at least 15,000 will leave this state [Missouri] alone and we think the balance of the states will swell the number to 50,000."

Ref: New York *Weekly Tribune,* May 25, 1850; St. Joseph *Gazette,* April 26, 1850; *The Daily Reveille,* St. Louis, March 15, 1850; *Missouri Republican,* St. Louis, April 29, 1850.

❧ April 27.—"Steamboats are coming into St. Joseph, three and four a day, each with three hundred or four hundred passengers California bound. The lower deck is filled as closely as they can stow them with horses and mules, and the upper decks with wagons and men. Some are playing cards, some fiddling, some drinking, others dying, all at the same time and on the same boat. The streets of St. Joseph are so thronged with men and animals that you cannot tell which way the mass is moving."—Emigrant Gershom B. Day, in a letter.

The St. Joseph *Adventure's* "Marine List" for the April 26-May 2 period was as follows:

	Arrived	From	Departed	For
April 26	El Paso	St. Louis	Monroe	St. Louis
	Minnesota	St. Louis		
April 27	Pocahontas	St. Louis	Minnesota	St. Louis
			El Paso	St. Louis
April 28	Highland Mary	St. Louis	Pocahontas	St. Louis
April 29			Highland Mary	St. Louis
April 30	Julia	St. Louis		
	Tuscumbia	St. Louis		
May 1	Pride of the West	St. Louis	Tuscumbia	Council Bluffs
	Bay State	St. Louis	Julia	St. Louis
May 2			Pride of the West,	St. Louis
			Bay State	St. Louis

Ref: M. E. D. Trowbridge, *Pioneer Days, the Life-Story of Gershom B. and Elizabeth Day* (Philadelphia, c1895), p. 96; *Adventure*, St. Joseph, May 3, 1850. The book on the Days links Gershom B. Day to the 1849 emigration, but there is ample evidence he crossed the plains in 1850, not 1849. The St. Joseph (Mo.) *Gazette* of April 19, 1850, noted the arrival of the Rev. G. B. Day, and four other men, from Michigan; the May 3 issue reported the departure of the Michigan company "of which Rev. G. B. Day is a member" for Old Fort Kearny on April 29; and the July 10 issue printed Day's May 27, 1850, letter from Fort Laramie.

❮ April 29.—An express from Fort Kearny (left on the 22d) arrived at St. Joseph, Mo., bringing word from Bvt. Maj. R. H. Chilton that supplies at Forts Kearny and Laramie were insufficient for the troops, and therefore not available to emigrants.

The detachment reported there was no grass when they left Fort Kearny; yet the first emigrants had passed the post in mid-April; and they met a great number on the road.

Ref: *Missouri Republican*, St. Louis, May 10, 1850 (from St. Joseph *Adventure*, May 3, 1850); St. Joseph *Gazette* extra, April 29, 1850.

❮ MARRIED: the Rev. Nathan Scarritt (principal of Western Academy, the high school at Shawnee Methodist Mission—*see* p. 776) and Matilda M. Chick (daughter of William M. Chick, deceased, and Ann Eliza Chick), on April 29, by the Rev. Thomas Johnson.

Ref: Jackson county, Mo., "Marriage Book" No. 3, p. 12. Whether this was a "Kansas" marriage, or a Kansas (City), Mo., one, is not recorded. Matilda Scarritt's mother—Ann Eliza Chick—taught at the Indian manual labor school in 1851 and perhaps in 1850, also.

❮ April-May.—The St. Joseph *Gazette* of May 3 reported: "Since our last paper [April 26] went to press some 8,000 emigrants have arrived at this place—mostly emigrants from Missouri. . . . More than half . . . who have crossed . . . [here], are going across the plains with horse teams. This we presume, is owing to the scarcity of mules and oxen in Michigan, Iowa, Wisconsin, Illinois and Indiana, where a large majority of the emigrants are from." ("Ralph Ringwood," in his April 23 letter, had written:

"The larger portion of the emigration go this year with American horses. How the experiment will succeed is doubtful.") The *Gazette* commented: "The flood of California emigrants has run grain and provender up to a high price. Corn is selling from 75 to 80 cents per bushel and wheat from $1.10 to $1.12½. We recollect of seeing corn sell at 10 cents per bushel in St. Joseph, and very dull even at that price. Quite a change." (The St. Louis *Intelligencer* of April 20, stated: "It is estimated that at least 17,500 emigrants will leave Missouri for California this year.")

On May 6 "Ralph Ringwood" wrote (from St. Joseph): "The great rush of emigration appears now to be over; yet still they are pouring in by thousands. . . . During the two weeks last past there were more arrivals than in any preceding ones. . . . Just across the Missouri—almost within stone's throw of us—there is now in the midst of the ["Kansas"] wilderness the hum and bustle of a great city. Not less than 10,000 emigrants are encamped in the woods on the opposite bank. The poor Kickapoos and Pottawatomies [a band of that nation living with the Kickapoos] . . . gaze upon the crowd and their doings with wonderment. . . . Since this letter was commenced, several hundred emigrants who had got out as far as 300 miles (beyond Grand Island), have returned, and are now recrossing with their teams. They report that they saw the 'Elephant,'—head, tail and all—large enough to satisfy them. To-morrow their teams will be sold at auction [and they will return home]. . . ."

Ref: St. Joseph *Gazette*, May 3, 1850; New York *Weekly Tribune*, May 25, 1850; New York *Daily Tribune*, May 21, 1850; St. Louis *Intelligencer*, April 20, 1850.

¶ April-May—In mid-April a company of Arkansans (and some Cherokees), headed by "Maj." Elias Rector, of Fort Smith, and "Col." Matthew Leeper, of Fayetteville, started for California, traveling up to Fort Scott ("Kan."), and thence out to Council Grove (by the trail opened in 1849?—*see* pp. 831, 832).

Mark L. Evans wrote from "Pacific Springs" (Continental Divide) on June 26, that "Many of our company were sick with diarrhoea on the Platte. I escaped. . . . Leeper, Ledford, Rector and Spring are behind us. Dr. Dean is with us, in good health. . . . Rollin and Eneas Ridge [Cherokees], Auchey Smith, Jack Stricklin, Jim Yoes and mess, also Moses Stout, are behind intending to pack. All well when we left them. . . ." Evans also stated: "The express mails from Salt Lake and the States [the Mormons' express; and the Estill & Co. express] that have just met here say the number of wagons ahead of us is 5,000, and are throwing away their wagons and are packing. I never have seen before in no place, such destruction of property. The most

I see is wagons, carriages, harness, axes, cooking stoves, mining tools, log chains, and horse shoes, and everything that is not essentially necessary. . . ."

Ref: Grant Foreman's *Marcy & the Gold Seekers* (1939), pp. 111-113.

❦ May 1-7.—"On the first day of May ice to the thickness of an inch formed in the Missouri, and in the vicinity of Council Bluffs boats experienced considerable difficulty in navigating, owing to the large masses of it floating in the river."—"Ralph Ringwood's" May 6 letter, from St. Joseph, Mo.

On May 7 Eleazar S. Ingalls (camped on the Missouri river bluffs in "Kansas" about six miles west of St. Joseph) wrote: "Had a bad night last night; it rained and snowed nearly all night. Had about two inches of snow on the ground this morning." (But the sky cleared; Ingalls' party made a start, and traveled 20 miles.)

Ref: New York *Daily Tribune*, May 21, 1850; Eleazar S. Ingalls, *Journal of a Trip to California in 1850-51* (Waukegan, 1852).

❦ May 3-9.—Steamboats arriving and departing St. Joseph, Mo., in this period (as listed in the *Adventure*) were:

	Arrived	From	Departed	For
May 3	Melodeon	Council Bluffs	Melodeon	St. Louis
	Tuscumbia	"Table Creek" (Old Fort Kearny)	Saranak	Council Bluffs
	Saranak	St. Louis		
May 4	Andrew Jackson	St. Louis	Tuscumbia	Council Bluffs
	Princeton	St. Louis		
	St. Ange	St. Louis		
May 5	Cora	Council Bluffs	Andrew Jackson	St. Louis
			Princeton	St. Louis
May 6	Anna	St. Louis	Cora	St. Louis
	Saluda	St. Louis	Anna	St. Louis
	Alton	St. Louis	St. Ange	St. Louis
	Robert Campbell	St. Louis		
May 7	Lightfoot	St. Louis	Alton	St. Louis
			Saluda	Council Bluffs
			Robert Campbell	Council Bluffs
May 8			Lightfoot	Council Bluffs
May 9	St. Paul	St. Louis		

The *Cora* (see May 5 above) had left Kanesville (Council Bluffs), Ia., on May 4. Her officers reported that the weather there had been disagreeable, with no signs of early vegetation; and that provisions were very high—corn selling at $2.00 a bushel.

On May 8, the *Sligo No. 2*, carrying a large number of California-bound emigrants "whom she had brought from Nashville, Tenn.," reached Kansas, Mo.—the debarking point for her passengers. Among the Tennesseans was Madison B. Moorman, who, in his journal, recorded their arrival at "Kansas, a new and seemingly growing little town." (By May 12 he had decided it was "New and flourishing.")

Ref: *The Daily Reveille*, St. Louis, May 2, 1850; Irene D. Paden, ed., *The Journal of Madison Berryman Moorman* . . . (San Francisco, 1948), pp. 1-7; *Adventure*, St. Joseph, May 10, 1850; St. Louis *Intelligencer*, May 11, 1850.

❦ On May 4 or 5 a company of First U. S. dragoons (picked up at Jefferson Barracks, Mo.; assigned destination, Fort Hall "Idaho") arrived at Fort Leavenworth aboard the *Anna*.

Ref: *Utah Historical Quarterly*, Salt Lake City, v. 20 (January, 1952), p. 34. Emigrant Robert Chalmers, a passenger on the *Anna* this trip, debarked at Wayne City (landing for Independence, Mo.) on May 4.

❦ May.—Emigrants westbound on the St. Joseph branch of the Oregon-California trail who kept diaries, or wrote letters, usually mentioned Wolf creek crossing, the Iowa, Sac & Fox Presbyterian Mission, or the Great Nemaha Subagency—all in Doniphan county of today (*see* April 7 entry). These were the comments of some travelers in 1850:

Thomas Woodward (May 5)—"Traveled over Dry Ridges To Wolf River which we crossed . . . Below the Sac & Fox village. The Indians has Built here a Rude log Bridge otherwise it would Be nearly impossible to cross They charged 50 cent . . . [three miles to a brook; and three miles more] To the Mission There was a good many Lazy Indians Lounging about here We Registered our names. . . . The Mission seems To be in a T[h]riving Condition. . . ." (Emigrant Francis White, who crossed the Wolf creek bridge early in May, 1852, recorded the toll as 50 cents per wagon.)

John Warnock (May 6)—"at Wolf creek is a log toll bridge built by the indians where they charge 25¢ for each wagon that crosses. The Keeper of the bridge says 1400 wagons had passed before us." (On May 7 Warnock "passed Iowa Mission.")

Lorenzo Sawyer (May 8)—"This morning we crossed Wolf creek 2 miles from our camp, on a toll bridge owned by the Indians. Several long trains were ahead of us, and the road as far as we could see, was lined with wagons on the march. Several trains came in on the Savannah road [the Missouri crossing point was near present Amazonia, Mo.] just as we passed the junction of the roads. . . . We saw a few log houses and some cultivated fields at the Mission this morning, the first seen since we left St. Joseph. . . . The bridge tender at the Missouri [*i. e.*, at the Mission?] said 1400 teams had crossed the bridge. The Savannah road comes in this side of the bridge, and several hundred teams must have come in by that road, so there cannot be less than 2000 wagons ahead of us on this road."

Joseph Price (May 10)—"came to wolf creek it is a small Stream 12 feet or 14 feet wide very deep and swift current with a tall Bridge blonging to the Iowa indians 25 cts for a wagon and team we then travled 6 miles and came to the Iowa mishion or agency it is a beautiful place there is a large Farm in a high state of cultivation established by the georvnament for the purpose of learning the Red men of the west to cultivate the Soil there

there is al so a School or mishionary establishment for teaching the children of those wild Sons of Adam."

N. A. Cagwin (May 11)—"In passing Wolf creek yesterday the banks of which are verry steep. We paid 2/-per wagon for the privilege of crossing on an old log bridge. . . . Here we saw some fine looking Indians remnants of Iowas, Sock and Fox tribes. . . . Five miles from Wolf creek is located the Indian Mission and a beautiful Site it is. Farm well fenced, houses cumfortable and neat, a good mill & etc. The land here is verry fertile and gently rolling."

"Old Boone" (May 19)—(From "Sac and Fox Territory, 57 miles from St. Joseph") "At the ferry at St. Jo. the Kickapoos demanded a toll of 10 cts per wagon, for crossing their territory, and at Wolf creek we had another 25 cts. to pay for crossing a bridge."

Dr. David S. Maynard (May 19)—"Traveled about 18 miles. Passed one grave. An Indian farm about four miles west of the toll bridge kept by the Sac and Fox Indians. Toll, 25 cents. Passed one of the most beautiful pictures of country I ever saw."

James Bennett (May 23)—"We arrived at Indian Agency to-day at 11 o'clock. Several white men were settled here with excellent farms under a high state of cultivation. The wheat, which was about knee deep, was the finest looking crop of the kind I have ever seen. I noticed several squaws very neatly dressed in the costume of the whites, sitting at work in the houses, while quite a number of Indian men, in their native dresses, were busily engaged in trading at a store."

Ref: *Wisconsin Magazine of History*, Madison, v. 17 (March, 1934), p. 348 (for Woodward); St. Joseph *Gazette*, April 10, 1932 (for data from Francis B. White's 1852 diary—original still privately owned?); John Warnock's letter of May 22, 1850, is in Western Historical Manuscripts Collection, University of Missouri, Columbia; Sawyer, *op. cit.*, pp. 20, 22; *Mississippi Valley Historical Review*, Cedar Rapids, Ia., v. 11 (September, 1924), pp. 246, 247 (for Joseph Price); N. A. Cagwin's "Diary" (*loc. cit.*); *Weekly Missouri Statesman*, Columbia, Mo., June 10, 1850 (for "Old Boone"); T. W. Prosch, *David S. Maynard and Catherine T. Maynard . . .* (Seattle, Wash., 1906), p. 8; Bennett, *op. cit.*, p. 12.

❑ May.—Below, are some descriptions of the Big Blue crossing (present Marysville area) on the St. Joseph branch of the Oregon-California trail, the country westward, and the travel situation, as recorded by emigrants of 1850:

A. H. Thomasson (May 4)—"came to big bliew this Stream is as prity a streem as I ever saw plenty timber butiful ford we traveled 1½ miles left the road on our left ¼ mile and camped here we found grass little better wood very scarce saw 3 dead horses 2 graves on each side of the big *bliew* very rocky the first rock we came to since we left St Joseph we orgenised to knight we have 39 men in our company at present our teemes consist of horses & mules. . . ." (Traveling, on the next three days, Thomasson noted that he saw three graves on the 5th, seven on the 6th, and three on the 7th— on which evening they camped on the Little Blue.)

William J. Cook (May 8)—"started early in the morning, travelled about 10 mi. to a stream . . . called Big Blue River; crossed the same without

any difficulty; travelled about 15 mi. further and encamped. . . . May 9th
. . . travelled about 15 mi., crossed an ugly little stream with a grave on
the east bluff, and two on the west. . . . [moved on five or six miles to
camp]." Cook wrote of the encampment: "in appearance a boundless prairie
and a remarkable sight of wagons and teams. I think they may be seen five
miles each way and the thickest places resemble little towns with white houses."

Lorenzo Sawyer (May 11)—"About eighteen miles brought us to the crossing
of the Big Blue river, a fine stream and fordable. Wood is plenty along its
banks. The country east of the river is beautiful prairie, gently undulating and
having a rich soil. On the west it is high rolling prairie. We took on wood
and water at the ford, and drove seven or eight miles and encamped. . . ."

Eleazar S. Ingalls (May 12—Sunday)—[Made 30 miles and reached Blue
river.] "Here we found a large city of tents, and preaching. There were probably 2000 men camped within two miles of the crossing; and here we found
wagons broken down last year, with irons of those burnt. . . . we found
some last year's graves, besides the usual amount of dead horses. . . .
Blue River, or as it is commonly called, the Big Blue, is a beautiful clear stream,
about eight rods wide, and at this time about three feet deep. . . . It has
a skirt of timber, mostly cotton wood, from 8 to 100 rods wide along its west
bank, and generally plenty of grass may be found. Sometimes however the
emigrant is detained here for two or three weeks by the high water, when his
only consolation is in hunting antelope and wild turkies, of which game there
is an abundant supply on this river, and in fishing."

N. A. Cagwin (May 14)—"We are now in the midst of Extensive ox trains
. . . we pressed on hoping by & by to get in advance of them all . . .
finally brought up for the night on the farther banks of the Big Blue River
[after a 27-mile day's trip] fording good." On the 15th Cagwin wrote: "The
scenery around and as you approach the Big Blue is highly pictoresque &
romantic. High bluffs   deep bottoms   extensive views of divide rising on
divide. . . . The blue is a clear rapid stream 125 feet wide   pebly bottom.
Face of the country quite rolling. Road dry and very dusty. Met two teams
on the retrigade track." On the 16th Cagwin wrote: "What a beautiful country. Like the long peaceful swell of an Old Ocean at rest. The soil being a
kind of blackish muck, is rich in the extreme as plainly indicative in the
luxuriance of the grass and other species of vegetation now   . . . shooting
up to maturity. . . . Game of all kinds seem quite abundant. Prairie
Hens and plover. The wolf and the badger, the Antelope, Elk and deer,
living streams of water are only to be met with, at long intervals. . . .
Passed by six graves today, but two of which were of this years emigration. . . ."

Joseph Price (May 16)—"travled 22 miles and camped on the east side of
the big Blue   it is a beautiful Stream a bout 40 yards wide and near three
feet deep   the crossing at this time is good   the water is clear with a bold
current." (On the 17th Price wrote: "cross the Big blue without any Difficulty
and as we arose the high Roaling Prairie on the west side the most beautifull
scenery the most pleasing land scape that I have ever seen. . . .")

W. R. R. (May 21)—From "Little Blue": "We left St. Joseph on the 9th.
. . . Even at this time the grass is quite short. . . . The Californians
generally, are in high spirits and good health. . . . Between the Big Blue

— 924 —

River and this place we have passed four 'newly made graves'—one of R. Melone of Huntsville, who accidentally shot himself through the head. . . . The crowd upon this route is perfectly astonishing. In travelling hours the wagons block the road as far as eye can see. It is impossible to camp within any short distance of the road without being surrounded with trains. . . . Last Friday [May 17] we passed the junction of the Independence and St. Joseph routes. The former from appearance has not been much travelled yet: And from gentlemen who came that way, I learn that over two-thirds of the emigrants from that point are yet behind. . . . We meet more or less returning Californians every day. . . . Nearly one half of the emigration upon the St. Jo route have horse teams. [W. R. R.'s company apparently had oxen]. . . ."

Dr. David S. Maynard (May 24)—"Camped at Blue river. One grave, child 11 years old. Forded the stream. Raised our loading. Got my medicines wet. Boys caught a meal of catfish. Fish were large and plenty, and included enough for tomorrow's breakfast."

James Bennett (May 28)—"Arrived at Big Blue river at 10 o'clock a. m. This stream favorable at all ordinary times, we now found very much swollen. About fifty wagons were already collected on the bank and several companies were occupied in crossing on rudely constructed rafts. We . . . drove on to a point a mile above and commenced constructing a couple of canoes. . . . There was a train of five wagons at this crossing, who had nearly completed a raft and proposed to us to join them in ferrying on it, which we agreed to do and abandoned the building of but one canoe." [They got the five wagons across on the 28th.] On the 29th: "When we launched our canoe this morning we found it capable of carrying a thousand pounds with perfect safety, although the stream was very rapid and apparently dangerous for so small a craft. We commenced placing our provisions and clothing in the canoe, while the empty wagons were crossed on the raft by means of ropes attached to each end of it and to the banks. [Except for a minor accident, all 14 wagons, and contents, were ferried across safely.] . . . after moving up the stream half a mile to the prairie we encamped." (George Keller, whose party forded the Big Blue on April 14, 1850, wrote: "Later in the season . . . this stream is swollen very much, and may detain a company several days, either in waiting for it 'to fall,' or in ferrying it.")

Calvin Taylor (May 31)—Made arrangements to cross "by means of a raft of logs to the centre of which is attached a stout rope, the other made fast to a tree on shore some distance above. To each side of the raft is attached smaller ropes by which the raft is drawn back and forth."

Ref: A. H. Thomasson's "Diary" (*loc. cit.*); Unionville (Mo.) *Republican and Putnam County Journal*, July 17, 1935 (for W. J. Cook); Sawyer, *op. cit.*, p. 25; Ingalls, *op. cit.*; N. A. Cagwin's "Diary" (*loc. cit*); *Mississippi Valley Historical Review*, v. 11 (September, 1924), p. 247 (for Price); *Weekly Missouri Statesman*, Columbia, June 14, 1850; T. W. Prosch, *op. cit.*, p. 9 (for Maynard); James Bennett, *op. cit.*, p. 13; Keller, *op. cit.*; *Nebraska History*, v. 50 (Summer, 1969), p. 129 (for Taylor).

⟪ May.—Several of the year's California-bound commercial passenger trains *originating at St. Louis* started their overland journeys either from St. Joseph or Weston, Mo., this month.

(1) McPIKE & STROTHER. John M. McPike and E. J. Strother, of Ashley, Pike county, Mo., had advertised in January, to start from St. Joseph, about April 25, a passenger train of 20 hacks (four mules to each, with extra mules and horses); passage $200; 50 pounds of baggage allowed; each passenger to provide his own arms and ammunition; proprietors to furnish provisions and cooking utensils. On May 3 the St. Joseph *Gazette* gave considerable space to the "Train of McPike & Strother," listing the officers (Dr. R. B. Ellis, St. Louis, captain; John W. Priest, Marion county, Ind., lieutenant; Dr. R. L. Ward, of Indiana, commissary; Dr. John L. Taylor, Palmyra, Mo., secretary), and the names of over 100 company members (Pike county, Mo., and Marion county, Ind., were well represented; but persons from Kentucky, Iowa, Ohio, Michigan, Indiana, Tennessee, Wisconsin, Illinois, Pennsylvania, and Ireland were on the roster). By May 11 McPike & Strother's train was west of the Big Blue. On May 27th E. S. Ingalls (who crossed the Platte's South Fork this day) heard that "McPike & Strother's train lost 25 mules and horses in a stampede last night." From Sacramento City on September 22, "C." wrote that "McPike & Strother left most of their wagons on the desert."

(2) JEROME, HANSON & SMITH. In March this company had advertised that their "Mississippi and Pacific Line" of spring wagons would leave from St. Joseph at the earliest practicable April date. On May 10 "Jerome and Hanson's" train was camped on the bluffs (in "Kansas"), opposite St. Joseph. Listing over 120 passengers (including, near the end of the roster, William C. Smith, Mrs. Smith, James H. Hanson, and M. Jerome), the St. Louis *Missouri Republican* of May 18 stated that "Messrs. Jerome, Hanson & Smith's train," on the 14th[?], had "struck out in earnest for Sacramento City." Later, a traveler from Fort Kearny reported at St. Louis that "Jerome and Hanson's train" had passed that post on May 17[?]. "C." wrote from Sacramento on September 22 that "Jerome, Hanson and Smith, left most of their wagons and packed."

(3) WILES & BENNETT (or, Wild? & Bennett). The *St. Paul*, which left St. Louis May 2 (and reached St. Joseph on the 9th) carried 300 California-bound emigrants and 500 tons of freight—including "Wiles & Bennet's California train" (12 wagons and 40 persons) "with their 'entire fixens'." Emigrant "C." (who reached Fort Kearny May 31) wrote that "Wild's & Bennett's train from St. Louis" had passed that post. On June 23, when "C." was west of Fort Laramie, he wrote: "When we were at Fort Laramie, Hall's train [*see* following], Smith, Jerome & Hanson, and Chadwick, Laveille & Co. [a train starting from Council Bluffs] had passed. Wilds & Bennett are either behind or they failed to report themselves [*i. e.*, had not registered at the army post]." From Sacramento, on September 22, "C." wrote: "Wiles and Bennett succeeded in crossing the desert with their wagons and got a part over the mountains."

(4) ALEXANDER & HALL. "Capt. Hall," St. Louis, and G. C. Alexander, Edwardsville, Ill., advertised in March to "start a line of light spring wagons" from St. Joseph "at earliest possible day" (after leaving St. Louis about April 20); fare $200; passengers to furnish part of their outfit. (Both Hall and Alexander had crossed the Plains in 1849.) On May 10 "Hall's train" was said to be camped at Weston, Mo. (Alexander, due to his wife's illness,

did not make the trip.) At the beginning of June, Alexander & Hall's train was on the Little Blue. On the 5th, the first of several deaths occurred. Captain Hall wrote from Chimney Rock on June 13 that four passengers had died of cholera (two young Allen brothers, and a Mr. Walker, all of Benton county, Mo., and Mr. Hill of Jackson county, Mo.), and Mr. Blum, with smallpox, had been left at Fort Kearny. Hall stated that the ladies of the party (Mrs. Hunter, Miss Rice, and Miss Hall) were in excellent health; and that the train was getting on very well. "C's" September 22 letter, from Sacramento, stated: "Hall's train arrived here with 16 wagons and ⅔ds of his animals."

Ref: For McPike and Strother: *Missouri Statesman*, Columbia, January 18, 1850; St. Joseph *Gazette*, May 3, 1850; Sawyer, *op. cit.*, pp. 22, 25; Ingalls, *op. cit.*; *Mississippi Valley Historical Review*, v. 11 (September, 1924), p. 254; *Missouri Historical Review*, Columbia, v. 25 (October, 1929), pp. 135-137 (for the curious "History of Joe Bowers"). For Smith, Jerome & Hanson: *Missouri Republican*, St. Louis, March 6, May 15, 18, August 7, 1850; St. Louis *Intelligencer*, June 14, 1850; St. Joseph *Gazette*, July 31, 1850. For Wiles & Bennett: *The Daily Reveille*, St. Louis, May 2, August 20, 1850; *Missouri Republican*, St. Louis, July 16, August 7, 1850. For Alexander & Hall: *The Daily Reveille*, St. Louis, March 23, 1850; *Missouri Republican*, St. Louis, March 6, 28, April 9, May 15, July 16, 30, August 7, 1850; St. Louis *Intelligencer*, June 14, 1850; St. Joseph *Gazette*, July 31, 1850. For "C.'s" letter, September 22, from Sacramento, Calif., see *Missouri Republican*, St. Louis, November 18, 1850.

❡ May 7.—"From Independence to this point [St. Joseph] the country is full of emigrants for California," wrote "B." (in a letter), "and here every nook and corner is crowded. Hundreds have left every starting point, anxious to be on their 'winding way,' though the grass is scarcely above the ground. Vehicles of almost every size and shape, from a wheelbarrow to an old hackney coach, have been put in requisition, with animals from the diminutive Indian poney, with a pack-saddle, to the spirited gelding. . . . The number of emigrants are variously estimated at from 20 to 40,000." ("B." thought 20,000 "higher than the reality.")

On May 3 the St. Joseph *Gazette* had stated: "From the best information we can obtain there are about 1500 emigrants at Independence, 1000 at Kansas, 3 or 400 at Weston and about 10,000 at Council Bluffs. Up to the present time, some 20,000 emigrants have arrived at this place by land and water and they still continue to arrive in large numbers." (The St. Joseph *Adventure* of May 3 asserted: "The whole number of emigrants that have reached the Missouri river at St. Joseph and the [Council] Bluffs and intermediate points may be safely set down at thirty-two thousand.")

On May 6 "Ralph Ringwood" (at St. Joseph) had written: "As yet no accurate estimate can be formed of the number of the overland emigration of the present season. It is thought that up to this date 2000 have rendezvoused at Independence, 1,000 at Kansas, 1,000 at Weston, 10,000 at Council Bluffs, and from 15,000 to 20,000 at this point. The total number to reach the Missouri at the points above named and other intermediate ones, will not fall short of 50,000. How many more yet remain behind?"

Ref: St. Louis *Intelligencer*, May 13, 1850; St. Joseph *Gazette*, May 3, 1850; *Adventure*,

St. Joseph, May 3, 1850; New York *Daily Tribune*, May 21, 1850. One "wheel barrow man" arrived at Fort Laramie on May 14 in good shape. He had left St. Joseph about 25 days earlier, it was said.—*Missouri Republican*, St. Louis, June 9, 1850.

❮ May 8.—"50 or 60 Cal[ifornia] wagons pass us," wrote Jotham Meeker at Ottawa Baptist Mission (some three miles east of present Ottawa, Franklin co.). As appears below, these were probably Missourians, following a route used (for the first time?) in 1849, which entered "Kansas," at, or near, present Louisburg, Miami co. This branch trail (the Harrisonville, Mo.-to-Council Grove route) lay "almost entirely on the ridge between the tributaries of the Kansas and Osage [Marais des Cygnes—in Kansas] rivers." In mid-May a military party, eastbound from Santa Fe, "met a large number of emigrants near Council Grove [quite possibly the train, or trains, noted by Meeker]. There was little or no grass on the Plains, which caused much distress among the emigrants, as most of their animals had given out for want of food."

The Boonville (Mo.) *Democrat*, in an early November(?) issue, stated that *in 1849* two companies of Cooper county, Mo., emigrants had taken a route by way of Georgetown, Warrensburg, and Harrisonville, Mo. "and from thence intersecting the main California [*i. e.*, Santa Fe] trail at or near Council Grove. Capt. Benj. McCullock's company took this route last spring [1849?], and were the second company to arrive at the mines—the other companies following close behind him. . . ." After reaching Council Grove, presumably the emigrants proceeded towards California by a route up the Arkansas past Bent's Fort (*see* pp. 854, 856, 857).

Ref: Jotham Meeker's "Diary" (in KHi); New York *Daily Tribune*, May 25, 1850; *Jefferson Inquirer*, Jefferson City, November 9(?), 1850 (for the Boonville *Democrat* information). The St. Joseph *Gazette* of April 12, 1850, carried an advertisement by one Meriwether Lewis, who offered his services as a guide to emigrants, stating he had "made the trip to the Gold mines last season, in Capt. Robert M'Cullock's company, (which was the second company to arrive in the mines). . . ." Were **Benjamin, and Robert,** McCullock co-leaders of a company?

❮ May.—A band of Pawnees, intent on stock-stealing, came down into the Pottawatomies' country, took some horses, and lost a few men in skirmishes with their enemies.

On May 8 emigrant James Mason wrote: "Passed Uniontowns. . . . Crossed Caw river & encamped 3 miles back got word that the Pottawatomes & the Pawnees was a ware some 16 miles. . . ." Next day Mason and party "passed the Catholic mishon [St. Mary's]. . . . Saw a lot of Indian warriors & the arrow that Kiled the Pawnees Saw them [the Pottawatomies] dance round the Scalp Saw a hand cut off. . . ."

On May 12 (according to the statement of "Dr. Garver, of Ohio") Pawnees raided a small California-bound emigrant train (in the Black Vermillion valley, apparently) of "some 30 or 40 head of horses and mules." "Wa-wa-sah" (a young Pottawatomie chief) proposed to pursue the Pawnees and rescue the stock for the whites. In a skirmish with the marauders two days later, the

Pottawatomies were victorious. "Wa-wa-sah . . . himself shot the Pawnee leader" (on whose person were found four white and nine Indian scalps, which "seemed to have been but recently taken"); and a number of the horses were recovered, "with their lariats and picket-pins."

Presumably referring to the above incident, a man wrote from "Union Post, Upper Crossing of Kansas River," on June 5: ". . . Three weeks ago some Pottawatomie horses were stolen immediately west of Catholic Mission, 12 miles from here, by Pawnees. The Pottawatomies pursued the thieves, killed 3 and brought in the scalps and recovered the horses. Since then several false alarms . . . [of Pawnees]. Parties of armed Pottawatomies, Sacs, and Foxes went out to scour the country and give them battle. They proceeded some sixty or seventy miles west of this, and returned reporting no Pawnees. . . . The Pottawatomies and their allies, the Sacs and Foxes, are on the alert. If the Pawnees should come down, they will meet with a warm reception!"

South of the Kansas river (in present Douglas? county), on May 13, emigrant Robert Chalmers "Met several Indians of the Caw [Kansa] tribe all armed. They had been at war with the Pawnees and were returning. Their heads were all shaved, but a small spot on the crown. It was braided and tied up. Their heads were painted red. They were large men, 6 feet and heavily built in proportion. . . . The weapons they used were a tomahawk, knife, spear seven or eight feet long, bow and arrow. They had taken three white scalps[?] which had belonged to two men and a boy."

See, also, May 30 annals entry.

Ref: *Nebraska History,* Lincoln, v. 33 (June, 1952), pp. 107, 108 (for James Mason); *Missouri Republican,* St. Louis, June 4 (for Garver), 16 (for "Union Post" letter), 1850; *Utah Historical Quarterly,* v. 20 (January, 1952), p. 36 (for Chalmers). See KHC, v. 14, p. 545, for a statement that "Kack-kack," chief of the Prairie band of Pottawatomies, who died in 1907, was "a famous warrior. . . . He planned the ambush by which the Pottawatomies defeated the Pawnees soon after the founding of the Catholic Mission at St. Marys. He killed some of the Pawnees. The scalps he had taken in all his fighting . . . were retained by him as long as he lived." See KHC, v. 17, pp. 457, 458, for other statements on the Pottawatomie-Pawnee skirmishes of 1850.

❧ May 9.—From "Grasshopper Creek," 50 miles out (from Weston, Mo., apparently), probably in Atchison county of today, "Dr. Mc-Adow" wrote to the Weston *Reporter* that cholera, "in its most malignant form," had broken out in the train of "Dr. Clark." Dead was C. H. Moore, of Milford, Ill.; two others were not expected to live; and one stricken man was recovering.

On the St. Joseph branch, Oregon-California trail, there were reports, later in May, of cholera deaths. As examples: John Herlinger, aged 36, of Ralls county, Mo., who died May 17 "on a branch of Wolf river," probably was a cholera victim. His grave, and several others—in the Big Blue vicinity—were noted by an emigrant. John A. Stauder, of La Grange, Mo., whose company camped east of the Big Blue ("Marysville") crossing on May 22, wrote that he was in sight of a camp where two men had died of cholera on the 21st (and where another succumbed on the night of the 22d). After fording the Big Blue, on May 23, Stauder saw, about a mile beyond, the graves of two brothers—John and Thomas Walker, from Illinois (dead of cholera?).

Beyond the confines of "Kansas"—out on the Platte—many emigrants of 1850 were carried off by cholera, or a malady with like symptoms. A traveler, writing June 9, from 110 miles west of Fort Kearny, stated: "That disease broke out about the same time in every train that was in Plum Creek Valley from the 1st to 7th June. . . . Up to this time I have counted forty graves, in sixty miles travel, and we have passed several trains where from one to six were sick, and probably two-thirds of them are dead ere this." "Cheyenne," in a July 1 letter from Fort Laramie, commented: "A man just from the frontier states he counted no less than 645 new graves along side the road." A week later "Cheyenne" concluded that 700 emigrants had died on the trail east of Fort Laramie. The toll may have been higher.

Ref: *The Daily Reveille*, St. Louis, June 1, 1850; St. Joseph *Gazette*, June 28, 1850; *Missouri Republican*, St. Louis, July 18, August 9, 1850; John A. Stauder's letter is in the Western Historical Manuscripts Collection, University of Missouri, Columbia.

❆ May.—This was the Kansas (Kaw) valley scene, in present Shawnee and Pottawatomie counties, as described by three Oregon-California trail travelers of 1850, each of whom ferried the river at a different crossing:

Joseph Rhodes' party ferried over, at the lower ("Topeka") crossing on May 3. Rhodes wrote: "Before we left the states we fell in company with 4 waggons from Cooper Co. Mo. We traveled on together to the Cansas river . . . where we fell in with 3 more waggons. We crossed over the river . . . went up the river one mile and camped. . . . On the 4th of May [the company now 30 men; eight wagons, and 30 yoke of oxen] we traveled 14 miles. . . . May 5th . . . 2 miles & crossed Cross Creek. A fiew miles further on we came to a saw and grist mill, 2 miles further we came to a French and Indian Town of about 100 houses, then on to where we camped."

Some five(?) miles upriver from the lower crossing was the Pottawatomie Baptist Mission—a little removed from the main trail. Madison B. Moorman's party, on May 20, "arrived at the 'Potawotamie Manual Labor School,' half a mile from the ferry of the Kanzas river. . . ." (Moorman noted that "Mr. Saunders"—the Rev. B. W. Sanders—was superintendent; that the site was "a most beautiful and healthy place"; that 54 pupils were in attendance—most of them "half breeds.") "An hour or two spent here [and] we moved on to the ferry, where we found an old boat upon which we made out to transport our wagons. The mules were swam over . . . we moved out a short distance and encamped for the night. . . ." On the 21st, after traveling eight or nine miles, this company of Tennesseeans came to "a creek with very steep and muddy banks [Cross creek] . . . exceedingly difficult of crossing, so much so that several hundred wagons had accumulated before we were off. In a distance of a few miles several other little creeks were passed over upon toll bridges. One belonged to some frenchmen, who had Indian wives.—They were well fixed, good farms and a sawmill. . . . [At one creek were two bridges, and two gaudily-dressed Indian youths; one asked five cents toll, the other ten.] About fifteen miles from the Baptist mission is one belonging to the Roman Catholics [St. Mary's] . . . [it] seems to be in quite a flourishing condition. A great many of the Potawotamies live around and have nice fields."

Nine miles above the Baptist mission was the upper (Union Town) crossing, where Dr. John F. Snyder's party ferried the Kansas the second week of May. Snyder wrote: "After leaving the Kansas ten miles, we arrived at the 'Pottawattamie Mission,' establ. here by the catholics [St. Mary's] . . . it is a very neat looking place, consisting of three, or four two story log houses belonging to the church, and about twenty small log huts. The indians here have large farms, and seem to be very industrious. Ten miles farther we camped at the 'Little [now Red] Vermillion.' I here found a Frenchman [apparently not Louis Vieux (or Jarveau) though he later resided at that location] with his family liveing in a small log house and was called in by him 'professionally' to see a sick child. . . . We met many Indians here in a tolerable state of civilization, being able to read & write. This nation (The Pottawattamies) number about 4000."

Ref: *Annals of Wyoming,* Cheyenne, v. 23 (January, 1951), p. 61 (for Rhodes); Paden, *op. cit.,* pp. 10-12; John F. Snyder's May 22, 1850, letter (photocopy in KHi); Joseph B. Thoburn, *A Standard History of Oklahoma* . . . (Chicago and New York, 1916), v. 5, p. 2168, in sketch of Jacob Johnson—who married Sophia Vieux (originally "*Jarveau*"), daughter of Louis Vieux, it is stated that Louis Vieux and family, moving to "Kansas" with the "Council Bluffs" Pottawatomies in 1847, settled at what became Indianola till 1857; *then* moved to the Vermillion, where Vieux kept a toll bridge. Louis Vieux (or, "Jarveau") was half French, half Pottawatomie; but so were a number of the Nation. Considering the ever-present threat of Pawnee raiders, the Little Vermillion was, in 1850, a frontier location for a Pottawatomie family.

❡ May.—Observations, and experiences of some emigrants in 1850, at Union Town (Pottawatomie trading post) and the upper Kansas crossing of the Oregon-California trail, were as follows:

Dr. John F. Snyder (May 8-10?)—"We then came into the 'Pottawattamie' nation, and passed through their trading post, called 'Uniontown,' at the crossing of the Kansas river This town consists of about fifty log houses, with a population of about 300, nearly all indians. The government has stationed at this post, a physician, two blacksmiths, a wagon maker, two gun smiths, and a circular saw mill. Crossing the Kansas, we encamped near the hut of a chief; who had the U. S. flag floating proudly over his miserable habitation. . . ."

Robert Chalmers (May 15)—"Went 12 miles, passed Union Town. A few Indian huts and two or three stores kept by traders were scattered along the way. Arrived at the ferry and camped, for there were so many wagons there that we could not get across till morning. We drove the cattle down to the river to drink and they all got mired. It proved quick sandy clay. . . . We unyoked them and drew them out with ropes." (On May 16 Chalmers' party: "Went 2 miles. Ferried our wagons and forded our cattle and laid up half a day to let our cattle recruit after their mire. . . ."

Cyrus C. Loveland (May 18)—"We . . . passed through a settlement called Union Village, situated on the Kaw or Kansas River one mile from Johnson's Ferry. Arrived there about noon. There we found twenty or thirty wagons to cross before we could. We grazed our cattle [some 721 head of loose cattle and 64 head of work steers] till near evening, then crossed, drove a few miles and camped." (Loveland was a cowboy in the party of cattle drover Walter Crow, who, accompanied by his four sons, and employees, was taking a large herd of Durhams to California.)

M. Littleton (June 2)—"now camped at Caw [Kansas river], which is about ¾ of a mile from a village called Union Village which is Situated on the Hill on a beautiful cite for a town There are about 25 or 30 Houses in it Dwellings Stores Bakerys Beer Shops etc. . . ."

(*See* May 14-20 entry for another Union Town item; and *see* pp. 795, 796, for some '49ers' comments on Union Town and the upper Kansas crossing.)

Ref: John F. Snyder's May 22, 1850, letter (photocopy in KHi); *Utah Historical Quarterly*, v. 20 (January, 1952), p. 37 (for Chalmers); Richard H. Dillon, ed., *California Trail Herd, The . . . Journal of Cyrus C. Loveland . . .* (Los Gatos, Calif., 1961), p. 58; M. Littleton's "Journal" (from typed copy, courtesy California State Library, Sacramento). W. W. Cone in his *Historical Sketch of Shawnee County, Kansas* (Topeka, 1877), p. 12, listed William Johnson as among the settlers in 1847, of Silver Lake township. Possibly he was the operator of "Johnson's Ferry," referred to by C. C. Loveland, above.

❡ May.—On the 9th, west of the Iowa, Sac & Fox Presbyterian Mission (present Doniphan county), emigrant Lorenzo Sawyer noted: "today we passed a large drove of cattle on their way to California." The St. Joseph *Adventure* of the 17th reported: "A drove of about eight hundred cows, destined for California, crossed the river at this place on Wednesday last [May 15]."

Perhaps it was the latter herd that diarist (and cowboy) Cyrus C. Loveland (of the Crow family cattle drive—*see* above) referred to in his May 24 entry: "we crossed Big Sandy [on the 23d they had forded the Big Blue at the "Independence" crossing—near Alcove Spring]. . . . While we were at the creek a Mr. Packwood came up with nine wagons and about 400 head of loose cattle. He told me he had lost sixty head and eight mares."

The Missouri river starting points of the herds mentioned below is not certain. Emigrant James Bennett, on June 26, west of Fort Laramie, wrote: "A train of forty wagons, Thompson's, stopped about a mile above us, late in the evening. They drove upwards of 200 head of loose cattle. Their herd of cattle in all numbered over 500." The mail from Salt Lake City (left September 11), brought to Independence, Mo. (on October 25), news that "Thompson's, and Brown's, and Waddle's lots of cattle, for California," had just started. At Lexington, Mo., on June 5, 1851, Robert Aull wrote to Siter, in New York, that "Bullard & Waddell will not be able to pay until they receive a remittance from California where they have taken [in 1850?] a large drove of oxen." On the 26th Aull wrote: "W. W. Waddell of Bullard & Waddell has heard from California I will endeaver to get your claim against them paid."

Ref: Sawyer, *op. cit.*, p. 23; *Adventure*, St. Joseph, May 17, 1850; Dillon, *op. cit.*, Bennett, *op. cit.*, p. 21; *Missouri Republican*, St. Louis, November 1, 1850; Missouri Historical Society, St. Louis, *Collections*, v. 5 (June, 1928), p. 310.

❡ May 10.—At St. Joseph, Mo., the *Adventure* reported: "great numbers [of emigrants] continue to arrive, the largest portion overland with their stock and wagons. They generally cross the river immediately and are ready to leave as soon as grass is sufficiently grown to support their teams. Many thousands have left during the past week, taking with them forage to feed their stock from ten to twenty days."

The *Adventure*, and *Gazette*, of May 10 concurred in projected estimates that the year's emigration would run from 25,000 to 30,000 at St. Joseph; from 10,000 to 15,000 at Missouri river points above; the over-all total perhaps 40,000.

On May 17 the *Adventure* stated: "California emigrants continue to arrive, overland with teams in great numbers. Those starting from St. Joseph may be set down at 30,000 persons, from points above, to Council Bluffs, about 10,000. The number of animals will average more than 2 to each person, say from 100,000 to 120,000 horses, mules and oxen, will be taken on the plains from the States this spring."

Ref: *Adventure*, St. Joseph, May 10, 17, 1850; St. Joseph *Gazette*, May 10, 1850.

❡ May 10-16.—At St. Joseph, Mo., according to the *Adventure's* "Marine List," these were the steamboat arrivals and departures:

	Arrived	From	Departed	For
May 10	J. L. McLean	St. Louis	St. Paul	St. Louis
	Mary Blane	St. Louis	J. L. McLean	Council Bluffs
May 11	Sacramento	St. Louis	Mary Blane	Council Bluffs
	Saranak	Council Bluffs		
May 12	Monroe	St. Louis	Sacramento	Council Bluffs
			Saranak	St. Louis
May 13	Julia	St. Louis	Monroe	St. Louis
	Saluda	Council Bluffs	Saluda	St. Louis
			Julia	St. Louis
May 14	Lightfoot	Council Bluffs	Lightfoot	St. Louis
	Robert Campbell	Council Bluffs	Robert Campbell,	St. Louis
	Highland Mary	Council Bluffs		
May 15			Highland Mary	St. Louis
May 16	J. L. McLean	Council Bluffs	J. L. McLean	St. Louis
	Tuscumbia	St. Louis		
	Pocahontas	St. Louis		

The *Saranak* (which had left Council Bluffs May 10) reached St. Louis on the 16th with some 30 mountain men and 600 packs of buffalo robes—returns of Harvey, Primeau & Co.—taken aboard from Mackinaw boats at Council Bluffs. (The company's Alexander M. Harvey, and James Russell—only survivors from a party of seven whose small boat capsized May 1 in the upper Missouri during a gale—had arrived at St. Louis on May 13.)

Ref: *Adventure*, St. Joseph, May 17, 1850; *Missouri Republican*, St. Louis, May 14, 17, 1850; St. Louis *Intelligencer*, May 20, 1850.

❡ May.—Various statements reporting on westbound traffic passing Fort Kearny ("Neb.") this month are listed below. These "statistics" cover only that part of the California-Oregon-"Utah" emigration which set out from points on the Missouri south of the Platte (Old Fort Kearny, "Neb.," Savannah Landing, Iowa Point, St. Joseph, Weston, Kansas, Westport, Independence—in Missouri, Fort Leavenworth—in "Kansas," and ferry crossings in between), to travel via South Pass. As will be seen, there are puzzling discrepancies in the wagon totals.

Despite the fact that spring was unusually backward in 1850, the first train bound for the gold regions reached Fort Kearny on April 13; and the emigration was, as one man put it, "full one month earlier than last year," or, as another opined, three weeks ahead of 1849.

May 3—According to John M. McGlashan, 300 wagons had passed the fort by this date.

May 10—Up to this date, 2,691 men, and 25 women, having with them 744 wagons, had passed—as stated in a Fort Kearny May 10 letter, published in the Chicago *Democrat.*

May 11—Dr. A. H. Thomasson wrote: "up to ten o'clock to day 960 waggons has past the fort. . . ."

May 13—James Abbey wrote: "Eleven o'clock passed by Fort Kearney   It is said that 'three thousand two hundred' [1,200?] wagons had passed the Fort before us, and 300 more are now in the vicinity."

May 13—The Rev. Gersham B. Day—under date of May 14—wrote: "We left Fort Kearney about 11 o'clock. Since the junction of the St. Joseph and [Old] Fort Kearney emigrations the road is lined for miles with wagons. On Monday [May 13] ours was the four hundredth that had passed that day, and there were no less than a one hundred behind us."

May 16—Samuel A. Lane (who reached Fort Kearny this day) later wrote: "Though we were almost at the head of the emigration that year [1850], a record kept at the fort showed that 1,952 wagons and 6,152 souls had preceded us."

May 19—Dr. J. S. Shepherd (whose company reached the fort and camped three miles beyond): "There have been 2,300 wagons passed Fort Kearney before us. . . ."

May 21—"Observer" (writing at the fort) stated that the number of wagons that had passed amounted to 2,754; that there had been an average of about 4½ men to each wagon (*i. e.,* above 12,000 men), and a total of about 76 ladies.

May 24—Up to this day there had passed 3,462 wagons; averaging 4½ men to the wagon (upwards of 15,000, by this estimate)—as reported by a Boone county, Mo., emigrant, in a May 26 letter.

May 29—Odon Guitar (at Fort Kearny) stated that 5,000 wagons had passed.

May 30—Cyrus C. Loveland (whose company passed "Fort Garney" at 11 A. M.) wrote: "Here we learned the number of teams and emigrants which had passed the Fort—4,500[?] teams, 21,287 emigrants, are now ahead of us."

May 31—"C." (writing on June 1 from "New Fort Kearny"): "Up to this time, 6,500[?] wagons have passed this point." He noted, also, that most were California-bound; that about 3,000 wagons (it was thought) had passed on the north side of the Platte—making "near 10,000" in all; and that each wagon averaged 4½ persons. "C." estimated the year's overland emigration to California, Oregon, and Salt Lake at little short of 50,000; and thought at least 20,000 were Missourians.

June 1—Reuben Knox (at Fort Kearny): "About 30,000 have already passed the fort upon this side of the river, and probably ¼ as many upon the north side. While resting here yesterday probably 1,000[?] wagons passed and very likely as many will pass today as there is one continual stream ever in sight almost."

Mid-June—Rouville Brunet (having brought a train of wagons loaded with buffalo robes from Fort Laramie to Fort Leavenworth) arrived at St. Louis in mid-June. The *Missouri Republican* of the 20th stated: "He puts the whole number of wagons at 13,000—pack animals 3,000—about 500 footmen, and three wheelbarrow men—one an Irishman, another a German, and a third a Scotchman. The health of the emigrants was very good—no cholera, and only a few cases of small pox and measles. He counted only six graves, four of which were filled by persons who had accidentally taken their own lives."

Ref: *Missouri Statesman,* Columbia, Mo., June 21 and July 12, 1850 (for April 13 and May 24 items); *Missouri Republican,* St. Louis, June 15, 1850 (for April 13 and May 21 items); New York *Daily Tribune,* June 28, 1850 (for Chicago *Democrat* item); Merrill J. Mattes, *The Great Platte River Road* (Lincoln, Neb., 1969), p. 201 (for McGlashan); A. H. Thomasson's "Diary," 1850 (typed copy, courtesy of California State Library, Sacramento, which has the original journal); Seymour Dunbar's *A History of Travel in America* (c1915), v. 4, p. 1302 (for Abbey); Trowbridge, *op. cit.,* p. 102 (for Day); Shepherd, *op. cit.,* Samuel A. Lane's *Fifty Years and Over of Akron and Summit County* . . . (Akron, 1892), p. 1116; *Missouri Statesman,* July 12, 1850 (for Guitar); Dillon, *op. cit.; Missouri Republican,* July 16, 1850 (for "C."); North Carolina *Historical Review,* v. 37 (April, 1960), p. 252 (for Knox).

❧ May 11.—The *El Paso* (John Durack, captain), under charter (at $1,200 per month) to the American Fur Company, left St. Louis for the upper Missouri, carrying about 100[?] employees and some 200 tons of freight. Passengers included the company's Fort Vermilion agent—Charles Larpenteur, and geologist Dr. John Evans (who went to Fort Pierre). The *El Paso* went by St. Joseph on May 17. The *Gazette* heard there were some 250 trappers and hunters aboard.

The *El Paso's* log stated: "On the 18th of May, when near the mouth of Wolfe [Wolf] River [present Doniphan county], we ran afoul of a snag which crashed our blacksmith shop, carrying overboard our bellows, &c. . . ." In May, also, there were six cholera deaths aboard.

On July 6 the *El Paso* returned to St. Louis, having achieved a "first" by going up the Missouri higher than any other steamboat (to a point, reached June 20, beyond the mouth of Milk river). Passengers on the down trip included Thaddeus A. Culbertson (*see* March 19-27 annals entry), Ferdinand Culbertson (apparently), and company agents Malcolm Clark, James Kipp, and "Mr. Disantel" (Desautel).

Ref: St. Louis *Intelligencer,* July 8, 1850; St. Joseph *Gazette,* May 24, 1850; *The Daily Reveille,* St. Louis, May 12, July 7, 1850; *Missouri Republican,* St. Louis, May 7, 15, July 8, 1850; Charles Larpenteur, *Forty Years a Fur Trader* (1898), v. 2, p. 289.

❮ About May 13 a detachment of U. S. troops (Third infantry, apparently) from Jefferson Barracks, Mo., destined for Santa Fe, arrived at Fort Leavenworth aboard the *Pocahontas.*

Ref: St. Louis *Intelligencer,* May 13, 1850.

❮ May-June.—At the Big Blue crossing on the Independence route Oregon-California trail (the ford not far from Alcove Spring; and about seven miles south of the St. Joseph route "Marysville" crossing) some emigrants of 1850 found the river fordable; others did not.

Dr. *George W. Read (May 13)*—"Passed the big Blue. A very beautiful stream. . . . We were very fortunate in passing it at low water. . . . We came into the St. Joseph road today."

Madison B. Moorman (May 24)—"Our camp [after fording] was on the left (west) bank of the Big Blue, a fine stream of excellent water full of nice fish. . . ."

M. Littleton (June 8)—"about 9 miles from the [Black] Vermillion arrived here Blue River (big Blue) about 2 o'clk. are now making a raft to cross the waggons on. This is a fine bold Stream and I Should think nearly 150 feet wide the curent rapid and now Swims the Horses it being up Some 3 to 5 feet I can not Say how much there is a ferry needed here badly there is a plenty of timber here for all purposes cotton wood Walnut ash etc. good water on Both Sides and wood but not much grass. haveing the appearance of many Emigrants laying here for Some time." (Littleton was one of the "Glenn & Co. train" passengers. So, also, was Henry A. Stine.)

Henry A. Stine (in a letter of June 17, after reaching Fort Kearny)—"At Big Blue River we stopped three days . . . [to repair wagons] and also to make a raft. The river being too high to ford and very rapid, we had to fix ropes from bank to bank and let the raft swing across by the action of the current, the first wagon [loaded with bacon] sunk the raft in about five feet of water, we got it out without damage. . . . the others crossed without difficulty. This was a Sunday [June 9] job. . . ." (The Glenn & Co. train set out again on June 11.)

Ref: Georgia W. Read, ed., *A Pioneer of 1850* . . . (1927), p. 27 (for G. W. Read); Paden, *op. cit.,* p. 14; M. Littleton's "Journal," and Henry A. Stine's letter of June 17, from typed copies, courtesy California State Library, Sacramento.

❮ May 14-20.—At Independence, Mo., on the 14th, a correspondent wrote: "Our town is yet quite crowded with emigrants; the numbers passing through greatly exceed our anticipations, and from every enumeration we can make we are firmly of the opinion, that they are more in number by one-third than passed through here last spring."

(In 1849—*see* p. 843—Independence had been the departure point—as appears—for at least 8,000 California-bound emigrants.)

On May 20 "H." (a Missourian) wrote from Independence: "The emigrants have nearly all left this point. For the last few days it seems as though the town was deserted." ("H.'s party—18 or 20 men—was piloted by David F. McClelland, making his third trip to California; and included James and Joseph Walker, who had crossed the plains before.)

From Union Town (near the "upper crossing" of Kansas river, on the Oregon-California trail's Independence route), a correspondent wrote, June 5, that no "regular records" had been kept at the Kansas river ferries, but from best estimates perhaps 2,700 wagons had crossed, and some 4,000 head of "loose cattle," in droves of from 150 to 500. At four persons per wagon (allowing for men with pack trains) it was thought around 11,000 persons had passed "through this neighborhood alone."

Ref: New York *Daily Tribune*, May 29, 1850 (from *Missouri Republican*); *Jefferson Inquirer*, Jefferson City, Mo., May 25, 1850; *Missouri Republican*, St. Louis, June 16, 1850. In 1849 (*see* annals, p. 796), about 700 wagons had crossed at the Kansas "upper" ferry near Union Town by May 18. What proportion of the 1849, or 1850, emigration crossed at the "lower" ferry ("Topeka") is not known. Not enough information is available to make a guess. Nor is there adequate information available on travel overland in 1850 from Independence, *via the Santa Fe trail*, to California.

❡ May 14-15.—Jas. M. Estill & Co's. "Express Mail Line for the California Emigration" left Weston, Mo. (home of Estill, and of his chief? associate James W. Denver), on the 14th, and St. Joseph, Mo., on the 15th—bound for Pacific Springs (South Pass), and for California, carrying letters (at 50c each; double letters in proportion; and U. S. postage prepaid by the sender) to emigrants on the Oregon-California trail (and to California).

Estill's express had been announced in the St. Louis *Reveille* of April 30, and the St. Joseph *Gazette*, Columbia *Missouri Statesman*, Liberty *Tribune* (etc.) of May 3. Agents to accept letters at 18 towns from St. Louis upriver to St. Joseph were listed. "We have bought 3 Spring Carriages and 24 fine horses, and are sending out daily by emigrant wagons, 5 bushels of oats for various posts on route," Estill wrote. One carriage was to go through to California; the others would bring mail back to the States. Estill's wagons would carry 24 mailbags (each stamped with a letter of the alphabet). An advance express, as it passed the emigrants, would hand out printed alphabetical lists of the letters in the mailbags. Stops would be made at Forts Kearny and Laramie, as well as on the trail.

The St. Louis *Reveille* of May 9 reported: "Capt. Denvers [James W. Denver] . . . leaves town today for the western border, thence enroute for California . . . [and] carries with him a special issue of our paper, containing a week's news from all portions of the country"; and next day announced: "Messrs. Ball,

Warren & Wood will receive letters until 10 o'clock this morning, to go by Estill's Express. . . ." However, it was May 20 when Denver's party left Fort Leavenworth. By rapid travel, he and his companions "came up with Col. Estill's train" before noon on May 24, west of the Big Blue. Four days later, the "express" party (Denver, "Judge Barnett," and others) separated from the "train" (and Estill) to push on ahead. With a mule team, horses and a carriage, they proceeded "very rapidly" up the Little Blue; arrived at Fort Kearny on May 29; left on the 30th. (Emigrant Robert Chalmers wrote on May 29: "The mail passed us for California. We arrived in sight of Fort Carnie.") Fort Laramie was reached June 8; and left on the 10th. Denver, and Robert Forsythe, preceding the rest of the "express" party (left on the 18th) reached Pacific Springs (Continental Divide) on June 20. This was "headquarters" till mid-July. James M. Estill (in the rear) in a letter dated June 23, 1850, from "North Fork of Platte," estimated, "having passed almost the whole . . . [emigration] in the express mail," that it (the emigration) would "reach about 60,000"; and expressed the opinion that a "semi-weekly mail" from St. Louis to San Francisco was feasible.

Emigrant Albert S. Holmes (about to cross South Pass) wrote his wife a letter on June 24, stating "I expect to send this . . . [by] the express for the emegrants and [it] is now recruiting five miles from here. Emigrant Joseph Price (who crossed South Pass on June 26) wrote a letter that day from "Sweet Water River," addressing it to "Mrs. Elizabeth Price Caloway Cty Mo. Fulton P O Estill Co Express." Emigrant L. M. Wolcott wrote from "South Pass" on July 4 (to Horace Greeley): ". . . 'Estell's Express and Mail' leaves for the States on the 7th inst. . . ." But the date was, instead, July 14. On that day Christopher Ritson and John T. Shortridge started from Pacific Springs with the Estill's express eastbound mail (to be "joined at Fort Laramie by E. S. Darlington"); and in the afternoon Denver and his party set out for California. On July 15 they "overtook Col. Estill's [westbound] train" (which apparently had started prior to July 14).

The St. Joseph *Gazette* of August 21 reported: "Estel's & Co's. express has returned from the Pacific Springs. They brought in upwards of 4,000 letters. . . ." (The arrival date was August 15, or 16—accounts vary.) Holmes' letter was cancelled at Weston on the 16th; the Price letter was postmarked "Weston Aug 19."

At Salt Lake City on July 27, Estill "laid before Pres. Brigham Young
. . . [and others] proposals for taking stock in a company organized for
carrying mail and passengers from Independence to San Francisco. . . ."
And from Mormon Tavern, Calif., on October 2, Estill addressed a letter to
Young on this subject (as he had done earlier—on July 10).

[L. A. Norton, at a later time recollecting details of his overland journey in
1852, said that his party met a relief train "sent out from California," in
Carson Valley; that "Gen. James Estil" was "first in command"; and that he
(Norton) was introduced to "Gen. J. W. Denver," the "issuing commissary,"
to "Gen. Price and some others. . . ."]

James W. Denver (for whom Denver, Colo., was named) served as acting
governor, and governor, of Kansas territory in the period between December 21,
1857, and October 10, 1858. (In California, Denver had served in the state
senate in 1852, and as secretary of state between 1853-1856.)

Ref: *Missouri Republican*, St. Louis, April 30, August 18, 1850; *The Daily Reveille*,
St. Louis, April 30, May 2, 3, 9, 10, July 20 (Estill's June 23 letter), 1850; Glasgow
(Mo.) *Weekly Times*, August 29, 1850; H. H. Bancroft's *History of California* (San Francisco, 1884-1890), v. 6, pp. 656 and 687 (for some items on Estill and Denver); [James
W. Denver] "Journal," 1850, typed copy, from James W. Denver Collection, Division of
Manuscripts, Library, University of Oklahoma; St. Joseph *Gazette*, May 3, 10, August 21,
1850; *The Weekly Tribune*, Liberty, Mo., March 22 (for a Denver item), May 3, August 23
(for Denver's July 18[?], 1850, letter), 1850; New York *Weekly Tribune*, September 14,
1850 (for Wolcott); *Utah Historical Quarterly*, v. 20, p. 38 (for Chalmers), v. 29, pp.
327-330 (for Estill at Salt Lake City; and the Holmes letter); *Mississippi Valley Historical
Review*, v. 11, pp. 252, 254 (for Price letter); L. A. Norton's *Life and Adventures* . . .
(Oakland, Cal., 1887), pp. 257-259 (for Norton); G. C. Barnes, *Denver the Man* (Wilmington, Ohio, 1949), p. 30. The New York *Daily Times* of September 6, 1852, via telegraphic
dispatch from New Orleans (where the SS *Daniel Webster*, from San Francisco, had arrived
on September 4, with "Panama dates to August 29"), reported: "Hon Edward Gilbert
has been killed in a duel with Gen. [James W.] Denver, in San Francisco." The *Missouri
Republican*, St. Louis, of September 20, 1852, published a letter from "Gen. [James M.]
Estill, dated "Rag Town, Carson River, Utah Territory, July 10th, 1852."

❏ May 15.—"This day Mr. Abelard Guthrie [of the Wyandot Na-
tion] and Company set [out] for California. . . ."—William
Walker's diary entry.

Of Wyandotte, Butte county, California, H. L. Wells' *History of Butte
County* states: "This place was first located in 1850, by a party of Wyandotte Indians, who were prospecting for gold. The diggings proved very
rich. . . . In 1850, there were at least two hundred miners in the
vicinity." Whether (as seems probable) the Wyandots were from the '49er
company—*see* p. 867—or from the above party, is not clear. Guthrie (and his
companions?) returned to "Kansas."

Ref: William Walker's "Journals," in W. E. Connelley's *The Provisional Government
of Nebraska Territory* . . . (1899); Harry L. Wells' *History of Butte County* [1882],
v. 2, p. 266—as quoted in Georgia W. Read and Ruth P. Gaines, editors, *Gold Rush—
The Journals, Drawings, and Other Papers of J. Goldsborough Bruff* . . . (New York,
1949), p. 667.

❏ May 15-20.—The *Highland Mary*, leaving St. Joseph, Mo., for
St. Louis, met, on the 15th, the *Tuscumbia* (at Smith's Bar), the
Pocahontas (at Iatan); on the 16th, the *Bay State* (at Parkville),
Pride of the West (in Kaw river bend), the *El Paso* (at Randolph);

on the 17th, the *Princeton, St. Ange, Anna, Melodeon;* on the 18th, the *Kansas, Alton, Cora;* and on the 19th, other boats below. Reaching St. Louis just ahead of the *Highland Mary* on the 20th was the *Saluda* (which had been to Council Bluffs).

Ref: St. Louis *Intelligencer,* May 20, 1850.

❧ Mid-May.—Bvt. Lt. Col. John M. Washington, of the Third artillery (New Mexico's military governor in 1849), and command, arrived at Fort Leavenworth overland from Santa Fe. In his party were Bvt. Lt. Col. Benjamin L. Beall (First dragoons), and son, Bvt. Capt. Thomas L. Brent (Fourth artillery), Bvt. Capt. Henry B. Judd (Third artillery), 2d Lt. Thomas G. Williams (First infantry), and a small troop escort. Also, there was a government train of 24 wagons ("Mr. Johnson's train," apparently).

Civilians traveling with Johnson included George Wethered, "Mr. Simons" (who, in advance, reached Independence on May 13), and E. W. Prewitt (who had left Santa Fe on April 17; and arrived at St. Louis May 21 or 22).

Ref: New York *Daily Tribune,* May 25, 29, June 6, 1850; *Missouri Republican,* St. Louis, May 19, 28, June 8, 1850.

❧ May 17.—Coming up from northeastern "Oklahoma" by way of the Cherokee trail (*see* p. 855), a California-bound company (principally Cherokee Indians, together with some 40 Arkansans and Missourians), captained by Clement V. McNair (a Cherokee), arrived at the Turkey creek junction with the Santa Fe trail (in present McPherson county). There were 37 wagons, and 132 persons (including 15 Negroes, and 12 females).

The May 17 journal entry of John Lowery Brown (a Cherokee) states: "today at 12 oclock Traveled 10 miles and came to the Santa fee Trail to Independence   Traveled about 8 miles after entering the Trace and camped on a small stream of water, Turkey creek. This morning the company devided. Part of the company, 19 waggons, started ahead, independent of Clem McNairs." (The faster-traveling separating group included many Cherokees, and had as secretary John H. Wolf.)

On May 20 Brown noted that two wagons from Wolf's company had rejoined his (the McNair) train—"we number 20 waggons & one Carryall . . . the other train passed on ahead." McNair's company camped this night at Cow creek. Brown recorded on the 25th that they "crossed Pawnee fork . . . camped on Ark[ansa]s River"; and next day (Sunday) while in camp "Captain T. F. Taylor's company consisting of eight horse waggons came up with us . . . [to join]." Still in camp on May 27, Brown noted that "a Train of ox waggons, 20 waggons, came up this evening." By the evening of the 30th, McNair's train had "passed the Ruins of Ft. Mann and camped 2 miles above on the Bank of the River." (The "Wolf company," on May 29, was already 30 miles above "Camp Mann.") On May 31 they "Traveled 25 Miles [by Brown's reckoning] came to the crossing of the Santa fee Road Maj. FitzPatrick, Indian Agent, was there paying out annuities to the different tribes." (Fitzpatrick, at St. Louis, in June, mentioned a company of about 200 Cherokees, with their 60 wagons, bound for California.)

The California-bound companies continued on up the Arkansas. "T. J. Mims & Co Caught up with the crowd 12 days from home," Brown noted on June 2. McNair's train reached Pueblo on the 13th; "found J. H. Woolfs company there preparing to 'Pack'. . . ." On the 14th "The ox Train [Captain Oliver's—which included some Cherokees] consisting [now] of 33 waggons came up and camped near. . . ."

Via the Cherokee trail followed in 1849 (with some variations) the trains continued the journey West. On a branch of Clear creek, six miles beyond the South Platte crossing, Lewis Ralston discovered gold on June 22; but there was no large "find," and the gold-seekers went on. The Continental Divide was crossed on July 9. Between July 25 and September 6 eight deaths occurred in the company with which Brown traveled. For two sick men, arrangements were made with James M. Estill (see p. 937) to haul them to California. In the Cherokee company there was much illness during the latter part of the journey.

Ref: John Lowery Brown's "Journal," in *Chronicles of Oklahoma,* Oklahoma City, v. 12 (June, 1934), pp. 177-213; Foreman, *op. cit.,* pp. 98-116; *Missouri Republican,* St. Louis, June 27, 1850; *The Colorado Magazine,* Denver, v. 36 (April, 1959), p. 84 (for Lewis Ralston).

❡ May 20.—The *Saluda,* arriving at St. Louis from the Missouri, reported that nearly all the emigrants to California had left St. Joseph; but that from that point up to Council Bluffs "they were scarcely out of sight of California tents and wagons," and at every landing the emigrants were "still crossing the river in considerable numbers."

Other steamboats reaching St. Louis on the 23d, also reported that nearly all the emigrants had "taken up the line of march" from St. Joseph, Independence and other area river points. St. Joseph seemed almost deserted "compared to its previous lively appearance."

Ref: St. Louis *Intelligencer,* May 20, 1850; *Missouri Republican,* St. Louis, May 24, 1850, or, New York *Daily Tribune,* June 3, 1850.

❡ May 21.—John S. Jones' train, freighting government supplies west under contract (see March 5 entry), left Fort Leavenworth en route to Fort Laramie. (His wagons undoubtedly traveled the new military route laid out by Ogden—see p. 908.)

William Grinstead, of Pettis county, Mo., was a teamster for Jones on this trip. His notebook jottings supply varied information —an itinerary of the journey; the names of some 43 fellow teamsters; items on mess rations; a brief table of distances traveled in eastern "Kansas." (From Fort Leavenworth to "California forks of road,"

14 miles; to "little grasshopper," 21 miles; to "second grasshopper," 4 miles; to "main grasshopper," 8 miles; to "West fork," 20 miles; to "Lemataw" [Nemaha], 13 miles.)

The train departed Fort Kearny June 13. Eastbound Jesse W. Crosby (whose Mormon party had crossed the South Platte on June 19), on June 21 noted in his journal: "Passed several heavy trains belonging to Government, bound for Fort Hall, also 100 mounted men, soldiers. . . ." Grinstead's record indicates Jones' wagons arrived at Fort Laramie (end of the trip) before July 10. On that date he (Grinstead) continued his journey to California. He had "Worked for John S. Jones fifty-four days $20 per month." Grinstead took Sublette's Cut-off on July 30; left Fort Bridger August 5; arrived at Salt Lake City August 11; departed on the 13th; arrived at Carson river September 19; and at "Weberville," Calif., on October 12.

Ref: William Grinstead's account book, 1850-1851 (microfilm in KHi); *Annals of Wyoming*, v. 11 (July, 1939), p. 190.

❧ May.—At least two of the year's St. Louis-originating commercial passenger lines to California left the frontier from the Independence, Mo., area this month.

(1) GLENN & Co. Messrs. Glenn (an "experienced 'prairieman'") and Ridgeway were the principal operators. (A statement that one of the company had "performed a through trip 7 times" doubtless referred to Glenn.) In January this line proposed to start from Independence; switched, in March, to St. Joseph; but, on April 14, was reported planning to leave Independence May 5, and to have room for more persons. The March "ad" had mentioned a $200 fare; elliptic spring light carriages; 50 pounds of baggage allowed; two good (riding) ponies for passengers of each carriage; six-mule-drawn baggage wagons; company-supplied provisions, tents, and medicines. This late-starting train finally got under way (from a camp southeast of Independence) on May 22. Diarist Henry A. Stine stated that the company consisted of 124 men (passengers?); and that several "handsome and strong Barrouches" had been added to the original outfit. On June 2 the train passed Union Town and went into camp, above, near the upper Kansas river ferry. From Union Town a correspondent reported, on June 5: "Glenn & Co.'s passenger train from Independence (39 wagons, 200 mules and horses, and 140 men) passed here on 2d inst. So did Patrick's[?] ox trains on the next day." The company reached the Big Blue on June 8, found it in flood; built a raft; crossed on the 9th and 10th. Glenn & Co. got to Fort Kearny on June 17. Before arriving at Salt Lake City (August 11), where the train broke up, two passengers and a teamster died.

(2) J. C. FAINE & Co. In March this "South-western Company" line advertised to leave St. Louis March 15; and to touch at Independence on April 10; fare $150. H. A. Stine (of the Glenn & Co. train) wrote on June 3 (when at Kansas river, above Union Town) "We passed [en route from Independence] the Ox train of J. C. Fane & Co. . . ." (Was this "Patrick's ox trains" referred to above?)

Ref: For Glenn & Co.: *Missouri Republican*, St. Louis, January 28, March 6, April 14, June 5, 1850; Henry A. Stine's "Letters and Journal . . . 1850" (from typed copy, courtesy California State Library, Sacramento); M. Littleton's "Journal . . . 1850" (from typed copy, courtesy California State Library); L. H. Woolley, *California, 1849-1913* . . . (Oakland, Calif., 1913), p. 3. For J. C. Faine & Co.: *Missouri Republican,* March 6, 1850; H. A. Stine's June 3, 1850, letter.

❡ Around May 23(?) one army officer with 50 troops, and their horses, reached Fort Leavenworth (from Jefferson Barracks) aboard the *Dr. Franklin.*

Ref: 31st Cong., 2d Sess., H. Ex. Doc. No. 23 (Serial 599), p. 21.

❡ May 24.—John Tecumseh Jones (half Chippewa), and family, moved from Pottawatomie creek (on the old Pottawatomie reserve) to a location on Ottawa creek, four miles north of Ottawa Baptist Mission (with which the Joneses were associated). (The mission was about three miles east of present Ottawa, Franklin co.)

Jones and his Maine-born wife—the former Jane Kell(e)y—had been adopted (about 1848) by the Ottawas, after severing connections with the Pottawatomies. (See p. 550; and *see, also,* portrait of Jones on p. 602.) The home that "Ottawa" Jones (a Free-State man) built in 1850(?) was destroyed by border ruffians in August, 1856. But a fine stone house he subsequently erected still stands.

Ref: Jotham Meeker's "Diary" (in KHi); *KHC,* v. 3, p. 329; Leslie A. White, ed., *Lewis Henry Morgan, The Indian Journals, 1859-62* (c1959), pp. 38, 39; *KHQ,* v. 23, p. 134.

❡ May 29.—"J. O. Sawyer" signed a contract (made with Bvt. Maj. E. A. Ogden, AQM) to (1) "continue the construction of a stone warehouse now commenced" at Fort Leavenworth, and complete it by August 1, for the sum of $5,500; (2) construct another stone warehouse for $5,175 (to be completed by October 1); (3) finish two frame buildings "now commenced," for $1,150.

The warehouse facilities were required because of Fort Leavenworth's new role as "an intermediate depot" from which "troops are marched and supplies transported by trains to the posts on the Oregon and Santa Fe routes and in New Mexico."

Ogden's 1851 report stated: "One of the warehouses [40' x 100'; three stories high] . . . is at the river side, and is used as a receiving store. It . . . [stands] against a lofty bank, with a graded landing in front. Wagons receive, from the third story on the side opposite to the river, the property delivered from steamers in the lower story. This is an exceedingly strong building. . . . The other storehouse [39' x 100'; three stories, with cellar] is on the hill adjoining the garrison. . . ." The two structures, with grading and excavation expenses, cost $13,973. But "in reality . . . cost the United States nothing. The funds were derived from sales of unserviceable horses and mules and a great mass of worn-out ox wagons and worthless property [relics of the Mexican War Volunteers' outfits]. . . . Sold, however, at a favorable time [the gold rush], it produced the handsome sum of $15,649.70. . . ." (For one such auction *see* April 9 annals entry.)

Ref: 31st Cong., 2d Sess., *H. Ex. Doc. No. 23* (Serial 599), p. 17; 32d Cong., 1st Sess., Sen. Ex. Doc. No. 1 (Serial 611), pp. 222, 290, 291. Both W. O. Goetzmann (in his *Army Exploration* . . . [New Haven, 1959], pp. 369, 422) and W. Turrentine Jackson (in his *Wagon Roads West* [Berkeley, 1952]—see p. 286, particularly) make reference to "James A. Sawyers," a civilian contractor, from Sioux City, Iowa, who built bridges for the army in Kansas territory in 1856. A "J. O. Sawyer" was superintending Fort Riley construction work in 1855 (*see KHC*, v. 7, pp. 101-105). (Could these all refer to the same man? Jackson, in *KHQ*, v. 17, pp. 42-44, listed the road contractor as "J. O. Sawyer.")

❏ May 30.—"Learn that a general war between the Pot[tawatomie], Kansas, Osage, Kickapoo, Delaware, Shawanoe, Sauk & Fox tribes on the one side, and the Pawnees on the other is being raised forthwith," wrote Jotham Meeker (at Ottawa Baptist Mission).

According to E. A. Tompkins, his train, on entering the Black Vermillion valley May 30, found the Pawnees and Pottawatomies engaged in battle. One dead, scalped Pawnee was seen, in a ravine.

Emigrant M. Littleton (in the Glenn & Co. train), encamped south of the Kansas river, and west of the Wakarusa, recorded in his journal June 1: "this evening there was 19 Indians came flying across the Road on a way chase from the best information they are the Pottowattimas fighting the pawnees. . . ." Another Glenn & Co. passenger—Henry A. Stine—(in a letter of June 3, near Union Town) wrote: "The other day 5 Potawatamies chased 8 Pawnees right through our train at the top of their horses speed and the next day we heard that they had killed two of the Pawnees."

At Fort Leavenworth, on June 1, the Hon. Henry J. Coke (an English visitor going up the Missouri via steamboat) learned that "This morning the Pawnees descended *en masse,* and had a brush with the Potowatamies."

William Walker (Wyandot) recorded in his diary on June 4: "Just heard of an onslaught by the Pawnees upon the Pottowattomies in which the latter repulsed their assailants with the death of their leader. . . ." On the 7th Walker wrote: "Just learned that Capt. Ketchum, the Chief of the Delawares, had informed our Chief that a band of Pawnees had attacked the Pottowattomies and were repulsed and that one had been captured and six scalps had been found in his possession, supposed to have been taken from some California emigrants."

Ref: Jotham Meeker's "Diary," *loc. cit.;* Irene D. Paden, *The Wake of the Prairie Schooner* (New York, 1943), p. 46 (for Tompkins); M. Littleton's "Journal," and Henry A. Stine's "Letters and Journal," from typed copies, courtesy California State Library, Sacramento; Henry J. Coke, *A Ride Over the Rocky Mountains* . . . (London, 1852), p. 86; William Walker's diary in Connelley, *op. cit.,* p. 310.

❏ May-June.—The *Robert Campbell* returned to St. Louis on June 3(?), having made the trip up to Council Bluffs and back (about 1,370 miles) in seven days and six hours running time—a speed surpassing that of any other boat (according to the *Reveille*).

On June 7 the *Robert Campbell* started up the Missouri again—bound for St. Joseph this trip.

Ref: *The Daily Reveille,* St. Louis, June 4, 7, 1850.

❏ June 1.—A letter Father John J. Bax, S. J., wrote from Osage Mission (present St. Paul, Kan.) contained a list of the Osage towns;

and stated, also, that the Osages numbered nearly 5,000 souls— 3,500 on the Neosho river, and the rest on the Verdigris.

According to Bax, these were the villages on the Neosho:

(1) Little Osages (1,500); 22 miles from the Mission.

(2) Village of Nanze-Waspe (600); 12 miles from the Mission.

(3) Big Chief (300); four miles from the Mission.

(4) Weichaka-Ougrin (500); three miles from the Mission. (Bax also wrote of the "village named Woichaka-Ougrin, or Cockle-Bird"—*i. e.*, cockleburs, apparently. [This settlement was called by Father Ponziglione—*see below*—"Briar's town."])

(5) Little Town (300); 30 miles from the Mission. (Bax, in a June 10 letter, mentioned "Cawva-Shinka, or Little Valley," 30 miles distant.)

The villages on the Verdigris (as listed by Bax):

(6) Big-Hill, or Passoi-Ougrin (600); 40 miles from the Mission.

(7) Les Chêniers, or Sanze-Ougrin (nearly 700); 55 miles from the Mission.

(8) The Black-Dog, or Skanta-Sape village (400); 60 miles from the Mission [near present Claremore, Okla.—*see below*].

(9) "There are, besides, other small villages, dispersed at a great distance from us," he wrote.

Some years later, Father Paul M. Ponziglione, S. J., in a manuscript on the Osages, listed the 17 villages existing in the time of George White Hair (principal chief, 1843-1852). The "Neosho district" towns he described as follows: the Little Osages (grouped by Bax) had four villages—(1) Wha-pe-ka, on Owl creek some eight miles above its mouth, the northern-most settlement; (2) Ugekzecta (Bax once mentioned it as "Huzegta"), about 10 miles below, "just on the spot now occupied by Chanute"; (3) and (4) Chiefs Nishumani and Numpevale had their towns (not far from each other) perhaps five miles on downstream.

Below the Little Osages' towns were the Great Osages' Neosho river villages: (1) Nantze-waspe, on the east bank, at present Shaw—"on almost the identical place"; (2) Pawhuska—Chief George White Hair's capital—on the west bank, on a range of small hills, nearly four miles west of present St. Paul (Osage Mission); (3) Briar's-town, five miles east of Pawhuska, on Flat Rock creek (*see* Bax's "Weichaka-Ougrin" above); (4) Beaver's town, on a high hill, at the headwaters of Hickory creek, eight miles southeast (of Pawhuska?); (5) Littletown—where George White Hair's brother was chief—on the west bank of the Neosho, where now is the "east end of Oswego"; (6) Chouteau's town, outside the Osage reserve, on the Cherokees' lands, several miles above the junction of the Grand Saline with the Neosho.

The Great Osages' "Verdigris District" villages: (1) Little Bear's town, in the northwest part of the reserve, some 10 miles above the junction of Fall river with the Verdigris; (2) Chetopa, at the headwaters of a creek called Chetopa, running west of the Verdigris; (3) Elk-town, on Elk creek; (4) Big Hill Town—called, by the Osages, "Pawnee-no-pah-tze" for the chief—the principal town of the district, located a few miles northwest of Big Hill creek's mouth, "where now is Independence"; (5), (6), and (7) On down the right bank of the Verdigris, "at a certain point between its junction with the Cana [Caney]," were three more villages "a few miles apart from one another"—called after their chiefs "Tally, Clearmor [Clermont] and Black Dog." "These were settled by a clan of nice looking Osages, all stalwart fellows, considered to be the bravest of the nation." (Black Dog's village—*see* p. 454—was near present Claremore, Okla. These three towns were outside the Osage reserve, on the Cherokees' land.)

Ref: Pierre-Jean De Smet's *Western Missions and Missionaries* (New York, 1859), v. 1, pp. 355, 357, 358, 365 (for Bax data); Garraghan, *op. cit.*, v. 2, pp. 501, 502.

❡ June 1.—The *St. Ange,* upbound from St. Louis, "Stopped four hours at Fort Leavenworth to discharge cargo" (as passenger the Hon. Henry J. Coke—brother of the Earl of Leicester—wrote in his 1852-published *A Ride Over the Rocky Mountains to Oregon and California*). Coke "walked up the hill and had a fine view of the Prairie."

Coke, his friend "Fred, a British parson," their five employees, and outfit of two wagons, nine mules, and eight horses, were aboard the *St. Ange.* After disembarking at St. Joseph, Mo., this party traveled northward to the Council Bluffs area before crossing the Missouri (on June 18); subsequently arrived at Fort Laramie on July 17.

Ref: Coke, *op. cit.*

❡ June 1.—Emigrant James Bennett, traveling up the Little Blue, recorded in his diary: "We met a company of dragoons today on their march from Ft. Kearney to Fort Leavenworth, having a number of baggage wagons in charge."

Ref: Bennett, *op. cit.*, p. 13.

❡ June 13.—Bound for Fort Laramie, Fort Leavenworth's commandant, Bvt. Col. Edwin V. Sumner, First U. S. dragoons, set out from his post with an escort of 50 mounted Sixth infantry troops (from "B" and "D" companies).

Except for the loss of one man (Private Mahoney) and a horse (both killed by lightning below Fort Kearny), Sumner's command reached Fort Laramie speedily and safely, in 21½ days (July 6, by official record).

On July 25 Sumner (and his escort) left Fort Laramie and marched southward—presumably by way of the established route along the base of the Rocky mountains—to the upper Arkansas river, where he would (under orders) select a site for a new military post. *See* p. 965. He arrived at the Arkansas on August 8. *See* p. 958.

Ref: *Missouri Republican*, St. Louis, August 9, 16, 1850; New York *Daily Tribune*, August 26, 1850; Glasgow (Mo.) *Weekly Times*, August 8, 1850; Fort Atkinson ("Kan.") post returns (microfilm of National Archives records, in KHi).

❡ June.—The *Jefferson Inquirer* of the 15th reported: "We learn from a man just from St. Joseph, that the emigration that has passed through that place, this season, amounts to at least 30,000 persons."

On June 18, from "Council Bluffs Nebraska Territory," a correspondent wrote: "The last company of California emigrants numbering near thirty men and some 50 or 60 horses left the Missouri river at this place the latter part of last week. . . . This brings up the rear of about 4,000 wagons, ten or twelve thousand persons and eighteen or twenty thousand head of horses, cattle &c."—all of this immense number "have crossed within a scope of twenty-five miles of this place, numbering near six times as much as the emigration of last year." This writer noted that the Mormons (encamped near the Platte's mouth) "take some 500 or 600 wagons and teams, besides large quantities of cattle, sheep, hogs, poultry &c."

Ref: *Jefferson Inquirer*, Jefferson City, Mo., June 15, 1850; St. Louis *Intelligencer*, July 11, 1850. *See* annals, p. 843, for some 1849 emigration statistics.

❦ June.—On the 16th, a few days in advance of Santa Fe trail co-travelers (left at Pawnee Fork), William O. Ardinger and Robert H. Smith arrived at Independence, Mo. (bringing first news of the massacre near Wagon Mound—*see* April 18 entry).

The company (of 20 or more men) with which Ardinger and Smith had set out about May 19 from Barclay's Fort, and on May 27 from Las Vegas, N. M., consisted of a mail party (apparently headed by "Mr. [Elliott] Lee,"); and the wagon trains of Hickman & Adams, and "Mr. Harley." From Las Vegas "to the crossing of the Cimarron," a military escort (headed by Bvt. 2d Lt. A. E. Burnside; including 2d Lt. P. W. L. Plympton, and 22 men) accompanied them. By June 18 the mail had reached Fort Leavenworth.

Leaving Santa Fe, originally, on May 14, the journey of these travelers had been interrupted and delayed when, on May 19, they came upon the massacre scene near Wagon Mound.

Ref: *Missouri Republican*, St. Louis, June 11, 1850; *The Weekly Tribune*, Liberty, Mo., June 21, 1850 (from Independence *Commonwealth* extra of June 17); New York *Daily Tribune*, July 1, 1850; or *The Daily Reveille*, St. Louis, June 21, 1850; McCall, *op. cit.*, pp. 493, 494; Calhoun, *op. cit.*, pp. 198-200, 206-208. The delayed mail (which was to have left on May 14) departed Santa Fe on May 24.

❦ In June these New Mexico-bound traders' and freighters' trains, and other Santa Fe trail travelers, were met by F. X. Aubry as he journeyed to the States (*see* July 3 entry):

June 21. At the lower crossing of the Cimarron: "a man with the mail, also Pike Vasques, Hatcher, Wood, Bransford and [Isaac?] McCarty," with 20 wagons.

June 22. Below the Middle Spring of the Cimarron: "Majors [Gouverneur?] Morris [Third infantry] and [Lawrence P.] Graham [Second dragoons] Capt. [Langdon C.] Easton [quartermaster's dept.] and several other officers and their families," also 100 recruits for the Third U. S. infantry.

June 23. At the Lower Spring of the Cimarron: "old Bob Brent, Spencer and lady [Charles E.] Kearney, Senecal, Fraser, Blanco, [William] Mitchel[l], Dalton, Guiterrez's [Gutierrez's] son-in-law." At Sand creek: "Mrs. C. McKnight and sister, and Patterson, with 22 wagons, and Messrs. Beech and [George] Estes, with 20 wagons."

June 25. At the crossing of the Arkansas: "[James J.] Webb with 22 wagons, Vasquez, Tom McCarty and [Charles] Kitchen, with 30 wagons, and Ewing with 100 cows."

June 27. Aubry *saw* (from the ridge road) six trains "on the lower [river] road." (Probably one belonged to Alexander Majors who, in his memoirs, stated: "In the early part of June, 1850, I loaded my train, consisting of ten wagons drawn by 130 oxen, at Kansas City, Mo., with merchandise destined for [merchants in] Santa Fe. . . ." Majors also related an adventure he had with Indians at 110-mile creek; mentioned Samuel Poteet as a faithful assistant on the trip; and recollected that he received $13,000 in Mexican silver dollars for this freighting job.)

June 28. Water-bound at Pawnee Fork: "Sims, with 30 wagons."

June 30. At Chaves creek: "[Cornelius] Davy, with 24 wagons, for Chihuahua.'

July 3. At 110-mile creek: "a quartermaster's train of 40 wagons."

Ref: *Missouri Republican*, St. Louis, July 8, 1850; Alexander Majors' *Seventy Years on the Frontier* (Chicago, 1893), pp. 128-139.

❧ June 30.—The "June" express from Fort Laramie, with mail dated up to the 11th from that post, arrived at Fort Leavenworth.

The preceding (or May) express from Laramie had been met on the Platte's South Fork on May 11 by a westbound emigrant company. Undoubtedly it reached Fort Leavenworth well before the end of May.

Ref: *The Weekly Tribune*, Liberty, Mo., July 12, 1850; Fawkes, *op. cit.*; Glasgow (Mo.) *Weekly Times*, July 11, 1850 (from Platte [Mo.] *Argus* of July 6).

❧ June.—The *Saluda* (returning from Council Bluffs) reached St. Louis on the 30th. Aboard were nearly 40 mountain men, and 2,047 packs of buffalo robes and furs belonging to the Union Fur Company, consigned to Messrs. Robert & William Campbell. Other passengers included several Mormon missionaries bound for England, or the European continent.

Ref: St. Louis *Intelligencer*, July 1, 1850; *Missouri Republican*, St. Louis, July 1, 1850.

❧ June-July.—The *St. Ange* (Joseph La Barge, captain) chartered by the Union Fur Company, left St. Louis June 13 for the upper Missouri. Aboard were partner Alexander M. Harvey, some 75 mountain men, and about 150 tons of freight.

The *St. Ange* arrived at the Yellowstone's mouth July 8; started back next day; and on July 19 reached St. Louis, having made the round-trip in 36 days—"it being by nearly one-third the quickest trip ever made." In her cargo were about 800 packs of buffalo robes; also skins and furs.

Ref: *The Daily Reveille*, St. Louis, June 12, July 20, 1850; *Missouri Republican*, St. Louis, June 8, July 20, 1850.

❧ July-November.—Licenses to trade with Indians in "Kansas," as granted by agents and subagents of the St. Louis superintendency, were:

Traders	Indians	Issued by	Rec'vd at St. Louis
David Waldo	[Tribes on the Arkansas river]	Sup't D. D. Mitchell	July
Duncan Macdonell	Iowas, and Sacs & Foxes (of the Missouri)	W. P. Richardson	July
John W. Forman	Iowas, and Sacs & Foxes (of the Missouri)	W. P. Richardson	July
John W. Polke	Pottawatomies	Luke Lea	August
(W. F.) Dyer & (S. G.) Mason	Delawares, Kickapoos, and Pottawatomies	Luke Lea	August
Duncan Macdonell	Pottawatomies	Luke Lea	August
Moses H. Scott	Pottawatomies	Luke Lea	September
Robert Robitaille	Pottawatomies	Luke Lea	September
(Michel) Giraud & (E. L.) Chouteau	Osages	Henry Harvey	September
(David) Waldo & (Jacob) Hall	Kansa	C. N. Handy	September
A. B. H. McGee	Sacs & Foxes (of the Mississippi)	C. N. Handy	November

Ref: SIA, St. Louis, "Records," v. 9, typed copy, pp. 442, 446, 455, 459, 462, 466, 468, 470, 471, 479, 481. "D. & T. D. S. Macdonell" opened a store in St. Joseph, Mo., in the autumn of 1849. Their "ad" in the *Gazette* first appeared in the October 26, 1849, issue; and *see* editorial comment in November 2, 1849, issue. In OIA, Letters Received from Fort Leavenworth Agency (National Archives Microcopy 234, Roll 303) is a Samuel G. Mason letter of December 26, 1849, stating: "I am here trading with the Kickapoo Indians with my wife's brother [*i. e.*, W. F. Dyer]. . . ." Robert Robitaille (a member of the Wyandot Nation), and family, were residents of Jackson county, Mo., in 1850 (U. S. census, 1850).

❧ July 1.—Departure from Independence, Mo., for Santa Fe, of Waldo, Hall & Co.'s first stagecoaches marked the beginning of a regular monthly U. S. post office department mail service between the States and New Mexico. Partners in the four-year mail contract enterprise were David Waldo, Jacob Hall, and William McCoy (all Independence residents; all connected with the Santa Fe trade, and government freighting).

On June 27, at Independence, "M." had written to Horace Greeley, of the New York *Tribune:* "The mail party [in charge of Bertram Spratt] which leaves here on the 1st prox. will consist of 10 men, well armed, all resolute fellows, except two young cadets from Fort Leavenworth, who have yet to be tried. If we meet the Apaches we are determined to give them h—ll or die in the attempt. If not scalped you will hear from me."

As reported by the Independence *Missouri Commonwealth,* two[?] six-mule, eight-passenger coaches (having "beautifully painted" and "water-tight" bodies), each with a four-man, well-armed guard, would start for [and leave from] Santa Fe on "the first of every month." "Each . . . [guard] has at his side, strapped up in the stage, one of Colt's revolving rifles; in a holster, below, one of Colt's long revolving pistols, and in his belt a small Colt revolver, besides a hunting knife; so that these eight men are prepared, in case of attack, to discharge *one hundred and thirty-six shots* without stopping to load!"

The *Commonwealth* account noted, also, that Waldo, Hall & Co. had "established a sort of depot at Council Grove," and had "sent out a blacksmith, a number of men to cut and cure hay, with a quantity of animals, grain and provisions"; and understood that they intended "to make a sort of traveling post there, and to open a farm. . . ." Jacob Hall testified in June, 1862 (at Washington, D. C.) as follows: "In the month of August [1850] . . . on my way to Santa Fe, in charge of about 60 wagons belonging to Waldo, Hall & Co., 35 of which were loaded with Government stores, and the balance with our own goods, and also in charge of the U. S. Mail, which Waldo, Hall & Co. were transporting as partners, I bought the house, field, corral &c., built [at Council Grove] by [William] Mitchell, from Mosier & Baker for the sum of four hundred dollars in cash, and where I established a mail station, and where I have kept one ever since. . . ." He stated, also: "Waldo, Hall & Co. . . . also took out a traders' license [*see* preceding entry] and kept an Indian trading house at Council Grove until 1854, when the first mail contract expired, and I became the contractor for the next four years. . . ."

Ref: *Missouri Republican*, St. Louis, June 4, July 26, September 3, 6, 1850; *The Western Journal*, St. Louis, v. 4 (September, 1850), pp. 414, 415 or, *see KHQ*, v. 18, p. 97; New York *Daily Tribune*, July 26, 1850; New York *Weekly Tribune*, June 29, 1850; *The History of Jackson County, Missouri* (1881), p. 644; *Hall vs. Huffaker* (brief in Circuit Court of U. S. for District of Kansas), in KHi library; SIA, St. Louis, "Records," v. 9, typed copy, pp. 442, 443, 465, 466 (re trading license for David Waldo); 33d Cong., 2d Sess., *H. Ex. Doc. No. 86* (Serial 789), pp. 318, 319 (for Jacob Hall's mail contract in 1854).

❧ July 1-5.—The *Robert Campbell* returned to St. Louis July 5, having left Council Bluffs on the first of the month. Passengers included Joseph V. Hamilton (American Fur Company agent at Fort Alexander, on the Yellowstone's headwaters), and over 50 company employees. Also aboard were 2,735 bales of buffalo robes and furs (the cargoes from 10 Mackinaw boats).

Ref: New York *Daily Tribune*, July 15, 1850 (from St. Louis *Intelligencer*, July 6); *The Daily Reveille*, St. Louis, July 6, 1850; T. A. Culbertson, *op. cit.*, p. 90.

❧ July 3.—Francis X. Aubry arrived at Independence, Mo., from Santa Fe (left June 12), four or five days in advance of his company (42 men, including traders Eugene Leitensdorfer and "Mr. Turley"; 10 wagons and 200 mules). He had left the train at Cottonwood Crossing (around 185 miles out) two days earlier; and "traveled 125 miles of this distance in *twenty hours and a half,* on the same yellow mare that did him such service . . . [in 1848—*see* p. 775]. On that occasion, this animal traveled 200 miles in twenty-six hours. . . ."

Aubry reported having met about 400 out-bound traders' wagons (*see* p. 947), also many Indians (friendly) in the Arkansas Crossing vicinity; and had thwarted, at Plum Buttes on June 29, an attempted raid by Osages on his mules.

Ref: St. Louis *Intelligencer*, July 8, 1850; *The Daily Reveille,* St. Louis, July 9, 1850; *Missouri Republican,* St. Louis, July 8, 1850; *The Weekly Tribune,* Liberty, Mo., July 12, 26, 1850, or, New York *Weekly Tribune,* July 20, 1850, or, St. Joseph *Gazette,* July 17, 1850—all from an account in the *Occidental Messenger,* Independence, Mo.

❏ Early in July 18 persons died of cholera at Kansas (City), Mo.— 17 of them Belgian emigrants recently arrived; the other, "Dr. Fulton," who had attended them.

Visitor John O. Wattles, writing from "Kansas, Mo.," in June, to Horace Greeley of the New York *Tribune,* had stated: "There are now just landing between 60 and 70 emigrants from the old country, (Florence) [*i. e.,* Belgium!] They are strong and able-bodied men and women. They settle in this State, within a few miles of this town. . . ."

Allen T. Ward, writing from Shawnee Methodist Mission (present Johnson county) on September 1, commented: "Our country . . . has . . . been perfectly healthy this summer, except some Belgians who settled two miles below Kansas were attacked with Cholera & some 15 or 20 died, the physician that attended them also died of the same disease. . . ."

Ref: *The Daily Reveille,* St. Louis, July 20, 1850; New York *Daily Tribune,* July 8, 1850; *Missouri Statesman,* Columbia, Mo., July 26, 1850; Allen T. Ward's letter (in KHi ms. div.) or, *see* KHQ, v. 33, p. 371; William Walker's "Diary," *loc. cit.* Walker recorded the death of "Dr. Fulton" as occurring on July 5, 1850. Under June 28 he had noted the cholera death, at Kansas, Mo., of "Mr. Walrond's black boy Arch." Wattles (a Yale graduate; active in the anti-slavery cause; friend of William Lloyd Garrison and Gerrit Smith) moved to Kansas territory in 1855, from Ohio, as did his brother Augustus. John O. Wattles, died in Linn county in 1859.—W. A. Mitchell's *Linn County, Kansas* . . . (c1928), pp. 135-140.

❏ July.—At Fort Leavenworth the ranking officer was Capt. Charles S. Lovell, Sixth U. S. infantry. Dragoon recruit James A. Bennett, who arrived at the post about July 27 wrote: "Garrisoned by 2 companies of [First] Dragoons, 2 companies of [Fourth] Artillery, and 1 company of [Sixth] infantry. The Fort swarmed with Indians."

Ref: Louis Pelzer's *Marches of the Dragoons in the Mississippi Valley* . . . (Iowa City, 1917), p. 170; *New Mexico Historical Review,* Santa Fe, v. 22 (January, 1947), p. 60.

❏ July 8.—Government contractor Joseph Clymer (*see* February 26 entry) started a train of 38 wagons from Fort Leavenworth for Santa Fe. The army freight totaled 196,275 pounds. (By early August Clymer's train had reached San Miguel.)

Ref: 32d Cong., 1st Sess., *Sen. Ex. Doc. No. 1* (Serial 611), p. 295; *Missouri Republican*, St. Louis, September 3, 1850.

❦ July 9.—A David Waldo 19-wagon train (carrying 97,592 pounds of government freight) set out from Fort Leavenworth for Fort Laramie. (*See* February 25 entry.)

Ref: 32d Cong., 1st Sess., *Sen. Ex. Doc. No. 1* (Serial 611), p. 295.

❦ July 10.—The *Robert Fulton,* reached St. Louis after a journey up to Council Bluffs. Both the *Saluda* (met at Wakendah Prairie) and *Highland Mary* (met above Glasgow) had cholera aboard. The latter had lost her first engineer by this disease.

Ref: *The Daily Reveille,* July 11, 1850.

❦ July.—From Fort Leavenworth, on July 10, Jones Creech's eight-wagon train (carrying 32,367 pounds of government freight) set out for Fort Kearny. On July 20 David Hunt's nine-wagon train (carrying 41,820 pounds of army supplies) left for the same destination.

Ref: 32d Cong., 1st Sess., *Sen. Ex. Doc. No. 1* (Serial 611), p. 295.

❦ July.—A Pottawatomie "National Ferry" was established on the Kansas river not far west of Union Town (and near what is now the Shawnee-Wabaunsee county line), with Lucius R. Darling as ferryman.

Darling's contract (dated July 10; signed by him, and by Agent Luke Lea; witnessed by John D. Lasley and Samuel Lewis) stipulated that he would "keep and attend a ferry," for the "use & benefit of the Potawatomie Indians," "on the Kansas river, . . . at or near said Darling's present habitation, within one & a half or two miles of [and upriver from] the trading post of Union Town, on the main emigrant route across said river." The ferryman's pay was set at $650 per year. (Darling operated the ferry till January, 1854, when John L. Ogee got the contract.)

Ref: OIA, Letters Received from Fort Leavenworth Agency (National Archives Microcopy 234, Roll 303). The land office plat of T. 11 S., R. 13 E. (in the state auditor's office) shows Darling's ferry-crossing in Section 15; the location being about three miles almost directly south of present Rossville, and about four miles east, and north, of present Maple Hill, in northeastern Wabaunsee county. John Wentworth's *Early Chicago: a Lecture . . . 1875* (Chicago, 1876), p. 37, states that Lucius R. Darling married (apparently in the 1830's) Elizabeth (Ouilmette) Welch, widow of Michael Welch (whom she had married May 11, 1830; and by whom she had a daughter, Mary Ann), and daughter of Antoine Ouilmette (a Frenchman with a Pottawatomie, or half-French wife). Lucius R. and Elizabeth Darling, by this account, had the following children: Mitchell, Lewis, Josette, Francis, Sophia, and Joseph. The family removed with the "Council Bluffs" Pottawatomies to "Kansas" in late 1847, presumably. SIA, St. Louis, "Records," v. 9, typed copy, pp. 821, 822 (for 1854 item).

❦ July 15.—H. H. White received $1,975 for building a saw and grist mill for the Miami Indians. Henry L. Hicks was the miller appointed August 1.

(On August 30, *1851,* Agent A. M. Coffey stated that the mill was "incomplete" when received from the contractor, and much of the work unsubstantial. As a result, "they [the Miamis] are unable to operate the saw, and the grinding is done slowly and imperfectly.")

Ref: 32d Cong., 1st Sess., *H. Ex. Doc. No. 103* (Serial 647), p. 616; OIA, Letters Received from Osage River Agency, 1849-1854 (National Archives Microcopy 234). *See KHQ*, v. 31, p. 143, for information on Miami village. 33d Cong., 1st Sess., *H. Ex. Doc. No. 37* (Serial 718), p. 361, states that Henry L. Hicks was miller "from Aug. 1, 1849 to Jan. 8, 1850"—a statement which evidently *should* read "from Aug. 1, 1850 to Jan. 8, 1851."

❡ July 15-16.—Bvt. Capt. Mansfield Lovell (also Lt. Albert L. Magilton and 2d Lt. Orlando B. Wilcox) and Company G, Fourth U. S. artillery, accompanied by Bvt. 2d Lt. Nathan G. Evans and 25 men from Company K, First U. S. dragoons, left Fort Leavenworth to travel the Santa Fe trail. They were to meet Bvt. Col. Edwin V. Sumner (*see* June 13 entry) on the Arkansas.

Early in August an eastbound party (which had left Santa Fe about July 16; and subsequently arrived at Fort Leavenworth August 15) met "Capt. Lovell, with a command of Lovell's Light Battery and Company K, [First] dragoons . . . at Jones's Fort[?], on their way to Big Timbers [the area originally designated for a new military post to protect the Santa Fe route]. . . . " (Evans and his First dragoons, on August 12, were detached to escort Santa Fe-bound government trains.)

It was on August 20 that Lovell's command joined Sumner. *See* August 8 entry.

Ref: 32d Cong., 1st Sess., *Sen. Ex. Doc. No. 1* (Serial 611), p. 298; New York *Daily Tribune*, August 27, 1850 (from *Missouri Republican*, St. Louis, August 18); *The Weekly Tribune*, Liberty, Mo., July 26, 1850; Fort Atkinson ("Kan.") post returns, August, 1850 (from National Archives; microfilm in KHi).

❡ From July 22 to August 5(?) an emigrating company of "Brewsterites" ("a society of dissenters from the Salt Lake Mormons" who planned to colonize in present Arizona, near the Gila river's mouth) camped on the Santa Fe trail, 20 miles west of Independence, Mo., making final travel preparations. There were (at one time) 98 persons (mostly women and children), with 27 wagons, about 200 head of cattle, and a few horses. On August 5 (or possibly as late as the 9th) these emigrants began their journey across "Kansas."

Coming overland from Illinois (Springfield; Fulton City) and Iowa (West Buffalo), separately, or in small groups, the Mormon "dissenter" families first had rendezvoused 10 miles south of Independence—the Royce Oatman family (of nine) arriving, in the van, June 29; and the James C. Brewster party (of 10), in the rear, July 13. Organizing on July 15, the company chose Jackson Goodale as leader (for one year). On the 22d the emigrants moved to the camp in "Kansas"—on the Shawnees' reserve. ("The Indians have farms about here, and raise things. . . . They bring string beans, green corn, blackberries and onions into camp," wrote one woman, on August 4. She stated, also: "We expect to start to-morrow for the plains.")

Apparently a signed-up member of the "Brewsterites" was Max. Greene (a roving Pennsylvanian; author, in 1856, of *The Kanzas Region*). In his book he stated: "In the close of the summer of 1850, I was [on the Santa Fe trail] one of a company bound on a gold-hunt, and the doubtful experiment of effecting a settlement among the pugnacious Jumas [Yuma Indians] at the head of the Gulf of California . . . [but] confess . . . I was personally merely on the lookout for novelty." Greene accounts for his own midsummer travels in a table of "thermometric observations . . . made by myself" which indicates he was at Fort Leavenworth on June 21, and as late as June 30, 1850; at Big John's Spring on July 4; at Cottonwood Grove on July 6 and 7; at Bend of the Arkansas on July 11; at Pawnee Fork on July 13 and 14; traveling along the Arkansas from July 16 to 30; and at Bent's Fort from July 30 to August 15.

Elsewhere in Greene's book is mention of "coming into the Santa Fe road [in the Pawnee Fork vicinity?; in early September?]," and of coming "to a halt within the white-tented circle of wagons of the party we[?] had arranged to join." He tells, also, of discord in the company; refers to the "untameable Wisconsan" Royce Oatman as "the nucleus of our troubles"; describes peacemaking efforts of a young printer (Max. Greene), whose speech to assembled members (at, or near the Arkansas Crossing) helped patch up (for a time) a split in the company.

The "Brewsterites" camped on September 12 at Sand creek (where, according to James C. Brewster, the mail coaches from Santa Fe "attended by a guard of ten well armed men" came up to them about 10 P. M., and continued the night journey eastward because of pursuit by Indians). Emigrant Mary Ann Lane, aged 16, died at Middle Cimarron Spring on the 16th.

The long-brewing split occurred at Las Vegas, N. M., on October 9. The Goodale-Brewster company, reduced to 32 persons, went to Socorro, N. M. The Royce Oatmans and "other malcontents" (11 families totaling some 50 persons) crossed the Rio Grande on October 19—still bound for the original destination. In February, 1851, the Oatmans, traveling ahead of others in their party (left at Pima Village), were attacked by a band of Yavapai. Except for three children (Lorenzo—left for dead; Olive and Mary—taken captive) the family was massacred. Lorenzo was rescued; Mary later died of starvation (among the Mohave Indians—to whom the two girls had been sold); Olive was ransomed in 1856.

Max. Greene (who left the "Brewsterites," perhaps at Santa Fe?) published in *The Kanzas Region* his "own table of distances on the Santa Fe trail," taken "with my own viameter . . . 1850." *The mileages are not compatible with those listed by Gregg and other travelers.* (Examples: Council Grove 152 miles from Independence, Mo.; Little Arkansas 250 miles; Walnut creek 293 miles; Pawnee Fork 319 miles; Caches 388 miles; Old Fort Mann 402 miles; "Fort Sumner" [Fort Atkinson] 406 miles; Ford of the Arkansas 416 miles; Jornada to Sand creek 465 miles; Middle Spring on the Cimarron 513 miles.) For comparisons *see* distance tables on pp. 814, 815.

Ref: *The Olive Branch,* Springfield, Ill., v. 2-4 (February, 1850-September, 1851), *passim* (microfilm, courtesy Utah Historical Society, Salt Lake City; from original file in the Huntington Library); Max. Greene's *The Kanzas Region* (New York, 1856); R. B. Stratton's *Life Among the Indians: Being an Interesting Narrative of the Captivity of the Oatman Girls, Among the Apache and Mohave Indians* . . . (San Francisco, 1857)— microfilm of a copy in the Edward Eberstadt & Sons collection; *California Historical Society Quarterly,* San Francisco, v. 41 (December, 1962), pp. 309-317; New York *Daily Tribune,* February 19, 1851 (has brief letter by "N. S.," from "Socoro, Dec. 21, 1850"); *Missouri Republican,* St. Louis, May 9, 1851. Old Fort Mann and Fort Atkinson were not over one mile apart. In *KHC,* v. 7, p. 365, George W. Martin wrote: "A tramp printer from the same office from which I started, the Hollidaysburg, Pa., *Register,* made a trip through this country in the early '50's, and wrote a glowing account of the Smoky Hill valley. His name was Max Greene." Frank L. Greene's *Descendants of Joseph Greene, of Westerly, R. I.* (Albany, N. Y., 1894) lists several "Maxson" Greenes. It seems likely that "Maxson" was Max. Greene's name. This same book also mentions intermarriages of Greenes with Oatmans.

❡ July 25-27.—Around 400 dragoon and infantry troops (329? of them recruits), bound for Santa Fe, debarked at Fort Leavenworth from the *St. Paul* and *Anna.* They brought with them cholera— which had become epidemic aboard both boats during the trip up the Missouri from Jefferson Barracks.

One man died on the *St. Paul;* seven(?) others succumbed after landing at the fort. Dragoon recruit James A. Bennett (a July 25 arrival) wrote: "Our sick [under the care of Asst. Surg. Elisha P. Langworthy] were placed in Hospital there while we moved 3 miles from Fort to Salt Creek and formed an encampment. Were joined [two? days later] by 200 [infantry] recruits from Newport, Ky." He also recorded, under date of August 3: "Cholera raging to an awful extent among us. Men at active pursuits one day . . .; the next day they are a loathsome mass, thrown coffinless into the yawning pit. We wrap 4 to 5 daily in their blankets, and throw their remains in the ground with a blessing or a prayer. No stone marks their last resting place . . . desertions continued in gangs from 3 to 8." Asst. Surg. Rodney Glisan (who was on the boat carrying the infantry recruits), in his *Journal of Army Life* (published 1874), wrote that "nearly every man in the command [except the officers] was taken sick with it [cholera], in some of its stages, before our arrival at Fort Leavenworth" where "we found this pestilence in full force. . . . None of the cases, however, proved fatal until the night we reached the fort, when several died." For a time, there was near-panic among the recruits.

Ref: 32d Cong., 1st Sess., *Sen. Ex. Doc. No. 12* (Serial 614), p. 18; Pelzer, *op. cit.,* p. 170; *New Mexico Historical Review,* v. 22 (January, 1947), pp. 60, 61 (for Bennett); Rodney Glisan, *Journal of Army Life* (San Francisco, 1874), pp. 11-25.

❡ July 26.—Government contractor David Waldo started a train of 45 wagons from Fort Leavenworth for Santa Fe. The army freight totaled 236,669 pounds.

Ref: 32d Cong., 1st Sess., *Sen. Ex. Doc. No. 1* (Serial 611), p. 295. *See, also,* annals entries for March 6, and July 1, 1850.

❡ Summer.—Two small Catholic chapels—out-stations of St. Mary's

(Pottawatomie) Mission—were completed during July and August, at sites south of Kansas river, in what is now Shawnee county. Thomas Macdonell superintended their construction.

One was on Mission creek, a little above its junction with Blacksmith creek (not far from the old Kansa Methodist Mission); the other—"St. Joseph's" (also known as "Mechgamiinak") was only a few miles west of present Topeka, near the Kansas river—between it and the Pottawatomie Baptist Mission.

Ref: Augustin C. Wand, *The Jesuits in Territorial Kansas 1827-1861* (St. Marys, Kan., 1962), pp. 20, 21; Garraghan, *op. cit.*, v. 2, p. 615.

❧ Summer.—Santa Fe-bound trains on the trail in the July-August period included the following:

Eastbound travelers who left Santa Fe in mid-July (and reached Fort Leavenworth in mid-August) met James J. Webb's train only 30 miles from Santa Fe; Samuel Wethered, James E. Sabine, E. Ross, and Hez. Harrison's train at Red river; McCauley's train at Rabbit Ear. Around August 1 they met Dr. Henry Connelly, James L. ("Squire") Collins, William C. Skinner, William O. Ardinger, and party, near Fort Mann; later met Connelly's train of wagons at Walnut creek; and Francis X. Aubry's train at Big Bend of the Arkansas. ("Messrs Crabbe and Edwards" were the "experienced" wagon masters of the Connelly and Skinner trains.)

The eastbound mail which left Santa Fe August 1 met Joseph Clymer's train at San Miguel; McCauley's near there; Cornelius Davy's and Lofland's train, close to Las Vegas; the train of Wells & Gutierrez at Upper Cimarron Springs; Francis X. Aubry's wagons at Lower Cimarron Springs; and Dr. Connelly near Sand creek. (Aubry reached Santa Fe some time in mid-August, in 36½ days from Independence. Of his round-trip it was reported: "The wagons were absent from Santa Fe 77 days being 21 days less than any previous trip." *For earlier mention of several trains above, see June entry, p. 947.*

Another eastbound company (which included P. M. Papin), which left Santa Fe August 16, met Connelly's train (and Skinner's?, stranded at Cedar Springs, on August 28. (On the 23d Indian raiders had carried off 84 mules.) On the Cimarron this party met Joseph Clymer's "about 100[?] wagons" with government freight (*see* July 8 entry); and met Oldham's wagons on the Jornada. (The mail party which left Santa Fe October 1 saw "Oldham's train and Oldham's company" at "Old Pecos," or, as another report stated: "Oldham and Thomson's train" was met at "Old Pecos Church.")

Ref: *The Daily Reveille*, St. Louis, August 18, October 3 (for Thomas D. Russell's August 24 letter from "Cedar Spring"), 1850; *The Weekly Tribune*, Liberty, Mo., August 30, 1850 (from St. Louis *Intelligencer*, August 19); *Missouri Republican*, St. Louis, August 18, September 3, November 1, December 7, 1850; New York *Daily Tribune*, August 27, September 16, 1850; New York *Weekly Tribune*, September 21, October 5, 12, 19, 1850; Calhoun, *op. cit.*, pp. 255, 256. Cornelius Davy died in Chihuahua in November, 1851.— *The Weekly Tribune*, Liberty, Mo., January 9, 1852.

❧ August 1.—As the Independence *Occidental Messenger* reported it: "On the 1st inst. commenced regular monthly [U. S. post office department] mail service between this point and Salt Lake. The mail is carried in light wagons drawn by mules. Under the man-

agement of its enterprising contractors James Brown and his associates [Brown, Woodson & Co.—as another account stated] . . .
the undertaking will no doubt be conducted with energy and
promptness. . . ." Manager "Thos. D. Scroggins" headed the
"August mail" party. He reached Fort Bridger September 5, and
Salt Lake City September 9; also he brought the first mail back to
Independence—*see* October 24 entry.

James Brown (government freighter) had obtained U. S. mail contract No.
4965—which called for transport of mail "From Independence, by Uniontown
[the Pottawatomies' Kansas river trading post], Fort Kearny, Fort Laramie and
Fort Smith [Bridger?], to Salt Lake City, and back, once a month, in four or
six-mule or horse stages." The mail was to "Leave Independence and Salt Lake
first day of each month, and arrive at the other end of the route on the last day
of the same month." (Annual pay for the contractor: $19,500.)

The September, October, and November mails (at least) departed Independence on schedule. Captain Stansbury met the September mail near Ash
Hollow on October 17. Around the end of October, other eastbound travelers
met the September mail at "Strawberry Creek" (a few miles this side South
Pass), in difficulty because of mules giving out. (On November 22 this carrier
reached Salt Lake City on foot, having lost all the animals.) The October mail
carrier went out to the Platte's South Fork; decided the road was impassable;
and returned (temporarily?) to Fort Kearny in November.

Ref: *The Frontier Guardian*, Kanesville, Ia., September 4, 1850; 32d Cong., 2d Sess.,
H. Ex. Doc. No. 62 (Serial 680), p. 750; *The Weekly Tribune*, Liberty, Mo., August 2,
1850; New York *Daily Tribune*, February 13, 1851; *Missouri Republican*, St. Louis, November 7, 14, 1850; St. Louis *Intelligencer*, November 13, 1850; New York *Daily Tribune*,
February 25, 1851; St. Joseph *Gazette*, December 25, 1850. Contract No. 4965 was transferred from "Jas. Brown" to S. H. Woodson, as of January 1, 1852 (but "Date of execution
of service: May 27, 1852")—as stated in a post office department "Report of contracts"
for the year preceding July 1, 1852. James Brown had died at Santa Fe late in December,
1850-—*see* September 4, 1850, annals entry.

❡ August 1(?)—Freighter John S. Jones (*see* March 5 and May 21
annals entries), direct from Fort Laramie (left July 20), arrived
at Independence, Mo., having performed "one of the quickest trips"
ever made from that post. He had averaged over 50 miles per day
on the 650-mile journey.

Aboard the *St. Paul*, Jones reached Lexington, Mo., August 1 (or 2?).
He (as reported) had met straggling California-bound parties—about 200
persons in all—the first few days out of Fort Laramie (but by July 20 the
main body of emigrants had passed that post); and he also had met trains
of Mormon emigrants en route to Salt Lake City.

Ref: *The Daily Reveille*, St. Louis, August 3, 1850.

❡ August 1.—"The [U. S.] mail from the States" (including St.
Louis newspapers up to July 23), which left Independence, Mo.,
this day (in Waldo, Hall & Co.'s coach[es]), reached Santa Fe on
August 28.

The U. S. mail which departed Santa Fe on August 1 (the first return trip under Waldo, Hall & Co.'s contract) arrived at Independence on August 28. The carrier—Bertram Spratt—had made the round trip in seven weeks and three days, stopping two or three days in Santa Fe. The outgoing and incoming mail stages had met at Arkansas Crossing.

Ref: Calhoun, *op. cit.,* p. 255; New York *Daily Tribune,* August 27, September 16, 1850; *Missouri Republican,* St. Louis, September 3, 6, 1850.

❦ August 3.—Isaac Preston obtained the contract (made with Capt. A. Morrow, AAQM) to furnish and deliver at Fort Scott, by September 20, 225 tons of "good, well-cured hay," for $6.90 per ton. (His sureties were George Douglass and A. F. Nelson.)

Ref: 31st Cong., 2d Sess., H. Ex. Doc. No. 23 (Serial 599), p. 21.

❦ August 8.—Bvt. Col. Edwin V. Sumner, First dragoons, and escort of 50 mounted Sixth infantry troops, arrived on the upper Arkansas river—after a journey from Fort Leavenworth (left June 13—*see* p. 946), by way of Fort Laramie (reached July 6; left July 25).

Sumner (according to mail carrier Bertram Spratt) subsequently arrived at the Arkansas Crossing on August 16 and "immediately moved the troops that were waiting [Bvt. Capt. Mansfield Lovell's command—*see* July 15-16 entry] higher up the river to the 'big timbers' " where a new military post was to be erected. (*See* September entry, p. 965, for the establishment of "New Post on Arkansas"—Fort Atkinson.)

Ref: *Missouri Republican,* St. Louis, August 16, September 3, 1850; Fort Atkinson ("Kan.") post returns, August, 1850 (from National Archives; microfilm in KHi).

❦ August 9.—Twelve wagons carrying a total of 50,978 pounds of government freight (Jones Creech, contractor) left Fort Leavenworth for "New Post Arkansas River"—or Fort Mackay (later Fort Atkinson).

Ref: 32d Cong., 1st Sess., Sen. Ex. Doc. No. 1 (Serial 611), p. 295; and *see* Erna Risch's *Quartermaster Support* . . . (c1962), p. 309.

❦ August 10-12.—Under command of 1st Lt. Henry B. Schroeder, Third U. S. infantry, a large contingent of infantry recruits left Fort Leavenworth (*see* July 25-27 entry) on the 12th, to march overland to Santa Fe. Two days earlier (it appears) 2d Lt. George H. Paige, Second U. S. infantry, and another detachment, had set out with the command's 16-wagon, mule-drawn supply train (and 18 teamsters) —perhaps headed by Charles White, Independence, Mo.

Travelers from Santa Fe reaching Fort Leavenworth about August 15 had met the "detachment of recruits under . . . Capt. Schroeder . . . near Stranger Creek, and several detached parties along the route." The "August" mail carrier from Santa Fe met (about the 23d?) "a company of soldiers at Council Grove"; and in the fore part of September, some 20 miles south of the Arkansas Crossing, another eastbound party "met a company of infantry on their way to Santa Fe, all in good health."

Ref: *New Mexico Historical Review*, v. 22 (January, 1947), p. 61 (for James A. Bennett's August 12 Fort Leavenworth journal entry: "Recruits destined for the infantry left us today."); 32d Cong., 1st Sess., *Sen. Ex. Doc. No. 1* (Serial 611), p. 298; *Missouri Republican*, St. Louis, August 18, September 3, 1850; New York *Weekly Tribune*, October 5, 1850; New York *Daily Tribune*, August 27, September 16, 1850. As stated by the *Missouri Republican's* Independence correspondent ("J. M.") the mail carrier had met "Charley White and U. States troops at Council Grove."

❡ August 14.—Contractor John Dougherty (sutler at Fort Kearny) started three wagons of government supplies (11,255 pounds) from Fort Leavenworth for Fort Kearny.

He forwarded (also under contract) one wagon with 3,058 pounds of freight on September 1; another with 4,465 pounds on September 24; and on October 14, a load of 2,284 pounds. Another contractor, E. Harrington, on September 18, started six wagons, with 28,177 pounds of supplies, from Fort Leavenworth to Fort Kearny.

Ref: 32d Cong., 1st Sess., *Sen. Ex. Doc. No. 1* (Serial 611), p. 295.

❡ August 14.—From Santa Fe (left in mid-July) Richard H. Weightman and S. Green reached Independence, Mo., on the 14th. From the same party, there arrived at Fort Leavenworth on the 14th, or 15th Bvt. Capt. Harvey A. Allen, Second artillery, Bvt. Capt. George Sykes, Third infantry, 2d Lt. Peter W. L. Plympton and Bvt. 1st Lt. William H. Tyler, of the Seventh infantry, Asst. Surg. Lewis A. Edwards, Dr. Carrol Thomas, Richard McKinney, the family of Capt. Alexander W. Reynolds, and an escort of 15(?) troops.

Weightman (senator-elect under New Mexico's provisional government) was bound for Washington, D. C., but did not reach St. Louis till August 23; Plympton, Tyler, Allen, and Edwards were aboard the *St. Paul* arriving at St. Louis on the 16th.

Ref: *Missouri Republican*, St. Louis, August 19, 1850, or New York *Daily Tribune*, August 27, 1850; *The Daily Reveille*, St. Louis, August 18, 24, 1850; St. Joseph *Gazette*, August 21, 1850; *The Weekly Tribune*, Liberty, Mo., August 30, 1850 (from St. Louis *Intelligencer*, August 19); New York *Weekly Tribune*, September 7, 1850; Glasgow (Mo.) *Weekly Times*, August 22, 1850.

❡ In mid-August 2d Lt. John L. Tubbs, trader John S. Tutt, "Mr. Ward," and four or five others, who had left Fort Laramie on July 6, arrived at Fort Leavenworth.

Aboard the *Kansas*, Tutt passed Glasgow, Mo., August 20. He reported they had met "Brown's express mail for Salt Lake" (*see* August 1 entry) on the Little Blue.

Ref: Glasgow (Mo.) *Weekly Times*, August 22, 1850; L. R. Hafen and F. M. Young's *Fort Laramie* . . . (1938), p. 166 (for quote from a July 11, 1850, letter by John S. Tutt).

❡ August 14.—Missionary Jotham Meeker (in present Franklin

county) wrote: "For the last ten days the mercury has risen every day to from 104 to 110 deg. above zero. On to-day it was to 108."

Ref: Jotham Meeker's "Diary," in KHi ms. division.

❦ August 15.—Expressman "Ormsby" set out from Fort Leavenworth for Santa Fe; reached his destination on the 30th with news from Washington, D. C., "as late as the 3d inst." (According to P. M. Papin, who met him at Cedar Springs on August 13, Ormsby had received a bonus of $300 to make the trip in 15 days.)

On August 14 or 15 an express *from* Santa Fe had reached Fort Leavenworth. It was reported "They brought sealed dispatches, and orders for 2,000 stand of arms" (for use in case of trouble with Texas over the disputed boundary matter).

Ref: *Missouri Republican*, St. Louis, August 18, 1850; Calhoun, *op. cit.*, p. 257; New York *Weekly Tribune*, October 12, 1850 (from St. Louis *New Era*); Boonville (Mo.) *Observer*, August 22, 1850; Glasgow (Mo.) *Weekly Times*, August 22, 1850. "Ormsby" possibly was "Owensby."

❦ In mid-August around 500 Seventh U. S. infantry troops arrived at Fort Leavenworth, aboard Missouri river steamboats, en route to Santa Fe.

On August 13, at St. Louis, contracts had been made with Joseph La Barge, Jr., of the *St. Ange*, and W. C. Jewett of the *Kansas*, to transport seven officers and 250 men, each, upriver to Fort Leavenworth. Other August St. Louis-Fort Leavenworth steamboat contracts were for small detachments (perhaps not all related to the Seventh infantry): the *Pocahontas*, August 5, "a detachment of U. S. troops" (one cabin, and four deck passengers), and 50 horses; the *St. Paul*, August 10, 125 horses, forage, and hired citizens; the *Highland Mary*, August 20, one officer, 14 men, and baggage; on the 22d the *El Paso* and the *Robert Campbell* each contracted to take five men, 40 horses, and 20 mules; on the 23d the *Anna* took aboard three officers and 70 men; etc.

In mid-September the Seventh infantry left Fort Leavenworth to march overland to New Mexico. The troops (and a 100-wagon supply train) had proceeded some distance down the Santa Fe trail when, about the end of September, an express arrived with an order cancelling the expedition. The secretary of war's report stated that the change of plans was due to the loss of a Missouri river steamboat (the *Julia?*) carrying supplies for the Seventh infantry, and to the "advanced state of the season."

See, also, October 11-12 entry.

Ref: 32d Cong., 1st Sess., Sen. Ex. Doc. No. 12 (Serial 614), pp. 16, 17, 19, 23; 32d Cong., 1st Sess., Sen. Ex. Doc. No. 1, p. 298; *Weekly Reveille*, St. Louis, August 26, 1850; St. Louis *Intelligencer*, July 8, 1850 (which reported the arrival of five Seventh infantry companies at Jefferson Barracks, from Tampa Bay, via New Orleans, on the *Cora No. 2*); 32d Cong., 1st Sess., Sen. Ex. Doc. No. 1 (Serial 611); New York *Weekly Tribune*, December 7, 1850; *Missouri Statesman*, Columbia, Mo., September 27, 1850 (from *Missouri Republican* of the 24th).

❦ August 21-22.—From Fort Leavenworth these contractors' trains set out with government freight for "New Post Arkansas River"—or

Fort Mackay (later Fort Atkinson): on August 21, A(rmistead) Dawson with six wagons (totaling 24,759 pounds); on the 22d Perry & Young's 10 wagons (with 46,146 pounds).

Ref: 32d Cong., 1st Sess., *Sen. Ex. Doc. No. 1* (Serial 611), p. 295; and *see* Risch, *op. cit.*, p. 309. In 1848 the St. Joseph *Gazette* carried an advertisement to the effect that Charles A. Perry, Elias H. Perry, and M. L. Young had associated themselves as "Perrys' and Young" (formerly Middleton, Perry & Co.), at St. Joseph and Weston, Mo. The firm's advertisement, dated March 7, 1849, in *The Frontier Guardian*, Kanesville, Ia., read "Perrys & Young," St. Joseph, Mo.

❡ August 25.—Bvt. Capt. Abraham Buford, First U. S. dragoons, and a large force of dragoon regulars and recruits marched out of Fort Leavenworth en route to New Mexico. Soldier James A. Bennett wrote: "Today our long cavalcade was put in motion. 250 men, over 1000 animals, and 70 wagons [40 drawn by eight mules each; 30 pulled by five yoke of oxen each] makes quite a show. . . ." Many of the wagons carried freight for "New Post on the Arkansas."

On September 5 Bennett recorded in his diary: "Cholera [*see* July 25-27 entry] has all disappeared from us. Arrived at Council Grove and Indian Mission. . . . 6 houses only. The Mission was established for the Caw or Kansas Indians. . . ." (*See* September 4 entry—the Kansa Methodist Mission building had been started the day before Buford's command reached Council Grove.) In mid-September, at Little Arkansas Crossing, eastbound travelers came up to the camp of Captain Buford's dragoon command "of two or three companies." Several officers were "on the sick list," but none dangerously ill; Buford was "awaiting the arrival of Brown's train" and its dragoon escort. A day or two later the States-bound party met Brown's train at Lost Spring. "He carried out machinery for the construction of a saw mill, provisions, &c. for Govt." About three miles west of Council Grove the same travelers met a second government train "freighted with building implements, building materials, and provisions destined for Mann's Fort" (*i. e.*, for the "New Post"—Fort Atkinson—located about a mile west of old Fort Mann).

Bennett, in a September 25 diary entry, wrote: "Arrived Fort Atkinson [the name must have been supplied later], garrisoned by 1 company." Buford and his dragoon command reached Las Vegas, N. M., on October 13. There, on the 22d, the recruits were assigned to companies. James A. Bennett joined Company I, First dragoons.

Ref: New Mexico *Historical Review*, v. 22 (January, 1947), pp. 61-67 (for James A. Bennett diary entries); New York *Weekly Tribune*, October 5, 12, 19, 1850; 32d Cong., 1st Sess., *Sen. Ex. Doc. No. 1* (Serial 611), p. 295 (shows that James Brown's train departing the fort on August 23, consisted of 30 wagons carrying 143,897 pounds of army freight), p. 298 (shows that Capt. A. Buford, on August 24, was assigned 30 teamsters, 10 horses, 138 mules, 23 wagons, one ambulance, and one traveling forge).

❡ September 1.—In charge of Jacob Hall (*see* July 1 entry), Waldo, Hall & Co.'s mail coach (with "an exceedingly heavy" mail) left Independence, Mo., for Santa Fe. The Independence *Commonwealth* commented: "This is already an important branch of the

U. S. mail service. . . . The Mail to the Salt Lake [see August 1 entry] is as yet a small one, though it is much needed."

On September 24, six days before due, the "September mail" from Santa Fe reached Independence.

Ref: *Missouri Republican,* St. Louis, October 1, 1850; St. Louis *Intelligencer, November* 1, 1850; *Jefferson Inquirer,* Jefferson City, Mo., September 28, 1850; New York *Weekly Tribune,* October 12, 19, November 9, 1850. The "October mail" from Santa Fe met Jacob Hall's "two trains" (see July 1 entry) in New Mexico—one at Wagon Mound, the second at Cottonwood. Hall, and the mail coach, presumably had arrived at Santa Fe before the end of September.

❆ September 4.—At Council Grove, Allen T. Ward, and a crew of about 25 men, began work on the Kansa Methodist Mission and manual labor school—a short-lived institution operated by the Methodist Episcopal Church, South (but paid for, and supported by the government).

By mid-December masonry work on the 35 by 50-foot, two-story, eight-room stone building was completed. Before the middle of February, 1851, carpenters finished the interior. (An accounting by the Rev. Thomas Johnson, of Shawnee Methodist Mission, dated February 11, showed that $3,102 had been expended on the mission—paid to B. T. Kezar and Allen T. Ward. Of this amount $3,000 was for the stone building; $25 for a log workshop, 18' x 20'; $50 for a hewn log smoke-house, 15' x 15'; and $27 for a 27'-deep well.)

Operating under supervision of Shawnee Mission's Thomas Johnson, the Kansa manual labor school was placed in charge of Thomas Sears Huffaker (b. 1825; from Clay County, Mo.; Shawnee Mission employee since 1849). "I, with H. W. Webster, took the contract for the management of the school and farm," Huffaker stated (in 1905?). "Webster was married; I was single [then—but was married, at the mission, in May, 1852]. Webster and family remained one year; he in charge of the farm, I in charge of the school. . . . I continued the school until 1854. . . . [It] averaged about thirty pupils, all boys. The branches taught were spelling, reading, writing, and arithmetic. None of them received instruction in the trades. The boys worked well on the farm." Huffaker also started a free elementary school for white children of the Council Grove vicinity in May, 1851; and continued it "for three or four years."

Agent F. W. Lea, in September, 1852, wrote: "Much cannot be expected from the Methodist mission among the Kanzas Indians, as it will take time to operate on their prejudices against schools." In August, 1855, Agent John Montgomery reported: "At present they [the Kansa] have no school, and it seems that what they have had has been only a dead expense to the government; those who have enjoyed the privilege of the school heretofore are now no more than common Kaws in dress, manners, and everything else."

About 1906—some 55 years after the Kansa Methodist Mission was built—

George P. Morehouse wrote: "The building is of stone, with two large fireplace chimneys in each gable. The walls are very thick, and the general appearance of the structure is solid and quaint and the surroundings are romantic. . . . [It] is still in good condition and is occupied as a dwelling. It has been used . . . as a schoolhouse, council-house, meeting-house, church-house, and during the Indian raids and scares of the old frontier days . . . [as] the place of refuge and stronghold. . . . It will always be pointed out as one of the oldest and most historic buildings in Kansas." (*See* views of the mission, p. 820.)

In 1951 the Kansas legislature authorized purchase of the 100-year-old "Old Kaw Mission" building and grounds, and since that time the property has been administered as a museum by the Kansas State Historical Society.

Ref: Allen T. Ward's September 1, December 21, 1850, and February 23, 1851, letters (in KHi ms. div.); 32d Cong., 1st Sess., *H. Ex. Doc. No. 103* (Serial 647), p. 974; *KHC*, v. 9, pp. 201, 202, 231-234; Comm'r of Indian Affairs, *Reports*, 1850-1855; *KHQ*, v. 20, pp. 24, 25. Though Huffaker stated (1905) that the school was discontinued in 1854, J. R. McClure, who took the census in that area in February-March, 1855, later wrote: "I was . . . entertained by . . . Huffaker [in a two-day stay at Council Grove] and was interested in observing his method of teaching the Indian children who attend his school."—*KHC*, v. 8, p. 234. Allen T. Ward's letters are printed in *KHQ*, v. 33, pp. 370-372.

❧ September 4.—Agent Luke Lea forwarded a contract, made with Frederick Kesler, for the erection of a $5,000 corn and flour mill, propelled by water power, on the Pottawatomies' reserve; and notified the Indian department that he had authorized Kesler (who had already hired laborers and ordered materials) to begin work, so as to have the milldam completed before winter. (Kesler received payment of $1,000 on November 15.) This "permanent" mill gave Mill creek (in present Wabaunsee county) the name by which it since has been known.

Agent Lea, in a July 20 letter, had described the chosen millsite (selected by him) as located about four miles (west) from Union Town on the south side of the Kansas river, and about three miles (west) from the Pottawatomies' national ferry (*see* July 10 entry). The site was within a few miles of Mill creek's mouth, in what is now Maple Hill township, Wabaunsee co.

Jake (or Jabez?) Durfee was employed as grist miller in 1851; in 1852 "Jabes" Durfee was listed as "grist miller," and Jude W. Bourassa (a mixed-blood Pottawatomie) was paid as "Keeper of the grist mill." It was Bourassa who subsequently ran the mill. The Whitman & Searl 1856 map of eastern Kansas shows the Indian settlement "Bursaw's Mills." In 1856, during his autumn tour of eastern Kansas territory, Gov. John W. Geary (coming downriver from Fort Riley, Manhattan, and Wabaunsee) on November 5 entered the Pottawatomie reserve "and [his executive minutes read] traveled rapidly through it, crossing Mill creek, a beautiful clear stream, abounding in fish. Stopped at Jude Bourassa's, an enterprising Indian, having a good mill [*i. e.*, it belonged to the Pottawatomies], and cultivating a rich farm. . . . They [the Indians] have quite a thriving town called 'Uniontown'. . . ." Max. Greene, in his *The Kanzas Region* (1856), under the heading "Notes on the Kansas River," wrote: "Next we have Uniontown, a village of log cabins, a mile to the south of the river. Then, Red Bluffs, taking name from the peculiar bright brown of the soil. . . . Darling's [Pottawatomie] Ferry is passed; and Mill Creek comes plashing and leaping in, like a little mountain river. . . . on it the Pottawatomies have erected a grist mill." Greene also remarked on the lovely scene in this area.

Ref: OIA, Letters Received from Fort Leavenworth Agency (National Archives Microcopy 234, Roll 303) for Agent Lea's letters; 32d Cong., 1st Sess., *H. Ex. Doc. No. 103* (Serial 647), p. 610; SIA, St. Louis, "Records," v. 9, typed copy, pp. 465, 470, 471; *KHC*, v. 4, p. 623 (for Geary's executive minutes quote); Greene, *op. cit.*, p. 43; 33d Cong., 1st Sess., *H. Ex. Doc. No. 37* (Serial 718), p. 446 (for Durfee and Bourassa, 1852). *See* annals, p. 482, for some earlier names for Mill creek, Wabaunsee co.

❡ September 4.—Brown, Russell & Co. (James Brown, William H. Russell, John S. Jones) signed a contract (made with Bvt. Maj. E. A. Ogden, AQM) to transport government freight from Fort Leavenworth to Santa Fe, in the amount of at least 600,000 pounds, for $14.33⅓ per hundred pounds. (Bond: $200,000; sureties: James W. Renick, W. H. Ewing, and E. C. McCarty.)

(This late-in-the-year large-scale movement of supplies over the Santa Fe trail—*see, also,* next entry—was necessitated by failure of an attempt to get army stores overland to Santa Fe by way of Texas; and because of the build-up of troop strength in New Mexico.)

Brown, Russell & Co.'s first train (30 wagons carrying 148,612 pounds) set out from Fort Leavenworth on September 14; a second 30-wagon train (total load 150,300 pounds) started on the 19th; a third 30-wagon train (with 154,875 pounds) left on the 22d; a fourth train (30 wagons; 151,979 pounds) departed on the 30th; and a fifth train (15 wagons; 78,868 pounds) got under way October 2. Many of the teamsters (it was said) were "Yorkers" bound for California. Senior partner James Brown headed the expedition. The first(?) train (met by eastbound travelers at Lost Spring in mid-September) carried "machinery for the construction of a saw mill [at New Post on Arkansas], provisions, &c. for Govt." (*See* September 19 entry.)

The "September mail" from Santa Fe, nearing Independence (in the latter part of the month) met "one of James Brown's government trains." ("Mr. Kephart, a Missionary sent out [to Santa Fe] by the Presbyterian Board of Missions," and his family, were traveling with this train.) The "October mail" from Santa Fe met "one of Brown & Co.'s [trains] at Big Bend of the Arkansas"; another at Turkey creek; and a third beyond Cottonwood Crossing. "Brown's train"(?) was reported to have passed "Fort Mann" (*i. e.,* "New Post on Arkansas") on November 2; and up to then had lost "about 20 cattle."

About November 25, at Pecos pueblo (within 45 miles of Santa Fe), a severe snowstorm stalled some of the trains. Brown, Russell & Co. subsequently suffered heavy loss of animals. James Brown (going in advance to Santa Fe) became ill; died on December 5. Charles O. Jones (brother of John S.) took charge, and, under army ultimatum, force-marched the supplies to their destination during December.

Later, "Russell & Jones" memorialized congress to obtain remuneration for the losses incurred. On July 29, 1854, an act was passed "for the relief of John S. Jones and William H. Russell, surviving partners of the firm of Brown, Russell, and Company." It stipulated that claims allowed should total not more than $38,800.

Ref: 31st Cong., 2d Sess., H. Ex. Doc. No. 23 (Serial 599), p. 22; 32d Cong., 1st Sess., Sen. Ex. Doc. No. 1 (Serial 611), p. 295; 32d Cong., 1st Sess., Sen. Com. Report No. 304 (Serial 631); U. S. Statutes at Large, v. 10, p. 802; New York Daily Tribune, February 25, 1851; New York Weekly Tribune, October 12, 19, 1850 (from St. Louis New Era); St. Louis Intelligencer, November 1, 1850; Daily Inquirer, Jefferson City, Mo., January 2, 1851; Missouri Republican, St. Louis, November 1, December 7, 1850.

❡ September 6.—David Waldo signed a contract (made with Bvt. Maj. E. A. Ogden, AQM) to transport government freight from Fort Leavenworth to Santa Fe, in the amount of 150,000 pounds at $14.33⅓ per 100 pounds. (Bond: $50,000; sureties: Jabez Smith and William McCoy.)

One David Waldo train of 30 wagons (carrying 156,050 pounds) left Fort Leavenworth for Santa Fe on September 18; and a second train (30 wagons; 153,725 pounds) started on October 4. The "October mail" from Santa Fe met the first "Waldo & McCoy" train at Big Bend of Arkansas; and the second at Lost Spring.

Ref: 31st Cong., 2d Sess., H. Ex. Doc. No. 23 (Serial 599), p. 22; 32d Cong., 1st Sess., Sen. Ex. Doc. No. 1 (Serial 611), p. 295; St. Louis Intelligencer, November 1, 1850; Missouri Republican, St. Louis, October 25, November 1, 1850.

❡ September.—On the Santa Fe trail, west of present Dodge City, "New Post on Arkansas" (later—June 25, 1851—officially named Fort Atkinson) was located by Bvt. Col. Edwin V. Sumner (who since August 8—see p. 958—had been on the upper Arkansas to accomplish this mission). The chronology below gives some perspective on the founding of short-lived Fort Atkinson ("Kan.").

The first week in September, eastbound P. M. Papin (and party) "met Col. Sumner, encamped about 4 miles from [abandoned-in-1848] Fort Mann." He and "several companies" were "awaiting the arrival of a company on detached service, who were escorting the train containing the building materials for a new Fort."

September 10—Bvt. Col. E. V. Sumner wrote the War Department that he had selected the place on the Arkansas where he then was encamped (and evidently he had moved a little downriver—see below) as the location of "New post on Arkansas." (The site, by present survey description, is within the "SW¼, Sec. 29, T 26 S, R 25 W, about two miles west of Dodge City and just south of U. S. 50.")

About mid-month the "September" mail carrier from Santa Fe (who passed Sumner and troops on the Arkansas) reported, at Independence, Mo.: "Col. Sumner has located the post just one mile from Fort Mann, instead of [at] the 'Big Timbers' [in eastern Colorado], and calls it Fort Mackay." (An army officer who traveled the Santa Fe trail in May-June, 1852, provided corroborative evidence on the relationship of the two posts: "Three-fourths of a mile below Fort Atkinson are still seen the ruins of old Fort Mann, which was also built of sods   .   .   .," he wrote.)

The fourth(?) week in September, contractors' trains, freighting construction equipment and supplies for "New Post on Arkansas," from Fort Leavenworth, began to arrive. (See August 9, and August 21-22 entries.)

September 24—Colonel Sumner turned over command at "New Post" to 2d Lt. Henry Heth—whose Company D, Sixth infantry (around 80 men) would garrison the fort.

September 25—Sumner, escorted by Bvt. Capt. Mansfield Lovell and his Fourth artillery troops (see July 15-16 entry) set out for Fort Leavenworth.

September 25—James A. Bennett (in Buford's command—see August 25 entry) wrote in his diary: "Arrived Fort Atkinson [he must have supplied the name later] garrisoned by 1 company   .   .   .   The company is in constant fear of an attack from a nearby camp of 1500 hostile[?] Indians. This company has to send 35 miles for firewood and are obliged to send 12 to 15 men in company to get it. Passed in sight of the Indians and crossed the Arkansas River.   .   .   ." (Asst. Surg. Aquila T. Ridgely, stationed at Fort Atkinson in 1851-1852, wrote: "It [the fort] is 26 miles below the 'crossing of the Arkansas,' and 74.07 miles above the crossing of the Pawnee fork.")

About October 1 passing eastbound travelers found the troops at "New Post on Arkansas" "progressing with their buildings pretty well."

In October's second week a party eastbound met the Santa Fe-bound "October" mail at "Fort Sumner"; and reported (on arrival at Independence) that "The troops were building pretty rapidly at the new fort, in preparation for winter." [Ridgely—quoted above—wrote: "The quarters   .   .   .   built of sod   .   .   .   were thrown up hastily (though not until one snow had whitened the uncovered walls), in order, as was supposed, to obtain shelter from the storms of one winter."]

In mid-October 34 wagonloads of supplies reached the new fort—freighted from Fort Leavenworth by Jones Creech, Charles McCarty, and Alexander Majors (see September 14 and 19 entries).

November 24—Bvt. Lt. Col. William Hoffman, Sixth infantry, arriving from Fort Leavenworth, assumed command at "New Post on Arkansas." The November return showed the garrison as consisting of Hoffman, Asst. Surg. Elisha P. Langworthy, 2d Lt. Henry Heth, and an aggregate 79 Sixth infantry troops.

December 16—The War Department's General Order No. 44 gave approval to the post site selected by Colonel Sumner, and to his recommendation that one-story stone buildings be erected. (But Fort Atkinson was constructed entirely of impermanent materials. One of the best descriptions was written by an army officer who saw it in June, 1852: "Our eyes were first greeted some ten miles distant from the post with a sight of the stars and stripes, waving over and among what appeared to be a close encampment of huge tents, but on nearer approach proved to be buildings of earth, the roofs of which were covered with tent canvass or duck, to keep out the drifting snow in winter and the dust in spring and summer. All the buildings at this post are constructed of heavy sods laid carefully with mortar of common surface soil, and are substantial and comfortable. All the defensive arrangements are constructed of this rude material, which gave it at first the name of 'Fort Sod.' The site of this post struck me as being exceedingly dreary and desolate; scarcely a tree is to be seen near it; all the fire-wood for the troops, and timber, are cut upon the upper branches of Pawnee Fork, twelve miles north of the Fort. . . .")

Ref: New York *Weekly Tribune*, October 12, 19, 1850; *Missouri Republican*, St. Louis, October 1, 25, November 1, 1850; "Fort Atkinson" (a one-page government circular; no imprint); Fort Atkinson post returns (from National Archives; microfilm in KHi); *New Mexico Historical Review*, v. 22 (January, 1947), p. 62 (for Bennett); 34th Cong., 1st Sess., Sen. Ex. Doc. No. 96 (Serial 827), pp. 163-167 (for Ridgely); New York *Daily Tribune*, February 4, 1853 (for quotes by the army officer, 1852); KHQ, v. 15, pp. 329, 330 (has an account of the "relocating" of the Fort Atkinson site), v. 23, p. 131 (for survey description); KHC, v. 4, pp. 363, 364 (has statement by P. G. Lowe: "The soldiers dubbed it [Fort Atkinson] 'Fort Sod,' and later on, 'Fort Sodom.' The walls were built entirely of prairie sod, partly covered with poles and canvas, and partly with poles, brush, and sod"). Lowe (a dragoon sergeant) first saw Fort Atkinson in 1852. *See, also*, Lowe's *Five Years a Dragoon, op. cit.* From the evidence given above, Fort Mann and Fort Atkinson were *not* on the same site (as has been stated in the past). Presumably it is the Fort Atkinson site that is known (and Fort Mann's location that remains to be found).

❧ September 10.—At "Delaware," on the north side of Kansas river, at the Fort Leavenworth-Fort Scott military road crossing (the Grinter ferry location, in present Wyandotte county), a post office was established, with James Findlay as postmaster.

An Oregon-bound emigrant of 1853 called the settlement on the Delaware crossing's north bank "Little St. Louis."

In mid-1854 Delaware was reported to contain "two or three trading-posts, a blacksmith shop, etc." The same writer stated the post office was 10 miles from the Kansas river's mouth. A contract for Star Mail Route No. 8909, let April 29, 1854, listed Delaware as 16 miles from Kansas City, Mo., and 24 miles from Fort Leavenworth. The name was changed February 1, 1856, to "Secondine" (James Findlay still the postmaster). Secondine post office was discontinued on April 14, 1859.

Ref: Robert W. Baughman's *Kansas Post Offices* (c1961), pp. 34, 156, 239; KHC, v. 1-2, p. 266; F. R. Holdcamper letter (from National Archives) of July 14, 1950 (in KHi ms. div.); annals, pp. 181, 182 (for the Grinter ferry). Whether Delaware was the fourth post office location in "Kansas," or the third, depends on the site of Crawford Seminary within the Quapaw reserve—*see* pp. 742, 772. "Secondine" was the name of a Delaware chief— *see* annals, p. 208. The 1860 census of Jackson county, Mo., p. 132, shows that two children (James W. and Maggie C., aged 8 and 7, respectively, in 1860) of James and Juliette Findlay were born in "Kansas." Probably their birthplace was Delaware. *Transactions of the Forty-sixth Annual Reunion of the Oregon Pioneer Association*, Portland (1918), for Celinda E. Hines' 1853 "Diary"—May 5, 1853, entry.

❧ September 14.—The nine-wagon train of Jones Creech, and

Charles McCarty's four wagons left Fort Leavenworth for "New Post Arkansas River"—Fort Mackay (later Fort Atkinson), carrying, respectively 38,714 and 22,240 pounds of army supplies.

Ref: 32d Cong., 1st Sess., Sen. *Ex. Doc. No. 1* (Serial 611), p. 295.

❡ September 16.—Nine persons reached St. Joseph, Mo., from California—the first overland party of 1850 to arrive.

In the company were Alexander Johnson (of St. Joseph?), Barnet Furnish and Pleasant Wilson, of Howard county, Mo., Squire Griffith and Henry Swearingen, of Nodaway county, Mo., Dr. Clemens, of Pike county, Ill., James and Aaron Anglin, of Arkansas, and Mr. Moore, of Kentucky. They had left Weaverstown July 1; and reached Salt Lake City on August 3. Their trip was made in 78 days.

Ref: St. Joseph *Gazette*, September 18, 1850; Glasgow (Mo.) *Weekly Times*, September 26, 1850.

❡ September.—A westbound William Bent train of eight wagons "on its way to trade with the Camanches," was met at Rock Creek (east of Council Grove) in mid-month by a party en route to Missouri.

Ref: New York *Weekly Tribune*, October 12, 1850 (from St. Louis *New Era*). P. M. Papin, one of the Missouri-bound travelers, reached St. Louis about September 27. William Bent, at, or near Fort Laramie in the early part of July, left (for the States?) prior to July 11—*see* Hafen and Young's *Fort Laramie*, p. 166.

❡ September 19.—Alexander Majors' train of 20 wagons (transporting 103,644 pounds of government freight) left Fort Leavenworth for "New Post Arkansas River"—Fort Mackay (later Fort Atkinson).

Majors (in his memoirs) stated: "I arrived in good time, with everything in good order, and when the Govt. freight were unloaded he [2d Lt. Henry Heth, then commanding officer] expressed a desire that I should take my entire train and go south about 25 miles, where there was some large timber growing near a stream called Cottonwood[?], for the purpose of bringing him a lot of saw-logs to make lumber for the building of his post. . . . I made the trip and brought him a fine lot of cottonwood and walnut saw-logs. . . ." Majors returned home (Jackson county, Mo.) "without losing any men or animals" on this trip.

Ref: 32d Cong., 1st Sess., Sen. *Ex. Doc. No. 1* (Serial 611), p. 295 (listed as "Fort Mackay" here); Majors, *op. cit.*, pp. 139, 140; New York *Weekly Tribune*, October 19, 1850 (from *Missouri Republican*, St. Louis).

❡ September 24.—Henry Hardy, "bearer of despatches to New Mexico," left Fort Leavenworth on, or about, this day. He had four teamsters, four horses, 12 mules, and two wagons. (Of his journey to Santa Fe, no mention has been found.)

Ref: 32d Cong., 1st Sess., Sen. *Ex. Doc. No. 1* (Serial 611), p. 298.

❡ September.—Around the 25th L. N. Ross' train, returning from

Santa Fe, reached Independence, Mo. Other incoming trains arriving at the Missouri border shortly thereafter included those of Joseph Clymer, Westport, Mo., and McCauley, of Independence.

P. M. Papin, of St. Louis, who reached home September 27 or 28, had left Santa Fe August 16, and traveled east "with a train of 30 wagons [not further identified], and in the company of Mr. Robert Ewing and other gentlemen."

Ref: New York *Weekly Tribune*, October 5, 12, 19, 1850; *The Weekly Tribune*, Liberty, Mo., October 4, 1850 (from St. Louis *Intelligencer*); *Missouri Republican*, St. Louis, September 28, 1850 (from St. Louis *New Era*).

❡ September 30.—The contract for U. S. mail route No. 4887 was transferred from Z. L. Price to John Frink. (It was to run till June 30, 1854; annual pay $750.) Originally this contract called for the carrier to start from Independence, Mo., at 6 A. M., tri-weekly (Monday, Wednesday, and Friday), go by way of Westport, to Kansas, Mo., by noon; and back between 1 and 7 P. M. Round-trip distance: 34 miles.

Apparently it was combined with another contract prior to July 1, 1850. An Independence resident wrote on June 17: "In a few days we shall have a tri-weekly mail stage to Fort Leavenworth"; and when, on November 12, 1851, more service ("Three additional weekly trips . . . in two-horse coaches"; Frink's allowance increased by $750) was ordered for route No. 4887, it was stated that this contract was for an "Independence to Fort Leavenworth" 46-mile route—to be covered "Three times a week with certainty, celerity, and security."

Ref: 32d Cong., 1st Sess., *H. Ex. Doc. No. 56* (Serial 643), p. 856; 32d Cong., 2d Sess., *H. Ex. Doc. No. 62* (Serial 680), pp. 822, 834; *Missouri Republican*, St. Louis, June 21, 1850. See annals, p. 624, for earlier Independence-Westport-Kansas, Mo., mail service.

❡ September 30.—James Wells left Fort Leavenworth with three wagon-loads (6,709 pounds) of government freight for Fort Scott.

On October 19 William Wells started out with three wagon-loads (6,708 pounds) also for Fort Scott. (The rate of pay, in each case, $2.00 per hundred pounds.)

Ref: 32d Cong., 1st Sess., *Sen. Ex. Doc. No. 1* (Serial 611), p. 295.

❡ In October, before the 12th, a military party arrived at Fort Leavenworth from Fort Laramie. It included these officers (who had spent the summer on court-martial, and court-of-inquiry duty at Forts Kearny and Laramie): Bvt. Lt. Col. William Hoffman, Lt. Col. Gustavus Loomis, and Capt. Henry W. Wharton of the Sixth infantry, Bvt. Maj. James H. Carleton, Bvt. Maj. Philip R. Thompson, both of the First dragoons, and Bvt. Capt. Alexander B. Dyer, U. S. ordnance. Company B, First dragoons, which moved to Fort Leavenworth, from Fort Kearny, in October, may have served as escort from that post.

Hoffman subsequently went out to "New Post on Arkansas"—Fort Atkinson, Wharton returned to Fort Kearny, and Thompson to Fort Scott—each as commanding officer.

Ref: *Jefferson Inquirer,* Jefferson City, Mo., November 9, 1850 (from *Missouri Republican,* October 23?); Lowe, *op. cit.,* p. 44.

❦ October 11-12.—The recalled Seventh U. S. infantry regiment (numbering around 500 men), coming in from the Santa Fe trail (*see* p. 960) arrived at Fort Leavenworth on the 11th. On the 12th the *St. Ange* and the *Anna* were chartered to carry some of the troops, their baggage, etc., downriver to Jefferson Barracks, Mo.

The steamboats (each carrying about 150 men, and between 30 and 40 tons of freight) had a difficult trip on the low-stage Missouri. It was October 22 when the *Anna* reached St. Louis. (She had struck a snag on the 19th.) Her passengers, besides Seventh regiment personnel, included Lt. Col. Gustavus Loomis (Sixth infantry), 2d Lt. John L. Tubbs (Sixth infantry), 2d Lt. Charles H. Ogle (First dragoons), and 2d Lt. Thornton A. Washington (First infantry). The *St. Ange,* detained by broken machinery, after going aground in Howard's Bend, finally arrived at St. Louis on October 25.

Four companies of the Seventh infantry, under command of Bvt. Maj. Theophilus H. Holmes, remained overwinter at Fort Leavenworth.

Ref: 31st Cong., 2d Sess., *H. Ex. Doc. No. 23* (Serial 599), p. 22; *Jefferson Inquirer,* Jefferson City, November 9, 1850; St. Louis *Intelligencer,* October 22, 26, 1850; *Missouri Republican,* St. Louis, October 17, 22, 23, 1850; Lowe, *op. cit.,* p. 44.

❦ October 12.—John R. Chenault, of Jasper county, Mo., was appointed in the place of Charles N. Handy, as head of Osage River Agency. (*See* p. 977.)

In a February 3, 1851, letter, Mrs. Robert Simerwell (wife of the Miamis' government blacksmith) wrote: "Mr. Chenault . . . with his wife and two small children board with us for a little while until they can get a house to live in."

Ref: 32d Cong., 1st Sess., *H. Ex. Doc. No. 103* (Serial 647), pp. 622, 624; Simerwell Collection (in KHi ms. div.); St. Joseph *Gazette,* November 13, 1850; *Missouri Republican,* St. Louis, October 16, 1850.

❦ October.—Waldo, Hall & Co's. mail stages, setting out from Independence, Mo., and from Santa Fe, N. M., on October 1, passed each other at "Fort Sumner" (the "New Post on Arkansas"—*see* p. 965) in mid-October.

Passengers leaving Independence with the mail on October 1 included the Rev. E. G. Nicholson, his wife, and daughter. Nicholson was going to New Mexico as missionary of the Methodist Episcopal Church, North, to the Indians and Mexicans of Santa Fe and vicinity.

The mail *from* Santa Fe, in charge of Bertram Spratt, arrived at Independence October 26—five days ahead of schedule.

Ref: St. Louis *Intelligencer,* November 1, 1850; *Missouri Republican,* St. Louis, November 1, 1850; *New Mexico Historical Review,* v. 39 (October, 1964), p. 310, for Nicholson's initials.

❦ Mid-October.—From New Mexico, a military party (five officers; 25? dragoons) headed by Bvt. Col. Charles A. May, Second dragoons, arrived at the Missouri border. (Bvt. Maj. John J. Peck, Lt. John O. Simpson, Bvt. Capt. Charles H. Humber, and Bvt. 2d Lt. Ambrose E. Burnside were with May.)

The "September mail," en route to Independence, Mo., had overtaken "Messrs. Wm. S. Messervy, Jerry [Jared W.] Folger, and party . . ." on September 3, near Moro, N. M.—then in company with Colonel May's detachment—but (as the mail carrier reported it) "For greater safety and certainty of trip, they [the civilian?] come by the 'Bent Fort route.' . . ."

A Las Vegas-bound military force which included dragoon recruit (and diarist) James A. Bennett, on October 4, while on the *Cimarron route* (having crossed the Arkansas September 26) "Met Col. May and several other officers returning from [New] Mexico. Stopped one hour. The colonel got pretty drunk: our officers also felt their brandy. . . ." (Bennett did not mention the presence of civilians with the military party.) Messervy, Folger, and companions—via Bent's Fort?—probably reached Missouri before month's end.

Ref: *New Mexico Historical Review,* v. 22 (January, 1947), p. 63 (for James A. Bennett); New York *Weekly Tribune,* October 19, 1850 (from *Missouri Republican*); *Missouri Republican,* St. Louis, October 28, 1850.

❦ October 18.—Isaac Lightner, Independence, Mo., "Mr. Domingo," of Chihuahua, and their small party, arrived at Independence from El Paso (left August 28), via Santa Fe (left September 13).

Ref: *Missouri Republican,* St. Louis, October 25, 1850.

❦ October.—On the 21st the *Highland Mary,* which had been up to Weston, Mo., reached St. Louis "with both her larboard and starboard guards much torn by snags encountered on her passage down. . . ." (The Missouri was said to be in the worst condition possible for navigation.)

On October 25 the *Robert Campbell* (which had left St. Joseph, Mo., on the 19th) returned to St. Louis. She had met the *Eureka* at Fort Leavenworth, the *Hamburg* at Parkville, the *El Paso* at Wayne City—all on the 19th; the *Lightfoot* and *Sacramento* on the 21st; and the *Saranak,* at Rocheport, on the 23d.

Ref: St. Louis *Intelligencer,* October 22, 26, 1850.

❦ October 24.—"Thos. D. Scroggins," and four companions, with the first (Brown, Woodson & Co.) U. S. monthly mail ("a heavy one") from Salt Lake City, reached Independence, Mo.—24 days behind schedule (*see* August 1 entry).

"Scroggins" had delivered the "August mail" from Independence at Salt

Lake on September 9; started back to Missouri on the 11th; reached Fort Bridger (110 miles) on the 15th; got to Fort Laramie on the 29th, and Fort Kearny on October 8. He had been delayed eight days (six by illness; two by shoeing mules, etc.).

This eastbound mail had met the "September mail" from Independence on September 28, 65 miles beyond Fort Laramie; and the "October mail" from Independence on October 10 at Fort Kearny.

Ref: *Missouri Republican*, St. Louis, November 1, 1850; St. Louis *Intelligencer*, November 1, 1850, or, St. Joseph *Gazette*, November 6, 1850.

❧ MARRIED: William Thorp [Tharp?] and Zerelda Roberts, on October 28, at the Osage River Agency (present Franklin county), by the Rev. Jotham Meeker.

Ref: Jotham Meeker's "Diary," in KHi ms. division.

❧ October 30.—Edward B. Horner's five-wagon train arrived at Independence, Mo., from Santa Fe. His party (12 men) included Samuel Wethered ("an old and wealthy trader"), of Baltimore, Newton Williams, of Boonville, Mo., Murray J. Tuley, George W. Martin, and Elias Brevoort.

They had left Santa Fe on October 2. Some 35 to 40 discharged government teamsters were in the party as far as "Cottonwood" (N. M.)—200 miles out. While encamped there, the night of October 12, Kit Carson, Capt. R. S. Ewell, and some 40 troops arrived with news of, and in time to forestall execution of, a plot by a teamster named Fox (and some cohorts) to rob and kill Wethered, Williams, and others. Horner's party, separating from the teamsters after this incident, pushed on ahead for the States.

Ref: *The Weekly Tribune*, Liberty, Mo., November 8, 1850 (from *Occidental Messenger*, Independence, Mo.); St. Louis *Intelligencer*, November 6, 1850; *Missouri Republican*, St. Louis, November 7, 1850.

❧ November 1.—The Ottawas' Baptist missionary, Jotham Meeker ("Kansas" resident for some 17 years) recorded in his diary: "Think I have never known so dry a season as we have now had."

He added: "The last rain we have had to swell any of the streams was early in May. In June the creeks stopped running, and have been gradually falling ever since. The holes in our creek are now about one foot lower than I have seen them since we came into the country."

Ref: Meeker "Diary," *loc. cit.* The Meekers came to "Kansas" in 1833.

❧ On November 1 Waldo, Hall & Co's. mail coach left Independence, Mo.; met the eastbound mail at Arkansas Crossing; reached Santa Fe the evening of November 26.

Ref: New York *Weekly Tribune*, February 8, 1851 (from *National Era*); *Missouri Republican*, St. Louis, December 7, 1850.

❧ November 6.—Capt. Howard Stansbury (U. S. topographical engineers) and party, returning from the expedition to the Valley of the Great Salt Lake of Utah (begun in 1849—*see* p. 868), arrived at Fort Leavenworth. From Fort Laramie (left October 12) to the Missouri, the train had been in Lt. John W. Gunnison's charge. (Stansbury, incapacitated by an injury, made the trip in a wagon.)

They had reached Fort Kearny on October 26; and arrived at the Big Blue crossing (the future Marysville) on November 2. Subsequently they followed the new military road laid out by Bvt. Maj. E. A. Ogden seven months earlier (*see* p. 908) in to Fort Leavenworth. These are some notes on the last section of their homeward journey from Captain Stansbury's report:

	Intermediate distance	*Day's march*
Nov. 2 [After traveling over 30 miles they came to the]		
Big Blue—Rolling country. Stream at low stage; 160 feet wide by 2½ feet deep. Thence a long ascent.		
Nov. 2 Vermilion—Cross a small branch half a mile from Big Blue.		31.52
Nov. 3 Junction—The old road, to the north is near the Vermilion; the new track keeps on the ridge, having the heads of streams frequent, with timber on either hand, at a short distance from the road.		
Branch—Supposed tributary to the Big Nemaha, 10½ feet wide by 2 inches deep.	24.05	
Creek—Runs south, into the Nemaha; the road passing between branches	12.08	36.13
Nov. 4 Nemaha Branch—We ascend, from the tributary to high ground; good road.	19.57	19.57
Nov. 5 Creek—Runs south.	7.60	
Creek—Runs south; has fine timber and grass in vicinity.	4.66	
Creek—Rising a long slope, and then descending from the ridge.	5.46	
Independence Creek—Road sinuous; on the dividing ridge between affluents of Kansas and Missouri Rivers.	14.89	32.61
Nov. 6 Fort Leavenworth—The road winds on the "divide" till within fourteen miles from the fort, and then descends and crosses several small streams, affluents of the Missouri.	22.74	22.74

In traveling from Fort Leavenworth to Fort Kearny in 1849 (by the "old" military road then in use), Stansbury recorded a journey of 311.013 miles. On the return trip the distance was set down as 289.68 miles. Ogden's road, shortening the section east of the Big Blue, by assumption, accounted for most of the nearly 21-mile improvement in 1850.

See, in this volume, the eastern "Kansas" segment from "Map of a Recon-
noissance between Fort Leavenworth on the Missouri River, and the Great Salt
Lake in the Territory of Utah, made in 1849 and 1850 . . . by Capt.
Howard Stansbury . . . aided by Lieut. J. W. Gunnison. . . . (The
map was drawn by Lieutenant Gunnison and Charles Preuss.)

Ref: Stansbury, *op. cit.,* New York *Weekly Tribune,* November 30, 1850.

❦ November 8.—The "new and elegant steamer *Isabel*" (W. B.
Miller, captain), making her first trip up the Missouri, arrived at
St. Joseph. She had left St. Louis October 28; and carried nearly
100 tons of cargo upriver despite a low stage of water.

On November 14 the *Isabel* returned to St. Louis with "a fair freight and a
goodly number of passengers."

Ref: St. Joseph *Gazette,* November 13, 1850; *Adventure,* St. Joseph, November 15,
1850; St. Louis *Intelligencer,* November 15, 1850; *Missouri Republican,* St. Louis, October
28, 1850. The *Isabel* had a 210-foot deck length; three boilers, 26 feet long, 40 inches
in diameter.

❦ November 12.—Dr. Wilson Hobbs, his wife Zelinda (Williams)
Hobbs, and family (Orville, aged 2½; Mary Z., 1 year old) arrived
at Kansas (City), Mo., by steamboat, en route to Shawnee Friends
Mission (reached on the 13th) where the Hobbs would serve, for
two years, as teachers.

(In June visitor John O. Wattles had written: "The Friends Mission is . . . sustained entirely by that body.—Thomas Wells
is Superintendent. This Summer there are but 18 or 20 children in
attendance. In the Winter it is much larger.")

Hobbs, in reminiscences, wrote: "We landed at Kansas City late in the
afternoon. . . . There was standing near the landing a large brick building which had the appearance of a hotel. I afterward learned that it was
built for such use during the more prosperous days of the early California
emigration, and had for some time [since spring?] been abandoned. We soon
learned there was but one hotel in the 'city.' This was a double, hewed-log
house on the bluff, a few hundred yards to the left of the old brick hotel. My
present recollection is that the population of the place did not exceed 500 or
600. It was a mere port for the debarkation of goods to Western points of
trade. . . . In the suburbs . . . we passed the saw mills of Mr.
McGee, and from there to Westport, four miles the way led through almost
unbroken forest. Westport was then a village quite as large as its more pre-
tentious neighbor, Kansas City, and had much the advantage in stir and busi-
nesslike appearance. . . . [From Westport, Mo., it was six miles to Shawnee Friends Mission.] We passed to the right of the elegant residence of
[Shawnee] chief Jo[seph] Parks, near . . . [Shawnee] Methodist mission,
leaving it on our left; near the [Shawnee] Baptist mission and church, leaving
them to our right, to the edge of the timber which skirted Turkey creek where
. . . [Shawnee Friends Mission lay]."

Ref: *KHC,* v. 8, pp. 251, 252; New York *Daily Tribune,* July 8, 1850 (for Wattles).

❡ In the latter part of November, a company of some 16 persons, overland from California, passed through Weston, Mo. They had left Sacramento City around September 1.

Ref: St. Louis *Intelligencer,* November 30, 1850 (from Weston [Mo.] *Reporter*).

❡ November 25.—The U. S. mail (Waldo, Hall & Co.) stage from Santa Fe (left November 1) reached Independence, Mo. "Mr. Caldwell, of Cincinnati," who had departed Santa Fe around October 20, traveled most of the way to Missouri as a passenger. (Caldwell debarked from the *Mary Blane* at St. Louis December 2.)

Five out-bound trains had been met—the last one ("Russell & Co's. of Lexington, Mo.") was at "Fort Expedient, near the crossing of the Arkansas" (still another name for "New Post on Arkansas"—subsequently Fort Atkinson). Incoming trains passed were three belonging to Waldo & Co.—one at Big Bend of Arkansas; another at Turkey creek; and the third at 114-mile creek.

Ref: St. Louis *Intelligencer,* December 6, 1850; *Missouri Republican,* St. Louis, December 7, 1850.

❡ MARRIED: Thomas Nesbit Stinson (Union Town trader), aged 32, and Julia Ann Beauchemie (daughter of Mackinaw Beauchemie), aged 16, on November 28, at the home of the bride's brother, Alexander Beauchemie, by a missionary of Pottawatomie Baptist Mission.

Ref: Statement by Julia Ann Stinson, April 21, 1906 (in KHi ms. div.); *KHC,* v. 9, p. 212; *Bulletin of the Shawnee County Historical Society,* Topeka, v. 2 (December, 1948), p. 114. Mrs. Stinson's statement is that she was married "in Auburndale" (within present Topeka). An account says the Alexander Beauchemie house was on what is now Franklin street. For other information on Stinson, and the Beauchemie family, *see* annals index.

❡ December(?)—Late in the year, "Mr. Martin" (a newcomer to the Santa Fe trade) left the Missouri border with "an ox train heavily laden with merchandise." By extraordinary good luck he made a "very successful" winter trip, reaching Santa Fe, in January, 1851.

Ref: *Missouri Republican,* St. Louis, March 12, 1851.

❡ December 1.—William H. Arnall (Brown, Woodson & Co. employee) left Independence, Mo., with the U. S. mail (in a wagon) for Salt Lake City. Though he got to Fort Kearny in 17 days, it was not until March 7, 1851, that he reached his destination (with over 200 pounds of mail matter).

An account stated Arnall had been detained several weeks in all, at several points, by storms and snow; that he lost a portion of his mules, but "persevered," and finally got through. West of Fort Laramie he used pack mules.

Ref: New York *Daily Tribune,* February 25, 1851 (from *The Frontier Guardian,* Kanesville, Ia.—which referred to the mail carrier as "Mr. Arnold . . . an old mountaineer"); Glasgow (Mo.) *Weekly Times,* June 5, 1851 (from an interview with

Arnall); L. R. Hafen and F. M. Young, *op. cit.,* pp. 171, 172 (from "Journal History," March 12, 1851, Mormon church archives).

❡ December 13.—Southwestern "Kansas"—the section south of the Arkansas river, and west of the 100th meridian—came under formal United States control. (Until 1822 it had been claimed by Spain; Mexico's claim was extinguished by the Mexican War settlement in 1848; from 1835, till November 25, 1850, Texas laid claim to the area.)

President Fillmore, in a special message, December 13, to congress, announced the acceptance by Texas (on November 25) of propositions offered in the act of September 9, for establishment of her northern and western boundaries, and relinquishment of her claims to lands exterior to those in the agreement.

Ref: J. D. Richardson, comp., . . . *Messages and Papers of the Presidents* . . . (1905), v. 5, pp. 94, 95; W. C. Binkley's *The Expansionist Movement in Texas 1836-1850* (Berkeley, Calif., 1925), pp. 207-218.

❡ December.—Fifteen men (including "Mr. Miligan's" U. S. mail party of four) arrived in the States this month, after a tedious, difficult (due to snow and cold weather) trip overland from Salt Lake City by way of South Pass, Forts Laramie and Kearny, and the Old Fort Kearny road to the Missouri.

In advance of Miligan's party (left at Scotts Bluff), 11 reached the Missouri together: Messrs. Livingston and Kinkead (whose destination was Council Bluffs), Oscar Middleton, Jeff. Thompson, W. E. Horner (these three in the employ of Middleton & Riley, St. Joseph), Mr. Cogswell, Doctor Barnes, of St. Louis, Mr. Waldon, Mr. Sledge, and Antonio Selman—who arrived at St. Joseph on December 17. It was reported they brought from $75,000 to $80,000.

"Miligan" and his companions, who had reached Fort Kearny before the 11 others departed that post, were expected at St. Joseph around December 21 or 22—they, too, traveling the Old Fort Kearny trail "it being impossible to get to Independence by the usual route along the Blue." This "October" mail from Salt Lake reached Independence on December 26—*see* next entry.

Ref: St. Joseph *Gazette,* December 25, 1850; *Adventure,* St. Joseph, December 20, 1850; *Frontier Guardian,* Kanesville, Ia., December 25, 1850, January 8, 1851; St. Louis *Intelligencer,* December 28, 1850.

❡ December 26.—Two U. S. mail parties (one delayed by snow, ice, and bad weather) from Salt Lake City, and the December U. S. mail from Santa Fe, arrived at Independence, Mo.

Two or three of the Salt Lake mail carriers (as reported) were "badly frostbitten." James E. Sabine, trader, brought the Santa Fe mail to the States (the scheduled carrier, "Mr. Borland," having died). "Mr. Moore," who joined Sabine's party at "new post at Arkansas" (Fort Atkinson), got "badly frosted" on the journey.

Ref: *Missouri Republican,* St. Louis, January 5, 1851.

ℭ Employed in "Kansas" by the Indian Department during all, or part of the year were the following persons:

FORT LEAVENWORTH AGENCY *[Kickapoos, Delawares, Shawnees, Pottawatomies, Stockbridges and Munsees]*—*Agent* Luke Lea; *Interpreters* Henry Tiblow and Joseph LaFromboise; *Physicians* Johnston Lykins, James B. Stone, and Archibald B. Earle—for the Pottawatomies; *Wagonmaker* Henry R. Samuel—for the Pottawatomies; *Gunsmith* James B. Franklin and *Assistant gunsmith* William H. Franklin—for the Pottawatomies; *Blacksmiths* Calvin Perkins—for Shawnees, Granderson T. Deering and James F. Mills—for the Pottawatomies, Isaac Mundy—for the Delawares; *Assistant blacksmiths* Lindsey T. Cook—for Shawnees, William H. Scruggs, William F. Deering, Thomas Evans, and Samuel Lewis—for Pottawatomies, Hugh Murdock—for Delawares; *Sawyer* John W. Tucker and *Assistant sawyer* Thomas G. Campbell—for Pottawatomies; *Ferryman* Lucius R. Darling—for Pottawatomies; *Laborers* (at Pottawatomies' saw mills) William H. Huffman (quit May 15), Thomas Merander, Peter Moose, Valentine C. Warden, Albion S. Ollcott, and Noah Daniels.

OSAGE RIVER AGENCY *[Sacs & Foxes of the Mississippi, Kansa, Ottawas, Chippewas, Weas, Piankeshaws, and Miamis]*—*Agent* Charles N. Handy, superseded by John R. Chenault (appointed October 12; arrived in mid-December); *Interpreters* John Goodell and Baptiste Peoria; *Blacksmiths* Alfred Laws and Matthew R. Johnson—for Sacs & Foxes, Robert Wilson ("removed") and Robert Simerwell (to replace Wilson)—for Miamis; *Assistant blacksmiths* Thomas C. Warren and Rolin McDaniel—for Sacs & Foxes, James A. Mitchell, Morris Baker, and Emanuel Mosier—for Kansa, James P. Wilson ("removed") and Luther Paschall—for Miamis; *Farmer* Amos H. Goodin—for Miamis; *Gunsmiths* Charles H. Withington and James E. Gray—for Sacs & Foxes; *Physician* F. McKnight—for Sacs & Foxes(?); *Miller* Henry L. Hicks—for Miamis.

GREAT NEMAHA SUBAGENCY *[Iowas, and Sacs & Foxes of the Missouri]*—*Agent* William P. Richardson; *Interpreters* John B. Rubite—for Sacs & Foxes, John B. Roy—for Iowas; *Blacksmiths* Newman York ("resigned") and John McCloskey—for Sacs & Foxes; *Assistant smith* Charles Eggers—for Sacs & Foxes; *Farmer and miller* James F. Forman—for Sacs & Foxes.

OSAGE SUBAGENCY *[Osages]*—*Subagent* Henry Harvey (A. J. Dorn of the Neosho Subagency was acting subagent till Harvey's arrival in April); *Interpreters* Charles Mongrain and Antoine Penn; *Blacksmiths* John R. McKinney ("removed"), Elijah Pennington, and George Tinker; *Assistant smiths* Joseph Captain (to July) and Francis Mitchell; *Millers* Augustus Captain (to July 11) and E. K. Howland (from July 11); *Assistant millers* Dodridge Barnaby, Peter Chouteau, and Joseph Captain (from July).

WYANDOT SUBAGENCY *[Wyandots]*—*Subagent* Thomas Moseley, Jr.; *Interpreter* William Walker; *Blacksmith* Charles Graham; *Assistant smith* Guilford D. Hurt.

Ref: 31st Cong., 2d Sess., H. Ex. Doc. No. 27 (Serial 599), pp. 3-6; 32d Cong., 1st Sess., H. Ex. Doc. No. 103 (Serial 647), pp. 355, 356, 604-607, 610-627, 701, 702, 705, 706, 715, 717, 718, 721, 780, 783, 784; SIA, St. Louis, "Records," v. 9, typed copy, pp. 413-416, 420, 434, 447, 448, 463, 470, 475, 476, 485, 492; OIA, Letters Received from Osage Agency, 1849-1854 (National Archives Microcopy 234); Jotham Meeker's "Diary," December 18, 1850, entry (for Chenault's arrival "some 4 or 5 days since").

1851

❖ January.—Capt. Frederick H. Masten (AQM), who left Fort Laramie January 2, arrived at St. Louis on February 2. (Whether his route from Fort Kearny to the Missouri border was by way of "Kansas" is not indicated.)

He had "suffered a good deal from severe weather" during the journey; had overtaken and passed "a mail from Salt Lake City"—the "November" mail, evidently, *see* second entry following. His trip was for the purpose of hiring mechanics to erect barracks at Fort Laramie.

Ref: *Missouri Republican,* St. Louis, February 3, 1851.

❖ January.—The Independence-to-Salt Lake "January" U. S. mail with which "Powell" (traveling with pack mules) started west on January 1(?), reached Fort Kearny on the 16th (and left there on the 22d). As reported: "The mail bags got wet at the 'Big Blue' [the Alcove Spring area crossing, present Marshall county], and when opened [at Fort Kearny] were in an *'awful condition.'* "

Powell reached Fort Laramie on February 8 (and a correspondent at that post wrote that "St. Louis dates of Jan. 9[?] were in the mail received"). On February 10 "Mr. Hackard"(?), who had set out January 4 and "packed through," arrived at Fort Laramie from the west, with the "January" Salt Lake-to-Independence mail. "Hackard" then returned to Salt Lake with the mail from the States; and Powell, having received the eastbound mail, started back to Missouri. Both left Fort Laramie on February 11.

By mid-March Powell was back in Independence. The Liberty *Tribune* of March 21 printed a letter (to the editor) from "Me," written at Fort Laramie on February 10; and in the March 28 issue, observed: "quite a large mail is brought down by Powell." "Winter's" letter of February 10 from Fort Laramie was published in the St. Louis *Republican* of March 22, 1851.

Ref: *The Weekly Tribune,* Liberty, Mo., March 21, 28, 1851; *The Frontier Guardian,* Kanesville, Ia., February 21, 1851; *Missouri Republican,* St. Louis, March 22, 1851. In L. R. Hafen and F. M. Young's *Fort Laramie* . . . (1938), p. 172, it is stated that "Ephraim K. Hanks led a party which set out from Salt Lake City with the mail [the U. S. mail?] early in January, 1851. From Fort Bridger they took a route to the south of South Pass and reached Fort Laramie, after traveling through the snow for 36 days." (The sources given are the "Journal History"—Mormon church archives, and the *Missouri Republican* item cited above.)

❖ Some time after mid-January, the "November" U. S. mail party from Salt Lake City, which had started east on November 24, 1850, reached Independence, Mo.

James Monroe (who left Salt Lake December 1, for the States, and overtook the eastbound mail wagon at Fort Bridger) was a cotraveler to Fort Laramie; and from that post to Fort Kearny "hired his passage with the mail." Via the Old Fort Kearny trail, alone, he reached Kanesville, Ia., on January 16.

Ref: New York *Daily Tribune,* February 13 (from St. Louis *Union* of February 1), and 25 (from *The Frontier Guardian,* Kanesville, Ia.), 1851. *Also, see, The Frontier Guardian,* May 16, 1851.

❡ January 26.—In charge of "Mr. [Jarvis] Streeter," and five days early, the "January" U. S. mail from Santa Fe arrived at Independence, Mo.

Streeter reported good travel conditions on the plains; the Arkansas clear of ice; and no Indians seen. The outbound "January" mail had been met on the 13th at "Fort Mackay"—the new military post on the Arkansas (*see* p. 965).

Ref: *Missouri Republican*, St. Louis, February 3, 1851.

❡ January-June.—Licenses to trade with Indians in "Kansas," as granted by agents of the St. Louis Superintendency were:

Traders	Indians	Issued by	Rec'vd at St. Louis
(J. M.) Simpson & (J. M.) Hunter	Pottawatomies	Luke Lea	March
Cyprian Chouteau	Delawares & Kickapoos	Luke Lea	March
Thos. D. S. Macdonell	Iowas, and Sacs & Foxes (of the Missouri)	W. P. Richardson	April
J. B. Scott	Sacs & Foxes (of the Mississippi)	J. R. Chenault	April
Polke & Macdonell	Sacs & Foxes (of the Mississippi)	J. R. Chenault	April
(A. G.) Boone & (W. R.) Bernard	Osages	Henry Harvey	April
John W. Forman	Iowas, and Sacs & Foxes (of the Missouri)	W. P. Richardson	June

Ref: Superintendency of Indian Affairs (SIA), St. Louis, "Records," v. 9, typed copy, pp. 499, 503, 505, 506, 510, 521. Beginning October 26, 1849, the St. Joseph (Mo.) *Gazette* carried an advertisement for the new store of "D[uncan] & T[homas] D. S. Macdonell Dry Goods, Grocery & Commission Merchants. . . ."

❡ February 1-11.—The U. S. mail party to Santa Fe which left Independence, Mo., at the beginning of the month, was joined at Diamond Spring by an express from Fort Leavenworth, which traveled in company to "New Post Arkansas River."

A letter from "Fort Sumner" (*i. e.*, another name for the new post), dated February 11, stated that the mailmen had sighted a mounted band of Pawnees on the morning of the 9th, at Walnut creek. The Indians, after discovering the party's size—"two carriages," and "out side riders"—disappeared; but in the afternoon, near Pawnee Rock, they chased mailman G. H. Williams (when he went back on the trail in search of a "broken-down mule").

By February 16 the mail coaches were at Middle Cimarron Spring.

Ref: *Missouri Republican*, St. Louis, March 11, 12, 1851.

❡ February 2.—Nine men—Robert Nesbitt, Solomon J. Spiegelberg, James Gilchrist, four teamsters, and two Mexicans (with three wagons)—who had left Santa Fe January 6, reached Independence, Mo.

Nesbit and Spiegelberg, ordered outfits from local merchants; then continued to the East to buy goods.

Ref: *Missouri Statesman,* Columbia, Mo., February 21, 1851; *Missouri Republican,* St. Louis, February 3, 1851 (in which it was stated that this party planned to bring, from Santa Fe, the remains of freighter "Judge" James Brown, and "Nesbitt"); New York *Daily Tribune,* February 25, 1851 (in which "A. Z. McK.," in a letter to Horace Greeley, from Santa Fe, January 5, 1851, wrote that "Government intend farming here, and have sent Mr. Nesbit to buy seeds and the necessary implements"). In 1856, Gilchrist was a cofounder of the short-lived Douglas county town, Prairie City. (Information from Mrs. Lola Christianson, Topeka; and *see KHC,* v. 12, p. 486.)

❈ February 16.—Martha J. Chenault (wife of Indian agent John R. Chenault) wrote, from "Osage River Agency" (to which the family had just moved): ". . . the Agency . . . is situated in a high prairie country . . . [The Chenaults were at the former Sac & Fox Agency * in present Franklin county—*see* p. 704] [we have] a good well of water we have three rooms and a passage below and two above stairs and upon the whole we have a comfortable house for an Indian Country we have here *six trading houses, two blacksmiths and two gun smiths.* most of them have families all white except one, the Sac & Fox Indians are wild looking people but I dont feel mutch afraid, they appear very much pleased with Mr. Chenault. . . .

"[Of our family] Felix, Sarah and Eliza are at fathers [in Jasper? county, Mo.] . . . we have James, William, Stephen and Emily with us."

Ref: Martha J. Chenault's letter, February 16, 1851, in KHi ms. division. A "Sac & Fox Agency" ❋ was reestablished as of July 1, 1851. John R. Chenault was assigned as agent, and remained till the spring of 1853. For note on abolishment of the original Sac & Fox Agency, in 1848, *see* p. 762. *Also, see* p. 970.

❈ February 17.—Jones & Russell (John S. Jones and William H. Russell, Lexington, Mo.) signed a two-year contract (made with Lt. Col. Thomas Swords, QM) to transport army stores from Fort Leavenworth to Santa Fe (rate: $8.59 per 100 pounds) and Albuquerque (rate: $9.50 per 100 pounds). Sureties for the $50,000 bond were: Elijah Rogers, W. W. Porter, Jonathan Hicklin, James W. Renick, G(eorge) R(appeen) Smith, and A. M. Forbes.

On May 15 Jones & Russell signed another two-year contract (made with Bvt. Maj. E. A. Ogden, AQM) for transporting army stores from Fort Leavenworth to New Mexico (Las Vegas, Moro, Rayado, etc.); delivery to be made between May 7 and August 1, in 1851, and 1852; rate $7.87½ per 100 pounds. E. Rogers, E. C. McCarty, T. M. Ewing, and J. H. Graham were the bondsmen.

Ref: 32d Cong., 1st Sess., *Sen. Ex. Doc. No. 12* (Serial 614), p. 22; 32d Cong., 2d Sess., *Sen. Ex. Doc. No. 18* (Serial 660), p. 7.

❈ A February 18 letter from Weston, Mo. (received at Boonville, Mo., on, or before the 22d), contained the far-from-accurate information that "Pawnees" had attacked the "Government [mail] Station" at Council Grove and "killed several persons"; and that a company of Fort Leavenworth's dragoons had set out for that place.

In mid-March the St. Louis *Republican* learned that the "Indian outrage" of some weeks back consisted of the theft, by "Sac" Indians, of a number of horses and mules from the Council Grove mail station; and that the Fort Leavenworth troops had captured part of the stolen animals (the rest were believed in the hands of the Osages), and had brought back to the fort "some of the principal men of the nation" as hostages for delivery of the unrecovered animals.

Percival G. Lowe (a corporal in Company B, First dragoons, in 1851) wrote, in his 1906-published *Five Years a Dragoon*, that "The Kaw [Kansa] Indians near Council Grove had been committing some depredations—stealing horses . . . [etc.]," and that in "January[?]" of 1851 Bvt. Maj. Robert H. Chilton, with about 50 dragoons, marched the 120 miles to Council Grove, "had a 'big talk,'" and brought back "four of the principal chiefs of the Kaw Nation" to Fort Leavenworth as prisoners. (Lowe described the troopers' hardships—for lack of winter clothing—on this trip; and recollected that about half the men were frostbitten to some extent, several severely.)

Lowe's account also stated that there was "Not a house between Fort Leavenworth and Papan's Ferry across the Kaw [Kansas], sixty miles, and none between the ferry and Council Grove. . . ." He was referring to the *new* (in 1850) *military road which linked Fort Leavenworth with the Santa Fe trail by a nearly direct route from the army post to a junction east of Council Grove.* (This was a refinement of the Fort Leavenworth-Union Town-Council Grove road which Capt. L. C. Easton had suggested in 1849—*see* p. 887—shortening it by utilizing the Kansas river "lower crossing" 15 miles below Union Town [the "Papin's ferry" crossing] at present Topeka.) In his book Lowe outlined the route as follows:

"The road from Fort Leavenworth to New Mexico ran through what is now Easton, at the crossing of Stranger Creek [which was known as "Dawson's crossing" in the early 1850's]; then through what is now Winchester, [and on to] Ozakee [Ozawkie] at the crossing of Grasshopper, now [called] Delaware River and [thence to] Soldier Creek, four miles north of where now stands Topeka. There [at Topeka] it crossed the Kaw on Papan's [Papin's] Ferry, about sixty miles from Fort Leavenworth, thence to Council Grove, sixty miles farther, intersecting the main Santa Fe trail from Independence, Missouri [at what became Wilmington, Wabaunsee co.], east of the Grove [and west of present Burlingame]."

A Santa Fe-bound army officer, traveling this route in May, 1852, referred to it as "the new road . . . which has been established and used for three years only." He (2d Lt. William D. Whipple?) also stated that it was 54 miles from the fort to the Kansas river; and that after crossing (*i. e.*, at Topeka) it was 17 miles to "Wah-ka-russi Creek"; and at "86 miles from Fort Leavenworth" the new road struck the "broad trace from Independence to Santa Fe."

Ref: *Missouri Republican,* St. Louis, February 24, March 13, 1851; New York *Daily Tribune,* March 28, 1851 (for the *Republican's* March 13 item); Percival G. Lowe's *Five Years a Dragoon* . . . (1906), pp. 33, 44-46; New York *Daily Tribune,* November 18, 1852 (for Whipple?). Bvt. Maj. E. A. Ogden, in his 1851 report (32d Cong., 1st Sess., Sen. Ex. Doc. No. 1, Serial 611), mentioned his own Spring, 1850, survey of the road from Fort Leavenworth towards Fort Kearny, and referred to the route "now used" towards Santa Fe "surveyed by Lieutenant Field [Bvt. 2d Lt. Charles W. Field]." Ogden implied that Field's survey was made in the spring of 1850, also. No diaries or journals for 1850 or 1851 have yet come to light which describe or even mention this route. (James A. Bennett, who must have been on this military pathway in August-September, 1850, with Buford's command—*see New Mexico Historical Review,* Santa Fe, v. 22, p. 61—did not report [in his diary] on the journey between Fort Leavenworth and Council Grove.) See *Bulletin of the Shawnee County Historical Society,* Topeka, v. 3 (March, 1949), pp. 23-36, for Paul Adams' article "The Old Trail Through Topeka." *Herald of Freedom,* Lawrence, April 14, 21, May 12, 1855, issues have items on the military road and geographical locations relating to it.

❡ February 18.—William Walker (Wyandot) recorded in his diary: "The Kansas river has about run dry; there not being water enough to float the ferry boat [the Wyandots' national ferry, near the Kaw's mouth—*see* p. 500], and consequently no ferrying. . . ." (By evening, the ferry was "passable.")

Ref: William Walker's "Journals," in W. E. Connelley, *The Provisional Government of Nebraska Territory* . . . (1899), p. 319.

❡ February 25.—Benjamin Holladay, Weston, Mo., obtained a two-year contract (made with Lt. Col. Thomas Swords, QM) to transport army stores from Fort Leavenworth to Forts Kearny and Laramie (for $3.80 per 100 pounds to the former; $6.80 per 100 pounds to the latter). J. M. Hughes and Joseph Charless were sureties for the $20,000 bond.

In 1851 the government-contract (*i. e.*, Holladay) wagon trains which set out from Fort Leavenworth for the two Oregon-California trail posts were (by official report) as listed below:

For Fort Laramie, on May 31   A(rmistead) Dawson with 11 wagons (52,926 pounds total)
For Fort Laramie, on June 10   F(rancis) C. Hughes with 17 wagons (86,815 pounds total)
For Fort Kearny, on June 24   A(ndrew) S. Hughes with 10 wagons (50,652 pounds total)
For Fort Kearny, on June 27   A(ndrew) S. Hughes with 4 wagons (21,200 pounds total)

Benjamin Holladay's own activities in 1851 received comment in the San Francisco *Placer Times and Transcript* of October 12: "Messrs. [Benjamin] Holladay & [Theodore F.] Warner, of Weston, near Fort Leavenworth, Missouri, have freighted this year nearly two hundred tons of merchandise, costing, landed at its destination, one hundred thousand dollars. They have an establishment at Salt Lake [William H. Hooper had charge of Holladay & Warner's store there—opened in 1850], from which Mr. Holladay has landed in California, with thirty large mule wagons, five hundred oxen and two hundred mules, brought to this city for sale, and a portion of them now to be seen at the horse market in this city. . . ."

A Salt Lake-bound "Holladay & Warner" train was met on May 11, by eastbound travelers, about 40 miles east of Fort Kearny—on the Old Fort Kearny road (the regular route—as appears—of their merchant trains). On June 8 and 9 this train was near Independence Rock. Before July 1 Benjamin Holladay had reached Salt Lake City.

The mail carrier who left Salt Lake City July 1 for the States, reported that he had met "Holladay's ox team[s]" at Fort Laramie; and their "second train [mule-drawn]" at Scott's Bluff. These, presumably, were the Dawson and Hughes trains which left Fort Leavenworth on May 31 and June 10, respectively (see above).

Ref: 32d Cong., 1st Sess., Sen. Ex. Doc. No. 12 (Serial 614), p. 20; 32d Cong., 1st Sess., Sen. Ex. Doc. No. 1 (Serial 611), p. 295; St. Joseph (Mo.) Gazette, May 21, 1851; Missouri Republican, St. Louis, July 15, 26, 1851; The Weekly Tribune, Liberty, Mo., July 11, August 1, 1851. For the Placer Times quote see St. Joseph Gazette, December 24, 1851, or, Missouri Republican, December 27, 1851; Glasgow (Mo.) Weekly Times, August 7, 1851; Orson F. Whitney's History of Utah . . . (Salt Lake City, 1892), v. 1, p. 498.

❧ February-March.—Down from Weston, Mo., "with a full cargo and a large number of passengers," the "fine steamer" Robert Campbell (William Edds, captain) reached St. Louis on February 28. "The Robert Campbell is the first steamboat arrival from Weston, or any point above Lexington this season," the Intelligencer stated.

On March 2 the "popular Missouri river packet" El Paso (T. H. Brierly, captain) "returned" to St. Louis from Weston, "being the second boat of the season" (according to the Intelligencer).

Upbound (for Weston?), the Highland Mary passed the Kansas river's mouth on March 5. The Mary Blane, on March 8, apparently was the first steamboat of the year to reach St. Joseph, Mo.

Ref: St. Louis Daily Intelligencer, March 1, 3, 1851; Adventure, St. Joseph, Mo., March 14, 1851; St. Joseph Gazette, March 12, 1851; William Walker's "Journals," loc. cit., p. 319.

❧ March.—The U. S. mail party leaving Independence, Mo., March 1(?), for Salt Lake City, got as far as the Big Blue (of "Kansas") crossing (in the Alcove Spring vicinity), where "in consequence of high water" a return was made to Missouri. (It appears the March mail trip then was cancelled.)

Ref: The Frontier Guardian, Kanesville, Ia., May 16, 1851.

❧ March.—The U. S. mail which left Independence, Mo., on March 1 for Santa Fe, reached its destination on the 24th. The mailmen, while en route, had "bluffed off" some Indians who "endeavored to approach them."

The "March" mail from Santa Fe did not start out till March 9. A disgruntled Santa Fe correspondent wrote that the "blame must be laid to the mail agent, [Jacob] Hall, a most unaccommodating man to the public generally."

Ref: New York Daily Tribune, May 7, 1851.

❧ About March 1 a "Brown, Russell & Co." (i. e., Jones & Russell)

28-wagon mule train, freighting government stores to Santa Fe, left Fort Leavenworth.

(C. E. Kearney, and party met the advance section at Bull creek early in the month; and on the 15th, west of the Little Arkansas, Major Cunningham—*see following*—met "Martin of Russell's mule train.")

At a "place near Chouteau's Island," on March 22, all the wagons (of the leading train?) were destroyed in a prairie fire (set, it was supposed, by Pawnees). The teamsters saved themselves by crossing the Arkansas. George Cranmer, assistant wagonmaster, carried news of the disaster back to Lexington, Mo.

Ref: *Missouri Republican*, St. Louis, March 12, 31, 1851; *Missouri Statesman*, Columbia, May 2, 1851 (from Lexington [Mo.] *Express* of April 5); 32d Cong., 1st Sess., *Sen. Ex. Doc. No. 1* (Serial 611), p. 222.

❧ March.—Insofar as information is available, these were the steamboats (from St. Louis) which reached Weston or St. Joseph, Mo., between March 7 and March 31:

Date	Arrived at	Name of boat	Left	For	Remarks
March 7	Weston	*Robert Campbell*	March 8	St. Louis	Arr. March 15
March 8	St. Joseph	*Mary Blane*	March 9	St. Louis	Arr. March 15
March (9?)	Weston	*Kansas*	March 10	St. Louis	Troops carried to Fort Leavenworth—*see* next entry
March 10	St. Joseph	*El Paso*	March 11	St. Louis	
March 11	St. Joseph	*Isabel*	March 12	Savannah Landing	Started back to St. Louis March 12; arr. March 18
March 13	St. Joseph	*St. Ange*	March 14		
March (17?)	Weston	*Saranak*	March 18	St. Louis	Arr. March 23(?)
March (19?)	Weston	*Highland Mary*	March 20	St. Louis	Arr. March 27
March 25	St. Joseph	*El Paso*°	March 26		

° Had aboard "a great number of English Mormons . . . *en route* for the Salt Lake Valley."—St. Joseph *Gazette*.

March 28	St. Joseph	*Isabel*	March 29	St. Louis	
March 28	St. Joseph	*St. Ange*	March 29		
March (29?)	(Weston?)	*Kansas* †			

† At St. Louis, March 20, the *Kansas* contracted to take up to Fort Leavenworth, one officer and 37 [*i. e.*, 87?] men.

March 29	**St. Joseph**	*Pocahontas* ‡	March 30		

‡ "The fine Missouri river trader *Pocahontas* left [St. Louis] yesterday for West Union, . . . 50 miles above St. Joseph with a heavy cargo . . . and many passengers."—St. Louis *Daily Intelligencer*, March 19.

Ref: *Missouri Republican*, St. Louis, March 4, 1851; St. Louis *Daily Intelligencer*, March 15, 17-19, 24, 27, April 5, 1851; St. Joseph *Gazette*, March 12, 19, 26; *Adventure*, St. Joseph, March 14, 21, 28; 32d Cong., 1st Sess., *Sen. Ex. Doc. No. 12* (Ser. 614), p. 25.

❧ March 8(?).—Lt. John W. Davidson, First dragoons, another officer, 84 "raw recruits," a few laundresses, some horses, and 30 to 40 tons of government freight, were landed at Fort Leavenworth from the steamboat *Kansas* (William C. Jewett, master).

The *Kansas*, heading for the Missouri, had passed St. Louis on March 2. "She had on board, including the soldiers, near 300 passengers," the *Intelligencer* reported (and the *Republican* concurred). On March 8, "above Parkville," the downbound *Robert Campbell* met the *Kansas* (which probably reached Fort Leavenworth the same day).

Ref: St. Louis *Daily Intelligencer*, March 3, 15, 1851; *Missouri Republican*, St. Louis, March 3, 1851; 32d Cong., 1st Sess., *Sen. Ex. Doc. No. 1* (Serial 614), p. 25.

❡ On or before March 9, 25 men (with five wagons) who had left Santa Fe on February 1, arrived at Independence, Mo. Among those in the party who boarded the *Highland Mary* and debarked at St. Louis March 11 were: Charles E. Kearney, Richard ("Dick") Owens, Joseph Mercure, Henry Grandjean, (Charles S.) Rumley, (J. W.?) Austin, "Edwards," "Parrott," (Elias) Brevoort, "Johnson," and "P. [Dr. Philippe] Masure."

Remaining at Independence were: J(oseph) D. Ellis, William Mitchell, John Fristoe, George Estes, and Francis Green (who, after accidentally shooting himself, near Turkey creek, had made the rest of the journey in Kearney's carriage).

Ref: *Missouri Republican*, St. Louis, March 12, 1851; St. Louis *Daily Intelligencer*, March 13, 1851. The federal census of Jackson county, Mo., 1850, listed (as at John Harris' hotel, in Kaw township, on August 9, 1850) "E. S. Johnson," a "Mexican trader," aged 28.

❡ March 10.—Perry & Young (of St. Joseph and Weston, Mo.) received a two-year contract (made with Lt. Col. Thomas Swords, QM) to transport army stores from Fort Leavenworth to "Fort Mackay" (subsequently named Fort Atkinson)—on the Arkansas, west of present Dodge City—for $4.23 per 100 pounds. A. W. Riley and W. Dickey were sureties for the $50,000 bond.

Ref: 32d Cong., 1st Sess., *Sen. Ex. Doc. No. 12* (Serial 614), p. 20.

❡ March.—On the 10th(?) Francis X. Aubry left Independence, Mo., with a merchandise train—apparently the first of the Santa Fe traders on the trail in 1851. About a week later he was at Lost Spring (where Major Cunningham's party—*see following*—met him).

On April 5 other Missouri-bound travelers met Aubry at "Whetstone Branch"; and on April 8 they met "Russell's train" (called both "Brown and Russel's train" and "Morton [Martin], Russell & Co's. train" by other eastbound travelers who also met it in New Mexico.) This train, it was reported, had left Missouri 15 days later than Aubry.

See, also, May 12 annals entry.

Ref: *Missouri Republican*, St. Louis, March 12, 31, April 28, 1851; New York *Daily Tribune*, May 19, 1851 (from St. Louis *Union*, May 7).

❡ March 18.—At Union Town (the Pottawatomies' three-year-old trading post, in present Shawnee county—*see* p. 737), near the "upper crossing" of Kansas river, on the Oregon-California road, a post office was established, with Robert Robitaille (of the Wyandot Nation; a licensed Indian trader) as first postmaster.

This short-lived station at Union Town (a designated point on the U. S. mail route from Independence, Mo., to Salt Lake City) was, for eight months, the westernmost post office in "Kansas" (but *see* p. 1049); and was the first in present Shawnee county. On December 16, 1852, it was discontinued.

Ref: Robert W. Baughman's *Kansas Post Offices* (c1961), pp. 130, 156, 239 (wherein Union Town should be listed under Shawnee county instead of Wyandotte county). For Robert Robitaille as an Indian trader, *see* annals, p. 949. The 1850 Jackson county, Mo., federal census listed Robert Robitaille (merchant, aged 46), and his children: Robert W. (12), Rosalie (10), Elizabeth (8); also, James (4) and Mary A. (2)—both born in "Indian Terr." (Kansas).

❧ Near the end of March, Maj. Francis A. Cunningham (army paymaster), C. H. Merritt (U. S. marshal of New Mexico ter.), "Mr. [John] Hatcher" ("late a resident of Rayado"), and "escort" of some 45 to 50 men, arrived at Independence, Mo., from Santa Fe (left February 17).

Ref: *Missouri Republican*, St. Louis, March 31, April 3, 1851.

❧ March-April.—The *Adventure* of April 11 reported that during the preceding two weeks several steamboats had reached St. Joseph, Mo., "having on board small companies of emigrants"—most of them destined for Oregon territory. "Many . . . who have arrived are agents for Companies that are to follow. . . . Several families have arrived here, over land. . . . This season . . . [is] several weeks more forward than last. . . ."

The St. Joseph *Gazette* of March 26 had stated: "From best information . . . but few persons will emigrate to California or Oregon this year. This time last year our town literally was crowded, but now very few are in the place. A few Oregon emigrants have passed through . . . who will camp a short distance from town to wait for grass. . . ." The *Gazette* of April 9 noted the arrival of a "number of emigrants"—mostly bound for Oregon; and among them "several missionaries sent out by the Baptist Home Missionary Society [*i. e.*, the Rev. George C. Chandler (president, 1843-1850, of Franklin College; Franklin, Ind.), his family, and the Rev. James S. Read (just graduated from Franklin College)]."

Ref: *Adventure*, St. Joseph, April 11, 1851; St. Joseph *Gazette*, March 26, April 9, 1851; *Oregon Historical Quarterly*, Salem, v. 17, pp. 314, 439; *Baptist Home Missions in North America . . . 1832-1882* (New York, 1883), p. 605.

❧ April.—Listed below are most of the steamboats that went up the Missouri to points beyond the Kansas river's mouth during the month:

Date	Arrived at	Name of boat	Left	For	Remarks
April 1	St. Joseph	*Alton*	April 1	St. Louis	
April 3	St. Joseph	*Saranak* °	April 3	St. Louis	Had aboard, for Fort Leavenworth, one officer, and 80 men.

° "The *Saranak* arrived yesterday having on board a large number of passengers with wagons and other outfits for a journey across the plains. We understand the most of them are bound for Utah and Oregon territories. This is the first arrival of any considerable number of emigrants for the plains this spring."—*Adventure*, St. Joseph, April 4.

April 3	St. Joseph (on return from upriver?)	*Anthony Wayne*	April 4	St. Louis	On down trip, sank above Liberty Landing.
April 7	St. Joseph	*El Paso*			
April 9	St. Joseph	*Cataract*	April 9		Emigrants aboard; *see* p. 990.
April (9?)	Weston	*Highland Mary*		St. Louis	Arr. April 13.
April (11?)	Weston	*Kansas* †	April 12	St. Louis	Arr. April 18.

† "The *Kansas* returned yesterday. . . . Her officers report the navigation of the Missouri extremely difficult, even more so than they ever saw it at this season. . . ." The *Kansas* had met the *St. Ange* above Parkville; the *Pawnee* at Kansas; and *Pocahontas* at Sibley; the *Isabel* was "hauling over Fishing River bar"; the *Saranak* was met at Waverly; the *Ben West*, the *Bay State*, and others, were met below. [Neither the *Pocahontas* nor the *Ben West* went as far as St. Joseph this trip.]—St. Louis *D. Intel.*, April 19.

| April 11 | St. Joseph | *Duroc* ‡ | April 12 | Council Bluffs | |

‡ The *Duroc* took up a large number of emigrants for Salt Lake and Oregon.—St. Louis *Times*, April 28.
   On April 27 the *Duroc* left St. Joseph on the down trip.—*Gazette*, April 30.

| April 13 | St. Joseph | *St. Ange* § | April 14 | Council Bluffs | |

§ Some 200 Mormons were aboard the *St. Ange* when she left St. Joseph for upriver.— *Gazette*, April 16.

| April 15 | St. Joseph | *Pawnee* | April 16 | | |
| April (17?) | Fort Leavenworth | *El Paso* ¶ | | | |

¶ On April 12 the *El Paso* was engaged to take three officers and 133 enlisted men from Jefferson Barracks to Fort Leavenworth.

April 17	St. Joseph	*Saranak*	April 17		
April 18	St. Joseph	*Isabel*	April 19		
April 19	St. Joseph	*Bay State*	April 20		
April 22	St. Joseph	*Sacramento* ° °	April 23	Council Bluffs	

° ° "400 Mormons passed up the Missouri this morning on *Sacramento*, destined for the Salt Lake."—St. Joseph *Gazette*, April 23.

April 23	St. Joseph	*Highland Mary*	April 23	St. Louis	Arr. April 27.
April (24?)	Weston	*St. Paul*			
April 25	St. Joseph	*Statesman* ††	April 26	Council Bluffs	

†† At Bellevue, in mid-May, R. F. Kurz saw the *Statesman* approach. "On the hurricane deck I could see wagon bodies painted blue and red wheels piled upon them—a sort of vehicle I had identified with Pittsburgh. . . ." Kurz learned the boat was bound for "Kanesville or Mormon Landing," 30 miles upriver.—Kurz' journal.

Ref: St. Louis *Daily Intelligencer*, April 19, 28, 1851; *Adventure*, St. Joseph, April 4, 11, 18, 25, 1851; St. Joseph *Gazette*, April 2, 9, 16, 23, 30, 1851; *Missouri Republican*, St. Louis, April 14, 28, 1851; New York *Daily Tribune*, May 7, 1851 (from St. Louis *Times*, April 28); 32d Cong., 1st Sess., *Sen. Ex. Doc. No. 1* (Serial 614), p. 28; *Oregon Historical Quarterly*, v. 25, p. 136*ff.*; Bureau of American Ethnology *Bulletin No. 115* (Kurz' "Journal"), p. 63.

¶ April.—The U. S. mail for Salt Lake City this month was placed in charge of "Mr. [Richard S.] Phelps, of Independence"—who was taking a train of goods over the Oregon-California trail. Phelps passed Fort Kearny on April 15.

Other westbound travelers at Fort Kearny in mid-April included William and T. Randell (en route to [Richard's] new North Platte river bridge) with groceries and provisions for emigrants; J. B. Nichols (for Fort Laramie); "Richards & Co." (trader John Richard's outfit) with provisions, &c.

On April 26 eastbound Michel Robidoux met "Phelp's train in charge of the mail for Utah" about 125 miles east of Fort Laramie.

Some travelers who left Salt Lake City April 8 for the States met "Childs [Chiles] & Phelps' train" near Fort Laramie. Mail-carrier Jarvis Streeter, who set out from Salt Lake on May 26, met the train of "Phelps & Chiles" 25 miles east of Salt Lake, "a long way in advance of any other traders." The next—"Cogswell"—was met 200 miles east of Fort Bridger. (Cogswell—of Independence—reached his destination before July 1.)

The mail carrier who left Salt Lake City July 1 (and reached Independence on the 24th) reported it was thought that the merchants and traders who had gone out "last Spring" would all lose money. "Messrs. Phillips [Phelps] and Chiles" had sold a portion of their stock at pretty fair profits," but had a lot left; and talked of taking the rest to California. "Messrs. Holiday [Holladay] & Warner [*see* p. 982] were speaking of boxing up theirs, and taking them to Oregon."

Ref: *The Frontier Guardian*, Kanesville, Ia., May 16, 1851; St. Joseph (Mo.) *Gazette*, February 26, 1851 (for "J. Richard's" advertisement that he would have "in the spring" 150 to 200 ponies for sale at Ash Point; and that he had "very nearly completed a bridge across the North Platte"); New York *Daily Tribune*, April 2, 1851 (for other North Platte bridge comment); *Missouri Republican*, St. Louis, June 25, July 15, 25, 1851; *The Weekly Tribune*, Liberty, Mo., July 11, 1851.

❡ On April 1 (it is said) Dr. Abraham Still (physician and minister) brought his family (from Missouri) to the log house and farm (near the Wakarusa's mouth) which he had prepared, during the preceding winter, as the Northern Methodists' mission for the Shawnees. This *fourth* Shawnee mission was located by present-day description) in Sec. 8, T. 13, R. 21 E., a mile south of Eudora, in northeastern Douglas co. It was described (at a later time, by Marovia Still Clark) as "a hewed log house with a clapboard roof there were four rooms two above and two below and the house stood out on a great broad prairie. . . ." (In 1854 Henry Harvey wrote that "a farm of about one hundred acres is under cultivation, and comfortable log buildings are erected.")

Contemporaneous data on the founding of Wakarusa Shawnee Methodist Mission have not been located. The autobiography (ca. 1921?) of Marovia Still Clark (a daughter of Dr. Abraham Still), is the chief (and so far as can be determined, reliable) source of information. She was, however, aged seven in the spring of 1851.

By Marovia Clark's account, her father was appointed missionary to the Shawnees in the fall of 1850 by the Methodist Episcopal (Missouri Annual) Conference. In October, 1850, Dr. Abraham Still went to the Shawnee reserve; spent the winter; fenced a 160-acre farm; built a log house (assisted by Cephas Fish—a young Shawnee, son of John Fish); and returned to Missouri early in 1851 for his family. The party he brought to the new mission on April 1 consisted of his wife, Mary P. (Moore) Still, his son Andrew T. (with wife, and two children), his daughters Marovia and Cassandra, and a man named "Mikel," "who came along to teach." (Notably, Mrs. Clark's account mentions that between Fishing river, in Clay county, Mo., and the Missouri river ferry at Kansas, Mo., they saw men "putting up a Telegraph pole . . ." which "was the last pole on a line." *See* pp. 1028 and 1043, for the telegraph line to, and out of Kansas, Mo., in 1851.)

The Abraham Stills were at Wakarusa Shawnee mission for three years (but the *Andrew T.* Still family may not have been there all the time). Of their neighbors Marovia Clark's account says Pascal Fish (Shawnee) was their "truest and best friend"; and that he lived "only a few hundred yards" from the mission. She mentions a white man "a little German by the name of Wm Grafenstein who kept a small store[?] on the Wakarusa at the Blue Jacket Ford," who "was an exile from his own country." This man, whom they called "Dutch Billy," had "been among the Indians for a number of years." The Stills later "lost track of this good friend." He was, undoubtedly, none other than the William ("Dutch Bill") Greiffenstein, who, in the 1860's had a ranch on Cowskin creek, west of Wichita; and in the 1870's was a prominent Sedgwick county figure.

Discussing the Shawnees' land-cession treaty of May 10, 1854, a correspondent (from "Kansas" territory) wrote the Milwaukee *Daily Sentinel,* in a November 6, 1854, letter, that "the Mission of Dr. Still was not recognized at the conclusion of the treaty, and in consequence he was made a trespasser upon their lands, and was obliged to break up his mission, sacrifice all his property except $800 which a brother [an Indian] . . . gave him for that . . . [which he could have taken free]."

Ref: The M. E. Church Missouri Annual Conference journal for 1851 (microfilm in KHi) shows, in connection with the above Shawnee Mission: (1) that a "communication from Bro. Pascal Fish and others was received on the subject of a school to be under the control of this conference in the Indian Territory"; (2) that the committee on education to which it was referred "made a final report" relating to the establishment of a Mission school in the Shawnee Nation, which was adopted; (3) and that the Committee on the Indian School was to be composed of G. W. Robbins (P. E. of the Platte District), Pascal Fish, and Thomas B. Markham. Marovia Marsden (Still) Clark's "Autobiography" (ms. in KHi ms. division); *KHC,* v. 7, p. 496, v. 9, pp. 191, 192, 230, v. 10, p. 215; Henry Harvey's *History of the Shawnee Indians* . . . *to 1854* (Cincinnati, 1855), p. 278; William H. Goode's *Outposts of Zion* . . . (Cincinnati, 1864), pp. 251-253; R. B. Woodworth, *The Descendants of Robert and John Poage* . . . (Staunton, 1954), v. 2, pp. 1206, 1207 (for data on Rev. Abraham Still, his wife, and their nine children—and the family's connections with Kansas history after 1854). For various mention of Greiffenstein, *see KHC,* v. 7, p. 48, v. 10, pp. 661, 664, v. 17, p. 361; and index to D. W. Wilder's *Annals of Kansas* (Topeka, 1886). According to *KHC,* v. 9, p. 192, the autobiography (1897) of Dr. Andrew Taylor Still (founder of osteopathy) states that he and his wife moved to Wakarusa mission "in May, 1853." *See KHQ,* v. 23, p. 189, for S. N. Wood's mention, in a "Kansas Territory, August 20, 1854," letter, of "Dr. [Abraham] Still, a true man, who also has a mission here." For the May 10, 1854, letter, *see* "Webb Scrapbook," v. 2, p. 3, in KHi library.

❧ April.—*"Kansas Public Ledger* is the title of a new [weekly] paper, published at Kansas, Mo., by [R. V.] Kennedy & [Charles] Epperson," reported the Glasgow (Mo.) *Weekly Times* of April 17. "It is a handsome sheet, neutral in politics. . . ." (The St. Joseph *Gazette* of March 12 had noted: "The *Independence Commonwealth* is to be removed to Kansas, Mo. . . .")

Copies of two 1851 issues (July 4 and August 29) of the first newspaper of

Kansas City, Mo., are in the Kansas City, Mo., Public Library. The *Ledger* was
a short-lived publication. The May 8, 1852, *Occidental Messenger,* Independence, Mo., noted that Epperson's paper "has ceased its labors."—*see* Liberty
Tribune, May 14, 1852.

Ref: The Glasgow, and St. Joseph, Mo., papers noted above; C. C. Spalding's *Annals
of the City of Kansas* (1858), p. 97; William H. Taft's *Missouri Newspapers* . . .
(Columbia, Mo., 1964), p. 80. *The Weekly Tribune,* Liberty, Mo., August 15, 1851,
reported the marriage "on Wed. week," of Mr. Charles Epperson, "one of the proprietors
of the *Kansas Public Ledger,*" to "Miss Mary Th[r]elkeld." R. V. Kennedy (editor; aged
28), and family, are listed in the 1850 federal census of Jackson county, Mo.

❨ April.—Aboard the *Cataract* (from St. Louis—left April 3) a
company of Indiana families (74 persons), bound for Oregon,
arrived at St. Joseph on April 9; landed their freight; set up their
wagons; and "encamped for the night on the wharf." Next day
they moved a mile east of town, to remain till April 25.

Among these emigrants was P. V. Crawford (one of the few 1851 diarists);
and, likely, the Baptist missionaries—*see* p. 986—were also of this party.

With 19(?) wagons the Indiana company crossed the Missouri on
April 25; traveled six miles westward; encamped till the 27th; then
set out on the road to Oregon. The night of April 27 they stopped
at Wolf river—which P. V. Crawford described as "12 feet wide
and 6 inches deep." Moving ahead slowly, it was May 7 before
these emigrants reached the Big Blue river (at present Marysville).
They found it "low enough to wade." Crawford wrote: "After
crossing, we got a seine from another company and went fishing.
Good camping and lots of fish, good grass and plenty of wood."

The Indianans reached Fort Kearny May 18. On June 1, near Chimney
Rock, the company divided, "6 wagons taking the advance; leaving 13 in the
rear." Crawford reached the Willamette Valley on September 20.

Ref: *Oregon Historical Quarterly,* v. 25 (June, 1924), pp. 136-169 (for P. V. Crawford's
journal); St. Louis *Daily Intelligencer,* April 1, 1851 (which reported: "The steamer *Baltic*
which arrived yesterday morning from the Ohio had on board 74 Oregon emigrants. . . .
They are from the interior of Indiana [etc.] . . .").

❨ On April 17 Richens L. ("Dick") Wootton of New Mexico
arrived (alone?) at Independence, Mo., in 15½ days from Santa Fe.
He had left there, on horseback, April 2, with Bvt. Maj. William
N. Grier, First dragoons, and a few others.

(It was Wootton's later *recollection* that he made this trip in "a little over
seven days, on a wager . . . with Colonel Greer." Grier "got laid up on
the way," so that Wootton "reached the end of our journey nearly two weeks
ahead of him.")

About April 25(?) the monthly U. S. mail from Santa Fe reached
Independence. Apparently Lewis D. Sheets and "Montmarguet,"
(who, as reported, left Santa Fe on April 1) were mail coach

passengers. Bvt. Maj. William N. Grier (*see above*) and others (making a party of some eight or 10 in all) had traveled in company from "Sumner's Fort" (new post on the Arkansas).

On April 27 the *Isabel* (down from St. Joseph) reached St. Louis. Among those aboard were Grier, Montmarguet, Sheets, and Wootton.

Ref: *Missouri Republican*, St. Louis, April 28, 1851 (two items); St. Louis *Daily Intelligencer*, April 29, 1851 (for mention of Wootton's 15½-day journey); H. L. Conard's *"Uncle Dick" Wootton* . . . (Chicago, 1890), p. 245.

❡ April 18.—Joseph Clymer (of Westport, Mo.) signed a two-year contract (made with Lt. Col. Thomas Swords, QM) to transport army stores from Fort Leavenworth to El Paso, Tex., and Dona Ana and Don Fernando de Taos, N. M. (Rates $12.84, $12.50, and $8.83 per 100 pounds; sureties for the $50,000 bond: David Waldo, Jabez Smith, and William McCoy.)

On May 16 Clymer's 30-wagon train (carrying 150,141 pounds of supplies) set out from Fort Leavenworth for El Paso del Norte.

Ref: 32d Cong., 1st Sess., *Sen. Ex. Doc. No. 12* (Serial 614), p. 23; 32d Cong., 1st Sess., *Sen. Ex. Doc. No. 1* (Serial 611), p. 295.

❡ April.—At "New Post on Arkansas" (Fort Atkinson-to-be) trader William Bent was engaged in collecting Indians of the Plains (for official talks relating to the Great Indian Council to be held at Fort Laramie later in the year).

Connelly's party, passing the post in mid-April, found Bent waiting for the Comanches and Kiowas, to whom he had "sent out a dispatch" to come in and trade. "Kit" Carson, traveling down the Arkansas in April, met friendly Arapahoes and Cheyennes; and at the "New Post" talked with Bent. (A Shawnee, in Bent's employ as a hunter, recently had been killed by a Cheyenne.)

See, also, May 4-5 annals entry.

Ref: New York *Daily Tribune*, May 19, 1851 (from St. Louis *Union*); *Missouri Republican*, St. Louis, May 15, 1851; St. Louis *Daily Intelligencer*, May 14, 1851.

❡ April 23.—"Quite a number of Oregon and California emigrants are now here," the St. Joseph *Gazette* reported. "Several wagons have crossed the ferry here and we learn that the ferries above have crossed upwards of 200 wagons."

One California-bound party ferrying over the Missouri at St. Joseph on April 23 was the "Mohican Gold Company," a well "fitted" party of some 40 men from Delaware and Ashland counties, Ohio, captained by Joseph Smith. It was their intention to start overland on April 24.

On April 23, and in the company of others who had crossed the Missouri at St. Joseph, the Rev. Neill Johnson family (overland from Mt. Pleasant, Ia., with three wagons) reached Wolf creek (in present Doniphan county), where they were joined by several more

Oregon-bound wagons. John L. Johnson (a son of Neill), an 1851 diarist, mentioned meeting on April 24, at the Iowa, Sac & Fox Presbyterian Mission, Captain Keeney's 12-wagon company, with a large drove of cattle, en route to Oregon.

Ref: St. Joseph (Mo.) *Gazette,* April 23, 1851; John L. Johnson's "Diary," 1851 (original in Yale University Library's Coe Collection; used by permission).

❆ April-May.—About one-fifth of the "Missouri" Sacs & Foxes (of northeastern "Kansas") died of smallpox. Agent W. P. Richardson, early in May, hired Dr. O. B. Knode to vaccinate the Great Nemaha Subagency Indians. The epidemic was checked before it spread to the Iowas. (But *see* p. 1002.)

Ref: Comm'r of Indian Affairs, *Report,* 1851 (Richardson's report, therein); SIA, St. Louis, "Records," v. 9, typed copy, p. 516; 33d Cong., 1st Sess., H. *Ex. Doc. No.* 37 (Serial 718), pp. 387, 392 (for payments of $100, and $50, to O. B. Knode).

❆ April-May.—Missionaries Gottlieb F. Oehler and David Z. Smith set out from "Westfield" (Munsee Moravian Mission, present Wyandotte county—*see* p. 338), the morning of April 22, on a "journey and visit" to the Pawnee Indians. Their joint narrative of the trip, and Dr. D. Z. Smith's "Description of the Manners and Customs of the Pawnee Indians," were published in the *Moravian Church Miscellaney of 1851-1852.*

"Br. Paul Oehler accompanied us to Weston, in order to take the wagon back," the missionaries wrote. On the way to Fort Leavenworth ("about 24 miles from Westfield") they stopped for a few minutes at "Briggs' Vale" (Delaware Baptist Mission—*see* sketch appearing on p. 816); then "soon struck the prairie," and the military road; met, on that pathway, a Fort Gibson-bound company of infantry (*see next entry*).

The missionaries remarked that Fort Leavenworth "is a place of considerable business, in the way of furnishing military stores for the more western forts. At the wharf a large storehouse has been built . . . for . . . depositing military stores. The premises are kept in a very neat and cleanly condition, and a large garden has been prepared near by, for the soldiers to raise vegetables for their use."

The Oehlers, and Smith, crossed the Missouri at Fort Leavenworth's ferry ("on a horse-boat, which is kept here at the expense of the Government"); and reached Weston ("a place of considerable trade, having about 1,700 inhabitants") towards evening. From Weston to Council Bluffs, their journey was by stage. They passed through St. Joseph, Mo. ("a town of about 3,000 inhabitants"), on April 23d; reached Bellevue ("Neb.") five or six days later.

On May 6, accompanied by trader Peter Sarpy, Samuel Allis (government teacher for the Pawnees), and a Loup Pawnee chief named "Gatarritatkutz (Big Axe)," Missionaries Oehler and Smith set out for the Pawnee villages. On the 7th, after crossing the Platte, they arrived at the Pawnee Loup's town ("Siskatuppe, the principal chief" was their host). On May 8 they traveled about 25 miles to the upper village (where their host was "Asseruregarrigu," chief of the Grand Pawnee band, and principal chief of the whole Pawnee nation). At councils held in this town, speechmakers included "Leezikutz" (chief of the Republican band) and "Terrericawaw" (chief of the "Topages"). The journey back to Bellevue, begun on May 9, was completed on the 11th.

Aboard the *El Paso,* on May 15, the two missionaries started down the Missouri; debarked on the 17th at Kansas, Mo. Next day they "proceeded to Westfield, eight miles on foot. . . ."

Dr. David Z. Smith's report on the Pawnees included information on their two villages, both south of the Platte, and both "situated on eminences." The lower village "lies about 50 miles from Bellevue, and about 10 or 15 miles above the mouth of the Elkhorn. . . . [It] consists of about 80 lodges, with a population of nearly 2,500." The upper village "is situated about 20 or 25 miles above the lower, nearly opposite the mouth of the Loup Fork of the Platte. . . . [In it] there are between 140 and 150 lodges, the population amounting perhaps to 3,500."

Ref: Gottlieb F. Oehler and David Z. Smith, *Description of a Journey and Visit to the Pawnee Indians Who Live on the Platte River* . . . to which is added *A Description of the Manners and Customs of the Pawnee Indians by Dr. D. Z. Smith.* Reprinted from the *Moravian Church Miscellaney of 1851-1852* (New York, 1914).

❡ April 22.—Maj. Theophilus Holmes, and four mounted companies of Seventh U. S. infantry, set out overland from Fort Leavenworth (after spending the winter of 1850-1851 at that post) for Fort Gibson ("Okla."). The Fort Smith (Ark.) *Herald* of May 16 reported the four companies had reached their destination.

Ref: St. Joseph (Mo.) *Gazette,* April 30, 1851 (from Platte *Argus*); *Missouri Republican,* St. Louis, May 26, 1851 (from Fort Smith *Herald*); Lowe, *op. cit.,* p. 44; 32d Cong., 1st Sess., *Sen. Ex. Doc. No. 1* (Serial 611), p. 299 (April 21 item *re* furnishing 2d Lt. P. W. L. Plympton [AAQM], Seventh infantry, nine horses, 96 mules, and 16 wagons, for trip from Fort Leavenworth to Fort Gibson).

❡ April 23.—"[J. S.] Lightner & Co's. train," in charge of (Wilson?) Hamilton, left the Missouri line, en route to New Mexico. These goods-laden wagons arrived at Santa Fe on May 30. (Hamilton, starting back June 3, reached home—Lexington, Mo.—on June 22.)

Ref: St. Louis *Daily Intelligencer,* June 24, 1851; James S. Calhoun's *Official Correspondence* . . ., ed. by Annie H. Abel (1915), p. 400, mentions "J. S. Lightner & Co." in 1851.

❡ Late in April, Dr. Henry Connelly, Dr. John M. Whitlock, and four Mexicans—José and Feliciano Gutierrez, Juan Perea, Vicente Otero—who had left Las Vegas, N. M., on April 6, reached Independence, Mo., in advance of their train, after "a delightful journey across the plains," in carriages. They took the *Saranak* to St. Louis; arrived there May 6.

Ref: New York *Daily Tribune,* May 19, 1851 (from St. Louis *Union,* May 7); St. Louis *Daily Intelligencer,* May 7, 8, 1851; *New Mexico Historical Review,* v. 16, pp. 104-106 (for Dr. John M. Whitlock).

❡ April 30.—The St. Joseph *Gazette* reported: "Since our last publication many companies have crossed the River and are now on the Plains"; and noted that emigrants were arriving in town daily.

Philip McGaughren, and four companions (all from Platteville, Wis.) had set out for California on April 28. An Oregon-bound company of "families" (46 persons) from Vermilion county, Ill., had started on April 29. Emigrants (five men, two women, and eight children) from Kaskaskia, Ill., planned to start for Oregon on May 1.

Ref: St. Joseph *Gazette,* April 30, 1851.

❮ April-May.—Supt. D. D. Mitchell, St. Louis, en route to the "Indian Country" on an inspection tour, arrived at Kansas, Mo., April 30, aboard the *Robert Campbell,* bringing with him B. Gratz Brown (as secretary), also a "carriage, driver, &c." Mitchell's travels in "Kansas" apparently ended May 11. (On May 12 he paid John Harris, Westport, Mo., innkeeper, for "boarding" his party overnight[?]; and took passage for St. Louis on a steamboat captained by W. S. Sprout.)

While in "Kansas," on May 1 Mitchell visited the Shawnee Methodist Mission and Indian manual labor school. He later reported: ". . . I found the school to consist of 21 Indian boys, and 4 White boys; in the female Dept, I found 25 girls, 3 of them white. . . . There was a separate room occupied exclusively by white boys & girls—28 in number; these latter were the children of frontier inhabitants whose education was paid for by their parents or friends. . . ." Neither the superintendent—Rev. Thomas Johnson, nor the school's principal teacher were on hand. Mitchell "regretted to learn . . . that but few of the boys ever acquired much knowledge of agriculture or the mechanical arts." Mitchell considered the mission farm "one of the finest and most productive in the Western Country," but was critical of the fact that its profits ("which are very great") enriched the mission's managers instead of benefitting the Indians whose money was being expended. He understood the superintendents "never fail to make fortunes" in a four or five-year period.

Ref: 32d Cong., 1st Sess., *H. Ex. Doc. No. 103* (Serial 647), p. 459 (for Mitchell's expenditures); SIA, St. Louis, "Records," v. 9, typed copy, pp. 517-519.

❮ On May 1 Jarvis Streeter left Independence, Mo., with the U. S. mail for Salt Lake City. He reached his destination on the 28th (in 25 days' traveling time).

A Salt Lake City correspondent wrote that Streeter's was the quickest trip yet on the route; and that he brought St. Louis newspapers "up to April 25."

Ref: *The Weekly Tribune,* Liberty, Mo., July 25, 1851.

❮ May 1.—Four steamboats at the Kansas (City), Mo., landing departed—three (the *Saranak, Pocahontas,* and *Alton*) for St. Joseph (where all arrived on May 2); and one (the *Robert Campbell*) for St. Louis (reached May 4 or 5).

The *Robert Campbell* had left St. Louis April 22, bound for Council Bluffs, having aboard (1) a number of gentlemen connected with Utah's territorial government, (2) Elder Orson Pratt and other Mormons, (3) several persons connected with Salt Lake Valley commerce, and (4) some Santa Fe traders.

Ref: *Missouri Republican*, St. Louis, April 23, May 5, 1851; St. Louis *Daily Intelligencer*, May 6, 1851; St. Joseph *Gazette*, May 3, 1851. The *Saranak* had aboard one officer and 50 enlisted men for Fort Leavenworth—*see* 32d Cong., 1st Sess., *Sen. Ex. Doc. No. 12* (Serial 614), p. 28.

❧ May 1.—"Kit" Carson, who had left Rayado, N. M., on March 17, arrived at Kansas (City), Mo. He had come in by way of Bent's Fort. Carson's own (later) account of the trip east was this: "I remained in Rayado till March and then started for St. Louis, took with me twelve wagons of Mr. [Lucien] Maxwell for the purpose of bringing out goods for him. Arrived at Kansas May 1. I proceeded to St. Louis. . . ."

The St. Louis *Republican* of May 15, reported: "Kit Carson . . . informs us that he started from the Rayada with a party of 16 Mexicans, on March 17. . . ." The preceding day's issue had noted that "Kit Carson, the celebrated mountaineer, reached our city yesterday, with several Mexicans on the steamer El Paso." According to the St. Louis *Intelligencer* of May 14, "Kit Carson . . . arrived yesterday on the Gen'l Lane, accompanied by Dr. East, a trader from Chihuahua. . . ." In the same issue was mention of the arrival of some 10 or 11 Mexicans "from the plains," including two brothers of one-time New Mexican governor Manuel Armijo, accompanied (from Independence?) by Richard Owens (as interpreter). It was stated the Mexican party had set out from Albuquerque on *April* 5.

Ref: *Missouri Republican*, St. Louis, May 14, 15, 1851; St. Louis *Daily Intelligencer*, May 14, 1851; Blanche C. Grant, ed., *Kit Carson's Own Story of His Life* . . . (Taos, N. M., 1926), p. 100. *See* annals, p. 486, for previous mention of "Dr. East." The "10 or 11 Mexicans" (including East?) doubtless traveled the Cimarron route to the States.

❧ At the beginning of May a pack party of seven Indiana and Illinois men left St. Joseph for California. A July issue of the *El Dorado News* announced the arrival at Placerville, Calif., on July 17, of these men—the first overland company of the year. They had traveled "from St. Joseph in seventy-seven days," by way of Sublette's Cut-off. (L. W. Keely, C. C. Crandell, W. Lemon, and John Hart were from La Porte, Ind.; H. and C. Carpenter, and N. Flax were from Joliet, Ill.)

On July 21 the year's second party of immigrants "packed in" to Placerville, having come from Kanesville, Ia., by way of Salt Lake, in 79 days.

Ref: *The Frontier Guardian*, Kanesville, Ia., October 3, 1851 (from an unidentified newspaper which reported the *El Dorado News* story).

❧ May.—The *Kansas*, leaving Weston, Mo., on May 2, with a light cargo, reached St. Louis safely on the 9th. Her captain—William C. Jewett—reported he had never seen the Missouri "as difficult and hazardous of navigation as it is at present."

At Howard's bend the *St. Paul* and *Mary Blane* were "laid up," and had paid off their crews. The downbound *Alton* (*see* May 1 entry), unable to get over the bar at Howard's Bend, had discharged her freight, and engaged to return upriver with the *St. Paul's* passengers, and some freight. Aboard the *St. Paul* were 120, or more, U. S. troops, who, when the *Kansas* passed by (on May 7?) were "engaged in transporting their baggage across the bar to the Alton in small flats." (The *Alton's* captain—W. H. Fulton—had agreed May 7 to transport these troops [one officer, and 135 men, as stated] from Howard's Bend to Fort Leavenworth for $1,250.)

About May 15(?), after a rise in the Missouri, the *St. Paul* "laden with Government stores" got over the bar (as reported by the downbound *St. Ange*).

Ref: St. Louis *Daily Intelligencer*, May 9, 19, 1851; 32d Cong., 1st Sess., *Sen. Ex. Doc. No. 12* (Serial 614), p. 29.

❡ May-June.—On May 3, 13 Perry & Young wagons, carrying government stores under contract (*see* March 10 entry) left Fort Leavenworth for "Fort Mackay"—Fort Atkinson, on the Santa Fe trail. A Perry & Young 12-wagon train was sent on May 19; 14 more wagons started on June 11; and on June 13, Jones Creech (sub-contractor?), with an eight-wagon train left for the same destination.

The 47 wagons sent to Fort Atkinson in 1851 carried a total of 248,052 pounds of army stores; and their transportation cost the government $10,492.60.

Ref: 32d Cong., 1st Sess., *Sen. Ex. Doc. No. 1* (Serial 611), p. 295; 32d Cong., 1st Sess., *H. Ex. Doc. No. 2* (Serial 634), pp. 295-297.

❡ May 3.—An Oregon-bound company (principally Ohioans?) which had outfitted at Weston, Mo., crossed the Missouri at Fort Leavenworth this day (according to the recollections of Denny H. McClure); and got under way on the 5th. "Our company consisted of 18 wagons, about 150 head of cattle, 8 women with their children and 40 men fit for duty," wrote Pennsylvanian Quincy A. Brooks (in a letter from Oregon ter., November 7).

(D. H. McClure—whose brother William McClure ran a Weston hotel—mentioned the names of Presley George and wife, Victor Trewitt, and Quincy A. Brooks, as members of the company. Brooks named Dr. Eggers, "Hardin" [a Weston lawyer], "Cartwright," and a Dutchman named "Shadel.")

Brooks wrote in his letter: "The first river we came to was the Big Blue; this we found so swollen that it was impossible to ford it. To work we all went cutting down trees and digging out canoes, and in two days we got safely across, taking our wagons and provisions in two canoes lashed together, and swimming our horses and cattle."

Oregon-bound Robert Robe, who crossed the Missouri on May 11, at Old Fort Kearny (Table creek), reached Fort Laramie June 14. In a diary entry of June 16 he wrote: "Resolved to pack through from this place—bought a pony in connection with Capt. Hardin of Weston" [the lawyer "Hardin" mentioned above?]; and on June 17, recorded: "Started with Hardin & Treoit [the Victor Trewitt above-mentioned?] expecting 3 others tomorrow."

Ref: *Oregon Historical Quarterly*, v. 15 (September, 1914), pp. 210-215 (for Q. A. Brooks' November 7, 1851, letter); Oregon Pioneer Association, *Transactions of the Twenty-third Annual Reunion . . . 1894*, pp. 50-52 (for D. H. McClure's recollections); *Washington Historical Quarterly*, Seattle, v. 19 (January, 1928), pp. 52-63 (for Robert Robe's diary).

❡ May 4-5.—Above "New Post on Arkansas" on May 4, eastbound F. X. Aubry "passed 30 lodges of Cheyenne Indians on their way to Fort Mackay." Next day, at the new army post, his party saw Comanches, Cheyennes, Arapahoes, Kiowas, and Apaches of the Plains, assembled to make peace with Bvt. Lt. Col. William Hoffman (commandant).

As reported: "Both sides of the river were crowded with lodges for at least fifteen miles. The principal Chiefs of each tribe were sitting in Council in Col. Hoffman's tent, and the ceremony of smoking the pipe of peace had taken place [when Aubry came on the scene]. Col. Hoffman had acted with prudence and care, and the Indians appeared to be well satisfied with him. . . ."

See annals entry of June 19 for Agent Fitzpatrick's council with these Indians.

Ref: *Missouri Republican*, St. Louis, May 18, 1851.

❡ May.—Jones & Russell, government contractors (*see* p. 980) started three large trains of supplies from Fort Leavenworth to New Mexico this month. By official report: on May 6, 27 wagons left the post for Santa Fe; on the 17th, 27 wagons set out for Ninth military department headquarters; and on the 31st, 30 wagons got under way for Albuquerque. (The 84 wagons carried a total of 424,690 pounds.)

The Independence *Occidental Messenger* of June 14(?) stated: "Messrs. Russell & Co., from Lexington, and Gen. Smith's trains [probably George R. Smith, connected with Jones & Russell—*see* February 17 entry] were much troubled, while loading at Fort Leavenworth on account of sickness, and we think are still delayed, not being able to get hands to take places of the sick." A telegraphic communication of July 31 from Independence stated: "Gen. Smith's train [the above train?] left Bull Creek, Sunday morning [July] 27th."

Ref: 32d Cong., 1st Sess., *Sen. Ex. Doc. No. 1* (Serial 611), p. 295; *The Weekly Tribune*, Liberty, Mo., June 20 (from Independence *Messenger* of June 14?); *Missouri Republican*, St. Louis, August 1, 1851.

❡ May 7.—The St. Joseph *Gazette* noted the departure of several emigrant companies in the preceding days of May: (1) a pack company of six men from Bedford, Ind., on May 1, for Oregon; (2) a company (upwards of 20 men and women) mostly from Rhode Island, on May 3, for California; (3) N. V. Sheffer's train (six men) from Warren county, Ia., on May 5 "passed through" St. Joseph; (4) William Macky and nine others (from Wisconsin and Illinois), on May 5, for California; Joseph Sander and wife, and 19 other Indianans, "a few days since," for California.

Ref: St. Joseph (Mo.) *Gazette*, May 7, 1851, or, *Missouri Republican*, St. Louis, May 16, 1851.

❦ May.—A man named Jones (perhaps Lewis Jones), headed a company of 14 men, with eight wagons, which set out for Oregon, from Kansas (City), Mo., in the early part of May (apparently).

In a letter dated June 4, from Fort Kearny, Jones wrote (to his brother Joseph Jones, of Kansas, Mo.) that Pawnees (10 to their one; and well armed) had "attacked" them "three days back," taking three cows. "They have perfectly stripped the companies behind us," he added. "The Troops are in pursuit of them."

Ref: St. Louis *Daily Intelligencer*, August 13, 1851. See annals, p. 836, for earlier mention of Lewis Jones.

❦ In the fore part of May, Capt. Stewart Van Vliet (quartermaster's department), his wife, and military escort, arrived at Fort Leavenworth, after a journey (reportedly of 17½ days) overland from Fort Laramie (left April 16).

En route they endured two heavy snow storms; at "O'Fallon Bluffs" encountered a war party of Cheyennes (amicable to whites) going to attack Pawnees; on May 2, near the "crossing of Little Blue" (*i. e.*, at the head of the Little Blue?) met the first emigrant train; and from that point to the frontier, met others "almost every day." "The main body of the emigration was for Salt Lake[?] . . . [Van Vliet] found, in all he passed, but two companies for California."

Ref: *Missouri Republican*, St. Louis, May 14, 1851; St. Louis *Daily Intelligencer*, May 14, 1851. The Van Vliets were aboard the *El Paso* which reached St. Louis on May 13. Under the circumstances it does not seem likely this overland march was accomplished in 17½ days. If they left Laramie on April 16, and were at Little Blue's head (the Little Blue was not *crossed* on the Oregon-California trail) on May 2, 17 days had elapsed by that time. If the *Big* Blue crossing was meant, the travelers still had several days' march ahead of them. It could be *speculated* that the party may have made the trip in about 25 days—reaching Fort Leavenworth perhaps May 8. The *El Paso* started downriver from St. Joseph, Mo., on May 9.—St. Joseph *Gazette*, May 14, 1851.

❦ May 10.—The *Utah*, purchased "for a ferryboat at St. Joseph," arrived from St. Louis. For lack of business, owner John Corby, St. Joseph, decided to operate her as a packet between that town and Kanesville, Ia.

Ref: *Missouri Republican*, St. Louis, April 23, 1851; St. Joseph *Gazette*, May 7, 14, June 18, 1851; *The Frontier Guardian*, Kanesville, Ia., July 11, 1851.

❦ May 11.—"Messervy's train" of 60 wagons (in charge of John "Simmons—[Sims, or Simms]" at Bridge (or Switzler's) creek, and William S. Messervy at 110-mile creek, were met by eastbound, fast-riding F. X. Aubry (*see* next entry). This same day he saw "Spalding of Los Vegas" on his way to New Mexico with "a drove of cows," (Preston) Beck & (Robert) Brent's 25-wagon train at Willow Point, and met some wagons "whose owners were not known" to him.

The rapid-traveling "May" mail party from Santa Fe, which reached Independence on the 19th, reported having met the following traders' and freighters' trains: Russell and Co's. at Arkansas Crossing; McCauley's train (freighting Messervy's goods) at Lost Spring; McCauley & Sons' second train at Cottonwood; the McCauley's third train "this side" of Cottonwood, where also was met "Pigeon's" train; and the McCauleys' fourth train at Lone Elm.

Ref: *Missouri Republican*, St. Louis, May 18, 1851; St. Louis *Daily Intelligencer*, May 14, 1851. The *Missouri Republican* of June 29, 1851, stated that the "June" mail party arriving at Independence June 22, from Santa Fe, had met "Messervy & Simms' train" at Cold Spring, and "Beck's" at Upper Cimarron Spring.

❆ May 12.—Francis X. Aubry, returning from Santa Fe (*see* p. 985), arrived at Independence, Mo., in 19 days' travel, and in advance of his wagon train. He had covered the approximately 200 miles from Cottonwood Crossing in two days and one hour.

Leaving the Santa Fe road two miles "this side" of Cold Spring (in the "Oklahoma Panhandle"), on April 29 (having left Santa Fe on the 23d), Aubry had "attempted a new route with the wagons"—hoping to find a better trail to the Arkansas. But this (apparently his first such attempt) was an unsuccessful exploration. An account in the *Missouri Republican* (based on Aubry's journal) included the following: "On the 2d [May] they arrived at the [Arkansas] river, their animals having been two days without water. The last day the party had no water to drink, and they traveled through sand and a hot sun, and had to drink the blood of the Antelope." Journeying downstream, it was not until May 5 that Aubry's party reached "Fort Mackay" (west of present Dodge City). *See* p. 1042 for Aubry's second exploratory trip between Cold Spring and the Arkansas.

Ref: *Missouri Republican*, St. Louis, May 18, 1851; *ibid.*, May 25, 1851, noted Aubry's arrival at St. Louis on May 24; *The Weekly Tribune*, Liberty, Mo., May 23, 1851 (from Independence *Messenger*).

❆ May.—Of travelers whose destination was New Mexico, an Independence, Mo., correspondent wrote, on May 12: "Maj. Weightman and family are here [Richard H. Weightman, one of four newly appointed Indian agents for New Mexico]; [also] Col. Cunningham [*i. e.*, Maj. Francis A. Cunningham, army paymaster], Mr. J[ohn] Greiner [another of the Indian agents], Mr. Smith and lady, the Baptist missionary to Santa Fe [the Rev. Lewis Smith and wife], Mr. Barkley [trader Alexander Barclay, of the Barclay & Doyle post on the Moro], and many others of some notoriety, who will start in a few days on their journey. Col. C. [Major Cunningham] goes out with the troops, of course. . . ."

Among the "many others" were Abraham R. Woolley and Ed. H.

Wingfield (the other Indian agents), Judge Grafton Baker (New Mexico chief justice), William E. Love, and Jared W. Folger, probably.

Some of the above travelers—perhaps all of them—were, for a time, with, or near, the command of Bvt. Col. Edwin V. Sumner (*see* p. 1003), as they journeyed to New Mexico. On May 20 it was reported from Independence: "Major Weightman and family, Mr. and Mrs. Smith (missionaries) and others, leave here today for Santa Fe." (In the fore part of July, the eastbound "July" mail carrier met "Missionary L. Smith and family . . . at Cold Spring, getting along finely—having left the troops [Sumner's] on account of cholera.") A letter from Santa Fe in July stated that "Chief Justice [Grafton] Baker, Maj. [Richard] Weightman, Mr. Postmaster Love, Maj. Cunningham, [John Greiner] and other gentlemen, arrived at Santa Fe on July 16." Gov. James S. Calhoun, in a July 30 letter, wrote that "Col. [Abraham R.] Woolley and Mr. [Ed. H.] Winfield arrived with the mail wagon on the 25th inst."

Ref: *Missouri Republican*, St. Louis, April 24, May 18, 25, July 28, September 1, 1851; New York *Daily Tribune*, September 9, 1851; Calhoun, *op. cit.*, pp. 388, 392; *Baptist Home Missions in North America* . . . 1832-1882 (New York, 1883), p. 599.

❡ May 13.—"Dr. Long," former St. Joseph, Mo., resident, crossed the Missouri at that place with a drove of 1,200 sheep, destined for market at the Mormon settlements in the Great Salt Lake valley.

Ref: Glasgow (Mo.) *Weekly Times*, May 29, 1851 (from St. Joseph *Adventure*, May 16?). Dale L. Morgan, Bancroft Library, suggests the possibility this may have been Dr. T. Pope Long, California immigrant of 1846.

❡ May 15.—Thomas N. Stinson, Indian trader at Union Town, Pottawatomie Nation, bought of Alexander and Margret Boshman (Beauchemie), "a certain Negro Man named Moses of the age of twenty-six years old [warranted to be sound and healthy] to be a slave for life."

The bill of sale (original in the Society's Stinson Collection) which the Beauchemies signed with X-marks, has the signature of Indian agent Luke Lea, as witness. Alexander Beauchemie's father—Mackinaw Beauchemie (*see* p. 355)—was of French and Chippewa ancestry; his mother (*see* p. 260) was half Shawnee and half English. The transaction took place in present Shawnee county. Stinson's wife was Alexander Beauchemie's sister.

Ref: T. N. Stinson Collection (in KHi ms. division).

❡ In mid-May, aboard the *Kansas* (which had left Jefferson Barracks on, or about May 12), four officers and some 200 troops arrived at Fort Leavenworth. Most of the men likely were recruits destined for New Mexico—*see* p. 1003.

Ref: 32d Cong., 1st Sess., Sen. Ex. Doc. No. 12 (Serial 614), p. 28.

❡ May 17 (or 18?)—Maj. Sackfield Maclin (army paymaster) set out from Fort Leavenworth (bound for Forts Kearny and Laramie) with a large sum of money, and a small military escort (a corporal and seven men from Company B, Sixth infantry; Corp. P. G. Lowe and three privates from Company B, First dragoons). The major's clerk ("Mr. Reed"), a servant, and three teamsters, made the party 18 in all. They had for transportation Maclin's "four-mule ambulance," and two mule-drawn wagons.

At the Big Blue (present Marysville) Maclin, and escort, were halted by high water. Work was commenced on a raft. But after a time "some large freight trains came along [as Lowe later recollected], stretched a rope across the river, lashed two large wagon beds together, and in a few days ferried over fifty wagons and their contents, and our little outfit—all the animals, oxen, mules and horses being compelled to swim." Trader John Dougherty (Fort Kearny sutler) who traveled with these trains, lost a servant at this crossing (the young Negro man fell in the river and drowned). Beyond the Blue, Maclin and party made good time.

(On the return trip, in July, Mrs. Rhett, wife of Bvt. Capt. Thomas G. Rhett, U. S. Mounted riflemen, and her two young children and a servant, traveled in company.)

Ref: Lowe, *op. cit.*, pp. 46-73 (Lowe gives the starting month as April); 32d Cong., 1st Sess., *Sen. Ex. Doc. No. 1* (Serial 611), p. 299 (wherein it is stated that on May 17, at Fort Leavenworth, Major Maclin was furnished three teamsters; 18 mules, two wagons, and one ambulance, for a trip to Forts Kearny and Laramie).

❡ May 19.—Twelve days ahead of contract time, the "May" U. S. mail from Santa Fe arrived at Independence, Mo. "Capt." W. T. Martin, of Martin, Russell & Co., Lexington, Mo., and three mail carriers were aboard the stagecoach.

Neville Stewart (recently editor of the Santa Fe *Gazette*) reached Independence, Mo., on May 19, but perhaps not with the mail party.

Ref: *Missouri Republican*, St. Louis, May 25, 1851; St. Louis *Daily Intelligencer*, May 24, 1851. Stewart (or Stuart?), because of "feeble health," started back to Santa Fe "instantly."

❡ May 20.—William H. Arnall (or Arnalls?) arrived at Independence, Mo., with the "April" U. S. mail from Salt Lake City. He (and others?) had started east on April 1.

Ref: Glasgow (Mo.) *Weekly Times*, June 5, 1851; Hafen and Young, *op. cit.*, pp. 171, 172 (from the "Journal History," Mormon church archives, March 12, 1851—which gives the carrier's name as "Arnalls"). *See, also*, annals entry of December 1, 1850 (for Arnall's December, 1850-March, 1851, journey with the "December" mail from Independence to Salt Lake City).

❡ May 20.—At Independence, Mo., a correspondent wrote that Olivares' train, for Chihuahua, "under care of Domingo," would set out on the Santa Fe trail "in a day or two"; that Joseph C. Irwin's, Mayer & Co's., and Ross & Wethered's trains "are now making active preparations to get off"; and McCauley's fifth train (*see* May 11 entry) "also goes in a few days."

Ref: *Missouri Republican*, St. Louis, May 25, 1851.

❡ May 21.—2d Lt. Joseph L. Tidball and a detachment of Sixth infantry recruits left Fort Leavenworth on, or about the 21st; and arrived at Fort Kearny on June 12. Chaplain James De Pui—another June 12 arrival—presumably accompanied Tidball on the march. Part of the recruits were destined for Fort Laramie.

Ref: 32d Cong., 1st Sess., *Sen. Ex. Doc. No. 1* (Serial 611), p. 299; New York *Daily Tribune*, July 30, 1851.

❡ May.—Some Mexican merchants "on a visit to the United States to purchase goods," were aboard the *Kansas*, "from the Missouri river," arriving at St. Louis on May 24. These men (who, presumably had reached the States a few days earlier) were: Narciso Santiestebeau, Juan Nepomasemo," "Gutieres" (Gutierrez), Juan Maria Baca, Simon Gallegres (Gallegos?), Guiseto Baca, Jose Maria Martinez, Jose Salazar, "Y." Otero (probably Miguel Otero).

It was reported they had left Santa Fe "about May 1." F. X. Aubry (who was also aboard the *Kansas*) had recorded in his "journal," that on April 29 he had passed five trains of States-bound wagons belonging to Mexicans (the above company?).

Ref: *Missouri Republican,* St. Louis, May 18, 25, 1851. William Walker's journal entry of June 22, 1851, states: "Mr. Miguel Otero from Mexico bro't Harriet home in his carriage from Kansas [City]."—Walker's "Journals" in Connelley, *op. cit.*

❡ May.—The "Mississippi" Sacs & Foxes (of present Franklin and Osage counties) numbered 2,660 souls at the spring enrollment. Later in May, a visiting "Missouri" Sac Indian broke out with smallpox (*see* p. 992); and the disease spread rapidly among the settlements.

By one account 110 Indians died before preventive measures could be taken. Agent J. R. Chenault hired Dr. Edwin R. Griffith; then persuaded some 1,700 Indians (nearly all the Sacs, and part of the Foxes) to accept inoculation ("with small pox virus, adulterated with new milk"). Of these, about 40 died (but all were ill before treated).

In September Chenault reported that a "large band of Foxes" (uninoculated) "are yet suffering from this disease, and have . . . scattered in every direction." He thought the Sacs & Foxes, from smallpox, "flux," and other diseases, had lost about 300 souls since the latter part of May. (But a year later—October, 1852—he wrote: "I am now convinced that the mortality last year was greater than I supposed. . . .")

Ref: Comm'r of Indian Affairs, *Reports,* 1851, 1852 (Agent Chenault's reports, therein); *Missouri Republican,* St. Louis, September 5, 1851; 33d Cong., 1st Sess., *H. Ex. Doc. No. 37*

(Serial 718), pp. 318, 326. Dr. F. McKnight was paid $833.33, on May 10, 1851, for "Services as physician" to the "Mississippi" Sacs & Foxes (in 1850 and 1851); and apparently departed before the smallpox outbreak.—*See* 32d Cong., 1st Sess., *H. Ex. Doc. No. 103* (Serial 647), p. 630.

❡ May-June.—Bvt. Col. Edwin V. Sumner, First dragoons (who had been selected April 1 to take over the Ninth military district command), set out May 26 on the Fort Leavenworth-to-Santa Fe road (*see* p. 981) for New Mexico. He headed a sizable expeditionary force.

(In April, while Sumner visited St. Louis "on short sojourn," the *Republican* reported: "Col. Sumner will take out with him six or seven hundred fresh recruits to fill up the companies now in [New] Mexico. He will also take out a supply of fresh horses for the Dragoon and Artillery service; and we learn that orders have been given to take out improved stock, bulls, cows, hogs, &c., and a large amount of seeds, grains, etc.—with farming implements, and appliances for irrigating, etc. . . .")

Officers in Sumner's command included Bvt. Maj. James H. Carleton and Bvt. Maj. Philip R. Thompson, with their First dragoon companies. Bvt. Maj. Ebenezer S. Sibley (AQM) was in charge of the accompanying wagon train. (On May 24, at Fort Leavenworth, Sibley had been assigned two "principal" teamsters and 67 others, 87 horses, 386 mules, 60 wagons, a traveling forge, an ambulance, a brood mare, 22 stallions, and two wagon floats.) Several officers took their families along. Lt. Col. Thomas Swords (QM), on special assignment to New Mexico, also was with Sumner. En route, a number of civilians (*see* p. 1000) joined the expedition, to travel all, or part of the way, under military escort. Following Sumner was a "supply train" (of Jones & Russell wagons?—*see* February 17 entry) under Bvt. Maj. Daniel H. Rucker (AQM); and about June 13 Capt. Isaac Bowen (commissary) left Fort Leavenworth for New Mexico, having been furnished one mule, 69 oxen, and 24 wagons. (Around July 15-19, the "July" mail-carrier from Santa Fe met several government trains "in charge of Rucker and others," between Pawnee Rock and Council Grove.)

Of this march, Sumner later reported: "The cholera had appeared in the command some days before I left [Fort Leavenworth], and remained in it till I reached the Arkansas. I lost one surgeon (Dr. [Alfred W.] Kennedy,) and about 35 men. My other surgeon (Dr. [William H.] Tingley,) was . . . unwell most of the time, and was left at the new post on the Arkansas. . . ."

Early in June news reached Missouri that cholera had "appeared when the troops were about 90 miles from Fort Leavenworth" (between the military road's crossing of Kansas river, at present Topeka, and the Santa Fe trail junction); that the victims included Asst. Surg. Alfred W. Kennedy, and his son; and that Mrs. Kennedy had gone back to Fort Leavenworth. Trader William Bent, passing along the Santa Fe trail (to Missouri) before Sumner's command reached the trail junction, heard that the troops were "at 110[?] . . . proceeding very slowly"; that "as many as eight or ten were dying daily, and . . . numbers were deserting." A Mr. Wolfe, who left Council Grove on June 10—after Sumner had reached that place—reported that during the cholera panic some 60 to 70 men had deserted, and 25 to 30 had died.

On June 20 Colonel Sumner and troops arrived at "New Post" on the Arkansas; encamped a mile and a half above the fort (not far from a large Cheyenne village); and stayed most of two days. Agent Thomas Fitzpatrick was amazed at the "unrestricted intercourse" allowed officers and men with the Indians. Sumner's report (dated October 24) took note of some restiveness on the part of the Cheyennes, but failed to mention that one of his officers grossly insulted them by whipping the son of a chief "without cause" (as a Santa Fe correspondent put it). Bvt. Lt. Col. William Hoffman sent Sumner information, the night before the troops' departure, that "it was thought" the Cheyennes "intended some act of hostility." "At the dawn of the day the next morning, I marched back with my whole command," Sumner wrote. "I assembled a number of the chiefs and head men, and said to them I had come back to meet them, as friends or enemies, it was for them to say which, but they must say it immediately. They at once disclaimed all intention of hostility, and I resumed my march."

Taking the Bent's Fort route, the command traveled the rest of the way to New Mexico without special incident. A Santa Fe correspondent wrote (on July 30): "Col. Sumner, Maj. Sibley and other officers of the new command, arrived here on the 19th inst. all well. The troops which came from the States with Sumner did not come to Santa Fe but were stationed in surrounding country." Sumner established a new post—Fort Union—"near the Moro River, and on the line of communication with the Missouri frontier," and removed Ninth military district headquarters there (from Santa Fe), for a time.

Ref: 32d Cong., 1st Sess., Sen. Ex. Doc. No. 1 (Serial 611), pp. 125, 235, 299; New York Daily Tribune, May 6, July 31, September 9, 23, 1851; Calhoun, op. cit., pp. 382, 383, 416, 417; Missouri Republican, St. Louis, June 10, 14, 16, July 14, 25, 28, 1851; Comm'r of Indian Affairs, Report, 1851 (Agent Fitzpatrick's report, therein).

¶ May 28.—At Fort Leavenworth, Bvt. Maj. E. A. Ogden (AQM) negotiated two-year contracts for the delivery of corn (quantities not to exceed 12,000 bushels in either year) at Forts Kearny and Laramie. Jones & Russell (of Lexington, Mo.) got the Fort Kearny contract (at $2.07 per bushel); David Waldo (of Independence, Mo.) received the Fort Laramie contract at $3.94 per 56-pound bushel). Deliveries were to be made before October 1 in each year. Sureties for Jones & Russell were: C. R. Morehead, Isaac Chanslor, and James W. Renick. David Waldo's bondsmen were Jabez Smith and William McCoy.

Two Waldo & McCoy wagons trains (one merchant, the other government, evidently) were on the Oregon-California trail in the spring and summer of

1851. About May 18(?) the first train was reported to be on the banks of "Little [i. e., Big] Blue," unable to cross because of high water. The second (in charge of "Cummings") was met on June 22 "at Little Blue" by the incoming mail carrier. The Independence *Occidental Messenger* of June 14(?) reported: "We understand that part of a train sent out by Waldo, McCoy & Co. to Fort Laramie & Salt Lake, was much delayed by sickness and the consequent dispersion of the hands; but timely aid sent out enabled them to get along without greater loss. Five of the men, who left here in the train, died [of cholera?]." (Jones & Russell trains had similar difficulties—*see* p. 997.)

Returning "Californians" who arrived at Independence August 13, had met a "Waldo & Co's train" four or five days' travel west of Fort Laramie; and their second train at the crossing of the Platte's South Fork.

Ref: 32d Cong., 2d Sess., *Sen. Ex. Doc. No. 18* (Serial 660), pp. 4, 7; *The Weekly Tribune*, Liberty, Mo., June 20, 1851 (from Independence newspaper); *Missouri Republican*, St. Louis, June 25, July 15, August 19, 1851.

℃ May 29-30.—At Kansas, Mo., on the 29th, a guest at the Union Hotel ("a commodious and roomy house . . . very well conducted by its proprietor, Mr. [William G.] Barclay") composed a letter to the St. Louis *Republican* which stated (in part): "I write you from a point which is getting to be more and more a favorite resort with those engaged in the Santa Fe trade. . . . It has the advantage of an excellent landing, accessible at all stages of the river, and is only four or five miles from the 'Plains,' with which it is connected by a road that, already good, is constantly improving. The Traders seem well pleased with the treatment they receive here. . . ."

The May 30 issue of the town's new newspaper—the Kansas *Public Ledger* —stated: "Most of the following gentlemen have either started or will this week start trains of wagons from Kansas for Santa Fe and other places in New Mexico. This list does not include any of the large number of trains which left here previous to this week. . . . [It] is made up from the register of the Union Hotel, where the persons named are stopping:

"Geo. H. Estes, Richard Owens, Kit Carson . . ., Gillard N. Dock, Maj. E. H. Wingfield (Ind. agent), Col. W[illiam] S. Allen (Sec. Ter. N. M.), B. F. Moseley, R. F[rancis?] Green, Chas. S. Rumley, Jas. E. Sabine, J. Wood, John Barker, [Charles L.] Spencer & [Henry] Grandjean, Chas. E. Kearney, P. H. Le Blanc, J. & H. Mercure, Elias Brevoort, Charles McCarty, Finis Y. Ewing, Judge J. B. Yager, Samuel Hays, C. D. Burnes, P[reston] Beck, Chas. H. Wild, J. M. Ferguson, Michael Carroll, Richard Wooten, James Wooten [i. e., Richens L. and James Wootton], Louis Debus, H. Hungerien, Placido Romero, Francisco Guterez [Gutierrez], Cristobal Lu[c]ero, Alexander Barclay, Ach. Earle [Dr. Archibald Earle—not a trader], L. M. Myers.

"We presume not less than 300 wagons have left Kansas [Mo.] this spring for the Plains, most of which have gone to Santa Fe. The trade between this point and N. M. is rapidly increasing. Already not less than 1,500,000 lbs. of freight for that country has been landed here and shipped for its destination, and there is much yet to arrive from St. Louis."

(In a February 23, 1851, letter, Allen T. Ward—Shawnee Methodist Mission employee—had written: "The Santafe trade now nearly all passes thro' Kansas [City], & that trade is rapidly increasing.")

Ref: *Missouri Republican*, St. Louis, June 3, 1851; Allen T. Ward's letter (in KHi ms. division). At Kansas, Mo., on May 3, 1851, Sup't D. D. Mitchell paid "Gillis & Barkly" for board—*see* 32d Cong., 1st Sess., H. Ex. Doc. No. *103* (Serial 647), p. 459. In 1858 "W. G. Barkley" was clerk of the steamboat *Ben Lewis*. A. T. Ward's letter is printed in *KHQ*, v. 33, p. 374.

❡ May 30.—Thomas Jefferson Sutherland (an eccentric and controversial man; sometime lawyer, politician, soldier under Bolivar, Canadian rebellion "hero," printer, phrenologist), who probably was—as described in 1854—"the first public advocate for, and overt actor in, the movement to organize and settle Nebraska [an area covering both Nebraska and 'Kansas']," wrote a letter headed "Independence Creek,° Nebraska Territory, May 30," which is quoted, in part, below:

"I pen this . . . [near] an Indian camp. The yellow skins have just received their annuities for the present year.

"I have just arrived here from Table Creek [Old Fort Kearny], distant about one hundred miles[?] above. The more I have traveled in the Nebraska Territory and observed the lands, and examined its resources, the higher has risen my opinion of the country; and I emphatically pronounce it as unequalled by any other section of the United States.

"I have taken pains to gain correct information of the number of emigrants who have this Spring set out for the Plains, and upon the best information I cannot state the number at more than 6,000, including men, women and children, and of these, by far the larger portion are bound for Oregon. The greatest number of wagons were crossed at Council Bluff and proceeded up the N. side of the Nebraska River—say seventeen[?] or eighteen hundred[?] wagons, each having about three persons. The number of wagons crossed at Table Creek, below the mouth of Nebraska [Platte] . . . was two hundred twenty. Of these, one hundred fifty-five were for Oregon, thirty-five for California and thirty for the Valley of the Great Salt Lake. The others crossed the Missouri at St. Joseph and Weston, and put out from Independence and Kansas. . . ."

° On May 29 Sutherland had written a letter (to the Cincinnati *Daily Nonpareil*) from Thule, Atchison co., Mo. (just south of the Iowa line) stating: "Since I wrote my last communication [May 3 from Table creek, Neb.] for your paper, I have perambulated much of the Territory of Nebraska. . . ." Obviously, to get from Thule to Independence creek's mouth (near present Doniphan, Kan.) in one day, Sutherland must have journeyed by steamboat.

Sutherland's May 29 letter also contained Oregon-California-Salt Lake emigration "statistics," adding the information that his source for the number of wagons crossing at Table creek [Old Fort Kearny] was Missouri river ferry operator John Boulware.

Ref: New York *Daily Tribune*, July 31, 1851 (from the Cincinnati *Commercial*), for the

May 30, 1851, letter—to which no name is given, but which can have been written by no one except T. J. Sutherland; James C. Malin's *The Nebraska Question, 1852-1854* (Lawrence, Kan., c1953), pp. 77-79; *Nebraska History*, Lincoln, v. 34 (September, 1953), pp. 181-214 (for James C. Malin's article on Sutherland); *Putnam's Monthly Magazine*, New York, v. 3 (May, 1854), pp. 457-460 (for editorial article "Nebraska. A Glimpse At It . . ." with comment on Sutherland, including quote in paragraph one, above); *The Weekly Tribune*, Liberty, Mo., October 31, 1851 (for item: "Thomas Jefferson Sutherland, the hero of Navy Island, is in [*i. e.*, has been in] Nebraska Territory. He proposes to found a settlement there . . ."); *The Frontier Guardian*, Kanesville, Ia., June 27, 1851, devoted most of two columns to the subject of T. J. Sutherland. (In a letter dated May 22, 1851, Sutherland had written Luke Lea, Comm'r of Indian Affairs, from Council Bluffs, to protest the Mormons' treatment of Indians west of the Missouri, and to denounce the *Frontier Guardian's* editor, Orson Hyde.)

❦ May 31.—John B. Miege, S. J. (Vicar-apostolic of the Indian territory east of the Rocky mountains; and a titular bishop) arrived at St. Mary's (Pottawatomie) Mission—the place he had selected as residential headquarters. Bishop Miege and his party were greeted by Father John B. Duerinck, Father Maurice Gailland, others of the mission, and a large crowd of Indians. (Next day—Sunday—a celebration was held.)

Accompanied by Father Paul M. Ponziglione, Brothers Sebastian Schlienger and Patrick Phelan, Bishop Miege had left St. Louis May 17, traveling by steamboat to St. Joseph, Mo. (reached May 24), where four days were spent. On the 28th the party crossed the Missouri and "started for the western plains." Bishop Miege and Father Ponziglione, on horseback, led the march; the two brothers, and two Creoles driving wagons, followed. They were "two days on the road and at noon of the 31st of May . . . reached St. Mary's Mission," according to Ponziglione's account.

"It is here at St. Mary's," Father Gailland wrote, "that the Bishop has fixed his place of residence; our little church is filled with pride and astonishment, to see itself raised at a bound to the rank of a cathedral. A wooden house . . . serves as palace for the bishop of the Indians." (Until 1855, when Bishop Miege removed to Leavenworth, the Catholic mission church of St. Mary's was a cathedral. Today the site is marked by an outside altar and plaque.)

Ref: G. J. Garraghan, *The Jesuits of the Middle United States* (New York, 1938), v. 2, pp. 635-648; Augustin C. Wand, *The Jesuits in Territorial Kansas 1827-1861* (St. Marys, 1962), pp. 23, 24, 45, 46; *KHC*, v. 9, pp. 25, 153-159; *KHQ*, v. 20, facing p. 512 (photograph of the St. Mary's Mission church which was a cathedral from 1851 to 1855).

❦ June.—The U. S. mail for Salt Lake City which left Independence, Mo., on June 1, passed Fort Kearny on the 10th; and was met by the incoming mail party on June 15 at a point 110 miles "this side (east) of Fort Laramie.

Ref: *The Frontier Guardian*, Kanesville, Ia., July 11, 1851; *The Weekly Tribune*, Liberty, Mo., July 11, 1851 (from Independence [Mo.] *Occidental Messenger* of July 5).

❦ June.—The Independence-to-Santa Fe "June" U. S. mail, in charge of "Mr. Griffith Williams," left the Missouri border (apparently) on June 3. Stagecoach passengers included the "Associate Judges [of New Mexico territory], Messrs. [Horace] Mower of Michigan and [John S.] Watt[s] of Indiana," also Caleb Sherman. As reported by the Santa Fe *Gazette*, the mail (an unusually large one) reached that place on June 26, "making the trip out in 23 days"—but in 18 traveling days, having been detained five days by high water.

Ref: New York *Daily Tribune*, August 8, 1851 (from Santa Fe *Gazette* of June 28); Calhoun, *op., cit.*, pp. 364, 407. Sherman served as a district court clerk in New Mexico ter.

❧ June.—"Kit" Carson, with 12 goods-filled wagons (Lucien Maxwell's—*see* May 1 entry), left Kansas, Mo., early in June, for Santa Fe. The company consisted of Carson, his daughter, Adaline, his niece, Susan (wife of Jesse Nelson), and 15 employees—Jesse Nelson, a French-Canadian, and 13 Mexicans.

Taking the "Bent's Fort route" ("on account of water and grass being in greater abundance thereon"), Carson's train, around the end of June, passed a Cheyenne village—at a point about 15 miles above the Arkansas Crossing. As Carson later recounted it: "They were at the time hostile . . . on account of one of the officers of Colonel Sumner's command (that was about ten days march in my advance) having flogged an Indian Chief of their tribe. . . . On me they intended to retaliate. [*See* p. 1004.]

"I had travelled about twenty miles from their village. They pursued me. I was encamped. They came to me by one, two, and threes till twenty arrived. . . ." Carson at first thought them friendly; but overheard talk which made him aware of a plot to kill him and his men. He ordered the Indians to leave; sent an express ahead for help; next day managed to bluff the Cheyennes so that they did not attack. Several days later, when Carson's train was "about twenty miles of Bent's Fort," troops (from Rayado, and from Sumner's command) arrived. Under their protection the Carson party reached Rayado safely.

Ref: Grant, *op. cit.*, pp. 100-104; Harvey L. Carter's '*Dear Old Kit,*' *op. cit.*, pp. 129-132; Edwin L. Sabin's *Kit Carson Days* . . . (New York, 1935), v. 2, p. 627; *Missouri Republican*, St. Louis, June 3, 1851.

❧ Up to June 6 there had passed Fort Kearny (as reported) 837 emigrant wagons, 1,156 men, 928 women, 799 children, 5,975 oxen, cows, horses, and mules. (By these statistics—837 wagons and 2,883 emigrants—the average was close to three and one-half persons per wagon.)

[Presumably, the above figures represent with fair accuracy the 1851 westbound emigration setting out from the Missouri at points below the Platte's mouth—*i. e.,* the various landings between Old Fort Kearny, "Neb.," and Independence, Mo. They have special value for a year in which very little information is to be found regarding the Oregon-California emigration crossing "Kansas."]

According to John Boulware (ferryman at Table creek—Old Fort Kearny), as stated by T. J. Sutherland (May 30 annals entry), the westbound emigration crossing at that point, up to late May of 1851, totaled 220 wagons. Subtracted from the Fort Kearny total of 837 wagons, the remainder—617—would represent the number of wagons crossing at all other points below. Probably between 500 and 600 emigrant wagons (and from 1,700 to 2,000 emigrants traveled west on the routes across "Kansas" (the "Independence" Oregon-California trail, up the Kansas river valley; the Oregon-California trail, St. Joseph branch; the increasingly used Fort Leavenworth-Fort Kearny military road).

Ref: *The Frontier Guardian*, Kanesville, Ia., July 11, 1851; or, St. Louis *Daily Intelligencer*, July 28, 1851. Since the emigration, except for its "Kansas" connections, is outside the scope of these annals, the following references (from which information was gathered, but not used) are noted here for their possible value to other researchers: *Missouri Republican*, St. Louis, June 25, August 15, 1851; *The Frontier Guardian*, August 8, 22, October 3, 1851; St. Joseph *Gazette*, September 17, December 31, 1851; New York *Daily Times*, September 22, 1851, and March 5, 1852. All these references relate to the size of the 1851 emigration.

❡ June.—On the *St. Ange* (which left St. Louis on the 7th, under charter to the American Fur Company) cholera broke out as she steamed up the Missouri. Aboard were 80, or more, company employees. Dr. John Evans (U. S. geologist), was a passenger; so, also, were Jesuit Fathers Pierre-Jean De Smet and Christian Hoecken. (The latter, long a missionary to Indians of "Kansas," had left St. Mary's Mission, on the Kansas river, early in the year.) One account states that the "wife and family" of Joseph La Barge, the *St. Ange's* captain, made this trip (". . . it is said she will be the first white female that has ever ascended the Missouri as far as the Yellowstone").

Before the steamboat reached Bellevue ("Neb."), on June 16, a number of deaths had occurred; the final toll was 14. One of the last cholera victims was Father Hoecken, who died on June 19 (De Smet says), or June 21 (Kurz' diary). Father De Smet fell ill, but recovered. From Fort Union he traveled overland to Fort Laramie, and attended the Great Indian Council in September.

The *St. Ange* went 40 to 50 miles above the Yellowstone's mouth; left Fort Union, on the return trip, July 15; arrived at St. Joseph's wharf July 27; returned to St. Louis on July 30 (with a large amount of furs for P. Chouteau, Jr. & Co.), having made the trip out and back in "just 53 days, 17 longer than she performed the same voyage last season."

Ref: *Missouri Republican*, St. Louis, June 21, July 12, 1851; *Jefferson Inquirer*, Jefferson City, Mo., June 14, 1851; St. Joseph *Gazette*, June 18, July 30, August 13, 20, 1851; St. Louis *Daily Intelligencer*, June 5, 22, July 12, 31, 1851; New York *Daily Tribune*, August 12, 1851; R. F. Kurz' "Journal," *loc. cit.*, pp. 69-79; H. M. Chittenden and A. T. Richardson, eds., *Life, Letters and Travels of Father Pierre-Jean De Smet* (New York, 1905), v. 1, pp. 61, 62, v. 2, pp. 638-642; Pierre-Jean De Smet, *Western Missions and Missionaries* . . . (New York, c1859), pp. 58-66; Wand, *op. cit.*, pp. 26, 50. For Father Hoecken's years of Indian missionary service in "Kansas," *see* annals index. H. M. Chittenden, in his *Early Steamboat Navigation on the Missouri River* (1903), v. 1, pp. 177-183, says Mrs. Joseph La Barge went to the Upper Missouri with her husband on the *Martha*, in 1847! (*See, also,* annals, p. 685.) Artist R. F. Kurz boarded the *St. Ange* on June 16, at Bellevue.

❡ June-August.—Cholera was prevalent in the Missouri river towns of Independence, Kansas, Weston, and St. Joseph; also, in the Indian country. These were some of the cholera situation reports:

—Up to June 12, according to an Independence correspondent, 16 to 18 persons had died there.—*Missouri Republican*, St. Louis, June 15, 1851.

—Between June 10 and 20, at Weston, 25 persons died.—*The Weekly Tribune*, Liberty, Mo., June 27, 1851. (Names of the victims were listed.)

—From June 13 to 20, at Independence, 19 persons died.—*Ibid.* (Names were listed.)

—In the week of June 21-27, at Independence, 8 persons died.—*Missouri Republican*, July 7, 1851.

—Between June 20 and 28, at Weston, 7 persons died; and in the same period, at St. Joseph, 4 died.—*The Weekly Tribune*, Liberty, Mo., July 4, 1851.

—From June 28 to July 4, at Independence, there were 10 deaths.—*Ibid.*, July 11, 1851.

—July 1. A telegram from Lexington, Mo., stated that the *Alton* (down from St. Joseph "yesterday") reported cholera abating at Weston; only two cases at Independence on "Saturday [28th]."—*Missouri Republican*, July 2, 1851.

—July 2. The Rev. John G. Pratt, wrote from Delaware Baptist Mission: "The cholera has made its appearance again in our neighborhood, and many of the most dissipated have died. The alarm is very general, but not so great as in the former visitation [1849]."—*The* (Baptist) *Missionary Magazine*, Boston, v. 31 (November, 1851), p. 427.

—July 4. The Kansas (Mo.) *Public Ledger* stated that cholera was "still raging" at Independence; Doctor Hockensmith, his wife, daughter, and four "blacks" of the household had died in a 30-hour period; another victim: E. K. Arnold.—*Missouri Republican*, July 9, 1851.

—July 7. News received at Lexington, via downbound steamboats, was that the health of Weston and Independence was "materially improving." —*Ibid.*

—July 12. "Cholera still raging in Independence."—William Walker's diary entry.

—July 15. At Bull creek three Shawnees died. (The telegraphic report said, erroneously, "Pawnees.")—*Missouri Republican*, July 25, 1851.

—July 15. "Six more deaths [at Independence] on Saturday [the 12th]."— Wm. Walker.

—July 16. William Walker learned that Charles Graham [government blacksmith for the Wyandots] had died of Cholera, probably the 14th inst. "Just as I predicted and repeatedly told him," Walker recorded in his diary.

—July 23-28. In this period, at St. Joseph, 13 persons died.—St. Joseph *Gazette,* July 30, 1851.

—July 26. "Several cases of cholera in Kansas [City, Mo.]."—Wm. Walker.

—In the week of July 20-26, according to the *Occidental Messenger,* Independence, several deaths had occurred at Kansas; cholera was prevailing in parts of Jackson county, Mo.; and Jacob Johnson and daughter had died on the 25th, near Independence.—St. Louis *Daily Intelligencer,* August 4, 1851.

—August 6. The St. Joseph *Gazette* stated there had been no local cholera cases in the week past.—*Gazette.*

—August 9. "John Johnston [of Kansas City?] lost his entire family—his wife and two children, by Cholera."—Wm. Walker's diary entry.

—August 11. "The Cholera is still carrying off its victims."—*Ibid.*

—August 25. Agent Thomas Moseley, Jr., in a letter, stated that the cholera deaths among the Delawares, Shawnees, Munsees, and Stockbridges, in the "last two months," totaled about 40.—Comm'r of Indian affairs *Report,* 1851.

—September 1. The Rev. Johnston Lykins, in his report, referred to the prevalence of cholera "now" among the Pottawatomies.—*Ibid.*

Ref: As indicated above; William Walker's diary, *loc. cit.*

❦ June.—Overland from "New Post" on the Arkansas, William Bent arrived at the Missouri border in the fore part of June. He, "Mr. Campbell," and "other gentlemen" reached St. Louis (via steamboat) on June 13.

Bent had been at the post on the Arkansas since early spring—*see* p. 991.

Ref: *Missouri Republican,* St. Louis, June 14, 1851. Presumably "Mr. Campbell" was of the St. Louis firm R[obert] & W. Campbell, but he is not further identified.

❦ June.—The Independence *Occidental Messenger* of June 14(?) reported news just received from Council Grove: ". . . All our [Independence] merchant trains are getting along pretty well—no sickness among them. They are detained however, by high water and bad roads. A good many of Mr. Major's [Alexander Majors'] cattle stamp[ed]ed in a hail storm beyond Council Grove, but we learn he has recovered most of them."

Majors, in his memoirs, stated: "In the year 1851 I again crossed the plains with a full outfit of twenty-five wagons and teams. This trip was a complete success; we met with no molestations, and returned home without the loss of any animals, but, owing to the cholera prevailing to some extent among the men who were on the plains, I lost two men by that disease."

Ref: *The Weekly Tribune,* Liberty, Mo., June 20, 1851 (from Independence *Messenger*); Alexander Majors' *Seventy Years on the Frontier* (Chicago, c1893), p. 140.

❦ June 15.—From Fort Kearny an army man wrote: "The emigrants are getting along finely—no sickness among them. . . .

"Within the last few days the Indians have been quite troublesome on the road from Fort Leavenworth to this place—so much so that two commands were sent out to protect the emigrant trains. A party of Rapehoo [Arapahoe] Indians from the Arkansas have been on the road along the little Blue River. Mr. Marshall of Ohio lost two horses by the Indians and some others lost provisions.

"Capt.[Henry W.] Wharton (C. O.) went out with one party and Lt. Foot [Rensselaer W. Foote] with another. F. has not returned. Capt. W. drove some 45 [Indians] across the [Little] Blue River and placed an escort with the trains that were along the road; scouted the river for some days—and returned yesterday to the fort. . . ."

Ref: New York *Daily Tribune*, July 30, 1851 (from Philadelphia *Ledger*).

❡ June 17.—Indian agent Luke Lea (aged 68?; head of the "Fort Leavenworth Agency" since October, 1849—*see* p. 891) was killed in a fall from his horse while riding from Westport, Mo., to his "residence at the old Agency [just west of the state line, in present Johnson county, Kan.]."

(As of June 30, 1851, in the Indian department reorganization, the "Fort Leavenworth Agency" was discontinued. Francis W. Lea, a son of the above Luke Lea, received appointment as agent of the newly created Pottawatomie Agency—*see* p. 1015—which his father would have headed.)

Ref: *Missouri Republican*, St. Louis, July 1, 1851, or *Jefferson Inquirer*, Jefferson City, Mo., July 5, 1851 (both from the Kansas *Ledger*); SIA, St. Louis, "Records," v. 9, typed copy, p. 527 (Sup't D. D. Mitchell's letter of June 24, 1851, to the Indian dep't announcing Agent Luke Lea's death); Kansas City chapter, Daughters of the American Revolution, comp., *Vital Historical Records of Jackson County, Missouri* (Kansas City, Mo., c1934), p. 416 (item on Luke Lea's headstone—giving year of birth as 1783—in the old Westport Cemetery); Zella Armstrong, comp., *Notable Southern Families* (Chattanooga, 1926), v. 3, pp. 71-83 (for Lea family); *U. S. Biographical Directory of American Congress* (has sketch of Luke Lea's career). The Indian agent Luke Lea, who died on June 17, 1851, was an *uncle* of the Luke Lea (b. 1810) who was commissioner of Indian affairs, from July, 1850, to April, 1853.

❡ June 17.—The marriage, this day, of "Mr. Daniel Dofflemyer, Indian Territory," and Mrs. Virginia Tutt, of Platte county, Mo., by the Rev. B. F. Russell, was noted in the Glasgow (Mo.) *Weekly Times* of the 26th.

(In the autumn of 1851 the Rev. Daniel D. Doffelmeyer was appointed as a Methodist Episcopal Church, South, missionary to the Shawnees, Delawares, and Wyandots, assisting the Rev. Nathan Scarritt; and in 1852 was "reappointed" to the Wyandots.)

Ref: Glasgow (Mo.) *Weekly Times*, June 26, 1851 (place of ceremony not given); *KHC*, v. 9, pp. 221, 229; William Walker's "Journal" (*loc. cit.*), October 2, 1852, entry. The name is variously spelled in the sources available: Dofflemyer, Doffelmyer, Doffelmeyer.

❡ June 19.—Agent Thomas Fitzpatrick, who had arrived from the States on June 1, held a council at "New Post on Arkansas" (Fort Atkinson), with leaders of the Plains Indian nations gathered there. (*See* May 4-5 entry.) Perhaps 3,000 Comanches, Kiowas, Cheyennes, Arapahoes (and Plains Apaches?) were camped in the vicinity (William Bent's advance estimate).

Agent John Greiner (en route to New Mexico), who was at the scene, wrote:

"It was a very grave assemblage, and many of their greatest warriors were present. Little Mountain Chief, of the Camanches, and Little Bear, are two of the most distinguished Indians of the Prairies, and possess more influence than any other Chiefs among them." Greiner's letter also noted that the Indians professed to want peace; that "a small amount of presents was distributed to them"; that Fitzpatrick was anxious to get the Indians to go 500 miles to Fort Laramie for the Great Council; but they (having heard reports of cholera and smallpox on the Oregon-California trail) feared to go.

Ref: New York *Daily Tribune*, July 31, 1851 (from *Ohio State Journal*); *Missouri Republican*, St. Louis, June 14, 1851 (for Bent); Comm'r of Indian Affairs, *Report*, 1851 (Fitzpatrick's report, therein). Fitzpatrick left on July 3 for the Fort Laramie council— see New York *Daily Tribune*, June 22, 1854, or *KHC*, v. 1-2, p. 265. "Little Mountain Chief" was the famed Kiowa chief "To-hau-sen" (or "Do-hau-sen"); and "Little Bear," *perhaps*, was the Kiowa war chief Sitting Bear (Satank).

❰ The June 19-25 period was event-filled at "New Post" [Fort Atkinson] on the Arkansas:

June 19—Bvt. Maj. Robert H. Chilton and his Company B, First dragoons, reached "New Post." (Though traveling behind Sumner's command—as appears—for the early part of the journey from Fort Leavenworth, Chilton's company—including Agent John Greiner, and other civilians?—preceded Sumner by one day to "New Post.")

June 19—Agent Thomas Fitzpatrick counciled with Indians gathered at "New Post" —*see* above entry.

June 20—Bvt. Col. Edwin V. Sumner and his New Mexico-bound command arrived; camped beyond the fort for about two days—*see* separate entry.

June 22—Sumner, after a showdown with offended Cheyennes, departed with his troops—heading up the Arkansas.

June 25—Bvt. Maj. Robert H. Chilton took over command of "New Post" from Bvt. Lt. Col. William Hoffman—who probably left this day for Fort Leavenworth, where he arrived July 9. (Hoffman, commandant since November 24, 1850, had been promoted; and reassigned to the Fifth infantry.) Chilton's tenure lasted 12 days—*see* below.

June 25—In Washington, D. C., General Orders No. 34, AGO, gave official name—Fort Atkinson—to "New Post." (Unofficially, during its short span of existence, this post on the Arkansas variously was known as Fort Mackay, Fort Sumner, Fort Sod, and even Fort Sodom.)

The June post returns showed the garrison to consist of Company B, First dragoons and Company D, Sixth infantry. Officers present were: Bvt. Maj. Robert H. Chilton, Asst. Surg. Elisha P. Langworthy, 2d Lt. Henry Heth (Sixth infantry), 2d Lt. David H. Hastings (First dragoons), and Asst. Surg. William H. Tingley ("Left sick at post since June 21, 1851").

On July 6, 2d Lt. Henry Heth assumed command of Fort Atkinson; and Bvt. Maj. Robert H. Chilton, with his First dragoons, left for Fort Leavenworth.

Ref: Fort Atkinson post returns (National Archives microfilm); *Missouri Republican*, St. Louis, June 16, July 14, 1851; St. Louis *Daily Intelligencer*, June 16, 1851; *KHC*, v. 4, pp. 363, 364; Lowe, *op. cit.*, pp. 72, 73; New York *Daily Tribune*, June 22, 1854 (or, *KHC*, v. 1-2, p. 265); 32d Cong., 1st Sess., Sen. Ex. Doc. No. 1 (Serial 611), p. 299.

❰ June 22.—Eight days before contract time, the "June" U. S.

mail from Santa Fe, in charge of William Allison, reached Independence, Mo. According to one report the mail was accompanied by four or five men, and three or four passengers—including "Mr. [Joseph] Mo[o]rehead, one of the engineers for the [U. S.-Mexican] Boundary Commission, and Mr. Duncan and lady from New York."

At "Fort Sumner" (Fort Atkinson) the Santa Fe-bound "June" mail, and Nesbit's train had been met. East of the fort other New Mexico-bound trains encountered were: Joseph Clymer's train (at Coon creek), a government mail train (at Pawnee Fork), Colonel Sumner's command (at Plum Buttes), Alexander Barclay's train (at Cow creek), Russell & Jones' (at Cottonwood), Joseph Irwin's, Ross', and Kit Carson's trains (at Lost Spring), F. Y. Ewing, C. E. Kearney & C. H. Merritt's train (at Council Grove). From Council Grove eastward the mail party had met "almost one continual line of Wagons." (For further mention of some of these trains *see* July entry, p. 1025.)

Ref: *Missouri Republican*, St. Louis, June 29, 1851; *The Weekly Tribune*, Liberty, Mo., July 11, 1851 (reprinting of the Independence *Messenger's* account, identifying the mail carrier as *William* Allison, and stating "We understand it [the mail coach] brought 6 passengers."); John R. Bartlett's *Personal Narrative* . . . (New York, 1856), p. 593 (for Joseph Moorehead).

❨ June 26.—The Rt. Rev. John B. Miege arrived (for a few weeks' visit) at Osage (Catholic) Mission (present St. Paul, Kan.), and vicinity, accompanied by Fathers Paul M. Ponziglione (who would remain), John B. Duerinck (who had been "guide" for the party), and a lay brother. (The four had set out from St. Mary's Mission, on horseback, in mid-June, apparently. They carried rations for five days, and the trip was around 160 miles.)

A processional met the bishop: "On the advance were marching the school-boys two and two with their teachers; next came the school-girls in the same order with the Sister; after all Father [John] Schoenmakers and Father John J. Bax. . . ."

On leaving Osage Mission, Bishop Miege journeyed to Fort Scott (some 40 miles northeast), accompanied by Father Bax.

Ref: *The Kansas Magazine*, v. 1 (June, 1872), p. 528 (in which the Rev. James H. Defouri gives the date of arrival as June 26); Garraghan, *op. cit.*, v. 2, pp. 510, 511 (wherein the arrival date is stated to be July 4); KHC, v. 9, pp. 19-32 (for an article on Father Ponziglione).

❨ June 27.—Jarvis Streeter, and party, with the "June" U. S. mail from Salt Lake City, arrived at Independence, Mo. The carriers had been detained four days by the illness of one man; and their journey—in 23 days' traveling time—was a rapid one. Streeter reported the road good "until they reached Kaw [Kansas] river."

Ref: *The Weekly Tribune*, Liberty, Mo., July 11, 1851 (from the Independence

Occidental Messenger). This account stated (evidently in error, considering the time element) that Streeter started east on May 26, but gave his traveling time as 23 days! Streeter had not reached Salt Lake City—*see* p. 994—till May 28 (with the mail *from* Independence).

❡ In late June(?) Francis X. Aubry started for New Mexico with his second merchandise train of the year. (*See* pp. 985, 999, for his earlier Santa Fe trail journeys in 1851.)

About July 19 the incoming "July" mail party met this trader east of Council Grove (at 142-mile creek); and reported (at Independence) that Aubry and hands "who were sick, are now well." When the "August" mail reached Independence (on August 23), a telegram sent to St. Louis stated: "Aubrey and Connelly were [met by the mail party] at the crossing of the Arkansas. The cholera had just left their trains." (The Independence correspondent of the *Missouri Republican* wrote that the mail had met Aubry's train 10 miles above Lower Cimarron Spring.) The *Republican* reported that a letter from Aubry's company, written on August 8, at Arkansas Crossing, "states they had suffered a good deal from cholera. There were 10 cases of it between Pawnee Fork and the Crossing, but only one died—a Shawnee hunter named Logan."

Lt. Col. Dixon S. Miles, Third U. S. infantry ("on his way to New Mexico where he will be second in command"), apparently was traveling with the Aubry or Connelly company when the "August" mail met the traders. He may have joined at Fort Atkinson (or earlier). Eastbound travelers reaching Missouri in the fore part of August mentioned having met "Maj. Miles at Turkey Creek."

See p. 1042 for Aubry's return to Missouri; and *see* p. 1046 for his third merchant train (of 1851).

Ref: *Missouri Republican*, St. Louis, July 25, 28, August 17, 28, 1851; *Missouri Statesman*, Columbia, Mo., August 29, 1851 (from St. Louis *Union*, August 19).

❡ Effective July 1 (in accordance with an act of February 27 providing for Indian department reorganization), the Superintendency of Indian affairs, St. Louis, was superseded by the Central Superintendency—headquarters continuing at St. Louis, and David D. Mitchell remaining as superintendent. Created within the Central Superintendency were these agencies governing Indians of "Kansas":

Pottawatomie Agency	Pottawatomies; Kansa	Luke Lea (d. June 17) would have headed this agency. His son, Francis W. Lea, got the job.
Sac & Fox Agency	Sacs & Foxes of the Mississippi; Ottawas; Chippewas	John R. Chenault, agent
Osage River Agency	Miamis; Weas; Piankeshaws; Peorias & Kaskaskias	Asbury M. Coffey, agent

Kansas Agency   Shawnees; Delawares;
                         Wyandottes; Munsees; Stock-
                         bridges; and Christian Indians Thomas Moseley, Jr.,
                                                            agent

Great Nemaha Agency   Kickapoos; Iowas; Sacs &
                         Foxes of the Missouri   William P. Richardson,
                                                            agent

Neosho Agency
   (based in northeast
   "Oklahoma")   Shawnees & Senecas;
                         Osages; Quapaws; Senecas   William J. J. Morrow,
                                                            agent

[Up to July 1 there had been the *Fort Leavenworth Agency* (for Kickapoos, Delawares, Shawnees, Pottawatomies, Stockbridges, Munsees, etc.), headed by Luke Lea; *Osage River Agency* (for Sacs & Foxes of the Mississippi, Kansa, Ottawas, Chippewas, Miamis, Weas, Piankeshaws, Peorias & Kaskaskias), headed by John R. Chenault; *Wyandot Subagency* (for Wyandots), headed by Thomas Moseley, Jr.; *Great Nemaha Subagency* (for Iowas, Sacs & Foxes of the Missouri), headed by William P. Richardson; and *Osage Subagency* (for Osages), headed by Henry Harvey.]

Ref: *U. S. Statutes at Large;* 32d Cong., 1st Sess., *H. Ex. Doc. No. 103* (Serial 647); 33d Cong., 1st Sess., *H. Ex. Doc. No. 37* (Serial 718). The Rev. Paul M. Ponziglione, of Osage Mission, in 1876 stated that the "Osage agency [Subagency] was moved . . . to Quapaw Nation, some four miles from the southeast corner of this state [Kansas] on a small brook called Lost Creek."—*Neosho County Journal,* Osage Mission, Kansas, July 5, 1876.

❡ July-December.—Licenses to trade with Indians in "Kansas," as granted by agents of the Central Superintendency, St. Louis, were:

Traders	Indians	Issued by	Rec'vd at St. Louis
C(yprian) & F(rederick) Chouteau	Kansa	J. R. Chenault	July
(A. G.) Boone & (W. R.) Bernard	Sacs & Foxes (of the Mississippi)	J. R. Chenault	July(?)
John D. Lasley	Pottawatomies	J. R. Chenault	August
James R. Whitehead	Iowas, and Sacs & Foxes (of the Missouri)	W. P. Richardson	August
William F. Dyer	Kickapoos	W. P. Richardson	August
Boone & Bernard	Pottawatomies	J. R. Chenault	August
Thos. D. S. Macdonell	Pottawatomies	J. R. Chenault	August
Moses H. Scott	Pottawatomies	J. R. Chenault	September
Allen B. H. McGee	Sacs & Foxes (of the Mississippi)	J. R. Chenault	September
Cyprian Chouteau & Co.	Sacs & Foxes (of the Mississippi)	J. R. Chenault	September
Harrison McDowell	Pottawatomies	J. R. Chenault	September
David Gillespie	Pottawatomies	J. R. Chenault	September
Hiram M. Northrup	Sacs & Foxes (of the Mississippi)	J. R. Chenault	September

[*Continued on p. 1025*]

BVT. MAJ. EDMUND A. OGDEN
(1811?-1855)

Stationed at Fort Leavenworth, 1849-1855, Ogden in October, 1852, headed the board of officers selecting the site for Fort Riley (established in May, 1853); then supervised construction of the new post's buildings till his sudden death, August 3, 1855, in Fort Riley's cholera outbreak.

36—4138

ITINERARY OF THE CENTRAL ROUTE.

From Westport, Missouri, to Los Angeles, California.

DATE.	CAMPS.	DIST-ANCE.	DISTANCE FROM W.	REMARKS.
May 15	Ind. Creek		12	Cottonwoods, willows, good grass.
" 16	Bull Creek	23	35	Some timber; good grass and water.
" 16	Garfish Creek	22	57	Nearest wood, half mile; water and grass.
" 17	"110"	23	80	Running stream; timber, good grass.
" 17	Dragoon Creek	12	92	" fine timber and grass.
" 18	Stream	10	102	Good water; timber and grass.
" 18	"	4	106	" " "
" 18	Hollow	6	112	Water in holes; grass.
" 18	Council Grove	10	122	Settlement; abundant timber; grass; water.
" 19	Hollow	17	139	Water; grass and timber abundant.
" 19	Lost Spring	15	154	Good water, not abundant; grass; no wood.
" 20	Cottonwood Creek	16	170	Large timber; running water; good pasturage.
" 20	Turkey Creek	19	189	Plenty of water and grass; no wood.
" 21	Pool	12	201	Grass and water; small bushes.
" 21	Little Arkansas	18	219	Good timber; grass and water.
" 21	Owl Creek	10	229	Timber and grass; no water, except after rains.
" 22	Great Bend of Ark.	35	264	Wood; grass and water.
" 22	Walnut Creek	7	271	" "
" 23	Pawnee Fork	31	302	Well wooded; grass and water.
" 23	Pond	9	311	Good pasturage; water; no wood; plenty "buffalo chips."
" 24	"	25	336	Water; grass.
" 24	Arkansas River	20	356	Water; grass; small bushes.
" 25	Fort Atkinson	5	361	" " "
" 26	1st Crossing of S. Fé trail	10	371	" " "
" 26	2d " "	5	376	" " "
" 26	Camp on Ark.	20	396	" " "
" 27	"	20	416	" coarse grass; no wood.
" 28	Island on Ark.	19	435	" " little wood.
" 28	Chouteau's Island	12	447	" coarse rank grass; driftwood.
" 29	Slough of Ark.	28	475	" wiry grass; no wood.
" 29	Arkansas River	8	483	" " "
" 30	Big Timbers	20	503	" coarse grass; large timber.
" 30	Arkansas River	12	515	Good water; abundant bottom grass; timber.
" 31	Lower Dry Creek	25	540	Scanty dry grass; water in pools, warm; wood.
" 31	Bent's Fort	7	547	Bottom grass; river Arkansas; wood.
" 31	Upper Dry Creek	7	554	" " "
" 31	Pond	6	560	Dry bunch grass; water; wood near river.

G. Harris Heap, journalist of Edward F. Beale's 1853 expedition (*see* p. 1152), compiled this Santa Fe trail (and Bent's Fort branch) table of distances, published in his *Central Route to the Pacific* (1854).

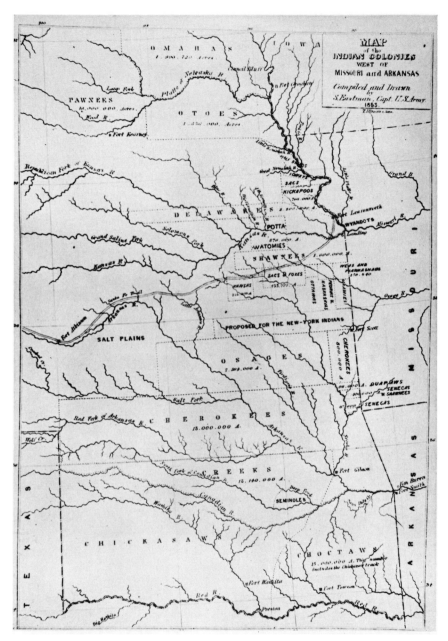

In the year preceding organization of Kansas and Nebraska territories the Indians held reserves as shown on Capt. Seth Eastman's map of 1853. Reproduced from Henry R. Schoolcraft's *Archives of Aboriginal Knowledge.*

KANSAS (CITY), MO.

In March, 1853, Celinda E. Hines wrote: "The village [of Kansas, Mo.] is situated on a high bluff rising from the river. The houses are very much scattered, extending over considerable space. . . . The houses are mostly log, with nice brick chimneys on the outside. The streets run every way without regard to form, and houses are scattered hither and thither over the hills and in the valleys."

Little of the *upland* town is depicted in the waterfront view shown above. See p. 1054, for another description; and see April 5, 1853, annals entry.

Views, 1853, of three Missouri river towns opposite the "Kansas" border. Reproduced from *The United States Illustrated*—a work issued serially in 1853 and published in two volumes before February, 1854, by Herrmann J. Meyer, New York. The artist is nowhere identified.

WESTON, MO.

ST. JOSEPH, MO.

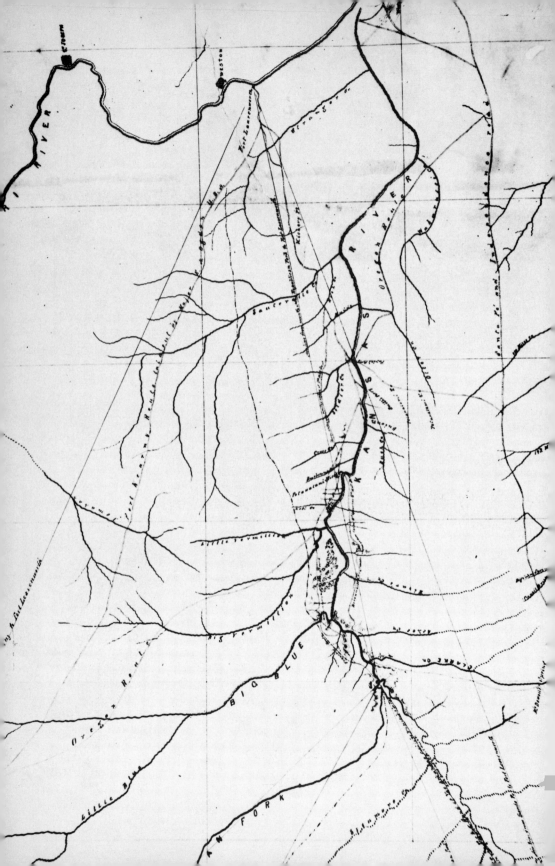

To accompany a board of officers' report, 1852, on selection of the future Fort Riley site (see p. 1131), Lt. Israel C. Woodruff, Topographical engineers (a board member), compiled the above "Chart"—also showing on it his own summer, 1852, reconnaissances in "Kansas" (made under orders of Bvt. Brig. Gen. Newman S. Clarke, Sixth military department head). See pp. 1103 and 1121.

Woodruff made some use of the Fremont and Emory maps. ("Wakarussi Cr.," "Otter Cr.," and "Buck Creek" [now Mill creek] derive from Fremont.) Higher up the Kansas, "Clarke Cr." (evidently named for the general), "Rivar's Cr.(?)," "Ashes Cr." (now McDowell creek), and "McDowell's Spring" relate to Woodruff's explorations. Note that downriver, "Union To[wn]," "Smith's Ferry" (established 1852), and "Papin's Ferry" (at present Topeka) are shown. "Site" labels the location of the future Fort Riley.

As stated in the introduction this study had to be broken with the year 1854, but the Westward migration continued in even greater flows. There were other gold-rushes. The Pony Express of 1860-1861 was yet to come. Huge freighting firms supplied interior army posts and settlements. And in the greatest influx came the homesteaders eventually by trainloads. One of the visitors who passed through in the spring of 1859 was Albert Bierstadt who made this glass-plate photograph of Wolf creek crossing in present Doniphan county, Kan., and the two on the following page. Bierstadt is best known for his magnificent paintings of Western scenes.

Emigrant wagons in Bellemont, Doniphan county, Kan.
Photos by Bierstadt.

Pike's Peak emigrants preparing to shove off from St.
Joseph, Mo., in 1859.

[*Continued From p. 1016*]

Oliver Polke & Robert Robitaille	Pottawatomies	J. R. Chenault	December
James Findlay	Ottawas	J. R. Chenault	December

Ref: SIA, St. Louis, "Records," v. 9, typed copy, pp. 529, 532, 541, 543, 544, 547, 552, 554, 560, 561, 585, 586; and *ibid.*, pp. 545, 560, 572 for (1) Henry Netherton as clerk for Josiah Smart (a Sac & Fox trader, licensed in 1850), (2) John B. Forman as clerk for A. B. H. McGee, (3) Francis M. Knight as clerk for Josiah Smart, and (4) W. H. Haskell as clerk for P. M. Chouteau (a licensed-in-1849 trader with the Miamis, Weas, etc.). See *KHQ*, v. 13, p. 28, for James R. Whitehead's statement that he settled on his claim, on the Missouri, on November 1, 1851. Joseph S. Chick, early day merchant of Kansas City, Mo. (reminiscing in 1908), stated: "Our clerk in charge at Uniontown was Harrison McDowell, our principal man. There were others who helped him. . . . We had a log store building. . . ." (J. S. Chick's recollections in KHi ms. division.)

❡ July.—Between the 1st and 22d the Santa Fe-to-Independence mail party (*see* July 22 entry) met much traffic on the Santa Fe trail. Listed below are the trains reported; also some notes from other sources.

Approximate date	Trains met; and place of meeting	Notes
[July 2]	Biggs' train, at Old Pecos	
[July 3]	Jones & Russell, at Mora	Probably preparing to return to Missouri.
[July 3]	McCauley & Sims' train, at Mora	Probably preparing to return to Missouri.
[July 4]	One of McCauley's trains, *returning*, was overtaken at Wolf creek	
[July 4]	Clymer's train, at Point of Rocks	Joseph Clymer's government train had set out May 16—*see* April 18 annals entry.
[July 5]	Beck & Brent ⎫ Doct. Massie ⎪ Barclay's ⎬ at Little Round Mound Majors' ⎭	Preston Beck; Robert Brent; Dr. Philippe Masure(?); Alexander Barclay, of Barclay's Fort; Alexander Majors.
[July 6]	Ewing, at Cold Spring (in the "Oklahoma Panhandle")	Finis Y. Ewing, presumably.
[July 7]	Another *returning* McCauley train was overtaken at Upper Cimarron Springs	
[July 7]	Ross & Meyers, at Upper Cimarron Springs	Both "E." and "L. N." Ross were in the Santa Fe trade. "Meyers" presumably was "H. Mayer & Co." (*See* under Ref: below.)
[July 8]	Irwin's, at Lower Cimarron Crossing	Joseph C. Irwin.
[July 8]	Spencer & Lipscomb's, at Lower Cimarron Crossing	Charles L. Spencer. (*See* under Ref: below.)

Approximate date	Trains met; and place of meeting	Notes
[July 9]	McCarty's, on the Jornada	
[July 9–10]	Several Mexican trains, on the Jornada	One of these was Otero's.
[July 14]	Creech & Hubble, at Pawnee Rock	Jones Creech—bound for Fort Atkinson; (Santiago L.?) Hubbell.
[July 15–19]	Several government trains, "in charge of Rucker and others," between Pawnee Rock and Council Grove	Bvt. Maj. Daniel H. Rucker (AQM).
[July 19]	Barnes, at Council Grove	
[July 19]	Aubry, at 142-mile creek	Francis X. Aubry—*see* p. 1015 —taking his second train (1851) to Santa Fe.
[July 20]	Jose Chaves, at Willow Spring	
[July 21]	McCaul(e)y's, at Lone Elm	
[July 22]	McCoy's and Waldo, at Missouri boundary line	

Between August 1-20 the "August" mail met the following trains which had left Missouri in June or July. (Some can be identified on the "July" list above.)

Lipscomb & Barnes' trains, at Bernal Springs, N. M.; at San Miguel, the mail *overtook* Ewing's and Majors' trains returning; two Mexican trains, at Ocate, N. M.; L. D. Sheets' train, at Red (Canadian) river; Jones & Russell's train, at Cold Spring; Aubry's train, 10 miles above Lower Cimarron Spring; three Mexican trains, at Sand creek (on the Jornada); Jones & Russell's second train, 10 miles below Arkansas Crossing; at "Fort Mackay" (Fort Atkinson), the mail *overtook* a returning Jones & Russell train; McCauley & Kirby's train, 8 miles west of Walnut creek; at Big Bend of Arkansas, McCaul(e)y & Lewis' train, returning, was *overtaken*; S(idney?) Bartleson's train, at Cottonwood; David Waldo & Co's train, at Lost Spring; "Hutton's" train ("Huston's—or Houston's?), at Council Grove.

Ref: *Missouri Republican*, St. Louis, July 25, 28, August 17, 28, 1851. The August 17 issue says that H. Barthel (who reached St. Louis August 16, from Santa Fe) had met: Russell & Jones' train at the Moro; Hubbell's at the Cimarron, also Spencer's there; Otero's at Rio Jornada; "Maj. Ruggles" (i. e., Rucker's) at Fort Mackay; Aubry's train at Big Cow creek. The *Missouri Statesman*, Columbia, Mo., August 29, 1851 (from St. Louis *Union*, August 19), printed a list of trains met by "Mr. Waldron" (also arriving at St. Louis on August 16, from Santa Fe). It is nearly the name as Barthel's list. Isaac Rippetoe, another arrivee (*see* the *Republican*, August 22 issue) reported that Indians had raided (and upset) Mayer's provision wagon at Upper Cimarron Springs; and that Lipscomb's train (met at "the Walnut Spring"—in N. M.?) had lost "the greater portion" of their cattle and were hunting for them. John M. Huston (Houston?) who returned from Santa Fe in August (*see* St. Louis *Daily Intelligencer*, August 13 issue) reported his train was the third to reach Santa Fe; and that on his return he met 47 trains "all in good health." Did he take a second train out in July?

❡ July-August.—The *Robert Campbell*, under partial charter to

Harvey, Primeau & Co., left St. Louis July 2 (with some 130 mountain men and about 200 tons of freight aboard) for the Upper Missouri.

At the end of July she reached the Yellowstone's mouth. The return trip was begun August 2. On the 17th the *Robert Campbell* (with buffalo robes and furs consigned to Messrs. R. & W. Campbell) returned to St. Louis, having made the round trip within a "few hours" of 48 days.

Ref: St. Louis *Daily Intelligencer*, June 30, July 2, 12, August 18, 1851; *Missouri Republican*, St. Louis, August 18, 1851; Kurz "Journal," *loc. cit.*, pp. 86, 89.

❧ July.—Eleven Missourians (from Platte, Cooper, and Howard counties) and one Virginian, who had left Hangtown, Calif., on May 15, and "packed through" with 34 mules, reached Missouri in mid-July (as reported by the Glasgow *Times* of July 24).

These men were among the early arrivals of a sizable "emigration fro·n California homeward bound" by way of the plains in 1851. They reported that another party—chiefly from Clay county, Mo.—would be in "in a few days"; and that "Col." Congreve Jackson (*see* p. 856) was to start home with a company on July 1. (John, James, and Thomas Jackson—all of Howard county—were in the above party of 12.)

Ref: Glasgow (Mo.) *Weekly Times*, July 24, 1851.

❧ July 22.—The "July" U. S. mail from Santa Fe, in charge of "Mr. [Griffith H.] Williams," arrived at Independence, Mo. (nine days ahead of contract time).

At the "Narrows" in New Mexico, there had been a skirmish with Indians which caused the mail party to fall back to "Beck's train of wagons," after killing one of the attackers.

While the mail carriers were at Fort Atkinson (in the July 12-14 period?), two soldiers (cholera victims) had been buried. But the health of "Fort Sumner" (with the exception of three [fatal] cases of cholera) was reported to be "remarkably good."

Ref: *Missouri Republican*, St. Louis, July 25, 28, 1851. The July 23 (telegraphic) account from Independence (published in the July 25 issue) gave the above "cheerful" report concerning Fort Atkinson; the "July 22" letter by the *Republican's* correspondent (in the July 28 issue) gave the erroneous information that "from one to three of the soldiers are dying daily [from cholera, at Fort Atkinson]." The *Republican* of August 17, 1851, stated that there had been a few cholera cases at "Fort Mackay" (Fort Atkinson), "only three of which were fatal."

❧ July 24.—"Mr. Wyrock," and party, with the "July" U. S. mail from Salt Lake City, arrived at Independence, Mo. They had started east on July 1; laid by two days en route; and traveled 22 days. The *Occidental Messenger* believed this to be "the quickest trip that has been made."

On the 13th, at Ash Hollow, the outbound July mail had been met.

Ref: *Missouri Republican*, St. Louis, July 26, 1851 (by telegraph—and with errors—

from Independence, July 25); *The Weekly Tribune*, Liberty, Mo., August 1, 1851; or, St. Louis *Daily Intelligencer*, August 4, 1851 (both from *Occidental Messenger*, Independence, Mo., of July 26).

❧ July 25.—A telegraph office (the St. Louis and Missouri River [Morse line] Telegraph Company; Tal P. Shaffner and Isaac M. Veitch, managers) was opened at Kansas (City), Mo. What was, apparently, the first telegraphic communication from that town read: "Kansas, July 25: Weather warm and pleasant. River is falling fast. The steamers Isabel and Saranak passed down yesterday." (The *Missouri Republican*, and *Daily Intelligencer*, were two St. Louis papers which printed this item, on the 26th.)

The *Republican* of the 27th, commenting on the opening of the Kansas, Mo., office, stated (in part): ". . . dispatches may be sent from this time forward. The office at Independence is also at work and so are the intermediate offices. . . . Mr. Vietch is at St. Joseph, making arrangements for the extension of the line to that town." (*See, also,* pp. 1043 and 1048.)

Ref: *Missouri Republican*, St. Louis, July 26, 27, 1851; St. Louis *Daily Intelligencer*, July 26, 1851. The Glasgow (Mo.) *Weekly Times* of May 29, 1851, noted that the telegraph line had been completed to Lexington, Mo., and that the *Express* editors had sent the first dispatch to St. Louis on May 23. (The *Republican* of February 24, 1851, published a February 22 telegraphic dispatch from Boonville, Mo.) The St. Joseph (Mo.) *Gazette* of July 23, 1851, stated: "Mr. Veitch, one of the builders of the St. Louis and Missouri River Telegraph Line, called on us to-day . . . [in regard to extending the line to that town]." For earlier, and later, history of this line *see* "The Early Telegraph in Rural Missouri, 1847-1859," in *Missouri Historical Review*, Columbia, v. 51 (October, 1956), pp. 42-53; and *see KHQ*, v. 25, pp. 32, 33.

❧ July 31.—A telegram sent from Independence, Mo. (to St. Louis), read: "The emigrants for the Mormon settlement on the Rio Colorado [in "Arizona"], from Keokuk Iowa and neighborhood, via Santa Fe, who passed through here a few days since, left their encampment on Bull creek [present Johnson county, Kan.] yesterday morning. Two more wagons, to join them, left this place today —in all 22 wagons, about 65-75 persons   men, women and children, and about 90 yoke of oxen. A few cholera cases among them, but no deaths."

(For account of the first—1850—Brewsterite movement company of Mormon "dissenters" *see* p. 953.)

From a camp in "Indian Territory, two miles west of the [Missouri] Line," John Clemerson (Clemenson?), of Harrisonville, Mo., had written, on July 22, a letter reporting his (and his family's) arrival "here" on July 11. He had joined three families (with six wagons), some of whom had "been here" two months. (These were the Andrew Patchin[g?], John W. Crandal, and Francis Wallis [or, Wallace?] families.) A few days later others had arrived: the Nathaniel Frampton and F. A. Trump (or, Troup?) families, with three wagons, on July 18; and on the 19th seven wagons of the "Rushville Branch" (the John Goodsel, and Lorenzo Cram families; and John Sigler's four-wagon party).

At a meeting on Sunday, July 20, the company had organized "into a Branch," electing John Sigler as presiding elder. Clemerson stated the party had no plan to go "where Bro. Brev ster is" (*i. e.,* Socorro, N. M.), but were bound for the "Colorado."

Ref: New York *Daily Tribune,* August 8, 1851 (from *Missouri Republican,* St. Louis, August 1); *The Olive Branch,* Springfield, Ill., v. 3, no. 7, v. 4, no. 2 (February and September, 1851).

❡ DIED: Hard Fish (a Sac chief), in July(?), or early August(?), on the Sac & Fox reserve. He was buried near the Sac & Fox Agency, in present Franklin county.

The month of his death is not known. On August 8, 1851, Thomas Owens was paid $30 for "Hauling corpse of Hard fish." The marble slab which marked his grave, subsequently, bore this inscription: "Sacred to the memory of Hard Fish   a Sac Chief   Born at Shock-o-ton in 1800. Died in 1851."

Ref: Edward McCoonse's August 24, 1875, letter (typed copy), written from Ottawa, Franklin co., to J. H. Pickering (in KHi ms. division); 33d Cong., 1st Sess., *H. Ex. Doc. No. 37* (Serial 718), p. 312. For earlier data on Hard Fish, *see* annals index. It could be that he died as early as May or June during the smallpox outbreak.

❡ August 1-12.—Under the heading "Indian Politics," the New York *Weekly Tribune* of August 23, published the following:

"In the *Kanzas (Mo.) Public Ledger,* of the 1st inst. we find the ticket of nominations recently made in opposition to the present Board of Chiefs of the Wyandot Nations:

Nominees	Votes	Present Incumbents	Votes
John Kayrohoo	[28]	Jas. Washington	[62]
John Manoncuo *	[37]	Jas. Rankin	[58]
John Arms	[45]	M[at.] Mudeater	[52]
J. S. Bearskin	[67]	J. W. Grayeyes	[52]

"Some of them (says *The Ledger* correspondent) 'have done the State some service,' but while doing so, were never suspected of possessing preeminent abilities.

"There will be no election of principal Chief, as that officer is elected every two years, and the term of the incumbent, G. J. Clark [*i. e.,* George I. Clark], will not expire till next August a year. . . ."

(William Walker, of the Wyandot Nation, in his August 12, 1851, diary entry, wrote: "Went to town [Wyandotte—now within Kansas City, Kan.] to attend the National Election. . . ." The votes he recorded are shown above. Instead of the name "John Manoncuo," * he listed "Towareh.")

Ref: New York *Weekly Tribune,* August 23, 1851; William Walker's diary, *loc. cit.*

❡ August-September.—Sup't David D. Mitchell (head of the Indian superintendency at St. Louis), en route to the Great Indian Council at Fort Laramie (where he, and Agent Thomas Fitzpatrick would serve as United States commissioners), arrived at Kansas (City), Mo., July 29, aboard the *Cataract.* Mitchell and his party —which included A. B. Chambers (the *Missouri Republican's* senior editor) and B. Gratz Brown, of St. Louis, Henry C. King, of Georgia, and J. H. Dillon, of England—spent a few days in the vicinity; then (without Dillon, and King?) began the overland journey, proceeding first to Fort Leavenworth.

Two letters (one dated "Uniontown, Pottawotomie Nation, August 6th, 1851"; the other "Snake Creek, in the Pawnee Country, July [*i. e.,* August] 11, 1851") written by A. B. Chambers, are quoted extensively here.

[Letter No. 1] "The trip from Westport to Fort Leavenworth [August 3] was one of great interest to me. A few miles from Westport we crossed the State line, and from thence the country is as beautiful, and as inviting for agricultural purposes, as any in the West. Capt. Parke's [Joseph Parks, Shawnee chief] farm on the State line, and the Methodist Mission farm adjoining, are, in extent and fertility, equal to any to be found in the State. During the ride through the country of the Shawnees, up to the Kansas river, we passed many large and well cultivated farms belonging to Indians. We stopped at the house of a Shawnee, Blue Jacket, and found his family as comfortably situated, and his children as intelligent, as are to be found among the frontier settlements of the whites.

"We crossed the Kansas (this river, up here, is universally called the *Caw*) river at the trading post called Delaware, the principal trading post of the Delawares. It is situated immediately on the bank of the river. There is a Post-Office here. . . . Here I saw Kitchum [Ketchum], or Tawhelaum, the principal chief of the Delawares. He is a large, intellectual looking man, seventy-seven years of age; now complaining of ill health. He was Tecumseh's second in command at the battle of the Thames, and an active and efficient warrior in the last war with England. He is said to be quite wealthy, and is a very exemplary man. I also saw a chief called Sarcoxie, the same after whom the town of that name in Missouri is called. . . . Mr. Tableau [Henry Tiblow], the Interpreter is an intelligent and educated Indian. At this place we had the pleasure of partaking of the hospitality of Mr. Finley, the P. M. [James Findlay, postmaster], and his lady.

"We arrived at Fort Leavenworth before sundown, and were at once taken care of by Mr. Rich [Hiram Rich, sutler] and his family. We called upon the commander of the post, Col. [Thomas T.]

FAUNTLEROY, and spent the next day most agreeably in intercourse with the officers stationed here. . . .

"We left the Fort, between nine and ten A. M. [August 4] for . . . [Union Town]; Mr. [William F.] Dyer, who has a trading house among the Kickapoos, traveling with us from his post. That day we reached the . . . Grasshopper [now Delaware], a beautiful tributary of the Kansas, about forty miles from the Fort. Here we encamped . . . and next day reached . . . [Union Town], a further distance of thirty-five miles. The country between the Fort and Uniontown is equal, in beauty and fertility, to any that we have passed over. The prairies are high and rolling, with good strong soil. . . . Between the Fort and this place there are the Stranger, Grasshopper, and Soldier, creeks of considerable magnitude. [Mitchell's party traveled the military road described on p. 981.]

"Uniontown is situated on a high prairie—a bleak, cold spot [surely not in August!], and about a mile and a half from wood and water. It is difficult to conceive what induced the selection of such a location [see p. 737]. . . . It is situated on the east [south] side; near the crossing of the Kansas river, and about the same distance from St. Joseph, [Mo.]. There are six trading houses here, each having a large stock of goods. [Mitchell stayed at trader T. D. S. Macdonell's place, it was reported.] . . ."

[Letter No. 2] "Here we are, eighteen miles beyond the [Big] Blue [on August 11] . . . We left Uniontown on Thursday evening [August 7] after sundown, crossed the Kansas, and joined our train at Cross Creek that night. . . .

"We reached the Big Blue yesterday evening, crossed it [Alcove Spring area], and encamped upon its banks. This morning, after a ride of about 18 miles, we came up to the encampment of [Bvt.] Major [Robert H.] Chilton, in command of the escort of Troop B, First Dragoons [from Fort Leavenworth]. They arrived here Saturday last [August 9], and have been waiting for us. We move forward tomorrow. The wagon trains [carrying the supplies and presents for the Indians at Fort Laramie] are all behind, and it is now certain that they cannot arrive at Laramie by the time expected. This will be a great disappointment to Col. Mitchell and a heavy loss to the contractors [Robert Campbell—R. & W. Campbell—St. Louis]. . . . [By report, the 27 wagons carrying provisions and presents, crossed the Kansas river—place not indicated

—on August 17. They did not reach the treaty grounds till September 20.]

"We have not yet been joined by the English and other gentlemen who were to have made a part of our company. [*See* pp. 1033, 1034.] . . ."

Mitchell and party reached Fort Laramie at the end of August. On September 8 (after the council site had been moved to Horse creek—30 miles distant) official talks were commenced. Comm'rs D. D. Mitchell and Thomas Fitzpatrick (the latter having come up from Fort Atkinson, on the Arkansas) "presented the features of the Treaty [peace, and mutual accommodations] to a Council composed of representatives of Sioux, Cheyennes, Arapahoes, Crows, Mongeurs, Shoshones or Snakes, Gros Ventres, Assineboines, Arickarees and smaller delegations from other tribes. . . . [There were] several thousand [Indian] men, women and children on the ground, with horses and dogs to match. . . ." The military force consisted of "a fragment of a company of [First] Dragoons, two companies of Mounted Riflemen, with a six-pound howitzer, all under command of [Bvt.] Major [R. H.] Chilton."

The Treaty of Fort Laramie was signed on September 17. Distribution of the provisions and presents (which arrived on the 20th) was completed on the 23d. On the 24th Bvt. Maj. R. H. Chilton (accompanied by Bvt. Lt. Col. Samuel Cooper, of the Adjutant general's dept.) and the First dragoons, in advance, started back to Fort Leavenworth; and, in the evening, Mitchell's party, in which were A. B. Chambers, B. Gratz Brown, Agent Thomas Fitzpatrick, Father Pierre-Jean De Smet, a delegation of Indians—16? in number—who were to visit Washington, Robert Campbell (apparently), Edmund F. ("Guesso") Chouteau, John Simpson Smith, Joseph Tesson Honore (and others?), also began the journey back to the States.

Ref: *Missouri Republican,* St. Louis, July 25, August 8, 13, 26, September 5, 25, 26, October 5, 17, 19, 24, 27, 29, November 2, 9, 23, 1851; St. Louis *Daily Intelligencer,* July 26, August 13, 14, 1851; New York *Daily Tribune,* July 26, August 2, 8, October 4, 10, 18, November 1, 1851; *The Weekly Tribune,* Liberty, Mo., October 10, 1851; *Jefferson Inquirer,* Jefferson City, Mo., October 11, 25, 1851; St. Joseph (Mo.) *Gazette,* August 13, 1851; P. G. Lowe, *op. cit.,* pp. 76, 77; Chittenden and Richardson, *op. cit.,* v. 1, pp. 61-65, v. 2, pp. 684-691; Pierre-Jean De Smet, *op. cit.,* pp. 58, 59, 99-120; SIA, St. Louis, "Records," v. 9, typed copy, pp. 498, 510, 511, 514, 522-524, 536, 538, 548, 558, 559, 570, 574-577; C. J. Kappler's *Indian Affairs. Laws and Treaties* (1904), v. 2, pp. 594-596; *New Mexico Historical Review,* v. 17, pp. 204-210; Kurz "Journal," *loc. cit.,* pp. 220, 221; G. J. Garraghan, *op. cit.,* v. 2, pp. 478, 479.

❡ August.—The U. S. mail party for Salt Lake City (*i. e., for Fort Laramie*) which left Independence, Mo., on the 1st, was met by eastbound travelers on August 6, 40 miles west of the Big Blue. The carriers had been obliged to abandon the rear section of their broken wagon, but were getting along "finely" with the fore wheels.

According to Whitney's *History of Utah,* in the summer of 1851 Samuel H. Woodson, of Independence (mail contractor on the Independence-Salt Lake City route), subcontracted with Feramorz Little (a Mormon) to carry the mail between Salt Lake and Fort Laramie for the balance (two years and 11 months) of Woodson's contract. Little's partners were his brothers-in-law—

Charles F. Decker and Ephraim K. Hanks. The carriers from Independence, and Salt Lake, were to meet at Fort Laramie on the 15th of each month. "Messrs. Little and Hanks" made their initial eastern trip, under this agreement, in August, 1851.

Ref: *Missouri Republican*, St. Louis, August 17, 1851; St. Louis *Daily Intelligencer*, August 18, 1851; Orson F. Whitney's *History of Utah* . . . (Salt Lake City, 1892), v. 1, p. 498. Woodson's contract ran to June 30, 1854.

❡ August.—The U. S. mail for Santa Fe which left Independence, Mo., at the beginning of the month, reached New Mexico's capital on August 29. Griffith H. Williams was the mail-carrier-in-charge, apparently.

Ref: Calhoun, *op. cit.*, p. 414. Williams carried the "July" mail *to* Independence; and he brought the "September" mail *from* Santa Fe.

❡ August 6.—Twenty-four Missourians (23 men and one woman), returning overland from Sacramento, Calif. (left June 2), reached St. Joseph (Buchanan co.), Mo. They had made the journey in 66 days.

In the party were three Harrison county men, five from Ray county, and these persons from Buchanan county: Thomas Waller, John and Charles Daily, Green Taylor, Thomas and Dudley Arrington, Henry and Washington Long, Henry and Zebediah Baker, Wood Ray, William Plank and wife, Pryor Plank, William Coker, Matthew L. Davis.

Ref: St. Joseph *Gazette*, August 6, 1851.

❡ August 7.—Detailed to escort Sup't D. D. Mitchell's party to Fort Laramie (*see* p. 1029), Bvt. Maj. Robert H. Chilton, and Company B, First dragoons, set out on the Fort Leavenworth-Fort Kearny military road. Accompanying Chilton was Bvt. Lt. Col. Samuel Cooper (Adjutant general's dept.).

By the night of August 9 they had reached, and encamped some miles west of Big Blue Crossing (present Marysville). Superintendent Mitchell's party, traveling the Oregon-California trail from Kansas river, joined Chilton's command August 11.

Ref: *Missouri Republican*, St. Louis, August 13, 14, 1851; St. Louis *Daily Intelligencer*, August 13, 1851.

❡ August 8.—The Kansas (Mo.) *Public Ledger* reported the arrival (August 6 or 7), aboard the *Saranak*, of Robert Campbell, St. Louis, George Wilkins Kendall, of the New Orleans *Picayune*, "Lord Fitz William of England," and his suite. (Kendall's party, according to the *Saranak's* officers, numbered 11 persons. The English "Lord" was Charles William Wentworth Fitzwilliam, son of Earl Fitzwilliam.) All were bound for Fort Laramie; and though some days behind Sup't D. D. Mitchell's company (*see* pp. 1029, 1030) they hoped to catch up with him.

Robert Campbell (successful bidder—over Pierre Chouteau, Jr. & Co.— to supply the Fort Laramie Indian Council's provisions and presents) may have joined Mitchell on the Oregon-California trail. He was at Fort Laramie when Father De Smet arrived—about September 10.

From Fort Kearny, on August 30 (when Mitchell's party was nearing Fort Laramie), George W. Kendall wrote: "We have finally reached this military post . . . at least ten days behind our time. For a week after leaving the Pottawattamie trading post [Union Town] on the Kansas, we were daily visited by drenching showers, swelling the small streams, cutting up the roads, and rendering our progress almost impossible. . . . The long train of wagons containing Indian presents is still behind, and can hardly reach Laramie before the 20th of September [the exact date of their arrival] . . ." Kendall's letter also (1) described a meeting with 14 Kansa Indians at the "crossing of the Vermillion" (the Kansa had been on an unsuccessful war expedition against the Pawnees; had also failed at hunting, and were very hungry); (2) reported that Mr. Dillon's fine gelding had been "spirited away by a Pawnee"; (3) commented on the many travelers met on the route ("far more than we expected. They have been mostly . . . returning Californians . . .").

"Mr. Polk," an express rider, who journeyed from Fort Laramie to Fort Leavenworth in 12 days—September 8 to 20, saw Kendall "and others of his party" at Fort Kearny (about the 15th?). "They had met with so many accidents and delays as to disgust them with the trip and Mr. Kendall, Mr. Yeatman, Mr. Dillon and others were on their return home. Lord Fitzwilliam and one or two others were determined to persevere in the journey."

Kendall (and companions) traveled eastward by way of the Pawnee villages; reached the Missouri at Council Bluffs; soon thereafter wrote a letter dated: "On board Steamboat Pocahontas, Independence, Mo., September 26, 1851." He reached St. Louis on the 30th.

Fitzwilliam did persevere; and was at Fort Laramie early in October. Paul Wilhelm, Duke of Wuerttemberg, in his later-written narrative, mentioned meeting "Lord Fitz-Williams, a daring traveller and globe-trotter," at a trading post near the fort. (In 1852 the New York *Times*' St. Louis correspondent wrote that "Mr. Fitzwilliam . . . is a modest, unassuming young man of fair intelligence and attainments. . . .")

Ref: St. Louis *Daily Intelligencer*, August 13, October 2, 1851; *Missouri Republican*, St. Louis, August 13, September 25, October 1, 1851; New York *Daily Times*, October 15, 23, 1851, June 10, 1852; De Smet, *op. cit.*, pp. 99, 100; *New Mexico Historical Review*, v. 17, p. 210.

❡ August 8.—The "new and splendid steamer" *Clara* (Joshua Cheever, captain), having made her first voyage up the Missouri, left Kansas (City), Mo., on the 8th, for St. Louis. William Walker (Wyandot), in his diary entry of August 8 wrote: ". . . our folks took the Steamer 'Clara' for St. Charles."

Advance notice had reported the Pittsburgh-built *Clara* would have a 183-foot deck, a beam of 31 feet, three 40-inch boilers, 26 feet long; and that her cabin would be "furnished in a style of comfort and elegance that will far excel that of any boat now plying above . . . [St. Louis]."

After this boat arrived at St. Joseph, Mo. (August 15), on her second run up the Missouri, the *Gazette* stated that the *Clara*, and the *Isabel*, would run as regular St. Joseph-St. Louis packets.

Other steamboats on the "middle" Missouri in the late summer, and autumn, included the *Buena Vista, Cataract, Duroc, Hermann, Sacramento, Saranak, St. Ange* ("refurbished," and now under Capt. Thomas Scott), *Elvira, Ben West, Pocahontas, Kansas, El Paso, Timour No. 2* (new in August), *Banner State, Highland Mary,* and *Robert Campbell.*

Ref: William Walker's diary, *loc. cit.;* St. Joseph *Gazette*, June 25, July 30, August 20, 1851; St. Louis *Daily Intelligencer*, July 25, August 18, 23, September 11, 13, 15, October 1, 2, *also*, November issues, 1851; *Missouri Republican,* St. Louis, August 18, 24, 25, 28, September 6, October 2, 1851; *KHC*, v. 9, p. 300 (where it is stated the above *Clara* was sunk by ice, at St. Louis, in 1856).

❦ August 11.—E. Denniston, Kalamazoo county, Mich., Lucius A. Booth, Terre Haute, Ind., and others, arrived at Fort Leavenworth, overland from Sacramento, Calif. (left June 1). They had made the journey in 70 traveling days (stopping three days at Salt Lake City).

Eleven persons (four, or five, of Jackson county, Mo.) from this party reached Independence, Mo. on August 13.

Ref: *Missouri Republican,* St. Louis, August 17, 19, 1851; St. Louis *Daily Intelligencer,* August 18, 1851.

❦ On August 11, at a camp 18 miles west of the Big Blue, "a train of 15 returning Californians" (mostly from Missouri), who had left the "mines on Weaver river on June 11," were met by Sup't D. D. Mitchell's Fort Laramie-bound company.

"They looked to be weary, and expressed themselves sick of the gold region," wrote A. B. Chambers (of Mitchell's party); and he also reported: "They had to divide their provisions with about 600 Pawnees who are encamped on the Little Blue about 50 miles in advance of us." The "Californians" presumably reached Missouri within a week.

Ref: *Missouri Republican,* St. Louis, August 26, 1851. Chambers misdated his letter written from the above camp, heading it "Snake Creek, in the Pawnee Country, July [*i. e.,* August] 11th, 1851."

❦ In mid-August (before the 16th) Isaac Rippetoe, who had been at "Barclay & Doyle's Fort on the Moro" (and had left there July 14 or 15, alone, on horseback), arrived at Westport, Mo., alone and afoot.

He had made his way to Fort Atkinson safely; and remained at the post five days to rest his pony. Setting out again, "in two days and two nights" of traveling Rippetoe reached the flooded Little Arkansas. In attempting to cross, he "lost his horse, provisions, gun and ammunition"; and walked the rest of the way to the States.

Ref: St. Joseph (Mo.) *Gazette*, August 27, 1851 (from Independence *Messenger* [of August 16]); *Missouri Republican*, St. Louis, August 22, 1851.

⟪ In mid-August, Paul Wilhelm, Duke of Wuerttemberg, accompanied by artist-adventurer Heinrich B. Möllhausen, and "Mr. Ziellinski," journeyed up the Missouri from St. Louis to Kansas (City), Mo. After further preparations, in late August the three men set out on the Oregon-California trail, with two light, horse-drawn wagons, and a saddle horse for Möllhausen (a former Prussian cavalry officer, "who was to do scouting duty during the expedition").

(For the Duke's earlier connections with "Kansas" history [1823; 1830], *see* pp. 110-113, 167, 168. *Also, see* his "photograph," p. 199.)

Duke Paul's narrative gives a few details of the journey westward across "Kansas" in 1851. He wrote: "I followed along . . . the regular California route. In passing along the first ninety miles I had to ford many deep creeks and small wooded rivers. At the end of this leg of the journey I reached a settlement . . . called Union-Town. Not far from this place I had my outfit ferried across the Kansas which at this point has a very strong current. . . .

"Ten miles farther on is the last settlement, a Catholic Mission [St. Mary's], about 130 miles distant from Kansastown. Here we met a number of people mounted on mules and horses who came from California. These had made the journey in 57 days.

"Here resides a titular bishop [the Rt. Rev. John B. Miege]. Indian children of both sexes are cared for and instructed at this mission in both religious and secular subjects. This institution is in a fairly prosperous condition and is spreading a good influence that is felt far and wide.

"From the Catholic Mission to the La Platte river it is about 240 miles, all of it a country undulating and crossed by deep brooks and small rivers. . . ."

It took the Duke and Möllhausen 19 days (from Missouri's border) to reach Fort Kearny. One of the wagons got wrecked on the way (and Ziellinski apparently was left with it).

(The travels of Duke Paul and Möllhausen from Fort Kearny to Fort Laramie are not included here. On that journey, in late September, they met the military and civilian parties returning from the Great Indian Council; and the Duke was overjoyed at meeting his old friend Father De Smet. They reached Fort Laramie on October 5; and in mid-month started back to the States. For the return trip *see* p. 1049.)

Ref: *New Mexico Historical Review*, v. 17, pp. 181-214; *KHQ*, v. 16, pp. 226-228; Chittenden and Richardson, *op. cit.*, v. 2, p. 685 (De Smet places the meeting with Duke

Paul at, or near the South Platte crossing; whereas the duke indicates they visited at
trading post "Fort John"); *South Dakota Historical Collections,* Pierre, v. 19, pp. 463, 464.

❡ August.—In mid-month(?), Bvt. Col. John Munroe (recently
Ninth military dept. head), Capt. Langdon C. Easton, and Capt.
Lafayette McLaws, who had left Santa Fe on July 29, reached the
Missouri border.

Ref: New York *Daily Tribune,* September 9, 1851 (for a July 30, 1851, letter from
Santa Fe, noting arrival of Bvt. Col. E. V. Sumner—new Ninth military dept. head—on
July 19; and departure "yesterday" of the above trio).

❡ August 23.—The "August" mail from Santa Fe, eight days ahead
of contract time, arrived at Independence, Mo. Six passengers were
aboard the stage: "Messrs. [S. P.] Sanford, [Henry C.] Cranston,
[Thomas] Dunn and [John S.] Stewart [Stuart]," of the U. S. and
Mexican Boundary commission, also "Mr. Wolfe, and Mrs. Forsythe." (Some of the men reached St. Louis August 27, aboard
the *Clara.*)

Ref: *Missouri Republican,* St. Louis, August 24, 28, 1851; Bartlett, *op. cit.,* pp. 595,
596 (for supplied names).

❡ August 24.—"Judge [Robert] Irwin" (who had gone to Oregon
in 1850) returned to St. Joseph, Mo., overland from Oregon City
(left in June). He (and others?) had made the trip in 60 days.

Ref: St. Joseph *Gazette,* August 27, 1851; *The History of Buchanan County, Missouri*
. . . (1881), pp. 134, 135 (for note on Irwin).

❡ August 29.—In 29 days from Salt Lake City, the "August" U. S.
mail arrived at Independence, Mo. The carriers had met, en route,
a large number of Indians on their way to the Fort Laramie treaty-
council; and Sup't D. D. Mitchell's party, 70 miles west of Fort
Kearny, in mid-August.

Ref: *The Frontier Guardian,* Kanesville, Ia., September 19, 1851 (letter by "H. L. S.,"
from Independence, August 30, 1851, to "Br. Mackintosh").

❡ August.—Some part-year statistics on the Santa Fe trade in 1851
were made available by the report William S. McKnight brought
to Missouri. (He arrived at St. Louis on September 6; he had left
Santa Fe on July 29.)

By his statement 120 traders' wagons had entered Santa Fe up
to July 29. En route to Missouri, McKnight met the following New
Mexico-bound trains:

Name(s)	No. of wagons	Name(s)	No. of wagons
"Ross and Ewings"	55	"Perea"	20
"Barn[e]s and Co."	7	"Baca"	9
"Jos. Armijo"	7	"Dr Connelly"	30
"N. Armijo"	10	"Armijo"	23
"Sarrisina" [Sarracina?]	17	"Otery" [Otero]	35
"McCarty"	24	"Barn[e]s"	21

"Guiteres" [Gutierrez]	8	"Moetaxa and Chaves"	19
"Gonzales"	9	"White"	20
"Hubble" [Hubbell]	10	"Waldo & Co."	12
"Sheets"	7	"Houston"	12
"Jones"	7	"Torres, Chavis and Perea"	40

Jose Chaves and Juan Perea's trains left Westport for Santa Fe on August 22. (*See* last entry on McKnight's list.) The wagons above total 402. Added to the 120 earlier ones, the count would be 522. McKnight's count was 527—a minor discrepancy, perhaps a printing error. Note that no *government* trains are included (with the possible exception of "Jones"—Jones & Russell?). For a "full" 1851 count, a number of later trains would have to be included—*see* September and October entries—which, conservatively estimated at 50 more, would swell the year's total to around 575 Santa Fe-bound traders' wagons.

Ref: *Missouri Republican*, September 7, 1851; and *ibid.*, August 28 issue (for Chaves and Perea).

❡ August-September.—A manuscript map "Sketch of the Route Pursued by [Bvt.] Capt. J[ohn] Pope Top. Eng'rs. From Fort Union N. M. to Fort Leavenworth Mo. in the months of August & September 1851 under Instructions from Col. J. J. Abert Chief Top. Eng'rs," perhaps reached Washington, D. C., in the autumn.

Pope (with escort?) set out from Fort Union on this reconnoiter after August 12; and by September 18 he was in St. Louis. Little is known of his journey, except that Pope lost his horses and mules (stampeded by Arapahoes) while on the Smoky Hill river (evidently early in September). In an October 24 report from Fort Union, N. M., Bvt. Col. E. V. Sumner stated: "Captain Pope . . . was sent to find a better and more direct route to Missouri, avoiding if possible the large arid plains. He found an excellent route to the Arkansas, intersecting that river at the 'Big Timbers,' Beyond that on the head waters of the Kansas, he was not so successful. He is however, to return by another line to the 'Big Timbers,' and I still hope he will find a good route up the valley of the Kansas river." (For mention of Pope westbound on the Santa Fe route, late in 1851, *see* December 13 annals entry.)

Lt. G. K. Warren, Top'l eng'rs, in his "Memoir" (1859), described Pope's path eastward in 1851: "Capt. Pope travelled on the Cimarron route [from Fort Union] as far as Cedar creek, where he turned north and struck the Arkansas at the Big Timbers. Crossing this river he took a northeast course to the Smoky Hill Fork, and came upon it near where Captain Fremont struck it in 1844 [*see* p. 521]. From this point he travelled down the stream. The map constructed by Capt. Pope would make it appear that what had been considered the source of Smoky Hill Fork . . . was probably that of the Big Sandy or some other tributary of the Arkansas."

Pope's map erroneously located "Fort Mackey" (Fort Atkinson) *east* of the 100th meridian. The post was west of present Dodge City (through which the 100th meridian runs).

[A year prior to Pope's trip there had been a military reconnaissance of a route between the Big Timbers and the Cimarron. The St. Louis *Republican's* Independence correspondent, in an August 28, 1850, letter, stated that Bvt. Col. E. V. Sumner had arrived at the Arkansas Crossing on August 16; and had moved troops up to the "big timbers"; and further reported: "A new route from that place has been surveyed across to old Santa Fe road, through the Cimarron country, shortening the distance and avoiding the 'jornada.' . . ." In 1851 Francis X. Aubry's explorations (*see* pp. 999 and 1042) also were directed to finding a route bypassing the Jornada.]

Ref: Copy of Pope's map (in KHi); W. H. Goetzmann, *Army Exploration in the American West 1803-1863* (New Haven, 1959), p. 247; Calhoun, *op. cit.*, pp. 417, 418; *New Mexico Historical Review*, v. 36 (January, 1961), pp. 39, 40; *Missouri Republican*, St. Louis, September 3, 1850; Lt. G. K. Warren's "Memoir" (p. 63 for quote above), is in the Pacific Railroad Explorations and Surveys series, 33d Cong., 2d Sess., Sen. Ex. Doc. No. 78, v. 11 (Serial 768); Carl I. Wheat, *Mapping the Transmississippi West*, v. 3 (1959), p. 18.

❡ September 7.—Overland from Sacramento, Calif. (left July 1), a company of some 42 persons (principally Missourians; Robert McCullock, Cooper county, acting captain) arrived at Weston, Mo.

Ref: *Missouri Statesman*, Columbia, September 19, 1851 (in which 42 names—supplied by company member Richard S. Willhite, Boone county—are listed).

❡ September.—Lt. Ambrose E. Burnside (bearer of dispatches from the U. S. and Mexican Boundary Commission, to Washington) arrived in St. Louis on September 11 after a journey overland from New Mexico to Fort Leavenworth (and thence by steamboat, presumably).

An account stated: "He was only 21 days from the Copper Mines—some 1,200 miles to Fort Leavenworth. With only 3 attendants he crossed the country of the Apaches to Socor[r]o, and thence to the U. S." But the 21-day journey evidently was from Santa Fe, for Burnside brought news from that place up to August 22.

Ref: New York *Daily Tribune*, September 23, 1851 (from *Missouri Republican*, St. Louis, September 13).

❡ September 11.—Five men, overland from Sacramento, Calif., in 62 days, arrived at St. Joseph, Mo. They were: Congreve Jackson (*see* p. 1027), B. F. Howard, John Cunningham, George Vance and son.

Three others (two from Illinois, one from Iowa) "who came from California by way of Oregon City," had joined the above five, on the road. (Probably they parted company at Fort Kearny and took the Old Fort Kearny trail to the Missouri.)

Ref: St. Joseph *Gazette*, September 17, 1851.

❡ September.—Overland from eastern Wisconsin (by way of Iowa and Missouri) some 640 Indians arrived in "Kansas"; and joined related tribesmen on the Pottawatomie (Kansas river) reserve.

A Milwaukee newspaper (of early August?) referred to the emigrants as the "Indians constituting the united tribes of Chippewas, Ottawas, and Pottawatomies, who had left their homes in Sheboygan and Manitouwoc Counties, Wis."; stated that the "whole number (640) including men, women and children passed through Beaver Dam on Thursday"; and remarked "a more motley-looking crew were never gathered."

The Madison (Wis.) *Statesman* subsequently reported: "On Saturday last [August 9?] a band of between 600 and 700 Indians passed around the Fourth Lake, and encamped over Sunday near the head of the Lake. . . ." They were, this newspaper stated, remnants of Pottawatomies, Menominees, and Winnebagoes; and "in charge of Mr. Coquellard [Alexis Coquillard]," government agent for their removal.

On August 22 the Fairfield (Ia.) *Ledger* reported that the emigrants ("remnants of the tribes Pottawattamies, Menominees and Winnebagoes, who have been scattered over Mich., Wis. and Ill.") "passed through our place on Wed. [August 20]." "There were some sixty or seventy wagons employed in their removal, besides a goodly number [hundreds the *Statesman* had said] of ponies belonging to the Indians."

Agent Thomas Moseley, Jr. (given special charge of the immigrants), journeyed, in September, to "Kansas" to receive the 639 Indians "under Alexis Coquillard and others" (Paul Junore, conductor; Francis Ross, temporary isssuing agent). He found them "a few miles West of Fort Leavenworth"; but before they could reach the Pottawatomie reserve (some 45 miles distant) cholera broke out and "some 12 died." The Indians "scattered to the 4 Winds in despite of all and every persuasion brought to bear." William D. Harris, on September 13, got the contract for "temporary subsistence" of the newcomers. Moseley (who returned to his agency on September 17) employed Edward Carter as issuing agent (but in the spring of 1852 Carter was removed for irregularities in the "survey out of these rations"; and replaced by Joseph N. Bourassa).

Ref: New York *Daily Tribune*, August 9, 22, 1851; *Missouri Republican*, St. Louis, August 26, 1851; SIA, St. Louis, "Records," v. 9, typed copy, pp. 544, 553, 557, 558, 562, 587, 620, 622; 33d Cong., 1st Sess., H. Ex. Doc. No. 37 (Serial 718), p. 407; Wand, *op. cit.*, p. 21; OIA, Letters Received from Kansas Agency (National Archives Microcopy 234, Roll No. 364).

❧ September 20.—At Fort Atkinson, 2d Lt. Alden Sargent, Company B, Sixth infantry, assumed command. (He, and Asst. Surg. Aquila T. Ridgely, had arrived at the post on the 19th.) Departing September 20 were 2d Lt. Henry Heth (on detached service), and Asst. Surg. Elisha P. Langworthy (transferred).

See, also, November 6 entry.

Ref: Fort Atkinson post returns (National Archives microfilm).

❧ September 21.—Lt. Col. Thomas Swords (who had accompanied

Sumner's command to New Mexico; and spent the July-August period "inspecting the affairs of the Quartermaster's Dept. in New Mexico"), returned to Fort Leavenworth. He had left (new) Fort Union, N. M., on September 1, and traveled the Santa Fe trail with a "small party of citizens 'en route' for Independence."

Swords continued eastward from Fort Leavenworth; and was at New York in October.

Ref: 32d Cong., 1st Sess., Sen. Ex. Doc. No. 1 (Serial 611), pp. 235-238 (for Swords' report of October 25, 1851).

❡ September.—Traders' and freighters' trains setting out from Missouri on the Santa Fe trail after mid-month were these:

"McCauslin's" (i. e., McCauley's?)—which eastbound F. X. Aubry met at the Little Arkansas on October 6. Apparently this was "Simms' train" which the McCabe party met in mid-October at Middle Cimarron Spring. The "November" mail, from Santa Fe, met "McCauley's train" early in November at the Moro, "getting along pretty well."

"Chiles's"—which Aubry met at Turkey creek on October 6. (The "September" mail from Santa Fe had met Chiles' train at the Missouri line—just starting out—on September 24.) McCabe and party met "Childs and Phelp's train" at Cold Spring in mid-October. The "November" eastbound mail reported having met Chiles' mule train at Cimarron Springs "out of corn and nearly out of provisions for the men."

"Mason and Dyer's"—which Aubry met on October 6 at Turkey creek. Samuel G. Mason and William F. Dyer's wagons were bound for Fort Atkinson, where Mason was sutler.

"Jones & Russell's—which Aubry met at Cottonwood, on October 6(?). (This Jones & Russell train, in charge of Wilson Hamilton, Lexington, Mo., had left Westport, Mo., on September 24; and it reached Santa Fe on November 10 Since it did not start from Fort Leavenworth, it probably was not a government train.) McCabe's party met "Russell, Jones & Co's." train at Lower Cimarron Spring in mid-October.

In addition to trains noted above, the McCabe party (see November 6 entry), on the trail eastbound in October, reported passing a (returning?) government train at Arkansas crossing; and encountering "Gotaris" (Gutierrez'?) train there, also. Aubry's train (see p. 1046) had been met west of Cottonwood Fork; and at Brush creek they had passed Perry and Young's (government) trains, returning (from Fort Atkinson).

Ref: Missouri Republican, St. Louis, October 13, November 18, December 12, 1851; The Weekly Tribune, Liberty, Mo., October 3, 1851; Missouri Statesman, Columbia, Mo., January 2, 1852 (for Hamilton).

❡ September.—Both the Kansas (Mo.) Public Ledger, and the St. Joseph (Mo.) Gazette, published the article quoted (in part) here:

"As the season is advancing when the representatives of the people will again assemble at our national metropolis . . ., we deem it not amiss to direct their attention, as well as the attention of the people themselves, to the importance of trying early measures for bringing into market much, if not all, of the beautiful and fertile lands lying within the Territory of Nebraska [*i. e.*, present Nebraska and Kansas] . . . Congress should, at an early day at the next session, authorize a treaty to be held with the various Indian tribes inhabiting this territory, with a view to the extinguishment of Indian titles, &c. . . ."

See, also, October 25 annals entry.

Ref: St. Joseph (Mo.) *Gazette*, September 24, 1851; *The Weekly Tribune*, Liberty, Mo., October 3, 1851 (from the Kansas *Ledger*); Malin, *op. cit.*, p. 79.

℃ September 25.—In charge of Griffith H. Williams, the "September" U. S. mail from Santa Fe (left on the 3d) arrived at Independence, Mo. Five stage passengers were men connected with the U. S. and Mexican Boundary Commission, who had come from the Copper Mines in New Mexico: Charles Radziminski ("principal assistant surveyor"), Alexander A. Camp, Theodore F. Moss, Fred D. Keller, and Robert Murphy.

These travelers reached St. Louis on September 30. Radziminski was reported to be "the bearer of dispatches from [the U. S. commissioner] Mr. [John R.] Bartlett to the Government at Washington."

Ref: *The Weekly Tribune*, Liberty, Mo., October 3, 1851 (from Independence *Messenger*); New York *Daily Tribune*, September 27, October 1, 1851 (telegraphic items from Independence); *Missouri Republican*, St. Louis, October 1, 1851; Bartlett, *op. cit.*, pp. 594-596; New York *Daily Times*, October 18, 23, 1851.

℃ September 28.—"Mr. Smith" with the "September" U. S. mail from Salt Lake City arrived at Independence, Mo. The mail party had left Fort Laramie September 16. En route, "Mr. Wyrock" (carrier-in-charge) had received an accidental gun wound, and could not complete the journey (but was expected to recover).

The Independence newspaper stated: "This mail now arrives and departs with great regularity, and the contractors [S. H. Woodson & Co.] deserve great credit. . . . On nearly every trip out and in they carry one or more passengers. . . ." (For explanation of the improved service, *see* p. 1032.)

Ref: *The Weekly Tribune*, Liberty, Mo., October 10, 1851 (from the *Occidental Messenger*, Independence, Mo.).

℃ October.—Francis X. Aubry, who (in advance of his train—62 men; 30 wagons; 300 mules) had come from Cottonwood Crossing to Westport, Mo., in a "little over two days" (at the rate of "a little over 100 miles per day"), on his "favorite mare 'Dolly'," arrived at Independence, Mo., on October 11 (as did some others of his party).

Setting out from Las Vegas, N. M., on September 19, Aubry (and train) had left the Santa Fe trail (about September 25?) at Cold Spring (in the Oklahoma Panhandle of today), and traveled "from 10 to 40 degrees east of North" to the Arkansas, finding (as reported) "an excellent wagon road, well supplied with water and grass, and avoiding the Jornada and Cimarone [Cimarron] trail altogether." (*See* p. 999 for Aubry's earlier attempt to locate a route which avoided the Jornada.)

Cotravelers on this journey included: William S. Messervy, "Delemater," (Charles L.) Spencer, "Dalamie[?]," B. F. Moseley, "Le Blanc"; and several men connected with the U. S. and Mexican Boundary Commission: "Dr. Mallory," (W. B.) Yerby, (C. N.) Simms, "Hoven" (Joseph Hoban?), and "Rainey."

Ref: *Missouri Republican*, St. Louis, October 13, 30, 1851; *The Weekly Tribune*, Liberty, Mo., October 17, 1851; or St. Joseph (Mo.) *Gazette*, October 22, 1851 (for Independence *Occidental Messenger* account); Bartlett, *op. cit.*, pp. 595, 596 (for Yerby, Simms, and Hoban). Aubry's date of arrival at *Westport* is not mentioned, but must have been early in October. On Aubry's April-May, 1851, exploratory trip, he was said to have left the "main road" two miles "this side" of Cold Spring, and to have traveled "from 20 to 30 deg. East of North."—*Missouri Republican*, May 18, 1851.

❡ October 4.—A telegraph office (St. Louis and Missouri River Telegraph Company) was opened at Weston, Mo.

(From Kansas, Mo.—*see* July 25 entry—the company's line had been extended across the Missouri, and thence up the river's left bank.)

Ref: *Missouri Republican*, St. Louis, October 5, 1851; *Missouri Historical Review*, v. 51 (October, 1956), p. 51.

❡ October.—Fort Leavenworth's extensive farming operation 1,332 acres in cultivation; around 30 hired men employed) was expected to result in a profit of $7,000 for the year (as against $6,300 in 1850), according to Bvt. Maj. E. A. Ogden's report of October 4.

The anticipated yield: some 18,000 bushels of corn (from 425 acres), 8,000 bushels of oats (from 356 acres), 528 tons of hay (from 373 acres in timothy), 500 bushels of buckwheat, 600 bushels of barley, 1,200 bushels of potatoes, "besides straw, corn-fodder, &c., pumpkins, turnips, and . . . wheat."

Ogden stated: "The implements used on the farm consist of ploughs of every variety, of St. Louis, Peoria, and Worcester (Mass.) manufacture, horse-power reaping and mowing machines, cultivators of different kinds, harrows, horse-rakes, and one-horse and one six-horse power threshing machines, fanning mills, corn shellers, seed drills, &c."

Ref: 32d Cong., 1st Sess., *Sen. Ex. Doc. No. 1* (Serial 611), p. 292.

❡ October.—Sup't David D. Mitchell's "good and numerous company" (De Smet) en route to the States from the Fort Laramie Indian Council (*see* p. 1032) escorted by two companies of U.S. Mounted riflemen, arrived at Fort Kearny on October 2. After a brief stop at this post (during which time Mitchell counciled with a "deputation of some twenty Pawnee chiefs and braves") there was a division of forces.

Mitchell, accompanied by Robert Campbell, A. B. Chambers, B. Gratz Brown, and others(?), together with (all?) the military escort, took the Old Fort Kearny road eastward to the Missouri. (A telegram dated Weston, Mo., October 18, stated: "Col. D. D. Mitchell and party passed down last night on the Clara, all in fine health. . . .")

Agent Thomas Fitzpatrick, with the Washington-bound Indian delegation (of 16?), also Edmund F. ("Guesso") Chouteau, interpreters John Simpson Smith and Joseph Tesson Honore, and accompanied by Father Pierre-Jean De Smet, took the "southern route"—the Oregon-California trail—to the Kansas river valley.

According to Father De Smet, the Indian deputies were: CHEYENNES—White Antelope, Red Skin, and Rides on the Clouds; ARAPAHOES—Eagle's Head, Tempest, and Friday; SIOUX—One Horn, Little Chief, Shell-man, Watchful Elk, and Goose ("a Blackfoot Sioux"); OTOES—Black Elk (and his wife), Black Bear (and his wife).

Father De Smet's account states: "We reached St. Mary's, among the Potawatomies, on the 11th of October. Bishop [John B.] Miege and the other Fathers of the Mission received us with great cordiality and kindness. To give the Indian deputies a relish for labor by the tasting of the various products of farming, a quantity of vegetables and fruits were set before them. Potatoes, carrots, turnips, squashes, parsneps, melons, with apples and peaches, graced the board. . . . The day after was Sunday, and all attended high mass. The church was well filled. The choir, composed of half-bloods and Indians, sang admirably. . . . The Rev. Father [Maurice] Gailland delivered a sermon in Potawatomi, which lasted three-quarters of an hour. . . . We spent two days visiting the mission. . . ." (The visiting Indians "painted their faces in various colours" and entertained with "war" and "hair" dances—their favorites.)

The rest of the journey—to Westport, and Kansas, Mo.—took three days. On October 18, William Walker (Wyandot) visited Kansas, Mo., and recorded in his diary: "A deputation of Sioux, Cheyennes, Arapahoes, Crows and Snake Indians headed by Major Fitz Patrick were at the 'Union Hotel' waiting for a Boat. They are on a visit by special invitation to Washington. . . . The Clara came down and they took passage on her."

The St. Louis *Republican's* list of the Indian delegation was as follows: CHEYENNES—The White Antelope, Little Chief, and Rides on the Clouds; ARAPAHOES—Eagle's Head, The Storm, and Friday; SIOUX—One Horn, Red Skin, Shell Person, and Elk on His Guard; ASSINIBOINES—Goose; OTOES—Black Elk (and his wife), Black Bear (and his wife). The disappearance, at Brunswick, Mo., of the Crow "brave" was noted.

Ref: Chittenden and Richardson, *op. cit.,* v. 1, p. 65, v. 2, pp. 684-691; De Smet, *op. cit.,* pp. 112-120; *Missouri Republican,* St. Louis, October 19, 27, 1851; St. Louis *Daily Intelligencer,* October 22, 1851 (reported the arrival of the *Clara,* "last night"); William Walker's "Journals," *loc. cit.,* p. 336; Garraghan, *op. cit.,* v. 2, p. 634.

For earlier mention of Friday (the Arapahoe) in "Kansas," *see* annals index, and for John Simpson Smith's previous connection with "Kansas" history (as commander—briefly—of Mann's Fort on the Arkansas), *see* p. 670. Edmund F. Chouteau (son of Francis G. Chouteau, who died in 1838) was a witness to the treaty of Fort Laramie; and his presence on the Oregon-California trail, homeward-bound with Fitzpatrick after the treaty, was noted

by Paul Wilhelm, Duke of Wuerttemberg (*see New Mexico Historical Review*, v. 17, p. 205).
He called him "Mr. G. Chouteau." "Guesso" was the name by which Edmund F. Chouteau
was commonly known—*see* Kate L. Gregg and J. F. McDermott, editors, *Prairie and Mountain
Sketches* . . . (Norman, Okla., c1957), p. xliv. For his travels across "Kansas" in
1843 (with Sir William D. Stewart) *see* annals, pp. 474, 498.

❡ October.—Bvt. Maj. Robert H. Chilton and his Troop B, First
dragoons, accompanied by Bvt. Lt. Col. Samuel Cooper, returning
from Fort Laramie (which they had left September 24—*see* p.
1032), reached Fort Leavenworth by, or before, October 15. On
October 17 Cooper and Chilton arrived at St. Louis "bringing letters
from the treaty ground."

Ref: *Missouri Republican*, St. Louis, October 17, 1851; P. G. Lowe, *op. cit.*, pp. 78-92;
New York *Daily Times*, October 18, 1851.

❡ October.—On the 17th(?) Capt. Thomas Duncan, Lt. Washington L. Elliott, and their companies C and E, U. S. Mounted riflemen,
overland from Fort Laramie (to Old Fort Kearny?) reached Fort
Leavenworth. (They had escorted Sup't D. D. Mitchell's party—
see p. 1043.)

While at the "Kansas" post, 29 men from Captain Duncan's company deserted; crossed the Missouri to Weston; represented that they had been forced
to do more duty "than is required of a soldier"; and persuaded a justice of the
peace (who "fancied himself authorized to act in the premises") to discharge
them. Subsequently, the "usual reward" was offered for these deserters. One
of them was arrested November 11 (at St. Louis?).

Arrangements were made at Fort Leavenworth on October 26
(by Bvt. Maj. E. A. Ogden, AQM) for the *St. Ange* (Thomas W.
Scott, captain) to transport the Mounted riflemen (three officers,
and 140 enlisted men), together with 100 horses, six laundresses,
with baggage, &c., down the Missouri (for $900). The *St. Ange*
reached Jefferson Barracks, Mo., on October 30.

Ref: 32d Cong., 1st Sess., *Sen. Ex. Doc. No. 12* (Serial 614), p. 31; Glasgow (Mo.)
Weekly Times, October 30, 1851; *Missouri Republican*, St. Louis, November 1, 1851; St.
Louis *Daily Intelligencer*, November 12, 1851.

❡ October.—2d Lt. Cuvier Grover, Fourth artillery, and a detail
of 20 Company B, First dragoons, left Fort Leavenworth in mid-
month for Union Town (some 70 miles distant), to serve as guard
during the Pottawatomie annuity payments.

Dragoon P. G. Lowe later recollected: "We crossed [the Kansas river] at a
rocky ford near Silver Lake. . . . We were . . . [at Union Town]
ten days in glorious Indian summer."

Ref: P. G. Lowe, *op. cit.*, pp. 92, 93.

❡ October 22-23.—From Santa Fe the "October" mail, in charge of
"Mr. [William] Allison, accompanied by Crawford M'Kenzie and
two others," arrived at Independence, Mo., on the 22d. Stage pas-

sengers were: Judge Grafton Baker, Indian agent E. H. Wingfield, "Messrs. [Thomas A.?] Hereford, Smoker, and Mrs. Branton."

On October 23 "Esquire [James L.] Collins and Rev. H[iram] W. Read and family," overland from Santa Fe, reached Independence. From the Moro, to (near?) the Missouri border, they had traveled in company with the mail party. Read (a Baptist missionary, and army chaplain), while at Council Grove, on October 19, wrote a letter telling of having met on October 14 (near "Fort Mackay on the Arkansas"), New Mexico-bound Baptist missionaries Rev. James M. Shaw and wife, traveling "in company with an ox-train."

Ref: *Missouri Republican*, St. Louis, October 24, 28, 1851; New York *Daily Tribune*, November 12, 1851 (letter by "Mack," from Independence, October 24); *New Mexico Historical Review*, v. 17, pp. 113-147 (article on Read—whose name was Hiram, not Henry); *Baptist Home Missions in North America* . . . 1832-1882 (New York, 1883), pp. 339, 599 (for items on Read, and Shaw). Heitman's army register lists the Rev. "Henry" W. Read as army chaplain from July 16, 1849, to March 15, 1852. The *Missouri Republican* editor (November 2 issue) noted greeting the "Rev. Mr. Reed, of the American Baptist Mission, direct from Santa Fe"; referred to him as "formerly Army chaplain"; and stated: "Mr. R. returns in the spring to Santa Fe."

❡ October 22.—"Aubrey's [30-wagon?] train will start from West-port tomorrow or next day," an Independence, Mo., correspondent reported. Francis X. Aubry was bound for Santa Fe with his *third* merchant train of the year.

A party from Santa Fe arriving at Independence November 6, had met Aubry's train 10 miles west of Cottonwood Fork, about the end of October. The "November" mail did not meet Aubry on the Santa Fe trail for he had "left the old for his new route, up the Arkansas." (That is, he was retracing the "excellent wagon road" he had discovered on his September-October trip east—*see* p. 1042.) However, while he was still traveling up the Arkansas, travelers coming downriver from Bent's Fort, met Aubry four miles above Chouteau's Island. (His new route apparently struck off southwestward from the river a little west of the Kearny-Hamilton county line of today.)

Early in December, the Missouri-bound mail party met Aubry at Barclay's Fort (on the Moro), "getting on well." A Santa Fe correspondent (writing on December 31) mentioned that Aubry "came through with heavy teams and without loss of an animal"; and further remarked: "He has now made 3 trips across the Plains in one year, with loaded wagons."

Ref: *Missouri Republican*, St. Louis, October 28, November 18, December 12, 14, 26, 27, 1851; New York *Daily Tribune*, February 16, 1852 (from *Missouri Republican*). An 1882 map of Hamilton county (then unorganized) shows a town "Aubrey," located on Sec. 25, T. 24, R. 39 W. (less than half a mile from the Kearny county line). In 1866, from January 24 to October 3, there was a Hamilton county post office "Fort Aubrey." Aubry had brought 30 wagons to the states in October; and took some (or all?) on departing again for Santa Fe.

❡ October 25.—The annual report of David D. Mitchell (head of the Indian superintendency, St. Louis) included the following recommendation: ". . . [the] border tribes . . . are gradually advancing in civilization, and a large majority of the families are now as intelligent, comfortable and well informed as their white neighbors. They have become very much intermixed and amalgamated with the whites . . . I beg leave to suggest, for the consideration of the Department, the following measures, viz,

the laying off of the Nebraska Territory, with the following boundaries: Commencing on the Missouri, at the mouth of the Kansas river, and running up the Missouri to the mouth of the L'eau qui court, or Running Water river; following up the Running Water river to its source, about 35 miles above Fort Laramie, where this stream issues from the base of the southern range of mountains, known as the Black-hill; from thence due south to the Arkansas river; thence along our established boundaries to the western line of the State of Missouri, to the place of beginning. This will give to the United States *all* of the agricultural lands south of the Missouri river that are considered exclusively Indian territory."

Mitchell also stated: "The force of circumstances will soon compel the Government to adopt some plan by which the fine agricultural lands (that form a large portion of Nebraska) will be thrown open to that class of American citizens that have always been found on our extreme western frontiers, forming, as they do, a kind of connecting link between civilized and savage life. The State south of the Missouri river is densely populated all along the western border, there being a continuous range of farms immediately on the line."

Ref: Comm'r of Indian Affairs, *Report*, 1851 (Mitchell's report, therein).

❦ Around the end of October "Major" Richard H. Weightman, "delegate elect to Congress from New Mexico," and his family, arrived at Independence, Mo., overland from Santa Fe (and en route to Washington).

Weightman (also E. H. Wingfield—*see* p. 1046; and "Capt. Smith," U. S. army) were aboard the steamboat *Ben West* which reached St. Louis on November 5.

Ref: *Missouri Republican*, St. Louis, October 24, 28, 1851; St. Louis *Daily Intelligencer*, November 6, 1851. The army officer probably was Capt. Andrew J. Smith, First dragoons.

❦ October 30.—The "October" U. S. mail from Salt Lake City arrived at Independence, Mo. Stage passengers were Richard S. Phelps (of Chiles & Phelps, traders), W. D. Boyer, both of Independence, and Mr. Foster (or Forster?), of England.

Phelps had made the journey from Salt Lake City; Boyer and "Foster" joined at Fort Laramie (reached October 16 by the mail party.) "Messrs. Gillan [Gillam?], Young, and Cogswell"—all of Independence—who had left the stage at the fort, would "be in, in a few days," it was reported.

News brought by the incoming party was that all the "U. S. officers" in Utah territory, except Gov. Brigham Young, had resigned, and "left for home"; and that "most of them" had reached Fort Laramie on October 16. [These officials— Chief Justice Lemuel G. Brandebury, Associate Justice Perry E. Brocchus, Secretary B. D. Harris, and Indian Agent Henry R. Day—did not cross "Kansas." They reached the Missouri at some point (Old Fort Kearny?) in "Nebraska"; and on November 9 "passed thro' " Savannah, Mo., and arrived at St. Joseph. On November 12 (en route to Washington) they boarded the *El Paso* for St. Louis.]

Ref: *Missouri Republican,* St. Louis, November 2, 6, 25, 1851; Savannah (Mo.) *Sentinel,* November 16, 1851; *Adventure,* St. Joseph, Mo., November 15, 1851; St. Joseph *Gazette,* November 12, 19, 1851; *The Weekly Tribune,* Liberty, Mo., November 14, 1851.

❮ November 1.—A telegraphic dispatch from St. Joseph, Mo., stated: "The office of Morse's line of telegraph westward [from St. Louis] has been opened at this point for a few days. . . . Weather has been fine for a few days past, and business has become quite brisk, owing to the large Indian trade since the payment of the annuities. River falling slowly. Clara arrived yesterday from below."

The Savannah (Mo.) *Sentinel,* v. 1, no. 1, issued on November 1, reported: "The Telegraph wires are extended to St. Joseph, and we learn from yesterday's *Adventure* that the office is now in operation at that place. . . ."

Ref: *Missouri Republican,* St. Louis, November 2, 1851; Savannah (Mo.) *Sentinel,* November 1, 1851.

❮ A November(?) issue of the *Occidental Messenger,* Independence, Mo., reported the prevalence of a "disease called Texas fever" among the cattle in Missouri's southern Jackson and northern Cass counties (bordering on "Kansas"); and stated that "great numbers" had been destroyed.

Ref: Savannah (Mo.) *Sentinel,* November 22, 1851 (from Independence *Messenger*).

❮ November 6.—Bvt. Capt. Simon B. Buckner, Sixth infantry (transferred from Fort Snelling; and newly arrived) took command at Fort Atkinson on the Arkansas.

Other officers at the post over the winter: 2d Lt. Henry Heth (who returned on November 3), and Asst. Surg. Aquila T. Ridgely.

Ref: Fort Atkinson post returns (National Archives microfilm).

❮ November 6.—Overland from Santa Fe in 18 days, these travelers arrived at Independence, Mo.: Dr. J. Keller McCabe, F. H. Glasscock, Edward Owensby, and Mr. McGomery. They reported the weather pleasant; had found the grass burned off "this side" of the Little Arkansas.

Ref: The *Occidental Messenger,* Independence, Mo., November 8, 1851, account—as reprinted in *The Weekly Tribune,* Liberty, Mo., November 14, 1851; the *Missouri Republican,* St. Louis, November 18, 1851; and the *Missouri Statesman,* Columbia, Mo., November 21, 1851.

℄ November 11.—At Fort Atkinson (on the Arkansas; west of present Dodge City) a post office was established, with Samuel G. Mason as postmaster. (*See* Mason & Dyer's wagon train mention, p. 1041.)

Ref: Baughman, *op. cit.*, pp. 45, 46, 156, 182. Presumably Mason was also Fort Atkinson's sutler.

℄ Mid - November.—Eastbound on the Oregon - California trail, while traveling down the Little Blue (with a wagon, horses, and a mule), Paul Wilhelm, Duke of Wuerttemberg, and his companion, H. B. Möllhausen, were overtaken by a blizzard on the night of November 14(?). They were, by the Duke's reckoning, "still 30 miles [but it must have been more] from the Big Blue and 120 miles from the Catholic Mission [St. Mary's]."

[Duke Paul and Möllhausen—*see* p. 1036 for their journey west—had left Fort Laramie for the States in October; and, from the outset, had experienced a series of misfortunes (including harrowing encounters with Indians), and hardships, which are not recounted here.]

By morning the storm was worse (and the temperature "down to about 30° below zero, Fahrenheit"). The chestnut mare had frozen to death; and only "the mule and the scrawny Indian pony" were left. Both men, but the Duke particularly, suffered with eye troubles (due to smoke, and to snow glare) in the three days spent at this camp. On the fourth day, the Duke's narrative says, "we dragged ourselves fifteen miles farther onward until it grew dark, setting up our miserable tent [now full of little holes from sleet] . . . on the bank of an almost dry and treeless creek."

Next morning—November 17—they hitched the two remaining "miserable beasts" to the wagon, but in spite of the "cruellest efforts" were able "to make an advance of only seven miles." On the 18th they managed to reach "Sandy Hill Creek" ("where it falls into the Big [*i. e.*, Little] Blue," Möllhausen's account said); only to be overtaken by another blizzard. For "eight unending days and nights" they were immobilized. (Their horse died, but the mule remained alive.)

On November 25, when the situation seemed hopeless, the "mail-stage from Fort Laramie came along [*see* p. 1055]. The driver and the passengers found us [says the Duke's account]. But there was scarcely enough room for one more person." In addition to a promised large payment, Duke Paul "had to give the mule and a saddle to the passenger who was to be incommoded." A coin was tossed by the Duke and Möllhausen; the former won and was taken along in the mail wagon. (Duke Paul was 54; Möllhausen was 26.)

It was Möllhausen's fate to remain at the "Sandy Hill Creek" camp, alone, from late November till early January, 1852, when some friendly Otoes came along. (The account of his ordeal—an extraordinary tale of survival—is omitted here.) With the Otoes he traveled eastward; and reached the Missouri at a new settlement called "Bethlehem," in February.

Of his journey from "Sandy Hill Creek" to Independence, Mo., Duke Paul says: "The succeeding ten days . . . were as hard as any through which I had passed before the mailcoach found me. The nights were terrible, exposed as we were to the deadly blasts of the gale. . . ."

Briefly, before the party reached "the Catholic Mission of the Putowatomies [St. Mary's]," the weather turned warmer. But the "reception by the Jesuit Brothers" was "cold and inhospitable"; and they showed no interest in sending help to Möllhausen. However, a "Canadian half-breed" volunteered to go (whereupon the "Anglo-Americans" present made up a purse of $200 for the man). "I learned later," the Duke's account says, "that he never found Möllhausen, and he himself was not seen again. . . ." Despite the "ill-concealed hostility" of their hosts, the travelers spent a night at St. Mary's Mission.

Next day they resumed the journey; came to, and crossed, the Kansas river. (There were "huge ice-floes . . . rushing down in the rising torrent that threatened a score of times to crush the sides of our frail, flatbottomed ferry-boat.") Presumably this was the regular crossing near (above) Union Town. The Duke's account says: "On the opposite side a Swede [named Gustaf Larson] was living on a lonely homestead[!]. This kindly fellow insisted that we stay with him until we had recovered our strength and spirits. . . . For the first time since my brief stay in Scott's Bluffs I had the blissful luck of sleeping in a comfortable bed." ("Gustaf Larson" is nowhere else found in "Kansas" historical records. But the Duke's narrative is reliable on proper names, in most cases.)

"The rest of the distance to Independence was again over slippery ice and through mountain-high snowdrifts." (The arrival date was December 4.) Duke Paul was in "critical" condition when he reached Missouri, but was well cared for at "lovable, hospitable Independence." Subsequently he journeyed in a post-wagon to Boonville where he recuperated for a time; then went on to St. Louis, and from there to New Orleans.

Ref: *New Mexico Historical Review*, v. 17, pp. 214-225, 294-344; *KHQ*, v. 16, pp. 226-231; St. Joseph (Mo.) *Gazette*, December 31, 1851; New York *Daily Tribune*, March 30, 1851; R. F. Kurz' "Journal," *op. cit.*, p. 335; *Chronicles of Oklahoma*, Oklahoma City, v. 31, pp. 392, 393.

❦ November 13.—"Four Caw and Kansas Indians[?] were arrested for fighting at a house of bad repute" in St. Louis.

"In the affray one of them received a pistol shot wound from the hɾnds of one of the others, who is not known. They promise, if released, to return immediately home," the *Intelligencer* reported. But on November 18 (as noted in a later issue) a "Caw and Kansas Indian were fined $10 each by the [City] Recorder   . . ." and sent to the work house, because "They have been loafing about the streets for some days, rendering the lives of citizens insecure by an imprudent use of fire-arms and other dangerous weapons."

Ref: St. Louis *Daily Intelligencer*, November 14, 19, 1851.

❦ November.—News received at Independence, Mo., on the 26th "confirmed" that "275 mules" belonging to an eastbound government train had been lost (*i. e.*, had died) during a "sleet and rain" storm at a point "60 miles" west of Council Grove; and that a Kentuckian (one of three men who had left the train "to come in in advance to Council Grove") had frozen to death within a few miles of that place.

The Kansas, Mo., *Ledger's* account (November 29 issue?) also gave the number of mules killed as 275; located the disaster scene as about 40 or 50 miles beyond Council Grove; noted that "The stock were some that Col. [E. V.] Sumner was sending to the States to be wintered in order to economize"; and stated that 25 of the "wagons and fixtures" had been left at Council Grove.

(Colonel Sumner, in his October 24 report, from Fort Union, N. M. ter., had written: "I have sent in to Fort Leavenworth, 71 wagons and 473 mules. The expense of wintering these animals, will be much less there. . . .")

Ref: *Missouri Republican*, St. Louis, November 29, December 8, 1851; *Missouri Statesman*, Columbia, Mo., January 2, 1852 (gives statement of Wilson Hamilton that 170 mules of the government train froze to death at "Cottonwood Grove"); Calhoun, *op. cit.*, p. 418 (for Sumner's report).

❦ November.—At the three army posts in "Kansas" (as stated in the secretary of war's report, dated November 29) these were the commanding officers, and troops:

Post	Commandant	Garrison
Fort Leavenworth (on the Missouri)	Col. Thomas T. Fauntleroy	1 co., First dragoons; 1 co., Fourth artillery; 2 cos., Sixth infantry. Aggregate: 11 officers; 166 men.
Fort Scott (on the "Marmiton")	Bvt. Maj. Albemarle Cady	1 co., Sixth infantry. Aggregate: 4 officers; 54 men.

Fort Atkinson
    (on the Arkansas)   Bvt. Capt. Simon B. Buckner 1 co., Sixth infantry.
                                                    Aggregate: 3 officers;
                                                    57 men.
        Ref: 32d Cong., 1st Sess., *Sen. Ex. Doc. No. 1* (Serial 611), pp. 194-196.

❡ December(?)—Published in Ohio, late in the year (by internal evidence) was a work compiled by Stephen L. Massey entitled: *James's Traveler's Companion. Being a Complete Guide Through the Western States.* . . .

The author's preface (dated "Cincinnati, May, 1851") stated "The following work was commenced about a year ago. . . . The materials . . . have been collected and arranged for publication, mostly during leisure hours. We have designed to have the work take a much wider range than any similar one yet presented to the public. . . ." The reference in Massey's book to St. Joseph, Mo.'s telegraph line (*see* following) seems to place the publication date as no earlier than November or December, 1851. Pages 175-187 of *James's Traveler's Companion* were devoted to "Route of the Missouri River," from which some excerpts are as follows:

"COUNCIL BLUFFS, on the west bank of the Missouri, in the Indian territory, is a high bluff bank, on which a celebrated Indian council was held [in 1825— *see* annals, p. 121]. It is a place of considerable notoriety, on account of its being about as far as steamboats ever ascend the river."

"COUNCIL POINT, situated opposite, in Iowa, is sometimes miscalled Council Bluff. It is the landing point for a Mormon town named KANESVILLE ["population of about 2,000"], situated about four miles in the interior. . . ." (The site of Council Bluffs, Iowa.)

"TRADERS' POINT, four miles below Council Point, in the same county, is a small French settlement. . . . It contains about 100 inhabitants."

"BELLEVUE, twenty-one miles below Traders' Point, on the west bank of the river, in the Indian territory, is an Indian missionary station. It is also the residence of the [Indian] agent. . . . It has a good landing for boats, and may some time become an important place."

"PLATTE RIVER . . . empties into the Missouri fifteen miles below Bellevue. . . ."

"IOWA POINT, one hundred thirty-five miles below the mouth of Platte river, [in] Holt county, Missouri, is the landing point for the town of Oregon ["population of about 500"] . . . situated ten miles in the interior. . . ."

"NODEWAY CITY, thirty miles below Iowa Point, in Andrew county, Missouri, is a small village . . . about 200 inhabitants. It is the landing point for Savannah, a town of 1,000 inhabitants, situated a few miles off the river. . . ."

"ST. JOSEPH, twenty-five miles below Nodeway City, in Buchanan county, Missouri, is a thriving and important town. It was settled only about seven years since [in 1843—*see* annals, p. 497]. . . . St. Joseph is now growing with amazing rapidity. . . . There has been a telegraph line established between this town and St. Louis [*see* November 1, 1851, annals entry], and there is in contemplation a railway to Hannibal, on the Mississippi. . . . St. Joseph . . . [has] a population of about 4,000. There are many emigrants constantly passing through this place . . . [for the West]. The principal routes to California and Oregon however, commence at Fort Leavenworth, Independence, and the mouth of Kansas river. . . ."

"WESTON, about 55 miles below St. Joseph, in Platte county, Missouri, is a fine flourishing place, and is rapidly improving. Many of the emigrants make this a stopping place, for laying in supplies, previous to starting out on the plains. It . . . [has] a population of 2,000."

"LITTLE PLATTE RIVER LANDING, three miles below Weston, is the landing point for Platte City, situated a short distance up the Little Platte river. . . ."

"FORT LEAVENWORTH, four miles below Platte River Landing, is situated on a high bluff of the Missouri, in the Indian territory. The situation is remarkably fine, the bluff being about 150 feet in hight, and composed principally of white limestone. There is an excellent landing for boats, and many other superior advantages, which warrant the belief that there will, some day, be at this place a large and flourishing town. There is usually[!] a small garrison stationed here, and it is the rendezvous for all United States' troops destined for Santa Fe, Oregon, and the frontier stations. One of the principal routes to California commences at this place." (The "Route from Fort Leavenworth to Sutter's Fort, California," which Massey gave, begins "To [Little] Blue river, 249 miles; to Big [Grand] Island, 35 miles . . . [etc.].")

"LITTLE PLATTE RIVER . . . empties into the Missouri twenty miles below Fort Leavenworth. . . ."

"PARKVILLE, situated one mile below the mouth of Platte river, in Platte county, is a fine flourishing little village. . . . It [has] a population of 260."

"KANSAS RIVER.—This is one of the largest tributaries of the Missouri. . . . Its entire length is about twelve hundred miles, for nine hundred of which it might be navigated. . . ."

"KANSAS RIVER LANDING, is a landing point for WYANDOTTE CITY, situated a short distance in the interior. It is also one of the principal starting points for emigrants going to Oregon." ["Wyandotte City"—now part of Kansas City, Kan.—was on the Wyandot Indians' reserve, at the mouth of Kansas river. Part-Wyandot William Walker, in a journal entry of June 9, 1847, had written: "My execrations upon the Captain of the steamboat '*Manona*' for landing my lumber on the point opposite Wyandott City, instead of our usual landing place." The size of this village in 1851 is nowhere given.]

(The "Route from Kansas River landing to Oregon City," in Massey's work, begins: "To Kansas river crossing, 75 miles; to Platte river, 220 miles . . . [etc.] . . . This route is generally considered as commencing at Independence, but the traveler does not actually take leave of civilization . . .

until he arrives at this point [Kansas River Landing]. Hence we have given the route from this place.")

"KANSAS, situated near the mouth of Kansas river, in Jackson county, Missouri, is a pleasantly situated town, standing on a high bank of the river, and commanding a view of the surrounding country for many miles. It has been settled about four years. . . . The business of the place is very extensive, there being an almost constant stream of travel passing through this region, on their way to . . . [California]. Kansas contains 1 Methodist, 1 Baptist, and 1 Presbyterian church, a large number of stores, and about 800 inhabitants." [Paul Wilhelm, Duke of Wuerttemberg, who saw Kansas, Mo., in August, 1851, described it (in a narrative for his countrymen): "Kansastown is quite picturesquely situated on some hills along the Kansas river near it junction with the much bigger Missouri. The main street is about thirty feet above the water level. The houses are of both baked brick and boards, the latter called 'frame' houses. It is a lively little place. Here most travellers bound for the West purchase what they require for their long overland journey. Moreover, the neighboring hordes of semi-civilized Indians buy their supplies here. . . ."]

"INDEPENDENCE, county seat of Jackson county, Missouri, is situated about four miles back of Wayne City; is a place of great importance, and is growing with amazing rapidity. . . . The business done here is immense. . . . [It has] a population of 2,500. . . . There is a large trade carried on between this place and Santa Fe. The goods are transported . . . in wagons, which are built very large and strong, and are usually drawn by oxen, from sixteen to twenty of which are attached to each wagon. . . . Independence derives its importance from being the point where most of the emigrants going the overland route to California and Oregon, get their last supplies, and, also, as being the point where the principal routes to these places commence. . . . Stages leave . . . once a month for Santa Fe." (Massey failed to mention that these were U. S. mail-carrying stages; and that a monthly U. S. mail also departed for Salt Lake City.)

(The "Route from Independence to Santa Fe," in Massey's work was derived from Gregg's table of 1844, and is not quoted here.)

Ref: Stephen L. Massey, *James's Traveler's Companion* . . . (Cincinnati, Published by J. A. & U. P. James, 1851); *New Mexico Historical Review*, v. 17, p. 196 (for Duke Paul's Kansas, Mo., description).

℃ December 1(?).—From Santa Fe, in charge of "Mr. Wallace," the "November" U. S. mail arrived at Independence, Mo. Stage passengers were "Mr. Porter and his wife."

It had been a difficult trip, due to "great depth of snow on the plains." A storm that "commenced upon the party at Cold Springs," lasted four days and nights; but the party had progressed slowly—until November 12, when "they lost all their animals except one, with which they were enabled to get a new supply from [80 to 100-mile distant] Fort Atkinson." Despite the delay they were en route again in time to "make the trip through to this point by Monday last"—according to the *Missouri Republican's* correspondent at Independence (writing on Tuesday, December 2). The New York *Times* published a telegram dated "St. Louis, Friday Dec. 5," which stated: "The Santa Fe mail arrived at Independence yesterday. . . . [Snow storm at Cedar Springs caused the loss of 14 mules.] The snow was 2 feet deep on the Plains to Fort Atkinson."

Ref: *Missouri Republican,* St. Louis, December 12, 1851; New York *Daily Times,* December 6, 1851.

❡ December 1.—On schedule, the mail for Salt Lake City left Independence, Mo. But it did not reach its destination until January 29, 1852—nearly a month late. *See, also,* January 24, 1852, annals entry.

The Salt Lake *Desert News* reported that the man who carried the mail from Fort Laramie westward "had to wait at Laramie 16 days for said mail, which was hindered by the Pawnee Indians."

Ref: New York *Daily Tribune,* April 20, 1852; *Deseret News,* February 7, 1852.

❡ December 4.—The "November" U. S. mail from Salt Lake City arrived at Independence, Mo., "having been much impeded in its progress by the snow," which was "in some places 15 inches deep." Stage passengers were John S. Tutt, trader (from Fort Laramie), and "Paul William, Prince of Wurttemberg," who had been "taken up" about 235 miles from the States. (*See, also,* pp. 1049, 1050.)

News from the Plains: Indians in the Fort Kearny area were troublesome; had "robbed the Farmer, Fox Booth"; and troops had been sent to his aid. The Cheyennes and Pawnees were at war. "Ward and Geary's [traders Seth E. Ward and William Guerrier] wagons were met by the mail party at Chimney Rock."

Ref: *The Frontier Guardian,* Kanesville, Ia., January 9, 1852; St. Joseph (Mo.) *Gazette,* December 31, 1851.

❡ December.—The *Kansas,* apparently the last steamboat operating on the "middle" Missouri in 1851, arrived at St. Louis December 10, from Weston.

The *Intelligencer* reported: "Several Salt Lake merchants were passengers. . . . Col. [Robert M.] Stewart [president of the Hannibal & St. Joseph Railroad] also came down, on his way to Washington."

Ref: St. Louis *Daily Intelligencer,* December 11, 12, 1851. The *Kansas* had been at Weston, previously, on December 2; and passed Arrow Rock, on the return trip, December 4. —St. Joseph *Gazette,* December 3, 17, 1851. Stewart was a resident of St. Joseph.

❡ December 10.—Maria Meeker, aged 17, born in "Kansas" in 1834 (*see* p. 276), was married to Nathan L. Simpson, of Westport, Mo.

(Their first child, and the first grandchild of Baptist missionaries Jotham and Eleanor Meeker [residents of present Franklin county], was born September 22, 1852.)

Ref: *Miscellaneous Genealogical Records From Kansas Society D. A. R.* [v. 3], p. 9 (family records from Maria Meeker Simpson's Bible), in KHi library. Mrs. Simpson died at Nebraska City, Neb., January 15, 1885.

❡ December 13.—A telegram from "Kansas" (City, Mo.) to St. Louis read: "Weather cold. River clear of ice. Capt. [Alexander

W.] Reynolds, Judge [Joab] Houghton, R[ichard] Owens and J[ames] H. Quinn, arrived this morning [from Santa Fe]. Met Aubrey 4 miles above Chouteau's Island; Capt. Polk [*i. e.,* Bvt. Capt. John Pope, Topographical engineers] at Pawnee Fork; Maj. Greer [Bvt. Maj. William N. Grier] and Capt. [Langdon C.] Easton at Bluff creek, with the [December] mail [party]." Also with the mail were Charles Radziminski (*see* p. 1042) and "Mr. Scott."

From Independence, a telegram of December 15, to St. Louis, stated (in part): "A. W. Reynolds and Company [evidently having come by way of Bent's Fort, since they had met F. X. Aubry at Chouteau's Island] arrived here at 7 . . . p. m. . . . Reynolds' party encountered no less than 20 snow storms on their way, which were very fatal to their animals." (Reynolds was en route to Washington where he would contest Richard Weightman's claim to the seat as delegate to congress from New Mexico.)

It had been reported that Reynolds was to leave Santa Fe for the States on October 20. The "November" eastbound mail overtook his party at Fort Atkinson in mid-November. It then was said to be composed of 10 to 16 persons, including Judge Houghton, Richard Owens, "Mr. Pilans, wife and two children."

The "January" (1852) mail met "Capt. Easton, Radiminsky, Maj. Grier, and party, on the 5th [January], at Wagon Mound [N. M.] getting along very well, and expecting to reach Santa Fe in 4 or 5 days. Their course . . . [had] been much retarded by the deep snows of the last month." But the "December" mail arrived at Santa Fe before year's end.

Ref: *Missouri Republican,* St. Louis, November 4, 18, December 12, 14, 15, 1851; New York *Daily Tribune,* November 8, 1851, February 10, 1852; *The Weekly Tribune,* Liberty, Mo., December 26, 1851.

❡ December 13-19.—The Independence *Occidental Messenger* of December 20 reported: "During the past week we have had quite a number of arrivals from Santa Fe." Listed were: Reynolds, Houghton, Owens and Quinn (*see* preceding entry); also, William McGrorty, "T. S. J." Johnson, Mr. Kennett, Lt. (John A.?) Brown, and John S. Jones (freighter).

Jones had left Santa Fe on November 27; in his company were a number of Jones & Russell employees. One of them—Wilson Hamilton—reached Lexington, Mo., on December 18. He told of their overtaking "Chiles' train" (mules worn out; 58 head lost) near Council Grove. Despite a severe snow storm, near Fort Atkinson, and cold weather on the plains, the Jones & Russell party's trip had been an "entirely successful" one (all hands well; but one mule lost). At "Crow [Cow?] Creek" they had met the Santa Fe-bound December" mail— "passengers and all in fine spirits." (*See* preceding entry.)

Ref: *The Weekly Tribune,* Liberty, Mo., December 26, 1851 (from Independence *Messenger,* December 20 issue); *Missouri Statesman,* Columbia, Mo., January 2, 1852 (from

Lexington *Express* of December 23, 1851). In Calhoun, *op. cit.*, p. 375, Johnson's initials are given as "J. S. T."

❏ Mid-December.—Smallpox broke out "in the village of St. Mary" (the Pottawatomie settlement around St. Mary's [Catholic] Mission). "For two months it raged with the greatest virulence," Father Maurice Gailland wrote. "Scarcely a day passed without a funeral, often three or four. . . . Death . . . carried off the elite of the village."

Earlier in the year (when smallpox was a threat) the missionaries twice had sent for "vaccine matter from the U. S., but the vaccination had no effect."

Ref: Garraghan, *op. cit.*, v. 2, p. 634.

❏ December 15.—R. D. Blackston(e) and Alexander Warfield began trading with the Osage Indians.

An extant ledger is titled (on its first page): "Blackston & Warfield Day Book Osage Mills Jan. 1852"; but also states: "Blackstone & Warfield commence business in Osage Nation Dec 15th 1851 Bill of merchandise Bo[ugh]t of Messrs Walker Boyd & Chick as per Invoice No. 1 $1843.60." The book notes that "John Mishell [Mitchell] Commenced as Interpreter Jan. 12th 1852 at $15.00 per month"; that "Thomas Rogers commences business with Blackston & Warfield as interpreter Feb 20, 1852 at $15 per month"; and that "Pleasant McGhee commenced work for A. Warfield Nov 23, 1852 at $25 per month." There are accounts for A. H. Hudson, J[ames] R. Edwards, Lafose Papin, Tall Chief, J. D. Childers, Robert Wan, Dodridge Barnaby, Aiken Brunt, Misho Bevenaw, John Bazziel, and R. Lumbey—among others.

Blackston(e) apparently quit before the end of 1852. In 1853 there is mention of Warfield & Boone; and another ledger has the title: "Boon & Warfield's Acct Book Big Hill Town Verdigris River, Osage Nation 1854." Still another has "J. R. Edwards" at the front; but in the middle of the volume is a page headed "Warfield & Edwards Account Book or J. R. Edwards & Co. Aug. 1855" (and the accounts here run on into 1859).

Ref: Ledgers of Indian traders with the Osages (as noted above), in the Kansas Collection of Kansas University library, Lawrence. The name "Bazziel," is to be found as "Brazil," or "Brazile" in other sources.

❏ December 24.—In charge of "Mr. [William] Allison," the "December" mail from Santa Fe (which had left that place on the 2d), arrived at Independence, Mo.

The party had found snow 12 to 14 inches deep on the Cimarron; had made their way through three storms—one at McNees' creek, another at Fort Atkinson (where the Santa Fe-bound "December" mail was met), and a third at Lost Spring. Lt. James N. Ward (passenger in the stage) had been left at Fort Atkinson, too ill to proceed.

Ref: *Missouri Republican*, St. Louis, December 27, 1851.

❏ Employed in "Kansas" by the Indian Department during all, or part of the year were the following persons (other than Indian agents—who are listed on pp. 1015, 1016). For the:

KANSA—John Brazil, *interpreter;* Morris Baker, *blacksmith;* Emanuel Mosier and James Tingler, *assistant smiths.*

POTTAWATOMIES—Abram Burnett, *interpreter;* John L. Ogee and John W. Brown, *blacksmiths;* James H. Crockett and James F. Mills, *assistant smiths;* Henry R. Samuel, *wagonmaker;* Lucius R. Darling, *ferryman;* Johnston Lykins ("removed") and Luther R. Palmer, *physicians;* Jake Durfee, *grist miller;* John Hardin, *sawmill laborer.*

"MISSISSIPPI" SACS & FOXES—John Goodell ("resigned"), Antoine Gokey, and George Powers, *interpreters;* Charles H. Withington ("resigned"), John Van Horn, James E. Gray, and James T. King, *gunsmiths;* Alfred Laws, Matthew R. Johnson, and James F. Mills, *blacksmiths;* Rolin McDaniel, John Tapscott, Andrew J. Beasley, and Thomas C. Warren, *assistant smiths;* F. McKnight and Edwin R. Griffith, *physicians;* Thomas Owens, *farmer.*

MIAMIS—Baptiste Peoria, *interpreter* (he served for the Weas, Piankeshaws, etc., also); Robert Simerwell, *blacksmith;* Luther Paschal, *assistant smith;* Amos H. Goodwin (or Goodin), *farmer;* James B. Chenault, *miller.*

WYANDOTS—William Walker, *interpreter;* Samuel Drummond and William McCown, *blacksmiths;* Guilford D. Hurt, Samuel Drummond, Isaac Baker, and H. C. Long (for one month), *assistant smiths.*

SHAWNEES—Joseph Parks, *interpreter;* Calvin Perkins, *blacksmith;* Lindsey T. Cook and Joseph A. W. Meador, *assistant smiths.*

DELAWARES—Henry Tiblow, *interpreter;* Isaac Mundy, *blacksmith;* Joshua Myers (to June 23; died), Julius Fairfield, William R. Ketchum, and J. G. Evans, *assistant smiths.*

"MISSOURI" SACS & FOXES—John B. Rubite, and Paschal Pensineau, *interpreters;* H. J. McClintock, Mansfield Carter, and James F. Forman, *farmers;* John McCluskey (or McClaskey) and John W. Forman, *blacksmiths;* Francis Dupree ("resigned"), Antoine Gravaille (or Granville?), and Isaac McCloskey (or McClaskey), *assistant smiths.*

KICKAPOOS—Peter Cadue, *interpreter.*

IOWAS—John B. Roy, *interpreter.*

OSAGES—Elijah Pennington ("resigned"), George Tinker, Akin Brant, Thomas J. Kennedy, and David M. Austin, *blacksmiths;* Francis Mitchell, Joseph Captain, and William Biet (or Beyett), *assistant smiths;* Egbert K. Howland and Robert Wan, *millers;* Dodridge Barnaby and Peter Chouteau, *assistant millers.*

Ref: 32d Cong., 1st Sess., *H. Ex. Doc. No. 103* (Serial 647), pp. 479, 630-632, 718, 721, 724, 725, 784, 786, 791; 33d Cong., 1st Sess., *H. Ex. Doc. No. 37* (Serial 718), pp. 311, 312, 314, 317, 318, 321, 386, 387, 390, 392, 393, 409-412; SIA, St. Louis, "Records," v. 9, typed copy, pp. 495, 496, 500-502, 509, 515, 516, 533, 534, 543, 545, 550, 566, 582, 587, 589, 599; OIA, Letters Received from Great Nemaha Agency (National Archives Microcopy 234, Roll 308). The last reference contains a certification, dated September 30, 1851, by Agent W. P. Richardson that he was born in Franklin county, Ky.; that James F. Forman was born in Bourbon county, Ky.; John McClaskey in Nelson county, Ky.; John B. Roy in St. Louis, and Peter Cadue in "Canada East."

1852

⸿ January-June.—Licenses (new and renewal) to trade with Indians in "Kansas," as granted by agents of the Central Superintendency, St. Louis, were:

Traders	Indians	Issued by	Rec'vd at St. Louis
William P. Burney	Delaware	Thomas Moseley, Jr.	January
(R. C.) Miller & (G. L.) Young	Delaware	Thomas Moseley, Jr.	January
William F. Dyer	Delaware	Thomas Moseley, Jr.	January
W. G(eorge) Ewing, Jr.	Delaware	Thomas Moseley, Jr.	January
Thomas D. S. Macdonell	Delaware	Thomas Moseley, Jr.	January
A. B. Sharp	Delaware	Thomas Moseley, Jr.	January
Josiah Smart	"Mississippi" Sac & Fox	J. R. Chenault	February
(R. A.) Kinzie & (J. H.) Whistler	"Mississippi" Sac & Fox	J. R. Chenault	February
(David) Waldo & (Jacob) Hall	Kansa	J. R. Chenault	February
(A. G.) Boone & (W. R.) Bernard	"Mississippi" Sac & Fox	J. R. Chenault	February
M. D. Richardville	Miami	A. M. Coffey	February
A. I. Baker	"Mississippi" Sac & Fox	J. R. Chenault	February
W. F. Dyer & Co.	Pottawatomie	F. W. Lea	March
Seth M. Hays	Kansa	F. W. Lea	March
Christopher Columbia	Kansa	F. W. Lea	March
R. L. McGhee	Pottawatomie	F. W. Lea	March
(P. M.) Chouteau & (W. H.) Haskell	Miami	A. M. Coffey	April
Cyprian Chouteau	Delaware	Thomas Moseley, Jr.	April
J. B. Scott	"Mississippi" Sac & Fox	J. R. Chenault	April
Robert C. Miller	Kansa	F. W. Lea	April
C(yprian) & F(rederick) Chouteau	Delaware	Thomas Moseley, Jr.	May
Hayden D. McMeekin	"Mississippi" Sac & Fox	J. R. Chenault	June
(A. G.) Boone & (W. R.) Bernard	Pottawatomie	F. W. Lea	June
Moses H. Scott	Pottawatomie	F. W. Lea	June

Ref: Superintendency of Indian Affairs (SIA), St. Louis, "Records," v. 9, typed copy, pp. 600, 604, 606, 607, 609, 611, 613, 617, 620, 621, 628, 635, 637; and *ibid.*, pp. 616, 619, 624, for (1) John D. Skidmore as teamster, and John W. Solomon as clerk for Seth M. Hays, (2) J. B. Forman as clerk for Josiah Smart, (3) Charles B. Randall as clerk for Boone & Bernard, (4) P. Baker as clerk for A. I. Baker, (5) B. D. Castleman as clerk for W. George Ewing, Jr.; and p. 956 for mention of the Indian department's refusal to renew Christopher Columbia's license in 1854. *KHC*, v. 10, p. 209, has biographical sketch of Columbia. In *ibid.*, v. 6, p. 106, is a biographical note on William P. "Birney"—*i. e.*, Burney.

❡ January 1.—Bishop Miege's letter, written at St. Mary's (Pottawatomie Catholic) Mission, present St. Marys, Kan., included the following statements:

"Cholera, fevers of every kind, and small-pox . . . have made great ravages among our Indians this year. . . . The Potowatomie tribe comprises 3500 Indians dispersed in small villages over thirty square miles of land. We count among them 1500 converted Indians distributed between three villages, the first and largest . . . is called St. Mary's. Here are found the schools, the farm, and the big folk of the countryside, namely the doctor, the horse-shoer, a few traders and a certain number of mixed-blood families who know a little of reading and writing. The Indian families who surround us have each their log house . . . their little herd of livestock and a field sufficient for their support . . . these [number] 600 or 700 simple and truly pious savages.

"In the two other villages [see p. 955] which are located only three miles from one another and twenty miles from St. Mary's, there is also a good number of zealous and fervent Christians. . . .

"At Soldier River [in Shawnee county of today], twenty-five miles from St. Mary's on the confines of the Delaware [Indians' land], we have another village, which can also be called Catholic. It is composed of half-breeds, nearly all of them Canadians, rangers of the mountains and plains, who have ended by marrying one or more Indian women. With the exception of one or two families who lead a good life, the rest are a perfect *canaille* in the matter of immorality, drunkenness, bad faith, stupid ignorance, indifference to all instruction . . . [etc.]." (The now-extinct town of Indianola—site of the Topeka Goodyear plant today—developed from this community.)

Ref: G. J. Garraghan's *The Jesuits of the Middle United States* (New York, 1938), v. 2, pp. 645, 646.

❡ DIED: on January 3, Eliza S. (Ewing) Witten, aged 53, wife of the Rev. James Witten, "northern" Methodist Episcopal church missionary to the Wyandot Indians.

It is said hers was the first burial in the "Old Quindaro Cemetery" (located at "intersection of the Louisa Smith, and Parallel roads," present Wyandotte county).

Ref: Grant W. Harrington's *Historic Spots* . . . *of Wyandotte County, Kansas* (Merriam, 1935), pp. 151, 152 (which says the burial marker shows her age was 53 years, 6 months, and 14 days); *KHC*, v. 9, pp. 222, 223.

❡ DIED: in January, at Wea Baptist Mission (present Miami county), the following: Sarah Ann Osgood (teacher), on the 7th; Abigail Ann (Webster) Lykins (wife of the Rev. David Lykins), on the 15th; an Indian pupil of the school, on the 17th(?); Charles Lykins, aged about eight (son of the Rev. David Lykins), on the 17th.

The school (of over 30 children) was suspended for a time; but in May, or June, Eliza McCoy (previously of Pottawatomie Baptist Mission), reopened it; and remained till June, 1853 (when she retired from missionary service).

Ref: Jotham Meeker's "Diary" (in KHi ms. division); American Indian Mission Association, *Proceedings of 9th Annual Meeting*, 1852, p. 18 (where Miss Osgood's death date is given as January 9), pp. 39, 40; Comm'r of Indian Affairs, *Report*, 1852 (David Lykins' report, therein); Calvin McCormick, *The Memoir of Miss Eliza McCoy* (Dallas, 1892), pp. 77-79. David Lykins called it the "Wea and Piankeshaw Mission."

❧ January.—"Quite a number of Delaware Indians on a trading expedition to the Camanches, were killed a short time since—some of them very influential members of the tribe." (As reported, February 3, by the *Missouri Republican's* Independence, Mo., correspondent, who probably heard it from F. X. Aubry, just in from Santa Fe.)

See, also, p. 1073.

Ref: *Missouri Republican*, St. Louis, February 16, 1852. It may be that the Delawares killed by the Comanches were from the band long residing in "Oklahoma" whose chief was Black Beaver.

❧ January 12.—"John Randolph Benton (only son of Col. T[homas] H[art] Benton) stops with us," wrote Jotham Meeker, of Ottawa Baptist Mission (present Franklin county); and on the 13th recorded in his diary: "Mr. Benton leaves at 10, A. M."

(Two months later—on March 17—at St. Louis, young Benton [aged 22 years and four months] died. Father Pierre-Jean De Smet commented "and yet, though so young, he had rambled over the greater portion of the United states, New Mexico, California and Oregon . . . [*see* p. 451, for the 12-year-old Randolph Benton accompanying Fremont's expedition of 1842]." De Smet mentioned, also, the recent [early in 1852?] return from New Mexico of the senator's son.)

Ref: Jotham Meeker's "Diary," in KHi ms. division; Pierre-Jean De Smet's *Western Missions and Missionaries* . . . (1859), pp. 373-377.

❧ January.—Fort Atkinson's commanding officer—Bvt. Capt. Simon B. Buckner—made a trip up the Arkansas to the Big Timbers. He found 20 lodges of Kiowas, hunting buffalo, encamped on the river 10 miles above Aubry's crossing (in present Hamilton county).

Ref: *Missouri Republican*, St. Louis, February 16, 1852 (the news was reported by F. X. Aubry, who saw Buckner at Fort Atkinson about January 22).

❧ January 18.—"Messrs. Nelson and Irwin," overland from Santa Fe, arrived at Independence, Mo. They had met the "December" mail for Santa Fe at Red river; and the "January" mail on the Arkansas.

William Allison was in charge of the "January" mail; and he reached Santa Fe on the 24th. (Presumably he had left Independence January 1.) The Santa Fe *Gazette* (of the 31st) commented: "Mr. Allison . . . has made the quickest trip, we believe that has yet been made [by the mail *from* Independence]."

Ref: *Missouri Republican*, St. Louis, January 19, 30, February 26, 1852.

❧ January.—The outbreak of smallpox among the Pottawatomies

"entirely arrested operations" at Pottawatomie Baptist Mission (present Shawnee county). Missionaries in residence at the time were the Rev. B. W. Sanders and wife.

In the spring Dr. Johnston Lykins (who had been in the East) returned; and with him came the Rev. Isaac F. Herrick and Mrs. Herrick to join the staff.

Ref: American Indian Mission Association, *Proceedings, 9th Annual Meeting,* 1852, pp. 20, 39, 40.

❡ A "Jan. 22 p. m." telegraphic dispatch from Independence, Mo., read (in part): "The Santa Fe mail ['Walker and Thruston,' carriers] is just in. We have news up to 2d inst. by it. Little or no snow on route. Weather quite cold. . . . Aubry with 12 wagons is on his way to States and expects to be here by Feb. 5."

Ref: *Missouri Republican,* St. Louis, January 23, 30, 1852; St. Joseph *Gazette,* January 28, 1852.

❡ DIED: on January 23, George White Hair, chief of the Great and Little Osages, aged about 48, of pneumonia. He was buried at Osage (Catholic) Mission, present St. Paul, Kan., on the 24th.

Indian sup't David D. Mitchell, St. Louis, who visited the Osages twice in 1851, had written in his autumn annual report: "The half-breeds and the principal chief, George Whitehair, have commenced farming with a commendable zeal. Whitehair's example will have great influence with the Indians . . . he has doffed the Indian costume, and now appears in the white man's dress. . . ." Following the chief's death, Mitchell stated that he had been "the most sensible and managing man in the whole tribe."

The Osages chose as George White Hair's successor his cousin Gratamantze (chief of Nantze-waspe, or Papin's town—some 12 miles from Osage Mission). George White Hair had no son; his two brothers were by-passed because one—Little White Hair—was in poor health, and the other—Tcio-cioanca, chief of Elktown—was a wild, mischievous man.

Ref: *The Kansas Magazine,* Topeka, v. 1 (June, 1872), p. 528; Osage Mission records (microfilm in KHi), v. 2 (burials at Osage Mission), p. 103; Comm'r of Indian Affairs, *Reports,* 1851, 1852 (Mitchell's reports therein); Sister Mary Paul Fitzgerald's *Beacon on the Plains* (Leavenworth, 1939), pp. 84, 85. George White Hair had been baptized by Father J. J. Bax on May 29, 1851. His home was some four miles west of Osage Mission— *see* annals, p. 945.

❡ January 24.—Over three weeks late, the "December" mail from Salt Lake City, "Mr. Darraugh, the conductor," reached Independence, Mo. The trip from Fort Laramie had been made in 18 days.

Westbound, in December, 1851, Darraugh had been detained some 10 days by starving Pawnee Loups, to prevent him, as they feared, from scaring the buffalo. On leaving their village (where he had been well treated) the mail carrier proceeded up the north side of the Platte to Fort Laramie. Eastbound in January, Darraugh met about 25 Cheyennes (with whom he had a smoke); also met the Pawnees, and learned Sioux had killed four of the band.

Ref: *Missouri Republican,* St. Louis, January 28, 1852; St. Joseph *Gazette,* February 11, 1852 (from *Occidental Messenger,* Independence, January 31); annals, p. 1055.

❡ January 29.—From Parkville, Mo. (across the Missouri from the Delaware reserve), this telegraphic dispatch was sent to St. Louis:

"Our town was thrown into a state of great excitement this evening, by the arrival of a band of Delaware Indians from a hunting expedition. They bring with them a quantity of gold dust, which has proved to be finer than the California gold. All we could learn from the Indian of whom we purchased the dust is, that he obtained it on this side of the Mountains, about 700 miles from this place. He refused an offer of $1,000 from one of our citizens, to show him the place."

Ref: *Missouri Republican,* St. Louis, January 30, 1852. *See* annals, p. 941, for item on a gold discovery in present Colorado in 1850.

❡ January 30.—About 15 miles "below" Council Grove, two or three Kansa were killed during a "drunken row."

Ref: *Missouri Republican,* St. Louis, February 16, 1852 (from news brought to Missouri by F. X. Aubry); New York *Daily Tribune,* February 27, 1852.

❡ February 2.—"Mr. Wrick" arrived at Independence, Mo., with the "January" mail from Fort Laramie. He brought none from west of that post as the mail party from Salt Lake City had not reached there up to January 17 when he set out. "Wrick" reported he had "high water and muddy roads to contend with" during his journey.

On February 14 "Mr. Darragh," who had left Independence February 1 with the mail for Salt Lake, returned. He had found the roads "excessively muddy," streams difficult to cross, and at Big Blue had been halted by high water (with no sign of a fall soon). The *Occidental Messenger* of the 21st stated: "We learn that the enterprising contractors have sent out hands, and expect to have a ferry in operation by the first of March, the time of the next starting." (No further mention of this proposed ferry for the Oregon-California trail crossing near Alcove Spring has been found.)

Ref: *The Weekly Tribune,* Liberty, Mo., February 13, 27, 1852 (from the Independence *Occidental Messenger* issues of February 7 and 21).

❡ February.—Several Missouri newspapers this month noted that a Lexington, Mo., company, captained by Ansel Martin, planned a cattle drive (2,000 head) "over the plains" to California in the spring; that employees would be furnished mules, saddles, guns, and provisions, and taken through "free of expense."

Early in June some men returning from California (having encountered the first westbound emigrant company "the other side" of Green river on May 31, and no other in between) met "Mr. Martin's party driving about 2,500 head of loose cattle." The Martin drive must have crossed "Kansas" (by which trail?) in April to have a position so advantageous in the 1852 westward trek.

(The *Missouri Republican,* St. Louis, May 8, 1854, noted the arrival at New York of the *Northern Light;* and that E(benezer) W. Pomeroy and James

Lightner, both of Lexington, Mo., and members of the firm of "Martin, Pomeroy & Co." were on this ship. "They were large adventurers in stock to California in 1851 [*i. e.*, 1852?]. They bring with them a net profit of one hundred thousand dollars, independent of losses sustained by the unfortunate death of Capt. Anderson[?] Martin, under whose superintendence the expedition was conducted. . . .")

Ref: Item from the *Brunswicker*, reprinted in *The Weekly Tribune*, Liberty, Mo., February 13, 1852, St. Joseph (Mo.) *Gazette*, February 18, 1852, etc. The *Gazette* of June 30, 1852, has the trail item.

❡ February 5.—Intrepid, indefatigable Francis X. Aubry, overland from New Mexico; arrived at Independence, Mo. He had left Santa Fe on December 31. His party included Lts. James N. Ward (Third infantry) and Charles W. Field, (Second dragoons). "His wagons, twelve in number, he brought with him, a thing rather unprecedented in prairie travel, during the winter," wrote an Independence man, "and although he had much severity of weather, he did not lose a single mule, either in going out [late in 1851] or returning."

After Aubry reached St. Louis (February 14) the *Missouri Republican* reported: "In his trip in he took a new route, ever varying from the one adopted on his last visit to the States. Very intense cold was experienced on the route, the thermometer on several occasions [particularly January 18 and 19] 20 degrees below zero. . . ." After encamping one night on an island in the Arkansas, the party "cut through two feet of solid ice without finding water"; and at several places during the journey they encountered snow to a depth of 18 inches. "He is certainly the most daring traveler on the prairies," the *Republican* commented. Aubry was said to have brought in "a large amount of specie."

Of the "new route" attempted on this trip, it was reported that Aubry turned off from Cold Spring (as before) but crossed the Arkansas river "higher up than usual [for him]; but thinks it not so good [a trail] as his former one."

See p. 1067 for return trip.

Ref: *Missouri Republican*, St. Louis, February 15, 16, 1852. For Aubry's explorations in 1851, *see* annals, pp. 999, 1042, and 1046.

❡ About February 5 a "Santa Fe express" arrived at Fort Leavenworth (after a 16-day journey), bringing news from New Mexico to January 20. The regular U. S. mail from New Mexico reached Independence on February 19.

Ref: *The Weekly Tribune*, Liberty, Mo., February 13, 1852; *Missouri Republican*, St. Louis, March 4, 1852.

❡ February 10.—The *El Paso*—first steamboat of the year—reached Weston, Mo. She was followed by the *Highland Mary* on the 16th, and the *Ben West* four days later. Also on the 20th, the *St. Ange* lay opposite the town, unable to approach Weston's landing because of ice. She finally made it on the 23d; and started downriver the same day.

February 26 arrivals at Weston were the *Timour No. 2*, and the *El Paso* (on her second trip). On February 27 the *Saranak* tied up at Weston. When she left for St. Louis on the 28th, the *El Paso* was reported to be at St. Joseph (the first steamboat arrival of the year there) with machinery broken.

The St. Joseph *Gazette* of March 3, commented that the Missouri "at this point has been filled with running ice," and reported that the *El Paso* "has been detained on account of [ice] . . . until this morning. This boat carries off a large amount of freight and a number of passengers." But on March 9 the crippled *El Paso* had to put her cargo ashore at Fort Leavenworth, and her passengers were transferred to the *Kansas* (which had reached St. Joseph on the 6th[?] and started downriver on the 7th).

Ref: *Missouri Republican*, St. Louis, February issues, and March 3, 6, 16, 1852; Savannah (Mo.) *Sentinel*, February 21, 1852; St. Joseph (Mo.) *Gazette*, March 3, 1852; H. Miles Moore's "Journal" (microfilm of original in Coe Collection, Yale University Library).

❡ The February 11 issue of the St. Joseph (Mo.) *Gazette* (using an item from the Pittsburgh *Gazette*) reported that a "company belonging to the Presbyterian Church" (about 60 persons, headed by the Rev. J. A. Hanna), which planned to leave Pennsylvania and "found a colony in Oregon," would rendezvous at Cincinnati on March 15, and at St. Joseph on April 15.

Emigrant Francis B. White, whose company (33 men, nine women, and 12 or 15 children) left St. Joseph in the fore part of May, "met" (*i. e.*, came up to) the Reverend Mr. Hanna's train on May 18 (near the Little Blue?). In his diary he noted that it contained 20 wagons and 40 men.

The Rev. J. A. Hanna, in a March 18, 1904, letter, reminisced: "Here [St. Joseph, Mo.] we convened as a Presbyterian colony and purchased our outfit for crossing the continent with ox teams and wagons. Our company consisted of about sixty persons and eighteen wagons. We endured the usual privations and hardships incident to such a journey—had some Indian scares but nothing serious. After five months we arrived in Oregon City. . . ."

Ref: St. Joseph *Gazette*, February 11, 1852, and April 10, 1932 (for data from Francis B. White's diary); *Oregon Historical Quarterly*, Salem, v. 15 (June, 1914), p. 95.

❡ Mid-February.—Crawford Seminary, the Methodist Episcopal Church, South, school for the Quapaw Indians (of southeastern "Kansas," and northeastern "Oklahoma"), closed. The Rev. Samuel G. Patterson "left the Indian country without making any arrangements for a successor."

Apparently the school had not been in operation since the spring of 1851. Agent William J. J. Morrow, in his 1851 report, remarked that Patterson had visited the chiefs and headmen several times (when he returned, in the summer?, after an absence) but no children arrived to attend the next scheduled session of school.

Ref: Comm'r of Indian Affairs, *Reports*, 1851, 1852 (Agent Morrow's reports, therein). For earlier information on Quapaw Methodist Mission, *see* annals, pp. 468, 472, and 772.

❡ February 14.—The Savannah (Mo.) *Sentinel's* editor wrote: "From all the indications, at home and abroad, it appears evident, that the rush across the plains, this season, will, at least equal, if not excel that of '50. The note of preparation is heard from every quarter, not in this State alone, but also in Iowa, Illinois, Indiana, Ohio, and even, some of the more Eastern States.

"*One hundred thousand,*—men, women and children,—will emigrate to the Pacific slope, during this year, most of whom, will take the trip over the plains. . . ."

Ref: Savannah *Sentinel*, February 14, 1852 (microfilm in KHi).

❡ February 16.—News reached the Central (Indian) Superintendency, St. Louis, that smallpox had "carried off fifty of the Potawatomies," and recently had broken out among the Delawares.

Ref: SIA, St. Louis, "Records," v. 9, typed copy, p. 606. *See, also,* annals, p. 1057.

❡ DIED: Kennekuk (the Kickapoo Prophet), of smallpox, at his home on the Kickapoo reserve (in present Leavenworth county), *probably early in the year* (but no record of the month, or day, has been located). Agent W. P. Richardson, in his September 30 report, noted that the Kickapoos had lost Kennekuk; referred to him as "their principal chief"; and commented:

"He exerted a most beneficial influence over a great portion of that tribe for some years before his death, in restraining, by all means in his power, the introduction and use of spirits. On the other hand, he was notorious for his superstitious quackery—a conjurer of the first water—and regarded by most of his people as possessing supernatural powers. . . ."

In a letter of 1848 (written in midyear), the Rev. Edmund Wright, of Weston, Mo., had stated: "Kenekuk, an Indian *prophet* has just been in town. Government built him a log church, about 30 feet square, several years since [*see* p. 298], and there it stands on a bluff, in the Kickapoo country, about 4 miles from Weston. It is in a dilapidated state, and I rejoice to learn that Kenekuk is abandoning his follies, and now meets in church with the Methodist Missionary, who is 'half breed.' [This was Paschal Fish, part-Shawnee.] For several years he has had a separate congregation every Sabbath, and has opposed the mission, pretending to be the Indians' Savior and deriving his authority from certain characters on a 'chip' which he has called his Bible. Kenekuk has persuaded scores of Indians to believe that white men killed Jesus Christ before he had made an atonement for the Indians, and that he, Kenekuk, has been appointed by the Great Spirit to supply the deficiency."

Ref: Comm'r of Indian Affairs, *Report*, 1852, p. 361; Bureau of American Ethnology, *Fourteenth Annual Report*, Part 2, pp. 692-700; *The Home Missionary*, New York, v. 21 (September, 1848), p. 102 (for Wright's letter); KHC, v. 9, pp. 186, 228 (for Paschal Fish). *See* annals, p. 234 (for Kennekuk's arrival in "Kansas," in 1833), and *see, also,* his portrait on p. 401.

❡ DIED: "The somewhat notorious Iowa ex-chief, White Cloud, and the [Iowa's] second chief, Ne-u-mon-ya, or Rain Walker [on the Iowa reserve, in present Doniphan county; *probably early in the year;* and *perhaps* about the same time]. . . . Both were men of decided talents, and the latter was particularly noted for shrewdness."—Agent W. P. Richardson (writing on September 30).

In a letter of February 16, *1853,* from "Ioway & Sac Mission," the Rev. S. M. Irvin wrote: "The Ioway Nation has diminished over one half since this mission was first commenced. There are now not over 400 living souls of 830 the number of the Nation 15 years ago. Of six chiefs then living and acting, but one survives, and of ten or a dozen braves but one yet lives. The Chief is No heart, the firm friend of the mission and the brave is Little Wolf a relative of No heart and a friend to us."

Ref: Comm'r of Indian Affairs, *Report,* 1852, p. 361 (Richardson's report stated only that the two Iowa chiefs had "died within the year"); Presbyterian Historical Society, American Indian Correspondence (microfilm in KHi), on reel labeled "Box 3, vol. 2." According to P. L. Gray's *Doniphan County History* (Bendena, Kan., 1905), pt. 2, pp. 27, 31, White Cloud was buried just below present Iowa Point, Kan., on a high point (bluff?) overlooking the Missouri. *See* annals, pp. 735 and 752, for earlier comment on the Iowa chief.

❡ About March 1 Francis X. Aubry "with his wagons," left Independence, Mo., for Santa Fe. (*See* February 5 entry.) Probably his was the first New Mexico-bound trader's train of the year.

Ref: *The Weekly Tribune,* Liberty, Mo., May 14, 1852 (from *Occidental Messenger,* Independence [May 8? issue]).

❡ March 3.—The St. Joseph (Mo.) *Gazette's* editor commented: "The city begins to throng with strangers, emigrants bound for California"; and estimated "perhaps there are not less than two hundred persons [westbound] in and about St. Joseph."

Ref: St. Joseph *Gazette,* March 3, 1852.

❡ March 5.—Francis J. Marshall's license to trade with the Pawnee Indians (issued by Agent John E. Barrow, in February?) was forwarded to Washington from the St. Louis Central Superintendency. This earliest-located item connecting him with "Kansas" history, and other evidence, tend to prove that Marshall established his (first, and only) trading post on the Big Blue (at present Marysville) not earlier than 1852. His site was at the crossing of the (1) Fort Leavenworth-Fort Kearny military road, and (2) St. Joseph branch of the Oregon-California trail.

In mid-1895 Marshall (in a letter) stated: "This undertaking [trading post and ferry] was commenced as early as the year 1852." He recalled that he had applied first to the Indian agent; and then had asked Bvt. Maj. E. A. Ogden (Fort Leavenworth quartermaster) for "a contract with the government to put in boats, build ware- and store-houses and to supply troops returning from the western forts in the winter time, and he [Ogden] protested [pointing out the danger from Indians, etc.]. . . . I expressed myself, however, as willing to arrange for my own protection, to which he afterward gave his consent. . . . I proceeded at once, bought a piece of artillery, mounted it, loaded my own wagons and was on the way to the Big Blue crossing at the point referred to within twenty-four hours after my contract. This arrangement was universally concurred in by the officers at Ft. Leavenworth. . . ." Marshall also noted: "Most of the time the river could be forded, but often even for six weeks at a time it could not be crossed except by means of the ferry." (His further statement of travel figures—"at least 5,000 to 10,000 people a day from April to July"— presumably was intended to read "5,000 to 10,000 people a *month* from April to July.")

Quoted here are excerpts from some emigrant diaries of 1852, describing experiences at the Big Blue (Marysville) crossing:

May 7 (Thomas C. Lewis)—"Friday fine morning Early start got to the Big Blue it had raised in the night ferried over charged $3 for each wagon 25 cts for each stock 25 [cts] Passengers. . . ."

May 7 (Jay Green)—"Wee arrived at big blue river this day at twelve o'clock and found its water so swolen from the heavy rains as to render it im posable to cross except in boats, and without delay wee prepared two wagon beds for the purpos of ferrying a line was made fast to eather end of the beds and they ware drawn from shore to shore by the men, and before dark wee ware all safe across wagons and baggage leaving our mules tied on the opisit shore as it was to late to cross them. . . ." [On May 8 Green wrote] ". . . wee still remain at blue the valley . . . is about two miles wide. . . . A trading post is cept here."

May 12 (William C. Lobenstine)—". . . arrived at this side of the Big Blue River. This is a very nice stream and bordered with willow, elm and walnut and some of the oak found on the hills. We crossed the river the next day [May 13] having but little difficulty, the river being low and the roads good. A starting house is to be found at the ferry this side of the river where emigrants can get what is most necessary on the journey. . . ."

May 16 (John H. Clark)—". . . From our camp to the [Big Blue] river it was six miles. . . . The road lay through an open country and the wind went howling over our heads and beating the rain directly in our faces and with such force that we could hardly stem the current. . . . We made the journey by nine o'clock, encamped near a drift wood pile, set fire to the concern, warmed ourselves and cooked breakfast.

"Here was a 'private' post office, trading post and ferry kept by a company of men who had established themselves to rob the emigrant of what little money he happened to have after leaving the States. Twenty-five cents for a glass of bad whiskey, one dollar for taking your letter to the States and three dollars for crossing each wagon. We gave neither, for we bought no whiskey, wrote no letters and drove our wagons through the 'drink.'

"There are many new graves on the banks of this river, some fifteen or twenty perhaps. We overtook a large company today. They had lost some fifteen since leaving the States."

[The May 16 entry from *another version* of the John H. Clark diary states (in part): "Upon the banks of this river is a post office, carried on, I believe, by private enterprise. There is also a store, groceries, and many articles whereby a person can refit. . . . The Big Blue river is quite a stream of water and when it is high has to be ferried. At the time of our crossing the water had fallen so as to be fordable. Although a cold and wet morning the boys took to water like young ducks. The ferry charges are $3 per wagon for crossing. . . . There are many new made graves upon the banks of this river, perhaps fifteen. We overtook a large train at the ferry. They have near 100 passengers and have lost (we have been informed) ten or fifteen. Put in wood and water and pushed out into the open prairie, and near good grass."]

[The May 16 entry from a *third version* of the John H. Clark diary contains other variations: "Six miles in six hours and we are on the banks of the Big Blue. . . . On the east bank of this river is located a private postoffice, a dramshop, hotel and a ferry, the business all under one roof. If we mail a letter we pay $1; if we take a dram of good whiskey, seventy-five cents; a square meal,(?) $1.50; if it is a wagon we want carried over the river, $4, and no grumbling. The proprietor is doing a rushing business. During our stay of two and a half hours he crossed forty wagons, his clerks were busy handing out whiskey and the cooks getting out bacon, biscuits and coffee. How many letters he received for transportation during the same time I am unable to say, but our company handed in fifteen or twenty. The 'boss' has a good thing just now; how long he will be able to keep it depends on the overland immigration. . . ."]

May 18 (Mrs. Lodisa Frizzell)—"Proceeded onward, crossed the Big Blue river   there was a ferry here, but we forded it, although it came near running into our waggon bed. . . ."

May 18 ("G.")—[Writing from "Fort Marshall"—*i. e.*, Frank Marshall's trading post]—"I am informed at this place, that twenty one hundred wagons [and thus probably well over 7,000 persons] have passed this ford. [Later?] Twelve miles from Big Blue, to the junction of the Independence and St. Joseph roads,   up to this place to this time, thirty-two persons have died. . . .   Game is plenty here, and I am now in one of the most beautiful valleys I ever saw, surrounded by high bluffs, covered with tall cedars. It is truly a romantic looking place. . . ."

May 24 (William Kahler)—"got to the big blew river   hear is a black smith shop and a sort of a store   this [stream] is a   bout 6 rods wide and is about 4 feet deep   we forded it by raising our wagon beads 2 inches   got over all safe. . . ."

Ref: SIA, St. Louis, "Records," v. 9, typed copy, p. 609 (for item on Marshall's license); Emma E. Forter's *History of Marshall County, Kansas* (Indianapolis, 1917), pp. 64-66 (Marshall's mid-1895 letter); Thomas C. Lewis "Memorandum" (manuscript, Yale University Library); Jay Green, *Diary* . . . (Stockton, Calif., 1955), p. 8; William C.

Lobenstine, *Extracts From the Diary of* . . . (1920), p. 20; John H. Clark "Diary" (from typed copy lent by California State Library, Sacramento); *KHQ*, v. 3, pp. 137, 138 (for second version of J. H. Clark May 16 diary entry), v. 11, p. 237 (for third version of J. H. Clark May 16 diary entry); Mrs. Lodisa Frizzell, *Across the Plains to California in 1852* (1915), p. 16; St. Joseph *Gazette*, May 26, 1852 (for "G's" May 18, 1852, letter); William Kahler's "Diary," original in Coe Collection, Yale University Library; Elizabeth P. Ellsberry, comp., *Marriage Records 1820-1850* . . . *of Ray County, Missouri* (lists marriage of Francis Marshall, Caldwell county, and Mary R. Williams, November 4, 1847); *The History of Clear Creek and Boulder Valleys, Colorado* (Chicago, 1880), p. 519 (states that Francis J. Marshall was born in Lee county, Va., April 3, 1816; that he emigrated to Caldwell county, Mo., in 1842; married in 1847; removed to "Kansas" in 1852). The statements in *KHC*, v. 7, p. 86, in Wilder's *Annals of Kansas*, and in some other sources, give erroneous information concerning Marshall's early activities in Kansas. In KHi (on microfilm, from National Archives) are some "Selected documents concerning the trading activities of F. J. Marshall and Albert Woodward," in connection with an 1854-1855 depredation claim of Marshall & Woodward against the Pawnees. In one affidavit (of 1860 date) Marshall stated: ". . . the price for which corn was sold at said Trading Post to the United States during the years 1852, '53, '54, '55, '56, '57 and 1858 was never less than two dollars per bushel and . . . corn during the year A. D. 1855 was sold by us to the California Emigrants as high as two dollars and fifty cents per bushel. . . ."

❦ March 10.—Charles A. and Elias H. Perry (merchants at Weston and St. Joseph) began advertising a passenger train to California— proposing to transport fares from Weston, St. Joseph, and Elizabeth- town (where they would cross the Missouri) and "thence direct through—starting about April 15."

For $150 (cash, in advance) they would include provisions, "good, new Tents and double Wagon Sheets" (but not bedding or blankets), and allow fifty pounds of baggage per person "free." Elias H. Perry would accompany the train through.

Probably the Perrys took a large number of passengers to California. It appears the train did not start till the second week in May. "B." ("a gentle- man in Perry's train") wrote to the St. Joseph *Gazette's* editor on May 15 from "Big Blue": ". . . so far we have had but little difficulty, except some sickness, and a few deaths from Cholera. I send you a list of those who have died in our train. . . . [May 13. James H. M'Kinney, Erie county, N. Y., Duncan Gilchrist, of Roxbury, Canada, Charles Kelsey, of West Wheeling, Ohio, J. J. Pearce, of Massachusetts; May 14: Thomas M. Sneed, Clay county, Ill., and John M'Calisters, of North Ireland; May 15: Mrs. Dawson, and a son of William Bedford, both of St. Joseph, Mo.]."

In the St. Joseph *Gazette* of May 19 the editor noted: ". . . Many of our citizens, to whom we were strongly attached, have left within the last ten days. . . ." He listed "Judge [Robert] Irwin and family, W. P. Lewis, two young McCorkles, L. Archer and wife, Wm. H. and Thomas J. Bedford and families, Mrs. Dawson and three daughters . . . [also 11 other persons]." Very likely all had set out in the Perrys' train. The May 26 *Gazette* reported nine persons of this train had died.

The Weston *Reporter* editor, in an August issue, noted letters had been received from persons with "Mr. Perry's train," dated Fort Laramie, June 19, stating that the company's "health is comparatively good, and that the emigrants are getting along well." But Thomas Clinton had died on June 14, "near Fort Laramie," of cholera.

Ref: St. Joseph *Gazette*, March 10, May 26, 1852; *The Weekly Tribune*, Liberty, Mo., May 28, August 20, 1852 (for Weston *Reporter* item); *Missouri Republican*, St. Louis, June 13, 1852. The Perrys' "ad" advised inquirers to apply to C. A. Perry at Weston, E. H. Perry, at St. Joseph, or E. Perry, at Elizabethtown. (Elizabethtown first appeared as a Missouri river crossing point in 1845—*see* annals, p. 539.) *The History of Andrew and DeKalb Counties, Missouri* (1888), p. 179, states that Elizabethtown, adjoining present Amazonia, Mo., on the northwest, "was laid out" as a small village, as early as 1850 or 1851, but its plat was never recorded; and that "about the same time" a store was started by "Messrs. Perry & Young, who, in addition to carrying on a mercantile business, operated a warehouse on the river. A landing was established early in the fifties." *The History of Buchanan County, Missouri* . . . (St. Joseph, 1881), pp. 414, 853, 854, contains information on the Perrys. On p. 854 it is stated that their freighting and mercantile business increased so rapidly that E. H. Perry "found it expedient in 1852 to move to California," to give personal attention to business, and that he stayed four years. The Perrys were merchants at Salt Lake City, also. *The History of Buchanan County, Missouri,* pp. 134, 135, has mention of Robert Irwin.

❡ March.—"At the Savannah Landings, there are two Ferries in constant operation . . .," the Savannah (Mo.) *Sentinel* of March 14 stated. A week earlier, "Bonifield & Roberts" had begun advertising their Savannah Landing ferry ("nine miles above St. Joseph"), announcing they had "two large boats for crossing Wagons and Teams. . . ."

As appears, the two Savannah landings (several miles apart) were: *Boston* (formerly Nodaway City; officially renamed in 1851) where Bonifield & Roberts were established; and *Elizabethtown* (*see* preceding entry). "Roberts" undoubtedly was Peter S. Roberts, to whom, in 1855, the Kansas territorial legislature gave authorization to keep a ferry opposite the town of Boston, Mo.

Emigrant Moses F. Laird, whose Oregon-bound, 16-wagon company left St. Joseph on May 3, crossed the Missouri on May 6 at a "Savanah landing" which he placed as 16 miles above St. Joseph. The ferry was an oar-propelled flat boat. In his diary he noted "there is a couple of houses here." On May 12 emigrant William Kahler ferried the Missouri at a landing 10 miles above St. Joseph—the Boston location, presumably. (He had spent most of May 11 in "Savanna.")

Ref: Savannah *Sentinel*, March 6, 14[?], 1852, *KHQ*, v. 2, p. 133 (for a reference to Peter S. Roberts' ferry); *History of Andrew and DeKalb Counties, Missouri* (1888), pp. 171-174, 179. Nodaway City (earlier Caples' Landing), it is said, adjoined present Amazonia, Mo., on the east. Moses F. Laird's "Journal," and William Kahler's "Diary," are in the Coe Collection, Yale University Library, and used by permission.

❡ March 18.—In 17 days from Santa Fe, the "March" U. S. mail reached Independence, Mo. Reportedly the trip was "the quickest ever made" by the contract mail carriers. (*See* January 18 entry.)

Ref: *The Weekly Tribune*, Liberty, Mo., March 26, 1852 (from Independence *Occidental Messenger*); *Missouri Republican*, St. Louis, March 20, 26, 1852.

❡ March.—These passenger trains *to California* were being advertised in the St. Louis *Missouri Republican:*

P. H. ELSWORTH (over the route before; now taking his family, and some others) announced he would start from St. Louis about mid-April or May 1, with an ox train, and "take with him a large drove of stock"; and that he would "take through," for $100 each, 35 to 40 passengers, who would be furnished provisions and transportation, but "be obliged to stand watch and do camp duty."

ALEXANDER PATTERSON (veteran of two overland trips) announced his train would start from St. Louis about April 20, and from St. Joseph between May 1 and 10. Passengers (limited to 40) would all go mounted; baggage wagons would be drawn by four mules each, and a "spring Hospital Wagon with medicines" taken along. Cost per person if providing his own riding animal, $150; or, $300 fare "with a horse furnished."

J. W. MALONE and R. P. LOCKE announced they were fitting out a "splendid passenger train for California," terms "easy." Passengers would be "shipped" by steamboat to St. Joseph, where the train would be ready to start about April 25. Contracts "have already been made with some 15 persons," their notice stated.

GEORGE HUGHES and JOHN DUFFY's passenger train was advertised to leave St. Louis about April 20, and to start from St. Joseph between May 1 and 10, with 16 light wagons "drawn by 6 or 8 head of cattle." Company limited to 30; fare $100, from St. Joseph. "He [Hughes?]," said the notice, "has made the trip (once) across the Plains in 1850, in 67 days."

"L. J. MINTURN & Co., PROPRIETORS" (who presumably advertised in March, also) had a notice in the April 13 St. Louis Republican stating that "All who are going with our passenger train [to California] must obtain their certification this week."

Ref: *Missouri Republican,* St. Louis, February, March, and April issues, 1852. Elsworth's "ad" first appeared on February 20; Patterson's on February 24; Malone and Locke's "ad" is in the March 20 issue, and still "in" on April 13; the same is true for Hughes and Duffy. For Minturn, *see* April 13, 1852, issue.

❆ The March 31 St. Joseph *Gazette* stated: The *Timour* [*No. 2*], *Kate Swinney,* and *Ben West,* have arrived and departed during the week, bringing to the city, several hundred emigrants, for California and Oregon."

(A Weston resident—H. Miles Moore—who saw the *St. Ange, Timour No. 2,* and *Kate Swinney* arrive at his town on March 26, wrote that the new steamboat *Kate Swinney* [a "Beautiful Craft"] was making her first trip—direct from Louisville, Ky., to St. Joseph, Mo. The *Ben West* had left St. Louis on March 24 "literally covered with passengers"—mostly bound for Independence and St. Joseph, it was reported.)

On March 31 the *Ben West* (heading homeward) passed the *Kansas* "lying up" at Columbus landing; next day met three upbound boats—the *Banner State at* Fort Leavenworth, the *Elvira* and *Pontiac No. 2* at Kansas (City), Mo. Ahead of the *Ben West* was the *Highland Mary,* which had started downriver from Kansas at noon on April 1.

Ref: St. Joseph *Gazette,* March 31, 1852; *Missouri Republican,* St. Louis, March 25,

April 3, 1852; H. Miles Moore's "Journal" (microfilm, from original in Coe Collection, Yale University library).

❡ March 31.—Three Salt Lake City firms of "merchants and trad-ers"—Livingston & Kinkead, O. H. Cogswell, and Holladay & Warner—in a joint advertisement, first published in the St. Joseph (Mo.) *Gazette* of this date, advised emigrants they would be able to purchase "every necessary article" at "fair remunerating prices" in Salt Lake City; and, if "well-disposed," could expect a "cordial reception" from the citizens.

(Holladay & Warner's Missouri headquarters was at Weston, Mo., Cogswell's was at Independence, Mo. Livingston & Kinkead trains set out from Iowa.)

Ref: St. Joseph *Gazette*, March 31, 1852.

❡ Spring.—"In their [the Delaware] hunting excursions this spring two of the sons of Captain Ketchum, their principal chief, were killed by a war party of the Sioux on the waters of the Platte, be-tween Forts Kearny and Laramie. All their furs, horses, traps, and blankets fell into the hands of the Sioux. Another Delaware Indian was shot through the leg but made his escape."—Agent Thomas Moseley, Jr., in his autumn report.

Moseley added: "The Delawares are brave, chivalrous, enterprising Indians. They hunt and roam throughout the length and breadth of the great western plains, some as far as California. It appears that quite a number of this tribe, engaged in the chase and trade on the plains, are annually killed by wild tribes, or die from great exposure." (*See, also,* p. 1061.)

Ref: Comm'r of Indian Affairs, *Report,* 1852 (Moseley's report, therein).

❡ At the beginning of April, eastbound Santa Fe travelers found William Bent trading with the Arapahoes, Kiowas, "Pawnees" (*i. e.,* Comanches!), and Cheyennes, on the Arkansas, five miles above Fort Atkinson.

The "April" mail carriers, not more than 10 days later on the route, reported that bands of Kiowas, Apaches, Arapahoes, and 400 lodges of Comanches were at Fort Atkinson (*i. e.,* in the vicinity).

Ref: *Missouri Republican,* St. Louis, April 14, 21, 1852.

❡ April.—Most of the steamboats which were on the "middle Mis-souri" this month are mentioned in the following chronology:

On April 3 the *Saranak* headed downriver from St. Joseph. She met the upbound *Elvira* and *Pontiac No. 2*—both "laid up"—not far below St. Joseph; and was detained four days, above "Columbus [Landing]," by "heavy running ice." Below that point the *Clara,* upbound, also was "laid up." On April 8 the *Saranak* left Weston; passed the *Alton,* "laying by," at Parkville; met the *El Paso* at Sibley, and the *Minnesota* below; at Lexington saw the *Isabel* and *Saluda;* reached St. Louis April 11.

(The *Saluda* "burst her boilers" at Lexington on the morning of April 9, killing and maiming many of her passengers—"most of whom were emigrants for

Utah." Possibly as many as 135 persons died as a result of the *Saluda's* explosion.)

On April 9 the *Clara* left St. Joseph; met the *Alton* (still "laying up"?) below Fort Leavenworth. By, or before, April 10 (after being detained five days by ice) the *Minnesota* reached St. Joseph. She left, downriver, on the 11th; met the *Isabel* (bound for Council Bluffs) 10 miles below, the *Sonora* (bound for St. Joseph) at "Independence Prairie," and other boats.

The *Sonora* started down from St. Joseph on April 13. She met the *Martha Jewett* (a new boat) at Iatan, the *St. Ange* at Weston, and the *Yuba* (earlier reported "crowded with Californians, and heavily freighted") near Weston, "hard aground."

The fast-moving *Robert Campbell* (with about 300 passengers aboard) which started upriver three days after the *St. Ange* (*see above*), overtook her below Lexington; also gained 60 hours on the *Martha Jewett* (*see above*); and apparently reached St. Joseph by April 14. On April 17 the St. Louis *Missouri Republican,* noting the *Robert Campbell's* return (on the 16th?), stated her running time from St. Joseph to St. Louis was 22 hours—"the quickest time we have ever seen reported."

On April 16 the *Highland Mary* ("with a large number of Californians aboard") reached Kansas, Mo. This same day, the *Isabel* (*see above*) started downriver from Council Bluffs. She met, on the 17th the *Banner State* at St. Joseph; later met the *Highland Mary* and *Clipper No. 2* at Iatan, the *J. S. Chenoweth* and the *Yuba* (still aground?) at Weston, the *Ben West* (bound for Kanesville, Ia.) at Liberty, and other boats, later. Two other steamboats en route to Kanesville (Council Bluffs) were the *Saranak* and *Delaware*. They, and the *Ben West,* were "in port" by the 25th.

On April 22 the *Clara* started down from St. Joseph. She soon met the *Monongahela* (at "Miller's Wood Yard") and the *El Paso;* below Iatan met the *Honduras,* and at Kansas, the *Timour No. 2.*

Both the *Timour No. 2* and *Honduras* left St. Joseph, bound downriver, on April 24. According to the latter's log, she met the *Minnesota* at Weston that day; on the 25th met the *Pontiac No. 2* at Parkville, the *Sonora* at "Upper Liberty," the *Midas* at "Lower Liberty," and the *Robert Campbell* a mile below.

An April 27 telegram from St. Joseph read: "Weather clear and cool. Delaware and Saranak down last night. [The *Saranak* had left Council Bluffs on the 25th; the *Delaware* on the 26th. Neither remained long at St. Joseph.] Robt Campbell, St. Ange and Sonora [all up from St. Louis] arrived this morning. The Pontiac No. 2 sunk 20 miles below here, at Smith's Bar—hull under water and broke in the middle, boat and cargo total loss. No lives lost. She had on board two hundred emigrants for California and Oregon; their outfits all lost. . . ."

The *Midas* also reached St. Joseph on the 27th; and started back down that evening, leaving the *Sonora* "in port." She passed the downbound *Delaware* (which was beside the wrecked *Pontiac No. 2*); on the 28th met the *Lewis Whiteman* and *Martha Jewett* at Fort Leavenworth, the *Brooklyn* (bound for Council Bluffs) and the *Isabel,* below Liberty. The *Midas* reached St. Louis April 30 (a day after the *Saranak*). The *Delaware* came in two days later, delayed by having spent 30 hours taking out the machinery, fixtures, etc., of the *Pontiac No. 2.*

On April 28 the "very heavily laden" *Martha Jewett* (*see* above) reached St. Joseph. She had left St. Louis on the 23d, with around 300 passengers (about two-thirds for California), some 100 head of livestock, also wagons, and other freight. Among the emigrants she carried were Mrs. Lodisa Frizzell (a California-bound emigrant who kept a diary), and "Major" John Stemmons, of Rocheport, Mo. (now en route to California with his family), author of an 1850-published guidebook (*see* p. 902) of which no copy is known to be extant.

On April 30 the *Isabel* started down from St. Joseph. She met the *Brooklyn* at "the Lost Lake," and the *Yuba* at Weston; on May 1 met the *Banner State* at Rialto (across from Fort Leavenworth), the *Clipper No. 2* at Wayne City, and other boats below.

Ref: *Missouri Republican*, St. Louis, April, and early May, 1852, issues; Frizzell, *op. cit.*, pp. 7-10; St. Joseph (Mo.) *Gazette*, April 14, 1852 (for account from [Lexington (Mo.)] *Journal* which, on information from the *Saluda's* clerk, stated there were some 175 persons aboard when the explosion occurred; that only 50 were known to be living; of that number, 20 were seriously, or dangerously, injured; and that the number of lives lost "will be found to be not less than" 135).

❡ Early April.—Black measles was epidemic at Osage (Catholic) Mission, present Neosho county; and spreading to the Indian towns. (Following the arrival of a fatally ill Quapaw, 45 boarding students had fallen sick within a four-day period.) Eleven boys and one girl of the mission children died. (However, seven had been taken from the school by relatives, "as the alarm spread," and failed to receive proper care.) On April 18 Father John J. Bax wrote: "We are obliged to interrupt the school for some time. . . . The contagion is spreading among the Indians, and mortality is very great. . . ."

Other diseases followed the measles outbreak. On June 14 Bax (himself a sick man; and at Fort Scott for treatment) wrote: "The measles, typhus fever and scurvy have made a dreadful havoc among our Indians. Everyone thinks that there died at least one-thousand since last January and there is not yet a stop. . . . [The Osages] went all at once in a kind of despair on their summer hunt without planting any corn, pumpkins, etc. and news has returned that every town loses 7 or 8 every day."

Bishop Miege (who visited the Osages in midsummer) stated in an August letter: "Small-pox [*i. e.*, black measles] visited the Osage towards the end of winter and carried off 12 of our school children and 1200 at least of our Osage, who were attacked at the same time by the scurvy and yellow fever. . . ." The Rev. John Schoenmakers wrote in a September 15 report: "no less than 1000 children or youths died within a few weeks. . . . Next to the measles and typhoid [typhus?] fever, followed the whooping cough." (But in 1876 Father Schoenmakers stated: "In . . . 1852 [the Osages] fell victims to disease and 800 died of measles. Scurvey . . . then appeared with its train of alarming effects, and of the 400 who lived near the Mission 40 died or this disease within one month. The tribe was also visited by small pox, some even suffering the third attack. . . .") Agent W. J. J. Morrow reported (October 1): "The Osages were unusually sickly last winter and spring.

It is estimated by many that not less than one thousand have died within the last twelve months."

Ref: De Smet, *op. cit.*, pp. 371, 372 (for Bax's April letter); Garraghan, *op. cit.*, v. 2, p. 513 (for Bax's June letter); Comm'r of Indian Affairs, *Report*, 1852 (Schoenmakers' and Morrow's reports, therein); *Neosho County Journal*, Osage Mission, Kan., June 7, 1876.

❡ April.—A notice headed "Kansas, Mo.! California!! Oregon!!," advertising the advantages of Kansas (City), Mo., as a starting point for emigrants, appeared in issues of the *Missouri Republican*, St. Louis, beginning about April 8.

The concluding paragraph read (in part): "Finally, They [the citizens of Kansas, Mo.] would say that all the largest and most celebrated jobbers in conducting trains across the Plains, universally start from Kansas as the best and most convenient starting point, from which to make their trips, speedily, comfortably and safely. Aubry, Messervy, Huston, Kit Carson, and all the celebrated voyagers, invariably select Kansas as their starting point. . . ."

Ref: *Missouri Republican*, St. Louis, April 8, and succeeding April, 1852, issues.

❡ April.—"Parkville [Mo.] is the best point to cross the Missouri," a notice in the Liberty *Tribune* of April 9 advised California and Oregon emigrants, "Because it is between the Independence and St. Joseph routes and you save the traveling over long muddy hills and crossing Kanzas river from Independence; or some 60 miles travel up to St. Joe. . . ."

The notice also stated: ". . . some three miles from Parkville you strike the divide between the waters of Kansas and the Missouri and keep it a short distance till you intersect the military road from Fort Leavenworth to Fort Laramie which has been surveyed by U. S. Eng[ineer]s, and is the best road in the world; or you may keep up the North side of the Kansas and intersect the Independence route in the Pottawatomie nation. Both are great highways and were much traveled in 1849, 1850 and 51. On the route up the Kansas Corn can be had at Burney's store [William P. Burney, licensed Delaware trader—*see* p. 1059], some 5 miles from the Missouri river, and at different points for some 70 miles. . . ."

Names "signed" to the notice were: R. G. Stevens, W. P. Burney, Thos. W. Davis, A. J. Goodyear, Dr. G. W. Barnes (all of Parkville), A. H. Scott, Buchanan county, and Jas. T. V. Thompson, of Liberty, Mo.

Ref: *The Weekly Tribune*, Liberty, Mo., April 9, 1852.

❡ April 9(?)—The St. Joseph *Adventure* commented as follows on the year's emigration:

"Within the past two weeks our City and vicinity present something like the appearance of the springs of '48 and '49 [*i. e.*, 1849 and 1850]. The Public houses are full, the streets thronged with strangers, bound for the West, waiting for the first appearance of grass. The landing [is] covered with wagons and other articles of outfit for a trip across the plains. Every boat that arrives brings great numbers of passengers, and from present indications the emigration will be as great as in any former year."

Ref: *The Weekly Tribune,* Liberty, Mo., April 16, 1852 (from the *Adventure* of April 9, probably).

❦ In mid-April parties of traders, and other travelers, from New Mexico reached the Missouri border.

A telegram from Independence, Mo., on April 13 announced that R(obert) Nesbit, "mayor of Santa Fe," who left the New Mexican capital March 13, had "just arrived."

"Another portion of the party from Santa Fe arrived in this city last night," it was reported at St. Louis on April 21. "Messrs. J. W. Whittelsy and J. H. Marshall, of the U. S. Army, and José Ply, a Mexican trader, were of the number." They had left Santa Fe on March 17; and reached Independence in 28 days—in company with a wagon train. (Lt. Joseph H. Whittlesey was, at this period, regimental adjutant of the First dragoons; and 2d Lt. Louis H. Marshall was in the Third infantry. Presumably they were the men referred to above.)

Aboard the *Clara* which tied up at St. Louis on April 25 (having left St. Joseph, Mo., on the 21st) were some 20 traders from New Mexico who (by report) bought $300,000 in specie, and planned to buy goods at St. Louis. Names given in the *Missouri Republican* were: R. L. Allen (*see* April 19 entry), J. Armijo, S. Del Gardo, F. Del Gardo, P. Del Gardo, T. Romero, N. Lucero, P. Trupello, S. D. Trupello, M. Armijo, D. Armijo, F. Armijo, T. T. Garrareno, D. Esquivel, M. Esquivel, J. S. N. Brehouse(?).

Ref: *Missouri Republican,* St. Louis, April 14, 26, 1852; New York *Daily Times,* May 1, 1852. "Del Gardo"—possibly Delgado?; "Trupello"—possibly Trujillo?

❦ April 15.—"Jos. O. Sawyer" by contract made with Bvt. Maj. E. A. Ogden, agreed to build a barn (for $2,565) and two cottages (for $1,520 and $1,280) on the government farm near Fort Leavenworth. Sawyer was to furnish all materials except hardware and stone.

Ref: 32d Cong., 2d Sess., *Sen. Ex. Doc. No. 18* (Serial 660), p. 11. *See* annals, p. 944, for comment on "J. O. Sawyer," "James A. Sawyers," as name variations.

❦ Dɪᴇᴅ: on April 15, John M. Armstrong, influential member of the Wyandot Nation, in Ohio, while en route to Washington, D. C.

In Wyandotte (present Kansas City, Kan.) at the Wyandots' Methodist "brick church" (the building occupied by the Church, South), on June 13 the Rev. James Witten (missionary of the "northern" Methodists) preached the funeral sermon for the late John M. Armstrong.

Ref: William Walker's "Journals" (in W. E. Connelley, *The Provisional Government of Nebraska Territory* . . . (1899), pp. 346, 347, 351. *See* annals, p. 521, for earlier mention of Armstrong.

❦ Dɪᴇᴅ: on April 17, Hester (Zane) Fish, a Wyandot, wife of Paschal Fish, a Shawnee.

William Walker (who entered the item in his journal) had, on October 14, 1847, recorded: "Mr Fish and Hetty were married." Hester (Zane) Fish was a cousin of John M. Armstrong—*see* preceding entry.

Ref: William Walker's "Journals," *loc. cit.*

❧ April 19.—The U. S. mail stage, which had left Santa Fe on April 1, arrived at Independence, Mo. "Messrs. [R. L.] Allen and Williams" were passengers.

Ref: *Missouri Republican,* St. Louis, April 21, 1852 (news by telegram of April 20 from Independence).

❧ April.—"For three or four days now past California emigrants have been passing," wrote Jotham Meeker of Ottawa Baptist Mission (east of present Ottawa), on April 21. On the 26th he recorded in his diary: "7 or 800 Cattle & perhaps 50 wagons pass for California—for 5 or 6 days past great numbers have passed us. Am compelled to watch my Cattle to prevent their being driven off." On the 27th he wrote: ". . . Watch and take care of my cattle. California emigrants are passing in great numbers. Four companies encamped near us last night with 1300 Cattle,—on this evening three more companies encamp with 700 Cattle—these are exclusive of probably 5 or 600 Oxen with about 60 or 70 Wagons."

Meeker conducted funeral services the evening of May 7 for the young daughter of "Mr. Gabriel & Mrs. Smith, emigrants to California from Ohio, who is buried in our Ch. yard." He recorded in his diary on May 8: ". . . Have religious talks with emigrants to California and Oregon almost every day. But few observe the Sabbath—some 30 or 40 wagons pass to-day."

On May 15 Meeker wrote: ". . . we think to this time about 800 wagons and 10,000 cattle have gone along this road. About 30 wagons & 300 cattle pass to-day."

Ref: Jotham Meeker's "Diary," in KHi ms. division. *See* annals, p. 928, for Jotham Meeker's mention of the 1850 emigration passing Ottawa mission, and for comment on this route.

❧ April 21.—"Every boat that arrives at our wharf, is crowded with California and Oregon emigrants," the St. Joseph (Mo.) *Gazette* stated. "During the past week, several hundred have landed at this place by water and overland, and still they come. From the best estimate we can make, we are inclined to the belief, that the emigration this year will be as large, if not larger, than at any previous spring since the discovery of gold. Almost half the emigrants are bound for Oregon, the majority of them taking their families. . . ."

By April 21 some (few?) parties already had begun the trek west from St. Joseph. The Sacramento *Union,* early in July, reported the arrival, on July 3, of the "first of the overland immigration . . . in this city"—a company of 26(?) Ohioans (captained by J. Clark; with mule-drawn wagons) which had "left Ohio on the 18th of March, and St. Joseph, Mo., on the 20th April." The account further stated: "At the latter place [*i. e.,* St. Joseph] a number of trains were ready to start [on April 20], but the bulk of the emigration was concentrated at Independence and Council Bluffs."

David W. Cartwright, in his later-written *Natural History of Western Wild Animals*, devoted a chapter to "A Tramp to California in 1852," in which he recollected that his company (33 Wisconsin men, captained by John Nutter), after traveling overland to St. Joseph, started west from that point on April 17.

Regarding the Oregon emigration, the New York *Times* of October 14, quoted an Oregon newspaper of September 10 as follows: "The emigration to Oregon this year is very large, 186 wagons having passed the 'Gate' on the other side of the mountains, and with them 750 persons, of whom 160 were females and 609 males. They had 1,000 head of cattle and 400 head of horses and mules. . . . As to the number of emigrants on the route we can form no estimate. The accounts conflict—ranging from 10 to 20 thousand all told." The Oregon *Statesman* of October 23 reported: "The number of this year's immigration is set down at ten thousand, and the proportion of women and families is much larger than in any previous year." A November issue of the same paper stated: "The immigration this year will probably reach 20,000."

Ref: St. Joseph *Gazette,* April 21, 1852; New York *Daily Tribune,* August 16, November 29, December 30, 1852; David W. Cartwright, *Natural History of Western Wild Animals* . . ., Second ed. (Toledo, 1875), pp. 165-237; New York *Daily Times,* October 9, 1852.

❡ April 24—At Savannah, Mo., the *Sentinel* editor reported: "The rush to California has now commenced in earnest." He noted that from 50 to 200 wagons, drawn mostly by oxen, were passing through town daily "bound for El Dorado"; that the "larger part" had families; and that some of the trains had large numbers of loose cattle.

Ref: Savannah *Sentinel,* April 24, 1852.

❡ April 26-28.—"R. B. L." wrote from St. Joseph on the 26th: "The influx of emigrants gives our thriving city a very animated appearance. . . . The emigrants are generally men of moral character, and have so far manifested but little of that spirit of recklessness and lack of restraint, that characterized so many of them in 1850 and 1851. . . ." He went on to say:

"The principal business street of our city is crowded with men from morning till night. . . . There seems to be a very large proportion of the gentle sex among the emigrants, and to diversify the matter, a few of those latterly assigned to an extra gender, Bloomers. . . .*

"Many of the emigrants are preparing to start in a few days, others have already gone, taking with them extra wagons, with feed. . . . The spring is unusually backward—vegetation is at least fifteen days behind that of last year or the year preceding. . . ."

A telegram sent from St. Joseph (to St. Louis) on April 27 (at 11 P. M.) stated, in part: "The emigrants are detained here by cold weather and scarcity of grass." The St. Joseph *Gazette* of April 28 reported: "Hundreds of California and Oregon emigrants, arrive in our city daily. . . . The ferries at this city, are crossing large numbers every day, who are making arrangements to leave in a short time. In ten days hundreds will be on the plains, but how their stock is to subsist, is a mystery to us, as there is not yet a particle of grass on the plains. . . ."

* The *Oregonian* of October 2 commented: "Quite a number of Bloomers—just over the Plains—have made their appearance in Oregon City, and being the first specimens of the genuine Bloomer costume ever seen here, of course attracted much attention."

Ref: *Missouri Republican*, St. Louis, April 28, May 2, 1852; St. Joseph *Gazette*, April 28, 1852; New York *Daily Times*, November 9, 1852.

⟪ April 27.—At Independence, Mo., the *Missouri Republican's* correspondent wrote: "Though overrun with California and Oregon adventurers still, yet the mass of them are finding their way out upon the wide prairies, and testing the realities of a camp life. . . . The character of those who have passed here this season has been of a better caste than ordinary. . . . From our town and its immediate vicinity, many of the very best of our population have determined and are already gone."

On May 1 (the same?) writer stated: "The number [of emigrants] passing out from and through here, has exceeded all the calculations we have ever made. Our streets have been crowded day after day with vehicles of every description, and people of all classes and conditions, are seen moving along. The mass of them are now passing out, and the road from here to Little Blue river [of "Kansas"] is lined with wagons. A short distance beyond that point, the first companies were met by the mail party [which left Fort Laramie in mid-April and reached Independence April 30]. . . ."

Ref: *Missouri Republican*, St. Louis, May 3, 5, 1852.

⟪ On Wednesday, April 28, the St. Joseph (Mo.) *Gazette* announced that "Blodget & Co's" (mail) express train, under the command of "Col. Blodgett," would leave for the plains "on Thursday next," taking 30 head of horses, and "everything necessary to make the trip."

The stated object of the express was "the conveyance of letters, &c., to the States," from three Oregon-California trail stations: (1) "Archambault's Fort," at Devil's Gate, (2) the South Pass, and (3) Goose creek—200 miles west of the continental divide. The partners (later identified as George E. Blodget and R. S. Raymond) were said to have "journeyed over the route several times," and to have "excellent stock along the whole line of Road, and light wagons."

The May 5 *Gazette* carried an advertisement headed "Blodgett & Co's Overland Express for Sacramento City[!]" (signed by "Major J. F. M. Case, Genl. agent"), which announced that stations had been established at Fort Kearny, Fort Laramie, North Fork of Platte, South Pass, Salt Lake City, and head of the Humboldt; that emigrants westbound would meet "an Express Messenger between each of these stations who will receive letters and deposit them in the P. O. at St. Joseph in the shortest possible time"; also that the company would "start a Passenger Train [10 wagons; 40 fares] from St. Joseph on the 10th June, via Salt Lake City." (The *Gazette* of June 2 reported that "Blodgett & Co's. Express Train" would not leave St. Joseph till June 15, because of "the great amount of sickness on the other side of the river." Perhaps no start ever was made.)

Early in September, partners Blodget and Raymond returned to St. Joseph. (Blodget had been as far as "Devil's Gate on Sweetwater River"; and had left there July 27.) The *Gazette* of September 8 carried their notice disclaiming any connection with (or knowledge of) the *passenger train* advertised by "one Maj. J. F. M. Case [who] has represented himself as our general agent. . . ."

Ref: St. Joseph *Gazette*, April 28, May 5, June 2, September 8, 1852. In the April 28 issue "Maj. J. F. M. Case" was listed as "Secretary," (and George A. Case as "ass't") for "Blodget & Co's" (mail) express train.

❬ April 29.—At St. Joseph, Mo., waiting by the ferry landing to cross the Missouri, Mrs. Lodisa Frizzell (a California-bound emigrant) saw a party of Indians removing to "Kansas," and wrote in her diary:

". . . some 200 Indians of the Pawtawattimees & Winnewbagoes came down the street. . . . They were verry dark complected, quite black, half clothed, & some few were ornamented; they had some 30 or 40 ponies which were laden as I should judge by the variety; with every thing that they possessed. . . . They were in a hurry to cross over and crowded down to the waters edge, the ferrymen would not take but a few of them at a time for there was not room for the waggons. . . ."

Ref: Frizzell, *op. cit.*, p. 9.

❬ April 30.—"Mr. Caldwell" with the "April" U. S. mail from Salt Lake City arrived at Independence. He had left Fort Laramie on the 17th.

The mail carrier reported that "it has been remarkably dry and cool on the plains . . . no grass is to be found beyond Fort Kearny"; between Kearny and Independence "there is grass for mule teams, but not for horned cattle . . ." (as stated in the *Occidental Messenger* of May 1).

Ref: *Missouri Republican*, St. Louis, May 5, 1852; St. Joseph *Gazette*, May 19, 1852 (from *Occidental Messenger*, Independence, May 1).

❬ May-July.—Statements and statistics below describe that part of the Oregon-California-Utah emigration which went by Fort Kearny ("Neb.") in 1852, after traveling west from the Missouri (across "Kansas," or "Nebraska") by routes south of the Platte.

On April 30 the first emigrant train passed Fort Kearny. Much earlier—on March 1, during a snowstorm—three Michigan men, afoot, had arrived at the post. (One enlisted; two went on, were robbed by Cheyennes, and "Capt. Wharton sent wagons and relieved them from starvation"; one then "returned," and the other, later, continued west.) On April 1 two more men on foot, from Michigan, reached the fort. They stayed "until wagons arrived."

Up to May 16 (according to "C. W. L.") 1,400 wagons had passed Fort

Kearny. His May 19 letter stated: "The general health of the emigrants is good, although there has been some few cases of small pox. The grass is very poor, or in fact, I can hardly say it is grass at all."

According to M. Fleming, who reached Fort Kearny on May 21 (in 11 days from Old Fort Kearny), 360 wagons had encamped within 15 miles of the fort "last night"; and, "Reports say over 2,000 have already passed here." He wrote, also, that "smallpox and cholera" were said to be on the St. Joseph and Independence roads—with "thirty or more deaths"; that roads and grass were good, and teams in fine condition; but the weather was stormy and uncomfortably cold. (A man who returned to St. Joseph on May 24 stated that he had counted 60 graves between the Big Blue and the Missouri; and that the disease which was causing "considerable sickness" among the emigrants was reputed to be cholera, "having part of the symptoms.")

"G. W. H.," who reached Fort Kearny May 24, wrote, on May 25, that the register of emigrants "this morning" showed 2,870 wagons with an average of four persons to each (*i. e.*, over 15,000 souls) had passed that point. In a postscript "G. W. H." listed the statistics for the emigration "up to May 22" (given him by Capt. Henry W. Wharton) as: 2,654 wagons, 8,174 men, 1,285 women, 1,786 children (11,245 persons in all), 3,533 horses, 2,316 mules, 26,269 head of cattle, 2,501 sheep, and one hog.

"S. M. B.," who quoted the same statistics, wrote from "In Camp, near Fort Kearney," on May 24: "The country we have crossed is principally prairie. We could see the road for miles ahead, showing one continuous line of covered wagons, while every ravine was filled with tents, and every bluff covered with flocks of sheep, or droves of cattle. The bulk of the emigration is behind us. Thousands are passing along the north side of the Platte. It is believed the emigration will be equal to that of 1849. . . ."

On May 26 Mrs. Lodisa Frizzell reached Fort Kearny. She wrote: "They kept a register here, of the number of waggons which passed, there had then passed 2657, & as many waggons pass without touching here, I do not think they can keep a correct account, & I do not think they try to get the number of those that pass on the north side of the river. . . ."

Probably about May 26 Seth N. Doty passed Fort Kearny. His letter (from 100 miles west of that post) written June 1, contained commentary on the Oregon-California trail scene ("the greatest show in the world"): "The train is estimated to be 700 miles long, composed of all kinds of people from all parts of the United States, and some of the rest of mankind, with lots of horses, mules, oxen, cows, steers and some of the feathered creation, moving along about 15 or 20 miles per day; all sorts of vehicles from a coach down to a wheel barrow; ladies on horseback, dressed out in full-blown Bloomers; gents on mules, with their Kossuth hats and plumes, galloping over the prairies, making quite an equestrian troupe and a show ahead of anything Barnum ever got up. The plains are a pleasant place to travel; excellent roads . . . and were it not for the sick and the dying, that everywhere meet our eye, and the vast number of graves along the road, the journey would be a pleasant one. As near as I can ascertain by observation, there are about 80 graves to the 100 miles so far; that is, new ones. . . ."

On May 28 emigrant Alpheus N. Graham recorded in his diary: "Passed

Fort Kearney today. There are 3,280 teams ahead of us on this side of the river and about 1000 on the other. . . ." (At four persons per wagon: 13,120 souls.)

"Up to the 31st of May," wrote Lewis B. Dougherty (from Fort Kearny, on June 3) "there has passed this Post on the South side of the Platte River:— Men 13,059. Women 2,562. Children 3,482. [This total of 19,103 persons would indicate about 4½ souls per wagon.] Horses 5,482. Mules 3,563. Cattle 43,788. Sheep 2,812. Hogs 1. Wagons 4,291. Donkeys 1. The cry is 'still they come.' There has been considerable sickness amongst the emigrants. . . . I was told by a lady emigrant, that she counted 45 graves between this and St. Joseph, all of cholera. . . ."

On June 10 Andrew Goodyear (who had left Independence, Mo., May 28, on his third trip overland to California) reached Fort Kearny. His estimate of the emigration passing the post up to June 10 (as reported after he reached Sacramento): about 7,000 wagons, 30,000 people, 8,000 horses, 5,000 mules, 100,000 cattle, 8,000 sheep. The Sacramento *Union* (of August 28?) also stated: "he [Goodyear] thinks the emigration on the north side [of the Platte] was fully as great. At this time [late May and early June] and point [Fort Kearny] much sickness existed among the emigration; he met some 400 wagons returning on account of sickness; one company of 72 men, with 9 wagons, had lost 24 out of their company, and on that day [June 19, apparently] had burried five, and had scarcely well men enough left to drive their teams. On the 19th of June he arrived at Fort Laramie . . . [where the troops were in good health—as was also true at Fort Kearny]. . . ."

Josiah Collins, who left Fort Kearny on May 29 and arrived at Independence, Mo., June 11, combined post statistics with those he compiled on his journey eastward (figures covering much of the military road, and St. Joseph route travel, as well as all the Independence trail traffic), to give these estimates: 5,325 wagons, 16,362 men, 3,242 women, 4,266 children (for a total of 23,870 persons), 6,538 horses, 4,606 mules, 59,392 cattle, 10,523 sheep, 1 hog, from 100 to 150 turkeys, 4 ducks, and 2 guinea fowls. The Independence man who interviewed Collins also wrote: ". . . it is known that very many more were on the routes North, those leading out from Council Bluffs [north of the Platte] and old Fort Kearney [south of the river]. . . ." Sickness among the emigrants was mentioned, too; and it was indicated Collins had counted some 70 graves while coming in (but only four were seen on the Independence route).

Final "statistics," from three sources, of the westbound emigrant traffic passing Fort Kearny in 1852, are given in the tabulation below. (1) "H." (a Mr. Harvey, connected with the St. Louis *Intelligencer*) stopped at Fort Kearny, eastbound, in November, 1852; and Capt. Henry W. Wharton gave him the post emigrant record book (containing records up to July 4,) (2) Corp. F. Longfield, of Company I, Sixth infantry, wrote a letter from "Fort Kearney, Nebraska Territory, Friday, Aug. 6, 1852," which included these observations: ". . . The great emigration of the present season is past and gone. The mighty throng, that crowded the roads from east to west is no longer seen; the murmuring of voices, the rattling of chains and wagons, the lowing of thirsty oxen, that daily passed our garrison, are heard no more." He listed figures which he stated represented the number of emigrants, etc. "which passed this post from the 1st May to the present time"; and noted that the emigration had passed "all in May, and beginning of June," except for a few Mormon trains. (*See* p. 1109.) (3) Thomas A. Stoddart left Fort Kearny on July 13 and reached Weston, Mo., on July 23. Presumably he traveled the Fort Kearny-Fort Leavenworth military road. It was said he had counted 600(?) fresh graves between Fort Kearny and Weston. The source of his emigration "statistics" is nowhere given.

Number of:	(1) Fort Kearny record*	(2) Longfield†	(3) Stoddart	Amount of variation between Fort Kearny record and Stoddart
Wagons	7,516	6,479[?]	8,166	650
Men	18,656	19,000	25,865	7,209
Women	4,370	4,400	7,021	2,651
Children	5,600	5,555	8,270	2,670
Total persons	[28,626]	28,955	[41,156]	[12,530]
Horses	7,783	7,800	8,483	700
Mules	3,983	5,000	5,853	1,870
Cattle	74,780	74,538	90,340	15,560
Sheep	23,980	23,980	24,230	250

* The post record noted, also, that 15 persons were traveling with hand carts, 111 as "packers," and 29 on foot.

† Longfield commented that the "emigration on the other side of the Platte is computed to be equal to the above." Was "6,479" wagons a printer's error, and intended to read 7,479?

Ref: St. Joseph (Mo.) *Gazette*, May 26, June 9, 1852; *Weekly Intelligencer*, St. Louis, July 6 and December 17, 1852 (for early emigration, and cholera deaths, items); St. Joseph *Gazette*, June 9, 1852 (for "C. W. L."); *Weekly Intelligencer*, July 6, 1852 (for Fleming; and for "G. W. H."); *Missouri Republican*, St. Louis, July 1, 1852 (for "S. M. B."); Frizzell, *op. cit.*; New York *Daily Tribune*, July 8, 1852, or *KHQ*, v. 11, p. 400 (for "Seth N. Doty" letter of June 1); *Kansas Magazine*, Manhattan, 1966, p. 54 (for A. N. Graham); *The Weekly Tribune*, Liberty, Mo., June 25, 1852 (for "Lieut. B. Daugherty"—i. e., Lewis B. Dougherty evidently); New York *Daily Tribune*, October 5, 1852 (for Goodyear); *Missouri Republican*, June 18, 1852 (for Collins); *Weekly Intelligencer*, December 17, 1852 (for "H."—Harvey); *Missouri Republican*, July 28, 1852 (for Stoddart); New York *Daily Tribune*, September 4, 1852 (for Longfield). The *Tribune* of October 14, 1852, published a letter dated "Larimee Peak, Rocky Mountains, June 29, 1852," by "Lem. Newell Doty." Presumably the writer was the same Doty in the annals item above—that is, Seth(?) N. Doty. "S. M. B." was S. M. Bowman. (See *Missouri Republican*, August 1, November 2, December 31, 1853).

¶ [May?].—Starting from Independence, Mo. (if the following can be credited as fact), was an emigrant bound for California with a large flock of turkeys.

The August mail from California contained a letter stating: "A man from Illinois has just arrived from Independence having driven the entire distance two thousand turkeys, all hale and heavy. They cost him about fifty cents apiece in the States. . . . He has been offered eight dollars apiece."

Ref: St. Joseph (Mo.) *Gazette*, October 13, 1852.

❧ May 1.—Temporarily camped across the Missouri river (in "Kansas") from St. Joseph, emigrant Mrs. Lodisa Frizzell observed: "Teams crossing the river all the while, but there is not half ferry boats enough here. . . . There is every description of teams & waggons; from a hand cart & wheelbarrow, to a fine six horse carriage & buggie; but more than two thirds are oxen & waggons similar to our own. . . . Most of the horses, mules & cattle, are the best the states afford. . . ."

At Savannah, Mo., the *Sentinel* editor reported (on May 1): "The rush continues as great as ever. Our streets are thronged with teams and vehicles of every description—bound principally for California, though sometimes the wagons are chalked 'for Oregon.' Many of our townsmen have left during the past week [he listed such names as Petree, Richasan, Rohrer, Holt, McCord, Clark, and Chambers]. . . ." (The *Sentinel* of May 15 gave the names of 105 heads of families who, taking their families, averaging eight to each, "have left this [Andrew] county for California and Oregon this spring.")

Ref: Frizzell, *op. cit.*, p. 10; Savannah *Sentinel*, May 1, 15, 1852.

❧ May.—Duncan's ferry, four miles above St. Joseph, Mo., was a much-used Missouri river crossing point, as it had been since 1849, or earlier. (*See* pp. 829, 863, and 875.)

Emigrant Jay Green "crost the Missouri river at Duncans ferry," on May 1. Emigrant William C. Lobenstine arrived there May 3. "The ferry being badly attended to by its owners travelers were obliged to stop here rather longer than if things were put in better condition with better men there to take care of it," he wrote. "We got across the river, however, after a 36-hour detention. . . ."

Ref: Jay Green's *Diary* . . . (Stockton, Calif., 1955), p. 7; Lobenstine, *op. cit.*, pp. 15, 16.

❧ May.—Most of the steamboats plying the middle Missouri during the month are listed in the following chronology:

On May 3 the *Alton* started downriver from Weston. (The *Kansas*—bound for Council Bluffs—was then "in port.") She met the *Clara* at Big Blue. The *El Paso* left St. Joseph on May 3. On her downward trip she met the

Kansas at Iatan; left the *Clipper No. 2* at Weston; passed the *Banner State* at Kansas, Mo.

The *Elvira* and *St. Paul* started upriver from St. Joseph on May 5. Another Council Bluffs-bound boat—the *Brooklyn* (*see* p. 1074)—was reported "hard aground below Savannah." The *Timour No. 2*, started down from St. Joseph on May 5. She met the *Saranak* (bound for Council Bluffs) and *Honduras* at Weston; on the 9th, met the *St. Ange* at Liberty and the *Delaware* (en route to Fort Leavenworth with troops, and then to Council Bluffs) below. (On the *St. Ange* this trip, one passenger died; and on the *Honduras,* reportedly, there were seven cholera deaths. Emigrant Seth N. Doty, on June 1, from 100 miles west of Fort Kearny, wrote: "The cholera is the general topic among the emigrants, spreading consternation and alarm from one train to another. . . . The cholera originated . . . among the emigrants, on board the steamboat Honduras, which lost some seven passengers on her [May] trip up to St. Joseph and some 20 or 30 died a few days after leaving here [*i. e.,* her]." The *Saranak* reached Council Bluffs—from St. Louis—in the record time of six days and 20 hours!)

On May 10 the *Honduras* started down from St. Joseph; met the *St. Ange* below Columbus (Landing); passed the *Delaware* at Weston; met the *Martha Jewett* at Kansas. (The *Delaware*—leaving Weston on the 10th—met the *Sonora* at Fort Leavenworth, and the *Martha Jewett* at Parkville.) On May 11 the *St. Ange* left St. Joseph for St. Louis.

From Council Bluffs, four steamboats—the *Kansas* and *Elvira* (which had left there on May 11), the *Saranak* and the *St. Paul*—all returned to St. Louis before the 17th. The *Saranak* had met the *El Paso* (bound for Council Bluffs) at "Eight Mile Bar," the *Isabel*, above Parkville, the *Banner State*, above Independence, the *Robert Campbell* and the *Clara* above Miami. (Fur trader Alexander Harvey, accompanied by his daughters, five and seven, came down on the *Kansas;* Alexander Culbertson, and other American Fur Company men were aboard the *St. Paul*.) The *Brooklyn* (*see above*) was reported "high and dry" on a sand bar some three miles above St. Joseph.

On May 16 the *Banner State* started down from St. Joseph; met the *Alton* (bound for St. Joseph, with "a host of emigrants on board for California") above Columbus Landing; on the 17th met the *Robert Campbell* (en route to Council Bluffs) at Weston, and the *Clara* at Fort Leavenworth. (As reported at St. Louis, a party of Mormon emigrants on the *Robert Campbell* had with them machinery for the manufacture of salt [sugar!].

Emigrants from Salem, Iowa (including the Caleb Richey family), were among travelers crossing the Missouri at Council Bluffs, on May 21. Caleb Richey later wrote: "I paid $20 for crossing the Missouri. We crossed on the Robt. Campbell. There are two steamboats ferrying, the other the Elpaco. They came up with provisions and found they could get almost any price for ferrying, as the ferryboats could not cross near all the emigration."

On May 21 the *Yuba* left St. Joseph, downbound, and reached St. Louis on the 25th. The *Timour No. 2* started down from St. Joseph at noon on May 22. She met the *Honduras* at Kansas, and the *Delaware* at Liberty (Landing). Both were bound for Kanesville, Ia.

The *Robert Campbell* (*see above*) returned to St. Louis from Council Bluffs on May 26. On the 27th the *St. Paul* started down from St. Joseph. She met the *Banner State* at Weston.

On May 28 the *Banner State* left St. Joseph; met the *Kansas* (en route to Council Bluffs) at Parkville; brought down fur returns (250 packs of buffalo robes, and some deer skins) for R. & W. Campbell, St. Louis.

The *Delaware* and the *Honduras* started down from Council Bluffs on May 28. The latter met the *Kansas* (noted above) at St. Joseph on the 30th, the *Alton* at Weston, and the *Clara* at Lower Liberty (Landing).

On May 31 the *Isabel* left Weston, for St. Louis; met the *Clara* at Wayne City.

Ref: *Missouri Republican*, St. Louis, May, and early June, 1852, issues; *Transactions of the Fortieth Annual Reunion of the Oregon Pioneer Association*, 1912, pp. 589, 590 (for Caleb Richey); New York *Daily Tribune*, July 8, 1852, or *KHQ*, v. 11, p. 400 (for Doty). As reported at St. Louis, the *Yuba's* clerk (on May 25) stated that the *El Paso* was engaged in ferrying passengers across the Missouri at St. Joseph (but instead was at Council Bluffs!) when the *Yuba* left there on May 21. The Richey statement clarifies this. Also, the St. Joseph *Gazette* of June 9, 1852, stated: "The El Paso on her recent trip up the Missouri was 4 or 5 days engaged in ferrying across the river at the Bluffs emigrants to California and Oregon. In the period named, the boat transported over 2,000 people, 500 wagons, 4,215 head of stock and received over $5,000. The emigrants were exclusively from the States of Iowa, Wisconsin, Illinois, and Indiana."

❡ May 5.—"The steam ferry boat, Eagle, which was advertised for the ferry at Council Bluffs, will be run at the Ferry at St. Joseph, during the emigration," stated the notice (dated May 5) of R. Middleton and P. L. McLaughlin, which appeared in the St. Joseph *Gazette*.

The *Gazette* of May 5 contained this comment: "California and Oregon emigrants are still coming in. Our streets are crowded, and every house in the town filled. The Steam ferry is crossing hundreds daily, and the crowd does not appear to get less. . . ."

Emigrant Theodore E. Potter, in his *Autobiography*, wrote: "Our train of nine wagons took its place in line on the night of the fifth of May [at St. Joseph], at least half a mile from the ferry, to await its turn and it was not until the afternoon of the next day that we were landed on the west bank of the raging Missouri." But he evidently was mistaken in recollecting that "The number of teams waiting to be ferried across the Missouri was so great that four steam ferry boats were kept busy transporting them." Emigrant John H. Clark, on May 6, at St. Joseph, wrote: "The Missouri river has to be crossed to-day. There are several boats and among them one steamboat to ferry over the crowd that is waiting their regular turn. . . ." Mrs. Lodisa Frizzell, on May 8, "walked up a hill which overlooks the town [of St. Joseph] & river, never saw such a bustle, there was a large drove of cattle filling the streets for some distance, which they were crossing . . . as fast as possible, with their little boats, where there should have been at least 2 good large steam ferry boats. . . ."

Ref: St. Joseph *Gazette*, May 5, 1852; Theodore E. Potter, *The Autobiography of . . .* (Concord, N. H., c1912), p. 29; *KHQ*, v. 11, p. 232; Frizzell, *op. cit.*, p. 11.

❡ May 5.—Emigrant "S. M. B." and companions, crossed the Kansas river at "Smith's Ferry, six miles below Uniontown." (This is the earliest known mention of Sidney Smith's ferry.)

"Mr. Sidney W. Smith moved to Uniontown, in 1848," says W. W. Cone's 1877-published *Historical Sketch of Shawnee County, Kansas.* "In March, 1852, he moved into . . . [Mission] township . . . [locating on the SE part of Sec. 30, T. 11, R. 15 E., just northwest of the Pottawatomie Baptist Mission farm]. He established a ferry across the Kansas, the same year, which he run for 8 years. The ferry crossing, on the S. bank was on the SW of 30-11-15. . . ."

Ref: *Missouri Republican,* St. Louis, July 1, 1852; Cone, *op. cit.,* p. 10 (which also says Smith was born in Orange county, Vt.; removed to Council Bluffs, Iowa, in 1838; thence to present Shawnee county in 1848; and that in 1877 he was still living there). "Smith's Ferry" is shown on Lt. Israel C. Woodruff's "Chart . . .," 1852 (reproduced on p. 1022). See *KHQ,* v. 3, pp. 15, 16, for other "Smith's ferry" information.

❡ May 6.—"This day the Oregon Company, consisting of Mr [William] McCowen [McCown], and family, Mr [Ira] Hunter family, Mr [William] Lynville and family, with various others, names unknown, set out on their long and lonesome journey. . . ."—William Walker's diary entry.

Lynville and Hunter (not Indians) had been in the Wyandot Indians' '49er company—*see* p. 867—and were Kaw's mouth area residents. William McCown had been blacksmith for the Wyandots in the last half of 1851, and in 1852, up to April.

Ref: William Walker's "Journals," *loc. cit.;* 33d Cong., 1st Sess., H. Ex. Doc. No. 37 (Serial 718), p. 422; Office of Indian Affairs (OIA), Letters Received from Kansas Agency (National Archives Microcopy 234, Roll 364) for Agent Moseley's employment of William McCown (native of Virginia).

❡ MARRIED: Thomas Sears Huffaker (teacher at Kansa Methodist Mission), and Eliza A. Baker (daughter of [Joshua W.?] Baker, one-time government blacksmith for the "Mississippi" Sac & Fox Indians), on May 6, at Council Grove, by the Rev. E. G. Nicholson (a "northern" Methodist missionary en route East from New Mexico —*see* p. 1089).

Ref: *KHC,* v. 9, pp. 202, 231, 234. Missionary Nicholson had gone out to Santa Fe in October, 1850—*see* annals, p. 970.

❡ May 7.—The scene on the uplands some six miles west of St. Joseph—in present Doniphan county—was described by emigrant Theodore E. Potter (later, in his *Autobiography*) as follows:

"When we reached the prairie we found that all the emigrants who had crossed the [Missouri] river during the five previous days had gone into camp waiting for the rain to cease. . . . It was a grand sight to look over the prairie as far as the eye could discern and see the new white-covered wagons and tents clustered here and there and the great number of horses and cattle, scattered in every direction, trying to get a bite of the short spring grass that had just started to grow. It was estimated at the time that at least 10,000 emigrants were camped within a distance of ten miles of this point. . . ."

Potter went on to say: "The morning of the eighth of May brought us good weather and the entire body of people and animals formed a great procession and started on the way. Previous to this time there had been but one trail over which the wagons could pass. But 10,000 people starting from the same locality on the same day made it necessary for more trails, which were very easily made on the open prairie, excepting when we came to a stream that had to be bridged. During the first day's march there were at least 12 roads for 12 teams abreast. Our roadometer . . . registered 15 miles for this first day's drive. . . ."

Ref: Potter, *op. cit.*, pp. 29, 30.

❧ May 8(?)—"Our friend and townsman, Mr. Henry Mayer, will arrive in a day or two from Chihuahua," the *Occidental Messenger*, Independence, Mo., reported. "Mr. Carethers [Carothers] accompanies him, they bring five wagons and a large amount of silver."

Ref: *The Weekly Tribune*, Liberty, Mo., May 14, 1852 (from *Occidental Messenger*— of May 8?). The news had been received on Wednesday (May 5?) by a man arriving in advance of Aubry's party, with which he had traveled from Santa Fe.

❧ About May 8 Santa Fe trader and route explorer Francis X. Aubry reached the Missouri border with his second wagon train of the year. (*See* February 5 entry.) "As a traveller . . . Aubry has not an equal in the Union," said the *Occidental Messenger*, Independence, Mo. Accompanying him (as this paper reported) were William S. Allen (recently New Mexico territory's secretary), "Major Pillan," "Senecal," and the Rev. E. G. Nicholson with his family.

Aubry's journey was notable for the fact that he and his party traversed a new route north of the Arkansas. One of his companions —Allen?—sent some "notes" on this exploration to the *Missouri Republican.* They are quoted, in part, below:

"Leaving Santa Fe, on the 11th ult [April], we pursued the usual route as far as Cold Spring [*see* annals, p. 999]. Two miles northeastwardly of that point we turned off, and shaping our course north by east, reached the Cimarone river at a distance of 7 miles from the Spring. Crossing it, we proceeded on a general course N. 25 E. to Bear Creek, touching it at a bend 25 miles from the crossing of the Cimarone. . . . [After following down Bear creek for some 20 miles] we crossed over to the Arkansas, in the direction N. 20 E., 15 miles distant, striking that river 12 miles above Chouteau's Island and 58 above the point where the Cimarone road crosses the Arkansas. . . . [This section of Aubry's route was said to eliminate all but about seven of the 60 miles of "heavy" travel—the "Jornada"—on the old Cimarron route.]

"Mr. Aubry being satisfied that a still further saving of distance could be made on this side of the Arkansas, determined to test the point, on his present journey, by leaving that river some miles below his crossing. The point chosen was five miles below Elk Island, and twenty-five miles above the Cimarone crossing.

"From this point we set out on the 25th ulto., our general course being N. 25 E. . . ." [After about 14 miles of travel they came to "a range of sand hillock, interspersed with trees, scattered thinly among them, but not a particle of water." The trees were large, and old. Next day they came to "Buffalo Creek," and met there a small party of Cheyennes; then came to another creek, and camped the night of the 27th on it. Three days later, after changing course several times (*e. g.*, on the 29th, 10 miles heading N. 80 E.; and then 10 miles S. 80 E.), they found themselves, not near the mouth of Pawnee Fork, as anticipated, but "at Big Bend of the Arkansas" some 36 miles east of the Pawnee Fork crossing; and learned the stream they had followed was Walnut creek. Pawnee Fork, the writer stated, had always been considered larger; now they had discovered that Walnut creek was "the more considerable of the two in respect to length and probably in the amount of timber on its banks."]

A table accompanying the Allen (?) notes gave these mileages for the regularly traveled "Arkansas Route":

	Miles
From Aubry's lower camp on Arkansas, to Cimarone crossing of Arkansas	25
From Cimarone crossing, to Fort Atkinson	25
From Fort Atkinson, to Jackson's Island [Jackson Grove—*see* annals, p. 619]	15
From Jackson's Island, to Coon Creek	47
From Coon Creek, to Pawnee Fork crossing	11
From Pawnee Fork crossing, to Big Bend Arkansas	35
Total miles	158
Saved by [taking] "Dry Route"	5
Total miles, by shortest Arkansas Route	153

By comparison, Aubry's party, on the "Walnut Creek Route," had traveled 20 miles on April 25, 16 miles on April 26, 19 miles on April 27, 18 miles on April 28, 20 miles on April 29, and eight miles on April 30, for a total of 101 miles. So that the estimated saving, on Aubry's new trail, was 52 miles!

Aubry (so the writer stated) believed these savings could be made on the Santa Fe trail: between Cold Spring and the Arkansas, 20 miles; between the Arkansas and Walnut creek, 15 miles; down Walnut creek, 44 miles; between Walnut creek and Cottonwood creek, 20 miles—total 99 miles. Comment was made that the road could be made much safer if the government would establish military posts at Walnut creek, and near Cold Spring.

See, also, August 25 annals entry.

Ref: *The Weekly Tribune*, Liberty, Mo., May 14, 1852 (from *Occidental Messenger*, Independence—of May 8?); *Missouri Republican*, St. Louis, May 18, 1852, and *see* issue of February 1, 1852, also.

❦ May.—From the Great Nemaha Agency (not far from present Highland, Doniphan county), James F. Forman (farmer for the Missouri Sacs & Foxes) wrote, on May 15: "There have been 7 deaths of Cholera, 1 of Small Pox, and 1 of whooping cough within two miles of this place, to my certain knowledge. All Emigrants." (He particularly noted the death, from cholera, on "Saturday morning"—the 15th, of Adeline Fowler, of St. Joseph, who had come to his home seeking employment.)

Emigrant Theodore E. Potter, in his *Autobiography,* wrote of an emigrant family (seven persons; from Virginia?) encamped about two miles west of the "Pawnee [*i. e.,* Iowa, Sac & Fox] Mission," in the fore part of May, all of whom died of cholera except the "oldest girl" (who, on May 10, had come to the Mission and "reported that her father, mother and two brothers were dead and that the two others were very sick"). Captain Joseph Smith and others of Potter's company (then passing by) volunteered to help. "We buried the six persons in one grave," Potter stated.

The St. Joseph *Gazette* of May 19 reported: "Several persons have died near the [Iowa, Sac & Fox] Mission, about 30 miles from this place, and still further on the road we have heard of several deaths." The *Gazette* also stated: "From the best information we can obtain, we suppose 35 or 40 immigrants have died in and near the city," some of them in camps across the river in "Kansas."

From May 10 to May 17, between St. Joseph and the Big Blue crossing (at present Marysville), emigrant Moses F. Laird counted 29 graves. Mrs. Lodisa Frizzell, who traversed the same section of trail between May 11 and May 18, wrote: ". . . we have not passed less than 100 fresh graves from St. Joseph to the Blue river. . . ."

Ref: St. Joseph *Gazette,* May 19, 1852; Potter, *op. cit.,* p. 31; Moses F. Laird's "Journal," in Coe Collection, Yale University Library (used by permission); Frizzell, *op. cit.,* p. 16.

℃ May 10.—Around 300 recruits ("intended for the Third infantry and the Third artillery in New Mexico," the *Missouri Republican* stated), under command of Bvt. Maj. Enoch Steen, First dragoons, arrived at Fort Leavenworth aboard the *Delaware.* (*See* next entry.)

Ref: *The Frontier Guardian and Iowa Sentinel,* Kanesville, Iowa, June 4, 1852 (from *Missouri Republican,* St. Louis); *Missouri Republican,* May, 1852, issues (for the *Delaware* on the Missouri in May). The *Missouri Republican* said there were 300 recruits. In 32d Cong., 2d Sess., *Sen. Ex. Doc. No. 18* (Serial 660), p. 10, the item on the May 5 contract (Maj. D. H. Vinton with W. W. Baker) to transport troops on the *Delaware,* from Jefferson Barracks to Fort Leavenworth, gives the number as eight officers and 318 men. On p. 21, in *ibid.,* is an identical item, except that the number of men is given as 380, instead of 318.

℃ May 12.—Bvt. Maj. Enoch Steen, First dragoons, and a command of recruits (183 men, by one report), set out from Fort Leavenworth for New Mexico, by way of the road running southwesterly to the Kansas river (in the present Topeka area) and on to a junction with the Santa Fe trail east of Council Grove. (A St. Louis newspaper said the recruits were "intended for the Third infantry and the Third artillery," but there may have been dragoon replacements, also.)

Other officers starting on this journey were Bvt. Lt. Col. Joseph H. Eaton, 2d Lt. Martin P. Parks, 2d Lt. William D. Whipple and (2d Lt.) Alexander E. Steen (all of the Third infantry), Bvt. 2d Lt.

Kenner Garrard, First dragoons, Asst. Surg. Eugene H. Abadie, and Asst. Surgeon Elisha P. Langworthy; and a contract surgeon, Dr. Thomas C. Henry. (Lieutenant Parks died on June 5; Steen—whose commission as a second lieutenant dated from June 30, 1852—accompanied his father's command to Fort Atkinson, then returned to Missouri.)

A rumor soon reached St. Louis that Steen's command "had suffered some loss previous to reaching Grasshopper Creek [now Delaware river]." At Fort Leavenworth, on May 17, a correspondent wrote: "From a report recvd from Major Steen last night, I learn that his march was arrested by the prevalence of cholera in his command. There had been 9 fatal cases, and yest. the surgeon reported 47 men under treatment for that disease."

Four long letters describing the march of Steen and troops, written from "Navajo Country, N. M.," in August, September, and November, 1852, by one of the above officers (almost certainly 2d Lt. William D. Whipple), were published in the New York *Tribune* in 1852 and 1853, without the writer's name. (In several other annals entries there are quotes from Whipple's? letters.)

It was May 29 when the command crossed Cottonwood creek (50 miles west of Council Grove); and June 3 when camp was made on Big Cow creek. On the night of June 7 Steen and troops were at Pawnee Fork.

"Between Pawnee Fork and Fort Atkinson [Whipple? wrote] there are, for about three-fourths of the distance, two routes—one known as the *river route,* the other as the *dry route.* . . . The fork of the road is in a ravine, three and a half miles beyond Pawnee Fork crossing. . . . At ten miles from Fort Atkinson the dry route strikes into the valley of the [Arkansas] river. By our computation, this route, which is near fifty miles long, saves in distance about ten or eleven miles—but the river route is certainly preferable, as it affords good grazing and an abundance of water. The Santa Fe mail riders, it is understood, always take this *dry route.*" Steen and troops, traveling it, found both water and grass in short supply; also "the whole prairie was literally alive with swarms of grasshoppers."

On June 10 the military command reached Fort Atkinson, "all in good health." But 20 (cholera) deaths had occurred on the journey. "This among 183 men is a heavy mortality," the *Missouri Republican* commented.

Leaving Fort Atkinson on June 13, Steen and troops headed up the Arkansas, *to take Francis X. Aubry's new route.* Fifteen miles above Chouteau's Island, and about 68 miles from the fort, they embarked on the "eighty-odd miles" of the new route. Whipple(?) later wrote: "Our only annoyance was in finding watering places, described by him [Aubry], completely dry and destitute of water, by which for twenty-four hours we suffered greatly. On the whole, however, we were satisfied that the new route . . . is greatly to be preferred to the eastern portion of the Cimmarron route."

Ref: *Missouri Republican,* St. Louis, May 4(?), 22, 27, June 5, 25, 1852; 32d Cong., 2d Sess., *Sen. Ex. Doc. No. 18* (Serial 660), pp. 10, 21, 27; New York *Daily Tribune,* June 4, 12, and for Whipple's(?) letters, the issues of November 18, December 25, 1852, and February 4, March 5, 1853; *Frontier Guardian and Iowa Sentinel,* Kanesville, Iowa, June 4, 1852 (from *Missouri Republican*).

℃ May 13.—"Heard yesterday that there were cases of Cholera in

Westport, and one death," William Walker (Wyandot) wrote in his journal. On May 14 he recorded: "The Cholera is in our land—several deaths near and in Westport. It is awfully destructive among the Mormon emigrants. . . ."

At Independence, Mo., on May 10, a correspondent reported that there were three cases "of a disease resembling cholera" in the family of an emigrant from Illinois, camped near town. The writer did not think the disease would spread.

Ref: William Walker's "Journals," *loc. cit.*

❚ DIED: on May 13, John Jackson, "chief counsellor" of the united Seneca & Shawnee Indians, of cholera, at Kansas (City), Mo. Wrote Agent W. J. J. Morrow: "He was an ornament to the Indian race."

Morrow's 1852 report disclosed that the Seneca & Shawnee band (emigrants to northeastern "Oklahoma" in 1832—*see* p. 224) had numbered 320 (68 men, 94 women, 158 children) at the last annuity payment.

Ref: William Walker's "Journals," May 14, 1852, entry (*loc. cit.*); Comm'r of Indian Affairs, *Report,* 1852 (Morrow's report, therein).

❚ May.—Some items on eastbound Santa Fe trail traffic, garnered from St. Louis newspaper items reporting Missouri river steamboat arrivals, are noted below:

On May 13 the *St. Ange* reached St. Louis. She had brought down from Kansas (City), Mo., 10 boxes containing some $20,000 in Mexican dollars (consigned to Messrs. Glasgow & Bro.), and two boxes containing about $4,000, belonging to "Mr. [William S.] Allen, a Santa Fe trader [*i. e.*, he had been New Mexico territory's secretary] on board." This money had been transported to Missouri by Francis X. Aubry "the celebrated Santa Fe courier." Allen had traveled in his party—*see* a preceding entry. Carried aboard the *St. Ange* from Kansas to Boonville, Mo., were the remains of two Santa Fe traders who had met violent deaths in New Mexico in 1851—Robert F. Brent (murdered by Apaches), and William C. Skinner (killed by one of the Armijo family).

The *Sonora* (arriving at St. Louis on May 15?) brought down about $125,000 in specie, part of which (the printed figure "$3,000" doubtless an error) was sent in by H. Mayer and J. Carothers (Chihuahua traders) for the purpose of buying goods.

On May 16(?) the *Kansas* reached St. Louis. She had aboard some $30,000 in gold consigned to various individuals of the city, and $6,000 ("$5 [$5,000?] in silver") consigned to Messrs. B. R. Pegram & Co.

The *Clara*, arriving at St. Louis May 21, brought about $10,000 in specie consigned to Messrs. Page & Bacon; and the "Messrs. Bean Santa Fe traders, who came down on her" carried about $50,000 in Mexican silver. "They come to buy goods," the *Republican* stated.

On the *Yuba* (reaching St. Louis May 25) was Father Renigno, a Mexican Catholic priest ("direct from Mexico City"), on his way to Rome; and having with him a "little Mexican girl about six" whom he was taking there to be educated.

The *Timour No. 2*, arriving at St. Louis May 26, had aboard about 80 cabin passengers, Among them were 10 Mexican traders (unacquainted with the English language) who had left Santa Fe on May 3, and had boarded the steamboat (about the 23d?) at Kansas, Mo. The *Republican* reported: "They bring $180,000 in Mexican silver and gold for purchase of goods and will remain here for some time for the purpose. . . . [Their names] so far as we could ascertain them: Salassaro, Otero, Perraf[?], Narcisso, Vallencia. . . ."

Ref: *Missouri Republican*, St. Louis, May 15-17, 22, 26, 27, 1852; *Missouri Statesman*, Columbia, May 21, 1852 (from St. Louis *Intelligencer* of May 15).

❦ In mid-May this was the scene at Papin's ferry crossing of Kansas river (present Topeka) as described (in an August 28 letter) by an army officer (2d Lt. William D. Whipple?) of Major Steen's Santa Fe-bound command:

"The [Kansas] river is crossed by the main traveled route from Fort Leavenworth to the Council Grove and by the Emigrant road from Independence to Oregon, &c., at the same point. Here we met hundreds of emigrants for California and Oregon, whose trains, and herds of cattle and sheep, lined the banks on either side. . . . I was surprised to find at the Kansas river Ferry a young Canadian Frenchman [one of the Papin brothers?], apparently proprietor of the ferry, who, with note-book in hand, was all day long busily occupied in taking down the number of wagons, horses, mules, sheep, &c., crossed over in his boats. Between the emigrant trains [crossing to the north side] and those belonging to our command [ferrying to the south bank] you may be sure he had a task to attend to. Beyond the Kansas some of our party met a drover who stated that he was driving ten thousand head of cattle before him to California. Whether he was able to drive such a number in one drove or only divided into several droves I cannot say. Such is the statement given to me, and it illustrates, better than anything else could, the amount of travel and trade in the direction of the Pacific shore the past season."

Ref: New York *Daily Tribune*, November 18, 1852. Though no name is given with the printed letter of August 28, 1852, from New Mexico, the evidence is that the writer was Whipple.

❦ May 19.—"Our streets which have been crowded with emigrants for several weeks, look quite bare at this time," the St. Joseph *Gazette* commented. "The number of emigrants that will cross the plains this spring, will greatly exceed that of 1850; while the amount of stock is six times as large."

Ref: St. Joseph *Gazette*, May 19, 1852.

❡ May 20.—2d Lt. Henry Heth, Sixth infantry, set out from Fort Atkinson (west of present Dodge City) "In charge of Prisoners ordered to Fort Leavenworth for trial."

At St. Louis, in a letter of June 14, D. D. Mitchell (Indian affairs superintendent) stated: "At my request, Genl Clark [Bvt. Brig. Gen. Newman S. Clarke, Sixth military department head] . . . has ordered Lt. Heath [Heth] to Washington for the purpose of explaining the condition of Indian Affairs on the Arkansas; and to urge upon the proper Dept the adoption of such measures as will be best calculated to preserve friendly relations. . . ."

For Heth's return to Fort Atkinson, see p. 1113.

Ref: Fort Atkinson post returns (microfilm from National Archives); SIA, St. Louis, "Records," v. 9, typed copy, p. 633.

❡ May 20.—Thomas C. Gordon got the contract (made with Capt. William T. Sherman, of the Army's Commissionary of subsistence office, St. Louis) to provide fresh beef for Fort Union, N. M.; delivery to be made by September 1.

In March the St. Joseph *Gazette* (and other papers) had carried Captain Sherman's advertisement inviting bids (until May 1, at St. Louis) for delivery at Fort Union (on, or before September 1) of 1,340 head of "Beef Cattle, on the hoof, composed of nearly equal proportions of steers and heifers, each being not less than three hundred and twenty-five pounds in weight, and not over four years old." The "ad" stated: "Fort Union is on the main road to New Mexico, 718 miles from Fort Leavenworth, and 167 miles this side of Santa Fe."

Ref: St. Joseph (Mo.) *Gazette*, March 24, 1852 (and later issues); 32d Cong., 2d Sess., Sen. Ex. Doc. No. 18 (Serial 660), p. 24. See annals, p. 669, for Thomas C. Gordon as Fort Leavenworth beef contractor, 1847.

❡ May.—Several thousand sheep were "on the plains," according to a man who came in to St. Joseph, Mo., from the Oregon-California trail on May 24.

At Savannah, Mo. (north of St. Joseph), the *Sentinel* of May 22 reported that a drove of 4,000 sheep "from Platte and Buchanan counties," en route to California, had passed through town "the other day." The issue of May 29 stated that 2,600 sheep "bound for California" had passed through Savannah on May 23, and a drove of 11,000, "principally from Platte county," had crossed town on the 28th.

Early in August, eastbound G. E. Blodget met James Moore, of Platte county, Mo., "about 5 miles this side of Fort Laramie, driving about 10,000 head of sheep, which, from bad water and continued travel, were dying at the rate of 40 to 45 daily. He aimed to winter at Salt Lake and not leave in the spring till after taking their fleece, which product he supposed would pay the expense and loss." (Moore's was the last company Blodget met on his way in.) In mid-July, the "July" mail carrier, coming from Fort Laramie, had met "Capt. Harper's drove of sheep for California," at Ash Hollow.

The San Francisco *Placer Times* of November 16 reported: "Mr. Newton Peters, Cooper, Co., Mo., recently made a handsome speculation. He started from home with 2500 head of sheep, driving them over the Plains and through the Mormon country to California. At Salt Lake he sheared them and sold the wool for $2500, and on reaching California with 2000 of them in good condition, was offered $18 per head, but refused, being sure of higher prices."

A November(?) issue of the Stockton (Calif.) *Journal* noted the arrival of "Messrs. Patterson & Co." in San Joaquin county with 1,600 head of sheep, "which they offer for sale at from $13 to $17 per head. They also brought 300 head of good American work oxen, together with 17 large wagons. They offer the wagons at $500 a piece. They brought freight to Salt Lake City at 12½ cents per pound, and cleared $12,000 by the operation." (Was this venture connected with the Alexander Patterson passenger train noted on p. 1072?)

See, also, August annals items, p. 1119.

Ref: St. Joseph *Gazette*, May 26, September 8, 1852; Savannah (Mo.) *Sentinel*, May 22, 29, 1852; *Missouri Statesman*, Columbia, Mo., September 10, 1852 (from St. Louis *Intelligencer*); *Missouri Republican*, St. Louis, December 9, 1852 (for Patterson & Co.); *Jefferson Inquirer*, Jefferson City, Mo., August 7, 1852 (for "Capt. Harper" item); *Weekly Intelligencer*, St. Louis, December 28, 1852 (for San Francisco item); *The Weekly Tribune*, Liberty, Mo., February 18, 1853.

❡ In the latter half of May, a Salt Lake-bound train variously referred to as "Holladay, Hughes & Co's," "Hughes, Holladay & Co." and "Holladay & Warner's," set out from Weston, Mo.

Early in June, from "Muddy Creek," some 80 miles out [present Nemaha? county], "Mr. Burnam," the train's wagonmaster, returned to Weston. "Several of his teamsters have died, and others have abandoned the trip and returned home," reported the Platte *Argus*. "We learn that $30 per month is offered for teamsters. Holladay & Warner's train has come to a halt for want of hands." The Weston *Reporter* said seven persons had died of "cholera," and some 10 or 12 others had been stricken; also, the train had lost 13 oxen (all dying suddenly; "all within an hour, and whilst they had their yokes on").

In mid-June news reached Weston that the sickness among the "Holladay, Hughes & Co's" teamsters had subsided, and that the train had resumed the journey (being at last report "five miles beyond Muddy Creek"). "From all we can learn," said the *Reporter*, "the seven persons who died (one of whom was a child of Mr. Burnam's, waggon master) were imprudent in eating of the cattle that died, which induced a disease very similar to milk sickness."

Ref: St. Joseph (Mo.) *Gazette*, June 9, 1852 (items from Platte *Argus* and Weston *Reporter*); *The Weekly Tribune*, Liberty, Mo., June 11, 18, 1852 (items from Independence *Occidental Messenger* of June [5], Platte *Argus*, and Weston *Reporter*). *See* annals, p. 982, for Benjamin Holladay's two-year contract (of February 25, 1851, date) to haul "army stores" to Forts Kearny and Laramie. The above train may, or may not have included wagons carrying government supplies.

❡ May.—Some of the traders whose trains set out from the Missouri border for New Mexico, or Chihuahua, this month, were mentioned by incoming travelers (in May, June, and July):

"Mr. Charles Spencer and Le Blanc . . . on their way to Santa Fe," were at Red river early in June, according to a mail coach passenger. Near Plum Buttes, about June 12(?), were "[Francis X.] Aubry's train . . . and several other companies." "There had been considerable sickness among those going out. . . . All the California and Santa Fe trains had suffered more or less," reported the *Missouri Republican* (from "Hockstadt's" information, and other sources). Cholera had been very bad in Aubry's train (some 17 cases breaking out at one time); however, "by careful attention to his men," Aubry "lost only one of them." [On June 1, Jotham Meeker, returning home, passed "a Santa Fe train (Aubrey's) 20 miles from Ottawa, with ten cases of cholera."]

The Independence (Mo.), *Occidental Messenger* of June 5(?), commented: "We neglected to state, at the proper time the departure of the trains of Jno. F. McCauly, L. M. Ross, and many others, from Westport during the past two weeks, for Santa Fe, and Francis McManus party to Chihuahua. . . . Mr. George Wethered, Johnson and McManus left for the prairies a few days ago." The arrival of "Hubble's" party (on June 3? or 4?), from Santa Fe, was noted in the same issue. This company had met Aubry "progressing very well, the sickness in his party having abated . . ."; and reported that "Ross, Wethered and party" were also getting along "very well, all in good health"; and that "Solomon Houck and company, as also all the others, barring bad weather, [were] getting along so so."

Principal trains met by the "June" mail from Santa Fe (which reached Independence on June 21) were these:

"Byrn's" and "some others"—"three trains" [altogether] at "Sand Hill."

"Wing's train"—at Middle Cimarron Spring.

"McCauley's train"—in the Jornada.

(*Passed* a [Brewsterite] Mormon train of four wagons and six men, *returning* from the Gila.)

"Aubry's train"—"between the Coon Creeks"; "getting along very well."

"Jones and Russell's [government] train"—near the Little Arkansas.

"McManna's [McManus'] party"—at Council Grove.

"Quite a number of Mexican trains were on the road, and some other Americans."

"Ross and Wethered's company"—"progressing finely now, since the rains are over."

The "July" mail from Santa Fe, which reached Independence on July 21, had met: Ross' train at Tucalote; McCauley's at Point of Rocks; Ewing's at "Big Cannon"; Houck's at old Pecos; McManus' at Sand creek; Jones and Russell's at Whetstone; Aubry's at Point of Rocks.

Ref: *Missouri Republican*, St. Louis, June 25, 26, 1852; *Weekly Tribune*, Liberty, Mo., June 11, 1852 (from *Occidental Messenger*—of June 5?); New York *Daily Tribune*, June 25, 1852; *Weekly Intelligencer*, St. Louis, August 10, 1852 (from *Occidental Messenger* of July 24). For Jones & Russell's 1851-signed, two-year government contract, *see* annals, p. 980.

℘ May-June.—Fur traders eastbound on the Oregon trail were met by travelers heading west.

Mrs. Lodiza Frizzell, who, on May 24, "passed over the 16 mile desert, to the head waters of the L[ittle] Blue   .   .   .," wrote in her diary: "Met a company of fur traders with 16 waggons loaded with buffalo robes, they were very singular in appearance looking like so many huge elephants, & the men, except 2, were half-breeds; & indians, & a rougher looking set, I never saw; & their teams which were cattle, looked about used up.   .   .   ."

Perry Gee (whose company had crossed the Big Blue, near Alcove Spring, on May 26), three days later "passed [*i. e.*, met] 14 loads of Buffalo roabs returning to the states from Fort Carny"; and on June 4 "passed 8 loads of Buffalo Robes and passed 6 graves, and camped that night on the north bank of Blew [Little Blue] River."

Ref: Frizzell, *op. cit.*, p. 17; Perry Gee's "Journal" (in the Coe Collection, Yale University library), used by permission.

❧ May-July.—Several thousand Mormons remaining, until now, in Kanesville, and other settlements on the Pottawatomie reserve in Iowa, removed to Utah. (This large-scale removal was planned as the terminal phase of the migration begun in 1847.)

Twenty-three separate emigrant companies, in trains averaging 60 wagons each, made the journey—some via the Mormon trail north of the Platte, others traveling on the Platte's south side. (Captain Foote's 105-wagon train, on the latter route "had serious trouble and suffered at least twenty-two deaths, mostly from cholera.")

Ref: Wallace Stegner, *The Gathering of Zion*   .   .   .   (New York c1964); Wain Sutton, *Utah a Centennial History* (New York, 1949), v. 1, p. 530.

❧ In late May this description of the Council Grove area was written by an army officer (2d Lt. William D. Whipple?) on his way to New Mexico:

"Big John Spring is the name of a creek which crosses the road between two and three miles before reaching Council Grove.   .   .   .   On the hills or swells of ground, near Big John Spring, there is a good prospect of the valley of the Neosho River, with the Council Grove green and beautiful on its opposite or western bank.   .   .   .   Its broad meadow-valley, handsomely bordered with rich foliaged groves of trees and dotted with the lodges of Kaw Indians, is one of the most picturesque and beautiful I have ever looked upon.   .   .   .   The Neosho is a quick-running stream, with a stony and gravelly bed, not over 30 feet wide at our crossing and not more than from 18 inches to 2 feet depth of water. On the opposite or west bank we found the small trading settlement of Council Grove, with a blacksmith shop, two or three stores, and about the same number of dwelling-houses or huts—all log buildings."

On August 8 William Carr Lane (en route to New Mexico where he would be territorial governor) reached Council Grove. "Here is a mail agent with his family, Charles H. Whittington [*i. e.*, Withington], two or three trading firms, a blacksmith and a Baptist [*i. e.*, Methodist Church, South] Mission school," he wrote.

Julius Froebel, traveling the Santa Fe trail with Henry Mayer's train, arrived at Council Grove on August 27. "[It] will unquestionably become one day an important place," he (later) wrote. "The situation is beautiful and possesses many advantages. At the time we visited it, this place consisted of about ten houses, inhabited by white men and Indian women. A little higher up the brook stood, detached, the Mission-house [Kansa Methodist Mission], a somewhat large stone building, surrounded by hedged-in-fields. . . . About a mile distant down the stream was a [Kansa] camp, composed of twelve to fifteen leather tents. The country around is rich in natural beauty on a small scale. The rivulets, bordered by trees and bushes, wind along through beautiful flowery valleys, between hills covered with grass."

Ref: New York *Daily Tribune*, November 18, 1852 (for Whipple?); Historical Society of New Mexico, *Publications No. 20*, pp. 28, 29 (for Lane); Julius Froebel, *Seven Years' Travel in Central America, Northern Mexico, and the Far West of the United States* (London, 1859), p. 251.

❡ May 27.—The U. S. mail stage from Santa Fe reached Independence, Mo. Little news was received, by it, from New Mexico.

An army officer (2d Lt. William D. Whipple?) who saw the "May" mail parties, wrote the following:

"The mail is transported in a heavy Jersey wagon, drawn by four mules; relays of mules are obtained at Fort Union, Fort Atkinson and Council Grove, and at these places supplies of corn for animals are also procured. The mail party consists of four men, together with such persons as are going to the States or to Santa Fe, and who take this means, by paying from $100 to $120, to travel with expedition. These mail carriers are well armed, and can at any moment, deliver, say, fifty shots, without stopping to reload. The mules move in a trot all day long and instead of stopping over night on the traveled road, are invariably driven off some distance from it, without looking for water —continuing the journey until some time after nightfall, so as to prevent their camp-ground being known to Indians. Here they remain until, perhaps, half or three-fourths of an hour before daylight, when they harness up and recommence the journey. This, you will see, sets the efforts of Indians to molest them by night completely at defiance; for, after dark of the evening, it is impossible for any hostile party to find them, except by accident; and if, by chance, they should discover the party, and should lie in wait for them, on the road, for the purpose of a morning attack, their intention is frustrated by the early start before day."

Ref: New York *Daily Tribune*, May 31, 1852, and February 4, 1853 (for Whipple?).

❡ May.—At Independence, Mo., on May 27, a correspondent wrote that the health of the town was "unusually good"; but that rains had been "unusually frequent," so that the "whole earth" there, and "to the west" was "completely saturated with water." Emigrants on the Oregon-California trails had not been able to make much progress; and because of delays and exposure, sickness had broken out "to a very alarming extent," as reported.

At Ottawa Baptist Mission (present Franklin county), on May 27, Jotham Meeker recorded in his diary: "Learn the Cholera is raging among the California emigrants. The rains, bad roads and Cholera are bringing perhaps unprecedented distress on the roads to California and Oregon."

On May 29 Meeker journeyed up to Shawnee Baptist Mission (in Johnson county of today), where he learned that "many of the Shawanoes, Emigrants & Citizens of Westport and Kansas [City, Mo.] are dying with Cholera & other diseases. . . ." About 50 Shawnees attended church services on Sunday, May 30. Meeker noted: "Two men take the Cholera at the Meeting." On May 31 Meeker rode to the Shawnee Methodist Mission and to Westport. "People are sick and dying at Westport & Kansas with Cholera," he recorded in his diary. "Br[other John G.] Pratt [of Delaware Baptist Mission, in present Wyandotte county] writes us [i. e., the Rev. Francis Barker, and Meeker] that one of his Ch[urch] members died on last Thursday, one this morning, and that another, Br[other] Hendrick [a Stockbridge Indian], is dying."

Two weeks later—June 15—back at Ottawa mission, Meeker wrote: "California emigrants are returning, fleeing from the Cholera—the[y] report that great numbers are dying with it on the Plains—they have two Cholera cases with them. . . ." On June 13, a Wyandot, William Walker had noted in his diary: "One death in K[ansas City] by Cholera last night—a stranger."

Ref: *Missouri Republican*, St. Louis, June 4, 1852; Jotham Meeker's "Diary," *loc. cit.*; William Walker's "Journals," *loc. cit.*

℄ About the end of May "Waldo and McCoy's" train set out from Independence, Mo., for Fort Laramie. Presumably the wagons carried corn—fulfilling the government (two-year) contract of May, 1851—*see* p. 1004.

The eastbound "July" mail carrier met "Dr. [David] Waldo & Co's" train "four miles this side of Fort Laramie."

Ref: *The Weekly Tribune*, Liberty, Mo., June 11, 1852; *Jefferson Inquirer*, Jefferson City, Mo., August 7, 1852.

℄ "DIED—of cholera on the 30th day of May, near the 'Big Blue' Nebraska Territory [in present Marshall? county], Mr. Isadore Robidoux, aged 60 years."

"C's" notice, published in both St. Joseph newspapers, mentioned that the deceased was a brother of the town's founder—Joseph Robidoux; that he had "been a mountain trader from early life, and was a noble specimen of his class"; and eulogized: "those who knew him will long remember his many virtues—he was brave, hospitable, honest and generous to a fault, no human being either white or red, ever entered his cabin on the frontier, or his camp in the mountains, and went away hungry."

Ref: Savannah (Mo.) *Sentinel*, June 12, 1852 (from *Adventure*, St. Joseph); St. Joseph *Gazette*, June 9, 1852.

℄ At the end of May a California-bound "party of Kentucky gentlemen, with wagons and a large herd of cattle," who had traveled the "Cherokee trail" across "Oklahoma" and southern "Kansas" (*see* pp. 853-855, for first use of this road), reached the Santa Fe trail at the Turkey creek junction (in present McPherson county), or, in that vicinity.

This party (not further identified) joined Bvt. Maj. Enoch Steen's New Mexico-bound command at the Little Arkansas, around June 1, and traveled in company to Fort Atkinson, or beyond. One of the military men (2d Lt. W. D. Whipple?) wrote: "They had purchased their stock in the State of Arkansas. . . . Their route [westward] would, therefore, necessarily be to Bent's fort, on the Upper Arkansas, thence northward to the South or Fremont's Pass, and thence into the Salt Lake settlement or California."

Other use, this year, of the "Cherokee trail," was indicated by emigrant-to-Oregon Wilson M. Tigard, who, with his family, in a company of about 120 other persons, left northwest Arkansas in mid-April. Tigard did not travel the "Cherokee trail," but in a letter of November 13, 1852, after his "long and tedious Journey of over six months" to Oregon, wrote: "After we struck on to bear river we fel in company with some of the companeys that went up the Arkansas river   at that time there had been little or no sickness amongst them but their suferings and losses on the latter part of the trip was equivelent to ours on the first part of the trip. . . ."

Ref: New York *Daily Tribune*, November 18, 1852 (for Whipple's letter of August 28, 1852, from New Mexico); *Oregon Historical Quarterly*, v. 45 (September, 1944), pp. 228-237 (for Tigard).

❧ June-September.—Several westbound travelers this summer wrote, with some awe, of the buffalo seen between the Little Arkansas and the Coon creeks, on the Santa Fe trail:

At the beginning of June an army officer (2d Lt. William D. Whipple?) arrived at the Little Arkansas, and later wrote: "On this day's march . . . we had the satisfaction of knowing that we had fairly reached the buffalo-range. A few buffalo were seen by our column at a distance before reaching the crossing of the [Little Arkansas] creek." On June 3 the military command traveled 20 miles to Big Cow creek. Whipple(?) had this to say: "As we approached Little Cow Creek [17 miles from the Little Arkansas], the entire surface of prairie plain and slope appeared black with countless numbers of the buffalo. . . . The antelope, also, were now more numerous, and in some instances ran almost into the column as it marched along."

". . . on leaving our [Big Cow creek] camp ground on the morning of the 4th June, we soon came in sight of thousands of buffalo spread over the prairies to the left and right of the road. After reaching the Plum buttes . . . 9 miles from Big Cow Creek, several herds of buffalo frightened and driven by our men, who were hunting, galloped across the road, giving us fine opportunities to observe their appearance and all their peculiar motions. . . . In company with others of our party, I mounted the *plumbutte* to the right of the road . . . and from it obtained a capital view of the prairies for 15 to 20 miles to the northeast[?] and west, covered black with immense herds of buffalo. . . . In the section of the country between the Little Arkansas and Pawnee-fork the buffalo seem now to be mainly included during the spring and winter months; scarcely any are found East of the former, or West of the latter stream. . . . In the winter season, however, the buffalo extend themselves over a greater belt of country east and west. They then are found near the Arkansas River and remain there to graze and to shelter themselves from snow storms under cover of the low bluffs or hills which line the bank of the river at from 200 to 400 yards distant from its margin. They have in this way afforded opportunities to kill them in winter from the doors and windows of the quarters at Fort Atkinson. These natives of the American desert are fast disappearing from the face of the earth; each successive year finds them diminished in numbers and their range more circumscribed. . . ."

On August 12 William Carr Lane, in the Santa Fe-bound mail stage, camped for dinner at Big Cow Creek. In his diary, he noted: "Since our last halt [at noon "at a mere puddle"], we have never been out of sight of buffaloes, and I dare say there are about 10,000 of them now in sight. They are by no means wild. . . ." In the night, after a long drive, the party camped on Walnut creek. On the 13th Lane wrote: "We passed through a succession of herds of buffalo yesterday evening for some 4 miles as long as we could see them and after night we were surrounded by them as was made manifest by the bellowing of the bulls until I went to sleep. To attempt to estimate their numbers would be idle. This morning vast numbers remain in sight attended by many wolves, some perfectly white. On the Arkansas saw a magnificent bald eagle." Later (in a letter of September 26), Governor Lane again referred to the buffalo seen on the Santa Fe trail: "& dare say I saw that number [i. e., "probably 100,000 Buffalo"], & probably double that number, in continuous Herds,— before we crossed the Arkansas,—near Fort Atkinson. After we crossed the Arkansas, I did not see a single Buffalo. . . ."

Tourist Julius Froebel, Chihuahua-bound with Henry Mayer's train wrote: "From September 1st [this day they nooned along the Little Arkansas] to the 8th we journeyed through [buffalo] . . . incessantly. . . . On the 6th, whilst moving along between Pawnee Fork and Coon Creek, the buffalo herds formed a close line at least eight miles long upon the northern heights. Doubtless this herd, which surrounded us for a week whilst traveling, consisted of millions of animals, and formed one body, journeying along in company. I must, with my own eyes, have seen hundreds of thousands."

Ref: New York *Daily Tribune,* December 25, 1852 (for Whipple?); Historical Society of New Mexico, *Publications No. 20,* p. 34, and *New Mexico Historical Review,* v. 3 (April, 1928), p. 187 (for Lane); Froebel, *op. cit.,* pp. 254, 255.

❧ **June.—Steamboats on the middle Missouri this month included the *Clara, Kansas, Sonora, El Paso, Yuba, St. Paul, Highland Mary, Timour No. 2, Isabel, Delaware, Honduras, Robert Campbell, Alton,* and *Elvira.***

The *El Paso* brought down Harvey, Primeau & Co., upper Missouri fur returns (the cargoes of three Mackinaw boats); and aboard the *Highland Mary* reaching St. Louis on June 14, were the contents from three more of this company's boats (786 bales of, and 440 loose buffalo robes, 99 packages of furs and skins, also a lot of buffalo tongues). Upper Missouri fur returns (1,024 buffalo robe bales, and 44 deer skin packs) of Pierre Chouteau, Jr. &

Co., were brought down from Council Bluffs by the *Honduras,* which left there June 20, and reached St. Louis on the 25th.

Ref: *Missouri Republican,* St. Louis, June, and early July, 1852, issues; St. Joseph *Gazette,* June 9, 1852; John E. Sunder's *The Fur Trade on the Upper Missouri, 1840-1865* (Norman, c1965), p. 146.

❡ June 3 or 4.—"Mr. Hubble" (Santiago L.? Hubbell), trader, and party of between 35 and 40 persons, "reached Westport and Kansas [Mo.]," overland from Santa Fe. New Mexico territory's associate justice, John S. Watts (en route to Indiana on a visit) was in the company.

Ref: *The Weekly Tribune,* Liberty, Mo., June 11, 1852 (from Independence *Occidental Messenger*—of June 5?).

❡ June.—The Independence *Occidental Messenger*—June 5 issue, apparently—noted: "Rev. Mr. Reed and family are at the [Shawnee] Baptist Mission, Indian Territory, making preparations to go out to Santa Fe. He is accompanied with assistants for establishing and building up a Mission Academy." In another item it was stated: "Judges Baker and Baird of New Mexico and Col. Wells[?], are here now, and will leave in a few days for the plains."

"Rev. Mr. Reed" was the Rev. Hiram W. Read, who had gone to New Mexico in 1849, both as missionary and as army chaplain; and had journeyed eastward over the Santa Fe trail, accompanied by his family, in October, 1851— see p. 1046. The Reads were still at Shawnee Baptist Mission on June 22. Missionary Jotham Meeker, on that day, stopped "at Bro. [Francis] Barker's," and noted that "Br. Reed & Company are their on their Mission to New Mexico." (On August 13 Read was at Barclay's Fort, N. M., traveling with J. B. Yager's train.)

"Judge Baker" was New Mexico territory's Chief Justice Grafton Baker, who had come east in the autumn of 1851, and now was returning to Santa Fe. "Baird" was Indian agent S. M. Baird.

Ref: *The Weekly Tribune,* Liberty, Mo., June 11, 1852 (from *Occidental Messenger*— of June 5?); Jotham Meeker's "Diary," *loc. cit.; Missouri Republican,* St. Louis, September 26, 1852.

❡ June 7.—Apparently on this day a military party from Fort Leavenworth arrived at St. Mary's (Pottawatomie) Mission—after a journey of some three, or four days? The diary of Father John B. Duerinck (in September) included the following:

Distances between Leavenworth & Catholic Mission as measured by Lieut [Israel C.] Woodruffs viameter in Major [Henry L.] Kendrick's Convoy, June 7th 1852
From Fort Leavenworth to junction of Oregon road [or road to]
    Santa Fe .... 7¾ miles
From Fort Leavenworth to Upper Crossing Stranger [creek] ...... 12 miles
From Fort Leavenworth to Creek ¾ mile west of Hickory P[oin]t ... 27½ miles
From Fort Leavenworth to Lower Crossing Grasshopper .... 37¼ miles

From Fort Leavenworth to Rock creek 44   miles
From Fort Leavenworth to Upper Crossing Soldier creek .... 54½ miles
From Fort Leavenworth to Cross creek Bridge at Lortons[?] ...... 69¾ miles
From Fort Leavenworth to Bourbonnais creek (saw mill) .... 73¾ miles
From Fort Leavenworth to Catholic Mission 75.88 76   miles

Woodruff spent the rest of the summer in "Kansas," exploring, under orders from the Sixth Military Department. Later, Lt. G. K. Warren, in his historical *Memoir* (1859) wrote: "Lieutenant I. C. Woodruff, Topographical Engineers, made a reconnaissance, in 1852, of a portion of the Kansas river; of Walnut creek; of Pawnee Fork; and of other streams lying between the Smoky Hill Fork of the Kansas and the Arkansas rivers. These examinations were made for the purpose of selecting proper sites for military posts. The map [*see* p. 1022, this volume], and report [which, in June, 1966, the National Archives reported could not be located] prepared by Lt. Woodruff have never been published. . . ."

From Woodruff's "Chart," it would appear that when he left St. Mary's Mission (labeled "Potawatamie Mission") in June, he crossed the Kansas and traveled south of the river to "Clarke Cr."; turned southward, after crossing near its mouth, and followed along its course to a junction with the old Santa Fe trail east of Lost Spring. For next mention of Woodruff, *see* August 24 annals entry.

Ref: John B. Duerinck's "Diary" (original at St. Louis University, St. Louis, Mo.); 33d Cong., 2d Sess., *Sen. Ex. Doc. No. 78*, v. 11 (Serial 768), pt. I, p. 64 (for Warren). See annals, p. 981, for identification of "Upper Crossing Stranger" as "Dawson's crossing"—subsequently, Easton; and "Lower Crossing Grasshopper" as the later Ozawkie—presumably.

℃ June 16.—"The emigrants are all gone, with the exception of a few straggling parties . . .," wrote the St. Joseph *Gazette* editor.

Information "a few days since," from a man just in from Fort Laramie, was that the road east of Fort Kearny to the forks of the Independence and St. Joseph roads had "one continued train of wagons and cattle"; that he had been compelled, after leaving Fort Kearny, "to leave the road, frequently five or six miles to get sufficient grass for his animals"; and that he estimated the emigration of 1852 to be one-third larger than in 1850.

Ref: St. Joseph *Gazette*, June 16, 1852.

℃ June 17.—At a Parkville, Mo., public meeting on the subject of "Nebraska Territory," it was resolved that congress should be petitioned:

(1) for "the immediate organization of the Territory of NEBRASKA," (2) for the "domiciling" of Indians "which claim lands lying therein," on "small parcels of land to be assigned to them for cultivation," and (3) "for the immediate settlement of the lands of the Territory from which the Indian title has been extinguished, by American citizens who may desire to emigrate . . . [there]."

Thomas H. Starnes called this meeting to order; William H. Summers presided; and Dr. Milton G. Young was appointed secretary.

Ref: *The Weekly Tribune*, Liberty, Mo., July 2, 1852; James C. Malin, *The Nebraska Question, 1852-1854* (Lawrence, c1953), p. 80. Sen. David R. Atchison, of Missouri presented the "Parkville petition" to the senate, July 7, 1852. Malin cites *Congressional Globe*, 32d Cong., 1st Sess., p. 1666.

❡ June-August.—"Bent, Chouteau and pleasure party of ladies and gentlemen" were met at Council Grove about June 18 by the east-bound mail party. A few days later, other incoming travelers met "Chouteau, King & Co's. party . . . all in good health," reportedly at "a place called Arkansas Crossings," but instead, probably at the Little Arkansas crossing.

In its May 26 issue the St. Joseph *Gazette* had noted (from a St. Louis source?) that "A party of ladies and gentlemen have left Savannah [Georgia] on a summer excursion to the great prairies of the north-west. They consist of Mr. Stephen Clay King, of Wayne co. Ga., his lady, two daughters and two sons, and Mr. Gignillat, of Glynn co. [Ga.], and perhaps 1 or 2 English gentlemen. A member of the party passed on some time since to St. Louis, to lay in provisions and private conveyances. From St. Louis the excursionists will take a boat up the Missouri for several hundred miles and at a convenient place disembark and strike out into the prairies. . . ." Equipment, the article stated, would include a wagon "so constructed as to swing a mattress in it to sleep on," two or three light carriages, one or more saddle horses, tents, servants, and all the conveniences of cooking, sleeping &c." Fort Laramie was to be included on the itinerary; and the party planned to return to St. Louis by the middle of October. "A son of Mr. King went over the same ground last year, with a party of gentlemen from New Orleans," the article further stated, "and derived so much benefit that his father has determined to take his family with him. All the gentlemen of the party will go armed. . . ." (*See* p. 1030, for mention of Henry C. King in "Kansas" in 1851.)

At Fort Atkinson, on August 1, "Kiowa" wrote in a letter: "I am sorry to say that the wife of Mr. King of Alabama [*i. e.*, Georgia] who came with his family to the plains for the benefit of their health died at this post a few days ago. About three weeks earlier a lovely and accomplished daughter died."

On August 2 or 3, Maj. Winslow F. Sanderson and a Mounted riflemen squadron left Fort Atkinson for Fort Laramie. Stephen Clay King and others of his party evidently traveled in company, not only to Fort Laramie, but eastward on the Oregon route to Fort Leavenworth. (*See* p. 1126.) The *Missouri Republican* of October 5, reported: "Mr. King and his party . . . came down on the Timour No. 2 yesterday evening. They all seem to be in fine health. . . ."

William Carr Lane, arriving at Fort Atkinson on August 15, noted in his diary: "Miss Chouteau and Caysan[?] here on a visit. Saw Mr. Hette[?]"; and on the 16th, leaving for Santa Fe with Bvt. Maj. James H. Carleton and his troops, Lane wrote: "We are escorted for some ten or twelve miles by Major Simon Bolivar Buckner and Miss Marie Chouteau on horseback with five dogs, a fair escort."

On August 24, when Lt. Israel C. Woodruff, accompanied by Bvt. Maj. Simon B. Buckner and detail, left Fort Atkinson, eastbound, "Mr. Chouteau's party" traveled with them. (*See* pp. 1121, 1122.)

The October, 1857, issue of *Harper's New Monthly Magazine*, contained an article entitled "The Siege of Fort Atkinson" (later identified as written by Charles Hallock) purporting to be a narrative of events at that post in July, 1852, and including a detailed, verisimilar account of the Bent-King caravan's arrival at Fort Atkinson.

According to Hallock, about 50 persons were in the William Bent and Stephen C. King caravan which reached the post on the Arkansas in the middle of July, after harassment by the Plains Indians then camped in the area. Five of the train's 14 wagons belonged to Bent, and were ox-drawn; nine others (mule-drawn), and two carriages were the outfit of "Mr. King's party" ("composed chiefly of young adventurers and valetudinarians"). Also, "Fitzwilliam had . . . joined company, and was along with his men— all the camp-equipage and accoutrements of his party being secured upon the backs of pack-mules, hunter fashion." [The departure of "Mr. Charles William Fitzwilliam, son of Earl Fitzwilliam," and his party, from St. Louis on May 30, for the West, had been noted by a correspondent in that city.]

Ref: St. Joseph (Mo.) *Gazette*, May 26, 1852; *Missouri Republican*, St. Louis, June 26, July 11, August 30, 31, October 2, 5, 1852; New York *Daily Tribune*, June 11, 1852; New York *Daily Times*, June 10, September 13, 23, 1852; Historical Society of New Mexico, *Publications No. 20*, pp. 37, 38 (for Lane); *Harper's New Monthly Magazine*, New York, v. 15 (October, 1857), pp. 638-648; William Walker's "Journals," *loc. cit.*, May 28, 1852, entry for item: "In the afternoon the girls came home from the party at the Union Hotel [in Kansas, Mo.], accompanied by W. Mulkey and a Mr. King from Georgia."

℄ June 21.—In charge of "Mr. [James] Rupe," accompanied by "Jones and Williams," the "June" U. S. mail from Santa Fe arrived at Independence, Mo. Passengers in the stagecoach were William Goldstein, "Hockstadter" (E. Hockstadt, in another account), and 2d Lt. Alexander E. Steen, Third infantry (who had joined at Fort Atkinson).

Ref: *Missouri Republican*, St. Louis, June 25, 26, 1852; *The Weekly Tribune*, Liberty, Mo., July 2, 1852. "E. Hockstadt" and "Lt. Stein [Steen]," reached St. Louis on June 24, aboard the *St. Paul*. James Rupe is identified in C. R. Morehead's recollections published in W. E. Connelley's *Doniphan's Expedition* . . . (1907), pp. 603-605.

℄ June 28.—Overland from Oregon, two Missourians (from Caldwell county) reached St. Joseph, after a journey (in company with 15 others; and with pack mules) of 56 traveling days. They had left Oregon City on April 16. J. C. Bell, of Weston (and others?) had "stopped at Fort Laramie," but would arrive in a few days.

On July 7 the St. Joseph *Gazette* commented: "Every day or two we see persons arrive across the plains from Oregon."

Ref: St. Joseph (Mo.) *Gazette*, June 30, July 7, 1852.

❈ DIED: on June 30(?), New Mexico territory's governor James S. Calhoun, while eastbound on the Santa Fe trail, somewhere between Council Grove and the Missouri border. His remains (placed in a coffin carried as baggage from New Mexico) were "brought in to Kansas [City, Mo.]" on the evening of July 1 (according to the Independence newspaper).

Governor Calhoun (very ill, and aware death was imminent) had set out from Santa Fe, on May 5, in a mule-drawn army ambulance. From Fort Union, where he stopped to rest, his party, with military escort, had resumed the journey on May 26. Persons mentioned as in Calhoun's company (when overtaken at Middle Cimarron Spring by the eastbound "June mail" party) were Abraham R. Woolley (Indian agent), David V. Whiting (Calhoun's secretary), W. Johnson, Esq., William E. Love (Calhoun's son-in-law), Asst. Surg. Thomas A. McParlin, and the military escort (under Bvt. 2d Lt. Robert Johnston—who had discretionary orders to go as far as Pawnee Fork). Also there were five Pueblo Indians (from Tesuque), en route East to visit the President. A later-day account says Calhoun's daughters—Martha Ann, and Carolina L. (Calhoun) Love, made this trip.

David V. Whiting, writing from Independence, Mo., on July 5, stated that Calhoun's remains had been "interred at Kansas, Mo." "We brought in five Pueblo Indians with us . . ." (Whiting continued), "they are now at Kansas, awaiting the arrival of a boat to conduct them to Washington. . . ." William E. Love, accompanied by 16 persons (including the five Pueblo Indians), reached St. Louis on July 14.

Ref: *Missouri Republican*, St. Louis, June 26, 1852; *The Weekly Tribune*, Liberty, Mo., July 9, 1852 (for item from Independence *Occidental Messenger* of July 3); James S. Calhoun's *Official Correspondence* . . ., ed. by Annie H. Abel (Washington, 1915), pp. 531-540, 548; William Walker's "Journals," *loc. cit.*, July 2, 1852, entry; William A. Keleher's *Turmoil in New Mexico* . . . (Santa Fe, c1952), pp. 60, 61; New York *Daily Times*, August 10, 1852 (from *National Intelligencer* of August 6); St. Joseph (Mo.) *Gazette*, August 11, 1852.

❈ July-December.—Licenses (new and renewal) to trade with Indians in "Kansas," as granted by agents of the Central Superintendency, St. Louis, were:

Traders	Indians	Issued by	Rec'vd at St. Louis
Isaac G. Baker	"Mississippi" Sac & Fox	J. R. Chenault	July
Samuel M. Cornatzer	Shawnee	Thomas Moseley, Jr.	July
John W. Forman	Iowa, and "Missouri" Sac & Fox	W. P. Richardson	July
Benjamin Harding	Kickapoo, Iowa, and "Missouri" Sac & Fox	W. P. Richardson	July
Thomas D. S. Macdonell	Pottawatomie	F. W. Lea	July
Oliver H. P. Polke	Pottawatomie	F. W. Lea	July
John D. Lasley	Pottawatomie	F. W. Lea	July
Thomas N. Stinson	Pottawatomie	F. W. Lea	July

Emanuel Mosier	Kansa	F. W. Lea	August
Harrison McDowell	Pottawatomie	F. W. Lea	August
R. L. McGhee	Pottawatomie	F. W. Lea	September
James R. Whitehead	Kickapoo, Iowa, and "Missouri" Sac & Fox	W. P. Richardson	October
Cyprian Chouteau	Kickapoo	W. P. Richardson	October
Waldo, Hall & Co.	Kansa	F. W. Lea	November
W. G. Ewing, Jr.	Delaware	Thomas Moseley, Jr.	December
(R. C.) Miller & (G. L.) Young	Pottawatomie	F. W. Lea	December
Milton P. Randall	"Mississippi" Sac & Fox	J. R. Chenault	December
Walker, Northrup & Chick	"Mississippi" Sac & Fox	J. R. Chenault	December
Robert Wilson	Kickapoo	W. P. Richardson	December
James F. Forman	Kickapoo, and "Missouri" Sac & Fox	W. P. Richardson	December

Ref: SIA, St. Louis, "Records," v. 9, typed copy, pp. 638, 641, 642, 646, 649, 655, 667, 683, 686, 687, 692-694; and *ibid.*, pp. 691 and 706 for John Robidoux (and wife) as employees of Isaac G. Baker, and Robert Polke as clerk for Baker.

❧ On, or about July 3, Maj. Winslow F. Sanderson, two companies of Mounted riflemen, and Company B, First dragoons (under 2d Lt. David H. Hastings) marched from Fort Leavenworth for Fort Atkinson, where (according to rumors and reports received) the several thousand Indians gathered in the area were threatening to destroy the post and "to perpetrate murders and outrages generally."

Reaching Fort Atkinson on July 19, Sanderson (as the ranking officer) assumed command at that post (from Bvt. Maj. Simon B. Buckner, Sixth infantry) on July 20. His squadron of Mounted riflemen (then, or later) went into camp "25 miles above," "for the benefit of grass." 2d Lt. David H. Hastings and Company B, First dragoons, meanwhile, were occupied in organizing and escorting the Santa Fe-bound trains on the trail.

Sgt. Percival G. Lowe, of Company B, later recollected that Hastings "compelled [the train] owners or managers to concentrate in large caravans and proceed with the greatest caution in double column" after they reached Walnut creek; and wrote of an incident on the march involving a Mexican train in the Pawnee Rock area. ("[Dragoons] charged in time to drive off the [Indian] robbers [from a laggard wagon], though a shower of arrows had already hit the wagon and slightly wounded the man. One pony was killed, and it was believed that some Indians were wounded, though all got away.") Company B, First dragoons, arrived at Fort Atkinson on August 1.

Ref: New York *Daily Times*, July 27, 1852; *Weekly Intelligencer*, St. Louis, August 10, 1852; *Missouri Republican*, St. Louis, August 30, 1852; Lowe, *op. cit.*, pp. 102-104; Fort Atkinson post returns (microfilm from National Archives).

❡ July 4.—From Fort Leavenworth a small Mormon company (including some families), headed by Elders John Taylor and Philip De LaMare, with a train of heavily-laden wagons carrying the Deseret Manufacturing Company's imported sugar-refining machinery, made an abortive start for Salt Lake City. An account says that this equipment (cost $12,500; import duty, $5,000), in five to nine thousand pound loads, was being transported in "new wagons built by Captain Russell," each drawn by four to eight oxen. Elias Morris (a Welshman, in whose charge the machinery had arrived at New Orleans) wrote: "The first day's travel was but four or five miles. In that distance four or five axle-trees were broken. The cattle were very wild; we teamsters very green; the wagons very badly made with bad and green timber; and the loads were very heavy."

(The refining equipment, and the party of [22?] Saints, had reached St. Louis, via steamboat from New Orleans, early in May. The *Missouri Republican* of May 15 commented: "Another party [of Mormons] now in the city will leave soon for . . . [Utah], with intention of engaging in manufacturing of sugar from beet root.")

The July 4 breakdowns made it necessary for De LaMare (in charge of the overland journey arrangements) to obtain other wagons. The account states that he "met Charles H. Perry from whom he purchased, on credit, some forty Santa Fe Wagons . . ."; and that he also bought on credit a large amount of flour, part of which was found to be worm-infested, and adulterated with plaster of Paris. At a later date in July the Mormon train finally got under way for Utah.

On September 3 the "company of Mormons, with the machinery and other materials for a Sugar Refinery" reached Fort Laramie. Later in September eastbound traveler "H." (who left Salt Lake City September 13) "met the last of Mormon trains on Sweetwater . . . quite a large train, intrusted with . . . machinery for the manufacturing of beet sugar, recently imported from France. . . ."

Early in November, after a hardship-filled journey, the Mormon company arrived at Salt Lake City, but some of the machinery did not reach there till later.

Ref: *Missouri Republican*, St. Louis, May 15, October 2, 20, 1852; New York *Daily Tribune*, December 22, 1852 (from St. Louis *Intelligencer*), for "H.'s" letter; Wain Sutton, editor, *Utah A Centennial History* (New York, 1949), v. 2, pp. 920-923 (for Morris quote, etc.). "Charles H." was Charles A. Perry, Weston, Mo.

❡ July.—Steamboats plying the middle Missouri this month included the *St. Paul, Delaware, St. Ange, Honduras, Isabel, Clara,* and *Kansas.*

The *St. Ange* (reaching St. Louis July 14, from "Lindens Landing"—left on the 11th) brought fur returns of 1,305 bales of, and 969 loose buffalo robes for Pierre Chouteau, Jr. & Co. The *Clara* (reaching St. Louis July 18, from St. Joseph—left on the 15th) had in her cargo 655 bales of buffalo robes (consigned to Riley & Christy) which had been taken aboard at Kansas (City), Mo., after being "brought from the plains in wagons." The *St. Ange* (reaching St. Louis on July 26, from Savannah—left on the 23d) brought down 93 bales of buffalo robes, of which 22 were consigned to Pierre Chouteau, Jr. & Co., 19 were for J. & E. Welsh, and 52 for Riley & Christy. The *Isabel* (down from Weston—left on the 26th—to St. Louis, on the 29th) had aboard 72 bales of buffalo robes and skins for Pierre Chouteau, Jr. & Co. The *St. Paul* (down from St. Joseph), arriving at St. Louis on July 31, brought 152 packs of buffalo robes (apparently for Pierre Chouteau, Jr. & Co.). The *Clara* (which left St. Joseph on July 30 and reached St. Louis August 3), had in her cargo 144 bales of, and 252 loose buffalo robes, for Pierre Chouteau, Jr. & Co.

Ref: *Missouri Republican,* St. Louis, July, and early August, 1852, issues; Sunder, *op. cit.,* p. 146.

❧ About July 14(?) Bishop Miege left his diocese headquarters— St. Mary's Mission—on Kansas river, to visit the Osages and Osage Mission. "I had a good carriage, two excellent horses, a prudent driver . . . a real Californian's outfit," Miege wrote. (However, his party had to contend with hot weather, high water, flies, mosquitoes, and fever.)

At Ottawa Baptist Mission (east of present Ottawa) the Rev. Jotham Meeker noted in his diary on July 15: ". . . the Catholic Bishop & servants from Potawatomie [arrive in the evening] to lodge for the night."

Bishop Miege was at Fort Scott on August 1, and as late as August 3. His visits to the Osage towns (in July?, or August?, or both) began (as he wrote in a letter) at "the village called Big Hill, the chief of which is called Great Man . . . a specimen about six feet six inches tall, who hides nothing nature gave him." Miege's conference with "Great Man" was followed by a banquet (the principal dish "buffalo meat boiled in water"), then by a ceremonial dance. The bishop's letter contained other commentary on the Osages, and such descriptive items as: "The villages are all built on heights within comfortable reach of wood and water. . . . And they do have something like streets and public squares—everything perfectly clean. They are guarded by seven or eight hundred ravenous dogs which make approach difficult in the day time and dangerous at night. . . ."

Ref: *KHQ,* v. 21, pp. 84-86 (for Miege's letter); Garraghan, *op. cit.,* v. 2, p. 514 (for Miege at Fort Scott); Jotham Meeker's "Diary," in KHi ms. division.

❧ July 21.—Overland from California in 66 days, seven men (out of a party numbering 21, which had set out May 16) arrived at St. Joseph, Mo.

These travelers had met the "greater part" of the westbound emigration in the vicinity of Fort Laramie. Among the seven were "Mr. Bliss of New York," "Mr. Smith of Erie Co., Ohio," "Mr. Cole of Iowa," "Mr. Hood, of Livingston Co., Mo.," and "Mr. Briggs of Hannibal."

Ref: St. Joseph *Adventure,* July 23, 1852.

❡ July 21.—In charge of William Allison, the U. S. "July" mail stage from Santa Fe reached Independence, Mo. Passengers were: Bvt. Maj. William N. Grier and Bvt. Capt. Oliver H. P. Taylor, First dragoons, Lt. Charles Griffin, Second artillery, "Dr. Hammond" (Asst. Surg. [William A.?] Hammond), and "Mr. Davidson."

Ref: *Missouri Republican,* St. Louis, July 23, 27, 1852; *Weekly Intelligencer,* St. Louis, August 10, 1852 (from *Occidental Messenger,* Independence, Mo., of July 24).

❡ In the last week of July the American Fur Company-chartered *Banner State* (James Gonsales [or Gunsollis?], captain; John B. Sarpy in charge of the expedition), which had been up to Fort Union with supplies, passed along the "Kansas" shore; and reached St. Louis July 31. The "returns" she brought for Pierre Chouteau, Jr. & Co., consisted principally of 1,400 bales of buffalo robes, furs, and skins.

On the trip up to the Yellowstone, the *Banner State* had left St. Louis about June 10. The round trip was variously reported as 52 days, and 53 days and a few hours.

Ref: *Missouri Republican,* St. Louis, May 24, July 31, 1852; New York *Daily Tribune,* August 11, 1852 (from St. Louis *Union*); New York *Daily Times,* August 11, 1852.

❡ July 29.—The "July" U. S. mail ("Mr. Van Eps," conductor) from Salt Lake City reached Independence, Mo. "Mr. Packard" (carrier of the "July" mail from Independence *to* Fort Laramie?) had been left at Fort Laramie (to come in with Captain Ketchum's party). "Van Eps," *it appears,* had carried the mail east from Salt Lake City (leaving there July 2).

Ref: *Jefferson Inquirer,* Jefferson City, Mo., August 7, 1852; *Weekly Intelligencer,* St. Louis, August 17, 1852.

❡ Late July(?)—Four army deserters, traveling eastward on the Santa Fe trail, journeyed for several days in company with two Delaware Indians (a young man of 18 or 20, and his "cousin" "Mar-mar-trish-ey," widow of recently deceased Jim Dickey, a Delaware hunter). The Indians were returning from the mountains with some 13 horses and mules, deer and elk skins, also other valuables (including about $450 in money).

One noon, at a camp five or six miles east of "Running Turkey Creek," the "young man was killed by these men, and the squaw was also supposed by these wretches to be dead, having had her throat cut badly and her head severely fractured."

The criminals made for the Missouri border with their loot; disposed of the animals as best they could; and three of them took a steamboat to St. Louis. Meantime "Mar-mar-trish-ey" recovered enough to travel; and a Kansa Indian assisted her to reach Council Grove. One of the deserters was arrested at Liberty; the other three at St. Louis.

The case stirred up considerable excitement among the Delaware Indians. At Liberty, Mo., a three-day hearing was held in mid-August. The *Missouri Republican* of August 18 reported the return of the four men to St. Louis, in charge of "Capt. J. E. D. Couzins and Officer Page," on August 17, under order of the U. S. District Court. A few of the stolen animals were returned to the Delaware woman.

In 1853 William Carr Lane stated that two of the criminals were hanged, one was acquitted, and the fourth "turned States evidence, and saved himself."

Ref: *Missouri Republican,* St. Louis, August 18, 1852 (or, New York *Daily Tribune,* August 27, 1852); Comm'r of Indian Affairs, *Report,* 1852 (Agent Thomas Moseley, Jr.'s report, therein); Historical Society of New Mexico, *Publications No. 20,* pp. 29, 30, 32; *New Mexico Historical Review,* Santa Fe, v. 39 (October, 1964), p. 318.

❦ Summer.—The Pottawatomies, "whilst on a buffalo hunt in the upper country," smoked a peace pipe with the Pawnee Indians, with whom they had warred since 1848 (*see* pp. 763, 928, and 944).

Father John B. Duerinck, St. Mary's Mission, reporting this development, wrote (on September 24): "The peace and harmony of this settlement is now seldom disturbed by war parties, or alarming reports of invasion." He remarked, also, that there had been no recent complaints of horses stolen by the Pawnees.

Ref: Comm'r of Indian Affairs, *Report,* 1852 (Duerinck's report, therein).

❦ July-August.—These were the events, and circumstances, at Fort Atkinson as July ended, and August began:

July 31. Maj. Winslow F. Sanderson (commandant since July 20 —*see* p. 1108) turned over command to Bvt. Maj. Simon B. Buckner, in preparation for an early departure.

July 31. Bvt. Maj. Robert H. Chilton, head of Company B, First dragoons, who had been on a long leave of absence, arrived at the post. He and a small escort had made the journey from Fort Leavenworth in 12 days.

August 1. "Kiowa," who wrote a letter this day from "Fort Atkinson, Santa Fe Route," stated that "most" of the "many thousands" of Indians who had been awaiting the arrival of Agent Fitzpatrick, had "gone back to their own territories," "greatly disgusted." "Some . . . still linger about here," he wrote, "and if F comes soon, he may succeed in conciliating their good opinion by ample presents." (It was the end of August before Fitzpatrick arrived—*see* p. 1114.)

August 1. 2d Lt. David H. Hastings and Company B, First dragoons arrived at the fort "from Plains."

August 1. Bvt. Maj. Robert H. Chilton (as ranking officer) assumed post command from Buckner; and took over command of his Company B, First dragoons. ("Kiowa," in his letter, stated: "The major remains here with his company of 25 or 30 men to keep the Comanches, Kiowas, Cheyennes, Osages, Crows[?] &c. in check.") Chilton was commandant at Fort Atkinson till September 27—after which time he and the dragoons returned to Fort Leavenworth.

Sgt. Percival G. Lowe, and dragoon D. C. Beam, of Company B. both later recollected incidents of the summer at Fort Atkinson. Beam referred to the post as "Fort McKey . . . dried mud shelters for the men and a trading post for Indians. Here we spent some two months or more with the Kiowas, camped near by. These Indians were great horsemen, and would run races, bet their tepees and everything they had on their favorite horse. Besides they were superb with the bow. . . ." Both Lowe and Beam referred to a week or 10-day trip higher up the Arkansas with Major Chilton. "We returned leisurely along the trail," wrote Lowe, "met F. X. Aubry, the champion rider of the plains, Colonel William Bent, of Bent's Fort, and [Lucien] Maxwell, of Riado [Rayado], New Mexico. All were of the opinion that the Indians would not return to the trail that season. From Pawnee Fork we made time for home —Fort Leavenworth."

August 2, or 3. Maj. Winslow F. Sanderson and his Mounted riflemen departed for Fort Laramie (by way of Bent's Fort, Pueblo, and the route along the base of the Rockies). *See, also,* September entry, p. 1126.

Ref: *Missouri Republican,* St. Louis, August 30, October 2, 1852; Fort Atkinson post returns (microfilm from National Archives); Percival G. Lowe, *Five Years a Dragoon* . . . (1906), pp. 105-121; Nebraska State Historical Society, *Transactions,* Lincoln, v. 3, pp. 292-294.

❡ Around August 1 goods valued at $30,000 (furnished by R. & W. Campbell) were turned over to Agent Thomas Fitzpatrick (at St. Louis) for distribution "among the Prairie tribes—parties to the Fort Laramie treaty [of 1851], and residing within his Agency." By Sup't D. D. Mitchell's direction, $6,000 worth were to be "distributed among the Comanches and Kioways on the Arkansas . . . inasmuch as they had been led to believe that they would receive presents during the summer [though not parties to the treaty]. . . ."

About August 7 eastbound travelers met "Lieut. Heath [2d Lt. John Heth] and Major Fitzpatrick with presents for the Indians at Diamond Spring"; and at Lost Spring (on the 18th?), Aubry's incoming train met "Major Fitzpatrick with Lieut. Heath. . . . They were making forced marches in order to deliver the presents . . . to the Comanches at an early day."

A Missouri-bound traveler arriving at "Fort Mackay" (Fort Atkinson) on August 29 found "about 2,000 Indians camped, waiting for Fitzpatrick." Next day he met the Indian agent—who, with the laden wagons, probably reached the fort on August 30, as did Lieutenant Heth. Later arrivals at the Missouri border (September 10) reported that "Lt. Heath and Mr. Fitzpatrick" were "engaged in distributing the presents for Camanches and other tribes," when they passed Fort Atkinson.

Ref: *Missouri Republican,* St. Louis, August 28, 31, September 26, 1852; New York *Daily Times,* September 23, 1852; Fort Atkinson post returns (microfilm from National Archives); SIA, St. Louis, "Records," v. 9, typed copy, pp. 650, 651.

❧ August 3.—At Fort Scott, A. G. Hale entered into a contract with Lt. D. D. Clark to deliver 75 tons of good hay (for $3.40 per 2,000-pound ton) at the post during the month.

Sureties for his $1,000 bond were H. J. Wilson and W. R. Miller.

Ref: 32d Cong., 2d Sess., Sen. Ex. Doc. No. 18 (Serial 660), p. 15.

❧ Died: on August 5, the Rev. John J. Bax, S. J., aged 35, of Osage Mission (present Neosho county), at Fort Scott (present Bourbon county). He was buried at the mission.

Agent Morrow (in his 1852 report) wrote: "This school, as well as the whole Osage people, has sustained an irreparable loss by the death of the Rev. Father Bax. . . ."

Ref: Garraghan, *op. cit.,* v. 2, pp. 513-515; Augustin C. Wand, *The Jesuits in Territorial Kansas, 1827-1861* (St. Marys, 1962), p. 41; Comm'r of Indian Affairs, *Report,* 1852 (Morrow's report, therein); Fitzgerald, *op. cit.;* p. 88.

❧ August.—When the "August" mail party left Independence, Mo., for Santa Fe on the 5th, William Carr Lane (newly appointed governor of New Mexico territory) was aboard the stagecoach. "I took passage with my servant Frank, and much extra baggage," wrote Lane (in the detailed, informative diary he kept of this journey). "The mail stage was drawn by six mules and the baggage wagon by four. The conductor, Mr. Wm. Allison, and his two assistants, rode horseback."

On August 6 the party breakfasted at Bull creek ("there are [here] some Shawnee farms with cabins"), after spending a night encamped on "a high prairie." On the 7th (following another night "upon a high prairie"), after a 20-mile journey, they crossed 110-mile creek ("after which there is a strip of heavy timber and a Shawnee settlement"); then traveled some 20 miles beyond to camp—on the prairie. They arrived at Council Grove on August 8, at 5 P. M. Lane "quartered" at the cabin of mail agent Charles H. Withington; and "became acquainted with Mr. Christopher Columbia and others." On August 10 (after two nights at Council Grove) the party set out at 7 A. M. ("6 mules to wagon as well as stage. Allison and Peter out-riders."). They lunched at Diamond Spring; supped at Lost Spring; camped "some 7 or 8 miles" beyond (after a day's trip of some 40 miles).

On the 11th they breakfasted at Cottonwood creek; stopped to rest, at 2 P. M., at "Running Turkey Creek"; went on, to camp on the prairie. They breakfasted, on August 12, at the Little Arkansas ("this point is said to be 90 miles from the [Council] Grove"); began to see buffalo as they continued westward; halted for dinner, at 4 P. M., at Big Cow creek; camped on Walnut creek "after a long drive," and after passing through numerous buffalo herds. On the 13th they stopped for dinner on Ash creek (having made a 36-mile trip); camped for the night west of Pawnee Fork; on August 14, took the dry route (as opposed to the river route). Early on Sunday morning, August 15, they arrived at Fort Atkinson.

Lane left the stagecoach at this point, and set out "with the command of Major [James H.] Carleton" on August 16, to take the Cimarron route. (The mail party traveled with, or near, the military company, for protection.) Lane's diary states: "Crossed the Arkansas about 18 miles from the Fort and had some difficulty in the transit." He subsequently reached Santa Fe on September 9 (and was inaugurated on the 13th), after a delay (due to his sudden illness on August 25) of some 12 days at Fort Union, N. M.

Lane recorded in his diary comment on the various trains met, or overtaken, during his August journey, and identified some of them:

August 7, at Switzler's creek—"passed five groups of ox-teams from ten to twelve in number, five yokes on each and twenty to thirty extra teams following."

August 8, at 142-mile creek—"Mr. Renick passed our encampment with some twenty ox-teams or more on his return from Fort Union, to which place he had transported government stores at $8.85 per cwt. . . . in his rear was another ox-team [i. e., train], also returning from Fort Union, making in all some fifty wagons. The average travel per day with six yoke is from eighteen to twenty miles. They return empty with five yoke in each and make from twenty to twenty-five miles in a day. Soon after we met Hawk's [Houck's] wagon train of some fifty great wagons with the same complement of oxen and the same number of extra ones in a drove following after." [James W. Renick was a "surety" for Jones & Russell's February 17, 1851, two-year government contract—*see* p. 1004. At Independence, on August 10, a correspondent wrote that "McCauley's and Houck's trains are on their return and will be here in a few days. Solomon Houck is returning himself with his train. Some other trains are also looked for shortly."]

August 8, at Council Grove—"Before bedtime Mr. _____ [Orrick], a citizen of Platte City, passed. He is the owner of an ox-train on its way to Fort Atkinson with army stores." [Orrick had had some oxen driven off by Kaw Indians a few days earlier. He recovered some; then, overtaking the thieves with the rest of the cattle, he met opposition —the Indians "took his pistols from him and shot at him, the bullet passing through his hat above his head. "He returns today to Fort Leavenworth to report the outrage and to demand assistance," wrote Lane.]

August 12—"We passed [overtook] Orrick's ox-team [train] on its way to Fort Atkinson with general stores east of the Little Arkansas." [Orrick may have been freighting for Perry & Young—who had the 1851-1852 Fort Atkinson contract (*see* p. 985); or, perhaps he carried goods for the sutler's store at that post.]

August 13, west of Pawnee Fork—"found . . . one train of 17 wagons from Santa Fe."

August 22, near the Upper Cold Spring [of the Cimarron]—"met an ox train of twenty wagons, with six yoke of oxen in each returning from Santa Fe empty and driving a large herd of extra oxen. There is also another train encamped at the Upper Cold Spring on their way into the states."

Ref: Historical Society of New Mexico, *Publications No. 20* (Santa Fe, 1917); *Missouri Republican*, St. Louis, August 17, 1852.

❡ August 5(?)—Accompanied by four Sisters of Loretto, the Rt. Rev. John B. Lamy, vicar apostolic of New Mexico, traveled from

Independence, Mo., to Willow Springs; there joined the rest of his party (15 to 20 in all, by report); and the company proceeded down the Santa Fe trail.

Six Lorettines had left St. Louis July 10 on the *Kansas*. Three were stricken with cholera. Mother Matilda Mills died July 16 aboard the steamboat. Sister Monica Bailey survived, but was too feeble for the trip overland. Sister Magdalen Hayden, who became ill while nursing Sister Monica, at Todd's Warehouse, Independence Landing, made a good recovery. The others who went to New Mexico were Sisters Catherine Mahoney, Rosanna Dant, and Roberta Brown.

On August 8[?] Bishop Lamy said mass "near an Indian hut on the banks of the Hundred and Ten [Mile] Creek." His party reached Council Grove on the 15th; left on the 16th; by August 22 had reached Pawnee Fork. While encamped, September 7, west of Fort Atkinson, about 400 Indians (not hostile) surrounded the wagons—a terrifying experience for the Sisters. On September 26 the Lorettines reached Santa Fe. In January, 1853, their boarding-school mission was opened.

Ref: *New Mexico Historical Review*, v. 13 (April, 1938), pp. 134-142; *Missouri Republican*, St. Louis, July 31, August 28, 1852; L. H. Warner's *Archbishop Lamy an Epoch Maker* (Santa Fe, c1936); J. B. Salpointe's *Soldiers of the Cross* (Banning, Calif., 1898), pp. 202-204. William Carr Lane, who left Independence, Mo., with the mail stage, on August 5, noted that they "passed the encampment of Bishop Lamy about 2 miles east of the State line."—Historical Society of New Mexico, *Publications No. 20*, p. 25. Elsewhere it is stated that Lamy's party set out from Independence on August 1. But it must have been no earlier than August 5. Bishop Lamy's party on the Santa Fe trail was met by eastbound travelers—as noted in the *Missouri Republican*, St. Louis, August 28, 1852; *St. Louis News*, August 31, 1852 (reprinted in New York *Daily Times*, September 15, 23, 1852), etc.

❡ August.—Steamboats on the middle Missouri this month included the *El Paso, Elvira, Clara, Kansas, Timour No. 2, St. Ange,* and *Isabel.*

At least two boats were at Council Bluffs in August. The *El Paso* left there August 7, and returned to St. Louis on the 11th. The *Kansas* left Council Bluffs on August 15, and reached St. Louis on the 21st. Port of destination for the other craft, from information available, was either Weston, or St. Joseph. The *Isabel* (which left Weston August 23) brought down 294 packs of buffalo robes consigned to R. & W. Campbell, St. Louis.

Ref: *Missouri Republican*, St. Louis, August, and early September, 1852, issues.

❡ August.—Messrs. Mayer and Co's. wagon train, bound for Chihuahua, left Independence, Mo., in mid-month. "Our caravan . . . consisted of eighteen or twenty waggons, each drawn by ten mules, with the requisite number for relays, and the complement of drivers, muleteers, &c.," wrote cotraveler Julius Froebel (in a letter dated "Chihuahua, Nov. 25, 1852"). "The whole party was under the conduct of a second partner of the Firm, Mr. H[enry] Mayer."

Froebel (having been invited by the firm's Samuel Kaufmann, in New York, to make this Santa Fe trail journey) had arrived at Independence, Mo., on July 5. In his later-published book—the English edition entitled *Seven Years' Travel in Central America, Northern Mexico, and the Far West of the United States*—"Book II" was devoted to the "Journey from New York by Missouri to the North of Mexico; stay at Chihuahua, and Return Through Texas." (Most of the material had been printed earlier—as letters written from Mexico during November and December, 1852—in the New York *Daily Tribune*, in 1853.)

His comments on Independence included these: "[It] . . . is a small town, with the character of a frontier place engaged in an extensive carrying trade. . . . The town is surrounded by wheelwrights' shops, large premises filled with new wagons, painted red, green, or blue, and the whole trade of the place consists in supplying the wants of trading and emigrant caravans, which start from this and from a few other stations on the Missouri, for New Mexico, Utah, California, and Oregon. . . . Formerly Independence had the exclusive benefit of this communication 'over the plains,' . . . but at the time of my visit Westport, lying twelve miles higher up the Missouri, disputed the monopoly. . . . Formerly oxen were here used . . . as draught-cattle for the journeys across the prairies; but mules have gradually superseded them. . . ." [He remarked that Missouri mules were "noted for their beauty, size, and strength, and although inferior to the small Mexican mules in briskness and endurance, they readily find purchasers even in Mexico, where they are sought chiefly for carriage teams."]

On August 17, in company with Henry Mayer and his bride (the wedding had taken place at Cincinnati late in June), Froebel set out to overtake the wagons, which had made an earlier start. It was August 27 when the Mayer train arrived at Council Grove; and September 3 when it reached the Great Bend of the Arkansas. (From September 1 to 8, the caravan was practically surrounded by buffalo.)

About September 9, while traveling the "river route" (rather than the "dry" one), the party met numerous bands of Comanches (hunting buffalo). Among the chiefs who visited the Mayer train were To-ho-pe-te-ca-ne (or, the "White Tent") and Way-ya-ba-tosh-a (or, the "White Eagle"), and a more important, older chief, Okh-akh-tzo-mo.

On September 10 Fort Atkinson was reached. "It is a group of adobe buildings, with canvas roofs—something between a house and a tent. . . . The word 'fort,' . . . here, merely signified a permanent camp of eighty foot-soldiers; but to all these posts is attached a well-stored magazine where clothing, saddlery, ironmongery, tinware, and provisions may be obtained, from the indispensable flour and bacon up to preserved oysters and champagne. . . . We were, however, so well provided with the chief delicacies, that we had, in these places, to sell—not to buy."

The Mayer caravan "halted a few miles above the Fort," and "numbers of the Kiowas" visited their camp. (Froebel commented on the flowers to be seen: "Yellow sunflowers, of various kinds, red Cinnias, blue Delphiniums and Salvias, white-leaved Euphorbias, and pigmy Asters, with small violet flowers;

elegant little mallows, with crimson and vermillion blossoms . . . [etc.].")

On September 12 the Mayer train crossed the Arkansas; left the banks of the Cimarron on September 23. Subsequently, after reaching Las Vegas, N. M., on October 5, the caravan set out for El Paso; and on November 23 left that place for Chihuahua.

Ref: Froebel, *op. cit.*, pp. 205-341; or, Julius Froebel's letters in the New York *Daily Tribune*, February 7, March 5, 11, April 16, 20, 1853; *KHQ*, v. 7, p. 326; Henry R. Wagner and C. L. Camp's *The Plains and the Rockies* . . . (Columbus, Ohio, 1953), pp. 377, 378.

❡ August.—As noted by the eastbound "August" mail party (arriving at Independence on the 23d), these were the trains "met on the road outward":

Jones & Russell's—at Point of Rocks.

Hubble's [*Hubbell's*]—on the Cimarron. ("Mr. Hotchleadter," who left Santa Fe on August 9, met [J. B.] Yager's train at Barclay's Fort on August 13; and met "Hubble's" train at Rabbit Ear on the 18th.)

Caruthers and Hueston's [*Houston's?*]—at Fort Mackay [Fort Atkinson]. (Baptist missionary Samuel Gorman, and family, traveled with the train headed by "Mr. Caruthers." Gorman's account says the trip from Kansas, Mo., to Las Vegas, N. M., took 12 weeks. At the Arkansas Crossing—west of Fort Atkinson, hordes of Comanches and Kiowas were encamped. The wagon train arrived on a Sunday, and stayed till Monday morning. By the wagonmaster's orders, Mrs. Gorman and the children had to remain all day in a carriage, under cover.)

Mayer & Kauffman's [Messrs. Mayer & Co's. train]—at Rock creek. (Another account says the mail party reported "H. Mayer and lady, and Mr. Wm. Stone and Jno. Flournoy" were "going along well.")

Bishop Lamy [The Rt. Rev. John B. Lamy's party—*see* pp. 1115, 1116]— near Council Grove.

Francis X. Aubry (who left Santa Fe July 31, and reached Independence August 25) had met Stone on the Arkansas; Preston Beck at Diamond Spring, and "Major [_____?] and lady at 110"—all after the middle of August.

"Mr. Hotchleadter" (or E. Hockstadt[er]—*see* June 21 entry), noted above, met Stone's train at Lower Cimarron on August 24, Beck's train at Pawnee Fork on September 2; "Meyer" [Mayer] on September 3 at "Crow" [Cow] creek.

The eastbound "September" mail party (arriving at Independence on the 20th) reported having met William Stone's train at Red river; Bishop Lamy's party at Willow Bar; Preston Beck's train at Lower Cimarron Spring; Henry Mayer's at Fort Atkinson (September 10 or 11); at Pawnee Fork had overtaken a Jones & Russell train "on the route home"; and had met Francis X. Aubry's Santa Fe-bound train near 110-mile creek.

Ref: *Missouri Republican*, St. Louis, August 28, 31, September 26, 29, 1852; *Weekly Intelligencer*, St. Louis, September 7, October 4, 1852; *Old Santa Fe*, Santa Fe, v. 1 (January, 1914), pp. 316, 317 (for Gorman).

❡ August 9.—A party of 12 to 15 "returned Californians" (mostly Missourians), traveling with pack mules, arrived at Independence after a 61-day journey over the Oregon-California trail.

Eleven were named: Allen and William White, Pleasant and Samuel Farris, Hiram Miller, William M. Dunn, James L. Dickerson, of Arrow Rock, Joseph W. Scott, Ohio, John McCart, Howard county, Mo., William H. Grant, Columbia, Mo., Samuel McClelland's black man, Jackson county, Mo.

Ref: Savannah (Mo.), *Sentinel*, August 28, 1852 (reprinted from the *Missouri Republican*, which had published the letter, from Independence, August 10, containing the information).

❧ Mid-August.—Capt. William S. Ketchum, Sixth U. S. infantry, accompanied by his wife, and a "large number of persons from . . . Fort [Laramie] and vicinity," reached the States. His party had been "detained some days at the Big Blue by high water." Ketchum arrived in St. Louis August 17. (By advance report he had expected, originally, to reach the Missouri border about August 6.)

Ref: *Missouri Republican*, St. Louis, August 18, 1852. The detention at Big Blue *suggests* the party did not come in via the "Marysville crossing" where Marshall's ferry presumably was in operation, although it was the military road crossing to Fort Leavenworth.

❧ August 17.—The proposed 200-mile Hannibal and St. Joseph railroad was put under contract (to John Duff & Co., Boston) by the president ("Col. R. M. Stewart") and directors of the company, at St. Joseph, Mo.

It was reported: "The whole work is to be completed, with cars, locomotives, and every thing in perfect order, within four years"; and that "Twenty-five miles of the road, at each end, will be commenced as soon as the location is made."

Ref: St. Joseph *Gazette*, July 14, August 18, 1852; *Jefferson Inquirer*, Jefferson City, Mo., August 28, 1852; *Missouri Republican*, St. Louis, August 25, 1852.

❧ August 20.—Fourteen Missourians, overland from California (they had left Placerville June 14) passed through Savannah, Mo., on their way home. One of these returnees was "Mr. Harman," of Andrew county.

Ref: Savannah (Mo.) *Sentinel*, August 21, 1852.

❧ About August 20 (by advance report) "Mr. Z. Rochan," of New York, and some 20 employees ("picked mountain men"), with a flock of 6,000 sheep, and a large number of cattle, horses, and mules, expected to leave the St. Joseph, Mo., area, bound for California but intending to winter on Green river, and complete the journey in 1853).

Ref: *Missouri Republican*, St. Louis, August 15, 1852. Rochan was said to have made the overland journey "several times," but not with large stock drives.

❧ August.—Leaving Independence on the 21st, and Westport on the 24th, was a small merchant train (four large mule-drawn wagons), in charge of Richard S. Phelps, which an Independence man referred to as a Holladay & Warner train. In this Salt Lake City-bound company were 13 men ("all armed"), two women, and an infant.

Phelps, his wife, and their four-weeks-old child, traveled in a "very commodious" mule-drawn carriage. In another mule-drawn vehicle were Benjamin G. Ferris (Utah territory's new secretary) and his wife. Also there was a small baggage-wagon. "Our train, when stretched out in the road, with its accompaniment of spare mules looks quite imposing," wrote Mrs. Ferris. "Our carriage has fairly become our domicil—our parlor, kitchen, and bedroom . . . [stowed in it are] blankets, buffalo-robe, shawls, umbrella, overcoat, port-folio, books, basket, carpet-bag, ham, pickles, pistols, and other things 'too numerous to mention'." The Ferris' "mess" included "Denton," "Morse," "Doc" (their driver), and "Doc's" relative "Mundy" (a "tall, gentlemanly man"). Aside from hired hands of the train, there were also two young men—one named "Pierce" (an "amateur traveler"; nephew of presidential nominee Franklin Pierce), the other, a young Virginia lawyer named "Stringfellow."

Mrs. Ferris' first travel letter was written August 25 from "Shawnee Country, eight miles from Westport." Her second letter, dated September 2, written at a camp near (east of) the "Big Vermillion," recounted the journey up the Kansas river valley. She wrote ". . . we approached the Kansas, which was lined with a beautiful belt of trees. We reached the river in advance of the train, and crossed in a ferryboat in season to encamp on the north bank. . . . It was low water; and, after leaving the boat, we crossed a troublesome sand level before reaching the grassy bank. The rest of the train came up, but not in time to cross [that day]. . . . [The Papin ferry, at "Topeka," probably.] The next day they went "many miles" out of the way to "find a convenient crossing over one of the affluents of the Kansas."

About September 3d(?) the train crossed the Big Blue [Alcove Spring area], and camped "a little out of the belt of tall trees, with which it is lined." The Little Blue was reached on September 7, and Fort Kearny on the 10th (where Mrs. Ferris wrote another letter). Her next one, on September 27, was from "Ward & Garay's Station" [the trading post of Seth E. Ward and William Guerrier], seven miles west of Fort Laramie. On October 10 (two days before the train entered South Pass) Benjamin G. Ferris wrote a letter mentioning the "sickness of myself, and others in the camp," and of trouble with inferior mules, etc. The Ferrises (and the train?) reached Salt Lake City on October 26.

Ref: *Missouri Republican*, St. Louis, August 3, 28, October 20, November 4, 1852 (B. G. Ferris' October 10 letter is in the November 4 issue); New York *Daily Times*, February 1, 1853 (for an October 30, 1852, letter by B. G. Ferris); Benjamin G. Ferris, *Utah and the Mormons* . . . (New York, 1856); Mrs. Benjamin G. Ferris, *The Mormons at Home* . . . (New York, 1856), pp. 1-84 (for the travel letters); *Putnam's Monthly Magazine*, New York, v. 6 (July-December, 1855), pp. 144-148, 262-266, 376-381, 501-505, 602-605 (for Mrs. Ferris' letters of "Life Among the Mormons"). It is likely that the "young Virginia lawyer named 'Stringfellow'" was James W. Stringfellow, resident of Atchison in 1856. He is described (in *KHC*, v. 14, pp. 135 and 139) as "of Virginia," and as a young man who "had had some mountain experience."

❡ August 23.—William Gilliss (connected with the history of Kansas [City], Mo., since 1830) advertised for rent his "Large Hotel or

Tavern" in Kansas, Mo., known as Union Hotel." (*See* p. 1005.)

His notice (in the St. Louis *Republican* of August 23, and later dates) stated: "The house is new, built of brick, and contains forty-six rooms, with a pump in the kitchen, and every room furnished. Its location is on the Missouri river, and immediately above where the Missouri steamboats land. The town of Kansas is, by this time, so well known as the starting point for New and Old Mexico, the Rocky Mountains, California and Oregon, that farther comment is unnecessary. Attached to the house is a large brick stable, 100 feet long, to which is attached a large cattle yard. Immediate possession can be given. . . ."

Ref: *Missouri Republican*, St. Louis, August 23, 1852, and succeeding issues; *see* annals index, for earlier references to William Gilliss. William G. Barkley (who, in 1851, had been running the Union Hotel—*see* annals, p. 1006—went into the Missouri river steamboat trade.

❡ August 23.—In charge of "Mr. [James] Rupe," the August mail from Santa Fe arrived at Independence, Mo. Those who accompanied it said the trip had been "a very agreeable one." "The mail party . . . tried Aubry's new route [from Cold Spring, on the Cimarron, to the Arkansas]," reported the *Occidental Messenger,* "and found it a most excellent one for summer and winter."

The Independence paper also commented: "Aubry deserves praise for marking it out so successfully, and in spite of all opposition and danger, opening up a way so useful to all who cross the plains. . . ." The *Missouri Republican's* Independence correspondent, on the 23d, noted that the mail party had overtaken Aubry's train en route east "at the crossing of Arkansas, on his own road. . . ." (*See* next entry.)

A "passenger," or traveler with the mail party, apparently was Charles L. Spencer. On August 14, 20 miles east of Fort Atkinson, William C. Lane (and the westbound "August" mail) "Met the returning mail stage at about 4 p. m., with a single passenger, a Mr. Spoven [*i. e.*, Spencer?] a native of Santa Fe in his private carriage drawn by two mules with which force he keeps up, with the stage. He goes to Missouri for his family." ("Mr. Spencer and lady" were among the "passengers" with the "September" Santa Fe-bound mail party.)

L. N. Ross, whose train had been overtaken at Plum Buttes, also "came in with the mail." (His wagons would reach Independence around the end of August.)

Ref: *Weekly Intelligencer*, St. Louis, September 7, 1852 (from *Occidental Messenger,* Independence, August 28); New York *Daily Tribune,* September 7, 1852 (from *Missouri Republican*); Historical Society of New Mexico, *Publications No. 20* (for Lane); *Missouri Republican*, St. Louis, September 26, 1852.

❡ August 24.—Lt. Israel C. Woodruff (topographical engineers) and his party (teamsters and wagons), escorted by Bvt. Capt. Simon B. Buckner (Sixth infantry), and detail of (six?) soldiers, set out eastward from Fort Atkinson. (*See* June 7 annals entry.)

From news via F. X. Aubry (who reached St. Louis near the end of

August), the *Missouri Republican* of August 31 reported: "Capt. Buckner
and Lt. Woodruff were to leave Fort Atkinson on the 25th for the States.
Mr. Chouteau's [pleasure] party would return with them. Lt. Woodruff has
explored the country north and south of the Arkansas River, and it is understood that he has reported in favor of a [Santa Fe trail] route along the
Pawnee Fork and Buckner's Branch to intersect the road made by Aubry
from Cold Spring to the Arkansas." (When William Carr Lane reached Fort
Atkinson on August 15, he mentioned Woodruff as one of the officers present.)

At St. Mary's (Pottawatomie) Mission, Father J. B. Duerinck
recorded in his diary: "On September 6th 1852 Lieutenant Woodruff, escorted by Captain Buckner with a party of six soldiers and
some teamsters and wagons reconnoitered the new road from the
mission to Rock Creek. Medard Beaubien & [Brother] Th[omas]
McNamara acted as Guides." "Lieutenant Woodruff, U. S. A. returns
today from his reconnoitering expedition to mouth of Republican
River and Fort Atkinson. From the mission to mouth of Republican
river, forty miles; to mouth of Clarke Creek, which will be recommended for the location of a new depot, 38 miles." (*See* portion
of Woodruff's "Chart" reproduced on p. 1022, on which can be seen
the "new" road which he reconnoitered on September 6, from the
mission eastward to Rock creek. It is labeled "Reconnoitered
under orders of 6th Mil[itar]y Dept." Though Woodruff may have
recommended the "mouth of Clarke Creek," as the site for a new
fort, the location selected by a board of officers appointed for that
purpose, of which he was one—*see* p. 1131—was higher upstream
at the Republican-Smoky Hill junction. As shown on his "Chart,"
p. 1022, the future Fort Riley is labeled "Site.")

Ref: *Missouri Republican*, St. Louis, August 31, 1852; J. B. Duerinck's "Diary," as
quoted in Garraghan, *op. cit.*, v. 2, p. 656, Fort Atkinson post returns (microfilm from
National Archives), for record of Buckner's departure from that post on August 24 "commdg
escort to Lieut Woodruff, Topl Engs."; Historical Society of New Mexico, *Publications
No. 20*, p. 37.

❡ August 24.—Capt. William Steele, Second dragoons, and a "detachment of mounted troops, near 100 strong" (by advance report
in Washington, D. C.), left Fort Leavenworth on the march overland to New Mexico.

The "October" eastbound mail party (reaching Independence on the 22d)
reported that "Capt. Steel, with his command, had lost 135 horses and mules
at Pawnee Fork, which were not all recovered. Those with the command
are scarcely able to stand the trip." And also reported that "[Francis X.]
Aubrey was met at Aubrey's crossing of the Arkansas; also [James L.?] Collins,
and Mrs. Steel, and Mrs. Sturges." Presumably the two ladies were the wives
of Captain Steele, and 2d Lt. Samuel D. Sturgis (Second dragoons).

Ref: *Weekly Intelligencer*, St. Louis, August 10, 1852 (from *National Intelligencer*);

Missouri Republican, St. Louis, August 28, 1852 (which had an Independence, Mo., August 23 telegram stating: "Major Steel and troops leave Fort Leavenworth for Santa Fe tomorrow"). The steamboat *Isabel,* leaving Jefferson Barracks, August 14 or 15, carried four officers and 69 men up to Fort Leavenworth; and likely they made up part of Steele's command.—32d Cong., 2d Sess., Sen. *Ex. Doc. No. 18* (Serial 660), p. 14. On June 25 the *St. Paul* had left St. Louis "having on board the large lot of [fine] dragoon horses purchased for the government by Thomas Gray. . . . They will cost Uncle Sam on delivery at Fort Leavenworth, $95[?] each."—*Missouri Republican,* St. Louis, June 26, 1852. (The combination of small newsprint, and microfilm, made the cost figure difficult to determine.)

❧ August 25.—Francis X. Aubry, "the fleet traveler of the Prairie," and party of some 50 men (including Bvt. Maj. Jefferson Van Horne, Third infantry, and "Messrs. [Charles E.] Kearney and [William F.] Dyer"), arrived at Independence, with 12 wagons, two carriages, and 250 mules, after a 25-day journey from Santa Fe— Aubry's *third* wagon train trip east of the year. As reported: "The sum of $25,000 in specie and $30,000 in drafts" was brought in by this party.

Aubry carried copies of the Santa Fe *Gazette Extra* of July 17, which contained "an article written by Mr. Aubry in reply to Mr. Pope [Bvt. Capt. John Pope, Topographical engineers], in defence of [being the discoverer of] the new road he laid out, in which a considerable cut off is made, from Cold Spring to the Arkansas River, on the Santa Fe route." The *Gazette's* comment was: "the probability is that civilians will generally call it Aubrey's Route, while the military will designate it as Pope's Route." (For Pope's exploration in 1851, *see* p. 1038.) The *Occidental Messenger,* Independence, of June 26(?) had stated: "We learn from our exchanges and other sources, that Captain Pope disputes with Aubry the right of discovery to his new route."

Ref: *Missouri Republican,* St. Louis, August 31, 1852; *Jefferson Inquirer,* Jefferson City, Mo., August 31, 1852; *The Weekly Tribune,* Liberty, Mo., July 2, 1852; New York *Daily Times,* September 13, 1852 (from St. Louis *News,* of August 31). Aubry had left Santa Fe on July 31. Dyer presumably joined the party at Fort Atkinson.

❧ August 28.—The "August" U. S. mail from Salt Lake City reached Independence, Mo. Stage passengers were "Messrs. Campbell, of St. Louis, and Rantall."

The mail carriers had made the trip out to Fort Laramie, and back, in 23 traveling days (on five other days they had been delayed by high water). West of Fort Kearny they had overtaken three parties of "returning Californians" who would reach the States shortly.

Ref: *Missouri Republican,* St. Louis, August 31, 1852, New York *Daily Tribune,* September 8, 1852.

❧ September 1.—In his annual report, Agent Asbury M. Coffey, head of the Osage River Agency (covering the tribes of the Marais des Cygnes river area), noted the (recent?) arrival of "about thirty of the Six Nations, or New York Indians, who are stopping temporarily within the bounds of this agency. . . ."

Coffey described them as poor, diseased, and destitute. "When able to travel they will join their brethren, whose territory is south of and continuous to that of the Miamis. This territory and people are not assigned to any agency."

Ref: Comm'r of Indian Affairs, *Report,* 1852 (Coffey's report, therein).

❢ September 1.—McCauley & Kirby (of Independence, Mo.?), by contract made with Capt. F. H. Masten, at Fort Leavenworth, agreed to deliver 600 bushels of corn ($2.33½ per bushel) at Fort Atkinson, "Santa Fe route," on or before October 25.

R. Kirby, William McCoy, and John McCoy were sureties for the $2,500 bond.

Ref: 32d Cong., 2d Sess., *Sen. Ex. Doc. No. 18* (Serial 660), p. 17.

❢ September 3.—In Washington, D. C., a 14-member delegation of "Mississippi" Sacs & Foxes paid a second visit to the Indian Bureau. Sac chief (Moses) Keokuk and Fox chief Powashiek headed the group. (These Indians probably had left their reserve in "Kansas" about August 9. When William Walker [Wyandot] went to Kansas [City], Mo., on August 11, he saw there "Agent Chenault, with a large deputation of Sacs and Foxes on their way to Washington.")

The speeches of Keokuk, Powashiek, Tackwauss, Waashawmeesaw (or young Black Hawk), Mahnwytook, Nakascowat, Monuss, and Mahnatooaa, were printed in the *National Intelligencer,* which reported, also, that the Indians seemed to have "no very distinct purpose in view, beyond perhaps the objects of complaining generally, and endeavoring to extract from the generosity or commisseration of the Government all that they can." Chief Powashiek, in his talk, mentioned that the Sacs & Foxes "had made a [peace] treaty with the Pawnees. . . ."

Ref: New York *Daily Times,* September 18, 1851 (from *National Intelligencer,* September 4); *Missouri Republican,* St. Louis, August 16, 1852; William Walker's "Journals," *loc. cit.* For mention of "young Black Hawk" as "Aw-tha-me-saw," see annals, p. 568. Wives of several Sacs were in the party. In 33d Cong., 1st Sess., *Sen. Ex. Doc. No. 69* (Serial 701), pp. 290, 291, Agent J. R. Chenault's accounts include items for payment (of $150) on August 15, 1852 (date of their arrival at St. Louis) to the *Elvira's* clerk for passage of the Sac & Fox delegation from Kansas to St. Louis; and payment, September 28, to clerk of the *Timour No. 2,* for return passage of the Indians. The Pawnee-Sac & Fox hostility dated back to 1848—see annals, p. 763.

❢ September.—The Santa Fe-bound "September" mail was met at Lost Spring on the 7th by an eastbound traveler. He reported the stage passengers were "Mr. [Charles L.] Spencer and lady, and Mr. [Solomon] Houck. . . ."

Ref: *Missouri Republican,* St. Louis, September 26, 1852.

❢ DIED: on September 7, "Gen." Thomas Jefferson Sutherland, at "Iowa Mission, Nebraska Territory" (near present Highland, Doniphan county), of typhus fever. (*See* annals—p. 1006—for earlier mention of his connection with "Kansas.")

In June the Weston (Mo.) *Reporter* had published Sutherland's notice (dated June 24) of a planned "tour in the eastern part of the Territory of

Nebraska for the purpose of topographical examination and search for minerals and mill-sites . . ."; he invited others to join him; suggested August 5 as the starting date; outlined a journey encompassing a trip either up the west side of the Missouri to the Big Nemaha's mouth, westward to its source, then across to the Big Blue, downstream to the Kansas, thence eastward along that river to Missouri, or, reversing the route.

On August 5 Bvt. Lt. Col. Benjamin L. Beall, from "Head Quarters Fort Leavenworth, N. T.," wrote a notice (published in the Weston *Reporter* of August 14—if not earlier) stating that he had "received a communication from . . . citizens of Platte co. [Mo.]," informing him of the proposed tour "in the Territory of Nebraska" of "one styling himself General Thomas Jefferson Sutherland"; and that such an expedition—unless fully sanctioned by proper authority—would be in violation of United States treaties with the Indian tribes. He warned that "it will become my duty to take such measures . . . as may be necessary to prevent the intrusion of whites into the Indian country, contrary to law. . . ."

Ref: Savannah (Mo.) *Sentinel*, September 25, 1852, or St. Joseph *Gazette*, September 29, 1852 (for the item on Sutherland's death); *Jefferson Inquirer*, Jefferson City, Mo., August 28, 1852 (for Beall's notice, reprinted from the Weston *Reporter* of August 14); New York *Daily Tribune*, October 7, 1852 (for biographical data, and commentary, on Sutherland); St. Joseph *Gazette*, June 30, 1852 (for Sutherland's June 24 notice, reprinted from the Weston *Reporter*); Malin, *op. cit.*, pp. 77-79; and his article on Sutherland in *Nebraska History*, Lincoln, v. 34 (September, 1953), pp. 181-214. Additional data on Sutherland can be found in the *Weekly Kansas Chief*, Troy, November 23, 1893 (or, see *ibid.*, in a bound clipping volume, pp. 403-406, in KHi library).

❡ DIED: on September 14(?), Calvin Perkins, government blacksmith for the Shawnees since 1844.

William Walker (Wyandot), on September 14, "Rec'd a dispatch . . . informing me of the death of Mr. Perkins, the Shawnee Blacksmith."

Ref: William Walker's "Journals," *loc. cit.*; KHC, v. 8, p. 256; annals, p. 533.

❡ In mid-September, Francis X. Aubry left the Missouri border for Santa Fe. About the 17th, or 18th, his train was met at 110-mile creek by the incoming mail party. (This was Aubry's last journey on the Santa Fe trail.)

He carried some government stores this trip. On September 3, in a contract made at St. Louis with Maj. D. H. Vinton, Aubry had agreed to transport 29 bales of clothing (at $12.50 per 100 pounds) from Westport, Mo., to Fort Union, N. M.

About October 10(?) the incoming "October" mail party met Aubry at "Aubrey's crossing of the Arkansas."

Ref: *Weekly Intelligencer*, St. Louis, October 4, 1852; 32d Cong., 2d Sess., Sen. Ex. Doc. No. 18 (Serial 660), p. 15; *Missouri Republican*, St. Louis, October 24, 1852. Gov. William Carr Lane, in a November 16, 1852, letter from Santa Fe, reported: "[Aubry] sets out tomorrow for California, via the Mexican state—Sonora, with a flock of sheep. He appears to be restless, when stationary, & only contented, when making these appalling journeys."—*New Mexico Historical Review*, v. 3 (April, 1928), p. 190.

❡ September.—Steamboats on the middle Missouri this month included the *St. Ange, Isabel, Clara, Timour No. 2, Banner State, Highland Mary, El Paso,* and *Kansas.*

The *Highland Mary*, upbound, was at St. Joseph on September 15; went on to Kanesville, Iowa; left there on the 21st; and returned to St. Louis on the 29th. The *Kansas*, upbound, left Weston, for Kanesville, on September 30. *Apparently,* no other boats made trips to Council Bluffs this month.

Ref: *Missouri Republican*, St. Louis, September, and early October, 1852, issues.

❦ September 20.—The "September" U. S. mail from Santa Fe, in charge of William Allison, reached Independence. New Mexico territory's associate justice, Horace Mower, eastbound to visit family and friends, was a stage passenger.

Ref: *Weekly Intelligencer*, St. Louis, October 4, 1852, or *The Weekly Tribune*, Liberty, Mo., October 1, 1852; *Missouri Republican*, St. Louis, September 29, 1852.

❦ September 20.—Overland from Oregon City (which they had left July 6), a small company of men arrived at St. Joseph, after a 72-day trip.

Missourians in the group were: D. B. Frost, Livingston county, James Sullivan, Mercer county, Thomas W. Harris of Weston, and William Lewis of St. Joseph. Others were from Illinois, Texas, Indiana, and Iowa.

Ref: St. Joseph (Mo.) *Gazette*, September 22, 1852.

❦ September 24.—In his report from "St. Mary's Pottawatomie Mission, Nebraska Territory" (present St. Marys, Kan.) Father John B. Duerinck stated that the mission farm ("a sort of 'model farm' for the Indians") consisted of 170 fenced acres, 95 under cultivation. "We have planted this year sixty acres in corn, twenty-five in oats, six in potatoes, and the balance in turnips, hemp, and buckwheat. We raise a great many cattle, as much for our own sake as for that of the Indians, hoping to induce them to follow our example. . . ."

(In March, 1852, Duerinck had ordered a "grass-mowing machine, propelled by horse-power" from Cody & Baker, Weston, Mo. He wrote manufacturer Cyrus McCormick, Chicago, in October, 1854: ". . . I believe that I have been the first man that has introduced your mowing machine in these prairies. We have met with success. One of your machines of 1852 used to be the wonder of this country: people have come 25 miles to see it in operation. . . .")

Ref: Comm'r of Indian Affairs, *Report*, 1852 (Duerinck's report, therein); Garraghan, *op. cit.*, v. 2, pp. 653, 654; *Illinois Catholic Historical Review*, Chicago, v. 11 (April, 1929), p. 291.

❦ Around September 25(?) Maj. Winslow F. Sanderson and two companies of Mounted riflemen arrived at Fort Leavenworth from Fort Laramie (left September 3), ending a long summer's march over the Santa Fe and Oregon trails. (*See* pp. 1105, and 1108.) Co-travelers included Stephen Clay King (*see* p. 1105), "Messrs. Gevelette and Weed of Georgia, Dr. Andrew of Kentucky, Mr. Rich of

Buffalo, N. Y., and Mr. Mason of St. Louis, all of whom have been travelling for their health."

The *Missouri Republican* (after Sanderson reached St. Louis aboard the *Clara,* September 30) described the journey as a march of over *2,000 miles;* and as one of the longest and most rapid marches ever made by U. S. troops. It was stated the riflemen had been *four months* in the saddle; and had lost only one man (accidentally run over by a wagon). [Sanderson and his men had set out from Jefferson Barracks in June, and apparently traveled overland across Missouri to Fort Leavenworth.]

On the September journey from Fort Laramie to Fort Leavenworth, these westbound outfits were met by the Mounted riflemen:

[R. & W.] Campbell's train (loaded with Indian presents)—on September 8, at Ash Hollow.

[Joseph] Bissenett's [Bissonette's] train—on September 12, at Cottonwood Point.

Holladay, Phelps and Warner's train for Salt Lake—on September 13, encamped at Plum creek; all the teamsters ill of chills and fever.

Robinson's train—on September 13, at Plum creek.

Three wagons laden with grain for the mail contractor at Fort Kearny—on September 18, at Little Blue.

Shaw's Ward's and Geary's trains [*i. e.,* John S. Shaw's; Seth E. Ward and William Guerrier's]—on September 21, at Snake creek.

A flock of 3,000 head of sheep, belonging to Mr. Reshaw [John Richard], bound for Salt Lake—September 21, at the St. Joseph-Independence roads junction.

Ref: *Missouri Republican,* St. Louis, October 2, 1852; or, New York *Daily Times,* October 11, 1852; or, New York *Daily Tribune,* October 11, 1852.

❡ Autumn(?)—Andrew B. Canville (and family) removed from Kansas (City), Mo., to the Osage reserve in 1852 and opened a trading post (in what is now Erie township, Neosho county) which he operated for nearly 20 years (1852-1871?). *See* p. 442, for earlier mention of this Frenchman.

His location was some three miles above the mouth of Canville creek (between it and the Neosho river), near a ford long used by the Osages. By survey description the site is described as in the NE¼ of Sec. 22, T. 28 S., R. 19 E. Accounts state Canville's place consisted (ultimately) of three houses—the store, the home, and an inn for travelers—each 25 by 40 feet, and solidly constructed of walnut logs laid in cement.

At Canville Trading Post in September, 1865, the Osages signed a treaty ceding a part of their reserve in Kansas. From June 13, 1866, to January 10, 1872, there was a "Canville" post office. Andrew B. Canville was the third of five postmasters who served during the six years. (He was appointed September 23, 1867; and his successor was appointed May 16, 1870.)

Probably the Canvilles removed to Indian territory in 1871. They were still in Canville township (since divided) when the 1870 census was taken in June. (Canville, his wife, Mary Louise [Terrien] Canville, and nine children, aged 5 to 22, were recorded therein.) In 1876, when A. B. Canville returned to Neosho county on a visit, his home was said to be "Just south of Elgin Kansas," in the Indian territory. He died two years later—in July, 1878. His wife was one-quarter Osage. She, and her children were on the Osage tribal rolls. Mary Louise (Terrien) Canville died after 1890, and prior to 1906 (when the last Osage roll was made).

Ref: W. W. Graves' *History of Neosho County* (1949), v. 1, pp. 125-127; L. W. Duncan's *History of Neosho and Wilson Counties Kansas* (Fort Scott, 1902), pp. 108, 109; R. W. Baughman's *Kansas Post Offices* (c1961), pp. 21, 210, and other data compiled from official post office records, in KHi; *Western Journal of Commerce*, Kansas City, Mo., August 14, 1858; U. S. census, 1870, Canville township, Neosho county, Kansas; *Neosho County Journal*, Osage Mission, June 14, 1876, and August 21, 1878 (which states: "A. B. Canville, who settled in 1852 above Erie . . . died about a month since in the Indian Territory, to which he removed a few years ago"). The relationship of Andrew B. Canville (native of France, according to four census records) to the Quennevilles who came earlier to Canada, and from there to Missouri and "Kansas," has not been determined. Among the employees of Trader James Aird who arrived at Prairie du Chien (Wis.) on September 11, 1816, was a Jean Canifell (Canville?).—SIA, St. Louis, "Records," v. 3, p. 34 (in KHi). A Francois Quenneville (American Fur Company employee) married Wihethtange (an Osage woman) about 1818(?). Their known children were Francois (b. 1819), Pierre (b. 1822?), Angelique (b. 1826), Andre (b. 1829), and Elizabeth (b. _____?), whose marriage, August 10, 1840, has been noted in these annals. *See* editorial note by Stella M. Drumm in John C. Luttig's *Journal of a Fur-Trading Expedition* . . . (1920), p. 60, for Quenneville data. *Also, see,* annals, p. 39. Mrs. Blanche O. Garrison, Bartlesville, Okla., a grandniece of Mrs. Andrew B. Canville, has been of much assistance in the compilation of data on the Canville family.

❮ October 1.—The stages carrying the U. S. mail for Santa Fe, and for Salt Lake City, left Independence, Mo., on schedule. Passengers in the Santa Fe-bound coach were New Mexico territory's associate justice John S. Watts, Indian agent Edward H. Wingfield, and the latter's servant. In the Fort Laramie-bound stage were Utah territory's recently appointed chief justice Lazarus H. Reid, of New York, and associate justice Leonidas Shaver, of Lexington, Mo.

Reid, on arriving at Fort Laramie, turned back because of ill health. On November 5, aboard the *Timour No. 2*, he reached St. Louis.

Ref: *Missouri Republican*, St. Louis, September 17, October 7, 1852; St. Joseph (Mo.) *Gazette*, October 20, 1852; New York *Daily Times*, October 21, 1852; New York *Daily Tribune*, November 16, 1852 (from St. Louis *Union* of November 6).

❮ October.—Plying the middle Missouri this month were the *Banner State, Isabel, Robert Campbell, Elvira, Highland Mary, El Paso, Clara, Kansas, Timour No. 2,* and three boats new to this river—the *Brunette, Polar Star,* and *Herald.*

The *Brunette* was at Kansas (City), Mo., on October 4. (William Walker, Wyandotte, in his diary, noted: "Went to Kansas and learned that Mr. Dawson and Sophia got off this morning at 4 o'clock on board the 'Brunette'.") The *Missouri Republican*, St. Louis, of September 18, had reported: "The Brunette has been permanently placed in the Missouri river trade. . . ." The new *Polar Star* was at Fort Leavenworth on October 13; and left St. Joseph (downbound) on the 14th. On her second(?) trip up the Missouri she left Weston (for St. Louis) on October 29. The *Herald* left Weston on October 16, for St. Louis, after her first(?) trip up.

Ref: *Missouri Republican*, St. Louis, September 18, October, and early November, 1852, issues; William Walker's "Journals," *loc. cit.* The *Brunette* had been completed at Louisville, Ky., in May, 1852—*see Missouri Republican, May 23, 1852.*

❧ MARRIED: Alexander Soule Johnson (aged 20; born in "Kansas" on July 11, 1832), of Kansas (City), Mo., and Prudence C. Funk, on October 7, at St. Joseph, Mo., by the Right Rev. Bishop Paine.

Ref: St. Joseph *Gazette*, October 13, 1852; *KHC*, v. 9, p. 190; annals, p. 217.

❧ October 12.—At the Wyandots' council-house (in present Kansas City, Kan.) 35 votes were cast for Abelard Guthrie (the only candidate) in an election for a delegate to represent "Nebraska Territory" at the second session of the 32d congress.

The Wyandots chose this course of action (earlier petitions having been ignored) to promote the organization of "Nebraska Territory." The men most active in this maneuver (it is said) were Guthrie (a Wyandot by adoption), Francis A. Hicks, George I. Clark, the Walkers (Isaiah, Joel, Matthew R., William), the Garretts (Charles B., Joel W., Russell), Matthew Mudeater, Silas Armstrong, and John W. Gray-Eyes.

Election voters (not all members of the Wyandot Nation) were: Benjamin N. C. Andrews, Isaac Baker, Isaac Brown, George I. Clark, Peter D. Clark, Thomas Coonhawk, Francis Cotter, Nicholas Cotter, Edward Fifer, James Garlow, Charles B., Cyrus, Henry, Joel W., and Russell Garrett, Wilson Gibson, Abelard Guthrie, Edward B. Hand, Francis A. Hicks, John W. Ladd, Henry C., Isaac, and James Long, John Lynch, Daniel McNeal, Presley Muir, Henry C. Norton, Jose Antonio Pieto, Henry W. Porter, Samuel Priestley, Samuel Rankin, William Trowbridge, Joel, Matthew R., and William Walker.

There had been advance notice of the election. The *Missouri Republican*, St. Louis, of September 30, for example, had an editorial on "Nebraska Territory," which stated (in part): "Another Territory is about to be added to the United States, by the organization of a local government, and the election of a delegate to Congress." Guthrie (in an 1862 address) said that Col. Thomas T. Fauntleroy, commanding officer at Fort Leavenworth, "threatened to arrest me if I should attempt to hold the [October 12, 1852] election."

See next entry, and October 21 entry, for counter measures by those opposed to the Wyandots' action.

Ref: *KHC*, v. 1-2, p. 262, v. 6, p. 102; Connelley, *op. cit.*, pp. 24-27, 58, 67, 79, 80; Malin, *op. cit.*, pp. 80-85.

❧ October 13-20.—The St. Joseph (Mo.) *Gazette* of the 13th stated: "We have been requested to announce John E. Barrow, at present Ind. Agent at Council Bluffs, as a candidate for Congress in . . . [Nebraska Territory]. . . ." In another item the *Gazette* noted: "Mr. Abelard Guthrie is announced as a candidate for Congress in the Nebraska territory." In the October 20 issue the editor commented: "We see from the last Weston Reporter, that Col. William T. Dyer [*i. e.*, William F. Dyer, Indian trader], is also a candidate for Congress, from Nebraska Territory. We hear of one or two other candidates, who will make themselves known at the proper time."

The *Missouri Republican*, St. Louis, of October 17 editorialized: "The people residing within this [Nebraska] Territory are determined to take the initiatory steps for organization, and for this purpose will, in a short time, hold an election for a Delegate to Congress. There are already some four or five candidates out for the office of Delegate.—The Government cannot avoid taking up the subject of organizing this territory. The people will not much longer be restrained from taking possession of it."

See, also, October 21 entry.

Ref: St. Joseph *Gazette*, October 13, 20, 1852; *Missouri Republican*, St. Louis, October 17, 1852; Malin, *op. cit.*, pp. 81-83.

❡ October 14.—Arriving at Independence, Mo., overland from the west, were Stephen B. Rose (Indian agent for the "Shoshones and Utahs"), John C. Waddell (Lexington, Mo., merchant)—both from Salt Lake City; and a few "returning Californians" (including W. S. Price and a Mrs. Phillips, widow—both of Michigan).

Rose reached St. Louis, aboard the *Polar Star*, October 19. He had left Salt Lake City on August 31; and arrived at Fort Laramie on October 2, reports stated. Rose's friend "D.," at St. Louis wrote: "He rode down twelve horses in coming in."

Ref: *Missouri Republican*, St. Louis, October 16, 20, 1852; New York *Daily Times*, October 21, 29, 1852.

❡ October 21.—At the settlement around St. Mary's Mission (present St. Marys, Kan.), on the Pottawatomie reserve, a "mass meeting of citizens of Nebraska Territory" was held "to take measures for the election of a Delegate to Congress, to urge the establishment of a regular Territorial Government."

David Gillespie was chairman; Robert C. Miller was appointed secretary. While a committee (composed of Francis J. Marshall, Thomas D. S. Macdonell, Alexander Peltier, James M. Hunter, and Dr. Luther R. Palmer) drafted resolutions "expressive of the sense of the meeting," and "to set forth the claims and interests of the Territory," addresses were made by "Col. A. M. Mitchell and others," who "spoke of the great and growing importance of the tract . . . known as the Nebraska Territory, and urged speedy and united action in regard to its interest."

Resolutions were passed calling for an election to be held on November 16 at five polling points (*see below*) to elect a delegate to congress. The candidate recommended was John E. Barrow. (*See* October 12, and October 13-20, entries.)

These election commissioners were appointed: for *Bellevue* ("Neb."): Stephen Decatur and S. B. Frost; for the *Great Nemaha Agency* (present Doniphan county): James Whitehead and William P. Richardson; for *Fort Leaven-*

worth: Hiram Rich and William F. Dyer; for *Delaware* (or, Grinter) *Crossing* (present Wyandotte county): James Findlay and Isaac Mundy; for *St. Mary's Mission*: E. G. Booth and Alexander Peltier. Hiram Rich (Fort Leavenworth sutler) was appointed "secretary of the Commissioners to receive and report the state of the polls at each of the elective precincts."

See, also, November 16 entry.

Ref: St. Joseph *Gazette*, October 27, 1852; Malin, *op. cit.*, p. 83; New York *Daily Tribune*, November 15, 1852.

❆ October 22.—The "October" mail from Santa Fe reached Independence, Mo. "Mr. Kennedy, from Cleveland" was a stagecoach passenger.

Ref: *Missouri Republican*, St. Louis, October 24, 1852 (by telegram of October 23, from Independence); New York *Daily Times*, November 6, 1852 (says the mail arrived on October 20).

❆ Late in October Bvt. Maj. Edmund A. Ogden and Capt. Langdon C. Easton (both of the quartermaster's dept.), Capt. Charles S. Lovell (of the Sixth infantry), and Lt. Israel C. Woodruff (of the topographical engineers)—the board of officers appointed (September 21) to select a site for a military post (the future Fort Riley) near the junction of the Smoky Hill and Republican rivers—set out from Fort Leavenworth on the assigned mission. They were escorted by Bvt. Maj. Robert H. Chilton, and about 15(?) of his Company B, First dragoons.

Sgt. Percival G. Lowe, at a later time, stated that "The Santa Fé Trail [*i. e.,* from Fort Leavenworth—*see* p. 981] was followed to the crossing of Soldier Creek, four miles north of Pappan's [Papin's] Ferry, thence to Silver Lake—up the Kaw [Kansas] through St. Mary's Mission, . . . thence fifty-two miles to the junction of the rivers. . . . A week was spent in that vicinity resulting in the location of the new post [first known as Camp Centre], afterwards named Fort Riley, about 130 miles from Fort Leavenworth. A band of Delaware Indians returning from a buffalo hunt said there were plenty of buffalo twenty-five miles west of the new post. We were never without turkey after reaching the Big Blue River until our return. It was a little late in the season, nights cold, but no rain or snow, and with big fires and plenty to eat, the trip was rather pleasant."

Dragoon D. C. Beam later recollected: "The . . . day [after passing St. Mary's Mission] I was ordered to take 5 men and 3 teams and go back to the mission for corn. . . . we had to work hard shelling corn for three days and only shelled 125 bushels. . . . Before we got back to camp we suffered much with cold, and snow had fallen six inches deep; but it was cheering to find the boys sitting around rousing fires, with numbers of wild turkeys strung up to roast and many hung on trees for future use. Our work was now done and the ground work of Fort Riley was laid. We broke camp and started for winter quarters [*i. e.,* Fort Leavenworth]." (The St. Mary's Mission records include the following: "October 29, 1852. Delivered to order of Major E. E. [Edmund A.] Ogden, now at the mouth of the Republican, the following articles: 60 bushels shelled corn; 45 bushels in ear, etc. etc. J. B. D[uerinck] furnished 41 sacks for the corn and potatoes. Major E. E. [E. A.] Ogden, 10 sacks.")

The report Ogden and the other board members submitted was dated November 10, 1852. It was approved by the secretary of war on January 7, 1853. Lt. Israel C. Woodruff's "Chart accompanying the report of the Board of Officers to select a site for a military post at the mouth of the Republican Fork of the Kansas River 1852" (a manuscript map) is reproduced, in part, in this volume. *See* pp. 1022, 1023.

Ref: W. F. Pride, *The History of Fort Riley* (c1926), p. 61; Lowe, *op. cit.*, pp. 121, 122; *KHC*, v. 4, p. 364; Nebraska State Historical Society, *Transactions*, v. 3, p. 294 (for Beam); Garraghan, *op. cit.*, v. 2, p. 656; *KHQ*, v. 18, p. 156 (for an item stating that Capt. Charles S. Lovell descended the Kansas river in a skiff, in the autumn of 1852—probably while returning from the above trip?). Woodruff's "Chart" is in the National Archives.

❡ October 29.—The "October" U. S. mail from Salt Lake City arrived at Independence, Mo. At Fort Kearny the mail carriers had overtaken a party of 70 States-bound Mormons, some of whom would come in to Independence, others to St. Joseph.

On October 30, merchants O. H. Cogswell (of Independence) and J. H. Kinkead, who had left Salt Lake City "the same day the mail did," reached Independence. Kinkead (of Livingston, Kinkead & Co., Salt Lake City) took the *Timour No. 2* to St. Louis, arriving there November 5.

Ref: *Missouri Republican*, St. Louis, November 2, 16, 1852; St. Louis *Intelligencer*, November 19, 1852; New York *Daily Tribune*, November 16, 1852.

❡ October-November.—"Captain Thomas [*i. e.*, Mr. William E. Love?] and the Pueblo Indians [the five who had come to the States with Governor Calhoun's party—*see* p. 1107—and gone on east to Washington, D. C.], Judge [Joab] Houghton and party, are here and at Westport and will leave for Santa Fe week after next."— Telegram, sent from Independence, Mo., on October 15.

"Captain Thomas and the Pueblo Indians are at Independence and Westport, and will leave for Santa Fe on the 10th or 12th of November."—Telegram, sent from St. Louis, October 16, 1852.

Ref: *Missouri Republican*, St. Louis, October 16, 1852; New York *Daily Tribune*, October 18, 1852; SIA, St. Louis, "Records," v. 9, typed copy, p. 662, has D. D. Mitchell's September 25, 1852, letter stating "I have this day placed in the hands of Mr. W. E. Love, the sum of $1200, for the outfit and travelling expenses of the delegation of Pueblo Indians in his charge, to their homes."

❡ November.—Steamboats on the middle Missouri this month included the following:

Highland Mary—Left Kanesville (Council Bluffs), Iowa, on October 30. River thence to St. Joseph "very low and difficult to navigate." Left St. Joseph on November 2; met upbound *Banner State* at "Devil's Half-acre," and the *Kansas* at Liberty Landing; reached St. Louis November 7.

Timour No. 2—Left Weston on November 1; reached St. Louis November 5.

Banner State—Left St. Joseph on November 3; reached St. Louis November 8.

Kansas—Left St. Joseph on November 6; weather cold and disagreeable; lost 24 hours as a result of breaking machinery; left Weston on the 8th; reached St. Louis November 12.

El Paso—En route down the Missouri on November 9. Reached St. Louis November 15. "W. C. B." wrote a letter aboard "Steamer El Paso, Sunday, Nov. 9th, 1852," which stated (in part): ". . . [we are] a medley mixture of Merchants and Mormons, Lawyers and Loafers, Loungers and Ladies. . . . We have had the usual amount of Euchre and Poker, of Whist and 'Seven up,' in the Social Hall; the Ladies have had their spirit rappings in the Ladies Cabin, where chairs and tables have danced about after the most approved spirit fashion; and to sum up all in a sentence we are having and have had 'a time of it.' . . . ." Among the passengers, he noted, were Orson Pratt and "some dozen other Elders of the [Mormon] Church, just in from the Valley," en route to missions abroad.

Clara—Left St. Joseph on November 14; "Ice in the river. Water falling very fast all the way down"; returned to St. Louis November 19.

Timour No. 2—Left Kansas, Mo., on November 17; reached St. Louis November 21.

Banner State—At Weston on November ___?; reached St. Louis November 27. *See* November 27 annals entry.

Highland Mary—Left Weston on November 22; met upbound *Kansas* at Parkville, Mo., and the *El Paso* at Liberty; reached St. Louis November 28.

Kansas—Left Weston on November 25; met *El Paso* same night at Fort Leavenworth. Weather quite cold at Weston. From Weston to Parkville, river "lower than at any time this season"; reached St. Louis November 29.

Ref: *Missouri Republican*, St. Louis, November, and early December, 1852, issues; St. Joseph (Mo.) *Gazette*, December 8, 1852 (for "W. C. B.'s" letter). The *Missouri Republican* of November 16 reported the *El Paso* brought down "nine Missionaries," "being a portion of a company of about 80 Mormon Elders, who left Salt Lake City on September 15. . . ."

℄ November.—At the three army posts in "Kansas" (as reported by the adjutant general, November 15) these were the commanding officers, and troops:

Post	Commandant	Garrison
Fort Leavenworth (on the Missouri)	Col. Thomas T. Fauntleroy	1 co., First dragoons; 1 co., Fourth artillery; 2 cos., Sixth infantry.
Fort Scott (on the "Marmiton")	Maj. Winslow F. Sanderson	2 cos., Mounted riflemen; 1 co., Sixth infantry.
Fort Atkinson (Crossing of Arkansas, Santa Fe route)	2d Lt. Henry Heth	1 co., Sixth infantry.

Ref: 32d Cong., 2d Sess., Sen. Ex. Doc. No. 1 (Serial 659), p. 56.

℄ November 16.—Votes were cast at Fort Leavenworth ("Kan.") and Bellevue ("Neb.")—and possibly at all five designated polling places—in the "second election" for a "Nebraska Territory" delegate to congress. (*See* October 21 entry.) Abelard Guthrie was the winner over John E. Barrow, but the circumstances are not entirely clear.

The St. Joseph *Gazette* of November 24 stated: "We learn from the Platte Argus, that Guthrie is elected delegate to Congress from the Nebraska Territory, beating Maj. Barrow 40 votes. Barrow withdrew some two weeks since, and was not a candidate. Guthrie is a democrat, and quite an accomplished politician. Barrow beats Guthrie 40 votes at the Belleview precinct."

Referring to the November 16 event, Guthrie wrote (in June, 1856): "This election was held at Fort Leavenworth, (the commanding officer having abandoned his opposition,) and resulted in a large majority for me—I think 54 to 16. This second election I gave no attention to . . . but my friends at the fort, (not soldiers,) having been prevented from voting at the first election [see October 12 entry], determined to remove all shadow of a right of my opponent to contest my claim to a seat in Congress, by giving me a very decided majority at this election also. But the judges never sent me the returns. . . . I was now universally admitted to be the rightfully elected delegate, and met with no further opposition."

Guthrie left for Washington on November 20; reached his destination before December 9. He did not gain a seat in congress. (His memorial to the house, asking to be admitted as a delegate was presented December 17.)

On December 13 Rep. Willard P. Hall of Missouri, introduced a bill to create the Territory of the Platte (boundaries: Missouri on the east; 43d parallel on the north; the Rocky Mountains on the west; 36° 30′ on the south). It was referred to the committee on territories.

Ref: St. Joseph *Gazette*, November 24, 1852; Connelley, *op. cit.*, pp. 28, 29, 67-77; Malin, *op. cit.*, pp. 83-85. The *Missouri Republican*, St. Louis, December 28, 1852, quoted this item from the Dayton (Ohio) *Journal*: "Abelard Guthrie, Esq., formerly a resident of this city, and now the delegate to Congress from Nebraska territory, intends taking his Indian wife [Quindaro Nancy (Brown) Guthrie—*see* annals, p. 520] with him to Washington. She will create a 'sensation' at the Capital."

❡ November 16.—"Doctor Clipper [*i. e.*, the Rev. M. T. Klepper], the Northern [Methodist] preacher, and his lady arrived [among the Wyandots]."

William Walker (Wyandot), whose sympathies were with the Methodist Church, South, added: "He succeeds Rev. James Witten as preacher in charge of the *pitiful faction here.*"

Ref: William Walker's "Journals," *loc. cit.*; KHC, v. 9, pp. 192, 222-224, 230 (for items on Witten and Klepper).

❡ Mid-November.—At Van Buren, Ark., to attend U. S. court for the Western District of Arkansas (on cases involving theft of horses by white men), were Osage chiefs Tally (head of Clermont's band), and "Wan-nah-sha," or Black Dog, together with other Osages, Agent W. J. J. Morrow, interpreter Charles Mongrain, and their counselors.

Ref: *Jefferson Inquirer*, Jefferson City, Mo., December 4, 1852 (from Van Buren

Intelligencer of November 19). *See* annals, p. 945, for location of Tally's and Black Dog's bands—in Oklahoma of today.

❡ Mid-November (about the 20th?).—Thomas Fitzpatrick, Indian agent, and four companions, arrived at St. Mary's (Pottawatomie Catholic) Mission, on Kansas river, en route from Fort Laramie to the States.

"H." (in a November 27 letter from Independence, Mo.) wrote that he had left Fort Laramie with Fitzpatrick, "Mr. Fitzhugh, of Alexandria, Va.," and two others, on October 23; that they had been "persecuted" on the journey by a "succession of rain and snow storms," but had been entertained hospitably at Fort Kearny by Capt. Henry W. Wharton and his wife.

In advance of the rest, "H." left St. Mary's Mission, after a stay of several days ("While there, I was kindly permitted, in company with Major Fitzpatrick and Mr. Fitzhugh, to examine the *female* school and establishment. . . . We were all highly pleased. . . .") Fitzpatrick, according to "H.", would "remain at the Mission some time longer," and "probably be in St. Louis early in the winter."

Ref: New York *Daily Tribune,* December 22, 1852 (for "H's" October 20 letter from Fort Laramie, telling of Fitzpatrick's councils with Indians on October 19 and 20, etc.); St. Louis *Intelligencer,* December 17, 1852 (for "H's" November 27 letter); New York *Daily Times,* October 21, 29, December 17, 1852; *Missouri Republican,* St. Louis, October 20, 1852 (for information that Fitzpatrick was, on October 2, out on the South Fork of the Platte with the Cheyennes and Arapahoes; and statement that the government train with the Indians' annuities had reached Fort Laramie before October 2—all supplied by Agent S. B. Rose). Though "H." left Salt Lake City on September 23, probably he was the "Harvey" mentioned in the *Missouri Republican* of October 20, as follows: "Messrs. Harvey, late of the [St. Louis] Intell'gr, and others, were at Salt Lake . . . and would leave on the 12th of October for the States." (The information came from Stephen Rose who left Salt Lake City on August 31.)

❡ November 27.—Later in the month than was customary, the mail from Santa Fe arrived at Independence, Mo. The party had been delayed "in consequence of frequent storms of rain, sleet and snow."

"At Fort Union [New Mexico], the snow had fallen to the depth of eighteen or twenty inches. On the Jornada, but little was to be seen. Nearer the States, the ground was covered, more or less, according to locality."—Telegram from Independence, 27th.

Ref: *Missouri Republican,* St. Louis, November 28, 1852.

❡ November 27.—Aboard the *Banner State,* arriving at St. Louis from the Missouri river, were 16 Delaware Indians, "all braves," bound for "the western part of Arkansas, for the purpose of spending the winter in hunting."

Ref: *Missouri Republican,* St. Louis, November 28, 1852. The *Banner State* had gone up as far as Weston, Mo., on this trip.

❡ Around the end of November(?) Maj. Francis A. Cunningham (army paymaster) and party (including Antoine Leroux), from Santa Fe, reached the Missouri border.

The major, and others, left St. Louis on December 13 for Washington, D. C.

Ref: *Missouri Republican,* St. Louis, December 9, 14, 1852. The issue of December 9 contained a letter by "W." written at Santa Fe on October 27, stating (in part): "Enclosed I send you a note from Mr. Leroux, one of the best guides. . . . He goes in with Major Cunningham. . . ."

❡ DIED: on December 1, James Washington, part-Wyandot, aged 65, at his home in the town of "Wyandott." He was a descendant of "the famous Chief, Half King"; and "one of the oldest Councilors" of the Nation.

Ref: William Walker's "Journals," *loc. cit.*

❡ December 4.—At a "large and respectable [Railroad] Convention" of the "citizens of Kansas [City, Mo.] and the surrounding region," Dr. Johnston Lykins (recently head of Pottawatomie Baptist Mission; now a Kansas, Mo., resident) was called to preside; Pierre Menard Chouteau and Henry B. Bouton were appointed secretaries.

In addition to endorsing the Pacific Railroad company's "great work," the Convention noted the earlier-held (October 27) railroad meeting at Platte City —a meeting "of the friends favorable to a rail road from Kansas [City, Mo.] to St. Joseph"—and pledged to "aid by every means . . . the speedy completion of the Kansas and St. Joseph railroad." Among other resolutions passed was one praising Sen. Thomas Hart Benton for his efforts "in promoting the interests of upper Missouri, and for his patriotic course on the subject to the Pacific road."

Ref: *Jefferson Inquirer,* Jefferson City, Mo., December 16, 1852 (has a column article on the December 4 convention); St. Joseph *Gazette,* October 27, 1852 (for item on the Platte city meeting); *Missouri Republican,* St. Louis, October 17, 1852 (for article from the Platte *Argus*).

❡ December 28.—The "December" U. S. mail from Salt Lake City arrived at Independence, Mo. J(ohn) M. Hockaday (said to be of the "topographical corps"?) was a mailcoach passenger.

Between Forts Laramie and Kearny the carriers had been delayed by storms; and found snow from 12 to 36 inches deep, so that they had to travel "just on the bank of the [Platte] river all the way." On December 16, at Fort Kearny, the temperature had been 18° to 20° below zero:

Ref: *Missouri Republican,* St. Louis, December 30, 1852. Later (in 1858) Hockaday became the Salt Lake mail contractor—*see KHQ,* v. 11, p. 302. From mid-1854 to mid-1858(?), Hockaday was associated with Jacob Hall in carrying the Independence-Santa Fe mail. See "Hockaday & Hall" "ad" in Santa Fe (N. M.) *Weekly Gazette,* e. g., March 3, 1855, issue. *Also, see* annals entry for April 29, 1854.

❡ Employed in "Kansas" by the Indian Department during all, or part of the year (so far as can be ascertained from available records) were the following persons:

KANSAS AGENCY [*Wyandots, Delawares, Shawnees, Munsees, Stockbridges*] —*Agent* Thomas Moseley, Jr.; *Interpreters* William Walker (for Wyandots), Henry Tiblow (for Delawares), Charles Bluejacket and Joseph Parks (for Shawnees); *Blacksmiths* William McCown (till April) and Samuel Priestley (for Wyandots), Isaac Mundy (for Delawares), Calvin Perkins (died September 14) and William Donalson (for Shawnees); *Assistant smiths* Isaac Baker (for Wyandots), William R. Ketchum (resigned), James H. Hines (resigned), and Silas A. Boyd (for Delawares), Joseph A. W. Meador (for Shawnees).

POTTAWATOMIE AGENCY *[Pottawatomies and Kansa]—Agent* Francis W. Lea; *Interpreters* Abraham B. Burnett (for Pottawatomies), John Brazil (left; went to Osages) and Clement Lessert (for Kansa); *Blacksmiths* John L. Ogee, John W. Brown, and Robert Wilson (for Pottawatomies), Jesse King (for Kansa); *Assistant smiths* James H. Crockett, John Anderson, James Wilson, and Samuel Lewis (for Pottawatomies), William King (for Kansa); *Millers* Jude W. Bourassa ("Keeper of the Grist mill") and Jabez Durfee (grist miller); *Gunsmiths* Newman York, Hugh M. Weldon, and James B. Franklin (for Pottawatomies), *Assistant gunsmiths* William H. Franklin, and William Rice (for Pottawatomies); *Physicians* A. B. Earle (resigned), George W. Bouton, and Luther R. Palmer (for Pottawatomies); *Wagonmakers* Henry Samuel, and Anthony A. Ward (for Pottawatomies); *Assistant wagonmaker* John B. Souce ("Susee") (for Pottawatomies); *Ferryman* Lucius R. Darling ("Ferryman for [Pottawatomie] nation").

SAC & FOX AGENCY *[Sacs & Foxes of the Mississippi, Ottawas, Chippewas]—Agent* John R. Chenault; *Interpreters* Thomas J. Connolly (resigned) and Antoine Gokey; *Gunsmiths* James T. King, James B. Franklin, John Van Horn; *Blacksmiths* James F. Mills, and Alfred Laws; *Assistant smiths* Thomas C. Warren, Andrew S. Beasley, Gilbert M. L. Wright, and Hiram G. Tharp; *Physician* Edwin R. Griffith. (All, except the agent, employed for the Sacs & Foxes, only.)

OSAGE RIVER AGENCY *[Miamis, Weas, Piankeshaws, Peorias & Kaskaskias]—Agent* Asbury M. Coffey; *Interpreter* Baptiste Peoria; *Blacksmith* Robert Simerwell; *Assistant smith* Luther Paschall; *Miller* James B. Chenault. (Except for the agent, and interpreter, employed for the Miamis only.)

GREAT NEMAHA AGENCY *[Iowas, Sacs & Foxes of the Missouri, and Kickapoos]—Agent* William P. Richardson; *Interpreters* Paschal Pensineau, and Francis Bricknelle (for Sacs & Foxes), John B. Roy (for Iowas), Peter Cadue (for Kickapoos); *Blacksmiths* John W. Forman, and John McCloskey (for Sacs & Foxes); *Assistant smith* Isaac McCloskey (for Sacs & Foxes); *Farmers* James F. Forman, and Harvey W. Forman (for Sacs & Foxes).

NEOSHO AGENCY *[Osages, Quapaws, Senecas & Shawnees, Senecas]—Agent* William J. J. Morrow. For the Osages: *Interpreters* Charles Mongrain and D. A. Penn. (No list of other employees for this year has been located.)

Ref: 33d Cong., 1st Sess., *Sen. Ex. Doc. No. 25* (Serial 695), *or*, 33d Cong., 1st Sess., *H. Ex. Doc. No. 37* (Serial 718); 33d Cong., 1st Sess., *Sen. Ex. Doc. No. 69* (Serial 701); SIA, St. Louis, "Records," p. 9, typed copy, pp. 582-708 *passim*.

1853

❡ January-June.—Licenses (new and renewal) to trade with Indians in "Kansas," as granted by agents of the Central Superintendency, St. Louis, were:

Traders	Indians	Issued by	Rec'vd at St. Louis
William P. Burney	Delawares	Thos. Moseley, Jr.	January
M. D. Richardville	Miamis	A. M. Coffey	January
W. H. Haskell	Miamis	A. M. Coffey	January
Gilham & McDaniel	Miamis	A. M. Coffey	January
Josiah Smart	Sacs & Foxes	J. R. Chenault	January
(R. A.) Kinzie & (J. H.) Whistler	Sacs & Foxes	J. R. Chenault	January
Arthur I. Baker	Sacs & Foxes	J. R. Chenault	January
J. B. Scott	Sacs & Foxes	J. R. Chenault	March
(R. C.) Miller & (G. L.) Young	Pottawatomies "on Soldier creek"	F. W. Lea	March
Seth M. Hays	Shawnees	Thos. Moseley, Jr.	April
Baker & Street	Shawnees	Thos. Moseley, Jr.	April
Seth M. Hays	Kansa	F. W. Lea	April
Cyprian Chouteau	Delawares	Thos. Moseley, Jr.	April
Joseph Robidoux	Kickapoos, Iowas, and Sacs & Foxes (of the Missouri)	W. P. Richardson	April
William Hughes	Kickapoos, Iowas, and Sacs & Foxes (of the Missouri)	W. P. Richardson	April
Cyprian & Frederick Chouteau	Kansa	F. W. Lea	May
John W. Forman	Iowas, and Sacs & Foxes (of the Missouri)	W. P. Richardson	May
Oliver H. P. Polke	Pottawatomies at St. Mary's Mission Pottawatomies at Union Town	F. W. Lea	June
Harker S. Randall	Sacs & Foxes	B. A. James	June
Baker & Street	Sacs & Foxes	B. A. James	June

Ref: Superintendency of Indian Affairs (SIA), St. Louis, "Records," v. 9, typed copy, pp. 696, 699, 700, 706, 707, 718, 720, 725, 734, 740, 745; and *ibid.*, pp. 739, 751, 811 for (1) E. M. Sewell as clerk for Arthur I. Baker, (2) Milton P. Randall as clerk for Seth M. Hays, (3) Harvey Forman as clerk for John W. Forman. Alexander Gilham and Thompson McDaniel advertised as wholesalers and retailers of dry goods, groceries, etc., in the Kansas City (Mo.) *Enterprise* in the mid-1850's. *See*, for example, February 9, 1856, issue. In 1856 John W. Forman testified he had been a "Kansas" resident since April, 1843; and moved to "Doniphan, where I now live in 1853."—34th Cong., 1st Sess., *H. R. No. 200* (Serial 869), p. 17.

❧ January 18.—On the Wyandot reserve (and within present Kansas City, Kan.) John Coon, Jr., was executed by a firing squad. He had been convicted December 19, 1852, in a Wyandot court, of "murder in the first degree" for the killing of Curtis Punch in a drunken brawl.

Of the jury's December decision, William Walker (prominent Wyandot) had commented: "This was wrong. . . . He could not be convicted of anything more than 'Manslaughter.' But such is the verdict."

Ref: William Walker's diary, in W. E. Connelley's *The Provisional Government of Nebraska Territory* . . . (1899), p. 371.

❦ January 19.—The January mail party from Santa Fe arrived at Independence, Mo., after a "fine weather" journey all the way. James Gilchrist was a stage passenger.

Immense numbers of buffaloes had been seen on the Cimarron river.

Ref: *Missouri Republican*, St. Louis, January 22, 1853; or, New York *Daily Times*, February 1, 1853; or, New York *Daily Tribune*, February 2, 1853.

❦ January 26.—Bvt. 2d Lt. John T. Shaaff assumed command, temporarily, at Fort Atkinson, while 2d Lt. Henry Heth and a Sixth infantry detachment went up the Arkansas "to examine the vicinity of Purgatory [Purgatoire] river I. T. per instructions from Dept. Head Quarters."

Heth was absent less than a month. The February post returns listed the officers at Fort Atkinson as Heth, Asst. Surg. Aquila T. Ridgely, and Shaaff.

Ref: Fort Atkinson post returns (microfilm from National Archives, in KHi).

❦ February.—The Independence-to-Santa Fe mail party, setting out February 1(?), in charge of "Mr. [John?] Jones," reached Santa Fe on February 25, having had good weather as far as Fort Union, N. M. (where the stage was detained by a heavy fall of snow).

Ref: New York *Daily Times*, April 5, 1853 (from Santa Fe *Gazette* of February 26); or, New York *Daily Tribune*, April 4, 1853.

❦ February 4.—The January "Salt Lake" mail, with dates as late as January 12 from Fort Laramie (but none from west of that point), reached Independence, Mo. Stage passengers were "Messrs. Meer and Mechelle" (according to a telegraphic dispatch).

Between Forts Laramie and Kearny the party encountered snow averaging 15 inches in depth, and had to follow the "meanderings of the [Platte] river, and pack their provisions and mail."

Ref: *Missouri Republican*, St. Louis, February 6, 7, 1853; *Missouri Statesman*, Columbia, Mo., February 18, 1853. Possibly "Meer" was H. F. Mayer—*see* September 1 annals entry.

❦ Died: on February 7, Edmund F. ("Guesso") Chouteau, eldest son of Kaw's mouth pioneer Francis G. Chouteau (d. 1838), in Jackson county, Mo.

Ref: William Walker's diary, *loc. cit. See* annals index for earlier references to Edmund F. Chouteau.

❦ Died: on February 14, John Hicks, "last of the hereditary Chiefs of the Wyandott nation," aged "upwards of 80 years," on the Wyandot reserve (present Wyandotte county).

Ref: William Walker's diary, *loc. cit.*

❦ February 16.—"Dougherty's Ferry," on the Missouri two miles above Sonora, Atchison county, Mo., was advertised (in the St.

Joseph *Gazette*) by proprietors O'Fallon Dougherty and George Borches.

The notice stated they were "fitting up two new Ferry Boats"; and that the Rev. R. Horn and John Hall (proprietors of Sonora) were "also putting in two fine Boats," to be completed "early in the Spring." Sonora was described as a "thriving little town"; and Linden, 10 miles distant, was said to be "well supplied with large stores. . . ." Via the Sonora route, emigrants would intersect the Old Fort Kearny road about 15 miles west of the old military Post.

Ref: St. Joseph (Mo.) *Gazette*, February 23, 1853.

❡ February 18.—"Story, Wagner, & Lewis, proprietors" began advertising "Story's Ferry across the Missouri river," located "about 9 miles below the mouth of the Nishnabotana river, in Holt co., Mo."

Their notice (in the St. Joseph *Gazette*) stated: "Once across [the Missouri] the emigrant will find a pleasant road along the high dry and level lands of ridge dividing the waters of the two Nemahaws, which will lead him into the main [Oregon-California] trail at the intersection of the Fort Leavenworth and St. Joseph roads, at a point about 50 miles from the ferry. . . . By this route the emigrant will avoid crossing Wolf River the Big Nemahaw, and their tributaries. . . ."

Ref: St. Joseph (Mo.) *Gazette*, February 23, 1853. The *Gazette* of March 8, *1854*, mentioned Mr. Story's ferry "at his landing on the Half Breed tract in Nebraska . . ." opposite Holt county.

❡ February 18.—"Bissonnette, Kenceleur & Co.," in a lengthy "Notice to Californians" of this date (first published in the St. Joseph [Mo.] *Gazette* of the 23d), announced they were constructing a "substantial" bridge across the North Fork of the Platte (110 miles above Fort Laramie) which would be ready "in time for the earliest trains."

Their advertisement also stated: "There will be at the Bridge two Black smith and Wagon maker's shops, for the accommodation of emigrants. The company will have a good Grocery Store and eating house, and all kinds of Indian handled peltries, also oxen, cows, horses, and mules at low prices. . . ."

"Bissonnette, Kenceleur & Co's." St. Joseph agent was R. L. McGhee.

Ref: St. Joseph *Gazette*, February 23, 1853. For earlier annals mention of trader Joseph Bissonette *see* index.

❡ February 20.—The *Robert Campbell* (intended destination Weston, Mo.), having discharged her freight at a point two miles below Fort Leavenworth, where a gorge of ice had formed, started downriver. She reached St. Louis on February 25.

Among the upbound steamboats she had met were the *El Paso* (at Camden, Mo.), the *Ben West*, the *Polar Star*, and the *Banner State*. The *El Paso* returned to St. Louis on February 28, from Parkville, Mo., having been unable to get higher up the Missouri than "Spar Island . . . six miles below Fort Leavenworth," because of the "very thick and heavy" ice jam at that point.

Ref: *Missouri Republican*, St. Louis, February 26, March 1, 1853.

❦ February 28.—The *Ben West*, apparently the year's first steamboat to reach Weston, Mo., left there for St. Louis; and soon met the upbound *Banner State*, at Parkville, Mo. Meantime, the *Polar Star* (which had steamed upriver not far behind the *Ben West*) went on above Weston to St. Joseph; reached there on, or about, the 28th. She was the year's first steamboat arrival at that town. (The *Polar Star* left St. Joseph March 1; returned to St. Louis March 4.)

The *Banner State*—second arrival at St. Joseph—reached, and left, there March 2; returned to St. Louis March 7. En route down, she met the *St. Ange* at Parkville (March 3), and other boats below.

Ref: *Missouri Republican*, St. Louis, March 3, 5, 7, 8, 1853; St. Joseph (Mo.) *Gazette*, March 2, 1853.

❦ February 28.—Ten Quapaw children were entered at Osage (Catholic) Mission school (present St. Paul, Kan.). By May 20, 24 were enrolled; and in July there were 28 Quapaw students.

Ref: W. W. Graves, *Life and Letters of Rev. Father John Schoenmakers* (Parsons, Kan., c1938), p. 40; Sister Mary Paul Fitzgerald, *Beacon on the Plains* (Leavenworth, 1939), p. 91. The Southern Methodist school for the Quapaws, on the Quapaw reserve, had closed in 1852—*see* p. 1065.

❦ March 2.—"Tutt & Dougherty" (John S. Tutt and Lewis B. Dougherty), "Sutlers at Fort Laramie," in a notice (first published in the St. Joseph *Gazette* of this date) announced that "having made extensive preparations last Fall for the supply of the emigration this Spring," they were prepared to provide emigrants with "every article that is needed on the trip, as well as luxuries, in the eating line that will please the most fastidious taste."

Emigrants would also find at Laramie "a large supply of Medicines" (and could avail themselves of the services of the "United States Surgeon stationed here"); blacksmith shops would be ready by spring; and flour and pork could be bought from post supplies "at cost and transportation," by those in distress.

Ref: St. Joseph (Mo.) *Gazette*, March 2, 1853; *Annals of Wyoming*, Cheyenne, v. 5 (July, 1927), p. 17.

❦ March 3.—The army appropriations act (for 1853-1854) included a provision authorizing the secretary of war:

"to employ such portion of the corps of topographical engineers, and such other persons as he may deem necessary," to make such explorations and surveys as he may deem advisable, to ascertain the most practicable and economical route for a railroad from the Mississippi River to the Pacific Ocean.

The sum of $150,000 was appropriated "to defray the expense of such explorations and surveys."

Ref: *Statutes at Large, 32d Cong., 2d Session.*

❡ March 7.—The February mail from Fort Laramie, in charge of "Messrs. [William] Allison and Smith," arrived at Independence, Mo., after a "very difficult and disagreeable" journey.

Ref: *The Weekly Tribune*, Liberty, Mo., March 18, April 15, 1853; New York *Daily Tribune*, March 28, 1853 (from *Occidental Messenger*, Independence, Mo., March 12, 1853).

❡ March 15.—W. P. Richardson, Great Nemaha Agency head, paid Henry Thompson $14.10 for "Ferriage of agent, &c." across the Missouri.

Later-day accounts say that Henry Thompson established a trading post, and ferry, on the "Kansas" side of the Missouri, opposite St. Joseph, in the fall of 1852. Daniel Vanderslice (Richardson's successor), in a December 6, 1853, letter, mentioned the house "in the bottom opposite St. Joseph which is occupied by Henry Thompson. . . ." Vanderslice said he had told Thompson to move, as the trading license issued to him by Richardson had been withheld or suspended; and Vanderslice was not going to grant him one. In 1855 the Kansas territorial legislature granted Thompson a 15-year ferry charter at the same location.

Ref: 33d Cong., 1st Sess., *Sen. Ex. Doc. No. 69* (Serial 701), p. 436; P. L. Gray's *Doniphan County History* (1905), p. 23; Office of Indian Affairs (OIA), Letters Received from Great Nemaha Agency (National Archives Microcopy 234, Roll 308), for Vanderslice's letter; *General Statutes, Kansas*, 1855, pp. 787-789; *KHQ*, v. 2, p. 126.

❡ In mid-March the *St. Ange* went up the Missouri to Council Bluffs; and left there on the 24th for St. Louis. As reported, she was "the first boat to arrive at and depart from Council Bluffs City" in 1853.

On her downward journey the *St. Ange* met the *Patrick Henry* (bound for Council Bluffs) 10 miles below St. Joseph; saw the *St. Paul* (hard aground) at Smith's Bar; met the upbound *Banner State* at Parkville, Mo., and other boats below. She reached St. Louis on April 3.

Ref: *Missouri Republican*, St. Louis, April 4, 1853.

❡ Mid-March.—"Mr. Stockton, of Pennsylvania," arriving at St. Joseph, Mo., said he had some 1,200 head of sheep, bound for California, which would cross the Missouri at that point.

"He informs us," reported the St. Joseph *Adventure*, "that the wool of these sheep will be taken off at this place."

Ref: *The Weekly Tribune*, Liberty, Mo., March 25, 1853 (from the *Adventure*).

❡ March 19.—A passenger in the mail stage, arriving at Independence, Mo., from Santa Fe, was Lt. Lloyd Beall, Second artillery. The party had encountered cold weather; and numbers of Indians had been seen on the route.

Ref: *Missouri Republican*, St. Louis, March 20, 1853.

❡ March.—The *Occidental Messenger,* Independence, Mo., of March 26(?) reported: "Emigrants for California and Oregon are beginning to arrive by land and by river. Those who come by land have already their quantum of stock. . . ."

"C. M. S." wrote (from Independence) on March 31: "There is a good number [of emigrants] here already, and others are arriving daily—yet I think there will not be as many here this spring as heretofore. The principal starting points are St. Joseph and Council Bluffs. . . ."

He described Independence Landing as "graded and set with stone, and accessible at all stages of water. The road up the bluff is also graded, and now nearly McAdamized."

Ref: *The Weekly Tribune,* Liberty, Mo., April 1, 1853; Alton (Ill.) *Telegraph,* April 9, 1853.

❡ April 5.—In her diary under date of "Wednesday, April 6," Oregon-bound Celinda E. Hines wrote: "On Tuesday Kansas [Mo.] was made a city and Dr. [Johnston] Lykins mayor."

At the town's first municipal election—on Monday, April 4—William Gregory had been elected mayor, Lykins, council president, T. H. West, W. G. Barkley, Thompson McDaniel, and M. J. Payne other council members. But Gregory had not lived at Kansas City, Mo., long enough to be eligible for office, so Lykins was named to replace him as mayor.

Ref: Oregon Pioneer Association, Portland, *Transactions of the Forty-sixth Annual Reunion,* . . . *1918* (for Celinda E. Hines' diary); *The History of Jackson County, Missouri,* reprint of 1881 edition (1966), pp. 413, 414; Perl W. Morgan's *History of Wyandotte County Kansas* . . . (1911), v. 1, p. 112; Daughters of the American Revolution, Kansas City chapter, *Vital Historical Records of Jackson County Missouri 1826-1876* (Kansas City, Mo., c1934), p. 439.

❡ April 6.—Jarvis Streeter with the March mail arrived at Independence, Mo., from Fort Laramie (which place he had left on the 21st). His party had found the weather "unusually pleasant" and roads "remarkably fine."

Streeter brought no Salt Lake mail; and reported that none had been received at Fort Laramie from the west "for the past five months owing as it is alleged to the fact of the frequent and unusual heavy snows which have fallen in that region.

Ref: St. Louis *Intelligencer,* April 15, 1853; or, Liberty (Mo.) *Weekly Tribune,* April 22, 1853.

❡ April 12.—At Fort Leavenworth a public auction of government property (horses, oxen, mules, wagons, harness, etc., etc.) was held.

A mid-April issue of the Platte (Mo.) *Argus* said the sale was well attended; and that on *this* occasion the tables were turned and "the Government speculated off of the citizens. . . ."

Ref: St. Joseph (Mo.) *Gazette,* February 2, 1853 (has "ad" for the sale, dated January

31, signed by L. C. Easton, AQM); Liberty (Mo.) *Weekly Tribune*, April 22, 1853 (from Platte *Argus*).

❡ April.—These were some newspaper items reporting Missourians' overland-to-California stock drives in 1853:

From Hannibal, Mo., on April 12, a company composed of "two eastern men and a few citizens," planned to start for California with 1,500 sheep, 500 cattle, 40 horses and mules.—*Weekly Missouri Sentinel*, Columbia, April 21, 1853.

On April 14 F. M. McLean of Randolph county was crossing a California-bound drove of 500 steers at Glasgow, Mo. They were said to be the best, out of some 5,000 head that had "passed up the river."—*Ibid.*

At the end of March, partners "Mr. Lagrave" and Joseph Bogy (who had made the trip before), were preparing to set out from Ste. Genevieve, Mo., with some 25 young drivers, about 500 cattle, and around 4,000 sheep.—St. Joseph *Gazette*, April 6, 1853.

Early in April, John Holloway and Dr. J. R. Pointer, with about 20 young men, left the Glasgow vicinity with a large number of cattle destined for California. Several other companies were soon to set out from the same area for the West.—*Missouri Republican*, St. Louis, April 12, 1853.

Early in May, the Springfield (Mo.) *Advertiser* reported that the year's emigration west from Greene county included 25 or 30 families, a great many young men, and at least 100 wagons; and that the number of cattle to be driven to California amounted to 6,630 head. One company was taking 1,500 sheep. In addition 1,600 steers had been driven to Independence and St. Joseph.—*Weekly Missouri Sentinel*, Columbia, May 12, 1853.

See, also, p. 1151, for Jackson county, Mo., stock drives west in 1853.

Ref: As noted above.

❡ April-May.—At St. Joseph, Mo., the *Gazette* of April 13 stated: "Emigrants for the plains, still continue to come, though they are not as numerous here as they were this time last year. From every indication we may still look for a large number."

The April 20 issue of the *Gazette* noted: "Many of the emigrants now here, are destined for Oregon, and still they come. They are mostly persons well fixed who are going there to settle permanently."

A late-April issue of the St. Joseph *Adventure* reported: "The emigration this spring, so far, is much greater at this point than was anticipated. Great numbers arrive daily, make their purchases and cross the river on the way to the plains. Not a day passes but large droves of stock are driven thro' our streets—the amount on the plains, if equal at each of the other starting points . . ., will be immense. Emigrants are encamped in every direction in and around the city; the streets are thronged, and business brisk."

At the beginning of May, for three days, the steamboat *Alton* ferried emigrants across the Missouri at St. Joseph. During that time she "took over 7,563 head of cattle, 382 head of horses, and 212 wagons."

A correspondent of the St. Louis *News,* writing from St. Joseph on May 5, stated: "For the past two weeks the roads leading to the city have been thronged with emigrant wagons, droves of sheep, cattle and horses, and our streets have been sometimes so crowded that it was with difficulty you could get along the sidewalks of the principal thoroughfares.—A good many have come by boats also, but the emigration so far, is not as large as that of last year, by one half. . . . I think the greater part of the wagons have crossed the river. Two flat-boats have been constantly engaged, and were not sufficient. The steamer Alton . . . ferried for three or four days. . . . There is a ferry about four miles above which has also been kept busy, and another eight miles above by land, has crossed a great many. . . ."

Ref: St. Joseph *Gazette,* April 13, 20, May 25, 1853; Liberty (Mo.) *Weekly Tribune,* May 6, 1853; *Missouri Republican,* St. Louis, May 10, 1853 (or, see *KHQ,* v. 10, p. 413).

❧ April.—On the 19th the April mail from Santa Fe, in charge of "Mr. [James] Rupe," reached Independence, Mo. Stage passengers were "Judge [Grafton] Baker" (recently New Mexico territory's chief justice, 1851-1853; now homeward-bound), James A. Lucas ("formerly of Independence"), and one other person.

En route the party had overtaken the Missouri-bound trains of Mexican traders Gutierrez (at McNees' creek) and Armijo (one at Sand creek, the other at Cow creek). They had met, near Fort Atkinson, the Santa Fe-bound April mail party; and at Council Grove, some dragoons.

The dragoons probably escorted Bvt. Maj. Edward Johnson, Sixth infantry, who, in April, was en route to Fort Atkinson—where he took over as commanding officer on April 26.

A party of Mexican traders reached St. Louis April 26, aboard the *Georgia.* It was said they brought "about $100,000, chiefly in gold and silver"; and that they were bound for New York "to buy goods, etc."

Ref: *Missouri Republican,* St. Louis, April 21, 27, 1853; Liberty (Mo.) *Weekly Tribune,* April 29, May 6, 1853; New York *Daily Tribune,* April 22, 1853; or New York *Daily Times,* April 22, 1853; Alton (Ill.) *Telegraph,* April 28, 1853 (from St. Louis *Evening News,* April 26); Fort Atkinson post returns (microfilm from National Archives, in KHi).

❧ April 19.—At Council Bluffs, Iowa, the steamboats *Patrick Henry* and *Highland Mary,* were ferrying emigrants across the Missouri (at 25 cents per head for cattle, and $2 each for wagons). Only a few companies had left the river-area camps to begin the journey west.

On May 11, when the *Patrick Henry* left Council Bluffs, the *Hindoo* and *Highland Mary* were "still engaged in ferrying emigrants across the river," but the "larger portion" had set out for the West. The *Hindoo* left Council Bluffs on May 13, for St. Louis. The *Highland Mary* started downriver June 5; returned to St. Louis June 9.

Ref: *Missouri Republican*, St. Louis, April 25, May 21, June 5, 10, 1853.

❡ April 20.—The St. Joseph (Mo.) *Gazette* (long published by William Ridenbaugh) appeared with the masthead of new owner- ship—"Lucian J. Eastin & Co."

(In late October, 1854, Eastin became a Kansas journalist—as editor of the Democratic and Proslavery *Kansas Weekly Herald*, Leavenworth).

Ref: St. Joseph *Gazette*, April 13, 20, 1853. Eastin, as a Mexican War volunteer (from Missouri), had crossed "Kansas" in 1846 and 1847—*see* annals index.

❡ April 20.—A company of 12(?) from Galena, Ill., and vicinity, captained by Isaac Evans, left St. Joseph, Mo., for California. They had four wagons and 25 "handsome" horses.

Their arrival, July 4, at Sacramento, was heralded by the *Union* as the "first of the great overland army of the present season." Evans was accounted "a famous overland traveler, this being his third trip since the gold emigration commenced."

Ref: Liberty (Mo.) *Weekly Tribune*, August 26, 1853. The New York *Daily Tribune*, August 24, 1853, quoted the Downieville (Calif.) *Echo* of [July?] 23d as follows: "On Saturday a pack train reached Sacramento from the Missouri river, having left St. Joseph on April 23d last. The company consists of five persons, all from Illinois."

❡ April 22.—The *Kansas* (Henry White, captain), bound for Coun- cil Bluffs, struck a snag "near Iowa Point" ("at Linden Landing" another report stated), and sank in 20 feet of water. "The boat, and freight which was large, total loss. No lives lost."

Built in 1847 (*see* p. 743), the *Kansas* "at one time a favorite Missouri river packet, . . . at the time of her sinking had seen her best days." White, and William W. Wilson (her clerk) recently had purchased the boat for $7,000. It was said the *Kansas* was not insured.

Ref: Liberty (Mo.) *Weekly Tribune*, May 6, 1853 (from St. Joseph *Adventure*); *Missouri Republican*, April 27, 1853 (via telegraphic dispatch from St. Joseph).

❡ April 22.—Fort Scott (founded 1842) was this day "broken up, pursuant to Dept Orders No. 9 of March 30, 1853, and the Garrison put *en route* for Fort L[eaven]worth." A sergeant was left in charge of the post.

Three companies of troops departed: "A" and "K" of the Mounted riflemen, "H" of the Sixth infantry. Officers present when the fort closed were: Capt. Michael E. Van Buren (commanding), Asst. Surg. Levi H. Holden, Bvt. Capt. Thomas Claiborne, Bvt. 1st Lt. George H. Gordon, 2d Lt. Darius D. Clark, 2d Lt. Eugene A. Carr, Chaplain (and Schoolmaster) David Clarkson.

Ref: Fort Scott records (microfilm from the National Archives, in KHi). The article on Hiero T. Wilson (Fort Scott's sutler), in *United States Biographical Dictionary, Kansas* (1879), pp. 39, 40, says Fort Scott, after being abandoned, was "left solely in charge of Orderly Sgt. David Reed" for 13 months; that on April 16, 1855, the buildings were auctioned; and that the government realized less than $5,000 of the $200,000(?) expended on improvements. Chaplain Clarkson's name is "David" on the Fort Scott post returns. Unaccountably, he is listed as "Daniel" in F. B. Heitman's *Historical Register* and *Dictionary of U. S. Army* (1903).

❦ April.—Alfred Cumming, "formerly of Georgia," and now of Missouri, was appointed to head the Central [Indian] Superintendency, St. Louis, replacing David D. Mitchell.

Ref: *Missouri Republican*, St. Louis, May 4, 1853 (from item in Washington [D. C.] *Union* of April 28).

❦ A late-April issue of the Weston (Mo.) *Reporter* stated: "Large numbers of Emigrants are daily crossing the Missouri river at this place, taking the great Military Road from Fort Leavenworth to California and Oregon."

Ref: Liberty (Mo.) *Weekly Tribune*, May 6, 1853.

❦ April 30.—The April mail from Fort Laramie, in charge of "Mr. Hobbs" (who had set out on the 15th), arrived at Independence, Mo. (No mail from Salt Lake had reached Laramie prior to his departure. *See* April 6 entry.)

Hobbs and party made the Fort Kearny-to-Independence segment in six days (averaging over 70 miles per day). West of the Big Blue they had met the advance emigrant parties—including Pitcher, Foulke & Co. of St. Louis ("at Little Blue" on April 25), and (Joel) Chiles & Co. of Independence (*see* p. 1151).

Ref: *Missouri Republican*, St. Louis, May 15, 1853; Liberty (Mo.) *Weekly Tribune*, May 13, 1853; or, New York *Daily Tribune*, May 24, 1853.

❦ May 1.—On schedule, the Santa Fe, and Salt Lake, U. S. mail parties set out from Independence, Mo. William S. Messervy (appointed secretary of New Mexico territory) was a passenger in the Santa Fe-bound coach; the Hon. John M. Bernheisel (Utah territory's delegate to congress) and Edward A. Bedell (new Indian agent for Utah) were aboard the Fort Laramie-bound stage.

Ref: *Missouri Republican*, St. Louis, April 26, May 15, 1853; Liberty (Mo.) *Weekly Tribune*, May 13, 1853; or, New York *Daily Tribune*, May 24, 1853.

❦ DIED: on May 1, Gabriel Philibert, aged 52, at, or near Kansas (City), Mo. He had been a resident of the Kaw's mouth area since the (late?) 1820's; and had lived in "Kansas"—as blacksmith to the Kansa Indians—from 1827 to 1831.

Ref: Kansas City chapter D. A. R., *Vital Historical Records of Jackson County Missouri 1826-1876*, p. 267. *See, also,* annals index.

❦ May 1-31.—These were the steamboat arrivals and departures at the "Port of St. Joseph [Mo.]," as reported by the *Gazette*:

Arriving	From	Date	Departing	For
St. Paul	St. Louis	May 1	Banner State	St. Louis
Alton	St. Louis	May 2	St. Paul	Council Bluffs
Honduras	St. Louis	May 3	Honduras	St. Louis
Ne Plus Ultra	Council Bluffs	May 3	Ne Plus Ultra	St. Louis
Timour No. 2	St. Louis	May 4		
Martha Jewett	St. Louis	May 4		
Clara	St. Louis	May 5	Martha Jewett	St. Louis
			Timour No. 2	St. Louis
		May 6(?)	Alton	St. Louis
Polar Star	St. Louis	May 7	Clara	St. Louis
		May 8	Polar Star	St. Louis
St. Paul	Council Bluffs	May 10	St. Paul	St. Louis
F. X. Aubrey	St. Louis	May 11	F. X. Aubrey	St. Louis
Bluff City	St. Louis	May 12	Bluff City	Council Bluffs
Sonora	St. Louis	May 13	Sonora	St. Louis
Patrick Henry	Council Bluffs	May 15		
		May 16	Patrick Henry	St. Louis
Honduras	St. Louis	May 18	Honduras	St. Louis
Bluff City	Council Bluffs	May 19		
Clara	St. Louis	May 20	Bluff City	St. Louis
Polar Star	St. Louis	May 21	Clara	St. Louis
		May 22	Polar Star	St. Louis
F. X. Aubrey	St. Louis	May 24		
		May 25	F. X. Aubrey	St. Louis
Sonora	St. Louis	May 26		
El Paso	St. Louis	May 27	Sonora	St. Louis
		May 27	El Paso	Council Bluffs
Robert Campbell	St. Louis	May 29	Robert Campbell	Mouth of Yellowstone
Honduras	St. Louis	May 31		

Ref: St. Joseph *Gazette*, May 11, 25, June 1, 1853. The *F. X. Aubrey* was a new boat (making her first trip in April). In *some* newspaper accounts she is listed as the *F. X. Aubry* (the correct spelling of the name), but more often as given here. Other boats were on the "middle Missouri" in May—for example, the *Isabel* (regular packet to Weston) arrived at Weston on May 2 and again on May 16; and the *Saranak* was at Weston on May 13.— *Missouri Republican*, St. Louis, May 5, 17, 20, 1853.

❢ May 4.—"Ward & Guerrier" (Seth E. Ward and William Guerrier), in a notice of this date (published in the St. Joseph *Gazette*), announced the establishment of their "Ferry across the North Fork of the Platte River," nine miles above Fort Laramie; also, "in company with others who have lived for the last twenty years with the Sioux, Shians, and Snake Indians," the construction of a toll bridge (charge: $5.00 per wagon) across the Platte "four miles below the old ferry or Mormon Crossing."

At the ferry Ward & Guerrier had a "large band of horses, mules, and oxen" for sale or trade; a blacksmith shop; also, "all kinds of Groceries, Dried Meat and other substantials for the plains."

Ref: St. Joseph (Mo.) *Gazette*, May 11, 1853 (but doubtless first published in the May 4 issue, which is lacking). *See Annals of Wyoming*, v. 5 (July, 1927), pp. 5-18 for some data on Ward & Guerrier as partners.

ℂ On May 5 a small Oregon-bound company captained by the Rev. Gustavus Hines crossed the Kansas river at Delaware (Grinter) Crossing (present Wyandotte county) to begin the journey overland. In this party were three Hines brothers, their families, and a Bryant family—all from New York, Ohioans Holden A. Judson, wife and daughter; also, three young men, and, for a short time, a Missouri family named Leonard.

Celinda E. Hines (daughter of Jedediah) kept a diary—a journal of special "Kansas" interest for her comment on local events and social life in the Missouri border-Shawnee Methodist Mission area (where the Hines families sojourned from late March till early May); and for the description (though brief) of a route up the north side of the Kansas river, which, "for the first hundred miles," was "away from the great line of emigrant travel."

"It took almost all day to ferry the teams and cattle across [the Kansas]," wrote Celinda on May 5. "Some of the cattle swam the river. . . . at length we were all safely landed in Nebraska[!] at Little St. Louis [Delaware trading post]."

Two days later, and some miles to the northward, a Delaware chief advised the Hines train to "take the divide route [heading west] instead of [continuing northward on] the government road by Ft. Leavenworth, as it is nearer and they say a better road." After three days on the "divide route," the company spent most of May 12 at Grasshopper (Delaware) river—which they crossed by ferry. ("The wagons had to be unloaded and let down the bank with ropes, it being so steep and high on both sides, and the river so deep that we could not ford it," Celinda wrote.) Just before night, on May 14, they "intersected the southern road which crosses the Kansas at the upper ferry" (at or near, present Topeka). On the 16th they passed the "Catholic Mission of the Pottawatamies [St. Mary's]."

The Hines train arrived at the "Middle Fork of the Blue" (the Alcove Springs area ford of the Big Blue) on May 19. The river was at flood stage. There were people "camped in every direction, waiting for the water to fall." Two days later the company decided "to go north to the ferry about seven miles." (The Francis J. Marshall ferry at present Marysville.) Going with them was the train of "Mr. Ferguson, a Santa Fe trader," who had "lived ten years in Mexico and crossed the plains six times." Celinda's May 23 diary entry says: "Remained in camp because our turn had not yet come to cross the Blue. Many camps in sight. Mr. Jones' company from Kansas [Mo.] arrived." On the 24th the Hines company ferried the Big Blue and swam the cattle over. ("I should think there were a hundred wagons in sight during the day," Celinda wrote.)

The Hineses and their cotravelers reached Oregon in September.

Ref: Oregon Pioneer Association, *Transactions of the Forty-Sixth Annual Reunion, 1918* (for Celinda E. Hines' diary); Phoebe G. Judson, *A Pioneer's Search for an Ideal Home* (Bellingham, Wash., 1925), for an account of the trip. The original Celinda E. Hines diary is in the Coe Collection, Yale University Library. Mrs. Judson's book makes mention of the fact that the Gustavus Hineses had adopted the Rev. Jason Lee's daughter; and that she (Lucy Ann Lee, aged 10) was one of the children in the party.

❆ May 6 and 7.—Sen. Thomas Hart Benton, of Missouri, made speeches at Kansas City, Westport, and Independence, Mo., on the subject of a railroad to the Pacific, and the advantages of the central route. He publicized the forthcoming overland expedition of Edward F. Beale (*see* p. 1159).

Ref: *Jefferson Inquirer*, Jefferson City, May 28, 1853; St. Joseph (Mo.) *Gazette*, May 11, 18, June 8, 1853. The senator had accompanied Beale up the Missouri on the *Clara*.

❆ May 7-17.—Leaving Fort Leavenworth on the 7th, Capt. Charles S. Lovell and command (Companies B, F, and H, Sixth infantry) marched overland by way of the old, and new, sections of military road leading from Fort Leavenworth to "Fort Riley" (*see* p. 1154); and reached their destination on the 17th.

In a June 15 letter (from "Camp Centre") a man commented on his journey over the Fort Leavenworth-"Fort Riley" road: ". . . it was the roughest and most disagreeable one that ever was traveled by white man or nigger since the days of Moses. It was an incessant crossing of creeks, sloughs, quagmires, swampy bottoms and rocky hollows, the entire route. . . . It will cost Government more than the new post to make that road practicable for general travel." (The army appropriations act of March 3 had allotted $11,725 for "bridges, establishing communications between Fort Leavenworth and the Republican Fork of the Kansas River." But most of the bridge-building came later. *See* an October annals entry, p. 1183, for first mention of the government ferry at the Big Blue crossing; and other comment on the military road.)

This table of distances, giving mileages from Fort Riley to Fort Leavenworth, published in Max. Greene's *The Kansas Region*, in 1856, from all appearances was compiled in 1853:

	Miles	Total miles
From Fort Riley to Wild Cat [creek]	12	
Big Blue [river]	7	19
Sargent's Creek	3	22
Rock Creek	14	36
Vermillion	4	40
Lost Creek	5	45
[St. Mary's] Catholic Mission	7	52
Soldier Creek	20	72
Grasshopper [Delaware] (crossing Bayou creek)	20	92
Hickory Point	10	102

Stranger Creek [river] 12   114
Salt Creek 9   123
Missouri State line 4   127

(In a January 12, 1855, letter Bvt. Maj. E. A. Ogden stated: "Fort Riley . . . is one hundred and thirty miles west of Fort Leavenworth. . . . It is connected with Fort Leavenworth . . . by a good road on the north side of the Kansas.")

Ref: W. F. Pride's *The History of Fort Riley* (c1926), p. 61; *Missouri Republican*, St. Louis, July 6, 1853; or, New York *Daily Tribune*, July 15, 1853; Max. Greene's *The Kanzas Region* . . . (New York, 1856), pp. 139, 140; U. S. Statutes at Large (for 1853); 33d Cong., 2d Sess., H. *Report No. 36* (Serial 808)—for Ogden, 1855. "Sargent's Creek" evidently was named for 2d Lt. Alden Sargent, Sixth infantry, stationed at Fort Riley in its early days.

❦ **May.**—The *Occidental Messenger,* Independence, Mo., of May 7, published an estimate of the livestock *owned by citizens of Jackson county, Mo., alone,* that would be driven across the plains [and across "Kansas"]; and noted that "some of the heaviest droves" were from "other portions of the State, or from different States, and hence . . . not included in the . . . list":

Owner(s)	Stock	Wagons	"Animals"	Number in party
John Cantrell's train	250 cattle	1	6	6
Finley, Johnson & McCabe [Findlay]	700 cattle	8	30	30
Cunningham & Asbury ["Asberry" in 1850 census] ..	2,200 sheep	4	10	10
John C. Chrisman	300 cattle	4	10	10
John Montgomery	300 cattle	5	15	35
Thomas G. Clarkson	400 cattle	22	15	35
William Clark ["Clarke" in 1850 census]	500 cattle	5	20	20
Charles S. Shortridge	13[0?] cattle	1	1	8
John Sims	800 cattle	8; and 1 carriage	35	35
Joel Chiles	400 cattle	5	20	20
Finis Ewing	300 cattle	4	15	15
Manna [?]	140 cattle	4	15	6
James and Thomas Rogers..	200 cattle	5	8	10
John Adams	150 cattle	4	10	10
Caldwell & Overton	110 cattle	4	6	6
Smart, Caldwell & Barnes ..	300 cattle	3	10	15
Joel W. Hudspeth	700 cattle	8	30	30
Smith, McCaul[e]y & Hereford	2,000 cattle	20; and 2 carriages	70	70
D[avid] Waldo & Co.	500 cattle	17	10	21
Enoch Moore	300 cattle	11	25	16

As the *Occidental Messenger* recapitulated it: Number of cattle, 8,263; Wagons, 143; Animals, 350; Men, 385; Carriages, 4; Sheep, 2,200. And added: "We feel satisfied that the whole number of stock that will be driven by the drovers of this county, and of those that will be taken in the trains of our citizens who are going to Oregon and California for the purpose of hunting homes, will equal, if it does not exceed, ten thousand head of cows and sheep." (The columns above add up to 8,480 cattle, 2,200 sheep, 143 wagons, 361 animals, and 408 persons.)

Ref: *Missouri Republican*, St. Louis, May 11, 1853. As quoted from the Independence paper by the *Weekly Missouri Sentinel*, Columbia, May 12, 1853, the figures *varied* slightly: 8,050 cattle, 2,200 sheep, 153 wagons, 4 carriages, 349 animals (horses and mules), and 373 persons. The *Sentinel* of April 21, 1853, quoted the *Occidental Messenger* of April 9, as stating that Joel Chiles, with the *first drove of the season*, had set out during that week. Returning Californian E. G. McClure (who reached Independence August 4) reported having met "Smith, Hereford & McCauley's train at South Pass, all well and getting along finely—as are the emigrants and drovers generally. . . ."—Liberty (Mo.) *Weekly Tribune*, August 12, 1853; or, *Missouri Republican*, August 12, 1853. Joel F. Chiles died February 6, 1855, at his home in Jackson county.—Liberty *Tribune*, February 16, 1855.

❡ May 10.—At St. Joseph, Mo., contracts were let for the first 25 miles of the Hannibal and St. Joseph railroad's western end.

Successful bidders were Messrs. Harding, Mills & Co., New York, for grading, and Messrs. Passmore & Newman, for heavy masonry and bridging.

On July 27 the *Gazette* reported: "There are now about sixty hands at work on this end of the Rail Road, and Mr. Kingsley has advertised for 200 more."

Ref: St. Joseph *Gazette*, May 18, July 27, 1853.

❡ May 11.—"Wm. Priddee, Presley Muir & Company set out from Wyandotte Territory [present Wyandotte county] for California, with nearly *two* hundred head of cattle."—William Walker.

Ref: William Walker's diary (*loc. cit.*). See pp. 867 and 939, for Wyandot expeditions to California in 1849 and 1850. On May 11, 1853, Walker "Wrote a long letter to the California Wyandotts"—which the above company presumably carried West.

❡ Mid-May.—From Westport, Mo., the overland (by a central route) light-traveling pack-train expedition of California's Indian affairs superintendent—Edward F. Beale (aged 31), got under way. Beale dispatched the train on May 10—to go as far as Council Grove. He, and his cousin G. Harris Heap (journalist of the trip), set out on May 15. Their path across "Kansas" would be the Santa Fe trail, and its Bent's Fort branch.

At the outset the party numbered 12. Cotravelers included three men from Washington—Elisha and William Riggs, William Rogers; the employees were Henry Young, J. Wagner, J. Cosgrove, Richard Brown (a Delaware), Gregorio Madrid, Jesus Garcia, and George Simms (cook).

Heap's journal notes that the first day's (12-mile) ride (May 15) was "over prairies enamelled with flowers." They camped on Indian creek. Of the habitations between Westport and Council Grove, Heap had these comments: (May 16) "at Bull Creek . . . we found two log-huts . . ."; (May 17—at 110-mile creek) "This hamlet is composed of a few log-houses situated in a hollow, near a small stream shaded by cottonwoods.

The inhabitants are Shawnees . . . the women appeared neat and respectable."

He described Council Grove (reached May 18) as "a settlement of about twenty frame and log houses, and scattered up and down the stream are several [Kansa] Indian villages. At a short distance from the road is a large and substantially built Methodist mission-house, constructed of limestone. . . ." (Elsewhere in Heap's 1854-published *Central Route to the Pacific* is the statement: "At Council Grove, there is a large, well-furnished store [run by Seth M. Hays], where a constant supply of everything required for the road is kept. Also, a good farrier and blacksmith [Emanuel Mosier?].")

Beale and his party set out from Council Grove on May 19. Their Santa Fe trail marches varied from 32 to 45 miles per day, and they passed many other westbound travelers (slower-moving emigrant trains—*see* p. 1159). At Turkey creek (May 20) they overtook Antoine Leroux (Taos-bound with his own wagon train) and Beale arranged to hire him as guide. (But Leroux developed pleurisy and was left at Fort Atkinson.)

It was May 25 when Beale and company reached Fort Atkinson. Bvt. Maj. Edward Johnson (commandant) gave them "a cordial reception." (William Riggs left the party at this place, to return home.)

On May 26 Beale's party (now 11) left Fort Atkinson to continue up the Arkansas. The night of May 28 was spent on Chouteau's Island. Bent's (old) Fort was passed on May 31. (*See* Heap's "Itinerary of the Central Route" from Westport, Mo., to Bent's Fort, on p. 1018.)

The rest of the journey is not chronicled here. G. Harris Heap summarized the Beale expedition's "central route" travels from Westport, Mo., to Los Angeles (reached August 22, "in exactly one hundred days"; total distance 1,852 miles) as follows:

"From Westport, Missouri, to Council Grove, 122 miles"; "From Council Grove to Fort Atkinson, Arkansas River, 239 miles"; "From Fort Atkinson . . . to mouth of Huerfano River, 247 miles"; "From the mouth of the Huerfano to Fort Massachusetts, 85 miles"; "From Fort Massachusetts to Coochatope Pass, 124 miles"; "From Coochatope Pass to Grand River, 134 miles"; "From Grand River to Green River, 154 miles"; "From Green River to Mormon Settlements near Las Vegas de Santa Clara, Utah Territory, 242 miles"; "From . . . [these] Settlements . . . to Mohaveh River, 374 miles"; "From Mohaveh River to Los Angeles, 137 miles."

Ref: G. Harris Heap's *Central Route to the Pacific* . . . (Philadelphia, 1854); G. Harris Heap's *Central Route to the Pacific* . . ., Edited by LeRoy R. and Ann W. Hafen (Glendale, Calif., 1957); St. Joseph (Mo.) *Gazette*, May 11, 1853, or, New York *Daily Times*, May 14, 1853; New York *Daily Tribune*, August 2, October 14, 1853. The *Weekly Missouri Sentinel*, Columbia, September 29, 1853 (for adventures, and return east of Elisha Riggs, who, with William Rogers, had left the party while at Taos, N. M.). Emanuel Mosier was blacksmith for the Kansa Indians in 1853, and a Council Grove resident.

ℂ Mid-May.—The California-bound emigrant company headed by Charles Albright, which included John B. Haas, arrived at the Big Blue crossing (present Marysville). They found the river bank full and "roaring like a millrace." There were "hundreds of tents and wagons" at camps in the vicinity.

As described by Haas (in a later-written account), the ferry (Frank Marshall's) was a "rough flat boat," just large enough for one wagon and a yoke of oxen. "A stout rope spanned the river, and upon it a block and tackle run the current, propelling the boat across. The ferry men crossed a wagon every fifteen or twenty minutes at five dollars a wagon . . . The approach to the ferry was in deep mud, and had to be constantly renewed by putting in logs and boughs. One man of the ferry crew had been drowned that day, carried down stream."

Ref: *Pony Express Courier*, Placerville, Calif., v. 5, no. 3 (August, 1938), p. 9.

❡ May.—Captained by "Bob" Smith, a company of Arkansas emigrants (57? persons; 18 wagons) crossed "Kansas" by way of the Cherokee and Santa Fe trails; followed up the Arkansas to Pueblo; then journeyed northward along the base of the Rockies to a junction with the Oregon-California trail—as recollected (in 1900) by Dillis B. Ward. (His family had started from "near Batesville, Ark.")

Emigrant J. S. Bowman (who traveled the Oregon-California trail) stated that a "large number of immigrants (not generally estimated in the aggregate of overland immigration,) from Arkansas, &c., via the Arkansas river; thence to the head waters of the Platte, came into the Salt Lake road this side of Green river. Their stock generally was in better condition than that which came by the Platte, though there were some complaints of sickness by this route."

Ref: *The Washington Historian*, Tacoma, v. 2, pp. 83-88, 124-133, 173-181; *Missouri Republican*, St. Louis, November 2, 1853. "L's" May 31, 1853, letter from St. Louis (published in the New York *Daily Times* of June 9, 1853) stated that Major Howe's party (*see* p. 1160), on the Santa Fe trail eastbound in May, had met "a number of large parties of emigrants to California from the Southern and S West'n States, who were driving out immense herds of cattle. Most of these emig's will pursue the El Passo route. Some were inclined to follow Sitgreaves path from Albuquerque. . . ." Another account (from Independence, Mo., May 25) said Howe's party had met "large parties of emigrants to California from Arkansas, and points south, with immense herds of cattle. The Pawnees[?] were a little troublesome to them. They had run off a hundred head of stock for Col. Hill of Batesville, Ark., and killed one of his teamsters. . . ."—New York *Daily Tribune*, June 3, 1853.

❡ May 17.—Capt. Charles S. Lovell, with Sixth infantry companies B, F, and H, arrived at "Camp Centre" (at the Smoky Hill-Republican rivers junction—*see* p. 1131) to establish the military post subsequently named Fort Riley. (The army appropriations act of March 3 had included the sum of $65,000 for "barracks and quarters at the Republican Fork of the Kansas River.")

An 1853 chronology of Fort Riley events and developments follows:

May 28. A train with quartermaster and commissary stores set out from Fort Leavenworth for Camp Centre. (Bvt. Maj. Edmund A. Ogden, AQM at Fort Leavenworth, and supervisor of construction at Fort Riley, was at "Camp Centre" in May, but left on June 1. He was back, briefly, early in July.)

May 31. News, via an express from "Camp Centre": "The place is   .   .   .

in good health, and officers stationed there are busily employed in making preparations for putting up the necessary buildings &c." (May post returns showed six officers present: Captain Lovell, Bvt. Major Ogden, Asst. Surg. Joseph K. Barnes, 2d Lt. Joseph L. Tidball, 2d Lt. Darius D. Clark, and 2d Lt. Alden Sargent. Besides the three Sixth infantry companies, there were 41 civilians [mechanics, teamsters, etc.] in quartermaster department employ.)

June 4. Capt. Thomas Hendrickson (arriving from leave) took over command of Company H, Sixth infantry.

June 15. From "Camp Centre" a correspondent wrote: "One set of quarters are about half up, and it is contemplated to commence the other in about a week. . . . The quarters are very capacious, being calculated to accommodate eighty-eight men, exclusive of the married portion; and there is also in it quarters for one laundress. The dimensions of the building are 36 by 86 feet. The lower or basement story is divided into seven apartments, to be occupied as a mess-room, kitchen, orderly room, laundress' quarters, pantries and store room. The upper part is to be in one apartment, the full size of the building, which will be occupied by the soldiers." (The "plan" called for barracks of stone for eight companies.) The writer also reported that everybody, except himself, had the "ague and fever, bilious fever, diarrhea, or some other agreeable complaint." (Asst. Surg. Joseph K. Barnes wrote [in August?] of the "large and unfailing" spring which had supplied troops with water during the summer. Of the buildings being erected, Barnes said they were, "judiciously situated . . . commodious and well ventilated with walls of porous limestone." He noted, also, that "since the 20th day of May, large quantities of timber" had been cut in the river bottoms by the troops.)

June 27. War Dept. General Order No. 17 gave a permanent name—Fort Riley—to the new military post. (Named for Maj. Gen. Bennet Riley whose death had occurred June 9, at Buffalo, N. Y.)

July 2. At "Camp Centre, Nebraska [*i. e.*, 'Kansas'']," (where news of the "Fort Riley" name had not yet been received) Bvt. Major Ogden negotiated a contract with J. A. Crump to "put up such masonwork of brick and stone, pertaining to the barracks at Pawnee [Republican] river, as may be required, for the sum of $488, and eight cents per cubic foot of work . . . [etc.]."

July 4. Capt. John W. Gunnison, and some members of his expedition, visited Fort Riley, briefly—*see* p. 1168.

August 1.—At Fort Riley, Charles Perry, Weston, Mo., signed a contract (made with 2d Lt. Alden Sargent, AAQM) to deliver 250 tons of hay (at $7 per ton) to the post by October 15. His bondsmen were Elias Perry and Robert Wilson.

August. According to post returns for this month, there were 26 civilian teamsters and 60 civilian mechanics at Fort Riley, in addition to the troops.

October 10. Bvt. Maj. Edward Johnson and Company D, Sixth infantry, arrived at Fort Riley from Fort Atkinson (*see* p. 1170). Asst. Surg. Aquila T. Ridgely, Lt. Henry Heth, and 2d Lt. John T. Shaaff were in this party. Johnson assumed command of the post (from Captain Lovell).

October 14. Bvt. 2d Lt. J. A. Smith joined Company F at Fort Riley.

October 26. Lt. Levi C. Bootes (joining from furlough on the 25th) assumed command of Company F. Bvt. 2d Lt. Augustus H. Plummer (from the military academy) arrived and joined Company D.

October (28?). John C. Fremont crossed the Republican near the post— *see* p. 1181.

November 14-15. Maj. Albemarle Cady, Sixth infantry (transferred from regimental headquarters) arrived at Fort Riley on the 14th; and on the 15th assumed command of the post (from Bvt. Major Johnson).

November. In his annual report, the quartermaster general stated: "Much labor has been done [at Fort Riley], and materials procured for future operations. A steam saw-mill is in operation, with shingle machine, lath saws, and mortising machine attached." But "quarters sufficient for the officers and men of [only] two companies, according to the plan [*see above*]," had been completed. They would, however, "during the winter, shelter the four [Sixth infantry] companies of which the garrison is now composed." November post returns showed an aggregate of 229 troops at Fort Riley; and there were some 40 civilians (32 mechanics; eight teamsters). Ten officers were present: Cady, Ridgely, Johnson, Hendrickson, Heth, Bootes, Sargent, Shaaff, Smith, and Plummer. (Lovell, Tidball, and Clark were "absent with leave"; Barnes had been transferred.)

Ref: Fort Riley post returns, 1853 (microfilm from National Archives); Pride, *op. cit.*, p. 61; New York *Daily Tribune*, June 29, July 15, 1853; *Missouri Republican*, St. Louis, July 6, 1853; 33d Cong., 1st Sess., *Sen. Ex. Doc. No. 37* (Serial 698), pp. 31 and 33 (for Perry, and Crump contracts): 34th Cong., 1st Sess., *Sen. Ex. Doc. No. 96* (Serial 827), pp. 167, 168 (for Barnes); 33d Cong., 1st Sess., *Sen. Ex. Doc. No. 1* (Serial 691), p. 131 (for quartermaster general's 1853 report); 33d Cong., 2d Sess., *Sen. Ex. Doc. No. 78* (Serial 758), p. 16 (for Gunnison); *U. S. Statutes at Large* (for army appropriations act). In KHi ms. division are some original quarterly muster rolls 1853-1855, of Company H, Sixth infantry. The death, by drowning in the Kansas river near Fort Riley, of Pvt. George W. Sewell, on October 18(?), 1853, is recorded therein.

❡ May 17.—In charge of "Mr. [John] Jones," the Santa Fe mail reached Independence, after a 17-day trip—pleasant except "for a few heavy rains and hailstorms. . . ." Stagecoach passengers were: A. H. Foster, J. B. Gardner (also referred to as "Sargeant Gardner"), and John Gwyn.

They reported that the Cheyennes (encamped about Fort Atkinson, awaiting arrival of Agent Fitzpatrick) were "remarkably friendly."

On the trail they had met "a great many large droves of cattle" en route to California (the drivers having "sustained some heavy losses" of cattle as a result of stampedes during hailstorms). Also met: California-bound (Indian) Sup't Edward F. Beale, Harris Heap, and company, at "Willow Spring," in "fine health and spirits. . . ."

Ref: Liberty (Mo.) *Weekly Tribune*, May 27, 1853 (from *Occidental Messenger*, Independence, Mo.); *Missouri Republican*, St. Louis, May 20, 1853; New York *Daily Tribune*, May 20, 1853 (by telegraph from Louisville, May 19); Alton (Ill.) *Telegraph*, May 21, 1853.

❡ Mid-May.—Oregon resident William H. Gray (who had traveled overland to Oregon in 1836 with the Whitman party; east to the states in 1837; and westward again in 1838), left the vicinity of Westport, Mo., on May 18, to drive a flock of sheep overland.

His small company (15 at the start) included four women and three children. Rebecca Ketcham of Gray's party kept a journal.

Most of the party ferried the Kansas river on May 25—Papin's(?), or Smith's(?) crossing (present Topeka area). Rebecca described the operation: "This is done by means of a strong rope fastened on each side of the river. They have a boat something like those they have on the canal called scows. This is fastened to the rope across the river by means of another rope and pulleys. One of the ox teams went on the boat first, then two saddle horses, then the ladies and children. . . . The current is very swift. The banks on one side are high, and it was quite difficult to get the teams on the boat, but everything came over safely." Gray's party camped near the river, after crossing, and temporarily minus their supply wagon, had to borrow a water pail from "the house of one of the ferrymen who lives on this [north] side the river."

Under way again, on the 27th, after delays, the company camped four miles beyond a stream Rebecca called "Vermillion Creek," but which must have been Cross creek (at present Rossville). There was a toll bridge, but they did not use it. On May 28 they traveled some 25 miles. Rebecca wrote: "We went over several hills that were *much* higher than the surrounding country, and once or twice had the most beautiful view I ever saw. We could see something like 20 miles before us and 12 or 14 behind us, and the same on each side." Her description (and the fact she made no mention of St. Mary's Mission) indicates Gray headed his company over the hills after fording Cross creek. Also, it *appears* he did not approach the Big Blue in the Alcove Springs area, but, rather went directly to the crossing at present Marysville, so as to use Marshall's ferry. "When we got to the river [on May 31] we found there were 20 or 30 wagons to be ferried over before we could go, and only one could go at a time," wrote Rebecca. Some hours later it was their turn. Her diary entry states: "The river is not very wide but quite deep and muddy. The bank where they cross is quite steep on both sides, and the mud was awful. The wagon in going down to the boat and out from it sometimes stood almost on end. We all walked down to the boat and stood on one end of [it] while we went over." There was trouble with the sheep; and it was next day before they were across (the sheep had to swim). Eleven days later the party arrived at Fort Kearny.

In September Gray's party reached Oregon.

Ref: *Oregon Historical Quarterly*, Salem, v. 62 (September and December, 1961, issues), pp. 237-287, 337-402.

❡ May 18.—The St. Joseph *Gazette* stated: "It is estimated that considerably upwards of ten thousand head of cattle alone have crossed the river at St. Joseph destined for California. . . . The number of cattle [to cross the Plains this spring] it is supposed will exceed *one hundred thousand head.*"

Ref: St. Joseph (Mo.) *Gazette*, May 18, 1853.

❡ May-August.—"Statistics," and other information on the year's westbound emigration passing Fort Kearny (on the south side of the Platte), from the post register, and a few other sources, are given below:

Up to noon of May 20: 3,348 men, 905 women, 1,207 children. (Total persons: 5,460.) 1,320 wagons, 34,151 cattle, 1,691 horses, 740 mules, 1,200 sheep.

Up to May 31: 4,937 [7,937?] men, 1,900 women, 2,630 children. (Total persons: ?) 2,084 wagons, 81,660 cattle, 4,360 horses, 1,637 mules, 11,000 sheep.

"Passing Fort Kearny [*on May 31*]: There has passed here 13,000 people, 3,000 wagons, and about 90,000 head of stock."—Agnes Stewart.

On June 4, at Fort Kearny: "The Captain informed Pa that there had passed here 85,000 head of cattle and 8,000 men who were crossing the plains this year, also that most of the emigration was going to Oregon."—Celinda E. Hines.

Up to June 4, from *estimates* supplied by Francis A. West (on returning to St. Joseph): 30,000 men, 8,000 women, 11,000 children. 17,000 horses and mules, 88,000 cattle, and sheep "without number." West had seen 12,000 sheep in one herd; 2,700 sheep belonging to a Holt county, Mo., doctor had drowned in crossing the Platte river.

Up to June 6: 8,746 men, 2,088 women, 2,892 children. (Total persons: 13,726.) 2,377 wagons, 91,493 cattle, 4,839 horses, 1,827 mules, 11,000 sheep. ("J. S. B."—who sent these post records to St. Louis—wrote: "On the roads from St. Joseph and Independence there must be at least 35,000 head more of cattle, and 50,000 head of sheep. These statistics relate only to the emigration south of the Platte, and may be safely estimated as not exceeding one half the entire emigration and stock, which are crossing the Plains this summer. As far as I can judge, the emigration this year will be considerably less, perhaps one-fourth [less], than that of last year, while the number of cattle and sheep will be twice as great.") Mountain man A. Archambault, arriving at St. Louis in June, direct from Devil's Gate, reported he had met 105,000 head of cattle *south of the Platte,* also, a large number of sheep, and a great many horses ("the finest he ever saw").

On July [4?]: 9,698 men, 2,248 women, 3,058 children. (Total persons: 15,004.) 3,000 wagons, 102,828 cattle, 5,415 horses, 2,131 mules, 40,125 sheep. [Probably it was 3,600 (not 3,000) wagons in the Post record.]

Up to July 5: 9,711 men, 2,247 women, 3,058 children. (Total persons: 15,016). 3,603 wagons, 102,846 cattle, 5,414 horses, 2,151 mules, 43,825 sheep.

Up to August 15: 9,909 men, 2,252 women, 3,058 children. (Total persons: 15,219.) 3,708 wagons, 105,792 cattle, 5,477 horses, 2,190 mules, 48,495 sheep. (The *Missouri Republican,* having at hand the Fort Kearny record book in quoting these figures, also stated: Of this number, as we understand the register, 1,661 males, 761 females and 1,085 children were destined for Oregon—making 3,507.")

Ref: For May 20: *Missouri Republican,* St. Louis, June 9, 1853, or, New York *Daily Tribune,* June 3 and 17, 1853; for May 31: *Mo. Rep.,* June 21, 1853; for Agnes Stewart: *Oregon Historical Quarterly,* v. 29 (March, 1928), pp. 83, 84; for Celinda E. Hines: Oregon Pioneer Association, *Transactions of the Forty-Sixth Annual Reunion, 1918;* for June 4: *Weekly Missouri Statesman,* Columbia, June 24, 1853; for June 6: *Mo. Rep.,* June 22, 23,

1853; for July [4?]: *Mo. Rep.*, July 27, 1853; for July 5: St. Joseph (Mo.) *Gazette*, August 3, 1853; for August 15: *Mo. Rep.*, November 4, 1853. The New York *Daily Tribune* of August 1, 1853 (from the *Missouri Republican*), quoted a Fort Laramie letter, dated June 28, 1853, as follows: "Up to this time there has passed about 6,000 wagons, 23,000 persons, and 150,000 cattle. Owing to cool weather and rain, cattle have got along finely, but few lame, and those are sold to the swarm of buyers that line the road at exhorbitant prices. We hear of no sickness, and I suppose there never were as many persons traveled the same distance who were so healthy. . . ." The *Tribune* of December 13, 1853, had news from Oregon as follows: "The overland immigration is nearly all in. From an account kept at 'U[ma]tilla,' by the Indian agent, it appears that the whole number of immigrants who have passed that point, is 6,449, of which 898 are wives, 1,408 sons, 1,513 daughters; leaving 2,630 men. . . ." The stock was given as: 9,077 oxen, 6,518 cows, 2,009 horses, 327 mules, 1,500 sheep; the wagons as numbering 1,269. The "comparatively few" immigrants on other routes, it was stated, would bring the total (for Oregon) to a little over 7,000 souls.

❡ May 20.—J. Soulé Bowman and companions (about 12?) set out from Kansas City, Mo., for California, taking the route up the Kansas valley. They crossed the river near Pottawatomie Baptist Mission (just west of present Topeka); reached Fort Kearny about June 7, and Fort Laramie on June 21(?); left Salt Lake City on July 29.

A San Francisco newspaper reported this party's successful journey "bringing in thirty-five fine horses and mules, without losing or laming an animal; and the entire company of men in good health. . . ." Bowman estimated the emigration to California at 25,000; and the Mormon emigration at under 10,000.

Ref: *Missouri Republican*, St. Louis, August 1, November 1, 1853; and *ibid.*, December 31, 1853, issue for item on Bowman's death on November 24 at San Francisco. He had made the journey west in 1852 as well as in 1853. *See* a mention of Bowman's 1853 trip in 33d Cong., 2d Sess., *H. Misc. Doc. No. 37* (Serial 807), p. 86.

❡ May.—California, or Oregon-bound traffic on the Santa Fe trail (across "Kansas," and up the Bent's Fort branch) was fairly heavy this month—as shown in the items below, quoted from the journal of G. Harris Heap (westbound with Beale's pack train party— *see* p. 1152).

May 22 (when west of Turkey creek, and east of Walnut creek): "We had already overtaken and passed several large wagon and cattle trains from Texas and Arkansas, mostly bound to California. With them were many women and children. . . ."

(While camped at Walnut creek, Heap wrote: "This is the point at which emigrants to Oregon and California, from Texas and Arkansas, generally strike this road. They prefer the route which leads them through the South Pass—to the one on the Gila, or Cooke's route. . . ." But *see* pp. 853-855.)

May 27 (above Fort Atkinson): "We passed during the morning several large parties of emigrants for California with cattle. Their stock was in good condition, and travelled steadily at the rate of fifteen miles a day. Encamped near an emigrant train at noon. . . ."

May 28 (at Chouteau's Island in the Arkansas): "On the left shore, opposite

to us, was a large emigrant train, whose cattle were in splendid condition.
. . ."

May 29 (on up the Arkansas): "A wagon and cattle train of emigrants encamped near us [at noon]. . . . In the evening, we had a large company of emigrants on each side of us."

May 30 (near the Big Timbers): "We passed this morning two wagon and cattle trains for California via Great Salt Lake. Washington Trainor, of California, with a large number of cattle, and about 50 fine horses and mules, camped near us."

May 31 (after passing Bent's [old] Fort): "The adobe walls . . . were covered with written messages from parties who had already passed here to their friends in the rear; they all stated that their herds were in good condition, and progressing finely."

Ref: Heap (1854), *op. cit.*, pp. 19-25. Possibly among the trains above was a company from Frankfort, Ky. (headed by Joseph Davis)—who died August 3 before reaching California), which was said to be driving cattle from Missouri and Arkansas.—St. Joseph *Gazette*, November 23, 1853.

❡ May 24.—Maj. Marshall S. Howe, Second dragoons, some other officers (among them Maj. George A. H. Blake, Lt. Harvey A. Allen, 2d Lt. James W. Robinson, 2d Lt. Nathan G. Evans), and 10 privates, arrived at Fort Leavenworth on, or about this day, from Santa Fe (left May 3).

As escort, Sgt. William McCleave and 13 Company K, First dragoons had traveled with them from Fort Union, N. M., to Fort Atkinson (and perhaps farther east?). The military party was accompanied by traders Albert Smith, Gutierrez, and one or two El Paso and Chihuahua merchants.

On May 20, west of Cottonwood crossing, Beale's party (*see* p. 1152) had met "Major [Daniel H.] Rucker, and Lieutenants Heath [Heth?] and [James W.?] Robinson on their way from New Mexico to Fort Leavenworth."

Ref: New York *Daily Tribune*, May 28, June 3, July 15, 1853; New York *Daily Times*, June 9, 1853; *Missouri Republican*, St. Louis, June 21, July 6, 23, 1853; *Weekly Missouri Sentinel*, Columbia, June 16, 1853; Fort Atkinson post returns, June, 1853 (microfilm in KHi, from National Archives); G. Harris Heap, *op. cit.*, p. 89.

❡ May 25.—The May "Salt Lake" mail party headed by William Allison, reached Independence, Mo., having traveled out to Fort Laramie and back in 25 days—the quickest trip on record. They brought the first mail "entirely through" from Salt Lake since November, 1852.

By report, the Salt Lake-Fort Laramie mail carrier had found his journey difficult, due to very deep snow in the mountains.

Allison's party, en route east, had met the first emigrants within five miles of Fort Laramie, and "from that point" to Fort Kearny, had found the road "crowded with living beings."

Ref: *Missouri Republican*, St. Louis, June 9, 1853; New York *Daily Tribune*, May 28, June 3, 17, 1853; New York *Daily Times*, May 28, 1853; Liberty (Mo.) *Weekly Tribune*, June 3, 1853.

❑ May 26.—California-bound Dr. Thomas Flint (on his way up to Council Bluffs aboard the *El Paso*) recorded in his diary:

". . . at Fort Leavenworth this A. M. Took a walk through the town. Mostly barracks and two old forts. Square lower story stone, upper wood with the corners projecting over the stone midway between stone corners. Making an octagonal facing to all sides. A few soldiers around. . . ."

Ref: *Annual Publications*, Historical Society of Southern California, 1923, v. 12, pt. 3, p. 75.

❑ From late May till June 14 a general court-martial was in session at Fort Leavenworth. High-ranking officers attending included Bvt. Brig. Gen. Newman S. Clarke (Sixth military department head) and Bvt. Lt. Col. Braxton Bragg.

The trial of Maj. Marshall S. Howe, on "charges preferred against him by Lieutenants Pleasanton [Alfred S. Pleasonton], N. G. Evans and company, of the 2d dragoons," opened on June 4. The court-martial adjourned on June 14, with Howe's case incomplete (the defendant having insisted that officers then in New Mexico be called as witnesses). The New York *Herald* of July 18 stated it had learned "from authority" that Major Howe had been "fully acquitted" of all charges, "and this, too, without the court waiting for any defence on the part of the Major."

Ref: *Missouri Republican*, St. Louis, June 15, July 6, 23, 1853.

❑ May 29.—The *Robert Campbell* (under charter to the American Fur Company) "came up [to St. Joseph, Mo.] and landed on the opposite side of the river, in Nebraska [*i. e.*, in 'Kansas'], with a flag flying from the mast, and floating beautifully in the breeze, with the name of P. Cho[u]teau on it, in large letters."

Carrying about 170(?) persons, and more than 300 tons of freight, this steamboat had left St. Louis May 21. Among the passengers: company agents Alexander Culbertson and John B. Sarpy, Alfred J. Vaughan (upper Missouri Indian agent), and Prof. Fielding B. Meek and Dr. Ferdinand V. Hayden (young scientists en route to the Bad Lands), Dr. John Evans and Dr. Benjamin F. Shumard (on a separate Bad Lands expedition), Lt. Andrew J. Donelson (corps of engineers) and party (Lt. John Mullan, First artillery, W. N. Graham, an astronomer, and six soldiers), en route to join Gov. Isaac I. Stevens' expedition; William Nicholas, Prince of Nassau, and his entourage (four persons).

The *Robert Campbell* went up the Missouri to 150 miles beyond the Yellowstone's mouth; and came downriver in July, bringing over 2,800 packs of robes, skins, and furs. On July 22 she passed St. Joseph, and stopped, briefly, at Parkville, Mo., to put ashore company agent James Kipp (resident of Platte county, Mo.); and on the 25th reached St. Louis.

Ref: St. Joseph (Mo.) *Gazette*, June 1, July 27, 1853; New York *Daily Tribune*, June 7, 1853 (from St. Louis *Intelligencer* of May 25); Liberty (Mo.) *Weekly Tribune*, July 29, 1853 (from Parkville [Mo.] *Industrial Luminary* of July 26); *Weekly Missouri Sentinel*, Columbia, Mo., August 4, 1853; *Missouri Republican*, St. Louis, July 26, November 17, 1853; John E. Sunder, *The Fur Trade on the Upper Missouri, 1840-1865* (c1965), pp. 151-155; 33d Cong., 1st Sess., *Sen. Ex. Doc. No. 37* (Serial 698), p. 28; 33d Cong., 2d Sess., *H. Misc. Doc. No. 37* (Serial 807), p. 82.

❡ MARRIED: at the Iowa, Sac & Fox Presbyterian Mission (in present Doniphan county), on May 30(?) William Zook and Sarah Ann Waterman, by the Rev. William Hamilton.

Ref: Highland Presbyterian Church Records, 1843-1890 (microfilm in KHi). The "Register of marriages," gives the date as May 30 (a Monday). However, the "Minutes" of May 23, 1853, state that Miss Waterman was married to Zook on "Tuesday following this meeting [of the 23d]," and that the Zooks, Hamilton (and family), left for "Otoe & Omahaw Mission this day." The Hamiltons had been present Doniphan county residents since late December, 1837—*see* p. 339.

❡ June 1.—"Whitehead's Ferry 4½ miles above St. Joseph . . . on the Missouri river . . . on the nearest and best route from St. Joseph to the Iowa Mission, Fort Kearney . . . [etc.]," was advertised by proprietor James R. Whitehead (in the St. Joseph *Gazette*).

His notice stated that he had "two good Boats in good order," and could cross "from 5 to 700 head of Cattle per day." In the same *Gazette* issue was a card signed by Simeon Mattingly, Jno. Johnstone, and Jno. W. Martin, stating that they—"bound for California, via the Plains, having over 800 cattle, horses, wagons &c—recommend[ed] Whitehead's ferry. . . ."

Ref: St. Joseph *Gazette*, June 1, 1853; 33d Cong., 2d Sess., Sen. *Ex. Doc. No.* 69 (Serial 756), p. 157 (for item on Agent Daniel Vanderslice's payment, August 31, 1853, of $3.95 to James R. Whitehead for "Ferriage").

❡ On, or around, June 1, Bvt. Maj. Robert H. Chilton and his Company B, First dragoons left Fort Leavenworth for soon-to-be-abandoned Fort Atkinson, on the Arkansas. Accompanying them down the Santa Fe trail were "teams and citizen teamsters to transport the government property from the Arkansas to the new [military] camp [near the mouth of Walnut creek]"—as recollected by Percival G. Lowe, in his 1906-published *Five Years a Dragoon*.

On arriving at the Plum Buttes (in present Rice county), the dragoons came upon the bodies of three Mexicans. As Lowe described it: "One was still breathing, and blood was trickling from the scalped heads. Away down towards the Arkansas was a large Mexican train. The dead men belonged to it, and were hunting antelope in the hills when killed. Ponies and arms were gone. They were evidently completely surprised. After following the Indian trail a short distance it was completely obliterated by countless thousands of buffalo tracks. The Mexican train was corralled on the plain below . . . but they had corralled to let the herds of buffalo pass by, and had not seen any Indians." (Lowe stated that the dragoons' travel was nearly blocked by buffalo from Cow creek to Coon creek.)

See p. 1169.

Ref: Percival G. Lowe, *Five Years a Dragoon* (1906), pp. 128, 129; *Missouri Republican*, St. Louis, June 15, 1853 (from Weston [Mo.] *Reporter* of June 2[?], or June 9[?]), which says the dragoons "left Fort Leavenworth on yesterday . . ."); or, *see* KHQ, v. 10, p. 203. D. C. Beam, in 1853 a Company B dragoon, in his reminiscences (*see* Nebraska State Historical Society *Transactions*, v. 3, p. 295) did not mention the Indian depredations described by Lowe, but told of an incident at Arkansas crossing that summer in which Plains

Indians tried to rob a Mexican train. They were run off by the First dragoons. This occurred before the treaty of July 27.

❡ June 3.—From Westport, Mo., the overland-to-California cattle drive (and scientific expedition?) of an Italian—Count Leonetto Cipriani—got under way. His companions included Alexander Garbi, Giuseppe Del Grande, "Gosto" (a servant), Mornard (a Frenchman), and Herman Reinke. According to Cipriani's later-written account, there were 11 covered wagons (carrying more than 20,000 pounds of freight), one "omnibus," 24 hired hands, 500 cattle, 600 oxen, 60 horses, and 40 mules.

(A Kansas City, Mo., man reported that the count had "three secretaries and a draughtsman, one engineer, one mathematician, a physician, a number of servants and many wagons to carry provisions, instruments, etc."; and that "His surveys will comprehend 15 miles wide the whole distance.")

Traveling up the Kansas valley, Cipriani's company camped the night of June 12 "near a cold-water spring surrounded by giant oak trees . . . a veritable oasis" (at present Big Springs, Douglas county); crossed "Chonguinnangii creek" (the Shunganunga) on the 13th; and on the 14th was delayed all day at the Kansas river (presumably at "Topeka") by the crossing of a 30-wagon military convoy (Chilton's?—*see* preceding entry) from "Fort Lawrence" (Fort Leavenworth), which preempted the ferry. Cipriani's account says the ferry was a flat-bottom boat which could transport two wagons at a time (for $2 per wagon, and 50 cents per horse).

On June 17 the count attended a special mass at St. Mary's Mission. His train reached the Big Blue ("Alcove Spring"-area crossing) on June 20; and by noon of June 21 the wagons, supplies, men, and animals were all safely across the river.

Count Cipriani reached California in October (after a journey by way of Salt Lake City). His wagons and cattle arrived a little later that month. It is said he realized "a moderate return on his investment."

Ref: *California and Overland Diaries of Count Leonetto Cipriani* . . . translated and edited by Ernest Falbo (Portland, Ore., c1962); *Weekly Missouri Sentinel*, Columbia, Mo., May 26, 1853 (from the St. Louis *Democrat*); G. Harris Heap (1854), *op. cit.*, p. 11, said he met the count at Westport; and that his party "consisted of eleven persons of education and science, and an escort of mountain men; and his outfit was in every respect well appointed and complete."

❡ June.—Headed by "Colonel Lander, of Kentucky," a California-bound company of 17 persons, driving with them a herd of 725 fine cattle, crossed "Kansas," after a journey northward from southern "Oklahoma."

Asst. Surg. Rodney Glisan, at Fort Arbuckle, "Okla.," wrote that Lander's party "passed through this place" on June 1; and that having "left the States in a hurry, without even supplying themselves with subsistence or clothing," the post commissary "issued them sufficient provisions to last to Fort Atkinson [on the Arkansas, in Kansas]; where they anticipate replenishing their stock for the entire trip." Glisan also stated: "The route they contemplate traveling is west of north, until striking the Santa Fe, or Independence road, at Fort Atkinson."

Ref: Rodney Glisan, *Journal of Army Life* (San Francisco, 1874), p. 116.

❡ In mid-June(?) a party of travelers which included Maj. Francis A. Cunningham (army paymaster), Charles S. Rumley (marshal of N. M. territory), Lt. Charles Griffin, Second artillery, 2d Lt. Louis H. Marshall, Third infantry, and "Lt. Bell [2d Lt. David Bell?]," left the States; and reached Santa Fe prior to July 16.

Ref: New York *Daily Tribune,* August 25, 1853 (from Santa Fe *Gazette,* via the New Orleans *Picayune* of August 18). Bell may have been Bvt. 2d Lt. George Bell, Fourth artillery.

❡ Between June 16 and 29 the *Bluff City* (John McCloy, captain) made an unusually fast run from St. Louis to Council Bluffs, Ia., and back. It was stated that she not only made the round trip in 13 days (including all lost time), but also "laid by" 36 hours at the Bluffs. (She left there on June 25.)

The *Bluff City* brought to St. Louis "several packages of gold and silver in the hands of a party of Santa Fe traders who came down on board."

Ref: *Missouri Republican,* St. Louis, June 30, 1853. Earlier in June when the *Bluff City* had made the same trip in "one day less than two weeks," the *Republican* (June 11 issue) had stated that 20 days was considered "very quick" for that round-trip journey. This steamboat burned at St. Louis on July 25.—*Ibid.,* July 26, 1853.

❡ June-July.—From Fort Leavenworth, on June 17, General Garland's New Mexico-bound command, temporarily in charge of Capt. Nathaniel C. McRea, Third infantry, set out for Council Grove. In this large cavalcade were more than 200 troops (mostly recruits), over 50 wagons, and a large number of horses.

According to the Weston (Mo.) *Reporter* the troops numbered 212 (125 dragoons; 87 artillerymen). Listed as making this trip were: Bvt. Maj. Oliver L. Shepherd, Bvt. Capt. William B. Johns, Lt. Henry B. Schroeder, Lt. William D. Smith, Asst. Surg. David C. DeLeon, 2d Lt. Horace F. DeLano, Bvt. 2d Lt. Matthew L. Davis, Bvt. 2d Lt. Charles H. Rundell, Bvt. 2d Lt. Alexander M. McCook. (Captain McRea's family accompanied him. Probably other families were along.)

On June 23 Bvt. Brig. Gen. John Garland (assigned to New Mexico as head of the Ninth Military dept.) left Fort Leavenworth (he had arrived on the 18th) for Council Grove. He was accompanied by Bvt. Maj. William A. Nichols, AAG; and perhaps by Maj. Cary H. Fry, army paymaster. (Fry did make the trip; and it was reported Garland had in charge $300,000 in coins.)

Before June 25 a small party of civilians (with carriages and wagons) reached Council Grove, from Westport, Mo., to join the military command. It was composed of New Mexico territory's newly appointed governor—David Meriwether, the new chief justice—James J. Davenport, new Indian agents

Edmund A. Graves and James M. Smith, Meriwether's son Raymond, a Doctor Jacobs, of Kentucky, and some employees.

On June 26 Col. Joseph K. F. Mansfield, inspector general, left Fort Leavenworth (where he had arrived on the 25th) to overtake General Garland. (2d Lt. Eugene A. Carr, and some Mounted riflemen, served as escort.)

About July 1(?) General Garland and his command got under way for New Mexico from the Council Grove encampment. (Beckwith's exploring party—see p. 1167—reaching Council Grove on June 30 found Garland's company, and the civilian party, there.)

On July 9 (having just arrived at Walnut creek) Lieutenant Beckwith wrote: "General Garland's command passed our camp at 11 o'clock, all in fine health; and we also parted here with Governor Merriwether and his party, in equally fine condition."

Garland must have passed Fort Atkinson about July 15; and it was perhaps on the 16th(?), near one of the Arkansas crossings, that the approach of his cavalcade put to flight a party of Kiowas intent on searching McCarty's merchant train for two young Mexican girls who had escaped from them. McCarty had given the girls refuge, and was determined to keep the Indians at bay. Except for the timely arrival of the troops a fight probably would have occurred.

Notably, Garland's command did not take the Cimarron route, but followed Aubry's route—continuing up the Arkansas to present Kearny county before crossing the river (on July 20). The general reached Fort Union, N. M., on August 2, and Santa Fe on August 7. Governor Meriwether arrived in Santa Fe on August 8; and was inaugurated the same day.

Ref: *Missouri Republican*, St. Louis, May 22, 30, June 13, 15, July 6, September 27, 1853; New York *Daily Tribune*, July 15, August 25, 1853; *Missouri Statesman*, Columbia, June 10, 1853; Liberty (Mo.) *Weekly Tribune*, June 3, 1853; Alton (Ill.) *Telegraph*, June 14, 1853; New Mexico *Historical Review*, v. 39 (October, 1964), pp. 284, 285; William W. H. Davis' *El Gringo; or New Mexico and Her People* (New York, 1857), pp. 249, 250; 33d Cong., 2d Sess., *Sen. Ex. Doc. No. 78* (Serial 758), pp. 20-22 (for Beckwith); David Meriwether, *My Life in the Mountains and on the Plains*, edited by R. A. Griffen (Norman, Okla., c1965), pp. 141-156; Chris Emmett's *Fort Union and the Winning of the Southwest* (Norman, Okla., c1965), p. 154. Emmett names these officers as accompanying Garland: Maj. Electus Backus, Lt. William D. Smith, Capt. Langdon C. Easton, Asst. Surg. David C. DeLeon, and Captain "McPai" (McRae). Backus and Easton are not on the Weston *Reporter* list.

℄ June 18.—From Westport, Mo., California-bound Charles W. McClanahan and partner "Mr. Crockett," with "a large number of sheep and some cows," set out to follow the Santa Fe trail, and the path of Gunnison's expedition. (Originally, these Virginians had taken their stock—purchased in Illinois and Missouri—to St. Joseph, Mo., for a start from that point.)

McClanahan's letter (written from Fort Massachusetts ["Colo."], August 28) told of cotravelers—"the two Mr. Ross's [brothers], of Iowa, with their families" (whom he had met at Westport), and "the two Mr. Burwells [brothers] of Franklin City, Virginia, with a large number of cattle" (whom he had met on the trail a few days out). It was reported by mountain man Dick Wootton (in an October 22 letter) that this McClanahan-headed train had "2,000 sheep, and from 3 to 400 head of cattle."

At Willow Springs, the night of June 26, "Mr. Ross" lost five horses (stampeded); and above Fort Atkinson, on the Arkansas, a "similar misfortune" resulted in the loss of several more riding animals, by some of the party.

Ref: 33d Cong., 2d Sess., *Sen. Ex. Doc. No. 78* (Serial 758), pp. 13, 20, 68 (for mention of these travelers in Beckwith's report of the Gunnison expedition); G. Harris Heap (1957), *op. cit.*, pp. 265-272 (for McClanahan, Wootton, etc.). The *Missouri Republican*, St. Louis, November 12, 1853, reprinted the McClanahan letter (from the *National Intelligencer*, Washington).

❡ June-July.—"Mr. Carrol Hughes" (Francis Carroll Hughes, of Platte[?] county, Mo.), while "stationed" at Independence Rock in late June and early July, saw the following Missouri trains pass. (All, or almost all?—had crossed "Kansas" by one branch or another of the Oregon-California trail.)

June 21.—Hudspeth's train from Jackson county. (*See* p. 1151.) "J." Hudspeth had been very sick, but was "nearly well." The stock were "all in fine order."

June 24.—Perry & Young's train. (They had lost "some few" cattle.) L. Younger's train, from Clay county. David James' train from Buchanan county.

June 26.—Dorris of Platte [county] with a large drove of cattle "all in good order."

June 27.—Andy Hughes from Caldwell county, "getting along fine."

July 4.—A big celebration was held at Independence Rock. Many emigrants had driven hard to get there for the Fourth. The Declaration of Independence was read; and an oration delivered.

July 5.—Peter Lovell and Mr. Davis of St. Joseph passed.

In mid-July Hughes began the journey back to Missouri. On the way he met the following trains:

July 14—At the bridge over the North Fork of the Platte, Coleman Younger and family, and Drury Malone, "getting along well."

July 18(?).—At a place not recollected, Rucker & Hopkins from Boone county. (The St. Joseph *Gazette* of June 22, 1853, had stated: "Messrs. Rucker & Hopkins, of Boone Co. Mo. passed here yesterday, with 4,000 sheep for California.")

July 27.—At Big Sandy, "D. McDonald" (Duncan Macdonell), of Weston, Harvey Jones, A. J. Morrow and Mr. Tiernan of St. Joseph. (*See* p. 1182.)

July (28? or 29?).—At Vermillion, McDonald's (Macdonell's) train, in charge of Brown, "all in good order."

Ref: St. Joseph (Mo.) *Gazette*, August 3, 1853. For Francis C. Hughes *see* annals index.

❡ June-July.—With a large wagon train of Indian goods, Agent Thomas Fitzpatrick (under commission this year to negotiate treaties with Plains tribes) left Kansas City, Mo., on June 20 to travel the Santa Fe trail. (At Bull creek on June 25, Captain Gunnison's party met and talked with Fitzpatrick and William Bent.) Two young St. Louis men—B. Gratz Brown and George M. Alexander—traveled with Fitzpatrick.

On delayed arrival (July 25?) at Fort Atkinson, Fitzpatrick found the greater part of the Comanche and Kiowa nations assembled "a short distance above the fort, and also a large number of Apaches near by. Others were daily arriving. . . ."

See also, July 27 entry.

Ref: Comm'r of Indian Affairs, *Report*, 1853 (Fitzpatrick's report, therein); *Weekly St. Louis Intelligencer*, June 28, 1853; *Missouri Republican*, St. Louis, August 9, 16, 1853; St. Joseph (Mo.) *Gazette*, August 31, 1853; 33d Cong., 2d Sess., *Sen. Ex. Doc. No. 78* (Serial 758), p. 13 (for Gunnison).

❏ June 21.—Stage passengers arriving at Independence, Mo., with the June mail from Santa Fe included John Greiner (late secretary of New Mexico territory), and "Mr. [W. T.?] Dalton, a merchant of Santa Fe."

Ref: *Weekly St. Louis Intelligencer*, June 28, 1853; New York *Daily Tribune*, July 2, 9, 1853. Greiner reached St. Louis June 23—*Missouri Republican*, St. Louis, June 24, 1853. "W. T. Dalton," of Santa Fe, is mentioned in James S. Calhoun's *Official Correspondence* . . . (1915).

❏ June 23.—Heading for the Santa Fe trail, Capt. John W. Gunnison's expedition (which would make explorations and surveys for a Pacific railroad route near the 38th and 39th parallels) got under way from a camp about five miles west of the Missouri border ("in the midst of the various Shawnee missions," and "in a fine grove near a spring"), where the party had been organizing since mid-June.

Captain Gunnison (U. S. topographical engineers) had as chief assistant Lt. Edward G. Beckwith, Third artillery. His "scientific party" was composed of Richard H. Kern (topographer and artist), Sheppard Homans (astronomer), Dr. Jacob H. Schiel (geologist and surgeon), Frederick Creutzfeldt (botanist), and James A. Snyder (asst. topographer). Charles Taplin (wagonmaster) headed the teamsters; and there were other employees. Bvt. Capt. Robert M. Morris, 2d Lt. Laurence S. Baker, and some 30 Mounted riflemen (who had come from Fort Leavenworth June 20) made up the escort. The expedition force totaled around 60 men; and in the train were 16 mule-drawn wagons (three teams per wagon), an instrument carriage, and an ambulance.

On June 26, from a camp on Bull creek (present Johnson county), Lieutenant Beckwith, most of the party, and the wagon train, continued down the Santa Fe trail—to go as far as Walnut creek, where Gunnison's detachment would rejoin them. (Beckwith's command reached the rendezvous on July 9.)

Capt. John W. Gunnison, accompanied by Kern, Homans, Captain Morris, some Mounted riflemen, a teamster, and a packer—a party of 16 in all—set out on June 26 for the Wakarusa, en route to the upper Kansas. They had one light horse-drawn vehicle. Their June 26 camp was on the Wakarusa (and on the Oregon-California trail). Gunnison's notes for June 27 included comment on the conspicuous landmark "Wahkarrussi [Blue] mound," the "wooded dell, called Coon Point," the 21-mile march from Coon Point to "Big spring" ("situated in a hollow, and there are several small jets from the bank"). On the 28th, his party "steered . . . towards a hill [now called Burnett's mound] fifteen miles from camp, and made, opposite to it, [Thomas N.] Stinson's trading-house, on Shunga Munga creek." ("Here," wrote Gunnison, "the road to California branches off to the middle ferry, which is three miles to the north-west.") They camped that night on a branch of Mission creek.

After a 7½-mile ride on June 29, they came to Union Town ("a street of a dozen houses"). At this point Gunnison's party left the thoroughfare, to continue up the south side of the Kansas—starting out by way of a trail. Three Delaware Indians (John Moses, guide; Wahhone, hunter; James Sanders, interpreter), hired earlier, joined them this day. Traveling on the upland, and sometimes far away from the Kansas river, Gunnison and his companions came, on July 2, to a high point where the distant new military post (Fort Riley) could be seen.

On July 3 the party crossed "Mahungasa [Clarke's—now Clark] creek" ("100 feet wide and 3 deep, with a swift current"). "It is rightly named Big Stone," wrote Gunnison, "for at the ford we found its bed covered with boulders." Two and a half miles beyond, they arrived on the bluff opposite the fort.

On the Fourth of July, about noon, Gunnison's party got across the Kansas river. (The horses swam the stream. The light vehicle upset as it was being floated over on an "India Rubber ponton.") Their stop at Fort Riley was brief. The same day they resumed the march—crossing the "Pawnee" (Republican) via a ferry. That night their camp was at a spring between the Republican and Smoky Hill.

Of his travels from June 26 to July 12, Captain Gunnison later (August 22) wrote: "I followed the Kansas River valley to the new fort (Riley) on Pawnee river, and crossing, took a very level and direct route on the northerly side; crossed the Nepeholla (Solomon's fork) and Saline rivers by ferrying on rafts of logs, as they were swollen by recent rains; and then, cutting off the southern bend of the Kansas at the Smoky Hill, passed in the same direction to the Walnut creek . . . [where the main expedition party was waiting]."

After the July 12 reunion at Walnut creek, Gunnison's expedition continued westward on the Santa Fe trail, on the 13th; reached (and camped a mile west of) Fort Atkinson on July 16. Beckwith's journal says 280 lodges of Comanches were along the Arkansas near by; and that on the river's southern bank, "the old men and the women and children of the Kioways were encamped." (The warriors had gone to fight Pawnees.) Shaved Head (principal chief of the Comanches) came to visit Captain Gunnison. They had a smoke and talk.

On July 19 the Gunnison expedition left Fort Atkinson to continue up the Arkansas. Their route, subsequently, was much the same as that traveled by E. F. Beale earlier in the year (see p. 1152). Three months after leaving "Kansas," while the party was again divided, Captain Gunnison, Richard Kern, Frederick Creutzfelt, William Potter (guide), John Bellows (employee), and three Mounted riflemen were massacred (October 26) by a band of Indians, on the Sevier river in Utah.

Ref: 33d Cong., 2d Sess., *Senate Ex. Doc. No. 78* (Serial 758); Jacob H. Schiel, *Journey Through the Rocky Mountains* . . . (Norman, Okla., c1959); Nolie Mumey, *John Williams Gunnison* . . . (Denver, 1955); Heap (1957), *op. cit.*, p. 303, Kern, Creutzfeldt, and Taplin had been with Fremont on his expedition of 1848; and Taplin on the 1845 trip, also. Two young St. Louis men—George Collier, Jr., and Ben. O'Fallon—apparently traveled in company with the Gunnison expedition for several weeks on the Santa Fe trail, leaving it at Fort Atkinson. (*See* Beckwith's July 19 journal entry, p. 26 of *Sen. Ex. Doc. No. 78* cited above.)

❡ June 25.—William Allison with the "June" Salt Lake mail reached Independence, Mo., having again made the trip to Fort Laramie and back in 25 days (*see* p. 1160).

Ref: *Missouri Republican*, St. Louis, July 11, 1853; or, St. Joseph (Mo.) *Gazette*, July 13, 1853.

❡ June-September.—These were some events at (or relating to) Fort Atkinson, on the Arkansas, during the last four months of its existence:

June 24.—Bvt. Maj. Robert H. Chilton and Company B, First dragoons, arrived from Fort Leavenworth. (*See* p. 1162.)

June 25.—Chilton assumed command of the post. Subsequently, Bvt. Maj. Edward Johnson and Company D, Sixth infantry, departed for the new military camp site on Walnut creek (near present Great Bend). (Orders had been received at Fort Atkinson in mid-May directing that the post be removed to Walnut creek.)

July 15(?).—Bvt. Brig. Gen. John Garland's command passed Fort Atkinson on, or about, this day. (*See* p. 1164.)

July 16.—Capt. John W. Gunnison's expedition (*see* p. 1167) arrived at the post; camped a mile above; departed on July 19 for the upper Arkansas.

July 25.—Sixth military department Special Order of June 28 was received at Fort Atkinson. It directed that all operations at Walnut creek be suspended.

July 25(?).—Agent Thomas Fitzpatrick arrived at the post with a wagon train of Indian supplies and presents. (*See* p. 1166.)

July 26-27.—Fitzpatrick counciled with leaders of the Comanches, Kiowas, and Plains Apaches on the 26th; and on the 27th a peace-and-friendship treaty was negotiated. (*See* p. 1174.)

July 28(?).—Distribution of presents was made by Agent Fitzpatrick to the Plains tribes, at a site two miles above the fort. (By the end of July the Indians had moved south of the Arkansas.)

August 4.—Bvt. Maj. Edward Johnson and Company D, Sixth infantry, returned to Fort Atkinson from Walnut creek.

August 6.—Bvt. Maj. Robert H. Chilton and Company B, First dragoons, set out on patrol of the Santa Fe road west of Fort Atkinson.

August 14.—Special Order No. 44 (dated July 29), from the Sixth military department, was received at the post. It directed that troops be removed from Fort Atkinson to Fort Riley. Also, there were instructions for the removal of public property to the new post on the upper Kansas river; and for Company D, Sixth infantry to remain at Fort Atkinson till mid-September.

August 22.—The U. S. post office at Fort Atkinson (established November 11, 1851—*see* p. 1049) was discontinued; and, according to post office department records, reestablished at Walnut creek (with Samuel G. Mason postmaster, as before).

August 30.—At Fort Leavenworth, Russell, Waddell & Co., contracted to transport 65,000 pounds of military stores from Fort Atkinson to Fort Riley (for $7 per 100 pounds).

September 22.—Fort Atkinson was abandoned. Johnson, and Company D, Sixth infantry, departed for Fort Riley; arrived there October 10.

October 1.—Returning from Santa Fe trail patrol (west of the post), Chilton and Company B, First dragoons, bound for Fort Leavenworth, left the Fort Atkinson area. Sgt. P. G. Lowe, stated (at a later time) that there remained "only heaps of broken sod leveled to the ground, so that from it the Indians could not ambush mail carriers . . . [and other travelers]."

October 17.—Trader William F. Dyer, arriving at Independence, Mo., from Fort Atkinson, reported that post "entirely abandoned, every thing having been removed to Fort Riley."

Ref: Fort Atkinson post returns (microfilm in KHi, from National Archives); "Fort Atkinson" (1 p.), in KHi library (in "Kansas History Pamphlets," v. 3, pt. 2); Lowe, *op. cit.*, pp. 128-137; *Weekly Missouri Statesman*, Columbia, Mo., October 21, 1853 (for Dyer); 33d Cong., 1st Sess., *Sen. Ex. Doc. No. 37* (Serial 698), p. 33; R. W. Baughman, *Kansas Post Offices* (Topeka, c1961), pp. 45, 135. Post office department records *apparently* show that the Walnut Creek post office was not discontinued till September 22, 1855! Except for the month of July, 1853, there was no military camp at Walnut creek during the 1853-1855 period. Was the post office discontinued, rather, on September 22, 1853—the date of Fort Atkinson's abandonment?

❧ June 27.—Maj. Sackfield Maclin (paymaster), accompanied by Bvt. 1st Lt. George H. Gordon and 10 Mounted riflemen, left Fort Leavenworth for Forts Kearny and Laramie.

The Weston (Mo.) *Reporter* of June 30 also stated that Capt. Michael E. Van Buren and two companies of Mounted riflemen were to "leave for the Plains" (from Fort Leavenworth), "in a few days, to protect the emigrants."

(Around October 6, on the Little Blue, a westbound traveler "met the company of Riflemen under Capt. Van Buren, returning after a tour of duty in the upper country.")

Ref: New York *Daily Tribune*, July 15, 1853 (from *Missouri Republican*, St. Louis, July 6; and originally from the Weston *Reporter* of June 30); *Missouri Republican*, November 7, 1853.

❡ June(?).—At Weston, Mo., a third edition, revised and enlarged, of the Rev. Leander Ker's *Slavery Consistent With Christianity*—a 36-page "lecture," described by its author as "a public defence of the Institution of Slavery on the word of God"—was printed by "Finch & O'Gormon, Reporter Office."

Ker (native of Pennsylvania; chaplain at Fort Leavenworth, 1842-1859—*see* p. 460) dated his seven-page revised preface to this edition: "Fort Leavenworth, June, 1853." His introduction included "a Notice of the 'Uncle Tom's Cabin' Movement in England."

Ref: A verifax copy of Ker's pamphlet, courtesy of David C. Skaggs, Bowling Green State University, Bowling Green, Ohio. The Library of Congress has copies of all three editions (Baltimore, Md., 1840; Jefferson City, Mo., 1842; Weston, Mo., 1853) of Ker's pamphlet. Apparently few others are extant. For more on Chaplain Ker's career *see* Professor Skaggs' "Military Contributions to the Development of Territorial Kansas" (unpublished M. A. thesis, University of Kansas, 1960), pp. 108-111.

❡ July-December.—Licenses (new and renewal) to trade with Indians in "Kansas," as granted by agents of the Central Superintendency, St. Louis, were:

Traders	Indians	Issued by	Rec'vd at St. Louis
Samuel M. Cornatzer	Shawnees	B. F. Robinson	July
James R. Whitehead	Kickapoos, Iowas, Sacs & Foxes (of the Missouri)	Daniel Vanderslice	July
John W. Robinson	Pottawatomies	J. W. Whitfield	August
Moses H. Scott	Pottawatomies	J. W. Whitfield	August
Emanuel Mosier	Pottawatomies	J. W. Whitfield	August
Benjamin Harding	Kickapoos, Iowas, Sacs & Foxes (of the Missouri)	Daniel Vanderslice	September
Simpson, Glenn & Co.	Miamis	A. M. Coffey	September
Harker S. Randall	Sacs & Foxes	B. A. James	September
Robert Wilson	Kickapoos	Daniel Vanderslice	October
E. G. Booth	Pottawatomies	J. W. Whitfield	October
James F. Forman	Kickapoos	Daniel Vanderslice	December
(David) Waldo & (Jacob) Hall	Kansa	J. W. Whitfield	December
Walker, Northrup & Chick	Pottawatomies	J. W. Whitfield	December
S. P. & W. H. Keller	Pottawatomies	J. W. Whitfield	December
R. L. McGhee	Pottawatomies	J. W. Whitfield	December
Hayden D. McMeekin	Pottawatomies	J. W. Whitfield	December

Ref: SIA, St. Louis, "Records," v. 9, typed copy, pp. 751, 757, 770, 778, 779, 781, 782, 784, 786, 790, 805-807; and *ibid.*, p. 853 for (1) G. W. Smith as clerk for James R. Whitehead, (2) Jackson Withrow as laborer for Whitehead, (3) M. P. Rively as clerk for Robert Wilson. In a December 6, 1853, letter, Agent Vanderslice noted that James F. Forman's trading post was on the Missouri about two miles above Independence creek; and that "Pensonneaux" (Paschal Pensineau, presumably) was his interpreter.—OIA, Letters Received from Great Nemaha Agency (National Archives Microcopy 234, Roll 308).

❡ July 1.—The mail parties for Salt Lake and Santa Fe left Independence, Mo. "Captain [James] Hutton" was a passenger in the Santa Fe-bound stage.

Ref: St. Joseph (Mo.) *Gazette*, July 13, 1853, or *Missouri Republican*, St. Louis, July 11, 1853—both from the *Occidental Messenger*, Independence, Mo. For James Hutton *see* September 19, 1853, annals entry.

❡ July 20.—Stage passengers arriving at Independence, Mo., with the July mail from Santa Fe were trader James J. Webb (of Messervy & Webb), Bvt. Maj. William H. Gordon, Third infantry, and "Mrs. Wells."

Except for "muddy roads and musquitoes" the trip had been a pleasant one. Met on the trail were a number of trains "bound for Old and New Mexico," getting along "very well." Overtaken at Cottonwood Fork: Colonel Sumner's party. (*See* next entry).

Ref: *Missouri Republican*, St. Louis, July 22, 1853; Liberty (Mo.) *Weekly Tribune*, July 29, 1853; New York *Daily Tribune*, August 1, 1853.

❡ Around July 24(?) Bvt. Col. Edwin V. Sumner, First dragoons (recently military commandant in New Mexico), and party, reached the States after a journey overland from Santa Fe (left June 30). Bvt. Maj. Peter V. Hagner, ordnance officer, Bvt. Maj. William W. Morris, Fourth artillery, his wife, and Lt. Joseph N. G. Whistler, Third infantry were in company; as were, also, some 20 or 30 discharged soldiers.

The night of July 12 Sumner's party had arrived at Walnut creek—where Bvt. Maj. Edward Johnson and his Sixth infantry troops were encamped (*see* p. 1169); and where, as it happened, the reunited Gunnison expedition party (*see* p. 1169) was also in camp.

Ref: New York *Daily Tribune*, August 1, 1853 (from St. Louis *Intelligencer*); Emmett, *op. cit.*, p. 154; 33d Cong., 2d Sess., *Senate Ex. Doc. No. 78* (Serial 760), p. 19.

❡ July 24.—A "big Indian fight" took place about 60 miles southwest of Fort Kearny (or, "50 miles beyond the Caw [Kansas] river"). The Cheyennes and their cohorts (over 1,000 in number) lost. A smaller force of Pawnees and allies (possibly 800?) won.

The Pawnees' account (as related by a Fort Kearny man) was that they (some 400 warriors, and their families) had collected together for the summer hunt. In the vicinity were about 30 Iowas, 85 Otoes, and 40 Pottawatomies, also hunting buffalo. An enemy force composed of "Arapahoes, Cheyennes, Comanches, Kiowas and a few Sioux" attacked the Pawnees while their friends were absent. The battle took place "in front of a ravine (in which were the Pawnee women and children)." They fought "from early morn till about 4 p. m.," when their "allies" came up. The Pottawatomies (armed with rifles) then took over, and routed the Cheyenne force "before dark." The Pawnees brought in 25 scalps; claimed to have killed "many more" of the enemy, and 170 horses. (They captured a number of horses, also.) Their own admitted losses: two men, two women, and two boys killed; one warrior taken prisoner; a number severely wounded.

Agent Whitfield reported the Pottawatomies had brought in some 20 to 30 scalps; and that they "lost in killed and wounded some four or five." Except for the timely aid of the Pottawatomies, the Pawnees would have been wiped out.

Trader John Sibille, who had information "from both sides," figured the killed and wounded as about 150 for the Cheyennes and allies, and about 30 for the Pawnees and their friends. The Pottawatomies' rifles had turned the tide of battle.

Still another account said that "Sacs and Pottawatomies" came to the Pawnees' rescue; that one Iowa, one Otoe, 13 Pawnee warriors and several women and children had been killed; also, four Iowas, 10 Otoes, two Sacs, four Pottawatomies, and about 20 Pawnees had been wounded, and several of the wounded later had died. From Fort Laramie came a report (confirmed "very nearly" by the Cheyennes) that of the attacking force 17 Cheyennes, five Arapahoes, two Kiowas, and 170 horses, had been killed.

Ref: *Missouri Republican*, St. Louis, August 12, 14, September 14, 1853; New York *Daily Tribune*, August 22, November 14, December 9, 1853; Liberty (Mo.) *Weekly Tribune*, August 12, September 3, 1853; St. Joseph (Mo.) *Gazette*, August 31, 1853; Comm'r of Indian Affairs, *Report*, 1853 (Whitfield's report, therein); The Dial (St. Mary's College), St. Marys, v. 3 (April, 1892), p. 121; *Mid-America*, Chicago, v. 36 (October, 1954), p. 240; Nebraska State Historical Society, *Transactions*, Lincoln, v. 3, p. 294.

❡ July 26.—At Parkville, Mo. (on the Missouri, 10 miles above the Kansas river's mouth), the first issue of the weekly *Industrial Luminary* was published by "Park and Cundiff." ("Park" was George S. Park, town founder.)

Ref: St. Joseph (Mo.) *Gazette*, August 3, 1853; W. M. Paxton's *Annals of Platte County, Missouri* . . . (1897), p. 171.

❡ July 26.—At the Wyandots' Council House (in present Kansas City, Kan.) a convention of "citizens of Nebraska Territory" was held. A "large collection" of the "habitans of Nebraska" attended.

(The published notice, or invitation, to attend, dated June 30, was signed by Samuel Priestly, E. B. Hand, and Isaiah P. Walker of Wyandotte precinct; W[illiam] P. Burney, M[oses] R. Grinter, and James Findlay, of Delaware precinct; W. F. Dyer, of Kickapoo precinct. According to Findlay, 150 copies of the notice were printed and sent to "central points" in the territory.)

Abelard Guthrie called the meeting to order; W. P. Burney was appointed president; William Walker, secretary; James Findlay, W. F. Dyer, and Silas Armstrong a committee to draft resolutions. Addresses were made by Missourians W. Claude Jones, Independence, and W. J. Patterson, Parkville.

A majority of those present resolved to elect a "Nebraska Territory" provisional governor, secretary, and a council-and-committee of three; and to nominate a delegate to the 33d Congress. Indian agent John W. Whitfield spoke for the minority opposition—those in attendance who "thought this convention premature," and believed "that treaties with the Indians should precede territorial organization." The Rev. Thomas Johnson spoke in an attempt to "appease the opposition."

Elected were: William Walker (a Wyandot) as provisional governor (over Robert Kinzie); George I. Clark (a Wyandot) as provisional secretary (after W. F. Dyer declined); Matthew R. Walker (a Wyandot), Robert C. Miller, and Isaac Mundy as the council committee. Nominated for delegate to congress was Abelard Guthrie (*see* p. 1129). (Thomas Johnson declined to be a nominee.)

On August 1 William Walker issued the proclamation for an election of a delegate to congress, to be held on the second Tuesday in October.

See, also, September 20, and October 11, annals entries.

Ref: St. Joseph (Mo.) *Gazette,* July 27, August 10, 1853; Liberty (Mo.) *Weekly Tribune,* August 5, 1853; *Missouri Republican,* St. Louis, August 5, 8, 1853; William Walker's diary, *loc. cit.,* July 25, 26, 28, August 1, 1853.

❡ July 27.—At Fort Atkinson (west of present Dodge City), a peace-and-friendship treaty was concluded between the Comanches, Kiowas, and Plains Apaches, and the United States (Thomas Fitzpatrick, U. S. commissioner). Article 6 provided for a 10-year annual payment of $18,000 (in goods, provisions, etc.) to the Indians.

Five chiefs (and 11 head men) signed the treaty: Wulea-boo (Shaved Head), Comanche; Ka-na-re-tah (One that Rides the Clouds), Southern Comanche; To-hau-sen (Little Mountain), Kiowa; Si-tank-ki (Sitting Bear), Kiowa war chief; Si-tah-le (Poor Wolf), Apache. Signing for the United States: Thomas Fitzpatrick, B. Gratz Brown (secretary), Bvt. Maj. Robert H. Chilton, First dragoons, B. T. Moylero; and as witnesses: B. B. Dayton, George M. Alexander, T. Polk, and George Collier, Jr.

It was reported the Indians "numbered 5 or 6,000," and that they were growing impatient before late-arriving Thomas Fitzpatrick reached the post on July 25(?) with the wagon train of supplies and presents. The councils began on July 26; and despite the difficulties which had to be surmounted (the "distant and suspicious bearing of the chiefs"; the lack of an interpreter who "understood their intricate languages"; the fact there was no one present "in whom mutual confidence could be reposed"; the inadequacies of the "sign language" for "matters of so much importance and delicacy"), agreement was reached next day.

It was ex-dragoon Percival G. Lowe's recollection, 50 years after the event, that 30,000(!) Indians were present. He wrote: ". . . The big ox train came in, the wily [Plains] Apaches . . ., the Kiowas and Comanches having assembled in full force, the goods were unloaded, boxes and bales opened, the nabobs of the tribes decorated in brilliant uniforms, medals and certificates issued, goods parceled out, winding up with plenty to eat, feasting, sham battles, etc. The Apaches were off their home ground and anxious to return. Major Fitzpatrick seemed equally anxious to have the job over with and kept his little working force and a couple of clerks pushing things. The long drawn out dignity of the Horse Creek [Fort Laramie] treaty [of 1851] was lacking. . . ." (Elsewhere, Lowe stated that the distribution of presents was made at a site two miles above Fort Atkinson.)

By the end of July the Indians had moved south of the Arkansas, leaving the Santa Fe trail clear. Agent Fitzpatrick set out for Fort Laramie on August 2.

Ref: Comm'r of Indian Affairs, *Report*, 1853 (Fitzpatrick's November 19 report, therein); C. J. Kappler, comp., *Indian Affairs, Laws and Treaties* (1904), v. 2, pp. 600-602; *Missouri Republican*, St. Louis, August 9, 16, 1853; *KHC*, v. 4, pp. 365, 366; Lowe, *op. cit.*, pp. 131-135. In F. W. Hodge's *Handbook of American Indians* . . . (Washington, 1907), v. 1, pp. 394, 395, is an article on "Dohasan" ("little bluff"), whose name appears above as "To-hau-sen (Little Mountain)." It is stated that he was "the greatest chief in the history of the Kiowa tribe"; and "ruled over the whole tribe from 1833 until his death on Cimarron river in 1866." Artist George Catlin painted his portrait in 1834— and called him "Teh-toot-sah." In Lowe, *op. cit.*, p. 131, is a description of the Kiowa war chief Satank (or, Sitank), whom he mistakenly called "Satanta."

❡ August.—About 80 Mormons from the vicinity of Galveston, Tex., crossed "Kansas" this month, en route to Salt Lake City. They had set out from the Gulf of Mexico area in May; and had reached Fort Arbuckle (in southern "Oklahoma") on July 21, after being "on the way" two months.

Asst. Surg. Rodney Glisan wrote that this company was "composed of men, women and children—rather more males than females." Four had died prior to July 21; and when at the post (where Glisan gave medical attention) there was still "much sickness" among them. "Mr. Thomas, the Elder" preached to the officers and men of Fort Arbuckle on three occasions.

On July 24 the Mormon party left—probably pursuing the pathway northward taken by the Lander party in June (*see* pp. 1163, 1164).

Ref: Glisan, *op. cit.*, pp. 120, 121. "These Mormons . . . had been gathered up from the divergent colony Lyman Wight established . . . [in Texas] in 1845."—Dale L. Morgan's statement, in notes sent to L. Barry.

❡ August 4-11.—Two small companies of returning Californians— all from Missouri, reached Independence, Mo., on the 4th, overland from the West. Most of them (18 names were listed) had left Hangtown around May 25. Nine more "Californians" arrived on August 11, "by the overland route, 60 days out."

(On July 24 a small party from Hangtown—left May 17—had reached Council Bluffs, Iowa. The *Bugle* reported: "A large number of Californians are returning to the States this season, overland. They think the number will reach 1200.")

Ref: Liberty (Mo.) *Weekly Tribune*, August 12, 1853; *Missouri Republican*, St. Louis, August 12, 13, 1853.

❧ **August 12.**—At "two minutes past 12 noon," the "magnificent steamer" *Polar Star* (Thomas H. Brierly, captain) arrived at St. Joseph, Mo., after a record-breaking two-day-and-20-hour run from St. Louis (left on August 9 at 4:23 P. M.). En route she had made "all her usual landings for freight and passengers."

The *Polar Star's* time to Lexington: 45 hours, seven minutes (10 hours ahead of the *Martha Jewett* whom she had challenged); to Liberty Landing 52 hours, 57 minutes; to Kansas City 55 hours, 25 minutes; to Parkville 57 hours, 25 minutes; to Fort Leavenworth 61 hours; to Weston 61 hours, 37 minutes; to St. Joseph 68 hours.

A "large pair of Elk Horns" was presented to the *Polar Star* at St. Joseph, where the "Robideaux Grays" turned out in full uniform to help celebrate the event. The inscription read: "SAINT JOSEPH/ TO/CAPTAIN BRIERLY/the fleetest Elk has shed them from his brow/ Fit emblem 'Polar Star' to deck thy prow."

(Earlier in the year—on May 21 and June 18—the *Polar Star* had reached St. Joseph after three-and-one-half-day trips from St. Louis. Both arrivals had been noted in the St. Joseph *Gazette* as fast runs.

Ref: *Missouri Republican*, St. Louis, August 12, 13, 15, 22, 1853; St. Joseph *Gazette*, May 25, June 22, August 17, 1853; Liberty *Weekly Tribune*, August 19, 1853; Walter Williams, ed., *A History of Northwest Missouri* (1915), v. 1, pp. 160-162. For an earlier race between the *Polar Star* and *Martha Jewett* (from St. Louis to Lexington) which the latter won, *see Missouri Republican*, July 29, 30, 1853.

❧ **August 22.**—"Mr. [Francis] Boothe" was in charge of the "August" mail from Santa Fe, arriving at Independence, Mo., this day.

Ref: Liberty (Mo.) *Weekly Tribune*, September 3, 1853 (from Independence *Occidental Messenger*).

❧ **August.**—The homeward-bound *St. Ange* (P. E. Hannum, captain), under charter to Robert Campbell & Co., and carrying St. Louis Fur Company proceeds, reached Council Bluffs, Ia., on August 22. (She had left the Yellowstone's mouth August 8.) On the 24th the *St. Ange* met the *Timour No. 2* at (George M.) Million's Landing and the *Clara* at Lost Lake; next day she met the *Honduras* at Kansas (City), Mo.; and on August 27 arrived at St. Louis, having made the round trip in 51 days and six hours.

Passengers on the down voyage were Capt. F. S. Everett (bearer of dispatches from Washington territory's governor, Isaac I. Stevens), and some eight ex-members of Stevens' North Pacific railroad exploration party.

Ref: *Missouri Republican*, St. Louis, August 29, 1853; Sunder, *op. cit.*, p. 150. In *KHQ*, v. 2, p. 117, it is stated that George M. Million started a ferry opposite present Atchison "about 1850"; and that he had "occupied the present site of East Atchison as a farm . . ." as early as 1841. The August, 1853, reference above is the earliest-located contemporaneous mention of Million. The *St. Ange* had started upriver from St. Louis on

July 7, with partners Alexander M. Harvey and Charles Primeau, and some 50 mountain men on board.

❧ **August 27.**—J. W. Stringfellow and "Nicholet" were passengers arriving at Independence, Mo., with the August Salt Lake mail party.

Some distance out of Fort Laramie the stage had broken down. Mail, provisions, driver and passengers then were "stowed upon the two wheels [remaining]" for the rest of the journey. Later the mail got thoroughly soaked in the crossing of a deep stream.

Ref: *Missouri Republican,* St. Louis, August 29, 1853. *See* annals, p. 1120, for earlier mention of Stringfellow.

❧ **Late August.**—Under orders to "determine the practicability of navigating the [Kansas] river by steamers or keel boats," 2d Lt. Joseph L. Tidball, Sixth infantry, accompanied by a steersman, descended the stream (at a very low stage of water) in a small craft, starting from a point "about a mile . . . nearly east of" new Fort Riley, and "about two miles below the junction of the Smoky Hill Fork and Pawnee [*i. e.,* Republican] river."

Tidball wrote in his report (dated at Fort Riley, October 10): "I am strongly impelled to the belief that there is a period of from two to four months of the year, dating from the first spring rise, during which boats can ascend to this point." He made mention of four Kansas river ferries: "Uniontown," "Weld's," "Papan's" [Papin's], and "Delaware" [or, Grinter].

Ref: *KHQ,* v. 18, pp. 146-158 (for Tidball's report). Notably Tidball did not mention Smith's ferry (*see* annals, p. 1088). W. W. Cone, in his *Historical Sketch of Shawnee County* . . . (1877), p. 12, stated: "Hiram Wells [Weld] and John Ogee established the first and undoubtedly the only deck ferry boat ever on the Kaw river. . . . They commenced running it in 1853. This ferry was located only a stort distance from Smith's ferry." "W. H. Weld" was a voter in the 12th election district (Soldier creek), November 29, 1854 (*see* original poll book in KHi archives).

❧ **September 1.**—In charge of "Mr. Bard" (or, Barr?), the Salt Lake mail party left Independence, Mo., for Fort Laramie. H. F. Mayer was a stage passenger.

(The arrival date at Fort Laramie was September 13; on the 14th the mail party *from* Salt Lake reached the post.)

Ref: *Missouri Republican,* St. Louis, October 7, 1853 ("Yankton's" September 15, 1853, letter from Fort Laramie).

❧ **September 1 (?).**—Passengers on the Santa Fe-bound mail coach leaving Independence, Mo., were John Greiner, of Columbus, Ohio (*see* p. 1167), and the Rev. E. G. Nicholson (*see* p. 1089).

Greiner (en route to New Mexico to buy mineral lands) had sent this doggerel dispatch to Independence, late in August, to hold the mail stage for his arrival: "Running fast and living well, /Greiner's on the Isabel,/ Bound to meet the mail, so he/ Can passage take to Santa Fé."

Ref: *Missouri Republican,* St. Louis, September 9, 15, 1853.

❧ From September 2 till October 11 Comm'r of Indian Affairs George W. Manypenny was in eastern "Kansas" and "Nebraska," on a tour of Indian reserves, "visiting and talking with various tribes." (He had been designated by the President to conduct negotiations leading to Indian land-cession treaties.) John W. Whitfield (Pottawatomie-Kansa agent) accompanied him "the greater part of the time." They had a mule-drawn carriage (hired at Shawnee Methodist Mission), and a driver (Samuel J. Huffaker).

In his report (of November 9) Manypenny stated: ". . . I held councils with the Omahas, Ottoes [September 19, at Bellevue, "Neb."], and Missourias, Sacs and Foxes of [the] Missouri [at Iowa, Sac & Fox Presbyterian Mission, September 12], Kickapoos, Delawares, Wyandotts [on September 6], Shawnees, Pottawatomies, Sacs and Foxes of the Mississippi, Chippewas of Swan creek and Black river, Ottowas, Peorias and Kaskaskias, Weas and Piankeshaws, and Miamies." (He stayed at "Ottawa" Jones' the night of September 30; and at Wea Baptist Mission on October 4.) The "aggregate population" of the above tribes was estimated at 14,384 souls; and the "aggregate quantity of land held by them" at 13,220,480 acres (or, about 920 acres to each soul). For lack of time, Manypenny did not visit the Pawnees, Kansa, Osages, Quapaws, Senecas & Shawnees, and Senecas, who were estimated to have an "aggregate population" of 11,597 souls, and an "aggregate quantity of land" estimated at 18,399,200 acres (or, about 1,586 acres to each soul). [For the practical results of these councils of 1853, *see* annals of 1854.]

Manypenny also wrote: "A civil government should be organized over the Territory. The intercourse act is almost a dead letter." . . . [But] The statements which appear in the press, that a constant current of emigration is flowing into the Indian country, are destitute of truth. On the 11th of October, the day on which I left the frontier, there was no settlement made in any part of [Kansas and] Nebraska. From all the information I could obtain, there were but three white men in the Territory except such as were there by authority of law, and those adopted, by marriage or otherwise, into Indian families."

Ref: 33d Cong., 1st Sess., *H. Ex. Doc. No. 84* (Serial 723); Comm'r of Indian Affairs, *Report*, 1853; St. Joseph (Mo.) *Gazette*, August 31, October 5, 1853; *Missouri Republican*, St. Louis, August 26, October 6, 15, 1853; William Walker's diary, *loc. cit.*, September 6, 1853, entry; New York *Daily Tribune*, October 11, 1853.

❧ September 15.—At Fort Leavenworth Russell, Waddell & Co., Alexander Majors, and J. B. Yager signed contracts (made with Lt. J. H. Whittlesey, AAQM) to transport to Fort Union, N. M., "such stores as may be turned over to them," for $16 per 100 pounds.

Sureties for Russell, Waddell & Co., were N. Conder, W. Morrison, J. Warder(?), and J. W. Rennick; for both Alexander Majors and J. B. Yager, Duke W. Simpson and James M. Hunter were the bondsmen.

Ref: 33d Cong., 1st Sess., *Sen. Ex. Doc. No. 37* (Serial 698), p. 34. *See* Alexander Majors' *Seventy Years on the Frontier* (c1893), p. 140, for his mention of the trip to Fort Union in 1853. Majors said he returned to his home near Westport, Mo., "late in November."

❡ September-October.—Traveling the Santa Fe trail to New Mexico was a military party headed by Lt. Col. P. St. George Cooke, Second dragoons.

On October 7 eastbound William Carr Lane (mail stage passenger) recorded in his diary: "During breakfast Col. St Geo Cook[e], & Major Rucker [Bvt. Maj. Daniel H. Rucker, AQM], & Dr Davidson & their families, came into camp [at Rabbit Ear creek, N. M.], from the E[ast]. They had left St Louis, on the 6th ult. [i. e., September]. Geo McGuinny accompanied sister, Clara, now Mrs. Davidson, & her babe. . . ."

Ref: *New Mexico Historical Review*, v. 39 (October, 1964), p. 308. Cooke was at Fort Union, N. M., when W. W. H. Davis (*see* his *El Gringo*, p. 48) passed there in November, 1853.

❡ September 19.—Stage passengers arriving at Independence, Mo., with the September mail coach from Santa Fe were: "Mr. [Elisha] Riggs of [Indian supt. Edward F.] Beale's party," Edward H. Wingfield (recently an Indian agent in New Mexico), Mrs. Spiegelberg, "Jacobs," and James Hutton and servant.

Ref: *Missouri Republican*, St. Louis, September 21, 1853; Liberty (Mo.) *Weekly Tribune*, September 30, 1853; New York *Daily Tribune*, September 27, 1853. Riggs and Hutton (of the firm of Ellis & Hutton, St. Louis) reached St. Louis September 23.—*Missouri Republican*, September 24, 1853. Possibly "Jacobs" was the Doctor Jacobs who had traveled to Santa Fe with Meriwether—*see* p. 1165.

❡ September 20.—At Kickapoo village (four miles above Fort Leavenworth), some "citizens of Nebraska" held a "Grand Barbecue and Mass Meeting" (*i. e.*, a bolting convention) to "secure the adoption of proper rules for the proposed election of a Delegate [to congress] in October," and to nominate their opposition candidate. (*See* July 26 entry.)

The convention's chairman was Francis J. Marshall. George B. Patten served as secretary. A committee of three (Robert C. Miller, of Soldier creek, E. G. Booth, of St. Mary's Mission, W. S. Yohe, of Fort Leavenworth) drafted resolutions. H. Miles Moore, Weston, Mo., made an address.

The Rev. Thomas Johnson (of Shawnee Methodist Mission), put in nomination by William F. Dyer, was "elected without opposition" as candidate for delegate to congress.

Resolutions adopted included one calling for the speedy organization of "Nebraska territory," but not prior to extinguishment of Indian land titles. Another proposed that the coming election of October 11 be held at these polling places: Great Nemahaw, Big Blue, Fort Leavenworth, Fort Riley, St. Mary's Mission, Union Town, Pottawatomie Baptist Mission, Soldier Creek, Wyandott City, Delaware Mission, Sac and Fox Agency, Story's Landing, Bellevue ("Neb."), Old Fort Kearny ("Neb."), and Council Grove.

See October 11 entry.

Ref: Liberty (Mo.) *Weekly Tribune,* August 12, 1853; *Missouri Republican,* St. Louis, September 29, 1853; St. Joseph (Mo.) *Gazette,* August 10, October 5, 1853; *Weekly Missouri Sentinel,* Columbia, October 6, 1853; *KHC,* v. 1-2, p. 262, v. 6, p. 109. *See map showing Kickapoo Village location, p. 408.*

℃ September 22.—From a camp (occupied since September 14) not far from Westport, Mo., John C. Fremont's fifth (and last) expedition to the West made a "trial start."

Fremont expected to demonstrate "the practicability of the [central] route [to the Pacific] during the season of snows." Both Beale (*see* p. 1152), and Gunnison (*see* p. 1167), earlier in the year, had traversed much the same pathway he would take.

The small cavalcade (mounted men and pack train) "started in excellent order and spirits," and camped the night of September 22 at "[Shawnee] Methodist mission, about six miles from Westport," according to S. N. Carvalho (artist). On September 23 the party "proceeded to the Shawnee [Baptist?] Mission, a few miles further, and camped for the night." Fremont, ill, returned to Westport, accompanied by Max Strobel (hired that day as assistant topographer).

In the party continuing the journey next day (24th)—traveling the Oregon-California thoroughfare up the Kansas valley—were W. H. Palmer ("passenger"), F. W. Egloffstein (topographical engineer), Oliver Fuller (ass't engineer), S. N. Carvalho (artist and daguerreotypist), and a few hired hands (muleteers, etc.). On September 27, in the vicinity of Union Town, they were joined by Captain Wolff and nine other Delaware Indians—including "Washington," "Welluchas," "Solomon [Everett]," and "[John?] Moses"— whom Fremont had hired on September 16. (They were, according to Carvalho, a "noble set of Indians . . . most of them six feet high, all mounted and armed *cap-a-pie.* . . .")

Until the end of September the party camped somewhere in the Union Town area. (Carvalho described this "principal town of the Pottawatomies" as a place of "Two or three stores with no assortment of goods, and about thirty shanties.") Then Max Strobel arrived with a letter from Fremont placing W. H. Palmer in charge, and directing that the expedition proceed "as far as Smoky Hills," and camp on the Saline (in the buffalo range), until joined by Fremont (who, meantime, had boarded the *Clara* and returned to St. Louis [on the 27th] to get medical attention).

Carvalho says Fremont's company (now 20? in number) "crossed the Kansas river at its junction with the Republican, within half a mile from Fort Riley, thence to Solomon's Fork. . . ." His statement, taken literally, would indicate the route they took from Union Town to Fort Riley was a pathway up the south side of the Kansas (and not the regularly-traveled military road north of the river); and that the crossing was made near the junction of the

Smoky Hill and Republican branches of the Kansas river. Out on the Saline (in present northeastern Saline county) the party set up camp, in the fore part of October, and spent the rest of the month awaiting Fremont's arrival. Twice they sent back to Fort Riley for supplies.

By October 30 prairie fires were all around them. (Carvalho described their campsite as "between Kansas [Smoky Hill] River on one side, Solomon's Fork on another, Salt Creek [the Saline river] on the third, and a large belt of woods about four miles   .   .   .   [distant] on the fourth.")

Fremont (on horseback), accompanied by "Doctor Ober [Ebers?]" (on muleback), also Fremont's cook, and one of the Delaware Indians, arrived on October 31.

(Fremont's "Memoirs" include items from the explorer's "notebook" for the dates of October 25-27, 1853. On the 25th he wrote: "Went to Uniontown and nooned. This is a street of log-cabins. Nothing to be had here. Some corn for our animals and a piece of cheese for ourselves. Lots of John Barleycorn which the men about were consuming. Uniontown is called a hundred miles from Kansas. About two o'clock [on October 26, he] reached the pretty little Catholic Mission of Saint Mary's. The well-built, whitewashed houses, with the cross on the spire showing out above them was already a very grateful sight. On the broad bottoms immediately below are the fields and house of the Pottawatomie Indians.   .   .   ." Fremont spent the night of the 26th at St. Mary's Mission. On the 27th he and his companions set out again. As Fremont stated it: "Prepared our luggage, threw into the wagon the provisions obtained here, and at ten o'clock took leave of the hospitable priests and set out.   .   .   ." Fremont traveled the military road out to Fort Riley; whereas his expedition party, earlier in October, probably went up the opposite [south] side of the Kansas.)

On November 1 Fremont and party (22? in all) left the Saline river camp; passed "through the fiery ordeal [of the prairie fire] unscathed"; and headed toward Walnut creek and the Great Bend of the Arkansas (as had Gunnison, in July). From there, they followed the Santa Fe trail, and its upper Arkansas branch to the "Big Timbers," and to William Bent's new fort. (Fremont dated a letter "Big Timber on Upper Arkansas, Nov. 26.") Carvalho's account says the Cheyenne village at the Big Timbers contained about 250 lodges and "probably" 1,000 souls. He described Bent's New Fort as "built of adobes, .   .   .   one story high, in form of a hollow square, with a courtyard in the centre.   .   .   ." "Doctor Ober [Ebers?]" left the company here.

Fremont and party continued westward on the foolhardy winter trip. Subsequently, the expedition came close to disaster from starvation and exhaustion. Fremont, in a letter of February 9, 1854, from Parawan (a Mormon settlement in southern Utah they had reached the day before) laconically wrote of their difficulties: "The Delawares all came in sound but the whites of my party were all exhausted and broken up and more or less frostbitten. I lost one [man].   .   .   ." Carvalho and Egloffstein left the expedition at Parawan. Fremont and the others went on to California.

Ref: Solomon N. Carvalho, *Incidents of Travel and Adventure in the Far West* (1857), pp. 17-75; John C. Fremont, *Memoirs of My Life* .   .   .   (1887), pp. 27, 28; *Missouri Republican*, St. Louis, September 9, 28, 1853; Liberty (Mo.) *Weekly Tribune*, October 21, 1853; New York *Daily Tribune*, April 13, May 16, 1854; G. J. Garraghan, *The Jesuits of the Middle United States* (1938), v. 2, p. 656; Heap (1857), *op. cit.*, p. 307; H. R. Wagner and C. L. Camp's *The Plains and the Rockies* . . ., third edition (1953), p. 307; *KHQ*, v. 19, pp. 369, 370; 58th Cong., 1st Sess., *Sen. Doc. No. 16* (Serial 4563), pp. 159, 160; Allan Nevins, *Frémont, Pathmarker of the West* (1939), pp. 408-420; Julia Ann (Mrs. Thomas N.) Stinson's statement, April 15, 1914 (in KHi ms. division). In 1853 the Stinsons were living on the Shunganunga near Burnett's mound (present Topeka). Mrs. Stinson recollected that Frémont (*i. e.* his party) camped north and east of their house "for a couple of weeks" (but it was only a few days?); and that he had many people(?) with him; etc. By steamboat, from New Orleans, Max Strobel and seven Delaware Indians arrived at St. Louis on June 5, 1854. The account stated that one Indian (John Smith) had died aboard the steamboat, and was buried "at B. F. Allain's plantation, Diamond Point, Arkansas."—*Missouri Republican*, St. Louis, June 6, 1854.

❡ September-October.—A Fort Laramie-bound man who had left the Missouri on September 22, wrote from Fort Kearny ("Neb.") October 10, of traffic met, or also westbound, on the Oregon-California trail.

At the "St. Joseph Mission" (Iowa, Sac & Fox Presbyterian Mission, present Doniphan county)—a "party returning from California having left July 27."

At the Big Blue—"Smith's freight train from Fort Laramie." (George Rappeen Smith?)

About 10 miles west of Big Blue—"McDonald of Weston, and Col. Tiernan" who had been on a summer's "slight reconnaissance of the South Pass route, with reference to the advantages for the Pacific Railroad." (Duncan Macdonell, and M. F. Tiernan, engineer, had left Weston in July on this mission. *See, also,* p. 1166.)

Between the Big and Little Blue—"one or two parties returning from Green River and Salt Lake."

On the "Lost Sandy"—"the Prince de Viede and Prince of Nassau [*i. e.*, William Nicholas, Prince of Nassau—*see* p. 1161]," returning from a pleasure trip.

At the point "where you touch the [Little] Blue"—Captain Van Buren and his Mounted riflemen, eastbound. (*See* p. 1170.)

"Near the same place"—overtook the "train having goods for the Sutler [John Dougherty] at Fort Kearny."

"At the point of leaving the Blue"—"Fitzpatrick Drips and party," eastbound. (*See* p. 1186.)

Ref: *Missouri Republican*, St. Louis, November 7, 1853; or, New York *Daily Tribune*, November 14, 1853; Liberty (Mo.) *Weekly Tribune*, July 29, 1853 (for Macdonell and Tiernan).

❡ Around September 25 a military party which had left Fort Union, N. M., on the 3d, arrived at Fort Leavenworth. Headed by Bvt. Lt. Col. Dixon S. Miles, Third infantry, the company included Bvt. Maj. Henry H. Sibley, Second dragoons, and wife, Bvt. Capt. Barnard E. Bee, Third infantry, Capt. William Steele, Second dragoons, and wife, the Misses Richardson and Shoemaker, and "a train of 40 teamsters."

Ref: *Missouri Republican*, St. Louis, September 21, 1853; or, New York *Daily Tribune*, September 27, 1853.

❧ DIED: on September 28, Pierre La Liberte, aged 61 years, at, or near Kansas (City), Mo. He had been a resident of the Kaw's mouth area since 1830, if not earlier.

Ref: Kansas City chapter D. A. R., *Vital Historical Records*, p. 267. For earlier mention, *see* annals index.

❧ September 28.—In charge of "Mr. Barr" (or, Bard?), the "September" mail from Salt Lake arrived at Independence, Mo., from Fort Laramie. Arrivals on the stage: Dr. John M. Bernhisel (Utah territory's delegate to congress), Samuel Brown, Theodore McKain, Louis Vasquez ("an Indian trader of much notoriety"), also a "Mrs. Wharton" (returning from Salt Lake City) and her two children.

Ref: Liberty (Mo.) *Weekly Tribune*, October 8, 1853.

❧ October.—An account of a trip overland from Parkville, Mo., to Fort Riley appeared in the *Industrial Luminary*—Parkville's newspaper, in late October, or early November. (The writer undoubtedly was publisher George S. Park.)

"On the 4th day of October, we left Parkville, on a tour of exploration; crossed the Missouri river at [James M.] Kuykendal[l]'s excellent Ferry at this place, and took the fine road westward used by the California and Oregon Emigrants, who prefer the Kansas valley route, on account of grass being two weeks earlier in the spring. . . . We crossed the Fort Scott and Fort Leavenworth road about ten miles from this place, and took nearly a westerly direction, on the same excellent road; crossing Stranger Creek, we came in sight of the Kansas river where it makes a bend in a southerly direction, about forty miles distant from Parkville. Crossed the Grasshopper and Soldier Creek—beautiful clear streams— . . . and about eight miles at [Robert C.] Miller's Trading Post [on the Pottawatomie reserve], struck the Military road from Fort Leavenworth to Fort Riley. We crossed the Independence and Oregon, and California Road, the Little and Big Vermillion rivers, the [Big] Blue river. . . . We here found Mr. Garland in charge of the Government Ferry, about five miles from the mouth of the Blue, and twenty-four miles below Fort Riley.—About five miles above this Ferry, we crossed a beautiful, well timbered creek [Wild Cat], and seven miles further another of like description [Seven Mile creek], wending our way through a rich and beautiful upland rolling prairie to the Kansas; about twelve miles further on we reached the New Fort, which has a commanding site at the junction of the Republican and Smoky-Hill forks of the Kansas, which is reported to be navigable at this point, by Lieut. Tidball of the Army [*see* p. 1177]. This is the centre of a country belonging to the U. S., on the direct central route to the great States and Territories lying west of the Missouri, a region of unsurpassed fertility, and the most picturesque and beautiful scenery. . . . [Compare Big Blue-Fort Riley distance given here with the table on p. 1150.]

"The best approach to Fort Riley is from Parkville, up the north side of the Kansas river, by the excellent carriage road we traveled up. [He also referred to it as "the direct and excellent waggon road to Fort Riley, one hundred and twenty miles from Parkville."] On the South side of the Kansas, the route is crooked and hilly, and can never be made so good a route; besides Parkville is the nearest point of departure, from the Missouri, and the best point for emigrants to land, coming to the Territory. . . .

"The officers at the Fort [Fort Riley] had no orders to drive settlers off the United States lands nor did they expect any, their orders only extended to the trespasses on Indian lands. We saw Pioneers making claims, and met others who had axes, and full equipments to make claims. They were all highly pleased.—We shall promptly keep our readers informed. . . ."

Ref: St. Joseph (Mo.) *Gazette*, November 9, 1853 (from Parkville *Industrial Luminary*); Paxton, *op. cit.*, p. 170 (for Kuykendall as ferry operator). Samuel D. Dyer was operator of the government's Big Blue river ferry, subsequently. Accounts have stated (incorrectly?) that he ran the ferry beginning in the fall of 1853. (*See KHC*, v. 17, p. 461, *KHQ*, v. 3, p. 120, and v. 21, pp. 87, 88, for some mention of Dyer.)

❡ October 11.—The election of a "Nebraska Territory" delegate to the 33d Congress was held at various polling places in the Indian Country west of Missouri and Iowa. (*See* July 26 and September 20 entries.)

In the Kaw's mouth area, according to a telegram sent from "Kansas, Missouri, October 13th," the voting was as follows:
At Delaware—Guthrie 0   Johnson 31
At Wyandotte—Guthrie 33   Johnson 18
At Shawnee—Guthrie 17   Johnson 80

On November 7 the "Territorial Council, Sec'y and Governor [*see* p. 1179] . . . proceeded to open the returns" for the official count and ascertained that the Rev. Thomas Johnson had received the most votes.

The entire vote for Abelard Guthrie was 82, and for Thomas Johnson 337, according to the *Missouri Republican,* St. Louis, November 7, 1853, issue. A third candidate—Hadley D. Johnson— received all the votes cast at Bellevue ("Neb."). The Council Bluffs *Bugle* said the Bellevue poll book was "not counted" in the final vote-counting at Kickapoo, but that Hadley D. Johnson (from Council Bluffs, Iowa) had received more votes than either of the other two candidates and was unquestionably the delegate elect.

Both Johnsons subsequently went to Washington, D. C. Hadley D. Johnson's later-written account tells of the two Johnsons being "incontinently bounced" from the House of Representatives (where each had taken a desk), and "relegated to the galleries."

Ref: William Walker's diary, *loc. cit.*, August 1, October 11, November 7, 1853, entries; *Missouri Republican*, St. Louis, October 14, 19, November 7, 1853; Liberty (Mo.) *Weekly Tribune*, November 18, December 2, 1853; New York *Daily Tribune*, November 7, 25, December 5, 1853; St. Joseph (Mo.) *Gazette*, December 21, 1853; *KHC*, v. 17, p. 427 (for H. D. Johnson's statement).

❡ October 22.—The month's mail party from Santa Fe (Francis

Boothe, conductor) arrived at Independence, Mo. William Carr Lane, St. Louis (recently governor of New Mexico territory; now homeward-bound), was a stage passenger. Others (as reported at Independence) were John M. Kingsbury (Messervy & Webb's clerk), and a "Mr. Sloan."

Lane's extensive diary of the trip included these items relating to Santa Fe trail travel, or to "Kansas":

October 9 (on the Cimarron).—"Passed Mitchells Train of Ox trains, freighted with army stores. . . ." (With Mitchell, he indicated, were the "Apostate [Benigno] Cardenas"—a former Catholic priest turned Methodist, and the Rev. E. G. Nicholson. But *see* September 1 entry.)

October 12.—"A few miles below the [Arkansas] crossing," they met the mail stage bound for Santa Fe. "Lts. [John C.?] Moore & [John S.?] Garland were passengers."

October 14.—"Stop'd upon Little Coon Creek, now drained dry, by the immense herds of Buffalo, which overspread the country, in every direction. We have passed a succession of Herds, for at least 10 miles & if I were to estimate their numbers, at many hundred thousand I presume I would not err. Many of the herds are composed of Bulls alone." They were "in the midst of vast Herds of Buffalo" until they reached Pawnee Fork. [See p. 1102, for Lane's comment on buffalo herds on the Santa Fe trail in 1852.]

October 15.—At Walnut creek they met Charles H. Withington (mail agent at Council Grove) who had brought corn for the mules. From him they learned that "2 German Noblemen, with their retainers, were encamped, a half a Mile up the Creek, hunting the Buffalo." Withington (who traveled back to Council Grove with the mail party) told Lane that he had "just bot 1000 Bu. Corn, which was raised by the Kansas Indians, at 66 cts per Bu in Mdze"; that the Kansa numbered "about 1320 Souls, & their annuity, per capita, is 6 & some cents each. Their numbers are s[ai]d to be on the increase; & their condition is improving. . . ." James Rogers ("a Cherokee"), of Withington's party, told Lane the Osage Indians numbered 4,800.

October 17.—West of Cottonwood crossing they met "Mr. Abram's [Abrahams'] train of 8-12 Ox Waggons, under the charge of Mr. Van Eppy [Van Epps] & Mr Thos Ackerman. They had 4 Span Oxen & three under the yoke looked well." (The Jackson county, Mo., 1850 U. S. census lists "A. M. Abrahams"—aged 39; merchant; also, "N. D. Vaneps"—aged 24; "stock driver.")

October 18 (At Council Grove).—"Found some 40 or 50 Lodges of Kaw Indians encamped South of the Town, & heard much complaint of their thieving, from the Whites."

October 19.—On the road they met "Mons. Cyprian Chouteau, with an Ox-train going to the Grove." [See p. 1138.]

October 20 (At 110-mile creek).—"This Settlement consisted of 3 families. The women were mixed breeds of the Shawnee Tribe. One of the men was also a Mixed breed, & the 2 other men were whites. Their Habitations exhibited industry. The Houses were well built Cabbins, & the Fences were substantial. . . . All spoke english, but Shawnee was the language in common use. Fever & Ague prevailed & the White men especially looked lean, sallow & miserable. The children were of uncommonly large size, but did not present a healthy look. The furniture in their Houses & their modes of living, were those of the Whites. . . ."

October 21 (At Bull creek.)—"halted at The Trading house of Baker & Street [*see* p. 1138] to bait the Mules." They saw "a patient with the Int[er-mittent] Fever, which disease prevails here."

The night of October 21 the mail party "Reached S[an]ta Fe [*i. e.*, New Santa Fe] which is on the Boundary line of Missouri & all camped. . . ." They arrived at Independence early on the afternoon of October 22.

Ref: *New Mexico Historical Review,* v. 39 (October, 1964), pp. 303-329; Lib rty (Mo.) *Weekly Tribune,* November 4, 1853.

❡ October-November.—Aground (since late August) at Smith's Bar (about 25 miles below St. Joseph), the *Timour No. 2,* in mid-October, lay "high and dry . . . not a drop of water within one hundred yards" of her.

"Messrs. Eads & Nelson," St. Louis, sent up a company of men and got the steamboat afloat early in November. It was said the expense incurred would amount to $6,000 in all—$3,000 of it due the company "putting her in the water." The *Timour No. 2* returned to St. Louis on November 8.

(On December 5 the trouble-plagued *Timour No. 2* sank about eight miles below Rocheport, Mo.; but was raised, and reached St. Louis on December 13, with a big hole in her bow, and leaking badly.)

Ref: St. Joseph (Mo.) *Gazette,* August 31, November 9, 1853; *Missouri Republican,* St. Louis, October 15, November 5, 9, December 8, 9, 14, 1853.

❡ October.—Late in the month, Agent Thomas Fitzpatrick, accompanied by Andrew Drips, and by three young St. Louis men— B. Gratz Brown, George M. Alexander, George Collier, Jr.— arrived at Westport, Mo., from Fort Laramie, after a "delightful" journey overland on the Oregon-California trail.

Brown, Alexander, and Collier reached home on October 31, reportedly in "greatly improved" health, after their summer on the plains. Fitzpatrick, "detained on the Upper Missouri" (at Westport?), was expected at St. Louis "in a few days." (He arrived November 9.)

Ref: *Missouri Republican,* St. Louis, November 1, 7, 1853; Comm'r of Indian Affairs, *Report,* 1853 (Fitzpatrick's report, therein).

❡ October 29.—The monthly mail from Salt Lake City arrived at Independence, Mo. Theodore Winthrop of New York, "direct from Puget's Sound," was a stage passenger.

At Devil's Gate the mail party had overtaken mountain man James (Jim) Bridger and his family, en route to Missouri: (Bridger, accused by the Mormons of furnishing arms and ammunition to the Utahs, had been forced to abandon his trading fort on Black's Fork of Green river.)

The mail party reported there were buffalo "in abundance" as far east as the Big Blue; and that on October 25 snow was four inches deep on the Nemaha.

Ref: *Missouri Republican*, St. Louis, November 5, 1853; New York *Daily Tribune*, November 8, 12, 1853; Liberty (Mo.) *Weekly Tribune*, November 25, 1853; *Weekly Missouri Statesman*, Columbia, October 7, 1853.

❧ November.—Francis Boothe conducted the Independence-to-Santa Fe mail party (six employees, and six fares, traveling in four mule-drawn vehicles), which left the Missouri border early in the month. One passenger was William W. H. Davis (U. S. attorney for New Mexico territory) who, in his 1857-published book *El Gringo* . . . (based on a diary), gave an account of the trip. The others were G. Rodman, Capt. Alexander W. Reynolds, U. S. A., his step-son "Mr. Ash, of Philadelphia," a Catholic priest—Father Donato, and a lay brother, Carlos. Boothe's assistants were "Converse," "Jones," "Mitchell," a black "outdriver," and a Mexican named Jose.

According to Davis, "the stump of the Lone Elm [famed landmark] furnished the necessary fire-wood," when they stopped at that point for breakfast on November 3. At Bull creek he noted the "small trading establishment [of Baker & Street]" on a hill near by. (The "old German woman" at the cabin refused to sell him milk.) When at 110-mile creek Davis observed: "Here . . . close to the road were the log cabins of a settler with an Indian wife." The night of November 5 was spent at Council Grove ("some half dozen log cabins and a trading house"), where mail agent Charles Withington offered hospitality.

West of Council Grove there was no longer any habitation (or military protection) until one reached Fort Union, N. M. But no hostile Indians were encountered on the journey. At Coon creek Davis and three others acquired bruises when runaway mules overturned a wagon. On the "Dry Route," the party "passed through immense herds of buffaloes all day"; and met the "down mail from Santa Fe" (one wagon in charge of four men). They passed "old Fort Atkinson, now in ruins"; subsequently forded the Arkansas at "the middle crossing." Davis described the waterless *Jornada* as a "stretch of nearly fifty miles of dead level, without a tree, or bush, or hill to break the evenness of the surface, and covered with buffalo-grass." They crossed it in 15 driving hours; and continued on to Santa Fe—arriving before the end of November.

Ref: Davis, *op. cit.*

❧ November.—Some traders' trains en route to New Mexico or Old Mexico were met on the Santa Fe trail by the eastbound "November" mail party. The report was that all of them would "be likely to get through," though "Russell's trains" were weak, and he was "losing many of his cattle daily." "Abraham J. Rosenthall's" (*i. e.*, Abrahams & Rosenthall's) company had taken the Bent's Fort route.

The "December" mail from Santa Fe brought news that "Hickman & Adams

[and] Carrol & Amberg, agents of Rosenthall," were at El Paso, "endeavoring to pass their goods." Amberg, it was said, "had his papers made out for three wagon loads, and ascertained the duties on them would be $8,000. He did not pass them of course."

Ref: Liberty (Mo.) *Weekly Tribune*, December 2, 30, 1853.

❡ November.—The monthly mail from Santa Fe, in charge of "Mr. [John] Jones," arrived at Independence, Mo., on November 20. Part of the journey had been made through snow one to four inches deep.

A November 23 telegram from Independence stated that Manuel Gallegos, the delegate elect to congress from New Mexico territory "did not come with the [mail] stage," but would arrive in a few days. An Independence dispatch of the 28th reported the arrival of "Padre [Jose-Manuel] Gallegos . . . with his Interpreter" on November 27.

Ref: *Missouri Republican*, St. Louis, November 24, 29, 1853; Liberty (Mo.) *Weekly Tribune*, December 2, 1853. See 33d Cong., 1st Sess., *H. Report No. 121* (Serial 742) for the Gallegos-Lane contested election in New Mexico.

❡ November 27(?).—The *Honduras,* last steamboat of the year at St. Joseph, Mo., started downriver. She reached St. Louis on December 8 (after being aground for three days, below Lexington, Mo.).

Ref: *Missouri Republican*, St. Louis, December 7, 9, 1853; St. Joseph *Gazette*, March 8, 1854. The *Republican* gave the St. Joseph departure date as the "17th ultimo," but also stated the *Honduras* was "over 10 days out," so she evidently started down on the 27th.

❡ November 28.—The Salt Lake mail (with news from that place up to November 1—including an account of the Gunnison party massacre) reached Independence, Mo.

Ref: *Missouri Republican*, St. Louis, November 29, 1853; Liberty (Mo.) *Weekly Tribune*, December 9, 1853.

❡ November 30.—The *Kate Swinney* left Weston, Mo. (she was probably the last steamboat at that town in 1853); and returned to St. Louis on December 6.

Ref: *Missouri Republican*, St. Louis, December 7, 1853.

❡ In mid-December the Independence-to-Santa Fe mail party, John Jones conductor, was "suddenly charged upon" at Pawnee Rock by a mounted band of 15 to 20 Osage Indians, who "succeeded in purloining from the back of one of the wagons, by cutting through the canvas, some articles of clothing. . . ." Jones, alone, pursued them; caught up with "the rascals"; drew a revolver and "made them give up the stolen articles."

"These Osages have lately been very troublesome, intimidating and robbing emigrants on their way to California and Salt Lake   . . .," said the Santa Fe *Gazette*.

Ref: New York *Daily Tribune,* February 2, 1854 (from Santa Fe *Gazette* of December 31[?].

❆ December 21.—Francis Boothe was in charge of the "December" mail from Santa Fe reaching Independence, Mo., this day. His party had been overtaken by a snow storm at Cottonwood Crossing.

Ref: Liberty (Mo.) *Weekly Tribune,* December 30, 1853; New York *Daily Tribune,* December 29, 1853; *Missouri Republican,* St. Louis, December 23, 1853.

❆ December 27.—At a meeting held at Great Nemaha Agency (present Doniphan county), delegates were chosen to attend a "Nebraska Convention" scheduled for January 9, 1854, at St. Joseph, Mo. Indian agent Daniel Vanderslice served as president, Harvey W. Forman as secretary. A committee composed of John McClaskey, Thomas J. Vanderslice, and R. P. Kelly drafted resolutions.

Delegates chosen were: John McClaskey, Harvey W. Forman, James R. Whitehead, Benjamin Harding, S. Story, J. B. Roy, Francis Bushnell, James Williams, Peter Cadue, Samuel McClaskey, Thomas J. Vanderslice, James F. Forman, William T. B. Vanderslice, John W. Forman, John G. Kelly, and Daniel Vanderslice.

Ref: St. Joseph (Mo.) *Gazette,* December 7, 1853 (for account of a Nebraska meeting held at St. Joseph on December 3), and January 4, 1854.

❆ December 29.—In charge of William Allison, the "December" mail reached Independence, Mo., from Fort Laramie. No mail from Salt Lake had arrived when he left that post on the 17th. "Bad weather and roads notwithstanding," the mail party had averaged 75 miles' travel per day.

Ref: Liberty (Mo.) *Weekly Tribune,* January 13, 1854.

❆ Employed in "Kansas" by the Indian Department during all, or part of the year (so far as can be ascertained from available records) were the following persons:

KANSAS AGENCY *[Wyandots, Delawares, Shawnees, Munsees, Stockbridges]* —*Agents* Thomas Moseley, Jr., replaced, in June, by Benjamin F. Robinson; *Interpreters* William Walker (for Wyandots), Henry Tiblow (for Delawares), Charles Bluejacket (for Shawnees); *Blacksmiths* Samuel Priestly (for Wyandots), Isaac Mundy (for Delawares), William Donalson, and James Mathews (for Shawnees); *Assistant smiths* Isaac Baker, and Orange D. Wilcox (for Wyandots), Silas A. Boyd (for Delawares), Levi Flint (for Shawnees).

POTTAWATOMIE AGENCY *[Pottawatomie and Kansa] Agents*—Francis W. Lea, replaced, in June by John W. Whitfield; *Interpreters* Abraham B. Burnett, Clement Lessert (for Kansa); *Blacksmiths* John W. Brown and Robert Wilson, Jesse King (for Kansa); *Assistant smiths* James Wilson and John Anderson, William King (for Kansa); *Gunsmith* Hugh M. Weldon; *Assistant gunsmith* William Rice; *Millers* Jude W. Bourassa, and V. C. Warden; *Laborers at mill* Albion Olcott and John Harden; *Wagonmaker* Anthony A. Ward; *Assistant wagonmaker* John Souce ("Susee," "Sousee"); *Ferryman* Lucius R. Darling;

Physicians Luther R. Palmer, George W. Bouton, H. W. Whitfield. (The above employed for the Pottawatomie, unless otherwise noted.)

SAC & FOX AGENCY *[Sacs & Foxes of the Mississippi, Ottawas, Chippewas]*— *Agents* John R. Chenault, replaced in May by Burton A. James; *Interpreter* Antoine Gokey; *Blacksmiths* Alfred Laws, James F. Mills (dismissed in August?), H. Bohl; *Assistant smiths* Hiram G. Tharp, and Huston Franklin (dismissed in August); *Gunsmiths* James B. Franklin, John Van Horn, Jacob H. Early; *Physicians* Edwin R. Griffith (resigned) and J. W. Ray (appointed in April?). (All, except agents, employed for Sac & Foxes.)

OSAGE RIVER AGENCY *[Miamis, Weas, Piankeshaws, Peorias & Kaskaskias]*— *Agents* Asbury M. Coffey, replaced in August by Ely Moore; *Interpreter* Baptiste Peoria; *Blacksmith* Robert Simerwell; *Assistant smiths* Luther Paschal, and John Robidoux; *Millers* James B. Chenault, Luther Paschal, Jack Hackley. (All, except agents, employed for Miamis.)

GREAT NEMAHA AGENCY *[Iowas, Sacs & Foxes of the Missouri, Kickapoos]*— *Agents* William P. Richardson, replaced in May by Daniel Vanderslice; *Interpreters* John B. Roy (for Iowas), Francis Bricknelle (for Sacs & Foxes), Peter Cadue (for Kickapoos); *Blacksmith* John McClaskey (for Sacs & Foxes); *Assistant smith* Isaac McClaskey (for Sacs & Foxes); *Farmer and miller* Harvey W. Forman (resigned) and Thomas J. Vanderslice.

NEOSHO AGENCY *[Osages, Quapaws, Senecas & Shawnees, Senecas]*—*Agents* William J. J. Morrow; replaced by Andrew J. Dorn; *Interpreters* (for Osages) Charles Mongrain, and Lewis Davis(?); *Blacksmiths* (for Osages) James A. Kennedy, John Finch, and Richard Price; *Assistant smiths* (for Osages) Francis Mitchell and Joseph Mitchell.

Ref: 33d Cong., 1st Sess., Sen. Ex. Doc. No. 69 (Serial 701); 33d Cong., 2d Sess., Sen. Ex. Doc. No. 69 (Serial 756); SIA, St. Louis, "Records," v. 9, typed copy, pp. 706-811, *passim.*; St. Joseph (Mo.) *Gazette*, May 11, June 1, 1853.

1854

❧ January-May.—Licenses (new and renewal) to trade with Indians in "Kansas," as granted by agents of the Central Superintendency, St. Louis, were:

Traders	Indians	Issued by	Rec'vd at St. Louis
W. G. Ewing, Jr.	Delawares	B. F. Robinson	January
Josiah Smart	Sacs & Foxes	B. A. James	January
(R. A.) Kinzie & (J. H.) Whistler	Sacs & Foxes	B. A. James	January
Walker, Northrup & Chick	Kansa	J. W. Whitfield	January
W. H. Haskell	Miamis	Ely Moore	February
M. D. Richardville	Miamis	Ely Moore	February
McHeeny & Feely	Miamis	Ely Moore	February
Gilham & McDaniel	Pottawatomies	J. W. Whitfield	February
M. P. (P. M.?) Chouteau, O. H. P. Polke & Fred. Chouteau	Miamis	Ely Moore	February
J. B. Scott	Sacs & Foxes	B. A. James	March

Baker & Street	Shawnees	B. F. Robinson	April
Ebenezer Blackston(e)			
(Blackiston?)	Kickapoos	Daniel Vanderslice	April
S. P. & W. H. Keller	Kansa	J. W. Whitfield	April
W. F. Dyer	Kickapoos	Daniel Vanderslice	May

Ref: Superintendency of Indian Affairs (SIA), St. Louis, "Records," v. 9, typed copy, pp. 820, 822, 823, 825, 830, 831, 845, 854, 857, 862, 869. In a January 21, 1854, letter Agent J. W. Whitfield stated he was sending the license granted to Walker, Northrup & Chick (the "successors and former partners of E. Mosier of Council Grove"); and that he had *not* included Mosier as clerk, as requested.—Office of Indian Affairs (OIA), Letters Received from Pottawatomie Agency (National Archives Microcopy 234, Roll 644).

❦ January 1.—At Union Town (Pottawatomie trading post), John L. Ogee signed a contract (with Agent J. W. Whitfield) "to keep and attend two Ferrys for the use and benefit of the Pottawatomie Indians . . . on the Kanzas river"—one to be located "at or near Smiths Ferry near the Baptist Mission"; the other, "at or near L. R. Darling place—near Union Town. . . ."

The ferries were to be operated daily from sunrise to sunset, Sunday not excepted. Ogee was to be paid $580 per year. John W. Brown and Anthony A. Ward witnessed the contract signing.

(In a November 13, 1854, letter, George W. Clarke, new head of the Pottawatomie Agency, wrote that he had discharged Ogee; and that a successor would not be appointed till the spring rise of the Kansas river in 1855.)

Ref: OIA, Letters Received from Pottawatomie Agency (National Archives Microcopy 234, Roll 679). *See* annals, p. 952, for L. R. Darling as operator of the first national Pottawatomie ferry.

❦ January 9-10.—At St. Joseph, Mo., several hundred persons (principally from northwestern Missouri and western Iowa) attended a Nebraska delegate convention. Resolutions were passed, and a memorial to congress was adopted, calling for immediate organization of the Nebraska territory, extinguishment of Indian land titles therein, and "liberal encouragement" to settlement.

Daniel Vanderslice (head of the Great Nemaha Agency) had an active role in the convention; Bvt. Maj. Edmund A. Ogden (Fort Leavenworth's quartermaster) was elected a vice-president. The latter's participation, subsequently, was criticized by R. S. Kelley (editor of the Liberty [Mo.] *Democratic Platform*).

Ref: St. Joseph *Gazette*, January 11, 18, February 15, 1854; James C. Malin's *The Nebraska Question, 1852-1854* (Lawrence, c1953), pp. 207-287 (for a comprehensive study of this Nebraska convention); and *see* Doctor Malin's "Aspects of the Nebraska Question, 1852-1854," in *KHQ*, v. 20, pp. 385-391.

❦ January 18.—The St. Joseph (Mo.) *Gazette* reported that congress was considering the organization of the large Nebraska territory into three territories, to be named "Cherokee," "Kansas," and "Nebraska."

In the extant newspaper files *of this area* the above is the earliest mention of a proposed *Kansas* territory.

Ref: St. Joseph *Gazette*, January 18, 1854; or, *KHQ*, v. 20, p. 450.

❧ January 18.—Wright Williamson & Co., in an advertisement for their "St. Joseph Steam Ferry Boat" (the *General Gaines*—brought upriver in late autumn, 1853), announced: "A splendid road is opened 100 feet wide from the [Missouri] River to the Bluff on the Nebraska [*i. e.*, "Kansas"] side, making it dry at all seasons." (Upwards of $6,000 had been spent on the steamboat, and in "fixing pastures for cattle, etc." the owners claimed.)

"The Boat . . . can cross the River in five minutes," their "ad" stated, "and carry each time two hundred head of cattle, and at least 12 waggons. . . . [The proprietors] have a large Hotel and commodious State Rooms on the Boat, sufficient to accommodate 125 persons comfortably with Boarding and lodging, which will be reserved for the emigrants."

Ref: St. Joseph *Gazette*, December 14, 1853, January 18, 1854; *Missouri Republican*, St. Louis, November 1, 1853 (the *F. X. Aubrey*, leaving St. Joseph October 27, met the upbound *General Gaines* at Spar Island, below Fort Leavenworth). The *Gazette* of September 6, 1854, mentioned the steam ferryboat (*General Gaines*) as still operating at St. Joseph.

❧ January 20.—The Santa Fe mail (in charge of [John?] Jones) arrived at Independence, Mo. John Greiner was a stage passenger. Also with the mail party was "Mr. [N. D.?] Van Epps," agent for "Abrahams & Rosenthall," who had left his wagon and hands at Council Grove.

Ref: Liberty (Mo.) *Weekly Tribune*, January 27, 1854 (from *Occidental Messenger*, Independence, Mo.); *Missouri Republican*, St. Louis, January 21, 1854.

❧ January(?).—The death of To-pe-ne-bee—a "Life Annuity Chief" of the Pottawatomies—was mentioned by Agent J. W. Whitfield in a January 21 letter. But he did not indicate when the event occurred. (On November 13, 1853, To-pe-ne-bee had been paid a $100 annuity for 1853.)

When To-pe-ne-bee came to "Kansas" in 1837 (*see* p. 337) Isaac McCoy referred to him as the "principal chief of the Pottawatomie nation."

Ref: Whitfield's letter, *loc. cit.*; 33d Cong., 2d Sess., *Sen. Ex. Doc. No. 69* (Serial 756), p. 219; 34th Cong., 1st Sess., *Sen. Ex. Doc. No. 19* (Serial 815), p. 94 (which lists "life annuity" chiefs Shah-beh-ney and Joseph LaFromboise—each receiving $200 on October 21, 1854).

❧ January 23.—Sen. Stephen A. Douglas, of Illinois, from the committee on territories, reported a revised Nebraska bill (substituted for one reported on January 4) which called for the creation of two territories—Nebraska and Kansas; repealed the Missouri Compromise (changes in the bill on February 6, 7, and 15 made it explicit), and introduced the principle of popular, or "squatter" sovereignty.

This bill, subsequently, passed both houses of congress, and became law when President Pierce signed the measure on May 30, 1854.

Ref: Malin's *The Nebraska Question,* pp. 288-351; also, his "Aspects of the Nebraska Question . . .," *loc. cit.;* Roy F. Nichols' "The Kansas-Nebraska Act . . .," in *Mississippi Valley Historical Review,* v. 48 (September, 1956), pp. 187-212.

❦ In a late January issue, the Savannah (Mo.) *Sentinel* commented: "The Cattle Trade, in this section, has been very active during the past few weeks. Drovers and speculators have made very extensive purchases for the plains. At least 5,000 head of cattle have changed hands since the new year.

"Prices have been high. Good work cattle, have commanded $100. Four and five year old steers, from $25 to $35. Cows from $18 to $25. Heifers $13 to $16; Yearlings $10 to $12. Good horses or mules, sixteen hands high are worth from $100 to $150."

Ref: *Weekly Missouri Statesman,* Columbia, February 10, 1854.

❦ January 31.—A telegram from Independence, Mo. (to St. Louis), announced the arrival (at 4 P. M.) of "Mr. K. W. [William] Allison" (from Fort Laramie) with the "December mail" from Salt Lake. (The January mail from Utah had not reached Laramie when he left there—on the 19th?)

As reported, Allison's party encountered snowstorms for six days; the animals all "broke down"; and Cheyennes took all the mail company's bedding and provisions (but Sioux Indians "gave them provisions and were more friendly").

Ref: *Missouri Republican,* St. Louis, February 1, 1854.

❦ January 31.—"River frozen hard here—foot passengers crossing on the ice all day."—dispatch from St. Joseph, Mo.

Ref: *Missouri Republican,* St. Louis, February 1, 1854.

❦ DIED: on February 7, at Washington, D. C., Thomas Fitzpatrick (b. 1799?), for 23 years a noted mountain man, and since 1846 agent for the Upper Platte and Arkansas Indians.

Ref: L. R. Hafen, *Broken Hand* . . . (Denver, 1931); *Daily Globe,* Washington, D. C., February 9, 1854.

❦ February 7.—Charles A. Perry, Weston, Mo., signed a contract (made at Fort Leavenworth with Bvt. Maj. E. A. Ogden, AQM) to "transport, per steamers, to Fort Riley," 7,000 bushels of corn in sacks (at $1.15 per bushel), and such "public stores" as might be turned over to him at Fort Leavenworth (at $1.25 per 100 pounds).

For Perry's successful Kansas river steamboat venture, and the first steamboat navigation of the Kaw for any distance, *see* April 22 entry.

Ref: 33d Cong., 2d Sess., *H. Ex. Doc. No. 68* (Serial 788), p. 7; *The History of*

Buchanan County, Missouri . . . (St. Joseph, 1881), p. 853 (for biographical sketch of Perry).

❡ February.—"Earl Fitzwilliam, a member of the English Parliament" (who had spent part of the winter at Taos, and Bent's Fort; and was now homeward-bound), crossed "Kansas" this month and arrived at Westport, Mo., by, or before February 23.

The "escorting party" (mentioned in the item about Fitzwilliam) may have been the company of Ceran St. Vrain, John L. Hatcher and Lucien Maxwell. "Kiowah," from Taos, N. M., on January 25, had written: "St. Vrain, Hatcher and Maxwell form a party for the States early in . . . [February]. They expect to return by June or July, with a large train of merchandise, &c. St. Vrain & Pley have purchased here a train of wagons, about 40 in number which they will send in about the time they start; the wagons in good repair, averaged them about $45 a piece."

Ref. St. Joseph (Mo.) *Gazette*, March 8, 1854; Liberty (Mo.) *Weekly Tribune*, March 10, 1854; *Missouri Republican*, St. Louis, February 24, March 2, 1854. For earlier mention of Fitzwilliam *see* annals, pp. 1033, 1106.

❡ February 23.—Delayed en route two days by a snowstorm in the Council Grove area, the Santa Fe mail (Francis Boothe, conductor) arrived at Independence, Mo. Aboard the stage were James L. Collins (Santa Fe *Gazette* proprietor), Murray F. Tuley (an Albuquerque lawyer), and G. Rodman (a Philadelphian).

Ref: Liberty (Mo.) *Weekly Tribune*, March 3, 1854; St. Joseph (Mo.) *Gazette*, March 8, 1854; New Mexico *Historical Review*, Santa Fe, v. 39, p. 205 (for an item on Tuley). *See* annals, p. 1187, for Rodman's trip to Santa Fe.

❡ February.—On his way to Rome, the Rt. Rev. John B. Lamy (vicar apostolic of New Mexico) traveled the Santa Fe trail this month; and reached the Missouri border near the end of February.

Those of Bishop Lamy's party also going abroad, as reported: the Rev. Jose E. Ortiz, Jesus Marie Ortiz (son of Don Francisco Ortiz y Delgado), a son of Don Santiago Gonzales of Corrales, and an Indian boy from Santa Clara.

Ref: Liberty (Mo.) *Weekly Tribune*, March 3, 1854; St. Joseph (Mo.) *Gazette*, March 8, 1854; *Missouri Republican*, St. Louis, February 24, 1854.

❡ March 1.—The *Polar Star* (T. H. Brierly, captain) reached St. Joseph, Mo.—the first steamboat arrival of the year. (She had left St. Louis February 21.)

The Liberty *Tribune* of March 3 noted that the *Polar Star*, and *Banner State* "passed up the river the other day, and are the first boats that have ascended this high the present season."

On March 7 the *Honduras* (which left St. Louis February 27) tied up at St. Joseph's landing—the second steamboat arrival of 1854.

Ref: St. Joseph *Gazette*, March 8, 1854; Liberty (Mo.) *Weekly Tribune*, March 8, 1854; *Missouri Republican*, St. Louis, February 21, 28, March 7, 1854. The *Polar Star* returned to St. Louis March 6. The *Banner State* perhaps did not go as far as Weston, Mo. She is not mentioned in Weston resident H. Miles Moore's "Journal" (original in Yale University Library; microfilm in KHi). Moore noted the early March arrivals of the *Polar*

Star, and *Honduras* at Weston (on March 1, and 7), and the arrival of the *El Paso* on March 8. The *El Paso* went up to Council Bluffs—the first steamboat to reach there in 1854.

❡ March 3.—William Allison with the "Salt Lake" mail (bringing news from Salt Lake up to January 1), arrived at Independence, Mo. He had left Fort Laramie on February 18.

In early(?) February some U. S. mail from Salt Lake had been brought to Austin, Fremont county, Iowa, by J. H. Jones, of St. Joseph, Mo. Jones (with two? traveling companions) had left Salt Lake City December 24, 1853, and reached Sydney, Iowa, after a journey of 35 traveling days.

Ref: Liberty (Mo.) *Weekly Tribune,* March 3, 17, 1854; *Missouri Republican,* St. Louis, March 6, 1854.

❡ March.—"Mules, Nebraska and cattle, and cattle, Nebraska and mules are the topics of the day . . .," said the *Missouri States-man,* Columbia, of March 3.

Ref: *Weekly Missouri Statesman,* Columbia, March 3, 1854.

❡ March 4.—At Fort Leavenworth, Charles A. Perry, of Perry & Young, Weston, Mo., was awarded the contract to provide 225 horses (sound animals; 15 to 16½ hands high; from 5 to 7 years old) for dragoon service, and to deliver them at San Francisco. Perry's bid was $270 per head. (Other bids ranged from $288 to $480 per animal.)

Ref: Liberty (Mo.) *Weekly Tribune,* February 3 (for Ogden's "ad" of January 27), March 24 (for award, and list of bidders), 1854. *See also,* Ogden "ad" in St. Joseph (Mo.) *Gazette,* February 8, 1854 (this one for "about sixty very superior saddle Horses fit for Dragoon service on the plains"—needed before May 10). A biographical sketch of Charles A. Perry (in the 1881 Buchanan county, Mo., *History—op. cit.,* p. 853) states that he went through to Salt Lake as sutler to the command of "Colonel Stephens [*i. e.,* Steptoe)," in 1854 (*see* June 1 annals entry for Steptoe; but George S. Park places Perry on the *Excel,* voyaging the Kansas river in mid-June, 1854 (*see* June 16-22 annals entry).

❡ Mid-March.—"We learn from the St. Louis papers, that there is quite a rush of travelers up the Missouri river, all the boats going up crowded to their utmost capacity. They are most of them emigrants for California, Oregon or Nebraska."

Ref: *The Daily* Alton (Ill.) *Telegraph,* March 16, 1854.

❡ March 21.—Passengers arriving at Independence, Mo., in the mail stage from Santa Fe were "Messrs. Wethered, Mitchell, and Mercure."

Ref: *Weekly Missouri Statesman,* Columbia, March 31, 1854 (from the *Western Dispatch,* Independence); Liberty (Mo.) *Weekly Tribune,* March 31, 1854 (from *Occidental Messenger,* Independence—which said *four* "gentlemen" were passengers); *Missouri Republican,* St. Louis, March 23, 1854 (by dispatch from Independence).

❡ March 21.—At St. Louis, Capt. Ralph W. Kirkham, quartermaster for the Sixth U. S. infantry, arranged (by contract with E. F.

Dix) for the *Timour No. 2* to transport one officer, 101 men, and two horses from Jefferson Barracks, Mo., to Fort Leavenworth.

Ref: 33d Cong., 2d Sess., *Sen. Ex. Doc. No. 46* (Serial 752), p. 14.

❑ **March 24.**—An Office of Indian Affairs "Statement of number of Indians in Kanzas & Nebraska," gave these statistics for eastern Kansas tribes:

Delawares	1,132	Sacs & Foxes of the	
Iowas	437	Mississippi	2,173
Kansa	1,375	Sacs & Foxes of the	
Kickapoos	475	Missouri	200
Miamis	250	Shawnees	931
Osages	4,941	Chippewas (Swan Creek	
Ottawas	247	& Black River)	30
*Peorias & Kaskaskias	255	*Weas & Piankeshaws	251
Pottawatomies	4,300	Wyandots	553
[Grand total			17,550]

° The *united* tribes of Weas & Piankeshaws, Peorias & Kaskaskias, numbered 259 according to the "Schedule of persons or families" appended to their May 30, 1854, treaty. The separate listings above constitute a duplication.

The Stockbridges, and the Munsee (or Christian) Indians—residing on the Delaware reserve—who totaled 278 souls in 1845, are not listed in the tabulation. Their number (diminished) would offset the duplication above (unless they were included with the Delawares?). A very few "New York" Indians also were in "Kansas" in March, 1854.

Ref: The "Statement" is to be found in Office of Indian Affairs, "Letters Received from Kansas Agency," 1854 (microfilm from National Archives in KHi). A notation says it is recorded in "Miscellaneous Records No. 8, p. 255"; and another (penciled) note reads: "Transmitted with letter to Hon Mr. Phillips 24 March 54." *See* C. J. Kappler's *Indian Affairs, Laws and Treaties* (1904), v. 2, pp. 640, 641, for the Wea (etc.) "Schedule."

❑ **March.**—The Rt. Rev. John B. Miege (who had gone to Rome in April, 1853) returned to St. Mary's (Pottawatomie) Mission. (*See* p. 1007.)

The gifts Bishop Miege brought back for his log cathedral included an organ (a source of amazement for the Indians), and a painting of the Immaculate Conception (said to be the work of Italian painter Benito), which is still at the parish church in St. Marys.

Ref: G. J. Garraghan, *The Jesuits of the Middle United States* (1938), v. 3, p. 1.

❑ **March 30.**—The Salt Lake mail arrived at Independence, Mo., from Fort Laramie, bringing, as the latest news from Utah, the *Deseret News* of February 2. On the last six days of the trip the mail party had endured "an unusual quantity of disagreeable weather."

Ref: Liberty (Mo.) *Weekly Tribune*, April 7, 1854.

❑ **April 7.**—"Capt. [Andrew] Wineland's magnificent floating palace Jas. H. Lucas, an entirely new boat, came to our wharf on Friday last," the St. Joseph (Mo.) *Gazette* of April 12 reported.

"She is the largest and most commodious boat in the [Missouri river] trade, and elegantly furnished, with a bridal chamber, and a Parlor in the Texas, suitable for tete-a-tete, and courting. Mr. Taylors Brass & Cotillion Band from St. Louis, came up on the Boat."

Ref: St. Joseph *Gazette*, April 12, 1854; *Missouri Republican*, St. Louis, April 14, 1854. The *Jas. H. Lucas* operated on the Missouri till midsummer. In the St. Joseph *Gazette* of August 16, Charles K. Baker advertised his boat, the *Admiral*, as a St. Louis-St. Joseph packet replacing the *Jas. H. Lucas*.

⊄ An April issue of the Fort Smith (Ark.) *Herald* stated: "Droves of cattle may be seen every day, in our city, for California. . . . The road to California will be filled with cattle from Arkansas for many miles. We have no doubt but 100,000 head will go from our State."

Maj. O. F. Winship (who, in the summer of 1854 traveled out to Fort Atkinson, and from there, by way of the upper Arkansas and the route along the base of the Rockies, to Fort Laramie), reported, after his return, that "during the past season" large droves of cattle "with attendant wagons &c.," had been taken "by emigrants and traders from Texas and Arkansas" over the route he had pursued—from Bent's Fort to Fort St. Vrain—whence they had "struck due west through Bridger's or Stansbury's Pass direct to the Salt Lake"; and that the number of cattle taken "over that road the past summer" was about 25,000.

Ref: *Weekly Missouri Statesman*, Columbia, May 5, 1854; *Kansas Weekly Herald*, Leavenworth, October 6, 1854.

⊄ April 11.—Two Indian delegations—Delawares and Shawnees—accompanied by Agent Benjamin F. Robinson, and the Rev. Thomas Johnson, left Kansas (City), Mo., aboard the *Polar Star,* en route to Washington, D. C. They were empowered to make land cession treaties.

A letter (by Agent B. F. Robinson?) dated "Delaware, N. T. [*i. e.,* 'Kansas'], April 5, 1854," stated that the writer had been "constantly engaged in attending a Council of the Indian Tribes," from late March till April 4; that the Shawnees had decided on March 31 to send a delegation of eight or ten; and the Delawares, on April 3, had determined to send nine delegates.

See, also, May 6 and 10 entries.

Ref: William Walker's diary, in W. E. Connelley's *The Provisional Government of Nebraska Territory* . . . (1899), pp. 401, and 403 (for May 22, 1854, entry: "The Delaware and Shawnee Chiefs returned"); *Weekly Missouri Statesman*, Columbia, March 31 (for Robinson? letter), April 28, 1854. The Kansas Agency papers in the John G. Pratt Collection (in KHi ms. division) include a May 11, 1854, letter from George W. Manypenny stating that John Ketchem and James Conner, Delawares, and Henry Tiblow, the Delawares' interpreter, would "visit their friends in Indiana on their return home [from Washington]."

⊄ April 12.—At Fort Riley, Thomas Simpson and Mary Joanne Riordon were married by the Rev. J. B. Duerinck, S. J., of St. Mary's (Pottawatomie) Mission.

(If not the first marriage at Fort Riley, it was the first of which there is record.)

Ref: St. Mary's Mission records, at St. Louis University, St. Louis, Mo. Witnesses to the ceremony were Edward Davis, and Anna McCarroll (the Fort Riley hospital matron).

❡ April 12.—"Lewis' Nebraska Ferry"—a "good Horse Boat" ferry —on the Missouri "at Hart's Point, about 15 miles above Weston," was advertised in the St. Joseph *Gazette*. The notice also stated that a good road leading from Columbus, Mo. (later renamed "Rushville") to the ferry "is now open."

Presumably the operator was Calvin Lewis, who, in 1855, obtained a charter for his ferry, from the Kansas territorial legislature.

Ref: St. Joseph *Gazette*, April 12, 1854. In *KHQ*, v. 2, p. 27, it is stated that (Calvin) "Lewis' Point" was about three miles above Kickapoo City, and just above Oak Mills, Atchison county. But that does not fit the "about 15 miles above Weston" description; nor does it relate to Columbus (or, Rushville), Mo.—which is above Atchison. *See* Sheffield Ingalls' *History of Atchison County, Kansas* (1916), pp. 127, 128 (for the Oak Mills location); and *The History of Buchanan County, Missouri* (1881), p. 372 (for Columbus— Rushville). Note, in June 17, 1854, annals entry that "Million's Ferry" is described as "about fifteen miles above Weston." Million's location was at "Atchison."

❡ April.—Reports of cholera (or, a disease resembling it) on the Missouri, reached St. Louis in mid-month.

The *News* of April 15 said that according to "arrivals last evening" a number of cholera (or cholera-like) deaths had occurred on the upbound *Australia*— which carried "a crowd of Mormons and other emigrants." (At Keokuk, Iowa, from 10 to 15 of the emigrants "with whom that town is flooded," had succumbed to cholera, or a similar complaint.)

Ref: *Weekly Missouri Statesman*, Columbia, April 28, 1854.

❡ April 15.—At Ottawa Baptist Mission (east of present Ottawa), Missionary Jotham Meeker noted in his diary: "The first California Emigrants arrived last evening—to-day several Companies pass with about 850 Cattle, besides work oxen."

On April 24 (after returning from a trip to Westport, Mo.) Meeker wrote: "Learn that during all of last week great numbers of Cattle have been passing every day. On yesterday morning about 1000 left here—they continued passing all day, on last night between 2200 & 2300 loose Cattle encamped within a mile of our house. Large droves still move onward through the day. About 1500 more encamp this evening within a mile of us. We have heard of over 2100 having passed and arrived to-day. Don't know how many more there have been." Meeker recorded in his diary on April 25: "Rode out to-day in the Road, half mile from our house, remained about a half hour—some 1600 Cattle passed me while there—others passed afterwards, and other droves arrive this evening."

See, also, May 27 annals entry.

Ref: Jotham Meeker's "Diary," in KHi ms. division.

❡ April.—These were the steamboats making one, or more, April trips to points on the Missouri above the Kaw's mouth: *Aleonia* (a Nashville and St. Louis boat; she made only one? run up the Missouri), *Australia, Banner State, Clara, F. X. Aubrey, Genoa, Herald, Honduras, Isabel, Jas. H. Lucas, Ne Plus Ultra, Polar Star, Sam Cloon, Sonora, Timour No. 2,* and *Tropic*.

Ref: Issues of the St. Joseph (Mo.) *Gazette* and *Missouri Republican,* St. Louis, and H. Miles Moore's "Journal" (*loc. cit.*), for April, and May, 1854.

¶ April 19.—Arrival of these Santa Fe travelers was reported at Independence, Mo.: Dr. Henry Connelly, New Mexico's Gov. David Meriwether, his son Raymond, Mrs. Louis Smith (wife of a Santa Fe Baptist missionary), William Cunningham, "Perea" (Juan? Perea), and "any number of Mexican traders." It was said they had been 23 days on the road. In a brush with Indians at Pawnee Fork, "a man named Montague" had been wounded in the neck by an arrow.

Governor Meriwether (en route to Kentucky on a visit; and to report in Washington) later recollected of this trip that he, his son, and Mrs. Louis Smith traveled in the train of Connelly and "Chaves"; that in the caravan there were three carriages, about 100 wagons, some 100 extra mules; and that (at his suggestion) Connelly's train crossed to the Arkansas by *Aubry's route* (which Meriwether had traveled in 1853—*see* p. 1165). At Council Grove, both the governor and Mrs. Louis Smith had expected to stay overnight at the Kansa Methodist Mission, but were turned away (says Meriwether) because of Mrs. Smith's Baptist affiliation.

Ref: *Missouri Republican,* St. Louis, April 21, 1854; *Weekly Missouri Statesman,* Columbia, April 28, 1854; Liberty (Mo.) *Weekly Tribune,* April 28, 1854; New York *Daily Tribune,* May 4, 1854 (from Santa Fe *Gazette* of March 25); David Meriwether, *My Life in the Mountains and on the Plains,* ed. by R. A. Griffen (Norman, c1965), pp. 174-186; *Old Santa Fe,* Santa Fe, N. M., v. 1 (October, 1913), p. 216 (for Perea).

¶ April 19-24.—"Quite a number of trains are here fitting out for California and Oregon."—report, April 19, from Independence, Mo. On the 24th it was stated: "California emigrants are leaving daily, all in good health."

(The first "Californians" passed St. Mary's Mission [at present St. Marys] on April 22.)

Ref: *Weekly Missouri Statesman,* Columbia, April 28, May 5, 1854; Garraghan, *op. cit.,* p. 657.

¶ April.—From Weston, Mo., Franklin B. Gilbert, John M. Guthrie, and B. F. Bishop set out for Salt Lake City with a load of goods. On their return home, August 26, it was reported that they "were the first in the valley, reaching there the 3d day of July."

Ref: *Missouri Republican,* St. Louis, September 9, 1854 (from Weston *Reporter*).

¶ April 20.—In the charge of "Mr. [J. H.?] Jones," merchants McLaughlin, Barrow & Jones, St. Joseph, Mo., started a "Goods and Groceries" train of 12 mule-drawn wagons (each with a 3,000-pound load), and eight ox-drawn wagons (carrying 3,800-pound loads) for Salt Lake City.

In mid-May eastbound travelers met "Jones' merchant train" near Fort Laramie.

Ref: St. Joseph *Gazette*, April 26, July 19, 1854. *See* March 3, 1854, entry for J. H. Jones.

❡ April 21.—Alexander Majors signed a government contract to transport army stores overland, during the summer, from Fort Leavenworth to Fort Laramie, at the rate of $7.90 per 100 pounds; and to furnish and deliver at Fort Laramie, by July 15, 1,000 bushels of corn (at $4.89 per bushel). J. M. Hunter and S. L. McKinney were sureties for his $15,000 bond.

See, also, April 28 entry.

Ref: 33d Cong., 2d Sess., *Sen. Ex. Doc. No. 46* (Serial 752), p. 11.

❡ April 21.—(M. G.?) Shrewsbury, (A. G.?) Woodward & Co. signed a government contract to transport army stores (received by June 15) overland from Fort Leavenworth to Fort Kearny, for $3.80 per 100 pounds; to furnish and deliver at Fort Kearny, by October 1, 2,000 bushels of corn (at $2.40 per bushel); and to furnish and deliver at Fort Laramie, by July 15, 1,000 bushels of corn (at $4.47 per bushel). Sureties for the $8,000 bond were C(harles) A. Perry and E(lijah) Cody.

Ref: 33d Cong., 2d Sess., *Sen. Ex. Doc. No. 46* (Serial 752), p. 11; *KHQ,* v. 28, pp. 448, 452, and following, for Elijah Cody (uncle of William F. "Buffalo Bill" Cody). In connection with the Marysville Town Company, the names of A. G. Woodward and M. G. Shrewsbury are mentioned in the Marshall county section of the A. T. Andreas-W. G. Cutler *History of the State of Kansas* (Chicago, 1883), p. 917.

❡ April-May.—"It is supposed that 3,000 head of cattle were passed by the [Salt Lake] mail between Laramie and this place."—report from Independence, Mo., May 5. (The mail reached Missouri May 3; presumably had left Fort Laramie about April 15.)

The Liberty (Mo.) *Weekly Tribune* of April 21 stated: "The number of cattle that will be driven over the plains this season will be considerable. We hear of droves from various quarters of . . . [Missouri] on the march."

In a mid-April issue, the Huntsville (Mo.) *Recorder* said: ". . . It is an every day affair, that from one to half dozen or more droves of cattle pass through our streets from counties east of this *en route* for the land of gold. Thomas L. Gorham, Dr. W. T. Lowery, Roberts & Terrill, H. C. Collins & Bro., B. Furnish and Jas. M. Turner, have each started from this [Randolph] county within the last few days, with large droves of cattle for the California market. Very many families are passing daily, with view of making their homes in the far West." (When Gorham crossed the Missouri at Glasgow on the 24th[?] it was reported he had "about 500 [large, fine] cattle.")

According to the Lexington (Mo.) *Chronicle* of April 22, these droves had passed Lone Jack in Jackson county (and were herded just above that place, while waiting for the grass to grow): a drove from Franklin county of 490 head, and 20 men; James Hackley, from the Dover vicinity, with 190 head, and seven men; Mr. Henning, also from the Dover area, with 90 head, and five men. The Lexington paper further stated that William (H.) Russell's stock was at

Lone Jack (and ready to start about April 25). His two droves of 450 cattle each were in the charge of R. W. Durham and Benjamin Shackelford. From Major Baird's, in Lafayette county, the train of Messrs. Upton B. Winsor and Charles L. Ewing, with nearly 600 head of cattle, horses, and mules, and 18 men, planned to start on April 25. In the week of April 16-22, on different days, in lots of 300 and more, a drove of upwards of 1,000 cattle from Osage county crossed the Missouri at Lexington. (The owners were three brothers—Germans—making their fifth trip across the plains. They were headed for St. Joseph, Mo.)

"Mr. Maupin of Boone co., Mo." set out in April(?) with a drove of 600 cattle. As later reported from California, he lost about 290 head en route, and all but three of 80 yoke of work steers in his train. Prior to April 14, Messrs. John S. and William F. Wilhite and Willis March of Boone county started for California with 400 head of cattle.

In mid-April Messrs. Cooper of Howard county, Mo., bound for California, passed through Glasgow with 2,000 head of sheep. (They expected to cross the Missouri at Council Bluffs.) Also in mid-April, Messrs. McKinney & Anderson, of the Glasgow area left for California with their train—10 men, one woman, five wagons, and 400 head of cattle.

On May 12, at St. Mary's (Pottawatomie) Mission, Father Duerinck wrote in his diary: "The Californians are driving a great deal of stock. We have bought of them forty-five head of cattle."

Mr. Lunt, who left Salt Lake City on July 7 and reached Independence, Mo., August 22, said that 100,000 and "probably" 150,000 head of cattle had been driven to California "this season." He had met only about 20,000—most of which would go by way of Salt Lake; but "far the greater number went by the cut-off and Fort Hall." "Great numbers of fine horses and mules, and numerous large flocks of sheep" were also on the route.

Ref: *Weekly Missouri Statesman,* Columbia, April 14, 28, May 5, 12, 1854; Liberty *Weekly Tribune,* April 21, 1854; *Missouri Republican,* St. Louis, April 29, August 31, November 2, 1854; Garraghan, *op. cit.,* v. 2, p. 657 (for Duerinck).

¶ April.—John W. Whitfield was appointed Indian agent for the Upper Platte Agency (in place of Thomas Fitzpatrick, deceased). Richard C. S. Brown, Van Buren, Ark., was appointed to the post Whitfield vacated—head of the Pottawatomie Agency (for the Pottawatomies and Kansa).

Brown arrived at Westport, Mo. (which he made his headquarters), about May 25(?). On June 22 he died of cholera. His replacement was George W. Clarke, also of Van Buren, Ark., who accepted the post on August 14. On November 25 Clarke wrote that he had established his agency at "Douglass" (Douglas), on the Kansas river about 50 miles west of Westport. (His home was a 14-foot square cabin; but he was erecting another cabin for an office.)

Proslaveryman Whitfield, on November 29, was elected delegate to congress from Kansas territory.

Ref: St. Joseph (Mo.) *Gazette,* April 26, 1854; OIA, Letters Received from Pottawatomie Agency (National Archives Microcopy 234, Roll 679), for Brown and Whitfield items.

❬ April 21.—Bound for Washington to make land cession treaties, the Iowa, Sac & Fox (of the Missouri), and Kickapoo Indian delegations, accompanied by Agent Daniel Vanderslice, were aboard the *Honduras* as she started downriver from St. Joseph, Mo. (They arrived in Washington on May 1. *See, also,* May 17 and 18 annals entries.)

"As soon as Vanderslice left, many [persons] flocked over [from Missouri] and made their claims by laying a foundation for a cabin and writing their names on a tree near by, and now [May 27] there is not a grease spot left unclaimed within my knowledge; and still claim hunters are passing daily. After thus locating their claims most of them go back and are now awaiting the results of the treaty. . . ."—"H. B.," in a letter dated May 27, from his "Spring Hill Farm [in] Nebraska, alias Kansas."

Ref: Howard Vanderslice and H. N. Monnett, *Van der Slice and Allied Families* (Los Angeles, c1931), p. 167 (from Daniel Vanderslice's diary, 1854); New York *Daily Tribune*, August 14, 1854 (reprinted from Reading [Pa.] *Gazette* of August 12) for "H. B.'s" May 27 letter. "H. B." (*i. e.*, "B. H.") was Indian trader Benjamin Harding. In *KHQ*, v. 13, p. 31, is a Harding letter dated "Spring Hill Farm Kansas Ter July 17th 1854." Since 1852 (*see KHC*, v. 10, p. 206) he had been located at the site of present Wathena, Doniphan county.

❬ April 21-26.—In present Doniphan county (and across the Missouri from St. Joseph) three meetings relating to "Kansas" squatters' land claims were held.

At the April 21 "assemblage" (place not indicated, but probably Henry Thompson's residence) "it was determined that all persons who had previous to that time designated particular spots or localities [in 'Kansas'] should hold them independent of all others who might come hereafter."

An opposition group, meeting April 24, near "the venerable Wauthena's wigwam" (at Benjamin Harding's trading post?) adopted rules and regulations for the mutual protection of squatters. Essentially, this gathering declared the decisions of April 21 null and void.

At Henry Thompson's, on April 26, a meeting was held to reaffirm the stand taken on April 21; and to counteract the "high handed" measures adopted by the April 24 assemblage, which, it was said, had resulted in many claims being jumped, or disputed. Lucian J. Eastin (St. Joseph *Gazette* editor) presided; Sidney Tennent was secretary; Messrs. Sykes, Mansfield, and Northcutt were resolutions committee members.

(On May 5 the adjourned meeting at Henry Thompson's [with T. Wildbahn as chairman; and Alfred Larzelere as secretary] passed more resolutions—one an endorsement of Douglas' Nebraska bill; adopted new rules for registration of claims; and appointed D. M. Johnston, St. Joseph, as register.)

Ref: St. Joseph *Gazette*, May 3, 10, 1854; *Missouri Republican*, St. Louis, May 8, 1854; Malin's *Nebraska Question* . . ., pp. 361, 362. "Wah-the-nah" was one of the Kickapoos' "leading men," according to Agent Daniel Vanderslice—*see* his "Diary" (*loc. cit.*), April 7, 1854, entry. He lived where the town of Wathena subsequently was established.

❬ April 22.—The "neat little stern-wheel steamer" *Excel* (owned by Charles A. Perry, and Messrs. Tutt & Baker, all of Weston, Mo.) started up the Kansas river. She carried government-contract supplies (principally, this trip, 1,100 barrels of flour, it is said); and reached her destination—Fort Riley—in two days (according to the recollection of passenger Hayden D. McMeekin).

The *Excel* was the first steamboat to enter the Kansas river since the flood year, 1844 (*see* p. 517), so far as known; and the first steamboat ever to go up the Kaw for any distance. She was the only steamboat on the Kansas in 1854; she made perhaps six trips to Fort Riley between April 22 and June 22; and was never on the Kansas again. These items provided some information on the *Excel* in 1854:

April 8.—"The little steamer Excel was sold on Saturday [April 8] for $7,500 to Capt. Baker, for the Kansas river trade."—*Mo. Rep.*, St. Louis, April 11.

April 19.—In the morning, the *Sonora* left Weston, and met the upbound *Excel* below Kansas (City), Mo. The *Herald*, later in the day, met the *Excel* at "Barker's landing" (somewhere above the Kaw's mouth).—*Ibid.*, April 23. The arrival of the *Excel* at Weston, on the evening of the 19th, was noted by resident H. Miles Moore.

April 21.—The Weston *Reporter* of April 20 announced that the *Excel,* owned by townsmen C. A. Perry, and Tutt & Baker, and commanded by Capt. Charles Baker, would "ply as a regular packet" between Weston and Fort Riley; and would leave on her first trip "to-morrow morning."—Liberty *Weekly Tribune*, April 28.

April 22.—The Liberty *Democratic Platform* of May 4 (Thursday) reported the *Excel* "started up the Kansas River last Saturday week [April 22], laden with Government freight from Fort Leavenworth, bound for Fort Riley."

April 29.—The Independence *Occidental Messenger* commented: "The Excel, commanded by Capt. Johnson, left the port of Kansas a few days since, but we are informed that she did not get up the Kaw, beyond six or eight miles, before she landed upon a sand bar . . . [apparently this was misinformation]. This effort of Captain Johnson is worthy to be recorded among the progressive events of the age, it is the commencement of steam navigation in the beautiful Nebraska Territory. . . ."—*Mo. Rep.*, May 5.

May 23.—From Kansas river, the *Excel* tied up at Weston in the afternoon.—H. Miles Moore.

June 3.—The *New Lucy* (downbound) left Weston; passed the *Excel* at Fort Leavenworth.—*Mo. Rep.*, June 7. (The *Excel* had left Weston on June 2.—Moore.)

June 8.—The *Excel* returned to Weston in the evening.—Moore.

June 9.—The *Excel* started down from Weston in the morning.—Moore.

June 13.—The *Excel* arrived at Weston in the morning.—Moore. The Parkville *Industrial Luminary* of June 20 stated: "Last week [*i. e.*, June 13?] the fine little steamer 'Excel' brought to the landing here a large lot of skins from Delaware Town [at the Delaware, or Grinter Crossing of Kansas river] in Kansas Territory, being the first exports after the passage of the Territorial Bill.

. . ."—"Webb Scrapbooks," v. 1, p. 44. The remains of a clipping which quoted the Weston *Reporter* of (June) 15th, read: "The fine little Weston and Fort Riley packet [*Excel*] came in [Tuesday morn]ing, as usual . . . on a pleasure . . . [trip up?] the smoky Hill. . . ." (Evidently the steamboat had made a run up the Smoky Hill tributary of the Kansas—as she did, again, about June 20—*see* June 16-22 entry.—*Ibid.*, p. 45.)

June 14.—H. Miles Moore, at Weston, indicated the *Excel* was to leave the levee on the 15th for Fort Riley. *See* June 15-22 entry for the *Excel's* last trip on the Kansas river.

Ref: Missouri newspapers as noted; *KHC*, v. 9, p. 322; "Webb Scrapbooks," KHi library, v. 1; New York *Daily Times*, August 30, 1854 (for reported *six* trips made by the *Excel*); H. Miles Moore's "Journal," *loc. cit.*

❡ April 23.—The mail from Santa Fe, in charge of Francis Boothe, reached Independence, Mo. Stage passengers were "Messrs. [Preston] Beck and [John?] Flournoy, of Santa Fe, and John Cece, of Las Vegas."

James Milligan ("one of the Fremont party") who reached Westport, Mo., on April 23 (as reported by dispatch from Independence) probably had been aboard the mail coach, also.

Ref: Liberty (Mo.) *Weekly Tribune*, May 5, 1854; *Weekly Missouri Statesman*, Columbia, May 5, 1854; *Missouri Republican*, St. Louis, April 26, 1854.

❡ DIED: the Rev. Joel Grover, aged 64, on April 24, at the Kickapoo Methodist Mission (present Leavenworth county), where he had been the Methodist Church, South, missionary from 1851 to 1853.

Ref: *KHC*, v. 9, p. 229 (for Grover's mission appointments). The item on Grover's death is from "Remsburg Clippings," v. 1, pp. 181, 182 (in KHi library). Remsburg stated that the missionary is buried in the National Cemetery at Fort Leavenworth; that Joel Grover, born in Conway, Mass., January 8, 1790, died April 24, 1854, aged 64; and noted that two sons (D. A. N. and Charles H.) afterwards were lawyers in Leavenworth. An article (written when?) published in the New York *Daily Tribune* of June 22, 1854, included reference to Kickapoo Village, and this statement: "There is but one trading-house in the village; and the mission now occupied by the Rev. Mr. Grover has no school. . . ."

❡ Between late April and mid-June, 19 officers and 481 troops arrived at Fort Leavenworth aboard steamboats (according to army quartermaster department contracts made with steamboat captains):

Contract with	Date	Steamboat	Troops	Taken aboard at
A(ndrew) Wineland	April 24	James H. Lucas	4 officers; 100 men	Jefferson Barracks
T. H. Brierly	May 1	Polar Star	1 officer; 32 men	St. Louis
Joseph La Barge	May 4	Sonora	1 officer; 100 men	Jefferson Barracks
P. M. Chouteau	May 8	Isabel	8 officers; 117 men	Alton, Ill.
G. W. Bowman	May 12	Edinburg	1 officer; 49 men	St. Louis
W. W. Baker	May 26	Delaware	3 officers; 48 men	Jefferson Barracks
J(oshua) Cheever	June 13	Clara	1 officer; 35 men	St. Louis

Ref: 33d Cong., 2d Sess., Sen. Ex. Doc. No. 46 (Serial 752), pp. 9, 10, 12, 13; *Missouri Republican,* St. Louis, May 6, 1854 (which reported that the *Sonora* would start "this afternoon" for Jefferson Barracks, to take on board over 100 troops, a number of officers, and 50 wagons, bound for Fort Leavenworth). P. G. Lowe, in his *Five Years a Dragoon* (1906), p. 157, stated "Toward the last of May [1854], 'D' Troop [First dragoons], Capt. John Adams, came [to Fort Leavenworth] from Fort Snelling by steamboat [the *Delaware?*]. . . ."

❧ April.—At St. Joseph, Mo., the *Gazette* of April 26 stated: "Our streets for the last week have been crowded with emigrants. Our Hotels are full, and still they come. The Steam Ferry Boat [*see* January 18 entry] is kept busy. An immense qua[n]tity of stock, will cross here."

On March 29 the Gazette had reported: "Emigrants for the plains are beginning to arrive. Every boat brings new arrivals. There is a prospect of a large emigration." And the April 19 issue had this comment: "Our city is now pretty well filled with emigrants for California and every Boat adds to the number. We hear of several thousand head of stock now on their way to this place. There are a greater number of emigrants here destined for Oregon. Several families from this place are preparing to go [including Baptist minister W. F. Boyakin]. . . ."

Ref: St. Joseph (Mo.) *Gazette,* issues as noted.

❧ April 26.—The Massachusetts Emigrant Aid Company was incorporated by act of the Massachusetts general assembly. Organization under this charter never was completed.

On July 24 Eli Thayer and other "interested parties" of Boston, and vicinity, organized an Emigrant Aid Company (unincorporated) to promote Free-State emigration to Kansas territory; and commenced fund-raising and colonization efforts. Thayer, Amos A. Lawrence, and J. M. S. Williams were the company trustees; Dr. Thomas H. Webb was secretary.

Between July 29 and the end of November, 1854, six Emigrant Aid Company parties (totaling fewer than 700? persons) reached Kansas territory. *See* rosters of these parties in *KHQ,* v. 12, pp. 115-155.

On March 4, 1855, the "non-corporate joint stock company" was superseded by the New England Emigrant Aid Company [incorporated]. Under its auspices, about 900? persons came to Kansas in 1855.)

Ref: Samuel A. Johnson's "The Genesis of the New England Emigrant Aid Company," in *The New England Quarterly,* Cambridge, Mass., v. 3 (January, 1930), pp. 95-122; *KHQ,* v. 12, pp. 115-155, 227-268.

❧ April 27.—Wells & Washburn's long-awaited "new, safe and commodious steam ferryboat"—for the traffic between Weston, Mo., and Fort Leavenworth, "Kan."—arrived at Rialto, Mo. (a mile below Weston), where, for 10 years, or longer, John B. Wells, Platte county, Mo., had operated a ferry across the Missouri.

Weston resident, H. Miles Moore, went down to see the steamboat on April 28; and crossed the river on it next day.

Ref: H. Miles Moore's "Journal" (*loc. cit.*); *Kansas Weekly Herald*, Leavenworth, September 15, 1854 (and later), for Wells & Washburn's advertisement; *KHQ*, v. 2, pp. 23-25; W. M. Paxton's *Annals of Platte County, Missouri* (1897), pp. 62, 172, 913, 914.

❧ April 28.—"Messrs. Alexander and Norton," and a large party of German emigrants (all men), from Illinois, set out from Weston, Mo., for California. The train (a passenger train, apparently) consisted of nine wagons and 40 "superior" horses.

The company reached Carson Valley on July 29. Alexander and Norton, arriving at Sacramento on August 4, reported the trip had been a pleasant one, with dry weather most of the way. At the Big Blue (present Marysville) the water "did not come above the horses' knees." The train had lost no stock; and there had been no Indian trouble.

Ref: *Missouri Republican*, St. Louis, September 13, 1854; New York *Daily Times* September 9, 1854.

❧ April 28.—(Alexander) Majors & (William H.) Russell signed a government contract to transport army supplies overland from Fort Leavenworth to Albuquerque, N. M., during the summer, at the rate of $10.83 per 100 pounds. (J. M. Hunter, J. B. Yager, and W. B. Waddell were sureties for the $75,000 bond.)

Majors, in his memoirs, stated that in 1854 he changed his business from freighting for merchants in New Mexico, to carrying government freights (*see, also*, April 21 entry), and added to his transportation "making 100 wagons and teams for that year, divided into four trains [some, evidently, going to Fort Laramie]."

James A. Little (fresh from Indiana, and a Majors & Russell employee with the New Mexico-bound train) later recollected that they set out from Fort Leavenworth on May 1. "Our wagons were nearly all loaded with sugar and we had some coffee, bacon and spices." he wrote (in his 1904-published *What I Saw on the Old Santa Fe Trail*). "We started with over 500 oxen. Six yoke pulled each wagon and we took a lot of extras for recruits. . . ." Little also stated: "Our train consisted of forty large prarier[*sic*] schooners. There were ten old wagons and thirty new ones sent out by the government for the use of the army post. Each wagon was as large as four ordinary wagons and carried a load averaging three tons."

During the return trip—dates not given—there was an outbreak of smallpox. Little (unvaccinated) left the train and arrived at Council Grove alone. (He stayed with trader Seth Hays.) When the party of "Armeho [Armijo], a very noted Mexican freighter," bound for Kansas City, came along, he traveled east in company. His account says: "With the [Armijo] train were four passengers, a single white lady, two young white men and a negro [Jordan]." According to

Little the two men were rivals for the young woman and he says she afterwards married one of them at Kansas City, Mo.

Ref: 33d Cong., 2d Sess., Sen. Ex. Doc. No. 46 (Serial 752), p. 11, or, 33d Cong., 2d Sess., H. Ex. Doc. No. 68 (Serial 788), p. 11; Alexander Majors, *Seventy Years on the Frontier* (1893), p. 140; James A. Little, *What I Saw on the Old Santa Fe Trail* . . . (Plainfield, Ind., c1904).

¶ April 28.—William S. McKnight signed two government contracts for the transporting of army supplies overland to New Mexico during the summer: (1) from Fort Leavenworth to Fort Fillmore, at $13.75 per 100 pounds; (2) from Fort Leavenworth to "El Paso, N. M.," at $14 per 100 pounds. (McKnight's bondsmen for both contracts were Robert Campbell and Kenneth McKenzie of St. Louis.)

Ref: 33d Cong, 2d Sess., H. Ex. Doc. No. 68 (Serial 788), p. 11; or, 33d Cong., 2d Sess., Sen. Ex. Doc. No. 46 (Serial 752), p. 11.

¶ April 29.—Among the four-year U. S. mail contracts (effective July 1) let at Washington, D. C., were these three with "Kansas" connections:

Route

No. 8912. Independence, Mo., to Santa Fe, N. M. ter. 885 miles, once a month, each way; in six-mule coaches. Contractor: Jacob Hall, Independence, Mo.; at $10,990 per year. [Hall had been connected with this mail service since its inception, July 1, 1850—*see* p. 949; and was, by his own statement, the sole contractor from July 1, 1854, till June 30, 1862. However, the Santa Fe *Weekly Gazette*, in 1854, and 1855, carried the advertisement of (John M.) Hockaday & (Jacob) Hall, *dated June 12, 1854,* informing Santa Fe traders and others, that Hockaday & Hall would carry the U. S. mail from Independence to Santa Fe for four years, beginning July 1, 1854. Fare: November to May 1—$150; May 1 to November, $125. Authorized agents: W. W. H. Davis, at Santa Fe; John S. Harris at Westport, Mo.]

No. 8911. Independence, Mo., to Salt Lake City, Utah ter. 1,150 miles (estimated), once a month each way; in four-horse coaches. Contractors: William M. F. Magraw and John E. Reeside, of Pennsylvania; at $14,400 per annum. [Magraw and Reeside underbid Samuel H. Woodson—a contractor on the route since beginning of service August 1, 1850 (*see* p. 956). Till now the mail carriers had traveled up the south side of the Kansas, on the old Oregon-California trail, crossing the river just above Union Town (trading post). The Magraw-Reeside route would be: Independence—Westport—Delaware Crossing (of Kansas river)—Fort Leavenworth—Big Blue Crossing (present Marysville)—Fort Kearny—Fort Laramie—Salt Lake City. On July 1, 1855, Magraw became the sole contractor. On August 18, 1856, he was allowed to terminate the contract.]

No. 8909. Independence, Mo., to St. Joseph, Mo. 75 miles, and back, daily. Contractor: Preston Roberts; at $4,400 per annum. Route: Independence—Westport, Mo.—Kansas (City), Mo.—Delaware (Kansas river crossing)—Fort Leavenworth—Weston, Mo.—Dekalb, Mo.—Sparta, Mo.—St. Joseph, Mo.

Ref: 33d Cong., 2d Sess., *H. Ex. Doc. No. 86* (Serial 789), pp. 316-319; 34th Cong., 1st Sess., *H. R. No. 6* (Serial 868); 34th Cong., 1st Sess., *H. Ex. Doc. No. 122* (Serial 860), p. 335; St. Joseph (Mo.) *Gazette*, June 14, 1854; F. R. Holdcamper letter, July 14, 1950 (in KHi ms. div.), re Star Mail Route No. 8909, as of 1854; *Hall vs. Huffaker* (brief in Circuit Court of U. S. for District of Kansas), in KHi library; Santa Fe (N. M.) *Weekly Gazette*, March 3, 1855 earliest issue available), for Hockaday & Hall advertisement.

❡ April-May.—The Independence (Mo.) *Western Dispatch* of May 19 commented: "We noticed several weeks since, the arrival of several wagons at Westport, loaded with wool from New Mexico. This is a new feature in the trade of that country, and we think if carried on properly, will be profitable. . . . Our traders who freight goods to that country every season . . . might find it to their interest to return loaded with wool . . . [instead of bringing back empty wagons]."

Ref: Liberty (Mo.) *Weekly Tribune*, May 26, 1854.

❡ April-May.—"Up to the first of May there had crossed the river at the St. Joseph [Mo.] Ferry, Cattle 7858, Waggons, 220, Horses and Mules 588, Men, Women and children 1120," said the *Gazette* of May 3. "As many more will yet cross here. A number stop here a while, and then cross at ferries above. It is believed at least 15,000 head of cattle will cross at this ferry. . . ."

In an article dated May 2, the *Gazette* commented: "The Emigration this season is much larger than we anticipated, our Steam Ferry Boat, is doing a land-office business, being busily engaged in transferring Emigrants with their families and their wagons, stock &c., to the Nebraska [*i. e.*, Kansas] side of the Missouri river. The grass is abundant . . . [for] the many thousand animals, that are weekly taken over, en route for California. . . . We understand that there are large numbers of . . . [emigrants] encamped upon the banks of many streams east of us, recruiting themselves, and teams, &c. preparatory to crossing the River. . . ."

On May 10 the St Joseph *Gazette* stated: "Emigration continues, and numerous waggons from Iowa, Illinois, Indiana, Ohio, Michigan and Wisconsin have passed through our streets. . . ." (Many were bound for California "but a large portion" also for Oregon.) "We also notice many families from southeast Missouri and especially large droves of cattle &c. from the same section . . . [crossing the river here]."

The Liberty (Mo.) *Weekly Tribune* of May 26 reported: "The stock and emigrants that have crossed at St. Joseph up to this time [May___?] sum up as follows. Loose cattle 16,500 head. Add, to this the yoke cattle, not counted in the droves and the number will reach 18,000 head. Horses and mules 1050; persons 2000, wagons, 500."

Ref: St. Joseph *Gazette*, May 3, 10, 1854; Liberty *Weekly Tribune*, May 26, 1854.

❡ April-June.—No register of westbound traffic was kept at Fort Kearny (Neb.) in 1854. Missouri newspapers published information on the emigrant, and merchant trains, as received from incoming travelers, and a Fort Kearny correspondent.

On May 12 the Weston *Reporter* stated that Duncan McDonnell (Macdonell) and Henry Adams "just in" from Fort Laramie, had met a good many trains and emigrants on the road (the first train was seen about April 27, on the north side of the Platte, some 20 miles east of Fort Kearny). They reported, also, that (1) Indians, except the Cheyennes, were "very friendly"; (2) a "good many" Mormons were on the route; (3) a great number of cattle and fine horses were being taken west; (4) all were getting along well. (On, or about May 12, the "advance train" of California-bound emigrants reached the North Platte crossing. An emigrant train from Wisconsin arrived at Salt Lake City on June 2.)

The first emigration passed Fort Kearny on May 3, according to "White Bear," in a May 20 letter from that post. He estimated the emigration would be "at least one third smaller" than in 1853—"particularly in the number of Cattle, and, in fact in all kinds of stock." (The stock was of "a very inferior quality," he thought, "compared with the last seasons.") Indians ("the Kaws of Kansas," he said), near the Big Blue, had given emigrants "considerable trouble from all accounts." (One Kansa? had been killed while driving off a cow.) Pawnees (by report) had stolen some cattle near Old Fort Kearny.

Emigrant J. M. Wright, in a May 12 letter (written while on the Little Blue) stated: "The emigration, I think, may be regarded as small, and almost one-half for Oregon, composed principally of horses and cattle, and some as fine as you ever saw. . . ." At Fort Kearny, on May 18, he wrote: "I now think it likely the emigration will be large. There is a perfect crowd here of cows; bells jingle all around."

After traveling in from Fort Laramie (to Independence) during the latter half of May, the mail party reported that (1) from the post to the States "trains of cattle and emigrant parties were visible almost every hour of the day; (2) in "one or two instances where the number was kept, as many as 10,000 head of cattle were passed, and them owned by only two or three companies" (stock on the road was estimated to be "as many if not more" than in 1853); (3) freighting operations to Salt Lake were "much increased" over 1853 (the first freight trains from Independence met by the mail party were those of Mr. Clarkson, and Mr. Patterson).

"White Bear," in a letter of June 19 from Fort Kearny, said the emigration was "much larger" than had been anticipated early in the spring. From "a rough calculation," he thought "not over half" as much stock had passed as in 1853 (when the count of cattle was 105,000 head). He noted "some [diarrhea] deaths here of the Emigrants and on the road" since his May 20 letter. ("Mr. Riley," of Independence—in charge of Liggett & Moore's train was one such victim. He died on May 12.)

The "mass of the emigration" had passed Fort Kearny before June 20—as reported by Captain Wharton (post commandant) arriving at St. Louis, on leave. Among the late-starting Mormons (*see* p. 1220) there had been some cases of cholera. (The cholera had started among the Mormon emigrants before they left the Westport, Mo., camps. As soon as they "were fairly on their way" it disappeared—according to eastbound Mormon "Mr. Lunt.") Wharton said a "very large quantity of stock" was crossing the plains.

After the "June" Salt Lake mail reached Independence (on June 29) an Independence correspondent commented: "It is estimated that not as many emigrants, other than Mormons, by one-half are on the road, nor as many cattle and horses by one-third or one-half."

Ref: St. Joseph (Mo.) *Gazette*, June 14, July 5, 12, 19, 1854; Liberty (Mo.) *Weekly Tribune*, June 9, 1854; *Weekly Missouri Statesman*, Columbia, June 9, 1854; *Jefferson Inquirer*, Jefferson City, June 17, July 22, 1854; *Missouri Republican*, St. Louis, May 17, June 2, July 9, August 13, 31, November 2, 1854. (The November 2 *Republican*, from a California source, stated: "The influx of immigrants over the plains this season is variously estimated between 18,000 and 20,000.") The New York *Daily Times*, September 9, 1854, from an Oregon news source, reported that J. B. Morgan, of Eddysville, Iowa, who arrived at Portland, overland, on July 25, said there were about 400 wagons on their way to Oregon, besides many droves of cattle.

℄ Spring.—Dr. Philo R. Hoy, "an ardent and successful naturalist of Racine, Wis.," who reached Lexington, Mo., in mid-April, subsequently "made various excursions, some of them into Kansas," and returned home in June—having gathered together "many species of birds, reptiles, and fishes. . . ."

Ref: 33d Cong., 2d Sess., *H. Misc. Doc. No. 37* (Serial 807), p. 88; or, *Ninth Annual Report* of the Smithsonian Institution.

℄ Spring-Summer.—Westport, Mo., merchants Charles E. Kearney and William R. Bernard (partners since 1853), this year (as later reported) outfitted 822 wagons at their establishment for the New Mexico and mountain trade.

(In 1853 it had been 600 wagons; in 1855 they outfitted 1,217 wagons.)

Ref: *History of Jackson County, Missouri* (1881), p. 352.

℄ May 1.—Joseph B. Chiles (one-time Jackson county, Mo., resident; and now of Napa, Calif.) left Independence, Mo., on his fourth *westbound* overland journey. (His previous trips *to* California had been made in 1841, 1843, and 1848.)

At the start, Chiles had "several loaded wagons," 72 work cattle, and 22 head of Durhams. On the road he brought more cattle; later had losses (both wagons and stock) on the Carson route. But he arrived at Sacramento on October 2 with 115 head of fine cattle.

Ref: *Missouri Republican*, St. Louis, November 30, 1854 (from Sacramento *Union* of October 3). In Helen S. Giffen, *Trail-Blazing Pioneer Colonel Joseph Ballinger Chiles* (San Francisco, 1969), p. 87, it is stated that "Chiles had a thousand head of sheep when he crossed the South Platte," and that he "lost almost the entire herd" while making the crossing.

℄ May 1.—An Ohio company (including John A. Martin of Dayton, and D. J. Storms of Franklin) left Independence, Mo., for California, driving "several hundred head" of cattle.

Up to arrival at Fort Laramie (on, or before June 13), they lost but two of the herd.

Ref: New York *Daily Tribune*, July 15, 1854 (from Dayton *Gazette* of July 11).

❡ May 2.—(Jones) Creech & (Armistead) Dawson signed a government contract to transport army supplies overland from Fort Leavenworth to Fort Union, N. M., during the summer, at the rate of $7.96 per 100 pounds. Sureties for the $50,000 bond were Elijah Cody, W. H. Bell, and Samuel Fernandis.

Ref: 33d Cong., 2d Sess., *Sen. Ex. Doc. No. 46* (Serial 752), p. 11; or, 33d Cong., 2d Sess., *H. Ex. Doc. No. 68* (Serial 788), p. 11.

❡ May 3.—Three days late (due to snow, rain, and swollen streams), the "April" Salt Lake mail (brought from Fort Laramie by "Mr. [John] Jamison") arrived at Independence, Mo. Passengers in the stage were the Hon. Lazarus H. Reid, recently chief justice of Utah territory, and 10 Mormons (some bound for the British Isles), on mission work.

Ref: *Missouri Republican*, St. Louis, May 5, 6, 1854; *Weekly Missouri Statesman*, Columbia, May 12, 1854; Liberty (Mo.) *Weekly Tribune*, May 12, 1854; New York *Daily Tribune*, May 9, 13, 1854. In the Liberty *Tribune* of September 15, 1854, the mail driver "Jamison," is identified as John Jamison—once a printer at Independence, Mo.

❡ May 5.—A party of California-bound Missourians, traveling up the Kansas valley with a large drove of cattle, decided to locate in what became Tecumseh township, Shawnee county. These early settlers (according to W. W. Cone's history) were the families of J. K. Waysman, A. D. Hand, H. Walker, Albert Byler, Joshua Sartain, and Nathaniel Hedrick.

Ref: W. W. Cone, *Historical Sketch of Shawnee County* (1887), p. 10.

❡ May 5.—From Independence, Mo., it was reported: "The merchandise trains to Salt Lake and the Mexican territory have left, or are daily getting away from this point, Westport and Kansas [City]."

The "June" mail party from Santa Fe (which reached Independence on the 17th) met the "first merchant trains [for Santa Fe] . . . going along well at the lower Cimarron Springs," and "from that point to the [Missouri] line they were met almost daily."

One train for Salt Lake City which left Independence in May was that of William K. Sloan and L. Stewart, whose goods were freighted by the Barnes brothers of Independence.

A party of travelers from Salt Lake City (left May 1) reaching Fort Leavenworth on May 26, reported that from the number of merchant trains met "it is thought goods will be plenty in the valley this season." (Weston, St. Joseph, etc., were other starting points for Salt Lake-bound trains. Note April entries pp. 1199 and 1209.)

Ref: *Weekly Missouri Statesman*, Columbia, May 12, 1854; Liberty (Mo.) *Weekly Tribune*, June 30, 1854; *Annals of Wyoming*, Cheyenne, v. 4 (July, 1926), p. 259; New York *Daily Tribune*, June 6, 1854 (from St. Louis *Daily Democrat*).

❡ May 6.—The Delaware Indians, by treaty made at Washington, D. C., ceded to the United States their lands (all lying north of

Kansas river) in "Kansas," except (1) a tract of about 275,000 acres, and (2) the 39 sections previously sold to the Wyandots.

They ceded, also, their interest in the Delaware "outlet," for $10,000, which was to be paid (in shares of $2,000, and at $250 per chief each year, until spent) to the Delawares' five old chiefs: Captain Ketchum, Sarcoxey, Segondyne, Ne-con-he-cond, and Kock-ka-to-wha.

Four sections of land were to be confirmed to the Munsee Indians, upon payment by them of $2.50 per acre.

Nine Delawares signed the treaty: Sarcoxey, Ne-con-he-cond, Kock-ka-to-wha, Qua-cor-now-ha (or, James Segondyne), Ne-sha-pa-na-cumin (or, Charles Journeycake), Que-sha-to-wha (or, John Ketchum), Pondoxy (or, George Bullet), Kock-kock-quas (or, James Ketchum), and Ah-lah-a-chick (or, James Conner). Among the witnesses: Thomas Johnson, Benjamin F. Robinson (Indian agent), and Henry Tiblow (interpreter).

Ref: Kappler, *op. cit.*, v. 2, pp. 614-618; annals, pp. 177, 179 (for origin of the Delaware outlet), and p. 338 (for Munsee Indians' location, 1854-1858); Annie H. Abel's "Indian Reservations in Kansas . . .," in *KHC*, v. 8, pp. 88, 89. The original treaty is preserved in the archives of the Kansas State Historical Society.

❡ May 8.—The Rev. Jotham Meeker of Ottawa Baptist Mission (east of present Ottawa) wrote: "Learn that many White families are breaking over the rules of the Government, and are actually settling and opening farms within from 12 to 15 and 25 miles' from us."

When Kansas became a territory, officially, on May 30, the news was not long in reaching Ottawa mission. In a June 1 diary entry, Meeker wrote: "Learn that Nebraska and Kansas Territories are organized, that the Shawanoes have sold their lands, and that emigrants are squatting around us in great numbers."

Meeker noted, on June 17, the brief visit of three Indiana families (Cart, Miner, and Shaw) who planned "to settle on the Peoria lands, some 5 or 6 miles S. E. of us"; and commented: "Learn that many others are coming—so that, all of a sudden, we are to be surrounded by White settlements. Next day (18th) he recorded: "Learn that among the settlers (Whites) adjoining the Ottawa line whiskey shops have been opened [where Sac Indians, and some of the Ottawas, too, were getting liquor]."

Ref: Jotham Meeker's "Diary."

❡ May 10.—The Shawnee Indians, by treaty made at Washington, D. C., ceded to the United States all of their estimated 1,600,000-acre reserve in "Kansas," out of which a 200,000-acre tract was re-ceded to them.

The diminished Shawnee reserve was bounded (as before) by the Kansas river on the north; the state of Missouri on the east; other Indian reserves on the south. But the new western limit was a line parallel to, and 30 miles west of, the Missouri state line.

Treaty terms provided for dividing much of the 200,000 acres by allotment in severalty (200 acres for each individual—including absentee, and adopted, Shawnees). Two Shawnee settlements—Black Bob's and Long Tail's—preferred to retain lands in common. For them, communal assignment of 200 acres per person was provided.

Specific grants of land were made to three Shawnee missions: 1,920 acres for the Methodist Church, South (to include the Indian manual labor school); 320 acres for the Friends' Shawnee labor school; 160 acres to the American Baptist Missionary Union. Also, five acres to the Shawee Methodist church, and two acres to the Shawnee Baptist church (including, in each case, a meetinghouse and graveyard).

Eight Shawnees signed the treaty: Joseph Parks, Black Hoof, George McDougal, Long Tail, George Bluejacket, Graham Rogers, Wa-wah-che-pa-e-kar (or, Black Bob), and Henry Bluejacket. Among the witnesses were Agent Benjamin F. Robinson, and Charles Bluejacket, interpreter.

Ref: Kappler, *op. cit.,* v. 2, pp. 618-626; *KHC,* v. 8, p. 93.

❡ May 11.—En route to Washington for land cession treaty-making, delegations of Miamis, and the confederated Wea & Piankeshaw and Kaskaskia & Peoria nations, accompanied by their agent Ely Moore, and Baptiste Peoria, interpreter, arrived at St. Louis. They continued their journey east on May 12.

Ref: OIA, Letters Received from Osage River Agency, National Archives Microcopy 234, Roll 644 (A. Cumming letter of May 12, 1854).

❡ May 13.—Bvt. Lt. Col. William R. Montgomery (also, Capt. Nathaniel Lyon, 2d Lt. Marshall T. Polk, and Bvt. 2d Lt. Robert F. Hunter) and two Second infantry companies ("B" and "C") arrived at Fort Riley (from Jefferson Barracks, Mo., by way of Fort Leavenworth). Montgomery assumed command of the post (from Maj. Albemarle Cady) on May 15.

At the end of May Fort Riley's garrison consisted of two Sixth infantry companies and two of Second infantry. *See, also,* May 27 annals entry.

Ref: Fort Riley post returns, May, 1854 (microfilm from National Archives, in KHi); New York *Daily Times,* April 15, 1854 (for Army General Orders No. 3, April 7, 1854). Asst. Surg. James Simons reached Fort Riley on May 21.

❡ May 13.—At Fort Riley, Alexander Lee signed a contract to "execute all the masonry of brick and stone for the barracks and quarters . . ." at the post. (He was to supply "a ration to each person employed, and their transportation from and to Fort Leavenworth.") *See* pp. 1155, 1156, for buildings erected in 1853.

Fort Riley was described in "Leavenworth's" September 8, 1854, letter:

"On one side stand the officers' quarters—houses a story and a half high, built of white limestone, with wide piazzas. They are spacious and tasteful structures. On two other sides of the square are the barracks for the soldiers. These are two stories high with porticos on either side. Connected with the garrison is a large and well cultivated garden. An object of no little interest here is the very copious and never-failing spring which supplies the inhabitants with all their water. . . ."

The November, 1854, quartermaster general's report stated: "Major Ogden, who has direction of the work [at Fort Riley] reports the erection of three double blocks of officers' quarters, and four sets of soldiers' barracks: two of the latter require shingling, flooring, and plastering. These buildings when completed will afford accommodation for four full companies." (Estimated cost of completing "the works at that post": $29,300.)

Ref: 33d Cong., 2d Sess., Sen. Ex. Doc. No. 1 (Serial 747), p. 73; 34th Cong., 1st Sess., Sen. Ex. Doc. No. 7 (Serial 815), p. 3; "Webb Scrapbooks," v. 1, p. 142a (in KHi library).

❧ May.—In addition to the *Australia, Banner State, Clara, F. X. Aubrey, Genoa, Honduras, Isabel, Jas. H. Lucas, Polar Star, Sam Cloon,* and *Sonora*—all of which also had been on the "middle Missouri" in April—these steamboats made one, or more, trips up the Missouri to points above the Kaw's mouth in May: *Delaware, Edinburg, Michigan,* and *New Lucy.*

In an October 9, 1854, letter, "St. Louis" commented that the *Polar Star* was the best and "fastest boat on the Missouri," usually making the St. Louis-to-Kansas (City), Mo., run in about three days. He listed the *New Lucy* and *F. X. Aubrey* as "next in rank," and rated the *Banner State, Edinburg,* and *Clara* as "very good."

Ref: Issues of the St. Joseph (Mo.) *Gazette* and *Missouri Republican,* St. Louis, and H. Miles Moore's "Journal" (*loc. cit.*), for May and June, 1854; "Webb Scrapbooks," v. 1, p. 172 (for "St. Louis").

❧ May 17.—The Iowa Indians, by treaty made at Washington, D. C., ceded to the United States 400 sections of land in northeastern "Kansas," but retained a diminished reserve bounded as follows:

"Beginning at the mouth of the Great Nemaha River where it empties into the Missouri; thence down the Missouri river to the mouth of Noland's Creek; thence due south one mile; thence due west to the south fork of the Nemaha; thence down the said fork with its meanders of said river to the place of beginning."

The treaty provided for a grant of 320 acres (including mission improvements), and a 160-acre timber tract, to the board of foreign missions of the Presbyterian Church; and for a grant of 320 acres ("to be selected by him in 'Wolf's Grove' . . .") to John B. Roy, interpreter for the Iowas.

Four Iowas signed the treaty: Nan-chee-ning-a (or, No Heart), Shoon-ty-ing-a (or, Little Wolf), Wa-moon-na-ka (or, Man who Steals), and Nar-ge-ga-rash (or, British). Witnesses included Daniel Vanderslice, agent and John B. Roy.

Ref: Kappler, *op. cit.,* v. 2, pp. 628-631; *KHC,* v. 8, p. 91.

❲ May 18.—The Sacs & Foxes of the Missouri, by treaty made at Washington, D. C., ceded to the United States their lands in northeastern "Kansas," reserving a tract of 32,000 acres (to be selected either within, or outside the limits of the ceded lands). Also, they were to retain, for two years, a section of land at "the site of their present farm and mill."

The treaty provided, also, for a grant of 160 acres to the board of foreign missions of the Presbyterian Church.

Five Sacs & Foxes signed the treaty: Pe-to-o-ke-mah (or, Hard Fish, Mo-less (or, Wah-pe-nam-mah, or Sturgeon), Ne-son-quoit (or, Bear), Mo-ko-ho-ko (or Jumping Fish), and No-ko-what (or, Fox). Witnesses included Agent Daniel Vanderslice, and Peter Cadue, interpreter.

Ref: Kappler, *op. cit.*, v. 2, pp. 631-633; *KHC*, v. 7, p. 91.

❲ May 18.—The Kickapoo Indians, by treaty made at Washington, D. C., ceded to the United States all their lands in northeastern "Kansas," except a tract of 150,000 acres in the western part of their old reserve.

The treaty provided that Peter Cadue, their "faithful friend and interpreter," was to have 640 acres of land (to include his home and improvements on Cadue's creek).

Five Kickapoos signed the treaty: Pah-kah-kah (or, John Kennekuk), Kap-i-o-ma (or, the Fox Carrier), No-ka-wat (or, the Fox Hair), Pe-sha-gon (or, Tug made of Bear Skin), and Ke-wi-sah tuk (or, Walking Bear, or Squire). Witnesses included Agent Daniel Vanderslice, and Peter Cadue.

Ref: Kappler, *op. cit.*, v. 2, pp. 634-636; *KHC*, v. 8, p. 90. The Kickapoos' head chief —Mah-she-nah—did not go to Washington. *See* Vanderslice's diary (*loc. cit.*, p. 172) for mention of Mah-she-nah as head chief in August, 1854.

❲ May 20.—The Santa Fe mail reached Independence, Mo. "Jones" was the conductor; W. F. Dever (or Deaver?) and "Kelly," were his assistants.

Cheyennes (some 40; armed with bows and arrows) had surrounded the mail party one noon (on the Arkansas?) and run off all the mules. When Jones aimed his gun "at the chief's head," the Indians became friendly; and were given the provisions they asked for—after the mules had been returned.

Ref: *Missouri Republican*, St. Louis, May 27, 1854; Liberty (Mo.) *Weekly Tribune*, June 2, 1854, and February 2, 1855 (for W. F. Dever); *Weekly Missouri Statesman*, Columbia, May 5, 1854.

❲ May 22.—The controversial Kansas-Nebraska bill passed in the house by a vote of 113 to 100. (The "aye" votes came from 44 free-state, and 69 slave-state representatives; 91 free-state, and nine slave-state members voted against the measure.)

Ref: *The Congressional Globe*, Washington; Daniel W. Wilder's *The Annals of Kansas* (Topeka, 1886), pp. 43, 44.

❦ May 25-26.—The U. S. senate passed the Kansas-Nebraska bill "at 1:15 a. m., May 26, but at the session of Thursday, May 25. Immediately a salute of 100 guns was fired from Capitol Hill. Intoxication and anger made memorable the night scenes in the Senate and House. . . ."—Wilder.

Ref: Wilder, *op. cit.*, pp. 44, 45 (for above, and additional data).

❦ May 26.—Arriving at Fort Leavenworth "by the mail stage" were Seth M. Blair (U. S. district attorney for Utah territory), "Gen." James Ferguson, and six Mormons en route to Europe on missionary service. (These gentlemen reached St. Louis May 30, aboard the *Sam Cloon*.)

Ref: *Missouri Republican*, St. Louis, June 2, 1854; St. Joseph (Mo.) *Gazette*, June 14, 1854; New York *Daily Tribune*, June 6, 8, 1854.

❦ May 27.—Jotham Meeker wrote in his diary: "California emigrants have passed [Ottawa Baptist Mission—*see* April 15 entry] more or less perhaps every day from April 15 until last Monday, May 22—Have not noticed any passing since until this evening— two or 3 wagons and a small drove of cattle encamp in front of our house. Several of my neighbors have tried to keep count of the number of loose Cattle that have been driven along this route during this spring, who make the number to be about 30,000."

In various May diary entries he had recorded some of the westbound traffic: *May 1*—"Am told that over 2000 loose Cattle and 30 Wagons passed here on yesterday for California—See three large companies pass on to-day with perhaps 12 or 1500. Drovers stop with us to-night." *May 2*—"Several Droves of Cattle pass." *May 13*—"Streams are all near overflowing their banks. Near 800 cattle pass for California—other droves are stopped by high water within hearing distance of us." *May 15*—"Some 5 or 600 Cattle pass, but the drovers think they are about the last of the emigration." *May 16*—"Several hundred Cattle encamp in front of our house." *May 17*—"Upwards of 600 Cattle leave here this morning, 2 or 300 pass to-day, and others are encamped near us." *May 18*—"See two companies of Cattle & Wagons pass to-day." *May 19*—"One company passes." *May 20*—"See one company pass to-day." *May 22*—"Two Wagons & some Cattle pass on this morning for the West." On *June 2* he noted: "Californians still pass occasionally."

Ref: Jotham Meeker's "Diary."

❦ May 27.—Maj. Albemarle Cady with a battalion of Sixth infantry (Companies F and H) left Fort Riley, under orders (of April 7) to proceed to the site of old Fort Atkinson (west of present

Dodge City), establish a temporary camp, and remain till "some time in October." His command (around 150 men) included these officers: Capt. Thomas Hendrickson, Asst. Surg. Aquila T. Ridgely, Lt. Levi C. Bootes, 2d Lt. Joseph L. Tidball, 2d Lt. Darius Clark, Bvt. 2d Lt. James A. Smith, and Bvt. 2d Lt. Augustus Plummer.

The battalion camped at Cottonwood creek on June 1 (probably having struck the Santa Fe trail at Cottonwood Crossing); left there June 2; reached old Fort Atkinson (*see* p. 1169) on June 13; and set up summer camp. When Fauntleroy's command passed there in July, it was reported that Cady's command ("quite comfortably situated") had "pitched their tents on the site of Fort Atkinson, which, by the bye, has all tumbled down since last fall."

(On October 2 Major Cady and command abandoned the site, and marched for Fort Riley; left that post October 23; arrived at Fort Leavenworth on the 29th; departed on October 30—for Jefferson Barracks—aboard the *Genoa*.)

Ref: Fort Riley post returns, May, 1854 (microfilm from National Archives, in KHi); Fort Atkinson post returns (microfilm from National Archives, in KHi); New York *Daily Times*, April 15, 1854 (for Army General Orders No. 3, April 7, 1854); Muster rolls of Company H, Sixth U. S. infantry, 1854 (originals in KHi ms. division); 33d Cong., 2d Sess., *Sen. Ex. Doc. No. 46* (Serial 752), p. 21 (for the *Genoa*); *Missouri Republican*, St. Louis, August 25, 1854. The September, 1854, post return for Fort Atkinson states: "This post abandoned Oct. 2/54 per G. O. No. 5 (H. Q. A.) Sept 6/54." *See* 33d Cong., 1st Sess., *H. Misc. Doc. No. 47* (Serial 741), and 33d Cong., 1st Sess., *H. Report No. 223* (Serial 743), for attempt to get Fort Atkinson reestablished.

❧ May 27.—"Kansas" resident "H. B. (Benjamin Harding), writing from his "Spring Hill Farm, Nebraska, alias Kansas," stated:

"I must say *candidly* that Nebraska is *one* of the greatest humbugs of the age. A small portion of the country near the Missouri River and along the various smaller streams which abound in the Territory can hardly be excelled in any portion of the world (that is where timber is not too scarce) and affords many very valuable locations for *stock raising;* and there are many places on the various emigrant roads where money can be made at corn-raising and otherwise. Aside from that the country is of little value. Hill lands are generally poor. Farther back the country grows more level and the high prairies produce good crops generally for many miles, say 50 to 150, still further on it grows poorer until it becomes a barren waste. The high grounds furnish very little timber."

Ref: New York *Daily Tribune*, August 14, 1854 (from Reading [Pa.] *Gazette* of June 12); or, "Webb Scrapbooks," v. 1, p. 92. *See* comment on "H. B.'s" identity in annals entry of April 21, 1854.

❧ May 28.—From Fort Leavenworth, A. H. Johnston (an Indianian on a visit to "Kansas") wrote:

"To-day, and for several days past, persons from Missouri have been landing from steamboats, and with their hatchets are marking off their claims in the Indian country, not knowing whether the '*bill*' has passed Congress or not. . . ."

Ref: "Webb Scrapbooks," v. 1, p. 42.

❡ May 29-31.—Arrivals at Independence, Mo., in this period included (1) the Salt Lake mail (in William Allison's charge), on May 29; and (2) from Salt Lake City the small party of Oliver H. Cogswell, merchant, which included his wife, and Isaac Rogers, on May 31.

Ref: Liberty (Mo.) *Weekly Tribune,* June 9, 1854.

❡ May 30.—The Kansas-Nebraska bill, which created, and opened to white settlement the territories of Kansas and Nebraska, was signed by Pres. Franklin Pierce. Three boundaries of Kansas were set as they are today: The 40th parallel on the north, the Missouri border on the east, the 37th parallel on the south. To the west, Kansas territory extended to the summit of the Rocky mountains.

"The Kansas-Nebraska act also repealed the Missouri Compromise of 1820, which had prohibited slavery in the area of the Louisiana Purchase north of the line 36° 30', with the exception of Missouri, and provided instead that the people of the territories might decide their own institutions for themselves. This was the principle of popular sovereignty which had been applied earlier to the territories of Utah and New Mexico in the Compromise of 1850."— *KHQ,* v. 21, p. 1.

Ref: *Statutes at Large,* 33d Cong., 1st Sess., 1854. See *KHQ,* v. 21, pp. 1-7 ("The Kansas Territorial Centennial").

❡ May 30.—The united tribes of Kaskaskias & Peorias, and Weas & Piankeshaws, by treaty made at Washington, D. C., ceded to the United States the larger part of their two small reserves in "Kansas," but retained a quantity equal to 160 acres for allotment in severalty to each member; and 6,400 acres as a national reserve.

The treaty provided for the grant of 640 acres to the American Indian Mission Association [for Wea Baptist Mission].

Seven united tribesmen signed the treaty: Kio-kaw-mo-zan, Ma-cha-ko-me-ah (or, David Lykins—white missionary, and adopted member), Sa-wa-ne-ke-ah (or, Wilson), Sha-cah-quah (or, Andrew Chick), Ta-ko-nah (or, Mitchel), Che-swa-wa (or, Rogers), and Yellow Beaver. Witnesses included Ely Moore, Indian agent, and Baptiste Peoria, interpreter.

Ref: Kappler, *op. cit.,* v. 2, pp. 636-639; *KHC,* v. 8, p. 92.

❡ June 1 (on, or about).—Bvt. Lt. Col. Edward J. Steptoe, Third U. S. artillery, and command, "under orders, by the plains, for California," set out from Fort Leavenworth on the military road to Fort Kearny.

Capt. Rufus Ingalls (assistant quartermaster) in his report, stated: "This command consisted of two companies of artillery, and about 85 dragoon recruits. In the Quartermaster's dept. there were some 130 citizen employés, as teamsters, ostlers, and herders; 450 mules, 300 horses, 70 wagons, &c. There were, on an average, 300 persons, soldiers and citizens, and nine officers." The 70 heavy baggage wagons were draw by six mules each; to the seven light wagons "were attached the horses, in strings of from 30 to 40."

After a 40-mile march, the command "was brought to a halt by the cholera, which raged rather fiercely for some days. It disappeared after some eight or ten had fallen victims." Subsequently "the whole command was unusually healthy." All the streams on the route were high. Ingalls stated: "We forded all until we reached the Big Blue, which had to be ferried."

Steptoe's command reached Fort Kearny on June 21; and arrived at Salt Lake City on August 31. The trip had required 92 days; the distance traveled was recorded as 1,216 miles. The command had marched on only 64 days— "making an average 19 miles per day." (Steptoe and troops remained in Utah over the winter, having orders to "secure the murderers of the late Captain Gunnison, if . . . practicable. . . .")

Ref: 34th Cong., 1st Sess., *Sen. Ex. Doc. No. 1* (Serial 811), pp. 152-156; *Missouri Republican,* St. Louis, October 17, 1854 (for report on Steptoe's command having arrived in Salt Lake City with "officers and men all well and stock in remarkably fine condition"; "only eight animals having been lost on the route").

℃ June.—At Westport, Mo., on the 3d, and at Independence, Mo., on the 5th, public meetings were held to organize for "mutual protection [of Jackson county Proslavery citizens] in claiming and holding lands in Kansas Territory, . . . in good faith and with a view to actual settlement. . . ."

The *Missouri Republican,* St. Louis, of June 14, editorialized: "They [the people of Jackson county] have as much right to go upon Kansas territory with their slaves and other property, as any fanatical son of New England and this right they will assert at all hazards. Their resolutions are calm but firm."

At the Independence meeting one resolution called for the appointment of a vigilance committee which would keep informed on progress of settlement in Kansas, and take "proper steps to prevent and resist" any infringement (or danger of) upon the "rights of Southern settlers."

Both at Westport and Independence, resolutions were passed urging citizens of other Missouri border counties to meet, organize, and take action to secure and guarantee the rights of southern emigrants to Kansas territory.

Free-State pioneer S. N. Wood, who arrived on the Missouri-Kansas border around June 20, later (1886) recollected: "The Pro-Slavery men from Missouri had met in Kansas and adopted a code of squatter laws, and the whole Territory seemed staked into claims. They had a register of claims, with an office at Westport, Missouri. One law of this remarkable code provided that Nebraska was for the North and Kansas for the South. One provision was, that every white-livered abolitionist who dared to set foot in Kansas should be hung.

Ref: "Webb Scrapbooks," v. 1, pp. 21, 21a (for clippings relating to the above meetings; one of which, if correctly dated, places the Independence meeting as on June 4); *Missouri Republican*, St. Louis, June 7, 14, 18; Malin's *The Nebraska Question . . .*, pp. 367, 368; *KHC*, v. 3, p. 428 (for S. N. Wood).

℄ June 5.—The Miami Indians, by treaty made at Washington, D. C., ceded to the United States all but 70,000 acres of their lands in eastern "Kansas."

The diminished reserve was to be apportioned as follows: 200 acres to be alloted in severalty to each tribal member, and, except for a 640-acre tract set aside for educational purposes, the remainder (some 20,000 acres) to be held in common, for the time being. There were treaty provisions applicable to the Miamis of Indiana, also.

Treaty signers were: Nah-we-lan-quah (or, Big Legs), Ma-cat-a-chin-quah (or, Little Doctor), Lan-a-pin-cha (or, Jack Hackley), So-ne-lan-gish-eah (or, John Bowrie), Wan-zop-e-ah; and five Indiana Miamis. Witnesses included Agent Ely Moore, and Baptiste Peoria, interpreter.

Kappler, *op. cit.*, v. 2, pp. 641-646; *KHC*, v. 8, pp. 91, 92.

℄ June.—Sir George Gore's "grand hunting company for the plains" was encamped west of Westport, Mo., in present Johnson county, on June 6, preparing to set out for Fort Laramie. A passerby wrote that he saw in the camp some 40 to 50 dogs ("mostly greyhounds and staghounds, of the most beautiful breeds"), a "large carriage, and probably a dozen large wagons [five yoke of oxen to each] to transport provisions, &c."; and that these, together "with the horses, men, &c.," made up "quite an imposing company."

Gore (who spent three years in the west) presumably got under way (to Fort Laramie) in June. It is said that Jim Bridger assisted in the outfitting; that Henry Chatillon and brother were with the English baronet when he set out; that when the company left Fort Laramie there were 41 men, four six-mule wagons, two three-yoke ox wagons, and 21 red-painted French carts, each drawn by two horses; that one wagon carried Sir George's guns (some 75 rifles; 12, or more, shotguns); that two wagons were loaded with fishing tackle and other sportsman's gear; that Gore had, also, such luxury items as a large linen tent, a collapsible brass bed, a portable iron table and iron washstand.

Ref: New York *Daily Tribune*, June 23, 1854; or, *KHQ*, v. 6, p. 316; J. Cecil Alter's *Jim Bridger* (Norman, Okla., c1962), p. 259; Montana Historical Society *Contributions*, Helena, v. 1 (1876), pp. 144-148, and v. 9, pp. 246-251.

℄ June.—Salt Lake-bound Mormons (immigrants from Wales, Scotland, England, and the Scandinavian countries, chiefly) were encamped in large numbers near Westport, Mo.

(In March it had been reported at Independence, Mo., that William Empey was in the area "buying cattle to out-fit some 6,000 [Mormon immigrants]";

that some 2,000 of them already had landed in the United States; and that the Mormons, this year "design making Westport and Kansas . . . their outfitting and starting points." Elder S. W. Richards, quoted in a London newspaper of June 2, 1854, stated: "At St. Louis, another agent of the Church co-operates with the agent sent from England. From thence the emigrants are forwarded still by steamboat to the camping grounds, which were last year at Keokuk in Iowa . . ., and this year at Kansas [City], in Jackson County, Missouri. . . . Here the emigrants find the teams which the agent has prepared. . . .")

The Chicago *Tribune* of June 6 contained this item: "A letter [of May __?] from Kansas [City] . . . states that the advance guard of the Mormon emigration over the plains this season, is encamped near that town. This body numbers 1,600 persons; they are chiefly Danes, Swedes, Norwegians, Welsh and English."

On his way from Independence to Fort Leavenworth on June 6, a traveler noted he "passed an encampment of 3,000[?] Mormons," between Kansas and Westport. ("They were in a fine forest. Some were sleeping in their wagons, but the most of them had tents, and the woods and fields adjoining in all directions were covered with these white and fragile dwellings . . . most of [these emigrants] . . . do not speak a word of English . . . The cholera is said to be among them. . . .")

The Independence *Occidental Messenger* of June 24(?) commented on "the Mormon Camp near Westport": "It looks like a great city built up in the beautiful prairie south of town. . . . They number now we believe about 1200, and still they come— every boat brings more or less of these infatuated beings. . . . It is the intention of those in charge of them, to start upon their journey across the plains this week, they are to move in bands, so that they will not impede the progress of each other."

Welshman John Johnson Davies (later) stated that his company of immigrants arrived in New Orleans March 18, 1854; got to St. Louis April 10; left on the 24th ("We had to stop a few times to bury the dead while going up the river"); and reached Kansas (City) in May. "After we got on shore," he wrote, "we camped close to the river. . . . The cholera was very bad among us by this time, and in a few days we moved to Mr. Magee's [Milton McGee's] plantation. . . . We buried quite a few of our brethren and sisters in this place [including Davies' in-laws]." (After six weeks "in these camps," they went to Westport and remained a few days making final preparations.) "We [a train of 50 wagons] started on the Plains on the 1st of July, 1854." (Mrs. Davies gave birth to a daughter between midnight and 1 A. M. the first night out, at Indian creek.) This Mormon train reached Salt Lake City in October. Davies recalled that a Danish train behind them, caught up near Fort Laramie;

and that it was the killing of a cow (by Sioux Indians) in the latter train that
led to the "Grattan massacre" of August 19.

See p. 1226 for large(?) Mormon camp west of Fort Leavenworth.

At Independence on June 30 the arrival "last night" of the Salt
Lake mail was reported. The account stated: "The first party of
Mormons were only out about 150 or 200 miles; *the other companies
of them go out by Fort Riley and open up a new road to Laramie.*"
(Italics supplied.)

This well may be the clue to the origin of the "Mormon trail"
which diverged northwestward (towards Fort Riley) from the
Santa Fe road's 110-mile creek crossing—a "Mormon trail" already
there when settlers arrived in the mid-1850's. Theodore Weichselbaum (in 1908) told of his journey from Kansas City to Ogden,
K. T., in December, 1857: "I followed the Santa Fe trail with my
three wagons until I reached the station at 110. From there I took
the Mormon trail . . . to Fort Riley. . . ." Questioned
about this trail, Weichselbaum said, "I only knew the road as the
Mormon road. Before and after I came to Ogden [just east of
Fort Riley] the Mormons traveled on that road, turning onto it
from the Santa Fe trail. They crossed the Kansas at Whisky Point
. . . and climbed the hill on the east side of where the hospital
now [1908] stands at Fort Riley, and thence across the country to
Fort Kearney, Neb., and from there to Salt Lake City. I don't
remember of any other emigration than the Mormons using that
road." Albe B. Whiting (who settled northwest of Fort Riley in
April, 1856) referred (in a 1910 address) to the "old Mormon trail,
said to have been made in 1846" (but this has no basis of fact),
which "left the Santa Fe trail at 110 Creek, in Osage county, and
bearing northwest crossed the Kaw at a ferry on the site of Pawnee
City. . . . Then the trail ran nearly due north till it met the
trails from Leavenworth and up-river towns, on the Little Blue.
. . ."

Incoming travelers brought various reports on the progress of the Mormon
trains of 1854. Out on the South Platte (in early August?) the Eldridge and
Pratt train had 120 head of cattle stampeded by buffalo. Travelers who reached
Weston, Mo., August 26 said they had met "a good many Mormons with freight
trains, getting along slowly; some even this side of Fort Kearny. . . ."
Eastbound Mormons (en route to Council Bluffs) who passed Fort Laramie a
few days after the "Grattan massacre" of August 19, said they had met "three
large trains of English, Danish, and other foreign emigrants on their way to
Utah, comprising in the whole, over two hundred wagons, besides many smaller
scattering companies. . . ." Samuel Machette (from Fort Laramie), who

started east August 16, reported at St. Louis that "the Mormon emigration this season is unusually large. . . ." "Mr. Lunt" (a Mormon) who reached Independence (from Salt Lake) August 22, estimated the 1854 emigration to Utah at about 4,000 souls. The Salt Lake mail party which started east on September 1 "met the last of the Mormon emigrants on the Sweetwater, doing well."

Ref: Liberty (Mo.) *Weekly Tribune*, March 17 (for Empey), June 30, 1854; E. W. Tullidge's *The History of Salt Lake City and Its Founders* [1886?], p. 655 (for Richards); Chicago *Daily Tribune*, June 6, 1854; New York *Daily Tribune*, June 23, 1854, or, *KHQ*, v. 6, pp. 315, 316 (for "3,000 Mormons . . .") ; *Utah Historical Quarterly*, Salt Lake City, v. 9 (July-October, 1941), pp. 159-161 (for Davies); *Weekly Missouri Statesman*, Columbia, July 7, 1854 (for June 30 item); *KHC*, v. 8, p. 239, v. 11, pp. 561, 569, v. 12, pp. 1, 2 (for Mormon trail in Kansas); *Jefferson Inquirer,* Jefferson City, Mo., September 16, 1854; *Missouri Republican,* St. Louis, August 31, September 9, October 17, 19, 1854; St. Joseph (Mo.) *Gazette,* September 20, 1854. See Charles Dawson's *Pioneer Tales of the ,Oregon Trail* (Topeka, 1912), pp. 66, 67, and 96, 97, for interesting, but undocumented statements about Mormon trails across Kansas. Not all the immigrant Mormons of 1854 outfitted on the western Missouri border. The Columbia *Weekly Missouri Statesman* of May 12, 1854, stated: "A train of twenty-one wagons belonging to Mormons from England and Wales passed through this place on Friday last [May 5]." There were, said this paper, 106 people (men, women, and children), and 125 head of cattle.

❡ June 6-7.—"Dakota" (going up the Missouri on a steamboat) wrote a letter in which were these comments:

Independence, Mo.—The Santa Fe business has "diminished there of late, and reverted to Westport, a thriving town. . . ."

Kansas (City) Mo.—"a place of about a thousand inhabitants situated on the high bluffs of the river. There is not very much business done there at present. . . ."

Fort Leavenworth, K. T.—"This is without exception the most beautiful place on the river. . . . [We] stepped on shore and ascended the hill to the barracks, about a quarter of a mile. . . . As far as the eye could reach on either hand, hill rose above hill in an almost endless series of undulations, beautiful streams were winding their sinuous course through fertile valleys, and the whole diversified with fine groves, gave to the view the air of enchantment. . . . At the foot of the landing is a large store-house, at which considerable business is done. On the summit of the bluff is a large plateau, on which the fort or rather village stands,—for it has far more the appearance of a beautiful village than fort. In the center are three or four large buildings much like 'city blocks,' in which the soldiers have their mess and lodge. At a little distance from these and at the several corners are a number of fine houses, the residences of the officers. In the rear is a splendid grove of elms, with their branches bending to the ground. . . . This is the promenade ground. This beautiful place is fixed upon as the seat of Government of Kansas Territory. . . ." [Gov. Andrew H. Reeder arrived at Fort Leavenworth on October 7, aboard the *Polar Star.* He made his headquarters at the post till November 23; then removed to the Shawnee Methodist Mission.]

St. Joseph, Mo.—"Here . . . the [Missouri's] current is doing extensive mischief in wearing away the banks and carrying downstream the finest portion of the city. . . . Within a year an hundred feet has been washed away from Main st., and in some places as many yards have fallen in. The inhabitants are beginning to build back on the hills. . . . St. Joseph contains about five thousand inhabitants, and is fast increasing in population." [In July "Philos" wrote of St. Joseph: "This certainly is a very remarkable place. Although the river has washed away its levee, and encroached far upon the town, taking away large warehouses, stores and dwellings, it is going ahead in business, prosperity and enterprise, and increasing in population, as if there had been no such calamity." "Plymouth," in a November letter, commented that the Missouri "has carried off whole blocks of fine stores [at St. Joseph], while at Weston it has taken the opposite course and left entirely—the landing being some distance below town, and the channel of the river nearly half a mile from the paved landing, where I saw steamboats lying when there in the spring."]

Ref: New York *Daily Tribune,* July 4, 1854, or "Webb Scrapbooks," v. 1, pp. 54a, 55; *Kansas Weekly Herald,* Leavenworth, October 8 and November 24, 1854 (for Reeder); *Missouri Republican,* St. Louis, July 12, 1854 (for "Philos"); *Weekly Missouri Statesman,* Columbia, December 1, 1854 (for "Plymouth's" November 21 letter, from St. Joseph).

℃ June.—The "Bridge on the Nemahah, will soon be in good order again for crossing," reported the St. Joseph, Mo., *Gazette* of June 7. "There are now at that place [*i. e.,* the vicinity of the Oregon-California trail St. Joseph branch ford of the Nemaha], about 40 [*i. e.,* 90] miles from the Missouri river, about 20 families." (As shown on the land office plats, the crossing was in the SE¼ of Sec. 23, T. 1 S., R. 12 E. This was some nine miles north of present Seneca.)

In his *History of Kansas: and Emigrant's Guide* . . . (Akron, 1855), p. 58, J. Butler Chapman (who spent some time in Kansas territory during the latter half of 1854) wrote: "In 1852 [*i. e.,* 1853?] Wallace B. Moore [*i. e.,* W(illiam?) W. Moore] made a descent upon the Nemehaw, settled at the crossing of the California road, and built a bridge . . . But his bridge was too low and was washed away. He has laid out a town at the old crossing, named Arbana [Urbana], but his own residence is all that now [late 1854?] graces the city, and that a log cabin, without a floor." (Chapman had been a guest of the Moores at some time in 1854.) An 1876 history states that W. W. Moore came from St. Joseph, Mo., in January, 1854, and located near the Nemaha crossing later known as Baker's Ford; that Walter D. Beeles came in February (settling "north of Moore's place"); and that other settlers followed. The Andreas-Cutler (1883) *History of Kansas* says that Moore and Beeles built a toll bridge about half a mile below the Baker's Ford point; and that they felled a large elm tree in the ford, forcing the public, for a time, to use their bridge; but in 1855(?) a flood carried the elm tree downstream, and it swept the bridge away!

The "house of W. W. Moore, where the St. Joseph road crosses the Nemaha," was named as the "place of election" for the 18th election district (erected by proclamation of Governor Reeder, February 24, 1855). The name generally applied to his location was "Moorestown." (On the Whitman & Searl "Map of Eastern Kansas," 1856, it appears as "Moorestown.") But *Urbana* was a post office from March 3 till June 19, 1855 (John Jett, postmaster).

In February, 1855, the 12th district, Kansas territory census-taker wrote of the persons residing "on the main Nemaha, and in the vicinity of the crossing of the St Joseph Road," as follows: "At this place a Town has been laid out by one Martin of St. Joseph but which is claimed by W. W. Moore who resides at the place. Several families have been residing in this vicinity since August 1853. The place is ninety miles from St. Joseph forty-five miles from Woodward and Marshall's on the Blue, three miles from the Nebraska line and between fifty and sixty miles from the Kansas River due North."—Written in original 1855 census (in KHi archives). Part of the 12th district was, by proclamation of Governor Reeder, February 24, 1855, included in the newly created 18th district.

Ref: St. Joseph (Mo.) *Gazette*, June 7, 1854; Andreas-Cutler, *op. cit.*, pp. 941, 942, and 950 (biography of James Parsons); J. Butler Chapman, *History of Kansas* . . . (Akron, 1855), pp. 58, 59; *KHC*, v. 3, pp. 248, 256; Robert W. Baughman's *Kansas Post Offices* (Topeka, c1961), pp. 131, 209; *Kansas Weekly Herald*, Leavenworth, October 20, 1855, and November 8, 1856 (wherein his name is given as William W. Moore); *Weekly Kansas Chief*, Troy, November 23, 1893 (*see* bound clipping volume of this issue in KHi library), which has account of Moore's connection with Thomas J. Sutherland's activities of 1852; Nemaha County "Clippings," v. 1, p. 35 (in KHi library); *Kansas Herald of Freedom*, Lawrence, August 18, 1855 (which notes: "W. W. Moore keeps a public house on the St. Joseph and California road . . ."). In the Andreas-Cutler history (*op. cit.*), p. 942, it is stated that Farmington, in Nemaha county, was located on the NW¼ of Sec. 26 and NE¼ of Sec. 27, T. 1 S., R. 12 E. "being southwest of old 'Urbana' a paper town started by W. W. Moon [Moore] at Baker's Ford. Thomas Smith and James Parsons succeeded W. W. Moon [Moore] at that point."

❡ June 7-8.—"The Genoa and Sonora passed up Wednesday [7th] and Thursday . . . for the mouth of the Yellowstone. They have gone up for the Fur Companies."—St. Joseph (Mo.) *Gazette*, June 14.

The *Genoa* (Capt. Joseph Throckmorton), chartered to Robert Campbell, St. Louis, carried Harvey, Primeau & Co. freight; and Indian annuity goods for the Upper Missouri tribes. (On her return, she passed St. Joseph July 12, apparently.)

The *Sonora* (Capt. Joseph La Barge), chartered to Pierre Chouteau, Jr. & Co., carried the American Fur Company's goods and supplies. (On her return, she passed St. Joseph about July 14.)

Ref: St. Joseph *Gazette*, June 14, 1854; *Missouri Republican*, St. Louis, June 3, 14, July 16, 1854; John E. Sunder's *The Fur Trade on the Upper Missouri, 1840-1865* (c1965), pp. 162, 163.

❡ June 10.—An Ohioan, after a journey from Independence, Mo., to Council Bluffs, Iowa, by stage, and by steamboat, made these comments in a letter from the latter place:

Kansas (City), Mo.—"is not a place of much importance. There are some good store-houses on the shore at the landing, but the site for the town is rough and not at all attractive. It is my judgment that it will *not* be a second St. Louis."

Westport, Mo.—"This is back from the river . . . but the California trade and outfit business has made it a point of some importance. There are several fine large brick buildings going up . . . it does not seem to me to have a great prospect."

Fort Leavenworth, K. T.—"the only things that look like forts being a pair of block-houses, with musket port-holes. The barracks are extensive and appear to be in fine order. The store-houses, &c., are also extensive, and are substantially built of stone. There is a farm of 1,000 acres that is cultivated by Uncle Sam. It is a beautiful tract and in a high state of cultivation. . . . The landing is of rocks, and is one of the finest and most substantial on the river. . . ."

Weston, Mo.—"is a flourishing place, and does an immense business in the hemp trade. It has about 3,000 inhabitants."

Ref: New York *Daily Tribune*, June 27, 1854, or, *see KHQ*, v. 6, pp. 315, 316.

❡ June 10.—Three miles west of Fort Leavenworth, in Salt creek valley, about 300(?) persons met to form a "Squatters' Association" for the regulation and protection of land claims. Lewis Burnes, Weston, Mo., was chairman, J. H. R. Cundiff, St. Joseph, Mo., served as secretary. The resolutions committee members were D. A. N. Grover, David Dodge, Dr. ___ ___ Bonifant, Henry Kitchen, and James N. Burnes.

Among the resolutions passed: (1) "That we are in favor of *bona fide* squatter sovereignty . . ."; (8) "That we recognize the institution of slavery as already existing in the territory, and recommend to slaveholders to introduce their property as fast as possible"; (9) "That we afford protection to no Abolitionists as settlers of Kansas territory"; (10) "That a 'Vigilance Committee' of thirteen be appointed by the chairman to decide upon all disputes in relation to claims. . . ." (The 13 appointees were D. A. N. Grover [as register of claims], Isaac Cody, Lorenzo D. Bird, Dr. G. W. Barnes, Charles H. Allen, John Freeland, J. H. McHolland, James Lewis, James J. Daneil, George W. Cooper, E. S. Wilkinson, James N. Burnes, and Samuel J. Finch.

On June 20 "Kansas" wrote that the Salt creek squatters' registry books had been open for "upwards of a week," and about 50 claims a day recorded.

Ref: St. Joseph (Mo.) *Gazette*, June 14, 1854; *Missouri Republican*, St. Louis, June 17, 19, 1854; *Weekly Missouri Statesman*, Columbia, June 23, 1854; *The Democratic Platform*, Liberty, Mo., June 29, 1854; or, *KHQ*, v. 6, pp. 97, 98 (where, by error, the date is given as June 19 instead of June 10); "Webb Scrapbooks," v. 1, pp. 43, 44, for clippings from *Industrial Luminary*, Parkville, Mo., June 20, 27, 1854; New York *Daily Times*, July 15, 1854 (for "Kansas'" comment). The Salt creek meeting place was M. Pierce Rively's trading post—formerly the post of Robert Wilson. "Leavenworth"—writing from Fort Leavenworth on June 13, 1854, said *over 100* persons attended the June 10 meeting.— *See* "Webb Scrapbooks," v. 1, p. 46.

❡ June.—"J. S.," writing from "Salt Creek Trading House, Kansas Territory, 3 miles west from Fort Leavenworth, June 10, 1854," reported: "The Mormon camp here has had a few cases of cholera. . . . Its number of wagons and emigrants are increasing daily. The advance party is expected to start on or about the 20th instant for Salt Lake City. . . ."

Ref: New York *Daily Times*, June 29, 1854 (reprinted from Baltimore *Sun* of June 28, 1854).

❡ June 13.—"It is estimated that over 2,000 people have already come into the territory to settle," wrote a correspondent from Fort Leavenworth.

"The most of them pass by here on the road leading to the prairies. There is almost a constant procession of them, some in wagons with their families, some on horses, with a bag and an axe. These, with the flood of Mormons on their way to Salt Lake City, would keep a tollgatherer—if there was one—quite busy. Of the number who come, many are from neighboring towns in Missouri, who go through the ceremony of entering a 'claim.' . . ."

Ref: "Webb Scrapbooks," v. 1, p. 46 ("Leavenworth's" letter—published in the Boston *Post*). From this reference to the Mormons, and the one in the preceding entry, it would *appear* that in 1854 a large number of them landed at Fort Leavenworth, and took the military road westward. But *see* the June, 1854, annals entry on p. 1220.

❦ June 13.—D. M. Chapman, writing from St. Joseph, Mo. (after making an extensive tour of Nebraska and Kansas territories), reported:

". . . you can scarcely imagine the state of things, not only in this city but all along the frontier line. The rush to California was nothing to it. Camps are formed, and tents are dotting all the hills and valleys. Thousands are waiting 'the permit' to cross. Large numbers have organized for mutual protection and defense, and have crossed the river, and are locating claims, and staking out farms. Trees are 'blazed' in every direction; and even now much of the choicest land is 'marked.' . . ."

Ref: "Webb Scrapbooks," v. 1, p. 58 (Chapman letter—published in the Troy [N. Y.] *Whig*). See KHQ, v. 13, pp. 18, 19, for a June 13, 1854, description from the *Industrial Luminary*, Parkville, Mo.

❦ June 13.—Thirty men (28 from Weston, Mo., or vicinity; two from Fort Leavenworth, K. T.) signed the original articles of agreement forming the Leavenworth Association. On June 12 G. W. Gist, his son, J. C. Gist, and Samuel Fernandis had staked off claims, totaling 320 acres, adjoining Fort Leavenworth's southern boundary (on Delaware trust land) for a proposed town. A decision on the name "Leavenworth" was made after June 13 and before June 20.

The 30 signers were: George W. Gist, Lorenzo D. Bird, D. H. Stephens, L. W. Caples, William H. Adams, Oliver Diefendorf, L. A. Wisely, Amos Rees, Samuel Norton, William S. Murphy, Samuel Fernandis, Merritt Johnson, George H. Keller, William G. Caples, H. Miles Moore, Joseph Murphy, John C. Gist, George B. Panton, Edward H. Mix, Joseph B. Evans, Malcolm Clark, John Bull, Frans. Impey, James F. Bruner, the Rev. Frederick Starr, J. D. Todd, A. Thomas Kyle, Maj. Sackfield Maclin, Bvt. Maj. Edmund A. Ogden, Dr. Samuel F. Few. (Later admitted as members: James W. Hardesty and W. S. Yohe.)

Some, or all, of the Leavenworth Association officers were elected at a June 22 meeting: George W. Gist, president; Joseph B. Evans, treasurer; H. Miles Moore, secretary. The original trustees were Bvt. Maj. E. A. Ogden, Maj. Sackfield Maclin, and Lorenzo D. Bird. (Ogden resigned August 30; was replaced by Amos Rees.)

"Out West"—in a July 17 letter from "Kansas Territory"—wrote that he was living at Fort Leavenworth. ". . . it has always been asserted that the Govt's land extended three miles South of here on the Missouri," he stated. "But now, a company composed partly of army officers and partly of citizens, have entered upon the lower part . . . and laid out a town, nineteen workmen have been employed the past week to clear away the brush and bushes, who are paid $1.50 per day each. and boarded. . . . The company have building frames already under way at St. Louis and other places, and will shortly erect them. . . ."

Ref: H. Miles Moore's, *Early History of Leavenworth City and County* (1906), pp. 17-25; H. Miles Moore's "Journal," and Leavenworth Association records in H. Miles Moore's papers (microfilm, from original in Coe Collection, Yale University Library); Leavenworth *Daily Times*, September 14, 1879 (*see* in Leavenworth county "Clippings," v. 1, pp. 87-90, in KHi library); "Webb Scrapbooks," v. 1, p. 76 (for "Out West's" letter).

❡ June 15.—Of Fort Leavenworth and environs, a Lexington, Ky., man (on a tour of observation; and writing from Kansas [City], Mo.) had this to say:

"This reservation is about six miles, meandering with the Missouri River, and extending three miles back. Outside of this for ten miles every foot of land has been taken, and tents and cabins are being erected all over the country. At the Western [*i. e.*, Weston] Ferry alone, in one half day up to noon, upward of 500 people crossed. The emigration is immense to all parts of the Territory. Associations are being formed for mutual protection. . . ."

Ref: New York *Daily Tribune*, July 12, 1854 (from Lexington [Ky.] *Observer and Reporter* of July 5).

❡ June 15-22.—The *Excel* made her last run from Weston, Mo., to Fort Riley, and back; and her last trip on the Kansas river. For the first time she carried women passengers on the Kaw. (*See* April 22 entry.)

Coowners Charles K. Baker (captain) and Charles A. Perry (also their families), and "Dixon" (clerk) were on the steamboat. George S. Park (who boarded at Parkville, Mo., on the 16th), in his "Notes of a Trip up Kansas River," listed as other passengers Asst. Surg. William A. Hammond (assigned to Fort Riley), his wife, and Mrs. Hammond's sister (Clara Nesbit), "Mr. [Thaddeus K.?] Mills" (paymaster's clerk), "Mr. Castelman," of Delaware, "Mr. McCann," of Virginia. (Some of our company joined us at Delaware [trading post, at Delaware, or Grinter's crossing of the Kansas]," wrote Park.)

In his account Park mentioned such points of interest as (Thomas N.) Stinson's Ferry, and his house (at the site of Tecumseh—laid out in August, 1854); "Pappan's [Papin's] Ferry," and his house; the "Great Crossing" (three ferries —Smith's, Ogee's, and Papin's); Union Town (the Pottawatomie trading post); "Darling's Ferry" (but operated by John L. Ogee—*see* January 1 entry); Fort Riley, and its fine stone buildings; the government bridge on the Republican (which another 1854 visitor described as "a substantial bridge, upwards of 200 feet long"); and the fort's saw mill (erected within the forks of the Republican and Smoky Hill).

After arriving at Fort Riley (on June 20?), the *Excel* made a short run up the Smoky Hill river (this tributary had no bridge, but there was a ferry). On Wednesday morning, June 21, the steamboat started back down the Kansas, and entered the Missouri early next day. (On the 22d, the *Clara,* downbound from Weston, met the *Excel* upbound on the Missouri.)

Ref: *Organization, Objects, and Plan of Operations of the Emigrant Aid Company* . . . (Boston, 1854), pp. 9-19; or, *Kansas Herald of Freedom,* Lawrence, October 21, 1854 (for George S. Park's "Notes"); W. W. Cone, *op. cit.,* p. 104; Walter S. Sloan's *History and Map of Kansas & Nebraska* (Chicago, 1855), p. 22 (for Republican river bridge quote); *Missouri Republican,* St. Louis, June 26, 1854 (for the *Clara*); Andreas-Cutler, *op. cit.,* p. 977 (for item on James Graham, young orphan, as a passenger on the *Excel,* debarking at St. Mary's Mission on June 17, 1854).

❦ Mid-June.—From Weston, Mo., a correspondent wrote the New York *Tribune* as follows:

"We are all crazy here about Nebraska [*i. e.,* meaning Kansas]. There are four hundred men in town to-day, from Platte County, ready to go into the new Territory. I think I can safely say there are over ten thousand people already in this Territory, exploring and making out claims and in less than two months there will be double that number. . . ."

Ref: New York *Daily Tribune,* June 29, 1854. The letter writer said that his party had united with about 20 others to found a village on the "Chicapa [Kickapoo] lands lying at the mouth of a large creek," about 15 miles from Fort Leavenworth.

❦ June 17.—Earlier in the month than usual, the Santa Fe mail (Francis Boothe, conductor) arrived at Independence, Mo. Stage passengers were Frank McManus, from Chihuahua, __ __ Stephenson (son of the El Paso merchant), and Lt. James A. Smith.

Ref: Liberty (Mo.) *Weekly Tribune,* June 30, 1854.

❦ June 17.—The *Occidental Messenger,* Independence, Mo., stated: "We learn that since the passage of the bill opening this [Kansas] Territory for settlement, some three thousand claims have been staked off, to be occupied by virtue of the bill. We are also informed that many difficulties and furious quarrels are arising among the claimants. . . ."

Ref: Liberty (Mo.) *Weekly Tribune,* June 23, 1854.

❦ June 17.—A squatters' meeting was held at a site in Kansas territory, described as "about fifteen miles above Weston, opposite Millions Ferry." (A little later in the year the town of Atchison was located at this point.) The Salt creek resolutions (*see* June 10 entry) were adopted (with the exception that 30 days, instead of two weeks, be allowed to make improvements on claims).

Thomas H. Christopher presided at this meeting; S. K. Welch was secretary. Eli C. Mason was appointed register of claims. Appointed as a vigilance committee were: Sidney Waters, Samuel Dickson, James M. Givens, J. Graves, B. G. Wells, Levi Boles, and James F. Forman.

Ref: St. Joseph (Mo.) *Gazette,* June 21, 1854.

❦ June 18-23.—"This fearful disease [cholera] made its appearance in our midst on Sunday morning last [18th]," said the Independence *Western Dispatch* of June 23, and has resulted fatally in thirty cases. Since Wed. morning [21st] but one or two new cases have occurred."

News reached St. Louis that several fatal cases had been reported at Weston and St. Joseph; and six or eight had died of cholera aboard the *Clara* and *Sam Cloon*.

At Ottawa Baptist Mission, on June 23, Jotham Meeker recorded in his diary: "Learn from emigrants the Cholera is raging at Independence, Kansas and Westport—and that several have died with it within a few days past at Bull Creek and Wahkaroosa."

Ref: Liberty (Mo.) *Weekly Tribune*, June 23, 30, 1854; New York *Daily Tribune*, June 27, 1854; St. Joseph *Gazette*, June 28, 1854 (for news of cholera at Independence and on the river, but nothing about the disease at St. Joseph); Meeker's diary, *loc. cit.*

❦ June 20.—Writing from Fort Leavenworth, "Kansas" commented in a letter he sent the New York *Times*:

"Two rambles, in different directions, into the interior . . . have afforded me a more extensive view of the Territory [of Kansas]. At every advancing step the prospect brightens. There are no very steep hills, but the land is rolling enough to appear beautiful, without being incapable of cultivation. Between these elevations wide fields are stretched along, with soil apparently two or three feet in depth. The brooks are numerous, and are lined with high trees and shrubbery. Wild fruits and flowers abound along the road-side. The real new England blackberry, and various roses of peculiar fragrance, thrive side by side. Thick groves, dotted all over the country, add to the splendor of the landscape. I would not, of course, give the impression that the scenery here is lovelier than in any other place. But I have yet to see the spot *where all the land can be used for agricultural purposes* that surpasses this in beauty. . . ."

Ref: New York *Daily Times*, July 15, 1854.

❦ June 24.—At James R. Whitehead's (trading post), some four miles above, and across the Missouri from St. Joseph, "a large and enthusiastic" group of the "Settlers of Kansas Territory" met and formed a Squatter Association.

"Col." A. M. Mitchell presided; James R. Whitehead was appointed secretary. On the resolutions committee were: "Col." W. Broadus Thompson, "Capt." John Whitehead, Benjamin Whorter (Whorton?), James B. O'Toole, and John R. Carter. The resolutions adopted were similar to those passed at Salt creek on June 10 (*see* p. 1226).

James R. Whitehead was appointed register of claims; the 13 vigilance committee members were: John H. Whitehead, Samuel P. Blair, Henderson Smallwood, James B. O'Toole, Thomas W. Waterson, Cary B. Whitehead, Anderson

Cox, John W. Smith, Sr., Samuel Montgomery, Benjamin Harding, John W. Smith, Jr., John (James J.?) Keaton, and Joseph Siceliff.

Ref: St. Joseph *Gazette*, June 21, July 5, 1854; *Missouri Republican*, St. Louis, July 1, 1854; Martha B. Caldwell, editor, "Records of the Squatter Association of Whitehead District, Doniphan County," in *KHQ*, v. 13, pp. 16-35. (The *Gazette* lists five resolutions committee members; in *KHQ*, v. 13, p. 22, the name James B. O'Toole is omitted.)

❦ June 26.—"Philos," writing from "Whitehead, Kansas Territory" (*see* preceding entry), stated: ". . . This city is as yet, of course, a prospective one. There are only several houses built, but they are well constructed and permanent. The site is about five miles from St. Joseph. . . .

"The country around is filling up with a most enterprising and intelligent people. Thousands have already come in, and thousands are still coming. The lands, for from ten to twenty miles back, have, with but few exceptions, been claimed by squatters. . . . They consist of some of the best stock of Virginia, Kentucky, Tennessee and Missouri. . . ."

Ref: *Missouri Republican*, St. Louis, July 1, 1854.

❦ June 27.—Free-State man Samuel N. Wood (who, with his family had arrived, from Ohio, on the Missouri border about June 20) wrote from Independence, Mo., to the Cincinnati *Columbian:*

"We have made one short trip over into the Indian country, and satisfied ourselves that a man can get almost just such a home as he pleases. I never saw richer land in my life; and it appears inexhaustible. . . . The only drawback is this slavery question. Missourians have already flocked to this Territory by hundreds; many slaves are already in the Territory. . . . A few missionaries thought in the start that they would regulate the settlement of this whole Territory. Northern men were ordered off; lynching was freely talked of, even by United States officers at Fort Leavenworth, merely because they happened to be born North of Mason and Dixon's line. Some Northern men were actually driven off; others were frightened away. All manner of lies were told, and misrepresentations made, in order to keep Northern men away. But now the charm is broken. A dozen families of Free Soilers drove ahead, and have commenced a settlement upon Kansas river. ["To reach here . . . cross the Shawnee Reserve thirty miles, to Wakarusa ferry and you come to the promised land," wrote Wood in an August 20 letter. His claim—as he later described it—was "on the California road, some three miles southwest of Lawrence."] A meeting is called on July 8, of those friendly to making Kansas a free State. Emigrants from Iowa, Illinois and Indiana are arriving daily. Ten days will not pass until the cabins of at least two hundred opponents of slavery will be in progress of construction. A few more, and we shall be invincible. All we want is, for every Northern man—every Northern family, who have their minds on this Territory, to come on at once. This slavery question must be met and decided *now.* . . ."

Ref: New York *Daily Tribune*, July 13, 1854 (for June 27 letter); *KHQ*, v. 23, pp. 181-190 (for other S. N. Wood letters of 1854); *KHC*, v. 3, pp. 426-431 (for Wood's address, 1886).

℘ June 29.—The "June" Salt Lake mail, brought from Fort Laramie in charge of William Allison, arrived at Independence, Mo. "The mail party had a hard time of it, owing to rains and high waters," said the *Occidental Messenger.*

The mail party reported there was "a good deal" of cholera on the route; and that some trains, "particularly the Mormons," had suffered severely from it.

(This was the last run under Samuel H. Woodson's expiring contract—*see* April 29 annals entry, and pp. 956, 957, 1032.)

Ref: Liberty (Mo.) *Weekly Tribune,* July 7, 1854.

℘ June-July.—The *Missouri Republican,* St. Louis, in its July 12 issue printed extracts from a letter written at St. Joseph, Mo. (in late June, or early July?), by "Philos," who stated:

". . . Within the last two weeks I have met persons here from almost every State in the Union, and from the Territories of Oregon, Utah, Nebraska and Kansas. They come by boats, stages, carriages, wagons, on horse-back and mule-back, and it is no unusual thing to see troops of hardy pioneers passing on foot, with their axes and knapsacks upon their backs, making their way into the forests of Kansas and Nebraska, to hew out a home. The emigration to these territories is unprecedented except in the history of California. Thousands of sturdy and enterprising men are flocking thither to select the choicest spots for their future homes. The ferry-boats here are busy transporting them from daylight until dark. They fire, thus far, all from slave States, except a few from Illinois and Indiana, and those are of slavery proclivities—at all events, they are not abolitionists. . . ."

Ref: *Missouri Republican,* July 12, 1854. "Philos" stated that there had been two deaths resulting from an argument over a claim—the claim jumper, and the original claimant (a man from near Weston, Mo.) had killed each other with axes.

℘ June 30.—The New York *Daily Tribune* listed the Kansas "Territorial Appointments":

Andrew H. Reeder, of (Easton) Pennsylvania, governor
Daniel Woodson, of Virginia, secretary
* Madison Brown, of Missouri, chief justice
Rush Elmore, of Alabama, associate justice
Sanders W. Johnston, of Ohio, associate justice
Andrew J. Isacks, of Louisiana, district attorney
Israel B. Donalson, of Illinois, U. S. marshal

* Brown did not accept the appointment. (Samuel D. Lecompte was appointed chief justice in his place.)

Over three months elapsed before Gov. Andrew H. Reeder arrived in Kansas territory. On October 7 he debarked at Fort Leavenworth (temporary seat of government) from the *Polar Star.*

Ref: New York *Daily Tribune,* June 30, 1854; *Kansas Weekly Herald,* Leavenworth, October 8, 1854. Reeder had been commissioned by President Pierce on June 29. He took the oath of office July 7.—*KHC,* v. 1-2, p. 146.

Index

Appendix

TRAILS, 1825-1854, AND SOME RELATED DEVELOPMENTS
(See Back Endpaper)

1825-1827   Santa Fe trail surveyed by Sibley and Brown. (Pages 122-124, 142, 143.) The *upper* (survey) crossing of the Arkansas (in Chouteau's Island vicinity) was used in early years. In the 1830's the *middle* crossing (near present Cimarron) became the established fording area. A *lower* crossing (near mouth of Mulberry creek) had limited use.

1827   "Sublette's Trace," pioneered in the winter, was retraced by fur trade party in the spring. This pathway, with some variations, became the "Independence" Oregon-California trail. (Pages 137, 139.)

1827   Kansa Agency established on Kansas river, some four miles below the Grasshopper's (Delaware's) mouth. (Pages 138, 139.) From 1829 up to 1838, this was the crossing point for "Sublette's Trace" travelers. (Pages 265, 323, and 474—for its use in 1843.)

1827   Cantonment Leavenworth established, on the Missouri's right bank, below mouth of Salt creek. (Page 141.)

1827   Independence, Mo., founded. (Page 144.) By 1832 it was the outfitting point for, and eastern terminus of, the Santa Fe trade.

1829   Sublette's pack-train, en route West by way of Independence, Mo., probably for the first time traveled out the Santa Fe trail some distance before turning northwest towards the Kansas river. This became the established Oregon-California trail route. (Pages 157, 171.)

1831   Council Grove (treaty point, 1825, and Santa Fe trail landmark) first used as rendezvous by a New Mexico-bound traders' caravan. (Pages 203, 204.)

1831   By this year (and perhaps in 1830) the lower Kansas river ferry known as Delaware or Grinter crossing was in use. The later-established Fort Leavenworth-Fort Gibson military road crossed the Kansas here. (Pages 175, 181.)

1834   Westport, Mo., established. (Page 261.) This inland town's access to the Missouri was at present Kansas City, Mo. (which, though lots were sold in 1838, did not begin to develop till 1846, and was better known as Westport Landing up to that time).

1834   Bent's Fort (Fort William), fur trade post on the upper Arkansas, established. (Page 256.) A Bent, St. Vrain & Company party (with wagons) eastbound from Santa Fe in the late summer, traveled by way of Taos and Raton Pass to Fort William; then came down the Arkansas to the Santa Fe trail—thus opening the Bent's Fort branch of the Santa Fe trail. (Pages 276, 277.)

1835   Dodge's expedition, on a summer tour, traveled from the South Platte down to the upper Arkansas by a route *along the base of the Rockies;* then followed downriver past Bent's Fort to the Santa Fe trail junction on the march back to Fort Leavenworth. (Pages 287, 293.)

1837   Weston, Mo., established. By 1839 it was prospering. (Page 375.)

1837-1839   Fort Leavenworth-Fort Gibson military road along Missouri-"Kansas" border located, surveyed, and constructed. (Pages 332, 357.)

1838   First use by an American Fur Company caravan of the Kansas crossing in present Topeka area. (Page 345; and *see* page 323.)

1839   Gregg's Santa Fe-bound party (from Van Buren, Ark.) traveled a north-of-the-Canadian route, but returning kept mostly to the south side. (Page 367.) Leavitt, in 1846 (page 573), some '49ers, and Marcy's expedition in 1849 (pages 798, 799, 804) also traveled west by north-of-the-Canadian routes.

1841   First emigrant wagon train for the Pacific. The Bidwell-Bartleson party's journey west was from Independence, Mo., via "Sublette's Trace" (or, the now developing Oregon-California trail). (Page 428.)

1842   Fort Scott established, at Marmaton crossing of the Fort Leavenworth-Fort Gibson military road. (Page 445.) Closed in 1853, on founding of Fort Riley.

1843   Troops from Fort Scott, heading for Council Grove, traveled a route described as generally on the divide between the Marais des Cygnes and Neosho rivers. (Page 481.)

1843   First mention of Papin's ferry at the "Topeka" crossing of Kansas river on the Oregon-California trail. (Page 476.) The Papins had moved there in 1840. (Page 409.)

1843   St. Joseph, Mo., established, on site of Robidoux's Blacksnake Hills trading post. (Page 497.) This town developed rapidly.

[1844?]   Before 1848 (and speculatively pioneered in 1844—the flood year) an Oregon-California trail cut-off route over the hills left the main trail five miles east of the Little (Red) Vermillion crossing, and rejoined it at the Big (Black) Vermillion. (Page 747, for mention in 1848; and page 1157, for 1853 mention.)

1844   St. Joseph branch of Oregon-California trail pioneered. (Pages 503, 508.) Because of difficult terrain, and attempts to make the road less circuitous, the route was not a fixed one in the beginning years. Street's 1850 table of distances (pages 911, 912) represents the established route.

1844   First use of route north of the Platte (from Council Bluffs) by westbound emigrants (the Stephens-Townsend-Murphy party). (Page 511.) In 1847 this became known as the Mormon trail.

1845   Kearny's expedition blazed a trail from Fort Leavenworth out to a junction, west of the Big Blue, with the "Independence" Oregon-California road. (Kearny's trail crossed the St. Joseph branch road east of the Big Blue, but did not travel it. Subsequently, the military road and the St. Joseph branch road *joined* east of the Big Blue, probably because the military road proved superior, and emigrants made use of it.) (Pages 546, 819, 899.)

1845   Kearny's expedition journeyed from Fort Laramie southward to the South Platte, and then *along the base of the Rockies* to the upper Arkansas; followed it downstream, past Bent's Fort, to the Santa Fe trail en route back to Fort Leavenworth. (Page 547.) In 1849 (and succeeding years) westbound emigrants (in increasing numbers) traveled the Santa Fe trail-Bent's Fort route to the upper Arkansas, and journeyed northward by a trail along the base of the Rockies up to the South Platte, and to Fort Laramie.

1845-1846   Kearny's expedition of 1845 left the Santa Fe trail east of Willow Springs and blazed a route northeastward to Fort Leavenworth, ferrying the Kansas, near the Wakarusa's mouth, on flatboats operated by Shawnee Indians. (Page 558.) In 1846 Kearny dispatched his Army of the West to New Mexico over this Fort Leavenworth branch of the Santa Fe trail. (Page 598.) Much-traveled in 1846, the road seems to have had limited use thereafter. Some '49ers traveled it. (Page 858.)

1846   Kansas (City), Mo. (originally started in 1838) was revitalized; and soon lost the appellation "Westport Landing." (Page 575.)

1846   Crossing points above St. Joseph, Mo., such as Iowa Point and Elizabethtown, used by Pacific-bound emigrants this year, and subsequently. (Page 575.)

1846-1848   Fort Kearny on Table creek established (and closed) in 1846. In winter of 1847-1848 some Missouri volunteers were quartered here. (Pages 586, 712, 805.) The south-of-the Platte branch of the Oregon-California trail which ran west from "old" Fort Kearny was referred to as the "central route between [the starting points of] St. Joseph and Council Bluffs." (Pages 586, 712, 805.)

1847   Mormon trail established north of the Platte, from Council Bluffs area to Fort Laramie. (Pages 672, 673.)

1847   At Council Grove, on the Santa Fe trail, Boone & Hamilton established a trading post. (Page 671.)

1847-1848   Mann's Fort (a stockaded government depot) was established in 1847 on the Santa Fe trail, some 21? miles below the Cimarron crossing of the Arkansas. It was occupied, briefly, in the spring and early summer by non-military personnel, and then was abandoned. In the fall Gilpin's battalion of Missouri volunteers arrived at Mann's Fort. Three companies remained over-winter; and till late summer, 1848, some, or all, of Gilpin's troops were quartered there. It was then abandoned. (Pages 669, 720, 721, 731, 778.)

1848   Fort Kearny established, at the head of Grand Island on the Platte. Its chief purpose: to protect the Oregon-California emigration. (Pages 755, 756.)

1848   Union Town (Pottawatomie trading post) established. (Pages 737, 738.) Many '49ers ferried or forded the Kansas at this new *upper* crossing, on the "Independence" Oregon-California trail. From August, 1850, to July, 1854, Union Town was on the Independence-Fort Laramie-Salt Lake mail route. (Page 957.)

1849   Road from St. Joseph, Mo., via Union Town, to Council Grove established. Easton, whose party, returning to Fort Leavenworth, traveled part of it, described the route. (Pages 886, 887.)

1849   A branch trail from the Missouri border by way of Fort Scott and the "Old Pottawatomie nation reserve" joined the road to Santa Fe east of Council Grove. (Pages 831, 832.)

1849   From Harrisonville, Mo., a new branch trail west joined the Santa Fe road east of Council Grove. Presumably the traffic passing Ottawa Baptist Mission (described by Missionary Meeker) was on this route. (Pages 928, 1078.)

1849   Some '49ers, coming from Fayetteville, Ark., and the Cherokee Nation, blazed a trail (the "Cherokee trail") up to a junction with the Santa Fe road at Turkey creek. (Page 853.)

1850   From Fort Leavenworth out to the Big Blue, Ogden's party improved and shortened, the Fort Leavenworth-Fort Kearny road. (Pages 908, 973, 974; and *see, also,* pages 546, 819, and 899.)

1850   Fort Atkinson established, on the Santa Fe trail some 20? miles below the Cimarron crossing of the Arkansas. It closed in 1853. (Page 965.)

1851   Aubry, in October (after a first attempt in May), found a good Santa Fe trail cut-off which avoided the Jornada. He turned off the established route near (or at) Cold Spring, on the Cimarron, and traveled "from 10 to 40 degrees east of North" to the Arkansas. (Page 1042; and *see, also,* pages 999, 1038, 1046.)

1852   Smith's Kansas river ferry established at a site a few miles above Papin's "Topeka" ferry. (Page 1088.)

1852   Marshall's trading post and ferry established (at Big Blue crossing —"Marysville") on St. Joseph branch of Oregon-California trail and Fort Leavenworth-Fort Kearny military road. (Pages 1067, 1068.)

1852   From Parkville, Mo., a road west on the north side of the Kansas was in use. (Year of origin not known.) (Pages 1076, 1183.)

1852   Road from Fort Leavenworth to St. Mary's Mission (76 miles) reconnoitered in June by Woodruff. (Page 1103.) This became part of the Fort Leavenworth-Fort Riley military road.

1853   Fort Riley established, at junction of Smoky Hill and Republican rivers. (Pages 1131, 1150.)

1853   Fort Leavenworth-Fort Riley military road in use. Rough and difficult to travel. Ferry in operation at Big Blue crossing, above present Manhattan. (Pages 1150, 1183.)

1854   Trail pioneered northwestward from 110-mile creek crossing of Santa Fe trail to Fort Riley, and from Fort Riley to a junction with the Oregon-California trail, by a party of Salt Lake-bound Mormons. (Page 1222.)

PRINTED BY
ROBERT R. (BOB) SANDERS, STATE PRINTER
TOPEKA, KANSAS
1972

33-4138

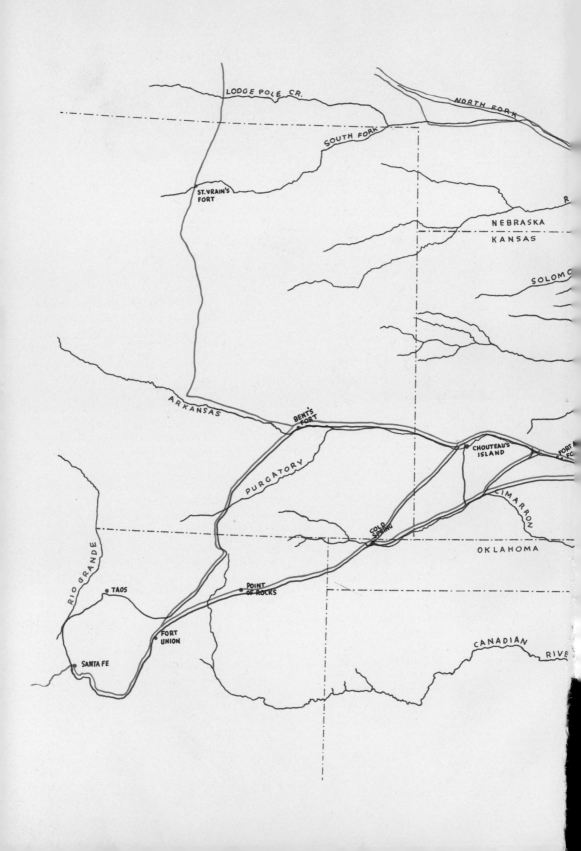